A
DICTIONARY OF MODERN MUSIC
AND MUSICIANS

Da Capo Press Music Reprint Series

GENERAL EDITOR

FREDERICK FREEDMAN

VASSAR COLLEGE

A
DICTIONARY
OF MODERN MUSIC
AND MUSICIANS

General Editor
A. Eaglefield-Hull

Editorial Committee
Sir Hugh Allen
Professor Granville Bantock
Edward J. Dent
Sir Henry J. Wood

𝄞 DA CAPO PRESS • NEW YORK • 1971

A Da Capo Press Reprint Edition

This Da Capo Press edition of
A Dictionary of Modern Music and Musicians
is an unabridged republication of the first
edition published in London and New York in 1924.

Library of Congress Catalog Card Number 78-139192

SBN 306-70086-7

Published by Da Capo Press
A Division of Plenum Publishing Corporation
227 West 17th Street, New York, N. Y. 10011

A
DICTIONARY OF MODERN MUSIC
& MUSICIANS

A
DICTIONARY
OF MODERN MUSIC
AND MUSICIANS

MUSIC IS IN THE SEA & AIR

MCMXXIV
LONDON & TORONTO
J. M. DENT & SONS LTD.
NEW YORK: E. P. DUTTON & CO.

The articles assembled in this Dictionary have all been specially written, and the copyright is strictly reserved by the Publishers.

PREFACE

BY THE

EDITORIAL COMMITTEE

THE political confusion which began in 1914, and from which Europe has not yet been able wholly to emerge, has affected the world of music in many ways. In some countries it has deeply intensified the desire for music and the will to create it; in others it has to some extent caused music to be laid aside as a matter of secondary interest. A sharply accentuated sense of nationalism, however valuable a stimulus it may have given in individual cases, has hindered that free international exchange of musical ideas which up to 1914 had been developing for generations. The English musical public has shown for centuries a healthy curiosity about the music of the whole civilised world; Dr. Burney's " General History of Music," published towards the end of the eighteenth century, and Grove's " Dictionary of Music and Musicians," begun a hundred years later, are both of them now recognised abroad as well as at home as pioneer works in their respective lines. The last thirty years have, in spite of all the damage caused by political events, brought about an enormous increase of interest in music in England and a growing consciousness that music can be, in the best sense, a form of national self-expression. It is, indeed, one of the healthiest signs of our new musical life that we still feel, no less than our predecessors, that vigorous curiosity about the music of other countries; but the normal sources of information have been obstructed, and the lover of music, not only in England but in all countries, has been cut off from knowledge.

The object of this new Dictionary is to supply the musician and the general musical reader with a concise and practical survey of all modern musical activities. Its backward limit has been fixed at or about 1880, the year in which Parry's " Prometheus Unbound " marked the beginning of what has been called the " English Renaissance." The period thus included covers, as regards the music of other countries, such outstanding landmarks of musical history as Wagner's " Parsifal," Verdi's " Otello " and " Falstaff," the later works of Brahms and César Franck, so that the reader may here find information not only about the music of

v

our own day, but may also trace the historical sources of its various styles. Since the beginning of the new century a remarkable change has come over our whole musical outlook, a change easily perceptible to the general music-lover no less than to the trained specialist. All aspects of this change, practical as well as theoretical, have been carefully considered and expounded in this new Dictionary.

The chief technical article is that on " Harmony," which has been written not by a single author, whose views, however interesting, might be one-sided, but by various contributors who have met several times as a committee[1] to discuss it by word of mouth, and have supplied material on various points to the General Editor. A special feature of the Dictionary is the series of critical articles on Opera, Symphony, Chamber Music, Songs, etc., in various countries. The numerous foreign contributors have been selected with great care by the Editorial Committee, who have desired to leave them as wide a latitude as possible in the expression of critical opinions. The proofs of the whole Dictionary have been read by all the members of this committee, and the general policy of the work has been determined by them.

HUGH P. ALLEN
GRANVILLE BANTOCK
EDWARD J. DENT
HENRY J. WOOD
A. EAGLEFIELD-HULL

[1] *Sir Hugh Allen, Mr. Béla Bartók, Mr. Arnold Bax, Mr. Eugène Goossens, Dr. Eaglefield-Hull, Prof. Tovey, Dr. Vaughan Williams, and Prof. Granville Bantock (Chairman of the Harmony Committee). The whole of the General Principles are endorsed by them.*

GENERAL EDITOR'S PREFACE

THE Editorial Committee's decision to follow the 1919 rulings of the Versailles Supreme Council in dealing with the various European countries was not so completely simple as it seemed at first. Little-known languages have now sprung into prominence, and great stress is laid on their exact usage by those concerned; many unfamiliar names of places have come into use again, and in 1922 a fairly complete European tour became necessary to meet the various committees personally, and to settle many questions on the spot. In 1923 I again visited most of the European countries to discuss the progress of the work. Even this did not prevent some overlapping in the names chosen and some omission of artists of thoroughly cosmopolitan habits. Most of these articles have subsequently been supplied by myself.

The necessary material has been obtained through National Sub-editors, some of whom have written the majority of the articles themselves (as, for example, Dr. Einstein and Germany, Dr. Alaleona and Italy); others have formed a National Committee, which has allotted the work in sections. Thus in France, Dr. Henry Prunières (Chairman), Mr. Cœuroy and Mr. Calvocoressi have written the articles on the composers; Mr. Scheeffner those on the conductors; Mr. Rigaud, on the singers; Mr. Lazarus, on the pianists and harpists; Mr. Raugel, on the organists; Mr. Pincherle, on violinists, cellists, etc., and Mlle. Pereyra, on musicologists, societies, etc. (see list on pages ix and x).

In the articles dealing with the recently freed countries of Poland, Hungary, Lithuania, Czecho-Slovakia, etc., the new names of places have been given, often with the more widely known name in brackets (see list on page xiii).

In the spelling of Polish names, Dr. Jachimecki has naturally followed the Polish spelling; but a few of the more widely accepted spellings have been retained. Leschetizky, for instance, looks strange in the Polish *Lezetycki*; but Polish names in general should never have the final " i " converted into " y." For the Polish pronunciation, as well as for other good advice, I am indebted to Mr. F. B. Czarnowski, of the Polish Legation in London. For the Russian accentuation, Mr. Victor Belaief, of the Russian State Music Publishing Department, Moscow, and Mr. M. D. Calvocoressi have made themselves responsible. For the titles of pieces, books, works, etc., various courses have been followed. Where the English translation is widely accepted, or where it may be translated back again with comparative safety, the English title alone has been given. Elsewhere, either the original title is given, or both the original and an English translation appear; for example:

Elementær Musiklære (Elementary Music Theory).

For the translation of all the French and German articles, Mr. W. H. Kerridge, M.A., Mus.Bac. Cantab., has been responsible. Miss E. J. Bray has undertaken all the Italian translations. Amongst the many helpers engaged in the production of the Dictionary I am specially indebted to Mr. Charles Lee, of Letchworth, for much valuable help and advice, and to Mr. E. F. Bozman, B.A., for many useful suggestions.

The newly revived languages have necessitated the manufacture of large numbers of special letters for their exact representation. In this matter, as in all others, the publishers, in their high esteem for music, have been most generous. It is the intention of the publishers that the Dictionary shall be brought well up to date in successive editions, and they have undertaken to keep the type standing, in order that all corrections and additions may be made in their proper places instead of being relegated to an appendix.

Additions, corrections, and all editorial matters relating to the Dictionary, should be addressed to me, c/o Messrs. J. M. DENT AND SONS LTD., 10-13, Bedford Street, London, W.C.2.

A. EAGLEFIELD-HULL

General Editor.

NATIONAL COMMITTEES AND SUB-EDITORS

ARGENTINA
Dr. Angelo Menchaca, Buenos Ayres

AUSTRALIA
Mr. Gibson Young, Melbourne
Mr. F. Bennicke Hart, Melbourne
Mrs. Louise B. M. Dyer, Melbourne

AUSTRIA
Dr. Egon Wellesz, Vienna
Dr. Hugo Botstiber, Vienna
Dr. Ernst Decsey, Vienna
Dr. Wilhelm Fischer, Vienna
Dr. Paul A. Pisk, Vienna
Dr. Paul Stefan, Vienna

BELGIUM
Dr. Charles Van den Borren, Brussels
Dr. Ernest Closson, Brussels
Mr. Joseph Jongen, Brussels

BRAZIL
Mr. J. Armstrong Read, Rio de Janeiro
Mr. Oscar Guanobarino, Rio de Janeiro

CANADA
Dr. A. S. Vogt, Toronto
Mr. H. F. Fricker, Toronto
Mr. Leo Smith, Toronto
Miss Helen Roberts, Chicago

CZECHO - SLOVAKIA (BOHEMIA, MORAVIA, SILESIA, SLOVAKIA)
Dr. Erich Steinhard, Prague
Dr. Václav Štěpán, Prague

DENMARK
Dr. Angul Hammerich, Copenhagen
Dr. William Behrend, Copenhagen

ENGLAND
Professor Sir Hugh Allen, London
Professor Granville Bantock, Birmingham

Sir Henry Wood, London
Mr. Edward J. Dent, London
Dr. Eaglefield-Hull, London

FRANCE
Dr. Henry Prunières, Paris
Mr. André Cœuroy, Paris
Mr. M. D. Calvocoressi, London
Mr. Marc Pincherle, Paris
Mlle. M. L. Pereyra, Paris
Mr. Henri Raugel, Paris
Mr. André Rigaud, Paris
Mr. André Scheeffner, Paris
Mr. Joseph Bonnet, Paris

GERMANY
Dr. Alfred Einstein, Munich
Dr. Hugo Leichtentritt, Berlin
Dr. Adolf Weissmann, Berlin

HOLLAND
Mr. William Pijper, Bilthoven, Holland

HUNGARY
Mr. Béla Bartók, Budapest
Mr. Zoltán Kodály, Budapest

INDIA
Mr. A. K. Coomaraswamy, Boston, U.S.A.

IRELAND
Mr. Hamilton Harty, Manchester
Dr. J. F. Larchet, Dublin
Professor William Starkie, Dublin

ITALY
Dr. Domenico Alaleona, Rome
Mr. Renato Fondi, Rome

JAPAN
Lord Raitai Tokuguwa, Tokio

LATVIA
Mr. K. Paucitis, Riga

NATIONAL COMMITTEES AND SUB-EDITORS

LITHUANIA
Mr. H. Rabinavičius, London

MEXICO, CUBA, CHILE, PERU
Mr. Frederick H. Martens, New York

NORWAY
Mr. Reidar Mjöen, Christiania
Mr. Jens A. Arbo, Christiania
Mr. Ulrick Mörk, Christiania
Dr. O. M. Sandvik, Christiania
Mr. Alfred Hurum, Christiania

POLAND
Professor Zdzisław Jachimecki, Cracow

PORTUGAL
Mr. Cecil Mackee, Lisbon

RUMANIA
Mr. Constantin N. Brailoiù, Bucharest

RUSSIA
Mr. Victor Belaief, Moscow
Mr. M. D. Calvocoressi, London
Mr. Boris de Schloezer, Paris
Mr. W. Bessell, Paris

SCOTLAND
Professor Donald Tovey, Edinburgh
Mr. Hugh S. Roberton, Glasgow
Mr. J. Petrie Dunn, Edinburgh
Mr. William Saunders, Edinburgh

SERBIA
Mr. T. F. Dunhill, London

SOUTH AFRICA
Prof. W. H. Bell, Cape Town
Mr. Theo Wendt, Cape Town
Prof. Percival Kirby, Johannesburg
Mr. H. Lyell-Taylor, Durban

SPAIN
Mr. Pedro G. Morales, London

SWEDEN
Dr. Patrik Vretblad, Stockholm

SWITZERLAND
Mr. Frederick Hay, Geneva

WALES
Sir Henry Walford Davies, Aberystwyth
Dr. D. Vaughan Thomas, Swansea

U. S. A.
Dr. Otto Kinkeldey, New York
Mr. Julius Mattfeld, New York

CONTRIBUTORS

The articles in this Dictionary appear over the initials of their contributors
according to the following list

A. B.	Arnold Bax, London
A. C.	André Cœuroy, Paris
A. CL.	Alfred Clark, London
A. E.	Alfred Einstein, Munich
A. H.	Angul Hammerich, Copenhagen
A. K. C.	A. K. Coomaraswamy, Boston, U.S.A.
A. M.	Angelo Menchaca, Buenos Ayres
A. N.	Antoon Nauwelaerts, Bruges
A. R.	André Rigaud, Paris
A. S.	André Scheeffner, Paris
A. S. V.	Augustus S. Vogt, Toronto
A. W.	Adolf Weissmann, Berlin
B. B.	Béla Bartók, Budapest
B. DE S.	Boris de Schloezer, Paris
C. L.	Charles Lee, Letchworth
C. M.	Compton Mackenzie, London
C. M. B.	C. M. Barbeau, Ottawa
C. N. B.	Constantin N. Brailoiù, Bucharest
C. V. B.	Charles Van den Borren, Brussels
D. A.	Domenico Alaleona, Rome
D. L.	D. Lazarus, Paris
D. T.	Donald Tovey, Edinburgh
D. V. T.	D. Vaughan Thomas, Swansea
E. C.	Ernest Closson, Brussels
E. D.	Ernst Decsey, Vienna
E. E.	Edwin Evans, London
E. G.	Edward German, London
EU. G.	Eugène Goossens, London
E.-H.	Eaglefield-Hull, *General Editor*
E. J. D.	Edward J. Dent, London
E. R. D.	Emily R. Daymond, London
E. S.	Erich Steinhard, Prague
EG. W.	Egon Wellesz, Vienna
F. A. H.	Frank A. Hadland, London
F. C.	Frederick Corder, London
F. G. S.	Frederick G. Shinn, London

F. H.	Frederick Hay, Geneva
F. H. M.	Frederick H. Martens, New York
F. K.	Frank Kidson, Leeds
F. R.	F. Raugel, Paris
G. B.	Granville Bantock, Birmingham
G. M. G.	Guido M. Gatti, Turin
G. O.	George Osborne, Huddersfield
G. Y.	Gibson Young, Melbourne
H. B.	Hugo Botstiber, Vienna
H. G.	Harvey Grace, London
H. H.	Herbert Howells, London
H. H. R.	Helen H. Roberts, Toronto
H. J. W.	Sir Henry J. Wood, London
H. L.	Hugo Leichtentritt, Berlin
H. P.	Henry Prunières, Paris
H. P. A.	Sir Hugh P. Allen, London
H. R.	H. Rabinavičius, London
H. S. W.	H. Saxe Wyndham, London
H. T. B.	H. T. Burleigh, New York
H. W.	Hadley Watkins, Bournemouth
H. W. D.	Sir Henry Walford Davies, Aberystwyth
J. A.	Jens Arbo, Christiania
J. A. F.	J. A. Forsyth, Manchester
J. B.	Joseph Bonnet, Paris
J. B. R.	J. B. Richardson, Toronto
J. C. M'L.	J. C. McLean, Aberystwyth
J. F. R.	J. F. Russell, Manchester
J. G.	James Graham, London
J. LL. W.	J. Lloyd Williams, Aberystwyth
J. M.	Julius Mattfield, New York
J. M'D.	J. MacDonagh, London
J. M. L.	J. Mewburn Levien, London
J. M. M.	J. M. Mitchell, Dunfermline
J. P. D.	John Petrie Dunn, Edinburgh
K. P.	K. Paucitis, Riga
L. F.	Louis Fleury, Paris
L. S.	Leo Smith, Toronto
L. S. J.	L. Stanton Jefferies, London

CONTRIBUTORS

M. Ba.	Maurice Barbleau, Toronto	S. G. S.	S. Geoffrey Smith, Buenos Ayres
M. B.	Maurice Bex, Paris	S. S. F.	S. S. Forsyth, Glasgow
M. D. C.	M. D. Calvocoressi, London		
M. K.-F.	Marjory Kennedy - Fraser, Edinburgh	T. F. D.	Thomas F. Dunhill, London
M. L. P.	Marie Louise Pereyra, Paris	T. H.	Toivo Haapanen, Helsingfors
M.-L.	H. H. Mischa-Léon, London		
M. P.	Marc Pincherle, Paris	U. M.	Ulric Mörk, Christiania
O. G.	Oscar Guanobarino, Rio de Janeiro	V. B.	Victor Belaief, Moscow
O. K.	Otto Kinkeldey, New York	V. St.	Václav Štěpán, Prague
O. M. S.	O. M. Sandvik, Christiania		
		W. A.	Wilfred Arlom, Sydney, Australia
P. B. R.	P. B. Richardson, Toronto	W. B.	William Behrend, Copenhagen
P. C. H.	Percy C. Hull, Hereford	W. F.	Wilhelm Fischer, Vienna
P. E. W.	Percy E. Watkins, Aberystwyth	W. H. B.	W. H. Bell, Cape Town
P. G. M.	Pedro G. Morales, London	W. H. K.	W. H. Kerridge, London
P. H.	Philip Heseltine, London	W. M.	William Murdoch, London
P. K.	Percival Kirkby, Johannesburg, S.A.	W. P.	Willem Pijper, The Hague
P. P.	Paul Pisk, Vienna	W. S.	William Saunders, Edinburgh
P. St.	Paul Stefan, Vienna	W. St.	Walter Starkie, Dublin
P. V.	Patrik Vretblad, Stockholm	W. W. S.	W. Wooding Starmer, Tunbridge Wells
R. F.	Renato Fondi, Rome	Zd. J.	Zdzisław Jachimecki, Cracow
R. M.	Reidar Mjöen, Christiania	Z. K.	Zoltán Kodály, Budapest
R. V. W.	R. Vaughan Williams, London		

LESS FAMILIAR PLACE-NAMES ADOPTED
SINCE 1918[1]

CZECHO-SLOVAKIA

Bratislava .	. Pressburg (Ger.), Pozsony (Hung.)
Brno . .	. Brünn
Budéjovice	. Budweis
Karlovy Vary	. Carlsbad
Marianshé Lázne	Marienbad
Olomouc .	. Olmütz
Plzeň .	. Pilsen

FINLAND

Åbo . .	. Turku
Hämeenlinna	. Tavastehus
Kaarina .	. St. Karins
Oulu . .	. Uleåborg
Pori . .	. Bjorneborg
Savonlinna .	. Nyslott
Tempere .	. Tammerfors
Viipuri .	. Viborg

GERMANY

Regensburg	. Ratisbon

JUGO-SLAVIA

Lublanjá .	. Laibach

LITHUANIA

Gardinas .	. Grodno
Klaipéda .	. Memel
Kaunas .	. Kovno
Šiauliai .	. Sharli
Tilžé . .	. Tilsit
Vilnius .	. Vilna

POLAND

Bydgoszcz .	. Bromberg
Lwów .	. Lemberg

RUMANIA

Cluj . .	. Klausenburg

[1] Except Regensburg.

ABBREVIATIONS

a.	alto
A.f.M.	*Archiv für Musikwissenschaft*
	(*Archive for Musical Knowledge*)
Acad.	Academy
acc.	accompaniment; accompanist
adj.	adjudicator
Amer.	American
arr.	arranged; arrangements
art.	article
b.	bass
b.	born
b.c.	bass clarinet
b.d.	bass drum
barit.	baritone
B.N.O.C.	British National Opera Co.
bsn.	bassoon
c	*circa,* about
c.a.	cor anglais
Cantab.	Cambridge
cath.	cathedral
cello	violoncello
cf.	compare
ch.	church
clar.	clarinet
coll.	collection; college
collab.	collaboration
comp.	composed
compn.	composition
compr.	composer
cond.	conducted
condr.	conductor
Cons.	Conservatoire
contr.	contralto
cpt.	counterpoint
d.	died
d.b.	double-bass
dir.	director
D.d.T.	*Denkmäler deutscher Tonkunst*
	(*Monuments of German Music*)
D.T.B.	*Denkmäler der Tonkunst in Bayern*
	(*Monuments of Bavarian Music*)
D.T.Ö.	*Denkmäler der Tonkunst in Österreich*
	(*Monuments of Austrian Music*)
Dunelm.	Durham

ed.	edited; editor; edition
educ.	educated
Eng.	English
establ.	established
fest.	festival
fl.	flute
Fr.	French
gen.	general
Ger.	German
Ges.	*Gesellschaft*
	(*Society*)
h.c.	*honoris causâ*
hon.	honorary
ib.	in the same place
id.	the same
I.M.G.	*Internationale Musik-Gesellschaft*
	(*International Society of Music*)
Inst.	Institute; Institution
instr.	instrument; instrumental
instrs.	instruments
Ital.	Italian
LL.D.	Doctor of Laws
m.-sopr.	mezzo-soprano
ma.	major
mi.	minor
ms.	manuscript
mss.	manuscripts
mus.	musical
Mus.Bac.	Bachelor of Music
Mus.Doc.	Doctor of Music
n.d.	no date
n.s.	new style
ob.	oboe
op.	opus
orch.	orchestra; orchestral
orgt.	organist

ABBREVIATIONS

orig.	original		stud.	studied
o.s.	old style		syll.	syllable
Oxon.	Oxford		symph.	symphonic
perf.	performed; performer		t.	tenor
pf.	pianoforte		tpi.	timpani
Ph.D.	Doctor of Philosophy		tpt.	trumpet
Philh.	Philharmonic		transl.	translated; translation
phon.	phonetic			
prod.	produced		unacc.	unaccompanied
prof.	professor		Univ.	University
pron.	pronounced			
publ.	published; publisher		v.	voice
			vla.	viola
Q.H.	Queen's Hall		vn.	violin
			vol.	volume
R.	Royal			
R.A.M.	Royal Academy of Music		Z.	*Zeitschrift*
R.C.M.	Royal College of Music			*(Journal)*
rev.	revised		Z.f.M.	*Zeitschrift für Musikwissenschaft*
R.M.C.M.	Royal Manchester College of Music			*(Journal for Musical Knowledge)*
Russ.	Russian			
			4tet	quartet
s.	soprano		5tet	quintet
sec.	secretary		6tet	sextet . . . and so on
Soc.	Society			
Span.	Spanish		4-v.	4 voices or parts
str.	string or strings		5-v.	5 voices or parts . . . and so on

A DICTIONARY OF MODERN MUSIC AND MUSICIANS

A

ABENDROTH, Hermann. Ger. condr. *b.* Frankfort-o-M., 19 Jan. 1883. Originally bookseller, became pupil of Ludwig Thuille (compn.) and Anna Langenhan-Hirzel (pf.); condr. of Munich Orch. Soc., of the Music-Lovers' Soc., 1903, and of Stadttheater, Lübeck (1905–11); dir. of music to Municipality of Essen, 1911; municipal dir. of music and dir. of Cons., Cologne, 1915, becoming gen. [mus. dir. 1918, and prof. in 1919. In 1922 he was condr. of Lower Rhine Festival; 1922–23 also of Symphony Concerts of Berlin State Opera. His conducting is remarkable for its rhythmic strength.—A. E.

ABERT, Hermann. Ger. musicologist; *b.* Stuttgart, 25 March, 1871. Stud. under his father, Johann Joseph Abert (1832–1915, for many years condr. of Court Orch. Stuttgart); also attended Stuttgart Cons. First stud. classical philology (securing his Ph.D. at Tübingen in 1897), after which took a 4-years' course in theory of music at Berlin Univ. In 1902 submitted thesis *The Æsthetic Principles of Mediæval Melody - construction,* and was formally admitted academic lecturer in theory of music at Univ. of Halle-o-S., being titular prof.-in-ordinary, 1909; prof.-in-ordinary, 1918. Has been prof. at Univ. of Leipzig in succession to Riemann since 1920. Declined a call from Univ. of Heidelberg in 1919, and has responded to later invitation to Berlin 1923. He is one of the most versatile investigators, in the field of music, in all Germany, having more especially mastered the history and theory of ancient and mediæval music, as well as the opera of XVII and XVIII centuries and that of Romantic music.

Die Lehre vom Ethos in der griechischen Musik (1899, Breitkopf); several contributions on *The latest Discoveries in Oxyrhynchus, A.f.M.* I and *Z.f.M.* IV; *The Concept of Music in Mediæval Times and its Principles* (Halle-o-S., 1905, Niemeyer); *Dramatic Music at Court of Duke Karl Eugen of Würtemberg* (1905); *Nicolo Jommelli as a Composer of Operas* (Halle, 1908, Niemeyer); *Joh. Jos. Abert* (1916, Breitkopf); *Goethe and Music* (Stuttgart, 1922, J. Engelhorn); *History of the Robert Franz Acad. of Singing in Halle* (1908); *Robert Schumann* (1903, 3rd ed. 1917, Berlin, Schlesische Verlags-Anstalt). His principal achievement is the re-writing of Otto Jahn's *Biography of Mozart* which thus becomes practically a new work (1920–1). Ed. a *Gluck Annual* (4 issues since 1914), and a *Mozart Annual* (from Munich, 1923, Drei Masken Verlag). He ed. Pergolesi's *La Serva Padrona* (Munich, Wunderhorn Verlag, now Tischer & Jagenberg, Cologne); in *D.d.T.* XXXII and XXXIII he ed. Jommelli's *Fetonte,* Carlo Pallavicino's *Gerusalemme Liberata,*

ballets by Florian Deller and J. J. Rudolph; in *D.T.B., Le Nozze d'Ercole e d'Ebe* by Gluck; in *D.T.O.,* the Italian version of Gluck's *Orfeo ed Euridice.*—A. E.

ABONNEMENT. A term used in connection with concert-tickets, in France, Germany and Switzerland. In Italy it is called *Abbonamento.* It is a subscription-ticket for a series, working out more cheaply than tickets for single performances.—E.-H.

ABRAHAM, Otto. Musical psychologist; *b.* Berlin, 31 May, 1872. Stud. medicine and natural science in Berlin, where he obtained M.D. in 1894. Since 1896 assistant to Prof. Carl Stumpf at Psychological Inst., Berlin, and is associated with Prof. Dr. E. M. v. Hornbostel in the direction of the latter's Phonograph Archives.

The Limits of Tone-Perception (with L. J. Brühl, *Zeitschr. für Psychologie u. Physiologie,* 1898); *On the Maximum Speed of Sound Progression* (with K. Ludolf Schäfer, 1899, *ib.*); *On the Discontinuance of Tone-Sensations* (1899, *ib.*); *Studies on Interruption-Tones* (with K. L. Schäfer, 1900–4 in *Archiv f. d. Ges. Physiologie*); *Absolute Sound-Perception* (*Sammelb. d. I.M.G.* III, i, and VIII, iii); *Studies on the Tone-System and Music of the Japanese* (*Sammelb. d. I.M.G.* IV, ii, 1904); *Phonographed Turkish Melodies; On Importance of Phonograph in Comparative Musical Science,* and *Phonographed Indian Melodies* (all with E. M. v. Hornbostel, 1904); *Phonographed Indian Melodies from British Columbia* (with E. M. v. Hornbostel, 1905, in fest. publication for Boas); *On Susceptibility to Harmonisation of Exotic Melodies* (with E. M. v. Hornbostel) in *Sammelb. d. I.M.G.* VII, 1906.—A. E.

ÁBRÁNYI, Emil. Hungarian compr. condr. *b.* Budapest, 1882. Was condr. at R. Hungarian Opera House; then at Municipal Theatre, Budapest.—B. B.

ACADEMIES, Colleges, *Conservatoires,* etc. *ARGENTINA.*—**Buenos Ayres :** Chief Cons. is that of *Alberto Williams* ; it has 92 branches in different parts of the Republic. The *Thibaud and Piazzini Cons.* is also important. There are many others : *Sta. Cecilia Cons.* dir. by H. Forino and C. Troiani ; the *Argentine School of Music,* under Julián Aguirre ; the *Beethoven Cons.* founded 1900 (Profs. Scolese and Flocco) ; the *Verdi Cons.* (A. Faleni); *Fontana's Institute of Music,* which has 10 branches in the provinces, etc. *AUSTRALIA.*—**Melbourne:** (i) *The Univ. Cons. of Music,* founded 1894; Dir. W. A. Laver, the Ormond Prof. of Music. (ii) *Cons. of Music,* Albert St., founded 1895; Dir. F. Bennicke Hart. **Sydney:** *N.S.W. State Cons. of Music,* founded 1914; Dir. W. Arundel Orchard,

I

from 1923. **Adelaide:** *Elder Cons. Univ. of S. Australia*; Dir. Dr. Harold E. Davies.

AUSTRIA.—**Vienna:** *Conservatoire (Akademie für Musik und darstellende Kunst)*, founded 1 Aug. 1817 by Gesellschaft der Musikfreunde as singing-school under Salieri. 1819, vn. class added under Joseph Böhm, the father of Vienna school of violinists (among his pupils were Ernst, Grün, Hellmesberger, Joachim); 1821, other instr. classes followed. Dir. by a committee of 16. 1844, Gottfried Preyer appointed first and sole Dir. Later on Joseph Hellmesberger sen. (1851–93) was Dir. Under his and Johann Nep. Fuchs's (1893–9) direction it reached its highest standard. A dramatic class was added. Chief professors were : Dachs, Door, Epstein, Fuchs, and Grün. Amongst the chief pupils were: Kreisler, Mahler, Mottl, Nikisch, Rosé, Schalk, Schreker, Hugo Wolf and Zemlinsky. The succeeding Directors were: Richard von Perger, Wilhelm Bopp, Ferdinand Loewe and now Dr. Josef Marx (from 1922). In 1908, the Cons. (formerly a private inst. supported by Gesellschaft der Musikfreunde) was taken over by the Government as a State institution.

BELGIUM.—There are 4 Royal Cons. which are State insts.: those of **Brussels,** (Dir. Léon Du Bois), **Ghent** (Dir. Martin Lunssens), **Liège** (Dir. Sylvain Dupuis), and **Antwerp** (Dir. Emil Wambach). This last bears the title of *Flemish Conservatoire (Vlaamsch koninglijk Conservatorium)*. The Brussels Cons. possesses a library of over 30,000 vols. and an instrumental museum of more than 3000 exhibits, of international importance. A large number of provincial towns (Bruges, Louvain, Mons, etc.), and of suburbs of large cities (St. Josse-den-Noode-Schaerbeek, St. Gilles, Ixelles, etc.), possess schools of music of which some have a very well-deserved reputation.

CANADA.—**Toronto:** (i) *Cons. of Music*, founded 1886 by late Dr. Henry Fisher. In 1919 the Cons. was acquired, by Act of Parliament, for the Univ. of Toronto, thus becoming in effect a State school of music. The Cons. grants 2 diplomas — Associateship and Licentiateship. The present Principal is Dr. A. S. Vogt and the Vice-principal is Dr. Healey Willan. (ii) *Toronto Coll. of Music*, founded 1888 by late Dr. Torrington. It was affiliated with the Univ. of Toronto. At founder's death in 1917, it was amalgamated with the Canadian Coll. of Music. (iii) *Canadian Coll. of Music*, founded 1911 under name of Columbian Cons. of Music. Amalgamated in 1917 with Toronto Coll of Music (see above). Grants 2 diplomas—Associate and Licentiate. Present Dir. F. S. Welsman. (iv) *Hambourg Cons. of Music*, founded 1911 by late Michael Hambourg. Present Directors, Jan and Boris Hambourg, the eminent players. **Montreal:** *The McGill Cons. of Music*, founded 1904. First mus. Dir. Dr. C. A. E. Harris, succeeded in 1908 by Dr. H. C. Perrin. It was generously endowed in 1917 by Sir William Macdonald. It gives degrees of Mus.Bac. and Mus.Doc. and also diploma of Licentiateship. **Hamilton:** *Cons. of Music*;

Principal, W. H. Hewlett; partly affiliated with Toronto Cons. **London (Canada):** *Inst. of Musical Art*; Principal, A. D. Jordan; partly affiliated with Toronto Cons. **Ottawa:** *The Canadian Cons. of Music*; Principal, H. Puddicombe. **Regina (Sask.):** *Coll. of Music*; Principal, F. G. Killmaster.

CZECHO-SLOVAKIA.—**Prague:** (i) *Prague Cons. of Music*, founded 1811 by Soc. for Cultivation of Music in Bohemia; supported by that Soc. until 1919; then taken over by new Republic of Czecho-Slovakia. Bears the stamp of a middle-school, on to which some advanced classes have been grafted. Directors during last 40 years : Anton Bennewitz (1881–1901); Antonín Dvořák (1901–4); Karel Knittl (1904–1907); Jindřich Kaàn de Albest (1907–18). Since then, it has elected its own dir. : Vítězslav Novák (1918–22); now Josef B. Foerster. The Administrative Principal, 1918–22, Fr. Spilka ; now Otakar Šín (*q.v.*). In 1922 there were 660 students. The Organ School was amalgamated with the Cons. in 1890. The Advanced School profs. include: J. B. Foerster, V. Novák, J. Suk, O. Ševčík, K. Hoffmann, K. Hofmeister, A. Mikěs, J. Burián, J. Klička. (ii) *German Acad. of Music and Descriptive Art*. The Prague Cons. of Music (founded 1811) was bi-lingual until 1918, when it was confiscated by the Czechs. The Germans founded the Acad. in 1920. It takes the status of a High School, although amalgamated with 3 *Meister-schulen*, to which are attached Conrad Ansorge, Henri Marteau and Alex. Zemlinsky, the last-named being Dir. from 1920. **Brno (Brünn):** *Cons.* founded 1919, after the political upheaval. Formed on the Organ School founded by Leoš Janaček, its first Dir. Taken over by State in 1921. Administrative Principal is Jan Kunc (*q.v.*). In 1923, it had 243 pupils.

DENMARK.—**Copenhagen:** *Royal Cons. of Music*; Dir. Otto V. Malling.

ENGLAND.—**London:** (i) *R. Acad. of Music*, founded 1822; Principal, John B. McEwen (from July, 1924); former Principals: Dr. Crotch, 1822–32; Cipriani Potter, 1832–59; C. Lucas, 1859–66; Sir W. Sterndale Bennett, 1866–75; Sir G. A. Macfarren, 1875–88; Sir Alexander Mackenzie, 1888–1924. (See special art. under R.) (ii) *R. Coll. of Music*, founded as National Training School, 1882; Royal Charter, 1853; R.C.M. Principals: Sir George Grove, 1883–94; Sir Hubert Parry, 1894–1918; Sir Hugh P. Allen from 1918. (See special art. under R.) (iii) *Guildhall School of Music*, founded 1880; Principals: Weist Hill, 1880–92; Sir J. Barnby, 1892–6; Dr. W. H. Cummings, 1896–1910; Sir Landon Ronald from 1910. (See special art. under G.) (iv) *Trinity Coll. of Music*, founded 1872; first Warden, Rev. H. G. Bonavia Hunt, Mus.Doc. ; present Chairman, Sir F. Bridge; Dir. of studies, Dr. C. W. Pearce; Dir. of examinations, Dr. E. F. Horner. (v) *Royal Coll. of Organists*, founded 1864; President (1924), Dr. Alan Gray. (See special art. under R.) **Manchester:** *Royal*

Manchester Coll. of Music, founded 3 Oct. 1893 ; first Principal, Sir Charles Hallé (till his death, 25 Oct. 1895); then Dr. Adolph Brodsky till present time. Royal Charter, 5 May, 1923. The Coll. is closely associated with Victoria Univ. (Owens Coll.), Manchester. **Birmingham:** *Birmingham and Midland Inst. School of Music,* founded 1854 ; present Director, Granville Bantock (from 1900). (See special article.) *FINLAND.*—**Helsingfors:** The mus. soc. *Helsingfors Musikförening* (founded 1882) opened in the autumn of same year a municipally subsidised Music Inst., a higher acad. of music. First Dir. was Martin Wegelius; after him, came Armas Järnefelt, 1906–7; Karl Ekman, 1907–11; Erkki Melartin, 1911–22; the present Dir. Armas Launis, from 1922. A large section of staff consisted originally of foreign teachers (best-known being Ferruccio Busoni); later, the staff was limited to native teachers. Nearly all the younger Finnish musicians have received their musical education at this Music Inst. Students, 49 in 1882, numbered in 1924, over 800. Regular concerts (chiefly chamber-music) are also given, and up to 1924 numbered over 500.

FRANCE.—**Paris:** (i) *Conservatoire national de Musique et de Déclamation.* For the history of its beginnings, consult Constantin Pierre's *Le Conservatoire national de Musique et de Déclamation* (Paris, 1910), and *Les anciennes Écoles de Déclamation dramatique* (*ib.* 1896). Housed from 1911 in an old school of expelled Jesuits, 14 rue de Madrid. Directors of recent years: Th. Dubois (1896–1905) ; Gabriel Fauré (1905–1920) ; Henri Rabaud (1920). On the staff (1924) are : Widor, Vidal (compn.) ; Gédalge, Caussade (cpt.) ; Chapuis, Dallier, etc. (harmony) ; E. Gigout (organ, voluntary) ; Lorrain, Engel, Hettich, Mlle. Grandjean, Guillamot (singing) ; H. Büsser (vocal ensemble) ; Chevillard, Capet, Tournemire (instr. ensemble) ; V. d'Indy (orch. class) ; Philipp, Cortot, etc. (pf.) ; Lefart, Rémy, Touche, etc. (vn.). (ii) *Schola Cantorum* (*q.v.*), founded by d'Indy in 1896. (iii) *École normale de Musique de Paris* (1919), dir. by A. Mangeot (founder and administrator), and the compr. R. Laparra ; complete curriculum of studies. (iv) *Cons. Rameau,* Dir. F. Delgrange. (v) *École supérieure de Musique et de Déclamation,* President, Ch. M. Widor. (vi) *École de Chant Choral,* an earlier foundation than (v) (Dir. H. Radigner), the mainspring of the *Association pour le développement du chant choral.* Its aim is to revive the tradition of serious popular artistic work and to make mus. education accessible to all. (vii) In addition to the 15 provincial branches of the Paris Cons. there are also in the departments and colonies of France, 22 National Schools, and 32 establishments called Municipal Cons., Municipal Schools, Free Schools, etc. (viii) *Conservatoire Américain,* founded in 1921 by Fragnaud and the compr. Francis Casadesus (*q.v.*). This school, called "des hautes Études musicales," has its abode in the palace of Fontainebleau, and is equipped for the reception of Amer. music-students. Managed by an Amer.

committee—on the board, among others, W. Damrosch—it has for Dir.-gen. of studies Ch. M. Widor and for technical dir. Max d'Ollone. It comprises classes in all subjects. Open each year from 25 June to 25 Sept. (ix) *École Niedermeyer,* founded in 1853 by Louis Niedermeyer (1802–61) under name of *École de Musique religieuse et classique* for training singers, orgts., orch. condrs. and comprs. by study of masters of xv, xvi, xvii centuries. Its founder intended it to continue the work of the *Institution royale de musique classique et religieuse* (created by Choron) which ceased in 1830. Among its students were Gabriel Fauré, Lecocq, André Messager, Eugène Gigout, Claude Terrasse, Henri Büsser, etc. Saint-Saëns was a prof. there. Its present Dir. is Henri Büsser (*q.v.*). Consult Gabriel Fauré, *Souvenirs* (*Revue Musicale,* Oct. 1922).

GERMANY.—**Berlin:** *Staatliche Akademische Hochschule für Musik* (Charlottenburg, Fasanen-Str. 1). Opened 1 Oct. 1869 under Joseph Joachim, primarily for vn. cello. pf.; now all subjects. Dir. Franz Schreker; Deputy-Dir. Dr. George Schünemann. Staff: L. Koch, P. Juon, R. Kahn, A. Moser, Hugo Becker, etc. (ii) *Sternsches Konservatorium der Musik* (Bernburger-Str. 11 and 22a, 23). Oldest Cons. in Berlin, founded 1850 by A. B. Marx, T. Kullak and Julius Stern; from 1857 conducted by Stern alone; Dir. (until 1915) G. Hollaender; now Alex. von Fielitz. Present staff includes R. M. Breithaupt, J. Kwast, W. Klatte, Max Schwarz, E. R. Mendelssohn, etc. (iii) *Klindworth-Scharwenka Konservatorium der Musik* (Genthiner-Str. 11). Founded 1881 by Scharwenka; amalgamated with Klindworth's school, 1893. Operatic and dramatic school attached; also a training-school for teachers. Dir. Robert Robitschek. Staff includes C. Ansorge, T. Lambrino, Hugo Leichtentritt, Erwin Lendvai, etc. (iv) By their dependence on the *Staatlichen Akademie der Kunste* (State Acad. of Arts), the following 2 insts. are connected with the *Akademische Hochschule* (Acad. High School): (a) The *Akademische Meisterschule* which gives further training in compn. It started in 1833. Present teachers, F. Busoni, Hans Pfitzner, Georg Schumann. (b) *Akademische Institut für Kirchenmusik;* since 1922 under name of *Akademie für deutsche Schul- und Kirchenmusik* (Acad. for Ger. School-and Church-music). Founded by Carl Zelter, a friend of Goethe. Carl Thiel succeeded Kretschmar as Dir. in 1922. Staff includes Max Seiffert, and Joh. Wolf. **Carlsruhe:** *Konservatorium,* founded 1884 by H. Ordenstein. Dir. from 1921, H. K. Schmidt. **Dresden:** *Konservatorium,* founded 1856. **Frankfort:** *Dr. Hoch'sche Konservatorium,* founded 1878 under Joachim Raff; raised to great esteem under dir. of Ivan Knorr (1908–16). Present Dir. Waldemar von Baussnern. **Hamburg:** *Konservatorium,* founded 1873 by Julius von Bernuth. Present Dir. R. Barth. **Leipzig:** *Konservatorium und Hochschule der Musik,* founded by Mendelssohn, 1843; from 1887 in Grassi-Str. Has numbered amongst its former teachers, Robert Schumann, Ferd. David,

M. Hauptmann, F. Hiller, N. W. Gade, I. Moscheles, H. Kretschmar, Max Reger. High school, 4 divs.; finishing classes (*Ausbildungsklassen*), 5 divs.; opera-school; church music institute. Present Dir. Stephan Krehl. Councillors: P. Graener, O. Lohse, K. Straube, R. Teichmüller. Consult *Festschrift* of 75th anniversary (Leipzig, 1918). **Munich:** *Akademie der Tonkunst.* State inst. (as is also the one at Würzburg), founded 1846 by Franz Hauser; reorganised by Hans von Bülow. Specially noted under dir. of Joseph Rheinberger and Felix Mottl. Present Dir. Siegmund von Hausegger. **Stuttgart:** *Konservatorium* (now Hochschule für Musik), founded 1856 by L. Stark, Lebert, Faisst; (*a*) Künstlerschule (Artists' School), (*b*) Dilettanten-Schule (amateurs). Dir. Max Pauer (from 1908). **Weimar:** *Konservatorium.* Dir. from 1872, Bruno Hinze-Reinhold. **Breslau:** *Institut für Kirchenmusik.* **Regensburg (Ratisbon):** The famous *Kirchenmusikschule*, founded by Father X. Haberl. In 1910 Carl Weinmann succeeded him as director.

HOLLAND.—**Amsterdam:** *Cons.* Dir. Julius Röntgen from 1913. **Rotterdam:** *Cons.* Dir. Woulter Huytschenruyter from 1917. **The Hague:** *R. Cons.* Dir. Johan Wagenaar from 1918. **Utrecht:** *Cons. of Music.*

HUNGARY. — **Budapest:** *Magyar királyi zenemüvészeti föiskola* (Hungarian R. High School) (Liszt Ferenc-tér, 12). Until 1919 called R. Hungarian State Acad. for Music (*Országos magyar királyi zeneakadémia*). Educational institution supported by the State. Founded 1875. Originally only 2 subjects were taught—pf. and compn. Now instruction is given in all subjects. Special tuition in cimbalom-playing (see HUNGARIAN MUS. INSTRUMENTS). First President was Franz Liszt, who up to his death gave pf.-lessons several months a year. Among its first professors was Robert Volkmann (compn.) until his death in 1883; then David Popper (cello), 1886–1913. First Dir. Franz Erkel (*q.v.*) until 1887; acted as pf. prof. until 1889. From 1887–1919 the Dir. was Ödön Mihalovich (*q.v.*); 1919–20 Ernst von Dohnányi. Present Dir. (since 1920) Eugen Hubay, (vn. prof. there from 1886). Present staff includes: Béla Bartók (pf.); Zoltán Kodály, Hans Koessler, Leo Weiner (compn.); Nándor Zsolt (vn.).

IRELAND.—**Dublin:** *R. Irish Acad. of Music.* In 1856 a committee was formed, and was substantially assisted by the Marquis of Downshire. In 1870, the British Govt. (under Gladstone) voted it an annual grant of £150, later increased to £300. There is apparently no Director. Signor Esposito has been head of the pf. section for over 40 years. The chief vn. profs. in the past have been Papini, Adolf Wilhelmj, Achille Simonetti. The present one is Joshua F. Watson. Chief singing prof. Adelio Viani; prof. of harmony, etc. Dr. J. F. Larchet.

ITALY.—**Rome:** (i) *Santa Cecilia* (*Regio Liceo Musicale di*). One of foremost teaching insts. in the world. Founded 1876 by the Acad. of same name, on which it depended for some time for support. Royal charter 1919, becoming directly dependent on State for support. Has a dramatic school attached. Situate in Via dei Greci. Dir. Marco Enrico Bossi till Nov. 1923, when Ottorino Respighi was appointed (ii) *Pontificia Scuola Superiore di Musica Sacra*, instituted by desire of Pope Pius X in 1910; opened Jan. 1911; officially sanctioned by Papal mandate in same year; proclaimed "Pontifical" 1914. The Dir., from its foundation until his death, was Padre Angelo De Santi (*q.v.*). Gives instruction in all subjects of music, but with special regard to sacred music and the organ, vocal polyphony, and Gregorian chant. Located in Piazza di Sant' Agostino; has a fine hall and an excellent organ. **Bologna:** (i) *Accademia Filarmonica di Bologna*, founded 1666; gives diplomas (Mozart won one), as well as tuition. Present President, Guglielmo Zuelli. (ii) *Liceo Musicale Gioacchino Rossini.* Belongs to municipality. Founded in 1804 by Padre Stanislao Mattei. Possesses a library of very interesting old music (see printed catalogue, 2 vols., publ. by Gaspari, formerly dir. of library); has a rich gallery of pictures of musicians, chiefly from collections of the famous Bolognese musician, Father Giambattista Martini. **Florence:** *Istituto Musicale Cherubini* (*Regio*). One of the 6 govt. insts. for teaching music. Its origin dates from 1814; but its real foundation took place in 1860. Possesses a rich library of old music. There is attached to it a school of acting and an Acad., which publishes monographs, and takes other steps for spread of mus. culture. **Milan:** (i) *Conservatorio di Musica* (*Regio*) *Giuseppe Verdi.* One of most renowned in Italy; founded by Napoleon I; inaugurated 1808. Possesses a rich library. Located in Via Giuseppe Verdi; has a beautiful concert-hall, the best in Milan. Present Dir. Ildebrando Pizzetti. (ii) *Scuola Municipale di Musica.* This school is divided into two branches: one for wind instrs. (males); the other for choral singing (mixed). The head of singing section is Filippo Brunetto; of wind section, Pio Nevi. Located at Castello Sforzesco. **Naples:** *Conservatorio di Musica* (*Regio*) *San Pietro a Maiella.* The oldest Ital. Cons., and the richest in glorious traditions. Possesses a valuable library. Present Dir. Francesco Cilea. **Palermo:** *Conservatorio di Musica* (*Regio*) *Vincenzo Bellini*, founded in XVII century. One of 6 present Ital. State Cons. Its last Dir., Guido A. Fano, was succeeded in 1923 by Giuseppe Mulè. **Parma:** *Conservatorio di Musica* (*Regio*) *Arrigo Boito*, founded 1888, on traditions of ancient *Regio Scuola di Musica Parmense.* Now an important school again, under dir. of Guglielmo Zuelli. Possesses a rich library. **Pesaro:** *Liceo Musicale Rossini.* Owes its foundation to a legacy and testamentary disposition of Rossini, who wished to pay a lasting tribute to his native town. Started its activity in 1882, Carlo Pedrotti being its first Dir. It flourished especially under Pietro Mascagni. Its present Dir. is Amilcare Zanella. **Turin:** *Scuola Municipale di Canto Corale*, founded and dir. in 1864 by Eugenio Tancioni, under title of *Scuola Sperimentale di Canto*. When, in 1867, the Liceo Musicale was instituted, this school was incorporated with it, and until 1905 continued its activity uninterruptedly, having as Directors after Tancioni: Filippo Angeleri, Maurizio Sciorati, Alessandro Moreschi, Oreste Pasquarelli, Delfino Thermignon, Faustino Del Marchi. After a short interruption from 1905 to 1914, it was reconstituted, and the direction was entrusted to Vittore Veneziani and then to Ettore Cordone and Giorgio Federico Ghedini. From 1921 to 1924 the direction was resumed by Delfino Thermignon. He was followed in 1924 by Franco Alfano. **Venice:** *Liceo Musicale Benedetto Marcello.* Supported by the municipality. Founded in 1878, under auspices of Concert Soc. of same name, still in existence. Present Dir. Mezio Agostini.

LATVIA.—**Riga:** *State Cons.* Dir. Jozefs Vitols.

LITHUANIA. — **Kaunas (Kovno):** *State School of Music;* Dir. J. Naujalis. (See LITHUANIAN MUSIC.)

NORWAY.—**Christiania:** *Cons. of Music,* founded 1883 by Peter Lindeman and L. M. Lindeman. Number of students, between 800 and 900. Receives from State and Municipality grants amounting together to Kr. 5000. **Bergen:** *Acad. of Music,* founded in 1905 by Torgrim Castberg with the support of Frithjof Sundt. Number of students, between 300 and 400. Receives from State and Municipality grants amounting together to Kr. 2500.

POLAND.—**Warsaw:** *Cons.* founded 1821 by Elsner; closed 1830; re-opened 1861 under Apoll. de Kontski; Dir. 1904, E. Młynarski; 1911, S. Barcewicz; 1919, Młynarski again; 1922, H. Melcer-Sczawinski. **Cracow:** *Cons.* founded 1888; Dir. Władysław Żeleński (*d.* 1921): **Lwów (Lemberg):** *Music School of the Galician Music Society;* Dir. K. Mikuli, 1858–98; Mieczysław Sołtys from 1899. **Posen:** *State Cons.* Dir. H. Opieński.

PORTUGAL.—**Lisbon:** *Conservatorio Real,* founded 1833 with Bontempo as Dir.; now under Guilhelme Cossoul.

RUMANIA.—**Bucharest:** *Cons. of Music.* Dir. from 1918, J. Norma Otescu. **Cluj** (formerly **Klausenburg**): Cons. founded by Governing Council of Transylvania in 1919; Dir. G. Dima (*q.v.*). **Jassy:** Cons. founded in 1836; State inst. since 1860. Suppressed by budget of 1876; but reorganised same year. Amongst its Directors have been Ed. Caudella (1892–1901) and G. Muzicescu (1901–3), both zealous propagandists of Rumanian music and comprs. of choruses and songs.

RUSSIA.—**Petrograd:** *Imperial Cons.* (now *State Cons.*), founded in 1862 by the Imperial Russ. Soc.; 1st Dir. Anton Rubinstein, 1862–7; Zaremba, 1867–71; Asantschevsky, 1871–6; K. Davidof, 1876–86; then again A. Rubinstein, 1887–91; Johannsen, 1891–6; A. Bernhardt, 1896; Alex. Glazunof from 1909. The

staff has included Auer (vn.), Essipof (pf.), Liadof (compn.). About 75 teachers, 870 students. **Moscow:** (i) *Imperial Cons.* (now *State Cons.*), founded by Nicolas Rubinstein 1866, its first Dir. (until 1881); Huberti, 1881–3; K. Albrecht, 1883–5; Tanéief, 1885–9; Safonof, 1889; Ippolitof-Ivanof from 1906. 40 teachers, 526 students. (iii) *Philharmonic Society's Music School,* founded by P. Schostakowski in 1878; had same official recognition as the Imperial Cons. Its Directors were: P. Schostakowski, 1883–96; S. Kruglikof, 1898–1901; W. Kes, 1901; Brandukof. 30 teachers, 482 students. In the **Russ. provinces** there are Cons. at Astrakan, Kirschnief, Kief, Nicolaief, Odessa, Kostof, Saratof, Tambof, Tiflis, Charkof.

SCOTLAND.—**Edinburgh:** *Univ. School of Music.* Originated with Reid Chair, founded and endowed by the late General Reid, an XVIII century amateur and flautist. Chair founded 1839. Treated as a sinecure for many years, and bulk of endowments diverted into other channels. Prof. Donaldson, who built the Music Class Room on scientific acoustical principles, took the University Court to law and recovered the misapplied endowments. Faculty greatly extended under *régime* of Prof. Niecks, and more so under Prof. Tovey, who succeeded the former as Reid Professor in 1914. Now fully equipped school for higher instruction in music. Former professors included Sir Henry R. Bishop and Sir Herbert Oakeley. **Glasgow:** *Athenæum (Incorporated) School of Music.* Establ. 1890. (See special article under G.)

SERBIA.—**Belgrade:** *Serbian State School of Music;* Dir. Joram Zorka, violinist, from 1920.

SOUTH AFRICA. — **Cape Town:** *South African College of Music,* founded 1909; govt. grant of £1000 per annum from 1911. Principal, W. H. Bell, F.R.A.M. Staff of 25 teachers; 600 students.

SPAIN.—**Madrid:** *Conservatorio de Música y Declamación (Real).* Official school of music, created by Royal decree, 15 July, 1830, on the initiative of Maria Cristina, the Ital.-born fourth wife of Ferdinand VII. Modelled on similar establishments in Italy, its 1st Dir. being the Ital. singer Francesco Piermarini. Its original name was *Conservatorio de Maria Cristina,* and has been called afterwards, at different periods (a school for acting being attached to it), *Escuela Nacional de Música y Declamación* and *Real Conservatorio de Música y Declamación.*

SWEDEN.—**Stockholm:** (i) *R. Cons. of Music;* Dir. Bror Beckman. (ii) *Richard Andersson's Music School;* Dir. Iven Lizell. (iii) *Stockholm Musikinstitut;* Dir. Sigrid Carlheim. **Malmö:** *Cons. of Music* (private), founded by Giovanni Tronchi, subsidised by the city, from 1909. **Lund:** *Sydsvenska Musikkonservatoriat.*

SWITZERLAND.—**Zurich:** *Konservatorium für Musik,* founded 1876; Dir. F. Hegar (1876–1914); 1894–1914, jointly with C. Attenhofer; from 1914, Volkmar Andreae; from 1919, jointly with C. Vogler. (*a*) Dilettantenschüle. (*b*) Berufsschule: (i) teachers, (ii) concert and orch.

players, (iii) opera-school. **Basle:** *Conservatoire,*
founded 1867; Dir. Selmar Bagge, 1867–96;
Hans Huber, 1896–1918; H. Suter, 1918–21;
now Willy Rehberg. In 1922, there were 58
teachers and 1363 pupils.
UNITED STATES OF AMERICA.—There
is as yet no official national school of music in
America, and no independent Cons. subsidised by
a national or State government. The nearest
approach to such an inst. may be found in some
of the State univs., like the Univ. of Michigan at
Ann Arbor, or the Univ. of Wisconsin at Madison,
which have a more or less completely organised
Cons. or school of music attached to the Univ.,
either as a separate branch of the Univ. complex
or as a department of the school of arts. A number of the larger univs. which are not State insts.,
like Harvard, Yale and Columbia, or Vassar,
Wellesley and Smith Colls., have music departments or schools of music in which, however, the
training in the practical or performing side of
the art is less emphasised than the theoretical
side and the teaching of musical compn., and
the more general training in the appreciation of
music. Still, other univs. and colls. have highly
developed mus. cons. like that of Oberlin Coll.
in Oberlin, Ohio, or the Music School of Northwestern Univ. at Evanston, Illinois. In some of
these cases, the higher instructors of the cons.
have full academic standing as professors, in
the faculty of Arts. The following are some of
the more important independent Cons. in the
U.S.A. **New York:** (i) *Inst. of Mus. Art,*
planned in 1904 by Frank Damrosch on the
basis of an initial endowment of $500,000
by James Loeb, with later additions. Opened in
1905. Present Dir. Frank Damrosch with a
faculty including Franz Kneisel, Percy Goetschius and other instructors of high repute. Its
financial independence enables it to be rigid in
its requirements for admission and graduation.
(ii) *David Mannes Music School,* cond. since 1916
by David and Clara (Damrosch) Mannes. (iii)
Metropolitan Cons. of Music, establ. 1886 by
Charles B. Hawley and Herbert W. Greene. In
1891 it was incorporated as the Metropolitan
Coll. of Music. In 1900 reorganised as the *Amer.
Inst. of Applied Music.* (iv) *National Cons. of
Music of America,* founded by Mrs. Jeanette
Thurber in 1885. Among the Directors were
Jacques Bouhy, Antonín Dvořák, Emil Paur, and
W. Safonof. (v) *Amer. Inst. of Applied Music,*
incorporated 1900. Dean, Kate S. Chitten-
den (1900). (vi) *New York Coll. of Music,*
founded 1878. Dir. Alexander Lambert, 1887–
1905, succeeded by Carl Hein and August
Fraemeke. **Baltimore:** *Peabody Cons.,* opened
1868. Dir.: Lucien H. Southard, 1868–71;
Harold Randolph, 1898. **Boston:** *New England
Cons. of Music,* establ. 1867 by Eben Tourkee.
Dir. Carl Faelten, 1891–97; George W. Chadwick, 1897. Wallace Goodrich is now Dean
of the Faculty. In 1902 the Cons. occupied the
present building. It contains a large auditorium
called Jordan Hall after the donor, Eben D.
Jordan, benefactor (at one time President of

Cons.). The total registration since its foundation is over 100,000. The faculty includes over
75 members. **Chicago:** (i) *Amer. Cons. of Music,*
organised 1886, incorporated 1887. Founder,
John J. Hattstaedt. Three present Directors
are John J. Hattstaedt, Karlton Hackett and
Adolf Weidig. (ii) *Cons. of Dramatic and Mus.
Art,* founded 1885 by Samuel Kayzer (1885–
1907). Present President, Walter Perkins, 1907.
(iii) *Mus. Coll.* founded 1867 by Florenz
Ziegfeld, incorporated 1877. President, Ziegfeld,
1867–1905–1906; present President, Borowski;
Vice-president, Carl D. Kinsey, 1905. **Cin-
cinnati:** (i) *Cons. of Music,* started 1867 by Clara
Baur, in charge 1867–1912, succeeded by her
niece Bertha Baur, 1912. (ii) *Coll. of Music,*
founded 1878. Endowed by Reuben R. Springer.
Dir. Theodore Thomas, 1878–80; George Ward
Nichols 1880–5; Peter Rudolph Neff, 1885–94;
Frank Van der Stucken, 1894–9; Arnold J.
Gantvoort, 1899–1920.—E.-H.

ACHTÉ, Irma. See TERVANI.

ACKTÉ, Aino. Finnish operatic singer; *b.*
Helsingfors, 23 April, 1876. Stud. under her
mother, the opera-singer Emmy Strömer-Achté,
and at Paris Cons. 1894–97. Engaged at Grand
Opéra, Paris, 1897–1904, where she proved herself to be an artist of the highest rank in many
rôles, notably as Marguerite in Gounod's *Faust.*
She appeared at Metropolitan Opera, New York,
1904–6, and went with the company on tours
throughout U.S.A. Up to 1913, undertook
extensive opera and concert tours in Europe
(Gewandhaus Concerts, Leipzig; Colonne and
Cons. Concerts, Paris; Queen's Hall, London).
Engaged 3 times at Covent Garden, London.
In Finland, she has perf. much as operatic and
concert-singer, and is one of most enthusiastic
promoters of Finnish opera (*q.v.*). In 1911 she
organised the annual Finnish Opera Fests. in
Savonlinna (Nyslott). 1901, married the senator
Dr. Heikki Renvall, and 1919 the minister
B. Jalander. Lives in Helsingfors.—T. H.

ADAJEWSKI, Ella von (real name, Schultz).
Russian compr. *b.* Petrograd, 10 Feb. 1846. Pf.
pupil of Henselt; after several years' concert-
touring, became (1862–6) pupil of Rubinstein, Zaremba, Dreyschock and Famintsin at
Petrograd Cons. Paid special attention to peculiarities of old Greek music. In 1882 she went
to Italy, collected national songs (among others
waltz songs of the Resianer (Rhætians) in 5-4
time); resided a long time in Venice; living
since 1909 in Germany at Neuwied on the Rhine.
Wrote several arts. on folk-music in *Rivista Musicale Italiana* (XVI, 143, 311; XVIII, 137; *La
Berceuse Populaire,* I, 240; II, 420; IV, 484; *Les
Chants de l' Église Grecque Orientale,* VIII, 43, 579).

Unacc. choruses for Russian Church; 1-act opera;
songs and duets; Greek Sonata, pf. and clar. (1880;
Tischer & Jagenberg, 1913); 4-act Russian folk-
opera, *The Dawn of Liberty* (1881); pf. pieces; vocal
chamber-music, etc.—A. E.

ADAMS, John. British t. singer; *b.* Paisley.
Stud. under Victor Beigel, London, and in
Munich. Sang in César Franck's *Beatitudes* with

Bach Choir, London, in 1912, and has sung often with them in *St. Matthew Passion, St. John Passion, Mass in B mi.*, etc. A fest. singer of serious aims.—E.-H.

ADAMS, Suzanne. Operatic s. singer; *b.* of Irish-Amer. parents in America. Stud. under Jacques Bouhy, Paris; *début* there as Juliette; principal oratorios and concerts in England; opera in America. Appeared at Covent Garden annually from 1899 to 1906; has lived in London since 1903; favourite rôles: Juliette, Marguerite, Euridice, Gilda, Micaela, Zerlina, Cherubino, Donna Elvira. Married the late Leo Stern, well-known cellist.—E.-H.

ADAMUS, Henryk (*phon.* Ahdahmoos). Polish cellist, compr. *b.* 19 Feb. 1880. Stud. Warsaw Cons.; then Leipzig under Krehl and Klengel. Was solo-player of Warsaw Philh. and Opera orch.; then manager of Mus. Soc. at Kalisz. Lately dir. of opera-chorus at Warsaw. His works give evidence of melodious skill and technical knowledge of modern style.

2 operas (perf. Warsaw): *Sumienie* (*The Conscience*) 1918; *Rey w Babinie* (comic opera about the first Polish poet), 1922; 2 symph. poems; *Solemn Overture*; some short instr. pieces.—ZD. J.

ADJUDICATORS. The British Federation of Musical Competition Festivals gives the following list of adjudicators: A. T. Akeroyd, Sir Hugh Allen, Sir Ivor Atkins, Frederic Austin, E. L. Bainton, Dr. E. C. Bairstow, Prof. Granville Bantock, F. H. Bisset, Acton Bond, Dr. Adrian Boult, Dr. A. H. Brewer, A. Collingwood, F. Corder, Dr. Henry Coward, Dr. Harold Darke, Sir Walford Davies, Frederick Dawson, T. F. Dunhill, Rev. Dr. E. Fellowes, Ernest Fowles, Harvey Grace, H. Plunket Greene, Madame Edith Hands, Julius Harrison, Hamilton Harty, Gustav Holst, Dr. A. Eaglefield - Hull, Granville Humphreys, Dr. T. Keighley, Miss Editha Knocker, Dr. E. Markham Lee, Dr. James Lyon, Dr. Charles Macpherson, Mrs. Tobias Matthay, Robert McLeod, Walter Nesbitt, Ernest Newman, J. Weston Nicholl, S. H. Nicholson, Dr. C. Palmer, Madame Denne Parker, Dan Price, W. H. Reed, H. S. Roberton, Dr. Caradog Roberts, E. Stanley Roper, Harold Samuel, Dr. Malcolm Sargent, C. Kennedy Scott, Cecil Sharp, Geoffrey Shaw, Dr. A. Somervell, W. Wooding Starmer, David Stephen, Felix Swinstead, Sir R. R. Terry, Dr. Vaughan Thomas, Dr. F. W. Wadely, Dr. W. G. Whittaker, Dr. Vaughan Williams, Dr. R. H. Wilson, Steuart Wilson, Dr. F. H. Wood.—G. B.

ADLER, Agnes Charlotte Dagmar (*née* Hansen). Danish pianist; *b.* Copenhagen, 19 Feb. 1865. Sister of Robert Hansen; pupil of Edmund Neupert and of R. Cons. of Music, Copenhagen. At 17, made her *début* under Niels W. Gade at Musikforening (Music Soc.), Copenhagen. Has toured extensively in Scandinavia, but only occasionally abroad.—A. H.

ADLER, Guido. Austrian musical historian; *b.* Eibenschütz (Moravia), Nov. 1855. Prof. of history of music at Vienna Univ. Leader and founder of Univ. Musikhistorisches Inst. Pupil of Anton

Bruckner. Founded (with Felix Mottl and Hugo Wolf) the Akademische Wagnerverein (Academical Wagner Soc.). LL.D. 1878; Ph.D. 1880. In 1885, prof. of history of music at Prague; 1898 at Vienna. To promote musico-historical study in Austria, he began to publ. important works from the XIV century to the classics, in *D.T.Ö.* Organised historical department and wrote catalogue for the Exhibition for Music and Theatre, Vienna, 1892; in 1909, for the Haydn Fest. and for Congress of Mus. History. Founded a new method of historical musical research.

Richard Wagner (1st critical biography and analysis of his works) (1904, Breitkopf; Fr. transl. by Laloy); *Der Stil in der Musik* (*Style in Music*) (1912, Breitkopf); *Methode der Musikgeschichte* (*Method in Mus. History*) (1919). Many vols. of the *D.T.Ö.* with valuable introductions.—EG. W.

AEROPHOR. A new appliance for enabling a wind-instr. player to sustain his notes *ad infinitum*; invented by Bernard Samuels, flautist in the orch. of the Grand Duke of Mecklenburg-Schwerin. The apparatus consists of a small bellows worked by one foot, with rubber tubing attached, terminating in a small metal reed fixed near the mouthpiece of the instr. played. The air from the player's lungs is prevented from passing into the bellows by a stop-cock in the tubing. First used in Richard Strauss's *Festliches Präludium*, written for the opening of the Concert House in Vienna, 19 Oct. 1913; used again in his *Alpine Symphony*.—E.-H.

AFANASSIEF, Nicholas (*accent 3rd syll.*). Russ. compr. *b.* Tobolsk, 1821; *d.* Petrograd, 22 May/ 3 June, 1898. After working for many years as a violinist and teacher, he devoted himself to compn.; in 1860 his str. 4tet *Volga* took 1st prize at competition organised by Russ. Mus. Soc. Wrote a quantity of chamber - music, several operas, 2 oratorios, a symphony, and other works, none of which has survived.—M.D.C.

AFFERNI, Ugo. Ital. pianist and condr. *b.* Florence, 1 Jan. 1871. Completed his studies in Florence; went to Germany; occupied important posts at Annaberg, Harzburg, Wiesbaden and other towns; organised concerts of chamber-music with his wife, the Eng. violinist, Mary Brammer. At the beginning of the 1914–1918 war he returned to Italy.—D. A.

AGENTEN-VERTRÄGE. Ger. contract-forms supplied by the agent to a singer, giving him (or her) particulars of a vacancy and an introduction to the dir. of an opera. The agent fills in the possible salary tentatively. The singer then signs the form and returns it to the agent. As a contract is worth nothing at all, until signed by the dir. of the opera-house concerned. Even then it is not valid until singer has sung, at the opera house concerned, as many trial performances as the contract calls for.—E.-H.

AGNEW, Roy E. Australian compr. *b.* Sydney, 1894.

Poem, orch. and voice; 7 pf. sonatas; 18 preludes, pf.; *Poema Tragico*; *Dance of the Wild Men*, for pf —E.-H.

AGOSTINI, Mezio. Ital. compr. and pianist; *b.* Fano, 12 Aug. 1875. Pupil of Liceo at Pesaro;

1900, teacher in same. Since 1909, dir. of Liceo Mus. Benedetto Marcello, Venice. Has given concerts as pianist and condr. Is author of various dramatic works (unpubl.) and chamber-music, pf. and other instruments.—D. A.

AGUIRRE, Julián. Argentine pianist and compr. b. Buenos Ayres, 1869. As boy, stud. at R. Cons. Madrid, under Karl Beck (pf.) and Emilio Arrieto (harmony). Returning to Argentina, was appointed secretary and prof. in Buenos Ayres Cons. upon its foundation. Was a founder-member of Music Section of the Ateneo and of National Committee of Fine Arts. His early pieces, the Barcarola, Idilio and Rapsodia española, show Span. influence. His later works are in two styles; Aires criollos, Aires populares, Tristes argentinos and Aires nacionales being purely Argentine: his Loin, Romanza, 5 Mazurkas and Las Intimas follow the Fr. school. Also publ. sonata (vn. and pf.), Ballad and Nocturne (vn.) and sonata (cello and pf.).—A. M.

AHNGER, Alexander. Finnish singer; b. Kuopio, 15 May, 1859. Stud. Helsingfors Music Inst., Dresden and Paris. Since 1906 teacher at Music Inst. Has appeared as concert, opera and oratorio-singer.—T. II.

AITKEN, George. Eng. pianist, compr. b. London. Stud. R.A.M.; prof. Guildhall School of Music; orgt. and choirmaster Hampstead parish ch. from 1895.

Pf. pieces: songs; church music (Augener; Ashdown; Boosey; Chappell; Elkin; Ricordi; Schott); book, Tobias Matthay and his Teachings (Field Press).—E.-H.

AKIMENKO, Feodor Stepanovitch (accent 2nd syll.). Russ. compr. b Kharkof, 8/20 Feb. 1876. Began his mus. education in Court Chapel School, Petrograd, under Balakiref, and continued it at Petrograd Cons. (1896–1901), where his compn. teacher was Rimsky-Korsakof. After a period at Tiflis as dir. of Music School, he was for a time principal of a music school at Nice (France), lived some time in Paris, and later was teacher of theory of Kharkof section of Imperial Russ. Mus. Soc.; then prof. at Petrograd Cons., a post he now holds.

His works are many, and consist chiefly of pieces for pf., pf. and vn., pf. and cello, songs; for orch. a Lyric Poem and a Russian Fantasy; his chamber-music comprises 2 sonatas (vn. and pf. and cello and pf.), a str. 4tet and a str. trio. Among his pf. pieces, the suite Uranie and the sets Récits d'une Ame rêveuse and Pages de Poésie fantasque are particularly characteristic of his favourite moods of poetic reverie and of his mus. style, which is quiet as a rule, but often very free and subtle, showing at times in its details, the influence of Scriabin. He has also written an opera, The Snow Queen (poem by M. D. Calvocoressi), and a ballet (both unpubl.), both of fantastic character. Publ. Belaief and Jurgenson.—M. D. C.

ALABARDEROS (Banda del Real Cuerpo de). Military band of the Real Cuerpo de Alabarderos (R. Corps of Halberdiers), the King of Spain's bodyguard, doing service only within the royal palace. During reign of Isabel II it consisted of 24 players. In 1875, on advent of Alfonso XII, after restoration of monarchy, the band was reorganised and increased to 40. Nearly all the soloists of the classical concert orchs. and the professors of wind-instrs. at Real Cons. de Música are amongst its members, forming one of most remarkable ensembles of its kind in Europe.—P. G. M.

ALALEONA, Domenico. Ital. compr. b. Montegiorgio (Piceno), 16 Nov. 1881. After having completed his first mus. activities as church orgt., and taking part in the band in his native place, he studied at the R. Liceo Mus. di Santa Cecilia, Rome (compn. under De Sanctis; pf. under Bustini and Sgambati; organ under Renzi). He has gained a place amongst modern Ital. musicians, as one of most national and most original composers. His productions can be divided into three groups: the first recalls the open air and distant places, the simple and frank people of his native place. To this group belong the Albe, the Melodie Pascoliane (on the poetry of that exquisite modern Italian poet, Giovanni Pascoli), and also the opera, Mirra, in which the profound and ingenuous sense of the myth, and the accents of potent but delicate passion, well out from the spirit of an author born and bred in a healthy, uncontaminated country atmosphere. To the second, which one might call the "city-group," belong, e.g., the collection of Stigmata for pf., styled La Città fiorita. There palpitates the nostalgia of one who, amidst the narrow life of cities and the tumult of machines, keeps alive and eager the memory of the pure, free and boundless air of the fields. The third group includes the collections of Canzoni italiane and Laudi italiane, for orch., str. 4tet and pf., in which, by reviving the songs of his people and identifying his spirit with the purest expressions in the Ital. musical heritage of the Golden Age, he has tried to reconstruct a basis for the symphony and for modern instrumental music, which should be genuinely Italian.

A. has also devoted his energies to conducting, both at theatre and concerts (Augusteo), and as dir. of choral societies (Choral Soc. Guido Monaco of Leghorn), giving special attention to propaganda of Ital. music, and the revival of the glorious heritage of the Ital. vocal symphony. We also owe to him some important studies of Ital. mus. history. His book on The Musical Oratorio in Italy, which contains much new and valuable research, was the thesis for his University degree.

To this national characteristic, he adds an absolutely modern and progressive spirit; the two articles New Horizons of Musical Technique and Modern Harmony (in Rivista Musicale Italiana, 1911) are amongst most daring precursory manifestations of their kind. A lecturer, writer, teacher of history and æsthetics of music at R. Liceo Mus. di Santa Cecilia, and mus. critic to daily newspaper Il Mondo, A. is one of most representative and combative modern Italian musicians.

Dr. Alaleona is responsible for most of the Italian articles in this Dictionary.

Compns.: *Mirra*, melodrama in 2 acts and an Intermezzo (on 2nd part of tragedy of that name by Vittorio Alfieri), 1st perf. Rome at Costanzi Theatre, 31 March, 1920, with success (Ricordi); *Albe*, 6 songs, v. and pf. (Rome, De Santis ed.) ; *Melodie Pascoliane*, v. and pf. (18 songs, divided into various sets, *Creature, Marine, Canti di neve e di primavera, Brividi, Meteore*) (Ricordi); *Canti di Maggio*, 6 songs, v. and pf. (*id.*); *La Città Fiorita*, 5 *Impronte* (*Stigmata*), pf. (*id.*); 2 *Canzoni italiane*, str., harp, celeste and tpi.; 4 *Canzoni italiane*, str. harp and some wind; 4 *Laudi italiane*, str. fl. and brass; 6 *Canzoni italiane*, str. 4tet; *Canto dell' amore, Il Tramonto*, 4-v. male choruses (all Ricordi).

Writings: *Studi su la storia dell oratorio musicale in Italia* (Turin, 1908, Bocca); *Le Laudi spirituali italiane nei secoli XVI e XVII, e il loro rapporto coi canti profani* (*Rivista Musicale Italiana*, 1909, No. 1); *I nuovi orizzonti della tecnica musicale* (*id.* 1911, No. 2); *L'Armonia modernissima : le tonalità neutre e l'arte di stupore* (*id.* 1911, No. 4); *Linguaggio materno e umanità musicale* (review *Harmonia*, Rome, 1914, No. 4); *Il libro d' oro del musicista*, physical, historical and æsthetic fundamentals of the art, 3rd ed. (Edizioni musicali Palestrina, Rome, 1923); *Educazione musicale del popolo e sua organizzazione nella scuola e nella vita cittadina*, lecture at Mus. Congress, Turin, Oct., 1921, publ. in Congress Records (Turin, Bocca).

Consult sketch of Alaleona (Milan review, *L'Eroica*, 1920, Nos. 8–10). Also: T. Ferriozzi, *Un' musicista d' avanguardia : D. A.* (review *Picenum*, 1921, No. 4); G. M. Gatti, in *Mus. Times*, London, Dec. 1921; E. G. Rovira, *La Mirra di D. A. nella sua spiritualità musicale* (*Musica* publ. house, Rome, 1920). R. De Angelis, *La Mirra di D. A. nei giudizi della stampa romana* (*Rassegna Italiana*, Rome, 1920); A. Eaglefield Hull, *Alaleona's New Theory of Harmony* (*Monthly Mus. Record*, London, Aug. 1922); and *The Pentaphonic Mode* (*id.* Sept. 1922).—R. F.

ALBANESI, Carlo. Ital. pianist, compr. *b.* Naples, 22 Oct. 1858. Recitals in Italy and in Paris; settled in London in 1882; gave recitals till 1893, in which year, was made prof. at R.A.M. Is Knight of the Crown of Italy; had many distinguished pupils amongst royalty. Has composed in many forms.

Orch. works; str. 4tet; pf. trio; 6 pf. sonatas (Ricordi); songs (*id.*).—E.-H.

ALBANI, Emma (Marie Cécile Emma Lajeunesse). Operatic and concert s. singer; *b.* Chambly, near Montreal, Canada, Nov. 1852. 1st s. at St. Joseph's Catholic Ch., Albany, New York, 1866. Subsequently became orgt. and choir-trainer there. Then stud. under Duprez in Paris and later under Lamperti in Milan. *Début* in Messina, Sicily (1869), in *La Sonnambula*. First sang in London at Covent Garden Theatre, May 1872. Since then in all European countries, America and the Colonies. Sang in oratorio at all the great Eng. fests. Decorated by Queen Victoria, King Edward VII, German Emperor, King of Denmark. Gold medal, Eng. R. Philh. Soc. Retired from public singing in 1911, and has devoted herself to teaching.—E.-H.

ALBENIZ, Isaac. Spanish pianist and composer; *b.* Camprodon (Gerona), 29 May, 1860; *d.* Cambo-les-Bains, 16 June, 1909.

The rather uncommon name of Albeniz appears more than once, with special significance, in the history of Spanish music. In 1802, Don Mateo Antonio Pérez de Albeniz attained distinction with his treatise *Instrucción metódica*

para enseñar a cantar y tañer la música moderna y antigua (*Methodical Instruction for the Teaching of Singing and Playing Modern and Ancient Music*), as well as for being one of the first to fight the Italian music invasion. To this end he wrote (with Carnicer, Saldoni and Piermarini) a lyric melodrama (*Los enredos de un curioso*) in the Spanish language, performed at Conservatorio Real de Música, founded two years before (1830). Next we have Don Pedro Albeniz (*b.* Logroño, 1795; *d.* Madrid, 1855), famous for his *Método completo de piano del Conservatorio de Música, Madrid*, for his piano works, and specially for being the founder in Spain of modern school of piano-playing, the knowledge of which he had acquired in Paris, where his father (music master and organist at Logroño, and later at San Sebastian) had sent him to study. There he became a prominent pupil and friend of Henri Herz, Kalkbrenner, Thalberg and Fétis.

Neither of these musical reformers are related to Isaac Albeniz, who was also, in larger measure, an innovator. With him came into existence the " new Spanish school," and his name as piano composer has now extended to all countries.

Isaac learned the piano as a child with his second sister, appearing in public, at the Teatro Romea, Madrid, when only four. At six he went to Paris, and after receiving tuition for 9 months from Marmontel, competed for admission at the Conservatoire. When the jury, astonished at the boy's ability, were about to decide in his favour, the " prodigy " produced a ball from his pocket, threw it at a looking-glass and smashed it to pieces. Obviously he was declared *too young* to be a pupil at that institution. In this incident we may see a symbolic announcement of the characteristic restlessness of his subsequent life: his several escapades (from his 11th to 15th years) as a concert-giver in the provinces and North and South America, with the police on his track; his joining the Leipzig Conservatoire, for a short time, with the savings from his concerts in California; his new escapade to North America from the Brussels Conservatoire, where he was studying under the auspices of King Alfonso XII; his return to Brussels and further escapade to follow Liszt to Weimar and Rome; his disastrous experiment in financial speculations, and flight to France; his failure as a musical-comedy *impresario*, and many other adventures that enhanced his life with a background of picturesque romance, but left their damaging influence on his career. Three persons exercised over him a definite influence at three cardinal stages of his life: the Conde de Morphy, the Spanish musicologist, his faithful adviser and protector when he was a youngster; the admirable lady he married, and Francis Money-Coutts (Lord Latymer), the poet, his Mæcenas and collaborator. Gevaert also took a fatherly interest in his education.

As pianist, Albeniz was specially famous for his rendering of the clavecinists, Bach, Chopin and Schubert. He had had lessons from many a teacher in Spain, from Marmontel (Paris),

Brassin (Brussels), Jadassohn and Reinecke (Leipzig), but none for long. He also received advice from Rubinstein and Liszt. Eventually he gave up the piano to devote himself entirely to composition. His musical output is astounding in quantity. It falls into two separate groups: his works from 1883 to 1890, approximately; and works from this date till his death. The first period covers over 200 works for the piano, including concertos and sonatas, but mostly pieces of a light character, revealing a distinctive personality and impeccable taste. They are the spontaneous outcome of an exuberant natural genius, for at the time Albeniz had not a conscious knowledge of composition, nor even full command of musical grammar. It was not until 1890 that he took up seriously the study of composition, under Vincent d'Indy and Paul Dukas in Paris, writing subsequently his operas *Pepita Jiménez, Henry Clifford, Merlin*, the orchestral suite *Catalonia* and the great piano works that have placed him in the forefront of modern musicians.

It seems to be the fate of the Spanish school that some of its most promising composers (like Usandizaga and Granados) die leaving their mission unaccomplished. Such is the case of Albeniz. Even in his most representative works, *La Vega, Albaicín* or the great piano suite *Iberia*, one finds the composer, only just reaching mature development, obviously delayed by unfortunate circumstances. The texture of his operas shows him unable to get away from piano idiom when composing for the orchestra (this is noticeable even in his rich scoring of first part of unfinished suite *Catalonia*). Monotony of form and technique can be detected in his production which is unconvincing, but disarms the critic by its magical colour and intensely sincere feeling, which conceals the author's occasional lack of constructive imagination. The style has been more than once denounced as French—an absurd assertion; for in its very essence it represents the antithesis of the eliminating process, characteristic of the French mind. Besides harmonic schemes based on the colour of the augmented triad, some of the technical devices common to Albeniz and the French modern composers are derivations from Spanish folk-music (specially evident in Debussy and Ravel). If comparison must be made, it would be nearer the truth to call Albeniz the Spanish Liszt; and this only on account of an external resemblance —the Slavonic pomposity of the one and the Mediterranean exuberance of the other. Psychologically they are totally different, to say nothing of the superiority of Liszt's musical achievements in general. Albeniz's greatness is based on a genius and personality forceful enough to shine in spite of unmethodical training. He continued the work of Chopin and Liszt as an explorer of pianoforte tone and colour possibilities, in accordance with the post-Wagnerian attitude. He revealed to the world the artistic significance of Spanish music, and awoke musical Spain to the reality of a modern sensibility.

Of the unnecessary difficulty of his piano writing, there is something to be said. He was the young hero destined to fight the last battle in Spain against the traditional tyranny of the C major chord and its near "relative keys." To cause its disappearance he may have gone at times so far as to disguise C major as B sharp major.

Pf.: *Chants d'Espagne* (5 pieces); *España* (6 album-leaves); *Suite española* (8 pieces); *Piezas características* (12 pieces); *Seis danzas españolas*; *Suite ancienne*; *Deuxième suite ancienne*; *Yvonne en visite*; *Iberia* suite (12 *nouvelles impressions*, in 4 books); *La Vega*; *Albaicin*. Posthumous works finished by Déodat de Séverac and Enrique Granados: *Azulejos*; *Navarra*. Orch.: *Catalonia, suite populaire* (1st part). Operettas: *The Magic Opal* (1st perf. Lyric Theatre, London, and Madrid); *San Antonio de la Florida* (perf. Brussels, Madrid). Operas: *Henry Clifford* (Barcelona, 1895); *Pepita Jiménez*, (*ib.* 1897; Paris, Opéra Comique, 1923); *Merlin*; *Lancelotte* (unpubl.). For v. and pf.: *To Nellie* (6 songs); *Quatre mélodies*; *Two Songs*; *Il en est de l'Amour*. At the time of his death, he was writing 3rd part of trilogy *King Arthur*, the 1st and 2nd of which are *Merlin* and *Lancelote*.

Publ.: Heugel; Durand; P. Girod; Rouart, Lerolle; Édition Mutuelle, Paris; Stanley Lucas & Hatzfeld, London; Juan Bautista Pujol y Compañia, Barcelona; Unión Musical Española, Madrid. —P. G. M.

d'ALBERT, Eugen (Eugène Francis Charles). Compr. and pianist; *b.* Glasgow, 10 April, 1864. Son of the dance compr. Charles d'Albert (*b.* of Fr. parents, 25 Feb. 1809, at Nienstetten near Altona; *d.* London, 26 May, 1886); stud. under Ernst Pauer, Stainer, Prout, and Sullivan in London, then with Hans Richter in Vienna and especially under Franz Liszt in Weimar. As a pianist, he called forth the astonishment of Hans v. Bülow on his first public appearance. His playing was distinguished by force and poetry of conception, and by greatness of construction; and even now, when he has become almost exclusively an opera compr. and no longer cultivates refinements of technique, he still maintains some of his former excellence. Was for a short time (1895) Court condr. in Weimar. Married several times: (1892–5) to celebrated pianist, Teresa Carreño; (1895–1910) to singer, Hermine Finck; (1910–12) to Ida Theumann. Now resides in Lucerne.

Pf. suite, op. 1; pf. pieces, op. 5; sonata, F sharp mi. op. 10; pf. pieces, op. 16; cadenzas to Beethoven's G ma. pf. concerto; 2 pf. concertos, B mi. op. 2, and E ma. op. 12; cello concerto, op. 20; overture; symphony; str. 4tet, A mi. op. 8, and another, E flat ma. op. 11; many songs, and chiefly the operas: *The Ruby* (Carlsruhe, 1893); *Ghismond* (Dresden, 1895); *Gernot* (Mannheim, 1897); *The Departure* (*Die Abreise*, a charming little 1-act comedy, Frankfort-o-M., 1898, publ. by Brockhaus); *Cain* (Berlin, 1900; *The Improviser* (Berlin, 1900); *Tiefland* (Prague, 1903), his most successful work (forms part of the stock repertory of all German theatres; it Germanises and improves the style of the Italian Verists); *Flauto Solo* (Prague, 1905, mus. comedy); *Tragaldabas* (Hamburg, 1907); *Izeyl* (Hamburg, 1909); *The Proffered Wife* (Vienna, 1912); *Love's Chains* (Dresden, 1912); *Dead Eyes* (Dresden, 1916); *The Bull of Olivera* (Leipzig, 1918); *The Wedding during the Revolution* (Leipzig, 1919); *Scirocco* (Darmstadt, 1921); *Mareike von Nymwegen* (Hamburg, 1923).—A. E.

ALBINATI, Giuseppe. Ital. musicologist; *b.* Milan, 2 Feb. 1856. One of oldest employés of publ. house of Ricordi, Milan. The compilation of important catalogues of this firm is due to him. His position has enabled him to exercise abundantly his passion for research and study of mus. history. His *Dizionario di opere teatrali, oratorii, cantate* (Milan, 1912, Ricordi) is noteworthy.—D. A.

ALBINI, Eugenio. Ital. cellist; *b.* Saludecio, near Rimini, 26 April, 1881. Stud. at Bologna under Francesco Serato; then in Germany under Hugo Becker. After having travelled abroad for some years, settled in Rome, where he has devoted himself to teaching and concerts. Is a noted player of viola da gamba. Took leading part in founding the Roman Società degli Amici della Musica (Society of Friends of Music) and started a quartet (Sandri, Zerti, Raffaelli, Albini). Author of several compns. and transcriptions for his own instr.—D. A.

ALCOCK, Walter Galpin. Eng. orgt. *b.* Edenbridge, Kent, 29 Dec. 1864. Stud. at National Training School for Music (now R.C.M.) under Sullivan, Stainer, Barnett; orgt. Holy Trinity, Sloane Square, 1895–1902; then of Chapels Royal, 1902–16; assistant-orgt. of Westminster Abbey, 1896–1916; organ prof. R.C.M. from 1893; orgt. and choirmaster, Salisbury Cath. from Jan. 1917. Orgt. at Coronations of King Edward VII (1902), and of King George V (1911). M.V.O. Mus.Doc. Dunelm. 1905.

A large amount of church and organ music; an excellent organ tutor (Novello); articles in *Mus. Times*; lectures in R.C.O. calendar.—E.-H.

ALDERIGHI, Dante. Ital. pianist; *b.* Taranto, July, 1898. Stud. under Sgambati; then at Leipzig. Acquired a good name amongst young Ital. concert-artists, and plays in principal towns, and at the Augusteo in Rome. Is also a good composer.—D. A.

ALDRICH, Richard. Amer. critic and author; *b.* Providence, R.I., U.S.A., 31 July, 1863. Graduated A.B. (1885) Harvard College, where he had stud. music under Paine. Began journalistic career on *Providence Journal*; 1889–91, private secretary to Senator Dixon in Washington, also wrote criticisms for *Washington Evening Star*. 1891–2, with *New York Tribune* in various editorial capacities, assisting Krehbiel with mus. criticisms. Mus. ed. of *New York Times*, and one of most respected music critics of metropolis. Associated with Krehbiel as Amer. contributor to revised ed. of Grove's *Dictionary*.

Guide to Parsifal (Ditson, 1904); *Guide to Ring of the Nibelung* (id. 1905); transl. of Lilli Lehmann's *How to Sing* (Macmillan, 1912).—O. K.

ALESSANDRESCU, Alfred. Rumanian compr. *b.* Bucharest, 14 Aug. 1893. Pupil of Castaldi (for pf. and compn.) at Bucharest Cons. and of Vincent d'Indy at *Schola Cantorum*, Paris. Took Enescu Prize in 1916. Condr. at Bucharest Opera House since 1921.

Dramatic overture, *Dido* (1911); symph. poem, *Actéon* (perf. Colonne Concerts, Paris, 1920); songs for v. and pf. (6 publ. by Rouart & Lerolle, Paris, 1922).—D. A.

ALEXANDER, Arthur. Pianist; *b.* Dunedin, New Zealand, 25 March, 1891. Stud. R.A.M. London under Tobias Matthay (pf.) and F. Corder (compn.). Macfarren and Chappell gold

medals for pf. playing; 1912, recitals Vienna, Berlin (with Leila Doubleday, Australian violinist); recitals in London, many 1st perfs. of Bax (2nd sonata) Scriabin (5th sonata) Metner, etc.; prof. Matthay Pf. School from 1912; prof. R.C.M. from 1920.

Songs with orch. (Patron's Fund concert); str. 4tet, etc.—E.-H.

ALEXANDROF, Anatole Nicolaevitch (*accent 3rd syll.*). Russ. compr. and pianist; *b.* Moscow, 13 May (o.s.), 1888. Son of prof. of Tomsk Univ.; pupil of Jiliaef, S. I. Tanéief and Vassilenko (theory) and Igumnof (pf.) at Moscow Cons. which he left in 1915. His music reveals influence of Metner and Scriabin. His inventive powers, technical skill and depth of thought place him with Miaskovsky and Feinberg in the first rank of contemporary Russ. comprs. He was appointed prof. at Moscow Cons. in 1923.

Str. 4tet, G, op. 7 (ms.); 5 pf. sonatas, op. 4, 12, 18, 19 (Russ. State Music Publ. Dept.), 22 (ms.); pf. preludes, op. 1, 10 (Gutheil); other pf. pieces, op. 6, 21; songs, op. 2, 5, 8, 11 (Gutheil), 13, 14, 15, 20 (R.S.M.P.D.); incidental music for Moscow Chamber Theatre.—V. B.

ALFANO, Franco. Ital. compr. *b.* Posillipo (Naples), 8 March, 1876. Stud. at Naples, then at Leipzig. After some attempts at dramatic works and ballets, began to acquire a solid reputation by his work *Resurrection* (from Tolstoy's novel), perf. Turin, 1904. He is one of best living Ital. musicians, from technical point of view. Dir. and prof. of compn. at Liceo Mus. at Bologna; from which he went to Liceo at Turin in 1923 as Director.

Dramatic works : *Resurrection* (1904); *Prince Zilah* (1907); *The Shade of Don Giovanni* (1914); *La leggenda di Sakuntala* (Bologna, 1922). Also *Romantic Suite* for orch. (1909); symphony in E (1912); 3 *Poems of Tagore*, v. and pf. (Ricordi, Milan). 4tets in D (1918) (publ. Pizzi, Bologna). Consult: G. M. Gatti, *F. A.*, in *Modern Musicians in Italy and Abroad* (Bologna, 1920, Pizzi) and in *Mus. Times* (London), March 1921; and Gajanus, *Contemporary Artists : F. A.*, in *Emporium*, Bergamo, March 1919.—D. A.

ALFONSO, Father José. Span. orgt. and compr. of religious music, *b.* Alcañiz, 1867. Orgt. at Valladolid Cath. and Segovia. Choirmaster at Cath. of Santiago de Compostela and later at Madrid.—P. G. M.

ALFVÉN, Hugo. Swedish compr. condr. *b.* Stockholm, 1 May, 1872. Stud. R. Cons. Stockholm, 1887–91, then vn. under Lars Zetterqvist, pf. under Johan Lindegren, 1891–7; then stud. in Germany, France and Belgium (César Thomson), 1900; sub-condr. under Kutzschbach in Dresden; prof. of compn. R. Cons. Stockholm, 1903–4; dir. of music, R. Univ. of Upsala, where he now lives as condr. of well-known students' glee club, " O. D." He has cond. also in music fests. at Dortmund (1912), Stuttgart (1913), Gothenburg (1915), Copenhagen (1918–19). Dir. fest. Upsala, 1911. Toured Germany, Denmark, Russia, Norway, with " O. D." Ph.D. *h.c.* Upsala, 1917; member R.A.M. Stockholm, 1908. His 2nd symphony (D ma.), and his rhapsody, op. 19, have both been perf. at Queen's Hall, London, under Sir Henry Wood.

Orch.: Symphony I, F mi. op. 7, ms.; II, D ma. op. 11 (Mayence, 1901); *Midsommarvaka*, rhapsody, op. 19 (Copenhagen, 1908); symph. poem, *En skär-gardssägen* op. 20 (Stockholm, 1921); Symphony III, E ma. op. 23 (*id.* 1913); *Upsala Rhapsody*, op. 24 (*id.* 1907); *Festspel* for theatre, op. 25 (*id.* 1908); *Drapa*, op. 27; *Den bergtagna*, ballet-pantomime, op. 37; Symphony IV, C mi. op. 39 (Vienna, 1922). Vs. and orch.: *The Bells* (barit. and orch), op. 13; *Ballade*, barit., male chorus, orch. op. 30; *Baltic Exhibition Cantata*, op. 33 (1914); Ode on *Gustavus Vasa*, soli, mixed vs., orch. op. 40. Chamber-music: sonata, vn. and pf. op. 1; *Romance*, vn. and pf. op. 3; *Élégie*, horn and pf. op. 5; pf. pieces; songs.—P. V.

ALIO, Francisco. Span. musician of Catalonian group. Author of a coll. of Catalonian folk-songs: *Cançons Populars Catalans* (Unión Musical Española, Madrid).—P. G. M.

ALLEN, Sir Hugh Percy. Director of Royal College of Music, London; *b.* Reading, 23 Dec. 1869. Began his musical career at Chichester Cathedral as assistant organist under Dr. F. J. Read; then became assistant music-master at Wellington College (under Dr. Alan Gray); organ - scholar, Christ's College, Cambridge; organist, St. Asaph Cathedral, 1897–8; Ely Cathedral, 1898–1901; proceeded to the Oxford Mus.Doc. 1898; organist, New College Oxford, 1901–18; later sub-warden and Fellow of the college; conductor, Bach Choir, London, 1901–20. He was appointed to the Heather Chair of Music in University of Oxford in 1918; followed Sir Hubert Parry as Director of Royal College of Music, London, 1918; and was knighted in 1920.

As the Professor of Music at Oxford, he has done extremely valuable work in widening the scope and practicality of the musical courses there. As a choral conductor he has always been highly successful, for he loves the broad phrase and the plasticity of massed sound, whether it be a small country cathedral choir, a large congregation of hymn-singers, a University chorus, the Bach Choir or the huge Royal Choral Society.

He was appointed to the Directorship of the Royal College of Music, the most influential academic post in England, at a time ripe for the unification of all the diverse and scattered musical developments in Great Britain. The British Music Society did much towards the consolidation of music in England; but no single man individually has done more than Sir Hugh to advance this purpose. His magnetic personality, strong driving force, broad outlook, unusual organising gifts, and entirely unprejudiced mind, have all combined to make him the most trusted musician in Britain.—E.-H.

ALLEN, Maud Perceval. Eng. s. singer; *b.* Ripley, Derbyshire. Trained under W. Shakespeare; *début* at Philh. London, 1905; has sung at many Eng. fests.; sang Brünnhilde in 1st Eng. perf. of Wagner's *Ring*, R. Opera Synd. Covent Garden, under Richter. World-tour with Quinlan Opera Co. as leading s. 1913–14; 3 tours in America with Chicago Orch.—E.-H.

ALLENDE, Humberto. Chilean compr. *b.* 1885. Stud. in Chile. His first pieces appeared in 1912. after a tour through Europe, where he was sent, by Government of Chile, to study teaching of music in primary schools. Debussy,

Pedrell and Massenet expressed high opinions of his compositions.

Choruses; many pf. pieces (Leipzig, Carisch; Barcelona, Astor). His cello concerto (1915), and his symph. poem *Escenas campestres* achieved a great success.—A. M.

ALLIN, Norman. Eng. opera concert singer; *b.* Ashton-u-Lyne, Lancs, 19 Nov. 1885. Stud. under John Acton (singing) and Dr. Walter Carroll (theory) in Manchester. Has a fine b. voice, which is particularly effective as Boris Godunof in Mussorgsky's opera and as Gurnemanz in *Parsifal*; has appeared at all the leading Eng. fests. A. was one of founders of British National Opera Co.—E.-H.

ALME, Waldemar. Norwegian pianist; *b.* Christiania, 10 Jan. 1890. Trained as pianist and orgt. at Lindeman's Music Cons. Christiania. *Début* there, 1909; Stud. afterwards in Berlin (theory, Tobias; pf., Barth). Teacher at Klindworth-Scharwenka Cons. in Berlin, 1916–1917; teacher in Helsingfors, 1919–21. Has given concerts in Scandinavia and Germany. Lives in Christiania.—U. M.

ALNÆS, Eyvind. Norwegian compr. orgt. condr. *b.* Fredriksstad, 29 April, 1872. Stud. first at Music Cons. Christiania (1889–92); afterwards in Leipzig (Reinecke and Ruthardt) and Berlin. Orgt. in Drammen, 1895–1907; from 1907 in Christiania; from 1916 orgt. and choirmaster at Our Saviour's Ch.; condr. of Holter's Choral Soc. from 1920, also of Christiania Craftsmen's Choral Soc. 1905–1920 and again from 1922.

As a compr. he became known by his Symphony in C mi. (Christiania Mus. Soc. 1898); in following year he cond. his Symph. Variations. His works show solid construction, capable treatment of cpt., and effective instrumentation. It is as a lyric compr. that A. has become widely known outside Norway; his songs and romances rank amongst the best productions of his native land. They have a simple, natural quality, often with a strong national tinge.

Symphony, C mi. (Leipzig, 1900; Christiania, 1898); *Variations Symphoniques* (perf. Leipzig, Copenhagen, Christiania); pf. concerto, D ma. (perf. Copenhagen, Christiania); Suite for vn. and pf.; male-chorus piece; pf. pieces; songs with piano (including famous *Sidste reis* (*Last Journey*).—J. A.

ALONSO, López Francisco. Span. compr. *b.* Granada, 9 May, 1887. Stud. there under Don Celestino Vila (music-master of Cath.). Founder and condr. of orch. and choir of Sociedad Filarmónica Granadina. Regimental bandmaster, before he turned to writing mus. comedies (*zarzuelas*) in Madrid, where he now lives. His successful stage works already exceed 60 in number. *Las Corsarias* has been perf. in Spain and Latin America, during last 3 years, over 10,000 times. One of its musical numbers, the March, known as *Paso doble de la Bandera* or *La Banderita* (*The Little Flag*), may be described as the Span. *Tipperary*. It has taken the place in popularity of that famous *Marcha de Cádiz* once officially proclaimed a national hymn (*himno nacional*). In Dec. 1922, the Granada County Council conferred upon him the freedom of the city, and in 1923 he received the Gran Cruz of Alfonso XII.

La Boda de la Farruca; *De Madrid al Infierno*; *Poca Pena*; *Cleopatra*; *Música, Luz y Alegría*; *El Secreto de la Cibeles*; *La Perfecta Casada*; *Las Corsarias*; *La Hora Tonta*. (Publ.: Antonio Matamala; Ildefonso Alier; Unión Musical Española, Madrid.)—P. G. M.

ALPAERTS, Flor. Belgian compr. condr. *b.* Antwerp, 12 Sept. 1876. Stud. at Antwerp Cons. under Benoit and Blockx. Prof. there in 1903. Condr. at symphony concerts of Zoological Soc. in 1919. Manager of R. Belgian Opera House, 1922.

Opera, *Shylock* (Antwerp, 1913). Orch.: *Psyché*; *Renouveau*; *Cyrus* (symph. poems); *Symphonie du Printemps*. *Het schooner Vaderland*, cantata, children's vs. and orch.; *Kinderlieder* (Children's Book), v. and pf. Author of a Solfeggio in 5 parts.—E. C.

ALTMANN, Wilhelm. Ger. mus. critic, author, historian; *b.* Adelnau, 4 April, 1862. Stud. history at Marburg and Berlin. Entered career of librarian in 1886, first Breslau, then Greifswald, where he devoted himself to music. Chief librarian Prussian State Library since 1900. In 1906 founded its *Deutsche Musiksammlung*, embracing nearly whole of modern published music. Since 1914 dir. of musical section, Prussian State Library.

Chronik des Berliner Philharmonischen Orch. (1902); *H. v. Herzogenberg* (1903); *Richard Wagner's Letters* (1905, Breitkopf: Index of 3143 letters); *Wagner's Correspondence with his Publishers*, 2 vols. (1911); *Brahms' Correspondence*, Vol. III (1907); *Index to Chamber-Music Literature* (1910, 3rd ed. 1923, Leipzig, C. Merseburger); *Catalogue of Orch. Literature* (Leipzig, 1919, Leuckart).—A. E.

ALTSCHULER, Modest. Russ. condr. cellist; *b.* Mogilef, Russia, 18 Feb. 1873. Stud. cello under Goebelt at Warsaw Cons. and Fitzenhagen and von Glen at Moscow Cons. where he was also a pupil of Arensky (harmony) and Tanéief (compn.), graduating in 1890. Went to America in 1895 as cellist and teacher. Condr. of Russ. Symphony Orch. from its organisation in 1903. In 1919, the regular subscription concerts in New York were abandoned, but A. still conducts his orch. regularly at music fests. in the Southern States. —O. K.

ÁLVAREZ, Carmen. Span. pianist; *b.* Madrid, 2 Dec. 1905. Has attained special distinction as exponent of works of modern Span. comprs. Stud. at R. Cons. de Música under José Tragó and Francisco Furter. Recitals in Madrid, Paris and London.—P. G. M.

ÁLVAREZ UDELL, Luis. Span. operatic t. singer; *b.* Seville, June 1866; *d.* there, May 1920. First prize for pf. at R. Cons. de Música, Madrid; stud. singing under Francisco Reynés, Seville. After a remarkable season at Lyric Theatre, Milan, when he sang in 22 perfs. of *The Barber of Seville* (with the sopr. Maria Barrientos), appeared at Petrograd and Moscow (with Sembrich and Nilsson), being entrusted by Rubinstein with principal rôle for first perf. of his opera *The Demon*.—P. G. M.

ALWIN, Karl. Ger. condr. and compr. *b.* Königsberg, 15 April, 1891. Stud. literature and philosophy in Berlin; music with Humperdinck and Hugo Kaun. Through Carl

Muck, went to Court Opera House, Berlin, as Korrepetitor; took part in Wagner fest. at Bayreuth, 1912. Assistant condr. Halle, 1913; condr. in Posen, 1914; condr. at Stadttheater, Düsseldorf, 1915–17; and Hamburg Stadttheater, 1917–20. Condr. at Vienna State Opera House since 1920. Cond. *Ring* and Strauss perfs. Grand Opera, Covent Garden, London, May 1924.

Numerous songs; also some orch. works. Married the celebrated lyrical s., Elizabeth Schumann, who was at Hamburg Stadttheater, and is now at Vienna State Opera House (chief parts: Susanne, Despina, Sophie in *Rosenkavalier*, etc.).—A. E.

AMATO, Pasquale. Singer; *b.* Naples, 1880. One of the most renowned Ital. baritones; well known on principal stages in Italy and America; assisted at Verdi Commemoration at Busseto Theatre 1913, under Toscanini, rendering *La Traviata* and title-rôle in *Falstaff*.—D. A.

AMELLI, Guerrino. Ital. historian and critic of sacred music; *b.* Milan, 18 March, 1848. Ordained in 1870; 1885, joined monks of San Benedetto at Montecassino, assuming name of Ambrogio; occupied positions of monastic prior and librarian; at present, is visitor to the Cassinese Congregation. One of most efficient and authoritative promoters in Italy of the restoration of sacred music; founded in 1881 the Associazione Italiana Santa Cecilia, for which he had been preparing since 1877 by his periodical *Musica Sacra*. In 1882, instituted at Milan a higher school of sacred music. The movement, already officially recognised by Pope Leo XIII in 1884 (by his *Regolamento per la Musica Sacra*), had its victorious crowning with the famous *Motu Proprio* of Pius X. In 1920, on the occasion of 50th anniversary of ordination of Padre Amelli, the Abbey of Montecassino publ. in his honour a coll. of *Various Writings in Ecclesiastical Literature*.

The Restoration of Sacred Music in Italy, lecture (Bologna, 1874, Felsinea); *St. Thomas and Music* (Milan, 1876); *Musica Sacra*, review of mus. liturgy (Milan, 1877–85); *The Psalms of Benedetto Marcello*, 5 vols. (Milan, 1880, Calcografia *Musica Sacra*); *Posthumous Works of Jacopo Tomadini*, with preface by G. Amelli, 2 vols. (Milan, 1882); *Repertory of Sacred Vocal Music*, 9 vols.; *Repertory of Sacred Music for the Organ*, 9 vols. (in Records of Associazione Santa Cecilia, Milan, 1884–6); *Aretium, Roma, Argentoratum: Oratio habita in generali cantus gregoriani studiosorum conventu* (Argentorati [Strasburg], 1900); *Guidonis Monachi Aretini Micrologus ad prestantiores codices exactus* (Rome, 1904, Desclée Lefèbvre); a specimen from the Complete Critical Ed. of the works of Guido d'Arezzo, prepared by Amelli, an ed. he was unable to publish for various various reasons; *From an Unpublished Writing of San Ludovico, Bishop of Toulouse, about Music* (in *Archivium Franciscanum*, Quaracchi, 1909); *Biblioteca Ceciliana* (Milan, 1907).—D. A.

AMER, Miguel. Span. musicologist; *b.* in the Balearic Islands. One of founders of Capella de Manacor (see NOGUERA). Author of *Reforma de la música religiosa* (Palma de Mallorca, 1900).— P. G. M.

AMES, John Carlowitz. Eng. compr. pianist; *b.* Westbury-on-Trym, nr. Bristol, 8 Jan. 1860. Educated Edinburgh Univ.; stud. Stuttgart Cons. under Pruckner (pf.), Goetschius and Faisst (compn.); later at Dresden Cons. under

F. Wüllner; *début* at Steinway Hall, London, 1881, playing his own compositions.

4-act opera, *The Last Inca*; 3 comic operas; incidental music to *Richard II* (Tree, at H.M. Theatre); incidental music to *Bonnie Dundee* (Lawrence Irving, Adelphi); orch. pieces; 2 pf. concertos; *Psalm CXXX*, chorus, soli, orch.; chamber-music; pf. pieces; songs, etc.—E.-H.

ANCELL, Sarah. Argentine pianist; *b.* Buenos Ayres, 4 Aug. 1896. Stud. under Alberto Williams at Buenos Ayres Cons. Has given many successful concerts, especially those in Argentine Centenary celebrations and a grand symph. concert in 1911. One of the first pianists to give concerts with an orch. in S. America. —A. M.

ANDERS, Erich. Ger. compr. *b.* Teutschental, near Halle-o-S., 29 Aug. 1883. First intended for banking; took up music on advice of Max Reger; entered Cons. Leipzig, and the Univ.; condr. Barmen Stadttheater, Heidelberg Stadttheater; teacher and reviewer, Berlin; 1916–19, Munich; 1919–20, Cologne; 1920, lector in music at Bonn Univ.; 1922, teacher of compn. at Klindworth-Scharwenka Conservatoire, Berlin.

Many songs, especially for children; choral pieces; chamber-music; pf. pieces. Operas: *Venezia* (Frankfort-o-M., 1917); *Anselmo* (not produced); *Death and Life* (spoken opera, Hanover, 1920) and *Mandragola* (not produced).—A. E.

ANDERSEN, Carl Joachim. Danish fl. virtuoso, condr. *b.* Copenhagen, 29 April, 1847; *d.* there 7 May, 1909. Member of R. Chapel of Copenhagen, 1869–78; of orch. of Ital. Opera, Petrograd; later of R. Chapel, Berlin, and of Philh. Orch. there. Engaged in conducting in Berlin and Bad Scheveningen, Holland. From 1894 till death, condr. of Tivoli Concerts in Copenhagen, and of popular Sunday Palace Concerts. Comp. studies as well as concerted pieces for flute.—A. H.

ANDERSEN, Hildur. Norwegian pianist; *b.* Christiania, 25 May, 1864. Pupil of Jadassohn, Weidenbach and Reinecke in Leipzig, and of Leschetizky in Vienna. As a brilliant interpreter, especially of classical works and chamber-music (a member of Gustav Lange's chamber-music ensemble), she has had an important influence on music in her native city.—J. A.

ANDERSEN, Sophus. Danish song-compr. *b.* 8 Dec. 1859; *d.* 19 Sept. 1923. Mus. critic of journal *Kóbenhavn* (*Copenhagen*). One of his chief pieces is a recitation to orch. acc. *Historien om en Moder* (*The Story of a Mother*), text from Hans Chr. Andersen and Stuckenberg.—A. H.

ANDERSEN WINGAR, Alfred. Norwegian compr. condr. *b.* Christiania, 15 Oct. 1869. Pupil of Alfred Paulsen, Johannes Haarklou, Jules Massenet and André Gédalge (Paris); Violinist in Christiania Theatre orch. (1890–9); vla.-player in National Theatre orch. (1901–5); from 1911, leader of Popular Symphony Concerts, partly supported by grant from municipality; from 1921, vla.-player in Philh. Orch. Christiania. His operas are written with dramatic talent. The comic opera seems to be his most natural field.

2 operas; 2 operettas; 2 symphonies; 2 vn. concertos; stage-music to O. Sinding's drama *Iraka*;

overtures to Ibsen's *Hedda Gabler* and *Master-Builder*; orch. fantasias, *Aus Norwegens Berg und Thal*, and *Les Naïades*; orch. suites, *La Vie* and *Les Sauterelles*; 2 Oriental Rhapsodies for orch.; songs with pf., etc.—J. A.

ANDERSSON, Otto. Finnish writer on music and choral condr. *b.* Vårdö, 27 March, 1879. Stud. at Helsingfors Music Inst. and Univ. (Ph.D. 1923). Founded (1906) Brage Soc. for cultivation of Swedish folk-music and folk-dance in Finland. Has written several special studies on mus. history and instrs. of Finland: *Inhemska Musiksträvanden* (1907); *Musik och Musiker* (1917); *Martin Wegelius* (1918); *J. J. Pippingsköld och musiklivet i Åbo 1808–27* (1922); *Stråkharpan* (1923).—T. H.

ANDERSSON, Richard. Swedish pianist; *b.* Stockholm, 22 Sept. 1851; *d.* 20 May, 1918. Stud. R. Cons. Stockholm, 1867–74; *début* R. Opera, 1872; stud. in Berlin (pf. Clara Schumann and H. Barth; compn. R. Würst, F. Kiel) 1876 *et seq.*; concert-pianist in Stockholm from 1884; founded his own pf. school there in 1884; prof. pf. R. Cons. 1912; member R.A.M. Stockholm, 1891. Amongst his pupils are W. Stenhammar, Knut Bäck, Astrid Berwald.

Pf. sonata (1889); *Schwedische Tänze* and other pf. pieces; 12 songs (1919).—P. V.

ANDERTON, Howard Orsmond. Eng. compr. author; *b.* Clapton, London, 20 April, 1861. Stud. at R.A.M. under Bannister, Macfarren and Prout. In 1908, took post at Midland Inst., Birmingham, with Bantock. 1923, librarian at London head-quarters for British Federation of Musical Competition Festivals.

Books: *Baldur* (Fisher Unwin); *Song of Alfred* (Constable); *Early English Music* (*Musical Opinion*); *Granville Bantock* (John Lane); *On Desert Islands* (Blackwell). Music: *Song of the Morning Stars* (Forsyth); *Baldur*, *Prelude and Death-March*; *English Sinfonietta*. Music to Euripides' *Trojan Women* and Sophocles' *Trachiniæ* (Greek text).—E.-H.

ANDOLFI, Otello. Ital. cellist and critic; *b.* Tivoli, 20 Feb. 1887. Cellist in quartet-concerts (with his brothers, Argeo, Uberto, and Goffredo); as soloist in concerts (together with his wife, Manolita de Anduaga-Andolfi). Critic on Rome paper *Musica*. Dir. of an Ital. Concert Agency.—D. A.

ANDRÉ, José. Argentine compr. critic; *b.* Buenos Ayres in 1891. Stud. under Alberto Williams at Buenos Ayres Cons.; Grand Prize for compn. 1909. His style is based on modern Fr. school. 19 songs (Fr. words), choruses and pf. pieces. Has establ. a mus. review, and is a well-known musical critic.—A. M.

ANDREAE, Volkmar. Swiss conductor, composer; *b.* Berne, 5 July, 1879. Studied in Berne; later pupil of Wüllner, Franke and Staub at Cologne Conservatoire (1897–1900). In 1902 conductor of the Gemischter Chor at Zurich and the Stadtsängerverein at Winterthur. Succeeded Fr. Hegar as conductor of symphony concerts at Zurich in 1906 and has since devoted himself entirely to the development of musical life in Zurich, where he directs the Conservatoire and delivers occasional courses of lectures at the University. An excellent conductor, he has been called to conduct symphony concerts in Germany, Holland, Sweden, Spain and Italy. 1914, Ph.D. *h.c.* Zurich University.

2 symphonies; *Charons Nachen,* for chorus and orch. op. 3 (Mayence, Schott); *Symph. Phantasy,* t. solo, chorus and orch. op. 7 (Leipzig, Hug); Suite for orch. op. 27 (Leipzig, Leuckart), perf. Queen's Hall Symph. Concerts and Proms. under Sir Henry Wood; opera, *Ratcliff,* op. 25 (Berlin, Fürstner); vn. sonata, op. 5 (Schott); str. 4tet and trio (Hug); numerous unacc. choruses and songs in op. 13–24 (Hug).—F. H.

ANDRÉE, Elfrida. Swedish orgt. and compr. *b.* Visby, Gottland, 19 Feb. 1844. Stud. in Stockholm, Copenhagen, Berlin. From 1867, orgt. Gothenburg Cath. where she has given recitals; from 1897 condr. of People's Concerts, Gothenburg; member R.A.M. Stockholm, 1879.

Opera, *Fritiofs saga* (libretto by Selma Lagerlöf); symphony; organ symphonies (1 publ. Augener); cantata, *Snöfrid,* with orch. (1879); *Swedish Mass* (1903); pf. 5tet (Ed. Mus. Konstföreningen); pf. trio (*id*); songs.—P. V.

ANDREOLI, Guglielmo. Ital. pianist and compr. *b.* Mirandola (Modena), 9 Jan. 1862. Belongs to a family of musicians. With his brother Carlo, now deceased, organised in Milan (1878–86) seasons of popular concerts, which left a strong impression on mus. life of Milan. Took vla. part in various quartets. Since 1891, prof. at Milan Conservatoire.

Compns. for pf. (Ricordi); a *Manual of Harmony* in collab. with E. Codazzi (Milan, Cogliati.). Consult G. Tebaldini, *A Family of Musicians : the Andreoli* (in the periodical *L'Arte Pianistica,* Naples, Oct. 1918).—D. A.

ANDREWS, W. Bowker. Eng. music-publ. *b.* Durham, 25 Feb. 1876. Head of firm of Swan & Co. London, which specialises in publ. music by British composers.—G. B.

ANDRIESSEN, Willem. Dutch pianist; *b.* Haarlem, 25 Oct. 1887. Stud. at Amsterdam Cons. (de Pauw, pf; Bernard Zweers, theory); 1908, *Prix d'excellence;* 1910–18, prof. of pf. R.A.M., The Hague; then teacher at Music School, Rotterdam.

Mass, chorus, soli and orch.; pf. concerto in D flat; numerous songs.—W. P.

ANFOSSI, Giovanni. Ital. pianist and compr. *b.* Ancona, 6 Jan. 1864. After activities as concert-player, founded in Milan a school named after Pasquale Anfossi, his ancestor. He directs and teaches pf. there.—D. A.

ANGELELLI, Carlo. Ital. pianist and compr. *b.* Florence, 5 Sept. 1872. Concert-player, teacher, compr. of pf., vn. and vocal works. His 2 songs to d'Annunzio's words took prize offered by journal *Il Tirso* (Rome).

Variations for organ (New York, Fischer); concert transcription of a little clavier piece of Bach (London, Schott); *Danze italiane del secolo XVI per liuto* (concert transcription for pf.).—D. A.

d'ANNUNZIO, Antonio. Ital. conductor; *b.* Pescara. Brother of the great poet. For many years he has lived in North America, engaged in conducting.—D. A.

d'ANNUNZIO, Gabriele. Italian poet, soldier, writer and thinker; *b.* Pescara, 12 March, 1864. An enthusiastic lover of the art of music, which he has always cultivated profoundly. The musical style of his writings,

orations and poetry is marvellous. Two of his beautiful *Laudi* are inspired by Bellini and Verdi. In his youth in Rome as journalist he wrote many mus. reviews. In 1917, he took the initiative in the *National Coll. of Ital. Music,* which with the technical co-operation of various musicians, was then publ. in Milan by the Istituto Editoriale Italiano.

Many lyrical works were inspired by his stage pieces. Franchetti set music to *La Figlia di Jorio,* Mascagni to *Parisina,* Italo Montemezzi to *La Nave,* Zandonai to *Francesca da Rimini,* Pizzetti to *Fedra.* Pizzetti wrote the mus. interludes for *La Nave* and *Pisanella;* and the music of the mystery *Le Martyre de St. Sébastien* was comp. by Debussy. Many of d'Annunzio's poems have given Ital. comprs. musical inspiration.

In the Statute of the Ital. Regency of Carnaro, promulgated by d'Annunzio in 1920, the last two paragraphs, with their noble sentiments, are dedicated to music. Therein he exalts mus. art as the supreme means of spiritual and civil education, and fixes the basis of what—in the divine remembrance of Ancient Greece—should be the mus. regulations of an ideal State. He is at present living at Gardone Riviera (Brescia). In 1924 he was ennobled by King Victor Emmanuel III.—D. A.

ANROOY, Peter van. Dutch condr. *b.* Zalt-Bommel (Guelderland), 13 Oct. 1879. Stud. in Utrecht under Dr. Joh. Wagenaar, theory; and G. Veerman, vn. In 1899 went to Willem Kes (formerly condr. of Concertgebouw Orch. Amsterdam) in Moscow, for vn. study and conducting practice. There stud. cpt. under Tanéief. 1901–2 violinist in Scottish Orch. Glasgow, and Tonhalle Orch. Zurich; 1902, 2nd condr. Lyric Theatre, Amsterdam; 1905, condr. Groningen Symph. Orch.; 1910, condr. Arnhem Symph. Orch.; 1917, dir. of Residentie Orch. The Hague (second best orch. in Holland—80 members). 1914, created Doctor *h.c.* Groningen Univ. An enthusiastic Brahms, Beethoven and Bach conductor.

Andante for wind instrs. (1895); Introduction and Scherzo for orch. (1896); 2 overtures for orch. (1897); 5tet, pf. and str. (1898); 2 cantatas for children's vs. (1898 and 1899): (*a*) *Zonneklaartje* (*Princess Sunshine*), publ. Lichtenauer, Rotterdam; (*b*) *In het Woud* (*In the Wood*), publ. Eggers, Leyden; Dutch Rhapsody, *Piet Hein,* for orch. (1901), well known in Holland and Germany (publ. Noske, The Hague); Ballad, vn. and orch. (1902); music to *Das Kalte Herz* (Wilh. Hauff).—W. P.

ANSELMI, Giuseppe. T. singer; *b.* Catania, 16 Nov. 1876. One of most renowned Ital. opera singers (*Traviata; Rigoletto; Barbiere di Siviglia; Cavalleria; La Bohème; Lucia; La Sonnambula*).—D. A.

ANSERMET, Ernest. Swiss condr. *b.* Vevey in 1883. First a teacher of mathematics in Lausanne; stud. compn. under Denéréaz (Lausanne), A. Gédalge (Paris), O. Barblan and E. Bloch (Geneva). In 1912, became condr. of orch. concerts in Montreux and, since 1913, of the Orchestre de la Suisse Romande in Geneva. A pioneer of modern music, which he conducts extremely well; has done a great deal to make known the music of the modern Russ. school, particularly Igor Stravinsky. Conducted the Russ. ballet in Paris and London.—F. H.

ANSORGE, Conrad. Ger. ɼianist and compr. *b.* Buchwald, near Liebau, Silesia, 15 Oct. 1862. Pupil of Leipzig Cons. and of Franz Liszt, 1885–6; recitals in America, 1887; settled in Weimar 1893, and in Berlin 1895 ; piano teacher there, 1898–1903, at Klindworth-Scharwenka Cons. A brilliant Liszt exponent and an impressive Beethoven interpreter. As compr., belongs to a mystic romantic circle, and in his time was the specially favoured musician among the associates of the poet Stefan George.

Songs; pf. works; 3 sonatas; pf. concerto (1922); 2 str. 4tets; str. 6tet; *Requiem* (with free text) male vs. and orch.; orch. pieces.—A. E.

ANTCLIFFE, Herbert. Eng. writer on music; *b.* Sheffield, 30 July, 1875. Writes for a large number of journals.

Books: *Living Music* (J. Williams); *Short Studies on Nature of Music* (Kegan Paul); *The Successful Music Teacher* and *The Amateur Singer* (Augener); short biographies of Brahms and Schubert (G. Bell); *The Chorus-Master* (W. Paxton). Transl. of Lenormand's *Étude sur l'harmonie moderne* (1912, J. Williams). Arr. for 2 v. and pf. of Dutch folk-songs with English words (Evans).—E.-H.

ANTOINE, Georges. Belgian composer; *b.* Liège, 28 April, 1892; *d.* Bruges, 15 Nov. 1918. Son of a choir-master of Liège Cath. Stud. at Liège Cons. and began to compose about 1910. Fought in the war (1914–18), discharged for sickness, rejoined army and died of fever at Bruges, in the moment of victory. Was a remarkably gifted musician with a culture above the ordinary, as witnessed by his articles in the review *Les Cahiers*, publ. on the Belgian front during the war. His *Veillée d'Armes*, perf. at Liège in 1919, and Brussels, 1922, revealed a temperament alien to Lekeu's, in its intense lyricism and richness of musical matter.

Sonata, pf. and vn. op. 3 (1912–15); pf. concerto, op. 5 (1914); 4tet, pf. and str. op. 6 (1916); *Veillée d'Armes*, poem for orch. op. 9 (1918); a dozen songs and some unfinished works.—C. V. B.

ANZOLETTI, Marco. Italian violinist; *b.* Trent, 4 June, 1866. Prof. at Milan Cons. Has composed many works for his own instrument. Is also a student of mus. history and a writer. He has written 4 unperf. operas: *Serbia* (1898); *Le gare* (1902); *Faida* (1912–15); *Belfegor* (1920). His writings include:

W. A. Mozart (Florence, *Rassegna Nazionale,* 1899); *Dom. Cimarosa* (*id.* 1901); *L'insegnamento del violino in Italia* (*id.* 1909); *Mozart* (scenes of home-life) in 4 parts (Milan, Cogliati, 1902); *Giuseppe Tartini* (crit. biog. study) (Milan review, *Italianissima,* 1917). —D. A.

APPIANI, Vincenzo. Ital. pianist and compr. *b.* Monza, 18 Aug. 1850. Has occupied for many years post of teacher at Milan Cons. Had a great reputation as concert-player; and founded the Milanese Trio, in which he took part, together with violinist Rampazzini and cellist Magrini. —D. A.

APPRECIATION, MUSICAL. The study of mus. appreciation as a separate branch is a recent addition to the syllabus of mus. education. Greater importance is ascribed to it, as such,

in the Anglo-Saxon countries than in any other; and practically all the books devoted to it are in the Eng. language. The principles upon which it is conducted aim at developing perceptivity and receptivity. They all fall under one of three headings: (*a*) aural training, (*b*) mind and memory training, (*c*) stimulating the imagination. Aural training, of course, is the very basis and *sine qua non*. It is generally conducted on the lines laid down by Lavignac in his *Cours de Dictée Musicale.* Many more or less complicated suggestions offered in books on appreciation are justified in so far as they make for aural training, but would be more useful if this point was made clearer.

The necessity of being able to listen not only discriminatingly, so as to perceive the very subtlest shades in details, but reconstructively, so as to acquire a conception of each work as a whole, calls for training of the memory, which retains the necessary data, and of the mind, which, consciously or unconsciously, organises these data into a whole. To this end, knowledge of the principles of construction, or familiarity with the main features of musical design and architecture, are useful. Hence, most books lay great stress upon technical information of various kinds as to the materials used and how they are used. It has been remarked (*Mus. Times,* July 1912, art. by H. P. S.) that " it is a mistake to lead the layman to the gates of music along the same path that the professional must traverse, supplying him with a rough technique only modified so that he may acquire it more easily." Ernest Newman (see *infra*) writes: " Scientific understanding of music has absolutely nothing to do with the ability to understand it as a language of the emotions." And M. D. Calvocoressi (*Monthly Mus. Record,* Nov. 1921–Jan. 1922, " On teaching Musical Appreciation," and " Labelling versus Appreciating ") expresses the fear that elementary knowledge of theory and technique may lead listeners very far astray. But as a rule, writers on mus. appreciation favour the opposite view.

Stimulating the imagination is a more direct contribution to that formation of mus. taste which is aimed at by all. This is generally done with the help of comments, direct or indirect. Direct comments refer to the music only. Indirect comment may be of two kinds. One is that which refers to associations, to emotional or dramatic suggestions, and to concrete imagery in connection with music. The other refers to historical and biographical facts, and to other elements of information outside the works considered. The latter is useful, but may tend to introduce circumstantial evidence of a misleading nature, *e.g.* when an artist's intentions, as revealed in his biography or writings, are confused with the actual achievements embodied in his music.

On the value of the other order of indirect comment, opinions vary greatly. Dr. F. H. Hayward (quoted by Scholes, see *infra*) writes: " If, hearing the first movement of Beethoven's Fifth Symphony, we do not hear the hammer-strokes of Fate knocking at Beethoven's door and saying 'You shall suffer, suffer, suffer—you shall be deaf as a stone—you shall never know domestic joys . . .' and our appreciation of the symphony is merely the appreciation of its musical make-up, we miss much that it is a thousand pities to miss." On the other hand, W. J. Turner, in *Music and Life* (London, 1921), writes: "The higher the type of music, the less it will suggest concrete images . . . the emotional listener really misses all that distinguishes music from any other art." Whoever feels the latter view to be true will agree that while direct comment provides a less easy path, it will lead further. The chief books on Appreciation are:

H. Antcliffe, *How to enjoy Music* (Kegan Paul); Clarence G. Hamilton, *Musical Appreciation* (Ditson, Boston); W. J. Henderson, *What is Good Music?* (Murray); Leigh Henry, *Music, what it means and how to understand it* (Curwen); E. Markham Lee, *On listening to Music* (Kegan Paul); Stewart Macpherson, *Music and its Appreciation* (J. Williams); Ernest Newman, *The Appreciation of Music* ("Art of Life" Courses); Arthur W. Pollitt, *The Enjoyment of Music* (Methuen); Percy A. Scholes, *Musical Appreciation in Schools* and *The Listener's Guide to Music* (Oxford Univ. Press); T. W. Surette and D. G. Mason, *The Appreciation of Music* (W. H. Gray, New York).—M. D. C.

APTHORP, William Foster. Amer. author, critic; b. Boston, Mass., U.S.A., 24 Oct. 1849; d. Vevey, Switzerland, 19 Feb. 1913. Early schooling in Dresden, Berlin and Rome. Graduated A.B., Harvard Univ. 1869. From 1863, stud. pf., harmony and cpt. under Paine; later pf. under B. J. Lang. 1874, teacher of piano and theory at New England Cons. Boston, until 1886. Lectured on æsthetics and history of music at Coll. of Music of Boston Univ. From 1872-7 music critic of *Atlantic Monthly*; 1881-1903, one of most influential of Boston music and dramatic critics, on *Evening Transcript*. 1892-1901, provided the analytical notes for the Boston Symphony programmes. Retired 1903 to Switzerland.

Musicians and Music Lovers (Scribner, 1894); *The Opera, Past and Present* (Scribner, 1901); translator of a selection of *Berlioz's Letters* (Holt, 1879). Ed. (with J. D. Champlin) of useful 3-vol. *Cyclopædia of Music and Musicians* (Scribner, 1880-90).—O. K.

ARAB FOLK-MUSIC. See BARTÓK.

ARACENA, Infanta Anibal. Chilean orgt. b. Chañaral, 1881. Stud. in Chile; in 1918, recitals in Buenos Ayres. Has publ. 72 pieces, mostly sacred.—A. M.

d'ARÁNYI, Jelly. Hungarian violinist; b. Budapest, 30 May, 1895. Stud. under Jenő Hubay at R. High School for Music, Budapest. For some time past has lived in England, where she is well known as a solo-violinist. Produced Bartók's 2 vn. sonatas in London (1st, March 1922; 2nd, May 1923).—B. B.

ARBO, Jens. Norwegian music critic; b. Kristiansand, 20 Aug. 1885. Engaged on *Nationen*, Christiania, and *Musikbladet* (1917-21), *Musikbladet og Sangerposten* (from 1922). Contributor to *Norges Musik-historie* (1921). Writer of several of the Norwegian arts. in this Dictionary.—R. M.

ARBÓS, Enrique Fernandez. Span. vn. teacher and condr. b. Madrid, 25 Dec. 1863. Pupil of Jesús Monasterio, Madrid; stud. in Brussels under Vieuxtemps, and Berlin under Joachim with whom he lived for some time. Stud compn. under Gevaert in Brussels and Herzogenberg in Berlin. He commenced his studies under auspices of H.R.H. the Infanta Doña Isabel. Taught vn. at Hamburg Cons. and, for many years, at the R.C.M. London. Former leader of Philh. Orch. Berlin, and Boston Symphony Orch. Has appeared occasionally as condr. in England, France and Russia; also as chamber-music player. Since 1908, condr. of the Orquesta Sinfónica in Madrid, where he now resides, and is vn. prof. at the R. Cons. de Música, a position he won by competition in the early days of his career. Is also a member of the orch. of R. Chapel, Commander of Order of Isabel la Católica, Knight of Order of Carlos III, *Légion d'Honneur*, and Santiago and Villaviciosa, Portugal.

Centro de la Tierra, mus. comedy, prod. Madrid about 1890; *Trois pièces originales dans le genre espagnol*, vn. cello and pf.; *Zambra*, *Tango*, and *Guajiras*, vn. and pf. (Bote & Bock, Berlin; Schott, Mayence).—P. G. M.

ARDITI, Luigi. Ital. violinist, opera-condr. and compr. b. Crescentino (Piedmont), 22 July, 1822; d. 1 May, 1903. Noted for his waltz-songs, among which the most celebrated are *Il Bacio* and *L'Estasi*.—D. A.

ARENSKY, Antony Stepanovitch (*accent 2nd syll.*). Russ. compr. b. Novgorod, 30 July/11 Aug. 1861; d. Terioki, Finland, 26 Feb./11 March, 1906. Stud. under Zikke, and later under Johansen and Rimsky-Korsakof, at Petrograd Cons. In 1882, appointed prof. of cpt. at Moscow Cons., and in 1892 his first opera, *A Dream on the Volga*, was successfully perf. in that city. His other chief works are the opera *Nal and Damayanti* (1899), the ballet *A Night in Egypt*, and cantata *The Fountain of Bakhchisarai*. He also comp. church music, pf. pieces, songs, 2 symphonies, a set of Variations for strings, on a theme of Tchaikovsky (often played at Q. H. London) and some chamber-music, among which a pf. trio (op. 31) enjoys a certain popularity. The greater part of his output is already forgotten. He is a compr. in most respects akin to Tchaikovsky, but with less inclination towards dramatic eloquence, and a far less efficient and less versatile technical equipment.—M. D. C.

ARIANI, Adriano. Ital. pianist and compr. b. Macerata, 1880. Stud. at Liceo at Pesaro, pf. under Vitali, compn. under Mascagni. Rapidly gained high reputation as concert-player, appearing in Rome (at Augusteo) and in many other towns. Several years ago he went over to New York, where he devoted himself also to conducting; in 1918, an oratorio *San Francesco* was perf. at Carnegie Hall under his bâton. In 1920, dir. a successful season of opera at the Brooklyn Acad. of Music theatre. Lately returned to Italy.—D. A.

ARÍN Y GOENAGA, Valentín. Span. teacher and compr. b. Villafranca (Alava), 3 Nov. 1854. One of first in Spain to adopt modern methods of studying and teaching harmony and cpt.

Until his recent death, he was teacher at R. Cons. de Música, Madrid, where, as pupil of Arrieta, he obtained 1st prize for compn. in 1877.—P. G. M.

ARKWRIGHT, Godfrey E. P. Eng. mus. writer and researcher; *b.* 10 April, 1864. Stud. under John Farmer (Balliol Coll. Oxford) and H. E. Wooldridge.

Ed. *Musical Antiquary* (magazine); *Old English Edition* (25 vols.) of old Eng. music; some vols. for Purcell Soc.; Eng. songs, *Lawes to Linley*; catalogue of ms. music in Christ Ch. Library, Oxford (not yet completed; 2 vols. publ.); *Studies in Modal Composition* (*Musica Antiquata*) with H. E. Wooldridge; 5 vols. songs.—E.-H.

ARKWRIGHT, Marian Ursula. Eng. compr. *b.* Norwich, 1863; *d.* 1922. Mus.Doc. Dunelm. 1913. Sister of the above. Has exercised a great influence on rural music.

Concert pieces, vla. and pf. (Breitkopf); *Requiem Mass* (Cary); *Dragon of Wantley*, female chorus (Cary); orch. suites; chamber-music for wood-wind instrs.; *Waterbabies*, operetta; *Last Rhyme of True Thomas*, chorus and strings.—E.-H.

ARLOM, Wilfred. Australian compr. *b.* Newcastle-on-Tyne. Lives in Roseville, N.S.W.

Many songs; anthems; pf. pieces (Newman; Allan & Co. Melbourne).—E.-H.

ARMÁNDOZ, Norberto. Span. orgt. and compr. *b.* Astizárraga (Guipúzcoa), June 1893. Stud. in Spain and in Paris; at age of 26, chief orgt. of Cath. of Seville, a position he still holds.

Church music; arr. Basque folk-songs (*Itiuna, Goixian On*, etc.).—P. G. M.

ARMBRUST, Walter. Ger. orgt. *b.* Hamburg, 17 Oct. 1882. Son of celebrated orgt. Carl F. A. (1849–96), whose pupil he was; then of W. Böhmer and P. Homeyer (Leipzig); 1903, orgt. and choirmaster of Heiligengeist Kirche, Hamburg; 1908, founded Brahms Cons. Hamburg; condr. of Philh. Orch. Dresden since 1920.—A. E.

d'ARNEIRO, Count. Portuguese compr. *b.* Lisbon, 1838; *d.* 1903. Stud. under V. Schira for compn. and singing, under Antonio José Soares for pf., on which instr. he became very proficient. He early migrated to Italy where he spent the rest of his life, but continually returned to Lisbon, where his early works, including his ballet *Ginn* (San Carlos Theatre), were given in 1866. In 1871 his *Te Deum* was given there; later it was transformed to a cantata and given in Paris under Léon Martin.

Opera, *Elisir di giovanezza*, 4 acts (Lisbon, 1876; Dal Verme, Milan, 1877); given later in a new version, as *La Derelitta* (San Carlos Theatre, Lisbon, 1885); *Don Bibas*, his last opera, took a prize in a competition in Italy; *Symphonie-Cantate* (*Te Deum*), chorus and orch.; many pf. pieces.—E.-H.

AROCA Y ORTEGA, Jesús. Span. compr. and musicologist; *b.* Algete (Madrid), Oct. 1877. Stud. pf. and compn. at R. Cons. de Música, Madrid. President of Asociación de Directores de Orquesta (Association of Orch. Condrs.), Spain. Also known as compr. of a number of small popular pieces and mus. comedies. As a mus. scholar, he renders valuable service to the reconstruction of mus. history of Spain. Amongst his works are *Cancionero musical y poético del siglo XVI*, transcriptions of song - book of Claudio de la Sablonara, containing music and biographical notes of Span. poets of the Golden

Age, such as Juan Blas de Castro, Mateo Romero, El Maestro Capitán, and Machado el Portugués (publ. in the Boletín de la R. Acad. Española); *Reseña histórica de la tonada*, mus. transcriptions from the XVI, XVII, and XVIII centuries (publ. by R. Velasco, Madrid).—P. G. M.

Incidental music for drama of Antonio J. de Linares, *Alma remota* (Teatro Español, Madrid); *Arrabales Castellanos*, suite for orch. (perf. in Madrid by Orquesta Sinfónica and Orquesta Filarmónica). (Publ.: Faustino Fuentes; Mateu; Unión Musical Española, Madrid.)—P. G. M.

ARREGUI GARAY, Vicente. Span. compr. *b.* Madrid, 3 July, 1871. Stud. at R. Cons. de Música, Madrid, being awarded 1st prize for pf. and compn. In 1899 was granted the Rome Prize by the Acad. de Bellas Artes. He does not follow any particular school, and in this sense may be considered a free-lance whose mus. output always exhibits those features of sobriety and solidity inherent in the Castilian temperament.

Str. 4tet; pf. sonata (1st perf. 1916, Sociedad Nacional de Música); orch. *Melodia religiosa* (1st perf. Orquesta Benedito, Gran Teatro, Madrid, Feb. 1917); *Oración y Escena de los Angeles* from oratorio *San Francisco*; *Historia de una Madre*, symph. poem based on story by Andersen (awarded prize in Concurso Nacional, 1910, and has been perf. many times by Orquesta Sinfónica and Orquesta Filarmónica, Madrid, and the Orquesta Sinfónica, Barcelona); *Sinfonía vasca*, 1st perf. Orquesta Sinfónica, March 1922); *El Lobo Ciego*, cantata (R. Opera House, Madrid, 1916); operas: *Yolanda*, 1 act, based on poem by Henry Hertz (awarded prize at Concurso Nacional del Estado, 1911; Teatro Real, Madrid, 1923); *La Maya*, 2 acts; *La Madona*, 2 acts; *El Cuento de Barba Azul* (*Story of Bluebeard*), 3 acts; Motet, 4 v.; Mass, 3 v. and organ acc.; 3 lyrical comedies for children, *Chao, Tatin*, and *La Sombra de Mariani* (Schott).—P. G. M.

ARRIETA Y CORERA, Emilio. Span. compr. *b.* Puente de la Reina (Navarra), 21 Oct. 1823. Prof. of compn. (1857) at R. Cons. de Música; dir. of same from 1858 until his death, 11 Feb. 1864, in Madrid. Member of the Acad. de Bellas Artes de San Fernando; counsellor to the Ministry of Education. At age of 15 went to Italy, stud. under Perelli and Mandanicci. Entered the Milan Cons. 1841, where he obtained 1st prize for compn. and wrote, whilst a pupil there, his opera *Ildegonda*, perf. later in Madrid (R. Opera House), and at several theatres abroad. He wrote cantatas and some religious music, but mostly *zarzuelas*, after the style of the Ital. operetta, for which he became famous. (*El Domino Azul* was written in 1853, and he made an operatic version of *Marina*, his most popular one, for R. Opera House, Madrid.)

Like his contemporary, Hilarión Eslava, he exercised greatest influence on public taste and mus. education of Spain. Both of them, owing to lack of sensibility, ignored or despised the Wagnerian ideas predominating at the time throughout the world. A. was an upholder of the Ital. tradition, and shares with Eslava the responsibility for delaying the advent of the Span. renaissance at least twenty years.

Opera, *Ildegonda*. Zarzuelas: *El Grumete*; *La Estrella de Madrid*; *Marina*; *El Planeta Venus*, *Llamada y tropa*; *La Guerra Santa* (Unión Musical Española, Madrid).—P. G. M.

ARRIOLA, José. Span. pianist. He appeared on concert platform at such an early age that his toys had to be placed on the piano in order to induce him to play. He is still known as *Pepito Arriola* (diminutive of *Pepe*, pet-name for José in Spain). Struck by the 9-year-old boy's talent, Nikisch undertook in 1908 the direction of his education at Leipzig Cons. He has toured occasionally in Germany, Spain and America.—P. G. M.

ARROYO. See PORTUGUESE OPERA.

ARTE DI STUPORE. An expression adopted by Domenico Alaleona (*q.v.*) in his arts. on modern harmony (publ. in *Rivista Musicale Italiana* in 1911) to indicate certain expressive effects of "neutral tonailty." (See TONALITÀ NEUTRE.)—E.-H.

ARTSYBUCHEF, Nicolas Vassilievitch (*accent 2nd syll.*). Russ. compr. *b.* Petrograd, 1858. Stud. under Rimsky-Korsakof. Made transcriptions of works of R.-K., Mussorgsky, Borodin; comp. songs and pf. pieces in pleasing melodic style; but eclectic. Reflects the influence of "the Five," and also of Chopin. 1908, president of Committee of Management of Russ. Mus. Soc. (Petrograd section), and in same year, succeeded R.-K. as president of committee founded by Belaief for encouragement of Russ. comprs. and executants. He carries out this function at the present time. In 1920 he settled in Paris where he dir. the firm of the Belaief Mus. Ed.—B. de S.

ARVESCHOUG, Albert. Norwegian barit. singer; *b.* Hamar in 1861; *d.* in Oregon, U.S.A., in 1913. Trained at Music Acad. in Stockholm. Went when young to New York, where he lived for many years, being a popular and admired singer. Made concert-tours in America, England and Norway. One of the most gifted vocalists Norway has possessed.—R. M.

ARVESEN, Arve. Norwegian violinist and teacher; *b.* Hamar, 12 Sept. 1869. Trained under Gudbrand Böhn, Christiania, at Cons. in Leipzig, under Marsick, Paris, and 1892–5 (State scholarship) under Eugène Ysaye in Brussels. *Début* 1890 in Christiania at concert given by Erika Nissen; leader of chief orchs. in Helsingfors, Åbo, Bergen and Gothenburg. Since 1904, in Christiania, as teacher and soloist. Founded in 1917 a chamber-music soc., whose string quartet (with A. as 1st vn.) has perf. in Paris, Copenhagen and Stockholm, as well as regularly in Christiania.—R. M.

ASHDOWN, Edwin, Ltd. Publishers. The orig. founder was Christian Rudolph Wessel (*b.* Bremen, 1797). Came to London and started publishing unknown foreign works in 1825, Chopin and Heller. The business was afterwards acquired by Edwin Ashdown and Henry J. Parry (both formerly in employ of Wessel). The publication of pf. pieces by Sydney Smith and Brinley Richards brought fame and fortune to the firm. On retirement of Parry, Edwin A. devoted himself to bringing out the classics and secured services of Walter Macfarren and Sterndale Bennett as editors. The firm is now (1924) conducted by two grandsons of late Edwin A.

and is largely devoted to modern teaching material.—E.-H.

ASHTON, Algernon Bennet Langton. Eng. compr. *b.* Durham, 9 Dec. 1859. Went to Leipzig 1863, remaining there for 17 years. Stud. at Cons. there (1875–9) under Reinecke, Jadassohn and E. F. Richter; later under Joachim Raff, Frankfort-o-M. Settled in London in 1881. Pf. prof. R.C.M. 1885–1910. A compr. of serious aims and sound scholarship. Has publ. over 150 works.

Pf. trios; 24 pf. sonatas; 5 vn. sonatas; 5 cello sonatas; 3 trios; 2 pf. 4tets; 2 str. 4tets; 2 pf. 5tets; 1 str. 5tet; 1 wind 5tet; 1 str. 6tet (Leipzig, Hofbauer); pf. pieces (Hofbauer; Erler; Simrock; Steingräber; Leuckart; Forberg; Schirmer; Chester; Stainer & Bell); songs (Simrock; Hofbauer; Erler); part-songs (Hofbauer; Erler); organ pieces (Novello). In ms.: 5 symphonies, overtures, marches, dances (orch.); pf. concerto; vn. concerto; songs; chamber-music. Has also publ. *Truth, Wit and Wisdom*, 525 Letters to the Press (Chapman & Hall, 1905); Vol. II, 656 Letters (*id.* 1908).—E.-H.

ASPESTRAND, Sigwardt. Norwegian compr. *b.* Fredrikshald, 13 Nov. 1856. Pupil of Dalback and Böhn (Christiania) in vn.; from 1881 pupil of Cons. in Leipzig, afterwards of High School in Berlin (Joachim). An injury to his hand forced him to abandon vn.-playing, whereupon he stud. compn.; during a residence of many years in Germany, comp. several operas to his own text. He has also written some chamber-music, etc. In style he has kept close to the classicists and Romanticists, especially Weber and Marschner, often with a popular and national mode of expression. Now lives in Christiania.

Operas : *Sjömandsbruden* (produced in Gotha, Coburg and Christiania); *Freyas Alter*; *Der Recke von Lyrskovheid*; *Die Wette*; *Im Göthezimmer*; *Le Baiser au Porteur*; *Robin Hood*; comic opera, *Pervonte*.—J. A.

ASSAFIEF, Boris Vladimirovitch (*accent 2nd syll.*). See GLEBOF, IGOR.

ATANASIU. See RUMANIAN OPERA.

ATKINS, Sir Ivor Algernon. Orgt. of Worcester Cath., England; *b.* Cardiff, 29 Nov. 1869. Assistant-orgt. under Dr. Sinclair at Truro and Hereford. Cond. fests. of the Three Choirs at Worcester, 1899, 1902, 1905, 1908, 1911, 1920, 1923. Mus.Doc. Oxon. 1920. Knighted 1921. Has ed. (with Sir Edward Elgar) Bach's *St. Matthew Passion* and the *Orgelbüchlein* of Bach's Weimar period, in Eng. form (Novello).

Hymn of Faith (libretto by Ed. Elgar); settings of *Magnificat and Nunc Dimittis*, chorus and orch.; part-songs; songs, etc.—E.-H.

ATONALITY. A new style of composing without conscious reference to any scale or tonic. The scale, under the mus. system at present in vogue, must of course be the dodecuple (*q.v.*). The desire to elude a fixed tonality (key) is at least as old as Mozart. The term was first given to the works of Arnold Schönberg. The sources can be traced through the chromatic harmony of Wagner's *Tristan*. The dissolution of fixed tonality had its first definite expression in Schönberg's 3 pf. pieces, op. 11 (1909). He refers to atonality in his *Harmonielehre* (Univ. Ed. Vienna, 1911). Atonality also came about through building up dissonances on every degree of the chromatic scale, so that each degree gains the function of a dominant. By this means, the predominance of the dominant and tonic of the older system is extinguished, and new laws have to be discovered empirically. Schönberg uses atonality in a contrapuntal way, often polytonally. Amongst the purely atonal writers are Béla Bartók, Arthur Honegger, Arthur Bliss, Stravinsky, Anton von Webern, Bernard van Dieren, Sorabji, Daniel Ruyneman, and many others. Debussy achieves atonal effects often through the use of the whole-tone scale. Amongst modern comprs. who resorted occasionally to atonality before 1911 may be mentioned Richard Strauss, Granville Bantock and Cyril Scott. See Chap. XI in Eaglefield-Hull's *Modern Harmony* (Augener, 1913). Also arts. in *Musical Opinion*, Oct. and Nov. 1922, and art. HAUER in this Dictionary.—EG. W. & E.-H.

ATTERBERG, Kurt M. Swedish compr. and condr. *b.* Gothenburg, 12 Dec. 1887; engineer in R. Patent Office; music critic *Stockholms Tidningen*. One of most talented of young Swedish comprs.

Op. 1, *Rapsodie*, pf. and orch. (1908; perf. Gothenburg, 1912); op. 2, *Adagio* and *Scherzo*, str. 4tet (1909; Stockholm, 1918); op. 3, Symphony No. I, B mi. (1909–11; Gothenburg, 1912); op. 4, concert-overture, A mi. (1909–11; Gothenburg, 1912); op. 5, symph. poem, barit and orch. (1912); Stockholm, 1913; op. 6, Symphony No. II, F (1911–13; Sondershausen, 1913); op. 7, vn. concerto (1913; Gothenburg, 1914); op. 8, *Requiem*, chorus and orch. (1914; Malmö, 1914); op. 9, pantomime-ballet, *Per Svinaherde* (1914; Gothenburg, 1916); op. 19, Symphony No. III, *Meeressymphonie* (Stockholm, 1916); op. 11, str. 4tet (Stockholm, 1918); op. 12, opera, *Härvard Harpolekare* (to own words; 1912–5; Stockholm, 1919); op. 13, prelude to *Perseus* (1918; Stockholm, 1919); op. 14, Symphony No. IV (*Piccola sinfonia*; 1918; Stockholm, 1919); op. 15, *Autumn Ballades*, pf. (1918–9; Ed. Nord. Musikföri.); op. 16, cantata for mining-school Jubilee (Stockholm, 1919); op. 17, orch. rhapsody, *The Foolish Maiden* (1920; Ed. Nord. Mus.); op. 18, music to a Shakespeare play; 2 orch. suites (Leuckart); op. 20, Symphony No. V (*Funèbre*; 1922); op. 21, cello concerto (1922); pf. pieces.—P. V.

AUBERT, Louis François Marie. Fr. compr. *b.* Paramé, 19 Feb. 1877. Stud. at Paris Cons., where his teacher of compn. was Gabriel Fauré. In 1901 the perf. (Concerts-Colonne) of his *Fantaisie* for pf. and orch. (comp. 1899) confirmed the excellent impression created in 1900 by his orch. *Suite Brève*. Until 1902 he was engaged in writing an important lyric score, *La Légende du Sang*, of which only two excerpts, the song *Hélène* and an *Invocation à Odin*, have appeared. In 1910 he completed a lyric fairy-play in 3 acts, *La Forêt bleue*, which was successfully produced at Geneva and at Boston (1913), but of which only concert performances have taken place so far in France. He has written a number of songs, among which the fine sets *Crépuscules d'automne* (1910) and *Poèmes arabes* (1917) stand foremost. Among his pf. works the picturesque set, *Sillages* (1911), deserves special mention. And his latest orch. work, *Habanera* (1919), has been hailed as particularly beautiful from both technical and poetic points of view. It was given in Queen's Hall, London in 1920 under Sir Henry Wood. Consult L. Vuillemin; *Louis Aubert* (Paris, Durand, 1921).—M. D. C.

AUBRY, Pierre. Fr. musicologist and historian; *b.* Paris, 14 Feb. 1874; was killed accidentally at Dieppe (Seine Inférieure), 31 Aug. 1910. Having obtained degrees in Letters and Law (1894, 1896), and diploma from l'École des Chartes, awarded for his thesis on the *Philosophie musicale des trouvères*, he taught at Catholic Inst. in Paris. Entrusted in 1901 with an official mission for musical research in Turkestan, he there collected documents in view of a comparative history of liturgic chant of Greek and Roman Churches. As he was specialist musician-palæographer of sacred and secular music of Middle Ages, his labours have brought to light a quantity of melodic notations of the period. His interpretations have been greatly disputed and have been in certain cases the object of sharp polemics. His numerous publs. are always of the greatest value. Of special interest are:

Estampies et danses royales: Les plus anciens textes de musique instrumentale du Moyen-Âge (1907); *Recherches sur les "tenors français" dans les motets du XIIIe siècle* (1907); *Le Roman de Fauvel*, 1907 (Reproduction of ms. in National Libr.); *Cent Motets du XIIIe siècle*, 3 vols., 1908 (Reproduction of Cod. Bamberg, E. D. IV, 6); *Chansons des Croisades*, 1909 (with J. Bédier); *Trouvères et troubadours* (*Les Marches de la musique*, Paris, Alcan, 1909); *Chansonnier de l'Arsenal* (1910), etc. He ed. *La Tribune de St. Gervais* with A. Gastoué and from 1903 to 1908 he wrote in the *Mercure Musical* a series of essays. He collaborated in 2 vols. of *Chansons* (*Chansons de troubadours, Chansons du XVe siècle*), with harmonies by V. d'Indy, Ch. Bordes, R. de Castéra, etc. (Paris, Rouart).—M. L. P.

AUDRAN, Edmond. Fr. compr. *b.* Lyons, 11 April, 1842; *d.* Lierceville (Seine et Oise), 17 Aug. 1901. After studies at École Niedermeyer, went to Marseilles at age of 20 and became orgt. there. From 1877, he lived in Paris and comp. operettas with success. His facile style, less laboured than Lecocq's, is praiseworthy for gaiety of melodies and freedom of rhythms. Operettas: *Le Grand Mogol* (1877); *La Mascotte* (1880); *Gillette de Narbonne* (1882); *Miss Helyett* (1890). The complete number of his works, almost all operettas, is over 40. There is a mass and an oratorio. All publ. by Choudens, Paris.—A. C.

AUDSLEY, George Ashdown. Scottish organ designer, writer; *b.* Elgin, 6 Sept. 1838. Educated as an architect. Became interested in organs and organ-building about 1865 and commenced writing on the subject in 1886. Went to U.S.A. in 1892.

The Art of Organ-building (Dodd, Mead, 1905); *The Organ of the Twentieth Century* (Dodd, Mead, 1919); *Organ-stops and their Artistic Registration* (Gray, 1921); contributions to *The English Mechanic* and *World of Science*, 1886–8.—J. M.

AUER, Leopold (von). Hungarian violinist; *b.* Beszprém, 7 June, 1845. Stud. at Budapest Cons. under Ridley Kohne; Vienna Cons. 1857–8 under J. Dont; later at Hanover under J. Joachim; in 1863 he was leader of orch. at Düsseldorf; in 1866 of orch. at Hamburg; 1868, Imperial Solo-violinist at Petrograd and prof. of vn. at Cons.; from 1887 to 1892 he led the concerts of the Russ. Imperial Music Soc.; in 1895, was ennobled; 1903, created Staatsrat. From 1911 he lived at Dresden, going back in

1914 to Petrograd; 1917 at Christiania; in Feb. 1918, went to New York, where he publ. *Violin Playing as I teach it* (1921). Has also written an autobiography, *My Long Life in Music* (London, 1924, Duckworth).—E.-H.

AUGÉ DE LASSUS, Lucien. Fr. writer on music and librettist; *b.* Paris, 1846; *d.* there, 1914. Wrote 5 comedies in verse, a drama in 5 acts, and libretti for 8 comic operas; a popular lecturer, and treated the most diverse subjects in mus. history with masterly ease; a personal friend of Camille Saint-Saëns and wrote 3 libretti for him (*Phryné, L'Ancêtre, La Gloire*); also devoted a book to him—*Camille Saint-Saëns* (Paris, 1914, Delagrave). Also publ. a volume on *Boïeldieu*; a history of the mus. soc. called La Trompette; *Un Demi-siècle de Musique de Chambre* (1911, Delagrave).—M. L. P.

AUGENER, Ltd. Publishers, founded 1853 in London, by late George Augener. In 1855, first cheap type-ed. of classics was produced; since that date the firm has been closely identified with cheap eds. of classics, and other educational music. Augener's Edition (over 6000 vols.) was commenced in 1867. In 1871 the publ. of *The Monthly Musical Record* was commenced. In 1878 the firm established a printing department in Lexington Street, Golden Square; superseded 1911 by modern printing works at Acton. In 1896 the trade-name of Robert Cocks & Co. (establ. 1823) was acquired. The business was converted into a company with limited liability in October 1904. The founder, George Augener, retired in 1910 and died in 1915. Almost from the outset the publ. of pf. music became a speciality, and the catalogue is remarkable for large number of names of British comprs. which it contains.—E.-H.

AUGUSTEO, The. Famous concert-hall in Rome, the most important in Italy both as regards size and artistic programmes. Built on ruins of the Mausoleum of Augustus, whence its name. During the last century, was used for popular spectacles; then closed for a long time. Some years ago the municipality of Rome made it into the present magnificent concert - hall, inaugurated 1908. The orch. and choral concerts, which had formerly taken place in Hall of Acad. of Santa Cecilia, were transferred here, and the Augusteo soon became the centre of the Ital. mus. movement, as far as symph. works are concerned. All the greatest condrs. and concert-artists have appeared there. The hall belongs to the municipality of Rome, and is managed by R. Acad. of Santa Cecilia. The concert-season is from Dec. to April. Bernardino Molinari (*q.v.*) is now the artistic dir. of the Augusteo.—D. A.

AULA GUILLÉN, Luis. Span. compr. and pf. prof. *b.* Saragossa, 1876. Stud. at R. Cons. de Música, Madrid. Prof. of pf. at Escuela Nacional de Música, Saragossa.

Double 5tet, str., wind and pf. (Filarmónica, Saragossa, 1915); *Añoranzas*, symph. poem (Orquesta Filarmónica, Madrid, 1919); *Cuadros poéticos*, suite for orch. (Orquesta Sinfónica, Madrid, 1922); *Trozo rapsódico* (*id.* 1923).—P. G. M.

AULAS, Francisque. Fr. compr. *b.* Lyons, 1884; *d.* during the war, 30 June, 1915. Pupil of Cons. Lyons; a compr. of considerable promise, of ardent temperament; was a fanatical follower of Berlioz. Left a certain amount of work unpublished:

Poème fantasque, orch.; *Le Crépuscule*, ob. and orch. (1904); pf. and vn. sonatas; pf. suite; songs (to composer's own words).—A. C.

AURIC, Georges. Fr. compr. *b.* Lodève (Hérault), 1899. Pupil of Caussade at Paris Cons.; of V. d'Indy at *Schola Cantorum*. Joined the so-called "Group of Six," of which he was the youngest member. Now mus. critic of the *Nouvelles Littéraires*.

Theatre: *Les Noces de Gamache*; *La Reine de cœur*; *Les Fâcheux*; *Les Pélicans*. Orch.: *Fox-Trot*; nocturne; suite. Pf.: 3 pastorals. Songs: *Les Joues en feu*; *Alphabet—Recueil de chansons pour enfants* (Songs for Children).—A. C.

AUSTIN, Ernest. Eng. compr. *b.* London, 31 Dec. 1874. Was in business until age of 33 when he took up profession of music. Received a few lessons from F. Davenport, but is practically self-taught. His *Vicar of Bray* variations for str. orch. (Novello) were perf. at Queen's Hall in 1918 (again 1919, 1920); *Hymn of Apollo*, Leeds Choral Union, 1918; *Stella Mary Dances*, (Queen's Hall, 1918); *Ode on a Grecian Urn* (R.C.M. Patron's Fund, 1922); a long cycle of works for organ founded on Bunyan's *Pilgrim's Progress*. His works are of modern type and show a considerable feeling for true poetical accentuation; some of his songs are without barlines. Has publ. a vol. of verses, *Songs from the Ravel* (Reeves).

Has compn. several sonatinas for children on national tunes, and a large amount of pf.-teaching music. Most of his works are publ. by J. H. Larway, London; a few by Novello; Stainer & Bell; Boosey; Chester. —E.-H.

AUSTIN, Frederic. Eng. barit. operatic singer and compr. *b.* London, 1872. Stud. singing under Charles Lunn; compn. and music in general under his uncle, Dr. W. H. Hunt. Sang at Gloucester Fest. 1904; since then at many of the chief fests.; and as principal barit. at R. Opera, Covent Garden; in Beecham's seasons at His Majesty's and Covent Garden; in Denhof's Eng. *Ring*, *Mastersingers* and other perfs.; also in Germany, Holland, Denmark; arr. and comp. a new version of Pepusch's *Beggar's Opera* (Hammersmith) which ran uninterruptedly in London from 6 June, 1920, to 17 Dec. 1923 (1463 times); also given in Paris, U.S.A., Canada, Australia. Later on he wrote a new mus. version of *Polly* (Gay's sequel to *Beggar's Opera*). His other stage works include music to *The Knight of the Burning Pestle* (1921), *The Insect Play* (1922), and Congreve's *Way of the World* (1924). His orch. works have been successful. In 1924 he was appointed artistic dir. of British National Opera Co.

Orch. works: Rhapsody, *Spring* (ms.), Promenade Concerts, Sir Henry Wood, 1907; symph. poem, *Isabella* (ms.), League of Music Fest. Liverpool, 1912; symphony in E (Balfour Gardiner Concerts, 1913); *Palsgaard*, Danish sketches (ms.), R. Philh. Soc. 1916; 3 songs with orch. *Songs of Unrest* (Augener), Birmingham League of Music Fest. 1913; 3 songs, *Love's Pilgrimage*, v. pf. str. 4tet (Enoch). *Songs in a Farmhouse*, soli, str. 4tet and pf. (Novello); pf. pieces (W. Rogers); *The Beggar's Opera* (Boosey); *Polly* (*id.*); 3 dances from *The Insect Play* (*id.*).—E.-H.

AUSTRIAN ORCHESTRAL MUSIC. The period at the end of xix and beginning of xx century, was most significant in Austrian music. Whereas opera was deeply influenced by Wagner, the symph. line was taken up by Bruckner from where Schubert had left it. Brahms, though important, is not thoroughly representative of Austrian art, which follows on from Beethoven's 9th symphony. The last movement of symphony becomes the problem. Bruckner connects it by bringing in principal theme of 1st movement at climax of last as a *leitmotiv*. Mahler does this in his 1st symphony, but in his 2nd, uses chorus. His 3rd symphony has 6 movements (4th, a solo; 5th, chorus). In last movement of his 4th symphony he uses a s. solo voice. The 5th, 6th, 7th are instrumental, and, in contrast to former, very polyphonic. The finale of 5th and 7th is a rondo; the finale of 6th is a symphony in itself (¾-hour). He solved Beethoven's problem by making his 8th symphony choral throughout. Mahler began a new style with his 9th symphony, instrumental throughout, leaving his former individual romantic line to open an objective period. Nothing further has been done in Austria. The younger men are trying to create a new dramatic style or work out the new chamber-music initiated by Schönberg in the *Kammersymphonie* and 2nd str. 4tet.—EG. W.

AUTERI - MANZOCCHI, Salvatore. Ital. compr. *b.* Palermo, 25 Dec. 1845; *d.* Parma, 1924. Compr. of several *mélodrames*, amongst which *Dolores* (perf. Florence, 1873) was especially successful. Many of his ballads became popular for their melodic richness and spontaneity.—D. A.

AVISON EDITION. An ed. of contemporary British music, publ. for the members of Soc. of British Comprs. by Cary & Co. The name was taken from an Eng. compr. Charles Avison (*b.* Newcastle-on-Tyne, about 1710) (see Grove's *Dictionary of Music*).—E.-H.

AXMAN, Emil. Czech compr. *b.* ˙Rataje, Moravia, 1887. Stud. at Prague Univ. under Vítězslav Novák; Doctor of Mus. Science, 1912; official of Nat. Museum, Prague, since 1913. Publ. a study, *Moravia in the Czech Music of XIX Century.*

Choral works, song-cycles: *Z Vojny (From the War); Duha (Rainbow)* 2 symph. poems: *Smutky a naděje (Mourning and Hope); Jasno;* 2 pf. sonatas (publ. V. Kotrba; J. Otto; E. Starý; F. A. Urbánek; Hudební Matice).—V. ST.

AXTENS, Florence E. Australian compr. *b.* London. Lives in Sydney.

Memory Sketches pf. (Novello); sets of Australian 2-part songs (Nicholson, Sydney; also New South Wales Education Board); vn. sonatina, ms.; solosongs, etc.—E.-H.

AZKUE, Father Resurrección María de. Span. compr. philologist and leading musicologist of Basque group; D.D.; dir. of Acad. de la Lengua Vasca (Basque Language Acad.), Bilbao.

Vizcaytik Bizkaira, 3-act *zarzuela; Pasa de chimbos,* 2-act *zarzuela; Eguzkia nora,* 2-act *zarzuela; Colonia inglesa,* 3-act comedy; *Sasi-eskola,* 1-act *zarzuela; Aitaren bildur,* 1-act *zarzuela; Ortzuri,* 3-act opera; *Urlo,* 3-act opera. Folk-lore: *La música popular vascongada; Música popular vasca; Cancionero popular vasco.* Church music: *Jesusen Biotzaren ila,* meditations; *Cánticos religiosos; Cánticos a Nuestra Señora; Coro y tres estrofas en honor de San José.*—P. G. M.

B

BACARISSE CHINORIA, Salvador. Spanish compr. *b.* Madrid,12 Sept. 1898. Stud. at R. Cons. de Música, Madrid, under Conrado del Campo. His works are modern in spirit and form.

2 Nocturnes, v. and orch. (poems by J. A. Silva); *La Nave de Ulises*, symph. poem; *Heraldos*, pf. (Unión Musical Española, Madrid).—P. G. M.

BACCARA, Luisa. Ital. pianist; *b.* Venice, 14 Jan. 1894. Stud. at Milan Cons., then at Vienna. She appeared successfully as concert-player; in 1918 played at Augusteo, Rome. Gabriele d'Annunzio dedicated various eulo-gistic writings to her.—D. A.

BACH, David Josef. Austrian writer on music; critic; *b.* Vienna, 13 Aug. 1874. Stud. philosophy and philology at Vienna Univ. Graduated Ph.D. at 23; went to Berlin, where he stud. under Helmholtz; later at Leipzig (under Wundt). At 26 began to study music, giving lessons and writing for newspapers. In 1900, returned to Vienna; wrote for *Frankfurter Zeitung, Die Zeit*, and finally for the *Arbeiter Zeitung* (Labour paper), where he is now chief critic. Instituted great Workers' Symphony Concerts in Vienna and leads mus. education amongst Viennese working classes. The great Music Fest. in Vienna, 1918, was due to him. He is also mus. adviser to municipality of Vienna. He was editor (with J. Bittner) of the *Merker*, 1918-22.—P. P.

BACH, Fritz. Swiss orgt. compr. *b.* Paris, 3 June, 1881. Stud. compn. in Paris under Vin-cent d'Indy and organ under Guilmant and Vierne. Since 1913, has lived at Nyon (Switzer-land), where he is orgt. and teacher of harmony.

Symphony in C mi.; pf. 5tet, A mi.; numerous choruses (Lausanne, Fœtisch) and organ pieces. —F. H.

BACH DE LLOBERA, Lea. Harpist; *b.* Paris in 1883. At 7, entered Cons. of Isabel II in Barcelona, where her parents had gone. Gained professional diploma with honourable mention here when 12 years old. Then went to Cons. Paris, under Hasselmans. 1st prize and pro-fessional diploma, 1907. In London was received and complimented by late King Edward VII. —A. M.

BACHELET, Alfred. Fr. compr. *b.* Paris, 26 Feb. 1864. Is one of the most remarkable opera-composers in modern French school; gained popularity only late in life; then only with one work, a lyrical drama called *Quand la cloche son-nera* in 1922. After brilliant studies at Conserva-toire, he obtained *Prix de Rome*, in 1890. He was then practically unheard of for 25 years, except among his composer friends. Very occasionally a song, lyrical scene, or symphonic poem from his pen was performed at concerts. In 1914, the Opéra performed *Scemo* (lyrical drama,

3 acts and 5 scenes; libretto by Charles Meré). This powerful and stormy piece aroused both enthusiasm and hostility, but it won the approval of musicians. During the war, as conductor of the Opéra orchestra, he successfully produced a ballet (libretto by Henry Prunières) into which he incorporated works of xviii century, which he had orchestrated with great verve and skill, *La Fête chez La Pouplinière*.

When appointed head of Conservatoire at Nancy (succeeding Guy Ropartz), Bachelet showed great initiative. He conducted the orchestra, and composed for it his lyrical drama, *Quand la cloche sonnera*, which was performed with phenomenal success at the Opéra-Comique in Nov. 1922. Although the libretto is most mediocre, it yet contains a dramatic situation of which the composer has taken excellent advantage. The music throughout is animated by a dramatic inspiration which carries the hearer away without even being able to analyse his sensations. This work is one of the most powerful produced on the French operatic stage for the last 30 years.—H. P.

BÄCK, Knut. Swedish compr. pianist; *b.* Stockholm, 22 April, 1868; stud. there and in Berlin; lives in Gothenburg; member R.A.M. Stockholm, 1912. Has comp. pf. pieces and songs.—P. V.

BACKER-GRÖNDAHL, Agathe Ursula. Nor-wegian pianist, compr. *b.* Holmestrand, 1 Dec. 1847; *d.* Christiania, 6 June, 1907. Pf. pupil of Otto Winter-Hjelm, Halfdan Kjerulf and Ludv. M. Lindeman; in 1866 of Kullak (Ber-lin); afterwards, for short time, of Bülow and Liszt. Gave concerts in 1871 with great suc-cess at Gewandhaus, Leipzig, and subsequently in the great cities of Europe. Bülow spoke very highly both of her gifts as a pianist and of her compositions in one of his letters to *Allg. d. Musikzeitung*. In compn. she was pupil of Würst in Berlin amongst others, and her 70 works secure for her the first place among Norwegian female composers.

As a pianist, she cultivated especially masters of Romantic school, and her romantic tempera-ment also stamps her pf.-pieces and songs. Her lyric vein flows richly and smoothly, and her songs have charm, and a fresh, natural feeling. B.-G. gave frequent concerts in her native land, where she was also highly esteemed as a teacher. In 1875 she married the condr. and teacher of singing, C. A. Gröndahl.

Songs with pf. (including popular and well-known cycles: *Flower Vignettes; Southwards; The Child's Spring Day; Songs from the Sea; Ahasuerus*, etc.); arr. of Norwegian folk-songs and folk-lays; pf. pieces (including several concert-studies); character-pieces; suites; fantasy-pieces; cycle, *In the Blue Mountains; Children's Pictures*; adaptations of folk-songs and dances, etc.—J. A.

BACKER-GRÖNDAHL, Fridtjof. Norwegian pianist, compr. *b.* Christiania, 15 Oct. 1885. Stud. pf. under his mother, the pianist and compr. Agathe Backer-Gröndahl (Christiania); afterwards under Rudorff, Barth and Dohnányi (Berlin), and theory under Iver Holter (Christiania), and Kahn (Berlin). Gave his 1st concert in Christiania, 19 Sept. 1903. Has given concerts in most of large cities in Europe. Has comp. several colls. of short pieces for pf. Has frequently played in London, where he is now living.—U. M.

BACKER-LUNDE, Johan. See LUNDE.

BACKHAUS, Wilhelm. Pianist; *b.* Leipzig, 26 March, 1884. Pupil of Alois Reckendorf, Leipzig, till 1899; then of Eugen d'Albert, Frankfort-o-M. Has toured as virtuoso pianist since 1900. Piano-teacher R. Coll. Music, Manchester, 1905; Rubinstein Prize, 1905. Is one of the most brilliant German pianists with an astounding and polished technique.—A. E.

BACKHOUSE, Rhoda. Eng. violinist; *b.* near Darlington, 17 June, 1889. Stud. under Editha Knocker (York) and Leopold Auer (in Petrograd, Dresden and Christiania). 1st publ. appearance 1917. Specialises in chamber-music, and leads her own str. quartet.—E.-H.

BAGIER, Guido. Ger. author and compr. *b.* Berlin, 20 June, 1888. Stud. under Max Reger and Hugo Riemann, Leipzig; Ph.D. 1910 (thesis, *Herbart and Music*); editor of the progressive publication, *Feuer,* since 1918. Wrote *Max Reger* (Stuttgart, 1923, Deutsche Verlags-Anstalt).

Songs; chamber and orch. music; pf. pieces; music to H. v. Bötticher's *Liebe Gottes* (Düsseldorf, 1919).—A. E.

BAGLIONI, Silvestro. Ital. physiologist and patron of the science of music; *b.* Belmonte Piceno, 30 Dec. 1876. Prof. of Physiology at R. Univ. Rome; applied himself with particular devotion to research and study in relation to music. Had constructed for his researches a harmonium with two keyboards, tuned to quarter-tones, which he calls an *enarmonium.*

The Psycho-physiological Basis of Musical Æsthetics (in *Review of Applied Psychology,* Vol. VI, 1910); *Contributions to the Knowledge of Natural Music* (in *Records of Roman Anthropological Soc.,* 1910 and 1911); *The Influence of Sounds on the Vocal Range of Language* (in *Review of Anthropology,* XIX, 1914, and *Italian Record of Otology,* XXV); *A New Tone-Meter* (*id.*); *Variations of the Vocal Register during the Various Hours of the Day* (*id.*).—D. A.

BAGNATI, Cayetano. Argentine pianist, compr. *b.* Tropea, Italy, in 1840; *d.* Buenos Ayres, 1904. Stud. at Naples under Fischietti and Ketten when 8 years old. Played in public at 9, when he was most enthusiastically received. Went to Cons. di San Pietro a Maiella, Naples, to complete his training. Appointed mus. dir. of Chapel of Bishop of Tropea at age of 19. Then went to Buenos Ayres with Melani, playing for first time in Buenos Ayres the 1st concerto of Martucci. Establ. Cons. of Almagro in 1890, which soon became a famous institution. Has publ. large number of pf. solos, trios, 4tets and some orch. music.—A. M.

BAINES, William. Eng. compr. *b.* Horbury, Yorks, 1899; *d.* 6 Nov. 1922. Showed mus. inclination at a very early age; practically self-taught; developed pneumonia in the army in 1918, and never fully recovered; comp. chiefly during the months when he was temporarily convalescent. Two striking pf. works, *Paradise Gardens* and *Seven Preludes* (Elkin), drew the attention of L. Dunton Green, and the writer, to the unusually fine character displayed by the then unknown compr. Frederick Dawson helped much by giving B.'s works special prominence in his programmes. The writer assisted him to further publication; but the composer's rich promise was broken before full maturity by his untimely death at the age of 23. A tablet is being erected in York Minster to his memory. In his remarkable pf. feeling he followed in the direct line of Field, Chopin, and Scriabin.

There is a pf. sonata left in ms.; also many songs, cello pieces, and much chamber-music. Amongst his other publ. pf. pieces are: *Tides* (Elkin); *Milestones* (*id.*); *Silver-Points* (*id.*); *Poems* (Augener); *Coloured Leaves* (*id.*).—E.-H.

BAINTON, Edgar Leslie. Eng. compr. *b.* London, 14 Feb. 1880. Won open pf. scholarship, R.C.M. London, 1896; Wilson Scholarship (compn.) 1899. Stud. compn. under Walford Davies, Sir Ch. Stanford, Ch. Wood. In 1912, principal of Cons. of Music, Newcastle-on-Tyne. Symph. poem, *Pompilia* (Queen's Hall, London, 1903); symphony, B flat (Bournemouth, 1903); overture, *Prometheus* (Newcastle Fest. 1909); *Celtic Sketches* (Queen's Hall, 1912); str. 4tet (London, 1912). Interned in Ruhleben, Germany, 1914-18. Cond. 2 concerts of British music in Holland with Mengelberg's orch. (Amsterdam, The Hague), Dec. 1918.

The Blessed Damozel, s. and t. soli, chorus and orch. (Breitkopf); symphony, *Before Sunrise,* contr. solo, chorus, orch. (Carnegie award; Stainer & Bell); *Sunset at Sea,* chorus and orch. (*id.*); *The Vindictive Staircase,* chorus and orch. (*id.*); *Song of Freedom* (Curwen); *Concerto-Fantasia,* pf. and orch. (Carnegie award, 1921; Stainer & Bell); Miniature Suite, pf. duet (Anglo-French Co.); pf. pieces (Augener; Anglo-French Co.); songs, etc. A sonata, vla. and pf. (1922), an *Eclogue,* orch. (1923) and a work for chorus and orch. *The Tower* (1923) are not yet published.—E.-H.

BAIRSTOW, Edward Cuthbert. Eng. orgt. compr. *b.* Huddersfield, 22 Aug. 1874. Pupil of Sir F. Bridge, 1893-6; amanuensis to him, 1896-9. Orgt. Wigan Parish Ch. 1899-1906; Leeds Parish Ch. 1906-13; York Minster, 1913. Condr. Leeds Philh. Soc., Bradford Fest. Choral Soc. and York Mus. Soc. Mus.Doc. Durham, 1900. He is one of the very finest of cathedral orgts. and choir-trainers. Has comp. many fine anthems, part-songs (Novello) and organ pieces (Augener; Stainer & Bell). His music is always very solidly constructed, scholarly and sincere. His sacred works have a strong church character. In his own perfs. he shows a great preference for music by native composers.—E.-H.

BAIXULI, Father M. Span. musicologist. Author of study on *Obras musicales de San Francisco de Borja* (in review *Razón y Fe,* Madrid, 1902). Pupil of José María Ubeda. Member of the Jesuit Order.—P. G. M.

BAJARDI, Francesco. Ital. pianist and compr. *b.* Isnello (Palermo), 23 April, 1867. One of best pianists of the Sgambati school. Concert-player and teacher of note; mus. prof. at R. Liceo Mus. di Santa Cecilia, Rome. Author of charming compns. for his instr. There are also a symphony, an overture and a suite for orchestra.—D. A.

BAKER, Dalton. British singer and orgt. *b.* Merton, Surrey, 17 Oct. 1879. Trained at R.A.M. London. Won the Mence Smith scholarship for singing. 1894, orgt. and choirmaster at the Guards' Chapel, Chelsea Barracks; 1894–6, held similar position at St. Mary Magdalene's, Munster Square. His *début* as a singer occurred at St. James's Hall Ballad Concerts in 1902, after which he appeared regularly at mus. fests. and at most important London and provincial concerts. Took part in 1st perf. of Bantock's *Omar Khayyám* (Birmingham Fest.) and 1st London perf. of Elgar's *The Kingdom.* In 1914 went to Canada and joined staff of Toronto Cons. as teacher of singing. In 1920 founded Toronto Orpheus Soc. He has frequently sung in U.S.A. and now lives in New York.—L. S.

BAKER, Theodore. American author and editor; *b.* New York, 3 June, 1851. Stud. in Leipzig from 1874 under Oskar Paul, and 1878 at Univ. Here received his Ph.D. with thesis on the music of the N. Amer. Indians, the result of studies made in 1880, on the Reservation of the Seneca Tribe in New York State, and at the Indian School at Carlisle, Pennsylvania. This was the first scientific attempt at fixing the music of the Indians, and was the source of a number of the themes used by Mac-Dowell in his *Indian Suite* for orch. (1896). Until 1890, B. lived in Germany. Since 1892, has been literary ed. of music-publishing firm of G. Schirmer in New York, for whom he has transl. innumerable songs as well as theoretical, pedagogical, historical, and æsthetic works by Paul, Bussler, Lobe, Jadassohn, Löwengard, Richter, Kullak, Bree, Lamperti, Weitzmann, d'Indy, Busoni, Istel and others.
Über die Musik der nordamerikanischen Wilden (Leipzig dissertation, 1882); *Dictionary of Musical Terms* (Schirmer, 1895; 18th ed. 1918); *Biographical Dictionary of Musicians* (Schirmer, 1900; 3rd ed. by Alfred Remy, 1919).—O. K.

BALAKIREF, Mily Alexeievitch (*accent 2nd syll.*). Russian composer; *b.* Nijny-Novgorod, 21 Dec. 1836/2 Jan. 1837; *d.* Petrograd, 16/29 May, 1910. The acknowledged leader of the so-called "Nationalist" Russian school which sprang up in the 'fifties, as much under his influence as under that of Glinka, whose direct continuator he always remained. According to his own statement (letter to N. Findeisen, 1903, published in *Russian Musical Gazette,* 1910, No. 41) his only teacher, apart from his mother under whom he started to study music and Dubuque (1812–97, a pupil of Field) from whom he received a few lessons, was Karl Eisrich, to whom his early *Fantasy on Russian Motives* for pf. and orch. (1852; unpubl.) is inscribed.

As a pianist he achieved fame early. Of his early compositions a few remain unpublished; others, such as the incidental music to *King Lear* (1861), the tone-poem *Russia* (1862), the overtures on Spanish (1851), Russian (1858), and Czech (1867) motives were only published many years after they were written, and often in much revised form (the last-named now bears the title *In Bohemia,* tone-poem). In 1861, he began to be acknowledged as the leader and educator of a number of budding musicians whom we see instinctively congregating around him; first Cui and Borodin (both of them his elders), then Mussorgsky, and a little later Rimsky-Korsakof. He exercised upon every one of them a great influence, not always easy to disengage clearly; and an influence of similar order made itself felt even on composers who were not his pupils, such as Tchaikovsky, who received from him a great many suggestions and often profited by these (see *The Correspondence between Balakiref and Tchaikovsky,* by M. D. Calvocoressi, *Musical Times,* Nov. 1912).

In 1862 he founded with Lomakin the Petrograd Free School of Music, and devoted much of his time to organising and conducting concerts at which many orchestral works by Russian composers were first performed. In 1869 he was appointed conductor of the Imperial Russian Musical Society and director of the Imperial Chapel. In 1874 he renounced his various posts and went to live in the country, where he remained in complete seclusion until 1881, when he re-appeared at Petrograd with the score of his symphonic masterpiece, the tone-poem *Tamara,* which he had started composing in 1867. In 1883 he was appointed director of the Court Chapel. In 1894 he retired on a pension, and devoted the remainder of his lifetime to revising his early works and writing new ones.

As a creative artist, he is extremely original, although much under the influence of Glinka, Chopin, Liszt and Schumann, and, to a lesser degree, of Berlioz. Nowhere has the combination of these influences (common to most great composers of his generation, especially Borodin and Rimsky-Korsakof) and of the direct influence of folk-music, Russian and Eastern, led to finer artistic results. His output is uneven and comprises (especially as regards pf. music) works whose artistic significance is very slight. But *Tamara,* the pf. fantasy *Islamey* and the tone-poem *Russia* (as well as some of his early songs) remain landmarks in the history of modern developments in music; and many other works of his, such as the two symphonies (one written in 1865 but published in 1897 only; the other published in 1909, immediately after its completion) are rich in poetic beauty of the highest order.

Orch.: *Tamara,* tone-poem (Moscow, Jurgenson); *Russia,* tone-poem (Leipzig, Zimmerman); *In Bohemia,* tone-poem (*id.*); incidental music to *King Lear* (*id.*); pf. concerto; *Islamey,* fantasy, for pf., recently scored for pf. and orch. (Jurgenson); pf. *scherzi,* mazurkas, waltzes (Zimmermann); pf. sonata (*id.*); 20 songs (1858–61) (Moscow, Gutheil); 10 songs (1895) (Jurgenson); 10 songs (1903) (Zimmermann).—M. D. C.

BALDANZA, Romana. Argentine singer; *b.* Tropea, Italy. Went to Buenos Ayres as a child, where she stud. at Almagro Cons. under Bagnati. Completed her training at Cons. in Naples; gained special prize offered by Ricordi, the Milan publ. After giving numerous concerts in Naples and Milan, went to Buenos Ayres in 1908. Her light s. voice has a very pure quality. Founded Buenos Ayres Academy of Singing, 1910.—A. M.

BALDASSARI, Rafael. Argentine cellist; *b.* Rome in 1861. Stud. under Quarenchi and Torriani at Milan Cons., becoming 1st cellist of La Scala, Milan. Visited S. America in 1896, settling down in Buenos Ayres as teacher. His *Hymn to Guemes* took gold medal in Salta competition, 1911. Has comp. songs and light instrumental pieces.—A. M.

BALFOUR, Henry Lucas. Eng. orgt. condr. *b.* Battersea, London, 1859. Scholar of National Training School of Music (now R.C.M.), 1876–82. Stud. under Sullivan, Stainer, Ernst Pauer, Brinley Richards, Cowen, Prout. Gen. condr. R. Albert Hall Choral Soc. from 1922.—E.-H.

BALL, George Thalben. Eng. orgt. *b.* Sydney, Australia, 18 June, 1896. Stud. R.C.M. London, under Sir H. Parry, Sir C. Stanford, Sir F. F. Bridge, Frits Hartvigson and Dr. Charles Wood; orgt. Temple Ch. London from 1919; prof. of organ, R.C.M. from 1919.—E.-H.

BALLING, Michael. Ger. condr. *b.* Heidingsfeld-o-M., 28 Aug. 1866. Pupil of Hermann Ritter at Würzburg Music School ; then as vla. player in Mayence; in Court Orch. Schwerin (1886–92); and fest. performances in Bayreuth. From Schwerin went to New Zealand. Founded the first music school in Australasia at Nelson. After world-tour of 2½ years came to England; in 1896 entered upon career of condr. as assistant at Bayreuth and in the autumn of same year was chorus-master at Hamburg Stadttheater; 1898, 1st condr. in Lübeck; then in Breslau and succeeded Mottl in Carlsruhe; 1906–14, was also engaged as mus. dir. Bayreuth. In 1911 went to Manchester (Hallé Orch.) as successor to Hans Richter, remaining there till outbreak of 1914 war. Gen. mus. dir. at Darmstadt since 1919. The complete edition of Richard Wagner's works, now being publ. by Breitkopf, is under his direction.—A. E.

BAND, Erich. Ger. condr. and compr. *b.* Berlin, 10 May, 1876. Stud. High School of Music and Univ. Berlin; condr. Mayence, Bremen, Rostock; mus. dir. and condr. Court Theatre, Stuttgart, from 1905.
Pf. pieces, op. 1 and 5; pf. sonata, op. 2; str. 4tet in A, op. 3; *Romanze* for cello and orch. op. 7; songs, op. 4 and 6. Has also done literary work.—A. E.

BANDA MUNICIPAL of Madrid. Spanish military band, of 88 first-class performers, founded by Madrid County Council; organised and cond. since its creation (June 1909) by Ricardo Villa (*q.v.*).—P. G. M.

BANDINI, Bruno. Argentine vla.-player; *b.* Faenza, Italy, in 1889. Went to Buenos Ayres as a child; stud. in Santa Cecilia Inst. under Galvani; obtained gold medal in open competition. Gave first vla. concerts in Buenos Ayres. Now devotes himself to teaching in government and private insts. Has publ. a Prelude for vla. solo.—A. M.

BANDROWSKI, Alexander. Polish t. singer; *b.* Lubaczow, 1860; *d.* Cracow, 1913. Excellent impersonator of Wagner's and Meyerbeer's heroes. From 1889 to 1901, permanently engaged at Frankfort Opera. Sang in nearly all the larger opera houses of Europe and America. Publ. transl. of some dramas of Wagner and wrote libretti to 2 Polish operas: *Stara Basn* (*An Old Fable*), for Władysław Żeleński (1907), and *Boleslaw Smialy* (*Boleslas the Bold*) for Ludomir Różycki (1909).—ZD. J.

BANG, Maja. Norwegian-Amer. violinist; *b.* Tromsö, 24 April, 1877. Trained at Leipzig Cons.; afterwards stud. under Marteau in Geneva and Auer in Petrograd. *Début*, Christiania, 1900. Establ. Oslo Music School, Christiania. Teacher at Auer's Acad. in New York, 1919. Wrote a *Violin Method* in 6 vols. (New York, 1922, Fischer). Married, in 1922, Baron Hoehn, New York.—U. M.

BANTOCK, Granville. English composer; *b.* London, 7 August 1868. Originally intended for Indian Civil Service, but soon turned to music; after a few lessons at Trinity College of Music, entered Royal Academy of Music in 1889, winning the Macfarren Scholarship after his first term there. During his student days a concert version of his *Cœdmar* (1-act opera staged at Olympic, 1892) was given. Between May 1893 and February 1896, he edited *The New Quarterly Musical Review* and toured the country as conductor of musical comedies and light music. After a world-tour with an operatic company, he settled again in London in winter of 1896, giving a concert devoted entirely to modern British composers (Bantock, Hawley, Hinton, R. Steggall, Wallace). In 1897, he was appointed musical director of the Tower at New Brighton, contenting himself with a military band for the first year, but inaugurating in the following year a series of concerts with bold and even adventurous programmes. In February 1900, he conducted a concert of British music at Antwerp. There his music was heard for the first time out of England.

In the autumn of 1900, he was appointed Principal of the School of Music attached to the Birmingham and Midland Institute, a post he still holds. To this great music-school he has given a character all its own; and he has been no less original in his modelling of the Faculty of Music at Birmingham University where (from 1908) he is the Professor of Music. He was appointed conductor of Liverpool Orchestral Society in 1904, and Sibelius paid his first visit to England (to conduct his first symphony and *Finlandia*) at Bantock's invitation. One of the most generous of men, numberless musicians and composers owe their first start to him. He was one of the earliest pioneers of contemporary

British music, and himself one of the foremost creators of it. He never composes without a programme, more or less defined; and much of his music is avowedly of a mimetic order. His *Omar Khayyám* for chorus and orchestra (Part I, produced Birmingham Festival, 1906; II, Cardiff Festival, 1907; III, Birmingham Festival, 1909) flung wide the gate to a new English choralism, a gate partly opened by Elgar with his *Gerontius* in 1900. Bantock enjoys his new domain in *Atalanta; The Great God Pan; Vanity; The Song of Songs* (1922-4), etc. His genius was of just the right calibre to stand in between the somewhat dry academicism and strongly German bias of the 'eighties and 'nineties in England and the younger XX century school. His original outlook and strong imagination, his pagan love of beauty in all forms, and his bold pursuance of it, brought an entirely new feature into English music. In addition, he has personally trained many young composers.

As a composer he has passed through many phases, and made valuable contributions in all —cult of the East, folk-music, and nationalism, modern choral development, socialistic music and a more universal style. He did not ignore the big figures of European music, and owes a good deal to Wagner, Strauss and the Russians. He is a great orchestral colourist. His best orchestral work is to be found in the *Hebridean Symphony*, frankly pictorial, and in *The Great God Pan*. He is a sturdy believer in the competition festival movement and one of its most active apostles. In 1923, with Plunket Greene, he visited Canada and started the competition movement there. His adjudicative work has reacted on his own compositions, inspiring him to write for unaccompanied choirs in an increasingly masterful way (*Atalanta; Vanity of Vanities*). Birmingham University bestowed on him M.A. and Edinburgh, Mus.Doc. *honoris causa*.

For chorus and orch.: *Omar Khayyám*, Parts I, II and III for c. t. and b. soli, chorus, orch. (Breitkopf): *The Great God Pan*, soli, chorus, orch. (Novello); *The Time-Spirit*, chorus and orch. (Breitkopf); *Sea-Wanderers*, chorus and orch. (Breitkopf); *Christ in the Wilderness*, for s. and b. soli, chorus and orch. (Breitkopf); *The Song of Songs*, in 5 parts, for soli, chorus and orch. (Swan); *The Seal-Woman*, a Celtic folk-opera, in 2 acts; etc. Orch. works: *Hebridean Symphony* (Stainer & Bell); *Pagan Symphony*; *Processional* and *Jaga-Naut* (Breitkopf); *The Pierrot of the Minute* (*id.*); *Dante and Beatrice* (*id.*); *Helena Variations* (*id.*); *The Witch of Atlas* (Novello); *Fifine at the Fair* (*id.*); *Overture to a Greek Tragedy* (Leuckart); *Russian Scenes* (Bosworth); *From the Far West* (Breitkopf); *Scenes from the Scottish Highlands* (*id.*); *Sapphic Poem* (Novello), etc. Unacc. choral works: *Villon*, ballade (Novello); *The Lost Leader* (Breitkopf); *The Twilight Tombs of Ancient Kings* (Curwen); *Cavalier Tunes* (Novello); *Atalanta in Calydon* (Breitkopf); *Vanity of Vanities* (Curwen); *A Pageant of Human Life* (Novello); *The Golden Journey to Samarkand* (Birchard); *The Grianan of Aileach* (Curwen); *Lucifer in Starlight* (Novello); *War-Song of the Saracens* (Curwen), etc. Vocal works: *Sappho* (Breitkopf); *Ferishtah's Fancies* (*id.*); *Hymn of Pan* (Swan); *Ghazals of Hafiz* (Breitkopf); *Songs of Arabia, Japan, Egypt, Persia, India, China*, 6 vols. (*id.*); *4 Pagan Chants* (Swan); *13 Dramatic Lyrics* (*id.*); *4 Songs of Arcady* (Curwen); *The March* (Chester); *Songs from the Chinese Poets*, 2 vols. (*id.*); *Songs from the Chinese* (Elkin); *Songs of Childhood* (*id.*); *The Vale of Arden* (Enoch), etc.

Chamber-music: Sonata in F for vla. and pf. (Chester); sonata in G mi. cello alone (*id.*); *Hambadil* and *Pibroch* for cello (*id.*), etc.; pf. pieces (Swan; Forsyth; Elkin). Miscellaneous: Music for *Electra* of Sophocles (Breitkopf); *Judith*, 2 vols. (Swan); *Lalla Rookh*, (2 vols. (*id.*); *Arabian Nights*, 4 vols. (*id.*); *Scottish Scenes* (*id.*), etc. Unison and 2-, 3-, 4-pt. songs; school songs; part-songs, etc. (Curwen; J. Williams; Novello; Arnold; Boosey).

Edited 100 *Folk-Songs of all Nations* (Oliver Ditson Co.); 100 *Songs of England* (*id.*); 60 *Patriotic Songs of all Nations* (*id.*); pf. Albums of Byrd, Bull, Farnaby (Novello).

Consult H. O. Anderton, *G. B.* (John Lane, 1915). —E.-H.

BARBI, Alice. Italian concert-singer; *b.* Bologna, 1862. Acquired great fame by her concerts in Italy and principal countries of Europe. An excellent interpreter of music of the past and present, which she sang in the orig. languages. Brahms wrote many songs for her, and Martucci composed *La Canzone dei Ricordi* for her. In 1897, B. married Baron Wolf-Stomersen. Sgambati, an admirer of B., publ. an art. about her in *Musical World*, London, 1885, p. 452.—D. A.

BARBIER, René Auguste Ernest. Belgian compr. *b.* Namur, 12 July, 1890. Stud. at Académie de Musique, Namur; later Liège Cons. (compn. under Sylvain Dupuis). 1st prize for cantata *La Légende de Béatrice*.

Yvette (opera, 1st perf. Namur, 1912); pf. and vn. sonata; 5tet; trio; pf. *Triptych* (publ. *L'Art Belge*, Brussels); concerto for Hans piano (*q.v.*) and orch.; Mass for 3 vs. and organ (Ledent-Malay, Brussels); *L'Épopée Belge*, patriotic cantata (perf. Namur); many songs.—C. V. B.

BARBIERI, Francisco Asenjo. Span. compr. condr. and musicologist; *b.* Madrid, 3 Aug. 1823; *d.* there, 19 Feb. 1894. In 1859 organised a series of Conciertos Espirituales at Madrid. In 1870 cond. symph. concerts at Lisbon. Fellow of Real Acad. de Bellas Artes. Holder of many Span. honours, including the Gran Cruz de Isabel la Católica. He started his career as a clar.-player in a band of the Milicia Nacional. He initiated the reconstruction of the history of Span. music, and the doom of the domination of the Ital. school in Spain. Having a natural bent for historical investigation he devoted himself, on his own initiative, to the research of *libros de cifra* (tablature), all kinds of ancient mus. documents, and especially the books of the *vihuelistas* [1] and the *Cancioneros* (collections of songs) of XV and XVI centuries. In these, he found the fundamental elements for regeneration of contemporary school and practical study of mus. folklore, a branch of knowledge which before him had in modern times been explored only by literary men such as Serafín Estébanez Calderón, José María Quadrado, Pablo Piferrer, Francisco Pelayo Briz, Manuel Mila y Fontanals (author of first book on Æsthetics publ. in Spain). The fruit of his research work is to be found in (*a*) the publication of the annotated transcriptions of the so-called *Cancionero de Palacio* and *Cancionero Musical de Barbieri* (1890), the pamphlet on the *Canto de Ultreja*, the much discussed Pilgrimage Chant (probably of foreign extraction), annexed

[1] Players of the old Span. instr. *vihuela*, not to be confused with the lute of the same period.

to the Codex of Calixtus II (XII century) (see OLMEDA); (b) the leading part he took in the religious reform initiated towards 1890; (c) the assistance he gave to Don Marcelino Menéndez Pelayo in relation to his great work *Historia de las Ideas Estéticas en España* (1881–91)—in which the artistic personality of the Jesuit Eximeno (see PEDRELL) was brought to light—and (d) the coll. of books and mss. now in the Biblioteca Nacional, Madrid.

As a compr. B. was distinguished from Eslava, the most important of his contemporaries, by working always, within the limits of his technique, in perfect agreement with his ideas on mus. nationalism. This attitude is the most eloquent proof of his strong individuality and solidity of character. His zarzuelas, *El Barberillo de Lava-piés* and *Pan y Toros*, show him, among his Italianised contemporaries, as the Spanish composer *par excellence*. In them, by far his most important work, he saved from oblivion a treasure of rhythmic and melodic elements characteristic of the national folk-lore of the XVIII century, thus laying the foundation of a national school with a physiognomy that distinguishes it from all the others. Never was a man of a studious nature, and possessor of rare knowledge, so free of pompousness and pedanticism. Joviality is ever present in his music, for it was a distinct feature of his character, well illustrated in "a humorous study dedicated to all dancers by one of them," entitled *Las Casta-ñuelas* (*The Castanets*). His *Barberillo de Lava-piés* and *Pan y Toros* have the greatest significance for Spanish music.

The following list contains but a few of his zarzuelas, of which he wrote over 70, in 1, 2, 3 or more acts:

Los Carboneros; Un loro y una lechuza; Triste Chactas; Ojo a la niñera; El Diablo Cojuelo; Los Chichones; Gloria y Peluca; Jugar con Fuego; Juan de Urbina; Chorizos y Polacos; La Vuelta al Mundo, etc. (publ. Unión Musical Española, Madrid). Many of his works are out of print, but the scores are in the possession of the Sociedad de Autores Españoles, Madrid.—P. G. M.

BARBLAN, Otto. Swiss orgt. compr. b. Scanfs (Engadine), 22 March, 1860. Began mus. studies at Chur (Switzerland). Entered Cons. at Stuttgart in 1878, pupil of Schuler and Alwens (pf.) and of F. Faisst (organ and compn.). Became condr. of mixed choir and male choir at Chur in 1885. Since 1887 orgt. at St. Peter's Cath. in Geneva, where he also conducts the Société de Chant Sacré (Oratorio Concerts) and teaches compn. at Cons. Among his compns. (written in Bach style) his choruses obtained great success.

For soli, chorus and orch.: *Post tenebras lux*, op. 8 (for jubilee of Calvin in 1909); festspiel, *Calvinfeier*, *Ode patriotique*, op. 20 (for inauguration of Swiss National Exhibition, Geneva, 1896); *St. Luke Passion*, op. 25; *Psalm CXVII* and *Psalm LXXV* and numerous other choruses. Organ: Passacaglia, op. 6; Chaconne on B.A.C.H. op. 10; Toccata, op. 23; Variations on B.A.C.H. op. 24; str. 4tet, op. 19. Mostly publ. by Hug, Leipzig.—F. H.

BARCEWICZ, Stanisław (*phon.* Bartsevich). Polish violinist; b. Warsaw, 16 April, 1858. Stud. under Hrimaly, Laub and Czajkowski at Moscow Cons. At 11, began to appear in public. For many years, undertook long tours in Europe. His playing is distinguished by an immense and beautiful tone and true Slavonic temperament. Since 1885, prof. Warsaw Cons. where he was dir. 1911–18. —ZD. J.

BARILLI, Bruno. Ital. compr. b. Fano, 14 Dec. 1880. In 1923 won the prize for a lyric opera, instituted by the Ital. Government, with the opera *Emiral* (Costanzi Th. Rome, March 1924). Was mus. critic of Rome newspaper *Il Tempo*; is now critic of the *Corriere Italiano*.—D.A.

BARINI, Giorgio. Ital. critic, historian, lecturer, teacher; b. Turin, 3 Aug. 1864. First wrote for the Rome newspaper *La Tribuna*, then for review *La Nuova Antologia*, and the newspaper *L'Epoca*.—D. A.

BARLOW, Arthur. Eng. b. singer; b. Wilmslow, 31 Aug. 1868. Prof. singing, Guildhall School of Music, London.—E.-H.

BARMOTIN, Simon Alexeievitch (*accent 2nd syll.*). Russ. compr. b. Petrograd in 1877. Began his mus. education under Balakiref and continued it under Rimsky-Korsakof. Has written a number of pf. works, among which are a sonata, a set of preludes and a Theme and variations; a sonata and a suite for vn. and pf.; and songs. —M. D. C.

BARNEKOW, Christian. Danish compr. b. 28 July, 1837; d. 20 March, 1913. President of Musikforening (Music Soc.), Copenhagen, 1895. Comp. chamber-music works, cantatas and many songs, both secular and religious.—A. H.

BARRATT, Edgar. British pianist, compr. b. Lincoln, 1877. The son of an accomplished musician, John Barratt, Mus.Bac. Oxon. (who became orgt. and choirmaster in Paisley Abbey in 1879). Stud. Leipzig Cons., pf. under Bruno Zwintscher and Robert Teichmüller; compn. under Schreck. Has appeared as soloist with Scottish Orch.; sole accompanist at Scottish Orch. concerts for many years. Has played with world-famous British and Continental str. and pf. quartets; acc. Albani and Dolores on extensive tours. Has comp. much pf. and vocal music, largely in the Scottish idiom. Is rapidly acquiring an assured position and popularity, not in Scotland alone, but in England as well, where most of his publ. works have appeared with Elkin.—W. S.

BARRATT, Mary Louise. Norwegian pianist; b. Bergen, 9 April, 1888. Pupil of Lindeman's Music School, Christiania. Stud. in Rome (Signorina Mettler and Sgambati), in London (Percy Grainger) and in Paris. *Début*, Christiania, 1908. Has given concerts throughout Scandinavia. Married in 1916 the Norwegian-Amer. violinist, Henrik Due, Christiania.—U. M.

BARRERA, Tomás. Span. compr. Lives in Madrid. Chief zarzuelas:
El Celoso Extremeño, Sueño de Pierrot, El Maño, Ideicas, La Vara de Alcalde, La Tajadera, La Manzana de Oro (publ. by Fuentes & Asenjo, Madrid). —P. G. M.

BARRIENTOS, María. Span. s. operatic singer; b. Barcelona, 10 March, 1885. At a very early age, entered Cons. at Barcelona, studying vn.

with distinction, and compn. as well as pf. Her exceptional coloratura voice was discovered at a private concert of students. Her solid mus. education proved a great asset to her, and, after receiving some lessons from the local singing master Bennet, she made her *début* at age of 14, with great success (Teatro de Novedades) in *L'Africaine*. She then stud. in Milan, appearing 12 months later in *Lakmé*. Was immediately engaged at La Scala; subsequently at all principal theatres of Europe and America. After a retirement of 3 years, she reappeared (1916) at Metropolitan Opera House, New York, which has practically monopolised her ever since.

Besides *The Nightingale* (Stravinsky), *El Abanico* (specially written for her by Amadeo Vives) and other modern works, her repertoire includes: *Puritani*; *Sonnambula*; *Barber of Seville*; *Lucia*; *Don Pasquale*; *Elisir d'Amore*; *Traviata*; *Rigoletto*; *Pêcheurs de Perles*; *Linda*; *Dinorah*; *Lakmé*; *Mignon*; *Hamlet*; *Martha.*—P. G. M.

BARRIOS, Angel. Span. compr. *b.* Granada, 1862. Began as orch. vn.-player; gave up vn. for study of guitar; became a very remarkable performer, though, in opposition to some famous guitarists, he excluded from his repertoire all transcriptions of orch. or pf. works, faithful to his feelings, as a genuine Andalusian, that the guitar is only suited to music known in Spain as *flamenco*. In this he followed the example of his father who, though a commercial man by profession, is very well known as a guitar-player and singer, being considered the greatest connoisseur of Andalusian songs and dances in Granada. B.'s ideas have attracted many musicians of greater technical capacity than himself. Was the founder (about 1900) of the once celebrated Trio Iberia (see CHAMBER-MUSIC PLAYERS). B. completed his mus. studies under Antonio Segura (Granada), Gédalge (Paris), and Conrado del Campo (Madrid).

Symph. poem, *Zambra en el Albaicín* (perf. by Orquesta Sinfónica at R. Opera House, Madrid); *Copla de Soleá* and *Danzas gitanas*, for orch.; several pf. pieces; incidental music for Moorish tragedy of Francisco Villaespesa (*Aben Humeya*) and Alejandro Mackinlay (*La Danza de la Cautiva*); *Granada mía*, 2-act *zarzuela*; 2 operas (in collab. with Conrado del Campo), *La Romería* (2 acts) and *El Avapiés* (3 acts) first perf. at R. Opera House, Madrid. —P. G. M.

BARTELS, Wolfgang von. Ger. compr. *b.* Hamburg, 21 July, 1883. Son of marine painter, Hans v. Bartels. Stud. under Anton Beer-Walbrunn, Munich, and André Gédalge, Paris (1904–1909). Lives in Munich. Comp. music of *The Little Dream* (John Galsworthy, Manchester, 1911); *Little Snowdrop* (nursery tale, text by Green, Manchester, 1911); *The Spanish Lovers* (Fernando de Rojas, adapted by Garnett, London, 1912); *The Persians* of Æschylus (Feuchtwanger, Munich Theatre, 1917); *Li-J-Lan* (text by Warden and Welleminsky, Cassel, 1918). Wrote a cycle of Old German Songs and *The 12 Songs of Li-Tai-Pe*, 1921.—A. E.

BARTH, Karl Heinrich. Ger. pianist, teacher; *b.* Pillau, near Königsberg, 12 July, 1847; *d.* Berlin, Dec. 1922. Pupil of Hans v. Bülow, Hans v. Bronsart and C. Tausig. Teacher at Stern's Cons. 1868; at R. High School of Music,

Berlin, 1871, of which he was head of pf. dept. in 1910 and *ex-officio* member of R. Acad. of Arts. Retired 1921. Formerly one of Barth Trio with de Ahna (vn.) and Hausmann (cello). As teacher was one of the most distinguished and successful in Germany.

Vn. sonata in D.—A. E.

BARTH, Richard. Ger. choral condr. and compr. *b.* Grosswanzleben, 5 June, 1850. First trained as violinist under Beck, Magdeburg, and Joachim, Hanover (1863–7); then concert dir. in Munster, in Crefeld, 1882; then dir. of music, Univ. of Marburg; 1895–1904, dir. Philh. Concerts, Hamburg, Acad. of Singing and other choral societies; dir. of Cons., Hamburg, since 1908. In 1904 Ph.D. *h.c.* Univ. of Marburg.

3 sonatas for vn. and pf. op. 14, 20, 23; pf. trio, op. 19; str. 4tet, G mi. op. 15; *Partita*, for vn. solo; *Ciacona*, vn. solo. Publ.: J. Brahms' correspondence with J. O. Grimm (*Brahms' Correspondence*, Vol. IV, Berlin, 1908, German Brahms Soc.); *Johannes Brahms and his Music* (1904).—A. E.

BARTHOLDY, Conrad Johan. Danish compr. *b.* 12 March, 1853; *d.* 6 Dec. 1904. Cantor, St. Matthew's Ch. Copenhagen; dir. of the Studenter-Sangforening (Univ. Students' Singing Soc.). Numerous vocal and orch. works.

Operas : *Svinedrengen* (*The Swineherd*), libretto based upon Hans Chr. Andersen; *Loreley*; *Dyveke* (produced R. Theatre, Copenhagen).—A. H.

BARTÓK, Béla. Hungarian composer, pianist and folk-song collector; *b.* Nagyszentmiklós, Hungary (now annexed by Rumania), 25 March, 1881. His mother first taught him piano in his 6th year. His father, director of the School of Agriculture (and a gifted musician), died in the boy's 8th year; so his mother had to earn her living as an elementary school-teacher. After working in small provincial towns, she was able to settle in Pozsony (now Bratislava, annexed by Czecho-Slovakia), where the active musical life helped in Bartók's development. Here 'he studied piano and harmony under László Erkel (son of well-known opera-composer, Franz Erkel). Became acquainted with classical music from Bach to Brahms, and also with Wagner's first operas. Began composition in his 9th year and finished a piano sonata (1897), a piano quartet (1898) and a string quartet (1899). In 1899, entered Royal Hungarian High School for Music, Budapest, studying composition under Hans Koessler and piano under Stephan Thomán. In the first two or three years, composition was in abeyance, B. being better known as a very promising pianist. A performance of Strauss's *Thus Spake Zarathustra* suddenly awoke his impulse for composition, and in a short time numerous works appeared: a *Scherzo* for orchestra, a fragment of a symphony already planned; a symphonic poem, *Kossuth* (1903), performed by the Budapest Philharmonic Society, and in Manchester under Hans Richter; a violin sonata (1903) and a piano quintet (1904), both performed in Vienna. The above-mentioned works (apart from the Funeral March from *Kossuth*) remain unpublished. Published works of this period include: 4 songs; 4 piano pieces;

Rhapsody, op. 1 (1904) with which he competed unsuccessfully for the Rubinstein Prize in Paris, 1905; and 1st Suite for orchestra, op. 3 (1905). A *Burlesque,* op. 2 (1904), for orchestra is still unpublished. All these works already show a pronounced individuality. Besides the influence of Strauss there is Hungarian colouring. A strong national movement, which also helped to encourage the expression of national character through art, was then at its height, and had its effect on Bartók. Not only do his musical themes show the undisguised use of Hungarian popular melodies, but the very programme of *Kossuth* itself was of a national and political nature. It was soon proved, however, that the possibilities of this so-called Hungarian folk-music, most of which arose in the xix century, had its limitations, and was unsatisfactory as a basis for a national style in music. It soon became known that there was a much older kind of peasant-music, up to that time uninvestigated, which was not to be obtained except on the spot. So Bartók—who had been engaged as teacher at the Budapest High School since 1907—set out on an exploration, which later extended to Slovakian and Rumanian territory, and brought to light a large number of old, traditional melodies. His style soon showed the effect of this archaic music, which is for the most part pentatonic and modal, with an extraordinary amount of rhythm. The 2nd Suite, op. 4 (1905–7), and *Two Portraits,* op. 5 (1907), marked a transition to a new style of expression, which in the *Bagatelles,* op. 6 (1908), becomes consistent and homogeneous. Inspired by this peasant-music, remote from conventional European forms, B. attains a melodic, rhythmic and harmonic freedom of a highly individualised kind. This new style, especially the frequent and unaccustomed employment of dissonance, called forth strong opposition. Whereas Bartók's first works earned unqualified success, he had now for a long time to forgo all outward success, and content himself with the intelligent appreciation of a small circle. The more characteristic works of this period are 1st string quartet (1908); *Deux Images* (1910); the *Nénies* (1910); and the opera *Duke Bluebeard's Castle.* This opera was rejected at a subsequent prize-competition. A Music Society under his direction had to be dissolved after only a short spell of activity. Disheartened by this and other failures, he withdrew more and more from public life. After a period of intensive production a pause set in, during which time he devoted himself to his folk-lore studies, the extent of which had by this time greatly increased. Thus in 1913 he travelled to Biskra and returned with a rich collection of Arab peasant music. The war put an end to all further ideas of travelling. Cut off as he was from the outer world, and living in a country where desperate conditions prevailed, he became more reserved and ended in complete isolation. The works of this period became more and more individual and subjective. Nevertheless, one of these was to mark a turn in popular favour for Bartók. The pantomime, *The Wooden*

Prince (magnificently performed in the Budapest Opera House in 1917 under E. Tango), at one stroke brought him recognition, which since that time could be no more in dispute. In 1918, followed the first performance of *Bluebeard,* and the new generation received his later works also with enthusiasm. These were the piano Suite, 2nd Quartet, and the Studies. The last big work of this creative period is the pantomime, *The Wonderful Mandarin,* which is not yet completed. The disturbances in the country in 1919-20 were not favourable to great productive work. In 1920 there appeared *Improvisations on Hungarian Folk-Songs.* In 1921 Bartók finished the Violin Sonata, op. 21, which he himself performed in England with Jelly d'Arányi in 1922. In the same year the Frankfort Opera gave his two works for the stage. In recent years Bartók has often accepted invitations to foreign countries to perform his own works. His 1st Suite has been perf. at Queen's Hall, London, and his *Deux Portraits* at Æolian Hall, both under Sir Henry Wood.

Mr. Bartók is responsible for the Hungarian articles in this Dictionary.

Dramatic works:
    Opera, *Duke Bluebeard's Castle,* op. 11
    Pantomime, *The Wooden Prince,* op. 13 (both
      publ. Univ. Ed. Vienna)
Orch.:
    Burlesque, op. 2 (ms.)
    1st Suite, op. 3 (Rózsavölgyi, Budapest)
    2nd Suite, op. 4 (Univ. Ed.)
    Deux Portraits, op. 5 (Rozsnyai, Budapest)
    Deux Images, op. 10 (Rózsavölgyi)
    Quatre Morceaux, op. 12 (Univ. Ed.)
    Dante-Suite (id.)
Chamber-music:
    1st str. quartet, op. 7 (Rózsavölgyi)
    2nd str. quartet, op. 17 (Univ. Ed.)
    Vn. sonata, No. I *(id.)*
    Vn. sonata, No. II *(id.)*
Vocal:
    4 songs (Bárd, Budapest)
    5 songs, op. 16 (Univ. Ed.)
Pf.:
    4 *Morceaux* (Bárd)
    Funeral March from *Kossuth* (Rozsnyai)
    Rhapsody, op. 1 (Rózsavölgyi)
    14 *Bagatelles,* op. 6 (Rozsnyai)
    10 easy pf. pieces *(id.)*
    2 *Élégies,* op. 8b *(id.)*
    2 *Danses roumaines,* op 8a (Rózsavölgyi)
    Esquisses, op. 9 (Rozsnyai)
    3 *Burlesques,* op. 8c (Rózsavölgyi)
    4 *Nénies (id.)*
    Allegro barbaro (Univ. Ed.)
    Suite, op. 14 *(id.)*
    3 *Études,* op. 18 *(id.)*
    Improvisations, op. 20 *(id.)*
Arr. of folk-songs:
    (i) Pf.: 3 Hungarian folk-songs (Rozsnyai)
      For children, 4 vols. *(id.)*
      15 Hungarian peasant-songs (Univ. Ed.)
      Roumanian folk-dances from Hungary *(id.)*
      Roumanian Christmas songs *(id.)*
      Sonatina on Rumanian themes (Rózsavölgyi)
    (ii) V. and pf.: 20 Hungarian folk-songs (with
      Z. Kodály; Rozsnyai)
      8 Hungarian folk-songs (Univ. Ed.)
    (iii) Chorus : Hungarian folk-songs for male
      vs. (ms.)
      Slovakian folk-songs for mixed vs. (ms.)
      Slovakian folk-songs for male vs. (Univ. Ed.)
Folk-lore publications: *Chansons populaires roumaines du département Bihar* (Academia Română, Bucharest, 1913). *Transylvanian Hungarian Folk-Songs,* 150 melodies with preface in Eng. and Fr., publ. by B. Bartók and Z. Kodály (Popular Literary Soc. Budapest, 1923). *Volksmusik der Rumänen von Maramures (Sammelbände für vergleichende Musikwissenschaft,* IV, Munich, 1923, Drei Masken Verlag). *Hungarian Folk-Music,* 340 melodies and critical notes

(Oxford Univ. Press, 1924). *Slovakian Folk-Tunes*, 2600 melodies with preface and notes in Slovak, French, English, German, (Slovenská Matica, Curčiansky-Svätý-Martin, 1924–5). *Der Musikdialekt der Rumänen von Hunyad (Z.f.M.* II, 489–522). *Die Volksmusik der Araber von Biskra und Umgebung (Z.f.M.* II, 352–360).
The greater part of the folk-tunes collected by B. (2700 Hungarian, 3500 Rumanian, and 200 Arab) remains unpubl. He has also written (in collab. with Alex. Reschofsky) a Pf. School, and has ed. many classical pf. works for teaching purposes. —Z. K.

BARTOŠ, František. Czech folklorist and philologist; *b.* Mlatcov, 1838; died there, 1906. After studying in Vienna, engaged mostly in Brünn. During his travels in Moravia for many years he collected folk-songs of his country and publ. collections (notation partly written by Leoš Janáček, *q.v.*). The Moravian folk-songs were collected in the fullest manner through his activity. Chief works (all in Czech):
New Moravian Folk-Songs (1882); 2nd coll. 1887–9; 3rd coll. 1901.—V. ST.

BARTOŠ, Josef. Czech writer on music; *b.* Vysoké Mýto, 1887. Stud. and graduated Ph.D. in Prague, where he lives as critic and teacher.
Anton Dvořák, 1913; *Zdenko Fibich*, 1913; *J. B. Foerster*, 1923; *Introduction to Musical Art*; *Introduction to Æsthetics*, 1922 (all in Czech).—V. ST.

BARY, Alfred E. von. Ger. t. opera singer; *b.* La Valetta, Malta, 18 Jan. 1873. Stud. medicine; M.D. 1898; assistant Mental Clinic of Leipzig Univ.; also stud. singing; 1902–12 at Court Opera, Dresden; 1912–18, Court Opera House, Munich. Retired from stage 1918 (owing to increasing eye-trouble) and returned to treatment of mental diseases. Sang Parsifal, Siegmund, Siegfried, Lohengrin and Tristan at Bayreuth from 1904.—A. E.

BAS, Giulio. Ital. theorist, orgt. compr. *b.* Venice, 21 April 1874. Director of music at S Luigi di Francesi, Rome. Has devoted himself specially to study of Gregorian chant.
Manual of Gregorian Chant (Düsseldorf, Schwann); *Ideas of Gregorian Chant* (Rome, Desclée); *A Renewal of Studies of Harmony and Counterpoint* (Schwann); *Harmonisation of Gregorian Melodies* (Desclée); *Method of Accompaniment of Gregorian Chant and of Composition in the Eight Modes* (Turin, S.T.E.N.); *Treatise on Musical Form* (Milan, Ricordi). All in Italian.—D. A.

BASABILBASO de Catelin, Henriette. Argentine dramatic s. singer. Stud. at Paris under Rosa Caron and Matilde Marchesi at Buenos Ayres under Maguilli. Sang at La Scala, Milan, 1906, and several times in Paris. She is one of the most distinguished amateurs of Buenos Ayres. —A. M.

BASQUE FOLK-MUSIC. See AZKUE; BORDES, CHARLES; DONOSTÍA; GASCÚE, F.

BASSI, Amadeo. Ital. t. singer; *b.* Montespertoli (Florence), 20 July, 1874. Known in principal opera houses in Europe and America. Was first to sing t. rôle in Puccini's *The Girl of the Golden West* at Costanzi Theatre, Rome, and at Covent Garden, London.—D. A.

BASTIANELLI, Giannotto. Ital. critic and compr. *b.* San Domenico di Fiesole (Florence), 20 July, 1883. Was mus. critic for newspapers *La Nazione* (Florence) and *Il Resto del Carlino* (Bologna). Has publ. a voluminous study on

The Musical Crisis in Europe (Pistoia, Pagnini ed.); a study on P. Mascagni (Naples, 1910, Ricciardi); *Musicians of To-day and Yesterday* (Milan, 1914); *The Opera and Other Musical Essays* (Florence, 1921, Vallecchi). Of his compositions the following have been performed:
Concerto for 2 pfs.; 4 sonatas for 2 pfs.; Poem for 2 vns. and pf.—R. F.

BATES, Frank. Eng. orgt., condr. *b.* March, Cambs, 13 Jan. 1856. Mus.Doc. Trin. Coll. Dublin. Orgt. and master of the choristers, Norwich Cath. Condr. Norwich Philh. Soc. (regular orch and choral concerts); Norwich Choral Soc.; Diocesan Choral Association; chairman, Norwich Competition Fest. Committee. Promoter of out-door music and folk-dances.—E.-H.

BATH, Hubert. Eng. compr. *b.* Barnstaple, Devon, 6 Nov. 1883. Stud. under Dr. H. I. Edwards and later at R.A.M. London (Goring Thomas Scholarship for compn.) under Beringer, R. Steggall and Corder. In 1913–14 was one of condrs. for Quinlan Opera Co. Condr. Royal Carl Rosa Opera Co. 1923–4. Was for some years condr. of opera class at Guildhall School of Music, and also mus. adviser to London County Council. In compn. he turns to the lighter kinds of music, which he writes very tastefully, with great skill and knowledge of effect, although he has achieved a measure of success with symph. work. His mus. settings of the works of Fiona Macleod are extensive and interesting.
Operas: *Bubbole*, 1 act (Milan, 3 Jan. 1920); *Young England*, comic opera (with G. H. Clutsam), Daly's Theatre, London, 1915; Drury Lane, 1916; *The Sire de Malétroit's Door*, 1 act; *The Three Strangers*, 1 act; *Trilby*, 3 acts. Orch.: *Orch. Variations* (Queen's Hall, 1905); *African Suite*; overture, *Midshipman Easy*; *Woodland Scenes*; *Visions of Hannele*, symph. poem (Queen's Hall, Feb. 1920), etc. Chorus and orch: *Wedding of Shon Maclean* (Leeds Fest, 1910); *Wake of O'Connor*, 1918; *Men on the Line*, male vs. (Albert Hall, 1913); *Jackdaw of Rheims*; *Look at the Clock*, etc. Incidental music to *Hannele* (His Majesty's Theatre, 1908); to *Light of Asia* (Kegan Paul). Numerous recitations to music, songs, pf. pieces, etc. *Freedom*, the first symphony ever written for a brass band, 1922.—E.-H.

BATKA, Richard. Austrian critic, musicologist; *b.* Prague, 14 Dec. 1868; *d.* Vienna, 24 April, 1922. Stud. at Prague (Ph.D.). Worked as musicologist from 1896. Critic of *Prager Tagblatt*. Did good work for contemporary music as mus. ed. of *Der Kunstwart*; founded the Dürerbund and awakened the public interest in historical as well as modern music. From 1908, B. worked as music-critic in Vienna for *Fremdenblatt*, then for *Allgemeine Zeitung*; for some time, ed. (with Richard Specht) the *Merker*. Was teacher of mus. history and of lute at Vienna Music Acad. Was a most diligent and successful writer, ed., translator and author of many opera-texts.
Biographies of Bach and Schumann (Reclam); a short handy biography of Wagner; *Geschichte der Musik in Böhmen* (1906); *Allgemeine Geschichte der Musik* (1908); *Gesammelte Aufsätze aus der Musik- und Theater-Welt* (1899); *Musikalische Streifzüge* (1908); *Kranz* (1903). He dir. the coll. *Hausmusik der Kunstwart* (from 1907); re-ed. Bach's *Notenbüchlein für A. M. Bach* (1904).—P. ST.

BATON, René. See RHENÉ-BATON.

BATTISTINI, Mattia. Italian baritone operatic and concert singer; *b.* Rome, 27 Feb. 1858. Known in all the principal theatres of the

world. His repertory includes 82 works, belonging to all periods, from Mozart's *Nozze di Figaro* and *Don Giovanni*, the *Barbiere*, *Rigoletto*, *Luisa Miller*, *Lohengrin*, *Carmen*, to Massenet's *Werther* (which the compr. specially re-set as a barit. part for him), Rubinstein's *Demonio* and Tchaikovsky's *Eugene Onegin*. A cultured and intelligent artist, he gives every care to the costumes and the interpretation of his parts. Has recently completed very successful concert - tours in Germany, Scandinavia and England. Is also the compr. of some ballads.
Consult Monaldi, *Celebrated Singers* (Turin, Bocca).—D. A.

BATTKE, Max. Ger. teacher and author; *b.* Schiffuss, East Prussia, 15 Sept. 1863; *d.* Berlin, 4 Oct. 1916. Pupil of R. High School and Acad., Berlin. Teacher at several cons. in Berlin. Founded a "Seminary for Music" in 1900, which became in 1910 "Seminary for School Singing." Founder of "Young People's Concerts." Wrote a whole series of widely circulated works on teaching music; publ. collections of songs and choral pieces.—A. E.

BAUER, Harold. Pianist; *b.* New Malden, near London, 28 April, 1873, of an Eng. mother and a Ger. father. Stud. vn. under father and Adolph Pollitzer in London; *début* as violinist in London in 1883. For 9 years after this, appeared frequently in various British towns as violinist. His pf.-playing, however, attracted the attention of Paderewski, who advised him to devote himself to this branch of the art. Accordingly he went to Paris in 1892, where he stud. under Paderewski for a year, supporting himself meanwhile by giving lessons. Paderewski was his only master. So great was his natural aptitude for the pf. that he has become one of the world's foremost virtuosos on this instr. Official *début* as pianist in 1893; 1893-4, made a concert-tour in Russia, followed by engagements on the Continent and in England. His Amer. *début* was made with Boston Symphony Orch. in 1900. Until the outbreak of the war he lived chiefly in Paris, where he establ. an enviable reputation as a teacher. After the outbreak of the war he settled in New York. Here he founded the Beethoven Association of which he is the President. This soc., with the co-operation of many artists and virtuosos of the first rank, began giving concerts in 1919, devoting itself in the beginning chiefly to the presentation of Beethoven's works in all forms, particularly those less often heard. It has become a powerful factor in the mus. life of New York City. A part of the proceeds of its concerts it devoted to the publ. (Schirmer) of the orig. Eng. version (in a revision and emendation by H. E. Krehbiel) of Arthur Wheelock Thayer's authoritative life of Beethoven, hitherto available only in its Ger. translation. It contributed materially to the establ. in the New York Public Library of a valuable coll. of works by Beethoven and books about this compr., and made a substantial contribution towards the erection of a new Festspielhaus at Salzburg.—O. K.

BAUER, Moritz. Ger. critic and historian; *b.* Hamburg, 8 April, 1857. Stud. medicine; then music at Leipzig. Ph.D. 1904; teacher at Hoch's Cons. Frankfort; prof. Univ. of Frankfort-o-M., 1914.
Contributions to the Understanding of Franz Schubert's Songs (1914, Breitkopf); *Ivan Knorr* (Frankfort, 1916) and other studies, *e.g.* on Schubert's friend, the poet Johann Mayrhofer (*Z.f.M.* V, 1922-3).—A. E.

BÄUERLE, Hermann. Ger. compr. and ed. of church music; *b.* Ebersberg (Würtemberg), 24 Oct. 1869. Stud. theology at Tübingen; also music under Emil Kauffmann and Haberl in Regensburg. Teacher in School of Church Music, Regensburg (Ratisbon), 1901; then vicar of Reutlingendorf. 1917, mus. dir. in Schwäbisch-Gmünd; dir. of a cons. in Ulm since 1921.
Church vocal music; masses, etc.; ed. of *a cappella* church music in modern notation.—A. E.

BAUSSNERN, Waldemar von. Ger. compr. *b.* Berlin, 29 Nov. 1866. Spent his youth in Transylvania, whence his family came. Pupil R. High School of Music, Berlin, 1882-8 (Kiel; Bargiel); chorus-master, Mannheim, 1891; Dresden, 1895; teacher in Cons. and condr. Cologne, 1903; dir. of Grand Ducal Music School, Weimar, 1908 (1910, prof.); dir. of Hoch's Cons. Frankfort-o-M. 1916; secretary of Berlin Acad. of Art, and teacher in Acad. for Church and School Music since 1923.
6 symphonies; chamber-music; pf. pieces; songs; operas: *The Poet and the World* (Weimar, 1897); *Dürer in Venice* (Weimar, 1901); *Herbort and Hilde* (Mannheim, 1902); *The Clog* (Frankfort-o-M. 1904); *Satyros* (after Goethe; Basle 1923); and especially the choral work *The Great Hymn of Life and Death*. He edited 2 of Peter Cornelius' operas and completed C.'s unfinished opera *Gunlöd* (perf. Cologne, 1906).—A. E.

BAUTISTA, Julián. Span. compr. *b.* Madrid, 21 April, 1901. Pupil of Conrado del Campo, Madrid. His works are conceived in accordance with the most advanced tendency of to-day.
Dos impresiones sinfónicas, orch.; *Interior*, 1-act lyric drama (Maeterlinck); *Dos canciones* and *La Flûte de jade*, v. and pf.; *Colores*, 5 pf. pieces; *La Fuerza*, ballet (publ. Unión Musical Española, Madrid).—P. G. M.

BAX, Arnold Edward Trevor. English composer; *b.* London, 6 Nov. 1883. Comes of a family, several of whose members have attained prominence in the public eye. He studied at the Royal Academy of Music, under Frederick Corder for composition and Tobias Matthay for piano (1900-5), and was one of the most brilliant students that that institute had known, astonishing everybody, in particular by the facility with which he read at the piano the most intricate of modern scores as they arrived. The same remarkable proficiency showed itself quickly in composition, and if the works belonging to this early period appeared over-elaborated it must be ascribed in part to this youthful exuberance which knew no difficulty. Most of these works were subsequently withdrawn or revised. It was not long before the process of simplification began to set in, and although the texture of Bax's music will always have a certain complexity of appearance, it had long since been clear in effect. Structurally it is diatonic, but the figuration is of a personal order of chromaticism, and every thematic idea is treated with a continuous flow of harmonic variants. At an early age he came under the influence of the Neo-Celtic movement, and he has taken an absorbing interest in Irish folk-lore and literature. This is clearly revealed in many of his works, and the mode of expression it has induced has frequently been described as the musical equivalent of W. B. Yeats's poetry. Omitting for the moment piano pieces and songs, of which there has been a continuous flow, the chronological order of his larger works indicates sufficiently the progress of his development. To 1906 belongs the trio for violin, viola and piano, which has ceased to be in any sense representative. The following year produced *Fatherland* for tenor solo with chorus and orchestra. The chief works of 1908 were the orch. poem *Into the Twilight*, since discarded, and a string 5tet, of which only an *Interlude* has been retained. With 1909 are reached the first works which survive the composer's criticism, chiefly the tone-poem *In the Faëry Hills*, and the Festival Overture, together with a setting, for two sopranos, chorus and orchestra, of a fragment from Shelley's *Prometheus Unbound* under the title *Enchanted Summer*. In 1910 he wrote the earlier version of his first piano sonata and commenced that of his first for violin and piano; all the four sonatas however, two for violin, and two for piano, have been subjected to such complete revision that they may practically be regarded as recent works. The years 1912–13 were prolific in large orchestral works. Their output comprises *Christmas Eve in the Mountains*; a suite of four pieces concluding with the *Dance of Wild Irravel*; two works inspired by Swinburne (the tone-poem *Nympholept* and the symphony in four connected movements *Spring Fire*); a symphonic scherzo; and another tone-poem, *The Garden of Fand*. The latter was given in Paris with great success under Kussevitzky (17 May, 1923). The outstanding work of 1914–15 was the piano quintet, one of Bax's greatest achievements. About the same time he completed the earlier version of both the violin sonatas and set six poems from *The Bard of the Dimbovitza* for voice and orchestra. The following year, 1916, was mostly occupied with the Symphonic Variations for piano and orchestra, performed five years later (by Harriet Cohen), the only other concerted work being the Elegy Trio for flute, viola and harp. In 1917 there was another outburst of orchestral activity. three tone-poems being completed in rapid succession; the as yet unperformed *In Memoriam*, followed by *November Woods*, and *Tintagel*, besides a ballet, *Between Dusk and Dawn*, an Irish tone-poem for two pianos, *Moy Mell* or *The Happy Plain*, and an Irish Elegy for cor-anglais, harp and strings. In 1918 appeared the string quartet in G. To 1919 belong the quintet for strings and harp, and the second piano sonata. In 1920 the composer was commissioned to write

the music for Sir J. M. Barrie's phantasy *The Truth about the Russian Dancers*, produced at the Coliseum with Mme. Karsavina in the principal part. In the same year he wrote the two carols, *Mater Ora Filium*, for unaccompanied double choir, and *Of a Rose. I sing*, for choir, harp, cello and double-bass. Next followed a concerto for viola and orchestra which was introduced at a Philharmonic Concert by Lionel Tertis. After that the composer was engaged for a time in the final revision of the four sonatas, which involved the writing of entirely new movements. 1921 saw the completion of yet another tone-poem, *The Happy Forest*, of relatively moderate dimensions. On 13 Nov. 1922, a concert, chiefly orchestral and choral, of his works was given with conspicuous success at Queen's Hall. During the same week Lionel Tertis and the composer gave the first performance of a new sonata for viola and piano. Both this work and the symphony in E flat were composed during 1922. The symphony was first perf. 2 Dec. 1922, revived with great success on 12 Jan. 1924 at Queen's Hall, London, under Sir Henry Wood, and given in Prague, 7 June, 1924. In 1923, a new choral work *To the Name above Every Name* was performed at the Worcester Festival.

The smaller piano pieces, of which about two dozen have been published, are very characteristic of the composer, especially in their mode of elaboration, for which he has found a very personal type of pianistic arabesque. Three of the best-known were inspired by a visit to Russia, and of these the most frequently performed is *In a Vodka Shop*. Those pieces which incline to the form of the nocturne, are remarkable for their delicacy. Of songs he has written a large number in all styles, besides harmonising many French and English folk-songs.

If it were necessary to find a label for Bax we might call him a Neo-Romantic. He has a strong feeling for beauty, both of line and of texture, and, contrary to a tendency prevalent among modern composers, he is not afraid to give it full play, whether in the fashioning of a poetic melody, or in a more prolonged flow of fantasy. In a certain sense of the word, he is one of the most musical of present-day composers, for music flows from him in a generous stream. The length of some of his works is due to this, and not to diffuseness, or the common practice of adopting the larger musical forms and filling them. Almost invariably this stream is lyrical. It sings in every mood, but always with a romantic inflection.

Orch.: Symphony in E flat (1921–2) (full score publ. by Murdoch & Co. London); *The Garden of Fand* (id.); *November Woods* (id.); *In the Faëry Hills* (id.); *Tintagel* (id.); vla. concerto (id.). Choir and orch.: *Enchanted Summer* (Murdoch); *Fatherland* (Chester); *To the Name above Every Name* (Worc. 3 Choirs, 1923; Murdoch); *St. Patrick's Breastplate* (1923), ms.; Male chorus, fl. pf.: *Now is the Time of Christymas* (id.). Small choir, harp, cello, db.: *Of a Rose I sing a Song*, 1921 (id.). *A cappella* motets: *Mater ora Filium*, 1921 (id.); *This World's Joy*, 1923 (id.). Unacc. male chorus, *The Boar's Head*. Chamber-music: 5tet, pf. and str. (Murdoch); 5tet, str. and harp, in 1 movement (id.); str. 4tet (id.); 4tet, in 1 movement, ms.; trio, fl. vla. harp (Chester); trio, pf. vn. vla. (*id.*); sonata, vn. and pf. in E (Murdoch); sonata, vn. and pf. in D (*id.*); sonata, vla. and pf. 1921 (*id.*); sonata, cello and pf. (1923), ms. (first perf. 26 Feb.1924 by Beatrice Harrison and Harriet Cohen); *Folk Tale*, cello and pf. (Chester); *Legend*, vn. and pf. (Augener); pf. sonata, F sharp (Murdoch); pf. sonata in G (*id.*); *Moy Mell*, Irish tone-poem, 2 pfs. (Chester); many pf. pieces and songs (Murdoch; Anglo-Fr. Co.; Augener; Chester; J. Williams; Enoch; Boosey). —E. E.

BAYREUTH. In 1872, on 22 May, Richard Wagner laid the foundation-stone of the Festival Theatre, which was formally opened on 13 Aug. 1876, with perf. of *The Nibelungen Ring*. Since that time it has remained the tutelar home of the authentic interpretations of Wagner's works. Towards end of 1914, it closed its doors, and did not re-open till 1924.—A. E.

BAZELAIRE, Paul. Fr. cellist; *b.* Sedan, 1886. Stud. at Paris Cons.; 1st prize for cello at age of 11. 1903–5, 1st prize for harmony, cpt. and fugue. Possesses a remarkable technique. Prof. of cello at Cons. Wrote works on technique, *e.g.*: *Quelques notes sur différents points importants de la technique générale de violoncelle* (Paris, Senart). As compr. is known by his pf. pieces, works for cello and clar., choral music.
Fantaisie for pf. (played London, 1899), *Le Colibri*, for solo vn. (played Manchester, 1908), etc. —M. L. P.

BAZZINI, Antonio. Italian violinist and compr. *b.* Brescia, 11 March, 1818; *d.* 10 Feb. 1897. From 1882 until his death, dir. of Milan Conservatoire.
Biblical cantata, *La risurrezione di Cristo*; overtures: *Saul*; *Re Lear*; *Francesca da Rimini*; str. 4tets; many pieces for vn.; vocal chamber-music; an opera.—D. A.

BEACH, Mrs. H. H. A. (*neé* Amy Marcy Cheney). Amer. compr. *b.* Henniker, N.H., U.S.A., 5 Sept. 1867. Stud. the pf. under E. Perabo and K. Baermann, and harmony under Junius W. Hill in Boston. In this city she made her *début* as pianist at age of 16. In succeeding years she appeared repeatedly with Boston Symphony Orch., the Thomas Orch. (in Chicago), the Pittsburgh and St. Louis Orchs., and also the Berlin Philh., and gave pf. recitals, often playing her own compns. in America and in Munich, Dresden and Breslau.

After her marriage in 1885 to Dr. Beach, she appeared less frequently, devoting herself more to compn., in which she was wholly self-taught. For her own use in her studies she made complete Eng. transl. (not published) of Berlioz's and Gevaert's classic works on instrumentation. After her husband's death in 1910 she spent several seasons concertising in Europe.

Her op. 1 (songs) was publ. by A. P. Schmidt in Boston in 1886, but she first really came into prominence as a compr. when her Mass in E flat, op. 5, was perf. by Boston Handel and Haydn Soc. in 1892. On 30 Oct. 1896 the Boston Symph. Orch. gave 1st perf. of her *Gaelic Symphony*, op. 32, and she played her C sharp mi. concerto for the pf. (comp. 1899) at a Boston Symphony concert on 7 April, 1900. Her *Festival Jubilate*, op 7, was written by invitation for the dedication of the Women's Building at the Chicago Exposi-

tion in 1893. For the Panama-Pacific Exposition in San Francisco in 1915 she wrote a *Panama Hymn*, op. 74, for chorus and orch. Her polished, at times much elaborated style, rooted in the Wagner - Brahms period, often displays an energetic daring and an unusual virility.
Gaelic Symphony, op. 32 (1897); pf. concerto, op. 45 (1900); Mass in E flat, op. 5 (1890); *The Minstrel and the King*, ballad for male vs. and orch. op. 16 (1892); *The Rose of Avontown* for female vs. op. 30; *Festival Jubilate*, op. 17 (1892); *Sylvania*, wedding cantata for mixed vs. op. 46 (1901); *The Chambered Nautilus*, cantata for female vs. op. 66 (1907); *Panama Hymn*, op. 74 (Schirmer, 1915); 5tet for pf. and str. op. 67 (1909); Theme and variations for fl. and str. 4tet, op. 80 (Schirmer, 1920); sonata for vn. and pf. op. 34 (1899); Variations on a Balkan theme for pf. op. 60 (1906); *Eskimos*, 4 pieces for pf. op. 64 (1907); 2 pieces for pf. op. 92 (Schirmer, 1922). Also church music, many pf. pieces and about 100 songs. Mostly publ. by A. P. Schmidt, Boston.—O. K.

BECHGAARD, Julius. Danish compr. *b.* 19 Dec. 1843; *d.* 5 March, 1917. Pupil of Cons. Leipzig; wrote numerous vocal pieces in large and small forms, all of distinctly national character. His opera *Frode* was produced at R. Theatre, Copenhagen, and at Prague,1893.—A.H.

BECK, Ellen. Danish singer; *b.* 3 Oct. 1873. Pupil of Algot Lange, Copenhagen, and Devilliers, Paris. Countless concerts in Scandinavia, also Paris and London. An excellent and most experienced vocal teacher. Has sung in England at Sheffield and other festivals.—A. H.

BECK, Reinhold J. Ger. compr. *b.* Hanover, 10 Jan. 1881. At first, pharmacist; then actor; took up music in Berlin, 1906. Compr. and lecturer on Science of Music at Herder High School and People's High School, Berlin-Harmsdorf.
Lyrical phantasy *On the Rhine*, for orch.; chamber concerto for vn. in suite form; *Serenade* for clar. and str. 4tet; 2 str. 4tets; songs; chamber-music; duets; choruses; music to Grillparzer's *Ahnfrau*; operettas, *Rivieraliebe* and *Berliner Rangen*.—A. E.

BECKER, Hugo. Ger. cellist; *b.* Strasburg, Alsace, 13 Feb. 1864. Stud. under his father, the celebrated violinist, Jean Becker (1833–84), Kanut Kündinger, Fr. Grützmacher, sen., Karl Hess in Dresden, Piatti and de Swert. Solo violinist Opera House Orch., Frankfort-o-M.; teacher, Hoch's Cons., 1890–1906; solo cellist from 1901 (in succession to Piatti) at the Monday Popular Concerts, London; teacher High School of Music, Berlin, since 1909. Formerly member of Heermann Quartet. At present, member of a trio with Carl Friedberg (formerly Arthur Schnabel) and Carl Flesch. Becker is the classical cellist of Germany. He has written a concerto (A ma. op. 10, Schott) for his instrument.—A. E.

BECKER, Reinhold. Ger. compr. *b.* Adorf, Saxony, 11 Aug. 1842. At first violinist; since 1870 in Dresden as compr. and dir. of Men's Choral Society (1884–94).
Many favourite songs and male choruses; 2 vn. concertos (A mi. and G mi.); symphony in C, op. 140; vn. sonatas; str. 4tets; symph. poem, *The Prince of Homburg*; operas: *Frauenlob* (Dresden, 1892); *Ratbold* (Mayence, 1896).—A. E.

BECKMAN, Bror. Swedish compr. *b.* Christinehamn, 10 Feb. 1866. Stud. under J. Lindegren (at pf. school of S. Carlheim-Gyllensköld), 1890–1902; member R.A.M. Stockholm, 1904; from 1910, dir. R. Cons. Stockholm.

Symphony in F (Stockholm, 1902); *Om lyckan* (*About Fortune*), orch. op. 10 (*id.* 1902); *I sommarnätter* (*Summer Nights*), str. orch. (1893); *Flodsänger*, v. and orch. (1897); *Ballade*, barit. and orch. (1906); stage-music; sonata, vn. and pf. op. 1; pf. pieces (3 symph. ballades, op. 14); songs.—P. V.

BEDFORD, Herbert. Eng. compr. and painter; *b.* London, 23 Jan. 1867. Has lectured on Modern Unacc. Song and publ. an essay on it (Oxford Univ. Press, 1923). Married Liza Lehmann (*q.v.*).

Opera, *Kit Marlowe*; symph. phantasy, *The Optimist*; suite, *Queen Mab*; overture, *Sowing the Wind*; *Vox Veris*, s. v. and orch. (all F. & B. Goodwin Library); *Mélodie Solennelle* for str. (Schott); songs with str. 4tet (Boosey; Chester); 8 unacc. songs (F. & B. Goodwin).—E.-H.

BEECHAM, Sir Thomas, Bart. Eng. condr. and operatic impresario; *b.* near Liverpool, 29 April, 1879. Educated Rossall School (where he had lessons in compn. from Dr. Sweeting) and Wadham Coll. Oxford (a few lessons from Dr. Varley Roberts); no further regular music tuition; 1889, he founded an amateur orch. at Huyton, near Liverpool, and at a concert given by his father, he deputised for Dr. Richter who was indisposed; 1902, engaged by Kelson Truman to cond. a touring opera co.; then stud. compn. for 12 months and comp. 3 operas (ms.); 1905, gave his 1st concert in London with Queen's Hall Orch. In 1906, founded New Symphony Orch. (severed his connection with it in 1908); then started Beecham Symphony Orch.; in 1910, took Covent Garden Theatre and gave a few series of old and new operas, including Strauss's *Elektra*, Ethel Smyth's *Wreckers*, Debussy's *L'Enfant Prodigue*, and the 1st production of Delius's *A Village Romeo and Juliet*; he gave a season of light opera in autumn of 1910 at His Majesty's Theatre and a second Covent Garden season in the winter, when he cond. Strauss's *Salome* and produced Clutsam's 1-act opera *A Summer Night*, Strauss's *Elektra*, Debussy's *Pelléas et Mélisande*, etc. In 1911, he cond. the Beecham Symphony Orch., the London Symphony and other orchs. and continued his determined advocacy of Delius by producing his *Appalachia*, *Paris*, and the *Dance Rhapsody*. Indeed, England owes more to B. than to any other man, for its knowledge of Delius. In 1913, he went to the relief of Denhof Opera Co. in the provinces (Wagner's *Ring*, etc., Strauss, under Balling and Cortolezi).

Between Jan. and March 1913, he produced largely Strauss and Wagner operas; from 27 May to 7 June, 1913, he co-operated with Sir Herbert Tree in producing at His Majesty's Theatre Molière's *Le Bourgeois Gentilhomme* with Strauss's *Ariadne in Naxos* (the play in English, the opera in German).

It was in June and July 1913 that his father, Sir Joseph, gave a 5-weeks' season of Russ. opera and ballet at Drury Lane Theatre: Mussorgsky's *Boris* (24 June) with Chaliapin in title-rôle; his *Khovanshtchina* (1 July); Rimsky-Korsakof's *Ivan the Terrible*, with Emil Cooper

as chief condr. The ballet was under Serge Diaghilef, the new ones being Stravinsky's *Le Sacre du printemps*, Florent Schmitt's *La Tragédie de Salome*, and a poem-dance, *Jeux*, by Debussy. In 1914, Sir Joseph gave a second Russ. season of opera and ballet with the singers from Imperial Opera, Petrograd, and Diaghilef's troupe. This included Borodin's *Prince Igor*; Rimsky-Korsakof's *Coq d'Or*, *Night of May* and *Ivan*; Strauss's *Rosenkavalier*; Mozart's *Die Zauberflöte*, and the 1st perf. on any stage of Stravinsky's *The Nightingale*. The ballets included Ravel's *Daphnis et Chloé*; Rimsky-Korsakof's *Antar* and *Scheherazade*; Steinberg's *Midas*; Tchaikovsky's *Le Lac des Cygnes*; Balakiref's *Tamara*; Rimsky-Korsakof's (with Glazunof) *Cléopâtre*; Tchérepnin's *Narcisse*; Stravinsky's *Petrushka* and *L'Oiseau de feu*, and the 1st perf. in England of Strauss's *Legend of Joseph*, which had been produced in Paris a few weeks previously. On 4 July, 1914, B. produced (1st perf.) Holbrooke's *Dylan*.

In Oct. 1915, at the Shaftesbury Theatre (with R. Courtneidge) Thomas Beecham cond. a season of opera in Eng.: Mozart, Puccini, etc.

Between May and July, 1916, he gave a Beecham Opera season at Aldwych Theatre: Mozart's *Flute* and Wagner's *Tristan* (in Eng.); Bach's *Phœbus and Pan*, Mussorgsky, Puccini, Verdi (*Otello*), Stanford's *The Critic*, Ethel Smyth's *The Boatswain's Mate*, etc. (He had been knighted by King George in 1914 and inherited the baronetcy in 1916.) In Oct. 1916 he gave an autumn season of opera in Eng. at the Aldwych: Mozart, Wagner, Saint-Saëns, Verdi, Puccini, Gounod (*Faust*; *Romeo and Juliet*), Charpentier (*Louise*). This season continued till 10 Feb. 1917.

In autumn 1917 (till Nov. 24), he removed to Drury Lane Theatre: Mussorgsky, Rimsky-Korsakof, Wagner (*Tristan*), Puccini, Bach, etc. The summer season (3 June to 27 July) of 1918 he gave at Drury Lane Theatre, and there again in 1919 (from 19 March) he gave a season (Wagner, Mozart, Verdi, Charpentier, Puccini, etc.), including Bizet's *Fair Maid of Perth*. At Covent Garden, in May and June of this year he revived Massenet's *Thaïs* and gave the first production in England of Massenet's *Thérèse*. In Nov.–Dec. of the same year the Beecham Opera Co. gave a season at Covent Garden which included Wagner's *Parsifal*, Wolf-Ferrari's *Susanna's Secret*, and Stravinsky's *Nightingale* (the last 2 in Eng. for 1st time). A fortnight of Russian opera brought the season to a close on 22 Dec. 1919.

On 24 Feb. 1920, the Beecham Co. were again at Covent Garden, and produced Delius's *A Village Romeo and Juliet* (19 March, 1920) and all the usual operas. On 10 May, under the Grand Opera Syndicate, Ltd., Sir Thomas dir. at Covent Garden Opera House, amongst other works, Bizet's *I Pescatori di Perle*, Debussy's *Pelléas*, Donizetti's *Don Pasquale*, etc., but the season ended in July. Since then Sir Thomas has only appeared occasionally as condr. at a few orch. concerts in London and in Manchester.

It goes without saying that B. has done more than any living man towards the establishment of grand opera in England. Without his good work the British National Opera Co. could not have made their fine beginning. As condr. he added a greater zest and a finer line to the works of Mozart. He rejuvenated the programmes of the R. Philh. Soc. concerts during the seasons when he was artistic director, 1916–17 and 1917–1918; and he did the same for the Hallé orch. concerts in Manchester.—E.-H.

BEER-WALBRUNN, Anton. Ger. compr. *b.* Kohlberg, Bavaria, 29 June, 1864. At first a teacher and orgt. in Eichstätt; then pupil at Acad. of Music (Rheinberger) in Munich; teacher of compn. there since 1901; prof. 1908. As compr. is a delicate and melodious romanticist.

Songs; Cycle of Shakespeare's Sonnets should be specially mentioned, op. 34 (own publication); chamber-music: vn. sonatas, D mi. op. 30, Tischer & Jagenberg; pf. 4tet, op. 8 (Peters); 4tet, G. ma. op. 14 (Peters); orch. pieces, the most orig. of the 3 Burlesques being *Cloud-Cuckoo-Town*, op. 40 (Cologne, Tischer & Jagenberg); vn. concerto; operas: *Atonement* (Lübeck, 1894); *Don Quixote* (Munich, 1908, Drei Masken Verlag); *Das Ungeheuer* (Carlsruhe, 1919); also music to *Hamlet* and *The Tempest*.—A. E.

BEETHOVEN ASSOCIATION, New York. See BAUER, HAROLD.

BEGGAR'S OPERA, The. Originally produced at John Rich's theatre, in Lincoln's Inn Fields, 29 Jan. 1728, with immense success. Written by John Gay with popular tunes for the songs; arranged with an overture by Dr. J. C. Pepusch. It ridiculed the Ital. Opera of that day, had political satire, drew attention to the bad system of prison discipline, and the payment of informers. Prior to the 1920 revival, it was last seen on the Eng. boards in 1886, with Sims Reeves as Captain Macheath. The 1920 reproduction at Lyric Theatre, Hammersmith, under auspices of Nigel Playfair, ran from 5 June, 1920, to 17 Dec. 1923 (1463 continuous perfs.). The airs were artistically harmonised by Frederic Austin, and the scenery designed by late C. Lovat Fraser. Some necessary "cuts" had to be made, owing to length of piece and other causes. See "POLLY."—F. K.

BEHM, Eduard. Ger. compr. *b.* Stettin, 8 April, 1862. Pupil at Leipzig Cons.; then of Härtel, Raif and Kiel in Berlin; resided in Vienna; then in Kiel as critic and condr.; sometime teacher at Acad. of Music, Erfurt; next dir. of Schwantzer Cons. Berlin, till 1901; prof. 1917.

Symphony; *Idyll of Spring* for orch.; pf. concerto; vn. concerto; pf. trio, E mi. op. 14; 5tet for clar. and str.; str. 6tet (with violotta); 2 vn. sonatas, A ma. op. 15 and D mi.; vn. suite, G. ma. op. 22; glees; songs; operas: *The Rogue of Bergen* (Dresden, 1899); *Marienkind* (1902); *The Vow* (1914).—A. E.

BEHN, Hermann. Ger. compr. *b.* Hamburg, 11 Nov. 1859. Jurist; became pupil of Anton Bruckner in Vienna, and Joseph Rheinberger in Munich, and Hermann Zumpe in Hamburg, where he has resided since 1887; has given lectures on musical history since 1897.

9 books of songs; pf. sonata, C mi. (Leipzig,

Fr. Kistner); arrangements of works of Wagner, Bruckner, Mahler, etc.—A. E.

BEHREND, Fritz. Ger. compr. *b.* Berlin, 3 March, 1889. Stud. under A. van Eyken, Ph. Rüfer and E. Humperdinck for compn., K. M. Breithaupt for pf.; was for a time Korrepetitor at Court Theatre, Brunswick; then once more in Berlin as compr. and teacher of compn. and pf. There is a Fritz Behrend Society engaged in spreading his works.

Songs, op. 11, 21, 27, 30 (Magdeburg, Heinrichshofen), 2, 14, 19, 23, 24 (Dresden, Aurora Verlag), and 1-act opera *King René's Daughter* (Magdeburg, Heinrichshofen). Unpubl.: Prelude to Kleist's *Penthesilea*; symphony; *Young Olaf* (ballad for barit. and orch.); other orch. works; 2 str. 4tets.—A. E.

BEHREND, William. Danish music historian, critic; *b.* 16 May, 1861. Stud. law at Univ. Copenhagen; has since occupied important positions under the magistracy of Copenhagen; mus. critic of several dailies and magazines; author of musico-historical works. Chief is *Illustrated History of Music* (*Illustreret Musikhistorie*, Vol. II, Copenhagen, 1905), 1076 pages, covering period from Gluck to present time; also biographies (Danish) of Niels W. Gade (1917) and J. P. E. Hartmann (1919).—A. H.

BEIGEL, Victor. *b.* London, 29 May, 1870, of Hungarian parents. Stud. in Vienna, later at Königliche Hochschule, Berlin (Wilhelm Berger, Anton Raif, W. Bargiel). Toured as pianist in Austria, Germany, Sweden, Norway, Poland, with the singers Eugen Hildach and Raimond von Zur Mühlen. 1896, prof. singing, Brooklyn School of Music, New York, teaching in London in the season. Settled in London in 1906 as teacher of singing. Famous pupils: late Gervase Elwes, Susan Metcalfe-Casals, Hubert Eisdell, John Adams, Yves Tinayre (Paris), Loritz Melchoir (Copenhagen Opera).—E.-H.

BEILSCHMIDT, Kurt. Ger. compr. *b.* Magdeburg, 20 March, 1886. Pupil of Schünemann and F. Kauffmann, Magdeburg; at Leipzig Cons., 1905–9; engaged in Brussels for short time; has lived in Leipzig since end of 1909 as composer, teacher and author.

Symphonietta *In May*, op. 17; *Zu einem Liebespiel* for orch. op. 31; *Serenade*, op. 33; pf. suite, op. 2; vn. sonatas, op. 3 and 34; cello sonata, op. 10; str. 4tet, op. 5; choruses; songs; and for stage: *The Adventure in the Wood*, op. 25 (Leipzig, 1918); the mus. comedy *Meister Innocenz*, op. 24; pastoral play, *Artful Cupid* (Leipzig, 1921).—A. E.

BEKKER, Paul. Ger. writer on music; *b.* Berlin, 11 Sept. 1882. At first, violinist in Philh. Orch. Berlin; then condr. in Aschaffenburg and Görlitz; writer on music since 1906, firstly as reviewer to *Berliner Neueste Nachrichten*, in 1909 to *Berliner Allgemeine Zeitung*, and 1911–1923 to *Frankfurter Zeitung*. Resides in Hofheim, Taunus. One of most influential critics and one of most stimulating writers on music in Germany; an advocate of progress and international fertility; champion of Mahler and Schreker. His controversy with Hans Pfitzner marked an era in German criticism.

Beethoven (Stuttgart, 1911, Deutsche Verlags-Anstalt); *Das deutsche Musikleben: Attempt at a Sociological Appreciation of Music* (1916, *id.*); *The Symphonies of Gustav Mahler* (1921, *id.*); *The*

Symphony from Beethoven to Mahler (1918, *id.*); *Franz Schreker* (1919); *Critical Sketches of the times* (collected essays, 1921 and 1923, *id.*).; *Sound and Eros*—A. E.

BEKKEVOLD, Frederik August. Norwegian barit. singer; *b.* Christiania, 18 May, 1830; *d.* there, 17 Jan. 1911. Stud. philology at Christiania Univ.; subsequently trained as vocalist; gained great popularity by his spirited lyrical nterpretation.—J. A.

BELAIEF, Mitrofan Petrovitch (*accent 2nd syll.*). Russ. music publ. *b.* Petrograd, 10/22 Feb. 1836; *d.* Petrograd, 10/23 Jan. 1903. A distinguished music-lover and generous patron, to whom musical Russia owes much. He founded (in 1885) the publ. firm which bears his name, and the Russian Symphony Concerts, devoted to the propagation of Russian music.—M. D. C.

BELAIEF, Victor Michaelovitch. Russ. writer on music; *b.* Uralsk (Ural Cossack govt.) 24 Jan./5 Feb. 1888. Pupil of Liadof, Wihtol, and Glazunof in .Petrograd Cons. (1908–14). Before finishing students' course became teacher of theory 1913, and prof. 1919. From 1917, secretary of Art Council of Petrograd Cons.; 1918–19, secretary of chief direction of Russ. Music Soc. In 1922, went to Moscow as member of council of Russ. State Music Publ. Dept. Has written for many papers and periodicals: *Muzika* (1911–16); *Mus. Contemporary* (1916–17); *Melos* (1917–18). Founded in 1923 (with V. Derjanovsky) the mus. monthly *Towards New Shores* (suspended 1924). Member of Russ. Acad. of Art-Sciences and of State Inst. of Mus. Science; 1923, prof. at Moscow Cons.

Short exposition, *Counterpoint and Mus. Forms* (1st ed. 1914; 2nd, 1922); biography, *A. K. Glazunof* (Vol. I, 1921); *Correspondence of Scriabin and M. P. Belaief* (1922); Russ. transl. of Prout's *Fugal Analysis* (1913).

Mr. Belaief has contributed a large number of the Russ. articles in this Dictionary.—E.-H.

BELGIAN CHAMBER - MUSIC. Is cultivated with a very special partiality. It is in this domain that Belgian comprs. of the last 20 years have brought forth their most significant works, notably Joseph Jongen and Victor Vreuls, in whom, spiritual links with Young Fr. school have inspired a style and mode of writing in perfect harmony with the exigencies of this species, distinguished among all others by its refinement and delicacy. Several groups of Belgian artists devote themselves with assiduity to the interpretation of chamber-music. See art. on CHAMBER-MUSIC PLAYERS.—C. V. B.

BELGIAN FOLK-MUSIC. See CLOSSON, ERNEST, and references under FLEMISH FOLK-MUSIC.

BELGIAN OPERA. Belgian works destined for the lyric stage do not show, as a whole, any very clear national characteristics. Apart from the operas of Jan Blockx, which have tendencies more or less towards folk-lore, but which are rather superficial, the Belgian comprs. of last 20 years are essentially indebted to Wagner, (Du Bois, Gilson, De Boeck). For the rest, one notices the infiltration of Fr. influences (Franck,

d'Indy, Massenet, etc.) or the Ital. Verism, sometimes unadulterated (Vreuls, Buffin), sometimes under forms more or less mixed (Thiébaut, Alb. Dupuis, Rasse, Lagye, etc.). Consult L. Solvay, *L'Évolution théâtrale*, Vol. II, *La Musique* (Brussels, 1922, Van Oest).—C. V. B.

BELGIUM, ORCHESTRAL CONCERTS IN. In Brussels the symphonic works find hospitality in three great concert insts. founded long ago: *Concerts du Conservatoire* (condr. L. Du Bois), for the exlusive perf. of the works of deceased musicians; *Concerts populaires de musique classique* (condr. Rühlmann; manager, Henry Le Bœuf), whose repertory tends more and more to enlarge itself in time and in space, extending from the music of the XVII century to that of the most daring masters of to-day; *Concerts Ysaye* (condr. Eugène Ysaye), which, pursuing their pre-war apostolate, continued to provide, in a generous eclecticism, the music of to-day and that of former times, until the beginning of 1924, when they were replaced by chamber-concerts. Their place in orch. work was consequently taken up by the *Concerts symphoniques Houdret*. In addition, there are the *Concerts Spirituels* (orch. condr. Joseph Jongen), more especially devoted to oratorio and cantata. In Ghent and Liège, *Concerts du Conservatoire*. In Antwerp there are also exceedingly good societies of symph. concerts dir. by excellent conductors (Alpaerts de Vocht, Mortelmans).—C. V. B.

BELL, George. British mus. ed. *b.* Lisburn, Co. Antrim, Ireland; *d.* Glasgow, 6 March, 1923. Presbyterian minister in Establ. Church of Scotland, who did much for furtherance of church music there. Educated at Trinity Coll. Dublin, where he graduated Mus.Bac., and (1888) Mus.Doc. He had been licensed by Irish Presbyterian Church in 1882, but in 1890 obtained admission to Church of Scotland; when inducted as 1st minister of parish ch. of St. Kenneth, Holmfieldhead, Govan, from very beginning he worked for attainment of a fully choral service, and musically his church was one of best in Scotland. Influential member of Church of Scotland Psalmody Committee. On his initiative, a general survey of position of psalmody in every church under their jurisdiction was made by the Gen. Assembly. Had much to do with preparation and publication of *Scottish Mission Hymn-book* in which several of his own tunes appear, and of *Classified List of Anthems.*—W. S.

BELL, William Henry. Eng. compr. *b.* St. Albans, 20 Aug. 1873. Stud. R.A.M. London, winning scholarship in 1889; prof. of harmony there, 1903; vacated it to take charge (as dir.) of S. African Coll. of Music at Cape Town. In March 1918, appointed to the newly-formed chair of music at Univ. of Cape Town. Latterly the S. African Coll. of Music has become part of Univ. with B. as Dean of the Faculty of Music. Practically all his earlier orch. works were produced in England between 1899 and 1912; first by Manns at the Crystal Palace, who presented a new work of Bell's nearly every year from 1899 onwards; and later by Richter, Sir T. Beecham and Sir H. Wood. The last works to be done in London were *A Song of Greeting*, symph. poem, under Sir H. Wood at R.A.M. centenary, Queen's Hall, July 1922; and the Symph. Variations, under the compr. (then in London on his only visit to this country since 1912) at a Philh. concert, Feb. 1921. All his later orch. work is in the repertoire of the Cape Town Municipal Orch. and is frequently played by them under Theo Wendt. B. cond. at the St. Albans Pageant, 1907 (for which he wrote the music), and at the Fest. of Empire, 1911. F.R.C.M. *h.c.* 1924.

Operas: *Hippolytus*, 3 acts (after Euripides), about 1920; *Isabeau*, 1 act (1922); symphonies: I, C mi. *Walt Whitman* (early); II, A mi. (1917); III, F ma. (1918); Symph. Variations (1916; perf. Philh. London, 1921); preludes for orch.: *The Canterbury Pilgrims* (Manns, Crystal Palace, 1899); *A Song in the Morning* (Gloucester Fest. and Queen's Hall, 1901); symph. poems: *The Pardoner's Tale* (Manns, 1900); *La Fée des Sources* (1912); *Mother Carey* (a) *In the Night Watches* (Philh. Soc.), (b) *In the Fo'c'sle* (Novello); *Love among the Ruins* (Beecham); *The Shepherd* (Queen's Hall); *The Portal* (1921); *Veldt Loneliness* (1921); *A Song of Greeting* (Sir Henry Wood, 1922); *Arcadian Suite*, 1909 (Avison Ed. Cary & Co.); music to St. Albans Pageant (*id.*); his most representative work, *Maria Assumpta* (Crashaw), s. v. double chorus, boys' chorus, orch. (1922; Stainer & Bell); vla. concerto, *Rosa Mystica* (about 1917); *Ballad of the Bird-Bride*, early work, barit. solo and orch. (1909; Richter, Queen's Hall); for chorus and orch.: *Hawke* (early); *The Baron of Brackley*, early (J. Williams); 3 vn. sonatas, E mi. F mi. D mi.; songs, 6 *Love Lyrics*, Henley (Novello); 16 songs from Bliss Carman's *Sappho*; 3 old Eng. songs, v. and orch.; music for Ben Jonson's masque *A Vision of Delight* (Kingsway Theatre, 1908); 5 *Mediæval Songs*, female vs. str. and pf. (2 sets); choruses from Shelley's *Prometheus Unbound* (1923), etc.

Consult arts. on the Symph. Variations and 2 symphonies by M. van Someren-Godfery, in *Mus. Times*, May, June, July 1920.—E.-H.

BELLA, Jan Levoslav. Slovak compr. *b.* St. Mikuláš, Slovakia, 1843. Stud. in Vienna; Catholic priest, devoting himself to church music, into which he introduced Slovak folksongs. Later, several years in Hungary; now at Cluj (Klausenburg), Rumania.

Motet *Tu es Petrus*; masses; church hymns; symph. poem, *Osud a Ideál* (*Fate and the Ideal*), 1875; songs; variations and transcriptions of Slovak folksongs.—V. ST.

BELLAIGUE, Camille. Fr. musical critic; *b.* Paris, 1858. Stud. law. Pupil of Paladilhe and Marmontel at Cons., Paris; 1st prize for pf., 1878. Wrote articles for *Correspondant*, *Figaro*, *Le Temps*, *L'Écho de Paris*, and is still writing for the *Gaulois*; mus. critic for *Revue des Deux Mondes* since 1885; gained *Prix Vitet*, 1894. The greater part of his work is contained in *L'Année musicale* (1886–91, 5 vols.) and *L'Année musicale et dramatique* (1892–93, 2 vols.), both publ. Paris, Delagrave.

Un Siècle de musique francaise; *Portraits et silhouettes de musiciens* (Eng. and Ger. transl.); *Études musicales* and *Nouvelles Silhouettes de musiciens* (also transl.); *Les Époques de la musique: Notes brèves* (Delagrave). Also *Mendelssohn* and *Gounod* (Paris, Alcan); *Mozart* and *Verdi* (Paris, Laurens), etc. Amongst latest publ.: *Propos de musique et de guerre*; *Souvenirs de musique et de musiciens* (1921).—M. L. P.

BELLENOT, Philippe. French compr. *b.* 24 Jan. 1860; pupil of École Niedermeyer,

then at Cons.; choirmaster Saint-Sulpice since 1884; *lauréat de l'Institut*; author of motets, masses, 2 dramatic works, *Naristé* and *Le Cœur dormant*, perf. Monte Carlo and Cannes, and Opéra-Comique, Paris.—F. R.

BELLINCIONI, Gemma. S. singer; *b.* Monza, 17 Aug. 1864. One of the most famous artists of Ital. singing of modern times. Her interpretations of Santuzza in Mascagni's *Cavalleria Rusticana* (of which she, with t. Roberto Stagno, was first interpreter), of Violetta in *La Traviata*, of Salome in Strauss's opera, are now memorable. Began her career by playing light and comic parts. The t. Tamberlik, having noticed her ability, engaged her to tour with him abroad; in 1881 she was in Spain and then in Portugal. From that time her fame grew continually, until she was known universally, and her successes aroused the highest enthusiasm. She became the favourite artist of the public and of the Royal Courts. She also establ. herself as an actress in stage-plays, the *Dame aux Camélias* being one of her greatest successes. She publ. her autobiographical memoirs in a book *Myself and the Stage* (*Io ed il Palcoscenico*) (Milan, Quintieri, 1920).

Consult: G. B. Baccioni, *G. B.* (Palermo, S. Biondo); O. Roux, *Illustrious Contemporaries* (Florence, Bemporad).—D. A.

BELLS AND CARILLONS. During recent times great developments have taken place in the making, hanging and tuning of bells. It has been established that there can be very little deviation from the most approved contour of the bell which has been arrived at by the practical experience of generations of bell-founders, without a very detrimental influence on the tone. The science of change-ringing, as regards the fundamental principles, remains the same, namely, that in ringing changes a bell may repeat its position or move one place up or down, but new methods have been evolved, adding interest to various modes in which different series of changes are obtained. The magnificent ring of bells at Exeter Cath. has recently been added to by the gift of two trebles, so that now it is possible to ring peals in 3 keys: B flat (12), E flat (8), and C mi. (8) (descending melodic scale). Great advances have been made in hanging of bells. Steel and iron have gradually taken place of wooden frame-construction, and by use of ball-bearings, bells which required four men to ring them can now be rung with comfort by one man. The development of art of tuning bells has been accomplished by much experimental work and by invention of necessary machines for taking out metal from inside of bell. Every good bell should contain 5 tones in accurate tune, thus:

From this it will be seen that the tuning-zone has a compass of 2 octaves. It will be noted that the tierce is minor and not major as is the case in the series of partial tones of strings and pipes. All these tones can be tuned to accuracy of a single vibration. Such accuracy of tune has never before been possible in the whole history of bells, although it is surprising how near to truth such a master as Hemony got in many of his bells. This finer tuning has greatly influenced the making of carillons with clavier tuned to equal temperament, and has greatly increased the love of bell-music, particularly as such bells can be used with excellent effect in chords of 3 or 4 notes, and can be played with great expression. Intense crescendos, delicate diminuendos, and strong rhythmic accent,· etc., are all possible to the skilled bell-player. The most famous continental carillons are: (i) in Holland, Rotterdam City Hall, Middelburg, Arnhem, Utrecht; (ii) in Belgium, Mechlin, Antwerp, Bruges. The most distinguished living carillonists are: Josef Denijn, Mechlin; Jules Van de Plas, Louvain; Antoon Nauwelaerts, Bruges; Antoon Brees, Antwerp; Gustav Nees, Mechlin. The following carillons with clavier have been erected during recent years in the British Isles: Bournville, 37 bells; Queenstown, 42; Armagh, 42; Parkgate, 37; Loughborough Foundry Tower 42; Loughborough War Memorial, 47; and in U.S.A.: Gloucester, 31; Birmingham, 25; Monistown, 25; Andover, 30, all made in England.—W. W. S.

BELLUCCI, Hector. Argentine condr. and teacher; *b*. Rome in 1855. Stud. vn. and pf. under Ettore and Oreste Pinelli. Orch. condr. at Reggio Emilia and Perugia, going to Buenos Ayres in 1878, where he formed part of the " First Quartet " with Cayetano Gaito, Enrique Bomon and Cayetano Ghignatti. Pf. prof. in Cons. Thibaud-Piazzini. One of pioneers of Ital. music in Argentina.—A. M.

BENDER, Paul. Ger. b. singer; *b*. Driedorf, Westerwald, 28 July, 1875. Son of clergyman; at first a physician, and at same time stud. singing under Luise Resz and Baptist Hoffmann. Stadttheater, Breslau (1900–3), since which time has been one of most prominent singers of National Theatre, Munich; also sang at Bayreuth from 1902 onwards. Equally distinguished in opera and concert music. In 1922 first voyage to America. Repertoire embraces: Sarastro, Osmin, Barber of Bagdad, Basilio, Ochs von Lerchenau, Marke, Gurnemanz, Hagen, Hans Sachs, Dutchman, Wotan.—A. E.

BENDIX, Victor Emanuel. Danish compr. *b*. 17 May, 1851. Pupil of R. Cons. Copenhagen, and of Niels W. Gade. A follower of Neo-Romantic school; several works have attained a place in international repertoire. Pianist and teacher; condr. of Folkekoncerterne (Peoples' Concerts), Philh. Concerts (1897–1901) and Dansk Koncertforening (Danish Concert Soc.) 1907–10.
4 symphonies; concerto, pf. and orch.; pf. trio; series of songs and romances of great individuality. —A. H.

BENDL, Karel. Czechoslovak compr. *b*. Prague, 16 April, 1838; *d*. there, 16 Sept. 1897. Pupil of Organ School, Prague (under Blažek and Zvonař); 1864, condr. of theatres in Brussels and Amsterdam; 1865–77, condr. of the choir *Hlahol*, Prague; 1879–81, condr. of private orch. of Baron Dervies in Nice, then in Milan. From 1881, again in Prague, devoting himself entirely to compn. His activity with amateur orchs. and choirs left its traces in his inclination to choruses, duets, songs with orch. His style is eclectic — older German romanticism, Italian suavity, influence of Smetana, Czech folksong, etc. In his operas, we even have verism. To-day his works are nearly forgotten, despite their good qualities — sincerity, tunefulness, cheerfulness.
Štědrý den (*Xmas Eve*), 1885 (chorus, soli, orch.); *Jihoslovanská rapsodie* (*Jugoslav Rhapsody*) 1881, orch.; str. 4tet; 2 masses; church compns.; *Ciganské melodie* (*Gipsy Songs*); 2 vols., Novello); *Cypřiše* (*Cypresses*); *Písně skřivánčí* (*Songs of the Nightingale*); *Písně z rukopisu Královdorského* (*Songs from Codex of Dvůr Králové*), v. and pf.; choruses. Operas: *Lejla*; *Břetislav*; *Starý ženich* (*The Old Bridegroom*), 1871; *Indická princezna* (*Indian Princess*); *Čarovný květ* (*A Magic Flower*); *Černohorci* (*Montenegrins*); *Švanda dudák* (1st in concert form; dram. form, 1891); *Karel Škréta* (1883); *Dítě Tábora* (*The Child of Tabor*), 1888; *Máti Míla* (*Mother Míla*); *Česká svatba* (*Czech Wedding-Day*), a ballet; publ. F. A. Urbánek; E. Starý, Prague; Novello, London.—V. ST.

BENGTSSON, Gustav Adolf Tiburtius. Swedish compr. *b*. Vadstena, 29 March, 1885. Stud. R. Cons. Stockholm, compn. under Johan Lindegren, and later, under Paul Juon and Hugo Riemann. Lives in Norrköping.
Symphonies: I, C mi. (1908); II, D mi. (1910); III, C mi. (1921); str. 4tet (1907); sonata, vn. and pf. (1905); pf. trio (1916); songs with pf.—P. V.

BENJAMIN, Arthur L. Australian pianist; *b*. Sydney, 18 Sept. 1893. Won open scholarship, R.C.M. London, 1911. Stud. there under Charles Stanford and Frederic Cliffe (pf.). In 1920, prof. of pf. State Cons. Sydney.
Orch: 3 *Dance-Scherzi*; Rhapsody on negro folktunes; 2 songs (Masefield), barit. and orch.; clar. 5tet, C mi.; Rhapsody in D, vn., cello, pf.; sonata, E mi. for vn. and pf.; *Scherzo* in B mi. clar. and pf.; 4 *Impressions*, m.-sopr. v. and str. 4tet; suite of songs, for barit. and pf. (xviii century poems); *Pastoral Fantasia*, str. 4tet (Carnegie award, 1924); all ms.—E.-H.

BENNER, Paul. Swiss orgt. condr. compr. *b*. Neuchâtel, 7 Sept. 1877. Stud. at Cons. in Frankfort, pupil of Ivan Knorr and B. Scholz (compn.). Since 1901, orgt. and condr. of Société Chorale (Oratorio Concerts) at Neuchâtel.
For soli, chorus, orch. and organ: *Requiem* (Lausanne, Fœtisch); *Poèmes de la Mer* (*id.*); Le *Baptême du Bourdon*; *Liber apertus est*. Numerous unacc. choruses publ. by the *Commission du Chant sacré de l'Église indépendante* (Neuchâtel). Chambermusic; songs with orch. and with pf.—F. H.

BENNETT, George John. Eng. orgt. compr. *b*. Andover, 5 May, 1863. Stud. R.A.M. London under Macfarren and Steggall, at Berlin under Kiel and Barth, and at Munich under Rheinberger. Orgt. Lincoln Cath. since 1895. Condr. Lincoln Mus. Fest. 1896–9; 1902–6–10; condr. Lincoln Mus. Soc. from its foundation in 1896. Mus.Doc. Cantab. 1893.
Church music; orch. suite in D mi.; organ music; manuals on *Combined and Florid Counterpoint* and *Elements of Music for Choir-boys* (Novello). A large number of good organ arrs. of orch. and other works, especially Wagner (mostly Novello).—E.-H.

BENNEWITZ, Kurt. Ger. compr. *b.* Magdeburg, 2 Feb. 1886. Assistant at Inst. of Chemistry and Physics, Berlin; stud. music under Bischof, the orgt., and Kauffmann, mus. dir. Magdeburg.
Pf. sonata, F mi. (Magdeburg, Heinrichshofen); pf. trio in D; songs.—A. E.

BENOIT, Pierre Léonard Léopold. Belgian composer; *b.* Harlebeke (Flanders), 17 August, 1834; *d.* Antwerp, 8 March, 1901. Born of a peasant family with musical and literary tastes, Benoit first studied under his father and the village organist. At fifteen he composed music for the village prize distribution. From 1851 to 1855, he attended Brussels Conservatoire, becoming later conductor at the Flemish Theatre and composing melodramas. Having won the *Prix de Rome*, 1857, he made the stipulated journey to Germany. In 1861 he went to Paris, where his opera *Erl King* was accepted but not played. Whilst there, he held the post of 2nd conductor at Offenbach's Bouffes-Parisiens. He settled in Antwerp in 1863 and there realised his ideal — the creation of a national Flemish art. During his travels in Germany, he published a work on the future of Flemish music. From 1867 to 1884 his Flemish pamphlets (many translated) appeared, asserting the objective existence of Flemish musical art. Thanks to his efforts, Antwerp became an important musical centre. He established a society for concert organisation and an association of musical artists. In 1867, he founded the Flemish School of Music (Vlaamsche Muziekschool) and induced the Government to take it over as the Royal Flemish Conservatoire in Antwerp, 1898.

He organised a Gounod Festival and was first to produce Berlioz's *Damnation de Faust* in Belgium. Benoit was a member of the Academy. An important society in Antwerp, the Benoit Fonds, propagates his works.

As composer he is deservedly reckoned as the Tyrtæus of the Flemish movement (which he, however, only considered as within the Belgian nationality). He dreamt of expressing his race under a concrete musical form; for although there had been Flemish composers, there had not been a Flemish musical art. He undertook to create one, and was completely successful. His own work is deeply imbued with Flemish genius. His songs become merged in the Netherland folk-songs. His historical significance, however, must be sought in his oratorios: *La Guerre, Lucifer, L'Escaut*, the *Rubens Cantata*, which, like real musical frescoes with broad lines, massive effects and decorative procedure, call to mind the great Flemish painters. His writing is simple, summary even; the style quite classic; the melody sometimes commonplace; but some of his inspirations are full of beauty and occasionally call to mind Beethoven, with whom, through the Bonn master's Flemish ancestry, he has points of resemblance. One of his distinctive characteristics is the felicitous use of children's choirs, which no one else had done with such striking effect. It is not sufficient to say that he was talented; he must be considered as one who just missed being a genius.
Stage pieces: *Het Dorp in 't gebergte* (1856); *Isa*, drama with lyrics (1864); *Willem de Zwijger, id.* (1876); *Juicht met ons*, cantata with popular scenes (1886); *Het Meilief*, pastoral play with songs (1893). Melodramas: *De belgische Natie* (1855); *Charlotte Corday* (1875); *Karel van Gelderland* (1891); *Pompeia* (1894); *Van Blek in 't jaar '30* (1897). Works for soli, chorus and orch.: *Le Meurtre d'Abel* (*Prix de Rome*); *Vlaanderen Kunstroem* (Rubens cantata); *Lucifer* (1866); *Paris* (1883); *Londres* (1883); *De Schelde*; *De Rhyn*; *De Oorlog*; *Feestzang*; *De Wereld in* (children's cantata); *Triomfmarsch*; *De Leie*; *Kinderhulde aan den dichter*; *Antwerpen*; *De Muze der Geschiedenis.* Sacred: a tetralogy comprising *Cantate de Noël, Messe, Te Deum, Requiem*; *Drama Christi* (sacred drama); *Messe brève*; 20 motets; *Ave Maria.* Tales and ballads, pf. and orch.; pf. concerto; fl. concerto; pieces for ob., clar., etc.; many songs, especially cycles *Dichterheil, Liefde uit Leven*; *Liefdedrama*; Tales and Ballads, pf. Consult: Eeckhoud, *P. B.*, 1897; Stoffels, *P. B.*, 1901; Gittens, *P. B.* (in *Nouvelle Revue Internationale*, 1901–2). Sabbe, *In Memoriam P. B.*, 1902; Blockx, *P. B.*, 1904; *P. B.'s Jaarboek* (Benoit Soc.), 1905, 1906, 1907.—E. C.

BEÑOS, Avelino. Uruguay cellist; *b.* Montevideo, 1887. Stud. at Cons. La Lira, Montevideo; completed his training at Brussels under César Thomson. On return to Montevideo, joined Vicente Pablo in founding the Cons. Uruguay. Many concerts; admirable technique.—A. M.

BENVENUTI, Giacomo. Ital. historian and compr. *b.* Toscolano (Brescia). Stud. at Liceo Mus. at Bologna under Bossi. Is author of some appreciated vocal compns. (Ricordi; Pizzi ed.), and some important reprints of old Ital. music.—D. A.

BEOBIDE, José María. Contemporary Span. orgt. of Basque group; *b.* at Zumaya. Stud. at Real Cons. de Música, Madrid. Former orgt. in Jesuit College, Quito (Ecuador); and prof. at Quito Cons. Lives at Zumaya.—P. G. M.

BERBER, Felix. Ger. violinist; *b.* Jena, 11 March, 1871. Pupil at Cons. Dresden and Leipzig; played in London, 1899; Konzertmeister in Magdeburg, 1891–6; Chemnitz, 1896–8; Gewandhaus Orch., Leipzig, 1898–1902; teacher in Acad. of Music, Munich, 1904, and in Hoch's Cons. Frankfort-o-M., 1905; Geneva Cons., 1908; returned to Munich 1912, where he has been prof. in Acad. of Music since 1920. Leader str. quartet (Berber, A. Huber, V. Härtl and Johannes Hegar).—A. E.

BERENS, Hermann. Ger. compr. *b.* Hamburg, 7 April, 1826; *d.* Stockholm, 9 May, 1880. Son of military bandsman, Karl Berens (1801–57), whose pupil he was; afterwards of Reissiger in Dresden. Accompanist to Alboni, in Stockholm, 1847; mus. dir. in Örebro, 1849; condr. of orch. Stockholm, 1860; cond. of Court Oper., teacher of compn. and prof. at Acad. Stockholm.
Operas and operettas; pf. and chamber-music. His *New Course of Agility* (pf. studies, op. 61) is well known.—A. E.

BERG, Alban. Austrian compr. *b.* Vienna, 7 Feb. 1885. Since 1910, teacher of theory and compn. From 1918, he was active in the Verein für Musikalische Privataufführungen (Association for Private Performances of Music), founded by

Arnold Schönberg. Arr. piano-score of Schönberg's *Gurrelieder* and Schreker's opera *Der ferne Klang*, as well as Mahler's 8th symphony for four hands. Author of Guide to the *Gurrelieder*, and a thematic analysis of Schönberg's *Kammersymphonie*. (All Univ. Ed. Vienna.) His own compns. are publ. by Schlesinger & Lienau (Berlin and Vienna): pf. sonata, op. 1 (1908); 4 songs for v. and pf. op. 2 (1919); str. 4tet, op. 3 (1909–10); 4 pieces for clar. op. 5 (1913). These works are of equal importance, in the history of modern music in Vienna, with those of Webern. Not yet publ.: 5 songs with orch. (words by Peter Altenberg), op. 4 (1912), and 3 orch. pieces (*Prelude, Dance, March*), op. 6 (1914). His opera *Wozzek* (finished 1922), publ. in piano-score, seems destined to open new paths in dramatic music. Each of the 15 scenes follows a special mus. form. Scene 1 is a suite; Scene 4, 21 variations on a theme; Act II a symphony in five movements; Act III a sequence of 6 inventions. Consult art. by E. Stein (*Chesterian*, No. 26).—P. St.

BERG, Maria. Argentine pianist; *b.* London, 1888. Stud. in England and under Bosch at Madrid Cons. Gave concerts in London and Madrid; went to Buenos Ayres in 1904, where she establ. the Cons. Beethoven in Quilmes.—A. M.

BERG, Natanael. Swedish compr. *b.* Stockholm, 9 Feb. 1879; stud. singing at R. Cons. there, 1897–1900; and compn. in Germany, France and Austria. President of Soc. of Swedish Comprs. from its foundation in 1918. One of the most eminent of younger Swedish composers.

Operas: *Leila* (1908–10; Stockholm, 1910); *Josua* (only partly written). Pantomime-ballets: *Älfvorna* (*Fairies*), Stockholm (1914); *Sensitiva* (1919); *Hertiginnans friare* (*The Duchess's Wooers*), 1920. Symph. poems, orch.: *Traumgewalten* (1911); *Alles endet was entstehet* (1913); *Varde ljus!* (*Fiat lux!*) 1914; *Årstiderma* (*The Seasons*) 1916; *Makter* (*Powers*) 1917; *Pezzo sinfonico* (1918); *Trilogia della passione* (1922). *Ballades*, v. and orch.: *Saul and David* (1907); *Eros' vrede* (*The Wrath of Eros*), 1907; *Predikaren* (*The Preacher*), 1911; *Die badenden Kinder* (1918). Chorus, soli, orch.: *Mannen och kvinnan* (*The Man and the Woman*), 1911; *Israels lovsång* (1915). Vn. concerto (1918); pf. 5tet (1917; Musikaliska Konst-föreningen); str. 4tet (1919).—P. V.

BERG-HANSEN, Johannes. Norwegian barit. concert-singer; *b.* Christiania, 5 March, 1882. Pupil of Schinckel in Munich, and of Lulle Haanshus in Christiania. *Début*, Christiania, 1904. Outside Scandinavian countries, has sung in Antwerp, Paris and London.—U. M.

BERGER, Francesco. Pianist, compr. *b.* of Ital. parents, London, 10 June, 1834. Stud. compn. at Trieste (under Luigi Ricci), pf. under Karl Lichl; later, Leipzig (pf. Moscheles and Plaidy; harmony, Moritz Hauptmann). For 27 years hon. sec. R. Philh. Soc. London. Pf. prof. at R.A.M. and Guildhall School of Music. His part-song *Night, Lovely Night* had a great vogue.

Overture and incidental music to *The Lighthouse*, and to *The Frozen Deep* (2 plays acted by Charles Dickens and his circle in 1856–7); over 100 pf. pieces (Novello; Augener); Chappell; Boosey; Enoch; Ashdown, etc.); nearly 100 songs, duets, trios, part-songs, to Eng. Ger. Fr. or Ital. texts. Author of *Reminiscences, Impressions and Anecdotes* (Sampson Low), and a *Musical Vocabulary in 4 Languages* (1922, W. Reeves).—E.-H.

BERGER, Wilhelm. Compr. *b.* Boston, U.S.A., 9 Aug. 1861; *d.* Jena, 16 Jan. 1911. Of Ger. descent; brought up in Bremen; pupil of Kiel and Rudorff at R. High School, Berlin, 1878–84; teacher at Klindworth-Scharwenka Cons. from 1888. Court Orch. condr. Meiningen, 1903; prof. and member of Prussian Acad. of Arts, 1903.

2 symphonies, in B flat, op. 71 (Breitkopf) and in B mi. op. 80 (Bote & Bock); Variations and fugue for orch. op. 97 (Leuckart); pf. works, including a sonata in B, op. 76 (O. Forberg); 3 vn. sonatas, op. 7, A ma. (Praeger), op. 29, F ma. (Peters), op. 70, G mi. (Simon); pf. trio, G mi. op. 94, with clar. and cello (Kahnt); pf. 4tet, op. 21 (Praeger); pf. 5tet, F mi. op. 95 (Kahnt); str. 5tet, E mi. op. 75 (Bote & Bock); choral works with orch.; choruses; some favourite songs. Consult list of his publ. works by W. Altmann (1920).—A. E.

BERGH, Rudolph. Danish compr. *b.* 22 Sept. 1859. Prof. of embryology at Univ. of Copenhagen, 1890; retired in 1903, to devote himself to music; settled at Godesberg-on-Rhine; has lately resided in Copenhagen.

3 choral works with orch. (*Requiem für Werther*; *Geister der Windstille*; *Der Berg des heiligen Feuers*); *Tragic -Symphony*; 3 orch. pieces; str. 4tet; 2 vn. sonatas; numerous songs and pf. pieces.—A. H.

BERGMANS, Paul Jean Étienne Charles Marie, Belgian writer on music; *b.* Gand (Ghent). 23 Feb. 1868. Stud. at Ghent Cons. and privately under Waelput. Doctor of philosophy and literature, Ghent Univ. 1887; assistant-librarian there, 1892; chief librarian, 1919; lecturer in music to Faculty of philosophy and literature, 1912; professor-extraordinary in same, 1919; member R. Belgian Acad. of Archæology, 1900; member of R. Acad. of Belgium, 1913. Dramatic and music critic of the *Flandre Libérale* (Ghent). Contributor to various reviews (*Guide Musical*, since 1884; *S.I.M.*; *Sammelb.` d. I.M.G.*, etc.). Author of numerous monographs, small in dimensions, but extremely rich in documentation and irreproachable in scientific exactitude. Amongst others:

P. J. Leblan, carillonneur de la Ville de Gand au XVIIIe siècle (Ghent, 1884, Van der Haeghen); *H. Waelput* (Ghent, 1886, Van der Haeghen), *Variétés musicologiques* (1st series, Ghent, 1891, Vijt; 2nd series, 1901, id.; 3rd series, Antwerp, 1920, Sécelle); *La Vie musicale gantoise au XVIIIe siècle* (music; Ghent, 1897, Beyer); *L'Organiste des archiducs Albert et Isabelle : Peter Philips* (Ghent, 1903, Vijt); *Les Musiciens de Courtrai et du Courtraisis* (Ghent, 1912, Vijt); *Notice sur Fl. Van Duyse* (Brussels, 1919, Hayez); *Henry Vieuxtemps* (Turnhout, 1920, Brepols); *Le Baron Limnander de Nieuwenhove* (Brussels, 1920, Hayez); *Quatorze lettres inédites du compositeur Philippe de Monte* (Brussels, 1921, Hayez); *Tielman Susato* (Antwerp, 1923), etc.—C. V. B.

BERINGER, Oscar. Pianist, teacher; *b.* Furtwangen, Baden, 14 July, 1844; *d.* London, Feb. 1922. Pupil of Ignaz Moscheles at Leipzig and of Carl Tausig, Berlin; from 1871 in London, where he had an acad. for advanced pf. playing; in 1885, prof. of pf. at R.C.M. London; in 1900, hon. member of same. Well-known pf. teacher and examiner in London.

Educational works for pf. (Bosworth; Augener); pf. concerto; songs. Wrote *Fifty Years' Experience of Pf. Teaching and Playing* (London, 1907, Bosworth).—A. E.

BERLIOZ, Louis Hector. French composer; *b.* Côte-Saint-André, near Grenoble (Isère), 11

Dec. 1803; *d.* Paris, 8 March, 1869. Although Berlioz died in 1869, and consequently does not come strictly within the limits of the present work, it is impossible not to devote some space to this great musician whose influence is felt, even to-day in European music, on what is most vital amongst contemporary musicians. There is nothing more French than Berlioz and nothing less related to the past, unless by that taste for vast musical frescoes which traverses the ages from Jannequin to Lully and Debussy to Ravel, and seems to be the appanage of French genius. Berlioz appears as a sort of phenomenon. Instead of slowly gathering up the efforts of preceding generations (as was the case for the most part with the German geniuses, Bach, Beethoven, Wagner, Brahms) he seems to draw everything from himself, to construct precociously a huge edifice of which certain parts were never finished, others quickly fell in ruin, but of which the rest leaves for musicians a fruitful source for meditation and invention.

Berlioz is really the origin of all that revolutionary movement which has been carried on, in the search for new forms, by the French musicians during the last half-century. He broke up all the traditional forms and conventions which stifled music, and he opened the door to the future. He offers an absolute contrast to Wagner. Whilst the latter slowly took possession of his genius and followed its ascension methodically and surely, Berlioz perpetually hesitated to follow along his road. It does not behove us to trace this *vie douloureuse*, full of uncertainties. In 1830 (three years after Beethoven's death) this young man of 27 had already composed the 8 Scenes from *Faust*, the overture *Waverley* and the *Symphonie Fantastique*, in which, breaking through the *milieu* of the symphony character, he gives us the prototype of the "symphonic poem." Liszt (who made in 1830 at Paris a piano-transcription of the *Symphonie Fantastique*) only progressed by systematising Berlioz's idea. Berlioz knew not what to do with his inventions; he sowed to the winds, but nothing was lost; and Liszt, Richard Strauss, Rimsky - Korsakof, Lalo, Saint - Saëns, profited largely by Berlioz's suggestions.

Berlioz was, above all, a marvellous inventor of orchestral sonorities. He reviewed all his discoveries of orchestral technique in his famous *Traité* of 1839, which lives even to-day as an important work on the subject. Instead of treating the orchestra in the mass (as did Beethoven and even Wagner) Berlioz placed a value on the sonority of pure isolated tone-qualities proceeding by juxtaposition of touches, as Delacroix was endeavouring to do at that time in painting. Although an admirable theorist in his art, Berlioz often appears guided by a kind of intuition. His orchestral writing is moreover so far removed from the usual procedure, that one cannot imagine the effect produced in performance by merely reading it.

Saint-Saëns noticed this apropos of the *Course à l'abîme* in the *Damnation*.

In the domain of musical architecture, as in that of orchestral colour, Berlioz was a prodigious innovator. Not only is his *Symphonie Fantastique* the original of the symphonic poem, but his admirable *Roméo et Juliette* (1839) is the first model of a new type—the dramatic symphony—of which musicians are still far from realising the full consequences.

His faults, very visible (the results of his impetuous temperament and his impatience of discipline), have turned away from him numbers of musicians who nevertheless profited from his discoveries. His clumsinesses of writing (often as potentially expressive as those of Mussorgsky) were denounced by purists, as much as by the representatives of the Impressionist school, Debussy, and Ravel. However, Berlioz is the father of musical Impressionism, just as Eugène Delacroix is the point of departure for all modern pictorial evolution, and musicians will end one day by acknowledging this.

Berlioz had the soul of a great poet. His fiery, romantic periods of genuine creation attained an admirable balance and transposed into the language of tone the harmonies brought to light by Virgil. *Les Troyens* contains sublime pages; unfortunately the whole is badly proportioned. Self-taught artists only make fragmentary and incomplete studies, and Berlioz escaped from the discipline of symphonic classicism which had already established itself strongly in Germany, and so avoided the contagion of the Italian opera. Admirer of Beethoven, he did not seek to imitate him, but, fully grasping the lesson of the 9th Symphony, courageously carried forward mus. progress in an age when all efforts were expected to be merely along the lines indicated by Haydn, Mozart, and Beethoven.

Consult Alfred Ernst's *L'Œuvre dramatique d'H. B.* (1884); Adolphe Jullien's biography of H. B. (1888); Berlioz's Memoirs and Letters, edited by Bernard; W. H. Hadow's *Studies in Modern Music* (Seeley, London, 1894); T. S. Wotton,*The Scores of B.*(*Mus. Times*,Nov.1915); W.J.Turner,*H. B.*(*New Statesman*,14 Oct.1916); J. G. Prod'homme, *Unpublished Berlioziana* (*Mus. Quarterly*, April 1918).—H. P.

BERNEKER, Konstanz. Ger. compr. *b.* Darkehmen, 31 Oct. 1844; *d.* Königsberg, 9 June, 1906. Pupil at Acad. Inst. for Church Music, Berlin; choirmaster in Berlin; cath. orgt. in Königsberg; dir. of Acad. of Singing, 1872; lector at Univ., and teacher at Königsberg Cons. One of most important musicians of East Prussia. A Berneker Society was founded in Königsberg (1907) which publ. his works.

Cantatas and oratorios (*Victory Festival*, 1871; *Judith*, 1877; *Hero and Leander*; *Mila the Heathchild*).—A. E.

BERNERS, Lord (Gerald Tyrwhitt). Eng. compr. *b.* Apley Park, Bridgnorth, 18 Sept. 1883. Entered diplomatic service as hon. attaché, 1909; appointed to Constantinople, 1909–11; to Rome,

1911–19; chiefly self-taught in music; stud. orchestration (for a time) under Stravinsky and Casella. His style is sometimes subtly complex, at others, daringly outspoken. He has chosen unusual paths in music. He ranges from caustic cynicism to witty musical parody, from mock-lyricism to amazing caricature, from pleasant fooling to biting sarcasm. His *Valses bourgeoises* for pf. duet were played at the Salzburg International Fest. Aug. 1923.

Le Carrosse du Saint-Sacrement, opera (1923); Fantaisie Espagnole, orch.; 3 pieces (Chinoiserie, Valse Sentimentale, Kasatchok); Fragments Psychologiques (Hatred, Laughter, A Sigh), pf.; The Goldfish, pf.; 3 Funeral Marches (For a Statesman, a Canary, a Rich Aunt); Valses bourgeoises, pf. duet; Lieder album (Ger. words); 3 songs (Eng.); 3 chansons (Fr.); Dialogue between Tom Filuter and his Man, by Ned the Dog-Stealer (all publ. by Chester).—E.-H.

BERNTSEN, Jens. Norwegian barit. singer and choral condr. *b.* Aalesund, 22 Aug. 1867. Took organist's examination at Christiania Music Cons. in 1889; then stud. singing. Teachers: Wilhelm Kloed and Thv. Lammers (Christiania), Arlberg (Stockholm), Prof. Ney and George Armin (Berlin). *Début* as opera-singer, 1893, old Christiania Theatre (no longer existing); took part in perf. at National Theatre, Christiania. Chief rôles: Mephistopheles (*Faust*); Don Juan and Leporello (*Don Juan*); Kaspar (*Freischütz*); Lothario (*Mignon*), etc. Leader of several choirs in Christiania. Teacher of singing, and publicist working for popularisation of Armin's method.—R. M.

BERR, José. Ger. compr. *b.* Regensburg (Ratisbon), 29 Dec. 1874. Pupil of Rheinberger and Kellermann at Acad. of Music, Munich; teacher at Acad. of Music, Zurich, 1901; establ. a cons. of his own there in 1913.

Choral pieces for male vs.; song-cycle, 4 vs. and pf.; mimodrama, Francesca.—A. E.

BERTELIN, Albert. Fr. compr.; *b.* Paris, 26 July, 1872. Stud. at Paris Cons. under Th. Dubois and Ch. M. Widor; 2nd *Grand Prix de Rome*, 1902. B. is skilful in harmony and vigorous in cpt.; he submits to classical discipline whilst expressing himself in very modern musical language.

Songs; poems (v. and orch.); sonatas; a 5tet (1922); Sakountala, a Hindoo legend (prize, Paris Competition); Goïtza, lyrical drama, 3 acts (1912); preludes and interludes on Christmas carols, organ; 2 oratorios, Sub Umbra Crucis (1917), In Nativitate Domini (1922), which were perf. at Church of St.-Eustache.—F. R.

BERTRAM, Georg. Ger. pianist; *b.* Berlin, 27 April, 1882. Pupil of Ernst Jedlicka (pf.) Hans Pfitzner and Ph. Rüfer; teacher at Stern's Cons. Berlin, since 1903. Excellent concert artist.—A. E.

BERTRAM, Madge. Scottish compr. *b.* Edinburgh, 8 Nov. 1879. Youngest of a family of 9, all of whom were musicians. Her father, James B., was a well-known Edinburgh bandmaster and concert-agent, and he was himself the mus. descendant of a long line of mus. ancestors. She stud. harmony under Grieve of Edinburgh and pf. under Mme. Krüger (a pupil of Clara Schumann). Composition came naturally, and she possesses a rich gift of melody. Has publ. many songs and pf. pieces, and has had some of her work orchestrated for use in local theatres.—W. S.

BERUTTI, Arturo. Argentine compr. *b.* San Juan, in 1862. Stud. at Leipzig under Reinecke and Jadassohn. Then went to Paris and Milan to study operatic compn. Returned to Buenos Ayres in 1896, his works from this period showing influence of the legends and airs of his native land.

Vendetta (1892), 3 acts (libretto by Domingo Crisapulli), perf. at Vere·lii and Milan (publ. by Demarchi); Evangelina (1893), 3 acts (libretto by Costella), perf. in Milan and afterwards in Bologna, Naples, Florence and Buenos Ayres (publ. by Demarchi); Tarass Bulba (1895), 4 acts (libretto by Guillermo Godio), perf. in Turin and later in Buenos Ayres, Montevideo and Mexico (publ. Ricordi); Pampa (1897), libretto by Guido Borra, the 1st lyrical compn. of a national character; produced at Opera of Buenos Ayres with great success; Yupanki (1899), 3 acts, libretto by Enrique Rodríguez Larreta, founded on Inca legend; Khrysé (1902), 4 acts (own libretto), perf. at Politeama Theatre, Buenos Ayres; Horrida Nox (1905), in 2 acts. Also pf. and vn. and pf. pieces.—A. M.

BERUTTI, Pablo M. Argentine compr. *b.* San Juan, in 1887. Stud. at Leipzig under Jadassohn. Was dir. of Argentine National Military School of Music. Received from late Emperor of Austria an hon. Doctorate and Grand Cross of Francis Joseph. Now inspector of bands of national army and dir. of a Cons. which he establ. in Buenos Ayres.

Opera, Cochabamba, in 3 acts (publ. by Oretti, Buenos Ayres); Mass; Funeral March; pf. pieces. —A. M.

BERWALD, Astrid. Swedish pianist; *b.* Stockholm, 8 Sept. 1886. Stud. pf. under Richard Andersson and at High School for Music, Berlin (under E. Dohnányi and G. Bertram). Frequently appears at Konsertföreningen in Stockholm and in Gothenburg. Teaches at R. Andersson's pf. School, Stockholm.—P. V.

BERWALD, William Henry. Amer. compr. *b.* Schwerin, Germany, 26 Dec. 1864. Stud. under Rheinberger, 1883–7; in Stuttgart under Faisst, 1887–88. Went to Libau, Russia, in 1889 as condr. of Philh. Soc. In 1892, prof. of pf. and compn. at Univ. of Syracuse, N.Y. where he is still active. B. has been a prolific compr., particularly of anthems, many of them very effective. Also over 70 pf. pieces. A dramatic overture and an overture *Walthari* (both still ms.) have been repeatedly perf. by American orchestras.—O. K.

BESCH, Otto. Ger. compr. and writer on music; *b.* Neuhausen, near Königsberg, 14 Feb. 1885. At first, stud. theology; then music with O. Fiebach, Königsberg, and Ph. Rüfer and E. Humperdinck, Berlin.

Orch. works: overtures (E. T. A. Hoffmann, 1920); chamber-music: str. 4tet in one movement, Mitsommerlied (Midsummer Song); pf. trio; Suite aus Ostpreussen. Ed. a biography of E. Humperdinck (1914, Breitkopf). Lives in Königsberg as a compr. and critic to Hartungschen Zeitung.—A. M.

BESLY, Maurice. Eng. condr. compr. *b.* Normanby, Yorks, 28 Jan. 1888. Stud. pf. and compn. at Leipzig Cons. 1910–12; pupil of Teichmüller (pf.), Schreck and Krehl (compn.), Ernst Ansermet (cond.); orgt. at Eng. Ch., Leipzig, 1910–12; assistant music-master Tonbridge School 1912–14; served in H.M. forces, 1914–19. Orgt. to Queen's Coll. Oxford, 1919;

condr. Oxford Orch. 1920; London *début*
Queen's Hall, 1922, with R. Albert Hall Orch.
One of condrs. of Scottish Orch. 1924. Ed. the
Queen's College Hymn Book.
Overture and incidental music to *Merchant of
Venice*; *Mist in the Valley*, Impression for orch.
(ms. Chester); *Chelsea China*, orch. suite (Boosey);
Bach's trio in C mi. and 2 chorale preludes, tran-
scribed for orch. (ms. Chester); *A Tune with Dis-
guises*, vn. and pf. (Boosey); *Nocturne*, vn. and pf.
(id.); organ transcriptions from Stravinsky's *Fire-
Bird* (Chester); *Phædra*, scena, s. v. and orch.
(Boosey); *The Shepherds heard an Angel*, s. v.,
chorus and c.a. (Curwen); 4 Poems, v. and pf.
(Boosey); songs (Boosey; Curwen; Enoch); anthems, motets (Curwen; Stainer & Bell).—E.-H.

BESSE, Clément. Fr. musicologist; *b.* Paris in
1870. *d.* 1923. Pupil of Ch. Planchet. Canon;
founder of Chorale des Franciscaines, Saint-Ger-
main-en-Laye; and prof. at Institut Catholique.
Numerous articles on interpretation of Gregorian
Chant, works of musicology, as follows:
*The Crisis of Religious Ceremonies and of Sacred
Music* (1914); *German Music in France* (1916);
author of religious songs set to music by Albert
Alain, orgt. of the Chorale.—A. C.

BIAŁKIEWICZOWNA, Irena. Polish singer,
pianist and compr. of many pretty songs. Born
in 1890. Heard chiefly in Ital. opera houses.—
Zd. J.

BIANCO-LANZI, Maria. Ital. pianist; *b.*
Turin, 3 Oct. 1891. Stud. at Bologna, Rome
(under Sgambati), Paris, and Berlin. Many
successful concerts both in Italy and abroad
(Paris, Berlin, Brazil, etc.).—D. A.

BIARENT, Adolphe. Belgian compr. *b.*
Frasnes-lez-Gosselies, 11 Oct. 1871; *d.* Mont-
sur-Marchiennes, 4 Feb. 1916. Stud. music in
Brussels and Ghent; *Prix de Rome*, 1901;
Teacher of harmony and cpt. at Acad. of Music,
Charleroi. In spite of brevity of his career,
Biarent left a considerable number of works
which occupy an honourable place in modern
Walloon school.
Orch.: *Conte d'Orient*, suite; *Trenmer*, a symph.
poem; *Légende de l'amour et de la mort*; *Rapsodie
wallonne*; *Poème héroïque*. Pf. 5tet; pf. and cello
sonata ; *Nocturne* for vs. pf. harmonium, harp,
horn; pieces for pf.; songs.—E. C.

BIE, Oscar. Ger. writer on music; *b.* Breslau,
9 Feb. 1864. Ph.D. in music; pupil of Philipp
Scharwenka ; lecturer on history of art at
Technical High School, Berlin; ed. of in-
fluential review, *Die Neue Rundschau* (S. Fischer,
publ.); reviewer to Berlin *Börsen Courier*. Is
a brilliant writer and a champion of Strauss,
Busoni, etc.
The Pf. and its Masters (Munich, 1898, Bruck-
mann; Eng. transl. by E. E. Kellett and E. W.
Naylor, J. M. Dent & Sons); *The Dance* (Berlin, 1906,
Bard, Marquardt & Co.); *The Opera* (Berlin, 1913, S.
Fischer), and smaller works.—A. E.

BIENSTOCK, Heinrich. Ger. compr. *b.* Mulhouse, Alsace, 13 July, 1894; *d.* Tübingen, 17
Dec. 1918. Pupil of Georg Haeser and Hans
Huber in Basle; then of conductors' class at R.
High School, Berlin; solo-repetitor in Carlsruhe.
Along with Rudi Stephan, he was one of the
greatest hopes of German musical life destroyed
by the war.
1-act opera, *Zuleima* (Carlsruhe, 1913); *Sandro
the Fool* (Stuttgart, 1916); the 4-act mimodrama
The Conquerors of Life (Drei Masken Verlag, not
yet produced).—A. E.

BIERNACKI, Michał Marjan. Polish compr.
and theorist; *b.* Lublin, 24 Nov. 1855. Pupil of
Roguski and Żeleński at Warsaw Cons. Dir. of
Mus. Soc. at Stanisławow (Galicia), 1880–97.
Prof. and dir. of Mus. Soc. Warsaw, 1902–5.
Among numerous compns. first place must be
given to symph. prologue, *The Vigil*; symph.
polonaise; symph. poem; 3 cantatas (one
received 1st prize at Brussels); 2 masses. His
songs, small instr. and choral pieces, like the
preceding, have the dignity of a conservative
style. Has publ. some works on theory and mus.
æsthetics.—Zd. J.

BIFONIA. New tonal effect, obtained by
dividing the octave into 2 perfectly equal parts,
expounded by Domenico Alaleona (*q.v.*) in his
I moderni Orizzonti della Tecnica Musicale (Turin,
1911, Bocca).—E.-H.

BILLI, Vincenzo. Ital. compr. *b.* Brisighella
(Romagna), 4 April, 1869. His pieces are of a
popular type. A pf. piece *Campane a sera* has
a tremendous success. Has also written several
successful operettas (*La camera oscura*, 3 acts)
(Ricordi, 1921).—D. A.

BINENBAUM, Janko. Compr. *b.* Adrianople,
28 Dec. 1880. Stud. theory at Munich Cons.
under Victor Gluth and Rheinberger. His first
works (songs, part-songs, 2 symphonies, and an
overture) were perf. in that city. His first str.
4tet was played at Paris in 1910; his 2nd in
1911; his pf. 5tet in 1912. The 2nd 4tet has
recently been perf. in New York, Boston and
Philadelphia. He has written a 3rd symphony,
a ballet *The Masque of the Red Death*, a *Poème
lyrique* for 8 str. instrs., a *Poème intime* for
pf. trio, songs, and pf. pieces.
His works have aroused great interest among
those who have heard them. He stands apart
from all classified tendencies of the present day,
and in some respects shows affinities with the
Ger. classics. His music is substantial, earnest,
often grim and terse in character, and altogether
original.—M. D. C.

BINYON, Bertram. Eng. t. singer; *b.* Capri,
1874. Educated Collegio Alfano, Naples; came
to England in 1892 to study architecture with
his uncle Brightwen B. at Ipswich; 1894,
entered Herkomer School of Painting at Bushey;
stud. under Prof. Herkomer for 2 years. Stud.
singing under Walter Austin at Guildhall School
of Music; and in 1897 under Bouhy in Paris for
3 winters; in 1900 sang with D'Oyly Carte's
Opera Co. on a special tour of *The Rose of Persia*.
1904, toured with Albani in England and Ireland; 1905, stud. under many masters, including
Jean de Reszke in Paris; sang (Don Ottavio) at
Mozart Fest. under Reynaldo Hahn; for 3
seasons at R. Opera, Covent Garden, in Grand
Opera season. Sang in Nigel Playfair's production of *As You Like It* in 1919 (Stratford-on-
Avon) and 1920 (Lyric, Hammersmith). Many
vocal recitals in London.—E.-H.

BIRBYNE. See LITHUANIAN MUSIC.

BIRD, Arthur. Amer. compr. *b.* Cambridge,
Mass., U.S.A., 23 July, 1856. Pupil of Haupt,

Loeschhorn and Rohde in Berlin,1875–7. Returning to America, was orgt. in Halifax, N.S. In 1881, again in Berlin studying compn. under Urban. In 1884–5, pupil of Liszt in Weimar. In 1886 during a visit to America he conducted at a Milwaukee music fest. Has resided since then chiefly in Berlin. B. has comp. much in all forms. During the past 20 years he has made a speciality of compn. for harmonium. A comic opera, *Daphne*, was perf. at a Bagby *musicale* at the Hotel Waldorf Astoria, New York, in 1897. One of his 2 decimettes for wind-instrs. (unpubl.) won Paderewski Prize, 1902.

Symphony, op. 8 (Hainauer, 1886); *Dritte Kleine Suite* for orch. op. 32 (A. P. Schmidt, 1892); *Eine Carneval - Scene* for orch. op. 5 (Hainauer, 1887); Gavotte for str. orch. op. 7 (C. F. Schmidt, 1899); pf. pieces (Hainauer, 1886–9); pf. pieces, 4 hands, op. 13, 16, 23 (*id.* 1886–7); organ pieces (Schirmer, 1903, 1905); harmonium pieces (Berlin, Köppen).—O. K.

BIRMINGHAM AND MIDLAND INSTITUTE SCHOOL OF MUSIC. Founded 1854, when collective singing-classes were instituted. These were dropped in 1861, but re-established in 1863, since when there has been continuous growth. In 1886 an hon. principal (Stockley) was appointed, resulting in appointment in 1900 of regular principal (Granville Bantock) who now holds office of dir. The Hon. Visitor is Sir Edward Elgar, O.M. At present this school provides tuition for over 1600 individual students; there are teachers in all branches of the art, with weekly classes for chamber and orch. music. Three open rehearsals are held every term; in addition to terminal concerts, an annual orch. concert is given in Town Hall. Examinations are held annually; diplomas of Associateship and Licentiateship are granted to successful candidates.—G. B.

BIRMINGHAM TRIENNIAL FESTIVAL. The original fests., initiated in 1768, played a considerable part in mus. life of city. In their time they acquired a valuable influence, and show a good record in the commissioning and production of new works, such as Mendelssohn's *Elijah*; Gounod's *Mors et Vita*; Dvořák's *Stabat Mater*; Elgar's *Gerontius*; Bantock's *Omar Khayyám*, etc. List of condrs. includes Crotch, Costa, Richter and Wood. Since the war, these triennial fests. have been discontinued, and a more important need is being met by the growing activities of the Midland Mus. Competition Fest. (*q.v.*).—G. B.

BIRNBAUM, Zdzisław. Polish violinist, condr. *b.* Warsaw, 1880; *d.* tragically in the neighbourhood of Berlin in 1921. Pupil of Eugène Ysaye. Worked many years at Paris with Claude Terrasse in his chamber-operettas; then Berlin and last 10 years (1991–21) Warsaw, as condr. of Philh. Orch.—ZD. J.

BISCHOFF, Hans. Ger. pf. teacher and ed. *b.* Berlin, 17 Feb. 1852; *d.* Niederschönhausen, 12 June, 1889. Pupil of Kullak and Würst; stud. philosophy and modern languages in Berlin; teacher at Kullak's Acad. in 1872; later at Stern's Cons. Is (with others) ed. of best

practical edition of Bach's pf. works (Steingräber).—A. E.

BISCHOFF, Hermann. Ger. compr. *b.* Duisburg-o-Rhine, 7 Jan. 1868; stud. at Leipzig Cons.; then in Munich, where he establ. a close friendship with young Richard Strauss. Is a landed proprietor at St. Georgen on the Ammersee, Upper Bavaria. As a compr. he is a talented but not prolific representative of the " Modern German " music.

2 symphonies, E ma. and D mi.; symph. poem *Pan*; *Gewittersegen* (solo and orch.; verses by Richard Dehmel); songs, partly in simple harmony; publ. *Das deutsche Lied* (1905, C. F. W. Siegel's Verlag).—A. E.

BISGAARD, Astri Udnæs. M.-sopr. operasinger; *b.* (of Norwegian parents) Bellingham, Wash., U.S.A., 22 Jan. 1891. Went to Norway in 1911. Stud. under Ellen Gulbranson and Mimi Hviid (Christiania), Valdis Zerener (Munich). *Début*-concert, Christiania, 1917. Was attached to Opéra-Comique, Christiania, as long as it existed (1918–21). Best rôles: Elizabeth (*Tannhäuser*); Tosca.—U. M.

BISPHAM, David Scull. Amer. opera and concert barit. *b.* Philadelphia, Pa., U.S.A., 5 Jan. 1857; *d.* New York, 2 Oct. 1921. A singer of unusually high intellectual attainments, and of high artistic ideals, who made his mark both on the operatic stage, where he exhibited marked talents as an actor in humorous as well as in serious parts, and on the concert platform. Of Quaker antecedents, his early training was very strict. Attended Haverford Coll. (Quaker inst.) and graduated A.B. 1876. In 1886, went to Milan and stud. under Vannuccini and Hall. 1887–90, stud. in London under Shakespeare and Randegger. Made his operatic *début* as Longueville in Messager's *Basoche*, at Covent Garden Opera House, London, 3 Nov. 1891. In 1892 sang Kurwenal at Drury Lane. Was particularly successful in Wagner's barit. rôles, notably Alberich and Beckmesser. Until 1909, divided his time between Covent Garden, London, and Metropolitan Opera, New York, numbering over 50 rôles. Created rôles of William the Conqueror in Cowen's *Harold*, Chillingsworth in Damrosch's *Scarlet Letter*, Benedick in Stanford's *Much Ado about Nothing*, Rudolph in Ethel Smyth's *Der Wald*. He was an excellent Mefistofele in Boito's opera, and Falstaff and Iago in Verdi's operas. First to sing Brahms's *Four Serious Songs* in England and America. After 1909, devoted himself to recital singing, and became an ardent advocate of singing all songs in English. 1916–17, he was associated with the Soc. of Amer. Singers in the revival of Mozart's *Bastien and Bastienne*, and *Der Schauspieldirektor* and other small operas in English. Also made a speciality of reciting to music, being particularly successful in Strauss's *Enoch Arden* and Schillings' *Hexenlied*. Wrote *A Quaker Singer's Recollections* (New York, 1920, Macmillan).—O. K.

BITTNER, Julius. Austrian compr. *b.* Vienna, 4 April, 1874. LL.D.; was a judge for a long time. Showed a ms. opera *Alarich* to Mahler, who sent him to Bruno Walter for training. His

Die rote Gred (1907) was very successful. Then followed *Der Musikant* (1910); *Der Bergsee* (*Peasants' War*), 1st perf. 1911 (new version, 1922); *Das höllisch Gold* (1st perf. 1916); *Die Kohlhaymerin* (1921); *Das Rosengärtlein* (1923). He wrote his own opera‑books; they are amongst the best in libretto literature. He also wrote dramas with incidental music: *Der liebe Augustin* (Raimund Prize); *Die unsterbliche Kanzlei*. Also a ballet, *Pantomime des Todes*. He ed. (with D. J. Bach) the *Merker* for 1918–22. Has an excellent, witty and enthusiastic pen. His music is both popular and original in the best sense. He is the greatest hope for the Ger. popular opera of our time.

Consult biography by R. Specht (Munich, 1922, Drei Masken Verlag).—P. St.

BIZZOZERO, Julieta. Uruguay pianist; *b.* Montevideo. Stud. at Cons. La Lira there. After a series of very successful concerts, she founded Cons. Chopin at Montevideo in 1916. A pianist of great artistic ability. In 1920, founded the Wagnerian Association which has received good support from music-lovers of Uruguay.—A. M.

BLACK, Andrew. Scottish barit. *b.* Glasgow, 15 Jan. 1859; *d.* Australia, Nov. 1920. Stud. under Randegger and in Milan; sang Crystal Palace concerts 1887; Leeds Fest. 1892; and later at many other fests.; sang Judas in 1st perf. *The Apostles* (Birmingham, 1903); toured Australia and settled there about 1913.—E.-H.

BLÁHA-MIKEŠ, Záboj. Czechoslovak compr. *b.* Prague, 1887. Pupil of V. Novák, A. Mikeš and F. Spilka. Chiefly vocal works.

Song-cycles: *Notturna*; *Hovory se smrtí* (*Dialogue with Death*); *Milostné písně* (*Love Songs*); *Veselá láska* (*Gay Love*); *Píseň Šalomonova* (*Song of Solomon*), female chorus and orch.); 3 melodramas in Tagore, acc. by chamber-ensemble; *Nocturnes* and *Visions* for pf.—V. St.

BLANCH, Pedro. Span. condr. Lives and works in Lisbon, where he teaches at the Cons. —P. G. M.

BLANCHET, Émile R. Swiss pianist, compr. *b.* Lausanne, 17 July, 1877. Son of well-known orgt. Charles B. of Lausanne; stud. pf. at Cons. Cologne, and under Busoni at Weimar. Settled at Lausanne, but lives during winter season in Paris. One of the most eminent Swiss pianists of day, possessing a masterly technique; also a compr. of great originality. His pieces (mostly for pf.), recall Chopin, as well as the modern Fr. school (Debussy). They have a very complex harmony and an extraordinarily rich colour.

Concert-piece, pf. and orch.; *préludes*; polonaises; *études*; variations; *Scherzo* and other pf. pieces (Ricordi).—F. H.

BLANCO, Pedro. Span. compr. Stud. at R. Cons. de Música, Madrid; establ. himself at Oporto (Portugal), where he died in 1920.

Orch., *Añoranzas*; pf. suites: *Hispania*; *Galanías* (*Imágenes de España*); *Heures romantiques* (*Impressions intimes*); *Dos mazurkas del amor y del dolor*; songs with Span. and Portuguese words; vn. and pf. pieces (publ. E. da Fonseca, Oporto).—P. G. M.

BLANCO RECIO, José Ramón. Span. compr. *b.* Burgos, 13 Sept. 1886. Though he practised music from his early youth, he did not adopt it as a profession until 1919, when he revealed himself practically as a self-taught compr. with

his symph. poem, *Égloga*, founded on a Basque subject (perf. by Orquesta Benedito, Madrid, 20 April; 2nd perf. by Orquesta Filarmónica, Madrid, under Pérez Casas, 5 March, 1920). On 11 Dec. 1921, the Orquesta Lassalle played for first time his 2nd symph. work, *Cinco Miniaturas*, and repeated it 1 Feb. 1922. He lives in Madrid, and has also written:

Faunalia, choreographic poem, full orch.: *Oración y Marcha fúnebres*, str. orch. and tpl.; *Fantasía apasionada*, pf. and cello; sets of Span. songs and children's songs; pf. pieces. (Publ.: Unión Musical Española, Madrid; Leduc, Paris).—P. G. M.

BLARAMBERG, Paul, Ivanovitch (*accent 1st syll.*). Russ. compr *b.* Orenburg, 14/26 Sept. 1841; *d.* Nice, 15/28 Feb. 1907. Received lessons from Balakiref, but chiefly self-taught; 1883–98, prof. of theory at Philh. Soc. School at Moscow. Several operas; orch. and choral music; many songs, most of which are in a facile vein.—M. D. C.

BLAUWAERT, Émile. Baritone singer; *b.* St. Nicholas (East Flanders) 13 June, 1845; *d.* 2 Feb. 1891. Stud. at Brussels Cons.; 1st prize for vn., one for trombone and one for singing. Joined orch. of Théâtre Flamand, Brussels, as 2nd vn.; soon devoted himself entirely to singing, which was always characterised by the purest taste and reverent deference to spirit of masters. He had an extraordinary compass; was principal interpreter of Benoit's great oratorios (*Lucifer*, 1868; *De Schelde*, 1869; *De Oorlog* [*War*], 1880; *De Pacificatie van Gent*). Taught singing at Bruges, Antwerp, and Mons Acad. From 1880 toured Holland, France, Germany, Austria, Russia and England, finally going to opera stage, distinguishing himself in Wagnerian opera, especially part of Telramund in the solitary perf. of *Lohengrin*, Paris, 1887, and part of Gurnemanz at Bayreuth.—C. V. B.

BLAŽEK, František. Czechoslovak theorist; *b.* Velešice, 1815; *d.* 23 Jan. 1900. Taught at Organ School, Prague (until 1895), where Bendl and Dvořák were his pupils. Wrote *Manual of Harmony*; *Figured Bass Exercises*, etc.—V. St.

BLECH, Leo. Ger. compr. *b.* Aix-la-Chapelle, 21 April, 1871; was at first in business; stud. music for a year in Berlin under Bargiel and Rudorff; in the winter months (1892–8) was engaged as condr. at Stadttheater, Aix-la-Chapelle (early operas: *Aglaja*, 1893, and *Cherubina*, 1894); continued his studies under Engelbert Humperdinck for 4 years during summer months. Called to Prague (1899) as first condr. to Deutsches Landestheater, and in 1906 to Berlin as condr. at the R. Opera House, where he has been gen. mus. dir. since 1913; first condr. Charlottenburg Opera, Berlin, since 1923.

Songs (op. 19, 21, 24); pf. pieces; symph. poems: *Die Nonne*; *Trost in der Natur*; *Waldwanderung*; choruses with orch.: *Von den Englein* (chorus for female vs.), *Sommernacht*. A 1-act comic opera, *Das war ich* (Dresden, 1902, words by R. Batka); *Cinderella* (*Aschenbrödel*), Prague, 1905, 3 acts; and *Versiegelt* (Hamburg, 1908, 1 act); also a new setting of Raimund's *Alpenkönig und Menschenfeind*, text recast by Batka, as a 3-act opera (Dresden, 1903); and the operetta *Die Strohwitwe* (*The Grass Widow*), Hamburg, 1920.—Λ. E.

BLEYLE, Karl. Ger. compr. *b.* Feldkirch (Vorarlberg), 7 May, 1880. 1894, private pupil of Hugo Wehrle and Samuel de Lange in Stuttgart; at Cons. there, 1897–99 (E. Singer, de Lange); then stud. three more years (1904–7) under Thuille in Munich, where he settled; at present living at Canstatt, near Stuttgart.

An den Mistral, op. 21 (for male vs. and orch., Nietzsche); male choruses, *a cappella,* op. 4 and 7 (Nietzsche); symphony in 1 movement, F ma. op. 6; *Learn to laugh,* op. 8 (for contr., barit., mixed chorus and orch., text from *Also sprach Zarathustra* put together by compr.); *Flagellantenzug,* op. 9 for orch. (Munich, 1908); vn. concerto, C ma. op. 10; *Mignon's Funeral,* op. 11 (mixed chorus, boys' vs., full orch.); *Musikalische Bausteine,* op. 12 (10 pf. pieces); *Heilige Sendung,* op. 13 (t. and barit. soli, mixed chorus, boys' vs. and orch., text by Fr. Lienhard); *A Bouquet of Flowers,* op. 14 (10 songs by Christian Wagner); *Gnomentanz,* op. 16 (full orch.); *Die Höllenfahrt Christi,* op. 17 (after Goethe: barit., male vs. and orch.); *Thousand and One Nights* (10 pf. pieces), op. 18; *Chorus Mysticus* (from *Faust*), op. 19 (mixed chorus, harmonium and pf.); *Ein Harfenklang,* op. 20 (contr. solo, male chorus, orch., 1911); *Victory Overture,* op. 21 (1913 Centenary Fest. of Battle of Leipzig); 4 duets, op. 22 (m.-sopr. and barit.); overture to Goethe's *Reineke Fuchs,* op. 23; *Lustiges A B C,* op. 24 (pf. variations); *Prometheus,* op. 25 (male chorus and orch., 1912); comic opera, *Hannesle and Sannele* (Stuttgart, 1923).—A. E.

BLIN, René. Fr. compr., orgt. *b.* Somfois (Marne), 13 Nov. 1884. Pupil of *Schola Cantorum;* orgt. St. Elizabeth Ch. Paris. Music with classical tendency.

En Champagne (suite for pf.; orch. in 1919); *Symphonie brève;* symphony in B flat; *Suite héroïque* (organ); many other organ pieces; songs.—A. C.

BLINDER, Naum Samoilovitch (*accent 1st syll.*). Russ. violinist; *b.* Eupatoria, Crimea, 6 June (o.s.), 1889. Pupil of Brodsky, 1910; now vn. prof. Moscow Cons.—V. B.

BLISS, Arthur. Eng. compr. *b.* Barnes, London, 2 Aug. 1891. Educated Pembroke Coll. Cambridge; stud. music at Cambridge under Dr. Charles Wood and at R.C.M. London under Sir Charles Stanford and Dr. Vaughan Williams; served in war, 1914–18; prof. R.C.M. 1921–2. B. was one of the most prominent comprs. in London from 1920–3, when he went to live in America. His *Rout* was perf. at Salzburg 1922 Fest. and establ. his reputation on the Continent; his *Rhapsody* was equally successful there in 1923. His so-called *Colour Symphony* was produced at Gloucester Three Choirs Fest. 1922, and later at Queen's Hall, London, under Sir Henry Wood, 10 March, 1923. Opinions differ about the relative value of the orch. and the chamber works, though all contain passages of undeniable interest. His style is decidedly modern, and owes much to the Fr. group known as *Les Six,* espec. to Honegger; his music shows a cheerful, humorous and occasionally ironic cast of mind. He played a part of some importance in extending the boundaries of Eng. music at a critical period.

Madam Noy, song for s. v. and 6 instrs. (fl. clar. bsn. vla. d.-b. harp), Chester; *Rhapsody,* s. and t. vs. fl. c.a. str. 4tet, d.-b. (Carnegie award), Stainer & Bell; *Rout,* s. v. and chamber-orch. (Goodwin & Tabb); 2 *Nursery Rhymes,* s. v. clar. and pf. (Chester); *Conversations,* vn. vla. cello, fl. (+ bass fl.) ob. (+ c.a.) (Goodwin); *Mêlée Fantasque,* full orch. (*id.*); 3 *Romantic Songs,* v. and pf. (*id.*);

symphony (*Colour*). Consult a booklet on A. B. by Percy A. Scholes (F. & B. Goodwin).—E.-H.

BLOCH, Ernest. Composer; *b.* Geneva, Switzerland, 24 July, 1880. Son of a Jewish merchant in Geneva. Stud under Jaques-Dalcroze (*solfège*) and Louis Rey (vn.) between 1894 and 1897. From 1897–9, attended the Conservatoire at Brussels, studying violin under Ysaye and composition under F. Rasse. From 1897–9. was pupil in composition of Ivan Knorr at Hoch's Cons. Frankfort-o-M. After a short time under Thuille in Munich, went to Paris and returned to Geneva in 1904, becoming a bookkeeper in his mother's shop and devoting his spare hours to composing.

Through the interest of Mme. Bréval, his opera *Macbeth* (written at 23) was brought out at the Opéra-Comique, Paris, 30 Nov. 1910. It aroused much opposition and some interest. The composer was declared a revolutionary. In 1909–10 he conducted orchestral concerts at Neufchâtel and Lausanne, and in 1910 produced his 1st symphony in C sharp minor (written 1901–3), which was warmly acclaimed by Romain Rolland. From 1911 to 1915 he taught composition and æsthetics at the Geneva Conservatoire. In 1915 he went to America as conductor for the dancer, Maud Allan. In 1917 he settled in New York as teacher at the David Mannes School of Music. In 1920 he was called to Cleveland, Ohio, as the head of the newly organised Cleveland Institute of Music.

His earlier works included two symphonic poems, *Vivre et Aimer* (1900) and *Printemps-Hiver* (1905). Besides these he wrote several Psalms for solo voice with orchestra. According to the composer's own statement his creative work entered upon a new phase with his *Trois Poèmes Juifs* for orchestra (1913). They were first performed by the Boston Symphony Orchestra, 23 March, 1916. Then his works gradually gained a hearing in America. At a concert of his own compositions arranged by the Society of the Friends of Music in New York on 3 May, 1916, he brought out his second symphony, *Israel* (begun 1914), and *Schelomo: a Hebrew Rhapsody* for cello and orchestra. His string quartet was first performed by the Flonzaley Quartet in New York, Dec. 29, 1916. A Suite for viola and piano won the Coolidge Chamber-music Prize in 1919, and was first performed at Pittsfield, Mass., 27 Sept. 1919. An arrangement for viola and orchestra was produced by National Symphony Orchestra in New York, 5 Nov. 1920.

Among the many composers of modern tendencies Bloch maintains a striking individuality. Frankly avowing his purpose of producing Jewish music, he does not rely upon the use of actual Oriental or Hebrew themes, but seeks to express the character and the spirit of his race in all its Old Testament dignity and grandeur. A dark, sombre spirit pervades much of his music. It is highly polychromatic, ofttimes barbarous, refractory and even cacophonous, but it displays much temperament and tragic passion, with a fantastic logic all its own. As a teacher Bloch is

47

by no means a revolutionary, requiring of his pupils a careful study of the masters of XVI century polyphony.

Opera, *Macbeth* (vocal score, Enoch). *Printemps-Hiver*, symph. poem (1918); *Trois Poèmes Juifs*, for orch (1918); *Schelomo : Hebrew Rhapsody*, cello and orch. (1918); str. 4tet (1919); Suite, vla. and pf. (1920); *Poèmes d'Automne*, v. and pf.(1918); sonata, vn. pf. (1921); *Psalms CXIV, CXXXVII*, for s. and orch. (full score, 1921); *Psalm XXII* for barit. and orch. (*id.* 1921; both also in vocal score). (All publ. by Schirmer.) Consult art. by Guido Gatti, *E. B.* in *Musical Quarterly* (New York, Jan. 1921); also Rosenfeld, *Musical Portraits* (Kegan Paul).—O. K.

BLOCKX, Jean (commonly called Jan Blockx). Belgian composer; *b.* Antwerp, 25 Jan. 1851; *d.* there 26 May, 1912. Son of a simple upholsterer; had a very hard childhood; learnt music at school and in churches as chorister; lost his father at 13, and had to support his family by giving music lessons, and studying during the night. Later he entered the Antwerp School of Music, then directed by Benoit, whose pupil he became. Organised a concert of his works in Antwerp, 1876; obtained prizes at competitions for composition of popular songs and overtures. 1879, went to Leipzig, studying under Reinecke at the Conservatoire. Appointed professor at Antwerp School of Music, and director of the Cercle Artistique, 1886; in 1901 followed Benoit as director of Antwerp Conservatoire. Blockx had never received any official distinction, and never entered for *Prix de Rome*. He was a member of the Belgian Academy.

He is directly connected with the Antwerp School, founded by Benoit, which evolved from the so-called " national " schools, giving musical expression to the soul of the race and drawing their inspiration from folk-lore. Blockx's artistic mission was the transference to the stage of Benoit's popular style. Benoit was more epic, nobler; Blockx, more of a realist. Benoit suggests Jordaens; Blockx suggests Rubens. Up to present he is the most popular of Belgian lyrical composers. Nevertheless, his composition, like Benoit's, is summary, his harmony rudimentary, his polyphony hollow. These defects are counterbalanced by a very keen instinct for stage requirements, the incisive and vigorous stroke with which he accentuates a dramatic situation. He is incomparable in popular scenes of a collective nature (Kermesses, etc.), arranged for him with great skill by his chief librettist, the Flemish poet Nestor de Tière.

Stage-works: *Iets vergeten*, comic opera (Antwerp, 1876); *Milenka*, ballet (Brussels, 1888); *Maître Martin*, opera (Brussels, 1892); *Saint-Nicolas*, pantomime (Brussels, 1894); *Herbergprinses*, lyric drama (Antwerp, 1896; Fr. version, *Princesse d'auberge*, Brussels, 1898); *Thyl Uilenspiegel* (*Till Owlglass*), lyric drama (Brussels 1900; new version completely rewritten by compr., finished by P. Gilson after B.'s death, Brussels, 1920); *De Bruid der Zee*, lyric drama (Antwerp, 1901; Fr. version, *La Fiancée de la mer*, Brussels, 1902); *De Kapel*, lyric episode (Antwerp, 1903); *Baldie*, lyric drama (Antwerp, 1908, rewritten under title *Liefdelied*, Antwerp, 1912). Of these the most appreciated are *Herbergprinses* and *De Bruid der Zee*, which with *Baldie* form a trilogy: the Flemish town, coast, and countryside (poems by de Tière). Cantatas: *Klokke Roeland*; *Het Vaderland*; *Scheldezang*; *Feest in den Lande*; *Jubelgalm*; *Een droom van 't paradijs*; oratorio; church music; unacc. mixed choruses and solo pieces. Orch.: *Rubens*

Overture; *Concert Overture*; *Kermisdag*; symph. poem in 3 parts; Flemish Dances; symphony in D; *Symph. Triptych*; Suite in ancient style. Pf. 5tet; *Albumblad* and *Humoresque*, str. 4tet; trio; songs, among which *Ons Vaderland* has become popular. —E. C.

BLOM, Eric. Eng. writer on music; *b.* 20 Aug. 1888. Attached to Queen's Hall Orch. as writer of analytical programme notes.—E.-H.

BLUMENFELD, Felix Michaelovitch. Russ. compr. pianist, condr. *b.* in govt. of Kherson, S. Russia, 7/19 April, 1863. Pf. pupil of his father, F. Stein, at Petrograd Cons. (1881–5); pupil of Rimsky-Korsakof (compn.). Made prof. at Petrograd Cons. 1885; 1895–8, chorus-master Maryinsky Opera House; 1898, condr. there; pf. prof. Petrograd Cons. till 1918, appearing as condr. of several concerts of Russ. Music Soc. and of Russ. Symphony Concerts (founded by M. P. Belaief); a fine pf. soloist, accompanist, and chamber-music player.

Symphony in C mi. op. 39; *Allegro de Concert*, pf. and orch. op. 7; str. 4tet in F, op. 26; *Sonata-Fantaisie*, pf. op. 46; many fine pf. pieces; songs, etc. (mostly Belaief).—V. B.

BLUMER, Theodor. Ger. compr. *b.* Dresden, 24 March, 1882. Pupil of his father (R. chambermusician) and of R. Cons. (Draeseke) in Dresden; Korrepetitor 1906–10 ; then condr. Court Theatre, Altenburg; back in Dresden since 1911.

Opera *Der Fünfuhrtee* (*Five o'clock Tea*, Dresden, 1911); *Carnival Episode* for orch.; symph. poem, *Erlösung* ; pf. 5tet ; vn. sonata, D mi. op. 33; *Serenade und Thema con variazioni* for wind 5tet, op. 34; 6tet for wind instrs. and pf. op. 45; an orch. work, *The Legend of Thais the Dancer*; songs; pf. pieces.—A. E.

BOCCACCINI, Pietro. Ital. pianist; *b.* Comacchio, 6 Nov. 1843. Was at the school of Liszt in Rome; then stud. in Naples under Beniamino Cesi, of whose method he became the champion. Devoted himself specially to propaganda and teaching. Wrote a voluminous book on *The Art of Playing the Pianoforte* (publ. by *Musica*, Rome, 1913).—D. A.

BOEHE, Ernst. Ger. compr. and condr. *b.* Munich, 27 Dec. 1880. Pupil of Rudolf Louis and Ludwig Thuille in Munich. Condr. of People's Symphony Concerts in the Kaimsaal; Court condr. in Oldenburg, 1913–20; dir. of Palatinate Symphony Orch. in Ludwigshafen since 1920. As a premature compr. of the so-called "Munich School" his productive power has quickly abated.

The Voyages of Ulysses (4 symph. poems); *Taormina*, op. 9; *A Tragic Overture*; *Symphonic Epilogue to a Tragedy*, op. 11; *Comedy Overture* ; also some songs.—A. E.

BOËLLMANN, Léon. Fr. orgt., compr. *b.* Alsace, 29 Sept. 1862; *d.* Paris, 11 Oct. 1897. Died too young to give his full measure, but promised great things. Pupil of École Niedermeyer; quickly became famous for the purity of his playing and was appointed titular orgt. of St.-Vincent-de-Paul in Paris.

Symphonic Variations, cello and ̃orch.; Fantasia in form of dialogue, organ and orch. (often played at Queen's Hall, London); *Heures mystiques* (collections for organ); pf. 4tet; pf. trio; cello sonata; pf. pieces. Consult P. Locard, *Boëllmann* (1901).—A. C.

BOEZI, Ernesto. Ital. compr. and orgt. *b.* Rome, 11 Feb. 1856. After distinguished

career as orgt. and condr. was elected in 1905
Master of the Cappella Giulia at St. Peter's,
Rome. Technical dir. of Pontifical School
of Sacred Music, (instituted under Pius X)
from its foundation till 1918. Member of the
R. Acad. of Santa Cecilia, of R. Philh. Acad.
and of Pontifical Commission of Sacred Music.
One of his operas, in 1 act, *Don Paez*, was perf.
in Venice, 1893. A distinguished compr. of
sacred music, a cultured man (a graduate in
law), he is held in great esteem in mus. world
of Rome.—D. A.

BOGHEN, Felice. Ital. compr. *b.* Venice,
23 Jan. 1875. Resides in Florence, where he is
prof. of harmony at Cherubini R. Inst. of Music.
Amongst his works are an opera *Alcesti* (not
yet perf.); 6 fugues for pf. (Ricordi); 6 *Paesaggi
musicali*; *Prelude and Choral*; *Aubade* (Carisch
ed.); *Momento capriccioso* (Paris, Noël). He
has also publ., in a modern ed. brought out
by himself, some works of Frescobaldi, some
colls. of old Ital. fugues and toccatas (Ricordi)
and of compns. of Bernardo Pasquini (Rome,
Musica ed.).—D. A.

BÖHN, Gudbrand. Norwegian violinist; *b.*
Nes in Romerike, 10 Nov. 1839; *d.* Christiania,
9 Jan. 1906. Pupil of Nils Ursin, Ullensaker,
Fredrik Ursin, Christiania; Léonard, Brussels
(1859 and 1861); Lauterbach, Dresden (1864).
For a whole generation he was leader of orch.
at Christiania Theatre and in Musikforeningen
(Mus. Soc.), besides being 1st vn. in well-known
str. quartet (Kunstnerkvartten) which during
many years gave chamber-music evenings every
season.—U. M.

BOHNEN, Michael. German bass singer; *b.*
Cologne, 1888. In Düsseldorf, 1910; Wiesbaden,
1911; since then at Berlin State Opera House.
Has undertaken many tours. Excellent both
as singer and actor.—A. E.

BOHNKE, Emil. Compr. *b.* Zdunska Wola,
Poland, 11 Oct. 1888. Pupil of Sitt and Krehl
at Leipzig Cons., and of Fr. Gernsheim, Berlin.
Teacher at Stern's Cons.; vla. player in Bandler
Quartet, and (1919–20) in Adolf Busch Quartet.
Then establ. in Berlin as compr. and mus.
dir. of modern tendencies; condr. of Symphony
Orch. Leipzig since 1923; at same time teacher
of vla. at High School of Music, Berlin.
    Str. 4tet, C mi. op. 1; pf. trio, op. 5 ; pf.
sonata, B mi. op. 10; pf. pieces, op. 4, 6, 8 ;
Symph. Overture, op. 2; vn. concerto, D ma. op. 11;
Theme with variations, full orch. op. 9.—A. E.

BOITO, Arrigo. Ital. compr. and poet; *b.*
Padua, 24 Feb. 1842; *d.* Milan, 10 June, 1918.
An extraordinary type, musician, poet, and
artist in the highest and most complete sense
of the word. He has exercised a profound and
beneficial influence in Italian musical spheres
of the last 50 years, especially on young
musicians, by the fascination of his noble personality and by the example of his culture and
fine intellectuality. This influence has been
much greater than one can judge from the
limited extent of his work as a composer. He
was son of Cavaliere Silvestro B. and Countess

Giuseppina Radolinski (a Pole); when he was
very young he went to Milan, where he was
admitted to the Cons. He had Mazzuccato as
a master, who understood his worth, and Franco
Faccio as a companion, in collab. with whom he
wrote the cantata *Il Quattro Giugno* (*The Fourth
of June*) and a mystery *Le Sorelle d' Italia*
(*The Sisters of Italy*), perf. at the Cons. in 1860
and 1861 respectively. Having obtained a
bursary in consequence, he travelled in France
and Germany, and also in his mother country,
Poland. He came back to Italy full of the
new ideas on musical art then agitating those
countries, particularly the appearance of Wagner,
and he returned with an acute desire for conquest
and rebellion.

There were then in vogue in Milan *cenacoli*
(meetings) at which artists and poets gathered
round Emilio Praga; artists who, with Boito,
loved a strange and nervous poetry, abounding
in realistic crudeness and verbal iridescence,
with bizarre metres and rhymes, and play on
words. It was in this atmosphere that B. grew;
here were born his first verses, his first theatrical
works, of which some were done in collab.
with Praga himself. Here the *Mefistofele* ger-
minated. (A parenthesis in the artistic activity
of B. and his friends occurred in 1866, when
they enrolled with Garibaldi.) The first perf.
of *Mefistofele* at La Scala on 5 March, 1868, can
well be included amongst celebrated first performances. The opera was a very long one, and
commencing at 7.30, it lasted, it is said, until
2 in the morning. The public, unwarned, and
imbued with the very different tastes prevailing at that time, gave the opera a most hostile
reception. Seven years later, *Mefistofele*,
revised and abbreviated, had a triumphant
revenge at the Teatro Comunale, Bologna, 4 Oct.
1875. B. published no other musical works, if
we exclude an *Ode to Art* (to verses of Giacosa)
perf. Turin, 1880 (a composition of little importance), and a few small pieces for v. and pf.

Between the first *Mefistofele* and the second
he turned his attention to gathering together
his poems, which he publ. under title of *Il
Libro dei Versi*. Whereas in the mus. field he
would not publish anything besides *Mefistofele*, he did not hide his activity as a writer
of operatic libretti. The affectionate friendship
which bound him to Giuseppe Verdi, for whom
he wrote *Otello* and *Falstaff*, is well known.
Hero and Leander, which he had begun to set
to music himself, and of which some parts had
been transferred into *Mefistofele*, was handed
over by him to Bottesini and Mancinelli. He
then wrote—mostly under the anagrammatic
pseudonym of Tobia Gorrio—*Pierluigi Farnese*
for Costantino Palumbo, *La Falce* (*The Scythe*)
for Catalani, *La Gioconda* for Ponchielli, *Hamlet*
for Faccio, *Un Tramonto* for Gaetano Coronaro,
Iram for Cesare Dominiceti, *Semira* for Luigi
Sangermano, *L'Inno delle Nazioni* for Verdi, and
Basi e Bote (in Venetian dialect), set to music
after his death by Riccardo Pick-Mangiagalli
(*q.v.*) (not yet perf.). There remains to be

49

mentioned *Nerone* (*Nero*), which B. had in hand for nearly forty years, without ever making up his mind to complete it, so that it has become almost a legend. In 1901 he publ. the poem, but the music (although the perf. of the opera was announced many times as imminent) was even at his death left incomplete, for which reason it was not possible for the work to be produced until 1 May, 1924, when it was given at the Scala, Milan, under Toscanini. But, even in his obstinate silence as a composer, B. continued to take an active part in Ital. mus. life, by giving his advice, and by acting on committees, particularly on the Permanent Commission for the Art of Music for the Ministry of Education. During his last years he was nominated Senator of the Kingdom. His memory will remain in the minds of modern Ital. musicians as a very high example of nobility and spirituality.

Poetic works, besides libretti above-mentioned: *Il Libro dei Versi*, *Re Orso* (1877, Turin; there are more recent reprints in existence); *The First Mefistofele* (reprint of libretto, Naples, 1916, Perrella); *Nerone* (Milan, 1901, Treves); *Novelle e riviste drammatiche*, with preface and bibliographic appendix by Gioacchino Brognoligo (Naples, 1920, Ricciardi); the comic libretto in Venetian dialect, *Basi e Bote*, was publ. in Milanese review *La Lettura* (Nos. 1 and 2, 1914).

Mus. works: Of the first *Mefistofele*, Ricordi publ. only two detached pieces, the *Sabba Classico* (*Classical Walpurgis-Night*) and the *Battaglia*, an intermezzo between Acts IV and V. The second *Mefistofele* is Ricordi's publication. Some minor compns. are publ. by other firms.

Consult: Camille Bellaigue, *A. B.* (*Revue des Deux Mondes*, 15 Aug. 1918); D. Alaleona, *A. B.* (in *Rassegna Italiana*, Rome, 15 July, 1918); A. Pompeati, *A. B.*, *Poet and Musician* (Florence, 1919, Battistelli); Corrado Ricci, *A. B.* (Milan, 1919, Treves).—D. A.

BOLIA, David. Argentine violinist; *b.* Mercedes in 1867. In 1880, stud. under Pinto at Cons. at Naples. Diploma in 1882. Returning to Buenos Ayres, continued studies under Pedro Melani. In 1886 appointed 1st violinist at the Colón; later at the Opera. Now devotes himself entirely to teaching, having founded the Cons. Melani, which he personally directs.—A. M.

BÖLSCHE, Franz. Ger. compr. *b.* Wegenstedt, 20 Aug. 1869. Pupil of R. High School, Berlin; teacher of theory of music, Cologne Cons. 1896; prof. 1911; ed. of Melchior Franck's instrumental works in the *D.d.T.*; author of a widely circulated exercise-book for study of harmony (1911).

Symphony, op. 30; overtures; chamber-music; songs; choral works.—A. E.

BOLSTAD, Per. Norwegian violinist; *b.* 7 Jan. 1899. Pupil of Ingebret Haaland, Christiania, and (with State scholarship) of Marsick in Paris. *Début*, Christiania, 1918. Outside own country, he has appeared in Copenhagen and Helsingfors.—R. M.

BOLZONI, Giovanni. Ital. compr. *b.* Parma, 14 May, 1841; *d.* Turin, 21 Feb. 1919. After a successful career as violinist and condr. he took up in 1889 position of dir. of Liceo Mus. G. Verdi, Turin, which post he held until his death. He tried opera but with small success; his

works for orch., and especially for str., are well known, and are written with simplicity and good taste.

Operas: *Giulia da Gazzuolo* (1869); *Il matrimonio civile* (1870); *La stella delle Alpi* (1871); *Jella* (1881). Many overtures and suites for orch.; symphony in E (1886); 6tet for ob. 2 clar. horn, 2 bsns.; Theme with variations, str. 4tet (Milan, Ricordi).—D. A.

BONAVENTURA, Arnaldo. Ital. mus. historian; *b.* Leghorn, 28 July, 1862. Prof. of history and mus. æsthetics and librarian of Cherubini R. Inst. of Music, Florence. National vice-president, (and Florentine section president) of Assoc. of Ital. Musicologists. He has published:

History and Literature of Pianoforte; *Manual of History of Music* (7th ed.); *Manual of Æsthetics of Music*; *Manual of History of Musical Instruments*; *Dante and Music*; *Historical Essay on the Italian Musical Theatre*; *The Personality and Art of Giuseppe Verdi* (all publ. by Giusti of Leghorn). *Music in the Works of Horace* (Florence, Franceschini); *Musical Life in Tuscany in the XIX Century* (Florence, Barbera); *Nicolò Paganini* (Genoa, Formiggini); *L'Anfiparnaso di Orazio Vecchi* (Florence, Tipografia Galileiana); *Boccaccio and Music* (Turin, Bocca); *Le Maggiolate* (*Merry May Songs*) (id.); *The Autographs of Nicolò Paganini* (Florence, Olschki); *On a Musical MS. of the Medici* (id.); *Verdi* (Paris, 1923, Felix Alcan).—D. A.

BONCI, Alessandro. Ital. singer; *b.* Cesena, 10 Feb. 1870. One of the most famous living tenors. Of humble origin, thanks to his beautiful voice he succeeded in entering the Liceo Mus. at Pesaro, where he stud. under Felice Coen. In 1892 admitted as 1st t. in choir of Basilica of Loreto, where he already gained wide renown. His operatic career began in 1893, at the Regio Theatre, Parma, with part of Fenton in *Falstaff*. His fame soon spread throughout the world. In certain operas, like *Sonnambula*, *Puritani*, *Favorita*, *Don Pasquale*, *Elisir d'Amore*, *Don Giovanni*, and *Ballo in Maschera*, B. is without a rival. He has appeared with triumphant success in all the theatres of Europe and America.—D. A.

BONFIGLIOLI, José. Argentine vla.-player; *b.* Bologna in 1851. Stud. under Carlos Veradi, going to Buenos Ayres as 1st vla.-player at the Colón, 1881–90. Formed part of the Melani, La Rosa and Cattelani Quartets. Joined staff of Cons. Melani.—A. M.

BONI, Livio. Ital. cellist; *b.* Rome in 1885. First a pupil of Forino in Rome; then of Francesco Serato at Bologna. Went to Germany, England and France, perfecting himself and giving concerts, until he gained reputation as one of most distinguished Ital. cello players. In Rome he has given important concerts at the Augusteo and at Acad. Hall of Santa Cecilia.—D. A.

BONICIOLI, Fruhman Ricardo. Argentine compr. *b.* Zara (Dalmatia) in 1853. Stud. at Milan. Now leader of orch. at Politeama Theatre, Buenos Ayres. 2 operas (*Marco Bozzari*, 1881; *Don Juan de Garay*, 1900); symph. poems, 4tets, etc.—A. M.

BONINSEGNA, Celestina. Ital. s. singer; *b.* Reggio Emilia, 26 Feb. 1877. Was a pupil of Liceo Mus. at Pesaro, when Mascagni was dir.

M. asked her to create the part of Rosaura in his opera, *Le Maschere.*—D. A.

BONNET, Joseph Élie Georges Marie. Fr. orgt. and compr. *b.* Bordeaux, 17 March, 1884. First taught by his father, Georges Bonnet, organist at Sainte - Eulalie, then by Charles Tournemire and finally by Alex. Guilmant at Paris Cons. First prize for organ by unanimous vote in 1906, and the same year was appointed, in open competition, orgt. of Saint-Eustache. Invited to all the European capitals, received in U.S.A. and Canada, this admirable virtuoso rapidly acquired universal celebrity, exciting everywhere great enthusiasm on behalf of classical organ music and organ music of Fr. school. The Univ. of Rochester (New York) entrusted to him the management of the teaching of organ in that famous school. He is the ideal interpreter of Bach and of César Franck, in the complete expression of whose ardent lyricism he excels; yet he is not less astonishing in the masterpieces of the early comprs., of whom he has publ. several collections carefully revised and annotated: *Historical Organ Recitals* (5 vols., G. Schirmer) and the *Fiori musicali* of Frescobaldi (Senart). As compr. he has written numerous pieces in various styles, from the austere paraphrase of the Gregorian chant to the grand concert fantasia, romantic and brilliant (3 vols. of pieces, Durand, Paris). We mention especially his *Poèmes d'automne,* his *Noëls,* his *Versets d'Hymne,* his *Légende symphonique,* and several motets for chorus or solo vs. He first visited England in 1910 and America in 1916. Has contributed articles on GREGORIAN CHANT and SOLESMES, and on GUILMANT, to this Dictionary. —F. R.

Consult arts. on him by A. Eaglefield-Hull, in *The Organ* (London, Oct. 1921).

BOOSEY & CO. Publishers. The following facts bring the history of firm, in Grove's *Dictionary,* up to date. During winter of 1865, late John Boosey instituted London Ballad Concerts. These have now run for 57 years without break. They were originally held at St. James's Hall and transferred to Queen's Hall when former building was demolished. In 1907, they removed to Albert Hall where they are now held. Among the post-war activities is foundation of Westminster Choral Society, in 1919, with Vincent Thomas as condr. In addition to music-publishing, they carry on manufacture of wind instrs. In 1868 they purchased business of Henry Distin. In 1879, manufacture of clarinets and other reeds, including saxophones, was added to brass and flute departments. Besides Pratten flutes and Clinton clarinets, the firm has patent compensating pistons for brass instrs. designed to correct sharpening effect of valves used in combination, and the "Solbron" valves introduced in 1908. Present partners are C. P. Boosey, L. A. Boosey and C. E. Boosey.—E.-H.

BOOTH, John. Eng. t. singer; *b.* Bolton, Lancs, 11 Sept. 1878. Stud. under John Acton at the R. Manchester Coll. of Music; also pf. and harmony there. 1916–19, active war service

in France and Flanders; then stud. in Milan under Cav. Ernesto Colli; also opera under T. C. Fairbairn in London. Well known as an oratorio singer with a large repertoire; toured S. Africa 1922–3.—E.-H.

BORCH, Gaston. Norwegian-Amer. cellist, compr. condr. *b.* Guines, Pas-de-Calais, France, 8 March, 1871. Son of Norwegian father and Fr. mother. Educated in Sweden. Stud. 3 years under Massenet, Paris; afterwards under Svendsen in Copenhagen. Condr. and music-teacher in Christiania and Bergen 1893–8. Went to America in 1899, where he has, amongst other things, been condr. of Symphony Orch. in Pittsburg and Carnegie Orch. in St. Louis; now condr. at Opera-House in Boston; had special engagements as condr. of a number of orchs. in Europe, mainly in 1906 and 1907. Made his 1st appearance as compr. in Christiania (1893) with a fragment of the orch. work *Geneviève de Paris* (perf. in its entirety in Europe and America, 1906). Has publ. a large number of works for pf., organ, vn., cello, and for orch. and voice. His more important works show influence of Wagner and of Italian Verists.

Opera, *Silvio,* a kind of sequel to *Cavalleria Rusticana* (1st perf. Eldorado Theatre, Christiania, 1897); music to fairy-comedy *Östenfor sol og vestenfor maane* (1906); symph. poem, *Quo vadis* (Philadelphia, 1909); several symphonies.—U. M.

BORCHMAN, Alexander Adolphovitch (*accent 1st syll.*). Russ. compr. *b.* 28 March, 1872. Chose medical profession; after a music course at Moscow Univ. became pupil of Gretchaninof and Glière (1904–7).

Symph. poem *Kusum* (after Tagore's *The Harbour Steps*); Variations on a White-Russ. theme, orch. (1909); str. 4tet in C (Zimmerman); pf. trio; vn. sonata (1914); songs (op. 11, 13, publ. by Russ. State Music Publ. Dept.).—V. B.

BORDES, Charles. French compr. *b.* La Roche Corbon, 12 May, 1863; *d.* Toulon, 8 Nov. 1909. Stud. in Paris, pf. with Marmontel, compn. with César Franck; but did not take up music professionally until 1887, when he accepted a small post as church-orgt. and choirmaster. In 1889 the French Ministry of Education commissioned him to collect folk-tunes in the Basque provinces; and the following year he was appointed choirmaster of St.-Gervais, Paris, where he soon organised the now world-famous choir, the Chanteurs de St.-Gervais. He also undertook the publication of his *Anthologie des maîtres religieux primitifs* and other old works. A little later he began to give concerts of Bach's music, and (1894) founded (with Guilmant and d'Indy) the *Schola Cantorum* as a soc. whose object was to raise the standard of music in Fr. churches by promoting return to true tradition of plainsong, to the music of old masters, and by the creation of a suitable repertory of church music by contemporary comprs. His exertions proved forthwith far-reaching in effect, and heralded the reforms introduced by Pope Pius X. Two years later, the *Schola Cantorum* organised the teaching of church-singing on a practical basis; and in 1900 it became a high school of music, of which Bordes, with his partners Guilmant and d'Indy, remained a dir. until his death. The following years of his life were devoted to ever-increasing activities in concert organising, conducting, teaching, and collecting, editing and issuing music old and new, sacred and profane, and also to composition. The catalogue of his works comprises a fair quantity of church music, songs, a few instr. works, among which a *Suite basque* for fl. and strs. (1887, Bornemann), a *Rapsodie basque*, pf. and orch. (1889, Rouart & Lerolle), and a lyric drama, *Les Trois Vagues*, left unfinished. As a compr. he occupies an honourable rank among the minor poets of his time. Considering the spirit and originality of some of his music, one may regret that his very devotion to propaganda work should have prevented him from asserting himself more fully as a compr. during the few years of his artistic maturity. But none deserves better than he the gratitude of his contemporaries for all that he has achieved or set in motion. His was one of the chief influences through which mus. art and science progressed in France during last decade of XIX and first of XX century. Consult Octave Seré, *Musiciens d'aujourd'hui* (Paris, *Mercure de France*, 1921).—M. D. C.

BORGATTI, Giuseppe. Ital. t. singer; *b.* Cento, 19 March, 1871. Of humble origin; stud. at Liceo Mus. at Bologna with Busi as master. By the quality of his voice and his intelligence succeeded in winning a place in the front rank, especially as a Wagnerian tenor. In Italy he was the first interpreter of *Siegfried*, and of other Wagner works, and his rendering of the characters has become a model one. His repertoire also includes the works of other composers, of which he has always been an individual and intelligent interpreter. Has visited principal theatres of Europe and South America.—D. A.

BORGSTRÖM, Hjalmar. Norwegian composer and musical critic; *b.* Christiania, 23 March, 1864. Studied violin under Martin Ursin, Christiania (a pupil of Léonard), theory and composition under the eminent Norwegian organist and contrapuntist Ludv. M. Lindeman, and instrumentation under Johan Svendsen. Likewise studied piano-playing. Went in 1887 to Conservatoire in Leipzig and in 1890 (State scholarship) to Berlin; was in these years greatly impressed by Wagner's music and instrumentation. Also went to London and Paris for study and returned in 1904 to Christiania, where he became musical critic, which occupation he has since pursued on various journals (from 1913 on staff of *Aftenposten*). His musical output is very great and includes: 2 symphonies; 2 operas (to own text); 5 symphonic poems; a choral work; a good deal of chamber-music (including a string quartet and a piano quintet); concerto for piano and orchestra; a considerable number of songs and piano pieces. In Berlin, Busoni has played his piano pieces, and the Berlin Philharmonic Orchestra has produced works by him. In his native land, his music is much cultivated and he is regarded as the most

eminent Norwegian composer after Christian Sinding.

The most important part of Borgström's production is represented by his last 4 symphonic poems: *Jesus in Gethsemane, Hamlet, John Gabriel Borkman* (after Ibsen's well-known play) and *Tanken (Thought)*. Of these, again, *Hamlet* (orchestra and piano) is undoubtedly the work which has made him most known, both within and outside of his own country. *Hamlet* was first performed in Christiania in 1903, with the composer's wife Amalie Müller at the piano. The symphonic poem *Tanken* is, however, regarded as his most important work. Borgström inclines to the modern programmatic tendency in music. Although in his treatment of the orchestra he is in close touch with the young German school, yet he is quite independent in his style and method of expression. The national element can be felt in his music, without being very strongly marked. Of older Norwegian composers, the programmatic compr. Johan Selmer is the one to whom he stands nearest.—R. M.

BORKOWICZÓWNA, Maria. Polish compr. *b.* Warsaw, 1886. Pupil of Urstein at Warsaw.
Pf.: *Incantagione; Idylle champêtre; Ghiribizzo; Plaintes des fleurs; L'ultimo canto* (Paris, Fromont). Vn. and pf.: *Romanza e Intermezzo boemo* (Ricordi); *Daphnis et Chloé.*—ZD. J.

BORODIN, Alexander Porphirievitch (*accent 3rd syll.*). Russian composer; *b.* Petrograd, 31 Oct./12 Nov. 1834; *d.* there, 16/28 Feb. 1887. Of this composer, it has been said that "no musician has ever claimed immortality with so slender an offering—yet, if there be, indeed, immortalities in music, his claim is incontestable" (*Edinburgh Review*, Oct. 1906); and a great majority of music-lovers will certainly subscribe to this opinion. He displayed from his early childhood an equal liking for music and for science. Professionally, his career was that of an expert in chemistry, but all his spare time he devoted to music. He first came under Balakiref's influence, and after a period of study wrote his first symphony (which betrays to a great extent the influence of Schumann but is in many respects characteristic of Borodin as we see him in his later works), and started to compose his opera *Prince Igor*, at which he worked at irregular intervals. This score, left unfinished, contains some of the finest music he wrote. His other works are: a second symphony (1877, Bessel), and a third, left unfinished (Belaief); two string quartets and a few minor pieces for the same combinations of instruments (Belaief); 2 episodes for an opera-ballet *Mlada* (Belaief); a little Suite and a pf. *Scherzo* (Bessel); a dozen songs, some of which are of great beauty (Jurgenson; Belaief; Bessel); and the orchestral tone-picture *In the Steppes of Central Asia*.

Among the chief characteristics of his music are, on the one hand, the exquisite quality of his melody, always individual, even when the influence of folk-lore is most obvious, and of his harmonies, simple but rich and effective; on the other hand, the gift he has—almost alone among Russians—for utilising equally simple, but remarkably apt and effective polyphonic combinations of these melodies (*e.g.* in the tone-picture *The Steppes* and in the famous *Polovtsian Dances* in *Prince Igor*).—M. D. C.

BOROWSKI, Felix. Compr., teacher; *b.* Burton, England, 10 March, 1872. Stud. vn. under Jacques Rosenthal. In 1887, went to Cologne Cons., studying under Japha (vn.), Heuser (pf.) and Gustav Jensen (compn.). From 1889, stud. vn. under Pollitzer and cpt. under Pearce in London. After 1892, taught in Aberdeen and London. In 1897, went to Chicago as teacher of compn. at Chicago Mus. Coll., where he has also taught vn. and history of music. Since 1916, President of this school. Between 1906 and 1918, wrote mus. criticisms for various newspapers (*Chicago Evening Post, Chicago Herald*). Since 1908, author of programme notes for the Chicago Orch. His pf. concerto was first perf. at a concert of the Symphony Orch. at Chicago, 27 April, 1914; while the Chicago Symphony Orch. produced an *Allegro de Concert* for organ and orch., 17 March, 1915, and an *Elégie symphonique*, 9 March, 1917. A pantomime-ballet, *Boudour*, produced by Chicago Opera Co., 25 Nov. 1919. A *Poème* for orch., *Le Printemps passionné*, 1st perf. at Chicago North Shore Fest. (Evanston, Ill.), 25 May, 1920. His *Youth* for orch. won $1000 prize of North Shore Mus. Fest. (perf. 30 May, 1923).

Pf. concerto, arr. 2 pfs. (Composers' Music Corp. 1921); 1st organ sonata (London, Laudy); 2nd organ sonata (Paris, 1906, Laudy); pieces for pf. and for vn. (Laudy; Gould; Presser; Ditson).—O. K.

BÖRRESON, Hakon. Danish compr. *b.* Copenhagen, 2 July, 1876. Pupil of Johan Svendsen. Awarded Anker Stipendium, 1901; went abroad for study. His vn. concerto was perf. under Nikisch; his overture *Normannerne* (*The Normans*) was produced in England under Safonof.

3 symphonies and some smaller orch. compns.; 2 str. 4tets; 6tet; numerous pf. pieces; songs; 2 operas : *Kongelige Gæst* (*The Royal Guest*), 1 act; *Kaddara* (3 acts). The latter opera, with its unique setting and subject from Greenland, was produced at R. Theatre, Copenhagen, 1921.—A. H.

BORWICK, Leonard. English pianist; *b.* Walthamstow, Essex, 26 Feb. 1868. Stud. pf. under Henry R. Bird; vn. and vla. under Alfred Gibson up to age of 16; then pf. under Clara Schumann at Hoch's Cons. Frankfort-o-M.; compn. under Bernhard Scholz and Ivan Knorr; vn. and vla. under Fritz Basserman. Made his *début* at Museum concerts in Frankfort (in Nov. 1889), with Beethoven's E flat concerto; in London, 8 May, 1890, at Philh. concert in Schumann's concerto; 1891, in Brahms's D mi. concerto in Vienna under Richter; since then, appeared regularly in all chief European countries. He belongs to the Clara Schumann school but adds a rhythmic force peculiar to himself. He was closely associated with Joachim in the latter's musical work in England.

Arrs. for pf. solo of Bach's smaller organ works (Augener); of Debussy's *L'Après-midi d'un Faune* and *Fêtes* (both Fromont, Paris).—E.-H.

BOSCH, Carlos. Span. music critic. Author

of *Impresiones estéticas* (García Rico & Co. Madrid), and other essays on mus. subjects. Lives and works in Madrid.—P. G. M.

BOSCHOT, Adolphe. Fr. writer on music; *b.* Fontenay-sous-Bois (Seine) in 1871. Wrote from 1897 onwards for *Revue de Paris, Revue Hebdomadaire.* Vice-pres. of *Cercle de la Critique*; mus. critic to *Écho de Paris* (from 1910) and *Revue Bleue* (from 1919); made important addition to literature on Berlioz in *Histoire d'un romantique (Berlioz)* 1906–13 (3 vols.) and *Une Vie romantique,* 1920 (transl. Eng.), both works crowned by Académie des Beaux-Arts and Académie Française (Paris, Plon - Nourrit). Wrote *Le Faust de Berlioz* (Paris, Costallat, 1910). His last work is *Chez les musiciens,* (Plon-Nourrit, 1922).—M. L. P.

BOSE, Fritz von. Pianist and compr. *b.* Königstein, Saxony, 16 Oct. 1865. Pupil of Leipzig Cons. and (1887–8) of H. v. Bülow in Hamburg. Teacher at Cons. Carlsruhe, 1893; in Leipzig since 1898. Prof. 1912. A refined and sensitive player; compr. of pf. pieces and chamber-music.—A. E.

BOSKOFF, Georges. Rumanian pianist and compr. *b.* Jassy, 1882. Stud. Cons. of Paris (L. Diémer's class). Many pf. pieces and transcriptions of Bach's organ works (Paris,Hamelle). Lives in Paris.—C. Br.

BOSQUET, Émile. Pianist; *b.* Brussels, 8 Dec. 1878. Received diplomas for virtuosity at Brussels Cons. 1898, and International Rubinstein Prize, Vienna, 1900; prof of pf. at Antwerp Cons. 1905; and at Brussels Cons. 1919; has rare intelligence, high culture, complete self-effacement in interpretation; as far back as 1895, devoted himself to making known classical works seldom played, and also modern music at recitals and chamber-concerts in Brussels, Paris, London, Petrograd, Vienna, Berlin, etc. Has written various instruction books for piano.—C. V. B.

BOSSI, Costante Adolfo. Ital. orgt. and compr. *b.* 25 Dec. 1876. Appointed orgt. of Milan Cath. in 1907; prof. of harmony and cpt. at Milan Cons. in 1914.

Opera in 3 acts, *Enoch Arden* (1913); *La mammola e l'eroe,* 1-act (1916); *Il marito decorativo,* 3-act operetta (1916); Requiem Mass (funeral of King Humbert I), 4–6 v. and orch. (1921); *Messa di gloria,* 4-v. (Böhm); numerous organ pieces.—D. A.

BOSSI, Marco Enrico. Italian organist and composer; *b.* Salò (Lake Garda), 25 April, 1861. One of the most esteemed musicians and composers of Italian music of the modern school, and a organist of world-wide fame. As a composer of concert-music he is regarded as one of the few within the last ten years of XIX century (other names are those of Sgambati and Martucci) who have devoted themselves in the highest way to the culture of symphonic, vocal, and instrumental music in Italy.

Bossi studied first at the Liceo Musicale at Bologna, and then at the Conservatoire, Milan. He then went abroad and formed an idea of the great inferiority of organ-study in Italy at that time, and resolved to make a reform in that branch, which he effected in the best way, by teaching and by example. In 1881 he obtained Diploma of Honour at Bonetti Competition with a 1-act opera called *Paquita*. In the same year he was appointed choirmaster and organist of Como Cathedral; in 1890, he went to Naples as teacher of organ and harmony at the Royal Academy of San Pietro a Maiella. From 1895 to 1902 he was director of the Liceo Musicale Benedetto Marcello, Venice. In 1902 he succeeded Martucci as director of the Liceo Musicale at Bologna, which he left in 1911 in order to spend a few years devoting himself entirely to composition. In 1916 he took up the direction of the Royal Liceo Musicale di Santa Cecilia, Rome, which he resigned in 1922. Member of the Permanent Commission of Musical Art attached to the Ministry of Instruction, and of numerous academies in Europe and America.

Choral works : *Canticum Canticorum*, biblical cantata for soli, chorus, orch. and organ (1st perf. in St. Thomas Ch. Leipzig, 1900); *Il Paradiso perduto* (*Paradise Lost*) vocal and instr. symph. poem (1st perf. Augsburg, 1903); *Giovanna d'Arco* (*Joan of Arc*), mystery for soli, chorus and orch. (1st perf. Cologne, 1914).

Operas: *Paquita* (Milan, 1881); *Il veggente* (*The Seer*) (Milan, Dal Verme Theatre, 1890); *L'angelo della notte* (*The Angel of the Night*) (not yet perf.).

B's. minor compns. are very numerous. Amongst his organ works: Concerto, organ and orch. op. 100; overture, op. 3; 2 *Scherzi* and Impromptu, op. 49; *Triumphal Hymn*, op. 53; suite, *Res severa magnum gaudium*, op. 59; fugue, *Fede a Bach*; Fantasia, op. 64; Processional March, op. 68; Symph. Study, op. 78. Other works: *Tota pulchra*, mixed chorus and organ, op. 96; Mass (of St. Mark) 3 v. and organ, op. 61; Requiem masses, op. 83 and 90; *Cantate Domino*; *The Wedding*, for organ, str. and harp; Symph. Suite, for orch.; *The Blind Man*, short poem for barit., chorus and orch. (to words by Giovanni Pascoli); *Mossa d'Averno*, cantata for 4 v. (to words by Pope Leo XIII); *Intermezzi goldoniani*, for str.; 2 trios, pf. vn. and cello; 2 organ sonatas; 2 sonatas, pf. and vn.

B.'s music is publ. by Lucca; Ricordi; *Musica Sacra* ed.; Pigna; Carisch, Milan; Perosino, Turin; Pizzi, Bologna; Izzo, Pisano, Naples; Durand, Lemoine, Paris; Augener, Laudy, Novello, London; Peters, Kistner. Breitkopf, Leipzig; Heinrichshofen, Magdeburg; Schirmer, Fischer, New York; Presser, Philadelphia; Hug, Zurich.

In collab. with Tebaldini (*q.v.*), he has publ. a *Method of Study for Modern Organ* (Milan, 1893–4, Carisch).—D. A.

BOSSI, Renzo. Ital. compr. *b.* Como, 9 April, 1883. Son of Marco Enrico Bossi. Stud. at Naples, Venice and then at Leipzig; successfully devoted himself to conducting and to pf.-playing. In 1913, prof. of organ and compn. at Parma Cons., whence he went to Milan Cons. in 1916.

Much vocal and instr. chamber-music; a symphony in A mi. (Leipzig, Rieter Biedermann); concerto, vn. and orch. (Bologna, Pizzi); several operatic works, amongst which *Passa la Ronda* was perf. Milan, 1919 (score printed by Chester, London).—D. A.

BOSWORTH & CO. Ltd. Founded Leipzig, 1889, by wish of Sir Arthur Sullivan for publication and advancement of his works on Continent. The firm has developed greatly, by purchase of catalogues of Leipzig, Stuttgart, Vienna and London houses, by its own initiative (Ševčík's vn. school, Beringer's, Graham P. Moore's,

Matthay's and other educational pf. works), and by an ed. of classics now numbering over 1000 vols. Total works publ. about 40,000. Has houses under its own management in London, Brussels, Leipzig, Vienna, Zurich and New York.—E.-H.

BOTSTIBER, Hugo. Austrian music historian; *b.* 21 April, 1875. Graduated at Vienna Univ. in law and philosophy; stud. at same time at Cons. under Robert Fuchs; later under Zemlinsky. In 1896, assistant of Mandyczewski at Library of Gesellschaft der Musikfreunde; in 1900, secretary of newly-founded Wiener Konzertverein; 1905 sec. of Vienna Cons. (since 1908 called Academy of Music and Dramatic Art); 1913, sole manager of Wiener Konzertvereins-Gesellschaft. The foundation and erection of the Wiener Konzerthaus is due to his efforts. 1904–11, ed. of *Musikbuch aus Österreich*. Wrote *History of the Overture* (Breitkopf); monograph *Haydn und das Verlagshaus Artaria* (Franz Artaria). Is now completing Pohl's unfinished biography of Haydn.—EG. W.

BOTTARO, Cav. Arnaldo. Singer and teacher; *b.* Genoa in 1871. Stud. under several masters without result for some years. Finally Tartini's methods developed his t. voice. Began operatic career at the Carlo Felice, Genoa. After singing in Spain, Turkey, Egypt, and Greece, went to Buenos Ayres Opera in 1907. Prof. of singing at Buenos Ayres Conservatoire.—A. M.

BÖTTCHER, Lukas J. Ger. compr. *b.* Frankfort-o-M., 13 Feb. 1878. Pupil of E. Humperdinck at Hoch's Cons.; black-and-white artist and pf. teacher in Frankfort till 1915; condr. at Stadttheater, Halle, 1916–17; at Bad Brückenau, 1917; then as composer in Bamberg.

Large choral works; ballads; songs; the rococopantomime *Der blaue Falter* (1917); operas: *Salambo* (Altenburg, 1920); *Hildebrand* (own text, 1921); *Lagunenfieber* (own text, 1921).—A. E.

BOTTI, Cardenio. Ital. bandmaster and compr. *b.* Magliano Sabino, 14 Dec. 1890. Began his mus. career at Sistine Chapel under Perosi; stud. vn. under Tagliacozzo and Fattorini, and band-orchestration under Alessandro Vessella at R. Liceo Mus. di Santa Cecilia, Rome. In 1914, he won by competition the post of bandmaster of 35th Infantry Regiment, with headquarters at Bologna. Recently he left to conduct the band at Valetta (Malta). Author of various instr. and vocal chamber-works (Bologna, Bongiovanni). Has contributed to reviews and mus. papers. —D. A.

BOUCHER, Maurice. Fr. compr. musicologist; *b.* Paris, 1886. Pupil of École Normale Supérieure; *Agrégé des Lettres*; in music, pupil of Savard and Witkowski; comp. str. 4tet; pf. pieces (*En Savoie*); songs (own words). Wrote *Albéric Magnard* (Les 2 Collines, Lyons, 1919); *La Musique moderne* (*ib.* 1919).—A. C.

BOUCHERIT, Jules. Fr. violinist; *b.* Moraix, 29 March, 1877. 1st prize, Paris Cons., 1892. Many tours, and has gained great success as soloist with symphony orchs. His extremely delicate and pure style inclined him from the outset towards the classics, particularly Mozart. Without forsaking his first ideals, now shows leanings towards romantic and modern schools. Schumann's sonata in D has no finer interpreter. —M. P.

BOUGHTON, Rutland. English composer; b. Aylesbury, Bucks, 23 Jan. 1878. Stud. R.C.M. London under Charles Stanford and Walford Davies (1900–1). From 1904–11 he taught singing at Birmingham Midland Inst. of Music (under Bantock). Started in Aug. 1914 a series of music-drama fests. at Glastonbury, Somerset, at first with the object of producing a cycle of music-dramas on Arthurian legends by the late R. R. Buckley to Boughton's own music. The prelude and 1st scene of *The Birth of Arthur* had been given at Bournemouth (with "human scenery") on 17–28 Aug. 1913, under Edgar L. Bainton. *Arthur of Britain* did not come to a perf. for want of a suitable building; but the Tintagel scene was given several times in Aug. 1914, and, in addition to various plays, 3 perfs. of the romantic opera *The Immortal Hour* (on play by Fiona Macleod) were given by the Glastonbury Players recruited largely from the locality (see *Mus. Times*, Oct. 1914). Boughton has always been a believer in amateur capacity in the arts, and his first Glastonbury venture ripened into the foundation of the Glastonbury Music School and the Glastonbury Fests. (*q.v.*). Up to 1923, nearly 300 perfs. were given, the greater number being operatic. His own *Alkestis* was given there in Aug. 1922. *The Immortal Hour*, when produced by Barry Jackson in London at the Regent Theatre in Sept. 1922, settled down into the longest run of any Eng. romantic opera. It had already been given at Bournemouth, Bristol, Birmingham, the "Old Vic." London (by the Glastonbury Players, 1920 [Gwen Ffrangcon-Davies as the Princess]) but it was not until presented by the Birmingham Repertory Co. that it became an establ. success. His *Bethlehem* was given at Regent Theatre, London, Dec. 1923–Jan. 1924, and his *Alkestis* by British National Opera Co. Covent Garden, 11 Jan. 1924. *The Immortal Hour* was revived again at the Regent in Feb. 1924. B. is essentially a compr. for the stage; and Eng. feeling and folk-song play a great part in his musical equipment.

Stage-works: *The Birth of Arthur* (1907–8, ms.); *The Immortal Hour* (1912–13, Stainer & Bell); *Snow-White* (1914); *Bethlehem* (1915, Curwen); *The Round Table* (1916); *Dawn at Agincourt* (1918); *The Moon-Maiden* (1919, Curwen); *Alkestis* (1920–2, id.). Choral works: *Midnight* (Birmingham Fest.; Novello); *The Invincible Armada*; *The Skeleton in Armour*; *Song of Liberty* (Curwen); Choral Variations on folksongs (Leeds Fest.; W. Reeves); 6 spiritual songs for unacc. chorus (Reeves); Choral Dances (unacc. Curwen). Vn. sonata (Goodwin & Tabb); *Celtic Prelude*, pf. vn. cello (1917); str. 4tets in A and F (1923). Song-cycles: *Songs of Womanhood* (Larway); *Symbol Songs* (Curwen); numerous songs and part-songs. Literary works: *Bach* (J. Lane); *The Glastonbury Festival Movement* (Somerset Folk Press); *The Death and Resurrection of the Mus. Festivals* (W. Reeves); *The Music-Drama of the Future* (id.); *A Study of Parsifal* (Mus. Opinion Office).—E.-H.

BOULANGER, Lily. Fr. compr. b. Paris, 21 Aug. 1893; d. Paris, 15 March, 1918. One of a family of musicians; showed signs, at early age, of extraordinary musical gifts. In spite of constant ill-health she worked at technique with as much facility as if she had known music before learning it. At 20 she gained *Prix de Rome* (never before awarded to a woman). Although suffering from a new and even more acute illness, she again set to work; her sublime resignation in the face of certain death seemed to bring forth the full beauty of her genius. The result was the production of *Deux Psaumes* (choir and orchestra), *Les Clairières du ciel* (collection of songs), a great deal of vocal music and religious works. The music is remarkable, not so much for its novelty, as for a certain sensitiveness and purity of feeling. Her nobility of soul and dauntless faith radiate through it. When this young musician died at the age of 24, the world lost a real genius.

Consult Camille Mauclair, *La Vie et l'œuvre de L. B.* (*Revue Musicale*, Aug. 1921).—H. P.

BOULNOIS, Joseph. Fr. compr. b. Paris, 1880; killed in action, Chalaines (Meuse), 1918. Operas, symphonies, chamber music, mostly unpubl.—A. C.

BOULT, Adrian Cedric. Eng. condr. b. Chester, 8 April 1889. Educated Westminster School and Christ Ch. Oxford (music under Sir Hugh Allen); Leipzig Cons. (Hans Sitt; Eugen Lindner; S. Krehl; and stud. the methods of Nikisch); on mus. staff, R. Opera, Covent Garden, 1914; since 1918, has cond. at R. Philh. Soc., Liverpool Philh. Soc., London Symphony Orch. and Queen's Hall Orch.; also a season of Russ. ballet at Empire Theatre, 1919; on teaching staff at R.C.M. London, 1919; teacher of conducting, condr. of orch. and of Patron's Fund concerts there, 1919; Mus.Doc. Oxon.; condr. of Birmingham Fest. Choral Soc. 1923. Has done fine work, especially for the younger Eng. school of composers.

Handbook for Conductors (Goodwin & Tabb).—E.-H.

BOURGAULT-DUCOUDRAY, Louis Albert. Fr. composer; b. Nantes, 2 Feb. 1840; d. Vernouillet, near Paris, 4 July, 1910. During his childhood he heard a good deal of chamber-music in his home. At 15 he wrote a small comic opera, produced at Nantes, 1859. The same year he went to Paris, and entered the Conservatoire, studying under Ambroise Thomas, obtaining the *Prix de Rome* in 1862. In Italy he developed an interest in the music of Palestrinian period and in folk-music. In 1869 founded at Paris a society for production of choral and orchestral works, ancient and modern, which during 5 years of existence rendered signal services. In 1874, his health having broken down in consequence of a wound received in Franco-Prussian War (awarded *Médaille Militaire* for conspicuous bravery), he was sent to Greece on an official mission. There he began his studies of Greek church-music and folk-music, thereby inaugurating an order of research which was to open new vistas in both musical science and musical art. In 1878, appointed professor of musical history at Paris Conservatoire. He held the post 30 years, exercising a far-reaching influence by his teaching which included æsthetics as well as history. His course on Russian music (1903) heralded the progress which this music was to make in France and subsequently in other countries.

As early as 1878 (in a lecture at Paris Universal Exhibition) he had pointed out how necessary it was to extend the vocabulary of music by resorting to " all possible modes, old or new, European or exotic." And what he preached he successfully practised in works such as the *Rapsodie cambodgienne* (1882) and *Le Carnaval d'Athènes* (1884) for orch., the operas *Myrdhin* (1905, unpublished) and *Thamara* (Paris Opéra 1891, revived in 1907), etc.

His other chief works are the operas *Michel Columb* (1877) and *Bretagne* (1888), both unpublished; a *Stabat Mater* (1862), an *Hymne à la Joie* (1864), *Prométhée* (1868) and many other choral cantatas or hymns; *L'Enterrement d'Ophélie* (1877) for orchestra, a little satirical play, *La Conjuration des fleurs* (1883), of which he wrote both words and music, and numerous songs.

He is a composer of high originality and genuine feeling, whose best works would certainly be popular among music-lovers if they were better known.

His collections of folk-songs, *Trente Mélodies populaires de la Grèce et de l'Orient* (1875) and *Trente Mélodies populaires de la Basse Bretagne* (1883), *Mélodies du Pays de Galles et d'Écosse* (1909), are classics of their kind; likewise his books, *Études sur la musique ecclesiastique grecque*, *La Modalité dans la musique grecque*, and *Souvenirs d'une mission musicale en Orient* (Paris, Hachette). He has also written a sound and instructive critical biography of Schubert (Paris, Laurens).

There is practically no literature on him except for notices of his opera *Thamara* and of a few other works, and obituary notices in the Paris Press.—M. D. C.

BOURIELLO, François. Fr. compr. *b.* Algiers, 1872. This blind compr. has long frequented Spanish and Algerian *milieux*, from which he has transcribed many popular songs. Formerly orgt. of grand organ at Algiers Cathedral.

Theatre: *Catherine de Sienne*; *Le Lys dans la vallée* (after Balzac); *Libération*. Cantata, *Le Cantique des Cantiques* (*Song of Solomon*). Pf. pieces: *Le Livre de la Jungle*; *Préludes*; *Tarentelles*, etc.—A. C.

BOUVET, Charles. Fr. writer on music; *b.* Paris, 1858. Archivist to the Opéra, succeeding Henri Quittard (*q.v.*). Founded and directed (1903–11) *La Fondation J. S. Bach*, a soc. specially devoted to perf. of old music. Then devoted himself to musicology. Wrote for various reviews, such as *Monde Musical*, *Courrier Musical*, *Bulletin de la Société française de Musicologie*.

Une leçon de G. Tartini et une femme violoniste au XVIIIe siècle (Paris, 1915, Senart); Une Dynastie de musiciens français : les Couperins (Paris, 1919, Delagrave) crowned by Acad. of Fine Arts. Also revisions of old works publ. under title Collection Charles Bouvet (Paris, E. Demets); 4 Inventions for vn. and pf. taken from La Pace by Antonio Buonyporti; Pièces de viole de F. Couperin (Paris, Durand).—M. L. P.

BOWDEN, Alfred H. E. Tasmanian musician; *b.* Glenorchy, near Hobart. Trained under A. Jackson Dentith at Hobart and Heinrich Dettmer, Victoria; for 14 years choirmaster, St. Andrew's Presbyterian Ch. Launceston, where he produced many oratorios; was for some years member of Philh. Soc. Orch. Melbourne. Has taught in Tasmania for 35 years; for 23 years, music critic of *Daily Telegraph*, Launceston (pen-name " Moderato "). Has publ. pieces for vn. and pf. In 1920, Trinity Coll. of Music, London, conferred on him the L.T.C.L. *h.c.* —E.-H.

BOWDEN, Mrs. Alfred H. E. Tasmanian pianist and teacher; *b.* Hobart. Stud. under her father, A. Jackson Dentith (who was at that time Hobart's most prominent musician, and had stud. with Costa in London, and Jacob Schmidt in Hamburg). Made many concert-appearances in Tasmania and in Melbourne. Has trained many prominent teachers in N. Tasmania.

Has publ. pf. pieces, songs, anthems, etc. (Allan & Co., Melbourne).—E.-H.

BOWEN, York. Eng. compr. and pianist; *b.* London, 22 Feb. 1884. Played a pf. concerto in public at age of 8½; was not allowed to appear as a prodigy; at 14, gained a 3-years' scholarship at R.A.M. and afterwards a further 2 years (pf. under Tobias Matthay; compn. under Battison Haynes and F. Corder); then pf. prof. there; has appeared regularly as soloist in chief London and provincial concerts. His 1st pf. concerto was produced Queen's Hall Promenades 1904; his 3rd concerto, G mi., there, 8 Sept. 1908. His symph. poem, *Lament of Tasso*, had been given there, 1 Sept. 1903. He is one of leading Eng. pianists of last 20 years; has a full rich tone, a wide mus. culture and a most brilliant keyboard technique. As a compr. he is at his best in pf. music; he derives from the Romantic school, and adds all the subtler nuances of a modern harmonic style. His earlier works show Wagnerian influence; his later ones are thoroughly original, Neo-Romantic in feeling, and quite untouched by Fr. Impressionism. His contributions to chamber-music, and especially to pf. music and vla. music, are particularly valuable.

2 symphonies (ms.); overture; suite; orch. poem, Eventide; 3 pf. concertos (ms.); vn. concerto, E mi. (Ascherberg); Rhapsody, cello and orch. (1923); At the Play, orch. (id.); 7tet, clar. horn, pf. and str.-(ms.); trio, vla. harp and organ; str. 4tet, No. 2, D mi. (Stainer & Bell; Carnegie award); No. 3 in G; id.); sonata, cello and pf. op. 64 (Schott, London); 2 sonatas and a suite, vla. and pf. (Schott); 5 suites for pf. (I, II and III, Anglo-Fr. Co.; IV and V, J. Williams); Polonaise (Anglo-Fr. Co.); pf. pieces (Swan; Ricordi; Ascherberg); pf. duets (Stainer & Bell); 12 studies, Bells (Ascherberg); Curiosity Suite (J. Williams); Hans Andersen, 4 books (Swan); pf. sonata, F mi. op. 72 (Swan); 7 songs, 1921 (id.); Chinese Lyrics (Enoch); Meg Merrilies, song with str. 4tet, 1921 (ms.); Songs of Elfland, op. 73 (Swan); 2 songs, op. 75 (id.).—E.-H.

BRAGA, Hernani. Portuguese pianist; *b.* about 1855. Pupil of Marmontel at Paris; taught for a long time at the Academia de Amados de Musica, Lisbon; introduced clavecin music into Lisbon, being the only Portuguese teacher who possessed one.—E.-H.

BRAHMS, Johannes. German composer; *b.* Hamburg, 7 May, 1833; *d.* Vienna, 3 April, 1897. Son of the double-bass player of Hamburg Stadt-theater, Johann Jakob, and of Henrika Christina, *née* Nissen. At first, pupil of his father for violin and cello, of Otto Fr. W. Cossel for piano and Eduard Marxsen for composition. First public appearance as pianist in Hamburg, 21 Sept. 1848. In April 1853, left his native town for a concert-tour with the Hungarian violinist Ed. Reményi. In May, met Joseph Joachim in Han-over, with whom he remained in lifelong friend-ship despite occasional disagreement. Later, became acquainted with Liszt, whose guest he was in Altenburg near Weimar; finally, in the autumn, met Schumann in Düsseldorf. Acquain-tance with Brahms's first compositions was the occasion of Schumann's enthusiastic introduc-tory article (*Neue Bahnen*) in the *Neue Zeit-schrift für Musik* (23 Oct. 1853), since the appearance of which Brahms's fame may be said to date. After several concert-tours, and visits to Clara Schumann and Joachim, Brahms settled in Detmold, Sept. 1857, as choral con-ductor and teacher to Princess Friederike. In 1860 Brahms returned to Hamburg, where he conducted a Ladies' Choral Society and com-posed the works op. 18–34. In Sept. 1862, settled in Vienna, which from henceforth to his death became his second home. In winter 1863, took over for a short time the conductorship of the Vienna Singakademie, and then led for several years a rather restless life, wandering from place to place. Returned to Vienna, how-ever, and, 1872–5, took over conductorship, this time of the Society of Friends of Music (Gesell-schaft der Musikfreunde). Since that time he lived as a creative musician without any fixed post, and only left Vienna for summer holidays and travels, of which those in Italy proved very fruitful for his creative work. Of honorary titles he received Mus.Doc. Cantab. 1877 ; Ph.D. Breslau Univ. 1879; Freedom of City of Hamburg, 1889; Foreign Member, Académie de Paris, 1896.

As a man, Brahms sought to conceal under a rough exterior an enormous fund of delicacy and impressionability. The purity and nobility of his character elevated him to a singularly lofty height. His historical position is deter-mined by his attitude as a musician of a " late " generation (*nachgeborenen Geschlechts*) towards the past and classical music. Contrary to his con-temporaries Liszt and Wagner, his ideals lay, not in the future but in the past. He began as a Romantic, somewhat in the stormy, youthful manner of Schumann; but he soon felt the necessity of establishing his own creative activity through a profound acquaintance with the crea-tive work of the classical composers, including Schubert. He was perpetually striving after the mastery of sonata and variation form by per-sonally assimilating harmonic, rhythmic and melodic modes of expression inherited from the past. As an artist in practice he became the greatest master of the XIX century. He may be truly called the " classic of the Classicists "; for he was the last who succeeded in putting content into classical forms which, in the hands of the Romanticists, had become weak, empty and purely formalistic. Through his posthumous masterpieces he succeeded, at the close of his life, in giving pure expression in music to the human element within him, and in transfiguring that element through the medium of art. In the lyricism of the 4 *ernste Gesänge*, in the final movement of the E minor symphony, in his chamber-music, in the clarinet quintet and the clarinet sonatas, he is the prophet of resigna-tion and pessimism, since he gives expression to a post-classical period that has lost something of its original fullness.

Orch.: *Serenade* in D, op. 11; in A, op. 16; Varia-tions on theme of Haydn, op. 56*a*; Symphony I, in C mi. op. 68; II, in D, op. 73; III, in F, op. 90; IV, in E mi. op. 98; *Academic Overture*, op. 80; *Tragic Overture*, op. 81. Pf. and orch.: Concerto I, in D mi. op. 15; II, in B flat, op. 83. 2 cadenzas to Beethoven's G ma. Concerto. Vn. and orch.: Vn. concerto in D op. 77; concerto for vn. and cello in A mi. op. 102. Pf.: Sonata I, in C, op. 1; II, in F sharp mi. op. 2; III, in F mi. op. 5; *Scherzo*, E flat mi. op. 4; Varia-tions on theme of Schumann, op. 9; *Balladen*, op. 10; Variations on orig. theme, op. 21*a*; on a Hun-garian song, op. 21*b*; on theme of Handel with fugue, op. 24; on theme of Paganini, op. 35; *Klavierstücke*, 2 books, op. 76; 2 *Rhapsodies*, op. 79; *Phantasien*, 2 books, op. 116; 3 *Intermezzi*, op. 117; *Klavierstücke*, op. 118, 119. Pf. duet: Variations on theme of Schumann, op. 23; *Waltzer*, op. 39; *Waltzer-Liebeslieder*, op. 52*a*; *Waltzer Neue Liebeslieder*, op. 65*a*. Pf. and vn.: Sonata I, in G, op. 78; II, in A, op. 100; III, in D mi. op. 108. Pf. and cello: Sonata I, in E mi. op. 38; II, in F mi. op. 99. Pf. and clar.: Sonata I, in F mi. op. 120*a*; II, in E flat, op 120*b*. Trios: Pf. vn. cello in B, op. 8; in C, op. 87; in C mi. op. 101; pf. vn. waldhorn in E flat, op. 40; pf., clar. and cello in A mi. op. 114. 4tets: Pf. vn. vla. cello G mi. op. 25; pf., vn. vla. cello in A, op. 26; pf. vn. vla. and cello in C mi. op. 60. Str.: I, in C mi. op. 51*a*; II, in A mi. op. 51*b*; III, in B flat, op. 67. 5tets: Pf. and str. F mi. op. 34; str.: I, in F, op. 88; II, in G, op. 111; clar. and str. in B mi. op. 115. 6tets: Str.: I, in B flat, op. 18; II, in G, op. 36. Organ: 11 *Choralvorspiele* (his last work) 2 books, op. 122; *Choralvorspiel und Fuge*, A mi. (without op. no.); Fugue in A flat mi. (*id.*). Unacc. mixed chorus: *Marienlieder*, op. 22; 2 motets, 5-v. op. 29; 3 *Gesänge*, 6-v. op. 42; 7 *Lieder*, op. 62; 2 motets, op. 74; *Lieder und Roman-zen*, 4-v. op. 93*a*; 5 *Gesänge*, op. 104; *Fest- und Gedenksprüche*, 8-v. op. 109; 2 motets, 4- and 8-v. op. 110. Unacc. female chorus: 2 *Geistliche Chöre*, op. 37; 12 *Lieder und Romanzen*, op. 44; 13 canons, op. 113. Unacc. male chorus: 5 *Lieder*, 4-v. op. 41. Chorus and orch.: *Ave Maria*, female chorus, op. 12; *German Requiem*, op. 45; *Rinaldo*, t. solo and male chorus, op. 50; *Rhapsodie*, contr. solo and male chorus, op. 53; *Schicksalslied*, mixed chorus, op. 54; *Triumphlied*, double chorus, op. 55; *Nänie*, mixed chorus, op. 82; *Gesang der Parzen*, 6-v. op. 89; *Begräbnisgesang*, mixed chorus and wind instrs. op. 13; *Gesänge*, female chorus, 2 horns and harp, op. 17; 2 *Lieder*, contr., vla. and pf. op. 91. 4 solo vs. and pf. op. 31, 64, 92, 112, 52, (*Liebes-lieder*), 65 (*Neue Liebeslieder*), 103 (*Zigeunerlieder*). Vocal duets and pf.: Op. 20, 61, 66 (all s. and a.); 28, a., barit.; 75 (*Balladen*); 84 (*Romanzen*). Songs (v. and pf.): Op. 3, 6, 7, 14, 19, 32, 33 (*Magelone*), 43, 46, 47, 48, 49, 57, 58, 59, 63, 69, 70, 71, 72, 84, 85, 86, 94, 95, 96, 97, 105, 106, 107, 121, and 4 *ernste Gesänge* (without op. no.). Consult: Max Kalbeck, *J. B.*, 4 vols. (1904–14) Walther Niemann, *J. B.* (Berlin, 1920); Heinrich Rei-mann, *J. B.* (1897); Gustav Jenner, *J. B. als Mensch*,

Lehrer und Künstler (1905); W. A. Thomas-San Galli, J. B. (Munich, 1912); Florence May, *The Life of J. B.* (Eng. 1905; Ger. 1912); J. A. Fuller-Maitland, B. (Eng. 1911; Ger. 1913); Ed. Evans, *Historical Description and Analytical Account of the Entire Work of J. B.* (London, 1912, Reeves); H. C. Colles, B. (Eng. 1908; Ger. 1913); H. Imbert, *J. B.* (1905); P. Landormy, *B.* (1920). Reminiscences: G. Henschel, *Personal Recollections of J. B.* (Boston, 1907); Albert Dietrich, *Erinnerungen an J. B.* (1898); J. V. Widmann, *J. B. in Erinnerungen* (1898); J. V. Widmann, *Sizilien und andere Gegenden Italiens, Reisen mit J. B.*; J. Ophüls, *Erinnerungen an J. B.* (1921); R. v. d. Leyen, *J. B. als Mensch und Freund* (1908). 15 vols. of B.'s correspondence have been publ. by the Brahms Soc. (Deutsche Brahmsgesellschaft). A thematic catalogue of the complete works of B. was issued in 1897 (2nd ed. 1902) by Simrock (Berlin) who publ. nearly all the music of B.—A. E.

BRAHY, Édouard. Belgian condr. *b.* Liège, 1 Sept. 1873; *d.* Brussels, 6 Nov. 1919. Stud. Liège Cons. in 1887. 1st prize for cello and chamber music, 1891. Went to finish his studies at Leipzig (under Jadassohn) and in Berlin where he stud. conducting under Bülow, Nikisch and Weingartner. Came back to Brussels (1896), one of founders of Zimmer Quartet in which he was cellist. 1898–1907, cond. symph. concerts at Anger, 1903–13, Winter Concerts at Ghent, 1906–18, the Brahy Concerts at Liège Cons. Having cond. concerts in Brussels with great success (1905, 1916, 1917), appointed condr. of Popular Concerts there in 1919. He had just cond. 1st concert of season when he died. He was extraordinarily talented as a condr.; he could conduct the most complicated works from memory and with the deepest lyrical appreciation.—E. C.

BRAITHWAITE, Sam Hartley. Eng. compr. and pianist; *b.* Egremont, Cumberland, 20 July, 1883. Stud. R.A.M. London; holder clar. scholarship, 1902; stud. compn. under F. Corder; clar. under George Clinton, pf. under Cuthbert Whitemore; mus. dir. Passmore Edwards Settlement, 1910–13; from 1917, living in Bournemouth on account of health. His pf. works, in particular, are well written for the instrument. Overture, military band (Pageant of Empire, Crystal Palace, 1911); orch. tone-poem, *On a Summer's Day* (Bournemouth Fest. 1923); tone-poem, *Snow-Picture* (a Carnegie award, 1923; Stainer & Bell); pf. music (Augener; Schirmer; Arnold). —E. H.

BRANBERGER, Jan. Czech writer on music; *b.* Prague, 18 Nov. 1877. Trained at Cons. there; 1905, Ph.D.; stud. under Kretzschmar, Wolf, Friedländer at Berlin Univ. From 1906 to 1918 secretary and prof. of mus. history at Prague Cons. Since 1919 official of the Ministry of Public Instruction. Wrote much for mus. periodical *Dalibor*. For a long time, critic for newspaper *Čas.*

Catechism of General Musical History; The Music of the Jews; Rhythm and Tone; History of Prague Cons.; (contin. of Ambros' work), all in Czech. In German: *Musical History of Bohemia*; 1922, publ. *Musical Almanac* of Czechoslovak republic.—V. ST.

BRANCOUR, René. Fr. musicologist; *b.* Paris, 17 May, 1862; custodian of Museum of Instrs. at Paris Cons. Has written some unpretentious chamber-music. As musicologist, represents the intractable party of opponents of the young school. Has publ. *Félicien David*, 1911; *Méhul*, 1912; *Bizet*, 1913; *Massenet*, 1923.—A. C.

BRANDELER, Henriette van Heukelom van den. Dutch compr. *b.* The Hague, 25 Sept. 1884. Stud. under Joh. Wagenaar, Dirk Schäfer, Bernard Zweers. Numerous songs and choral works, perf. several times in Holland. (Publ. Alsbach, Amsterdam; De Algemeene Muziekhandel, Amsterdam; Noske, The Hague.) Consult arts. in Dutch reviews: Nolthenius in *Weekblad voor Muziek* (23 Jan. 1909); Marie Berdenis van Berlekom in *De Vrouw en haar huis* (1917); Henriette van Lennep in *De Amsterdammer* (17 June, 1916); Herman Rutters in *Het Muziekcollege* (July, 1917).—W. P.

BRANDT - RANTZAU, Rolf. Norwegian pianist; *b.* Sarpsborg, 21 May, 1883. Pf. pupil of Paolo Gallico in New York, 1892–1901; gave his first concert in that city in 1898; afterwards pupil of Agathe Backer-Gröndahl, Xaver Scharwenka and Busoni. B.-R. has developed into a virtuoso of European dimensions, and he has given concerts in Berlin, Stockholm, Gothenburg, Copenhagen and in most Norwegian towns. He is a highly-esteemed pf. teacher and is resident in Christiania, to which city he has also made valuable contributions of chamber-music performance.—J. A.

BRANDTS-BUYS, Jan. Dutch compr. *b.* Zutphen (Guelderland), 12 Sept. 1868. Stud. at Frankfort; comp. several operas well known in Germany (*Das Veilchenfest*, Berlin, 1910; *Das Glockenspiel*; *Die Schneider von Schönau*; *Der Mann im Mond*; *Mi-Carême*); 3 concertos, pf. and orch.; suite, str., harp and horn; 4tet; 5tet (str. and fl.); trio; numerous songs with pf. and with orch.; pf. pieces (*Études*; Leipzig, Cranz). Lives in Vienna.—W. P.

BRANDTS-BUYS, Johan Sebastian. Son of Ludwig Felix; 1910–18 mus. critic of *Utrechtsch Dagblad*; pioneer of modern music; 1918, went to Java and stud. Javanese music; has written an extensive brochure, *De ontwikkelingsmogelijkheden der inlandsche muziek op Java (Position of Javanese Music)*. Lives in Solo, Java.—W. P.

BRANDTS-BUYS, Ludwig Felix. Dutch choirtrainer and compr. *b.* Deventer, 20 Nov. 1847; *d.* Velp, 29 June, 1917. Comp. several choral works, songs and smaller pieces.—W. P.

BRANDTS-BUYS, Marius. Dutch choirtrainer; brother of Jan B.-B.; comp. choruses; operettas for children's voices; numerous songs.—W. P.

BRANSCOMBE, Gena (Mrs. John F. Tenney). Canadian compr. *b.* Picton, Ontario, 4 Nov. 1881. Stud. pf. at Chicago Mus. Coll. under Ziegfeld and Friedheim, and compn. under Borowski, 1897–9. Later, pf. under Ganz and compn. under von Fielitz and Humperdinck. A faculty for pleasing melodic invention has won many admirers for her numerous songs and choruses. One of her most popular songs is *Hail ye Time of Holie Dayes* (Schmidt). A *Festival Prelude* for orch. was perf. at MacDowell Fest. in Peterboro, N.H. in 1914.

Pf. pieces (A. P. Schmidt); songs (Schmidt; Schirmer; Ditson); 2 song-cycles: *A Lute of Jade*; *The Sun-Dial* (Schmidt, 1913); *Carnival Fantasy*, vn. and pf. (*id.* 1920).—O. K.

BRANZELL, Karin Maria. Swedish contr. operatic and concert-singer; *b.* Stockholm, 24 Sept. 1891; stud. under Thekla Hofer, Mantlen, Louis Bachuen (Berlin). *Début* 1911; member Stockholm R. Opera, 1912–18; then Berlin and Vienna operas as guest; many other Ger. operas and Zurich. Rôles: Amneris, Azucena, Carmen, Brünnhilde, Erda, Fricka, Ortrud, Brangäne, Leonora, Martha, etc.—P. V.

BRATT, Thora. Norwegian pianist; *b.* Christiania, 8 Oct. 1892. Stud. at R. Music Cons. in Copenhagen, 1907–10; at High School in Berlin under Dohnányi, 1911–14; *début,* Christiania, 1914.—U. M.

BRATZA, (real name, Milan Yovanovitch). Serbian violinist; *b.* Novi Sad, 12 May, 1904. Trained as violinist by Prof. Ševčík at Vienna Imperial Acad. of Music. His development was very rapid; finished his studies at Vienna in 1918, when only 14. Since then B. has played and achieved extraordinary success in the principal European capitals. ·He now resides in London, where he is frequently heard. Both technically and temperamentally he ranks with the greatest players of the day. Has made a special success with Tchaikovsky's concerto.—T. F. D.

BRAUNFELS, Walter. Ger. compr. *b.* Frankfort-o-M., 19 Dec. 1882. Pupil of J. Kwast, Frankfort-o-M., Leschetizky and Navrátil, Vienna, and Ludwig Thuille in Munich, in which town he has resided since 1903, distinguishing himself as a pianist (Beethoven and Bach). As a compr. he alike approaches the classicism of a Brahms, the feeling for the grotesque of a Berlioz and the romanticism of a Schumann. Songs, op. 1, 2 (folk-style, ms.), 4, 7 (*Fragmente eines Federspiels*), 13 (*Echoes of Beethoven's Music*), 24 (after Eichendorff and Goethe, ms.); pf. pieces, op. 5, 10 (Studies); *Rondo,* op. 9; Variations for 2 pianos, op. 21; *Hexensabbat* (*Witches' Sabbath*) for pf. and orch. op. 8. For orch.: Variations on children's song, op. 15; *Ariel's Song,* op. 18; *Serenade,* op. 20; *Fantasia* on theme of Berlioz, op. 25 (Univ. Ed. Vienna); choral work, *Revelation of St. John, Chap. VI,* t. solo, chorus and orch., op. 17; *Te Deum,* op. 32 (Univ. Ed. Vienna); *Neues Federspiel,* vs. and orch.; *Die Ammenuhr,* boys' chorus and orch., op. 28; orch. songs, op. 15, 26, 27; music to *Twelfth Night,* op. 11, and *Macbeth,* op. 14 (ms.). Operas: *Falada,* op. 3 (ms.); *Der Goldene Topf* (unfin. ms.), op. 6; *Princess Brambilla,* op. 12 (Stuttgart, 1909); overture as *Carnival Overture,* op. 22); *Till Eulenspiegel,* op. 23 (Stuttgart, 1913); the very successful *Die Vögel* (*The Birds*), op. 30 (Munich, 1920; Univ. Ed. Vienna); *Don Gil von den grünen Hosen* (Munich, 1924).—A. E.

BRAUNSTEIN, Pierre. Fr. compr. *b.* Alsace, 1888; *d.* during war, 16 Sept. 1914. Exceptionally gifted, he stud. rather late under Michel Karren. Left 2 symphonies. The 2nd, left unfinished, was orchestrated by Florent Schmitt. First part of it ends on night preceding mobilistion of 1914.—A. C.

BRAZILIAN OPERA. See GÓMEZ, A. C.; MIGNONE, FRANCESCO.

BRAZYS, Theodore. Lithuanian priest and compr. *b.* Pabirze, in Birziai district, 20 Nov. 1870. Educated at Bauskis, Courland. Orgt.; then priest in 1900 at Batstoge. In 1905, entered Haberl's Church Music School, Ratisbon. Awarded diploma for 4-v. Mass and Fugue.

From 1907–17 teacher of singing at Vilna and dir. of Cath. choir, where he reformed the Gregorian chanting. Removed from Cath. post for having written a memorandum against Polish policy of aggression towards Lithuania.
    Masses; responses; vespers; *Completium* (4-v. *faux-bourdon*); *Dominica Resurrectionis* (*id.*); *Te Deum*; cantata *Nurimki Tevyne* (*Be tranquil, Fatherland*); Cantata of Commemoration on return of hostages from Bolshevik captivity; *Salute to the Lithuanian Flag*; coll. of Lithuanian songs; a Singing Manual (*Giedojimo mokykla*); Guide to Harmony (*Muzikos Teorija*) in Lithuanian; etc.—H. R.

BRECHER, Gustav. Ger.-Czechoslovak condr. compr. and author; *b.* Eichwald, near Teplitz, 5 Feb. 1879. Stud. in Leipzig. Has been condr. at Stadttheater, Leipzig; dir. of R. Opera, Vienna, 1900; then Hamburg Theatre, 1903; producer of opera in Cologne, 1911, and Frankfort-o-M., 1916.
    Symph. poem, *Rosmersholm*; social symphony, *Aus unsern Zeit*; str. 5tet op. 50; pf. sonata F mi. Biography of *Richard Strauss*; a remarkable book, *On Translations of Operas* (1911).—E. S.

BREITHAUPT, Rudolf Maria. Ger. pf. teacher; *b.* Brunswick, 11 Aug. 1873. Stud. law, philosophy, psychology, art and the science of music at Jena, Leipzig and Berlin; also pupil at Leipzig Cons. 1897, and lived in Vienna for a while; from 1901 has settled in Berlin as a writer on musical subjects and an authority on pf. teaching. From 1918 has been Martin Krause's successor as teacher at Stern's Cons.
    Natural Pf. Technique (1904, 3d ed. 1912); and, as second part of same, *The Principles of Pf. Technique* (1907; Fr. ed. 1908; Eng. ed. 1909); and third part, *Practical Studies* (1919); *Practical Exercise Book* (1914, 2 parts); also *Topical and Controversial Matters* (Collected Essays, 1908).—A. E.

BREMA, Marie. Eng. operatic singer; *b.* Liverpool. *Début* at Popular Concerts, 1891, after studying 3 months under George Henschel; stage *début* as Adrienne Lecouvreur at Oxford; operatic *début* 1891 at Shaftesbury Theatre under Lago; at R. Ital. Opera, London (under Grau), in 1892, sang Gluck's *Orfeo,* and Brünnhilde; in New York, the *Ring, Tristan,* at the Metropolitan under Mottl, Seidl, and others. First Eng. singer to sing at Bayreuth; sang in Brussels and Paris; 1911, produced *Orpheus* at Savoy Theatre with great success; in March 1912, toured provinces with Denhof Opera Co. Is now teaching at R. Coll. of Music, Manchester.—E.-H.

BRENET, Michel (Marie Bobillier). Fr. musicologist; with Romain Rolland and André Pirro, one of the great names in contemporary French musicology; *b.* Lunéville, 11 April, 1858; *d.* Paris, 4 Nov. 1918. Although an invalid, she worked with a patient and intelligent perseverance which cannot be sufficiently admired. She undertook deep and systematic research of old archives, and the thousands of jottings and notes left by her to the Bibliothèque Nationale are an inexhaustible treasure-trove for musicologists. She especially devoted herself to the history of sacred music in France; death struck her down before she could achieve the great work on the *Royal Choirs of the Kings of France* for which she had been amassing notes for over 30 years. M. B. was one of the first musicologists in France to apply to the history of music the systematic methods of research and classification now generally adopted in the study of general history documents. Her vast labour on archives have made possible a complete reconstruction of French musical life of the XVI and XVII centuries, and her notes will be consulted with advantage by musicologists for many years to come.

The Musicians of the " Sainte Chapelle" (1910, Picard); *Concerts in France under the Old Régime* (1900, Fischbacher); *Palestrina* (1910, Alcan); *Haydn* (1909, Alcan); *Military Music* (1917, Laurens); *Handel* (1903, Laurens); *Notes on the History of the Lute in France* (Turin, 1899, Bocca); *The Musical Library in France from 1653 to 1780* (Leipzig, 1907, Breitkopf), etc.—H. P.

BRET, Gustave. Fr. compr. *b.* Brignoles (Var), 1875. Pupil of Ch. M. Widor for organ at Cons., and of V. d'Indy at *Schola Cantorum.* Taught there himself, until 1908, lyric declamation, organ and improvisation. Called to replace his master Widor at organ of St.-Sulpice (1898–1903), he founded at Paris in 1904 the Société J. S. Bach (see SOCIETIES). Is now music critic of newspaper *L'Intransigeant.*

Oratorio in 2 parts, *Les Pèlerins d'Emmäus* for soli, chorus and orch. (Paris, Rouart), perf. 1903, Amsterdam, under Willem Mengelberg; unacc. choruses; songs, etc.—M. L. P.

BRETAGNE, Pierre. Fr. compr. *b.* Épinal, 1881. Pupil of Guy Ropartz at Cons. Nancy.

Str. 4tet; cello sonata; overture for play *Les Caprices de Marianne* (after Musset).—A. C.

BRETÓN, Abelardo. Span. compr.; son of famous *maestro* Tomás Bretón. Compr. of *Fantasía Gitana,* and other orch. works perf. by Orquesta Sinfónica and Orquesta Filarmónica, Madrid. Teaches harmony at R. Cons. de Música, Madrid.—P. G. M.

BRETÓN, Tomás. Span. compr. *b.* Salamanca, 29 Dec. 1850; *d.* Madrid, 2 Dec. 1923. Former condr. of orch. Unión Artístico-Musical (founded 1876), of the R. Opera House, Madrid, and the Soc. de Conciertos (now Orquesta Filarmónica); ex-dir. and lecturer of R. Cons. de Música, Madrid (1901); fellow of R. Acad. de Bellas Artes (1896). Honours: Cruz y Encomienda de Carlos III; Encomienda de Número de Alfonso XII; Golden Palms, Fr. Acad. Stud. under Arrieta at Madrid Cons.; 1st prize for compn. in 1872. Received grants from King Alfonso XII and the R. Acad. de Bellas Artes for study in Rome, Paris and Vienna. Of very humble parentage, he started to earn his living as an orch. player in Salamanca, when only ten. At 15, went to Madrid, played in cafés, theatres, toured with a mus. comedy company, and acted at Retiro Theatre as leader, and assistant-condr. to the celebrated waltz-compr. Olivier Metra. As condr. of Unión Artístico-Musical, he had to fight against establ. traditions, in order to introduce new works, amongst them the *Danse macabre* of Saint-Saëns, which had been rejected at rehearsals for its modernity by the veteran orch. Soc. de Conciertos. In 1891, Isaac Albeniz introduced B. to the London public as a condr. at two concerts at St. James's Hall. In one of these he perf. two works of his own, a symphony on classical lines and a minor work of Span. character. One of the leading critics advised him to

abandon the imitation of the classics and devote his talents to the music of his country. B. took the hint in the right spirit, for no Span. musician has ever worked with more fervour for the establishment of the Span. opera as a national institution, nor came so near to bringing it to a successful end. No lyric work in modern times has gone so deep into the Span. heart as his 1-act *zarzuela, La verbena de la paloma,* dealing with a typical aspect (picturesque and sentimental) of Madrid life. His most successful works, besides this, are the operas: *Los Amantes de Teruel,* 5 acts (1889), perf. throughout Spain and in Vienna and Prague, under compr.'s baton; *Garin,* 4 acts (1891), Spain and Prague; *La Dolores,* 3 acts (1895). *La Dolores* received 63 consecutive perfs. in Madrid, and 112 in Barcelona. It was also perf. with equal success in S. America, and was produced 11 years later at Milan and Prague. At the perf. of *Los Amantes de Teruel* at Prague, B. was invited to succeed Karl Muck as condr. of the Opera House Orch. He was often his own librettist, and wrote and lectured widely in favour of the establishment of Span. national opera.

Zarzuelas in 1 act: *Los dos caminos* (1874); *El 93* (1875); *El inválido* (1875); *Un chaparrón de maridos; Vista y sentencia* (1886); *Cuidado con los estudiantes* (1877); *Las señoritas de Conil* (1881); *El grito en el cielo* (1886); *La verbena de la paloma* (1893); *El Domingo de Ramos* (1894); *Las nieves* (1895); *El Guardia de Corps* (1897); *El Puente del Diablo; El reloj de Cuco* (1898); *Botín de guerra; La bien plantá* (1902); *El caballo del señorito; La Cariñosa* (1899); *La Generosa; Piel de oso* (1909); *Al alcance de la mano* (1911); *Las Percheleras* (1911); *Los Húsares del Czar* (1914); in 2 acts: *El alma en un hilo* (1874; in collab.); *El viaje de Europa* (1874); *María* (1875); *Los dos leones; Huyendo de ellas* (1877); *El bautizo de Pepín; Bonito país;* in 3 acts: *El Campanero de Begoña* (1878); *El Barberillo de Orán; Corona contra corona* (1879); *Los amores de un príncipe* (1881); *El clavel rojo* (1899); *Covadonga* (1901); *Las cortes de amor* (1916). Operas in 1 act: *Guzmán el Bueno* (1876); *El Certamen de Cremona* (1906); in 3 acts: *La Dolores* (1895); *Tabaré* (1913); *Don Gil* (1914); in 4 acts: *Garin* (1891); *Raquel* (1900); *Farinelli* (1901); in 5 acts: *Los Amantes de Teruel* (1889). Choral works: *Flors del Orta; Vizcaya; Eructavit cor meum; Oquendo; La primavera* (female vs. orch. and pf.); *El Apocalipsis,* oratorio. Chamber-music: pf. trio; 3 str. 4tets; pf. 5tet; 6tet, pf. fl. ob. clar. bsn. and horn. Orch.: *En la Alhambra; Los Galeotes,* symph. poem; *Salamanca,* symph. poem; *Elegía y Añoranzas;* suite, *Escenas Andaluzas;* vn. concerto (first perf. Queen's Hall, London, 21 Aug. 1923, by Angel Grande under Sir Henry Wood). (Unión Musical Española, Madrid).—P. G. M.

BRETON MUSIC. Collection by Maurice Duhamel (Rouart & Lerolle), who has also written a brochure, *Les 15 Modes de la Musique Bretonne.* See also BOURGAULT - DUCOUDRAY; CELLIER, LAURENT.—E.-H.

BREUNING-STORM, Gunna. Danish violinist; *b.* Copenhagen, 25 Jan. 1891. Pupil of Anton Svendsen, Copenhagen, and Henri Marteau. Made her *début* at an early age; toured extensively in Scandinavia and Germany. Since the war, has resided in Copenhagen, where she is the 1st-vn. member of the Copenhagen Str. Quartet (see CHAMBER-MUSIC PLAYERS).—A. H.

BRÉVAL, Lucienne (real name Lisette Schilling). Fr. s. singer; *b.* Berlin, 4 Nov. 1869. At 17, 1st prize for pf. at Geneva Cons. In Paris, 1890, 2nd prize (singing) and 1st prize (opera).

Her voice was rich and particularly warm in tone, and her imposing physique made her an admirable interpreter of lyrical rôles. For 30 years, she helped to maintain the fame of the Opéra in Paris. Her name will particularly be remembered by the numerous rôles she created in Wagnerian operas, e.g. Brünnhilde (*Valkyrie*); Eva (*Mastersingers*); also Chimène in *Le Cid* (Massenet), *Griseldis, Ariane, Pénélope* (Fauré), *Monna Vanna, La Burgonde, Pallas Athéné, Amy Robsart*.—M. B.

BRÉVILLE, Pierre Onfroy de. Fr. compr. *b.* Bar-le-Duc, 21 Feb. 1861. Stud. harmony at Paris Cons. under Théodore Dubois; soon afterwards went to César Franck for cpt., fugue and compn. Since then, he has divided his time between compn. and other mus. activities. For several years, taught cpt. at *Schola Cantorum*; and during the war took charge of a chamber-music class at Paris Cons. Has long been, and still is, one of most industrious members of committee of Société Nationale de Musique. For a time was mus. critic of *Mercure de France*; has written (jointly with H. Gauthier-Villars) an instructive booklet on d'Indy's *Fervaal*. As a creative artist he holds, among Fr. comprs., a place very much his own. His music has given rise to no discussion, but is held in high esteem. It is instinct with poetic feeling and sôber originality, and remarkable for its exquisite proportions and finish, as well as for the quiet intensity of its tone and colours.

Lyric drama, *Éros Vainqueur* (perf. Brussels, 1910); incidental music to Maeterlinck's *Sept Princesses*; a variety of vocal works (among which are *Sainte Rose de Lima* for s. solo and female chorus, *Hymne à Vénus* for 2 vs., wind and harp; a mass, and 2 books of songs); orch. suite, *Stamboul*, in 4 parts, also in pf.-solo form); overture for *La Princesse Maleine* for orch.; a few organ pieces; vn. sonata (Rouart); pf. sonata (*id.* 1922).—M. D. C.

BREWER, Alfred Herbert. Eng. orgt. and compr. *b.* Gloucester, 21 June, 1865. Educated Cath. School, Gloucester; Exeter Coll. Oxford; first organ scholar, R.C.M. London. Appointed orgt. and master of the choristers, Gloucester Cath. 1897; cond. Three Choirs Fest. 1898, 1901, 1904, 1907, 1910, 1913, 1922; instituted organ recitals in Gloucester Cath for elementary school children. Mus.Doc. Cantuar. 1905. His muse turns naturally to cheerful subjects.

Orch. Service in C (Glos. Fest. 1895); *Psalm XCVIII* (*id.* 1898); *Emmaus* (*id.* 1901); Dedication Ode (Worc. Fest. 1902); *The Holy Innocents* (Glos. Fest. 1904); *A Song of Eden* (Worc. Fest. 1905); 3 *Elizabethan Pastorals* (Hereford Fest. 1906); *Sir Patrick Spens* (Cardiff Fest. 1907); *In Springtime* (Leeds Fest. 1907); *England, My England* (Worc. Fest. 1908); *Age and Youth*, orch. (Queen's Hall Prom. 1908). *Summer Sports* (Glos. Fest. 1910); *Jillian of Berry* (pastorals), Hereford Fest. 1921 (mostly Novello); a large number of songs; pf. pieces; organ pieces (Novello; Boosey; Augener). —E. H.

BREWER, John Hyatt. Amer. compr. *b.* Brooklyn, N.Y., U.S.A., 18 Jan. 1856. For ten years a pupil of Dudley Buck. From 1871 to 1873, orgt. at various churches in Brooklyn. An orig. member of Apollo Club (male chorus) founded in 1877; its accompanist until death of Buck, whom he succeeded as condr. in 1903. 1899–1906, prof. of music, Adelphi Coll. Brooklyn.

One of founders of Amer. Guild of Orgts. in 1896. Mus.D. *h.c.* New York Univ. 1914. Over 200 anthems; 40 songs and cantatas (Schmidt; Schirmer; Ditson).—O. K.

BREWSTER-JONES, H. Compr. Lives at Adelaide, S. Australia. Founded his own orch. in Adelaide, which has given most of his orch. works.

3-act opera, *Deirdre of the Sorrows* (1915–17); 5-act mus. drama, *Jesus of Nazareth* (1918–23); 2-act mus. drama, *Undine* (started 1918, unfin.). Orch.: *Scherzo* in E mi. (1915; perf. by Brewster-Jones Symphony Orch.); ballet-music to *Call of France* (1917; Gala Review, Adelaide); *Nightingale Suite* (Adelaide, 1919); *Anzac Suite* (1917); *Rhapsody* (1918). *Pastoral Concerto*, pf. and orch. (1921); str. 4tet (1921); sonatas for pf. and cello; for pf. and vn.; for pf. and vla. (all 1921); many pf. pieces and songs, 4 books (Allan and Co. Melbourne).—E.-H.

BREZOVSCHEK, Ivan. Serbian opera-condr. *b.* Celje (Slovenia), 3 July, 1888. Stud. at Cologne Cons. under Steinbach; under Friedmann for pf. One of principal condrs. at National Theatre (New Opera House) in Belgrade.—T.F.D.

BRIAN, William Havergal. Eng. compr. *b.* Dresden, Staffs, 29 Jan. 1877. Stud. harmony under T. Hemmings, Stoke-on-Trent; otherwise self-taught; attended Richter's concerts as critic for the *Musical World*, just then (1905) revived. On 12 Jan. 1907, B.'s 1st *English Suite* was produced by Leeds Municipal Orch. under compr.; in Sept. same year by Sir Henry Wood at Queen's Hall. His *Festival Dance* (1908) was produced by Bantock in Birmingham in 1914; by Beecham in London, June, 1915. *Dr. Merryheart* (comedy-overture) was produced at Mus. League Fest. (1913) in Birmingham under Julius Harrison, and in following October by Sir Henry Wood at Queen's Hall. *For Valour* concert-overture (1907) was rewritten and perf. by late Coleridge-Taylor at a Crystal Palace Empire concert, 1910, and at a Strauss concert under Beecham in Birmingham, 1911; *Fantastic Variations*, perf. by Lyell-Taylor in Brighton, 1920; *In Memoriam* tone-poem, under Sir Landon Ronald with Scottish Orch. at Edinburgh, Dec. 1920. An *English Suite* No. 3 was produced by Sir Dan Godfrey, Jan. 1922. His music is highly original and often daring. He has even made excursions into Expressionism (pf. pieces). His choral writing is of a high order. The works mentioned above are all publ. by Breitkopf, Leipzig. Other works:

5 symph. dances and symph. variations from opera *The Grotesques* (ms.); choral works: *By the Waters of Babylon* (Breitkopf); *Cleopatra* (Bosworth; Southport Fest. 1909); *Die Wahlfahrt nach Kevlaar* (Heine; ms.); 8 pf. works (4 *Miniatures*, etc.), Augener; *Illuminations* (Chester); songs (Breitkopf; Enoch); part-songs (finest are publ. by Augener).—E.-H.

BRIDGE, Frank. Eng. compr. *b.* Brighton, 26 Feb. 1879. Trained at R.C.M. London as a vn. student; gained scholarship in compn. 1899, and stud. under Sir Charles Stanford for 4 years; in 1903, was already well known as a vla.-player; took part in Joachim Quartet on Wirth's indisposition in 1906. Cond. Marie Brema's opera seasons 1910–11, at Savoy Theatre, London; in autumn season of 1913 was one of condrs. of Raymond Roze's Eng. Opera season at Covent Garden; later, as condr. at Queen's Hall

Symphony Concerts and R. Philh. Soc. He cond. at Rochester, U.S.A. in 1923. His reputation as a chamber-music compr. dates from 1904. He is amongst the foremost Eng. chamber-music comprs. He always writes very finely for the strings; and takes high rank as a vla.-player both as soloist and in the English Quartet. He rose to a prominent position with his songs, when public opinion in 1916-17 awoke to recognition of the new xx century Eng. school of compn. F.R.C.M. *h.c.* 1924.

Orch.: Symph. poem, *Isabella* (ms.); *Dance Poem* (ms.); *Dance-Rhapsody* (ms.); tone-poem, *Summer*, written 1914 (Augener); 2 *Poems* (Richard Jefferies), orch. written 1915 (Augener, 1923); suite *The Sea* (Stainer & Bell). Str. orch.: *Lament*; Suite (1920; F. & B. Goodwin). Chamber-music: str. 6tet (Augener); pf. 5tet; str. 4tets, E mi. and G mi. (the latter known as *Boulogne 4tet*); also 3 *Idylls*; 3 *Novelletten* (id.); *Sally in our Alley*; *Cherry Ripe*; *Irish Melody* (*Londonderry Air*); *A Christmas Dance* (*Sir Roger De Coverley*)—all for str. 4tet (Augener); an orch. version of *Sir Roger* was played at the Queen's Hall; pf. 4tet; *Phantasy Trio*, pf. vn. cello; sonata, cello and pf. (W. Rogers); *Mélodie* and *Élégie*, cello and pf. (F. & B. Goodwin); *Morning Song*, id. (W. Rogers); *A Prayer* (Thomas à Kempis), chorus and orch.; sonnet, t. v. and orch. *Blow out, ye Bugles* (Rupert Brooke); numerous songs, pf. pieces, etc. (W. Rogers; Augener, etc.).—E.-H.

BRIDGE, Sir Frederick. Eng. orgt. compr. condr. *b.* Oldbury, Worcs, 5 Dec. 1844; *d.* London, 18 March, 1924. Choir-school, Rochester Cath.; orgt. Trinity Ch., Windsor, 1865-9; Manchester Cath. 1869-75; Westminster Abbey, 1875-1918; Gresham prof. from 1890; condr. R. Choral Soc. 1896-1922; King Edward prof. of music, London Univ. from its foundation 1902; Mus.Doc. Oxon. 1874; knighted 1897; M.V.O. 1902; C.V.O. 1911. Chairman of Trinity College of Music, London. Mus. dir. of the Madrigal Soc. London. His books on counterpoint had a wide vogue. He was very popular as a lecturer on mus. subjects. He composed in all branches, from dignified church music to humorous glees for male voices.

Oratorios: *Mount Moriah*; *The Repentance of Nineveh* (Novello). Cantatas: *Boadicea*; *Callirhoë* (Novello); *Hymn to the Creator*; *The Inchcape Rock*; *The Cradle of Christ*; organ sonata; male choruses; mixed choruses; church music; glees; 2 manuals: *Counterpoint*; *Double Counterpoint and Canon* (mostly Novello; some Bosworth). Books: *A Shakespeare and Music Birthday Book* (Bosworth, 1900); *Shakespearean Music* (Dent & Sons, 1923); *Samuel Pepys, Lover of Music* (1904); *A Westminster Pilgrim* (Novello, 1919); *The Old Cryes of London* (id. 1921).—E.-H.

BRIDGE, Joseph Cox. Brother of the above. Eng. orgt. *b.* Rochester, 1853. Organ scholar Exeter Coll. Oxford; orgt. Chester Cath. from 1877; condr. Chester Triennial Fest. 1879-1900; founder and condr. (31 years) Chester Mus. Soc.; Mus.Doc. Oxon. 1884; Mus.Doc. Dunelm. 1908; prof. of music, Univ. of Durham, from 1908.

Oratorio, *Daniel*; cantatas; *Requiem*; organ works; church music; part-songs; *Song of Horns*; *Chester Madrigalists*; *Recorders*; *Ludlow and the Masque of Comus*, etc.—E.-H.

BRITISH CHAMBER-MUSIC FROM 1880. Chamber-music made very little headway in England between 1880 and 1900. Parry had written his pf. 4tet in F minor in 1879, and followed it up by his string 4tet in G minor. A little later he wrote a str. 5tet in E flat and a 4tet for wind instruments. His chamber-music belongs mostly to the earlier part of his long career. Stanford, who was by far the ablest writer of chamber-music in this period, published his early str. 4tets in Germany (Eulenberg), his later 4tets in England, and his 7th and 8th (1919-20) still remain in ms. His great admiration for Brahms shows itself repeatedly in his chamber-works, and his personality is least marked in this kind of music; but his impeccable workmanship, found here as elsewhere, is eminently suited to this genre, and he shows great aptitude for the chamber-music style. But on the whole, chamber-music was little cultivated in England at that time, and native composers received small encouragement to write in this form.

Delius wrote his first str. 4tet in 1893, but it has not been heard in England. His other chamber-music belongs to a later period of his career—2nd str. 4tet, 1916-17; sonata for vn. and pf. 1915; sonata for cello and pf. 1917—all highly original and interesting works. Elgar only turned to chamber-music late in life. The year 1919 saw the production of his sonata for pf. and vn. op. 82, his str. 4tet, E mi. op. 83, and his 5tet for pf. and strings, A mi. op. 84. Although these three works are written in the style of German classicism, notably Schumann and Brahms, he yet retains his individuality—most in the vn. sonata, and least in the pf. 5tet.

W. H. Hurlstone was the first to break away from the German classical manner, though he falls unduly at times under the spell of the Bohemian, Dvořák. His early sonata for pf. and vn., the one for cello and pf. and his string 4tet in E mi. were produced in 1897-8-9; his 5tet for pf. and wind, the suite for clar. and pf. and the 4tet for pf. and str. waited till 1904 for a hearing. He stands at the beginning of the remarkable school of modern British chamber-music composers.

Walford Davies wrote many quartets between 1890 and 1895, but did not achieve popularity in this form until his *Peter Pan* str. 4tet of 1909. His delightful *Pastorals* for 4 solo voices, strings and pf. however had appeared in 1897. Ernest Walker has written some refined works for pf. and strings and for strings alone. Vaughan Williams's chief contribution is his characteristic song-cycle *On Wenlock Edge*, for tenor voice, strings and pf. (1909), very English in feeling, yet with the delicacy of French Impressionism. Joseph Holbrooke (*b.* 1878) provided more exciting matter in his approach to chamber-music, of which his titles give some indication: 5tet, pf. and str. (*Diabolique*) op. 44; *Miniature Suite* for wind instrs. op. 33; 4 dances for str. 6tet; *Pickwick* 4tet; *Russia* and *Belgium*, etc. His chamber-music is amongst his best work.

Tovey inclines to the older schools, especially that of Brahms, in his trio for pf. clar. and horn, his string 4tets, his *Air and Variations* (str. 4tet), *Elegiac Variations* (cello and pf.), etc. They are none the less valuable, for he is one of the most erudite of living musicians. Cyril Scott has contributed some very interesting pieces, a pf. 4tet, a surprisingly virile str. 4tet, a free-metre sonata for vn. and pf. and a charming *Pastoral Idyll* for voice, ob. and cello.

John B. McEwen has always cultivated chamber-music very assiduously and to good purpose, in his Phantasy 5tet and his 14 str. 4tets, the two most played being *Threnody* and *Biscay*. York Bowen is another composer to whom the concerted forms come very gratefully (7tet, 2 str. 4tets, 2 sonatas for vla. and pf., etc.). Rutland Boughton has also composed some chamber-works, which, however, cannot be classed with his more important stage-works. T. F. Dunhill's chamber-music is always pleasantly written, leaning to the intellectual side of music.

In 1915, John Ireland sprang to fame with his 2nd sonata for vn. and pf., one of the finest written since César Franck's of 1886. His 1st vn. sonata is a charming work in a lighter vein. His other chamber-music is all deeply felt and tensely expressed (2 pf. trios; a 4tet, etc.). Frank Bridge is another composer whose muse is well suited to this form, and his knowledge of strings is profound. Joseph Speaight created a *genre* of his own in his series of *Shakespearean Sketches*. The viola music of B. J. Dale, like that of York Bowen, is of the greatest importance. The latter has also written some fine str. 4tets and a 4tet for 4 violas. Amongst other gifted composers of this period are James Friskin (Quartet Phantasy, Trio Phantasy, pf. 5tet in C mi.), Arthur Hinton (pf. 5tet; pf. trio), Norman O'Neill, Waldo Warner, Ernest Austin, and many others. Nor is the slightly later generation less rich. First amongst these is Arnold Bax, with a charming pf. 5tet, a 5tet for str. and harp (1919), two picturesque and romantic vn. sonatas. Then mention must be made of Goossens, with his short picturesque pieces, *Jack o' Lanthorn*, *By the Tarn*, etc., Herbert Howells, J. N. Hay, W. J. Fenney, Armstrong Gibbs, J. R. Heath and E. J. Moeran (str. 6tet). Arthur Bliss is adventurous, even here; his chamber-music and pieces for clar. and voice, and other combinations, are amongst the finest works of the modern school. Almost alone at present, stands a young and promising composer in the cosmopolitan atonal manner, W. T. Walton, whose str. 4tet played in London and Salzburg in 1923 showed him well able to hold his own amongst the younger Continental writers.

Amongst women composers, Ethel Smyth holds easily the first place. She is not at her best in chamber-music, and her early string quartets, recently revived in England, sound outmoded and not very individual.

The taste for chamber-music, even more than the taste for the intimate forms of poetry which awakened at the same time, has undergone a sudden and remarkable growth in Britain since 1914, and a whole school of gifted and interesting native composers responded to the stimulus. No nation is now more richly endowed with chamber-music players and composers, and this form of music appears to be well adapted to the racial characteristics of Britons.—E.-H.

BRITISH MUSIC SOCIETY. Founded in 1918 by Dr. Eaglefield-Hull. Its aims are to fight for a recognised place for music in education, to stimulate appreciation of music by lectures and concerts, to champion the cause of British comprs. and performers at home and abroad, to encourage the establishment of music libraries, to co-ordinate all musical activity in the United Kingdom for greater strength. Headquarters in London with Sir Hugh Allen as chairman; numerous active centres and branches throughout the world. The central London office (3 Berners St. W. 1) is also the official home of the International Soc. for Contemporary Music. Monthly journal, the *Music Bulletin*. Gen. Sec. Arthur Reade, M.A.—G. O.

BRITISH ORCHESTRAL MUSIC FROM 1880. Up to within ten years before the birth of the xx century, orchestral composition in Britain was the least cultivated form of the musical art. The reason for this is to be found in the great poverty of orchestras. The North of England and the Midlands have still to draw on Leeds and Manchester for wood-wind and other players; all Scotland is dependent chiefly on the Scottish Orchestra, centred in Glasgow, notwithstanding the establishment by Prof. Tovey of the efficient Reid Orchestra in Edinburgh. The Three Choirs and other festivals in the South and West of England draw their orchestras from London, which city, together with Manchester (Hallé Orchestra), affords the only opening for orchestral composers. The pioneers amongst these were Parry, Stanford and Mackenzie. Parry's orchestral works (4 symphonies, including the *English* Symphony of 1889; Symphonic Variations [1897]; overtures, etc.) were important not so much for what they achieved in themselves, as for what they made possible. Elgar, for instance, owes more to Parry than is usually acknowledged. Mackenzie introduced the national and the topical into his well-scored works (*Scottish Rhapsody, Canadian Rhapsody, Britannia Overture, London Day by Day, Pibroch, Scottish* pf. concerto, etc.). Stanford, with a still finer style, also struck the national note, in his 7 symphonies (the 3rd, called the *Irish*) and 5 Irish Rhapsodies.

The most Scottish of composers, Hamish MacCunn, supplied 3 very picturesque overtures, *The Land o' the Mountain and the Flood* (1887), *The Dowie Dens of Yarrow* (1888) and *The Ship o' the Fiend* (1888). The works of Delius were mostly produced in Germany some years before their performance in England; but they quickly secured a firm hold through their charming originality and delightful scoring, though the moods are rather long-drawn-out at times. His *Appalachia* was written in 1896, *Paris* in 1899, *Brigg Fair* in 1907, 1st *Dance Rhapsody* 1908, the 2nd, 1916, *North Country Sketches* 1913–14. William Wallace wrote tone-poems, *The Passing of Beatrice* (1892), *Wallace* (1905), *Villon* (1909) and called his symphony of 1899 *The Creation*. Elgar's finest orch. work is his *Enigma Variations* (1899). His 2 symphonies (No. 1, A flat, 1907–8; No. 2, E flat, 1911) contain much fine material, splendidly scored, but raise the question as to the suitability of the symphony form to his muse. His overtures (*In the South, Cockaigne, Froissart*) are thoroughly successful. His tone-poem *Falstaff* seems somewhat hampered by its over-elaborate programme. His concertos for vn. and for cello are amongst the finest of modern works. Nor must his early *Serenade* and his *Introduction and Allegro* for strings be overlooked.

Granville Bantock's orchestral works were the most advanced of his time in technique and handling. He began with tone-poems—*Thalaba* (1900), *Dante and Beatrice* (1902), *Fifine at the Fair* (1912), *The Witch of Atlas* (1902), *The Pierrot of the Minute* (1908). His finest orch. work is the *Hebridean Symphony* (1914).

Another powerful composer of programmatic tendencies is Holbrooke. *The Raven* was produced under Manns at Crystal Palace in 1900; his *Ulalume* at a London Symphony Orchestra concert in 1904, his *Queen Mab* at Leeds in the same year and *The Bells* at Birmingham in 1906. His *Apollo and the Seaman*, given under Beecham at the Queen's Hall in 1907, followed the poem (by Trench) closely, having it thrown on a lantern screen, verse by verse.

A composer of a very different type is Vaughan Williams whose *London Symphony* has been as much played abroad as at home. It was first heard in the spring of 1914. It waited until 1922 (2 Jan.) for its successor, *A Pastoral Symphony*, a much finer work. *The Lark Ascending* for vn. and orch. was first played at a British Music Society concert in 1921, with Marie Hall as soloist. After him, the two outstanding orchestral composers are Holst and Bax. The former wrote his *Beni Mora* in 1910, but made his great success with his suite *The Planets* (1915–16) produced in part at a R. Philh. concert in 1919, but in full at the British Music Society congress in 1921 under Adrian Boult. Arnold Bax is one of the leading figures in British music of to-day. He is a composer of pure, absolute music. His 1st symphony was produced by Albert Coates at a London Symphony Orchestra concert in Dec. 1922. His 2nd symphony, *Spring Fire* (1912–13) still awaits performance. His *Garden of Fand* (1912–13) has been repeatedly played in England. It was given in Paris under Kussevitzky with great success in May 1923. His *Tintagel* and *Symphonic Variations* for pf. and orch. are also important.

Hamilton Harty, the condr. of the Hallé Orchestra, has contributed some valuable works —*With the Wild Geese, Comedy Overture*, and a fine vn. concerto. Cyril Scott has written a *Christmas Overture*, 2 *Passacaglias, La Belle Dame sans Merci, Aubade*, etc. and a characteristic pf. concerto. John Ireland has only written two orch. pieces, *A Forgotten Rite* (1912) and the symphonic rhapsody, *Mai-Dun* (1921), both very fine works.

Arthur Bliss's Colour Symphony made a sensation at the Worcester Festival of 1922 (London, 1923) by its daring harmony, polyphony and orchestration. It is a very virile work, in the Neo-classical style, and his migration to America in 1923 was a great loss to English music. Goossens's *Eternal Rhythm* (1920) and his *Sinfonietta* (Feb. 1923) show a masterly handling of the orchestra as well as of material. In 1923, McEwen's *Solway Symphony* was successfully produced. Amongst other gifted orch. composers are Frederic Austin, Hubert Bath, W. H. Bell, York Bowen, Havergal Brian, Frank Bridge, Howard Carr, Eric Coates, E. Bristow Farrar, John Foulds, Balfour Gardiner, Julius Harrison, James Lyon, Norman O'Neill, Montagu Phillips, Roger Quilter, Cyril Rootham, Arthur Somervell, Joseph Speaight, and others.

Although the remarkable impetus given to chamber-music in Britain seems to have temporarily diverted many composers from the orchestral forms, yet the galaxy of British orchestral composers, ranging from Elgar, Delius and Bantock on the one hand, to Bax and Bliss on the other, can by no means be said to be lacking in its contribution to the finest orchestral music of the world.—E.-H.

BRIUSSOVA, Nadejda Jacevlovna (*accent on the U*). Russ. pianist and writer on music; *b.* Moscow, 7/19 Nov. 1881. Sister of the poet Valery Briussof. Pupil of S. I. Tanéief (theory), and Igumnof (pf.); teacher of theory at People's Cons. of Music, Moscow (1906–16) and at Shaniavsky Univ. there (1917–19); now prof. at Moscow Cons. (from 1921) and its pro-rector (from 1922) As theorist, she is a follower of Javorsky. Member of Russ. Acad. of Art-Sciences and of State Inst. of Mus. Science. Wrote *Musical Science; Temporal and Extensional Construction of Form*, etc.—V. B.

BROADCASTING. See WIRELESS MUSIC.

BROCKWAY, Howard A. Amer. compr. *b.* Brooklyn, N.Y., U.S.A., 22 Nov. 1870. Stud. pf. (1890–5) under Barth and compn. under Boise in Berlin. Gave a concert, 23 Feb. 1895, in Berlin, including pf. pieces of his own compn., a symphony in D mi. op. 12 (played in America by Boston Symphony Orch., 5 April, 1907) and a vn. sonata. 1895–1903, teacher in New York. 1903–10, taught pf. and compn. at Peabody Inst. Baltimore. From 1910 again in New York; pf. teacher at David Mannes School. Excellent workmanship and refined mus. taste mark his works. He is a member of the National Inst. of Art and Letters.

Vn. sonata, G mi. op. 9 (Schlesinger, 1894); *Cavatina*, vn. and small orch. op. 13 (*id.* 1895); *Romanze*, for vn. and pf. op. 18 (*id.* 1897); *Sylvan Suite* for orch. op. 19 (Schirmer, 1900); *The Minstrel's Curse*, ballad for 8 vs. unacc. op. 27 (*id.* 1902); *Sir Olaf*, ballad for mixed chorus and orch. op. 37 (*id.* 1913); pf. pieces; vn. pieces (Church); songs (Church; Novello). With Lorraine Wyman, 2 colls. of folk-songs; *Lonesome Tunes* (Gray, 1916); 20 *Kentucky Mountain Songs* (Ditson, 1920). Consult Hughes, *Contemporary American Composers* (pp. 298–304).—O. K.

BRODER, Annie Glen. British pianist and writer; *b.* Agra, India. Trained at National Training School and R.C.M. London. On completing her studies, gave considerable attention to art of accompanying. Her book *How to Accompany* (Robert Cocks) was first textbook publ. on this subject. Lectured extensively on this subject; adjudicator at R.A.M. for Santley Acc. Prize and Heathcote Song Prize. After her marriage in 1900, left England for Western Canada where she has accomplished much valuable work of a pioneer nature. In addition to her teaching, she has acted as special correspondent for the *Toronto Globe*, *Manitoba Free Press* and other papers. Lives at Calgary, Canada.—L. S.

BRODERSEN, Friedrich. Ger. barit. singer; *b*. Bad Boll (Würtemberg), 1 Dec. 1873. Distinguished stage and concert singer. Was intended for an architect, but stud. singing at same time under Heinrich Bertram (Theodor Bertram's father). In 1903 went to the Stadttheater, Nuremberg ; from there he was engaged by E. v. Possart in 1903 for Munich Opera House, to which he is still attached (1907, private Court singer), and in which he has played all the lyric, dramatic and character parts of a baritone's repertoire. In songs has distinguished himself as interpreter of Strauss and Schubert (*Winterreise*). His daughter, Linde Brodersen (*b*. Munich, 22 June, 1903), assists him as his accompanist.—A. E.

BRODSKY, Adolph. Russ. violinist; *b*. Taganrog, 21 March, 1851. Stud. Vienna Cons. 1860-6; member of Vienna Court Orch.; 2nd vn. of famous Hellmesberger (his teacher's) Quartet; toured in Russia 1870-4; condr. of Kief Symphony Orch. 1878-80; toured Austria, Germany, England, 1880-3; appeared in London at Richter concerts, 1882, 1883; head-prof. Leipzig Cons. (where he formed his famous Brodsky Quartet, 1883-91; toured U.S.A. and Canada, 1891-4; principal R. Manchester Coll. of Music since 1895; leader of Hallé Orch. and temporary condr. after Hallé's death; founded Brodsky Quartet in Manchester in Oct. 1895. A powerful master of the vn.; was first to play his friend Tchaikovsky's vn. concerto. In 1902, Mus.Doc. *h.c.* Victoria Univ. Manchester.—E.-H.

BROGI, Renato. Ital. compr. *b*. Sesto Fiorentino, 25 Feb. 1873. Stud. at Florence and Milan. When 23 he gained the Steiner Prize of Vienna with a 1-act opera, *La prima notte*, perf. successfully in Florence, 1898. He subsequently comp. two other operas: *Oblio*, and *Isabella Orsini*; the latter was perf. in Florence in 1920 and then in Rome and South America.
Vn. concerto; str. 4tet, B mi.; pf. trio, B mi.; several song albums; 2 books of valses.—R. F.

BROMAN, K. Natanael. Swedish pianist and compr. *b*. Kolsva, 11 Dec. 1887. Stud. R. Cons. Stockholm, 1902-12 (pf., compn.), then pf. under Ignaz Friedman (1912-13), compn. under Carl Kämpff. Excellent concerto, ensemble and acc. player.
Symph. poem, *Fritiof och Ingeborg* (Gothenburg, 1912); ballad, *Kung Lif och Drottning Död* (Stockholm, 1913); sonata, vn. and pf.; *Romance*, vn. and pf.; songs; pf. pieces.—P. V.

BRONDI, Maria Rita. Ital. guitar concert-player; *b*. Rimini, 5 July, 1889. Gained a special reputation in Italy and abroad as a guitar-player on account of the artistic character with which she invests her perfs., which aim

at reviving the old local and national music and songs. She has also studied the lute.—D. A.

BRONSART, Hans von. Ger. compr. *b*. Berlin, 11 Feb. 1830; *d*. Munich, 3 Nov. 1913. Pupil of Dehn in Berlin and Franz Liszt in Weimar; at first a concert pianist. Dir. of Euterpe Concerts in Leipzig, 1860-2, and of Concerts of Soc. of Friends of Music, Berlin, 1865-6; manager of Court Theatre, Hanover, 1867; gen. manager in Weimar in 1887. Retired in 1895. In 1898 at Achensee, Tyrol, but spent his last years in Munich. He was one of last survivors of great "New-German" period in music. Married in 1862 the pianist and compr. Ingeborg Starck (1840-1913).
Pf. concerto, F sharp mi. (played by v. Bülow); pf. trio, G mi. op. 1; *Phantasy of Spring*, orch.; symphony with chorus, *In den Alpen*; dramatic tonepoem, *Manfred* (Weimar, 1901); str. 6tet; cantata, *Christnacht*; pf. works.—A. E.

BROOME, Edward. Brit. orgt. choral condr. compr. *b*. Manchester in 1868. At an early age he went to live in N. Wales and received his early instruction at Bangor. Chorister at Bangor Cath.; assistant-orgt. there; orgt. of Bangor Choral Soc. and condr. of Penrhyn Male Chorus. In 1893, visited Chicago and won Eisteddfod Prize at World's Fair. From there, went to Canada, and, after living some time in Brockville, went to Montreal, as orgt. at Amer. Ch. and condr. of McGill Univ. Glee Club. 1896, went to Toronto to succeed Dr. A. S. Vogt as orgt. at Jarvis Street Baptist Ch., and in 1898 became condr. of Toronto Oratorio Soc. (see CHORAL SOCIETIES), which position he now holds. Has publ. over 70 works, chiefly anthems, motets, songs, etc. (Novello). Has won 8 National Eisteddford prizes in compn., last one being £50 prize for best dramatic cantata awarded at Cardiff in 1900. Holds degree of Mus.Doc. Trinity (Toronto) University.—L. S.

BROTHIER, Yvonne. Fr. light operatic singer; *b*. St.-Julien l'Ars (Vienne) 6 June, 1889. Entered Cons. 1910; 1913, 1st prize (singing), also 1st prize (*opéra-comique*). Engaged by La Monnaie Theatre, Brussels, 1914; 1915, went to Opéra-Comique, Paris; *début* in *Lakmé*. Sang usual repertoire; created rôles in *Ping-Sin* (1917), *Le Sauteriot* (1920), *Masques et Bergamasques* (1920). Possesses a voice of even quality and great purity, sufficiently versatile for her varied repertoire.—A. R.

BRUCH, Max. German composer; *b*. Cologne, 6 Jan. 1838; *d*. Berlin-Friedenau, 2 Oct. 1920. Pupil of Karl Breidenstein. Mozart Foundation Scholar, 1853-57, and as such, became the special pupil of Ferdinand Hiller, Karl Reinecke (till 1854) and Ferdinand Breunung. After a short stay in Leipzig, lived as music teacher (1858-61) in Cologne, where he produced his first dramatic composition, a musical play by Goethe, *Scherz, List und Rache* (op. 1). In 1861 he entered upon an extended tour for the purpose of study, which ended in Mannheim (1862-64). Here his opera *Loreley* (op. 16) was produced in 1863. The text was taken from that written by Geibel for Mendelssohn. In 1864–5 he was again on his travels. Musical director in Coblence, 1865–7, Court-conductor at Sondershausen, 1867–70. After 5 years (1873–8) in Bonn, entirely devoted to composition, with two journeys to England for the production of his works, he was appointed director of the Stern Choral Society, Berlin (on Stockhausen's retirement) in 1878. In 1880 he succeeded Benedict as director of the Philharmonic Society in Liverpool. He married Klara Tuczek the Berlin singer in 1881 (she died at Friedenau, end of Aug. 1919). In 1883 he gave up his position in Liverpool to take over the directorship of the Orchestral Society in Breslau (in succession to Bernhard Scholz), remaining there till the end of 1890. In 1891 he received the title of Professor, when placed at head of an academic advanced class in composition at the Berlin Academy. In 1893, the University of Cambridge conferred on him Mus.Doc. h.c., and in 1898 he was elected a corresponding member of the French Academy of Arts. Bruch was for a long period the President of the Music Section of the Senate of the Royal Academy of Arts, Berlin (since 1913, honorary member), and member of the board of management of the Royal High School for Music. In 1908 he received the Prussian Order of Merit for Arts and Sciences. In 1918 he was granted the Th.D. and Ph.D. (Berlin). In the autumn of 1910, he retired and settled at Friedenau, near Berlin.

For mixed chorus and orch.: *Schön Ellen*, op. 24 (1867); *Odysseus*, op. 41 (1872); *Arminius*, op. 43 (1875); *Das Lied von der Glocke*, op. 45 (1878); *Achilleus*, op. 50 (1885); *Das Feuerkreuz*, op. 52 (1889); *Moses*, op. 67, sacred oratorio (1894); *Gustav Adolf*, op. 73, secular oratorio (1898); *Nal und Damajanti*, op. 78 (1903); *Jubilate, Amen*, op. 3; *Die Birken und die Erlen*, op. 8; *Die Flucht der heiligen Familie*, op. 20; *Rorate Cœli*, op. 29; *Römische Leichenfeier*, op. 34; *Kyrie, Sanctus and Agnus Dei*, op. 35, double choir; *Lied vom Deutschen Kaiser*, op. 37; *Dithyrambe*, op. 39, 6-v.; *Gruss an die heilige Nacht*, op. 62; *Hymne*, op. 64; *Easter Cantata*, op. 81; *Die Macht des Gesanges*, op. 87; 5-v. choral songs with organ, op. 69; mixed chorus *a cappella* op. 38 and op. 60; *The Voice of Mother Earth* (with orch. op. 91); *Trauerfeier für Mignon* for double chorus, soli and orch. op. 93.

For female vs., soli and orch.: *Frithjof auf seines Vaters Grabhügel*, op. 27; *The Flight into Egypt* and *Morgenstunde*, op. 31; *The Priestess of Isis*, op. 30 (contr. and orch.); *Christkindlieder* for female chorus, soli and pf. op. 92; female chorus, *a cappella*, op. 6; 3 duets for s. and contr. op. 4 (with pf.).

For male chorus and orch.: *Römischer Triumphgesang*; *Das Wessobrunner Gebet*; *Lied der Städte* and *Scotland's Tears*, op. 19; *Song of the Three Holy Kings*, op. 21; *Frithjof*, op. 23 (1864; the choral work which first made his name known); *Salamis*, op. 25; *Normannenzug*, op. 32; *Thermopylæ*, op. 53; *Leonidas*, op. 66; *Der letzte Abschied des Volkes*, op. 76; and the choral songs, op. 19 (*a cappella*), op. 48 (*id.*), op. 68 (with orch.), op. 72 (*a cappella*), op. 74.

Songs with pf.: *Scotch Songs*; *Hebrew Melodies*, and op. 7, 13, 15, 17, 18, 33, 49, 54, 59, 90.

Instr. works: Vn. concertos, op. 26, G mi. dedicated to Joseph Joachim (C. F. W. Siegel, Leipzig, his most celebrated work), op. 44 and 58 (both in D mi.); *Konzertstück*, vn. with orch. op. 84; *Romance*, vn. op. 42, A mi.; *Scottish Phantasy*, op. 46; *Adagio appassionato*, op. 57; *In Memoriam* (*Adagio*, op. 65); *Serenade*, op. 75, all with orch.; *Swedish Dances*, op. 63; *Swedish and Russian Songs and Dances*, op. 79, for vns. and pf. (also for orch.).

For cello and orch.: *Kol Nidrei* (Hebrew melody), op. 47; *Canzone*, op. 55; *Adagio on Celtic Melodies*,

op. 56; *Ave Maria*, op. 61; and for cello and pf., 4 pieces, op. 70.

Symph. works: 3 symphonies: op. 28, E flat, op. 36, F mi. and op. 51, E ma.

Chamber-music: 2 str. 4tets, op. 9, C mi. and op. 10, E; trio, op. 5, C mi.; for pf. op. 2, 11, 12, 14.

Operas: *Scherz, List und Rache*, op. 1 (Cologne, 1858); *Hermione*, op. 40 (Berlin, 1872).—A. E.

BRUCKEN-FOCK, Gerard von. Dutch compr. and painter; b. Middelburg (Zeeland), 28 Dec. 1859. Stud. music in Utrecht under Richard Hol and in Berlin under W. Bargiel.

Oratorio, *Christ's Return*; a grand symphony; numerous songs and pf. pieces.—W. P.

BRUCKNER, Anton. Austrian composer; b. Ansfelden (Upper Austria), 4 Sept. 1824; d. Vienna, 11 Oct. 1896. One of the most important Austrian composers; came of a family of village schoolmasters. The deepest impressions, for his future evolution, can be traced back to his childhood, when he received decisive impulses from the church-music which still cultivated the traditions of the baroque and classical periods. As a boy of 10, he played the organ in public, and the influence of this instrument may be seen in nearly everything he wrote, particularly in scoring. After his father's death in 1837, he came to St. Florian monastery as choir-boy. There he learned the violin and piano. From 1837 to 1840 he studied at Linz for teaching, and took his first appointment in 1841 at Windhag, and 1843 at Kronsdorf, where he received his first harmony lessons. In 1845 he returned as teacher and assistant-organist to St. Florian, where a very famous organ deepened his knowledge of playing. Although in 1853 he went to Vienna to be examined on the organ, extemporising a double fugue to Simon Sechter (the famous counterpoint teacher), he had not then decided to follow music. But in 1855 he became organist at Linz, where he played until 1868. Although he had already attained a masterly theoretical technique, he took counterpoint lessons from Sechter in Vienna during his holidays, for five years. At the examination, one of the examiners, Herbeck, spoke the famous words, " He should have examined us." In 1861–3, Bruckner studied formal analysis and instrumentation under Otto Kitzler at Linz, and wrote his 1st symphony, in F minor (unpublished). At this time, he heard *Tannhäuser* at Linz and studied the score; his admiration for Wagner, and the influence of Wagner's instrumentation on him, then began. In 1865–6 he composed his 2nd symphony, in C minor (publ. as first symphony; first performance, Linz, 1868). After Sechter's death in 1867, Bruckner was nominated organist at the Court Chapel, professor at Vienna Conservatoire, lector for theory at the University in 1875, a Doctor (h.c.) of the University in 1891. He composed the greater part of his works in Vienna. The symphonies, 3rd (dedicated to Wagner), 4th (*Romantic*), 7th (with so-called Funeral Music to Wagner's memory) and the unfinished 9th (his *Te Deum* for mixed choir is usually performed as *Finale*) are the most famous. Of his church music, his Masses in E minor and F minor are the best-known.

As a symphonic composer, Bruckner continues the line of the Austrian classical period. One can see very plainly a continuation from Schubert. The proportions of the movements are greater than usual; the instrumentation is richer. In the *Adagios* of the 7th, 8th, and 9th symphonies he uses the 4 Wagner-tubas. His first movements represent a heroic feeling of struggle, in the manner of Beethoven. The *Scherzi* are often in the style of peasant-dances. Bruckner gives his best in the *Adagios*, especially those of 4th, 7th and 8th symphonies, where there is a deeply religious feeling and a beautiful body of tone. (See AUSTRIAN ORCHESTRAL MUSIC; CHORALE-SYMPHONIE; GERMAN ORCHESTRAL MUSIC.)

Bruckner was very late in obtaining a name as a composer and his works have been ignored by the greater public, on account of the animosity of his followers towards those of Brahms. Musical life in Vienna at the end of the XIX century was divided by the open conflict of the *Brucknerianer* and *Brahmsianer*, and even now this divergence continues. Nikisch, and Hermann Levi, made Bruckner's name known in Germany. In Vienna it was the sustained work of Ferdinand Löwe and Franz Schalk, who edited and revised the scores and made piano arrangements, which rendered him famous.

9 symphonies; str. 5tet in F; 3 masses; *Te Deum*; *Psalm CL*; several vocal compns. (Univ. Ed.). Biographies: R. Louis, *A. B.* (1905); Franz Graflinger (1911); consult also A. Halm, *Die Symphonien A. Bs.* (1914).—EG. W.

BRUGNOLI, Attilio. Ital. pianist and compr. *b.* Rome, 7 Sept. 1880. Was pupil at Naples Cons. (under Rossomandi for pf. and Serrao for compn.). After having gained high reputation as concert-player, entered in 1906 the Parma Cons. as teacher, whence he went in 1920 to the R. Music Inst. Florence. Has comp. several works specially for his own instr.; also occupies himself with writing didactic propaganda in the principal reviews.—D. A.

BRÜLL, Ignaz. Moravian compr. *b.* Prossnitz, 7 Nov. 1846; *d.* Vienna, 17 Sept. 1907. Pupil of Julius Epstein (pf.) and Johann Rufinatscha and Otto Dessoff (compn.); was concert pianist till quite old age. 1872-8, pf. teacher at Horak's Pf. School, Vienna; 1881, co-dir. of same. He belonged to Viennese Brahms circle; cultivated as pf.-compr. a pleasing late-romantic style, and as opera-compr. paid special attention to *Spieloper*.

Overture to *Macbeth*, op. 46; overtures, *In the Forest* and *Overture Pathétique*, op. 98; 3 orch. serenades, op. 29; symphony E mi. op. 31; vn. concerto, op. 41; 2 pf. concertos; *Konzertstücke*, pf. and orch. op. 88; chamber-music and several pieces for pf; especially operas: *The Beggar of Samarkand* (1864); *The Golden Cross* (1875) (his most successful work); *Der Landfriede* (1877); *Bianca* (1879); *Queen Mariette* (1883); *Glory* (1886); *The Stone Heart* (1888); *Gringoire* (1892); *Checkmate* (1893); *The Hussar* (1898); ballet, *A Tale of the Champagne* (1896). Consult Hermine Schwarz, *Ignaz Brüll and his Circle* (Vienna, 1922).—A. E.

BRUMAGNE, Fernand. Belgian compr. *b.* Namur, 11 Nov. 1887. Pupil of Léon Du Bois at Brussels Cons., and of d'Indy (*Schola Cantorum*, Paris); wrote *L'Invasion*, lyric drama

(Brussels, 1919); *Judith of Bethulia*, ballet; *Le Miracle de Saint-Antoine*, miracle-play.—E. C.

BRUN, Fritz. Swiss condr. and compr. *b.* Lucerne, 18 Aug. 1878. Stud. at Cologne Cons. (1896-1901) and after being teacher at Dortmund Cons. for pf. and theory, became condr. of Symphony Concerts at Berne, where he has been dir. of the Cäcilienverein (mixed choir) and the Liedertafel (male choir) since 1907. His compns. although influenced by Brahms, show a very personal style and, particularly in the slow movements of his symphonies, he attains the highest degree of expression. In 1921, the Univ. of Berne gave him the Doctorate, *h.c.*

3 symphonies (2nd in B, publ. in Swiss National Ed.); symph. poem, *Aus dem Buche Hiob* (*From the Book of Job*); vn. sonata; numerous songs (Zurich, Hüni).—F. H.

BRUNCK, Constantin. Ger. compr. *b.* Nuremberg, 30 May, 1884. Pupil of Municipal School of Music, Nuremberg; 1904 of Humperdinck and Rüfer, Berlin; dir. of German Male Choral Soc., Milan; chorus-master in Nuremberg since 1911, as well as critic to the *Fränkischen Post*. As writer, he occupied himself largely with social questions affecting the profession. The Soc. for the Publ. of Composers' own Works—the Meistersingerverlag in Nuremberg—is a result of his endeavours, and has been under his direction since 1920.

Numerous songs (23 publ.) and some pf. pieces; *Overture to a Rococo Play* for small orch.—A. E.

BRUNEAU, Louis Charles Bonaventure Alfred. Fr. compr. *b.* Paris, 1 March, 1857. Stud. cello and compn. (under Massenet) at Paris Cons. which he left in 1881 after having obtained 2nd *Grand Prix* for compn. He has written a few symph. works, among which the best-known are tonepoem, *La Belle au Bois Dormant* (1884) and *Penthésilée* for v. and orch. (1888); songs, and a *Requiem* (1889). But it is almost solely as a writer of dramatic music that he has made his mark. His first important score, *Le Rêve* (whose libretto was written by Louis Gallet after Zola's novel) was produced at Opéra-Comique in June, 1891. It is a work of striking originality and power, which has exercised a great influence upon the development of the modern Fr. school. From that time on he worked in increasingly close co-operation with Zola. Louis Gallet wrote the libretto of *L'Attaque du Moulin* (1893) after Zola's story, but Zola himself was responsible for poems of *L'Ouragan* (1901), *L'Enfant Roi* (1905) and of the unpubl. *Lazare* (1905). After Zola's death, Bruneau himself adapted *La Faute de l'abbé Mouret* (1907) and *Naïs Micoulin* (1907) for the stage. Another work on a poem by Zola, *Les Quatre Journées*, remains unpubl. Critics of his works are unanimous in praising *Le Rêve*, but there is no such agreement as regards his later works. He has many enthusiastic admirers (such as Arthur Hervey in England), but in some quarters there is a tendency to consider his technique rather crude. His uncompromising genuineness, however, has never been questioned. He has acted as mus. critic to *Le Figaro* and since 1904 writes in *Le Matin*. 3

vols. of essays by him have appeared: *Musiques d'hier et de demain* (1900); *La Musique française* (1901); *Musiques de Russie et Musiciens de France* (1903).

Consult: Bibliography in Octave Séré (*q.v.*); Arthur Hervey, *A. B.* (London, J. Lane); Julien Tiersot, *Un Demi-siècle de musique française* (Paris, 1918, Alcan).—M. D. C.

BRUNOLD, Paul. Fr. pianist; *b.* Paris, 14 Oct. 1875. Pupil of Raoul Pugno and of Xavier Leroux at Cons. Paris; later, of Marmontel and Paderewski. He specialises in ancient music, which he plays on a harpsichord of XVIII century. Publ. (in collab. with Henry Expert) anthology of *Maîtres françaises du clavecin des XVII*e *et XVIII*e *siècles* (Senart). Is titular orgt. of Grand Organ, St.-Gervais, the instr. of the Couperins.—F. R.

BRUSSELMANS, Michel. Belgian compr. *b.* Paris (Belgian parentage), 12 Feb. 1886. Stud. at Brussels Cons. under Paul Gilson. Prize from the *Morgendstar* in 1910 (for song) and at the *Concours de Rome* in 1911. In 1914, obtained Agniez Prize for symph. poem. Became prof. of harmony and compn. Since 1922, has been editing the Jamin publications in Paris. Public attention was drawn to B. mainly after perf. at Ysaye Concerts in Brussels (1913) of his *Kermesse flamande*, a set of symphonic pictures. These are quite original and decidedly modern in tone, and depict the visions of Breughel the Elder. His music, although extraordinarily independent in style, yet shows a purely Flemish temperament. His sure instinct, however, leads him to seek inspiration outside the frontiers of his country, thus widening and refining it.

Rapsodie, on a popular air (Antwerp, 1911); *Ouverture fériale* (Brussels, 1912); *Kermesse flamande* (1913); *Hélène de Sparte*, symph. poem on Emile Verhaeren's tragedy (Brussels, 1915); *Les Néréides*, tone-picture, vn. harp and orch. (1915); pf. and vn. sonata, B mi. (1915, Senart); sonata, cello and pf. (1916, *id.*); numerous songs and organ pieces.—C. V. B.

BRUSSELS, THÉÂTRE DE LA MONNAIE (Royal Opera-House). Goes back to 1700; has won a position of first rank in world, especially under the brilliant management of Dupont and Lapissida, and of Kufferath and Guidé (1900–14). At La Monnaie were produced works, celebrated, or at least of undeniable merit, with which Paris would at first have nothing to do: *Hérodiade*, Massenet (1881); *Sigurd*, Reyer (1884); *Gwendoline*, Chabrier (1886); *Salammbô*, Reyer (1889); *Fervaal*, d'Indy (1897); *Le Roi Arthus*, Chausson (1903); *L'Étranger*, d'Indy (1903); *Éros Vainqueur*, de Bréville (1910); *Le Chant de la Cloche*, d'Indy (1912). It welcomed the Wagnerian repertory at a period when it was still the subject of much debate (see Evenepoel, *Wagnerism outside Germany* [1891]).—C. V. B.

BRUSSELS CONSERVATOIRE MUSEUM. See MAHILLON, VICTOR CHARLES.

BRYSON, (Robert) Ernest. Scottish compr. *b.* Glasgow, 30 March, 1867. His music is modern in texture and finished in style.

Opera, *The Leper's Flute* (on Ian Colvin's play (1923); 1st symphony in D (Goodwin & Tabb); 2nd symphony in C (a Carnegie award); *Voices*, orch. study (Goodwin); *Vaila*, fantasia for str. (*id.*); str. 4tet in E (1923).—E.-H.

BRZEZIŃSKI, Franciszek (*phon.* Bjezinski). Polish compr. *b.* Warsaw, 6 Nov. 1867. Stud. under Kleczynski, then under Krehl, Max Reger and Richard Hoffmann at Leipzig. His characteristic trait is the polyphonic cast of his ideas. Cultivates particularly the writing of fugues, which are found in nearly all his works. Was music critic of *Kurjer Warszawski* at Warsaw. Polish Consul, Breslau, 1922.

Pf. concerto, G mi. (played by Ignacy Friedman); vn. concerto; *Polish Suite*, pf. op. 4; Introduction and Polonaise in form of fugue; *Oberek* (Polish dance), Intermezzo and Krakowiak; Triptych, op. 5: *Le Doute*, prelude and fugue; *Noël en Pologne*, prelude and fugue; *Devant le Sphinx*, prelude and fugue (awarded prize at competition at Chopin Centenary, 1910, Lemberg); Toccata, op. 7, etc.—ZD. J.

BÜCHER, Karl. Ger. political economist; *b.* Kirberg, near Wiesbaden, 16 Feb. 1847. Prof. of political economy, Leipzig, since 1892; retired 1916. His work *Arbeit und Rhythmus* (1896, 5th ed. Leipzig, 1919, E. Reinecke) entitles him to a notice in this work, since it maintains the origin of music to lie in the rhythmically ordered singing of labourers at work.—A. E.

BUCHMAYER, Richard. Ger. pianist; *b.* Zittau, 19 April, 1857. Pupil at Dresden Cons.; after 4 years in Russia, teacher at Cons. Dresden (to 1890); teacher Dresden School of Music, 1892; no official post at present. Prof. 1917. Not only is he a specialist in interpretation of older clavier music, but also an excellent investigator of music of this branch, which owes to him some discoveries of the greatest importance (Christian Ritter, Georg Böhm, one of whose cantatas he publ.). He is opposed to Wanda Landowska on question of the *Cembalo versus Pianoforte*.—A. E.

BUCK, Percy Carter. Eng. mus. educationist; *b.* West Ham, Essex, 1871. Stud. at Guildhall School of Music under Dr. C. J. Frost and F. Davenport; later at R.C.M. (scholar) under Sir Hubert Parry, Sir Walter Parratt, and Dr. C. H. Lloyd; Mus.Doc. Oxon. 1899; orgt. Worcester Coll. Oxford, 1891–5; Wells Cath. 1895–9; Bristol Cath. 1900–1; mus. dir. of Harrow School from 1901; prof. of music, Trinity Coll. Dublin (succeeding Ebenezer Prout), 1910–20; first Cramb lecturer, Glasgow Univ. 1923.

3 organ sonatas (Breitkopf); several choral works and school songs; 2 organ manuals (Stainer & Bell); *Unfigured Harmony* (Clarendon Press, Oxford, 1911); *Acoustics for Musicians* (*ib.* 1918).—E.-H.

BUCKLEY, John. British barit. singer; *b.* Ewloe, Flintshire, Wales, 14 Dec. 1888. Stud. at Guildhall School of Music, London; at London School of Opera; repertoire under Sir Henry Wood and Victor Beigel; *lieder* under Mme. M. Rosenberg. He has a fine legato style as well as great dramatic powers of interpretation.—E.-H.

BUFALETTI, Federico. Ital. pianist; *b.* Naples, 1 March, 1866. Gained much fame by his concerts in Italy, Spain, France, Greece, Turkey, etc. Having settled in Turin as prof. of pf. at Acad. of Music, he conducted an important series of symphony concerts and founded a mus. soc. which has given many memorable perfs. Has written many compns. for his own instrument.—D. A.

BUFFIN, Victor (Baron). Compr. *b.* Chercq, near Tournai, 19 July, 1867. Stud. compn. at first with De Boeck, but gave up his mus. work to become a soldier. He worked his way through all ranks until he became a general, in command of a cavalry division, a post he holds to-day. After an interruption of ten years, he resumed his mus. career under H. Waelput (harmony, cpt., fugue); then became pupil of J. Jongen. Eugène Ysaye first made his works known, and Kufferath and Guidé (managers of La Monnaie) urged him towards opera. His style is of the Fr. school, but his modernism is temperate.

Opera, *Kaatje* (Brussels, 1913); orch.: Suite (1906); *Lovelace,* symph. poem (1911); *Les Villages de la Côte* (on a work of Verhaeren), 1921; *Poème,* vn. and orch. (1922); sonata, vn. and pf. (1908); *Poème,* vn. and pf. (1912); songs.—E. C.

BUHLIG, Richard. Amer. pianist; *b.* Chicago, 21 Dec. 1880. Stud. in native city, and from 1897–1900 under Leschetizky in Vienna. Thereafter (1901) teacher in Berlin and extended tours in Europe and U.S.A. (Amer. *début* 5 Nov. 1907, with Philadelphia Symphony Orch.). From 1918–20, teacher at Inst. of Mus. Art, New York.—J. M.

BULL, Ole Bornemann. Norwegian violinist; *b.* Bergen 5 Feb. 1810; *d.* there, 17 Aug. 1880. Attended Christiania Univ. but abandoned his studies and devoted himself to the vn., in which his teachers were a Danish chamber-musician, Paulsen, and a Swedish violinist, Lundholm (pupil of Baillot). Became at 19 condr. at theatre in the capital ; but went same year to Cassel to study under Spohr. Broke off his studies there, as Spohr's Ger. method did not please his taste. Went in 1831 to Paris, where he was strongly affected by Paganini's style, and in following year gave his first concert with the assistance of Chopin, Ernst and other celebrities. After concerts in Italy, which aroused much attention, he again in 1835 gave a concert in Paris, this time in the great Opera House. From then onwards he was one of the world's famous artists. After that, he made constant tours through England, France, Germany, Russia, Sweden, everywhere hailed with enthusiasm as Paganini's equal and loaded with distinctions from royal courts, from mus. societies and from the great celebrities of music. Went in 1843 to America, where he reaped still greater triumphs than he had ever gained in Europe and earned huge sums. With greater part of this money, B. founded in 1852 a Norwegian settlement in Pennsylvania and called it Oleana. There he wished to offer Norwegian emigrants good and free conditions of life under the "Stars and Stripes." Oleana turned out a disappointment for B., for there were swindlers at work and B. lost the whole of his fortune. In Pennsylvania a fund is now being raised for a monument to the great virtuoso.

America became B.'s second fatherland. Here he married in 1872 his second wife, Sarah Torp, daughter of Senator Torp of Madison, his first wife, Alexandrine Félicité Villeminot, of Paris, having died in 1862. His death occasioned universal grief in Norway. At his graveside

Edvard Grieg and Björnstjerne Björnson spoke. In 1901 there was unveiled in Bergen a statue of B., designed by Stephan Sinding.

His best-known compn. is the song *Paa solen jeg ser* (*Upon the Sun I gaze*).—R. M.

BULLOCK, Ernest. Eng. orgt. compr. *b.* Wigan, 15 Sept. 1890; trained under Dr. E. C. Bairstow at Leeds Parish Ch.; orgt. St. Michael's, Tenbury, for a short time in 1919; appointed, in Dec. of that year, to Exeter Cath. Mus.Doc. Dunelm. 1914. His compns. have solidity and dignity, sound workmanship and poetic feeling.

Organ music (Augener); church music (Novello; Stainer & Bell; Oxford Univ. Press); songs (Ashdown; Curwen; Cramer; Enoch); school songs (Oxford Univ. Press).—E.-H.

BÜLOW, Hans Guido, Freiherr von. German pianist and conductor; *b.* Dresden, 8 Jan. 1830; *d.* Cairo, 12 Feb. 1894. Son of the author, Eduard v. Bülow. Learnt piano under Fr. Wieck in 1839; harmony from Max Eberwein, Dresden. From 1836 to 1846 the family lived in Stuttgart, where Bülow already played in public. In 1848 he studied law at Leipzig and also counterpoint under Moritz Hauptmann. He went to Berlin in 1849, where he became an advocate of Wagner's ideals. A performance of *Lohengrin* at Weimar in 1850 finally determined him to devote himself entirely to music, and in spite of his parents' opposition, he hurried to Wagner at Zurich, under whom he learnt conducting. After making his first attempts at conducting in Zurich and St. Gallen, he visited Liszt in Weimar, from whom he received the final inspiration for his piano playing, which had already attained a high degree of masterly achievement. In 1853 he undertook his first concert tour through Germany and Austria. A second tour was undertaken in 1855, terminating with his appointment as principal pianoforte teacher at Stern's Conservatorium (in Th. Kullak's place). In 1857 he married Liszt's daughter Cosima (*b.* 1837). He was appointed Court pianist in 1858, and was granted the degree of Ph.D. *h.c.* by the Jena University in 1863. Conducted the concerts of the " Friends of Music " in Berlin for a time. In 1864 he received a call to Munich from R. Wagner as Court pianist at first, but later as Court Orchestra conductor, and director of the Royal Music School in course of reconstruction, after he had spent some time in Basle giving concerts and teaching. After his divorce from his wife, who followed Wagner to Triebschen, he settled in Florence, where he influenced the dissemination of German music in Italy by organising regular concerts and performances of chamber music. In 1872 he again changed his place of residence (1875–6 in America). Conductor of the Hanover Court Theatre from 1877 to 3 Nov. 1879 (provisionally appointed at first; definitely 1 July, 1878). From 1880 to 1885 he was musical director to the Duke of Saxe-Meiningen and soon raised the Court Orchestra to a first-rank model orchestra, with which he undertook a series of concert tours through Germany.

He was next engaged in conducting the Philharmonic Concerts in Petrograd, Berlin, etc., and gave a month's tuition at the Raff Conservatorium, Frankfort-o-M., in the summer of each year. In July 1882, he married his second wife, Marie Schanzer, the Saxe-Meiningen Court actress. From 1887 he settled in Hamburg, where he had been conducting since 1886 the Abonnement Konzerte, a new concert institution, founded by Hermann Wolff. Bülow is the prototype of the modern interpreter, both as conductor and pianist. His alliance with Wagner was dissolved later by a close intimacy with Brahms, which was not quite unclouded.

Pf. works; songs and orch. pieces; music to *Julius Cæsar.* Symph. poems, *Des Sängers Fluch,* op. 16; *Nirvana,* 4 characteristic pieces, op. 23; *Mazurka Phantasie,* op. 13 for pf. The editions of classical works ed. by him have a certain educational value, though this is increasingly disputed (Beethoven's Pf. Works, from op. 35 on; Studies from Cramer and Chopin). The edition of his letters and writings in 8 vols. may be considered as the best source for biographical information (1895-1908, Breitkopf).—A. E.

BULTHAUPT, Heinrich. German writer on music; *b.* Bremen, 26 Oct. 1849; *d.* Bremen, 21 Aug. 1905. Has written a whole series of oratorio and opera-texts for Bruch (*Achilleus*), E. d'Albert (*Cain*) and others. Best known by his *Dramaturgie der Oper* (1887, 2 vols.).—A. E.

BUNGERT, August. Ger. compr. *b.* Mühlheim-o-Ruhr, 14 March, 1846; *d.* Leutesdorf-o-Rhine, 26 Oct. 1915. Pupil of F. Kufferath, Mühlheim; 1860-2 at Cologne Cons.; Paris till 1868; condr. Kreuznach, 1869; then resided Carlsruhe, Berlin, 1873-81 (stud. under Kiel); mostly at Pegli, Riviera, from 1882. Later Berlin and Leutesdorf; prof. 1911. He attempted a cycle of Homeric operas on the lines of Wagner's *Ring,* a hopeless task. In 1911 a Bungert Union was founded to disseminate his works. Consult Max Chop's *A. B.* (1916).

Comic opera, *Die Studenten von Salamanka* (Leipzig, 1884); music-drama tetralogy, *Homerische Welt* (*Kirke* [*Circe*], 1898; *Nausikaa,* 1901; *Odysseus' Heimkehr,* 1896; *Odysseus' Tod,* 1903); mystery-play, *Warum? Woher? Wohin?* (1908); orch. works; songs (many with words by Carmen Sylva, Queen of Rumania).—A. E.

BUNNING, Herbert. Eng. compr. condr. *b.* London, 1863. On leaving Oxford, was for 2 years a subaltern in 4th Hussars; started mus. study 1886 (Hanover and Milan); as mus. dir. at Lyric Theatre 1892-3, he produced Albeniz's *Magic Opal,* and Goring Thomas's *Golden Web;* condr. Prince of Wales's Theatre, 1894-6.

Opera, *La Princesse Osra* (Covent Garden, July 1902); *Sir Launcelot and Queen Guinevere,* t. scena, Norwich Fest. 1905; incidental music to *Robin Hood,* 1906.—E.-H.

BURBURE DE WESEMBEEK (le Chevalier Léon Philippe Marie de). Belgian compr. musicologist; *b.* Termonde, 16 Aug. 1812; *d.* Antwerp, 8 Dec. 1889. LL.D. Ghent Univ. 1832. Lived at Termonde, later at Antwerp. During first part of his life comp. many mus. works which he left to Antwerp public library. Then took up research in gen. history of art, particularly music. Member of R. Acad. of Belgium, 1862. With the exception of his article on *Jan van Ockeghem, zijne geboorteplaats en zijn verblijf*

in Antwerpen (Antwerp, 1856, and Termonde, 1868), his publications have all appeared in the *Bulletins de l'Académie de Belgique.*

Summary of Ancient Societies of Instrumentalists at Antwerp (1862); Notes on Harpsichord and Stringed-instrument makers in Antwerp (1863); Two French Virtuosi of Antwerp—Episode in Musical Customs of XVI Century (1880); Charles Luython, Composer to Imperial Court 1550-1620: his Life and Works (1880); Study of a XVI Century MS. (songs for 3 and 4 vs., etc.), 1882.—C. V. B.

BURIÁN, Karel. Czechoslovak singer, heroic t. *b.* Rousinov, 1870. Stud. at Wallerstein, Prague. *Début* National Theatre, Brno (Brünn), 1891. After long engagement in Dresden, sang in chief musical centres of world, chiefly Wagnerian rôles. Sang Parsifal at Bayreuth.—V. St.

BURLEIGH, Cecil. Amer. violinist; *b.* Wyoming, N.Y., U.S.A., 17 April, 1885. Stud. vn. in Berlin under Gruenberg and Witek, theory under Leichtentritt. Continued vn. at Chicago Mus. Coll. under Sauret and Hugo Heermann, compn. under Borowski. 1907-9, gave concerts in the U.S.A. and Canada. 1909-19, vn. instructor in various Western colleges; 1919-21, lived in New York. Since 1921, head of vn. department of the Univ. of Wisconsin. Comp. more than 110 pieces for vn. and pf., some 40 songs and 20 pf. pieces (Fischer; Schirmer; Ditson).—O. K.

BURLEIGH, Harry Thacker. Amer. negro spiritual and art-song singer, compr. *b.* Erie, Pa., U.S.A., 2 Dec. 1866. His maternal grandfather was a slave. B. was the first native American negro to win recognition as a compr. After working as stenographer for a few years, B. went to New York in 1892, and through the interest of Mrs. MacDowell (mother of the compr.) obtained scholarship in National Cons. of Music, then under dir. of Dvořák, who never tired of hearing him sing the old plantation songs of his boyhood. Appointed principal barit. of St. George's Episcopal Church, New York. He sang for many years at concerts and at home, and only took up compn. about 10 years ago.

Over 100 songs, of which best are: Five Songs of Laurence Hope, The Grey Wolf (Arthur Symons), The Young Warrior, and Passionale. Among the best spirituals are Deep River (Coleridge-Taylor's favourite), Swing Low, Go down Moses, My Lord, what a morning (publ. by Ricordi). See art. on NEGRO SPIRITUALS.—E.-H.

BURLIN, Natalie Curtis. See CURTIS, NATALIE.

BURMESTER, Willy. Ger. vn.-virtuoso; *b.* Hamburg, 16 March, 1869. Pupil R. High School, Berlin (Joachim); professional tours since 1886; Konzertmeister in Sondershausen, 1890; lives in Berlin. Arranger of small virtuoso pieces. Composed a *Serenade* for str. 4tet; D ma.—A. E.

BURNETT, Robert. Scottish barit. singer; *b.* Lasswade, Midlothian, 1875. Received his early mus. training as chorister in Duke of Buccleuch's private chapel at Dalkeith. It was with great diffidence, and only after long and careful consideration, that he resolved to enter the mus. profession. His first teacher endeavoured to make him a t., but as his voice matured, there could be no doubt of its barit. calibre. Stud. first under Signor Ricci of Edinburgh; afterwards under Randegger, and Sir Henry J. Wood in London. Began his vocal career as member of a once-famous Edinburgh male-v. quartet, "The Harmonists." His first real step into popular favour was on a certain New Year's Day, when the barit. engaged to sing in the Edinburgh R. Choral Union annual perf. of *Messiah* was detained by a railway breakdown occasioned by a snowstorm, and failed to appear. B. stepped out of the chorus, and sang the solos with tremendous success. He thus became famous in a day, and has since appeared as soloist with nearly every choral soc. of note in Great Britain, and also sung at London Symphony, Queen's Hall, Hallé, Liverpool Philh., London Ballad, and Scottish Orch. Concerts. He is a great protagonist of Scottish folk-song, and (with David Stephen, principal of Dumfermline Carnegie School of Music) has ed. several valuable colls. of such (Glasgow, Paterson Sons).—W. S.

BURROWS, Benjamin. Eng. orgt. and compr. *b*. Leicester. Stud. under Dr. C. H. Kitson; Mus. Doc. London, 1921. His pf. works are written in a very graceful, poetic style (Augener).—E.-H.

BURSA, Stanisław (*phon.* Boorsah). Polish compr. and choral condr. *b*. Obertyn, Galicia, 22 Aug. 1865. Publ. some hundreds of choral compns. adapted by himself and some orig. solo songs. Music critic and organiser of Professional Syndicate of Musicians and Music-teachers (*Polski związek muzyczno-pedagogiczny*) at Cracow.—ZD. J.

BURZIO, Eugenia. Ital. dramatic s. singer; *b*. Turin, 20 June, 1872; *d*. Milan, 1922. Won a high reputation by means of her forceful temperament. Sang in principal European and Amer. opera houses (Massenet's *Navarraise*; *Gioconda*; *Cavalleria*; *The Girl of the Golden West*; Pacini's *Saffo*; Alfano's *Resurrezione*. —D. A.

BUSCH, Adolf. Ger. violinist and compr. *b*. Siegen, Westphalia, 8 Aug. 1891. Brother of Fritz; taught vn. by his father, by Anders, Duisburg, and Bram Eldering, Cologne; pupil Cologne Cons. and of Hugo Grüters (compn.) in Bonn. After extensive tours, succeeded Marteau at High School of Music, Berlin, 1918–20; formed str. quartet, 1919, with Karl Reitz, Emil Bohnke and Paul Grümmer (now G. Andreasson, Karl Doktor, P. Grümmer).

Sonata for vn. and 1 for cello-solo; Prelude and fugue for vns. and cello; Variations on theme of his own for pf.; Variations on theme of Schubert for 2 pf.; Passacaglia for 2 vns. and pf. (Berlin, Simrock); vn. sonata, G ma. op. 21 (Breitkopf); cello sonata, op. 48; *Serenade* for str. quartet (Simrock); songs with pf.; *Fantasie* for organ, op. 19 (Breitkopf); *Konzertstück*, vn. and orch.; vn. concerto, A mi. op. 20 (*id.*); pf. trio, A mi.; Variations on Mozart theme for small orch.; Variations on Radetzky March for orch.; overture to *King Œdipus*; symphony in D mi.; choral, *Darthulas Grabgesang*. Also ed. new series Bach's sonatas and scores for vn. (1919).—A. E.

BUSCH, Fritz. Ger. condr. *b*. Siegen, Westphalia, 13 March, 1890. Eldest son of Wilhelm Busch, vn. maker. Pupil Leipzig Cons. (Steinbach, Böttcher, Uzielli, Klauwell); condr. Riga, 1909; chorus-master, Mus. Soc. Gotha,

1911–12, and Court-condr. and dir. of Kurhaus concerts in summer (1910–12) at Bad Pyrmont; mus. dir. Aix-la-Chapelle, 1912; 1918, followed Max Schillings as chief condr. Stuttgart; dir. Opera House, 1919; dir. Dresden (following Reiner). Also made name as pianist.—A. E.

BUSONI, Ferruccio Benvenuto. Ital. compr. and pianist; *b*. Empoli, near Florence, 1 April, 1866. His early musical training was due to his father, Ferdinando Busoni, a well-known clarinet virtuoso, and to his mother, Anna Weiss-Busoni, an accomplished pianist of German descent. His early years were spent chiefly in Trieste. At 9 he was introduced to the musical world by a concert in Vienna. Not only by his piano-playing, but also by his compositions and his gift of improvisation, he excited the admiration of the severe critic, Eduard Hanslick, who wrote enthusiastically about him. A few years later, he studied composition with Wilhelm Meyer-Remy at Graz; but in piano-playing he was never taught by an acknowledged master. As a youth of 15 he made a successful concert-tour in Italy, was honoured by admission as member (the youngest one since Mozart) of the Bolognese Philharmonic Academy and had his most ambitious work (a long cantata for solo voices and orchestra, *Il Sabato del Villaggio*, to Leopardi's poem) performed in Bologna. The next years were spent in Vienna and Leipzig. In 1889 he was appointed professor at the Helsingfors Conservatoire. The close contact with the northern art of Scandinavia, Finland, and Russia had an important effect on the development of his art. In 1890 he won the Rubinstein Prize in Petrograd for his *Konzertstück* for piano and orchestra, op. 31a. The years 1891–4 he spent in America, giving concerts and teaching for some time at the New England Conservatory in Boston. From 1894 to 1914 he resided in Berlin. In these years his international celebrity was founded by his concerts in almost all European countries. 1901–2, he held summer-courses for advanced pianists in Weimar, thus continuing in a certain manner the work of Liszt. For many years he conducted orchestral concerts in Berlin devoted exclusively to new and rarely heard works. In 1911 he gave 6 Liszt recitals (Liszt's birth-centenary) which marked an epoch in the growth of pianistic art. In 1910–11 he was in America; in 1913 he gave a series of historical concerts in Italy and was appointed director of the Liceo Musicale in Bologna. This position he resigned a year later. After the outbreak of war in 1914 he left Berlin for America in 1915, and could not return to Germany after Italy had entered into the war. 1915–19 he spent in Switzerland, living in Zurich in a sort of self-chosen exile, and manifesting his independent, international, neutral position by refraining from all concerts in the countries engaged in the war. In 1920 he returned to Berlin, where he is residing at present. The Berlin Academy of Arts put him in charge of a *Meisterklasse* for composition. The pianist Busoni is universally acknowledged to have the most powerful individuality and the greatest technical mastery since Liszt and Rubinstein, a technical mastery never displayed for its own sake, but made subservient to a most powerful intellect, and a cultured mind. There is an elevation, a spiritual force, an utter absence of materialism in his playing which renders it unique. The astounding boldness and clearness of his polyphonic playing, the vehemence and elementary force of his brazen octaves and chords, his sweeping passages, the fascinating elegance of his ornamental work, the elasticity and precision of his rhythms, the surprisingly new and admirable treatment of the pedal, create marvels of sound, the like of which have never been heard before. The profundity which is the metaphysical background of his playing does not interfere with its musical qualities. He started with universal tendencies, interpreting almost the entire piano literature. In his middle years, however, he evinced a marked predilection for Bach and Liszt, and the latest phase is characterised by his passionate love for Mozart, whose concertos he plays in a truly creative manner, discovering them, as it were, anew for our time.

As a composer Busoni has been busily active since his childhood. In the middle of his career, however, there is a gap of about ten years (about 1890–1900). These were the years in which his pianistic mastery came to full development. The composer, however, was silent during these years and slowly began to evolve the new ideas which characterise his mature art. The works from 1877 up to 1892, comprising about op. 1–32, the products of his youth, are no longer fully recognised by him. Nevertheless they contain much fine music, and several have appeared in a second, revised edition, such as the *Konzertstück*, op. 31*a* (piano and orchestra), written in 1890 for the Rubinstein Prize and rounded off into a concertino in 1921 by addition of a charming *Romanza e Scherzoso*. Similarly the Second Orchestral Suite (*Geharnischte Suite*) received its final shape years after. His second, mature period may ·be dated from the violin sonata, No. 2, op. 36*a*, which shows his peculiar mixture of Southern temperament with mystic and fantastic Northern traits. The art of his earlier years is summed up in the monumental piano concerto, op. 34, which occupies a place of its own by reason of its novel conception of the concerto-idea, by grandeur of construction and wealth of musical invention. After this magnificent climax his style begins to change. In every new work he seems to be different, always intent on entering further into unknown regions and pursuing this research with a passionate mental activity. To enumerate these compositions is to show most interesting examples of the manifold tendencies of modern music. The charming and clever *Turandot Suite*, op. 41 (1906), with its fantastic oriental colouring continues a series including Borodin's *Asiatische Steppenskizze*, Rimsky-Korsakof's *Scheherazade*, Delius's *Appalachia*. The touching and unique *Berceuse élégiaque*, op. 12, and the closely-knit *Nocturne*

symphonique, op. 43, show the new harmonic and contrapuntal treatment which he develops in a certain parallelism with Schönberg. The *Indian Sketchbook* and the *Indian Fantasia* for piano and orchestra, op. 44, follow the trend of modern folk-lore research. The second sonatina, perhaps the most problematic of his works, is a most remarkable predecessor of the boldest revolutionary attempts of the present time in its disdain of triads, tonality, and bar-notation. Lately he has entered a new phase. The immense experience, skill and culture acquired he now intends to apply to a neo - classical style, in which form and expression are perfectly balanced. Specimens of this style are offered by his later sonatinas, the *Divertimento* for flute and orchestra, *Sarabande* and *Cortège* from the *Faust* music.

In dramatic art, he objects to the veristic conception of opera, as also to the Wagnerian methods, and sees as fit objects for musical treatment only those based on the supernatural, magical, mythical, fantastic, or the mere " play." His three operas corroborate these ideas very logically and strongly. In all of them he has been his own librettist. *Die Brautwahl* (first performance 1912, Hamburg), takes its plot from a fantastic tale by E. T. A. Hoffmann. *Turandot*, after Gozzi's drama, and *Arlecchino* (Zurich, 1918) are a direct continuation of the old Italian *commedia dell' arte*. For years he has been occupied with the composition of his opera *Doctor Faust*, which he considers his chief work.

The art of arrangement he has brought to a perfection surpassing even Liszt's efforts. His *Bach Studies* fill 7 extensive volumes, including the edition of the *Well-tempered Clavichord*. His numerous literary essays, which give him a rank also as a writer, have lately been collected into a volume entitled *Von der Einheit der Musik* (Max Hesse, Berlin). His essay *Entwurf einer neuen Ästhetik der Tonkunst* (1907; 1916) has been translated into Russian and English.

His compositions have been published almost entirely by Breitkopf & Härtel. The list of his mature works comprises:

Operas: *Die Brautwahl*, op. 45; *Turandot*, a Chinese fable (without op. number); *Arlecchino*, a stage *capriccio*, op. 50.

For pf.: Variations and fugue on Chopin's C mi. Prelude, op. 22; 4 *Balletszenen* (op. 6, 20, 30, 30*a*); 6 elegies; 6 sonatinas; *An die Jugend*; *Indianisches Tagebuch*; *Fantasia contrappuntistica* (on parts of Bach's *Art of Fugue*).

For 2 pianos: New version of *Fantasia contrappuntistica*; *Improvisation on a Bach Chorale*: *Duettino concertante* (on themes from a Mozart concerto).

For pf. and orch.: *Konzertstück*, op. 31*a*, supplemented by *Romanza e Scherzoso*, op. 54; concerto, op. 39; *Indian Fantasy*, op. 44.

Chamber-music: 2 str. 4tets, op. 19, 26; 2 vn. sonatas, op. 29, 36*a*.

For orch.: Symph. tone-poem, op. 32*a*; *Lustspiel-Ouvertüre*, op 38; *Symph. Suite*, op. 25; *Geharnischte Suite*, op. 34*a*; *Turandot Suite*, op. 41; *Brautwahl Suite*, op. 45; *Berceuse élégiaque*, op. 42; *Nocturne symphonique*, op. 43; *Rondo arlecchinesco*, op. 46; *Gesang vom Reigen der Geister*, op. 47; *Sarabande, Cortège*, op. 51 (from the *Faust*-music); *Tanzwalzer*, op. 53.

Various: Vn. concerto, op. 35*a*; *Concertino* for clar. and orch. op. 48; *Divertimento*, fl. and orch. op. 52. Various songs (op. 1, 2, 15, 18, 24, 31, 32, 35). Numerous cadenzas to concertos by Beethoven,

Brahms, Mozart. Arr. from Bach (collected in 7 vols. of *Bach Studies*); ed. of *Well-tempered Clavichord*, D mi. Concerto, *Goldberg Variations*, etc. *Entwurf einer neuen Ästhetik der Tonkunst* (Leipzig, Insel Verlag); Eng. transl. by Th. Baker, *The New Æsthetic of Music* (New York, 1911, Schirmer). Biographies: H. Leichtentritt, *F. Busoni* (Leipzig, 1916, Breitkopf); G. Selden-Goth, *F. Busoni* (Vienna, 1922, E. P. Tal). ESSAYS: H. Leichtentritt, *F. Busoni as a Composer* (*Musical Quarterly*, New York, Jan. 1917); J. Chantavoine, *F. Busoni* (*Revue Hebdomadaire*, Paris, 17 April, 1920); Busoni number of *Anbruch*, Vienna, 1920; *Il Pianoforte* (Turin, June 1921), and various articles by E. J. Dent in the *Athenæum*, London, 1919–21.—H. L.

BÜSSER, Henri. Fr. compr. orch. condr. *b.* Toulouse, 16 Jan. 1872. *Prix de Rome* 1893 (for cantata, *Amadis des Gaules*); orgt. St.-Cloud; then chorus - master, Opéra - Comique, Paris; finally at Cons. and condr. at Opera. His compns. are carefully worked out and have an official touch.

Daphnis et Chloé, 1897 (*opéra-comique*); *Colomba*, 1920 (opera); *Les Noces Corinthiennes*, 1922 (opera); *La Ronde des Saisons*, 1905 (ballet).—A. C.

BUSTINI, Alessandro. Ital. compr. and pianist; *b.* Rome, 24 Dec. 1876. A musician greatly esteemed in Roman mus. circles. Was pf. pupil of Sgambati. Is teacher at R. Liceo Mus. di Santa Cecilia in Rome. Has comp. several operas, of which *Maria Dulcis* was perf. at the Costanzi in Rome in 1902. Also chamber-music and concert pieces. Has publ. a study on *The Symphony in Italy* (Rome, 1904, Roux & Viarengo).—D. A.

BUTHS, Julius. Ger. pianist and condr. *b.* Wiesbaden, 7 May, 1851; *d.* Düsseldorf, 12 March, 1920. Son and pupil of Karl Buths (oboist); pupil of W. Freudenberg, and at Cologne Cons. 1860–70 (Hiller, Gernsheim); 1872, under Friedrich Kiel, Berlin; Meyerbeer Travelling Scholarship, Italy, 1873, Paris, 1875; pianist and condr. Breslau, 1875–9; dir. Concert Soc. Elberfeld, 1879–90; mus. dir. Düsseldorf, 1890–1908; dir. of Cons. from 1903. Translated Elgar's *Apostles* and *Dream of Gerontius* into German. The latter work he cond. for first time in Germany in May 1902 (Lower Rhine Fest.).

Pf. concerto; pf. 5tet; str. 4tet.—A. E.

BUTT, Dame Clara. Eng. contr. singer; *b.* Southwick, Sussex, 1 Feb. 1873. Stud. R.C.M. London, under late Henry Blower; *début* in R.C.M. students' perf. of Gluck's *Orfeo* at Lyceum Theatre, 5 Dec. 1892; further study under Duvernoy and Bouhy in Paris; under Mme. Etelka Gerster in Italy. The most popular contr. in Britain of present day; confines herself chiefly to ballad-songs. Married Kennerley Rumford (*q.v.*), 1900.—E.-H.

BUTTERWORTH, Clara. S. singer; *b.* Manchester. Stud. at R.A.M. under Agnes Larkcom; *début* Queen's Hall, London, March 1908; made her appearance on light opera stage with great distinction in 1914; *A Country Girl* (revival Daly's, 1914); *Young England* (*ib.* 1916); *The Lilac Domino* (Empire, 1918); *Medorah* (Alhambra, 1920); *The Rebel Maid* (Empire, 1921); *Lilac-Time* (Lyric Theatre, 1922–4). Married Montague Phillips, the composer.—E.-H.

BUTTERWORTH, George S. Kaye. Eng. compr. *b.* London, 1885; lived in Yorkshire, 1891–1909; fell in Somme battle, 5 Aug. 1916. His first serious compn. was written whilst at school at Eton (*Barcarolle* for orch.); took a Classical Honours degree at Oxford; stud. music chiefly privately, though for a short time he was at R.C.M. London. Threw himself whole-heartedly into the folk-song and dance movement. In his songs and orch. pieces is heard a particularly pure English strain. His *Shropshire Lad*, tone-poem, raised high hopes which were frustrated by the war. His songs are amongst the finest of the xx century composers.

Two Folk-Song Idylls (Oxford, 1912); *A Shropshire Lad*, orch. tone-poem (Leeds Fest. under Nikisch, 1913); *The Banks of Green Willow*, idyll for small orch. (Liverpool, 1913); cycle of 4 songs, *Love Blows as the Wind Blows*, barit. and str. 4tet (1912, Novello); cycle of 6 songs from *A Shropshire Lad* (Augener); another cycle, *Bredon Hill* (*id.*); *Folk-Songs from Sussex* (*id.*); single songs (Augener); *Country-Dance Tunes* (8 parts, 1906–16, Novello); *The Morris Book* (5 parts, 1907–13, *id.*); part-song (t.t.b.b.), *We get up in the Morn* (Augener).—E.-H.

BÜTTING, Max. Ger. compr. of chamber-music; *b.* Berlin, 6 Oct. 1888. Stud. under Arnold Dreyer, Berlin orgt., Paul Prill, Klose and Courvoisier, Munich, where attended the Univ.; resident in Berlin since 1919.

Unfinished mass, op. 6; songs with orch. or chamber- orch., op. 1–5; 4 str. 4tets, op. 8, 16, 18, 20 (1st 3 publ. by Tischer & Jagenberg); str. 5tet, op. 10; solo sonatas for vn. in 5 movements, op. 11; pf. 4tet, op. 14; str. trio, op. 15; cello concerto, op. 19; chamber-symphony, op. 21; 5tet for ob. clar. vn. vla. and cello, op. 22; str. 5tet with d.b. op. 24; chamber-symphony for 13 instruments, op. 25.—A. E.

BÜTTNER, Paul. Ger. compr. *b.* Dresden, 10 Dec. 1870. Pupil of Draeseke (Dresden Cons.); teacher there 1896–1907; also engaged as critic. As a symphonist, has been somewhat influenced by Anton Bruckner.

4 symphonies in F, G, D flat ma. (his best-known work) and B mi.; symph. phantasies; overture to *Napoleon's Tomb*; *Saturnalia*, drums and wind instrs.; chamber-music (vn. sonata; str. 4tet, G mi. publ.); male choruses; 2 stage works, *Anka* and *Das Wunder der Isis*.—A. E.

BUTTYKAY, Ákos. Hungarian compr. *b.* Halmi, Hungary (now annexed by Rumania), 1871. 1907–22, teacher at R. High School for Music, Budapest.—B. B.

BYE, Erik. Norwegian barit. opera-singer; *b.* Drammen, 20 March, 1883. Stud. singing under Zur Mühlen (London); 1909–12, in Milan, Paris and Berlin. *Début*, Christiania, 1913. Engaged at Breslau Stadttheater 1914–17; subsequently gave special performances at National Theatre and Opéra–Comique, Christiania. Best rôles, Don Basilio, Amonasro, Wolfram. Since 1921, engaged at the Capitol Kino-Theatre, New York.—U. M.

BYK, Ryszard. Polish pianist; *b.* Brody, Galicia, 1892. Pupil of Friedmann and Leschetizky in Vienna. Stud. music history under G. Adler and theory under Carl Weigl. Is much appreciated in Germany, Poland and Rumania. Lives in Dresden.—ZD. J.

C

CABALLERO, Manuel Fernández. Span. compr. *b.* Murcia, 1835; *d.* 26 Feb. 1906. Was youngest of family of 18. Pupil of Indalecio Soriano Fuertes at Murcia; of Pedro Albeniz and Hilarión Eslava at R. Cons. de Música, Madrid; 1853–86, in Spain, Portugal, Cuba and S. America as theatre- and concert-condr.; 1891, elected Fellow of R. Acad, de Bellas Artes; 1903, received Grand Cross of Alfonso XII; hon. member of many foreign literary and musical societies. He was equally popular in Spain and America as a compr. of mus. comedies, some of which were perf. in Italy and Portugal. Besides many songs and much church music, he wrote nearly 200 works for stage, in 1, 2, 3 or 4 acts. Not only as a compr. but also as an impresario, he contributed to the maintenance of the dignity of Span. lyric art against detrimental influences and fashions. Amongst his best-known works, some of which were comp. and dictated during several years of total blindness, are:

La jardinera, Un cocinero, Frasquito, El loco de la guardilla, Luz y Sombra, El primer día feliz, La gallina ciega, Las nueve de la noche, La Marsellesa, El siglo que viene, Los sobrinos del capitán Grant, El salto del Pasiego, Las dos princesas, El lucero del alba, Las mil y una noches, Curriya, Para casa de los padres, Château Margaux, Los zangolotinos, La choza del diablo, Los aparecidos, Triple alianza, El dúo de La Africana, Los dineros del sacristán, El cabo primero, El padrino del Nene, La viejecita, El señor Joaquín, Gigantes y cabezudos, El traje de luces, La diligencia, La trapera, La manta zamorana, María Luisa, La cacharrera, El lego de San Pablo (Unión Musical Española, Madrid).—P. G. M.

CÄCILIENVEREIN (Ger.). A choral society for mixed voices.—E.-H.

CADMAN, Charles Wakefield. Amer. compr. *b.* Johnstown, Pa., U.S.A., 24 Dec. 1881. Received his mus. education entirely from Pittsburgh teachers (Walker, Oehmler, Steiner, von Kunits) 1899–1909. Mus. critic *Pittsburgh Despatch*; orgt of East Liberty Presbyterian Ch. One of the Amer. musicians who have sought inspiration from the music of the Indians. The first results of this interest are laid down in *Four Indian Songs*, op. 45 (1907), one of which, *The Land of the Sky-Blue Water*, has become very popular in America and has been sung by singers of note. After his removal from Pittsburgh he was orgt. in Denver and since then has made his home chiefly in Los Angeles. He has travelled much as lecture-recitalist, assisted in recent years by an Indian m.-sopr., Princess Tsianina Red-feather. His lecture on Amer.-Indian music was given in 1910 in Paris and London.

Cadman's compns. are numerous. Not all are in the category of Indian music. He adhered consistently to a comparatively simple style. His most important work is 1-act Indian opera, *Shanewis (The Robin Woman)*, 1st perf. Metropolitan Opera, New York, 23 March, 1918. An earlier 3-act opera, *The Land of the Misty Water* (completed 1912), and a later work in 1 act, *The Garden of Mystery*, have not been perf. A suite for orch., *The Thunderbird*, originally written as incidental to Norman Bel Geddes' drama of same name, 1st played by Los Angeles Symphony Orch. 9 Jan. 1917. An Oriental suite, *Omar Khayyám*, 1st perf. San Francisco Symphony Orch., Los Angeles, Aug. 1922.

Shanewis (The Robin Woman) (1918); *To a Vanishing Race*, str. 4tet (John Church Co. 1917); *The Vision of Sir Launfal*, cantata, male vs. (Schirmer, 1910); pf. trio, D ma. op. 56 (1914); *The Legend of the Canyon*, vn. and pf. op. 68 (1920); *Idealised Indian Themes*, op. 54 (1912); pf. sonata, op. 58 (1915); *Thunderbird Suite*, pf. op. 63 (1917); pf. suite, *The Rubáiyát of Omar Khayyám*, op. 75 (1921); *Four Indian Songs*, op. 45 (1908); *From Wigwam and Tepee*, Indian song-cycle, op. 57 (1914); *Sayonara*, Japanese song-cycle (1913); *The Willow Wind*, Chinese song-cycle (1922). Mostly publ. by White Smith Co., Boston. Other pf. pieces publ. also by Presser; Hatch; Willis. Other songs (Presser; Willis; Ditson; Summy).—O. K.

CAHNBLEY, Ernst. Ger. cellist; *b.* Hamburg, 3 Sept. 1875. Pupil Hamburg Cons. and Hugo Becker; teacher Würzburg Cons. from 1909; member of Schörg Quartet since 1918. Prof. 1919. Wrote cello pieces and studies; songs. —A. E.

CAHNBLEY-HINKEN, Tilly. Ger. s. singer; *b.* Bremen, 12 June, 1880. Ernst Cahnbley's wife; pupil of Bussjäger and Rössler (Bremen); Wolff and Wüllner (Cologne Cons.); Ducal chamber-singer; teacher of singing, Würzburg Cons. Esteemed singer in oratorio.—A. E.

CAHN-SPEYER, Rudolf. Mus. research scholar; *b.* Vienna, 1 Sept. 1881. Stud. natural sciences, Vienna; music under Jadassohn, Krehl, Riemann, Nikisch, science of music with Sandberger, theory under Thuille and Beer-Walbrunn; condr. in Kiel, 1908, in Hamburg, 1909–11; teacher at Klindworth-Scharwenka Cons. Berlin; President of council, Union of Ger. Concert Artists, (since 1913), a professional organisation having for its object the suppression of agents.

Franz Seidelmann as a Dramatic Composer (Leipzig, 1909, Breitkopf); *Handbuch des Dirigierens* (Leipzig, 1919, Breitkopf).—A. E.

CAIROS-REGO, Rex de. Australian compr. *b.* Sydney, 25 Sept. 1886. Teaches in Sydney.

Many songs; pf. solos; *Humoresque*, vn. and pf. (all Shrimpton & Sons, 101 Leadenhall St. London); vn. sonata (ms.); *Fantaisie-Sonata* in 1 movement, pf. and cello; ballad, *Killed at the Ford* (Longfellow), male chorus and orch.—E.-H.

CALAND, Elizabeth. Pf. teacher; *b.* Rotterdam, 13 Jan. 1862. Stud. 1884–6 under Ludwig Deppe, Berlin, theory under J. Rebiček; 1898, pf. teacher in Berlin; 1915 at Gehlsdorf, near Rostock. Publications (all by Heinrichshofen, Magdeburg):

Quick Instruction in Pf. Playing, 1897; 4th ed. 1912 (also in English, Fr., Dutch and Russian);

74

Technical Advice to Pf. Players, 1897; 4th ed. 1912; *The Application of Weight in Pf. Playing*, 1904–5; *Artistic Pf. Playing*, 1910; 2nd ed. 1919; *Practical Course of Instruction*, 1912; 2nd ed. 1919; *Important Facts for controlling Proper Arm-movements*, 1919.—A. E.

CALLEJA, Gómez Rafael. Span. compr. *b.* Burgos, 23 Dec. 1874. Choirboy at Burgos Cath.; then stud. at R. Cons. de Música, Madrid, where he distinguished himself in compn. under Arrieta. Has held at different times the position of condr. at nearly all principal theatres in Spain, Portugal and Latin America. Besides works on national folk-lore, orch. and vocal pieces, he has written 287 mus. comedies and revues, all of which have been perf. He lives in Madrid.

Colección de canciones populares de la provincia de Santander; Colección de canciones populares de Galicia y Asturias; Cantos de la Montaña, symph. poem for orch. Mus. comedies and revues: *El Arbol de Bertoldo; Las Alondras; El As; Aires Nacionales; El Abanico de la Pompadur; La Araña Azul; Las Bribonas; El Conde de Lavapiés; Copito de Nieve; Frou-Frou; El Genio de Velázquez; La Ilustre Fregona; La Maja Desnuda; Maese Figaro; El Principe Carnaval; El Mozo Crúo*, etc. (Publ.: Unión Musical Española; Faustino Fuente; Ricardo Rodríguez; Antonio Matamala, Madrid; Salabert, Paris.) —P. G. M.

CALMUS, Georgy. Ger. mus. research scholar; *b.* Berlin, 10 Sept. 1874. Pupil of Berlin R. High School of Music (Joachim) and the Univ. (Kretzschmar, Friedlaender, Fleischer, Wolf).

Die ersten deutschen Singspiele von Standfuss und Hiller (Leipzig, 1908, Breitkopf); new ed. of Lesage's *Télémaque* and Gay's *Beggar's Opera* (Berlin, Liepmannssohn); articles on *Opera in England* (*S.I.M.G.*).—A. E.

CALVÉ, Emma. French operatic singer; *b.* Madrid (of Fr. parents) in 1864. Pupil of Marchesi and Puget; first appeared at a charity concert at Nice. *Début* in Brussels, 1882 (Marguerite in *Faust*). Toured in Rome, Paris, London and in America. Created rôles of Bianca in *Aben Hamet* (Dubois), Santuzza in *Cavalleria Rusticana*, also in *La Navarraise, Sapho, La Carmélite, Messaline*. Famous for her interpretation of *Carmen*. Not content with possessing a very fine voice and perfect technique, she always endeavoured, by intense study, to interpret each of her rôles with the greatest realism. She lived the life of a gipsy at Granada, dressing and dancing like one, in order to enter more deeply into the sources of inspiration of Bizet and Mérimée.—M. B.

CALVOCORESSI, Michael D. Mus. critic; *b.* Marseilles, 2 Oct. 1877. Both parents Greek. Educated in Paris; stud. harmony under Xavier Leroux at Paris Cons.; otherwise self-taught in music. Stud. literature and classics under Gabriel Vauthier and philosophy under André Lalande. Began writing criticism at end of 1901; correspondent to many foreign papers and periodicals; 1905–14, lectures, at Paris École des Hautes Études Sociales, on modern music, abundantly illustrated, introduced many works of various schools (Bartók, Kodály, Stravinsky, Schönberg, Wellesz); also lectures on mus. criticism; 1914–19, served in British Military Intelligence. Has transl. into Eng., Fr. or Ger. countless works of various comprs. (Balakiref, Mussorgsky, Rimsky-Korsakof, Debussy, Du-

parc, Bartók, Stravinsky, etc.) and books on music; has contributed to Eng. papers, *Morning Post, Daily Telegraph, Musical Times, Monthly Musical Record, Glasgow Herald, Music and Letters*, etc. Is devoted to the dissemination of contemporary music, especially Russ., Fr., British and Hungarian. Collab. with Diaghilef, 1907–10. Has lectured in Britain, Belgium, and France. C. has an exceptionally clear, well-balanced style of musical criticism. Contributor of many articles on Fr. and Russ. musicians, etc., to this Dictionary.

Books (in Fr.): *Liszt* (Laurens, 1905); *Mussorgsky* (Alcan, 1908; Eng. 1917; Span. 1919; Ger. 1922); *Glinka* (Laurens, 1911); *Schumann* (Michaud, 1912). Pamphlets on *Russian Music* (1907); *British Music* (1911). In Eng.: *The Principles and Methods of Musical Criticism* (H. Milford, 1923).—E.-H.

CAMETTI, Alberto. Ital. historian of music; *b.* Rome, 5 May, 1871. At present condr. of the Choir of San Luigi dei Francesi in Rome. Member of many acads. and of the Pontifical Commission of Sacred Music. Has devoted himself specially to interesting researches regarding Roman mus. history. As compr. has written pf. and organ pieces, songs, and especially sacred music.

His chief monographs are on Frescobaldi (Milan, 1895, Ricordi); *Bellini in Rome* (Rome, 1900, Cuggiani); *Mozart in Rome* (Rome, 1907, Union Coop. ed.); and numerous articles on these and other subjects (Corelli, Rossini, Donizetti, etc.) in the *Rivista Musicale Italiana* (Turin, Bocca) from 1899 to present time (1923).—D. A.

CAMPANINI, Cleofonte. Ital. condr. *b.* Parma, 1 Sept. 1860; *d.* Chicago, 19 Dec. 1919. Eminent condr. who helped to maintain, both in Italy and abroad, the prestige of Ital. art. Started his career at Parma in 1883, conducting a series of perfs., in which his brother, Italo, the celebrated t. singer, participated. In 1884 C. stayed in Turin, conducting a series of symphony concerts. He immediately passed on to the principal theatres in Italy and abroad (La Scala, Milan; Municipal Theatre, Nice; Colón and Opera, Buenos Ayres; Lyceum, Barcelona; San Carlos Theatre, Lisbon; R. Theatre, Madrid; San Carlo Theatre, Naples; Covent Garden, London). In 1913, on occasion of Verdi Centenary, he cond. a cycle of Verdi's works at Parma. He then went to North America and linked his name with the foundation of the McCormack - Campanini annual competition among Ital comprs. for an Ital. opera. During his last years he was the artistic and administrative dir. of the Chicago Opera Association, and in that post he greatly contributed to spreading the repertoire of Ital. operas.—D. A.

CAMPBELL, George. Scottish barit singer; *b.* Westmorland, 1873. Choirboy at Carlisle Cath. Stud. singing under Hugo Beyer, pf. under W. Thomson, organ under Scott Jupp. For many years, choirmaster, St. Peter's R.C. ch. Edinburgh. Has sung widely in oratorios and concerts. Orgt. at several Edinburgh churches. In 1886 entered music-selling firm of Messrs. Townsend and Thomson, one of oldest businesses in Edinburgh. In 1894, became sole owner.—W. S.

CAMPBELL-McINNES, James. Brit. barit. singer; *b*. Holcombe, Lancs, 23 Jan. 1874. Stud. at R.C.M. London; also under M. Bouhy in Paris; Sir George Henschel, Sir Charles Santley and William Shakespeare in London. First appeared at a song-recital in St. James's Hall. His fine interpretation of the songs of Brahms in 1899 brought him to notice of Joseph Joachim, who introduced him to various concert societies, resulting in many important provincial engagements. One of the orig. members of the Soc. of Eng. Singers, London; became known as one of the finest of Bach singers. After several years of war service he resumed his profession (1919) in Toronto, Canada, where he now resides. Has helped a large number of British comprs. to a hearing; a great number of modern representative Eng. songs have been comp. or dedicated to him. His most characteristic feature is his fine musicianship and great diversity of style, this permitting him to interpret equally successfully the humorous folk-songs on the one hand and the *Christus* of Bach on the other.—L. S.

CAMPO Y ZABALETA, Conrado del. Span. compr. *b*. in Madrid, 28 Oct. 1879. One of chief figures in modern Span. music. Started his mus. education at Real Cons. Madrid. On entering the compn. class, his professors found themselves dealing with a personality they could not control or understand. He had developed through his own efforts a mentality superior to that prevailing in his environment. Nevertheless Campo adopted a compromising attitude and finished his studies brilliantly. Thenceforth he became a free lance, an uncompromising and expert adept in modern technique. He was soon declared unfaithful to the Span. traditions and a fanatical follower of the Ger. school—an unjust accusation, for the works of his most advanced pupils prove that he is equally familiar with the methods of modern Fr. comprs. He is the possessor of a complex mus. mind that might give grounds for describing him as the " Spanish Strauss," but he differs from Strauss in a very essential way; there is a sincerity of purpose in Campo which is nearly always absent in Strauss. For this, Campo is also accused of being a Romantic, nowadays a deprecatory term he accepts with pride. He is a modern progressist who abhors all kinds of unruly extravagance in art and professes the doctrine that without feeling there is no conception worth the name, and that perfect expression cannot be attained without a complete mastery of technique. The existence in Spain of such a personality is unsuspected abroad, though he is the most prolific Span. compr., and one who excels in chamber and symph. music, two styles of compn. which, unlike theatrical works, are free from limitations in regard to universal meaning. The list of his works speaks for itself; all have been perf. in Spain, many of them having won prizes; but very few are publ. up to now. They constitute an invaluable asset to the modern Span. school. His activities as prof. of harmony at Madrid R. Cons., private teacher in compn., member of the

Cuarteto Francés, Quinteto de Madrid, and a brilliant writer on mus. subjects, are a powerful element in the mus. regeneration of the country. He it was who in his early youth told Madrid of the supreme beauty of Beethoven's latest quartets, then neglected there as the incomprehensible failures of a deaf man. Campo has been for many years the vla. soloist at Madrid R. Opera House and the Orquesta Sinfónica, of which he is a founder, as well as of the other two chamber-music organisations above mentioned.

Operas: *La Dama Desconocida*, 3 acts (book by Tomás Borras; *Leonor Teller* (book by M. Mezquita); *Don Alvaro*, 4 acts; *Tragedia del Beso*, 2 acts; *Romeo y Julieta*, 4 acts; *Dies Iræ*, 4 acts; *Avapiés*, (in collab. with Angel Barrios); *La Culpa* (not yet perf.); *La Flor del Agua* (in preparation). Orch.: *La Divina Comedia*; *Granada*; *Danza del Niaou*; *Kasida*; *Don Juan de España* (suite from incidental music to M. Sierra's play of same title). *Aires, Airiños, Aires*, for orch., s. v. and chorus. Mass for orch. and double chorus. Str. 4tets: *Asturiano*; *Cristo de la Vega* (with recitation, of poem of same name by José Zorrilla); *Caprichos románticos*; *Oriental*; 2 4tets in E ma. (one a prize one); another in C mi.; *Las Horas de Nietzsche*. Publishers: Unión Musical Española (Madrid); Schott (Mayence).—P. G. M.

CAMPODONICO, Armanda. Argentine singer; *b*. Rosario. Stud. at Milan under Benvenuti, and at Brussels under Warnotz. Began operatic career at Barcelona in *Samson and Delilah*. After singing in Italy and Russia, returned to S. America in 1900 to fill engagements in Chile and Buenos Ayres. Now teaches in Buenos Ayres Conservatoire.—A. M.

CAMUSSI, Ezio. Ital. compr. *b*. Florence, 16 Jan. 1893. Stud. in Rome and Bologna; then in France under Massenet. Is noted for two melodramas which were perf. with a certain amount of success, *La Dubarry* (Lyric Theatre, Milan, 1912), and *I Fuochi di San Giovanni*, based on Sudermann's work (Dal Verme Theatre, Milan, 1920).—D. A.

CANAL, Marguerite. Fr. compr. Gained 1st *Grand Prix de Rome* (by unanimous vote), 1920, for her dramatic poem, *Don Juan*; also 1st prizes for harmony, acc. and fugue, at Paris Cons., where she pursued her studies and where she is to-day a titular professor.

About 100 songs; 5 vn. pieces; some pf. pieces; cello pieces; vn. sonata; *Don Juan* (orch.). (All publ. by Jamin.)—A. C.

CANALES, Marta. Chilean violinist and compr. Stud. in Chile where she has gained an eminent position on concert-platform. Is even better-known as compr., especially of a *Funeral March* and a *Berceuse*.

Orch. works; pieces for vn. and pf.; choruses, etc.—A. M.

CANONICA, Pietro. Ital. compr. *b*. Turin, 1 March, 1869. Is best known as a very clever sculptor, but is also passionately devoted to music. Has comp. various works, one of which, *La sposa di Corinto (The Bride of Corinth)*, has been perf. at the Argentina, Rome, 1918.—D. A.

CANTELOUBE, Jean. Fr. compr. *b*. Montauban, 1875. Pupil of *Schola Cantorum*; a "regional" musician of the artistic family of Déodat de Séverac, finding his inspiration in the popular songs of Languedoc, of which he is a native.

Many songs, melodies and a very lively opera, *Le Mas*, based on æsthetic charm of regional inspiration.—A. C.

CANTOR. The name for a choirmaster in Germany.—E.-H.

CANTRELLE, William. Fr. violinist; *b.* Paris, 20 Nov. 1888. Pupil of Rémy at Paris Cons.; 1st prize 1905; first became known at Concerts Rouge, which had seen *début* of Jacques Thibaut. Remained here as soloist, 1908–12; then appeared at Touche Concerts, 1913–21; solo vn. Colonne and Lamoureux orchs., united in 1917 and 1918; 1922, soloist at Colonne Concerts. His technical ability is extraordinary. The repertory of Heifetz and Elman is well known to him, but his orch. work has given him a complete general culture and a style which is as pure in the classics as it is fanciful in Paganini or Wieniawski. He may be placed, with Thibaut, Capet and Boucherit, as a violinist of first rank.—M. P.

CAPELL, Richard. Eng. mus. critic; *b.* Northampton. Critic of *Daily Mail*, London, since 1911. Has an interesting style and a penetrating insight. Puts great emphasis on native art.—E.-H.

CAPELLEN, Georg. Ger. writer on theory of music; *b.* Salzuflen, 1 April, 1869. Jurist. Since 1901, theorist in harmonics and acoustics, with special reference to exotic influences.

Harmony and Melody in Wagner's Works (*Bayreuther Blätter*, 1901); *Is Simon Sechter's System a Suitable Point of Departure for Theoretical Wagner Research ?* (1902); *Musical Acoustics as the Basis of Harmony and Melody* (1903): *The Freedom or Want of Freedom of Tones and Intervals as a Criterion in Part-writing* (1904); *Interdependence* (*Abhängigkeitsverhältnisse*) *in Music* (1904); *The Future of Musical Theory* (1905); *A New Style in Exotic Music* (1906); *Progressive Course of Harmony and Melody* (Leipzig, 1908).—A. E.

CAPET, Lucien. French violinist ; *b.* Paris, 1873. Pupil of Morin at Cons.; 1st prize, 1893. Appeared as soloist for all the great symphony societies, especially Concerts Lamoureux. Taught at Cons. Bordeaux (1899–1903) and at Paris (1907 onwards). Excels as teacher, and his book *Technique de l'Archet* (*Technique of the Bow*) is authoritative. Has comp. 3 4tets. Mainly celebrated in connection with the quartet he founded, with Giron, H. Casadesus, Touret (replaced by Carcanade); this quartet (composed in 1903 of L. C., Touret, Bailly [Carcanade], Hasselmans; in 1910 of L. C., Hewitt, Benoît, Delobelle) has reached the highest points of perfection. Although it devotes a few performances each year to modern music, it is mainly concerned with the execution of the 17 quartets of Beethoven.—M. P.

CAPLET, André. Fr. compr. condr. *b.* Le Havre, 27 Nov. 1879. Began to study music in native city under Henry Woollett; in 1897 entered Paris Cons., where his teachers were Leroux and Lenepveu. *Prix de Rome*, 1901; at that time had already made his mark as condr. at the Odéon. On his return from Rome, extended his activities in this capacity to Germany, and later to United States (Boston Opera) and to England (Covent Garden).

Pf. 5tet; *Legend*, harp and small orch. (after Poe's *Masque of the Red Death*); *Suite persane*, wind instrs.;

7tet, 3 female vs. and strs.; mass, 3 female vs.; sonata, v., cello and pf.; a number of songs and part-songs. They evince ingenuity and an original imagination as well as technical skill. As a creative artist, he has much in common with the school of Gabriel Fauré.—M. D. C.

CAPPELEN, Christian. Norwegian compr. and orgt. *b.* Drammen, 26 Jan. 1845; *d.* Christiania, 11 May, 1916. Received his mus. training at Cons. in Leipzig and in Dresden; afterwards orgt. in Drammen. From 1887, L. M. Lindeman's successor as orgt. to Our Saviour's Ch. Christiania, where he acquired a name as Norway's greatest church musician after the death of his predecessor. His fame as orgt. extended beyond his own country and his dominant personality gave his art a noble and lofty character. His improvisations were famed for their deep religious spirit. As a compr. he belongs to the older school, but all his 32 works show taste, excellent form and clever cpt. with restrained characterisation.

Cantatas; organ pieces; unacc. choral works for mixed chorus (6 *Geistliche Lieder*, perf. in Leipzig); pf. pieces; songs.—J. A.

CARABELLA, Ezio. Ital. compr. *b.* Rome, 1891. Compr. of symph. works (perf. at the Augusteo), and of operettas, perf. with success.

Impressione sinfonica, small orch. (1913); *Preludio*, full orch. (1916); *Variazioni sinfoniche* (1921) incidental music to Fraschetti's *Fortunello* (Rome, Teatro dei Piccoli, 1921); *Don Gil dalle calze Verdi*, operetta (Rome, 1922).—D. A.

CARBONELL DE VILLAR, Manuel. Singer; *b.* Alicante in 1856. Stud. under Fasenga at Madrid Cons. and under Antonio Selva at Padua. First appeared at the Dal Verme, Milan (in *Favorita*). Sang throughout Europe and N. America for 30 years, in company with the greatest singers. On leaving opera stage, was appointed prof. of singing at Regio Cons. Barcelona, and later at Imperial Cons. Petrograd. Went to Buenos Ayres in 1910, where he founded a successful school of singing. Author of a book giving the careers of the principal opera-singers, and a work dealing with operatic scenery and stage-setting.—A. M.

CARELLI, Emma. Ital. s. singer; *b.* Naples, 12 May, 1877. Pupil of her father, Beniamino Carelli, a noted teacher of singing. Owing to her ability and uncommon artistic qualities, she rapidly gained a position in front rank of Ital. operatic world. She was a very capable interpreter of the title - rôle in Mascagni's *Iris* in company with Caruso; she created the title-rôle in *Elektra* (Strauss) in Italy. At the age of 35, she gave up her career to devote herself to operatic enterprises, with her husband, Walter Mocchi, and she took over the management of the Costanzi Theatre (*q.v.*) as representative of a company which also runs various theatres in South America under Mocchi's management.—D. A.

CAREY, Francis Clive Savill. Eng. compr. and b. singer; *b.* Sible Hedingham, Essex, 30 May, 1883; educated Sherborne and Clare Coll. Cambridge; stud. R.C.M. under Sir Charles Stanford (compn.); singing under James H. Ley, London, and Jean de Reszke, Nice; member of

"The English Singers" ensemble. C. is a fine singer, a good actor and an intelligent producer. Incidental music to *The Blue Lagoon* (London, 1920); *The Wonderful Visit* (London, 1921); *All Fools' Day* (Glastonbury, 1921); songs (Stainer & Bell; Boosey; W. Rogers); 10 *English Folk-Songs* (Curwen); folk-song and dance arrs. in *The Esperance Morris Books* (2 vols., Curwen).—E.-H.

CARILLO, Julián. Mexican compr. *b.* 1875. Has comp. operas, symphonies, chamber and choral music, and written a treatise *Tratado sintético de Harmonía* (1913–15).—F. H. M.

CARILLON. See art. on BELLS.

CARILLON MUSIC is rarely published. Most of it is in ms. An important vol. consisting of a selection of preludes, fugues, minuets, etc., from the works of Matthias van den Gheyn (1721–85) was printed by Schott in 1862 and ed. by X. van Elewyck in collab. with Lemmens, the well-known orgt. This is out of print; the plates have been destroyed, and the few existing copies are only to be found in the most important libraries. A contemporary compr. of Van den Gheyn was Pothoff of Amsterdam. In recent times Josef Denijn and J. A. F. Wagenaar have written music specially for the carillon. Sir Edward Elgar comp. a special *Memorial Chime* for opening ceremony of Loughborough carillon, 1923. The compr. must have an exact appreciation of special characteristics of bell-tone as well as an intimate knowledge of the clavier technique. Two-part writing with clearly defined harmonic suggestion is perhaps the most effective. In the upper octaves of the clavier, chords of 3 or more notes can be freely used, in which case it is desirable to keep the bass part distant. A school of carillon-playing has recently (1922) been inaugurated at Mechlin with Josef Denijn as dir. The premises are granted free by the city authorities and are conveniently situated near the carillon tower. The complete course of study extends over a period of 3 years and provides carefully-graded work, first for attainment of manual dexterity; then the addition of a simple pedal part; finally elaborate manual and pedal technique. In England a bold and comprehensive course has been adopted by Prof. Granville Bantock at Birmingham Univ. A special lectureship has been instituted in campanology, including bell - making and tuning, acoustics of bells, carillons and carillon music, chimes, chime-tunes, the composing of bell-music, etc., together with practical demonstrations of the carillonist's art. The subject is included in the requirements of the Honours Mus.Bac. degree. The Bournville carillon is being completed by making the compass 3 octaves chromatic (37 bells) and will be available for students. There will also be a practice clavier—an exact replica of the carillon one—for the purpose of individual study. The Birmingham Univ. scheme is the only one of its kind in the world.—W. W. S.

CARL, William Crane. Amer. orgt. and teacher; *b.* Bloomfield, N.J., U.S.A., 2 March, 1865. Stud. chiefly in New York. Was for 2 years a pupil in organ and theory of Guilmant in Paris. A founder in 1896 of Amer. Guild of Orgts. Establ. a Guilmant Organ School in New York in 1899. Has travelled far and wide in U.S.A. as a concert orgt. *Officier de l'Instruction Publique* in 1909, and in 1911 Mus.D. *h.c.* New York Univ. Has comp. organ pieces and ed. several large colls. of organ works (Schirmer; Boston Music Co.; Ditson).—O. K.

CARLHEIM-GYLLENSKÖLD, Sigrid. Swedish pianist; *b.* Väjö, 9 May, 1863. Stud. R. Cons. Stockholm (Hilda Thegerström) and Leschetizky (Vienna). Founded Stockholm Musikinstitut, which enjoys a good reputation. Member R.A.M. Stockholm, 1912.—P. V.

CARLSON, Bengt. Finnish compr., choral condr. *b.* Ekenäs, 26 April, 1890. Pupil of Helsingfors Music Inst. and of Vincent d'Indy, Paris. Since 1920, condr. Swedish Students' Choir (Akademiska Sångföreningen) and recently of Swedish Oratorio Choir in Helsingfors. Has comp. chamber-music, choral songs, etc.—T. H.

CARNEGIE UNITED KINGDOM TRUST. The musical policy of the Trustees falls under the following heads: (1) Music Publication Scheme; (2) Tudor Music Editions; (3) rural concert and dramatic (largely mus.) tours: (4) miscellaneous grants. Grants to churches towards purchase of organs are definitely discontinued. Altogether the Trust has honoured promises to the number of 540.

(1) Each year the Trustees publish new compns. by British comprs. residing within United Kingdom (maximum number 6). The works eligible are: (*a*) Concerted chamber-music for 3 or more instrs.; (*b*) concerto for one or more solo instrs. with acc. for large or small orch.; (*c*) choral work, with acc. for large or small orch.; (*d*) symphony or other orch. work of an important nature; (*e*) opera or mus. drama, including incidental music to plays. In chief works in classes *c, d* and *e*, the full score is not normally publ., but a sufficient number of ms. copies of full score and parts are provided to facilitate performance ; in classes *c* and *e* an edition of the vocal score is printed. Works must be submitted by 21 Dec. each year; awards are announced about 4 or 5 months later. The works published up to Dec. 1923, are:

Before Sunrise, symphony, contr. solo, chorus, orch. (Edgar L. Bainton); *The Hebridean Symphony*, orch. (Granville Bantock); *The Immortal Hour*, music drama (Rutland Boughton); *The Sea*, symph. suite, orch. (Frank Bridge); 4tet in A mi. pf. vn. vla. cello (Herbert Howells); *The Travelling Companion*, 4-act opera (Charles V. Stanford); *A London Symphony*, orch. (R. Vaughan Williams); *Poème Symphonique*, orch. (L. A. Collingwood); str. 4tet in A ma. (E. N. Hay); 4tet in C mi. pf. vn. vla. cello (Alfred M. Wall); 3 *Rhapsodies*, str. 4tet (George Dyson); *The Hound of Heaven*, fantasy for bart. solo. chorus and orch. (W. H. Harris); *The Hymn of Jesus*, 2 choruses, semi-chorus, orch., pf. and organ (Gustav T. Holst); 6tet for str. in G mi. (P. H. Miles); *The Magic Harp*, rhapsody, orch. (Ina Boyle); *Tam o' Shanter*, concert-overture (Learmont Drysdale); *English Pastoral Impressions*, suite, orch. (Ernest B. Farrar); *Rhapsodic 5tet*, clar. 2 vns. vla. cello (Herbert Howells); *Chamber Rhapsody*, No. 2, fl. c.a. str. 4tet and 2 vs. (Arthur Bliss); *Brown Earth*, chorus, semi-chorus, and orch. (Cyril Bradley Rootham); *Prince Ferelon*, 1-act mus. extravaganza (Nicholas Gatty); *Among the Northumbrian Hills*, pf. 2 vns. vla. cello (W. G. Whittaker); str. 4tet No. 2 in D mi. 2 vns. vla. cello (York Bowen); *Fan-*

tasy, str. orch. (R. O. Morris); *The Nymph's Complaint for the Death of her Fawn*, poem for ob. (or
vn), vla. and pf. (Felix White); *Fantasy-Overture*,
orch. (Edward Mitchell); *Solway*, symphony, orch.
(John B. McEwen); *St. Dominic*, mass for choir,
soli and orch. (Harry Farjeon) (vocal score only);
Nativity Hymn, solo, chorus, and orch. (Cyril Scott)
(vocal score only); *L'Allegro ed il Pensieroso*, symphony No. 5 in D ma. orch. (Charles V. Stanford);
Snow Picture, tone-poem (S. H. Braithwaite); *The
Curlew*, t. v. fl. c.a. str. 4tet (Peter Warlock), poem by
Yeats; *Hymn to the Virgin* and the *White Island*,
men's vs. str. pf. organ (Leslie Woodgate). All
inquiries to Messrs. Stainer & Bell, Ltd. 58 Berners
Street, London, W.1.

Recommended for publication, 1924 (7 works):
Pastoral Fantasia, str. 4tet (Arthur Benjamin); *A
Severn Rhapsody*, chamber orch. (Gerald Finzi); *The
Blue Peter*, comic opera (C. Armstrong Gibbs); *The
Western Playland*, song-cycle on works by A. E. Hous-
man (Ivor Gurney); 5tet, pf. and str. (Cyril Scott);
4tet, pf. and str. (W. T. Walton); *A Lyke-Wake Dirge*,
chorus and orch. (W. G. Whittaker).

(2) A quarto ed. of 10 vols. containing compns.
by Elizabethan comprs. is in course of publication. Vol. II (*Byrd : English Church Music*,
Part I) appeared in autumn of 1922, Vol. I
(*Taverner*, Part I) in Dec. 1923, and Vol. III
(*Taverner*, Part II) in March 1924. The remaining vols. will contain further compns.
of Byrd, and also of Orlando Gibbons (Vol.
IV), Robert White, Thomas Tallis, Thomas
Tomkins, John Merbecke, Thomas Morley,
Thomas Weelkes and John Ward. For convenience of choirs, 50 characteristic works are being
separately publ. in 8vo at popular prices. All
inquiries to Oxford University Press, Amen
House, Warwick Square, London, E.C.

(3) The Trustees have assisted, by grants and
guarantees, the Village and Country Town Concerts Fund and the Arts League of Service, to
arrange tours in small towns and villages, mainly
under the auspices, locally, of county education
committees. The former body, during 1922, gave
roughly 500 concerts in 20 counties of England
and Scotland.

(4) The Trustees have assisted the formation
and early development of the British Federation of Mus. Competition Fests. They are setting
up gradually an Orch. Loan Library for the use
of smaller orch. societies. They publ. in 1921 a
Report on British Music by Sir Henry Hadow.—
J. M. M.

CARNEVALI, Vito. Ital. pianist; *b.* Rome,
4 July, 1888. Stud. at R. Liceo Mus. di Santa
Cecilia (pf. Bajardi and Sgambati; compn.
Falchi and Respighi). Favourably known as a
concert-player. Now lives in New York.—D. A.

CAROL-BÉRARD. Fr. compr. *b.* 1885. Pupil
of Albeniz; stud. especially Chinese, Arabic
and negro music; directs his researches towards
the utilisation in music of *noises* of modern
life (factories, stations, etc.). He publ. numerous
articles to defend his theories, notably the
Couleur en mouvement (*Revue Musicale*) and
*Instrumentation par le système des bruits enre-
gistrés*; also several vols. of verses and essays
(under the name of Olivier Réaltor). He helped
to found Union Syndicale des Compositeurs de
Musique (of which he is gen. secretary), and is
planning the creation of a *Maison des Musiciens.*
His mus. output (very abundant and almost entirely

unpubl.), comprises: *Symphonie dansée*; suite, *Pro-
vence*; incidental music for *Semiramis* of Peladan;
little ballet, *Les Amants de Tong-ho*; a piece,
L'Oiseau des Iles; fragments for a film, *La Terrasse
de Babylone*; many pf. pieces; songs.—A. C.

CARPENTER, John Alden. Amer. compr. *b.*
Park Ridge (Chicago), Ill., U.S.A., 28 Feb. 1876.
Stud. pf. under Amy Fay, later under Seeboeck
in Chicago. His theoretical studies he continued
at Harvard Univ. under J. K. Paine. After
his graduation (A.B. 1897), entered his father's
business (mill, railway and shipping supplies).
In 1909, became Vice-President of the corporation organised by his father. He did not, however, abandon his mus. studies. In 1906 he came
into contact for a short time with Edward Elgar
in Rome. Between 1908 and 1912 he continued
the study of mus. theory under Bernhard Ziehn
in Chicago.

His first publ. works of any significance were
Improving Songs for Children (Schirmer, 1907).
A sonata for pf. and vn. was 1st perf. in public
at a concert of the *Schola Cantorum* in New York,
11 Dec. 1912. He became better known after
the publication in 1914 of his *Gitanjali*, a song-
cycle of poems by Tagore. A humoristic orch.
suite, *Adventures in a Perambulator*, was 1st perf.
by the Chicago Orch. 19 March, 1915, and was
perf. in London at B.M.S. Congress in June
1921. His 1st symphony, *Sermons in Stones*
(written 1916-17), was first played at Litchfield
County Choral Union Fest. (Norfolk, Conn.), 5
June, 1917. A ballet-pantomime, *The Birthday of
the Infanta* (after Oscar Wilde), was brought out
by the Chicago Opera Co. 23 Dec. 1919. His
latest work is a ballet *Krazy Kat* (described as a
"jazz-pantomime"), founded on a series of popular newspaper cartoons. The music was played
by the Chicago Orch. 23 Dec. 1921.

In 1921 C. was decorated with the Cross of the
Fr. Legion of Honour. He received the degree of
M.A. *h.c.* from Harvard Univ. 1922. As a compr.
he follows modern tendencies entirely, although
he has not yet joined the extreme ultra-
modernists. His work exhibits great variety and
skill in the handling of the orchestra.

Adventures in a Perambulator for orch. (1917);
Concertino for pf. and orch. (1920); *Krazy Kat*,
ballet, pf. arr. by compr. (1922); sonata for vn. and
pf. (1913); *Gitanjali : Song-Offerings*, poems by
Rabindranath Tagore (1914); *Water Colours: four
Chinese Tone-Poems* (songs) (1916). (All publ. by
Schirmer.)—O. K.

CARPI, Fernando. Ital. operatic t. singer;
b. Florence, 1881. Stud. singing at Liceo
Mus. at Bologna, and at the same time stud.
law at the Univ. Rapidly gained a wide reputation for the exquisite qualities of his light
lyric voice. Has appeared at all the principal
opera-houses, especially in North America.
Repertoire:
*Rigoletto, Barbiere, Sonnambula, Don Pasquale,
Elisir d' amore, Bohème, Manon, Mefistofele, Tosca,
Werther, Zazà*, etc.—D. A.

CARRAUD, Gaston. Fr. compr. critic; *b.* Paris,
1869; *d.* there, 1920. *Grand Prix de Rome*,
1890; put at service of mus. compn. a nature
as literary as musicianly; has always oscillated
between compn. and criticism, and the latter has
finally triumphed. (This is the case with Émile

Vuillermoz also.) Critic for journal *La Liberté*, he has shown for 20 years a free mind, the judgment of a historian, and real talent also. Author of *Albéric Magnard* (Paris, 1921).

Songs, *Soirs moroses* (1891); symph. poem, *La Chevauchée de la Chimère* (1905); dramatic symphony, *Buona pasqua*.—A. C.

CARREÑO, María Teresa. South Amer. pianist; *b.* 22 Dec. 1853 at Caracas (Venezuela) where her father was Minister of Finance; *d.* New York, 12 June, 1917. Stud. under L. Gottschalk in Caracas and later under G. A. St. C. Mathias in Paris; then under Rubinstein. At the age of 9 appeared as pianist in New York and toured through the States. She toured England, and the Continent, 1865–74. She appeared (1875–82) on the operatic stage; reappearing as pianist in 1889. Her fame as one of the most brilliant and powerful of pianists dates from her European tour of 1889–90. She married 4 times —1872, the violinist Sauret; 1875, the baritone Giovanni Tagliapietra; 1892, the pianist d'Albert; 1902, Arturo Tagliapietra.—E.-H.

CARROLL, Walter. Mus. Adviser to Manchester Education Committee since 1918; *b.* Manchester, 4 July, 1869. Stud. privately and at Univ. of Manchester; Mus.Doc. Manchester, 1900; formerly prof. of harmony, compn. and art of teaching, R. Manchester Coll. of Music; formerly lecturer in music and examiner, Univ. of Manchester. Has done much to advance the cause of musical appreciation in schools, and to improve methods of teaching music.

Large amount of children's music (Forsyth; 1909–23); book, *The Training of Children's Voices*. —E.-H.

CARSE, Adam. Eng. compr. *b.* Newcastle-on-Tyne, 19 May, 1878. Stud. in Germany, 1893; R.A.M. London under Corder and Burnett, 1894–1903 (Macfarren Scholarship; Musicians' Co. Medal; Lucas Medal; Dove Prize); assistant music-master, Winchester Coll. 1909–22; now prof. of harmony and cpt. R.A.M. London. Has a pleasant and well finished style of writing, which concerns itself more with sound construction than original or atmospheric effects. Has written much educational music.

Orch.: Miniature suite, *Boulogne* (J. Williams); *The Merry Milkmaids* (1922, Augener); *Barbara Allen*, variations for str. orch. (Novello); *Norwegian Fantasia*, vn. and orch. (J. Williams). Two sketches, str. orch. (1923; Augener); sonata, C mi. vn. and pf. (*id.*); *Judas Iscariot's Paradise*, ballad for chorus, barit. solo and orch. (1922, *id.*); *The Lay of the Brown Rosary*, dramatic cantata (Novello); many part-songs; numerous songs, pf., vn. and other pieces; pf. studies, exercises. Books: *Summary of the Elements of Music* (Augener); *Practical Hints on Orchestration* (*id.*); *Harmony Exercises*, 2 books (1923, *id.*).—E.-H.

CARUSO, Enrico. Italian operatic tenor singer; *b.* Naples, 25 Feb. 1873; *d.* Naples, 2 August, 1921. This celebrated artist, who gained, especially in North America, such a superlative degree of celebrity that he commanded the salary of $10,000 a night, started his career in a very humble and uncertain way. At the age of 10 he was singing in church choirs; then he set himself to study, passing under various masters, none of whom knew how to appreciate his extraordinary qualities; only

quite late did he discover, in the masters Lamperti, Concone and Lombardi, teachers who set him seriously on the high road of art. He started his career in his native town; then appeared at the Lyric, Milan, with a clamorous reception; from then onwards his successes became continuous and triumphant. He took part in the first perfs. of *Fedora* (Giordano) and of *Germania* (Franchetti). His repertoire was vast, and included almost all the lyric and dramatic Fr. and Ital. operas, from *Sonnambula* to *L'Africana*, *Don Giovanni* to *Il Trovatore*, *L'Elisir d' amore* to *Cavalleria* and *Pagliacci*, *La Gioconda* to *La Bohème* and the *Fanciulla del West*, *Pescatore di Perle* and *Samson and Delilah* to *Faust* and *Manon* (Massenet). C. was gifted with an exquisite artistic sense in other directions also; he was an enthusiastic collector of pictures and works of art; he amused himself also by drawing and was a capable caricaturist (see *Caruso's Book, being a collection of caricatures and character-studies from original drawings of the Metropolitan Opera Company*, 1906). He publ. a book on the art of singing, entitled *Wie man singen soll* (Mayence, 1914, Schott).

Consult: Onorato Roux in *Illustrious Italian Contemporaries* (Florence, Bemporad); Wagenmann, *Enrico Caruso und das Problem der Stimmbildung*; Pierre V. Key, *E.C.* (London, Hurst & Blackett, 1923); also innumerable articles published in America during his stay there, and everywhere on the occasion of his death.—D. A.

CARYLL, Ivan (real name Felix Tilkin). Compr. condr. *b.* Liège, Belgium, 1861; *d.* New York, 28 Nov. 1921. Stud. Liège Cons. Comp. mus. comedies.

Duchess of Dantzig (1903); *Earl and the Girl* (1904); *New Aladdin* (1906); *Our Miss Gibbs* (1909); *The Pink Lady* (1911), etc.—E.-H.

CASADESUS, Francis. Fr. compr. *b.* Paris, 1870. 1918–22, dir. Fontainebleau School of Music for Amer. teachers and advanced students. He was followed there by Max d'Ollone in 1923.

Cachaprès, 3-act opera, 1914; *Le Moissonneur*, 5-act, 1918; *Au beau jardin de France*, 1-act, 1918; symphony, E mi.—A. C.

CASALS, Enrique. Span. violinist and compr. *b.* Vendrell (Barcelona) Leader of the Pau Casals Orch. Barcelona. As a compr. he specialises in Catalonian popular music, best known for his *sardanas*. Brother of celebrated cellist, Pablo Casals.—P. G. M.

CASALS, Pablo. Span. cellist and condr. *b.* Vendrell (Catalonia), 30 Dec. 1876. His father, the local orgt., taught him to play several wind and str. instrs., which he abandoned for the cello, taking lessons with José García. First public perf. in 1889 at Barcelona, where he remained until his 17 year. Under patronage of Queen María Cristina, he entered the R. Cons. de Música, Madrid, attending the chamber-music classes of the late Monasterio. At 19, he joined the Brussels Cons. for a short time, but did not actually receive any tuition there, returning to Barcelona, where he became prof. at the Cons. and founded a str. quartet with his colleague, the Belgian violinist, Crickboom. Made his *début* in Paris, at Lamoureux Concerts; and in London,

Crystal Palace (1898). His rise to fame was preceded by years of patient struggle. In 1919 he founded in Barcelona the Orquesta Pau Casals, and gave several series of concerts. As a condr. he is looked upon as a stimulating force, opposed to that pseudo-virtuosity of the bâton, into which the Nikisch tradition seems to be degenerating. He is a remarkable pianist and has comp. pieces for orch. and chamber-music. C. is recognised as one of the epoch-making figures in the contemporary history of art. Guided by an unusual inborn understanding of the abstract meaning of music, he has developed the resources of cello technique and expression to a limit of unsuspected possibilities. No cello exponent of the present generation can remain immune to his influence, the title of founder of a new school of cello-playing being due to him. An uncompromising and incorruptible attitude in matters of mus. interpretation is the foundation-stone of his incomparable art, in which he exhibits the robust sobriety characteristic of the Span. creative genius of Velásquez, Victoria, Morales, Zurbarán, Fray Luis de León and Herrera. He has restored to the concert repertoire Bach's unaccompanied compositions for the cello, thus saving from complete deterioration that standard of refinement in execution and sense of extreme subtlety of nuance which are essential to the accurate rendering of the classics. In 1906 he married Guilhermina Suggia (q.v.)—P. G. M.

CASAUX, Juan. Span. cello virtuoso; b. San Fernando (Cadiz), 28 Dec. 1889. First prize at Paris Cons.; lives in Madrid, where he is senior prof. at the R. Cons. de Música. —P. G. M.

CASELLA, Alfredo. Italian pianist and composer; b. Turin, 25 July, 1883. Son of a teacher at the Turin Liceo; studied piano first under his mother; then went at the age of 13, on Martucci's advice, to Paris Cons., under Diémer, (pianoforte) and Fauré (composition) He then toured successfully as a pianist, appearing under famous conductors (Colonne, Lamoureux, Monteux, Hasselmans, Mengelberg, etc.). From 1912 he directed the Concerts Populaires at the Trocadéro, Paris, and for 3 years directed a piano class at the Paris Conservatoire. From 1915 to 1923 taught at the Royal Liceo Musicale di Santa Cecilia, Rome. Musical critic to journals *Monde Musical*, *S.I.M.*, the Paris daily *Homme Enchaîné*; Italian correspondent for *Courrier Musical* (Paris) and *Musical America* (New York). In 1917 he founded in Rome the Società Nazionale di Musica (afterwards the Società Italiana di Musica Moderna; refounded, 1923, as the Corporazione delle Musiche Nuove [Italian section of the International Society for Contemporary Music]). Gifted with powers of memory and analytical faculties of assimilation that are truly prodigious, Casella is the accomplished type of European musician. He knows all styles, and practises them on occasion with an unheard-of virtuosity. He submitted in turn to the most contradictory

influences—Debussy, Mahler, Ravel, Stravinsky and Schönberg. These influences may be recognised in all his works; those of his youth particularly (symphony; cello sonata; Suite in C; *Couvent sur l'eau* [ballet]; *Notte di Maggio*) have caused certain people to deny to Casella a strictly original talent. This is unjust. His personality appears in his first compositions, and manifests itself brilliantly in his more recent works: *Pagine di guerra*, *Elegia eroica*, *L'Adieu à la vie* (to poems of Tagore), *A notte alta* (piano concerto). He there manifests a sombre soul haunted by funereal visions, expressing, in a new and original manner, his sense of mystery and of the beyond. One finds also in certain works a singular humour and a truly ferocious sense of the grotesque. From the purely technical point of view, he is without doubt the most able of Italian composers of the day. His *Elegia eroica* and his *Pagine di guerra* reveal a surprising orchestral virtuosity. In 1924, he published an interesting book, *The Evolution of Music* (Italian, French and English texts; Chester, London).

Pf.: *Toccata*, 1904 (Ricordi, Milan); *Berceuse triste*, 1909 (Mathot); *Barcarola*, 1910 (Ricordi); *Sarabanda*, 1910 (Mathot); *Nove pezzi*, 1914 (Ricordi); *Pagine di guerra*, 1915 (pf. duet) (Chester, London); *Pupazzetti*, 1916 (pf. duet) (*id.*); *Sonatina*, 1916 (Ricordi); *A notte alta*, 1917 (*id.*); *Inezie* (3 easy pieces); 2 *Contrastes* (*Grazioso*; *Antigrazioso*), 1918 (Chester); 3 pieces for pianola (Æolian Co. London) *Undici pezzi infantili*, 1920 (Univ. Ed. Vienna); *Fox-trot* (pf. duet) 1920 (*id.*).
Songs: *Cinque liriche*, 1903 (Mathot); *Soleils couchants*, *Soir païen*, *En ramant*, 1906 (*id.*); *Sonnet*, 1910 (*id.*); *Il bove*, 1913 (Ricordi); *L'Adieu à la vie* (4 funeral songs from Tagore), 1915 (Chester).
Chamber-music: *Barcarola e scherzo*, fl. and pf. 1904 (Mathot); sonata, pf. and cello, 1907 (Mathot); *Siciliana e burlesca*, pf. vn. and cello, 1914 (Ricordi); 5 pieces for str. 4tet (*Preludio*; *Ninna-nanna*; *Valse ridicule*; *Notturno*; *Fox-trot*), 1920 (Univ. Ed.).
Orch.: 1st *Sinfonia* in B mi. 1905 (Mathot); 2nd *Sinfonia* in C mi. (1908–10); *Italia* (rhapsody) 1900 (Univ. Ed. Vienna); Suite in C ma. (much perf.) 1909 (*id.*); *Notte di maggio* (Colonne Concerts, 1914), v. and orch. (Ricordi); *Le Couvent sur l'eau* (1911–12), suite symph. (Monteux Concerts, 1914) (Ricordi); *Elegia eroica*, 1916 (Univ. Ed.); *Pagine di guerra* (1917), 5 " films " (Chester). Stage-work: *Le Couvent sur l'eau* (commedia coreografica) in 2 acts. Arr. Mahler's 7th symphony for 4 hands (Univ. Ed.)
Consult G. M. Gatti, *A. C.* (in *Critica Musicale*, Florence, July 1918) and *Mus. Times* (London) July 1921.—H. P.

CASIMIRI, (Monsignor) Raffaele Casimiro. Ital. compr. and condr. of sacred music; b. Gualdo Tadino (Umbria), 3 Nov. 1880. After having occupied various positions in seminaries and chapels in several Ital. cities, in 1911 he was called to conduct the choir of St. John Lateran, Rome, which post he still occupies; at the same time he is teacher at the Pontificia Scuola Superiore di Musica Sacra, and member of various commissions. Author of much sacred music (publ. Capra, Turin; Bertarelli, Milan; Schwann, Düsseldorf, etc.). Has cond. concerts of sacred music of XVI century, with the Società Polifonica Romana (q.v.), with which soc. he has toured in America, England and other countries. Has publ. numerous studies in various Ital. mus. reviews, especially regarding the history of sacred music in Rome. His

vol. on *Codex* 56 *of the Lateran Musical Archives*
(the only known autograph of Giovanni Pierluigi da Palestrina) is important. In 1907,
founded in Perugia the *Psalterium*, a review of
sacred music, which he soon transferred to Rome,
where it is still publ. under his direction.—D. A.

CASSADÓ, Gaspar. Span. cello virtuoso; *b.*
Catalonia, 1898. Pupil of Pablo Casals; tours
Spain, France, Germany and America.—P. G. M.

CASSADÓ, Joaquín. Span. contemporary
compr. *b.* in Catalonia. Lyric drama, *Lo Monjo
Negre*; cello concerto; *Sinfonía Macarena*; *His-
pania*, piano and orch. (first perf. in London,
Promenade Concerts, Queen's Hall, 1923, soloist
José Iturbi, under Sir Henry Wood); smaller
works for orch., for cello, etc. Lives in
Barcelona.—P. G. M.

CASTBERG, Torgrim. Norwegian violinist;
condr. of the Music Acad. in Bergen; *b.* Skien
in 1874. Stud. 1893–6 in Paris; 1896–1900 in
Berlin. In 1905 he founded (with splendid
assistance from the art-patron, Frithjof Sundt,
and with the support of Edvard Grieg, J. L.
Mowinckel, Joachim Grieg and Under-Secretary
of State Haugen) the Music Acad. in Bergen, of
which he has since been director.—R. M.

CASTELNUOVO-TEDESCO, Mario. Compr.
b. Florence, 3 April, 1895. Stud. at Cherubini
R. Inst. of Music there, under Del Valle (pf.)
and I. Pizzetti (compn.). As one of the young
Ital. school, he is noted for his interesting work.
Orch: *Cielo di settembre* (1910). Pf.: *Il raggio
verde*; *Alghe*; *I naviganti*; *Cantico*. V. and pf.:
Fuori i barbari; *Le Roi Loys*; *Ninna Nanna*; *Stelle
cadenti*; *Coplas*; *Briciole*; *Cera Vergine*; *Il libro di
Dolcina*; *Girotondo dei golosi*; *Star*. Vn. and pf.:
Signorine (1918); 3 *Canti* (1919); *Ritmi* (1920);
Capitan Fracassa (1920). V. and orch.: 2 *Liriche*
(from Tagore) (1917); 3 *Fioretti di San Francesco*
(1919). Unacc. 4-v. chorus: 2 *Madrigali a Galatea*
(1914); 2 *Canti Greci* (1917). Mostly publ. by
Forlivesi (Florence). Also 5 *Songs of Shakespeare*
(Chester, 1923).
Consult Guido M. Gatti, *M. C.-T.* (*Musicisti
moderni, d' Italia e di fuori*: Bologna, 1920, Pizzi),
and *Mus. Times* (London) Feb. 1921.—D. A.

CASTÉRA, René de. Fr. compr. *b.* Dax,
3 April, 1873. Inclined at first towards agriculture; stud. music from 1897 onwards; pupil
at *Schola Cantorum*; contributed in 1902 to
foundation of Soc. of Édition Mutuelle, which
has publ. greater part of productions of *Schola*
pupils.
Pf. trio; vn. sonata; symph. poem, *Jour de fête au
pays basque*; pf. pieces; some songs.—A. C.

CASTILLON, Alexis de. Fr. compr. *b.* Chartres,
13 Dec. 1838; *d.* Paris, 5 March, 1873. Entered
military school of Saint-Cyr; left to devote himself to mus. compn. At first, pupil of Victor
Massé, then of César Franck, to whom Duparc
introduced him in 1868. Died suddenly in 1873,
having had time, however, to draw up the
statutes of the Société Nationale de Musique
(founded 1871) of which he was secretary.
Symph. music: pf. concerto (played by Saint-
Saëns, March 10, 1872, at Pasdeloup Concert; hissed
by public not then accustomed to serious music);
chamber works: pf. 5tet; 2 str. 4tets; 2 trios for
pf. vn. and cello; pf. and vn. sonata; pf.: *Pièces
dans le style ancien*; 2 suites; 6 *Valses humoristiques*;
Pensées fugitives; songs. Consult Hugues Imbert,
Profils d'artistes contemporains (1897).—A. C.

CASTRO, Ricardo. See MEXICAN OPERA.

CATALANI, Alfredo. Ital. opera - compr. *b.*
Lucca, 19 June, 1854; *d.* Milan, 7 Aug. 1893.
Stud. first under his father in his native city,
afterwards under Bazzini in Paris, then for 2
years at Milan Cons. under Bazzini, where in
1875 his eclogue in 1 act, *La Falce*, was perf.
His *début* as opera-compr. was made in Turin,
1880, with *Elda*. In 1883 *Dejanire* was produced
at La Scala; in 1886 *Edmea* in same theatre; in
1890, in Turin, *Loreley* (a revision of *Elda*); in
1892 *La Wally*. In 1885, he wrote the symph.
poem *Ero e Leandro*. He was also an esteemed
teacher at Milan Cons. His work has had a
marked influence on the Ital. comprs. who succeeded him (Mascagni, Puccini, etc.).—D. A.

CATHIE, Philip. Eng. violinist; *b.* Manchester,
1874. Stud. at R.A.M. London under Sainton
and Sauret; *début* as boy-violinist; later at St.
James's Hall in R.A.M. concert, 1891, when he
introduced Goldmark's concerto into England;
prof. R.A.M. in 1897. Since 1914, had been dir.
of music in various London theatres.—E.-H.

CATOIRE, George Lvovitch (*pron.* Catuár,
accent on 3rd syll.). Russ. compr. *b.* Moscow,
15/27 April, 1861; pupil of Klindworth (pf.)
and Vilborg, Rüfer (Berlin) and Liadof
(theory); took mathematical course at Moscow
Univ. His early works drew Tchaikovsky's
attention, and showed his influence; but
gradually he evolved an individual style, fine and
elaborate, especially in his pf. 4tet, op. 31, 5tet,
op. 28, and later songs, op. 32, 33 (all Russ.
State Music Publ. Dept.). His pf. concerto
(E flat) was perf. at Q. H. London in 1920. In
1923 he completed a manual of harmony, founded
on the dodecuple scale (*q.v.*). Is prof. of compn.
at Moscow Conservatoire.
Symphony, op. 7; symph. poem, *Mzyri* (after
Lermontof), op. 13; pf. concerto, op. 21; str. 5tet,
op. 16; pf. 5tet, op. 28; pf. 4tet, op. 31; pf. trio,
op. 14; 1st vn. sonata, op. 15; 2nd vn. sonata, *The
Poem*, op. 20; many songs; choruses; pf. pieces.
—V. B.

CATTELANI, Ferruccio. Argentine violinist;
b. Parma in 1867. Stud. at Cons. of Parma under
Mantovani and Dacci. In 1897, vn. soloist at the
Opera and Colón theatres in Buenos Ayres.
Prof. of vn. for 14 years at Argentine Cons. of
Music (dir. by Pallemaerts). Set himself the un-
grateful task of educating mus. taste in Argen-
tina; founded Cattelani Quartet 1897 (with
Alessio Morrone, José Bonfiglioli and Tomás
Marenco). In 1900, formed a Symphony Concert
Company, which after 4 years had to be dis-
solved through lack of support. After unceasing
efforts, re-established the company 3 years later.
Its 4 concerts each year have proved very
successful.
Atahualpa, 4-act opera; symphony in E; 8tet;
5tet; 4tet; vn. pieces; numerous songs; 6 vn.
studies.—A. M.

CATTERALL, Arthur. Eng. violinist; *b.*
Preston, Lancs. Stud. under Willy Hess in 1894;
under Adolph Brodsky at R. Manchester Coll.
of Music, 1895; played at all Cosima Wagner's
mus. evenings at Bayreuth in season 1902;

appeared at a Hallé concert in Tchaikovsky's concerto, 1903; leader of Queen's Hall Promenade concerts, 1909; prof. of vn. R. Manchester Coll. of Music, 1912; leader of Hallé Orch. and of quartet under his name (Catterall, Bridge, Park, Hock).—E.-H.

CAUDELLA, Ed. See RUMANIA in art. ACADEMIES.

ČELANSKÝ, Ludvík Vítězslav. Czech compr. and condr. *b.* Vienna, 1870. At first a teacher, at Prague Cons. 1892; also at singing schools. Condr. at several theatres (Plzeň, Zagreb, Lwów, Prague) and of several orchs. (Prague, Lwów, Warsaw, Kief). Organised several orchs. personally, but did not remain long at their head. 1907–8, opera-dir. at Town Theatre, Vinohrady, Prague; then some time in Paris (Châtelet); 1918–19, in Prague with Czech Philh., and is now living there. One of best Czech condrs., distinguished by verve and intensity of expression. His rendering is characterised by numerous *rubati.* His talent is great, but he is without the necessary perseverance to utilise his gifts adequately.

Opera, *Camilla* (1907). Orch. melodramas: *The Earth; The Ballad of Jan Neruda's Death; The Bells.* Symph. poems: *Adam; Noah; Moses; Hold slunci* (*Homage to the Sun*).—V. ST.

CELESTA. See MUSTEL.

CELLI, Edoardo. Ital. pianist; *b.* Rome, 2 Feb. 1888. Pupil of Giovanni Sgambati at R. Liceo Mus. di Santa Cecilia; diploma in 1904; then went to Vienna to the Sauer and Leschetizky school. Has given concerts with the greatest success at the Augusteo, Rome, and in Paris, Boston and New York (where he resided for 2 years.)—D. A.

CELLIER, Alexandre. Fr. compr. orgt. *b.* Molières-en-Cèze (Gard), 1883. Pupil of Diémer, Leroux, Guilmant and Widor; orgt. and choirmaster.

Symph. suite, organ; 2 str. 4tets; Impromptus, pf.; cello sonatas; *Paysages cévenols,* pf. duet; songs. Author of an important work on the modern organ, *L'Orgue moderne* (1913).—A. C.

CELLIER, Laurent. Fr. compr. *b.* Metague, 1887. Pupil of Roger-Ducasse, Gédalge, Vierne. Has coll. 1200 Breton songs in Morbihan.

Pf. duets; *Prélude,* pf.; *Barcarolle,* pf. Also a monograph on his master, Roger-Ducasse (1920, Durand).—A. C.

CERNIKOF, Vladimir. Pianist; *b.* Paris, 2 May, 1882. Stud. Geneva, Malta, Berlin. *Début* 17 Oct. 1905, Mülhausen, Alsace; 1st London appearance, Feb. 1908; tours widely.—E.-H.

CESARI, Gaetano. Ital. music critic; *b.* Cremona in 1870. At first a d.-b. player; then, having gone to Germany, he stud. at the Arnold Krug School in Hamburg, and in Munich under Mottl, Sandberger and Kroyer. Returned to Italy and taught mus. history at the Istituto Superiore Manzoni. Now critic for the daily *Corriere della Sera,* and librarian at the Liceo Mus. G. Verdi; was a member of the permanent commission for mus. art at the Ministry of Education. Has given some of his best work to the preparation of a complete ed. of the works of Claudio Monteverdi (which will

appear shortly). Publ. following important studies in *Rivista Musicale Italiana:*
The Origins of XVI Century Madrigal; Giorgio Giulini as a Musician (contribution to history of symphony); *The " Orfeo " of Claudio Monteverdi, at the Association of the Friends of Music at Milan; Six Nocturne Sonatas of Giambattista Sammartini.*—D. A.

CESI, Beniamino. Ital. pianist; *b.* Naples, 6 Nov. 1845; *d.* there, 19 Jan. 1907. A distinguished concert-player and teacher. The most esteemed living pianists of the Neapolitan school have been his pupils, and his influence has been very wide and beneficial. He was at first his father's pupil, then Albanesi's. When Thalberg heard him, he made him one of his favourite pupils. At 20, he won the competition for pf. prof. at R. Cons. di San Pietro a Maiella in his native town.

His career as concert-player began at 18, and he very quickly gained a first-class reputation, not only in Italy but in all principal cities of Europe. He appeared in London in 1886, with great success. He was a great interpreter of old Ital. music, as well as Bach, Beethoven, Chopin, Schumann.

Anton Rubinstein esteemed Cesi, to such a degree that when Rubinstein was appointed dir. of Cons. of Petrograd, C. was asked by him to direct the pf. schools there. C. went to Petrograd in 1885, and remained there until 1891, when he was obliged to return to Italy on account of paralysis, which quickly reduced him to immobility, leaving, fortunately, his intelligence and his right hand untouched. In 1894 he was re-admitted as a teaching official in Cons. of Palermo, from whence, a few years after, he was able to return to the Naples Cons. in charge of a chamber-music class which he superintended until his death. His educational works have great importance.

Metodo, per pianoforte, in 3 large parts to be used contemporaneously: 1. Exercises and studies; 2. Polyphonic works: fugues, canons, legato style; 3. Pieces: sonatas, trios, 4tets, concertos, etc. (Ricordi). Many other colls. of pf. music, excellently revised. Consult a biography by Alessandro Longo (in review *L'Arte pianistica,* Naples, 1 Jan. 1914). —D. A.

CESI, Cecilia. Ital. pianist; *b.* Palermo, Dec. 1903. Daughter and pupil of Napoleone Cesi (*q.v.*). Showed a precocious aptitude as a pianist, worthily continuing the traditions of her family. At 6, made her *début;* at 8, gave a concert at the Sala Maddaloni, Naples, with great success. She had similar welcomes in Rome, Milan and other Ital. cities.—D. A.

CESI, Napoleone. Ital. pianist and compr. *b.* Naples, 6 Aug. 1867. Eldest son of Beniamino, whose pupil he was; with his younger brother Sigismondo (*q.v.*) he carried on the traditions and artistic heritage of his father. As a compr. he won several important competitions, and has publ. various works, especially for piano.—D. A.

CESI, Sigismondo. Ital. pianist and compr. *b.* Naples, 24 May, 1869. Second son of Beniamino. With his brother Napoleone he continued his father's teachings and traditions. Founded in Naples, 1908 (together with Ernesto Marciano) the Liceo Musicale, a private teaching institute which rose later to notable development and importance. C. has given successful concerts in principal Ital. cities, and is an esteemed teacher.

Numerous revisions of classical pf. music, and also *Appunti di storia e di letteratura del pianoforte*; also (in collab. with Marciano) a *Prontuario di musica* (*Handbook of Music*) (Ricordi).—D. A.

CHABRIER, Alexis Emmanuel. French composer; *b.* Ambert, 18 Jan. 1841; *d.* Paris, 13 Sept. 1894. Showed from early childhood a marked disposition for music, but was not allowed to study with view of taking it up professionally. Whilst pursuing his classical studies at Paris, received piano lessons from Eduard Wolf, and later lessons in harmony and counterpoint from Semet and Hignard. He also came into contact with César Franck's circle. In 1877 the success of his operetta *L'Étoile* (performed at Bouffes-Parisiens) marked the first step in his artistic career. It was followed by another operetta (in one act), *L'Éducation manquée* (1879) which attracted much notice. A journey to Munich, in company of Duparc, brought Wagner's music to Chabrier's notice, and exercised a decisive influence upon him. Soon afterwards he had the good fortune to find a post as assistant choirmaster to Charles Lamoureux, and henceforth he was able to devote all his time to music. Successively his orchestral rhapsody *España* (1883), his *Sulamite* for mezzo-soprano and female chorus (1885), and fragments of his lyric drama *Gwendoline* were performed under Lamoureux; and meanwhile various other works, such as his 10 *Pièces pittoresques* for pianoforte (1881) and *Valses romantiques* for 2 pianofortes (1883) were being published.

Gwendoline was produced at Brussels in 1886, but its run was cut short by the manager becoming bankrupt. A year later, the comic opera *Le Roi malgré lui* was produced at Paris Opéra-Comique, the first performance taking place a bare week before that theatre was destroyed by fire. Both these works were produced in Germany, but first performance of *Gwendoline* at Paris took place only at end of 1893, at a time when the composer's health had finally failed him.

His later works were the *Bourrée fantasque* for pianoforte, a few songs, and a choral ode, *A la Musique*. When death came, he was engaged in composing an opera, *Briséis*, of which the first act, which he had completed, was given at the Concerts Lamoureux in 1897 and produced at the Opéra in 1899 (publ. Enoch).

He died long before having given his measure, and, most unfortunately, before having come to his own for what he had achieved. Endowed with a wonderfully original imagination and with an instinct which enabled him to acquire, unassisted, the full measure of technique which he needed for self-expression, he is now regarded as one of the most significant French composers of his time. In picturesque and humorous effects he remains unsurpassed, and he has exercised a considerable influence upon contemporary developments in French music.

Consult: J. Desaymard, *E. Ch.* (Clermont Ferrard, 1908); R. Martineau, *E. Ch.* (Paris, 1910); G. Servières, *E. Ch.* (Paris). Further bibliography in Séré (*q.v.*).—M. D. C.

CHADWICK, George Whitefield. Amer. compr. *b.* Lowell, Mass., U.S.A., 13 Nov. 1854. Came of a New England family in which the love for music and some practical skill in singing or playing was common. At 15 he played the organ in a church in Lawrence, Mass. He entered his father's insurance business; but did not put aside music, studying at the New England Cons. in Boston, where Dudley Buck taught him theory, and George E. Whiting the piano. Later Eugene Thayer became his organ-master. After teaching for a year in 1876 at Olivet Coll. (Michigan), he entered the Leipzig Cons., studying theory under Jadassohn and pf. under Reinecke. His graduation work, an overture, *Rip Van Winkle*, was perf. at the Cons. in Leipzig (June 1879) and later in America (11 Dec. 1879) by Harvard Mus. Association. In the winter of 1879 he stud. organ and compn. under Rheinberger in Munich. Returning to America, Chadwick became the orgt. of the South Congregational Ch. in Boston in 1880, and in 1881 joined the teaching staff of the New England Cons. with which he has been connected ever since. In 1897 he became its dir. and has made of this inst. one of the most solid and most highly respected schools in U.S.A. He cond. J. K. Paine's music at the perf. of Sophocles' *Œdipus Tyrannus* at Harvard Univ. in 1881. His work with choral organisations in Boston and with the Amateur Boston Orch. Association led to his engagement by the Hampden County Fest. Association as condr. of their Springfield Fests. (1889–99). From 1898 to 1901 he cond. the better-known Worcester (Mass.) Fests. An achievement of no little significance was his organisation and conducting of the Cons. orch., which under C.'s direction began giving public concerts in 1902. The orch. raised the quality of its performances steadily up to the present day. He relinquished the bâton in 1919. In 1901 he went to England to study the organisation of typical Eng. music schools such as the R.C.M., R.A.M. and Guildhall School. In 1905 he made a similar trip to the Continent.

From the very beginning his compns. found a ready hearing. His first symphony was perf. by Harvard Mus. Association 23 Feb. 1882. On 13 Jan. 1883 the Boston Symphony Orch. played his overture *Thalia*. His second symphony, B flat, was perf. by the Boston Symphony Orch. 11 Dec. 1886. The overture *Melpomene* followed, 23 Dec. 1887, and in Feb. 1888, the Kneisel Quartet played his 5tet for pf. with strs. Thus his reputation as a compr. was establ., so that in 1892 the managers of the World's Columbian Exposition, held in Chicago in 1892, turned to C., when they sought a compr. for the *Columbian Ode* which was to commemorate the occasion, and which, in C.'s setting, was perf. by a chorus of 3000 singers with an orch. of 300 under Theodore Thomas.

As a compr. C. is a fine type of the native Amer. musician, who, like MacDowell, although trained in Europe, raised the standing of the Amer. compr. by giving evidence of a capacity for original work and a masterly technical equipment. Although true to the principles of Postclassic and Romantic schools which he had imbibed in his European training, he was not entirely oblivious to new movements. A loyal member of the conservative Old Guard, his later works show occasional evidences of the assimilation of new ideas, both in technique and in matters of style. Liberal and versatile in his tastes, his chief qualities are fluent melodic invention, and a fine mastery of classical forms. In 1897 he received A.M. *h.c.* from Yale Univ.; in 1905 LL.D. from Tufts Coll. He is at present (1924) the only musician in the Amer. Acad. of Arts and Letters, where he is the successor of MacDowell.

Symphony in F, No. III (Schmidt, 1896); *Melpomene*, dramatic overture (*id.* 1891); *Euterpe*, concert overture (*id.* 1906); *Aphrodite*, symph. fantasy (*id.* 1912); *Sinfonietta* (Schirmer, 1906); *Symphonic Sketches*, orch. suite (Schmidt, 1907); *Suite symphonique*, E flat (*id.* 1911); *Tam O'Shanter*, symph. ballad (Boston Music Co. 1917); *The Pilgrims*, for chorus and orch. (Schmidt, 1890); *Noel*, for chorus, soli and orch. (H. W. Gray, 1909); *Judith*, lyric drama for soli, chorus and orch. (Schirmer, 1901); *Everywoman*, a morality (T. B. Harms, 1911); many songs (Schmidt; Ditson); *Manual of Harmony*, (Boston, 1897, B. F. Wood).—O. K.

CHAILLEY, Marcel. Fr. violinist; *b.* Paris, 1881. Pupil of Bertheliez at Cons., which he left in 1902 with a prize. Since 1905, has devoted himself entirely to chamber-music playing. His quartet, which has changed several times, now consists of Chailley (1st vn.), Guilevitch (2nd vn.), Pascal (vla.), and Diran Alexanian (cello). This party, relatively little heard in France, enjoys great popularity in Holland, where it has produced important works (Voormolen's 4tet, etc.), and in Brazil where it made a brilliant tour. C. married the pianist Céliny Richez, who obtained 1st prize at Paris Cons. and was one of favourite pupils of Raoul Pugno.—M. P.

CHAINS OF IRON. Used for instr. effect by A. Schönberg in 3rd part of *Gurrelieder* (*Wilde Jagd* chorus).—EG. W.

CHAIX, Charles. Compr. *b.* Paris, 26 March, 1885. Stud. 1 year at the École Niedermeyer, Paris (1903); entered Geneva Cons. (organ); prof. of harmony there from 1909. His comprs., very poetically conceived and admirably clear in texture, show the influence of the school of César Franck.

Scherzo for orch. op. 2 (Swiss National Ed.); symphony in D, op. 3 (Geneva, A. Henn); 6 *Chorals figurés* for organ, op. 1 (Leipzig, Leuckart); 2 motets, unacc. chorus, op. 4 (Paris, Huguenin); *Poème funèbre*, chorus and orch. op. 5 (written in Macedonia during the war).—F. H.

CHALIAPIN, Feodor Ivanovitch. Russian operatic bass singer; *b.* Kazan on the Volga, 15 Feb. (o.s.) 1873. Sang as choir-boy; at 17, joined a provincial opera-company, beginning as the Stranger in Vertovsky's *Askold's Tomb*; on its dissolution, became a porter, a hunter, and a street-sweeper in turn; later, travelled with a Malo-Russ. company as singer and dancer, visiting the Caucasus; Ussatof, a well-known

singer, offered to teach him, and secured for him an engagement at Tiflis Opera House; in summer of 1894, he sang at Summer Theatre of Aquarium, Petrograd; then at Maryinsky, and at Imperial Opera House in following season (Ivan the Terrible in Rimsky-Korsakof's *Maid of Pskof*); he visited Milan; but received his most important schooling in Mamantof's company (Miller in Dargomisky's *Russalka*, Salieri in Rimsky-Korsakof's *Mozart and Salieri*, Mephistopheles in Gounod's *Faust*, etc.). In 1899, appeared as guest-artist at Imperial Opera, Moscow, and at Maryinsky, Petrograd (title-rôle in Rubinstein's *The Demon*; Holofernes in Serof's *Judith*, etc.). In Boito's *Mefistofele* he appeared 10 times in Milan in 1901. Two of his favourite parts are Don Basilio (Rossini's *Barber*) and Leporello (Mozart's *Don Giovanni*). On June 24, 1913, C. appeared for first time in England, in Sir Joseph Beecham's season of Russ. opera and ballet; appeared also in the 1914 season and created a *furore*. Since 1918 his London appearances have been confined to song-recitals in the Albert Hall.—E.-H.

CHAMBERLAIN, Houston Stewart. Wagnerian author; *b.* Portsmouth, 9 Sept. 1855. Pupil of Cheltenham College; stud. natural sciences at Geneva, 1879–81; 1885, Dresden; 1889, Vienna; 1908, Bayreuth; married Eva, daughter of Cosima Wagner. Chamberlain, a naturalised German, through his chief work, *The Foundations of the Nineteenth Century*, was with Gobineau the originator of the view that the Germanic race is the race *par excellence* —the modern Germans in particular. Or, negatively expressed, he held that the Hebrew race was both inferior and disintegrating.

Richard Wagner's Drama, 1892; *Richard Wagner's Genuine Letters to Ferdinand Praeger*, 1894; *Richard Wagner*, 1896 (Eng., 1897; Fr., 1899): *First Twenty Years of Bayreuth Festival Plays*, 1896. Consult his autobiography *Lebenswege meines Denkens* (Bruckmann, Munich, 1919).—A. E.

CHAMBER-MUSIC in Belgium, in Britain, in Finland, etc. See under headings of various countries—BELGIAN CHAMBER-MUSIC, BRITISH, FINNISH, etc.

CHAMBER-MUSIC PLAYERS. *ARGENTINA.* —Buenos Ayres: (i) *Primer Cuarteto.* The first str. quartet party formed in Argentina under this name, was the Gaito party, founded 1874. Cayetano Gaito, Bellucci, Ghignatti and Melani. Toured S. America in 1879. Pedro Melani joined as 1st vn. in 1880. (ii) *Buenos Ayres Str. Quartet*, founded 1886. Hercules Galvani, Forino, Bonfiglioli, Scarabella. (iii) *Cattelani Str. Quartet*, founded 1879. Ferruccio Cattelani, Alessio Morrone, José Bonfiglioli, Tomás Marenco. (iv) *Argentina Soc. of Chamber-Music*. Directed by León Fontova and Antonio López-Naguil.

AUSTRIA.—*Rosé Str. Quartet* (Vienna). Arnold Rosé, Anton Rušizka, Paul Fischer, Anton Walter.

BELGIUM.—(i) *Schörg Str. Quartet* (Brussels). F. Schörg, H. Daucher, P. Miry, Jacques Gaillard (toured Europe and America for 15 years).

Zimmer Str. Quartet (Brussels). A. Zimmer, F. Ghigo, L. Baroen, J. Gaillard. (iii) *"Pro Arte" Str. Quartet* (Brussels), founded 1922. Alphonse Onnou, Laurent Halleux, Germain Prévost, Robert Maas. (iv) *Mathieu Crickboom Quartet.*

CZECHO-SLOVAKIA.—(i) *Czech Quartet* (formerly *Bohemian Quartet*), founded in Budapest in 1892 by pupils of Hanus Wihan of Prague Cons. Karel Hoffmann, Josef Suk, Oskar Nedbal, Otto Berger (*b.* 1873, *d.* 1897). Wihan took Berger's place. Nedbal left in 1906, replaced by Jeří Herold (*b.* 1875). Wihan left in 1913, replaced by Ladislav Zelenka (*b.* 1881). Tours Europe repeatedly, especially with Smetana's and Dvořák's quartets. Noted for their warm tone and fiery rhythms. In 1922 the 4 members were appointed profs. at Prague Cons. Consult Boleska's *Ten Years of Czech Quartet* (Prague, 1902, M. Urbánek). (ii) *Ševčík-Lhatsky Str. Quartet* (late Ševčík Quartet), founded at Warsaw, 1903; the leader Bohuslav Lhatsky (*b.* Libochovice, 1879), Karel Procházka, Karel Moravec were all pupils of Ševčík. The cellist Bohuslav Váska was replaced in 1911 by Ladislav Zelenka and after the latter's removal to the Czech Quartet by Antonio Fingerland. Toured Russia, 1904; then settled in Prague; later toured Europe regularly.

DENMARK. — (i) *Copenhagen Str. Quartet,* founded 1916. Gunna Breuning, Gerhard Rafn, Ella Faber, Paulus Bache. Tours in Denmark, England, Germany, Sweden, Finland. (ii) *Copenhagen Trio.* Peder Möller (vn.), Louis Jensen (cello), Agnes Adler (pf.).

ENGLAND.—(i) *London Str. Quartet,* formed in 1908. First concert 26 July, 1910; have given hundreds of concerts, toured England, America, France, Germany, Spain, Portugal, Canada; world-tour Nov. 1922–April, 1924. James Levey, T. W. Petre, H. Waldo Warner, C. Warwick Evans. (ii) *Philharmonic Str. Quartet* (London). Frederic Holding, Cecil Bonvalot, Raymond Jeremy, Cedric Sharpe. (iii) *English Str. Quartet* (London). Marjory Hayward, E. Virgo, Frank Bridge, Ivor James. (iv) *Mandeville Str. Quartet* (London). William J. Fry, Henri Peros, Vera L. Henkel, Elsa Martin. (v) *Spencer Dyke Str. Quartet.* (vi) *Kendall Str. Quartet.* (vii) *Chamber-Music Players, The* (London). William Murdoch (pf.), Albert Sammons (vn.), Lionel Tertis (vla.), Cedric Sharpe (cello). (viii) *Catterall Str. Quartet* (Manchester), founded 1912. Arthur Catterall, John S. Bridge, Frank S. Park, Johan C. Hock. (ix) *Edith Robinson Str. Quartet* (Manchester). Edith Robinson, Gertrude Barker, Hilda Lindsay, Kathleen Moorhouse. (x) *M'Cullagh Str. Quartet* (Liverpool), founded 1920; first London appearance 1921; played at Salzburg International Fest. Aug. 1923. Isobel M'Cullagh, Gertrude Newsham, Helen Rawdon Briggs, Mary M'Cullagh.

FRANCE.—(i) *Capet Str. Quartet* (Paris). Originally Lucien Capet, Giron, H. Casadesus, Furet; in 1903, Lucien Capet, Touret, Bailly, Hasselmans; in 1910, Capet, Hewitt, Benoît, Delobelle. (ii) *Chailley Str. Quartet* (Paris).

Marcel Chailley, Guilevitch, Pascal, Diran Alexanian. (iii) *Hayot Str. Quartet.* Maurice Hayot, André, Denayez, Salmon. (iv) *Soc. de Musique de Chambre pour Instruments à Vent,* founded 1879 by Paul Taffanel, flautist and condr.; is unique of its kind; its repertoire consists of all the 6tets, 5tets, 4tets, trios, duos, and solos for wind instrs. with or without the pf., of both ancient and modern schools. Present players: René le Roy (fl.), Louis Bas (ob.), Achille Grass (clar.), Jules Vialet (horn), Leir Letellier (bsn.). (v) *Société Moderne d'Instruments à Vent.* See special article.

GERMANY.—(i) *Busch-Quartett.* Adolf Busch, Gösta Andreasson, Karl Doktor, Paul Grümmer. (ii) *Klingler-Quartett.* Karl Klingler, Richard Heber, Fridolin Klingler, Max Baldner. (iii) *Amar-Quartett.* Licco Amar, Walter Casper, Paul Hindemith, Maurits Frank. (iv) *Wendling-Quartett.* Carl Wendling, Philipp Neeter, Hans Michaelis, Alfred Saal. (v) *Havemann-Quartett.* Gustav Havemann, Georg Kniestädt, Hans Mahlke, Adolf Steiner. (vi) *Gürzenich-Quartett.* Bram Eldering, C. Körner, A. Zimmermann, Emanuel Feuermann. Nos. ii and v specialise in the propaganda of contemporary music.

HOLLAND.—(i) *Hollandsch Quartet* (Dutch Str. Quartet), formed at Amsterdam, 1911. Herman Leydensdorff, Julius Röntgen, jun., Bram Mendes, Thomas Canivez. Reconstituted in 1922: Herm. Leydensdorf, Jul. Röntgen, jun., Bram Mendes, Thomas Canivez. Plays in Holland, Belgium, Germany, Denmark and Sweden. Has given a very large number of first perfs. of modern works. (ii) *Amsterdam Str. Quartet,* formed 1912. Louis Zimmerman, Joh. Herbschleb, Herman Meerloo, Frits Gaillard. Since 1920, cello, Marix Loevensohn. (iii) *Haagsch Quartet,* formed at The Hague, 1918. Sam Swaap, Adolphe Poth, Jean Devert, Charles van Isterdael. Produced many Dutch works: Schäfer, Voormolen, van den Sigtenhorst Meyer, Oberstadt, Blitz, Brandts-Buys, Diepenbrock, Zagwijn, van Anrooy, etc. Perf. also for first time in Holland quartets of Milhaud, Migot, Honegger, Tailleferre, Esplá, Turina, Franco Alfano, Respighi, Malipiero, Casella, Enesco, Procházka, Suk, Stravinsky and Stan Golestan. (iv) *Concertgebouw Sextet,* formed at Amsterdam, 1909. Evert Cornelis (condr. pf.), N. Klasen (fl.), G. Blanchard (ob.), P. Swager (clar.), G. S. de Groen (bsn.), H. Tak (horn). Gives in nearly every Dutch town classic and modern chamber-music for wind instrs. First Dutch perfs. of Magnard's 5tet, op. 8; Roussel's 6tet; Debussy's sonata, fl. vla. harp; Ravel's 7tet; Goossens's *Holiday Impressions*; chamber-symphonies of Schönberg, Juon, Wolf-Ferrari, Sekles (in connection with other players) and Ravel's *Poèmes de Stéphane Mallarmé.* Works by Averkamp, Dopper (6tet), Sem Dresden (three 6tets and a trio), Diepenbrock, Ingenhoven, Willem Pijper (7tet), Röntgen and Henri Zagwijn were specially written for them. (v) Societies of wind-instrs. also exist at The Hague (*Haagsch Sextet*) and at Utrecht.

HUNGARY.—(i) *Hungarian Str. Quartet* (Budapest). Emeric Waldbauer, Egon Korstein,

Jean de Temesváry, Eugene de Keynely. (See WALDBAUER.) (ii) *Budapest Str. Quartet.* Hauser, Pogany, Ipolyi, Son. (iii) *Lehner* (sometimes spelt *Léner*) *Str. Quartet.* J. Lehner, J. Smilovits, S. Roth, I. Hartmann.

ITALY.—(i) *Quartetto Romano* (str. quartet), founded by Oscar Browning in Rome in 1921. Formerly the Spada Quartet (Spada was drowned in 1922). Armando delle Fornaci, Ettore Gandini, Giuseppe Matteucci, York Zuccaroli. Giuseppe Cristiani often joins them at the pf. (ii) *Quartetto di Roma* (str. quartet), founded in Rome in 1923, from leading players of Augusteo orch. Oscar Zuccarini, Francesco Montelli, Aldo Perini, Tito Rosati. (iii) *Società fra Strumenti a Fiato per la Musica da Camera*, founded in Rome in 1922. Alberto Veggetti (fl.), Riccardo Scozzi (ob.), Carlo Luberti (clar.), Marsilio Ceccarelli (horn), and Gino Barabaschi (bsn.) Has given many concerts at Reale Accademia Filharmonica. (iv) *Doppio Quintetto Torinese*, founded in Turin in 1920, and formed by the best professors of Liceo Municipale, of Symph. Concerts and of Teatro Regio. The quintet is composed of 5 str. instrs. (2 vns. vla. cello and d.-b.), and 5 wind instrs. (fl. ob. clar. bsn. horn) in addition to a harp and pf. The present players are: Maurizio Vico, Italo Vallora, Angelo Lissolo, Gaetano De Napoli, Angelo F. Cuneo, Ulrico Virgilio, Ermete Simonazzi, Leonardo Savina, Carlo Giolito, Ezio Nicolini, Clelia Aldovrandi (harpist), Luigi Perrachio (dir. and pianist). The soc., which has a governing board, is domiciled at Piazza Castello No. 1. It gives 3 concerts annually in Turin, and it has won many successes also in other Italian cities. (v) *Quartetto Bolognese.* Federico Barera, Giorgio Consolini, Angelo Consolini, Dante Serra. (vi) *Quartetto Napoletano.* Cantani, Parmiciano, Scarano, Viterbini; Alessandro Longo often joins them at the pf. (vii) *Quartetto Polo* (Milan); leader, Enrico Polo (*q.v.*). (viii) *Trio Nucci* (Florence). (ix) *Quintetto Senese di Violoncelli*; leader, Arrigo Provvedi. (x) *Trio Consolo-Serato-Mainardi*. (xi) *Trio Casella-Corti-Crepax*.

NORWAY.—*Arvesen Quartet* (Christiania). Arvesen, Haaland, Vitols, Yrjö Selin.

SCOTLAND—*Horace Fellowes Str. Quartet.* See FELLOWES.

SPAIN.—(i) *Cuarteto Francés* (str. quartet), founded in Madrid, 1902, for development of national chamber-music. Julio Francés, Odon González, Conrado del Campo, Luis Villa. During 8 years they toured all over Spain, including small villages, the result being, in many cases, the creation of Philh. Societies which now exist in almost every one of 49 Span. provinces. To their initiative is also due the writing of 17 chamber-works, dedicated to them by Ricardo Villa, Ruperto Chapí, Bartolomé Pérez Casas, Vicente Zurrón, and one of its members, Conrado del Campo. (ii) *Cuarteto Vela* (str. quartet), founded in Madrid, 1908, by the violinist Telmo Vela. In 1911, owing to absence of two of its members, it was reorganised and renamed *Cuarteto Español.* (iii) *Cuarteto Español* (see CUARTETO VELA above).

(iv) *Trio Iberia*, composed of plucked str.-instrs. bandurria, lute and guitar; founded (about 1900) by Angel Barrios (*q.v.*), in collab. with R. Deovalque and C. Artea, the object being to spread a knowledge of Andalusian music. Their success in Paris, London and Rome, not to mention Spain, exceeded all expectations. They gave several perfs. before the royal families of England and Spain, and, at the time, contributed more than any other mus. organisation of higher standard to awake the interest of foreign peoples in the works of Albeniz, Granados, Bretón, Falla and others then hardly known outside Spain. As their real end was study and propaganda, when they considered their aims fulfilled, they refused many tempting offers and dissolved the organisation. They handed their repertoire and their tradition to the *Trio Albeniz*, a similar ensemble of players, well known in Spain at present. (v) *Trio Albeniz* (see TRIO IBERIA above). (vi) *Sociedad de Instrumentos de Viento*, founded in Madrid, 1910, by Mariano San Miguel (*q.v.*).

SWEDEN.—(i) *Svon Kjellström Str. Quartet* (Stockholm). Sven Kjellström, Gösta Björk, Einar Grönwall, Carl Christiansen. (ii) *Julius Ruthström's Str. Quartet* (Stockholm). (iii) *Society of Chamber-Music* (Malmö). (iv) *Gothenburg Str. Quartet.* (v) *Mazerska Kvartett "Uskapet,"* founded by Johan Mazer's bequests of 1841 and 1846. The members cultivate chamber-music, in closed meetings.

U.S.A.—(i) *Kneisel Str. Quartet* founded 1885, disbanded 1917 (see special art.). (ii) *Flonzaley Str. Quartet* (New York), founded 1902 (see special art.). (iii) *Olive Mead Str. Quartet* (New York), founded 1904. Olive Mead, Vera Fonarof, Gladys North, Lillian Littlehales. (iv) *Margulies Trio* (New York), founded 1904 (see special art.). (v) *Philharmonic Ensemble of New York* (str. quartet), founded 1913. (vi) *Letz Str. Quartet* (New York), founded 1917, after dissolution of Kneisel Quartet. Hans Letz, Sandor Harmati, Edward Kreiner, Gerald Maas. (vii) *New York Chamber Music Soc.*, str. and wind, formed 1914 by Miss Carolyn Beebe (pf.) and Gustave Langenus (clar.). Incorporated 1919; about a dozen players. (viii) *Adamowski Str. Quartet* (Boston), founded 1888. Timothée Adamowski, E. Fiedler, D. Kuntz, Giuseppe Campanini. Reconstituted in 1890: T. A., A. Moldauer, Max Zach, Joseph Adamowski. (ix) *Longy Club* (Boston) of wind instrs., to which was added in 1910 the similar Barrère Ensemble of New York. (x) *Kortshak Str. Quartet* (Chicago), founded 1915; name changed to *Berkshire S. Q.* 1916.—E.-H.

CHANTAVOINE, Jean. Fr. musicologist; *b.* Paris, 17 May, 1877. Pupil of Friedländer, Berlin; dir. of the *Collection des Maîtres de la Musique* (Alcan, Paris). Formerly critic of *La Revue Hebdomadaire* and of *Excelsior*. Since 1923, gen. secretary of Paris Conservatoire.

Beethoven, 1905; *Nibelungen Ring* (transl. of Pochhammer's commentaries), 1911; *Liszt*, 1912; *Musiciens et Poètes*, 1912; *De Couperin à Debussy*, 1921. Also a transl. of a selection of Beethoven's letters, and ed. of 12 Beethoven minuets, for orch. —A. C.

CHAPÍ, Ruperto. Span. compr. *b.* Villena, 23 March, 1851; *d.* 25 March, 1909. A son of the local barber, he started as a piccolo-player in his native town; became afterwards a brilliant executant on the cornet; in 1867 went to Madrid, on his own initiative, as student at R. Cons. de Música, carrying with him only a few pounds, and relying for support on his cornet-playing, which proved injurious to his health. In 1872, he won the post of regimental band-master; in 1873, the Rome award of the R. Acad. de Bellas Artes; in 1878, obtained a special grant for study in Paris, which he renounced (1879) and returned to Spain. He conducted the Sociedad Artístico Musical in 1881, and in 1882 rose definitely to fame with his *zarzuela La Tempestad,* the book being a version of the *Juif polonais* of Erckmann-Chatrian. In 1892 he had sufficient authority and means to start alone a campaign of the utmost importance for the mus. profession in Spain. In his endeavour to become independent of the patronage of publishers, he had always refused to part with the right of reproduction of the orch. parts of his works. There was at the time a very well known *acaparator,* who had acquired the rights of practically every work produced in Spain, by paying ridiculous sums to the needy comprs. He offered Chapí not less than 1,000,000 pesetas for the orch. material of his works. Chapí not only refused the offer, but started a library of his own in opposition to the powerful monopoliser. The latter tried to boycott Chapí, to whom the doors of practically every theatre were closed for a time. But the people missed Chapí's music, and on one occasion, the attraction of his name was considered indispensable to prevent the closing of the Teatro de la Zarzuela before the season was over. So he was called upon to write in three days a new play, which he did (*Mujer y reina,* 1895), obtaining a phenomenal success. This and his triumph with *El Tambor de Granaderos* made him the sole master of the situation.

Almost simultaneously with the foundation of his library, he founded the Sociedad de Compositores y Editores Propietarios de Obras Musicales, which in 1893 extended its scope to dramatic authors, as the Soc. de Autores, Compositores y Editores de Música. The object of the Soc. was to organise, protect, and administrate the *petit droit,* until then unknown in Spain; but C.'s idea was that the Soc. should control all kinds of authors' rights. This was accomplished (with the co-operation of the author Sinesio Delgado) by the establishment of the Soc. de Autores Españoles (Span. Soc. of Authors), 1899, which all the authors and comprs. in Spain joined in 1901. In 1899, C. was elected fellow of the R. Acad. de Bellas Artes, but he declined the honour. His death, the day after the production of his *Margarita la Tornera* at the Teatro Real (R. Opera House), called forth a popular demonstration of mourning in Madrid, where his memory is honoured by a statue in the Jardines del Retiro.

Many claim for Chapí the place given in the history of Span. music to Isaac Albeniz, and never was a Span. compr. discussed with so much intemperance, both by his admirers and critics. The composer, scholar and academician, Manuel Manrique de Lara, proclaims Chapí the founder of the Span. opera, and the inspiring reformer, " thanks to whom Span. contemporary music is in closer relationship to that of Mozart, Weber, Beethoven and Wagner than it ever was to that of Rossini, Meyerbeer, Donizetti or Mercadante. So the logical evolution of the mus. art that started with the *Magic Flute, Freischütz* and *Fidelio,* leading through Spontini to *Tannhäuser* and *Lohengrin,* has its manifestation in Spain in the master-works of Chapí, his *Curro Vargas, Circe,* and *Margarita la Tornera.*"

Henri Collet, the eminent Fr. critic and historian, an authority on old and modern Span. music, expresses himself on Chapí (*Encyclopédie de la Musique et Dictionnaire du Cons.*):

Up to his death, he flooded Spain with compositions *aussi détestables que faciles*; amongst them 4 ridiculous str. 4tets, 2 unsubstantial orch. poems, motets devoid of any originality, commonplace pf. pieces and songs, and zarzuelas like *La bruja, Curro Vargas, El rey que rabió, La revoltosa,* that cannot be compared in value to Charles Lecocq's operettas. His unfortunate attempts in *Circe* and *Margarita la Tornera* to speak a more serious mus. language are not worth mentioning.

Julio Gómez, the compr., scholar and librarian of the R. Cons. de Música, considers Chapí's 4tets " four master-works that will for ever stand as the foundation and origin of pure Span. music." Rafael Mitjana, in his book *Para música vamos,* writes:

In the history of Spanish art, Chapí will always have his place as the most genuine representative of a period, not so much of decadence as of singular degradation.

A man who was the object of such divergency of views must have been a personality of no mean order. In fact, he left the mark of talent on every page of music he wrote. Considering as a whole his prolific production, the conclusion is that he possessed what is generally called mus. genius. His facility for work brings to mind the name of Schubert; but undoubtedly he was the victim of his own gifts combined with the exigencies of a public that expected from him mus. comedies (chiefly of 1 act) in profusion, many of which had to be written at a stretch in one or two days. From the point of view of modern music, his works offer little interest to the student in general, but they must not be ignored by those concerned in the evolution of Span. music.

The following are some of his 168 works for the stage:

Operas in 1 act: *Las naves de Cortés; La hija de Jefté; La muerte de Garcilaso; La serenata*; in 3 acts: *Roger de Flor, La Bruja, Circe, Margarita la Tornera.* Zarzuelas in 1 act: *Música clásica; Las doce y media y sereno; Los alojados; Las tentaciones de San Antonio; La leyenda del Monje; Las campanadas; La czarina; El tambor de granaderos; La gitanilla; La revoltosa; Pepe Gallardo; La chavala; El puñao de rosas; La venta de Don Quijote; El amor en solfa; La patria chica*; in 2 acts: *Los lobos marinos; Las hijas del Zebedeo*; in 3 acts: *Dos huérfanas; La tempestad; El milagro de la Virgen; El rey que rabió; Mujer y reina; Curro Vargas; La cortijera.* Orch.: Moorish fantasia, *La Corte de Granada*; symphony in D mi.; symph. legend, *Los Gnomos de la Alhambra*;

symph. poem, *Escenas de capa y espada*; *Scherzo*, on an episode of *Don Quixote*; *Polaca*; fantasia, *Recuerdo a Gaztambide*; *Marcha de recepción*; *Jota*, for vn. and orch. Chamber-music: 4 str. 4tets (G; F; D ma.; D mi.); *Allegro* and *Scherzo*, pf. trio; *Romanza*, vn. and pf. For pf.: *Zarabanda*; *Danza Morisca*; *Marcha de los trovadores*; *Hoja de Album* (*Album-Leaf*). V. and pf.: *Seis melodias*. Oratorio, *Los Angeles*; Motet for 7 vs.; *Veni Creator*, double chorus and orch.; *Ave Maris Stella*, vs. and orch.; military band: *Marcha heroica*; *Himno militar*. (Unión Musical Española; Faustino Fuentes, Madrid.)—P. G. M.

CHAPLIN, Kate. Eng. vla.-d'amore player; violinist; *b.* London 3 July, 1865. Stud. under Adolph Pollitzer at London Acad. of Music; later under Eugène Ysaye in Brussels. Her vla. d'amore was made by G. Saint-George.—E.-H.

CHAPLIN, Mabel. Eng. vla.-da-gamba player and cellist; *b.* London, 19 Oct. 1870. Stud. under Pezze at London Acad. of Music; also for 3 years under E. Jacobs at Brussels Cons. Stud. vla. da gamba alone. Her gamba is by Barak Norman, dated 1718.—E.-H.

CHAPLIN, Nellie. Eng. harpsichordist; *b.* London, 11 Feb. 1857. Stud. at London Acad. of Music under Dr. Wylde; also Deppe method under Frl. Timm and Virgil system under A. P. Virgil. She was the pioneer in the revival of the old dances including the Allemande, Courante, Sarabande, Chaconne (1st perf. 1904); first to revive old Eng. folk-dances from Playford's *Dancing-Master* (after a lapse of 200 years).

Playford's Dances, with Steps (Curwen); *Court Dances* (id.); *Music and Steps of the Dances of the Suite* (i.d.), etc—E.-H.

CHAPUIS, Auguste. Fr. compr. *b.* Dom-pierre-sur-Salon (Haute Saône), 1858. Dir. of mus. instruction in schools of City of Paris and prof. of harmony at Cons. Several times *lauréat* of Cons. and of Inst.; pupil of César Franck for compn.; orgt. at churches of Notre-Dame-des-Champs and of St.-Roch, Paris; made a name as compr. by the dramatic works:

Enguerrande (*opéra-comique*), Paris, 1882; *Les Demoiselles de St.-Cyr* (Monte Carlo, 1921); *Yannel*, lyric drama in 3 acts. Has had perf. a symphony; *Tableaux flamands*; pf. and cello sonata; pf. and vn. sonata (Paris, Durand); orch. pieces; pf. pieces; songs; choruses; and about 20 volumes of solfeggi. —M. L. P.

CHARPENTIER, Gustave. Fr. compr. *b.* Dieuze (Lorraine), 25 June, 1860. Stud. at Lille Cons.; granted by town of Tourcoing an annual pension of 1200 fr., allowing him to come to Paris (1881); entered Paris Cons.; *Grand Prix de Rome*, 1887 (with cantata, *Didon*); founded in 1900 *Cons. populaire de Mimi Pinson*, with free courses of popular music and classical dancing. The art of Gustave Charpentier is directed to the people. He takes as his basis a naturalistic æstheticism and seeks to translate social questions into music. One discovers in him also traces of romanticism, deliberately grandiloquent, and of lyricism, often verbose but full of fire and conviction.

Impressions d'Italie (1890), symph. poem; *La Vie du Poète*, symph. drama, 3 acts (1892); *Louise*, mus. romance, 5 tableaux (1900); *Julien*, lyric drama 5 acts (1913). Songs: *Poèmes chantés* (1894); *Les Fleurs du Mal* of Baudelaire, v. and orch. (1895); *Impressions fausses* of Verlaine (1895). He was elected *Membre de l'Institut* in place of Massenet, in

1912. The 500th perf. of *Louise* took place in Jan. 1921. Consult: Alfred Bruneau, *La Musique française* (1901); André Himonet, "*Louise*" *de Charpentier* (1922); D. C. Parker, *G. C.*, *Mus. Opinion*, Oct. 1915 and *Mus. Standard*, 23 Sept. 1916.—A. C.

CHAUMONT, Émile. Belgian violinist; *b.* Liège, 29 March, 1878. Entered Liège Cons.; vn. medal, 1896. Two years in Berlin as pupil of Halir and Max Bruch. Came to Paris and became 1st vn. at Lamoureux Concerts. Settled in Brussels as virtuoso and vn. teacher. 1909, taught at Liège Cons.; 1919, at that of Brussels.

36 *Studies in Transcendental Execution*, 1913; some songs with pf.—E. C.

CHAUSSON, Ernest. Fr. compr. *b.* Paris, 21 Jan. 1855; *d.* Limay (Seine et Oise), 16 June, 1899. Started mus. study rather late, after having passed his law examinations. At first pupil of Massenet at Cons. (1880); then of César Franck. Was secretary of the Société Nationale de Musique. Died from a bicycle accident. In the group of pupils round Franck, he possessed the greatest sensibility. His symph. writing is remarkable and always betrays a sentiment from the heart. His music reveals, however, traces of the influence of Franck and Wagner.

Numerous songs (the best-known: *Le Colibri*; *La Caravane*); choruses: *Hymne védique*; *Chant nuptial*; *Chant funèbre*. Chamber-music: pf. trio; concerto, pf. vn. and orch.; pf. 4tet; str. 4tet (unfinished). Symph. music: *Viviane* (1882); symphony, B flat (1890). *Poème*, vn. and orch. (1896); *Poème d'Amour et de la Mer* (v. and orch.). For theatre: *La Tempête*; *La Légende de Sainte-Cécile*; dramatic music: *Jeanne d'Arc* (1880); *Le Roi Arthus* (6 tableaux; Carlsruhe, 1900; Brussels, 1903).—A. C.

CHELIUS, Oskar von. German composer; *b.* Mannheim, 28 July, 1859; *d.* Munich, 12 June, 1923. Pupil of Emil Steinbach (Mannheim). Symots (Heidelberg), Reiss (Cassel), Jadassohn (Leipzig); then a soldier, 1911; major-general, aide-de-camp to William II; 1914, military attaché, Petrograd.

Songs; pf. pieces; symph. poems *Und Pippa tanzt* (after Gerhart Hauptmann); *Requiem* (text by Friedrich Hebbel), chorus and orch.; *Psalm CXXI*. Operas: *Haschisch* (Dresden, 1897); *The Infatuated Princess*, text by Otto Jul. Bierbaum (Wiesbaden, 1905); *Magda-Maria* (Dessau, 1920).—A. E.

CHENAL, Marthe. Fr. operatic s. singer; *b.* Saint-Maurice (Seine), 24 Aug. 1881. Stud. at Cons. in 1901 under MM. Martini and Melchissédec; 1905, 2 1st prizes for singing and operatic work. *Début* at Opéra 1905, in *Sigurd* as Brunehilde; then in *Freischütz*, *Tannhäuser*, *Faust*, *Ariane*. Went to Opéra-Comique in 1908 and sang in *Aphrodite*, *La Tosca*, *Le Roi d'Ys*, *Sanga* (1909), *On ne badine pas avec l'amour* (1910). Created rôles in *Bacchus Triomphant* (Bordeaux, 1909); *La Sorcière* (Opéra-Comique, 1912); *L'Aube Rouge* (Rouen, 1912); *Le Tambour* (Opéra-Comique, 1915); *Goyescas* (Opéra, 1919); *Les Trois Mousquetaires* (Cannes, 1921); *La Mégère apprivoisée* (Opéra, 1922).—A. R.

CHESTER, J. & W. Ltd. Publishers, establ. Brighton in 1860. London house opened in 1915 as a centre for modern music and agency for foreign publications. The firm's bulletin *The Chesterian*, publ. in 1919 as a mus. review, has now an international circulation.—E.-H.

CHEVALLEY, Heinrich. Ger. mus. writer and critic; *b.* Düsseldorf, 19 May, 1870. Pupil Leipzig Cons.; started the *Redenden Künste* journal, Leipzig; 1896 in Hamburg, where he has been mus. ed. since 1897 of *Hamburger Fremdenblatt*; ed. of the *Monats Musikzeitschrift* since 1920. Compr. of songs and pf. pieces.—A. E.

CHEVILLARD, Camille. Fr. compr. and condr. *b.* Paris, 14 Oct. 1859; *d.* Paris, 30 May, 1923. Son of Alexandre Chevillard (prof. of cello, Cons. Paris, and founder of Soc. des Derniers Quatuors de Beethoven). Pupil of G. Mathias for pf.; choral condr. of Concerts Lamoureux; son-in-law of Charles Lamoureux, whose official successor he became in 1899. In that year, he founded the Société de Fondation Beethoven, and in 1903 the trio Chevillard, Hayot and Salmon. 1907, prof. of instr. ensemble class at Cons.; also, since 1914, dir. of mus. studies at the Opéra.

Ballade symphonique; Le Chêne et le Roseau (symph. poem) 1890; *Fantaisie symphonique* (1893); 5tet, pf. and str.; str. 4tet; pf. trio; pieces for pf. and vla.; sonata, vn. and pf. Consult Romain Rolland, *Musiciens d'aujourd'hui* (1908) (Eng., Kegan Paul, 1915).—A. C.

CHILESOTTI, Oscar. Italian musicologist; *b.* Bassano (Veneto), 12 July, 1848; *d.* there, 1916. Publ. (Ricordi) interesting transcriptions of ancient pieces for lute; author of important works, such as *Evoluzione della musica* (Turin, Bocca), also arts. on mus. history and theory in *Rivista Musicale Italiana*, etc.—D. A.

CHINESE MUSIC. See LALOY, LOUIS.

CHLUBNA, Osvald. Czechoslovak compr. *b.* Brno (Brünn), 1893; pupil of Leoš Janáček in compn.; teacher of Cons. in Brno. Some orch. compns. perf. in Prague and Brno:

Do pohádky; Dvě pohádky (Fairy-Tales); *Píseň mé touhy (Song of Longing)*. For vs. and orch.: *Tiché usmíření (Quiet Consolation)*; *Sumařovo dítě (The Musician's Child)*. Opera, *Pomsta Catullova (The Revenge of Catullus)*, book by Vrchlický.—V. ST.

CHOJNACKI, Roman (*phon.* Hoynatski). Polish theorist and writer; *b.* Warsaw, 1880. Pupil of Noskowski at Warsaw Cons. Teacher of mus. theory. Ed. of mus. periodicals (*Nowa muzyka* and *Przeglad muzyczny*) at Warsaw. In 1918, became manager of Warsaw Philh. Orch. (see ORCHESTRAS).—ZD. J.

CHOP, Max. Ger. mus. writer and critic; *b.* Greussen, 17 May, 1862. Journalist; ed. of *Signale für die Musikalische Welt* since 1920; well known through his *Erläuterungen von Meisterwerken der Tonkunst* in Reclam's Universal Library. Publ., *inter alia*, F. Delius (1907); August Bungert (1899 and 1906).—A. E.

CHORAL MUSIC in England, France, etc. See ENGLISH CHORAL MUSIC, FRENCH CHORAL MUSIC, etc.

CHORAL SOCIETIES, etc. *AUSTRALIA.*—(i) *Melbourne Philh. Soc.* founded 1853. Present condr. Alberto Zelman. Has a brilliant record (see George Peake's *Historical Souvenir*. Melbourne, 1913, Peacock Bros.). (ii) *Royal Victorian Liedertafel* (formed from amalgamation of Melbourne Liedertafel and Royal Metropolitan Liedertafel, Aug. 1905). Present condr. Mansley Greer.

CANADA.—These are relatively of great importance and so far mark the highest achievement of purely Canadian musical endeavour. (i) The unique position of the *Mendelssohn Choir of Toronto* is due primarily to it founder and condr. Dr. A. S. Vogt. Beginning in 1895 with *a cappella* works, the scope was soon enlarged by the co-operation of Amer. symphony orchs., and since then, the 4 or 5 concerts, given usually in Feb. each year, have constituted the most important feature of the Toronto mus. season. Important tours in U.S.A. have gained for Toronto a fine reputation for choral-singing. Its present condr., H. A. Fricker, succeeded Dr. Vogt in 1917 and has most successfully piloted the organisation over a difficult period due largely to war and post-war conditions. The choir now averages about 250 voices. (ii) The *National Chorus of Toronto*, founded and cond. by Dr. Albert Ham, has given concerts in that city for 20 years. It gives a concert in Jan. each year. Formerly programmes were given with Amer. symphony orchs.; lately the policy has been more directed to *a cappella* works, and in this respect much fine music has been introduced to Canadian audiences. The choir averages 200 voices. (iii) The *Oratorio Society* (Toronto), founded and cond. by Dr. Edward Broome, has given concerts in that city since 1898. Beginning with the standard oratorios, the policy of late has been to co-operate with one of the big Amer. symphony orchs. and to give a fest. of 2 or 3 concerts with performances devoted largely to modern works. This choir averages 240 voices. (iv) The *Elgar Choir* of Hamilton, Ontario, organised in 1905 by Bruce Carey, gives concerts in Hamilton and occasionally in Toronto. It has an excellent reputation in *a cappella* singing. The present condr., W. H. Hewlett, was appointed in 1922. (v) There are also the *Winnipeg Male-Voice Choir*, condr. Hugh Ross, which has a fine reputation in Winnipeg and in certain U.S.A. cities; the *Orpheus Society* (Toronto), condr. Dalton Baker, now in its 3rd season; and the *Toronto Male-Voice Choir*, cond. by E. R. Bowles.

CZECHO-SLOVAKIA.—(i) *Choral Union of Prague Teachers* (*Pěvecké sdružení pražských učitelů*), founded in 1908 by Frant. Spilka (*q.v.*). After months of methodical preparation it made a most successful appearance, subsequently meeting with quite exceptional appreciation abroad (France, England, Germany). Along with its Moravian prototype, this choir represents the highest grade of the great national choir-cultivation; it has assisted the productivity of modern choral composition. Method Doležil (prof. at the Prague Cons.) has been dir. since 1922. He had before founded an equally notable Choral Union of Prague Lady-teachers. (ii) *Choral Union of Moravian Teachers* (*Pěvecké sdružení moravských učitelů*), founded by Ferdinand Vach (*q.v.*) in 1903 from his pupils at teachers' school in Kroměříž. Their centre is now Brno (Brünn). The beauty of the voices and the mus. intelligence of the members helped Vach to attain a high standard of technical efficiency. True intonation, strong rhythmic feeling, clear declamation, perfect balance of tone, dramatic graduation and purity of style are united to the feat of memorising their large repertory. In Czecho-Slovakia this association marked a new epoch in choral singing, the Czechoslovak comprs. now writing, in consequence, choral pieces of great difficulty. The choir has made successful tours in Europe. It appeared in London in 1919. From 1914 a choir of lady-teachers (*Sdružení moravských učitelek*) has been connected with it, being one of the best female choirs in Czecho-Slovakia. (iii) The *Smetana Choir* (Prague), condr. K. Černý. Approaches the Prague Teachers' Choir in importance. (iv) The *Křížkovský*, male choir (Prague). (v) The large choral soc. *Hlahol* (Prague), founded 1861; now conducted by A. Herle.

DENMARK.—(i) *Danish Choral Soc.* (Copenhagen); condr. Georg Höeberg. (ii) *Studenter-Sångforening* (Univ. Students' Choral Soc.), Copenhagen.

ENGLAND.—(i) *Royal Albert Hall Choral Society* (London); condr. Sir Hugh Allen. (ii) *Bach Choir*; condr. Dr. Vaughan Williams. (iii) *London Choral Society*; condr. Arthur Fagge. (iv) *Oriana Madrigal Choir*; condr. C. Kennedy Scott. (v) *Philharmonic Choir*; (vi) The *Novello Choir*; condr. Harold Brooke. (vii) *South London Philharmonic Society*, founded 1912; present condr. William H. Kerridge. Pioneer soc. of decentralisation, arranging lectures and recitals in addition to its own choral and orch. concerts. Has its headquarters at Goldsmiths' College, New Cross.

There are also large choruses in connection with the fests. at Birmingham, Leeds, Sheffield, Three Choirs (Gloucester, Worcester, Hereford); and large choral societies at Bradford, Cambridge, Halifax, Huddersfield, Nottingham, Newcastle, Oxford (Bach Choir, etc.), Wolverhampton; and in connection with the Hallé Orch. at Manchester, and the Philharmonic at Liverpool, where there is also the Welsh Choral Union (condr. T. Hopkin Evans).

FINLAND.—(i) Choral soc. *Suomen Laulu*; condr. H. Klemetti (*q.v.*) who also cond. the *Ylioppilaskunnan Laulajat* (Students' Choir), Helsingfors. (ii) *Swedish Oratorio Choir* (Helsingfors); condr. B. Carlson (*q.v.*). (iii) *Kansallis-Kuoro* (Helsingfors); condr. A. Maasalo (*q.v.*).

FRANCE.—(i) *Les Chanteurs de Saint-Gervais.* Choral association, created in 1892 by Charles Bordes (*q.v.*), precentor of St.-Gervais in Paris; for perf. of sacred and secular polyphonic music of XV and XVI centuries, and of Gregorian chant. Its origin was an attempt to organise the singing of the responses in Holy Week (1891). Since 1909, it has been cond. by Léon Saint-Réquier. This choir (60 in number) sings regularly in church of Saint-Gervais only 6 times a year (Christmas, Purification, Maundy - Thursday, Good Friday, Easter and Pentecost). Since their creation, over 600 other concerts have been given. Their repertoire extends from Gregorian pieces

of XII century to modern works. This association has powerfully contributed to the renewal in France of the taste for ancient polyphonic art. (ii) *Concerts Spirituels de la Sorbonne*, founded in Paris in 1898 by P. de Saunières, and cond. by him; gives every year in the Church of the Sorbonne oratorios and other sacred works. (iii) *Manécanterie des Petits Chanteurs à la Croix de Bois*. *Manécanterie* (from Latin *mane cantare*, to sing in the morning) formerly meant a singing school attached to a cathedral. Founded in Paris in 1907; both a school of liturgic singing and a centre for Christian education. This choir of boys and young men is trained both in unison-singing and polyphonic music, and is heard in churches and at concerts. Condr. Abbé Rebufat. (iv) *Chorale Universitaire* (*Univ. Choral Soc.*). Founded 1918 by Mlle. Bonnet, principal of the Maison des Étudiantes, with H. Expert (*q.v.*) as choirmaster, and E. Borrel, prof. in *Schola Cantorum*. First composed only of girls, it became later a mixed choir by amalgamation with a young men's soc. in 1920. Although its repertoire mainly consists of Renaissance masters and the whole of Fr. choral work excluding modern comprs., it also produces from time to time works of the Ital., Ger. and Span. Renaissance as well as foreign works of other periods. Its President is H. Lichtenberger (*q.v.*). (v) *Chœur Mixte de Paris (Paris Mixed Choir)* of 70 voices, founded in 1921 by M. de Ranse, prof. at the *Schola Cantorum*, and cond. by him. Its programmes consist of works by the great Renaissance masters, classical and modern compns. and works of contemporary comprs. (G. Fauré, Fl. Schmitt, Ravel, Inghelbrecht, etc.). (vi) *Société Griset-Saintbris*, founded in Paris, 1865. Present condr. Étienne Millot. 110 singers. 2 concerts a year.

HOLLAND.—*Madrigaalvereeniging.* A cappella choir of 9 solo-singers, founded 1914 by Sem Dresden (*q.v.*). The present singers are: Kubbinga-Burg, Van Raalte-Horneman, Van der Linde (s.); Evekink Busgers, Dresden-Dhont (a.); J. van Kempen, R. van Schaik (t.); W. Ravelli, H. Kubbinga (b.). First concert 8 Nov. 1915, Amsterdam; 100th concert 13 Oct. 1922. Concerts in Paris, Dec. 1919; Brussels, 1922.

IRELAND.—(i) *University of Dublin Choral Soc.* founded 1837; at first, Handel's works; 1845, Mendelssohn's *Antigone.* First condr. Joseph Robinson (until 1847); then Sir Robert Stewart till 1894; C. Marchant till 1920; present condr. Dr. G. P. Hewson (orgt. St. Patrick's Cath.). Up to 1870, choristers of the 2 caths. took treble parts; then ladies. (ii) *Hibernian Catch Club*, oldest existing mus. soc. in Europe. Founded 1679 by vicars-choral of St. Patrick's and Christchurch cathedrals.

ITALY.—(i) *Accademia di Canto Corale Stefano Tempia* (Turin). One of oldest and most famous Ital. choral institutions ; founded in 1785 by Stefano Tempia, who dir. it until his death. After him, the condrs. were Giulio Roberti, Delfino Thermignon, Michele Pachner, and Ettore Lena. Up to 1922, it had given 234 ordinary and 68 special concerts, taking part also in massed performances, and tours. It has also inaugurated choral competitions and possesses a rich mus. library. In 1923, it was merged with the other Turin choral soc. of more recent foundation, the *Palestrina*, thus forming the new *Società Corale Stefano Tempia-Palestrina*. (ii) *Orfeonica* (Bologna). Male choral soc. founded in 1868. (iii) *Euridice* (Bologna). Male choral soc. founded in 1880. (iv) *Euterpe* (Bologna). Male choral soc. founded in 1905. (v) *Guido Monaco* (Leghorn). One of the most important choral socs. in Italy. Is composed only of male singers and numbers about 50 voices. Under the dir. of Domenico Alaleona (*q.v.*), it has made successful appearances in Marseilles, Florence and at the Augusteo in Rome. (vi) *Società Polifonica Romana* (Rome); see special article. (vii) *Coro di Varese* (Milan); condr. Romeo Bartoli.

NORWAY.—The principal male choirs in Christiania are: *The Students' Choral Soc.* (founded 1845; present condr. Emil Nielsen); *The Mercantile Association's Choral Union* (founded 1845 [or 1847]; present condr. Leif Halvorsen); *The Artisans' Choral Union* (founded 1845; present condr. Eyvind Alnæs); *The Workmen's Choral Union* (founded 1864; present condr. Alfred Russ); *Guldberg's Choir* (founded 1916; present condr. Ansgar Guldberg). The principal mixed choirs are: *The Cecilia Soc.* (founded 1898; present condr. Leif Halvorsen); *Holter's Choir* (founded 1898; present condr. Eyvind Alnæs). Ladies' choir: *The Female Students' Choral Soc.* (founded 1895; present condr. Per Winge). In Bergen: *The Choral Union*, founded 1891 by Ingolf Schjött.

SCOTLAND.—(i) *Edinburgh Royal Choral Union*, founded 1858. First condr. Charles J. Hargitt; first work, Sterndale Bennett's *May Queen*. From 1862–4, James Shaw cond. and William Howard (1864–6). In 1866 a theory-class was started in connection with it, and this has continued up to the present day. From 1866 to 1883 Adam Hamilton cond. and brought the choir up to a high state of efficiency. Dr. T. H. Collinson, who cond. 1883–1913, was followed by Herr Feuerman, and in 1915 by W. Greenhouse Allt. It received Royal recognition, 10 Aug. 1911. (ii) *Glasgow Orpheus Choir*; condr. Hugh S. Roberton. One of the finest choral bodies in the United Kingdom. (iii) *Glasgow Choral Union.*

SPAIN.—Choral singing flourishes more extensively in Spain than is generally known, though its practice is mostly confined to the Basque and Catalonian provinces. (i) *Sociedad Coral* (Choral Soc.), founded in 1922 by the Asociación General de Profesores de Orquesta, Madrid. Condr. Julio Francés. (ii) *Orfeó Català* (Barcelona), founded in 1891 by its condr. the compr. Luis Millet. It has been acknowledged by Richard Strauss and Vincent d'Indy as one of the leading choral bodies of the world. It sings in the magnificent hall, Palau de la Musica Catalana. Appeared in Paris and London (Albert Hall), 1914. (iii) *Sociedad Coral* (Bilbao), founded

in 1886 under the name of *Orfeón Bilbaino*, and consisting then of male voices only. Has obtained many prizes in national and international competitions. In 1906, reconstituted as a mixed chorus, giving the first perfs. in Spain of César Franck's *Béatitudes* in 1907 and Brahms's *Requiem* in 1913. It also took part in first perf. of Basque operas *Mendy-Mendiyan* by Usandizaga, *Mirentxu* and *Amaya* by Guridi, pastoral *Maitena*, *Lide ta Izidor*, etc., thus helping the Basque lyric-theatre's ideal. Zabala cond. 1886–99; then Aureliano Valle; from 1910, the compr. Jesús Guridi. It is one of the most important choral societies in Spain; appeared with distinction at Verviers (Belgium) in 1905. (iv) *Orfeó Donostiarra* (San Sebastian), founded in 1896 by its condrs. Norberto Luzurriaga and Miguel Oñate. One of the most important of its kind since 1902, under dir. of Secundino Esnaola (*q.v.*). It was composed exclusively of male voices until 1906, when it was enlarged to a mixed chorus of 220, including children's voices. Has won prizes at international competitions in Paris; is recognised in Madrid and Barcelona as a first-class choir (first perfs. in Spain of Mass in D and Ninth Symphony of Beethoven, Brahms's *Requiem*, etc.). (v) *Coros Clavé* (see CLAVÉ, JOSÉ ANSELMO). (vi) Of other choral societies, the most important are: *Orfeó Manresa*; *Orfeó Gracienc*; *Orfeó Tarragoni*; *Orfeó Villafranqui*; *Escola Coral*; *Orfeón Euskaria*.

SWEDEN.—(i) *Musikföreningen* (Stockholm), founded 1880 by Ludvig Norman and Vilh. Svedbom; condr. Victor Wiklund. (ii) *Musikaliska Sällskapet* (Stockholm), founded as *S.S.U.H. Choir*, 1908, newly organised 1915; condr. David Åhlen. (iii) *Stockholms Madrigalsällskap*, founded 1917; condr. Felix Saul. (iv) *Stockholms Allmänna Sångförening*. (v) *Sjung, sjung* (Stockholm) male choir. (vi) Glee-society *Par Bricole* (Stockholm). (vii) *Philh. Sällskapet* (Sundsvall). 1st concert in Feb. 1922; condr. A. Wahlberg. (viii) *Motett- och Musikförening* (Christianstad); condr. O. Wadborg. (ix) *Musikförening* (Falun); condr. Joel Olsson. (x) *Allmänna Sångföreningen* (students of the Univ. at Upsala); condr. the mus. dir. of the Univ. (xi) *Göta Par Bricole* (glee-soc. of Gothenburg); (xii) *Lunds Studentsångförening* (glee-soc. of Lund); condr. the mus. dir. of the Univ. (xiii) *Svenska Sångarförbundet*, a national federation of 22 provincial glee-clubs, comprising about 6000 singers.

SWITZERLAND.—(i) *Basler Gesangverein*. The most eminent mixed choir of Switzerland, admirably trained. Founded at Basle in 1824. Condrs.: Ferd. Laur (1824–45); E. Reiter (1845–1875); Alfred Volkland (1875–99); Hans Huber (1899–1903), and from 1903, H. Suter. Consists at present of 380 active and 420 subscribing members. Gives 2 oratorio concerts every winter. (ii) *Basler Liedertafel*. Best Swiss male choir, every member being a professional singer. Founded in 1852. Condrs.: E. Reiter (1852–75); A. Volkland (1875–1902), and now H. Suter. This choir of 180 singers gives every winter one *a cappella* concert and one with orch. (iii) At

Berne, there is the *Cäcilienverein* cond. by Fritz Brun. (iv) At Geneva, the *Soc. de Chant du Cons.* cond. by F. Hay. (v) Also *Soc. de Chant Sacré*, condr. O. Barblan.

U.S.A.—Of all forms of mus. activity cultivated in the U.S.A. to-day, apart from the church music, choral-singing can look back upon the longest continuous history. Before the end of the XVIII century, sacred concerts by the church choirs came into vogue. New England was the chief scene of activity. (i) One of these singing-schools, led by the tanner-composer, William Billings, in Stoughton, Mass., was organised in 1786 as the *Stoughton Mus. Soc.* and under this name has maintained an uninterrupted existence up to the present day. (ii) Not quite so old, but still active and more ambitious, is the *Handel and Haydn Soc.* of Boston, founded 1815 with Thomas S. Webb as mus. dir. The most striking figure among its early leaders was Lowell Mason (1792–1872) who cond. from 1827–32. Later condrs. were Carl Zerrahn (1854–95), B. J. Lang (1895–7), R. L. Herman (1898–9) and Emil Mollenhauer (from 1899).

Consult Charles G. Perkins and John S. Dwight, *The History of the Handel and Haydn Society* (Boston, 1893).

(iii) The *Cecilia Soc. of Boston* was founded 1874 as a subsidiary of the Harvard Mus. Association, but became independent in 1876. Its condrs. were B. J. Lang (1874–1907), Wallace Goodrich (1907–10), Max Fiedler (1910-11), Arthur Mees and Henry Gideon (1911–15), Chalmers Clifton (1915–17), and then Arthur Shepherd, Ernest Mitchell and Georges Longy in rapid succession. (iv) The most important choral organisation in New York City is the *Oratorio Soc.* founded in 1873 by Leopold Damrosch. Its condrs. were Leopold Damrosch (1873–85), Walter Damrosch (1885–99), Frank Damrosch (1899–1912), Louis Koemmenich (1912–17), Walter Damrosch (1917–1921) and Albert Stoessel (from 1921).

Consult H. E. Krehbiel, *Notes on the Cultivation of Choral Music and the Oratorio Society of New York* (New York, 1894); and his continuation of this history in the Festival Programme Book for 1920.

(v) The *Mus. Art Soc.* of New York, organised by Frank Damrosch in 1894, consisted of selected professional singers and cultivated particularly the older masters of *a cappella* music. It ceased its activity in 1920. (vi) The *Schola Cantorum* of New York was organised by Kurt Schindler in 1909, originally under the name of *The MacDowell Chorus*. Its present name was adopted in 1912. It sings *a cappella* music as well as choral works with orch. (vii) Among the male choruses, two of the Ger. singing societies were for many years factors in the mus. life of New York. The *Liederkranz* was organised in 1847. Its recent condrs. have been R. L. Herman (1884–9), Heinrich Zoellner (1890–8), Paul Klengel (1898–1903), Arthur Claassen (1903–14) Otto Graf (1914–17), E. Klee (1917–20) and O. Wick (from 1920). (viii) The *Arion*, founded in 1854, was raised to a high artistic level by Leopold Damrosch (1871–84). Frank van der Stucken, who cond. 1884–94, took the society on a European tour in 1892. His successors were Julius Lorenz (1895–

1911) and Carl Hahn (1913–18). The society united with the Liederkranz in 1920. (ix) The *Mendelssohn Glee Club* (male chorus) was founded in 1866. Among its condrs. were Edward MacDowell (1897–9), Arthur Mees (1899–1909), Frank Damrosch (1904–9), Clarence Dickinson (1909–13), Louis Koemmenich (1913–19), N. P. Coffin (from 1919). (x) The *St. Cecilia Club* (female vs.) has been cond. from 1902 by Victor Harris; and a similar organisation, (xi) the *Rubinstein Club*, is cond. by William R. Chapman. (xii) The *Brooklyn Oratorio Soc.* organised in 1893 and cond. since then by Walter Henry Hall, gives 2 concerts yearly. The *Apollo Club* (male chorus) of Brooklyn was founded in 1877 by Dudley Buck. He was succeeded as condr. in 1903 by J. H. Brewer, the present condr. (xiii) The *Oratorio Soc.* of Newark, N.J., was organised in 1878 by Louis Arthur Russell, who is still its condr. (xiv) The *Mendelssohn Club* of Philadelphia began its activity in 1874 under W. W. Gilchrist, who died in 1916 and was succeeded by N. Lindsay Norden. It became a mixed chorus in 1879. (xv) The *Oberlin* (Ohio) *Mus. Union* had its beginning in 1860. It was cond. from 1871 to 1900 by Fenelon B. Rice, and since 1900 by George W. Andrews. (xvi) The *Apollo Mus. Club* of Chicago was organised in 1872 by Silas G. Pratt and George P. Upton. Originally a male chorus, it was later transformed into a mixed chorus. Its condr. from 1875–98 was William L. Tomlins, and since 1898 Harrison M. Wild. (xvii) The *Mendelssohn Club* (mixed voices) of Chicago had Frederick W. Root for its first condr. (1894–95). Since 1895 Harrison M. Wild is the leader.

For the Bethlehem Bach Choir, the Hampden County Musical Association and the Litchfield County Choral Union, see U.S.A. MUSIC FESTIVALS.—E.-H.

CHORALE-SYMPHONIE. Name given to 5th symphony of Anton Bruckner, which introduces a chorale-tune in last movement. It is played at end of symphony by a band of 11 brass instrs. placed in gallery of concert-hall—a reminiscence of the old baroque tradition. B. derived the idea from the perf. of masses in Austrian monasteries. Mahler has also introduced chorale-tunes in last movement of his 1st symphony, augmenting the brass instrs. for this purpose; and also in his 2nd (*Resurrection*) symphony. Like Bruckner, Mahler introduced (end of 1st and 2nd parts of 8th symphony) a special band (4 tpts. 3 trombones) playing in the gallery.—EG. W.

CHRISTIANSEN, F. Melius. Norwegian-Amer. condr. compr. *b.* Eidsvold, 1 April 1871. Pupil of Oscar Hansen (orgt. condr. Larvik). Went to America in 1888. Took examination at North-western Cons. 1894, stud. at Cons. in Leipzig, 1897–9, 1906–7; mus. dir. at St. Olaf Coll. Northfield, Minnesota, from 1903. Leader of the students' band. His numerous concert-tours in the Northern States with St. Olaf Choir have exercised great influence on the public's interest in church singing.

Practical Modulation (1916); *Reformation Cantata* (1917); *The Prodigal Son*, cantata (1918); *St. Olaf*

Choir Series (I, 1920, mainly classical compns., also some Norwegian; II, 1921, mainly his own compns.) (Minneapolis, Augsburg Publ. House).—U. M.

CHRISTIE, Winifred. Eng. pianist. Played in public at age of 6; stud. later at R.A.M. London, under Oscar Beringer, and harmony under Stewart Macpherson; later pf. under Harold Bauer; tours in Germany, England, Holland, France; 1915–19 in America; toured with Boston Orch. In 1921, gave recitals in London on Emmanuel Moór's new Duplex-Coupler pianoforte, which she considers has effected a complete regeneration of pf. interpretation.—E.-H.

CHRYSANDER, Friedrich. Ger. mus. research scholar; *b.* Lübtheen, 8 July, 1826; *d.* Bergedorf, 3 Sept. 1901. Stud. philosophy at Rostock; lived a long time in England; settled in Bergedorf, near Hamburg. Not only was he indefatigable ed. of complete ed. of Handel's works (1859–94), but also universal worker in field of musical research in Germany; endowed with great brilliancy and force of character, even though the depth of his specific qualities as a musician has been somewhat challenged owing to his *Practical* ed. of Handel's works.

Yearbooks of Musical Science, 1863 and 1867; ed. of *Allgemeine Musikalische Zeitung,* containing a quantity of his essays, 1868–71 and 1875–82; joint ed. of the *Vierteljahrsschrift für Musik-Wissenschaft,* a quarterly publication from 1885–94. *Inter alia* publ. all Corelli's works and Couperin's *Pièces de Clavecin* (London, Augener, 4 books). Chief work is the biography *G. F. Händel,* which remains a monumental work (Breitkopf, 1858–67; unaltered reprint 1919).—A. E.

CHUBB, John Frederick. Eng. orgt. *b.* Hastings in 1885. Educated principally at St. John's Choir School, St. Leonards and Cambridge Univ. Organ appointments: St. John's, St. Leonards, 1898–1903; Ely Cath. assistant orgt. 1903–6; Christ's Coll. Cambridge, 1906–10; Christ Ch. Harrogate, 1910–12. In 1912, went to Canada and has been orgt. at Christ Ch. Vancouver, B.C., since that time. Has exercised much influence on mus. education in Vancouver. He holds degrees of B.A. Cantab. and Mus.Bac. Oxon.—L. S.

CHUECA, Federico. Span. compr. *b.* Madrid, 5 May, 1848; *d.* 20 June, 1908. Generally reputed as a musician who had no knowledge of music. He did know it, but in a very small measure. Perhaps this is the reason why he nearly always worked in collab. with the compr. Joaquín Valverde, the association being known as *Chueca y Valverde.* His father intended him for a doctor, but he was determined to be a musician, and a musician he became, in spite of his poor training, winning fame and fortune with his numerous mus. comedies. His popularity went as far as to convert him at one time into a powerful influence for municipal and political propaganda in Madrid. He had an inborn gift for appealing to the man in the street. He was destined by the gods to be the barrel-organ of his generation. *La Gran Vía,* his revue-like mus. comedy, took Spain by storm, passed the frontiers and attained almost equal success in foreign countries, though its

subject—a satire on the municipal affairs of the Madrid of that period—could not be understood outside Spain. The magic power of his melody was the attraction; for he might not have been able to compose, in the real sense of the word, but he could invent tunes, and nobody else ever got such results from a simple tonic-and-dominant system of harmony. He even succeeded in interesting, though in a negative sense, the proudest of modern philosophers. On hearing the famous *Jota de los Ratas* (*Pick-pockets' Song*) from *La Gran Vía,* Nietzsche exclaimed: " The people that has produced this music is beyond salvation." In London the music of *La Gran Vía* failed to gain the same vogue as in other parts of Europe. The English theatrical manager's customary treatment robs the continental importations of their character. Chueca's music was introduced in a show arranged · *ad hoc,* entitled *Castles in Spain.* It was neither English nor Spanish. A march from his mus. comedy *Cádiz* imposed itself on Spain as a national hymn, and was proclaimed so by the Government. It is still in the repertoire of all the military bands in the world.

La Abuela, A la exposición, El año pasado por agua, Los Arrastraos, Cádiz, La Gran Vía, Los Barrios Bajos, El Bateo, La Canción del Amor, Los Caramelos, La caza del oso o el tendero de comestibles, La Corrida de Toros, De Madrid a París, Lección conyugal, El Chaleco Blanco. (Unión Musical Española, Madrid.) —P. G. M.

CHVÁLA, Emanuel. Czech critic and compr.; *b.* Prague, 1851. Stud. under Josef Foerster and Zdenko Fibich. For over 30 years (until 1917) one of most noted Czech critics. Wrote (in Czech) for *Národní Politika*; (in Ger.) for *Politik*; also later for *Union.* Lives in Prague. At his own expense he publ. *A Quarter of a Century of Bohemian Music* (1886).

Opera, *Záboj*; orch.: *Sousedské*; overture, *At the Kermesse* (*O posvícení*); str. 4tet; songs.—V. ST.

CHYBIŃSKI, Adolf (*phon.* Hybinski). Polish music-historian; *b.* Cracow, 29 March, 1880. Student of Ger. philology. Pf. pupil of Jan Drozdowski (Jan Jordan). Stud. science of music at Munich under Sandberger and Kroyer. Ph.D. 1908, with dissertation *Beiträge zur Geschichte des Taktschlagens.* In 1912, lecturer; 1917, prof.-extraordinary; 1921, prof.-in-ordinary at Lemberg Univ. Industrious contributor to many Polish and Ger. music periodicals. Many reviews in *Z. der I.M.G.* His treatises, dealing with history of Polish music, are:

Bogurodzica (oldest Polish church song) *in relation to the History of Music* (1907, Polish); *Materials for the History of the Rorantic Chapel in R. Castle Vavel at Cracow from 1540 to 1700* (1910, Polish); *The Tablature for Organ of Johannes de Lublin from 1540* (published 1912–13 in periodical *Kwartalnik Muzyczny*). Elaborated Polish part for Polish ed. of Karl Weinmann's *Geschichte der Kirchenmusik* and transl. (with Josef Reiss) Hausegger's *Musik als Ausdruck.* —ZD. J.

CILEA, Francesco. Ital. compr. *b.* Palmi, 26 July, 1866. A representative of the Ital. lyric, veristic school of period of Mascagni and Puccini. He is specially noted for his opera, *Adriana Lecouvreur,* first perf. in 1902 (Lyric Theatre, Milan) with great success, which has gone round the principal theatres of the world. Before this opera, C. had comp. *Gina* in 1889; *Tilda* (perf. Florence, 1892); *Arlesiana* (Lyric, Milan, 1897). It was at first perf. of *Arlesiana* that the t. Caruso revealed himself in Milan. C.'s last opera was *Gloria* (perf. at Scala, Milan, 1907). He has comp. some elegant chamber-music, pf. pieces and songs. At present C. is dir. of Cons. of San Pietro a Maiella, Naples, having gone there from Palermo, where he was also dir. of the Cons. Previously he was a teacher in Naples and Florence.—D. A.

CIMBALOM. See HUNGARIAN MUS. INSTRS.

ĈIURLIONIS, Mikalojus Konstantinas. Lithuanian compr. *b.* Varena, Vilna government, 10 Sept. 1875; *d.* near Warsaw, 28 March, 1914. His father was an orgt. At 14, the boy entered the music-school attached to Prince Oginski's orch. at Plunge. The Prince sent him to Warsaw Cons. In his fifth year there, he was leading pupil of Noskowski's compn. class. In 1901, his symph. poem for orch. *Miškas (The Forest)* took 1st prize at Zamojski competition at Warsaw. It was perf. at Kaunas in 1921. For his second orch. work, *Polonez*, he received from Prince Oginski an award of 1000 marks towards cost of mus. study in Leipzig. After a year there under Reinecke, he returned to Warsaw and gave mus. lectures. He spent a year at the Strabrausti art school (1903–4) and wrote symph. poem *Jura (Ocean)*. He proposed to turn this into an opera, but left the work unfinished, though his wife Sofija (Kymantaite) had written the libretto, *Jurata (Queen of the Ocean)*. During his later years, whilst living at Vilna, he wrote mostly for pf. and for chorus. Through his efforts, the Vilna people first heard a properly trained Lithuanian choir. His cantata *De Profundis* (1899–1900) is still perf. Together with the artists A Žmuidzinaviĉius and P. Rimŝa, he founded in Vilna the Lithuanian Art Association and exhibited many of his own pictures. For an account of his pictorical art, see Rosa Newmarch's *The Russian Arts* (Jenkins) under heading *Chourlianis (sic)*, pp. 271–3.—H. R.

CLARINET in E flat. Modern symph. music gives this instr. great importance. Gustav Mahler uses it in all his symphonies and in the *Lied von der Erde*, and gives instructions *to double the part* in *ff* passages. Mahler uses the clar. in E flat not for tone-colour but to strengthen the intensity of the melody when the full orchestra is playing.—E.-H.

CLARKE, Rebecca. Eng. compr. vla.-player; *b.* Harrow, England, 27 Aug. 1886. Stud. compn. under Sir Charles Stanford at R.C.M. At his advice, took up vla., which she has played professionally ever since. 1916, went to New York, and played much in solo and chamber-music in America.

Her vla. sonata tied with a piece by Ernest Bloch for the Mrs. F. S. Coolidge Prize, in 1919. The donor decided on the Bloch piece. It was produced at the Pittsfield Fest. that year, played by Harold Bauer and Louis Bailly. Since perf. in Europe by herself, Lionel Tertis, and others. In 1921 her trio (pf. vn. cello) again took the second Coolidge Prize (perf. London, 3 Dec. 1922, by Myra Hess, Marjorie Hayward, May Mukle). Was commissioned for a cello and

pf. work for Mrs. Coolidge's Pittsfield Fest. 1923. Two songs (*Shy One*; *The Cloths of Heaven*) are publ. by Winthrop Rogers; the vla. sonata by Chester; the trio by Murdoch.—E.-H.

CLARKE, Robert Coningsby. Eng. songwriter; *b.* Old Charlton, Kent, 17 March, 1879. Educated Marlborough Coll.; articled pupil of Sir F. Bridge at Westminster Abbey; orgt. Trinity Coll. Oxford; B.A. (jurisprudence), 1902.

Popular songs and ballads, and pf. pieces (Chappell; Boosey; Cramer; Church; Newman; Ascherberg, etc.).—E.-H.

CLAUSETTI, Carlo. Ital. writer; *b.* Naples, 17 Oct. 1869. A graduate in law; devoted from early youth to music; active member, for 6 years, of Concert Soc. founded by Martucci; then in Naples assisted in founding the Quartet Society. Finally, developing Martucci's idea, founded a new concert soc. which took Martucci's name, and gave important series of concerts. Founded the review *Symphonia*. Until 1912, C. was manager of Ricordi's at Naples; in 1919, joined Renzo Valcarenghi in the management of the Ricordi head-office at Milan. Publ. 2 illuminating books on Wagner's *Tristan* and *Twilight of the Gods*; wrote the legend *Sumitra*, set to music by Riccardo Pick-Mangiagalli (*q.v.*).—D. A.

CLAVÉ, José Anselmo. Span. musician; *b.* Barcelona, 21 April, 1827; *d.* there, 1872. Founder of famous Coros Clavé of Barcelona, a choral soc. of great importance in the education of Catalonian working classes; for it he wrote numerous works of an adequate, but somewhat obsolete, character. His memory is honoured by a statue in the Rambla de Cataluña, Barcelona.—P. G. M.

CLAVICEMBALO. See LANDOWSKA, WANDA; BUCHMAYER, RICHARD.

CLAVIOR. A little apparatus made of aluminium for stretching the hand. Invented in July 1922 by Ennemond Trillat.—E.-H.

CLEATHER, Gabriel Gordon. Eng. timpanist; *b.* Manchester, 3 May, 1846. 1882, gen. manager of Crystal Palace; has played under most of the famous condrs.; has lectured widely on the drums, especially on their use in churches in combination with the organ. Played the Tausch concerto for 6 drums with Thomas Orch. in New York.—E.-H.

CLEGG, Edith Kate. Eng. operatic singer; *b.* London. Stud. under Hermann Klein, London; Bouhy, Paris; John Acton, Blackburn; operatic *début* in Liza Lehmann's *Vicar of Wakefield*; sang in grand opera seasons, R. Opera, Covent Garden, Suzuki (*Butterfly*); Mother (*Louise*); Maddalena (*Rigoletto*), etc. Toured Australia, S. Africa, Canada with Quinlan Co.; member of Beecham Opera Co. (in above, and also in *Boris*, *Falstaff*, *Tales of Hoffmann*). Now member of the British National Opera Co.—E.-H.

CLERICE, Justino. Argentine compr. *b.* Buenos Ayres in 1863; *d.* Paris in 1900. After studying in Argentina, went to Paris Cons., under Pessard and Delibes. Devoted himself to comic operas and operettas. His 1st piece, *Le Meunier d'Alcalá*, was given at Trinidad Theatre, Lisbon,

1887. In 1889, produced several pieces at Paris theatres, which were warmly received by the public.

Le Meunier d'Alcalá, 3-act opera, libretto by Garrido and Lafrique; *Figarella*, 1-act comic opera, libretto by Grandmougin and Méry; *Monsieur Huchot*, 1-act vaudeville, libretto by Férésand (Bouffes-Parisiennes, 1889); *Au pays noir*, 2-act ballet (Theatre Royal, Antwerp, 1891); *Le 3e Houssards*, 3-act operetta (Gaieté, Paris, 1894); *Les Œufs de Pâques*, lyrical comedy; *Colibri*, ballet (in collab. with Noël); *La Petite Vénus*, 3-act opera; *Margarred*, 4-act comic opera; *Flagrant Délit*, comic opera; *La Dame de cœur*, 2-act ballet (in collab. with Mars); *Ordre de l'Empereur*, operetta (a large number of perfs.). Many songs and pf. pieces.—A. M.

CLEVE, Berit Winderen. Norwegian pianist; *b.* Vestre Aker, near Christiania, 10 Feb. 1878. Stud. pf. in Christiania under Ida Lie, in Berlin under Raif, Jedliczka and Carreño. *Début* in Christiania in 1902. Married (1904) the compr. Halfdan Cleve.—U. M.

CLEVE, Halfdan. Norwegian compr. pianist; *b.* Kongsberg, 5 Oct. 1879. Stud. pf. and compn. under Otto-Hjelm in Christiania. Lived (1898–1909) in Berlin, where his teachers were O. Raif and the brothers Scharwenka. *Début* as compr. in 1902 at Singakademie in Berlin where 2 of his pf. concertos were perf. as well as some pf. pieces. Critics foretold a brilliant future for him. Three years later, gave a successful concert of his own compns. in the same hall, with Philh. Orch. In 1907, at a concert which Grieg gave with the Berlin Philh., C. played brilliantly the pf. part in Grieg's concerto. Has frequently appeared as soloist in his native land and abroad. Stands in the first rank of younger Norwegian comprs. His pf. pieces are especially brilliant.

5 pf. concertos; vn. sonata; over 20 pf. pieces; songs with orch.—R. M.

CLIFFE, Frederic. Eng. pianist; b. Lowmoor, near Bradford, 2 May, 1857. Orgt. at various churches at a very early age; 1873–6, orgt. to Bradford Fest. Choral Soc.; 1883, prof. of pf. at R.C.M. London (now senr. prof. of pf. there); orgt. Bach Choir, 1888–94; and of Ital. opera, Drury Lane, about same time. His orch. works met with success.

Symphony I, C mi. (Crystal Palace, 1889); II, E mi. Leeds Fest. 1892); *Coronation March* (Westminster Abbey, King George V); vn. concerto (Norwich Fest. 1896); *Cloud and Sunshine*, orch. poem (R. Philh. 1890); *Ode to North-East Wind*, chorus and orch. (Sheffield Fest. 1905); scena, *Triumph of Alcestis* (Norwich Fest. 1902); church music; many songs.—E.-H.

CLIFFORD, Julian. Eng. compr. condr. pianist; *b.* London, 28 Sept. 1877; *d.* Hastings, 27 Dec. 1921. Stud. Leipzig Cons., also under Sliwiński and Sir W. Parratt; condr. Birmingham Symphony Orch.; Yorkshire Permanent Orch., Leeds; mus. dir. Harrogate Corporation and Eastbourne Corporation. Cond. frequently in London. A particularly fine condr. of Tchaikovsky's music. His son succeeded him as condr. at Eastbourne.

Orch. pieces; cantata; pf. pieces; songs (Schott). —E.-H.

CLIFTON, Chalmers. Amer. condr. *b.* Jackson, Miss., U.S.A., 30 April, 1889. Stud. at Cincinnati Cons. 1903–8. Graduated A.B. at Harvard 1912, with highest honours in music. Cond. 1st MacDowell Fest. in Peterboro, N.H., in 1910;

1912–14, a pupil in Paris of d'Indy and Gédalge (as holder of a Sheldon Fellowship of Harvard Univ.). In 1914 again a condr. at MacDowell Fest. Comp. and cond. the music for Lexington (Mass.) Pageant in 1915. Condr. of the Cecilia Soc. in Boston (1915–17) and Plymouth Pageant, 1921. Now dir. of a well-accredited training orch. of the Amer. Orch. Soc. of New York. Publ. *Adagio* for orch. (Schirmer, 1919).—O. K.

CLOSSON, Ernest. Belgian mus. critic, musicologist; *b.* Brussels, 12 Dec. 1870. Stud. under various profs., notably Léopold Wallner. In 1896, appointed curator of instr. museum of Brussels Cons. In 1912 became prof. of general culture and mus. history there. In 1917, prof. of mus. history at Mons Cons. Since 1920, music critic of *L'Indépendance Belge* (Brussels). Is also famous for his mus. lectures and numerous transl. into Fr. of Ger. and Ital. mus. works. Member of commission for publ. old Belgian masters. Collab. with C. Van den Borren for the Belgian articles in this Dictionary.

Siegfried (1891); *Edvard Grieg* (1892); *Music and the Plastic Arts* (1896); *Folk-Songs of the Belgian Provinces* (1905, 2nd and 3rd ed. 1911 and 1920); *Franco-Walloon Folk-Songs* (taken from the former coll. 1913); *Old French Christmas Carols* (1911); ms. of *Les Basses-Danses de la Bibliothèque de Bourgogne* (1912); *Folk-Songs in Belgium* (1913); *Elements of Musical Æsthetics* (1916); *Musical Æsthetics*, 1921 (all publ. Brussels); monographs on Lassus and Grétry (Turnhout, 1919 and 1920); colls. of old Belgian harpsichord music (Paris, Durand). Contributed to *Guide Musical* (1892–1914), to *Biographie Nationale*, and to following newspapers and periodicals: *Echo Musical, Libre Critique, Jeune Belgique, Durendal, Le Soir* (Brussels); *Wallonia* (Liège); *La Terre Wallonne* (Charleroi); *Weekblad voor Muziek* (Amsterdam); *S.I.M., Revue Musicale, Courrier Musical* (Paris); *Z.* and *Sammelbände* of *I.M.G.*; *Signale* (Leipzig); *Österreichische Musik- und Theater-Zeitung*, etc.—C. V. B.

CLUTSAM, George H. Australian compr. music critic; *b.* Sydney, New S. Wales, 1866. Toured New Zealand as a prodigy-pianist; in 1890, India, China, Japan, and then settled in London, rapidly becoming known as an accompanist; music critic for *The Observer*, 1908–18.

Operas: *The Queen's Jester* (Leipzig, 1896); *A Summer Night*, 1 act (Beecham's seasons, 1910); *The Quest of Rapunzel*, cantata (Queen's Hall, 1911); *After a Thousand Years*, 1 act (Tivoli); *The Pool*, fantastic melodrama (Alhambra); *King Harlequin* (Berlin, Nov. 1912); *Young England* (with Hubert Bath), 1916; light operas: *Gabriella* (with A. Joyce), 1921; *The Little Duchess* (1922); *Lilac-Time* (arr. of Schubert themes), Lyric Theatre, 1923. Orch. suites, pf. music and many songs.—E.-H.

COATES, Albert. Eng. condr. *b.* in Petrograd in 1882, of Eng. parents. At age of 12, sent to Liverpool for education; at 18, office-work in Thornton Woollen Mills, Petrograd; later stud. pf., cello, compn. at Leipzig Cons.; joined Nikisch's conductors' class in 1904; assistant to N. at Leipzig Opera House; 1909, senior-condr. and artistic dir. Imperial Opera, Petrograd; in 1914, cond. at Covent Garden, London, for 1st time, during Wagner season; re-engaged for Grand season, sharing work with Nikisch (N. *The Ring*; C. *Tristan, Mastersingers, Parsifal*). When Czar's opera-dir. resigned in the 1917 revolution, C. was elected president of Opera House, by the managing committee; Bolsheviks confirmed the opera autonomy. Illness

96

forced him to leave Russia, through Finland. In May 1919, engaged by Beecham as senior condr. and artistic co-dir. for the English Opera. Since then has cond. opera (Beecham; R.N.O.C. and orch. concerts [Leeds Fest. 1922], etc.) continuously in England and America. In 1923 and 1924, took conducting classes, at Eastman Inst. Rochester, U.S.A. C.'s thorough mastery of orch. effect, great control of orch. and tireless rhythmic energy, place him amongst the greatest conductors of to-day.—E.-H.

COATES, Eric. Eng. compr. b. Hucknall, Notts, 27 Aug. 1886. Stud. in Nottingham under Georg Ellenberger (vn.) and Dr. Ralph Horner (compn.); 1906, gained scholarship at R.A.M. London. Stud. vla. under Lionel Tertis, compn. under F. Corder. 1907, toured S. Africa with Hambourg Str. Quartet. At one time, member of Cathie and Walenn Str. Quartets; 1912, principal vla. Queen's Hall Orch. for some years, during which he comp. several light orch. works which were produced under his direction at the Promenade Concerts and have since become widely played. In 1918, devoted himself entirely to composition.

Miniature Suite (Boosey); *Countryside Suite* (Hawkes); *Summer Days Suite* (Chappell); *Joyous Youth Suite* (id. 1921); *The Merry-makers*, miniature overture (id. 1923); *Moresque, Dance Interlude* (id.); valsette, *Wood-Nymphs* (id.). Song-cycles with orch.; *Lace and Porcelain* (Boosey); *Four Shakespeare Songs* (id.); *The Mill o' Dreams* (Chappell); also numerous songs.—E.-H.

COATES, John. Eng. song and operatic t. singer; b. near Bradford, 29 June, 1865. Came of a mus. family on both sides, for generations; stud. in Yorkshire under J. G. Walton, Robert Burton, Dr. J. C. Bridge; in London, under W. Shakespeare, and T. A. Wallworth; in Paris under Bouhy. 1st London appearance (as barit.) Savoy Theatre, 1894; for 5 years sang comic opera and mus. comedy in England and America; as t. at Globe, London, 1900; 1st appearance R. Opera, Covent Garden, 1901 (Faust; and created Claudio in Stanford's *Much Ado*); Gürzenich Concerts and Opera, Cologne, 1901; Leipzig, etc.; Berlin R. Opera House and Hanover R. Opera House, 1902; Dresden, Hamburg, Frankfort, Mannheim, Paris, Cincinnati Fest. 1906; Holland, 1910; 1st fest. engagement Leeds, 1901; since then, all the chief Eng. fests.; Covent Garden, Eng. seasons, Moody Manners Co.; Carl Rosa, 1909; Beecham spring, summer and winter seasons, 1910; production of Ethel Smyth's *The Wreckers*, 1909; Denhof *Ring* perfs., both Siegfrids, 1911; Quinlan tour United Kingdom, S. Africa, Australia, 1911-13; 4 years war-service, in France, 1916-19; resumed prof. career 1919. Very many song-recitals (especially all Eng.), concerts, etc., 1920 till now. He unites to a fine tenor voice, wide culture, perfection of vocal declamation and high dramatic attainments.—E.-H.

COBBETT, Walter Willson. Eng. music patron; an amateur violinist and chamber-music player; b. Blackheath, 11 July, 1847. Inaugurated 1st Cobbett Competition in 1905, under auspices of the Musicians' Company, for a new,

short form of str. 4tet, *Phantasy*, the modern analogue of the old-time *Fancy*. The winner of the 1st prize (50 gs.) was W. H. Hurlstone. In 1908, C. offered further prizes for a Phantasy-Trio (1st prize taken by Frank Bridge); in the 1909 competition (international, 134 entrants), the 1st prize went to John Ireland, for sonata vn. and pf. (No. 1; publ. since by Augener). In 1914 a competition for str. 4tet prize of 50 gs. was won by Frank Bridge. A Folk-song-Phantasy competition in 1916 resulted in 1st prizes to J. Cliffe Forrester for Phantasy Trio and H. Waldo Warner for Phantasy-Quartet; York Bowen took the 1st prize in 1918 for a Phantasy for vla. and pf.; in 1919, dance-measures were introduced and the 1st prize for a Dance-Phantasy for str. and pf. went to C. Armstrong Gibbs. In 1921, Mr. Cobbett offered 50 gs. in prizes to students and ex-students of R.A.M. and a similar prize to R.C.M. He has also, at various times, commissioned 18 British comprs. to write pieces in Phantasy form for various combinations of instrs. He also gave prizes at R.A.M. (1922) and R.C.M. (1920-21-22-23) for best quartet-teams amongst the students, playing a work of their own choice. He ed. a chamber-music supplement to the *Music Student* (for 3½ years). Has contributed to many journals. Wrote 60 arts. for Grove's *Dictionary of Music*. Has planned (1924) an International Encyclopædia of Chamber-music.—E.-H.

COCCHI de SANCTIS, Eduardo. Compr. b. Rome in 1868. Stud. under Serrao at Cons. of Naples, and under De Sanctis, dir. of R. Liceo Mus. di Santa Cecilia in Rome. Went to Buenos Ayres in 1906, where he establ. the Cons. which he now directs.

Funeral Mass for King Charles Albert (perf. R. Palace of Superga). Orch. marches, *Tripoli* and *Libya*; some sacred pieces and chamber-music.—A. M.

COCHRANE, Sir Stanley H., Bart. One of foremost Irish patrons of music in Dublin; b. 19 Sept. 1877. Has on many occasions most generously aided the cause of orch. music. In 1913-14 he engaged London Symphony Orch. (under Hamilton Harty) for concerts in concert-hall at his residence, Woodbrook, near Dublin; organised chamber-music concerts there, at which Esposito, Simonetti and Clyde Twelvetrees perf. complete set of Beethoven trios. Chiefly owing to his generous patronage, the Quinlan Opera Co. perf. entire *Ring* of Wagner in Dublin, 1914. With Esposito, he founded the " C. & E. Edition " for publishing music.—W. ST.

COCORASCU, Scarlat. See RUMANIAN OPERA.

COCQ-WEINGAND, Amelia. Chilean pianist; b. 1884. Began stud. at Santiago; in 1900 went to Paris and stud. under Raoul Pugno. Returning to Chile in 1905, gave a series of most successful concerts. In 1914, settled in Buenos Ayres, with her husband, the violinist Edmundo Weingand, with whom she continues her concert career.—A. M.

COERNE, Louis Adolphe. Amer. compr. b. Newark, N.J., U.S.A., 27 Feb. 1870; d. Boston, Mass., 11 Sept. 1922. Received his early schooling in Germany and France. Then attended Boston (Mass.) Latin School and (1888–90) Harvard Coll., taking mus. theory under Paine. At the same time, a vn. pupil of Franz Kneisel; 1890–3, stud. the organ and compn. under Rheinberger in Munich. Here his symph. poem, *Hiawatha*, op. 18, was perf. in 1893. He cond. this work with Boston Symphony Orch. 4 April, 1894. After acting as a choral dir. and as church orgt. in Buffalo, N.Y. (1894–7), and in Columbus, Ohio (1897–9), he returned to Germany where he remained until 1902. 1903–4, was associate-prof. of music at Smith Coll., Northampton, Mass. Having devoted himself for some time to mus. research work, he received the degree of Ph.D. from Harvard Univ. in 1905, the first mus. degree of this kind to be conferred by an Amer. Univ. His thesis, *The Evolution of Modern Orchestration*, was publ. by Macmillan, New York, 1908. Then followed 2 more years in Germany, 1905–7. During this time his opera *Zenobia* was brought out in Bremen, the first opera by a native American to be produced in Germany. After this he was mus. dir. in Troy, N.Y. (1907–9). From 1909 to 1910, head of the mus. cons. of Olivet Coll. Michigan, from which inst. he received the degree of Mus.D. in 1910. From 1910 to 1915, head of music department of Univ. of Wisconsin in Madison, and from 1915 until death, prof. of music at Connecticut Coll. for Women at New London.

Although he was an industrious compr. of the old school—his opus numbers are close to 200, of which more than half are publ.—his larger compns. have not been often heard in America.
Mass in D mi., 6-v. unacc. op. 53 (Leuckart); *Swedish Sonata*, vn. and pf. op. 60 (Hofmeister); pf. trios, op. 62, 64 (Bosworth; André); *Zenobia*, 3-act opera, op. 66 (Seemann). Cantatas (all Ditson): *Until the Day Break*, op. 124; *A Song of Victory*, op. 125; *Skipper Ireson's Ride*, op. 131; *The Landing of the Pilgrims*, op. 135; *The Man of Galilee*, op. 141 (Schirmer). Many anthems and choruses (Ditson) and pf., organ and vn. pieces.—O. K.

CŒUROY, André. Fr. musicologist; *b.* Dijon, 24 Feb. 1891. Former pupil of École Normale Supérieure, Paris; *Agrégé de l'Univ.* Paris; music pupil of Max Reger; stud. specially the connections of music with literature in Europe. Has publ. *La Musique française moderne* (Delagrave, 1922); studies and analysis of *La Walkyrie* and *La Tosca* (1923); *Essais de musique et de littérature comparées* (Bloud & Gay, 1923, with preface by Maurice Barrès); *Weber* (Alcan, 1924). As compr. has produced (under name of Jean Belime) a trio for vla. and clar. and a 5tet. Contributed in 1920 to the foundation of *La Revue Musicale*, of which he is ed.-in-chief. Music critic of *La Revue Universelle*. Collab. with Henry Prunières (chairman), M. D. Calvocoressi, D. Lazarus, M. Pincherle, M. L. Pereyra, Félix Raugel, André Rigaud and A. Scheeffner for the Fr. articles in this Dictionary.—H. P.

COHEN, Dulcie M. Australian compr. Lives at Sydney.
Zuleika, small orch.; *Chanson d'Éviradnus*, tone-poem, solo, v. and orch.; cantatas; educational pf. and chamber-music; many songs.—E.-H.

COHEN, Harriet. Eng. pianist; *b.* London. Stud. at R.A.M. under Tobias Matthay; 1st recital, June 1920, Wigmore Hall (with John Coates); has toured widely, and given the 1st perfs. of most of Arnold Bax's pf. works, in which she is heard at her best. She also gives very sensitive readings of the Russ. and Ger. xviii and xix century classics.—E.-H.

COLAÇO, Alexandre Rey. Portuguese pianist and teacher; *b.* about 1850. Stud. at Cons. at Madrid and in Paris under G. Mathias and T. Ritter; also at Berlin, for a short time, under Barth and Rudorff for pf., Härtel for cpt. and Spitta for history. Was a for long time the most fashionable pf. teacher in Lisbon, and occupied a chief place at the Cons. He contributed largely to the introduction of chamber-music in Lisbon. Comp. numerous *fados* and other popular songs. Consult *Encyclopédie de la Musique* (Paris, 1920, Delagrave).—E.-H.

COLERIDGE-TAYLOR, Samuel. Eng. compr. *b.* Holborn, London, 15 Aug. 1875; *d.* Croydon, 1 Sept. 1912. Was of Negroid race, and later on in life became an enthusiastic apostle of colour; early vn. training under Joseph Beckwith of Croydon; stud. R.C.M. London, 1890–7, at first with vn. as chief study; later, on advice of Sir Charles Stanford, placed compn. first. In 1893 gained a 3-years scholarship at R.C.M., later renewed for a further year. Joachim led a perf. of C.-T.'s clar. 5tet, op. 10, in Berlin, 1897. His great achievement was his strikingly original setting of *Hiawatha's Wedding Feast* (Longfellow) for soli, chorus and orch. It was first perf. at the R.C.M. 11 Nov. 1898. The compn. of the 2 other parts, *Death of Minnehaha* and *Hiawatha's Departure*, followed. A long string of works for chorus and orch. led on to his next chief success along this line, the cantata *A Tale of Old Japan*, op. 76 (London Choral Soc. Queen's Hall, 1911). His pf. and his vn. works are also very characteristic. As is the case with many other comprs. there is some dross amongst the gold; but of his original creative gift there is no doubt. A believer in the folk-song element in art, his aim was to do for the negro music, what Dvořák had done for the Bohemian, and Grieg for the Norwegian. The overture to the *Song of Hiawatha* is built upon the Jubilee Singers' song, *Nobody knows the trouble I see, Lord!* His visit to U.S.A. in 1904 was successful in every way. His works were given at Washington (2 evenings C.-T. Fest.) New York, Chicago, Baltimore and Philadelphia.
Op. 1, 5tet in G mi. pf. and str. (ms.); 2, nonet in F mi. pf., wood-wind, str. (ms.); 3, *Suite de Pièces*, vn. and organ (Schott); 4, *Ballade* in D mi. vn. and orch. (Novello); 5, *Fantasiestücke*, str. 4tet; 6, *Little Songs for Little Folk* (Boosey); 7, *Zara's Ear-rings*, v. and orch. (Imperial Inst.); 8, symphony, A mi. (R.C.M. St. James's Hall, 1896); 9, 2 romantic pieces (Augener); 10, 5tet in A (Breitkopf); 11, *Dream-Lovers*, operatic romance (Boosey); 12, *Southern Love-Songs* (Augener); 13, str. 4tet in D mi. (ms.); 14, *Legend*, vn. and orch. (Augener); 15, *Land of the Sun*, part-song (*id.*); 16, *Hiawathan Sketches*, vn. and pf. (*id.*); 17, *African Romances*, pf.; 18, church service in F (Novello); 19, 2 *Moorish Pictures*, pf. (Augener); 20, *Gipsy Suite*, vn. and pf. (*id.*); 21, part-songs, s.s.a. (*id.*); 22, 4 characteristic waltzes,

orch. (Novello); 23, *Valse-Caprice* (Augener); 24, *In Memoriam*, vs. and pf. (*id.*); 25, missing; 26, *Gitanos*, cantata-operetta (*id.*); 27, 28, missing; 29, songs (Augener); 30, *Song of Hiawatha* (Novello); 31, *Humoresques*, pf. (Augener); 32, missing; 33, *Ballade*, A mi. orch. (Novello); 34, missing; 35, *African Suite*, pf. (Augener); 36, *Nourmahal's Song and Dance*, pf. (*id.*); 37, 6 songs; 38, *Silhouettes*, pf. (*id.*); 39, *Romance* in G, vn. and orch. (Novello); 40, *Solemn Prelude*, orch. (Novello), Worc. Fest. 1899); 41, *Scenes from an Everyday Romance*, orch. (Novello, Phill. Soc. 1900); 42, *The Soul's Expression*, contr. and orch. (Novello), Hereford Fest. 1900; 43, *Blind Girl of Castél-Cuillé* (Novello) Leeds Fest. 1901; 44, *Idyll*, orch. (Novello); 45, *American Lyrics*, v. (Novello); 46, *Toussaint L'Ouverture* (Novello), Queen's Hall, 1901; 47, incidental music to *Herod* (Augener); 47 ii, *Hemo Dance*, orch. (Novello); 48, *Meg Blane*, cantata (Novello), Sheffield Fest. 1902; 49, incidental music to *Ulysses*; 50, *Song-Poems* (Enoch); 51, *Ethiopia saluting the Colours*, march (Augener); 52, *Novelletten*, str. orch., tambourine, triangle (Novello); 53, *The Atonement*, cantata (Novello), Hereford Fest. 1903; 54, Choral Ballad, barit., chorus, orch. (Breitkopf); 55, *Moorish Dance* (Augener); 56, *Cameos*, pf. (*id.*); 57, 6 *Sorrow Songs* (*id.*); 58, 4 *African Dances*, vn. and pf. (*id.*); 59, 24 negro melodies (Ditson, Boston); 60, *Romance*, vn. and pf. (Augener); 61, *Kubla Khan*, cantata (Novello) (Handel Soc. London, 1906); 62, incidental music to *Nero* (Novello); 63, symph. variations on African air, orch. (*id.*); 64, *Scènes de ballet*, pf. (Augener); 65, *Endymion's Dream*, 1-act opera (Novello), (Brighton Fest. 1910); 66, *Forest Scenes*, pf. (Augener); 67, part-songs (*id.*); 68, *Bon-Bon Suite*, chorus and orch. (Novello); 69, *Seadrift*, unacc. 8-v. chorus (*id.*); 70, incidental music to *Faust* (Boosey); 71, *Valse Suite*, pf. (Augener); 72, opera, *Thelma* (ms.); 73, *Ballade*, G mi. vn. and pf. (Augener); 74, *Scenes from an Imaginary Ballet*, pf. (Schirmer); 75, *The Bamboula* (Hawkes) (Norfolk Fest. Conn. U.S.A. 1911); 76, cantata, *A Tale of Old Japan* (Novello); 77, *Suite de Concert* (Hawkes); 78, 3 Impromptus, organ (Weekes); 79, incidental music to *Othello* (Metzler); 80, vn. concerto, G mi. (*id.*); 81, 2 songs, *Waiting* (Boosey), *Red o' the Dawn* (Augener); 82, *Hiawatha* ballet, orch. (ms.). Various pieces without opus no. and numerous arrs. Consult biography by W. C. Berwick Sayers (Cassell, 1915).—E.-H.

COLLEGES OF MUSIC. See ACADEMIES.

COLLES, Henry Cope. Eng. music critic; *b.* 1879. Stud. R.C.M. London; Worcester Coll. Oxford (organ-scholar); music critic to *The Academy*, 1905; assistant-critic to *The Times*, 1906; followed J. A. Fuller-Maitland as chief mus. critic of *The Times* in 1911; joined the staff of R.C.M. as lecturer in mus. history and form, 1919; dir. of music, Cheltenham Ladies' Coll. 1919. His criticisms are sound, logical and scholarly. In 1923, was entrusted with the editing of the new ed. of Grove's *Dictionary of Music and Musicians*. Wrote in New York as a guest-critic for the *New York Times* for 3 months, in 1923.

Books: *Brahms* (1908); *The Growth of Music* (Part I, 1912; II, 1913; III, 1916; Milford); edited Parry's *R.C.M. Addresses*.—E.-H.

COLLET, Henri. Fr. musicologist, compr. *b.* Paris, 5 Nov. 1885. LL.D. Has publ. some studies relating to Spanish music, *Le Mysticisme musical espagnol au XVIᵉ siècle* (Alcan, 1913); *Vittoria* (1914). Has comp. some chamber-music in a style imitated from the Spanish.—A. C.

COLLINSON, Thomas H. Scottish orgt. condr. *b.* Alnwick, Northumberland, 1858. From his great-grandfather, who was a remarkable mathematician, and from his father who for 47 years was headmaster of Alnwick School, he inherited abilities and energy of exceptional order. Commenced study of organ at 9, and played his first

service in church at 10. Possessed a good alto voice, and while training as chorister proved to have exceptional reading abilities, and the gift of absolute pitch. In 1871 articled to Dr. Armes, orgt. of Durham Cath.; also stud. under Dr. Dykes there. Mus.Bac. Oxon. in 1877; in 1878, orgt. and choirmaster of new Episcopal Cath. of St. Mary, in Edinburgh. There he has laboured for nearly 50 years with unqualified success. For 31 years, condr. of Edinburgh R. Choral Union; 24 years, cond. Edinburgh Amateur Orch. Soc.; since 1898, official orgt. to Univ. of Edinburgh. He has publ. many services, anthems, and organ pieces.—W. S.

COLLISSON, Rev. William Alexander Houston. Irish compr. *b.* Dublin, 20 May, 1865; *d.* Hawarden, 31 Jan. 1920. Educated at Trinity Coll. Dublin; Mus.Bac. 1804; Mus. Doc. 1890; orgt. St. Patrick's, Trin. 1881; held appointments at Rathfarnham and St. George's, Dublin. Owing to his energy, the Dublin Popular Concerts were started in 1885; also organised some in Belfast and London; 1898, ordained; 1899, assistant - priest, St. Tudy's, Cornwall; remained there until 1901, when he went to London; devoted all his leisure time to mus. compn.; wrote many popular songs of a humorous character.

Comic operas: *The Knight of the Road*; *Strongbow*; *Midsummer Madness*. Cantatas: *St. Patrick*; *The Game of Chess*; *Samhain*. *Noah's Ark*, operetta; *Rosaleen*, Irish suite; songs (*Maguire's Motor-Bike*, *Mountains of Mourne*, etc.). Book, *Dr. Collison in and on Ireland*.—W. ST.

COLONNE, Édouard Judas. Fr. orch. condr. *b.* Bordeaux, 23 July, 1838; *d.* Paris, 28 March, 1910. Pupil of Cons., Paris. Founder of the Concert National (1873), which quickly took the name of Concerts Colonne (see below).—A. C.

COLONNE CONCERTS, Paris. Founded 2 March, 1873, at Odéon Théatre by Édouard Judas Colonne (*q.v.*), who specialised in the works of Beethoven and Berlioz, whose *Damnation de Faust* was perf. there over 200 times. The concerts are now given at Théâtre du Châtelet. On death of Colonne in 1910, Gabriel Pierné became condr. The concerts are given on Saturday and Sunday afternoons and the audiences consist chiefly of students and business people.—A. C.

COLONNESE, Elvira. S. singer; *b.* Naples. Stud. at Cons. there. *Début* at La Scala, Milan, as *prima donna* in *Les Huguenots*. For 20 years, continued singing at all the principal theatres in Italy, at Madrid, Barcelona, London, Budapest, Petrograd, Moscow, and Vienna. Went to S. America in 1887 to sing in opera at Montevideo and Buenos Ayres. Her greatest part was Desdemona in Verdi's *Otello*. Franchetti chose her for Queen Isabel in his *Christopher Columbus*. Establ. herself as teacher in· Buenos Ayres, where she founded Acad. Magistral of Singing, which supplies a complete finishing school for Argentine students.—A. M.

COMBARIEU, Jules. Fr. writer on music; *b.* Cahors (Lot), 1859; *d.* Paris, 1916. Lectured on history of music, 1904–10, at Collège de France. Appointed Inspector of Lycée Choirs. Specially interested in advancement of choral singing; publ. many colls. of songs for school use. While a pupil of J. Langlade at École Niedermeyer and of Spitta in Berlin, he was struck by lack of instruction in mus. matters at Fr. Univ. In the effort to remedy this need, he assisted in founding the *Revue Musicale*, of which he became ed. in 1904. The object of the review was to further musicological study.

Les Rapports de la Musique et de la Poésie, considérées au point de vue de l'expression, thesis for Doctorate (Paris, 1894, Alcan); *De parabaseos partibus et origine* (1894); *Théorie du rythme dans la composition musicale moderne* (Paris, 1897, Picard); *Éléments de grammaire musicale historique* (*Revue Musicale*, 1905–6); *Le Chant Choral* (Paris, Hachette); *La Musique, ses lois, son évolution* (Paris, 1907, Flammarion; Eng. London, Kegan Paul); *La Musique et la Magie* (Picard); *Histoire de la Musique*, 3 vols. (Paris, A. Colin), etc.—M. L. P.

COMBE, Édouard. Swiss compr. musicologist; *b.* Aigle, 23 Sept. 1866. Pupil of Guilmant in Paris, where he was secretary to Lamoureux, 1891–3. Thanks to his initiative and to his great efforts, the Association of Swiss Musicians (Schweizerische Tonkünstlerverein) was founded in 1899, of which he remained member of committee for 18 years. Lecturer on mus. history at Lausanne (1902–14); now gen. ed. and mus. critic of *Tribune de Genève*.

Symph. poem, *Les Alpes*; *Serenade* and Overture (*Guillaume Tell*), orch.; ode, *Moisson* (Verlaine), chorus, orch. and organ. Numerous unacc. choruses; songs (Lausanne, Fœtisch).—F. H.

COMETTANT, Oscar. Fr. musicologist; *b.* Bordeaux, 18 April, 1819; *d.* Havre, 24 Jan. 1898. Although he composed a large number of religious works and pf. pieces, he is known to-day solely on account of his literary labours. He was rather a brilliant chronicler than a genuine musicologist. There are interesting gleanings here and there in his numerous writings.

Adolphe Sax (1860); *La Musique, les Musiciens et les Instruments de Musique chez les différents peuples du monde* (1869); *Un Nid d'autographes* (1885), etc. —H. P.

CONCERTAL. See MUSTEL.

CONCERT-MEISTER. See KONZERTMEISTER.

CONCERTS ROUGE, Paris. Founded 1889 to supply classical music at moderate prices. Situated in the Univ. quarter of Paris, they recruited greater part of their audiences from the student world. These popular concerts are at present suspended. They have been replaced by concerts on a larger scale, with higher aims, in Paris and the provinces, by the condr. Léon Loicq.—M. L. P.

CONDUCTORLESS ORCHESTRA. See ZEITLIN, LEF, and GRAINGER, GEORGE PERCY.

CONN, John Peebles. Scottish violinist, pianist and condr. *b.* Penicuik, Midlothian, 15 Sept. 1883. Stud. under MacKenzie, Townsend, and Prof. Niecks in Edinburgh; won Bucher scholarship in 1902, and entered the Cons. of Cologne, where Eldering and Steinbach were his teachers (1905–6); stud. under Ševčík in Prague. Subsequently leader of Dortmund Philh. Orch.; later leader and sub-condr. of Bielefeld Municipal Orch. (1909–14). Was a prisoner of war at Ruhleben. Deputy-leader of Scottish Orch.

1919–22. Now teacher at the Athenæum, Glasgow, and condr. of Greenock and Glasgow Amateur Orch. Societies.—J. P. D.

CONRADI, Johan Gotfried. Norwegian compr condr. historian; *b.* Tönsberg, 7 April, 1820; *d.* Christiania, 29 Sept. 1896. Began to study medicine, but soon went over to music. Formed in 1843 a 4-v. singing-club of students and artisans in Christiania; founded in 1845 the Haandverkersangforening (Artisans' Glee Soc.) in the same city. Started singing-clubs in several smaller Norwegian towns. C. thus shares with Johan D. Behrens the credit for the great interest roused in Norway for 4-v. male choirs; 1875–93, condr. of Christiania Trades' Union Choral Soc.; also did important work for Norwegian orch. music; 1853–4 cond. orch in the Norwegian Theatre, Christiania. He then stud. music in Germany (chiefly Leipzig), 1855–6; in 1857–9, held subscription concerts, which afforded Christiania an opportunity of hearing for first time fine interpretations of the orchestral masterpieces.

Kortfattet historisk oversigt over musikens utvikling og nuværende standpunkt i Norge (*Historical Survey of Development and Present Position of Music in Norway*) (Christiania, 1878, Carl Warmuth), which forms a thorough preparation for later investigations regarding Norwegian music. Music to Christian Monsen's drama *Gudbrandsdölerne* (Norwegian Theatre, 1861); 4-v. songs for male chorus.—U. M.

CONSERVATOIRES OF MUSIC. See ACADEMIES.

CONSOLO, Ernesto. Pianist; *b.* London, of Ital. parents, 15 Sept. 1864. One of most esteemed among Ital. pianists; Stud. at R. Liceo Mus. di Santa Cecilia, Rome, under Sgambati; then in Leipzig under Reinach. Has given concerts in principal cities, of Europe and America. Lives at present in Florence, being prof. at Cherubini R. Inst. of Music.—D. A.

CONUS, George Edwardovitch. Russ. compr. and theorist; *b.* Moscow, 18/30 Sept. 1862. Pupil of his father (a pf. teacher) and of S. I. Tanéief and Arensky (theory) in Moscow Cons. From 1891 to 1899, prof. of harmony and orchestration there; from 1902, prof. at Music School of Moscow Philh.; then prof. and dir. of Saratof Cons. After the 1918 revolution returned to Moscow; now prof. at Cons. and dean of theoretical faculty there. Member of Russ. Acad. of Art-Sciences and of State Inst. of Mus. Science. A gifted theorist, with orig. theories on metric-technical analysis of musical form. His chief books on these ideas are not yet published.

Ballet, *Daita*; suite, *From Child-life*, chorus and orch. op. 1; symph. poem, *From the World of Fancy*, op. 23; symph. poem, *The Forest is rustling* (after Korolenko), op. 33; songs; pf. pieces; manual of Harmony, 1894; *1001 Exercises in Mus. Theory*; *Add. Exs.* to same; Russ. transl. of Guiraud's *Instrumentation*.—V. B.

CONVERSE, Frederick Shepherd. Amer. compr. *b.* Newton, Mass., U.S.A., 15 Jan. 1871. Educated at Harvard Univ. where he stud. music under Paine. Graduated A.B. 1893 with highest honours in music. His op. 1, sonata for vn. and pf. (Boston Mus. Co.), was produced in 1909. From 1894 to 1896, stud. under Baermann and Chadwick in Boston; 1896–8, under Rheinberger at Cons. in Munich, where his symphony in D mi. op. 7, was perf. in 1898. From 1898 to 1901, taught at New England Cons. in Boston. From 1901 to 1904 instructor in music, from 1904 to 1907 assistant-prof. at Harvard. In 1907, resigned to devote himself to compn. At present (1924) prof. in theory and compn. at New England Cons. His opera, *The Pipe of Desire*, was first work by Amer. compr. perf. at Metropolitan Opera, New York (1910).

Festival of Pan, orch. romance, op. 9 (1st perf. Boston Symphony Orch. 1900; publ. Boston Music Co. 1904); *Endymion's Narrative*, orch. romance, op. 10 (Boston Symphony Orch. 1903; H. W. Gray, 1909); *La Belle Dame sans Merci*, for barit. and orch. op. 12 (Schirmer, 1902); *The Mystic Trumpeter*, orch. fantasy, op. 19 (1st perf. Philadelphia, 1915; Schirmer, 1907); *The Pipe of Desire*, romantic opera in 1 act (1st perf. Boston, 1906; H. W. Gray, 1907); *Job*, dramatic poem for soli, chorus and orch. op. 24 (1st perf. Worcester [Mass.] Fest. 1907; Gray, 1907); *Ormazd*, symph. poem (1st perf. St. Louis Orch. 1912; Gray, 1913); *The Sacrifice*, 3-act opera (Gray, 1910); *The Peace Pipe*, cantata (Birchard, 1915).—O. K.

COOK, Edgar Thomas. Eng. orgt. *b.* Worcester, 18 March, 1880. Became assistant-orgt. of Worcester Cath. (under Sir Ivor Atkins) in 1904; since 1907, orgt. and dir. of music at Southwark Cath. London, where he has instituted choral and orch. perfs. of the greatest modern oratorios as well as early English music.

Anthems; services; part-songs (Weekes; Stainer & Bell; Faith Press; Novello).—E.-H.

COOLIDGE PRIZE. See U.S.A. MUS. FESTS. (ix).

COOLS, Eugène. Fr. compr. *b.* Paris, 1870. Gained the *Prix Cressent* in 1906. His music is modern in style but based on a groundwork of solid classicism. Has comp. for the stage:

Musique pour Hamlet (1920); *Le Jugement de Midas* (1922). Also some chamber-music.—A. C.

COOMARASWAMY, Ananda K. Writer on art and music; keeper of Indian and Mohammedan Art in Museum of Fine Arts, Boston, Mass. Educated Wycliffe Coll., Stonehouse, Glos; Univ. Coll. London; D.Sc. London; 1910, assisted in founding the Indian Soc.; lecturer on history of Indian art, and general æsthetics, sociology, metaphysics. Author of many books. Dr. Coomaraswamy is the author of the Indian articles in this Dictionary.—E.-H.

COQUARD, ARTHUR. Fr. compr. *b.* Paris, 25 May, 1846; *d.* Noirmoutiers (Vendée), 20 Aug. 1910. After successful law studies, took lessons with César Franck and became his disciple. From that date a series of orch. works appeared: *Ballade des Épées* (1875); *Héro* (1881); *Ossian* (with harp obblig.), 1880; *Cassandre*; *Hai-Luli*; *Andromaque*; *Christophe Colomb*; *Jeanne d'Arc*; *Le Meurtrier*. Appeared as dramatic compr. in 1884 with *L'Épée du Roi*; then *Le Mari d'un Jour* (1886); *La Jacquerie* (1895); *Zahel* (1900); *Philoctète*; *La Troupe Jolicœur* (1902). He is sentimental, emotional, picturesque and of classical tendency. Has written as critic in *Écho de Paris*. Author of a biography of César Franck, and a *History of French Music since Rameau* (only a sketch).—A. C.

CORBANI, Francisco. Teacher and compr. *b.* Cremona in 1871. Stud. at Cons. of Bergamo; went to Buenos Ayres in 1896. Singing-master

of National School for Blind. Has publ. pf. transcription of *Andrea Chénier.*—A. M.

CORBELLINI, César. Condr. teacher; *b.* Genoa in 1856; *d.* Buenos Ayres in 1912. Stud. at Civic Inst. of Music, Genoa. Selected by Ceferino Alassio to conduct his opera *Il Sindaco Babbeo* at theatre of R. Palace, Genoa. Went to Buenos Ayres in 1884, to give concerts. Joined Santa Cecilia Inst. there; establ. a mus. acad. in Barracas, which he dir. up to his death.—A. M.

CORDER, Frederick. Eng. compr. teacher cf compn. *b.* London, 26 Jan. 1852. Stud. under G. A. Macfarren at R.A.M. London, and under Ferdinand Hiller at Cologne Cons. First appearance as condr. at Brighton Aquarium 1880; prof. of compn. at R.A.M. London, from 1888 till now. Curator there from 1890. His opera *Nordisa* was perf. by Carl Rosa Co. at Liverpool, 1887. He founded the Soc. of British Comprs. in 1905 (disbanded in 1915) and formed many British composers.

Opera, *Nordisa* (Forsyth, 1886). Cantatas: *The Bridal of Triermain* (Novello, 1886); *The Sword of Argantyr* (Forsyth, 1889); *Margaret* (female vs.) (Williams, 1888); overture, *Prospero* (Novello, 1885); Elegy for 24 vns. and organ (*id.* 1908); 24 pieces for a 2nd pf. composed to Czerny's Studies (Williams, 1899); *Rumanian Dances*, 2 books, vn. (Breitkopf, 1883); numerous songs and part-songs. Books: *The Orchestra* (Curwen, 1895); *Modern Composition* (*id.* 1909); *History of the Royal Academy of Music* (Anglo-Fr. Co. 1922). Principal works are unpubl. —E.-H.

CORDER, Paul W. Eng. compr. *b.* London, Dec. 1879; son of Frederick C. (*q.v.*). Stud. at R.A.M. London as pianist and compr.; prof. of harmony and composition there from 1907.

2 operas (ms.); *Dross*, music-drama without words; ballets; *A Song of Battle*, chorus and orch.; 4 *Sea-Songs*, barit. and orch.; pf. pieces; *Transmutations* of an orig. theme; 9 preludes; *Heroic Elegy*, etc. (Ricordi; Anglo-Fr. Co., etc.).—E.-H.

CORNELIS, Evert. Dutch condr. and pianist; *b.* Amsterdam, 5 Dec. 1884. Pupil of Amsterdam Cons. (de Pauw, pf. and organ). In 1904, *Prix d'excellence* for organ. 2nd condr. of Concertgebouw Orch. (Amsterdam) 1910-19. In 1922, condr. of Utrechtsch Stedelijk Orch. Was condr. of Concertgebouw Sextet (see CHAMBER-MUSIC PLAYERS) and orgt. Lutheran Ch. Amsterdam. As a pioneer of modern music, he has played in Holland, Belgium, France, Germany, Austria, India and Australia.—W. P.

CORNELIUS, Peter. Ger. poet and compr. *b.* Mayence, 24 Dec. 1824; *d.* Mayence, 26 Oct. 1874. It was only after his death that the influence of this refined and sensitive poet-composer spread and took root. The publication of his literary works brought to light his fine mental personality (Vols. I and II, *Selected Letters*, ed. by his son, C. M. Cornelius, 1904-5; III, *Essays on Art and Music*, ed. by Edgar Istel, 1904; IV, *Poems*, ed. by Adolf Stern, 1905, Breitkopf). The complete ed. of his musical works in 5 vols. by Max Hasse (Breitkopf), has had the practical result of his first and most charming operatic work, *The Barber of Bagdad*, being again performed in its orig. version, whereas it had only been heard before in a fully-orchestrated Wagnerian version, which misrepresented,

though it may not have injured, the orig.
form. Consult:

Max Hasse, *P. C. und sein Barbier von Bagdad*,
(1904); Edgar Istel, *P. C.* (Leipzig, 1904, Reclam);
Max Hasse, *Der Dichtermusiker, P. C.*, 2 vols. (Leipzig,
1922, Breitkopf).—A. E.

CORNELIUS, Peter. Danish t. singer; *b.*
4 Jan. 1865. Stud. in Copenhagen and Paris.
Début in 1892 as barit. at R. Theatre, Copenhagen
(Toreador in *Carmen*). Later sang *Don Juan*
(Mozart). After renewed study abroad, he went
over to leading t. roles, in which he immediately
came to front rank (Samson in Saint-Saëns's
Samson and Delilah; Pedro in d'Albert's *Tief-
land*), and especially in Wagner's operas, having
repeatedly sung these parts at Bayreuth and
Covent Garden, London. He still sings at R.
Theatre, Copenhagen. Not to be confused with
P. C. the Ger. compr. (*q.v.*).—A. H.

CORONARO, Gaetano. Ital. compr. and
teacher at Milan Cons.; *b.* Vicenza, 18 Dec. 1852;
d. 5 April, 1908. Belonged to a distinguished
family of musicians (his brothers Antonio and
Gellio-Benvenuto were comprs.). His best operas
are *Un tramonto*; *La Creola*; *Enoch Arden*; also
symph. works and chamber-music. Consult E.
Oddone, *G. C.* (Rome, 1922, Ausonia).—D. A.

CORTI, Mario. Ital. violinist; *b.* Guastalla,
9 Jan. 1882. Performer and teacher of repute.
Stud. vn. at Bologna under Massarenti, and
compn. under Martucci and Bossi. As leader
of Mugellini Quintet, C. carried out several
tours in Italy and abroad, achieving great
success everywhere. At age of 24, he competed successfully for post of prof. at Parma
Cons.; in 1914, went to Scharwenka Cons.
Berlin (as substitute for Arrigo Serato); in
1915 prof. at R. Liceo Mus. di Santa Cecilia
in Rome, a post which he still holds. Has
publ. (Milan, Carisch) a coll. of little-known
works by XVII century musicians, entitled
Classical Italian Violinists.—D. A.

CORTOLEZIS, Fritz. Ger. condr. *b.* Passau,
21 Feb. 1878. Army officer, 1899; pupil of
Ludwig Thuille and Bussmeyer, Munich; 1907,
Court condr., Munich, under Felix Mottl; dir.
of Wagner-Strauss operas in England, 1911;
condr. of Kurfürsten Opera House, Berlin, 1912;
Court music dir. Carlsruhe, since 1913.

Compr. of operetta *Rosemarie*, Bremen, 1919.—A. E.

CORTOT, Alfred. French pianist; *b.* Nyon
(Switzerland) of French parentage. While still
a child he came to Paris with his family. Began
studying pianoforte under his sisters. At the Conservatoire his first master was Decombes (an old
pupil of Chopin); later, studied under Diémer
and in his class carried off a brilliant 1st prize
in 1895. At this time he was passionately devoted to Wagner whose operas he used to play at
private performances to a select audience. After
being appointed Korrepetitor at Bayreuth, he
founded a Concert Society in Paris, to which
he gave his name and in which he conducted
the orchestra. In 1902, he conducted at Théâtre
du Château d'Eau, *Götterdämmerung, Tristan,
Parsifal*, Beethoven's *Mass*, Liszt's *St. Elizabeth*,

Brahms's *Requiem* (all first performances in
Paris). At the Société Nationale, he directed
many first performances, without ceasing to
appear allover Europe as a soloist. In 1905, he
founded (with Jacques Thibaut and Pablo Casals)
the trio which is to-day undoubtedly the best in
the world. At the age of 30, he was appointed
head of the highest pianoforte course at the
Conservatoire (in place of Pugno).

The war interrupted his artistic activities.
When he was again at liberty to follow his profession, he submitted himself to a rigorous
course of study and re-appeared on the concert
platform in possession of an astounding facility
of execution, which, with his deep sensitiveness
and an intuition which amounts to genius, easily
puts him first among French pianists.

Of late years his reputation has steadily increased in both the continents through which he
tours. If his playing appears at first to lack that
brilliant force which strikes one in Busoni, he
none the less captivates his audience with his
soul-penetrating grace and tenderness. His tone
gives an effect of inexpressible transparency, yet
retains its vigour. What one reads about Chopin's
touch from his contemporaries might easily be
applied to Cortot, but the latter has a force
which the ailing genius lacked. After devoting
himself to German classics and romantics, he
has for some years given the French school pre-
eminence in his programmes. He is without
equal in his interpretation of the works of César
Franck, Debussy, Fauré and Ravel. He has
published a student's edition of Chopin's *Études*
(Senart), and important articles on piano compositions of Debussy and Gabriel Fauré (*Revue
Musicale*, Dec. 1920; Oct. 1922). The Debussy
articles are published in English by Chester,
London. Each spring, Cortot gives a course of
musical interpretation at École Normale de
Musique.—H. P.

COSTA, Alessandro. Ital. compr. *b.* Rome,
19 March, 1857. Took an important part
in Roman mus. life from 1880 to 1900,
especially as founder of Bach Soc., which gave
fine renderings of Bach's works. The Soc.,
which first perf. at the Sala Costanzi, and
later at hall of same name in Via Gregoriana,
was at that time the centre of the most select
portion of the Roman mus. world. As composer, C. publ. a 5tet (Kistner); *La Leggenda
dell' anima* and an *Allegretto* from a Fantasia
for orch. (Rome, Cristiano); *Presso una
fontana*, v. and pf. (Berlin, Simrock); *Danza
degli Scheletri, Ondine*, v. and pf., *Canzone della
bajadera*, from opera *Sumitri* (Bologna, Tedeschi).
Costa has also written arts. on music, and
about the doctrines of Buddha, of which he
is a convinced devotee. For many years he has
lived in solitary retirement at Mompeo, a little
place in Umbria.—D. A.

COSTA, Pasquale Mario. Ital. compr. *b.*
Naples, 24 July, 1858. Popular for his numerous
songs to Ital. and Neapolitan words, and for
his pantomime *L'Histoire d'un Pierrot*, which
he almost improvised in Paris at quite a

difficult period of his life (1892–3). It was such a success that it has been reproduced countless times in theatres all over the world. After having stud. at Naples Cons., in 1881 he went to London, where he won fortune and popularity by his songs, which he sang himself as a tenor. He now lives in Rome.

Best-known songs are *Luna nova, Napulitanata, Catari, Un organetto suona per la via, Scetate!* For the stage, in addition to the *Histoire d'un Pierrot*, he wrote various other pantomimes and 3 operettas: *Il Capitan Fracassa* (Turin, 1909), *Posillipo* (Rome, 1921), and *Scugnizza* (1923). Mostly publ. by Ricordi, Milan.—D. A.

COSTA CARRERA, Francisco. Span. violinist; b. in Barcelona, Feb. 1891. Stud. at Barcelona Municipal School; 1908, the Barcelona County Council made him a grant for mus. study at R. Cons. Brussels, where he obtained high distinction. Appeared as soloist in 1914, with Granados, at the concert when the latter gave 1st perf. of his *Goyescas*. Former leader of Pierre Monteux's orch. concerts, Dieppe. Has toured extensively in America, Egypt and Spain. Lives in Barcelona.—P. G. M.

COSTANZI, Teatro. The foremost opera-house in Rome, and one of most important in Italy, in spite of its quite recent origin. Built by initiative of Domenico Costanzi, a native of Macerata, who went to Rome in 1851, devoting himself at first to the hotel business; he constructed and managed several hotels, amongst them the Albergo del Quirinale. He conceived the bold idea of giving to Rome a great theatre, which the Ital. capital was then in need of, as the Argentine and Apollo theatres (latter now demolished) were insufficient; and in 18 months he succeeded in realising his dream. Its construction was entrusted to the engineer Sfondrini. The theatre is one of the largest and most beautiful in Italy. The pictures are by Brugnoli. Inaugurated 27 Nov. 1880, with Rossini's *Semiramide*. From that year onwards opera seasons have followed, gaining for it the wide fame it now enjoys. Amongst the most important events are the 1st perfs. of Mascagni's *Cavalleria Rusticana, L'Amico Fritz, Iris* and *Le Maschere*; Puccini's *La Tosca* and the triptych *Il Tabarro, Suor Angelica* and *Gianni Schicchi*. Between the opera seasons the theatre is used for plays and operettas; there have been some important symphony-concerts there also. A fine concert-hall is annexed. The theatre has always remained private property, privately managed. At present it is in the hands of a company, and the management is entrusted to Signora Emma Carelli (q.v.), herself a well-known operatic singer. The municipality of Rome allows the undertaking a considerable grant, imposing certain obligations. Consult Matteo Incagliati, *The Costanzi Theatre, 1880–1907* (Tipografia editrice Roma, 1907). —D. A.

COTOGNI, Antonio. Ital. barit. b. Rome, 1 Aug. 1831; d. Rome, 15 Oct. 1918. One of the greatest and most popular lyric artists of Italy during latter half of XIX century. His greatness was due both to beauty of voice and cleverness and versatility as interpreter. Of humble origin, he stud. first at Hospice of San Michele; then he stud. under Faldi, Capocci, Mustafà, and Aldega. C. gained his first success in the Oratory of the Filippini in the Chiesa Nuova. He appeared on stage for first time in Rome in 1852, and his fame grew rapidly. The greatest theatres vied with each other for him; he returned to Petrograd for 26 seasons, to London for 23 seasons, and appeared at all the principal theatres of Europe in the course of his long career. His repertoire included 157 operas, from *Don Giovanni* and *Magic Flute* to modern ones like *Pagliacci* and *Manon Lescaut*. He was a great interpreter especially of *Ballo in Maschera, Ernani, Linda di Chamounix, Faust, Elisir d' amore* and *Barbiere*. In Italy he was the first to interpret Verdi's *Don Carlos* at Bologna, and in this opera he was, in Verdi's opinion, unrivalled. He created many importants parts in new operas. During his sojourn in Russia, at Rubinstein's invitation, he accepted the directorship of school of singing at the Cons. of Petrograd, which he held for 4 years, and had to abandon in consequence of a serious illness. He left the stage in 1904, and took over dir. of school of singing at R. Liceo Mus. di Santa Cecilia, Rome, where he passed the last years of his life, beloved by his many pupils and all who knew him.

Consult: Nino Angelucci, *Ricordi di un artista: A. C.* (Rome, 1907, Soc. Ed. Teatrale); Onorato Roux, *A. C.* (Florence, Bemporad).—D. A.

COUNTERPOINT. The bringing together of two or more melodic lines. Also called Polyphony. See art. on HARMONY.—E.-H.

COURVOISIER, Walter. Compr. b. Riehen, near Basle, Switzerland, 7 Feb. 1875. Medical man. Musician since 1902, pupil of Ludwig Thuille in Munich, whose son-in-law he became later. Assoc.-condr. of People's Symphony Concerts in the Kaimsaal, 1907; teacher of compn. at Acad. of Music, 1910; prof. 1919. He is a tasteful representative of the so-called "Munich School."

Many songs, including cycle of 52 sacred songs, op. 29 (Cologne, Tischer & Jagenberg); choral works with orch. op. 5, 11, 12; *Funeral Service* for soli, choir and orch. op. 26; 6 suites for vn. solo, op. 31; symph. prologue to Spitteler's *Olympischer Frühling*, op. 10; Variations and fugue for pf. op. 21; opera, *Launcelot and Elaine* (Munich, 1917, Drei Masken Verlag); 1-act comedy, *Die Krähen* (Munich, 1921, Drei Masken Verleg).—A. E.

COUTTS, D. J. Prof. Univ. of Music, Melbourne, Australia; d. 1923. Has comp. orch. overture; cantata, *Lord Ullin's Daughter*, chorus and orch.; album of 5 songs (Allan & Co., Melbourne); 3 songs by J. E. Brown (F. Harris Co., London); many pf. pieces.—E.-H.

COVENT GARDEN, Royal Opera House. See ROYAL OPERA HOUSE.

COVIELLO, Ambrose. Eng. pianist; b. Brixton, London, 30 Jan. 1887. Stud. under Oscar Beringer and Frederick Corder at R.A.M.; gained Thalberg Scholarship and Macfarren Gold Medal. Prof. (1914) and Fellow (1922) of R.A.M. Contributed arts. to *Music Student* (1920), *Monthly Musical Record*, etc. (1921–2). —E.-H.

COWARD, Henry. Eng. chorus-trainer and choral condr. *b.* Liverpool, 26 Nov. 1849. Began training singing-classes at 18 ; cond. 1st concert at 19; became a school teacher at 22; left scholastic prof. in 1888; in 1889 (at age of 40) took Mus.Bac. Oxon.; and in 1894 the Doctorate. His 20 years' work as condr. and trainer passed unnoticed till the 1st Sheffield Fest. proved his choral prowess. This has resulted in choral music being raised to a higher plane in technique and expression. In this and succeeding fests. (1902, 1905, etc.), he opened a new epoch of choral singing. He conducts choruses at Sheffield, Leeds, Huddersfield, Newcastle, Glasgow, Barnsley, Hull, Derby (each averaging 350 members); toured with his Sheffield choir in Germany (twice); with Yorkshire chorus in Canada and round the world. Is lecturer in music at Sheffield Univ. which has conferred on him the degree of M.A. Is a well-known adjudicator at mus. competition fests.

Numerous cantatas; anthems; glees; part-songs; songs; books: *Choral Technique and Interpretation* (Novello, 1914); *Reminiscences* (Curwen, 1919); many articles in mus. journals. Consult J. A. Rodgers, *The Pioneer Choirmaster* (J. Lane, 1911).—E.-H.

COW-BELLS as mus. instrs. Used by Mahler in *Adagio* of his VI (*Tragic*) Symphony, behind the platform, to express feelings of a man in the high mountains, whom no human sound reaches. He only hears the dispersed sounds of cow-bells. The effect differs absolutely from their use in *Scherzo* of R. Strauss's *Alpine Symphony.* —EG. W.

COWEN, Sir Frederic Hymen. British compr. and condr. *b.* Kingston, Jamaica, 29 Jan. 1852. Brought to London at age of 4; placed at age of 8 under Benedict for pf. and Goss for harmony; in 1865, competed successfully for the Mendelssohn Scholarship, which was relinquished as his parents did not wish to surrender the control of their son; stud. at Leipzig Cons. under Moscheles, Reinecke and Hauptmann, 1865–6; and in Berlin, under Kiel, 1867–8. Amongst his unpubl. works are an operetta, *Garibaldi* (written when 8); 2 trios, pf. vn. and cello (A ma.; A mi.) a str. 4tet in E flat; a 4tet for pf. and str. in C mi.; a sinfonietta in A; 2 symphonies (C mi.; F ma.); an overture in D mi.; an oratorio, *The Deluge.* As condr. he has held many of the chief positions in London and the provinces: Promenade Concerts at Covent Garden 1880, and again in 1893; R. Philh. Soc. 1888–92 and 1900–7; Hallé Concerts, Manchester, 1896–9; Liverpool Philh. 1896–1912; Bradford Fest. Choral Soc. 1897–1915; Scottish Orch. Glasgow and Edinburgh, 1900–10; Cardiff Fests. 1902–4–7–10; Handel Fests., Crystal Palace, 1903–6–9–12–20–23. Was *maestro-al-piano* at Ital. Opera, under Mapleson, 1871–9; made many tours with Titiens, Trebelli, Christine Nillson; also toured with Trebelli in Scandinavia. His 3rd symphony, *The Scandinavian*, in C mi., was first perf. at one of his own concerts in Dec. 1880. It was played in Vienna by Richter in Jan. 1882. In 1888, went to Melbourne as condr. of Centennial Exhibition where he received from the Victorian Government the largest fee (£5000) ever paid to a condr. for six months' service. Was condr. at Queen's Hall at its *inauguration* in Dec. 1893, and during the season of choral concerts given there the same winter. Mus.Doc. *h.c.* Cambridge Univ. 1900; also Edinburgh Univ. in 1910; received knighthood in 1911.

As a compr. he has turned chiefly to the lighter side of music. His orchestration is always refined.

Operas: *Pauline* (Carl Rosa Co. Lyceum Theatre, 1876); *Thorgrim* (*id.* Drury Lane, 1890); *Signa* (Milan, 1893; Covent Garden, 1894); *Harold* (Covent Garden, 1895). Oratorios: *Ruth* (Worcester Fest. 1887); *The Transfiguration* (Gloucester Fest. 1895); *The Veil* (Cardiff Fest. 1910). Cantatas: *The Rose Maiden* (1870); *The Corsair* (Birmingham Fest. 1876); *St. Ursula* (Norwich Fest. 1881); *Sleeping Beauty* (Birmingham Fest. 1885); *Song of Thanksgiving* (Melbourne Exhibition, 1888); *St. John's Eve* (Crystal Palace, 1889); *The Water Lily* (Norwich Fest. 1893); *Ode to the Passions* (Leeds Fest. 1898); *Coronation Ode* (1902); *John Gilpin* (Cardiff Fest. 1904); *The Sleep* (*ib.* 1907); *Monica's Blue Boy*, playlet without words (Pinero) (New Theatre, 1917); *Cupid's Conspiracy*, ballet (Coliseum, 1917); *Dream of Endymion*, scena for t. v. and orch. (Philh. Soc. 1897). Orch.: Symphony No. III (*Scandinavian*) in C mi. (St. James's Hall, 1880); IV (*Welsh*) in B flat mi. (Philh. Soc. 1884); V, in F (Cambridge, 1887); VI (*Idyllic*) in E (Richter Concerts, 1897); ballet suite, *Language of Flowers* (1880); suite, *In Fairyland* (1896); *Four Old English Dances* (1896); *Concertstück*, pf. and orch. (1898); overture, *The Butterflies' Ball* (1900); orch. poem, *A Phantasy of Life and Love* (1901); *Coronation March* (1902); *Indian Rhapsody* (1903); *Four Old English Dances*, 2nd set (1905); *Language of Flowers*, 2nd suite (1914); *The Enchanted Cottage*, 2 entr'actes (1922). Many pf. pieces; part-songs; cantatas for female vs.; anthems; about 300 songs.—E.-H.

CRAS, Jean. Fr. compr. *b.* Brest, 1879. The sea has its representatives not only in Fr. literature (with Loti, Farrère and Avesnes) but also in music — Albert Roussel, Bloch, Mariotte and Jean Cras. The latter stud. compn. under Henri Duparc, whose friend he is. Among his works are a str. 4tet; a sonata, pf. and cello; 3 collections of pf. pieces; 3 collections of songs; and *Âmes d'enfants* (symph. poem). His lyric drama *Polyphème* (after Samain) obtained the *Grand Prix de la Ville de Paris* in 1922.—A. C.

CREMONINI, Eligio. Ital. cellist; *b.* Persiceto, 1854. After having taken part as leading cellist in the most important orchestras, in 1895 was elected, by competition, prof. at Liceo Mus. at Turin. From there he passed in 1896, to the Rossini Liceo at Pesaro, where he has remained, training a large number of very capable pupils. He took part in the Pesarese Trio with the violinist Frontali and the pianist Vitali.—D. A.

CRICKBOOM, Mathieu. Belgian violinist and compr. *b.* Hodimont (Liège), 2 March, 1871. One of Ysaye Quartet, 1888–94; 1894–6, leader of a quartet at Société Nationale, Paris (under management of V. d'Indy). Principal of Acad. of Music and of Philh. Soc. of Barcelona, 1896–1905. Prof. of vn. Liège Cons. 1910, and at Brussels Cons. 1919. As a violinist he is perfect in technique and poetical interpretation. His instructive works are models of their kind (*Le Violon théorique et* *pratique,* 5 vols.; *La Technique du Violon,* 4 vols.). As a compr. he does not claim any great originality, but his work is distinguished by a certain serious elegance.

Vn. and pf.: *Esquisses* (Baudoux); sonata (Schott, Brussels); *Romance, Ballade, Poème.* Cello and pf., *Chant élégiaque.* Songs.—C. V. B.

CRIMI, Giulio. Ital. lyric and dramatic t. singer; *b.* Paternò (Catania), 10 May, 1885. Began career at Teatro Sociale at Treviso, in Catalani's *Wally;* then appeared at all principal European and Amer. theatres (Covent Garden, London; Opéra, Paris; Colón, Buenos Ayres; Metropolitan, New York; etc.). He created t. part in Zandonai's *Francesca da Rimini* (Turin), and in Puccini's *Tabarro* and *Gianni Schicchi* (New York).—D. A.

CRISTIANI, Giuseppe. Italian pianist; *b.* Anagni, 19 March, 1865. Stud. at R. Liceo Mus. di Santa Cecilia in Rome, under Eugenio Terzini for compn. and Sgambati for pf. In 1886 won a competition offered by Orch. Soc. in Rome, for a symphony. Then founded and cond. the Roman Quintet (Cristiani, Zuccarini, Tignani, Rosa and Magalotti), which revealed many modern compns. to Rome. In 1915, won by competition a position as teacher in Liceo Mus. di Santa Cecilia, Rome. Amongst his works we mention a sonata for vn and pf. (Leipzig, Jurgenson).—D. A.

CRITICISM, Musical. The history of music criticism runs parallel with that of mus. philosophy and æsthetics, and in the present state of our knowledge should begin with the study of the doctrines of Pythagoras, Aristoxenes, Plato, and Aristotle. At the very outset, two opposite conceptions are to be observed, Pythagoras holding that music is to be judged from the point of view of the mind, and Aristoxenes that it is to be judged from the point of view of the ear —a matter upon which controversy is not yet altogether a thing of the past.

In point of fact, musical criticism remained either dogmatic or empirical (and correspondingly tentative, erratic, and, at its best, very vague) until the XIX century, when the desirability of method (as opposed to systems), of discipline, and of specificness, began to be realised, in accordance with the modern progress of the art and science of criticism in general and of musical æsthetics. It is now almost universally admitted that "the true critic is simply the most enlightened listener: not standing aloof with a manual of arrogant imperatives, but taking his place among us to stimulate our attention when it falters, and to supplement our knowledge where it is deficient" (Hadow, *Edinburgh Review,* Oct. 1906); and increasing attention is given to the part played by imagination in the appraisement of music.

The first attempt towards laying the foundation of a specific method in musical criticism is Hadow's (*Studies in Modern Music;* London, Seeley, first series, 1895), who disengages the 4 main principles—vitality, labour, proportion, and fitness—from the existence of which,

estimates of musical works can be arrived at. Frédéric Hellouin (*Essai de Critique de la Critique Musicale;* Paris, 1906, Joanin) tends to favour a purely deductive method; "criticism," he writes, "ascertains whether the characteristics of beauty, as determined by æsthetics, exist in a given work," but he qualifies the assertion by showing that criticism should be partly objective and partly subjective. M. D. Calvocoressi ("La Critique Musicale, ses devoirs, ses méthodes," in *Courrier Musical,* Paris, 1910; and *Principles and Methods of Musical Criticism* [Oxford Univ. Press, 1923]) advocates a method founded, in the main, upon the general principles of criticism disengaged by J. M. Robertson (*New Essays towards a Critical Method;* London, J. Lane, 1891) and Hennequin (*La Critique Scientifique;* Paris, Perrin, 1888), these principles being modified only so far as required by the special conditions governing music. Dogmatism and inconsistency, he writes, will be further avoided by doing away with the looseness of conception of which the prevailing ambiguity of the critical vocabulary is a sign.

Among endeavours to provide practical tuition in musical criticism should be mentioned the classes at the Royal College of Music, London (H. C. Colles), at the Berlin Seminar für Musik (Dr. W. Altmann), and at the Paris École des Hautes Études Sociales (1904, F. Hellouin; 1909–1914, M. D. Calvocoressi).

Various other points of principle and methods will be found in the following articles: J. Bradford, *Musical Criticism and Critics* (*Westminster Review,* Nov. 1894); M. D. Calvocoressi, *Can Musical Criticism be Taught?* (*Musical Times,* May 1911) and *Towards a Method in Musical Criticism* (*Musical Quarterly,* Jan. 1923); A. Hervey, *Concerning Musical Criticism* (*Musical Times,* June 1911); E. Newman, *A School for Musical Critics* (*Musical Times,* Jan. 1911). —M. D. C.

CUBAN OPERA. See MEXICAN AND CUBAN OPERA.

CUBILES, José. Span. pianist; *b.* Cadiz, 1896. Pupil of Pilar de la Mora, Madrid, and of Diémer, Paris. ˙ Prof. at R. Cons. de Música, Madrid. —P. G. M.

CUCUEL, Georges. Fr. musicologist. *b.* Dijon, 14 Dec. 1884; *d.* 28 Oct. 1918. One of the most able of the young French musicologists trained by Romain Rolland. He died at the age of 34, of trench fever. His Doctorate thesis, *La Pouplinière et la Musique de Chambre au XVIII° siècle,* is a veritable monument of research on that musical renaissance, of which Paris, no less than Mannheim, was the active centre. His *Études sur un orchestre au XVIII° siècle* add much of importance to the history of the origin of symphony in France, and also contain important notes on the horns, clarinets and harp which made their appearance in orchestras of that period. He wrote a little book full of facts and ideas on the *Founders of the French Opéra-Comique* (Alcan, 1914); also *Documents on the Musical Library of the XVIII Century* (*Sammelbände der I.M.G.,* 1912); *Le Baron de Bagge et son temps* (*Année Musicale,* 1911); *Operas of Gluck according to the*

Parodies of XVIII Century (posthumous, *Revue Musicale*, March–April, 1922). He had in preparation a work on Italian *opéra-bouffe*, when the war cut short his activities. He possessed a fine power of synthetic construction, added to erudition that considered no detail insignificant.—H. P.

CUI, César Antonovitch (*pron.* Quee). Russian composer; *b.* Vilna, 6/18 Jan. 1835; *d.* Petrograd, 1/14 March, 1918. Received his first lessons in music from Polish composer Moniuszko; but did not start to study composing until 1857, when (after having completed courses at Petrograd School of Military Engineering) he joined forces with Balakiref in taking the lead of the "Nationalist" movement which followed the advent of Glinka. He did not altogether practise what he preached, and the resemblances between his works and those of his comrades are few. He was particularly impressed by Dargomisky's innovations in the province of melodic recitative, and at times he followed this master's methods, although more often he inclined to abide by the tenets of operatic style proper. His music shows no trace of the folk-song influence which is so great on practically all his contemporaries; and he was never attracted towards the realms of picturesque and fantastic poetry from which other Russian composers derived so many felicitous inspirations. He even evinced small interest in national history, legend, or fiction as subjects for lyric treatment, and most of his operas after his early *Captive of the Caucasus* (1859) are written on libretti of foreign origin: *Angelo* (after Hugo, 1876); *Le Flibustier* (by Richepin, 1889); *The Saracen* (after Dumas, 1889); *Mam'selle Fifi* (after Maupassant, 1903); *Matteo Falcone* (after Mérimée, 1908); the only two exceptions are the short *Feast at the Time of the Plague* (1859) and *The Captain's Daughter* (1911), both after Pushkin. He wrote many songs, a few choral works, 4 orchestral suites, a small amount of chamber-music, and a few pf. pieces. His music is often ingenious and graceful, but reveals no great degree of creative imagination.

He was active as a writer of articles and essays on music (chiefly on Russian music). A book of his in French, *La Musique en Russie*, appeared in 1880 (Paris, Fischbacher), and constitutes a curious document as to his outlook.—M. D. C.

CULWICK, James C. Orgt. and condr. *b.* West Bromwich, 28 April, 1845; *d.* 1909. Trained at Lichfield Cath. as chorister and assistant-orgt.; orgt. of Parsonstown, 1866; of Chapel Royal, 1881; prof. of pf. and harmony, Alexander Coll. Dublin; Mus.Doc. *h.c.* 1893; an excellent lecturer on mus. subjects. His most successful work was choral-conducting, and it was through his enthusiasm that the Orpheus Choral Soc. became best choir in Dublin. After his death, his daughter, Miss Culwick, carried on the excellent work.—W. St.

CUMBERLAND, Gerald. Eng. critic and writer on music; *b.* Eccles, 7 May, 1881. Mus. critic of *Manchester Courier*, 1909–12; *Daily Citizen*, 1912–15; prolific contributor to Eng. and Amer. papers. Author of *Imaginary Conversations with Great Composers* (W. Reeves); *Set Down in Malice* (Grant Richards, 1918); *Written in Friendship* (*id.* 1923); editor of Musician's Handbook Series (*id.*).—E.-H.

CUMEYAS RIBÓ, José. Span. compr. of choral, religious and popular music; *b.* Barcelona, 1875. Cond. of Orfeó Catalá. Choirmaster at San Felipe de Neri's Ch. Barcelona.—P. G. M.

CUMMINGS, William Hayman. Eng. t. vocalist, condr. mus. antiquarian; *b.* Sidbury, Devon, 22 Aug. 1831; *d.* Dulwich, 10 June, 1915. Sang at many fests.; in opera from 1865; prof. R.A.M. 1879; joined newly-formed Guildhall School of Music, London, 1880; condr. Sacred Harmonic Soc. 1882; Principal of Guildhall School of Music, 1896 till death. Mus.Doc. Dublin, *h.c.* 1900.—E.-H.

CUNDELL, Edric. Eng. compr. and condr. *b.* London, 29 Jan. 1893. Began as Fr.-horn player; played in Covent Garden opera season 1912; pf. scholarship, Trinity Coll. of Music; appointed to teaching staff there, 1914; condr. of Westminster Orch. Soc. 1920. Gained the Hammond Endowment Grant (£200) for composition in 1920.

Suite for str. orch. (Goodwin); symph. poem, *Serbia* (1919; Robert Goodwin Libr.); Poem, *The Tragedy of Deirdre*, op. 17 (1922, ms.); Sonnet, *For Dead*, t. v. and orch. (Goodwin Libr.); pf. 4tet, op. 15 (1922, ms.); str. 4tet, op. 18 (1922, Goodwin); *Valse Fantasque*, op. 16 (1922, Paxton); *The Water Babies*, Parts I and II (pf. pieces for young) (Paxton); numerous songs (Chappell).—E.-H.

CUP-BELLS. 25 copper-bells, with chromatic range of 2 octaves, from c^1 to c^3. Surprisingly beautiful tone, which mixes well with other instrs. The lower ones possess a heavy tone-quality; the upper ones sound like flageolets. The instr. was cast by J. Taylor & Co., Loughborough, England. Used for 1st time by Dutch compr. Daniel Ruyneman (*q.v.*) in his *Hieroglyphs*.—E.-H.

CURTIS, Natalie (Mrs. Paul Burlin). Writer on Indian and negro music; *b.* New York; *d.* Paris, 23 Oct. 1921. Stud. pf. in New York under Arthur Friedheim, and abroad under Busoni (Berlin), Giraudet (Paris), Wolf (Bonn) and Kniese (Wagner-Schule, Bayreuth). Returned to America as pianist, but sojourning with her brother in Arizona became interested in the music of the Indians and visited their encampments. The first result of her studies here is her *Indians' Book*, a coll. of 200 songs, culled from 18 tribes. Her success brought the invitation to undertake similar investigations in negro music which she pursued among the students of Hampton (Va.) Inst. and elsewhere. Married the artist Paul Burlin, 1917. Died in Paris after an automobile accident.

Songs of Ancient America (Schirmer, 1905); *The Indians' Book* (Harper, 1907); *Negro Folk-Songs*, 4 series (Schirmer, 1918–19); *Songs and Tales from the Dark Continent* (Schirmer, 1920); songs and choruses (Wa-Wan Press; Schirmer; Dilworth).—J. M.

CURWEN, Annie Jessie. British didactic writer; *b.* Rathmines, Dublin, 1 Sept. 1845. Stud. at R. Irish Acad. of Music, Dublin, under Joseph Robinson, Fanny Robinson, and Sir Robert Stewart; well-known educationist; has done much to raise standard of teaching in the elementary grades, striving to do for the pf. teacher what John Curwen did for the teacher of class-singing, by the application of the same educational principles. Wife of J. Spencer Curwen.
The *Child Pianist* (now known as the *Curwen Pianoforte Method*) a practical course in elements of music (Curwen, 1886); *Psychology applied to Music Teaching* (*id.* 1920).—E.-H.

CURWEN, J. & SONS, Ltd. Music publishers and general printers, founded by John Curwen in London about 1850. Succeeded by John Spencer C. F.R.A.M. in 1881, and Kenneth C. in 1916. The original aim was to publish music in Tonic-Solfa notation. Spencer Curwen developed it on choral and educational side to a position of great strength. Kenneth C. while following this tradition, is also devéloping the work of youngest school of British comprs. The firm owns *Musical News and Herald*, a weekly newspaper, and *The Sackbut*, a monthly mus. review. It also controls the London and Continental Mus. Publ. Co. Ltd. which holds agency for Univ. Ed. of Vienna. It amalgamated F. & B. Goodwin, Ltd. Jan. 1924.—E.-H.

CURWEN, John Kenneth. Eng. mus. publ. *b.* Upton, Essex, 1881. Educated Abbotsholme and New Coll. Oxford. Man. dir. J. Curwen & Sons, 1914; President, Tonic Solfa Assoc. from 1919; editor *Mus. News and Herald* from 1922 to 1924.—G.-B.

CURWEN, John Spencer. Eng. journalist; writer on mus.-educational subjects; *b.* Plaistow, Essex, 30 Sept. 1847; *d.* London, 6 Aug. 1916. Stud. at R.A.M., under Ebenezer Prout, Sir Arthur Sullivan and Sir George Macfarren. Devoted his life to the Tonic Solfa movement,

the cultivation of sight-singing in schools and the general development of choral music. Continued his father's (Rev. John C.) work. President of Tonic Solfa Coll. 1880; establ. first competitive mus. fest. (an adaptation of the Welsh Eisteddfod) 1883 at Stratford, London, E. Visited and inspected chief continental, Canadian and Amer. schools; promoted conferences of music-teachers throughout Great Britain. Ed. *Musical Herald* from 1866.
Studies in Worship Music (1880); 2nd series (1885); *Memorials of John Curwen* (1882); *School Music Abroad* (1901) (all publ. by Curwen).—E.-H.

CURZON, Henri de. Fr. musicologist. *b.* Le Havre, 1861. D.Litt.; musicographer and mus. critic; keeper of National Archives. Wrote *L'État sommaire des pièces et documents concernant le théâtre et la musique, conservés aux Archives Nationales* (1899); regular contributions to papers and reviews such as *Le Guide Musical* (1894–1918), which he managed, *La Gazette de France* (1889–1914), *Le Bulletin de a Société de l'Histoire du Théâtre* (1902–22), etc. Since 1889, when he wrote *La Légende de Sigurd dans l'Edda. L'Opéra d'E. Reyer*, his researches extended in many directions.
Musiciens du temps passé (1893); *Croquis d'artistes* (1897); *Les Lieder de F. Schubert* (1899); *Les Lieder et airs détachés de Beethoven* (1905); *Essai de bibliographie Mozartine* (1906); *Documents inédits sur le " Faust " de Gounod* (with Albert Soubies) (1912, Paris, Fischbacher), etc. Has written a *Mozart*, a *Rossini* (Paris, Alcan, 1914, 1920), *Grétry, Meyerbeer* (Paris, Laurens, 1907, 1910). Transl. letters and writings of Mozart, Schumann and Hoffmann.— M. L. P.

CUYPERS, Hubert. Dutch compr. *b.* Roermond (Limburg), 26 Dec. 1873. Pupil of Bernard Zweers, Amsterdam. His 3 melodramas *Terwe* (*Wheat*), *Die Wallfahrt nach Kevlaar* (from Heine), and *Das Klagende Lied* (*The Complaint*) are well known in Holland.—W. P.

CZECH FOLK-MUSIC. See KUBA, LUDVÍK; MALÁT, JAN.

D

D'AGUILLO, Corradino. Argentine compr. *b.* Agnone, Campobasso, Italy, in 1868. Stud. at Naples Cons. Went to Buenos Ayres in 1888. Here he set to music *Il Leone di Venezia*, given at the Politeama, Buenos Ayres. Then returned to Italy, for 4 years, again coming to Buenos Ayres. as prof. of cpt. and harmony at Cattelani Cons. Now pf. prof. at Santa Cecilia Inst. His other opera, *La Zingara*, is in 1 act (libretto by his uncle, Nicolas d'Aguillo the poet).—A. M.

DAHL, Viking. Swedish compr. *b.* Osby, 8 Oct. 1895. Stud. Cons. of Malmö and of Stockholm; then in London and Paris (under Vidal, Ravel, Viñes), dancing under Isadora Duncan. Composes in most modern style and shows great interest in the dance-pantomime.

Suite orientale, ballet (1917; Stockholm, 1919); *Maison de fous*, ballet-pantomime (1920, Théâtre des Champs-Elysées, Paris; 1921, London); *Pastorale*, concert-piece, ob. and orch. (Copenhagen, 1922); symphonietta; str. 4tet; pf. trio; suite, vn. and pf.; studies; songs; pf. pieces.—P. V.

DAHMS, Walter. Ger. music critic; *b.* Berlin, 9 June, 1887. Violinist in orch.; stud. under Adolf Schultze, Berlin; music critic of *Kleine Journal*. Lived in Berlin, now in Rome.

Schubert (1912, Deutsche Verlags-Anstalt); *Schumann* (1916, *ib.*); *Mendelssohn* (1919, *ib.*); *Die Offenbarung der Musik*, an Apotheosis of Friedrich Nietzsche (Munich, 1922, Musarion Verlag).—A. E.

DAINO. See LITHUANIAN MUSIC.

D'ALBERT, Eugen. See D'ALBERT.

DALCROZE. See JAQUES-DALCROZE.

DALE, Benjamin James. Eng. compr. *b.* Crouch Hill, London, 17 July, 1885. Educated privately, and afterwards at R.A.M. under Frederick Corder, Evlyn Howard-Jones, H. W. Richards, E. H. Lemare. His best-known work is the pf. sonata op. 1 (Novello), on which a full art. on which (by F. Corder) see *Mus. Times*, April 1918. His music is of the Neo-Romantic order.

Op. 2, Suite, vla. and pf. (Novello); op. 3, *Night-Fancies*, pf. (Ricordi); op. 4, *Phantasy*, vla. and pf. (Schott); op. 7, *Before the Paling of the Stars*, chorus and orch. (Hereford Fest. 1921) (Novello); op. 9, 2 songs from *Twelfth Night*, for male v. with vla. obbligato (Novello); op. 10, *English Dance*, vn. and pf. (Anglo-Fr. Co.); op. 11, vn. sonata (Augener); op. 12, *Song of Praise*, chorus and orch. (Novello); *Prunella*, vn. and pf. (Augener); (with K. Dale) 6 pieces by Couperin, freely arr. vn. and pf. (*id.*); op. 6, Carols: *In Bethlehem* (Novello); *The Holy Birth* (*id.*); *The Shepherd and the Mother* (Stainer & Bell). Unpubl.: op. 5, *Fantasia* for 6 vlas. (see *Mus. Times*, Oct. 1917, p. 446); op. 11, sonata, vn. and pf. (played Rowsby Woof and York Bowen, Wigmore Hall, 27 Oct. 1922).—E.-H.

DALLA RIZZA, Gilda. One of best living Ital. s. singers; *b.* Verona, 1892. Appeared chiefly in Rome and S. America. Created s. parts in Puccini's *La Rondine*, *Suor Angelica*, *Gianni Schicchi* (1st perf. in Italy); Mascagni's *Il Piccolo Marat* and Zandonai's *Giulietta e Romeo*. —D. A.

DALLEY-SCARLETT, Robert. Australian orgt. and compr. *b.* 16 April, 1887. Lives as teacher at Brisbane, Queensland.

Cantatas with orch.: *Christmas Cantata*; *The Armada*; *Psalm XXIV*; Mass in E flat; anthems; choruses; 2 sonatas, vn. and pf. (in D; in A); many songs and pf. pieces, all ms.—E.-H.

DALLIER, Henri. Fr. orgt., compr. *b.* Rheims, 1849. Cath. orgt. at age of 16; stud. under Bazin and César Franck at Paris Cons.; 1st prize for fugue and organ-playing; prof. of harmony at Cons. 1908; orgt. at St.-Eustache, Paris, 1878–1905, in which year he succeeded G. Fauré as orgt. at the Madeleine.

Allegro (Paris, Mennesson); *Andante* in G (Paris, Leduc); offertories; preludes for All Saints' Day, etc. Has written 2 masses; 3 cantatas; choruses; chamber-music (including a trio in C mi. awarded a prize by Institut [Paris, Fromont]); pieces for v. and pf., etc.—M. L. P.

DAMERINI, Adelmo. Ital. writer and compr. *b.* Cormagnano (Florence), 11 Dec. 1880. Resides in Rome, where he teaches singing in the Amer. Methodist Inst. Author of various vocal and instr. compns. Has publ. many articles in journals and reviews on mus. subjects; a study on the score of *Ercole in Tebe*, by Jacopo Melani (1623–76) in the *Bollettino storico pistoiese*, XIX, parts 1, 2); and a work on *The Origin and Development of the Symphony* (Pistoia, 1920, Pagnini).—R. F.

DAMROSCH, Frank Heino. Amer. condr. educator; *b.* Breslau, Germany, 22 June, 1859. Son of Leopold Damrosch, brother of Walter; educated in New York City schools. Stud. pf. under Joseffy, Jean Vogt, Pruckner and Von Inten; compn. under father and Moritz Moszkowski. In 1879, went to Denver, Col., where from 1882–5 he cond. Denver Choral Club, and from 1884–5 supervised music in public schools. Returned to New York as chorus-master at Metropolitan Opera House until 1891. In 1892, organised the People's Singing Classes, later developed into People's Choral Union, which has accomplished much for popular training in choral singing in New York City. This work is being carried on by D.'s assistants. In 1893 founded Mus. Art Soc., an organisation of about 60 selected professional singers, which gave concerts, largely of *a cappella* music, old and new, with a degree of finish and style not heard in America before or since. This remarkable organisation ceased its activity in 1920 for want of financial support. 1898–1912, condr. of Oratorio Soc. of New York, founded by his father in 1873; 1898–1918, cond. Symphony Concerts for Young People. 1897–1905, supervisor of music in New York public schools. In 1905 organised the Inst. of Mus. Art, which (well endowed by James Loeb) has become one of the best music schools in America. He received the degree of Mus.D. *h.c.* from Yale Univ. in 1904. *A Popular Method of Sight-Singing* (Schirmer, 1894); *Some Essentials in the Teaching of Music* (*id.* 1916).—O. K.

DAMROSCH, Walter Johannes. Amer. condr. compr. *b.* Breslau, Germany, 30 Jan. 1862. Son of Leopold Damrosch, brother of Frank; came to America, when 9, with his father. Educated in public schools of New York; stud. pf. under Von Inten, Boekelmann and Pinner in New York, and theory under his father, then under Rischbieter and Draeseke in Dresden, later with Urspruch in Frankfort-o-M. and under Bülow.

While still a young man, he acted as his father's assistant as condr. at Metropolitan Opera House in New York. When Leopold Damrosch died in 1885, the task of continuing his work, not only with the opera, but with Oratorio Soc. and with Symphony Soc. of New York, devolved upon his 23-year-old son, who cond. Oratorio Soc. 1885–98 and again 1917–21. In 1895 he organised the Damrosch Opera Co. which toured the country for 4 years, being the first to make Wagner operas really well known in America. With this company he also produced his own opera, *The Scarlet Letter* (1st perf. in Boston, 10 Feb. 1896). Another opera, *Cyrano de Bergerac*, was produced at Metropolitan Opera, 27 Feb. 1913. His chief claim to fame rests on his work with the orch. of the Symphony Soc. He has been its leader since 1885, and is thus the doyen of Amer. orch. condrs. With this organisation and the Oratorio Soc. he gave the 1st perf. in America of *Parsifal* in concert form (1896). First in America to perform Tchaikovsky's fifth and sixth, Brahms's fourth, Elgar's first and second, Sibelius' fourth and d'Indy's third symphonies, and Elgar's *Falstaff*, Ravel's *Daphnis and Chloe* and Delius's *Summer Night on the River*, and *On Hearing the First Cuckoo*. In 1920 he made an extended tour through Europe with the Symphony Orch., the first Amer. orch. to visit Europe. In 1902–3 he also cond. the concerts of the New York Philh. Orch. and in 1900–2 cond. the Wagner operas at the Metropolitan under Maurice Grau's management. In June 1921 he cond. a programme of Amer. music at the British Music Soc. Congress in London. Beside the compns. listed below he has comp. incidental music to Euripides' *Medea* and *Iphigenia in Aulis* (1915) and to Sophocles' *Electra* (1917). Mus.D. *h.c.* Columbia Univ. New York, 1914; is a trustee of the Amer. Acad. in Rome, and a member of National Inst. of Arts and Letters.

The Scarlet Letter, opera (Breitkopf, 1896); *Cyrano de Bergerac*, opera (Schirmer, 1913); *The Dove of Peace*, comic opera (*id.* 1912); *Manila Te Deum*, chorus and orch. (J. Church Co. 1898); *The Virgin Mary to the Child Jesus*, 2 motets for 6 vs. a cappella (*id.* 1899); sonata for pf. and vn. op. 6 (*id.* 1899). Many songs (among them the popular " Danny Deever," op. 2, No. 7; Church, 1897). Publ. *My Musical Life* (Scribner, 1923).—O. K.

D'ANDREA, Cav. Gennaro. Argentine pianist; *b.* Naples in 1860. Stud. at Naples Cons. under Cesi. First concert at Naples at 15. In 1896, made concert-tour, playing in Paris, Nice and Monte Carlo. Went to Buenos Ayres in 1898, where his concerts were so successful that he remained as teacher. Dir. Cons. Fracassi - D'Andrea, which he founded with Fracassi. In 1906, the Ital. Government awarded him the Cross of the Crown of Italy. Cesi, in his *Appunti di Storia e Letteratura del Pianoforte*, mentions him with high praise.—A. M.

DANEAU, Nicolas Adolphe Gustave. Belgian compr. *b.* Binche, 17 June, 1866. Stud. at Acad. of Music, Charleroi, then at Ghent Cons.; 1895, obtained in Rome Competition the 1er *second prix*; 1896, became dir. of Acad. of Music, Tournai; 1919, succeeded Van den Eeden at Mons Conservatoire.

Linario, 3-act lyric drama (Tournai, 1906); *Myrtis*, opera-idyll, 4 acts; *The Sphynx*, 3-act opera; *Chasse du Roy*, lyric vaudeville, 3 acts; *La Brute*, 1-act opera. Choral works for male vs.; songs with pf.; pf. pieces; str. 4tet and a 5tet, etc.—E. C.

D'ANGELI, Andrea. Ital. historian and music-critic; *b.* Padua, 9 Nov. 1868. Teacher of mus. history in the Rossini Liceo Mus. at Pesaro, and lecturer on same subject at Univ. of Padua. Has publ. interesting studies, some in review *Cronaca Musicale* (dir. by him in Pesaro from 1907 until outbreak of 1914 war); others in vols., a sketch of Giuseppe Verdi (Formiggini, Rome), and a study on *Music in the Greek Drama* (Loescher, Turin). He is also the author of some libretti for operas, and of various compositions.—D. A.

DANISH FOLK-MUSIC. See LAUB, T. L.; THUREN, HJALMAR.

DANNREUTHER, Gustav. Amer. violinist; *b.* Cincinnati, Ohio, U.S.A., 21 July, 1853; *d.* New York, 19 Dec. 1923. Brother of Edward, at whose instance he went to the Berlin Hochschule in 1871, studying there until 1874, vn. under De Ahna and Joachim. Lived in London until 1877, then went to Boston and after playing for 3 years with the Mendelssohn Quintet Club became a member of the new Boston Symphony Orch. in 1880. From 1882 to 1884 was dir. of the Buffalo (N.Y.) Philh. Soc. (chamber-music). In 1884, went to New York and organised the Beethoven String Quartet, which, from 1894 to 1917, when it disbanded, was known as the Dannreuther String Quartet. For three years was leading violinist in New York Symphony Soc. orch., but from 1899 devoted himself exclusively to church music and to teaching. From 1907, instructor-in-music in Vassar Coll., Poughkeepsie, N.Y. *Violin Scale and Chord Studies* (Breitkopf).—O. K.

DARBO, Erica. Norwegian opera- and operetta-singer (s.); *b.* Christiania, 23 May, 1891. Pupil of Ellen Gulbranson, Christiania (1914), and Mme. Cahier. *Début* at concert in Christiania, 1913. Has been engaged at different theatres in Christiania, and at Opéra-Comique, 1919–21; afterwards at Mayol Operetta Theatre. Starred in Copenhagen in 1921–2.—U. M.

D'ARIENZO, Nicola. Ital. compr. and teacher of compn. in Naples Cons. *b.* Naples, 24 Dec. 1843; *d.* there, 25 April, 1915. Was pupil of Mercadante. Author of several operas, and interesting studies on Neapolitan comic opera (*Rivista Musicale Italiana*).—D. A.

DARKE, Harold E. Eng. orgt. and compr. *b.* Highbury, London, 29 Oct. 1888. Scholar R.C.M. (organ and compn.); winner of Tagore Gold Medal. Stud. under Sir Walter Parratt (organ), Sir Charles Stanford (compn.), Herbert Sharpe (pf.). For 10 years assistant-orgt. Temple Church; now orgt. St. Michael's, Cornhill, and condr. of St. Michael's Singers, a choral soc. for city clerks (100 vs.). Prof. of harmony, cpt. and vocal ensemble at R.C.M. Mus.Doc. Oxon. 1919. Has given a complete series of Bach organ recitals and conducted many modern British choral works.

Choral cantata, *The Kingdom of God* (Stainer & Bell); cantata, *As the Leaves fall* (s. v., female chorus, small orch.); *Ye Watchers*, female chorus and orch. (1923, Stainer & Bell); part-songs (Stainer & Bell; Novello; Curwen); *5 Miniatures*, pf. (Stainer & Bell); *Rhapsody*, organ (*id.*); *3 choral preludes*, organ (Novello); *Morning and Evening Service in F* (Stainer & Bell); songs: *Uphill*; *Three Songs of Innocence*; *Baby Songs* (Stainer & Bell).—E.-H.

D'ATRI, Nicola. Ital. music critic; *b.* Foggia. Was, from its foundation until 1914, the much appreciated music critic of Roman newspaper *Il Giornale d'Italia*, in which position he exercised an effective influence on the Ital. mus. movement, contributing, especially in Rome, to the foundation of the concerts at the Augusteo. In 1908, he gave a lecture on *The Future Genius of the Italian Opera*, and in 1913 another on *Giuseppe Verdi*. Has served on the permanent commission for mus. art for the Ministry of Education, and also on other commissions. Is a Councillor of the R. Acad. Mus. di Santa Cecilia, and member of the concert-board at the Augusteo.—D. A.

DAURIAC, Lionel, Fr. musicologist; *b.* Brest, 19 Nov. 1847; *d.* 1923. Pupil of École Normale Supérieure, Paris; hon. prof. of philosophy; reseaches in æsthetics: *La Psychologie dans l'opéra français* (1897); *Essai sur l'esprit musical* (1904); *Rossini* (1907); *Le Musicien-poète R. Wagner* (1908). He founded the Fr. Soc. of Musicology (1904).—A. C.

DAVELLI, Marthe. Fr. lyrical s. *b.* Lille, Stud. under M. Duvernois; *Début in La Tosca*, Opéra-Comique, 1912; sang in 1st perf. of *Marouf, Savetier du Caire*, 1914; also in *Madame Sans-Gêne* (1915); *Les Quatre Journées* (1916); *La Rôtisserie de la Reine Pédauque* (1920); *Dans l'ombre de la Cathédrale* (1920). Engaged at Paris Opéra, 1922; sang in revivals of *Griseldis* and *Magic Flute*. Apart from her extraordinarily pure-toned voice. she has real talent as an actress.—A. R.

DA VENEZIA, Franco. Ital. pianist and compr. *b.* Venice 2 Nov. 1876. Left the Milan Cons. with diplomas for pf. and compn.; won various competitions, amongst them, with his opera *Il Domino Azzurro* (*The Blue Domino*), that offered by publisher Sonzogno in 1904. He lives at present in Turin, as teacher in Acad. there. Ricordi, Hug, Carisch, Rieter-Biedermann and others, have publ. many of his

pieces, especially for pf. He also writes for the musical journals.—D. A.

DAVEY, Henry. Eng. mus. historian; *b.* Brighton, 29 Nov. 1853. Was in business for some years; did not begin to study music seriously until 1874 (Leipzig Cons., under Reinecke, Jadassohn, Richter, and Weidenbach). Returned to Brighton, 1877, as teacher and journalist. Retired, 1903, from practical music. Did a great service to early Eng. music by his research work in libraries.

History of English Music (Curwen, 1895; rev. and enlarged ed. 1921); *Student's Musical History* (*id.* 1891; 8th ed. 1920); *Handel* (in "Masterpieces of Music" series), 1912; numerous arts. in London and foreign mus. press. Eng. corrector of Eitner's *Quellenlexikon*.—E.-H.

DAVICO, Vincenzo. Compr. *b.* Monaco Principality, of an Ital. family, 14 Jan. 1889. Stud. first at Turin, then at Leipzig under Max Reger. He is very well known amongst young Ital. comprs. for numerous orch. symph. works, pf. music and songs. His opera, *La Dogaressa*, was perf. at Monte Carlo in 1920; *The Temptation of St. Antony* (after Flaubert), soli, chorus, orch., was given in 1923.

Impressioni romane, orch. suite (1913); *Poema erotico* (1913); *Impressioni pagane*, orch.; *Polifemo*, orch.; also a Requiem (4-v.). Consult: E. Jenco, *V. D.* (Naples, 1917); M. Gaglione, *V. D.* in vol. *I giovani*; G. M. Gatti, *I giovani sinfonisti* (Rome, Orfeo).—D. A.

DAVID, Karl Heinrich. Swiss compr. *b.* St. Gall, 30 Dec. 1884. Stud. at Cologne Cons. and under L. Thuille (compn.) at Munich. Teacher of theory at Cons. Basle, 1910–14. Since 1917, has lived at Zurich.

Tredeschin (Bundi), opera; *Aschenputtel* (*Cinderella*), fairy-opera; *Das Hohe Lied Salamonis* (*The Song of Songs*), female chorus and orch. (Swiss National Ed.); *Schnitterlied*, chorus and orch.; *Gessnerlieder*, s. and orch.; vn. concerto; str. 4tet. Mostly publ. by Hug, Leipzig.—F. H.

DAVIES, Ben. British t. singer; *b.* Pontardawe, Wales, 6 Jan. 1858. Stud. R.A.M. London, under Randegger and Signor Fiori. 3 years with Carl Rosa Opera Co. Sang title-rôle in *Ivanhoe*; and then took a leading position in concerts, festivals, etc.—E.-H.

DAVIES, E. T. Welsh orgt.; *b.* Dowlais, S. Wales, 1879. Stud. pf. and organ; acc.; condr.; 1900, toured U.S.A. with a small concert party; organ recitalist; opened over 100 new organs in Wales; succeeded late Harry Evans in Merthyr Tydfil in 1906; well-known adjudicator; dir. of Mus. Univ. Coll. Bangor, 1920; choral, orch. and regular chamber-music classes with lecture-notes; lectures on mus. history; organised and cond. Anglesey Choral and Orch. Fest. (1000 vs.), 1921–22, and cond. (jointly with Sir Walford Davies) Harlech Mus. Fest. 1922. Keen folk-song enthusiast and a firm believer in knowledge of Welsh language and study of Welsh literature and poetry for Welsh comprs. Successful compr. in lighter form of instr. and vocal music.

Series of Welsh miniatures, vn. cello, pf.; also for str. 4tet; very popular part-songs: *When Summer's Merry Days*; *Y deryn Pur* (*The Gentle Dove*); *The Winds*.—D. V. T.

DAVIES, Fanny. Eng. pianist; *b.* Guernsey, 27 June, 1861. Stud. privately in Birmingham, and at Leipzig Cons. under Reinecke and Oscar Paul; and under Mme. Schumann at Frankfort. Appeared in Birmingham at 6 years of age; Crystal Palace, 1885; Sat. and Mon. Popular Concerts, 1885; Philh. 1886; Berlin 1887; Gewandhaus, Leipzig, 1888; Rome, 1889; Beethoven Fest. Bonn, 1893; Vienna Philh. 1895; Milan, 1895 and 1904; Paris, 1902, 1904, 1905; Holland, 1920, 1921; Prague, 1920, 1922; Spain, 1923. Has lectured and written articles (Schumann's music, *Musical Times*, Aug. 1911; teaching the pf. etc.). As a player, she is particularly fine in Beethoven, Schumann, Brahms, and the early schools; she was, however, very early in the field in introducing the works of Debussy and Scriabin to London. Consult *Mus. Times*, art. on F. D., June 1905.—E.-H.

DAVIES, Harold E. Mus.Doc. Orgt. and teacher, Univ. Adelaide, S. Australia. Head of Adelaide Cons. Founder and condr. of S. Australian Orch. from 1922. Brother of Sir Walford Davies. Compr. of anthems and songs (Novello).—E.-H.

DAVIES, Sir Henry Walford. Dir. of music in the University of Wales from 1919 ; *b.* Oswestry, Shropshire, 6 Sept. 1869. Chorister, St. George's Chapel, Windsor, 1882; assistant-orgt. to Sir Walter Parratt, 1885–90; compn. scholar R.C.M. London (1890–4), stud. under Parry, Rockstro and Stanford; orgt. St. Anne's, Soho, 1890–1; Christ Ch. Hampstead 1891–8; teacher of cpt. R.C.M. 1895; condr. London Bach Choir 1903–7; London Church Association 1901–13; orgt. Temple Ch. London, 1898–1919, holding the post nominally, with an acting orgt. until 1923; organising dir. of music to Royal Air Force, 1918–19; prof. of music, Univ. Coll. of Wales, Aberstywyth, from 5 June, 1919; chairman of the National Council of Music, Univ. of Wales, from 1919. He was knighted in 1922. Mus.Doc. Cantab. 1696; LL.D. *h.c.* Leeds, 1904; F.R.A.M. *h.c.* 1922; F.R.C.M. *h.c.* 1924.

As a compr. the weightiest part of his work has been in oratorio and cantata form. Since 1902, when *The Temple* was produced at Worcester, he has written important choral works regularly for the Eng. fests. In *The Temple* he first showed himself a master of construction, and introduced an innovation in the use of a solo str.-quartet for certain parts. His morality *Everyman* was produced at Leeds in 1904, and has since been widely perf.; a choral symphony, *Lift up your hearts*, at Hereford 1905; an *Ode on Time* for the Milton celebration in 1908; *Noble Numbers* followed in 1909; the *Five Sayings of Jesus* at Worcester in 1911; *Song of St. Francis* for Birmingham Fest. 1912. There was a short *Requiem* in English in 1915. The *Dante Fantasy* of 1914 was prod. at Worcester in 1921. *Heaven's Gate* was prod. at the People's Palace, London, in 1916. His chief orch. works are the *Holiday Tunes* (Queen's Hall Promenades, 1907); *Parthenia* Suite (1911); *Wordsworth* Suite (1913); *Conversations*, pf. and orch. (1914). In songs for and about children, he has a niche all his own, and such

things as *A Child's Grace*, the song *When Childher Play*, the *Peter Pan* Suite for str. 4tet (1909) testify to remarkable gifts in this direction. He was a pioneer in England in certain forms; the 6 Pastorals for vocal 4tet, str. 4tet and pf. were written in 1904. He has never abandoned organic form for "programme music," but is a great believer in "pictorial" or illustrative music (*Peter Pan* Suite, etc.), and sometimes constructs his musical themes on the rhythms of verbal sentences. He invariably secures a fine texture, good workmanship, simplicity and directness ; and with him it is ever "art for life's sake." As an organiser and inspirer, he has always been a great force, whether as trainer of the Temple Choir, organiser in the Royal Air Force, adjudicator, a pioneer of community singing, or the director of music in the Welsh Univ. and schools. In the elementary and secondary schools he makes much use of the pianola and the gramophone.

Orch.: Variations in A flat (1891); *Dedication Overture* in G (1893); symphony in D (1894); overture, *A Welshman in London* (1899); *Holiday Tunes* (1907, Curwen); *Solemn Melody* (1908, Novello); *Festal Overture* in 4 movements (1910, Goodwin MS. Library); *Parthenia* Suite (1911, *id.*); symphony in G (1911, *id.*); *Wordsworth* Suite (1912, *id.*); Memorial Suite in C (Queen's Hall Promenades, 18 Oct. 1923; *id.*); *Conversations*, pf. and orch. (1914, *id.*).

Chorus and orch.: *The Future* (1889); *Nativity* (1892); *Music* (an ode), 1893; *Hervé Riel* (1894, Novello); *Days of Man* (1897); *God created Man*, motet, double chorus and organ or orch. (1898, Novello); *Jovial Huntsmen* (1902, *id.*); *The Temple* (1902, *id.*); *Everyman* (1904, *id.*); *Lift up your Hearts* (1906, *id.*); *Ode on Time* (1908, *id.*); *Noble Numbers* (1909, *id.*); *Sayings of Jesus* (1911, Curwen); *St. Francis* (1912, Curwen); *Heaven's Gate* (1916, *id.*); *Dante-Fantasy* (1914, *id.*). Pf. and chorus: *Jovial Huntsmen* (1902, Novello); *Humpty Dumpty* (1907, *id.*); *Merry Heart* (1910, Curwen); *Eight Nursery Rhymes* (1905, Boosey); *New Nursery Rhymes* (1908, Chappell).

Chamber-music: Str. 4tet in D mi. (1890); str. 4tet in D ma. (1892); pf. 4tet in E flat (1893); pf. 4tet in D mi. (1893); str. 4tet in C (1895); pf. 4tet in C (1895); *Peter Pan* 4tet (1909, Curwen); pf. trio in C (1897); *Quiet Tunes*, pf. vn. and cello (1906); *Songs of Nature* (1909, Goodwin MS. Library). Pf. pieces: Suite in G, 2 pfs. (1914); 6 sonatas, pf. and vn.: G (1889); E flat (1893); A (1893); E mi. (1894, Novello); D mi. (1896, *id.*); F (3 movements) (1899–1902); sonata in F (1891) pf. and horn; *Prospice*, 5tet for vs. and str. (1894, Novello); *Psalm XXIII*, t. v., harp and str. (1896, *id.*); *Psalm XXIX*, t.v., harp and str. (1896); *Six Pastorals*, 4 vs., 4 str. and pf. (1897, Curwen); *Psalm XIII*, t. v., harp and str. (1898); *Songs of a Day*, vs. and instrs. (1908); over 100 songs; numerous part-songs; ed. *Fellowship Song Book* (1915, Curwen); *Thirty Songs Old and New* (1915, *id.*); *Fifty-two Hymn Tunes* (1915, *id.*); ed. *Hymns of the Kingdom* and *Students' Hymnal* (both Oxford Univ. Press, 1923). Consult *Musical Opinion*, March 1920.—E.-H.

DAVIS, John David. Eng. compr. and pianist; *b.* Edgbaston, Warwickshire, 22 Oct. 1870. Stud. at Raff Cons. in Frankfort-o-M. under Max Schwarz; then for 3 years at Brussels Cons. where his teachers were Jules de Zarembski and Arthur de Greef (pf.), Ferdinand Kufferath (cpt.) and Leopold Wallner (privately) for compn. Has been prof. at Guildhall School of Music, Birmingham and Midland School of Music, and prof. of theory and *solfège* at the now-defunct International Cons. (London).

The Maid of Astolat, symph. poem, orch. (Novello); *Pro Patria*, orch. march (*id.*); cello concerto, op 73 (ms.); *Song of Evening*, str. 5tet (Novello); *Summer*

Eve at Cookham Lock, str. 4tet (Hawkes); trio, pf. vn. cello, op. 76 (ms.); sonata, pf. and cello, op. 74 (ms.); Fantasia and fugue, organ (Novello); pf. and vn. pieces (*id.*); pf. pieces (Schott; Boosey; Bosworth).—E.-H.

DAVY, Ruby C. E. Australian compr.; correspondence pupil of Dr. Eaglefield-Hull; took Mus. Doc. at Adelaide Univ.
Overture in B flat; pf. concerto in C mi.; oratorio; str. 4tet in A mi.; pf. and str. 4tet in C; trio in B flat, pf. and str.; sonata, vn. and pf.; many pf. pieces; songs, etc. (all ms.).—E.-H.

DAWSON, Frederick. Eng. pianist; *b.* Leeds, 16 July, 1868. Chief appearances: Hallé Concerts, Manchester, 26 Dec. 1890; Monday Popular Concerts, 9 Jan. 1893; Saturday Popular Concerts, 21 Jan. 1893; Inaugural Concert, Queen's Hall, London, 2 Dec. 1893; Crystal Palace Concerts, 23 Feb. 1895; Philh. Concerts, 20 March, 1895; Promenade Concerts, Queen's Hall, 1st season, 1895 (6 times); Sheffield Fest. 12 Oct. 1899. Also lectures widely on music. An enthusiastic exponent of Debussy, Ravel and Scriabin. A warm friend and eager propagandist of the works of the late William Baines (*q.v.*). —E.-H.

DAWSON, Peter. Barit. singer; *b.* Adelaide, Australia, 13 Jan. 1882. Stud. under Sir Charles Santley, 1903-7. Well-known as an operatic and concert-singer.—E.-H.

DE ANGELIS, Alberto. Ital. writer on music; *b.* Rome, 4 Sept. 1885. Journalist; ed. of daily paper *La Tribuna*, Rome. Has devoted himself to publ. biographies and monographs, especially on Ital. mus. life in XIX and present centuries. Among his principal arts. publ. in reviews are:
Franz Liszt in Rome (*Rivista Musicale Italiana*, Vol. XVIII); *Contemporary Italian Musicians: Giovanni Sgambati* (*ib.* Vol. XIX); *Cosima Wagner* (*ib.* Vol. XX); *The Mission of the Orchestral Soc. in Rome* (in *Harmonia*, 1914); *Alessandro Vessella* (*The Roman Review*, 1914); *Alberto Gasco* (in the *Corriere del Teatro*, Milan, 1916); *The Memoirs of Luisa Mancinelli* (in *Noi e il Mondo*, Rome, 1920).
He is also the author of the vol. *L'Italia musicale d' oggi* (*Musical Italy of To-day: Dictionary of Musicians*) (1st ed. 1918; 2nd ed. 1922). He then conceived the idea of writing a series of biographies of Ital. musicians of present time, and of monographs regarding the Ital. mus. movement of recent years, which work he directs for the publ. firm *Ausonia* —D. A.

DE ANGELIS, Nazareno. Ital. b. singer; *b.* Rome, 17 Nov. 1881. One of most distinguished living Ital. singers, remarkable both for his magnificent voice and his skill as an interpreter. Of humble origin, he pursued his first mus. studies at a monastic school in Rome. Later, on account of his beautiful voice, he was persuaded to take up singing and stud. under various masters; but he perfected himself chiefly by his own efforts. He began his operatic career at Aquila in *Linda di Chamounix*, and his reputation made rapid strides, until it placed him in the first rank. He has appeared at the principal theatres in Europe and America. His repertoire includes 42 operas. His interpretations of *Mefistofele*, *Mosè* (Rossini), *Valkyrie* and

Parsifal are splendid. He created the b. parts of operas *Gloria* (Cilea), *L'Amore dei tre re* (Montemezzi) and *Mirra* (Alaleona).—R. F.

DEARTH, Harry. Eng. b. singer; *b.* London, 1876. Stud. singing at R.C.M. Principal bass, Westminster Abbey, 14 years; 3 years with Beecham Opera Co.; 3 years light opera with the late George Edwardes and Robert Courtneidge. All principal concerts in Britain.—E.-H.

DE BOECK, Auguste. Belgian compr. *b.* Merchtem (Brabant), 9 May, 1865. Stud. at Brussels Cons. under J. Dupont (harmony), Mailly (organ), Kufferath (cpt.). Now teacher of harmony at Brussels Cons.; and dir. of Acad. of Music in Malines. He has a temperament profoundly Flemish, loving colour heavily applied and rich orch. effects. His impetuosity is not always sufficiently controlled by self-criticism. He is, essentially, a theatrical musician, loving action and the picturesque. Yet Wagnerian (and occasionally Russ.) influence have been so strong that he has not been able to give to his mus. ideas a really original stamp.
For theatre: *Théroigne de Méricourt* (1901, Opéra Flamand, Antwerp); *Een Winternachtsdroom* (1903, *id.*); *De Rijndwergen* (1906, *id.*); *Reynaert de Vos* (1909, *id.*); *La Phalène*, ballet (1914, Théâtre de la Monnaie, Brussels); *La Route d'Émeraude* (1921, Théâtre Royal, Ghent); *Cendrillon*, ballet (ms.). Many songs; pf. pieces; symph. music (*Rapsodie dahoméenne*, etc.); religious music (masses, motets); choruses, cantatas, etc.—C. V. B.

DEBOGIS, Marie Louise. Swiss s. singer; *b.* Geneva, 15 Aug. 1879. Stud. singing at Geneva under Leopold Ketten, after having won 1st prize in pf. competition at Lyons; *début* at Opera in Geneva; soon rose to fame after a recital in Berlin. Siegfried Wagner engaged her (1909) for the fest. at Bayreuth. Triumphal tours through America and Europe. A natural musician with a wonderful voice and an intensely sympathetic rendering. Lives in Geneva.—F. H.

DE BONDT, Louis. Belgian compr. orgt. teacher and theorist; *b.* Puers, 5 July, 1877; *d.* Brussels, 23 Sept. 1920. Stud. at Brussels Cons. where he was sub-prof. of harmony 1899, of organ 1903, and prof. in 1910; 1901, orgt. and choirmaster at Notre-Dame, in Laeken, near Brussels (a royal parish). Inspector of mus. educ. in secondary State schools; teacher in School of Religious Music in Malines.
Incidental music for drama *Robrecht van Eync*; *Marche religieuse* for orch.; Mass. Author of a Preparatory Course of harmony (Breitkopf), and a complete course of harmony.—E. C.

DEBRNOV. Pseudonym of Josef Srb (*q.v.*).

DEBUSSY, Claude Achille. French composer; *b.* St. Germain-en-Laye, near Paris, 22 August, 1862; *d.* Paris, 26 March, 1918. The personality of Debussy dominated the whole history of music, not only in France, but in Europe for a quarter of a century. A musician of extraordinary powers, he regenerated every form of musical art: symphony, lyrical drama, song, chamber-music and pianoforte composition. One may differ from this great composer in musical ideals, but it is impossible to deny his stupendous originality. His genius, like that of Berlioz, is somewhat elusive. It is essentially intuitive—he allows himself to be guided by instinct rather than reason, and with him the most astonishing technical ability was always the slave of sensibility.

He came of a family entirely unacquainted with musical matters. His talent, however, soon became evident and his parents sent him at the age of eleven to the Conservatoire. Here he obtained several prizes for pianoforte and accompaniment, and in 1884, under the tuition of Massenet, carried off the *Prix de Rome,* for his cantata *L'Enfant Prodigue.*

It was in the shades of the Villa Medici in Rome that he began to meditate on his art. He endeavoured to forget the formulas that he had learnt, in order to fashion for himself new laws which should fulfil the requirements of his temperament. One finds in his earliest compositions evidence of the influence of Massenet, Wagner, and later Mussorgsky, Lalo and Chabrier. The work he sent from Rome, an orchestral suite *Printemps,* caused a veritable scandal in the Institut on account of its harmonic audacities. *La Damoiselle Élue* (Rossetti's *Blessed Damozel*), composed about the same time (1887), was not produced until five years later.

On his return to Paris, Debussy, with his sureness of instinct, set about acquiring the literary culture which he lacked. He was immediately attracted by the school of Symbolists, and frequented the house of Mallarmé. No doubt artistic discussions on symbolism and impressionism had a very great influence on him; but he had a far wider vision than Mallarmé, who was immersed in the Wagnerian cult. Debussy, like Erik Satie, realised that music must follow an evolution parallel to that of literature and painting, and repudiating the rhetoric of the Romantics, find more direct means of interpreting impressions and feelings. This inner development of ideals took place imperceptibly, without Debussy being fully conscious of it. Still groping for means of expression, he produced his adorable *Ariettes oubliées,* the first collection of *Fêtes galantes* on some lines of Verlaine, his *Cinq Poèmes de Baudelaire,* and for the piano, his *Arabesques* and *Suite Bergamasque.*

Between 1892 and 1894, Debussy composed the Prelude to *L'Après-midi d'un Faune,* a symphonic poem inspired by an eclogue of Mallarmé. It was of its kind as original and epoch-making a work as the *Symphonie fantastique* of Berlioz in 1829. Not only did Debussy introduce methods of composition which were entirely new, but his style of harmony, his orchestration, his rhythm, in short the whole thing, produced an atmosphere hitherto unknown. This was music ardent, sensuous, profound, that developed not in accordance with a certain necessary dogma, but simply and logically in accordance with the feeling which it sought to express.

From this time forward, masterpieces followed in quick succession: in 1893 a marvellous quartet entirely new in form and yet classic in tone and inspiration; in 1894 the *Proses lyriques* for which he had written delightful words; in 1898 the *Chansons de Bilitis* and *Nocturnes* for orchestra, a set of impressionist tone-pictures calling forth sensations which, up to then, music had been powerless to interpret. Finally, in 1902, the Opéra-Comique produced *Pelléas et Mélisande* before an audience which came to laugh and stayed to jeer. A few years later *Pelléas* was to become almost a popular success! Abandoning archaic forms of opera and the Wagnerian lyrical drama, Debussy instinctively returned to the pure traditions of French musical drama introduced by Lully, according to which, recitative should consist of a simple but well-marked declamation, while the orchestra weaves an atmosphere of melody around the action. Debussy from the outset succeeded in producing a perfect balance between poetry and music. He could interpret, with a sort of fine restraint, the most poignant emotions that rend the human soul; he could evoke by the simplest means the most delicate impressions, the most fleeting sensations—the fragrance of flowers, the coolness of the evening, the stillness of water.

In spite of several attempts, Debussy was not destined to leave behind him any other opera. He wrote nothing more for the stage except the incidental music to d'Annunzio's *Martyre de Saint Sébastien* and a ballet, *Jeux,* composed for Diaghilef's company; but even this is very important, and contains some of his finest inspiration. He devoted himself to orchestral and chamber-music, producing, in succession *La Mer, Rondes de printemps, Iberia,* several collections of songs and pianoforte pieces, instrumental sonatas, etc.

The criticism has sometimes been made that his two books of *Préludes* contain less spontaneous work than his first collections. One is certainly conscious of a greater attention to details of style and technique; but who can deny the poetry of such compositions as *La Cathédrale engloutie, Ce qu'a vu le vent d'ouest,* and *La Terrasse des audiences du clair de lune?* These are worthy of a place side by side with the most perfect emotional efforts of Chopin, who shared, with Mozart, Debussy's sincerest homage.

Although in the grip of an incurable disease, Debussy struggled on for years, heroically composing works of astonishing freshness, such as the sonata for flute, viola, and harp, or the sonata for violin and the one for cello.

Debussy accomplished a complete revolution in musical art. He ended the reform in harmony that Chabrier, Lalo and Gabriel Fauré had begun; he invented new ways of associating chords hitherto regarded as discords, and used them to produce exquisite and delightful harmonies, and he disengaged the separate *timbres* of the orchestra by making one accentuate the value of another, instead of combining them in confused masses. In this respect his method is that of an impressionist painter who lays on his canvas primary colours, side by side, instead of mixing them on the palette. In short, Debussy violated all conventional formulas, replacing them by new ones no less beautiful, and far more suitable for the expression of those transient sensations and delicate emotions which he loved above all to portray. He was the incomparable painter of mystery, silence and the infinite, of the passing cloud and the sunlit shimmer of waves—subtleties which none before him had been capable of suggesting. His power of expression is not less real for being always restrained and intolerant of excess and over-emphasis, but its force is under the surface, like that of Racine. One must realise to the full the French genius in order to understand that there may be as much force in *Phèdre* as in *Macbeth*.

The figure of Debussy so overshadows those of his contemporaries in music that the following quotation from M. André Suarès does small injustice to his masters and himself: "If it is a fact that French music is to-day an example and an ornament to Europe, as it was in the vital Middle Ages, and in the tempestuous times of the first Renaissance, Debussy and Debussy alone is responsible." He visited London on 27 Feb. 1909, conducting the Queen's Hall Orchestra in the 3 *Nocturnes* and the prelude *L'Après-midi d'un Faune*. The 2nd Nocturne and the prelude were encored.

Pf.: 2 *Arabesques* (1888, Durand); *Ballade* (1890, Froment); *Danse* (1890); *Suite Bergamasque* (1890); *Pour le Piano* (1901); *Estampes* (1903); *L'Isle Joyeuse* (1904); *Masques* (1904); *Images* (Set 1, 1905; Set 2, 1907); *Children's Corner* (1908); *La plus que lente* (1910); 12 *Préludes* (1910); 12 *Préludes* (1913); *La Boîte à Joujoux* (1913); *Berceuse héroïque* (1914); 12 *Études* (1915); pf. duet: *Marche écossaise* (1891); *Petite Suite* (1894); 6 *Épigraphes antiques* (1915); 2 pfs. (4 hands) *En blanc et noir* (1915). V. and pf.: *Ariettes oubliées* (1888); *Cinq poèmes* (Baudelaire), 1890; *Mandoline* (1890); *Fêtes galantes* (1892 and 1904); *Proses lyriques* (1893); *Chanson de Bilitis* (1898); *Trois chansons de France* (1901); *Trois ballades de François Villon* (1910); *Le Promenoir des deux Amants* (1910); *Trois poèmes* (Mallarmé), 1913; *Noël des enfants qui n'ont plus de maison* (1915). Vocal 4tet, *Trois chansons* (1908); v. and orch.: *Le Jet d'eau*; *Deux proses lyriques*. Chamber-music: str. 4tet (1893); sonata, vn. and pf.; sonata, cello and pf.; sonata, fl. vla. harp; *Rapsodie*, clar. and pf. (1910). Orch.: *Prélude à l'Après-midi d'un Faune* (1892); 3 *Nocturnes* (*Nuages*: *Fêtes*; *Sirènes* [with female chorus]), 1899; *Danse profane*, *Danse sacrée* (harp and orch.), 1904; *La Mer* (1905); *Images* (3rd set), 1909. Cantata (female chorus), *La Damoiselle Élue* (1887). Stage-music, *Le Martyre de St. Sebastien* (d'Annunzio), 1911. Dramatic: *L'Enfant Prodigue* (1884); *Pelléas et Mélisande* (Durand, 1902); *Jeux*, ballet (1912).

Consult: Louis Laloy, *Claude Debussy* (Dorbon); *La Revue Musicale*: Special number devoted to Debussy, Nov. 1920 (articles by Suarès, Robert Godet, Cortot, Falla, etc.); Romain Rolland, *Musicians of To-day* (Fr. ed. Hachette; Eng. transl. Kegan Paul); G. J.-Aubry, *La Musique et la Nature* (Chester). Articles by Debussy have lately appeared (Dorbon) and *Nouvelle Revue Française*) under title chosen by himself: *M. Croche anti-dilettante*.—H. P.

DECAGRAMA. See Notations; also Guervós

DECAUX, Abel. Fr. orgt. *b.* Auffay (Seine Inférieure), 1869. Stud. at Cons. Paris; then at *Schola Cantorum*, under Alexandre Guilmant;

since 1898 organ prof. at that school. From 1903 onwards, orgt. at Sacré-Cœur, Montmartre.

La Lune blanche, song (1899, Senart); 4 pf. pieces, *Clairs de lune* (Paris, 1900-7, Chapelier), played at Société Nationale, 1913; a *Fuguette on Ave Maris Stella* (in *Maîtres contemporains de l'orgue* of Abbé Joubert).—M. L. P.

DECHERT, Hugo. Ger. cellist; *b.* Dresden, 16 Sept. 1860. Pupil High School of Music, Berlin (Robert Hausmann); after concert tours, cellist in opera orch. Berlin, 1881; solo cellist, 1894. Member of Halir Quartet, then of Hess Quartet.—A. E.

DECIMETTE. A composition for 10 solo instruments, usually wood-wind. See Bird, Arthur.—E.-H.

DECKERT, Willy. Ger. cellist; *b.* Naumburg, 4 June, 1870; *d.* Berlin, Feb. 1923. Stud. under Louis Schröder, Friedrich Grützmacher, Dresden, and Julius Klengel, Leipzig. First cellist Liszt Soc. and Acad. Orch. Concerts, Leipzig; Komische Oper, Berlin; then independent soloist.

Ed. and arranger of old classical cello music.—A. E.

DECSEY, Ernst. Austrian mus. author; critic; *b.* Hamburg, 13 April, 1870. Stud. at Vienna Acad. of Music (pupil of Bruckner); took doctor's degree (law) at Univ. of Vienna. Went to Graz as government-official, where he became critic of *Tagespost*, and subsequently chief editor (1908). Since 1921, music critic of *Neue Wiener Tagblatt*. He made his name through his definitive biography of *Hugo Wolf* (1903–6) —originally 4 vols.; revised ed. in 1 vol. 1919. A deeply human spirit is shown in his work on *Bruckner* (1919). His book on *Johann Strauss* (1922) is an entirely poetical version of the life. D. is author of several novels, chiefly describing the charms of Old Vienna; also a splendid description of the time of Franz Josef (all publ. by Schuster & Loeffler). *Musiker-Anekdoten*, publ. by Tal, Vienna, 1922.—P. St.

DE FILIPPIS, Eduardo Angel. Argentine violinist; *b.* Santa Fé, Argentina, in 1887. Stud. at Cons. Safafecino, Santa Fé, where he now dir. Cons. Mozart, founded by him. Has publ. manual of vn.-playing (awarded prize, Liceo Rossini, Milan, 1911).—A. M.

DEGNER, Erich Wolf. Ger. compr. and teacher; *b.* Hohenstein-Ernstthal, 8 April, 1858; *d.* Berka, 18 Nov. 1908. Stud. Ducal Music School, Weimar, and R. School, Würzburg. Teacher, Regensburg and Gotha Music Schools; dir. Music School, Pettau (Steiermark), 1885; teacher, Ducal Music School, Weimar, 1888; dir. Steiermark Mus. Soc. Graz, 1891; dir. Music School, Weimar, 1902.

Symphony, E mi. organ and orch.; overture, E mi. organ and orch.; *Serenade*, G mi. for small orch.; Theme and variations for org.n; choral variations, songs, choral works; pf. pieces; oratorio, *Maria als die Mutter*, for soli, chorus and orch. Consult R. v. Mojsisovics, *E. W. D.* (1909).—A. E.

DE GREEF, Arthur. Belgian pianist, compr. *b.* Louvain, 10 Oct. 1862. Pupil of Louis Brassin at Brussels Cons.; of Liszt at Weimar. Pf. prof. at Brussels Cons. 1885. Toured in England, France, Holland, Germany,

Italy, Spain, Russia, Sweden and Norway. As a pianist he combines force and grace, emotion and style. Specialises on works of Grieg, whose personal friend he was. Originator and chief perf. of Durant Concerts, founded in Brussels before the war by Félicien Durant. As compr. he combines a Flemish generosity of inspiration with a Latin distinction of style.

Ballade en forme de variations, str. orch. (Peters); Fantaisie, pf. and orch.; Suite, orch.; Symphonie; Four old Flemish Songs, orch. (Chester) produced Queen's Hall, London, under compr. 4 Oct. 1896; Chants d'Amour, v. and orch.; Menuet varié and Concerto in C, pf. and orch. (produced Queen's Hall, London, under Sir Henry Wood, with compr. at pf. 6 Sept. 1921), etc. Pf. pieces; songs.—C. V. B.

DE IRIGOYEN, Bernardo Manuel. Argentine cellist; b. Buenos Ayres in 1883. Stud. in Europe. Whilst in Brussels, was member of Van Necke Quartet. Well known in Argentina as a concert player.—A. M.

DEITERS, Hermann C. O. Ger. philologist and mus. research scholar; b. Bonn, 27 June, 1833; d. Coblence, 11 May, 1907. Secondary schoolmaster at Bonn, Düren, Konitz, Posen. Chief inspector Provincial Education Dept., Coblence, 1885. In his writings he opposed Wagner and championed Brahms, on whom he wrote a short study (1880).

Revision of 3rd and 4th ed. of Otto Jahn's Mozart and revision of Beethoven's Biography by A. W. Thayer (from 1866).—A. E.

DE KOVEN, Reginald. Amer. compr. b. Middletown, Conn., U.S.A., 3 April, 1859; d. Chicago, Ill., U.S.A., 16 Jan. 1920. His family removed to England in his early youth. Graduated at St. John's Coll. Oxford, 1879. After graduation, stud. a year under Lebert (pf.) and Pruckner (theory) at Stuttgart. After half a year in compn. under Hauff in Frankfort, went to Florence where Vannuccini was his singing-master. Also enjoyed instruction of Genée in Vienna and Delibes in Paris. After a year as music critic of Evening Post in Chicago, was 1891–7 music critic of New York World; then of Journal (1898 to 1900) and again of the World, 1907 to 1912. In 1902 organised a Philh. Orch. in Washington, D.C.; cond. it until 1905. Possessed of facile melodic invention, he was a prolific compr. in the lighter style. His opus numbers run to 411, including more than 130 songs. He composed no fewer than 20 comic operas, beginning with The Begum (Philadelphia, 1887). The most successful were Robin Hood, brought out in Chicago, 1890, and perf. in London, under the title of Maid Marion, 1891; The Highwayman (New Haven, 1897). Also The Knickerbockers (Boston, 1893), Rob Roy (Detroit, 1894). A grand opera, The Canterbury Pilgrims, was first perf. at Metropolitan Opera, New York, 8 March, 1917, and another, Rip van Winkle, was brought out by the Chicago Opera Co., 2 Jan. 1919.

The Canterbury Pilgrims (J. Church Co. 1916); Rip Van Winkle (Schirmer, 1919). His comic operas were publ., up to 1897, by Schirmer; after that by Harms, Church, Stern, Remick and Schubert. King Witlaf's Horn, ballad for male chorus and t. solo, with pf. (Church, 1915). Most famous song, O Promise Me, op. 50 (Schirmer, 1889). A setting of Kipling's Recessional for male and for mixed chorus (Church) is very popular.—O. K.

DELACROIX, Auguste. Fr. compr. b. Marseilles, 27 Dec. 1871; pupil of Taudon and Guiraud; several songs; symph. poem Les Roses.—A. C.

DELAGE, Charles Maurice. Fr. compr. b. Paris, 13 Nov. 1879. Stud. harmony, cpt. and compn. under Maurice Ravel, and Indian music during a visit to the East. His publ. works (Durand) are 2 books of songs; Quatre Poèmes hindous, v. and small orch.; Ragamalika, v. and full orch.; and Schumann, pf. The unpubl. comprise a choreographic poem on Indian themes and a tone-poem Conté par la Mer. His music has great delicacy of colour.—M. D. C.

DE LAMARTER, Eric. Amer. critic, condr. b. Lansing, Mich., U.S.A., 18 Feb. 1880. Stud. pf. under Mary Wood Chase in Chicago, organ under Fairclough in St. Paul, and Middelschulte in Chicago; pupil of Guilmant and Widor in Paris, 1901–2. Was orgt. of the New England Congregational Ch. in Chicago until 1912. Mus. critic of Chicago Record-Herald 1908–9, then of the Tribune, and after 1910 of the Inter-Ocean. From 1911 to 1913, cond. Mus. Art Soc. Made assistant-condr. of Chicago Symphony Orch. in 1918. His symphony in D was first perf. by Chicago Orch. 23 Jan. 1914; Serenade for orch. in 1915 at Gunn's Amer. Concerts. Several overtures and suites have been played by Chicago Orch. and on 2 April, 1920 (with compr. as soloist) his 1st organ concerto was brought out. A 2nd organ concerto followed on 24 Feb. 1922.—O. K.

DE LARA, Isidore. Brit. compr. b. London, 9 Aug. 1858. At 13 appeared in public as pianist; at 15 stud. in Milan under Mizzucati (compn.) and Lamperti (singing); settled in London as singer, compr. and condr. Gave many series of British chamber-music concerts in London in 1915–16. His operatic style is founded on that of Saint-Saëns and Massenet. He is Chevalier of the Legion of Honour and Commander of the Crown of Italy.

Operas: The Light of Asia, a cantata converted into an opera (Covent Garden, 1892); Amy Robsart (Covent Garden, 1893); Moïna (Monte Carlo, 1897); Messaline (ib. 1899); Soléa (Cologne, 1906); Sanga (Opéra-Comique, Paris, 1908); Naïl (Théâtre de la Gaieté, Paris, 1910; Covent Garden, 1919); The Three Masks (Marseilles, 1912); The Three Musketeers (Cannes, 1920).—E.-H.

DELCROIX, Léon. Belgian compr. b. Brussels, 15 Sept. 1880. Pupil of Joseph Wieniawski (pf.), Alphonse Mailly (organ), V. d'Indy and Théo Ysaye (compn.). Leader of orch. at Théâtre Royal, Ghent, 1911; at Tournai Theatre, 1912; now at Trocadéro, Brussels. His compns. are marked by an elegant and graceful style which is full of distinction.

Orch. works: Symph. suite, op. 18; symphony, op. 19 (crowned by R. Acad. of Belgium, 1909); Le Roi Harald, op. 26; Çundçépa, op. 65; Soir d'été à Lerici, op. 66, symph. poems; Rhapsody of Langue doc, op. 27. Chamber-music: pf. 4tet, op. 1 (crowned by R. Acad. 1903); str. 4tet, op. 35; trio, op. 4 (Brussels, Schott); 5tet, op. 23; sonata, vn. and pf. op. 34 (Paris, Evette & Schaeffer); sonata, cello and pf. op. 67. Opera, Le Petit Poucet (Tom Thumb) (Brussels, 1913); La Bacchante, ballet (Ghent, 1912). —C. V. B.

DELHASSE, Félix. Belgian musicologist; b. Spa, 5 Jan. 1809; d. Brussels, 4 Nov. 1898.

Gave up commercial career to devote himself to sociology and music. Founded the *Guide Musical* (1854) to which he long contributed, as well as to *Diapason*, *La France Musicale*, etc.; author of an anonymous *Annuaire Dramatique* (1839–47); biography of Vieuxtemps; Gallery of Belgian artists' portraits, etc. Gave much material, intellectual and moral assistance to writers, artists and institutions. Both rich and generous, he used his fortune to benefit others; many made their *début* through him. Several eminent musicologists and artists owed their position to him. His unflagging love of collecting documents enabled him to provide valuable materials to Van der Straeten, Kufferath, Grégoir, Pougin for their works. His memory was encyclopædic.—E. C.

DELIBES, Léo. French composer; *b.* St.-Germain du Val (Sarthe), 21 Feb. 1836; *d.* Paris, 16 Jan. 1891. This charming musician, after having terminated his studies at the Paris Conservatoire, appeared, when 19, with an operetta *Deux Sous de Charbon* at the Folies-Nouvelles. He then gave at Théâtre-Lyrique, *Maître Griffard* (1857) and *Le Jardinier et son Seigneur* (1865). But it was at the Grand Opéra that he knew his greatest triumphs with his ballets *La Source* (1865), *Coppélia* (1870), *Sylvia* (1876). At the Opéra-Comique he achieved a great success with *Le Roi l'a dit* (1873), *Jean de Nivelle* (1880), and especially *Lakmé* (1883), which is still in the repertoire. From 1881 he taught harmony at the Conservatoire, and was elected a member of the Institut in 1889. Delibes practised in music the *écriture artiste* which Goncourt made the fashion in literature. His music, entirely superficial, is gracious and supremely elegant. He knew all kinds of refinements. His light music seems truly "winged," and suits the classical ballet perfectly. He contributed to the enrichment of the musical language, and his influence has been very real on musicians of the generation of Gabriel Fauré. Even to-day it is to Delibes that Henri Rabaud pays allegiance in *Marouf*.—H. P.

DELIUS, Frederick. British composer; *b.* Bradford, Yorkshire, 29 Jan. 1863. Son of Julius D. who became a naturalised British subject in 1850. He was educated at Bradford Grammar School and at International Coll., Spring Grove, Isleworth (1876–9). Parental opposition at first prevented him from devoting himself exclusively to music, but after a few years of business in the north of England—pleasantly relieved by occasional trips to Scandinavia—he persuaded his father to purchase an orange-grove in Florida. Here he had ample opportunity to develop in the most congenial surroundings. After six months of solitude, which he regards as the decisive period of his career, he was fortunate enough to encounter an admirable musician, Thomas F. Ward, who came to live with him and proved a sympathetic friend as well as a valuable teacher. But Delius soon began to feel the need of a definitely musical environment and begged his father to allow him to go to Germany. His request was refused. In August 1885, he left the orange-grove and secured a post as music teacher in Danville, Virginia, with the object of becoming financially independent. He was very successful in this capacity and his abrupt and long-unexplained disappearance from Florida seemed to convince his parents of the futility of their attitude towards his ambition. In the following year he went to Leipzig where he learned nothing from the Conservatorium but a great deal from his association with Grieg, who was at that time living in the town. On leaving Leipzig in 1888, he settled in Paris, where, as he never allied himself to any clique or coterie of musicians, his work was—and is still—completely ignored. Publicity, however, meant little to him; he wrote much, but published nothing and had no work performed until he had attained maturity. In 1893, he withdrew at the last moment, on purely self-critical scruples, an opera which had been accepted for production at Weimar, and it was not until 1899 that he ventured to give a concert of his own works. This took place in London at the old St. James's Hall, and attracted so much attention (as may be seen from the press notices) that it is astonishing to find that no further performance of any of his works took place in England during the next eight years. Germany was more active in her recognition of his genius. Hans Haym in Elberfeld, Julius Buths in Düsseldorf and Busoni, Oskar Fried and Fritz Cassirer in Berlin supported their belief in him by performing his orchestral works, and his reputation was still further enhanced by the production of *Appalachia* at the Lower Rhine Musical Festival in 1905, and *Sea-Drift* at the Tonkünstlerfest of the united German musical societies in 1906. In England we have to thank Sir Thomas Beecham, more than any other conductor, for familiarising us with all his works.

Delius is one of the very few composers who have learnt much from Wagner without being overwhelmed by him. The early works of Delius are clearly Wagnerian, with touches here and there of Chopin and Grieg; but from the very first there was always more Delius than Wagner, or anyone else, and the traces of external influence gradually diminished until, by 1900, Delius's individuality completely asserted itself. He is the sunset of that period styled Romantic, of which Wagner may be regarded as the high noon. Delius's art is retrospective, in the sense of being compact of " emotion recollected in tranquillity." It is therefore the reverse of impressionistic. Nature is interpreted not as a series of external phenomena, but rather as an integral part of the soul itself. Neither in his orchestral works nor in his operas and other compositions constructed upon a poetic basis is there any programme other than a purely spiritual one. Taking his text as a starting-point, Delius extracts what is universal from the particular details of his subject and leaves one wondering at the way in which minute particulars seem to be contained and individually expressed in an all-embracing synthesis. His greatest work, *A Mass of Life (Zarathustra)* — inspired by Nietzsche the poet rather than Nietzsche the philosopher—is an epic of initiation, of the bringing to birth of God in Man: the most essentially religious work of our time, consequently one of the most neglected—a work which in its grandeur, its breadth of vision, and its wealth of beauty, is unsurpassed by the most monumental achievements in music. In his technique Delius relies mainly, but by no means exclusively, upon an almost kaleidoscopic interplay of harmonies. Though historians might compare him on the one hand with Gesualdo, on the other with some composers of the present day, his work bears no trace of any contemporary influence and its peculiarly individual qualities are elusive and unanalysable. The letter without reference to the spirit is a thing of naught. But his personal style is as clear and distinguished in a little unaccompanied chorus like *On Craig Ddu* as in the operas and the great works for chorus and orchestra. Delius lives at Grez-sur-Loing, Seine-et-Marne, France.

Operas: *Koanga* (1897); *A Village Romeo and Juliet* (1901; produced Berlin, 1907; London, Beecham Opera Co. 1910; revived 1919); *Fennimore* (1910). Choral works: *Appalachia* (1902); *Sea-Drift* (1903); *A Mass of Life* (1905; produced London, 1909); *Songs of Sunset* (1906); *Song of the High Hills* (1912). Orch. works: *Paris* (1899); *Brigg Fair* (1907); *In a Summer Garden* (1908); *Dance Rhapsody* (1908); *On hearing the First Cuckoo in Spring* (1912); *North Country Sketches* (1914); *Eventyr* (1917). Pf. concerto (1906); vn. concerto (1916); double concerto for vn. and cello (1916); cello concerto (1921). Incidental music to James Elroy Flecker's play, *Hassan: or the Golden Journey to Samarcand* (1920; produced His Majesty's Theatre, London, 1923); many songs and a few part-songs. Publ. chiefly Univ. Ed. Vienna, and Augener, London. Consult book on D. by the writer, publ. by J. Lane, 1923. —P. H.

DELMAS, Jean François. Fr. operatic b. singer; *b.* Lyons, 14 April, 1861. *Début* in opera at small theatres of suburbs of Paris. Stud. at Cons., Lyons; also at Paris under Busine and Aubin. 1881, 1st prize for singing in *Semiramis*, and 1st prize for opera in *Œdipe à Colone*, *Robert le Diable* and *Les Huguenots*. Created rôles in *Le Dame de Montmartre*, 1888; *Lohengrin*, 1891; *Salammbô*, 1892; *Valkyrie*, 1893; *Thaïs*, 1894; *Messidor*, 1897; *The Mastersingers*, 1897; *Les Barbares*, 1901; *Paillasse*, 1903; *L'Étranger*, 1904; *Armide*, 1905; *Ariane*, 1906; *Hippolyte et Aricie*, 1908; *Götterdämmerung*, 1908; *Monna Vanna*, 1909; *Rhinegold*, 1909; *La Forêt*, 1910; *Roma*, 1912; *Parsifal*, 1914; *La Légende de St. Christophe*, 1920; *Antar*, 1921; *La Fille de Roland*, 1922. He possesses a voice of exceptional range and purity which enables him to take a variety of parts, ranging from operatic barit. to b. His singing is a model of mus. declamation and the nobility of his style has made him one of the most respected of operatic singers for the last 30 years. In the opinion of the Wagner family he is the most perfect Wotan ever heard.—A. R.

DELMAS, Marc. Fr. compr. *b.* St. Quentin, 28 March, 1885. Pupil of X. Leroux, Caussade, Lenepveu, and Paul Vidal; *Prix de Rome*, 1919.

His lyric legend *Anne-Marie* gained the *Prix Rossini* (1911); *Les Deux Routes* (symph. poem) gained the *Prix A. Thomas*. The *Prix Chartier* was awarded to him in 1919 for his chamber-music works: a trio; *Legende et Danse* for str. 4tet; pf. pieces: *Impressions d'Ariège*; *Nostalgie*; *Suite française*. The *Prix Cressent* has rewarded his lyric drama, *Iriam*. He is the typical musician-laureate.

Jean de Calais (1907); *Stéphanie* (1910); *Laïs* (1909); *Camille* (1921); *Anne-Marie* (1922). Symph. music: *Les Deux Routes* (1913); *Au pays wallon* (1914); *Le Poète et la Fée* (1920); *Du Rêve au Souvenir* (1919); *Le Bateau turc*; *Penthésilée*.—A. C.

DE LUCA, Giuseppe. Ital. barit. singer; *b.* Rome, 25 Dec. 1876. One of the most celebrated living artists of Ital. song. Stud. in Rome at R. Liceo Mus. di Santa Cecilia (under Persichini). At *début* at Piacenza, 1897 (in *Faust*), his fame was immediately assured, and he became sought after by chief theatres of Europe and America. Amongst his finest interpretations are those of *Damnation of Faust*, *Rigoletto*, and *Parsifal*. He created parts of Michaunnet in *Adriana Lecouvreur* (Cilea), of Gualberto in *Notte di Leggenda* (Franchetti) of Sharpless in *Madama Butterfly*, and title-rôle in *Gianni Schicchi* at its first perf. in New York.—D. A.

DE LUCIA, Fernando. Ital. t. singer; *b.* Naples, 11 Oct. 1860. Celebrated for his unique qualities as singer and interpreter. Stud. at Cons. in his native town, where he made his first appearance at the San Carlo in *Faust*. Rapidly gained a footing and laid the foundations of a most brilliant career. In *Carmen*, in the *Pescatori di Perle*, in *Iris*, he has remained unsurpassed. Created *L'Amico Fritz* and *I Rantzau* (Mascagni). Lives at present in Naples, where he teaches singing at the Cons.—D. A.

DEL VALLE DE PAZ, Edgardo. Pianist, compr. *b.* Alexandria (Egypt), of Ital. parents, 18 Oct. 1861; *d.* Florence, 5 April, 1920. Was prof. of pf. at Cherubini R. Inst. of Music, Florence. Very capable teacher and concert-player; gave many concerts in Italy and abroad. In 1886, made a tour with violinist, César Thomson. Is the compr. of orch., vocal and pf. music (Ricordi and Augener) and of interesting educational works. In 1896, founded in Florence *La Nuova Musica*, which he directed until his death.—R. F.

DELVINCOURT, Claude. Fr. compr. *b.* Paris, 12 Jan. 1888. Studied at Conservatoire, Paris, under Widor. In 1913, carried off brilliantly *Prix de Rome*, with cantata *Faust et Hélène* (Legouix). His labours were interrupted by the war, in which he was severely wounded and lost an eye. This highly gifted musician has taken up composition again after an interval of 8 years. He has written songs (Senart); vocal quartets (Legouix); and an extremely interesting sonata for pianoforte and violin (Senart, 1923).—H. P.

DE MALEINGREAU, Paul. Belgian orgt. compr. *b.* Trélon en Thiérache, 23 Nov. 1887; entered Brussels Cons. 1905; stud. compn.

there under Edgar Tinel; lecturer in harmony there, 1903; lecturer in organ classes, 1921. Revived primitive and classic compns. for organ, gave remarkable perf. at Brussels (1921–2) of the entire Bach organ works. As compr. he combines a keen perception of modern harmony with a marked predilection for fine form and architecture. His works (not numerous) are marked by a characteristic aspiration after depth and perfection.

Pf.: Suite; *Sonatine*; *Angelus de Printemps*. Organ: 2 *Triptyques*; 2 symphonies; 20 liturgical pieces (Lauwerijns, Brussels); suite, op. 14 (Durand); *Opus Sacrum* (Chester). Sonata, cello and pf. (Lauwerijns, Brussels).—C. V. B.

DEMÉNY, Dezső. Hungarian compr. *b.* Budapest, 29 Jan. 1871. Over 100 songs; orch. and especially choral works. Condr. at St. Stephen's. —B. B.

DEMEST, Désiré. Belgian singer; *b.* Liège, 16 Sept. 1864. Pupil of Bonheur and Carman at Liège Cons. Sang t. parts at concerts, notably in oratorios; teacher of singing, Brussels Cons. since 1893, where he has trained some well-known artists: Swolfs, Ansseau (ts.), Dufranne (barit.), and Huberty (b.). Author of *Manual of Singing Exercises* (12th ed.).—E. C.

DE MOL, Guillaume. Belgian compr. *b.* Brussels, 1 March, 1846; *d.* Marseilles, 7 Sept. 1874. Remarkably gifted artist; brother and nephew of musicians; stud. at Brussels Cons. *Prix de Rome,* 1871, for cantata *Columbus Droom.* After the prescribed journey abroad, went to Marseilles, where his brother was orgt. and there died prematurely at age of 28.

Symphony, *La Guerre*; oratorios: *Levenstijden*; *Laatste Zonnestraal*; songs on Flemish poems, one of which, *Ik ken een lied vol melodij,* acquired a well-earned popularity, owing to its extreme simplicity and its deeply expressive emotion.—C. V. B.

DE MURO, Bernardo. Ital. t. singer; *b.* Tempio Pausania, Sardinia, 1881. Much appreciated dramatic singer. Stud. in Rome; *début* at the Costanzi. Has since sung in principal theatres of Italy and S. America. At Scala in Milan, created part of Folco in Mascagni's *Isabeau.*—D. A.

DEMUTH, Leopold. Ger.-Czechoslovak singer (barit.); *b.* Brünn, 2 Nov. 1861; *d.* Bernwoitz, 4 March, 1910. Kammersänger at Vienna R. Opera, 1897.—E. S.

DE NARDIS, Camillo. Ital. compr. *b.* Orsogna (Chieti), 26 May, 1857. Teacher of fugue and compn. and vice-dir. of Naples Cons. A skilful compr. of operas and much instr. and vocal music. Especially interesting are his orch. works inspired by Abruzzi melodies. Was dir. of San Carlo Theatre and (as substitute for Martucci) condr. of orch. of the Quartet Soc. Has publ. several educational works and transcriptions of music, notably of XVIII century Neapolitan school.

Bi ba bu, comic opera (1880); *Un bacio alla Regina,* id. (1890); *Stella,* serious 3-act opera (1898); *Camoens* (unpubl.); *I Turchi in Ortona,* oratorio (1884).—D. A.

DENÉRÉAZ, Alexandre. Swiss orgt. compr. musicologist; *b.* Lausanne, 31 July, 1875. Stud. at R. Cons. Dresden (1891–5) under F. Draeseke

(compn.), C. H. Döring (pf.) and Jannsen (organ). Became orgt. at St. Francis' Ch. in Lausanne and prof. of compn. and organ at Cons. Since 1918, lecturer at Univ. where he delivers courses on mus. philosophy (*Symbolique des principes acoustiques et du principe tonal*). Has written (with C. Bourguès) a most important book *La Musique et la Vie interieure: Histoire psychologique de l'Art musical* (Paris, Alcan). As supplement,. he publ. *L'Arbre généalogique de l'Art musical* (Alcan), illustrated, representing the continuity of mus. technique from 4000 B.C. till Strauss, Debussy and Stravinsky (about 1200 comprs. grouped according to their melodic and harmonic relationship, and 27 colours help to distinguish the various kinds of national movements).

3 symphonies (C ma., C mi., E mi. with organ); 2 symph. poems, *Le Rêve* and *Les Saisons*; *Épopée symphonique* (visions of war, 1914–18) for full orch.; symph. variations, *Scènes de la vie de cirque*; symph. pieces, *Autour du monde*; vn. concerto, D ma. (1st perf. by Jacques Thibaut). Works for chorus, soli and orch.: *Aurores lointaines*; *La Chasse maudite*; *Cantate d'inauguration*; *Mil huit cent trois, cantate patriotique* (Lausanne, Walbach); 2 str. 4tets, E and D (Lausanne, Fœtisch); incidental music to *La Dime* (Morax); unacc. choruses; songs with orch. and with pf.—F. H.

DENIJN, Jef. Belgian carilloneur; *b.* Malines, 19 March, 1862. Succeeded his father, Adolphe Denijn, municipal carilloneur of Malines, 1881, when latter became blind. Officially appointed Jan. 1887. Since 1892 organised Carillon Concerts in Malines, famous to-day. Has given concerts in various cities in Belgium, Holland and England. Introduced technical carillon improvements not only in Belgium but in France and Holland. Comp. for carillon (publ. in *Journal of R. Soc. of Arts,* Vol. LXIV, No. 3291, 17 Dec. 1915, an article *Technique et mécanismes de carillon).* A congress of *L'Art du Carillon* was organised in Malines, April 1922, on his 35th year of office. D. is the herald of the art of carillon - playing. His world-wide fame is due to his astonishing skill and to the great variety of his repertoire. Thanks to the Carillon School, which he directs at Malines, he forms pupils who will maintain and develop his ideas.—C. V. B.

DE NITO, José. Argentine compr. *b.* Rosario de Santa Fé, in 1887. Stud. at Cons. of Naples under Serrao, De Nardis, Longo, Cotrufo and Napoli. Returned to Argentina in 1910, where he establ. an Inst. of Music, which he now directs. Pieces for pf.; vn. and pf.; songs.—A. M.

DENKMÄLER DER TONKUNST IN BAYERN (*Monuments of Music in Bavaria*). A parallel publication to *Denkmäler Deutscher Tonkunst*; supported by Bavarian Government; under dir. of Adolf Sandberger. The works publ. since 1900 are: I and IX 1, Dall' Abaco, *Selected Works* (Sandberger); II 1, Johann and W. H. Pachelbel, *Clavier Works* (M. Seiffert); II 2, J. K. Kerll, *Selected Works,* Part 1 (Sandberger); III 1, VII 2, and VIII 2, *Symphonies of Bavarian Palatinate School—Mannheim Symphonists* (H. Riemann); III 2, Ludwig Senfl's Works, I (Theodor Kroyer); IV 1, Johann Pachelbel, *Organ Compositions* (Seiffert); IV 2, Organ Compositions of Chr. Erbach, H. L. Hassler and Jakob Hassler (E. v. Werra); V 1, *Notes for Biography of H. L. Hassler and his Brothers*, etc. (Sandberger); V 2, Works of H. L. Hassler, Part 2 (Rudolph Schwartz); VI 1, *The Nuremberg Masters of 2nd Half of XVII Century* (Seiffert); VI 2, Agostino Steffani, *Selected Chamber Duets* (Alfred Einstein and Ad. Sandberger); VII 1 and VIII 1, Johann Staden, *Selected Works* (Eugen Schmitz); IX, Leopold Mozart, *Selected Works* (Seiffert); X 1, G. Aichinger, *Selected Works* (Kroyer); X 2, Ad. Gumpeltzheimer, *Selected Works* (O. Mayer); XI 2, Agostino Steffani's opera *Alarico* and particulars of all his operas (H. Riemann); XII 1, Ag. Steffani, *Selection from his Operas* (H. Riemann); XII 2, Anton Rössler (Rosetti), *Symphonies* (O. Kaul); XIII, J. Erasmus Kindermann, *Selected Works* (Felix Schneider); XIV 1, Traetta, *Selected Works*, I (H. Goldschmidt); XIV 2, Gluck, *Nozze d'Ercole e d'Ebe* (Abert); XV–XVI, *Mannheim Chamber-Music of the XVIII Century* (Riemann); XVII, T. Traetta, *Selected Works*, II (H. Goldschmidt); XVIII, Joh. Krieger, Murschhauser, J. Ph. Krieger, *Selected Works* (Max Seiffert); XIX and XX, Pietro Torri, *Selected Works*, I (H. Junker).—A. E.

DENKMÄLER DER TONKUNST IN ÖSTERREICH (*Monuments of Music in Austria*). Annual publ. of old Austrian compns., from time of Minnesänger period up to classical era. Founded 1894 by Guido Adler (*q.v.*). Up to 1924, 56 vols. were publ.—*a cappella* works from the 6 Trentine Codices (Dufay, Binchois, Dunstable, etc.), complete operas of baroque period (Cesti's *Il pomo d'oro*; Fux's *Constanza e Fortezza*), a rococo opera (Gassmann's *La Contessina*), and Umlauf's *singspiel Bergknappen*. A 2nd series has started on Gluck's works (only *Orfeo*, after orig. score of 1762, done so far). In 1913, Adler commenced admirable studies on these comprs.; so far 9 vols. publ. in the *Denkmäler*. Chief are: *Gluck's Early Operas* (by E. Kurth), *XVII Century Masses in Austria* (by G. Adler), *Operas and, Oratorios in Vienna 1660–1708* (E. Wellesz), *The Trentine Codices* (Finker and Orel). The *Denkmäler* was at first publ. by Artaria; now by Univ. Edition.—EG. W.

DENKMÄLER DEUTSCHER TONKUNST (*Monuments of German Music*). An extensive publication of older works, supported by Prussian State and ed. by Commission for History of Music under dir. of R. von Liliencron (*d.* 1912, succeeded by H. Kretzschmar), Leipzig, Breitkopf & Härtel. Since 1892 have been publ.: I, S. Scheidt, *Tabulatura nova* (M. Seiffert), and after long delay in 1900, when better materials had been taken in hand, there followed in quick succession: II, H. L. Hassler, *Cantiones Sacræ* 4–12 *vs.* (H. Gehrmann); III, Fr. Tunder, *Gesangswerke* (M. Seiffert); IV, J. Kuhnau, *Clavier Works* (K. Päsler); V, J. R. Ahle, *Selected Vocal Works* (Joh. Wolf); VI, Math. Weckmann and Chr. Bernhard, *Solo Cantatas and Chorales with Instr.* (M. Seiffert); VII, H. L. Hassler, *Masses 4–8 vs.* (Joseph Auer); VIII–IX, J. Holzbauer,

opera *Gunther von Schwarzburg* (H. Kretzschmar); X, J. K. F. Fischer, *Journal du Printemps*, and D. A. Schmicorer, *Zodiacus Musicus* (E. v. Werra); XI, D. Buxtehude, *Instrumental Works* (K. Stiehl); XII–XIII, Heinrich Albert, *Arias* (Ed. Bernoulli); XIV, D. Buxtehude, *Abend-Musiken and Cantatas* (M. Seiffert); XV, K. H. Graun, *Montezuma* (Mayer-Reinach); XVI, Melchior Franck and Valentin Hausmann, *Selected Instr. Works* (Fr. Bölsche); XVII, Johann Sebastiani and Johann Theile, *Passion Music* (Fr. Zelle); XVIII, Johann Rosenmüller, *Chamber Sonatas of 1670* (Nef); XIX, Ad. Krieger, *Arias* (Alfred Heuss); XX, Hasse, *Conversione di S. Agostino* (Arn. Schering); XXI–XXII, Fr. W. Zachow's Works (Seiffert); XXIII, Hieronymus Prætorius, *Selected Church Music* (H. Leichtentritt); XXIV–XXV, H. L. Hassler, *Sacri concentus 4–12 vs.* (Joseph Auer); XXVI–XXVII, J. G. Walther, *Organ Pieces* (Seiffert); XXVIII, Telemann, *The Day of Judgment* (text by Alers), and Ramler–Telemann, *Ino* (Max Schneider); XXIX–XXX, *Instrumental Concertos of German Masters* (Pisendel, Hasse, Ph. Em. Bach, Telemann, Graupner, Stölzel, Hurlebusch) (A. Schering); XXXI and XLI, Ph. Dulichius, *Centuriæ* (Rudolf Schwartz); XXXII–XXXIII, Jommelli, *Fetonte* (Hermann Abert); XXXIV, Rhaw, *New German Sacred Songs* (Johannes Wolf); XXXV–XXXVI, Sperontes, *Singing Muse* (E. Buhle); XXXVII–XXXVIII, Keiser, *Cræsus* and selection from *L'inganno felice* (M. Schneider); XXXIX, Johann Schobert, *Selected Works* (Hugo Riemann); XL, Andr. Hammerschmidt, *Selected Works* (Leichtentritt); XLII, Ernst Bach and Valentin Herbing, *Songs* (Kretzschmar); XLIII–XLIV, *Ballets* by Fr. Deller and J. J. Rudolph (Abert); XLV, *Elmenhorst's Sacred Songs*, comp. by J. W. Franck, G. Böhm, P. L. Wockenfuss (Kromolicki and Krabbe); XLVI–XLVII, Erlebach, *Harmonic Joy* (O. Kinkeldey); XLVIII, Johann Ernst Bach's *Passion* (Kromolicki); XLIX–L, *Thuringian Motets of 1st Half of XVIII Century* (Max Seiffert, 93 nos. from ms. 13661 in Univ. Library, Königsberg); LI–LII, *North German Symphonies*, 1 vol. (M. Schneider and B. Engelke) LIII–LIV, J. Ph. Krieger, 21 *Selected Church Compositions* (M. Seiffert); LV, B. Pallavicino, *Gerusalemme liberata* (H. Abert); LVI, J. Chr. Fr. Bach's *The Children of Jesus* and *The Awakening of Lazarus*—texts by Herder (G. Schünemann); LVII, G. Ph. Telemann, 24 *Odes* and Görner's *Collection of New Odes and Songs* (W. Krabbe).— A. E.

DENSMORE, Frances. Writer on Amer. Indian music. Author of *Chippewa Music* (Bureau of American Ethnology, Washington, D.C., 1910); *Teton Sioux Music* (id. 1918); *Northern Ute Music* (id. 1922).—J. M.

DENT, Edward Joseph. English writer on music; *b.* Ribston, Yorks, 16 July, 1876. Studied composition under C. H. Lloyd at Eton and under Charles Wood and Stanford at Cambridge, but from 1900 onwards devoted himself to historical research, for which he obtained a

Fellowship at King's College, Cambridge, in 1902. He lectured on musical history at Cambridge for several years; in 1919 became musical critic of *The Athenæum*. First chairman of the International Society for Contemporary Music (*q.v.*). *Alessandro Scarlatti, his Life and Works* (1905, E. Arnold); *Mozart's Operas, a critical study* (1913, Chatto & Windus); transl. into Ger. by Dr. Anton Mayer, Berlin, 1923); a chapter on Fr. music (from Josquin des Prés to Ravel) in Arthur Tilley's *Modern France* (Cambridge, 1922); a chapter on Eng. music since 1880 in Guido Adler's *Handbuch der Musikgeschichte* (1924); arts. in Grove's Dictionary and *Encyc. Brit.* chiefly on Ital. opera-comprs. of XVIII century; several papers, chiefly on Ital. opera of XVII and XVIII centuries, in *Sammelbände der Internationalen Musik- Gesellschaft, Musical Antiquary, Monthly Musical Record, Musical Quarterly* (New York) and *Music and Letters*; transl. of Mozart's *Magic Flute* (Cambridge, 1911), *Nozze di Figaro* (1920, Old Vic. London); *Don Giovanni* (1921, *ib.*); Wagner's *Liebesverbot* (Breitkopf, 1922).—E.-H.

DENZA, Luigi. Ital. compr. *b.* Castellamare di Stabia, 24 Feb. 1848; *d.* London, 1922. A noted compr. of songs and pf. pieces. Over 500 songs to Ital., Neapolitan, Eng. and Fr. words. Together with those of Tosti, Rotoli and others, these constituted a type of ballad and Ital. song greatly in vogue during the last 10 years of XIX century. In 1897 he settled in London; was one of directors of London Acad. of Music. 1898, prof. of singing at R.A.M. London. In 1876, his opera *Wallenstein* was perf. at Mercadante Theatre, Naples, with only moderate success. At Naples Cons. he had stud. compn. under Mercadante and Serrao. —D. A.

DENZLER, Robert F. Swiss condr. compr. *b.* Zurich, 19 March, 1892. Stud. pf. and compn. at Cons. Zurich; pupil of Volkmar Andreae; 1911, became condr. of symphony concerts at Lucerne; since 1915, condr. of opera and choral concerts at Zurich. His music shows the influence of R. Strauss; his symph. poems were particularly appreciated at fests. of Swiss Music Society.
Totentanz and *Richmodis*, symph. poems for full orch.; *Bergpsalm*, symph. poem, chorus, soli and full orch.; 16 songs in op. 2, 5, 10 and 12 (Zurich, Hüni); suite for 2 vns. (Hüni).—F. H.

DEPANIS, Giuseppe. Ital. writer, mus. organiser; *b.* Turin, 5 April, 1853. In his native town, D. has been a valuable promoter of mus. activity, and took an effective part in organisation of symphony concerts during Exhibitions of 1884, 1898 and 1911. Especially memorable were those of 1884, to which the following orchs. contributed: Turin, cond. by Pedrotti; Milan, cond. by Faccio; Naples, cond. by Martucci; Bologna, cond. by Mancinelli; Rome, cond. by Pinelli; Parma, cond. by Campanini. To D. (and to Carlo Pedrotti) is due the credit for this musical awakening, which placed Turin ahead of other Ital. cities in organisation of symphony concerts. D. was one of first propagandists of Wagner's art in Italy. His book, *Popular Concerts and the Regio Theatre of Turin, 1872–86 (Fifteen Years of Musical Life)*, 2 vols. (S.T.E.N., Turin, 1914–15), is a very interesting mine of records. He has publ. also a book on the *Nibelung Ring* (Roux & Frassati, Turin, 1896), and various

other writings, especially on Wagnerian subjects.—D. A.

DÉRÉ, Jean. Fr. compr. *b.* Niort, 1886. Pupil of Diémer, Caussade, and Widor; just missed *Prix de Rome* in 1919; author of stagemusic for Marlowe's *Dr. Faustus*; several songs; pf. pieces.—A. C.

DE RENSIS, Raffaello. Ital. mus. writer; *b.* Casacalenda (Campobasso), 1880. Founded in Rome in 1908 the periodical *Musica* and the publ. firm connected therewith. As ed. of the paper, he has taken an active share in Ital. mus. life of last 15 years. Publ.: *Anime musicali* (*Musical Souls*), psychological essays on writers and poets (1913); *Rivendicazioni musicali* (*Musical Vindications*), a vol. of historical criticism and controversies. Has helped to recall to mind forgotten figures of Ital. musicians. Is mus. critic of Rome daily paper *Il Messaggero*, and contributor to many reviews.—D. A.

D'ERLANGER, Baron Frederic. Compr. *b.* Paris, 1868. Spent his youth and completed his literary and mus. studies in Paris; he resides in England, the country of his adoption; has been for many years one of the dirs. of Covent Garden Opera. His opera *Tess* (on Hardy's novel) was first produced at San Carlo, Naples, and afterwards at Dal Verme Theatre, Milan. Its first London perf. was in 1909 (with Emma Destinn as heroine).
4 operas: *Jehan de Saintré* (Fr., 2 acts; Aix-les-Bains, 1893); *Ines Mendo* (Fr., 4 acts; *id.* 1893; Covent Garden, London, 1897); *Tess* (Ital. 4 acts; Naples, 1906); *Noël* (Fr., 2 acts; Théâtre Municipal, Nice, 1912); orch. works; vn. concerto; pf. concerto; 5tet, pf. and strings; pf. pieces; vn. pieces; songs (Eng. and Fr.), etc. (Schott; Augener; Ricordi, Milan; Rouart & Lerolle, Paris).—E.-H.

DE ROGATIS, Pascual. Argentine violinist, compr. *b.* Naples in 1883. Went to Buenos Ayres as a child. Stud. at Buenos Ayres Cons. In 1906, the Cons. gave a concert devoted entirely to his symph. works.
3 orch. poems: *Marko y el Hada*; *Belkiss en la Selva*; *Zupay*. Other pieces are *Preludes*; *Suite arabe*; *Danza de las Driadas*; *Paisaje Otoñal*; *Romance* for vn.; 2 vn. concertos; 2 cello concertos; songs; pf. pieces.—A. M.

DE RUBERTIS, Oreste. Ital. pianist; *b.* Naples in 1893. Coming from the Rossomandi School at Naples Cons., he gained a good reputation as a concert-player and teacher. Founded in Naples the Società Amici della Musica (Friends of Music). Prof. of pf. at R. Liceo Mus. di Santa Cecilia in Rome. Has comp. orch. and chambermusic.
Leggenda indiana, orch.; *Ægyptia*, orch.; sonata for vn. and pf.—D. A.

DE SABATA, Victor. Compr. *b.* at Trieste, of Ital. parents, in 1892. Is noted amongst young Ital. musicians for his opera *Il Macigno*, perf. at Scala in Milan, 1916, and for various symph. works: 2 overtures, a suite, a symph. poem *Juventus* (publ. by Ricordi, Milan), vocal works and instr. chamber-music. Is also a good conductor.—D. A.

DE SANTI, Father Angelo. Ital. writer and propagandist of sacred music; *b.* Trieste, 12 July, 1847; *d.* Rome, 28 Jan. 1922. When very young, entered Jesuit Order, and devoted himself to music, especially the teaching of singing. Called to Rome by Pope Leo XIII, he found there a vast field for propagating his ideas on reform of sacred music in Italy, and became one of most efficient collaborators of the movement started for that purpose by the priest Guerrino Amelli (q.v.). By his activities as teacher in Roman seminaries and as a writer, particularly for Jesuit review *La Civiltà Cattolica*, he exercised a very great influence, which aroused not a little opposition from those attached to the decadent and theatrical taste to which sacred music in Italy had been reduced. This reform, initiated by Pope Leo XIII, was brought to fulfilment by Pius X. De S. had not only the satisfaction of seeing his ideas triumph; he succeeded also in effecting another project of his—the foundation of the Pontificia Scuola Superiore di Musica Sacra (see ACADEMIES). He publ. a memoir on the first 10 years of its activity. In 1909, at National Congress of Sacred Music at Pisa, he was elected Gen. President of the Associazione Italiana di Santa Cecilia, and again at succeeding congress held at Turin in 1920. He publ. a very large number of historical and polemical articles on sacred music and Gregorian chant in the *Civiltà Cattolica*, in *Rassegna Gregoriana* (which he founded in 1902 together with Monsignor [now Card.] Respighi) and in other reviews.—D. A.

DESMOND, Astra (Mrs. Thomas Neame). Eng. contr. singer; *b.* Torquay, 10 April, 1893. Stud. under Blanche Marchesi; took B.A. honours classical degree at Westfield Coll. London in 1914. Has given many recitals in London and the provinces. Is a fine interpreter, particularly of the contemporary Eng. and Fr. songs.—E.-H.

DESSAU, Bernhard. Ger. violinist; *b.* Hamburg, 1 March, 1861; *d.* May 1923. Stud. under Schradieck (Hamburg and Leipzig), Joachim and Wieniawski; Konzertmeister in Görlitz, Ghent, Königsberg, Brünn, Prague and Rotterdam (where he taught at Cons.), Bremen (Philh.); has been Konzertmeister at the R. Opera, Berlin; for a time also teacher at Stern's Cons.; R. prof. 1906.

Numerous works for vn. (op. 9–16, 20; vn. concerto *In the Old Style*, op. 55), etc.—A. E.

DESTINN, Emmy (family name Kittel). *b.* Prague, 1878. Received her vocal training and her professional name from Marie Destinn-Löwe. Engaged Berlin Court Opera, 1898. After series of star performances in Prague, was granted hon. membership of Prague National Theatre, 1908. Her world-wide reputation dates from 1901. Bayreuth, Paris, London and New York are the stages of her artistic career. Whilst abroad she was a keen advocate for Smetana's operas. Now confines herself to star tours in opera and concert platform; lives on her estate in Stráž, Bohemia. Her voice is remarkable for its smooth silvery timbre and its great carrying power. A superior singing technique and dramatic plasticity are further characteristics.—V. ST.

DETT, Robert Nathaniel. Amer. compr. *b.*

Drummondville, Ontario, Canada, 11 Oct. 1882. A remarkable coloured musician, of high attainments. Graduated Niagara Falls Collegiate Inst. 1903. Early mus. education at Oliver Willis Halstead Cons., Lockport, N.Y., later at Oberlin, Ohio. Continued his studies at Columbia Univ. and elsewhere until 1915. At various times, mus. dir. of several educational insts. for coloured people—Lane Coll., Jackson, Tex. (1898–1903), Lincoln Inst., Jefferson City, Miss. (1908–11). Since 1913 has been connected with the Hampton (Va.) Inst. and dir. of its excellent Choral Union. Won the Bowdoin Prize of Harvard Univ. with an essay, *The Emancipation of Negro Music*, 1920; and the Francis Boott Prize at Harvard for a Motet on a negro theme, *Don't be Weary, Traveller*. Has comp. also *Magnolia Suite* for pf. (Summy, 1912); *Juba Dance* (*id.* 1921); many motets, negro spirituals and songs (Church; Schirmer).
—O. K.

DEUTSCH, Piet Hermann. Swiss singer; *b.* Richterswyl, Switzerland, 21 Feb. 1876. Started singing in 1907, after having stud. law and practised as lawyer in Winterthur (Switzerland). Pupil of Paul Reimers in Berlin; gave first concerts there in 1910. Since 1914 in Switzerland; soon rose to fame and became prof. at Cons. in Basle and Winterthur. A perfect musician with an admirably trained voice. Has written an important essay, *Über Stimmbildung* (Winterthur, A. Vogel).—F. H.

DE VOCHT, Louis. Belgian compr. condr. *b.* Antwerp, 21 Sept. 1887. Precentor Antwerp Cath. since 1912; dir. of *Cecilia* mixed choir; prof. of harmony, Antwerp Cons. and condr. of Nouveaux Concerts, 1921.

Avondschemering (Evening Twilight); Lentemorgen (Spring Morning); Meizangen (May Song); Ballingschap (Exile); symph. poems; choruses; songs.—E. C.

DIACK, John Michael. Scottish musical editor, *b.* Glasgow, 26 June, 1869. Manager of the publ. dept. of Paterson Sons & Co. Glasgow.

Vocal Exercises in Tone-Placing and Enunciation; Song Studies; Five Minutes Daily Exercises on Vocal Technique; arr. *New Scottish Orpheus,* Vol. I (100 songs) and *The Burns Song Book* (50 songs); Eng. transl. of Bach's *Peasant Cantata* (all Paterson).
—E.-H.

DIAGHILEF, Serge Pavlovitch (*accent on the long A*). Russ. ballet producer. Born in the government of Novgorod (Russia), 19 March, 1872. Stud. law at Univ. of Petrograd, and worked at mus. theory and singing at same time under Cotogni, Sokolof and Liadof. He began as critic of journal *Les Nouvelles* in 1897, and in that year organised the first exhibition in Petrograd of Eng. and Ger. water-colourists. The following year he arr. an exhibition of Scandinavian art. In 1899 he founded review, *Le Monde de l'Art,* which ran for 6 years, helped materially by the Emperor Nicholas II. It played a great part in the artistic and intellectual life of Russia. During the following years, D. organised numerous exhibitions in Russia and abroad. In 1904 he issued an important work on the painter Levitzky. His theatrical and mus.

activity, which was destined to be so fruitful—thanks to his organising and inspiring talents, his energy and his rich artistic culture—dates from 1907. He then came to Paris and organised a series of concerts of Russ. music in which the greatest artists from Moscow and Petrograd took part. In 1908, helped financially by the Grand Duke Vladimir, he produced at the Grand Opéra in Paris, Mussorgsky's *Boris Godunof*, with Chaliapin and the chorus of Imperial Opera from Petrograd; then, in 1909, he gave Rimsky-Korsakof's *La Pskovitaine* and the first season of Russ. ballet with Nijinsky, Pavlova, Karsavina, Fokin, etc. The following years, he effected a veritable renaissance of theatrical and choreographic art. Grouping round himself the most remarkable comprs., painters and interpreters, he produced opera and ballet-spectacles in Paris, Rome, Berlin, London, Madrid and America. The war slackened his activity without paralysing it and during recent years he has undertaken new ventures (seasons in Paris, London, Monte Carlo, Brussels, etc.).—B. DE S.

DIANOF, Antony Michaelovitch (*accent 2nd syll.*). Russ. compr. *b*. 7/19 Feb. 1882. Pupil of G. Conus, Javorsky, and Korestchenko (theory). Graduated Musico-dramatic School of Moscow Philh. in 1912. From 1920, dir. of Technicum (music school, grade II), founded in honour of Mussorgsky, in Moscow.

Lyric Fragments, vn. and pf. op. 10; pf. sonata, op. 12; 2 *Lyric Suites*, pf. op. 6; songs, op. 2, 3, 8; pf. pieces, op. 1, 4, 5, 7, 9, 11, 13, 14.—V. B.

DIAPHONY. A primitive form of harmonising a melody in parallel consecutive fourths, or even in fifths. The name has been applied to certain technical procedures in modern harmony. See art. on HARMONY.—E.-H.

DICKINSON, Clarence. Amer. compr. *b*. Lafayette, Ind., U.S.A., 7 May, 1873. Mus. training from Cutler, Wild and Weidig in Chicago. Was pupil of Singer and Reimann (organ) in Berlin, and later of Guilmant (organ), Moszkowski (pf.) and Vierne (compn.) in Paris. Founded the Mus. Art Association in Chicago and was its condr. for 3 years. A light opera, *The Medicine Man*, was produced in Chicago, 1895. In 1909, settled in New York as orgt. of the Brick Presbyterian Ch. and of Temple Emanu-El. In 1912, made prof. of ecclesiastical music at Gen. Theological Seminary, New York. Here his historical recitals and concerts with lectures attracted wide attention. Has given organ recitals in U.S.A., Canada, France, Germany and Spain. Has comp., arr., ed. and publ. many choruses, sacred and secular songs and organ music.

Storm King, symphony for organ (1920); *Historical Recital Series* (about 100 to date); author of *Technique and Art of Organ Playing* (1921); joint-author with his wife, Helena Adele Dickinson, of: *Excursions in Musical History* (1917); *Songs of the Troubadours* (1920); all publ. by H. W. Gray, New York. —O. K.

DICKINSON, Edward. Amer author, educator; *b*. West Springfield, Mass., U.S.A., 10 Oct. 1853. Stud. music at New England Cons. in Boston, 1871–2. Later, 1878–9, was an organ pupil of Eugene Thayer in Boston. After holding organ

positions in Northampton, Mass., and Springfield, Mass., became dir. of Elmira (N.Y.) Coll. of Music from 1883 to 1892. During this period he went to Europe several times and attended the lectures of Spitta at Univ. of Berlin and of W. Langhans, 1885–6, 1888–9, 1892–3. In 1893, prof. of mus. history and criticism at Oberlin (Ohio) Coll., where he did much to raise the standard of general mus. education and intelligent appreciation. Retired from active teaching in 1922.

Music in the Western Church (Scribner, 1902); *The Study of the History of Music* (id. 1905; 2nd augm. ed. 1908); *The Education of a Music-Lover* (id. 1911); *Music and the Higher Education* (id. 1915).—O. K.

DIDUR, Adam. Polish *b*. singer; *b*. Sanok, Galicia, 24 Dec. 1874. In 1892, stud. singing under Wysocki at Lemberg. In 1893, pupil of Emerich at Milan, where he sang shortly afterwards *b*.-solo in Beethoven's Ninth Symphony under Lamoureux. Began opera career in Rio de Janeiro, 1894. Then at Cairo and, for 4 years, at La Scala, Milan. From 1899–1903 at Warsaw Opera. After that, Petrograd, Moscow, London, Barcelona, Madrid, Buenos Ayres. For last 15 years, 1st b. at Metropolitan Opera, New York. Principal parts: Mephistopheles (Gounod), Mefistofele (Boito), Wotan (Wagner), Boris (Mussorgsky), Kezal (Smetana's *Bartered Bride*) Don Basilio (Rossini), Figaro (Mozart), etc. D. sings in Polish, Ital., Eng., Fr., Russ. and German.—ZD. J.

DIEPENBROCK, Alphons. Dutch compr. *b*. Amsterdam, 2 Sept. 1862; *d*. there, 5 April, 1921. Most important Dutch compr. between 1890 and 1920; self-taught; teacher of classical literature at Amsterdam Grammar School. His first compns. show Wagnerian influence; his later style is noble and original. A characteristic is its uninterrupted and continually modulating melodic flow.

Mass, male vs. and organ (1891); incidental music to Joost van den Vondel's *Gijsbrecht van Aemstel* (1896); *Te Deum*, chorus and orch. (1897); *Stabat mater dolorosa* and *Stabat mater speciosa*, unacc. chorus; *Les Elfes*, chorus (1897); *Hymne an die Nacht* (1899), s. and orch.; *Abendmahlshymne*, s. and orch.; *Die Nacht* (Hölderlin), contr. and orch.; 1902 and 1904, 2 long barit. solos with orch: *Vondels Vaart naar Agrippina* (Alberdingt Thijm), 1902, and *Im grossen Schweigen* (Nietzsche), 1904; *Hymne*, vn. and orch. (written for famous Dutch violinist Louis Zimmerman), 1905; *Hymne aan Rembrandt* (1906); music to *Marsyas* (comedy by Balthazar Verhagen), 1911; music to *Faust* (Goethe); *The Birds* (Aristophanes); *Electra* (Sophocles). Numerous songs. His works are publ. chiefly by Noske (The Hague).—W. P.

DIEREN, Bernard van. Compr. *b*. in Holland, 27 Dec. 1884. Father Dutch, mother Fr. Stud. science, but began to devote himself exclusively to music about his 20th year. In 1909, came to England as mus. correspondent to the *Nieuwe Rotterdamsche Courant* and has continued to reside in London.

His position in the musical world is somewhat paradoxical; for while his methods of expression are sufficiently novel to earn him the title of "revolutionary" from those who must needs find a label and a category for every composer, his art is too firmly based upon the best traditions of the past to win him a welcome in those circles where the term *iconoclast* is considered the highest possible compliment. The letter of his music offends neo-classicists, while its spirit repels some "ultra-moderns." Those whose conception of personal style in art demands the reappearance in each new work of the same elements that were apparent in its predecessors will certainly be baffled by the apparent multiplicity of van Dieren's methods. He has not, like Schönberg or Debussy, evolved a strictly personal system of expression only to become himself enslaved by it. He adapts his style to his conceptions, or rather each fresh conception conditions and creates its own appropriate style. Pre-eminently a contrapuntal writer whose methods are the reverse of impressionistic, his harmonic basis has become gradually simpler; and all his works reveal a concentration upon organic development and unity. The compns. of his maturity include:

Six Sketches for Piano (1911; Univ. Ed. Vienna); 4 str. 4tets (1912, 1917, 1919 and 1923 respectively, of which the 2nd was perf. at a " Sackbut " concert in London, Oct. 1920, by the Pennington Str. Quartet, and at the Donaueschingen Mus. Fest. 1922); a symphony for soli, chorus and orch., based on Chinese poems (1914); a Diaphony for chamber-orch. and barit. solo, on 3 sonnets of Shakespeare (Nos. 28, 30 and 43), and an overture to an imaginary comedy for chamber-orch. (1916; these 2 works were perf. under the compr.'s direction at a concert given in London by Cecil Gray, Feb. 1917); The Tailor, an opera buffa in 3 acts (scored for small orch.) to a libretto by Robert Nichols (1917); Les Propous des Beuveurs, introit for full orch., after Rabelais (Promenade Concerts, 1921); several songs, of which the most important are These are the Sorrows (from De Quincey's Levana) and False Friend (from Shelley's The Cenci) for v. and str. 4tet, Fair Eyes (No. 7 of Spenser's Amoretti) for v. and chamber-orch., and Verlaine's Spleen for v. and pf., and two recitations with str. 4tet—a Ballade of Villon and a Sonnet of Baudelaire. All these works, except the pf. pieces, are still in ms. Van D. has also written a book on the sculpture of Jacob Epstein (J. Lane).—P. H.

DIMA, G. Rumanian compr. *b.* 1847. Dir. of Cons. of Cluj (formerly Klausenburg). See RUMANIA in art. ACADEMIES. Has comp. many songs, religious and secular choruses, masses, etc. (Leipzig, Kahnt; Bucharest, Feder). —C. BR.

D'INDY, Vincent. See D'INDY.

DI PIETRO, Pio. Ital. compr. and teacher of singing; *b.* Rome, 3 Aug. 1862. Stud. in Rome under Eugenio Terziani. In 1889, won a competition organised by Ministry for Interior, with a Requiem Mass (soli, chorus and orch.). This Mass was performed in 1891 at Pantheon in Rome, in commemoration of King Victor Emmanuel II. Di P. is the author also of a few operas, some esteemed songs and vocal studies (Ricordi). Since 1914, prof. of singing at R. Liceo Mus. di Santa Cecilia. Some of the very best pupils have come from his school. —D. A.

DITSON COMPANY, OLIVER. The oldest of the still existing music publishing firms of America. Its founder, Oliver Ditson (*b.* Boston, 20 Oct. 1811; *d.* 21 Dec. 1888), began copyrighting and publishing under his own name in 1835. The next year, however, he joined in partnership with an older Boston publ., Samuel H.

Parker, under the name of Parker and Ditson. In 1842 Parker was bought out by Ditson who continued under his own name. In 1857 the firm became Oliver Ditson and Co., by the admission to partnership of John C. Haynes. On death of founder in 1888 the firm was incorporated with Haynes as president. In 1907, Haynes died and Charles H. Ditson, son of Oliver, became president. A New York branch, which still exists, was establ. in 1867 under name of Charles H. Ditson and Co.

The firm of Ditson has publ. various mus. periodicals. In 1858 it took over *Dwight's Journal of Music*, which it continued until 1878. This was followed immediately by *The Monthly Musical Record*, which changed its name in 1898 to *The Musical Record*. From 1903 until 1918 *The Musician* was publ. by Ditson's. Its most notable recent achievement is the publication (beginning in 1903) of an admirably selected and edited series of newer classic vocal and instr. compns. under the general title of *The Musician's Library.*

Consult William Arms Fischer, *Notes on Music in Old Boston* (Ditson, 1918).—O. K.

DI VEROLI, Manlio. Ital. pianist and compr. *b.* Rome, 12 April, 1888. Stud. pf. under Sgambati at R. Liceo Mus. di Santa Cecilia, Rome. In 1911 settled in London, where he became a well-known as accompanist at concerts. Comp. instr. pieces and songs.—D. A.

DIXTUOR A CORDES LÉO SIR. An ensemble of 10 str. instrs. created by Léo Sir, vn.-maker at Marmande (France) to constitute a complete family of str. instrs. with new timbres. Besides the four usual ones, we find: (1) the *Sursoprano* (tuned a fourth above the vn.); (2) the *Mezzosoprano* (tuned like the vn. but of the sonority of a vla.); (3) the *Contralto* or *Haute-contre* (a new timbre, and playing an octave below the written note); (4) the *Tenor* and (5) the *Baryton* (both tuned an octave below the vla.); (6) the *Sousbasse* (below the cello, tuned 2 octaves lower than the vn., and playing a fourth higher than the written note). The timbre of this last is very touching and mournful. It is the only one which appears to present a real acquisition to chamber-music. Several young comprs. (A. Honegger, Darius Milhaud, O. Ygouw) have written suites for *dixtuor.*—A. C.

DŁUSKI, Erazm. Polish compr. *b.* Podolien, 1858; *d.* Warsaw, 1922. In 1877, pupil of Sołoviev and Rimsky - Korsakof at Petrograd Cons. First prize, 1886. Remained in Petrograd till 1920, teaching theory, singing and compn. In 1920, became prof. of opera classes at Warsaw Conservatoire.

Operas: Romano, 4 acts; Urwasi, 2 acts (perf. 1902, Lemberg and Warsaw); The Bride of Corinth. Has also publ. 63 popular songs; 2 sonatas for pf. (played by Anton Rubinstein); pieces for cello; symph. works.—ZD. J.

DÖBBER, Johannes. Ger. compr. *b.* Berlin, 28 March, 1866; *d.* Berlin, 26 Jan. 1921. Pupil Stern's Cons.; concert pianist at first, then theatre orch. condr. in Berlin (Kroll), Darmstadt, Coburg and Hanover. In Berlin since 1908 as compr., teacher of singing, music critic to *Volkszeitung*.

Dolzetta; *The Blacksmith of Gretna Green* (Berlin. 1893); *The Rose of Genzano* (Gotha, 1895); *Die Grille* (Leipzig, 1897); *The Three Roses* (Coburg, 1902); *Der Zauberlehrling* (Brunswick, 1907); fairy ballet, *Der verlorene Groschen* (Hamburg, 1904); operetta, *Die Millionen-Braut* (Magdeburg, 1913). An opera, *Die Franzosenzeit* (text by Ad. Döbber after Fritz Reuter), awaits performance; also symphony, op. 34, and a great number of songs.—A. E.

DOBICI, Cesare. Ital. compr. and teacher; *b.* Viterbo, 11 Dec. 1873. A capable contrapuntist and compr. of polyphonic music. Several masses, str. 4tets, pf. pieces, songs, an unpubl. opera *Cola di Rienzo*. Teacher of harmony and fugue at R. Liceo Mus. di Santa Cecilia, Rome.—D. A.

DODECAFONIA. A tonal effect, expounded by Domenico Alaleona (*q.v.*) in his arts. on modern harmony (*Rivista Musicale Italiana*, 1911). Compare art. DODECUPLE SCALE.—E.-H.

DODECUPLE SCALE. A name invented by A. Eaglefield Hull, for a scale which divides the octave into 12 equal parts. The name is now widely adopted in European treatises. See art. on HARMONY.—G. B.

DOHNÁNYI, Ernst von (Ernő). Hungarian composer, pianist and conductor; *b.* Pozsony, Hungary (now Bratislava, annexed by Czecho-Slovakia), 27 July, 1877. Studied piano when six years old under his father (Friedrich), professor at Gymnasium; and began to compose soon after. His training was continued under the Cathedral organist, Karl Förstner. On presenting himself at the Royal High School for Music, Budapest, in 1893, he already brought with him 3 string quartets, 1 string sextet, a Mass (written for the pupils of the Gymnasium), a large number of piano pieces, and a piano quintet (perf. in Vienna, 1893, with compr. as pianist). 1893-7, studied in Budapest (composition, Hans Koessler; piano, Stefan Thomán). In summer 1897, received some instruction from Eugen d'Albert. In autumn of the same year began his travels as concert-pianist, visiting Austria, Hungary, Germany, England, North America; later, Scandinavia, France, Spain, Italy and Russia, winning success everywhere. 1905, appointed piano professor, Royal High School for Music, Berlin. Engaged thus till 1915, since which time he has lived in Budapest. From 1916 till 1919, piano professor at High School for Music, acting for a time as director. Since 1919, president and conductor of Philharmonic Society; 1922, Ph.D. *h.c.* University of Kolozsvár. His orch. Variations in F sharp mi. are in the permanent repertoire of Queen's Hall Orch. London.

Pf. 5tet, op. 1; 4 pf. pieces, op. 2; valses for pf. duet, op. 3; Variations and fugue for pf. op. 4; pf. concerto, op. 5 (Bösendorfer Prize, 1899); Passacaglia for pf. op. 6; 1st str. 4tet, op. 7 (all publ. Doblinger, Vienna); cello sonata, op. 8 (Schott); symphony, op. 9 (Schott); Serenade for vn., vla. and cello, op. 10 (Doblinger); 4 Rhapsodies for pf. op. 11 (*id.*); Concertstück, cello and orch. op. 12 (*id.*) perf. Q. H. London, with Hugo Becker as cellist; Winterreigen for pf. op. 13 (*id.*); songs with pf. op. 14 (*id.*); 2nd str. 4tet, op. 15 (Simrock); songs with pf. op. 16 (Doblinger); 5 Humoreskes for pf. op. 17 (Simrock); The Veil of Pierrette, pantomime in 3 scenes, op. 18, text by Arthur Schnitzler (Doblinger), 1st perf. Dresden,

1910; Suite for orch. op.19(Doblinger), Q. H. London, 9 Oct. 1913; Aunt Simona, 1-act comic opera, text by Victor Heindl, op. 20 (Simrock),1st perf. Dresden, 1912; sonata for vn. and pf. op. 21(Simrock); 2 songs for barit. with orch. op. 22 (*id.*), 3 pieces for pf. op. 23 (*id.*); pf. suite in olden style, op. 24 (*id.*); Variations on a child's song, for pf. and orch. op. 25 (*id.*), perf. Q. H. Symph. Concert, in 1922 with compr. at pf.; 2nd pf. 5tet op. 26 (*id.*) : vn. concerto, op. 27 (Alberti, Berlin): 6 concert studies, op. 28 (Rózsavölgyi, Budapest); Variations on a Hungarian folk-song for pf. op. 29 (*id.*). The grand opera The Castle of Woiwoden (text by H. H. Ewers), op. 30, 1st perf. Budapest, 1922, is still in ms. Fest-ouvertüre, for orch. op. 31 (ms.). At present D. is working on a comic opera, The Tenor (text by E. Goth).—E.-H.

DOHRN, Georg. Ger. condr. *b.* Bahrendorf, near Magdeburg, 23 May, 1867. Educated at Magdeburg and Leipzig, where he stud. law, also in Munich and Berlin, taking LL.D. Took up music, attending Cons. Cologne, 1891-5. First engagement Munich (Korrepetitor Court Opera, 1897); Flensburg (condr. Stadttheater); Weimar (deputy assistant condr. 1898); Munich (assistant dir. Kaim Orch.); now dir. Orch. Soc. and Acad. of Singing in Breslau (1901).—A. E.

D'OISLY, Maurice. Operatic t. singer; *b.* Tunbridge Wells, Kent, 2 Nov. 1882. Stud. under Maurice Noël at Blois; and at R.A.M. under Tobias Matthay (pf.), Fred. King (singing); *début* Covent Garden 1909 as David in Die Meistersinger; appeared there 1910–11–12 seasons; principal t. Quinlan Opera Co. worldtour (1913–14); favourite part Rudolfo (La Bohème). Married (1920) Rosina Buckman, operatic soprano.—E.-H.

DOLCI, Alessandro. Ital. t. singer; *b.* Bergamo in 1888. Capable dramatic t., known in Italy and America. One of his best interpretations is that of Rossini's *Mosè*.—D. A.

DOLEŽIL, Method. See CZECHO-SLOVAKIA in art. CHORAL SOCIETIES.

DOLMETSCH, Arnold. Fr. expert on old instrs. and their music; *b.* Le Mans, 1858. Stud. vn. under Vieuxtemps in Brussels, also at R.C.M. London; then became a teacher, Dulwich Coll. London; became interested in old instrs., collected and repaired them and learned to play them; was at Chickering factory in Boston, U.S.A., 1902–9; had a department in Gaveau factory, Paris, 1911–14; returned to London 1914; has installed a workshop at Haslemere, Surrey.

Select English Songs and Dialogues of XVI and XVII Centuries (2 books, Boosey, 1912); The Interpretation of the Music of the XVII and XVIII Centuries (Novello, 1915).—E.-H.

DOLMETSCH, Hélène. Fr. cellist and viol-da-gamba player; *b.* Nancy, 14 April, 1880. Stud. in London and in Germany; *début* 1887 as child-cellist.—E.-H.

DOŁZYCKI, Adam (*phon.* Doljitski). Polish condr. *b.* Lemberg, 1886. Stud. first at Lemberg Cons.; then in Berlin. In 1912, worked at Warsaw Opera; 1915–17, in Russia; then again at Warsaw, and in 1919 became dir. of opera at Posen (Poland). Resigned this post, Feb. 1922. Distinguished by an extraordinary temperament and the greatest refinement. Is equally brilliant both in opera and symphony.—ZD. J.

DOMANIEWSKI, Bolesław. Polish pianist and teacher; *b.* Gronowek, 1857. Stud. under Lorer and Jozef Wieniawski at Warsaw Cons.; then at Petrograd under Liadof and Solovief. 1878–1887, travelled as pf.-virtuoso; then for over 10 years prof. Cracow Cons. In 1900, went to Warsaw, where he teaches at the school of the Music Soc., of which he became dir. in 1906. Has publ. a few pf. pieces.—ZD. J.

DOMSELAER, Jacob van. Dutch compr. *b.* Nijkerk (Veluwe), 15 April, 1890. Pupil of Joh. Wagenaar. Comp. (1913–16) *Proeven van Stijlkunst* (modern harmonic studies) for pf. (publ. De Nieuwe Kring, Amsterdam); (1916–22) 6 sonatas for pf.; also a symphony (ms.).—W. P.

DONALDA, Pauline (real name, Lightstone). Canadian operatic and lyric s. singer; *b.* Montreal, 5 March, 1884. Stud R. Victoria Coll. there; won Strathcona Scholarship of Montreal; stud. under Edmond Duvernoy at Paris Cons.; *début* at Nice, 30 Dec. 1904 (title-rôle in *Manon*); then at Théâtre de la Monnaie, Brussels; R. Opera, Covent Garden; Manhattan, New York (*début* there, May 1905, Micaela in *Carmen*); Opéra-Comique, Paris, 1907, etc. In addition, has toured nearly all the European countries. —E.-H.

DONAUDY, Stefano. Ital. compr. *b.* Palermo, 21 Feb. 1879. Known for his operas *Sperduti nel buio* (Palermo, '1907), *Ramuntcho* (Milan, 1921), and *La Fiamminga* (Naples, 1922); also for some vocal and instr. chamber-pieces, all publ. by Ricordi, Milan.—D. A.

DONAUESCHINGEN FESTIVAL. The castle-residence of the Princes of Fürstenberg in the Black Forest has ancient and celebrated mus. traditions. Chamber - music fests. have been held there annually in Aug. since 1921 under the patronage of the prince, for encouragement of contemporary music.—A. E.

DONIZETTI, Alfredo. Compr. *b.* Smyrna in 1867. Stud. at Cons. of Milan. His first work, *Nama*, 1-act opera, was given at Philodramatic Theatre, Milan, obtaining a great success. His symph. works were given at Ital. orch. concerts in Berlin. In 1896, obtained a greater success with his 1-act opera, *Dopo l' Ave Maria*, produced in Milan and many other towns in Italy. Went to Mexico, Havana and Brazil as orch. condr. and to Buenos Ayres in 1901. Then returned to Europe; cond. in Vienna, Egypt, London, Italy. In 1906, returned to Argentina and establ. the Cons. Donizetti at Rosario. His *Nozze delle Tindáridi* for children's vs. obtained diploma of honour at Rome Exhibition.—A. M.

DONOSTÍA, Fray José Antonio de. Span. musician and folk-lorist of Basque nationalist group. Author of *Euskel Eres-Sorta*, a work on Basque folk-music, awarded a prize in 1912. Member of the Capuchin Order. Publ. Unión Musical Española, Madrid.—P. G. M.

DOPPER, Cornelis. Dutch compr. *b.* Stadskanaal (Friesland), 7 Feb. 1870. Self-taught for the greater part; stud. some years at Leipzig Cons.; chorus-master; opera-condr.; travelled

for 2 years in U.S.A. and Canada; from 1908, 2nd condr. Concertgebouw Orch. Amsterdam. His compositions are well known in Holland.

4 operas: *The Blind Girl of Castell-Cuillé; Frithjof; Het Eerekruis* (perf. Amsterdam, 1894, 1896 and 1910); *William Ratcliff* (perf. Weimar, 1912). 7 symphonies, very often perf. Concertgebouw, Amsterdam, under Mengelberg (No. 5, choral symphony on 1st book of Homer's *Iliad*, perf. 1916; No. 6, *Amsterdam* —very often played—also in Berlin under R. Strauss, 1918, and in San Francisco, 1920; No. 7, *Zuiderzee*, (1st perf. 1919); concerto, cello and orch. (introduced by Gérard Hekking); concerto for 3 tpi., tpt. and orch., very often played, Amsterdam; 2 overtures, *Paäns*, 1918: *Chaconna gothica* (1920), played Amsterdam and New York. Many choral songs and works for children's vs. and orch. Numerous songs; chamber-music, pf. pieces; sonatas for pf. and vn.; pf. and cello; a str. 4tet (1st prize of Toonkunst 1914, but never perf.). D. is now (1922) at work on his 8th ymphony and a rhapsody, *Paris*.—W. P.

DORET, Gustave. Swiss compr. *b.* Aigle, 20 Sept. 1866. First stud. medicine; soon took up music entirely; stud. at Paris Cons. 1888, under Dubois and Massenet (compn.) and Marsick (vn.); 1893–4, cond. Concerts d'Harcourt and Concerts de la Société Nationale de Musique in Paris. Now lives in Switzerland (Lausanne), where he ranks amongst best Swiss comprs. of our day. His compns. show relationship with the Fr. school, but possess a distinctly personal style. Extremely melodious, poetically conceived and finely orchestrated, his works are greatly appreciated in France, Italy and Switzerland. Is also a well-known essayist, whose books on music and musicians are widely circulated.

Oratorio, *Les Sept Paroles du Christ* (Paris, Rouart); 2 *Festspiele*, *La Fête des vignerons* (1905), *Le Peuple Vaudois* (Lausanne, Fœtisch); cantata, *Voix de la Patrie* (*id.*); operas: *Les Armaillis*, *drame alpestre* (Paris, Choudens); *Le Nain de Hasli* (Fœtisch); *La Tisseuse d'Orties; Loÿs* (*drame lyrique*); incidental music to *Tell* and *La Nuit des Quatre-temps* from Morax (Fœtisch); *Julius Cæsar* (Shakespeare) and *Aliénor* (Rouart). Choruses and songs, partly coll. in *Chansons, airs, couleurs du temps* (Rouart) and *Ailleurs et jadis* (Fœtisch).—F. H.

DOUŠA, Karel. Czech compr. *b.* Zlonice, 1876. Stud. Prague Cons.; prof. there; choirmaster, St. Veit's Cathedral, Prague. Comp. church music; pf. pieces; songs.—V. ST.

DRAESEKE, Felix. Ger. compr. *b.* Coburg, 7 Oct. 1835; *d.* Dresden, 26 Feb. 1913. Pupil Leipzig Cons., especially of Rietz (compn.); first lived in Leipzig, Berlin and Dresden. Adherent of Liszt in Weimar and friend of H. v. Bülow. Teacher Lausanne Cons. 1864–74, with a break, 1868–9, undertaking in the latter year a long tour in France, Spain and Italy. After a stay in Geneva, moved to Dresden, 1876, where he succeeded Wüllner as teacher of compn. at Cons. 1884; prof. 1892; 1898, Hofrat; 1906, Geheimer Hofrat; 1912, Ph.D. *h.c.* of Berlin Univ. From a partisan at first of the "New German School," he later developed into an opponent.

4 symphonies: op. 12, G ma.; op. 25, F ma.; op. 40, C mi. (*S. tragica*) and E mi. (*S. comica*); *Serenade* for orch. op. 49, D ma. (1912); symph. prelude to *Das Leben ein Traum*, op. 45, and *Penthesilea*, op. 50; *Jubilee Overture* (1898); *Funeral March*, op. 79; 3 str. 4tets, C mi., E mi. and C sharp mi.; pf. concerto, op. 36; pf. 5tet, op. 48 with horn; 2 str. 5tets (one, the *Stelzner Quintet* with vla., remained in ms., the other, op. 77, with 2 cellos, publ. Simrock); clar. sonata, op. 38; cello sonata, op. 51; pf. sonata, op. 6; smaller pf. pieces (op. 14 *Twilight Dreams*; op. 21

What the Swallow Sang; op. 43 *Looking Back*; op. 44 *The Setting Sun*); also some in legato style (*Ghaselen*, op. 13; fugue, op. 15; canons for 2 hands, op. 37; canons for 4 hands, op. 37, 42); also large vocal works: op. 60, Mass in F sharp ma.; op. 85, *Missa a cappella*; op. 22, *Requiem*, B mi.; op. 30, *Advent Hymn* for soli, chorus and orch.; op. 60, mystery play *Christus* (Prologue [*The Lord's Birth*] and three oratorios [I. *Dedication of Christ*, II. *Christ the Prophet*, III. *The Lord's Death and Victory*], publ. 1905); op. 39, Easter Scene from *Faust* (for barit. solo, orch. and mixed chorus); op. 52, cantata *Columbus* (solo, mixed chorus and orch.). Many songs and ballads, *Pausanias* (barit. and orch.). Male, female and mixed chorales: *Salvum fac regem*, 4-v. op. 55; *Psalm XCIII*, for 6, 4 and 8 v., op. 56; Offertory, 4-v., and graduals for 6, 5 and 4 v., op. 57; also operas *Gudrun* (Hanover, 1884); *Herral* (Dresden, 1892); fragments of an older opera *Sigurd*, given at Meiningen, 1867. As ms. there remained: 3-act opera, *Bertrand de Born*; 1-act, *Fisher and Caliph*; *Merlin* (upon Immermann's myth, produced in Gotha, 1913), and an orch. piece *Der Thuner See*. Theoretical works: *Directions for Artistic Modulation* (1876); *The Removal of the Tritone* (1878); *Humorous Lecture on Harmony, in Verse* (1884, 2nd ed. 1892); *Der gebundene Stil*, text-book on counterpoint and fugue (1902, 2 vols.), and a polemic, *Confusion in Music* (1907).—A. E.

DRĂGULINESCU-STINGHE. See RUMANIAN OPERA.

DRAMATURG. A special member of the staff in a Ger. theatre who, amongst other things, chooses the plays, acts as literary adviser, reads mss., and frequently co-operates with, and advises the producer in actual rehearsal. —W. H. K.

DRANGOSCH, Ernesto. Argentine pianist; *b.* Buenos Ayres in 1862. Stud. at Buenos Ayres Cons.; afterwards in Berlin under Bruch and Humperdinck. Gave several concerts there (playing at Philh. Concerts) and also at Stettin. In 1905, became prof. at Buenos Ayres Cons. An enthusiastic supporter of music of his native land.

Pf. concerto; a sonata; 2 Spanish Sonatas; Fantasia, and many pf. pieces and studies; 2 sets of songs (Ger. words).—A. M.

DRDLA, Frans. Hungarian violinist; compr. *b.* Saar, 28 Sept. 1868. Stud. under Hellmesberger at Vienna Cons.; in Vienna Opera orch. 3 years; then leader of orch. Theater an der Wien; then condr. Carl Theatre; then concert tours. Now lives in New York.

Many vn. pieces and songs (Schott, etc.).—E.-H.

DRESDEN, Sem. Dutch compr. condr. and pianist; *b.* Amsterdam, 20 April, 1881. Stud. harmony under Bernard Zweers (Amsterdam) and Pfitzner (Berlin). 1905–14, choirmaster at Laren, Amsterdam and Tiel; 1914, founded the Madrigaalvereeniging *a cappella* choir of 9 solosingers (see CHORAL SOCIETIES). From 1915 has lectured on mus. subjects in Holland and Belgium; 1918, founded (with Daniel Ruyneman and Henri Zagwijn) the Soc. of Modern Dutch Composers (now defunct); 1921, lectured at Art Congress, Paris; 1919, teacher of compn. Amsterdam Cons. Writes for many periodicals. Wrote an extensive brochure, *Het muziekleven in Nederland sinds 1880* (*Dutch Music since 1880*) (Amsterdam, 1923). The most authoritative pioneer of modern Dutch music. His later style, in the sonata for fl. and harp and 3rd sextet, is both original and progressive.

Sonata, vn. and pf. (Carl Flesch, violinist, and the compr., Amsterdam, 1905); 6tet for str. and pf.

(perf. June, 1911, Amsterdam); 3 6tets for wind instrs. and pf. (perf. 1912, 1914, Amsterdam); trio for 2 ob. and c. a. (1912, Amsterdam); *Duo* for 2 pf. (perf. 31 Jan. 1914, Amsterdam, Sisters Roll); Variations for full orch. (perf. 29 March, 1914, Concertgebouw Orch., Amsterdam, under Willem Mengelberg); sonata, cello and pf., perf. Jan. 11, 1918, Arnhem, Thomas Canivez and the compr. (Paris, Senart); sonata, fl. and harp, perf. 6 Nov. 1918, The Hague, Rosa Spier and Klasen (Paris, Senart); *Wachterlied*, unacc. chorus, perf. 27 Oct. 1919, Amsterdam, Madrigaalvereeniging (The Hague, Noske); 2 songs with pf. or orch. (The Hague, Noske); songs with pf., and pf. pieces (Noske). Now working on Suite for full orchestra.

Consult Arthur Petronio, *Un Compositeur Moderne* (*De Kroniek*, Dec. 1918), and in *La Revue Musicale* (Paris, Jan. 1922).—W. P.

DROZDOWSKI, Jan. Polish pf.-teacher; *b.* Cracow, 1857; *d.* in 1916. Began mus. studies under Płachecki at Cracow; then under Dachs, Epstein and Anton Bruckner at Vienna Cons. 1889, became prof. Cracow Cons. Remained in this post till end of his life. Publ. practical works on pf. pedagogy, in which he developed his own observations, based on physiological facts:

Preparatory Exercises for Piano-playing (Polish, 1886); *Systematic School of Piano Technique* (Polish and Ger.; 2nd ed. 1899, Munich (under pseudonym of Jan Jordan); a *General Music Instruction* (1897), and a popular *History of Music* (2nd ed. 1913). —ZD. J.

DRYSDALE, Learmont. Scottish compr. *b.* Edinburgh, 3 Oct. 1866; *d.* there 18 June, 1909. One of most representative Scottish comprs. He could trace his lineage on both sides back to early Middle Ages. His mother, a Learmont who claimed descent from Scottish poet and seer of XIII century, Sir Thomas Learmont of Ercildoune, better known as " Thomas the Rhymer," was a lady of the old school, who had always at her command a perfect mine of old Scots songs and fairy-tales, and she it was who constituted the greatest formative influence upon his life. D. was educated at Edinburgh R. High School, and for some years after leaving it, stud. architecture. During this period he was orgt. in Greenside Parish Ch. At Edinburgh Industrial Exhibition of 1886 he gave organ recitals, and in 1887 became sub-orgt. of All Saints', Kensington, when he finally abandoned architecture, and took up music. In Sept. 1888, entered R.A.M. London, taking compn. and pf. as his principal subjects. He also stud. most of the orch. instrs. His first orch. work, *The Spirit of the Glen*, was successfully perf. in St. James's Hall, in 1889. In his 2nd year at R.A.M. he won Charles Lucas Medal with an overture to a comedy, which he wrote in 4 days. With another concert-overture, written in less than a week, he won prize of 30 guineas offered by Glasgow Soc. of Musicians, 1890. This was the famous *Tam o' Shanter* which under August Manns had quite a vogue, both in Glasgow and London. A dramatic cantata, *The Kelpie*, followed (perf. Dec. 1894, at a Paterson Orch. Concert in Edinburgh, by the late Mr. Kirkhope's choir and the Scottish Orch.). This was succeeded by several cantatas, operas, and orch. pieces, all of them more or less permeated with Scottish idiom. For one season (1906–7), was condr. of famous Glasgow Select Choir for which he comp. 2 choral ballads. He collab. with late Duke of Argyll in an ode, and an opera, *Fionn and Tera*; comp. and arr. many Scottish songs; mus. ed. of well-known Dunedin Coll. Most of his best work (including 10 operas) remains unpubl., and many of his most important mss. have been lost trace of. The Kelpie, dramatic cantata; *Tamlane*, chorus and orch.; *Barbara Allan*, choral ballad; many pf. pieces; songs; arrangements.—W. S.

DRZEWIECKI, Zbigniew (*phon.* Jevyelski). Polish pianist; *b.* Warsaw, 8 April, 1890. Began study under his father; then stud. under Oberfeldt and Pilecki at Warsaw. After matriculation, went to Vienna, where he remained 1909–1914, studying under Mme. Prentner, assistant of Leschetizky. In 1916, became prof. of advanced pf.-classes at Warsaw Cons. Has given many recitals in Polish towns, in Vienna, Prague and Berlin.—ZD. J.

DU BOIS, Léon. Belgian compr. *b.* Brussels, 9 Jan. 1859. Stud. at Brussels Cons. under Mailly (organ), J. Dupont (harmony), F. Kufferath (cpt.) and Gevaert (compn.). *Prix de Rome*, 1885. Leader of orch. in Nantes theatre (1889–90); also at La Monnaie Theatre (1890–1891), Liège (1891–2), Brussels (1892–7). Principal of École de Musique, Louvain, 1899; succeeded Tinel as principal of Brussels Cons. 1912. His music is related to the Walloon school, showing only a slight tendency towards the Modernist school. Most characteristic is *Le Mort*, a mimodrama (based on celebrated novel of Lemonnier, written in a mus. form rarely cultivated).
Operas: *Son Excellence ma femme*, 1884; *La Revanche de Sganarelle*, comic opera (Nantes, 1890); *Smylis*, ballet (Brussels, 1891); *Le Mort*, mimodrama (*id.* 1894); *Edénie*, lyrical tragedy (Antwerp, 1912); *Vers la Gloire*, dramatic ode (Brussels, 1919). *L'Aveugle-né*, oratorio (1922), male vs.; songs, etc. —E. C.

DUBOIS, Théodore. Fr. compr. *b.* Rosnay, 24 Aug. 1837; *d.* Paris, June 1924. Two years younger than Saint-Saëns, he stud. at Rheims; then at Paris Cons.; *Prix de Rome*, 1861; then orgt. of Ste.-Clotilde and of Madeleine. At Cons. he occupied post of prof. of harmony, then of compn.; became finally dir. (1895–1905) in succession to Ambroise Thomas. He is known chiefly by his completion of the Harmony Course of Reber; but his orch. and dramatic works are numerous. The correctness of their style is irreproachable. It is excellent professorial music.
Opéras-comiques: *La Guzla de l'émir* (1873); *La Lilloise ou le Pain bis* (1879); *Xavière* (1895). Operas: *Aben Hamet* (1884); *Fritjof* (1892). Ballets: *L'Enlèvement de Proserpine*; *La Farandole* (1893). Oratorios: *Les Sept Paroles du Christ*; *Le Paradis perdu*. Orch.: *Adonis*; *Notre-Dame de la Mer*; *Symphonie française*. Pf. pieces; songs; masses, etc.—A. C.

DUCASSE. See ROGER-DUCASSE.

DUDA. See HUNGARIAN MUS. INSTRS.

DUKAS, Paul. Fr. composer; *b.* Paris, 1 Oct. 1865. He studied at the Conservatoire under Guiraud; gained a 2nd *Prix de Rome*, 1888. Produced (Lamoureux Concerts) an Overture for Corneille's *Polyeucte* in which he depicts the agony and triumph of the martyr. It shows evidences of the influence of Wagner who at that time fascinated the young musicians of Europe. Dukas, however, understood the dangers of the Wagnerian cult and submitted himself to the rigour of classical form. In 1896 he composed his symphony in C, then a sonata in E flat, of gigantic proportions. At this period he reached the zenith of his powers, producing his dazzling symphonic scherzo on Goethe's ballad, *L'Apprenti Sorcier* (1897). For 10 years after this he devoted himself to his lyrical drama *Ariane et Barbe-Bleue* (Opéra-Comique, 1907). This work shares with Debussy's *Pelléas* the honour of ranking as the masterpiece of contemporary French opera. But the conception of Dukas is very different from that of Debussy. There is no longer a perfect balance between music and poetry (as in Debussy)— here music resolutely usurps the first place. Each act is constructed symphonically, like a grand finale of Mozart. The melodic ideas, of a rare plastic beauty, are developed as the drama progresses, according to the method of variations peculiar to Dukas, excellently exemplified in his *Variations, Interlude et Finale* for piano on a theme of Rameau (1903).

In 1911, Dukas published *La Péri*, a ballet interpreted in 1912 by Mlle. Trouhanowa at the Châtelet Theatre. It is not a ballet, but a symphonic poem. The music creates around the mime an atmosphere of voluptuous languor. The conclusion, which expresses the distress of the Hero in the face of Night and Death who surround him, is profoundly moving.

Besides these great works, he published practically nothing except a charming *Villanelle* for horn (1906), and a very beautiful pianoforte composition *La Plainte au loin du Faune* for the *Tombeau de Debussy* (published by *Revue Musicale*, 1920). For some years he has been working on a great symphony in 3 parts on Shakespeare's *Tempest*. He is also engaged in revising the works of Rameau and Scarlatti (Durand) and has shown himself an able critic in the *Revue Hebdomadaire* and the *Gazette des Beaux Arts*, and, after an interruption of 20 years, in the *Revue Musicale and* the *Quotidien*. He has become more and more exacting as far as his own composition is concerned. Always discontented with what he has written, he only consents to give it to the public when he realises that he is incapable of making it more perfect. This conscientiousness and honesty in his art have made of Dukas one of the noblest figures in contemporary music. He has never sought official honours or popularity. He lives a solitary life, surrounded by a small circle of affectionate and devoted friends, avoiding salons, coteries, and concert-halls. He has never begrudged either his advice or his services to those who may appeal to him. One can hardly judge the degree to which Albeniz is indebted to him—Dukas was certainly the mentor to his budding genius. Dukas' influence on the modern school is great, because his works have revealed to them the rarest secrets of instrumentation. His music is dazzling; the most delicate tones and the rarest shades are contrasted with vigorous and warm brush-work—it is an irresistible wizardry of colour. But he is also a great artist who knows how to create in the hearts of his audience that delightful unrest, that total abandonment to music's sway, which is the hall-mark of real creative genius. Consult Samazeuilh's *Dukas* (Durand), O. Séré (*q.v.*) and A. Cœuroy (*q.v.*). —H. P.

DUMAS, Louis. Fr. compr. *b.* Paris, 1877. Pupil of Leroux, Caussade and Lenepveu; *Prix de Rome*, 1906, with cantata *Ismail.* Since 1919, dir. of Cons. at Dijon. Since 1920, orch. condr. of Concert Soc. of Dijon Conservatoire.

Symphonie romaine (orch.); overture and incidental music to *Stellus*; *La Vision de Mona* (2-act opera); fantasia, pf. and vn.; sonata, pf. and vn.; str. 4tet.—A. C.

DUNHILL, Thomas Frederick. Eng. compr. *b.* Hampstead, London, 1 Feb. 1877. Entered R C.M. London, in 1893 (pf. under Franklin Taylor, compn. under Sir Charles Stanford). Won open scholarship for compn. in 1897; for several years a music-master at Eton Coll.; prof. at R.C.M. in 1905; gave concerts of chamber-music, The Thomas Dunhill Concerts, in London for 12 years from 1907, at which prominent chamber-music by British comprs. was perf. He has written fine chamber-music and some widely-known songs; his music is pleasant and opti-mistic, always scholarly, and frequently on educational lines; he gave a concert of music by British comprs. in Belgrade in 1922; and has contributed several arts. on Serbian musicians to this Dictionary.

Orch.: *The Wind among the Reeds,* t. v. and orch. (Stainer & Bell) (1st perf. by Gervase Elwes, R. Philh. 1912); overture, *The King's Threshold*; Dance Suite for str. (Curwen) (perf. Promenades, Queen's Hall); Variations on an old English tune, cello and orch. (Goodwin & Tabb) (produced by May Mukle, Queen's Hall); *The Chiddingfold Suite,* str. orch. (Novello); Elegiac Variations, in memory of Parry (ms.) (Gloucester Fest. 1922); symphony in A mi. (ms.) (produced under compr., Belgrade, Serbia, 28 Dec. 1922). Chamber-music: 4tet in B mi., pf. and str. (Novello); 5tet in E flat, pf., wind and str. (Rudall, Carte); Phantasy-trio, pf. vn. and vla. (Stainer & Bell); Phantasy str. 4tet (Cramer); sonatas, vn. and pf.: No. 1 in D (Stainer & Bell); No. 2 in F (Augener); numerous songs and part-songs; 3 children's cantatas (*John Gilpin; Sea Fairies; The Masque of the Shoe*; all publ. Year-Book Press); many pf. pieces, mostly for children (J. Williams; Lengnick; Curwen; Anglo-Fr. Co.; Ashdown; Augener, etc.); pieces for vn.; for cello, etc.; a book, *Chamber Music,* for students (1913, Macmillan).—E.-H.

DUNN, John. Eng. violinist; *b.* Hull, 10 Feb. 1866. Started playing at 8; stud. Leipzig Cons. when 12; after 3 years there under Henry Schradieck and others, appeared at age of 16 at Promenade concerts, Covent Garden. Intro-duced Gade's concerto at Crystal Palace in 1887; first to play Tchaikovsky's concerto in London (1900); first Eng. player to perf. Elgar's concerto (Queen's Hall, London, spring 1911). D. has a fine tone, a superlative technique, and is gener-ally regarded as one of the finest violinists Eng-land has produced.

Soliloquy, vn. and pf. (Hawkes); *Berceuse,* vn. and pf. (Schott); sonatina in D, pf. (Lengnick); manual, *Vn. Playing* (Strad Library, 2 Duncan St. E.C.). —E.-H.

DUNN, John Petrie. Scottish pianist and author; *b.* Edinburgh, 26 Oct, 1878. Stud. theory under F. Niecks at Univ. of Edinburgh; awarded Bucher Scholarship in 1899; pupil of Max Pauer and S. de Lange at Stuttgart Cons.; 1902, teacher of pf. there; 1909–14, principal pianist and latterly vice-dir. of Cons. of Kiel; 1920, appointed lecturer on music at Univ. of Edin-burgh. Numerous concert-tours, including one with Kubelik in West Germany. Educational works: *Das Geheimnis der Handführung beim Klavierspiel* (Leipzig, Kahnt); *Ornamentation in the Works of Frederick Chopin* (London, Novello). Has contributed some of the Scottish articles to this Dictionary.—E.-H.

DUNSTAN, Ralph. Eng. writer and compr. *b.* Carnon Downs, Truro, 17 Nov. 1857. Self-taught; Mus.Doc. Cantab. 1892; has done valuable work in spreading sight-singing; as a compr. adheres mainly to the older classical methods.

Services; anthems; school cantatas; school songs, etc. (various publs.); 21 polyphonic settings of plainsong masses; *Missa de Angelis* for female vs. (Curwen). Treatises and textbooks: *Basses and Melodies* (Novello); *Diatonic Modal Counterpoint* (id.); *A Manual of Music* (13rd ed. 1918); *Cyclo-pædic Dict. of Music*; *Composer's Handbook*; *Organ-ist's First Book*; *ABC of Musical Theory*; *Voice Production Exercises*; *First Steps in Harmony* (all Curwen). *Sight-Singing through Song* (6 books, harmonised ed., and Cape Union Ed. with 200 additional songs); *Modern Music Reader* (4 books) (all Schofield & Sims, Huddersfield).—E.-H.

DUPARC, Henri Fouques. Fr. compr. *b.* Paris, 21 Jan. 1848. One of the best pupils of César Franck; mingled, at an early age, in Fr. mus. life. Closely connected with almost all the musicians of his generation; contributed to foundation of Société Nationale de Musique; but from 1855 his health obliged him to abandon mus. compn. He is celebrated for his songs (16 in number), written 1868–77, in his early youth. They illustrate clearly César Franck's saying of Duparc, that he was the best-organised of his generation as "discoverer of musical ideas." The songs have made a name through their musical virtues alone.

Songs: *La Romance de Mignon*; *Sérénade*; *Extase*; *Soupir*; *L'Invitation au voyage*; *La Vague et la Cloche*; *Le Manoir de Rosamonde*; *Phidylé*; *Lamento*; *Élégie*; *La Vie antérieure*; *Au pays où se fait la guerre*; *Galop*; *Sérénade florentine*; *Testament*; *Chan-son triste.* Other works: Symph. poem (Wagnerian), *Lénore* (1875); *Aux étoiles* (short nocturne for orch.); *Feuilles volants* (pf.). Duparc has destroyed a sonata for pf. and cello, a *Poème nocturne,* and a suite of *Ländler* for orch. (Publ. Rouart, Lerolle; Demets.) Consult O. Séré, *Musiciens français d'aujourd'hui* (*Mercure de France*); A. Cœuroy (*q.v.*).—A. C.

DUPÉRIER, Jean. Swiss compr. *b.* Geneva, 1896. Stud. compn. at Cons. Geneva, where he teaches harmony. His works show influence of modern Fr. school by their sensitiveness and form, but are full of original ideas.

Vn. sonata (Paris, Ed. Mutuelle); *Le Mignard Luth,* v. and pf. (Paris, Demets); *3 Sonnets pour Hélène,* s. and orch. (Geneva, Henn); *Musique à deux sous,* suite for small orch. and pf. (id.); *Concert pour Ninette ou Ninon,* full orch. (id.); *Concert pour le mois de Marie,* full orch.; *Concert pour le Roi,* full orchestra.—F. H.

DUPIN, Paul. Fr. compr. *b.* Roubaix, 14 Aug. 1865. Son of a musician of Ypres and of a poetess of Rennes; pupil at Coll. Roubaix 1873-1876; at Inst. Mell-lès-Gand, Belgium, 1876–81; at *Arts et Métiers*, Tournai (1882–85). There he took up work with a builder. In Aug. 1887, set out for Paris, where he worked alone, studying the treatises of Bazin, Reber and Gevaert. Driven by need, was an accountant from 1894 to 1911, when he was enabled by friends to give his whole time to mus. study. The music of Dupin strikes popular taste. It is free, and flows from the fountain-head; it does not ally itself to any school. His production is extremely abundant, but few works are published.

Canons (370, 3- to 12-v., partly publ. by Durand, Paris); 40 *Poèmes*, str. 4tet; sonata, pf. and vn.; sonata, sonatina, pf.; *Esquisses fuguées*; lyrical stage-piece, *Marcelle* (4-act); a *Symphonie populaire* (dedicated to King and Queen of the Belgians). Consult: André Cœuroy, *La Musique français moderne*; Ch. Kœchlin, *Dupin* in *Revue Musicale*, Jan. 1923.—E. C.

DUPONT, Auguste. Belgian compr. pianist; *b.* Ensival, 9 Feb. 1827; *d.* Brussels, 17 Dec. 1890. Stud. under father, orgt. at Ensival; entered Liège Cons. 1838 (pf. under Jalheau). Concert tours in foreign countries; but his inclination drew him to teaching. In 1852, prof. for pf. Brussels Cons. (together with Mme. Pleyel). At first in charge of men's course, but when Brassin was appointed (1869), D. became prof. of ladies' course. He carried out his duties with passionate zeal for 30 years, and considerably influenced Belgian school of pianists. His pf. compns. are to-day somewhat out-moded, as belonging to Romantic school; but are well written and reveal an exceptional melodic gift. The *Chanson de jeune fille, Chanson hongroise, Toccata, Marche nocturne*, enjoyed a long popularity. His ed. of the classics (with Gevaert and Sandré) is excellent.

Cromwell, opera (unfinished); *Brussels R. Cons. Pf. Tutor* (Leipzig, Breitkopf); 4 concertos (best-known, F mi.); Polonaise, pf. and orch.; *Rondes ardennaises*, pf. duets; *Fantaisies concertantes*; studies; pf. pieces; songs.—E. C.

DUPONT, Gabriel. French composer; *b.* 1878; *d.* 1914. His destiny was tragic. When quite young he tasted success and artistic fame, when his first opera *La Cabrera* carried off the Sonzogno Prize in Italy. But then the lung disease which was to cause his death made its appearance. From that time he waged a desperate battle against death. Gabriel Dupont who in *La Cabrera* (Milan, 1904) and once more in *La Glu* (Cannes, 1910), showed himself above all pre-occupied with external effects, retired within himself. He wrote a collection of piano pieces, *Les Heures dolentes*, where he clearly showed his obsession about the death which prowled around him. He scored four of these and had them performed at the Concert Colonne, where they were hissed on account of their daring experiments in instrumentation. A symphonic poem, *Le Chant de la Destinée*, was not much better received by the public at large. His health improving, he wrote a comic opera, the *Farce du Cuvier* (Brussels, 1912), but soon the malady reappeared. He then composed *Antar*, an opera into which he put all

his heart. He dreamt of seeing it produced, but in August, 1914, the war interrupted the rehearsals. Completely crushed, Dupont resigned himself to die. *Antar* was produced in 1921 with real success. It is a courageous, brilliant, sumptuous work, full of life and colour. It has the defects of its species of opera, but it may be said that it is perhaps the best modern "*opéra*" produced in France since *Samson et Dalila*.—H. P.

DUPONT, Joseph. Belgian condr. *b.* Ensival, 3 Jan. 1838; *d.* Brussels, 21 Dec. 1899. Brother of Auguste Dupont. Stud. at Liège and Brussels Cons. *Prix de Rome*, 1863; at once took up conducting; engaged with an Ital. opera company, which he dir. in Warsaw, 1867, and at Imperial Theatre, Moscow, 1871. Returned to Brussels, 1872, prof. of harmony at Cons. and condr. at La Monnaie Theatre. 1872–6, cond. under successive dir. of Avrillon, Campotasto, Stoumon and Calabresi; dir. of La Monnaie, 1886–9 (with Lapissida), retaining his position of condr. Followed Vieuxtemps as condr. of Concerts Populaires (1873 till death, 26 years in all). Cond. concerts of Association des Artistes Musiciens; was engaged for several seasons at Covent Garden, London. If as a condr. he was not gifted with exceptional talent or marked personality, he had experience, and enjoyed a great prestige. In Belgium he was the most active propagandist of Wagner's works. In 1873 he cond. at La Monnaie the 1st perf. (after its set-back in Paris, 1861) of Fr. version of *Tannhäuser*, and in (1885) of *Master-singers*. He organised (1887) 1st perf. of *Valkyrie* on Bayreuth lines (darkened house, submerged orch.) which created an enormous sensation. His success at the Concerts Populaires was even greater, and this institution had a most valuable educational influence; it is to him the Belgian public owes in great measure its recognised characteristics of artistic receptivity. He it was who introduced them to Brahms, the young Russ. school, Richard Strauss and many Belgian comprs., besides securing visits from Richter, Mottl, Lévy, and others. As a compr. he was hardly gifted, and none of his works has survived him.

Ribeiro Pinto, opera (Liège, 1858); *Paul et Virginie* (cantata, *Prix de Rome*); *Hector*, overture; sacred music.—E. C.

DUPRÉ, Marcel. Fr. organ-virtuoso and compr. *b.* Rouen, 3 May, 1886, of a family of musicians and organists. Pupil of his father, Albert Dupré, chief orgt. at St.-Ouen, Rouen; later stud. under Guilmant, Diémer and Widor. Carried off innumerable 1st prizes at Paris Cons.; pf. (1905); organ (1907); fugue (1909); *Grand Prix de Rome* (1914). Succeeded Widor as orgt. at St.-Sulpice and Louis Vierne at Notre-Dame. His inexhaustible imagination in polyphonic compn. makes him one of the greatest improvisators that have existed; his power of memory is no less extraordinary than his gifts as a virtuoso. In 1920 he gave a series of 10 organ recitals at the Paris Cons., devoted to

works of J. S. Bach, all played from memory—
a performance without precedent. He has toured
frequently in England and America.

Sonata B mi. (pf. and vn.); 3 preludes and fugues
(organ) of very curious composition both technically
and musically; *Fantaisie* (pf. and orch.); motets;
psalms; a magnificent collection of 15 *Versets-Préludes* for organ. See *Mus. Times*, London, Dec.
1920; *Mus. News*, 18 Dec. 1920.—F. R.

DUPUIS, Albert. Belgian compr. *b.* Verviers,
1 March, 1877. An infant prodigy. At first
attended the pf., vn. and fl. courses at Verviers
School of Music; then entered Paris *Schola
Cantorum* (compn. under d'Indy; organ under
Guilmant). *Prix de Rome*, 1903. Successive
posts were: choirmaster at d'Harcourt Concerts, Paris; precentor St. Quentin; dir. of
Verviers School of Music, a position which he
holds to-day. As compr. devoted more especially
to lyric stage. He belongs really to modern
Walloon school, but, at same time, has a share
in Belgian group of young Fr. school (C. Franck
tradition); he is more eclectic than anything
else.

Stage-works: *L'Idylle* (Verviers, 1896); *Bilitis* (Verviers, 1899); *Jean-Michel* (Brussels, 1903, his best
work); *Martille* (Brussels, 1906); *Fidelaine* (Liège,
1911); *La Chanson d'Halewyn* (Antwerp, 1913;
adaptation for stage of *Prix de Rome* cantata); *Le
Château de la Bretèche* (Nice, 1914); *La Passion*
(Monte Carlo, 1915); *La Délivrance* (Lille, 1921);
La Victoire (Brussels, 1923). Unperf.: *La Captivité
de Babylone*, biblical drama. Various: *Les Cloches
nuptiales* (*Wedding Bells*), *Prix de Rome* cantata;
Œdipe à Colone, lyric cortège; symph. pieces; a
symphony; concertos for cello; vn.; horn; pf.;
str. 4tet; trio; sonata; songs.—E. C.

DUPUIS, Sylvain. Belgian compr. condr. *b.*
Liège, 9 Oct. 1856. Comes from a family of
musicians. Pupil of Liège Cons. *Prix de Rome*,
1881; prof. of harmony, Liège Cons. 1886;
dir. of celebrated *La Legia* choral soc. 1887;
1888, founded Société des Nouveaux Concerts
at Liège; condr. of Théâtre de la Monnaie and
of Concerts Populaires, Brussels, 1900, continuing
these until made dir. of Liège Cons. 1911.
Member of Belgian Acad. and of Commission
for publ. works of old Belgian comprs. His
compns. do not belong to any specific school,
and are of a temperate modernism.

Stage-works: *Coûr d'Oignoñ* (Walloon regional
opera); *Moina*. Cantatas: *Chant de la Creation*
(for *Prix de Rome*), *La Cloche Roland*, *Camoëns*;
Judas (lyric episode). Orch.: an overture; 2 suites;
Macbeth (symph. tableau). Many male-v. choruses,
Le Retour, *Le Chant du Cygne*, *Les Cloches*, etc.;
songs; pf. pieces; pieces for vn.; cello; organ; an
ob. concertino.—E. C.

DUREY, Louis. Fr. compr. *b.* Paris, 1888.
Pupil of Léon Saint-Réquier. Formerly one of
group of young comprs. called "Les Six." Since
1914, his compns. number 30, of which 7 have
been publ.:

Carillons; *Neige*; *Romance sans paroles* for pf.
(4 and 2 hands) (Paris, 1920, La Sirène Press; 1919,
Demets). For v. and pf. or orch.: *Images à Crusoé*;
Inscriptions sur un oranger; *Le Bestiaire* (London,
1920, Chester); *4 Epigrammes de Théocrite*; 3
Poèmes de Pétrone (Paris, 1919, Durand). Among his
unpubl. works, 2 trios, 2 str. 4tets, songs on poems
of Verlaine, Francis Jammes, André Gide, Tagore,
etc. Is preparing a 5-act opera, *Judith* (F. Hebbel)
and *Le Chant de la Nuit* (Nietzsche). Has written for
Écho Musical, *Courrier Musical*, *Chesterian*, etc.—
M. L. P.

DURIGO, Ilona (Kacics). Hungarian m.-sopr.

concert and oratorio singer; *b.* Budapest,
13 May, 1881. Stud. at R. High School for
Music, Budapest. At present teacher of singing
at Zurich Conservatoire.—B. B.

DUSCH, Alphons. Dutch orgt. pianist and
compr. *b.* Zutphen (Guelderland), 13 July, 1895.
Started pf. study at very early age; then stud.
at Aix-la-Chapelle Cons.; later at Amsterdam and
Utrecht under Wagenaar, Röntgen and Evert
Cornelis; 1913–14, lived in New York; 1918,
pf.-teacher Rotterdam Cons. His mus. style is
influenced by César Franck and the *Schola
Cantorum*.

Songs; sonata, vn. and pf. (1915); 2 sonatas, cello
and pf. (1917, 1919), perf. Amsterdam, 1919, by
Marix Loevensohn and compr.; str. 4tet (1917);
Introduction and fugue for organ (1917); smaller
pf. pieces (1918); *Jeux fantasques*, for pf. (Amersfoort,
L. Klein); *Hymnus*, for vn. and pf. (1919); choral
works, and Mass with organ.—W. P.

DUTCH FOLK-MUSIC. See Antcliffe,
Herbert; Röntgen, Julius; Van Duyse,
Florimond.

DUX, Claire. Ger. s. stage and concert singer;
Member of Berlin State Opera; chamber-
concert singer. In America, 1921.—A. E.

DVOŘÁK, Antonín. Czech composer; born
of humble parents in Nelahozeves, 8 Sept.
1841; died at Prague, 1 May, 1904. Like
his father he was to have become a butcher,
but his extraordinary talent for music so impressed his first teacher that he was sent to the
Organ School at Prague, where he stud. 1857–9.
Later he became viola-player in the orchestra
of the Czech Theatre, Prague, 1862–73, and
organist at the church of St. Adalbert, 1873–6.
Already during this period Dvořák was diligently
composing, and for a time was under the strong
influence of Richard Wagner. However, his
works were not performed, and it was not until
the year 1873 that the attention of the Czech
public was drawn to him, when he had great
success with his *Hymnus* for chorus and orchestra, the text by Vítězslav Hálek. Other
countries first heard of him through the influence
of Brahms and Hanslick, who, as members of
the Viennese jury for State music subsidies,
had become acquainted with his compositions.
They recommended him to the editor Simrock,
and through the publication of his *Moravian
Duets*, and especially of his *Slav Dances* (1878),
Dvořák's fame became world-wide. Well-known
conductors, like Richter and Bülow, the famous
quartet-players, Joachim, Becker and Hellmesberger, later also the Bohemian String Quartet,
acted as propagandists for his ever-increasing
works, which Simrock and other editors rapidly
published. Moreover, responsible critics like
Hanslick and Ehlert spread abroad his fame.
Thus, of all Czech composers, Dvořák became
the best-known in foreign countries. From 1884
to 1887 he visited England five times in order
to conduct *The Spectre's Bride*, *St. Ludmila* and
the *Requiem*, at the several music festivals then
being given. In 1890 he became professor of composition at the Prague Conservatoire. In 1892
he was called to New York as director of the

National Conservatoire. From this time dates the influence of negro folk-music on the melodic and rhythmic structure of his themes. On his return to Prague he became professor once more, and in 1901, director of the Conservatoire. In his later years Dvořák turned more to the symphonic poem and opera, whereas before his abundant activity had been concentrated on symphony and chamber music. His music is *simple* in the sense that it reveals the feelings of a simple-hearted man. His love for God, mankind and all creation, his fundamental joyousness, his blissful confidence, openheartedness and purity are the finest sides to his character. His work owed nothing to reflection on the ways and means of musical development, on his own position in that development, or on the idea of Art as such. It had its origin in the exuberant creative wealth of his own personality and was guided by artistic intuition. His music is *not* simple if by simplicity we mean a superficial outlook on life and a lack of seriousness. On the contrary, in his music is often to be found the expression of a certain melancholy, which sometimes deepens into indefinable pain and suffering. His genuine religious fervour was remarkable among the music of his day. Since intellectual control was a subordinate element in all his creative activity, it occasionally happens that his naïve, elemental joyousness leads him to the very borders of triviality, or causes him to lose the balance between fidelity to his programme and unity of form and purpose—in the symphonic poems, for instance. Yet in the enormous range of his works these slight blemishes form but a small part which in no way diminishes the value of the whole.

The spirit of his creative activity, unlike that of the neo-romantic Smetana, had leanings towards the classical school. In the sixties of the XIX century he passed through a Wagner period, but soon found that the tender melodiousness of Schubert, the grace of Haydn, the architectonics of Beethoven and the strict logic of Brahms were much closer akin to his personality, and therefore he tended more and more in that direction. In oratorio the monumental simplicity of Handel was his model. The form of his instrumental music is strictly classical, though the content is new, not alone in the matter of the composer's personal qualities, but also on account of its national individuality and the rigorous, conscious accentuation of it. Along with Smetana, Dvořák belongs to that generation for which nationality means the striving after the creation of a national style, distinguishing himself also externally from the others. Although his conception does not extend to the prophetic power of Smetana, nevertheless his racial freshness is enriched by other Slav influences. In many works he combines harmoniously his own national feeling with the melodic and rhythmic characteristics of other Slav nations (opera *Dimitrij*, *Slav Dances*, *Rhapsodies*, *Dumky*, etc.). Dvořák had his hardest struggle in dramatic music and in the

symphonic poems, for his chief faculty, spontaneous musicality, often tempted him to exceed the necessary dramatic and architectonic conciseness. Nevertheless, through the depth and earnestness of his feelings and through his luxuriant inventive power, he has succeeded in creating, even in these departments, works that are quite extraordinary—the operas *The Jacobin* and *Rusalka*. Smetana and Dvořák represent in modern Czech music the typically national-classical generation. Smetana added glory to the Czech nation, for which and about which he wrote; Dvořák created his works out of the inmost feelings of the nation, of which he was just a simple member. Thus he conquered, for Czech music, provinces hitherto neglected, *i.e.*, chamber-music, symphonies, etc., into which he infused the new characteristic folk-element.

Chamber-music. Str. 4 tets: A mi. op. 16 (1874); E ma. op. 80 (1876); D mi. op. 34 (1877); E flat ma. op. 51 (1878); C ma. op. 61 (1881); F ma. op. 96 (1893); A flat ma. op. 105 (1895); G ma. op. 106 (1895). Pf. trios: B flat ma. op. 21 (1875); G mi. op. 26 (1876); F mi. op. 65 (1883); *Dumky Trio*, op. 90 (1890–1). Pf. 4 tets: D ma. op. 23 (1875); E flat ma. op. 87 (1889). Pf. 5 tet, A ma. op. 81 (1887). Str. 5 tet, E flat ma. op. 97 (1893). Str. 6 tet, op. 48 (1878). Vn. sonatas: F ma. op. 57 (1880); G ma. op. 100 (1893).

Orch. works. Symphonies: E flat ma. (1873); D mi. (1874); D ma. op. 60 (1880); D mi. op. 70 (1884); F ma. op. 76 (1885); G ma. op. 88 (1889); E mi. *From the New World*, op. 95 (1893); overtures, *Husitska*, op. 67 (1883); *Nature*; *Carnival*; *Othello*, op. 91–93 (1891); *Scherzo capriccioso*, op. 66 (1883); 3 Slav rhapsodies, op. 45 (1878); Slav dances (2 series), op. 46 and 72 (1878; 1886); *Legends*, op. 59 (1881); Symph. Variations, op. 78 (1877); Suite, op. 39 (1879); 2 serenades. Symph. poems: *The Waterman*; *The Noon-day Witch*; *The Golden Spinning-wheel*; *The Forest Dove*, *The Song of the Hero*, op. 107–111 (1896). Concertos: Vn., op. 53 (1879–80); pf., op. 33 (1876); cello, op. 104 (1894–5).

Pf. works: *Poetic Tone-pictures* (1889); humoreskes (1894); valses (1879–80); mazurkas (1880). Voice and pf.: *Moravian Duets* (1876); *Biblical Songs* (1894); *Gipsy Songs* (1880); *Love Songs* (1865); *Folk-Songs* (1886); *Four Songs* (1887). Cantatas, oratorios: *Hymnus* (1872); *Stabat Mater* (1876–7); *The Spectre's Bride* (1884); *St. Ludmila* (1885–6); *Requiem* (1890). Operas: *King and Charcoal-burner* (1874); *Wanda* (1875); *The Thick-heads* (1874); *The Peasant-Rogue* (1877); *Dimitrij* (1882); *Jacobin* (1887–8); *The Devil and Kate* (1898–9); *Rusalka* (1900); *Armida* (1902–3).

Chief publishers: N. Simrock, Berlin; F. A. Urbánek, E. Starý, Hudební Matice, Prague; Bote & Bock, Berlin; Novello, Lengnick, London; Schlesinger, Hainauer, Hofmeister, etc.

Consult O. Šourek, *Life and Work of Dvořák* (Czech), 2 vols. so far, Hudební Matice, Prague. Also: *Dvořák's Works: Thematic Catalogue* (Ger. and Czech), Simrock, 1917; Bartoš, *A. D.* (Prague); *A. D.: Collection of Studies* (Prague, Hudební Matice, 1912).—V. St.

DWELSHAUVERS, Victor Felix. Belgian writer on music; *b.* Liège, 20 Feb. 1869; *d.* there, 22 Feb. 1915. Pupil of Liège Cons.; Ph.D. Leipzig Univ. (1891). Author of various researches, which, if of limited dimension, nevertheless reveal an undeniable scientific spirit and æsthetic sensibility.

Monographs on *R. Wagner* (1889); *Tannhäuser* (1892); *The Flying Dutchman*; *Les Précurseurs de la neuvième symphonie de Beethoven* (1901); *Contribution à l'étude du " Tempo " musical* (1907); *A propos de l'op. 1 de Hamal* (1908); *La Symphonie pré-haydnienne* (1908); *Bach's St. John Passion* (1908), etc.—C. V. B.

DYCK, Ernest van. See VAN DYCK.

DYCK, Felix. Ger. pianist; *b.* Bremen, 14 Jan. 1893. Stud. under Mayer-Mahr, Berlin, and Diémer, Paris. Awarded Blüthner Prize, 1909, and first prize Paris Cons. 1912. Pianist and compr. in Berlin.—A. E.

DYGAS, Ignacy. Polish heroic t. singer; *b.* Warsaw, 28 July, 1881. Began study as barit. His teacher, Prof. Alexandrowicz, discovered t. qualities and developed them accordingly. In 1905, made 1st appearance in Moniuszko's opera *Halka* at the Warsaw Opera. In 1907, began to sing in Italy (Turin, Padua, Genoa, Milan, Rome, Naples); then in Spain, Russia and America. Also sang often in Warsaw. During the war, sang at Moscow. Since 1919, 1st dramatic t. at Warsaw Opera House.—ZD. J.

DYGAT, Zygmunt. Polish pianist; *b.* Cracow, 1894. Stud. under Mme. Czopp-Umlaufowa at Cracow; then under Jerzy Lalewicz at Vienna Cons. From 1919, has given recitals in Poland, and France (especially Paris and Monte Carlo), where he is well known.—ZD. J.

DYKE, Spencer. Eng. violinist; *b.* St. Austell, 22 July, 1880. At age of 17 won the Dove Scholarship at R.A.M. London; prof. there from 1907; chiefly occupied with chamber-music, teaching and editing; leads the well-known quartet bearing his name.

Vn. pieces; studies; eds. of classics and a book of Scales (Boosey; Bosworth; J. Williams).—E.-H.

DYMMEK, Zbigniew. Polish pianist, compr. *b.* Warsaw, 29 March, 1896. Pupil of Michałowski and Melcer at Warsaw; then of Mme. Zurmühlen at Petrograd. Stud. theory under Paul Graener at Leipzig. In 1919, 1st prize at Paderewski competition for pianists at Lublin (Poland). A serious talent and splendid technique balanced with earnest endeavours in compn. Has publ. some well-written works for pf. and orch. and many songs.—ZD. J.

DYSON, George. Eng. compr. *b.* Halifax, Yorks, 28 May, 1883. Scholar R.C.M.; then Mendelssohn Scholar; dir. of music, R. Naval Coll. Osborne; then Marlborough Coll.; later Rugby School, and now dir. of music, Wellington College. Mus.Doc. Oxon. 1918. Lectures on modern harmony (publ. in *Music and Letters*, 1923). His 3 rhapsodies for str. 4tet won a Carnegie award, 1920.

Suite for small orch. *Won't you look out of your Window* (ms.); 3 *Rhapsodies*, str. 4tet (Stainer & Bell); *Epigrams*, pf. (Schott); songs; part-songs; services; educational pieces (Curwen; Arnold; Stainer & Bell, etc.); book, *The New Music* (H. Milford, 1924).—E.-H.

DYSTHE, Carl Schoyen. Norwegian merchant and author; *b.* Ostre Toten, 20 July, 1871. Publ. (1897) historical account of Christiania Mercantile Association's Choral Union from 1847 to 1897. In 1907, an account of same union's activities at home and abroad from 1897 to 1907. In 1914, an historical review of male-choir singing in Norway.—U. M.

E

EAMES, Emma. Operatic s. singer; b. Shanghai, 13 Aug. 1867, of Amer. parentage. Stud. in Paris under Mathilde Marchesi; appeared at Grand Opéra, Paris, 13 March, 1889 (heroine in Gounod's *Romeo and Juliet*); first appeared as Marguerite (*Faust*), R. Covent Garden Opera, 7 April, 1891; later in that year, appeared in grand opera, New York (under Messrs. Abbey and Grace), with the brothers de Reszke). Her triumphs in America were great. London season 1892 (De Lara's *The Light of Asia*, etc.) and regularly after that in London and America. Has lately resided in Rome.—E.-H.

EBEL, Arnold. Ger. compr. b. Heide (Schleswig), 15 Aug. 1883. Teacher and orgt. at Tingleff (N. Schleswig); went to R. High School of Music and the Advanced School of Max Bruch for further study from 1906-9. Since then, orgt. and choirmaster of Knights of St. John, Berlin; President Soc. of Berlin Musicians since 1920; also of Amalgamated Pedagogic Unions; in 1921 succeeded Egidi as orgt. to Paul Gerhardt Ch., Berlin-Schöneberg.

Songs; duets; choral songs, op. 3, 10 (men's) and op. 9 (mixed); *Requiem*, op. 17, for s. solo, chorus and orch. (after Hebbel); *Die Weihe der Nacht*, op. 19 (barit., chorus and orch.).—A. E.

ECCARIUS-SIEBER, Artur. Ger. pf. teacher; b. Gotha, 23 May, 1864; d. Berlin, 30 June, 1919. Pupil Gotha Cons. (Patzig); music teacher in Zug, 1886; Zurich, 1888, where he founded Swiss Acad. of Music, 1891. Moved to Düsseldorf, 1916, and lived in Berlin from 1916 as pf. teacher and music critic to *Signale*. Ed. *Kammermusik* from 1897 to 1901 (Heilbronn, C. F. Schmidt), and a number of educational works for pf. and vn.:

Vn. Method, 1891; *Vn. Positions*, 1892; *Sonata Album* (vn., 2 vols.); *Album of Studies* (vn., 3 vols.); *New Elementary Method for Pf.* (1897, Simrock); *Course of Instruction. for Pf.*; also one for vn. (both by Simrock); *Master System for Pf.* (Litolff); *Handbook of Pf. Teaching* (Vieweg); *Pf. Teaching as it should be* (1895) (1896); *Musical Ear-Training* (1898) (1902); *Handbook of Vn. Teaching* (1903); *Guide through Vn. Literature*. Also ed. Moscheles' *Études*, op. 95 (Steingräber).—A. E.

ÉCOLE CLASSIQUE D'ORGUE. A coll. of ancient and classical pieces for the organ ed. by Alexandre Guilmant. It comprises 25 books, including works of d'Englebert, S. Bach, Ph. E. Bach, W. R. Bach, Buxtehude, Bruhns, Czernokoesky, Frescobaldi, Handel, Kerll, Krebs, Kopriwa, Martini, Muffat, Murschhauser, Roberday, Pachelbel, Sweelinck, Scheidt, Walther, Zipoli.—A. C.

ÉCORCHEVILLE, Jules. Fr. musicologist; b. Paris, 17 March, 1872; fell in battle, 19 Feb. 1915. One of finest of contemporary French musicologists, who has done more than any other to interest the general public in works of the past. After literary studies in Paris, he studied music under César Franck, and later under Hugo Riemann at Leipzig. In 1904 he joined Lionel Dauriac and J. G. Prod'homme in founding the French section of the International Society of Music (S.I.M.). His great energy and power of organisation enabled him to bring into contact musicologists who up to that time had worked in ignorance of each other. He helped to circulate among them modern methods of research in archives, publication of manuscripts, etc. In 1907 he founded the *Bulletin français de la Société Internationale de Musique* which before long absorbed the *Mercure Musical*, the *Courrier Musical* and the *Revue Musicale*. The *S.I.M.* was from 1907 to 1914 the most up-to-date and interesting organ of musical criticism in Paris. In 1905 he wrote a brilliant thesis (for Doctorate), *De Lully à Rameau, l'Esthétique musicale*; also *Vingt Suites d'orchestre du XVIIe siècle français*. Was preparing various works on lute music, history of the sonata, and musical iconography, and editing an enormous catalogue of the musical contents of the Bibliothèque Nationale, Paris. The catalogue appeared in 8 vols. just after the war, but without the 2 vols. of supplements and errata which were to complete it.

As President of the S.I.M. he was really the soul of the congress in Paris in 1914 of nearly 600 musicologists of all nations. Some months after this manifestation of international co-operation the war broke out and, as an officer in the Reserves, Écorcheville fell while leading his company in an assault in Champagne.—H. P.

EDDY, Hiram Clarence. Amer. organ virtuoso; b. Greenfield, Mass., U.S.A., 23 June, 1851. Pupil of Dudley Buck in Hartford. Went to Berlin, 1871; pupil of Haupt (organ) and Loeschhorn (pf.). Settled in Chicago 1874. Orgt. of various churches. The oldest and, until late in life, one of the most active concert-orgts. of America. After playing at Vienna Exhibition of 1875 he has played at almost all Amer. exhibitions up to present day; also at Paris Exhibition 1889. Head of organ department of Chicago Mus. Coll. Hon. member of R. Accad. di Santa Cecilia in Rome. One of founders of Amer. Guild of Orgts. 1896. Has comp. and ed. many organ pieces; transl. Haupt's *Theory of Counterpoint and Fugue* (Schirmer, 1876).—O. K.

ÉDITION MUTUELLE. A Fr. publ. society, founded in 1902 at the *Schola Cantorum*, Paris, to publ. at small expense the greater part of the works of pupils, disciples and friends of the *Schola*. It has publ. works of Albeniz (which form the most important part of its coll.), of Bret, Bordes, P. de Bréville, Chausson, Castéra, Dupuis, Jongen, Magnard, de Polignac, Sérieyx,

Le Flem, de Séverac, Ryelandt, Vreuls, Blanche Selva, L. Saint-Réquier, Tournemire. Since the 1914 war, the Soc. has ceased to work.—A. C.

EDSTRÖM, Liva. See JÄRNEFELT, LIVA.

EDVINA, Marie Louise. Operatic s. singer; *b.* Quebec of Fr. Canadian parentage. Stud. under Jean de Reszke, Paris, 1904–8; *début* Covent Garden, London, as Marguerite (*Faust*), 15 July, 1908; also title-rôles in Debussy's *Pelléas et Mélisande*; Charpentier's *Louise*, etc. Married (1914) the Hon. Cecil Edwardes; in 1919, N. Rothesay Stuart-Wortley.—E.-H.

EGGAR, Katharine E. Eng. compr. and pianist; *b.* London.

Two Sketches, pf. (Avison Ed.); *Tarantella*, pf. (Stainer & Bell); *Idyll*, fl. and pf. (Rudall, Carte); *Remember Me, my Dear*, v. and pf. (Chappell); *Curtsey to the Moon* (*id.*); *Wolfram's Dirge* (Avison Ed.); a considerable amount of chamber-music; songs; trios, etc., in ms.—E.-H.

EGGELING, Georg. Ger. compr. and teacher; *b.* Brunswick, 24 Sept. 1866. Son of Duke of Brunswick's Konzertmeister, Theodor Eggeling. Attended Prof. Emil Breslaur's Piano Seminary (Kalischer, Wilhelm Wolf, Grunicke, Frank), 1885–90; private pupil of Eduard Frank, 1889–91; teacher at Breslaur's school (pf., theory and method), 1890–1900. Since 1900 Inst. of his own in Berlin.

Studies for Pf. (2), op. 21; op. 58 (100 *Modulations*); op. 90 (18 *Studies in Octaves*); op. 122 (50 *Studies in all the Major and Minor Keys*); op. 170 (25 *Melodious Studies*); op. 172 (7 *Exercises for practising Extended Chords*); op. 175 (10 *Melodious Studies*); op. 176 (35 *Tuneful Studies for Young People*); op. 184 (7 *Studies in Octaves*); op. 185 (12 *Tuneful Studies for Lower Intermediate Class*); 12 *Tuneful Studies for Grace and Rapidity*; studies in octaves; large number of instructive pf. pieces; *Music in Lighter Vein*; and books, *Musician's Lexicon* and *Young People's Musical Reference Book*.—A. E.

EGGEN, Arne. Norwegian compr. orgt. condr. *b.* Trondhjem, 28 Aug. 1881. Stud. at Cons. in Christiania and in Leipzig. Obtained a State scholarship in 1909. 1908, orgt. Bragernaes Ch. Drammen. Has given numerous concerts of church music throughout the country, and in Sweden. Condr. of Drammen Symphony Orch. Gave in 1910 and 1915, successful concerts of his own compns. in Christiania. They have a national tinge, and yet are stamped with individuality. They are characterised by combination of broad, manly strength with tender, lyrical feeling.—R. M.

Symphony, G mi.; choral work, *Mjösen*; incidental music to fairy-play *Liti Kirsti* (text by Hulda Garborg); 2 vn. sonatas; *Chaconne* for organ; numerous songs.—R. M.

EGGEN, Erik. Norwegian music research scholar; *b.* Trondhjem, 17 Nov. 1877. Matriculated in 1904; graduated in philology 1914; headmaster since 1917; went to England for study in 1903, to Denmark in 1908. Has written numerous studies on national music. Has publ. a biography of Edvard Grieg in Norwegian peasant-dialect. Lives at Voss, near Bergen. —J. A.

EGIDI, Arthur. Ger. compr. and organ-recitalist; *b.* Berlin, 9 Aug. 1859. Attended R. High School and Kiel and Taubert's Acad. Advanced School. Teacher Hoch's Cons. Frank-

fort, 1885–92; orgt. of St. Paul's Ch. Berlin, 1913–21, of the Paul Gerhardt Ch., and teacher at Inst. for Church Music.

Psalm LXXXIV for 6-v. choir; songs and choruses; organ pieces; orch. and stage works.—A. E.

EHRENBERG, Carl E. Th. Ger. compr. and mus. dir. *b.* Dresden, 6 April, 1878. 1894–8, pupil Dresden Cons. (Rischbieter, Draeseke); condr. Stadttheater, Dortmund, 1898; Würzburg, 1899; Posen, 1905; Augsburg, 1907; Metz, 1908; Korrepetitor, Court Theatre, and condr. Orch. Soc. Munich, 1900–4; 1909–14, dir. Symphony Orch. Lausanne; dir. of Opera and Municipal Orch. Augsburg, 1915–18; Homburg, 1918; condr. Berlin State Opera, 1922.

Tone-poem *Youth*, op. 19; *Nachtlied*, for vn. and orch., op. 14 (Leipzig, Leuckart); *Suite d'Orchestre*, No. 1 *From German Legends* (1900); No. 2 (1914); 2 pieces for str. band, op. 15; *Prologue, Melodrama and Epilogue* for National Memorial Play (1916); *Burlesque in form of Waltz* (1911); *Sunrise* for 5-v. chorus and orch. (1901); sonata for vn. and pf. (1906); str. 4tet in E mi. (1912); songs with pf. acc. op. 3, 4, 7, 9, 10; *Songs of Heine*, op. 12; *Liebesleben*, for v., vn. and pf. op. 13; 4 songs with orch. op. 16 (Leuckart); *Liebeshymnen*, s. and orch. op. 17 (*id.*); *Ernste Gesänge*, contr. and orch. op. 18 (*id.*); opera, *Anneliese* (Düsseldorf, Musicians' Fest. 1922); pf. pieces. Early works: 2 str. 4tets; 2 symphonies; overture to *Maria Stuart*; symph. bagatelles; pf. trio; pf. pieces, op. 6, 8; opera, "*Und selig sind . . .,*" etc.—A. E.

EIDE, Kaja Hansen. Norwegian concert- and opera-singer (s.); *b.* Horten, 26 April, 1884. Pupil of Ellen Gulbranson, Christiania, and Zur Mühlen, London. Has given many concerts in Norway and appeared in many operas at National Theatre, Christiania (*Mignon*; *Madame Butterfly*; *Barber of Seville*; *Onegin*; *Lakmé*, etc.).—U. M.

EINHEITSPARTITUR. An attempt made by Hermann Stephani (*q.v.*) to introduce a unified notation, by using the treble G clef only, with octave signs.—E.-H.

EINSTEIN, Alfred. Ger. musicologist; *b.* Munich, 30 Dec. 1880. Stud. science of music (Sandberger) and compn. (A. Beer-Walbrunn) in Munich; study-tours in Italy, 1901, 1905, 1908, 1909; in London, 1905; critic in Munich (on *Münchener Post* since 1917). Ed. of Hugo Riemann's *Musik-Lexikon* from 1919; ed. of *Zeitschrift für Musik-Wissenschaft* from 1918. His principal field for research is the vocal and instr. music of the XVI and XVII centuries (madrigals, cantatas, sonatas), on which he has publ. a large number of works.

On German Literature for the Vla. da Gamba (Leipzig, 1905, Breitkopf); *Biography of Agostino Steffani* I (*Kirchenmusikalisches Jahrbuch*, 1910); *History of Music* (1917; 2nd ed. 1920, Leipzig, B. G. Teubner); *Benedetto Marcello's "Teatro alla Moda,"* Ger. transl. (Munich, 1917, G. Müller).

Ed.: *Selected Chamber Duets by Ag. Steffani* (*D.T.B.* VI, ii); *Benda's "Ariadne"* (Leipzig, C. F. W. Siegel); *Lives of German Musicians: Hiller, Neefe, Gyrowetz* (Leipzig, 1914, C. F. W. Siegel); *Palestrina, Missa Papæ Marcelli* (Munich, 1920, Drei Masken Verlag).

Dr. Einstein is responsible for nearly all the German articles in this Dictionary.—E.-H.

EISDELL, Hubert Mortimer. Eng. tenor singer; *b.* Hampstead, London, 21 Sept. 1882. Exhibitioner, Caius Coll. Cambridge; stud. singing under Victor Beigel; has appeared at R. Philh., Hallé Orch. concerts, Queen's Hall, etc.; toured U.S.A., Canada and Australasia.—E.-H.

EISENBERGER, Seweryn. Polish pianist; b. Cracow, 1876. Pupil of Leschetizky in Vienna. From 1914–21, prof. Cracow Cons. In 1922, moved to Vienna. One of the finest pianists of the day. As interpreter of Schumann and Brahms few can be compared to him.—ZD. J.

EITNER, Robert. Ger. musicographer; b. Breslau, 22 Oct. 1832; d. Templin, 2 Feb. 1905. Pupil of M. Brosig, Breslau, music-teacher in Berliñ from 1853; founder and dir. of music school, 1863; founder of the Gesellschaft für Musikforschung, for publishing older music, and a journal, *Monatshefte für Musikgeschichte* (1869–1904). Lived at Templin from 1882. Prof. 1902.
Bibliography of Musical Compilations of the XVI and XVII centuries (Berlin, 1877, Liepmannssohn, in conjunction with Haberl, Lagerberg and Pohl); *Dictionary of Biographical and Bibliographical Sources* in reference to musicians and mus. research scholars, 10 vols. (Leipzig, 1899–1904, Breitkopf).—A. E.

EITZ, Carl A. Ger. teacher of music; b. Wehrstedt, 25 June, 1848. Lives at Eisleben; inventor of the *Tonwortmethode*, which uses intelligently conceived syllabic notation as basis of elementary teaching of singing, and which has met with as much violent opposition as it has found support from ever-increasing numbers during the last few years. His method has been introduced into Bavaria and lately (1922) into Prussia.
Bausteine zum Schulgesangunterricht im Sinne der Tonwortmethode (Foundations for teaching Singing in Schools by the " Tonwort" Method) (Leipzig, 1911); *Teaching of Singing as Foundation of Musical Education* (Leipzig, 1914).
Consult: G. Borchers, *C. Eitz* (Würzburg, 1908); O. Messmer, *C. Eitz' Tonwortmethode* (Würzburg, 1911); Frank Bennedik, *Historical, Psychological and Musical Investigations in relation to the Eitz Tonwort Method* (Langensalza, 1914).—A. E.

EKMAN, Ida (*née* Mordauch). Finnish concert-singer; b. Helsingfors, 22 April, 1875. Stud. Helsingfors Music Inst. 1891–2; Vienna, 1892–5; and (with a State scholarship) in Paris, 1898–9. Nuremberg Stadttheater, 1896–7; soloist in Paris tour of Helsingfors Philh. Orch. 1900; concerts with her husband, Karl Ekman (*q.v.*) in Finland and abroad. Famous as a singer of songs. Now living in Helsingfors as a teacher of singing.—T. H.

EKMAN, Karl. Finnish pianist, condr. b. Kaarina (St. Karins), 18 Dec. 1869. Stud. Helsingfors Univ. and Music Inst. 1889–92; (with State stipend) in Berlin and Vienna 1892–5; later in Paris and Rome. Dir. of Helsingfors Music Inst. 1907–11; condr. of orch. at Abo (Turku), 1912–20. For many years, has arranged chamber-music concerts in Helsingfors; critic and teacher and condr. in Helsingfors. Arr. of folk-music. Married the singer Ida Ekman in 1895.—T. H.

ELDERING, Bram. Dutch vn.-virtuoso; b. Groningen, 8 July, 1865. Pupil of Christian Poortman (Groningen), Jenő Hubay (Brussels), and Joseph Joachim (Berlin); 1887–8, vn. teacher, Budapest; vla.-player, Hubay-Popper

Quartet; 1891–4, Konzertmeister of Berlin Philh.; 1895–9, R. Konzertmeister at Meiningen; 1899–1903, teacher Amsterdam Cons.; 1903, at Cologne Cons.; Konzertmeister of Gürzenich Orch. and leader of the excellent Gürzenich Quartet. He was personally closely acquainted with Brahms and excels in Brahms' chamber-music.—A. E.

ELECTROPHONE. An instr. consisting of various electric bells, giving a rapid, trembling sound. Also effect of a heavy shower of gold and silver. The instr. can be played from a keyboard. Was invented by the Dutch compr. Daniel Ruyneman (*q.v.*).—E.-H.

ELGAR, Sir Edward. English composer; b. Broadheath, near Worcester, 2 June, 1857; son of W. H. Elgar (orgt. R.C. church, and music-seller of Worcester); educated in close touch with the Three Choirs festivals, the glee clubs and local chamber-music. In 1877 he visited London for a few violin lessons with Pollitzer, the last actual lessons he ever had. For 5 years (1879–84) he was a bandmaster at the County Lunatic Asylum, and member of Stockley's orch. at Birmingham, when an *Intermezzo* of his was played in 1883. In 1882 he visited Leipzig for a few weeks. On his marriage in 1889 he came to London but withdrew to Malvern two years later, removing to Hereford in 1904. His first really characteristic work, *Scenes from the Saga of King Olaf*, was produced at the N. Staffordshire Fest. in 1896. A short oratorio, *The Light of Life*, was given at the Worcester Fest. 1896. Two of his best works, the *Enigma* orch. variations (Richter concerts, 19 June) and his *Sea Pictures* (Clara Butt, Norwich), were perf. in the year of their completion, 1899. His finest and most individual work, *Gerontius*, was produced at Birmingham in 1900; it had taken him years to compose. He did not, however, rise to general importance until this work had received the honour of a German performance (Lower Rhine Fest. Düsseldorf, May 1902, under Julius Buths) when Strauss publicly praised the rising English composer. The work has since been more frequently performed in England than any other oratorio save *Messiah* and *Elijah*. In March 1904, Covent Garden Theatre was taken for a 3-days Elgar festival (*Gerontius, Apostles*, a new overture *In the South*, etc.). The Coronation of King Edward VII (1902) inspired Elgar's 2 military marches, *Pomp and Circumstance*, and the *Coronation Ode* (A. C. Benson). The tune *Land of Hope and Glory* which occurs in the Ode, as well as in the second march, became so popular that for years it has ranked next to *God Save the King* as a national song. *The Apostles* (B'ham Fest. 1903) was followed by its sequel *The Kingdom* (B'ham Fest. Oct. 1906). The 1st symphony, A flat, was produced by Richter at Manchester in 1908, the 2nd symphony, E flat, in 1911 and the tone-poem *Falstaff* at Leeds in 1913. In 1916 his *Spirit of England, To Women* and *For the Fallen* revealed the same touching and consoling power. Indeed, the highly individual art of the early *Serenade* for str. orch. op. 20 is still as strongly in evidence as ever in the later vn. concerto, op. 61 (Kreisler, 1910), and cello concerto, op. 85 (Queen's Hall, 1919). This individuality is remarkable enough to shine through a technique already fully developed by the great German masters.

In 1919 he produced some chamber-music, a sonata for vn. and pf. a str. 4tet and a 5tet in A mi. for pf. and strings; but he is not at his best in these works and, although one of the greatest living orchestrators, he never writes with a real understanding of the piano.

Elgar is the most widely known of all English composers. He has received many orders and decorations, the chief being the O.M. in 1911. He was knighted in 1904. Received Mus.Doc. *h.c.* Cantab. 1900; Dunelm. 1904; Oxon, 1905; Yale, U.S.A. 1905. F.R.C.M. *h.c.* 1924. In Nov. 1923, he left England for a South American tour, journeying to Manaos, 1000 miles up the river Amazon. He conducted the massed choirs and bands at State opening of British Empire Exhibition at Wembley, 23 April, 1924, when his Imperial March and *Land of Hope and Glory* were performed before King George V and an audience of 100,000. Appointed Master of the King's Music, May 1924.

Op. 1, *Romance*, vn. and orch.; op. 2, Motets, 1 publ. (*Ave Verum*); op. 3, *Allegretto*, vn. and pf.; op. 4, 2 pieces, vn. and pf.; op. 5, 2 songs; op. 6, wind 5tet (ms.); op. 7, *Sevillana*, orch.; op. 8, str. 4tet (ms.); op. 9, sonata, vn. and pf. (ms.); op. 10, 3 pieces for orch. (*Mazurka*; *Sérénade Mauresque*; *Contrasts—the Gavotte, 1700 and 1900*); op. 11, *Sursum Corda*, for str. brass and organ; op. 12, *Salut d'amour*, vn. and pf.; op. 13, 2 pieces, vn. and pf.; op. 14, organ voluntaries (easy); op. 15, 2 pieces (*Chanson de Nuit* and *Chanson de Matin*) for vn. and pf., subsequently scored for small orch.; op. 16, 3 songs; op. 17 *La Capricieuse, morceau de genre* for vn.; op. 18, *O Happy Eyes*, part-song; op. 19, *Froissart*, concert-overture; op. 20, *Serenade* for str. orch.; op. 21, Minuet for pf.; op. 22, missing; op. 23, *Spanish Serenade*, chorus and orch.; op. 24, missing; op. 25, *The Black Knight*, cantata; op. 26, 2 3-v. songs, female chorus, with vn. obbligato, orchestrated in 1904; op. 27, *Scenes from the Bavarian Highlands*, for chorus and orch.; op. 28, organ sonata in G; op. 29, *The Light of Life* (*Lux Christi*), oratorio; op. 30, *Scenes from the Saga of King Olaf*, soli, chorus and orch.; op. 31, missing; op. 32, *Imperial March* (Diamond Jubilee, 1897); op. 33, *The Banner of St. George*, cantata; op. 34, *Te Deum and Benedictus*, in F; op. 35, *Caractacus*, cantata; op. 36, Variations for orch.; op. 37, *Sea Pictures*, contr. solo and orch; op. 38, *The Dream of Gerontius*, oratorio; op. 39, 2 military marches, *Pomp and Circumstance*; op. 40, *Cockaigne* (*In London Town*), concert-overture; op. 41, missing; op. 42, incidental music and funeral march for *Grania and Diarmid* (by George Moore and W. B. Yeats); op. 43, *Dream Children*, 2 pieces for small orch.; op. 44, *Coronation Ode*, 1902; op. 45, 5 part-songs for male vs. from the Greek Anthology; op. 46–8, missing; op. 49, *The Apostles*, Parts I and II; op. 50, overture, *In the South*, for orch.; op. 51, *The Kingdom*; op. 52, part-songs, *A Christmas Greeting*, for mixed vs.; op. 53, 4 part-songs; op. 54, part-song, *Reveillé*, for male vs.; op. 55, symphony I, in A flat (1908, Manchester); op. 56, 57, part-songs, *Angelus* and *Go, Song of Mine*; op. 58, *Elegy*, for str. orch.; op. 59, 6 songs; op. 60, 2 songs; op. 61, concerto in B mi. for vn. (1910); op. 62, *Romance* for bsn. and orch.; op. 63, symphony II, in E flat (1911); op. 64, 65, Coronation Offertorium and March (1911); op. 66, masque, *The Crown of India* (1912); op. 67, Psalm XLVIII, *Great is the Lord*; op. 68, symph. study, *Falstaff* (1913); op. 69, ode, *The Music-Makers*, for contr. chorus and orch. (1912, Birmingham); op. 70, *Sospiri*, adagio for str., harp and organ; op. 71–3, choral songs (*The Shower*; *The Fountain*; *Death on the Hills*; *Love's Tempest*; *Serenade*); op. 74, anthem, *Give unto the Lord*; op. 75, *The Carillon*, recitation with orch. (1914); op. 76, symph. poem, *Polonia*

(1915); op. 77, *Une Voix dans le Désert*, recitation with music; op. 78, suite, *The Starlight Express*, for pf. (1915); op. 79, *The Belgian Flag*, recitation with music; op. 80, choruses, *The Spirit of England* (*To Women*; *For the Fallen*) (1916); op. 81, *The Fan*, ballet, only for a private charity performance; op. 82, sonata for vn. and pf. (1919); op. 83, str. 4tet (1919); op. 84, 5tet in A mi. pf. and str.

Consult: E. Newman, *Elgar* (J. Lane, 1906); R. J. Buckley, *Sir Edward Elgar* (J. Lane, 1912); J. F. Porte, *Sir Edward Elgar* (Kegan Paul, 1921).—E.-H.

ELKIN & CO. Ltd. Publishers, founded 1903 in London, by W. W. A. Elkin. Its publications consisted, for a time, mainly of " popular " music; but works of more serious scope, especially by Eng. comprs. soon began to be included, and the " popular " side of output is now negligible. Elgar, Cyril Scott, Bantock, Quilter, Albert Coates, William Baines have all contributed to the firm's catalogue. It also owns copyright for Great Britain and Colonies of majority of works of Edward MacDowell.—E.-H.

ELLBERG, Ernst Henrik. Swedish compr. *b.* Söderhamn, 11 Dec. 1868. Stud. R. Cons. Stockholm, 1886–92; attached as violinist to R. Chapel 1887–1905; from 1904, teacher of compn. at R. Cons.; 1916, prof.; member R.A.M. Stockholm, 1912.

Opera, *Rassa*; *Askungen* (*Cinderella*), pantomime-ballet (1906; perf. 1907); *En sommaridyll* (*Summer Idyll*), ballet (1898); concert overture, *Vårbrytning* (*Breath of Spring*), perf. 1906; symphony in D (1897); overture (1892); Introduction and fugue, str. orch.; str. 5tet (1895); str. 4tet, E flat (1890); male 4tets; choruses for male voices.—P. V.

ELLING, Catharinus. Norwegian compr. and folk-music collector; *b.* Christiania, 13 Sept. 1858. Took his examination in philology in 1883. Stud. music in Leipzig (1877) and Berlin (1886 and following years). Teacher of theory and compn. at Lindeman's Cons. Christiania. Has had since 1899 a State grant for collection and adaptation of Norwegian folk-music.

Opera, *Kosakkerne* (*The Cossacks*) (Eldorado Theatre, Christiania, 1897); modern oratorio, *Den forlorne Sön* (*Prodigal Son*) (Christiania, 1897); choral work, *Gregorius Dagssön* (*ib.* 1898); symphony; chamber-music; stage-music; about 200 solo and choral songs; pf. and vn. pieces. Treatises: *Our Folk-Melodies* (1909); *Our Ancient Lays regarded from a Musical Point of View* (1914); *Our Tunes* (1915); *Norwegian Folk-Music* (1922), etc.—U. M.

ELLINGFORD, Herbert Frederick. Eng. concert orgt. *b.* London, 8 Feb. 1876. Stud. at R.C.M. under Sir Walter Parratt, Dr. F. E. Gladstone, Sir J. F. Bridge, M. Barton; exhibitioner, 1894; open scholar, 1895. A.R.C.M.; F.R.C.O.; Mus.Bac. Oxon. Orgt. St. George's Hall, Liverpool.

A Primer of Scales and Arpeggios, systematised for organ (Novello, 1917); *The Organ:* a study of its principles and technique, Part I (*id.* 1919); *Transcribing for the Organ* (H. W. Gray Co. 1922). Comp.: songs; choral works; organ pieces and arrs.; pf. pieces.—E.-H.

ELMAN, Mischa. Russ. violinist; *b.* Stalnoje, South Russia, 20 Jan. 1892. First lessons on vn. from his father, a schoolmaster. Played in public at 6. Stud. under Fidelman at Odessa until 10. Then Leopold Auer, hearing his phenomenal playing, procured for him a dispensation from prohibition which forbade enrolment of Jews at Petrograd Cons., and here taught him from 1902 to 1904. He appeared in public, Petrograd

1904, and 15 Oct. 1904 in Berlin. After playing in Dresden, Copenhagen and other cities, was heard in London, 21 March, 1905. Amer. *début* with Russ. Symphony Orch. 10 Dec. 1908. Toured Far East and Orient, 1920–1. Has publ. a series of excellent vn. transcriptions of older and more modern pieces. (Schirmer; Carl Fischer).—O. K.

ELSON, Louis Charles. Amer. author, lecturer and teacher; *b.* Boston, Mass., U.S.A., 17 April, 1848; *d.* there, 14 Feb. 1920. Stud. singing under Kreissmann in Boston and theory under Gloggner-Castelli in Leipzig. In 1880 ed. of organ-journal, *Vox Humana*, also ed. of *Musical Herald* at this time. For several years, mus. ed. of *Boston Courier*; after 1888 of *Advertiser*. From 1881 until death, prof. of mus. theory and history of music at New England and Cons. For 7 years city lecturer on music in Boston (240 lectures). Delivered two series of Lowell Inst. lectures. Comp. operettas and songs, transl. and arr. over 2,000 pieces.

Curiosities of Music (Ditson, 1880); *History of German Song* (New England Cons. 1888); *The Realm of Music* (essays) (*id.* 1892); *Great Composers and their Works* (Page, 1898); *The National Music of America and its Sources* (*id.* 1900); *Shakespeare in Music* (*id.* 1901); *History of American Music* (Macmillan, 1904); *Music Dictionary* (Ditson, 1905); *Mistakes and Disputed Points in Music* (Presser, 1910); *Woman in Music* (Univ. Soc. Inc. 1918); *Children in Music* (Univ. Soc. 1918). *Folk-Songs of Many Nations* (Church, 1905); *University Encyclopædia of Music*, 10 vols. (Univ. Soc. 1912).—O. K.

ELWES, Gervase. Eng. t. singer; *b* Billing Hall, Northants, 15 Nov. 1866. Killed in train accident at Boston, U.S.A., 13 Jan. 1921. Trained for the diplomatic service, in which he served 1891–5. Whilst in Vienna, stud. harmony under Mandyczewski. Stud. singing in Paris under Bouhy, and in London under Henry Russell and Victor Beigel. He made his 1st public appearance with the Handel Soc. in Humperdinck's *Pilgrimage to Kevelaar* at Westmorland Festival, Kendal, in May, 1903, and rose suddenly to fame with Elgar's *Gerontius*, the chief part of which he sang over 100 times. He was equally fine in Bach's *St. Matthew Passion*, and sang in these two works in Britain, Germany, Holland and America. His voice had no unusual strength, but was managed with superb skill. His chief virtue lay in his perfect musicianship and intensely sympathetic renderings. These qualities were especially revealed in his singing of Brahms' *lieder* as well as of English songs. Several of the more serious of the Eng. song-composers of his time owe much to him for the introduction of their songs. After his death a memorial fund was started for the benefit of needy musicians. A tablet and bust have been erected to his memory in Queen's Hall, London.—E.-H.

EMMANUEL, Maurice. Fr. compr. musicologist; *b.* Bar-sur-Aube, 2 May, 1862. Pupil (at Paris Cons.) of Bourgault-Ducoudray, Delibes, Savard, and (at Brussels) of Gevaert. Was mus. dir. of Ste.-Clotilde. Since 1909, has taught mus. history at Cons. in chair of Bourgault-Ducoudray. Has composed:

Vn. sonata; 2 str. 4tets; 6tet, *Airs rythmés à l'antique*; *Oriental Suite*, pf. and vn.; *Prométhée*; *Pierrot peintre*; songs; choruses.

His work in musicology is much more important: *The Greek Orchestra* (1895); *The Education of the Greek Dancer* (1895); *History of Musical Language* (1911); *Treatise on the Modal Accompaniment of the Psalms* (1912). Many articles in the reviews: *The Conservatoires of Germany and Austria* (*Revue de Paris*, 1898); *Le Chant à l'École* (*Grande Revue*, 1910); *Music at the German Universities* (*Revue de Paris*, 1910); *Treatise on Greek Music* (in Lavignac's *Encyclopédie*).—A. C.

ENARMONIUM. See BAGLIONI, SILVESTRO.

ENCYCLOPÉDIE DE LA MUSIQUE. This Fr. work, which bears as sub-title, "Dictionnaire du Conservatoire," was begun in 1912. Its direction was entrusted by the Government to Albert Lavignac; then, on the death of the latter, to Lionel de la Laurencie. The work will contain 3 parts, each consisting of several vols. The first part treats of *l'Histoire de la Musique*; the 2nd will treat of *Technique, Pédagogie et Esthétique*; the third, a *Dictionnaire*, will recapitulate the two first in alphabetical order. The authors of the principal contributions are: Maurice Emmanuel (Ancient Greece); Amédée Gastoué (Byzantine music and Gregorian chant); Henry Expert and P. M. Masson (XVI century); R. Rolland and André Pirro (XVII century); de la Laurencie (XVIII century); J Rouanet (Arabian music), etc. The first part only has appeared so far (5 vols. Delagrave).—A. C.

ENEHJELM, Alexis af. Finnish opera-singer (t.); *b.* Hämeenlinna (Tavastehus), 2 Oct. 1886. Stud. at Helsingfors Univ.; music and singing in Munich (1908) and Vienna (1909–13); teacher at Helsingfors Music Inst. 1914–18; engaged at Finnish Opera House until 1921, when he went to Darmstadt Opera House. Is much admired as an excellent singer and artist; has sung in Vienna, Petrograd, and other places; also frequently at concerts in Finland. Has publ. songs and a collection of tales.—T. H.

ENESCU, George. Rumanian violinist, composer and conductor; *b.* Liveni (Moldau, Rumania), 19 Aug. 1881. From 7th to 11th year, studied at Vienna Conservatoire, at first under Bachrich, later under Hellmesberger; composition under Robert Fuchs. On leaving the Conservatoire in his 11th year, received the highest award—the *Gesellschafts-medaille*. When 13, went to Paris under the patronage of Queen Elizabeth of Rumania. At the Paris Conservatoire, studied violin under Marsick, composition under Gédalge, Massenet and finally Fauré. In 1899, 1st prize for violin-playing. When 16, made his first public appearance as composer with *Poema Româna* (*Rumanian Poem*) performed in Paris by Colonne, who also performed Enescu's 1st Suite for orchestra in 1903, and his 1st symphony (E flat, op. 13) in 1906 (pub. Enoch, Paris). Enescu then travelled through Europe as violin virtuoso. In order to encourage music in his native land, he founded in 1912 a National Prize for works by younger Rumanian composers (awarded successively to Otescu, Cuctin, Alessandrescu, Tora, Enacovici and Stan Golestan). As conductor Enescu has appeared chiefly in Bucharest, where during recent years he has given many orchestral concerts of modern works. His first Suite was first given in Queen's Hall in 1911, and his *Orch. Rhapsody* was given there in 1921. His 2 *Rumanian Rhapsodies* (No. 1 in A, No. 2 in D) are in the permanent repertoire of the Queen's Hall Orch. He visited London in 1922, playing Lalo's *Symphonie Espagnole* and conducting his own 2nd Rhapsody with great success.

Important works, besides those mentioned, include:

1st and 2nd sonatas, pf. and vn., ops. 2 and 6; str. 4tet, op. 7; str. 8tet, op. 7. *Symphonie Concertante*, cello and orch. op. 8; 2 pf. suites, op. 3 and 10; Variations for 2 pfs. op. 5; *Chansons de Clément Marot* for v. and pf. op. 15 (all Enoch, Paris). Some later works—2nd symphony in A, op. 17 (1905), 2nd Suite for orch. op. 18—are not yet publ., as the mss., in the political confusion, found their way to Moscow, where they have since remained. His last two works are 3rd symphony in C, orch. pf. organ, chorus (perf. Bucharest, 1919; Paris under Pierné, 1920); and a str. 4tet. He has in hand a lyric drama *Œdipus* (poem by Edmond Fleg).—C. BR.

ENGEL, Carl. Amer. compr. librarian; *b.* Paris, 21 July, 1883. Stud. at Univs. of Strasburg and Munich. Pupil in compn. of Thuille in Munich. Went to America in 1905 and from 1909–21 was ed. and mus. adviser for Boston Music Co. Since Jan. 1922, chief of music division of Library of Congress, Washington, D.C.

Triptych, vn. and pf. (Boston Music Co. 1920); pf. pieces and songs (Boston Music Co.; Schirmer; C. Fischer); author of *Alla Breve, from Bach to Debussy* (Schirmer, 1921).—O. K.

ENGLISH CHORAL MUSIC FROM 1880. In the year 1880, musical England was still largely under the sway of the Handelian and Mendelssohnian traditions. In sacred music, the legacy left behind by Spohr (*Last Judgment*, Norwich, 1830; *Calvary*, *ib.* 1839) still lingered in a taste for sugary chromatics, despite the fact that two delightfully English works—Sterndale Bennett's *May Queen* (1858) and his *Woman of Samaria* (1867)—had shown the way to better things. In 1882, French operatic taste had been imported into English oratorio with Gounod's *Redemption* (written for the Birmingham Fest.); and even in 1898, Sullivan could not banish the secular stage feeling from his sacred music (*Golden Legend*, Leeds Fest.). Yet it was the year 1880 in which was first heard a cantata sounding again the real English note. This was Parry's *Prometheus Unbound*, produced at the Gloucester Three Choirs Fest. Parry's long and regular series of festival oratorios and cantatas, from *Prometheus* onwards, slowly but surely established a thoroughly English choral type, one which bowed less and less to Handel and Mendelssohn, and was only slightly touched at times by Wagner (*Saul*, 1894). Parry's broad sweep, his mastery of choral effect and his skill in building up huge climaxes are all seen at their best in his 8-part chorus, *Blest Pair of Sirens* (1887), and in *Job*.

It must be remembered that the great choral festivals (Birmingham, Leeds, Sheffield, The Three Choirs, Norwich, etc.) then offered the only field open to British composers. All Stanford's choral works were written for these meetings (*The Revenge*, Leeds 1886; *Eden*, Birmingham

1891; *Phaudrig Crohoore*, Norwich 1896; *Stabat Mater*, Leeds 1907). Mackenzie wrote his *Rose of Sharon* for Norwich 1884, his *Story of Sayid* for Leeds 1886; his cantata with reciter, *The Dream of Jubal*, which contains some of his best work, was produced at a Liverpool Philh. concert in 1889. Cowen's *Rose Maiden* was written in 1870; but his *St. John's Eve* of 1899, written for Melbourne, is of stronger material most skilfully orchestrated and his *Ruth* is a charming work. The choral works of Delius include *Appalachia* (Lower Rhine Fest. 1905), *Sea-Drift* (1906), *A Mass of Life* (London, 1909), *Song of the High Hills* (London, 1912) and his *Requiem* (produced London, 1920).

Since Parry, the outstanding figure in oratorio is Elgar. After several prentice works (*The Black Knight*, *The Light of Life*, *Caractacus*, etc.) came *Gerontius* (1902), produced in England and, shortly after, in Germany. It was an epoch-making work in the sense that no one had ever made the complex mass of modern chorus and orchestra the vehicle for so strong an expression of personal faith and feeling. He followed it up with *The Apostles* (Birmingham, 1903), *The Kingdom* (*ib.* 1906), and in 1916 produced his intensely felt *Spirit of England* to Laurence Binyon's war-poems.

Granville Bantock in his *Omar Khayyám* (an epoch-making work in its way, like *Gerontius*), his *Atalanta in Calydon*, his *Vanity of Vanities* (both for unacc. chorus) and *The Great God Pan*, carried the banner of progress and enrichment still further. Other landmarks were Walford Davies's *The Temple* (Worcester Fest. 1902) in which he tried the effects of chamber-music interspersed amongst the orch. portions, and his *Everyman* (Leeds Fest. 1904), Coleridge-Taylor's *Hiawatha* (1906), and Vaughan Williams's *Sea-Symphony* (Leeds, 1910). John H. Foulds's *A World Requiem* (Albert Hall, London, 11 Nov. 1923) was conceived on so colossal a scale, and in so sincere yet austere a mood, that it could hardly be fully appreciated at a first hearing.

The taste seems now to be turning in the direction of shorter works and a greater variety of subjects and treatments. Chief amongst these is Holst's *Hymn of Jesus* (London, 25 March, 1920, R. Philh. Soc. concert). His *Choral Hymns from the Rig Veda* (1908–12), his *Two Psalms*, his *Ode to Death*, his choruses to *Alkestis*, and his choral peroration to the orch. suite *The Planets*, are all remarkable.

Amongst prominent writers of shorter choral pieces are Arnold Bax, Herbert Brewer, Havergal Brian, B. J. Dale, Balfour Gardiner, Hamilton Harty, Cyril Rootham, Peter Warlock, W. J. Whittaker and others.

The choral bodies of the country have never been in a more efficient state and, in consequence, many new fields are being opened to the choral composers. For this healthy state of things, the growing mus. competition movement is largely responsible.—E.-H.

ENGLISH FOLK-MUSIC. See BUTTERWORTH, GEORGE; CAREY, FRANCIS; CHAPLIN, NELLIE;

ERLEBACH, RUPERT; GRAINGER, GEORGE PERCY; KIDSON, FRANK; MOERAN, E. J.; SHARP, CECIL; VAUGHAN WILLIAMS, RALPH; also art. FOLK-SONG SOCIETIES.

ENGLISH OPERA FROM 1880. The year 1880 found Balfe's *Bohemian Girl* (written 1843) and Wallace's *Maritana* (written 1845) still in the field of popular favour, whilst Sullivan had just commenced his brilliant series of comic operas, with *Pinafore* in 1878. The successful revival in 1920 of the early Eng. *Beggar's Opera* (1727) has revealed a distinct link with Sullivan's work. Mackenzie made a beginning with *Colomba* in 1883 and followed it with *The Troubadour* (Drury Lane, Carl Rosa, 1886) and *The Cricket on the Hearth* (R.A.M. 1914). Like Hamish MacCunn's *Jeannie Deans* (Edinburgh, 1894) and *Diarmid* (London, 1897), though melodious, they were too old-fashioned in form to gain a firm hold on the boards. The operas of Cowen (*Pauline*, 1876; *Thorgrim*, 1890; *Signa*, Milan, 1893, Covent Garden, 1894; *Harold*, 1895) had only a fleeting success. Stanford's works were of stronger material. The first two were produced in Germany—*The Veiled Prophet of Khorassan* (Hanover, 1881) and *Savonarola* (Stadttheater, Hamburg, 1882). The latter was given at Covent Garden under Richter with the Ger. Opera Co. in 1884. His *Canterbury Pilgrims* was produced by the Carl Rosa Co. at Covent Garden in 1884, and *Shamus O'Brien* at the old Opéra-Comique, London, in 1896. His *Much Ado About Nothing* deserves mention. *The Critic* (produced by Beecham at Shaftesbury Theatre, Jan. 1916) shows considerable knowledge of stage-craft. His last opera, *The Travelling Companion* (written 1918–19), still awaits performance.

Ethel Smyth's *Der Wald* was produced at Dresden in 1901 and Berlin in 1902. Her *Strandrecht* (*The Wreckers*) produced at Leipzig in 1906, sounded old-fashioned when first heard in England (under Beecham) in Jan. 1909. Her *Boatswain's Mate* is more characteristic. It was produced by Beecham in Jan. 1916. Her 1-act *Fête Galante* (British National Opera Co. 1923) proved an unequal work. Delius found a keen supporter in Beecham, who produced his *Village Romeo and Juliet* in 1910. It had already been given in Berlin in 1907. His *Koanga* (produced Elberfeld, 1904) and his *Fennimore and Gerda* (Frankfort, 1919) have not yet reached the English boards. Isidore de Lara, whose *Amy Robsart* had been given at Covent Garden in 1893, had his *Nail* given there in 1919. It was originally written to French words, and derives largely from the school of Massenet. His *Messaline* has been given several times, and his *Three Musketeers*, prod. by the Carl Rosa Co. in 1923, was given in London in May 1924. Edward W. Naylor's *The Angelus* secured the Ricordi Prize in 1910 and was produced several times at Covent Garden. It was written avowedly on Italian lines.

The only composer in the light opera lineage of Sullivan was Edward German. He turned the balance more on to the musical side in *Merrie England, Princess of Kensington, Tom Jones,* and *Fallen Fairies.*

In 1904, Richter had taken charge of the Wagner performances at Covent Garden, and his influence on English composers cannot be ignored. The two, on whom Wagner's spell is most deeply shown were Holbrooke and Boughton. Both are romantic. Holbrooke's *The Children of Don* was given at Hammerstein's ill-fated London Opera House in 1912 under Nikisch, and his *Dylan* at Drury Lane Theatre in 1913 under Beecham. *Bronwen*, which completes the trilogy, still awaits performance. Debussy's *Pelléas et Mélisande* (1902) had been given at Covent Garden in 1909, without any direct influence on English opera. Richard Strauss's operas (*Salome, Elektra, Rosenkavalier, Ariadne, Feuersnot*) also made a strong impression on English composers, which was strengthened by the brilliant seasons of Russian opera and ballet which Sir Joseph Beecham organised in 1913 and 1914 (Mussorgsky's *Boris*, and *Khovanstchina*; Rimsky-Korsakof's *Coq d'Or* and *Ivan the Terrible*; Stravinsky's *Petrushka, Sacre de printemps*, etc.).

Meanwhile Rutland Boughton had been organising his Festival School at Glastonbury, a tiny town in Somerset; and had brought his players up to the "Old Vic." London, with his *Immortal Hour*. It was not, however, till this opera was presented at the Regent Theatre by Barry Jackson, that it scored the longest run of any romantic opera in England. His *Bethlehem* was also successful at the same theatre in 1923–4. An unfortunate first performance of his *Alkestis* (28 Jan. 1924) by the British National Co. did not give the work a fair start; but they performed it in the provinces with considerable success. It is an earlier work than *The Immortal Hour*. The chief figure of the "nineteen-twenties," next to Boughton, is Gustav Holst. His *Perfect Fool*, a one-act piece, a light-hearted mixture of the romantic and the parodic, made a decisive success for English opera, which is bound to bear fruit in the future. His *Savitri*, an *opera da camera* (written 1908) was too intimate for Covent Garden, but is a great favourite in the British National Opera Co.'s provincial tours.

Nicholas Gatty has produced 4 of his operas at minor theatres—*Greysteel* (Sheffield, 1906), *Duke or Devil* (Manchester, 1909), *The Tempest* (Surrey Theatre, London, 1920), *Prince Ferelon* (Old Vic. London, 1921), of which the last was the most successful. He is one of the very few English composers with a real sense of the stage. Reginald Somerville's *David Garrick* (Carl Rosa, 1920) inclined more to the form of the light opera, lyrical in design and tuneful in expression. Cyril B. Rootham's *The Two Sisters* (produced Cambridge, 1921) is founded on folk-themes. James Lyon's *Sea-Wrack*, given by the Carl Rosa Co. in Liverpool in 1921, revealed considerable dramatic power.

Altogether the period from 1900 to 1920 did not contain so many or such weighty works as the period from 1880 to 1900. This can only be explained by the diminished opportunities for native works in this period. With the foundation of the British National Opera Company in 1921 the door was immediately opened again to native composition, and composers were not slow to avail themselves of the chance.—E.-H.

ENGLISH ORCHESTRAL MUSIC. See BRITISH ORCHESTRAL MUSIC.

ENGLISH SINGERS, The. A vocal sextet party in London, which has specialised on the Tudor madrigalian music: Flora Mann, Winifred Whelen, Lillian Berger, Steuart Wilson, Clive Carey and Cuthbert Kelly. Many recitals in London and provinces. Sang in Prague, 1920; Vienna and Berlin, 1922–3.—E.-H.

ENGLISH SONG FROM 1880. The Mid-Victorian period produced singularly few English songs of any value. A few names, such as Loder and Macfarren, are mentioned with respect by historians, but Hatton's *To Anthea* is practically the only song of those days which is still admitted to serious singers' programmes. Sterndale Bennett wrote a small number of songs which show his invariably polished craftsmanship, but they are more German than English in style. Sullivan might have become a great song-writer, but generally speaking his songs are addressed, like those of his forgotten contemporaries, to a much lower standard of musical intelligence than his other works. The English song, even at its best, was a mere drawing-room amusement. Parry and Stanford, prolific in other branches of composition, wrote few songs compared with the song-output of Schumann and Brahms; and in their earlier days their songs were little known or appreciated. Maude Valérie White, starting from the drawing-room level, set out to raise the standard gradually. Her songs are in no case great works of art, but she chose words with discrimination and set them with something more than mere refinement. Almost up to the end of the XIX century the songs of Schubert, Schumann and Brahms formed the main repertory of self-respecting English singers, and there were few English singers indeed to whom this epithet could be applied. Except for the songs of Maude Valérie White, there was a clear line of cleavage between the popular drawing - room song, called in the music-trade a "ballad," and the "classical" song, to which even the best English composers contributed but few examples. Towards the end of the century, Arthur Somervell, a disciple of Stanford and Parry, began to make a name as a writer of English songs that were both artistic and attractive. About the same time he published *Songs of the Four Nations*, a collection of English, Scottish, Irish and Welsh traditional songs, to which he supplied scholarly accompaniments in the artistic idiom of the day. This volume, which at once obtained immense popularity, paved the way, along with the equally scholarly Irish collections of Stanford and Charles Wood, for the folk-song revival (see FOLK-SONG SOCIETIES), the influence of which on contem-

porary English song-composition has been far-reaching. Parry's output of songs became more copious, as singers became more willing to sing English songs, and a younger generation of composers carried the tradition further. Vaughan Williams, heart and soul in the folk-song movement, edited collections of East Anglian songs with daring harmonic treatment, besides producing many original songs (*The House of Life* [Rossetti], *Songs of Travel* [Stevenson], and *On Wenlock Edge* [A. E. Housman]) of singular beauty. More in the line of Maude Valérie White is Roger Quilter, a song-writer of very individual grace and charm. French influences of the older school made themselves felt on Goring Thomas and Amherst Webber; the later influence of Debussy brought not merely new harmonic ideas but a more supple and delicate declamation of English. The composers who thus raised English song to an artistic level were all men and women of real literary culture. It is safe to say nowadays that no English song is worth looking at at all unless the words of it can claim respect as poetry; unfortunately it cannot always be said that a good poem guarantees an equally good musical setting. Various composers who are distinguished in instrumental music are hopelessly betrayed in their songs by their want of literary feeling. Among contemporary song-writers of note may be named, in addition to those already mentioned, John Ireland, Arthur Bliss, "Peter Warlock," Armstrong Gibbs, R. O. Morris, Clive Carey, Malcolm Davidson, Martin Shaw, Cyril Rootham, and the late W. Denis Browne.— E. J. D.

From an editorial point of view, in order to complete the survey of contemporary English song, many other names must be mentioned: Granville Bantock, for his *Sappho* set, the *Browning Songs*, his Eastern songs, etc.; Ernest Walker for such highly finished works as *Diaphenia, Bluebells from the Clearings*, etc.; William Wallace (*Freebooter Songs*, etc.); Sir Edward Elgar (*Sea Songs*, etc.); Cyril Scott, Hamilton Harty, Joseph Holbrooke, Julius Harrison, Donald Tovey, Arnold Bax, E. Bristow Farrar and George Butterworth. The latter, during his short career, wrote some English songs of the finest order.—E.-H.

ENNA, August. Danish compr. *b.* 13 May, 1860. Of Ital. descent, his grandfather, a soldier of Napoleonic period, having emigrated to Denmark. E. learned the shoemaker's trade; then engaged in business; stud. music unaided in his free time. At 20, went to Finland, where he was engaged in an orch. as violinist and drummer. Later returned to Denmark and joined a travelling theatrical company, for whose performances he furnished the necessary incidental music. He then wrote several operettas, which foreshadow his later development. The successful production of an orch. suite at the Tivoli, Copenhagen, drew attention of Niels W. Gade, who assisted Enna in procuring a government stipendium to help him continue his studies abroad. Upon his return, his opera *Hexen (The Witch)* was produced at R. Theatre, Copenhagen, 1892. This speedily obtained a hearing in Prague, Berlin, Magdeburg, Weimar, Hanover, Königsberg, Stockholm, Amsterdam, etc. He followed up this first success by a whole series of operas: *Cleopatra*; *Aucassin and Nicolette*; *Lamia*; *Prinsessen paa Ärten* (*The Princess and the Peat*); *Nattergalen* (*The Nightingale*): *Den lille Pige med Svovlstikkerne* (*The Little Match-Girl*) (last 3 texts from Hans Chr. Andersen); *Gloria Arsena* (subject from Fr. Revolution); *Komedianter* (*The Comedians*), libretto from Victor Hugo's *L'Homme qui rit.* Also ballets, *Hyrdinden og Skorstensfejeren* (*Shepherdess and Chimney-Sweeper*) and *St. Cecilias Guldsko* (*St. Cecilia's Golden Slippers*); *The Story of a Mother* (Hans Chr. Andersen) for chorus; 2 symphonies; vn. concerto; pf. pieces; songs; incidental music to Strindberg's *Kronebruden* (*The Crown-Bride*) and to a couple of pantomimes.

Of his voluminous productions, the dramatic works rank highest, his Ital. blood finding full vent in these forms, both vocally and instrumentally. He has kept well abreast of the times, his 1st opera, *The Witch*, following Verdi traditions; the latest, *The Comedians*, follows "Verism."—A. H.

EPSTEIN, Richard. Austrian pianist; *b.* Vienna, 26 Jan, 1869; *d.* New York, 1921. Stud there under his father at Cons.; then for 2 years in Berlin and Dresden; prof. at Vienna Cons.; settled in London, 1905; later lived in America.—E.-H.

EQUAL TEMPERAMENT. A method of tuning by slightly flattening the naturally pure "fifth," which leaves all the 12 keys equally tuned. It is the tuning now universally adopted for all keyboard instrs., and the harp. Compare UNEQUAL TEMPERAMENT.—E.-H.

ERB, Joseph Marie. Fr. compr. *b.* Strasburg, 23 Oct. 1860. Pupil at École Niedermeyer; later under Widor; now prof. of organ and compn. at Cons. Strasburg; orgt. at Church of St.-Jean. Has publ. organ sonatas and suites which rank among masterpieces of modern organ compns.; also numerous motets and masses which present a new ideal in church music; 4 operas (produced at Strasburg); symph. poems; many choral works.—F. R.

ERDMANN, Eduard. Pianist and compr. *b.* Wenden (Latvia), 5 March, 1896. Stud. under Bror Möllersten (pf.), Jean de Chastain (pf.) and Harald Creutzburg (harmony and cpt.), in Riga. Removed to Berlin, 1914; stud. compn. under Heinz Tiessen and pf.-playing under Conrad Ansorge. As compr. he is an exceptionally daring, temperamental and high-spirited artist; but in spite of enterprising flights into harmonic realms, he still keeps to a tonal basis. As pianist he is a pioneer of the little-heard works of the older, as well as of the more recent composers.
An den Frühling, vn. op. 1 (Ries & Erler); songs (*id.*); pf. pieces; *Rondo*, orch. op. 9 (Jatho Verlag); symphony, op. 10, (Steingräber); sonata for vn. alone, op. 12 (Jatho Verlag).—A. E.

EREMINAS. See LITHUANIAN MUSIC.

ERGO, Émile. Belgian theorist; teacher; *b.* Selzaete, 20 Aug. 1853. Acc. parents to Holland, to Terneuzen; returned to Belgium, 1883, to Antwerp. Cond. choral soc. (1898–1900 Ant-

werpia, a Ger. soc.; 1900–3 *Antwerpener Rubenskring*). Taught for some time in School of Music at Ixelles. As a musicographer, he became the representative in Belgium of the theory of harmonic dualism of von Öttingen-Riemann, on which he wrote a pamphlet. The works of V. Mahillon had likewise some influence on his book *Dans les propylées de l'instrumentation*. Contributor to mus. reviews, especially *Weekblad voor Muziek* (Amsterdam). His writings are characterised by their very enthusiastic, sometimes aggressive tone. He gave numerous lectures.
Eene ingrijpende Hervorming op musikaal Gebied (1887); *Le Dualisme harmonique* (1891); *Muziek diktaat* (1890); a Flemish transl. of *Harmonielehre* of Riemann (1894); *Leerboek voor het contrapunkt* (1896–1902); *Themaboek voor contrapunkt* (1897), *Verhandeling over de Sequenzen* (1898); *Elementaarmuziekleer* (1903); *Leerboek voor het muzieklezen* (1905–6); *Dans les propylées de l'instrumentation* (1908); *Uber R. Wagners Harmonik und Melodik* (1914).—E. C.

ERIKSSON, Josef. Swedish compr. *b.* Söderfors, 8 Dec. 1872. Stud. R. Cons. Stockholm; then compn. under Ruben Liljefors. Choirmaster and orgt. in Upsala, where he lives as composer.
Songs with pf. (13 nos.); male-v. choruses; pf. pieces (op. 22, *Sonatine*); organ (op. 1, 7); *Air*, vn. and pf. op. 15; suite, *Bukolika*, str. 4tet, op. 27. (Publ. Lundqvist; Elkan & Schildknecht [Emil Carelius]; Hansen; Dahlström.)—P. V.

ERKEL, Franz. Hungarian opera compr. condr. *b.* Békésgyula, 7 Nov. 1810; *d.* 15 June, 1893. Stud. in Pozsony (now Bratislava, Czecho-Slovakia). From 1837, opera-condr. at Hungarian National Theatre, Budapest. 1853, founded Budapest Philh. Soc. (dir. until 1875). Dir. and pf. prof., R. High School, Budapest, 1875–89. Operas: *Hunyadi László* (1st perf. 1844); *Bánk bán* (1st perf. 1861), both still favourite repertoire-pieces of R. Hungarian Opera House. Last operas: *Névtelen Hősök* (1st perf. 1880); *István király* (1st perf. 1885). Comp. melody of Hungarian National Anthem, 1875.—B. B.

ERLANGER, Camille. Fr. compr. *b.* Paris, 1863; *d.* 1919. Pupil of Delibes. *Grand Prix de Rome* 1888, with cantata *Velléda*. His music is derived from Massenet and from Italian verism. Chiefly for stage.
Le Juif polonais, 1900; *Le Fils de l'Étoile*, 1904; *Aphrodite*, 1906; *Forfaiture* (posthumous work, unworthy of his talent, 1920); *La Chasse fantastique*, orch. 1893; *St. Julien l'Hospitalier*, 1894; some songs.—A. C.

ERLEBACH, Rupert. Eng. compr. pianist; *b.* Islington, London, 16 Nov. 1894. Stud. R.C.M. under Sir Charles Stanford and Vaughan Williams(compn.); Franklin Taylor and Howard-Jones (pf.); has comp. in all forms, and believes in making the fullest use of folk-songs.
Orch.: *Before Dawn*, op. 22 (1922); *A Memory*, op. 25 (1923); *2 Folk-song Poems* for small str. orch. op. 24; *Rhapsody*, fl. ob. (c.a.) vn. vla. cello, op. 17 (1921; a Carnegie award in 1922); *Moods*, str. 4tet, op. 19; *2 Legends*, vn. and pf. (Curwen); sonata, cello and pf. (folk-song) in C, op. 8, No. 1 (*id.*); *Mystic Pieces*, vn. and pf. op. 21 (Goodwin); *Folk-song Suite*, Set I, op. 14a, organ (Stainer & Bell); *Folk-Carol Suite*, op. 29, organ (1923, *id.*); songs; choruses; etc. (Goodwin; Curwen).—E.-H.

ERNST, Alfred. Fr. musicologist; *b.* Périgueux, 9 April, 1860; *d.* Paris, 15 May, 1898.

Helped considerably Wagner's fame in France; produced transl. of his works.

L'Œuvre dramatique d'Hector Berlioz, 1884; *Richard Wagner et le drame contemporain*, 1887; *L'Art de R. Wagner*, 2 vols. 1893.—A. C.

ERSHOF, Ivan Vassilievitch (*accent 2nd syll.*). Russ. t. singer; *b.* district of Don Cossacks, 1868. Stud. Petrograd Cons.; later in Italy. In 1894–5, sang in opera co. at Charkof; from 1895, at Maryinsky Opera House, Petrograd; a brilliant heroic t., especially in Wagner's works.—V. B.

ERTEL, J. Paul. Ger. compr. *b.* Posen, 22 Jan. 1865. Pupil of Ed. Tauwitz, Posen ; stud. pf. under Louis Brassin, later with Liszt; came out as pianist. Stud. law in Berlin from 1886; after State exam. devoted himself to compn. LL.D. 1898; teaches music in Berlin (Born's Pädagogium and Petersen's Acad.). Music critic to Berlin *Lokalanzeiger*. From 1897 to 1905 ed. *Deutsche Musikerzeitung*.

Symphony, *Harald*; symph. poems: *Maria Stuart*, op. 1 (1896); *Belsazar*, op. 12; *Pompeji*, *Die nächtliche Heerschau* (*Night Review*), op. 16, 1908; *Der Mensch*, op. 9 (with organ, 1905); *Hero and Leander*, op. 20 (1909); double fugue for orch. and organ; vn. concerto; str. 4tet on Hebrew melodies, op. 14, D mi.; 2 suites for vn. and pf. op. 38; and *La Suisse* (olden style); sonata for pf. and vn. C mi. op. 50; ballads for barit. and organ and str. 4tet, *Die Wallfahrt nach Kevlaar* and *Des Sängers Fluch* (*The Singer's Curse*); harmonium 4tet: 2 Passacaglias (D mi., C mi.), for organ; prelude and double fugue on *Wachet auf*, organ; operas, *Gudrun* and *Die heilige Agathe*; pf. pieces; songs.—A. E.

ESAFONIA. New tonal effect, obtained by dividing the octave into 6 perfectly equal parts, expounded by Domenico Alaleona (*q.v.*) in his *I moderni Orizzonti della Tecnica Musicale* (Turin, 1911, Bocca).—E.-H.

ESLAVA Y ELIZONDO, Father Hilarión. Span. compr. *b.* Burlada (Navarra), 21 Oct. 1807; *d.* Madrid, 23 July, 1878. Choir-boy at Pamplona Cath. (1816); violinist of Chapel orch. there (1824). Choir-master at Cath. of Burgo de Osma (1828) and at Seville Cath. (1832). Mus. dir. at Royal Chapel, Madrid (1844). In 1854, prof. of compn. at Real Cons. de Música, Madrid; later, dir. of same. Knight of Gran Cruz de Isabel la Católica, and María Victoria; Commander of Order of Carlos III; founder of the *Gaceta Musical de Madrid* (1855). Stud. under Sebastián Prieto and Francisco Secanilla.

A hard Northerner, lacking imagination and artistic sensibility, Eslava, the most influential musician in his country during the 3rd quarter of xix century, used his activities in contradictory directions, indifferent to æsthetic ideals. He joins the Church in Seville and writes operas that raise an uproar of protest among the clergy. He introduces Span. numbers of the *flamenco* style in his Ital. operas, to please all sections of the public; founds the *Gaceta Musical de Madrid* and publishes the *Lyra Sacro-Hispana* and the *Museo Orgánico Español* to encourage the development of a national school, and at the same time flatters the perverted taste of the public with his operas, his religious music and even his educational works, all conceived after the pattern of the dominating Ital. school, of which he was the staunchest upholder. Had he not absorbed,

through his master Secanilla, the teachings, so fatal for Spanish religious music, of Francisco Javier Garcia, known in Naples as "Lo Spagnoletto" ? (*b.* 1750).

Eslava's operas were failures; but his church music, which he produced in profusion, was in his days accepted by all as beyond criticism. He establ. a wrong tradition. Some of his *Motetes a cappella* are not devoid of merit, but the rest do not offer any point of technical interest and in their very essence are the negation of mysticism. The most representative specimen is the theatrical *Miserere* (vs. and orch.) known as *Miserere Grande*. The t. part demands a singer with exceptional compass and dexterity. It is customary, since the days of Gayarre, to engage at a big fee a leading operatic tenor for its perf. at Seville Cath. during Holy Week. The importance of Eslava in public life was so great that numerous theatres, cafés, piano factories and editorial enterprises were, and still are, named after him throughout the country. It is curious to note, as a sign of the ill fate of the Span. school, that Eslava followed as mus. dir. of the R. Chapel, Madrid, an enlighted man who never exercised any influence among his contemporaries—the compr., condr. and singer Don Mariano Rodríguez de Ledesma (*b.* Saragossa, 1779). Ledesma was the herald in Spain of modern music and the antithesis of the unromantic, anti-progressivist, utilitarian Eslava, who, in point of character, was but a shrewd, hard-working, practical-minded man who would have succeeded in any profession he might have chosen. With the publication of the *Lyra Sacro-Hispana* he atoned in a certain measure for his artistic sins. His music to-day is the exclusive patrimony of an old-fashioned set of church-goers and an unprofessional section of the clergy, mostly in the south. The brilliant church comprs. and musicologists belonging to the Valencian, Catalonian and Basque groups, owe but little to him. They participate more of the spirit of Pedrell and Olmeda, and many of them have learned César Franck's gospel at the *Schola Cantorum*.

Lyra Sacro-Hispana, 7 vols.; *Museo Orgánico Español y Breve Memoria Histórica de los Organistas Españoles*; *Memoria Histórica de la Música en España*. Text-books. *Escuela de Armonía y Composición*; *Método Completo de Solfeo*. Operas: *Il Solitario* (Cadiz, 1841); *La Tregua de Ptolomaida* (Cadiz, 1842); *Pietro il Crudele* (Seville, 1843). Church music: 2 *Misereres*; 6 *Lamentations*; *Requiem Mass*; *Te Deum*; *Mass in A*; motets; *Bailes de Seises*, etc. (Publ. Unión Musical Española, Madrid.)—P. G. M.

ESNAOLA, Secundino. Span. prof. of singing and condr. Ex-music-master of Seminario, Salamanca. Since 1902, condr. of Orfeón Donostiarra, a choral soc. of San Sebastian which under his direction has attained great efficiency (see CHORAL SOCIETIES). His activities as a pioneer of mus. culture in Spain, have been rewarded with the Cross of Alfonso XII, the highest distinction conferred for literary and artistic merit in the country.—P. G. M.

ESPLÁ, Oscar. Span. compr. *b.* Alicante, Aug. 1886. Stud. engineering and philosophy in

Spain; stud. music, very early in life, in his native town; though later he stud. music in Germany under various masters, he may still be considered a self-taught compr. His training in abstract and exact science is not without influence on his mus. output, which gives evidence, at every stage of his progress, of his high intellectual qualities. He is one of the three leading Span. comprs., with Conrado del Campo and de Falla, representing the three different and well-defined tendencies in Span. modern school, since the advent of Pedrell and Albeniz. He is not a colourist, nor a Romantic. He has for basis the characteristic features of the popular music of Eastern Spain (*región levantina*), which has nothing in common with the current notions of so-called Oriental music, but he deals only incidentally with folk-lore picturesqueness in his music. He speaks with native feeling, in a universal language. This attitude led him to adopt a scale of his own formation, from which he evolves the harmonic system that gives to the texture of his music its regional character, without using any definite folk-melody. The scale is as follows:

This technical device appears in his works gradually, starting from op. 15, *Crepúsculo* and other works composed after his residence in Germany, reaching its full development in his 3 latest orch. works, *Ámbito de la Danza*, *Cíclopes de Ifach* and *Las Cumbres*, and the pf. *Confines*. These exhibit at the same time his highest technical achievement and mastery in the expression of his personality. Another aspect of his æsthetic principle is the tendency to use the elements of Impressionism within the broader boundaries of classical lines. He lectures and writes on music and philosophical subjects. His two most important literary works are *El Arte y la Musicalidad* and *Las actividades del espíritu y su fundamento estético* (Barcelona, Ed. Minerva).

Opera, *La Bella Durmiente* (*The Sleeping Beauty*). Orch.: Suite (1st prize International Competition for Symph. Works, Vienna, 1909); symph. poem, *El sueño de Eros*, perf. Munich,and Madrid; *Poema de niños*; fantasia-scherzo, *Ámbito de la danza*; symph. poem, *Las Cumbres*; choreographic poem, *Cíclopes de Ifach*. Chamber-music: pf. 5tet; sonata, vn. and pf. (1st perf. in England at concert of modern Span. music under Pedro G. Morales; Birmingham, March 1920); *Preludio*, organ and pf. Pf.: *Estudio fugado*; *Impresiones musicales*; *Cantos sin palabras* (*Songs without Words*); *Scherzo*; *Crepúsculo*, op. 15; *Crepúsculos*, op. 17; sonata; *Confines* (2 series). Choral work, *Coral religioso*. (Unión Musical Española, Madrid; Iberia Musical, Barcelona.)—P. G. M.

ESPOSITO, Michele. Compr. and pianist; *b.* Castellamare, near Naples, 29 Sept. 1855. Entered Cons. of Naples as pf. pupil of Cesi; and stud. compn. under Serrao for 8 years there; 1878, went to Paris for some years; 1882, chief pf. prof. R. Irish Acad. of Music. In his 40 years' residence in Dublin, he has devoted his energies to the encouragement of classical music in Dublin. Through his organisation, the R. Dublin Soc. chamber-music recitals were successful from the first. He has given pf. recitals for it every year. In 1899, he establ. Dublin Orch.

Soc. and cond. till its disbandment in 1914; also condr. of Sunday Orch. concerts (discontinued 1914). When the L.S.O. visited Woodbrook in 1913 and 1914, E. cond. some of concerts, and (under Hamilton Harty), played solo-part of his new pf. concerto. His cantata *Deirdre*, his *Irish Symphony* and his str. 4tet in D were awarded prizes by the Feis Ceoil (Irish Music Fest.). His sonata in D, cello and pf., was awarded a prize by the Incorporated Soc. of Musicians, London, 1899. His sonata in E mi., vn. and pf., gained prize in 1907 offered by La Société Nouvelle, Paris. His str. 4tet in C mi. gained prize offered by the Accademia Filarmonica, Bologna. With Sir Stanley Cochrane, he founded the " C. & E. Edition " for publishing music.

Deirdre (book by T. Rolleston), cantata for soli, chorus and orch. (Breitkopf); *The Tinker and the Fairy* (book by Douglas Hyde), 1-act opera (Dublin, C. & E. ed.); *The Post Bag* (book by A. P. Graves), 1-act opera (London, Boosey); *Irish Symphony*, orch. op. 50 (1902); *Poem* for orch. op. 44 (1899); *Irish Suite*, orch. op. 55 (C. & E. ed.); *Neapolitan Suite*, str. orch. op. 60 (*id.*); str. 4tet in D, op. 33 (Breitkopf, 1899); str. 4tet in C mi. op. 60 (C. & E. ed.); sonata in G, vn. and pf. op. 32 (Schott); sonata in E mi. vn. and pf. op. 46 (Paris, 1907, Astruc); sonata, vn. and pf. op. 67 (*id.*); sonata in D, cello and pf. op. 43 (Breitkopf).—W. St.

ESSIPOVA, Anna Nicolaievna. Russ. pianist; *b.* Petrograd, 19 Jan./1 Feb. 1851; *d.* there, 17 Aug. (n.s.), 1914. Stud. under Van Ark and Leschetizky at Petrograd Cons. Gold medallist 1870. Appeared in London 1874; Paris 1875; America 1876, etc. Married her former teacher, Leschetizky, in 1880; divorced 1892. From 1893 till death, prof. of pf. Petrograd Cons. She created her own school of playing; amongst its younger representatives are S. Prokofief and A. Borovsky.—V. B.

ETTINGER, Max. Compr. *b.* Lemberg, 27 Dec. 1874. Prevented from studying music early in life owing to ill-health. Received first instruction in harmony in Berlin in 1899. Passed through Cons. Munich, where he has since been living.

Vn. sonata, op. 10; cello sonata, op. 19; 5tet for 4 wood-wind and pf. op. 20; Suite after old English masters for full orch. op. 30; *Dreams*, 3 songs without words, full orch. op. 31; *Wisdom of the East* (Omar Khayyám), for soli, chorus and orch. (Nuremberg Fest. 1921); many songs; 1-act tragicomedy (from Boccaccio) *Der eifersüchtige Trinker* (*The Jealous Drinker*); tragic opera in 3 acts, *Judith*, op. 28 (after Hebbel; Nuremberg, 1921; publ. Die Schmiede, Berlin).—A. E.

EVANS, David. Welsh compr. and adjudicator; *b.* Resolven, Glamorganshire, 1874. Educated Arnold Coll. Swansea; Univ. Coll. Cardiff, and privately under late Prof. Ebenezer Prout. Graduated Mus.Bac. at Oxford, 1895; and later Mus.Doc. Orgt. New Jewin Presbyterian Ch., London, 1900–3; lecturer in music and head of department, Univ. Coll. of S. Wales and Monmouthshire, 1903. Prof. of music, Univ. Coll. Cardiff, 1909; examiner Central Welsh Board, 1908–20; ed. *Y Cerddor* (*The Musician*), Jan. 1916 to Dec. 1921. Condr. of Psalmody Fest. (*Cymanfaoedd Canu*) and of the Eryri Mus. Fest., Carnarvonshire.

Orch. suite (prize, Merthyr National Eisteddfod, 1901); orch. overture (Carnarvon National Eisteddfod Concerts, 1906); cantata, *Llawenhewch yn yr Ior (Rejoice in the Lord)* (Carnarvon National Eisteddfod Concerts, 1906); dramatic cantata, *The Coming of Arthur* (Breitkopf) (Cardiff Triennial Mus. Fest. 1907); ode, chorus and orch., *Deffro, mae'n ddydd* (opening of Coll. Buildings, Cardiff; and at Aberystwyth and Carnarvon National Eisteddfodau); ode, chorus and orch., *Carmen* (1909); operetta for children, *Bro y bugeiliaid* (Dewi Sant concert, Cardiff; Barry National Eisteddfod concert, etc.). Ed. of *Moliant Cenedl*; part-songs; choruses; anthems; church services, etc.—D. V. T.

EVANS, Edwin, sen. Eng. orgt. and writer; *b.* 1844; *d.* London, 21 Dec. 1923. Trained as an organist; best known as a writer. Nearly all his works are publ. by W. Reeves, London.

Beethoven's 9 Symphonies, Vol. I, 1923; Vol. II, 1924; *Handbook to the Vocal Works of Brahms; Modal Accompaniment of Plainchant; Wagner's Teachings by Analogy; How to compose; How to accompany at the Piano;* transl. of Wagner's *Opera and Drama.* He arranged a large number of opera overtures for the organ.—E.-H.

EVANS, Edwin, jun. Eng. writer on music, lecturer; *b.* London, 1 Sept. 1874. Son of Edwin E. sen.; general education at Lille, 1883–5; Echternach, Grand Duchy of Luxemburg, 1885–9; musically self-taught, except elementary lessons from E. E. sen.; followed many occupations before returning to music; cable telegraphy, 1889–1893; Stock Exchange and banking, 1895–1908; financial journalism, 1908–13; since then, music solely; began writing on music from 1901; series of arts. on modern Russ. comprs. 1902; on modern British comprs. 1902–3; subsequently lectured extensively on modern Fr. music; among the first in this country to draw attention to Debussy; lectured at R.A.M. on eve of 1st perf. of *Pelléas et Mélisande* in London. May 1914 to Nov. 1923, critic of *Pall Mall Gazette*; another series on modern British comprs., *Mus. Times,* 1919–20. Ed. of *Mus. News and Herald,* 1921–2; transl. several operas (*Louise, Pelléas et Mélisande*); intimately associated with Russ. Ballet; produced Barrie's fantasy *The Truth about the Russian Dancers* at Coliseum with music by Arnold Bax and *mise-en-scène* by Paul Nash; took part (1922) in discussions at Salzburg which led to creation of new International Soc. for Contemporary Music; has contributed copiously to leading Eng. reviews and also to mus. journals. As a critic E. E. combats claims to exclusive authority for any one kind of music; he admires both old and new music; confesses to a feeling of surfeit for the giants of the XIX century, but turns with great affection to XVIII century (Bach; Scarlatti; Mozart) and with great sympathy and curiosity to the XX century. In Jan. 1923, he was presented with his portrait by a group of young British comprs. and, in Dec. of same year, received the *Palmes Académiques* for his services to French music.

Tchaikovsky (J. M. Dent & Sons, 1921); transl. Jean-Aubry's *French Music of To-day* (Kegan Paul, 1919).—E.-H.

EVANS, Harry. Welsh choral condr. *b.* Dowlais, Glam., Wales, 1 May, 1873; *d.* Liverpool, 23 July, 1914. Resigned school-teaching for music in 1893, training choruses; chief choral prize, Welsh Nat. Eisteddfod, 1905; for male-v. choir, Liverpool Nat. Eist. 1900; acted fre-

quently as adjudicator; in 1902 became condr. of Liverpool Welsh Choral Union; 1906, orgt. Gt. George St. Congregational Ch., Liverpool. His *Victory of St. Garmon* was produced at Cardiff 1904 Fest. He was condr. of Liverpool Univ. Choral Soc.; dir. of music at Bangor Univ.; choral condr. of Liverpool Philh. Soc. With the Welsh Choral Union, perf. many modern works— Elgar's *Gerontius, Apostles*; Bantock's *Omar, Atalanta, Vanity of Vanities,* etc. Consult *Mus. Times,* Aug. 1907.—E.-H.

EVANS, Lindley. Compr. *b.* Cape Town, 1895. Now living in Sydney, N.S.W.

Trio, pf. vn. cello; sonata in old style, vn. and pf.; pf. pieces; many songs.—E.-H.

EVANS, T. Hopkin. Welsh condr. adjudicator, lecturer and compr. *b.* Resolven, Glamorganshire, 1879. Stud. under Dr. David Evans (Cardiff), Dr. Kitson and Granville Bantock; one of the most prominent of Welsh choral and orch. condrs.; condr. Neath Choral Soc., Liverpool Welsh Choral Union (successor of late Harry Evans), and Wrexham Choral and Orch. Soc.; graduated Mus.Bac. at Oxford, in 1913. Adjudicator at National Eisteddfodau and Eng. fests.

2 str. 4tets (prize); orch. overture, *Brythonic*; cantatas: *Cynon* (a tale of the Gododin), soli, chorus and orch.; *Ode to the Passions,* soli, chorus and orch.; choral song, *Fleur-de-lys,* s.m.-sopr.c.t.b.b.; *Ingeborg,* m.-sopr. solo and orch.; 6 songs, from Dryden; many part-songs; choruses; songs; pf. pieces.—D. V. T.

EVENEPOEL, Edmond. Belgian musicographer, *b.* Brussels, 23 March, 1846. An official at Ministry of Interior, now on retired list. 1880–1914, music critic of *La Flandre Libérale* (Ghent). Contributed to *Revue Wagnérienne* and to *Guide Musical*; wrote *Le Wagnérisme hors d'Allemagne* (Brussels, 1891).—E. C.

EVETTS, Edgar Thomas. Eng. singer, compr. *b.* Oxford, 20 Dec. 1864. Solo-boy at Cowley St. John's there; in 1879 went to America as solo-boy, St. Clement's, Philadelphia; 1882–5, in India; 1884–85, orgt. St. Peter's, Mazagon, Bombay; stud. singing at R.A.M. London, 1885–90; choirmaster at Holy Trinity, Sloane Sq., St. Mary's, The Boltons, S. Kensington, and Berkeley Chapel, Mayfair, 1889 (all 3 simultaneously); lecturer, London Acad. of Music, from 1910; founded operatic class there, 1920, in which year he became a dir. of the academy.

Songs (Augener; Lengnick); ed. Sieber's Solfeggios (18 books); Marchesi's; Panofka's; Vaccai's; etc. (Augener).—E.-H.

EVSEIEF, Serge Vassilievitch (*accent 2nd syll.*). Russ. compr. and pianist; *b.* Moscow, 25 Jan. (n.s.), 1894. Pupil of L. Conus (pf.), N. Metner (theory) and at Moscow Cons. under Goldenweiser (pf.), G. Catoire and S. I. Tanéief (theory). From 1922, teacher of theory at Moscow Cons.

Symphony, F sharp mi. op. 4; pf. trio, *Heroic Poem,* op. 7; pf. sonata, G mi. op. 2; 3 Russ. folk-songs with pf. op. 6; pf. pieces, op. 3, 5; 4 songs, op. 1 (op. 1, 2, 3, 5, 6, Russ. State Music Publ. Dept.). —V. B.

EXPERT, Henry. Fr. musicologist; *b.* Bordeaux, 12 May, 1863. Pupil of École Niedermeyer; advised by Reyer, César Franck and Gigout. In 1909 2nd librarian of Paris Cons.;

senior librarian since 1920. Prof., for a time, at École des Hautes Études Sociales. Since 1894, has publ. the magnificent coll. of *Maîtres Musiciens de la Renaissance française*, 23 vols. (*q.v.*); *Bibliographie thématique*; *Anthologie Chorale*; *Les Théoriciens de la Musique de la Renaissance*; *Sources du Corps de l'Art de Musique franco-flamande des XVe et XVIe siècles*; *Commentaires*; *Extraits des Maîtres Musiciens*. Also:

The Huguenot Psalter of XVI Century; *The Songs of France and Italy*; *The Harpsichord Masters of XVII and XVIII Centuries*; *The Diversions of the French Musicians of XVIII Century*; *Repertoire of Religious and Spiritual Music*. Has ed. the analytical notes in the Édition Nationale (Senart).—A. C.

EXPRESSIONISM. A term given to a new form of pictorial or mus. art, the chief exponent in painting being Kandinsky the Munich painter and, in music, Schönberg the Viennese compr. Consult *The Art of Spiritual Harmony* by Wassily Kandinsky (transl. by M. T. H. Sadler; Constable, 1914), and Egon Wellesz's book, *Arnold Schönberg* (J. M. Dent & Sons, 1924).—E.-H.

EYKEN, Heinrich. Ger. compr. *b.* Elberfeld,

19 July 1861; *d.* Berlin, 28 Aug. 1908. Pupil of Papperitz at Leipzig Cons., then of Herzogenberg at Berlin Acad. Teacher of theory at R. High School, 1902. As compr. became chiefly known through effective songs.

Judith's Song of Victory, contr. and orch.; *Icarus*, barit. and orch.; *Schmied Schmerz*; *Song of the Valkyrie*; *Stille Tröstung* (*Silent Consolation*); male choruses; a Psalm; *Serenade*. His chief work is the working-out of Liliencron's *Chorordnung* (4 vols. with 324 choral numbers in the strict style). A Harmony Tutor in ms. was publ. posthumously by H. Leichtentritt and O. Wappenschmidt in 1911.—A. E.

EYSLER, Edmund. Austrian operetta compr. *b.* Vienna, 12 March, 1874. Stud. a short time at Vienna Cons.; wrote many stage works, with a pronounced local note. He had a great success, chiefly because Girardi, the great Viennese actor, played the principal characters in his operettas.

Frauenfresser (1912); *Der berühmte Gabriel* (1916); *Der liebe Schatz* (1918); *Pufferl*; *Bruder Straubinger*, 1901 (his best work); *Vera Violetta* (1906). —P. P.

F

FABERT, Henri, (really Fabre). Fr. operatic t. *b.* 1881, of commercial family of Drôme; trained for business. Stud. law at Marseilles; then came to Paris. Attracted by the stage, played comic rôles in revues at music halls, and took up study of singing. *Début* in *La Fille de Madame Angot* at Gaîté-Lyrique; then sang in *La Vivandière* and *L'Attaque du Moulin.* Went to Opera-House, Monte Carlo, then to Opéra, Paris, where he gave brilliant perf. (Mime; Loge) in Wagner's *Ring* cycle. Also sang in operetta in Lyons, Brussels, Paris, Marigny. Formally engaged at Opéra, 1921, he sang in *L'Heure Espagnole, Rhinegold* (1922), *Falstaff, Magic Flute* and *Padmavati.* Began as 2nd t., later became 1st t. He excels as an actor. Gives fine renderings of songs of Schubert, Schumann and Mussorgsky, Ravel and Debussy.—A. R.

FACCIO, Franco. Ital. condr. *b.* Verona, 8 March, 1840; *d.* Monza, 21 July, 1891. After death of Angelo Mariani, F. was considered the foremost Ital. condr. Stud. at Milan Cons. (Mazzuccato School), where he was fellow-pupil with Arrigo Boito; F. was prof. in same Cons. from 1868. Comp. operas, *I Profughi fiamminghi* and *Amleto* (the latter on Boito's libretto); also a symphony and a 4tet. As a condr. he had a very grand style; during last years of his life, left impress of his personality on the seasons at La Scala, Milan, and at other theatres which competed for his services.—D. A.

FACH. The proper range of parts in Ger. theatres and operas. The chief *Fachen* are the Heldentenor (heroic tenor) corresponding to the Young Hero of the drama; High Dramatic Soprano, a Young Dramatic, a Coloratura-singer, and Opera Soubrette (all sopranos); a Leading Contralto, a Second Contralto, a " Comic Old Woman," a volunteer Soprano to do Pages, etc.; the Heroic Tenor, the Lyric Tenor, a Tenor-buffo, with sometimes a special Operetta Tenor; two baritones, *Heldenbariton* and Lyric; a serious and a comic Bass.—E.-H.

FACHIRI, Adila (*née* Arányi de Hunyadvár). Hungarian violinist; *b.* Budapest, 26 Feb. 1889. Early mus. education at R. Acad. of Music, Budapest. Began vn. at 10 under Hubay; at 17, artists' diploma, the highest distinction in Hungary; then stud. in Berlin under Joachim, her great-uncle (until his death), being the only private pupil he ever accepted. He left her one of his Stradivarius violins. She has played in public in chief cities of Hungary, Austria, Germany, Italy, France and Holland. First came to England in 1909. In 1915, married Alexander Fachiri, an Eng. barrister, living in London. Appears regularly at London concerts.—E.-H.

FÄHRMANN, E. Hans. Ger. orgt. and compr. *b.* Beicha, 17 Dec. 1860. Pupil of C. A. Fischer, Hermann Scholtz and J. L. Nicodé in Dresden; cantor and orgt. at Johanniskirche, Dresden, 1890; teacher of organ at Cons. Married Julie Bächi, contr. singer.

11 organ sonatas; organ concerto with orch., op. 20; other organ pieces; a symphony, C ma. op. 47; str. 4tet, op. 20; 2 pf. trios (op. 37, B ma.; op. 43, C sharp mi.); pf. sonata, op. 6; songs.—A. E.

FAIRCHILD, Blair. Amer. compr. *b.* Belmont, Mass., U.S.A., 23 June, 1877. Stud. at Harvard Univ. (A.B. 1899); mus. instruction from J. K. Paine and W. R. Spalding. Then went to Florence, studying pf. under Buonamici. After short business career, entered U.S. diplomatic service, and between 1901 and 1903 was stationed at Constantinople and in Persia. Many of his Eastern impressions bore fruit in his later compns. 1903, settled in Paris to devote himself entirely to music, studying under Widor and Ganaye. Since then, has resided alternately in Paris and in New York. Has comp. much in all forms, following, on the whole, classic models. His symph. poem *Zal,* op. 38, perf. in Paris, 1918. The ballet-pantomime *Dame Libellule,* op. 44, had its *première* at Opéra-Comique, Paris, 7 Dec. 1921.

East and West, poem for orch. op. 17 (Durdilly, 1908); str. 4tet, op. 27 (Demets, 1911); *Concert de Chambre,* vn. pf. and str. 4tet, op. 26 (Augener, 1912); 2 Bible Lyrics for chorus, s. solo and orch. op. 29: I, *From the Song of Songs;* II, *David's Lament* (H. W. Gray, 1911); *Tamineh,* sketch for orch. after a Persian legend (Augener, 1913); *Shah Féridoûn,* mus. picture for orch. op. 39 (*id.* 1915); sonata, vn. and pf. op. 43 (Durand, 1919); *Dame Libellule,* ballet-pantomime, op. 44 (pf. score Paris, Ricordi, 1919; full score *id.* 1921); *Étude symphonique,* vn. and orch. op. 45 (Durand, 1922); *Canti popolari italiani* (Tuscan *stornelli*) (Boston, W. C. Thompson, 1901–7). Op. 26 and op. 45 also publ. for vn. and pf.—O. K.

FAIRLESS, Margaret. Eng. violinist; *b.* New-castle-on-Tyne, 10 Nov. 1901. Stud. at Vienna Acad. under Ševčík (vn.), Rosé (chamber-music); London *début* at R. Albert Hall Sunday concerts followed by R. Philh. Soc. concerts and Queen's Hall Orch. concerts.—E.-H.

FALCHI, Stanislao. Ital. compr. *b.* Terni, 29 Jan. 1851; *d.* Rome, 17 Nov. 1922. 1902–15, dir. of R. Liceo Mus. di Santa Cecilia, Rome, which grew and flourished under his leadership; he had previously filled, in same Inst., the posts of teacher of choral singing and of compn. His output as a compr., inspired by a fine yet severe taste, includes the operas *Lorhélia* (Argentina Theatre, Rome, 1877), *Giuditta* (Apollo Theatre, Rome, 1887), *Il Trillo del Diavolo* (Argentina Theatre, Rome, 1899); a *Requiem,* an overture to Shakespeare's *Julius Cæsar* and much vocal and instr. chamber-music (publ. by Lucca; and Ricordi, Milan).—D. A.

FALCONER, Frederick James. Scottish violinist; *b.* Edinburgh, 2 May, 1885. Stud. under Prof. Wünsch in Brunswick in 1904; at the Prague Cons. in 1904; and at R.A.M. London, 1906–8. Has given successful recitals in Edinburgh, where he is now settled as a teacher.

Fantaisie for 4 vns.; pieces for pf.; and for vn. and pf.—W. S.

FALENI, Arturo. Argentine compr. *b.* Chieti, Italy, in 1877. Stud. at Genoa. Went to Buenos Ayres in 1897 and founded Verdi Inst. of Music. Practically self-trained, his compns. have been highly praised by Puccini, Mancinelli, Toscanini, and Mugnone.

Overture in D; Fantasia; *Romance sans paroles*; Fugue; music-poem, *Il Terremoto (The Earthquake)*; large number of songs and pf. pieces. Didactic works: *El Piano* (1910); *Compendio de historia de la música* (3rd ed. 1910); *Estética y psicología musical* (1907); *Biographical Notes of the Great Composers and Musicians* (2nd ed. 1911); *Teoria de la música* (5th ed. 1912; awarded diplomas at Exhibitions of St. Louis, U.S.A. 1904, and Milan, 1906).—A. M.

FALL, Leo. Operetta compr. *b.* Olmütz (Moravia), 2 Feb. 1873. Stud. at Vienna Cons. under Fuchs. Was 1st condr. at theatres in Berlin, Cologne and Hamburg. Comp. various operas. 1904, returned to Vienna and became one of most successful operetta writers. His sound training and pleasing invention place him on a level with Lehár.

Famous operettas (all publ. by Doblinger, Vienna): *Der fidele Bauer (The Merry Peasant)* perf. Mannheim, 1907; *Die Dollarprinzessin (The Dollar-Princess)* Vienna, 1907 (600 perf.); *Die geschiedene Frau (The Girl in the Taxi)* Vienna, 1908; *Das Puppenmädel (Doll-Girl)* Vienna, 1910; *Der liebe Augustin*, Vienna, 1911; *The Night Express*, Vienna, 1913; *The Student-Duchess*, Berlin, 1913; *Young England*, Berlin, 1914; *Der künstliche Mensch (The Artificial Man)*, 1915; *Der goldene Vogel (The Golden Bird)*, 1920; *Brüderlein fein* (1-act); and (for London) *The Eternal Waltz*, 1912.—P. P.

FALLA, Manuel de. Spanish composer; *b.* Cadiz, 23 Nov. 1876. Received first music lessons from his mother, an accomplished pianist. Lessons from Eloisa Galluzzo, Alejandro Odero and Broca, the well-known bandmaster, followed, until he went to Madrid and studied piano under José Tragó and composition under Felipe Pedrell, winning a special prize for piano-playing at the Real Conservatorio de Música. In 1905, he won the prize in a national opera-competition organised by the Real Academia de Bellas Artes, with *La Vida Breve*, the work destined to be the foundation of his world-wide fame. Previously he had composed, against his natural inclination, other works of a lighter character for the Spanish stage, which never provided him with the much-needed financial help and have been withdrawn by the author. *La Vida Breve* was not staged at the time, although this was stipulated in the competition conditions, and so remained unknown until 2 April, 1913, when it was produced with great success at the Municipal Casino, Nice; subsequently at Opéra-Comique, Paris, 29 Jan. 1914; Madrid, 1915, etc.

In 1907 he went to Paris, where he lived several years, devoted to the study of his art, with no other aid than his meagre earnings as an obscure music-teacher. It was then, whilst living under such discouraging circumstances,

that he refused the tempting offer from one of the most influential operatic concerns in Europe, to write Spanish operas after the conventional pattern, with libretti selected for him. It was then, too, that he declined the invitation from certain quarters in Paris to adopt French nationality as the sure means of finding there the facilities for producing his works, denied to him in his own country. Almost immediately on his arrival in Paris he was favoured by Debussy, Ravel, Dukas and other famous composers, with friendship, advice and encouragement, a distinction he always appreciated, and for which, as in the case of Albeniz, Turina and others, Spain will always be indebted to France.

On the outbreak of the 1914–18 war, he had to leave France for Spain, taking up residence at Granada. There, near the Alhambra, his contemplative character and modesty found suitable surroundings for an existence entirely ruled by the ethical and æsthetic principles which form his philosophical system. For de Falla is a philosopher, though, as often with Southern minds, his philosophy arises from emotions of different character, and has expression in some form of art. " God, Art and Country " are the words which enclose the philosophical synthesis of his life. From this principle, he not only derives his inspiration, but even evolves his technique. But de Falla, though already considered the foremost figure in the modern Spanish school, and one of the torch-bearers of musical progress in the world, has not yet fully revealed himself.

He is fastidious and painstaking to an extreme. To the demands of his subtle feelings and æsthetic sensibility he willingly sacrifices all natural gift and facility. His works are criticised, put away, recast over and over again, before being given to the public. He imposes upon the impulse of his mind a discipline which seems to follow in inverse order the motto we have attributed to him. In other words: a discipline meant to start from the popular (*El Amor Brujo*, *The Three-cornered Hat*, etc.), then to attain the æsthetic ideal, and rise finally to the metaphysical. *Noches en los jardines de España* *(Nights in the Gardens of Spain)*, is already a manifestation of high achievement in the second stage of his life's programme. Of his possibilities in a higher order of thought we can only conjecture, from dim indications in his known works, and an intimate knowledge of his personality. Though he is not the artist from whom a powerful creation of passionate or heroic character may be logically expected, yet he is one gifted to elevate himself to the supreme sphere of an intense musical mysticism.

How his feelings and ideas on religion and patriotism can form the basic elements of his music will be better understood by some of his written and verbal public declarations:

" The wonderful musical treasure previous to J. S. Bach is systematically ignored and despised as if the art of sound had not had a worthy existence until the arrival of the great Cantor. Beethoven employs the Lydian mode in his *Canzona* to give it a religious character, since it is written as a thanksgiving to

Divinity. Wagner also makes use of modal formulæ, and even themes from the Catholic liturgy, in *Parsifal*. Yet he does not abandon the Protestant tradition—that tradition of ill omen which has been the principal, if not the only, cause of the contempt that the music of the so-called classical period had for that of the XVII century. . . . In spite of narrow conservatism, music continues to detach itself from academical routine, false rhetoric, obsolete formulæ, and the forthcoming composers will follow the steps of those who have forced their way on the road of truth and liberty that leads to the domains of pure beauty, where music will triumph by itself, redeemed at last by the work and even martyrdom of some men of good will. . . . Mussorgsky was the true initiator of the new era in music; and, thanks to him, Rimsky-Korsakof, Balakiref and Borodin, the melodic forms and ancient scales that, despised by the composers, had taken refuge in the church and the people, were restored to musical art. . . . It is a widespread error, the belief that modernity in music depends on a prodigality of harmonic dissonances. This is to such an extent untrue that I make bold to declare that the modern spirit in music can subsist in a work in which only consonant chords are used, and, what is more, in music consisting only of an undulating melodic line. . . . The modern spirit resides mostly in the three fundamental elements of music, rhythm, modality and melody, used as a means of evocation. This does not mean that the harmonic discoveries have only a relative value; their value is absolute and great, but not unique; so much so that Debussy, from whom has arisen in a definite manner the innovating movement, has a distinct predilection for consonant chords. This, like every innovating movement recorded in the history of humanity, had been prepared gradually, not by technical treatises but by the work of other composers. Nevertheless, the spirit, the æsthetics and technique of modern music were not established in a precise, lasting and definite manner until the appearance of the *Nocturnes*, the G minor quartet, *L'Après-midi d'un Faune, Pelléas et Mélisande*. . . . The music of Schönberg particularly is ' atonal ' (keyless), and to this grave error is due the unpleasant effect produced by some of his music. But, fortunately, the majority of modern musicians observe the laws of tonality, considering them rightly as immutable. . . . Glinka made a journey to Spain in 1847, stopping specially in Granada. There he knew the celebrated guitarist, Francisco Rodríguez (*El Murciano*), with whose assistance he tried in vain to write, in musical notation, some of the popular songs typical of the style called *cante jondo* or *flamenco*, in which he found no end of interest and delight. Then, influenced by the music of Spain, he wrote his *Souvenir d'une nuit d'été à Madrid* and *Caprice brillant sur la jota aragonesa*, in which he arrived at certain new orchestral effects. On his return to Russia, he blended what he had learned in Spain with the elements of the Russian folk-songs, thus giving origin to the style that later on was taken up and developed by Rimsky-Korsakof and the other members of the well-known group, ' The Five.' . . . Stravinsky has also been so interested in Andalusian popular music as a possible source of original devices, that he has announced his intention of composing a work in which all the values of the said popular style will be used. The influence of the Andalusian *cante* is also to be found in Debussy, since he became acquainted with it at two world-exhibitions held in Paris. This shows the importance of the *cante jondo* as an æsthetic value, for Debussy's work represents the foundation-stone of the greatest revolution in modern musical art. There is ground to believe that we have to look to Glinka's journey to Spain for the origin of the modern orchestra."

How far the set of laws implied in these declarations will take the composer, no one can predict. The danger might lie in his giving undue importance to the folk-lore element.

The following is a complete list of de Falla's published works:

Ballets: *El Sombrero de Tres Picos* (*The Three-cornered Hat*); *El Amor Brujo* (*Love the Magician*). Operas: *La Vida Breve*; *El Retablo de Maese Pedro* (first perf. in Seville and shortly after at Princess Ed. Polignac's, Paris, 25 July, 1923). Pf. and orch.: *Noches en los jardines de España, impresiones sinfónicas*. Concerto for clavicembalo (or pf.), fl. ob.

ciar. vn. and cello. Pf.: *Pièces espagnoles*; *Fantasia Bætica*. V. and pf.: *Trois mélodies* (Fr. text, Théophile Gautier); *Siete canciones populares españolas*. Guitar: *Homenaje, pour le tombeau de Claude Debussy*. (Chester, London; Max Eschig; Durand; Rouart, Lerolle, Paris.) For a description of *El Retablo*, see *Chesterian*, London, Oct. 1923.—P. G. M.

FALTIN, Richard. Ger.-Finnish compr. *b.* Dantzig in 1835; *d.* Helsingfors in 1918. Stud. in native town, later in Dresden and Leipzig. In his youth, settled in Finland, beginning at Viipuri (Viborg); 1869, went to Helsingfors as successor to Frederick Pacius (1809–91; likewise a Ger.-born promoter of mus. life in Finland), thus becoming mus. dir. at Helsingfors Univ., orgt. of St. Nicholas Ch., and orch. condr. A skilled compr., ed. of a hymn-book, condr. of large choral works, and of the Finnish Opera House, teacher and arranger of Finnish folk-songs, he was a worthy successor to Pacius; became leader in Finnish mus. life, especially up to the 'eighties, when a movement rose in favour of native talent and the development of modern Finnish music.—T. H.

FALTIS, Evelyn. Ger.-Czechoslovak compr. *b.* at Trautenau. Her ancestors immigrated in XIX century from Bilbao (Spain). She stud. in Florence, Rome, Paris, Vienna (Rob. Fuchs, Mandyczewski), Dresden (Draeseke), Munich (Sophie Menter); became repetitor of solo parts at Stadttheater, Nuremberg, and at Theatre Royal, Darmstadt; in 1914 she was assistant at Bayreuth Festival.

Op. 1, pf. trio, D ma.; op. 2 (*a*) fantastic symphony, (*b*) *Hamlet*, symph. poem (orch.), (*c*) songs; op. 3, pf. concerto; op. 4, pf. trio, G mi.; op. 5, vn. and pf. sonata; op. 6, Andante and Slav dance, vn. pf.; op. 7, 3 songs; op. 8, 7 songs; op. 9, *Invocation*, 4-part mixed chorus (unacc.); op. 10, 6 songs; op. 11, 2 sacred songs, v., organ; op. 12, Fantasy and double fugue, with *Dies Iræ*, organ; op. 12(*a*), *Gipsy Songs*, op. 13(*a*) str. 4tet, (*b*) mass for organ.—E. S.

FANELLI, Ernest. Fr. compr. *b.* Paris, 27 June, 1860; *d.* there, 1919. This musician had a sad destiny. Although a pupil of Alkan and Delibes at the Cons. he worked almost entirely alone. Very poor and without relations, he had to earn his living as a drummer in an orch., without hope of ever being heard as a compr. In 1912 at age of 52 he had the joy of hearing perf. his *Tableaux Symphoniques*, comp. in 1882. The critics were unanimous in appreciating the orchestral colouring of this work, which, had it been performed at the time of composition, would have astonished by its novelty. In 1914 the Colonne Concerts produced his *Impressions pastorales*. Fanelli died a little after the Armistice, without having succeeded in revealing to the public his finest work, part of which remains in ms. This work is particularly interesting for the orchestral feeling which it reveals, a feature which made Fanelli a true precursor.

Tableaux Symphoniques, 6 suites for orch. on Théophile Gautier's *Roman de la Momie* (1882); *Impressions Pastorales*; *Suite rabelaisienne*; *Les Humouresques*; str. 5tet, etc.—H. P.

FANO, Guido Alberto. Ital. compr. and pianist; *b.* Padua, 18 May, 1875. In 1912 elected dir. of Parma Cons., whence he passed in same year to directorship of Cons. San Pietro a Maiella, Naples; subsequently to Palermo

Cons. As compr. he is known for a symph. poem, *The Temptation of Jesus*; an *Introduction, Lento Fugato e Allegro Appassionato* for orch., perf. at Augusteo, Rome; also two pf. sonatas; author of a still unpubl. operatic trilogy inspired by the origins of Rome. As pianist, became known through several tours in Italy and abroad. Publ. books dealing with mus. subjects: *Thoughts on Music* (Bologna, 1913, Beltrami & Cappelli) ; *The Life of Rhythm* (Naples, 1916, Ricciardi). Resigned direction of Palermo Cons. and is now pf. teacher at Milan Conservatoire.—D. A.

FARA, Giulio. Ital. folk-lorist; *b.* Cagliari, 4 Dec. 1880. Noted for his studies in mus. history and criticism; and especially in the folk-lore dealing with popular songs and instrs. of his native Sardinia, a most interesting country in this respect and one which has been very little studied. His writings are publ. mainly in the *Rivista Musicale Italiana*, Turin, in the *Cronaca Musicale,·*Pesaro, in the *Critica Musicale*, Florence. Books: *G. Rossini : Genio e ingegno musicale* (Turin, 1915, Bocca); *L'anima musicale d'Italia : La canzone del popolo* (Rome, 1921, Ausonia). Compr. of some *Sardinian Songs* (Rome, 1917, *Musica* ed.), and of an opera *Elia* (unpublished).—D. A.

FARJEON, Harry. Compr. *b.* Hohokus, New Jersey (of Eng. parents), 6 May, 1878. Stud. under Landon Ronald 1892; Storer 1893; at R.A.M. London under Haynes, F. Corder, E. Webbe, 1895–1901. F. is chiefly a compr. for pf. Most of his pieces have a sweet, refined sentiment. Into his later works has crept a desire for a freer melodic material and a greater elasticity of rhythmic outline, with a freer barring. Most of his earlier pf. pieces are publ. by Augener.

Orch. works (ms.): 2 tone-poems, 2 pf. concertos, 2 suites, variations; 2 str. 4tets; pf. trio; choral works: Mass, St. Dominic's, Carnegie award (Stainer & Bell); Singing Game for children (unison) (Augener); organ pieces; pf.: sonata in E (Ashdown, 1923); variations; tone-pictures; suites; 2 free fugues (Bosworth); idylls, etc.; *Album-leaves*, pf. duet; vn. pieces (Boosey; Augener; Schott; Goodwin); vla. pieces (Schott); 2 cello sonatas (ms.); songs (Chappell; Goodwin; Augener; Boosey); 2 Chapbooks of Rounds (J. M. Dent & Sons); recit. music, *La Belle Dame sans Merci*, and *Christ's Eve* (Augener); *The Art of Pf. Pedalling* (J. Williams, 1923).—E.-H.

FARNAM, Lynnwood. Canadian orgt.*b.* Sutton, Quebec, 13 Jan. 1885. Received his early mus. training at Dunham, Quebec. In 1900, won Montreal Scholarship given by Lord Strathcona and Lord Mount Stephen which gave him 4 years of study at R.C.M. London, under Franklin Taylor and Herbert Sharpe (pf.), and James Higgs, F. A. Sewell and W. S. Hoyte (organ). Returning to Canada in 1904, became orgt. at St. James's Methodist Ch., Montreal, and afterwards at St. James the Apostle in same city. Subsequent organ appointments: Christ Ch. Cath. Montreal (5 years), Emmanuel Ch. Boston (5 years), Fifth Avenue Presbyterian Ch. New York (1 year). In 1920, orgt. at Ch. of Holy Communion, New York. His organ recitals, given in U.S.A. (especially those at the Panama-Pacific Exposition, San Francisco, in 1915), have

proved him a brilliant player and a fine interpreter of the best organ music.—L. S.

FARNETI, Maria. Ital. s. singer; *b.* at Forlì. One of most celebrated contemporary Ital. operatic artists, known at all principal theatres of Europe and N. and S. America. Has a very extensive repertoire; amongst her most admired creations we mention *Iris* and *Isabeau* (Mascagni), and *Madama Butterfly* (Puccini). Pupil of Liceo at Pesaro, where she stud. under Boccabadati.—D. A.

FARRAR, Ernest Bristow. Eng. compr. *b.* Blackheath, 7 July, 1885; killed in action, 1918. His orch. suite, *English Pastoral Impressions*, received a Carnegie award. He inclined strongly to national subjects.

Orch.: Rhapsody I, *The Open Road*, op. 9 (ms.); II, *Lavengro*, op. 15 (ms.); symph. poem, *The Forsaken Merman*, op. 20 (ms.); *English Pastoral Impressions*, op. 26 (Stainer & Bell); *Heroic Elegy*, op. 36 (ms.); prelude on the Angelus, str. orch. op. 27 (Goodwin & Tabb); 3 spiritual studies, str. op. 33 (ms.); cantatas: *The Blessed Damozel*, solo v. chorus and orch. op. 6 (Stainer & Bell); *Out of Doors*, chorus and orch. op. 14 (Stainer & Bell); *Vagabond Songs*, barit. v. and orch. op. 10 (Stainer & Bell); *Summer*, s. v. and orch. op. 35; Choral Suite with orch. op. 14; Variations on an old British sea-song, pf. and orch, op. 25; *Celtic Impressions*, str. 4tet, op. 31; organ pieces (Stainer & Bell; Augener; W. Rogers); vn. and pf. (ms.); *Celtic Suite*, vn. and pf. op. 11 (Novello); pf. pieces (Augener; J. Williams; Chester; Ashdown); songs (Novello; Augener; E. Arnold); part-songs (J. Williams; Stainer & Bell).—E.-H.

FARRAR, Geraldine. Operatic s. singer; *b.* Melrose, U.S.A., 1882. Stud. under Trabadello in Paris and Lilli Lehmann in Berlin; *début* as Marguerite in *Faust*, R. Opera, Berlin, 15 Oct. 1901; since then has sung in all principal cities; engaged regularly at Metropolitan Opera House, New York.—E.-H.

FARRE, William. Norwegian musician; *b.* Trondhjem, 1 Aug. 1874. Took initiative in 1901 in establ. of first boys' band at the elementary schools in Christiania. Has since started similar bands in elementary schools in many Norwegian towns.—U. M.

FARWELL, Arthur. Amer. compr. *b.* St. Paul, Minn., U.S.A., 23 April, 1872. Graduated 1893 in electrical engineering from Massachusetts Inst. of Technology. Stud. music under Homer Norris in Boston, Humperdinck and Hans Pfitzner in Germany and Guilmant in Paris. From 1899 to 1901, lectured on music at Cornell Univ. (Ithaca, N.Y.). In 1901, establ. the Wa-Wan Press at Newton Centre, Mass., for publication of works of Amer. comprs., giving special prominence to works founded on, or inspired by, the music of the N. Amer. Indian, the Amer. negro and Amer. folk-lore. The series, continuing until 1908, included 54 works by about 25 Amer. comprs. (J. F. Beach, H. F. Gilbert, L. Gilman, E. B. Hill, E. Stillman Kelley, H. W. Loomis, C. Troyer and others). The publications are now issued by G. Schirmer of New York. From 1903 to 1904 F. travelled extensively in the Western states, studying music of Indians. 1909 to 1915, was on staff of weekly journal *Musical America* in New York; 1915–18, dir. of Music

School Settlement in that city; 1918 and 1919, acting head of mus. department of Univ. of California; 1921–2, holder of a compr.'s fellowship of Pasadena (Cal.) Music and Art Association. Since 1916 he has devoted himself much to compn. of music for masques (*Caliban* for Shakespeare Centenary, 1916; *The Evergreen Tree*, 1917; *A Pilgrimage Play*, 1921); and music for community choruses. An orch. arr. of the Indian piece, *The Domain of Hurakan* (orig. pf.) was played by San Francisco Symphony Orch., Los Angeles, Cal., 30 July, 1922.

Pf. (publ. Wa-Wan Press): *American Indian Melodies* (1901); *Folk-Songs of the West and South, Negro, Cowboy and Spanish Californian* (1905); *From Mesa and Plain : Indian, Cowboy and Negro Sketches* (1905); *Impressions of the Wa-Wan Ceremony of the Omahas* (1906); *Ichibuzzhi*, op. 13 (1902); *The Domain of Hurakan*, op. 15 (1902). *The Evergreen Tree : a Christmas Community Masque of the Tree of Light for Community Singing and Acting* (John Church Co. 1917). Songs (Ditson); community choruses and songs (Church).—O. K.

FASSBÄNDER, Peter. Ger. compr. *b.* Aix-la-Chapelle, 28 Jan. 1869; *d.* Zurich, 27 Feb. 1920. Pupil of Cologne Cons. From 1890, choirmaster in Saarbruck; from 1895 town mus. dir.; condr. and head of music school in Lucerne; 1911, condr. of choral soc. in Zurich. His daughter Hedwig is a violinist.

8 symphonies; 3 pf. concertos; 2 vn. concertos; cello concerto; chamber-music; songs; choral works; 4 operas.—A. E.

FATTORINI, Roberto. Ital. violinist; *b.* Rome, 1 Nov. 1870. First-class performer and teacher. Took part in important quartets and quintets in Rome, with Giovanni Sgambati and Luigi Gulli; for a long time leading violinist in foremost Roman orchs. Teacher at Istituto Nazionale di Musica; member of R. Acad. of Santa Cecilia.—D. A.

FAURÉ, Gabriel Urbain. French composer; *b.* Pamiers (Ariège), 13 May, 1845. In 1854 he was sent to Paris to study music at École Niedermeyer, where his teachers were Niedermeyer, Dietsch, and Saint-Saëns (who exercised a great influence upon him). In 1866 he accepted a post as organist at Rennes in Brittany. In 1870 he returned to Paris. While continuing to exercise similar functions at various churches, from Notre-Dame de Clignancourt to the Madeleine, he was successively professor at the École Niedermeyer, professor of composition at the Conservatoire (1896) and principal of the latter institution (1905). Countless official distinctions have been conferred upon him, culminating in the altogether unusual honour of an " Hommage National " which was paid to him at the Sorbonne, October 1922.

During the early 'seventies, various works of his were performed at Paris: the *Cantique de Racine* (1873), the *Lamento* (1873) and an *Orchestral Suite* (1874; unpublished), among others. In 1876, his violin sonata in A inaugurated the series of his significant chamber-music works; and his first pianoforte quartet appeared in 1879.

Since then he has continued writing leisurely, but steadily, evincing a marked preference for expressing himself in the media of song and chamber-music, but sometimes producing orchestral works, such as the incidental music to Dumas's *Caligula* (1888) and Haraucourt's *Shylock* (1883), the suite *Pelléas et Mélisande* (1898), the *Ballade* (1881) and the *Fantaisie* for piano and orchestra (1919), and a certain quantity of piano music. In 1900 appeared the important score of *Prométhée*, written for performance on the open-air stage of Béziers, and in 1913 the lyric drama *Pénélope*, performed at Monte Carlo and Paris. His beautiful *Requiem* is dated 1887.

Opinions as to the importance of his achievements vary far more than might be expected, considering the perspicuity of his music. But in France he is unanimously acknowledged not only as one of the greatest composers of to-day, but as a pioneer and leader. All that could be said on this point is summed up as follows in an article by the French critic Vuillermoz (*Revue Musicale*, Oct. 1922):

Some day people will wonder why, at a time when a Charpentier or a Bruneau were denounced as musical anarchists, Fauré escaped the ire of the conservatively-minded critics. For long before any other, he spoke a prophetic language. He created an altogether modern, logical, well-thought-out style, never sacrificing to passing fashions, but steadily tending towards greater serenity and simplicity. The easy grace of his art is deceptive: never did a creative artist present us with subtler and more powerful achievements.

Measure and balance, exquisite finish, quietness and purity of utterance, these essentially " classical " features of Fauré's music, contribute to render his most daring innovations unobtrusive; but this is no reason why the intense originality and eloquence of his music should be denied. They are fundamental characteristics of the ideals which he never ceased to assert during his evolution which, from the earliest songs to *La Bonne Chanson* and thence to the beautiful set *L'Horizon chimérique* (published 1922) or from the violin sonata of 1876 to the second quartet and to the quintet of 1921, affords a wonderful example of continuity and consistency.

As a teacher, Fauré has rendered no lesser services; the list of his pupils comprises, among others, Ravel, Kœchlin, Florent Schmitt, Louis Aubert, Ladmirault, and Roger-Ducasse.

Orch.: Ballade, pf. and orch. op. 19 (Hamelle); incidental music for *Caligula* (Dumas), op. 52 (*id.*); incidental music for *Shylock* (Haraucourt), op. 57 (*id.*); Suite, *Pelléas et Mélisande*, op. 80 (*id.*); Fantaisie, pf. and orch. op. 111 (Durand). Chamber-music: 1st vn. sonata, op. 13 (Breitkopf); 1st pf. 4tet, op. 15 (Hamelle); 2nd pf. 4tet, op. 45 (*id.*); 1st pf. 5tet, op. 89 (Schirmer); 2nd vn. sonata, op. 108 (Durand); 1st cello sonata, op. 109 (*id.*); 2nd pf. 5tet, op. 115 (*id.*); 2nd cello sonata, op. 117 (*id.*). Pf.: 6 impromptus; 13 nocturnes; 13 barcarolles; Theme and variations, op. 73 (Hamelle); *Huit Pièces Brèves*, op. 84 (*id.*); *Neuf Préludes*, op. 103 (Heugel). Dramatic music: *Prométhée* (3 acts), op. 82 (Hamelle); *Pénélope* (3 acts) (Heugel). Choral: *Cantique*, op. 11 (Hamelle); *Les Djinns*, op. 12 (*id.*); *La Naissance de Vénus*, op. 29 (*id.*); Requiem, op. 48 (*id.*). Songs: 4 books of songs (*id.*); *La Bonne Chanson*, op. 61 (*id.*); *La Chanson d'Eve*, op. 95 (Heugel); *Le Jardin clos*, op. 106 (Durand); *L'Horizon chimérique*, op. 118 (*id.*). Consult bibliography in Séré (*q.v.*), and special Fauré-number of *La Revue Musicale* (Paris, Oct. 1922) containing articles by the aforenamed pupils of his, Cortot, and others.—M. D. C.

FAVARA MISTRETTA, Alberto. Ital. compr. *b.* Salemi (Trapani), 1 March, 1863; *d.* Palermo,

1923. Teacher of compn. at R. Cons. Palermo. Operatic work, *Marcellina*, won a prize in the Sonzogno Competition 1884, and was perf. in that year in Milan; another, *Urania*, was given at Scala Theatre in 1918. Has also comp. secular and sacred music; gained reputation specially for his efforts in revival of Sicilian song. His *Land and Sea Songs of Sicily* (coll. by him and publ. Ricordi, Milan) are most interesting; also *Traditional Tunes of the Valley of Mazzara* (lecture at International Congress of Historical Sciences).—D. A.

FAZER, Edward. See FINNISH OPERA.

FEDELI, Vito. Ital. compr. and writer; *b.* Foligno, 19 June, 1866. Since 1904, dir. of Brera Mus. Inst. at Novara. Compr. of several operas and sacred music; is better known as writer of publications on history and propaganda. Has been active at various congresses of music, both Ital. and international. In 1911, commissioned by Government to represent Italy at International Mus. Soc. Congress in London. —D. A.

FEINBERG, Samuel Eugenievitch. Russian compr. and pianist ; *b.* Odessa, 14/26 May, 1890. Pupil of Jensen and Goldenweiser (pf.) and Jilaief (theory); graduated Moscow Cons. as pianist in 1911, as compr. has had no systematic tuition. With Miaskovsky and Alexandrof, F. is a representative of the foremost group of Russ. comprs. One of the most remarkable pf. comprs. after Scriabin, whose follower he is, without being an imitator. He acquired first rank as compr. and pianist in a very short time, from 1915 onwards.

6 pf. sonatas, op. 1 (ms.), 2, 3 (ms.), 6, 10 (ms.), 13 (ms.); 2 pf. fantasias, op. 5, 9; pf. pieces, op. 8, 11, 15; songs, op. 4, 7 (Russ. State Music Publ. Dept.).—V. B.

FEINHALS, Fritz. Ger. barit. singer; *b.* Cologne, 14 Dec. 1869. At first a mechanical engineer; pupil of Alb. Giovannini and Alb. Selva in Milan; after engagements in Essen and Mainz engaged since 1898 as barit. (Sachs, Wotan, Dutchman, Telramund, Amonasro), Munich Court Opera; Court chamber-singer. —A. E.

FEIS CEOIL (Irish Music Festival). Inaugurated in 1897 at Dublin. Started by Dr. Annie Patterson; originally intended that only Irish music should be performed. Owing to enterprise of Miss Edith Oldham (Mrs. Best), one of first secretaries, the fest. was extended to include all music. It takes place annually in May and occupies one week. There are competitions in choral and solo singing, in ensemble and solo instr. playing which are judged by well-known musicians. There are special competitions for playing traditional airs on the Irish pipes. The association has endeavoured to collect and publ. the ancient music of Ireland. Competitions are also held in mus. compn. and works by Esposito and Hamilton Harty have been awarded prizes. The fest. has been one of the strongest forces towards improving mus. conditions in Ireland. There is a separate Feis Ceoil at Lon-

donderry and one at Sligo, both modelled on the Dublin Feis.—W. S.

FELLOWES, Rev. Edmund Horace. Eng. writer, editor; *b.* London, 11 Nov. 1870. Stud. vn. under Charles Fletcher and Ludwig Straus; harmony and cpt. under Dr. Percy C. Buck and F. Cunningham Woods. Mus.Doc. *h.c.* Trinity Coll. Dublin, 1917; precentor of Bristol Cath. 1897-1900; minor-canon, St. George's Chapel, Windsor Castle, 1900 to present day. Librarian St. Michael's Coll. Tenbury, 1918. Dr. Fellowes has perf. a great national service in editing and publishing, entirely on his own responsibility, the whole of the works of the Eng. madrigal comprs. He is also co-editor of the Carnegie Ed. of *Tudor Church Music* (Vols. I, II and III, Taverner and Byrd only published).

English Madrigal Verse (Clarendon Press, 1920); *The English Madrigal Composers* (*id.* 1921); *W. Byrd* (*id.* 1923); *The English Madrigal School*: the complete madrigal works of Thomas Morley, Orlando Gibbons, John Wilbye, John Farmer, Thomas Weelkes, William Byrd, Henry Lichfild, Henry Ward, Thomas Tomkins, Giles Farnaby, Thomas Bateson, John Bennet, George Kirbye, etc. (Stainer & Bell, 1913 onwards), complete in 36 vols; *The English School of Lutenist Song-writers*: complete works of John Dowland, Thomas Campion, Thomas Ford, Francis Pilkington, etc. (Winthrop Rogers, 1920 onwards); *The 3 Masses of William Byrd* (Stainer & Bell, 1922); 2 Fantasias for str. (Byrd; *id.* 1922).—E.-H.

FELLOWES, Horace V. British violinist; *b.* Wolverhampton, 26 May, 1876. Stud. at Cons. of Cologne under Willy Hess and Fritz Steinbach; 1913, leader of Beecham Orch. in Russ. ballet and opera-season; 1915, leader of Scottish Orch. Has frequently cond. both in Germany and Great Britain. Gives chamber-concerts in Glasgow and surrounding districts. Principal teacher of vn. at Carnegie School of Music, Dumfermline; condr. of Athenæum Orch. Glasgow; leader of Horace Fellowes Quartet.—J. P. D.

FENNEY, William J. Eng. compr. *b.* Handsworth, Birmingham, 1891. Self-taught; then for some years a student at Midland Inst. Birmingham, under Granville Bantock.

In Early Spring, suite for small orch. (Chester); *Prelude, Aria and Tarentella*, suite for str.; pf. trio in G (*id.*); songs (Chester; Boosey); part-songs (Stainer & Bell; Curwen); pf. pieces (Chester; Swan & Co).—G. B.

FENNINGS, Sarah. Eng. violinist; *b.* Essex. Stud. under Hollaender, Wilhelmj, Ševčík; recital St. James's Hall, 1891; toured with Foli and Emma Nevada; prof. Trin. Coll. of Music, London.—E.-H.

FERNÁNDEZ BORDAS, Antonio. Span. violinist; *b.* Orense, 1870, where he stud. law and music simultaneously. At 10, won a vn. prize, under the adjudication of Sarasate; at 23, obtained LL.D.; and after a post in Civil Service, he devoted himself to mus. career. As a vn. virtuoso he attained great success; perf. frequently with Sarasate, Monasterio, Casals, Saint-Saëns, Bauer, Hekking, Malats, Granados and many others. He deputised for his famous master, Don Jesús de Monasterio, as leader of R. Chapel orch. Madrid, as well as senior vn. prof. at R. Cons. de Música. To fill this position, he sacrificed his career as a concert-giver abroad. *Officier d'Instruction Publique*; *Légiond'Honneur*(France); manySpan. honours; Knight of the Order of Carlos III; member of R. Acad. de Bellas Artes, Madrid. Dir. of R. Cons. de Música since retirement of famous compr. Tomás Bretón.—P. G. M.

FERRARI, Rodolfo. Ital. condr. *b.* Staggia (Modena), 1865; *d.* Rome, 10 Jan. 1919. Enjoyed a high reputation amongst Ital. condrs. of recent times. After studying at Bologna Acad. under Busi, immediately devoted himself to career of condr. and distinguished himself both in opera and on concert-platform. In 1891, he created the *Amico Fritz* of Mascagni in Rome; was engaged as condr. at the Comunale Theatre, Bologna, for 11 seasons. Dir. many orch. concerts in N. America and in chief Ital. cities, and at Augusteo, Rome.—D. A.

FERRARI FONTANA, Edoardo. Ital. t. singer; *b.* Rome, 8 July, 1878. *Début* at Regio Theatre, Turin, in 1910 with *Tristan* and *Ratcliff*; then gained a high reputation especially as Wagnerian tenor; his interpretations of *Tannhäuser* and *Tristan* are famous. In Pesaro he created the opera *Aura* (Zanella); at La Scala, *L'amore dei tre re* (Montemezzi). Has appeared at principal theatres of Europe and N. and S. America. Is also an esteemed concert-singer.—D. A.

FERRARI-TRECATE, Luigi. Ital. compr. orgt. *b.* Alessandria (Piedmont), 25 Aug. 1884. Was orgt. at Loreto; then at Basilica of Valle di Pompei. Subsequently pf. teacher at Scuola Musicale Comunale, Rimini; at present, prof. of organ and compn. for organ in R. Cons. Parma. Author of various operas (*Il piccolo montanaro*; *Pierozzo*; *Ciottolino*; *Belinda e il mostro*), and many sacred and chamber-music works.—D. A.

FERRERO, Willy. Ital. condr. *b.* Portland (Maine), U.S.A. of Ital. parents, 21 May, 1906. Has interested people for several years and obtained great successes as prodigy-conductor. He started at age of six: in 1912 gave his first concert at Costanzi Theatre, Rome, immediately winning public favour; subsequently, several times cond. difficult programmes in Rome at the Augusteo itself, also in other cities of Italy and abroad. Later, gave up touring (in which he had been accompanied by his father, a musician who taught and advised him) and has devoted himself to regular mus. studies. In addition to obtaining, as an infant prodigy, enthusiastic success with the public, for his memory, clearness and style, and for his facility and instinctive sureness, F. also claimed the interest of the critics, musical and psychological, who devoted much attention to him. He now lives in Turin. —D. A.

FERRETTI, Paolo. A Benedictine monk, and a profound scholar in Gregorian studies; *b.* Subiaco, 3 Dec. 1866. Called to Rome by Pope Pius X to take up the teaching of Gregorian chant in Higher Pontifical School of Sacred Music. Amongst his works are: *Theoretical and Practical Principles of Gregorian Chant* (Rome,

1905, Desclée); *The Metric Flow and Rhythm of Gregorian Melodies*, 1913 (Tipografia del Senato). Has taken active part in reform of sacred music in Italy, both by his writings and by his public speeches.—D. A.

FERRONI, Vincenzo. Ital. compr. and teacher; *b.* Tramutola (Potenza), 17 Feb. 1858. Since 1888, prof. of compn. at R. Cons. Milan, where he succeeded Ponchielli. He made his name as a compr. in 1889, when he was one of the 3 winners of the Sonzogno Competition with his opera *Rudello*; this contest also brought to light Mascagni's *Cavalleria Rusticana*, and the third winner was Spinelli with his opera *Labilia*. Whereas *Cavalleria* had a world-wide success, the other two operas, although favourably received, were very soon forgotten. Nor did either of Ferroni's successive operas, *Ettore Fieramosca* (Como, 1896) and *Il Carbonaro* (Lyric, Milan, 1900), meet with better success. F. is the compr. of much concert music (symphonies, symph. poems) and chamber-music (a 4tet, 2 trios, sonatas, vn. concerto, vocal and pf. music).—D. A.

FEST, Max G. Ger. orgt. *b.* Altenburg, 7 Jan. 1872. Pupil Leipzig Cons.; orgt. of Nathanael Ch. Leipzig-Lindenau, from 1897; singing - master at Oberrealschule; concert organist.—A. E.

FÉVRIER, Henri. Fr. compr. *b.* Paris, 1876. Not to be confused with Henri Louis Février, of Abbeville, who publ. (in XVIII century) 2 books of harpsichord pieces. The present musician, the son of an architect, has specialised in dramatic music to good purpose. He is mus. critic of *La Renaissance*.

Comic operas: *Le Roi aveugle* (1906); *Agnès dame galante* (1912); *Carmosine* (1913). Operas: *Monna Vanna* (1909); *Ghismonda* (1918).—A. C.

FIBICH, Zdeněk. Czech composer; *b.* Všebořice, 21 Dec. 1850; *d.* Prague, 15 Oct. 1900. Son of a forest ranger. Studied at a gymnasium; Leipzig Conservatorium, 1865-7 (Moscheles, Richter, Jadassohn); one year in Paris, and in Mannheim under Lachner, 1869-70. Except for two years, 1873-4 (in Vilna), he lived in Prague from 1871. Second conductor National Theatre, 1875-8; conductor at Russian Church, Prague, 1878-81. With these exceptions he occupied no public position but devoted himself to composition and private instruction. Towards end of his life, he filled position of dramaturg to the National Theatre.

Fibich is the first cosmopolitan among Czech musicians, after the typically national generation (Smetana-Dvořák). He forms the intermediate link between them and the more modern composers, Suk and Novák. A romanticist by disposition, he inclined to the style of Weber and Schumann, and the works of his first period are in the spirit of these masters. He did not, however, sink to the level of an epigonistic imitator; the trend of his ideas and his musical expression always preserve their independence. His predilection for the ballad style has its origin in this romanticism, which also influenced his stage works. After his first two operas he found an outlet for his tragic expression in the *Bride of Messina*, for which Otakar Hostinský (*q.v.*) wrote the libretto after Schiller. Wagner's principles and declamatory style are consistently embodied in this work, though not without clearly restraining the melodic freshness. The final consequence of those principles was to draw him into scenic melodrama, a spoken tragedy, accompanied by a symphonically conceived orchestra. This form was realised in his trilogy *Hippodamia*, on three dramas by Jaroslav Vrchlický. The difficulties of a good production and the dramatic faults of the libretto prevented the wider dissemination of this work, to which its music is undoubtedly .entitled. His meeting with Anežka Schulzová, the authoress, and their artistic collaboration meant a sudden change, manifested in a preponderance of subjectivity, a more intimate susceptibility and an extremely rich and flowing melodic inventiveness, as against the objectivity of expression hitherto apparent. During this period he makes entries in his musical diary in the form of short piano pieces, these inspirations being also introduced into his larger works. (376 compositions under the heading of *Moods, Impressions and Reminiscences*.) In the music-dramas of this epoch his principal interest is a passionate eroticism both happy and tragic, and to this he gives full expression, thus reaching his highest development. Born in the midst of a forest, to the forest he always reverts with new variations in his instrumental music. Fibich has not the racial outspoken peculiarites nor the directness of Smetana or Dvořák; he is more of a cosmopolitan and an aristocrat, and for that reason he is not so celebrated as either of them. Nevertheless, his importance for the development of Czech music is in no way second to that of those two masters.

Operas: *Bukovin* (1871); *Blaník* (1877); *The Bride of Messina* (1888); *Storm* (1894); *Hedy* (1895); *Šárka* (1896); *Pád Arkuna* (*Arcona's End*, 1890); melodramatic trilogy: *Pelops'Wooing*(1889); *Tantalus' Reconciliation* (1890); *Hippodamia's Death* (1891). Orch.: 3 symphonies; tone-poems, overtures: *Othello*; *Záboj, Slavoj i Luděk*; *Toman a lesní panna* (*Toman and the Wood Fairy*); *Storm*; *Dawning*; *The Spring*; *Vigiliæ*; *A Night on Karlštejn* (given Queen's Hall, London, under Sir Henry Wood); *Oldřich a Božena*; *Komenský*; *Dojmy z venkova* (*Rural Impressions*, suite). Cantatas: *Melusine*; *The Romance of Spring*. Chamber-music: vn. sonatina; pf. trio; str. 4tet; pf. 4tet; wind instr. 5tet. Pf.: *Z hor* (*From the Mountains*); sonata for pf. duet; *Moods, Impressions and Reminiscences*; *Studies on Pictures*; concert melodramas (*Štědrý den*; *Vodník*; ; *Věčnost*; *Hakon*); song collections; ballads, *Jarní Paprsky*, etc. (all publ. by F. A. Urbánek, Prague, mostly with Czech and Ger. texts).

Chief publishers: Fr. A. Urbánek; M. Urbánek; Hudební Matice; E. Starý; Univ. Ed.; Bosworth; Schott, etc.

Consult: C. L. Richter, *Z. F.* (Ger., Prague, 1900); Josef Bartoš, *Z. F.* (Prague, 1914); O. Hostinský, *Reminiscences of Z. F.* (Prague, 1909, both in Czech).—V. ST.

FIEBACH, Otto. Compr. *b.* Ohlau (Silesia), 9 Feb. 1851. Orgt. and mus. dir. at Univ. Königsberg, and dir. of an Inst. of Music; R. mus. dir. Wrote *Physiology of Music* (1891) and *Theory of Strict Counterpoint* (1921).

Operas: *Prince Dominic* (Dantzig, 1885); *Lorcley*

(Dantzig, 1886); *Bei Frommen Hirten* (Dresden, 1891); *Robert and Bertram* (Dantzig, 1903); *The Queen's Officer* (Dresden, 1900); *The Duchess of Marlborough*, and an oratorio, *The Nine Muses.*—A. E.

FIEDLER, A. Max. Ger. condr. *b.* Zittau, 31 Dec. 1859. Stud. Leipzig Cons. as stipendiary of Holstein Foundation. From 1882 teacher; 1903, dir. Hamburg Cons.; also condr. of Philh. Concerts, 1904; in 1908 accepted invitation to Boston as dir. of Symphony Concerts. Returned to Germany, 1912, taking up residence in Berlin. Has been mus. dir. in Essen since 1916. Has undertaken short tours as conductor.

Pf. 5tet; str. 4tet; symphony, D mi. (1886); *Comedy Overture* (1914); songs; pf. pieces.—A. E.

FIELITZ, Alexander von. Condr. and compr. *b.* Leipzig, 28 Dec. 1860. Of Polish descent. Pupil of Julius Schulhoff, K. Banck and Edm. Kretschmer in Dresden; condr. at theatres, Zurich, Lübeck and Leipzig; for his health's sake lived for a time at Capri; then for some time teacher at Stern's Cons. Berlin. In 1905 went to Chicago as teacher at Siegfeld's Cons.; 1906, condr. Chicago Symphony Orch.; 1908, returned to Germany, teaching at Stern's Cons., in the directorship of which he succeeded Gustav Hollaender at end of 1915.

Operas: *Vendetta* (Lübeck, 1891); *The Silent Village* (Hamburg, 1900); songs.—A. E.

FIGUŠ-BYSTRÝ, Viliam. Slovak compr. *b.* Bánská Bystrica, Slovakia, 1875, where he is orgt. Collected and harmonised Slovak folk-songs (publ. by V. Kotrba, Prague); comp. a series of songs and choral works; pieces for vn. and pf.; a pf. 4tet, etc. Chief work, cantata *Slovenská pieseň* (*The Slovak Hymn*) for soli, chorus, orch. (1913).—V. ST.

FILIASI, Lorenzo. Ital. compr. *b.* Naples, 25 Aug. 1878. In 1902 won the Sonzogno Competition with his opera *Manuel Menendez*, perf. at Lyric Theatre, Milan, 1904, with great success. A second opera, *Fior di neve*, perf. at Scala, Milan, 1911, met with little success. F. is also compr. of orch. works and of vocal chamber-music.—D. A.

FILIPPI, Filippo. Ital. mus. critic; *b.* Vicenza, 13 Jan. 1830; *d.* Milan, 25 June, 1887. For 28 years on Milan newspaper *La Perseveranza*. Was one of Wagner's apostles in Italy. Also publ. some books of mus. culture and some small pieces.—D. A.

FILIPPONE - SINISCALCHI, Tina. Italian pianist; *b.* Naples, Feb. 1903. A clever perf., well known for important concerts given at the Augusteo in Rome, and in other cities in Italy and abroad. Was pupil of Ernesto Marciano in Naples.—D. A.

FILKE, Max. Compr. *b.* Steubendorf-Leobschütz (Silesia), 5 Oct. 1855; *d.* Breslau, 8 Oct. 1911. Chorister Breslau Cath.; pupil of Brosig. In 1877 attended Regensburg (Ratisbon) Church Music School (Haberl); cantor in Duderstadt, 1878-9; then pupil of Leipzig Cons. (Piutti); choir-master at Straubing, 1881, dir. of Singers' Circle, Cologne, 1890; cath. choir-master in Breslau, 1891; from 1893 also teacher R. Acad. Inst. for Church Music; R. mus. dir.

1899. An influential compr. of Catholic Church music with progressive ideas.

Masses with orch.: op. 47 (*B.V.M.*, 4-v.); E flat ma. op. 58 (4-v.); E mi. op. 55 (4-v.); G ma. op. 80 (4-v.); F ma. op. 87 (*Lourdes*, 4-v.); D ma. op. 90 (*Sti. Antonii de Padua*, 3-v.); *Oriens ex alto*, op. 106 (a., choir and orch.); *Requiem*, op. 111; *Te Deum*, op. 101; *Lauretanian Litany*, op. 98; 4 *Corpus Christi* hymns and *Pange Lingua*, op. 79; *Regina cœli* and *Salve Regina*, op. 102; *Ave maris stella*, op. 88, and others.—A. E.

FINCK, Henry Theophilus. Amer. author, critic; *b.* Bethel, Mo., U.S.A., 22 Sept. 1854. Lived during youth in Oregon. Graduated A.B. at Harvard in 1876 with highest honours in philosophy and a fellowship for European study. While at Harvard, attended mus. history and theory classes of J. K. Paine. Was present at 1st Bayreuth fest. 1876. From 1878–81, stud. at Univs. of Berlin, Heidelberg and Vienna, chiefly comparative psychology, writing meanwhile for Amer. journals (*The Nation*; *New York World*; *Atlantic Monthly*) on various subjects including music. In 1881, returned to America and joined staff of *New York Evening Post*, with which he has been connected ever since as mus. critic and editorial writer. One of most advanced critics of day, quick to recognise and proclaim progressive representatives of the art. A warm advocate of Wagner, the German transl. of his excellent biography has found great favour in Wagner's native land. Did much for appreciation of Grieg in America and was one of MacDowell's earliest champions. Besides books, has written on *Foods and Flavours, Romantic Love and Personal Beauty*, and gardening.

Chopin and other Musical Essays (Scribner, 1889); *Wagner and his Works*, 2 vols. (id. 1893); *Anton Seidl* (id. 1899); *Songs and Song-Writers* (id. 1900); *Grieg and his Music* (J. Lane Co. 1909); *Success in Music and how it is won* (Scribner, 1909); *Massenet and his Operas* (J. Lane Co. 1910); *Richard Strauss* (Little, Brown & Co. 1917); ed. of selections of Schubert songs, Grieg songs and *One Hundred Songs by Ten Composers* in *The Musician's Library* (Ditson).—O. K.

FINKE, Fidelio. Ger. - Czechoslovak compr. *b.* Josefsthal, near Gablons, 22 Oct. 1891; pupil of Vítězslav Novák at Prague; dir. of School of Comprs. and prof. at Ger. Acad. of Music and Art, Prague; inspector of music. His technical development follows on from Brahms to Reger and finally to Schönberg (Expressionism). Many prizes have been awarded to his works. His latest works attain a supreme height of expression, and notwithstanding their "atonality" (*q.v.*) are never lacking in feeling, and are always strictly logical in construction.

Poetic symphony, Pan; operatic fragment, Die versunkene Glocke (The Sunken Bell, from Gerhard Hauptmann); orch. song-cycle, Spring (with Franz Werfel's Farewell as finale); Variations and fugue for chamber-orch.; suite for str. orch.; pf. 5tet, D ma.; 4tet for orch. D. ma. (1st perf. 2nd fest. of chamber-music, Donaueschingen, 1922); 7 str. trios; songs.—E. S.

FINNISH CHAMBER-MUSIC. Chief works are the str. 4tet *Voces Intimœ*, op. 56, of Sibelius, the 4 str. 4tets and vn. sonata of Melartin, pf. trio in A ma. of Kuula, pf. 5tet of Furuhjelm, pf. 5tet and str. 4tet of Raitio, sonata for vn. and pf. of Madetoja, pf. 4tet of J. Hannikainen, and the trio of Linko.—T. H.

FINNISH CHORAL MUSIC. The chorus, especially for male-v. choirs, is a characteristic Finnish mus. form. Amongst the chief comprs. are Kajanus, Sibelius (words by Kivi, from folk-lore poetry, etc.), Järnefelt, Palmgren (of outstanding merit), Kuula (*e.g. Song of Kullervo*, of orch. grandeur), Madetoja, Melartin, Ikonen, Kotilainen, Klemetti. Excellent male-v. choruses have also been written by Emil Genetz, Axel Törnudd (compr. and successful teacher, *b.* 1874; *d.* 1923), and P. J. Hannikainen. Pieces for mixed choir have been written by Kuula (large unacc. works), Madetoja, Krohn, Klemetti (also excellent arrs. of historical and folk-music), Maasalo, Ikonen, and many others. (See arts. on these comprs.).—T. H.

FINNISH FOLK-MUSIC. See KAJANUS, ROBERT; KROHN, ILMARI; LAUNIS, ARMAS; SCHINDLER, KURT.

FINNISH OPERA. The first period falls into years 1873–9, when, under dir. of Dr. K. Bergbom, creator of Finnish National Theatre, about 30 of best-known operas were given in Finnish, for the most part with Finnish artists (Emmy Strömer - Achté, Ida Basilier - Magelsen, Alma Fohström and others). For some time after, only occasional perfs. were given. Of these, worthy of special mention, are those of Emmy Achté, Maikki and Armas Järnefelt, as also those of the opera-condr. Arturo Vigna. In 1911, the annual opera fest. perfs. were founded in Savonlinna (Nyslott) by Aino Ackté, and in the same year Edward Fazer, Aino Ackté and others founded a "Native Opera," which had continued its activity since 1914 under dir. of Edward Fazer and under name of Finnish Opera (*Suomalainen Ooppera—Finska Operan*). Since 1918, when an opera-house (the former Alexanderstheater) was given by Finnish State to the opera company, its activity has been greatly extended and the repertoire much enlarged (through Wagner perfs. etc.). Opera is given 4 or 5 times a week. The dir. is Edward Fazer (*b.* 1861); condrs., Oskar Merikanto (1911–22), the Ger. gen. mus. dir. Franz Mikorey, since 1919, and recently also Tauno Hannikainen; producer, Hermann Gura. Artists, Väinö Sola (t. and producer), A. af Enehjelm (*q.v.*), William Hammer, Eino Rautavaara and Oiva Soini (barit.), Y. Somersalmi (b.); also Erna Gräsbeck, Jennie Costiander (s.), Greta von Haartman, Lahja Linko (m.-sòpr.), Elbe Nissinen (contr.).

The first native compns. were the operas of Fredrik Pacius (*King Charles' s Chase* was produced 1852 in Helsingfors with great enthusiasm by an amateur company), and the fairy song-play, *The Princess of Cyprus* (texts by Z. Topelius). The folk-epic *Kalevala* had provided material for the latter work, and it has often inspired subsequent comprs. of opera. Oskar Merikanto's *Pohjan neiti*, Erkki Melartin's *Aino* (a *Kalevala* mystery) and Armas Launis's *Kullervo* are based on stories from the *Kalevala*. Of a romantic and historical character are Palmgren's *Daniel Hjort* (on drama of J. J. Wecksell), and Merikanto's *Queen of Emmeritz*. Merikanto's *Elinan surma* is based on a folk-ballad. A comedy by Aleksis Kivi has been drawn upon for Launis's *Seitsemän veljestä*. As yet unperf. (1924) are the biblical scene *Tuhotulva (The Flood)* by Ilmari Krohn, the opera *Aslak Hetta* by Launis (based on a Lapland story), the *Pohjalaisia* (East Bothnian folklife) by Levi Madetoja, and others. Mention must also be made of Krohn's oratorio *Jkiaartehet.* (See arts. on these composers).—T. H.

FINNISH ORCHESTRAL MUSIC. J. F. von Schantz was the pioneer of modern Finnish orch. music. His *Kullervo Overture* (1860) was the first to treat a national theme orchestrally. R. Kajanus appeared in 1880, and later, with some folk-song rhapsodies and other works of national content (*Aino* Symphony; *Kullervo* Funeral March). After the 'nineties, when Jan Sibelius comp. his first important works, Finnish music began to make great strides. A large part of Sibelius' orch. works, especially that part inspired by the old Finnish sagas, consists of symph. poems. Whereas up to the beginning of this century his creative activity was concentrated chiefly on national music and patriotic tone-poems, his tendency since that time has been towards absolute instr. music, including his last symphony (No. 6). At the same time the elemental power of his music, which rises to its greatest height in the 2nd symphony (1902), becomes more tranquil in character and gives place to an introspective art. The six symphonies of Sibelius represent the true characteristics of his development. In his works an important place is taken by the vocal works with orch. Besides Sibelius, other comprs., contemporaries and younger writers, have produced music in which national as well as individual characteristics are reflected, influenced more or less by the lines upon which contemporary music has developed: Ernst Mielck (a talented compr. who died young, 1877–99), Melartin (5 symphonies), Madetoja (2 symphonies), Furuhjelm (symphony), Ikonen (2 symphonies), Raitio (symphony), A. Merikanto (symphony), Kaski (symphony) — also the Symphonietta by Kajanus, a later work. Symph. poems have been written by Järnefelt (*Korsholm*), Melartin (*Siikajoki* [*Dream-vision*]), Kuula (*Will-o'-the-Wisp* from *East Bothnian Suite*, etc.), Madetoja (*Kullervo*), Raitio (*Fantasia estatica*; *Antigone*, etc.). Suites and smaller orch. works: Järnefelt, Kajanus (*Lyric Suite*; overture), Melartin (3 suites, etc.), Palmgren (*From Finland*, etc.), Kuula (2 *East Bothnian Suites*), Madetoja (*East Bothnian Rhapsody*; several suites), Furuhjelm (*Romantic Overture*). Solo works with orch.: Palmgren (pf. concertos, *The River* and *Metamorphosis*), Melartin (vn. concerto), Linko, Hannikainen, Merikanto (pf. concerto), and others. Comprs. of vocal works with orch.: Kuula, Melartin, Madetoja, Krohn, Ikonen, Maasalo. (Consult arts. on these comprs.) —T. H.

FINNISH SONG. Nearly all Finnish comprs. have shown special affection for songs. Among chief songs are those of Sibelius (to words by Runeberg, Wecksell, Tavaststjerna, Fröding, Josephson, and others), which are most valuable, sometimes rising to the height of classic beauty; the inspiring lyrics of Armas Järnefelt; the prolific songs of Erkki Melartin; the expressive songs of Toivo Kuula; the refined songs of Palmgren and Madetoja; the original and expressive lyrics of Kilpinen; the popular folk-song production of Merikanto, and the songs of Hannikainen and Kotilainen.—T. H.

FINO, Giocondo. Ital. compr. b. Turin, 2 May, 1867. Is a priest; but has devoted himself more to operatic than to church music, gaining considerable success with his opera *Il Battista*, perf. Turin, 1906, and later in various theatres. His successive operas, *La festa del grano, Debora, Campane a gloria*, did not gain lasting success. Also comp. a biblical cantata, *Ruth and Naomi*; a str. 4tet and various orch. works.—D. A.

FISCHER, Edwin. Swiss pianist; b. Basle, 6 Oct. 1886. Pupil at Basle and at Stern's Cons. Berlin, where he has been teacher since 1905. He is one of most distinguished present-day musicians, combining elementary force with delicate feeling; prominent as a Bach and Beethoven player.—A. E.

FISCHER, Emil. Ger.-Czechoslovak compr. *b.* Wteln, near Brno (Brünn), 1872; pupil of Dvořák.

Symph. poem, *Indian Legend* (from Rabindranath Tagore); *Vision*; pf. 5tet, *Forest Tales*; symphony, E mi.; songs to words by Vietzsch.—E. S.

FISCHER, Wilhelm. Austrian music historian; *b.* Vienna, 19 April, 1886. Stud. theory under Hermann Graedener and Guido Adler; Mus.D. 1912. Chief librarian of Inst.; now prof. in Univ. for mus. history; member of commission for Austrian State music examinations. Most accurate in scientific research, especially in history of different styles and mus. forms. Publ. many little brochures and scientific arts. in newspapers. Ed. some vols. of the *D.T.Ö.* (*Viennese Instr. Music*, about 1750, Vol. XIX, 2). Is now working on a compendium of music history.—P. P.

FISCHER, William Arms. Amer. compr. ed. *b.* San Francisco, Cal., U.S.A., 27 April, 1861. Stud. pf., organ and theory under J. P. Morgan in Oakland. Later stud. singing in New York and (1892) under Shakespeare in London. After this a pupil in New York of Horatio Parker (theory) and Dvořák (compn.). In 1895 became ed. and publication-manager for Oliver Ditson Co., Boston. Many songs, choruses (Ditson; Schirmer). Author of *Notes on Music in Old Boston* (Ditson, 1918).—O. K.

FISHER, Edward. Orgt. choral condr. mus. dir. *b.* Jaimaca, Vermont, U.S.A., 11 Jan. 1848; *d.* Toronto, 31 May, 1913. Student of Boston Cons.; occupied at early age many organ positions in that city. In 1874, went to Berlin, studying under Haupt and Loeschhorn. On returning to America, was offered mus. directorship at Ottawa Ladies' Coll. which he held for several years. 1879, came to Toronto as orgt.

and choirmaster at St. Andrew's Ch. Organised Toronto Choral Soc. in 1878. In 1886, began the work with which his name is now so closely associated—the founding of Toronto Cons. of Music (see ACADEMIES), of which he remained mus. dir. until his death in 1913. His successes very materially helped to give to Toronto its pre-eminent position as the educational centre, musically speaking, of the Dominion.—L. S.

FITELBERG, Grzegorz. Polish compr. condr. *b.* Dinaburg (Livonia, formerly a Russ. province), 18 Oct. 1879. Son of a Russ. army bandmaster; pupil of Barcewicz (vn.) and Noskowski (theory); became by residence and culture completely identified with the Polish nation. In 1896, won 1st prize in international competition at Leipzig for sonata for vn. and pf., and in 1901 Count Zamoyski's prize for trio at Warsaw. Became solo-player at Warsaw Philh. in 1902, and was condr. 1907–11. In 1912, cond. concerts of Polish music (especially Karol Szymanowski), and became condr. of Imperial Opera House at Vienna but soon gave up, and returned to Warsaw; and was in Petrograd during the war and revolution, working as condr. of opera and symphony. Worked also as condr. of Russ. ballet company, with Pavlova and Fokin.

A pioneer of modern Polish music and a bold progressive, his works show the evolution from pseudo-classical decay to Impressionism, the best exhibiting bold and complicated harmony and richly-coloured orchestration. In 1905, founded, with Karol Szymanowski, Ludomir Różycki and Apolinary Szeluta, the Soc. of Young Polish Comprs. which has issued many remarkable compositions.

Symphony, E mi. op. 16; symph. poems: *The Song of the Falcon* (from Gorky), op. 18; *Protesilaus and Laodamia* (from Wyspiański), op. 24; vn. concerto, op. 13; two overtures, op. 14, 17; pf. trio, op. 12; 2 vn. sonatas, op. 2, 13; songs, op. 19, 21, 22, 23.—ZD. J.

FLAMENT, Édouard. Fr. compr.; also pf. and bsn. virtuoso; *b.* Paris, 1888. Ex-condr. of Concerts Rouges, of Trianon-Lyrique; of opera houses of Algiers and of Lille. Has comp. symph. poems, chamber-music, and songs.—A. C.

FLECK, Fritz. Ger. compr. *b.* Schwetz (W. Prussia), 24 Oct. 1880. Pupil of Arno Kleffel, Paul Geisler and Hans Pfitzner; lives in Cologne.

Songs (some with vn., others with orch.); chamber-music; fairy opera, *The Princess on the Pea-stalk* (Crefeld, 1918); pantomime, *Aischa* (Elberfeld, 1920); mus. comedy, *Prince Labakan*; symbolic story, *Psyche.*—A. E.

FLEISCHER, Oskar. Ger. musicographer; *b.* Zörbig (Saxony), 2 Nov. 1856. Stud. philology at Halle, 1878–83; then till 1885, under Spitta, science of music, and, after some years' travel for study, was entrusted with the installation, the preparation of catalogues, and direction of R. Collection of Ancient Musical Instruments, Berlin. In 1892 lector in mus. science, Berlin Univ.; in 1899 founded International Music Soc. (Internationale Musik-Gesellschaft) (*q.v.*), whose journal and compilations he ed. till 1904 (with Joh. Wolf).

Notker's Accentuation System in his "Boëthius"

(1883); *Denis Gaultier* (a study of lute music) in *Vierteljahrsschrift für Musik-Wissenschaft* (1886); *Guide to Royal Collection of Ancient Musical Instruments* (1892); *The Importance of the International Music and Theatre Exhibition* (1892) in *Vienna* (1893); *Studies in Neum Notation* (4 vols., 1895, 1897, 1904, the latter with facsimiles of late Byzantine notation); 1923, Vol. 4 under title *Die germanischen Neumen als Schlüssel zum altchristlichen und gregorianischen Gesang* (1923). *Biography of Mozart* (1899, *Moderne Geisteshelden*, Vol. 33); *Guide to the Bach Exhibition* (Berlin, 1901).—A. E.

FLEMING, W. P. Scottish pianist; *b.* Dundee. Commenced pf. study under John Kinross and Henry Nagel in Dundee. In 1883, stud. in Leipzig, pf. under Zwintscher, organ under Pappertz, harmony under Jadassohn, singing under Fräulein Heinemeyer. Was one of soloists at Bach Ges.; was influenced by Carl Reinecke, in study of ensemble-playing. Returned to London in 1885, and continued pf. studies under Miss Fanny Davies. Returned to Dundee as teacher, No one has exercised greater influence on music in Dundee than he has done. Was condr. of Dundee Choral Union, and of Newport Orch. Soc. for several years, and has been the means of bringing to Dundee most of the world's greatest string quartets.—W. S.

FLEMISH FOLK-MUSIC. See FRIENDENTHAL, ALBERT; VAN DUYSE, FLORIMOND.

FLESCH, Carl. Violinist; *b.* Moson, Hungary, 9 Oct. 1873. Began vn. when 6 years old; 1886–?, pupil of Grün, Vienna Cons.; 1890–4, pupil of Sauzy, Paris Cons.; also of Marsick, to whose school he professes to belong. Unanimously awarded 1st prize, 1894; 1896–1901, prof. R. Cons. Bucharest, and led the Queen of Rumania's Quartet. 1902, left Rumania; 1903–8, prof. Amsterdam Cons. Since 1908 has lived in Berlin. Dir. of special courses, State High School of Music, Berlin, since 1921. Joined Hugo Becker and Arthur Schnabel (now Carl Friedberg) to form an eminent Pf. Trio. Publ. *First Studies* and an extensive educational work, *The Art of Violin-Playing*. Ed. *Kreutzer's Studies* (Simrock), *20 Studies from Paganini* (Kahnt) and (with Schnabel) *Mozart's Vn. Sonatas*. Pupils: Alma Moodie, Willem de Boer, Josef Wolfsthal and others.—A. E.

FLETA, Miguel. Leading Span. operatic t. singer; *b.* in Aragón. After singing in Italy, Austria and Hungary, attained position he holds to-day by his *début* at Madrid R. Opera House in 1920. Has sung at La Scala, Milan; Metropolitan Opera House, New York; Liceo, Barcelona.—P. G. M.

FLETCHER, Alice Cunningham. Writer on Amer. Indian music; *b.* Boston, Mass., U.S.A., 1845. Active in Indian welfare work and special agent of the U.S. government to the Omaha, Winnebago and Nez Percés tribes. Since 1882 assistant in ethnology, Peabody Museum of Amer. Archæology and Ethnology; holder of the Thaw fellowship since 1891.

The Study of Omaha Indian Music (Peabody Museum, 1893); *Indian Story and Song from North America* (Small, Maynard. 1900); *Indian Games and Dances* (Birchard, 1915); papers in *Bureau of American Ethnology* (Peabody Museum), *American Anthropologist, Journal of American Folk-Lore.*—J. M.

FLEURY, Louis. Fr. flautist; *b.* Lyons, 1878; was pupil of P. Taffanel at Paris Cons.; 1st prize, 1900; dir. (since 1905) Société Moderne d'Instruments à Vent, and of Société des Concerts d'Autrefois (1906); displays great activity and travels incessantly over Europe as soloist or with one of his societies. Frequent visits to England; has devoted himself particularly to spreading knowledge of Eng. music on the Continent. Stud. assiduously the ancient music of the flute; has produced remarkable editions of the sonatas and other ancient pieces of Blavet, Naudat, Purcell, J. Stanley and other masters of XVIII century. Has contributed to Fr. and British mus. reviews. The article on modern Flute-Music in this Dictionary is by him.—M. L. P.

FLOCCO, Armando. Pianist, compr. *b.* Naples in 1885. Stud. at Naples Cons. Was orch. condr. at San Carlo and Bellini Theatres, being asked by Mugnone to cond. the opera *Salome* at the Costanzi Theatre, Rome, on its 1st production. Went to Buenos Ayres (under contract with Opera Theatre there) in 1908. Now devotes himself to teaching and choral singing. Has comp. some chamber- and pf.-music.—A. M.

FLODIN, Carl. Finnish writer on music and compr. *b.* in 1858. Stud. under Faltin and Jadassohn; also at Univ. (Ph.M. 1886). A much esteemed critic, working in Helsingfors until 1908, when he settled in Buenos Ayres. His two chief literary works are *Finska musiker* and a large biography, *Martin Wegelius* (1922). Has again been living in Finland for some years. F. has comp. mostly songs and pf. pieces; also cantatas and a lyric scene with orch. *Helena.*—T. H.

FLONZALEY QUARTET was the creation of Éduard J. de Coppet of New York, who in 1902 engaged Adolfo Betti, Alfred Pochon, Ugo Ara and Ivan d'Archambeau, to devote themselves entirely to quartet-playing, not originally with a view to giving regular concerts in public. Rehearsals began at de Coppet's summer residence, "Flonzaley," near Lausanne, Switzerland. After several years of practice, the quartet ventured upon a European tour and aroused great admiration by the perfection of its ensemble and the artistic finish of its work. In the autumn of 1904 it was heard in private in New York and at several charity concerts. Its first official public concert in America was given in New York on 5 Dec. 1905. Since then the quartet has appeared regularly in Europe and in America. Its members, adhering to the orig. principle of devoting themselves wholly to their quartet, accepting no outside engagements and no pupils, have made for this unique organisation a position of acknowledged superiority among the chamber-music ensembles of the world. In 1917 the vla.-player, Ara, who joined the Ital. army, was replaced by Louis Bailly. Since the death of Éduard de Coppet in 1916, the quartet has been maintained by his son, André.—O. K.

FLOOD, William Henry Grattan. Irish compr. and writer; *b.* Lismore, Co. Waterford, 1 Nov. 1859. Educated at Mt. Malhray, All Hallows, Catholic Univ., St. Kieran's Coll. and Carlow Coll. (Ireland). Self-taught in music, save for some lessons by mother and aunt and Sir Robert Stewart. Mus. prodigy at 9, when he played before H.R.H. Duke of Connaught. At various times, school-teacher, condr. of provincial operatic companies; bandmaster of Old 104th Regt.; condr. of many choral and orch. socs. in England and Ireland. Took minor orders for R.C. priesthood, but relinquished through scruples. Mus. Doc. *h.c.* National Univ. of Ireland (1907); Knight of the Order of St. Gregory. Cross *pro Ecclesia et Pontifice*; orgt. and choirmaster of Thurles Cath.; of Monaghan Cath.; and of Enniscorthy Cath. since 1895. Aims at a high standard in church music and making known best polyphonic compositions.

Numerous masses, motets, part-songs, solo-songs, pf. and orch. arr. Author of: *History of Irish Music* (1900; 3rd ed. 1913); *Story of the Harp* (1908); *Story of the Bagpipe* (1911); *Memoir of W. Vincent Wallace* (1912); *Memoir of John Field* (1919); *Introductory Sketch of Irish Mus. History* (1921). Ed. of: *Moore's Irish Melodies* (1910); *Spirit of the Nation* (1911); *Armagh Hymnal* (1918); *Selected Songs and Airs of O'Carolan* (1923). Contributor to leading continental, Eng. and Amer. mus. magazines; to Grove's Dictionary; to *Dictionary of National Biography*, etc.—W. ST.

FLORIDIA, Pietro, hereditary Barone Napolino di San Silvestro. Compr. condr. teacher; *b.* Modica, Sicily, 5 March, 1860. Stud. at Liceo di San Pietro a Maiella, Naples, 1873–9, under B. Cesi (piano), Paolo Serrao and Lauro Rossi (theory), and Polidori (æsthetics and history); later pf. with Hans v. Bülow. Produced Naples (7 May, 1882), successful comic opera, *Carlotta Clepier*, the score of which he destroyed. For a time 1st prof. of pf. at Palermo Cons.; 1885–90, toured as concert-pianist. For 3 years, with Boito and Toscanini, member of commission of three on Conservatoire diplomas. In 1889 won 1st prize, Società del Quartetto, Milan, with a symphony. Settled in U.S.A., 1904. Teacher at Cincinnati (O.) Coll. of Music, 1906–8. Now living in New York.

Operas: *Maruzza* (Ricordi), Venice, 23 Aug. 1894; *Colonia Libera* (Ricordi), Rome, 7 May, 1899; *Paoletta* (Feist, N.Y.), Cincinnati, 29 Aug. 1910. Suite in olden style, op. 8, and other pf. pieces (Ricordi; Carl Fischer). Songs (Ditson; Schirmer); ed. of *Early Italian Songs and Airs* (Ditson, 1923, 2 vols.).—J. M.

FLUTE AND FLUTE-PLAYING. The flute, more than any other instrument, appears to be in its definitive state. From end of XVII to middle of XVIII century, artists and manufacturers have sought constantly to improve it. The happy discovery of Boehm (1831) perfected the instrument. During the last 40 years especially no further development has taken place. The majority of the Eng. flautists use the "1867" system; elsewhere, especially in France, the so-called Boehm system is adopted. All the researches since that time have only led to the addition of superfluous keys which complicate the mechanism without appreciable advantages. Great Britain, Germany and Northern Europe remain faithful to the wood flute. In Belgium and the Latin countries, the silver flute is nearly exclusively used. In the U.S.A. also, many artists who have settled there, have establ. the use of the metal flute. The use of the bass-flute in the orch., though rare, is growing. Of the various forms, the best is the one in G. The technique of the flute certainly reached its highest point at the beginning of the xix century, although the flautists sought only success in virtuosity, often indeed at the expense of the music. If the harmonic complexities of modern music demand more purely mus. qualities (especially more speed in reading), it is not that they demand more technically than they were able to accomplish before. The difficulties have merely changed their form. Let us mention however, on the score of curiosity, the introduction into the technique of the *flatterzunge* (flutter-tongue, an innovation of R. Strauss), a kind of rolling of the tongue on the palate, and Ravel's very frequent use of " harmonic " notes (they can be obtained in the third octave, playing then a fifth lower, and even in certain cases 2 octaves lower), although these two innovations can only be used very exceptionally. What characterises the modern methods of treating the flute is the more frequent use of the low octave. This is explained by the revival of the interest in the flute music of the xviii century, the golden age of the flute. A study of the works of Bach, Handel, Blavet, etc., shows that these masters never used the flute above g³ and made large use of the first (lowest) octave, the sonority of which was so rich and full. Modern comprs. have attempted to restore to the flute its pastoral character, so tender and pathetic, and to avoid the embellishments of the chief works of the xix century. The great concertos of the rococo period have completely gone out of fashion. Besides, this literature was entirely virtuoso-work. Outside of Germany, where this tradition is preserved, the flautists, instead of composing themselves, appear to have inspired and encouraged the comprs. to enrich the flute literature, which has, during the last 40 years, reached notable proportions. Musicographers have brought many neglected treasures of the xviii century to the light again, notably the sonatas and pieces of Blavet, Naudot, La Barre, Quantz, Marcello, Stanley, Vinci, etc. On the other hand, at the suggestion of the virtuosi in search of new music, contemporary comprs. have written important works for flute and pf. and for flute in combination with other instruments. The following necessarily incomplete list only indicates a few of the more characteristic of these works:

Reinecke's sonata, *Undine*, fl. and pf.; Gernsheim's *Serenade*, fl. and str.; Tovey's Variations on a theme of Gluck, fl. and str.; Cyril Scott's *Scotch Pastoral*, fl. and pf. (Hansen); F. S. Kelly's *Sérénade*, fl. and small orch. (Schott); Peter Benoit's Suite, (Schott); Debussy's *La Flûte de Pan*, fl. alone (ms.); Saint-Saëns's *Romance* (Durand); Widor's Suite (Hamelle); Hahn's Variations; Huë's *Nocturne* and *Gigue*; Henschel's *Variations* (Leduc); pieces by Gaubert, Chaminade, Fauré, Casella, Enesco, Mouquet, Bréville, Milhaud, Kœchlin; Debussy's sonata, fl. vla. harp; Goossens's trio; Bax's trio; Charles Bordes's *Suite basque*, fl. and str. (Bornemann).

In accordance with the new developments, there has been an important output of tutors,

studies, etc. Especially notable are several books of studies by Andersen (Zimmermann, Hansen, Cranz), Moijse (Leduc), P. Camus (Senart), a *Tutor* by Prill (Berlin), and the very important *Méthode* by Taffanel-Gaubert (Leduc, 1923).

In modern orchestration the quality of agility of the flute cannot be ignored. Rimsky-Korsakof has made great use of it in cadenzas (*Grand Pâque russe*; *Capriccio espagnol*); R. Strauss has raised it to the rôle of chief soloist in the *Dance of the Veils* in *Salome*. The *airs de ballet* in Saint-Saëns's *Ascanio* and Lalo's *Namouna* are veritable acrobatic solos. Ravel in *La Flûte enchantée* (*Schéhérazade*) has given a new impulse to the song with flute *obbligato*. But it is perhaps Debussy (in *L'Après-midi d'un Faune*) who has defined for this generation the ideal use of the flute in orchestration, and brought into full light its special qualities of expressive and penetrating charm.—L. F.

FOERSTER, Josef. Czechoslovak compr. *b.* Osenice, 1833; *d.* Prague, 3 Jan. 1907. Stud. at Organ School in Prague; choirmaster in several churches; from 1866 at St. Adalbert's; since 1886 St. Veit's Cath., Prague; prof. at Organ School, later at Cons. (harmony). Successful in propagating classical reform of ecclesiastical song in Bohemia, though in his own works he followed more modern ways. Wrote *Theory of Harmony*—well developed but rather mechanical.

Missa de Beata; *Sti. Adalberti*; *Jubilei Solemnis*; 2 *Te Deums*; 2 Requiems, *Collection of Pange lingua*, *The Catholic Organist*. Publ. J. Hoffmann; Fr. A. Urbánek, Prague.—V. St.

FOERSTER, Josef Bohuslav. Czech compr. *b.* Prague, 30 Dec. 1859. Son of Josef F. (*q.v.*). He first stud. mechanics, but turned to music; trained in Organ School, Prague. Till 1893 orgt. and choir-master in Prague, when he accompanied his wife, the celebrated singer Bertha Foerster-Lauterer, to Hamburg, and again to Vienna in 1903. He remained there until 1918, returning to Prague after the political overthrow. 1918, prof. at Cons.; 1920 at Master-School of Compn.; 1922, dir. of Cons. Besides working at compn., he also taught compn. in Hamburg Cons. (1901-3), Vienna Acad. of Music (1904-18); music critic for *Národni listy*, Prague (1884-93); also in Ger. later on (*Die Zeit*), when living in Hamburg and in Vienna. He lives in Prague and is at the head of several mus. organisations. In technique F. belongs to transition period between the national classical (Smetana, Dvořák) and the modern (Novák, Suk) generation, hence by the side of Fibich (*q.v.*). On the other hand the fundamental ideas and the content of his music, his melody and harmony, especially during the last 10 to 15 years, have been permeated by the elements of a modern style. Subjectivism and psychological interest are the salient features of his works. We find a tender and delicate lyricism, sympathy, a spiritual conception of love in which erotic passion plays no part, devotion and humility, not force or daring, a tendency to melancholy which sometimes reaches actual pessimism, discreet and soft nuances. He does not always escape the danger of one-sidedness in mood or of a certain lack of colour, especially as his rhythmic and melodic types are often very similar. He opposes this danger with other characteristics. In the first place comes his inclination for nationality, not in the colourist folk-lore sense but as an expression of the deep significance of country life. This quality lends to his choral works a special, sometimes tragic, beauty, and for that reason these compns. are among his finest and best known. In his chief works his religious temperament finds expression, not in the ecclesiastical sense, but in the sense of a metaphysical deepening of thought and conception. In the operas the subjective point of departure threatens to obscure the individualisation of the characters and of the *milieu*, but the expressive power is all the warmer and more intimate wherever the scene reflects the author's own mood. His art was for a long time disputed by Czech critics; now the attitude towards F. is beginning to take the form of universal esteem for his work, which is neither revolutionary nor advanced, but pure, noble and deeply conceived.

Operas: *Deborah* (1891), *Eva* (1897), *Jessica* (1904). *Nepřemoženi* (*The Unconquered*, 1906); *Srdce* (*The Heart*, 1922); 4 symphonies. Symph. works.: *Mé Mládí* (*My Youth*); *Jaro a Touha* (*Spring and Yearning*); suites: *Cyrano de Bergerac*; *Shakespeare Suite*; *Spring*; *Legend of Happiness*; choir and orch.: *Angel's Hymn*; *Stabat Mater*; *A Legend*; *Spring Night*; *Bridge of Sighs*; *To the Dead Brethren*; *Four Heroes* (all Czech). Chamber-music: 3 str. 4tets; 3 pf. trios; cello and vn. sonata; 5tet for wind instrs.; 2 vn. concertos. Song-collections: *Erotikon*; *Remembrances*; *Songs of Twilight*; *Love*; *Spring Evening's Dream*; ballads; *Passiflora*; *Demon Love*; *Tagore* cycle; *The Story of the Long Desire*; *Clear Morning*; etc. Melodramas: *Amarus*; *Faustulus*, etc. Pf. pieces including the collections: *Reveries*, *Roses of Remembrance*; *And the Apple-trees are in bloom*; *Eros' Masquerades*, etc.; incidental music to *Princess Pampeliška*; *Trilogy of Samson*; *The Fool and Death*; much choral music. Publ: for F. A. Urbánek; M. Urbánek; Hudebni Matice; E. Starý; Foersterova Spolecnost; Univ. Ed.; Bosworth; Schott, etc.
Consult: Zdeněk Nejedlý, *J. B. F.* (Urbánek, 1910), Josef Bartoš, *J. B. F.* (Manes, 1923), both in Czech.—V. ST.

FOGG, Eric. Eng. compr. *b.* Manchester, 21 Feb. 1903. Chorister at Manchester Cath. 1912–1917; orgt. St. John's Ch. Manchester, 1917–19; stud. under his father, C. H. F. (35 years' orgt. Hallé Soc.); in 1920, stud. under Granville Bantock. The very free, modern style of the works with which he first came before the public, when quite young, has lately been simplified and the individuality has become clearer in consequence.

Sea-Sheen, small orch. (Ascherberg); *The Hillside* (Tagore) s. and barit. soli, chorus, orch. (ms. 1921); overture to *Comedy of Errors* (ms. 1922); orchestration of Schumann's *Études* in form of a canon (1922); str. 4tet, A flat; *Poem*, cello and pf. (Elkin, 1922); *Phantasy*, cello and pf. (Bosworth); Suite, vn. cello and harp (or pf.) (London & Continental); *Songs of Life and Life* (Tagore) (Elkin, 1921); *The Little Folk*, song-cycle (Leigh Henry) (Bosworth); *Three Chinese Songs* (Leigh Henry) (Curwen); also other songs (Elkin; Curwen; London & Continental; Bosworth); pf. pieces (Bosworth; Elkin; Murdoch); part-songs (Curwen; Novello).—E.-H.

FOHSTRÖM, Alma. Finnish coloratura singer; *b.* Helsingfors, 2 Jan. 1856. Stud.

in Helsingfors, Petrograd under Nissen-Saloman, and in Italy under Lamperti and Della Valle. First attracted attention in Helsingfors, particularly in opera, as well as in Petrograd; 1878, engaged at Kroll Theatre, Berlin, where she appeared for some time with great success. Then followed concert and opera tours in Scandinavia, Italy, Russia, Finland, Rumania, England, Austria, Switzerland, Germany, N. and S. America. After her marriage with Basil von Rode, captain of Russ. Gen. Staff (later Division-Gen.), she undertook an extensive concert-tour throughout Russia; engaged in 1890 as prima-donna at Imper. Court Opera, Moscow, where she remained till 1904. 1909, prof. at Petrograd Cons. After the Russ. revolution in 1917 she lived for a time in Helsingfors. Is now at Stern's Cons. Berlin.—T. H.

FOHSTRÖM, Ossian. Finnish cellist; *b.* Helsingfors, 21 Nov. 1870. Stud. at Helsingfors Music Inst. and (1894–5) at Brussels Cons.; later (with a State scholarship) in Belgium and Germany. Solo cellist in Helsingfors Philh. Orch. 1898–1903; and in the Municipal Orch. since 1914. Teacher at Helsingfors Orch. School 1899–1908, 1911–14, and Music Inst. 1895–6, and (since 1914) at these two amalgamated institutions. Soloist at concerts in Finland, Russia, Germany and England. Was condr. 1908–11 of orch. in Vasa, and has cond. concerts and opera performances.—T. H.

FÖLDESI, Arnold. Hungarian cellist; *b.* Budapest, 20 Sept. 1882. Stud. under David Popper.—B. B.

FOLESCU, G. See RUMANIAN OPERA.

FOLEY, Allan James. Irish b. singer; *b.* Cahir, Tipperary, 7 Aug. 1835; *d.* Southport, 1899. Stud. singing at Naples under Bisaccia; then sang in northern cities of Italy and in Paris. In 1865, *début* London in *The Huguenots*. For many years, a great favourite in London, where he sang in Ital. or in Eng., and was famous for his rendering of parts of Il Commendatore, Sparafucile, and Daland; appeared also in oratorio at the principal fests.; sang in opera and at concerts in America, Austria, Russia. His voice was powerful, but of beautiful quality and great compass. He was always known as " Signor Foli."—W. ST.

FOLK-MUSIC. See arts. under headings of various countries.

FOLK-SONG SOCIETIES.—*The English Folk-Song Society* was establ. 16 June, 1898, for publ. of Eng. traditional song; commenced with 110 members and now numbers 230; has publ. 26 journals, consisting of folk-songs gathered by its members in different parts of country; has done much to draw attention to great wealth of Eng. melody which exists, but which has hitherto been unnoticed. The success of Eng. Folk-Song Soc. led to establishment of *Irish Folk-Song Soc.* May 1904, which has issued a similar class of journal. *The Welsh Folk-Song Soc.* was formed at Llangollen, Sept. 1908. Up to present it has publ. 7 journals. In Scotland there are several societies which make the publ. of folk-music part of their programme—the *Rymour Club*, Edinburgh; the *Buchan Field Club* has devoted at least one of its *Transactions* to folk-song in Buchan.—F. K.

FOLVILLE, Juliette. Belgian compr. *b.* Liège, 5 Jan. 1870. First stud. under her father; then worked at vn. under Musin and César Thomson; at compn. under Th. Radoux. Came forward in triple rôle of pianist, harpsichord player and orch. condr. 1898–1914, pf. teacher in Liège Cons. At beginning of war, she settled in Bournemouth, England, where she devoted herself to teaching. Her music is skilfully written and in good style.

Opera, *Atala* (Lille, 1892); *Noce au village*, solo, chorus and orch.; symph. poem, *Oceano Nox*; 3 orch. suites; *Esquisse symphonique*; vn. concerto; *Morceau de concert*, cello; pf. concerto (perf. Bournemouth Fest. April 1924); pf. 4tet; *Poème*, cello and pf.; *Suite poétique*, vn. and pf.; church music with orch. and also unacc.; *Eva*, dramatic pieces, chorus and pf.; 2 pf. sonatas; 24 organ pieces; songs.—E. C.

FONDI, Enrico. Ital. musicologist; *b.* Rocca di Papa, 20 June, 1881. Wrote *La vita e l'opera letteraria del musicista Benedetto Marcello* (1909) and publ. a new ed. of Marcello's *Teatro alla moda* (1913).—D. A.

FONDI, Renato. Ital. writer and music-critic; *b.* at Pistoia. Contributor to newspapers and reviews, showing uncommon qualities of perspicacity and competence. Has publ. a vol. on *Ildebrando Pizzetti e il dramma musicale italiano d' oggi* (Rome, 1919, Biblioteca dell' *Orfeo*). —D. A.

FONT Y DE ANTA, José. Span. violinist; *b.* Seville, 1898. First lessons from his father, (violinist and bandmaster); on recommendation of Sarasate, received a grant from Seville County Council to continue his studies in Brussels, where he became a distinguished pupil of César Thomson; 1914, won highest prize at competitions at Brussels Cons. Author of *En el Jardín del Misterio*, book of art-songs, a form of compn. very little cultivated up to present by Span. comprs. Has given concerts in Belgium, Germany and Spain. Lives and teaches in Madrid. —P. G. M.

FONT Y DE ANTA, Manuel. Span. compr. and opera-condr. *b.* Seville, 1895. Stud. under his father and Don Vicente Ripollés; also compn. under Joaquín Turina in Madrid, and Sibelius in America. As condr., has toured S. America for several years, with opera companies. He is a compr. with a dual personality. Those who know him as the author of hundreds of examples of that style of popular song in Spain called *cuplés*, as well as many delightful, piquant numbers of dance-music, could hardly reconcile him with the compr. of chamber-music and symph. works. He is equally important in both aspects; for while in some of his serious works, modern and Franck-like in style, he reaches a degree of depth and intensity alien to the Southern temperament, his light works entitle him to be saluted as a reformer. In fact, his *cuplés*, devoid of the illiteracy traditional in every country, and bear-

ing often the mark of the author's technical efficiency, coupled with an exceptional sense of the popular touch in music, have created a new genre. For this, he enjoys wide fame and popularity.

Misa Coral Unisona, with organ acc.; vn. and pf. sonata; *Andalucía*, suite for pf.; scherzo, *Impresiones Aragonesas*; *Perchel*, symph. variations, orch. Light operas: *La Viuda Astuta* (2 acts, based on a play of Goldoni's); *El Preceptor* (3 acts); many popular songs; marches, etc. (Ildefonso Alier; Unión Musical Española, Madrid.)—P. G. M.

FONTOVA, Conrado. Argentine compr. *b.* Barcelona in 1865; *d.* Buenos Ayres, 1923. Brother of violinist León Fontova. Stud. in Brussels under Van Dam and De Greef. Cond. the Blankenbergen orch. concerts. In 1888 the massed military band played his symph. ode *Austria-España* at Universal Exhibition of Barcelona. Decorated with Cross of Isabel la Católica for this work. Put aside his own art for some years to act as accompanist to his brother. Then again devoted himself to compn. Publ. *La Caixeta de las Animas*, many songs, pf. and choral pieces.—A. M.

FONTOVA, León. Argentine violinist; *b.* Barcelona in 1875. Son of the well-known artist. Was a mus. prodigy, giving his 1st concert, in Liceo Theatre, Barcelona, when 6 years old. In 1888 the Queen Regent, Maria Cristina, heard him play at Universal Exhibition, Barcelona, and took upon herself the cost of his training for 5 years. Entered R. Cons. Brussels, where he stud. under Colyns, gaining *Grand Prix* when 15 years old. Returning to Spain, was appointed Musician of the Queen's Chamber. For next few years, gave concerts in Spain and abroad, being applauded for his marvellous execution. At 21, went to Argentina, repeating his triumphs at various concerts. In 1905, founded, with his brother Conrado, the Fontova Inst. and recently establ. the successful Argentine Soc. of Chamber-Music, which he dir. in collab. with the violinist López Naguil.—A. M.

FOOTE, Arthur William. Amer. compr. *b.* Salem, Mass., U.S.A., 5 March, 1853. Educated at Harvard Univ. (A.B. 1874). Granted degree of M.A. for work in music in 1875. Stud. pf. under B. J. Lang and theory under S. A. Emery and J. K. Paine. He received his whole mus. training in U.S.A. 1878–1910, orgt. of First Unitarian Ch. Boston; 1909–12, President of Amer. Guild of Orgts. First notable appearance as orch. compr. was in a popular concert of Boston Symphony Orch. 15 May, 1886, with his first Suite for str. in D, op. 15. Since then his orch. works have found their way into programmes of all larger Amer. orchs. Among later orch. works may be noted the *Four Character Pieces after Omar Khayyám* (transcription made in 1900, of 4 of 5 Poems for pf. after Omar Khayyám), first perf. Chicago Orch. under Frederick Stock, 20 Dec. 1907. Third Suite for str. in E, op. 63 (written in 1907–8), first perf. Boston Symphony Orch., 7 April, 1909, was played Queen's Hall, London, 25 Aug. 1910.

His chamber-music has been even more successful. Pf. 5tet, op. 38 (first perf. Kneisel Quartet in 1898) has been played often in America. He has produced works in all vocal and instr. forms except opera.

F. is the Nestor of that group of living New England comprs., which includes G. W. Chadwick, Mrs. H. H. A. Beach, and the somewhat younger F. S. Converse, which represents the classic, conservative or academic element in present-day Amer. mus. life. Refined and dignified in every respect, his music is characterised by originality and an imaginative quality which have done much to sustain its popularity. Is member of National Inst. of Arts and Letters; 1919, Mus.D. h.c. Trinity Coll. Hartford.

Overture, *In the Mountains*, op. 14 (1887); prologue, *Francesca da Rimini*, orch. op. 24 (1892); *Serenade* in E, str. op. 25 (1892); Suite in D, str. op. 21 (1886); Suite in D ml., orch. op. 36 (1896); Suite in E, str. op. 63 (1909); *Four Character Pieces after Omar Khayyám*, orch. op. 48 (1912); pf. 5tet, op. 38; *Tema con Variazioni* for str. 4tet, op. 32 (1901); str. 4tet, op. 70 (1911). About 100 songs (op. 13, No. 2, *I'm wearing awa'* and *Irish Folk-Song*); about 30 sacred vocal works (best-known anthems *Still, still with Thee* and *God is our Refuge*); about 20 organ works (*Festival March*, op. 29, No. 1); many pf. works (2 suites, op. 15 and op. 3). Almost all publ. by A. P. Schmidt, Boston. Author of: *Modulation and related Harmonic Questions* (Boston, Schmidt, 1919); *Some Practical Things in Pianoplaying* (*id.* 1909); joint author (with W. R. Spalding) of *Modern Harmony in its Theory and Practice* (*id.* 1905).—O. K.

FORCHHAMMER, Einar. Danish t. operasinger; *b.* 19 July, 1868. B.A. *Début* 1895 in Lübeck (Lohengrin); 1896–1902, connected with Dresden Opera; later with Operas of Frankfort-o-M. and Wiesbaden, where he sang the leading rôles in Wagner's music-dramas.—A. H.

FORD, Walter. Eng. lecturer and singing-teacher; *b.* London, 20 March, 1861. Scholar King's Coll. Cambridge, 1st class in Classical Tripos, 1883; stud. under H. C. Deacon in London, Sieber in Berlin, and Ronzi in Milan; numerous recitals in London and elsewhere; author of art. on *Song and Folk-Song* in *Encyclopædia Britannica*.—E.-H.

FORGERON, Charles. Pseudonym of Karel Kovařovic (*q.v.*).

FORINO, Ferdinando. Ital. cellist; *b.* Naples, 1837; *d.* Rome, 7 July, 1905. Stud. at Naples Cons. (in Ciandelli's class); in 1863 was called to Rome by the violinist Tullio Ramacciotti, to take part in concerts of chamber-music. From 1867, 1st cellist in Orchestra Romana; from 1875 to 1901, prof. at R. Liceo Mus. di Santa Cecilia, in which post he was succeeded by his son. He took part in the Court Quintet, with Sgambati, Monachesi, Masi (then De Sanctis) and Jacobacci. F. had a robust tone and a facile, graceful execution. Wrote a Method for cello, and many pieces for that instr., amongst which a *Tarantella* (Andrè) is particularly well known.—D. A.

FORINO, Hector. Pianist; *b.* Rome in 1875; *d.* Buenos Ayres, 1917. Stud. under Sgambati. Went to Buenos Ayres in 1899 to assist his brother Luigi in Cons. Santa Cecilia, which the latter founded in 1894. He gave a series of successful concerts there. Made the Santa Cecilia Cons. one of the most important schools of music in Argentina; then directed it in collab. with Galvani and Troiani. In 1906, Ital. Government bestowed on him title of Knight of Crown of Italy.—A. M.

FORINO, Luigi. Ital. cellist; *b.* Rome, 20 Aug. 1868. Prof. of cello at the R. Liceo Mus. di Santa Cecilia, Rome, having succeeded to that post after his father Ferdinando, of whom he was a pupil. From his youth he played in in the Consolo Quartet in Rome; then went to Buenos Ayres, where he taught harmony, cpt. and cello at National Cons. of Music; and then became dir. of Cons. of Santa Cecilia at Buenos Ayres. From 1901–6, played in the Regina Margherita Quintet in Rome. Compr. of several works for cello and for orch., and following educational publications: *La tecnica razionale e progressiva del violoncellista*, 3 vols. (Ricordi, Milan); *Il violoncello, il violoncellista ed i violoncellisti* (Hoepli, Milan).—D. A.

FORNEROD, Aloys. Swiss compr. *b.* Montet-Coudrefin, 16 Nov. 1890. Stud. vn. and compn. at Cons. in Lausanne and at *Schola Cantorum* in Paris; ed. of *Feuillets de pédagogie musicale* and mus. critic of *Tribune de Lausanne* and *Semaine Littéraire de Genève*. Teaches cpt. at Cons. in Montreux and at Institut de Ribaupierre, Lausanne.

2 symphonies (op. 1 and 8); 6 motets (Geneva, Henn); *4 Interludes dans les tons grégoriens*, organ (Paris, Roudanez); *La Nuit*, chorus (Henn).—F. H.

FORRESTER, James Cliffe. Eng. compr. *b.* Burslem, Staffs, 10 May, 1860. Stud. at National Training School with Minton Campbell Scholarship, 5½ years; pf. under A. O'Leary; organ under Sir F. Bridge; for 20 years, condr. of Ealing Choral Society.

Cantatas: *England, my England*, barit. solo, chorus and orch. (Cary); *The Kalendar*, female vs. (Novello); fantasy-trio, pf. vn. cello (1st prize, Cobbett competition, 1917) (*id.*); pf. pieces (Novello; Cary; Murdoch; Stanley Lucas); vn. pieces (Lucas; Cary); song-cycles (Cary; Lucas; Novello); numerous single songs; part-songs (Novello; Stainer & Bell; Forsyth); *Anthems Ancient and Modern* (Novello); numerous anthems (*id.*).—E.-H.

FORSELL, C. John J. Swedish barit. and concert-singer; *b.* Stockholm, 6 Nov. 1868; entered army 1888; stud. R. Cons. Stockholm, 1892–4 (under Julius Günther); *début* at R. Opera, Stockholm, 1896; engaged there 1896–1909; Metropolitan, New York, 1909–10; then appeared as opera-singer in London, Berlin, Vienna, and chief Ger. cities, Stockholm, Copenhagen, Christiania, Helsingfors, Amsterdam. As concert-singer, toured Europe and America. His voice is a high barit. finely modulated and very flexible. He is also an excellent actor and has done great work as pioneer for Swedish song-comprs. Lives in Stockholm as teacher; member R.A.M. Stockholm, 1906; R. Court singer, 1909. Chief opera-rôles:

Don Giovanni; Almaviva; Figaro; William Tell; Luna; Rigoletto; Iago; Amonasro; Dutchman; Wolfram; Telramund; Sachs; Beckmesser; Wotan; Amfortas; Tonio; Scarpia; Escamillo; Jochanaan (*Salome*); Sebastiano; Nevers; Mephistopheles; Onegin; Hans Heiling; Francesco (Schillings' *Mona Lisa*); also in Swedish operas, *Tirfing Valdemarsskatten, Arnljot*, etc.—P. V.

FORSYTH, Wesley Octavius. Canadian pianist; *b.* near Toronto in 1863. Stud. in Toronto, Leipzig and Vienna, under Zwintscher, Krause, Jadassohn and Julius Epstein. Since 1902, has lived in Toronto where he was some time dir. of Metropolitan School of Music; now member of advisory board of Canadian Acad. of Music. Is widely known as a teacher throughout Ontario; has publ. 60 pieces and many songs; has contributed to numerous magazines; mus. critic for many years of *The Week.* He has done much in moulding public opinion towards a better understanding of modern works.—L. S.

FORSYTH BROTHERS, Ltd. Publishers, establ. in Manchester in 1857; shortly afterwards a publ. branch was opened in London. Specialise in educational music, under editing of Sir Charles Hallé; later of Dr. Carroll.—E.-H.

FOSS, Hubert James. Eng. music critic; *b.* Croydon, 2 May, 1899. Mus. critic *New Witness,* 1922–3; *Daily Graphic,* 1923; mus. ed. Oxford Univ. Press (H. Milford), from March, 1921; contributor to *Music and Letters, Mus. Times, Daily Telegraph, Manchester Guardian,* etc.—E.-H.

FOSTER, Ivor. British barit. singer; *b.* Pontypridd, S. Wales, 1 March, 1870. Won barit. competition National Eisteddfod, Carnarvon, 1894; stud. 4 years at R.C.M. London, under Henry Blower and Sir Charles Stanford; has sung for all the chief choral societies and at the Boosey Ballad Concerts for 25 consec. seasons; created Don Pedro in Stanford's opera *Much Ado* (Covent Garden). His daughter, Megan, made a successful *début* as singer in 1920.—E.-H.

FOSTER, Muriel. Eng. contr. singer. Stud. R.C.M. London. Frankfort Museum concert, 1901; Düsseldorf, 1902; Lower Rhine Fest. (*Gerontius* in Ger.); Bach's B mi. Mass), 1902; Worcester Fest. (*Gerontius,* etc), 1902; Dresden; Zurich, Berlin, Cologne, Holland with Mengelberg orch.), 1903; in that year, created part of Mary Magdalene (Elgar's *Apostles*) at Birmingham Fest.; 1904, Leeds Fest. and 1st U.S.A. tour; 1905, Worcester Fest. and 2nd U.S.A. tour; 1906, Hereford and Birmingham Fests.; in concerts continuously; in 1906 married Ludovic G. Foster (Goetz, afterwards Foster) and retired from public life, save for a few occasional recitals in London. Has a voice of beautiful quality and a highly finished style.—E.-H.

FOSTER, Myles Birket. Eng. compr. *b.* London, 29 Nov. 1851; *d.* 18 Dec. 1922. Stud. under J. Hamilton Clarke; and then at R.A.M. under Sullivan and E. Prout; pf. under Westlake; cello, Pettitt; ob. Horton; clar. Lazarus. Founded R.A.M. Club in 1889; orgt. at various churches; dir. of music, Foundling Hospital, Hospital, 1880–93; composed chiefly church music and children's music.

Cantatas: *Ode to Music; Eudora,* male chorus, orch.; *The Making of a Rose,* s.s.a.; *Cinderella; Beauty and the Beast; Lampblack* for children (Weekes); *Agincourt; Golden Slippers* (Hammond); *Children's Summer Day and Winter Day; Snow Fairies; Fisher Maidens; Coming of the King* (Novello); *Elsa's Fairy* (Boosey); *Anthems of all Nations* (Boosey); duets, pf. (Weekes); vocal duets (Hammond); 2- and 4-part songs (Boosey; Weekes; Hammond; Metzler;

Novello; Curwen; Cramer; Rogers; Williams); unison songs (Novello; Weekes); songs (Weekes; Novello; Moutrie; Ashdown; Cary; Boosey); *A Day in a Child's Life; The Children's Christmas* (Weekes). —E.-H.

FOULDS, John Herbert. Eng. compr. and condr. *b.* Manchester, 2 Nov. 1880. Son of F. F. (member of Hallé Orch. for many years); in theatre-orch. at 14; member of Hallé Orch. at 20 (till 30); then condr. of stage-music, under Richter, regularly visiting continental cities for opera experience; compd. much music for stage-production; during war, gave weekly concerts at Ciro's Club for the forces; 1918, mus. dir. London Central Y.M.C.A. (Saturday orch. concerts, lectures, etc.); 1921, condr. Univ. of London Mus. Soc. His *Vision of Dante,* op. 7, completed in 1904, still awaits perf. It is for solo, chorus and orch. and is described as a concert-opera; the narrative and lyrical portions are set and sung, interspersed with purely orch. passages (in the manner of a symph. poem) descriptive of the poet's journeying through the various spheres. His *Epithalamium,* op. 10, and other "music-poems" are constructed in stanzas like a poem. In several works, particularly in his orch. *Music Pictures,* op. 33, he secures new shades of mus. colour by the use of quarter-tones for this very effective programme - music (see article on NOTATIONS). His choral work, *A World Requiem,* op. 60, was produced (on the recommendation of the British Music Soc.) at the Albert Hall, on Armistice Day, 11 Nov. 1923, with the Prince of Wales present. It is a musician's commentary on the war; laid out for soli, chorus, boy's choir, orch. and organ; in 2 parts, each of 10 numbers, each part taking about an hour in performance.

Chief serious works: *Music-Pictures,* op. 1; *Variazione,* pf. op. 4 (Novello, 1905); *Epithalamium,* op. 10 (perf. Sir H. J. Wood, 1906); cello concerto, op. 22 (1st perf. Carl Fuchs, at Richter's farewell concert, Manchester, 1911); *Music Pictures* (group 3), op. 33, orch. (Sir Henry Wood, 1913); *Mood-Pictures* (3 songs, v. and pf. op. 51 (Curwen); 72 essays in the modes, pf. op. 78; *A World Requiem,* op. 60 (Paxton) (see above); *Music Pictures* (group 1), op. 30, pf. trio. Also music for stage-productions: *Wonderful Grandmamma,* op. 34; *The Whispering Well,* op. 35; *Julius Cæsar,* op. 39; *Sakuntala,* op. 64; *The Trojan Women,* op. 65; *Deburau,* op. 72; *The Fires Divine,* op. 76. Lighter works: *Holiday Sketches,* suite, small orch. op. 16 (Bosworth, 1908); *Suite Française,* small orch. op. 22 (Hawkes); cello pieces, op. 25 (*id.*); *The Eastern Lover,* scena, contr. v. and orch. (Enoch); *Keltic Suite,* orch. op. 29 (Hawkes); vn. pieces, op. 40 (*id.*); *Idyll,* str. orch. op. 42 (*id.*); *Music-Pictures* (group 4), str. orch. op. 55 (Hawkes); *Gaelic Dream-Song,* small orch. op. 68 (*id.*); *Suite Fantastique,* from music to Pierrot play *Deburau,* op. 72 (*id.*).—E.-H.

FOURDRAIN, Félix. Fr. compr. *b.* Nice, 1880. Succeeds more easily in a light, clever style than in serious opera.

La Légende du Pont d'Argenton (1907); *Écho* (1907); *La Glaneuse* (1909); *Vercingétorix* (1912); *Madame Roland* (1913); *Les Contes de Perrault* (1913); *Les Folies amoureuses* (1920); *Dolly* (1922). Also some pf. pieces and songs.—A. C.

FOX-STRANGWAYS, Arthur Henry. Eng. mus. journalist and writer; *b.* Norwich, 14 Sept. 1859. Educated at Wellington Coll. and Balliol, Oxford; stud. pf. and cpt. at High School of Music, Berlin, 1882–4; assistant-master Wellington Coll. 1887–1910; dir. of music there,

1893–1901; two visits to India, 1901 and 1910, spent in studying Indian music; publ. *The Music of Hindustan* (Clarendon Press, 1914); founded the Eng. quarterly *Music and Letters* in 1920, which he still edits. With the *Revue Musicale* (Paris) and the *Musical Quarterly* (New York), it is one of the 3 finest mus. quarterlies in the world. On the mus. staff of *The Times*. Contributor to *The London Mercury*.—E.-H.

FRACASSI, Almérico. Argentine compr. *b.* Lucito, Campobasso, Italy. Went to Buenos Ayres as a child. In 1890, went to Naples Cons. under Rossomandi and D'Arienzo. Began concert-work in 1896, at Milan, Naples and Monte Carlo. In 1899, returned to Buenos Ayres; obtained a great success as pianist. In 1890, concerts in Europe. Returning to Buenos Ayres in 1903, devoted himself to compn. and teaching, taking over Cons. of Almagro (on death of founder, Bagnati). He now directs it with the Cavaliere Gennaro d'Andrea. An able teacher, he brought to Argentina the taste and technique of Cesi's school.

5 pf. studies; Suite and concerto for pf. and orch.; sonata for pf. and vn.; 4 Argentine Anthems, of which the *Himno al Centenario* obtained the gold medal awarded in open competition by the Argentine Goverment.—A. M.

FRANCÉS, Julio. Span. violinist, compr. and condr. Pupil of Ysaye; prof. of vn. at R. Cons. de Música; leader of R. Theatre orch., of Orquesta Sinfónica and of the Quinteto de Madrid; founder of Quarteto Francés; condr. of Sociedad Coral del Palacio de la Música; founder and condr. of Orquesta de Cuerda, Madrid.

2 orch. suites: *Chiquilladas*; *Escenas Madrileñas*, *Balada*, s., t., mixed chorus and orch. (Unión Musical Española).—P. G. M.

FRANCHETTI, Alberto. Ital. compr. *b.* Turin, 18 Sept. 1860. One of most renowned contemporary comprs., both in operatic and instr. fields. Belongs to a very prominent and gifted family, being the son of Baron Raimondo Franchetti and Baroness Luisa Rothschild. He had to struggle against his father's wishes in order to be able to follow his mus. inclinations; stud. first under obscure masters in Venice and Padua; then perfected himself in Germany, at Munich under Rheinberger and at Dresden under Draeseke and Rieschbieter. Wrote symph. poem *The Loreley*; Variations for str. 4tet and various overtures; became known by his symphony in E mi., perf. first in Dresden, 1886, then in many other cities.

Operatic works: *Asrael* (subject taken from Flemish legend of the XIV century and from an episode in Moore's *Loves of the Angels* (1st perf. Reggio Emilia, 1888); *Christopher Columbus*, written for Municipality of Genoa on 4th centenary of discovery of America (1st perf. Genoa, 1892); *Fior d'Alpe* (Scala, Milan, 1894); *Il Signor di Pourceaugnac* (Scala, Milan, 1897); *Germania* (Scala, Milan, 1902); *La figlia di Jorio* (Scala, Milan, 1906); *Notte di leggenda* (Scala, Milan, 1915); *Glauco* (San Carlo, Naples, 1922). Also operetta, *Giove a Pompei*, written in collab. with Giordano (perf. Rome, 1920); symph. impression, *Nella selva nera*; and biblical idyll, *Moabita*. Nearly all these are publ. by Ricordi, Milan.—D. A.

FRANCHETTI, Luigi. Ital. pianist; nephew of Alberto. Educated at Eton and Oxford; now lives at Munich.—E.-H.

FRANCK, César August. Belgian composer; *b.* Liège, 10 Dec. 1822; *d.* Paris, 8 Nov. 1890. César Franck came, on his father's side, of a family which had lived for generations at Gemmenich, in that corner of Belgium which is formed by the junction of the provinces of Liège, Dutch Limburg and the Prussian Rhineland. His mother was German and came from Aix-la-Chapelle. Both had settled in Liège before the birth of César in 1822. He studied first of all at the Liège Conservatoire. In 1835 his parents settled in Paris, where he received private lessons from Reicha (*d.* 1836). He entered the Conservatoire in 1837 and gained in succession the *Grand Prix d'honneur* for pianoforte (1839), a 1st prize for fugue (1840) and a 2nd prize for organ (1841). As his father had decided that his career was to be that of a virtuoso pianist, he left the Conservatoire in 1842, spent in Belgium two years (of which we have little information) and returned to Paris in 1844. From thenceforth he led an extremely laborious life, mainly in giving lessons in order to support himself and his parents; his brother Joseph, also a musician, followed the same occupation. But in the meantime César was composing. On 4 Jan. 1846, his biblical eclogue *Ruth* was first performed in public and attracted some notice. On 22 Feb. 1848, in mid-Revolution, he married an actress, daughter of the tragedian Desmousseaux, and left his father's house. He now devoted himself even more assiduously to the teaching of music, without, however, losing sight of the necessity for cultivating his own mental powers, for "reserving a thought-period" (according to the fine expression which Vincent d'Indy attributed to him).

He was organist at Notre-Dame de Lorette, then at St.-Jean-St.-François, finally at Ste.-Clotilde (where he had been choirmaster since 1858)—thus gradually he saw his financial position becoming more secure and his reputation as a soloist established. His improvisations on the organ left on those who had the good fortune to hear them the impression of something absolutely unique and profoundly moving. From 1850 to 1870 he composed practically nothing—he seems to have been concentrating and crystallising his forces in preparation for the final blossoming of his genius. Between 1869 and 1879 he composed the *Béatitudes*, his most famous work, of which only a fragment was produced during his lifetime (1887). In 1872 he was appointed organ-professor at the Paris Conservatoire, where his modest class soon became the nucleus of the glory and talent of the modern French school. The infinite kindliness, breadth of vision and skill of Franck, together with his generosity in instruction, gathered round him, whether at the Conservatoire or in the privacy of his home, a regular constellation of young enthusiasts whose names alone suffice to show that his efforts were not fruitless: Duparc, de Castillon, d'Indy, Chausson, de Bréville, Ropartz, Bordes, Lekeu . . . In 1873 he became a naturalised Frenchman.

The same year marks the first performance of the *Rédemption*. The last ten years of his life (1880–90) produced an almost uninterrupted succession of masterpieces—the *Variations Symphoniques*, the violin and piano sonata, *Psyché*, the symphony, the string quartet, and three great organ *Chorals*. This extraordinary creative activity was interrupted at its very height by a fatal attack of pleurisy, which caused his death on 8 Nov. 1890.

During his lifetime Franck was very little appreciated except by a select public who divined his genius and instinctively realised how many fresh beauties he was adding to the æsthetic patrimony of Europe. In official circles he was regarded merely as one teacher among many thousands of his kind. At the present time that opinion is absolutely reversed and he is venerated as one of those inspired masterminds who have inaugurated fresh eras in the history of music. No one wishes to assert that all of Franck's work is perfect—he took a considerable time to realise himself and educate his style. It is obvious that during the first part of his career (1840–70) he responded, albeit rather passively, to the detestable musical atmosphere in which he lived. Again, if later on during his prime, one or two of his works show occasional weakness, one must attribute this fact to a certain lack of critical judgment which allowed him to accept as subjects for inspiration, literary texts that are sometimes worse than mediocre. His operas, *Hulda* and *Ghiselle*, suffered most in this respect, and the *Béatitudes* and *Rédemption* do not wholly escape any more than some of his songs. On the other hand, one cannot fail to recognise that the genius of Franck restricts itself to the expression of a limited order of sentiment. His inability to depict evil has often been commented upon—when his music is forced to interpret such, owing to the character of the libretto, it becomes conventional, sometimes almost vulgar. One freely admits this fact, in order to point out that his genius is not suitable for human drama and for purely objective psychology as represented on the stage. His own domain is lyricism pure and simple, the outward projection of his own innermost dreams. In this he is without equal, and it is because he succeeded in clothing this inward idealism in new forms of music that he occupies so elevated a position among the great ones of musical evolution. No one in the xix century expressed better than he the sense of communion between man and God; no one has interpreted as he the agony of the modern soul beset by the tormenting problems of life, and seeking its deliverance in ardent faith, and confidence in an absolute ideal of beauty and perfection. The critics of the past have not sufficiently appreciated the delicacy of his interpretations of nature, nor realised that certain of his works, such as *Les Éolides*, *Psyché*, and parts of *Hulda*, by the subtlety of their harmonic colouring were already paving the way for the Impressionist school.

The principal method employed by Franck in order to realise his ideal of musical lyricism consists in the use of a melodic form of very delicate contour whose force of expression is increased by a characteristic harmony based on a system of figuration capable of the most exquisite *nuances*. César Franck develops chromatic modulation, already in embryo in classical harmony, to its fullest extent—so that to proceed further it was necessary to contradict the principles laid down by Rameau and consider that discords no longer existed, in fact that there were only concords. This last step was accomplished by Debussy. On the other hand, Franck re-established the rights of polyphony which had been neglected in the xix century, particularly in France. Lastly, he was the first to produce systematically the " cyclic form " in pure music. This procedure, which consists of unifying a symphony or piece of chamber-music by reuniting all the principal themes at the end, has been rather abused of late. But his merits in the pursuit of homogeneity in purely musical works do not stop there. The manner in which he conceives the thematic work contributes in a large part to the cohesion between the different movements, a cohesion which Beethoven himself only achieved in a limited measure: By combining in a hundred different ways his themes and his counter-themes, by preparing their chief entries by fugitive suggestions and bringing them back later on under the form of reminiscences which echo them in the most delicate manner possible, Franck introduces into the veins of the old sonata form, an art of infinitely free and subtle variations which renews its substance completely. Thanks to this absolute equilibrium between the substance and the form, he has carried, so it seems, the symphony and chamber-music to the point of perfection, in such a way that it may be asked, as was asked by Wagner apropos of Beethoven, " if he has not exhausted all their resources." The future alone will show if this thesis is sound.

In orchestration he was no innovator, and the ideas, which give an illusion of originality, he borrows from organ composition alone.

3 concert trios (1841); 4th trio (1842); *Ruth* (1843–6); 2 masses (1858 and 1860); 6 organ pieces, 1860–2; *Panis angelicus* (1872); *Rédemption* (1871–72); *Les Éolides* (1876); 3 organ pieces (1878); 5tet (1878–9): *Les Béatitudes* (1869–79): *Rébecca* (1881); *Le Chasseur maudit* (*The Accursed Hunter*), 1882; *Les Djinns* (1884); *Prélude, choral et fugue*, pf. (1884); *Hulda*, opera (1882–5, perf. at Monte Carlo, 1894); Symph. Variations (1885); vn. sonata (1886); *Prélude, aria et final*, pf. (1886–7); *Psyché* (1887–88); symphony, D mi. (1886–8); 4tet, D ma. (1889); *Ghiselle*, lyrical drama (1888–90; produced at Monte Carlo, 1896); 3 chorals for organ (1890).

The principal work on C. F. is that of Vincent d'Indy (Paris, Alcan). It contains all necessary bibliographical information. Consult also the art. on F. in J. Tiersot's *Un Demi-siècle de musique française* (Paris, Alcan).—C. V. B.

FRANCK, Richard. Ger. compr. *b.* Cologne, 3 Jan. 1858. The son of compr. Eduard Frank (1817–93). Pupil of Stern's Cons. Berlin, R. Cons. and Univ. Leipzig. 1880–3 teacher General Music School, Basle; Kullak's Acad. Berlin, and Magdeburg. Again in Basle, 1887–1900; then

(1900–9) dir. of Teachers' Choral Soc. Cassel. Now living in Heidelberg. R. mus. dir. 1903.

Overture (*Waves of the Sea and of Love*), orch., op. 21; *Dramatic Overture*, op. 37; *Symphonic Phantasy*, op. 31; suite, op. 30; *Cupid and Psyche*, op. 40, tone-poem, full orch.; *Words of Love* (chorus and orch); 2 pf. trios, op. 20 and 32; pf. 4tets, op. 33 and 41; vn. sonatas, op. 14 and 35; vn. concerto, op. 43; pf. concerto, op. 50; pf. sonata, op. 51; over 50 pf. pieces; some songs; male choruses, etc.—A. E.

FRANCKENSTEIN, Clemens, Freiherr von. Ger. compr. *b*. Wiesentheid (Lower Franconia), 14 July, 1875. Whilst a student at Munich, was pupil of Thuille, then of Knorr at the Frankfort-o.-M. Cons. Next went to America. Condr. in London, 1902–7; Wiesbaden Court Theatre 1907; from there R. Theatre Berlin. In 1912–18 Court mus. dir., Munich; gen. mus. dir. 1914 until the Revolution.

Numerous songs and orch. works. *Festival Music*, op. 35; Variations for full orch. on a theme of Meyerbeer; 4 orch. pieces (1922). Operas: *Griseldis* (Troppau, 1898); *Fortunatus* (Pesth, 1909); *Rahab* (Hamburg, 1911); *The Emperor's Poet* (*Li-Tai-Pe*), text by Rud. Lothar, Hamburg, 1920; pantomime, *Die Biene*, op. 37.—A. E.

FRANCMESNIL, Roger de. Fr. compr. pianist; *b*. Paris, 2 Dec. 1884; *d*. there, 1 Jan. 1921. Pupil of Diémer at Paris Cons. 1st prize, pf. 1905.

Chant de la Victoire (orch.); *Évocation symphonique* (orch.); chamber-music for vn., fl. and cello; str. 4tet; a collection of songs.—A. C.

FRANCO Y DE BORDONS, José María. Span. compr. and pianist; *b*. Irun, 1893. One of leading accompanists in Madrid; compr. of art-songs.

Rimas de Becquer: De un jardín de Andalucía; Rimas de Consuelo Gil Roesset; Pequeños poemas de R. Tagore, etc.; pieces for pf.; for vn.; for guitar (Romero & Fernández, Buenos Ayres).—P. G. M.

FRANKO, Sam. Amer. violinist, condr. *b*. New Orleans, La., U.S.A., 20 Jan. 1857. Stud. vn. under Blecha in Breslau and de Ahna in Berlin. At 10 appeared in public with orch. in Breslau. At 12 gave 1st concert in America at Steinway Hall, New York; 1876–8, stud. in Berlin under Joachim (vn.) and A. Hollaender (compn.); 1878–80, pupil of Vieuxtemps and Léonard (vn.) in Paris; 1880, member of Thomas Orch. in New York, leading violinist 1884–91; 1891–7, principal vla. New York Philh. Orch. In 1883, toured U.S.A. and Canada as solo-vn. of Mendelssohn Quintet Club of Boston; 1893–1901, gave concerts in New York with his own chamber-music organisation; 1894, organised the Amer. Symphony Orch. (65 native players); 1900–9, attracted much attention in New York with his Concerts of Old Music (XVII and XVIII centuries). These he continued after 1909 in Berlin where at Stern's Cons. he also taught advanced vn. pupils and cond. the orch. class. Returned to New York in 1915 for further concerts of old music, also series of chamber-music concerts for People's Inst. (1919–20) and cond. perfs. of Soc of Amer. Singers (Mozart's *Bastien and Bastienne*, and *The Impresario*. Has publ. vn. transcriptions and arr. of older orch. works (Jungnickel; C. Fischer; Ries & Erler), notably Pergolesi and Vivaldi *Concerti Grossi* (Schirmer, 1909, 1916). Many pieces for vn. and pf.—O. K.

FRANQUIN, Merri. Fr. tpt. soloist; *b*. Lançon

(Bouches du Rhône), 17 Oct. 1848; prof. of class of tpt.-playing at Cons. Paris. Author of *Grande Méthode de Trompette et de Cornet à Pistons* (used at Cons.); also invented the new modern tpt. with 5 pistons.—F. R.

FRANSELLA, Albert. Solo flautist; *b*. Amsterdam of Dutch parentage, but Ital. extraction. Son of a flautist; trained by his father and de Jong; appeared in public at 15; played under Brahms at 16; first appeared in London under Rivière at promenade concerts; principal fl. Scottish Orch. and at Crystal Palace under Manns; R. Philh. and Queen's Hall Orch.; prof. at Trinity College of Music, London.—E.-H.

FRANZ (real name Franz Gautier). Fr. heroic tenor, *b*. Paris, 1876. Started as railway clerk; Made many unsuccessful attempts to pass entrance exam. for Cons. In 1908 the newspaper *Comœdia* organised a competition for ts.; he entered under name of Franz, and gained 1st prize with aria from *La Juive*. After many trials, Messager and Broussan (then managers of Opéra) engaged him in 1909. *Début* in *Lohengrin*; thereafter sang in all the repertoire. Principal rôles in *Parsifal*, 1914; *La Légende de St. Christophe*, 1920; *Antar*, 1921; *Les Troyens*, 1921; *La Fille de Roland*, 1922. Has also sung in London, Italy and South America. A very rich t. voice, especially strong in middle register; for this reason, is one of finest singers of Wagnerian and modern opera.—A. R.

FREDERIKSEN, Tenna. Danish opera-singer (s.); *b*. Copenhagen, 16 May, 1887. Prima donna of R. Theatre, Copenhagen; Court-singer; trained under opera-singer J. L. Nyrop and Osta Schottländer (Copenhagen), Padilla and Jean de Reszke (Paris). *Début* (Elsa in *Lohengrin*), 4 April, 1906. Principal rôles: Tosca; Traviata Margaret (*Faust*); Madame Butterfly; Musette (*Bohème*); Tatjana (*Eugene Onegin*); Iolanthe (Tchaikovsky); Fidelio; Myrtocle (*Die toten Augen*); Louise (Charpentier).—A. H.

FREMSTAD, Olive. Norwegian-Amer. dramatic s. singer; *b*. Stockholm in 1872 of Norwegian father and Swedish mother. Went to Norway when 3 years old; to America when 12. Pupil of Lilli Lehmann, Berlin. *Début* in Berlin, 1895; sang in Bayreuth, 1896; Vienna, 1897; subsequently in Munich and at Covent Garden, London. Engaged at Metropolitan, New York, 1903–14, and from 1917. Has there sung most of leading parts in Wagner's operas, as well as Santuzza, Salome, etc.—U. M.

FRENCH CHAMBER-MUSIC FROM 1880. Saint-Saëns (trio in F, 1865), Gabriel Fauré (1st 4tet, 1878) and César Franck (sonata for pf. and vn. 1886; 4tet, 1889) were the pioneers of modern French chamber-music. Since the end of the XVIII century in France, as in Italy, the forms of pure music were disdained and could only be applied at the Opera. Only the great German classics were played at concerts, which for various reasons were few in number and reserved for the *élite*. These three musicians succeeded from the very first in supplying models truly French in style. Saint-Saëns with his eclectic talent and his incomparable constructive ability, Franck with his science and eloquent lyricism, Gabriel Fauré with his charming sensibility and delicate poesy, are the real creators of the French school of chamber-music.

César Franck's disciples—Vincent d'Indy (4tet; trio with clar.; sonata for pf. and vn.), Ernest Chausson (4tet; concerto)—claimed their freedom from the beginning. Chausson at the end of his life, which was very short (he died in 1899), felt himself drawn towards an ideal very close to that of Debussy. On the contrary, the tendencies of the "Scholistes" were manifested forcefully in the works of Albéric Magnard (trio, 1904; 4tet; 5tet for pf. and wind instrs.; vn. and pf. sonatas; sonata for cello and pf.), of which the tumultuous force bears witness to chivalrous generous feeling and full-blooded emotion.

Guy Ropartz's trio, Albert Roussel's trio and vn. sonata, and Witkowski's 4tet, are amongst the best productions of the "Scholistes," with whom we must rank Gabriel Pierné (5tet; trio) he seems to be influenced more by the school of Fauré. The influence of Fauré is indeed very considerable on all the French school, and it counteracts that of César Franck. We must not forget that although Fauré was one of the first in France to compose chamber-music (about 1880), he continues to produce, even now, works of astonishing freedom and extreme sensibility (5tet, 1921; trio, 1923; 2nd sonata for cello, 1921).

Debussy's influence is also considerable, and the day when his str. 4tet was first played is a landmark in the history of French music (1893). He completely renovated the style of the str. 4tet, arriving at the point of transforming it into a veritable orchestra, writing for the instruments with marvellous freedom and constructive knowledge. Towards the end of his life Debussy returned to chamber-music and wrote his vn. and pf. sonata, his cello and pf. sonata, and his charming trio for fl. vla. and harp, which is one of the most perfect of his compositions.

Although not entirely escaping the influence of Debussy, it is to Fauré and Saint-Saëns that we must attach Maurice Ravel in his str. 4tet, his pf. trio, and his sonata for vn. and cello. He has dared to open up new ways, albeit preserving a cyclic plan of surprising severity.

Florent Schmitt's 5tet, of immense cyclic construction, and his vn. and pf. sonata in two linked parts, bear witness to the power of this vigorous musician. The combined influence of Fauré and Debussy is felt in the works of Louis Aubert, Charles Kœchlin, André Caplet, Jean Huré, and other excellent musicians.

Relatively neglected by the musicians of the previous generation, who preferred the orchestra, chamber-music is now strongly in favour with the younger French composers, who very frequently find it a suitable vehicle for their experiences. Darius Milhaud has already composed five 4tets and numerous instr. sonatas of very daring material; Arthur Honegger, several sonatas for vn. vla. and cello, and str. 4tet; Germaine Tailleferre, a 4tet, a delicious vn. sonata; Durey, a 4tet; Poulenc, some pieces for wind instrs. and Georges Migot, several instr. pieces, very original in form.

In the music for piano is to be found one of the richest treasures of the French school. Whereas César Franck started to apply the colours of the organ to the piano, Gabriel Fauré and Chabrier gave the first models of those new pianistic effects of precious sonorities of harmony and subtleties of texture which seem to characterise the technique called "impressionist." Satie, in his *Gymnopédies* (1883) and his *Sarabandes*, had already made use of clusters of notes inexplicable according to scholastic rules. Already before Debussy, Ravel in his first piano works (1901) revealed models of the new pianistic style, derived from Chabrier, Fauré and Satie. In an analogous language, but with characteristic procedures, Debussy wrote, from the year 1902, his masterpieces. One can say that the school of modern French piano composition is related to Fauré, Debussy and Ravel, if we except the "Scholistes," who continue to compose sonatas according to traditional rules. Lately Darius Milhaud and Poulenc have applied their polytonal innovations to piano composition and have obtained some very interesting results.—H. P.

FRENCH CHORAL MUSIC FROM 1880. The difficulty of forming choirs in France is such that choral works are rarely performed, notwithstanding they have such a wonderful work as the *Beatitudes* by César Franck. Amongst modern French composers Saint-Saëns has assiduously cultivated this form under the most varied aspects: 4-part choruses; double choruses; soli and mixed chorus; unacc. mixed choruses; canons for children's voices, etc., and especially his cantatas for soli, chorus and orch.: *Le Déluge, La Lyre et la Harpe, Nuit Persane, La Gloire de Corneille*, etc. Massenet has competed with him in numerous 4-part male choruses (*La Caravane perdue, Moines et Forbans, Le Sylphe, Alerte*, etc.), 2-part female choruses (*Aux étoiles, La Chevrière, Chansons des Bois d'Amaranthe, Poème des fleurs*, etc.) and some cantatas (*Narcisse, Biblis*). Gabriel Fauré about 1880 made use of this form, but has renounced it since. We may mention his *Cantique de Racine* and *Les Djinns* for 4-part chorus; Madrigal for vocal 4tet; *La Naissance de Vénus*, soli, chorus and orch. Bizet, whose music still lives, wrote a 4-part chorus, *Saint Jean de Pathmos*, and various solos with chorus: *Chanson du rouet, Le Golfe de Baia*. One of the best-known works of 1890 period is the celebrated *Ode à la Musique* by Chausson (poem by Edmond Rostand) for female voices with solo and orch. It followed his *La Sulamite* (1884) on a poem by Jean Richepin. The choruses with soli by Gustave Charpentier (*Poèmes chantés, Impressions fausses*) are now little heard, no more than the choruses of Chausson (*Hymne védique, Chant nuptial, Chant funèbre*). The predominance of intimate lyrics and of the delicately chiselled *lied* adds to the difficulty of choruses for modern composition. Debussy has only written for chorus *Trois chansons* (Charles d'Orléans) for 4-part mixed unacc. voices. The third of his Nocturnes called *Sirènes*, which requires some singers, is hardly ever played, and the *Damoiselle élue* (on Rossetti's poem) for female voices, chorus and orch. is not often given. Of the choruses which Paul Ladmirault has written (*Les Berceaux, Printemps, Âmes de la forêt, Hymne de la Saint-Jean d'Été*) only the last is published. Roussel has written 2 madrigals for 4 voices, but neither Ravel, Duparc nor Dukas has written any choral music. The only contemporary composers who have seriously cultivated this form are Florent Schmitt and Gabriel Pierné, the former with excellent four-part songs, unacc. choruses, some choruses with orch. (*Danse des Devadasi, Chant de guerre, Hymne à l'Été*), the latter with some choruses for female voices in 2, 3 and 4 parts (*Le Printemps, Hymne à la Vierge, Le Repos en Égypte, Rondes des fées*, etc.). Some composers who act as inspectors of music in schools have written for children's voices—for instance Roger-Ducasse and his *Joli Jeu de furet*, but this is an exception. Choral music is not in decay in France, only resting. The younger composers use it intermittently and with great caution, like Darius Milhaud in some passages in *L'Homme et son désir.*—A. C.

FRENCH DRAMATIC MUSIC FROM 1880. French dramatic music has not known the discredit which paralysed symphonic music in France during the last half-century. The "Grand Opéra" was completely devoted to following the models of Rossini, Meyerbeer and Halévy, producing works both banal and stereotyped. Gounod alone wrote living music of a captivating charm. He must be considered the point of departure for modern French dramatic school and his influence on his successors was considerable. The revival started with Bizet's *Carmen* (1875) and Saint-Saëns's *Samson and Dalila* (1877). After that it had to wait till 1884 for the birth of two truly interesting works, Massenet's *Manon* and Reyer's *Sigurd*. Massenet gave in *Manon* a perfectly successful example of a melodic style, caressing, voluptuous, facile, with a very sure hold on the public. He became the chief of a whole school and his influence was immense. One traces it again in the work of Bruneau, Charpentier, Xavier Leroux, Henri Rabaud, Laparra, Levadé, etc. His *Werther* (1886) and his *Jongleur de Notre Dame* (1902) are living models of the type which he created.

One of his disciples, Alfred Bruneau, distinguished himself by seeking out popular and homely subjects. His first work, *Le Rêve* (1891), viewed from the point of harmonic style, gave an admirable promise which unfortunately was not fulfilled. Charpentier derived directly from Massenet and Bruneau. An admirably gifted musician, without critical spirit and without depth, he really wrote only one great work, *Louise* (1900). One can even attach to this school the very interesting works of Gabriel Dupont (*Antar*, 1922),

of Laparra (*La Habanera*, 1903), and Henri Rabaud's charming *Marouf* (1913) which renewed the traditional type of the Opéra-Comique.

All these musicians are essentially men of the theatre; but one can state without paradox that the most original and most interesting theatre works have been composed by musicians who only approached it, as it were, accidentally. This was the case with Chabrier, whose opera *Gwendoline*, produced in 1886, is from the harmonic and orchestral point of view of singular novelty, although touched with Wagnerism; and with Lalo, whose *Roi d'Ys* was staged in 1888, ten years after it was finished. In 1897, Vincent d'Indy, who had already composed *Le Chant de la cloche*, gave *Fervaal*, followed in 1903 by *L'Étranger* and in 1900 by *La Légende de St. Christophe*. This musician, essentially symphonic, remained faithful to the Wagnerian conception of the lyric drama, but proved himself truly French by his clarity and lyricism. Two other disciples of Franck, Albéric Magnard and Guy Ropartz, conceived their works (*Bérénice*, 1911; *Le Pays*, 1913) in the same spirit.

In 1902 Claude Debussy had brought about, with his *Pelléas et Mélisande*, a veritable dramatic revolution, and created a finished model of a French opera in which music and poetry were perfectly balanced. No longer a laborious development of the *leit-motiv*, with its far-fetched relationship of themes, was needed to secure unity of the drama. The result of this revolution was considerable, even on those theatre musicians whose habits were set and who wrote for a public which cared little for innovations, no less than on the younger composers. In 1907 Paul Dukas produced his *Ariane et Barbe-Bleue*, which presented another solution of the dramatic problem, one in which music prevails over poetry. In 1911 Ravel revived the *opéra-bouffe* with his striking *Heure Espagnole*. Gabriel Fauré, who always kept aloof from the theatre, gave in 1913 his *Pénélope*, a masterpiece of feeling; nobility, and simple grandeur.

The younger musicians appear to take no interest in the theatre. The form of the lyric drama appears to them worn out. They seek another way which they have not found yet and, whilst waiting, prefer to compose for the ballet, a more musical and supple form. In 1923 Albert Roussel gave at the Opéra, his *Padmavati*, a ballet-opera, a work essentially symphonic and choral, where the soloists play a very insignificant part. It is the most interesting attempt at revival which has occurred in France during the unquiet and tortured years since 1914.—H. P.

FRENCH FOLK-MUSIC. See CLOSSON, ERNEST; TIERSOT, JULIEN; WECKERLIN, J. B.; and arts. on BRETON MUSIC and FRENCH SONG.

FRENCH ORCHESTRAL MUSIC SINCE 1880. Under this general title we must speak of two rival schools, one of classical and conservative tendency, which has cultivated the symphony; the other, newer in tendency, following the way opened up by Berlioz and Liszt, and seeking freer and more varied constructive procedures.

Saint-Saëns' C mi. symphony with organ (1886) and César Franck's D mi. symphony (1887) mark the point of departure of the contemporary French symphonic school. In 1886, the best disciple of Franck, Vincent d'Indy, appeared with his luminous *Symphonie cévenole*. After him, Ernest Chausson, Albéric Magnard, Paul Dukas, Guilmant, Witkowski, who reveal creative power, sincere lyric feeling and constructive science. The school called "Scholiste" or "Franckist" has played a considerable part in French musical evolution. It prepared the public, in which it developed the taste for pure music, to understand and appreciate the infinitely more subtle art of Debussy and Ravel. It preserved the cult of counterpoint, despite the attacks of the "Impressionists," in such a way that it is with them that the majority of the musicians of the vanguard, who use a contrapuntal rather than a harmonic language, seem to be connected. Following a parallel route, and connecting themselves more with Saint-Saëns than with Franck, the Neo-classic school has produced a number of interesting works (Widor, Rabaud, Vierne, etc.).

The school called "Impressionist" was derived from Berlioz through Lalo and Chabrier. Lalo's *Namouna* (1882) and Chabrier's *España* (1883) exercised a deep influence on the newer generation in revealing a beautifully coloured art, brilliant and full of nuance. This music corresponds very closely to Manet's pictorial art. In 1894, Debussy produced his *Prélude à l'Après-midi d'un Faune* which brought a completely new vision to the universe of sound.

Amongst the classicists, Florent Schmitt (*Tragédie de Salomé*, 1911), Louis Aubert, Roger-Ducasse, André Caplet, Charles Kœchlin, Inghelbrecht, Ladmirault, Grovlez, Jacques Ibert and others, with their different temperaments, are related more or less directly to this school. After the 1914-18 war, a desire for reaction against the procedures of the school of Debussy and Ravel was manifested. The poet Cocteau exclaimed, "Après la musique à l'estompe, la musique à l'emporte-pièce!" Apparently musicians had grown tired of a too-refined and subtle art, and felt the need for stronger colours, and something even of brutality. Their harmonies were disposed in the systematic manner of superimposed tonalities, or remained completely atonal. These new tendencies appear in the least works of Albert Roussel (*Prélude pour une Fête de Printemps*, and symphony in G mi.). They are forcefully revealed in the works of Arthur Honegger (*Horace Victorieux*, 1921), Darius Milhaud (*Protée*, 1920), Auric (*Les Fâcheux*, 1924), Francis Poulenc, Daniel Lazarus and others.—H. P.

FRENCH SONG FROM 1880. The renaissance of the *mélodie* (song with pf. or orch. acc.) was established in France after the dawn of literary symbolism. The symbolists inspired by musical principles enriched French poetry. Intellectual intercourse of musicians and poets followed. The intimate communion of music and poetry which began the magnificent renaissance of the *lied*

with Henri Duparc, fixes a decisive stage in literary development as well as in musical taste. Duparc is the initiator. Although a pupil of Franck, his music retains a characteristic originality. His production has been very restricted, but his 16 songs, each one a little masterpiece (the best are settings of Baudelaire) have helped, with those of Fauré, to create in modern French music a kind which is only comparable in Germany with the romantic *lieder*.

If Duparc is more lyrical, Fauré is more sensitive. Melody has been the chief source of inspiration for him. He made for the song a complete, definite, and perfect form. He has selected his poems exquisitely and surrounded them with the musical atmosphere which best suits them. They are miracles of balance between musical and literary inspiration.

The success which rewarded Duparc and Fauré caused composers to follow on their lines. The more the musician cultivated and felt the poem, the nearer the result approached perfection. Debussy is the most convincing example of this with his *Ariettes oubliées* by Verlaine, the 5 *Poèmes* by Baudelaire, the *Chansons de France* by Charles d'Orléans or the *Trois Ballades* by François Villon. He himself wrote the words of four *Proses lyriques*. He made use of Leconte de Lisle (*Le Colibri*), Verlaine (*Apaisement*), and Maeterlinck (*Serres chaudes*). Folksongs also claimed attention. Here the researches of Charles Bordes in the Basque provinces and of Vincent d'Indy in the Vivarais have borne fruit. The *lieder* of Bordes constitute the best part of his work. He makes use of Verlaine and of Francis Jammes. D'Indy has composed very few songs, but his books of folksongs collected in the Vivarais and the Vercors have had a happy influence. Paul Ladmirault followed his example, and collected some Breton and Vendean songs which have influenced his own *lieder* for which Verlaine has provided the words. The songs of Languedoc inspired Déodat de Séverac, notably in *Flors d'Occitania* to Languedocian words.

For that refinement and musical delicacy which reveals high culture, the songs of Ravel to poems by Clement Marot, Mallarmé and Jules Renard, of Roussel to poems by Henri de Régnier, of Florent Schmitt, of André Caplet, are notable.

The younger French musicians continue along the lines of the delicate and refined *lied* of Saint-Saëns, Massenet, Honegger, Milhaud, Poulenc, Auric. Roland Manuel has set some subtle harmonies to poems not less subtle, by Mallarmé, Kahn and XVI century poets.—A. C.

FREY, Emil. Pianist and compr. *b.* Baden, 8 April, 1889. Stud. music in Basle, Zurich and Geneva; entered Paris Cons. 1904; pupil of Louis Diémer (pf.) and Ch. M. Widor (compn.); 1st prize, 1906, for pf.; settled in Berlin. Gave series of concerts in Germany, Rumania, Austria, France, Belgium, Russia, Finland. In 1910 won 1st prize in the Rubinstein Competition at Petrograd, and obtained honorary degree as pianist.

Engaged (1912) at Imperial Cons. in Moscow, where he stayed till 1917. Now living in Zurich, where he is leader of the master-classes for pf. at the Cons. Frey is considered to be one of the great pianists of our day.

Cello sonata, op. 8, and vn. sonata, op. 22 (Berlin, Simrock); *Sonata dramatica*, pf. op. 27; 2nd sonata, pf. op. 36 (Swiss National Ed.); pf. pieces, op. 1, 33, 38 (Simrock), op. 12 (Paris, Durand), op. 10 (Lausanne, Fœtisch), op. 14 (Paris, Heugel), op. 20 (Berlin, Ries & Erler); songs, op. 15 (Fœtisch), 45, 46 and 49 (Simrock).—F. H.

FRICKER, Herbert Austin. Eng. condr. orgt. *b.* Canterbury, 12 Feb. 1868. Educated at Cath. Choir School, Canterbury. At 16 deputy-orgt. of Canterbury Cath.; 1891, orgt. and choir-master, Holy Trinity Ch. Folkestone. Between 1898 and 1917 he lived at Leeds, becoming successively city - orgt., orgt. and chorus-master of the Leeds Mus. Fest.; founder and condr. of the Leeds Symphony Orch. and condr. of choral soc. at Bradford, Halifax and Morley. He exercised great influence on the appreciation of fine music in the West Riding of Yorkshire and introduced many notable new works. In 1917, went to Toronto as orgt. to Metropolitan Ch. and condr. of the Mendelssohn Choir (see CHORAL SOCIETIES). Holds the degrees of M.A. Leeds; Mus. Bac. Durham; Mus. Doc. *h.c.* Toronto, and F.R.C.O. In Toronto his influence has been very important, and, since visit of Mendelssohn Choir to U.S.A., his reputation has increased materially as a choral condr. He has publ. many organ arrs. from orch. scores.

Organ works: Concert-Overture, C ml.; *Cantilène Nuptiale*; *Adagio* in A flat; Fantasie Overture, G ml.; cantatas: *The Shield of Faith*; *A Song of Thanksgiving*; *The Hermit*; church music: anthems; Magnificat and N.D. in G, etc. (Novello).—L. S.

FRIED, Oscar. Ger. condr. and compr. *b.* Berlin, 10 Aug. 1871. Pupil of Humperdinck and Philipp Scharwenka; dir. of Stern Choral Soc. 1904–10; condr. also of Soc. of Friends of Music, Berlin, from 1907.

Choral piece, *Song of Intoxication* (Nietzsche), op. 11; *Harvest Song* (Dehmel), op. 15; preludes and double fugues for large str. orch., op. 13; piece for 13 wind instrs. and 2 harps, op. 2; songs (op. 1, 3, 4, 5, 7, 13); *Radiant Night*, soli and orch. (Dehmel), op. 9; female choruses, op. 12, 14. Consult Paul Bekker's *O. F.* (1907), and Paul Stefan's *O. F.* (1911, transl. into Eng.).—A. E.

FRIEDBERG, Carl. Ger. pianist; *b.* Bingen-on-Rhine, 18 Sept. 1872. Pupil of Louwerse (Bingen), Kwast, Knorr, Scholz and Clara Schumann at Hoch's Cons., Frankfort-o-M.; also attended Heidelberg Univ. Gave successful concerts as pianist in both solo and chamber music. From 1904 advanced teacher for pf. Cologne Cons.; went to America in 1914, but since 1918 has lived in Munich. He is pianist in a trio with Flesch and Becker. His wife, Frau Gerda Friedberg, is a concert singer.—A. E.

FRIEDENTHAL, Albert. Ger. pianist and writer; *b.* Bromberg, 25 Sept. 1862; *d.* Batavia, 17 Jan. 1921. Pupil of Th. Kullak, Berlin. Travelled as a pianist in Europe, N. and S. America, Africa, Australia, the Far East, etc., finally taking up residence in Berlin. As a compr., produced only songs and pf. music. Author of:

Voices of the Nations (Berlin, Schlesinger, 5 parts); *Woman in the Life of the Nations* (2 vols., 1911);

Music, Dancing and Poetry amongst the American Creoles (1913, with musical examples); *The Flemish Folk-Song* (Berlin, 1918, 5 parts and (6) supplement).—A. E.

FRIEDHEIM, Arthur. Pianist, condr. compr. *b.* Petrograd, 26 Oct. 1859. Appeared in public at 9; pupil of Anton Rubinstein; then pupil and close friend of Liszt, in the interpretation of whose music he excels. From 1894, teacher and player in N. America; then London (from 1889; later pf. prof. R.C.M. Manchester (till 1904); toured Europe. His opera *Die Tänzerin* was perf. by Carl Lohse at Cologne (1904) and by Nikisch in Leipzig (1907). In 1908–10, conducting in Munich; took part in many Liszt Centenary perfs. (1911). In 1921 went to Toronto as pf. prof. Canadian Acad. of Music. As a player, leans toward XIX century comprs. rather than modern Fr. or Russ. with whom he has little sympathy. Is engaged on a psychological study of Liszt. Decorated by Pres. Taft at White House in 1912. Now lives in New York.

Pf. concerto, B flat (1890); American March *E Pluribus Unum* (1894); operas: *Die Tänzerin*; *The Christians* (unfin.); *Giulia Gonzaga* (unfin.). Has orch. 4 Hungarian Portrait-Sketches (Liszt) and arrd. Liszt's 2nd Rhapsody for pf. and orch.—L. S.

FRIEDLAENDER, Max. Ger. b. singer and musicographer; *b.* Brieg (Silesia), 12 Oct. 1852. Stud. singing under Manuel Garcia in London, and J. Stockhausen in Frankfort-o.-M. *Début* at Monday Popular Concerts, London, 1880. Resided in Frankfort, 1881–3; since then in Berlin, where under Spitta's direction he devoted himself more and more to historical studies. Obtained his Ph.D. at Rostock and submitted *Contributions to Franz Schubert's Biography* as his thesis. In 1914 acad. lecturer on music, Berlin Univ.; prof. and acad. dir. of music, 1903; Geheimer Regierungsrat, 1908; prof.-in-ordinary, 1918. In 1911 he went as an exchange prof. to Harvard Univ., giving lectures at 20 American universities; granted LL.D. *h.c.* at Madison (Wisc.). Made important biographical discoveries about Schubert; publ. a series of unprinted Schubert songs. After Rochus v. Liliencron's death became President of Editorial Commission for the *Book of National Songs for Men's Choirs*, suggested by Emperor William II; also ed. *Book of National Songs for Mixed Choirs*. Together with Joh. Bolte and Joh. Meier, is at present collecting all the German folk-songs still existing.

New eds. of the songs of Schubert, Schumann and Mendelssohn, and of Beethoven's Scotch songs. Also critically revised *Students' Song Book*; *Choral Manual*; *Collection of hitherto unpublished Folk Songs*. He contributed to Stockhausen's *Technique of Singing*; wrote large number of essays on recent musical history in the *Goethe Annual*, the *Vierteljahrsschrift für Musik-Wissenschaft*, and also independently: *Goethe's Poems in Music* (1891); *Poems of Goethe in the Compositions of his Contemporaries* (1896 and 1916, the latter under the title of *Poems of Goethe in Musical Compositions*); *Brahms' Lieder* (Simrock, 1922). His chief work is *The German Song in the XVIII Century* (2 vols., Stuttgart, 1902, J. G. Cotta).—A. E.

FRIEDMAN, Ignacy. Polish pianist, compr. *b.* Cracow, 14 Feb. 1882. While studying at State school, learned pf. under Mme. Grzywinska in Cracow. In 1900, stud. theory under Hugo Riemann at Leipzig; then proceeded to Vienna

FRISKIN   FUGÈRE

to study under Leschetizky. Began to give concerts in 1904; soon made himself known in Europe and America as a most brilliant pianist. A fertile compr. for pf., his works amounting to over 90. Some of his works are very popular, notably:

Elle danse and *Tabatière à musique*; Passacaglia, op. 44; *Fantasiestücke*, op. 45; Studies on a theme of Paganini's, op. 47; *Polnische Lyrik*, op. 53, 60, 72; Suite, op. 70; *Tema con variazioni*. Transcriptions of Rameau, Grazioli, Dandrieu, Beethoven, Scarlatti, Dalayrac, etc. D. lives in Berlin.—ZD. J.

FRISKIN, James. Scottish compr. and pianist; *b.* Glasgow, 3 March, 1886. Stud. pf. there under Alfred Heap until 1900; at R.C.M. London under Dannreuther (pf.) and Sir Charles Stanford (compn.), 1900–7; settled in New York, Oct. 1914.

5tet, pf. and str. (Stainer & Bell); 5tet-Phantasy in F mi. (*id.*); Phantasy in E mi. pf. vn. cello (Novello); *Ballade* in C, pf. (Stainer & Bell); *Nocturne* (*id.*); sonata in G. vn. and pf. (*id.*); a pf. sonata in ms.—E.-H.

FROMM-MICHAELS, Ilse. Ger. pianist and compr. *b.* Hamburg, 30 Dec. 1888. Stud. Berlin, R. High School of Music, and with J. Kwast, Berlin, and Carl Friedberg, Cologne; compn. under Hans Pfitzner and Steinbach. Married a judge at Cuxhaven, 1915, and lives at Bergedorf, near Hamburg.

Round Dance Waltzes; *Sonata Sketches*; pf. variations.—A. E.

FRUGATTA, Giuseppe. Ital. pianist and compr. *b.* Bergamo, 26 May, 1860. From 1891, pf. teacher at R. Cons. Milan, succeeding his master, Carlo Andreoli. Many distinguished pupils have come from his school. Compr. of many pf. pieces and some chamber-music for str. His educational works (Ricordi) are held in high esteem.—D. A.

FRYER, George Herbert. Eng. pianist; *b.* Hampstead, London, 21 May, 1877. Stud. R.A.M. under O. Beringer, 1893–5; R.C.M. under Franklin Taylor, 1895–1900; compn. under Walford Davies and Sir Charles Stanford; under Busoni in Weimar, summer 1900; in Berlin, 1901. Since then he has toured considerably; teaches at R.C.M. London; in 1924 he visited Canada (with Dr. James Lyon) adjudicating at four festivals.

Pf.: Suite in old-forms (Schott); *Country-Side Suite* (*id.*); *Country Life Suite* (Bosworth); *Tunes for Totola* (*id.*); 6 little variations on a Rigadoon of Purcell (Schott); Purcell transcriptions (*id.*); 4 transcriptions of old Eng. melodies (Boosey); 5 *English Love Lyrics* (Schirmer); *Virgin's Cradle Hymn* (Schott); book, *Hints on Piano Practice* (Schirmer).—E.-H.

FRYKLÖF, Harald Leonard. Swedish compr. *b.* Upsala, 14 Sept. 1882; *d.* Stockholm, 11 March, 1919. Stud. R. Cons. Stockholm; compn. under Johan Lindegren (1901–5), pf. under Rich. Andersson, 1904. Teacher at Andersson's pf. school, 1905. Stud. under Philipp Scharwenka (Berlin), 1905. Sub-prof. 1908, and from 1911 prof. (harmony) at the R. Cons. Stockholm. From 1908, orgt. Nicolai Ch. Stockholm. Member R.A.M., Stockholm, 1915.

Concert overture (1907); songs with orch.; pieces for organ and for pf.; *Sonata à la Legenda*, vn. and pf. (publ. Musik. Konstföreningen); church anthems. Publ. a book: *Koralharmonisering—Kyrkotonarterna* (*Chorale-Harmony: Church Tones*), 1915.—P. V.

FUCHS, Carl. Cellist; *b.* Offenbach-o-M., 3 June, 1865. Stud. at Frankfort-o-M. under Riedel and B. Cossmann; played the Schumann concerto at his farewell perf. (in presence of Clara Schumann); went to Petrograd at Davidof's invitation to take lessons with him; after many concert-tours, settled in Manchester; 1st cello-prof. at R. Manchester Coll. of Music; one of founders of Brodsky Quartet; for many years, principal cellist, Hallé Orch. (under Hallé, and Richter); frequently played at Saturday Popular Concerts, St. James's Hall, London; prof. of cello, in addition to R. Manchester Coll., at the Huddersfield and Newcastle Colleges of Music.

Violoncello Method (Schott); a series of standard works for concert and educational purposes (*id.*); easy cello pieces (Augener).—E.-H.

FUCHS, Carl D. J. Ger. pianist and writer; *b.* Potsdam, 22 Oct. 1838; *d.* Dantzig, 27 Aug. 1922. Stud. theology in Berlin, 1859; at same time pupil of Hans v. Bülow, Weitzmann and Kiel; teacher at Kullak's Acad., 1868; orgt. in Stralsund, 1869; pianist in Berlin, 1871; condr. in Hirschberg, Silesia, 1875; pianist, critic and condr. in Dantzig from 1879. Championed Riemann's aspirations in phrasing and rhythmics.

Preliminaries to a Criticism of Music (1870); *The Future of Musical Expression* (1884); *The Freedom of Musical Expression*; *Artists and Critics* (1898); *Time and Rhythm in Chorales* (1911); *The Correctly-barred Chorale* (1923).—A. E.

FUCHS, Robert. Austrian compr. *b.* Frauenthal (Styria), 15 Feb. 1847. Stud. at Vienna Cons.; orgt. at Imperial Chapel and prof. of compn. at Vienna Cons. His many pupils included Gustav Mahler, Alexander Zemlinsky and Franz Schreker. He belonged to the circle around Brahms, who was very fond of his *Serenades*.

Many chamber-works; Mass; 2 symphonies; 5 serenades for str. orch. and 2 horns (one on themes by Johann Strauss); several other pieces for orch.; for chorus; for pf.; 2 operas (*Die Königsbraut* and *Die Teufelsglocken*).—H. B.

FUČÍK, Julius. Czechoslovak compr. *b.* Prague, 1872; *d.* during Great War in Berlin. Pupil of Dvořák; bandmaster of Austrian 86th and 92nd regiments. Author of 240 compns. of a light kind, chiefly dances, marches, notably *Gladiators*.—V. ST.

FUENTES, Eduardo Sanchez. See MEXICAN AND CUBAN OPERA.

FUGÈRE, Lucien. Fr. operatic barit. *b.* Paris, 22 July, 1848. Stud. first as sculptor, with his elder brothers, then went to Cons. but failed at his examination. Finally made *début* at Ba-ta-clan, 27 Feb. 1870, with two songs, *Au clair de la marjolaine* and *Vendanges*; remained there for 2 years; then (1873) at Bouffes-Parisiens (in *La Branche cassée*). Sang chief rôle in *La Jolie Parfumeuse* (1874); *Les Mules de Suzette* (1875); *Le Moulin du Vert-Galant* (1876); *La Boîte au Lait* (1876); revived *Madame l'Archiduc*. *Début* at Opéra-Comique, 8 Sept. 1877, *Les Noces de Jeannette*; and afterwards sang regular repertoire. Created parts in *L'Amour médecin* (1883); *Le Roi malgré lui* (1887); *La Basoche* (1893); *Les Folies amoureuses* (1891); *Les Troyens* (1892); *Phryné* (1893);

170

La Vivandiére (1894); La Vie de Bohème (1898); Louise (1900); Griseldis (1901); Le Jongleur de Notre Dame (1904); Le Bonhomme Jadis (1906). Then went to Gaîté-Lyrique for chief rôles in Don Quichotte (1910); Carmosine (1912); returned to Opéra-Comique in La Basoche. On 8 March, 1920, the Opéra-Comique gave a gala performance to celebrate 50th anniversary of his début. Consult H. Curzon, Croquis d'artistes. F. is an example of one of the longest and most successful careers in operatic singing. Naturally gifted with a fine semi-barit. voice. he gradually increased his possibilities, both as an operatic barit. and bass and also in the creation of comic characters, for which he evolved a variety of methods of voice-production which were called Fugères after him.—A. R.

FUGÈRES. Various comical methods of voice-production, invented by Lucien Fugère (q.v.)—A. R.

FULLER-MAITLAND, J. A. Critic and writer on music; b. 1856. Chief music critic for The Times (1889–1911).

Life of Robert Schumann (1884); Masters of German Music (1894); English Carols of XV Century; The Musician's Pilgrimage (1899); English Music of XIX Century (1902); The Age of Bach and Handel (for Oxford History of Music) 1902; Johannes Brahms (1911); The Consort of Music (1915). Editor of Grove's Dictionary of Music, 2nd ed. (1904-10); transl. (with Mrs. C. Bell) of Spitta's Life of Bach; English Country Songs (with Lucy Broadwood); The Fitzwilliam Virginal Book, 2 vols., with W. Barclay Squire (Breitkopf, 1899).—E.-H.

FUMET, Victor. Fr. compr. Pupil of Guiraud. Orgt. of Ste. Anne's Church, Paris. Writes symph. music with a spiritualistic tendency, all very carefully composed.

L'Âme du Feu; L'Âme des Eaux; Conciliabule des Fleurs; Cantique du Firmament.—A. C.

FURLOTTI, Ricardo. Argentine condr. b. Parma. Stud. cello at R. School of Music, Parma, then at Milan. Leader of orch. at many theatres in Italy, Germany and England. In 1885, went to Buenos Ayres to conduct orch. at former Colón Theatre. Settled down as music-teacher in Normal Schools. Founded the Popular Concerts which have been a great success in Buenos Ayres.—A. M.

FURTER VIRTO, Francisco. Span. pianist and compr. b. Valencia, 5 March, 1887. Stud. at Cons. de Música, Valencia, and R. Cons. de Música, Madrid, where he stud. under famous pianist, José Tragó; 1st prizes for pf. and compn.; gold medal in mus. competition, Valencia, Exposición Regional, for his Oberturas para Orquesta; now senior pf. prof. at Cons. de Música, Bilbao. —P. G. M.

FURTWÄNGLER, Wilhelm. Ger. condr. b. Berlin, 25 Jan. 1886. Son of univ. prof. (archæologist), Adolf Furtwängler; in Munich from his 8th year. Stud. under A. Beer-Walbrunn, chiefly under Rheinberger, later under M. Schillings. Condr. at several theatres, Zurich, Strasburg, Lübeck (4 years; succeeded Abendroth); in 1915 succeeded Bodansky in Mannheim; also dir. Viennese Musical Artists' Orch. from 1919; dir. of symphony concerts of Berlin State Opera Orch. as successor to Richard Strauss, 1920; in 1922 also, for a time, of Frankfort Museum Concerts (in succession to W. Mengelberg) and of concerts of Friends of Music Soc. Succeeded Nikisch as condr. of Gewandhaus Concerts, Leipzig (1922) and of Berlin Philh. Concerts. Has appeared in Berlin, Hamburg, Frankfort, Vienna, etc., as visiting condr. Only two of his compositions have been given as yet—a symphony and a Te Deum (mixed choir, soli, orch. and organ). First cond. in England in Jan. 1924 at R. Philh. Soc. and London Symphony Orch. concert. Consult R. Specht, W. F. (Vienna, 1922).—A. E.

FURUHJELM, Erik. Finnish compr. b. Helsingfors, 6 July, 1883. Stud. in Helsingfors, Vienna (with a State scholarship) under Robert Fuchs, Munich and Paris. Since 1907, theory and compn. teacher, and later, member of directorate of Helsingfors Music Inst. Critic and writer on music; has written a monograph on Jean Sibelius.

5tet; symphony; Romantic Overture, orch., etc. —T. H.

FURULYA. See HUNGARIAN MUS. INSTRS.

G

GABIOLA, Fernando de. Spanish organist; *b.* Durango, 1880. Pupil of Mailly and Edgar Tinel at Brussels Cons., where he obtained 1st prize for organ. In 1906 mus. dir. to County Council, San Sebastian.—P. G. M.

GABRILOWITSCH, Ossip Salomonowitsch. Russ. pianist, condr. *b.* Petrograd, 7 Feb. 1878. Stud. pf. under Tolstof and Rubinstein at Petrograd Cons. (1888–94); compn. under Lia-lof and Glazunof. Winner of Rubinstein Prize, 1894; 1894–6, stud. at Vienna under Leschetizky (pf.), Navrátil (compn.). *Début* in Berlin, Oct. 1896; then toured Germany, Austria, Russia, France and England. In 1900, 1901, 1906 and 1909 visited U.S.A.; 1909, married Clara Clemens (contr.), the daughter of Mark Twain, with whom he has since often given joint-recitals. 1909–14, lived in Munich where he cond. concerts of Konzertverein. His recital-tours in Europe, 1912–13, with a series of historical programmes attracted considerable attention. After leaving Europe for America in 1914, a similar series in Boston, New York and Chicago was equally successful. In 1917 he cond. orch. concerts in New York, and the same year was chosen condr. of Detroit Symphony Orch. Has comp. songs (Bote; Zimmerman; Rózsavölgyi); *Elégie,* cello and pf. (Zimmerman); pf. pieces (Rózsavölgyi).—O. K.

GADE, Axel. Danish violinist, compr. *b.* Copenhagen, 28 May, 1860; *d.* there 9 Nov. 1921. Son of the compr. Niels W. Gade; pupil of Danish R. Cons., and of Valdemar Tofte (Copenhagen), and Joseph Joachim (Berlin). From 1884, member of R. Chapel (Copenhagen); from 1910, leading violinist of same; vn. prof. at R. Cons. of Music; later one of its directors.
Opera, *Venezias Nat (Venetian Night),* perf. R. Theatre, Copenhagen, 1919; 3 vn. concertos; chamber-music pieces; many songs.—A. H.

GAGLIARDI, Cecilia. Ital. s. singer; *b.* Rome; stud. at R. Liceo Mus. di Santa Cecilia. Enjoys high reputation amongst Ital. dramatic soprani; has appeared at principal European and Amer. opera-houses. Took part in the Verdi season (1913) at La Scala, Milan, singing *Aida, Nabucco* and the *Requiem Mass.* She created rôle of Vanna in Franchetti's *Notte di Leggenda.*—D. A.

GAGNEBIN, Henri. Compr. orgt. *b.* Liège (Belgium), 13 March, 1886. Stud. organ and compn. in Berlin, Geneva and at *Schola Cantorum,* Paris (under Vincent d'Indy, Louis Vierne and Blanche Selva). Became orgt. at Church of Redemption, Paris; since 1916 at St. John's Ch. Lausanne, where he is also lecturer on mus. history at Cons. His works show relationship to the modern Fr. school, and are full of outspoken originality.

Symphony in F; *Les Vierges folles,* symph. poem; str. 4tet (Swiss National Ed.); vn. sonata; cello sonata; pf. sonata; *Pastorale,* harp and woodwind.—F. H.

GAILLARD, Frits. Dutch cellist; *b.* The Hague in 1875. From 1905–20, 1st solo cellist of Amsterdam Concertgebouw. His playing in R. Strauss's *Don Quixote* is very fine. Lives in Los Angeles, U.S.A.—W. P.

GAILLARD, Jacques. Belgian cellist; *b.* Ensival, 4 April, 1875. Stud. Verviers School of Music, and Brussels Cons. Lived in Paris and Geneva, where he was prof. of solfeggio at Cons. (1896–7); prof. of cello at Mons Cons. (1898–1902). Member and founder of Schörg Quartet (Brussels Quartet: F. Schörg, H. Daucher, P. Miry, J. Gaillard), which toured in Europe and America for 15 years; also toured as soloist. Prof. of cello at Liège Cons. (1912–21), and chamber-music, Brussels Cons. (1922). Now member of Zimmer Quartet (A. Zimmer, F. Ghigo, L. Baroen, J. G.).—E. C.

GAILLARD, Marius François. Fr. pianist; *b.* Paris, 1900. Pf. prize at Paris Cons. 1916. Specialises on Debussy's music.—A. C.

GAITO, Cayetano. Argentine violinist; *b.* Naples in 1852. Stud. at Naples Cons. under Fernando Pinto. 1874, went to Buenos Ayres, where he founded the first str. quartet in Argentina, with Bellucci, Ghignatti and Bomon. This quartet played with Bottesini on his famous tour in S. America in 1879. After giving concerts in Montevideo, he now dir. (with his son) the Gaito Conservatoire.—A. M.

GAITO, Constantino. Argentine compr. *b.* Buenos Ayres in 1878. Publ. 1st compn. when 11; two further vn. pieces, written 2 years later, were played with great success. Showed such promise that he was sent to the Cons. of Naples, where he stud. under Platania. Made a successful concert-tour through Italy. Returning to Buenos Ayres in 1900, devoted himself to compn. and dir. of Gaito Institute.
Operas: *Strapas* in 1 act (libretto by Ferruccio); *Doria,* in 3 acts (libretto by Crucinio); *Cajo Petronio* in 3 acts (libretto by Romanelli). Overture in D; Suite for orch.; many songs and pf. pieces.—A. M.

GÁL, Hans. Austrian compr. *b.* Brünn, 5 Aug. 1890. Pupil of Mandyczewski (theory) and Robert (pf.); Ph.D. (music history) 1913; 1915, government prize for 1st symphony. From 1918, teacher of harmony and cpt. at Vienna Univ. A voluminous compr. who combines a slightly modern harmonic equipment with the Brahms style, and finds much success through his pleasant melodies.
Operas: *Der Arzt der Sobeide (The Physician of S.)* perf. Breslau, 1919; *Die heilige Ente (The Sacred Duck)* perf. Düsseldorf, 1922; stage music to *Ruth* (Levetzof) perf. Vienna, 1920; overture to Grillparzer's *Weh' dem der lügt!; Serenade;* Symph.

Phantasy; Overture to a tragedy; chorus, *Von ewiger Freude* (*Eternal Joy*); Phantasy on poems from Rabindr. Tagore; chamber-music; songs; pf. pieces (15 works publ. Leuckart, Leipzig; Tischer, Cologne; Simrock, Berlin; Univ. Ed. Vienna).—P. P.

GALEFFI, Carlo. Ital. barit. operatic singer; *b.* in Rome. An able and esteemed singer; remarkable for beauty of voice, striking figure and artistic qualities. Known at principal opera-houses in Europe and America. Created parts of Rinaldo in Mascagni's *L'Amica* and title-rôle in Puccini's *Gianni Schicchi* at Costanzi Theatre, Rome.—D. A.

GALL, Jan (*phon.* Gahl). Polish compr. *b.* Warsaw, 1856; *d.* Lemberg, 1912. Stud. theory under Franz Krenn in Vienna; then under Rheinberger at Munich. After a long tour through Italy, became condr. of the choral soc. *Andante,* and music critic at Leipzig. In his later travels in Italy, was pupil of Mustafa at Rome and Lamperti, sen., at Cernobbio. Finally, settled at Lemberg and became dir. of choral soc. *Echo,* besides writing music criticism. His compns. are almost entirely vocal. His songs are widely popular in Poland and in Germany.

Amongst his 300 choral compns. (mostly for male chorus), 40 are orig. pieces, the others being transcriptions of the songs of Moniuszko and of popular Polish, Ruthenian, Ital., Span., Rumanian and Slovakian songs. His numerous solo-songs (about 70) represent the best qualities of the Polish song-style in the period from Moniuszko's death (1872) till 1905.—Zd. J.

GALL, Yvonne Irma (real name Galle). Fr. operatic first s. *b.* Paris, 6 March, 1885. In 1904 came out first of 300 candidates for entrance to Cons. Stud. under Dubulle; in 1907 1st prize for singing in *Freischütz;* 2nd operatic prize in *Iphigénie en Tauride*. Début at Opéra (1908) in *William Tell*. Sang in 1st perf. of *Hippolyte et Aricie,* 1908; also in *Twilight of the Gods,* 1908; *Déjanire,* 1911; *Parsifal,* 1914; *Scemo,* 1914. Toured in Spain (1917), South America (1918), and United States where she sang in *Le Chemineau, L'Heure Espagnole, Le Tabarro* and *La Jacquerie* at Chicago Opera House. Engaged at Opéra-Comique, Paris, 1921; sang in *Les Noces Corinthiennes* (1st perf.) 1922.—A. R.

GALLARDO, Javier Rengifo. Chilean compr. *b.* Santiago, 1879. Stud. in Chile; publ. his first piece, *Amor Plebeyo,* in 1896. Was attached to Chilean Legation in Belgium in 1904, where he seized the opportunity to continue his studies. His works have been highly appreciated both in France and Belgium, and he has frequently cond. them himself. Has publ. many pf. pieces and several waltzes. His *Pastoral Poem* (produced in Paris), is his best-known work.—A. M.

GALLI, Amintore. Ital. compr. historian and critic; *b.* Talamello (Rimini), 12 Oct. 1845; *d.* Rimini, 8 Dec. 1919. One of the musicians who, during the last 50 years, have contributed most to the progress and propaganda of mus. culture in Italy. Stud. at Milan Cons. under Mazzuccato; after some years as bandmaster in a provincial town, settled in Milan, where he showed indefatigable energy as compr., teacher, historian and critic. Entered the firm of Sonzogno (*q.v.*). Also exercised good influence as

teacher of history and æsthetics of music at R. Cons. Mus. G. Verdi, and as critic for newspaper *Il Secolo*.

Compns.: *David,* opera, on own libretto (perf. Milan, 1904); *Stabat Mater;* 2 masses; 5tet, E mi.; 2 overtures; *Inno dei lavoratori* (*Hymn of the Workers*), words by Filippo Turati, which became the popular hymn of the Ital. Socialists.

G. also completed several Fr. operas, setting parts originally in prose-dialogue to music as recitatives. He also translated into Ital. many libretti.

Books: *Storia e teoria del sistema musicale moderno* (*History and Theory of Modern Musical System*) (Ricordi, Milan); *Piccolo lessico del musicista* (*Little Lexicon for the Musician*) (id., 1891); *Trattato di contrappunto e fuga* (*Treatise on Counterpoint and Fugue*) (id.); *Strumenti e strumentazione* (*Instruments and Instrumentation*) (Sonzogno, Milan); *Estetica della musica* (*Æsthetics of Music*) (Bocca, Turin).—D. A.

GALLICO, Paolo. Amer. pianist; *b.* Trieste, 13 May 1868. Stud. at the Vienna Cons. under Julius Epstein; at 18 1st prize (gold medal) and Gesellschafts medal. Toured Italy, Austria, Germany. Since 1892, teacher and mus. ed. in New York. Won the $5,000 prize of National Federation of Music Clubs with his dramatic oratorio, *The Apocalypse* (Schirmer, 1922), first sung at their 12th biennial convention, Rock Island, Ill., 7 June, 1921. Also an operetta, *Johannistraum,* and an opera, *Harlekin*. Pf. pieces, studies (Schirmer).—J. M.

GALLI - CURCI, Amelita. Ital. coloratura singer; *b.* Milan, 18 Nov. 1890. Educated as pianist under Appiani at Milan Cons.; self-taught in singing; *début* at Costanzi Theatre, Rome, as Gilda (*Rigoletto*) 1910; sang at various European and S. Amer. opera-houses; U.S.A. *début* 18 Nov. 1916 (Chicago Opera Co. under Campanini). Since then, opera chiefly in New York and Chicago. Toured Gt. Britain, 1924-5. Has a remarkable vocal range rising to G in alt. Chief rôles: Butterfly, Gilda, Juliette, Lucio, Mimi, Rosina, Violetta, and Manon Lescaut (Massenet).—E.-H.

GALLIGNANI, Giuseppe. Ital. compr. *b.* Faenza, 9 Jan. 1851; *d.* Milan, 14 Dec. 1923. Stud. at R. Cons. Milan; first part of his career was passed as condr.; 1884, won by competition, post of Master of the Choir, Milan Cath., where 1886-94, he dir. periodical *Musica Sacra;* 1891, became dir. of R. Cons. at Parma; 1897 till death, dir. of Cons. at Milan. Has made notable contribution to development of this Inst., giving its large concert-hall, inaugurated 1908, on occasion of centenary fest. of Cons. promoted by himself. Has written much sacred and vocal chamber-music; also several operas, amongst which are: *Il grillo del focolare* (*The Cricket on the Hearth*) (Genoa, 1873); *Atala* (Milan, 1876); *Nestorio* (Scala, Milan, 1886); *Quare?* (Scala, Milan, 1903); *In alto!* (Trieste, 1921). G. gave particular care to improving singing methods in his Conservatoire.—D. A.

GALLOIS, Victor. Fr. compr. *b.* Douai, 1880. *Prix de Rome,* 1905; dir. of Douai Cons.; condr. of Grands Concerts at Lille. Has comp. chamber-music, amongst which is a seriously written 4tet for pf. and str. (1906).—A. C.

GALLON, Jean. Fr. condr. and compr. *b.* 26 June, 1878. Condr. of Concert Soc. at

Cons. (1906–14), at Opéra (1909–14); prof. of harmony at Cons. 1919. Has comp. songs, a Mass, motets, ballet *Hansli le Bossu*, (perf. Opéra, 1914), written in collab. with his brother, Noël Gallon.—F. R.

GALLON, Noël. Fr. compr. *b.* Paris, 11 Sept. 1891. Stud. at Cons.; 1st prize, pf. 1909; *Grand Prix de Rome*, 1910. Produced (Gaieté Theatre, Paris) lyrical drama, *Paysans et Soldats* (1911); a ballet (at Opéra) *Hansli le Bossu* (1914), written in collab. with his brother, Jean.—F. R.

GALLOTTI, Salvatore. Ital. compr. of sacred music; dir. of choir of Milan Cath.; *b.* Gallarate (Milan), 19 April, 1856. Diploma at Milan Cons. in 1878. For several years choirmaster of Church of San Carlo; in 1884, vice-dir. of choir of Milan Cath., succeeding Gallignani as dir. in 1892. In addition to an opera and symph. works, has written much sacred music—Masses, Hymns, Vespers. Specially noteworthy is his *Funeral Mass* (6-v.) in memory of King Humbert (perf. at Rome, 1911).—D. A.

GALPIN, Rev. Canon Francis William. Eng. mus. antiquary; orch. performer and collector; *b.* Dorchester, 25 Dec. 1858. Stud. organ under Prof. Sterndale Bennett and at Trin. Coll. Cambridge, under Dr. Garrett; librarian of Univ. Mus. Soc. and 1st clar. Univ. Orch. under Sir Charles Stanford; canon of Chelmsford Cath. 1917; president of Essex Archæological Soc. 1921. Particularly interested in history, evolution and mechanism of all mus. instrs. Encourages orch. and vocal music in village life, and specialises on the music of Elizabethan age.
Descriptive catalogue of the European mus. instrs. in Metropolitan Museum of Art, New York (1902); *The Mus. Instrs. of the Amer. Indians of N.-W. Coast* (1903); *Notes on a Roman Hydraulus* (1904); *The Evolution of the Sackbut* (1907); *Old Engl. Instrs. of Music* (Methuen, 1910); ed. new ed. of Stainer's *Music of the Bible* (Novello, 1914); arts. in Grove's Dictionary, *The Times*, etc.—E.-H.

GALVANI, Hercules. Argentine violinist; *b.* Bologna in 1863. Stud. at Liceo Rossini, Bologna, under Verardi. When 13, formed a quartet with the brothers Rondini and Turli, which had a notable success. After playing as solo and 1st vn. at several theatres in Italy, went to Vienna, to study under Hellmesberger at R. Cons. for 18 months. Returned to Italy and gave concerts at Trieste, Paris and Barcelona. Went to Buenos Ayres in 1883, where he organised concerts. In 1886, founded the Buenos Ayres Quartet with Forino, Bonfiglioli and Scarabelli. Now devotes himself to teaching, being co-dir. with Forino and Troiani of Santa Cecilia Inst., one of leading conservatoires of Argentina. Has trained a students' orch. (the first establ. in Buenos Ayres), with remarkable success.—A. M.

GANZ, Rudolph. Amer. pianist, condr. compr. *b.* Zurich, Switzerland, 24 Feb. 1877. Stud. at Zurich Cons. under R. Freund (pf.), Joh. Hegar (cello); at Lausanne under his uncle, Eschmann-Dumur (pf.) and Blanchet (compn.); later under Blumer (pf.) in Strasburg and Busoni (pf.) and Urban (compn.) in Berlin. At 10, appeared in Zurich as cellist, at 12 as pianist. 1901-5, head

of pf. department, Chicago Mus. Coll. Played in concert with the leading orchs. In America, he introduced many Fr. pf. works (Debussy, Ravel, d'Indy). Since 1921, condr. of St. Louis Symphony Orch. Has comp. a symphony, a *Konzertstück* for pf. and orch. (written 1902, 1st played at a commencement-concert of Chicago Mus. Coll. 17 June, 1902, and by Theodore Thomas Orch. in Chicago, 29 Dec. 1911).
Konzertstück, arr. 2 pianos (Schmidt, 1902); Symph. Variations on theme by Brahms for pf. op. 21 (Composers' Music Corp. 1921); 2 concert-pieces for pf. op. 29 (Composers' Music Corp. 1922). Over 200 songs: op. 2, 6, 11, 17, 20 (Schmidt, 1908); op. 13 (Schlesinger, 1910); op. 7, 8 (Summy, 1904, 1903).—O. K.

GARBIN, Edoardo. Ital. tenor; *b.* Padua. One of best singers of his time; known at all principal opera-houses of the world. Created part of Guevara in Franchetti's *Cristoforo Colombo*, and that of Loewe in same compr.'s *Germania*. By Verdi's wish, he was the 1st interpreter of *Falstaff* at La Scala. He took part in perf. of *Falstaff* and *La Traviata* at Busseto, under Toscanini, in the Verdi centenary year (1913).—D. A.

GARBUSIŃSKI, Kazimierz. Polish orgt. compr. *b.* Opatowiec, 25 Feb. 1883. From 1904-8, he was pupil of Władysław Żeleński at Cracow Cons. In 1909, became orgt. and dir. of choir of St. Anne's Church.
5 masses for male choir, 100 preludes for organ (publ. Zalewsky, Chicago) and some other pieces, of which 2 received prizes. The Oratorio Soc. at Cracow (founded by him) perf. his *Seven Words of Christ* and *Pastoral Suite*.—ZD. J.

GARCIA, Albert. Eng. barit. singer; teacher; *b.* London. Son of Gustave G.; grandson of Manuel G.; stud. at R.C.M. London under his father; then in Paris under his great-aunt, Viardot G., and Edmond Duvernoy, and Paul Lhérie; has sung at Covent Garden Opera and chief London concerts; also in Germany and France; prof. at Guildhall School of Music and R.C.M. London.—E.-H.

GARCIA MANSILLA, Eduardo. Argentine compr. Chargé d'affaires for Argentina in Petrograd. Stud. under Massenet in Paris, and under Rimsky-Korsakof in Petrograd.
Chant Hivernal and other symph. works; 34 songs with Fr. words; Fugue for 3 vs.; *Heure Matinale* for vn.; several pf. pieces.—A. M.

GARDEN, Mary. Amer. operatic s. singer; *b.* Aberdeen, Scotland, 20 Feb. 1877. Went to U.S.A. at age of 6. After living in Chicopee, Mass., and Hartford, Conn., her family settled in Chicago in 1888. At the age of 6 she began studying the vn., at 12 the pf. At 16 took part in an amateur perf. of *Trial by Jury*; 1896, in Paris where she stud. singing under Trabadello, Chevallier and Fugère. First appeared on stage at Opéra-Comique, when on 12 April, 1900, although she had had only a day's warning, she was called upon to relieve Mlle. Rioton, who was ill, in the 3rd act of Charpentier's *Louise*, singing the title-rôle, a part in which she has been very successful since. Later sang in London, Brussels and Paris. Her Amer. *début* she made in *Thaïs* at Manhattan Opera House, New York, 25 Nov. 1907. Since 1910, member of Chicago Opera Company, her most successful rôles, besides *Thaïs* and *Louise*, being *Mélisande* and *Salome*. 1921-2, gen. dir. of Chicago Opera.—O. K.

GARDINER, H. Balfour. Eng. compr. *b.* London, 7 Nov. 1877. Began to play at 5 and to compose at 9; at 17 stud. for 1 year at Hoch's Cons. Frankfort-o-M. under Ivan Knorr (compn.) and Uzielli (pf.); 1895, New Coll. Oxford; back to Frankfort; then Sondershausen; music-master at Winchester Coll. for a short time. Now lives principally in the country. His *Shepherd Fennel's Dance* has a wide vogue with orchestras. In 1912 he gave a series of orch. concerts devoted to the works of British comprs. He has a bold, masculine touch in composition.

Symphony; orch. suite in A ma.; overture, orch.; str. 5tet; str. 4tet; pf. pieces (Forsyth); songs; choral works, etc.—E.-H.

GARIEL, Eduardo. Mexican compr. *b.* 1860. Prominent as an educator and writer on music. His *New System of Harmony* is based on four fundamental chords.—F. H. M.

GARRATT, Percival. Eng. compr. and pianist; *b.* Little Tew Grange, Oxon, Whit-Monday, May 1877. Stud. in Vienna under Louis Rée and in Berlin under Klindworth. Was a foundation-scholar at Marlborough Coll. Has given pf. recitals in Bösendorfer and Ehrbar Halls, Vienna; Mus. Acad. Stockholm; Salle Gaveau, Paris; and chief London halls. 80 concerts in S. Africa; many tours with Clara Butt, Elman, Maaskof, Zacharewitsch, Louis Godowsky. Married Eve Lechmere, violinist, pupil of César Thomson. As a compr. his works show true Eng. national characteristics, with a strongly individual strain.

Pf.: sonata in A mi. op. 6; *Scherzo* op. 7; 4 *Bagatelles*, op. 9; *Waltz-Idyll*, op. 12; *Pageant Piece*, op. 13; *Scherzo-Toccata*, op. 14; *Rondel*, op. 15; 2 *Lyric Fancies*, op. 18; *Tempo di Ballo*, op. 19; *Momento Giocoso*, op. 20; 2 *Miniatures*, op. 22; *Toccatina*, op. 23; *Hunting-Piece*, op. 29; *Night-Piece and Musette*, op. 31; *Arabesque and Grotesque*, op. 32; Concert March, op. 33; *Impressions*, op. 44; *Helston Furry Dance*; 2 *Epigrams*, op. 46 (1923), etc. Vn. and pf.: *Arietta*, op. 2; *Minuet*, op. 17; *Pastoral Song*, op. 24; *Prayer*, G str. melody, op. 26; *Duo Barocco*, op. 47; *Preludio Fugato*, op. 48. V. and pf.: songs, op. 8, 10, 21; 3 *Punjab Lyrics*, op. 16; 2 Serbian songs; 2 Southern Slav songs; *Lullaby*, op. 30; *Infantile Conceits*, op. 45; 8 songs; *A Cartload of Villains*, pantomime, 3 acts; *Cherry-stones*, mus. play for children. (Chief publ. Ashdown; Ascherberg; Boosey; Chappell; Cary; Chester; Curwen; Cramer; Larway; Leonard; Novello; Rogers; Weekes; Whitehall Music Co.)—E.-H.

GÄRTNER, Eduard. Austrian barit. singer; *b.* Vienna, 15 Jan. 1862; *d.* there 2 July, 1918. Singing pupil of Sattler; also vn. and pf. player. Originally a provincial opera-singer; only later became recital and oratorio singer. Notable for helping many new Vienna comprs. to a hearing. First to sing songs by Hugo Wolf, Arnold Schönberg and Joseph Marx in public. Stöhr, Lafite, Braun, were also first perf. by him. As well known in Germany as in Austria. With Dr. Heinrich Schenker he ed. cantatas by J. S. Bach. Comp. a lyric opera (perf. 1900, Vienna) and many songs. Pupils: Leone Fumagalli, Alex. Varnay (Copenhagen), Lucy Weidt (Vienna Opera House), Béla Környey (t.

Budapest), Mizzi Günther (operetta singer), Hedy Iracema Brügelmann, Lorle Meissner, Dr. Lothar Riedinger.—P. P.

GASCO, Alberto. Ital. compr. and music-critic; *b.* Naples, 3 Oct. 1879. Graduate in law; completed mus. studies in Rome under Raffaele Terziani. Is a clear and simple compr., noted for opera *La leggenda della sette torri* (libretto by Ottone Schanzer) perf. successfully at the Costanzi, 1913 (Sonzogno, Milan). Author of several estimable works for v., pf. and vn. Songs, the *Poemi della notte e dell' aurora*; pf. works, *Le danzatrici di Jodhpur*, *Primavera fiorentina*; vn. music, *La visione di Sant' Orsola*, *La vergine alla culla*, *Maria di Magdala*; str. 4tet, *La Venere dormente*, inspired by the famous picture by Giorgione; several of his other works were inspired by pictures. Orch works: *Scherzo orgiasti co* poem, *Alle fonti del Clitunno*; prelude, *Buffalmacco*, all perf. with success in Rome, at Augusteo and elsewhere (Ricordi, Milan). As critic, G. has nobly exercised his activities for many years, writing for *La Tribuna*. He spoke at Turin Mus. Congress, Oct. 1921, on *The Lyric Theatre*. Consult Alberto De Angelis, *A. G.*, in *Corriere del Teatro*, Milan, 1916.—D. A.

GASCÚE, F. Span. musicologist and civil engineer; author of *Las gamas célticas y las melodías populares euskaras* (*The Celtic Scales and Basque Folk-Tunes*), 1919, Madrid; *Origen de la música popular vasca* (*Origin of Basque Popular Music*), publ. in *Revue Internationale des Études Basques*, 7th year. Died at Bilbao, 1920.—P. G. M.

GASPERINI, Guido. Ital. historian and palæographer of music; *b.* Florence, 7 June, 1865. Stud. in Florence under Sbolci (cello) and Tacchinardi (compn.). Then devoted himself to study of mus. history, and to holding conferences and auditions. Since 1902, has been librarian and prof. of mus. history at R. Cons. Parma. Founder and inspirer of the Associazione dei Musicologi Italiani, over which he presided. It undertook publication of the *General Catalogue of Ancient Music in existence in the Libraries of Italy*, and of interesting eds. of old Ital. musical masterpieces.

Storia della musica (*History of Music*). Lectures (Florence, 1899, Lastrucci); *Dell'arte di interpretare le scritture della musica vocale nel cinquecento* (*On the Art of Interpreting Writings of Vocal Music in XVI Century*) (Florence, 1902, Seeber); *Storia della semiografia musicale* (Milan, 1905, Hoepli); *I caratteri peculiari del melodramma italiano nell' opera dei predecessori e in quella di Giuseppe Verdi* (*The Peculiar Characteristics of Ital. Melodrama in Works of Predecessors of Giuseppe Verdi and of Verdi himself*) (Parma, 1913); *Cenni storici sul Conservatorio musicale di Parma* (*Historical Notes on Cons. Musicale of Parma*) (Parma, 1913).—D. A.

GAST, Peter. Pseudonym of Heinrich Köselitz. Ger. compr. *b.* Annaberg (Saxony), 10 Jan. 1854; *d.* there, 15 Aug. 1918. Private pupil of E. Fr. Richter in Leipzig and of Friedrich Nietzsche at Basle Univ. During this period he assisted Richter by reading to him and writing from dictation, remaining later as Nietzsche's most faithful friend. From 1878, was mostly travelling, chiefly in Italy; 1900-8 in Weimar (occupied with Nietszche Archives); finally in Annaberg.

Operas: *Willram* (1879); *König Wenzel* (1888); *Orpheus and Dionysus*; *The Secret Marriage* (Dantzig, 1891, publ. 1901 in pf. ed. as *The Lion of Venice*); mus. comedy, *Scherz, List und Rache* (1881); fest. play, *Walpurgis* (1903, in Mountain Theatre on Witches' Dancing Ground, Harz); symphony, *Helle Nächte*; str. 4tet; overtures; choral works; songs, etc. The songs, op. 1–9, were publ. by Hofmeister; op. 3, *Lethe* (poem by C. Ferd. Meyer), barit. and orch.; duet, *Nachfeier*, s. and b. Gast (with A. Seidl) ed. Vol. I of *Nietzsche's Letters*; and, with Frau Förster-Nietzsche, *Nietzsche's Correspondence with Hans v. Bülow* (1905, Ges. Ausg. [Complete Ed.], Vol. III, ii); Vol. IV of Nietzsche's correspondence gives his letters to Peter Gast (1908).—A. E.

GASTALDON, Stanislao. Ital. compr. *b.* Turin, 7 April, 1861. Famous as author of ballad which met with great success (200,000 copies), called *La musica proibita*. Other ballads also had large sale. Compr. of 10 stage works; one of them, *Mala Pasqua* (on same subject as Mascagni's *Cavalleria Rusticana*, perf. at Costanzi, Rome, in 1890, then in other theatres. For a time, mus. critic of the *Nuovo Giornale*, Florence.—D A.

GASTOUÉ, Amédée. Fr. musicologist; *b.* Paris, 13 March, 1873. Pupil of A. Deslandres; attended lectures on harmony at Cons. in Paris. Early attracted by study of liturgical chant, and music of Middle Ages, devoted himself entirely to those studies. Precentor, orgt., and teacher of Gregorian chant at *Schola Cantorum*, and at Catholic Inst. Appointed in 1904 to take part in Pontifical Gregorian Commission; engaged on Vatican ed. of Gregorian Chant. His works, which are of the greatest importance on this subject, are in correlation with all those undertaken in France, during last 30 years, for renovation of plain-chant.

Histoire de Chant Liturgique à Paris (1904), *Cours théorique et pratique de Plain-Chant Romain Grégorien* (Schola Cantorum, 1904); *Les Origines du Chant Romain* (crowned by Acad. of Inscriptions and Belles-Lettres) (1907); *Les Anciens Chants liturgiques des églises d'Apt et du Comtat, Catalogue des manuscrits de musique byzantine* (1908); *L'Art Grégorien* (Paris, 1910, Alcan); *Le Graduel et l'Antiphonaire romains* (Lyon, 1913); *Les Primitifs de la musique française* (Paris, 1922, Laurens), etc. Educational works on plain-chant, and a Classic Method for Piano (Paris, 1917). Also motets, *Missa Paschalis*, *Messe en l'honneur de Jeanne d'Arc*, etc., harmonisations of ancient Christmas carols, etc.—M. L. P.

GASTSPIEL. In German theatres, where there is a permanent company, a visiting performer is called a "guest" (*Gast*), hence the words *Gastspiel* (performance of a guest) and *gastieren* (to perform as a guest). The nearest ordinary Eng. equivalent is the word "star"; but *Gast* includes many performers who are in no sense "stars" and it does not necessarily imply the less reputable associations of the Eng. word. *Gastspiel* also covers visits of an entire company or orchestra.—E. J. D.

GATO. See SOUTH AMER. DANCES.

GATTI, Guido Maria. Ital. writer on music; *b.* Chieti, 1893. Stud. the vn. and pf. and, at same time, completed studies as engineer; devoted himself to mus. criticism and literature, especially contemporary music. 1913–15, chief

editor of Turin review *La Riforma Musicale*; recently (at the instance of the Fabbrica Italiana di Pianoforti) founded the review *Il Pianoforte*, and directs the publication of it. Contributes to principal Ital., Fr. and Eng. reviews. Amongst his publications are a *Guida musicale* (Musical Guide) to Bossi's *Giovanna d' Arco*; monograph on Bizet (Turin, 1915, *Riforma Musicale*); vol. on *Musicisti moderni d'Italia e di fuori* (*Modern Musicians in Italy and Abroad*) (Bologna, 1920, Pizzi). Has also organised interesting concerts of modern music.—D. A.

GATTI-CASAZZA, Giulio. Ital. opera dir. *b.* Ferrara, 3 Feb. 1869; completed studies at Univ. in his native city and at R. Scuola Superiore Navale in Genoa. Leaving as graduate in engineering, devoted himself enthusiastically and successfully to organisation of opera perfs. From 1898 to 1908, was artistic dir. of Scala Theatre, Milan. In 1908, was nominated general dir. of Metropolitan Theatre, New York, which position he still occupies. Has acquired a high reputation for the results obtained in his various managements.—D. A.

GATTY, Nicholas Comyn. Eng. opera compr. *b.* Bradfield, Sheffield, 13 Sept. 1874. Educated Downing Coll. Cambridge; and R.C.M. (compn. under Sir Cnarles Stanford, Dr. Charles Wood); orgt. Duke of York's R. Military School, Chelsea, for some years; mus. critic *Pall Mall Gazette*, 1907–14; In compn. works chiefly in opera. His *Greysteel* was produced by Moody-Manners Co. Sheffield, 1906; his *Duke or Devil* by the same company, at Manchester, 1909; *The Tempest* by Fairbairn-Milne Co. Surrey Theatre, London, 1920; *Prince Ferelon*, at Old Vic. London, 1921.

Duke or Devil (Cary); *Prince Ferelon* (Stainer & Bell; a Carnegie award); *Macbeth*, tragic opera, 4 acts, ms. Chorus and orch.: Milton's ode *On Time* (Forsyth); 3 *Short Odes* (Novello); orch. variations on *Old King Cole*. Vn. and pf.: sonata in G (Cary); *Variations* (Novello); *Romance* (Stainer & Bell); 2 sets of pf. waltzes (Cary); songs (Cary; Novello).—E.-H.

GAUBERT, Philippe. Fr. compr. flautist, condr. *b.* Paris, 1879; pupil of Taffanel. Condr. of Soc. Concerts of Cons. and of the Opéra. He writes almost entirely for orch. and chamber combinations. His music is neo-classic, but threatened with modernism.

Rhapsody on Popular Themes (1909); *Philotis* (ballet), 1914; *Le Cortège d'Amphitrite* (1911); *Poème Pastorale* (1911); *Jours tragiques et glorieux* (1917); *Josiane* (with choruses). His only work for stage is *Sonia* (1913). Chamber-music: *Légende* (harp); *Lamento* (cello and pf.); sonata, vn. and pf. (1917); some songs.—A. C.

GAUTHIER-VILLARS, Henry (called Willy). *b.* Villiers-sur-Orge (S. et O.), 1859. A very witty musical chronicler, who played an important part in diffusion of Wagnerism in France. Afterwards interested himself in young French school and defended Debussy and Ravel. His criticisms, where technical terms are in close proximity to puns and allusions to events of day, have entertained several generations of music-lovers and of musicians. They have been collected in volumes: *Lettres de l'Ouvreuse*, *Bains* *de Son, Accords perdus*, etc. He has also written a book on *Bizet* (*Musiciens Célèbres*, Laurens).—H. P.

GAUTHIEZ, Cécile. Fr. compr. *b.* Paris, 1873. Stud. under Léon Saint-Réquier, G. Bret and especially under V. d'Indy in compn. at *Schola Cantorum*, where she has been prof. of harmony since 1920. Writes mainly religious music.

Mass, *Ancilla Domini*, 2-part children's voices (Paris, 1917, Schola Bureau d'édition); motets, *Communione calicis, Benedicta es tu* (*Schola*), *In me gratia omnis viæ, Hodie Christus natus est* (Paris, Hérelle). Also organ solos; suite for pf. *Sur les chemins*; songs; choral works; str. 4tet, etc.—M. L. P.

GAVET, André. Fr. compr. *b.* Saint-Jean de Losnes, 1887. Pupil of Cons. of Dijon, of Nancy, and of Paris.

Stage music for *Pulcinella*; and for *Les Heures Blanches*; *Suite rapsodique* on Serbian airs; *Elégie funèbre* (orch.); coll. of old French songs harmonised.—A. C.

GAWROŃSKI, Wojciech. Polish compr. condr. *b.* Sejmony, 27 June, 1868; *d.* 1913. Stud. under Strobl (pf.) and Noskowski (theory) at Warsaw Cons. Was condr. in Vilna; afterwards dir. of Music School in Orel, Russia. From 1903, lived in Warsaw.

Operas: *Marya* (one of several Polish operas based on subject of Malczewski's romantic poem; libretto by well-known author Stan. Przybyszewski); *Pojata*. Symphony; 4 str. 4tets (the 1st received prize in Paderewski competition, Leipzig, 1892; the 2nd, at Moscow competition, 1903); 20 pf. pieces; 30 songs.—ZD. J.

GAY, María. Span. contr. singer; *b.* Barcelona. A leading contemporary opera-singer, specially famous for renderings of *Orfeo* and *Carmen*. Metropolitan Opera House, New York; Covent Garden, London; Teatro Colón, Buenos Ayres; Liceo, Barcelona; also Madrid, Milan, Paris, etc.—P. G. M.

GAYARRE, Julián Sebastián. Span. t. singer; *b.* Roncal (Navarra), 9 Jan. 1844; *d.* at end of XIX century. Formerly a blacksmith. Whilst singing in amateur chorus, his exceptional voice was detected by compr., Father Hilarión Eslava. Entered R. Cons. de Música 1869; *début* at Teatro Varese (Lombardy), Italy, with opera *Elixir de amore*. Thus began an ever-increasing success till his death, whilst in full possession of his wonderful faculties. He was the Caruso of his day; sang in every great opera house in Europe. The authorities of the Grand Opéra, Paris, felt justified in making an exception to the rule of the inst. concerning the Fr. language, and engaged Gayarre to sing in Ital. His renderings of *Il Trovatore* and *La Favorita* are always referred to as unequalled achievements in the art of singing.—P. G. M.

GAZTAMBIDE, Joaquín. Span. compr. *b.* Tudela (Navarra), 7 Feb. 1822; *d.* about the end of XIX century. In 1847, went to Paris as condr. of troupe of Span. actors, singers and dancers. Impressed by the characteristics of the Fr. light opera, he conceived the idea of creating a similar *genre* in the Span. language. This led to the complete development of the lyric plays known in Spain as *zarzuela grande* (see ZARZUELA), which for a long period bore the mark of its Fr. origin (specially in the

libretti), the music being a compromise between Fr. and Ital. influences. For this purpose, on the initiative of G., and in view of the success of his play *La Mensajera* (1849), the Teatro de la Zarzuela was constructed in 1856. He wrote many plays for the stage in 1, 2, 3 and 4 acts, amongst which the most representative are *En las astas del toro* (1 act); *El Valle de Andorra, Catalina, El Juramento, Las Hijas de Eva* (3 acts); *Los Magiares* (4 acts).—P. G. M.

GAZUL, Freitas. See PORTUGUESE OPERA

GÉDALGE, André. Fr. compr. *b.* Paris, 27 Dec. 1856. An estimable composer, an incomparable teacher. From his counterpoint class at the Paris Conservatoire have come forth the best musicians of the young French school. It is thanks to his instruction that they have acquired that virtuosity of writing, which is one of their characteristics. Ravel and Florent Schmitt, like Honegger and Darius Milhaud, learned their *métier* under his direction. He was rather late in devoting himself to music. He entered the Conservatoire in 1884 and studied composition with Guiraud. Two symphonies, an orchestral suite, a quartet and an *opéra-comique* reveal his skill as a contrapuntist and his art of construction rather than his natural gifts. His principal work is his *Traité de la Fugue* (1904).—H. P.

GEEHL, Henry Ernest. Eng. compr. pianist and condr. *b.* London, 28 Sept. 1881. Chiefly educated in music by his father; also under R. Orlando Morgan. As a compr. G. is chiefly known for his educational pf. music and songs (Augener; Ashdown; Gould). Some music for various other instrs. is publ. by Rudall, Carte, and Hawkes & Co.

2 operas (ms.); symphony in D mi. (ms.); vn. concerto; pf. concerto; 3 orch. suites (Novello; Boosey; Ashdown); *Cromwell*, military band.—E.-H.

GEISLER, Paul. Ger. compr. *b.* Stolp (Pomerania), 10 Aug. 1856; *d.* Posen, 3 April, 1919. Pupil of his grandfather, mus. dir. in Marienburg; also for a time of Konstantin Decker. Korrepetitor Leipzig Stadttheater, 1881–2; at Angelo Neumann's Wander-Theater, 1882–3; condr. in Bremen (with Anton Seidl), 1883–5; then resided in Leipzig and Berlin; finally in Posen, where he establ. a Cons. and cond. concerts of Posen Orch. Association; dir. of choral soc. of the province, 1899–1903; R. mus. dir. 1902.

Operas: *Ingeborg* (Bremen, 1884); *Die Marianer* (*The Knights of Marienburg*) (Hamburg, 1891); *Hertha* (Hamburg, 1894); *Psalm* (Lübeck, 1893); *Warum*; *Fredericus Rex* (*We are Victorious*), Berlin, Theater des Westens, 1899; *Princess Ilse* (Posen, 1903); *Wikingertod* (*Death of a Viking*), dramatic episode with music; publ.: *The Piper of Hamelin* (perf. by Allgemeine Deutsche Musikverein of Magdeburg, 1880), and *Till Eulenspiegel*; also cycles for soli, chorus and orch., *Sansara* and *Golgotha*; also songs; pf. pieces (*Monologue* and *Episodes*); 4 symphonies (*Symphonic Frescoes*), ms.—A. E.

GENETZ, Emil. Finnish compr. *b.* Impilahti, 24 Oct. 1852. Stud. at Helsingfors Univ.; later both music and dramatic art at Dresden Cons. Subsequently teacher of languages in several towns in Finland; afterwards head of Theatre School at Finnish National Theatre. His patriotic male choruses *Herää Suomi* (*Awake,*

Finland), *Karjala* (*Karelia*), and *Terve Suomeni maa* (*Hail to thee, Finland!*) have secured a prominent place among patriotic Finnish songs for male voices.—T. H.

GEORGE, André. Fr. musicologist; *b.* Algiers, 1890; mus. critic of Catholic review, *Les Lettres*. Has written studies on modern music in *La Nouvelle Journée* and the *Revue Musicale*; he collab. in the standard Fr. transl. of Richard Wagner's *My Life*.—A. C.

GEORGES, Alexandre. Fr. compr. *b.* Arras, 25 Feb. 1890. Former pupil of École Niedermeyer; then prof. there; has devoted himself principally to operatic and vocal music, of superficial effect and purposely grandiloquent. Especially well-known are the songs taken from *Miarka la Fille à l'Ours* (1905) (words by Jean Richepin). Also:

Le Printemps (1890); *Poèmes d'amour* (1892); *Charlotte Corday* (1901); *La Passion* (1902); *Myrrha* (1909); *Sang et Soleil* (1912).—A. C.

GEORGESCU, Georges. Rumanian condr. *b.* Sulina in '1887; first stud. cello at Cons. of Bucharest, taking a 1st prize; then in Berlin, under Hugo Becker; for 3 years, member of the Marteau Quartet. In 1918, on account of leftarm trouble, G. became condr. after studying under Arnold Tcleffel. After having, in that year, cond. a series of concerts at Berlin with the Philh. and also the Blüthner Orch., he returned in 1919 to Bucharest and was appointed condr. of the newly-created Filarmonica Orch. In 1922, was appointed gen. dir. of the Rumanian Opera House (see RUMANIAN OPERA).—C. BR.

GEORGII, Walter. Ger. pianist; *b.* Stuttgart in 1887. Pupil Stuttgart Cons. (Max Pauer); teacher (1910–13) Imperial Russ. School of Music, Woronesch. Obtained Ph.D. at Halle, 1914 (with dissertation *C. M. v. Weber as a Pf. Composer*). Ed. Weber's D mi. sonata (1920), and since 1911 has secured recognition in Germany as a pianist who makes a special feature of modern South Ger. music. Teacher Cologne Cons. since 1914.—A. E.

GERHARD, Robert. Compr. and pianist; *b.* Vals (Tarragona), Spain, 1896. Stud. compn. in Barcelona under late Felipe Pedrell, being last pupil of this famous master. Is always considered, in spite of his Swiss descent, as belonging to the modern Span. school, with which he is identified as well by temperament as by affection.

For voice and pf.: *L'Infantament maravillós de Schaharazada*; *El Verger de les Galanies*; *Amour et Paysage*; 2 pf. trios; *Dos apuntes*, pf. (Unión Musical Española, Madrid; Senart, Paris).—P. G. M.

GERHARDT, Elena. Ger. s. singer; *b.* Leipzig, 11 Nov. 1883. Pupil at Leipzig Cons., especially of Madame Hedmondt; from 1903 much helped by Arthur Nikisch; 1912, accompanied him to America. One of the most sensitive concert-singers in Germany; above all, unsurpassed as a singer of Brahms' songs. Well known in England and America for her classical song-recitals.—A. E.

GERMAN, Edward. Eng. compr. *b.* Whitchurch, Shropshire, 17 Feb. 1862. In 1880 entered R.A.M. London, taking organ as chief study, under Dr. Steggall. In 1881, took vn. as chief study under Weist Hill and Alfred Burnett. (Henry Wood and E. H. Lemare were fellow-students with G. at the R.A.M.) In 1885, won Charles Lucas Medal with *Te Deum* for chorus and organ. Whilst at Acad., wrote operetta *The Rival Poets* (perf. St. George's Hall, 1886). Left the R.A.M. in 1887, playing as 2nd vn. in theatres (in Sullivan's *Pirates of Penzance* and *Princess Ida*); 1888, mus. dir. of Globe Theatre, with band of 30. When Richard Mansfield produced Shakespeare's *Richard III* there, G. wrote the overture, entr'actes and incidental music. This, far above the standard of theatre music of the time, proved most successful. The overture was perf. shortly afterwards at Norwich Fest., Leeds Fest., Crystal Palace, and Philh. Concerts. In 1890, produced his symphony in E mi. at the Crystal Palace. In 1892, wrote the music for Sir Henry Irving's *Henry VIII* at Lyceum. The 3 dances perf. during Wolsey's reception at York Place (Act I) became immensely popular. Since then he has written:

Gipsy Suite (1892); music for *Romeo and Juliet* (Lyceum, 1895); *As You like It* (St. James's, 1896); *Much Ado* (ib., 1898); H. A. Jones's *The Tempter* (Haymarket, 1893); Duchess of Sutherland's *The Conqueror* (Scala, 1915); Anthony Hope's *Nell Gwynn* (Prince of Wales's, 1900). His orch. works include Symphony No. I in E mi. (Crystal Palace); No. II in A mi. (Norwich Fest.); Symph. Suite in D mi. (Leeds Fest.); Fantasia on march-themes (Philh. London, 1897); symph. poem, *Hamlet* (Birmingham Fest. 1897); symph. suite, *The Seasons* (Norwich, 1899); *Welsh Rhapsody* (Cardiff, 1904); *March Rhapsody* (Brighton); Coronation March and Hymn (King George V, Westminster Abbey, 1911); Theme and 6 Diversions (R. Philh. Soc., 1919); *The Willow Song* (R.A.M. Centenary, London, 1922).

In 1901, he collab. in music of *The Emerald Isle* (Savoy). Sullivan had left only 2 completed numbers, and for many others nothing but melodies without basses, while 13 numbers were untouched. Then followed light operas from German's own pen, *Merrie England*, *A Princess of Kensington*, *Tom Jones*, *Fallen Fairies* (libretto by W. S. Gilbert). He has also written a large number of songs and part-songs. In Edward German, the melodist and the scholar are happily combined. His music has a character all its own, albeit it stands in the direct lineage of Sullivan, and apart from his symph. works, has a strong old-English flavour in its melodic turn, its sprightly rhythms and its straightforward diction.—E.-H.

GERMAN CHAMBER-MUSIC FROM 1880.

The development of Ger. chamber-music has been accomplished with far greater ease and more directness than was the case with the opera or symphony. Neo-Romanticism leaves chamber-music to the domain of the classicists, under which head Johannes Brahms is regarded; He comp. a succession of important chamber-works in his last 15 years: pf. trios, op. 87 and 101; 5tets, op. 88 and 111; the 2 last vn. sonatas, op. 100 and 108; 2nd sonata for cello, op. 99; and the last and most mature works: op. 114 (clar. trio), 115 (clar. 5tet) and 120 (clar. sonatas) in which he has brought his utterance to the purest formula, his brooding view of life to the clearest expression. Only a few musicians of the " New German" branch have occupied themselves with chamber-music. Richard Strauss only considered it in a few youthful works, of which the vn. sonata, op. 18, and the pf. 4tet, op. 13, are the most important. Of Hugo Wolf, there is only the D mi. str. 4tet, a youthful work; of Heinrich Klose a str. 4tet in E flat ma.; of Schillings a str. 4tet and str. 5tet; whilst a musician like Walter Braunfels has completely ignored chamber-music in its real sense. Only Hans Pfitzner of this group has not merely importance, but a deep significance for chamber-music; he begins the list of his works with a sonata for cello, and his str. 4tet, pf. trio, pf. 5tet (not so, his vn. sonata) belong to his strongest lyrical utterance. Besides Pfitzner, the Neo-Romanticists who chiefly belong to the Munich school must be mentioned: Ludwig Thuille, August Reuss (4tet, 8tet), Julius Weismann, Heinrich Kaspar Schmid (4tet, vn. sonata, wind 5tet). The remaining Ger. chamber-music comprs. join on to Brahms and fill the classical form with more or less romantic subject-matter. It must suffice to mention the most prolific: Heinrich Herzogenberg, Arnold Mendelssohn, Robert Kahn. There are not only strict followers of Brahms, like Ewald Straesser, but also others who combine intimate expression with free impressionistic elements, like Paul Graener and Hermann Zilcher (pf. 5tet). One could divide these epigoni according to their regional origin: a Ger. group which would also include the Ger.-Swiss with their important master H. Suter, a S. Ger. Rhenish, Saxon-Thuringian, N. Ger., with their various relationships to Slav music. The most important master, who has gone farthest away from Brahms, is Max Reger; one can say that chamber-music is the apex of his music, not so much from the number of works (5 str. 4tets. str. 6tet, 2 pf. trios, 2 pf. 4tets, 7 sonatas for vn. and pf., 11 sonatas for vn. solo, etc.), as from their harmonic sensitiveness and audacity. His chamber-music is the dividing point for modern comprs., a testimony to absolute music (not inspired by poetry or exterior impulses), as well as the boundary line of atonal expression (even when his tonality is fixed). Reger has a number of direct disciples, of whom some lead back into the romantic style (Josef Haas), some step over all boundary lines (H. Grabner). Besides Reger, Arnold Schönberg and also Ferruccio Busoni lead modern chamber-music along the same roads of spirituality, abstraction and "expressionism," as do contemporary comprs. of modern chamber-music in Russia, England and France. Naturally such followers belong to the younger schools: Heinrich Kaminski, (who in his 4tet and 5tet has followed Bruckner), Arthur Schnabel, Hermann Scherchen, Max Butting, Eduard Erdmann, Ludwig Weber, Frank Wohlfahrt, Paul Hindemith, and others.—A. E.

GERMAN FOLK-MUSIC. See FRIEDLAENDER, MAX; JANIEZEK, JULIUS; MEERSMAN, HANS.

GERMAN OPERA (since Wagner). It is natural that so extraordinary a phenomenon as Wagner should at first compel practically the whole of Ger. opera-production to be dominated by him. The very content of Ger. opera became, in part at least, dependent on Wagner; hence numbers of post-Wagnerians have written dramas of " redemption," making the mistake of adopting the style of Wagner's third period (*Tristan, Parsifal*) with a display of pathos and the employment of orchestral, harmonic, and polyphonic means commensurate with the greatness of Wagner's own creations, and justifiable in their case alone. One of the most elegant, if not the most original, of these composers is Max Schillings. One of the most individual and logical is Hans Pfitzner, who in his first legend-opera, *Der arme Heinrich*, despite its obvious derivation from the *Tristan* style, was able to strike a note of his own; thus passing by way of his extremely musical fairy-play, *The Rose from the Garden of Love*, to the ascetic style of his essentially individual artist-legend, *Palestrina*. Another path leads from Wagner to the fairy-opera, whose most fecund representative is Wagner's own son, Siegfried Wagner, the most successful representative being Engelbert Humperdinck. All these works, however, are loaded with a heavy ballast of modulation and instrumentation out of harmony with their material content. Another branch of these fairy-operas takes on the character of the " adolescent style " (Thuille's *Lobetanz*; *Gugeline*), and becomes involved in mawkish ornamental sentimentality. To this group belongs the *Feuersnot* of Richard Strauss, which is derived from Ernst v. Wolzogen's *Überbrettl* (*q.v.*) and combines the comedy-style with the Wagnerian. Alexander Ritter has written some of the most individual of these post-Wagnerian comedies.

Yet another branch of opera, imitative of Wagner, attaches especially to the *Mastersingers*; *e.g.* Hugo Wolf's *Corregidor*, despite its Spanish theme. Another stream, arising from the *Mastersingers*, leads to the *Volksoper*, which adopts a human strain (Kienzl's *Evangelimann*), and also to Julius Bittner (*Der Musikant, Der Bergsee*), though the ideal of strength and dignity striven after is not attained.

Besides the Wagner operas, those of the Italian Verists have also had their imitators. The most successful is Eugen d'Albert with his *The Lowlands* (*Tiefland*). He writes the most natural and easy-going theatre-music in Germany, without always troubling much about the artistic level it attains. To his school belong musicians like Ermanno Wolf-Ferrari, who, like d'Albert, devotes part of his creative ability to the lighter form of opera derived from the Italian *Intermezzo*, and part to the Verist music-drama. Of such kind also is E. W. Korngold (*The Ring of Polycrates; The Dead City*). Strauss goes his own way. Proceeding from his symph. poems, which allow of his painting the most detailed " programmes," he writes his orchestral operas (*Salome*; *Elektra*) to ready-made libretti, passing by way of the melodious comedy (*Rosenkavalier*) to a synthesis of orchestra and melody in opera, e.g. *The Woman without a Shadow*. His fine parody-opera, *Ariadne*, may be regarded as a progressive work, embodying the "music of the future." Along with Strauss, there stands Schreker, who imparts, to some extent, to the fairy-opera erotic, sexual, psycho-analytical intensity, makes a kaleidoscopic "sound-vision" the central point of his creative activity. Walter Braunfels has struck a side-path and an outlet, with his fantastic, Neo-Romantic opera *The Birds*, without however producing anything of outstanding musical originality.

In contradistinction to all this music, which in some way proceeds either with or counter to Wagner, there is to be reckoned that of a group of musicians entirely independent of Wagner. Its most mature representative is Busoni, who turns into music the combination of ordinary practical life and fantasy to be found in E. T. A. Hoffmann's creations. The latest disciple is probably Paul Hindemith with his three one-act plays, which present types for expressionist and burlesque stage-plays with music.—A. E.

GERMAN ORCHESTRAL MUSIC FROM 1880. The development of Ger. orch. music of the last 40 years may be characterised best as the complete triumph, and later the complete decline, of programme music. The music of the Neo-Romantics, the modern Germans in particular, prepared the way for the triumph of programme music. Berlioz, with his symph. and semi-dramatic works, exercised an influence in Germany rather than in France. In another department, the music-drama, Wagner had created the mightiest. instrument yet known for symph. work, an entirely new orch. language, and an entirely new world of expression. Finally, it was Franz Liszt who found for the poetic and philosophical ideas that had invaded the music of his time the right setting, which in each case was quite free and variable though none the less true to formal principles. No contemporaneous musician represents the triumph of programme music in the form of the symph. poem more completely than Richard Strauss, the most successful of them all. Brought up on classic ideals, proof of which are his two symphonies and an overture, he was early won over to programme music and freedom of form by Alexander Ritter, a nephew of Wagner, and himself a compr. of six estimable symph. poems. His first effort was a half-impressionist, half-sentimental symphony or suite, *Aus Italien*, in the old form; this was followed by a series of symph. poems from *Don Juan* (1889) up to the *Alpine Symphony* (1915), in which the orch. skill of Berlioz, Liszt's constructive facility, and Wagner's *leit-motiv* idiom are combined with much temperament, sensuous charm, and extraordinary talent, superior to that of all three; in which also the prevailing ideas of the time (certainly nothing more exalted than the ideas of that time) are expressed with much boldness and vigour. Musicians who found a place beside Strauss moved in the same direction—Hugo Wolf (*Penthesilea*), Siegmund von Hausegger (*Barbarossa*; *Wieland der Schmied*), Reznicek (one

of the most orig. of them all), Gustav Brecher, the Swiss V. Andreae, K. Bleyle, E. Boehe, H. G. Noren, C. Ehrenberg, P. Ertel, August Reuss, G. Mraczek, O. Besch, and a hundred other Ger. comprs. of overtures and symph. poems. In the last 20 years, however, comprs. while taking full advantage of the orch. and artistic achievements of the Neo-Germans, have not utilised them to illustrate naturalistic and programme music, or the problems of philosophy. Comprs. of orch. music like Engelbert Humperdinck, Nicodé, Sekles, Kämpf, Braunfels, Hans Tiessen, P. Scheinpflug, Max Trapp, are more or less Straussian in the means they employ, but not in their thought and feeling. Their orch. music is picturesque and often inclined to impressionism, but it has a deeper and more expressive intellectual value. It is concerned neither with sensuous feeling, pathos and rhetoric, nor with the solving of problems that stand outside music.

In marked contrast to the music of the "progressive" comprs., who hail chiefly from S. Germany, is the symphony of Johannes Brahms, the classical nature of which tends to "classicism." Brahms's influence, which has steadily increased even in S. Germany, has almost completely paralysed the influence of the symph. writer Liszt. Progressing in the opposite direction to Richard Strauss, Felix Draeseke, and also Felix Weingartner, originally Neo-Germans, have become more and more conservative. Of similar tendencies are the many N. Ger. "academic" comprs.: Rudorff, Bruch, Gernsheim, Koch, Berger, Schumann, Kaun, Juon, and Straesser. Only Felix Woyrsch, Hermann Zilcher and, above all, Max Reger have struck out on independent lines for themselves. In his orch. works (*Sinfonietta*, Hiller, Mozart and Beethoven variations, overtures, suites, concertos, etc.), Reger has attempted a new synthesis of "absolute" music in classic form, but with the most daring devices of modern harmony and polyphony. In a later but short period of creative activity Reger, through his Böcklin and Eichendorff suites, gave evidence of a leaning towards Impressionism, which phase of art, however, never gained a devoted band of followers in Germany. Paul Graener (in a few of his works) might be described as a disciple of the Impressionists. With Reger there arose a new and original school, including imitators (H. Unger) and also symphonic writers of individual character. Among the latter are the Romanticist, Josef Haas, the gifted Gottfried Rüdinger, Hermann Grabner and others. Reger, who could no longer create in "large form," and who was really a miniaturist, and the destroyer of expression as such, has naturally much in common with those who are in search of new means of expression.

Although only part of his creative activity falls within the last forty years, Anton Bruckner himself exercised a great influence during that period. In Bruckner's symphonies it seemed, and still seems, as if the mus. aspirations of the time had been fulfilled—absolute music, having religious faith as its source and folk-music as its basis, modern yet classical, the unity of which has found many zealous defenders. The talented imitators of Bruckner in Germany include H. Bischoff, Richard Wetz, Paul Büttner, Wilhelm Petersen. Friedrich Klose, a personal pupil of Bruckner, has been more strongly influenced by Berlioz and Wagner. Gustav Mahler is also, to a certain extent, a disciple of Bruckner. Mahler's symphonic writing, which was at first miscalled " programme-music," employs the expressive power of voice and chorus to the utmost possibility. In Bruckner this striving to expression leads to unity; but whereas Bruckner's religious and mus. feeling do ultimately find this unity, Mahler is unable to overcome the dualism that affects both man and artist, and the discord in his personality cannot be harmonised. With Reger it is the same.

Mahler, in his 9th symphony, as well as in the technical sense, is the father of the " modern German" comprs. . The "moderns " vigorously oppose all Romanticism; they are antagonistic to programme-music; they are intent on pure music alone, and they hold in horror all excessive orch. means, contenting themselves, as is the case all over Europe, with the " chamber orch." The foremost of these in Germany is R. Stephan (music for orch., music for vn. and orch.). Such music strives beyond pathos towards pure expression, and endeavours to pass beyond duality to unity, and beyond the artificial to what is truly natural. It reflects the spirit of the age with fanatical, self-destructive, and contemptuous fury (E. Erdmann, *Symphony*; Hindemith, *Music in* 1921). It seeks inspiration from times of greater stylistic power, as in the case of Busoni, who draws on Bach and the masters of the Rococo period; it hopes with still more polyphony to realise the new Gothic style, *e.g.* Heinrich Kaminski and Ernst Křenek. But these musicians have not yet discovered the unity after which they are striving, nor is this unity to be discovered along the side-track of Impressionism, Neo-classicism or parody, as attempts in other countries have shown.—A. E.

GERMAN SONG FROM 1880. The development may be considered under two aspects—the cultural and social, and the musical and formal. Under either aspect the songs of Brahms form the central point; since they are to a certain extent the continuation of the great Romantic heritage of Schubert and Schumann, which by no means came to a sudden end in 1880. Brahms's songs from op. 84 up to the *Vier ernste Gesänge*, op. 121, actually fall in this later period. They are the songs of concentration, of sustained feeling, of inwardness, of home life and particularly of intimate and small circles. It is highly significant that Brahms, through his German Folk-Songs published in 1894, and through his pf. accompaniments, made popular as household music the simple Ger. folk-song, which had hitherto had its natural setting either as unacc. song or as chorus. Thus arose two types of song with characteristics strongly differentiating them from the Brahms song of sentiment:

(1) songs of companionship and open air, and (2) songs for the concert-hall. There are many points of connection between these two types; and numerous songs stand midway. The type we have called songs of companionship, which is sung by groups of people on excursion in the open air, is a specific phenomenon of last 30 years. Arising out of Ger. folk-song, it has become the lute or guitar song, and primarily the song of young people. Along with the reproduction and adaptation of old masters, there has arisen a body of orig. song by such comprs. as Robert Kothe and Fritz Jöde. The chief feature is its simple, national character. In this connection should be mentioned Ger. choral music, both for mixed and male vs. Music for mixed vs., in so far as it is not the reproduction of xvi and xvii century works, or of the Romantic school (Mendelssohn, Schumann, Silcher), has in latter times been cultivated by only a small number of minor comprs. (Arnold Mendelssohn; Erwin Lendvai). Male-voice choruses cultivate partly the simple form of song; partly also (as a consequence of institution of singing competitions), the more elaborate and picturesque choral ballad, of which the Ger. Swiss, Friedrich Hegar, has written the best-known examples. The whole repertoire of choral music, sung in Germany to-day, has been compiled in the so-called *Kaiser-Liederbücher* (*Emperor Song Books*) for male chorus (1906), and for mixed chorus (1915). The concert-song approximated more to the Brahms song of sentiment. Its first great representative was Hugo Wolf. The lyrical intimacy suffers somewhat through the consideration for dramatic characterisation, which demands declamation and requires a public. The song with orch. acc., which began with Hugo Wolf who himself orchestrated a number of his songs, strives for greater lyrical or pseudo-dramatic expansion, and to it almost all the Ger. symphony-writers have turned their attention (Mahler, Strauss, Hausegger, Pfitzner, Braunfels). Quite recently a preference for lyrical expression with chamber-music acc. and in cyclic form has shown itself. The feeling and desire for a new intimacy have reasserted themselves.

From the mus. and formal standpoint the contrast between Brahms and Wolf is as interesting and instructive as the contrast between Brahms and Liszt. Brahms's songs are on the basis of song in verses, with a clear-cut melody intimately connected with the bass; the accompaniment, while giving character, is not unduly prominent. In Wolf also a clear-cut melody and the verse-form are to be found; but in his hands the accompaniment is as worthy and important as the melody. It is conceived symphonically and constructed on " motives," and its function is to provide characterisation and tonal painting. The clear-cut nature of the song is preserved, not so much through the melody as through the " motival " unity in the accompaniment. Wagner's influence even penetrates to Ger. song: in its declamatory and harmonic tendency nearly every one of Wolf's songs, although Wolf himself did not write the words, became a musico-poetic work of " combined" art, which attained " redemption" in a six-four chord. In marked contrast to Brahms was Franz Liszt; for he rejected the song-form, and adopted a rhapsodic freedom for his song which recognised as its only law the lyrical declamation that went hand in hand with the text.

All three tendencies have further developed in the Ger. song, but they have not preserved their original independence, having largely intermingled Wolf alone has found direct imitators, among them Joseph Marx, Theodor Streicher, Otto Vrieslander. On the other hand, the individuality of the Liszt song, transmitted by Alexander Ritter, who has written some highly original songs, despite their declamatory and motival simplicity, has been entirely transformed by Richard Strauss. In addition to the passionate swing of his melody and the wealth of colour and motive in his accompaniment, Strauss in his later works has sought to produce songs of a " coloratura" style. In company with Strauss stands the founder of the Munich school, Ludwig Thuille, in whose train as song-comprs. are to be found Beer-Walbrunn, Schillings, Boehe, Walter Courvoisier, and H. K. Schmid. Max Reger stands quite apart; for he despises a directly illustrative accompaniment, preferring an organic one, frequently overloaded, and allowing the melody to dissolve into melodic " prose." Hans Pfitzner likewise stands by himself. He goes back to the intimate form of lyric associated with Schumann, only he pushes it to the extreme of romantic and introspective ecstasy. The Swiss compr. Othmar Schoeck even goes back to the Schubert style of song. A kind of protest against the harmonic and motival over-refinement and complexity of the post-Wagnerian song is to be observed in the deliberate return to the verse-song and its simplicity, as manifested by Alfred Heuss, Armin Knab, Hermann Bischoff, and to a certain degree by Gustav Mahler. Occupying an intermediate position are the countless song-writers — and there is no Ger. musician who has not written songs—who have chiefly cultivated the declamatory song, the most prolific and talented among them being Paul Graener, Felix Weingartner, Hermann Zilcher, Julius Weissmann, Richard Wetz, Erich J. Wolff, Hans Hermann, Robert Kahn, H. Kaun.

Characteristic of modern Ger. song is its attitude towards modern Ger. poetry. Hugo Wolf, in contrast to Brahms, who, with exquisite taste, culled from the garden of the whole of Ger. literature, turned to a few favourite poets alone—among them, Mörike, Goethe, Eichendorff—and also to Span. and Ital. folk-song. The mus. generation of Richard Strauss " discovered" the modern lyric as represented by Richard Dehmel, Mackay and others, whereas Reger exercised no taste in his selection. The ultra-modern group of poets such as Mombert, R. M. Rilke, Stefan George, Werfel and Trakl correspond once again to the modern song-

writers, the best representatives of which are Conrad Ansorge, the late Rudi Stefan, and Arnold Schönberg. In such songs, little account is taken of depth of feeling, or of that kind of atmosphere which may be created by picturesque and illustrative means of harmony, melody and rhythm; direct connection with the text is discarded. Indeed, the text serves as stimulus to a kind of " absolute" musical activity. Hence arises a fusion of lyric with chamber music. As example may be cited the song-cycle *Die junge Magd* by Paul Hindemith.—A. E.

GERNSHEIM, Friedrich. Compr. *b.* Worms, 17 July, 1839; *d.* Berlin, 11 Sept. 1916. Pupil Leipzig Cons. 1852; went to Paris for further instruction, 1855; mus. dir. Saarbrücken, 1861; teacher Cologne Cons. 1865–74; appointed prof. by Duke of Saxe-Coburg-Gotha, 1872; dir. Maatschappij Concerts, Rotterdam, 1874; teacher Stern's Cons. 1890–7; till 1904 dir. of Stern Choral Soc. Berlin, and also condr. of *Eruditio Musica*, Rotterdam, from 1897. Member of Senate of R. Acad. of Arts, Berlin, 1897; President of an academical advanced school for composition, 1901.

Chamber-music: 3 pf. 4tets, op. 6, 20, 47; 2 pf. 5tets, op. 35 and 63; trios, op, 28, 37; 3 vn. sonatas, op. 4, 50, 64; 2 cello sonatas, op. 12, 79; str. 4tets, op. 25, 31, 51, 66, 83; str. 5tet, op. 9; 4 symphonies, op. 32 (G mi.), op. 46 (E flat), op. 54 (C mi., *Miriam*), op. 62 (B flat); overtures, *Waldmeisters Brautfahrt* (op. 13), and *Zu einem Drama* (op. 82); pf. concerto, op. 16; 2 vn. concertos (op. 42, D; op. 86, F); *Introduction and Allegro*, vn., op. 38; cello concerto, E mi. op. 78; choral works: *Salamis* (male chorus, barit. and orch.); *Northern Summer Night*, op. 21 (soli, chorus, orch.); *Hafiz* (soli, chorus, orch); *Odin's Sea Ride* (barit., male chorus, orch.); *Watchmen's Song* from *New Year's Eve* 1200 (male chorus and orch.); *The Grave in Busento* (male chorus, orch.); *Prize Song*, op. 58 (Biblical text, for soli, chorus and orch.); *Norn's Lullaby*, op. 65 (chorus, orch.); *Phœbus Apollo* (for same); *Agrippina*, op. 45 (scena for contr. solo, chorus, orch.).—A. E.

GEROLD, Théodore. Fr. musicologist; *b.* Strasburg, 1866; pursued his mus. studies at municipal Cons. there; attended Univ. lectures of Prof. Jacobsthal on musicology. Received lessons from Stockhausen in singing, Humperdinck and A. Urspruch in compn. In 1892, came to Paris to work with R. Bussine, A. Giraudet and Ch. Bordes. Ph.D. of Ger. Univ. of Strasburg (1909); appointed lecturer on musicology at Univ. of Basle (1914–18). Having sustained his thesis for D.Litt. (1921), he now teaches mus. history at Univ. of Strasburg and also in Faculty of Protestant Theology. He has supplied an important contribution to history of ancient song.

Kleine Sängerfibel (Mayence, 1908, 1912, Schott); *Das Liederbuch einer französischen Provinzdame um 1620* (Frankfort-o-M. 1912); *Chansons populaires des XVe et XVIe siècles; Les Psaumes de Clément Marot et leurs mélodies*, with introduction and critical notes (*Bibliotheca romanica*, Strasburg, 1913, 1919, Heitz); *L'Art du Chant en France au XVIIe siècle* (1921); *Le Manuscrit de Bayeux, chansons du XVe siècle* (1921) (Publications of Faculty of Letters, Strasburg), both crowned by Acad. des Beaux-Arts. A vol. on *Schubert* is in preparation (Alcan).—M. L. P.

GESAMTAUSGABEN (Complete Editions). Of the comprs. who come within the scope of this Dictionary, complete editions have been issued as follows: Johann Strauss (sen.) 1887; Berlioz,

1900; Cornelius, 1905; Liszt, 1907 (unfinished); Wagner, 1914.—A. E.

GESELLSCHAFT DER MUSIKFREUNDE (Soc. of Friends of Music). The most important and oldest mus. corporation of Vienna. Founded at instigation of Ignaz v. Sonnleithner, Burgtheater dir. in 1812. First president was Prince Josef Lobkowitz; protector, Archduke Rudolph. This union created (1817) the Cons. for mus. study (now the State Acad. of Music) whose first dir. was the famous Salieri. The second institution of the Soc. was the Singverein, a mixed amateur chorus (now the best in Vienna), founded 1859; and the orch. of the Soc. (amateur too, but afterwards replaced by professionals). These concerts started in 1840; regularly held only from 1859. The present condr. is Leopold Reichwein. The orch. now named Orchesterverein still exists and is cond. by Julius Lehnert. (1) *Concerts.*—1880-4, condr. Wilhelm Gericke (1st perf. Liszt's *Dante Symphony*; Berlioz's *Requiem*). In 1884 Gericke was called to Boston. His place was taken by Hans Richter (1885-90) (1st perf. Bach's B mi. Mass and *Xmas Oratorio*; Weber Centenary Fest. 1886; Handel's *Theodora*). In 1890 Gericke returned and was re-engaged till 1895 (Mozart Fest. 1891; great music and theatre exhibition in Vienna, 1892; 1st perf. Bruckner's F mi. Mass). Succeeded by R. v. Perger, the Rotterdam condr. who preferred mixed programmes. He cond. the memorial concerts for Brahms, Bruckner, Joh. Strauss and the Empress Elizabeth. Ferdinand Löwe cond. 1900-4; then Franz Schalk till 1921 (Centenary Fest. of Soc. 1912, Beethoven Fest. 1920, etc.). In 1922 Leopold Reichwein and Wilhelm Furtwängler cond.; the latter with Schubert Fest. Nov. 1922. The new building, raised by Theophil Hansen in 1870, was damaged by fire in 1885. In 1902 the organ was renovated; in 1907 a new one was built by Rieger (Jägerndorf). In 1912 the architect Richter enlarged the concert-hall. There are also 2 small halls for chamber-music.

Consult: C. F. Pohl, *Die Gesellschaft der Musikfreunde* (1871); A. v. Böhm, *Geschichte der G.d.M.fr.* (1908); R. v. Perger and R. Hirschfeld, *Die G.d.M.fr.* (1909); E. Mandyczewski, *Die 100 jährige G.d.M.fr.* (1912); *Zusatzband für G.d.M.fr.* (1912).

(2) *Other Activities.*—In 1885 the Soc. convened an International Tuning Conference, at which the Vienna normal tuning (A equals 435) was accepted. 1880, the monument of Beethoven (erected by the Soc.) was unveiled; 1888, the body of Beethoven was exhumed and buried in the new central churchyard. The monument of Brahms was also due to the Soc. The library of the music-historian Gerber was bought in 1819; the Spann-Witteczek Schubert coll. and Köchel's Mozart mss. were added in 1877. Brahms left his library to the Soc. (1897); and Nikolaus Dumba, the autographs of Schubert's symphonies (1900). The archive has 35,000 vols. (printed works of XVI and XVII centuries, etc.). The library has 8000 vols.; the museum has colls. of mus. autographs, letters, pictures and mus. instrs. The autographs include some fragments by J. S. Bach, sketch-

books and mss. of Beethoven, 43 mss. of Brahms, pieces by Haydn, Mozart, Schubert and Schumann. The present curator is Eusebius Mandyczewski.—P. P.

GEVAERT; François Auguste. Belgian musicologist, compr. *b.* Huysse (near Oudenarde), 31 July, 1828; *d.* Brussels, 24 Dec. 1908. Of very humble origin. His father was a baker with 10 children; and when quite a child, G. tended cattle. His first mus. education was obtained at church; to this he attributed great importance for his special comprehension of liturgic chant. At 9, he tried his hand at mus. compn. At 10, was sent to Ghent Cons. to study pf. When 15, settled in Ghent as pf. teacher and orgt. 1841, appointed orgt. of Jesuit Church; 1847, obtained successively prize for compn. from Société des Beaux-Arts of Ghent, and *Prix de Rome*. Was allowed to postpone journey prescribed by conditions, and wrote his first two operas. 1859-61, lived in Paris, then a year in Spain, travelled through Italy and Germany, returning in 1862 to Ghent, but soon settled down in Paris. There devoted himself to compn. of several comic operas, which brought him into notice immediately. 1867, repetitor at Grand Opéra (a post created for him and suppressed after his departure). At same time, began to handle mus. literature (theory, history, æsthetics), and soon devoted himself to it exclusively. The war of 1870 caused his return to Belgium, and Fétis having died the following year, he succeeded him as dir. of Brussels Cons., a post which he held till his death (for he had made permanency a condition of acceptance). G. is certainly the man who exercised the preponderating influence on the development of music in Belgium in XIX century. As compr. his rôle was not very great. Most of his works belong to the old Fr. comic opera. He is remarkable, less for inspiration, which in him is not abundant, than for soundness of compn. based on study of classics superior to average of contemporary Fr. works. His happiest mus. idea consisted in development of a popular Franco-Netherlandish melody of XVI century, which he utilised successively in cantata *Jakob Van Artevelde*, in overture to *Capitaine Henriot* and hymn *Vers l'Avenir*. But the importance of G. lies, above all, in his activities as musicologist, organiser of mus. instruction, publ. of ancient works, and finally as orch. conductor. He reorganised tuition in Brussels Cons., and was able to gather round himself a teaching staff of first rank. Thanks to him, the fame of the establishment spread through the whole world. His musicological activity is not less important, and its significance is naturally more durable. To the hypothetical assertions and bold, venturesome conclusions of Fétis, he opposes documentary conscientiousness and compact reasoning. In contrast to Fétis he knew how to restrict the object of his labours and busied himself especially with ancient music and liturgic chant. His works on ancient music may have proved to be erroneous on points of detail, but he had the merit of being the first to transfer these studies from the purely literary and documentary domain, to the firm ground of facts and experiment. In his studies on liturgic chant his dominant idea was to show in Christian art a direct emanation from Greco-Roman music. After *Traité d'Orchestration* of Berlioz, which is rather of an æsthetic character, G.'s is the first work of its kind, drawn up in a really practical way. All the same, his *Traité d'Harmonie* is rather historical and æsthetic than really practical, and the absence of exercises, as well as its novelty, prevent its extensive use. All his writings are to be commended also on account of conciseness, precision and elegance of style, which gives them a real literary value. He brought to light numerous forgotten or unappreciated works. His practical editions of ancient works, with figured-bass parts worked out, hints on expression and performance, historical prefaces, etc., are distinguished by exactness, ingenuity and taste, but disfigured by arbitrariness and by audacious liberties taken with the originals. The effect obtained was more important in his eyes than fidelity to text. The same characteristics of fantasy and arbitrariness naturally marked the concerts of Brussels Cons. under his direction. They were not any the less remarkable from the point of material perfection and expressive warmth of interpretation. Through these concerts (a continuation of Fétis's work) the public of Brussels was brought into contact with all the great works. As a man, G. was distinguished by exceptional intelligence, a prodigious memory and faculty for work (which age could not weaken), by coolness, clear judgment, diplomatic skill, opportunism, inflexible firmness of purpose, implacable will and tyrannical despotism. No other Belgian musician wielded such a power. G. was member of the Acad.; bore the title of Precentor to the Court: in 1907 he was made a Baron.

Orig. compns.: Stage-works (where no indication to contrary, *opéra-comique* is to be understood): *La Comédie à la Ville*; *Hugues de Zomerghem*, opera (1848); *Georgette* (Paris, 1853); *Le Billet de Marguerite* and *Les Lavandières de Santarem* (Paris, 1855); *Quentin Durward*, opera (Paris, 1858); *Le Diable au Moulin* (Paris, 1859); *Le Château Trompette* (Paris, 1860); *La Poularde de Caux* (in collab., Paris, 1861); *Le Capitaine Henriot* (Paris, 1869). Vs. and orch.: *Belgie*; *Le Retour de l'Armée* (for fest. of Napoleon III at Opéra, 1859); *Jacques Van Artevelde*; *Super Flumina*; *Requiem*; Mass, children's vs., and other religious works. About 30 male choruses, unacc., *Fantaisie espagnole*, orch., and *Flandre au Lion* (brass band).

Transcriptions and eds.: *Transcriptions classiques*, for small orch. (Durand); *Chorals latins et français*, 4-v. unacc. (Lemoine); *Les Gloires de l'Italie*, choral pieces of XVII and XVIII centuries, transcribed with acc.; *Répertoire classique du chant français*, a vast collection of Fr., Ger. and Ital. airs (Lemoine); scores from Gluck; Bach's *St. Matthew Passion*, with acc.

Theoretical and other works: *Vade Mecum de l'Organiste* (Ghent, n.d.); *Leerboek van den Gregoriaenschen zang* (Ghent, 1858); *Méthode pour l'enseignement du plain-chant et la manière de l'accompagner* (Ghent, 1857); *Traité général d'instrumentation* (Paris, 1863), which became later on the *Nouveau Traité d'instrumentation* (1885); *Histoire et théorie de la musique de l'antiquité* (Ghent 1875–81); *Les*

Origines du chant liturgique de l'Église latine (ib. 1890); *La Mélopée antique dans le chant de l'Église latine* (ib. 1895); *Id. Appendice* (1896); *Les Problèmes musicaux d'Aristote* (Paris, 1899); *Traité d'harmonie* (Paris, 1905–7); reports, memoirs, prefaces, addresses and articles.—E. C.

GEWANDHAUS CONCERTS, Leipzig. See SOCIETIES.

GEYER, Stefi (Schulthess). Hungarian violinist; *b.* Budapest, 23 June, 1888. Stud. under Hubay at R. High School for Music, Budapest.—B. B.

GHIGNONI, Alessandro. Ital. churchmusician; a Barnabite monk; *b.* Rome, 1857; graduated in 1885 at Univ. in that city. A scholar in matters relating to sacred music, he took an important part in reform movement which led to new direction marked by the *Motu Proprio* of Pope Pius X. G. assisted by first founding in Genoa a soc. for that purpose, and then by starting in Florence a periodical entitled *Palestrina*. Many publications by G. relating to music in general, and to sacred music in particular.—D. A.

GIANNEO, Miguel. Violinist; *b.* Buenos Ayres in 1888. Stud. at Cons. there. Founded (with Carabelli and Schirmi) the first genuine Argentine trio, now a famous one.—S. G. S.

GIBBS, Cecil Armstrong. Eng. compr. *b.* Great Baddow, Essex, 10 Aug. 1889. Educated Winchester Coll. and Trin. Coll. Cambridge. Stud. under Edward J. Dent and Dr. Charles Wood at Cambridge; later, under Dr. Vaughan Williams and Dr. Adrian Boult at R.C.M. London. G.'s music is pleasing, scholarly and well-finished. It has sensitiveness and delicate imagination; is obviously out of sympathy with the revolutionary tendencies of many contemporary comprs.; in spirit it shows a curious similarity to the work of Howells (*q.v.*) who has done for chamber-music what G. has done for song (especially with de la Mare's poems).

Music to Æschylus' *Oresteian Trilogy* (Cambridge, 1921; Goodwin & Tabb); incidental music to Maeterlinck's *The Betrothal* (Gaiety Theatre, London, Jan.–April, 1921; B. Feldman & Co.); music to *Crossings*, fairy-play by de la Mare, 1919; *The Blue Peter*, comic opera, op. 50, book by A. P. Herbert (Carnegie award, 1924); *Midsummer Madness*, op. 51, a mus. play by Clifford Bax, 1923; *A Vision of Night*, symph. poem, orch. (ms. 1922); concerto, ob. and orch. op. 48 (1923); *Before Dawn* (de la Mare), chorus, str. orch. organ (Boosey, 1923); *The Enchanted Wood*, str. op. 25 (Cobbett Prize, 1920); *Pastorale*, str. (1916); *Dance Rhapsody*, str. and pf. (Cobbett Prize, 1920); 5 str. 4tets: G mi. (1 movement); A mi. (both ms.); E ma. (Goodwin); C (*Pastoral*), ms.; *Country Magic*, vn. cello, pf. (Goodwin, 1923); *Phantasy*, vn. and pf. (1915, Goodwin); vn. sonata (1919). Pf.: *Essex Rhapsody* (ms.); *Everyday Doings* (Stainer & Bell); 3 Sketches (Elkin); *Five o'clock* and *Cuckoo Flowers* (Goodwin). Many part-songs; over 40 songs (mainly Walter de la Mare). (Publ. Curwen, Elkin, Enoch, Goodwin, Boosey.)—E.-H.

GIBERT, Vincens María de. Span. orgt. and compr. *b.* Barcelona, 1879. Stud. under Luis Millet, Barcelona, and at *Schola Cantorum*, Paris. Prof. of Orfeó Catalá; author of church music, songs, *Marines* (full orch.).—P. G. M.

GIEBUROWSKI, Waclaw. Church musician and writer; *b.* Bydgoszcz, Poland (formerly Bromberg in province of Posen, Germany), 6

Feb. 1876. Becoming a priest, stud. church music in Ratisbon under Haberl and Haller, and afterwards history of music in Berlin under Wolf and Kretzschmar and in Breslau under Otto Kinkeldey. Ph.D. 1914. In 1914, condr. of the Cath. choir in Posen and prof. of church music at the Theological Seminary there, and also condr. of the Oratorio Society.

Musica Magistri Szydlovite, a Polish mus. treatise of xv century (1915, Ger.); *Gregorian Chorals in Poland in the XVI and XVII Centuries*, with special reference to the Medicean, Vatican and Piotrkov choral eds. (1922). Comp. motets and cantatas for church use.—ZD. J.

GIESEKING, Walter. Pianist; *b*. Lyons, 5 Nov. 1895. Son of a German medical practitioner; was brought up on Fr. and Ital. Rivieras; received first systematic instruction in pf. from Karl Leimer at Hanover Cons., his parents having removed to that town in 1911, in which he now lives as a highly gifted concert-pianist and especially as an interpreter of modern Impressionist and Expressionist composers. First London appearance, Oct. 1923. His songs, pf. pieces and a 5tet for pf. and wind instrs. are in ms. —A. E.

GIGLI, Beniamino. Ital. tenor singer; *b*. Recanati, 20 March, 1890. Pupil of R. Liceo Mus. di Santa Cecilia, Rome, under Enrico Rosati and Antonio Cotogni. *Début* at Rovigo, 1914, in *Gioconda*; then went to La Scala, Milan; thence to principal theatres in Europe and America. One of best and most noted of living Ital. tenors. At present, his activities are chiefly centred in U.S.A.—D. A.

GIGOUT, Eugène. Fr. orgt. and compr. *b*. Nancy, 23 March, 1844. Pupil of École Niedermeyer, where he knew Saint-Saëns, who became his organ-teacher. Having married the daughter of Niedermeyer, he became prof. in the latter's Inst. At the same time, became titular orgt. of church of St.-Augustin (1862). 1886, founded a school of organists, subsidised by the State. Has publ. a large number of organ works for concert use and for church service, notably *Album Grégorien* (300 interludes) and 100 pieces in the old modes for service use.—A. C.

GILBERT, Henry Franklin Belknap. Amer. compr. *b*. Somerville, Mass., U.S.A., 26 Sept. 1868. Stud. in Boston in 1888 under Mollenhauer (vn.), Howard and Whiting (theory); 1889–93 under MacDowell (compn.). Engaged for some years in business and foreign travel; returned to more serious mus. activity about 1901, following in his compns. the national folk-music movement, inaugurated by the projectors of the Wa-Wan Press, making use of Indian and still more of negro themes. G. has frankly and avowedly adopted " rag-time " rhythm as a medium of art expression. *The Dance in Place Congo*, a ballet-pantomime of old New Orleans, was produced at Metropolitan Opera, New York, 23 March, 1819. His orch. suite *Six Indian Sketches*, 1st perf. by Boston Symphony Orch., 4 March, 1921. Also:

2 Episodes for orch. op. 2 (Gilbert, 1897); *Negro Rhapsody* (1st perf. Norfolk [Conn.] Fest., June 1913) (Gray, 1915); *Uncle Remus*, American dance for

orch. with pf. (Boston Mus. Co. 1919); symph. prologue, *Riders to the Sea* (1st perf. Peterboro [N.H.] Fest., 20 Aug. 1914) (Schirmer, 1919); *Comedy Overture* on negro themes (comp. 1906; revised, 1909, 1st perf. by Kaltenborn at Central Park, New York, 17 Aug. 1910) (Gray, 1912); *Humoresque* on negro minstrel tunes, for orch. (*id.* 1913); *Five Negro Dances* for pf. (*id.* 1914); songs (Wa-Wan Press). —O. K.

GILBERT, Jean. Pseudonym of Max Winterfeld. Ger. operetta compr. *b*. Hamburg, 11 Feb. 1879. Pupil of Xaver Scharwenka; condr. Bremerhaven, 1897; Hamburg, 1899; later Apollo Theatre, Berlin. Since 1910 has devoted himself entirely to composing operettas and burlesques, many of which have been extensively perf. (*Polnische Wirtschaft*, Berlin, 1911). His *Lady of the Rose* had a long run at Daly's, London, 1922–3.—A. E.

GILL, Allen. Eng. condr. *b*. Devonport. Stud. cello at R.A.M. London; now prof. there; condr. Alexandra Palace Choral and Orch. Soc.; Nottingham Sacred Harmonic Soc.; prof. of singing. Has done much fine work with choruses and orchestras in and around London.—E.-H.

GILLES, Constantin. Fr. compr. Pupil of Xavier Leroux and Paul Vidal; finished his studies at *Schola Cantorum*.

Orch.: *Suite pastorale* (1899); *Titania* (1903); *Funérailles d'Imogène*; *La Tempête* (after Shakespeare); *La Revue Nocturne* (after Zedlitz); opera, *La Mort du Duc d'Enghien*; sonata, vn. and pf. (1909); songs.—A. C.

GILMAN, Lawrence. Amer. author, critic; *b*. Flushing, New York, 5 July, 1878. Self-taught in mus. theory, history, pf., organ and compn. Music critic of *Harper's Weekly*, 1901–13; its managing ed. 1911–13. Since 1913, connected with *North American Review* first as mus. and dramatic critic, later as associate-ed., replacing its ed. Col. George Harvey, when the latter went to England as ambassador of the United States in 1921. In April 1923, appointed mus. critic to *New York Tribune* (in succession to late H. E. Krehbiel). In addition to his books, G. has written attractive and illuminating programme notes for the concerts of Soc. of Friends of Music, New York, for National Symphony Orch. (1919-1921); since 1921 for Philadelphia Orch. and from 1922 for Philh. Orch. in New York as well. Member of National Inst. of Arts and Letters.

Phases of Modern Music (Harper, 1904); *The Music of To-morrow* (Lane, 1907); *Stories of Symphonic Music* (Harper, 1907); *Guide to Debussy's Pelléas and Mélisande* (Schirmer, 1907); *Aspects of Modern Opera* (Lane, 1908); *Life of Edward MacDowell* (Lane, 1909), an expansion of his vol. in Lane's series; *Living Masters of Music* (1906); *Nature in Music* (Lane, 1914).—O. K.

GIL-MARCHEX, Henri. Fr. pianist; *b*. Saint-Georges d'Espéranche (Isère), 1895. The chief hope of the younger school of Fr. pianism. Stud. at Paris Cons.; pupil of Diémer and Cortot. After an Amer. tour in 1913, appeared as soloist at Lamoureux and at Pasdeloup concerts, Paris, and at Queen's Hall, London. Was the interpreter of Fr. works at Salzburg International Festival of Chamber-music, 1923. —A. C.

GILSE, Jan van. Dutch compr. *b*. Rotterdam, 11 May, 1881. Stud. under Franz Wüllner in

Cologne, 1897–1902; 1902, prize of Beethoven-Haus, Bonn, with his 1st symphony; 1902, stud. in Berlin under Humperdinck; 1905–8, condr. of Opera House, Bremen; 1908–9, condr. at Amsterdam; 1909, won Michael Beer Prize, Acad. of Arts, Berlin, with 3rd symphony. Lived in Rome, Munich, Amsterdam, Utrecht (1917–22, condr. of Utrecht Symph. Orch.).

5 symphonies: No. I, comp. 1900 (perf. Cologne, 1900); No. II, 1903 (perf. Amsterdam, Concertgebouw, 1904); No. III, 1905–6 (perf. Munich, 1908); No. IV, 1914 (perf. Amsterdam, 1915; publ. Kistner Leipzig); No. V (1922–3); cantata *Sulamith (The Sulamite)*, chorus and orch. (1902), perf. Arnhem, 1903; *Eine Lebensmesse* (R. Dehmel), 1904, perf. Arnhem, 1911 (publ. Kistner, Leipzig); Variations on a St. Nicholas song, orch. (1909), perf. Amsterdam, 1910 (publ. Noske, The Hague); overture (1899), perf. Cologne; opera, *The Widow of Stavern* (1911–13); nonet for str. and wind (1916); songs with pf. and with orch.; 2 small studies, *Problem of a National Dutch Opera* and *Holland and Correct Performances*.—W. P.

GILSON, Paul. Belgian composer; *b.* Brussels, 15 June, 1865. His parents then removed to village of Ruysbroek, near Brussels, where he learnt elements of music from the village organist, coming under the tuition of Duyck, a teacher of the Fétis school, with whom he completed his theoretical studies. In 1886 Gevaert undertook his final tuition. Awarded 1st *Prix de Rome*, 1889. His real popularity dates from the performance of his symphonic poem, *La Mer*, in 1892. Appointed professor of practical harmony at the Brussels Conservatoire, 1899, and of harmony at the Antwerp Conservatoire in 1904, resigning both (1909), to become inspector of musical education in Belgium. Musical critic of *Soir* (1906–14) and musical review *Le Diapason*. One of the most distinctive personalities of the Flemish school of the present day. During one period his work showed signs of the dual influence of the Neo-Russian school (*La Mer*) and of Wagner (oratorio, *Francesca da Rimini*). Since then he has affirmed his right to be considered a truly Flemish artist, by the vigour of his expression and the richness of his polyphony, as also by a certain reserve, which distinguishes the Flemish musicians from their Walloon contemporaries, in their relation to musical modernism, especially as regards form and harmony. A distinctive feature of Gilson's art is the skilful and sumptuous orchestration.

Stage-works: *Prinses Zonneschijn* (Antwerp, 1903); *Zeevolk* (Antwerp, 1905); *Rooversliefde* (Antwerp, 1906); *Mater Dolorosa*. Melodramas: *Liefdebloed*; *Alvar*. Ballet: *La Captive* (Brussels, 1904); *Légende Rhénane*. Soli, chorus, orch.: *Sinaï (Prix de Rome* cantata, 1889); *Francesca da Rimini* (1892); *Que la lumière soit* (1896); *Inaugural Cantata* (1897); Cantata for 50th aniv. of Brussels *Cercle artistique* (1889). Orch.: Scotch Dance and Rhapsody; *Andante and Presto* on Brabant theme; *Canadian Rhapsody*; *La Mer* (symph. sketches), 1890; Inaugural fanfare; 3 overtures; 8 suites; *Italia, La Destinée* (symph. poems); Festival March; *Slavonica* (2 dances); *Cavatine*; *Ballet Suite*; *Rustic Suite*; Variations; Symph. Variations; Inaugural Symphony (1912). Str. orch.: 3 Scotch melodies; *Pizzicati*; *Zabava*; *Sérénade de Torcello*; 2 Flemish melodies; *Prelude and Scherzo*; Elegy; *Alla Marcia* (rhapsody). Many works for brass instrs. (fanfare) or military band (several for combined brass instr. classes of Brussels Cons.); Fantasia in Gavotte form; *Scherzo Fantastique*; Variations; *Fackelzug (Torch-light Procession)*; 2 str. 4tets; *Rural Scenes*, str. 4tet; *Les*

Saisons; trio. Recitations with orch. or pf.: *Christine*; *Le Feu du Ciel*; *De Harpspeelster (Harp-player)*; *Wie klopt aan de deur ? (Who knocks at the door ?)*; *Wiegenlied (Cradle-song)*. Chorus and orch.: *Chant de la Forge*; *Derniers rayons*; *Clairières*; 6 Fr. ballads. Unacc. choruses: *Marine*; *French Ballad*. Many songs. Pf.: *Rustic Suite*; *Suite nocturne*; sonatina, etc. Pieces for vn. and pf.; cello and pf.; suite for harp; 2 books of preludes, harmonium; *Norwegian Melody* and 2 *Humoresques* for wood-wind and horns; *Concertstück et Scherzo* in form of a trio for tpts. alone; 2 concertinos for saxophone and orch.; Concertino and *Fanfaluca*, fl. and orch. Educational works: *Les Intervalles*; *Le Tutti orchestral* (studies in the dynamics of the orch.); *Quintes et Octaves*; *Traité d'harmonie* (2 vols.); *Traité de lecture musicale* (4 vols.).—E. C.

GINER Y VIDAL, Salvador. Span. compr. *b.* Valencia, 19 Jan. 1832; *d.* there, 3 Nov. 1911. Prof. and founder (1880) of Valencia Cons.; later, director of same.—P. G. M.

GIORDANO, Umberto. One of most noted Ital. comprs. of operas of last generation; *b.* Foggia, 27 Aug. 1867. Stud. at Naples Cons. under Paolo Serrao. Whilst still young, gave proofs of uncommon aptitude; in Sonzogno Competition, 1888, received mention for an opera called *Marina*. Afterwards there followed the opera *Mala Vita* (perf. in Rome, 21 Feb. 1892); then *Regina Diaz* (Naples, 1894). But it was *Andrea Chénier* (libretto by Luigi Illica) which completely revealed the master; this work had great success at La Scala, Milan, 26 March, 1896, and from that time began his successful round of theatres all over the world. *Fedora* succeeded *Andrea Chénier* in 1898; *Siberia*, 1903; *Marcella*, 1907; *Mese Mariano*, 1910; *Madame Sans-Gêne*, 1915. Finally, in collab. with Franchetti, G. wrote an operetta of the mythological parodical kind, called *Giove a Pompei* (Rome, 1921). His music is publ. by Sonzogno, Milan. In 1924, he completed an opera on *La Cena delle beffe* by Sem Benelli.

Consult: A. Galli, G. Macchi, G. C. Paribeni, *Umberto Giordano nell'arte e nella vita* (Milan, Sonzogno); A. Della Corte, *Madame Sans-Gêne di U. G.*, in the *Rivista Musicale Italiana*, Turin, 1915.—D. A.

GIRALDONI, Eugenio. Ital. barit. singer; *b.* Marseilles, 1871, of parents who were both celebrated singers. For his father, Leone, Verdi wrote *Boccanegra* and *Un Ballo in Maschera*; his mother, Carolina Ferni, was first interpreter in Italy of *L'Africana*. Début at Barcelona, 1891, in *Carmen*; subsequently gained well-deserved fame as one of most skilful and intelligent Ital. actor-singers. Created part of Scarpia in Puccini's *La Tosca*, and that of Lazaro di Roio in Franchetti's *Figlia di Jorio*.—D. A.

GLASENAPP, Karl Friedrich. Ger. Wagnerian author; *b.* Riga, 3 Oct. 1847; *d.* there, 14 April, 1915. Stud. philology and comparative philology at Dorpat; lecturer on German language and literature at Riga Polytechnikum.

Richard Wagner's Life and Work, 2 vols. 1876–7; 3rd ed. under title, *Life of Richard Wagner : presented in Six Books*—I, 1813–43 (1894); II, 1843–53 (1896); III, 1853–62 (1899); IV, 1862–72 (1904); V, 1872–7 (1907); VI, 1877–83 (1911); in English by W. A. Ellis (1900 onwards). He also wrote *Wagner Lexikon, Fundamental Ideas on R. Wagner's Art and View of Life* (with H. v. Stein, 1883); *Wagner Encyclopædia*,

Chief Events in History of Art and Culture in the Light of Wagner's Views (2 vols. Leipzig, 1891, E. W. Fritzsch); *Siegfried Wagner* (1906); *Siegfried Wagner and his Art* (1911); new sequel, *Schwarzschwanenreich* (1913); new sequel II, *Sonnenflammen* (1919): also *Letters of Wagner* (*Bayreuther Briefe*, 1871–83), 1907; *Family Letters to R. Wagner*, 1832–74 (1907). Glasenapp was a contributor to the *Bayreuther Blätter*.—A. E.

GLÄSER, Paul. Ger. compr. *b.* Untermarxgrün (Vogtland), 22 March, 1871. Pupil of his father (cantor in Erlbach near Markneukirchen); at first scholar of Markneukirchen Advanced School of Music under dir. Carl Sachse; then of seminary in Plauen (Lohse and Reissmann); teacher for 3 years in Schöneck; then attended the Leipzig Cons. (Reinecke, Piutti, Homeyer, Zwintscher and Wendling); returned to teaching at Unterlauterbach (Vogtland); since 1901 cantor at Grossenhain (Saxony); has become favourably known by a largely-planned oratorio in a prologue and 4 parts, *Jesus* (soli, chorus, orch. and organ). Also:

3 numbers *Schlichte fromme Weisen* (s. and organ): some numbers of choral preludes and some motets for mixed choirs. A 3-act opera, *The Little Church on the Lake*, was perf. in Altenburg, 1922.—A. E.

GLASGOW ATHENÆUM SCHOOL OF MUSIC. Establ. 1890; the first school of music in Scotland, and is yet the only school in the country under the management of a public board of governors, with the single exception of the Carnegie School in Dunfermline. The curriculum provides a high-class mus. education for those who study the art for pleasure, as well as for those desirous of following it as a profession. While the school has no endowments, it has a number of scholarships, including the Mary Jane Murray Scholarship, which entitles two students to a grant of £100 per annum. A scheme of examinations has been established, on the results of which diplomas and certificates of various grades are awarded. The school is in close association with the R.A.M. London, which co-operates in the appointment of examiners. There is a staff of over 70, and 2436 students matriculated in session 1922–3.—S. S. F.

GLASS, Louis Christian August. Danish compr. and condr. *b.* Copenhagen, 23 March, 1864. Pupil of his father, who was an excellent musician and compr.; later of Niels W. Gade and Cons. Brussels under Zarembski and Servais. A fertile and versatile compr. in all fields of music—chamber, orch., dramatic, besides being an eminent pianist. As compr. he belongs to the conservative wing of modern school, following Bruckner and César Franck. His later works show a strong and vigorous development. They have been given in Stockholm, Christiania, Helsingfors, Berlin, Petrograd (Safonof), Wiesbaden as well as in Copenhagen. He was condr. of Dansk Koncertforening (Danish Concert Association), Copenhagen, 1914–17; chairman of Danish Mus. Artists' Soc. and of Music Teachers' Soc. Copenhagen.

Orch.: *Sinfonia svastica*, op. 57; suite, *Sommerliv* (*Summer Life*), op. 27; fantasy, *Havets Sang* (*Song of the Sea*), op. 54; str. 6tet, op. 15; str 4tet, op. 36; pf. trio, op. 19; sonatas, pf. and vn. op. 7, 29; pf. sonatas, op. 6, 25, 35; music to poem of J. P. Jacobsen, op. 16; numerous pf. pieces and songs (all publ.

Hansen, Copenhagen). Also 4 symphonies; Fantasy, pf. and orch.; 3 str. 4tets (unpubl.).—A. H.

GLASTONBURY FESTIVAL. Founded by Rutland Boughton (*q.v.*), Aug. 1914, in Somerset village of this name. From the inauguration to the end of 1922 311 stage perfs. have been given in addition to concerts and lectures, the greater number of the latter having been on Sunday evenings and without charge for admission. The stage productions have included the following:
1914: *·The Immortal Hour* (Fiona Macleod—Rutland Boughton) (3); *The Travelling Man* (Lady Gregory) (2); *The Night-Shift* (Wilfred Gibson) (2). 1915: *Dido and Æneas* (Purcell) (7); *·Oithona* (Edgar L. Bainton) (4); *The Immortal Hour* (7); *·Bethlehem* (Rutland Boughton) (4). 1916: *Iphigenia in Tauris* (Gluck) (6); *Snow-White* (Margaret Morris—Rutland Boughton) (4); *Everyman* (5); *The Immortal Hour* (3); *·The Round Table* (Reginald Buckley—Rutland Boughton) (3); *·The Sumida River* (Marie Stopes—Clarence Raybould) (3). (School closed from Sept. 1916 to Feb. 1919.) 1919: *The Immortal Hour* (6); *·The Moon-Maiden* (choral ballet by Rutland Boughton) (7); *The Round Table* (3); *The Sumida River* (3); *Everyman* (4); *Cupid and Death* (mask by Matthew Locke and Christopher Gibbons) (3); *Bethlehem* (11); *Snow-White* (4). 1920: *Venus and Adonis* (mask by John Blow) (7); *The Immortal Hour* (12); *The Round Table* (4); *·The Birth of Arthur* (Buckley—Boughton) (4); *Dido and Æneas* (6); *·Music Comes* (choral ballet by P. Napier Miles) (10); *The Moon-Maiden* (4); *·The Children of Lir* (ballet by Adela Maddison) (6); *Bethlehem* (13). 1921: *Dido and Æneas* (14); *Music Comes* (14); *The Moon Maiden* (16); *The Immortal Hour* (16); *·All Fools' Day* (Baretti—Carey) (3); *·The Fairy* (Housman) (3); *·The Death of Columbine* (Boughton) (3); *Spreading the News* (Gregory) (3); *Bethlehem* (7). 1922: *The Trachiniæ* (Sophocles) (2); *·Alcestis* (Boughton) (6); *Venus and Adonis* (3); *Bethlehem* (14).
The figure in parentheses indicates number of perfs. The asterisk (*) shows the 1st perf. of the work.—E.-H.

GLAZUNOF, Alexander Constantinovitch (accent *3rd syll.*). Russ. compr. *b.* Petrograd, 29 July/10 Aug. 1865. Became in 1879, upon Balakiref's recommendation, a pupil of Rimsky-Korsakof, and during the first period of his studies and creative activities (for Glazunof, one of the most precocious comprs. that ever lived, began to write music, and music of a kind which compelled attention, almost as soon as he began to study the theory and practice of his art) he received a good deal of advice from Balakiref himself. In 1882 Balakiref cond. at Petrograd the 1st perf. of his symphony in E (op. 5); at that time he had already written a str. 4tet, a pf. suite (op. 2) and an orch. overture on Greek folk-tunes (op. 3; a second, op. 5, was written in 1883), all of which evince an extraordinary maturity of technique and outlook. Three years later, he had completed his tone-poem *Stenka Razin* (op. 13), a suite and several other orch. works, a second str. 4tet, and an overture for Shakespeare's *Tempest*, besides other things which were publ. later only. His splendid second symphony (op. 16) was finished in 1886; and among his other early works, special mention should be given to his *Oriental Rhapsody* (op. 29).

In all these works G. is seen subscribing to the ideals of the school of Glinka and Balakiref, strongly influenced by Borodin, and at times not a little by Wagner (as shown for instance, by his tone-picture *The Sea* [op. 28]). Later, he came under various influences, among them, perhaps, that of the Ger. school of " pure " symphonists.

The result is that there exists a marked difference of character between the early part of his output and the later. He evinces a growing interest in the possibilities of " working-out," at which he was from the outset an adept, as shown by his early symphonies and by *Stenka Razin*, for instance; and, almost alone among Russ. comprs., he likes to exploit, at least occasionally, the " cyclic form " (*e.g.* in his 2nd pf. sonata). He no longer writes tone-poems, but chiefly symphonies (of which 8 exist), and chamber-music. Instr. music of all kinds (including 3 ballets, *Raymonda* [op. 57], *Ruse d'Amour* [op. 61] and *Les Saisons* [op. 67], and incidental music to Wilde's *Salome* and to *The King of the Jews*, a play by the Grand Duke Constantine) occupy the chief place in his output. In 1900 he was appointed prof. at Petrograd Cons., and in 1906 dir. of that inst. His works are publ. by Belaief. Consult V. Belaief's *A. C. G.* (Russian, 1923).—M. D. C.

GLEBOF, Igor (*accent 1st syll.*). Pen-name of Boris Vladimirovitch Assafief. Russ. mus. writer and compr. *b.* 29 July (n.s.), 1887. Pupil of Liadof. Stud. history and philology at Petrograd Univ. and art history under V. Stassof. G. is most brilliant mus. writer in contemporary Russia, and has a deep philosophical foundation. Librarian at music library of State Opera House, Petrograd; dean of mus. faculty of Art History Inst.; lecturer on mus. history, Petrograd Univ.

Symphonic Études (coll. of essays on Russ. operas, etc.); *Scriabin*; *Tchaikovsky*; *Chopin*; *Rimsky-Korsakof*; many booklets for opera and concert perfs. (State Petrograd Opera House and Philh.) Contributor to *Muzika*; *Mus. Contemporary*; *Melos* (Petrograd) of which he was ed.; *Towards New Shores.* Has comp. a ballet, *White Lily*; songs; incidental music for plays.—V. B.

GLEESON-WHITE, Cicely. Eng. operatic s. singer; *b.* Christchurch, Hants. Stud. under Anna Williams at R.C.M.; sang in 1st perfs. in Edinburgh and Glasgow in *Apostles* at Elgar's recommendation; Three Choirs fests. 6 years in succession; R. Opera, Covent Garden, 1906–7 (Wagner; Gluck); chief choral fests.; R. Carl Rosa season; Covent Garden, 1909; Beecham season, 1910; Denhof tour, 1911; Quinlan opera, 1912; Beecham tour, 1913 (Kundry in *Parsifal* under Balling at Manchester). Chief rôles: Isolde, Brünnhilde, Elektra, Princess (*Rosenkavalier*), Senta (*Flying Dutchman*), Elizabeth, Fidelio, Donna Anna. Married Lieut. George Miller (dir. mus. Grenadier Guards). —E.-H.

GLENCK, Hermann von. Compr. condr. *b.* Zurich in 1883. Stud. compn. at High School for Music, Berlin, under R. Kahn. After a short activity as opera-condr. at Weimar and Metz, devoted himself entirely to compn. Lives at Zurich. His works show relationship to Strauss and Reger, are finely orchestrated, and give proof of great musical imagination.

Variationen-Suite, full orch.; symph. poem; vn. concerto; str. 4tet; numerous songs and pieces for vn. and pf.—F. H.

GLIÈRE, Reinhold Moritzovitch (*accent on È*). Russ. compr. *b.* Kief, 30 Dec. 1874/11 Jan.

1875. Pupil S. I. Tanéief and Ippolitof-Ivanof, Moscow Cons. (1894–1900); gold medal. For some years, dir. of Kief Cons.; now prof. of compn. Moscow Cons. His str. 6tet, op. 1; *The Sirens*, op. 33; 3rd symphony, op. 42, *Ilia Murometz*, episodes from Vladimir cycle of Russ. ballads (perf. Bournemouth, Sir Dan Godfrey), won Glinka prizes. He is one of the outstanding representatives of the "New Russian" school.

1st symphony, E flat, op. 8; 2nd symphony, C mi. op. 25; 3rd symphony (*Ilia Murometz*) op. 42; symph. poems: *The Sirens*, op. 33, *Trizna* (*Old-Slav Funeral-Feast*); op. 54, *Zaporojzi* (on Repin's picture); str. 8tet, D, op. 5; 1st str. 6tet, C mi. op. 1; 2nd str. 6tet, B mi. op. 7; 3rd str. 6tet, C ma. op. 11; 1st str. 4tet, A ma. op. 2; 2nd str. 4tet, G mi. op. 20; many widely-known songs; pf. pieces. Now at work on ballet *The Sheep's Spring* (after Lope de Vega's *Fuente ovechuna*). (Mostly publ. by Belaief, or Jurgenson.)—V. B.

GLIŃSKI, Mateusz. Polish condr. compr. *b.* Warsaw, 1892. From 1909 to 1913, pupil of Barcewicz (vn.) and of Statkowski and Surzynski (theory) at Warsaw Cons.; 1913-14, under Riemann and Schering in Leipzig; 1914–16, under Glazunof and Tchérepnin in Petrograd. Has worked as condr. in Petrograd and Warsaw. Finished Liszt's ballad *The Blind Singer*. Numerous songs and pf. pieces. Now lives in Warsaw.—ZD. J.

GLOVER, James Mackey. Condr. *b.* Dublin, 18 June, 1861. Deputy-orgt. Dublin Cath.; in France, 1879; mus. dir. at Olympic Theatre, London, 1881; Empire Music-hall, 1885; Palace, 1893; engaged at Drury Lane, and Covent Garden (under Sir Augustus Harris); subsequently condr. Drury Lane for 30 years, and wrote 2 ballets for the Alhambra; comp. and arr. all the Drury Lane pantomimes; now ed. of *The Performing Right Gazette, Theatrical Managers' Journal* and *The Concert World.*—E.-H.

GLYN, Margaret Henrietta. Eng. research scholar and writer on music; *b.* Ewell, Surrey, 28 Feb. 1865. Stud. under Dr. C. J. Frost and Dr. Yorke Trotter (compn.; organ; vn., vla.); has done good work along the lines of natural intuitive rhythmic growth, and also in popularising the Elizabethan virginal music, which she claims as best foundation for school of instrumental composition. She is one of the best authorities on Tudor keyboard music.

Theoretical works: *The Rhythmic Conception of Music* (1907); *The Evolution of Musical Form* (1909); *About Virginal Music* (Reeves, 1924). Pf. ed.: *Simple Eng. Classics* (Lengnick); *Elizabethan Virginal Composers* (I, Gibbons; II, Bull) (J. Williams, 1922); *William Byrd*, Vol. I (W. Rogers, 1923); *Byrd Organ Book*, 2 vols. (Reeves, 1923).—E.-H.

GNECCHI, Vittorio. Italian compr. *b.* Milan, 17 July, 1876. Stud. privately in that city under Saladino, Coronaro and others. Operas: *Virtù d'Amore* (1896); *Cassandra*, (perf. 1905, Comunale Theatre, Bologna, under Toscanini); *Rosiera*, publ. like the others, by Ricordi; not yet perf. There are interesting discussions about *Cassandra*, in connection with several striking similarities between many of the mus. themes in it, and the themes of Strauss's *Elektra*, which was posterior to it. Giovanni Tebaldini publ. in *Rivista Musicale*

Italiana an interesting art. about this, which stirred up much controversy.—D. A.

GNIESSIN, Michael Fabianovitch (*accent 2nd syll. ES*). Russ. compr. *b.* 1883. After studying music at Petrograd Cons. he settled at Rostof-on-the-Don. Then he was for some time at Palestrina and Berlin ; now living in Moscow. His earliest works—and especially the orch. tone-poem *From Shelley*, which bears as epigraph 5 lines from *Prometheus Unbound*—displayed forthwith his sense of style and the strong romantic turn of his imagination. Among the publ. works (Jurgenson) some of the songs and the *Sonate-Ballade* for cello and pf. are very characteristic.—V. B.

GODFREY, Sir Dan. Eng. condr., dir. of music to Bournemouth Corporation since 1893; *b.* London, 20 June, 1868. The Godfrey tradition has been intimately associated with British music for 4 generations. It began with Charles Godfrey, bandmaster Coldstream Guards (1825–63), who left 3 musician sons: the eldest, Dan, bandmaster of Grenadier Guards (1856–96), was the first army bandmaster to receive a commission. The 2nd son, Fred, was bandmaster Coldstream Guards (1863–82). The 3rd son, Charles, was bandmaster Scots Fusilier Guards (1859–68), R. Horse Guards (1868–1904); M.V.O. 1902), 2nd army bandmaster to receive a commission. Dan left 2 sons, the elder, Dan (the subject of this art.), and Harry, bandmaster West Kent Yeomanry. The Godfrey tradition may be said to have culminated in Sir Dan, who was knighted in July 1922 for his services to British music. Sir Dan was educated at King's Coll. School, completing his course in Germany. Entered R.C.M. London in 1884; stud. under Lazarus (clar.), Alfred Caldicott (harmony); remained 3½ years. He also had the advantage of his father's tuition, and stud. under John Hartmann, an expert in military band-orchestration. In 1890, gained bandmastership diploma at R.A.M. Appointed condr. of London Military Band and Corps of Commissionaires Band (appointments held simultaneously). Toured S. Africa in 1891 as mus. dir. to the Standard Opera Co.; later, condr. Globe Theatre, Johannesburg. Returned to England, providing orch. for " Venice in London." 1892. Mus. adviser to Olympia, Ltd., 1893. Contracted with Bournemouth Corporation to supply band of 30 performers for summer and winter season of 1893. Appointed resident mus. adviser and dir. of music, Bournemouth, 1894. Municipality took over control of music in 1896 when " Dan Godfrey's Band " was converted into the Bournemouth Municipal Orch., the first of its kind establ. in England. His permanent settlement in Bournemouth severed his extensive London connection with exception of Covent Garden balls and military band-arrs. for London publishers. The mus. reputation of Bournemouth is based mainly on the high standard of his Symphony Concerts, establ. in 1893. These have been continued together with a series of classical and Popular Concerts, for 28 consecutive seasons (to May 1923) without a break. Total number of symphony and classical concerts given, 1588; works perf. 4428; works by British comprs. 1350, a large proportion being 1st perfs. The foregoing figures relate only to works perf. at the symphony and classical concerts which cover the winter season. Flat pitch was adopted in 1912. Visits of British comprs. to conduct perfs. of own works have been a feature since 1897, when Edward German was first to do so. The Municipal Orch. now numbers 39 permanent members, increased to 50 for special perfs. In May 1911 the Municipal Orch. gave a 1st London concert at the Crystal Palace in the Fest. of Empire. On the same day Sir Dan was entertained at a public dinner in London, given by British composers, Sir Alexander Mackenzie presiding, supported by Sir Hubert Parry and Sir Charles Stanford. The repertoire of the Bournemouth Orch. contains practically every classical symphony, overture, and concerto, with a completely representative selection of modern works. Sir Dan, who is responsible for the complete administration of municipal music in the county borough, controls an expenditure of some £30,000 per annum. In addition to the Municipal Orch. there is also a military band of 22 which plays in the gardens and on the pier. The most ambitious undertaking was the Easter Fest., 1922, when a most important series of concerts resulted in a substantial financial profit. Sir Dan is widely known as a lecturer on music and is an acknowledged authority on military band-transcription. By the long and consistent support given to native comprs., he has done much towards building up the modern renaissance of music in England. During 30 years' work in Bournemouth, has been consistently sympathetic towards British comprs. In 1924, elected Hon. Fellow of R.C.M., and publ. his *Memories and Music* (Hutchinson). An account of 1st 21 years of municipal music in Bournemouth was publ. by the writer of this article in 1914.—H. W.

GODFREY, Gavin. Scottish orgt., condr. *b.* Edinburgh, 1870. Orgt. and acc. to Edinburgh R. Choral Union; teacher of its theory classes which have over 1100 enrolments annually. Ed. of Victorian Ed. of pf. music, and of Edinburgh Ed. of Scottish part-songs.—W. S.

GODFREY, Percy. Eng. compr. *b.* Derbyshire, 1859. Stud. under Macfarren and Prout; gained Lesley Alexander Prize for pf. 5tet, 1900; Musicians' Company Prize for Coronation March, 1902; prize choral ballad, Dover Fest. 1904; military band suite, played by Souza; music-master King's School, Canterbury.—E.-H.

GODOWSKY, Leopold. Polish pianist; *b.* Vilna, 13 Feb. 1870. Stud. pf. in his native city, and, at the age of 9, appeared in public. After brief tour of Russia and Poland, stud. from 1881–4 under Rudorff at Hochschule, Berlin. Toured in U.S.A. 1884–5; went to Paris in 1886 and stud. under Saint-Saëns 1887–90. From 1890 to 1900 teacher and concert-pianist in U.S.A.; then for 9 years in Berlin and, in

1909, dir. of Klaviermeisterschule, Vienna. Since 1912 in U.S.A.

3 concert studies, pf. op. 11 (Schirmer); Studies on Chopin's *Études* (Schlesinger, 1904); pf. sonata (*id.* 1911); *Renaissance*, free transcriptions of old music for pf. (*id.*); *Triakontameron* (30 Moods and Scenes), pf. (Schirmer, 1920); 3 *Symphonic Metamorphoses of Themes of Johann Strauss*, pf. (Cranz); 24 *Walzermasken* (Schlesinger). Ed. of Educational Adaptations for Pf. (St. Louis, 1915, Art Publication Soc.).—J. M.

GOEDICKE, Alexander Fedorovitch. Russ. compr. pianist, orgt. *b.* Moscow, 20 Feb./3 March, 1877. Son of pf. teacher at Moscow Cons. and orgt. of Fr. Ch.; pupil of Pabst and Safonof (pf.), Moscow Cons. (1892–8), gold medal; 1900, Rubinstein Prize, Vienna, for his *Concertstück* for pf. and orch. From 1907, pf. prof. Moscow Cons. His music follows classical lines, but reveals a new pathos and concentration of thought.

Opera, *Virinea* (4 acts, ms.). Orch.: 4 pieces, op. 4 (ms.); dramatic overture, C mi. op. 7; 1st symphony, op. 15; 2nd symphony, op. 16; 3rd symphony, op. 30 (ms.); 6 *Improvisations*, op. 26 (ms.). Pf. 5tet in C, op. 21 (ms.); pf. trio, G mi. op. 14; vn. sonata in A, op. 10; 12 Russ. folk-songs for v. pf. vn. cello, op. 29; many pf. pieces; songs; pieces for various instrs.—V. B.

GOEPP, Philip Henry. Amer. author; *b.* New York, 23 June, 1864. Early schooling and pf. instruction in Würtemberg, Germany. Organ and theory under P. B. Sparks in New York. Graduated A.B. Harvard, 1884, where he took all of Paine's courses in music; and LL.B. Univ. of Pennsylvania, 1887. Since 1892, teacher and orgt. in Philadelphia; 1892, a founder of Philadelphia Manuscript Soc.; 1900–21, wrote programme notes for Philadelphia Orch. A vn. sonata, organ and pf. pieces are still in ms.

Fairy opera, *The Lost Prince* (1910); songs (Presser). Author of *Symphonies and their Meaning*, 3 vols. (Lippincott, 1898, 1902, 1913); ed. of L. C. Madeira's *Annals of Music in Philadelphia* (Lippincott, 1896). —O. K.

GOETSCHIUS, Percy. Amer. author; *b.* Paterson, N.J., U.S.A., 30 Aug. 1853. From 1873–8 stud. under Lebert and Pruckner (pf.), Faisst and Doppler (theory) at Stuttgart Cons., where he taught harmony (1876–85) and history and theory (1885–90). Returning to America, prof. of history, theory and pf. at Coll. of Fine Arts of Syracuse (N.Y.) Univ. 1890–2. Teacher of compn. at New England Cons. Boston, 1892–6. Private teacher in Boston, 1896–1905, and orgt. First Parish Ch., Brookline, Mass., 1897. Since 1905, teacher of compn. at Inst. of Mus. Art, New York. As a teacher he enjoys a well-deserved reputation. His books are works of a conscientious, painstaking thinker, and embody original thought and research. Received title of R. Würtemberg Prof. 1885; and Mus. Doc. *h.c.* Syracuse Univ. 1892.

Sonata in B, pf. (Schirmer, 1908); preludes and fugues, pf. op. 3 and 12 (Bosworth); anthems and *Te Deums* (Schirmer; Woolhouse). Author of: *The Material Used in Musical Composition* (Schirmer, 1889; 14th revised enlarged ed. 1913); *The Homophonic Forms of Musical Composition* (*id.* 1898); *Exercises in Melody Writing* (*id.* 1900); *The Larger Forms of Musical Composition* (*id.* 1915); and other works on cpt., tone-relations, etc. (Schirmer; Boston Music Co.).—J. M.

GOETZE, Marie. Ger. operatic m.-sopr. *b.* Berlin, 2 Nov. 1865; *d.* there, 16 Dec. 1922.

Pupil of Jenny Meyer at Stern's Cons. Sang at Kroll Opera House and at R. Opera House in Berlin; later in Hamburg, New York, Vienna; returning in 1892 to Berlin R. Opera House, to which she belonged till 1920. R. Prussian Court singer.—A. E.

GOETZL, Anselm. Ger.-Czechoslovak compr. *b.* Prague, 20 Aug. 1876; pupil of Fibich in Prague; of Schalk and Adler in Vienna; Ph.D.; since 1912 resident in America.

Opera, *The Ornamental Dolls* (Prague, 1907); operetta, *Madame Flirt* (Prague, 1909); str. 4tet; pf. 4tet; songs.—E. S.

GÖHLER, K. Georg. Ger. compr. condr. and music critic; *b.* Zwickau, 29 July, 1874. Attended Univ. Leipzig, and Cons.; graduated Ph.D. with study on *Cornelius Freundt the composer* (*c.* 1535–91). Deputy-condr. 1897; condr. 1898 of Riedel Soc. In 1903 succeeded W. Stade as Court Orch. condr. Altenburg; 1907–9, Court condr. Carlsruhe; 1909, returned to conductorship of Riedel Soc. and of orch. concerts of newly-founded mus. soc. in Leipzig; 1913, went to Hamburg as dir. to New Opera House and as dir. of Teachers' Choral Union. Condr. symphony concerts of Philh. Choir, Lübeck; 1922, went to Altenburg as opera condr. at Stadttheater.

2 symphonies; orch. suite (G ma.); 3-act comic opera, *Prince Night-Watchman* (191ɔ); many songs; male-voice choruses.—A. E.

GOLDENBERG, Franciszek. Pianist; *b.* Medan-Deli, Sumatra, of Polish parents, 7 Nov. 1896. Stud. under Hans Hermanns, Hamburg, and Arthur Schnabel, Berlin; later, under Demetrius de Messyng, Poland. Début 1915, under Mengelberg; concerts in Holland and Germany; in England 1922–3.—E.-H.

GOLDENWEISER, Alexander Borisovitch. Russ. pianist and compr. *b.* Kishinef, 26 Feb. 1875. Pupil (1889–97) of Pabst and Siloti (pf.), Arensky, S. I. Tanéief, and Ippolitof-Ivanof (theory); 1904–6, prof. at music-school of Moscow Philh. Soc. From 1906 till now, prof. at Moscow Cons.; from 1922, its director. Was a friend of Leo Tolstoy; has written a diary of days spent with him; has publ. many songs. —V. B.

GOLDMARK, Karl. Austrian compr. *b.* Keszthely, 18 May, 1830; *d.* Vienna, 2 Jan. 1915. Started in Vienna as a violinist; attracted attention with an overture, *Sakuntala* (1865). His great success was the opera *The Queen of Sheba* (1875), great in melodic qualities and remarkable for its independent style and exotic colour. Not so free from influences of the time (especially Wagner) was the next opera *Merlin* (Vienna, 1886), nor the later operas, which had no success. A symphony, *Ländliche Hochzeit* (1887), and some of his overtures (*Penthesilea*; *In the Spring*; *In Italy*) have had a great vogue.—EG. W.

GOLDMARK, Rubin. Amer. compr. *b.* New York, 15 Aug. 1872. Nephew of Karl Goldmark. Attended Coll. of City of New York for 3 years. Then went to Vienna, where he heard (1889–91) lectures on philosophy at the Univ. and stud. music under Door (pf.) and Fuchs (compn.).

After his return to New York was a pupil of Josefffy (pf.) and Dvořák (compn.) at National Cons. (1891-3), also teaching pf. and theory at the school. In 1895, went to Colorado Springs for his health, and until 1901 was dir. of Cons. of Colorado Coll. Since 1902, composing and teaching in New York.

His overture *Hiawatha*, comp. 1896, was 1st perf. by Boston Symphony Orch. 12 Jan. 1900. A symph. poem, *Samson* (completed 1913), was also brought out in Boston, 14 March, 1914 (Schirmer, 1916). Another symph. poem, *The Gettysburg Requiem*, was 1st perf. by New York Philh. Orch., 30 Jan. 1919. His latest work, a *Negro Rhapsody* for orch., was produced by New York Philh. Orch., Dec. 1922. In 1910, won Paderewski Prize for chamber-music with pf. 4tet.

Requiem (suggested by Lincoln's Gettysburg Address) for orch. (Schirmer, 1921); 4tet in A for pf. vn. vla. cello, op. 12 (*id.* 1912); trio, D mi., pf. vn. cello, op. 1 (Breitkopf, 1896); vn. sonata, op. 4 (*id.* 1900); pf. pieces (Ditson, 1904, 1908; Schirmer, 1915); songs (Breitkopf, 1900; Ditson, 1904).—O. K.

GOLDSCHMIDT, Adalbert von. Austrian compr. *b.* Vienna, 5 May, 1848; *d.* there, 21 Dec. 1906. The most famous of the Wagner followers, who imitated the exact structure of the music-dramas of that master and achieved great success in the period of the strongest Wagnerian enthusiasm. His chief work is the musico-dramatic trilogy *Gäa*, perf. at Vienna Opera House in 1888. One of his last scenic works was *Die fromme Helene*, comic opera (after W. Busch), perf. Hamburg, 1897. Consult E. Friedegg, *Briefe an einen Komponisten* (*A. G.*), 1909.—P. P.

GOLDSCHMIDT, Hugo. Ger. writer on music; *b.* Breslau, 19 Sept. 1859; *d.* Wiesbaden, 26 Dec. 1920. Stud. jurisprudence, graduated 1884; but left State service same year. Took singing lessons from Stockhausen in Frankfort, after which he gave himself up to studies in music history under dir. of E. Bohn in Breslau. 1903-5, assoc.-dir. of Scharwenka-Klindworth Cons., Berlin. R. prof. 1918. Spent his last years in Nice, on Lake Geneva, and finally Wiesbaden. Was one of the foremost authorities on history of opera in XVII and XVIII centuries.

Italian Vocal Methods of XVII Century (Breslau, 1892); *Vowel System of New High German Professional Singing and of Stage Language* (1892); *Handbook of German Singing Pedagogy* (1st part, 1896); *Studies for the History of Italian Opera in XVII Century* (1901-4, Breitkopf), in 2 vols.; Monteverdi's *Incoronazione di Poppea*; *The Theory of Vowel Ornamentation*, Vol. I, XVII and XVIII centuries to time of Gluck (Charlottenburg, 1907, P. Lehsten); *Wilhelm Heinse as Musical Æsthetician* (1909, in Riemann Fest. Publ.); *History of Musical Æstheticism in XVIII Century* (Zurich, 1915, Rascher); also essays in mus. journals: *Cavalli as a Dramatic Composer* (*Monatsch. für M. Ges.*, 1893, Nos. 4-6); *The Cembalo in the Orchestra of the Italian Opera of Second Half of XVIII Century* (1910, in Liliencron Fest. Publ.); *Introduction of Church Melodies in the Middle Parts of J. S. Bach's Cantatas* (*Z.f.M.* 1920). Also edit. selections of T. Traetta's operas (*D.T.B.* XIV, i, 1914, and XVII, 1917).—A. E.

GOLESTAN, Stan. Rumanian compr. and condr. Winner of the National Prize founded by George Enescu and awarded annually to young Rumanian composers.—C. Br.

GOLOVANOF, Nicolas Semenovitch (*accent 3rd syll.*). Russ. compr. and condr. *b.* 9 Jan. 1891. Stud. at Moscow Synodal School of Music; and at Moscow Cons. (under Vassilenko; gold medal and prize of 1000 roubles for his cantata *The Princess Yurata*; as condr. of Synodal Choir, appeared in Moscow, Berlin and Warsaw; from 1915, chorus-master of Moscow Grand Theatre; from 1819 its condr. Over 32 compositions.

2 operas; symphony, B mi.; symph. works; songs; choruses; church music.—V. B.

GOLSCHMANN, Vladimir. One of the youngest Fr. condrs. *b.* Paris, 16 Dec. 1893, of Russ. parentage. Stud. in Paris (pf., vn., harmony, cpt.); belonged to various orchs. as violinist. In 1919, founded the Concerts Golschmann which have popularised most modern works of Fr. school at the Salle des Agriculteurs, at Salle Gaveau, and at Champs-Élysées Theatre. He came to public notice by producing Milhaud's *Bœuf sur le Toit* (1920) and by his masterly rendering of polytonal music. He cond. perf. in Paris of the *Ballets russes* of Diaghilef (revival of *Sacre du Printemps*, 1920), of Pavlova and of Loie Fuller. Conducts an orch. class at the Sorbonne.—A. S.

GOLTHER, Wolfgang. German Wagnerian author; *b.* Stuttgart, 25 May, 1863. Prof.-in-ordinary of German philology in Rostock. Besides works on history of literature, he wrote:

The Legend of Tristan and Isolde (1887); *Legendary Groundwork of Richard Wagner's " Ring " Poem* (1904); *Bayreuth* (1904); *R. Wagner as a Poet* (1904, English by Haynes, 1907); *Tristan and Isolde in Mediæval Poems and in those of more recent times* (1907); *Wagner's Letters to Mathilde Wesendonk* (Berlin, 1904, A. Duncker), and *to Otto Wesendonk* (1905); *Correspondence between Robert Franz and A. Freiherr Senfft von Pilsach* (Berlin, 1907, A. Duncker.)—A. E.

GOMEZ, Antonio Carlos. Brazilian compr. *b* 1839; *d.* 1896. Amazon-Indian tunes are used in his opera, *Il Guaraney* (Milan, 1870); also comp. opera *O Condor* (Milan, 1891), the national hymn *Il saluto di Bresile* and a cantata *Colombo* (for Rio de Janeiro Columbus Fest. 1892). —F. H. M.

GÓMEZ, Julio. Span. compr. and musicologist; *b.* Madrid, 20 Dec. 1886. Stud. at R. Cons. de Música; former dir. of Museo Arqueológico, Toledo, and Music Department of Biblioteca Nacional. Librarian at R. Cons. de Música, Madrid. Author of historical essays on Span. music of XVI, XVII, and XVIII centuries.

Songs: *Tres melodías*; *Remembranza*; *Coplas de Amores*; *Esperanza*; *Corazón inquieto*. Orch.: Suite in A. (Ildefonso Alier; Faustino Fuentes; Harmonía; Imprenta Clásica; Unión Musical Española, Madrid.) —P. G. M.

GÓMEZ, Manuel. Span. clarinettist; *b.* Seville about 1860; *d.* London, 1920. Stud. his instr. in Seville under Antonio Palatin. Pensioned by Diputación Provincial to continue studies at Paris Cons. Early in his career, took up residence in London. First clarinettist for many years in Covent Garden and Queen's Hall orchs.; also in London Symphony Orch. of which he was a founder. Taught clar. at Guildhall School of Music and elsewhere. He always used a B-flat clar. specially constructed for him, with an extra key (his own device) which, by means of transposition, enabled him to dispense with the other clarinets in playing.—P. G. M.

GOMNÆS, Fredrik Wilhelm. Norwegian compr. condr. *b.* Ringerike, 4 April, 1868. Cello pupil of Hennum (Christiania); harmony of Iver Holter, High School in Berlin (Hausmann and Härtel). For several years, cellist in Christiania Theatre Orch.; 1898, bandmaster in Hamar; 1911, bandmaster (rank of lieutenant) 4th Division, Bergen; 1920, to 2nd Division, Christiania. G. has been instructor of male-v. choral societies (Hamar, Gjövik and Bergen); in 1921, condr. of Christiania Craftsmen's Choral Union.

Symphony, A mi. (National Theatre, 1908); pieces, *Tord Foleson*; *Aasgaardsreien*, etc., for male chorus; songs; fugues for organ; military marches. Has also coll. Norwegian folk-melodies, and his compns. have frequently a national tinge.—J. A.

GONZÁLEZ, Odón. Span. violinist; *b.* Población de Campos (Palencia), 1849. Stud. under José Hierro at R. Cons. de Música, Madrid. Member and founder of Quinteto de Madrid and Cuarteto Francés. Lives and teaches in Madrid. —P. G. M.

GONZÁLEZ AGEJAS, L. Span. musicologist, author of a study on *The Seven Species of Greek Octaves (Las Siete Especies de Octavas Griegas)*, (Madrid, 1908).—P. G. M.

GOODHART, Arthur Murray. Eng. compr. *b.* Wimbledon, 14 June, 1866. A classical assistant-master and House Master at Eton Coll.; stud. music under Sir Joseph Barnby, Dr. G. M. Garratt, W. S. Rockstro, Dr. C. W. Pearce; Cecil Forsyth, Frank Bridge. Works for mus. appreciation amongst boys, by adopting methods of training to capacity, talent and future career of the individual. Believes in the extensive use of gramophone and pianola at school recitals. His music has a fine, manly swing and an easy and good melodic flow. His organ pieces, in particular, are marked by a highly individual taste in tone-qualities and their blending, and he leans towards unusual time-signatures.

Orch.: *Elegy*; *Greek March*; *Concert-Waltz*; *Mowing the Barley*. Choral ballads: *Earl Haldan's Daughter*; *Arethusa*; *Sir Andrew Barton* (all Novello); ode, *Founder's Day* (id.); many part-songs (Novello; Chappell); anthems; carols; hymns; 25 organ pieces (mostly Novello; some by Augener); pf.: 2 sets of variations on *Tipperary*; 7 variations on *The Good-bye of the Berkshires*; works for military band; school songs; solo-songs; etc.—E.-H.

GOODRICH, John Wallace. Amer. orgt. *b.* Newton, Mass., U.S.A., 27 May, 1871. Stud. pf. under Petersilyea in Boston, then at New England Cons. under Dunham (organ) and Chadwick (compn.), then under Rheinberger and Abel at Acad. in Munich, 1894–5. From 1895–6, stud. under Widor in Paris, and from 1896–7 was coach and ballet-condr. at Stadttheater, Leipzig. Returning to America, organ-teacher at New England Cons. Since 1907 Dean of the Faculty, and since 1919 Chadwick's successor as condr. of the excellent orch. of this school. Orgt. of Boston Symphony Orch. 1897–1909, appearing as soloist at its concerts; 1902–9, orgt. Trinity Ch. Boston. 1902–7, chorus–condr. at Worcester (Mass.) fests. Founded Choral Art Soc. of Bos-

ton, 1901, and cond. it until 1907. From 1907–10, condr. of Cecilia Soc.; 1909–12, regular condr. of Boston Opera Co.

The Organ in France (Boston Music Co. 1917); transl. of A. Pirro's *J. S. Bach* (Schirmer, 1902); and of Niedermayer and d'Ortigues' *Gregorian Accompaniment* (Novello, 1905).—O. K.

GOODSON, Katharine. Eng. pianist; *b.* Watford. Stud. R.A.M. London, under O. Beringer; later 4 years under Leschetizky in Vienna; *début* 16 Jan. 1897, at Saturday Popular Concerts; at Richter's London concert, 20 May, 1901 (Tchaikovsky concerto); numerous highly successful tours in Europe and America. Is one of the finest Eng. pianists. She married the compr. Arthur Hinton in 1903.—E.-H.

GOODWIN, Amina Beatrice. Eng. pianist; *b.* Manchester, 1867. Stud. at Leipzig Cons. and with Liszt as a child; later won a scholarship at Paris Cons.; finally under Clara Schumann, becoming a strong disciple of her school; *début* Crystal Palace concert under Manns; toured Italy, England, Holland, Germany with great success; founded the London Trio in 1904 (vn. Pecskai; cello, Whitehouse). A remarkable pianist with a powerful technique.

Book, *Practical Hints on Technique and Touch in Pf.-Playing* (Augener).—E.-H.

GOODWIN, F. & B. Ltd. Publishers. See CURWEN & SONS.

GOOSSENS, Eugène. Belgian condr. *b.* Bordeaux, France, 1867. Early in his career, he settled in England and became well known as an operatic condr. notably for the Carl Rosa Opera Co. In 1922–3 he took *The Beggar's Opera* on tour; in 1924, *Polly*.—E.-H.

GOOSSENS, Eugène. Eng. condr. and compr. *b.* London, 26 May, 1893. The son of a condr. (see above) who, though of Belgian origin, was actually born in France, and settled long ago in England, where all his children were born. He entered the Bruges Conservatoire in 1903, and the Liverpool College of Music in 1906. There he won a scholarship which brought him to the Royal College of Music in London, where his masters were Sir Charles Stanford, Dr. Wood, Rivarde and Dykes. From 1911 to 1915 he was a member of Sir Henry Wood's orchestra. He also played in the Philharmonic String Quartet, and has dedicated his Op. 14 to his three colleagues. In 1915 began his close association with Sir Thomas Beecham which continued until the interruption of the latter's musical enterprises in 1920. One of his first appearances as conductor was in January 1916, when he directed Stanford's *The Critic*, in the character of Mr. Linley of Bath. In the summer of 1921 he formed his own orchestra of carefully picked players, with whom he gave a concert of modern music which established his reputation among the foremost conductors of the day, arousing so much interest that the programme was repeated at the following concert. Since then his services have been in constant demand. He has conducted the British National and Carl Rosa Opera Companies, the Russian Ballet, the London Symphony Orchestra, and many other organisations. He made his first visit to U.S.A. in autumn of 1923, when he conducted the newly formed Symphony Orch. at Rochester. As conductor he combines clarity and precision with brilliance, and his best efforts are produced constructively rather than by impetus. This gives him a wide range of styles. In the spring of 1924, he organised a series of chamber concerts in London.

As a composer his evolution has been remarkably rapid. His first works were performed in 1912 and 1913, but of this early period little remains. He first attracted attention in 1915, chiefly with two trios, one a suite for flute, violin and harp, the other, *Five Impressions of a Holiday*, for piano, flute and cello, both composed during the two preceding years, and already then less representative of him than the Fantasy for string quartet of 1923.

The following year (1916) appeared in rapid succession the Rhapsody for cello and piano, the string quartet in C, the two sketches, *By the Tarn* and *Jack o' Lantern*, which have remained his most frequently played works, and a number of songs. Then followed a change of style which was more apparent than real, for the *Kaleidoscope* and *Four Conceits* (1918) were an amplification of one aspect of his previous work rather than a departure from it, and the violin sonata and piano quintet (1919) which followed them proved that other aspects had been merely in abeyance. With the symphonic poem *The Eternal Rhythm* (1920) this stage may be said to have reached its culmination. Its rapid transitions were only in part due to the throwing off of various early influences. Like all young composers of his generation he absorbed what his seniors, of all schools, had to teach him, but he quickly gave it a personal expressiveness. The apparent vacillation of style had more to do with temperament than with method. Compressed within an unusually short period, the process of finding himself naturally presented sharper effects of action and reaction. His recent works, however, suggest that this process is ended for the present, and that his progress is taking a definite direction. They also refute the charge sometimes made against him that the cold brilliance of some of his earlier works indicated an absence of deep emotion. It was inevitable, and it showed discernment on his part, that he was at first deterred by the turgid emotionalism which had run riot in music, and cautious to avoid its pitfalls, but once sure of himself he soon gave lyrical expression to a vein of personal emotion. His harmonic sense is very keen, and he favours alike a chromatic texture, and the broad strokes of harmonic colouring obtained by the copious use of parallels. Though such works as the sonata reveal a strain of lyrical melody, in most of his songs he subordinates this to the declamatory values of the text, which are enhanced by the accompaniment. His style is at least as much European as it is English, but the humour of such works as *Kaleidoscope* has a national

quality. Though distinctly modern in his musical outlook, he is no revolutionary; or, if he is one, he favours constitutional in preference to subversive methods. Consequently he has found no "ism" nor is he likely to found one; but without inventing special theories he handles his material of sound with a wealth of ingenious resource. His latest works comprise a *Sinfonietta* whose first movements reveals a leaning towards a personal interpretation of Neo-classicism, and a sextet for strings, commissioned for and performed at the Berkshire (U.S.A.) Festival of 1923. Some new pf. pieces, harp pieces and a work for wind instrs. and pf. were produced at his London concerts in April and May, 1924.

Orch.: Variations on a Chinese theme, op. 1 (ms.); *Perseus*, op. 8 (ms.); Symph. Prelude on a poem of Ossian, op. 11 (ms.); *Tam o' Shanter*, op. 17a; *Four Conceits*; *Philip II Prelude*; *The Eternal Rhythm* (ms.); *By the Tarn*; *Silence*, poem for chorus and orch. Suite for fl. vn. and harp, op. 6; *Five Impressions of a Holiday*, pf., fl. or vn. and cello; *Fantasy*, str. 4tet; str. 4tet, op. 14; 2 sketches for str. 4tet (*By the Tarn* and *Jack o' Lantern*); 5tet for pf. 2 vns. vla. and cello; 3 songs for medium v. and str. 4tet; sonata, vn. and pf.; *Lyric Poem*, vn. and pf.; Rhapsody, cello and pf. Pf.: *Concert Study*; *Kaleidoscope*; *Four Conceits*; *Nature Poems*; *Hommage à Debussy*; *L'École en Crinoline* (ballet). Songs: *Deux Chansons*, op. 9; *Deux Proses Lyriques*, op. 16; *Persian Idylls*, op. 17b.; *Afternoon*; *Epigram*; *Tea-Time*; *The Curse*; *The Appeal*; *Melancholy*; *Philomel*. Arr. of folk-songs: *Variation sur Cadet Rousselle*; *Behave yourself before folk*; *I'm ower young to marry yet*. (Nearly all publ. Chester.)—E. E.

GOOVAERTS, Alphonse Jean Marie André. Belgian compr. writer on music; *b.* Antwerp, 27 May, 1847; *d.* Brussels, 25 Dec. 1922. Intended for a commercial career, which he soon abandoned for music. Librarian to City of Antwerp, 1866; and Keeper of the State Archives at Brussels, 1887. His compns. are thrown into the shade by his musicological works, especially by his *Histoire et Bibliographie de la Typographie musicale dans les Pays-Bas* (1880). Though not quite perfect in some respects, this work, and the records it embodies, are very valuable. Other works:

La Musique d'Église (1876); *De muziekdrukkers* (music publishers) *Phalesius en Bellerus* (1882); *Un Opéra français composé en 1770 pour le Théâtre de la Monnaie* (1891); *Le Chevalier L. de Burbure* (1891), etc.—C. V. B.

GORDON-WOODHOUSE, Violet (*née* Gwynne). Eng. harpsichordist and clavecinist; *b.* in Sussex. Stud. pf. under O. Beringer and Schönberger; but gave it up on becaming acquainted through Arnold Dolmetsch with the harpsichord and realising its possibilities in shades and combinations of tone. Played on the instruments for which they wrote, her renderings make the Elizabethan comprs.—Bull, Byrd, Morley—live again. Purcell, Couperin, Rameau, Scarlatti acquire with her a new meaning; but it is as an interpreter of J. S. Bach that she particularly excels. She possesses an xviii century harpsichord, restored by Dolmetsch; but she plays either on one made by him for Gaveau of Paris, or on an equally fine one by him belonging to Lord Howard de Walden. Her 3 clavichords were all made by Dolmetsch.— E.-H.

GOSPEL HYMNS. See SANKEY.

GOSS-CUSTARD, Reginald. Eng. organ recitalist; *b.* St. Leonards-on-Sea, 29 March,
1877. Stud. under his father, Walter G.-C.
Followed Edwin H. Lemare as orgt. St. Margaret's, Westminster, 1902, and carried on his
organ-recitals; resigned 1914; orgt. Bishopsgate
Foundation same year; toured widely; appointed
to St. Michael's, Chester Square, London, Nov.
1922. Toured America 1916. Is one of the
most brilliant and finished of concert-orgts.
—E.-H.

GOSS-CUSTARD, Walter Henry. Eng. orgt.
b. St. Leonards-on-Sea, 7 Feb. 1871. Stud. for
a short time under E. H. Lemare; orgt. Liverpool Cathedral from 1917.—E.-H.

GOUDOEVER, H. D. van. Dutch cellist and
compr. *b.* Utrecht, 12 Nov. 1898. Stud. at
Utrecht Music School (1907–17) under J. Wage-
naar (theory), E. Ferrée (cello); in Paris under
Gérard Hekking (1918–21). Became soloist at
Amsterdam Concertgebouw, 1922.

Allegro for orch. (1916); *La Fête bleue*, cello and
orch. (1917); 3 wordless songs, s. and orch. (1917)
(all perf. Utrechtsch Stedelijk Orch. under Jan Van
Gilse); *Sphynx*, nocturne for orch. (1919); *Impression*, orch. (perf. Amsterdam Concertgebouw Orch.
under Mengelberg, 1920); Suite, cello and orch.
(1922; first perf. New York Philh. Soc. under Mengelberg; solo played by compr.).—W. P.

GOULA, Juan. Condr. compr. *b.* San Felin
de Guixols, Barcelona, in 1843; *d.* Buenos
Ayres, 1915. Commenced his career as choir-
trainer and orch. condr. in Barcelona, and later
in principal theatres of Germany, and at Petrograd and Moscow. Prof. at R. Court of Lisbon.
Dir. the choral soc. Enterpenas de Barcelona
(600 choristers) which he conducted with
brilliant success during a tour through Spain.
Went in 1902 to Buenos Ayres, and establ. a
now famous school of singing. Has publ. a
Catalan opera, *A la voreta del Mar*, perf. at
Teatro Principal, Barcelona.—A. M.

GOUNOD, Charles. Fr. compr. *b.* Paris,
17 June, 1818; *d.* St.-Cloud, 18 Oct. 1893. A
pupil of Halévy, Paër, and Lesueur at Paris
Cons. In 1839 he won *Prix de Rome*, and in
1851 inaugurated his career as opera-compr.
with *Sapho*. *La Nonne Sanglante* followed (1854),
and in 1859 came *Faust*. *Mireille* (on Provençal
poem by Mistral) was produced in 1864, and
Roméo et Juliette in 1867.

Although he has written church music and
other works of religious character (among which
are the oratorios *Redemption* and *Mors et Vita*,
composed with a special view to the British
public and first perf. at Birmingham, 1882, 1885),
his fame rests chiefly upon a few operas, and
especially *Faust*. But other works of his—the
songs, for instance—are equally characteristic
of the highly original trend of his musical
imagination. This imagination is essentially
lyric; and, although somewhat narrow in outlook and, in a measure, subject to surrounding
influences which made for certain trivialities of
style and encouraged his tendency towards sentimentality, it led to happy results by virtue of

which his influence played a leading part in the
further evolution of French music. It is noticeable not only in the music of Fauré and Saint-
Saëns, but in many a feature of Debussy's.

This originality of Gounod, indeed, proved
too much for some of his contemporaries. It is
instructive to note that in 1862, the critic of
the *Revue des Deux-Mondes* branded him as "a
composer who, in company with all the bad
musicians of modern Germany, be they Liszt,
Wagner, Schumann, or even (for certain equi-
vocal things in his style) Mendelssohn, have
drunk at the tainted spring of Beethoven's
last quartets."

Operas: *Faust* (1859); *La Reine de Saba* (in London
as *Irene*), 1862; *Mireille* (1864); *La Colombe, opéra-
comique* (1866); *Roméo et Juliette* (1867); *Cinq-Mars*
(1877); *Polyeucte* (1878); *Le Tribut de Zamora* (1881).
Oratorios: *Gallia*; *Tobias*; *The Redemption* (Eng.),
1882; *Mors et Vita* (1885). *Messe solennelle Ste.-
Cécile* (1882). Symphony, *La Reine des Apôtres*;
Marche funèbre d'une marionnette, etc.—M. D. C.

GOW, George Coleman. Amer. teacher, author;
b. Ayer Junction, Mass., U.S.A., 27 Nov. 1860.
Graduated A.B. Brown Univ. 1884, and in 1889
from Newton Theological Seminary. Stud. music
in Pittsfield under B. C. Blodgett, and in Worcester (Mass.) under E. B. Story. From 1889,
taught harmony and pf. at Smith Coll., Northampton, Mass.; 1892–3, under Bussler in Berlin. Since 1895, prof. of music at Vassar Coll.
(for women) at Poughkeepsie, N.Y. Spent his
vacation year 1922–3 in Europe. Received
degree of Mus.Doc. *h.c.* 1903, from Brown Univ.
Author of *The Structure of Music* (Schirmer,
1895).—O. K.

GRAARUD, Gunnar. Norwegian tenor singer;
b. Holmestrand in 1888. Matriculated in 1906.
Stud. singing mainly in Germany. *Début* in
Christiania, 1920. Appeared in several foreign
opera-houses, at Dresden as *Parsifal* (Wagner),
and in various leading parts at Grosse Volksoper,
Berlin.—R. M.

GRABERT, Martin. Ger. orgt. and compr. *b.*
Arnswalde (Neumark), 15 May, 1868. Pupil of R.
Inst. for Church Music, Berlin, (under H. Beller-
mann, Bargiel); Meyerbeer Stipendium, 1891;
Mendelssohn Stipendium, 1894; condr. theatre
orch. in Rostock, 1894–5. Has since lived in Berlin
as orgt., first at Kaiser-Wilhelm-Gedächnis-
Kirche, then (1898) at Dorotheenstädtischen
Kirche.

Sacred choral music; organ phantasy, C mi. op. 44;
organ variations, E mi. op. 40; pf. 4tet, op. 22; sonata
for ob. and pf., G mi. op. 52.—A. E.

GRABNER, Hermann. Austrian compr. *b.*
Graz, 12 May, 1886. Stud. in his native town at
Cons. of the Steiermark Mus. Soc. At his father's
desire, he also stud. jurisprudence, passing in
1909. In 1910 went to Leipzig Cons. as pupil of
Max Reger (compn.) and Hans Sitt (conducting).
Received Nikisch Prize for his test-works (a
str. trio and a concerto for vn. vla. orch.). In
1912, removed to Meiningen as Reger's assistant;
1913, head-teacher of theory at Strasburg
Cons. After the war and his expulsion from
Alsace, he settled in Heidelberg, as head-teacher
of theory and compn. at Music Acad. and at

High School of Music, Mannheim. He also takes part in concerts as vla.-player.

Numerous songs and choral works; concerto in olden style for 3 violins; Prelude and fugue for organ; a great choral work, *Psalm CIII*; *Funeral Cantata*; Prelude for orch.; 5 vn. and pf. pieces; Variations and fugue on a Bach theme, for orch.; Prelude and fugue, str. 4tet; trio-sonata, vn. vla. and pf. Also wrote essay, *Regers Harmonik* (Munich, 1920, Halbreiter) and *Die Funktionstheorie Hugo Riemann's* (1923).—A. E.

GRACE, Harvey. Eng. orgt., writer, etc. *b.* Romsey, 25 Jan. 1874. Stud. under Dr. Madeley Richardson, Southwark Cath. Ed. of *Mus. Times* (Novello) from 1918 (succeeding Dr. McNaught). His organ music has a strong style, free from sentimentality, without dispensing with poetic sensitiveness.

Organ pieces (2 books, Schott, 1922; Novello; Stainer & Bell; Reid); songs (Stainer & Bell; Reid); part-songs (Novello; Stainer & Bell; E. Arnold); books: *The Complete Organist* (Grant Richards, 1921); *French Organ Music, Past and Present* (H. W. Gray, New York, 1919); *The Organ Works of Bach* (Novello, 1922).—E.-H.

GRÄDENER, Hermann. Ger. compr. *b.* Kiel, 8 May, 1844. Pupil of father, Karl G. P. Grädener (1812–83) and of Vienna Cons. Orgt. at Gumpendorf, 1862; violinist in Vienna Court orch. 1864; teacher of harmony at Horák's Pf. School, 1873; from 1877 at Cons. of the Friends of Music; condr. Viennese Acad. of Singing and of Orch. Soc. for Classical Music, 1892–6; lector in harmony and cpt. at Univ., 1899; pensioned in 1913 as prof. of the Acad.

Capriccio and *Sinfonietta*, op. 14, orch.; Variations, organ, strs., tpt. (1898); vn. concerto, D ma.; cello concerto, E mi. op. 45; pf. concerto, D mi.; str. 8tet; 2 pf. 5tets; str. 4tets, op. 33, 39; 2 trios, op. 16, 19; pieces for trio, and for pf. and vn.; sonata for 2 pfs.; pf. pieces; songs; rhapsody, *The Minstrel* (soli, chorus, orch., 1905); *Saint Zita* (Vienna, 1918), etc.—A. E.

GRAENER, Paul. Ger. compr. *b.* Berlin, 11 Jan. 1872. Sang as boy in R. Cath. Choir. Passed Askanische Gymnasium leaving-examination and entered the Univ., but went over to music. Condr. of theatre orchs. (Bremerhaven, Königsberg, Berlin; London, Haymarket, 1896). Was for some years on staff of R.A.M. in London; then went to New Cons. in Vienna; dir. of the Mozarteum in Salzburg, 1910–13. Next lived in Munich, being appointed prof. in 1920, in which year he succeeded Reger at Leipzig Conservatoire.

Symphony, D mi. op. 39 (*Schmied Schmerz*), orch. (Vienna, Univ. Ed.); *Sinfonietta*, op. 27, str.-band and harp (Vienna, Univ. Ed.); *From Pan's Domain*, op. 22; suite for orch. (Leipzig, Kistner); string 4tets, op. 33 (Vienna, Univ. Ed.) and 54 (Bote & Bock); *Music at Eve*, 3 pieces for orch. op. 44 (Berlin, Eos Verlag); *Romantische Phantasie*, orch., op. 41 (Copenhagen, Wilhelm Hansen); *Kammermusikdichtung*, op. 20, for pf. trio, after W. Raabe's *Hungerpastor* (Leipzig, Kistner); pf. trio, op. 61 (Peters); pf. pieces (3 *Impressionem; Aus dem Reiche des Pan; Wilhelm Raabe-Musik*, op. 58 [Berlin, Bote & Bock]); songs, op. 3, 4, 6, 11, 12, 15, 16, 21, 29, 30, 40, 43a, 43b (*Gallows Songs*), 45, 46, 47, 49, 52, 57; choral songs (*Notturno*, op. 37); Rhapsody for contr., str. and pf., op. 53 (Berlin, Bote & Bock); sonata for vn. and pf. op. 56 (Bote & Bock); Variations on Russian folk-song, orch., op. 55 (Bote & Bock). Graener has been most successful as an opera compr. A mus. comedy, *Der Vierjährige Posten*, op. 1, was never performed (London, Cecilia Music Co.). An opera, *Das Narrengericht (Fool's Tribunal)*, op. 38 (Munich, Drei Masken Verlag), was perf. Jan. 1913, at Volksoper, Vienna. *Don Juan's Last Adventure*, op. 42 (Drei Masken Verlag), Leipzig, June 1914 (and often elsewhere); *Theophano*, op. 48 (Munich, Drei Masken Verlag), in Munich (re-cast as *Byzanz*, Leipzig, 1922); *Schirin und Gertraude*, op. 51 (Berlin, Eos Verlag), Dresden, 1920. Consult Georg Graener's *P. G.* (Leipzig, 1922).—A. E.

GRAF, Ernst. Swiss orgt. compr. *b.* Schönholzersvilen, Canton Thurgau, Switzerland, 26 June, 1886. Stud. (1904–7) modern philology and history at Basle Univ. At same time stud. pf. under Hans Huber, theory under Edgar Munzinger and Georg Häser, organ under Adolf Hamm at Basle Cons., later (1912) under Karl Straube (Leipzig). Since 1912 has given in Berne regular organ recitals with historical programmes; since 1920 has given perfs. of brass instr. music on the Cath. tower, thus reviving the mediæval custom of the *Turmmusiken*; 1917, founded a scientific music library (Students' Library of the Berne Music Soc.). 1922, President of the Vereinigte Ortsgruppe Bern-Friburg-Solothurn of the New Swiss Music Soc. Lecturer on church music to Evangel. Theol. faculty, Berne.

Unacc. choruses (Latin and Ger.) (Leipzig, Leuckart); songs with pf. (Zurich, Hug). Educational works: *Principles of Organ Technique*, 1916–22; *Elementary Tutor of Trio-playing*, 1921 (Verlag des Bern. Organistenverbands, Berne).—F. H.

GRAF, Max. Austrian writer on music; *b.* Vienna, 1 Oct. 1873. Teacher of mus. æsthetics at Acad. of Music, Vienna; LL.D.; critic of many Viennese newspapers, *Neue Wiener Journal, Die Zeit, Allegemeine Zeitung, Der Tag*, since 1900. His arts. are marked by an acute and witty style and by a special emphasis of the Viennese note in music. Introduced the psychoanalysis of Freud into mus. æsthetics in his study on Wagner's *Flying Dutchman*.

Publ. books: *Deutsche Musik im 19 Jahrhundert (German Music in XIX Century)*, 1898; *Wagner Probleme und andere Studien (Wagner Problems and other Essays)*, 1900; *Die Musik in Zeitalter der Renaissance (Music at Renaissance Period)*, 1905; *R. Wagner im Fliegenden Holländer (Wagner in his " Flying Dutchman ")*, 1905; *Die innere Werkstatt des Musikers (The Inner Workshop of the Musician)*, 1904. Publ. transls.: Romain Rolland's *Paris musical* (1905); Alfred Bruneau's *Musiciens françaises* (1904); *La Musique de Russie* (1904).—P. P.

GRAINGER, George Percy (uses name Percy Aldridge G. as compr.). Australian pianist, compr. *b.* Brighton, Victoria, 8 July, 1882. Stud. pf. 5 years under his mother, a professional teacher; then under Louis Pabst in Melbourne, J. Kwast in Frankfort-o-M. and afterwards under Busoni. First public appearance in recital at 11 in Melbourne. Concertised in Germany during 1900; went to London and appeared there and in other Eng. towns from 1901 onwards in recitals and with orchs. Became an intimate friend of Grieg whom he met in London in 1906; visited Copenhagen in the same year and played Grieg's concerto at Leeds Fest., Oct. 1907, at compr.'s request. Toured in Europe, New Zealand and South Africa. Appeared in America for 1st time, New York, 11 Feb. 1915, and since then has been identified with Amer. mus. activities.

As a compr. and pianist G. introduced many of his own works at the Balfour Gardiner and Queen's Hall Concerts (London) and elsewhere, as well as in America, and also did much to spread the works of Debussy, Ravel, Cyril Scott,

Röntgen, Albeniz and other modern comprs. The rhythmic exuberance of his brilliant pf. playing finds a counterpart in the sincere and hearty character of his compns. Grieg's enthusiasm for national music stimulated G.'s interest in the subject, and he publ. in the *Journal of the Folk-Song Soc.* (No. 12, May 1908) a coll. of 27 British folk-tunes which have become the bases of many of his compns. He has always turned to small groups of instrs. rather than to the orch. which, he considers, suppresses the individuality of the separate players too much. On the other hand, he has never composed directly for a solo instr. His inclinations towards irregularly-barred music of 1899, *et seq.* have now developed into the desire for a "beatless" music of no standard pulse—the same kind of liberation as Schönberg has brought to harmony.

Orch.: Suite, *In a Nutshell* (Schirmer, 1916); *Molly on the Shore* (*id.*); *Colonial Song* (Schott, London, 1913); *Shepherd's Hey* (*id.*). Str. orch.: *Irish Tune from County Derry* (*id.*); *Mock Morris* (*id.* 1911). Pf. and str. orch.: *Clog Dance,* " *Handel in the Strand* " (*id.* 1912); 8tet: *My Robin is to Greenwood gone* (*id.*). Wind 5tet: *Walking Tune* (*id.*). Pf.: Paraphrase on the *Flower Waltz* from Tchaikovsky's *Nutcracker Suite* (*id.*); *Hill Songs* for 2 pfs. (Schirmer, 1922). Chorus and orch.: *Marching Song of Democracy* (Schirmer, 1916); *The Merry Wedding* (Ditson, 1916); *Father and Daughter* (Schott, London); *Sir Eglamore* (*id.*); *The Camp* (*id.*); *The March of the Men of Harlech* (*id.*); *The Hunter in his Career* (*id.*); *The Bride's Tragedy* (*id.* 1914). Chorus and brass band: *I'm Seventeen come Sunday* (Schirmer); *We have fed our Seas for a Thousand Years* (Schott, London, 1912); Marching Tune (*id.*). Chorus unacc. (all Schott, London): *Brigg Fair*; *The Inuit*; *Morning Song in the Jungle*; *A Song of Vermland*; *At Twilight*; *Tiger, Tiger,* etc. Also pieces for cello and pf. and songs.

Consult: D. C. Parker, *P. A. G. : a Study* (Schirmer, 1918); Cyril Scott, *P. G. : the Music and the Man* (*Mus. Quarterly*, 1916, Vol. II, pp. 425–33). —E.-H.

GRAMOPHONE. An instrument for reproducing, from discs of a reasonably hard and durable material, sounds of any nature which have been recorded. It is distinguished from the phonograph through the latter having become generally known as an instr. reproducing sound recorded on a wax-like cylinder. Thomas A. Edison, the orig. inventor of the phonograph, mentioned in his earlier patents the possibility of recording sounds on wax discs as well as on wax cylinders, but at that period there was no suggestion of means for multiplying the record so made. This essential of the modern gramophone originated with Emile Berliner of Washington, D.C., U.S.A., who in 1887 invented a process whereby the orig. record was made in zinc by etching. From this zinc a copper matrix was obtained by electrolysis, and this copper matrix used to press records in almost unlimited quantities.

Berliner was prominent during the seventies and eighties of the last century in research work on the then infant telephone, and after his invention of the gramophone, which name he himself gave to the instr., he did little to perfect it, turning his attention to other fields of research. His etching process proved to be not entirely satisfactory, as many of the fine sound-waves were eaten out by the acid, and in 1896 Eldridge R. Johnson, of Camden, N.J., U.S.A., turned his attention to the perfection of the gramophone, and invented a process of recording on a wax plate from which an electrolytic copy was obtained. It is this process, perfected from time to time, which is universally used. Johnson's improvements included the perfection of the spring motor, as well as the tone-arm and the enclosed horn, which so radically changed the aspect of the instr., the present-day gramophone having few points of similarity with that originally built by Berliner. The gramophone has enabled permanent records to be made of Their Majesties the King and the Queen, as well as of every great mus. artist, and copies are now held in the British Museum and the Museum of the Opéra in Paris, for the use of future generations. —A. CL.

GRAMOPHONE IN MUSICAL CULTURE will contribute as much to mus. education as the printing-press has contributed to the spread of knowledge. The effect of putting such a work as Beethoven's *Emperor* Concerto complete in the hands of an amateur, and thereby making great music an incident of his daily life, is incalculable. Moreover, the average man is becoming familiar with the sound of an orchestra through his gramophone. It must be remembered that such a one begins by disliking the sound of an orchestra. Music, as he understands it, is represented by the cornet, the piano, or the violin played with an exaggerated *tremolo*. Let him grow accustomed to the sound of an orchestra, and he is as willing to listen to a symphony of Beethoven as to a cheap waltz. One hesitates to suggest that the recording companies should issue records of the cornet in such melodies as the *Andante* from the C mi. symphony of Beethoven; but there is no doubt that by such a trap a still larger public as yet unmoved might be caught in the spell of great music. Meanwhile, let musicians pay as much attention to the gramophone as a wise mother pays to her children's nurse.

The greatest success of the gramophone is with the human voice, the flute and the violin; but the public should beware of composition diaphragms which often turn strings into woodwind. Mica is the best. The greatest failure of the gramophone is with the timpani. The piano was atrocious until lately, but the recording of it is improving every month. The cor anglais is usually flat, and the B-flat clarinet is liable to drown the rest of the orch.; but the horns, until recently execrable, are now splendid, which gives one hope for some of the other instrs. The brass, as might be expected, is most successful, but many orchestral records are spoilt by using tubas instead of double-basses. The following may be taken as examples of the gramophone at its best: for orch., Elgar's *Enigma Variations* (Gramophone Co.); for the violin any record of Hubermann's (Brunswick Cliftophone Co.); for the piano Moiseiwitsch playing Chopin's nocturne in E mi.; and for chamber-music any of the

Flonzaley Quartet's excerpts (Gramophone Co.). The best surface on records is the Columbia's.—C. M.

GRANADOS, Eduardo. Spanish composer; *b.* Barcelona, 28 July, 1894. Stud. compn. at Acad. founded in 1900 by his father, the famous and ill-fated pianist and compr. Enrique Granados; later on under Conrado del Campo, Madrid. Gave pf. lessons for 6 years at the Granados Acad.; dir. there 1916–19. Conducted occasional concerts of his father's and his own orch. works in Spain and France.

Bufón y Hostelero, 2-act zarzuela (Teatro Victoria, Barcelona, 1917); *La Princesita de los Sueños Locos*, 1 act (Teatro Cómico, Barcelona, June 1918); *Los Fanfarrones*, 1 act (Teatro Tívoli, Barcelona, Nov. 1920); *La Niña se pone tonta*, 1 act (Teatro Ruzafa, Valencia, May 1921); *La Ciudad Eterna*, 2 acts (Teatro Cervantes, Madrid, 1921); incidental music for Catalonian version of *Iphigenia in Tauris*; minor works for vn. and for v. with pf. (Unión Musical Española.)—P. G. M.

GRANADOS CAMPINA, Enrique. Spanish pianist and composer; *b.* Lerida, 29 July, 1867; *d.* 24 March, 1916. Son of an army officer, he received as a child his first musical tuition from bandmaster, Captain Junceda. Afterwards studied piano under Francisco Jurnet and the celebrated Catalonian master, Juan Bautista Pujol, Barcelona; composition under Felipe Pedrell. Later on, he studied the piano under de Bériot in Paris. Founder and conductor (1900) of the Sociedad de Conciertos Clásicos, and of the Academia Granados (1901). Knight of the Spanish Order of Carlos III; *Légion d'Honneur* and Officer of Public Instruction in France. The tragic circumstances of his death, in the sinking of the *Sussex* by a German submarine in the English Channel (24 March, 1916), after the production of his opera *Goyescas* at the Metropolitan Opera House, New York, gave universal prominence to his name; but more in reference to his talent as a composer than as a pianist. Yet it was in the latter capacity that he could be counted amongst the greatest virtuosi of any country. Owing to certain circumstances of temperament and environment, he limited his activities as concert-player mostly to France and Spain. In New York in 1915, his rare merits and unique personality, as a pianist, obtained prompt and complete recognition. Possessor of a fine technique, he only used it as a means, his real object being neatness, elegance and depth of expression, three distinctive features which are in evidence in his works. In general his prolific output, which must be studied in two groups, is free from French and German influence. In those works previous to the *Goyescas* (pf.), marking his first period, Grieg and Chopin seem to be the models. In the second period the influence of Albeniz is evident, though the similarity to these composers is to be found only in details of external order. In another direction, Granados has, in common with Albeniz, that special gift of excelling in the expression of the musical idiom and feeling of Spanish provinces that are quite distinct in character from that of their own

origin, Catalonia. Albeniz's extreme sensitiveness for the music of the South has its parallel in Granados' assimilation of the Castilian temperament, as shown in the piano *Goyescas*, his best-known and by far his most important works. In these, he has illustrated in musical terms that picturesque period of Madrid life, perpetuated on canvas by the genius of Francisco Goya. (The opera *Goyescas*, an afterthought, is a dramatic version of the piano works of the same title with some new material.) His deficiency in part-writing is particularly in evidence in his orchestral works, in which, as in his production in general, the melodic interest is superior to that of harmony and form. The Spanish composers' peculiar tendency (of folk-lore origin) to abuse the upper register of the human voice, appears specially accentuated in his case. As with Albeniz and certain Russian musicians, many of his piano pieces are a constant source of attraction for orchestrators and dancers. The great asset and redeeming point of Granados, as a composer, is his undeniable personality, even when dealing with borrowed materials, the grace and elegance of his piano-writing and the faculty of reaching at times a moving intensity of emotion. Rarely has the Spanish soul manifested itself so clearly in cultured music as in the initial theme of *Quejas o la Maja y el Ruiseñor* (*Goyescas*), an original melody, almost classic in character.

Pf.: *Danzas Españolas* (12 dances in 4 vols.); *Danza Gitana*; *Danzas para cantar y bailar*; *A la cubana*; *Seis piezas sobre cantos populares españoles*; *Rapsodia Aragonesa*; *Capricho Español*; *Morisca*; *Canción Arabe*; *Miel de la Alcarria*; *Escenas románticas*, 6 pieces; *Escenas poéticas*, 3 pieces; *Libro de horas*, 3 pieces; *Valses poéticos*; *Valses de amor*; *Carezza*; *Paisaje*; *Allegro de Concierto*; *Impromtu*; *Romeo y Julieta*; *Fantasía*; *Marcha militar*; *Dos marchas militares*, 4 hands; *Bocetos*, 5 pieces; *Elisenda* (*El Jardín*); *Seis estudios expresivos*; *Cuentos para la juventud*, 10 pieces; *Goyescas*, 1st part: *Los requiebros*, *Coloquio en la reja* (dúo de amor), *El fandango del candil*, *Quejas o la Maja y el Ruiseñor*; 2nd part: *El Amor y la Muerte* (balada), *Epílogo* (*Serenata del espectro*); *El Pelele* (escena goyesca). *Sonatas inéditas de Domenico Scarlatti* (26 transcriptions). Two vns. and pf.: *Serenata*. Cello and pf.: *Madrigal*; *Elisenda*, little suite; *Trova*. Ob. and strs.: *Oriental*. Pf. and orch.: Re-orchestration of Chopin's F minor concerto. Chorus, organ and pf.: *Cant de les estrelles*. Songs with pf.: *Colección de canciones amatorias* (7); *Colección de tonadillas* (10); *Elegía eterna*; *La Boira*; *L'Ocell profeta*. Pf. trio. Orch.: *Dante*, poem; *Elisenda*, suite; *Navidad*, suite; *Suite Arabe*; *Suite Gallega*; *Marcha de los vencidos*; *La Nit del Mort*, symph. poem; *Serenata*; *Tres danzas españolas* (scored by J. Lamote de Grignon). Operas: *Petrarca*; *Follet*; *María del Carmen*, 3 acts; *Goyescas*, 3 scenes. Zarzuelas: *Picarol*; *Gaziel*; *Liliana*; *Ovillejos*, 2 acts; *Miel de la Alcarria*. (Unión Musical Española, Madrid; Schirmer, New York.)—P. G. M.

GRANDE, Angel. Span. violinist; *b.* Madrid, 1894. Stud. at R. Cons. de Música, Madrid, and at Brussels Cons. under César Thomson. Concert tours in Spain, Belgium, England and Germany.—P. G. M.

GRANFELT, Lillian Hanna von. Finnish singer; *b.* Sakkola, 2 June, 1884. After studying in Helsingfors and Paris (Duvernoy), was engaged as prima-donna at Mannheim Court Theatre, 1909, and at Imper. Theatre (now State Opera) Berlin (since 1915). She adds to a fine voice, highly skilled technique and expressive interpretation. Her tours include:

1909, Bulgarian and Rumanian Court Operas; 1913, Covent Garden Opera, London (title-rôle in Raymond Roze's *Joan of Arc*); 1917, Mozart tours, cond. by Richard Strauss, in Switzerland; 1921, National Opera, Barcelona; 1923, Holland, (Amsterdam, Rotterdam, The Hague, Haarlem, Utrecht, Dordrecht). Her best rôles are Elsa (*Lohengrin*), Elizabeth (*Tannhäuser*), Countess (*Figaro*), Donna Anna (*Don Giovanni*), Pamina (*Magic Flute*), Octavian, Marschallin (*Rosenkavalier*); Salome, Ariadne, Empress (*The Woman without a Shadow*) in the Strauss operas; Mona Lisa (Schillings), Blanchefleur (Kienzl's *Kuhreigen*), Leonore (*Il Trovatore*), Marguerite (*Faust*), etc. Oratorio rôles: *Judas Maccabæus, Messiah* (Handel), *Stabat Mater* (Schubert), *Requiem* (Brahms). As concert-singer has appeared frequently in Finland, Germany and Scandinavia.—T. H.

GRANDJANY, Marcel. Fr. harpist; *b.* Paris, 3 Sept. 1891. Stud. at Paris Cons. where he obtained a 1st prize for harp and harmony. He now teaches harp-playing at American Cons. at Fontainebleau. Has written many songs, and harp pieces; his style of compn. is modern in sentiment and very delicate in tone.—F. R.

GRASSI, E. C. Fr. compr. *b.* Bangkok (Siam), 5 July, 1887. Having come to France when young, he stud. literature at the Sorbonne and music under Vincent d'Indy (1905) and Bourgault-Ducoudray (1910). Returned to Siam (1910–13) to study the folk-lore, on which his musical inspiration is principally founded. Has lived in Paris since 1913. His *Cinq mélodies siamoises* (written for pf. 1910) have attained popularity in their orch. form (1919). His art, at once subtle and direct, makes use of the exotic only so far as it expresses an inward thought. By the union of Siamese orientalism with most modern processes of Fr. school, his music displays an originality which is very rare. All his works are a "Siamese Confession" and by no means a virtuoso display of local colour.

Trois poèmes bouddhiques (1918), for vs. and orch.; *Poème de l'Univers* (1919), orch.; *Les Équinoxes* (1921), pf.; *Chanson nostalgique* (1921), vs. and pf.; also a masque for theatre (*La Fête du Zamkoukon*) for Bernstein's tragedy, *Judith* (1922).—A. C.

GRASSOT DE GOULA, Isabel. S. singer; *b.* Barcelona. After studying at Liceo Cons., Barcelona, made her *début* as dramatic s. at San Carlos Theatre, Lisbon (Elizabeth and Venus in *Tannhäuser*). At Barcelona created part of the Condesa de Foix in Pedrell's opera *Los Pirineos*. On her marriage with Goula (*q.v.*) she completely renounced her artistic career.—A. M.

GRAY, Alan. Eng. orgt., compr. *b.* York, 23 Dec. 1855. Educated St. Peter's School, York, and Trinity Coll. Cambridge. Stud. under Dr. E. G. Monk; mus. dir. Wellington Coll. 1883–92; orgt. Trinity Coll. Cambridge from 1892; condr. C.U.M.S. 1893–1912; Mus.Doc. Cantab. 1889; President R.C.O. London, 1922–3. His music is of a refined and lofty order. His organ pieces are among his best works. He is one of the finest of organists. Several of his lectures on organ construction and organ-playing appear in the R.C.O. Calendars.

Cantatas: *Arethusa*; *The Rock Buoy Bell*, 1914 (Novello); *Odysseus in Phæacia* (out of print) (Riorden); church music, many anthems and services (Novello; Stainer & Bell; Laudy); organ music: 4 sonatas and many pieces (Novello; Stainer & Bell;

Augener; W. Rogers); part-songs, etc. (Novello; Laudy; Stainer & Bell); sonata, vn. and pf. (Laudy); *A Book of Descants* (Cambridge Univ. Press); *Old National Airs with Descants* (Woodall, Minshall, Thomas & Co.).—E.-H.

GRAY, Herbert Willard. Music publ. *b.* Brighton, England, 3 Sept. 1868. Amer. representative (New York) of Novello and Co., London, since 1894; founder of the H. W. Gray Co., New York (sole agents for Novello), 1906. Publ. of *New Music Review*, and since Sept. 1921 of the *American Organ Monthly*.—J. M.

GRAY, Isabel Winton. Scottish pianist and teacher; *b.* Dundee, 14 Sept. 1898. Pupil of W. P. Fleming, Dundee, till 17, when she went to R.A.M. London. There she stud. pf. under Claude Pollard, compn. under J. B. McEwen; singing under Mme. Clara Samuel. Left Acad. in 1918; gave 1st recital in Wigmore Hall, Nov. 1918. Has since given several recitals there, and in Queen's Hall with Sir Henry Wood's orch. Elected to prof. staff of R.A.M. in 1920. Has played at Queen's Hall Promenades annually, Edinburgh, Glasgow and Dundee. Recently perf. Sir A. C. Mackenzie's Scottish Concerto at R.A.M. Centenary orch. concert in Queen's Hall.—W. S.

GRAY, William Craig. Scottish condr., orgt. *b.* Dalkeith, 10 April, 1861. Both his father and grandfather were precentors of old Scottish Presbyterian type. At 8, he became a choirboy, and an orgt. at 14. Orgt. of Congregational Ch. Dalkeith for over 20 years; afterwards at West Parish Ch. of that town. It is as a producer and condr. of Gilbert and Sullivan operas that he will continue to be remembered. In 1905 he produced *The Pirates of Penzance* in Dalkeith, and has gone on producing both in his native town and in Edinburgh with great success ever since. Lives in Edinburgh.—W. S.

GREEN, Gertrude Huntley. Canadian pianist; *b.* St. Thomas, Ontario, July, 1889. Stud. at Detroit, London (Ontario), and Paris (France) under Paul Viardot and Albert Geloso (vn.); Moszkowski and Leopold Godowsky (pf.). She has lived latterly in Victoria, B.C., where she has given many pf. recitals, and very materially helped the growth of mus. appreciation in Western Canada.—L. S.

GREEN, L. Dunton. Music critic; *b.* Amsterdam, 22 Dec. 1872. Stud. under C. Armbrust in Hamburg (harmony); Mangin, and Bondon (singing, pf.) in Paris; mus. ed. *Arts Gazette*; contributor to *Chesterian*; *Revue Musicale* (Paris); *Il Pianoforte* (Turin).—E.-H.

GREENE, Harry Plunket. Irish barit. singer; *b.* Dublin, 24 June, 1865. Stud. under Arthur Barraclough in Dublin; then at Stuttgart Cons. for 2 years; later at Florence; but singing chiefly under Alfred Blume in London. *Début* in London, 1888 (*Messiah*). Appeared at Covent Garden, 1890; but was always more attracted to recital-singing. In his recitals with Leonard Borwick, he rose to fame with the great songs of Schumann and Brahms. Many of Sir Hubert Parry's lyrical works were written for him. He has done great service to British folk-music by his illustrated song-lectures. His voice is not big, but is used with admirable taste, and his interpretations are most musicianly. With Granville Bantock as co-adjudicator, he visited Canada in 1923 and started the musical competition movement on sound lines there. Married Sir Hubert Parry's daughter. Author of *Interpretation in Song* (Macmillan).—W. St.

GREGOIR, Édouard Georges Jacques. Belgian compr. writer on music; *b.* Turnhout, 7 Nov. 1822; *d.* Wyneghem, near Antwerp, 28 June, 1890. Stud. pf. under Chr. Rummel at the same time as his brother, Jacques Mathieu Joseph. After touring as virtuoso, settled in Antwerp, where he devoted himself to compn. and musicological work. Only in latter field has he left any lasting works. He was an indefatigable compiler, but of mediocre intelligence and utterly lacking in scientific intuition. He brought together, in a whole series of volumes, innumerable facts and details about present and past musicians. Unfortunately, he omits to quote the sources of such information.

Biographie des artistes néerlandais (Netherlands) des XVIIIe et XIXe siècles et des artistes étrangers résidant ou ayant résidé en Néerlande à la même époque (1864); *Histoire de la facture et des facteurs d'orgue (Organ Building and Builders)*, 1865; *Documents historiques relatifs à l'art musical et aux artistes musiciens* (4 vols. 1872–6); *Panthéon musical populaire* (6 vols. 1876–7); *Bibliothèque musicale populaire* (3 vols. 1877–9); *Des gloires de l'Opéra, et la musique à Paris* (3 vols. 1878–81); *L'Art musical en Belgique sous les règnes de Léopold Ier et de Léopold II* (1879); *Grétry* (1883); *Souvenirs artistiques* (3 vols. 1888–9); *Les Artistes musiciens belges au XVIIIe et au XIXe siècles* (3 vols. 1885–90).—C. V. B.

GREGORIAN CHANT. " The chant proper to the Roman Church, the only chant she has inherited from the Ancient Fathers, which she has jealously guarded for centuries in her liturgical codices, which she directly proposes to the faithful as her own, which she prescribes exclusively for some parts of the Liturgy, and which the most recent studies have so happily restored to their integrity and purity " (Pope Pius X, from *Motu Proprio on Sacred Music*, 22 Nov. 1903). This chant was already in use in the early days of Christianity and was fixed in its definitive form under the Pontificate of St. Gregory the Great, from which it took its name. The Gregorian chant is distinguished from modern music by its essentially religious character arising from its purely diatonic tonality, and its natural rhythm. Admirably expressive, it contains wonders of the highest quality, and many musicians do not hesitate to place it in the first rank of mus. art. After a long period of decline, it has recovered its authentic and ancient form, and its full beauty, thanks to the works and researches of the Solesmes Benedictines. In 1904, Pius X established a commission to give an official ed. which was called *The Vatican Edition*. The Gradual, the Antiphonary, the Matins of Holy Week have already appeared. All these books, publ. in Rome at the Vatican Press, have been reproduced by the Solesmes Benedictines in their rhythmic editions. (See Solesmes.)

See also: Amelli, Guerrino; Bas, Giulio; Besse, Clément; De Santi, Angelo; Ferretti, Paolo; Gastoué, Amédée; Gevaert, F. A.; Gieburowski, W.; Houdard, Georges; Motu Proprio; Rue, A.; Shore, S. A.; Springer, Max; Suñol, Gregorio; Tinel, Edgar; Uriarte; Weinmann, Carl.—J. B.

GRESSE, André. Fr. b. singer; *b.* Lyons, 23 March, 1868, son of an operatic singer. First of all took up painting, although his father wished him to be an engineer. While doing military service he sang at a concert, and the success he obtained gave him the idea of going on the stage. Stud. at Cons. under Taskin, Duvernoy and Melchissédec; 1896, 2nd prize, *opéra-comique*, and honourable mention for singing and opera. Engaged by Carvalho at Opéra-Comique where he made *début* (1896) in *Don Juan*. He created rôles in *Le Spahi* and *Sapho* in 1897–8; in *Fervaal, Beaucoup de bruit pour rien* (1900) and in *Juif Polonais*. Engaged at Opéra, 1900; created rôles in *L'Enlèvement au sérail* (1903), *Tristan et Isolde* (1904), *Hippolyte et Aricie* (1908), *Bacchus* (1909), *L'Or du Rhin (Rhinegold)* (1909), *Don Quichotte* (1910), *Le Miracle* (1910), *Parsifal* (1914), *Scemo* (1914), *Mademoiselle de Nantes* (1915), *Iphigénie en Tauride* (1916), *Briséis* (1916), *Prométhée* (1917), *Castor et Pollux* (1918), *Le Retour*, and *Boris Godunof* (1919). Possesses a voice of great range, which allows him to add to his repertoire some of the b. rôles which made his father famous. Has been a famous member of the Paris Opéra company for 23 years.—A. R.

GRETCHANINOF, Alexander Tikhonovitch (accent *3rd syll.*). Russ. compr. *b.* Moscow, 13/25 Oct. 1864. Pupil of Safonof (pf.) at Moscow Cons. 1890; of Rimsky-Korsakof (theory) Petrograd Cons. 1893. Essentially a compr. of vocal music, as versatile as he is prolific. The main characteristics of his songs are refinement, easy grace, and sentiment which at its best owes little to sentimentality. He won a prize of Petrograd Chamber-Music Soc. for his 1st str. 4tet in 1894 and 2 Glinka prizes (establ. by M.P. Belaief) for his 2nd (1914) and 3rd (1916) str. 4tets.

Operas: *Dobrynia Nikititch*, 3 acts, op. 22; *Sister Beatrice* (after Maeterlinck), op. 50; music to Ostrovsky's *Snow Maiden*, op. 23; 1st symphony, B mi. op. 6; 2nd symphony (*Pastorale*, A mi.), op. 27; 3rd symphony (1921–2, ms.); 4th symphony (1923, ms.). 3 str. 4tets (I, G ma. op. 2; II, D mi. op. 70; III, C mi. op. 75); 1st pf. trio, C mi. op. 38; 2nd pf. trio, op. 60; vn. sonata, op. 87; cello concerto, op. 28 (ms.). 3 *Liturgies of St. John Chrysostom* (I, op. 13; II, op. 29; III, *id.* [on old Russ. sacred melodies], op. 79); many songs; very many choruses; pf. pieces.—M. D. C.

GREVILLE, Ursula. Eng. singer. Stud. from age of 6 under many masters; further studies in Italy, 1923; concert *début*, Æolian Hall, 4 March, 1920; operatic *début*, Covent Garden (Queen of Night, *Magic Flute*), 29 March, 1920. Her vocal range is from D in bass stave to G in alt; started with Ger. *lieder* and coloratura rôles; at present specialises in songs of young school of British comprs. with which she has toured the Continent and America. Editor of *The Sackbut* from Aug. 1921.—E.-H.

GREVILLIUS, Nils. Swedish condr. *b.* Stockholm, 7 March, 1893. Played vn. from 6 years of age; stud. vn. at R. Cons. Stockholm (under Book) and at Cons. of Sondershausen. First violinist of R. Chapel (opera-orch.), Stockholm, 1911–14; 2nd condr. of Konsertföreningen, 1914–20; continued studies as condr. in Germany, Austria, England, France, Italy and Belgium. Guest-condr. at concerts in Paris, Berlin, Vienna, Prague, etc. In the 1922–3 season, attached as condr. to R. Opera, Stockholm; also guest-condr. of Konsertföreningen, and at symphony concerts of Tonkünstler Orch. Vienna.—P. V.

GREW, Sydney. Eng. writer on music; b. Birmingham, 13 Aug. 1879. Engaged variously in business, and in farming in Manitoba, 1890–1900; stud. music at Birmingham and Midland Inst. 1899–1910, under Granville Bantock, George Halford, C. W. Perkins, W. F. Newey, and Joseph Morris; expenses of study borne in part by Earl Beauchamp from 1903–6; teacher of music and church orgt. 1902–10; mus. journalist from 1909; contributor to Eng. and Amer. monthly and quarterly periodicals.

Art of the Player-Piano (Kegan Paul, 1921); Our Favourite Musicians from Stanford to Holbrooke (T. N. Foulis, 1922); Our Favourite Musicians from John Coates to Albert Sammons (id. 1923); A Book of English Prosody (Grant Richards, 1924); Polymetric Ed. of xvi century vocal music (Curwen, 1922).—E.-H.

GRIEG, Edvard. Norwegian composer; b. Bergen, 15 June, 1843; d. there, 4 Sept. 1907. His musically gifted mother, Gesine (née Hagerup), gave him instruction in piano-playing from his sixth year. On the advice of Ole Bull he was sent to the Conservatoire in Leipzig in 1858, where he studied diligently until 1862. His opus 1, Four Piano Pieces (written during his last years in Leipzig), shows clearly that Schumann and Chopin were his ideals. These charmingly fashioned pieces reveal the unfolding of a singular individuality. It was, however, the study of Norwegian folk-music that first awakened his youthful genius, and the Humoresques (op. 6) already show that he had found himself. It is especially the character-peculiarities of the "Hardanger-violin," that he here tries to transfer to the piano. In quick succession now follow several of Grieg's masterpieces; in 1865 the piano sonata (op. 7) and the violin sonata in F (op. 8). In 1867 he married his cousin, Nina Hagerup (see below), a brilliant vocalist, who with consummate art has interpreted his songs. Already in op. 5 we find such gems as To brune öine (A Pair of Brown Eyes) and Jeg elsker dig (I Love Thee). In Christiania, Grieg worked with the greatest energy as pianist, conductor of the Philharmonic Society and choral leader. In 1868 during a summer holiday in Denmark he wrote his piano concerto in A minor (op. 16). This work is instinct with inspiration, with beautiful themes, characteristic rhythm, original harmony and warmly-coloured instrumentation. In 1871 he founded the Musical Society in Christiania, of which he was condr. for four years. The first Lyrical Pieces, the violin sonata in G (op. 13), the chorus Landkjending and the music to Björnson's Sigurd Jorsalfar also saw the light in this Christiania period. In 1874, Grieg was commissioned by Ibsen to write music to Peer

Gynt. Two years later, this music was performed for the first time in Christiania (24 Feb. 1876). The work was performed 36 times during the first year. At the same time as the Peer Gynt music, he wrote his second great piano work, the Ballade in G minor (op. 24). This is in the form of variations on a Norwegian folk-melody which Grieg found in L. M. Lindeman's collection. These works were written in Bergen. Afterwards he went to live at Lofthus in Hardanger. Here he created four new masterpieces, the string quartet in G minor (op. 27), Album for male voices (op. 30), Den Bergtekne (op. 32) and Vinje Songs (op. 33). The quartet is partly built upon a theme which we also find in the first song of. op. 25. This work like the Ballade, belongs to the most passionate and expressive of Grieg's compositions. Not less thrilling is Den Bergtekne, for baritone solo with string orchestra and 2 horns. The songs to texts by the poet A. O. Vinje mark perhaps the highest development of Grieg's capacity as a song-composer. The Album for male voices showed Grieg to be one of the finest composers in the North for male-voice choirs. Norwegian folk-melodies form the basis of these songs. The cello sonata in A minor dates from the same period.

In 1880–82 Grieg was leader of the musical society Harmonien in Bergen and was responsible for the production of a number of great works. The Holberg Suite and his 3rd violin sonata in C minor (op. 45) date from the 'eighties. The suite is a portrayal, instinct with character, of the rococo period.

Of dramatic works Grieg has, besides the Peer Gynt music, written Scener av Olav Trygvason (op. 50), to an uncompleted work by Björnson, as well as the melodrama Bergliot (op. 42), to words by the same author. This latter piece contains a fine funeral march.

By the 'eighties, Grieg had become a world-renowned master. To this result the great interest taken in him and his work by his publisher Dr. Abraham (C. F. Peters, Leipzig) contributed to an essential degree. As an excellent pianist and an inspiring conductor, Grieg was frequently engaged in concert-tours in Scandinavia, Germany, Austria, England, France, Poland, etc. In 1888 he conducted for the first time in London and Birmingham; in 1889 at Colonne's in Paris. The Peer Gynt music doubtless opened the way for him, but the fact that he has won such favour in homes far and wide is due to his long series of Lyrical Pieces and to his delightful songs. The Lyrical Pieces are character-sketches in the spirit of Schumann, concise and graphic, fresh in melody and characteristic in sonorous ring. They are often distinctively Norwegian in effect. As examples may be mentioned op. 12 (with Folk-Song), op. 43 (with Erotik), op. 57 (with Nostalgy), op. 68 (with Evening in the Mountains). Of the same character is op. 19, with Brudefölget drager forbi (The Bridal Procession goes by). By degrees Grieg lost courage to pursue the greater forms of composition. His health had always been feeble; ever since he had had an attack of pleurisy in his youth, he had to exist with only one lung. Of works produced in his later years we may point to some that stand on a level with his best productions. The songs to texts by Garborg, *The Haugtussa Songs* (op. 67), can undoubtedly be compared with op. 33. Deeply moving is his last work, *Four Hymns* for mixed chorus, *a cappella* (op. 74). Finally may be mentioned *Slaatter* (*Folk-Tunes*), op. 72, for piano, adaptations of Norwegian Hardanger-violin pieces collected by Johan Halvorsen, in which Grieg's keen vision has transferred to the piano all the strange rhythmic subtleties of these melodies, their peculiar intervals and their luxuriance of embellishment.

Thus it was Norwegian folk-melodies that finally occupied Grieg's mind, and his art cannot be sundered from this, its fountain-head. From them he drew his deepest inspirations, and none can, like Grieg, illumine Norwegian folk-music. Almost everything that has been created in this field under the name of "transcriptions" pales in comparison with Grieg's treatment. He penetrates into the core of the melody and draws out all that is most essential in it. Characteristic is op. 66 (19 Folk-Songs), which is based upon collections made by Frants Beyer, but which to some extent has become more Grieg than folk-music, the melodies being so absorbed by the composer's harmonisation. What renders him the naturally-appointed interpreter of Norwegian folk-music is his close kinship with the Norwegian national character. His own original melodies are of the same mould.

A new element of tunefulness has been contributed to music by the melodies of Grieg. Something similar may be said of his harmony, which is undoubtedly strongly influenced by the Norwegian Hardanger-violin. Grieg fashions his own rules, guided by a sense of tone that is both refined and richly coloured, and instinct with noble austerity. This combination of magnificent, semi-archaic melody with refined harmonisation has also influenced foreign masters of music. Grieg's importance must be designated as international.

Consult: Ernest Closson, *Edvard Grieg et la Musique Scandinave* (1892); Gerhard Schjelderup, *Edvard Grieg og hans Værker* (Copenhagen, 1903); H. T. Finck, *Edvard Grieg* (London and New York, 1906); G. Schjelderup and Walter Niemann, *Edvard Grieg* (Leipzig, 1908); Erik Eggen, *Edvard Grieg i Norges Musikhistorie* (Christiania, 1921); Richard H. Stein, *Grieg* (Berlin, 1921).—O. M. S.

GRIEG, Nina (*née* Hagerup). Norwegian singer; b. Bergen, 24 Nov. 1848. Stud. singing under Karl Helsted in Copenhagen, where she lived with her parents until she married her cousin the compr. Edvard Grieg in 1867. Since the latter's death in 1907 she has chiefly lived in Copenhagen. Nina Grieg won a name for herself as interpreter of her husband's songs. Many of Grieg's best songs were composed for her.—R. M.

GRIFFES, Charles Tomlinson. Amer. compr. b. Elmira, N.Y., U.S.A., 17 Sept. 1884; d. New York, 8 April, 1920. One of the most promising of the younger Amer. comprs., who had just begun to come into his own, when his career was cut short by his untimely death. Educated at Elmira Acad. and stud. pf. under Mary S. Broughton in Elmira, then for 4 years under Jedlicka and Gottfried Galston in Berlin. In theory he was a pupil of Klatte and Loewengard, and in compn. of Ph. Rüfer and Humperdinck in Berlin. For a time, gave lessons in Berlin, and in 1904 appeared there in a pf. recital, playing among other things an unpubl. pf. sonata. Returned to America in 1907 and became music-master at the Hackley School for boys at Tarrytown, N.Y., also giving private lessons in New York.

His earlier works (several sets of songs (Schirmer, 1909 and 1910) were written in the style to which he had been brought up. This he abandoned and adopted the new idiom, in which, without going to extremes, he struck a distinctly personal note.

A dance-drama *The Kairn of Koridwen*, for 5 wind instrs., celesta, harp and pf. (unpubl.), was brought out at Neighbourhood Playhouse in New York, 10 Feb. 1917. The same year saw the production of *Shojo*, a Japanese mime-play for 4 wind instrs., 4 muted str., harp, tam-tam, Chinese drum and tpi., by A. Bolm's Ballet Intime at Booth Theatre, New York. His reputation as an orch. compr. of high rank was establ. by the perf. of his symph. poem *The Pleasure-Dome of Kubla Khan* (after Coleridge) by Boston Symphony Orch. 28 Nov. 1919. Three songs for s. with orch. had been perf. at concert of Philadelphia Orch. 24 March, 1919.

Fantasy Pieces, pf. op. 6 (1915); *Four Roman Sketches* for pf. (after poems by William Sharp), op. 7 (1917); *Five Poems of Ancient China and Japan*, for v. and pf. op. 10 (1917); *The Pleasure-Dome of Kubla Khan*, symph. poem (1920); sonata for pf. (1920); 2 Sketches for str. 4tet, based on Indian themes (1922). All publ. by Schirmer.
Consult art. by W. T. Upton in *Mus. Quarterly*, July, 1923.—O. K.

GRIFFITH, Morgan William. Welsh compr. and orgt. b. Clydach, near Swansea, 1855. Stud. at Univ. Coll. of Wales, Aberystwyth, under the late Dr. Joseph Parry (1876); music-master at Dr. Williams' School, Dolgelley, from 1879; orgt. and choirmaster, parish ch. Dolgelley, 1885. Has comp. anthems, part-songs and several Welsh songs.—D. V. T.

GRIMSON, Annie. Eng. pianist; b. London. Stud. at R.C.M. (gold medal); then under Tobias Matthay; *début* Covent Garden Promenade Concerts, 1899.
Nocturne, cello and pf. (Augener); waltz, full orch. (Phillips); pf. pieces (Goodwin & Tabb).—E.-H.

GRIMSON, Jessie. Eng. violinist. Stud. under her father, S. Dean G. (member of Holmes Str. Quartet, one of 1st permanent parties to tour England); open scholarship, R.C.M. London; *début* at Crystal Palace under Manns; founded Grimson Str. Quartet (Monday and Saturday Popular Concerts, Broadwood Concerts, provinces).—E.-H.

GRÖNDAHL, Olaus Andreas. Norwegian singing-master, condr. compr. b. Christiania, 6 Nov. 1847. Matriculated in 1866; pupil of Cons. in Leipzig 1870–3. In 1873, pupil of

Lindhult in Cologne. In 1890, teacher of singing at Military School; in 1899 at Univ. in Christiania. Founded in 1878 Gröndahl's Choir, which has given masterly performances of ecclesiastical and secular works for mixed choir. Condr. of Craftsmen's Choral Soc. 1884–90; of Students' Choral Soc. 1888–1912; of Merchants' Choral Soc. 1888–1902. Has conducted concert-tours at home and abroad (Students' Choral Soc. Amer. tour, 1905; combined choir of different societies, Paris, 1900, etc.). As leader of male choirs and as instructor in singing his name is known all over the country. He was State Inspector of Singing. Married the pianist and compr. Agathe Backer-Gröndahl.

Foran Sydens Kloster (Before a Southern Cloister), for soli, chorus and orch. (text by Björnson); compns. for male choirs (including the poetical *Young Magnus*).—J. A.

GRÖNVOLD, Hans Aimar Mow. Norwegian writer on music; *b.* Saude (Telemark), 26 June, 1846. Under-Secretary of State (Department of Public Works) 1885–1905; from 1905 cabinet secretary to King Haakon VII. Mus. critic to Christiania journals *Aftenbladet,* 1867–81, and *Aftenposten,* 1881–6. Has written *Frederic Chopin* (Christiania, 1878); *Norwegian Musicians* (Christiania, 1883) and the section on Norwegian music in *Norway in the XIX Century* (1900–2).—U. M.

GROSZ, Wilhelm. Austrian compr. *b.* Vienna in 1894. Ph.D. (musicology) at Vienna Univ. 1920. Pupil of Franz Schreker at Acad. of Vienna 1920–1; condr. at National Theatre, Mannheim. Now lives in Vienna. A musician of great knowledge, with conservative leanings and a marked tendency towards the grotesque.

Many songs; pf. pieces (*Symphonische Variationen,* op. 9, and a very pleasing *Dance-Suite*); orch.: *Serenade,* op. 5, and a *Dance,* op. 7. Scenic music for Werfel's *Spiegelmensch* (afterwards made into Suite, op. 12). All publ. in Univ. Ed.—P. ST.

GROVLEZ, Gabriel. Fr. compr. *b.* Lille, 4 April, 1879. Stud. at Paris Cons. 1st prize for pf. 1899 (Diémer's class); harmony with Lavignac; cpt. and fugue with Gédalge; compn. with Gabriel Fauré. Started his career as pf. virtuoso; prof. for 10 years, of advanced pf. course at *Schola Cantorum;* chorus-master and condr. at Opéra-Comique; then mus. dir. Théâtre des Arts for mus. plays of Jacques Rouché; condr. at Paris Opéra since 1914; in 1921 spent a season as condr. of Chicago opera.

Symph. works: *Madrigal lyrique; La Vengeance des Fleurs; Le Reposoir des Amants.* Dramatic works: *Cœur de Rubis; La Princesse au jardin* (1920); *Maïmouna* (ballet, 1921); *Au vrai arbre de Robinson* (ballet, 1921, Chicago); *Le Marquis de Carabas* (*opéra-bouffe*); *Psyché* (lyric drama). Sonatas for pf. and vn.; many pf. pieces (*L'Almanach aux images; London Voluntaries* [Augener]); songs.—A. C.

GROZ, Albert. Fr. compr. *b.* Lyons, 1873. Was pupil of Eugène Gigout and V. d'Indy at *Schola Cantorum,* where he taught cpt. (1905–13). From 1905–10, produced 5 works at Société Nationale.

Heures d'été, 6 preludes and melodies (1902–3; *Cantique des Créatures de St. François d'Assise* (b. voice and orch.), produced under V. d'Indy (Paris, Rouart & Lerolle); *Epithalame,* pf. sonata (Paris, Demets, 1905); pf. and vn. sonata; *Les Amours de Marie,* 6 songs (Rouart & Lerolle).—M. L. P.

GRÜNFELD, Alfred. Hungarian pianist; *b.* Prague, 4 July, 1852; *d.* Jan. 1924. Taught in Prague and Berlin before settling down in Vienna, and becoming one of the most Viennese of artists. Many concert-tours. Some pf. compns.; operetta, *Der Lebemann* (Vienna, 1903); comic opera, *Die Schönen von Fogaras* (perf. 1907). His charm of touch and poetical rendering showed best in Schubert, Liszt, and Schumann. On his 70th birthday he was publicly fêted.—P. ST.

GRUODIS, J. See LITHUANIAN MUSIC.

GRUSZCZYŃSKI, Stanisław (*phon.* Grooshchynski). T. singer; *b.* Warsaw, 1890. Till 1915 he was a waiter in a hotel-restaurant in Warsaw. His voice was discovered by chance; 1 year later, was enabled to appear as Lohengrin and Canio at Warsaw, Berlin and Hamburg. Became an eminent singer, and appeared in Milan, Madrid, and other cities.—ZD. J.

GUARNIERI, Antonio. Ital. condr. *b.* Venice, 1881. Was condr. with Arturo Toscanini at La Scala, Milan. Came from a family of musicians and, whilst very young, completed his studies in cello, pf. and cpt. in his native city. First part of career was that of cellist; gave numerous concerts in Italy and abroad; also belonged to Martucci Quartet. Having gained a footing subsequently as one of the best of the younger condrs., he rapidly won a high reputation both in the theatre and concert world. Is also good compr.; some of his vocal chamber-music has been publ. by Ricordi.—D. A.

GUARNIERI, Francesco. Ital. violinist; *b.* Venice, 1867. Brother of Antonio Guarnieri. Before being appointed prof. in Liceo Mus. Benedetto Marcello, Venice, he resided for a long time in France, where he had stud. at Paris Cons. under César Franck; also lived in England and Russia, making successful concert tours and taking part in quartets. In Paris, founded the International Soc. of Chamber-music. Comp. 2 operas, a sonata and vn. concerto. Undertook for Ricordi the editing of classical vn. works.—D. A.

GUDAVIČIUS, J. See LITHUANIAN MUSIC.

GUDEHUS, Heinrich. Ger. operatic t. *b.* Altenhagen, near Celle (Hanover), 30 March, 1845; *d.* Dresden, 9 Oct. 1909. At first a schoolteacher in Kleinlehnen, Celle and Goslar, in which last town he was also orgt. at St. Mark's Ch. When at Goslar he took singing lessons from Frau Schnorr von Carolsfeld in Brunswick, by whom he was recommended to von Hülsen, gen. manager of Berlin R. Opera House, who engaged him in 1870 for that theatre. He made a successful *début* as Nadori (*Jessonda*), but left stage after 6 months, to study further under Luise Resz in Berlin. Not till 1875 did he again appear, when he sang successively in Riga, Lübeck, Freiburg-i-Br., Bremen (1878). From 1880 to 1890 member of Court Opera Company (Court chamber singer), Dresden; at the German opera in New York, winter of 1891; appeared (1895–6) at Court Opera, Berlin. Latterly he lived in retirement in Dresden. He created the part of Parsifal in Bayreuth (1882).—A. E.

GUERRERO, Alberto Garcia. Chilean pianist and compr. b. Serena, 1886. Self-taught; has a marvellous technique; toured U.S.A. (New York, New Orleans, Philadelphia, etc.). His pieces are mostly for pf. His *Valse triste* is known throughout N. and S. America. In 1918, he accepted invitation of Jan Hambourg, dir. of Toronto Cons. to take charge of pf. section there, where he continues to work.—A. M.

GUERRINI, Paolo. Ital. priest, and patron of studies in sacred music; b. Bagnolo Mella, near Brescia, 18 Nov. 1880. In review *Santa Cecilia* of Turin, he has publ. important studies of liturgical and mus. history; an Ital. ed., with index, of Cardinal Katschthaler's *History of Sacred Music*; biographical studies of Luca Marenzio, Gregorio, Francesco and Giulio Cesare Turini and other composers of Brescia.—D. A.

GUERVÓS, José María. Span. pianist and compr. b. Granada. First lessons from his father (orgt. and compr.), continuing studies at R. Cons. de Música, Madrid; 1st prize for pf. 1899. Founder, in collab. with famous cellist Pablo Casals, of chamber-music soc. in 1895. Pianist of the Cuarteto Francés in 1909. Has attained great distinction as an accompanist and soloist in concert-tours with Gayarre, Sarasate, Antonio F. Bordas and others. Since his 22nd year, prof. at R. Cons. Madrid, teaching vocal ensemble, opera and pf. Since 1917, prof. of pf. acc. there. Author of a new system of mus. notation in which the two staves, used for pf. and organ music, are united in one of ten lines called *decagrama*. The treble and bass staves are unified by one C clef on the 6th line. The full system, which extends to new classification of scales, key-signatures, etc., would demand a lengthy exposition. As a compr. he is specially noted for refinement of style in songs and pf. pieces previous to the Albeniz period.

Musical comedies: *Piquito de Oro*, 1 act; *Aretino* (both in collab. with the compr. Tomás Barrera); *La Buenaventura*, 1 act (in collab. with compr. Amadeo Vives); *A estudiar a Salamanca*; *El Lagar*, 1 act (in collab. with the compr. Carbonell). For pf.: *Allegro de Concierto*; *Pensamientos*, in 3 books. (Unión Musical Española, Madrid.)—P. G. M.

GUERVÓS, Manuel. Span. pianist and compr. b. Granada, 1863; d. 1902. Like his brother José María, received first lessons from his father; stud. later at R. Cons. de Música, Madrid, where he obtained 1st prize for pf.-playing. Started career as soloist at 12, touring afterwards with Isaac Albeniz and with Sarasate, of whom he was the favourite accompanist. Wrote many pf. pieces (influenced by Albeniz's early works); coll. of mazurkas in Chopin's style. His Span. pieces show a delightful ingenuity and spontaneity which accounts for their lasting popularity. (Unión Musical Española, Madrid.) —P. G. M.

GUGLIELMI, Filippo. Ital. compr. b. Ceprano, 15 June, 1859. Stud. at Naples under D'Arienzo, then in Rome under Eugenio Terziani; in his youth, enjoyed friendly intercourse with Liszt.

Made himself known by several symph. works, passing then to the theatre with his operas *Atala, Pergolese, Matelda*, and *I figli della gleba*. His most noted opera is *Le Eumenidi* (libretto by Fausto Salvatori; perf. Treviso, 1905). His symph. poems, *Pellegrinaggio a Monte Autore* and *Tibur*, have been perf. at the Augusteo, Rome. A study on G. was publ. by A. De Angelis in review *La Nuova Antologia*, Aug. 1912.—D. A.

GUI, Vittorio. Ital. condr. and compr. b. Rome, 14 Sept. 1885. Completed his literary studies, and at the same time went through his mus. studies at the R. Liceo Mus. di Santa Cecilia. Started his career as condr. 1907 at Teatro Adriano, Rome, whence he went on immediately to the Regio Theatre, Parma, the Regio at Turin and the San Carlo at Naples. *Début* as concert-condr. at the Augusteo, where he returned many times. 1922–3 was engaged at Costanzi Theatre, Rome. G. is an admired compr. of orch. works and vocal chamber-music, an able writer and critic, as well as one of most esteemed of the younger Ital. condrs.—D. A.

Scherzo fantastico, Ombre Cinesi (Rome, Casa Musicale Italiana); *Quattro Canti della morte, Commiato, Ritorno* (Bologna, Pizzi).—D. A.

GUIDÉ, Guillaume. Belgian oboist; b. Liège, 7 April, 1859; d. Brussels, 19 July, 1917. Pupil of Liège Cons.; prof. of ob. at Brussels Cons. from 1885. Dir. of Théâtre de la Monnaie (with Maurice Kufferath) from 1900 to death. A first-class oboist (V. d'Indy dedicated to him his *Fantasia* for orch. and ob.), he occupied a leading place in Belgian mus. life from 1890 to 1914.—C. V. B.

GUILDHALL SCHOOL OF MUSIC, London.— In 1879 an orchestral and choral society, chiefly amateur, gave occasional concerts in the Guildhall. From these beginnings in Sept. 1880, the G.S.M. commenced operations in an empty wool warehouse in Aldermanbury, with Weist Hill, Principal, and 62 students; at end of that year there were 216 pupils, taught by 29 professors. In 1885 the scholars had increased to a surprising extent, and it became absolutely necessary to provide a building specially adapted for music-teaching purposes. In July 1885, the Chairman of the Music Committee laid the foundation-stone of the present school in Tallis Street. It was opened for students in 1887. It contains 42 class-rooms, a concert-room, necessary offices, and a suite of 5 rooms, now used by the professors as a club. From 1892–96 Sir Joseph Barnby was Principal. In the latter year Dr. Cummings was appointed on the death of Barnby. Sir Landon Ronald was appointed in 1910. In 1898 a further increase of students rendered yet more accommodation necessary, and the Music Committee obtained permission from the Corporation to build an annexe on land in John Carpenter Street, adjoining the old building. This includes a theatre, fitted with a stage. There are over 100 professors on the staff which during the last 40 years has included many famous musicians: Prout, Stainer, Cusins,

Barnett, Gadsby, Sauret, Wolff, Sims Reeves, Cowen, and others. A large number of students are received for a complete musical education, though the bulk of the students are amateur. Among the most famous pupils have been Myra Hess, Carrie Tubb, Gladys Ancrum, Thorpe Bates, Sybil Thorndike and Edna Best. There are about 120 scholarships vacated annually. —H. S. W.

GUILMANT, Alexandre. French organist and composer; *b.* Boulogne - sur - Mer, 12 March, 1837; *d.* Meudon, near Paris, 2J March, 1911. Son of organist of St. Nicholas' Ch., Boulogne. Alexandre cultivated organ-playing at an early age, and in 1857 he took his father's place, after having had a short term of office at St. Joseph's. The greater part of his vocal and religious compositions date from this period. He spent part of his time in teaching in schools and privately, and in organising classical concerts, playing violin or viola therein. But the organ attracted him, and in 1860 a journey to Paris enabled him to meet Lemmens, the celebrated organ-teacher of the Brussels Conservatoire who had come to France to open the organ at Rouen Cathedral. Lemmens heard Guilmant play, and suggested that Guilmant should study under him at Brussels. He did this and after a month's work of 6 to 8 hours a day, he was able, to use Lemmens's expression, " to fly with his own wings." His course was now quite plain. Between 1862 and 1870 no new organ, however unimportant, was inaugurated without the Boulogne organist. Amongst these instruments, two, without peers, gave him the opportunity of displaying his talent in all its fullness, the organ of St.-Sulpice, and of Notre-Dame, Paris. On the death of Chauvet, Guilmant was called to succeed him at La Trinité, and his talent entered on a new phase. Admiration for the old masters took a complete hold of him. The year 1878, in which the immense organ of the Trocadéro was built, saw him still more renowned. He was appointed member of the Exhibition Commission, and in-augurated the great organ concerts at which all the chief organists agreed to play, and for which, César Franck wrote his three well-known pieces: *Fantaisie in A, Cantabile, Pièce héroïque.* It was intended that the Trocadéro should be demolished at the end of the Exhibition, but Guilmant took steps to preserve the organ and retain the hall to carry on the concerts alone. He popularised good music there for many years. He toured widely; but England and America attracted him most. He was received for several days by Queen Victoria at Windsor Castle; in Rome, he was received by Leo XIII and decorated with the Order of St. Gregory the Great. He was created Chevalier of the Legion of Honour, Corresponding Member of the Royal Academy of Stockholm, and Mus.Doc. (*h.c.*) of Manchester University. Besides the recitals already mentioned, he was heard at the Concerts Lamoureux, in Russia at Riga Cathedral, in Belgium at Laeken

(before the King of the Belgians) at Barcelona, Spain; in Italy, etc. In Paris, he founded, together with Charles Bordes and Vincent d'Indy, the *Schola Cantorum*, where he accepted the post of organ professor. He occupied a similar post at the Paris Conservatoire (1896). Amongst his most famous pupils were A. Decaux, G. Jacob, J. Bonnet, Poillot, M. Dupré, Achille Philip, Alex. Cellier, and in America, William Carl and J. H. Loud.

As composer, he added to organ music many unsuspected and valuable qualities.

2 symphonies, org. and orch.; 25 books of pieces in different styles; 12 parts of the *Practical Organist*; 10 parts of *Liturgical Organist*; 8 sonatas (2 with orch.) He ed. a repertoire of the Trocadéro Concerts, the Historical Organ Concerts, the *École Classique de l'Orgue*, and the *Archives des Maîtres de l'orgue*, which latter (with the prefaces and notes by André Pirro) will be his chief glory. In it, he brought to light the great masters whose music Bach so much admired and copied out with his own hand. Messrs. Schott & Co., London, now publ. all Guilmant's works, many of them in a new ed. Consult A. Eaglefield-Hull, *The Organ Works of Guilmant* (*Monthly Mus. Record*, Sept. Oct. Nov. 1914).—J. B.

GUIMARAES. See PORTUGUESE OPERA.

GUIRAUD, Ernest. Fr. compr. and teacher; *b.* New Orleans, 23 June, 1837; *d.* Paris, 6 May, 1892. A compr. too little remembered, who gained the *Prix de Rome* at 22. His music, picturesque and full of colour, has had some influence on the generation of the eighteen-eighties. His best-known work is the ballet *Gretna Green* (1873). But he has written many other dramatic works, especially some *opéras-comiques*:

Sylvie (1864); *Le Kobold* (1870); *Madame Turlupin* (1872); *Piccolino* (1876); *La Galante Aventure* (1882). Operas: *En prison* (1869) and *Frédégonde* (finished by Saint-Saëns and perf. 1895). For orch.: Suite; overture; Caprice for vn. *Practical Treatise on Instrumentation* (posthumous) has summed up the lessons which he gave at the Cons. from 1876, when he was prof. of harmony class, and afterwards (1880) of compn. class, in succession to Victor Massé.—A. C.

GUITAR MUSIC and Players. See BARRIOS, ANGEL; BRONDI, MARIA; FALLA, MANUEL DE; MORENO TORROBA; PUJOL, EMILIO; SEGOVIA, ANDRÉS; TÁRREGA, FRANCISCO.

GULBRANSON, Ellen. Norwegian dramatic m.-sopr. singer; *b.* Stockholm, 8 March, 1863. Since 1890, living in Christiania, being married to Major Hans P. Gulbranson. Trained at Cons. in Stockholm, afterwards under Mme. Marchesi in Paris. *Début* in 1886 in Paris at a concert of her own. Her 1st appearance in Scandinavia was at chamber-music *soirée* given by Grieg in Christiania in 1888. As an operatic singer, she appeared for first time at R. Opera House in Stockholm as Amneris in *Aida*. Appeared in following years in Stockholm and Copenhagen as Ortrud (*Lohengrin*), Elizabeth (*Tannhäuser*), Brünnhilde (*Valkyrie*) and other rôles. Her real fame as a star of the first magnitude was won in 1896 and following years, when she for the first time sang Wagner at the Bayreuth Fest., after having stud. the parts under Cosima Wagner herself. Became permanently attached to this theatre as one of its best performers. By degrees her powers of impersonation became more and more concentrated upon the commanding figure

of Brünnhilde, a rôle which she filled with all the power and greatness of her personality, both vocally and histrionically. In this character from the ancient Norse saga she won her world-wide fame. Twenty years ago she was regarded as the most successful Brünnhilde of the day. In Bayreuth she appeared for last time in 1914. As a Wagnerian singer she has won triumphs in Berlin, Vienna, London, Paris, etc. Owing to the unsatisfactory state of affairs as regards opera in Norway, she has had no opportunity of appearing in her chief rôles in that country; but in the concert-halls in Christiania and all over the country, she has been greatly appreciated.
—R. M.

GUND, Robert. Compr. b. Seckenheim (Germany), 18 Nov. 1865. Stud. at Leipzig Cons., then Vienna Cons.; pianist and teacher of singing, Vienna, till 1913; Switzerland till 1922; then returned to Vienna. His style is unpretentious yet melodious. His wife, Elizabeth Gund-Lauterburg, gave many concerts of his songs in Germany and Austria. One of his pupils is Ernst Kurth, the famous Swiss writer on music.

Romantic Suite, pf. and vn.; 4tet, pf. vn. vla. cello; str. 4tet; many songs; collection of Swiss folk-songs (Univ. Ed. 1921).—P. P.

GURICKX, Camille. Belgian pianist; b. Brussels, 29 Dec. 1848. Pupil of Auguste Dupont at Brussels Cons. His first appearances as a pianist were so brilliant that the Belgian Government granted him a subsidy, with which he was to visit Germany. In Weimar Édouard Lassen presented him to Liszt, who took a liking to him, called him "mon petit Belge," and continually advised him. Début in Paris in Vieuxtemps' salons, 1874. After several concerts in that city, made a tour in Russia. In 1876 Rubinstein invited him to give a recital at his house, which led to his giving a whole series of concerts in England. He next worked at compn. in Paris under Saint-Saëns. Appointed prof. of pf. at Mons Cons. Played in New York at Philh. Soc. On death of Auguste Dupont, succeeded him as prof. of pf. at Brussels Cons. A pianist of the best school, a high-class teacher, giving equal attention to interpretation and technique, he trained several of the best lady Belgian pianists: Amélie Pardon, Swaels-Wauters, Claire Preumont, Tambuyser, Van Neste and Simonard.—C. V. B.

GURIDI, Jesús. Span. compr., orgt.; b. Vitoria, 25 Sept. 1886. Prof. of organ at Acad. de Música Vizcaína, also at Cons. Vizcaíno (organ and compn.). Orgt. at the Basílica del Señor, Santiago, and condr. of the Soc. Coral de Bilbao. Amongst his ancestry is to be found a prominent figure in the history of Span. mus. decadence of XIX century — his great-grand-father, the compr. and orgt. Don Nicolás Ledesma, who died in 1883 at the advanced age of 92. Jesús G. made his début as a compr. at 13. His real career did not commence until he received serious tuition from Maestro Basabe, of Bilbao; in 1904, he left Spain, under the patron-

age of the Count of Zubiría, to study successively with d'Indy at the Schola Cantorum, Paris, Joseph Jongen at Brussels, and Otto Neitzel at Cologne. This diversity of influences did not eradicate from him the characteristic faith of his native province in the traditional ideals of the Basque country. Foreign influence is only detected in his technique—on which the Schola Cantorum has left the deepest mark—his music being mostly based on Basque themes or inspired by Basque legends. This is perhaps why, in association with Isasi and the late Usandizaga, he is hailed by some as one of the founders of a modern Basque school, as distinct from the rest of Span. comprs. Whether or not the mere difference in choice of thematic material affords solid ground to establish that distinction, the fact remains that G. is one of the chief figures amongst contemporary Spanish symphonists.

For pf.: Ocho cantos vascos; Tres piezas breves; for v. and pf.: Nere Maitia; Melodías populares; Paysage; Tres miniaturas; Canción de niño. Vs. unacc.: Tres series de cantos populares vascos, 4, 6 and 8 vs. Children's chorus with pf.: El Príncipe triste; Día de campo. Children's chorus and orch.: Así cantan los chicos. Solo v. and orch.: Saison des semailles. Organ: Fantasía; Improvisación; Preludio; Fantasía; Villancico. Vn. and orch.: Elegía. Orch.: Égloga, Leyenda Vasca, Una Aventura de Don Quijote. Orch., chorus and corps de ballet: Escena vasca. Operas: Mirentxu, 2 acts; Amaya, 3 acts and epilogue, first perf. Bilbao, 22 May. 1920; Madrid, 1923. (Unión Musical Española; Revista Sacro-Hispana, Madrid; Maison Beethoven, Brussels; Schott.)—P. G. M.

GURLITT, Willibald. Ger. writer on music; b. Dresden, 1 March, 1889. Son of fine-art historian, Cornelius Gurlitt, he passed out of the Annen-schule, Dresden, to Leipzig Univ., where he stud. mus. science (Riemann), and graduated Ph.D. (biography and bibliography) with first part of a comprehensive work on Michael Prætorius (Leipzig, Breitkopf). Assistant of Mus. Science Inst. of Univ. Leipzig. Wounded at Battle of the Marne, Aug. 1914 ; prisoner of war in France till 1919. In the autumn, 1919, lector in mus. science at Univ. of Freiburg-i-Br.; 1920, prof. in ordinary and dir. of seminary of mus. science. Latterly he has devoted himself specially to study of mediæval (Gothic) music.
—A. E.

GURNEY, Ivor Bertie. Eng. compr. b. Gloucester, 28 Aug. 1890. Choir-boy at Cath. there; scholar R.C.M. London, under Sir Charles Stanford, Herbert Sharpe, W. G. Alcock and Vaughan Williams. As compr. G. cultivates the smaller forms and achieves a fine, clear, English style, which is marked by an absence of the set-phrase thraldom, as well as by a respect for the classical school. G. is a keen student of the Elizabethan drama.

Orch.: Gloucester Rhapsody; War Elegy; str. 4tets: I, D mi. (1911–12); II, A mi. (1922); III, E (1922); pf. preludes; Ludlow and Teme, v. and str. 4tet (Carnegie award); numerous songs, including song-cycle on works by A. E. Housman (Carnegie award, 1924).—E.-H.

GUSTAVSON, Oscar, Norwegian violinist; b. Horten, 3 Jan. 1877. Pupil of Gudbrand Böhn (Christiania), Anton Witek (Berlin). 1st violinist at National Theatre, Christiania, 1899–1907.

Has lived for some years in Switzerland as teacher and concert-giver.—U. M.

GUTHEIL-SCHODER, Marie. Opera-singer; *b.* Weimar, 10 Feb. 1874. 1891–1900 at Hof-theater, Weimar; since then at Vienna Opera. Much influenced by Mahler. Together with Anna Bahr-Mildenburg she is the chief representative of his style. A brilliant singer of Mozart (Elvira, Susanna, Cherubino). Excels in all kinds of parts (*Iphigenia in Aulis, Carmen, Manon,* Nedda, Marie, *Der Waffenschmied*), *Frau Fluth, Rote Gred* (Bittner), *Salome, Elektra,* Octavian (*Der Rosenkavalier*), Potiphar (*Joseph's Legend*). Her husband was Gustav Gutheil (1868–1914), compr. and condr. at Weimar and Vienna (1900–1910) and popular concerts of Konzert-Verein. Consult L. Andro, *Marie Gutheil-Schoder,* in coll. *Die Wiedergabe* (Vienna, 1923).—P. St.

GUŻEWSKI, Adolf. Polish compr. *b.* Dyrwiany, Kovno; *d.* in Russia, 1917. Stud. at Milan and Riga, then at Petrograd Cons. under Sołovief (theory) and under Dubassof (pf.). After 1900, completed his studies under Noskowski in Warsaw. Prof. at Warsaw Cons. 1906–15.

Operas: *The Maiden of the Glaciers* (Andersen's tale); *Atlantide.* 2 sonatas for pf.; sonata, pf. and vn.; *Polish Rhapsody* for orch.; Variations for orch.; symphony in A ma. (the 2 last works received prizes at Warsaw competitions); numerous songs. Has publ. a practical manual of orchestration.—ZD. J.

GUZMÁN, Father Juan Bautista. Span. orgt. and compr. *b.* Aldaya (Valencia), 19 Jan. 1846; *d.* 18 March, 1909. Pupil of José María Ubeda. In 1872 orgt. at Cath. of Salamanca and later in same year of Real Colegiata de Nuestra Señora de Covadonga. In 1875, choirmaster at Avila Cath.; 1876, held same position at Valladolid, and in 1877 at Valencia. In 1889 became a Benedictine, adopting name of Father Manuel de Guzmán. He comp. religious music of slight value. In 1889 publ. an annotated full-score ed. of *Obras musicales del insigne maestro español del siglo XVII, J. B. Comes.*—P. G. M.

GYLDENKRONE, Lona Gulowsen (Baroness of Gyldenkrone). Norwegian operatic and concert-singer (s.); *b.* Christiania, 30 Jan. 1848. Pupil of Henrik Meyer, Christiania, and Pauline Viardot, Paris. *Début,* Stockholm, 1876. Won great recognition for her artistic singing and intelligent interpretation. Since her marriage in 1882 has lived in Copenhagen.—U. M.

H

HAALAND, Ingebret. Norwegian violinist; b. Stavanger, 8 Aug. 1878. Became in 1892 pupil of Music Cons. in Christiania; took in 1896 the organ examination; scholarship from Houen's Bequest; stud. vn. under Florian Zajič in Berlin. Became leading violinist in orch. of National Theatre in Christiania, where he worked for 15 years; besides being orgt. at Akershus Slotskirke, and teacher of vn. at Music Cons. in Christiania. Repeated concert-tours as violinist; violinist in Arvesen Quartet at concerts in Copenhagen, Stockholm and Paris. Has comp. pieces for pf., pf. and vn., mixed and male chorus.—J. A.

HAAPANEN, Toivo. Finnish musicologist; b. 1889. Stud. in Helsingfors Univ. (Ph.M. 1918) and Orch. School; and 1921 as scholar in Germany. Has made researches in mediæval Finnish music. Publ. *Verzeichnis der mittelalterlichen Handschriftenfragmente in der Univ. Bibl. zu Helsingfors, I, Missalia* (1922). A musical critic by profession, he has appeared as orch. condr. in Helsingfors and other towns in Finland. Dr. Haapanen is responsible for all the Finnish articles in this Dictionary.—E.-H.

HAARKLOU, Johannes. Norwegian compr. and orgt. b. Förde, Söndfjord, 13 May, 1847. Pupil of Cappelen (organ), Ludv. M. Lindeman (cpt.). Stud. at Cons. in Leipzig 1873–6, in Berlin 1877–8 (Kiel, Bungert and Haupt); orgt. at Gamle Akers Ch. Christiania, 1880–1920. Cond. (1883 and 1885–8) symphony concerts at popular prices, first of kind in Norway, partly with support of grants from State. The Parliament granted him in 1889 a travelling scholarship; in same year cond. his symphony in B ma. in Leipzig. His orch. works have frequently been perf. in Christiania and Leipzig. A clever contrapuntist; 1895–6, teacher at Music Cons. in Christiania. Music critic for many years on daily press. Granted a composer's pension by Parliament; member of the Commemorative Council for Culture.

As a compr. his rare polyphonic endowment has found expression in symphony, sonata and oratorio. Also as a music-dramatist he holds a prominent place. Like so many other Norwegian musicians of the Leipzig school, in his works he bridges the romantic and the classical, while emphasising the national element. In the minor forms the specifically Norwegian has unfolded itself most freely; for example the fine male-choruses *Varde* and *Fenrir*.

5 operas (*From Olden Days*; *The Varangians in Miklagaard*; *The Emigrant*; *Marisagnet* (*The Marian Legend*); *Tyrfing*); 3 symphonies (B ma., D mi., C ma.); oratorio, *Skabelsen* (*The Creation*); vn. concerto; pf. concerto; orch. suite, *In Westminster Abbey*; *Legend of St. Olav*; minor orch. pieces;

cantatas; male choruses; vn. sonata; pf. pieces; organ pieces; songs. Mostly publ. by Reinecke, Leipzig.—J. A.

HAAS, Joseph. Ger. compr. b. Maihingen (Bavaria), 19 March, 1879. Pupil of Max Reger in Munich and of Leipzig Cons. From 1911, teaching compn. at Stuttgart Cons. (prof. 1916). At Music Acad. Munich, since 1921. An excellent compr., and his reliance on Reger brought him individuality, a true musical humour and the cultivation of Post-Romantic feeling.

Pf. works: op. 2 (Bote & Bock); op. 9 (Boston, A. P. Schmidt); op. 10, *Kinderlust* (Leuckart); op. 16, *Loose Leaves*, 10 pieces (Rahter); *Joyous Moods* (Rahter); op. 27, *The Little Hobgoblin* (Tischer & Jagenberg); op. 35, *Home Fairy Tales* (Tischer); op. 36, *Joys of Youth* (Forberg); op. 39, *Till Eulenspiegel Medley* (Tischer); op. 42, *Nameless Days of Old* (Tischer); op. 43, *Home Fairy Tales* (Tischer); op. 46, sonata, A mi. (Leuckart); op. 51, *German Ring Dances and Romances* (Tischer); op. 55, *Farces and Idylls* (Mayence, Schott); op. 61, i and ii, sonatas. Organ works: op. 3, 10 choral preludes (Forberg); op. 11, 3 preludes and fugues (Forberg); op. 12, sonata, C mi. (Forberg); op. 15, 8 organ pieces (London, Augener); op. 20, suite, D mi. (Robt. Forberg); op. 25, suite, A ma. (Leuckart); op. 31, Variations on original theme (Regensburg, Coppenrath). Also 2 sonatinas, vn. and pf. op. 4 (Bote & Bock); sonata, vn. and pf. B mi. op. 28 (*A Ghostly Hour, Pixy Freakishness*) (Tischer); suite, vn. and pf. op. 40, *The Blue Devils* (Tischer); *Divertimento*, str. trio, op. 22 (Kistner); suite, ob. and pf., *A Little Garland* (Tischer); sonata for horn and pf. op. 29 (Tischer); chamber trio for 2 vns. and pf., op. 38 (Tischer); str. 4tet, *Divertimento*, op. 32 (Tischer); str. 4tet, A ma., op. 50 (Tischer); *Serenade* for orch., op. 41 (Tischer); Variations and rondo on old German folk-song, orch., op. 45 (Leuckart). Songs: op. 1 (Bote & Bock); op. 5 (Forberg); op. 7 (Berlin, Dr. Heinrich Lewy); op. 13, sacred songs for v. and organ (Leuckart); op. 24 (Leuckart); op. 33, *Rum-bi-di-bum*, 10 children's songs on texts by Hoffmann v. Fallersleben (Tischer); op. 37, 5 *Cuckoo Songs* (Tischer); op. 47, *Trali-Trala*, 12 children's songs (Tischer); op. 48, 6 songs on text of Cäsar Flaischlen (Tischer); op. 49, 6 Christmas songs; symph. suite, v. and orch., *Day and Night*, op. 58; choruses, op. 4, 7. 18, 26, 44.—A. E.

HAAS, Robert Maria. Ger. - Czechoslovak compr. b. Prague, 15 Aug. 1886; stud. under Kretzschmar, Riemann, Adler, Rietsch; condr. in Münster (Westphalia), Erfurt, Constance; 1911, Korrepetitor at R. Opera, Dresden; then secretary of *Corpus Scriptorum de Musica* and of *D.T.Ö.* in Vienna. Curator of music collection at National Library, Vienna.

A new ed. of I. Umlauf's *Bergknappen*; F. L. Gassmann's "*La Contessina*" in *D.T.Ö.*; F. L. Gassmann in Adler's *Studies in the Science of Music* (in collab. with G. Donath); in *New Archives of Saxon History* 1913 (J. M. Schürer); other scientific essays in volume of *I.M.G.* for its 3rd Congress: trio-suite; str. 4tets; pf. 5tets; vn. sonata; cello sonata; songs.—E. S.

HÁBA, Alois. Czechoslovak compr. b. Vyzovice (Moravia), 1893. Stud. compn. at Prague Cons. under Vítězslav Novák; at Mus. Acad. in Vienna; at High School, Berlin, under Franz Schreker. Stud. acoustics in Berlin Univ.

207

In 1921 took Mendelssohn Prize. Is now living in Prague. His first compns. attracted attention in Germany, his *Symphonic Phantasy* for pf. and orch. being played at Düsseldorf Fest. 1921. He has lately become interested in the theory of quarter-tones, and in this system he is composing now. His pamphlet *The Theory of Quarter-tones in Harmony* is publ. by Hudební Matice Umělecké Besedy. He uses the quarter-tones both melodically and harmonically.

Pf. sonata; 3 str. 4tets (the second and third ones in quarter-tones); orch. overture; *Symph. Phantasy*, pf. and orch.; phantasy for vn. solo; symph. music for chamber-orch. in quarter-tones; 7 compns. for quarter-tone harmonium. (Publ. mostly in Univ. Ed. Vienna; some by Hudební Matice, Prague.)—V. ST.

HADLEY, Henry Kimball. Amer. compr. *b.* Somerville, Mass., U.S.A., 20 Dec. 1871. Educated in the Somerville public schools. His father, a musician, gave him his first lessons on pf. and vn. Later he was student at New England Cons. in Boston under Stephen Emery and G. W. Chadwick. In 1893-4 he toured America with Schirmer-Mapleson Opera Co. as condr. He made his *début* as an orchestral compr. in 1894, when an overture, *Hector and Andromache*, was perf. for the Manuscript Soc. in New York under bâton of Walter Damrosch. The same year he went to Vienna to study cpt. under Mandyczewski. In 1895 he returned to America and was engaged as music-master at Cath. School of St. Paul's in Garden City, Long Island, N.Y. Here he taught pf. and vn. and was orgt. and choirmaster as well. He remained in Garden City until 1902, composing much church music and some orch. works. His 1st symphony, *Youth and Life*, op. 25 (unpubl.), was perf. at a concert of the Manuscript Soc. in New York by an orch. cond. by Anton Seidl, 16 Dec. 1897. In 1901 his 2nd symphony, *The Seasons*, op 30, won 2 prizes, the Paderewski Prize and the Prize of the New England Cons. of Music. In 1899 his cantata *In Music's Praise* gained a prize offered by the publ. house of O. Ditson in Boston, and was produced by the People's Choral Union of New York under Frank Damrosch.

The years 1904-9 were spent in Germany, where he gave concerts in many cities, performing his own works. In 1908-9 he was a condr. at the Stadttheater in Mayence, where he brought out his 1-act opera *Safie*. He returned to America in 1909 to conduct the 1st perf. in Chicago of his Rhapsody for orch., *The Culprit Fay*, which had won the $1000 prize of the National Federation of Women's Clubs. Then from 1909-11 he cond. the Symphony Orch. in Seattle, Washington, and from 1911-15 he held a similar position in San Francisco. After this he returned to the East. On 18 Dec. 1917, his opera *Azora* was produced by Chicago Opera Co. In 1918 his 1-act opera *Bianca* won a prize of $1000 offered by Mr. Wade Hinshaw, by whose Soc. of Amer. Singers the work was first sung in New York, 18 Oct. 1918. On 31 Jan. 1920, the Metropolitan Opera in New York produced his op. 90, *Cleopatra's Night*, an opera in 2 acts. A symph. poem, *The Ocean* (op. 99), was first perf. by the Philh.

Orch. in New York, 17 Nov. 1920, and a Christmas cantata, *Prophecy and Fulfilment*, was sung at a children's concert of Philadelphia Orch. in Dec. 1921. His *Resurgam* (op. 98) for soli, chorus and orch. was perf. at Cincinnati Mus. Fest. 1923, and by the London Choral Soc. at Queen's Hall, 8 April, 1924, when *The Ocean* was also given under the compr. Since 1920 he has been associate-condr. of New York Philh. Soc.

H. is one of the most active and prolific of living Amer. comprs. He has cultivated all the large and small forms. His style, though showing a natural evolution and development as the years went by, has been remarkably consistent and unified. He has made no violent attempt to borrow new or startling effects from the representatives of revolutionary tendencies in art. Fertile melodic invention, freshness and manly straightforward expression in the idiom in which he had been brought up and solid technical acquirements mark his work from beginning to end.

Symphonies: No. II, *The Seasons*, op. 30 (A. P. Schmidt, 1902); No. IV, *North, East, South, West*, 1st perf. Norfolk (Conn.) Fest. 1911 (Schirmer, 1912); Symph. Fantasia for orch. op. 46 (*id.* 1907); *Salome*, tone-poem for orch. op. 55 (Berlin, Ries & Erler, 1906); rhapsody, *The Culprit Fay*, op. 62 (Schirmer, 1910); overture, *Othello*, op. 96 (*id.* 1921); 5tet in A mi. for pf. and str. (*id.* 1919); concert-piece for cello and orch. op. 61 (*id.* 1909); *Azora*, 3-act opera, op. 80 (*id.* 1917); *Bianca*, 1-act opera (New York, Flammer, 1918); *Cleopatra's Night*, 2-act opera (Ditson, 1920); *In Music's Praise*, cantata, op. 21 (Ditson, 1900); *Ode to Music*, lyric drama for soli, chorus and orch. op. 75, 1st perf. Worcester (Mass.) Fest. 1917 (Schirmer, 1917); *The New Earth*, ode for soli, chorus and orch. op. 85 (Ditson, 1919); 2 pieces for vn. and pf. op. 36 (Schirmer, 1909); *A Prayer*, vn. and pf. op. 86 (C. Fischer, 1920). *Resurgam*, op. 98 (Ditson, 1922). About 150 songs. —O. K.

HADOW, Sir William Henry. Eng. writer and lecturer on music; Vice-Chancellor, Sheffield Univ. (from 1919); *b.* Ebrington, Glos, 1859. Educated at Worcester Coll. Oxford, of which he became Fellow; ed. *Oxford History of Music*. Knight 1918; C.B.E. 1920; Mus.Doc. of Oxford, Durham and Wales; LL.D. St. Andrews. His books on music rank with the finest critical literature. He is also an able lecturer on music.

Pf. sonata (1884); str. 4tet (1885); song-albums (1897; 1889; 1903; 1912); incidental music to Robert Bridges' *Demeter* (1905); etc. Books: *Studies in Modern Music* (Seeley & Co.), 1st series 1894; 2nd, 1895; *Sonata-Form* (Novello, 1896); *A Croatian Composer* (J. Haydn), 1897; *The Viennese Period* (*Oxford History of Music*), 1904; *British Music*, a Report, for the Carnegie United Kingdom Trust, 1921.—E.-H.

HAGELSTAM, Anna (*née* Silfverberg). Finnish singer; *b.* Åbo, 20 Nov. 1883. Stud. singing in Berlin (1907-10) and Paris (1911-16). Since 1911, has toured successfully in Finland, Paris, Monte Carlo, Denmark, Norway and Sweden; 1919-20, appeared at Finnish Opera House. Married the writer Wenzel Hagelstam in 1913. —T. H.

HÄGG, Gustav W. Swedish orgt. compr. *b.* Visby (Gottland), 28 Nov. 1867. Stud. R. Cons. Stockholm, 1884-90; compn. under Joseph Dente. In 1898, stud. in Germany and France; 1893, orgt. at St. Clara, Stockholm; 1904, sub-prof. (harmony), R. Cons.; from 1908, prof.

(organ). Has given many organ-recitals and also played with orch. Member R.A.M. Stockholm, 1906.

Organ: 4 *morceaux*, op. 12 (Leipzig, Kistner); *Meditation*, op. 16 (Gehrman); 5 pieces, op. 22 (Univ. Ed.). Pf.: 6 pieces (1890; Hirsch); sonata, op. 19, etc. Pf. trio. Vn. and pf.: *Romances*, op. 23, E mi. (Hofmeister); E ma. (Gehrman); *Liebeslied*, op. 27 (Hofmeister); *Adagio* with organ, op. 34 (Junne). Harmonium pieces; songs; Swedish folk-tunes for pf.; choruses. In ms.: symphony in D; str. 6tet; str. 4tet; 2 cantatas, soli, chorus, orch. (1906; 1907).—P. V.

HÄGG, Jakob. Swedish compr. *b.* Östergarn, Gottland, 27 June, 1850. Stud. at R. Cons. Stockholm; orgt. dipl. 1867; member R.A.M. Stockholm, 1917. Lives in Hudiksvall (Sweden).

Orch.: Suite, op. 3; concert-overtures, op. 26, 28; *Concert-Allegro*, op. 52; 3 pieces, op. 62 (all comp. 1871); sonata, vn. and pf. (Dresden, 1872); sonata, cello and pf. op. 1 (1871); pf. trio, op. 15; str. 4tet; songs; pf. pieces.—P. V.

HAGMAN, Carl. Norwegian operatic t. singer; *b.* Larvik, 16 Sept. 1874. Pupil of Fritz Arlberg and John Forsell, Stockholm. *Début* in 1897. Engaged at various opera houses; amongst others, National Theatre, Christiania, 1900–4, 1908–12 (*Il Trovatore*, Don José, Pinkerton, Lohengrin, Radamès, etc.).—U. M.

HAHN, Reynaldo. Fr. composer; *b.* Caracas (Venezuela), 9 Aug. 1874. Having come to France at age of 3 he belongs to the French school. At the Paris Conservatoire he was pupil of Massenet and Lavignac. In his early youth it might have been believed that he would one day be an amazing musical genius, so extraordinary were the signs which he gave of artistic precocity, composing sonatas and symphonies with astonishing harmonic accuracy at an age when his fellow-pupils were toiling over exercises on figured-bass. Unfortunately, these precocious gifts did not develop with age and he remained a fine musician, very culti-vated, profoundly artistic, but without great originality. Hahn has a most enthusiastic admiration for Mozart and has revived on the stage at the opera several of the master's operas —*Seraglio, Magic Flute.* During the winter he directs the opera in Cannes.

Opéra-comique, La Carmélite, 1902; ballets: *Le Bal de Béatrice d'Este* (1909); *Le Dieu Bleu* (1911); music for stage; pf. 5tet: pf. pieces, and especially some songs of great charm, admirably written for voice, of which several are deservedly popular: *Chansons grises, Idylles latines,* etc. (Heugel).—H. P.

HÅKANSON, Knut Algot. Swedish compr. *b.* Kinna, 4 Nov. 1887. Stud. compn. under Johan Lindegren in Stockholm, 1906–8; under Ruben Liljefors, 1913–14; pf. under Knut Bäck. Condr. of Orch. Soc. of Borås; lives in Rydbo-holm, near Borås.

Orch.: *Sérénade dramatique*, with vn. solo, op. 2 (1913); 2 festival marches, op. 3 (1915); concert overture, op. 9 (1917); music to ballet *Mylitta* (Copenhagen, 1918); *Romance*, with vn. solo (1918); 2 *Intermezzi*, op. 12 (1921); Suite, op. 14 (1922). Songs with pf. and with orch.; pf. pieces; choruses; chamber-music, etc. Publ. a remarkable arr. of the songs of C. J. L. Almqvist (Ad. Bonnier, 1916).—P. V.

HALE, Philip. Amer. author, critic; *b.* Nor-wich, Vt., U.S.A., 5 March, 1854. Admitted to the Bar at Albany, N.Y., 1880. Had stud. music under Dudley Buck and in 1882 abandoned law, going to Germany, where he was pupil of Haupt,

Faisst and Rheinberger (organ) of Raif and Scholz (pf.), and of Urban, Bargiel and Rhein-berger (compn.). After this, stud. organ and compn. under Guilmant in Paris. Returning to America in 1887, he was orgt. of St. John's, Troy, N.Y. In 1889, settled in Boston and was orgt. of the First Religious Soc., in Roxbury, Mass., from 1889–1905; and music critic for *Boston Post* (1890–1), for the *Journal* (1891–1903) and since 1903 for the *Herald*. Since 1901, has ed. the programmes of Boston Symphony Orch. These programmes form annual vols. that run from 1400 to almost 2000 pages, and contain, beside the annotations on the comprs. and the biographical sketches of the comprs. and the soloists, a great many *Entractes*, essays on topics of general mus. interest. They have become a veritable cyclopædia of music and a perfect treasure-house of information on Amer. concert-life of the past 30 or 40 years. They have furnished valuable data for the Amer. articles of this Dictionary.—O. K.

HALEY, Olga. Eng. m.-sopr. singer; *b.* Huddersfield, 10 Nov. 1898. First stud. under parents, both musicians; then at R.C.M. London and in Switzerland (1912–13); *début* Albert Hall, London, 30 Sept. 1916; almost immediately came to front rank as a singer of the finest songs, especially those of contemporary Fr. and Eng. comprs.; also made her first appearance in opera as Carmen, Covent Garden, B.N.O.C., June 1922.—E.-H.

HALFFTER ESCRICHE, Ernesto. Spanish compr. *b.* Madrid, 16 Jan. 1905. Pupil of the critic Adolfo Salazar, Oscar Esplá and Manuel de Falla. With the perf. of some of his works in 1922-3 he revealed himself as a promising artist of the school of Ravel and Stravinsky.

Chamber-music: str. 4tet (1923); *Sonatina-fan-tasia* (1923); *Dos bocetos* (1923); *Homenajes* (1923), str. 4tet; 10 pieces, pf. vn. and cello. Pf.: *Crépus-cules* (1918); *Trois pièces enfantines* (1922); *Marche joyeuse,* 4 hands (1922). Voice: 5 songs by Heine (1918); *Automne Malade* (Apollinaire), 1923; 2 pre-ludes, pf. and v. without words (1923). *Suite ancienne,* wind instrs. (1919). Orch.: *Dos bocetos; Dos retratos* (1923). For stage, *El amor alicorto.* (All unpubl.)— P. G. M.

HALFFTER ESCRICHE, Rodolfo. Spanish compr. *b.* Madrid, 30 Oct. 1900. According to the critic Adolfo Salazar, he differs from his brother Ernesto in revealing Schönbergian tendencies.

Natures mortes (1922), for pf.; *Piezas,* for str. 4tet (1923).—P. G. M.

HALL, G. W. L. Marshall. Eng. compr. *b.* London, 1862; *d.* 19 July, 1915. Educated King's College London and at Oxford; stud. at R.C.M. and in Germany and Switzerland; condr. in London Organ School; Ormond Prof. of Music, Melbourne Univ. Australia; resigned later, but reappointed in 1914; founded Cons. of Music in Melbourne; and in 1903 the Marshall Hall Symphony Orch. His opera *Stella* was produced in London in June 1914 at the Pal-ladium.

3 operas; orch. works; str. 4tets; songs; etc. —E.-H.

HALL, Marie. Eng. violinist; *b.* Newcastle-on-Tyne, 8 April, 1884. First lessons by her father (harpist in Carl Rosa Opera Co.); appeared as child-artist; heard by Sauret, he recommended her to go to R.A.M. London, but the project failed; later she had some lessons from Wilhelmj in London; and Max Mossel in 1898; in 1901, under Ševčík in Prague; *début* in Prague, Nov. 1902; Vienna, Jan. 1903; London, St. James's Hall, 16 Feb. 1903; has toured Great Britain and the Continent repeatedly; also U.S.A., Canada, Australia, New Zealand, India and S. Africa.—E.-H.

HALL, Pauline. Norwegian compr. *b.* Hamar in 1890. Pupil of Cath. Elling, Christiania. Stud. in Paris, 1912–13; in Dresden, 1913–14, under E. Kauffmann-Jassoy (harmony). Her chief work, Suite for orch. (to poem by Verlaine), produced in Christiania, 1920, displays, like her pf.-pieces and songs, a fine and dainty artistry, somewhat influenced by the Fr. Neo-Impressionists.—R. M.

HALL, Walter Henry. Amer. choral condr. *b.* London, 25 April, 1862. Pupil of Harold Thomas (pf.), Steggall (organ) and Banister (theory), for 4 years, at R.A.M. London. Went to America 1883; orgt. St. Luke's, Germantown, Pa., 1884–90; St. Peter's, Albany, N.Y., 1890; St. James's, New York, 1896–1913. In 1893 founded Brooklyn (N.Y.) Oratorio Soc., of which he is still condr. Since 1901, lecturer on music at Columbia Univ., N.Y.; since 1913, prof. of church and choral music and condr. of the Univ. chorus. Author of *Essentials of Choir-boy Training* (Novello, 1906).—J. M.

HALLÉ ORCHESTRA. Owed its inception to intelligent anticipation of Committee of Art Treasures Exhibition, Manchester 1857, when they invited the late Sir Charles Hallé (then Mr. Hallé), and invested him with plenary powers to form an orch. to give perfs. of best music in hall of Exhibition Buildings. The venture (in those far-off days a very remarkable one) proved such a success that Hallé was encouraged to take up his permanent residence in Manchester, and to give a series of orch. concerts on his own account in the Free Trade Hall. Thus there came into being " Mr. Charles Hallé's Grand Orchestral Concerts," which were continued by him without interruption until his death on 25 Oct. 1895, after having completed his 37th annual series of weekly orch. concerts (20 each season). It is on record that at the conclusion of the first season the business-manager presented Hallé with ten threepenny-bits, this sum being the net profit of the winter's work. Hallé died suddenly a few days before the first concert of the 1895–6 season. Fortunately for orch. music in the north of England a committee of 3 public-minded citizens determined to carry on Hallé's work, and the Hallé Concert Soc. was formed. This Soc. is a limited company, and as such is registered at Somerset House, with guarantors instead of shareholders. Each guarantee is for £100, the liability of which is terminated by death of guarantor. Calls are made only in case of loss, and by the vote of a majority of the guarantors. By this unique and excellent scheme

the Soc. has at call a large sum of money, the list of guarantors being kept up to about 200. Following the death of their founder, the concerts were at first cond. by guest-condrs. (Sir Arthur Sullivan, Sir Charles Stanford, Sir Joseph Barnby, Sir Frederick Bridge, Sir Frederick Cowen, Sir Alexander Mackenzie, Dr. Brodsky, Sir George Henschel). During 1896–9 Sir Frederick Cowen cond., after which Dr. Hans Richter was appointed resident-condr., and remained in charge 11 years, retiring eventually in 1911 owing to ill-health. During Richter's régime the orch. attained a high pitch of perfection, and a reputation travelling as far afield as Scotland and Ireland. It visited most of the large towns in the north of England. Even London was invaded, and a most successful fest. of Elgar's works was given. Richter's successor was Michael Balling, and he remained condr. until outbreak of war, 1914. Another season of guest-condrs. followed, and in 1915 Sir Thomas Beecham became artistic adviser and condr. On his resignation in 1920, owing to his many other activities, Sir Thomas was succeeded as permanent condr. by Hamilton Harty. During each winter season, the orch. gives, in addition to some 30 concerts at its headquarters, Manchester, between 40 and 50 concerts in other towns including Bradford, Bolton, Middlesbrough, Newcastle, Hull, Derby, Hanley, Leicester, Leeds, Belfast and Dublin. —J. A. F.

HALLÉN, Johan Andréas. Swedish compr. and condr. *b.* Gothenburg, 22 Dec. 1846. Stud. there, also Leipzig (1866–8), Munich (1869), Dresden (1870-2); singing-master and music critic in Berlin, 1880–3; condr. of Philh. Soc. Stockholm, 1885–95; at R. Opera, 1892–7; of South-Swedish Philh. (Malmö) 1902–7; teacher of compn. at R. Cons. Stockholm, from 1909; prof. 1915; music critic, from 1909, to *Nya Dagligt Allehanda.* H. is one of most important Swedish comprs. in last decade of XIX century. His orch. works and operas show dramatic power, with a tuneful and harmonic flow. He is considered a follower of Wagner but has his own style. As condr. he has given in Sweden many great choral works of Bach, Mendelssohn, etc.

Operas: *Harald Viking* (Leipzig, 1881; Stockholm, 1884); *Häxfällan* (Stockholm, 1896); *Valdemarsskatten* (*ib.* 1899); *Valborgsmassa* (*ib.* 1902). Stage-music to *Saga of Gustavus Vasa* (1896; arr. as suite), *Over Evne,* etc. For orch.: 2 concert overtures; 2 rhapsodies; 4 suites; symph. poems: *A Summer-Saga; In the Autumn; Toteninsel; Sphärenklänge.* Chorus and orch.: 4 ballades; cantatas: *Trollslottet; Styrbjörn Starke; Sverige; Requiescat; Dionysos).* Christmas Oratorio (1904). Ballads and songs with small orch. or pf.; pf. 4tet, op. 3; *Albumblätter* for pf. Wrote a book, *Musical Causerics* (1904).—P. V.

HALLER, Michael. Ger. compr. *b.* Neusaat (Bav. Upper Palatinate), 13 Jan. 1840; *d.* Regensburg, 4 Jan. 1915. Entered seminary for priests at Regensburg Cath. Canonry (choir-boys' Inst.); stud. church music under Schrems. In 1867, inspector of R. Inst., taking over the orch. at same; 1899, elected to a capitular canonry. Haller was an excellent compr. and wrote:

4 5-v. masses; 6-v. *Missa solemnis*; 8-v. mass, op. 92; 8 4-v. masses; 5-v. *Lamentations*; several volumes 4- to 8-v. motets, psalms, litanies, offertories, *Ave Maria*, *Te Deum*. Some secular music (*Youth's Garland of Songs, Youth's Treasure*, etc.); songs (op. 111): melodramas; str. 4 tets, etc. Essays for Haberl's *Kirchenmusikalisches Jahrbuch*; *Composition Manual for Polyphonic Church Singing* (1891); *Vademecum for Vocal Instruction* (1876, 12th ed. 1910); *Modulations in Church Modes*; collection of *Exempla polyphoniæ ecclesiasticæ*.—A. E.

HALM, August. Ger. author, compr. *b.* Gross-Altdorf (Würtemberg), 26 Oct. 1869. Theological student at Univ. of Tübingen; then to R. School of Music, Munich (Rheinberger, Bruckner, Abel, Hieber, Lang); teacher of music at Landerziehungshiem Haubinda (1903–6); then Free School of Wickersdorf till 1910. Dir. of male choral soc. of Ulm, 1910–11; teacher of music at Higher City Schools there, 1912. In 1913 held similar position in Stuttgart. In Ulm during the war; now back at Wickersdorf.

Text-book, *Harmonielehre* (No. 120, Göschen Coll.) vn. manual; pf. tutor, and the able works: *On Two Cultures of Music* (Munich, 1913, Georg Müller); *The Symphonies of A. Bruckner* (*ib.* 1914); *The Frontiers and Countries of Music* (*ib.* 1916); *J. S. Bach's Concerto Form* (*Bach Year-Book*, 1919). Pf. pieces; str. 4 tet, B flat ma.; 3 serenades, str. trio; 3 sonatas, vn. alone; a symphony for str. orch.; one for full orch.; pf. concerto, etc.—A. E.

HALSTEAD, Philip. Eng. pianist; *b.* Blackburn, 23 May, 1866. Stud. at Leipzig, 1885–8, under Zwintscher, Carl Reinecke, Jadassohn. Awarded bursary and Mozart Prize. Played at opening concert of new Cons. Leipzig. Further studies in Paris and Weimar (under Stavenhagen). Settled in Glasgow. Played frequently with orch. under Manns, and with Scottish Orch. Founded series of chamber-music concerts for Art Inst. in Glasgow, 1913 (still successful). Teacher at Glasgow Athenæum School of Music; Carnegie School in Dunfermline. As performer, his chief successes are in Mozart and other classics.—J. P. D.

HALVORSEN, Haldis. Norwegian singer; *b.* Dale, Söndfjord, 22 Sept. 1889. Stud. singing at home under Marie Irgens, Ellen Gulbranson and Grace Morris, and abroad under Mme. Reuss-Belce and Louis Bachner. After having given concerts in Christiania and Bergen, made repeated concert-tours in her native country; 1918–21, s. in grand opera at Opéra-Comique, Christiania. Her most important rôles are: Elisabeth (*Tannhäuser*), Recha (*The Jewess*), Delilah (*Samson and Delilah*). In 1922, gave concerts in Berlin. Married the violinist and conductor, Leif Halvorsen.—J. A.

HALVORSEN, Johan. Norwegian compr. *b.* Drammen, 15 March, 1864. Trained as violinist at Cons. in Stockholm and Leipzig, also under César Thomson in Liège. Numerous concerts in Norway and abroad; teacher of violin with Philh. Soc. in Aberdeen and at Cons. in Helsingfors; leading violinist for Norwegian and Swedish orchestras. 1893–9, condr. of orch. at theatre in Bergen and leader of concerts of mus. soc. Harmonien; 1899, condr. at new National Theatre in Christiania, a position he still holds. As leader of the symphony concerts in this theatre, he has for many years occupied a pro-

minent position in the mus. world in Christiania. Has occasionally cond. abroad, in Petrograd, Helsingfors, Stockholm, Copenhagen, Berlin, Paris. His orch. suite founded on *Vasantasena* was produced at Queen's Hall, London, by Sir Henry Wood in 1898.

His compns. consist for the most part of theatre-music, written for various Norwegian and foreign plays that have been produced at National Theatre. Arranged for concert performance, this music has won recognition far beyond his own country (music to play *Gurre* [Holger Drachmann], especially music to ancient Indian play *Vasantasena*). There is also a large number of works for orch., for male chorus, for v. and vn. A work of his youth, *Bojarernes indtogsmarsch* (*Entrance-March of the Boyards* (1893), is played as march-music all over the world. Favourite concert-pieces are *Suite ancienne* and the Passacaglia for vn. and vla. Two *Norwegian Rhapsodies* (1920 and 1921) have also been produced with success in Christiania.

H.'s music shows some influence from his great compatriots, Grieg and Svendsen, but nevertheless maintains its personal and national character side by side with these comprs. By his compilations and adaptations of folk-songs and dances, he has done good service.—R. M.

HALVORSEN, Leif. Norwegian violinist and compr. *b.* Christiania, 26 July, 1887. Pupil of Cons. in Christiania; scholarships for study in Berlin, Paris and Petrograd (under Witek and Leopold Auer). Concerts in Scandinavia. Leader at Opéra-Comique, Christiania, 1918–21. Since 1920, condr. Cecilia Soc., Christiania; since 1921, condr. of Mercantile Association's Choral Union in same city. As compr. attracted attention with his songs, pf. pieces and a couple of orch. works (*Légende rustique*), as well as music to Knut Hamsun's *Growth of the Soil*.—J. A.

HAM, Albert. British orgt. condr. compr. *b.* Bath, England, in 1858. Boy-chorister and assistant orgt. St. John's Ch.; later orgt. All Saints', Bath; of Ilminster Parish Ch.; of St. John's, Taunton. In 1898, went to Toronto to be dir. of music at St. James's Cath.; also lecturer and examiner in Toronto Univ. Founded National Chorus of Toronto, which he has cond. for 21 years (see CHORAL SOCIETIES). He is also examiner in Univ. of Bishop's College, Lennoxville, Quebec; ex-president of Empire Club; holds degrees of Mus.Doc. Trinity Coll. Dublin; Mus.D. *h.c.* Toronto.

Cantata, *Solitudes of the Passion*; part-songs; anthems; organ pieces (Novello); Pedal and Arpeggio Studies; text-books: *Musical Rudiments*; *Elementary Harmony*; *Graces and Embellishments of the Bach-Handel period.*—L. S.

HAMBOURG, Boris. Russ. cellist; *b.* Voronez, S. Russia, in 1884. Third son of late Michael Hambourg and brother to Mark, distinguished pianist, and Jan, distinguished violinist. Began his studies in London when 8 years old. After devoting some time to piano, decided to make cello his chief study, and took lessons from Herbert Walenn and later from Hugo Becker. In 1903, made concert tour in Australia and New Zealand; 1904, appeared in Pyrmont, Germany, at first Tchaikovsky Fest. held in that country. 1904–5 in Belgium as guest of Eugène Ysaye, from whom he received valuable hints in interpretation and style. London *début*, 1905. In

1910, came to America, and, after appearing as soloist in many cities, made his headquarters in Toronto, taking part in founding the Hambourg Cons. of Music of which he is now mus. dir. Has appeared as soloist with Queen's Hall and London Symphony Orch. besides many leading orchs. in Europe and U.S.A.—L. S.

HAMBOURG, Jan. Violinist; *b.* Voronez, S. Russia, 27 Aug. 1882. Brother of Mark H.; stud. London (Wilhelmj, Sauret), Frankfort (Hikeerman), Prague (Ševčík), Brussels (Ysaye); *début* Berlin, 1905; has toured widely.—E.-H.

HAMBOURG, Mark. Pianist; *b.* Bogutchar, S. Russia, 1 June, 1879. Stud. under his father in London and in 1895 under Leschetizky in Vienna; *début* Moscow Philh. March 1888; since then, with all leading orchs.; several tours to America, Canada, S. Africa, and one world-tour. One of the best-known of contemporary pianists.—E.-H.

HAMERIK, Asger. Danish composer; *b.* Copenhagen, 8 April, 1843; *d.* Frederiksburg, Denmark, 13 July, 1923. Stud. under Gade and Haberbier, subsequently (1860–3) under Bülow and (1863–7) under Berlioz. In 1872, became dir. of Peabody Cons. of Music, Baltimore, U.S.A., holding post till 1898, founding a fine orch. there. Retired to Copenhagen in 1898, being knighted by King of Denmark in 1890. His opera *La Vendetta* was perf. Milan in 1870.

7 symphonies; 2 choral trilogies; 4 operas; a Requiem; much chamber-music, including a pf. 4tet.—E.-H.

HAMILTON, Clarence Grant. Amer. educator; *b.* Providence, R.I., U.S.A., 9 June, 1865. Educated at Brown Univ.; A.B. 1888; A.M. 1890. Stud. music under Edward Hoffman, H. C. MacDougall, Foote, Chadwick, Edward Dannreuther and Tobias Matthay. 1889–1904, orgt. and teacher in his native city; 1904, associate-prof. of music at Wellesley (Mass.) Coll.; since 1918, prof. During 1917–18 also lectured at Boston University.

Piano Teaching, its Principles and Problems (Ditson, 1910); *Sound, and its Relation to Music* (*id.* 1912); *Outlines of Musical History* (*id.* 1913); *Music Appreciation, based upon Literary Criticism* (*id.* 1920); 9 chapters in Baltzell's *History of Music* (Presser, 1905); ed. of *The School Credit Piano Course* (Ditson, 1918–19).—J. M.

HAMM, Adolf. Orgt. *b.* Strasburg in 1882. Stud. organ under Prof. Münch, Strasburg, and Karl Straube, Leipzig. Since 1906, orgt. of Basle Cath., where he cond. the Bach Choir (1911–22, founded by him) and the Basler Männerchor (1915–20). One of best orgts. in Switzerland and is also greatly appreciated in Germany.—F. H.

HAMMER as mus. instr. Used by Mahler at climax of *Finale* to his 6th (*Tragic*) symphony. The effect is generally carried out there by a blow of a wooden hammer on a kind of large drum.—EG. W.

HAMMER, Birger. Norwegian pianist; *b.* Bergen, 6 March, 1883. Pupil of Martin Knutzen, Christiania, Arthur Schnabel and Wilhelm Klatte, Berlin. *Début*-concert, Christiania 1902. Extensive concert-tours, especially in Central

Europe. Teacher at J. Petersen's Pf. Acad. Berlin.—U. M.

HAMMERICH, Angul. Danish mus. historian; *b.* Copenhagen, 25 Nov. 1848. Brother of Asger H. (who spells his name—Hamerik). While pursuing cello study from youth, he was prepared for an official career, and took degree in political science at Univ. Copenhagen; abandoned this calling to devote himself to mus. criticism and mus. history. In 1880 became member of editorial staff of the great daily *Nationaltidende*, Copenhagen, and is still the leading critic of that journal. But mus. history gradually became his absorbing interest. He wrote (with V. C. Ravn) the monograph commemorating Jubilee of the Musikforening (Music Soc.) in 1886; in 1892, a similar work upon Jubilee of R. Cons. Copenhagen. In 1892, he published his exhaustive and fundamental work upon *Music at the Court of Christian IV*, and received degree of Ph.D. at Univ. Copenhagen. Extracts from this work (transl. into Ger. by C. Elling) appeared in 1893 in *Vierteljahrsschrift für Musik-Wissenschaft*. In 1896, was appointed prof.-extraordinary in mus. history at Copenhagen Univ. He founded the Musico-Historical Museum in Copenhagen, 1898, of which he issued an illustrated catalogue (in Danish and Ger.). Besides a long list of critical essays in Danish, Swedish, Ger. and other foreign magazines, and his important treatises on the famous ancient Danish Lures (horns) of the Bronze Age, the old historical organ at Frederiksborg Castle, the sojourn of Gluck in Copenhagen, there are the following books: *Mediæval Musical Relics of Denmark*, copiously illustrated with facsimiles of mss. (1912); Eng. transl. by Margaret Williams Hamerik; Leipzig, Breitkopf); *J. P. E. Hartmann*, biography (1916), and *Danish Musical History until about* 1700 (1921), the first exhaustive scientific history of earlier period of Danish music. His pioneer work has been most significant for the progress of mus. research in Denmark. Dr. Hammerich is the chief contributor of Danish articles (including the one on LURES) for this Dictionary.—W. B.

HAMMERSTEIN, Oscar. Amer. impresario; *b.* Berlin, in 1847; *d.* New York, 1 Aug. 1919. The most industrious *entrepreneur* and builder of large opera-houses known in the history of opera. Came to New York penniless in 1863 and gained his livelihood as a cigar-maker, an inventor of cigar-manufacturing machinery, and as ed. of a tobacco-trade journal. Began theatrical career in 1870, but did not build his 1st theatre until 1888 (Harlem Opera House). For next 20 years his activities as a manager were combined with those of a builder of theatres (Columbus Theatre, Harlem Music Hall, Murray Hill Theatre, the [1st] Manhattan Opera House, Olympia, Victoria, Republic and Harris, all built in New York). The second Manhattan Opera House, a large theatre still used from time to time for opera perfs., was built in 1906. Here for 4 years H. was a dangerous rival of the Metropolitan Opera, laying stress on Fr. opera,

and introducing a number of works not known in America (*Thaïs, Pelléas and Mélisande, Louise;* also Strauss's *Elektra*). In 1908 he built and managed the Philadelphia Opera House. In April 1910, he sold his interests to his rivals for $2,000,000, agreeing not to produce opera in the cities in which the Metropolitan Opera was accustomed to giving performances. Thereupon he built the London Opera House, which opened on 13 Nov. 1911, with Nouguès's *Quo Vadis ?* and where he also produced Holbrooke's *Children of Don.* The season ended in disaster, and he sold the theatre. Returning to America, he built Amer. Opera House (now Lexington Opera House), New York. His company had been engaged and the opening announced, when the Metropolitan secured an injunction and performances were not begun. Was planning resumption of activities when death interfered.
Consult H. E. Krehbiel, *Chapters of Opera* and *More Chapters of Opera.*—O. K.

HANFSTÄNGL, Marie (*née* Schröder). Ger. s. singer; *b.* Breslau; 30 April, 1848; *d.* Munich, 5 Sept. 1917. Operatic singer, pupil of Viardot-Garcia in Baden-Baden. At Théâtre Lyrique, Paris, 1866; returned to Germany on outbreak of war in 1870; engaged at Court Opera House, Stuttgart, 1871. Married the photographer Hanfstängl in 1873. In 1878 stud. further under Vannucini in Florence; engaged at Stadt-theater, Frankfort-o-M. In 1895 teacher of singing at Hoch's Cons. there. Retired 1897, spending her last years in Munich. Wrote *My System of Teaching Singing* (1902).—A. E.

HANNIKAINEN, Ilmari. Finnish pianist; *b.* Jyväskylä, 19 Oct. 1893. Son of P. J. Hanni-kainen. Stud. at Helsingfors Univ. and Music Inst. 1911–13; continued studies at Musik-akademie, Vienna (Paul de Conne and Franz Schreker), 1913–14; and under Siloti in Petro-grad, 1915–17; principal pf. teacher at Hel-singfors Music Inst. 1917–19, and again since 1922. Has appeared with much success at con-certs in Finland, Vienna, Paris, London, Copen-hagen, Petrograd, Stockholm, and Riga. Has comp. pf. concerto; pf. 4tet; pf. pieces; songs. —T. H.

HANNIKAINEN, Pekka Juhani. Finnish compr. *b.* Nurmes, 9 Dec. 1854. Until 1917, music-lecturer at Seminary, Jyväskylä. 1st condr. of Finnish students' choir Ylioppilas-kunnan Laulajat, 1882–5; ed. of 1st Finnish mus. paper, *Säveleitä,* 1887–91. Compr. of choruses and songs. Lives at Helsingfors.—T. H.

HANNIKAINEN, Tauno. Finnish cellist, condr. *b.* Jyväskylä, 1896. Son of P. J. Hanni-kainen. Stud. in Helsingfors and abroad. Since 1922, 2nd condr. Finnish Opera House, Hel-singfors.—T. H.

HANS, Pierre. Mus. instr. inventor; *b.* Wasmuel, near Mons, Belgium, 14 Feb. 1886. Stud. various instrs. Pupil of C. Smulders for compn. Electrical and chemical engineering at Liège Univ. Invented *clavier-Hans* (Hans keyboard). This consists of an attachment to pf. of 2 keyboards situated one behind the other. The first is an ordinary keyboard. The second is the same in construction, but is tuned a semitone higher than first. The aim is to simplify pf. technique. The black notes of first keyboard may be substituted in playing for white notes of second keyboard and vice versa. (See BARBIER; SMULDERS.)—E. C.

HANSEN, Robert Emil. Danish cellist, compr. *b.* Copenhagen, 25 Feb. 1860. Made his *début* as cellist at age of 11. At 14 became a pupil of R. Cons. Copenhagen; at 17 a member of R. Chapel. Here he remained until called to Ge-wandhaus Orch. Leipzig, where he soon advanced to solo cellist and became known as talented compr. of symph. works in larger forms and orch. condr. Returned to Denmark during the war; at present dir. of Philh. Concerts, Aarhus (Jutland).
Sonata, pf. and vn. op. 1; *Deutsche Lyrik,* op. 2; fantasy-pieces, ob. and pf. op. 3; cello concerto, op. 5; Suite, str. and 2 horns (Copenhagen, Hansen); *Im Mai,* male chorus and pf. (Leipzig, Leuckart); trio, fl. vn. and cello, op. 13 (Leipzig, Zimmermann); *Johannesrosen,* s. solo, male chorus and pf. op. 11 (Leipzig, Kahnt); cello pieces; songs.—A. H.

HANSLICK, Eduard. Austrian musicologist; *b.* Prague, 11 Sept. 1825; *d.* Vienna, 6 Aug. 1904. Stud. music in Prague under Tomaschek, and law at Vienna Univ.; took LL.D. degree 1849; became state official and at same time (1848) music-critic (*Wiener Zeitung; Presse,* and, from 1864 to death, of *Neue Freie Presse*). From 1856 also private lecturer in æsthetics and history of music, Univ. of Vienna; 1870–95, regular prof.; since 1886 an aulic councillor, with title Hofrat. His book *Vom Musikalisch Schönen : ein Beitrag zur Revision der Ästhetik der Ton-kunst* (1854), repeatedly re-ed. and transl. into several languages (1891 into English), quickly made him known. In it, conforming to the ideas of his time (especially those of Zeller and F. Th. Vischer), he has thrown into relief the formal elements. Turning entirely away from the mus. æsthetics of the Romanticists (Wagner, Liszt), music was for him intrinsically the "art of beautiful sounds." Against him were ranged F. v. Hausegger (*Musik als Ausdruck*) and many others. His *Geschichte des Konzert-wesens in Wien,* 2 vols., appeared in 1869–70; his autobiography, *Aus meinen Leben,* in 1894. As critic of the *Neue Freie Presse,* which at once became the most influential paper, Hanslick made for himself a position quite unique of its kind—*Der Musikpapst.* The success of Brahms, as well as the humiliation of Hugo Wolf and Anton Bruckner for many years, were chiefly due to him. He fought bitterly against Richard Wagner, and the latter's Beckmesser was originally to have been called *Hans Lick.* But Hanslick was the ideal of his readers—a well-trained, clear, witty, often brilliant, stylist; never too deep, always amusing, especially when indulging in satire. His criticisms and essays, interesting even now, were publ. in colls.: *Aus dem Konzertsaal* 1848–68 (1870); *Konzertvirtuosen und Komponisten der letzten Jahre* (1870–85); *Die moderne Oper,* 9 vols. (period 1878–1900); *Suite* (1884).—P. Sᴛ.

HARBURGER, Walter. Ger. compr. and writer on music; *b.* Munich, 26 Aug. 1888. Lives in Munich.

Symphony, F mi.; mass, F mi.; *Stabat Mater*, Harmonic series.

8-v., *a cappella*; 3 str. 4tets; pf. trio; sonata, vn. and pf.; sonata, cello and pf.; 3 sonatas and 2 suites, pf.; suite for clavichord; sonatina for pf.; 4 inventions and fugues; 3 scherzi; Variations and fugue, G mi.; Waltz-Phantasy (concert-piece), pf.; organ pieces: Phantasy and fugue, C mi.; Introduction, adagio and triple fugue, D ma. Also music to 2 pantomimes, *The Magician and his Shadow*, *The Decline of the West* (ms.). As a musical theorist, he attempted an a-prioristic derivation of the laws of harmony, which partly encroaches upon the domains of mathematics and logic. Publ.: *Outline of Musical Form* (Munich, 1912); *Metalogics: Logic in Music as a Separate Section of an Exact Phenomenology* (Munich, 1919, Verlag für Kultur und Politik); also an essay on political economy, *The State without a Rudder* (1919).—A. E.

d'HARCOURT, Eugène. Fr. compr. condr. *b.* Paris, 1861; *d.* March 1918. After his studies at Cons. in Paris, attended lectures at R. Acad. of Music in Berlin, till 1890. Having devoted himself to mus. propaganda, which he cond. with tireless energy, his object being to educate the public, he built in 1892 a concert-hall in Paris, which bore his name. He there directed the *Concerts éclectiques populaires*, which continued for nearly 3 years, and there the public could hear the works of the great masters for 50 centimes. Resumed in 1900, under another form, *Les Grands Oratorios à l'église St.-Eustache* in Paris. Their career did not last long. Was planning the foundation of *Concerts Populaires du Jeu de Paume*, when he died. First appeared as compr. with a Mass (Brussels, 1876).

3 symphonies, of which one, *La Symphonie néoclassique* (Paris, Durdilly), while badly received in Paris, had a certain success abroad (Antwerp, Wiesbaden, 1907, 1910). His opera *Le Tasse* (Durdilly), was played in Monte Carlo (1903), Bordeaux, Antwerp, Ghent, etc. Has written 2 4tets, some songs, cantatas, 2 ballets, etc., and unpubl. lyrical drama, *Severo Torelli*.—M. L. P.

HARDING, Harry Alfred. Eng. orgt. *b.* Salisbury, 25 July, 1855. Stud. under Drs. Corfe, Iliffe, Haydn Keeton; Mus.Doc. Oxon. 1882; borough orgt. Bedford; dir. of music, Bedford School; hon. secretary of Royal College of Organists (*q.v.*).

Church music; songs; cantata, *Mucius Scævola* (Weekes) etc. Books: *Analysis of Form in Beethoven's Pf. Sonatas* (Novello); *Musical Ornaments* (Weekes); *Allusiveness in Mus. Compn.* (R.C.O. Calendar, 1908). —E.·H.

HAREIDE, Olaf. Norwegian compr. and orgt. *b.* Brunlanæs, 24 Oct. 1880. Matriculated at Univ. in Christiania 1900; pupil of Music Cons. Christiania; stud. under Catharinus Elling; afterwards at High School in Berlin. H. is working as a pianist and music-teacher in Skien. A fine lyrical talent is revealed in his pf. pieces, op. 1–3 (Norsk Musikforlag).—J. A.

HARMONICS (Overtones). Those sounds resulting from the vibration of the string, pipe,

etc. in fractions of its length, halves, thirds, quarters, fifths, etc. They exist simultaneously with the ground tone. The following shows the series up to the sixteenth harmonic:

HARMONY. (A) HISTORICAL INTRODUCTION. The science of harmony seeks to discover the principles which order the artistic relations of successive groups of simultaneously sounded notes.

The first step towards harmony was the simultaneous singing of the same melody by voices of different range. Melodies were reduplicated at the octave and also at the fourth and fifth; but this cannot properly be called "harmonisation." Nor can the singing of a melody against a single sustained note be considered as "harmonisation," though the principle holds a certain place in harmonic practice. Artistic harmony arose from the combined singing of different melodies, through which certain intervals came to be recognised as having various degrees of pleasantness, by which certain emotional values might be expressed.

Intervals having once been distinguished as consonant or dissonant, it was felt that dissonances required "resolution" by being followed by the nearest available consonance. It was found that when a dissonance was approached from a consonance by oblique motion, and followed by another consonance (preparation—percussion—resolution) an effect of stress was created. Hence the adoption of the term "percussion."

In mediæval music, which was mainly in quantitative rhythms, the suspension produced a new kind of rhythmic value, or stress, which was therefore used especially at cadences. The change which took place in Western music about 1600 (though it may be traced back at least a century before) was in the first place a change in rhythmical outlook. The development of instruments (more especially those with plucked strings, the tone of which caused them to approximate to instruments of percussion) led to the habitual assumption of stress at recurrent periods, indicated in writing by bar-lines, the first beat of a bar being strongly accented. Simultaneously there grew up the habit of placing the principal melody in the uppermost part.

The system prevalent from about 1600 to 1900, basing music on the major or minor modes of a single scale that can be presented in a number of different transpositions, depends on the assumption of periodic stresses. The key-system as exemplified in the works of J. S. Bach is unthinkable apart from a system of equal bars, with a strong beat at the beginning of each. This rhythmical system once adopted, dissonances ceased gradually to have stress values, since the percussive stress of instruments, imitated by voices with the help of consonants when singing words, was much stronger. In this way, there developed an elaborate sense of the emotional value of dissonances. Hence the gradual abandonment of the system of "preparation"; for dissonances needed none as they became familiar. But the more familiar they became, the more their emotional value declined. One by one, they passed into the category of consonances, and newer and harsher dissonances had to be invented. Noticeable landmarks are the use of the "diminished 7th" as an unprepared chord, for the sake of emotional colour, about 1700 (see Alessandro Scarlatti's works), the use of the "augmented 5th" in the same way about 1850 (Liszt and Wagner), and the use of the "augmented 4th" about 1910 (Scriabin and Debussy). The diminished 7th, once regarded as an intense emotional thrill, has now lost all emotional value and is practically obsolete.

The rhythmical key-system established in the time of J. S. Bach not merely disregarded the stress values of dissonances, but regarded the rhythmic beat as sufficiently powerful to justify dissonances which earlier composers would have thought necessary to prepare, provided that they arose out of the melodic line. (Cf. the rules for dissonances on 1st beat in counterpoint, and use of dissonances in sequence, in the text-books of Cherubini's time.)

By Beethoven's time, the key-system is so completely established that emotional effects can be obtained by deliberate attempts to destroy it. (See also art. on ARTE DI STUPORE.) Certain chords, such as "diminished 7th" and "augmented 5th," destroy the sense of key, because they can belong to any key (cf. Liszt's Faust Symphony). This effect is allied to Atonality which will be discussed later.

Modern music has concentrated more and more attention on the values of single chords for the sake of their emotional colour (in Grieg and Delius, for instance). The "added 6th," originally reached by purely contrapuntal means, regarded later on as an unprepared discord, has now come to be regarded as a positive consonance (cf. Gounod's Dodelinette, and Borodin's Berceuse, for the pleasurable colour of the major 2nd). The beginnings of this feeling may be seen as far back as Domenico Scarlatti (see his sonatas, Longo's edition, Ricordi), though the curious dissonances are no doubt often acciaccature written as if they were part of the main chord.

Under the classical key-system, chords vary in æsthetic value according to their rhythmical position. In the previous period a prepared discord created a strong beat; in the classical period an unprepared dominant discord often comes on a weak beat and by its dissonance intensifies the élan of the arsis. A theory of harmony which ignores rhythm is useless. The change which took place in the general musical outlook about 1900, was like the change of 1600, largely a rhythmical one. The new harmonisation of old rhythms, begun mainly under the influence of Grieg, is only a small part of it; the influence of

Debussy, who is the most outstanding figure in the history of the new movement, is more fundamentally rhythmical. Modern music tends to break down the old symmetry of rhythm, though we may note that German music, on the whole, clings more closely to regular 4-4 rhythm than that of France, Italy or England. Plain-song, non-European influences in melody, and a certain reaction towards the music of the Middle Ages, are amongst the many causes which make for freer rhythms.

If chords are to be considered by themselves, apart from all rhythm, then any chord, whether major common chord or extreme modern discord, is an arbitrary selection of notes producing a single blend of colour (Klangfarbe, timbre). Resolution of a discord implies movement of parts, that is, counterpoint. To many listeners at the present day certain "discords" used by themselves in modern music still suggest imaginary resolutions remembered from older music, though withheld by the modern composer; but in many cases, probably increasing as time goes on, it would be unsafe to assume that the composer intended these chords to be so interpreted. The "juxtaposition of unrelated sonorities," as some modern theorists call it, seems to imply a franker recognition of the purely physical effects of sounds than theorists of the school of Hanslick would have been willing to countenance.—E. J. D.

(B) GENERAL PROCEDURE. Definitions. (1) Harmony is the simultaneous sounding of two or more musical sounds. (2) Counterpoint (Polyphony) is the bringing together of two or more melodic lines. (3) A Scale is a series of notes arranged in ascending or descending sequence. (4) The term Mode should apply to the arrangement of intervals—tones and semitones—in the scale. (5) Enharmonic Modulation is of two kinds—real and false. In real enharmonic modulation, there is a change of pitch. False enharmony only exists on paper, and is a matter merely of musical spelling. (6) Atonality is a style of music which abolishes the tonic or keynote, either temporarily, or throughout an entire movement or composition. (7) Temperament is the method of tuning; the manner in which the distance between a sound and its octave is divided.

Preliminary. Some system of explaining the practice of modern harmony is desirable, not only for the student who would compose, but also for a proper appreciation of music by the listener. The theories of most of the current text-books stop with Wagner's music, not even attempting to explain all that is found there. A proper system of harmony should claim no more than to be an observation and generalisation of the facts. It should not lay down a priori rules and prohibitions.

Contemporary harmony is the logical outcome of the practice of preceding generations. When we are not dealing with the highly developed and specialised technique of any particular instrument, harmony and counterpoint are practically the same thing; but one of the modern phases of harmonic development seems to have occupied itself more with the harmonic (perpendicular) view than with the contrapuntal (horizontal) one.

Temperament. Whereas the majority of composers now adopt the equal temperament unreservedly with all that it involves, yet there are some (Bantock, Tovey and others) who claim that the chief system of modern harmony should be based on the practice of voices or strings, understanding thereby *Just Intonation.* Whilst recognising the usefulness of the pianoforte, they do not choose to forget its imperfections of tuning. (See the definition of Enharmonic Modulation above.)

Scales. The number of Scales to which contemporary music is referred is very much larger than the number used by the preceding generation, and the number is continually increasing. There is, indeed, no limit to the variety of scales, upon which modern music may be founded, provided that the composer can hear them himself and can correct them in performance if played or sung falsely.

Amongst the scales in use, a few are shown here. C has been used as the starting-point or keynote.

Ex. 1.   DIATONIC

Ex. 2 (*a*).   DODECUPLE

or this:

Ex. 2 (*b*).

Ex. 3.   18-NOTE SCALE (*Tertia-tonal*)

Ex. 4.   21-NOTE SCALE

(See also art. on HÁBA).

A more multiplex scale would give several forms to each of our alphabetical notes: thus, C flat, D double-flat, C natural, C sharp, C double-sharp; or

Ex. 5.

Dodecuple Scale. In consequence of the wide acceptance of the Equal Temperament, the so-called Chromatic Scale is now nearly always dealt with as a Dodecuple Scale; that is, as one which divides the octave into 12 perfectly equal parts (in just the same way as a foot-measure is divided into 12 inches). In this scale, each note exists by its own right, having no derivation by chromatic inflection from a contiguous sound, and therefore no special duties towards it. It is indifferent whether the notes be written with sharps or flats. A much simpler notation is badly wanted. In this connection, it is not generally known that Beethoven followed the practice shown in the following extract from the autograph score of his F sharp ma. sonata, op. 78:

Ex. 6.

Nearly all editions print the bass part thus:

Ex. 7.   tr

And the same applies to the return of this subject in the recapitulation. A similar case may be seen in Mozart's *Don Giovanni*, Act I, No. 2, bars 72–74, at the words *Cor mio deh senti* (vocal score).

The dodecuple scale is generally used with a definite keynote, that is, along the lines of a fixed tonality. When the system of harmony used with it abandons a fixed keynote entirely, the procedure is called Atonality. There is nothing to prevent Atonality being used with other scales; but the only published examples at present occur in whole-tone practice.

Whole-Tone Scale. The Whole-Tone Scales fall only into two groups, the one group beginning, say, on C, and the other on C sharp. In each of these groups, all the scales consist of the same notes. The two groups, being a semitone apart, never coincide.

Ex. 8.

I.   or   or   or

II.

This scale is sometimes used with a note definitely selected as tonic or keynote. The following dance takes C as its central note:

Ex. 9.   RÉBIKOF, *Fête*, No. 6.

Vivo.

Often, the effect is atonal, or keyless. In either case, the same scale is seldom used for whole pieces. Rébikof has done so; but Debussy rarely remains in any one whole-tone scale, as in *Cloches à travers les feuilles*. In his *Voiles* from the second book of *Préludes*, he flies for relief, near the end of the piece, to a pentatonic scale. Modulation from one group of the whole-tone scales to the other group is of course available, and any note may be freely used as a "pedal-note."

Ex. 10.   BANTOCK, *Pan.*

Presto.

Chord-Construction. In harmonic analysis, although the classification of chords built up by thirds predominates in the older practice, chords may be constructed by 4ths, 5ths (perfect, augmented, diminished), 2nds (major or minor), etc. The following extract from Debussy's *Pour le piano* set makes great use of the "second" in chord-formation:

Ex. 11.   DEBUSSY.

Erik Satie seems to have been the pioneer in this direction. The following extract shows chords built up by 4ths:

Ex. 12:   SATIE.

Scriabin's 6th pf. sonata, op. 62, is built up on the following chord of 4ths:

Ex. 13.

and for the harmonic foundation of his 9th sonata, op. 68, he takes the following structure of 5ths:

Ex. 14.

(See also art. on SCRIABIN, where the "synthetic chord" is discussed.)

The following chord from Stravinsky's *Le Sacre du Printemps* is interesting:

Ex. 15.

STRAVINSKY.
(p. 71, pf. duet arr.)

The practice of teaching "inversions" of chords is referable only to the older system. The teaching of harmony by "figured-bass" is not in accordance with modern practice; for harmony may be built upwards on a bass, downwards from the uppermost part, or around an inside part.

Part-Writing. In part-writing, there are no forbidden progressions, but all progressions must be justified by their suitability. The only acceptable definition of "resolution" is that of the behaviour of a chord being justified either æsthetically, emotionally, or logically. There is no fundamental difference between a concord and a discord; it is merely a difference of degree. Finality is only a relative term; a piece may end on any combination of notes. Puccini's opera, *Madame Butterfly* (1910), finishes with an "added 6th" chord. The first act of Debussy's *Pélleas* ends with this cadence:

Ex. 16.

DEBUSSY.

pp presque plus rien.

The modern practice of over-lining or under-lining a melody at various intervals is simply a matter of duplication.

Ex. 17.

BAX, Vn. Sonata in E.
Allegro vivace.

VIOLIN.

PIANOFORTE.

f

Ex. 18.

SCRIABIN,
Études, Op. 65, No. 2.

p dolce.

&c.

Ex. 19.

SCRIABIN,
3 *Études,* Op. 65, No. 1.

pp

&c.

(Progression by 7ths is no new thing. We find it in the vocal music of Machault in the XIV century. In the XIX century it created an outcry, when Hermann Goetz's *Frühlings-Ouvertüre* was played in London at the Philharmonic, and it occurs again in the music of Stravinsky, Scriabin and others.)

From this, it is but a step to outlining by whole chords. This may be of 3 kinds: (*a*) exact as to intervals (major, or minor, etc.):

Ex. 20.

RAVEL, *Sonatine.*
*Animé,
très marque.*

ff

(*b*) diatonic as to intervals:

Ex. 21.

DEBUSSY,
La Soirée dans Granade.

&c.

(See also the *Choral* in *La Cathédrale engloutie*.)

(*c*) mixed:

Ex. 22.

GOOSSENS,
Nature Poems II, p 14.

In the first case, it has some analogy to the "mixture-stop" of the organ; and in the second case, to the mediæval "diaphony." Here is the same kind of thing, applied as it were on two tonal planes:

Ex. 23.

STRAUSS,
Electra, p. 23, Voc. Sc.

Omnitonality. This term is used to express a more fluid way of moving amongst the various keys than is afforded by the usual modulating methods of older classical procedure. The following extract from César Franck's *Prélude, Aria et Finale* (*Prélude*, bars 79–83) is a good example of this:

Ex. 24.

Risoluto. ♩ = 116.

C. FRANCK.

It is difficult to say what key the passage is in at any given point. This stage of harmonic development is a step towards Atonality.

Polytonality. This name was given by French theorists to the device of making more than one key heard simultaneously.[1] The superimposition of one key on another was probably arrived at through 3 channels: (*a*) through the use of superimposed streams of highly coloured diaphony, in other words, a counterpoint of harmonic streams:

Ex. 25.

BERNERS, *Un Soupir.*

(*b*) through empirical means in counterpoint:

Ex. 26.

STRAVINSKY,
Les Cinq Doigts.

Lento.

[1] J. Leroux in the *Revue Musicale* for Oct. 1921 debates the suitability of the term.

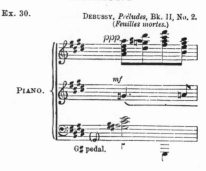

Ex. 30.

DEBUSSY, *Préludes*, Bk. II, No. 2.
(*Feuilles mortes*.)

PIANO.

G♯ pedal.

Ex. 27.

Sostenuto.

BARTÓK,
Bagatellen, No. 6.

or (*c*) from a pedal chord sustained. The primitive "drone" led to the pedals, further to elaborated pedals, then to a whole chord sustained as a pedal-sound, whilst the parts move on different lines.

and so on to four planes:

Ex. 28.

Poco lento.

MALIPIERO, *Ballata*.

Ex. 31.

Andantino.

CASELLA,
Berceuse Puppazetti, p. 6.

Ex. 29.

KODÁLY,
7 Pieces, Op. 11, No. 5.

I

II

This device when elaborated on structures of *basso ostinato* (ground-bass) may produce double tonality (see Debussy's *Jardins sous la pluie*, Busoni's *Berceuse élégiaque*, etc.). From two simultaneous keys (bi-planal harmony) to three (tri-planal) is a simple step:

Or even more, as in this example:

Ex. 32.   STRAVINSKY, *Renaud*,
                  Voc. Sc., p. 28.

But planal harmony can be indulged in without superimposed keys:

Ex. 33.   STRAVINSKY, *Le Sacre du Printemps.*
              Pf. Duet arr. p. 24.

Ex. 34.   R. VAUGHAN WILLIAMS,
           On Wenlock Edge (No. 5),
           Pf. arr. p. 28.

Ex. 35.   HOLST, *Hymn of Jesus*,
            Full Sc. p. 45.

Example 36 (on p. 222) from Arnold Bax's *Garden of Fand* illustrates two different points, (*a*) superimposition of unrelated harmonies and (*b*) superimposition of various triads. It will be seen that the three "diminished 7ths" are grouped together (with the exception of the A flat in the second. The harshness of the combination of the first and second is, in actual effect on the ear, mitigated by the "ictus" of the third which distracts the attention until the resolution of the second and third on the first, which has predominated throughout, owing to the insistence of the figure on the strings.

Elision. There is no doubt that some special chords were suggested in the older harmonic technique, by leaving discords as it were "in the air," *i.e.* without their expected resolution. But the theory that the newer chords of modern harmonic technique are accounted for in this way only arose from habits formed by listeners thoroughly inured to the older technique. The idea of its acceptance as an explanation of the newer kinds of harmony is scouted by the contemporary composers themselves.

Super-Harmonics. A more acceptable explanation of many of these chords, is the use of the higher and lesser-known harmonics. For their

FROM "THE GARDEN OF FAND"

Arnold Bax.

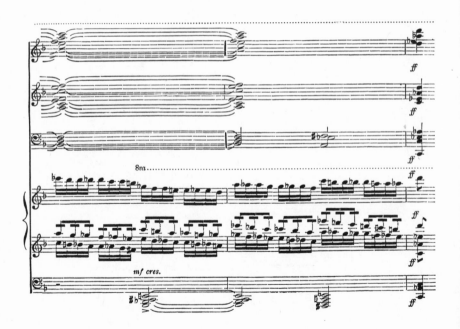

best effect they must be widely spaced from the ground-tone. The following treble chords show such a relationship to the deep bass D flat:

J. IRELAND, *Island Spell.*

Ex. 37.

It is even conceivable that the following extract from Strauss's *Elektra* (page 78, vocal score) may be explained in this way. Here the spacing has been reduced in order to increase the strangeness of effect:

STRAUSS, *Elektra,* Voc. Sc., p. 78.

Ex. 38.

Atonality. The harmonic method which dispenses with the hold on a definite tonality (as the term is at present understood) has attracted numerous composers in all countries. Its invention has been wrongly attributed to Arnold Schönberg. It is far older and more universal than this; but it certainly seems to be the most suitable technique for the particular style of "Expressionism" adopted by Schönberg and his pupils.

Ex. 39.   A. WEBERN, Op. 7, (4 Stücke), Vn. & Pf.

Ex. 40.   SCHÖNBERG, *Pierrot Lunaire,* Op. 21 (No. 3).

Spacing and Tone-Colour. This brings us to the questions of spacing the notes, the balance of the relative strengths of the various sounds, and the arrangement of the tone-qualities in orchestration, all of which have a most important bearing on harmony, a bearing, however, for the discussion of which there is no room here.

General Principles. Certain principles will be found which are fundamental to all Western music from the Middle Ages up to the present day. These are the principles of rhythm, shape and construction in the first instance, and they affect harmony more and more as time goes on.

Consult: D. Alaleona, *I moderni orizzonti della tecnica musicale* (Bocca, Turin, 1911); E. Lechter Bacon, *Our Musical Idiom* (Chicago, 1917); F. Busoni, *Entwurf einer neuer Ästhetik der Tonkunst* (Schmidl, Trieste, 1907); A. Cœuroy, *La musique française moderne* (Delagrave, Paris, 1922); H. Walford Davies, art. *Some New Scales and Chords* in *Mus. Times,* Nov. 1922; E. Goossens, *Modern Tendencies in Music* (Arts League of Service Lecture, 1919); A. Eaglefield-Hull, *Modern Harmony : its explanation and application* (Augener, London, 1913), and arts. in *Mus. Opinion*, London, 1922 and 1923; E. Kurth, *Romantische Harmonik* (Max Hesse, 1923); L. Laloy, *The Future of Music* (Reeves, Eng. transl. 1915); R. Lenormand, *L'Harmonie Moderne* (Fr. comprs. only); A. Potter, *Modern Chords Explained*, a pamphlet (Reeves, 1910); A. Schönberg, *Harmonielehre* (Univ. Ed. Vienna, 1911; rev. ed. 1922, very little altered); A. Vinée, *Principes du système musical* (Hamelle, Paris, 1909); A. Weissmann, *Die Musik in der Weltkrise* (Eng. transl. by Pfister, J. M. Dent & Sons, 1924); Egon Wellesz, *Arnold Schönberg* (Eng. transl. by W. H. Kerridge, J. M. Dent & Sons, 1924). Also the double number of *Melos* (Berlin, Aug. 1922) and arts. by A. Hába in *Der Auftakt* (Prague). See also arts. in this Dictionary under ATONALITY, EXPRESSIONISM, PENTAFONIA, WHOLE-TONE SCALE, etc., etc.—A. B., B. B., D. T., EU. G., E.-H., E. J. D., H. P. A., R. V. W.

HARRIS, Clement Antrobus. Eng. orgt. and writer; *b.* York, 2 April, 1862. Stud. under Dr. E. G. Monk there; for many years, orgt. and choirmaster in Scotland; has contributed widely to reviews, magazines, mus. journals, etc.; in 1921, left Scotland for Australia where he now resides in Blackwood, near Adelaide occupied in teaching, conducting and writing.

A Chronological Chart of Mus. History (Reeves); *How to Write Music* (mus. calligraphy) (Weekes); *Curios of Mus. History* (Vincent; now W. Rogers); *The Story of British Music* (Kegan Paul,1919).—E.-H.

HARRIS, William Henry. Eng. orgt. *b.* London, 28 March, 1883. Early mus. education, St. David's Cath.; organ scholar, R.C.M. London, under Sir Walter Parratt (organ), Sir Walford Davies (compn.); orgt. and accpt. London Bach Choir, 6 seasons; assistant-orgt. Lichfield Cath.; teacher of harmony Birmingham and Midland Inst.; orgt. New Coll. Oxford, 1919; Mus.Doc. Oxon. 1910.

The Hound of Heaven, fantasy for barit. solo, chorus and orch. (Stainer & Bell; a Carnegie award, 1919); Fantasy on Campion's tune *Babylon's Streams*, organ (*id.*); church-music; songs; part-songs (Stainer & Bell; Faith Press).—E.-H.

HARRISON, Beatrice. British cellist; *b.* Roorkee, N.W. India. Stud. at R.C.M. London; then under Hugo Becker and at High School of Music, Berlin; 1910, Mendelssohn Prize; *début*, Bechstein Hall, Berlin; played Elgar's cello concerto, 1921 (Hereford Three Choirs Fest.), the 1st perf. after its production in London; is one of leading British cellists; has toured in Europe and America; first to play Delius's concerto. —E.-H.

HARRISON, Julius. Eng. compr. and condr. *b.* Stourport, Worcestershire, 26 March, 1885. Stud. under Granville Bantock at Birmingham Midland Inst., having won a Worcester County Council scholarship. One of condrs. of Beecham Opera Co. for 5 years. Cond. the Scottish Orch. (*q.v.*) for 3 seasons. Is one of condrs. of British National Opera Co. Folk-song and folk-theme have played a part in his mus. compn. though he never allows them to interfere with real invention. He has drawn his inspiration from Worcestershire scenery and fairy-lore, and turns more naturally to the cheerful than to the tragic.

Orch.: Variations, *Down among the Dead Men* (ms.); *Rapunzel*, poem (1917, ms.); *Worcestershire Pieces* (1919; pf. score, W. Rogers). Chorus and orch.: *Cleopatra*, dramatic cantata (1907, Breitkopf); *Rosalys*, a dream-poem (1912, ms.); *Requiem of Archangels* (1919, Curwen). Chamber-music: *Widdicombe Fair*, str. 4tet (Hawkes); 5tet, harp and str. in G flat (1912); str. 4tet. D mi. (1910, ms.). Two

church cantatas (Novello). Many songs (Rogers; Boosey; Enoch; Curwen); pf. pieces (Rogers; Enoch; Elkin; Ascherberg); organ (Rogers; Lengnick); part-songs (Boosey; Williams; Novello; Curwen; Rogers). An opera, *The Canterbury Pilgrims*, is partly composed.—E.-H.

HARRISON, May. Brit. violinist; *b.* Roorkee, N.W. India. Stud. R.C.M. London, under Arbós and Rivarde; then under Leopold Auer, Petrograd; *début* St. James's Hall, London, when 13 years old; has played in all the chief European cities.—E.-H.

HART, F. Bennicke (Fritz Hart). Eng. compr. *b.* Brockley, Kent, 1874. Now Dir. of Cons. of Music, Albert St. Melbourne, Australia. A concert devoted entirely to his music was given in London in Oct. 1923. F.R.C.M. *h.c.* 1924.

Operas: *Pierrette*; *Malvolio* (from Shakespeare's *Twelfth Night*); *The Land of Heart's Desire* (Yeats); *Riders to the Sea* (Synge); *Deirdre of the Sorrows* (Synge); *The Fantasticks* (Rostand); *The Travelling Man* (Lady Gregory); *Ruth*, a biblical opera. For orch.: Suite; *Impressions* from Maeterlinck's *Blue Bird* (Melbourne, Verbruggen's Orch.); Fantasy-overture, *From the West Country*; 3 ballads, chorus and orch.; *To a Primrose* (Herrick), s. v. and orch.; 3 vols. of Herrick songs; 3 vols. of Blake's songs (7 in each); 3 vols, 20 Henley songs; many other vols. (Fiona Macleod; Hubert Church; Æ [George Russell]); many separate songs (Stainer & Bell; Curwen; Boston Music Co.; Elkin); pf. pieces (5 folk-song fantasies; 14 Miniatures; *Old English Suite*; 3 books of folk-song settings (Stainer & Bell), sonata for vn. and pf.; Suite, vn. and pf. —E.-H.

HARTMAN, Thomas Alexandrovitch. Russ. compr. *b.* 1883. Pupil of Arensky and Essipof. Worked also with Mottl in Munich, where H. cond. the opera for a time. In 1907, he prod. at Imperial Opera, Petrograd, his ballet *La Petite Fleur Rouge*, which has a great success. The ideas of the dancer, Alexander Sakharof, whom he knew in Munich, had a great influence on him, and turned his researches towards a closer union of music and gesture which he attempted in his 2nd ballet, *Fra Mino* (after Anatole France's story *St. Satyre*). The Russ. revolution caused H. to fly to Constantinople. He settled in Paris in 1921, teaching music and rhythmics at Gurdjief's choreographic institute.—B. DE S.

HARTY, Agnes (*née* Nicholls). Eng. oratorio and operatic s. singer; *b.* Cheltenham, 14 July, 1877. Stud. R.C.M. London, under Alberto Visetti; afterwards under the late John Acton. Has appeared at all the principal fests., at the R. Covent Garden Opera, the Beecham Opera, Denhof Opera Co. and Quinlan Opera Co.'s world tour. She was the first Brit. artist to sing Brünnhilde in all the 3 sections of *The Ring*. Created the part of Mary in Elgar's *Kingdom*. One of the finest oratorio and operatic singers of the present time. Honoured with the O.B.E. 1923. Married Hamilton Harty, the orch. conductor.—E.-H.

HARTY, Hamilton. Irish compr. and condr. *b.* Hillsborough, Co. Down, Ireland (where his father was orgt.), 1880. He was mainly self-taught. At 12, he was appointed orgt. at Magheracoll Ch. Co. Antrim. At a later date he came down to Dublin and came under the influence of Signor Esposito at the R. Irish Acad. of Music. On his arrival in London in 1900 he speedily became famous as an accompanist. The success which he obtained in the composers' competitions at the Feis Ceoil (Irish music fest.) encouraged him to continue producing works, and it was not long before he was generally recognised as one of the most individual of the younger comprs. His wife, Mme. Agnes Nicholls, was chiefly instrumental in making his songs popular. His setting of Keats's *Ode to a Nightingale* was sung by her with great success at the Cardiff Fest. 1907. In 1909, the production of his vn. concerto at Queen's Hall, London, when Josef Szigeti took the solo part, aroused great enthusiasm. He has also written a good deal of chamber-music. H.'s works at first showed strong influences of Irish folk-melodies, especially in his *Irish Symphony* and *The Wild Geese*; but in later years there is a tendency towards the cosmopolitan ideas of modern music. His chief energies have been taken up lately by conducting. His concerts with the London Symphony Orch. proved him one of the most brilliant condrs. in England. Since his appointment as permanent conductor of the Hallé Orch. at Manchester, he has done much to bring him into the front rank of European condrs. A notable feature has been his encouragement of ensemble for wind instrs. For the past few years he has given recitals in Dublin and other cities, devoting the programme to works for pf. and wind instrs. He is also one of the condrs. of the B.N.O.C. He was elected F.R.C.M. *h.c.* 1924.

Irish Symphony, orch.; *Comedy Overture*, orch. (Schott); *Ode to a Nightingale*, s. v. and orch. (Breitkopf); vn. concerto in D mi. (C. & E. Publ. Co. Dublin); pf. concerto (*id.*); *Fantasy Scenes*, orch. (*id.*); *The Mystic Trumpeter*, barit. solo, chorus and orch. (Novello); *With the Wild Geese*, symph. poem (*id.*); *Water-Music of Handel*, transcribed for modern orch. (Murdoch); *Romance and Scherzo*, cello solo (Boosey); 3 pieces for ob. and pf. (Stainer & Bell); pf., vn., cello and harp solos (Augener; Schott; Novello); *Rhapsody*, fl. and pf. ms. (1924); numerous songs (Boosey, Novello).—W. St.

HARWOOD, Basil. Eng. orgt. and compr. *b.* Woodhouse, Glos, 11 April, 1859. Stud. pf. under J. L. Roeckel; organ under G. Riseley; theory under Dr. C. W. Corfe; fugue under Jadassohn and compn. under C. Reinecke at Leipzig; orgt. Ely Cath. 1887–92; Christ Ch. Cath. Oxford, 1892–1907; precentor of Keble Coll. 1892–1903; condr. of Oxford Bach Choir, 1896–1900; Choragus of Univ. of Oxford, 1900–9; mus. ed. *Oxford Hymn Book*, 1908. Most widely known through his organ works and church services.

2 organ sonatas: No. 1, C. sharp mi. op. 5 (Schott); No. 2, F sharp mi. op. 26 (Novello); many organ pieces (fantasia, *Christmastide*, op. 34; *Rhapsody*, op. 38 [Novello, 1922]); organ concerto in D, op. 24 (Gloucester 3 Choirs Fest. 1910); *Song on May Morning*, cantata, op. 27 (Leeds Fest. 1913; Novello); *Inclina Domine*, op 9 (Gloucester 3 Choirs Fest. 1898); songs; part-songs; church music (mostly Novello). —E.-H.

HASELBECK, Olga. Hungarian m.-sopr. operatic singer; *b.* 1884. Stud. at R. High School for Music, Budapest. Since 1908, member of R. Hungarian Opera House.—B. B.

HASSE, Karl. Ger. compr. condr. *b.* Dohna, (Saxony), 20 March, 1883. Attended Thomas School, Leipzig ; stud. at Univ. there (Kretz-

schmar, Riemann) and at Cons. (Krehl, Nikisch, Straube, Ruthardt); then at Munich Acad. (Reger and Mottl). Ph. Wolfrum's assistant at Heidelberg ; condr. of acad. choral soc. and str. orch. (*Collegium Musicum*); orgt. and cantor of Johannis Ch. Chemnitz, 1909; from 1910 condr. of mus. soc. and teachers' choral soc. in Osnabrück, where, on 1 Feb. 1919, he instituted that town's Cons. with a High School for Music. Mus. dir. Univ. of Tübingen, 1919.

Variations for 2 pianos, op. 1; 3 elegies, pf. op. 2; *Romantic Suite*, pf. op. 26; choral preludes, organ, op. 4, 7, 13; *Serenade*, str. orch. op. 5; 3 phantasies and fugues, organ, op. 6; 6 organ pieces, op. 9; suite, organ, op. 10; *Missa brevis*, 8-v. choir *a cappella* and 4 solo vs., op. 8; *Suite in Olden Form*, orch. op. 11; pf. trio, op. 15; 2 organ preludes on *A Stronghold Sure*, op. 14; *Little Sacred Songs*, 4 vs. *a cappella*, op. 12; songs ; *Hymn for female chorus*, solo and orch. op. 24; *Psalm LXXX*, chorus and orch. ; symph. variations (full orch.) on song, *Prince Eugen the Noble Knight*; vn. sonata; 2 organ sonatas; overture, *From Courland*, op. 20; a monograph, *Max Reger* (Leipzig, 1921, C. F. W. Siegel). —A. E.

HASSE, Max. Ger. author and ed. *b.* Buttelstedt, near Weimar, 24 Nov. 1860. Music critic, *Magdeburger Zeitung*, since 1904.

Peter Cornelius and his "Barber of Bagdad" (1904, against Mottl and Levi's arrangement); *The Poet-Musician Peter Cornelius*, 1st part, 1922, 2nd part, 1923 (Breitkopf). Ed. complete series of P. Cornelius' works (Breitkopf), 5 vols.: I, Songs; II, Choruses; III, *The Barber of Bagdad*; IV, *The Cid*; V, *Gunlöd* (completed and scored by W. v. Baussnern).—A. E.

HASSELMANS, Louis. Fr. cellist; *b.* Paris, 1878. 1st prize Paris Cons. 1893. At first, cellist of Concerts Lamoureux; afterwards successful as condr. Engaged in Paris and abroad, notably U.S.A. Now attached to Opéra-Comique, Paris.—M. L. P.

HAST, Harry Gregory. Eng. singer; *b.* London, 21 Nov. 1862. One of founders of the Meister Glee-Singers (1890); sang with them until 1898, when he gave his 1st recital in May at Queen's Hall; toured U.K., Continent and U.S.A. many times; now teaches.—E.-H.

HATCHARD, Caroline. Eng. operatic and concert s. singer; *b.* Portsmouth. Stud. at R.A.M. under Agnes Larkcom; *début* at R. Opera, Covent Garden (1907), in Eng. perf. of Wagner's *Ring*; created parts of Madame Hertz in Mozart's *Impresario* (His Majesty's, London, 1911); Sophie in Strauss's *Rosenkavalier* for 1st perfs. in Eng. (Denhof and Beecham, 1913), and Tilburina in Stanford's *The Critic*, Shaftesbury Theatre, 1916. A notable singer of oratorio.—E.-H.

HAUDEBERT, Louis. Fr. compr. *b.* in Brittany, 1877. Pupil of J. Pillois. His music is of an intimate nature, animated with a religious spirit.

Collections of songs; *Dans la Maison* (words by his wife); pieces for vn. and pf.—A. C.

HAUER, Josef Matthias. Austrian compr. and musical theorist; *b.* Wiener Neustadt, 19 March, 1883. Has lived in Vienna since 1914, occupied with compn. and with elaboration of his system of atonal music. Starting with Goethe's *Farbenlehre*, he is constructing tone-colour pictures, and from these comes the purely atonal *melos*, neither consonant nor dissonant, which he entrusts to the human voice or to the " tempered " instrs. alone (such as pf. and harmonium). Str. and wind-instrs. he considers unsuitable for the purpose. The atonal melody is the result of the working of the *Bausteine* (building-materials), which characterise each type of melodic experience. Their logical, strictly lawful and impersonal development results in a composition. All possible combinations of the 12 sounds of our scale can be divided into groups (*Tropen*). The latent forces of an interval lie within each *Tropus* and cause the further development of the latter as regards sound and rhythm. This sole kind of perfectly and absolutely atonal melody can only be reproduced by means of homophony. Hauer rejects every kind of polyphony. Yet his recent works (such as *Barock-studie* publ. in the periodical *Anbruch*, IV, 5–6) seem to admit a certain modification concerning this point. Hauer thus intends to return to the music of Eastern nations, especially of the Chinese. To him the development of European music seems to have been an error. His theories are demonstrated in the three pamphlets: *Über die Klangfarbe, Vom Wesen des Musikalischen* (Vienna, 1920, Waldheim & Eberle), and *Deutung des Melos* (1923, Tal).

Whatever may be the opinion concerning Hauer's theories, some of his compns. certainly make a strong impression. Amongst these are *Nomoi* for piano, an *Apocalyptic Fantasia* for Kammerorchester (which means a combination of pf. and several harmoniums, according to needs), the *Hölderlin-Lieder* (sung by Anna Bahr-Mildenburg), choruses out of Sophocles' tragedies. Most of these works have been publ. by Goll, Vienna. The compr. uses a special kind of atonal notation in some of them. The *Barockstudien*, 12 new Hölderlin songs and 20 atonal pieces for piano are in ms. Interesting essays (*Melos und Rhythmus* and *Sphärenmusik*) by him have been publ. in the periodical *Melos*. Consult: Stefan, *Neue Musik und Wien*; M. Marton, in *Anbruch*, IV, 5–6.—P. St.

HAUG, Gustav. Ger. compr. *b.* Strasburg, 30 Nov. 1871. Pupil of Cons. in Strasburg. In Switzerland since 1895, first as music teacher in Rorschach; orgt. and choirmaster in Gais; since 1904 in St. Gallen, where he is orgt. at St. Leonhard's, condr. of the Herisau Orch. Soc., and of male choral soc. *Harmonie*. He has made a name chiefly as prolific compr. of choral works:

Swiss Prayer, op. 50, male chorus, s. solo and orch.; *The Infinite*, op. 57, male chorus, s., orch. and organ; *Divico*, op. 64, ballad, male chorus, barit. solo and full orch. (Zurich, Hug & Co.).—A. E.

HAUSEGGER, Friedrich von. Austrian writer on music; *b.* St. Andrä (Carinthia), 26 April, 1837; *d.* Graz, 23 Feb. 1899. Stud. law at Vienna. One of the most enthusiastic propagandists of Wagner.

Musik als Ausdruck (Vienna, 1885); *Richard Wagner and Schopenhauer* (2nd ed. 1892); *Vom Jenseits des Künstlers* (1893); *Unsere deutschen Meister* (1901).—EG. W.

HAUSEGGER, Siegmund von. Austrian compr. *b.* Graz, 16 Aug. 1872. His first works, a Mass (1899), an opera *Helfrid*, perf. at Graz; his second opera, *Zinnober* (1898), at Munich. His first great success was *Dionysische Phantasie*, a symph. poem in Liszt style, finely orchestrated, perf. with Kaim Orch. at Munich. His best work is the symph. poem *Barbarossa* (1900), one of most inspired works of South-Ger. school of this epoch. In his later works—*Wieland der Schmied* (1904), his choruses, the *Natursymphonie* (1911) and *Aufklänge* (1919), variations on a simple folk-tune—he shows no further evolution. Hausegger is an excellent condr. He started 1895–6 at Graz, and has cond. especially at Munich, Frankfort, Berlin and Hamburg. —EG. W.

HAUSER, Emil. Hungarian violinist; *b.* Budapest, 17 May, 1893. Stud. at R. High School, Budapest. Founder and leader of Budapest Str. Quartet (Hauser, Pogány, Ipolyi, Son). —B. B.

HAUSMANN, Robert. Ger. cellist; *b.* Rottleberode (Harz), 13 Aug. 1852; *d.* Vienna, 18 Jan. 1909. Pupil of Theodor Müller (cellist of old-establ. Müller Quartet) till 1869; Berlin High School till 1871; then pupil of Piatti, London; since then teacher at R. High School, Berlin; also a member of the Joachim Quartet (from 1879 till Joachim's death in 1907).—A. E.

HAUTSTONT, Jean. Belgian compr.; theorist; *b.* Brussels, 13 Dec. 1867. Devoted himself to compn. and reform in notation. Invented new system of notation which he uses in his works, the *Notation Autonome* (Paris, 1907), and which he explains in his *Solfège*, publ. 1913. Summoned to China in 1912–13 to found a Cons. based on his reformed system, but civil wars interfered. In 1921 founded in Brussels a soc. for publ. music with this notation. The system is based on the classification of sounds according to the number of their vibrations, and the state of physiological development of the ear. It avoids all the difficulties of diatonic notation which are mainly the result (according to H.) of the increasing accumulation of chromatic accidentals in contemporary music.

Lidia, lyrical drama (Oertel, Brussels); *Hymne national de la République chinoise* (Chinese National Anthem), comp. at request of Sun-Ya-Tsen Government and perf. in Pekin at official opening of Parliament 1913 (publ. at Monaco by Institut Professionel); *Hymne triomphal et prophétique de la Commune Mondiale* (under pseudonym of Ivan Bourié-Vestnik; the ed. in autonomous and diatonic notation was seized by the Fr. Government in 1922).—C. V. B.

HAVEMANN, Gustav. Ger. violinist; *b.* Güstrow, 15 March, 1882. Pupil of father of brother-in-law, Parlow, and of Bruno Ahner; then of Berlin High School of Music (Markees and Joachim). Hofkonzertmeister Darmstadt, 1905; teacher Leipzig Cons., 1911; Konzertmeister of Saxon State Orch. Dresden, from 1 Nov. 1915. Is now in Berlin at High School and leader of a str. quartet (H., Kniestädt, Mahlke, Steiner).—A. E.

HAWLEY, Stanley. Eng. compr. and pianist; *b.* Ilkeston, Derbyshire, 17 May, 1867; *d.* there, 13

June, 1916. Stud. at R.A.M. London, 1884–92; *début* St. James's Hall (1887) with Grieg's concerto; from then appeared frequently both as pianist and accompanist. Hon. sec. R. Philh. Soc. till his death. Wrote much music for recitation and piano.

Music to E. A. Poe's *The Bells* (1894); *The Raven* (1896); *Elizabethan Love-Lyrics*, etc. (Bosworth, 1903) 1903); *Dramatic Poems* (Novello); recitation music series, 25 nos. (Bosworth).—E.-H.

HAY, Edward Norman. Irish compr. and orgt. *b.* Faversham, 19 April, 1889. His father was a native of Coleraine; stud. under Dr. F. Koeller (condr. Belfast Philh.) 1904–11; Mus.Doc. Oxon. 1919 (qualified 1915); orgt. and choirmaster Coleraine parish ch. 1914–16; now of Bangor Abbey, Co. Down. His compns. are classical in style, and show a refined and poetic individuality.

Folk-song Phantasy, str. 4tet (Cobbett prize, 1916); str. 4tet in A; (Carnegie award, 1918) Stainer & Bell); overture, *The Gilly of Christ* (ms.); tone-poem, *Dunluce* (ms.); organ piece (Augener).—E.-H.

HAY, Frederick Charles. Condr. and compr. *b.* Basle, 18 Sept. 1888. First stud. medicine (till 1908), but soon devoted himself entirely to music; pupil of Hans Huber at Basle, of Ch. M. Widor and Debussy in Paris and of R. Fuchs and Schalk in Vienna. Condr. of Opera at Berne in 1912, where he also cond. symphony concerts and numerous choirs. Since 1920, dir. of Société de Chant du Conservatoire (oratorio concerts) and of Orchestre de l'Université at Geneva; lecturer on mus. history at Univ. His compns. show relationship to the modern Fr. school (Debussy) as well as to the Brahms-Reger type; are finely orchestrated and attain a great height of intensity and expression.

Mr. Hay has been responsible for all the Swiss arts. in this Dictionary.

Symph. poem, *Heaven and Earth* (Byron); *Psalm CXXI*, mixed chorus and orch.; *Hymne* (Tagore), female chorus, orch. and organ; str. 4tet; pf. concerto; songs with orch. and with pf.—E.-H.

HAYDON, Claude M. Australian compr. *b.* South Yarra, Melbourne, 8 Nov. 1884. His 5-act opera *Paolo and Francesca* (book by compr.) was produced at the Playhouse, Melbourne, 6 and 7 May, 1920. It was written in 1919. Now resides in Wellington, New Zealand.

Incidental music for Aristophanes' *The Wasps* (for Melbourne Univ. Jubilee) 1906); *Serenade*, pf. and str. orch. (1915); *Phantasie-trio*, pf. vn. cello (1907); str. 4tet, D mi. (1914); str. trio suite (6 pieces), 1918; pieces for cello and pf.; sonata, vn. and pf.; pf. pieces; many songs.—E.-H.

HAYE, R. de la. Brit. orgt. condr. *b.* Brecon, South Wales, in 1878. A notable personality in the mus. life of Edinburgh. Stud. under J. Roper of Collegiate Ch. Wolverhampton (a pupil of S. S. Wesley), and in 1893, at the age of 13, became assistant there; stud. vn. under Henry Hayward, Wolverhampton, and T. M. Abbot, of Birmingham; orchestration and orch. playing at Birmingham and Midland School of Music, under Dr. Iliffe and George Halford; later, pf. under Fred Westlake, and vn. under Gompertz. Appointed orgt. and choirmaster at West Parish Ch. Galashiels, in 1897, at age of 19; 1900, orgt. and choirmaster at Lauriston Place U.F. Ch. Edinburgh. Condr.

of St. Andrew Amateur Orch. Soc. (1908), Southern Light Opera Co., Edinburgh (1910), Edinburgh (Grand) Opera Co. (since its foundation in 1920).—W. S.

HAYES, Roland. Tenor singer; *b.* Curryville, Georgia, U.S.A., 3 June, 1887. One of foremost t. concert-singers of day; has toured in classical concerts, America, England, France, Germany, Italy, Austria, Czecho-Slovakia; stud. under W. A. Colhoun (a Negro) for 9 months and then under Miss Jennie Robinson (Fisk Univ. Nashville, Tenn., U.S.A.) for 4 years; and under Arthur J. Hubbard (Boston, U.S.A.) for 8 years; has specialised in negro music, particularly the Spirituals. Has a very pleasing voice of real tenor quality and is a thoroughly finished artist. —E.-H.

HAYNE, Eric. Australian violinist: *b.* Ipswich, Queensland. Stud. at High School of Music, Berlin, and later privately under Willy Hess. Played for 2 years in Boston Symphony Orch. under Carl Muck: toured U.S.A. with Evelyn Scotney: now teaches in Brisbane.—G. Y.

HAYOT, Maurice. Fr. violinist; *b.* Provins, 8 Nov. 1862. Took a brilliant 1st prize at Paris Cons. (1883) where he was pupil of Massart. Made successful tours in France and abroad; appointed vn. prof. at Paris Cons. 1893. Founder of one of most famous Fr. quartets, his partners being F. Touche (since replaced by M. André), Denayez and Salmon. This quartet was a regular collaborator in the famous soirées of La Trompette (see Societies), a private society which did much during the last century for the popularisation of chamber-music.—M. P.

HAYWARD, Marjorie. Eng. violinist; *b.* Greenwich, 14 Aug. 1885. Stud. under Jessie Grimson; then at R.A.M. London, under Émile Sauret (1897–3) and Otakar Ševčík (1903–6). She has a very powerful style; now leads the English String Quartet.—E.-H.

HAZLEHURST, Cecil. Eng. compr. *b.* Higher Runcorn, 22 May, 1880. Stud. Liverpool Coll. of Music; exhibitioner, Victoria Univ. Manchester; Mus.Doc. Manchester, 1906. Lives in London. Has a neat, tuneful style, founded on Romanticist models.

1-act opera, *Cleopatra*, op. 18; comic opera, *The Prince Elect*, op. 1; children's operetta, *The Dream*, op. 15; orch. pieces; choral ballad; str. 4tet, C mi. op. 23; str. 4tet on folk-songs, op. 40; pf. 5tet, *The Masque of Fear*, op. 47 (Cobbett bracketed-prize, 1920); organ fugue on theme of Elgar's, op. 36; pf. pieces (Elkin; Lengnick); songs (Weekes; Evans; Enoch; Curwen; Cramer; Novello).—E.-H.

HEATH, John Rippiner. Eng. compr. *b.* Edgbaston, Birmingham, 4 Jan. 1887. Mainly self-taught; a medical practitioner at Barmouth, Wales; condr. Barmouth Choral Union; writes for small combinations of instrs. in a modern style which eliminates all literary and philosophical interest and relies on the purely musical appeal.

Orch.: 3 *Characteristic Dances*, str. and tpi. (Goodwin & Tabb); 3 *Picturesque Pieces*, orch. (ms.). Chamber-music: *Serbian* str. 4tet (Chester); 3 *Macedonian Sketches*, vn. and pf. (*id.*); poem, *In the Heart of the Country*, vn. and pf. (*id.*); *The Lamps*, chamber music-drama (*id.*); *Il Bosco Sacro*, 3-part female vs., str. 4tet and harp (*id.*). Pf: 6 *Inventions*

(W. Rogers); *Reflexions (id.)*; 4 *Humoresques* (Enoch); suite, *A Child's Night (id.)*; *A Rune (id.)*. Songs: 3 *Welsh Landscapes*; 3 *Short Love-Songs*; *A Summer Song* (Robert Nicholls); *The Enchanted Hour*, etc. (mostly Enoch).—E.-H.

HEBER, Judith. Norwegian compr. pianist; *b.* Gol, Hallingdal, 27 June, 1880; *d.* Christiania, 7 Oct. 1919. Pupil of Agathe Gröndahl and Dagmar Walle-Hansen, Christiania, and of Jedliczka and Scharwenka, Berlin. *Début* as pianist in Christiania, 1907; as compr. in same city, 1911. Best known for her songs.—U. M.

HEBREW MUSIC. See IDELSOHN, A. Z.

HEBRIDEAN MUSIC. See SONGS OF THE HEBRIDES.

HECKELPHONE. See art. on OBOE FAMILY.

HEERMANN, Hugo. Ger. vn. virtuoso; *b.* Heilbronn, 3 March, 1844. Attended Brussels Cons. for 5 years under Meerts, de Bériot and Fétis; then 3 years in Paris for further study. After some concert tours, was called to Frankfort-o-M. as Konzertmeister and became first teacher of vn. engaged at Hoch's Cons. since its foundation (1878); also leader of Frankfort Str. Quartet (with Bassermann, Naret-Koning, Hugo Becker). In 1904 gave up position at Cons. and founded his own vn. school. Edited new ed. of Bériot's *Vn. Tutor* (1896).—A. E.

HEGAR, Friedrich. Swiss conductor, composer; *b.* Basle, 11 Oct. 1841. Studied in Leipzig, violin and theory (1857–61), pupil of David, Hauptmann, Rietz and Plaidy. For a short time 1st violinist Bilse's Orchestra, Berlin, and conductor in Gebweiler (Alsace); then engaged as leading violinist at opera-house in Zurich (1863); 2 years later, conductor of Symphony and Oratorio Concerts. During his 40 years of artistic activity, he founded in 1875 the Conservatoire, which he directed till 1915. A friend of Brahms, he did much to popularise the work of the German master. 1889, Ph.D. *h.c.* Zurich University; elected Hon. President of Association of Swiss Musicians. 1907, director of Royal Academy of Music, Berlin (as successor of Joachim). Hegar assured himself a name in the history of music by his numerous compositions for male chorus. He was the first to employ voices in the " tone-painting " manner, producing original orchestral effects. His choruses show an invention of great intensity, much character and excellent word-setting. His instrumental pieces, too, are of considerable importance. His oratorio *Manasse*, and his ballad *The Heart of Douglas* (tenor and baritone soli, chorus and orchestra), rank amongst the best compositions of his time.

Male choruses, unacc.: *Morgen im Walde*, op. 4; *In den Alpen*, op. 11; *Rudolph von Werdenberg*, op. 15; *Totenvolk*, op. 17; *Schlafwandel*, op. 18; *Hymne an den Gesang*, op. 20; oratorio, *Manasse* (J. V. Widmann); *Das Herz von Douglas*, op. 36; Festal Cantata, for inauguration of new building of Univ. (Zurich, 1914); Festal Overture, full orch.; vn. concerto; cello concerto; str. 4tet, F sharp mi. op. 46; numerous songs (Leipzig, Hug).—F. H.

HEGEDUS, Ferencz. Violinist; *b.* Fünfkirchen, Hungary, 26 Feb. 1881, of Hungarian father and Span. mother. Stud. at Budapest Cons.; later at R. Hungarian Acad. of Music; condr. Lustspiel Theatre, Budapest, 1899;

visited London, 1900; has toured all chief European cities.—E.-H.

HEGER, Robert. Condr. and compr. *b.* Strasburg (Alsace), 19 Aug. 1886. Stud. at Town Cons. Strasburg (Franz Stockhausen); then in Zurich (L. Kempter); lastly in Munich (Max Schillings). Engagements as condr.: 1907, Strasburg; 1908, Ulm; 1909, Barmen; 1911, Vienna Volksoper; 1913, Nuremberg, where he also cond. Philh. concerts; 1921, Munich.

The Jewess of Worms (melodrama); pf. trio, op. 14; songs; 3-act opera, *A Festival at Haderslev* (Nuremberg, 1919). Unpubl. works: *Hero and Leander*, symph. drama, full orch., op. 12; vn. concerto, D ma. op. 16; symphony, D mi.; a choral work, *A Song of Peace*, soli, chorus, orch. and organ.—A. E.

HEGGE, Odd Grüner. Norwegian pianist, compr. *b.* Christiania, 23 Sept. 1899. Pupil of Music Cons. in Christiania, of Nils Larsen and Backer-Gröndahl (pf.) and of Gustav Lange (compn.). As compr. he has attracted attention by his marked polyphonic talent and strong creative powers. His chamber-music works are distinguished by pleasing melodious invention and modern harmony. Member of committee of Norwegian Composers' Association.

Sonata for vn. and pf.; pf. suite; trio for vn. cello and piano.—J. A.

HEIDE, Harald. Norwegian violinist and condr. *b.* Fredrikstad, 8 March, 1876. Trained as violinist under Gudbrand Böhn (Christiania), César Thomson (Brussels), and Zajič (Berlin). Has given concerts in N. America and England. Orch. condr. to the theatre *Den Nationale Scene*, and to the mus. soc. *Harmonien* in Bergen. Has comp. a large number of works, especially for theatre.—U. M.

HEINS, Francis Donaldson. Brit. violinist; *b.* Hereford, England, 19 Feb. 1878. Stud. at Leipzig Cons. under Hans Sitt (vn.), Carl Bering (pf.), Gustav Schreck (harmony), Richard Hoffmann (orch.). In 1897, began work as teacher and player in Hereford, continuing his vn. studies under Wilhelmj. 1902, went to Ottawa, Canada, where he now resides. Condr. of Ottawa Symphony Orch. since 1903. Though not entirely a professional orch. its concerts have become a prominent feature of Ottawa mus. life. The Earl Grey Trophy offered for best orch. playing has been won 4 years in succession by this orch.—L. S.

HEISE, Peter Arnold. Danish compr. *b.* Copenhagen, 11 Feb. 1830; *d.* Taarbäk, suburb of Copenhagen, 12 Sept. 1879. B.A. 1847. Stud. music in Copenhagen under A. P. Berggreen, and under Hauptmann, Leipzig. His speciality as a compr. was in the romance form, for which he had a peculiar gift. The complete collection of his romances and songs fill 3 vols. in the new ed. and stand as a noble monument to the high development of Danish music in latter half of XIX century. This essentially lyric compr. in his last years turned to dramatic forms in his 2 operas, *Paschaens Datter* (*The Pasha's Daughter*), 1869, and *Drot og Marsk* (*King and Marshal*), 1878. The latter is a Danish-historical work of the grand opera type, and its appearance gave promise of rich development, the fulfilment of which was, however, prevented by his premature death.—A. H.

HEKKING, André. Fr. cellist; b. Bordeaux, 30 July, 1866. Stud. solely under his uncle, Charles Hekking, himself a remarkable artist. Début, when very young, as soloist to all the chief Fr. Symphony Concerts—Cons., Colonne, Lamoureux. In 1919, became teacher at Cons. at École Normale de Musique and at Amer. Cons. at Fontainebleau. He is remarkable for the firmness and power of his tone, especially in those passages of a concerto of Lalo or Brahms where the soloist had to sustain his part against a full orchestra.—M. P.

HEKKING, Gérard. Fr. cellist; b. Nancy, 1879, One of the foremost cellists of modern Fr. school. 1st prize, Paris Cons. 1899; after short probation at the Opéra, began brilliant career as soloist and 4tet-player. Has played as soloist with all chief Paris orchs.; at Cons.; Colonne and Lamoureux Concerts; and Société Nationale. Has often appeared abroad in Belgium, Holland, Russia, Spain and Germany under Eugène Ysaye, Safonof, Mengelberg and Mahler. He has often been chosen to perform formerly unsuccessful works, such as 2nd sonata of J. Fauré, the 2nd quintet (Fauré), trio of J. Pierné, sonata of Paul Paray, many works of A. Cellier, J. Boulnois, Thirion, Dirk Schäffer, etc. His extremely versatile talent, coupled with a rare technique, permits him to essay works of widely diverging schools with incomparable confidence of style.—M. P.

HELFERT, Vladimír. Czechoslovak music critic, historian; b. 1886. Pupil of O. Hostinský at Prague Univ.; Ph.D.; from 1921 teacher of mus. science, Brno Univ. Great historical works: The Musical Baroque at Bohemian Castles (Hudební barok na českých zámcích), 1916; Music at the Castle of Jaroměřice (Hudba na zámku jaroměřickém). Even his smaller works are chiefly about Czech music in the XVIII century. Æsthetic works: Smetanovské kapitoly (Essays on Smetana); Naše hudba a český stát (Our Music and the Czechoslovak State). He is critic of several reviews and papers.—V. ST.

HELLER, Gordon. Eng. barit. singer and writer; b. Bradley, Yorks, 18 June, 1857. Stud. under Santley, J. Rubini, Henry Blower, Fred Walker, Hugo Heinz; Fräulein Keller. Prof. of singing at Huddersfield Coll. of Music, from 1908. Author of The Voice in Song and Speech (Kegan Paul, 1917).—E.-H.

HELLMESBERGER, Joseph, sen. Austrian violinist; b. Vienna, 3 Nov. 1828; d. there, 24 Oct. 1893. Son of Georg Hellmesberger, the teacher of Joachim; dir. of Ges. des Musikfreunde in Österreich (Soc. of Friends of Music in Austria); condr. of Soc. concerts and of Cons. Since 1851, prof. of vn. at Cons. In 1860, leader of Opera orch.; 1863, solo vn. of Hofkapelle; 1877, Hofkapellmeister. A famous teacher of generations of violinists.—EG. W.

HELLMESBERGER, Joseph, jun. Austrian

violinist; b. Vienna, 9 April, 1885; d. there, 26 April, 1907. From 1870, member of his father's quartet; 1878, solo vn. of Opera orch.; prof. of vn. at Cons.; condr. of comic opera; also of ballet-music at Opera. 1900–2, 1st Hofkapellmeister; 1902–5, condr. at Stuttgart. Comp. various operettas (perf. 1880–1906 at Vienna, Munich and Hamburg), of which Das Veilchenmädel is best known.—EG. W.

HELMHOLTZ, Hermann Ludwig Ferdinand von. Ger. physicist; b. Potsdam, 31 Aug. 1821; d. Charlottenburg (Berlin), 8 Sept. 1894. Stud. medicine in Berlin; assistant at Charité Hospital, 1842; army surgeon at Potsdam, 1843; teacher of anatomy for artists, and assistant in anatomical museum, 1848; prof. of physiology, Königsberg, 1849; prof. of anatomy and physiology, Bonn, 1855; prof. of physiology, Heidelberg, 1858; prof. of physics, Berlin, 1871.

Sensations of Tone as a Physiological Basis for Theory of Music, a work of the greatest importance for the mathematical, physical and physiological foundation for the theory of music (1863; 6th ed. 1913; Fr. by Guéroult, 1868 [1874]; Eng. by Ellis, 1875 [1885]). Consult: E. Mach, Introduction to Helmholtz's Theory of Music (1866, popular ed. for musicians); J. Broadhouse, The Student's Helmholtz (1890); Ludwig Riemann, Popular Outline of Acoustics in their Relation to Music (1896); S. Epstein, Helmholtz as Man and as Scientist (1897); Leo Königsberger, Hermann v. Helmholtz (1903, 3 vols.; popular ed. in 1 vol. 1911); E. Waetzmann, On Helmholtz's Resonance Theory (Breslau, 1907); Sedley Taylor, Sound and Music. Helmholtz's lectures on The Mathematical Principles of Acoustics were publ. by A. Könitz and L. Runge (1888).—A. E.

HELSTED, Gustav Carl. Danish compr. and orgt. b. Copenhagen, 30 Jan. 1857. Comes of a well-known family of musicians; pupil of R. Cons. of Music, Copenhagen; also stud. later on Continent. Prominent orgt.; at present filling the position at Vor Frue Kirke (Church of Our Lady), Copenhagen. Prof. of cpt. at R. Cons. Copenhagen. His numerous chamber - music pieces, larger orch. and choral works, all reveal talent of high order and great originality. Chairman of Dansk Koncertforening (Danish Concert Soc.) and of Dansk Komponistsamfund (Danish Composers' Club), Copenhagen.

Pf. trio, op. 6; str. 4tet, op. 33; 2 sonatas, pf. and vn. op. 13, 20; cello concerto, op. 5; Romance, vn. and orch. op. 11; vn. concerto, op. 27; Our Fatherland, soli, chorus, orch. op. 30; Dance-Music, female chorus and pf. op. 28; pf. pieces; songs (Copenhagen, Hansen).—A. H.

HELY-HUTCHINSON, C. V. Born Cape Town, S.A. Educated at Eton and Balliol Coll. Oxford (Nettleship Scholarship in music) and R.C.M. London; lecturer in music, S. African Coll. of Music and Cape Town Univ. 1922.

Orch. suite; 2 dances, str. orch. and pf.; vn. sonata; Blake's Songs of Innocence, female chorus and str. orch.; songs.—W. H. B.

HEMPEL, Frieda. Ger. dramatic and coloratura operatic s. b. Leipzig, 26 June, 1885. Pupil of Leipzig Cons. and of Stern's Cons. Berlin; pupil of Frau Nicklass - Kempner. Début, 1905; engaged Schwerin, 1905–7; R. Court Opera, Berlin, 1907–12; Metropolitan Opera House, New York, since 1912.—A. E.

HENDERSON, Archibald Martin. Scottish orgt. condr. b. Glasgow, 1879. One of the most notable mus. personalities in West Scotland, and a dynamic force in artistic life of Glasgow. Stud. at Klindworth-Scharwenka Cons. Berlin; later at Paris under Pugno, Widor, and Cortot. At present orgt. to Univ. of Glasgow, and condr. of Glasgow Bach Choir. Lectures on modern music, chiefly Russian. Glasgow correspondent for *Scottish Musical Magazine* till 1923; has ed. 5 vols. of Russ. pf. music; 5 vols. of standard organ classics; 3 vols of pf. transcriptions from Bach; and 2 vols of old Eng. classics for pf. Has also transl. and ed. a series of Russ. church compns. for English choirs (Bayley & Ferguson).—W. S.

HENDERSON, William James. Amer. critic and author; *b.* Newark, N.J., U.S.A., 4 Dec. 1855. Graduated A.B. Princeton, 1876; A.M. 1886. Pupil at Princeton of Carl Langlotz (pf.) 1868–73. Stud. singing under A. Torriani, 1876–7. Began as journalist in 1883; from 1887–92 music critic of *New York Times*; since 1902, of *Sun* (now *The Herald*). 1899–1902, lectured on music history at New York Coll. of Music; since 1904, on development of vocal art at Inst. of Mus. Art. Author of libretto of Damrosch's *Cyrano* and several light operas. Besides his numerous and widely-read books on music, has written on the subject of navigation. Member of National Institute of Arts and Letters.

The Story of Music (Longmans, 1889, and many later eds.); *Preludes and Studies* (id. 1891); *How Music Developed* (Stokes, 1898); *What is Good Music ?* (Scribner, 1899); *The Orchestra and Orchestral Music* (id. 1899); *Richard Wagner, his Life and Dramas* (id. 1901); *Modern Musical Drift* (Longmans, 1904); *The Art of the Singer* (Scribner, 1906); *Some Fore- runners of Italian Opera* (Holt, 1911); *Early History of Singing* (Longmans, 1921); a vol. of verse, *Pipes and Timbrel* (Badger, 1905), and a musical novel, *The Soul of a Tenor* (Holt, 1912).—O. K.

HENKEL, Lily. Eng. pianist; *b.* Nottingham. Stud. in England and abroad; finally under Mme. Schumann at Frankfort; *début* in Nottingham; has played with chief orchs. and toured in France, Germany, Holland, Spain; 1910, founded Henkel Quartet (pf. and str.) (A. Beckwith, R. Jeremy, J. Mundy).—E.-H.

HENNEBERG, C. V. A. Richard. Swedish condr. compr. pianist; *b.* Berlin 5 Aug. 1853. Stud. under W. Rust; acc. for Malinger and de Swert, 1870; for Conrad Behrens (Norway and Sweden); condr. in Berlin; of *Harmonie*, Bergen, 1873; attached to Covent Garden Opera, London, 1875; then at theatres in Stockholm; condr. R. Theatre (opera), 1885; R. Court Musicmaster, 1894; dir. of orch. in Berne saloons, 1907–12; condr. popular concerts at Malmö, 1912; retired on pension; lives in Malmö. Member R.A.M. Stockholm, 1885. Introduced Wagner's operas in Sweden.

Opéra-comique, Droteningens vallfart (*The Queen's Pilgrimage*) 1882; music for Ibsen's *Brand*, and for Shakespeare plays; to ballet *Undina*; pf. 5tet and other chamber-music; songs; choruses; pf. music and orchestrations of various works.—P. V.

HENNERBERG, Carl Fredrik. R. Swedish Court orgt. *b.* Ålgarås (Sweden), 27 Jan. 1871. Stud. R. Cons. Stockholm, 1899–1907; teacher of harmony at Cons. from 1904; also of pf. from 1905; choirmaster at Chapel of R. Castle,

1906–8; orgt. there from 1909; librarian of R.A.M. Stockholm from 1908, where he systematised and catalogued the library. Made travel-studies in Germany, Switzerland, France (1910); England and France (1911). Member R.A.M. Stockholm, 1915.

Orgelns byggnad och vård (*Structure and Care of the Organ* (1912). List of compns. of Gunnar Wennerberg (1918); transl. of Carl Locker's *Orgelregister*. H. has written for many foreign music-journals: *Mus. News* (London); *Zeitschrift der I.M.G.*; *Bulletin de la Soc. française de musicologie*; and *Kongressberichte der I.M.G.* (Vienna, 1909; London, 1911).—P. V.

HENNUM, Johan. Norwegian cellist, condr. *b.* Christiania, 26 Aug. 1836; *d.* there, 13 Sept. 1894. Pupil of the chamber-musician Kuhlau, Copenhagen (1854–6) and of Servais, Brussels (1859–60). Orch. condr. at Christiania Theatre, 1866–94. For a time also condr. of popular concerts. Both as an eminent condr. and a fine player of chamber-music he was, during a generation, one of the corner-stones of mus. life in Christiania.—U. M.

HENRIQUES, Fini Valdemar. Danish compr. violinist; *b.* Copenhagen, 20 Dec, 1867. Pupil of Valdemar Tofte (Copenhagen), of Joachim (Berlin) and in compn. of Johan Svendsen (Copenhagen). Member of R. Chapel, 1892–6. His talent, exuberant and full of temperament, has found expression in nearly every form—songs, chamber-music, orch. pieces, symphonies, dramatic works. Of these, special mention must be made of *Völund Smed* (Holger Drachmann's text) and the ballet *Den lille Havfrue* (*The Little Mermaid*), based upon Hans Chr. Andersen's tale. These two works were produced at R. Opera, Copenhagen.

Suite for ob. and orch. op. 13; *Romance*, vn. and orch. op. 12; pf. trio, op. 31; sonata, pf. and vn. op. 10; pf. pieces, op. 1, 4, 6, 7, 11, 15, 19, 21, 28 30, 32; romances and songs, op. 2, 3, 8, 9, 18, 22, 23, 29, 33 (Copenhagen, Hansen).—A. H.

HENRY, Leigh Vaughan. Eng. compr. and critic; *b.* Liverpool, 23 Sept. 1889. Son of John Henry (compr., barit. soloist of Covent Garden and voice specialist); showed early interest in music, commencing to study pf. at age of 7. Destined for profession of architect, but always continued music as a side-study. At 13, became pupil of Charles Ross, ex-prof. of Leipzig Cons. (pf.) and of A. W. Locke (harmony); later of Walter Bridson, Liverpool (harmony and cpt.). At 16, some of his work attracted attention of Granville Bantock, to whose advice he attributes greater part of his mus. development. At 23, was appointed dir. of music in Gordon Craig's School for the Art of the Theatre, Florence. In that city, gave numerous lectures at the Fenzi Palace, together with recitals of modern music, and condd. Anglo-Ital. Choral. Invited to Germany, arrived there to be interned at commencement of war. At cessation of hostilities, returned to England, and contributed to several mus. publications. In 1921, created and became ed. of *Fanfare*, a mus. review of advanced tendencies, which ran for only six months; has lectured in France, Italy, Germany and Russia.

The Rogueries of Corviello, comedy-ballet after the *Commedia dell' arte* (1914; revised 1920–1) (New York Composers' Music Corp.); 3 pieces for fl. clar. and bsn. (*id.*); *Catawba: plaisanteries pour piano* (1910) (*id.*); *Les Heures intimes: préludes pour piano* (1911–12) (*id.*); *A Celtic Poem*, male chorus *a cappella* (1911) (Goodwin); choric poems for solo speaking-voice and declamation chorus (1914–15) (Curwen); songs: *Mousmé no O-dori* (poem by compr. from Japanese text), 1911 (*id.*); *Spring Morning* (P. H. Evans), 1910 (*id.*); *Pleasaunces*, fl. ob. vn. vla. cello (ms.); *Cymric Poem*, small orch. (from *Mabinogion*) (ms.); *Sheen of Waters*, pf. and orch. (ms.). Books: *Music: Its growth in Form and Significance* (Oxford Culture Manuals); *Music: What it means and how to understand it* (Curwen); *Stravinsky*, monograph, authorised by composer (Chester).—E.-H.

HENSCHEL, Isidor Georg (Sir George). Concert barit. and compr. *b.* Breslau, 18 Feb. 1850. Of Polish descent. Pupil of Franz Götze (singing) and Richter (theory) at Leipzig Cons. (1867–70); continuation studies from Ad. Schulze (singing) and Ḳiel (compn.) in Berlin. Cond. symphony concerts in Boston, 1881–4; went to London, 1885, where he directed London Symphony Concerts till 1886; first condr. of Scottish Orch., Glasgow; teacher of singing at R.C.M., 1886–8; naturalised in Britain, 1890; knighted by King George V in 1914. His first wife was a s. concert singer, Miss Lillian Bailey (*b.* 17 Jan. 1860, in Ohio; *d.* 5 Nov. 1901, in London), pupil of her uncle, Charles Hayden, of Mme. Viardot, and lastly of Georg Henschel himself, whom she married in 1881, and accompanied from that time on his concert-tours.

Canon suite for str. orch.; *Psalm CIII*, chorus, soli and orch.; *Stabat Mater* (Birmingham Fest., 1894); *Hamlet* music (London, 1892); operas: *A Sea Change* (*Love's Stowaway*, 1884); *Frederick the Fair* and *Nubia* (Dresden, 1899); *Requiem*, op. 59 (1903); str. 4tet, E flat ma. op. 55; many songs (from Scheffel's *Trompeter von Säckingen*, etc.); choral songs, etc. Wrote *Personal Recollections of Brahms* (1907); and his own reminiscences, *Musings and Memories of a Musician* (Macmillan, 1918). Has resided for many years in Scotland at Allt-na-Criche, Aviemore.—A. E.

HENSEL, Walter. Pseudonym of Julius Janiezek (*q.v.*).

HENSELT, Adolf von. Ger. pianist and compr. *b.* Schwabach (Bavaria), 12 May, 1814; *d.* Warmbrunn (Silesia), 10 Oct. 1889. Stud. some time as R. Stipendiary, under Hummel, Weimar, and 2 years (theory) under Sechter, Vienna, where he lived for some years. First concert tour was to Berlin in 1836. Married in Breslau in 1837, and in 1838 took up his residence in Petrograd, where he was appointed Court virtuoso to Emperor and music-master to the princes. Appointed inspector of mus. instruction at the girls' schools of the empire, and honoured with the Order of Vladimir; Imperial Russian Councillor of State.

Pf. concerto, F mi.: concert studies, op. 2, op. 5, *La Gondola*, op. 13; *Poème d'Amour*, op. 3; *Song of Spring*, op. 15; *Impromptu*, op. 17; *Ballade*, op. 31; concert paraphrases; trio; a "Second-Piano" arr. for *Cramer's Études*; in all 39 works with opus numbers, and 15 unnumbered. Ed. an excellent ed. of Weber's pf. works (with variants); also wrote *Exercises préparatoires*, etc.—A. E.

HERBERT, Victor. Amer. compr. condr. and cellist; *b.* Dublin, 1 Feb. 1859. A grandson of Samuel Lover. Was sent to Germany at the age of 7 to study music. Stud. cello particularly under B. Cossmann (1876–8). After appearing as a soloist in Germany, France and Italy, was 1st cellist of Strauss's Orch. in Vienna

(1882) and then of Court Orch. in Stuttgart (1883–6). In Stuttgart, stud. compn. under M. Seifriz; wrote a Suite for cello and orch. op. 3, (Zumsteeg, 1884), and a still unpubl. cello concerto. Went to America, 1886, as 1st cellist of Metropolitan Opera in New York; later in Theodore Thomas's orch. and with Anton Seidl; also acted as assistant-condr. to Seidl. Played solo-part in 1st perf. of his 2nd concerto for cello, with Philh. Orch. in New York, 10 March, 1894. In 1889–91, associate-condr. at Worcester (Mass.) fests. and for these fests. wrote a cantata for soli, chorus and orch. *The Captive*. After being bandmaster of 22nd Regiment, New York National Guard, for 4 years, he cond. Pittsburg Symphony Orch. 1898–1904. After 1894, devoted himself more to the compn. of light operas, of which he has produced more than 35. A serious opera in 3 acts, *Natoma* (Philadelphia, 21 Feb. 1911), and another in 1 act, *Madeleine* (Metropolitan Opera, New York, 24 Jan. 1914), have not held the stage. An unpubl. symph. poem, *Hero and Leander*, op. 33 (1st perf. by New York Philh. Orch. 30 Jan. 1904), and an orch. suite, *Woodland Fancies* (1st perf. Pittsburg, 1902), have been frequently played in America. Member of National Inst. of Arts and Letters.

Serenade for str. orch. op. 12 (Leuckart, 1889); 2nd cello concerto, op. 30 (Schuberth, 1898); *Suite Romantique* for orch. op. 31 (Simrock, 1901); *Irish Rhapsody* for orch. (Schirmer, 1910). Operas: *Natoma* (Schirmer, 1911); *Madeleine* (*id.* 1914). Comic operas: *Prince Ananias* (Schuberth, 1894); *The Wizard of the Nile* (*id.* 1895); *The Serenade* (*id.* 1897); *The Idol's Eye* (*id.* 1897); and many later ones (publ. by Witmark; some by Schirmer). Also pf. pieces and songs.—O. K.

HEŘMAN, Jan. Czechoslovak pianist; *b.* Neveklov (Bohemia), 1886. Pupil of A. Mikeš in Prague. As a young man, toured in America with violinist Miss M. Herites. For some years teacher of piano in Russia; from 1914 prof. at Cons. of Prague. Has played in Paris and London. Together with K. Hoffmann he is systematically cultivating the perf. of vn. sonatas.—V. Sᴛ.

HERMANN, E. Hans G. Ger. compr. *b.* Leipzig, 17 Aug. 1870. Pupil of W. Rust, E. Kretschmer and H. v. Herzogenberg; contrabassist in several orchs. 1888–93; teacher at Klindworth-Scharwenka Cons. Berlin, 1901–7; now living in Berlin as compr. Is above all a song writer.

Ballads; songs, op. 64; songs in popular strain (Löns); *Solomon's Great Song in Minnelieder*, op. 61; 17 songs, op. 63; *Christmas Songs*; *Wisdom of Omar Khayyám*, op. 60, barit. and pf.; 2 mus. comedies, *Judgment of Midas* and *The Scarlet Pimpernel*; symphony in D mi. (*Life's Episodes*); 2 str. 4tets (G mi.; C ma.); suite (sonata), pf. and vn.; 4 pf. duets; clar. and pf. pieces; pieces for cello and pf., and for vn. and pf.—A. E.

HEROLD, Vilhelm. Danish opera-singer (t.); *b.* Hasle, Isle of Bornholm, 19 March, 1865. After his studies in Copenhagen and Paris (Devillier) made *début* at R. Theatre, Copenhagen (Gounod's *Faust*); later sang Tristan in Tchaikovsky's *Iolanthe*; pursued this success in *Carmen, Cavalleria Rusticana, Pagliacci, Werther, Bohème, Tiefland, Lohengrin, Mastersingers* etc., not alone on Danish, but also international stages (Covent Garden, London, Berlin, Prague, Chicago). Dramatic energy, refinement, the possession of a finely trained voice of exquisite quality, made him the popular idol of the Danish R. Opera until his retirement in 1915. He resumed his relations with that inst. in 1922 as dir. In his leisure he has cultivated with success a considerable talent as sculptor.—A. H.

HERSENT, Simone. Fr. violinist; *b.* St. Jean d'Angély, 18 Aug. 1895. *Prix d'honneur* for vn., Paris Cons. 1917. One of the best hopes of vn.-playing in France.—A. C.

HERTZ, Alfred. Amer. condr. *b.* Frankfort-o-M., 15 July, 1872. Stud. in Frankfort under Max Schwartz (pf.) and Anton Urspruch (theory). Assistant-condr. at Halle Stadttheater, 1891–2, and condr. at various Ger. theatres until 1902, when he came to New York as condr. of Ger. and Eng. opera at Metropolitan Opera House. Here he cond. the 1st scenic production of *Parsifal* outside of Bayreuth (1903) and 1st perf. of Parker's *Mona* (1912), Damrosch's *Cyrano* (1913) and Parker's *Fairyland* (Los Angeles, Cal., 1915). Cond. at Covent Garden, London, 1910; since 1915, condr. of San Francisco Symphony Orch. Received Order of Art and Science from King of Saxony.—J. M.

HERWEGH, Marcel. Virtuoso violinist; *b.* Zurich, 1860. A naturalised Frenchman; pursued his mus. studies at Stuttgart Cons. under E. Singer, the Hungarian violinist. Founded in 1896 the Société des Petites Auditions. Has ed. the Concertos of Leclair and written (with Élie Poirée) a psychological analysis of Beethoven's Sonatas.—A. C.

HERZFELD, Conrado. Argentine pianist and compr. *b.* Berlin in 1845. Stud. under Brest and Feschner. After touring in America, settled in Buenos Ayres in 1866 as teacher. Founded the Cons. La Capital in 1899. Has publ. pieces for orch. several marches (one, a funeral march, highly praised by Chrysander). His song (poem by Stecchetti) *Quando tu sarai vecchia* is a truly inspired work.—A. M.

HESELTINE, Philip. Eng. compr. critic and writer; *b.* 30 Oct. 1894. Stud. under Colin Taylor at Eton and informally under F. Delius and Bernard van Dieren. Founded the *Sackbut* (May 1920) and edited it until May 1921. Has written a book on Delius and has arr. many of the orch. works of Delius for pf. (Augener and Univ. Ed.). Composes under the pen-name of Peter Warlock. His songs are amongst the finest written since 1900. Contributor of several articles to this Dictionary.

An Old Song, fl. ob. clar. horn and divided str. (Chester); *Serenade* for str. orch. (*id.*); *The Curlew,* song-cycle, t. v. fl. c.a. str. 4tet (a Carnegie award, 1923; Stainer & Bell); *Folk-song Preludes,* pf. (Augener); song-cycles: *Lillygay* (Chester); *Saudades* (*id.*); *Peterisms* (*id.*); *Candlelight,* 12 nursery jingles (Augener); *Corpus Christi,* unacc. chorus (Curwen); numerous separate songs (Augener; W. Rogers; Boosey; Curwen; Enoch; H. Milford); editions of 150 old Eng. airs (with Philip Wilson) (Enoch; Novello; Chester; H. Milford; Harold Reeves). Books: *F. Delius* (J. Lane, 1923); *The English Ayre* (H. Milford).—E.-H.

HESS, Ludwig. Ger. t. singer and compr. *b.* Marburg, 23 March, 1877. From 1895 to 1900, pupil of Berlin High School of Music (R. Otto, Bargiel, Wolf, Heymann) and of Melch. Vidal in Milan (1901), after which he made a name as a concert singer. In Munich, 1907–10, as condr. of concert soc. for choral singing; then in Frankfort-o-M. as music teacher. Concert tour in U.S.A., Mexico and Canada, 1912–14; settled in Berlin as concert and oratorio singer, teacher and compr. From 1917 to 1920 condr. of mus. acad. of Königsberg Teachers' Choral Soc., and of symphony concerts of Königsberg Concert Soc., after which he returned to Berlin.

2 symphonies (*Hans Memling's King of Heaven,* B mi., and C sharp mi.); pf. 6tet; choral work, *Ariadne;* choruses: *Joyous Harvest, A Fresh Morning, Pirates, Summer Evening Rest, Burial Hymn, Midsummer Night, Newly-Found Happiness, In the Evening, Of Undying Love* (sacred chorus); vocal pieces for female chorus, op. 61; many songs with pf. (*Songs of Hafiz*). Also wrote a lively comic opera, *Abu und Nu* (Dantzig, 1919).—A. E.

HESS, Myra. Eng. pianist; *b.* London. Stud. at R.A.M. under Tobias Matthay; has toured Gt. Britain, France, Belgium, Holland, and (1922–3) America and Canada.—E.-H.

HESS, Willy. Ger. violinist; *b.* Mannheim, 14 July, 1859. Stud. (after having travelled several years) with Joachim in Berlin (1876–8). Engaged as Konzertmeister in Frankfort-o-M.; 1886, in Rotterdam; 1888, in Hallé Orch. Manchester; 1895, condr. of Gürzenich Orch. and vn.-teacher at Cons. in Cologne; 1903, succeeded Sauret as vn.-teacher, R.A.M. London; 1904, went to Boston as dir. of Symphony Orch., and leader of str. quartet of which Alwin Schröder was cellist. In 1910 followed Halir as teacher at R. High School, Berlin, and first violinist of Halir Quartet; also a member of the Schumann Trio.—A. E.

HESSE-LILIENBERG, Davida Augusta. Swedish s. operatic and concert-singer; *b.* Gäfle, 29 Jan. 1877. Stud. R. Cons. Stockholm (under J. Günther) 1897–1901; *début* as Zerlina, R. Opera, Stockholm, 1904; regularly engaged there, 1904–9; stud. in Berlin (Frau Emmerich), 1909; then appeared in operas and concerts in Stockholm. Chief parts: Mimi, Butterfly, Gilda, Iolanthe, Eurydice, Mignon, Rosina (*Il Barbiere*), Marcellina (*Fidelio*), Greta. Married Erik Lilienberg, Kristianstad, Sweden. —P. V.

HESSLER, Gustaf Emil. Swedish clarinettist and military band condr. *b.* Stockholm, 23 Feb. 1873. Stud. R. Cons. there, 1888–97; solo-clar. R. Chapel from 1894; prof. of clar. and ensemble R. Cons. from 1904; condr. of 1st Guards (*Svea Lifgarde*) military band; captain, 1922; member R.A.M. Stockholm, 1921. Comp. 15 marches for band.—P. V.

HEUSS, Alfred Valentin. Ger. musicographer and compr. *b.* Chur, 27 Jan. 1877. 1896, pupil Stuttgart Cons.; 1898, at Munich Acad. and stud. philosophy at Univ. Finished univ. course under Kretzschmar in Leipzig, 1899–1903; Ph.D. 1903, with a thesis *The Instrumental Parts of "Orfeo" and the Venetian*

Opera Symphonies. Ed. *Journal of the International Soc. of Music* (1904–14), contributing many spirited articles to it; compiled new ed. of Adam Krieger's *Arien* in *D.d.T.* (Vol. XIX); wrote valuable programme-books for Bach Fest. in Leipzig (1904, 1907, 1908, 1914); also J. S. Bach's *Passion according to St. Matthew* (1909); *Beethoven : a Delineation* (1921); *The Dynamics of the Mannheim School* (1909, in *Riemann Fest. Journal*). The explanatory comments, prepared for People's Chamber-Music Concerts arranged to take place in Albert Hall, Leipzig, he publ. in 1919 under title *Chamber-Music Evenings.* Took part in formation of Union of German Music Critics, and was its first president. Concert reporter to *Signale* (1902–5); opera and concert reporter to *Leipziger Volkszeitung*; 1912–18, held same position on staff of *Leipziger Zeitung.* In 1921 took over chief editorship of *Zeitschrift für Musik.*

His analyses of the works of Bach, Handel, Pergolesi, Beethoven, Liszt and Bruckner appeared in the *Kleine Konzertführer*, publ. by him and Breitkopf. Since 1915, has shown marked preference for musical compn. Songs (op. 2–5, op. 7–15); *Chorus of the Dead*, op. 6; *Psalm II*, op. 16 (all Breitkopf).—A. E.

HEWLETT, William Henry. Canadian orgt. teacher, choral condr. *b.* Bath, England, in 1873. Stud. pf. and organ under Dr. A. S. Vogt in Toronto; theory under Arthur Fisher, Albert Ham and Sig. D'Auria. Later, went to Berlin and London, being pupil successively of Ernest Jedliczka, Hans Pfitzner and Vladimir Cernikof. Returning to Canada, took degree of Mus.Bac. (Trinity), Toronto; appointed orgt. Carlton Street Methodist Church. 1903, orgt. Centenary Ch. Hamilton, which position he now holds. Has been associated for some years with Hamilton Cons. of Music, of which he has been Principal since 1918. In 1922, condr. of Elgar Choir (see CHORAL SOCIETIES) in succession to Bruce Carey.—L. S.

HEY, Julius. Ger. teacher of singing; *b.* Irmelshausen (Lower Franconia), 29 April, 1832; *d.* Munich, 22 April, 1909. Attended Munich Acad. of Painters, but turned to music and stud. harmony under Franz Lachner and singing under Friedrich Schmitt. Through King Ludwig II, became acquainted with Wagner, who suggested to him the reform of singers' training, by imparting to it a German national character. He worked for this idea as first teacher of singing at R. Music School, Munich, which had been founded in 1867 on Wagner's plan, and was placed under the dir. of H. v. Bülow. He resigned his appointment in 1883; removed to Berlin in 1887; in 1906 returned to Munich.

German Singing Instruction, 4 parts, 1886 (I, Phonetic; II, Tone and Voice Formation of Women's Voices; III, V.F. of Men's Voices; IV, Textual Explanations). He publ. songs and duets (some comic); also a favourite collection of 16 *Children's Songs* for first instruction. Wrote *R. Wagner as a Teacher of Elocution*, 1911, publ. by his son, Hans Erwin Hey.—A. E.

HEYDRICH, R. Bruno. Ger. singer and compr. *b.* Leuben (Saxony), 23 Feb. 1863. Pupil of Dresden Cons. (1879–82). Contrabassist, Dresden and Meiningen Court Orch. On Wüllner's advice, took singing-lessons from

Scharfe in Dresden, Hey in Berlin, Feodor v. Milde in Weimar, and Schultz-Dornburg in Cologne. First appearance in Sondershausen, 1887. Engaged as lyric t. or *tenore robusto* at Weimar, Stettin, Aix-la-Chapelle, Cologne, Magdeburg and Brunswick. Now living in Halle-o-S. as dir. of Music Cons., which he founded.

Songs; duets; trios; choruses; solfeggi; also orch. and chamber music (symphony, D, op. 57; pf. trio, op. 2 ; clar. sonata, op. 14; str. 4tet, op. 3 ; pf. 5tet, op. 5). Pf. pieces; choruses with orch.; operas: *Amen* (1-act, Cologne, 1895); *Chance* (4-act, Mayence, 1907); *Chance* (1-act, Halle, 1914); folk-opera, *The Hurdy-gurdy Girl* (not yet perf.).—A. E.

HEYERDAHL, Anders. Norwegian compr. *b.* Urskog, 29 Oct. 1832; *d.* 18 Aug. 1918. For many years violinist in the Norwegian Theatre, Christiania, but was compelled, owing to a nervous affection, to give up music for a considerable time. Has won recognition as a collector of Norwegian folk-tunes; publ. a coll. entitled *Slaatter* (*Folk-Songs*). The national element also plays an important part in his compns., which include a symph. overture, 2 str. 4tets, a pf. 5tet, *Huldre-eventyr* (*A Fairy Tale*), etc.—J. A.

HEYERSCHES MUSIKHISTORISCHES MUSEUM (*Heyer's History of Music Museum*), Cologne. Founded 1906 by Wilhelm Heyer (*b.* Cologne, 30 March, 1849; *d.* there, 20 March, 1913; founder of firm of Poensgen & Heyer, wholesale paper-merchants). The museum contains over 2600 instrs. and accessories (the chief constituents being the second De Wits coll., the Krauss coll. [Florence] and von Ibach's in Barmen), the autographs of nearly 20,000 musicians, 3500 portraits, and a specialised mus. library containing numerous rare prints. The present curator (since 1909) is Georg Kinsky (*q.v.*), who edits the comprehensive catalogue of which 3 vols. have already appeared.—A. E.

HEYNER, Herbert. Eng. barit. singer; *b.* London, 26 June, 1882. Stud. singing under Frederick King and opera rôles under Victor Maurel; first important London appearance at Promenade Concerts, Queen's Hall, 1907; sings at leading festivals.—E.-H.

HIDALGO, Elvira. Span. coloratura s. singer. Teatro Real, Madrid; Liceo, Barcelona; La Scala, Milan; Metropolitan Opera House, New York. First appeared in England, Covent Garden, B.N.O.C. Feb. 1924.—P. G. M.

HIERRO, José. Span. violinist; *b.* Cadiz. Stud. with great distinction at the Cons.; played in Paris; then establ. himself in Madrid, where he appeared occasionally as soloist and in quartets with Sarasate. Ex-leader of Sóc. de Conciertos (now Orquesta Sinfónica). First vn. of R. Chapel Orch.; prof. of vn. at R. Cons. de Música, in which capacity he has contributed in great measure to the recognised high standard of the Madrid orchs. Amongst his pupils are Antonio Piedra, Rafael Martínez and Manuel Quiroga.—P. G. M.

HILDACH, Eugen. Ger. barit. singer; *b.* Wittemberge-o-Elbe, 20 Nov. 1849. It was only when 24 that he was able to enter on his training as singer. In 1878 married Anna Schubert (*b.* Polkitten, E. Prussia, 5 Oct. 1852, a fellow-pupil of his under Frau El. Dreyschock in Berlin). Went to live in Breslau; but in 1880 Fr. Wüllner invited them both to join teaching staff of Dresden Cons., where they remained till 1886. They then devoted themselves entirely to concert platform; in 1904 opened school of singing in Frankfort-o-M. In 1909 H. was appointed a R. prof. Anna Hildach possessed a rich m.-sopr. Comp. songs, duets and choruses.—A. E.

HILDEBRAND, Camillo. Condr. and compr. b. Prague, 31 Jan. 1876. Pupil of Prague Cons., under Bennewitz. Teacher of opera class, Hoch's Cons., Frankfort-o-M., then condr. of theatre orchs. in Heidelberg, Mayence, Aix-la-Chapelle and Mannheim. Condr. 1912–19, Berlin Philh. Orch.; 1919–20, dir. of opera, condr. town symphony concerts and choral soc. Freiburg-i-Br. Since 1921, condr. of Blüthner Orch. Berlin. Married operatic singer, Henni Linkenbach.

Songs; choruses; pf. pieces; orch. works: opera, *Promise* (Rostock, 1909); fairy-play, *Firlefanz* (Freiburg, 1919).—A. E.

HILL, Alfred. Australian compr. b. Melbourne, 1869. Now prof. State Cons. of Music, Sydney, N.S.W.

Operas: *A Moorish Maid*, comic-romantic (perf. Australia and New Zealand); *Tapa*, a Maori opera (id.); *The Weird Flute*, short Maori opera (no chorus); *The Rajah of Shinapore* (perf. Australia); *Don Quixote*; *Giovanni*, short grand opera (perf. Australia); *Auster*, a spectacular fantasy, grand opera. Cantatas on Maori legends: *Hineoma* (perf. Australia and New Zealand); *Tawhaki*. For orch.: *A Maori Symphony* (perf. London under Cowen, Empire concert); sonata for tpt. and orch. in B flat; *Maori Rhapsody*; *Valse, Retrospect, Berceuse, Satyr*, for orch.; 5 str. 4tets (I, Maori, in B flat; II, Maori, in G mi.; III, *The Carnival*, in A mi.; IV, C mi.; V, E flat; the first two are publ. by Breitkopf, Leipzig); 5tet, E flat, for str. and pf. (with 8 solo vs.); 3 sonatas, and a sonatina, vn. and pf. (Aug. Wild); vn. solos (Paling, Sydney; Nicholson, Sydney); pf. pieces (Nicholson, Sydney); Maori Songs (Chappell; Boosey, London; McIndol, Dunedin, N.Z.); many other songs.—E.-H.

HILL, Carmen. Scottish m.-sopr. singer; b. Aberdeen, 5 May, 1883. Stud. R.C.M. under Frederick King; *début* St. James's Hall, Dec. 1903; has sung widely at ballad concerts.—E.-H.

HILL, Edward Burlingame. Amer. compr. b. Cambridge, Mass., U.S.A., 9 Sept. 1872. Son of a Harvard prof., he stud. at Harvard, and was graduated A.B. in 1894 with highest honours in music, having attended Paine's classes in music during his coll. course. Stud. compn. under F. F. Bullard in Boston and Widor in Paris; then orch. under Chadwick in Boston. 1908–18, instructor in music at Harvard; since 1918, assistant-prof. In 1920 lectured on music for Lowell Inst. in Boston. His Op. 18, *The Nuns of the Perpetual Adoration* (Boston, Music Co. 1909), cantata for female vs. and orch. (1st perf. in Boston, 1908) was sung in Birmingham, England, in 1911. A pantomime for full orch., *Jack Frost in Midsummer*, was played by Chicago Orch. in 1908. A similar compn., *Pan and the Star*, op. 19, was produced at MacDowell Fest., Peterboro, N.H., 1914. A symph. poem, *The Parting of Lancelot and Guinevere*, op. 21, was first played by St. Louis Orch. 1915. His latest larger work, a symph. poem, *The Fall of the*

House of Usher, op. 26 (after Poe), was brought out by Boston Symphony Orch. 29 Oct. 1920. His orch. compns. have remained in ms. H. is a member of National Inst. of Arts and Letters.—O. K.

HILLEMACHER, Lucien and Paul. Fr. comprs. Lucien, b. Paris, 10 June, 1860; d. 2 June, 1909; Paul, b. Paris, 29 Nov. 1852. Two brothers, both *Prix de Rome* winners, who have always collab. and signed their works with the single name *P. L. Hillemacher*. Paul had the prize for his cantata *Judith* (1876), Lucien, for his cantata *Fingal* (1880). In collab. they had, in 1882, the *Prix de la Ville de Paris* for their *Légende symphonique, Loreley*. Chief works in common:

Orch.: *La Cinquantaine*, 1898; *One for two*, 1894; *Héro et Léandre*, 1894. For theatre: *Le Drac* (3-act, 1886); *Circé* (3-act, 1907); *Saint Mégrin* (4-act, 1886); *Aventure d'Arlequin* (1888); *Le Régiment qui passe* (1886); *Orsola* (1902). Oratorios: *La Passion*; *Sainte Geneviève* (1887).—A. C.

HINDEMITH, Paul. Ger. vla.-player and compr. b. Hanau, 16 Nov. 1895. Devoted himself to music from his 11th year, more especially to vn.-playing. His teachers in compn. were Arnold Mendelssohn and Bernhard Sekles at Hoch's Cons. Frankfort-o-M. Since 1905 has been chief condr. of Opera House Orch. in Frankfort. As a compr. he is one of the freshest and most earnest of Young Germany's talented musicians. Messrs. Schott, Mayence, have publ. the following works:

2 vn. sonatas, op. 11 (E flat; D); sonata for vla. and pf. op. 11, iv; str. 4tet, F mi., op. 10; sonata for cello and pf. op. 11, iii; song-cycle (*Melancholy*) for contr. and str. 4tet; ballad-cycle, *The Young Maiden* (G. Trakl) op. 23b; a *Kammermusik*, op. 24, i; 3 other str. 4tets; pf. 5tet; 5tet for wind instr. op. 24, ii; sonata, vla. alone, op. 11, v; cello alone, op. 26, iii; 2nd sonata, vla. and pf. op. 26, iv; ballad-cycle, *Das Marienleben*, op. 27; 5tet, clar. and str., etc. Also three 1-act operas: *Murderer, Women's Hope* (text by Oskar Kokoschka); *The Nusch-Nuschi* (Franz Blei); *Sancta Susanna* (Stramm). The first two were produced Stuttgart, 1921; all three in Frankfort-o-M., 1922.—A. E.

HINTON, Arthur. Eng. compr. b. Beckenham, Kent, 20 Nov. 1869. Stud. vn. under Prosper Sainton and Sauret at R.A.M. London; then at Munich under Rheinberger; then Vienna and Rome; Eng. provincial tours; has visited Australia and New Zealand twice. Married Katharine Goodson, pianist (q.v.).

2 symphonies (ms.); dramatic romance, *Porphyria's Lover* (Patron's Fund concert, Queen's Hall; ms.); orch. suite, *Endymion* (Fischer, New York); pf. concerto (id.); scena, *Epipsychidion*, t. v. and orch. (ms.); scena, *Semele*, m.-sopr. and orch. (ms.), perf. R. Philh. Soc. 1923; *Romance*, cello and orch. (J. Williams); pf. 5tet (Elkin); trio, pf. vn. cello (Rahter); vn. sonata (Chester); suite, vn. and pf. (Novello); *White Roses* song-cycle (Schmidt, Munich); *Schmetterlinge* (2 bks., Ries & Erler); songs, part-songs (Breitkopf; Fischer); vn. and pf. pieces (Fischer); operettas: *The Disagreeable Princess* (Bayley & Ferguson); *St. Elizabeth's Roses* (Curwen).—E.-H.

HJELLEMO, Ole. Norwegian compr. b. Dovre, 22 March, 1873. Pupil of Böhn (vn.), Ole Olsen and Iver Holter (compn.); teacher of vn., harmony and compn. at Music Cons. in Christiania.

Symphony in E ma. (National Theatre, 1912); Suite for orch. (The Young Composers' concert in 1920); *Springleik*; *Sang*; *Slaat*; military music. —J. A.

HOBDAY, Alfred Charles. Eng. vla.-player; b. Faversham, 19 April, 1870. Stud. R.A.M. London; has played in leading quartets (St. James's Hall, with Joachim, Lady Hallé, Ries, Strauss, Piatti; has given many vla. recitals with his wife, Ethel Sharpe; solo vla. R. Covent Garden Opera, 1900–14; leading vla. R. Philh., Goossens Orch., L.S.O. (since its inception, 1905) and chief festivals.—E.-H.

HOBDAY, Claude. Eng. d.b.-player; b. Faversham, Kent, 12 May, 1872. Stud. R.C.M. (1888–92); has played in leading orchs. (R. Eng. Opera under Sullivan; Glasgow Choral Union under Manns; Scottish Orch. under Henschel; Richter Concerts, London; London Symphony Orch.; R. Philh. Soc.); prof. of d.b. at R.C.M. from 1902.—E.-H.

HÖBER, Lorenz. Ger. vla.-player, compr. b. Frankfort-o-M., 30 Dec. 1888. Pupil Hoch's Cons. (vn. Anna Hegner and Ad. Rebner; compn. I. Knorr); afterwards of Willy Hess, Berlin High School. Solo vla. Philh. Orch. Berlin. As compr. has principally distinguished himself in chamber-music: a flute trio; 2 str. 4tets.—A. E.

HÖEBERG, Georg. Danish compr. violinist, condr. of the R. Chapel; b. Copenhagen, 27 Dec. 1872. Stud. R. Cons. Copenhagen. Stipendium, 1898. Prof. of vn. at R. Cons. 1900–14; condr. of Dansk Koncertforening (Danish Concert Soc.) 1910–14. Since 1914, condr. of R. Opera, Copenhagen, and from 1915 chief dir. of the united Danish Choral Society.

Opera, Bryllup i Katakomberne (The Wedding in the Catacombs), R. Opera, Copenhagen, 1909; ballet, Paris Dom (The Judgment of Paris), op. 17; sonata, pf. and vn. op. 1; Romance, vn. op. 3; songs; pf. pieces (Copenhagen, Hansen).—A. H.

HOEHN, Alfred. Ger. pianist; b. Oberellen near Eisenach, 20 Oct. 1887. Pupil of Hoch's Cons. (Prof. Uzielli), Frankfort-o-M. Secured Rubinstein Prize, 1910. An energetic and virile player. Also known as compr. of a str. 4tet and a Psalm for barit. and full orch.—A. E.

HOESICK, Ferdynand. Polish writer; b. Warsaw, 1869. Publ. in 1911 a most conscientious biography of Chopin (Polish, in 3 vols., Warsaw) and in 1912 Chopin's Correspondence.—ZD. J.

HOESSLIN, Franz von. German condr. and compr. b. Munich, 31 Dec. 1885. Pupil of Max Reger and Felix Mottl. Condr. since 1907; Opera, Dantzig; St. Gall; condr. Riga, 1912–14; 1919–20, concert-dir. Lübeck; orch. condr. Mannheim National Theatre, 1920–2; condr. of Berlin People's Opera; since 1923 condr. of opera at Dessau. Comp. 3 Kammerstücke for orch. (Berlin, Bote & Bock). —A. E.

HOFFMANN, Karel. Czechoslovak violinist; b. Smíchov, 1872. Pupil of Bennewitz, Prague Cons. In 1892 founded, with fellow-pupils, the Bohemian Quartet (see CHAMBER-MUSIC PLAYERS); from 1922, vn. prof. at Prague Cons. He has remarkable personality, a strongly expressive tone and a fine classical style.—V. ST.

HOFFMANN, Rudolf Stephan. Austrian composer and critic; b. Vienna, 21 Aug. 1878.

Degree as doctor of medicine in 1902; combines medical work with music. Pupil of Zemlinsky. Many songs and an opera (none publ.); transl. opera-texts of Manen, Respighi, Ethel Smyth. Widely known as clever and spirited critic (Merker; Anbruch; Neue Musikzeitung). Monographs on Franz Schreker (1920) and E. W. Korngold (1923).—P. ST.

HOFFMEISTER, Karel. Czechoslovak pianist and writer; b. Libice, 1868. Stud. at Univ. and Cons., Prague (pupil of J. Káan); 1890–98 prof. in Ljubljana; then at Cons. Prague. Has given concerts (Bohemian Trio), comp. songs and pf. pieces (Urbánek, Prague) and written critiques and analyses of modern Czechoslovak music; works on piano method and on Bach's clavier pieces. Chief works: Bedřich Smetana (Prague, 1915, Zlatoroh); The Piano: Its Methods and Masters (Prague, 1923, Hudební Matice). With Stecker, ed. Hudební Revue, 1908–20.—V. ST.

HOFMANN, Josef Casimir. Polish pianist; b. Podgorze, near Cracow, 20 Jan. 1876. His father, a pf.-teacher and orch. condr., was his first instructor. Toured Europe as a child-prodigy and went to America in 1887. His public concert career was interrupted by the Soc. for the Prevention of Cruelty to Children. In 1888 the family settled in Berlin, where Josef continued his pf. studies under his father and M. Moszkowski, and stud. compn. under H. Urban; 1892–4 under A. Rubinstein in Dresden. Resumed his brilliant concert career in 1894, returning to America in 1899, since which date he has spent much of his time in America. He is now one of the profoundest and most powerful of pianists. Eng. tour, 1924.

Is credited with 5 early unpubl. pf. concertos. Under the name of Michel Dvorsky he produced Chromaticon, a symph. duologue for pf. and orch., at concert of Cincinnati Symphony Orch. 24 Nov. 1916; a symph. narrative, The Haunted Castle, Philadelphia Orch. 7 Nov. 1919, and Three Impressions for pf. (Schirmer). Early pf. pieces (Hainauer). Author of Piano Questions Answered (Doubleday, 1909) and Piano Playing, with Piano Questions Answered (Presser, 1920).—O. K.

HOFOPER, HOFTHEATER (Ger.). A Court theatre or opera-house, i.e. one subsidised by the sovereign and forming part of the Court establishment. Up to the Ger. Revolution of 1918, the King of Prussia subsidised 12 opera-houses, some of which belonged to States, such as Hanover, which were annexed by Prussia. Since the Revolution the numerous Court theatres of Germany have been taken over by States or municipalities, and the name of Hofoper, with all the subsidiary titles derived from it, has become extinct. —E. J. D.

HOHENEMSER, Richard. Ger. writer on music; b. Frankfort-o-M., 10 Aug. 1870. Stud. 1892–6, Berlin (history of music, Ph. Spitta, H. Bellermann and O. Fleischer more especially); then philosophy in Munich, 1896–9 (psychology and æsthetics, Lipps; mus. science, Sandberger). Here he graduated Ph.D. (thesis: What effect did the Revival of the older Music in the XIX Century have upon German Composers?, Leipzig,

Breitkopf). Lived in Berlin from 1905; since 1919 in Frankfort-o-M.

Luigi Cherubini, His Life and Works (Leipzig, Breitkopf, 1913).—A. E.

HOLBROOKE, Joseph. Eng. compr. *b.* Croydon, 5 July, 1878. Prepared for the mus. profession by his father; later at R.A.M. London; 1st appeared St. James's Hall as solo pianist, June, 1896; toured with Arthur Lloyd, 1898; pantomime condr. on tour, 1899; condr. Woodhall Spa Orch. 1900; has since appeared regularly at leading concerts as pianist or condr. His orch. tone-poems have always provoked great interest. The one entitled *Apollo and the Seaman*, to Herbert Trench's words, was given with the words thrown on to a lantern sheet, section by section. His opera *Pierrot* was given 5 times at His Majesty's in May 1909. His opera-trilogy, *The Cauldron of Anwyn*, to words by T. E. Ellis (Lord Howard de Walden) consists of: I, *The Children of Don*; II, *Dylan*; III, *Bronwen*. The *Children of Don* was first given at the London Opera House (Hammerstein), 12, 14, 18 June 1912, under Nikisch and Holbrooke; *Dylan* at Drury Lane Theatre, 15, 18, 23 June 1913, under Beecham; *Don* was perf. at Volksoper, Vienna, 5 times in April 1923 under Weingartner, and at Salzburg 3 times in 1923 under Kaiser. *Bronwen* has not yet been produced. Some of his chamber-music is amongst his finest work. He has always been a great champion of the British composer, both at his own concerts, on his many tours (Continent, U.S.A., Jamaica, etc.) and in the Press. He is a writer of great vigour, and regularly and fearlessly engages in exposing the futility of newspaper criticism as at present practised. His music is unequal, often rising to heights of great inspiration, but at times dropping near to the commonplace. On the whole, it has the grand manner well sustained, and it is always finely orchestrated. His work is more closely allied to the older schools than to the newer ones. His early style showed relationship to Wagner; his middle to Richard Strauss; this does not detract from his originality, as he has a remarkable fertility of ideas.

Operas: *The Children of Don*; *Dylan*; *Bronwen*; *Pierrot and Pierrette*, op. 36 (His Majesty's, 1909); *The Wizard* (Chicago, 1915); *The Snob*, 1-act comic opera, op. 49 (not yet perf.). Tone-poems: *Byron*, ode, chorus and orch. op. 39 (Leeds Choral Union, 1906; Novello); *Queen Mab*, orch. and chorus, op. 45 (Leeds Fest. 1906); dramatic choral symphony, *Hommage to E. A. Poe*, chorus and orch. op. 48 (Leeds Choral Union, 1908); *The Bells*, chorus and orch. op. 50 (Birmingham Fest. 1907; Chester); *Apollo and the Seaman*, a dramatic symphony with choral ending (Queen's Hall, London, 1909; Novello). *Marino Faliero*, barit. and orch. (Chester); *Annabel Lee*, ballad, t. or barit. and orch. (Boosey). Orch. tone-poems: *The Raven*, op. 25 (Crystal Palace, 1901); *The Viking*; *Ulalume* (Queen's Hall, 1904); *Masque of the Red Death*; variations on *Three Blind Mice*; on *The Girl I left behind me*, op. 37; on *Auld Lang Syne*, op. 60; *Les Hommages* (3rd suite), op. 40; ballets: *The Moth*, op. 62; *Coramanthe*, op. 61; ballet-suite, *Pierrot*, str. orch. op. 36; *Pontorewyn* (Welsh suite), small orch. op. 17 (Chester); pf. concerto (*Song of Gwyn ap Nudd*), op. 52 (Chester); vn. concerto, op. 66 (Ricordi); military-band arrs.: *The Girl I left*; *Sérénade Sicilienne*; brass-band pieces: *Scherzo*, *A Hero's Dream*; *A Fantasie*; vn. concerto. ▶ Chamber-music: trio, pf. vn. horn, op. 36 (Rudall, Carte); *Fairyland*, pf. vla. ob. d'amore, op. 57

(Chester); str. 4tet in 1 movement, op. 17*b*; str. 4tet, No. 2, *Impressions*, op. 59; No. 3, *The Pickwick Club*, in 2 parts, op. 69; pf. 4tets: I, G mi. op. 21; II, D mi. op. 31; 2 5tets, str. and clar. op. 27, i and ii; 5tet, pf. and str., *Diabolique* (Novello); miniature suite for 5 wind instrs. op. 33*b* (Rudall, Carte); 6tets: I, 4 dances, op. 20 (Ricordi); II, str. op. 43; III, pf. and wind, op. 33*a*; IV, pf. str. d.b. *In Memoriam*, op. 46 (Chester). *Serenade* for 5 saxophones, s. flügel-horn, barit., ob. d'amore, corno di bassetto, clar. vla. harp, op. 52*a* (Rudall, Carte); *Nocturne*, pf. vla. clar. (Chester); numerous songs (Boosey; Enoch; Larway; Leonard; Novello; Cramer); pf. pieces (Hammond; Weekes; Enoch; Schirmer; Chester); Prelude and fugue, organ (Chester); vn. and pf. pieces (Larway; Boosey; Novello, etc.); clar. and pf. (Hawkes; Novello; Ricordi); part-songs (Novello; Cary; Bosworth, etc.).—E.-H.

HOLLAENDER, Alexis. Ger. pianist and compr. *b.* Ratibor (Silesia), 25 Feb. 1840. Pupil of R. Acad. Berlin, and privately of K. Böhmer. Teacher, Kullak's Acad. 1861; condr. of Cäcilienverein, 1870; teacher of singing at the Victoria School, 1877; prof. 1888. Lecturer at Humboldt Acad. 1903.

Pf. 5tet, G mi. op. 24; pf. pieces; songs; choral songs; *a cappella* 5-v. choruses.—A. E.

HOLLAENDER, Gustav. Ger. violinist; *b.* Leobschütz (Upper Silesia), 15 Feb. 1855; *d.* Berlin, 4 Dec. 1915. Pupil of Leipzig Cons. (David), 1867–9; and of R. High School, Berlin (Joachim and Kiel), 1869–74. Appointed to Court Opera orch., 1874, as a R. chamber-musician; and at same time, head vn. teacher at Kullak's Acad. Accompanied Carlotta Patti on concert tour in Austria in 1874. Establ. subscription concerts for chamber-music with X. Scharwenka and H. Grünfeld in Berlin, 1878–81; condr. of Gürzenich Concerts and teacher at Cologne Cons., 1881; and also leading condr. at Stadttheater. On the retirement of Japha, led the "Professors' Str. Quartet," to which he had already belonged, taking 1st vn. alternately with Japha. Dir. of Stern's Cons. Berlin, from 1895.

4 vn. concertos; suite; sonata; *Romanza*, vn. and orch. op. 19; pf. and vn. pieces, op. 15, 20, 22, 67; str. orch. pieces, op. 3, 38*a*.—A. E.

HOLLAENDER, Viktor. Ger. compr. *b.* Leobschütz (Upper Silesia), 20 April, 1866. Gustav Hollaender's brother; pupil of Kullak; condr. Metropol Theatre; 1908, Neues Operetten Theatre, Berlin, where he now lives as a compr.

Mus. comedy, *Schneider Fips* (Weimar, 1908); operettas: *Carmosinalba*; *The Sun Bird* (1907); vaudeville, *The Regiment's Papa* (Dresden, 1914); operas: *San Lin* and *Trilby*. Pf. pieces.—A. E.

HOLLINS, Alfred. Eng. orgt. and compr. *b.* Hull, 11 Sept. 1865. Though blind from his birth, H. is one of finest organ recitalists of the present time; his facility in extemporising is very great; stud. at the R. Normal Coll. for the Blind, Norwood, pf. under Frits Hartvigson and and organ under Dr. E. J. Hopkins. At age of 13, he played Beethoven's "Emperor" pf. concerto under Manns at Crystal Palace; stud. for a year in Berlin under Bülow; held various organ posts in London; toured America in 1886 and 1888, playing with leading orchs. In 1904, went to Australia to give recitals on the Sydney Town Hall organ; toured S. Africa in 1907 and 1909; and in 1916 opened the large instr. in Town Hall, Johannesburg. For many years past has been

orgt. and choirmaster of St. George's Free Ch. Edinburgh. Mus.Doc. *h.c.* Edinburgh Univ.
Concert-overtures, organ: I, C ma. (Weekes); II, C mi. (Novello); III, F mi. (*id.*); a large number of other popular organ pieces (Novello; Stainer & Bell); pf. pieces (*id.*).—E.-H.

HOLMES (HOLMÈS), Augusta Mary. Compr. *b.* Paris, 16 Dec. 1847; *d* there, 28 Jan. 1903. Came of well-known Irish family; began as mus. prodigy; stud. compn. at Versailles, when she lived, under Henry Lambert, orgt. of Cath.; 1875, pupil of César Franck and, under his magnetic influence, began to compose; 1877, produced at Concerts du Châtelet an *Andante Pastorale* from a symphony called *Orlando Furioso*. In 1878, at mus. competition of city of Paris, she was placed next to the winners, Dubois and Godard. In 1880, *Les Argonautes* received honourable mention at a competition and was perf. by Pasdeloup in 1881. In 1882, at the Concerts Populaires, she produced a symph. poem called *L'Irlande*, on which her chief claim to fame rests. Her music is characterised by great virility and passion. She was more influenced by the ideas of Wagner than by those of César Franck and her fault lay always in overloading her orchestration. In *L'Irlande*, her most complete work, we get faint reminiscences of melodies of her native race. At Paris Exhibition 1889, *Triumphal Ode* for soli, choruses and orch. was perf. At Florence in 1890, in honour of Dante Fest., her *Hymn to Peace* was given with great success. In 1895, her opera *La Montagne Noire* was given at Grand Opéra, Paris.—W. St.

HOLMSEN, Borghild. Norwegian compr. and pianist; *b.* Christiania, 22 Oct. 1865. Pupil of Reinecke and Jadassohn in Leipzig, of Albert Becker in Berlin. *Début* with concert of her own compns. in Christiania, 1890. Has comp. pf. pieces; a vn. sonata, many songs. Teacher at Acad. of Music in Bergen.—U. M.

HOLST, Gustav Theodore. English composer; *b.* Cheltenham, 21 Sept. 1874. Of Swedish extraction on his father's side, English on his mother's. The Holst family migrated from Sweden to Russia early in the XVIII century, and a 'member of the family (the great-grandfather of the composer) came to England about 1808. Holst was originally intended for the career of a pianist, but symptoms of neuritis in early youth prevented this possibility. His father then decided to make him an organist (as he was himself) and before he was 18, he became organist and choirmaster at Wyck Rissington in Gloucestershire. Here he laid the foundations of his knowledge of choral effect, and of his powers as a teacher; for Holst is a great teacher as well as a great composer.

In 1893 he went to R.C.M. London as a student and in 1895 obtained a scholarship in composition. By a lucky accident he added the trombone to his other studies while at the College. His teachers there were Stanford (compn.), Sharpe (piano), Case (trombone), Hoyte (organ) and Rockstro (theory). On leaving the College in 1898, Holst decided to take up the career of a

trombonist, and was for some years a member of the Scottish Orchestra. Never was a decision more lucky, because Holst is essentially an orchestral composer, and this experience of the orchestra from the inside helped to give him that sure touch which distinguishes all his orchestral writings. This lasted till 1903, when a new phase opened, and he became music-master at Edward Alleyn School, Dulwich, 1903–19, Passmore Edwards Inst. 1904–7, St. Paul's Girls' School from 1905, Morley Coll. from 1907, Reading Coll. 1919–23, and compn. teacher R.C.M. from 1919. He visited America in 1923. In 1924 he was elected Fellow of R.C.M. *h.c.* In spite (or perhaps because) of his busy life Holst has never ceased to compose; but he has had to wait many years for recognition and this recognition has coincided with the full maturity of his powers. *The Planets,* the *Hymn of Jesus,* the *Ode to Death* and *The Perfect Fool* are the culmination of a long series of strivings after the same ideal, often in early years not reached, but never lost sight of, and now come at last to complete fruition. (See also arts. on British Orch. Music; Eng. Choral Music; and Eng. Opera.)

1895 *The Revoke*, 1-act opera, op. 1.* †
1896 *Fantasiestücke,* ob. and str. op. 2 * †; 5tet, pf. and str. op. 3 * †; songs, op. 4: *Soft, Soft Wind*; *Margaret's Slumber Song* (Laudy); *Soft and Gently* *; *Awake, my Heart* (Schmidt, Boston).
1897 *Clear and Cool*, 5-part chorus and orch. op. 5.
1898 *Ornulfs Drapa,* scena for barit. and orch. op. 6 *†
1899 *Walt Whitman* overture, op. 7.* †
1900 5 part-songs: *Love is Enough*; *Sylvia* (Novello); *Autumn*; *Come away, Death*; *Love Song* Laudy); *Ave Maria*, 8-part female vs. (Laudy); *Cotswolds* symphony, op. 8 (perf. Bournemouth, 1902); Suite in E flat, op. 10 (Patron's Fund), called *Ballet Suite* (Novello).
1902 *The Youth's Choice,* opera, op. 11 * †; part-songs, op. 12: *Ye Little Birds*; *Dream Tryst* (Novello); *Her Eyes the Glow-worm lend Thee*; *Now is the Month*.
    6 barit. songs, op. 15: *Invocation to Dawn*; *Sergeants' Song*; *Fain would I*; *In a Wood*; *I will not let thee go*; *Between us now*; 6 s. songs, op. 16: *Calm is the Morn*; *My True Love*; *Weep no more* (Stainer & Bell); *Lovely, Kind*; *Cradle Song*; *Peace.*
1903 *Indra,* symph. poem, op. 13 * †; 5tet for wind, op. 14.* †
    King Estmere, ballad, chorus and orch. op. 17 (Novello).
1904 *The Mystic Trumpeter,* s. solo and orch. op. 18 (Patron's Fund).
1905 *Song of the Night*, vn. and orch. op. 19, No. 1.* †
1906 Songs without words, op. 22: *Marching Song*; *Country Song*, small orch. (Novello); *Sita*, 3-act opera, op. 23.* †
1907 *Songs of the West*, orch. op. 21a (selection of West Country songs); * *Somerset Rhapsody*, orch. op 21b (produced by Edward Mason).*
    Hymns from the Rig-Veda for solo v. op. 24: *Dawn*; *Varuna*; *Creation*; *Indra*; *Maruts*; *Frogs*; *Faith*; *Vac*; *Varuna* (II) (Chester); *The Heart worships*, s. song (Stainer & Bell).
1908 *Savitri, opera di camera,* op. 25 (produced 1916) (Curwen).
1908–12 *Choral Hymns from the Rig-Veda,* op. 26 (Stainer & Bell).
    Group 1, mixed chorus and orch. (1908).
    Group 2, female vs. and orch. (1909).
    Group 3, female vs. and harp (1910).
    Group 4, male vs. and orch. (produced in London by Edward Mason) (1912).
1909 Incidental music to *A Vision of Dame Christian* (a masque at St. Paul's Girls' School), op. 27a *; Incidental music to Stepney Pageant (for children) op. 27b *; First Suite, military band, op. 28a (Boosey).

    * ms.   † not performed.

1910 Oriental Suite in E mi. orch. *Beni Mora,* op. 29, No. 1 (produced at Balfour Gardiner concerts) (Curwen).
The Cloud Messenger, ode for chorus and orch. op. 30 (Balfour Gardiner concerts) (Stainer & Bell); *Christmas Day,* chorus and orch. (Novello); 4 Whittier songs, *Part-Songs for Children (id.).*
1911 *Invocation,* cello and orch. op. 19, No. 2 * (May Mukle, Queen's Hall, 1911); songs from *The Princess* for female vs. op. 20*a* (Novello); 4 carols, mixed vs. op. 20*b* (Bayley & Ferguson).
Second Suite, military band, op. 28*b* † (Boosey).
Two Eastern Pictures, part-songs, female vs. and harp (Stainer & Bell); *Hecuba's Lament,* from *The Trojan Women,* op. 31 No. 1; a. solo, female chorus and orch. (*id.*).
Fantastic Suite for orch. *Phantastes,* op. 29, No. 2 (Patron's Fund concert).*
1912 2 Psalms, chorus, str. and organ (Augener).
1913 *Hymn to Dionysus,* s. and a. chorus and orch. op. 31 No. 2 (Balfour Gardiner Concerts) (Stainer & Bell).
St. Paul's Suite for str. orch. (Curwen).
1914 *Dirge for Two Veterans,* part-song, male vs. and brass (Curwen).

1915 and 1916 { Mars / Venus / Mercury / Jupiter / Saturn / Uranus / Neptune } The Planets, suite for large orch. op. 32 (produced at R. Philh. concert, 1919, with the exception of *Venus* and *Neptune*) (Goodwin & Tabb).

1916 *Japanese Suite* for orch. op. 33 (produced at Coliseum, 1916, and Queen's Hall Promenades, 1919) (Hawkes).
Part-songs for mixed vs. op. 34: *To-morrow shall be my Dancing Day* (Augener); *Lullay* (Curwen); *Bring us in Good Ale (id.);* *Terly Terlow* (Stainer and Bell).
4 songs for v. and vn. op. 35: *Jesu Sweet; I sing of a Maid; My Soul has Nought; My Leman is so True of Love* (Chester).
Choruses from *Alcestis* for female vs., harp and flutes (Augener).
3 hymns for chorus and orch. op. 36 (Stainer & Bell):
(1) *Let all Mortal Flesh keep Silence;* (2) *Turn back, O Man;* (3) *A Festival Chime.*
6 choral folk-songs, op. 36 ii (Curwen):
The Seeds of Love; The Blacksmith; I love my Love; Matthew, Mark; Swansea Town; There was a Tree.
1917 *Hymn of Jesus* for 2 choruses and semi-chorus, orch. pf. and organ, op. 37 i (Stainer & Bell, for the Carnegie Trust).
Part-songs for children, op. 37 ii: *A Dream of Christmas* (Curwen); *The Corn Song* (Arnold); *Song of the Lumbermen (id.).*
1918 Ballet for orch. to opera *The Perfect Fool.* (Novello).
1919 *Ode to Death,* chorus and orch. (words by Walt Whitman), Leeds Fest. 1921 (Novello).
1921 *The Perfect Fool,* opera (Novello). Produced B.N.O.C. Covent Garden, spring, 1923.
1922 Fugal overture, op. 40 i (Novello).
1923 Fugal concerto, fl. and ob. with str. acc. op. 40 ii (Novello); Prom. concerts, 1923; choral symphony, op. 41.

R. V. W.

HOLTER, Iver Paul Fredrik. Norwegian compr. condr. *b.* Østre Gausdal, 13 Dec. 1850. Matriculated in 1869. Passed medical examination and at same time played vn. or vla. in Mus. Soc. Orch. under Grieg and Svendsen; stud. theory of music under Svendsen. Broke off medical studies in 1876; became pupil of Cons. in Leipzig. Gave in 1882 his first independent concert; became same year condr. of *Harmonien* (Bergen); 1886, condr. of Mus. Soc. in Christiania until 1911. A highly appreciated condr. of male-v. choirs: 1890–5, leader of Artisans' Choral Union; 1905–19, of Mercantile Choral Soc. Founded in 1897 Holter's Choral Soc.

* ms.   † not performed.

which he led until 1921. Has appeared as condr. in Stockholm, 1897; Paris, 1900; Helsingfors, 1908; Antwerp, 1910; Rouen, 1911. He was teacher of theory at Music Cons. Christiania, 1887–91; critic on *Dagbladet,* 1881–2; ed. the *Nordisk Musikrevy,* 1900–6; committee-member for administration of bequests and member of a departmental committee for regulation of teaching of singing in schools.

Greatly occupied as H. has been in practical fields, he has not developed any great productivity as compr. His versatile and sterling works have their roots in the romantic and classical ideals. They are firmly moulded, but more cosmopolitan than national in tone. Symphony in F (Christiania, 1882; Leipzig, 1885); orch. suite, *Götz von Berlichingen;* cantatas; vn. concerto (Christiania, 1920; Helsingfors, 1921); str. 4tet (Leipzig, 1877); *St. John's Eve* (idyll for str. orch.); Romance, vn.; male-v. choruses; pf. pieces; songs with pf., etc.—J. A.

HONEGGER, Arthur. Composer; *b.* Le Havre, 1892. Studied under Gédalge and Widor in Paris; thus belongs to French school, although he kept the nationality of his Swiss parents, Zurich merchants, who had settled in Normandy. Was at first violently attracted by Debussy, and later by Florent Schmitt. Wagner, Richard Strauss and Schönberg also influenced him; but he soon found out how to develop, from these widely-diverging influences, an æsthetic style peculiar to himself. In him (as in Florent Schmitt whom he resembles somewhat) the best qualities of the French and German schools meet and blend. His music, which is wholly atonal, is based entirely on counterpoint. Simple melodies, with natural inflections, develop one from another. Each instrument in his chamber-music, and each group of instruments in his orchestral scores, seems to have its individual life, and speak its own language. There sometimes result dissonances that are rather painful, a harshness that is cruel but never useless. One does not feel in this music, as in that of Darius Milhaud, any *a priori* system or arbitrary technique. The only reproach against it is that it verges sometimes on scholastic pedantry. Perhaps as a necessary reaction against the airy, but forceful, constructions of Debussy and Ravel, Honegger naturally uses classical forms. At times he seems to introduce fugue into subjects that hardly seem to call for it. This use of antiquated forms is in strange contrast to the boldness of his contrapuntal inspiration.

He has already composed many works of value: Sonatas for violin, for viola, and for cello; str. 4tet (Senart); compositions for wind instruments; for pianoforte; and songs (Chester). One of his first orchestral pieces, *Le Chant de Nigamon,* testifies to his precocious talent and knowledge of instrumentation. The promise contained in it was fully justified in the *Pastorale d'Été* (Senart), in his incidental music to *Dit des Jeux du Monde* (Vieux Colombier, 1918), in *Ste. Alméenne* (Max Jacob), in a magnificent oratorio *Le Roi David* (publ. Fœtisch, Lausanne), given at Mézières in 1921, and especially in his " mimed

238

symphony " *Horace Victorieux* (Composers' Music Corporation, New York, 1922), which is of epic inspiration. All his works leave an impression of assured power, of seriousness without austerity and of a healthy balance, that leads one to expect much of this young musician.

Consult: Chalupt, in *Revue Musicale*, Jan. 1922; André Cœuroy, *La Musique française moderne.* —H. P.

HOPEKIRK, Helen. Scottish pianist, compr. *b.* Edinburgh, 1868. Stud. there under Lichtenstein and Sir A. C. Mackenzie, and in Vienna under Leschetizky. She also spent 2 years at Leipzig Cons., where she made her *début* as a pianist, 28 Nov. 1878. For some years after, played with great success throughout England and Scotland. In 1882, she married a well-known Scottish merchant, Mr. William Wilson, and with him emigrated to America in 1883. Her success there as pianist exceeded even that of her early days in Britain. From 1887-91, she resided in Vienna, whence she made several tours throughout Germany. From 1891-7, she toured U.S.A., Canada, France, and Britain; in latter year, settled in Boston, U.S.A., where she has since won a phenomenal success as teacher, first in North-East Cons. of that city, and afterwards as private teacher. Her compns. are very numerous, and consist chiefly of songs and pf. pieces, some of which are in the larger forms.—W. S.

HORÁK, Antonín V. Czechoslovak compr. *b.* Prague, 1875; *d.* Belgrade, Serbia, 1910. Condr. in Bohemia and Jugo-Slavia.

Operas: *Na večer bílé soboty (On Easter Eve)* 1898; *Babička (Grandmother)* 1900; melodrama, *Nosáček* (1908); cantata, *První májová noc (First Night in May).*—V. St.

HORBOWSKI, Mieczysław. Singer and teacher; *b.* Warsaw, 1850. He has worked many years at Moscow Cons.; later in Cracow; Milan; lastly in Vienna. Has introduced many eminent singers.—Zd. J.

HORN, Camillo. Compr. and writer on music; *b.* Reichenberg (Bohemia), 29 Dec. 1860. Stud. in Vienna under Anton Bruckner. Condr. of Orchesterverein Haydn; prof. of harmony at State Acad.; critic of the *Deutsches Volksblatt.* In Vienna and Graz the Camillo Horn Soc. was founded, which produces his works. His style is rather conservative, dwelling in the lower territories of the old Romanticism (Ger. national song). Chief works (publ. by Kahnt, Leipzig):

Symphony, F mi. (perf. 25 times). Chamber-music: 5tet for 3 vns. vla. cello; Phantasy for vn.; sonata for horn and pf.; many songs and duets; male choruses: (*Deutsches Festlied*; *Gotenzug*; *Teufel und Engel*; melodrama, *Graf Walter.* Also a book of his own poems (Vienna, 1922).—P. P.

HORNBOSTEL, Erich M. von. Austrian music researcher; *b.* Vienna, 25 Feb. 1877. Stud. chemistry, physics and philosophy, Vienna and Heidelberg; Ph.D. Vienna, 1900; then went to Berlin, where he devoted himself exclusively to psychological and mus. science, especially mus. psychology. In 1905-6 was Stumpf's assistant at Psychological Inst., and travelled in N. America in 1908 for purpose of making psychological and musico-scientific studies of Indian races, more especially the Pawnees. Professor, 1917.

He is publishing (from 1922) *Sammelbände für die vergl. Wissenschaft*, in the first of which (1922) he contributes his translation of A. J. Ellis's *On the Musical Scales of Various Races*, and collects a series of his studies already published by him since 1903 (Munich, Drei Masken Verlag).—A. E.

HORNEMAN, Christian Frederik Emil. Danish compr. *b.* Copenhagen, 17 Dec. 1841; *d.* there, 8 June, 1906. He and his friend, Edvard Grieg, stud. together at Leipzig Cons. under Moscheles. Plaidy, Hauptmann and Jul. Rietz. Upon his return to native city, he shared in the mus. life there with an ardour that never diminished, founding (together with Grieg and Godfred Matthison-Hansen) the mus. soc. *Euterpe.* Later, was leading spirit in weekly popular Saturday Soirées; when after some years this had fulfilled its mission, he and Otto Malling formed a new and larger soc. the Koncertforening (Concert Soc.). Later, also founded a Cons. (1879) which bore his name He still found time to achieve a position as one of the most important of contemporary Danish comprs. He possessed great originality and a fiery temperament, coupled with rare productive ability, of which his later works especially bear ample witness. Prominent among these stand:

Opera, *Aladdin* (text by Oehlenschläger), R. Theatre, Copenhagen (1888) in celebration of Jubilee of Christian IX; *University Cantata, in memoriam* of the same king (1906); music for Gjellerup's antique drama *Kampen med Muserne (The War with the Muses)*, 1st perf. in 1908 (R. Opera, Copenhagen) after compr.'s death. Also the dramas *Esther* (Drachmann); *Kalanus* (Paludan-Müller); pf. pieces; songs (Copenhagen, Hansen).—A. H.

HORVÁTH, Attila. Hungarian compr. *b.* Nustár, 11 Aug. 1862; *d.* Budapest, 1920.—B. B.

HORWITZ, Carl. Austrian compr. *b.* Vienna, 1 Jan. 1884. Stud. music history at Vienna Univ. (Ph.D. 1906). Pupil of Arnold Schönberg (1904-8). Until 1914, condr. at various theatres, Trier, Breslau, Prague. Now lives in Vienna. His mus. style was formerly influenced much by Schönberg. He is now finding his own expression and style. We find solid technical ability and a refinement of mood-painting.

Symph. overture, for orch. (perf. Düsseldorf Fest. 1922); *Vom Tode (Death)* an overture and 3 orch. songs for barit.; 2 str. 4tets; many songs, the latter perf. at Donaueschingen Fest. 1921; Salzburg Fest. 1922.—P. P.

HOSTINSKÝ, Otakar. Czechoslovak musicographer; *b.* Martinoves, 1847; *d.* Prague, 1910. Stud. at Prague Univ. Tutor in aristocratic families. After much travelling, became lecturer in mus. history and æsthetics at Prague Univ.; prof. from 1892. Lecturer at Painting Acad. and Art Industrial School; from 1894, history of art at Univ. Chairman of committee for Czech folksongs; also of Philosophers' Club, etc. In æsthetics he built on Herbart's and Hanslick's formalism, but only as regards inter. music. In dramatic music he refutes Hanslick and inclines to Wagner (see *Das musikalische Schöne vom Standpunkte der formalen Ästhetik*, 1877, Ger.). He influenced the Czech school by his admiration for Gluck and Wagner and by his friendship for Smetana and Fibich. For Fibich he wrote a libretto from Schiller's *Bride of Messina*; for Roškozný's *Cinderella*. He espoused Smetana's cause when his art was only slowly finding its way to Bohemia. At that time H. was solving the pressing problems arising in the national music. He wrote *On the present Position and Tendency of Bohemian Music*, 1885; *On Czech Musical Declamation*, 1886 (Czech). His studies on Smetana have been publ. under the title *Bed. Smetana a jeho boj o moderní českou hudbu* (*Frederick Smetana and his Fight for Modern Czech Music*, 1901). He not only directed Fibich to a pure declamatory style, but also to the scenic melodrama. H.'s significance is not only in his founding of Czech mus. criticism, but also in his deeply influencing the development of Czech music itself.—V. ST.

HOUDARD, Georges. Fr. musicologist and compr. *b.* Neuilly, 30 March, 1860; *d.* Paris, 28 Feb. 1913. Pupil of L. Hillemacher and Massenet. Specialised in study of *neumes* (plain-chant notation), and advocated the theory of *neume-temps*. Each *neume*, whatever its melodic content, is equal to one beat. His doctrine has been taken up by Canon Clément Besse. It has been violently opposed by the Benedictine School, notably by Père Mocquereau. But certain authors (*e.g.* Laloy) make between the two theses a difference of degree only and not of nature. As compr. H. has written religious works (masses, offertories). His theoretical work is considerable:

L'Art dit grégorien d'après la notation neumatique (1897); *Le Rythme du chant dit grégorien* (1898); *L'Évolution de l'Art musical et l'Art grégorien* (1902); *La Richesse rythmique musicale de l'antiquité* (1903); *La Question grégorienne en 1904* (1904); *La Cantilène romaine* (1905); *La Science musicale traditionnelle* (1906); *La Rythmique intuitive* (1906); *Vademecum de la rythmique grégorienne des Xᵉ et XIᵉ siècles* (1912).—A. C.

HOWELL, Dorothy. Eng. compr. and pianist; *b.* Handsworth, 25 Feb. 1898. Stud. at R.A.M. London under Percy Waller and Tobias Matthay (pf.) and J. B. McEwen (compn.) 1914–19. Her symph. poem *Lamia* was played at the Queen's Hall, 10 Sept. 1919. An orch. *Ballet* was produced at Queen's Hall Promenades.

Pf. concerto, D mi. (1923, ms.); *Lamia* (Novello); orch. ballet, *Koong Shee* (1921); *Rosalind*, vn. and pf. (Anglo-Fr. Music Co.); pf. pieces (*id.*); songs (Boosey; Curwen; Cramer).—E.-H.

HOWELLS, Herbert. Eng. compr. *b.* Lydney, Gloucestershire, 17 Oct. 1892. 1905, pupil of Dr. Herbert Brewer, Gloucester; 1909, articled pupil at Gloucester Cath. until 1911; May 1912, open scholarship, R.C.M. London (compn. under Sir Charles Stanford; organ under Sir Walter Parratt; other subjects under Sir Hubert Parry, Sir Walford Davies, and Dr. Charles Wood). Left the Coll. 1917; appointed to staff of R.C.M. 1920; became ed. of *R.C.M. Magazine* in that year.

He has a remarkable facility and a sure touch in all forms (except the opera, which he has not attempted); his muse is best suited to the more intimate forms, chamber-music and songs. He has written some very fine organ music and some unacc. church pieces in the old modes.

Op. 1, organ sonata in C mi. (1911); op. 2, *Missa sine nomine* (for Westminster Cath.) (1912); op. 3, Variations for 11 solo instrs. (1914); op. 4, pf. concerto in C mi. (1913); op. 5, 5 male-v. part-songs (Stainer & Bell, 1912); op. 6, *Sarum Sketches* (Augener, 1917); op. 7, 3 dances, vn. and orch. (1915); op. 8, *Comedy Suite*, clar. and pf. (1913); op. 9, 4 Anthems of the B.V.M. (1915); op. 10, 5 songs, high v. and orch. (1915); op. 11, 5 part-songs (Curwen, 1916); op. 12, 3 rondeaux, v. and pf. (Stainer & Bell, 1913); op. 13, *The B's*, orch suite (1915); op. 14, 3 pieces for pf. (Ascherberg, 1919); op. 15, Elegy for strs. (Goodwin, 1917); op. 16, 2 pieces, str. orch. (1917); op. 17, 3 rhapsodies, organ (Augener, 1918); op. 18, 1st sonata in E, vn. and pf. (W. Rogers, 1917); op. 19, str. 4tet, *Lady Audrey's Suite* (Novello, 1916); op. 20a, *Puck's Minuet*, 20b, *Merry Eye*, orch. (Goodwin & Tabb, 1918); op. 21, 4tet in A mi. pf. vn. vla. cello (Stainer & Bell, 1916); op. 22, 4 songs, (W. Rogers, 1915); op. 23, *Sir Patrick Spens*, choral ballad with orch. (1916), publ. by Stainer & Bell; op. 24, 3 part-songs (E. Arnold, 1920); op. 25, Phantasy str. 4tet (Goodwin, 1916); op. 26, 2nd sonata, E flat, vn. and pf. (1918); op. 27, Phantasy Minuet, for pianola (Æolian Co. 1919); op. 28, 3 pieces (Stainer & Bell, 1919); op. 29, 4 French *chansons* (Chester, 1919); op. 30, *Snapshots*, pf. (Swan & Co. 1919); op. 31, Rhapsodic 5tet, clar and str. (Stainer & Bell, 1920); op. 32, 3 psalm-preludes, organ (Novello, 1920); op. 33, *Peacock Pie*, songs, medium v. and pf. (Goodwin, 1919); op. 34, str. 4tet, *In Gloucestershire* (1922); op. 35, *Procession*, orch. (Ascherberg, 1922); op. 36, *Sine Nomine*, phantasy, 2 solo vs. chorus, organ and orch. (Gloucester Fest. 1922); op. 37, 3rd sonata, vn. and pf. (1923); op. 38, *Pastoral Rhapsody*, orch. (1923); op. 39, pf. concerto in C (1923).—E.-H.

HOYER, Karl. German orgt. and compr. *b.* Weissenfels-o-S., 9 Jan. 1891. Stud. Leipzig Cons. under Reger, Straube, Krehl and Pembaur; went to Reval in 1911 as orgt. of Cath.; in 1912 chief orgt. of St. James's Church, Chemnitz.

Introduction and chaconne, orch. and organ; organ sonata, D mi. op. 19; Concertino in olden style, organ and str. orch.; Introduction and double fugue for 2 pfs.; sonata, vla. and pf. A ma. op. 30; a large number of organ, pf. and choral works.—A. E.

HŘÍMALÝ, Vojtěch. Czechoslovak compr. *b.* Prague, 1842; *d.* Vienna, 1908. Worked in Rotterdam, Gothenburg, Prague; from 1874 in Černovice.

Opera, *Zakletý princ* (*The Enchanted Prince*), 1872; *Svanda dudák* (1885), etc.—V. ST.

HUBAY, Eugen (Jenő). Hungarian violinist, compr. and vn. teacher; *b.* Budapest, 15 Sept. 1858. 1871–5, stud. under Joachim. 1882, became Wieniawski's successor at Brussels Cons. In 1866, called to Budapest as teacher of vn. at R. High School for Music, which post he still holds, becoming dir. Oct. 1919. Nearly all the most important Hungarian violinists of the present day have been his pupils; among them: Stefi Geyer; Franz Vecsey; Emil Telmányi; Jelly d'Arányi; Josef Szigeti; Emerich Waldbauer; Erna Rubinstein.

2-act opera, *The Violin-maker of Cremona*, perf. Budapest, 1894; then on many foreign stages. *Scènes de Csárda* for vn.—B. B.

HUBER, Hans. Swiss composer, conductor; *b.* Schönenwerd, 28 June, 1852; *d.* Locarno, 25 Dec. 1921. An excellent pianist when 10 years old. Studied at Conservatoire, Leipzig (1870–74); for 2 years piano-teacher in Wesserling (Alsace); since 1876 at Conservatoire in Basle, of which he was director till 1918. One of most eminent musicians, Huber was no doubt the master-spirit in the evolution of Swiss music during the last 50 years (*i.e.* from 1870 to 1920 broadly). A splendid teacher of piano and composition, an excellent conductor of large choruses (his *Festspiele* including about 1000 executants) and an extraordinarily active musician, he did everything possible to develop musical education in his country. In 1892, the University of Basle honoured him with the Doctorate *h.c.* A prolific composer, many of his compositions have become very popular in Switzerland. Influenced by Schumann and Brahms, his works (particularly the two *Festspiele*) contain passages of real originality and although his music is not very deep, it gives proof of great musical imagination and temperament.

Der Basler Bund 1501, festspiel, chorus, soli, orch. (Leipzig, Hug); *Klein-Balser Gedenkfeier*, festspiel for mixed chorus, soli, orch. (*id.*); *Der heilige Hain*, oratorio (*id.*); *Weissagung und Erfüllung*, oratorio (*id.*); *Aussöhnung*, oratorio. Operas: *Kudrun* (*id.*); *Simplicius* (*id.*); *Weltfrühling* (*id.*); *Die schöne Bellinda* (*id.*); *Frutta di mare*; 7 symphonies: I, *Tell*; II, *Böcklin*, op. 115 (*id.*); III, *Heroic*, op. 118 (*id.*); IV, *Der Geiger von Gmünd*; V, *Academic*; VI, in A (Leuckart); *Swiss* (Hug, National Ed.); 2 serenades for orch.; 2 overtures; 2 pf. 4tets; 2 pf. 5tets; 5 trios; 11 vn. sonatas; 4 cello sonatas; 4 pf. concertos; vn. concerto; 3 pf. sonatas; numerous choruses, songs and pf. pieces. Mostly publ. by Hug or Breitkopf.
Consult: E. Refardt, *H. H.* (Zurich, Hug); W. Merian, *Basels Musikleben* (Basle, 1920, Helbing & Lichtenhahn); Kretzschmar, *Führer durch den Konzertsaal*, I and II; E. Segnitz, *Ästhetisch-analytische Einführung in die Symphonie op.* 115 (Hug).—F. H.

HUBERMANN, Bronisław. Polish violinist; *b.* Częstochowa, near Warsaw, 19 Dec. 1882. Pupil of Michałowicz in Warsaw, and of Lotto in Paris; 1892, stud. under Joachim in Berlin; 1893, concert-tour as esteemed virtuoso. Lives in Berlin. Wrote *Aus der Werkstatt des Virtuosen (From the Virtuoso's Workshop).*—E.-H.

HUBERTI, Gustave. Belgian composer ; *b.* Brussels, 14 April, 1843; *d.* Schaerbeek (Brussels), 28 June, 1910. Son of painter Édouard Huberti; stud. at Cons. Brussels. Obtained four 1st prizes in 1858—pf., organ, chamber-music and harmony; 1859, 1st prize, compn.; 1865, 1st *Prix de Rome* for cantata *La Fille de Jephté.* Then travelled 3 years in Germany and one in Italy. Coming back to Belgium, was attracted by ideas and works of chief Flemish compr., Peter Benoit; although Fr. by education, H. collab. with poet Emmanuel Hiel in a whole series of works on Flemish libretti. An ardent admirer of Wagner, he took an active part in the Wagnerian controversy. Dir. of Acad. de Musique, Mons, 1874; resigned in 1877 in consequence of a conflict with municipal administration of town which involved his artistic honour and conscience; 1879–88, inspector of singing to schools of Antwerp. 1888, returned to Brussels where he taught harmony at Cons. In 1893, dir. of School of Music at St.-Josse-den-Noode-Schaerbeek (2 suburbs of Brussels). Member of R. Acad. of Belgium, 1891. Huberti's hatred of conservatism was shown in his speech on *Routine*, before the Acad. in 1903. His first songs, a delightful *Meilied* and *Sonnet de Ronsard* (comp. at beginning of his career) betray the healthy influence of Ger. Romanticism. Later, he be-

came disciple of young Flemish school with its freshness of inspiration; towards end of life he fell under sway of modern Fr. school, manifested in 6 remarkable songs (Brussels, Imprimerie Nationale de Musique), and an orch. work of great delicacy which he comp. as *mélodrame* to poem *Christine* by Leconte de Lisle. However, he was not especially apt at expressing anything save the picturesque and graceful, and, generally speaking, the half-tones of emotion. Where he is more ambitious (as in *Symphonie funèbre*) he becomes tedious and pompous.

Chorus, soli and orch.: *Een laatste Zonnestraal*; *Kinderlust en Leed*; *Bloemardinne*; *Cantate inaugurale des Eaux du Bocq*, etc. *Symphonie funèbre*, 1880; *Christine*, melodrama; many songs. Consult pamphlet on G. H. by Lucien Solvay (Brussels, 1919, Hayez.)—C. V. B.

HUË, Georges. Fr. compr. *b.* Versailles, 5 May, 1858. Pupil of Reber and Paladilhe. *Prix de Rome*, 1879. His music has always an elevated and limpid style.

Stage works: *Les Pantins* (1882); *Titania* (1903); *Le Roi de Paris* (1901); *Le Miracle* (1910); *Dans l'Ombre de la Cathédrale* (1922). Orch.: *Rubezahl* (1887); *Résurrection* (1893); *Jeunesse* (1893); *Scènes de Ballet* (1897). *Thème varié* for vla.: Fantasia, vn. and pf. Some songs, of which certain have been very successful.—A. C.

HUGHES, Edwin. Amer. pianist; *b.* Washington, D.C., U.S.A., 15 Aug. 1884. Stud. pf. under Joseffy in New York, 1905–6, and Leschetizky in Vienna, 1907–10, becoming his assistant in 1909. Début as concert-pianist, Knabe Hall, Baltimore, 16 Feb. 1903, and toured Germany and America. Head of pf. department of Ganapol School of Music, Detroit, Mich., 1911–12. Settled in Munich 1912, but returned to U.S.A. 1916. From 1919–22, teacher at Inst. of Mus. Art, N.Y. Songs and pf. pieces (Schirmer).—J. M.

HUGHES, Herbert. Irish compr. and critic; *b.* Belfast, 16 March, 1882. Orgt. of St. Peter's, Belfast, 1896; entered R.C.M. London, 1901, studying under Sir Walter Parratt, Gustave Garcia, Herbert Sharpe, Dr. Charles Wood. H. was one of founders of Irish Folk-song Soc. 1904; co-editor (with late Mrs. Milligan Fox) of its early journals. After contributing for some years, on mus. subjects to *The New Age* and various Irish journals, joined music-staff of *Daily Telegraph*, London, 1911. Has contributed largely by direct research to present-day knowledge of Irish folk-song; songs from his own coll. were introduced to Britain by Plunket Greene and into America by John McCormack. He ed. *Irish Country Songs* (2 vols. Boosey); and *Historical Songs and Ballads of Ireland* (Metzler). He visited America in 1922 and contributed special arts. on music in U.S.A. to *Daily Telegraph*. 1924, gen. ed. *Boosey's Modern Festival Series* of unison and choral songs. Married at Jersey City, N.J., Suzanne McKernan of the Irish Players from the Abbey Theatre.

Songs from Connacht (Padraic Colum), v. and pf. (Boosey); *Rhymes*, studies in imitation (2 vols. *id.*); three XVIII century songs (ed. and arr.; *id.*); *Parodies*, s. and orch. (2 vols. Metzler); *Shockheaded Peter*, song-cycle, s., barit. and pf. (*id.*); *Brian Boru's March*, pf. (*id.*); 3 *Satirical Songs*, vn. fl. clar. bsn. (Enoch); many other songs.—E.-H.

HUGHES, Rupert. Amer. author; *b.* Lancaster, Mo., U.S.A., 21 Jan. 1872. A.B. Adelbert Coll. (Western Reserve Univ., Cleveland, O.), 1892; A.M. 1894; A.M. Yale, 1899. Stud. compn. under Wilson G. Smith in Cleveland, 1890–2, under E. S. Kelley in New York, 1899, and under C. W. Pearce in London, 1901–2. Has been music critic and assistant-ed. of several Amer. magazines (Godey's *Current Literature, The Criterion*); also on the New York staff of *Encyclopædia Britannica.* Has comp. a number of songs, and has written numerous novels and plays. Is now engaged in the production of moving-pictures.

Cain, vocal scena for barit. and pf. (Schirmer, 1920); songs (*id.*). Author of: *Contemporary American Composers* (Page, 1900); enlarged ed. by Arthur Elson (1914); *Love Affairs of Great Musicians* (Page, 1903); *The Musical Guide,* 2 vols. (McClure, 1903); rev. ed. with title *Music-Lover's Cyclopædia* (Doubleday, Page, 1913); *Zal,* a mus. novel (Century, 1905); ed. of *Songs by Thirty Americans* (in Ditson's *Musician's Library,* 1904).—O. K.

HULL, Arthur Eaglefield-. Eng. writer on music, recital-organist, lecturer and musical organiser; *b.* Market Harborough, 10 March, 1876. Trained under Dr. C. W. Pearce (theory) and Tobias Matthay (pf.) London; Mus.Doc. Oxon. 1903; study-tours in France, Germany, Italy, Russia, etc.; choirmaster and condr. in London and Hertfordshire; founded Huddersfield Coll. of Music (for advanced musical training in Yorkshire) in 1908; has given many first perfs. there by leading continental 4tets, etc.; founded Huddersfield Chamber-Music Soc. in 1900 (now the H. Music Club); founded British Music Soc. 1918, and was its hon. dir. 1918–21, personally founding over 20 of its chief branches; founded Advisory Board for Composers, 1920 (disbanded 1923); founded and ed. *British Music Bulletin* (now *Music Bulletin*); ed. first *British Music Catalogue* (400 pp. 1920); organised the Three Arts Conference, May, 1921, in which leading painters, musicians and writers discussed contemporary art-activities; editor of the *Monthly Musical Record* (Augener) from 1912. Ed. the complete organ works of Bach for the Augener Edition. Ed. *Music Lovers' Library* (Kegan Paul). General Editor of this Dictionary.

His book *Modern Harmony : its Explanation and Application* is a valuable contribution to the literature of musical theory in its recent developments; it was the first serious effort in this country to examine this complex subject in a practical manner. H. has a forceful personality with power of initiative and a talent for organisation. His wide knowledge, his broad sympathies and sound judgment make him a successful editor and critic. He has contributed articles to all the leading Eng. dailies and musical journals, and is also widely known as a lecturer.

Overture in A, orch. (ms.); 3 *Shakespeare Songs,* v. and str. 4tet (Augener); organ and pf. pieces (Augener; Lengnick); organ tutor (Augener, 1923). Books: *Modern Harmony* (Augener; 1st ed. 1914; 3rd. ed. 1923; transl. into Span. and Russ.); *Organ-Playing : Its Technique and Expression* (*id.* 1st ed. 1911; 6th ed. 1923); *Scriabin* (Kegan Paul; 1st ed. 1916; 3rd ed. 1923); *Cyril Scott* (*id.* 1914); *Students' Harmony* (with Dr. Charles Macpherson) (Augener, 1914); numerous translations, etc.—G. B.

HULL, Percy Clarke. Eng. orgt. *b.* Hereford, 27 Oct. 1878. Stud. under Dr. G. R. Sinclair; orgt. and choirmaster Hereford Cath. from 1918; Mus.Doc. Cantuar. 1921; condr. Hereford Three Choirs Festival, 1921, 1924.—E.-H.

HULLEBROECK, Émile. Belgian compr. *b.* Gentbrugge (near Ghent), 20 Feb. 1878. Stud. at Ghent Cons. under Ad. Samuel. Comp. Flemish oratorio *Kunstvisioen;* several symph. choral works and pieces for various instrs. Widely known for his Flemish folk-songs. Toured in Europe, Asia and Africa as singer and composer.—E. C.

HUMBERT, Georges. Swiss writer on music; *b.* Ste.-Croix (Vaud), 10 Aug. 1870. Known by his Fr. transl. of Riemann's *Music Lexicon,* the *Simplified Harmony* and the *Elements of Musical Æsthetics.* Was dir. of numerous choirs in Geneva and Lausanne (1892–1918); cond. symphony concerts in Lausanne (1893–1901); orgt. at Notre-Dame Ch., Geneva (1892–6); and at the Temple, Morges (1898–1918). In 1918, organised and directed the Cons. at Neuchâtel, and brought it to a position of great esteem.—F. H.

HUMMEL, Ferdinand. Ger. pianist and compr. *b.* Berlin, 6 Sept. 1855. Stud. 1868–71 at Kullak's Acad. and then till 1875 at R. High School of Music and at the Compn. School of the Acad. (Rudorff and Grabau, Kiel and Bargiel). R. mus. dir. 1897.

4 cello sonatas; pf. 5tet; pf. 4tet; vn. sonata; horn sonata; suite for pf. duet; overture, op. 17; symphony, D ma. op. 105; the choral works: *Columbus; The New Master Olaf;* ballads: *Young Olaf; March of the Teutons; The Phantom Army;* male choruses; female choruses; *Tuscan Songs; Konzertstück,* pf., op. 1; pf. concerto, B flat mi. op. 35; many pf. solos; also pf. and other instrs.; a series of unpretentious works for stage.—A. E.

HUMPERDINCK, Engelbert. German composer; *b.* Siegburg (Rhineland), 1 Sept. 1854; *d.* Neustrelitz, 27 Sept. 1921. Pupil of Cologne Conservatoire; Mozart Stipendiary, 1876, and, as such, pupil of Royal Music School, Munich; Mendelssohn Stipendiary, 1879, enabling him to study in Italy till 1881, in which year he gained the Meyerbeer Stipendium. Teacher at Barcelona Conservatoire, 1885–7, when he returned to Cologne; 1890, teacher at Hoch's Conservatoire, Frankfort-o-Maine; title of Royal Prussian Professor, 1896. Lived for some time at Boppard on Rhine, composing; 1900, head of an academical school (*ex officio* member of Senate of Royal Academy of Arts; 1913, deputy-president of same). Retired 1920. He obtained his greatest success with his fairy opera, *Hänsel and Gretel,* which clothes the best-known German children's story half in homely folk-song melodies, and half in the somewhat pretentious garb of Wagnerian orchestration. Its success is not to be explained away by its forming such a contrast to realistic operas of Mascagni and Leoncavallo, which were at the time filling the stages of every country, even Germany, since it still meets with universal acceptation. Artistically *Hänsel and Gretel* is surpassed by *The King's Children* (text by Elsa Bernstein, pseudonym Ernst Rosmer, the Munich poetess). H. is in any case one of the most charming of post-Wagnerians, and possessed of the greatest wealth of technique in composition.

Choral ballads: *Luck of Edenhall*: *The Pilgrimage to Kevelaar*; orch. work, *Moorish Rhapsody* (Leeds Fest. 1898); orch. and choral pieces; str. 4tet, C ma. More especially works for stage: *Hänsel and Gretel* (fairy tale in 3 tableaux, text by Humperdinck's sister, Frau Adelheid Wette, Weimar, 23 Dec. 1893); *The King's Children* (melodrama, 1898, text by Ernst Rosmer; retouched 1908 and converted into tuneful complete opera, which has met with increasing estimation since its presentation in New York, 1910, and in Berlin, 1911); fairy play, *The Sleeping Beauty* (Frankfort-o-M., 1902); 2-act opera, *The Canteen Girl* (Cologne, 1914); ballad-opera *Gaudeamus* (Darmstadt, March 1919); comic opera, *The Unwilling Marriage* (Berlin, 1905); music to Aristophanes' *Lysistrata* (Berlin, 1908); Shakespeare's *Winter's Tale*, *The Tempest* (Berlin, 1906), *Twelfth Night* (1907), *Merchant of Venice* (1905); Maeterlinck's' *Blue Bird* (1910); Vollmöller's *Miracle* (1911).—A. E.

HUNEKER, James Gibbons. Amer. author, critic; *b.* Philadelphia, Pa., U.S.A., 31 Jan. 1860; *d.* Brooklyn, N.Y., 9 Feb. 1921. Graduate of Roth's Military Acad. Philadelphia. Stud. law for some time; pf. pupil of Michael Cross in Philadelphia. In 1878 went to Paris where he stud. pf. and theory under Leopold Doutreleau. Later he stud. at the National Cons. in New York under Joseffy. As the assistant of Joseffy, taught pf. at National Cons. 1888–98. From 1891–5, mus. and dramatic critic of *New York Recorder*; 1895–7, of *Morning Advertiser*; 1900–1912, wrote on music, drama and art for *New York Sun*. 1912, mus. critic of *New York Times*; 1919 until his death he again wrote for the *Sun*. H. was one of the most brilliant and most popular writers on music, literature and art that America has produced. To his mus. interests he added an intimate acquaintance with modern Fr. literature and with modern art in general. Gifted with an unusually facile pen and a ready wit, he sometimes (particularly in his later writings) sacrificed his more sober judgment in the interest of his fascinating style.

The following works are all with one exception publ. by Scribner, New York:

Mezzotints in Modern Music, 1899; *Chopin : the Man and his Music*, 1900; *Melomaniacs*, 1902; *Overtones : Music and Literature*, 1904; *Iconoclasts : a Book of Dramatists*, 1905; *Visionaries : Fantasies and Fiction*, 1905; *Egoists : a Book of Supermen*, 1909; *Promenades of an Impressionist : Studies in Art*, 1910; *Franz Liszt : a Study*, 1911; *The Pathos of Distance*, 1913; *Old Fogy*, *His Musical Opinions and Grotesques* (Philadelphia, Presser), 1913; *New Cosmopolis*, 1915; *Ivory*, *Apes and Peacocks*, 1915; *Unicorns*, 1917; *Bedouins*, 1920; *Steeplejack* (H.'s memoirs, 2 vols.), 1921; *Letters*, 1922. Also *The Philharmonic Society of New York and its 75th Anniversary* (New York, the Society, 1917). Ed. several vols. of songs and pf. pieces in Ditson's *Musician's Library*.—O.K.

HUNGARIAN FOLK-MUSIC. The expert investigation and study of this subject did not begin until the latter years of the XIX century, for the earlier collections had been made by *dilettanti* and were unsatisfactory from a scientific point of view. The more important collectors include: Béla Vikár, folk-lorist, 1500 melodies (1898–1910); Zoltán Kodály (*q.v.*), compr., 3500 melodies (1904–22); Béla Bartók (*q.v.*), compr., 2700 melodies (1904–1918); László Lajtha, compr., 500 melodies.

The whole material, about 8200 melodies, mostly unpubl., falls into three main groups:

(*a*) Melodies of the older style (about 10 per cent. Chief characteristic: 4-lined isometric strophes (the majority 8- or 11-syllable lines, also 6-. 7-, 10-, 12-syllable lines). Rhythm mostly *parlando-rubato*; scale pentatonic:

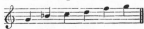

or Æolian or Dorian scales derived from the pentatonic (major and minor excluded). Not architectonically constructed (the lines of the strophe can be represented by ABCD). Apparently many centuries old; only known by old people.

(*b*) Melodies quite new in style, having arisen within the last 70 years (about 30 per cent.). Chief characteristic: 4-lined isometric, or heterometric derived from isometric, strophes (generally 11- and 12-syllable lines, sometimes also 6–22 syllables). Rhythm mostly *tempo giusto*:

$$\frac{4}{4}\, \downharpoonleft \quad \downharpoonleft\,\downharpoonleft\,\downharpoonleft. \;\| \text{ or } \downharpoonleft\,\downharpoonleft.\quad \downharpoonright \;\|$$

or more elaborate formulæ derived from the former. Scales, mostly major, Æolian, Dorian, also Mixolydian (seldom minor, never Lydian). Architectonic construction: AA⁵A⁵A, ABBA, AA⁵BA, AABA. Cultivated only by the younger generation.

(*c*) Melodies with no uniform characteristics (about 60 per cent.). Whereas the two preceding groups comprise melodies specifically Hungarian in formation, this group contains elements that have arisen under different, possibly foreign, influences. Of actual common characteristics there are none. Heterometric strophe-construction is frequent; also the use of major and minor scales.—Of the larger colls. already in print there are only the following: *Transylvanian Hungarian Folk-Songs*, publ. by Béla Bartók and Z. Kodály (Budapest, 1923, Popular Literary Soc.), 150 melodies with Eng. and Fr. preface; Bartók, *Hungarian Folk-music*, 340 melodies and critical notes (Oxford Univ. Press, 1924).

Consult also: Bartók, *La Musique populaire hongroise*, in *Revue Musicale*, Paris, 1 Nov. 1920 (with 11 examples); and Bartók, *Hungarian Peasant Music* (*Ungarische Bauermusik*), in *Musikblätter*, Vienna, June, 1920, Nos. 1 and 2 (with 26 examples).—B. B.

HUNGARIAN MUSICAL INSTRUMENTS

(a) ART INSTRUMENTS

1. *Cimbalom.* In early times and in its primitive form this instr. was in use in many different countries, but it became localised in Hungary and neighbouring districts during the last two or three hundred years. On a horizontal board, the steel wires are spread out like the strings on a piano; but they are not all placed in order of pitch. The compass is one of 50 notes:

from F sharp onwards in chromatic succession. The wires are struck with two wooden sticks, the striking end being covered with cloth. In 1874 Josef Schunda, a manufacturer of these instrs., invented a pedal-damper for the *cimbalom*, similar to the right pedal on a modern piano, and since that time it has been attached to the instr. Until comparatively recently, the *cimbalom* was used exclusively by gipsies; but latterly many Hungarian comprs. have used it, even in serious orch. music, in order to give local colour to their works. (The Russ. compr. Igor Stravinsky used it in his stage-work *Le Renard*, 1917).

2. *Tárogató.* A wood-wind instr. with double reed, originally found all over Hungary; probably of rustic origin, but now entirely disappeared from among the people. On models of the old instr., W. T. Schunda constructed (1900) a new form with only one reed, so that it now belongs to the clarinet family. Its tone resembles the cor anglais. Its compass:

generally used in B flat, sounding a major second lower. Often used as an orch. instr. by Hungarian comprs., and occasionally used as substitute for cor anglais. (Mahler used it at Vienna and Budapest for shepherd-boy's tune in 3rd act of *Tristan*.)

(b) POPULAR (PEASANT) INSTRUMENTS

There are no *special* Hungarian instrs. of this kind; those used by the peasant-folk now, as well as formerly, are of international character, Those mentioned below are, and were, played by peasant country-folk (never by gipsies).

1. *Duda* (bag-pipe). The bag is made of goat- or dog-skin. 3 pipes; the lowest gives the drone:

The two other pipes form practically a double pipe, made out of one piece of wood, of which lower pipe has only one finger-hole, and can thus produce only two notes:

The chanter has 6 finger-holes of normal size, pierced in upper side of pipe, operated by 4th, 3rd, 2nd fingers of both hands. There is also a hole for highest note, placed on under side of pipe, played by thumb of right hand. With this arrangement it is possible, even in rapidest passages, to make frequent use of the highest note as a kind of *acciaccatura*. The scale of this chanter is:

Nevertheless the pitch of the intervals does not correspond exactly to that of diatonic scale; e.g. the 3rd and 6th on many instruments are considerably flatter, the 4th somewhat sharper.

The 3 pipes have each a single reed. The piquant tone of the 2 higher pipes is reminiscent of oboe. Formerly known all over the country, the *duda* is now only found in northern districts, where Hungarian is spoken (recently become Czecho-slovak territory). Apparently the *duda* was confined to dance-music. Hungarian bagpipe-music, taken unaltered from a phonograph record and provided with an accompaniment, is to be found in Bartók's *15th Peasant Song*.

2. *Furulya* (a kind of shepherd's flute). A long wooden pipe, about 30–35 cm. Has a mouth-piece, sound-hole and 6 finger-holes. Compass (with similar deviations as in case of *duda*):

Is not used for dances, but chiefly among shepherd folk. *Furulya* music, recorded unaltered by phonograph and provided with acc., is to be found in Bartók's *42nd piece, A gyermekeknek*, and in *Chansons populaires hongroises*, arr. for pf.

3. *Tilinkó.* A long wooden pipe about 50–60 cm. in length. Has neither sound- nor finger-holes; hence only notes of the natural scale can be played on it. Apparently in use only among the Szekler Hungarians in Transylvania (since annexed by Rumania). Now obsolete.

4. *Kanásztülök.* The hollowed-out horn of the so-called Hungarian or Russian ox, about 70–80 cm. long. Thus a kind of trumpet, capable of producing only notes of natural scale, of which only

are possible. The fundamental note invariably sounds out of tune (lower, generally about F.

It is used exclusively by cowherds and shepherds to call their herds and flocks together, etc. They produce extraordinary effects, blowing short motives in *rubato* rhythm.

5. *Tekerő.* Corresponds exactly to the hurdy-gurdy (Fr. *vielle*) formerly spread all over Europe. An instr. with a sound-box like a cello, without neck and somewhat smaller. Has 4 strings, set in vibration by a disc turned by a handle.

Wooden keys are attached to the 4th string, whereby the notes of chromatic scale can be produced. Compass about 2 octaves. Formerly in general use; in the last decade confined to Szentes (Hungary). Was used to accompany dancing.—B. B.

HUNGARIAN OPERA, PANTOMIME AND BALLET. After the attempts of Franz Erkel to create a national opera, little was done in this direction for a long time. Operas (mostly on Wagnerian lines) were perf. at Budapest Opera House in the latter years of the last century, among them Mihalovich's (*q.v.*) *Toldi szerelme* and Hubay's (*q.v.*) *The Violin-maker of Cremona* (1894), also Mihalovich's *Eliana* (1908). Later were perf. Dohnányi's (*q.v.*) pantomime, *The Veil of Pierrette*; Bartók's (*q.v.*) fairy ballet, *The Wooden Prince* (1917), and his 1-act opera, *Duke Bluebeard's Castle* (1918), and Dohnányi's grand opera, *The Castle of Woiwoden* (1922).—B. B.

HURÉ, Jean. Fr. compr. *b.* Gien (Loiret), 17 Sept. 1877. Pursued his mus. studies in Angers (Maine et Loire). Went to Paris in 1898. A remarkable pianist, he gave many concerts there, in the provinces, and in Austria, Rumania, etc. Founded Normal School of Music for training of pianists, orgts. and comprs. His music has sincerity and force, showing also tendencies towards the investigation of modern forms and harmonies. Many educational works:
La Technique du Piano, La Technique de l'Orgue, l'Esthétique de l'Orgue, etc. A compr. of talent, the Odéon and the Opéra-Comique have produced his *Fantasio, Le Bois Sacré.* Has written a pf. and vn. sonata (1901); 5tet (1907-8); 2 str. 4tets; *Sérénade* for pf. vn. and cello ; 2 pf. and cello sonatas (1903, 1906) (Paris, Mathot; Senart), etc.—M. L. P.

HURLSTONE, William Yeates. Eng. pianist and compr. *b.* London, 7 Jan. 1876; *d.* there, 30 May, 1906. Hardly any early instruction; yet at 9 he publ. a set of 5 pf. valses and at 18 gained an R.C.M. scholarship. There he stud. under Stanford (compn.), A. Ashton and E. Dannreuther (pf.). Ill-health prevented an active pianist's career. In May 1904 his *Fantasie-Variations on a Swedish Air* were produced at the first R.C.M. Patron's Fund concert (just then founded by Sir Ernest Palmer). His pf. concerto in D was played by himself, at St. James's Hall in 1896. His chamber-music is important, as it stands on the threshold of the renaissance of the Eng. chamber-music school (Bridge, Dale, Ireland, York Bowen, McEwen, etc.). In it, he did not completely free himself from undue foreign influences (notably Dvořák); but he gave impetus to the new movement, and his early death was greatly deplored. Many of his chamber works were produced at the British Chamber Concerts in St. James's Hall, 1897-8-9.
Ballad, *Alfred the Great*, chorus and orch.; orch. variations (1904); fairy-suite, *The Magic Mirror*; pf. concerto (1896); 5tet, pf. and wind instrs.; 4tet, pf. and str. (Patron's Fund concert, 1904); str. 4tet, A mi.; pf. trio in G; sonata in F, vn. and pf.; 4 Eng. sketches, vn. and pf.; 2 sonatas, cello and pf. (in F; in D); 4 characteristic pieces, vla. and pf.; suite, clar. and pf.; pf. pieces (*Capriccio*, B mi.; 5 *Miniatures*, etc.); many songs.—E.-H.

HURUM, Alf. Norwegian compr. *b.* Christiania, 21 Sept. 1882. Pupil of Martin Knutzen (pf.), Iver Holter (harmony). Stud. 4 years at High School in Berlin (Rob. Kahn, Max Bruch and José Vianna da Motta); afterwards in Paris and Petrograd (orch. under Maximilian Steinberg). 1916, concert-tour in his own country; concerts in Stockholm in 1914. *Début* as condr.

in 1921 in *Harmonien*, Bergen. Is secretary and chairman of committee of Norwegian Musicians' Association.

H. has won recognition as one of the most talented younger Norwegian comprs. belonging to a modern tendency which seeks to deepen the national mus. elements through a restrained and yet individual employment of the modern means of expression. His melodic talent is conspicuous, his harmonisation is daring, full of imagination and rich in colour, with its frequently quite impressionistic mode of expression, and he has a masterly control of the orch.
2 sonatas, vn. and pf. (op. 2, D mi., 1st perf. 1911; op. 8, A mi., 1st perf. Bergen, 1916); str. 4tet (Christiania, 1914); male-chorus work, *Lilja*, op. 15 (after Norse poem; partly perf. in Trondhjem, 1921); *Exotic Suite* for orch. op. 9 (1st perf. Christiania, 1918); orch. suite, *Fairyland*, op. 16 (Christiania, 1921); minor orch. pieces; songs with pf. op. 11-14; pf. pieces: *Impressions*, op. 4; suites, op. 3, 10; *Aquarelles*, op. 5; *Gothic Pictures*, op. 17; *Norse Suite*, op. 18. symph. poem, *Bendik and Aarolilja* (Bergen, Christiania, 1923). All his works have been issued by his own publ. firm in Christiania.—J. A.

HUSS, Henry Holden. Amer. compr. *b.* Newark, N.J., U.S.A., 21 June, 1862. Stud. theory under Boise; 1882-5 in Munich under Giehrl (pf.) and Rheinberger (organ and theory). His graduation exercise, *Rhapsody* for pf. and orch., perf. after his return to America by Boston Symphony Orch., 30 Oct. 1886 (compr. at pf.). First pf. concerto with same orch. 29 Dec. 1894. It has often been played in other cities. A dramatic scene (s. with orch.), *Cleopatra's Death*, was first perf. New York Philh. 1 April, 1898. His chamber-music has also been frequently perf. by notable artists (Kneisel Quartet, Hambourg, May Mukle and others). His *Seven Ages of Man* for barit. and orch. (still in ms.) was effectively sung by Bispham. H. has been a successful teacher and concert-pianist in New York, and since 1905 has given many joint-recitals with his wife (Hildegard Hoffmann), a soprano singer.
Concerto in B, op. 10 (Schirmer, 1898); str. 4tet, op. 31 (Soc. for Publication of Amer. Music, Schirmer, 1912); vn. sonata, op. 19 (Schirmer, 1903; 2nd ed. 1920); *Ave Maria* for female chorus, solo and orch. op. 4 (Novello, 1890). Many pf. pieces and songs (Schirmer; Schmidt; Ditson).—O. K.

HUSSEY, Dyneley. Eng. music critic; *b.* Deolali, India, 27 Feb. 1893. Educated Corpus Christi Coll. Oxford; writes for *The Times* and *Saturday Review*.—E.-H.

HUSSLA, Victor. Portuguese teacher, violinist and condr. *b.* 1857; *d.* 1899. In 1887 appointed condr. of the orch. of Academia de Amadores de Musica (founded 1884 by a group of music-lovers). He taught many brilliant vn. pupils, both privately, at the Acad. and also at the Cons. With Colaço and others he made known in Portugal the masterpieces of chamber-music. Composed many works for his orch. of amateurs, notably the *Rapsodies portugaises*.—E.-H.

HUTCHENS, Frank. New Zealand pianist and compr. *b.* Christchurch, N.Z. in 1892. Prof. State Cons. of Music, Sydney, N.S.W. Gave successful pf. recitals in London, 1922.
Orch. overture, *Song of Victory* (ms.); cantata, *Psalm XXIII* (Novello); trio in 1 movement, F sharp mi. vn. cello, pf.; *Elegy*, vn. and pf.—E.-H.

HUTCHESON, Ernest. Australian pianist; b. Melbourne, 20 July, 1871. First pf. lessons from Vogrich and Torrance in Australia, where he appeared as child-prodigy. At 14, went to Leipzig, stud. pf. under Reinecke and Zwintscher, compn. under Jadassohn. 1890, went to Stavenhagen in Weimar. In 1898, appeared in Berlin as a pianist, also as condr. and compr. Went in 1900 to America as head of pf. department of Peabody Inst. in Baltimore. Resigned in 1912 to devote himself to concert work. 1912–1914 in Europe. Settled in New York, 1914. Has been heard as concert-pianist in England and Russia as well as in Australia, and has played in America with almost all the large orchs. Has comp. several orch. pieces, a pf. concerto, concerto for two pfs. and a vn. concerto (all ms.). Several pf. pieces (Composers' Music Corporation). Author of *Elektra by Richard Strauss : a Guide to the Opera* (Schirmer, 1910).—O. K.

HUTSCHENRUYTER, Wouter. Dutch condr. b. Rotterdam, 15 Aug. 1859. 2nd condr. Concertgebouw, Amsterdam (1890–2), then condr. Symph. Orch. Utrecht; resigned 1917 and became dir. of Music School, Rotterdam, which post he still occupies. During his Utrecht conductorship he was a pioneer of Dutch and little-known foreign music.

Op. 1 and 2, pf. duets; op. 3, sonata, pf. and vn. (Schott); op. 4, sonata for pf. and cello (Hamburg, Cranz); op. 5, concerto pf. and orch. (given frequently by Willem Andriessen); op. 6, overture for orch.; op. 7, *Festival March*, wind orch. (Paris, Evelle & Schoeffer); op. 8, *Suite in Ancient Style*, orch.; pf. works (2 and 4 hands). Wrote biographical studies on Mozart, Strauss, Weingartner, etc.—W. P.

HUUS-HANSEN, John Wilhelm. Norwegian orgt. b. Christiania, 23 Sept. 1894. Stud. organ-playing under Eyvind Alnæs, theory under Gustav Lange and Iver Holter. *Début* as orgt. in Christiania in 1915; regular concerts in that city and in provinces. Chairman of Christiania Organists' Association since 1919.—J. A.

HVIID, Mimi. Norwegian singer and teacher; b. Christiania. Appeared in 1906 as Mimi in *La Bohème*; 1907 Santuzza in *Cavalleria* at National Theatre. From 1910, one of Christiania's most valued teachers.—R. M.

HVOSLEF, Agnes Eveline Hanson. Norwegian m.-sopr. singer; b. Christiania, 4 April, 1883. Pupil of Ellen Gulbranson, Christiania, and Mme. Materna, Vienna. *Début* as concert-singer, Christiania, 1905; as operatic singer in National Theatre, Christiania, 1909. Engaged at Hofoper in Dessau, 1913; sang at Bayreuth in 1914. Lives at Drammen.—U. M.

HWYL, Welsh. Ordinarily, *hwyl* means eloquence and fervour in public speaking. In a more restricted sense it denotes the musical cadences employed by many Welsh speakers, particularly certain Nonconformist preachers, when speaking under the influence of deep emotion, or of intense conviction. This interesting phenomenon is not peculiar to Wales, but, to a greater or less degree, is common in other countries; and the reason for it is partly physical,

partly psychological. Military commands and street cries, for instance, tend to become musical tones, because regular vibrations are more resonant, and carry further, and are produced, with less effort than the irregular vibrations of ordinary speech. On the psychological side is the well-known fact that a dignified poetical passage or an emotional appeal cannot be recited without employing a non-conversational " tone "; and this often resolves itself into cadences which are almost, if not quite, musical.

The tendency towards this kind of quasi-musical speech is very strong in the Welsh people, but it has been accentuated by the religious movements of the close of XVIII century, and beginning of XIX. The *hwyl* tradition has persisted to the present day. In many cases it is quite spontaneous, the transition into it being so gradual and natural that neither speaker nor listener is conscious of it.

Hwyl, when genuine, reveals some interesting features that have a bearing on the early history of music. The most striking is the mode, which, instead of being minor, as is generally supposed, is invariably Dorian. Though the development of the *hwyl*, from its initiation to its climax, varies, the following is typical of the majority of cases. Firstly, the sounds seem to crystallise into a note of a definite pitch on which all the emphatic words are delivered, the others forming indeterminate inflections above or below. As the feeling intensifies another declamatory note appears, generally a minor third above, but sometimes below. In any case the lower note becomes the " final " of the mode. The intermediate note is at first vague in tonality and only employed as a kind of passing-note. When the fourth makes its appearance it often does so with thrilling effect, completing a well-defined tetrachord, to which the fifth is soon added. Should the sixth be introduced, the interval between it and the note below, though not well defined, is always greater than a semitone. The same is also true of the interval below the tonic. Both these notes are mainly used for non-emphatic words, the declamatory notes being the tonic, third, fourth and fifth; and the choice of notes and the consequent colour and effect of the musical cadences depends on the personality of the speakers. The octave above is never reached; occasionally the fourth below may be lightly touched but not so as to justify one in regarding the mode as Hypo-Dorian. The Amen cadence invariably descends from the supertonic to the tonic.

Some writers maintain that *hwyl* represents fragments of ancient church music traditionally handed down. It is, however, difficult to understand how people unversed in the niceties of the modes, and who hardly ever hear any music other than major and minor, should, in their *hwyl*, strictly confine themselves to the Dorian mode. It is probably more correct to regard it as having all originated from a psychological source. We may regard the steps in development of *hwyl*, from its commencement as a monotone to its full compass of about a sixth, as recapitulating the earlier stages in the evolution of the scale (tetrachord, hexachord, etc.); of mus. notation (one line, three lines, etc.), and of the chant. The melodies of many old Welsh hymn tunes and anthems are full of *hwyl* formulæ.

A genuine *hwyl*, when judiciously introduced, is very effective; but were attempts made to systematise it and to teach it from printed records according to formulated rules, it would probably degenerate into a mechanical exercise, sung in strict time, and there would be the same difficulty in securing a " live " rendering, as is now so frequently experienced in plain-song and the chant.—J. Ll. W.

HYDE, Walter. Eng. operatic t. singer; *b.* Birmingham, 6 Feb. 1875. Stud. at R.C.M. London under Gustave Garcia, Sir Walter Parratt and Sir Charles Stanford; elocution under Cairns James; *début* in light opera, *My Lady Molly* (Terry's Theatre, 1905); concert work and another light opera; then Siegmund in *Valkyrie*, Covent Garden, Eng. *Ring* under Richter; since then in nearly all Wagnerian t. roles; first Eng. t to sing Pinkerton in *Butterfly* at Covent Garden; toured U.S.A.; sang at Opera, Budapest; 1921–3, British National Opera, London and provinces. H. is one of the very finest of operatic tenors.—E.-H.

I

IBERT, Jacques. Fr. compr. *b.* Paris, 1890. Pupil of the Cons. (*Prix de Rome*, 1919). This admirable musician seems already to have fallen under the influence of Maurice Ravel. His works have a delicate and refined sensibility and an extremely able technique.

La Ballade de la Geôle de Reading (1920); Persée et Andromède (1921); Escales (1922); 4tet for wind instrs. (1922); Le Jardinier de Samos (1923); songs with pf. La Verdure dorée (1924, Leduc).—H. P.

IBSEN, Bergljot Björnson. Norwegian concert-singer; daughter of the poet Björnstjerne Björnson. Born Aulestad, Gausdal, 16 June, 1869. Pupil of Désirée Artôt, Paris. Extensive concert-tours at home and abroad. Has of late years given chiefly sacred concerts.—U. M.

IDELSOHN, A. Z. Ger. writer on music; *b.* Filzburg, near Libau (Courland), 14 July, 1882. Pupil of Stern's Cons. and of Jadassohn, Krehl, and H. Zöllner at Leipzig Cons. Went to Johannesburg, S. Africa, 1905, and to Jerusalem in 1907, devoting himself to study of Oriental music.

The Makamets of Arabian Music (Sammelb. d. I.M.G. XV, i), Remains of Ancient Hebrew Music (Ost und West, 1912–13), Synagogal Singing in the Light of Oriental Music (Monatsbl. des deutschen Kantoren-Verbandes, 1913), Parallels between Gregorian and Hebrew-Oriental Melodies (Z.f.M. IV, 9, 10, 1922); coll. in several vols. of Hebrew-Oriental Treasury of Melodies is being publ. by Breitkopf; 3 vols. publ. up to 1923. Also publ. Songs of Zion (with pf.) (Jerusalem, 1908); Synagogal Music (Berlin, 1910); Song Book (100 Hebrew Songs for School and Home, Berlin-Jerusalem, 1912); also Manual of European and Oriental Music (Jerusalem, 1910).—A. E.

IGUMNOF, Constantine Nicolaievitch. Russ. pianist; *b.* Liebedian, govt. of Tambof, 19 April/1 May, 1873. Stud. under Zvieref, and at Moscow Cons. under Siloti and Pabst; 1898–9, pf. teacher at Tiflis music-school of Russ. Music Soc. From 1899 till now, prof. at Moscow Cons.—V. B.

IKONEN, Lauri. Finnish compr. *b.* Mikkeli (St. Michel), 10 Aug. 1888. Stud. in Helsingfors Univ.; Ph.M. 1910. Stud. music in Helsingfors and Berlin (Paul Juon), 1910–12. Since 1923, ed. of the mus. paper *Suomen Musiikkilehti.*

2 symphonies (No. I named Sinfonia inornata); vn. sonata; choral works; songs.—T. H.

IMBERT, Hugues. Fr. musicologist; *b.* La Nièvre, 1842; *d.* Paris, 1905. He had his hour of celebrity, but to-day his works are of little interest. He represented the old style of criticism, anecdotal, incapable of synthetic views.

Profils de Musiciens, 3 vols. (1888–97); Portraits et Études (1894); Médaillons contemporains (1902).—A.C.

IMPRESSIONISM. A term which has been borrowed from the criticism of painting and recently applied in a not very clearly defined sense to music. The chief modern exponent of musical "impressionism" was Debussy, and the term seems generally to be applied to music intended to convey some suggestion of landscape, or of a picture in which colour is more important than outline, the melodic line in such cases being ill-defined and fragmentary, while sub-sidiary figures of accompaniment are much developed, often in rapid movement, the object of which is to produce a general effect of timbre rather than a clearly intelligible succession of notes. Similar effects are also obtained by slow harmonies based on chords which an older generation would have regarded as discords, but which the present day regards as agreeable consonances. The germs of "impressionism" can be traced far back; they may be found in the madrigals of Luca Marenzio and others; Torre-franca finds them in the harpsichord sonatas of Galuppi and Platti; Edward Carpenter has pointed out similar tendencies in the pianoforte sonatas of Beethoven. Liszt shows frequent examples; among living composers Delius is one of the most successful "impressionists."—E. J. D.

INCAGLIATI, Matteo. Ital. writer on music; *b.* Salerno, 1873; graduate in law; devoted himself to mus. criticism. Collaborated in Rome in the periodical *Musica*; then founded and dir. (for 10 years) periodical *Orfeo.* At present, is mus. critic of *Giornale d' Italia.* Has publ. *Storia del Teatro Costanzi* (Rome, 1907).—D. A.

INDIA, MUSIC IN. Apart from the folk-music (lullabies and songs of labour, etc.) and from processional and wedding-music, the music of India is either devotional or chamber-music. The devotional music includes on the one hand that of the ancient Saman chant, which has probably come down essentially unchanged during three millenniums, and on the other an infinite variety of hymns addressed to the Deity under various names. Chaitanya, in the xv century, in effecting a revival of Vaishnava faith by his impassioned hymns, was only repeating the methods of the Buddhist Ashvaghosa 1400 years earlier. In the South the great collection of Saiva hymns known as the *Tevāram*, and the songs of Mānikka Vācagar, are sung in temples, and those who hear these songs are moved to tears. Art-music remains almost entirely in the hands of an hereditary profession, consisting of *ustads*, or "masters" (of whom the most famous was Tān Sen in the xvi century), and of dancing-girls. These are maintained by aristocratic patrons or engaged on special occasions. The public concert is unknown, and music is a professional art, not a social accomplishment; nevertheless it may be said with truth that for every person in Europe in whose life music is an essential experience, there are, or have been until recently, ten in India. The masters are often the composers of their own songs (poetry and song are inseparable ideas). The words of art-songs are short lyrical compositions depicting a single emotional situation and always of high literary merit; but words are used more as a vehicle for the music than for their own sake—words are composed to music rather than music

248

to words. In any case, every performance is in some degree an improvisation; the musician plays or sings in accordance with certain rules and in given modes, but not from a fixed score.

The nearest analogues for the psychic effects of Indian music may be found in plain-song, in troubadour music, mediæval music generally, and in Bach. The music is devoted to the utterance of a given emotional experience, which is analysed and dwelt upon with overpowering intensity. But, however impassioned, it has none of the *Sturm und Drang* of Beethoven, or the romantic longings of Wagner; it is born of a clear understanding of life. As Fox-Strangways has said, writing from a Western point of view, " we do not know what to make of music which is dilatory without being sentimental, and utters passion without vehemence."—A. K. C.

INDIAN MUSIC. The Indian scale consists of 22 notes (16 only in the Southern system), of which 7 correspond to the white notes of the piano, if we imagine the piano tuned in a just and not a tempered scale. The 7 notes are known by the names *Sa, Ri, Ga, Ma, Pa, Dha, Ni, Sa,* used in the same way as the syllabic names in the Solfa system. The other notes are sharps or flats of these, and are distinguished by qualifying adjectives. All Indian music is modal, and only a selection of not more than 7 of these notes can be used in any one composition, except as grace-notes. All Indian music is melodic; without actual or implied harmony, other than the tonic note or drone which remains constant in all modes, and is pitched to suit the singer's voice. A characteristic use of grace-notes and sliding progressions produces a colour-variation such as is obtained in harmonised music only by varying degrees of assonance.

The fundamental conception in Indian music is that of *Rāga*, a word meaning passion or colouring. In the usual classification there are 6 *Rāgas*, each with 5 *Rāginis*, the *Rāgini* being a modification of the *Rāga*. The term is best translated as " melody-mould "; this melody-mould consists of a selection of 5, 6, or 7 notes distributed over the scale, employing certain characteristic progressions, and laying particular stress on one note, which however, is not to be regarded as a " key-note." Every song or composition must conform to and adhere to the peculiarities of the *Rāga* or *Rāgini* in which it is made. The form of the *Rāga* being known, the simple names *Sa, Ri,* etc., suffice for teaching or notation. Notation is little used; singing or playing is never from fixed scores, and every performance is in part an improvisation within the given limits. The *Rāgas* are proper to particular seasons and hours, and have definite emotional and ethical associations (*ethos,* as in ancient Greek music). These associations are described in sets of verse called *Rāgmālās,* and illustrated in pictures.

The second essential in Indian music is *Tāla* or time-measure. These measures are inseparably connected with the metres of verse (in the East, all poetry is sung or chanted, and never read in

a speaking voice); and are therefore based on quantity and not on accent (words are set to music, rather than music to words). Over 100 *Tālas* are known, but by no means all are in use. All are combinations of 1, 2, 3, 5, 7 or 9 time-units, each of which may be split up into smaller component parts. The art of the drummer is developed to a point unknown in the West.

Consult: A. H. Fox-Strangways, *Music of Hindustan* (Oxford, 1914); Ratan Devi, *Thirty Indian Songs* (London, 1913); E. Clemens, *Introduction to the Study of Indian Music* (London, 1913); H. A. Popley, *The Music of India* (Calcutta and London, 1921), and references in art. on INDIAN MUS. INSTRS.—A. K. C.

INDIAN MUSICAL INSTRUMENTS. The voice, in India, is regarded as the chief and noblest of instruments: vocal music therefore has a higher relative valuation than in the West, and is more highly developed.

Next in importance to the voice is the classical *vinā*, a kind of lute with 7 long metal strings and 24 frets. Of these strings, 3 are placed on one side and only used to make a drone accompaniment, and to mark time. A common tuning is CGC, and GCG₁. The *vinā* is a superb instr. with a vibrant ringing tone, not very loud. Equally with the human voice it is capable of very subtle inflections and graces, inasmuch as whole passages, especially the elaborate trills, shakes and slides which are an essential part of the melodic structure of Indian music and the most obvious vehicle of its peculiar appeal, can be played by a deflection of the long strings, without fresh plucking. In these deflections a range of as much as 4 semitones may be covered, and they lend themselves especially to *pp* effects. A Bengali instr., similar in principle but deeper in tone, is the *surbahār*.

The *tambura* is a similar instr. without frets, tuned GCCC₁. Pieces of silk are placed between the bridge and the strings to produce the buzzing tone, which is like a swarm of bees or the sound of an electric fan. All of the strings are struck by the fingers in rapid succession, so as to produce a continuous drone; this continuous drone is very rich in overtones, and sounds almost like a combination of instrs., never becoming monotonous. The *tambura* is used exclusively as the background of song, with or without the drum.

The instrs. played with a bow (*sitār, esraj, sārangī,* etc.) though they have been in use for many centuries, are mainly North Indian, and probably of Persian origin. The *sārangī* is something like a viola in effect; but has from 15 to 20 sympathetic strings, and is mainly used to accompany dancing, together with the drum.

The flute (*venu, murali*) is one of the most ancient of Indian instrs., and has an important place in literature in connection with the Krishna legends, where its sound represents the call to " leave all and to follow Me."

Drums are of very many kinds and uses. The drum provides the tonic to which other instrs. must be tuned. In certain varieties one or both heads are loaded with special compositions to produce the required tonal effects.

Ensemble consists as a rule of voice, *tambura*

and drum, or of *vīnā* and drum. More numerous orchestras in which wind instrs. (including the oboe) and drums are conspicuous are used in processional, wedding and martial music. Bands of this type are usually stationed at palace gates, and play all day.

Consult: C. R. Day, *Music and Musical Instrs. of Southern India and the Deccan* (London, 1891); C. Sachs, *Die Musikinstr, Indiens und Indonesiens* (Berlin, 1914); A. M. Meerwarth, *Guide to the Collection of Musical Instrs. in the Indian Museum* (Calcutta, 1917), and references in art. on INDIAN MUSIC.—A. K. C.

d'INDY, Paul Marie Théodore Vincent. French composer; *b.* Paris, 27 March, 1851. The foremost of César Franck's pupils, and the acknowledged leader of the school often called " Franckist," but which owes a good deal to the influence of his own music, personality, and teaching.

At an early age he began to study the pianoforte under Diémer and Marmontel, and, a little later, harmony under Lavignac. In 1872 or 1873 he was admitted into César Franck's organ class at the Conservatoire, and it is under Franck's guidance that he studied the classics and the technique of composition. He completed his professional education by practical work as organist, choirmaster and timpani player at the Concerts Colonne (1876-8).

As a composer he began to assert himself early, with a variety of works, the first of which was the *Piccolomini Overture* for orchestra (performed in 1874) which ultimately became the second part of his fine orchestral triptych *Wallenstein* (the other two parts were played in 1880). His tone-poem *La Forêt Enchantée* was written in 1878. His *Symphonie sur un thème montagnard français*, one of his greatest achievements, appeared in 1886; in 1885 his *Chant de la Cloche* was awarded the grand prize of the city of Paris. In 1897, he accepted the post of teacher of composition at the *Schola Cantorum* (founded by himself, Ch. Bordes, and Guilmant) which he still holds besides that of Principal.

As a composer, he came very strongly under the influence of Wagner and César Franck and a little later under that of folk-song and Gregorian chant. The degree of Wagner's influence, (an influence mainly obvious in the early works and especially in *Le Chant de la Cloche*) has been emphasised, not without exaggeration, by various writers, while others have maintained that the adoption, in their general lines, of Wagner's methods (*e.g.* in his lyric drama *Fervaal*) has not interfered in the least with the display of far-reaching originality. The influence of folksong is ever present, and discernible in the quality of the motives, the rhythmic structure, and the colours of his music. That of Gregorian chant, more gradual, is noticeable in parts of *Fervaal* and assumes a paramount importance in *La Légende de Saint Christophe*. He is typically French in his love of clarity. logical order and definite outline. He revised and systematised Franck's methods of construction and followed their logical development.

No French composer of to-day has been discussed more freely and more passionately; and the time has not yet come when a measure of agreement will decide how far his admirers and his detractors (whose chief argument is that his music is often remarkable more from the point of view of science than from that of inspiration) are right or wrong. But most critics endorse Romain Rolland's view that he is " one of the master-musicians of contemporary Europe as regards dramatic expression, orchestral colour, and science of style." Issue has chiefly been joined around *Fervaal*; and later, around various points referring more to d'Indy's theories, ideals, and utterances as a critic and teacher, than to the actual quality of his music.

His teaching, essentially founded upon the historical study and thorough analysis of artforms from their origin to the latest stages of their evolution, is summed up in the *Traité de Composition* (2 vols. publ.; Durand). His pupils number many notable musicians : de Séverac, Samazeuilh, Le Flem, M. Labey, Canteloube, etc. He has also written a critical biography of César Franck (Paris, 1906, Alcan), and a book on Beethoven (Paris, 1902, Laurens). He is (since 1890) president of the Société Nationale de Musique. He has edited, or co-operated in the editing of many classics of various schools (Monteverdi's *Orfeo* and *Incoronazione di Poppea* [Schola Cantorum]; Rameau's *Dardanus* and *Hippolyte et Aricie* [Durand]).

Dramatic works: *Le Chant de la Cloche*, dramatic legend (1883, Hamelle); *Fervaal*, lyric drama (1895, Durand); *L'Étranger*, lyric drama (1901, *id.*); *La Légende de St. Christophe* (1915, Rouart, Lerolle). Orch.: *Symphonie sur un chant montagnard français* (called *Symphonie cévenole*) (1886, Hamelle); 2nd symphony (1903, Durand); 3rd symphony (*De Bello Gallico*) (1919, Rouart, Lerolle); *Poème des Rivages* (1921, *id.*); *Wallenstein*, a trilogy (1873–81, Durand); *La Forêt enchantée* (1878, Heugel); *Saugefleurie* (1882, Hamelle); *Istar*, symph. variations (1896, Durand); *Jour d'été à la montagne* (1905, *id.*); *Souvenirs* (1906, *id.*). Chamber-music: Pf. 4tet (1888, Durand); 1st str. 4tet, in D (1890, Hamelle); 2nd, in E (1897, Durand); trio, pf. cello, clar. (1887, Hamelle); sonata, pf. and vn. (1904, Durand). Pf.: *Poème des montagnes* (1881, Hamelle); *Schumanniana* (1887); *Tableaux de voyage* (1889, Leduc); sonata (1907, Durand). Songs; church music, etc. Consult bibliography in Séré (*q.v.*), and: A. Sérieyx, *V. d'I.*; M. D. Calvocoressi, *V. d'I.* (*Mus. Times*, Nov. 1912), and *The Dramatic Works of V. d'I.* (*id.* May–Sept. 1921.—M. D. C.

INFANTE, Manuel. Span. compr. *b.* Osuna, Seville. Since the 1st perf. of his clear and graceful pf. works in Paris (1921) by the pianist José Iturbi, his compns. have attained an immediate and increasing success. Lives in Paris.

Pf.: *El Vito*; *Variations sur un thème populaire et danse originale*; *Sevillana*; *Guadalquivir*, nocturne; *Gitanerias*. For 2 pfs.: *Trois danses andalouses*; *Ritmo*; *Gracia*; *Sentimiento*. (A. Z. Mathot; H. Gregh. Paris.)—P., G. M.

INGENHOVEN, Jan. Dutch compr. *b.* Breda (N. Brabant), 19 May, 1876. Stud. under Ludwig Felix Brandts-Buys and Felix Mottl; cond. orch. concerts in Munich, Mannheim, Paris, The Hague, in Switzerland and Italy. Lives in Paris. Comp. numerous works for orch. and chamber-music (4 str. 4tets, etc.).—W. P.

INGHELBRECHT, D. E. French composer;

b. Paris, 17 Sept. 1880. One of the friends of Debussy during the last period of his life. As orchestral conductor, Inghelbrecht was particularly distinguished in the production of Debussy's works and in the revival of the earlier ones. He is a distinguished composer. His delicious albums for piano *The Nursery* (Mathot), his sonata for flute and harp, his *Cantique des créatures de Saint François* (chorus and orch.), especially his ballet *El Greco* (perf. by the Swedish Ballet Troupe), reveal in him a harmonic science, a sense of orchestral colour and a remarkable melodic invention.—H. P.

INSTITUTES OF MUSIC. See ACADEMIES.

INSTRUMENTS INVENTED or modified since 1880. The period from 1880 has seen various improvements in orchestral and military band instrs., due to the unceasing ingenuity of makers in overcoming technical drawbacks. These, however, are limited to minor details, and the working out of sundry problems was, of course, interrupted during the years of war. The orch. has remained in its broad outlines unchanged. The perfecting of valves of brass instrs. is perhaps the most noticeable of the various improvements in that department. While there is no type of wind instr. that can properly be regarded as new, there have been some changes in the customary instrumentation of military music, notably in growing rise of saxophones and B flat soprano trumpet. With percussion instrs. the case is slightly different. Various models of xylophones, chimes, etc. are now in frequent use, and these used to be regarded as quite exceptional. There are also other so-called instrs., which are not much more than noise-making contrivances, used in the modern dance and "jazz" bands. In the exclusive department of military bands, at a conference held at Kneller Hall, 7 Dec. 1921, in dealing with bands numbering from 21 to 50 players, the following instrs. were declared obsolete: E flat alto clar.; b.-c. (except in bands of 50 or more); D flat flute (E flat military), the concert-flute to be substituted; E flat tpt.; baritone; circular bass (except in cavalry units). It was further recommended that at least 25 per cent. of clars. in a band should be of the Boehm pattern. The extraordinary vogue of the saxophone is quite a recent feature, although the invention of the instr. dates back to days of Adolphe Sax, who settled in Paris in 1842. It achieved early acceptance in military bands, and its sudden leap to popularity a few years ago gave the impression in some quarters that it was a new instr. It has actually obtained a very limited footing in the orch., exemplified in some of Joseph Holbrooke's compns. In America small saxophone-bands are substitutes for an organ in a few churches, but its use in dance music is the chief feature of its revival. As regards the organ and pf., the period since 1900 has produced many improvements in the details of construction. Perhaps the most interesting feature of the period under review has been the rise of the pianola. Although patented in America in 1897, its employment in England may be said to date from

about 1903, and its manufacture on a large scale a few years later. The value of the instr. was not rated highly until, in 1912 at a concert at the Albert Hall, cond. by Nikisch in conjunction with London Symph. Orch., the piano-part in various concertos was played by the pianola; and another memorable event was the playing by pianola of Harold Bauer's interpretation of Saint-Saëns' concerto in G mi. by the Duo-Art reproducing type of instr., with Queen's Hall Orch. cond. by Sir Henry Wood. The player-piano had in its early days received the support of Chaminade, Leopold Godowsky, Josef Hofmann, Jan Kubelík, V. de Pachmann, Paderewski, Hans Richter, and later of many world-famous pianists. Works especially designed for the instr. have been written by Stravinsky, Casella, Howells, Malipiero and Goossens. The conservative attitude taken up by musicians with regard to the pianola has now largely given way to a recognition of its capabilities; of course with the reservation that the direct touch of an artist must always remain supreme. The player-piano has been fully treated of by Edward Schaaf, M.D. of Newark, New Jersey, in a series of arts. which appeared in *The Music Trades Review* (July 1922 to Sept. 1923), followed by another series by Sidney Grew. The idiom of the instr. and its technical possibilities, freed from the limitations of the hand, are therein fully discussed. On 25 Nov. 1923, the Duo-Art electrical reproducing piano was heard at Queen's Hall, when records by Cortot and Hofmann, taken by the new process, acc. by London Symphony Orch. under Felix Weingartner, were heard. The programme included Variations on a Beethoven theme, by Saint-Saëns, for two pianos, one played by the Duo-Art from a Cortot record on one instr., the other played by Clara Evelyn. The gramophone had a much harder battle to win the approval of musicians. Its association with imperfect reproduction and bad tone caused many musicians to hold aloof from it; but improvements have brought about its recognition as a useful medium for educational purposes and a means of carrying music to people who would otherwise be entirely deprived of opportunity of hearing the best things. (See art. GRAMOPHONE.) In 1921 the advent of a new pf. invented by Emanuel Moór (a Hungarian by descent but Eng. by nationality, residing at Mont Pélerin, Switzerland) created much interest among pianists. Up to the present its acceptance is not very general. The forces of conservatism have to be reckoned with, and the possibilities of this means of simplifying pf. technique and extending its range must be further discussed and demonstrated.[1] The invention was fully treated of by Prof. Donald Tovey in *Music and Letters* (Jan. 1922; reprinted by Æolian Co.). This instr., which claims to give more adequate renderings of Bach, Mozart, and Chopin, is worth attention. A second

[1] For full details the specifications in the Patent Office, 161549, 1 Feb. 1922, and 180633, 17 Aug. 1922, may be consulted.

keyboard with a duplex coupler, sounding an octave higher, constitutes its main principle, and a contrivance is added which by pressing a button converts the instr. into a harpsichord with a fuller tone than its prototype. (See also: MENCHACA KEYBOARD; RENDANO INDEPENDENT PEDAL; HANS; JANKÓ; MUSTEL; ORSI.)—F. A. H.

INTERNATIONAL SOCIETY FOR CONTEMPORARY MUSIC. Founded at Salzburg at the end of the chamber-music fest. of Aug. 1922. Has now nearly 20 branches, with its headquarters at the British Music Society's office, 3 Berners St. London. Chairman (1923–4) Edward J. Dent. In 1923, there was a 6-day fest. of chamber-music at Salzburg; in 1924 an orch. fest. was given at Prague (May) and a 2nd chamber-music fest. at Salzburg in August.—E.-H.

INTERNATIONALE MUSIKGESELLSCHAFT. See SOCIETIES.

INZENGA, J. Contemporary Span. musician of the old school, author of *Cantos y bailes populares de España*, an unfinished coll. of dances and songs preceded by explanatory notes on folk-lore of their respective provinces, and *Colección de aires populares para guitarra*. Was a prof. at the Real Cons. de Música, Madrid, and Fellow of Real Acad. de Bellas Artes.

Zarzuela (1-act). *Batalla de Amor*. (Antonio Romero; I. Castro y Campo, Madrid.)—P. G. M.

IPPOLITOF-IVANOF, Michael Michaelovitch *(accent 3rd syll.)*. Russ. compr. *b.* Gatchina, 7/19 Nov. 1859. A pupil of Rimsky-Korsakof at Petrograd Cons. 1876–82; from 1882–93, dir. of music school of Russ. Mus. Soc. at Tiflis and chief condr. Tiflis Opera House; from 1893 till present time, prof. of compn. Moscow Cons.; from 1905–22 he was a dir. of it. In 1923, he celebrated his 40th artistic anniversary and received title of People's Artist of Republic.

Operas: *Ruth*, op. 6; *Asia*, op. 30; *Asra* (1890); *Treachery* (1909); *The Spy* (1912); *Ole the Norseman* (1916). Orch. works: overture on Russ. themes, *Jar-Khmel*, op. 1; *Symph. Scherzo*, op. 2; suite, *Caucasian Sketches*, op. 10; suite, *Iveria*, op. 42; symphony, E mi. op. 46; *Armenian Rhapsody*, op. 48; symph. poem, *Mzyri* (after Lermontof), op. 54; pf. 4tet, op. 9; str. 4tet, A mi. op. 13; vn. sonata, op. 8; Liturgy of S. John Chrysostom, op. 37; songs, etc.—V. B.

IRELAND, John. Eng. compr. *b.* Inglewood, Bowden, Cheshire, 13 Aug. 1879. Son of Alexander Ireland, sometime ed. of the *Manchester Examiner and Times*, and author of *The Book-Lover's Enchiridion*, who included among his friends Carlyle, Leigh Hunt, and Emerson. The family hails from Fifeshire. His mother belonged to a Cumberland family; so that he is of Northern descent on both sides. He was educated at Leeds Grammar School, and entered the R.C.M. London in 1893, where he stud. pf. for 4 years under Cliffe, and compn. for the 4 following years under Stanford, emerging from studentship in 1901. From that year to 1908, he was engaged in forming his style by means of a number of compns., all of which he has since discarded as being unrepresentative. It is, however, important to remember that the two well-known vn. sonatas had two predecessors, that *The Forgotten Rite* was a long way from being his 1st

orch. work, and that he had written a large amount of concerted chamber-music. The earliest works which he now acknowledges are the Phantasy-Trio in A mi. (1908), and *The Songs of a Wayfarer* (1910), after which there occurs a break in his output, which is not resumed until 1913, when a marked advance in the compr.'s style is immediately apparent. Except that he spent a holiday during 1912 in Jersey, impressions of which are recorded in *The Island Spell* (*Decorations*) and in *The Forgotten Rite*, nothing has transpired as to the reason of this interruption in his activities. For the rest, like most comprs. he has to devote much time to other than creative work, and he lives in Chelsea. In the ordinary sense, his career has not been eventful. Its most memorable day was in 1917 when Albert Sammons and William Murdoch gave the 1st perf. of a work which had the immediate effect of establishing his reputation, the 2nd vn. sonata. The sequel was remarkable for the times in which it occurred. Whereas formerly violinists had fought shy of English works, most of them now felt it incumbent upon them to play this sonata, and even the conviction of publishers that sonatas were white elephants was shaken, for the first edition of this one was sold out before it left the press. Soon after the sonata, and before the latter was performed, he composed a one-movement trio in E mi. Since then, his most important works have been the pf. sonata in E (1920), and the Symphonic Rhapsody, *Mai-Dun* (1921). Meanwhile his shorter works for pf. and his songs have attained a fairly large number, although his output has not at any time been rapid. The reason for this is his unusually severe self-criticism. He has a passion for revision, and is scrupulous almost to excess.

His style is diatonic as to its foundation, which does not prevent it from having a chromatic appearance, owing to his method of enriching the harmonic texture. In form he stands closer than most modern composers to the orthodox tradition, but one has only to compare his work with that of the epigoni to see to which camp he belongs. Apart from a very characteristic harmonic sense, the chief features in his work are a feeling of austerity which has at times committed him to harshness, but has never impeded lyrical beauty, and a robust sincerity of purpose, both of which qualities proceed from that same artistic probity which causes him to scrutinise his work so closely before allowing it to go forth. Modern as he is, he is proof against the temptation of employing a device for its own sake, or inventing one as a "stunt." It is perhaps for this reason that, except the vn. sonata, which appeared to meet some psychological need of the moment, his best works have been slow to make their way in popular favour, though they have generally won in the end. It is the same with his songs, the most remarkable being rarely sung in comparison to numerous lyrics which have acquired popularity. Yet his most successful song happens to be also one of his best, the setting of Masefield's *Sea Fever* (Augener). He was elected Hon. Fellow of R.C.M. in 1924.

Orch.: *Symph. Rhapsody* (Augener, 1921); *The Forgotten Rite* (*id.*). Chamber-music: Phantasy-trio, pf. vn. cello (*id.*); trio No. II, in 1 movement (*id.*); sonata No. I, vn. and pf. (*id.*); sonata No. II, in A mi. vn. and pf. (W. Rogers). sonata, cello and pf. (Augener, 1924). Pf.: sonata in E mi. (Augener, 1920); *Rhapsody* (W. Rogers); 5 preludes (*id.*); *Decorations*; *London Pieces*; *For Remembrance*; *Amberley Wild Brooks*; *Soliloquy*; *On a Birthday Morning* (all Augener). Songs: *Songs of a Wayfarer* (Boosey); *Marigold*, song-impression (W. Rogers); *The Land of Lost Content* (6 songs from *A Shropshire Lad*) (Augener); numerous songs publ. singly; part-songs, etc.—E. E.

IRISH FOLK-MUSIC. See HUGHES, HERBERT; PATTERSON, ANNIE; STANFORD, C. V.; WOOD, CHARLES; also art. FOLK-SONG SOCIETIES.

ISAACS, Edward. Eng. pianist; *b.* Manchester, 14 July, 1881. Stud. at R. Manchester Coll. of Music; then Berlin, Leipzig, Vienna; appeared as soloist (under Richter) Manchester, 1905; has given over 60 " Midday Pf. Recitals " in Manchester. Founder of Edward Isaacs Chamber Concerts.

Pf. concerto (ms.; played under Richter; and Sir Henry Wood); pf. trio (ms.); vn. sonata.—E.-H.

ISASI, Andrés. Span. compr. *b.* Bilbao, 1890. Stud. compn. in Berlin under Humperdinck. Lives at Bilbao. One of leading figures of modern Span. school. Amongst his works, including pf. sonatas, vn. and pf. sonatas, str. 4tets and Ger. *lieder*, the following must be mentioned:

Zharufa, symph. poem (prize at International Competition, Malmö, Sweden), 1914; *Amor Dormido* (1st perf. Blüthner Orch. Berlin, 1914; Orquesta Filarmónica, Madrid, 1919); Second Symphony (1st perf. Orquesta Sinfónica, Madrid, 1918).—P. G. M.

ISTEL, Edgar. Ger. compr. and author; *b.* Mayence, 23 Feb. 1880. Pupil of Fritz Volbach; went to Munich, 1898, to finish his mus. education under Thuille; at same time attended Univ. Graduated Ph.D. 1900 (dissertation, *J. J. Rousseau as the Composer of " Pygmalion "* (*I.M.G.* Suppl. I, 1901). Removed to Berlin in 1913 as lecturer on music at Humboldt Acad.; and in 1919 at Lessing High School. Has been living in Madrid since 1920. Writings:

The German Christmas Play and its Rebirth from the Spirit of Music (Langensalza, 1900) (Vol. I of Rabich's *Musikalisches Magazin*); *Richard Wagner in the Light of a Contemporary's Correspondence* (Esser to Franz Schott, 1902); *Peter Cornelius* (1906, biography); *Origin of German Melodrama* (1906); *The Comic Opera* (historico-æsthetic study, 1906); *The Efflorescence of Musical Romanticism* (1909; 1920); *The Libretto* (1914); *Richard Wagner's Art Work* (1910); *Modern Opera since Wagner* (Leipzig, 1914, Teubner); *Paganini* (1919); *Revolution and Opera* (1919); *Book of the Opera* (Hesse, 1919; 1920). Also *P. Cornelius' Collected Essays* (1905); *E. T. A. Hoffmann's Musical Writings* (1907, in *Bücher der Weisheit und Schönheit*, also Regensburg, 1922, 2 vols., Bosse); *H.'s Musical Novels* (1910); *Poet and Composer* and *Kreisleriana* (1913); *Dittersdorff's Autobiography* (1909). Songs; 4-part mixed choruses in canon form, op. 12; *Musical Comedy Overture*, op. 17; 3 songs from Goethe with orch. op. 15; music to Küssner's *Magic Kettle* (originally *The Swineherd*) (Munich, 1908); *Hymn to Zeus* (chorus and orch.); music to Goethe's *Satyros* (Munich, 1910); adaptation of Rousseau's *Pygmalion* (Munich, 1904); romantic comic opera, *The Travelling Scholar* (Carlsruhe, 1906); *The Tribunal's Decree* (Mayence, 1916); romantic comic opera *The Glamour of May* and *Forbidden Love* (Gera, 1919); romantic opera burlesque, *Alone at Last* (Schwerin, 1920); musical

comedy, *If Women Dream* (Opéra Comique, Berlin, 1920); still in ms. romantic comic opera, *Don Toribio's Search for a Wife.*—A. E.

ISTERDAEL, Charles van. Cellist; *b.* Bergen (Belgium), 22 May, 1878. Stud. under Servais and Jacobs; 1894, soloist at Fr. Opera, Brussels; 1903, went to Holland; soloist of Residentie Orch. The Hague; teacher R. Cons. of Music. Toured in France, Belgium, Germany, Spain ; 1918, founded The Hague Str. Quartet (see CHAMBER-MUSIC PLAYERS).—W. P.

ISTRATTY, E. See RUMANIAN OPERA.

ITALIAN FOLK-MUSIC. See ADAJEWSKI, ELLA VON; ALALEONA, D.; FARA, G.; FAIRCHILD, BLAIR; FAVARA MISTRETTI, A.; ODDONE SULLI-RAO, E.; SADERO, G.; SINIGAGLIA, L.

ITURBI, José. Span. pianist; *b.* Valencia, 1896. Revealed himself as one of leading contemporary pianists at concerts of Colonne Orch. under the condr. Pierné, and at Salle Gaveau, Paris. He stud. at the Paris Cons., where he obtained first prize. Former prof. of pf. at Geneva Cons. Made his first appearance in England, with unusual success, at Promenade Concerts, Q. H. London, Sept. 1923. Lives in Paris.—P. G. M.

IVALDI, Filippo. Ital. pianist and compr. *b.* of an Ital. family in Alexandria, Egypt, 10 Dec. 1874; pupil of Giuseppe Martucci at Liceo of Bologna. Having gained his diploma, he left in 1908, but returned again in 1911 as prof. of pf. Many concerts both in Italy and abroad.

Pf. pieces; songs (Ricordi); ed. pf. classics.—D. A.

IVANOF-BORETSKY, Michael Vladimirovitch (*accent 2nd sylls.*). Russ. compr. and mus. historian; *b.* Moscow, 14/26 June, 1874. Pupil of Klenovsky (Moscow), A. Scontrino and A. Falconi (Florence), and Rimsky-Korsakof (Petrograd). Finished law course at Moscow Univ. in 1896; stud. XVI and XVII century mus. history in Ital. museums and libraries in 1901–2 and 1906. 1921, member and secretary of scientific council of State Inst. of Mus. Science; and, 1922, prof. of mus. history, Moscow Cons.

Operas: *Aphrodite* (after P. Louÿs); *The Sorceress* (after Chirikof); str. 4tet, op. 16; str. trio, op. 9, vn. sonata, op. 24; songs; choruses; pf. pieces.—V. B.

IVIMEY, John William. Eng. compr. and orgt. *b.* Stratford, Essex, 12 Sept. 1868. Stud. at Guildhall School of Music; mus. dir. S.W. Polytechnic, 1896–1902; orgt. Dulwich Coll. 1906–10; L.C.C. lecturer on music, 1913; dir. of music, Cheltenham Coll. 1915; Marlborough Coll. 1915; Mus.Doc. Oxon. 1916.

Grand opera, *The Rose of Lancaster*; 20 light operas; church and chamber-music, etc.—E.-H.

IVIMEY, Joseph. Eng. violinist and condr. *b.* Stratford, Essex, 21 July, 1867. Stud. under Alfred Gibson, 1882–92; prof. of vn. and condr. at Guildhall School of Music and Trinity Coll. London; condr. Strolling Players Amateur Orch. Soc. and Great Western Railway Mus. Soc.—E.-H.

IVOGÜN, Maria. Hungarian coloratura singer; *b.* Budapest, 1890. Pupil of Irene Schlemmer-Ambros at Vienna Acad. from 16th year. Member of Munich National Opera Company since 1913, also an important concert singer. Married (1921) Karl Erb, the Munich t. singer.—A. E.

J

JACCHIA, Agide. Ital. condr. *b.* Lugo (Romagna), 5 Jan. 1875. Stud. at Cons. in Parma, Milan and Pesaro. *Début* 1898–9, at Teatro Grande, Brescia. Until 1907 followed his profession in Italy; then went to U.S.A., where he was successively dir. of Montreal Opera Company, the Century Opera Company of New York, and the Boston Opera Company. Since 1917, has been dir. of concerts of Boston Symphony Orch.; since 1919, dir. of a mus. inst. in Boston. Comp. several works.—D. A.

JACHIMECKI, Zdzisław. Polish compr. and music historian; *b.* Lemberg, 7 July, 1882. Pupil of Stan. Niewiadowski (theory) in Lemberg Cons. In 1902, became pupil of Guido Adler at Vienna Univ. (history of music) and of Grädener and Schönberg (cpt.). Ph.D. 1906; went same year to Cracow; 1911, unsalaried lecturer on mus. science; 1917, prof.-extraordinary; 1921, prof.-in-ordinary at Cracow Univ. Has worked for 16 years as music critic for several Cracow newspapers. Condr. symph. concerts at Cracow.

Mozart, monograph (1906); *Polish Music* (1907); *Hugo Wolf* (1908); *Haydn*, monograph (1910); *Italian Influences on Polish Music from 1540 to 1640* (1911); *Richard Wagner* (1911); *The Tablature for Organ of Kraśnik of 1548* (1913); *The Evolution of Polish Musical Culture* (1914); *Music at the Court of King Władisław Jagiełło in Cracow 1424 to 1430* (1915); *The History of Polish Music* (1920); *Stanisław Moniuszko* (1921); *Richard Wagner* (1922); revised ed. of book of 1911). Also many treatises in mus. periodicals in Poland and foreign papers. His compns. include numerous songs, a symph. fantasia and other pieces in modern style.

Dr. Jachimecki has contributed all the arts. on Polish musicians in this Dictionary.—E.-H.

JACKSON, Roland. Eng. t. singer; *b.* Birkenhead, 26 March, 1879. Stud. under Korbay and Raimond von Zur Mühlen.—E.-H.

JACOB, Georges. Fr. compr. *b.* Paris, 17 Aug. 1877. *Lauréat* in Guilmant's class at Paris Cons. Since 1922, orgt. at Société des Concerts, in succession to Joseph Bonnet. Has written many organ works, also pf. pieces. Has also organised recitals which have been epoch-making.—F. R.

JACOBI, Viktor. Hungarian operetta compr. *b.* Budapest,22 Oct.1883; *d.* in America, 1921.—B. B.

JACZYNOWSKA, Katarzyna (*phon.* Yachynovska). Pianist; *b.* Stawle, Kowno, Poland, 1875; *d.* Warsaw, 1920. Pupil of Anton Rubinstein at Petrograd Cons. in 1884, and afterwards under him at Dresden in 1893. Also stud. for a short time under Leschetizky in Vienna. Played much in Poland, Germany and Russia. In 1912, prof. of advanced pf. classes, Warsaw State Conservatoire.—ZD. J.

JADASSOHN, Salomon. Ger. compr. and teacher; *b.* Breslau, 13 Aug. 1831; *d.* Leipzig, 1 Feb. 1902. Pupil Leipzig Cons. (1848), of Liszt in Weimar (1849–51), of Hauptmann in Leipzig in compn. specially. Music-teacher in Leipzig; dir. of *Psalterions* Choral Soc. 1866; condr. Euterpe Concerts, 1867–69; appointed teacher in theory, compn. and instrumentation at Cons., 1871; corresponding member R. Acad. Florence, etc. Ph.D. *h.c.* from Leipzig Univ. 1887; R. prof. 1893. J. was a typical academic composer and teacher.

4 symphonies; 2 overtures; 4 serenades; 2 pf. concertos, op. 89; concerted piece for fl. and orch. op. 97; 4 pf. trios; 3 pf. 5tets.; 2 str. 4tets.; preludes and fugues for pf., etc.; for choir and orch.: *Psalm C* (8-v. with contr. solo, op. 60); *Forgiveness* (with s. solo, op. 54); *Promise* (op. 55); *Hymn of Solace* (with organ *ad lib.* op. 65); for male chorus and orch.: *To the Hurricane* (op. 43); *Psalm XLIII* for 8-v. choir; *St. John's Day* for soli, female chorus and pf.; motets; choral songs; pf. pieces, etc.; orch. serenades, op. 35 and 42; pf. serenades, op. 8 and 125; pf. duet, *Ballet-Music*, op. 58; vocal duets, op. 9, 36, 38, 43. Instruction books: *Harmony Instructor* (1883, 23rd ed. 1922, also Eng., Fr., Dutch and Ital. eds.; *Commentary* on same, 1886); *Elementary Course of Harmony* (1895); *Counterpoint* (1884, 6th ed. 1917, Fr: by Jodin 1897, Ital. by Perinello1898,Commentary 1887); *Canon and Fugue* (1884, 3rd ed. 1913); *Forms in Musical Works* (1889, 4th ed. 1910, Ital. by Schinelli 1906, Fr. by Montillet 1900); *Manual of Instrumentation* (1889, 2nd ed. 1907, also in English); *Art of Modulating and of Playing Preludes* (1890, 3rd ed. 1916); *Tone Apperception* (1899); *Science of Musical Form* (1889); *Commentary on the Fugues and Canons contained in J. S. Bach's Art of the Fugue* (1899); *Introduction to Music of Bach's St. Matthew Passion* (1889); *Methodical Manual of Instruction in Musical Theory* (1898); *The Essence of Melody in Musical Art* (1899); *The Figured Bass* (*Instructions for Playing the Continuo*) (1901). Jadassohn's wife Heene (*d.* 31 Dec. 1891) was a teacher of singing.—A. E.

JAHN, Wilhelm. Austrian conductor; *b.* Hof (Moravia), 24 Nov. 1835; *d.* Vienna, 21 April, 1900. Condr. at Agram, Amsterdam, Prague (1857–64); Wiesbaden (till 1881). Chief condr. and dir. of Viennese Court Opera House 1881–97 (succeeded by Mahler). Excellent condr. (especially for Italian and *buffo* operas), fine judge of singing, brilliant scholar and stage-manager. Consult: Wallaschek, *Das Wiener Hofopern-theater*; R. Specht and Paul Stefan, *Wiener Opernbücher.*—P. ST.

JANÁČEK, Leoš (pronounced Leosh Janátcheck). Czechoslovak composer; *b.* Hukvaldy, Moravia, 1854. Taught for a year at the Teachers' School in Brno (Brünn). Studied for a year in Prague, for a short time in Leipzig, and Vienna. On his return, he became conductor of the Philharmonic Society (Filharmonická Beseda) in Brno, 1881–8. Founded and directed the Organ School whilst teaching music (until 1903) at Teachers' School. From 1919 until 1920, directed newly-founded Conservatoire in Brno, where he is also professor of Master-School of Composition.

254

His first pieces are entirely based on folk-lore. He is an ardent collector of Moravian folk-songs, of which he is an enthusiastic interpreter. He maintains that song lives by and in the melody of speaking, and that the whole spirit of the nation is manifested in its speech. He created his music in this way. At this period he was helping F. Bartoš with his folk-song collecting, making pianoforte arrangements (*Kytice lidových písní moravských—A Nosegay of Moravian Popular Songs*). He wrote a book on *The Musical Structure of National Songs* (Czech Academy, 1901) and composed a series of dances in the national manner. Later on, he worked much in musical theory and wrote *On Chords and their Connections* (Fr. A. Urbánek). His chief work, the opera *Její pastorkyňa* (*Her Stepdaughter*; German translation known as *Jenufa*), was written as late as 1902. It is a drama in prose, taken from Moravian country-life by Gabriela Preissová. Like Mussorgsky, Janáček rejects all intellectual elements in musical composition; he uses no polyphony, no thematic construction and development. He is convinced that the melodic and rhythmic line of the living language, with its emotion and all the moods of the person speaking, are the most effective and dramatic factors. Janáček does not cease to collect the "melodies of language" (*nápěvky*), and is entirely inspired by them both melodically and rhythmically. His passion and dramatic touch, penetrating and concise, accomplish amazing effects, especially when the *milieu* of the drama is so near to him as in *Her Stepdaughter* and *Katja*. The former, first given in Brno (1904), had a great success in Prague (1916), then Vienna (1918) and elsewhere. His *Diary of a Vanished Man* (*Zápisník zmizelého*, a cycle of 22 songs for tenor, with female choir behind the stage) also attracted great attention. It was prod. in London (Wigmore Hall) by Mischa-Léon in 1922. In his instrumental works, Janáček's point of view brings about much discord and scatters the musical phrase; but in his vocal and dramatic works, he is the most significant figure amongst the contemporary Czechoslovak composers.

Operas: *Počátek románu* (*The Beginning of a Romance*); *Její pastorkyňa* (*Her Stepdaughter*); *Osud* (*Fate*); *Výlety pana Broučka* (*The Excursions of Mr. Brouček*), based on Svatopluk Čech's satire, in 2 parts: (i) *Mr. Brouček's Excursion to the Moon*, (ii) *Excursion in the XV Century*; *Katja Kabanova*, on the Russian Ostrovsky's book *Burja* (*The Storm*); *Liška bystrouška* (*Quick-eared Foxey*) an animal opera; chorus and orch.: *Amarus*; *Na Soláni Cárták*; *Otčenáš* (*Paternoster*). Chorus: *Seventy Thousand*; *Maryčka Magdónova* (words by Bezrnč). Symph. poem, *Šumařovo dítě* (*The Musician's Child*; prod. Queen's Hall London, 3 May, 1924, under Sir Henry Wood). Song-cycle, *Zápisník zmizelého*. Publ.: Hudební Matice, Prague; Univ. Ed. Vienna; O. Pazdírek, Brno.—V. Št.

JANIEZEK, Julius (pseudonym, Walter Hensel). Ger.-Czechoslovak musician; *b.* Mähr Trüban, 1887. Ph.D. Ed. of old Ger. folk-songs; publ. of sacred and secular collections of folk-music.—E. S.

JANKÓ, Paul. Hungarian pianist; *b.* Tata, 2 June, 1859; *d.* Constantinople, 17 March, 1919. Educated Vienna, Berlin. Inventor of Jankó Keyboard, which consists of 6 rows of keys arr. in terraces (here in the compass of an octave) as follows:

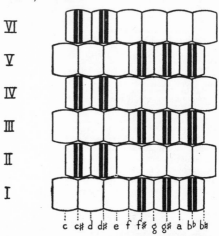

The length and breadth of the surface of a single key is about the same as that of the broad part of a white key on a normal keyboard. The single keys which correspond to one another in rows I, III, V (C, D, E, F♯, G♯, A♯) on the one hand, and in rows II, IV, VI (C♯, D♯, F, G, A, B) on the other, are duplicates; *e.g.* if one presses down key C in row III, the corresponding C's of rows I and V go down also. The Jankó keyboard facilitates considerably the playing of wide intervals (the stretch of an octave is reduced by the extent of a normal key); the relative pitch of the notes is more logically represented than in the normal keyboard; and all scales can be played with the same position of fingers. Unfortunately this invention proved to be impracticable, chiefly because each triple key having three separate positions from which it could be struck, the length of the lever was not uniform, and consequently the force necessary to play the key varied considerably according to the particular row in which that key happened to be. For instance, to produce the same amount of tone, the touch in row I required far less strength than in VI. Mr. J. C. Ames introduced it to England at Portman Rooms, London, in June 1888. See Jankó's pamphlet *Eine neue Claviatur* (Vienna, 1886, Weltzer).—B. B.

JAQUES-DALCROZE, Émile. Composer; *b.* Vienna, 6 July, 1865. Studied at Conservatoire in Geneva and in Vienna under R. Fuchs and A. Bruckner; pupil of Delibes in Paris. Lives in Geneva, where he became professor at Conservatoire in 1892 and where he worked out his famous educational method, the *Gymnastique rythmique*, a system of musical and gymnastic training, now known all over the world. At Hellerau, near Dresden, the first institute for teaching his system was built (1910–14); since then, others in Geneva, Paris and London have been opened. He is also one of most popular Swiss composers and has written, besides his charming and original songs, numerous compositions of great value, interesting especially as regards rhythm and melodic invention.

Festival Vaudois, chorus, soli and orch. (Lausanne, Fœtisch); *Fête de Juin*, chorus, soli and orch. (*id.*); operas: *Sancho* (Paris, Jobert); *Jumeaux de Bergamo* (Paris, Heugel); *Bonhomme Jadis* (*id.*); *Janie* (Leipzig, Siegel); vn. concerto C ml. (Amsterdam, Alsbach); 2nd vn. concerto (Simrock), played by Daisy Kennedy at Queen's Hall, London, under Sir Henry Wood; *Kermesse*, for orch. (Fœtisch); *Poème alpestre*, orch. (Geneva, Chouet & Gaden); str. 4tet (Paris, Enoch); numerous pieces for vn. and pf. (Paris, Rouart; London, Augener); songs, partly coll. in *Chansons populaires romands* (Fœtisch) and *Chansons et Rondes pour enfants* (*id.*).—F. H.

JARECKI, Henryk (*phon.* Yaretski). Compr. condr. *b.* Warsaw, 1846; *d.* Lemberg, 1918. Pupil of Stanisław Moniuszko in Warsaw. Condr. of opera in Lemberg, 1872; worked there till 1900. Composed and produced several operas: *Hedwiga*; *Barbara*; *Mindowe*; *The Father's Return* (after the ballad of Mickiewicz). Many songs and choral works. An excellent orgt., his works are full of national feeling.—ZD. J.

JARECKI, Tadeusz. Polish composer; *b.* Lemberg, 1889. Pupil of his father, Henryk J.; then of Niewiadowski, Jaques-Dalcroze and Tanéief in Moscow. Worked as teacher at Dalcroze Inst. Moscow, 1912–13; went to America; officer in Polish army in France (1918) and on Polish-Russ. front (1919-20); went back to New York and became naturalised Amer. citizen. Is dir. of Chamber Ensemble of New York (Louise Llewellyn-Jarecka and the Del Pulgar Trio). Publ. songs with trio acc.; pf. sonata, op. 19; 3 str. 4tets, op. 12, 16, 21 (op. 16 received 1st prize at Berkshire Fest. U.S.A. 1918, and from Polish Acad. of Science, Cracow, 1923; publ. by Soc. for Publication of Amer. Music); 3 trios, op. 11, 22, 23; orch. preludes and sketches, op. 14, 26. J. belongs to the advanced school of composers and makes free use (3 poems, op. 24) of polytony and polyrhythm.—ZD. J.

JARNACH, Philipp. Compr. *b.* Noisy, France, 26 July, 1892, son of the Catalonian sculptor, E. Jarnach. Educated at Nice and from 1907 received mus. training under Risler (pf.) and Lavignac (harmony) in Paris; but mostly self-taught. Lived in Switzerland from 1914. Teacher Zurich Cons. 1918–21, since then in Berlin.

Songs; pf. pieces; ballad and sonata for pf. and vn.; sonata for vn. alone (Munich, F. Zierfuss); fl. sonata, op. 12; str. 4tet. In ms.: str. 4tet, op. 16; sonatina for cello and pf.; *Winter Scenes*; *Prologue to a Tournament*; *Prelude to Prometheus*; *Sinfonia brevis* in 1 movement, orch. op. 14; *Sinfonietta*, orch. op. 18; Prelude, Prayer and Sacred Dance to *Wandbild* (orch. and female chorus).—A. E.

JÄRNEFELT, Edvard Armas. Finnish compr. condr. *b.* Viipuri (Viborg), 14 Aug. 1869. Stud. in Helsingfors (compn. Wegelius); Berlin (pf. Busoni and Alb. Becker), and Paris (Massenet). Korrepetitor, Stadttheater, Magdeburg, 1896; Düsseldorf, 1897; and orch. condr. Viipuri, 1898–1903. Cond. Helsingfors Opera, 1904. Dir. of Helsingfors Music Inst. 1906–7. Since 1907, condr. of R. Opera, Stockholm; 1911, Hofkapellmästare, Stockholm, where he now lives. One

of the creators of Finnish national music, J. in his works shows a smooth and skilful technique and a lyrical character of Northern colouring.

Orch.: symph. poem, *Korsholm* (1894, Breitkopf); *Heimatklang*, symph. fantasy (1895); 2 suites; 2 overtures (*Lyric* and *Fest.*); *Serenade*; *Präludium* to drama *Det forlovade landet* (*The Promised Land*); Chorus and orch.: *Laulu Vuoksella*; *Suomen synty*; *Abo slott* (*Abo's Castle*); *Betlehems stjärna* (*Star of Bethlehem*); male choruses; songs; pf. pieces.—T. H.

JÄRNEFELT, Liva (*née* Edström). Swedish operatic singer (m.-sopr.); *b.* Vänersborg, 18 March, 1876. Stud. singing at R. Cons. Stockholm from 1894 (under J. Günther); then under Köster and Gillis Bratt; *début* 1897–8, R. Opera, Stockholm; then regularly engaged there. Amongst her parts are Carmen, Azucena (*Trovatore*), Lola (*Cavalleria*), Venus, Ortrud, Magdalena (*Mastersingers*), Brangäne, Erda, Fricka, Isolde. Married Armas Järnefelt, 1910.—P. V.

JÄRNEFELT-PALMGREN, Maikki. Finnish operatic and concert-singer; *b.* Joensuu, 26 Aug. 1871. Stud. in Helsingfors, Paris and Berlin; later in Italy. Since 1895, engagements in opera in Breslau, Berlin (New R. Opera House), Magdeburg and Düsseldorf. Opera tours, Bremen, Vienna, Copenhagen and Stockholm, chiefly in Wagner rôles; 1899, in Bayreuth. Later, concert-tours in Finland and European music-centres. Took part in opera perf. in conjunction with Armas Järnefelt at Helsingfors; 1906, R. Opera, Turin; later at Opera, Rimini. Married (1893) Armas Järnefelt, (1910) Selim Palmgren (*q.v.*). Now living (1923) with her husband in United States.—T. H.

JAVANESE MUSIC. See BRANDTS-BUYS, JOHAN SEBASTIAN.

JAZZ MUSIC. A special kind of nigger dance music of American origin, which lays great stress on distorted rhythms. It is dance music with an exaggerated syncopation.—E.-H.

JEAN-AUBRY, G. Fr. writer on music; *b.* Havre in 1885. Writes works on contemporary music: *La Musique française d'aujourd'hui* (1915), Eng. transl. by E. Evans (Kegan Paul, 1919); *La Musique et les Nations* (1922), Eng. transl. Rosa Newmarch (Chester, 1923). Has lectured in Scandinavia. Present editor of the *Chesterian* (London). Some of his verses have been set to music.—A. C.

JEHIN, Léon. Belgian condr. *b.* Spa, 17 July, 1853. Son of Antoine Jehin, dir. of École de Musique at Spa. Stud. vn. and compn. at Liège and Brussels Cons.; assistant-prof. of harmony, then prof. of orch. class at Brussels Cons. Leader of orch. at La Monnaie Theatre, 1882–4; held same position to Soc. of Artistes Musiciens; 1888, leader of orch. at Opéra, Paris; at Casino, Royan (1889–93); at Covent Garden, London (1891–2); at Aix-les-Bains (1894–1911). Has cond. the theatre orch. at Monte Carlo since 1914. Is naturalised Frenchman. Married singer Mlle. Deschamps (*b.* Lyons, 1857; *d.* 1923; pupil at Lyons Cons.; sang regularly at La Monnaie, Brussels; Opéra and Opéra-Comique, Paris).

Lison, ballet; *Marche jubilaire*; *Scherzetto symphonique*, etc.—E. C.

JELMOLI, Hans. Swiss pianist, compr. *b.* Zurich, 17 Jan. 1877. Stud. at Cons. in Frankfort, under Ivan Knorr, B. Scholz and E. Humperdinck (compn.) and E. Engesser (pf.). Became opera-condr. at Mayence and Würzburg. Now lives in Zurich, where he teaches compn. and is known as an excellent pianist. His works, in the Brahms style, show a great depth of expression; he rose to fame especially with his Swiss folk-songs *Canti Ticinesi,* for solo v. or for unacc. chorus; mus. critic of *Zürcher Post* and *Schweizer Musikzeitung.*

Operas: *Sein Vermächtnis,* lyrical comedy; *Prinz Goldhaar und die Gänsehirtin,* fairy - play; *Die Schweizer* (Konrad Falke); incidental music to *Marignano* (C. Wiegand) and to *Am Lebensquell* (Bühler); mus. comedies: *Die Badenerfahrt; Das Gespenst auf dem Petersturm* (Aarau, Sauerländer); cantata, *Aus des Knaben Wunderhorn,* for t., chorus and orch.; pf. pieces, unacc. choruses (Leipzig, Hug; Geneva, Henn) and songs (Hug; Hüni, Zurich). Has written *Studien und Landschaften* (Zurich, Schulthess). Consult biography by Franz Curti (Schulthess).—F. H.

JEMNITZ, Alexander. Hungarian compr. *b.* Budapest, 9 Aug. 1890. Stud. at R. High School for Music, Budapest (under H. Koessler) and then in Leipzig (under Reger and Straube). Korrepetitor at Bremen Opera; condr. Czernowitz Municipal Theatre; then lived in Berlin, and now in Budapest.

Prelude, passacaglia and fugue for organ, op. 1; songs, op. 2, 6, 15; pf. Bagatelles, op. 5; pf. sonata, op. 8; 2 sonatas, vn. and pf. op. 10; sonata, vn. alone, op. 18; sonata, cello and pf. op. 17; chamber and orch. songs; male and female choruses; an organ 4tet; str. 4tet; str. trio; a fl. and an ob. trio; orch. works (Wunderhorn Verlag).—B. B.

JENSEN, Adolf. Ger. compr. *b.* Königsberg Prussia), 12 Jan. 1837; *d.* Baden-Baden, 23 Jan. 1879. Mainly self-taught; had only 2 years' instruction from Ehlert, Marpurg and Liszt. Music-teacher in Russia, 1856; condr. Stadttheater Posen, 1857; went to Gade, Copenhagen, 1858, returning to Königsberg, 1860; teacher at Tausig's School for advanced pf. playing in Berlin, 1866. To Dresden in 1868; then Graz (1870); spent last years of his life in Baden-Baden. A sensitive compr. of songs and pf. pieces with a somewhat feminine strain.

6 songs, op. 1; 7 songs, op. 11; *Dolorosa* (Chamisso's *Thränen*), op. 30; *Gaudeamus* (12 songs by Scheffel), op. 40; 2 books of songs from the *Spanish Song Book* of Geibel and Heyse (op. 4 and 21); *Romances and Ballads* (Hamerling), op. 41, etc.; choral pieces, op. 28, 29; 2 choral pieces with 2 horns and harp (or pf.), op. 10; pf. pieces: *Inward Voices* (op. 2); *Roving Sketches* (op. 17); *Idylls* (op. 43); *Erotikon* (op. 44); *Wedding-Music* (op. 45, pf. duet); sonata, F sharp mi. (op. 25); *German Suite* (op. 8); studies (op. 32); phantasies, dances, romances, nocturnes, etc. Larger works: *Jephtha's Daughter* for soli, chorus, and orch., and *The Disciples' Journey to Emmaus,* chorus and orch.; an opera, *Turandot* (arr. by W. Kienzl). Consult Niggli, *A. J.* (Zurich, 1895), and same author's biography of J. in Reimann's *Celebrated Musicians* (1900). P. Kuczinski publ. some of J.'s letters (1879).—A. E.

JEREMIÁŠ, Bohuslav. Czechoslovak compr. *b.* Restoky, 1859; *d.* Budějovice, 1918. Attended Organ School; from 1887–1906, choirmaster; later, condr. of choral society *Gregora* and dir. of music-school in Písek. Dir. of music-school in Budějovice from 1906 to his death. Chiefly choral compositions (Urbánek).—V. St.

JEREMIÁŠ, Jaroslav. Czechoslovak compr.

b. Písek (Bohemia), 1889; *d.* Budějovice (Bohemia), 1919. Son of Bohuslav J. Stud. at Prague Cons. (Stecker); later under Vít. Novák. Condr. at Lublanjá (Jugoslavia); teacher at Budějovice and Prague; likewise active as pianist. His fragmentary work is proof of a great inventive talent and high artistic conception. His style is based on the Smetana tradition, and is hardly touched by the new tendencies.

Symph. idyll, *Letní den (A Summer Day); Jarní romance (A Spring Romance);* sonata for vla.; opera, *Starý král (The Old King);* mystery-play, *Rimoni;* a number of songs, some with orch.; oratorio, *Jan Hus.* (Publ. Hudební Matice.)—V. St.

JEREMIÁŠ, Otakar. Czech compr. (son of Bohuslav J.); *b.* Písek, 1892. Pupil of Prague Cóns. and of Vít. Novák. Dir. of Music School at Budějovice. His music has a natural freshness, serious thought and a deliberate avoidance of modern tendencies, going back to tradition of Smetana.

2 symphonies; *Spring,* overture; *Phantasy,* orch. and chorus; pf. 4tet; str. 5tet; song-cycle, *Love,* with orch.; male chorus, *The Wolf's Track* (all Czech; ms.).—V. St.

JERITZA, Marie. Austrian opera-singer; *b.* Brünn. Roused public attention at Vienna Volksoper by her uncommon singing; since 1913 at Hofoper; 1921, in America. Her s. voice of high dramatic powers and great beauty, supported by recklessly passionate acting, best fits the " adventuresses " amongst the female opera characters: Carmen, Tosca, Violanta, the Dancer (in *Die tote Stadt*). She is also a brilliant performer of Santuzza, Elsa (*Lohengrin*), Ariadne.

Autobiography, *Sunlight and Song* (Appleton, 1924). Consult Wymetal, *M. J.,* in coll. *Die Wiedergabe,* Vienna, 1922.—P. St.

JERVIS-READ, Harold Vincent. Eng. compr. *b.* Powyke, Worcs, 14 March, 1883.

Prelude, *Variations and Coda,* vn. cello, orch. (ms.); *The Hound of Heaven,* t. boys' vs. chorus, orch. organ (Weekes, 1923); *Dream Tryst,* chorus and small orch. (rev. ed. 1922, Ashdown); *That Land (id.); To the Daughter of Earth (id.); High Tide,* contr. solo, chorus and orch. (Rogers); pf. pieces and songs (Elkin; Murdoch; Rogers; Weekes).—E.-H.

JILAIEF, Nicolas Sergevitch (accent on the *A*). Russ. writer on music; *b.* 18 Nov (n.s.), 1881. Pupil of S. I. Tanéief and Ippolitof-Ivanof at Moscow Cons. (1904). Teacher of comprs. of younger generation—Stanchinsky, Alexandrof, Feinberg. Member of Russ. Acad. of Art-Sciences and of State Inst. of Mus. Science. Has written many essays.—V. B.

JIMÉNEZ, Jerónimo. Span. compr. *b.* Cadiz; *d.* Madrid, 1923. Stud. comp. at Paris Cons. Afterwards condr. for a time of Sociedad de Conciertos (now Orquesta Filarmónica), Madrid. His production consisted chiefly of mus. comedies, of which he wrote a great number. Fragments from them are sometimes played at symph. concerts, with unfailing success, owing to their popularity. The most characteristic works of the compr.'s graceful style are *El Baile de Luis Alonso* and its sequel *La Boda de Luis Alonso.* —P. G. M.

JINDŘICH, Jindřich. Czechoslovak compr. *b.* Klenč, 1876. Compn. pupil of Vít. Novák.

is a schoolmaster in Domažlice (Bohemia). Mostly vocal compn. under influence of Vít. Novák, with a touch of sentimentality.

Song-cycles: *Love Dreams, Spring, In Memoriam Jaroslav Vrchlický, Heyduk's Songs, Sova's Songs*; many choruses (Fr. A. Urbánek; Mojmír Urbánek). —V. ST.

JIRÁK, K. Boleslav. Czechoslovak compr. *b.* Prague, 1891. Stud. compn. at Univ. under Novák and J. B. Foerster; 1915-8, condr. at Hamburg Opera; later, in Brno and Ostrava (Moravia); 1920-1, condr. of *Hlahol* Choir, Prague, with which he made a successful tour in Jugoslavia. From 1920, prof. of compn. at Prague Cons. Occasional guest-condr. of Czech Philh. Orch. The development of his work began with a conscious traditionalism. His music is characterised by a well-sounding polyphony, is closely built, occasionally rather bitter in feeling, but more often strong, energetic. By the extent and value of his best works he ranks as one of the most important of the younger generation.

Opera *Apollonius of Tyana*; 2 symphonies; overture to a Shakespeare comedy; *Psalm XXIII*, chorus and orch.; str. 6tet; str. 4tct; sonatas for cello and vn.; 2 pf. suites and other pf. pieces. Song-cycles: *Tragikomedie; Meditace (Meditations); Mijivé stešti (Short-lived Happiness); Tři zpěvy domova (3 Songs of Home); Večer a duše (Evening and the Soul).*—V. ST.

JIRÁNEK, Josef. Czech pianist; *b.* Ledeč, 1855. Pupil of Smetana, 1866-73, and at Prague Organ School; pf. prof. at Charkof (Russia), 1877-91; since then prof. at Prague Conservatoire.

Orch.: *Ballade, Scherzo fantastique*. Pf. 5tet. Instructive: *Double Scales: School of Chord-playing; New Scale Manual*; studies, etc. Publ.: Univ. Ed., Vienna; Bosworth, London.—V. ST.

JOACHIM, Joseph. Hungarian violinist and compr. *b.* Kittsee, near Pressburg, 28 June, 1831; *d.* Berlin, 15 Aug. 1907. Pupil of Serwaczinski, of I. Böhm, 1838; Vienna Cons. and in Leipzig from 1843. Appeared in London (on recommendation of Mendelssohn) 1844, as he did 1847-9, and often afterwards. In 1849 he took up the position of Konzertmeister at Weimar and was long an intimate of the Liszt circle. In 1853 he gave up this position to take over that of R. Konzertmeister in Hanover (1859, concert dir.). There he married in 1863 the contr. concert-singer Amalie Weiss (real name Schneeweiss; *b.* Marburg, Styria, 10 May, 1839; *d.* Berlin. 3 Feb. 1898. Divorced 1884; later teacher of singing at Klindworth-Scharwenka Cons.). Soon after 1866 moved to Berlin, where J. was placed in charge of the newly formed High School for Music in 1868, an institution which grew to ever greater dimensions from year to year. The organisation of this institute was altered later and J. became chairman of the board of directors and head of orch. instr. department. Appointed R. prof. and condr., member of the senate of the R. Acad. of Arts, of which he became later on the vice-president. He was a Dr. *h.c.* of the Univs. of Cambridge, Glasgow, Oxford and Göttingen. Afterwards only came into public notice as leader of his celebrated quartet (de Ahna [Kruse, 1897

Halir], Wirth, Hausmann). For many years J. was the attraction of every London Season, not only at the Crystal Palace Concerts but also at those of the Philh. Soc. and at the Saturday and Monday Popular Concerts.

3 vn. concertos: op. 3, G mi. (Breitkopf), op. 11, *In the Hungarian Style (id.)*, and G ma. (1889, Bote & Bock); Variations for vn. and orch.; *Andantino and Allegro* with orch. op. 1; 6 pieces with pf., op. 2 and 5; *Notturno* for vn. and orch. op. 12; *Hebrew Melodies* for vla. and pf. op 9; Variations on orig. theme for same, op. 10; overtures: *Hamlet, Demetrius, To the Memory of Kleist*, to a *Comedy of Gozzi*; 2 orch. marches; *The Marfa Scene* (Schiller's *Demetrius*) for contr. solo and orch. A. Moser publ. J.'s correspondence with Brahms (1908, Deutsche Brahmsgesellschaft), and, in collab. with Johannes Joachim, *Letters to and from J.* (3 vols. Berlin, 1911-13, Bard Marquardt). Consult: Andreas Moser, *J. J.* (1898, enlarged to 2 vols. 1907-10, also in English by L. Durham, 1900); Olga Plaschke, *Amalie J.* (1889); Fuller-Maitland, *On J. J.* (1906); L. Brieger-Wasservogel, *Short Memoir of J. J.* (1907); A. Kohut, *J. J.* (1891).—A. E.

JOHANNESSEN, Karl. Norwegian violinist. *b.* Sarpsborg, 11 April, 1869; *d.* Ledbury (Worcs.), 5 Dec. 1904. When only 11, was engaged as violinist at Opera House, Stockholm; later made successful concert-tours in Germany and Scandinavia; condr. of concerts in Bergen. On Joachim's recommendation, appointed prof. at Cons. in Leicester, England, where he won for himself a distinguished position, amongst other things, as leader of a str. quartet.—J. A.

JOHANSEN, David Monrad. Norwegian compr. *b.* Vefsen, Nordland, 8 Nov. 1888. Pupil of Karl Nissen (pf.), and of Catharinus Elling (harmony); continued his studies at High School in Berlin (Robert Kahn and E. Humperdinck). First independent concert as pianist, 30 Jan. 1910; 15 Feb. 1915, concert of his own compns. Concert-tours in Norway; took part in Northern Mus. Fest. at Helsingfors in 1921. Ed. of *Norsk Musikerblad*, 1918-19; critic on *Norske Intelligentsedler*, 1916-18. J. is one of most talented of younger Norwegian comprs.; has thoroughly stud. not only classical music but also the various phases of modern music. He aims at developing the typically national music on basis of modern harmony, rhythm and treatment of melody. His imaginative adaptation of Norwegian folk-melody in his lyric works gives them a charming poetic freshness and wealth of colour.

Sonata, vn. and pf.; 13 songs (some of them to words from old Norwegian folk-poems); 17 pf. pieces (Suite No. I, *Two Portraits from the Middle Ages*, op. 8; Suite No. II, *From Gudbrandsdalen*, etc.) (Copenhagen, Hansen); *Draumkvœdet (The Dream-Song)*, for male chorus; Suite for orch.; adaptation of Fr. troubadour-songs with harp and fl. acc.—J. A.

JOHNSON, Basil. Eng. orgt. *b.* Oxford, 5 April, 1861. Acad. clerkship in Magdalen choir, Oxford; stud. R.C.M. London, under Sir Walter Parratt (organ), Sir Charles Stanford (compn.); mus. dir. Rugby School, 1886-1914; precentor and orgt. Eton Coll. from 1914.—E.-H.

JOHNSTONE, J. Alfred. British writer on music; *b.* Co. Cork, Ireland, 1861. Educated Dublin Univ.; went to Australia in 1882; settled in Melbourne as pf. teacher; author of a series of educational works on music.

The Art of Expression in Pf. Playing (Weekes);

Rubato, or the Secret of Mus. Expression (Ashdown); *Hints on the Interpretation of Beethoven's Pf. Sonatas* (Allan, Melbourne); *The Metronome and Bach* (J. Williams); *Art of Teaching Pf. Playing* (W. Reeves); *Phrasing in Pf. Playing* (Ashdown); *How to use the Pedal* (*id.*); *Muscular Relaxation, Weight Touch, and Rotary Movement* (Allan, Melbourne); *The Beginner's Harmony* (J. Williams); *Octave and Wrist Technique* (Ashdown); etc.—E.-H.

JONAS, Alberto. Amer. pianist; *b.* Madrid, 8 June, 1868. Stud. under Olave and Mendizabel and at Madrid Cons.; under Gevaert and De Greef at Brussels Cons., winning 1st prize in pf.-playing in 1888; and under Rubinstein in Petrograd in 1890. *Début* in Brussels, 1880, and toured extensively in Europe, England, U.S.A., Canada, and Central America. 1894-8, head of pf. department at music-school of Univ. of Michigan; 1898-1904, dir. of Michigan Cons. of Music, Detroit, Mich. Thereafter for 10 years a successful teacher in Berlin. Since 1914, teacher in New York.

Pf. pieces (Schirmer; Ditson; Wagner & Levien, Mexico City); *Pianoscript Book* (Presser, 1918); *Master School of Modern Piano-Playing and Virtuosity* (Fischer, 1922); a transl. of Gevaert's *Treatise on Instrumentation* into Spanish (1903).—J. M.

JONES, Dilys. Operatic and oratorio singer of Welsh parentage. *Début* in *Elijah*, Royal Choral Soc. London, 1908; in grand opera, Covent Garden, 1911 (minor rôles in *Ring*); and leading fests. Appeared in *King Henry IV* (His Majesty's Theatre) 1914. Specialises in Bach's works (*St. Matthew Passion*, Westminster Abbey, 1913, etc).—E.-H.

JONES, Evlyn Howard. Eng. pianist; *b.* London, 1877. Stud. R.C.M. and later in Germany under Jedliczka and d'Albert; chiefly known as a Brahms and Bach player. Took a leading part in establishing the Federation of Music Clubs in London. Prof. pf. R.C.M.—E.-H.

JONES, Sidney. Eng. compr. and condr. *b.* Leeds, 1869. Comp. chiefly light operas and burlesques; cond. at various theatres (Gaiety, Empire, Prince of Wales's, Whitney, etc.).

A Gaiety Girl; *The Geisha*; *My Lady Molly*; *Persian Princess*.—E.-H.

JONGEN, Joseph. Belgian composer; *b.* Liège, 14 December, 1873. Studied at Liège Conservatoire. As early as 1893, the Royal Academy of Belgium awarded him a prize of 1000 francs for his first attempt at chamber-music, a string quartet. He competed twice for *Prix de Rome*; won the first prize in 1897 for his cantata *Comala*. About the same time he received a further prize from the Academy of Belgium for a piano trio. Assistant-prof. of counterpoint class, Liège Cons. 1891-8. After obtaining his *Prix de Rome*, he travelled in Germany, France and Italy. During this time he composed his symphony and his quartet for piano and strings, performed for the first time at the Société Nationale, in Paris, 1903. Having returned to his own country, he was promoted to the rank of professor of harmony at Liège Conservatoire. On the invasion of Belgium by the Germans, he and his family sought refuge in England, where he remained for the duration of the war (1914-18). Returning to Belgium in January 1919, he was appointed

teacher of counterpoint and fugue at Brussels Conservatoire (Oct. 1920).

With Guillaume Lekeu and Victor Vreuls, Jongen represents, in most characteristic and brilliant fashion, the generation of Belgian artists born about 1870 and nourished on the ideas of César Franck. From the time of his first works, more especially the pianoforte quartet, he showed himself a thorough musician, in whom an admirable technique is coupled with a sensibility as delicate as generous. All his subsequent evolution tends in the direction of a growing refinement. He is, indeed, influenced by the innovations of Debussy, more especially as regards orchestration, whose lightness and transparency he accepts with whole-hearted joy; but he never falls into that servile imitation, which transforms the most spontaneous intuitions into "mannerisms." Even when he yields himself to impressionism, he never loses sight of the exigencies of musical construction nor forgets that he is always a fervent disciple of chamber-music. From the purely expressive point of view, he soars, in most of his work (especially in slow movements), in an atmosphere of nostalgic reverie or cheerful well-being, in full accord with his own character and with the idealism of his native soil.

Orch.: Symphony (Concerts Ysaye, Brussels, 1900); *Fantaisie sur deux Noëls wallons*, op. 24 (Durand); *Lallah-Rookh*, op. 28 (Chester); *Impressions d'Ardenne*, op. 44 (Chester); *Pages intimes*, op. 55 (Chester); *Tableaux pittoresques*, op. 56 (Chester). Chamber-music: 1st str. 4tet, C mi. (Eulenburg); pf. trio; pf. 4tet, op. 23 (Durand); 1st vn. sonata, op. 27 (Schott); trio, pf. vn. and vla. op. 30 (Durand); 2nd vn. sonata, op. 34 (Durand); cello sonata, op. 39 (Durand); 2nd str. 4tet, A, op. 50 (Chester); 2 serenades, str. 4tet, op. 61 (*id.*); 3rd str. 4tet (ms.); cello concerto, op. 18 (Durand); 1st *Poème*, cello and orch.; 2nd *Poème*, cello and orch. op. 46 (Chester). Pf. pieces: *Le Crépuscule au lac Ogwen*, op. 52 (Chester); *Suite en forme de Sonate*, op. 60 (*id.*); a dozen songs (Brussels, *Art Belge*).—C. V. B.

JONGEN, Léon. Belgian compr. *b.* Liège, 2 March, 1884. Younger brother of Joseph (*q.v.*) from whom he received his first lessons in music. Stud. at Liège Cons.; 2nd *Prix de Rome*, 1907, for cantata, *Geneviève de Brabant*; again 2nd prize, 1909, for *La Légende de St. Hubert*. Finally, after a period of waiting, during which he settled in Paris, gained 1st prize, 1913, for *Les Fiancés de Noël*. During the war (1914-18), served in Belgian army. Since then has devoted himself preferably to dramatic composition. In contrast to his brother Joseph, Léon has an essentially dramatic temperament. His cantatas for *Prix de Rome* already showed a nature fitted for movement, colour, and active emotion. His supreme mastery and high inspiration entitle him to be ranked among the best Belgian composers.

L'Ardennaise, 2-act opera; *Le Rêve d'une Nuit de Noël*, a musical adaptation of war-drama by J. Fonson (Théâtre des Champs-Élysées, Paris, March 1918); *Thomas l'Agnelet*, 4-act opera (with Claude Farrère); many pf. pieces, songs, str. 4tet.—C. V. B.

JONSON, George C. Ashton. Eng. lecturer on mus. appreciation; *b.* London, 22 July, 1861. For 30 years, a member of London Stock Exchange; first appeared as lecturer in 1893, and has since lectured in Gt. Britain and America. Author of handbook on Chopin's works (Heinemann, 1895).—E.-H.

JONSSON, Josef Petrus. Swedish compr. *b.* Enköping, 21 June, 1887. Self-taught; lives in Norrköping as teacher and music critic.
Orch.: Suite, op. 9 (1914–15); concert overture, op. 12 (1916–17); symphony, *Nordland*, op. 23 (1919–22); symph. poem, *Korallrevet*, barit. chorus and orch. (1915–16); Stockholm, 1918; publ. Musik. Konstföreningen). Cantata, male vs. and organ (1919); *Ballade*, barit. and orch. (1919); cantata (1920); *The Dream and Life*, barit. and orch. (1921); pf. 5tet; songs; pf. pieces.—P. V.

JORDAN, Albert D. Canadian orgt. and condr. *b.* Seaforth, Ontario, 28 July, 1877. Stud. under Dr. F. H. Torrington in Toronto. 1896–1903, orgt. Brant Avenue Methodist Ch. Brantford, Ontario. In 1903, went to live in London, Ontario, where he now resides. Is condr. of Mus. Art Soc. Choir and Orch.; founded London Inst. of Mus. Art (see ACADEMIES); also condr. of Schubert Choir, Brantford, Ontario.—L. S.

JORDAN, Arthur. Eng. t. singer; *b.* Dudley, Worcs, 6 July, 1886. At first, a barit. singer; stud. under Rutland Boughton. One of the founders of Glastonbury School (*q.v.*); first appeared there; stud. Wagnerian t. rôles under Hermann Grünebaum. Sang *Siegfried* at Covent Garden (B.N.O.C. 1922); in *Mastersingers*, 1922–1923, and *Twilight of the Gods*, 1923.—E.-H.

JORDAN, E. B. R. Australian orgt.: *b.* Brisbane, 1885. From 1897–1917 orgt. of St. Paul's, East Brisbane: then of City Tabernacle, and Ann St. Presbyterian Ch.: 1911, condr. of Brisbane Operatic Soc.: 1913, condr. of Austral Choir: 1913, accompanied John McCormack on his Australian tour.—G. Y.

JORDAN, Jan. Pseudonym of Jan Drozdowzki (*q.v.*).

JORDAN, Sverre. Norwegian compr. pianist; *b.* Bergen, 25 May, 1889. Stud. 1907–14 in Berlin under W. Klatte, da Motta, Govtatowski and Conrad Ansorge. Lives in Bergen. Choral condr. for mus. soc. *Harmonien*; mus. critic on journal *Morgenavisen*. His works include pf. pieces; vn. pieces; vn. sonata; orch. suite *Norwegiana*; melodrama, *Feberdigte* (*Fever Poems*), to poem-cycle by Knut Hamsun; incidental music to Björnson's play *Halte-Hulda*; 60 songs. These latter have attained a wide circulation in Scandinavia, to some extent also in Germany, where his orch. suite has been perf. with success in Berlin and other cities. Besides Bergen and Christiania, *Feberdigte* has been produced in Finland, with declamation by compr.'s wife, the talented actress Magda Blanc. J. combines a bright and pure vein of melody with richly coloured instrumentation. The influence of Grieg is evident, but he reveals a quite individual inspiration.—R. M.

JOSEFFY, Rafael. Amer. pianist; *b.* Hunfalu, Hungary, 3 July, 1852; *d.* New York, 25 June, 1915. Son of a Jewish rabbi; pupil of Brauer at Budapest, of Wenzel and Moscheles at Leipzig Cons. (1866–8), of Karl Tausig in Berlin (1868–1870), and in 1870–1 of Liszt in Weimar. After his *début* in Berlin, 21 Nov. 1871, with Chopin's E mi. and Liszt's E flat concertos, he was hailed as Tausig's successor. First appearance in America, playing the same concertos with an orch. under Leopold Damrosch in Chickering Hall, New York, 13 Oct. 1879. Settled in New York as concert-pianist and teacher. His astounding technique and broad catholicity of taste brought him an unusually large number of engagements. Made a speciality of Chopin, but was also one of 1st exponents of Brahms in America. Had almost completed an ed. of Chopin's pf. works for publ. house of Schirmer when he died. As a teacher also, J. was in great demand. From 1888 to 1906 was prof. of pf. at National Cons. in New York. He exercised a far-reaching influence on the present generation of American pianists.
School of Advanced Piano Playing (Schirmer, 1902; Ger. transl. publ. Hofmeister). Many early pf. pieces. Besides his Chopin, he ed. pf. studies by Czerny, Henselt, Moscheles, Schumann, etc. Consult Edwin Hughes, *Rafael Joseffy's Contribution to Piano Technic*, in *The Musical Quarterly*, July, 1916.—O. K.

JOTEYKO, Tadeusz. Polish compr. *b.* in Ukraine, 1872. Stud. under Noskowski in Warsaw and Gevaert in Brussels. In 1895, publ. his 1st symphony (played in Berlin and Warsaw). Now lives in Warsaw.
Operas: *Grajek* (*The Player*), perf. Warsaw, 1919; *Sigismund Augustus* and *Fishermen*, unperf.; cantata, *Widziadto* (*The Phantom*); concert overture; str. 4tet; pf. pieces. Has also written some theoretical works.—ZD. J.

JOUHI-KANTELE. See KANTELE.

JOURET, Léon. Belgian compr. *b.* Ath, 17 Oct. 1828; *d.* Brussels, 6 June, 1905. Brother of Théodore Jouret. Started as chorister and orgt. in native town. Entered Brussels Cons. 1840, making a name as compr. of songs, male choruses, church music, and 2 comic operas, *Quentin Metsys* and *Le Tricorne Enchanté* (*Magic Three-cornered Hat*), Brussels, 1865, 1868; 1873, prof. of part-singing at Brussels Cons. Ed. a coll. *Chants populaires du pays d'Ath*, the authenticity of which appears doubtful.—E. C.

JOURET, Théodore. Belgian compr. mus. critic; *b.* Ath, 11 Sept. 1821; *d.* Bad Kissingen, 16 July, 1887. Prof. of chemistry, Brussels Military School. Comp. songs, male choruses, and a comic opera, *Le Médecin turc* (1845), collaborating with Meynne, then turned to mus. criticism (*Guide Musical, Revue Trimestrielle*.)—E. C.

JOURNALS, Musical. See PERIODICALS.

JUARRANZ LÓPEZ, Eduardo. Span. compr. *b.* Madrid, 1844; *d.* 1897. Stud. compn. under Arrieta at R. Cons. de Música, Madrid. Music dir. of 3rd Regiment of R. Engineers from 1876–1896, when he was appointed, after competition, condr. of Banda del Real Cuerpo de Alabarderos (see ALABARDEROS). Under his dir., the R. Engineer's band won the 1st prize at international competition in Paris, against some of most famous military bands in Europe. As a compr. he produced some religious music; but is best known, both in Spain and abroad, for his numerous works for military band, and as the creator of the typical Span. marches, based on melodies of Andalusian character, called *pasodobles*. Of these *La Giralda*, popular all over the world, stands as model. (Unión Musical Española, Madrid.)—P. G. M.

JUHÁSZ, Aladár. Hungarian pianist; *b.* Budapest. 1856; *d.* there in 1918. Pupil of Liszt.—B. B.

JULLIEN, Adolphe. Fr. musicologist; *b.* Paris, 1 June, 1845. Representative of old school of mus. criticism, author of vivid and picturesque works on the music of the XVIII century. One of his chief merits is his recognition of Berlioz and Wagner and his having prepared the way for them. Among his innumerable works one may cite: *Hector Berlioz* (1882); *Richard Wagner, sa vie et ses œuvres* (1886); *Musiciens d'aujourd'hui*, 2 vols. (1891–4); *Weber à Paris en 1826*; *La musique et les philosophes du XVIIIe siècle* (1873); *L'Opéra secret au XVIIIe siècle* (1880); *Paris dilettante au commencement du siècle* (1884). Critic of *Journal des Débats*.—A. C.

JÜNGST, Hugo R. Ger. compr. *b.* Dresden, 26 Feb. 1853. Stud. Dresden Cons. (Rietz), 1871–7. Founded Dresden Men's Choral Soc., which he cond. till 1904. Also cond. Julius-Otto-Bund from 1878. Dir. *Erato* Academical Choral Soc., 1895; mus. dir. and prof.; condr. Ger. choral soc. festivals, Dresden 1895, Weimar 1906, and others.

Choral works, male and mixed choirs; choral cycles; pf. and orch. works. Ed. of a coll. of national songs of foreign countries arr. for chorus (op. 87, about 80 numbers).—A. E.

JUON, Paul. Russ. compr. *b.* Moscow, 8 March, 1872. Stud. vn. playing under Johann Hrimaly and compn. under Tanéief and Arensky in Moscow, 1894 under Bargiel in Berlin. Theory instructor Baku Cons. (on Caspian Sea); returned to Berlin 1897, and has since lived there as teacher of compn. at R. High School of Music since 1906. Member of Berlin Acad. since March 1919.

3 str. 4tets (op. 5, D; op. 29, A mi.; op. 67, C); vn. sonatas (op. 7, A; op. 69, F); vla. sonata, op. 15, D; cello sonata, op. 54, A mi.; pf. trios (op. 17, A mi.; op. 60, G); *Trio Caprice*, A mi. op. 39; *Lisaniæ*, pf. trio, op. 70; *Trio Miniaturen*, op. 18, op. 24; *Silhouettes*, 2 vns. and pf. op. 9; *Divertimento* for clar. and 2 vlas. op. 34; *Rhapsody*, str. trio and pf. op. 37; pf. 6tet, C mi. op. 22; 8tet, op. 27 (pf. vn. cello, vla. ob. clar. horn and bsn.); also as 7tet (pf. and str. 6tet); pf. 5tet, op 33; pf. 4tet, op 50; 5 pieces for str. orch. op. 16; str. 5tet, op. 31; vn. concertos, B mi. op. 42 and A ma. op. 49: orch. phantasy, *Wächterweise*, on Danish folk-songs, op. 31; orch. serenade, op. 40; orch. suite, *Aus einem Tagebuch*, op. 35; 2 symph. ballet suites from the dance-poem. *Psyche*; pf. pieces (op. 1, 9, 12, 14, 18, 20, 26, 30, 41 65, 74); songs, op. 21. Publ.: *Practical Harmony Manual* (1901); *Handbook on Harmony* (1920); and Ger. transls. of Modeste Tchaikovsky's biography of his brother (2 vols. 1904).—A. E.

JÜRGENS, Fritz. Ger. compr. *b.* Düsseldorf, 22 April, 1888; killed in action in Champagne, 25 Sept. 1915. Educated Düsseldorf, went to Hamburg to enter business but soon turned to mus. studies, mostly self-taught. His meeting with Gustav Falke, the poet, was of decisive importance. He was a promising compr. and set 45 songs of Falke, and 36 of Martin Greif to music (Schott).—A. E.

K

KAÀN DE ALBÉST, Jindřich. Czechoslovak compr. *b.* Tarnopol, Galicia, Poland, 1852; son of an Austrian officer; pupil of V. Blodek and Skuherský at Organ School in Prague. Well known as a pianist; 1876–84, private tutor in an aristocratic family; 1889, prof. of pf. at Prague Cons. From 1907–18 he was dir. of it, leading it along conservative lines. After the revolution he was obliged to leave the school, which was conducted from this time in a new modern spirit. His compns., in which he very often uses his experience as a pianist, are derivative and eclectic.

Sakuntala; Eclogues of Spring for orch.; pf. trio (prize of Mus. Soc. in Lyon); 3 vn. sonatas; organ sonata; 3 pf. concertos; many studies; melodrama, *Toman and the Fairy*; concert transcriptions from Smetana's works; operas: *On the Flight; Germinal* (1902); ballets: *Bajaja* (1888); *Olim* (1902). Publ. mostly by Fr. A. Urbánek, Prague.—V. ST.

KABOS, Ilona (Zsigmondi). Hungarian pianist, *b.* Budapest, 7 Dec. 1893.—B. B.

KAČANAUSKAS, A. See LITHUANIAN MUSIC.

KACSÓH, Pongrácz. Hungarian compr. *b.* Budapest, 15 Dec. 1873. Songs, choral and pedagogic works. His operetta *János vitéz* (*Knight John*) has been given over 500 times in Budapest.—B. B.

KAEHLER, Willibald. Ger. compr. *b.* Berlin, 2 Jan. 1866. Pupil Berlin High School for Music (Kiel, Herzogenberg, Gustav Engel); condr. Hanover, Freiburg-i-B., Basle, Regensburg, Rostock; successor to Rezniček in Mannheim. Court Orch. condr. Schwerin; prof. 1911. Was also assist condr. at Bayreuth fest. 1896–1901.

Songs; male choruses; pf. works; *Elegy* for vn. and orch; symph. prologue to Kleist's *Prince of Homburg* (1910); music to Goethe's *Faust*.—A. E.

KAEMPFERT, Max. Ger. condr. *b.* Berlin, 3 Jan. 1871. Trained in Paris and Munich, where he was Konzertmeister and occasional condr. of the Kaim Orch.; condr. Eisenach 1898; Frankfort Palmengarten 1899; R. mus. dir. 1912.

Folk-opera, *The Sultan's Treasure*; 3 orch. rhapsodies; sonatas; trios; 4tets; songs; light orch. pieces. His wife, Anna, is a s. oratorio singer (*b.* Stuttgart, 25 May, 1877).—A. E.

KAHN, Esther. Compr. *b.* London; now lives in Kensington, N.S.W., Australia. Comp. a piece called *Illuminations*, a Fantasy in Polychrome, especially for A. B. Heeld's new colour-instrument.

Pf. pieces (many publ. Paling & Co.); sonata, vn. pf.; over 50 songs (Paling & Co.; Nicholson, Sydney; Beale, London). Many are set to words by Wrenn Sutton.—E.-H.

KAHN, Robert. Ger. compr. *b.* Mannheim, 21 July, 1865. Pupil of Vincenz Lachner, Mannheim; Kiel, Berlin (1882); and Rheinberger, in Munich (1885); in Vienna with Brahms, then to Berlin. Condr. of Ladies' Choral Soc. in Leipzig,

1890–3. Teacher of compn. at Berlin High School of Music from 1897. R. prof. 1903.

Str. 4tets, A ma. op. 8, A mi. op. 60; pf. 5tet, C mi. op. 54; 3 pf. 5tets, op. 14, 30, 41; trios, op. 19, 33, 35, 72; clar. trio, G mi. op. 45; *Serenade*, pf. ob. horn, op. 73; 3 vn. sonatas, op. 5, 26, 50; vn and pf. suite, op. 69; pf. pieces, op. 67; 2 cello sonatas, op. 37, 56; concerted piece for pf. and orch.; *Mahomet's Chant*, op. 24, for chorus and orch.; *Storm Song* (for same); songs (op. 2, 3, 6, 7, 12, 16, 20, 22, 23, 27, 31 [with orch.], 34, 38, 39, 40, 42, 46 [with trio acc.], 47, 48, 51, 52, 55, 57, 61); mus. comedy, *Summer Evening*, op. 28; duets (op. 21 and 43); glees for female chorus (op. 10, 4-v. and orch.; op. 15, 4-v. *a cappella*; op. 17, 3-v.; op. 70, 3-v. and pf.) and for mixed choir (*a cappella*, op. 9, 49; op. 32, 71 with pf.) Consult E. Radecke, *R. K.* (1894).—A. E.

KAJANUS, Robert. Finnish compr. condr. *b.* Helsingfors, 2 Dec. 1856. After studying in his native town, at Leipzig Cons. 1879–80, and in Paris under the Norwegian compr. Svendsen, K. founded in 1882 a new orch. in Helsingfors (Orchesterföreningen, later Philh. Soc.), which became of great importance for mus. life of Finland, and which (since 1914 under name of Municipal Orch.) has been in regular activity with K. as condr., the repertoire being both classical and modern. With this orch. were amalgamated an Orch. School (1885) and a Symphony Choir (1888). As compr. K. became the first important representative of Finnish national music, by taking (as J. F. von Schantz had already done in his *Kullervo Overture*, 1860), material from the Finnish folk-sagas and treating them in his orch. works, and also by arranging Finnish folk-music orchestrally. With his orchestra's tour in West Europe in year of Paris Exhibition, 1900, he did a great service in making Finnish music known, especially the early works of Jean Sibelius. K. frequently appeared abroad as condr. Since 1897, music dir. in Helsingfors Univ.; also professor.

Funeral march for orch. *Kullervo* (1st at Leipzig, 1881); symphony with final chorus, *Aino* (1885, for Jubilee of Finnish folk-epic *Kalevala*); 2 *Finnish Rhapsodies* (1882, Dresden; 1886, Helsingfors); orch. suite, *Memories of Summer*; symphonietta; cantatas; songs; choral works (among others *Sotamarssi* [*War March*] for male chorus).—T. H.

KALBECK, Max. Austrian musicologist; *b.* Breslau, 4 Jan. 1850; *d.* Vienna, 4 May, 1921. Stud. music at Munich. 1875, music critic of *Schlesische Zeitung* and assistant-dir. of museum of Breslau. Came to Vienna in 1880, upon Hanslick's recommendation, first as critic of *Allgemeine Zeitung*; then, from 1886 to his death, of *Neue Wiener Tagblatt*, where he acquired a most influential position. Like Hanslick, he was a bitter enemy of Richard Wagner (see his publs. about the *Nibelungen, Parsifal*, the Bayreuth music-festivals), of Bruckner and Hugo Wolf, and an enthusiastic friend of Brahms, whose biography he wrote (his chief work, 4 vols., the

2nd and 4th in 2 parts each, 1904–14), which is in spite of its partiality a very remarkable work. K. also publ. several vols. of Brahms's Letters and the Correspondence of Gottfried Keller with Paul Heyse (1918). Colls. of his critical essays: *Wiener Opernabende* (1885), *Opernabende* (2 vols. 1898). Many revisions and transl. of opera-texts: *Die verkaufte Braut* (Smetana), *Falstaff* (Verdi) and many others. All these are written in an elegant and tasteful style, Kalbeck being a poet himself. He wrote new texts to Mozart's *Bastien und Bastienne*; *Finta giardiniera*; Gluck's *Maienkönigin*; revised and re-adapted *Don Giovanni* and *Figaro* for Gustav Mahler (*Figaro : Bearbeitung des Wiener Hof-Operntheaters* [Peters]). He wrote some libretti himself (*Yabuka* for Johann Strauss, etc.). —P. ST.

KÁLIK, Václav. Czechoslovak compr. *b.* Opava (Silesia), 1891. Pupil of Vít. Novák and Jar. Novotný; was choirmaster of various singing-clubs; now of the Singers' Club of South Bohemian Teachers (*Pěvecké sdružení jihočeských učitelů*).

Choruses (publ. by M. Urbánek); vn. sonata; pf. suite; phantasy, vn. and pf.; 5tet with solo voice.—V. ST.

KALINNIKOF, Vassily Sergevitch (*accent 2nd syll.*). Russ. compr. *b.* Orel, 13 Jan. 1866; *d.* Yalta, 29 Dec. 1900/11 Jan. 1901. Educated at the Music School of the Moscow Philh. Soc., where his teachers were Ilyinsky and Blaremberg. Consumption, following upon the hardships of his early years, made his career a brief one; but even during his short span of life he enjoyed a measure of artistic success. His reputation rests chiefly on his 1st symphony, which is a fine and orig. work, with traces of Borodin's influence soundly assimilated. The list of his works includes a 2nd symphony and a few other examples of orch. music; a str. quartet; a few songs and pf. pieces.—M. D. C.

KALISCH, Alfred. Eng. mus. critic; *b.* London, 13 March, 1863. Educated King's Coll. School and Balliol Coll. Oxford; critic for *Daily News* and other papers; contributor to many mus. journals; transl. libretti of Strauss's *Elektra, Rosenkavalier, Ariadne in Naxos*, Mascagni's *Iris*, etc., into Eng. for perfs. at R. Opera, Covent Garden; revised Ger. text of Strauss's *Salome* for Eng. perf.; wrote libretto (both Eng. and Ger.) of Colson's opera *She Stoops to Conquer* (Baden-Baden, Sept, 1923). —E.-H.

KALISCH, Paul. Operatic tenor; *b.* Berlin, 6 May, 1855. Son of David K. the farce-writer. Pupil of Leoni in Milan. Sang in Italy, then joined Berlin Court Opera Company (1884–7). Sang in New York, where he followed Lilli Lehmann (*q.v.*), whom he married in 1888. Sang in Vienna, Cologne and Wiesbaden and made " star " tours through Europe and North America.—A. E.

KALLENBERG, Siegfried Garibaldi. Ger. compr. *b.* Schachen, near Lindau, 3 Nov. 1867. Stud. Stuttgart Cons. (Speidel, Faisst); 1890, Munich Acad. of Music. Dir. of private cons.,

Stettin, 1892, then in Königsberg, Hanover and Munich. His works either strike a popular note or are early evidences of the Ger. Expressionist school.

Toccata for pf. (Tischer & Jagenberg); 6 song albums. In ms.: 300 songs; choral works, mixed and female choruses; 3 s. and t. duets; 2 duets with small orch.; *Dance Song*; 6-v. female chorus with orch.; ˙*Requiem* (Hebbel), mixed chorus and orch.; *Psalm XC* for 8-v. choir and organ; *Germania to her Children* (Kleist) for chorus, orch. and s. solo; 2 symphonies, C mi. and D mi.; orch. music on a Tieck fairy-tale; 2 pf. sonatas; vn. and pf. sonata, B mi.; str. 5tet; str. 4tet; 2 pf. trios, B flat ma. and C mi.; pf. concerto; pf. pieces. 2 operas: *Sun Liao* (publ. 1918), *The Golden Gate* (1919–20). A Kallenberg Soc. was formed in Munich in 1921, to popularise his works.—A. E.

KALLSTENIUS, Edvin. Swedish compr. *b.* Filipstad, 29 Aug. 1881. Stud. privately; passed through theory course at Leipzig Cons. 1904–7. His style is of the modern Impressionist order. Lives in Stocksund, near Stockholm.

Op. 1, str. 4tet, No. I, G mi. (1904); op. 2, str. 4tet No. II, B flat (1905; Leipzig, 1905); op. 3, 2 songs (1908; Nord. Musikförlaget); op. 4*a, Andante pastorale*, organ; op. 4*b, Scherzo*, str. 4tet (1907); op. 5, *Allegro sinfonico*, orch. (1907; Stockholm, 1916); op. 6, sonata, pf. and cello, in D (1908); op. 7, sonata, pf. and vn. in E mi. (1908); op. 8, str. 4tet No. III, C mi. (1914); op. 9, 4 songs (Nord. Musikförlaget, 1921); op. 10, *Summer Night*, serenade, orch. (1916; Gothenburg, 1920); op. 11, cantata (1919); op. 12, pf. concerto in C (1922); songs, etc.—P. V.

KÁLMÁN, Emerich. Hungarian operetta compr. *b.* Siófok, 24 Oct. 1882. Stud. compn. at R. High School, Budapest, under Hans Koessler. Chief works: *Herbstmanöver; Der kleine König; Zigeunerprimas; Csárdásfürstin; Faschingsfee; Hollandweibchen; Die Bajadere.* Lives in Vienna. —B. B.

KALNINS, Alfreds. Latvian compr. and orgt. *b.* Cesis (Latvia), 23rd Aug. 1879. Stud. (1897–1901) Petrograd Cons. organ (Homilius), pf. (Czerny) and compn. (Liadof and Solovief). His works have the true national colouring, except, perhaps, his latest ones, written in modern idiom.

Opera, *Banuta*; orch.: *Song of the Native Country*; *Ouverture solennelle*; symph. poem, *Latvia*; pf. and organ pieces; 146 songs with pf. acc.; many part-songs, *a cappella*; 4-part arrs. of folk-tunes.—K. P.

KALVAITIS. See LITHUANIAN MUSIC.

KAMIEŃSKI, Lucjan. Polish writer and compr. *b.* Gniezno, 7 Jan. 1885. Pupil of Filke and Dercks at Breslau; then stud. in Berlin under Kahn and Bruch (theory) and Kretzschmar and Wolf (mus. science). Ph.D. 1910, with dissertation *Die Oratorien von Johann Adolf Hasse* (Leipzig, 1912). 1909–19, music critic of *Königsberger Allgemeine Zeitung*; 1920, 2nd dir. of State Music Acad. in Posen (Poland); 1922, prof.-extraordinary of history of music at Posen Univ. Arts. in many periodicals. Has also publ. 60 *Labour Songs* to his own words (Berlin, 1905–10); and brought out an operetta *Tabu* in Königsberg, 1917. In 1923 published *Fantaisie sur des Noël Polonais*, op. 17, a sonata for vn. and pf. op, 18, and *Polish Folk Songs*.—ZD. J.

KAMINSKI, Heinrich. Ger. compr. *b.* Thiengen, near Waldshut, 4 July, 1886. Son of an Old Catholic clergyman. Pupil of Wolfrum in Heidelberg and Klatte, Kaun and Juon in Berlin. K. may be briefly described as a musician of the Neo-Bach "Gothic" stamp, one of the most important musicians in Germany.

Motet, 8-v. and org.; *Psalm CXXX*, 4-v. op. 1a; 4tet for clar. vla. cello and pf.; str. 4tet (publ.); str. 5tet, F sharp mi. (Munich, O. Halbreiter); orch. suite; *Concerto grosso*, double-orch. (1923); music to W. Schmidtbonn's imitation of an old Fr. passion-play (Munich Künstlertheater, 1920); *Psalm LXIX* for soli, chorus and orch.; *Introit and Hymn* for orch., soli and small chorus.—A. E.

KAMMERSINFONIE (*Chamber - Symphony*). One of the chief works of Schönberg, marking the transition from the enlarged classical form to his new style. Written for 15 solo instrs. First perf. Vienna, 1907, by Rosé Quartet, and the Wind Instr. Association of the Opera. Afterwards Schönberg made a 2nd ed. for large concert halls, with a doubling of the strings.—E. W.

KÄMPF, Karl. Ger. compr. *b*. Berlin, 31 Aug. 1874. Pupil of Frau Olbrich-Poppenhagen, A. Sormann and Friedrich E. Koch in Berlin.

Symph. work, *Eichendorff's Early Days*; symph. march, *Neidhohle*; symphony, *The Power of Song*, male-chorus, contr. solo, orch. and organ; orch. suites: *Hiawatha* (after Longfellow); *From Baltic Lands, Andersen's Fairy Tales*; cycle, *On the Lake of Geneva* (after Franz Brendel); 2 melodies for str. orch.; *Legende* for cello and orch.; ballad for harmonium and str. orch.; *A Sea Fable, From Life and Nature, Gaudeamus Songs* (after Adolf Jensen) for male chorus and orch.; vn. sonata, E mi.; *Pathetic* sonata, op. 62, for cello and pf.; songs; duets; male and female choruses; cello and pf. pieces; compns. for *Normal-Harmonium*.—A. E.

KANÁSZTÜLÖK. See HUNGARIAN MUSICAL INSTRUMENTS.

KANKLES. See LITHUANIAN MUSIC.

KANTELE. Finnish national instr. with three-cornered sound-box, made of wood, the strings, played with the finger-tips, being of wire, though according to popular tradition originally of horse-hair. The oldest models had 5 strings tuned as follows: G, A, B (or B flat or an intermediate note), C, D. The modern forms show a great increase in number of strings. Essentially a folk-instrument, it is still found in East Finland, Karelia and among the Finnish peoples in Russ. territory. Even so late as XVIII century it was in general use throughout Finland. Recently it has been employed to some extent as a concert-instr., and of late a new invention (by P. Salminen), by which all scales are easily played, having greatly extended its possibilities. The *Jouhi-Kantele* is an entirely different instr., similar to the precursors of the vn. It has 3 strings woven out of hair and played with a bow. It shows close relationship to the Welsh *crwth*; and is found now only in certain outlying districts in Finland. —T. H.

KAPELLMEISTER (Ger.). Condr. of an orch. Not to be confused with *Konzertmeister*, who is the leading 1st vn. of an orchestra.—E.-H.

KAPP, Julius. Ger. writer on music; *b*. Steinbach, Baden, 1 Oct. 1883. Stud. Marburg, Berlin and Munich; graduated Ph.D. 1906. Founded (1904) and ed. (with Thyssen) till 1907 the *Literarische Anzeiger*. Since then has written mus. biography:

Richard Wagner and Franz Liszt (1908); *Franz Liszt* (biography, 1909; illustrated ed. 1911); *Liszt-Breviary* (1910); *Catalogue of Liszt's Collected Writings* (1909); *Richard Wagner* (biography, 1910); *Wagner*

as a Young Man (1910); *Liszt and Women* (1911); *Richard Wagner and Women* (1912); *Nicolo Paganini* (biography, 1913, Deutsche Verlags-Anstalt); *Richard Wagner's Collected Writings and Letters* (computed at 24 vols. from 1914, 2 vols. of letters already publ.); *Hector Berlioz* (Leipzig, 1914); *The Triple Star, Berlioz-Liszt-Wagner* (1920); *Meyerbeer* (1920, Deutsche Verlags-Anstalt); *Franz Schreker* (Munich, 1921, Drei Masken Verlag); *Present-day Opera* (1922); *Weber* (1922, Deutsche Verlags-Anstalt).—A. E.

KAPRÁL, Václav. Czechoslovak compr. *b*. Určice (Moravia), 1889. Pupil of Organ School in Brno and of A. Mikeš; lives in Brno as pf. teacher.

2 pf. sonatas (Pazdirek, Brno); a suite, *Lullabies of Spring*, pf.—V. ST.

KARATIGUIN, Vacheslaf Gabrilovitch (*accent 3rd syll.*). Russ. compr. and writer on music; *b*. 17 Sept. (n.s.), 1875. Well-known music critic in general and mus. papers (*Musical Contemporary*, etc.). Ed. some posthumous songs of Mussorgsky; is now prof. of mus. history at Petrograd Cons. of Music. Has comp. a number of songs.—V. B.

KAREL, Rudolf. Czech compr. *b*. Prague, 1881, where he studied at Univ. and also at Cons., devoting himself later entirely to music. He was Dvořák's last pupil in compn. He lived in Prague till 1914. During the war he was interned in Russia and was some time teacher at the Taganrog Music School there, and at the Cons. in Rostof. After the Bolshevist Revolution in 1917 he joined the Czech Legion, in which he founded a Symphony Orch., conducting it for a year and visiting the Czech garrisons in Russia. In 1920 he returned to Bohemia. Full of exuberant musicality, K. attained a style of his own, characterised by great wealth of expression, broadly elaborated themes, condensed polyphony, and large, extended forms, together with an earnest, manly energy and a massive sonority. His starting-point is Antonín Dvořák's classical formalism, Reger's polyphony and Brahms's earnestness. His development took the line of a continuous struggle for the formal and intellectual control of his own musical fecundity. Whenever he succeeds in doing so—*e.g.* in the violin sonata and in *The Demon*—he takes his place among the most important individualities of modern Czech music.

Opera, *Ilsea's Heart*; song-cycle, *In the Glow of the Hellenic Sun*; 2 symphonies; symph. compns.: *Ideals, The Demon*; str. 4tet; vn. sonata. Pf.: *Notturno*, variations, sonata, valses, burlesque. Publ.: N. Simrock, Berlin; Hudebni Matice, Prague. (Third symphony, a pf. 4tet and a vn. concerto, as yet unknown, remain in ms. in Russia.)—V. ST.

KARG (-ELERT), Sigfrid. Ger. compr. *b*. Oberndorf-on-Neckar, 21 Nov. 1879. Attended Teachers' Seminary at Grimma; then devoted himself entirely to music; became pupil of Leipzig Cons. (Reinecke, Jadassohn, Tamme, Homeyer, Wendling, Reisenauer); teacher at Madgeburg Cons.; then returned to Leipzig as instructor for compn., theory and pf. at Cons. in 1919. He is a devotee of "Tone-impressionism." A large number of his works have come from Carl Simon's publishing house ("Harmonium-haus," Berlin), and are intended more especially for the *Kunstharmonium*. He was elected Hon. Fellow of R.C.O. London in 1913. His music was much helped in England by Dr. Eaglefield-Hull.

Theoretical and Practical Elementary Tutor; The Art of Registering, op. 91 (for players of all kinds of harmoniums); *Advanced School of Legato Playing*, op. 94; *First Fundamental Studies*, op. 93; *Technique of Harmonium (Gradus ad Parnassum)*, op. 95. Orig. compns.: 3 sonatinas, op. 14; 2 sonatas, B mi. op. 36, and B flat mi. op. 46; *Partita*, op. 37; 8 pieces, op. 26; *Aquarelles*, op. 27; *Scènes pittoresques*, op. 31; 5 *Monologues*, op. 33; *Improvisations*, op. 34; *Madrigals*, op. 42; orch. studies, op. 70; *Intarsien*, op. 76; duets for pf. and harmonium, op. 29 (*Silhouettes*), op. 35 (*Poems*); also organ compns.: *Passacaglia*, op. 25 (also for harmonium); *Phantasy and fugue*, D ma. op. 39 (also for harmonium); *Choral Improvisations*, op. 65; 3 symph. chorals, op. 87; 20 preludes and postludes, op. 78; *Sanctus and Pastoral* (with vn.), op. 78; pf. pieces: sonata, F sharp mi. op. 50; 3 sonatinas, op. 67; *Travel Sketches*, op. 7; *From the North*, op. 18; *Scandinavian Airs*, op. 28; *Swabian Home*, op. 38; *Waltz Scenes*, op. 45; *Decameron*, op. 69; *Aphorisms*, op. 51; 10 bagatelles, op. 17 and 77; vn. sonata, E mi. op. 88; *Partita*, D ma. for vn. alone, op. 89; sonata, E mi. vn. alone, op. 89, i; vn. duets, op. 90; cello sonata, op. 71; orch. suite, op. 21 (*Jeux d'enfants*, after Bizet); sacred songs with organ and vn. op. 66, 81, 82; pf. songs, op. 11, 12, 40, 54, 56, 62, 63. Works issued by other publs.: 3 *Symph. Canzonas* for organ (Leuckart); 3 *Pastels* (Augener); Sonata-Chaconne-Fugue trilogy (quadruple fugue); choral with tpt. finale; 3 *Impressions* (Novello); *Impressions* for harmonium, op. 102; *Idylls*, op. 104; *Romantic Pieces*, op. 105; for the pf.: 2 sonatas, B flat mi. op. 80; concerto, D flat ma. op. 106; 28 preludes, op. 111 (Peters); pieces, op. 21–23 (Hofmeister); pieces, op. 16, 17, 45; *Symph. Legend* for vn.; songs, op. 20 (Kistner), op. 19, 24, 52, 53 (Bote & Bock); 5tet for ob. clar. horn and bsn. C mi. op. 30 (Kahnt); str. 4tet, op. 100, ms.; *Chamber Symphonietta*, A ma. (prize, Dresden, 1919), ms.; *The Christian Church Year* (12 motets); 8-v. *Whitsunday Hymn*; 12-v. *Requiem Æternam*. Consult: Hanus Avril, *S. Karg(-Elert)*, a monographic sketch; also articles by A. Eaglefield Hull, *Mus. Times* (Feb., March, 1913).—A. E.

KARŁOWICZ, Mieczysław. Polish compr. *b.* Wiszniewo (province of Vilna), 11 Dec. 1876; *d.* in the Tatra mountains, near Zakopane (Galicia), crushed by an avalanche, 10 Feb. 1909. Stud. at Warsaw under Barcewicz (vn.) and Noskowski (theory), 1890–5, and 1895–1900 in Berlin under Urban. His first compns. (several songs, op. 1, 3, 4), did not reveal his future evolution as a compr. Then followed larger and deeper works: pf. sonata; Prelude and double fugue; *Serenade* for str.; symphony in E mi. op. 7; violin concerto, op. 8. He found his finest expressive force in the form of the symph. poem, in which he came right to the front. In the first, *Returning Waves*, op. 9 (1904), he was still under the influence of Wagner (especially *Tristan*). Then he came nearer to Richard Strauss. Subsequent works in this form were *Three Eternal Songs*, op. 10 (1907); *A Lithuanian Rhapsody*, op. 11; *Stanislaw and Anna Oswiecinowie*, op. 12; *A Sorrowful Tale*, op. 13; *A Drama at a Masked Ball* (unfinished; completed by Grzegorz Fitelberg). These are distinguished by a great wealth of pathetic ideas and a variety of orchestral colour.

K. began a new epoch in Polish music in the sphere of the symphony, which had remained, till his appearance, at a lower level than solo instr. music and opera. From 1904–6 he was dir. of the Warsaw Soc. of Music. Then he went to Zakopane, where he remained till his death. Publ. in 1903 *The Hitherto Unknown Reminiscences of Chopin.*—ZD. J.

KARPATH, Ludwig. Hungarian musical author and critic; *b.* Budapest, 4 April, 1866. Stud. at Budapest Cons.; then went to America. Since 1894, music critic of *Neue Wiener Tagblatt*; contributor to several musical periodicals (including the *Musical Courier*); 1910–17, chief editor of the *Merker*; president of Association of Music-Critics of Vienna. His books are: *Siegfried Wagner* (1902); *Zu den Briefen Richard Wagners an eine Putzmacherin* (Notes on the Letters of Richard Wagner to a Milliner), 1906; *Richard Wagner als Schuldenmacher* (*Wagner as Contractor of Debts*), 1914. K., a nephew of Goldmark, was one of the intimates of the Wahnfried family and spent much time in the company of Brahms, Richard Strauss and other important musicians. He possesses many souvenirs and letters of the last decades of Vienna. He is now preparing his memoirs.—P. ST.

KASACHENKO, Gregory Alexeievich (*accent 3rd syll.*). Russ. compr. *b.* Petrograd, 3/15 March, 1858. Studied at Petrograd.

Operas: The Silver Prince; Pan Sotkin (both produced at Petrograd, 1892); symphony; 2 orch. suites.—M. D. C.

KASCHMANN, Giuseppe. Ital. barit. singer; *b.* Lussinpiccolo (Istria), 14 July, 1850. From boyhood, showed very marked ability for singing. His parents set him to study law, but he abandoned it in order to take up his favourite career. Stud. in Milan under Giovannini. *Début* in 1874–5 season at Regio Theatre, Turin, in *La Favorita.* He rapidly gained high fame, and sang in all the principal theatres of the world, distinguishing himself as an intelligent interpreter, passing from one opera to another in a very extensive repertoire. He sang in Ital., Fr., Ger. (Wagner Theatre, Bayreuth), Latin and Serbian. Is a remarkable interpreter of Perosi's oratorios. Of recent years, has devoted himself especially to concert-work, frequently singing at the Augusteo, and interesting himself in revival of old music. Is now a celebrated singing teacher.—D. A.

KASE, Alfred. Ger. barit. singer; *b.* Stettin, 28 Oct. 1877. Started as engraver in Munich, where Em. Kroupa discovered his voice, and sent him to Acad. of Music. After a first engagement at Cassel, 1902–7, Volkner engaged him for opera at Leipzig, to which he still belongs (since 1920, contract as visiting singer).—A. E.

KASKEL, Karl, Freiherr von. Ger. compr. *b.* Dresden, 10 Oct. 1866. Pupil of Reinecke and Jadassohn in Leipzig, of Wüllner in Cologne. Lives in Munich.

Operas: Wedding Morn (Hamburg, 1893): *Sjula* (Cologne, 1895); *The Beggar of the Pont des Arts* (Cassel, 1899); *Dusle and Babeli* (Munich, 1903); *The Prisoner of the Czarina* (Dresden, 1910); *The Nightingale* (Stuttgart, 1910); *The Kentish Locksmith* (Dresden, 1916); operetta, *The Station of Fortune*; also *Ballad* for orchestra.—A. E.

KASKI, Heino. Finnish compr. *b.* Pielisjärvi, in 1885. Stud. at Orch. School, Helsingfors and (with a State scholarship) in Berlin (pupil of Paul Juon).

Suites for orch.; symphony; pf. pieces; songs, etc.—T. H.

KASTALSKY, Alexander Dmitrievitch (*accent 2nd syll.*). Russ. compr. *b.* Moscow, 16/28 Nov. 1856. Pupil of Tchaikovsky and Tanéief (theory) at Moscow Cons. (1876–82). 1887, pf. teacher in Moscow Synodal School of Church Music, which became the People's Choral Acad. in 1918, and was closed down in 1923. He was dir. of this acad. from its foundation till its close. He is the chief representative of the new line of Russ. sacred music. He used the old church-tunes, and the strictest cpt. in accordance with the style. His *Requiem* was given in England by the Fest. Choral Soc. at Birmingham, under Sir Henry Wood in 1921.

Very many unacc. sacred choruses; secular choruses; opera, *Clara Militch* (after Turgenieff); *Georgian Suite.* His symphony *From the Agricultural Life,* for orch. and solo vs. singing Russ. folk-songs (illustrating various occupations), is still in ms. The Russ. State Music Publ. Dept. publ. in 1923, his important treatise on *The Folk's Harmonisation of the Russ. Folk-Songs.*—V. B.

KATILA, Ewert. Finnish music critic; *b.* 16 Nov. 1872. At first, stud. geology at Helsingfors Univ., but later turned to music; was student in Orch. School. Critic in Helsingfors since 1899. Has also appeared as compr. of choral works.—T. H.

KAUDER, Hugo. Austrian composer and violinist; *b.* Tobitschau (Moravia), 9 June, 1888. Has lived since 1905 in Vienna. A self-taught musician; 1910–17, first vn. then vla. player in Viennese Konzertverein Orch. Now devotes himself entirely to composing. In his works we find resignation, economy of effects and deep melancholy. He does not belong to modern group of mus. innovators.

2 symphonies (1921, 1922); *Phantasie,* vn. and orch. (1917); cello concerto (1917); *Gipsy Song* (from Goethe) for contr., chorus and orch. (1912); chamber-music; sonatas; Passacaglia for organ; 24 pf. pieces; 80 songs acc. by orch. or str. 4tet.—P. P.

KAUN, Hugo. Ger. compr. *b.* Berlin, 21 March, 1863. Stud. under Grabau and Fr. Schulz at R. High School, then under horn-player Karl Raif and his son O. Raif (pf.), also compn. under Fr. Kiel; 1887–1902, lived in Milwaukee as teacher, dir. and compr.; since 1902 in Berlin; member of R. Acad. of Arts; 1922, teacher of compn. at Klindworth-Scharwenka Conservatoire.

4 str. 4tets, op. 40, 41, 74, 114; 1 str. 5tet, op. 28 (as a pf. 5tet, op. 39); 2 pf. trios, B flat ma. op. 32, and C mi. op. 58; 8tet, F ma. op. 34; 8tet for wind instrs. op. 26; sonata for vn. and pf. op. 32; 3 symphonies (*To my Fatherland,* D ma. op. 22; C mi. op. 85; E mi. op. 96, 1914); overture, *The Rhine,* op. 90; *Märkische* orch. suite, op. 92; *Ceremonial Entrance March,* op. 99; several symph. poems (*Minnehaha and Hiawatha,* op. 43); pf. concerto, E flat mi. op. 50; festival march, *The Star-spangled Banner,* op. 29; symph. prologue, *Mary Magdalene,* op. 44; orch. humoreske, *Falstaff,* op. 60; *Hanne Nüte* for orch. op. 107; choruses: *The Norman's Farewell,* op. 20, for male vs. and orch. with barit. solo; *Mother Earth* for soli, chorus and orch.; pf. pieces and songs; 3 operas: *The Devotee* (*Oliver Brown*) 1 act; *Sappho* (Gera, 1917, under Lohse); *The Stranger* (Dresden, 1920).—A. E.

KEEL, James Frederick. Eng. barit. singer and compr. *b.* London, 8 May, 1871. Entered choir of Wells Cath. as chief solo-boy, 1883; stud. at R.A.M., singing under Frederic King and Frederick Walker, compn. under Frederick Corder; 1896, went to Milan for singing-study under

Federico Blasco; 1897 at Munich, under Eugen Gura. *Début* in London at Queen's Hall, 1898, at one of William Carter's concerts. Has sung in numerous concerts in London and the provinces, and given many recitals. Has made a special study of old and traditional songs; hon. secretary Folk-Song Soc. 1911–19; ed. of the Society's journal; lecturer and prof. of singing at R.A.M. London. Has publ. some pieces for vn. and pf. (Schott), songs, and ed. 2 books of Elizabethan songs.—E.-H.

KEÉRI-SZÁNTÓ, Imre. Hungarian pianist; *b.* Budapest, 15 Jan. 1884. Stud. at R. High School under Stephan Thomán. Since 1918, pf. prof. at same institution.—B. B.

KEFER, Louis. Belgian compr. and condr. *b.* Jambes-lez-Namur in 1842. Stud. at Brussels Cons. In 1873, on formation of École de Musique at Verviers, was appointed dir., a post he held for 45 years with admirable conscientiousness and a most progressive spirit. As condr. of Société d'Harmonie of Verviers, and Concerts Populaires and the Nouveaux Concerts (founded by him) in that town, he cond. in 35 years over 1400 concerts. The programmes show the most clear-sighted eclecticism combined with a most generous-minded proselytism. To him are due the 1st perf. of the various works of Lekeu, a personal friend for whom K.'s admiration bordered on a fervent cult.

Cantata for inauguration of Barrage de la Gileppe (1877–8); symphony in D (1889), crowned by Belgian Acad. and rewritten since, a work full of life and youthful freshness; *Caprice* for orch.; trio, pf. vn. cello; *Tantum Ergo,* choir and orch.; male choruses, etc.—C. V. B.

KEIGHLEY, Thomas. Eng. lecturer and writer on music; *b.* Stalybridge, 15 Oct. 1869. Stud. privately and at R. Manchester Coll. of Music (1895–8). Mus.Doc. Manchester, 1901; orgt. Albion Congregational Ch. Ashton-u-Lyne, from 1897; prof. of harmony, R. Manchester Coll. of Music, from 1898; lecturer in compn. at Univ.; condr. Stockport Vocal Union.

Rudiments of Music; 5 books of Graded Questions; *Harmony* treatise; 5 books of Questions; *Manual of Music* (Longmans); *Unfigured Basses* (Stainer & Bell); *Harmony Exercises for Strings* (W. Rogers); numerous part-songs and anthems; pf. pieces (Bayley & Ferguson; Forsyth; West; Banks, etc.).—E.-H.

KEIL, Alfredo. Portuguese compr. *b.* 1850; *d.* 1907. One of the finest representatives of modern Portuguese music. His operas met with much success in Lisbon. His style is somewhat daring and never banal, according to M. Lamber-tini's extensive study of Portuguese music, in Lavignac and Laurencie's *Encyclopédie de la Musique,* Vol. V, pp. 2401 *et seq.* (Paris, 1920). His song *A Portugueza* was adopted as the official national anthem by the new Republic.

Operas: *Don Branca* (22 perfs. at San Carlos Theatre, Lisbon); *Irene,* 4-act lyric drama (Turin, 1893; San Carlos, Lisbon, 1896); *Serrana* (Turin, 1899, 1900; Colyseu, Lisbon, 1901); and his mus. sketches *India* and *Simão o Ruivo.*—E.-H.

KELLERMANN, Berthold. Ger. pianist; *b.* Nuremberg, 5 March, 1853. Stud. under Ramann in Nuremberg and during summer months of 1873–8 under Liszt in Weimar; 1875–9, teacher at Kullak's Acad.; 1876–8 at Stern's Cons.; 1878

in Bayreuth in Wagner's *Nibelungen* Bureau, and
teacher to Wagner's children. Till 1881 also dir.
of Bayreuth orch. concerts; teacher at R. Acad.
of Music, Munich, since 1882; 1893-4, also
cond. Academic Choral Society.—A. E.

KELLEY, Edgar Stillman. Amer. compr. and
author; *b.* Sparta, Wis., U.S.A., 14 April, 1857.
Stud. under F. W. Merriam (1870-4), then under
Clarence Eddy and Ledochowski in Chicago
(1874-6). From 1876-80, pupil at Stuttgart
Cons. of Krüger and Speidel (pf.), Finck (organ),
and Max Seifriz (compn.). After his return to
America, orgt. in Oakland and San Francisco,
Cal., and then came East as condr. with a comic-
opera company, 1890-1. From 1896-1900, lived
in New York, teaching at New York Coll. of
Music; 1896-7, lectured on music for Univ.
Extension of Univ. of New York. 1901-2, acting-
prof. of music at Yale Univ. From 1902-10,
teacher in Berlin. Since 1910, prof. of compn. at
Cincinnati (Ohio) Cons.; is holder of a fellowship in compn. of Western Coll. for Women at
Oxford, Ohio. Degree of Litt.D. from Miami
Univ. 1916; LL.D. from Univ. of Cincinnati,
·1917. First came into prominence with incidental music to stage-production of Lew Wallace's *Ben Hur,* 1899. Also written music to
Macbeth and to *Prometheus Unbound.* His 1st
symphony, a humorous compn. on *Gulliver—His
Voyage to Lilliput,* op. 15, is unpubl. His 2nd
symphony, *New England,* op. 33, was 1st perf.
at Norfolk (Conn.) Fest. 1913. His op. 37, *The
Pilgrim's Progress,* Miracle Play for soli, chorus
and orch., was given at Cincinnati May Fest.
1918. A pf. 5tet and a str 4tet have been
frequently played in U.S.A.

Aladdin, Chinese suite, orch. op. 10 (Schirmer,
1915); *Puritania,* comic opera, op. 11 (Church, 1893);
Ben Hur, op. 17 (New York, Towers & Curran, 1902);
5tet, pf. and str. op. 20 (Berlin, Stahl, 1907); str.
4tet, op. 25 (*id.* 1907); *New England Symphony,*
op. 33 (Schirmer, 1915); *Pilgrim's Progress,* op. 37
(Ditson, 1917). Of his songs *The Lady picking
Mulberries* has been sung often (Schirmer, 1890).
Author of *Chopin, the Composer* (Schirmer, 1913).
—O. K.

KELLY, Frederick Septimus. Australian composer; *b.* Sydney, 29 May, 1881; killed in action,
Beaucourt, on the Ancre, France, 13 Nov. 1916.
At age of 5 played Mozart's pf. sonatas by heart;
educated at Eton and Balliol Coll. Oxford; stud.
music under Dr. C. H. Lloyd at Eton and under
Donald Tovey at Oxford; then at Hoch's Cons.
Frankfort-o-M., compn. under Ivan Knorr, pf.
under Eugesser. On his visit to Australia in 1911,
he gave some concerts in Sydney, and in 1912 he
gave a series of concerts in London at Æolian
Hall, and one with orch. A memorial concert of
his works was given at Wigmore Hall, 2 May,
1919. His brief career as a compr. was sufficient
to prove that here was a career cut short which
was destined to achieve something unique and
complete. The *Elegy* has a lofty, controlled expression that is Greek in spirit and truly inspired.
In the popular mind, he is associated with his
prowess as an athlete. He rowed in the Eton
eight in 1899; in Oxford eight 1903; won the
Diamond Sculls 3 times (1902-3-5) and rowed

for England in the Leander eight at Olympic
Regatta, 1908.

Serenade, op. 7 (5 movements), for fl. horn, harp
with str. (Schott); *Elegy, in memoriam Rupert
Brooke* (comp. in hospital at Alexandria, 1915), str.
and harp (ms.); str. trio; sonata in G, vn. and pf. (1st
perf. Jelly d'Arányi and Leonard Borwick, Classical
Concert Soc. 3 Dec. 1919); prelude for organ (1915);
Cycle of Lyrics, pf. (1907–8); 5 *Monographs,* pf.;
Allegro de Concert, pf. (Schott); Theme, Variations
and Fugue for 2 pfs. (*id.*); songs, etc.—E.-H.

KELTERBORN, Louis. Compr. and condr. *b.*
Boston (U.S.A.), 28 April, 1891. Stud. at Basle;
then at Geneva Cons. under Joseph Lauber (pf.
and compn.) ; teacher of theory and mus. history
at Wolff Cons. at Basle; Since 1918, condr. of
Oratorio Concerts and orgt. at Burgedorf;
author of important essay, *Tonkunst und
Schweizer Bühne.*

Amon (Kelterborn), mus. drama (publ. by compr.);
oratorio, *Hiob (Job);* *Hérode,* for barit., chorus and
orch.; *Penthesilea and Sylvius,* m.-sopr. and orch.
(Geneva, Henn); str. 4tet (Basle, Pohl); cello sonata
and sonata for vn. and pf. (*id.*); numerous songs
(*id.*).—F. H.

KEMPFF, Wilhelm. Ger. pianist, orgt. and
compr. *b.* Jüterborg, 25 Nov. 1895. Stud. pf. with
H. Barth, compn. with R. Kahn at Berlin High
School; 1917, gained both Mendelssohn prizes.
since 1916 has given organ and pf. recitals, sometimes as soloist, with Berlin Cath. Choir; in
Germany and Scandinavia, famous as impro-
visor on given themes.

Orch. suite, F sharp mi. (with 3 *cembali*); symphony in E flat ma.; overture to Kleist's *Hermann's
Battle,* orch., 3 old Ger. trumpets, male chorus; pf.
concerto, B flat mi. (*Dies Iræ*); sonatas; variations;
fantasy for pf.; sonata for vn. C sharp ma.; female
choruses; orch. songs.—A. E.

KENIG, Włodzimierz. Compr. and condr. *b·*
Suwałki, Poland, 1 April, 1883. In 1908, re-
ceived 1st prize at Warsaw Cons. as pupil of
Barcewicz (vn.) and Noskowski (theory). Then
stud. in Munich under Fr. Klose (theory) and
Bussmayer (conducting). In 1915–16, 1st condr.
of Warsaw Philh. Also known as condr. in
Germany.

3 symphonies (the 1st obtained a prize in Warsaw,
1912); 2 symph. poems; many songs and vn. and
cello pieces.—ZD. J.

KENNEDY, Daisy. Australian violinist; *b.*
Burra-Burra, near Adelaide, of Scotch and Irish
parentage. Three years Elder scholar at Ade-
laide Cons. Stud. for a year privately under
Ševčik in Vienna, then 2 years in the Meister-
Schule there. Has toured in Austria, Australia,
U.S.A. and England; married Benno Moisei-
witsch, the pianist.—E.-H.

KENNEDY, Margaret. Scottish contr. singer;
b. London, 27 March, 1865. Stud. at R.A.M. London; sub-prof. of harmony; stud. interpretation of Fr. and Ger. songs under Raymond von
Zur Mühlen. Toured in U.S.A., Canada, Australia, New Zealand, and Great Britain.
Specialises now in Hebridean songs.—J. P. D.

KENNEDY-FRASER, Marjory. Scottish singer
and folk-song collector; *b.* Perth, Scotland (of
Celtic parentage), 1 Oct. 1857; daughter of
David Kennedy, famous singer of Scots songs.
Childhood in Edinburgh and London. At 12,
toured with father as pf. accompanist. At 14,
sailed with him in a clipper ship round Cape of

Good Hope to Australia for world-tour lasting 4½ years. Vocal training from father, but at age of 22 went to study opera at Milan, and later in Paris under Mathilde Marchesi. On father's death, married A. J. Fraser, mathematician and headmaster of Alan Glen's school, Glasgow. On death of her husband, returned to Edinburgh and there taught and lectured on mus. subjects. Lecturing at Summer Meeting on Celtic music, she came across Ducoudray's Breton songs. Continued public lecture-recitals on all the great art-song writers, from Schubert to Hugo Wolf. In 1905, made 1st visit to Outer Hebridean Isles. Since then, has specialised in Celtic music-research and original work, converting the treasure of national melody preserved by the Island Gaels into art-songs, without in any way sacrificing the original character of the melodic material. Has given lecture-recitals throughout England and Scotland; has twice visited the U.S.A., having been invited first to New York by the MacDowell Club in 1913. Gives many recitals of Hebridean songs in London, Edinburgh, Glasgow, etc. C.B.E. 1924.

Songs of the Hebrides (3 vols., 1909, 1917, 1921, Boosey); albums of Lyrics and Sea Pieces, pf. (id.); Hebridean Suite, cello and pf.; albums with harp acc.; Scots Folk-Tunes; Suite for pf.; numerous songs (publ. separately); 10 Unison Songs for Schools (2nd ed.); 3 fest. handbooks on (a) Laws of Interpretation and Hebridean Song, (b) Lowland Scots Song, (c) Pronunciation of Lowland Scots.—E.-H.

KENNEDY-FRASER, Patuffa (Mrs. Hood). Scottish singer and harpist; b. Edinburgh, 10 June, 1888. Stud. pf., harp and singing in London and Edinburgh. Toured in U.S.A. and British Isles with the Songs of the Hebrides.—J. P. D.

KERNER, Stephan. Hungarian condr. b. Máriakéménd. Since 1885 at Budapest Opera House, first as vla.-player, later as condr. Condr. of Budapest Philh. Soc.—B. B.

KERPELY, Eugen (Jenő). Hungarian cellist; b. Budapest, 1 Dec. 1885. Member of Hungarian Str. Quartet (see CHAMBER-MUSIC PLAYERS). Stud. under David Popper, R. High School, Budapest. Teacher of cello there, 1913–20.—B. B.

KERR, Grainger. Scottish contr. singer; b. near Dundee. Stud. under Caravoglia, Anna Williams and Ffrangçon Davies; has sung at leading London concerts, Brussels, Frankfort, Egypt, Palestine, etc. Specialises in modern music.—E.-H.

KERREBIJN, Marius. Dutch pianist; b. The Hague, 1 Oct. 1882.

Symph. poem for orch., barit., chorus and organ, Lux in Tenebris, perf. Jan. 1918, Concertgebouw, Amsterdam, under Mengelberg; numerous smaller pieces.—W. P.

KES, Willem. Dutch condr. and violinist; b. Dordrecht, 16 Feb. 1856. Pupil of Reinecke, Wieniawski, Joachim and Kufferath; 1876, soloist of Park Orch. Amsterdam; 1883, condr. of same orch.; 1888, condr. of new Concertgebouw Orch. Amsterdam; 1895, resigned; condr. Scottish Orch., Glasgow, 1896–8; then till 1900, Philh. Soc. Moscow. Is now dir. of Music Inst. Coblence.

Symphony; vn. concertos; cello concerto; overture; sonatas, vn. and pf.; ballade, Der Taucher,

soli, chorus, orch.; songs. Arr. Schumann's Sinfonische Études for orch.—W. P.

KESTENBERG, Leo. Writer on music and organiser; b. Rosenberg, Hungary, 27 Nov. 1882. Pupil of Franz Kullak and Busoni (pf.), Draeseke (compn.). Teacher in Klindworth-Scharwenka Cons; an excellent Liszt player in Berlin; since 1918 official mus. assessor in Prussian Ministry of Culture; 1921, prof. at Academic High School, Berlin. Wrote Musical Education (Berlin, 1921, Quelle & Meyer).—A. E.

KESTEVEN, Horace. Eng. pianist; b. London, 6 Aug. 1870. Stud. at Leipzig Cons. under Bruno Zwintscher and Carl Reinecke; later under Saint-Saëns in Paris; recitals in England and Germany; now dir. of studies, Incorp. London Acad. of Music.—E.-H.

KETÈLBEY, Albert William. Eng. compr. and condr. b. Birmingham. Stud. Trinity Coll. of Music, London (pf., harmony, compn., horn, cello, organ); condr. at several London theatres; for some time, mus. ed. for Chappell's; mus. dir. Columbia Graphophone Co.

Comic opera, The Wonder Worker (Grand Theatre Fulham, 1900); Caprice, pf. and orch.; Concert-stück, pf. and orch.; overture, orch.; Suite de ballet (Queen's Hall, April 1913); pf. and wood-wind 5tet (Costa Prize); etc. Many popular pieces under penname of Anton Vodorinski.—E.-H.

KEUSSLER, Gerhard von. Ger. condr. and compr. b. Schwanenburg, Livonia, 6 July, 1874. First stud. natural science; 1900, turned to music; visited Leipzig Cons. and graduated as Ph.D. at Leipzig Univ. with The Limits of Æsthetics. Cond. Ger. Choral and Symph. Concerts of Music Soc. at Prague; 1918–21, cond. Acad. of Singing at Hamburg; 1920–1, also Hamburg Philh. Concerts.

Symph. poems: The Hermit; Eastern Fantasy; Resurrection and Last Judgment; oratorios: Before the High City: The Death; Jesus of Nazareth (Prague, 1917); melodramatic symphony, To Death; choral work, The Mother (Hamburg, 1919); operas: Prisons (Prague, 1914, German Landestheater); The Scourge Drive. Tone Symbolism in Beethoven's Masses (Peters' Annual for 1920).—A. E.

KEY-NAMES IN VARIOUS LANGUAGES. C major (Eng.), Do maggiore (Ital.), Ut majeur (Fr.), C dur (Ger.); A minor (Eng.), La minore (Ital.), La mineur (Fr.), A moll (Ger.); G major (Eng.), Sol maggiore (Ital.), Sol majeur (Fr.), G dur (Ger.); E minor (Eng.), Mi minore (Ital.), Mi mineur (Fr.), E moll (Ger.); D major (Eng.), Re maggiore (Ital.), Ré majeur (Fr.), D dur (Ger.); B minor (Eng.), Si minore (Ital.), Si mineur (Fr.), H moll (Ger.); A major (Eng.), La maggiore (Ital.), La majeur (Fr.), A dur (Ger.); F sharp minor (Eng.), Fa diesis minore (Ital.), Fa dièse mineur.(Fr.), Fis moll (Ger.); E major (Eng.), Mi maggiore (Ital.), Mi majeur (Fr.), E dur (Ger.); C sharp minor (Eng.), Do diesis minore (Ital.), Ut dièse mineur (Fr.), Cis moll (Ger.); B major (Eng.), Si maggiore (Ital.), Si majeur (Fr.), H dur (Ger.); G sharp minor (Eng.), Sol diesis minore (Ital.), Sol dièse mineur (Fr.), Gis moll (Ger); F sharp major (Eng.), Fa diesis maggiore (Ital.), Fa dièse majeur (Fr.), Fis dur (Ger.); D sharp minor (Eng.), Re diesis minore (Ital.), Ré dièse mineur (Fr.), Dis moll (Ger.); C sharp major (Eng.), Do diesis maggiore (Ital.), Ut dièse majeur (Fr.), Cis dur (Ger.); A sharp minor (Eng.), La diesis minore (Ital.), La dièse mineur (Fr.), Ais moll (Ger.); F major (Eng.), Fa maggiore (Ital.), Fa majeur (Fr.), F dur (Ger.); D minor (Eng.), Re minore (Ital.), Ré mineur (Fr.), D moll (Ger); B flat major (Eng.), Si bemolle maggiore (Ital.), Si bémol majeur (Fr.), B dur (Ger.); G minor (Eng.), Sol minore (Ital.), Sol mineur (Fr.), G moll (Ger.); E flat major (Eng.), Mi bemolle maggiore (Ital.), Mi bémol majeur (Fr.), Es dur (Ger.); C minor (Eng.), Do minore (Ital.), Ut mineur (Fr.), C moll (Ger.); A flat major (Eng.), La bemolle maggiore (Ital.), La bémol majeur (Fr.), As dur (Ger.); F minor (Eng.), Fa minore (Ital.), Fa mineur (Fr.), F moll (Ger.); D flat major (Eng.), Re bemolle maggiore (Ital.), Ré bémol majeur (Fr.), Des dur (Ger.); B flat minor (Eng.), Si bemolle minore (Ital.), Si bémol mineur (Fr.), B moll (Ger.); G flat major (Eng.), Sol bemolle maggiore (Ital.), Sol bémol majeur (Fr.), Ges dur (Ger.); E flat minor (Eng.), Mi bemolle minore (Ital.), Mi bémol mineur (Fr.), Es moll (Ger.); C flat major (Eng.), Do bemolle maggiore (Ital.), Ut bémol majeur (Fr.), Ces dur (Ger.); A flat minor (Eng.), La bemolle minore (Ital.), La bémol mineur (Fr.), As moll (Ger.).

KIDDLE, Frederick B. Eng. pianist and orgt. *b.* Frome, Somerset. Stud. at R.C.M. London under Sir W. Parratt, Rockstro and Higgs. Accompanist and orgt. to Queen's Hall concerts over a long period. Pf. accompanist to Gervase Elwes throughout his musical career.—E.-H.

KIDSON, Frank. Eng. mus. antiquary; *b.* Leeds 15 Nov. 1855. A foundation member of Folk-Song Soc. and one of the editors of its Journals. Contributed largely to new (1904) ed. of Grove's Dictionary; has written much in mus. journals; lecturer on music; contributor of articles on ballad-operas in this Dictionary.

Old English Country Dances (1890); *Traditional Tunes* (coll. of folk-songs from Yorkshire and borders of Scotland (1891); *British Music Publishers from Q. Elizabeth's Reign to George IV* (1908); *English Folk-Song* (Cambridge Univ. Press, 1900); *The Beggar's Opera, its Predecessors and Successors* (*id.* 1922). Ed. of *The Minstrelsy of England; The Minstrelsy of Childhood; English Songs of the Georgian Period; Songs of Britain; Dances of the Olden Time; Children's Songs of Long Ago,* etc.—E.-H.

KIENZL, Wilhelm. Austrian composer; *b.* Waizenkirchen (Austria), 17 Jan. 1857. Stud. at Graz, Prague, Leipzig and Vienna, where he took his degree as Ph.D. with thesis *Die musikalische Deklamation.* Influenced by the works of Wagner he went to Bayreuth in 1879 and lectured in 1880 at Munich. 1883–93, condr. at Amsterdam, Crefeld, Graz and Hamburg; then domiciled at Graz. 1917, removed to Vienna.

Music-dramas· *Urvasi* (1886); *Heilmar* (1892); *Der Evangelimann* (1895); *Don Quixote* (1898); *Der Kuhreigen* (1911, Vienna); 1914, Liverpool); *Das Testament* (1916). *Der Evangelimann* had great success at Vienna, being one of the first veristic Ger. operas.—EG. W.

KIESLICH, Leo. Ger. compr. *b.* Wiese (Neustadt), 15 Sept. 1882. Attended Breslau Academic Inst. for Church Music; pupil of Emil

Bohn; then singing-teacher and choral-condr. in Neustadt.

More than 100 songs; choruses of every description; pf. music; orch. works; 3 masses; *Hymns to Mary; Tantum ergo;* 2 Singspiels; a ballet; 3 oratorios: *Der Schöpfung Marienlob,* op. 39; *May Devotions,* op. 63; *Barabbas,* op. 65.—A. E.

KIESSIG, Georg. Ger. compr. *b.* Leipzig, 17 Sept. 1885. Stud. at Leipzig Cons. (Krehl, Wendling) and till 1910 under Richard Hagel. Solo-repetitor at the Leipzig Opera till 1910, condr. at the theatres of Arnstadt and Rudolstadt. Now devotes himself entirely to compn.

For orch.: *Eichendorff Suite* (1914); symph. poem, *Ahasuerus* (*The Wandering Jew*) (1914); *My Fatherland* (1915); *A Dance of Death* (1916); songs with orch. and pf. acc.; chamber and pf. music; choruses; 3-act opera, *Anselm* (words by Lothar Körner, 1918–20); music to Goethe's *Faust* (Leipzig, 1923).—A. E.

KIHL, Viggo. Danish pianist; *b.* Copenhagen, 11 Nov. 1882. Stud. Leipzig Cons. under Teichmüller. *Début* at Copenhagen, 1901. In 1903 went to London where he lived for 10 years; soloist at Æolian Hall, Queen's Hall and many other concerts. Went to Canada in 1913 to Toronto Cons. of Music, as pf. prof. His extensive concert-work in Canada has done much to promulgate European mus. traditions.—L. S.

KILPINEN, YRJÖ. Finnish song-compr. *b.* Helsingfors, 4 Feb. 1892. Stud. at Helsingfors Music Inst.; also in Vienna and Berlin. Up to present, has confined himself almost exclusively to song; has produced songs revealing strong individuality and depth of expression; among them, whole series of poems by Finnish writers (Larin Kyösti, Hugo Jalkanen, Eino Leino, V. A. Koskenniemi) as well as Swedish poets (Ernst Josephson, Bo Bergman, Pär Lagerqvist and others). Lives in Helsingfors. His songs are publ. by Breitkopf, Leipzig (31 songs to poems by Jalkanen), and by Wilhelm Hansen, Copenhagen (12 songs to poems by Leino).—T. H.

KING, Frederic. Eng. barit. singer, teacher of singing; *b.* Lichfield, 3 Jan. 1853. Stud. under Visetti, E. Faning, Prout and Kemp; first appeared at a ballad concert, St. James's Hall, 1878; then at all the leading fests. Created part of Lucifer in Sullivan's *Golden Legend* (Leeds Fest. 1886). Prof. of singing R.A.M. 1890. Amongst his pupils are Maurice D'Oisly, R. Radford, Herbert Heyner, Carmen Hill.—E.-H.

KINSKY, Georg. Ger. writer on music; *b.* Marienwerder (West Prussia), 29 Sept. 1882. Self-taught musician. On recommendation of Kopfermann, under whom he worked for a short time at Berlin R. Library, W. Heyer (of Cologne) entrusted him with cataloguing of his Musical-Historical Museum, of which he is curator. In 1921, he was elected teacher of science of music at Cologne Univ. His large catalogue of the Museum contains valuable information on history of instruments and study of manuscripts. (Vol. I, ·*Keyed Instruments,* Leipzig, 1910; Vol. II, *Plucked and String Instruments,* 1912; and Vol. IV, *Music-Autographs,* 1916.) In 1913, publ. a catalogue of the collections of instrs. full of historical notes. (See HEYERSCHES MUSIKHISTORISCHES MUSEUM.)—A. E.

KIRIAC, Demetri, G. Compr. and condr. of Rumanian Choir; *b.* Bucharest, 18 March, 1866. Stud. first there; then at Cons. of Paris under Pessard (harmony), Dubois (cpt.); later, at *Schola Cantorum,* Paris (under d'Indy). Prof. at Cons. of Paris (under d'Indy). Prof. at Cons. of Bucharest since 1900. Founder of choral soc. *Carmen* (1900). An assiduous folk-lore collector.

Many religious choruses (5 vols. Bucharest, J. Feder). Popular songs harmonised (Bucharest, Ed. Margaritescu); *Coronation Hymn,* for Rumanian sovereigns Alba-Julia (Bucharest, 1922, Filip). —C. BR.

KISTLER, Cyrill. Ger. compr. *b.* Gross-Aitingen, near Augsburg, 12 March, 1848; *d.* Kissingen, 1 Jan. 1907. Received his mus. training at Munich (Rheinberger); 1878, teacher at Sondershausen Cons.; 1885 at Kissingen as music-master. Kistler was a devoted follower of Wagner whom he popularised.

Romantic opera, *Kunihild* (Sondershausen, 1884); comic opera, *Eulenspiegel* (Würzburg, 1889); *Poor Little Elsie* (Schwerin, 1902); *Rosebud in the Hedge* (Elberfeld, 1903); *The Governor at Mühlstein* (Düsseldorf, 1904); *Baldur's Death* (Düsseldorf, 1905); 3-act opera, *The German Provincial* (publ. but unperf.); symph. poem, *Witch's Kitchen* (*Faust,* Part II); *Harmony Manual* (1879, 2nd ed. 1903); *Elementary Musical Instructor* (1880); *Singing and Music Lessons for Public Schools* (1881); *Simple Counterpoint and Fugue* (1904); *Triple and Multiple Counterpoint* (1908); *Choral Song Manual* (2nd ed. 1908); *Board School Teachers' Music Dictionary* (3rd ed. 1887); independent monographs; *Modern Musical Questions; The Passion-play at Oberammergau* (1880); *Beyond the Music Drama* (1888); *Franz Witt* (1888); *Originality in Music* (1894, 2nd ed. 1907).—A. E.

KITSON, Charles Herbert. Writer on music; *b.* Leyburn, Yorks, 13 Nov. 1874. Organ scholar Selwyn Coll. Cambridge; De Grey exhibitioner. Mus.Doc. Oxon. (1901); late orgt. of Christ Ch. Cath. Dublin; late prof. of music, Univ. Coll. Dublin (Nat. Univ. of Ireland); prof. of music, Dublin Univ. (from 1920); prof. of harmony, R.C.M. London.

Art of Counterpoint (new ed. 1924); *Evolution of Harmony; Applied Strict Counterpoint; Studies in Fugue; Elementary Harmony* (3 parts); all publ. by Oxford Univ. Press.—E.-H.

KJELLSTRÖM, Sven. Swedish violinist; *b.* Luleå, 30 March, 1875. Stud. R. Cons. Stockholm, 1889-92 (vn. under J. Lindberg); attached to R. Chapel 1890-3. Stud. 3 years under Rémy (Paris); 1st vn. Colonne Orch. 1900-5; member of Viardot Str. Quartet, concerts in Paris, London, etc.; also with the Swedish pianist Alfred Roth (London). Living from 1909 in Stockholm as teacher; some years leader of the Concert Soc.; founded a well-known str. quartet and (together with Erik Lidforss) the Chamber-Music Soc. (1911). Member R.A.M. Stockholm, 1912.—P. V.

KJERULF, Charles. Danish mus. critic and compr. *b.* Copenhagen, 22 March, 1858; *d.* Elsinore, 22 Aug. 1919. His brilliant musical critiques in *Politiken,* Copenhagen, gained wide notice and influence; he wrote an excellent biography of Niels W. Gade (1917), and an Autobiography in 2 vols. (1916-17) which gives a vivid description of mus. life in Copenhagen. His interest in the theatre gave impulse to the compn. of several operettas: *Keiserens nye Klæder (The Emperor's New Robes),* text

after Hans Chr. Andersen; *Madamernes Jens (The Missus's Tommy); Kreolerinden (The Creole),* etc.; music to several dramas, amongst others Drachmann's *Dansen paa Koldinghus (The Dance at Koldinghus).* He transl. Bellman's Swedish songs, *Fredmans Epistles,* into Danish.—A. H.

KLATTE, Wilhelm. Ger. author and teacher; *b.* Bremen, 13 Feb. 1870. Stud. in Leipzig; went to Weimar to Richard Strauss and worked at theatre there; was dir. in different places; since 1897, first music critic for Berlin *Lokalanzeiger;* and since 1904, teacher of theory at Stern's Cons. (1919, prof.); in 1900, married contr. singer, Clara Senfft of Pilsach. Since 1909, on committee of General Soc. of Ger. Music.

With Arthur Seidl, K. wrote a character-sketch of R. Strauss (1895). For R. Strauss's coll. *Music,* he wrote *History of Programme-Music* (vol. 7) and *Franz Schubert* (vols. 22–23, 1907); biographies; analyses of modern mus. works; exercises in simple cpt.; *Grundlagen des mehrstimmingen Satzes (Course of Harmony)* 1923.—A. E.

KLAUWELL, Otto. Ger. author and teacher; *b.* Langensalza, 6–7 April, 1851; *d.* Cologne, 11–12 May, 1917. Nephew of music-teacher, Adolf Klauwell (1818–79). Stud. mathematics at Leipzig Univ.; turned to music, 1872. Pupil at Leipzig Cons. under Reinecke and Richter (theory and compn.); 1874, Ph.D. 1875, pf. teacher Cologne Cons.; 1884, dir. of pf. training classes arr. by Fr. Wüllner; 1895, deputy dir. of Conservatoire.

Overture, *Vision,* op. 19 (str. orch.); pf. trio, G mi. op. 20; *Evening Peace* (mixed chorus and orch.); pf. pieces; 2 operas, *Lady of the Lake* (Cologne, 1899) and *The Secret Judges* (Elberfeld, 1902); songs. Books: *The Historical Development of Musical Canon* (1874, dissertation; 1876 as independent book); *Musical Points of View* (1881; 2nd ed. as *Musical Confessions,* 1892); *Expression in Music* (1883; Eng. 1892); *Fingering in Pf. Playing* (1885); *The Forms of Instr. Music* (1894; 2nd ed., ed. by W. Niemann, 1918); *History of the Sonata* (1899); *Beethoven and the Variation-Form* (1901); *Life and Works of Theodor Gouvy* (1902); *Studies and Recollections; Essays on Music* (1904); *History of Programme-Music* (1910, Breitkopf).—A. E.

KLEIN, Herman. Eng. mus. critic and teacher of singing; *b.* Norwich, 23 July, 1856. Stud. singing under Manuel Garcia, 1874–7; began journalism in 1875; critic of *Sunday Times,* 1881–1901; *Illustrated London News,* etc.; lived in New York, 1902–9; returned to London, 1909; mus. critic for *Saturday Review,* 1917–21.

Thirty Years of Musical Life in London (New York, 1903, Century Co.); *Unmusical New York* (London, 1910, John Lane); *The Reign of Patti* (New York, 1920, Century Co.); *The Bel Canto* (H. Milford, London 1923); co-ed. of Manuel Garcia's *Hints on Singing* (1894, Ascherberg); *Musical Notes* 1886–9 (Novello). *Lieder in English,* over 60 transls. of songs by Schubert, Schumann and Brahms (Metzler); etc.—E.-H.

KLEIN, Walter. Austrian composer and writer on music; *b.* Brünn (Moravia), 23 June, 1882. Trained in law; lived since 1900 in Vienna, stud. under Kitzler (teacher of Anton Bruckner). Wrote a very sound manual of harmony (Innsbruck, 1922, Wagner). Songs with pf.; songs with str. 4tet; *Scherzo,* pf. (all Breitkopf). Vn. sonata (publ. by compr.). His works are very artistic and sound in technique.—P. ST.

KLEINMICHEL, Richard. Ger. compr. and pianist; *b.* Posen, 31 Dec. 1846; *d.* Charlottenburg, 18 Aug. 1901. First pf. lessons with father (Friedr. Heinrich Hermann K. *b.* 26 May, 1817; *d.* Hamburg, 29 May, 1894; military-bandmaster, Posen, Potsdam, Hamburg; later dir. of music at Stadttheater, Hamburg). 1863–6, stud. at Leipzig Cons.; teacher of music in Hamburg; 1876, dir. of music at Stadttheater, Leipzig, then at Magdeburg; lived finally in Berlin. K. appeared several times as pianist, but was best known as compr. He made many pf. arrs. of Wagner's and Humperdinck's operas.

Works for pf. (excellent studies); sonata for cello, D ma. op. 36; *Spanish and Italian National Music* (for pf.); songs; chamber-music; 2 symphonies; 2 operas, *The Piper of Dusenbach* (Hamburg, 1891); *The Castle of Lorme* (Dantzig, 1885).—A. E.

KLEMETTI, Heikki. Finnish choral condr. *b.* Kuortane, 14 Feb. 1876. Studied at Helsingfors Univ. (Ph.M. 1899), and in local Orch. School; later at Stern's Cons. and Acad. for Church Music, Berlin. As condr. of Finnish Students' Choir (Ylioppilaskunnan Laulajat) since 1898, and of choral soc. Suomen Laulu (founded by him in 1900 first as a male choir; since 1907 enlarged to mixed choir), K. has greatly spread the art of choral singing in Finland, especially by raising technique and expression to a very high level. In concerts given by the Suomen Laulu, great choral works (many in a Finnish translation) have been perf. besides the native repertoire. The choir toured abroad, in 1900–1, 1906 and 1913, visiting Scandinavia, Germany, Holland, Belgium, Hungary and England. K. is also a compr. (choral songs, arr. of folk-songs and old music), a historian and writer (*Musiikin historia*; as yet, 2 vols.), as well as a teacher of singing.—T. H.

KLEMPERER, Otto. Ger. condr. and compr. *b.* Breslau, 15 May, 1885. Stud. at Hoch's Cons. in Frankfurt-o-M., finishing in Berlin (Ph. Scharwenka and Pfitzner). 1907, condr. at Ger. National Theatre in Prague (on Mahler's recommendation); 1909, first condr. in Hamburg; thence to Bremen, Strasburg, and (1917) Cologne. Now dir. Grosse Volksoper, Berlin.

Missa Sacra in C, for soli, choir, children's choir, organ and orch.; *Psalm XLII*, *b.* solo, organ and orch.; *Coloratura Aria*, as extra number in Rossini's *Barber*; songs.—A. E.

KLENAU, Paul von. Danish compr. *b.* Copenhagen, 11 Feb. 1883. Pupil of Hilmer (vn.) and Otto Malling in Copenhagen; then of Halir (vn.) and Max Bruch (compn.) in Berlin; and of Ludwig Thuille in Munich. In 1907, stage-dir. Freiburg-i-Br.; 1908 to Stuttgart, where he stud. under Max Schillings; 1914, again to Freiburg for short time as first condr.; since then, devoted to compn. in Copenhagen. He is a musician with a great feeling for harmony, and a strongly developed sense of form.

3 symphonies; symph. poem, *Paolo and Francesca* (Univ. Ed.); ballad, *Ebbe Skammelsen* (barit. and orch.); *Talks with Death* (6 songs for contr. with orch.); *The Shulamite* (1-act, Munich, 1908; Univ. Ed.); Pantomime-dance, *Little Ida's Flowers* (after Andersen) (Stuttgart, 1916); opera, *Kjartan and Gudrun* (Mannheim, 1918; Univ. Ed.); str. 4tet, E mi.; 9 pf. pieces, *Stories of the Four-year-old* (Schott); songs.—A. E.

KLENGEL, Julius. German cello-virtuoso; *b.* Leipzig, 24 Sept. 1859. Brother of Paul Klengel;

pupil of Emil Hegar and Jadassohn (theory); 1886, first cellist in Gewandhaus Orch., teacher at Leipzig Cons.

3 cello concertos; 2 str. 4tets; Suite for 2 celli; cello sonata; 3 cello suites; pf. trio; *Serenade* for str. orch.; pieces for 2 and 4 celli; solo pieces for cello; Practical Teaching Pieces in Expression.—A. E.

KLENGEL, Paul. Ger. violinist and compr. *b.* Leipzig, 13 May, 1854. Graduated at Leipzig Univ.; Ph.D. (dissertation, *Æsthetic in Music*, 1876); 1881–6, condr. Euterpe Concerts at Leipzig; 1887–91, second Court-condr. Stuttgart; 1892–8, condr. of *Arion* and the Acad. of Singing, Leipzig; 1898–1902, condr. Ger. Choral Union, New York; returned to Leipzig as condr. of *Arion.*

Songs and pieces for pf.; 2 suites, vn and pf. op. 38, 40; pieces for vla. and pf. op. 46.—A. E.

KLEVEN, Arvid. Norwegian compr. flautist; *b.* Trondhjem in 1900. Pupil of Gustav Lange, Christiania (theory and compn.). Stud. in Paris, 1921–2. Flautist in National Theatre Orch. 1919; then in Philh. Soc. Orch. Christiania. His early talent for compn. has won recognition, especially through his orch. works, which show a considerable sense for form and a sure mastery of modern orchestral expression. He is strongly influenced by Fr. and Eng. Impressionism.

Lotusland, poem for orch. (Christiania, Young Norwegian Composers' concert, 1922); *To akvareller* (*Two Aquarelles*) for orch. (perf. 1923); *Poema*, op. 3, for vn. and pf. (Christiania, 1923).—J. A.

KLIČKA, Josef. Czechoslovak compr. *b.* Klatovy, 1855. Pupil of Skuherský at Organ School. Was orgt. in Prague; 1876–81, condr. at theatre; 1891–8, choirmaster of *Hlahol*, Prague; 1906–20, public inspector of music in Bohemia. Prof. at Cons. (first at Organ School) since 1885; from 1920 prof. at its Master-School. His compns. in a conservative style are well adapted for instrs.; the best are for chorus and organ.

Oratorios: *Funeral on the Kaňk*; *The Czechs' Arrival at Říp*; opera, *The Beautiful Miller-girl*; mixed chorus: *Hymn*; *Two Psalms*; *Ballad of Bohemian Music*; *Polka comes*; *Lumír's Bequest* (with orch.); *Our Pearls*, etc.; 6 female choruses; 9 masses, 3 concert fantasies, organ; concert fantasia on chorale *St. Václav* and *Legenda* (both in *Les Maîtres contemporains d'orgue*, Paris); organ sonata, F sharp mi.; many pieces for harp; 2 str. 5tets; 5tet for wind-instrs. and pf.; 2 str. 4tets; trio; 6tet.—V. ST.

KLINDWORTH, Karl. German pianist and teacher; *b.* Hanover, 25 Sept. 1830; *d.* Stolpe, near Oranienburg, 27 July, 1916. Pupil of Liszt at Weimar; 1854–68, lived in London; 1861–2, arranged orch. and chamber-music concerts; 1868–84, prof. at Moscow Cons.; moved to Berlin to conduct Philh. Concerts with Joachim and Wüllner; opened (with Hans v. Bülow) a pf. school; 1893, combined with Scharwenka Cons.

Pf. pieces and songs; pf. arr. of Wagner's *Nibelungen* tetralogy; a complete Chopin Edition; Beethoven's Sonatas, etc.—A. E.

KLINGENBERG, Alf. Norwegian-American pianist; *b.* Trondhjem, 8 Sept. 1867. Pupil of Erika Nissen in Christiania and of Hochschule in Berlin. *Début* in Christiania, 1896. Went to America in 1903. Since 1919, dir. of Eastman School of Music at Univ. of Rochester.—U. M.

KLOED, Wilhelm Cappele. Norwegian tenor singer; *b.* Christiania, 26 July, 1855. Matriculated in 1874. Pupil of Thv. Lammers in Christiania. Afterwards stud. in Paris and Munich. *Début* in 1879 in Stockholm; engaged for several years in that city as singer and actor at a number of theatres. In 1887, dir. of Vasa Theatre. 1890–9, at Christiania Theatre as opera-singer and actor; subsequently at National Theatre. Leading rôles: *Faust*, Don José (*Carmen*), Hoffmann (*Tales of Hoffmann*), Turiddu (*Cavalleria*), etc. Has publ. a book on singing and a number of pieces for v. and pf.—R. M.

KLOSE, Friedrich. Swiss composer; *b.* Carlsruhe, Germany, 29 Nov. 1862. Studied composition under V. Lachner; then in Geneva under A. Ruthardt; pupil of A. Bruckner in Vienna (1886–9); returned to Geneva, where he wrote many of his best works; engaged at Basle Cons. 1906–7; soon after at R. Acad. Munich (succeeding Thuille). Resigned 1920; now lives at Thun, Switzerland. K. has achieved his greatest successes in purely lyric and dramatic works. He may be classed as a Post-Romantic. His works have been strongly influenced, not only by Wagner, but by Berlioz and Liszt. He resembles Bruckner in many ways, in rich orchestration, and sincerity of expression; but his music shows more sustained effort and a more carefully constructed scheme than those of Bruckner. Those passages of K. which sing in a pure, classical vein, are most lovely and attractive. In his Mass, his str. 4tet, his oratorio *Der Sonne-Geist*, his melody is superbly rich and voluptuous.

Mass, op. 6, soli, chorus, orch., organ (Magdeburg, Heinrichshofen); *Elfenreigen*, orch. (Leipzig, 1892, Leuckart); *Festzug*, orch. (Univ. Ed.); *Das Leben ein Traum* (*Life a Dream*), symph. poem, 3 parts, for orch. organ, female vs. reciter, brass instrs. 1899 (Univ. Ed.); *Ilsebill* (*The Fisher and his Wife*) dramatic symphony (or opera), poem from Hugo Hoffmann (Munich, Drei Masken Verlag; perf. Carlsruhe, 1903); oratorio, *The Sun Spirit* (*Der Sonne-Geist*) 6 solo vs. chorus, orch. organ, 1918 (Univ. Ed.); *Die Wallfahrt nach Kevlaar* (*Pilgrimage to Kevelaar*) reciter, chorus, orch., organ (Leuckart); *Ein Festgesang Neros* (*Festal Song of Nero*) (Victor Hugo), t. solo, chorus, orch. organ (Leipzig, Kahnt); Prelude and double fugue for organ—4 tpts. 4 trombones at end (Peters); *Elegy*, vn. and orch.; str. 4tet, E flat (1911, Peters); song-cycle; songs; choruses (Hug; Kahnt; Leuckart; Univ. Ed.).
Consult his own *Mein Künstlerischer Werdegang* in *Neue Musikzeitung*, 6 June, 1918 (Stuttgart, Grüninger); R. Louis, *F. K.* (Berlin, Schuster); *Ilsebill von F. K.* (Carlsruhe, 1907, H. Kuntz); *F. K. and his symph. poem Life a Dream* (1905, G. Müller); H. Knappe, *F. K.* (Munich, 1921, Drei Masken Verlag); H. Reinhardt, *F. K. Der Sonne-Geist*, thematic guide (Univ. Ed.).—F. H.

KLUGHARDT, August Friedrich Martin. Ger. compr. *b.* Köthen, 30 Nov. 1847; *d.* Dessau, 3 Aug. 1902. Pupil of Blassmann and Ad. Reichel, Dresden, theatre mus. dir. at Posen, Lübeck and Weimar. 1873, became Court mus. dir. at Neustrelitz, 1882 at Dessau; 1900, Ph.D. *h.c.* Erlangen University.

Overtures: *In the Spring*, op. 30; *Sophonisbe*; 2 *Festival Overtures* (op. 54, A ma. and op. 78); *Concert Overture*, op. 45; *Victory Overture*; 5 symphonies (*Leonore*, op. 27; *Forest Life*, D ma. op. 37; 5th and 6th C mi.); 2 suites for orch. op. 40, A mi. (6 parts) and op. 67 (*Wandering*); Capriccio, Gavotte and Tarantella for orch. op. 87; 3 pieces for str. orch. op. 14; pf. 5tet, G mi. op. 43; pf. 4tet, D ma.; trio, B flat ma. op. 47; str. 6tet, D ma. op. 68; 2 str. 4tets (F ma.; D ma.); 5tet for wood-wind, C ma. op.

79; ob. concerto; vn. concerto; cello concerto; vn. *Romance*, G ma.; 3 oratorios: *The Burial of Christ*; *The Destruction of Jerusalem*, op. 75 (1899); *Judith* (1901); *The Holy Night*; *Psalm C* (for chorus, b. and orch.); *Psalm LI* (vs. with orch.). Operas: *Miriam* (Weimar, 1871); *Iwein* (Neustrelitz, 1879); *Gudrune* (Neustrelitz, 1882); *The Monk's Wedding* (Dessau, 1886; then as *Astorre*, Prague, 1888). *Fairy Poems* for female chorus, soli and pf., *Bremen Town Musicians* and *Cinderella*; *Schilflieder* (fantasy pieces after Lenau for pf. ob. vla.); songs (*Old German Love Song*, op. 80).—A. E.

KNAPPERTSBUSCH, Hans. Ger. condr. *b.* Elberfeld, 12 March, 1888. Stud. philosophy at Bonn; 1909, went to Cologne Cons. (Steinbach, Lohse). 1912–13, cond. Wagner Fest. Plays in Holland; 1913–18, opera dir. at Elberfeld; 1918, chief condr. at Leipzig Stadttheater; 1919, opera dir.; 1920, gen. mus. dir. at Dessau; 1922, opera and gen. mus. dir. Munich Opera (in succession to Bruno Walter).—A. E.

KNEISEL, Franz. Violinist; *b.* Bucharest, Rumania, 26 Jan. 1865. Son of a German bandmaster in Bucharest; stud. under his father, and at Bucharest Cons.; a 1st prize in vn.-playing at 15 years. 1879–82, at Vienna Cons. under Grün and Hellmesberger. Made *début* with Vienna Philh. Orch. 31 Dec. 1882, playing Joachim's *Hungarian Concerto*. After a year as leading violinist in orch. of Hofburg Theatre, Vienna, then of Bilse Orch. in Berlin in 1884; the next year went to America as leading violinist of Boston Symphony Orch. Remained until 1903, acting as assistant-condr. for many years; 1892–1908, associate-condr. of Worcester (Mass.) fests. 1907, one of judges for vn. class at annual competition of Paris Cons. Since 1905, head of vn. department of Inst. of Mus. Art. in New York. Received Mus.D. *h.c.* from Yale Univ. 1911, and from Princeton, 1917. His chief claim to fame rests on his organisation and direction of Kneisel Quartet (*q.v.*).

Grand Étude de Concert (Schirmer); *Advanced Exercises* for vn. (Schirmer, 1910). Compiler of Kneisel Collection for Violin, 3 vols. (Church, 1900).—O. K.

KNEISEL QUARTET was organised in Boston, in 1885, by Franz Kneisel (*q.v.*). Orig. members: Kneisel, E. Fiedler, Louis Svečenski, and Fritz Giese. Kneisel was 1st vn. throughout its entire existence of 32 years. Its later 2nd vns. were Otto Roth (1887–99), Karl Ondriček (1899–1902), J. Theodorowicz (1902–7), Julius Röntgen (1907–12), and Hans Letz (1912–17). Svečenski was the only vla. Its later cellists were Anton Hekking (1889–91), Alwin Schroeder (1891–1907), Willem Willeke (1907–17). In 1903 the quartet transferred its headquarters to New York. For many years the quartet was recognised as by far the best organisation of its kind in America. It gave concerts in Europe, where it was compared favourably with the most notable European quartets. Owing to the increased demand made upon Kneisel's time by vn. pupils, the quartet ceased its activity in 1917. Farewell concert in New York, 3 April.—O. K.

KNITTL, Karel. Czech music-teacher, conductor; *b.* Polná, 1853; *d.* Prague, 1907. Stud. at Organ School, Prague; since 1890, prof. of Harmony at Prague Cons. 1878–90 and 1897–1901, condr. of Prague choral soc. *Hlahol*; 1901, administrative dir. of Cons.; reformed methods there by accentuating general and theoretical training. Vocal works (all early) publ. by F. A. Urbánek.—V. ST.

KNOCKER, Editha G. Eng. violinist; *b.* Exmouth, 2 March, 1869. Persistent neuritis broke off her concert-playing; spent several years teaching in the N. of England; founded a symphony orch. in York and one at Newcastle (now cond. by H. Harty); now teaches in London. Amongst her pupils are Rhoda Backhouse, Sybil Eaton, Murray Lambert.
The Making of a Violinist (Goodwin & Tabb); *Analysis of the Art of Practising* (*id.*); *The Violin* (fest. booklet; Paterson, Glasgow).—E.-H.

KNORR, Ivan. Russ. compr. and teacher; *b.* Mewe, West Prussia, 3 Jan. 1853; *d.* Frankfort-o-M. 22 Jan. 1916. Stud. at Leipzig Cons. (Reinecke, Richter); 1874, music-master at Charkof, South Russia, and dir. of theoretical instruction in department of Imperial Mus. Soc.; was called, 1883, to Hoch's Cons. Frankfort-o-M. as teacher of theory and compn.; dir. 1908.
Exercises for Instruction in Harmony (1903); *Text-book of Fugue Composition* (1911); *Fugues of the Well-tempered Clavier pictorially represented* (1912); *Biography of Tchaikovsky* (1900); and *Analysis* for the *Musikführer*. Orch. and chamber-music (pf. 4tet, E flat ma. op. 3; pf. trio, op. 1); *Variations* on an Ukraine national song for orch. op. 7 (greatly esteemed by Brahms); 8 songs, mixed chorus, op. 11; *Ukraine Love Songs* for mixed 4tet and pf. Operas: *Dunja*, perf. Coblence, 1904; *Through the Window*, Carlsruhe, 1908.
Consult: M. Bauer, *I. K.* (Frankfort-o-M. 1916); article by Cyril Scott, *I. K.*, *Monthly Mus. Record* (Sept. 1916); also C. Scott's *My Years of Indiscretion* (Mills & Boon, 1924).—A. E.

KNOSP, Gaston. Belgian compr. musicologist; *b.* Milan, 29 May, 1879. Pupil of Massenet and Lavignac. 1898–1904, in charge of an official mission for comparative study of music of the Far East in Fr. Indo-China (report publ. at Brill's, Leyden). Wrote art. and monographs on music of Far East for Lavignac's *Encyclopédie*. As compr. specialised in operatic works on Oriental subjects:
Le Yakounine; La Jeune Fille d'Ohçaka; Les Amants de Yeddo; Sharah-Sultane; L'Impromptu persan. Also *Cydalise*; *Le Poète et sa Femme* (incidental music to play by F. Jammes, perf. Brussels, 1914). —C. V. B.

KNOWLES, Charles. Eng. operatic barit. *b.* Leeds. Stud. under Santley, Randegger and Henry J. Wood; sang Leeds Fest. 1898, in Elgar's *Caractacus*; London Mus. Fest. 1899; since then, all the leading fests. Hagen in the Eng. perf. of *Ring* under Richter, Covent Garden, and Denhof, Beecham tours 1912–13; toured S. Africa 1913; tours, from 1918.—E.-H.

KNUTSEN, Dagny. Norwegian pianist; *b.* Christiania, 30 Nov. 1890. Pupil (pf.) of Anna Ø[slash]lstad and Fridtjof Backer-Gröndahl, afterwards of High School in Berlin (pf. Heinrich Barth), as well as of Cortot and Lortat in Paris. First independent concert in Christiania, 1914; has since frequently given concerts there and elsewhere in her own country, as well as in Stockholm. A gifted pianist, who, besides Brahms and Reger, has especially cultivated the French Impressionists.—J. A.

KNUTZEN, Martin. Norwegian pianist; *b.* Drammen, 24 May, 1863; *d.* Christiania, 9 Dec. 1909. Pupil of Chr. Cappelen, Drammen, Agathe Gröndahl, Christiania; of Barth, Berlin, and Leschetizky, Vienna. *Début*, Christiania Mus. Soc. 1887. Gave concerts mainly in Scandinavia and Germany. Regarded as finest Norwegian male pianist of his time.—U. M.

KOCH, Friedrich E. Ger. compr. *b.* Berlin, 3 July, 1862. 1883–91, cellist of R. Court Orch.; mus. dir. Baden-Baden; 1901, member of Berlin Acad.; 1917, dir. of department for theory at R. High School of Music, Berlin.
2 symphonies (*From the North Sea*, op. 4; G ma. op. 10); symph. fugue, C mi. op. 8; *German Rhapsody*, op. 31 (vn. concerto); *Romantic Suite*, op. 37, for pf. and orch.; organ work, *Gethsemane*; madrigals, 4- to 6-v. mixed chorus, op. 45; *Fantasy Pieces*, op. 20, pf. vn. and cello; str. trio, op. 9; 4 songs, barit. and orch.; songs, op. 6 and 38; oratorio, *Daytime*, op. 29; *The Flood*, op. 32; 5 Schiller Poems, op. 39; *German Motets*, op. 34; *The Prophecy of Isaiah*, chamber cantata, op. 42; choral works: *The Captivated Stream*, op. 29; *The German Fir Tree*, op. 30; symphonietta, *Forest Idyll*; 3 operas: *Die Halliger*; *Lea*; *The Mill on the Hill* (Berlin, 1918, Ger. Opera House).—A. E.

KOCH, Richert Sigurd Valdemar von. Swedish compr. *b.* Ångnö (on island near Stockholm), 28 June, 1879; *d.* Stockholm, 16 March, 1919. Stud. compn. under Johan Lindegren, and in Berlin; pf. under Richard Andersson.
Orch.: *Romance and Serenade*, vn. and orch. (1914; perf. 1915); *Impressions of the Sea* (1917; perf. 1918); *In the Fields of Pan*, lyric phantasy (1917; perf. 1917); *Ballade*, pf. and orch.; sonata, vn. and pf. (1913; perf. 1914); sonata, cello and pf. (1914; perf. 1915); pf. 5tet (1916; perf. 1916); songs; pf. pieces (publ. Elkan & Schildknecht; Nordiska Musikförlaget; Wilh. Hansen).—P. V.

KOCHANSKA-SEMBRICH, Marcelina. Polish coloratura singer; *b.* Wisniowczyk, Galicia, 1858. Stud. pf. at Lemberg Cons. when a little girl under W. Stengel (later her husband); then under Epstein in Vienna. In 1875, began to study singing under Rokitanski in Vienna, then under Lamperti, at Milan. From 1877, appeared as a singer and soon attained world-wide fame. —ZD. J.

KOCHAŃSKI, Paweł. Polish violinist; *b.* Odessa, 1887. At 7 years, pupil of Emil Młynarski. In 1901, when 14, played 1st vn. in Warsaw Philh. In 1903, went to Brussels Cons., where, after four months, he received the *Premier prix avec la plus grande distinction*. From this time he gave concerts in all the chief cities of Europe. In 1907, became prof. at Warsaw Cons. During the war he played much in Russia. From 1919, has been travelling in America, England and France. (Paul K. should not be confused with the other fine Polish violinist, Wacław K.).—ZD. J.

KOCHAŃSKI, Wacław. Polish violinist; *b.* in 1884. Pupil of Ševčik. Has played much in Poland, Germany and elsewhere. Was first to give vn. recitals without acc., playing the solo works of Bach and Reger. Now lives in Warsaw.—ZD. J.

KOCIÁN, Jaroslav. Czechoslovak violinist; *b.* Ústí, near Orlicí, 1883. A pupil of O. Ševčik at Prague Cons. After Kubelik he was first to draw the world's attention to the pedagogic supremacy of his teacher. His numerous tours led him to all parts of the civilised world. His sweet, soft tone and eminent skill in all problems of vn. technique are the most remarkable features of his playing. Has composed some orch., church and vn. pieces. Lives in Prague.—V. ST.

KOCZALSKI, Raul. Polish pianist, compr. *b.* Warsaw, 1885. Stud. under his father, and in very early childhood began to give concerts. Is well known in many countries. Has publ. more than 70 pf. works of virtuoso character, of which many are based on Polish national and popular airs. He also brought out 2 operas on the Ger. stage: *Rymond* (Elberfeld, 1902) and *Die Sühne* (1909). Lives in Berlin.—ZD. J.

KOCZIRZ, Adolf. Music historian; *b.* Wierowan (Moravia), 2 April, 1870. Stud. at Olmütz; came to Vienna and took mus. degree at Univ. in the Musikhistorische Institut of Guido Adler; Ph.D. 1903. His special study is the lute and its music. Ed. (in *D.T.Ö.*) *Österreichische Lauten-musik in 16 Jahrhundert* (XXXVII) and *Öster-reichische Lautenmusik 1650–1720* (L). His system of translating the lute-tablatures was accepted by the International Lute Commission at Congress of I.M.G. at Vienna.—EG. W.

KODÁLY, Zoltán. Hungarian compr. folk-song collector, and music critic; *b.* Kecskemét, 16 Dec. 1882. Stud. compn. (1900) at R. High School for Music, Budapest, under Hans Koessler. In 1905, turned his attention to the study of Hungarian folk-music, which he has pursued to this day with enthusiasm, and has founded a coll. of Hungarian pea-sant-tunes (about 3500), some noted down from the mouths of the peasants, others recorded by phonograph. Most of them were taken from regions on the confines of Hungary most remote from urban culture, and least influenced by it. A large number of these are still in ms. Since 1906, teacher of compn. at Royal High School for Music, Budapest, acting as deputy-dir. from Feb. to Sept. 1919. As critic, has been active on several Budapest papers (*Nyugat, Pesti Napló*), and is at present Hungarian correspondent for the *Revue Musicale* (Paris), *Musical Courier* (New York), and *Il Pianoforte* (Italy). His style of compn. owes much of its character to the individual mus. idiom he has created for himself out of the Hungarian peasant-music he has personally collected.

Op. 1, 16 songs with pf., Hungarian words, Eng. transl. (1907–9, Budapest, Rózsavölgyi); op. 2, 1st str. 4tet (1908; *id.*); op. 3, 9 pf. pieces (1909, *id.*); op. 4, sonata, pf. and cello (1909–10, Vienna, Univ. Ed.); op. 5, 2 songs with orch. acc. (1912–13, *id.*); op. 6, 7 songs with pf. acc. (1912–13, *id.*); op. 7, duo, vn. and cello (1914, *id.*); op. 8, sonata, cello solo (1915, *id.*); op. 9, songs with pf. acc. (1914–15, *id.*); op. 10, 2nd str. 4tet (1916–17, *id.*); op. 11, 7 pf. pieces (1917–18, *id.*); op. 12, *Serenade*, 2 vns. and vla. (1919–20, *id.*). *Psalm LV*, chorus, t. solo and orch. (1923, *id.*). Without opus numbers (in collab. with Bartók), 20 Hungarian folk-songs with pf. acc. (Budapest, 1906, Rozsnyai). Hungarian folk-songs with pf. acc. (Vienna, Univ. Ed.). Folk-lore publications: *Ungarische Totenklagen* (1924, Rózsavölgyi); *Transylvanian Hungarian Folk-Songs* (with Eng. and Fr. preface), publ. by Bartók and Kodály (Budapest, 1921, Popular Literary Soc.); *The Pentatonic Scale*

in the Hungarian Folk-Music of Zenei Szemle, 1st year-book (Temesvár, 1917).
Consult: *Hungarian Music of To-day* (*Monthly Musical Record*, Feb. 1922); *Z. K.* (*Musical Times*, May 1922); *Della Musica in Ungheria* (*Il Pianoforte*, July 1921); *The Development of Music in Hungary* (*Chesterian*, Jan. 1922).—B. B.

KOEBERG, F. E. A. Dutch compr. *b.* The Hague, 15 July, 1876. Stud. under Nicolai, Viotta and, in Berlin, under Scharwenka and Gernsheim. His choral works are in a pseudo-classical style, but later he was somewhat influenced by French Impressionism.

3 symphonies; symph. poems: *Zeelandia*; *Avond-muziek*; *Zotskap*; *Zevenzot*; *Lénore*; *Plato*; overtures; triple fugue for str. 4tet; pieces for vn.; pf.; ob.; a choral work with reciter, *Alianora*.—W. P.

KŒCHLIN, Charles. Fr. compr. *b.* of Alsatian parents at Paris, 27 Nov. 1867. After receiving the usual courses of classical and scientific education, he entered the École Polytechnique. In 1890 he renounced mathematics and entered the Paris Cons., where he stud. cpt. under Gédalge and compn. under Massenet and Fauré. He did not enter the *Prix de Rome* competition, and left the Cons. without diploma or award of any sort. Since that time, his career has been uneventful, marked only by hard work and scant recognition. He is very retiring in disposition, and has never taken any steps to speed the performance or publication of his numerous works. It is only lately that some of these were publ., and that a few critics began to call attention to his music.

The works so far available in print are:

Pf.: 5 *Sonatines* (Mathot); *Paysages et Marines*, 12 pieces (*id.*); 4 books of short pieces (Senart). Chamber: 1st vn. sonata (*id.*); sonata for fl. and pf. (*id.*); sonata for 2 fls. (*id.*); 1st str. 4tet (*id.*). sonata, cello and pf. (*id.*); sonata for 2 fls. (*id.*). Vocal: songs. 3 books (Rouart, Lerolle); rondels, 3 books (*id.*); *L'Abbaye*, solo vs. choir and organ (Janin).

It is hardly possible to form an estimate of his individuality without taking into account his considerable orch. output and his unpubl. chamber-music. The former especially, which comprises big works such as *Les Saisons*, *Études Antiques*, *La Forêt Païenne*, Chorales for orch., reveals aspects of his imagination which are not to be known from his publ. works. But the publ. works suffice to show the keenness and versatility of his imagination, the loftiness of his ideals, and the excellence of his technique.

The Sonatinas alone will show that he can be no less original and eloquent while employing an idiom which would have been found legitimate in the days of Haydn, than he is when resorting to the most daring polytonal combinations.

He contributes articles of mus. philosophy and criticism to various Fr. periodicals. His little book, *Étude sur les Notes de Passage* (Paris, *Monde Musical*, 1922), is an invaluable contribution to the study of cpt. and its harmonic consequences.

Consult: E Vuillermoz, *K.* (*Musiques d'aujour-d'hui*); H. C. Oliphant, *The Songs of Ch. K.* (*Mus. Quarterly*, April, 1921); M. D. Calvocoressi, *Ch. K.* (*Mus. Times*, Nov. 1921–Jan. 1922).—M. D. C.

KOEGLER, Hermann. Ger. compr. *b.* Lódž, 2 Feb. 1885. Pupil of Vienna Blind Institute

(Wotawa, Lafite); 1904–9 of Leipzig Cons. (Teichmüller, Krehl, Richard Hofmann); lives at Leipzig.

Pf. fantasy, op. 6; *Romantic Serenade* (pf. harmonium and cello) op. 17; *Easter Hymn* (mixed chorus, orch. and organ) op. 38; *Whitsuntide Prayer* (mixed chorus and organ) op. 39; *Psalm XXX* (mixed chorus *a cappella*) op. 40; male and female choruses; songs; the following in ms.: symphony, G mi.; concert overture; vn. concerto; str. 4tet; pf. trios; vn., cello and pf. sonatas; pf. suites and variations; *Ukraine Fantasy*; Prelude and fugue, pf.; pf. pieces; cantatas; songs, etc.—A. E.

KOEMMENICH, Louis. Amer. choral condr. *b.* Elberfeld, Germany, 4 Oct. 1866; *d.* New York, 14 Aug. 1922. Stud. pf., vn., theory under Krause, Kranzel and Blättermann in Barmen, and in Berlin (1885–7) under Kullak, Bussler, Pfeiffer, Hollaender and Tappert at Kullak's Acad. Settled in U.S.A. 1890 as condr. of various choral socs., among them the New York Oratorio Soc. (1912–17) and the Mendelssohn Glee Club (1913–19). Comp. male choruses, songs (Dieckman; Hug; Leuckart; Schuberth; Schirmer). —J. M.

KOENNECKE, Fritz. Compr. *b.* New York, 19 June, 1876. Son of Ger. parents; went to Munich at 16; devoted himself to music, 1896; under Rheinberger, Schmidt-Lindner and Thuille.

Songs; duets; opera, *Cagliostro* (words by Albert Sexauer, 1907); dramatic-mus. version of Shakespeare's *Tempest* (1909, ms.); carnival play, *The Travelling Scholar in Paradise* (from Hans Sachs; Carlsruhe, 1913); 1-act pastoral play, *Rococo* (publ. 1915); 3-act opera *Magdalena* (Charlottenburg, 1919); music to Max Reinhardt's fest. play *King Saul and King David* (1917, not performed).—A. E.

KOESSLER, Hans. Ger. compr. teacher; *b.* Waldeck (Fichtelgebirge), 1 Jan. 1853. 1871, orgt. at Neumarkt (Upper Palatinate); 1874–7, pupil of Rheinberger at R. School of Music, Munich; 1877, teacher at Dresden Cons. of theory and choral singing, and condr. of Choral Union; 1881, condr. at Cologne Stadttheater; 1882, called to National Mus. Acad. Budapest, as teacher of organ and choral singing, and after Robert Volkmann's death, 1883, took compn. classes. Retired 1908; 1919, went to Ansbach; 1920, dir. of advanced school for compn. at Music Acad. Budapest.

Psalm XVI (prize, Vienna Music Soc.); *New Year's Eve Bells* (chorus, solo, orch. and organ); 2 str. 4tets; str. 5tet; str. 6tet; vn. sonata; 2 symphonies; symph. variations, orch.; vn. concerto, A mi. in passacaglia form; *Waltz-Suite*, pf.; 2 Psalms; Mass, female vs. and organ; *Hymn to Beauty*, male chorus and orch.; chamber-songs with ob. horn and str. 5tet; opera, *Der Münzenfranz* (Strasburg, 1902). —A. E.

KOHMANN, Antoni. Polish t. singer. *b.* in Cracow, 1879. Stud. under Stockhausen, and later under Horbowski. Lives in Frankfort-o-M. Well known in Germany, France, Holland, Denmark, Poland, and Sweden; particularly eminent in oratorios and in songs.—Zd. J.

KOLAR, Victor. Amer. violinist, condr. *b.* Budapest, Hungary, 12 Feb. 1888. Son of Bohemian parents, stud. at Prague Cons. under Dvořák. In 1904, went to America as violinist in Chicago Orch.; 1905, joined Pittsburg Orch.; 1907–19, member of New York Symphony Orch.; acting as assistant-condr. after 1915. Now assistant-condr. of Detroit Symphony Orch. His symph.

poem *Hiawatha* was perf. by Pittsburgh Orch. 31 Jan. 1908. A symph. poem, *A Fairy Tale,* perf. by New York Symphony Orch. (16 Feb. 1913); symph. suite, *Americana* (25 Jan. 1914). Symphony in D by the same orch. (28 Jan. 1916), and *Slovakian Rhapsody* for orch. at Norfolk (Conn.) Music Fest. 7 June, 1922.

Americana, orch. op. 20 (Schirmer, 1914); 3 *Humoresques*, vn. and pf. (*id.* 1914); 3 songs, op. 18 (C. Fischer, 1912).—O. K.

KOLDERUP, Amunda. Norwegian operatic s. singer; *b.* Furnes, Hedemarken, 15 Dec. 1846; *d.* Christiania, 28 Sept. 1882. Pupil of Baroness A. Leuhusen (Stockholm), R. Levy (Vienna), and San Giovanni (Milan). *Début* as concert-singer in Stockholm, 1874; as opera-singer at Olmütz, 1875. Sang more than 20 leading rôles in Ger. and Austrian opera houses (Elizabeth, Elsa, Fidelio, Countess [*Marriage of Figaro*], Margaret, Aïda, etc.). One of most brilliant of Norwegian vocalists.—U. M.

KOLLER, Oswald. Austrian music historian; *b.* Brünn, 30 June, 1852; *d.* Klagenfurt, 10 June, 1910. Collab. of Guido Adler at Vienna Music and Theatre Exhibition in 1892; worked especially on-mediæval music. Ed. (in *D.T.Ö.*) the songs of the Austrian troubadour Oswald von Wolkenstein (IX, 1) and (in collab. with G. Adler) first selection of the famous Music Codices of Trent (South Tyrol, now Italy), one of the best sources of music of xv century.—Eg. W.

KONTA, Robert. Austrian compr. and writer on music; *b.* Vienna, 12 Oct. 1880. Ph.D. Vienna Univ.; pupil of Vítezslav Novák (famous Czech compr.). Since 1911, teacher of music-theory at New Vienna Cons. Critic of *Mittags-zeitung.* As dramatic compr. tries to combine folk-song style with a simple fairy-tale manner. Writes his own opera-books.

Operas: *Das kalte Herz* (*The Cold Heart*), perf. at Düsseldorf, 1908; *Der bucklige Geiger* (*The Hump-backed Fiddler*) perf. Prague, 1910; *Kohlenpeter* (*Charcoal-Burner*) perf. Vienna, 1916; *Jugunde*, perf. Prague, 1922; *Verirrt*, not yet perf. Also 1st symphony (perf. Prague, 1909); vn. concerto; songs; music to accompany recitation.—P. P.

KONUS. See Conus.

KONZERTMEISTER (Ger.). The leading first violinist in an orchestra.—E.-H.

KOPSCH, Julius. Ger. compr. *b.* Berlin, 6 Feb. 1887. Stud. law, at same time pupil (1905-11) of W. Klatte (compn.) and Arno Kleffel (conducting); 1911, mus. dir.; now dir. Landes-orchester and chief mus. dir. National Theatre, Oldenburg.

Tone-poem, *Comedians*, 1914; str. 4tet, 1916 pf. concerto, 1917; vn. and pf. sonata, 1919; symphony, 1920; songs.—A. E.

KOPYLOF, Alexander Alexandrovitch (*accent 3rd syll.*). Russ. compr. *b.* Petrograd in 1854; *d.* there 7/20 Feb. 1911. Pupil of Gunke, Liadof and Rimsky-Korsakof.

Symphony; concert overture; 2 str. 4tets; choral music; pf. pieces.—M. D. C.

KORESHTCHENKO, Arseny Nicolaevitch. Russ. compr. *b.* Moscow, 6/18 Dec. 1870. Pupil of Tanéief and Arensky at Moscow Cons.

Operas: *Balthazar's Feast* (1892); *The Angel of Death* (1895); *The Ice Palace* (1900); a symphony; 2 suites and other orch. pieces; songs; pf. music; a small quantity of chamber-music.—M. D. C.

KÖRLING, J. Felix A. Swedish compr. *b.* Kristdala 17 Dec. 1864. Stud. R. Cons. Stockholm, 1884–6; orgt. and choirmaster in Halmstad from 1889; condr. of choral societies. Well known as compr. of children's songs; songs for male vs. and operettas: *Guldgruvan* (*The Gold-Mine*) (Stockholm, 1912); *Rubber* (Gothenburg, 1917); *Jockeyen* (*The Jockey*) (Stockholm, 1918).—P. V.

KORNAUTH, Egon. German - Czechoslovak compr. *b.* Olmütz, 14 May, 1891. Pupil in Vienna of R. Fuchs and Fr. Schreker; 1900, accompanist in N. America; 1912, won Austrian State prize for vla. sonata, op. 3; 1915, Vienna, Ph.D. under Guido Adler; 1917–18, solorepetitor at R. Opera, Vienna; 1919, won the Gustav Mahler Foundation. Since that time has been travelling.

Symphonietta G mi., orch.; Fest. Prelude, E flat ma. full orch.; songs for orch.; str. 6tet, A mi.; pf. 4tet, E mi.; pf. trio, B mi.; sonata, vla. and pf. C sharp mi.; pf. sonata, A flat; sonata, clar. and pf. F mi.; sonata, vn. and pf. E mi.; pf. fantasia, E flat mi.; Fantastic Scherzo, fl. and pf.; *Evening Music*, str.; songs with fl.-obbligato; pf. music; choruses.—E. S.

KORNGOLD, Erich Wolfgang. Composer; *b.* Brünn, May 29, 1897. Son of well-known music-critic (now on the *Neue Freie Presse*), Dr. Julius Korngold. Showed precocious talent as a composer. Pupil of Fuchs and Zemlinsky. All his works (symphonic, chamber-music, songs and 3 operas) have been given in the chief cities of Europe and America in rapid succession and have remained in the repertoire. Korngold often conducted his operas and concerts himself with great ability, and was conductor in Hamburg for a short time. He lives in Vienna now, devoted entirely to composition.

His first works were the ingenuous pantomime *Der Schneemann* (performed at Vienna Opera House, 1908, with Zemlinksy's instrumentation) (Univ. Ed.); piano trio, op. 1, and a few piano pieces without opus number (*Don Quixote*). Written at age of 11 years, they are very remarkable for their vigorous melody and bold harmony. His other works (Schott)—second piano sonata, op. 2 (1910), *Märchenbilder* (pf.) op. 3; *Schauspiel-Ouvertüre*, op. 4—show already his orchestral mastery; also *Sinfonietta*, violin sonata, op. 6, string sextet, op. 10. A string quartet, op. 16, and a piano quintet, op. 15, are in preparation. The symphonic overture, *Sursum Corda* (orch.), *Einfache Lieder*, op. 9, and *Lieder des Abschieds*, op. 14, are often performed. His operas, *Der Ring des Polycrates*, op. 7 (*buffa*) and *Violanta*, op. 8 (tragic, from the Renaissance period), were great stage successes, yet eclipsed by *Die Tote Stadt* (after Rodenbach's *Bruges la morte*). Korngold's entire production holds fast to tonality. In his operas he shows a quick and infallible perception for both stage and musical effects. His dramatic accents are often enrapturing and his recognition of the rights of the singing-voice has a pleasing effect. Korngold is not only one of the most remarkable phenomena in the history of music, but, mature as he is now, he may be of great importance to the future

shaping of musical drama. Consult: Stefan, *Neue Musik und Wien*; R. St. Hoffmann, *E. W. K.* (*Anbruch*, IV, 5–6), and same author's book about this composer (1923, Stephenson).—P. St.

KORNGOLD, Julius. Austrian musicologist; *b.* Brünn, 24 Dec. 1860. Took law degree in Vienna. Became a lawyer and music critic in his native town. Was called in 1902 by Hanslick to *Neue Freie Presse*; worked there first with Hanslick, then as his successor. K. renounced the anti-Wagnerian tendencies of his predecessor and endeavoured to do justice to modern times, supporting Gustav Mahler most enthusiastically. His collected essays, *Deutsches Opernschaffen*, Vol. I, appeared 1920; *Die romanische Oper der Gegenwart*, 1922. Other colls. are in preparation. His son is Erich Korngold, the compr.—P. St.

KORNSTEIN, Egon. Hungarian vla.-player of the Hungarian Str. Quartet (led by Waldbauer). Pupil of Hubay, at R. High School for Music, Budapest.—B. B.

KÖRNYEY, Béla. Hungarian t. singer; *b.* Perőcsény, 18 May, 1875. Member of R. Hungarian Opera House, Budapest, with few interruptions, 1907–22.—B. B.

KOROLEWICZ-WAYDOWA, Janina. Polish coloratura and dramatic s. singer; *b.* Warsaw, 1875. Pupil of Wysocki and Alexander Myszuga in Lemberg. Appeared very early (1893) and sang at Warsaw, Lemberg, Cracow, in Italy, America, Australia, Russia; now sings chiefly in concerts.—Zd. J.

KÓSA, Georg. Hungarian compr. *b.* Budapest, 24 April, 1897.—B. B.

KÖSELITZ, Heinrich. Real name of Peter Gast (*q.v.*).

KOTHE, Robert. Ger. lute-singer; *b.* 6 Feb. 1869. Stud. law and music at Munich; practised as lawyer, but turned to music; stud. old Ger. national songs and lute-playing; since 1903 appeared as lute-singer. Lives in Munich, carrying on movement to revive national songs, especially appreciated by the Ger. *Wandervögel* students.

Poems: *Trot, my Steed, trot* (1910); *Mother, give me thy son* (1915); 12 text-books of songs with lute acc.; 1 for lute and viol da gamba; 1 with lute and female chorus; Tutor for guitar- and lute-playing (Magdeburg, Heinrichshofen). Consult Fritz Jöde, *R. K.* (1916).—A. E.

KOTHEN, Axel, Baron von. Finnish barit. singer; *b.* Hamina (Fredrikshamm), 15 Aug. 1871. Also teacher of singing and compr. Stud. music in Rome, Petrograd, Vienna, Paris, Berlin, Munich. Prof. at R. Liceo Mus. di Santa Cecilia, Rome, 1900; teacher of singing at Helsingfors Music Inst. Has comp. cantatas, orch. and choral works and songs.—T. H.

KOTILAINEN, Otto. Finnish compr. *b.* Heinävesi, 5 Feb. 1868. Stud. at Helsingfors Music Inst. and Orch. School; later abroad, chiefly in Germany. Teacher at Helsingfors Music Inst. Has comp. orch. works, stage-music, choral works, and songs.—T. H.

KOUBA, Josef. Czech compr., violinist; *b.* Prague, 1880. Stud. Prague Cons. under

Ševčík and Bennewitz; Konzertmeister at German Theatre, Prague. Took private lessons in compn. from Vítězslav Novák.

Str. 4tet; vn. sonata, pf. and vn. pieces (publ. Chadim; Hudebni Matice, Prague).—V. ST.

KOVÁCS, Sándor. Hungarian pianist and teacher; *b.* Budapest, 24 Jan. 1886; *d.* there, 1917. Has written several books on music-teaching.—B. B.

KOVAŘOVIC, Karel. Czechoslovak compr. condr. *b.* Prague, 1862; *d.* there, 1920. Stud. harp and clar. at Cons. there; up to 1885 member of orch. at National Theatre, Prague. Pupil in compn. of Zd. Fibich (1878–82); condr. to theatres of Plzeň (Pilsen) and Brno (Brünn), 1886–8; 1895, condr. symphony concerts at Ethnographic Exhibition, Prague. Appointed chief condr. of opera at National Theatre in 1900, when its management was modernised. He held this post till his death. In 1919 was condr. of Czechoslovak Fest. in London, Paris, and Switzerland. He created the ideal type for perf. of Smetana's operas, did much for the stage-works of Dvořák, helped Janáček's success, besides giving Wagner's later operas, Strauss's new works and French operas of the Massenet type. He polished his orch. performances up to chamber-music perfection. In his own works there is a mixture of Smetana's cheerfulness with French grace and the sentimentality of a Massenet. His last two operas are simple, melodious, eloquent and therefore popular.

Operas: *Ženichové* (*The Bridegrooms*) 1882; *Cesta oknem* (*The Way through the Window*) 1885; *The Night of Simon and Jude* (1891); *Psohlavci* (*Dog-heads*), 1896, libretto by K. Šipek after Jirásek's novel; *Na starém bělidle* (*At the Old Bleaching-ground*), 1900, libretto by Šipek after B. Němcová. Melo-dramas: *The Orphan*; *The Golden Spinning Wheel*; 7 ballets (3 under pseudonym Charles Forgeron); symph. poem, *Persefona*; 3 str. 4tets; vn. sonata; pf. concerto. (Last 2 operas publ. by Hudebni Matice; other works by F. Urbánek, Prague.)—V. ST.

KRALIK, Heinrich von. Austrian mus. author and critic; *b.* Vienna, 27 Jan. 1887. Son of Richard Kralik, the well-known historian and poet. Stud. mus. science at Vienna Univ. His dissertation for Ph.D. degree was a treatise on *Dittersdorf's Symphonies*. Mus. critic of *Wiener Zeitung*; since 1918 of *Neue Wiener Tagblatt*.—P. ST.

KRAMER, Arthur Walter. Amer. compr. *b.* New York, 23 Sept. 1890. Graduated A.B., Coll. of City of New York, 1910. Stud. in New York under Karl Hauser and Richard Arnold (vn.) and James Abraham (pf.). Since 1910, on staff of weekly journal *Musical America*. Two Sketches for orch. op. 37*a* (ms.), were perf. by New York Philh. Orch. 27 Feb. 1916.

Elegy, str. 4tet (Boston Music Co.); *Eklog*, vn. (Schmidt); other vn. and pf. pieces and many songs (C. Fischer; J. Fischer; Schirmer; Ditson; Boston Music Co; Church); choruses (Ditson; Church; J. Fischer); *Concert Prelude*, organ (Church).—O. K.

KRASA, Hans. Ger.-Czechoslovak compr. *b.* Prague, 1895. Pupil of A. Zemlinsky. Adopts the atonal style of Stravinsky.

Songs with orch. to words by Christian Morgen-stern.—E. S.

KRAUS, Felix von. Austrian b. singer; *b.* Vienna, 3 Oct. 1870. Stud. music Vienna (Ph.D. 1894); pupil of Stockhausen for 2 months, then self-taught; 1899 at Bayreuth as Hagen and

Gurnemanz; 1908, singing-teacher at R. Acad. of Music, Munich. His wife, Adrienne (*b.* Buffalo, North America, 1873), pupil of Auguste Götze and of her husband, is contr. opera- and concert-singer.—A. E.

KRAUSE, Emil. Ger. teacher and compr. *b.* Hamburg, 30 July, 1840; *d.* there, 5 Sept. 1916. Stud. under Hauptmann, Rietz, Moscheles, Plaidy and Richter at Leipzig Cons.; Hamburg 1860, teacher of pf. and theory; 1864–1907, music critic of *Fremdenblatt*; since 1885 teacher and prof. at Hamburg Conservatoire.

Contributions to Technique of Piano-playing, op. 38 and 57; *New Gradus ad Parnassum*, op. 95; *Exercise-Book for Harmony* (1869, 8th ed. 1908; chamber-music; 3 cantatas; *Ave Maria*, 6-v. double choir; a Requiem, *Den Heimgegangenen*, chorus and orch. op. 119 (Hebbel); songs; educational pamphlets; *Guide to Mus. History* (1906).—A. E.

KREBS, Carl. Ger. musicologist; *b.* Hanse-berg, near Königsberg, Neumark, 5 Feb. 1857. Stud. natural science, then music at R. High School of Music, Berlin, science of music at Univ. (Spitta); Ph.D. Rostock, 1895, with *Girolamo Dirutas Transilvano* (*Vierteljahrs-schrift für M.W.*, 1892); teacher of musical history at R. High School of Music; critic for *Vossische Zeitung*, *Moderne Kunst*, *Deutsche Rundschau* and *Tag*.

Women in Music (1895); *Haydn, Mozart, Beet-hoven* (1906, 3rd ed. 1920); *Dittersdorfiana* (1900); *Creation and Reproduction of Music* (1902); *Pré-eminent Conductors* (1920); Ph. E. Bach's *Sonatas for Connoisseurs and Lovers* (1895); *Beethoven's Sonatas in Original Form* (1898); *Des jungen Kreislers Schatzkästlein* (1908, for Brahms Soc.).—A. E.

KREHBIEL, Henry Edward. Amer. critic, author; *b.* Ann Arbor, Mich., U.S.A., 10 March, 1854; *d.* New York, 20 March, 1923. The most influential Amer. music critic of his time. Educated in public schools of Michigan and Ohio; stud. law in Cincinnati, 1872–4. Aban-doned law for mus. journalism, writing (1874–80) for *Cincinatti Gazette*. Then went to New York as ed. of *New York Musical Review* and critic for *New York Tribune*. For this latter newspaper he wrote reviews and criticisms up to the time of his death. Widely known as lecturer on mus. topics, and no small part of his educative influence was exerted through the illuminating analytical notes which for many years he provided for the programmes of Philh. Soc., the Oratorio Soc., the Mus. Art Soc. and other concert organisations. He was the chief Amer. contributor to the revised ed. of Grove's Dictionary.

An interested student of folk-music, an enthu-siastic lover of the classics with a wide know-ledge of older and newer music, K. was always a carefully discriminating critic, ready to wel-come what he considered good in new comprs. and performers, and by his sane criticisms and commentaries he did much for the growth of an intelligently appreciative attitude on the part of the Amer. mus. public. He was interested in opera in English, and made perf. transl. of Nicolai's *Merry Wives*, Paderewski's *Manru*, and Wagner's *Parsifal*.

In 1900, was member of international jury at

Paris Exposition; awarded Cross of the Legion
of Honour 1901. In 1909, received degree of
A.M. *h.c.* from Yale University.

Notes on the Cultivation of Choral Music and the
Oratorio Soc. of New York (New York, E. Schubert
& Co. 1884); Studies in the Wagnerian Drama (N.Y.
Harper, 1891); The Philharmonic Society of New
York (N.Y. Novello, 1892); How to Listen to Music
(N.Y. Scribner, 1896); Music and Manners in the
Classic Period (N.Y. Scribner, 1898); Chapters of
Opera (N.Y. H. Holt & Co. 1908); A Book of Operas
(N.Y. Macmillan, 1909); The Pianoforte and its
Music (N.Y. Scribner, 1911); Afro-American Folk-
Songs (Schirmer, 1914); A Second Book of Operas
(N.Y. Macmillan, 1917); More Chapters of Opera
(N.Y. H. Holt & Co. 1919). Ed. of A. W. Thayer's
Life of Ludwig van Beethoven, ed., rev. and amended
from orig. ms. and Ger. ed., New York. Publ.
for Beethoven Association (G. Schirmer), 1921.
3 vols.—O. K.

KREHL, Stephan. Ger. compr. *b.* Leipzig,
5 July, 1864. Stud. Leipzig and Dresden Cons.;
1889, teacher of pf. and theory Carlsruhe Cons.;
1902, at Leipzig Cons.; 1907, member of educational council; 1910, professor.

Vn. sonata, A ma. op. 8; cello sonata, F ma. op.
20; str. 4tet, A ma. op. 17; clar. 5tet, op. 19; pf.
trio, D ma. op. 32; symph. introduction to Hauptmann's Hannele, op. 15; cantata, Consolation (solo,
chorus and orch. op. 33); pf. pieces; songs. Wrote
for Göschen Coll. Practical Instruction in Form
(1902); General Music Instruction (1904, 1910);
Counterpoint (1908, 1912); Explanations for Fugal
Composition (1909); Harmony Instructor in 3 parts;
Theory of Mus. Art and Compn. Consult Fritz Reuter,
S. K. (1921).—A. E.

KREISLER, Fritz. Austrian violinist; *b.*
Vienna, 2 Feb. 1875. Stud. at Cons. there under
Hellmesberger; under Massart and Delibes in
Paris. In 1915, went to U.S.A. Wrote *Four
Weeks in the Trenches* (1918). From 1919, has
given concerts in Europe and America.

Operetta, Apfelblüten (New York, 1919); str.
4tet, A mi.; a large number of arrs. of classical
pieces for vn. and pf.—E.-H.

KREJČÍ, Miroslav. Czechoslovak compr.
b. Rychnov, near Kněžnou, 1891. Pupil of
Vítězslav Novák; prof. in Prague.

2 str. 4tets; 5tet clar. and str.; choruses; pf.
cycles; orch. suite, King Lávra. (In ms. or publ.
Hudební Matice.)—V. ST.

KŘENEK, Arnošt (Ernest). Czechoslovak
compr. *b.* Vienna, 1900. Stud. under Fr. Schreker in Vienna and Berlin; lives (since 1920) in
Berlin. His energetic music, formed by strictly
a linear part-writing, is guided more by the
musical idea and its development than by any
attempt at intensity of feeling. His free polyphony leads him to the atonal style.

3 symphonies; 2 str. 4tets (1st one, Univ. Ed.,
Vienna); pf. sonatas (Univ. Ed.); vn. sonata; Concerto Grosso for str. solo instrs. and str. orch.; symph.
music for 9 solo instrs.; dramatic cantata, Zwingburg.
—V. ST.

KREPS, Joseph. Belgian orgt.; writer on
music; *b.* Antwerp, 23 May, 1886. Orgt. at
Mount César Abbey, Louvain; stud. music
under Léon Du Bois, Joseph Jongen, and
Lodewijk Mortelmans. Various organ pieces;
songs on Flemish texts. His most characteristic
work is that composed for ceremony of laying
foundation-stone of the new Louvain Univ.
Library, built by the U.S.A. (28 July, 1921).
There is in it a curious blending of Gregorian
chant with acc. of brass instrs., chimes and
military tpts. As a scholar he has specialised

in study of music of Middle Ages and the de-
ciphering of neums, especially of the so-called
romaniens. He wrote an excellent work on the
Unifying Rôle of the Liturgical Organist.—C. V. B.

KRETZSCHMAR, A. F. Hermann. Ger. writer
on music; *b.* Olbernhau (Erzgebirge), 19 Jan.
1848; *d.* 10 May, 1924. Attended Kreuzschule,
Dresden; stud. philology at Leipzig; took doctorate with Latin essay Musical Signs before Guido
d'Arezzo, 1871; at same time pupil and teacher
at Leipzig Cons.; till 1876 condr. at Leipzig;
then theatre condr. at Metz; 1877, Univ. mus.
dir. Rostock; 1880, municipal mus. dir.; 1887,
at Leipzig Univ. mus. dir. and condr. of " St.
Paul's," and Univ. lecturer for mus. literature;
1888, condr. of Riedel Soc.; 1890, started Academical Orch. Concerts (with historical programmes) which lasted till 1895; 1898, owing
to ill-health, gave up positions, retaining only
academical lecturing post, and became lecturer
in mus. history at Cons.; 1904, given newly-
created degree of Prof.-in-ordinary of music at
Berlin Univ.; 1907-22, dir. of R. Inst. for
Church Music; 1909-20, dir. of R. High School.
K. was, with Riemann, Germany's leading
music researcher.

Concert Guide (Division I: symphony and suite,
1887, 5th ed. 1919; Division II: religious works,
1888, 4th ed. 1918; oratorios and choral works,
1890, 4th ed. 1920); last vol. (46th) Bach ed., J. S.
Bach's Handwriting in chronologically ordered reproduction. Essays in Musikalisches Wochenblatt, Grenz-
bote (Present-day Mus. Questions; also separately,
1903); Vierteljahrsschrift für Musikwissenschaft, and
Jahrbuch der Musikbibliothek Peters. Collection of
Essays appeared 1911 (Vol. I from Grenzboten; Vol.
II from Peters' Jahrbuch); 1st vol. History of New
Ger. Songs, 1912; History of Opera, 1919; Introduc-
tion to Mus. History, 1920 (Bach-Kolleg, 1923).
Ed. of Holzbauer's Gunther von Schwarzburg and
Vols. VIII and IX of D.d.T.; Songs of Ernst
Bach and Val. Herbing, D.d.T. XLII.—A. E.

KREUTZ, Edvard Sylou. Norwegian pianist;
b. Christiania, 7 May, 1881. Stud. under Agathe
Gröndahl, Iver Holter and Catharinus Elling in
Christiania; also for several years in Berlin and
Vienna. First concert in Christiania, 1910. Concert-tours in Norway. Has worked with zeal
for improvement of position of Norwegian
musicians, especially of music-teachers.—U. M.

KREYN, Alexander Abramovitch. Russ. cellist,
compr. *b.* Nijny-Novgorod, 1883. Stud. cello at
Moscow Cons. Self-taught as regards compn.

Symphony; Lyric Poem for orch.; pieces for pf.;
for vn.—M. D. C.

KREYN, Gregory Abramovitch. Russ. compr.
b. Nijny-Novgorod, 1880. Stud. cpt. under P.
Juon and fugue under Glière; but his compns.
show no trace of their influence.

Str. 4tet; pf. 4tet; pf. sonata; other pf. pieces;
songs.—V. B.

KRIBEL-VANZO, Anna. Norwegian s. singer;
b. Trondhjem, 20 Aug. 1863. Pupil of Mme.
Marchesi, Paris. Gave concerts with great success in native land, in Paris and in Germany.
Married in 1891 Count Vittorio Vanzo, at that
time orch. condr. at La Scala, Milan.—U. M.

KŘIČKA, Jaroslav. Czechoslovak composer;
b. Kelč (Moravia), 1882. Stud. first at Univ.;
1902-5, Prague Cons. under Stecker for compn.
After a year's study in Berlin, he was (till 1909)

prof. of compn. in Ekaterinoslav (Russia); then in Prague; first as choirmaster of *Vinohradský Hlahol* (until 1911), then of *Hlahol*, Prague (until 1920). His work as choirmaster was remarkable for perfection of rendering, as well as for novelty of programmes. 1920, prof. of Cons. Prague. After having been eclectic in his youth, K. inclined later to Russ. music; later still, to V. Novák. His very own world is that of a subjective lyricism, sometimes passionate and thrilling, sometimes smiling, and full of mischievous humour. His simplicity and his love · for children are shown in his compns. for children by their originality, expressiveness and merriment. His later works show depth of thought and feeling and a growing mastery of climax.

Song cycles: *Severní noci* (*Northern Nights*); *O lásce a smrti* (*Love and Death*); *Písně rozchodu* (*Farewell Songs*). Choral works: *Zrození pramene* (*The Birth of the Fountain*); *Slovensku* (*Slovakia*); *Záblesky* (*Lightning*); *Pozdrav* (*Greeting*); *Ve východní záři* (*In Eastern Light*). For orch.: *Venkovské scherzo* (*Idyllic Scherzo*); *Modrý pták* (*The Blue Bird*, overture); *Adventus*; *Pokušení* (*The Temptation*, a cantata for chorus, soli and orch.). Opera, *Hippolyta* (*Hippolita in the Hills*; on Hewlett's story). Pf. cycles: *Intimní skladby* (*Intimate Pieces*); *Lyrická suita* (*Lyrical Suite*). For children: operetta, *Ogaři*; songs: *Tři bajky* (3 *Fables*); *Jaro pacholátko* (*Fellow Spring*); *Dětem* (*To Children*). Mostly publ. by N. Simrock, Berlin; Hudební Matice, Prague; Fr. A. Urbánek; M. Urbánek, Prague.—V. ST.

KŘÍDLO, Bedřich. Czech compr. *b.* Kopidlno, 1876; *d.* 1902. Stud. Prague Cons.; prof. at Cons. in Kischenef.

Symph. poem, *Arrival of Spring*; str. 4tet; pf. trio; pf. pieces; songs; choral works. (F. A. Urbánek, Prague.)—V. ST.

KRIJANOVSKY, Ivan Ivanovitch (*accent the OV*). Russ. compr. *b.* 8 March (n.s.), 1867. Pupil of Rimsky-Korsakof at Petrograd Cons. Physician by profession. Imprisoned in Germany during war. Now prof. at Medical Inst. Petrograd.

Pf. concerto; vn. concerto, op. 10; vn. sonata, E mi. op. 4; cello sonata, op. 2; *Ballade*, vn. and pf. op. 11; many songs; pieces for organ and for other instrs. (publ. by J. H. Zimmerman; Belaief; Russ. State Music Publ. Dept.)—V. B.

KRILOF, Paul Dmitrievitch (*accent 2nd syll.*). Russian composer; *b.* Tver, 6/18 Feb. 1885. Finished Moscow Univ. course, 1907; pupil of Korestschenko in music-school of Moscow Philh. Soc. (1909–12); 1920, appointed prof. at Moscow Cons. His works are mostly unpublished.

Opera, *The Fountain of Bakhchisaray*; symphony in C mi.; symph. poem, *The Spring*; 3 pf. sonatas (D mi.; B mi.); choruses, etc.—V. B.

KŘÍŽKOVSKÝ, Pavel. Czechoslovak compr. *b.* Holasovice (Silesia), 1820; *d.* Brno (Brünn), 1885; priest in Brno and Olomouc (Moravia). Ed. popular songs; Fr. Sušil pointed out his way to the national music. K. wrote choruses on popular words, wherein for the first time, even before Smetana, the native tones are touched. He cond. the Filharmonická Beseda (Philh. Soc.) in Brno, which he founded.

Chief choruses: *Utonulá* (*The Drowned Girl*); *Dar za lásku* (*A Gift of Love*); *Odpadlý od srdce* (*The Unfaithful*); cantata, *St. Cyril and Methodius*, for choir and brass band.—V. ST.

KROEGER, Ernest Richard. Amer. pianist, compr. *b.* St Louis, Mo., U.S.A.,ₚ10 Aug. 1862. One of few Amer. musicians of note who have obtained their whole mus. training in U.S.A. Stud. pf. under Froelich, Malmene, and Kunkel; theory under Malmene, Golder and Anton; vn. under Spiering and orch. under L. Mayer, all in St. Louis. Began giving concerts, including his own·works, in 1886. Has establ. a repertoire of 1000 pieces played from memory. Since 1887, head of coll. of music of Forest Park Univ. (for women), St. Louis. In 1904, also establ. a school of his own. Has held a number of organ positions; at present (1922) orgt. of Delmar Baptist Ch. Cond. the Morning Choral Club (female vs.) 1893–1903, and Amphion Club 1910–12.

His unpubl. overtures, *Sardanapalus*, *Hiawatha*, *Atala*, *Thanatopsis* and *Endymion*, have been perf. in America. His latest orch. work, *Festival Overture*, to commemorate Missouri Centennial, was perf. by St. Louis Symphony Orch. 6 Nov. 1921. Pf. 4tet played Philadelphia, 1889; pf. 5tet, Detroit, 1890. These and 4 str. 4tets are in ms. In 1904 made *Officier de l'Académie*. Since 1915, member of National Inst. of Arts and Letters.

12 *Concert Études*, pf. op. 30; vn. sonata, op. 32; pf. sonata, op. 40 (all Breitkopf); *Romance*, pf. op. 63, No. 3 (Willis). Many pf. pieces, songs, choruses (Ditson; Schmidt; Church; Presser).—O. K.

KROGH, Erling. Norwegian dramatic t. singer; *b.* Christiania, 12 Sept. 1888. Trained under Ellen Schytte-Jacobson (Christiania), Peter Cornelius (Copenhagen); also stud. (with a scholarship) in Paris. *Début* at concert in 1915. From 1918–21, was one of leading performers at the short-lived theatre Opéra - Comique, Christiania. Chief rôles in *Tannhäuser*; *Pagliacci*; *Cavalleria Rusticana*; *Samson and Delilah*; *The Jewess*, etc. Gave concerts in Copenhagen which won great favour. Highly - esteemed concert - singer in Christiania.—R. M.

KROHN, Ilmari. Finnish musicologist and compr. *b.* Helsingfors, 8 Nov. 1867. Ph.M.; prof. of science of music at Helsingfors Univ. As the first ·representative of modern mus. science in Finland, K. has specially devoted his studies to folk-song and music theory. His chief scientific contributions are the systematised ed. of Finnish folk-melodies (*Suomen kansan sävelmiä*, I–III, 1893–1912), the dissertation *Über die Art und Entstehung der geistl. Volksmelodien in Finnland*. (*The Nature and Origin of Religious Folk-Song in Finland*), and a large compendium of theory of music, *Musiikin teorian oppijakso*, of which 3 vols. have appeared: *Rytmioppi* (*Rhythm*); *Säveloppi* (*Melody*); and *Harmoniaoppi* (*Harmony*). K. was made foreign member of R. Inst. for Music Research, Bückeburg, Germany. Is a fertile compr. Stud., among other places, in Leipzig, 1886–90; collab. with Mikael Nyberg and H. Klemetti in editing church music.

Oratorio, *Ikiaartehet* (*The Eternal Treasures*), 1912; opera, *Tuhotulva* (*The Flood*), 1919; songs; choral works, secular and sacred; folk-songs and chorales; a cantata, etc.—T. H.

KROMOLICKI, Józef. Polish music-historian and church music dir. *b.* Posen, 16 Jan. 1882. Pupil of Haberl and Haller in Ratisbon; then of Pfitzner, Kretzschmar and Wolf in Berlin. 1905, condr. of St. Michael's Ch. choir in Berlin; 1909, Ph.D. with treatise *Die Practica artis musicæ des Amerus*. In 1910 dir. of a church-music school in Berlin. He has publ. in *D.d.T.* 2 vols. of the compns. of J. W. Franck and J. E. Bach. Lives in Berlin.—ZD. J.

KRONKE, Emil. Ger. pianist and compr. *b*. Dantzig, 29 Nov. 1865. Pupil at Leipzig (Reinecke, Piutti, Paul) and Dresden Cons. (Nicodé, Th. Kirchner, Draeseke). 1917, became prof. Lives in Dresden.

Pf. pieces; orch. and chamber-music; instructive pf. pieces, op. 23; Chopin Studies, op. 17; *Virtuoso Arpeggio-Playing*, op. 44; *Modern Technique*, op. 77; *Advanced Exercises for the Fourth and Fifth Fingers*. Ed. Chopin's works for Steingräber.—A. E.

KROYER, Theodor. Ger. writer on music; *b*. Munich, 9 Sept. 1873. Stud. theology at Munich, then music (Sandberger) at R. Acad. of Music, cpt. (Gluth, Rheinberger) and pf. (Lang). Graduated Ph.D. at Univ. Munich, 1897; succeeded Max Zenger as mus. critic of Munich *Allgemeine Zeitung*, 1897; 1900, teacher of mus. history at Kaim's Music Inst.; 1902, honorary lecturer on mus. science at Univ.; 1920, prof. at Heidelberg; 1923, at Leipzig.

Beginning of Chromatics in Italian Madrigals (Breitkopf, 1902); *Joseph Rheinberger* (1916); *A cappella and Concerto* (1918); *The Speculative Music of Master Erasmus Heritius* (1918); 1st vol. of a complete ed. of Ludwig Senfi's works (*D.T.B.* III, ii, 1903); *Select Works of Gr. Aichinger* (*D.T.B.* X, i).—A. E.

KRUG, Arnold. Ger. compr. *b*. Hamburg, 16 Oct. 1849; *d*. there, 4 Aug. 1904. Son and pupil of Diedrich Krug (1821-80); 1868, pupil at Leipzig Cons.; 1869, Mozart scholar; pupil of Reinecke and Kiel (1871), pf. (Ernst Frank); 1872-7, pf. teacher at Stern's Cons. Berlin; 1877-8, won Meyerbeer scholarship and went to Italy and France. Later resided at Hamburg, cond. own Choral Soc.; since 1885 teacher at Cons. and condr. of Altona Acad. of Singing.

Symphony; symph. prologue to *Othello*, op. 27; *Margaret in Prison* (for full orch.); orch. suite, *Times of Travel*; *Roman Dances* for orch.; *Love News*, op. 14; *Italian Travel Sketches*, op. 12, for vns. and str. orch.; vn. concerto; str. 4tet, F ma. op. 96; choral works with solo and orch.; choral works with pf.; pf. 4tet, op. 16; trio; str. 6tet, D ma. op. 68; duet; waltz for pf.; pf. pieces; songs; choral songs; psalm.—A. E.

KRUG, Joseph (Krug-Waldsee). Ger. compr. *b*. Waldsee (Oberschwaben), 8 Nov. 1858; *d*. Magdeburg, 8 Oct. 1915. Stud. Stuttgart Cons.; 1882-9, condr. of Stuttgart New Choral Soc.; 1889-92, chorus-dir. at Hamburg Opera House, then condr. at Stadttheater Brünn, Augsburg; 1899, condr. of Privatkapelle at Nuremberg; 1901 at Magdeburg, condr. of symphony concerts and soc. concerts of town orch.; also condr. of Teachers' Singing Club, and a mixed choir; 1913, R. Prussian professor.

Choruses and songs; choral works: *Harald, King Rother, Violinist of Gmünd, Sea Views* (1894), *The Buried Song, Icarus*; symphony, C mi. op. 46; 4tet, D mi. op. 56; pf. and vn. suite, A ma. op. 43; overture to Schiller's *Turandot*; *Symph. Prologue* for orch.; symph. poem, *The Waves of the Sea and Love*, op. 4; operas: *The Procurator of St. John* (Mannheim, 1893, 1 act); *Astorre* (Stuttgart, 1896); *The Scarlet Cloak* (Augsburg, 1898).—A. E.

KRYGELL, Johan Adam. Danish compr. *b*.

Nœstved, 18 Sept. 1835; *d*. Copenhagen, 27 July, 1915. At desire of his parents he learned a trade, but in his leisure he turned to his violin, and as a violinist added to his means of sustenance. It was not till he was 32 that he succeeded in entering the R. Cons. Copenhagen, though he had already filled the position of orgt. at Herlufsholm, the renowned boys' school at Nœstved. His contrapuntal gift soon asserted itself and he became a most productive compr. in both larger and smaller forms: an oratorio, a Mass, a Requiem, organ works, chamber-music (str. 4tets), opera, *King Saul* (never staged). From 1880 till death, orgt. St. Matthew's Ch. Copenhagen.

Organ (publ. Hansen, Copenhagen): *Moll og Dur (Minor and Major)*, 24 fugues in all the keys, op. 64; sonata, op. 57; Toccata and fugue, op. 65; concerto, op. 112; shorter pieces. Also songs with pf. His mss. are placed in R. Library, Copenhagen.—A. H.

KUBA, Ludvík. Czech musician and painter; *b*. Poděbrady, 1863. Stud. at Organ School, Prague, and Teachers' Inst. Kutná Hora; then became teacher. Next attended Acad. of Painting, Prague, Paris and Munich, in which town he lived for 6 years; now lives in Prague. Chief mus. work, collection of folk-songs of all Slavonic nations; his life-work is the collection *Slovantsvo ve svých zpěvech* (*Slavdom in its Songs*; Hudební Matice, Prague), of which 10 vols. have appeared, containing many thousands of folk-songs of the Russians, Ruthenians, Czechs, Moravians, Slovenes, Slovaks, Serbs, Croats, Montenegrins, etc.—V. ST.

KUBELÍK, Jan. Czechoslovak violinist; *b*. Michle, 1880. Pupil of Ševčík, whose fame as a teacher he establ. K.'s playing is the climax of technical perfection; his tone is very noble and full; his expression distinguished but not deep. In 1914 he made a world-tour. After then he has been less frequently heard, devoting himself to compn. Has written 4 vn. concertos (Starý, Prague). Lives on his estate in Slovakia.—V. ST.

KUDIRKA, Vincas. See LITHUANIAN MUSIC.

KUFFERATH, Hubert Ferdinand. Belgian compr. *b*. Mülheim (Ruhr), 10 June, 1818; *d*. Brussels, 23 June, 1896. At first a violinist; stud. under his brother, Johann Hermann, then at Cologne Cons.; finally at Leipzig under David. From this moment, he turned more towards pf. and compn., which he stud. under Mendelssohn. Returning to Cologne, he there directed (1841-4) the Männer - Gesang - Verein. Settled in Brussels, 1844; 1872, teacher of cpt. and fugue at Cons. there, an appointment he held till his death. Comp. a symphony and many works for chamber-music, pf. and v., written in learned, serious style. Author of *École pratique du choral*.—E. C.

KUFFERATH, Maurice. Belgian musicologist, theatrical manager; *b*. Brussels, 8 Jan. 1852; *d*. there, 8 Dec. 1919. Son of preceding (Hubert Ferdinand). Stud. cello under François and Joseph Servais; but, destined for the bar, he stud. law at Univ. of Brussels (1873) and Leipzig (1874). Then returned to Brussels and in 1875 joined staff of *L'Indépendance Belge*, whose political bulletin he wrote for 25 years. At the same time he wrote in the *Guide Musical*, of which he soon undertook the management, retaining it for 30 years, till moment when war put an end to this, the principal mus. review in Belgium. In 1900, assumed, with G. Guidé, the management of Théâtre de la Monnaie, which he still held in 1914. Surprised in Switzerland by war, he there busied himself for 4 years in patriotic and philanthropic work. Returned to Brussels in 1918 and, Guidé having died, resumed with new colleagues the management of La Monnaie, and held it till death. He was a member of the Acad. from 1913. He was one of most active elements in Belgian mus. life, in last third of XIX century. A prolific writer, a remarkable stylist and formidable controversialist, he produced great quantity of arts. which were widely quoted as authorities. Under his management the Théâtre de la Monnaie attained its greatest brilliance. His erudition enabled him to restore to the productions of certain works their real character. Several, like *Fidelio*, *Magic Flute*, and *Parsifal*, were given in his translations. He inaugurated cycles of Wagnerian productions (in Ger., with Ger. artists and condr.) K.'s name will remain especially connected with the Wagnerian movement, of which he was one of the most active propagandists in Belgium and France, by his excellent works of exegesis publ. under the general title, *Le Théâtre de R. W.*, de *Tannhäuser à Parsifal*: *La Walkyrie*, *Siegfried* and *Lohengrin* (1891); *Parsifal* (1893); *Tristan et Iseult* (1894); *Les Maîtres Chanteurs* (1898). Unfortunately *Tannhäuser*, *Rhinegold*, and the *Twilight of the Gods* are missing. Other works: *R. W. et la neuvième symphonie, Berlioz et Schumann* (1879); *H. Vieuxtemps* (1883); *La Walkyrie* (1887), a pamphlet for propaganda, distinct from the 1891 work; *L'Art de diriger l'orchestre* (1891); *Musiciens et philosophes* (1894); *Les Abus de la Société des Auteurs* (1897); *Salomé de Strauss* (1908); *Fidelio* (1912). Also 2 vaudevilles, *Les Potiches de Damoclès* and *Le Propriétaire par Amour*. To the lyrical adaptations mentioned above, add lighter works, such as *Mikado* (Sullivan), *La Guerre Joyeuse* and *L'Étudiant pauvre*. Consult *L'Éventail* (Brussels), 14 Dec. 1919, and E. Closson, *Introduction à la Walkyrie de M. K.* (3rd ed. Brussels, 1921).—E. C.

KUILER, Kor. Dutch condr. and compr. *b.* Kinderdijk (S. Holland), 21 April, 1877. Stud. at Amsterdam Cons. (Zweers and Röntgen); 1910, condr. of Groningen Symphony Orchestra.
Cantatas for children's vs.; numerous songs; sonata for pf.; sonata, vn. and pf.; pf. pieces (publ. Noske, The Hague; Alsbach, Amsterdam); educational pf. music.—W. P.

KULLAK, Adolf. Ger. pianist and author; *b.* Meseritz, 23 Feb. 1823; *d.* Berlin, 25 Dec. 1862. Brother of Theodor Kullak; stud. philosophy at Berlin; then music under Agthe and Marx; joined staff of Berlin *Musikzeitung* and taught in his brother's acad. Besides pf. works and songs, he publ. books:
The Beautiful in Music (1858) and *Æsthetics of Pf. Playing* (1861); 2nd and 3rd ed. by H. Bischoff, 1876 and 1890; 4th ed. revised by Walter Niemann, 1906; 5th ed. 1916 (Kahnt, Leipzig).—A. E.

KULLAK, Franz. Ger. compr. and author; *b.* Berlin, 12 April, 1844; *d.* Berlin, 9 Dec. 1913. Son of Theodor Kullak; trained at his father's

acad., after whose death he took over its direction (suddenly dissolved 1890); 1883, R. prof.; made himself well known through careful eds. of classical pf. concertos, instructive works.
First Pf. Lessons; *Progress in Pf. Playing*; *Harmony at the Pf.*; songs; pf. pieces; *Expression in Music at End of XIX Century* (1897); *Jubilee Overture*; opera, *Ines de Castro* (Berlin, 1877).—A. E.

KULLAK, Theodor. Ger. pianist and teacher; *b.* Krotoschin, Posen, 12 Sept. 1818; *d.* Berlin, 1 March, 1882. Stud. under A. Agthe, Posen, and at Berlin, where he also stud. harmony (Dehn); 1842, continued mus. studies at Vienna under Czerny, Sechter and O. Nicolai; 1843, teacher at Berlin; 1850, establ. with J. Stern and A. B. Marx the Berlin Stern Cons.; 1855, withdrew and establ. the New Acad. of Music.
School of Octave Playing, op. 48 (Augener); *Materials for Elementary Teaching* (3 books); practical part to pf. method of Moscheles and Fétis (2 books); nearly 130 separate works, mostly for pf. Consult: O. Reinsdorf, *Th. K. and his New Acad. of Music*, Berlin (1870); H. Bischoff, *In Remembrance of Th. K.*—A. E.

KUNC, Jan. Czechoslovak compr. *b.* Doubravice (Moravia), 1883. Attended Teachers' School; stud. music at Organ School in Brno, and Cons. in Prague. Compn. pupil of L. Janáček and V. Novák. Administrator of Cons. at Brno. His compns. never leave the traditional line and have a rich mus. foundation, sometimes energetic, even aggressive, sometimes sweetly lyrical. His choral works grew by the side of Janáček's, but are nearer the virtuosity of the Moravian Teachers' Choir.
Male choruses, 2 collections (the chief is *Ostrava*); female chorus, cycle, *The Garden*. Many arrs. of national songs (Mölinburkian, Slovakian); *Sedmdesát tisic* (*Seventy Thousand*), chorus and orch.; 2 str. 4tets; symph. poem, *Píseň mládí* (*Song of Youth*); ballad for a. and orch. *Stála Kačenka u Dunaja* (*Katherine at the Danube*). (Hudební Matice; M. Urbánek, Prague; V. Novotný, Brno.)—V. ST.

KUNITS, von. See VON KUNITS.

KÜNNEKE, Eduard. Ger. compr. *b.* Emmerich-o-Rhine, 27 Jan. 1885. Stud. at R. High School, Berlin (Bruch).
Suite for orch. op. 4. Operas: *Robin's End* (Mannheim, 1909); *Ace of Hearts* (Dresden, 1913); fest. play, *Circe* (Munich, 1912, Artist Theatre); mus. play, *Village without Bells* (1919); operetta, *Love's Awakening* (Berlin, 1920); *The Well-beloved* (1920); *The Cousin from Nowhere* (1920; London, 1922); *Marriage in a Circle* (1921); music for film *Pharaoh's Wife*; operetta, *Lovesick People* (Berlin, 1922); all publ. by Drei Masken Verlag.—A. E.

KUNWALD, Ernst. Austrian condr. *b.* Vienna, 14 April, 1868. Stud. for Bar at Vienna; then turned entirely to music; attended Leipzig Cons. (Jadassohn) took up condr.'s career as Korrepetitor, Stadttheater Leipzig, Sondershausen, Essen, Halle-o-S.; then condr. at Rostock; cond. 1900-1 *The Ring* at Madrid; 1902-5, acted as opera-condr. at Frankfort; 1905-6, cond. Kroll Summer Opera at Berlin; 1906 at Stadttheater, Nuremberg; 1907-12, cond. Philh. Orch. Berlin; 1912, went to Cincinnati as condr. of Symphony Orch. and dir. of May Fest.; 1920, took over dir. of Symphony Concerts at Königsberg (Prussia).—A. E.

KURTH, Ernst. Musicographer; *b.* Vienna, 1 June, 1886. Ph.D., Vienna, 1903; lecturer at Univ. in Berne, 1912, where he founded and directs the *Collegium Musicum* and the Academic Orch.; since 1920, has been prof.-in-ordinary. He is famous in Switzerland and Germany, and ranks amongst most outstanding writers on music of our day; his book *Grundlagen des linearen Kontrapunkts* is a most important work.

Die Jugendopern Glucks (dissertation, 1908); *Zur ars cantus mensurabilis des Franko von Köln* (1907); *Die Voraussetzungen der theoretischen Harmonik* (Berne, 1913, Paul Haupt); *Grundlagen des linearen Kontrapunkts* (Berlin, 1922, Max Hesse); *Bachs melodische Polyphonie* (1917, Haupt); *Romantische Harmonik und ihre Krise in Wagners Tristan* (1920, Haupt; Berlin, 1923, Hesse).—F. H.

KURZ, Selma. Austrian coloratura singer; *b.* Bielitz (Silesia). Frankfort-o-M. Opera House; then Vienna Hofoper under Mahler, to whom her great advance is largely due. Many star-performances in Europe and America.—P. St.

KURZ, Vilém. Czechoslovak pianist; *b.* Německý Brod (Bohemia), 1872. Pupil of J. Holfeld at Organ School, Prague; 1898–1919, prof. of pf.-school at Cons., Lwów (Lemberg); from 1919, prof. at Czech Cons. Brno (Brünn). Made many tours in Czecho-Slovakia, Austria Germany and Poland. Lives in Brno.—V. St.

KURZOVÁ, Ilonka. Czech pianist; *b.* Lwów (Lemberg), Poland, 1899. Daughter and pupil of Vilém Kurz. Very successful from age of 10 in her pf.-recitals. Tours in Germany, Austria, Poland, Holland, etc.—V. St.

KUSSEVITZKY, Serge Alexandrovitch. Russian conductor and contrabassist; *b.* Tver in 1864. His father, an orchestral musician, destined him, from a child, for a musical career, and at 9, he played in the local theatre orchestra, making his first *débuts* there, two years later, as conductor. In 1878, went to Moscow to pursue his musical education, entering the École Philharmonique and studying the double-bass under Rambauseck. His success as a contrabassist dates from 1896. He gave in Russia and abroad a series of concerts which established his reputation as a great virtuoso with a pure and noble style, and an impeccable technique. But it was the orchestra which attracted him. He was in the conducting class at High School in Berlin under Nikisch. In 1909 he realised his dream, organising his own orchestra in Russia and founding at the same time a music-publishing house, the Russian Musical Edition, devoted specially to the publication of compositions of modern Russians (Scriabin, Stravinsky, Metner, Rachmaninof, etc.). His symphony concerts in Petrograd, Moscow, and later in the Russian provinces, achieved very great success, and had a deep influence on musical life in Russia, no less through the novelty of the programmes than by the excellence of the playing. The war, followed by the revolution, scattered Kussevitzky's orchestra, and his publishing house was confiscated by the State. Placed by the Soviet Government at the head of the State Orchestras (the older, unworthy orchestras), Kussevitsky succeeded finally in leaving Russia in 1922. He cond. series of concerts in Paris at the Grand Opera, then Mussorgsky's *Boris Godunof* (which he also cond. at Barcelona), then Tchaikovsky's

La Dame de Pique. In 1921–4 he cond. in London, Rome, Berlin, Paris; appointed condr. Boston Symph. Orch. 1924. He is an artist of the forceful, dynamic type. Gifted with a strong artistic temperament, it is particularly the active, impassioned side of music which he throws into relief. His very searching interpretations, fully detailed and highly coloured, never imperil the unity and general outline. They are very subjective, yet consequent, logical and overflowing with life. He is both lyrical and romantic, and in this respect approaches Nikisch.—B. de S.

KUTZSCHBACH, Hermann Ludwig. Ger. condr. *b.* Meissen, 30 Aug. 1875. Son of music-master; stud. at Dresden Cons. (Kluge, E. Krantz, Draeseke); 1895, Korrepetitor at Dresden Court Theatre, to which he belonged till 1906, except for short absences (1898, Cologne and Berlin, New R. Opera House); from 1898, 3rd condr. (with Schuch and Hagen); 1906-9 at Mannheim as 1st condr.; returned to Dresden, succeeding Hagen; 1913, 2nd condr.; since Schuch's death, 1st condr. with Fritz Reiner; then co-operated with Fritz Busch.—A. E.

KUULA, Alma. Finnish s. singer; *b.* Petrograd, 1884. Stud. at Helsingfors Music Inst., Milan and Paris. Concert and oratorio singer, chiefly in Finland, also in Petrograd and recently in Germany. In 1914, married Toivo Kuula (*q.v.*).—T. H.

KUULA, Toivo. Finnish compr. *b.* Vaasa, 7 July, 1883; died a tragic death (murdered) during the Finnish War of Independence, 1918. Stud. compn. at Helsingfors Music Inst., in Bologna (Bossi), also in Paris, and proved in his compns. to be one of the most intense personalities in Finnish music. His works evince strong national character, solid contrapuntal construction and rich colouring; they are drawn for the most part from the folk-music of his native country in southern East Bothnia.

2 *East Bothnian Suites* for orch. (among which are several admirable tone-paintings); vocal works with orch.: *Orjan poika* (*The Slave's Son*), *Merenkylpijäneidot* (*The Sea-Nymphs*), *Stabat Mater*; magnificent large unacc. choruses; trio, pf. vn. cello; sonata, vn. and pf.; songs; pf. pieces.—T. H.

KUYPER, Elisabeth. Dutch compr. and condr. *b.* Amsterdam, 13 Sept. 1877. Stud. at High School, Berlin, and under Max Bruch. Was teacher at Stern's Cons. Berlin. She cond. her ladies' orch. in Berlin and London. Now lives in New York where she has also organised a ladies' orch. As a compr. her orch. works are in the classical style, reflecting Brahms and Bruch.—W. P.

KVAPIL, Jaroslav. Czechoslovak compr. *b.* Fryštát (Moravia), 1892. Pupil of L. Janáček, later in Leipzig of Max Reger and Teichmüller (pf.); prof. of pf. and compn. at Cons. Brno; condr. of choir Filharmonická Beseda (Philh. Soc.). His compns. were at first strongly built contrapuntally and architecturally; later on, they are a kind of contemplative improvisation.

2 symphonies; orch. variations and fugue; pf. trio; pf. 5tet; str. 4tets; 3 song cycles (Hudební Matice, Prague, and Club of Friends of Art, Brno); pf. variations (Barvič and Novotný, Brno); 2 vn. sonatas; cello sonata; pf. sonata; 2 pf. cycles.—V. St.

L

LABAUCHI, Andrés José. Argentine singing-master, compr. *b.* Naples in 1856. Stud. at Cons. of Naples under Savoja, Correggio and Mercadante, pf. under Cesi. For 6 years, dir. of chorus and condr. at several theatres in Italy. Then devoted himself to the art of singing, making special scientific studies at the Univ. of Naples and at Lombardini's famous school of singing. Founded Primaria Scuola di Canto Italiano in 1880. Publ. monograph *Dell' arte del canto in Italia* (1880), and was music critic for several theatrical papers. In 1911, went to Buenos Ayres, where he establ. the Santa Cecilia Inst., his introduction of the Ital. school of singing into Argentina being attended with complete success.

Del canto corale e della ginnastica nella scuola popolare; Della laringologia, and other technical works. Sacred pieces; songs for voice-training; chamber-music; pieces for pf. and vn.—A. M.

LABEY, Marcel. Fr. compr. *b.* Le Vésinet, near Paris, 1875. Pf. pupil of Breitner and Delaborde; for harmony of René Lenormand. Entered *Schola Cantorum* in 1898 (cpt. under d'Indy). Until 1914, prof. of higher pf. class at *Schola* and tutor of orch. class. Member of Société Nationale de Musique from 1902-14, and since 1920.

Sonata, pf. and vn. (1901); sonata, vla. and pf. (1904); pf. 4tet (1911); pf. suite (1914); str. 4tet (1919); 2 pieces, fl. and pf. (1920); songs. Orch.: *Fantasia* (1900); 2 symphonies (1903 and 1908); *Overture for a Drama* (1920). *Berengère* (3-act opera, awarded prize at *Concours de la Ville de Paris,* 1921).—A. C.

LABIA, Maria. Ital. soprano singer; *b.* Verona, 14 Feb. 1889. Stud. singing under her mother, the Countess Cecilia Labia. First devoting herself to concerts, made her *début* on the stage at the Teatro Filarmonico, Verona, with great success. Subsequently went on a long concert-tour in Russia; was engaged at the Opera, Stockholm, where she remained 2 years; then went to Komische Oper, Berlin, where she remained for 5 years, gaining great success, especially in *La Tosca* (Puccini) and in *Tiefland* (d'Albert), and interpreting a wide repertoire in Ger., Fr. and Ital. Went to U.S.A. and, on returning, toured again in Russia, Germany, Hungary. Finally came back to Italy, and took part in important seasons at principal theatres; at La Scala, Milan, she interpreted *Salome*; at Costanzi, Rome (1918-19 season), she created the part of Giorgetta in Puccini's *Il Tabarro.*—D. A.

LABOR, Josef. Ger.-Czechoslovak compr. *b.* Horowitz, 29 June, 1842. He became blind; stud. in Vienna; made European concert tours; then became Court organist in Vienna.

Instr. and vocal works. Ed. Cesti's *Pomo d' Oro* and Biber's vn. sonatas for *D.T.Ö. (q.v.).*—E. S.

LABROCA, Mario. Ital. compr. *b.* Rome, 22 Nov. 1896. Pupil of Respighi and Malipiero. Compr. of interesting chamber-music (Suite and *Ritmi di marcia* for pf.; sonatina, vn. and pf.; Suite, vla. and pf.; str. 4tet). Musical critic for the Roman newspaper *L'Idea Nazionale.*—D. A.

LABUŃSKI, Wiktor. Polish pianist; *b.* Petrograd, 1895. Stud. under Felix Blumenfeld (pf.) and Wihtol (compn.) at State Cons. in Petrograd. Began recitals in 1916. In 1919 received a prize at pianists' competition in Lublin (Poland) and became prof. at Cons. in Cracow, where he lives. Plays much in Poland, Germany and in Vienna. Appeared in Glasgow (Scottish Orch.) 1924.—ZD. J.

LACERDA, Francisco de. Portuguese condr. *b.* Lisbon, 1869; received a government grant for tuition and stud. in Paris under d'Indy; there he establ. a good reputation as orch. conductor.—E.-H.

LACH, Robert. Austrian writer on music and compr. *b.* Vienna, 29 Jan. 1874. Pupil of Robert Fuchs at Cons.; 1902, Ph.D.; 1911, curator of music coll. in Court Library (now National Library); 1918 teacher, 1920 prof. of Vienna Univ. and member of Acad. of Science. He works especially at comparative and ethnological music history and folk-lore (commended by Prof. Wallaschek), and the style and *melos* of the Wagner music-drama. A very productive compr., but without pronounced individuality. Author of many books.

Book, *Studien zur Entwicklungsgeschichte der ornamentalen Melopoeie* (1913). Comp.: symphony, D mi. (1895); 3 overtures; Mass; music to Schönherr's *Königreich* (1906); songs; chamber-music.—P. P.

LACHNER, Vincenz. Ger. condr. and compr. *b.* Rain (Bavaria), 19 July, 1811; *d.* Carlsruhe, 22 Jan. 1893. Brother of Franz and Ignaz Lachner; was for a time tutor at Posen; then joined his brothers at Vienna; succeeded Ignaz, 1831, as orgt. of Protestant church, and Franz, 1836, as Court-condr., Mannheim, where he officiated till 1873; 1884, taught at Carlsruhe Conservatoire.

Overtures to *Turandot*, op. 33, *Demetrius,* op. 44; *March-Overture,* op. 54, etc.; male 4tets.—A. E.

LACHOWSKA (LAHOVSKA), Aga. Polish m.-sopr. singer; *b.* Lemberg, 1886. Well known and appreciated in Poland, Spain and Italy, especially as heroine in *Carmen* and *Samson and Delilah.* Also an excellent concert-singer.—ZD. J.

LACROIX, Eugène. Fr. orgt. and compr. Pupil of Gigout; 1896-1914, chief orgt. at St.-Merry, Paris, where he succeeded Paul Wachs. Comp. many organ pieces of very fine style: also chamber-music; symphony; mass; lyrical drama, *Nominoé.*—F. R.

283

LADMIRAULT, Paul Émile. Fr. compr. *b.*
Nantes, 8 Dec. 1877. Began to study music in
his native city. At 15, comp. a 3-act opera,
Gilles de Retz, which was produced there. He
then entered the Paris Cons., where his teachers
were Taudou for harmony, Gédalge for cpt., and
Fauré for compn. Among his chief publ. works
are the *Esquisses* for pf. (1909, Demets), *Variations* and *Musiques Rustiques* for pf. duet (1906–
1907, Demets), a *Gaelic Rhapsody* for pf. duet
(1909, Leduc), part-songs, songs, and instr.
excerpts from his lyric drama *Myrdhin* (Rouart).
The vocal score of this, his symphony (1910), and
his principal chamber-music works, are so far
unpubl. He is at his best in moods of poetical,
almost childlike, reverie, whose dictates he expresses with delightful originality.
Consult Séré (*q.v.*).—M. D. C.

LAFITE, Carl. Austrian pianist, compr. *b.*
Vienna, 29 Oct. 1872. Son of a well-known
painter. Stud. Vienna Cons. (1st prize for
compn.). After concert - touring returned to
Vienna; secretary of Gesellschaft der Musikfreunde (1911–21). His compns. are well known
in Vienna, but have little artistic value. He likes
the operetta style and wrote *Hannerl,* using
melodies by Schubert, but accentuating the
Viennese note. Successful writer of choral
works and esteemed accompanist (especially for
Schubert).
Die Stunde (from Leo Feld); opera, *Der Musen-
krieg* (written for 5th Centenary Fest. of Leipzig
Univ.); many popular songs.—P. P.

LA FORGE, Frank. Amer. pianist, song-writer;
b. Rockford, Ill., U.S.A., 22 Oct. 1879. Stud.
harmony and pf. under Harrison M. Wild,
Chicago, 1896-1900, and in 1900–4 pf. under
Leschetizky and compn. under Labor and
Navrátil, Vienna. As accompanist of Marcella
Sembrich, toured Germany, France, Russia and
U.S.A. for 6 years. Since then active as accom-
panist (Schumann-Heink, Alda, Matzenauer,
etc.).
Songs, *To a Messenger, Sanctuary, Like the Rose-
bud,* etc. (Schirmer; Ditson; Flammer); pf. pieces
(Schirmer).—J. M.

LAGO, Pura. Span. pianist; *b.* Villaviciosa
(Asturias), 1894. Stud. with distinction at R.
Cons. de Música, Madrid. By her 1st perf. as a
solo pianist, in Sweden, Denmark, Germany,
Italy and South America, of works by Albeniz, de
Falla and Manén, she has rendered valuable ser-
vice to the cause of modern Span. music.—P. G. M.

LA GYE, Paul. Belgian compr. *b.* St. Gilles
(Brussels), 8 June, 1883. Prof. of mus. science
at École Normale, Brussels. Many symphonies,
choral works, pf. pieces, songs, but specially
operas: *Franchimont* (1905), *Le Chevalier
Maudit* (1908), *L'Apercevance* (1908–9, Brussels,
Lauwerijns), *Le Rédempteur* (Bourse Theatre,
Brussels, 1916), *La Victoire d'Aphrodite,
Madeleine, L'Ennemi, L'Imposteur, Aisha, La
Marquise de Fontenay,* etc. He is a typically
eclectic musician, assimilating all influences
of his time (Wagner, d'Indy, Massenet, Puccini),
and utilises them, either singly or by combination according to necessities of his varied
subjects.—C. V. B.

LAJTHA, László. Hungarian compr. and folk-
lorist; *b.* Budapest, 30 June, 1891. Stud. compn.
at R. Hungarian High School for Music under
Viktor Herzfeld. Soon after this, he turned to
study of Hungarian folk-lore, and coll. valuable
material for Ethnographical Department of
Hungarian National Museum. Now curator of
Folk-lore Department in Museum, and also
teacher of compn. at National Cons. Budapest.
Des écrits d'un Musicien, pf. (Budapest, 1912,
Rózsavölgyi); *Contes,* pf. (Budapest, Harmonia
Verlag); pf. sonata (*id.*). Consult: *Modern Hun-
garian Composers* (*Musical Times,* March 1922);
Della Musica Moderna in Ungheria (*Il Pianoforte,*
July 1921); *The Development of Art-Music in Hun-
gary* (*Chesterian,* Jan. 1922).—B. B.

LA LAURENCIE, Lionel de. Fr. musicologist;
b. Nantes, 24 July, 1861. Pupil of Reynier (vn.)
and of Bourgault-Ducoudray. Being related to
Vincent d'Indy, he has devoted himself to the
study of XVIII century music on the one hand,
and the history of the vn. on the other. Contributor to principal Fr. and foreign reviews.
At present ed.-in-chief of the *Encyclopédie de
la Musique* (Delagrave). Hon. President of the
Fr. Soc. of Musicology.
Histoire du goût musical en France (1905); *L'Académie de musique et le concert de Nantes* (1905);
Documents sur J. Ph. Rameau et sa famille (1907);
Rameau (1908); *Les Bouffons* (1912); *Le Créateur de
l'Opéra français* (1920); *L'École française de violon
de Lully à Viotti* (1922-3).—A. C.

LALEWICZ, Jerzy (George). Polish pianist; *b.*
Suwalki, 1877. Pupil of Annetta Essipova (pf.),
Rimsky-Korsakof and Liadof (theory) at Petrograd Cons. where he finished in 1901 with gold
medal. Was then pf. prof. at Odessa State Music
School; 1905–11, at Cracow Cons.; 1912, prof.
at State Acad. of Music in Vienna; 1918, returned to Poland (Lemberg). Then went to
Paris and later to Buenos Ayres where he is now
prof. at Cons. Has played with great success in
Europe and America.—ZD. J.

LALIBERTÉ, Alfred. Canadian pianist and
composer; *b.* St. Johns, Quebec, Canada, 10
Feb. 1882. Stud. in Montreal; later in Berlin,
under Lutzenke (pf.), Baeker (harmony), Klappe
(compn.). Won scholarship from Ger. Government and played at Imperial Court, Berlin,
before Emperor Wilhelm II. In 1905, resumed
work in Montreal; in 1906 he met Scriabin, who
persuaded him to resume studies in Europe. He
stud. for a year under Teresa Carreño in Berlin,
after which he joined Scriabin in Brussels. Devoting himself to the study of Scriabin's works,
he became imbued with their characteristics
and received many tokens of friendship from
that compr., including mss. of *Poème de l'Extase,*
the 5th Sonata, etc. He returned to Canada by
way of Paris and London, where he gave
recitals, being probably the first Canadian to
fulfil an entire programme in those cities. Since
1911, has been actively engaged in teaching in
Montreal and has devoted himself also to the
playing of Scriabin's music which was hitherto
scarcely known in Canada.
3-act opera, *Sœur Béatrice* (Maeterlinck); cycle of
15 songs from *Chansons d'Été;* many folk-songs of
Canada.—L. S.

LALO, Édouard. French composer; *b.* Lille, 17 Jan. 1823; *d.* Paris, 22 April, 1892. He settled in Paris about 1840 to continue his work as a composer. He had already written several pieces of chamber-music, but at the period this type of music was out of favour with the public who were only interested in the operas of Meyerbeer and Halévy. It was not until 1865 that he succeeded in attracting a little public attention by an opera, *Fiesque,* which was however refused by the judges in an operatic competition. The work, which was written on classic lines, was nevertheless conceived in the style of symphonic music, which scandalised the judges. Lalo then composed a concerto in F, *Le Divertissement,* and the dazzling *Symphonie Espagnole,* which were well received at the Concerts Pasdeloup and at the Société Nationale. At the same time he was working on the *Roi d'Ys.* He encountered enormous difficulties in trying to produce the *Roi d'Ys,* but finally the manager at the Opéra consented to find him a *corps de ballet. Namouna,* another opera, had very few performances, but yet remains Lalo's master-work. His music, vivid, warm and colourful, full of fine, bold harmonies and extraordinary novelty in orchestration, appeared uncouth to the spoilt audiences of opera in 1882, but aroused great enthusiasm among the younger musicians. Debussy, Paul Dukas, and Vincent d'Indy knew the score of *Namouna* by heart and played it unceasingly. Lalo's influence on these three musicians was very great; he contributed to the harmonies of Debussy and to the orchestration of d'Indy and Dukas. He nearly died while finishing *Namouna.* When he had recovered from his illness, he plunged again into composition and produced successively the *Russian Concerto* (1883), and symphony in G minor (1885). Then, at last, the *Roi d'Ys* was performed, and, contrary to all expectations, gained a unanimous approval. Yet this work, in spite of some remarkable passages, is far from possessing the musical qualities of *Namouna* and certain orchestral works (*e.g.* the *Norwegian Rhapsody*). Lalo was the true precursor of the modern French School, and his influence in the formation of Debussy and Dukas is indubitable. His music is a delight to the ear—however often repeated it remains as vivid and colourful as when heard for the first time.

For full list of works and bibliography, consult *Revue Musicale,* March 1923, dedicated to Lalo with articles by P. Dukas, Pierre Lalo, etc.—H. P.

LALO, Pierre. Fr. music critic; *b.* Puteaux (Seine), 6 Sept. 1866; son of Édouard Lalo (*q.v.*). After contributing for several years to *Journal des Débats,* made his first appearance in music criticism with an article which attracted much notice, on V. d'Indy's *Fervaal.* This article (*Revue de Paris,* 15 May, 1898), procured for him the succession to J. Weber (1818–1902), as music critic to *Le Temps* (Oct. 1898). Endowed with rare penetration and great rectitude of judgment, his articles always bear the impress of genuine artistic and mus. understanding. A well-chosen style and language make them very attractive to read. He has publ. a coll. entitled *La Musique,* 1898–9 (Paris, Rouart).—M. L. P.

LALOY, Louis. Fr. musicologist; *b.* Grey (Haute Saône), 18 Feb. 1874. After a brilliant university career and submitting his thesis for Doctor of Letters (1904), abandoned education to devote himself to history and criticism of music. Contributed to *Revue Musicale,* 1901–3; then founded (with Marnold) the *Mercure Musical* (1905), which was transformed into the *S.I.M. Bulletin* (1907). In 1906, gave course of lectures at Sorbonne in place of Romain Rolland, who was on leave. A writer of great talent and vast culture, he was one of the first champions, in France, of Claude Debussy, to whom he devoted a book (Dorbon) which is a masterpiece of penetrating and comprehensive criticism. He has likewise published a remarkable book in popular style on Rameau (Alcan, 1902), but he has specialised, above all, in study of Greek music (*Aristoxène de Tarente,* 1904), and of music in the Far East, *La Musique chinoise* (Laurens, Paris). Appointed, in 1921, to give a course of lectures at the Sorbonne on Chinese music. Also gen. sec. of Grand Opéra, Paris. —H. P.

LA MARA. See LIPSIUS, MARIE.

LAMB, Carolina E. Scottish mezzo-s. singer; *b.* Kirkpatrick Fleming, Dumfriesshire, 28 May, 1901. Trained under Ernesto Colli, Milan. Made successful *début* as Azucena in *Il Trovatore* in Edinburgh, Nov. 1922.—W. S.

LAMBETH DEGREES. The Archbishop of Canterbury, by virtue of an old custom, bestows amongst other degrees, " Mus. Doc. Cantuar." *honoris causa.* The most recent mus. list is: William Lemare, 1894; Henry Faulkner Henniker, 1889; James Kendrick Pyne, Manchester, 1900; Thomas Barrow Dowling, Cape Town Cath. 1903; Alfred Herbert Brewer, Gloucester Cath. 1905; Charles A. E. Harris, Montreal, 1906; Percival John Illsley, 1912; Percy Clarke Hull, Hereford Cath. 1921; Charles H. Moody, Ripon Cath. 1923; Rev. G. R. Woodward, 1924. The fees for this degree are estimated in Grove's Dictionary at £63.—E.-H.

LAMBRINO, Télemaque. Pianist; *b.* Odessa, 27 Oct. 1878. Of Greek descent; pupil of Klimof at Imperial School of Music, Odessa; then at Munich Acad. of Music (Kellermann, Anton Beer-Walbrunn, and Rheinberger), and with Teresa Carreño in Berlin. From 1900, lived in Leipzig; 1908, teacher at Cons. Moscow; 1909, back to Leipzig; whence he also directs advanced class at Erfurt Cons. and (since 1914) a class at Klindworth-Scharwenka Cons. Berlin. —A. E.

LAMM, Paul Alexandrovitch. Russ. pianist; *b.* Moscow, 15/27 July 1882. Finished pf. course, Moscow Cons. 1911; 1907–13, accompanist and colleague of famous Russ. singer, Olenina d'Alheim (singer of Mussorgsky and

founder of House of Song); 1917–18, dir. of
Russischer Musik-Verlag of S. Kussevitsky).
After Russ. 1918 revolution, dir. of Russ. State
Music Publ. Dept. Since 1918, he has been the
centre of a group of contemporary Russ. comprs.
containing Miaskovsky, Goedicke, Feinberg,
Alexandrof, Borchman, Shenshin, Pavlof,
Evseief, and others. He has arr. symph. works
of Borodin, Glazunof, Stravinsky, S. I. Tanéief,
Goedicke, Miaskovsky, Scriabin, for 2 pfs., 8
hands.—V. B.

LAMMERS, Mally (Maria Katarina), *née* Sars.
Norwegian singer; *b.* Mangor, 22 June, 1850.
Pupil in singing of C. A. Gröndahl, Thorvald
Lammers and Désirée Artôt de Padilla. Engaged
in teaching singing (for about 35 years). Took
part in oratorio perfs. in her native land; gave
together with her husband, the singer Thorvald
Lammers (*q.v.*), numerous song and folk-song
concerts at home and abroad. For about 15
years she was condr. of the choir of the Female
Teachers' Soc. Her vocal gifts and her fine
artistic personality have won for her a wide
recognition.—J. A.

LAMMERS, Thorvald Amund. Norwegian
b.-barit. singer, condr. compr. *b.* Modum, 15 Jan.
1841; *d.* Christiania, 8 Feb. 1922. Graduated in
law in 1865 ; practised as a lawyer. In 1870
went over to music. Teachers : Fritz Arlberg,
Stockholm (1870–1); Francesco Lamperti, Milan
(1871–4). Was for short time attached to one
or two opera houses in Italy; came home and
gave in 1874 his first concert; 1874–7, attached
to Christiania Theatre; sang, amongst other
rôles: Leporello (*Don Juan*), Figaro (*Marriage
of Figaro* and *Barber of Seville*), Marcel
(*Huguenots*), Mephistopheles (*Faust*). After the
burning of the theatre in 1877, L. made several
concert-tours. Continued training in Leipzig,
especially song-singing. In 1879 founded Choral
Union in Christiania, which in 1902 took name
" Cæcilia Soc." Under his leadership (until 1911)
it became a most important factor in mus. life
of that city by its excellent perfs. of sacred and
secular choral works. L. also gave concerts at
home and abroad, sometimes together with his
gifted wife, the singer Mally Lammers, *née* Sars
(*q.v.*). For nearly a generation L. enjoyed a
great reputation as Norway's most distinguished
singer, closely connected wth the first performances of Norwegian songs. In 1896 he gave his
1st folk-song concert in his native land, and
his brilliant rendering of the ancient folk-
poem *Draumkvædet* (*The Dream Song*) and
other folk-melodies marks a triumph for the
position of folk-song in Norwegian executive
music. Has frequently given concerts in Stockholm, Copenhagen, London (1878), Paris (1889),
Berlin (1885) etc. As teacher of singing, he has
been working for 35 years, and as writer on
music he has also been active (see the work
Great Musicians).

Oratorio, *Fred* (*Peace*) (words by Björnson); *At
Akerhus*, solo, chorus and orch.; mixed choruses;
male choruses; songs; Norwegian refrains; folk-
songs in adaptation, etc.—J. A.

LAMOND, Frederic. British pianist; *b.* Glasgow, 28 Jan. 1868. Stud. in Glasgow, Frankfort-
o-M. under Schwarz, and under Bülow and Liszt;
début, Berlin and Vienna 1885, London 1886;
lived in Germany; London again, 1890–91; has
toured extensively; 1917, prof. of pf. at The
Hague Cons. Many tours. Renowned especially
as a Beethoven player.—E.-H.

LAMOTE DE GRIGNON, Mestre. Span. condr.
and compr. *b.* Barcelona, 1872. Condr. of the
Banda Municipal; condr. and founder of the
Orquesta Sinfónica, Barcelona.

Poema Romantic; *Scherzo*; *Quatre cançons populars*;
Reverie (cello and orch.); *Dotze cançons*, with orch.;
La Nit de Nadal; *Andalusia*, symph. picture. (Unión
Musical Española.)—P. G. M.

LAMOUREUX CONCERTS, Paris. Founded
1881 by Charles Lamoureux (*b.* 1834) and cond.
by him until his death in 1899, when his son-
in-law Camille Chevillard (*q.v.*) succeeded him.
Chevillard died in 1923, and was succeeded by
Paul Paray (*q.v.*) who had been deputy-condr.
from 1921. The concerts were originally given in
theatre of Château d'Eau, then at the Éden,
later at the Cirque d'Été. The Association des
Nouveaux Concerts was formed in 1897 and the
concerts were again given at the Château d'Eau;
1900–6 at Nouveau Théâtre; then at Théâtre
Sarah Bernhardt; now they are settled at the
Salle Gaveau.—A. C.

LAMPE, Walter. Ger. pianist and compr.
b. Leipzig, 28 April, 1872. Since 1920 teacher
of adv. pf.-playing at Acad. of Music, Munich.
Received training at Frankfort-o-M. (I. Knorr)
at Berlin (Herzogenberg and Humperdinck);
lived at Munich as compr. and pianist; then at
Weimar; now at Munich.

Trio, op. 3; cello sonata, op 4; str. 4tet, D ma.
(1923); Tragic tone-poem for orch. op. 6; *Serenade*
for 15 wind-instrs. op. 7; pf. pieces, op. 8.— A. E.

LANDORMY, Paul. Fr. musicologist and
compr. *b.* Issy - les - Moulineaux, 3 Jan. 1869.
Former pupil of École Normale Supérieure, Paris;
Agrégé des lettres. For music, pupil of Sbriglia
and of Plançon, whose niece, a perfect pianist, he
married. Ed.-in-chief of *Collection des chefs-
d'œuvre de la musique* for which he has written
a *Faust*, 1922. Also studies on *Brahms* (1921),
Bizet (1923), and numerous articles on modern
music. Has comp. many songs and pf. pieces
(*En Alsace*).—A. C.

LANDOWSKA, Wanda. Polish pianist; *b.*
Warsaw, 1877. An intelligent apostle and
finished performer of ancient clavicembalo works
on the orig. instr. Stud. under Michalowski and
Noskowski at Warsaw Cons. and completed her
studies under G. Urban in Berlin. 1900–13,
teacher of clavicembalo at the *Schola Cantorum*
(Vincent d'Indy) in Paris. Then went to Berlin
as prof. of that instr. at R. Music School, and
after the war returned to Paris. She has publ.
two books for the propaganda of clavicembalo-
playing and for the true interpretation of ancient
music, namely: *Bach et ses interprètes* (1906);
La Musique ancienne (1908). L. played at the
concerts of the Music Congress at Vienna in 1909,
and at the Bach Fest. of 1910.—ZD. J.

286

LANDRÉ, Willem. Dutch music critic and compr. *b.* Amsterdam, June 12, 1875. Pupil of Bernard Zweers, Amsterdam; 1899, critic of *Oprecht Haarlemsche Courant* (Haarlem); 1901, critic of *Nieuwe Courant* (The Hague); since 1906, chief critic of *Nieuwe Rotterdamsche Courant.*

Opera, *De Roos van Dekama*; *Erklärung*, barit. and orch.; *Nocturne*, orch. (perf. Amsterdam, 1921, under Mengelberg); *Requiem* for orch.; chamber-music; pf. 5tet; cello sonata; *Stabat Mater* for unacc. vs.; songs.—W. P.

LANDSHOFF, Ludwig. German writer and condr. *b.* Stettin, 3 June, 1874. Stud. under Thuille (Munich), Heinrich Urban (Berlin), Max Reger (Munich), Sandberger, Friedlaender and O. Fleischer; 1900, degree in philosophy at Munich, with *Study of Joh. Rud. Zumsteeg* (publ. 1902); temporary condr. at Kiel, Würzburg, Breslau, Hamburg; 1918, condr. Bach Society, Munich.

Polyphonic Accomp. and Figured-Bass (Sandberger Fest. Number, 1919); *Chorales of J. S. Bach with Figured-Bass written out in full* (Leipzig, Breitkopf, 1905); 2 vols. *Old Masters of Bel Canto* (Leipzig, 1912 and 1915, Peters); *Arias and Songs of J. Chr. Bach and Jos. Haydn* (Munich, 1923).—A. E.

LANE, Brand. Eng. choral condr. and teacher; *b.* London, 1854. Settled in Manchester (1875) as teacher of singing; founded Manchester Philh. Choir 1880 (at first, in 3 graded sections); gave first of his long series of concerts at Free Trade Hall in 1881, and has introduced the world's greatest artists to Manchester public. In 1914, he divided his annual series into 12 vocal and instr. concerts and 12 orchestral, engaging Sir Henry Wood as permanent condr. Together they have done almost as much as the Queen's Hall London Promenade Concerts, in bringing popular orch. music to the people.—E.-H.

LANG, Margaret Ruthven. Amer. compr. *b.* Boston, Mass., U.S.A., 27 Nov. 1867. Daughter of Benjamin J. Lang (1837–1909), noted Boston musician. Stud. pf. under father and Ph. Scharwenka; vn. under Louis Schmidt, Boston; 1886–7 under Drechsler and Abel, Munich; compn. under Victor Gluth. Returning to America, continued her studies under Paine, Chadwick and J. C. D. Parker in Boston. Began composing at 12 (5tet in 1 movement, pf., str.); several larger works in ms.: overture, *Witichis*, orch. op. 10, perf. by Thomas in Chicago, 1893; *Dramatic Overture*, E mi. for orch. op. 12, perf. Boston Symphony, 7 April, 1893; *Sappho's Prayer to Aphrodite*, contr. and orch., New York, 1895; concert aria, *Armida*, op. 24, with Boston Symphony, 10 Jan. 1896; overture, *Totila*; *Ballade*, perf. in Baltimore (Md.) 1901; str. 4tet, etc. Her songs have met with much success.

The Jumblies, cantata for barit. solo, male chorus and 2 pfs.; *Petit Roman en Six Chapitres*, suite, pf. op. 18; Rhapsody in E mi. pf. op. 21; 5 Norman songs, op. 19; 6 Scotch songs, op. 20 (all by A. P. Schmidt); about 50 songs (A. P. Schmidt; Church; Schirmer; Ditson; Enoch). Consult R. Hughes and A. Elson, *American Composers* (pp. 432–9, 520–1).—J. M.

LANGAARD, Borghild Bryhn. Norwegian concert and operatic s. singer; *b.* Kongsvinger, 23 July, 1883. Pupil of Oselio Björnson (Christi-

ania), Nina Grieg, Zur Mühlen (London). *Début* as concert-singer at a Grieg concert in Christiania in 1906, as opera-singer at Covent Garden, London, in 1907. Numerous concerts, mainly in Scandinavia and America; has sung in National Theatre and Central Theatre, Christiania, at Covent Garden and in the opera houses in Stockholm, Vienna and Chicago. Several Wagner-rôles (Elizabeth, Venus, Elsa, Brünnhilde), Carmen, Aïda, Butterfly, Tosca, etc. Lives in Christiania.—U. M.

LANGE, Daniel de. Dutch critic; *b.* Rotterdam, 11 July, 1841; *d.* Point Loma, California, 30 Jan. 1918. 1855–6, stud. cello under Ganz and Servais (Brussels); 1859, played (with his brother Samuel) in Galicia and Rumania; 1860–1863, teacher Cons. Lemberg (Lwów); 1864, teacher, Rotterdam; 1865, went to Paris; 1870, returned to Holland; 1878–1911, the most authoritative Dutch mus. critic (*Het Nieuws van den Dag*); 1895–1913, dir. of Amsterdam Cons.; 1914, went to California.

2 symphonies (1865 and 1880); opera, *De Val van Kuilenburg*; incidental music to Frederik van Eeden's *Lioba*) 1905). Numerous songs (Dutch, Fr., Ger. and Ital. words). Consult pamphlets by Henry Viotta, *Onze hedendaagsche toonkunstenaars, D. d. L.* (Amsterdam, 1894, Van Holkema & Warendorf); Ant. Averkamp, *Levensberigt van D. d. L.* (Leyden, 1918, Brill); also the *Theosophical Field*, March 1918.—W. P.

LANGE, Gustav Fredrik. Norwegian violinist and compr. *b.* Fredrikshald, 22 Feb. 1861. In 1878, pupil of Cons. in Stockholm; passed organ examination there. Afterwards stud. vn. first in Stockholm (under Lindberg), then in Paris and Berlin (under Sauret). From 1890, violinist in orch. of Christiania Theatre; from 1899, concert-master in National Theatre's Orch. Lange enjoys a great reputation as a violinist in his native land. Since 1890, teacher of vn., ensemble-playing and harmony at Music Cons. in Christiania. In 1899, establ. a str. quartet, which has during a number of years given concerts in Norway. Since 1919, leading violinist in Philh. Orch. in Christiania. Of his publ. pf. pieces, songs, and vn. compns., many are intended for teaching purposes; *A Practical Violin-Instructor* (3 parts), the most widely-used vn.-instructor in Norway; technical studies; *Practical Instruction in Harmony* (new ed. 1917).—J. A.

LANGE-MÜLLER, Peter Erasmus. Danish compr. *b.* Copenhagen, 1 Dec. 1850. M.A. 1870. Pupil of Gotfred Matthison-Hansen and Neupert; also 1 year at Copenhagen R. Cons. He himself declares he is essentially self-taught, resembling in this regard his great countryman, J. P. E. Hartmann. Received the Anker Stipendium, 1879, and spent much time in study and travel in Germany, Austria, France and Italy. His *début* as compr. of song-cycle *Sulamite and Solomon* (1874) and suite *In Alhambra*, revealed a talent of great originality and purely national character. These traits he has consistently preserved in his entire production. The wealth of imagination and value of his mus. ideas has constantly enriched Danish music with each new work. He easily takes front rank and is the most Danish of all his contemporaries. In his music for the plays of contemporary Danish poets (Kaalund, Holger Drachmann, Sophus Bauditz, Ernst von der Recke, Einar Christiansen) he has shown a peculiar gift of adapting himself with the most sensitive mental flexibility to every subtle phase. This is perhaps most plainly evident in Holger Drachmann's mediæval drama *Der var engang* (*Once upon a Time*), a genuine national Danish play, given innumerable times at R. Theatre, Copenhagen. Also each of his operas— the Danish *Tove*, with its dreamy character, *Spanske Studenter* (*Spanish Students*), *Fru Jeanna* (*Madame Jeanne*)—has its special mood; and, not least, his most recent opera upon an old Norse theme, *Vikingeblod* (*Viking Blood*). All of them belong to repertoire of R. Theatre. Some have been produced abroad.

A fine cantata was written for opening of Industrial Exhibition, Copenhagen, 1888, another for festival of Centenary of the Peasants' Freedom. Other choral works are 3 Psalms (*De profundis*); *Madonna Songs*; *Agnete and the Merman*; *Niels Ebbesen*; 2 symphonies; pf. trio; vn. concerto; *Romance*, vn.; many pf. pieces; finally a great number of songs in which he probably reaches the pinnacle of his art, the peculiarly characteristic production of a highly poetic nature. (Nordisk Musikforlag, Copenhagen.)—A. H.

LAPARRA, Raoul. Fr. compr. *b.* Bordeaux, 13 May, 1876; *Prix de Rome* in 1903. His music is founded on Spanish and Basque folk-lore, with a veristic technique.

Operas: *Peau d'Âne* (1899): *La Habañera* (1908); *La Jota* (1911). Orch.: *Danses basques*, given at Queen's Hall, London, 1921, with compr. at pf.; stage-music for *Amphitryon*; a str. 4tet.—A. C.

LAPEYRETTE, Ketty. Fr. operatic m.-sopr. *b.* Oloron (Basses-Pyrénées), 23 July, 1884. Entered Cons. Paris, 1903, under Masson, Hettich, and Bouvet. 1907, 1st prize for singing in *Sapho* and also in *Le Trouvère*. Engaged at Opéra by Messager and Broussau; *début* in *Samson et Dalila*, 1908. Sang in 1st perf. of *La Forêt*, 1910; *Les Sept Chansons*, 1919; *Goyescas*, 1919. Possesses a voice of very fine timbre, particularly in the middle register.—A. R.

LARCHET, John F. Irish compr. condr. *b.* Dublin, 1885. Stud. at R. Irish Acad. of Music. After very successful career as student, obtained diploma of Licentiate of Acad.; matriculated at Trinity Coll. Dublin; 1915, Mus.Bac.; 1917, Mus.Doc. During his Univ. career, was pupil of Dr. Kitson. For past 15 years, dir. of orch. music at Abbey Theatre, Dublin, and has made the mus. interludes one of the features of that theatre. As condr. he has given choral and orch. recitals of important modern works. He is undoubtedly the most promising of the younger Irish comprs.; for he is adapting his native mus. idiom to modern harmonic development. Since his appointment to the Professorship of Music in the National Univ. he has striven to encourage mus. compn. based on folk-music. Many of his songs (*Padraic the Fiddler*; *An Ardglass Boat-Song*) are true evocations of the Irish spirit. His tone-poem, *A Lament for Youth*, has been perf. with great success in Dublin by an orch. under his direction in 1923.

The Legend of Lough Rea (*Lagerniensis*), Stainer

& Bell; many songs to words by W. B. Yeats, Shelley, Longfellow, Padric Gregory. Arr. of Irish folk-tunes (Pigott, Dublin); coll. of Irish airs (for str. orch.); *Believe me, if all these endearing young charms,* unacc. female chorus; *A Lament for Youth* (C. & E. Ed. Dublin).—W. ST.

LA ROTELLA, Pasquale. Ital. compr. and condr. *b.* Bitonto, 28 Feb. 1880. Stud. compn., organ and pf. at Naples Cons. In 1902 won, by competition, post of dir. of *Schola Cantorum* at the Basilica di San Nicola, Bari, where he remained until 1913, composing much sacred music, and participating in movement for reform of sacred music taking place at that time. His first opera, *Ivan*, gained great success at Bari in 1900, and was immediately reproduced in Milan. A second opera, *Dea*, was produced in 1903 for opening perf. at new Teatro Petruzzelli at Bari. A third, *Fasma* (libretto by Arturo Colautti, written at instance of publisher Sonzogno), was perf. in Milan at Dal Verme Theatre, 1908. In the meantime, he gained a good reputation as orch. condr.; in that capacity he travelled successfully, appearing at most important theatres in Italy and abroad.—D. A.

LARREGLA, Joaquín. Span. pianist and compr. *b.* Lumbie (Navarra) in 1865. After obtaining his B.A. degree at Pamplona, went to Madrid, where he stud. pf. under Zabalza and compn. under Arrieta, at R. Cons. de Música, in which inst. he is now a prof. of pf. Member of R. Acad. de Bellas Artes. Well known in Spain as pf. soloist; author of a very large number of pf. pieces; orch. works; mus. comedies; a lyric drama in 3 acts, *Miguel Andrés*. (Unión Musical Española, Madrid.)—P. G. M.

LARROCHA, Alfredo. Span. cellist and condr. *b.* Granada, 1866. Started his mus. education as a choir-boy (*seise*) at the Cath. of his native town, under the choirmaster Celestino Vila. After becoming an efficient player on vn., vla., cello and d.b., he devoted himself to cello-study under Mireski, at R. Cons. de Música. In 1888, won a 1st prize and went to Paris, becoming a pupil of Delsar. Lives in San Sebastian, where he is dir. of Acad. de Música de la Sociedad de Bellas Artes, and condr. of its orch. As teacher of str. instrs. at Acad. Municipal, San Sebastian, has contributed in great measure to the development of mus. culture in that town, where he holds (since 1904) also the position of permanent condr. of the orch. of the Gran Casino. —P. G. M.

LARSEN, Nils. Norwegian pianist; *b.* Christiania, 7 June, 1888. Pupil of pianist Martin Knutzen, of J. Vianna da Motta and Rudolph Ganz. Since 1905, numerous concert-tours in his native land, and concerts in Gothenburg, Copenhagen and Danish provincial towns. Has gained a reputation for refined, poetical pf.-playing; has published pf. pieces, songs, an adaptation of Christoph Graupner, 2 Norwegian Dances, etc.—J. A.

LARWAY, Joseph H. Eng. publisher. His first activities date back to about 1890 when he personally began to build up his business by the sale of the then popular religious song which the

288

public of that day greatly liked. The publication of educational works and tutors for various instrs. brought some added prosperity. In course of time he began publishing popular ballads of a rather intimate lyrical type. Personal love of good music and keen interest in the difficult careers of young British comprs. led him about 1907 to publish many works by Joseph Holbrooke, and later by Ernest Austin.—E.-H.

LARYNGOSTROBOSCOPE. See SCRIPTURE, EDWARD W.

LA SALVIA, Antonio Santos. Argentine pianist and compr. *b.* Buenos Ayres, 1877. Toured through Argentina, Uruguay, Chile. Founded Cons. La Nación, Buenos Ayres. Pieces for orch. and for vn. and pf. Also text-book *Teoria de la Música*, a standard work in S. America.—S. G. S.

LASSALLE, José. Span. condr. *b.* Madrid, 1874. Ph.D. and D.Litt. Collab. with Benavente, Azorín, Maeztu and others in the *Revista Nueva*, herald of the Spanish intellectual upheaval of to-day. In 1900, went to study music in Germany. In 1903, made his *début* as condr. with the Kaim Orch. Munich; travelled as condr. with the Munich Tonkünstler Orch. in an extensive tour through Europe. Lives in Madrid, where he conducts an orch. founded by him, called Orquesta Lassalle.—P. G. M.

LASSERRE, Pierre. Fr. musicologist; *b.* Pau, 1867. Enthusiastic writer on music. Has also comp. some songs. Has written:
Les Idées de Nietzsche sur la Musique (1907); *L'Esprit de la Musique française* (1919); *Philosophie du goût musical* (1922).—A. C.

LASSON, Per. Norwegian compr. *b.* Christiania, 18 April, 1859; *d.* there, 6 June, 1883. A precocious talent. Stud. harmony for some time under Svendsen. His works include half a score pf. pieces and a vol. of songs (texts by Henrik Wergeland and Björnstjerne Björnson). He died at the age of 24; but the fresh melody and sincerity of his compns. have preserved several of them from oblivion. Thus, the pf. piece *Crescendo* is played almost all over the world. —R. M.

LATTO, David. Scottish pf. accompanist and concert organiser; *b.* Edinburgh, 24 Jan. 1878. Pupil of James A. Moonie and Nicol J. Affleck, in Edinburgh. One of most accomplished, and most unassuming, accompanists in Edinburgh. For Messrs Paterson Sons & Co., for 30 years has successfully organised more concerts than any other concert-giver in Scotland.—W. S.

LATTUADA, Felice. Ital. compr. *b.* Caselle di Morimondo (Milan province), Feb. 1882. Pupil of Ferroni at Milan Cons.; author of a sonata, vn. and pf.; a 4tet; vocal chamber-music; opera, *La Tempesta* (from Shakespeare), perf. Milan, 1922. His works are publ. by Ricordi. —D. A.

LAUB, Thomas Linnemann. Danish musician, writer, orgt.; *b.* Langaa, near Nyborg, 8 Dec. 1852. M.A. 1871. Pupil of R. Cons. Copenhagen (1873–6); orgt. at Ch. of The Holy Ghost, Copenhagen (1884–91) and at Holmens Ch. since

1891. Spent some time studying in Italy. Leader of national movement for restoration of the old Danish folk-songs and church tunes to their orig. form in rhythmic and tonal relations. His literary works on these subjects are:
Om Kirkesang (Church Song), 1887; *Luthersk Kirkesang (Lutheran Church Song)*, 1891; *Vore Folkemelodiers Oprindelse (Origin of Our Folk-Melodies)*, 1893, and his principal work, *Musik og Kirke (Music and the Church)*, 1920. Also his ed. of the old tunes in restored form: *80 rytmiske Koraler (80 Rhythmic Chorals)*; *Kirkemelodier (Church Tunes)*; *Salmemelodier i Kirkestil (Psalm Tunes in Church Style)*; *Danske Folkeviser med gamle Melodier (Danish Folk-Songs with Old Tunes)*. He designed the chimes of the Copenhagen City Hall.—A. H.

LAUBER, Joseph. Swiss compr. *b.* Lucerne, 25 Dec. 1864. Stud. pf. and compn. under Gustav Weber, Rob. Freund and Fr. Hegar at Zurich, and was pupil of Rheinberger at Munich and of Massenet in Paris; teacher at Zurich Cons. for a short time; then prof. of compn. at Cons. in Geneva; also 1st condr. of opera there for 2 years; known as excellent teacher; has comp. many pieces, remarkable for construction and orchestration, and full of real mus. imagination and temperament.
2 festspiele, *Neuchâtel Suisse* and *Ode lyrique*, soli, chorus, orch.; 2 oratorios, *Weltendämmerung* and *Ad gloriam Dei*; *Te Deum*, soli, chorus, orch.; 5 symphonies; *Humoresque* for orch. (Swiss National Ed.); symph. poems: *Sur l'Alpe*; *Chant du Soir*; *Le Vent et la Vague*; 2 pf. concertos; 2 vn. concertos; chamber-music and numerous songs. Mostly publ. by Fœtisch, Lausanne, and Hug, Leipzig.—F. H.

LAUNIS, Armas. Finnish musicologist and compr. *b.* Hämeenlinna (Tavastehus), 22 April, 1884. Stud. Helsingfors Univ. (Ph.D. 1913) and at Orch. School; made several journeys abroad in interests of art and science, and coll. folk-songs (among other places, in Lapland). Scientific works: *Die Lappischen Juoigos-Melodien* (1908); *Über Art, Entstehung und Verbreitung der estnisch-finnischen Runenmelodien* (1910); *Suomen kansan sävelmiä*, IV (see KROHN). Later devoted himself entirely to operatic compn. In 1922 L. founded People's Cons. in Helsingfors, and in same year became dir. of Music Inst. there. The chief characteristic of his operas consists in the development of a Finnish recitative style and in the artistic introduction of elements of primitive folk-music. Perf. up to the present:
Seitsemän veljestä (The Seven from the Jochenhof) after comedy by Aleksis Kivi (1st perf. 1910), and *Kullervo* (subject from folk-epic *Kalevala*), 1917. Both operas are publ. in full. ed. with Finnish and Ger. text.—T. H.

LAURENS, Edmond. Fr. compr. and teacher. Pupil of Duprato and Guiraud at Paris Cons.
Stage music for *Sylvie* (Abel Hermant); 4tets; *Mascarades*. He has publ. a *Cours d'Éducation musicale du pianiste*; *L'Art du Correcteur*; *Traité de Notation musicale*.—A. C.

LAVATER, Hans. Swiss compr. *b.* Zurich, 1885. Stud. at Cons. in Zurich and Cologne, particularly under Fritz Steinbach. Lives at Zurich. His works written in an Neo-classical style, attain great intensity of expression.
Bergpsalm (Scheffel), barit., chorus, orch. and organ; *Zauberleuchtturm*, ballad for male chorus and orch.; pf. concerto; pf. 5tet; vn. sonata; numerous songs and unacc. choruses.—F. H.

LAVATER, Louis. Australian pianist and teacher: *b.* St. Kilda, Melbourne, 1867. Stud.

pf. under O. Linden, theory under Pascal Needham and Dr. McBurney, orchestration under
Hamilton Clarke. Now teaches in Melbourne.
Has comp. 2 short orch. pieces, and some chamber
music (4tet, trio), pieces for vn. and pf.—G. Y.

LAVIGNAC, Albert. Fr. musicologist and
teacher; b. Paris, 21 Jan. 1846; d. there, 28
May, 1916. Prof. at Cons. (after having been
a pupil there); has specialised in study of
Mus. Dictation (on which he has written a
Complete Theoretical and Practical Course (1882),
and of Solfeggio. His other works do not not
rise above the level of good popularisation. The
best-known is:
Le Voyage Artistique à Bayreuth (1897) (Eng. transl.
by E. Singleton, under title of The Music Dramas of
R. Wagner). Also La Musique et les Musiciens (1895);
L'Éducation musicale (1902); Notions scolaires de
musique (1905); Les Gaîtés du Conservatoire (1906).
Until his death, ed. the Encyclopédie de la Musique
(q.v.), now ed. by Lionel de la Laurencie.—A. C.

LAVIÑA, Facundo. Span. compr. Orch.:
Sierra de Gredos; Indith, symph. poems, etc.
(perf. Orquesta Filarmónica, Madrid).—P. G. M.

LAW OF THE NEAREST WAY (Gesetz des
nächsten Weges). A harmonic term, used by
Anton Bruckner and others, to describe the
method of part-writing which takes every note
to its nearest one, in order to produce the most
perfect connection of the chords. Arnold Schönberg adopts the term in his Harmonielehre (3rd
ed. 1922, page 44).—EG. W.

LÁZARO, Hipólito. Span. t. b. in Catalonia.
One of leading opera singers of present day.
Teatro Real, Madrid; Liceo, Barcelona; Metro-
politan Opera House, New York; La Scala,
Milan, etc.—P. G. M.

LAZARUS, Daniel. Fr. compr. b. Paris, 1898.
Stud. at Cons.; 1st prize for pf. 1915. Shows
a precocious mastery of his art and a sureness
of touch that augur well; he does not hesitate
to strike out on new lines for himself.
Symph. poem; 3 ballets; pf. preludes; vn. and pf.
sonata; fantasy for cello and orch.—H. P.

LAZARUS, Gustav. Ger. compr. b. Cologne,
19 July, 1861; d. Berlin, June 1920. Pianist;
pupil at Cologne Cons. (Seiss, G. Jensen, Wüllner); 1887, teacher at Scharwenka Cons. Berlin;
after death of Emil Breslaur, took over his
Music School.
Over 170 works of all kinds, especially agreeable
pf. pieces; many pieces with character-titles; sonatina,
op. 19; Modern Pianist (4 books); duets for 2 pfs.
op. 39 (Ländler; Waltz; Scherzo).—A. E.

LAZZARI, Sylvio. Compr. b. Bozen, 1 Jan.
1858. French naturalisation at a very early
age; entered (after studies in Bavaria and
Austria), Paris Cons., where he was a pupil
of Guiraud and of César Franck. His music,
which is founded on Wagnerism, preserves a
seductive personality which recalls its origin
on Adriatic shores. Until 1894, he was the
Wagnerian committee's representative in Paris.
Stage works: Armor (1898); La Lépreuse (1912);
Le Sauteriot (1921). Orch.: Ophélia; Effet de Nuit
(after Verlaine); Impressions d'Adriatique; Rapsodie Espagnole; Fantaisie (vn. and orch.); pf. concerto. Chamber-music: vn. sonata; trio; 4tet;
8tet; choruses; duets; songs.—A. C.

LEANDER-FLODIN, Adée. Finnish s. singer;
b. 1873. Began studies in Helsingfors, continued
in Paris, 1893-8; appeared 1897-8 at Paris
Opéra-Comique. Toured in Norway and S.
America. Married the musical writer and compr.
Karl Flodin; since 1908, for some time, teacher
of singing in Buenos Ayres.—T. H.

LEBANO, Felix. Argentine harpist; b. Palermo
in 1867; d. Buenos Ayres, 1916. Stud. under
Scotto at Cons. San Pietro a Maiella, Naples.
Succeeded to professorship on Scotto's death.
Concert tours throughout Europe. Decorated
by Queen Isabel II, King Edward VII,
King Humbert I, and King Luis of Portugal.
His harp bears the autographs of many famous
musicians and painters. (Sardou wrote on it the
words: "C'est un corps sec et froid, sans chaleur
et sans flammes. Lebano sonne, et c'est une
âme.") Touring S. America, he came to Buenos
Ayres in 1887, and definitely settled down,
devoting himself to teaching. Organises an
annual series of concerts. In 1890 went to Paris
to give a concert there with Paderewski.—A. M.

LE BORNE, Fernand. Belgian compr. b.
Charleroi, 10 March, 1862. Pupil of Saint-
Saëns, Massenet and César Franck. Having
settled in Paris, he became mus. correspondent
of Le Soir, Brussels. Music critic of Petit Parisien.
Stage works: Daphnis et Chloé, pastoral drama
(Brussels, 1885); Mudarra, mus. drama (Berlin,
1899); Hedda, Scandinavian legend (Milan, 1898);
Fête bretonne, ballet (Nice, 1903); L'Idole aux yeux
verts, ballet (1902); L'Absent, music for theatre
(Paris, 1904); La Catalane, lyric drama (Paris, 1907);
Les Girondins, lyric drama (Lyons, 1906); Cléopâtre,
mus. drama (Rouen, 1914); La Brune et la Blonde,
music for theatre (Paris, 1921); Néréa, lyric drama;
Les Borgia, mus. drama. V. and orch.: Patria,
inaugural cantata for Exhibition, 1900; Temps de
Guerre, symph. tableaux with choruses; L'Amour
de Myrto, poem, vs. and orch.; L'Amour trahi, and
L'Amour d'une Parisienne, id.; songs, vs. and orch.;
2 masses. Orch.: Dramatic Symphony; symphony-
concerto, vn. and orch.; symphony with organ;
3 orchestral suites; 2 overtures; Aquarelles, small
orch.; Fête bretonne; L'Invasion; Poème légendaire
and Rêverie, vn. and orch. Chamber-music: str. 4tet;
trio; vn., pf. and cello, and pf. sonatas. Songs;
pf. pieces.—E. C.

LEBRUN, Paul Henri Joseph. Belgian compr.
b. Ghent, 21 April, 1863; d. Louvain, 4 Nov.
1920. Was entering Univ. of Ghent as civil
engineer when he suddenly decided to give all
his time to music; entered Cons. at Ghent
(under Karel Miry and Adolphe Samuel);
obtained (1881-6) most brilliant distinctions.
Entered Rome Competition three times in
succession and gained a 1st Grand Prix in 1891
for cantata Andromède (his rival was Guillaume
Lekeu, who only obtained a 2nd prize). Prof.
of harmony at Ghent Cons., 1890, and of chamber-music in 1892, and gained a reputation as
a devoted teacher of generous vision; 1913,
dir. of École de Musique, Louvain (until death).
His works show a very pure inspiration and
technique, also a tendency towards harmonic
originality in spite of a decided respect for
classical tradition.
Str. 4tet, D mi. (crowned by R. Acad. 1885);
Andromède, 1891; symphony, E mi. (crowned by
R. Acad. 1891); La Fiancée d'Abydos (2-act opera,
Ghent Theatre, 1896); Marche Jubilaire (full orch.),

1905; *Sur la Montagne*, symph. poem (1st perf. Ostend, 1911); *Ons Belgie vrij* (*Belgium Liberated*) lyrical poem celebrating liberation of Belgium, 1918 (Louvain, 1919).—C. V. B.

LECOCQ, Charles. Fr. operetta compr. *b.* Paris, 3 June, 1832; *d.* there, Oct. 1918. The most fertile and cleverest representative of the Fr. *opérette.* Pupil of Bazin, Halévy and Benoist at Paris Cons. where he was for a long time prof. himself. His music is always extremely carefully written, orchestrated with taste, and of perfect melodic grace. The rhythm sometimes lacks variety. Has produced some songs, some pf. pieces, an ed. of Rameau's *Castor et Pollux*; but nearly the whole of his production (about 100 works) is composed of operettas. The first, *Le Docteur Miracle*, carried off, at the same time as Bizet, a prize offered by Offenbach (1857). All the succeeding works, up to 1868, had no success; nor were they of great interest. But *Fleur de Thé* (1868) was a triumph, and thenceforth most of L.'s operas were celebrated; notably:

Le Testament de M. de Trac (1871); *Les Cent Vierges* (1872); *La Fille de Mme. Angot* (1872); *Giroflé-Girofla* (1874); *La Petite Mariée* (1875); *Le Petit Duc* (1878); *Le Jour et la Nuit* (1881); *Le Cœur et la Main* (1882).

After this period of full flower, his works, whilst being equally carefully written, did not recapture the sprightliness of former days.—A. C.

LEDESMA, Father Dámaso. Span. orgt. and compr. *b.* Ciudad Rodrigo (Salamanca), 3 Feb. 1868. Author of many choral works, religious and secular. Has attained a great reputation for his research work on national folk-music, a branch of study much neglected in Spain up to present. Of his several important works on this subject, his *Cancionero Salmantino* has received a special award from the R. Acad. de Bellas Artes, Madrid. It is the only one published. He lives at Salamanca.—P. G. M.

LEE, Ernest Markham. Eng. lecturer and compr. *b.* Cambridge, 8 June, 1874. Organ scholar, Emmanuel Coll. Cambridge; stud. under Dr. Charles Wood and others; originator of Woodford Green Chamber Concerts; Univ. extension-lecturer of Oxford, Cambridge and London. Has composed much sound and tuneful educational music.

The Story of Opera (Walter Scott Co.); *The Story of Symphony* (*id.*); *Tchaikovsky* (John Lane); *Grieg* (Bell); *Tchaikovsky* (*id.*); *On Listening to Music* (Kegan Paul); *Brahms* (Sampson Low); *Musical Theory and Knowledge* (Lengnick, 1923); numerous educational pieces and books of pieces for pf.; preludes, *Hesperis, Serapis*, pf. (Murdoch); *Modern Suite*, pf. (Lengnick); vn. pieces (J. Williams); church music (Novello); songs (Chappell; Murdoch); cantatas (Novello), etc.—E.-H.

LEE-WILLIAMS, Charles. Eng. orgt. *b.* Winchester, 1 May, 1853. Chorister New Coll. Oxford; tutor and orgt. St. Columba's Coll. Ireland; orgt. Llandaff Cath.; Gloucester Cath.; cond. 3 Choirs Fest. from 1882-97. Toured as examiner for Associated Board of R.A.M. and R.C.M. (Canada, Australia, etc.) 1897-1923.

Church music; short cantatas; part-songs (Novello). Ed. *Annals of the Three Choirs.*—E.-H.

LEEDS MUSICAL FESTIVAL. The first fest. formed part of opening of Leeds Town Hall

by Queen Victoria in 1858 (first perf. of Sterndale Bennett's *May Queen*); 2nd fest. in 1874 (Costa conducting); 1877 (Costa), Macfarren's *Joseph*; 1880 (Sullivan), *Martyr of Antioch*; 1883 (Sullivan), Macfarren's *King David*; 1886 (Sullivan), *Golden Legend*, Mackenzie's *Story of Sayid*, Stanford's *Revenge*, all 1st perf.; 1889 (Sullivan), Parry's *St. Cecilia's Day*, Corder's *Sword of Argantyr*, Creser's *Sacrifice of Freia*, Stanford's *Voyage of Maeldune*, all 1st perf.; 1892, Alan Gray's *Arethusa*, and symphony by F. Cliffe; 1895, Parry's *Invocation to Music*, Somervell's *Forsaken Merman*; 1898 (last one cond. by Sullivan), Stanford's *60th Year, Queen Victoria, Te Deum*, Elgar's *Caractacus*, Cowen's *The Passions*; 1901 (Stanford cond.), Coleridge-Taylor's *Blind Girl of Castél Cuillé*; 1904 (Stanford), new works by Mackenzie, Walford Davies, Charles Wood, Holbrooke, Stanford (5 *Songs of the Sea*); 1907 (Stanford cond.), Stanford's *Stabat Mater*, Somervell's *Intimations of Immortality*, Vaughan Williams's *Towards the Unknown Region*, etc., Boughton's 2 *Folk-Songs, with Variations*, Bantock's *Sea Wanderers* (all 1st perf.); 1910 (Stanford cond.), new works: Vaughan Williams's *Sea Symphony*, Rachmaninof's symphony, Stanford's *Songs of the Fleet*; 1913 (condrs. Elgar, Nikisch, Allen), new works: Elgar's *Falstaff*, Butterworth's *A Shropshire Lad*, Harty's *Mystic Trumpeter*; 1916-19, no fests.; 1922 (condrs. Allen and Coates), new work, Holst's *Poem of Death*. The choir is recruited from Leeds, Huddersfield and other towns of West Riding. Chorus-master, Dr. A. C. Tysoe; succeeding H. A. Fricker (*q.v.*); secretary, Charles F. Haigh.—E.-H.

LEFEBVRE, Charles. Fr. compr. *b.* Paris, 19 June, 1843; *d.* there, 1917. *Prix de Rome* in 1870. Gained the *Prix Chartier* in 1884 and 1891. Prof. of elementary classes at Cons. His art is Neo-classic.

Operas: *Zaïre* (1887); *Le Trésor* (1890); *Djelma* (1894); *Judith* (chorus and orch.); *Eloa* (chorus and orch.). *Scènes lyriques* : *Toggenburg* (after Schiller); *Dalila*; *La Messe du Fantôme.* A symphony; some chamber-music.—A. C.

LE FLEM, Paul. Fr. compr. *b.* Lézardieux (Côtes-du-Nord), 1881. Commenced his studies in music at Paris Cons.; finished them at Schola Cantorum, where he is now prof. Stud. harmony under Lavignac, cpt. under Albert Roussel, compn. under Vincent d'Indy. Much more cultured than the average of comprs., he is *licencié-ès-lettres*, and of a philosophic turn of mind. His music, however, has nothing intellectual about it, but draws its inspiration deliberately from the popular airs of Brittany.

Sonata, pf. and vn. (1905); symphony in 4 parts (1906); *Par Landes* and *Par Grèves*, pf. (1907); *Aucassin et Nicolette*, song-fable (1908); 5tet, pf. and str. (1910); *Les Voix du Large*, symph. poem (1910); songs; pf. pieces. Consult André Cœuroy, *La Musique française moderne.*—A. C.

LEGGE, Robin Humphrey. Eng. music critic; *b.* Bishop's Castle, Shropshire, 28 June, 1862. Read law at Cambridge; stud. music and languages at Leipzig, Frankfort-o-M., Florence, Munich; assistant music critic on *Times* for 15 years; joined staff of *Daily Telegraph*, London, 1906; now mus. ed. therof. Has written *Annals of the Norwich Fests.* and many biographies for *Dictionary of Nat. Biog.*, Grove's *Dictionary of Music*, besides numerous articles.—E.-H.

LEGINSKA, Ethel (real name Liggins). Eng. pianist; *b.* Hull, 13 April, 1890. Gave pf. recitals at age of 7, proving herself no ordinary child-prodigy by her improvisations on given themes. In 1900, won a scholarship at Hoch's Cons. Frankfort-o-M. Stud. there under Kwast (pf.) and Sekles and Ivan Knorr (theory); then for 3 years under Leschetizky. At age of 17, made 1st of several European concert-tours, later going to America. In New York, stud. harmony under Rubin Goldmark and compn. under Ernest Bloch. Her compns. are modern in style. She gave a concert of her pf. works in London, 8 July, 1922, and of her orch. music, Queen's Hall, 22 Nov. 1922.

Symph. poem, *Beyond the Fields we know*, orch.; fantasy, *From a Life*, for 2 fls. piccolo, ob. 2 clar. bsn. str. 4tet and pf.; *4 Poems*, str. 4tet; *6 Nursery Rhymes*, s. v. and small orch.; pf. pieces; songs. —E.-H.

LEHÁR, Franz. Hungarian operetta compr. *b.* Komarom, 30 April, 1870. Stud. partly in Vienna, partly in Prague; then became condr. of an Austrian military band. Later he cond. Vienna Tonkünstler Orch., but resigned and lives only for compn. He began with serious works (opera *Kukuska*, perf. 1896, Leipzig) but soon changed his style and is now one of the most famous operetta-writers living. His success is founded on his melodious material, ideas, and ingenious orchestration. He was the first to introduce special dancing parts for the actors after each song or duet. Also the influence of South-Slav folk-song is felt. About 30 operettas; best-known is *Die lustige Witwe* (*The Merry Widow*), 1905. His later pieces, by curtailing the dialogue, approach more closely to the comic opera.

Der Rastelbinder (1902); *Der Göttergatte* (1904): *Das Fürstenkind* (1909); *Der Graf van Luxemburg* (1909); *Zigeunerliebe* (1910); *Eva* (1911); *Endlich allein* (1914); *Wo die Lerche singt* (*Where the Lark sings*) (1918); *Die blaue Mazur* (1920); *Frasquita* (1921); *The Three Graces* (London, 1924); *Clo-Clo* (1924).—P. P.

LEHMANN, Lilli. Ger. s. singer; *b.* Würzburg, 24 Nov. 1842. From 1870, coloratura s. on Berlin stage; 1878, became singer of R. Chapel, but broke contract; went to America; took up dramatic singing, and married the t. Paul Kalisch (*q.v.*); 1890, returned to Germany, accepted star engagements; 1892 in Berlin. Has directed every summer the singing-courses of the Salzburg Mozarteum. Famous Wagner and Mozart singer, remarkable for her powerful acting (Fidelio, Isolde).

Study of Fidelio (1904); *How to Sing* (1902; Eng. by R. Aldrich 1903; Fr. by Edith Nägeli, 1910; revised Eng. ed. Macmillan, 1922); *My Way* (1913). Consult: Wangemann, *L. L.'s Secret of Vocal Cords* (1906); L. Andro, *L. L.* (1908). Her sister, Marie, *b.* 15 May, 1851, s. singer, was 1881–1902 member of Vienna R. Opera; now living near Berlin. —A. E. & EG. W.

LEHMANN, Liza. Eng. song-compr. *b.* London, 1862; *d.* there, 19 Sept. 1918. First

stud. under her mother (Mrs. Rudolf Lehmann, who comp. songs and arr. others of a classical type, under the initials " A. L."); then under Randegger; compn. under Raunkilde at Rome, Freudenberg at Wiesbaden, and Hamish MacCunn in London. Made her *début* as a singer at a Monday Popular Concert, St. James's Hall, London, 23 Nov. 1885. Retired from concert-platform on her marriage to Herbert Bedford in 1894. Her first great success was the song-cycle *In a Persian Garden* (Metzler, 1896); soon followed by *The Daisy Chain*.

Romantic light opera, *The Vicar of Wakefield* (Boosey, 1906); morality play, *Everyman* (ms.); stage-scenes: *Good-night, Babette* (Boosey); *Secrets of the Heart* (*id.*); orch. works (ms.); *Endymion* (J. Church Co.); *Molly's Spinning Song*, v. and orch. (Boosey); Suite, vn. and pf. (Keith, Prowse); incidental music (Chappell; Elkin; Boosey); song-cycles and songs (Chappell; Boosey; Schott; Metzler, etc.).—E.-H.

LEHNER, Eugen (Jenő). Hungarian violinist; *b.* Szabadka, Hungary (now annexed by Jugo-Slavia), 24 June, 1894. Stud. at R. High School for Music, Budapest. Founder and leader of Lehner Str. Quartet (Lehner, Smilovits, Roth, Hartmann).—B. B.

LEICHTENTRITT, Hugo. Ger. musicologist and compr. *b.* Pleschen (Posen), 1 Jan. 1874. Lived in America from 1889; stud. under J. K. Paine (Harvard Univ.); finished mus. training 1895–8 at Berlin High School; took Ph.D. 1901 at Berlin (dissertation, *Reinhard Keiser in his Operas*); joined staff of Klindworth-Scharwenka Cons. Dr. Leichtentritt is the author of the article on BUSONI in this Dictionary.

Chopin biography (1905 in Reimann's *Celebrated Musicians*, 2nd ed. 1913); short *History of Music* (*Hillger's Illustrated Popular Books*); *History of the Motet* (Leipzig, 1908, Breitkopf); *Lessons on Mus. Form* (1911, 2nd ed. 1920, Breitkopf); *Erwin Lendvai* (1912); *Ferruccio Busoni* (1916); *Analysis of Chopin's Pf. Works*, 2 vols. (1920, Max Hesse); *Handel* (1924, Deutsche Verlags-Anstalt); Revision of 4th vol. of Ambros's *Mus. History* (1909); in *D.d.T.*, he publ. *Selected Works of Hieronymus Prætorius* (vol. 23), and *Selected Works of Andreas Hammerschmidt* (vol. 40); for the Soc. for Dutch Mus. History, Amsterdam, revised the *Scherzi Musicali of Johann Schenk* (100 pieces for the gamba with figured-bass); in *Masterpieces of Ger. Art*, he publ. 35 part-songs of old German masters (for practical use); *12 Madrigals of Monteverdi* (Peters); *Ger. Home-Music of Four Centuries* (Berlin, Max Hesse, 1906, 2nd ed. 1922). Publ. compns.: str. 4tet, F ma. op. 1; songs, op. 2; op. 3 (13 songs to old Ger. words); op. 4 (*Chinese-German Days and Seasons*, Goethe). In ms.: *Hymns and Songs of Hölderlin*; 20 songs, op. 8 (Richard Dehmel); 6 romantic songs, op. 9; symphony in A, op. 10; symph. poem, *Hero and Leander*, op. 6; *A Summer Day*, op. 11 (female chorus, s., chamber orch.); str. 5tet, op. 7; suite for cello solo, op. 12; vla. sonata, op. 13; pf. 5tet, op. 14; vn. concerto, op. 15; play, *The Sicilian* (with dances), from Molière (Freiburg-i-Br. 1920).—A. E.

LEISNER, Emmy. Ger. contr. Appeared 1912 at Hellerau near Dresden as Orpheus; 1912–21, member of Berlin National Opera, since then prominent concert-singer (Brahms.)—A. E.

LEKEU, Guillaume. Belgian composer; *b.* Heusy, near Verviers, 20 Jan. 1870; *d.* Angers, of typhoid fever, 21 Jan. 1894. Until 9 years old, lived in his native town, where he studied solfeggio and violin. In 1879, he accompanied his parents to Poitiers, where he attended the high school till 1888, all the time continuing to study piano and violin. Coming into contact with the works of Beethoven, he was greatly attracted by musical composition, at which he worked alone for some time. In 1888, he settled with his family in Paris, where he took the degree of Ph.D. Th. de Wyzewa dissuaded him from entering the Conservatoire and brought him into touch with G. Vallin, under whose direction Lekeu completed his musical education. In 1888 he made the acquaintance of César Franck who, captivated by his exceptional gifts, took him as pupil. This instruction had hardly begun when Franck died and Lekeu put himself under d'Indy. On d'Indy's advice Lekeu took part, in 1891, in the competition for *Prix de Rome*, in Brussels, where he gained 2nd prize. After this period Lekeu wrote the sonata for piano and violin dedicated to Ysaye; the *Trois Poèmes* for voice; the orchestral *Fantaisie sur deux airs populaires angevins*. In 1892 he started a pianoforte quartet which death did not allow him to finish; it was completed by d'Indy. The concert of his works held in Paris shortly after his death was a revelation. Since then, his works form part of the stock repertory.

Other works: *Adagio*, str. orch.; 2 symph. studies on *Hamlet*; one on the second part of *Faust*. The following works: *Chant de triomphale délivrance*, orch.; pf. trio; cello sonata; pf. sonata; some pf. pieces and songs, are in part youthful works and less interesting. A fairly large number of works remain in ms. especially *Épithalame* for str. 5tet, 3 trombones and organ; *Introduction and Adagio* for solo tuba with brass band; a *Chant Lyrique* for singers and orch.; fragments of a lyrical comedy entitled *Barberine*, etc.

Lekeu may be considered the chief of the Belgian branch of the young French school. His style shows the outward characteristics of the style of Franck, but he adds to it an entirely original personality, recognisable among all others and all the more remarkable in that it appeared to be already entirely independent at the time of Lekeu's premature death, while that of Franck only freed itself entirely when old age was approaching. It is likewise interesting. owing to the fact that Lekeu was a real Walloon of the country of Liège, in contrast to the Germanic origin of Franck. His music bears the characteristic marks of the art and poetry of Liège: dreaminess, gentle nostalgia, an alternation of penetrating melancholy and wild transports, of an ideal and immense aspiration. If, in Franck, musical science seems at times to have no other end but itself and even shows a certain ostentation, in Lekeu it is exclusively at the service of expression, which reaches in him an intensity which was never surpassed by any musician and which was rarely attained. His inspiration is purely melodic, his themes are striking and, once heard, are never forgotten. His favourite master was Beethoven, whom he resembles at times in depth of feeling and ardent spontaneity. A

weakness in his art was the form, which lacks consistency and homogeneity. He was too young to have mastered this superior element of art. Franck was enraptured with the abundant gifts of Lekeu, whom d'Indy calls "a quasi-genius." The undersigned is convinced that Lekeu, had he lived, would have become an artist superior to Franck himself and the greatest master of the transition from the XIX to XX centuries.

Chief works: Pf. sonata (1891, Rouart, Lerolle); songs, 3 *Poèmes* (1892); *L'Ombre plus dense* (Liège, 1893); sonata, pf. and vn. (1892); sonata, pf. and cello (finished by d'Indy); str. 4tet (finished by d'Indy) (Rouart). 2 symph. *Études* (1889–90); *Introduction and Adagio*, brass band with tuba solo (1891); *Fantaisie sur 2 airs populaires angevins* (1892, Rouart) perf. Queen's Hall, London, under Sir Henry Wood, 18 Aug. 1903; *Chant lyrique*, chorus and orch. (1891); etc. Many in ms. Consult: O. G. Sonneck, *Miscellaneous Studies in History of Music* (1921); A. Tissier, *G. L.* (Verviers, 1906); Séré, *French Musicians of To-day* (Paris, 1922); *Lekeu's Letters* in *Courrier Musical* (1 Jan., 1 and 15 Feb., 1 and 15 March, 15 Sept., 1 and 15 Oct., 15 Dec. 1906); *Notes of Lekeu on 15th Quartet of Beethoven (Courrier Musical* of 15 Dec. 1906).—E. C.

LEMARE, Edwin Henry. Eng. orgt. compr. *b.* Ventnor, Isle of Wight, 9 Sept. 1865. Stud. organ under his father; 1876, won John Goss Scholarship at R.A.M. where he stud. for 6 years under G. and W. Macfarren, Steggall and Turpin. 1882–1903, orgt. successively at St. John's, Finsbury Park, London; Parish Church and Albert Hall, Sheffield; Holy Trinity, Sloane Square, London; St. Margaret's Westminster, establishing a great reputation as a concert-orgt. In 1900 toured in U.S.A. and Canada; orgt. of Carnegie Inst., Pittsburgh, Pa., from 1902–15. Recitals at the Panama-Pacific Exposition (San Francisco, 1915) and municipal orgt. of San Francisco 1917–21. Since 1921, municipal orgt. of Portland, Me. L. specialised for many years on rendering Wagner's music on the organ, and this originated a certain style of registering and organ-scoring which had a marked influence on his own compns. and arrs. He has done much to develop the taste for the modern side of organ tone-qualities.

2 symphonies for organ, G mi. and op. 50, D mi. (Novello); Sonata No. 1 in F, Toccata and fugue (both Schott), etc.; also many colls. of organ pieces and transcriptions of modern orch. works (Schott; Novello; Weekes; Augener; Gray).—J. M.

LEMMENS, Nicolas Jacques. Belgian orgt. compr. *b.* Zoerle-Parwijs (near Westerloo), 3 Jan. 1823; *d.* at Château de Linterpoort sous Sempst (near Malines), 30 Jan. 1881. Pupil of Fétis at Brussels Cons. and of Herse at Breslau; 2nd *Prix de Rome*, 1847; prof. of organ, Brussels Cons., 1849; founded School of Church Music at Malines in 1878. Married (1857) the English singer, Helen Sherrington (*b.* Preston, 4 Oct. 1834), who was appointed prof. of singing in 1881 at the Brussels Cons. and in 1891 at R.A.M. London. From that time Lemmens frequently resided in England.

Organ Tutor; *Method for accompanying the Gregorian Chant*; symphonies; many organ pieces; church music. Breitkopf issued 4 vols. of his unpubl. works in 1883.—E. C.

LENDVAI, Erwin. Hungarian compr. and teacher; *b.* Budapest, 4 June, 1882. Lives in

Germany. Opera, *Olga*; 3 str. trios (Bote & Bock); str. 4tet; choruses.—B. B.

LENEPVEU, Charles. Fr. compr. and teacher; *b.* Rouen, 4 Oct. 1840; *d.* Paris, 16 Aug. 1910. Turned his attention somewhat late towards music. *Prix de Rome*, 1866; *Membre de l'Institut*, 1880. Has written little, and always in classic style; but was an excellent teacher and trained numerous *Prix de Rome* winners. Having succeeded Guiraud as prof. of harmony, then of comp., he publ. in 1898 some *Leçons d'Harmonie*. *Le Florentin* (1874), *opéra-comique*; *Velléda* (1882), opera; and a *Requiem*.—A. C.

LÉNER. See LEHNER.

LENORMAND, René. Fr. compr. *b.* Elbeuf, 1846. Up to 14 he received from his mother an extensive mus. education; but, destined for a commercial career, he had to renounce music—only in appearance, however; for at night a little harmonium, enveloped in coverings, permitted him to work. His essays in compn. reached the coterie formed by Berlioz, Damcke and Stephen Heller, who brought him to Paris in 1868. He has specialised in the *lied*, and belongs to that little group of artists which constitutes the modern French *lied* school. Founded and directs the soc. *Le Lied en tous pays*. Publ. an *Étude sur l'harmonie moderne* (Paris, *Monde Musical*, 1913; Eng. Joseph Williams, 1915).
About 150 songs; pf. pieces; vn. pieces; sonatas; trio; 5tet; pf. concerto (Lamoureux Concert, 1903); *Le Lahn de Mabed* (Dresden, 1901); *Le Voyage imaginaire* (*tableaux symphoniques*) (Monte Carlo); *Le Cachet Rouge*, lyric drama (in collab. with his son, the dramatic author); *La Nuit de juillet*, mimodrama by Pierre Veber.—A. C.

LEON, Claudio Arrau. Chilean pianist; *b.* Chillan, 1903. After perf. at concert in Santiago before President of Republic, he was sent to Germany to study, where he worked under Martin Krause in Berlin. When he returned to Chile, he was most successful as a concert-player.—A. M.

LEONCAVALLO, Ruggero. Italian opera-composer; *b.* Naples, 8 March, 1858; *d.* Bagni di Montecatini, 9 Aug. 1919. One of the principal representatives of what was called the " young school " of Ital. opera-comprs., together with Mascagni, Puccini, and Giordano. Owes his popularity chiefly to a 2-act opera (own libretto), *Pagliacci*, whch was first produced at Dal Verme Theatre, Milan, 17 May, 1892, under the direction of Toscanini.

He made his mus. studies at Naples Cons. and his literary studies at Univ. of Bologna (during time of Giosuè Carducci), obtaining a degree in Letters. The first part of his life was adventurous; he toured abroad as a pianist; was music-master at the Egyptian Court; lived in the atmosphere of the café-concert. To the interest of the celebrated baritone Maurel, he owed his introduction to the Milanese publishing world. The clamorous success of *Pagliacci* made him famous; from that time onwards, his operas easily made their way. At the Dal Verme Theatre, Milan, on 10 Nov. 1893, *I Medici* was perf.; on 10 March, 1896, *Chatterton*

at the Nazionale Theatre, Rome. At the instance of Emperor William II of Germany, he wrote *Rolando di Berlino* (perf. at Court Theatre, Berlin, 13 Dec. 1904). These operas did not meet with much success. More fortunate were: *La Bohème* (Venice, 6 May, 1897); *Zazà* (Milan, 10 Nov. 1900); also *Maià* (Costanzi Theatre, Rome, 1910); *Zingari* (Hippodrome, London, 1912); and the operettas, *Malbruk* (Rome, 1910); *La Reginetta delle rose* (Rome, 1912); *Are you there ?* (London, 1913); *La Candidata* (Rome, 1915); *Prestami tua moglie* (Montecatini, 1916); *A chi la giarrettiera ?* (Rome, 1919). He also wrote *Goffredo Mameli* (Carlo Felice Theatre, Genoa, 1916). He left an *Edipo Re*, and an unfinished 3-act opera, *Tormenta*, on a Sardinian subject. Also comp. some chamber and concert works. (Sonzogno, Milan.)
Consult: Onorato Roux, *R. L.*, in *Memorie giovanili autobiografiche*; also study of his opera *I Medici*, publ. in the *Rivista Musicale Italiana*, 1894.—D. A.

LEONHARDT, Karl. Ger. condr. *b.* Coburg, 2 Feb. 1886. Stud. Coburg (August Langert), 1903–7 at Cons. (Nikisch, Pembaur, Sitt, Krehl, Noë, Seidl) and Univ. Leipzig (Riemann, Schering); 1907–20, solo-repetitor, since 1912 condr. at Hanover; 1909, 1911–12, assistant at Bayreuth Fest.; 1920–2, principal condr. Ger. National Theatre, Weimar; 1921, prof.; 1922, gen. mus. dir. of Würtemberg National Theatre, Stuttgart.—A. E.

LEONHARDT, Otto. Ger. compr. *b.* Hildesheim, 8 Oct. 1881. Stud. under Max Reger (theory and compn.) and Alois Reckendorf at Leipzig Cons.; now living at Hanover.
Symphony, C mi.; symph. poem (words of Clemens Brentano); 3 pieces for full orch.; str. 4tet, B mi.; pf. and vn. sonata, A ma.; songs.—A. E.

LEROUX, Xavier. *b.* Valletri, 11 Oct. 1863; *d.* Paris, 2 Feb. 1919. Fr. compr. though born in the Papal States. Pupil of Massenet at Paris Cons. *Prix de Rome*, 1885. From Massenet, he acquired his passionate and exuberant mus. language. His numerous operas are designedly grandiloquent and " written for effect ":
Evangéline (1895); *Astarté* (1900); *La Reine Fiammette* (1903); *Vénus et Adonis* (1905); *William Ratcliff* (1906); *Theodora* (1906); *Le Chemineau* (1907); *Le Carillonneur* (1913); *La Fille de Figaro* (1914). A dramatic overture, *Harald*; a cantata, *Endymion*. Stage-music for *The Persæ* (Æschylus), 1896; *Plutus* (Aristophanes), 1898; *La Sorcière* (Sardou), 1903; *Xantho chez les Courtisanes* (1910).—A. C.

LE ROY, René. Fr. flautist; *b.* Paris, 4 March, 1898. Pupil at Cons. of Hennebains and Gaubert; succeeded latter as leader of Société des Instruments à Vent. This young soloist is recognised as the most brilliant flautist of the present generation in France, and earns this place through the exceptional purity and fullness of his tone.—H. P.

LERT, Ernst Joseph Maria. Austrian Opera Intendant; *b.* Vienna, 12 May, 1883. Stud. mus. history at Univ. under Guido Adler, and history of the theatre. Powerfully stimulated by *mise-en-scène* of Gustav Mahler and Roller. 1909, started as a *régisseur* and dramaturg (*q.v.*) at Breslau; 1912, *régisseur* at Leipzig, working with Otto

Lohse at Opera and at the Stadttheater; 1919, dir. of Stadttheater, Basle; 1920-3, worked at Frankfort as Intendant of Opera. Became famous by perf. new operas and by his excellent *mise-en-scène* of Gluck and Mozart. His chief work is a profound study on the *mise-en-scène* of Mozart's operas, *Mozart auf dem Theater* (1918; 3rd and 4th ed. 1921). Has also written a biography of Otto Lohse (1918, Breitkopf). —EG. W.

LESCHETIZKY, Theodore. Pianist and piano - teacher ; *b.* Lançut, Poland, 22 June, 1830; *d.* Dresden, 14 Nov. 1915. Pupil of his father (an eminent Vienna teacher), of Carl Czerny and Simon Sechter. Went to Petrograd in 1852. One of founders of Imperial Russ. Music Soc. Prof. at Cons. there till 1878, when he settled at Vienna as a teacher of pf. and achieved a world-wide reputation by his new method, based on the principle of the "rounded hand" (*Kugelhand*). Paderewski was his most famous pupil. L. was married four times: (1) concert-singer Friedeburg, (2) Annette Essipoff, (3) Donimirska Benislavska, (4) Marie Gabr. Rozborska. Publ. pf. music, mostly elegant, effective little pieces, and a comic opera *Die erste Falte* (*The First Wrinkle*), 1st perf. Prague, 1867.

Biographies: Comtesse Angèle Potocka (1903); Annette Hullah (John Lane, 1906). Consult also Mary Unschuld von Melasfeld, *Die Hand* (1901), and Malvine Brée, *Die Grundlage der Methode Leschetizkys* (1902).—H. B. & ZD. J.

LETOCART, Henri. Fr. orgt. *b.* Courbevoie (Seine), 6 Feb. 1866. Pupil of C. Franck and Ernest Guiraud. Since 1900, orgt. at St.-Pierre, Neuilly - sur - Seine. Founded a soc. *Amis des Cathédrales*, which he conducts. Among his compns. are 4 colls. of organ pieces; motets; songs (with pf.); suites for orch., all fine symph. works. Has also rev. many old compns. of M. A. Charpentier, Lulli, and La Lande (played at historic concerts given by *Amis des Cathédrales*).—F. R.

LETOREY, Ernest. Fr. compr. *b.* Rouen, 2 Nov. 1867. Pupil of Pessard; *Prix de Rome*, 1895. Compr. of instr. works for orch. Numerous songs. Has been an orch. conductor.—A. C.

LETT, Phyllis. Eng. contr. singer; *b.* Redbourne, Lincs. Stud. at R.C.M. London, 1903- 6 under Visetti; *début* 1 Nov. 1906, R. Albert Hall, (*Elijah*, R. Choral Soc.); since then, at all the chief festivals.—E.-H.

LETZ QUARTET. See CHAMBER - MUSIC PLAYERS (U.S.A).

LEVADÉ, Charles. Fr. compr. *b.* Paris, 3 Jan. 1869. *Prix de Rome*, 1899; Pupil of Massenet, and has his languorous melody, but relieved by a certain irony.

Several orch. suites; *Cœur de Margot* (pantomime); music for *Hortense couche-toi* of Courteline (chorus of furniture-removers); *L'Amour d'Héliodore* (opera, 1903); *Les Hérétiques* (opera, 1905); *La Rôtisserie de la Reine Pédauque* (after Anatole France, *opéra-comique*, 1919).—A. C.

LEVEY, Richard Michael (real name, O'Shaughnessy). Irish condr. *b.* Dublin, 1811; *d.* 1899. Member of Theatre Royal Orch. 1826; for many years, set the music to pantomimes;

was a great friend of Balfe and Wallace; cond. 1st perf. of some of Balfe's operas. Sir Robert Stewart and Sir Charles V. Stanford were amongst his pupils. The R. Irish Acad. in its early years owed much to him. He did much to encourage ensemble-music in Dublin, by his formation of quartet societies (especially the Monthly Popular Concerts, 1868–71). His book, *Annals of the Theatre Royal*, contains many anecdotes about artists who came to Dublin. In 1880, the old Theatre Royal was burnt, and L. lived to see the opening of the new one in 1897.—W. ST.

LEVIEN, John Mewburn. Eng. barit. singer; teacher. Stud. under H. C. Deacon and Manuel Garcia; also under Vannuccini and Salzédo; sang at Crystal Palace under Manns; has taught many well-known singers; is hon. secretary of R. Philh. Soc. London. Has contributed to many periodicals on theory and practice of old Ital. school of singing. Contributed art. on SANTLEY to this Dictionary.—E.-H.

LEVITZKI, Mischi. Amer. pianist; *b.* Krementschug, Russia, 25 May, 1898. Pf. lessons as a child from A. Michałowski in Warsaw (1905-6). At 8, came to New York. 1907-11, pupil at Inst. of Mus. Art, New York, where his pf. master was Sigismund Stojowski. 1911-15 at Hochschule, Berlin, studying under Ernst von Dohnányi. 1913, 2nd Mendelssohn Prize; 1914 the 1st. In March 1914, appeared as recitalist in Berlin, and gave concerts in several Belgian towns. 1915-16, appeared in Germany, Austria-Hungary and Norway. Made his New York *début*, 17 Oct. 1916. Toured Australia, ·1921. —O. K.

LEVY, Ernst. Swiss pianist, compr. *b.* Basle, 18 Nov. 1895. Eminent pianist; began mus. studies at Cons. Basle, under Hans Huber; also under Raoul Pugno at Paris. Became prof. of master-classes for pf. at Basle Cons. 1916, succeeding Hans Huber. Since 1921 has lived in Paris; plays in concerts in all European towns. Publ. numerous songs (Leipzig, Hug), and a small Ger.-Fr. and Fr.-Ger. Dictionary of musical-technical terms (*id.*).—F. H.

LEVY, Michel Maurice. Fr. compr. *b.* Ville-d'Avray, in 1883. Stud. pf. and compn. with Lavignac, Leroux, Ch. René; medallist at Paris Cons. 1898. Was tutor of singing-classes at Opéra-Comique and Opéra; then dir. of singing at Gaîté-Lyrique and at Châtelet. Among his works, rather limited, but carefully done:

Collections of songs. Stage-music for *Le Clottre* (Verhaeren); for *La Grève des femmes* (Jacques Richepin); for *La Courtisane* (Arnyvelde, his brother). He is now appearing in music-halls under the name of Betove.—A. C.

LEY, Henry George. Eng. orgt. *b.* Chagford, Devon, 30 Dec. 1887. Chorister, St. George's Chapel, Windsor Castle; mus. scholar, Uppingham School (P. David; W. Greatorex); exhibitioner, R.C.M. London (under Sir W. Parratt, Sir Charles Stanford, Dr. Charles Wood, Marmaduke Barton; organ scholar, Keble Coll. Oxford;

Precentor, Radley Coll.; orgt. Christ Church Cath. Oxford; Choragus, Oxford Univ.; prof. of organ R.C.M. London. Mus. Doc. Oxon. 1914. He is one of the finest of organists.

Orch. variations on theme of Handel (ms.); str. 4tet in F mi. (ms.); sonata, vn. and pf. in C mi. (ms.); church music (Faith Press; Novello, etc.); songs (Acott, Oxford; Stainer & Bell); part-songs (Year-Book Press; Oxford Univ. Press; E. Arnold; J. Williams; Stainer & Bell; Novello).—E.-H.

LEZETYCKI. Polish spelling of Leschetizky (*q.v.*).

LIADOF, Anatol Constantinovitch (*accent 2nd syll. A*). Russ compr. *b.* Petrograd, 29 April/ 10 May, 1855; *d.* there, Aug. 1914. Received his mus. education from his father and (at the Petrograd Cons.) from Rimsky-Korsakof. He was appointed assistant-teacher at this inst. in 1878 and, later, prof. He may be described, in many respects, as a minor poet of the National Russ. school, endowed with genuine and genial imagination, who wisely refrained from over-ambitious efforts, and wrote the charming music which he was intended by nature to write. His most characteristic works are brief tone-poems such as *Kikimora* and *Baba-Yaga*, a number of pf. pieces, songs, and a few choral compns. But in the last years of his life he wrote a tone-poem entitled *From the Book of Revelation* which appears to betoken a remarkable change of out-look, its tone being more grim and more intro-spective than that of any of his previously known works.—M. D. C.

LIAPUNOF, Serge Michaelovitch (*accent 4th syll. OF*). Russ. compr. *b.* Yaroslav, 18/30 Nov. 1859. A pupil of the Moscow Cons. and nowadays (1923) the foremost living representative of nationalist tendencies as exemplified in the works of Balakiref (whose close friend he was) and his contemporaries. He devoted much of his time to collecting folk-songs in various parts of the Russ. Empire, of which he has publ. a valuable coll. in 3 vols. (Imperial Geographical Soc.). His pf. music is often of unusual interest, technically and artistically (especially his 12 *Études d'Exé-cution Transcendante*).—M. D. C.

Orch.: Symphony, B mi. op. 12; *Ballade*, op. 2; Solemn Overture on Russ. folk-tunes, op. 7; symph. poem, *Telazova Vola* (in mem. of Chopin), op. 37; Eastern symph. poem, *Hashish*, op. 53; 1st pf. con-certo, op. 4; 2nd, op. 38; Rhapsody on Little Russ. folk-tunes, pf. and orch.; vn. concerto; pf. 6tet; pf. pieces; songs, etc.—V. B.

LIBERT, Henri. Fr. orgt. and pianist; *b.* Paris, 15 Dec. 1869. Titular orgt. to R. Basilica of St.-Denis; prof. of organ at Amer. Cons. Fontainebleau. Pupil of Marmontel and Diémer for pf., of C. Franck and Ch. M. Widor for organ. First in France to popularise Bach's Chorales. With Widor at Cons. as prof. of cpt. and fugue, he was instrumental in training Gabriel Dupont. Has comp. for both pf. and organ (*Variations Symphoniques, Chorales, Pre-ludes et fugues*). In style he revives and de-velops the older constructional forms and adds thereto his own picturesque method of ex-pression.—F. R.

LIBRARIES OF MUSIC. *AUSTRIA.*—**Vienna:**

For the Library of the Gesellschaft der Musik-freunde see special article under G.

GREAT BRITAIN. — **London:** (i) The British Museum houses the enormous collection of music deposited there under the Copy-right Act. It is also rich in mss. The famous musical library of Buckingham Palace (con-taining 87 vols. of Handel autographs) is now housed at the British Museum. (ii) The Library of the Royal College of Music, based on the nucleus of the Sacred Harmonic Society, is almost equally valuable. It includes the Library of the Concerts of Antient Music (given by Queen Victoria), hundreds of dupli-cates from the British Museum, about 300 from the Victoria and Albert Museum, chamber-music from Ferdinand Ries' library, etc. (iii) The Royal Academy of Music Library. (iv) The Royal Philharmonic Society's Library. (v) The Library of the Royal Society of Musicians, Gerrard St. **Cambridge:** (i) The Fitzwilliam Museum has a fine musical library, including the famous *Fitz-william Virginal Book*. (ii) St. Peter's College and Magdalen have also valuable collections. **Oxford:** (i) The Bodleian Library contains inter-esting collections of early music. (ii) The library at Christ Church College is rich in early music, English and foreign. **Manchester:** The Henry Watson Library contains 38,000 volumes, with 100,000 part-songs, anthems, etc. (See special article, WATSON MUSIC LIBRARY.) **Leeds:** The Leeds Public Library possesses some rare works from the Taphouse and other col-lections. **Other Cities:** Birmingham, Liverpool, Sheffield, Huddersfield, Newcastle - on - Tyne possess large music departments in their Public Libraries. **Tenbury:** St. Michael's College possesses the library of its founder, Sir F. A. Gore Ouseley. Over 2000 volumes. **Bourne-mouth:** The library bequeathed by J. C. Camm is very serviceable and of considerable size, con-taining many orchestral scores. **Edinburgh:** (i) Library of the University contains bequests by General Reid, Professor Thompson and others, a full collection of modern scores and some old printed music. (ii) The Advocates' Library con-tains a music collection. **Glasgow:** The Library of the University was founded on W. Ewing's collection of ancient music and T. L. Stillie's collection of modern works. **Aberdeen:** The University Library contains over 2500 musical works. **Aberystwyth:** The National Library is of comparatively recent foundation. It specialises in Welsh and other Celtic works, and also benefits by the Copyright Act.

FRANCE.—**Paris:** (i) The most remarkable collection is that of the Bibliothèque Nationale, consisting of the old Bibliothèque du Roi to which numerous bequests and purchases have been added. Since time of Revolution it has received all publ. compns. There is a catalogue in 8 vols. (see ÉCORCHEVILLE). (ii) The Biblio-thèque Ste.-Geneviève and (iii) the Biblio-thèque Mazarine contain precious old mss. Of exclusively musical libraries, there are (iv) the Bibliothèque du Conservatoire, the inestimable riches of which are almost inaccessible, owing to the lack of a printed catalogue, and (v) the Bibliothèque de l'Opéra, founded by Nuittier, containing opera scores from the XVII century onward. (vi) The Sorbonne possesses works from the libraries of Pierre Aubry and Guilmant. **Versailles:** The library contains some valuable old mss.

IRISH FREE STATE.—**Dublin:** (i) Trinity College receives all music entered at Stationers' Hall. (ii) The Irish Academy of Music has valuable mss. and printed works.

U.S.A.—**Washington:** Music Division of the Library of Congress. See SONNECK. **New York:** The Public Library contains a valuable Beethoven collection. See BAUER.—E.-H.

LICHTENBERG, Emil. Hungarian condr. *b.* Budapest, 2 April, 1877. Dir. of Choral and of Orchestral Soc. Has cond. the Oratorio Concerts for many years.—B. B.

LICHTENBERGER, Henri. French musicographer; *b.* Mulhouse (Haut-Rhin), 1864. Prof. in Faculty of Letters, Nancy, 1887; prof. of Ger. language and literature in Univ. of Paris, since 1905. For several years taught history of music at Nancy Cons. (then dir. by J. Guy Ropartz). Until 1914 wrote mus. criticism in *L'Opinion.* His work is a valuable contribution to the music of Wagner, to whom he devoted a detailed study (crowned by Académie Française), called *Richard Wagner poète et penseur* (Paris, 1898, Alcan), and a vol. *Wagner* (1909, *id.*). —M. L. P.

LIE, Sigurd. Norwegian compr. condr. violinist; *b.* Drammen, 23 May, 1871; *d.* 30 Sept. 1904. Pupil of Gudbr. Böhn (vn.) and Iver Holter (compn.). Matriculated in 1889; afterwards stud. at Cons. in Leipzig (Arno Hilf, Rust and Reinecke) and under Heinrich Urban (Berlin). 1895-8, leader of orch. to *Harmonien* in Bergen; condr. of Mus. Soc. and of several choirs in same city. Leader of Central Theatre Orch. in Christiania, 1898-99; stud. in Berlin (scholarship from Houen's Bequest) from 1902; condr. of Mercantile Association's Choral Union, 1902-4.

L. was one of ablest talents in Norwegian music in latter part of last century. Already, at 25, a fully-trained musician, a highly cultivated violinist, a mature contrapuntist and an expert condr. of choir and orch. His activities as a practising musician made such demands upon his powers that his rich gifts as compr. had not before his early death attained that individual maturity which characterised his mus. labours otherwise. L. has produced, in the most widely-differing classes of music, good and interesting works; all reveal a highly-developed sense of sonority, a rare capacity for original characterisation (to which especially his songs and male-v. choruses bear witness) and a considerable constructive and orch. ability in the larger works (symphony, chamber-music, etc.). In the purely technical use of the national element in harmonic and rhythmic construction, he is to some extent dependent upon Grieg; but in the main points he nevertheless preserves his own original style, without being estranged from the new tendencies.

Symphony, A mi. (1st perf. Bergen, 1901); *Oriental Suite* for orch.; choral work, *Erling Skjalgsön*; pf. 5tet; str. 4tet; concert-piece for vn.; vn. sonata; pf. pieces; songs; male-v. choruses, etc.—J. A.

LIEBICH, Frank. British pianist; *b.* London, 1860; *d.* there 1922. Stud. at Cologne Cons. under F. Hiller and Isidore Seiss; then at Dresden under E. Kretschmer and Bülow; *début* 1867, R. Pavilion, Brighton; many recitals and chamber-concerts; specialised on modern music, especially Debussy's.—E.-H.

LIEBLING, Georg. Ger. pianist and compr. *b.* Berlin, 22 Jan. 1865. Stud. under Kullak and Liszt; theory under Würst, Albert Becker, Urban; *début*, 1884; travelled till 1893; 1894-7, own Pf. School, Berlin; came to England (1898), teacher at Guildhall School of Music; 1890, Ducal Court-pianist (Coburg); from 1908, own School of Music at Munich; now lives in Switzerland.

Pf. pieces; concertos, op. 22; vn. sonatas, op. 28 and op. 63; pieces for pf. and vn., and pf. and cello; songs; orch. works, ms.; opera, *The Wager* (1908, Dessau); a mystery, *Saint Katharine* (1908, Cologne).—A. E.

LIED (Ger.). The German word *Lied* signifies a song in every sense of the Eng. word, but since Ger. songs at the beginning of the XIX century developed into a highly artistic form in the hands of Schubert and others, the Ger. word has been used in other countries, especially in England and France, to signify songs of an artistic type, as opposed to the "ballads," "romances" and "mélodies" of a simpler and more popular kind, although the Ger. word still implies naturally the most elementary form of song. The normal *Lied* is the folk-song of which the tune remains the same in all verses; the song in which different verses are set to different music is called a *durch-komponiertes Lied.* Many songs by Brahms and others are called *Gesänge* to distinguish them from their more simple *Lieder.* The word *Lied-form* was used by certain theorists to designate simple ternary form (A-B-A); but it was found unsatisfactory and is now seldom used. Eng. journalism often uses the expression "*Lieder*-singer" to denote a singer of what are unpleasantly called "art-songs."—E. J. D.

LIEDERTAFEL (Ger.). A choral society for male voices.—E.-H.

LIEPE, Emil. Singer and compr. *b.* Potsdam, 16 Jan. 1860. Stud. at Schwantzer Cons. Berlin; 1878, Leipzig Univ.; 1879-82, Leipzig Cons. (Rebling, Jadassohn, Reinecke; 1882-3 at Vienna Cons. (Gänsbacher) as singer (barit.); 1884, engaged at different theatres as b.-barit. (1891-2, Bayreuth); from 1902, concert-work; 1903-7, singing-master Cons. Sondershausen; (1904, Kammersänger); since 1907 at Berlin.

Songs; overture and entractes to *Narciss* (Regensburg, 1895); symph. poem, *Fate* (1891); 1-act opera, *Colomba* (Dantzig, 1894), own words; symph. poem, *Looking Back* (1905); symphony, C mi. (1913); publ. Wagner albums (songs and pf.); new ed. of Erk's *Treasury of Song.*—A. E.

LIERHAMMER, Theo. Baritone singer; *b.* Lwów, Poland, 18 Nov. 1866. Stud. medicine in

Vienna; then music at Cons. there; later under Padilla in Paris and Stockhausen in Frankfort; *début* in joint recital with Hubermann, 1896; toured Germany, Russia, Poland, France, 1898–1900; London *début*, 20 Nov. 1900; prof. R.A.M. London, 1903–14; 1914–15, prof. Cons. Berlin; served as a doctor in Galicia, 1915–18; on resurrection of Poland, became Polish citizen; 1918–1920, tours through Austria, Czecho-Slovakia, Jugo-Slavia; resumed concerts and teaching in London from 1922.—E.-H.

LILJEBLAD, Ingeborg. Finnish m.-sopr. and contr. singer; *b.* Helsingfors, 1887. Stud. in Berlin and Paris. Engaged Court Theatre, Mannheim, 1911–13; at New Opera, Hamburg, till 1914. Also appeared as concert-singer.—T. H.

LILJEFORS, Ruben Mattias. Swedish compr. condr. *b.* Upsala, 30 Sept. 1871. Stud. Leipzig Cons. 1895–6, 1897–9; condr. Students' Glee Soc. Upsala, 1902; and of glee-club in Gothenburg, 1902–9; stud. under Draeseke, Max Reger and H. Kutzchbach, 1909–11; condr. of Orch. Soc. of Gäfle (Sweden) from 1912; member R.A.M. Stockholm, 1908.

Symphony, E flat (1905–6; Gothenburg, 1906); pf. concerto, F mi. (1899; Leipzig, 1899), publ. for 2 pf. 1922 (Raabe & Plothow); *Intermezzo* (1903); music to drama *Fritiof and Ingeborg* (Norrköping, 1908); *Summer Suite* (1920); *Festival Overture* (1922); *Romance*, vn. and orch.; cantatas; songs with orch. and with pf.; sonata, vn. and pf. (1896; publ. 1897, Abr. Hirsch); songs for male vs.; pf. pieces, etc. —P. V.

LINDBERG, Helge. Finnish barit. singer; *b.* 1 Oct. 1887. At first, stud. vn. at Helsingfors Music Inst.; from 1907 singing, in Munich and in Florence; later settled in Stuttgart as teacher of singing, finally proceeding to Vienna. For the last 5 years L., who in the meantime had furthered his studies as a singer, has been appearing with marked success as an artistic singer in Austria, Hungary, Germany, and the countries of the North, attracting attention as much by his magnificent voice and highly developed vocal technique, as by his deep power of expression. Has specialised in the old classical repertoire of Handel and Bach. 1923, concert-tours in France, England, etc.—T. H.

LINDBERG, Oskar Fredrik. Swedish compr. *b.* Gagnef (Dalarne), 23 Feb. 1887. Stud. R. Cons. Stockholm (compn. under E. Ellberg and Andr. Hallén), then in Sondershausen (under Corbach and Grabowsky); from 1914, orgt. at Engelbrekt Ch. Stockholm; from 1919, teacher at Royal Conservatoire.

Orch.: 3 *Dalamålningar* (*Pictures from Dalarne*) 1908; 3 concert overtures (E flat, 1909; B mi., 1911; D ma., 1921); symph. poems: *Vildmark* (*Wilderness*) (1912); *Flor and Blancheflor* (1914); *From the Great Forests* (1917); symphony in F (1916); suite, *Färdeminnen* (*Travel Memories*) (1919); cantata, chorus, soli and orch. (text by H.R.H. Prince Wilhelm of Sweden) (1918); *Requiem*, chorus, soli and orch. (1922); songs with orch. and with pf.; pf. pieces.—P. V.

LINDEGREN, Johan. Swedish composer; *b.* Ullared, 7 Jan. 1842; *d.* Stockholm, 8 June, 1908. Stud. at R. Cons. Stockholm, 1860–5; from 1884, choirmaster Nicolai Ch. Stockholm. Among his pupils were Hugo Alfvén, Bror

Beckman, Harald Fryklöf, S. von Koch. Member R.A.M. Stockholm, 1903.

Pf. sonata; fugue, pf.; str. 5tet (Stockholm, 1906); church hymn-book (1905); *Journal of Church-Music*. —P. V.

LINDEMAN, Ludvig Mathias. Norwegian compr. and orgt. *b.* Trondhjem, 28 Nov. 1812; *d.* Christiania, 23 May, 1887. Matriculated in 1835. Began to study theology, but went over to study of music. 1840, orgt. of Our Saviours' Ch. in Christiania; 1849, teacher of church-singing at Univ. Theological Seminary. Together with his son, Peter Lindeman (*q.v.*), he establ. in 1883 a music school which afterwards developed into Christiania Cons. In 1871 he visited London on an invitation to take part in the inauguration of the new organ in the Albert Hall, and gave on that occasion a number of concerts.

Lindeman has done great service for Norwegian music. He was one of the principal collectors of folk-melodies. Already in 1840 he had publ. a large coll. harmonised for the pf. And from 1848 onwards, he made regular journeys in this connection over the whole country. He publ. over 600 of these melodies in the monumental work *Older and Newer Norwegian Mountain Melodies*, for pf. with accompanying text. From this source our comprs., including Grieg, Svendsen, etc., have been able to derive much material. But L. was also a distinguished compr. equipped with deep learning, and highly gifted as a melodist. His fugues on the theme B.A.C.H. are masterly. The same applies to the superb mixed chorus *Draumkvædet* (*Dream Chant*),with themes from folk-tunes. His chief work is the *Chorale Book for the Norwegian Church*, introduced in 1877 and still used in Norwegian churches. In this we find a number of his own melodies, of which *Kirken den er et gammelt hus* (*The Church is it an ancient house*) is one of the finest of Norwegian hymn-tunes.—O. M. S.

LINDEMAN, Peter. Norwegian orgt., dir. of Christiania Music Cons. *b.* Christiania in 1858. Matriculated in 1877. Took in 1880 organists' examination at Stockholm Cons.; stud. further in Dresden, 1884–5. Since 1880, orgt. to Uranienborg Ch. Christiania. In 1883, he founded, together with his father, Ludvig L. (*q.v.*) a Cons. in Christiania, which still exists and which was 1st important inst. of the kind in Christiania. Pieces for organ, v., pf., vn.; organ tutor; manual on Modulation.—R. M.

LINDEMANN, Fritz. Ger. pianist; *b.* Wehlau (East Prussia), 22 July, 1876. Stud. Berlin (Xaver and Philipp Scharwenka, Wilhelm Beyer); acted there, after temporary conductorship, as accompanist at Berlin Opera House (among others, from 1903, of Lilli Lehmann); chamber-music player.—A. E.

LINDEN, Cornelis van der. Dutch opera-condr. *b.* Dordrecht, 24 Aug. 1839; *d.* 28 May, 1918. Founded 1888 the first Dutch national opera (1888–1904).

Cantatas; many songs; 7 overtures for full orch.; 2 operas; part-songs for male, female and mixed choirs; pf. pieces.—W. P.

LINDHOLM, Eino. Finnish pianist; *b.* 16 Oct. 1890. Stud. at Helsingfors Music Inst. and in Germany (Breithaupt; Carreño). Has given recitals in Finland and abroad. Pf. teacher at Helsingfors Music Inst. 1912–18 and since 1920.—T. H.

LINDNER, Edwin. Moravian condr. *b.* Brünn, 29 Oct. 1884. Stud. under P. de Conne and H. Grädener, (Vienna Cons.); and Reisenauer and Nikisch (Leipzig). After acting as pianist and condr. in Holland and Belgium, took charge, 1913, of Robert Schumann Acad. of Singing, Dresden, which he changed, 1914, by combining it, together with several other societies establ. by him, into Dresden Acad. of Singing. He founded the Dresden Philh. Orch. in 1915.—A. E.

LINKO, Ernst. Finnish pianist and compr. *b.* Tampere (Tammerfors), 14 July, 1889. Stud. at Helsingfors Music Inst. 1909–11; in Berlin, 1911–13; and in Petrograd, 1914–15. Teacher of pf. at Helsingfors Music Inst. since 1915. In summer of 1920, toured with the Finnish operatic t., Väinö Sola, in the U.S.A., visiting the districts inhabited by Finns.

2 pf. concertos; pf. trio; pf. pieces; songs.—T. H.

LIONCOURT, Guy de. Fr. compr. *b.* Caen, 1 Dec. 1887. Stud. at *Schola Cantorum* under Vincent d'Indy. Has been prof. of cpt. at *Schola* since 1914 and gen. secretary since 1915; former member of Committee of the Société Nationale de Musique. Gained in 1918 the *Grand Prix Lasserre* for his mus. fairy-play in 3 tableaux: *La Belle au Bois dormant.* Other works:

Hyalis (lyric tale, after Samain); *Jean de la Lune* (mus. drama in 3 acts and 9 tableaux); *Les Dix Lépreux*; several choral and instrumental works. —A. C.

LIPPS, Theodor. Ger. psychologist and æstheticist; *b.* Wallhalben (Palatinate), 28 July, 1851; *d.* Munich, 17 Oct. 1914. First stud. theology, then natural science and philosophy at Erlangen, Tübingen, Utrecht, Bonn; settled at Bonn, 1877; 1889, became prof.-extraordinary for philosophy, Bonn; 1890, prof.-in-ordinary, Breslau; 1894, Munich. Lipps made *Einfühlung* the basis of his æsthetic system.

Theory of Melody (Zeitschrift für Psychologie, 1901); *Psychological Studies,* II; *Nature of Musical Harmony and Discord* (1885, 2nd ed. 1905); *Affinity and Blending of Tone* (1899, in *Zeitschrift für Psychologie und Physiologie); Ästhetik,* 2 vols, 1903–6.—A. E.

LIPSIUS, Marie ("La Mara"). Ger. mus. authoress; *b.* Leipzig, 30 Dec. 1837.

Heads of Musicians, sketched (1868–82, 5 vols., several times reprinted, since 1911 publ. singly); *Mus. Gedanken Polyphonie,* collection of sayings of celebrated musicians about their art (1873); *Beethoven* (1870, 2nd ed. 1873); *Bayreuth Festivals* (1877); *Pauline Viardot-Garcia* (1882); *Musicians' Letters of Five Centuries* (1886, 2 vols.); *Classic and Romantic in the Mus. World* (1892); *Beethoven and the Brunswick Family* (1920); *Liszt's Letters* (1893–1905, 8 vols.), *Letters of Celebrated Contemporaries of Franz Liszt* (1895–1904, 3 vols.); *Letters between Franz Liszt and Hans v. Bülow* (1898); *Letters from H. Berlioz to Princess Karolyne of Sayn-Wittgenstein* (1903); *The Wonderful Weimar-Altenburg Period*—photographs and letters from life of Princess K. Sayn-Wittgenstein (1906); *Letters from Marie of Mouchanow-Kalergis, née Duchess Nesselrode, to her Daughter* (1907, 2nd ed. 1911); *Liszt and Women* (1911); *Exchange of Letters between Franz Liszt and Grand-Duke Karl Alexander*

of Saxony (1908); *Letters from Franz Liszt to his Mother* (1918); autobiography, *Through Music and Life, in promotion of the Ideal* (1917).—A. E.

LIPSKI, Stanisław. Polish pianist and compr. *b.* Warsaw, 9 April, 1880. From 1892, stud. pf. and theory under Żeleński. In 1900, went to Berlin to study pf. under Jedliczka and cpt. under Leichtentritt. Later, was pupil of Leschetizky and Robert Fuchs in Vienna. In 1910, became teacher of pf at Cracow Cons. Has publ. many songs and pf. pieces in an elegant style, and several works for male chorus. L.'s music is of a charming simplicity.—ZD. J.

LISSENKO, Nicolas (accent *1st syll.*). Russ. compr. *b.* Grinky, 10/22 March, 1842; *d.* Kief, 29 Oct./11 Nov. 1912. Brought up in the very centre of Ukraine, he began to study the country's folk-music, even before taking up music as a profession. Later he stud. theory at Leipzig under E. F. Richter. In 1874 he received lessons in orch. from Rimsky-Korsakof at Petrograd Cons. In 1876 he settled at Kief. His output comprises, besides his invaluable coll. of Ukrainian songs (6 vols., 1869–95) and choral arrs., 2 operettas, 3 operas, a *Ukrainian Rhapsody* for vn. and orch.; songs and a quantity of pf. music, mostly on Ukrainian themes. Hardly any work of his has yet crossed the borders of his native country. Consult his autobiography in *Russkaya Muzykalnaya Gazeta,* 1912, No. 48.—M. D. C.

LISZT, Franz. Hungarian composer and pianist; *b.* Raiding, near Sopron (Oedenburg), Hungary, 22 October 1811; *d.* Bayreuth, 21 July, 1886. It is well-nigh impossible adequately to set forth, within the limits of this article, the importance of the part played by Liszt as a pianist, a composer, a conductor, a propagandist and educator whose sympathies and understanding were keen and wide, and whose tireless activities were for ever at the service of all causes which needed them.

All works of reference show the division of his life into three periods. From his early childhood to 1847 his career was that of a pianist. He acquired world-wide fame, and began to write not only music of the kind expected from a virtuoso, but music in which the greater creations of the Weimar period were in many respects foreshadowed. This Weimar period (1848–51) was entirely devoted to composition and to propaganda of the finest order by which practically all Liszt's great contemporaries benefited. After 1861 he lived for some years in Rome, and after that divided his time between Rome, Weimar and Budapest, besides visiting Paris, London and other cities. During this third period he continued to devote his activities to composition and to education.

He received his first piano lessons from his father, Adam Liszt, appeared in public at the age of nine, studied the piano under Czerny and theory under Salieri in Vienna, and later received lessons from Paer and Reicha in Paris. He appeared as a pianist in that city in 1824. and the following year his opera *Don Sanche* was performed there. From 1830 onwards he devoted himself to piano-playing and to composition. Enthusiasm for the music of Beethoven, Berlioz and Chopin led him to study it with fruitful results, and Paganini's violin music further stimulated him to researches in the domain of technique. Towards 1837, with the *Études d'Exécution Transcendante*, the *Paganini Études* and the *Fantasia quasi Sonata*, his individuality as a composer stood clearly revealed. His transcriptions of orchestral works by Berlioz and Beethoven were the first earnest of his zeal for artistic propaganda. In 1843, the orchestral concerts, which he conducted at Weimar, heralded his activities during the years 1848–61 when he introduced *Lohengrin*, *Tannhäuser*, Schumann's *Genoveva* and *Manfred*, Berlioz's *Cellini*, Cornelius's *Barber of Baghdad*, and numerous classical operas, as well as many important symphonic works old and new. This was the time when he wrote most of his masterpieces; the twelve tone-poems, the *Faust* Symphony, the *Dante* Symphony, the *Graner Messe*, etc. From 1861 to 1870 he lived in Rome, writing *Christus, St. Elizabeth of Hungary* and other works of religious inspiration. He was heard in public as pianist for the last time in 1877. In April 1886 he visited London and Paris. He died at Bayreuth, where he lies buried.

All biographers and critics have paid due tribute to his genius as a pianist and to the beneficial result of his activities as a propagandist. On the value of his compositions, opinions vary far more than in the case of any other composer; and nearly two-score years after his death, the question is still debated. Some people consider that his creative genius was of the highest order; others would admit no single work of his among the masterpieces of musical art; and many hold that he heralded a good deal and opened many new paths, but fell short in actual achievement. That he heralded a good deal is unquestionable. He stands at the fountain-head of all the new developments which the second half of the XIX century brought. As regards form, idiom, and workmanship, his influence was universal. We see it chiefly upon Wagner and Strauss, upon practically all the best of the French school, from Franck and Saint-Saëns to Ravel, upon all the Russians (beginning with Balakiref and Borodin) and upon the Hungarian school of to-day.

He entered the field of composition at a time when the need for some new principle in musical architecture had already asserted itself, to a degree in Beethoven's music, and more definitely in that of Berlioz. Wagner's utterances upon the strife between the dictates of poetic imagination and those of formal practice apparent in the third *Leonore* overture will be remembered. But Beethoven rested content with outlining the struggle. Berlioz threw all old conventions aside, but without any definite attempt towards rebuilding. But, as Saint-Saëns wrote: "Liszt understood that in order to invent new forms, it was imperative to make it felt that they were needed. He boldly entered

the path which Beethoven and Berlioz had shown but hardly entered, and he created the symphonic poem." This creation was rendered possible by his conception of motives as plastic units capable of undergoing endless transformations in the course of a work whose general form is, in Wagner's words, "in every instance that which is necessary."

Meanwhile his contributions to the extension of the technical resources and colour-range of his art (a field in which Schubert, Weber and Chopin had been, with or before Berlioz, the first modern pioneers), considerable from the outset of his career, assumed an ever-increasing importance. One reason why his actual achievements are often underrated may be the enormous quantity of indifferent and bad music which he has left, and which is far better known than his fine works. Another is that (as pointed out by the French critic, Jean Marnold) his apologists and foes agree in considering him as a champion of programme-music. The alleged distinction—or rather opposition—between "programme" music and "pure" music has always been a stumbling-block, and has created a good deal of confusion either way. The matter can hardly be dealt with here; but to show the disturbing effect of the idea upon certain types of mind, one may adduce on one hand all the arguments piled up to show that the Scherzo, storm-music and finale of Beethoven's Pastoral Symphony are not real programme-music, and on the other, assertions such as Klauwell's (*Geschichte der Progr. Musik*, p. 79) that in Beethoven's op. 81a (*Les Adieux* sonata) "the encounter of the Tonic sixth (G–E flat) and the Dominant fifth (B flat–F) can be understood only in the light of a programme."

Should that initial cause of misconception be done away with, it is possible—especially given the present period's tendency towards a revision of art-values and tenets—that a sense of that greatness of Liszt as a pure musician which his admirers are steadfastly proclaiming will become more general.

Religious, choral, and vocal: *Missa quatuor vocum* (Haslinger); *Missa Solemnis* (Graner) (Schuberth); *Ungarische Krönungs-Messe* (Schuberth); *Requiem* (Kahnt); *Missa Choralis* (*id.*); *Christus*, oratorio (*id.*); *St. Elizabeth*, oratorio (*id.*); 57 songs (*id.*).

Orch.: 12 symph. poems: *Héroïde funèbre*; *Tasso*; *Les Préludes*; *Hungaria*; *Ce qu'on entend sur la montagne*; *Mazeppa*; *Prometheus*; *Festklänge*; *Orphée*; *Die Hunnenschlacht*; *Die Ideale* (Breitkopf); *Eine Faust-Symphonie* (Schuberth); *Symphonie zu Dantes Divina Commedia* (Breitkopf); *Zwei Episoden aus Lenaus "Faust"* (Schuberth); pf. concerto No. I (Haslinger); No. II (Schott); *Totentanz* for pf. and orch. (Siegel).

Pf.: *Harmonies poétiques et religieuses* (Kistner); *Années de Pèlerinage* (3 vols. (Schott); *Album d'un voyageur* (3 vols.) (Haslinger); *Études d'exécution transcendante* (Breitkopf); sonata (*id.*); *Hungarian Rhapsodies* (various); *Two Legends* (Rózsavölgyi).

Organ: Fantasia and fugue on the chorale *Ad nos salutarem undam* (Breitkopf); Prelude and fugue on the name B.A.C.H. (Schuberth); Variations on Bach's theme *Weinen, Klagen* (Peters).

Bibliography: L.'s complete works publ. by the Liszt-Stiftung are procurable at Breitkopf's, Leipzig. The same firm has publ. his coll. writings on music and musicians in 6 vols. and his correspondence in 15 vols.

Consult: L. Ramann, *Fr. L.* 3 vols. (Breitkopf);

J. Kapp, *Fr. L.* (Berlin, Schuster & Löffler) (contains an extensive bibliography); R. Louis, *Fr. L.* (Berlin, Bondi); M. D. Calvocoressi, *Fr. L.* (Paris, Laurens); F. Niecks, *Programme Music* (London, Novello); O. Klauwell, *Geschichte der Programm-Musik* (Breitkopf).; H. F. Chorley, *Modern German Music* (London, Smith, Elder); E. Newman, *Musical Studies* (John Lane, 1905). Also L. Rellstab, *Fr. L.* (1842); Richard Pohl, *Fr. L.* (1883); A. Habets, *Borodin and Liszt* (1885), Eng. transl. Rosa Newmarch (Digby, Long); Aug. Göllerich, *Fr. L.* (Berlin, 1908); K. von Schlözer, *Römische Briefe* (1864–9) (1913); B. Schrader, *Fr. L.* (Leipzig, 1914); E. Reuss, *Fr. L. ein Lebensbild* (1898) and *Fr. L.'s Lieder* (1907).—M. D. C.

LITHUANIAN MUSIC. From the earliest times the Lithuanians have been renowned for their songs (*dainos*) and dances, the instr. acc. for which was furnished by the *trimitas* (trumpet) *ragas* (horn), *birbyne* (pipe), *skudutis* (a kind of fife), and *kankles* (a kind of harp). The *birbyne* and *ragas*, in heathen days, served as altar accessories; the *trimitas* was used in war; the *skudutis* by shepherds, and the *kankles* as an accompaniment of song and story. The *kankles* was most frequently played by wandering old men who visited the estates of the great magnates and attended popular gatherings. Most of these ceremonies have now perished; the *kankles* players have disappeared, but the immortal *dainos* still remain.

In the XVI and XVII centuries, we find the *kanklininkas* (*kankles*-player) predominant, in close association with the *daina*, which was kept alive by aural transmission. Very little music has been committed to paper in Lithuania itself; but there are few important libraries in Europe which do not possess Lithuanian *dainos* in ms. form, or museums without Lithuanian musical instruments. Unfortunately this labour has been carried out not by Lithuanians but by foreigners, because the serfdom conditions of national life in Lithuania, under Poles or Russians, have not permitted the people in the past to become literate. But in 1883 the national voice again made itself heard. The cultural movement, whose spokesman was the famous periodical *Ausra* (*Dawn*), laid the first serious foundations of the coming renascence. After the Lutheran chorales (printed in Lithuanian) and the XVII century church melodies, the first Mass, written in Lithuanian, appeared in 1886 with music by Kalvaitis, a former orgt. of Kaunas (Kovno) Cathedral.

Nearly 10 years later, Vincas Kūdirka publ. 2 male-chorus books containing over 50 *dainos*, chiefly popular songs harmonised by Polish comprs. They included the air now used as the Lithuanian national hymn, *Lietuva Tevyne musu*, together with the famous waltz *Varpelis* (*The Bell*). This was probably the 1st appearance of the national hymn in print.

A little later, Ereminas publ. his collection of choral songs, which only contained a few purely Lithuanian, all the rest being from German words and music. About the same time, songs by an unknown compr. in blue hectograph printing, for mixed chorus, were disseminated. Amongst them were *Miškas užia* (*The Forest rustles*), *Sudiev Lietuva* (*Farewell, Lithuania*),

Eina garsas nuo rubežiaus (*The Sound comes from the Border*). These were in great vogue up to the war in 1914.

Juozas Naujalis (*q.v.*) published 8, and later 15 songs for chorus, several solos, and duets with pf. acc. Some of his songs appeared in Lithuanian and Esperanto. He was the first amongst Lithuanians to acquire a higher mus. education and to spread the Gregorian chant amongst Lithuanian churches. Česlovas Sasnauskas (*q.v.*) was the second during this period to acquire a higher mus. training. He lived in Petrograd. Mikas Petrauskas (*q.v.*), the third Lithuanian to graduate from the Petrograd Cons., has won fame in America where to-day Lithuanian-Americans owe their choir-leaders and singers solely to his propaganda. These three men, scattered over the world, constitute a famous triad in Lithuanian music from which has arisen an entire series of trained comprs. Stankevičius, a military band-condr. at Riga, has comp. many pieces. A. Kačanauskas has publ. pf. pieces. In 1921 the Švyturys Publ. Co. issued his unacc. choral works and songs, and in 1922 the Dirva Co. publ. his choral coll. *Lietuvos garsai* (*Sounds of Lithuania*).

Stasys Šimkus (*q.v.*) began to publish popular choral songs and orig. compns. whilst still at the Cons. Juozas Talat-Kelpša (*q.v.*) issued Lithuanian music in his Cons. days. Early in XX century, Julius Starka publ. a *Solemn Mass* for 1 v. with organ. Theodore Brazys (*q.v.*) played a great part in developing musical culture. J. Žilevičius publ. choruses. The most solid symph. and pf. works of Čiurlionis remain in ms. Vidunas has publ. school collections for 2, 3 and 4 vs. J. Gudavičius, a military band-condr., has also publ. choruses and songs, with material from Žemaitija sources. J. Gruodis brought out in 1921 orig. compns. based on popular melodies for pf. and chorus. These have a distinctly modern tendency which differentiates him sharply from other Lithuanian comprs. Great importance must be attached to Sasnauskas's cantata *Broliai*, Šimkus's *Sudiev Lietuva*, Gruodis's pf. variations and the operettas of M. Petrauskas.

Choral societies are thriving; there are good music-classes in all the towns. Bell-music was instituted in the Military Museum tower in 1922. The free public lectures on music, illustrated by a symphony orch. in the Military Museum, attract three or four thousand listeners.

About 1883, Prince Bagdonas Oginski at Rietavas, in order to have his own symphony orch. and choir, took the children of poor parents and had them taught to play orch. instruments. A similar school was establ. by his brother, Nicholas Oginski, at Plunge. At Rokiški, there was the Limanas Organ School, from which a number of fairly well-trained orgts. graduated. J. Naujalis at Kaunas (Kovno) Cath. had dozens of organ pupils who went as far afield as America and Russia. Recently his school was taken over by the State, and to-day has arisen therefrom the State Music School, Naujalis himself as director. In April 1923 a music school for children, the head of which is E. Gailevičius, began to function under the St. Cecilia Association.

The most prominent writers on music are V. Zadeikas, a really serious critic, and J. Žilevičius, the mus. historian.

Opera was founded on 31 Dec. 1920, through the efforts of a council of four members of the Association of Lithuanian Art Promoters — Kipras Petrauskas (former soloist of Russ. Imperial Marie Theatre, Petrograd, and brother to M. Petrauskas), Stasys Silingas (ex-President of Lithuanian State Council); Juozas Talat-Kelpša (dir.) and Juozas Žilevičius (administrator). They conducted the opera until it passed under government jurisdiction (20 Feb. 1922) as the Lithuanian State Opera. A symphony orch. (organised 1923) is maintained by J. Žilevičius. —H. R.

LIUZZI, Ferdinando. Ital. compr. b. Bologna, in 1884. Stud. pf. and compn. at Bologna, then perfected himself at Munich under Reger and Mottl. Now prof. of harmony and cpt. at the Music Inst., Florence. Compr. of various vocal and instr. works; a sonata for vn. and pf.; a fairy opera L'Augellin bel verde, perf. Rome, Teatro dei Piccoli. Also writer and critic.—D. A.

LIVENS, Leo. Eng. pianist and compr. b. Beckenham, Kent, 24 May, 1896. Pf. prof. R.A.M. London, 1922. His music is interesting and effective.

Pf. works (Anglo-Fr. Music Co.; Rogers; J. Williams, London) include sets of Impressions, preludes, studies, nature suites, Egyptian Phantasies, pf. sonata in C, preludes of various technique. In ms.: orch. poems; a ballet in 1 movement on Arabian Nights tale Alnaschar; pf. 5tet; str. 4tets, etc. —E.-H.

LJUNGBERG, Göta. Swedish operatic s. singer; b. Sundsvall, 4 Oct. 1893. Stud. in Stockholm. Chief parts : Elizabeth, Elsa, Sieglinde, Eva, Venus, Gudrune; Tosca, Santuzza, Margaret (Faust), Myrtocle (Die toten Augen), Eurydice (Orphée aux enfers). Married H. Stangenberg, the operatic producer, 1912. Sang in Ring and Salome, perfs. R. Opera, Covent Garden, London, May 1924.—P. V.

LLACER, María. Contemporary Span. operatic s. singer; b. Valencia. Besides her success at many European and Amer. opera houses, she has given, in provincial towns of Spain, with the Orquesta Sinfónica, the first performances of Parsifal and other Wagnerian operas.—P. G. M.

LLEÓ, Vincente. Span. compr. of light mus. comedies. He hailed from Valencia and, after a long stay in S. America, died in Madrid at the end of 1922. By the piquant character of his works he enjoyed great popularity, attaining the highest mark of his fame with the zarzuela La Corte de Faraón.—P. G. M.

LLOBET, Miguel. Span. guitarist; b. Barcelona, 18 Oct. 1878. Started life as a painter, but the call of the Span. national instr. made him abandon his former profession; became the favourite pupil of the great Tárrega. He is recognised as the most eminent player of the present day, being called the " Casals of the guitar."

The admiration and friendship for him of Vincent d'Indy, Debussy, Ravel, Dukas, de Falla, the late Granados and Albeniz and many other leading modern comprs. is not only due to his technical ability but also to his talent as interpreter of all styles of music. De Falla's Homenaje, for the Tombeau de Debussy, was specially written for him.—P. G. M.

LLOYD, Charles Harford. Eng. orgt. b. Thornbury, Glos; d. Eton, 16 Oct. 1919. Orgt. Gloucester Cath. 1876 (following S. S. Wesley); cond. Three Choirs Fest. 1877, 1880; orgt. Christ Church Cath. Oxford, 1882; prof. of organ, R.C.M. London, 1887–92; precentor at Eton, 1892 till death (succeeding Sir George Barnby).

Cantatas: Hero and Leander (1884); Andromeda (1886); Song of Judgment (1891); church music, organ pieces, madrigals, etc. (mostly Novello).—E.-H.

LLOYD, David de. Welsh compr. condr. b. Skewen, S. Wales, 1883. Educated at Univ. Coll. of Wales, Aberystwyth; graduated B.A. (1903) and B.Mus. (1905), being the first mus. graduate of Univ. of Wales; later took degrees of Mus.B. (1913) and Mus.Doc. (1914) at Dublin Univ.; continued mus. education at Leipzig Cons.; compn. under Zöllner, Schreef and Hoffmann. Held post on staff of Woolwich Polytechnic Secondary School; orgt. and condr. Zion Chapel, Llanelly; cond. several modern choral works; assistant-master at Llanelly County Intermediate School; 1919, lecturer in music at Univ. Coll. Aberstwyth. He is a firm believer in the Tonic Solfa system, and holds the marked distinction of being appointed, when a boy of 11, to accompany late J. Spencer Curwen on his lecture-tours in British Isles for public demonstrations of higher development of the Tonic Solfa system. He has played, from Tonic Solfa, short pf. pieces by Scriabin which he himself transcribed for benefit of a class of students, to illustrate the possibilities of the system for orch. purposes; has also transcribed 3 movements of Ravel's Mother Goose suite. Was one of principal contributors to a tune-book ed. by Haydn Jones, M.P.

Part-songs for s.s.a.; anthems; dramatic chorus for male voices.—D. V. T.

LLOYD, Edward. Eng. t. singer; b. 1845. Chorister at Westminster Abbey; member of both Trinity and Kings' Coll. chapels, Cambridge, 1866; St. Andrew's, Wells St. (under Barnby), 1869; then Chapel Royal, 1869–71; in 1871, sang at Gloucester Fest. and in following years created many t. parts in oratorios of Gounod, Sullivan and Elgar; retired in 1900. —E.-H.

LOEFFLER, Charles Martin Tornov. Amer. composer, violinist; b. Mülhausen (Alsace), 30 Jan. 1861. Studied violin under Léonard and Massart in Paris; under Joachim in Berlin; composition under Guiraud in Paris and Kiel in Berlin. After playing for a time in Pasdeloup's Orchestra in Paris, joined private orchestra of Baron de Dervies in Nice and Lugano; 1881, went to America; second principal violin in Boston Symphony Orchestra, often appearing as soloist at its concerts. 1903, devoted himself to teaching and composing, living since then in or near Boston.

With his orchestral compositions Loeffler holds a prominent place among modern American composers, being one of the earliest exponents in America of the " Impressionist " style. First appearance as orchestral composer 21 Nov. 1891, playing solo-part in his Suite for violin and orchestra *Les Veillées de l'Ukraine* at Boston Symphony concert. This was followed in 1894 by a *Fantastic Concerto* for cello. In these he clearly displayed traces of the striking harmonic originality which was to become more marked in his later works. With the *Divertissement* in A minor, for violin and orchestra, first performed in Boston in 1895 (composer as soloist), his style had become fairly well crystallised. It is characterised by its harmonic freedom, by a fascinating play of orchestral colour and unusual rhythmical invention. As a colourist Loeffler is prominent among the older generation of American composers. A symphonic poem, *La Mort de Tintagiles* (after Maeterlinck), was originally written with two *obbligato* viole d'amour, and was 1st performed thus, 1897. A later version uses only one viola d'amour. His fondness for unusual combinations is further evinced in his two Rhapsodies for oboe, viola and piano (produced 1901). His best-known work is probably the *Villanelle du Diable*, composed with another orchestral piece, *La Bonne Chanson*, in 1901, first performed in Boston, 12 April, 1902. A *Pagan Poem* (after Virgil) was originally a chamber-work, performed in Boston, 1901. The orchestral version was brought out by Boston Orchestra in 1907. Of his latest works, *Five Irish Fantasies* for voice and orchestra (poems by Yeats), three were sung for first time by John McCormack at a Boston Symphony concert, 10 March, 1922. Loeffler is an *Officier de l'Académie* and an *Officier d'Instruction Publique*.

La Mort de Tintagiles, symph. poem, orch. and viole d'amour (1905); *La Villanelle du Diable*, orch. (1905); *A Pagan Poem*, orch. op. 14 (1909); 2 Rhapsodies, ob. vla. and pf. (1905); Psalm for female chorus with organ, harp, 2 fls. and cello obblig. op. 3 (1907); *Ode for One who fell in Battle*, 8-v. mixed chorus unacc. (1911); 4 *Poèmes*, v. vla. and pf. op. 5 (1904) all publ. by Schirmer; music for 4 str. instrs. (Soc. for Publ. of Amer. Mus. 1923); many songs. —O. K.

LOESCHHORN, Albert. Ger. pianist and teacher; *b.* Berlin, 27 June, 1819; *d.* there, 4 June, 1905. Pupil of Ludwig Berger; then at R. Inst for Church Music; teacher there from 1851.

Pf. studies; sonatas; sonatinas; suites; brilliant salon pieces; pf. 5tet. Wrote *Guide to Pf. Literature* (1862; 2nd ed. 1885).—A. E.

LOEVENSOHN, Marix. Belgian cellist; *b.* Courtrai, 31 March, 1880. Stud. at Brussels Cons. (Jacobs); 1st prize 1898. *Début* in London same year; toured through England with Adelina Patti, Albani, Katherine Goodson. Became successively cellist of Wilhelmj, Marsick, Ysaye and Thomson Quartets; played in Paris, Rome, Madrid, Lisbon, Vienna, Amsterdam, Bucharest, Athens, Constantinople; toured as soloist with Colonne Orch. in 1905, visiting Rio de Janeiro, Montevideo, Buenos Ayres, Santiago

de Chile; 1906, with Ysaye in Berlin; remained in Germany till 1914 (Loevensohn's Modern Chamber-music Concerts in Berlin); 1914–16, in Belgian army; 1916, became soloist of Concertgebouw Orch. Amsterdam; 1920, appointed 1st prof. of cello at Brussels R. Cons.; now holding the two positions at Amsterdam and Brussels. Belongs also to Amsterdam Str. Quartet (see CHAMBER-MUSIC PLAYERS). Many comprs. have dedicated works to him, *e.g.*, Flora Joutard's Concerto; Henriette Bosmans' Concerto; Scharrès' *Poème*, Granville Bantock's *Elegiac Poem*; sonatas cello and pf. by Bosmans, Pijper, Dusch, Skauwen, Brusselmans. He lives in Amsterdam.

Many works for cello; about 50 songs (ms.); wrote a brochure, *Chamber-music of Belgian Masters* (publ. *Open Weg*, Amsterdam).—W. P.

LOEWENGARD, Max Julius. Ger. critic and teacher; *b.* Frankfort-o-M., 2 Oct. 1860; *d.* Hamburg, 19 Nov. 1915. Pupil of Raff, Frankfort; acted as condr.; 1890–1, teacher at Cons. Wiesbaden; then at Scharwenka Cons., Berlin (till 1904), and at same time mus. ed. of *Börsenzeitung*; 1904, succeeded Sittard as mus. ed. of *Correspondent*, Hamburg; till 1908, teacher at Hamburg Conservatoire.

Text-book on Harmony (1892, 6th ed. 1906; Eng. ed. Peacock, 1904; Liebing, 1907; Th. Baker, New York, 1910); *Lessons in Harmony* (1902, also Eng.); *Canon and Fugue* and *Lessons in Form* (1904); *Practical Instructions for Figured-Bass Playing, Harmony, Transposition and Modulation* (1913). He comp. songs and a comic opera *Die 14 Nothelfer* (*The 14 Rescuers*), Theater des Westens, Berlin.—A. E.

LÖHR, Hermann Frederic. Eng. song-compr. *b.* Plymouth, 16 Oct. 1872. Many songs, best-known being *Little Grey Home in the West* and *Where my Caravan has rested*.—E. H.

LOHSE, Otto. Ger. condr. *b.* Dresden, 21 Sept. 1858. Pupil of Draeseke, Wüllner, H. J. Richter (pf.) and Fr. Grützmacher (cello); 1877–9 in Dresden Court Orch.; 1880–2, pf. teacher at Imperial School of Music, Vilna; 1882–9, cond. Wagner Soc. and Imperial Russian Mus. Soc., Riga, also 1st condr. of Stadttheater, 1889–93; 1893–5, chief condr. Hamburg Opera House; 1894, manager of London opera season; 1895–7, cond. Ger. Opera (Damrosch Company) America; 1897–1904, principal condr. of Strasburg Stadttheater; 1901–4, manager of Ger. Opera season, Covent Garden, London; 1902, visiting condr. Symphony Concerts, R. Theatre, Madrid; opera dir. of combined Stadttheater, Cologne, 1904; 1911, opera dir. Brussels; 1912–23, opera dir. at Stadttheater, Leipzig; 1916, R. professor.

3-act play-opera *Der Prinz wider Willen* (Riga, 1890); numerous songs. Consult E. Lert, *O. L.* (1918, Breitkopf).—A. E.

LONGO, Alessandro. Italian pianist and composer; *b.* Amante (Cosenza), 30 Dec. 1864. Stud. pf. at Cons. di San Pietro a Maiella, Naples, under Beniamino Cesi, and compn. under Paolo Serrao. His first post was to deputise for Cesi as pf. prof. at the Cons.; in 1897 he succeeded him, and still occupies that position. Founded and dir. in Naples some important mus. insts.; played in the Ferni Quartet. Has gained a high reputation as concert-pianist. Since 1914, has dir. a review, *L'Arte Pianistica*. Is author of many compns. for his own instr., of a 5tet and various suites (Breitkopf; Hug; Kistner; Schmidt; Ricordi). He also published the Complete Works for Harpsichord of Domenico Scarlatti (in 11 vols. Ricordi) and of other important eds. of old pf. music, in addition to educational works.—D. A.

LOOMIS, Harvey Worthington. Amer. compr. *b.* Brooklyn, New York, 5 Feb 1865. Stud. pf. under Madeline Schiller; compn. under Dvořák at National Cons. New York. Five operas; several mus. pantomimes and incidental music for plays. Especially worthy are his songs for children.

Hungarian Rhapsody, pf. op. 53, No. 2 (Ditson, 1900), and other pf. pieces (Ditson; Witmark); *Lyrics of the Red Man*, op. 76 (Wa-Wan, 1903-4), and other songs, part-songs (Ditson; Gray); 2 recitations with pf. acc.: *The Song of the Pear* (Werner, 1913); *The Story of a Faithful Soul* (*id.* 1915); *Song Flowers for Children to gather*, 2 books (Fischer, 1911); *Toy Tunes* (*id.* 1911).—J. M.

LÓPEZ CHAVARRI, Eduardo. Span. compr. and musicologist. Stud. in France and Germany. Lives in Valencia, his native town, where by his work as a writer and prof. of history of music at the Cons. he has become a prominent figure in the musical revival of the country. He advocates nationalism in music.

La Trilogia Wagneriana; *El Anillo del Nibelungo*; *Historia de la Música*; *Vademecum Músico*; *Gabriel Fauré y su obra* (transl. from Louis Vuillemin's work); *Wagner* (transl. from Henri Lichtenberger, Liszt and others). Compns.: *Acuarelas*, str. orch. or 4tet; *Canciones para la juventud*, v. and pf.; *Cuentos líricos* and *Tierras Levantinas*, orch. (Unión Musical Española.)—P. G. M.

LÓPEZ-NAGUIL, Antonio. Argentine violinist; *b.* Buenos Ayres in 1885. Commenced studies in Buenos Ayres; then Paris in 1905 under Georges Enesco. Vn. soloist in Barcelona Mus. Soc. Returned to Argentina in 1909, after tour in France, Spain and Uruguay. Now dir. (with León Fontova) Argentine Soc. of Chamber-Music. Awarded gold medal of *Bien Public* by Fr. Government.—A. M.

LORENZ, Alfred Otakar. Austrian condr. *b.* Vienna, 11 July, 1868. Stud. law at Jena, Leipzig, Berlin; then music under Robert Radecke, mus. science under Spitta; condr. at Königsberg, Libau, Elberfeld, etc.; R. condr. at Coburg; 1917, gen. mus. dir.; till 1919 dir. of Coburg Mus. Soc.; resigned 1920. Lives in Munich.

Opera, *Helge's Awakening* (Schwerin, 1896); music to Æschylus's *Orestes* trilogy (Coburg, 1906).—A. E.

LORENZ, Julius. Ger. choral condr. and compr. *b.* Hanover, 1 Oct. 1862. Stud. at Leipzig, Cons. (Reinecke, Jadassohn, Paul); 1884-95, condr. of Acad. for Singing, Glogau; 1895, condr. of male choir *Arion*, New York; 1899, undertook long concert tour with *Arion* through America; was also master at College of Music; 1903, R. Prussian Music-dir.; since 1911 at Glogau.

Mass (D mi. for soli, chorus and orch.); *Psalm XCV* (choir and orch.); str. 4tet; trio, B flat ma. op. 12; overtures; pf. pieces; songs; opera, *Dutch Recruits*; Festival Cantata for Jubilee of *Arion* (1904).—A. E.

LORENZONI, Renzo. Ital. pianist; *b.* Padua, 10 Oct. 1887; in 1908 diploma for pf. at Cons.

di San Pietro a Maiella, Naples. Degree in law at Univ. of Padua, 1909. Immediately began a successful career as concert-pianist. Played all the Beethoven sonatas at concerts at Padua. In 1919 elected, by competition, prof. of pf. at Tartini Cons. Trieste. Besides being a much esteemed pianist, he is also a distinguished compr. and writer.—D. A.

LOŠŤÁK, Ludvík. Czech compr. and author; *b.* Nová Mitrovice, 1862; *d.* Prague, 1918. Stud. at Prague Cons.; 1888-91 in London; then in Prague.

Operas: *Selská Bouře* (*Peasants' Revolt*); *Furianti*; orch.: *Poem of Victory*; 2 overtures; *Rispetti, etc.* Writings: *The Chromatic Storm*; *Victorious Democracy* (both in Czech).—V. ST.

LOUIS, Rudolf. Ger. musicologist; *b.* Schwetzingen, 30 Jan. 1870; *d.* Munich, 15 Nov. 1914. Stud. at Geneva and Vienna; took degrees at Vienna; pupil of Friedrich Klose; stud. under Mottl at Carlsruhe; cond. theatre orch. at Landshut and Lübeck. From 1897, resided at Munich as teacher and concert-critic for *Münchner Neueste Nachrichten*.

Contradiction in Music (1893); *R. Wagner as Mus. Æsthetist* (1897); *World Opinion of R. Wagner* (1898); *Franz Liszt* (Berlin, 1900); *Hector Berlioz* (Leipzig, 1904); *Anton Bruckner* (Munich, 1905, Georg Müller); *Ger. Music of To-day* (1909, 3rd ed. 1912); propaganda pamphlets on Pfitzner and Klose. Publ. Hausegger's *Our Ger. Masters* (1903); wrote (with Ludwig Thuille) *Harmony Instructor* (1907, 6th ed. 1919, Stuttgart, Grüninger).—A. E.

LOUS, Ast.id. Norwegian m.-sopr. operatic singer; *b.* Kristiansund, 12 April, 1876. Stud. first as an actress; engaged as such in Bergen and Christiania, 1894-1900. Stud. singing in Berlin and Paris in 1899 and 1903. Engaged in Ger. opera houses (Senta, Sieglinde, Elizabeth, Venus, Fidelio, Recha, etc.).—U. M.

LÖWE, Ferdinand. Condr. *b.* Vienna, 19 Feb. 1865. Stud. at Vienna Cons. (Oskar Dachs, pf.; Anton Bruckner, compn.). The young man soon won the friendship of Bruckner and publ. (together with Josef Schalk and Cyril Hynais) pf. arr. of most of Bruckner's symphonies. Later on, he cond. much of Bruckner's music. In 1883, prof. of the Vienna Cons. (choral singing, later pf.). Then became a condr. 1897 and from 1908-14 in Munich (Kaim Orch. and Konzertverein), and in Vienna (Singakademie) to 1898, concerts of Soc. of Friends of Music (Ges. der Musikfreunde) to 1904, and Konzertverein Orch. since foundation. Also cond. regularly in Budapest and Berlin. In succession to Wilhelm Bopp, was elected in 1919 1st dir. of State Acad. of Music, Vienna (resigned 1922 on account of bad health). Lives now in Vienna, conducting only the Konzertverein.—P. P.

LÖWENBACH, Jan. Czechoslovak music critic; *b.* Rychnov, 1880. Stud. for Bar, took his degree, and practises as lawyer in Prague; stud. music at Univ. and privately; wrote for *Dalibor*; became ed. of *Hudební Revue*; correspondent of *Lidové Noviny*; is an expert in matters of copyright. Besides transls. of mus. texts into Ger., has publ.: *Ludevít Procházka*; *Gluck and Bohemia* (Hudební Matice) ; satirical poems: *Musical All Souls* (Srdce) ; *Correspondence of Procházka and Smetana.* Notable for his work in the organisation of mus. life and his able propaganda of modern Czechoslovak music abroad.—V. ST.

LUALDI, Adriano. Ital. compr. *b.* Larino (Campobasso), 22 March, 1887. Stud. at R. Liceo Mus. di Santa Cecilia, Rome, then in Venice under Wolf-Ferrari. Is known for his opera *Figlia di re,* which was successful in the McCormack competition in 1917, perf. at Regio Theatre, Turin, in 1922. Other operatic works are: *Le nozze di Haura, Le furie d'Arlecchino, Guerrin Meschino;* the last-mentioned work was intended for marionettes, and was perf. at Teatro dei Piccoli in Rome. Author of orch. works and vocal chamber-music. (Publ. Ricordi, Milan.) L. is also a writer, contributing to the principal mus. reviews. Now critic to *Il Secolo* of Milan.—D. A.

LUBIN, Germaine. Fr. operatic s. singer; *b.* Paris, 1 Feb. 1890. Stud. at Cons. (1908) under M. Martin. In 1912, 1st prize (singing) in *Oberon;* 1st prize (*opéra-comique*) in *La Navarraise*; 1st prize (opera) in *Faust. Début* at Opéra-Comique (1912) in *Les Contes d'Hoffmann.* Sang usual repertoire and created a rôle in *Le Pays,* 1913. Engaged at Opéra by M. Rouché 1914. 1919, created rôles in *Le Retour, La Légende de St. Christophe* (1920); also sang in *Valkyrie* and *La Fille de Roland.* Wife of poet Paul Géraldy. Possesses a rich, well-trained voice, very suitable for heroines in grand and modern opera, and is also a good actress.—A. R.

LUCIANI, Sebastiano Arturo. Ital. music critic; *b.* Acquaviva (Bari), 1884.
La Rinascita del dramma (The Rebirth of the Drama (Rome, Ausonia); *Verso una nuova arte : il cinematografo (Towards a New Art: the Cinematograph (id.* 1920). Has also publ. important studies and articles in *Rivista Musicale Italiana,* and other reviews.—D. A.

LUDLOW, Godfrey. Australian violinist; *b.* Newcastle, Australia, 19 Sept. 1893. Left Sydney at age of 14 to study under Ševčík in Vienna and Auer in Petrograd; when 17, toured through Greece and Turkey; interned in Ruhleben during the war; *début* in London with Sir Henry Wood's orch. 1919; concerts in Berlin, Holland, London, etc.; 1924, tour in U.S.A. —E.-H.

LUDWIG, Franz. Ger.-Czechoslovak compr. *b.* Graslitz, 1889. Pupil of Rietsch, Riemann, Reger. Prof. at Sondershausen Conservatoire.
Comedy-Overture, full orch.; *Serenade* in 5 movements for brass band; pf. concerto; pf. sonatas; horn concerto; songs.—E. S.

LUDWIG, Friedrich. Ger. musicologist; *b.* Potsdam, 8 May, 1872. 1890, stud. at Marburg and Strasburg, history and mus. science (Jacobsthal); 1899, undertook many long voyages for purposes of study; 1902, Potsdam; 1905, settled at Strasburg as Univ. teacher of mus. science; 1911, became prof.-extraordinary; 1920, prof.-in-ordinary at Göttingen; Ludwig is specialist for music of XIII and XIV centuries.
Besides articles in periodicals, he publ.: *Repertorium organorum recentioris et motetorum vetustissimi*

stili, 1 vol.; *Catalogue raisonné* of sources (Halle, 1910) and important articles on music of Middle Ages in *Z.f.M.* and *A.f.M.*—A. E.

LUDWIG, William. Irish barit. singer; *b.* Arran Quay, Dublin. In 1877, chief barit. of Carl Rosa Opera Co. From the outset, became famous as Wagnerian singer and continued for most of his career to sing in these operas. Not only was his big voice suited to parts such as Wotan, Dutchman, Hans Sachs; but his declamation and acting were splendidly dramatic. He also sang Claude Frollo in Goring Thomas's *Esmeralda* at Drury Lane in 1883; took part in 1st perf. of Mackenzie's *Colomba.* Was also justly famous for his oratorio and concert singing.—W. ST.

LUNA, Pablo. Span. compr. of light stage-music. One of the best-known and most popular amongst his contemporaries. Though not devoid of modern Ital. operatic mannerism and a touch of universal impersonality, when required by the dramatic situation he writes also with unfailing success in the Span. vein. Some of his numerous works are perf. in Italy. He hails from Aragon and lives in Madrid.
Molinos de Viento; El Niño Judío; El Rey Flojo; La Conquista de la Gloria; El Sapo Enamorado and *El Asombro de Damasco* (produced for 1st time in England at Harrogate, under title *The First Kiss,* Jan. 1923). (Unión Musical Española.)—P. G. M.

LUND, Signe. Norwegian compr. *b.* Christiania, 15 April, 1868. Trained in Berlin, under Wilhelm Berger, afterwards in Copenhagen and Paris. Belongs to well-known Norwegian artist-family. Lived abroad for 20 years, chiefly in America, where she has won a name as compr., especially after she was victorious in 1917 in a great competition arranged by the National Art Club on occasion of America entering into the war. The title of this piece is *The Road to France,* written to words of a war-poem by Daniel Henderson. She comp. by request, music for Björnson Memorial Concert in Chicago, 1910; in 1914, a cantata for Norwegian-Americans for the celebration of the centenary of Norway's constitution. Numerous pieces for pf., for v. and vn., cantatas and minor orch. works. Has given concerts of her own compns. in her own country, in America, London, Paris, Copenhagen and Vienna. Her music shows some influence from Grieg. It is, in the best meaning of the word, popular and tuneful.—R. M.

LUNDBERG, Lennart Arvid. Swedish pianist, compr. *b.* Norrköping, 29 Sept. 1863. Stud. at R. Cons. Stockholm; then pf. under Ehrlich (Berlin), Dubois and Paderewski (Paris). Pf. teacher at R. Cons. Stockholm, from 1903. Prof. 1913; Member R.A.M. Stockholm, 1904. As compr. has a modern Impressionist style.
Pf.: 3 sonatas; 9 sets of ballades; 7 sets of *Marins;* nocturnes; impromptus; preludes; legends; 9 sets of songs.—P. V.

LUNDE, Johan Backer. Norwegian pianist, compr. *b.* Havre 6 July, 1874. Pupil of Agathe Backer-Gröndahl and Busoni (pf.), of Iver Holter and Urban (compn.). Concert-tours in Norway, Sweden, Denmark, England and Germany. As compr. has won great popularity with his lyrical pieces (over 200 songs). His 3 symphonies and

16 orch. pieces are more lyrical than symphonic
in form and design, but they reveal solid theoretical knowledge and a capacity for effective instrumentation. Lives in Christiania, where he is
much in demand as an accompanist.—J. A.

LUNN, Louise Kirkby. Eng. operatic contr.
singer; b. Manchester. Stud. R.C.M. London,
under Visetti; début there; 1st appearance
Opéra - Comique, London (Nora in Shamus
O'Brien; on tour with Augustus Harris in grand
opera, 1896; Carl Rosa Co. 1896–99; Covent
Garden, 1901; Queen's Hall orch. concerts
from 1899. R. Opera 1902–1915 (Wagnerian and
other rôles). Dalila (Samson), Carmen and Orfeo
(Gluck) are her best parts. Has sung at Budapest
and Metropolitan, New York, for many seasons.
First to sing Kundry in English in U.S.A.
—E.-H.

LUNSSENS, Martin. Belgian composer; b.
Brussels, 16 April, 1871. Stud. Brussels Cons.
under J. Dupont, Huberti, F. Kufferath,
Gevaert. Prix de Rome, 1895. Travelled for
3 years in France, Italy, Germany. Leader of
orch. in Lyric Theatre, Antwerp (1901–2).
Prof. of harmony at Brussels Cons. (1911).
Dir. of École de Musique, Louvain (1921).
Appointed dir. of Ghent Cons. Jan. 1924, in
succession to Matthieu.

Stage works: Colette et Lucas, incidental music for
play by Prince de Ligne (Belœil, 1914); Saint-Amand,
incidental music for play of Delbeke. V. and orch.:
Callirhoé, cantata, Prix de Rome; Cantate Jubilaire
(1905); Ode to Music; Marche inaugurale (Antwerp
Exhibition, 1894); songs, orch. acc. Orch.: 4 symphonies; symph. poems (Roméo et Juliette; Timon
d'Athènes, Jules César, Le Cid); overtures: Ouverture de Concert; Phèdre. Chamber-music.—E. C.

LURE. A large, curved, ancient Scandinavian
bronze horn found through archæological ex-
cavations in Scandinavia and the countries
bordering upon southern shores of Baltic Sea,
especially upon the Danish Islands. The origin
lies in remote days of later Bronze Age (about
1000 B.C.). Quite a number of them are perfectly preserved and in condition to be played
upon to-day, which gives them an interest altogether unique. They represent an isolated
voice from the distant past which, so far as music

is concerned, is otherwise silent. The most remarkable find was made at a little village called
Lynge, about 29 kilometres north of Copenhagen.
A little over 100 years ago 6 large beautiful
lures were dug up out of a bog at one time. They
are in splendid condition and may with a little
practice be played upon; these lures are in
the National Museum, Copenhagen, and from
the balcony of this building it has been the
custom in recent years to celebrate Midsummer

Day by playing upon them, whilst thousands
crowd the adjoining streets to listen in awe and
respect to these mighty, resounding tones from
the past. In Denmark, about 30 specimens have
been found; the majority of these are also in the
National Museum, Copenhagen.

Their length ranges from 2·38 metres to 1·51
metres. The tube shows remarkable dexterity of
working. It is conical in shape; consists of sections, each fitting accurately into its extension;
smooth inside and out; so thin (1 to 1½ mm.) that
present-day foundries cannot produce this result;
the mouthpiece is similar to our trombone; the
finish and ornamentation is remarkable. The
compass of notes is extensive, including all the
first 12 natural open-tones, thus ranging over 3¼
octaves besides the 10 pedal-tones. The tube
responds easily to a ringing ff, or soft caressing
tones, the lower tones being clear and metallic,
whilst the upper notes approximate to the French
horn. They are invariably discovered in pairs,
tuned in unison.

Consult: Angul Hammerich, Bronze lurerne i
Nationalmuscæet i Kφbenhavn (Aarbog for Nordisk
Oldkyndighed, Copenhagen, 1893; Ger. ed. in Vier-
teljahrsschrift für Musikwissenschaft, Vol. X, Leipzig,
1894; Fr. ed. in Mémoire de la Société des antiquités
du Nord, Copenhagen, 1894); also Hubert Schmidt,
Die Luren von Daberkow (Prähistorisches Zeitschrift,
No. VII, Berlin, 1915).—A. H.

LUSTGARTEN, Egon. Austrian compr. b.
Vienna, 17 Aug. 1887. Stud. at Vienna Cons.
Now teacher of theory at New Vienna Cons.
A lyrical compr., he attracts attention by his
broadly conceived al fresco songs and his peculiar
manner of treating the chamber-orchestra, which
he prefers in his works, without showing any
other reforms in style.

Symphony for soli, chorus and orch. (1921); 4tet,
str. and pf.; Sonata-capricciosa, vn. Many songs,
mostly in cycles (acc. by str. and wind orch.).—P. P.

LUTE MUSIC and Players. See BATKA;
RICHARD; BRENET, MICHEL; BRONDI, MARIA;
CHILESOTTI, OSCAR; KOCZIRZ, ADOLF; KOTHE,
ROBERT; QUITTARD, HENRI; SCHMID, H. K.;
VIEUX, MAURICE.

LUTKIN, Peter Christian. Condr. orgt.
compr. b. Thompsonville, Wis., U.S.A., 27
March, 1858. Stud. at Chicago under Eddy
(organ) and Gleason (theory); 1881–3 at Hochschule, Berlin, under Raif (pf.), Haupt (organ)
and Bargiel (theory); at Leschetizky School,
Vienna 1883, and under M. Moszkowski in Paris
(1884). Orgt. of Cath. of St. Peter and St. Paul,
Chicago, 1871–81; of St. Clement's, Chicago,
1884–91; of St. James's, 1891–96; 1888–95, head
of theory department of Amer. Cons. Chicago;
1891, prof. of music and (1897) dean of school
of music at North Western Univ. (Evanston, Ill.),
which position he still holds. Since 1909, a
regular condr. at Chicago North Shore music
fests. held at Evanston. In 1900 Mus.D. h.c.
Syracuse Univ. Church music (Gray; Novello;
Summy). Author of Music in the Church (Milwaukee, The Young Churchman, 1910).—O. K.

LÜTSCHG, Waldemar. Russ. pianist; b.
Petrograd, 16 May, 1877. Son and pupil of Karl
Lütschg (pf. teacher 1839–99); first lived in Ber-

lin; then till 1906 teacher at Mus. College, Chicago; returned to Germany; 1st pf. teacher at Cons. Strasburg; now in Berlin; since 1920, teacher at Public High School for Music.—A. E.

LUTZ, Ernst. Ger.-Czechoslovak compr. *b.* Schönbach, 1887.

Symph. poem, *In Memoriam*; Symph. Prologue; *Märchensuite.*—E. S.

LYELL-TAYLOR, H. Eng. condr. *b.* London, 28 March, 1872. 1st vn. Carl Rosa Co. and Covent Garden Opera; leader of 2nd vns. Queen's Hall Orch.; later condr. of 2nd part of Promenade concerts there; condr. Colwyn Bay orch. (till 1907); then Buxton orch.; Derby orch.; Wolverhampton fest. choir; Nat. Sunday League concerts; Birmingham Symphony orch.; then condr. to corporation of Brighton; now Durban orch. S. Africa.—E.-H.

LYON, James. Eng. compr. *b.* Manchester, 25 Oct. 1872. Self-taught, except for a few organ lessons from Dr. T. W. Dodds, when an undergraduate at Queen's Coll. Oxford; Mus.Doc. Oxon. 1905. A fertile compr. with a strong feeling for the stage, and a Neo-Romantic style. He has also written much educational music. Has done much examining in Ireland. In 1924, visited Canada as adjudicator, with Herbert Fryer.

Operas: *The Palace of Cards*, op. 56; *Stormwrack*, 1-act, op. 64; *Fiametta*, 3-act, op. 77; *La Sirena*, 4-act, op. 79. Melomimes: *Toinette*, tragedy, op. 70; *The Necklace*, op. 74; *Madame s'amuse*, op. 79. Orch.: 4 suites, op. 14, 27, 32, 42; Welsh poem, *Gwalia*; Poem on Manx tunes; prelude, *Aucassin and Nicolette*, op. 53; *Idyll*, str. orch. (W. Rogers); *Ballade*, vn. and orch. op. 38 (Stainer & Bell); cantatas (W. Rogers); Fantasy 4tet, op. 46; trio in D mi. pf. vn. cello, op. 35; songs (Stainer & Bell; Rogers; Larway); pf. pieces (Lengnick; Novello; Ashdown); organ pieces, 3 sonatas, 2 suites, albums, etc. (Donajowski; Augener; Stainer & Bell; W. Rogers); pieces for vn. and pf. (Stainer & Bell); part-songs (Weekes; Ashdown; Stainer & Bell; Novello); educational works, sight-reading tests, etc. (Ashdown; Weekes; Stainer & Bell).—E.-H.

MAASALO, Armas. Finnish choral condr. compr. *b.* Rautavaara, 28 Aug. 1885. Stud. at Helsingfors Univ. (Ph.M. 1911), and at Music Inst.; 1919–20 (with State scholarship) in Paris. At present, teacher of music at Finnish Normal Lyceum; since 1923 dir. of Helsingfors Church Music Inst.; orgt. and condr. of mixed choir Kansallis-Kuoro in Helsingfors.

Orch. Suite; *Karelian Rhapsody,* orch.; works for chorus and orch.; choral works, songs, etc.—T. H.

MACAN, Karel Emanuel. Czechoslovak compr. *b.* Pardubice, 1858; stud. at Organ School; compn. under Fibich. Became blind when 22. From 1891, teacher at Blind Asylum in Prague; then chief organiser of the printing for blind.

Str. 4tet; 2 masses; melodrama, *Amarus*; many choruses, chiefly male (*Prague*); songs (publ. Fr. A. and M. Urbánek; Otto); children's songs (publ. Kotrba; Storch, Prague).—V. St.

MACCARTHY, Maud. British violinist, writer, lecturer; *b.* Clonmel, Co. Tipperary, Ireland, 4 July, 1882. Stud. under Arbós; appeared as a child at Crystal Palace, and Queen's Hall with Beethoven, Tchaikovsky and Brahms concertos; many appearances on Continent; toured U.S.A. with Boston Symphony Orch. twice; numerous London recitals. At 23, owing to neuritis, she gave up solo-playing and went to India with Mrs. Annie Besant, where she stud. metaphysics and Indian music, on which subjects she has lectured widely. She has appeared in theatrical productions. In 1915, she married the compr. J. H. Foulds (*q.v.*).—E.-H.

MACCUNN, Hamish. Scottish compr. and condr. *b.* Greenock, 22 March, 1868; *d.* London, 2 Aug. 1916. Stud. under Sir Hubert Parry at R.C.M. Condr. with Carl Rosa Opera Co. 1898–9; Moody Manners Opera Co. 1900–1; Savoy, 1902–4; Lyric, 1904–7. Assisted Beecham at Covent Garden and His Majesty's from 1910, and at Shaftesbury Theatre from 1915; in 1912, prof. of compn., and dir. of opera-class at Guildhall School of Music. He was the most Scottish of the Scots comprs. His 4-act opera *Jeanie Deans* was produced in Edinburgh in 1894; his *Diarmid* in London in 1897. His concert-overtures *The Land of the Mountain and the Flood, The Dowie Dens o' Yarrow,* and *The Ship o' the Fiend* are his best works. His mus. comedy *The Golden Girl* was produced in Birmingham in 1905.

Jeanie Deans (Joseph Bennett), grand opera in 4 acts (Augener); *Diarmid* (Duke of Argyll), grand opera in 4 acts (Boosey); *Breast of Light* (Duke of Argyll), grand opera (unfinished), ms.; *The Golden Girl* (Captain Basil Hood), light opera, 2 acts (Chappell); *Prue* (Chas. Taylor), light opera, 3 acts (unfinished), ms.; *The Masque of War and Peace* (Louis N. Parker) (Sir H. Beerbohm Tree, 1900); *The Pageant of Darkness and Light* (John Oxenham), stage pageant in 6 episodes (Weekes). Dramatic cantatas and ballads for chorus and orch.: *The Lay of the Last Minstrel* (Scott—J. MacCunn) (Novello, 1888); *Lord Ullin's Daughter* (Campbell) (*id.* 1888); *Bonny Kilmeny* (Hogg—J. MacCunn) (Paterson,

1888); *The Cameronian's Dream* (Hyslop) (*id.* 1890); *Queen Hynde of Caledon* (Hogg—J. MacCunn) (Chappell, 1892); *The Wreck of the Hesperus* (Longfellow) (Novello, 1905); *The Death of Parcy Reed* (traditional), male chorus and orch. (Weekes); *Kinmont Willie* (traditional) (*id.*); *Lambkin* (traditional) (*id.*); *The Jolly Goshawk* (traditional) (*id.*), produced by Sheffield Amateur Mus. Soc. under Sir Henry Wood, 1920; *Livingstone the Pilgrim* (Sylvester Horne) (*id.*); *Psalm VIII* (1890). Orch.: *Cior Mhor*, overture (ms.); *The Land of the Mountain and the Flood*, overture (Novello); ballad, *The Ship o' the Fiend* (Augener); ballad, *The Dowie Dens o' Yarrow* (*id.*); suite, *Highland Memories* (*By the Burnside*; *On the Loch*; *Harvest Dance*); dances (ms.): *Entente Cordiale*; *Mazurka*; *Harlequin*; *Columbine*; *Hornpipe*. Str. 5tet (ms.); pf. pieces (Augener); 3 pieces, cello and pf. (*id.*); very many songs (Augener; Chappell; Metzler; Beal; Novello; Cramer; J. Williams; Paterson; Methven Simpson; Weekes); part-songs (Augener; Novello).—E.-H.

MACDOWELL, Edward Alexander. Amer. compr. pianist; *b.* New York, 18 Dec. 1861; *d.* there, 23 Jan. 1908. Remains up to the present day the most striking figure among native American composers. Although his position as a world-composer has been greatly overrated by some and underrated by others, his contribution to the art as a whole, and his services to the cause of the American composer as such, cannot be dimmed or forgotten. He was first native American musician to receive the unhesitating recognition and admiration of his European colleagues, both as a composer and as an executant.

He was of Scotch-Irish-Quaker descent. His early training in piano-playing he received from Juan Buitrago, P. Desvernine and Teresa Carreño in New York. The last-named remained his staunch supporter to the end of her days. She was one of the first virtuosos to play his piano compositions in American recitals, and often played his second piano concerto in America and Europe.

From 1876–8 MacDowell studied at the Paris Conservatoire, the piano under Marmontel and theory under Savard. In 1878 he went to Germany and after studying the piano for a time under Louis Ehlert, he became the pupil of Karl Heymann on the piano and of Raff in composition. The latter became his warm personal friend and exercised a great influence upon the development of MacDowell's art.

MacDowell's talent as a pianist was recognised, and he secured an appointment as teacher of piano-playing at the Darmstadt Conservatoire, where he stayed from 1881–2. In 1882 he was introduced by Raff to Franz Liszt, who became interested in his compositions and through whose influence he was given an opportunity to play his first piano suite on 11 July, 1882, at the 19th annual festival of the Allgemeine Deutsche Musikverein held in Zurich.

With an interruption in 1884 for a short visit to America, where he married a former pupil,

Miss Marion Nevins, he remained in Germany until 1888, living until 1885 in Frankfort, and after that in Wiesbaden, where he devoted himself chiefly to composition. The works of this period reached the opus number 35, including two piano concertos and three tone-poems for orchestra.

His name had already been made known in America and England. On 8 March, 1884, Teresa Carreño played his second piano suite at a recital in New York. In March 1885 two movements from the first suite were heard at an " American Concert " in Prince's Hall, London. On 30 March, 1885, the second and third movements of his first piano concerto were played in New York at one of Frank van der Stucken's " Novelty Concerts."

In the autumn of 1888 MacDowell returned to America and settled in Boston. His first public appearance as a pianist in America was with the Kneisel Quartet in Boston, 19 November, 1888. At this concert he also played three movements from his own first piano suite. On 5 March, 1889, Theodore Thomas brought out his second piano concerto (D minor, written 1884–5) in New York with the composer as soloist. On 11 January, 1890 the Boston Symphony Orchestra played his symphonic poem, Lancelot and Elaine. From this time on, his larger compositions were played in Boston under Nikisch or Emil Paur as soon as they were completed. His most popular orchestral work, the second (Indian) suite for orchestra, was first performed by the Boston Orchestra at a concert in New York, 23 January, 1896.

In 1896 he was called to Columbia University in New York to take charge of the newly organised department of music. This was an entirely new field of work for MacDowell. Although not a gifted pedagogue, MacDowell's sincerity, his love and respect for his art, his high ideals and frank enthusiasm communicated themselves with lasting effect to all his students. His activity as a piano virtuoso and recitalist was restricted, but the next five or six years saw the production of his ripest and most important piano compositions. Much of his composing he did at his summer home in Peterboro, New Hampshire. From 1897–9 he also conducted the Mendelssohn Glee Club (male chorus) in New York.

In 1902 his health began to fail. A vacation year made no change in his condition. He resigned from his University position in 1904. In the autumn of 1905 undoubted signs of mental derangement manifested themselves. This sad condition grew worse and ended in his death three years later.

As a composer MacDowell did his best work for the piano and for the orchestra. As with Robert Schumann, his groups of shorter piano pieces exhibit his romantic spirit with all its intimate tenderness and his fine, thoroughly original harmonic sense at their best, while the depth and strength of his larger conceptions are exhibited with increasing force and conviction in the succession of four piano sonatas.

MacDowell was honoured during his lifetime by the degree of Mus.D. h.c. from Princeton University, 1896, and from the University of Pennsylvania, 1902. In 1904 he was elected to the American Academy of Arts and Letters.

Op. 42, first suite, orch. (Schmidt, 1891); op. 48, second (Indian) suite, orch. (Breitkopf, 1897); op. 22, Hamlet—Ophelia, tone-poem for orch. (Hainauer, 1885); op. 25, Lancelot and Elaine, symph. poem (id. 1888); op. 30, Die Sarazenen—Die schöne Alda, 2 fragments for orch. (Breitkopf, 1891); op. 15, pf. concerto, A mi. (id. 1911); op. 23, second pf. concerto, D mi. (id. 1907); op. 10, Erste Moderne Suite, pf. (id. 1883); op. 14, Zweite Moderne Suite, pf. (id. 1883); op. 45, Sonata Tragica, pf. (id. 1893); op. 50, Sonata Eroica, pf. (id. 1895); op. 57, third sonata (Norse), pf. (Schmidt, 1900); op. 59, fourth sonata (Keltic), pf. (id. 1901); op. 51, Woodland Sketches, pf. (Jung, 1896); op. 55, Sea Pieces, pf. (id. 1898); op. 61, Fireside Tales, pf. (Schmidt, 1902); op. 62, New England Idyls, pf. (id. 1902).

Of his smaller earlier pf. pieces, the Hexentanz, op. 17, No. 2, and Twelve Études, op. 39 (Schmidt, 1890), are best known. The works originally publ. by Jung are now publ. by A. P. Schmidt of Boston.

An excellent bibliography of MacDowell's compns. was publ. by the Library of Congress under the title Catalogue of the First Editions of E. MacD. by O. G. Sonneck (Washington, 1917). Consult also: L. Gilman, E. MacD.: a Study (New York, 1909, John Lane) (an expansion of a monograph by the same author in the series Living Masters of Music (London, 1906); E. F. Page, E. MacD.: his Work and Ideals; J. F. Porte, A Great American Tone Poet, E. MacD. (London, 1922, Kegan Paul).—O. K.

MACH, Ernst. Austrian prof. of physics; b. Turras (Moravia), 18 Feb. 1838; d. Haar, near Munich, 22 Feb. 1916. Stud. at Vienna Univ.; elected prof. of physics in 1861. Famous by his works on acoustics.

Einleitung in die Helmholtzsche Theorie der Musik (1866); Zur Theorie des Gehörorgans (1872); Beitrag zur Geschichte der Musik (1892); Die Analyse der Empfindungen und das Verhältnis des Physischen zum Psychischen (very valuable æsthetically).—EG. W.

MACHADO, Augusto. Portuguese compr.; dir. of Cons. at Lisbon; b. Lisbon in 1845. Stud. under E. Lami and J. G. Daddi for pf. and M. d'Almeida for compn.; in 1867, took a few lessons from A. Lavignac in Paris; appointed administrative and artistic dir. of San Carlos Theatre, Lisbon; dir. of the Lisbon Cons. where he also taught singing. He was one of most interesting of Portuguese musicians. His operas are frankly in the style of Massenet; but it was with his operettas (over 20) that he was most successful. His first was O sol de Navarra, 3 acts, in 1870; his last O Espadachim do Outeiro, which had many representations at Theatre Trindade in 1910. See art. PORTUGUESE OPERA.

Operas: Laureana (San Carlos Theatre, Lisbon, 1883); Os Dorias, 4 acts (ib. 1887); Paola Vicente, 4 acts; Triste Viuvinha, 3 acts; Rosas de toda o anno, 1 act; many operettas and mus. farces; a ballet, Zeffiretto (Lisbon, 1869); a symph. ode, Camões e os Luziadas (Milan, 1881); numerous smaller works.—E.-H.

MACKENZIE, Sir Alexander Campbell. Scottish compr. b. Edinburgh, 22 Aug. 1847. Came of a mus. family; his forbears for several generations having been professional musicians. His great-grandfather is known to have belonged to the Forfarshire military band, his grandfather was a violinist in Aberdeen and Edinburgh and his father was a popular Edinburgh musician, leader of the orch. of the Theatre Royal, Edinburgh, and a successful song-writer. Alexander

Campbell's early education was received at Hunter's School, and he learnt the vn. as soon as he was big enough to hold the instrument. By the advice of a musical friend, a cellist named Günther Bartel, the boy was sent, at the age of 10, to the care of Bartel's parents in Germany. M. sen. took his son to Schwarzburg-Sondershausen, a town near Weimar, and returned to Edinburgh, dying soon afterwards at the early age of 38. The young Alexander remained in Sondershausen about 5 years, learning vn. from K. W. Ulrich and harmony from Ed. Stein. In his 4th year of stay he was allowed to play 2nd vn. in the Ducal orch., thus forming a valuable acquaintanceship with the works of Wagner, Liszt and Berlioz. In 1862, ambition drove him to London with the view of obtaining instruction from his father's old teacher, Prosper Sainton. This worthy, upon seeing the lad's attempts at compn. recommended him to enter for one of the King's scholarships at the R.A.M. This he won and thus his mus. education was assured at the capable hands of Sainton, Charles Lucas and F. B. Jewson, these last two teaching him harmony and pf. respectively. Like most of his fellow-students he helped to maintain himself by occasional engagements in theatre bands, a rough but very valuable experience. In 1865, at the age of 18, he was considered sufficiently equipped and returned to his native city with the view of following in his father's footsteps. Then ensued 14 years of arduous professional work, including solo-playing, the giving of chamber concerts, pf. teaching at schools and conducting choirs—the routine labour of the British compr.—during which he yet found time to comp. songs and pf. pieces, besides 2 Scottish Rhapsodies for orch., works of marked originality. The first compn. to bring him fame was the pf. 4tet, op. 11, which he publ. in Germany at his own expense. The orch. pieces were introduced to the public by the ever generous August Manns, who did so much for British art. In 1879, Mackenzie, finding himself in a position to resign the uncongenial drudgery of his profession, retreated to Florence, where he lived for some years in peace, devoting himself to compn. Here his earliest and freshest works of importance were written, the cantata The Bride (Worcester Fest. 1881), Jason (Bristol Fest. 1882), and the opera Colomba, libretto by Franz Hueffer (Drury Lane, Carl Rosa Co. 1883), the latter placing its compr. in the forefront of British comprs. Thenceforward not a year has passed without a considerable work from this prolific and tireless pen. A beautiful and rarely-heard work is the orch. ballad, La Belle Dame sans Merci; another is The Dream of Jubal. By 1888 his position was such that, on the Principalship of the R.A.M. becoming vacant. through the death of Sir George Macfarren, he was appointed to the post, and then only was the strength of his personality revealed to the world. Under his able control, the inst. progressed by leaps and bounds. Still the composer never faltered or slackened in his output; the

same untiring hand that conducted the orch. and choral classes of the Acad. directed the Novello Choir and the R. Choral Soc., the R. Philh. (1892–99) and other important bodies; the pen, busy with The Pibroch (1889), the Britannia overture and the Scottish concerto (1897) found time to write numerous lectures and monographs on mus. subjects, and all this has gone on with scarcely any intermission for 35 years. In 1903 M. undertook a concert-tour in Canada, giving orch. concerts of British music in all the important towns of the Dominion, sometimes two in one day. In 1911 he saw the result of his able direction of the R.A.M. culminate in the rebuilding of that inst. on an imposing scale at York Gate. In the spring of 1924 he retired from the Principalship, and was succeeded by J. B. McEwen (q.v.).

Principal honours and decorations: 1862, King's Scholar, R.A.M.; 1884, Gold Medal for Art and Science, Hesse Darmstadt; 1886, Mus.Doc. h.c. St. Andrews; 1890, Mus.Doc. h.c. Edinburgh; 1893, member of Order of Art and Science, Saxe-Coburg and Gotha; 1893, Pencerdd Alban (Welsh Bard); 1893–7, President, R. Coll. of Orgts.; 1895, Knight Bachelor of Great Britain; 1898, member of R. Swedish Acad.; 1901, D.C.L. Glasgow; 1903, D.C.L. McGill Univ.; 1903, Mus.Doc. Toronto Univ.; 1904, LL.D. Leeds; 1908–12, Gen. President, International Mus. Soc. (including Congresses, Vienna, 1909, London, 1911); 1913, hon. member, Accademia di Santa Cecilia, Rome; 1914–16, President, R. Coll. of Orgts.; 1922, K.C.V.O.

Publ. compns. (chiefly Novello; J. Williams; Augener; Ricordi; Bosworth): op. 1–7, songs and pf. pieces; op. 8, 7 part-songs; op. 9, Rustic Scenes, pf.; op. 10, Larghetto and Allegretto, cello; op. 11, 4tet, pf. and str. E flat (Classical Chamber Concerts, Edinburgh, 1878) (Kahnt, Leipzig); op. 12, songs; op. 13, 5 pf. pieces (Novello); op. 14, 3 songs by H. Heine (Kahnt, Leipzig); op. 15, 3 morceaux, pf. (Novello); op. 16, 3 songs; op. 17, 3 songs by Christina Rossetti; op. 18, 3 songs; op. 19, 3 anthems; op. 20, 6 pf. pieces; op. 21, Scottish Rhapsody No. 1, orch. (Glasgow, under Manns, Jan. 1880); op. 22, 3 vocal trios; op. 23, In the Scottish Highlands, pf.; op. 24, Burns, Scottish Rhapsody No. 2 (Glasgow, under Manns, 1881); op. 25, cantata, The Bride, transl. from Ger. of R. Hamerling (Worcester Fest. 1881); op. 26, cantata, Jason (Bristol Fest. 1882); op. 27, 3 organ pieces; op. 28, opera, Colomba (Drury Lane, Carl Rosa Co. 1883); op. 29, orch. ballad, La Belle Dame sans Merci (Philh. 1883); op. 30, oratorio, The Rose of Sharon (Norwich Fest. 1884); op. 31, 5 songs; op. 32, vn. concerto (Birmingham Fest. 1885, by Sarasate); op. 33, opera, The Troubadour (Drury Lane, Carl Rosa Co. 8 June, 1886); op. 34, cantata, The Story of Sayid (Leeds Fest. 1886); op. 35, 3 songs of Shakespeare; op. 36, Jubilee Ode (Crystal Palace, 1887); op. 37, 6 pieces, vn. (including Benedictus) (Monday Pop. Concerts, 1888, by Lady Hallé); op. 38, ode, The New Covenant (Glasgow Exhib. 1888); op. 39, The Cottar's Saturday Night, chorus and orch.; op. 40, overture, Twelfth Night (Richter Concerts, 1888); op. 41, cantata, The Dream of Jubal (Liverpool Philh. 1889); op. 42, suite for vn. Pibroch (Leeds Fest., by Sarasate, 1889); op. 43, prelude, entr'actes and songs for Marmion (Glasgow, 1889; songs only publ.); op. 44, Spring Songs; op. 45, music to Ravenswood (Lyceum Theatre. 1890); op. 46, Veni Creator, chorus, soli and orch, (Birmingham Fest. 1891); op. 47a, Highland Ballad. vn. and orch. (Westminster Orch. Soc. 1893); op. 47b, Barcarolle and Villanelle, vn.; op. 48, 2 choral odes (from Buchanan's Bride of Love) (1893); op. 49, oratorio, Bethlehem (R. Choral Soc. 1894); op. 50, 3 Shakespeare sonnets; op. 51, Phœbe, comic opera (B. C. Stephenson) (not perf.); op. 52, overture, Britannia (R.A.M. commemoration concert, 17 May, 1894); op. 53, From the North, 9 pieces, vn. and pf.; op. 54, 3 songs; op. 55, Scottish Concerto, pf. and orch. (Philh. 1897, by Paderewski); op. 56, comic opera, His Majesty (F. C. Burnand and R. C. Lehmann) (Savoy, 20 Feb. 1897); op. 57, overture, entr'actes and incidental music The Little Minister (Haymarket

Theatre, 6 Nov. 1897); op. 58, 3 preludes and vocal music to *Manfred* (for Lyceum Theatre, but not produced; Nos. 2 and 3, *Pastoral* and *Flight of Spirits*, London Mus. Fest. 1889; No. 1, *Astarte*, perf. at Arthur Newstead's concert, 12 Dec. 1904); op. 59, 5 recitations with pf. acc. (J. Williams); op. 60, 6 *Rustic Songs*; op. 61, incidental music, *Coriolanus* (Lyceum, 15 April, 1901); op. 62, opera, *The Cricket on the Hearth*, 3 acts (overture at Philh., 2 July, 1902; opera, R.A.M. 6 June, 1914); op. 63, *Coronation March* (Westminster Abbey, 26 June, 1902); op. 64, orch. suite, *London Day by Day* (Norwich Fest. 1902); op. 65, operetta, *The Knights of the Road* (Palace Theatre, 27 Feb. 1905); op. 66, cantata, *The Witch's Daughter* (Leeds Fest. 1904); op. 67, *Canadian Rhapsody*, orch. (Philh. 1905); op. 68, Suite, vn. and orch. (L.S.O. 18 Feb. 1897, by Mischa Elman); op. 69, cantata, *The Sun-God's Return* (Cardiff Fest. 1910; Vienna.Singakademie, 1911); op. 70, Fantasia, pf.; op. 71, 4 part-songs; op. 72, *La Savannah, air de ballet*, orch.; op. 73, 3 trios, female vs.; op. 74, *Tam o' Shanter, Scottish Rhapsody* No. 3 (International Mus. Congress, London, 30 May, 1911); op. 75, *An English Joy-Peal*, orch. (Coronation, Westminster Abbey, 22 June, 1911); op. 76, *Invocation*, orch. (Philh. 21 March, 1912); op. 77, *Perfection*, part-song; op. 78, *The Walker of the Snow*, song for barit.; op. 79, songs by Tennyson; op. 80, dance-measures, vn.; op. 81, *English Air* with variations, pf.; op. 82, *Ancient Scots Tunes*, str. orch.; op. 83, *Odds and Ends*, pf.; op. 84, *Jottings*, pf.; op. 85, 3 school part-songs; op. 86, 6 easy impromptus, vn.; op. 87, 1-act opera, *St. John's Eve* (Ascherberg; B.N.O.C. Liverpool, early in 1924); op. 88, *Varying Moods*, pf. (J. Williams); op. 89, *Distant Chimes*, vn. and pf. (Novello, 1921); op. 90, *Youth, Sport, Loyalty*, orch. overture (J. Williams), for R.A.M. centenary, 1922.

At the Royal Institution, the R.A.M., and other places, he has delivered lectures on following subjects; the figures showing the number of lectures, where a series: *The Overture : Progress of Instrumentation* (4); *The Historical Elements of Music* (4); *Hänsel and Gretel*; *Verdi's Falstaff* (transl. into Ital.) (3); *A National School of Music*; *The Bohemian School of Music* (3); *Russian Music*; *Franz Liszt* (3); *Tchaikovsky*; *Brahms*; *Arthur Sullivan* (3); *Mendelssohn* (also in Ger.) (2); *Chamber-Music* (3); *The Latest Phases of Music* (3); *Form, or the Want of it* (2); *The Beginnings of the Orchestra*; *A Revival of Chamber-Music* (2); *War-Music, Past and Present* (3); *Hubert Hastings Parry, his Work and Place among British Composers* (Royal Institution); *Beethoven* (2) (Royal Institution). There have also been 2 monographs on *Liszt* and *Verdi* (Jack's *Masterpieces of Music*), and many contributions to the Press.—F. C.

MACLEAN, Alick (Alexander Morvaren). Eng. compr. and condr. *b.* Eton, 20 July, 1872. Son of Charles Donald Maclean. Educated at Eton, destined for army; comp. 3-act comic opera *Crichton* at age of 20; and 3-act opera *Quentin Durward* at 21; in 1912, mus. dir. Spa Co. at Scarborough; 1915–23, condr. Queen's Hall Light Orch. which played at the Chappell Ballad Concerts; dir. and condr. Scarborough Mus. Fest. 1920.

Operas: *Petruccio* (Moody-Manners Prize), produced June 1895, at Covent Garden (Wilcocks); *Die Liebesgeige* (produced Easter Sunday, 1906, Mayence); *Maître Seiler* (produced 20 Aug. 1909, Lyric Theatre, London, Moody-Manners Co.); *Die Waldidylle* (Ger. version; produced April 1913, Mayence); *Quentin Durward* (produced 13 Jan. 1920, Theatre Royal, Newcastle-on-Tyne, Carl Rosa Opera Co.); *The Hunchback of Cremona* (awaiting production). Choral: *The Annunciation* (produced 15 Feb. 1909, at Richter Concert, Sheffield Choral Union) (Novello); *Choral Song* (poem by Louis N. Parker); *Lament* (Alfred Hyatt, from Saadi); *At the Eastern Gate* (produced by Sheffield Choral Union under Coward, at Sheffield, March 1923; publ. by Ascherberg); incidental music to *The Jest* (Louis N. Parker); to *The Mayflower* (Prelude was produced at Harrogate Symphony Concerts under Howard Carr, 1923); to *Cyrano de Bergerac* (Sir Charles Wyndham's production); songs; choruses; orch. suites, etc.—E.-H.

MACLEAN, Charles Donald. Eng. compr. and

orgt. *b.* Cambridge, 27 March, 1843; *d.* London, 23 June, 1916. Orgt. Exeter Coll. Oxford; stud. at Cologne under Hiller; Mus.Doc. Oxon. 1865; music dir. at Eton Coll. 1871–5; concert-orgt. in London; 22 years' residence in India as a civil servant; from 1893 in London. From 1899, Eng. ed. of *I.M.G.*; from 1908, gen. secretary of that soc.; in 1912, ed. their polyglot "Report Volume"; in 1914, wrote *History of Modern Eng. Music* for Paris *Encyclopédie de la Musique* (Delagrave, not publ. till 1921), a summary which is by no means satisfactory.

Pageant march, orch.; pf. concerto in F; symph. poems: *Laodameia*; *Songs of Selma*; *Penthesilea*; *Iona*; character-piece from Bavaria; oratorio, *Noah*; Gaelic cantata, *Salmalla*; trio, pf. vn. cello, in B, etc.—E.-H.

MACMILLAN, Ernest. Canadian orgt. compr. *b.* Mimico, Ontario, Canada, 18 Aug. 1893. Began his mus. studies in Toronto, but afterwards went to Edinburgh to study organ under Alfred Hollins and theory under Prof. Niecks. His 1st appointment was orgt. of Knox Ch. Toronto. In 1911, F.R.C.O. and Mus.Bac. Oxon.; 1911–14, student at Univ. Toronto. In 1914, he left for a course of study in Europe, but, being at Bayreuth when war broke out, was interned, first at Nuremberg and afterwards at Ruhleben. Whilst in Ruhleben, he wrote setting of Swinburne's *England* which was approved by the Univ. of Oxford for degree of Mus.Doc. Returned to Canada (1919) and became orgt. of Eaton Memorial Ch. In 1920, appointed member of advisory board of Canadian Acad. of Music. His ode *England* was perf. by Toronto Mendelssohn Choir in 1920. His other compns., already numerous, are not yet published.—L. S.

MACPHERSON, Charles. Organist of St. Paul's Cathedral, London; Scottish composer; *b.* Edinburgh, 10 May, 1870. Early education mostly at St. Paul's Choir School (1879–87); the mus. side being under late Sir George C. Martin. For latter half of 1887, trained boys at St. Clement's, Eastcheap, and stud. cpt. under Dr. C. W. Pearce, then orgt. of church; stud. organ under Sir George Martin. Became orgt. at St. David's, Weem, Aberfeldy, Perthshire, end of 1887 till beginning of 1889; orgt. at private chapel of Luton Hoo, Beds (the late Mme. de Falbe); student at R.A.M. 1890–5, Charles Lucas Medal for compn. 1893; sub-orgt. St. Paul's Cath. 1895; orgt. in 1916. Mus.Doc. Dunelm. *h.c.*; cond. London Church Choirs Association from 1913.

Orch. overture, *Cridhe an Ghaidhil* (ms.); *Highland Suite*, orch. (ms.); 6tet for wind instrs. (ms.); Suite, military band (ms); *Hallowe'en*, orch. (Novello); pf. 4tet, E flat (ms); Prelude and fugue, A flat, organ (J. Williams); 144 accs. to Scots songs (Pentland, Edinburgh, 8 books publ:); *By the Waters of Babylon*, chorus, organ and orch.; *Thanksgiving Te Deum* for signing of Peace 1918, chorus, orch. organ; church music, organ pieces and arrs., part-songs, etc. (Novello). Book, *Short History of Harmony* (Kegan Paul, 1917).—E.-H.

MACPHERSON, Stewart. British mus. educationist, compr. *b.* Liverpool, 29 March, 1865. Entered R.A.M. London as Sterndale Bennett scholar in 1880; stud. compn. under Sir G. A. Macfarren, pf. under Walter Macfarren, vn.

under W. Frye Parker. During his studentship, cond. the newly-formed Westminster Orch. Soc. (until 1902). Ultimately became prof. of harmony and compn. in R.A.M., an appointment he still holds. Was created Associate of the Acad. in 1887 and Fellow in 1892. Is an examiner for the Associated Board of the R.A.M. and R.C.M., in which capacity he has visited Canada, Australia, New Zealand and S. Africa. Prof. of compn. at R. Normal Coll. for Blind 1903–20; member of board of musical studies in Univ. of London. Was instrumental in founding (1908) Music Teachers' Association, the first body of its kind to insist (i) upon the fact that aural training must be the basis of all mus. education worthy of the name, (ii) the need for definite *training in teaching* for those who intend to follow the teacher's career. Has been a pioneer in this country of the " Appreciation" movement in mus. education, and has devoted much of his time to its propagation, by means of lecturing and writing. His book *Music and its Appreciation* was the first work on the subject to be issued in England.

Ballade, orch. (Novello); *Notturno*, orch. (Williams); Mass in D, s. solo, chorus and orch. (*id.*); *Romance*, ob. and pf. (Rudall, Carte); *Suite de Valses*, pf. (Ashdown); part-songs, services, etc. (Novello; Williams); 6 Scotch songs and 6 Iroquois songs (Williams); songs (Boosey; Weekes), etc. Books: *Practical Harmony* (transl. into Ger.); *Appendix* to same: *Rudiments of Music*; *Practical Counterpoint*; *Form in Music* (1908); *Music and its Appreciation* (1910); *Aural Culture based upon Musical Appreciation* (with Ernest Read) Part I (1912), Part II (1914), Part III, (1918); *Studies in Phrasing and Form* (1911); *Musical Education of the Child* (1915); *Melody and Harmony* (1920); *The Appreciation Class* (1923), etc. (all publ. by Williams). Has ed. (J. Williams) a complete Analytical Ed. of Beethoven's pf. sonatas; is ed. of an important series of educational handbooks on music (*id.*).—E.-H.

MACRAN, Henry Stewart. Irish writer on music. Educated at Wesley Coll., Trinity Coll. Dublin, and Balliol Coll. Oxford; Fellow of Trinity Coll. in 1892. In 1901, prof. of moral philosophy; has done research work on Greek music (see his art. on Greek music in Grove's Dictionary). In 1902, publ. a critical ed. of *The Harmonics of Aristoxenus* in which he develops his theories on Greek music.—W. ST.

McALPIN, Colin. Brit. compr. and author; *b.* Leicester, 9 April, 1870. Stud. R.A.M. London; and privately under Sir George Henschel, Sir F. Bridge and Prof. Prout; gained prize for best British opera 1903 with *The Cross and the Crescent* (Covent Garden, London, and provinces). Wrote a remarkable study in comparative æsthetics, *Hermaia* (J. M. Dent).

Operas: *The Cross and the Crescent*; *King Arthur* (Leicester, 1896); *The Vow* (Nottingham, 1916); other operas not yet produced; cantata, *The Prince of Peace* (Cary); songs (*id.*); arts. in journals.—E.-H.

McCORMACK, John. Irish t. singer; *b.* Athlone, 1884. Won gold medal for t. solo at Feis Ceoil (Irish Music Fest.), 1903; member of Dublin Catholic Pro-Cath. (under direction of Vincent O'Brien); toured in America with this choir in 1904; went to Milan and stud. under Sabbatini. In 1907, sang at Ballad Concerts in London and made his *début* in opera as Turiddu in *Cavalleria Rusticana*. Appeared with great success in sub-

sequent seasons at Covent Garden, especially with Tetrazzini; also sang in oratorio in London and provinces. After singing at San Carlo, Naples, went to America where his success was immediate. Went on a world-tour, taking with him Vincent O'Brien as acc. His voice is not unusually big, but is of a very beautiful quality. His singing of Irish folk-songs has made him famous all over the world.—W. SR.

McEWEN, John Blackwood. Scots compr. *b.* Hawick, Roxburghshire, 13 April, 1868. M.A. Glasgow Univ.; stud. music at R.C.M. London; prof. of harmony and compn. R.A.M. London, 1898–1924; appointed Principal on Sir Alexander Mackenzie's retirement, 1924. His compns. are of the Neo-Romantic order, very soundly constructed, and Scottish characteristics are at times strongly marked. His chamber-music has great value. His *Solway* symphony was given at the R. Philh. Soc. concert, 22 Feb. 1923.

Orch.: Symphonies: I, C mi.; II, F mi.; III, F sharp mi.; IV, A mi ; V, C sharp mi. (*Solway*); 2 overtures, *Comedy*, *Tragedy* (Anglo-Fr. Co); Concert-overture, E mi.: 3 Border Ballads (*Coronach*, *Demon-Lover*, *Grey Galloway*) (Anglo-Fr.); *Comala*, symph. poem; Suites: 1 in F; II in E, small orch.; vla. concerto; 3 Highland Dances, str. orch.

Chamber-music: Phantasie-5tet, E mi. str.; str. 4tets: No. I in G; II, C mi.; III, G mi.; IV, A; V, F mi.; VI, F; VII, E flat; VIII, A mi. (Novello); IX, 2 studies; X, E mi. (Ricordi); XI, C mi. (Hawkes); XII, *Nugæ*, bagatelles (Hawkes); XIII, in A, *Biscay* (Anglo-Fr. Co.); XIV, E flat, *Threnody* (*id.*). Sonatas, vn. and pf.: I, E flat; II, F mi. (Anglo-Fr. Co.); III, G; IV, A (Anglo-Fr. Co); 6 Highland Dances (Novello).

Cantatas: *Hymn on the Morning of Christ's Nativity* (Milton); scene from *Hellas* (Shelley), s. solo, female chorus, orch.; *The Victim* (Tennyson); *The Last Chantey* (Kipling); *Psalm XXIV*, chorus, organ, pf.; *Psalm CXXX*, chorus and organ; incidental music for Empire Pageant (3 scenes), chorus and military band (Crystal Palace, 1910).

Pf.: Sonata in E mi. (Novello); 4 sketches (Ricordi); *Vignettes from La Côte d'Argent* (Anglo-Fr. Co.); sonatina (*id.*); 3 preludes (*id.*); comic opera, *The Royal Rebel*; melodrama, *The Gamekeeper*: acc. for *Grath my Mree* (str. 4tet, pf., drums); music for Romney's *Remorse*; songs (Avison Ed.; Ricordi; Chappell; J. Williams; Anglo-Fr. Co.).

Books: *Text-Book of Harmony and Counterpoint* (Ricordi); *Elements of Music* (*id.*); *Primer of Harmony* (*id.*); *Exercises on Phrasing in Piano-playing* (*id.*); *The Thought in Music*: an inquiry into the principles of musical rhythm, phrasing and expression (Macmillan); *Principles of Phrasing and Articulation in Music* (Augener).—E.-H.

McGUCKIN, Barton. Irish t. singer; *b.* Dublin, 28 July, 1852; *d.* 17 April, 1913. Choir-boy in Armagh Cath. Received instruction there in singing, organ, vn. and pf.; 1st t. at St. Patrick's Cath. Dublin, 1871; pupil of Sir Joseph Robinson. Made *début* at Crystal Palace Concerts, 1875; stud. at Milan under Trevulsi; first appeared in opera under Carl Rosa, Birmingham, 1880; remained in Rosa's company in London and provinces until 1887, and achieved great success both for his brilliant singing and acting. Sang opera in America 1887–8, and returned to Carl Rosa Co. 1889, remaining until 1896. Chief parts: Lohengrin, Faust, Don José, Des Grieux (*Manon*), Eleazer (*La Juive*); also well known as oratorio and concert-singer; sang at Philh., Monday Popular, and Handel and provincial fests. In 1905, dir. of an amateur operatic soc. in Dublin; condr. of orch. concerts at Irish Exhibition, 1908.—W. ST.

McLEOD, Robert. Scottish teacher, musical organiser and compr. *b.* Glasgow, 20 June, 1879. Completed full qualifying course as an ordinary teacher under the Scottish Education Department, before he commenced giving instruction in music. He stud. the theory of music privately; later, organ under Dr. Peace. In 1903, decided to devote his whole time to music, and soon began to give evidence of possessing a high degree of originality in his methods. He was one of the joint-discoverers of the value of teaching mus. appreciation, and a pioneer of its use in Scotland, as a special course; 1907, Mus.Bac. Univ. of Durham; the same year was promoted by Edinburgh School Board from teacher of singing in 4 schools to post of superintendent and organiser of mus. instruction in large schools; in 1912, became dir. of music, with 4 assistants. Is now dir. of mus. studies for teachers, under National Committee for the Training of Teachers. He is a most stimulating lecturer and adjudicator. Is a Fellow of the Tonic Solfa College.

Pictures in Song (2 vols.); numerous songs and part-songs (Novello; Curwen; Stainer & Bell; West & Co.; Ascherberg; Bayley & Fergusson); many arts. in educational and mus. journals.—W. S.

McNAUGHT, William Gray. Eng. writer on music; *b.* Mile End, London, E. 30 March, 1849; *d.* London, 13 Oct. 1918. Stud. R.A.M 1872–6; Mus.Doc. Cantuar.; assistant-inspector in music to Board of Education, 1883–1901; ed. Novello's *School Music Review;* mus. dir. Bow and Bromley Inst. 1876–1900; well-known adjudicator at choral competitions; ed. of *Musical Times* (Novello) 1910–18.—E.-H.

MADEIRA, Joaquim d'Azevedo. Portuguese pianist and teacher; *b.* Lisbon, 1851; *d.* 1891. His chief pupil is José Vianna da Motta.—E.-H.

MADETOJA, Leevi. Finnish compr. *b.* Oulu (Uleåborg), 17 Feb. 1887. Stud. at Helsingfors Univ. (Ph.M. 1910) and at Music Inst. under Järnefelt and Sibelius; later in Paris (d'Indy) and Vienna (Fuchs). 1912–14, 2nd condr. Philh. Orch. Helsingfors; 1914–16, condr. of orch. Viipuri (Viborg); since 1916, teacher of compn. and later also member of directorate at Helsingfors Music Inst. M. is one of most gifted of younger Finnish comprs., having remarkable feeling for orch. and vocal compn. and pronounced individuality as a symphony writer.

2 symphonies (1915 and 1918); symph. poems: *Kullervo; Dance Visions;* overtures; cantatas; *Sammon ryösto (Conquest of Sampo),* male chorus and orch.; *Stabat Mater,* female chorus, str. orch. and organ; *Väinämöisen kylvö (Väinämöinen sows),* solo v. and orch.; choral songs for male chorus; for mixed chorus; songs; pf. trio; *Lyric Suite,* cello solo; sonatina, vn. and pf.; pf. pieces; pieces, vn. and pf.—T. H.

MAESTRO-AL-PIANO (Ital.). The pianist retained by an opera company to rehearse with the solo singers at the piano.—E.-H.

MAGELSSEN, Ida Basilier. Finnish-Norwegian s. singer; *b.* Uleåborg, Finland, 10 Sept. 1846. Stud. at Paris Cons. 1867–70; under Mme. Nissen-Saloman in Petrograd, 1871. *Début* in Stockholm Opera House, 1871. Concert-tours throughout Europe, especially in Finland; has sung in many opera houses, chiefly in North Europe (Rosina, Philine, Lucia, etc.). Attached to Christiania Theatre, 1875–7. Married in 1878 in Christiania, where she is still active as a teacher of singing.—U. M.

MAGNANI, Aurelio. Clarinettist and compr. *b.* Longiano (Romagna), 26 Feb. 1856; *d.* Rome, 25 Jan. 1921. Gained diploma for clar. and compn. at Liceo Mus. at Bologna. After having for some years taught clar. at Liceo Mus. Benedetto Marcello, Venice, in 1888 he occupied a similar position at R. Liceo Mus. di Santa Cecilia, Rome, where he remained until his death. All the best living Ital. clarinettists have come from his school. He played in chief European and Amer. orchs.; also as soloist in Court Quintet of Queen Margherita. As compr., besides numerous pieces for his own instr., he has left several orch. works. His 2 operas are not yet published.—D. A.

MAGNARD, Albéric. French compr. *b.* Paris, 9 June, 1865; killed at Baron (Oise), 3 Sept. 1914. Stud. for a time at Paris Cons.; later, privately with Vincent d'Indy. From the outset of his career, he concentrated upon his work, courting neither success nor even publicity. He was never known to more than a small fraction of the mus. public in France and Belgium. In other countries he remains practically unknown. His mus. ideals were lofty and uncompromising. In instr. music he devoted his utmost attention to forms, aiming at achieving new forms without infringing any of the traditional principles in which he steadfastly believed. He attempted to introduce into dramatic music something of the logic and restraint inherent in the principles of the symphony. In either order, his style and aims reveal a spirit of impassioned austerity and of unflagging earnestness. And it is likely that in proportion as his works become better known, the number of his admirers will increase.

4 symphonies (op. 4, 1890; op. 6, 1893; op. 11, 1896; op. 21, 1913); orch. pieces: *Chant Funèbre,* op. 9; *Hymne à la Justice,* op. 14; *Hymne à Vénus,* op. 17; dramatic scores: *Yolande,* op. 5 (1891); *Guercœur,* op. 12 (1900); *Bérénice,* op. 19 (1909); 5tet, wood-wind and pf. op. 8 (1894); vn. sonata, op. 13 (1901); str. 4tet, op. 16 (1903); pf. trio, op. 18 (1905); cello sonata, op. 20 (1910); songs, op. 3 and 15. (Publ. Rouart & Lerolle.) Consult Gaston Carraud, *La Vie, l'Œuvre et la Mort d'Albéric Magnard* (Paris, 1921, Lerolle), a review of which, with additional remarks, appeared in *Mus. Times,* London, Oct. 1921.—M. D. C.

MAGNETTE, Paul. Belgian writer on music; *b.* Liège, 16 Jan. 1888; *d.* Paris, Oct. 1918. Stud. in native town and in Leipzig under Hugo Riemann; was expelled from Univ. of Leipzig for Germanophobia in 1912; in 1913, prof. of history and mus. æsthetics at Acad. of Music, Liège; was deported to Germany during the war (1914–18) but escaped and died in France, during a lecture tour. He left a number of small works of minor importance:

Les Grandes Étapes dans l'œuvre de H. Berlioz: I. La Symphonie fantastique (1908); *Contribution à l'histoire de la symphonie post-beethovénienne* (1909); *A. Bruckner* (1910); *Glazunof* (1911); *Litolff* (1914). He has publ. also a Fr. transl. of autobiography of Dittersdorf (1910) and a curtailed and annotated edn. of Grétry's *Mémoires ou essais sur la musique* (1915). Contrib. to *Guide Musical, Courrier, S.I.M., Die Musik, Rivista Musicale Italiana,* etc.—C. V. B.

MAGRI, Pietro. Ital. priest and compr. *b.* Vigarano Mainarda (Ferrara), 1873. Known by his 2 oratorios, *La Regina dei Pirenei* and *La Regina delle Alpi*, which have been perf. successfully. Author of church music. Was choirmaster first at Venice, then at Bari, Lecce, Molfetta and Vercelli. Since 1919 chief orgt. at Basilica del Santuario, Oropa.—D. A.

MAGRINI, Giuseppe. Ital. cellist; *b.* Milan, 6 Sept. 1857. Since 1880, prof. of cello at R. Cons. Giuseppe Verdi, Milan. For 25 years, 1st cellist at La Scala. A very skilful concert-artist; compr. of several works for his own instrument.—D. A.

MAHILLON, Victor Charles. Belgian musicologist; *b.* Brussels, 10 March, 1841; *d.* St.-Jean Cap Ferrat (France), 17 June, 1924. Director of Mahillon and Co., mus. instr. makers, a firm founded by his father. Chief curator of Museum of Brussels Cons., which he initiated in 1877. The Cons. Museum coll. is the most remarkable of its kind, not only on account of the number of the exhibits (over 3,500 at end of 1922), but also by their judicious selection. There is a complete coll. of old models of every type of instr., showing evolution from the remotest prototype. Space is also given to exotic instrs., especially of primitive races. This coll. has been brought together as the result of gifts and of very advantageous purchases. M. also rendered the greatest service to musicology by publ. the *Catalogue descriptif et analytique du Musée*. This work, a truly scientific achievement, is marked by its objective and positive character. The author is not satisfied with book-learning, but analyses the instr. itself. By this process he has modified this branch of musicology and has founded the objective science of mus. instrs. The documentary side is less extensive, but is characterised by severity and exactness.

Elements of Musical Acoustics (Brussels, 1874); *Catalogue descriptif et analytique de Musée du Conservatoire Royal de Musique de Bruxelles*, Vols. I–V (Ghent and Brussels, 1880–1922); *Étude sur le doigté de la flûte Boehm* (Brussels, 1882; transl. into Eng.); *Amsterdam Exhibition*, 1883, *Mus. Instrs. Class, Report* (Brussels, 1883); *Le Matériel sonore des orchestres de symphonie, d'harmonie et de fanfare* (Brussels, 1897); *Études expérimentales sur la résonance des colonnes d'air* (extract from Vol. III of above catalogue, Ghent, 1900; transl. into Eng.); *Quelques expériences sur la vibration des tuyaux à bouche, à anche et à embouchure* (Brussels, 1910); *Notes théoriques et pratiques sur la résonance des colonnes d'air* (Beaulieu, 1921); *Les Instruments de musique du Musée du Conservatoire Royal de musique de Bruxelles: I. Le Trombone; II. Le Cor; III. La Trompette* (Brussels, n.d.); *Guide pour l'accord des instruments à pistons (id.)*.—E. C.

MAHLER, Alma Maria (*née* Schindler). Austrian compr.-author. Daughter of the painter Emil Jakob Schindler. Stud. compn. under J. Labor; married Gustav Mahler in 1902. Five songs (Vienna, Univ. Ed.) witness to the strong nature of her art. She is preparing an ed. of Gustav Mahler's Letters.—P. St.

MAHLER, Gustav. Austrian composer and conductor; *b.* Kalischt, 7 July, 1860; *d.* Vienna, 18 May, 1911. A few months after his birth (in Dec. 1860) the family removed to Iglau, where he received his first music lessons at the age of six. In 1875 he came to Vienna Conservatoire (piano under T. Epstein; harmony under R. Fuchs; composition under Th. Krenn). Having carried off the Conservatoire prize in 1873, he attended the University for philosophy, general and musical history for 2 years. The works of this period (quintet for strings and piano; violin sonata; opera *Ernst von Schwaben*) were destroyed later on by the composer. He came into close contact with Anton Bruckner, who influenced his style more than any other composer. Mahler made an excellent piano arrangement of Bruckner's 3rd symphony. In the summer of 1880, he took his first engagement as conductor at Hall and finished his first work *Das Klagende Lied*, for soli, chorus and orchestra (revised 1898, published 1899). The orchestral score was rewritten after 1900. The poem of this cantata was written by Mahler in 1878. The first part is not published; the ms. is in possession of Mahler's sister, Justine, who married Arnold Rosé. This work shows already a fully developed style and technique. It marks the beginning of his first period, literary tendencies influenced by romantic poems, especially by the *Lieder aus des Knaben Wunderhorn*. This period ends 1900 with the composition of the 4th symphony.

During the winter season 1881–2 Mahler conducted at Laibach. An opera *The Argonauts* (written and composed 1880) was unfinished and finally destroyed, also a fairy-tale *Rübezahl* (1882) and a *Northern Symphony*. 1882–3, conducted at Olmütz Theatre, then chorus-master of an Italian season at Vienna. 1883 he composed his first volume of songs (published 1885). In the summer went to Bayreuth to hear *Parsifal* and went for the season 1883–4 to the Cassel opera. In Dec. 1883, composed *Lieder eines fahrenden Gesellen* and began his 1st symphony. In 1885 he was 2nd conductor at German Theatre, Prague, and in summer of 1886 was with Nikisch at Leipzig Opera. He adapted and completed Weber's opera-fragment *The Three Pintos* (1st performance, Leipzig, 1888). In 1888 was director of Royal Opera in Budapest and finished his 1st symphony (1st performance Budapest, 1889; published 1898). Began composition of songs from *Des Knaben Wunderhorn*. In 1891 he was 1st conductor, Hamburg Opera. In summer 1892, conductor of German opera performances at Drury Lane, London. He finished 2nd symphony in 1894 (1st performance Berlin, 1895; published 1896). In 1896 finished 3rd symphony (1st performance of the 3rd movement 1896, Berlin; publ. 1898; 1st complete performance 1902). 1897, director of Vienna Opera; began a great reformation of the repertoire; new *mise-en-scène* of operas of Gluck, Mozart, Wagner. This was the greatest period of the Vienna Opera House. 1899–1900, composed 4th symphony (1st performance Munich, 1902; published 1900).

The second period began in 1900 with songs of Rückert, *Kindertotenlieder* (all songs with chamber-orchestra), 1900–1902. *Five Songs,*

1901–2 (publication and 1st performance 1905);
1902, 5th symphony finished (1st performance
Cologne, 1904; published 1905). Whereas these
2nd, 3rd and 4th symphonies have solo or chorus
in the last movement, the symphonies of second
period (except 8th symphony) are entirely
instrumental. In 1904 he married Alma Maria
Schindler. 1903–4, composed 6th symphony
(published 1905, 1st performance Essen, 1906);
1904–6, 7th symphony (published 1908; 1st
performance Prague, 1908). 1906–7, 8th symphony, in 2 parts (with soli and double chorus);
1st part, Hymn *Veni, Creator Spiritus* as a
sonata first movement with double fugue; 2nd
part, the last scenes of Part II of *Faust* in form
of an *Adagio*, *Scherzo* and *Finale* (published 1908;
1st performance Munich, 12 Sept. 1908, as
Symphony of the Thousand).

After a period of 10 years' work he left his
post as director of Vienna Opera in 1907 and
went to America where he conducted (in New
York) operas of Mozart and Wagner, and many
concerts. During summer 1908 he finished *Lied
von der Erde* (1st performance Munich, 1911,
under Bruno Walter. This work is for alto and
tenor voice with orchestra, after Chinese poems.
It marks the beginning of a third period. 1908–
1919, concerts in America; composition of 9th
symphony (published 1912, 1st performance
Vienna 1912, under Bruno Walter). 1909–10,
sketches of 10th symphony (unfinished). 1910–
1911, last season in America (21 Feb. conducted
last concert); attacked by fatal malady; returned to Vienna, where he died. His fame
increased rapidly after his death. He is the last
in the line of Viennese "classical" composers.
He completes the Romantic symphony form,
handed on to him by Schubert and Bruckner.
(See AUSTRIAN ORCH. MUSIC; GERMAN MUSIC;
CHORALE-SYMPHONIE.) All 9 symphonies (except
5th, Peters, Leipzig) and many songs with
orch. are publ. in Univ. Ed. The 10th was 1st
perf. 6 June, 1924 (Prague) under Zemlinsky.
There is a portrait in bronze by Rodin. Consult books on Mahler by R. Specht, P. Stefan
(Eng. Schirmer, 1913), G. Adler. A large work
by P. Bekker (*Mahler's Symphonies*).—EG. W.

MAILLY, Alphonse Jean Ernest. Belgian
orgt. *b.* Brussels, 27 Nov. 1833; *d.* there, Jan.
1918. Prof. organ at Brussels Cons. from 1861.
An orgt. of the very first order, he rapidly
acquired an international reputation both as
a virtuoso and a teacher and trained a number
of excellent pupils, following the sound and
high-minded traditions of Lemmens, his predecessor in the organ class at Brussels Cons.
His talent as compr. is entirely overshadowed
by his merits as teacher and virtuoso.—C. V. B.

MAINARDI, Enrico. Ital. cellist; *b.* Milan,
19 May, 1897. Pupil in Milan of Prof. Magrini;
perfected himself at Berlin under Becker. Also
gained his diploma in compn. Has acquired a
wide renown as concert-player.—D. A.

MAITLAND, Robert. Eng. opera and concert
singer; *b.* Ulverstone, Lancs, 22 Nov. 1875.
Stud. at Edinburgh under T. H. Collinson,

1895–9; then in Paris under E. Delle Sedie.
Wagner concerts, Queen's Hall, under Wood;
Ring, Covent Garden, under Richter; recitals
Berlin, Hamburg, Brussels, Antwerp, Holland,
Manchester London, America, France, Italy,
etc.—E.-H.

MAÎTRES MUSICIENS (Les) de la Renaissance française. A Fr. mus. collection, dir. since
1894 by Henry Expert, librarian of Paris Cons.
comprising about 30 vols. It includes the *Mes-
langes* of Orlando de Lassus, Psalms of Goudimel,
and works by Costeley, Jannequin, Brumel,
Mouton, Fevin, Mauduit, Le Jeune, Gervais,
du Tertre, Caurroy, Sermisy, Courtois, etc.—A. C.

MALAMBO. See SOUTH AMER. DANCES.

MALÁT, Jan. Czechoslovak compr. singing-
teacher; *b.* Starý Bydžov, 1843; *d.* Prague, 1915.
Publ. (with Fibich) a *Piano School* (1884);
a *Violin School*; a manual of harmony and
a musical dictionary. Harmonised Bohemian
national songs in a simple, tasteful way.
Česky národní poklad (*Bohemian National Treasure*)
containing 700 songs; *Zlatá pokladnice* (*The Golden
Treasure Book*) 200; *Perly českého zpěvu* (*Pearls of
Czechoslovak National Songs*) and *Růže stolistá* (*The
Hundred-leaved Rose*) each 100 songs. Original works:
operas *Stáňa* (1899); *Veselé námluvy* (*Merry Wooing*)
1908. Orch.: *Maličkosti* (*Miniatures*); *Taneční rej*
(*The Dancing Roundelay*); *Furiant*; *Notturno*. Many
vocal, choral and pf. pieces; Bohemian 4tets; Moravian 4tets. (Fr. A. Urbánek, Prague.)—V. ST.

MALÁTS, Joaquín. Span. pianist, *b.* in Catalonia. Stud. at Barcelona under J. B. Pujol, and
at Paris Cons. under de Bériot. One of the first
exponents of Albeniz's latest works. Died in
Barcelona at the end of the XIX century.—P. G. M.

MALCOLM, Philip. Scottish barit. singer; *b.*
Edinburgh, 29 July, 1884. Stud. singing under
Vittorio Ricci, an Ital. who taught with marked
success in Edinburgh for about 15 years. M. has
sung oratorio rôles for all the leading Scottish
societies; has lately appeared with conspicuous
success in Edinburgh opera—*Faust*, *Trovatore*,
Pagliacci, and *Cavalleria Rusticana*. Has a voice
of exceptional range.—W. S.

MALEINGREAU. See DE MALEINGREAU.

MALHERBE, Charles Théodore. Fr. music
critic and historian; *b.* Paris, 21 April, 1853;
d. Cormeil (Eure), 1911. Stud. under Dan-
hauser, Wormser and Massenet. 1896, appointed
archiviste-adjoint to Paris Opéra, and in 1899
succeeded Nuitter (1895–11) as archivist. He
definitely completed the organising of the Opéra
Museum. His private collection of mus. autographs was one of the richest in the world. This
he left to the Paris Conservatoire.
Catalogue bibliographique des œuvres de Donizetti
(1897); *L'Œuvre dramatique de R. Wagner* (with
A. Soubies; 1886); *Précis d'histoire de l'Opéra-
Comique* (1881); *Histoire de la seconde Salle Favart*
(2 vols. 1892–3; crowned by the Institut). Collab.
with Saint-Saëns in complete ed. of Rameau's works
(Durand). Comp. several *opéras-comiques* and incidental music to *Les Yeux clos* (Odéon, 1896).—M. L. P.

MALHERBE, Edmond. Fr. compr. *b.* Paris,
1870. Pupil of Massenet and G. Fauré at Cons.
Prix de Rome, 1899.
Str. 4tet; 6tet for wind instrs.; Wedding March;
pf. pieces: *Valses Études à la manière de Chopin*;
Pièces enfantines; *Danses anciennes* (Paris, Heugel).
—M. L. P.

MALINOWSKI, Stefan. Polish compr. *b.* Warsaw, 1890. Publ. several pf. pieces and songs. Obtained a prize at the Smit competition in Paris, 1923. His operetta *Fernflower* was successful in Warsaw and Cracow.—ZD. J.

MALIPIERO, Gian Francesco. Ital. compr. *b.* Venice, 18 March, 1882. A cultured, combative musician of fertile inspiration. His name is better known in intellectual mus. circles abroad than in Italy, where his music has met with but scant success. Stud. at Liceo Mus. at Bologna, where he had Bossi as master; then went to Germany, studying under Max Bruch. At present, is teacher of compn. at Parma Cons. An intellectual artist, whose opinions have also been expressed in various articles. As compr. he has tried all kinds of music, from vocal and instr. chamber-music, to symph. and operatic poems.

For theatre: *Canossa*, 1-act opera, perf. without success at Costanzi, Rome, 1914; *Pantea*, symph. drama; *Sette canzoni*; *Baruffe Chiozzotte*, 1-act mus. comedy; *Orfeo*, 1-act mus. scene. (These works, except first, are publ. by Chester, London.) For orch.: *Sinfonie del silenzio e della morte* (Rahter, Leipzig); *Impressioni dal vero* (Pt. 1, Senart; Pt. 2, Chester; Pt. 3, Prague, 1924); *Pause del silenzio* (Pizzi, Bologna); *Ditirambo tragico* (Chester); *Armenia* (Senart); *Per una favola cavalleresca* (Ricordi, Milan); *Oriente immaginario*, small orch. (Chester). For pf.: *Six Pieces* (Carisch, Milan); *Poemetti lunari* (Senart, Paris); *Preludi autunnali* (Rouart, Lerolle, Paris); *Poemi asolani*, *Barlumi*, *Maschere che passano*, *Omaggi*, *La Siesta* (Chester); *Risonanze* (Pizzi). For voice and pf.: *I sonetti delle fate* (Carisch, Milan); *Cinque poesie francesi* (Senart, Paris); *Tre poesie di Poliziano* (Chester); *Sonetti del Berni* (Ricordi). For str. 4tet: *Rispetti e strambotti* (Coolidge Prize, America; Chester, London); *Stornelli e ballate*. Various: Sonata for cello and pf. (Schmidl, Trieste); *San Francesco*, mystery, (perf. New York, 1922). Booklet, *The Orchestra* (Chester); *The Theatre* (Bologna, Zanichelli, 1920); and various arts. in *Rivista Musicale Italiana*. M. has ed. some ancient Ital. music for the coll. publ. by Istituto Editoriale Italiano, Milan.

.Consult: Guido M. Gatti, in *Modern Musicians of Italy and Abroad*; Henry Prunières in *Musical Quarterly*, New York, July 1920; *Mercure de France*, May 1919. There is also a booklet on him publ. by Chester.—R. F.

MALISHEFSKY, Vitold Josephovitch. Russ. compr. *b.* Moghilef-Podolsk, 8 Sept. 1873. Stud. under Rimsky-Korsakof at Petrograd Cons. For some time, principal of Odessa Cons. Now lives in Poland. His music, in its main features, is of the eclectic order.

3 symphonies; 4 str. 4tets; vn. sonata; songs. —M. D. C.

MALISZEWSKI, Witold. Polish compr. condr. *b.* Mohylow Podolski, 8 July, 1873. In 1898, began to study theory under Rimsky-Korsakof at Petrograd Cons.; 1908–21, dir. of Imperial Music School, Odessa; at present lives in Warsaw. In 1923 received a prize for cello pieces at Smit competition in Paris.

3 symphonies; *Lustige Ouvertüre*; 3 str. 4tets (all publ. Belaief, Moscow). Has also written a Manual of Modulation (1905).—ZD. J.

MALLING, Jörgen Henrik. Danish compr. *b.* Copenhagen, 31 Oct. 1836; *d.* there, 12 July, 1905. With his op. 2, *Melodier til skotske Folkesange* (*Tunes to Scotch Folk-Songs*), he aroused attention as a compr. while quite young, received a stipendium and went abroad for study. In Paris he became interested in Chevé's method of singing, and warmly advocated its introduction

into his native city, an effort that for a time was successful. Later he resided in Sweden, then settled in South Germany where for many years he taught and composed. Besides shorter pieces there are several chamber-works; a concert-piece *Tonernes Sejr* (*The Triumph of Tones*); *Küwala* (from Ossian), and the operas *Frithiof* and *Lisinka*.—A. H.

MALLING, Otto Valdemar. Danish composer, organist; *b.* Copenhagen, 1 June, 1848; *d.* 5 Oct. 1915. Brother of Jörgen Malling. Master of Arts, 1866. He took the course at Royal Conservatoire, Copenhagen. Director of University Students' Singing Society, 1871–84; at same time dir. of the Koncertforening (Concert Society) where newer music found a hearing. Orgt. from 1878, succeeded to the post at the Church of Our Lady, Copenhagen, following the death of the elder Hartmann. Appointed professor at the Royal Conservatoire of Music, Copenhagen, 1885, later its director. His compositions cover nearly every form except opera.

Larger works for soli, chorus and orch.: *Prolog til Den gyldne Legende* (*Prologue to The Golden Legend*); *Snefald* (*Snowfall*); *Det hellige Land* (*The Holy Land*); *Knud den helliges Död* (*The Death of St. Canute*); *Absalon*; *Folkeviser* (*Folk-Songs*). For solo vs. and orch.: *Kvindens Skabelse* (*The Creation of Woman*); *Reveille*; *Ved Allehelgenstid* (*All Saints*); *Mirza Schaffys Lieder* (*Mirza Schaffy's Songs*). For orch.: symphony; concert overture; 2 suites; pf. concerto, 2 fantasies for vn. and orch. Chamber-music: str. 4tet; str. 8tet; pf. trio; pf. 5tet. His organ suites *Christus*, *Jomfru Marie* (*The Virgin Mary*) and *Kirkeaarets Festdage* (*The Festivals of the Church Year*) have also made their way into the outside world. Most of his works are publ. by Wilhelm Hansen, Copenhagen. He also wrote an educational work on Instrumentation in the Danish language (1884).—A. H.

MALLINSON, James Albert. Eng. song-compr. *b.* Leeds, 13 Nov. 1870. Choirboy under Dr. Creser at Chapel Royal, St. James's; orgt. St. Chad's, Leeds; his health necessitated change —Australia 1891; there he married the Danish soprano Anna Steinhauer; 1896, toured Europe; London recitals of songs, 1900–2–6–7; 1908, toured Australia and New Zealand; since 1914, have lived in Denmark, where they have given many recitals. His songs are soundly written and very effective, in late-Romantic style.

Cantata, *Tegner's Drapa* (Melbourne Male Choir; Sydney Philh.); *Battle of the Baltic*, solo and male chorus (perf. Melbourne Metropolitan Choir): pf. 4tet in D mi.; pf. trio in G mi. (Leeds); sonata, E mi.-vn. and pf. Over 300 songs (mostly publ. by John Church Co.).—E.-H.

MALTEN (real name Müller), Therese. Ger. operatic singer; *b.* Insterburg, East Prussia, 21 June, 1855. Pupil of Gustav Engel, Berlin; 1873, 1st appearance Dresden; immediately engaged for principal rôles; 1882, sang first Kundry at Bayreuth. Till 1903, belonged to Dresden R. Opera; now lives at Neu-Zschieren, near Dresden.—A. E.

MANACOR, Capella de. See NOGUERA, ANTONIO.

MANCINELLI, Luigi. Ital. compr. and condr. *b.* Orvieto, 5 Feb. 1848; *d.* Rome, 2 Feb. 1921. One of greatest and most popular Ital. condrs. of recent times; known all over the world. At first he was a cellist (studied cello at Florence under Sbolci and compn. under

Mabellini); in 1875, at Apollo Theatre, Rome, he began his career as condr., rapidly passing on to Spain, Paris and elsewhere, obtaining great successes both as a theatre dir., and concert condr. In 1881 he was entrusted with direction of Liceo Mus. at Bologna, in which city he succeeded Angelo Mariani as dir. of Teatro Comunale; at same time he occupied post of choirmaster of San Petronio. He also founded in that city the Società del Quartetto (Quartet Soc.); the Bologna Orch., under his conductorship, gained a high degree of perfection and a great reputation. He left Bologna in 1886 and went to London, where from 1887 to 1905 he was condr. of Covent Garden Opera, where he conducted some memorable performances of Wagner's operas. From 1886 to 1893 he also spent much time in Madrid, where he was condr. of Teatro Real and of Sociedad de Conciertos. From 1893 to 1901 he conducted, in addition to the London seasons, the Metropolitan Theatre of New York, which was inaugurated by him. He also inaugurated the Teatro Colón in Buenos Ayres, where he cond. from 1907 to 1911. In 1892, at San Carlo Felice Theatre in Genoa, he produced for the first time Franchetti's *Cristoforo*. As a concert condr. he appeared at the Augusteo, Rome; Philh., London; in Vienna, Hamburg, and the principal cities of all countries, always with great success. As compr. he occupies a conspicuous place amongst Italians of second half of xix century. His music, although always leaning towards modern progress, has a clearness of line, and a vigour of style which are purely Italian; it embraces all branches, from opera, orch. concert-music, to oratorio, cantata, sacred music and vocal chamber-music.

Overture to *Messalina* of Pietro Cossa (1876); overture and intermezzi to *Cleopatra* of same author (1877); *Inno a Guido Monaco*, to words by Boito (1882); *Tizianello*, short melodrama (1882); *Isora di Provenza*, 3-act opera (Bologna, 1884); *Isaias*, sacred cantata, words by Giuseppe Albini (Norwich Fest. 1887); *Scene veneziane* for orch. (1890); *Ero e Leandro*, 3-act opera by Boito (perf. as oratorio at Norwich Fest. 1896; on stage, Teatro Real, Madrid, 1897); 4 songs, v. and pf.; *Sancta Agnes*, cantata, words by G. Albini (Norwich Fest. 1905); *Paolo e Francesca*, 1-act opera, book by Arturo Colautti (Bologna, 1907); *Ouverture romantica*, written for Philh. London (1908); 6 songs, v. and pf. (1912); *Prière des oiseaux*, from Rostand's *Chantecler*, for contr., female chorus and orch. (Rome, at Augusteo, 1916); *Frate Sole*, oratorio, orch. and chorus, for cinematograph representation (1918); *Giuliano l'Apostata*, vocal and instr. poem, for cinematograph perf. (1920); *Sogno di una notte d'estate (Summer Night's Dream)*, 3-act opera on book by Fausto Salvatori (publ. but not perf.). Mostly publ. by Ricordi, Milan; *Isaias* is publ. by Chappell, London; *Ero e Leandro*, Novello, London; *Sogno di una notte d'estate* by Pizzi, Bologna. Consult Giacomo Orefice, *L. M.* (Rome, 1921, Ausonia).—D. A.

MANDL, Richard. Ger.-Czechoslovak compr. *b.* Prossnitz, 9 May, 1859; *d.* Vienna, 31 March, 1918. Stud. at Vienna Cons.; then under Delibes in Paris, where he lived for over ten years. 1900, returned to Vienna in bad health; died there after illness of many years, without having obtained recognition. In his music we find deep and sincere feeling, and a remarkable combination of the style of Brahms's successors and the

agile manner of writing and precise harmonies of the Fr. comprs. His orch. works reveal a special instrumental refinement.

Comic opera, *Rencontre imprévue* (*Nächtliche Werbung*), Rouen, 1888 (Prague, The Hague); opera, *Parthenia*; symph. poem, *Griseldis* (1909); overture for Gascony Tournament (1910); *Hymn to the Rising Sun* (given in 1917, Queen's Hall, London, under Sir Henry Wood); str. 5tet, G ma.; songs.—P. P.

MANDYCZEWSKI, Eusebius. Austrian writer on music; *b.* Czernowitz (Rumania), 18 Aug. 1857. Stud. under Nottebohm and Fuchs at Vienna Cons. 1887; condr. of Vienna Singakademie and archivist of Soc. of Friends of Music. 1897, prof. of music history and scientific knowledge of mus. instrs. at Acad. 1916, privy councillor. One of best experts of mus. literature. His scientific works are distinguished by solidity and accuracy.

Complete ed. of Schubert's works (1897); of Haydn's (Breitkopf); trios from J. S. Bach (with instrs.) (publ. by Bach Soc.); cadenzas to Mozart's pf. concertos; *Haydn's Scotch Songs* (1922, Univ. Ed.) Supplement to *History of Viennese Soc. of Friends of Music* (1912).—P. P.

MANÉN, Juan. Span. violinist and compr. *b.* Barcelona, 14 March, 1883. His is one of the not too frequent cases in which a child-prodigy develops into a great artist. Revealing his remarkable facility as pianist at 6, as compr. at 13, and being recognised as a great master of the vn. at 20, he has gradually attained the universal reputation he enjoys to-day as a virtuoso and compr. In both subjects he may be considered self-taught. A natural disposition of the scientific type, so much in evidence in his most representative works, has always enabled him to learn from the work of others. The intellectuality he reveals as a compr. is not the characteristic of his style as an interpreter, the outstanding feature of his playing being the purity and perfection of a vn. technique which baffles all expectations.

The publication of his works dates as far back as 1899, when he was only 16; as a minor he had no say in the matter of publ. of the numerous pieces produced for the next five years. It was not until he was 22 that he was able to protest against it, sparing no effort or expense to withdraw from circulation what he considered immature. For this reason, he has since adopted the device of marking, with the letter A in front of the opus number, those works which have his approval. Since early youth he has travelled throughout the world as virtuoso, having his fixed residence in Barcelona.

Operas (own libretti, orig. in Catalan dialect): *Neron y Acte* (perf. over 80 times at Leipzig, Dresden, Cologne, Wiesbaden, etc.); *Camino del Sol*, stage symphony (prologue, 3 acts and epilogue). Symphony, *Nova Catalonia* (Orquesta Sinfónica, Madrid; Philh. Orch. Berlin, under Fritz Reiner); *Spanish Concerto*, vn. and orch.; 4 Caprices, vn. and orch.; *Juventus*, concerto grosso, 2 vns. pf. and orch. (perf. Wiesbaden under Otto Lohse; Vienna, Weingartner; Amsterdam and The Hague, Mengelberg); Suite, pf. and vn. with orch.; *Pequeña suite española* (*Little Spanish Suite*), vn. and pf. Rev. ed. (with new pf. parts) of Paganini's complete works; transcriptions for vn. from old masters. (Univ. Ed. Vienna; Simrock; Bote & Bock; Zimmermann.)—P. G. M.

MANKELL, Henning. Swedish compr. *b.* Härnösand, 3 June, 1868. Stud. R. Cons. Stockholm (1889–95); then pf. under Lennart

Lundberg, 1895-9; many years musical critic on
Stockholm papers; from 1899, pf. teacher in
Stockholm. Member R.A.M. Stockholm, 1917.
Among his 50 works in modern style are:

Pf. concerto, op. 30; ballad with orch. *Flor and
Blancheflor*, op. 13; *Legende*, op. 14; pf. 5tet, op. 22;
pf. trio, op. 23; str. 4tets, op. 21, op. 48; sonatas,
pf. and vn. op. 2; vla. and pf. op. 28; *Andante* and
Berceuse, vn. and pf. op. 32; many pf. pieces:
Ballades (Breitkopf); *Intermezzi*; *Preludes* (Nord.
Musikförlaget), etc.—P. V.

MANN, Arthur Henry. Eng. orgt. and choirmaster; b. Norwich 16 May, 1850; chorister
there under Dr. Zachariah Buck; orgt. St.
Peter's, Wolverhampton 1870, Tettenhall 1871,
Beverley Minster 1875; orgt. and dir. of choir,
King's Coll. Cambridge, from 1876 till present
time. He made the King's Coll. Chapel services
famous for their music. He was choirmaster
of Norwich Fest. for some years, from 1902.
With Ebenezer Prout he recovered the orig.
wind-instr. parts of Handel's *Messiah* at the
Foundling Hospital and used them at King's
Coll. in the same year (1894). Mus.Doc. Oxon.
1882. Elected Fellow of King's Coll. 1922.

Church music, anthems, services, etc. Edited
Church of England Hymnal (1895); edit. Tallis' Motet
for 40 vs.; co.-edit. (with Fuller-Maitland) of the
Fitzwilliam Music Catalogue.—E.-H.

MANN, Josef. Polish t. singer; b. Lemberg,
1879; d. 5 Sept. 1921, during his last appearance
in the Berlin State Opera House, after 2nd act
of *Aida*, in which he sang as Radamès. After
his univ. training at Lemberg he became a judge.
Began singing as barit.; but his teacher (Dr.
Kicki in Lemberg) discovered t. qualities. Sang
at Lemberg Opera. In 1910 went to Milan to
finish his studies; 1912-16, sang in Vienna at
the Volksoper, and then to Berlin as member
of Imperial Opera House. He was an artist of
highest rank, both as singer and musician.—
Zd. J.

MANNERS, Charles (real name, Southcote
Mansergh). Opera bass singer and manager; b.
London, son of Col. J. C. Mansergh, R.H.A. and
J.P. for Tipperary and Cork. Stud. at R.A.M.
London; then in Florence; created parts in
comic opera (Willis in *Iolanthe*, Savoy); for 2
years principal bass, Carl Rosa Opera Co.; 4
years in Sir Augustus Harris's Ital. opera seasons,
Covent Garden; managing dir. Moody-Manners
Opera Co. (founded 1897, dissolved 1913);
gave £100 for best opera (without chorus) by a
British compr. 1895; £250 and 5 per cent.
takings for grand opera with chorus. Married
Fanny Moody (*q.v.*).—E.-H.

MANOYLOVITCH, Kosta P. Serbian compr.
condr. b. Krnjevo, 3 Dec. 1890. Stud. music
at Munich, Belgrade and Oxford (England)
where he took Mus.Bac. degree in 1919. Condr.
of the Belgrade Choral Soc.; prof. at School of
Music in that city.

By the Waters of Babylon (Eng. and Serbian
words) for barit. solo, double chorus and orch.; str.
5tet; *Danse Fantastique*, pf.; several songs and pf.
pieces of shorter character.—T. F. D.

MANRIQUE DE LARA Y BERRY, Manuel.
Span. compr., soldier and writer; b. Cartagena,
24 Oct. 1863. At 16, was gazetted lieutenant in

R. Marines, where he now holds rank of briga-
dier-gen. Took part, with great distinction, in
the war with U.S.A., for which he volunteered
in 1898, and in Morocco, at the head of a regiment from 1918 to 1922. Devotes considerable
time to literary and folk-lore research, having
collected over 200,000 verses and more than 500
melodies of traditional Span. ballads, amongst
the Jewish communities of Morocco, Greece,
Asia Minor, Palestine and Egypt. Began
his musical studies at 20, having only one
master, the great compr. Ruperto Chapí, who,
in his turn, had no other pupil in his whole life.
An ardent pioneer of Wagnerism in Spain, his
attitude is that of the orthodox Ger. pro-
gressivist. Member of the R. Acad. de Bellas
Artes de San Fernando, Madrid. Awarded many
civil and military decorations.

La Orestiada, mus. trilogy (1st perf. Sociedad de
Conciertos, Madrid, 1890); symphony in E mi. (1st
perf. Orquesta Sinfónica, Madrid, 1915, under Saco
del Valle); str. 4tet, E flat; *El Ciudadano Simón*,
3-act comic opera (1st perf. Madrid, 1900); *Alfonso y
Jimena*, symph. fragment, from his opera *El Cid*
(own libretto; perf. Orquesta Sinfónica, Madrid,
under Fernández Arbós).—P. G. M.

MANTECÓN, Juan José. Span. contemporary critic and lecturer on modern music.
Writes for *La Voz*, one of most important newspapers in Madrid, where he lives.—P. G. M.

MANTICA, Francesco. Italian composer; b.
Reggio Calabria, 23 Dec. 1875. Dir. of Regia
Biblioteca Musicale di Santa Cecilia, Rome.
Stud. compn. at R. Liceo Mus. di Santa Cecilia
under Stanislao Falchi; became favourably
known by various compns. of instr. and vocal
music; has also written several operas (ms.).
A distinguished writer and student of mus.
history. To him we owe the publ. of facsimile
of orig. ed. of the *Rappresentazione di Anima e
Corpo* by Emilio de' Cavalieri (1600).—D. A.

MANTOVANI, Tancredi. Italian historian,
musical critic; b. Ferrara, 27 Sept. 1865. Stud.
at Bologna under Busi and Torchi. In 1904,
prof. of history and æsthetics of music at Liceo
Mus. Rossini at Pesaro. Then went to Rome;
since 1919, prof. of poetic and dramatic literature
at R. Liceo Mus. di Santa Cecilia.

Estetica della musica (Trieste, 1892, Schmidl);
Carlo Pedrotti (Pesaro, 1894, Nobili); *Orlando di
Lasso* (Milan, 1895, Ricordi); *Rossini a Lugo* (Pesaro,
1902, Federici); *Cristoforo Gluck* (Rome, 1914, For-
miggini); *Angelo Mariani* (Rome, 1921, Ausonia);
Guide to the " Damnation of Faust " by Berlioz
(Milan, 1923, Caddeo).—D. A.

MANUEL, Roland (real name, Lévy). Fr.
compr. b. Paris, 22 March, 1891. Stud. under
Albert Roussel and Maurice Ravel.

Pf. trio (1917, Senart); *Idylles*, pf. (1918, Durand);
comic opera, *Isabelle et Pantalon* (perf. 1922, Paris,
Trianon-Lyrique; publ. Heugel); a book of songs,
Farizade au sourire de rose (Durand). Mus. critic,
Paris *Éclair*; has written an excellent little book
on *Maurice Ravel*.—M. D. C.

MANZIARLY, Marcelle de. Compr. b. 15 Oct.
1899. One of most highly-gifted of young Fr.
musicians. Since age of 12, has been a pupil of
Nadia Boulanger. Has comp. a sonata for pf.
and vn. (1918) in classical form and a trio (1922)
which is highly individual.—A. C.

MAORI MUSIC. See Hill, Alfred.

318

"MAPLE LEAF FOR EVER." The popular song of Canada. Words and music by Alexander Muir, a native of Scotland, and publ. in 1860. Has been taught and sung in the public schools of Ontario since 1887; is regarded as the national song of Canada by that section of population which dislikes *O Canada* on account of its French and Roman Catholic sentiment. The words have been altered since its first appearance, but inasmuch as they glorify the Eng. general, Wolfe, there is little hope that the song will ever be acceptable to Fr. Canadians. Another set of words, written by one Godfrey, was used for some time and is interesting because the writer depicted Canada as the antithesis of Rudyard Kipling's "Our Lady of the Snows." The version now used in Ontario schools is revised one by Muir. In a discussion on the merits of the compn. which appeared in the Toronto *Empire* in 1890, it was pointed out that the tune suffered a little owing to its reminiscence of the Scottish air *Low Down in the Broom*, used by Burns in his *My Love is like a Red, Red Rose*, also to the fact that the words were somewhat suggestive of *The Land of Cakes for Ever.*—L. S.

MARCHESI, Blanche. Operatic and concert singer; *b.* Paris. Came of an old Sicilian family named Castrone, both father and mother being famous singers, and both pupils of Manuel Garcia II. M. has lived for 25 years in England; now devoted to teaching; her best rôles were Isolde (*Tristan*) and Leonore (*Il Trovatore*). As an interpreter of songs in many languages she has few rivals. She has written her reminiscences, *Singer's Pilgrimage* (Grant Richards, 1923).—E.-H.

MARCHETTI, Filippo. Italian compr. of operas and vocal chamber-music; *b.* Bolognola (Camerino), 26 Feb. 1835; *d.* Rome, 18 Jan. 1902. Principally known for his opera *Ruy Blas* (Milan, Scala, 1869). Other works are: *Giulietta e Romeo*; *Gustavo Wasa*; *Don Giovanni d'Austria*. In 1881, was appointed dir. of Liceo di Santa Cecilia, Rome, a post he occupied until his death. Publ. (Ricordi) a series of popular songs.—D. A.

MARCHISIO, Barbara. Ital. contr. *b.* Turin, 6 Dec. 1833; *d.* Mira, 19 April, 1919. Together with her sister, Carlotta (1835–72), B. M. was one of most famous Ital. singers of second half of XIX century. Began with concerts; immediately afterwards, appeared on opera stage, where she gained great successes in *Il Barbiere*; *Il Trovatore*; *Cenerentola*; *Linda*; *Norma*; *Lucrezia Borgia*, and, in company with her sister, in *Matilde of Shabran*, in *William Tell* and in *Semiramide*. Rossini wrote especially for the Marchisio sisters the *Petite Messe Solennelle*, given in Paris in the salon of Count Pillet-Will, under dir. of the compr., 14 March, 1864. The career of B. M. continued triumphantly for many years at all the principal European theatres. After death of her sister, she almost completely retired from her profession. From 1892 to 1914, she occupied a special post as teacher of singing at R. Cons.

of Naples, where she trained some excellent pupils.—D. A.

MARCILLY, Paul. Fr. compr. and orgt. *b.* Paris in 1890. Has been *maître de chapelle* (precentor) at Church of St.-Gervais, Paris. *Prières*, organ; *Rayons intérieurs*, pf.; *Suite pastorale*, pf. trio; *Étude symphonique*, 3 parts.—A. C.

MARCONI, Francesco. Ital. t. singer; *b.* Rome, 14 May, 1855; *d.* there 5 Feb. 1916. One of most renowned and esteemed singers of last fifty years; noted for beauty of his voice and spontaneity of his talent. Of humble origin, in his early youth he became a carpenter. Ottavio Bartolini, an esteemed singing-master, whose attention was drawn to him, educated him in singing. M. made his *début* at Teatro Real, Madrid, in *Faust*. His interpretations of *I Puritani*, *Stabat* (Rossini), *Lucrezia Borgia*, *Ballo in Maschera*, *Rigoletto*, *Traviata*, *Aida*, *Requiem* (Verdi), *L'Africana*, *Huguenots* and *Lohengrin* will not easily be forgotten. He triumphantly visited all the greatest theatres of the world. He always retained his original simplicity, and remained attached to his native city, where he sang innumerable times.
Consult Giorgio Barini, *In Morte di Fr. M.* (in review *La Nuova Antologia*, Rome, 1916).—D. A.

MARCZEWSKI, Lucyan. Polish compr. *b.* Warsaw, 1879. Pupil of Noskowski. Publ. several charming songs. Has lived in Warsaw as proprietor and dir. of a music school.—ZD. J.

MARÉCHAL, Henri. Fr. compr. *b.* Paris, 22 Jan. 1842. Pupil of Paris Cons.; *Prix de Rome*, 1871. His style is Neo-classic. Has written his Memoirs under the titles: *Rome* (1904), *Paris* (1907), *Lettres et Souvenirs* (1921).
Comic operas: *Les Amoureux de Catherine* (1876); *La Taverne des Trabans* (1881); *L'Étoile* (1889); *Daphnis et Chloé* (1899). Operas: *Deïdamie* (1893); *Calendal* (1894). Ballet, *Le Lac des aulnes* (1907). Oratorio, *Le Miracle de Naïn* (1887).—A. C.

MARÉCHAL, Maurice. Fr. cellist; *b.* Dijon, 3 Oct. 1892. Scarcely had he left the Paris Cons. (1st prize, 1911) before he commenced one of the most rapid and brilliant careers in musical history. 1912, soloist for summer season at Lamoureux Concerts; 1919, regular soloist; soloist at Cons. 1920; Société Philharmonique in 1921; then member of Cons. board of examiners. His tours abroad have justified the judgment of the Fr. public. His talent is characterised by a very rare vigour and fullness of tone which, joined to his deep musical feeling, has won for him the honour of giving 1st perf. of many works (*e.g.* Duo of Maurice Ravel; Trio of Guy Ropartz) at the Société Nationale. Was chosen by Jacques Thibaut and Alfred Cortot, in their last series of trio concerts.—M. P.

MAREK, Czesław. Polish compr. and pianist; *b.* Przemysl, Galicia, 1891. Pupil of Niewiadowski, Lemberg; of Leschetizky, Vienna, and finally of Hans Pfitzner, Strasburg. 1914, prof. Lemberg Cons. Then went to Zurich, where he now teaches pf. and theory. Is much esteemed as pianist. His compns. are mode. ⌐ in character.
3 fugues, pf. op. 2; *Italian Serenade*, orch. op. 7; *Scherzo*, orch. op. 8; sonata, vn. and pf. op. 4; many songs and pieces for male chorus.—ZD. J.

MARGULIES TRIO. Founded in 1890 by Adele Margulies (*b.* Vienna, 7 March, 1863), a concert-pianist and teacher of high standing in New York. Leopold Lichtenberg was vn. and Victor Herbert, cello. The trio in this form lasted several years. It was revived in 1904 with Leo Schultz as cellist. Schultz was replaced by Alwin Schroeder in 1915. The trio has introduced much new chamber-music. It has given no concerts for the past 5 years.—O. K.

MARIANI GONZÁLEZ, Luis Leandro. Span. compr. *b.* Seville, 1868. Stud. there under the choirmaster of the Cath. Don Evaristo García de Torres, receiving also his literary education from his uncle, the philologist Don Emigdio Mariani. At 20, publ. *Un Nuevo Acorde*, a study in the theory of harmony which provoked at the time a good deal of controversy, bringing on the author the disapproval of Verdi, Massenet, Ponchielli, Gevaert, Gounod and Saint-Saëns, who considered him a daring revolutionist against the orthodox science of harmony of the period. Such a disposition of mind is hardly detected in his early works, the popular pf. pieces *Al pié de la reja, Claveles Rojos, Noche de luna*, etc., which have to be considered as productions detached from the author's mus. output of later stages of his career. Lives in Seville, where he is orgt. at the Cath. and conducts a school of music.

Operettas: *Aurora*, 3 acts; *Agustina de Aragón*, 2 acts; *Los Dragones*, 2 acts; *El talismán de la suerte*; *El corral de la Pacheca*; *Picci*; *Diamantito*; *Chicharra*; and *El Joven de las Trinitarias*, 1 act. Orch.: *Año Nuevo*, overture; *Suite infantil*, orch. and chorus; *Fantasia coral*, mass, 4 vs. and orch.; str. 4tet; *Tres Preludios y Fugas*, organ. Pf.: sonata; *Alma Andaluza* (5 pieces); *Tres Tonadillas*; many smaller works. (Publ.: Unión Musical Española; Ildefonso Alier, Madrid; Mundial Música, Valencia; Música Sacro-Hispana, Comillas; Z. du Wast, Paris; Schott).—P. G. M.

MARINI MURILLO, María. Contemporary Span. m.-sopr. (concert and operatic). Toured in Italy, Portugal, Spain.—P. G. M.

MARINUZZI, Gino. Ital. compr. and condr. *b.* Palermo, 24 March, 1882. One of best living Ital. condrs. *Début* at the Massimo, in Catania; rapidly rose to high reputation, conducting at Teatro Real, Madrid; at Opéra-Comique, Paris; and at Scala, Milan, where he remained for three years. He then went to South America. For three years he occupied post of dir. of Liceo Mus. at Bologna, which position he gave up in 1918 in order to devote himself more freely to his career as condr. In 1919 he was at the Costanzi in Rome; in 1920 succeeded Cleofonte Campanini in artistic direction of Chicago Opera Association, which he continued until 1921. He then returned to South America, and thence went to the Regio Theatre, Turin. He is also an esteemed compr., having written the operas *Barberina* (Palermo, 1903) and *Jacquerie* (Buenos Ayres, 1918), also various instr. and vocal concert-works.—D. A.

MARIOTTE, Antoine. Fr. compr. *b.* Avignon in 1875. Destined for navy; but retired with rank of midshipman in 1897. Entered the

Schola Cantorum, Paris. Since 1920, dir. of School of Music, Orléans. Chief stage-works: *Salomé* (Lyons, 1908; Paris, 1910); *Le Vieux Roi* (Lyons, 1913); *Nele Dooryn*; *Gargantua*; *Esther.*—A. C.

MARNOLD, Jean. Fr. writer on music; *b.* Paris, 1859. Music critic for *Mercure de France* from 1902 onwards. Founder and ed. (1905–7) of *Mercure Musical*.

Les Sons inférieurs et la Théorie de M. Hugo Riemann; Les Fondements naturels de la musique grecque antique (*I.M.G.* 1909; Leipzig, Breitkopf); *Musique d'autrefois et d'aujourd'hui* (Paris, 1911, Dorbon); *Le Cas Wagner* (Paris, 1918, Crès); *Nature et Evolution de l'art musical* (publ. *Rivista Musicale Italiana*); also a Fr. transl. of Nietzsche's *Origin of Tragedy in Music* (Mercure de France, 1881).—M. L. P.

MARRACO, Sancho. Contemporary Span. compr. of the Catalonian group. Lives in Barcelona, where he is choirmaster of San Agustín Church. Author of many religious, choral and orch. works, mostly based on Catalonian folk-music: *Ballet de Solsona, Tres Cançons Populars*; and *Tres Gloses de Cançons Populars.*—P. M.

MARSCHALK, Max. Ger. critic and compr. *b.* Berlin, 7 April, 1863. Pupil of Heinrich Urban; 1895, mus. critic of *Vossische Zeitung*, Berlin.

1-act opera, *In Flames* (Gotha, 1896); song-ballad, *Aucassin and Nicolette* (Stuttgart, 1907); operas: *Lobetanz*; *The Hero of Oggersheim*; *The Little Fellow*; *The Adventurer*; music to fairy-play, *The Naughty Princess* (1904, after Gabriele Reuter); to Gerhard Hauptmann's *Hannele* (Berlin, 1893); *The Sunken Bell*; *And Pippa dances* (Berlin, 1906); *Schluck and Jau*; *The White Saviour* (Berlin, 1920); dramatic legend, *Sister Beatrice* (Berlin, 1904; Maeterlinck); orch. works and songs.—A. E.

MARSCHALKÓ, Rózsi (Székelyhidy). Hungarian m.-sopr. operatic singer; *b.* Nagyszombat, Hungary (now annexed by Czecho-Slovakia), 23 Aug. 1887. Stud. in Budapest. Since 1912, member of R. Hungarian Opera House.—B. B.

MARSOP, Paul. Ger. writer on music; *b.* Berlin, 6 Oct. 1856. Pupil of Ehrlich and Bülow; since 1881 at Munich. Founded Popular Musical Libraries, which operate splendidly; first one was opened at Munich, 1902; up to the present about 20 exist in the country and abroad.

Pamphlets: *New Ger. Kapellmeister-music*; *Prospects of Wagnerian Art in France*; *Fundamental Wagner Questions*: *The Uniform Thought in Ger. Music*; *The Social Position of Ger. Orch. Musicians* (1905); *Why are we in need of the Reform-Stage?* (1907); *Socialisation of Music and Musicians* (1919); *Musical Essays* (1899); *Essays of a Musician* (1903, 2nd ed. *New Struggles*, 1913).—A. E.

MARTENS, Frederick Herman. Amer. writer on music; *b.* New York, 6 July, 1874. Stud. pf. in New York under H. C. Timm and Wm. Barker, and theory under Max Spicker. Since 1907 a writer on mus. topics, translator of libretti, choral works and songs into Eng. and author of lyrics.

Leo Ornstein: the Man—his Ideas—his Work (New York, 1918, Breitkopf); *Violin Mastery: Talks with Master-Violinists and Teachers* (1919, Stokes); *The Art of the Prima Donna and Concert Singer* (Appleton, 1923); *String Mastery: Talks with master violinists, viola players and violoncellists* (Stokes, 1923); and *Little Biographies* of Handel, Mendelssohn, Paganini, Rachmaninof, Rimsky-Korsakof and Rubinstein (1922, Breitkopf).—J. M.

MARTEAU, Henri. Violinist and compr. *b.* Rheims (France), 31 March, 1874. Stud. vn. under Léonard and Sivori; then under Garcin (Paris

Cons., 1st prize, 1892), and compn. under Th. Dubois. As soloist and ensemble-player, M. is one of most important artists of to-day. Tours over all Europe and America; 1900, teacher at Cons. of Geneva; 1908, succeeded Joachim at High School of Music, Berlin; 1921, head of the master-class at the Ger. Acad. of Music in Prague. As compr. shows modern influences. After the 1914–18 war he became a naturalised Swede. Member R.A.M. Stockholm, 1900.

Symphony; *Serenade*, wind instrs.; vn. concerto; Suite, vn. and orch.; mus. comedy *Meister Schwalbe*; str. 5tet (with clar.); 3 str. 4tets; str. trio; 3 fugues and Passacaglia, organ; Phantasy, organ and vn.; 2 *Caprices*, vn. (with pf.); vn. pieces and studies; songs (publ. Steingräber; Simrock; Siegel; Harting). —P. V.

MARTIN, Frank. Swiss compr. *b.* Geneva in 1890. Stud. compn. under Joseph Lauber at Geneva. He is one of most talented of young Swiss composers.

Les Dithyrambes (Pierre Martin), chorus, soli, orch. (1918); Suite, orch. (1913); *Esquisse*, small orch. (1920); pf. 5tet (Swiss National Ed.). *Pavane couleur du temps*, str. orch. (Geneva, Henn); vn. sonata (Leipzig, Hug); numerous songs.—F. H.

MARTIN, Friedrich. Ger. compr. *b.* Wiesbaden, 18 Jan. 1888. Stud. at Leipzig Cons. (Straube, Paul, Reger), 1916; town-orgt. at Weimar; teacher of organ, theory and mus. history at State School of Music. Since 1922, custodian of Max Reger archives at Weimar.

Popular *Short Songs* (1913); *From the Little Garden of Roses* (Hermann Löns, 1915); *Nursery Songs* (1915); ms. songs for contr. (Hesse); songs from Max Dauthendey's poems; *Ger. Songs to Virgin Mary* (s., organ and harp); male chorus; organ compns.; religious works.—A. E.

MARTIN, Sir George Clement. Eng. orgt. and compr. *b.* Lambourn, Berks, 11 Sept. 1844; *d.* London, 23 Feb. 1916. Stud. under Sir John Stainer; Mus.Doc. Cantuar. 1883; Oxon. *h.c.* 1912; orgt. St. Paul's Cath. London, 1888–1916; prof. of organ, R.C.M. 1883; at R.A.M. 1895. Knighted in 1897, having cond. the Diamond Jubilee service at St. Paul's, for which he comp. a special Te Deum. This was perf. outside the western entrance; the Cath. F bell "Great Paul" was used to form part of the orchestration. M. was solely a church musician; he wrote no secular music at all. A new style of church accompaniment came into being with him. His way of treating tone in huge masses evidently grew out of the acoustics of the vast edifice in which he worked. It had a special effect on his compns., too; of these he left a large number: services, anthems, hymns (nearly all publ. by Novello.) See arts. by various students in *Mus. Times*, April 1916, and also July 1897; by A. Eaglefield Hull, in *Monthly Mus. Record*, July 1916.—E.-H.

MARTINELLI, Giovanni. Ital. tenor singer; *b.* Montagnana (Padua), 1888. *Début* in *Ernani*, and immediately after was engaged by Toscanini and Puccini for the first perf. of the *Fanciulla del West* (*Girl of the Golden West*) at Costanzi in Rome, 1911. Has sung with continued success in Paris, Monte Carlo, Covent Garden, London, and New York.—D. A.

MARTÍNEZ DEL CASTILLO, Rafael. Span.

violinist; *b.* La Almunia de Doña Godina (Saragossa), 5 April, 1896. Pupil of Hierro at R. Cons. de Música, Madrid, 1920, appointed prof. of vn. at Escuela Municipal de Música, Saragossa. Solo vn. of Orquesta Filarmónica, Madrid. Has given many recitals in Spain.—P. G. M.

MARTUCCI, Giuseppe. Ital. compr. pianist, condr. *b.* Capua, 6 Jan. 1856; *d.* Naples, 1 June, 1909. One of noblest and most conspicuous figures in Ital. mus. life of last period. Took large part in propaganda of higher mus. forms, and in education of public taste for symph. music, at a time when Italy seemed to be turning all her musical attention to opera. After leaving the Naples Cons. he was, from 1886, dir. of Liceo Mus. at Bologna; in 1902 became dir. of the historic Neapolitan Cons. where he had been a student. He occupied this office until his death. His activities as pianist, teacher and condr. (he was a profound interpreter of Wagner's works) were most stimulating, and met with continuous success. He also reaped effective results from his propaganda. He introduced the music of Parry and Stanford to Italy. As a compr. he devoted himself exclusively to concert and chamber music. He was, with Sgambati and then Bossi, amongst the first in XIX century to cultivate this branch of music in Italy.

2 symphonies, D mi. op. 75 (1895), and F, op. 81 (1904); concerto, B flat mi., for pf. op. 66; pf. 5tet, op. 45; a large number of other minor instr. works (especially for pf.); also vocal chamber-music (publ. partly by Ricordi). Consult a study by Luigi Torchi, in *Rivista Musicale Italiana* (XVI, p. 660). Torchi also publ., in same review, two articles on the 2 symphonies of Martucci—1st Symphony, III, p. 128; 2nd, XII, p. 151.—D. A.

MARTY, Georges. Fr. compr. *b.* Paris, 16 May, 1860; *d.* there, 11 Oct. 1908. Pupil of Massenet. *Prix de Rome*, 1882, with cantata *Edith*; dir. of ensemble classes at Cons. 1892; successor of Taffanel as cond. of Cons. concerts (1903). He died without having shown his fullest measure.

Orch. works: *L'Enchanteur Merlin*; overture, *Balthazar*; *Les Saisons*; *Suite romantique*; *Ballade d'hiver*; *Matin de Printemps*; pantomime, *Lysis* (1888); operas, *Le Duc de Ferrare* (1899) and *Daria* (1905).—A. C.

MARTYN, Edward. Irish dramatist; *b.* Masonbrook, Co. Galway, 31 Jan. 1857; *d.* Dec. 1923. Educated in Dublin, and at Christ Church, Oxford. One of founders of the Irish dramatic movement of 1899; one of chief patrons of music in Ireland; founded Palestrina Choir (men and boys at Dublin) with object of reforming liturgical music. (This choir in 1903 became the *Schola Cantorum* of the Archdiocese, in Dublin.) A prominent patron of the Feis Ceoil (Irish Music Fest.) and the Dublin Orch. Society.—W. Sr.

MARX, Joseph. Austrian compr. *b.* Graz (Styria), 11 May, 1882. Pupil of Degner; stud. history of fine arts, then music; Ph.D. (dissertation, *The Functions of Intervals in Harmony and Melody for the Comprehension of Time-complexes*), 1st prize, Faculty of Philosophy. Lived till 1914 in Graz, since then in Vienna, as prof. at State Acad. of Music. In 1922 became dir. of the Acad. (succeeding

Ferdinand Löwe). Between 1900–11 publ. about 100 songs. His music started with popular manner (like Robert Franz's), then was influenced by Hugo Wolf. Later he found his own style, which is characterised by the free treatment of the voices, and, by his melodies, which stand between long-drawn *cantilena* and *recitativo*. Later, he wrote chiefly absolute music —chamber-music and orchestral works. All his compns. have a clearly marked local colour (*e.g.* Styrian scenery and popular elements), bold part-writing, polyphony, abundant feeling and richly coloured orchestral sound. The harmony is complicated and interesting, but not novel. His style belongs to the transition-period between Brahms, Wolf, and Schönberg. He may well be called a pure Romanticist.

Orch.: *Romantic Concerto*, pf. (1919); *Herbstsymphonie* (*Autumn Symphony*), perf. Vienna, 1922, at Phil. Concerts with great disturbance; then at Graz with great success. Chamber-music: pf. 4tet (*Ballade, Rhapsody* and *Scherzo*), 1911; *Trio Fantasie* (vn. cello, pf.), 1910; vn. sonata; cello sonata; pf. pieces. Choral: *Herbstchor an Pan* (*Chorus to Pan in Autumn*), 1911; *Abendweise* (*Evening Song*), 1910; *Morgengesang* (*Morning Song*); *Neujahrshymnus* (*Hymn for the New Year*); 120 songs (also *Italian Song-book*, from Paul Heyse), acc. by pf. or str. and wind (*Kammermusiklieder*).—P. P.

MASCAGNI, Pietro. Ital. opera compr. *b.* Leghorn, 7 Dec. 1863. He is a very popular musician; his activities are numerous and fervid, having not only devoted himself to compn. but also, no less successfully, to conducting and teaching. Born in humble circumstances, he began his mus. studies in his native city under Pratesi and Soffredini. Through the liberal patronage of Baron de Lardarel, of Leghorn (to whom M. dedicated *Cavalleria*), he was enabled to go to Milan Cons., having as teachers Saladino and Ponchielli. But he abandoned the Cons. before completing his studies, in order to take up a wandering life as condr. of an operetta company. He then went to Cerignola, in Apulia, where he establ. himself, giving lessons in pf. and conducting the band. In the meantime, he had set to music *Guglielmo Ratcliff* and *Cavalleria Rusticana*. The latter was perf. at one of the opera competitions arranged by Sonzogno (*q.v.*) and was successful. On 1 May, 1890, it was given at the Costanzi Theatre, Rome, and gained a memorable success, through which it started on its triumphant course through all the theatres of the world, suddenly raising the name of Mascagni to great celebrity.

Cavalleria was followed by the operas, *L'Amico Fritz* (Costanzi, Rome, 31 Oct. 1891); *I Rantzau*, (Teatro della Pergola, Florence, 1892); *Guglielmo Ratcliff* (Scala, Milan, 1895); *Silvano* (same theatre and year); *Zanetto* (Pesaro, 1896); *Iris* (Costanzi, Rome, 1898); *Le Maschere* (perf. simultaneously in 7 Ital. theatres on evening of 17 Jan. 1901); *L'Amica* (Monte Carlo, 1905); *Isabeau* (Teatro Coliseo, Buenos Ayres, 1911); *Sì*, operetta in 3 acts (Teatro Quirino, Rome, 1919); *Il piccolo Marat* (Costanzi, Rome, 1921). His operas (except *Iris* which belongs to Ricordi, and *L'Amica*, publ. by Choudens, Paris) have all been publ. by Sonzogno of Milan.

Apart from opera, M. has written interludes for Hall Caine's drama, *The Eternal City* (London, 1902); also a *Messa funebre*, in memory of King Humbert (Pantheon, Rome, 1900); *Rapsodia Satanica* for cinematographic perf. (Rome, 1915); *A Giacomo Leopardi*, cantata for orch. and s. solo, written for centenary of Leopardi (Recanati, 1898); and some chamber-music.

Mascagni's music in his first period had popular, genial and spontaneous characteristics; in later years it acquired high harmonic interest, especially in the opera *Iris*.

As condr. he is very skilful, and directed some important opera seasons and concerts. He was also a teacher and dir. of mus. institutes. From 1895 he held for several years the direction of Liceo Mus. Rossini, Pesaro; then became dir. of Scuola Nazionale di Musica, Rome. In latter Inst. he taught compn. and trained some excellent pupils. Amongst his many activities, M. also includes that of writer and lecturer. He took part in important commissions; was member of the permanent mus. commission attached to Ministry of Education.

Consult: Giannotto Bastianelli, *P. M.* (Naples, 1910, Ricciardi); Edoardo Pompei, *P. M. nella vita e nell'arte* (Rome, 1912); and numberless publications of a controversial character, and arts. in newspapers and reviews.—D. A.

MASCHERONI, Edoardo. Ital. condr. *b.* Milan, 4 Sept. 1859. Began his career in 1883 at Goldoni Theatre, Leghorn. For twelve years, dir. perfs. in the two foremost theatres in Rome, the Argentina and the Apollo. In 1885, President of Società Musicale Romana, for which he cond. concert perf. of Spontini's *Olimpia*. He then went to La Scala, Milan, where he succeeded Franco Faccio, remaining there for four years. M. enjoyed the esteem and friendship of Verdi, whose opera *Falstaff* he cond. at its 1st perf., then taking it on a triumphal tour through Italy. Verdi called him "the third author of *Falstaff*." M. has also cond. at principal theatres abroad, Madrid, Lisbon, Barcelona, Buenos Ayres, etc. Is, in addition, a distinguished compr. having written two operas—*Lorenza*, in 3 acts, book by Luigi Illica (Costanzi, Rome, 1901) and *La Perugina*, 4 acts, book also by Illica (San Carlo Theatre, Naples, 1909) (both publ. by Ricordi). Also several masses, and works for orch., pf. and voice.—D. A.

MASINI, Angelo. Ital. t. singer; *b.* Terra del Sole (Forlì), 1845. *Début* at Finale (Modena) in 1867 in *Norma*. His fame began to grow by his interpretation of Verdi's *Aïda* and *Requiem Mass*, completing a triumphal tour in latter work under direction of the compr. He then sang at principal theatres of Russia, France and England. Had a very extensive repertoire, and into every opera he infused the marks of his own personality and the great beauty of his voice. —D. A.

MASINI-PIERALLI, Angelo. Ital. b. singer; *b.* San Giovanni Valdarno, Tuscany, 1877. *Début* at Sesto Fiorentino in 1898 in *La Sonnambula*. Rapidly rose to principal theatres of Europe and America. During Verdi Centenary commemoration season, he gained special successes in *Don Carlos* and in *Oberto, Conte di San Bonifacio.* Is an excellent interpreter of part of Mefistofele.—D. A.

MÁSLO, Jindřich. Czechoslovak compr. *b.* Čistá, 1875. Pupil of B. Vendler and B. Křídlo.
Educ. works for pf. (F. Chadim; A. Neubert); symphony; pf. trio; 2 str. 4tets (all ms.).—V. ST.

MASON, Daniel Gregory. Amer. compr. *b.* Brookline, Mass., U.S.A., 20 Nov. 1873. Grandson of Lowell Mason; nephew of noted Amer. pianist William Mason. A.B. Harvard, 1895. Stud. music at Harvard under Paine. A pupil in Boston with C. Johns and E. Nevin, later of A. Whiting (pf.), Goetschius (theory) and Chadwick (compn.), also in Paris of d'Indy (compn.). Since 1900, teacher and lecturer in New York. Has lectured for Amer. Univ. Extension Soc.; delivered over 250 lectures for Board of Education of New York. Since 1910, connected with music department of Columbia Univ. in New York; associate-prof. since 1914.

In his compns., grounded in Brahms, d'Indy and the classics, M. displays a solid technique and a marked formal talent. Never reactionary, he has gone his own way without allowing himself to be unduly influenced by the extremes of modern innovators. His books also are characterised by calm judgment, thorough mastery and a sane, forcible presentation of his subjects. His op. 11, a symphony in C mi., was brought out by Philadelphia Orch. on 18 Feb. 1916. A songcycle, *Russians,* op. 18, barit. and orch., was 1st sung by Werrenrath at New York Symphony concert, 25 Jan. 1920. A string 4tet on negro themes was 1st perf. by Flonzaley Quartet in New York, 20 Jan. 1920.
4tet, str. and pf. op. 7 (comp. 1914) (Schirmer, 1917); *Pastoral,* pf. vn. and clar. op. 8 (Mathot, 1913); sonata, pf. and vn. op. 5 (comp. 1913) (Schirmer, 1913); sonata, clar. and pf. op. 14 (Soc. for Publ. of Amer. Music; Ditson, 1920); 3 pieces, op. 13, fl. harp and str. 4tet (Soc. for Publ. Amer. Music 1923); *Elégie* in free variation form, pf. op. 2 (Metzler, 1902); other pf. pieces (Church; Breitkopf; Ditson); Passacaglia and fugue, organ, op. 10 (Gray, 1913); *Russians,* song-cycle, barit. and pf. op. 18 (Schirmer, 1920); other songs (Ditson; Church; Schirmer; Boston Music Co.). Author of: *From Grieg to Brahms* (Outlook Co. 1902); *Beethoven and his Forerunners* (Macmillan, 1904); *The Romantic Composers* (*id.* 1906); *The Appreciation of Music,* Vol. I (with T. W. Surette) (Baker-Taylor, 1908); Vol. II, Great Modern Composers (Gray, 1916); Vol. III, Short Studies of Great Masterpieces (*id.* 1918); Vol. IV, Music as a Humanity (*id.* 1921); *Contemporary Composers* (Macmillan, 1918). Ed.-in-chief of *The Art of Music,* 14 vols. (National Soc. of Music, 1915–17).—O. K.

MASON, Edward. Eng. cellist and condr. *b.* Coventry, 24 June, 1878; killed in action 9 May, 1915. Stud. at R.C.M. under W. E. Whitehouse, Dr. Charles Wood and Dr. Walford Davies; London *début* as cellist, Bechstein Hall, 1900; cond. New Symphony Orch. on their 1st appearance at Queen's Hall, 1906; condr. Edward Mason Choir; member Grimson Str. Quartet. Married the violinist Jessie Grimson (*q.v.*).—E.-H.

MASSARANI, Renzo. Ital. compr. *b.* Mantua, 26 March, 1898. Stud. in R. Liceo Mus. di Santa Cecilia, Rome, under Respighi. He is compr. of interesting pieces for v. and pf. (Pizzi, Bologna; Ricordi); and of an Intermezzo, *Bianco e nero,* perf. in Rome, Teatro dei Piccoli, 1923. M. is musical critic for the Roman newspaper *L'Impero.*—D. A.

MASSAU, Alfred. Belgian cellist; *b.* Verviers, 12 Sept. 1847. Pupil at Liège Cons. of Léon Massart (cello), elder Massart (cpt.), H. Léonard (quartet-playing). Prof. at Verviers Cons. 1873–1920; ex-prof. of Liège Cons. and the School of Music at Maestricht. Author of *Méthode de Violoncelle,* widely used in Europe and America. Some of his many pupils are of first rank (Jean Gérardy, Jacques Gaillard, L. Reuland, J. d'Archambeau, P. Kéfer, Jean Schwiller, etc.).—C. V. B.

MASSÉ, Victor. Fr. compr. *b.* Lorient, 7 March, 1822; *d.* Paris, 5 July, 1884. *Prix de Rome,* 1846 (with cantata, *Le Renégat de Tanger*), after studying with Zimmermann for pf. and Halévy for compn. Celebrated during the Second Empire for his *romances,* then for his *opérascomiques,* of which the following are still played: *Les Noces de Jeannette* (1853); *Galatée* (1852), and sometimes *Paul et Virginie* (1876). He was an agreeable melodist who aroused the interest of Saint-Saëns. In 1872 he succeeded Auber at the Institut.—A. C.

MASSENET, Jules. French opera-composer; *b.* Montaud, near St.-Étienne (Loire), 12 May, 1842; *d.* Paris, 13 August, 1912. The case of this composer is very strange. His originality at first sight does not seem very striking. He appears rather to be an eclectic, skilled in turning to his own account all that happens around him. Nevertheless he has created for himself a style that is very characteristic, since he is imitated unceasingly even to this day.

He studied harmony at the Paris Conservatoire under Bazin and Reber, and composition under Ambroise Thomas. After his *Prix de Rome* in 1863, he met with some difficulties in obtaining recognition, but the success of *Marie-Magdeleine* (1873) opened all doors to him. Five years later, at 36, he entered the Institut and taught composition at the Conservatoire, where he was to have among his numerous pupils the young Claude Debussy. Massenet had a very feminine sensibility. Possessed with the necessity of fascinating, he delighted in easy lyrical effusions whose success with the great public was immense. His very voluptuous music has not the nobility of Gounod's, from which, however, it is derived. It is redolent of perfumes and powder of indifferent quality. One quickly tires of those transports, of those avowals, of those embraces, of those artificial swoons. However, one cannot without injustice deny to his melody qualities of grace and arresting charm. Debussy was indulgent to him; besides, did he not himself yield in his youth to the seduction of this charming master? We find traces of this, even in *Pelléas.*

A lover of the theatre, Massenet excelled in composing a dramatic scene or a love-duet. He never allowed the action to be overwhelmed by the music. It may be said that of their class *Manon, Werther, Le Jongleur de Notre Dame* are masterpieces. In them, he practises the art of half-tints, light and fine, transparent and voluptuous, in which he excels. Unfortunately, towards the end of his life he wished to vie with the composers of Germany and especially with the Italian Verists, and his last operas, from *Ariane* (1906) onwards, are noisy, vulgar and pretentious and had no lasting success.

Massenet was often handicapped by his insufficient knowledge of the orchestra. The works of this rival and contemporary of Lalo, Saint-Saëns, Bizet and Chabrier are subdued; the crescendos never result in the expected outburst. He had, however, a very fine harmonic sensibility; but it is his melody, sinuous and caressing, with languorous inflections, which is characteristic of his style.

It is in reality to the school of Massenet, more than to any other, that we owe this sickliness of melodic taste, this music of thrills, all this basely sensual art which has triumphed in the theatre as in the café-concert. It would, however, be unjust to hold him responsible for the excesses of his imitators. Rather let us salute in him a distinguished musician and acknowledge that he was able to find accents capable of throwing hearts into a delightful agitation.

He was professor of composition at the Paris Conservatoire from 1878 to 1896. His chief pupils were Alfred Bruneau, G. Charpentier, G. Pierné, X. Leroux, P. Vidal, G. Marty, L. Hillemacher, and A. Savard.

Chief operas: *Hérodiade* (Brussels, 1881); *Manon* (Opéra-Comique, 1884); *Le Cid* (Paris, Grand Opéra, 1885); *Werther* (Vienna, 1892); *Thaïs* (Paris, 1894); *Sapho* (Opéra-Comique, 1897); *Le Jongleur de Notre Dame* (Monte Carlo, 1902). His orch. *Scènes pittoresques* were written in 1874 (Heugel). Consult: L. Schneider, *M.* 1908; René Brancour, *M.* (Alcan, 1923); and Octave Séré, *Musiciens français d'aujourd'hui* (Mercure de France, 1911), for complete catalogue of his works.—H. P.

MASSON, Paul Marie. Fr. writer on music; *b.* Cette (Hérault), 1882. Pupil at École Normale Supérieure, then member of the Fondation Thiers. Devoted himself to mus. history and æsthetics under Romain Rolland; also stud. compn. under V. d'Indy at *Schola Cantorum*. Prof. at Institut Français, Florence, 1910; dir. of Institut Français, Naples, 1919. Most of his works on music have appeared in various musical reviews.

Les Odes d'Horace en musique au XVIᵉ siècle (*Revue Musicale*, 1906); *Les Brunettes* (*Sammelbände der I.M.G.* 17th year); *Lullistes et Ramistes* (*Année Musicale*, 1912), etc. He re-ed. *Florentine Carnival Songs of the time of Lorenzo the Magnificent*; publ. a vol. on *Berlioz* (Paris, 1923, Alcan). A study in historical criticism, *L'Opéra de Rameau*, is in preparation. Comp. *Marche à la Justice* (perf. 1917); pf. pieces.—M. L. P.

MASZYŃSKI, Piotr. Polish compr. condr. *b.* Warsaw, 1855. Stud. pf. in Warsaw under Michałowski and Noskowski. Went to Constance, Switzerland, in 1878, becoming 2nd condr. of choral soc. *Bodan*. In 1886, returned to Warsaw and founded famous choral soc. *Lutnia*; 1890, prof. at Cons. Besides some pf.

pieces and mus. illustrations of dramatic scenes, he writes chiefly songs and very effective choral compns. Ed. of popular music editions and transl. of opera libretti. Is one of the most active music-organisers and pioneers of musical culture in Warsaw.—Zd. J.

MATERNA, Amalia. Austrian opera singer; *b.* St. Georgen (Styria), 10 July, 1845; *d.* Vienna, 18 Jan. 1918. 1865, opera-soubrette at Graz (Styria); principal operetta-singer at Carl Theatre, Vienna; 1869–97 at Court-Opera. Since 1902, well-known singing teacher. A famous Wagner-singer, highly esteemed by Wagner himself. The first Brünnhilde at Bayreuth Fests. 1875. In 1882 was the first Kundry there.—P. St.

MATHIEU, Émile Louis Victor. Compr. *b.* Lille (of Belgian parents), 18 Oct. 1844. 2nd *Prix de Rome*, 1869 and 1871; prof. Louvain School of Music, 1867; of same, 1881. Dir. Ghent Cons. 1896; retired Jan. 1924. Member of Belgian R. Acad. and of Commission for publ. of works of old Belgian masters. His musical style is very conservative.

Stage works: *L'Échange, opéra-comique* (own words) (Liège, 1863); music to V. Séjour's drama *Cromwell* (Paris, 1874); *Les Fumeurs de Kiff*, ballet (Brussels, 1876); *Georges Dandin*, comic opera (Brussels, 1877); *La Bernoise*, comic opera (Brussels, 1880); *Richilde*, lyric tragedy (also text) (Brussels, 1888); *Bathyle*, comic opera (Brussels, 1893); *L'Enfance de Roland*, opera (also text) (Brussels, 1895); *La Reine Vasthi*, biblical opera (also text). Chorus and orch.: *La Dernière Nuit de Faust* (1869); *Le Songe de Colomb* (1871), *Torquato Tasso's Death* (1873), cantatas for *Prix de Rome*; *Te Deum*; *Debout, peuple!* (inaugural cantata); *Le Hoyoux, Freyhir*, and *Le Sorbier*, lyric and symph. poems (also text). Orch.: *Noces féodales*, *Le Lac, Sous bois* (symph. poems); vn. concertos; *Paysages d'automne*, pf. and orch. 6 songs on André Van Hasselt's poems; 6 Goethe ballads; 3 Heine ballads; *Le Roi Harald Harfagar* (Heine), etc. Choruses for female, male, and mixed choirs.—E. C.

MATTHAY, Tobias. Eng. pf. teacher, writer and lecturer; *b.* Clapham, London, 19 Feb 1858. Stud. at R.C.M. under Sterndale Bennett, Arthur Sullivan, E. Prout and W. Macfarren. Prof. of pf. at R.A.M. 1880 to present time; founded the Matthay School, 1900. He was the first to elucidate the laws underlying good and bad pf. technique, and to demonstrate the nature of mus. rhythm as "progressional movement." Amongst his pupils are Gertrude Peppercorn, Harriet Cohen, Myra Hess, Irene Scharrer, Désirée MacEwan, Arthur Alexander, York Bowen, Vivian Langrish, Felix Swinstead, Percy Waller.

Concert-piece No. I, A mi. op. 23 (Ricordi); 4tet, pf. and str. (Anglo-Fr. Co.); numerous pf. pieces, including *Love-Phases*, op. 12 (J. Williams); *Monothemes*, op. 13 (Forsyth); *Lyrics* (Paterson); Prelude, op. 16 (Weekes); *Bravura*, op. 16 (Ricordi); *Elves* (Weekes); *Sketch-books*, op. 24, 26 (Anglo-Fr. Co.). 31 variations on orig. theme, op. 28 (Augener); *On Surrey Hills*, op. 30 (Anglo-Fr. Co.); 3 *Lyric Studies*, op. 33 (*id.*). Books: *The Act of Touch* (Longmans, 1903); *Musical Interpretation* (J. Williams, 1913); *Method in Teaching* (Anglo-Fr. Co.); *Relaxation Studies* (Bosworth, 1907); *First Principles* (Longmans, 1905); *The Child's First Steps in Pf.-playing* (J Williams); *Pianist's First Music Making*, 3 bks. (Anglo-Fr. Co.).—E.-H.

MATTHEWS, Thomas Appleby. Eng. condr. *b.* Tamworth, 30 Aug., 1884. Stud. Birmingham and Midland Inst. under J. D. Davis and Granville Bantock; dir. and condr. City of Birmingham orch. since foundation Jan. 1920 (succeeded by Boult, 1924); dir. and condr. Birmingham Repertory Theatre's operatic productions, including unparalleled success of Boughton's *Immortal Hour*, Regent Theatre, London.—E.-H.

MATTHEY, Ulisse. Ital. orgt. *b.* Turin, 1876. Stud. organ at Turin at Liceo Mus.; then fugue and compn. with Prof. Ferroni in Milan. Perfected himself in organ-playing under Guilmant in Paris. From 1902, orgt. Basilica of Loreto. Has given many concerts with success. —D. A.

MATTHISON - HANSEN, Gotfred. Danish compr. orgt. *b.* Roskilde, 1 Nov. 1832; *d.* Copenhagen, 14 Oct. 1909. Belonged to one of Denmark's best-known musical families (his father, Hans M.-H., was the noted orgt. of Roskilde Cath.); M.A. 1850; stud. law at Univ. Copenhagen for 3 years. After a successful *début* in 1856 as orgt. he decided in favour of music as a profession. In 1859, orgt. at Frederiks Ch. Copenhagen; later advanced successively to posts at St. John's and Trinity, Copenhagen. In 1867, prof. at R. Cons.; 1900, member of its board of governors. Extensive concert-tours in Scandinavia and Germany, where he made quite a name for himself, as also in Copenhagen, through his regular organ recitals at Trinity Ch. In his own music (principally organ and chamber-music) he manifests an interesting personality.

Pf. trio, op. 5; Novellettes, pf. and cello, op. 12 (Leipzig, Breitkopf); sonata, pf. and vn. op. 11; sonata, pf. and cello, op. 16; numerous pf. pieces (op. 1, 2, 6, 10, 13, 14); organ pieces; sacred songs with organ acc. (Copenhagen, Hansen). There are a str. 4tet, a pf. 5tet, a pf. sonata and *Drapa* for orch. in ms.—A. H.

MATTIESEN, Emil. Ger. song compr. *b.* Dorpat, 24 Jan. 1875. Stud. philosophy and natural sciences at Dorpat and Leipzig, 1892–6; 1896, Ph.D.; 1898–1903, travelled in Asia and America; 1904–8, scientific work at Cambridge, England; 1908–15, in Berlin; till 1922 at Rostock. Through inducement of Karl Muck and Paul Müller he has appeared as compr. since 1910.

Ballads to the Dead (op. 1); songs and ballads, op. 2–12 (Peters). His compns. have been made known through a Mattiesen Soc. (establ. 1921).—A. E.

MATTIOLI, Guglielmo. Italian compr. *b.* Reggio Emilia, 14 Oct. 1859. Stud. at Bologna under Busi; took diploma for organ at Liceo Mus. of that city. Specially devoted himself to teaching. After having occupied various positions, he settled in 1908 in Bologna as prof. of cpt. compn. and organ in the Liceo Mus. there. Is author of several operas, and much vocal and instrumental music.—D. A.

MAUGUÉ, Fernand. Fr. compr. *b.* at Nancy. Pupil of Cons. of Nancy and of Paris. *Lauréat* of the Institut.

Le Sphinx, orch.; *Site agreste*, orch.; str. 4tet; double 5tet for wind instrs.; sonata, pf. and vn.; Theme, ob. and orch.—A. C.

MAUKE, Wilhelm. Ger. compr. and critic; *b.* Hamburg, 25 Feb. 1867. First stud. medicine, then music under Hans Huber and Löw at

Basle, and 1892–3 at Munich Acad. of Music. Mus. critic, till 1919 opera reporter at Munich, finally of *Münchner Zeitung.*

Songs and hymns; symph. poems: *Solitude*, op. 4 (after Nietzsche); *Liliencron*, op. 54; *Sursum corda*, op. 59; *Ora pro nobis*, op. 62 (dramatic scena for s. and orch.); *Romantic Symphony*, op. 63; symphony with chorus and solo, *Gold*; oratorio, *Expulsion from Paradise*, op. 78; opera, *The Good-for-Nothing* (after Eichendorff, 1905); operettas: *The Virtuous Prince* (Munich, 1907); *Fanfreluche* (Munich, 1912); *The Last Mask* (mimodrama, Carlsruhe, 1917); *Laurin's Garden of Roses* (romantic opera); *Festival of Life* (tragic opera, op. 73); *Thamar*, op. 76 (Stuttgart, 1922). Consult Wilibald Nagel, *W. M.* (1919).—A. E.

MAUREL, Victor. Fr. operatic barit. singer; *b.* Marseilles, 17 June, 1848; *d.* New York, Oct. 1923. Stud. at Paris Cons. under Faure; *début*, at age of 20, at Paris Opéra, as Nevers in *Huguenots*; first London appearance at Covent Garden, 21 April, 1873, as Renato in *Ballo in Maschera*. In 1875 he sang Telramund (*Lohengrin*) and in 1876 Wolfram (*Tannhäuser*) at first perfs. in England of those works. He created the part of Amonasro in *Aida*, Cairo, 1880. In 1883–4 he managed an opera season at Théatre des Nations, Paris, producing Massenet's *Hérodiade*. His most famous creations were Iago in *Otello* (Milan, 1887; Lyceum Theatre, London, 1889) and Falstaff in Verdi's last opera (Milan, 1893). In his later years he devoted himself to teaching. M. had a fine stage-presence and a powerful voice, and his performances were remarkable for their intense dramatic force. In 1897 he publ. a book of reminiscences, *Dix Ans de Carrière.*—C. L.

MAURICE, Pierre. Swiss compr. *b.* Allaman, 13 Nov. 1868. Stud. compn. at Paris Cons. under A. Gédalge, Massenet and G. Fauré (1890–8); lived in Munich, 1899–1917; now at Allaman (on Lake of Geneva). His music, finely orchestrated and very poetically conceived, shows relationship to Massenet and Fauré, and his works are greatly appreciated in Germany and Switzerland.

4 operas (Fr. and Ger. text): La Fille de Jephté, biblical drama (Paris, Enoch); Le Drapeau blanc, lyric drama (Stuttgart, Feuchtinger); Misé Brun, lyric drama (Berlin, Bote & Bock); Lanval, 3 acts, founded on poem by Marie de France (Leipzig); Arambel (J. Ravina), mimodrama, 4 acts; symph. poem, Françoise de Rimini; Pêcheur d'Islande (Pierre Loti), suite for orch. (Munich, H. Lewy); Gorm Grymme (Th. Fontane), barit. chorus, orch.; fugues for 2 pfs. (New York, Ditson); unacc. choruses (Geneva, Henn); songs (publ. Rouart; Hachette; Henn; Fœtisch).—F. H.

MAUS, Octave. Belgian musicologist; *b.* Brussels, 12 June, 1856; *d.* Lausanne, 26 Nov. 1919. LL.D. Univ. Brussels; first practised at the bar, later devoted himself entirely to his love of art and propaganda of new ideas in Belgium. 1881, founded weekly review *L'Art Moderne*; 1884, with an advanced group of painters and sculptors, the *Cercle des XX* and *La Libre Esthétique* (1894). A staunch admirer of Wagner from the first, he was present at the public rehearsals at Bayreuth in 1876 (see his booklet *Le Théâtre de Bayreuth* [Brussels, 1888], and his charming work *Les Préludes* [Brussels, 1921, Sand, publ. posthumously]). From 1888 onwards he brought to the notice of the public

the works of César Franck and of the modern
Fr. school at the *Concerts des XX* and the
Concerts de la Libre Esthétique. Thus he was
responsible for 1st perf. in Brussels of César
Franck's sonata (played by Eugène Ysaye), also
of works of Fauré, d'Indy, Chausson, and
sonata of Lekeu, 1892; 1894, devoted concert
to Debussy; 1905 to Cyril Scott; 1910 to
Poldowski, etc. Music lectures and many
arts. in *L'Art Moderne* (up to 1914). He was
wholly artistic, yet human, eminently fitted
to undertake the æsthetic regeneration of
Belgium with lasting results.—C. V. B.

MAWET, Fernand. Belgian composer; *b.*
Vaux-sous-Chèvremont, near Liège, 7 April,
1870. Stud. pf., organ at Liège Cons.; orgt.
and teacher there.

Religious compns., organ pieces, choruses for male
vs., songs, works in Fr. and in dialect of Liège,
notably *Li Fordjeu* (Liège, 1908), *Noël sanglant*
(1910), *Colas Boncour* (1911). Theoretic works:
Théorie analytique des accords; *Tableaux synoptiques
des intervalles.*—E. C.

MAYER, Max. Pianist and compr. *b.* Vechta,
Oldenburg, Germany, 31 May, 1859. Stud. pf.
and compn. in Stuttgart; later under Liszt
in Weimar; settled in Manchester, April 1883;
for 25 years gave regular chamber-concerts there;
1908, one of chief pf. profs. at R. Manchester
Coll. of Music, which post he still holds. Became
a naturalised British subject in 1900; his compns.
include pf. pieces for 2 and 4 hands and a great
number of songs (mostly Schott & Co.).—E.-H.

MAYR, Richard. Austrian singer; *b.* Henndorf,
near Salzburg. As student was heard by Gustav
Mahler in 1902 and appointed to Vienna Opera
House, where he has sung ever since. One of
the best b.-barits. of Ger. stage and brilliant
and original actor, an excellent King Mark,
Hans Sachs, Leporello, Figaro, Ochs von
Lerchenau. Also a fine concert-singer. Consult
biography by H. J. Holz (1923, Wila).—P. St.

MAZZOLENI, Ester. Operatic s. singer;
b. Sebenico (Dalmatia). *Début* at Costanzi in
Rome in *Il Trovatore*; rapidly gained high
reputation, visiting principal theatres of Europe
and America. A great interpreter of Bellini's
Norma.—D. A.

MEALE, John Arthur. Eng. orgt. *b.* Slaithwaite, Huddersfield, 18 Dec. 1880. Mus. dir. and
orgt. Central Hall, Westminster, from 1912.

Numerous songs; anthems; and organ pieces.
—E.-H.

MEDINS, Janis. Latvian compr. *b.* Riga,
27 Feb. 1890. Self-taught; fairly modern in
tendency. The most talented of the younger
generation of Latvian comprs.

2 operas; a symphony; a str. 4tet; 2 trios; a cello
concerto; pf. pieces; vn. and pf. works; many solo
songs and 4-pt. unacc. songs.—K. P.

MEDTNER, Nicolas. See METNER.

MEERENS, Charles. Belgian acoustician,
musicologist; *b.* Bruges, 26 Dec. 1831; *d.*
there, 14 Jan. 1909. Stud. cello privately
at Bruges and Antwerp (where he founded a
mus. soc. and also dir. a publishing firm for some
time). Stud. also at Brussels Cons. Then gave up
playing in order to devote whole time to acous-

tics and mus. physiology. He was entirely
opposed to idea of physical laws interfering
with physical effects of music, which he claims
to be entirely result of psychology. Also inventor of a metronome, based on oscillation of
a pendulum, and of system of notation in which
he replaced the clefs by the order-number of
different octaves. Also questioned acceptance
of 870 vibrations for normal diapason, preferring the number 864. His ideas only attracted
temporary attention and are entirely disregarded
to-day. Publ. booklets, mainly extracts from
his articles:

The Metronome (1859); *Elementary Instruction in
Musical Calculation* (1864); *Musico-psychological
Phenomena* (1868); *Tribute to the Memory of M.
Delezenne* (1869); *Diapason and Musical Notation
Simplified* (1873); *Notes on Diapason* (1877); *Ed-
mond Van der Straeten*, biog. (1877); *The Musical
Octave, Major and Minor* (1890); *Musical Acoustics*
(1892); *Real Relationships of Musical Sounds* (1894);
Catalogue of Musical Instruments of César Snoeck;
Future of Musical Science (1894); *Scheibler's Tono-
metre* (1895); *On the Old Melopœia in Singing in the
Latin Church of Gevaert* (1896); *Handbook for Rapid
Instruction in Music and Pianoforte* (all publ. Brus-
sels). Also wrote for the *Guide Musical* and the
Fédération Artistique.—E. C.

MEES, Arthur. Amer. condr. *b.* Columbus,
Ohio, U.S.A., 13 Feb. 1850; *d.* New York, 26
April 1923. Stud. under Kullak (pf.), Weitzmann (theory) and H. Dorn (cond.) in Berlin,
1873–6. Condr. of Cincinnati (O.) May Fests.
1880–6; Worcester (Mass.) Fests. 1908–19, Norfolk (Conn.) Fest. from 1900 to 1921. Assistant-condr. of Amer. Opera Co., 1888–1911, and
to Theodore Thomas with Chicago Symphony
Orch. 1896–8. Wrote analytical programmes of
New York Philh. Soc. 1887–96, and Chicago
Symphony Orch. 1896–8, Worcester Fest. 1908–
1921. Author of *Choirs and Choral Music*
(Scribner, 1911). Received Mus.Doc. *h.c.* Alfred
Univ., Alfred, N.Y.—J. M.

MELANI, Pedro. Argentine violinist; *b.* Salerno,
Naples, 1854; *d.* Buenos Ayres in 1900. Stud.
under Lambiase and Pinto at Naples. After concert tour through Italy, was 1st vn. at R. Theatre,
Cairo. Thence to Berlin, where he stud. under
Joachim for 3 years. Returning to Naples, he
set out upon a brilliant career, which (acting
under mistaken advice) he renounced in 1880 to
establish himself in Buenos Ayres. Argentina
was at that time no country for an artist of his
talents. He gave many concerts, and then
joined, as 1st vn., the Primer Cuarteto (First
Quartet) of Buenos Ayres, which soon became
famous. In 1888 he founded a Cons., but the
artist's child-like and simple nature was unable
to cope with the necessary business administration, and he closed it at the end of the year.
He then joined the Buenos Ayres Cons., but
his health began to fail, and he died in
1900.—A. M.

MELARTIN, Erkki. Finnish compr. *b.* Käki-
salmi, 7 Feb. 1875. Stud. at Helsingfors Music
Inst. and abroad (Vienna, Rome, Berlin);
1908–10, condr. in Viipuri (Viborg); 1911–22,
dir. of Helsingfors Mus. Inst. One of the most
prominent Finnish comprs.; has produced representative works in almost every department of

music. Characteristic of his music is an emotional lyricism which often draws on folk-song melody; his style shows modern Impressionist and Expressionist tendencies. M. has appeared as condr. in Stockholm, Copenhagen, Riga, Petrograd, Moscow, etc.

5 symphonies; symph. poems (*Dream Visions*, etc.); 3 orch. suites (*Impressions de Belgique*, etc.); vn. concerto; 4 str. 4tets; vn. sonata; pf. sonata; pf. pieces; cantatas with orch. (*Vardtrādet*); stage music (Topelius's *Prinsessan*, *Törnrosa*, Hauptmann's *Hannele*, etc.); an opera, *Aino* (a *Kalevala* mystery); about 200 songs; choral works, etc. (publ. in Helsingfors, Leipzig, Copenhagen, London).—T. H.

MELBA, Dame Nellie. Operatic s. singer; *b.* Melbourne, Australia. Daughter of a Scotch colonist; in 1885, sang at concert of Melbourne Male Choir, and was so largely successful, that she proceeded to England for study (1886). Wilhelm Ganz arr. for her to sing at a concert in Prince's Hall, London; she then stud. under Mathilde Marchesi in Paris. Made her stage *début* at La Monnaie, Brussels (Gilda in *Rigoletto*), 12 Oct. 1887, with immense success; first London appearance, 1 June, 1888, as heroine in *Lucia di Lammermoor*, a rôle which became her favourite one; then Paris Opéra in Ambroise Thomas's *Hamlet*; heroine in Gounod's *Roméo et Juliette*, Covent Garden (with Jean de Reszke, June 1889); then Paris again (Marguerite, Juliette, Ophélie, Lucia, Gilda); also in Russia, Sweden, Italy, Holland. She appeared in special performances of the B.N.O.C. London, 1922–3. Her career has been one of the most brilliant in the history of opera. Of late years, she has taken great interest in mus. education in Melbourne, where she is president of the Conservatoire. —E.-H.

MELCER-SZCZAWIŃSKI, Henryk. Polish pianist, compr. *b.* Kalisz, 21 Sept. 1869. Stud. under Strobl (pf.) and Noskowski (theory) at Warsaw Cons., and under Leschetizky in Vienna. 1895, prof. at Lemberg Cons.; in 1900 (not having obtained the position of dir.) left Lemberg for a short time; 1901–2, condr. of Lemberg Philh.; 1903–6, prof. at Vienna Cons. From 1908, has lived in Warsaw where he first cond. the Philh. Concerts, and then became prof. at State Cons. In 1922 was appointed dir. of Warsaw Cons. M. is one of the best Polish pianists.

Opera, *Maria* (after Malczewski), perf. Warsaw, 1904; 2 pf. concertos, E mi. (1st Rubinstein Prize, Vienna, 1895) and C mi. (Paderewski Prize, Leipzig, 1898); sonata, vn. and pf. G ma.; songs (in modern style); pf. transcriptions of Moniusko's songs. —ZD. J.

MELCHERS, H. Melcher. Swedish compr. *b.* Stockholm, 30 May, 1882. Stud. R. Cons. Stockholm, 1896–1902; then compn. under Johan Lindegren, 1904–5; stud. further at Cons. at Paris, 1908–12; taught in Paris, 1905–19. Gave teaching courses in Brussels and Sondershausen, 1921. Lives now in Stockholm, as private teacher.

8 *Zigeunerlieder*, m.-sopr. and orch. (1910; W. Hansen); cantata (1913); *Swedish Rhapsody*, orch. (Stockholm, 1914); symph. poems: *The Nixie* (1916); *La Kermesse* (1919; Stockholm, 1920); *Elégie* (1920; Sondershausen, 1921); songs with orch.; *Poem*, vn. and orch. (1922).—P. V.

MELIS, Carmen. Italian soprano singer; *b.* Cagliari, 14 Aug. 1885. Pupil of Antonio Cotogni. *Début* at Novara in *Iris* in 1905; immediately after, started on a brilliant career. Amongst her best parts are the *Fanciulla del West* and *Madama Butterfly* (Puccini) and *Manon* and *Thaïs* (Massenet).—D. A.

MELKIKH, Dmitry Michaelovitch. Russ. compr. *b.* Moscow, 31 Jan./11 Feb. 1885; pupil of B. L. Javorsky at People's Cons. Moscow.

Symph. sketches: *By the Sea*, op. 1; *The Contrasts*, op. 7, orch.; *Sonata Nocturne*, pf. (Russ. State Mus. Publ. Dept.); 2nd pf. sonata; songs (op. 1, Jurgenson; others R.S.M.P.D.); pf. pieces.—V. B.

MELLING, Einar. Norwegian orgt. compr. *b.* Lindaas, near Bergen, 16 Jan. 1880. Pupil of Music Cons. in Christiania and of Cons. in Leipzig. Appeared in 1900 as compr. and pianist at own concert in Christiania. From 1903, orgt. of Ullern Ch. near Christiania; since 1910, at different churches in Christiania, where he frequently gives organ-recitals. As compr. M. has only cultivated the minor forms of music, pf. pieces, male choruses and songs. These exhibit a bright and charming lyrical quality, influenced (in later works) by modern Impressionism. In spite of his being blind from birth, his exceptional mus. talent has raised him to a high artistic level.—J. A.

MELSA, Daniel. Polish violinist; *b.* Warsaw, 14 Aug. 1892. Stud. under Carl Flesch in Berlin; *début* at Lódź, Feb. 1901; in London, 15 Jan. 1913; since then has played in nearly every capital in Europe and toured extensively (Australia, New Zealand, Canada, U.S.A.).—E.-H.

MENCHACA, Angel. Argentine writer on music; *b.* Asunción del Paraguay, 1855. Stud. law and was a pioneer in stenography in Argentina. First dir. of government organ, *El Boletín Oficial*. His love for music drew him to scientific study of mus. notation. This resulted in publ. of his widely known work *Nuevo Sistema teórico-gráfico de la Música*, printed in 1904 by the Buenos Ayres provincial government (Pleyel, Lyon & Co.), who sent him to Europe to disseminate his new system, and to lecture on emigration (London, Madrid, Paris, Barcelona, Genoa, Milan, Berlin). Returning to Buenos Ayres, he started a series of courses on his new notation and the new keyboard connected with it. M. was the first to lecture and write extensively on the inconsistencies of the present notation, especially of the sharps and flats. He took the first steps towards a real dodecuple notation (see art. on NOTATIONS). At present, he occupies the chairs of history and literature in the National Coll. Mariano·Moreno. Has publ. many comedies, songs and school choruses.—S. G. S.

MENCHACA KEYBOARD, for pf., organ, harmonium, etc.; termed Continuous; formed of white and black keys in *regular* sequence. The black keys are on a slightly inclined plane and 2 mm. narrower at their extremities, the greater space thus given to the white keys making the fingering easier. The white keys go to the same level as the black at their ends in a width of 2 cm.; this allows of chromatic *glissando* which is of all sounds the most brilliant. The keyboard facilitates fingering. Was exhibited some years ago in Paris by its inventor,

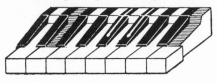

GENERAL VIEW

Angel Menchaca; and is in use to-day in Buenos Ayres, La Plata and Montevideo. See also art. NOTATIONS.—E.-H.

MENDELSSOHN, Arnold. Ger. compr. *b.* Ratibor, 26 Dec. 1855. Son of cousin of Felix Mendelssohn; stud. jurisprudence at Tübingen, then music in Berlin, under Haupt (organ), Grell, Wilsing, Kiel, Taubert, Loeschhorn; 1880-3, orgt. and Univ. teacher at Bonn; mus. dir. Bielefeld; 1885, teacher at Cologne Cons.; 1890, church choir-master, Darmstadt; 1899, Grand-Ducal Prof.; 1917, Ph.D. *h.c.* Heidelberg Univ.; 1919, member of Berlin Acad. of Art. He is a compr. of late-Romantic tendencies, his works being of delicate feeling and perfect in form; has distinguished himself by improving Protestant church music.

For mixed chorus, soli and orch.: *Evening cantata* (1881); *Der Hagestolz* (1890); *Spring Festival* (1891); *Paria* (1905); for male chorus, solo and orch.: *Pandora* (1908); *Tailor's Descent into Hell* (1897); cantata, *In Deepest Need* (s., mixed chorus and orch.), 3 5-v. madrigals, words from Goethe's *Werther*; many songs and small choral works for un-acc. choirs, op. 14, 32, 33, 42, 44, 59, 69, 81, 87, 89, 90; 6-v. *Zur Beherzigung* (Goethe); 8-v. *Funeral Song* (Shakespeare) and *God and the World* (Goethe); 4-v. *Bridal Dance* (Sim. Dach); symphony, E flat ma. op. 85; vn. concerto, op. 88; pf. sonatas, op. 2i and 66; str. 4tets, op. 67 and op. 83; cello sonata, op. 70 (1916); vn. sonata, op. 71; trio for 2 vns. and pf. op. 76; *Modern Suite* for pf. op. 77. —A. E.

MENGELBERG, Willem. Dutch conductor; *b.* Utrecht, 28 March, 1871. Started musical education at very early age; studied under Rich. Hol and M. W. Petri at Utrecht Music School; 1888-1891, in Cologne under Franz Wüllner and Isidor Seiss; conductor Lucerne (Switzerland), 1892-5; returned to Amsterdam, from 27 October, 1895. Conductor of Concertgebouw Orchestra, the chief orchestra of Holland (about 100 members).

M. cond. concerts at Bergen (Norway), 1898, Belgium (1900), London (1903), Frankfort (Museum Concerts) (1907-17), France (1907), New York, Rome, Milan, Petrograd, Moscow, Berlin, Vienna; 1913-14, condr. of Royal Philh. Soc. London; 1898, condr. of Toonkunst, Amsterdam (choral soc.); his perfs. of the Mahler symphonies are noteworthy (see Mahler biography by R. Specht, 1921).—W. P.

MENGES, Isolde. Violinist; *b.* 1894. Stud. under her father, and later under Leopold Auer in Petrograd (1909); her first orch. concert in

London was on 4 Feb. 1913, with Lyell-Taylor's Brighton Municipal Orch. Tours widely in Europe and America.—E.-H.

MENTER, Sophie. Ger. pianist; *b.* Munich, 29 July, 1846; *d.* Stockdorf, near Munich, 23 Feb. 1918. Pupil of Fr. Niest (Munich), Tausig, Bülow and Liszt; 1872, married cellist Popper (1886 divorced); 1883-7, prof. at Petrograd Cons.; lived finally (undertaking occasional concert-engagements) at her country seat, Itter in the Tirol, or at Stockdorf, near Munich. Comp. *Gipsy Songs,* pf. and orch. Her sister and pupil, Eugénie Menter (*b.* Munich, 19 May, 1853), stud. under Bülow.—A. E.

MENU, Pierre. Fr. compr. *b.* Paris, 1896; *d.* there, 16 Oct. 1919. Pupil of Roger-Ducasse at Paris Cons. Promised much for the young Fr. school. Left important works:

Pf. 4tet; sonatina for 4tet; fantasia for chromatic harp, *Dans l'ambiance espagnole* (1917); songs.—A. C.

MERIKANTO, Aarre. Finnish compr. *b.* Helsingfors, 29 June, 1893. Son of Oskar M. Stud. at Leipzig Cons. 1912-14 and in Moscow 1916-17. His compns., which have lately shown a marked colouristic tendency, include 2 symphonies, a pf. concerto, and symph. poems, etc.—T. H.

MERIKANTO, Oskar. Finnish orgt. operacondr. compr. prof. *b.* Helsingfors, 5 Aug. 1868; *d.* there, 17 Feb. 1924. Stud. at Leipzig Cons. and in Berlin. Orgt. of St. John's Ch. Helsingfors, from 1892. As condr. of the Finnish Opera (1911-22) and opera compr. did much for development of operatic art in Finland. His abundant production of songs contains some of the most popular in Finnish music. He was noted as an unusually fine accompanist.

3 operas: *Pohjan neiti* (*The Daughter of Pohja*), taken from *Kalevala* (1899); *Elinan surma* (*The Death of Elina*; from a national ballad); *Queen of Emmeritz* (from drama by Topelius); several examples of popular *singspiel*; pieces for organ; for pf.; for vn.; choral works; numerous songs.—T. H.

MERKEL, Gustav Adolf. Ger. orgt. and compr. *b.* Oberoderwitz, near Zittau, 12 Nov. 1827; *d.* Dresden, 30 Oct. 1885. Pupil of J. Otto (cpt.) and J. Schneider (organ) at Dresden; indebted to K. Reissiger and R. Schumann for further help. Teacher at Dresden School, then orgt. at Orphanage Church; Church of the Cross; 1864, R. orgt. at Catholic Court Church; 1867-73, condr. of Dreyssig Acad. of Singing; 1861, teacher at Dresden Conservatoire.

9 organ sonatas: op. 30 (organ duet with double-pedal), 42, 80, 115, 118, 137, 140, 178, 183; Organ Tutor (op. 177); 30 pedal studies; 3 organ fantasias; many choral preludes, fugues, etc; pf. pieces; songs; motets. Consult P. Janssen, *G. M.* (1886).—A. E.

MERKEL, Johannes Gottfried. Ger. teacher and compr. *b.* Leipzig, 25 Sept. 1860. Pupil at Cons. and Univ. Leipzig, and of Franz Liszt; 1888-92, pf. teacher at School of Music, Riga; 1892, at Berlin, Eichelberg Cons.; 1898, at Leipzig R. Cons.; 1918, R. professor.

Pf. sonata; vols. of pf. pieces; *Course of Instruction in Cpt.* (1917); ms.: pf. concerto, symphony, concert overture, str. 4tet., also fugues, canons and other contrapuntal pieces for pf.—A. E.

MERRICK, Frank. Pianist, compr. and teacher; *b.* Clifton, Bristol, 30 April, 1886, of

Eng. father and Irish mother. Stud. pf. under both parents, and compn. under father (Frank Merrick, Mus.Doc. Dublin); pf. under Leschetizky in Vienna 1898–1901, and again in 1905. 1st public appearance, recital in Clifton, Bristol, Nov. 1895.; 1st London appearance, recital Bechstein Hall, March 1903. Married (1911) Hope Squire, compr., pianist and teacher. Stud. with her many little-known works for 2 pfs., which have made up the programmes of their joint concerts. 1911, prof. of pf. at R. Manchester Coll. of Music.

Symphony, D mi. (ms.): *Celtic Suite*, small orch. (Blackburn, 1923); *A Dream-Pageant*, str. orch. (ms.); trio, F sharp mi., pf. vn. cello (ms.); *Chorus of Echoes* for unacc. choir (Shelley's *Prometheus Unbound*) ms.; pf.: *An Ocean Lullaby*; *Variations on a Somerset folk-song, The Bonnie Bluebell*; *Rhapsody in C mi.; paraphrase (in the Bach style) on a Somerset folk-song, *Hares on the Mountains*; pf. acc. in contemporary style to sonatas for vn. and figured bass, in D mi. and E mi. by Veracini and G mi. by Purcell. The works starred in list above formed a programme of orig. compns. which gained a diploma of honour at International Rubinstein Competition, Petrograd, Aug. 1910.—E.-H.

MERSMANN, Hans. Ger. musicologist; *b.* Potsdam, 6 Oct. 1891. Stud. philology at Munich; then went to Leipzig and Berlin (Kretzschmar) where he passed through compn. and condr. classes at Stern's Cons.; 1915, assistant at mus. history training - college of Berlin Univ.; at same time teacher at Stern's Cons. and critic for *Allgemeine Musikzeitung*; 1921, settled at Technical High School, Berlin; 1917, was entrusted with arrangement and administration of a department by Prussian National Song Commission, which was to collect and make scientific use of all Ger. folk-songs. The result of this labour has laid the foundation for mus. folk-song research (*A.f.M.* IV, ii, 1922). He also wrote *The Phenomenology of Music.*

Beiträge zur Ansbacher Musikgeschichte (1916); Kulturgeschichte der Musik in Einzeldarstellungen (1922).—A. E.

MERTENS, Joseph. Belgian compr. *b.* Antwerp, 17 Feb. 1834; *d.* Brussels 30 June, 1901. Prof. of vn. Antwerp Cons.; 1st solo vn. in orchs., especially at Rhenish festivals. 1882, settled in Brussels as inspector of State Schools of Music. Of his numerous operas (Flemish and Fr.) in an old-fashioned style, not one survives.

Stage works: *De Vrijer in de strop* (Antwerp, 1866); *De Vergissing* (ib. 1869); *Thecla* (ib. 1874); *Le Capitaine Robert* (ib. 1875); *Liederik* (ib. 1875); *Le Capitaine noir* (The Hague, 1877), his principal work, played also in Hamburg. An oratorio, *Angelus*; instr. music and choruses.—E. C.

MERZ, Victor. Ger.-Czechoslovak compr. *b.* Brünn, 1891.

Orch. and chamber-music; songs.—E. S.

MESSAGER, André. French operetta composer; *b.* Montluçon (Allier), 30 Dec. 1853. He may be regarded as the only pupil whom Saint-Saëns completely moulded. His master developed in him the taste for an impeccable style. Although an organist of talent and author of a symphony, he has become famous through his light music. His operettas and comic operas, *Les P'tites Michu* (1897), *Véronique* (1898), *Les*

Dragons de l'Impératrice (1905), *Fortunio* (1907), *L'Amour masqué* (1923), are justly celebrated. He has been able to preserve a moderation, an aristocratic distinction, in treating the most commonplace subjects. His melodies charm by their agreeable and sparkling grace. He seems to be the last of the composers of comic operas according to the pure French tradition made illustrious by Auber, Audran and Lecocq. He conducted the orchestra at Covent Garden, London (where he was chief director for several seasons), and made numerous tours in America and Europe. Although his tastes are entirely classic, he is sympathetic to the new school and helped to bring about the acceptance at the Opéra-Comique of the score of *Pelléas et Mélisande*, which he was the first to conduct and which is dedicated to him by Debussy. From 1907 to 1914 he was artistic director of the Opéra in Paris.—H. P.

MESSCHAERT, Johannes. Dutch baritone; *b.* Hoorn, 22 Aug. 1856; *d.* Zurich, 9 Sept. 1922. Stud. vn. at Arnhem; 1877, took singing as principal study at Cologne Cons. (Karl Schneider); 1879, at Frankfort under Julius Stockhausen; 1881, returned to Holland; rose suddenly to fame with Schubert songs and Bach cantatas. His part of Christ in Bach's *St. Matthew Passion* was incomparable. Consult brochure by Franziska Martienszen, *Die echte Gesangskunst, dargestellt durch J. M.* (Berlin, Behrs).—W. P.

MESTDAGH, Karel. Belgian composer; *b.* St.-Pierre, near Bruges, 23 Oct. 1850. Pupil of Waelput, Van Gheluwe and Gevaert. Dir. of Bruges Cons. since 1900. Member of R. Belgian Acad., of committee of mus. art instituted by Government, of council for perfecting teaching of music in Belgium, and of commission for publ. of old Belgian masters.

Jubilee Cantatas for chorus and orch.; marches; overtures; popular episodes for orch.; a 2-v. mass; motets; a prelude and other organ pieces; *Divertissements* and *Ballades*, pf.; many songs and poems for v. and orch. and with pf.—E. C.

METNER, Nicolas Razlovitch (*accent 1st syll.*). Russ. compr. *b.* Moscow, 1879. Stud. pf. under Safonof at Moscow Cons.; but as regards compn. is chiefly self-taught. Prof. of pf. at Moscow. Has written a quantity of pf. music and songs, as well as a few works for vn. and pf. and a pf. concerto. He is one of the chief exponents in Russia of the traditional classical tendency, and his music owes nothing to the influence either of the Nationalist movement or of more modern tendencies such as Scriabin's. His affinities with Brahms have often been commented upon. Consult arts. in Russ. by Sabaneief (*Muzyka*, 1912, No. 63), and by Miaskovsky (*id.* 1913, No. 119); in Eng. by Alfred Swan (*Mus. Times*, Sept. 1922).

Pf. concerto, C mi. op. 33; pf. sonata, F mi. op. 5; Sonaten-Triade, pf. A flat ma., D mi., C mi. op. 11; pf. sonata, G mi. op. 22; 2 pf. sonatas, C mi., E mi. op. 25; Sonata-Ballade, F sharp ma. pf. op. 27; pf. sonata, A mi. op. 30; vn. sonata, B mi. op. 21; many pf. pieces (*Improvisations, Arabesken, Dithyramben, Märchen, Novelles*, etc.); songs; vla. pieces.—M. D. C.

METZGER-FROITZHEIM, Ottilie. Ger. contr. singer; *b.* Frankfort-o-M. 15 June, 1878. Pupil of Mme. Nicklass - Kempner, Georg Vogel, Emanuel Reicher, Berlin; 1st engagements Halle-o-S. and Cologne; 1903, at Hamburg Opera House; 1902, married author Clemens Froitzheim (1908 divorced); 1910, married Theodor Lattermann, b.-barit. Hamburg. Gave concerts in America.—A. E.

MEULEMANS, Arthur. Belgian compr. *b.* Aerschot, 19 May, 1884. Pupil of Tinel; prof. of harmony at School of Religious Music, Malines; at the present time, principal of Limburg Organ and Singing School at Tongres. Has comp. many works, some romantic in tendency, others modern.

Opera, *Vikings*; oratorios: *Sacrum Misterium*; *De Zeven Wezen*; cantatas: *Verheerlijking*; *Aan zee*; *Beatrijs*, legend for solo, chorus and orch.; 4 masses; religious choral works; orch. overture, *De Kerels van Vlaanderen*; preludes, small orch.; *Esquisses*, symph. poem in 3 parts; organ sonata; fl. sonata; pieces for vn., cello, pf.; songs (including 2 cycles *Zonnesluimer* and *Verlangen*).—E. C.

MEXICAN AND CUBAN OPERA. The chief Mexican opera - comprs. are Melesio Morales (*q.v.*), *Ildegonda*; Aniceto Ortega (*Guatimozin*, 1867); Ricardo Castro (*Atizzamba*, 1900); Carlos Samaniego (*Netzahuacoyotl*); Julián Carillo (numerous operas). In Cuba, Eduardo Sanchez Fuentes's *Doreya* was produced in Havana in 1918.—F. H. M.

MEYER-OLBERSLEBEN, Max. Ger. compr. *b.* Olbersleben, near Weimar, 5 April, 1850. Pupil of Weimar Grand-Ducal School of Music and of Munich Acad. (P. Cornelius, Rheinberger, Wüllner). 1876, for short time teacher of theory, Weimar; teacher at R. School of Music, Würzburg, and condr. of Würzburg Choral Union; 1907, dir. of R. School of Music; 1920, retired; R. councillor.

Choral works: *The Buried Song*, op. 40; *An Old Story*, op. 65; songs; male choruses; pf. pieces; chamber-music; operas, *Clare Dettin* and *The Battle of Bonnets at Würzburg* (Munich, 1902).—A. E.

MEYROWITZ, Selmar. German condr. *b.* Bartenstein, East Prussia, 18 April, 1875. Pupil at Leipzig Cons. (Reinecke, Jadassohn) and Berlin Acad. School (Max Bruch); 1896, engaged for Carlsruhe by Felix Mottl; taken by him to Metropolitan Opera House, New York; travelled all over America with Gadski as concert-accompanist; 1905, went to Prague, Ger. Public Theatre; then to Berlin Komische Oper; after short engagement at Munich Court Theatre, 1st condr. of Hamburg Stadttheater, 1913; since 1917 wholly devoted to concert-work, especially concerts of Berlin Philh. Orch.; 1920-1921, condr. of Blüthner Orch. Berlin.—A. E.

MIASKOVSKY, Nicolas Jacovlevitch (*accent the O V*). Russ. compr. *b.* at the fortress Novo-georgievsk (now in Poland), 8/20 April, 1881. Son of a general of engineers of Russ. army. Pupil of Glière and Krijanovsky and of Rimsky-Korsakof and Liadof in Petrograd Cons. (1906-1911). Before this he was trained for an army career. In 1914 he was mobilised and fought on Austrian front; left army in 1920. From 1921, prof. of compn. at Moscow Cons. of Music. He is the greatest of living Russ. symphonists after Glazunof. His music shows profound skill,

masterly form, deep feeling and dramatic vigour. It has been perf. outside Russia (Berlin, New York, London) as well as Petrograd and Moscow. It is publ. by Russ. Music Co. Berlin, by Jurgenson and by Russ. State Music Publ. Dept. Moscow.

7 symphonies: I, C mi. (1908, unpubl. but recently revised by compr.); II, C sharp mi. (1911, unpubl.); III, A mi. (1913-14, unpubl.); IV, E mi. (1917, unpubl.); V, D ma. (1918) perf. Q. H. London under Sir Henry Wood, 8 March, 1924; |VI, E flat ma. (1922-3, unpubl.); VII, B mi. (1922, unpubl.). Symph. poem, *The Silence* (after E. A. Poe, 1909-11, unpubl.); *Alastor* (after Shelley, 1912-13), perf. Q. H. Prom. Concert, London, 1923; cello sonata, D ma. (1911); 3 pf. sonatas, D mi. (1907-10), F sharp mi. (1912), C mi. (1920); many fine songs; pf. pieces. Many essays in *Muzika* on Russ. mus. events (publ. by Derjanovsky, Moscow, 1910-16).—V. B.

MICHAŁOWSKI, Alexander. Polish pianist, teacher, compr. *b.* Kamieniec Podolski, 17 May, 1851. From 1867, pupil of Moscheles, Coccius and Reinecke at Leipzig Cons.; 1869, went to Berlin to study under Tausig; 1870, went to Warsaw, where he now lives; 1891-1918, prof. of concert pianists' class, Warsaw Cons. Is celebrated both as teacher and player, having a powerful technique; 35 pf. works (short pieces of brilliant character); also an instructive ed. of Chopin's works.—ZD. J.

MIDDELSCHULTE, Wilhelm. Amer. orgt. *b.* Werne, near Dortmund, Germany, 3 April, 1863. Stud. at Academic Inst. for Church Music in Berlin under Haupt, Loeschhorn, Alsleben, Commer and Schröder. Orgt. (1888-91) of Lukaskirche in Berlin. 1891-5, orgt. at Cath. of the Holy Name, Chicago. Since 1899, orgt. of St. James's Ch. 1894-1918, orgt. of Thomas Orch. in Chicago and since 1918 prof. of organ at Wisconsin Cons. Milwaukee. Has given many recitals; is a specialist in Bach.

Organ: *Kanonische Fantasie* on B.A.C.H. and Fugue on 4 themes of J. S. Bach (Kahnt); Toccata on *A Stronghold Sure*; concerto on a theme by Bach (Kahnt); Passacaglia in D mi. (Siegel). —O. K.

MIDGLEY, Samuel. Eng. pianist; *b.* Bradford, 22 Dec. 1849. Apart from one year at Leipzig (1873-4) was self-taught. Made a special feature of chamber concerts in Bradford at which the works of living Eng. comprs. have been given—*e.g.*: vn. concerto (G. A. Macfarren), 1877; pf. 4tet (A. C. Mackenzie), 1878; trio in E mi. (C. H. H. Parry), 1879; cello sonata, op. 9 (C. V. Stanford), 1880. Instituted, through the generosity of private friends in 1911, an annual series of six Free Chamber Concerts at which only the finest chamber-music of all countries is given entirely by local professionals, all performers to be paid the same fee. Admission to be entirely free (no seats reserved, room seating 1100, always full).

Handbook to Beethoven's Sonatas for Pf. and Vn.; *Scales and Arpeggios fully explained*, etc.; *A Future for British Music*; *Music and the Municipality*; *Russian and other Operas*, etc. Lectured on *Beethoven's Sonatas and a 5-octave Keyboard*.—E.-H.

MIDLAND MUSICAL COMPETITION FESTIVAL. Instituted 1912; instantly sprang into front rank of such organisations; nearly 7000 entries in first year. Held biennially in Birmingham, as the focus of the Midland area. The movement has grown steadily in spite of suspension during the war. At 1922 fest. entries numbered 11,000 and included 161 children's choirs—a record for the country. Began with competitions occupying an entire week, but now extends to a full fortnight. Classes for organ, pf. vn. orch. instrs. chamber-music, vocal solos, duets, quartets, choirs (male, female and mixed), elocution, drama, opera, folk-dances, dances in rhythmic expression, theory, and compn. An intermediate, or children's fest., taking 3 days, is held in intervening years. The Univ. of Birmingham offers an entrance scholarship in music to the competitor who is judged worthy of distinction.—G. B.

MIELCK, Ernest. See FINNISH ORCH. MUSIC.

MIGNONE, Francesco. Young Brazilian compr. Has written an opera, *The Diamond Contractor*, based on historic XVIII-century exploitation of the Brazilian diamond-mines.—F. H. M.

MIGOT, Georges. Fr. compr. *b.* Paris, 27 Feb. 1891. A pupil of Widor at the Paris Cons. He displays a most versatile activity as a compr. as a painter, and as a writer on æsthetics, musical and general. His works and views are giving rise to heated discussion in his native country. He has been awarded various important prizes for his pf. trio (1918), his pf. 5tet (1919) and other compns. In 1922 were perf. at Paris his *Paravent de Laque aux Cinq Images* (for 2 vns. vla. and pf.), his *Mouvements d'Eau* (for str. 4tet), his *Dialogue* (cello and pf.) and his *Agrestides* (orch.); at Monte Carlo, his ballet *Hagoromo* (Senart). His *Essais pour une Esthétique Générale* (Paris, 1919), and his *Apoggiatures non résolues* (*ib.* 1921) throw interesting lights upon his views on art.—M. D. C.

MIHALOVICH, Ödön. Hungarian compr. *b.* Feričance (Slavonia), 13 Sept. 1842. Stud. in Leipzig under Hauptmann and Jadassohn. Was in close intimacy with Bülow, Liszt and Wagner; zealous propagandist for the latter, whom he took as model in his operas; 1887–1919, dir. R. High School for Music, Budapest. Operas: *Toldi*; *Eliana.*—B. B.

MIKOREY, Franz. Ger. condr. *b.* Munich, 3 June, 1873. Son of the Munich tenor, Max M.; pupil of H. Schwartz, L. Thuille, Levi (Munich), and of Herzogenberg (Berlin); 1894, assistant-condr. Bayreuth and Munich; then condr. at Prague, German Theatre; at Regensburg, Elberfeld and at Vienna R. Opera; 1902–19, succeeded Klughardt as Court condr. Dessau; 1912, gen. mus. dir. ; 1919, opera condr. at Helsingfors.

<small>Pf. concerto (A ma.); *Songs to Spring*, for t. and orch.; *Sinfonia Engiadina*, orch., chorus, soli and organ; operas: *King of Samarkand* (Dessau, 1910); *Phryne*; *Echo of Wilhelmstal.*—A. E.</small>

MILDENBURG, Anna von. Austrian operatic singer; *b.* Vienna, 29 Nov. 1872. Pupil of Rosa Papier, Vienna. Started as dramatic s. at Hamburg. 1908–17, one of best singers at Vienna Opera, especially in the Mahler epoch. Chief rôles: Brünnhilde, Isolde, Leonore, Kundry, Klytemnestra. Married in 1909 the Austrian writer Hermann Bahr. Ed.

with him *Bayreuth and the Wagner Theatre* (1912; Eng. transl. T. W. Makepeace). Recently publ. her *Memoirs*. Settled in Munich as a singing prof. and *régisseur* of the Opera. Consult biography by Dr. Paul Stefan (Vienna, 1922, Wila).—EG. W.

MILES, Philip Napier. Eng. compr. *b.* Shirehampton, Glos, 21 Jan. 1865. Stud. under Draeseke, Schreyer (compn.), Roth (pf.); also in England privately under Sir Hubert Parry (compn.), Dannreuther (pf.).

<small>Operas: *Westward Ho !* grand opera in 3 acts, op. 4 (E. F. Benson, on Kingsley's novel); *Queen Rosamond*, 1-act, op. 6 (John Pollock); *Markheim*, 1-act, op. 10 (on story by R. L. Stevenson); *Fireflies*, 1-act (1923); lyric overture in G, *From the West Country*, orch. op. 2; Fantasia, orch. op. 15; *Hymn before Sunrise* (Coleridge), barit. solo, chorus and orch. op. 1 (Boosey); 2 songs, barit. with orch. op. 3; choral dance, *Music Comes* (John Freeman), op. 11 (Glastonbury Fest.; publ. Boosey); *Ode on a Grecian Urn*, 5-v. chorus and orch. op. 14; v. and pf.: *Battle Songs*, 1st set, op. 7 (Acott); 2nd set, op. 9 (ms.); *West Wind* (Masefield), op. 8 (Acott); part-songs (Stainer & Bell).—E.-H.</small>

MILHAUD, Darius. French composer; *b.* Aix-en-Provence, 4 Sept. 1892. Although he belonged to a Jewish Provençal family, he pursued all his musical studies from 1910 to 1919 at the Paris Conservatoire, taking composition and fugue with Gédalge. He is, without doubt, one of the most interesting and most gifted musicians of the young French school. He has an extraordinary creative energy and began to compose when very young. At 30, his works comprise several lyrical dramas, scores for dramatic performance, symphonic works, 5 quartets, pieces for violin, for piano, and for wind instruments, and songs. All these works are of very unequal value and he often pays the penalty of his facility, by falling into vulgarity; but alongside of indifferent or poor compositions, are found works which give evidence of valuable qualities of vigour and boldness. We must mention especially the *Euménides* (ms.), *Protée*, the 4th quartet (Durand), the *Poèmes juifs* (Demets). He has undergone contradictory influences. He is connected to a certain degree with the contrapuntal tendency of the *Schola Cantorum*, especially with Albéric Magnard; but that he has not escaped the attraction of Debussy is shown in *Alissa*. Stravinsky, Schönberg, Béla Bartók, opened to him other paths. He sought new means of expression in the superpositions of melodic lines, each working in a different tonality. His "polytonal" works have caused great offence to many people. In our opinion there is room for distinguishing between those which show signs of purely intellectual activity (like the 5th quartet), and those preserving the qualities of life, vigour, and spontaneity which form the real value of his best compositions, whatever system of writing he may adopt.

The momentary influence exercised on him by the æsthetic theories of the poet Jean Cocteau must not deceive us as to the real nature of Milhaud's inspiration. He is a follower of the romantic tradition, and his music often expresses a serious and religious feeling which is likewise found in Honegger, but which is entirely foreign to the preoccupations of the other musicians of the so-called "Group of Six" (q.v.). His most recent production (May 1924) is a ballet, *Le Train Bleu*.

Consult: Darius Milhaud. *Polytonalité et Atonalité* (*Revue Musicale*, Paris, 1923); Henry Prunières, *D. M.* (*Nouvelle Revue Française*, 1920); André Cœuroy (q.v.).—H. P.

MILLÁN, Rafael. Contemporary Span. compr. of *zarzuelas*, having a certain affinity with the traditional style of the operetta. His most famous works are *La Dogaresa* and *El Pájaro Azul* (libretti by Antonio López Monís) (Unión Musical Española).—P. G. M.

MILLAR, Charles Webster. Eng. singer; b. Manchester; d. London, 23 June, 1924. Studied at R.M.C.M. under John Acton; later under Santley, William Shakespeare and Victor Maurel; 1st appeared at Hallé Concerts under Richter, 1902 (Bach's B mi. Mass); then Sir Henry J. Wood secured him many appearances until 1910; then in mus. comedy under George Edwardes; in 1915 joined the Opera Commonwealth at the Shaftesbury, afterwards taken over by Sir Thomas Beecham; sang for him till 1920.—E.-H.

MILLENKOVICH, Max von. Real name of Max Morold (q.v.).

MILLET, Luis. Span. compr. condr. and musical scholar. One of the leading forces in the mus. progress of Catalonia, his native land. Lives in Barcelona, where he is the condr. of the Orfeó Catalá (see CHORAL SOCIETIES). His compns. include choral works of religious and secular character, pf. pieces, songs, and *Catalanescas* and *Eglogue*, for orchestra.—P. G. M.

MILLS, Robert Watkin. Eng. barit. singer; b. Painswick, Gloucestershire, 4 March, 1856. Began as boy-chorister and attracted attention of Dr. Samuel Wesley. Subsequently stud. in London under Sig. Randegger and Sir Joseph Barnby, and in Italy under Sig. Blasco. *Début* Jan. 1885 (in *Messiah* with Patti and Edward Lloyd). After that he sang in opera and oratorios and made frequent appearances at chief fests. Visited U.S.A. and Canada many times and, a few years ago, settled in Winnipeg, where he was actively engaged as teacher and concert-singer until 1922, when he went to Toronto where he now lives.—L. S.

MILNER, Augustus. Irish barit. singer; b. Cork. First trained for medecine; then stud. singing in Prague and Zurich for 4 years; in Zurich appeared as John the Baptist (Strauss's *Salome*) under the compr. Sang in Beecham Opera Co. (Iago, Boris, Amfortas) and later with B.N.O.C. London (in *Aida* and title-rôle in *The Goldsmith of Toledo*; gave a remarkable rendering of Shylock in Adrian Beecham's boyhood opera *The Merchant of Venice*.—E.-H.

MILONGA. See SOUTH AMER. DANCES.

MILOYEVITCH, Miloye. Serbian compr. condr., music critic; b. Belgrade, 15 Oct. 1884. Stud. in Belgrade; later in Munich (at the Acad.; also at Musikwissenschaft Univ.).

Is assistant-prof. of mus. science at Belgrade University.

Antique Legend (*Creation of Man*) in 4 movements, 3 solo vs., chorus and orch. ; symph. poem, *Smrt Majke Jugovica* (*Death of the Mother of Jugovitch*), orch.; music to drama *Kraljeva Jesen* (*The King's Autumn*); Suite for str. 4tet; *National Melodies of Serbia*, v. and pf. (also for pf. solo); *Serbian Dance*, vn. and pf.; *Legende*, cello and pf.; numerous part-songs and smaller pf. works.—T. F. D.

MINGARDI, Vittorio. Ital. condr. b. Bologna, 1860; d. Milan, 25 Nov. 1918. Pupil of Luigi Mancinelli. Establ. himself by conducting important seasons at leading theatres—Costanzi in Rome; San Carlo in Naples; at Barcelona and Buenos Ayres. Then for some years, held the directorship, both artistic and administrative, of La Scala, Milan, where he promoted important revivals of Ital. operas, such as Spontini's *La Vestale* and Cherubini's *Medea*.—D. A.

MIRY, Karel. Belgian compr. b. Ghent, 14 Aug. 1823; d. there, 5 Oct. 1889. Stud. at Ghent Cons., where he became prof. on Fr. and Flemish libretti: *Bouchard d'Avesnes*, 1864, *Le Mariage de Marguerite*, 1867; *Le Poète et son Idéal*, etc. Also songs, one of which, *De Vlaamsche Leeuw*, has become the national hymn of the Flemish.—C. V. B.

MISCHA-LÉON, Harry Haurcwitz. Danish t. operatic and concert-singer; b. Copenhagen, 9 Dec. 1889. Stud. Cons. there (singing, pf., literature, history, organ, harmony); singing under V. Lincke (Copenhagen), A. Heinemann (Berlin), E. Duvernoy (Paris), Jean de Reszke (Nice), Sir George Henschel (London); stud. stage-science and plastics, R. Opera School, Copenhagen; *début* there in *Fra Diavolo* and *Carmen* (Don José); chosen by Puccini to create t. rôle of Dick Johnson in *The Girl of the Golden West* (New York) ; extensive tours in U.S.A., Canada and Mexico; later leading t. Canadian National Opera, and in Boston, Chicago, San Francisco, and Spain; 1914, at Charlottenburg Opera, Berlin, Havana Opera (Cuba) ; 1915, prof. of singing at Minnesota Univ.; 1917, leading t. at Monte Carlo and Grand Opéra, Paris. Chief rôles: Don José; Romeo; Samson; Hoffmann; Werther; Lohengrin; Loge; Walther v. Stolzingen. Sings regularly in London at recitals. Since 1919, continuously touring Great Britain, Ireland and Continent (National Opera, Prague, 1923, etc.). Trans - American tour, 1924-5. Married Pauline Donalda (q.v.).

Numerous songs (Augener; Elkin).—E.-H.

MITJANA Y GORDON, Rafael. Span. musicologist, scholar and diplomatist; b. Málaga, 6 Dec. 1869; d. Stockholm, 15 Aug. 1921. As a member of the diplomatic corps, he held important positions in Sweden, Russia, Turkey and Morocco. Pupil of Eduardo Ocón (Málaga), Felipe Pedrell (Madrid), and Saint-Saëns (Paris). He wrote some works for theatre and for the orch. amongst them an opera, *La Buena Guarda*, with words from Lope de Vega, Zorrilla and Verlaine. His importance lies mainly in his critical and historical works, amongst which (besides his contributions to the *Encyclopédie du Cons. de Paris*, and many Span. and foreign periodicals) are the following:

Juan de la Encina, músico y poeta; Ensayos de Crítica Musical; Discantes y Contrapuntos: En el Bagreb-el-Aska (journey through Morocco); L'Orientalisme musical et la musique arabe; Cancionero de Upsala; El Maestro Rodríguez de Ledesma; Estudio sobre el arte musical contemporáneo en España; Lettres de Prosper Mérimée à Estébanez Calderón; Catalogue critique et descriptif des imprimes de musique des XVI et XVII siècle de la Bibliothèque de l'Université d'Upsala; Claudio Monteverdi y los orígenes de la ópera italiana; Mozart y la psicología sentimental; Francisco Soto de Langa; Don Fernando de las Infantas, teólogo y músico; Estudios sobre algunos músicos españoles del siglo XVI: Para música vamos. (Publ.: Academiska Bokforlaget, Upsala; Centro de Estudios Históricos, Málaga; F. Samper & Co. Madrid.) —P. G. M.

MJÖEN, Reidar. Norwegian musical critic; *b.* Gjövik, 6 July, 1871. Engaged on *Dagbladet*, Christiania. Writer of several of the Norwegian articles in this Dictionary.—E.-H.

MŁYNARSKI, Emil. Polish conductor, violinist, compr. *b.* Kibarty, 18 July, 1870. Stud. vn. under Auer and theory under Rimsky-Korsakof at Petrograd Cons.; gave a recital in London (Prince's Hall), 1890; 1893, condr. at Warsaw Opera; 1894–7, vn. teacher at Music School of Imperial Russ. Mus. Soc. in Odessa; 1899–1903, 1st condr. Warsaw Opera. From that time he co-operated in founding Warsaw Philh., becoming its 1st dir. and condr. 1901–5. In 1907, went to England to cond. symphony concerts in London and other towns. In 1910, became dir. of the Glasgow Orch. Union (Scottish Orch.); gave symphony concerts in London, June 1914, and a concert of British comprs. in 1915. In 1915, returned to the Continent and during the war lived in Russia. In 1919, became dir. of State Opera and Cons. in Warsaw. He relinquished the latter position in 1922, after having introduced some important innovations in the curriculum. He may be counted among the best conductors of our time.

Symphony in F, op. 14, with many Polish national themes (e.g. the ancient religious Polish song Boga Rodzica); vn. concerto in D mi. (1st prize, Paderewski competition, Leipzig, 1898. In 1923 his opera A Summer Night was perf. in Warsaw. Consult art. in Mus. Times, May 1915.—ZD. J.

MÖCKEL, Paul Otto. Ger. pianist; *b.* Strasburg, Alsace, 14 April, 1890. First lessons from M. J. Erb; stud. at Cons. Strasburg and Cologne; won Ibach Prize, 1908; distinguished himself afterwards as concert-pianist specialising on modern pf. music; 1912, married violinist Catharina van Bosch; dir. of training-classes at Zurich Cons.; 1922, called to Würtemberg High School of Music, Stuttgart.—A. E.

MOCQUEREAU, (Dom) André. See SOLESMES.

MOERAN, Ernest John. English compr. *b.* Osterley, near London, 31 Dec. 1894. Comes of an Irish family, but has lived much in Norfolk since his childhood. Educated at Uppingham where he began to compose at age of 17. Practically self-taught as regards music, but spent 18 months at the R.C.M. London, 1913–14. Served in the army, 1914–19. Has collected a large number of folk-songs in Norfolk, some of which were publ. in the Folk-Song Society's

journal, 1922. Gave a concert of his works at Wigmore Hall, London, 1923.

Rhapsody for orch. (Hallé concert, Manchester, by Hamilton Harty, 1924) (Chester); str. 4tet (*id.*); sonata, vn. and pf. (*id.*); *Toccata* and *Stalham River*, pf. (*id.*); songs v. and pf. (*id.*); Variations, pf. (Schott); 3 books of pf. pieces (*id.*); 6 folk-songs from Norfolk, arr. for v. and pf. (Augener). In ms.: 4 str. 4tets; 2 vn. sonatas; 2 trios for pf. vn. and cello; *Serenade-Trio* for str.; *Cushinsheean*, symph. impression for orch.; *Lonely Waters*, for small orch.; a large number of songs and pf. pieces.—E.-H.

MOESTUE, Marie. Norwegian writer on music and teacher of singing; *b.* Nes, Romerike, 28 July, 1869. Stud. singing under Mally Lammers, Wilma Monti and Désirée Artôt de Padilla; compn. under Sigurd Lie and Prof. Grunicke. 1911–14, stud. history of music in German libraries. Amongst her musico-historical works may be mentioned *Sangkunstens historie (History of Art of Singing)* (Christiania, 1917, Aschehoug), as well as numerous arts. in Norwegian periodicals. As compr. she has publ. pf. pieces, songs and female choruses. Represented Norwegian Music Teacher's Association at 1st International Congress of Music-Teachers, held in Berlin 1913, which subsequently led to establishment of Norwegian Music-Teachers' National Union, of which she was President until 1918.—J. A.

MOFFAT, Alfred. Scots compr. and arranger; *b.* Edinburgh, 4 Dec. 1866. Stud. in Berlin under Bussler, 1884–9; resided there, working for Ger. publ. firms, 1889–99; came to London 1899. An indefatigable arranger and editor. His work in editing and issuing old violin music, especially old Eng. pieces, is of great importance. His *Meister-Schule der alten Zeit* (Simrock) contains 36 vn. sonatas, unknown before, including many Eng. ones. Indeed he discovered a genuine school of XVII and XVIII century Eng. comprs. for vn. His *Kammersonaten* (Schott) contains 26 vn. sonatas. Schott's also publ. 24 XVIII century Eng. pieces, and Novello's, 14 works.

Pf. 4tet, C mi. (perf. Berlin, 15 Nov. 1886); many colls. of folk-songs, and arrs. of old music (Schott; Augener, etc).—E.-H.

MOGER, Gladys. Eng. s. singer; *b.* Bath, 17 Sept. 1889. Stud. R.C.M., privately, and in Paris. Has large repertoire of standard and modern works. Many recitals in England and on Continent. Created leading rôles in the Eng. operas: *The Tempest*, N. Gatty (Ariel); *The Two Sisters*, C. Rootham (Ellen); *Prince Ferelon*, N. Gatty (the Princess).—E.-H.

MOHAUPT, Franz. Ger.-Czechoslovak compr. *b.* Friedland, 1854.

Operas; orch. works; chamber-music; songs.—E. S.

MOISEIWITSCH, Benno. Russ. pianist; *b.* Odessa, 22 Feb. 1890. Stud. at Imperial Mus. Acad. Odessa, and at age of 9 won Rubinstein Prize; when 14, stud. under Leschetizky for 4 years; *début* in England, Town Hall, Reading, 1908; in London in spring of 1909 at Queen's Hall, when he achieved an instantaneous success. Has made 3 tours of U.S.A. and Canada; 2 of Australia and New Zealand, and many through United Kingdom, France, Belgium, Austria and

Germany. In 1914, married Daisy Kennedy, the Australian violinist (q.v.).—E.-H.

MOLIN, Georg Conny Hjalmar. Swedish barit. operatic singer; b. Norra Sandsjö, 9 Nov. 1885. Stud. R. Cons. Stockholm; then under F. Boyer (Paris) and von Zur Mühlen (London), 1912–13; from 1914, attached to R. Opera, Stockholm, where he has successfully perf. rôles of Wolfram, Kurvenal, Gunther, Amfortas, Luna, Germont, Escamillo, Amonasro, Arnljot. His voice has great volume, a pleasing quality, and a wide compass.—P. V.

MOLINARI, Bernardino. Italian condr. b. Rome, 11 April, 1880. From 1912, artistic dir. at Augusteo (q.v.) in Rome, where he has distinguished himself as a very able condr. There he has cond. important concerts; also in principal Ital. cities; and at Paris, Prague, and Liverpool. Also successful as a theatre-condr. Was pupil of R. Liceo Mus. di Santa Cecilia, Rome, where he stud. harmony and organ under Remigio Renzi, and compn. under Falchi. M. has made several interesting transcriptions of old Ital. music, for modern perf., amongst which we mention the *Sonata sopra Sancta Maria* of Monteverdi (publ. by Ricordi).—D. A.

MÖLLER, Peder. Danish violinist; b. Brönderslev, a small village in Jutland, 28 Feb. 1877; showed a pronounced talent for vn. while quite a young child. At 12, was sent to Copenhagen, where he stud. under Fr. Hilmer. When 18, made his *début* as violinist under the happiest auspices and, shortly after, left for Paris to study under Marsick and Berthelier. Engaged in solo and orch. work in Paris for a period of 15 years. In 1910, returned to native land, and was, for short time, member of orch. of R. Opera, Copenhagen. However, it is as a brilliant and temperamental solo-violinist that he has become famed through his numerous concert-tours in Germany, Sweden and Denmark. In 1918, was appointed Musician of the R. Chamber. He is the violinist of the noted Copenhagen Trio (Agnes Adler, pf.; Louis Jensen, cello).—A. H.

MOLNÁR, Anton. Hungarian compr. music writer; b. 7 Jan. 1890. From 1910–13, was vla.-player in Hungarian Str. Quartet (Waldbauer-Kerpely).—B. B.

MOMPOU, Federico. Span. compr. b. Barcelona, 1895. Stud. at one time under F. Motte Lacroix, but has evolved by himself an individual style of music, free from bar-divisions, key-signatures and cadences, described by compr.'s own term, *primitivista*. His ideal is apparently a return to the Primitives, taking the present-day conditions as point of departure. He aims at the utmost simplicity of means of expression and, according to a Fr. critic, some of his music could be dictated in words without making use of any conventional music-writing method. He has a great number of admirers and followers in Paris. His works, which are all written for the pf. are, with one or two exceptions, in the suite-form.

*Canço i Dança; Impressions intimes; Cants Magics; Scènes d'enfants; Suburbis; Pessebres; Festes Llun-*yanes; *Carmes; Trois variations.* (Unión Musical Española, Barcelona; Senart, Paris.)—P. G. M.

MONALDI, Gino. Ital. historian and music critic; b. Perugia, 2 Dec. 1847. Stud. at R. Cons. Milan, under Mazzuccato and Fumagalli. He then devoted himself to mus. criticism in newspapers and reviews, and to publications about historical subjects and mus. anecdotes, recording in them the rich and interesting memories of his past life. He participated (as an impresario also) in the most important events of Ital. mus. life of his time, in connection with the most famous musicians.

Verdi : la vita e le opere (Turin, Bocca); *Memorie d'un suggeritore* (id.); *Le prime rappresentazioni celebri* (Milan, 1910, Treves); *Le Regine della danza nel secolo XIX* (Bocca); *Cantanti celebri* (id.); *Impresari celebri del secolo XIX* (Rocca San Casciano, 1918, Cappelli); *Cantanti evirati celebri del teatro italiano* (Rome, 1920, Ausonia).—D. A.

MONASTERIO Y AGÜEROS, Jesús. Span. violinist; b. Potes (Santander), 21 March, 1836. Received his 1st lessons on vn. from his father; completed his artistic education at the Brussels Cons. under the famous violinist Ch. de Bériot; under Lemmens, Fétis and Gevaert for theory and compn. In 1852, awarded the *Prix d'Honneur*, against rules of Cons. on account of his tender age. On his way back to Spain he was introduced to Gounod in Paris, who acquainted him with a *Meditation* for vn. on Bach's First Prelude (which later on became the popular *Ave Maria*). In 1854, was elected hon. member of R. Chapel, Madrid, as well as hon. member of Accad. Pontificia, Rome. Toured with great success as a virtuoso in England and Scotland. In 1856, member of R. Chapel and prof. of vn. at R. Cons. Madrid, where he remained until 1861, when he left for a concert-tour in Belgium, Holland and Germany. During this tour the Grand-Duke of Weimar offered him the position of 1st vn. and condr. of the Court concerts, in collab. with Lassen and Liszt. On his visit to Brussels, Fétis asked him to take up de Bériot's vacated post at the Cons. M. declined in both cases, feeling that his duty was to give to his country the benefit of his experience and knowledge. He began his task immediately, creating at his class at the Cons., Madrid, an admirable school of vn.-playing, the tradition of which has been continued to the present day by José Hierro, Julio Francés and his pupil Fernández Bordas. As condr. (1869–76) of Sociedad de Conciertos, Madrid (now Orquesta Sinfónica), he establ. an orch. discipline till then unknown in Spain. In 1863, founded the Sociedad de Cuartetos to educate the public taste in the masterpieces of Beethoven, Haydn, and Mozart, of which even the educated classes of Madrid had at the time a very incomplete and imperfect knowledge. He laid the foundation of the mus. culture and efficient orch. playing so noticeable to-day. Was for some time dir. of the R. Cons. de Música, a position he resigned. He died in Madrid at the end of XIX century.

Orch.: Scherzo fantástico; Marcha Fúnebre; Andante religioso, str. orch.; vn. concerto in B mi.; Grand Fantasia on popular Spanish airs, vn. and orch.; *Estudio de Concierto,* harp, ob. clar. horn and str.; piece for vn. and pf. *Adiós a la Alhambra*, once very popular; 20 *Artistic Concert Études* for vn., adopted in 1878, and still in use, in curriculum of Brussels Cons. (Schott, Brussels; Unión Musical Española, Madrid.)—P. G. M.

MONCKTON, Lionel. Eng. compr. of light operas; *b.* London, 1862; *d.* there, 15 Feb. 1924. A prominent amateur actor of Oxford Univ. Dramatic Soc. His first compns. were heard at the Gaiety under George Edwardes. Contributed many songs to *The Shop Girl, The Greek Slave, San Toy, The Cingalee.* Part-compr. of *The Toreador* (1901), *The Spring Chicken* (1905), *The New Aladdin* (1906), *The Girls of Gottenburg* (1907), *Our Miss Gibbs* (1909), *The Arcadians* (1909), *The Mousmé* (1911). Sole compr. of *The Quaker Girl* (1910); *The Dancing Mistress* (1912). Married the operetta singer, Gertie Millar.—E.-H.

MONK, Cyril. Australian violinist: *b.* Sydney, 1882. Stud. in London under Guido Papini. Toured Australia and New Zealand. Settled in Sydney: founded Australian String Quartet, which introduced modern Fr. music to Australia (Franck, Debussy, Ravel, Lekeu, Michaud, Ropartz). Prof. at New South Wales State Cons. and leader of State Orchestra.—G. Y.

MONRAD, Cally. Norwegian s. singer; *b.* Sande, Romsdal, 31 July, 1879. Taught by Wilhelm Kloed, Christiania. *Début* there, 1898, at concert given by pianist Martin Knutzsen; aroused attention by her not especially powerful but exceptionally beautiful voice and her soulful interpretation; continued her studies under Frau Schuch-Proska, Dresden; 1st appearance as operatic singer in Christiania, 1903 (*Hänsel and Gretel*). Has since sung at R. Opera Houses in Stockholm and Berlin; was for some years permanently attached to last - named opera house. Her rôles were: Carmen, Orpheus, Tosca, Butterfly, Mimi (*La Bohème*), Nedda (*Pagliacci*), etc. Her highest art is displayed in song. She has made concert-tours in Norway, Denmark and Sweden; is author of 2 vols. of poems and a novel.—R. M.

MONTEFIORE, Tommaso. Ital. compr. and critic; *b.* Leghorn, 1855. Has comp. several operas—*Un bacio al portatore* (Florence, 1884), *Cecilia* (Ravenna, 1905); has gained a wide reputation as a critic, contributing to newspapers and reviews, interesting himself in the greatest problems of Ital. mus. life.—D. A.

MONTEMEZZI, Italo. Ital. opera compr. *b.* Vigasio (Verona) 31 May, 1875. Pupil of Ferroni and Saladino at Milan Cons.; made 1st appearance at Regio Theatre, Turin, with his opera *Giovanni Gallurese* in Jan. 1905. This was followed by *Hellera* (same theatre, 1910) and then *L'Amore dei tre re* (Scala, Milan, 1913) which had a very great success, and is the opera to which M. owes most of his reputation. It has been given at all the great theatres of Europe and N. America. His last work is *La Nave*, written on tragedy by d'Annunzio, and perf. at La Scala, Milan, 3 Nov. 1918. There is also a *Cantico dei cantici* for chorus and orch. (Milan, 1900). He is one of the most esteemed amongst Ital. opera comprs. of the years following the Mascagni-Puccini period—D. A.

MONTES, Juan de. Span. orgt. compr. *b.* Lugo. He remained unknown until Pedrell's campaign in favour of national folk-lore brought forward the importance of his compns. in relation to the popular music of Galicia, his native country. He sank again into obscurity and died unnoticed. Held at one time the position of music-master of Lugo Seminary, of which he had been a pupil in his youth. He wrote a *Te Deum* for orch. and a *Requiem Mass*, vs. and orch. His most representative work, in spite of its simplicity, is his *Seis Baladas Gallegas*, v. and pf. (The folk-lore of Galicia is, of all Span. popular music, the richest and least-known abroad.) About 1900 there was a move to erect at Lugo a monument to his memory. Other works are: *Fantasía sobre aires populares gallegos*, for orch. and *Sonata descriptiva*, for str. 4tet.—P. G. M.

MONTESANTO, Luigi. Ital. barit. *b.* Palermo, 23 Nov. 1887. A very capable singer and interpreter. *Début* at Conegliano Veneto in 1909 in *Carmen*. Since then, has appeared with continued success at principal theatres of the world. At La Scala, Milan, he interpreted Schumann's *Faust.*—D. A.

MONTEUX, Pierre. French conductor ; *b.* Paris, 4 April, 1875. Stud. at Cons. Paris; 1st prize for vn. 1896. Belonged to orchs. of Opéra-Comique and the Concerts Colonne (2nd leader of vlas.). Condr. to Russ. Ballet of Diaghilef, where he gained fame by producing *Daphnis et Chloé* (Ravel, 1912), the *Jeux* (Debussy, 1913), and the *Sacre du Printemps* and the *Rossignol* (Stravinsky, 1913–14). He noticed the indifferent place held by modern Fr. and foreign music in the programmes of Paris symph. concerts; to remedy this, founded in Feb. 1914, at Casino de Paris, the Société des Concerts Populaires, to which his name is still attached. Here he gave the first full concert-perf. of Stravinsky's *Petrushka*. On 5 and 26 April, 1914, he had the courage to include in his programme the *Sacre du Printemps*, scarcely a year after the scandal caused by that work at the *Ballets russes*; these two dates are celebrated in annals of Parisian music. During the war, he was recalled from the front, and sent to U.S.A. to carry on a mus. propaganda in favour of the Allied nations. He has now definitely settled there and conducts the Boston Symphony Orch. in that town or in New York. His programmes are still a model of eclecticism. His interpretations still gain in delicacy of detail—those of Debussy especially benefit by a fine gradation of nuances and a sensitive appreciation of the value of each group of instruments.—A. S.

MOODY, Fanny. Eng. operatic s. singer; *b.* Redruth. 1881, stud. in London under Mme. Sainton-Dolby; appeared 4 years later at a concert given by her; joined Carl Rosa Co. 1887 (*début* as Arline [*Bohemian Girl*]); in London as Micaela (*Carmen*). Her favourite rôle was *Butterfly*; sang Marguerite (*Faust*) under Lago at Covent Garden; many Wagner rôles; at Drury Lane and Covent Garden under Sir

Augustus Harris. In 1894, formed with her husband Charles Manners (*q.v.*) the Moody-Manners Opera Co. In 1896-7. toured Canada and S. Africa.—E.-H.

MOONIE, James Anderson. Scottish condr. teacher, compr. *b.* Edinburgh, 17 July, 1853; *d.* South of France, March 1923. Has probably done more to influence and develop the mus. life of Edinburgh than anyone else. His influence as a teacher has filtered into every corner of Scotland. He stud. under William Townsend in Edinburgh and attended classes of late Prof. Oakeley of the Univ. for 2 sessions. He then proceeded to London where he stud. under Alberto Randegger, J. B. Walsh, and Stanley Rivers. Returning to Edinburgh, he held successive posts as orgt. in Trinity College, St. Leonard's, and Hope Park U.F. churches; also cond. Hope Park Mus. Association; Moonie's Male-V. Choir; Univ. of Edinburgh Mus. Association, and Moonie's Choir, which he continued to conduct till his death. Introduced many choral works to Edinburgh—*Beatitudes* (César Franck); *Requiem* (Verdi); *The Blessed Damozel* (Debussy); the *Hiawatha* trilogy, *Bon-Bon Suite,* and *A Tale of Old Japan* (Coleridge-Taylor); *The Water Lily, The Sleeping Beauty, Ode to the Passions,* and *John Gilpin* (Cowen); *The Revenge, Songs of the Fleet,* and *Songs of the Sea* (Stanford); *The Mystic Trumpeter* (Harty); *Hymns from the Rig Veda* (Holst); *Atalanta in Calydon* (Bantock). Has given perfs. of works by Palestrina, di Lasso, Astorga, Leo, Elgar, Max Bruch, Goring Thomas, Rimsky - Korsakof, Gernsheim, and W. B. Moonie, as well as standard classical works. For many years singing-master, Edinburgh Ladies' Coll., George Watson's Coll., George Heriot's School, Daniel Stewart's Coll., James Gillespie's School, Normal School, and John Watson's Inst. Thus practically every secondary-school boy and girl in Edinburgh for years, came under his care. He was also lecturer in music to Provincial Coll. for Training of Teachers. Retired from educational work under the Government superannuation scheme in 1919. Was one of founders of Edinburgh Soc. of Musicians and its president for a number of years. Also one of founders of Competitive Fest. movement in Edinburgh.
Cantatas: *Killiecrankie;* *A Woodland Dream;* *Precept and Practice* (all Novello); *Gems of Highland Song* (Paterson). Many part-songs and arrs. Ed. of Concert Edition of Scots songs (Bruce Clements & Co.).—W. S.

MOONIE, William B. Scottish compr. *b.* Stobo, Peeblesshire, 29 May, 1883. Stud. pf. under A. W. Dace, and compn. under Prof. Niecks at Univ. of Edinburgh. In 1905, gained Bucher Scholarship there, and proceeded to Hoch's Cons. Frankfort-o-M., where he stud. under Ivan Knorr (compn.) and Uzielli (pf.); had several works produced with some success. Returning to Edinburgh 1908, took up music-teaching. Is at present engaged upon an opera on a Scottish subject. He generally affects the Scottish idiom, although he does not restrict himself to that. As a condr. also he is rapidly

attaining an assured position. On the death of his father, appointed condr. of Moonie's Choir.
Chorus and orch.: *Caledonia,* ode, Burns (Paterson); *Glenara,* ballad (Townsend & Thomson); pf. pieces (*Perthshire Echoes, Deeside Memories,* etc.); *Highland Suite,* vn. and pf.; songs (*Finland Love-Song; The Lads that were,* etc.).—W. S.

MOÓR, Emanuel. Compr. *b.* Hungary, 1862. Stud. in Budapest and in Vienna; toured U.S.A. as dir. of Concerts Artistiques; played his own pf. music in London 1894; invented the Duplex-Coupler piano on which recitals and lectures were given in London by Tovey, Winifred Christie, and Max Pirani in 1921. (See art. INSTRUMENTS INVENTED.)
Operas: *Die Pompadour* (Cologne, 1902); *Andreas Hofer* (*ib.* 1902); *Hochzeitglocken* (Cassel, 1908); *Der Goldschmid von Paris*; 7 symphonies (D mi. op. 45; VI, E mi. op. 65; VII, C ma. op. 67); Rhapsody, vn. and orch. op. 84; pf. concerto, op. 85; *Concertstück,* pf. and orch. op. 113; Rhapsody, orch. op. 93; chamber-music; pf. pieces; songs (all Mathot, Paris).—E.-H.

MOOR, Karel. Czech compr. *b.* Bělohrad, 1873. Stud. Prague Cons. and in Vienna. Music-teacher, critic and condr. in Prague; with Czech Philh. 1902; then condr. at several theatres in Bohemia, Trieste and Jugo-Slavia.
Operas: *Hjördis* (1899); *Vij* (1901); *Ratcliff; Český Honza.* Operetta, *The Professor in Hades.* Overture to Hauptmann's drama *Weber.* Symph. works: *Polonia; The Sea; Life; Requiem.* Str. 4tet; pf. trio; melodrama, *Marytka Magdonova;* pf. pieces (publ. V. Kotrba, Prague). Wrote a Czech novel on musical life, *Karel Martens* (1905).—V. ST.

MOORE, Bertha. Eng. s. singer and teacher; *b.* Brighton, 10 Jan. 1862. Stud. R.A.M. London, under W. H. Cummings, and later under Florence Lancia. Has sung and lectured widely. Was honoured with O.B.E. for organisation of a very large number of war-concerts.—E.-H.

MOORE, Frederick. Eng. pianist; *b.* London, 27 Feb. 1876. Prof. and lecturer at R.A.M. London; pf. recitalist.—E.-H.

MOOS, Paul. Ger. music æsthetician; *b.* Buchau, Oberschwaben, 22 March, 1863. Stud. at R. Acad. of Music, Munich (Thuille, Rheinberger, Giehrl, Bussmayer, Hieber, Abel); then lived at Berlin as writer on music; 1899, settled at Ulm after a long sojourn in Italy.
Modern Musical Æsthetics in Germany (1902); 2nd ed.: *The Philosophy of Music from Kant to Hartmann* (1922); *Richard Wagner as Æsthetician* (1906); *Ger. Contemporary Æsthetics with special consideration of Musical Æsthetics* (1909).—A. E.

MORALES, Melesio. Mexican compr. *b.* 1838; *d.* 1908. Founded Mexican Cons. Comp. the opera *Ildegonda.*—F. H. M.

MORALES, Olallo Juan Magnus. Compr. *b.* Almeria (Spain), 15 Oct. 1874. Stud. R. Cons. Stockholm; then in Berlin, 1899-1901 (Urban; Teresa Carreño); condr. of Orch. Soc. of Gothenburg, 1905-9; then music critic in Stockholm; teacher at R. Cons. there, and secretary of R.A.M. there from 1918; member 1910; prof. 1921; 1921, publ. (with Tobias Norlind) commemorative essay on 150-years' Jubilee of R.A.M.
Symphony, G mi.; concert overture, *Försommar* (*Early Summer*); *Andante lugubre* and *Serenade,* orch.; str. 4tet in D; pf. sonata, D flat; Suite, pf.; vn. pieces; songs.—P. V.

MORALES, Pedro García. Span. compr. poet and critic; *b.* Huelva, 1879. B.A. Seville Univ.

Stud. R.C.M. London. Of a non-prolific, over-critical artistic disposition, he devotes his activities as a musician to the creation of the Span. art-song, the least cultivated type of compn. in his country, and advocates the use of the Span. language in singing, being opposed to translations in general, as essentially detrimental to colour and rhythm. He works for the cause of modern Span. music outside his country, being responsible for the first concerts (orchestral and chamber-music) in England, entirely of Span. comprs., at which he appeared as condr., vn. and vla. player (London, Cambridge, Birmingham, 1918–20). Contributor to Span. and Eng. publications on music, literature and art. As a poet he is acknowledged a true representative of the modern Span. literary renaissance (*Cambridge Readings in Spanish Literature*, J. Fitzmaurice-Kelly). In his music, as well as in his poems, he shows himself possessed of the introspective rather than the external characteristics of the Andalusian (Van Vechten's *Music of Spain*, Eng. ed.). Mr. Morales is responsible for all the Spanish articles in this Dictionary.

Songs with orch. or pf.: Span.: *Mañana de primavera*; *El sol en sus ojos arde*; *Hoy la tierra y el cielo me sonrien*; *Por una mirada un mundo*; *Ven aqui tu, pastor lindo*; *Cuando las penas miro*; *Canzonetta*; *Porque cuaja en el aire la dulzura de Abril*; *Tus ojos*. Eng.: *You call me still, my Life*; *This is the place.* Ital.: *Quando cadran le foglie*; *O fiorellin di siepe*; *Nell' aria della sera*; *Un organetto suona per la via.* Vn. and orch.: *Esquisse Andalouse* (1st perf. Fritz Kreisler, London, 1911). Vn. and pf.: *Bagatelle* (1st perf. Fritz Kreisler, London, 1912). (Publ. Schott, Mayence; Pueyo, Madrid.)—E.-H.

MORAVIAN FOLK-MUSIC. See BARTOŠ, FRANTIŠEK; JANAČEK, LEOŠ; KUBA, LUDVÍK.

MORAWSKI, Eugeniusz. Polish compr. *b.* Warsaw, 1 Nov. 1876. Pupil of Noskowski at Warsaw Cons. Since 1908, has lived in Paris. His orch. compns. appear in programmes of Colonne-Lamoureux Concerts in Paris. At the outset, he composed under the influence of R. Strauss; but to-day he shows a character and style of his own.

Promethean Symphony (with choruses); symph. poem, *Vœ victis* (1910); *Fleurs du Mal* (after Baudelaire); *Don Quixote* (perf. 1912); *Nevermore* and *Ulalume* (1918, after Poe).—ZD. J.

MORCMAN, Oscar. Norwegian composer; *b.* Bergen in 1892. Engaged in business until a few years ago; developed his mus. gifts by his own efforts alone. *Début* in Christiania, 1921, with symph. overture *Euripides*, an astonishingly mature and technically sound work. The great expectations it aroused were not disappointed by his next work, a symph. poem *King Lear*, a broadly designed, powerful and characteristic work, produced in 1923 by Philh. Soc. in Christiania.—R. M.

MORELLI, Alfredo. Ital. condr. *b.* Rome, 1885. Stud. at R. Liceo Mus. di Santa Cecilia, Rome, under Stanislao Falchi; gained high reputation as condr. both in theatre and at concerts (San Carlo Theatre, Naples; Augusteo, Rome). He is also a good composer.

Symph. impression, *Consalvo* (on poem by Leopardi); *Rêverie*; *Novelletta all' antica* (str. orch.); numerous songs.—D. A.

MORENA, Berta (real name Meyer). Ger. s. singer; *b.* Mannheim, 27 Jan. 1878. Dramatic singer, especially of Wagner rôles; pupil of Sophie Röhr-Brajnin and of Orgeni; 1898, joined Munich Opera, to which she belonged till 1923, with short visits to America, England and Spain.—A. E.

MORENO TORROBA, Federico. Span. compr. *b.* Madrid, March 1891. Received his mus. education at R. Cons. de Música and stud. compn. under Conrado del Campo. His works bear the mark of the progressive schools of mus. art. Like Manuel de Falla, he advocates the re-establishment of the guitar as a national instr. He has written some pieces for it.

Orch.: *La Ajorca de Oro*; *Capricho Romántico*; *Loraida*; *Cuadros Castellanos* (perf. by Orquesta Sinfónica and Orquesta Filarmónica, Madrid; publ. Schott). Guitar: *Fandanguillo*; *Arada*; *Danza.*— P. G. M.

MORERA, Enrique. Span. compr. and critic; *b.* in Catalonia. The favourite pupil of Pedrell and one of the best technicians in the country. His music gives evidence of a close acquaintance with the modern Fr. and Belgian schools.

Operas: *Emporium*, *Bruniselda*; *La Fada*. Zarzuelas: *La canción del náufrago*; *La alegría que pasa*. Symph. poems: *La Vesta*; *La Atlántida*. Pf.: *Danzas españolas*. Songs: *Am Tu*; *Ausencia*; *Vetlla d'Amor*; *Enterro*; *Plor*; *L'Hibern*. (Publ.: Rouart, Paris; Unión Musical Española, Madrid.)— P. G. M.

MORGAN, Robert Orlando. English pianist, compr. *b.* Manchester, 16 March, 1865. Stud. at Guildhall School of Music, London, under J. F. Barnett, Henry Gadsby, Dr. Warwick Jordan; 1st prize and gold medal in Grand Concours International de Composition Musicale, Brussels, 1894; prof. of pf., harmony and compn. at Guildhall School of Music from 1887. As a compr. has a refined and graceful piano style.

Comic opera, *Two Merry Monarchs* (Savoy Theatre, London, 1910); cantatas, female vs.: *Zitella* (Curwen); *The Legend of Eloisa* (Augener); song-cycle, 4 solo vs., *In Fairyland* (*id.*); pf. sonata (Ashdown); *Modern School of Pf. Technique*, 6 vols. (*id.*); book, *The Rules of Harmony* (*id.*); numerous songs, pf. pieces, part - songs, etc. Annotated editions of Beethoven's pf. sonatas; of Bach's 48 Preludes and Fugues, Italian Concerto, and Chromatic Fantasia and Fugue (Ashdown).—E.-H.

MÖRIKE, Eduard. Ger. condr. *b.* Stuttgart, 16 Aug. 1877. Grand-nephew of poet E. M.; stud. at Leipzig Cons. (Ruthardt, Piutti, Sitt); theatre condr. in America, at Rostock, Kiel, Stettin, Halle; also assisted at Bayreuth Fest. and at Paris *Salome* performance, 1907; cond. Halberstadt Fest.; till 1923 condr. at Ger. Opera House; Univ. teacher at Lessing High School; pianist at Charlottenburg.—A. E.

MORIN, Henri. Fr. condr. *b.* Grenoble, 17 Aug. 1883. Stud. under Riemann at Leipzig; dir. orch. at special school there; also passed through the *Schola Cantorum*; at 26, condr. at Cologne; then 1st condr. at theatre in Nantes, at same time directing there the Concerts Henri-Morin, and those of the Nantes *Schola Cantorum*; engaged by Diaghilef to conduct his ballets on tour; afterwards condr. of Fr. repertoire at Chicago Opera (1920–1), at New York and in Brazil (1922).—M. L. P.

MORITZ, Edward. Compr. *b.* Hamburg, 23 June, 1891. First violinist; received training as compr. at Paris and Berlin (Paul Juon); now wholly devoted to composition.
Choral suite, *Conception*; vn. and pf. sonata; str. 4tet with s. solo, op. 10; *Burlesque* (often perf.) for orch. op. 9; symphony, C mi.; *Gitanjali*, symphony for contr. and orch.; pf. and vn. works; numerous songs (Schott).—A. E.

MÖRK, Ulrik. Norwegian writer on music; *b.* Trondhjem, 6 Oct. 1865. Graduate in philology; senior master at Christiania School of Navigation; stenographic revisor in Parliament House. Stud. vn. under Gudbrand Böhn and Severin Svensen, Christiania; singing under Thorvald Lammers, Christiania. Mus. critic on *Trondhjems Adresseavis*, 1885–6; on *Örebladet*, Christiania, since 1900. Has written numerous articles in Norwegian journals on mus. fests., male-choir meetings and tours. Wrote *Musical Life in Christiania from the 'Eighties to our own Day* in *Norges Musikhistorie* (1921). Writer of several of the Norwegian articles in this Dictionary.—R. M.

MOROLD, Max (real name Max von Millenkovich). Austrian musicologist; *b.* Vienna, 16 March, 1866. Lately a high official of Ministry of Education; 1918–19, dir. of Vienna Burgtheater; music critic of several Viennese newspapers. Wrote libretto to Reiter's opera *Der Bundschuh* (1895), a monograph on Reiter (1903), short pamphlets on Bruckner and Hugo Wolf for Breitkopf's collection (1912).—P. ST.

MORPHY, Conde de. Span. musicologist; descended from an old Irish family; author of *Los Vihuelistas españoles del siglo XVI* (Breitkopf, Leipzig). Tutor of King Alfonso XII before he was enthroned, when he became his private secretary, in which capacity he was of great assistance to the cause of music. Died Madrid at advanced age, at end of XIX century. —P. G. M.

MORRIS, Margaret. Eng. dancer and mus. educationist; *b.* London, 1891, of Welsh, Irish and Eng. descent. Lived in France till 5 years old; 1st engagement on the stage at 8 as principal fairy in pantomime at Plymouth; joined the Ben Greet Co., playing such parts as Puck, Boy in *Henry V*, and dancing. At 17 met Raymond Duncan, stud. his reconstruction of Greek dancing, and finally gave up the Ital. ballet technique, finding the Greek technique fundamentally sound, and a far better basis for the development of dancing. First ballets produced were for Marie Brema's production of *Orpheus* at Savoy Theatre, 1910. In 1912, founded Dancing School and the Margaret Morris Theatre, giving seasons of 2 and 3 weeks from time to time, including Children's Christmas Seasons with all parts played by children. 1915, first produced songs by Debussy, Ravel, Stravinsky and others with dance interpretations. Started the Margaret Morris Club for artists, musicians, and writers, for perfs. of orig. work. About 1915, first began to comp. music; 1st ballet *Angkorr*, in 3 movements, fl. ob. drums, and 2 vns. (produced at own theatre; later at Coliseum). 1917,

set to music the poem *En allant vers la ville* by Henri de Régnier (perf. at own theatre). A singer told story at side of stage, dancers also singing in places. Since then, comp. songs and ballets (unfin.). In 1920, founded school for general education and study of arts in relation to one another.—E.-H.

MORROW, Walter. Eng. tpt.-player; *b.* 15 June, 1850. Stud. at R.A.M. under Thomas Harper. Played with all the leading orchs.—E.-H.

MORS, Richard. Ger. compr. *b.* Mannheim, 18 Aug. 1873. Stud. law; became pupil of Ludwig Thuille, Munich; 1898–1906, condr. at different theatres; since then at Munich as compr. teacher and critic; 1907–8, temporary condr. of Bach Soc. Nuremberg.
Symph. poem, *Give Grief its Right* (1905); *And Pippa dances*; str. 4tet; vn. sonata; *Requiem*, chorus and orch.; many songs.—A. E.

MORTELMANS, Lodewijk. Belgian compr. *b.* Antwerp, 5 Feb. 1868. Stud. at École de Musique, Antwerp, under Peter Benoit. 1st prize R. Acad. of Belgium, 1891 (for symphony). and in 1893, 1st *Prix de Rome* for cantata *Lady Macbeth*. Now prof. of cpt. at Vlaamsch Koninklijk Conservatorium (R. Flemish Cons.) at Antwerp (since 1902); also president of Soc. of Flemish Comprs.; member of council for advancement of music at Ministry of Science and Arts. His tendencies are mainly towards tradition and Romanticism; but he exercises an exquisite and natural taste, rather rare among Belgian comprs. His style is truly lyrical and his inspiration, always restrained by severe self-criticism, never runs to vulgarity or extravagance.
Many songs, mostly to words of Guido Gezelle (Flemish poet); symph. poems, notably *Hélios* (1894) and *Mythe du Printemps* (1895); *Symphonie homérique* (1898–9); cantatas, *Jong Vlaanderen*, children's vs. (1907); 3 *Elegies*, orch. (*In Memoriam*, 1917; *Elévation du Cœur*, 1917; *Solitude*, 1919); opera, *De Kinderen der Zee* (*The Children of the Sea*), produced at Lyric Theatre, Antwerp, 27 March, 1920; pf. pieces, etc.—C. V. B.

MOSER, Andreas. Violinist and author; *b.* Semlin-on-Danube, 29 Nov. 1859. Pupil of Joachim at Berlin R. High School; then Joachim's assistant; 1888, prof. at R. High School.
Wrote biography of *Jos. Joachim* (1899, enlarged 1908, 2 vols., publ. by Brahms Soc.); *Correspondence of Brahms and Joachim* (1908); in collab. with Johannes Joachim, *Letters from and to Joseph Joachim* (1911–12, 3 vols.); publ. with Joachim a vn. tutor in 3 vols. (Fr. by Marteau; Eng. by Moffat); *Method of Violin-playing* (2 vols.). Ed. ancient vn. music.—A. E.

MOSER, Hans Joachim. Ger. writer on music; singer; compr. *b.* Berlin, 25 May, 1889. Son and pupil of Andreas Moser; also pupil of H. van Eyken, G. Jenner, Robert Kahn, of Oskar Noé and Felix Schmidt (singing); 1907, stud. music, Germanics and history at Marburg, Berlin, Leipzig; graduated Ph.D. Rostock, 1910 (dissertation, *Musical Associations in German Middle Ages*); 1919, lecturer for music and theory at Halle; 1923, professor.
In collab. with Oskar Noé: *Technique of Ger. Art of Song* (Göschen Coll., 1911); *History of Ger. Music* (2 vols. 1920, 2nd ed. 1922); a little *Dictionary of Music* (1923, Taubner). New arr. of Weber's *Euryanthe*, with new text, *The Seven Ravens*, by

Moser, was perf. at Berlin, 1915. Comp. a scena, *Song of Vestal Virgin* (contr. and orch., Berlin, 1912); publ. (1913) 5 books of songs (op. 1–5); male choruses, op. 8; 5-v. motets, op. 10.—A. E.

MOSER, Rudolf. Compr. *b.* Niedernzwil (Switzerland), 7 Jan. 1892. Stud. first theology, since 1912 devoted himself entirely to music; stud. under Max Reger (compn.) and H. Sitt (vn.) at Leipzig Cons. (1912–14); since 1921 leader of Vereinshauschor and teacher of cpt. at Basle.

3 str. 4tets; vn. sonata; songs (Leipzig, Hug) and unacc. choruses (Stuttgart, Missions Verlag); Prelude and fugue, fantasy and rhapsody for organ.—F. H.

MOSSEL, Isaac. Dutch cellist; *b.* Rotterdam, 22 April, 1870; *d.* Dec. 1923. Started vn. study when 3 years old; soon took cello as principal study; 1885, cellist Philh. Orch. Berlin; 1888–1904, soloist Concertgebouw, Amsterdam; from 1890 teacher at Conservatoire, Amsterdam; and had many famous pupils.—W. P.

MOSSEL, Max. Violinist; *b.* Rotterdam, 25 July, 1871. Stud. under Willy Hess and Sarasate; *début* Oct. 1876, at Bommel (Holland) Orch Soc.; in England, Crystal Palace Sat. concerts, 5 July, 1892; numerous wide tours; dir. of Max Mossel Concerts in chief cities of Gt. Britain; prof. Guildhall School of Music, London. —E.-H.

MOSZKOWSKI, Moritz. Polish pianist and compr. *b.* Breslau, 23 Aug. 1854. Stud. at Breslau and Dresden; then at Stern's Cons. and Kullak's Cons., Berlin; later, teacher at latter; 1873, concert-pianist; 1897, left Berlin for Paris; 1899, became member of Berlin Acad.; now lives in Paris. His characteristic pieces once had a very great vogue, and his ballet music is still frequently played.

2 concert pieces and *Scherzo* for vn. and pf.; 3 pf. and cello concert-pieces; pf. concerto, E ma. op. 59 (1898); 2 orch. suites (op. 39 and 47); *Fantastic Procession* for orch.; orch, suite, *Aus aller Herren Länder*, op. 23; 6 orch. pieces to Grabbe's *Don Juan and Faust*, op. 56; symph. poem, *Joan of Arc*, op. 19; Prelude and fugue, op. 85 (str. orch.); vn. concerto (op. 30); pf. pieces (especially *Spanish Dances*); 3 concert-studies; concert-waltz; gavotte, etc; songs. Opera, *Boabdil* (Berlin, 1892); ballet, *Laurin* (1896). —A. E.

MOTE, Arnold R. Australian compr. Lives in Sydney, N.S.W.

Orch.: *March of Triumph*, op. 68, prize-march (Curwen); *The Triumph of Liberty*, op. 55; overture, *On the Blue Mountains*, op. 57 (ms.); pieces for small orch.; 8tet, str. fl. clar. bsn. horn; str. 4tet, C mi. (New South Wales prize); trio, C. mi. pf. vn. cello; choruses (Novello; Curwen); organ pieces; pf. pieces; cantatas; songs; book, *Examples in "How to Score"* (Ambrose Elliot, London).—E.-H.

MOTTA, Vianna da. Portuguese pianist; *b.* in African island of St. Thomas in 1868, and taken to Lisbon a year later; stud. at Cons. there, and at 14, sent by King Ferdinand to study in Germany (under Sophie Menter and Xaver Scharwenka [pf.], and Philipp Scharwenka [compn.]; then under Liszt at Weimar [1885], Karl Schäffer at Berlin [1886] and Bülow in Frankfort [1887]). In 1902 toured Europe and S. America with great success. Lived in Berlin for some time as Court-pianist; 1915–17 as successor of Stavenhagen at Acad. at Geneva, and since then, has been dir. of National Cons. and Symph. Orch. at Lisbon.—E.-H.

MOTU PROPRIO. The decree issued by Pope Pius X on 22 Nov. 1903 for the purification of music in R.C. churches all over the world. It enforced the restoration of the Gregorian chant and the rejection of all music not specially composed for the Church. In 1910, a special school of church music was opened in Rome, and in 1912 it was given the title of Pontifical School of Church Music. This movement of purification had already been started by Leo XIII in his *Regolamento per la Musica Sacra* in 1884. See arts. AMELLI, GHIGNONI. Consult art. in *The Month*, Sept. 1919.—E.-H.

MOULAERT, Raymond. Belgian compr. *b.* Brussels, 4 Feb. 1875. Stud. at Cons. Brussels. 1898–1912, pianist, orgt. and assistant condr. at La Monnaie Theatre. Teacher at École de Musique at St.-Josse, then dir. at École de Musique, St.-Gilles (near Brussels), 1913; teacher of harmony Brussels Cons. (since 1896).

Organ sonata; *Variazioni quasi sonata*, pf.; sonata, F sharp (pf.); *Mei Sotterneye*, opera (not yet perf.); many songs, including *Poems of Old France* (2 vols.); 20 *Mélodies et Poèmes*; 4 *Chinese Poems*.—E. C.

MRACZEK, Joseph Gustav. German-Czechoslovak compr. *b.* Brünn, 12 March, 1878. Stud. at School of Music, Brünn, and Cons. at Vienna (Hellmesberger, Löwe). Dir. of Munich Künstler Theater, of Stadttheater, Leipzig, and Dresden Philh. Orch. Lives in Dresden.

Operas: *The Glass Slipper* (Brünn, 1902); *The Dream* (Berlin, 1912); *Aebelö* (Breslau, 1915); *The Love Council*; *Ikdar*; music for *Kismet* (Oriental sketches for chamber orch.). Symph. poems: *Max and Moritz*; *Eva*. Pf. 5tet; instr. music; songs. —V. ST.

MUCK, Carl. Ger. condr. *b.* Darmstadt, 22 Oct. 1859. Stud. philology at Heidelberg and Leipzig, at same time attending Cons.; 1880 Ph.D., also first appearance as pianist at Gewandhaus; condr. theatres at Zurich, Salzburg, Brünn, Graz; 1886, engaged by Angelo Neumann as first condr. of Prague Ger. Public Theatre; cond. the *Nibelungen* there, at Petrograd and Moscow, 1889; and summer season at Lessing Theatre, Berlin, 1891; became condr. of Berlin R. Opera House, 1892; music dir. 1908. M. very often cond. Symph. Concerts of R. Orch.; 1894–1911, Schleswig Music Fests.; 1899, Ger. Opera, London (Covent Garden); 1903–6, Philh. Concerts of Court Opera Orch., Vienna (alternately with Mottl); Seasons 1906–8, the Symph. Concerts, Boston, U.S.A.; 1912, definitely gave up Berlin engagement and accepted conductorship of Boston Symphony Orch.; 1919, returned to Europe; first engaged as visiting condr. (Munich, Amsterdam, etc.); 1922, cond. Philh. concerts, Hamburg. Muck is a brilliant condr., possessing rhythmic certainty and powerful constructive ability.—A. E.

MUGNONE, Leopoldo. Ital. condr. *b.* Naples, 29 Sept. 1858. Stud. there at R. Cons. di San Pietro a Maiella under Serrao and Cesi. He rapidly establ. himself, as an artist full of the fire and impetuosity of the South, and visited the principal theatres in Italy and abroad. He cond. a tour with the famous d.b.-player Bottesini.

During exhibition of 1899, he dir. a Grand Ital. Season in Paris. Was first to cond. Mascagni's *Cavalleria Rusticana* at the Costanzi in Rome (1890). He also acquired fame for his excellent revivals of important operas, *Orfeo* of Gluck, *Guglielmo Tell* of Rossini, *The Damnation of Faust* of Berlioz in its orig. form of oratorio. A very fine interpreter of *Falstaff*, having the esteem and admiration of Verdi. In the Verdi centenary year, he cond. at La Scala, Milan, important perfs. of Verdi's operas including *Nabucco*. He is one of most esteemed and famous Ital. condrs.—especially of opera—of the period 1900–20. As a capable concert-condr. he has gained important successes at Augusteo in Rome, and elsewhere. Amongst his works are the operas *Il Biricchino*, 1-act (Venice, 1892) and *Vita brettona* (Naples, 1905).—D. A.

MÜHLFELD, Richard. Ger. clarinettist; *b.* Salzungen, 28 Feb. 1856 ; *d.* Meiningen, 1 June, 1907. Stud. theory under Emil Büchner; 1873, member of Meiningen Court Orch.; then violinist; 1876, 1st clarinettist (self-taught). He was 1st clarinettist at Bayreuth Fest. 1884–1896. His playing induced Brahms to compose his opp. 114, 115 and 120.—A. E.

MUKLE, May Henrietta. Eng. cellist; *b.* London, 14 May, 1880. One of a large mus. family; stud. at R.A.M. under Pezze. Started on career as soloist at age of 9; has toured British Isles, France, Belgium, Italy, Germany, Austria, Hungary, Canada, S. Africa, Australia, U.S.A. and Hawaiian Islands. Has publ. 2 fancies for cello and pf. (Schirmer, New York).—E.-H.

MULÈ, Giuseppe. Ital. compr. *b.* Termini Imerese, 28 June, 1885. Pupil of R. Cons. Palermo, of which he is at present the dir. He is an appreciated compr. of various operas: *La Baronessa di Carini* (perf. Teatro Massimo, Palermo, 1912); *Al lupo* (Teatro Nazionale, Rome, 1919); *La Monacella alla fontana* (Trieste, 1923). These are publ. by Ricordi. He has also written symph. works, and the music for the *Bacchœ* of Euripides, perf. on revival of that tragedy at Greek theatre of Syracuse in 1922.—D. A.

MULET, Henri. Fr. orgt. *b.* Paris (Montmartre), 17 Oct. 1878; *lauréat* of the organ class of Guilmant at Cons. Paris; now prof. of organ at École Niedermeyer and orgt. at Saint-Philippe du Roule. Comp. a vol. of organ pieces, *Esquisses byzantines*, and 5 symph. poems of solid construction and richly original orchestration.—F. R.

MÜLLER-BORGSTRÖM, Harriet Amalie. Norwegian pianist; *b.* Trondhjem, 2 June, 1868; *d.* Christiania, 19 Sept. 1913. Pupil of Martin Ursin, Christiania, 1881–90; of Erika Nissen, same city, 1890–2; afterwards of Hollaender and Barth, Berlin. *Début* in Christiania, 1897. Married, 1904, the compr. Hjalmar Borgström. —U. M.

MÜLLER-HARTMANN, Robert. Ger. compr. and critic; *b.* Hamburg, 11 Oct. 1884. Stud. at Stern's Cons. and with Eduard Behm, Berlin; engaged as teacher of theory, Bernuth Cons.

Hamburg; 1923, lecturer Hamburg Univ. Several years mus. critic for Hamburg *Correspondenten*; later on for *Hamburger Fremdenblatt*.
Variations and fugue on own theme, orch.(Simrock); songs, op. 4; sketches for pf. op. 6 (Rahter); vn. sonata, op. 5; pf. pieces, op. 8; songs, op. 12. In ms.: str. 4tet, D mi.; symph. overtures; orch. variations on pastoral theme; and overture to *Leonce und Lena*.—A. E.

MÜLLER-REUTER, Theodor. Ger. condr. and compr. *b.* Dresden, 1 Sept. 1858; *d.* there, 14 Aug. 1919. Pupil of Friedrich and Alwin Wieck (pf.) and L. Meinardus, Julius Otto, Bargiel (compn.); 1878–9 at Hoch's Cons. Frankfort-o-M. (Clara Schumann, J. Stockhausen, Raff); 1879, pf. teacher at Strasburg Cons.; 1887, went to Dresden; 1888, condr. of Orpheus Male Choral Union; 1889, of orch. soc. and of Dreysing's Acad. of Singing; 1892, teacher at R. Cons.; 1893–1918, condr. of Concert Soc. Crefeld; 1902, dir. of Town Cons.; 1897, R. mus. dir.; 1907, professor.
Songs; female choruses (op. 15) with pf.; male choruses; 2 operas: *Ondolina* (Strasburg, 1882); *The Angry Earl* (Nuremberg, 1887); choral works: *Ruth*; *Song of the Storm*, op. 23 (double chorus and orch.); orch. suite, *In the Country*; pf. trio D mi. op. 19; pf. pieces (op. 6, 8, 18, 25; studies, op. 20). Wrote: *Study on Beethoven's C mi. Symphony*; *50 Years' Mus. Life on the Lower Rhine*; *Introduction to Liszt's "Legend of St. Elizabeth"* (1905); *Dictionary of Ger. Concert-Literature* (1 vol. 1909).—A. E.

MULLINGS, Frank. Eng. t. singer; *b.* Walsall, 10 May, 1881. Trained at the Birmingham and Midland Inst. *Début* in 1907 at Coventry (Gounod's *Faust*); Queen's Hall, London, 1911. In 1913, one of principal ts. in Denhof Opera tour (*Tristan*, etc.); British National Opera, Covent Garden, 1922–24. One of the finest of Eng. tenors.—E.-H.

MUNTHE-KAAS SANDVIK, Elisabeth. Norwegian concert-singer (s.); *b.* Havre, 12 June, 1883. Stud. singing in Christiania (Gina Hille), Berlin, Munich, London. *Début* in Christiania, 1906; numerous concerts at home and abroad, including many great cities of Europe. Has frequently sung in England (London and elsewhere). Lives in Christiania.—U. M.

MUNZINGER, Carl. Swiss condr. compr. *b.* Balsthal, 23 Sept. 1842; *d.* Berne, 16 Aug. 1911. Stud. at Basle under A. Walther, then at Leipzig Cons. (1854–60); dir. of Liedertafel (male choir) at Solothurn; in 1869 of Berne Liedertafel; 1884–1909, also cond. Symphony and Oratorio Concerts at Berne. Ph.D. *h.c.* Berne Univ.
2 cantatas, *Murtenschlacht* and *Natur und Mensch*; *Die Freischarbuben*, male chorus and orch.; songs and unacc. choruses.—F. H.

MURALI. See INDIAN MUS. INSTRUMENTS.

MURDOCH, MURDOCH & CO. London. The mus. department was establ. about 40 years ago. 15 years later they added the publishing of elementary school songs and easy music for small orch. and pf. In 1915 they began to issue music of a more important character, beginning with *Mayfair Classics*, about 200 pf. and vocal selections, from old masters (ed. by F. Corder and F. Swinstead). Since then, they have become noted for their comprehensive list of works of Arnold Bax, including large orch. works (*The Garden of*

Fand; *November Woods*; symphony in E flat; vla. concerto); pf. 5tet in G mi.; str. 4tet in G; 5tet, str. and harp, etc.—E.-H.

MURDOCH, William Daniel. Australian pianist; *b.* Bendigo, Victoria, 10 Feb. 1888. First recitals in London, end of 1910 and beginning of 1911; toured S. Africa 1911; Australia and New Zealand, 1912-13; United States and Canada, 1914; Scandinavia twice in 1918 and once in 1919. Writer of article on PIANOFORTE MUSIC in this Dictionary.—E.-H.

MUSICAL APPRECIATION. See APPRECIA-TION.

MUSICAL COMPETITION FESTIVALS. About 200 are held annually throughout the British Isles and Dominions. These do not include the Welsh Eisteddfodau, which embrace many things besides music and demonstrate national char-acteristics. No other mus. movement has grown so rapidly or has shown such widespread mus. enthusiasm. First fest. was that begun at Strat-ford, London, by late J. Spencer Curwen in 1882. Miss A. M. Wakefield, in 1885, began the rural or county type of fest. which brought village-choirs together to compete and to unite in per-forming large works which singly they never would have heard. Other fests. endeavour to cover all branches of music and conclude with a perf. of the chief prize-winners. The fests. seek to raise the standard of perf. and choice of music in the home, the school, the church and the choir or orch. Adjudicators criticise and advise the performers. The promoting workers and the listening audiences encourage the com-petitors. Talent is discovered, and in other ways the country is being made musical in the most practical and permanent fashion. The move-ment now has headquarters at 3 Central Build-ings, Westminster, and issues a Year Book and other literature, which can be had from the Secretary, British Federation of Musical Com-petition Festivals. A central board looks after the interests of the affiliated fests. and ad-ministers grants in aid from a fund subscribed by the Carnegie Music Trust. The following are a few of the larger fests. (with year of foundation):

Bedfordshire Eisteddfod Competitive Mus. Fest. Bedford (1920); Belfast M.C.F. (1908); Berks, Bucks and Oxon C.M.F. (1903), held alternately in each county (*q.v.*); Blackpool M. F. (1901), one of the largest (*q.v.*); Bristol Eisteddfod (1903); Buxton (revived in 1922); Carlisle and District M.C.F. (1895); Coventry M.F. (1922); Edinburgh M.C.F. Association (1920); Feis Ceoil Association!(1897); Irish Mus. Fest. Dublin (*q.v.*); Glasgow M.F. Association (1911) for West Scotland; Leamington and County Open C.M.F. (1911); Leeds C.M.F. (1922); London M.C.F. (1905) held at Central Hall, Westminster; Lytham M.F. (1901); Manx Competition, Douglas (1892); Mary Wakefield (Westmorland) Fest. Kendal (1885), biennial; Midland M.C.F. Birmingham (1912)—a great fest.; Mrs. Sunderland Mus. Competition, Huddersfield (1889); Mid-Somerset M.C., Bath (1901); Morecambe M.F. (1892), focuses Lancashire and Yorkshire choirs; Northern Counties of Scot-land Fest. Inverness (1921); North London M.F. (1920), held at Holloway; North of England Mus. Tournament, Newcastle-on-Tyne (1919); Notting-ham M.C.F. (1902); People's Palace M.F. London (1908), mainly choral; Perthshire Mus. (Competition) Fest. Association, Perth (1920); Plymouth M.F. (1914), open to Devon and Cornwall; Portsmouth

M.C.F. (1923); Renfrewshire M.C.F. (1913), Greenock; Stirlingshire Mus. (Competition) Fest. Association (1920); South-East London M.F. (1920), held at Bermondsey; Southern Area M.F. (1922), held at Wandsworth; Stratford and East London M.F. (1882), held at Stratford; Wharfedale Competition M.F. (1907), held at Ilkley; Worcestershire M.C. (1896); Canadian fests. for Manitoba, Alberta, Sas-katchewan and Ontario; Australia and New Zealand have many fests.; National Eisteddfod Association, London, directs Welsh national eisteddfodau.—J. G.

MUSICAL CRITICISM. See CRITICISM.

MUSICAL FESTIVALS. See BAYREUTH, BIRMINGHAM, DONAUESCHINGEN, FEIS CEOIL., GLASTONBURY, LEEDS, OIREACHTAS, SALZBURG, THREE CHOIRS, U.S.A. MUS. FESTS., etc.

MUSICAL JOURNALS. See PERIODICALS.

MUSICAL PITCH. See PITCH.

MUSIN, Ovide. Belgian violinist; *b.* Naudrin (Liège), 22 Sept. 1854. Graduated R. Cons. at Liège, 1868. Pupil of Léonard in Liège and in Paris. In 1883, toured with own con-cert company in U.S.A., Canada and Mexico; 1899 to 1908, prof. at Liège Cons. In 1908 founded a vn. school in New York.

Vn. pieces (Fischer); *The Belgian School of Violin*, 4 vols. (Musin Publ. Co. 1916) (contains studies by Léonard and Musin); author of *My Memories* (Musin Publ. Co. 1920).—O. K.

MUSSORGSKY, Modest Petrovitch (*accent 1st syll.*). Russian composer; *b.* Karevo, 16/28 March, 1839; *d.* Petrograd, 16/28 March, 1881. As a child, he was taught the pianoforte first by his mother, and afterwards by a teacher named Herke, and achieved proficiency as a pianist. He started composing at an early date, without preliminary training. An autograph ms. book (now in the library of the Paris Conserva-toire), containing original, unrevised versions of 15 songs, written by him between 1857 and 1866, shows him from the very outset making giant strides towards the independence and pregnancy of musical idiom, the intensity and directness of expression, which characterise his later master-pieces. Towards the end of 1857 César Cui in-troduced him to Balakiref, with whom he began to study theory and technique. He had pre-viously become acquainted with Dargomisky, whose creed that " the object of music was truth in expression rather than formal beauty " he promptly made his own.

He devoted himself chiefly to the writing of songs and of operas and lyric comedies or dramas. The songs, about sixty in number, comprise examples of purely lyric order among which a few are of slight interest, but others, such as the set *Sunless*, are of supreme beauty. When he aims at characterisation as well as at poetic expression—as he does in most of his peasants' or childrens' songs—he achieves wonderful results in the vein of tragedy as well as in that of comedy.

His first attempts at opera-writing were purely tentative; but in 1863 he began to write a *Salammbô* (after Flaubert's novel) which he relinquished after having written many scenes (some of the music partly utilised in *Boris Godunof*). In 1868 he started setting to music Gogol's comedy *The Marriage Broker*, but gave up the notion after having written one act (which is delightfully racy and original), and began a first draft of *Boris Godunof*. The final draft of this work, considerably longer, was completed in 1872, and produced at Petrograd in Jan. 1874. Despite its success, *Boris Godunof* was withdrawn after a score of performances. Long after Mussorgsky's death, a " revised " edition, in which all the alleged instances of " irregularity and clumsiness " had been severely dealt with by Rimsky-Korsakof, appeared; and until 1923, when a reprint of the genuine edition began to be issued in London (Chester), it was extremely difficult to know *Boris Godunof* as Mussorgsky had written it (the original orchestral score was never published).[1]

After having contributed a few scenes to an opera-ballet, *Mlada*, which was to be written by several composers jointly (the scheme eventually collapsed), he began, upon Stassof's suggestion, to write *Khovanshtchina*, at which he worked, somewhat fitfully, until the end of his life. In 1875, he started writing another work, this time of humorous character, *The Fair at Sorotchinsi* (after a tale by Gogol). He gave up this scheme after having written several scenes (some of which are now published) and he concentrated on *Khovanshtchina*. But at his death, he had only completed a provisional version in a rough draft, which was overhauled and finished by Rimsky-Korsakof.

Mussorgsky's instrumental works are few, and by far the least significant in his output. The principal are the tone-poem *A Night on the Bare Mountain* (very much overhauled by Rimsky-Korsakof) and the pf. suite *Pictures from an Exhibition*.

The much-debated questions, how far Mussorgsky's alleged technical shortcomings are to be accounted for by his very conception of his art (summed up in this excerpt from a letter of of his to Stassof: "The quest of mere beauty of shape and matter is a crude and childish stage of art; the true task of the artist is to aim at disengaging the subtle features which characterise individuals and masses ") ; and how far the " revisions " of his works were justified in principle or may lead to misconceptions as

[1] The first to protest was Pierre d'Alheim in his epoch-making book. In 1908, when *Boris Godunof* was produced in Paris, many French critics followed suit. See also an article by R. Godet in the *Revue Musicale*, 1922, No. 6.

regards his capacities and achievements, are still under discussion.

Songs: 7 publ. by Belaief, 1 by Gutheil, all the rest by Bessel
Pf. music: *Pictures from an Exhibition* for pf. (Bessel) (orch. versions, by Tukhmalof, Sir Henry Wood, and Maurice Ravel respectively, have been written)
Various pieces (Bessel, Jurgenson)
Vocal scores: *The Marriage Broker* (1 act only) (Bessel)
  Boris Godunof, original version (Bessel, 1875; now reprinting Chester, 1923)
  Boris Godunof, revised versions (Bessel, 1896 and 1908)
  Khovanshtchina (Bessel). New version of the final chorus, after M.'s rough draft, by I. Stravinsky (*id.*)
  The Fair at Sorotchinsi, fragments, ed. by V. Karatyghin (*id.*)
Orch. music: *A Night on the Bare Mountain* (*id.*)
Choral music: *The Defeat of Sennacherib* (1867) (Belaief)
  Joshua Navin (1877) (*id.*)
  Female chorus from *Salammbô* (1866) (*id.*)
  Mixed chorus from *Œdipus* (1860) (*id.*)
  Four unacc. part-songs on folk-tunes, for male vs. (Jurgenson)
Consult P. d'Alheim, *M.* (Paris, 1896, Mercure de France); M. Olénine d'Alheim, *Le Legs de M.* (*ib.* 1908, Rey); M. D. Calvocoressi, *M.* (*ib.* 1908, Alcan; rev. 1911; Eng. transl. by A. E. Hull, London, 1913, Kegan Paul); M. D. Calvocoressi, *The Unknown M.* (*Music and Letters*, July, 1922); *M.'s Letters to his Friends* (*Mus. Quarterly*, July 1923); R. Godet, *Les Deux Boris* (*Revue Musicale*, April, 1922). Further bibliography is to be found in aforenamed books and articles.—M. D. C.

MUSTEL, Alphonse. Fr. mus. instr. inventor; *b.* in 1873. Dir. of the famous factory of organs with " double expression," founded in Paris in 1853 by Victor Mustel (1815–90); later directed by his sons Charles (1840–93) and Auguste, who invented the *Celesta* (pf. with steel plates) which added a new and valuable element of sonority to modern instrumentation. The *Celesta* made its 1st appearance at the Opéra-Comique, Paris, in 1886; since then many comprs. have used it. A. Mustel, son of Auguste, invented in 1894 the *Prolongement* or pedal-point, and in 1907 the *Concertal*, a model of Swell organ with electric bellows which can be operated either by the fingers of the player or by an automatic system of perforated rollers. A. Mustel is also the author of a large work, *Méthode d'orgue expressive* (1902) which treats the instr. from all points of view—history, description, and instruction in playing.—F. R.

MUZICESCU, G. See RUMANIA under art. ACADEMIES.

N

NACHÉZ, Tivadar. Hungarian violinist; *b.* Budapest, 1 May, 1859. Stud. there under Sabathiel, leader of Opera orch.; won the approval of Liszt; then stud. under Joachim in Berlin; afterwards Léonard in Paris; played at foundation of Bayreuth theatre; appeared Hamburg 1881; first appeared England, Crystal Palace, 9 April, 1881; after that, continuous concerts and tours, England and elsewhere. Played his 2nd vn. concerto London Philh. 17 April, 1907; again at Landon Ronald's New Symphony Orch. concert, 27 Jan. 1910; lives in London.

Zigeunertänze; vn. concerto, E mi. op. 30; Polonaise, op. 26; ed. 2 vn. concertos of Vivaldi (A mi., G mi.).—E.-H.

NAGEL, Wilibald. Ger. musicologist; *b.* Mülheim-o-Ruhr, 12 Jan. 1863. Son of *lieder*- and oratorio-singer Siegfried Nagel (*d.* 1874); stud. Germanics and music (Ehrlich, Karl Treibs, Spitta, Bellermann), Berlin; Univ. teacher of mus. literature, Zurich; then went to England where he stud. old Eng. music; 1896, returned to Germany; 1898–1913, Univ. teacher of mus. theory and science at Technical High School, Darmstadt; 1917–21, ed. of *Neue Musik-Zeitung*, Stuttgart.

History of Music in England (2 vols. 1894 and 1897, Strasburg, Trübner); On the Dramatico-musical Arr. of Genoveva Legend (1888); Johannes Brahms; Beethoven and his Pf. Sonatas (2 vols. Langensalza, 1903–5); Chr. Graupner as Symphonist (1912); Pf. Sonatas of Joh. Brahms; Æsthetico-technical Analyses (Stuttgart, 1915); Wilhelm Mauke (1919).—A. E.

NANI, Enrico. Ital. barit. *b.* Parma, 4 Nov. 1873. Known at all the principal theatres in Europe and America. Stud. in Rome under Antonio Cotogni, and made his *début* in 1909. His repertoire extends from *L'Africana* to *L'Elisir d'amore*; is a good interpreter of Verdi and Wagner operas.—D. A.

NANNY, Édouard. Fr. d.b. soloist; *b.* St.-Germain-en-Laye in 1872. Has taught at Cons. Paris since 1920. Author of *Method of Double-Bass* (2 parts) (used at Cons.). Also wrote 60 Studies for same. Has given concerts throughout Europe.—F. R.

NANSEN, Eva Helene (*née* Sars). Norwegian singer; *b.* Christiania, 7 Dec. 1858; *d.* Lysaker, near Christiania, 9 Dec. 1907. Stud. under Thorvald Lammers and Désirée Artôt de Padilla. Concert-tours in her native land; also sang at Stockholm, Upsala, Gothenburg, Copenhagen and Helsingfors. Won great recognition for her soulful interpretations, especially in oratorio; highly-esteemed teacher of singing. In 1889 she married famous explorer Fridtjof Nansen.—J. A.

NAPOLEÃO, Arthur. Portuguese pianist; *b.* Oporto, 1843. Toured Europe and N. and S. America as brilliant pianist; then settled in Rio de Janeiro as proprietor of a pianoforte business.

In 1907, the city commemorated the jubilee of his first concert there. He comp. over 90 works (pf. fantasias, songs, hymns, marches, studies, etc.); also a lyric drama *O remorso vivo*.—E.-H.

NAPOLI, Gennaro. Ital. compr. *b.* Naples, 19 May, 1881. After having gained his diploma in compn. at R. Cons. Naples, he won in 1906 in Rome the *Pensionato Nazionale per la Musica*. He then returned to Naples; became teacher at Liceo Mus.; then at R. Cons. Of his compns., there must be mentioned a str. 4tet, a symphony, cantatas, songs and pf. pieces (Ricordi) and a 3-act opera *Jacopo Ortis*; also a theoretical work, *Bassi imitati e fugati* for cpt. (Ricordi, 1915).—D. A.

NAPPI, Giovanni Battista. Ital. music critic; *b.* Milan, 15 Jan. 1857. He has occupied for many years the post vacated in 1885 by the illustrious Filippo Filippi on newspaper *La Perseveranza* of Milan. Amongst his publications may be mentioned: *Cinquanta anni di musica drammatica* (1861–1911), for the book *Mezzo secolo di vita italiana* (Milan, Vallardi); *Della necessità di una biblioteca popolare di cultura musicale*, in Records of the Educational Musical Congress held on centenary of Cons. of Milan. (1908).—D. A.

NAPRAVNÍK, Eduard F. (*accent 2nd syll.*). Russ. compr. of Czech origin; *b.* Bejšt (Bohemia), 1839; *d.* Petrograd, 28 Oct./10 Nov. 1915. Stud. 1852–4 at Organ School, Prague, where he was next a music-teacher. In Russia from 1861, first as dir. of Prince Yussipof's orch.; then as 2nd, and from 1869 1st, condr. Court Opera House, Petrograd. From 1869 to 1887 cond. the concerts of the Russ. Mus. Soc., of Red Cross and of Patriotic Soc., enjoying great esteem in Russia both as compr. and condr. His whole bent and his inclinations place him among the Russ. comprs., his less important works belonging to the Czech period.

Operas: Nižegorodci (1868); Harold (1886); Dubrovsky (1895); Francesca di Rimini (1903); 4 symphonies; symph. works: Damon; Orient; Ouverture Solennelle; suite, dances and marches for orch. 3 str. 4tets; 2 trios; pf. 4tet; vn. sonata; 2 suites, cello and pf.; pf. concerto; 2 phantasies on Russian folk themes for pf. and orch.; id. for vn. and orch.; suite, vocal pieces with orch.; songs; choral works, etc. Consult: Weymarn, E. F. Napravník (1888); Findeisen, E. F. N. (1895), both in Russian (Petrograd). Most of his works are publ. by Jurgenson.—V. St.

NAT, Yves. Fr. pianist; *b.* Beziers in 1890; *lauréat* in Diémer's class at Cons. Paris, 1906. Has comp. pf. preludes, and a sonatina in which he revolutionises pf. technique, and gives it an added grandeur and force.—F. R.

NATIONAL COUNCIL OF MUSIC FOR WALES. In Feb. 1918, the Royal Commission on Univ. Education recommended that the Univ.

should (a) establish a music directorship, (b) set up a National Council of Music, to act as the supreme consultative body on all matters concerned with mus. education in Wales, (c) make an annual grant to the Council funds. Within 3 months of issue of report, an endowment fund, placed at disposal of Univ. by anonymous benefactors, enabled the Univ. to proceed at once to appoint a dir. of music. The first appointment was accepted by Dr. H. Walford Davies (now Sir Walford Davies),who was concurrently appointed prof. of music at Univ. Coll. Aberystwyth. The dir. took up his duties in April 1919, and first meeting of Council was held in June 1919. The Council consists of the dir. (chairman ex-officio), the profs. of music at constituent colleges of Univ., representatives of various educational bodies, with a limited number of co-opted members. The work already accomplished by the Council includes the compilation and issue of a coll. of Welsh hymns and tunes, a school and college hymnal with anthems and carols, church festival books, memorandum on music-teaching, and music in secondary schools; the organisation of illustrated lectures on chamber-music (mainly for secondary schools), of first-class orch. fests. and of a summer school in music; the placing of gramophones and records of lectures and illustrations in elementary and secondary schools; the establishment of weekly college concerts at the colleges of Univ., and the general stimulation of musical activity throughout the Principality. For the illustrated lectures on chamber-music, a trio of instrumentalists is made available at each of Univ. colleges for paying visits to surrounding schools, etc. The trio is accompanied by a lecturer. Already some 400 visits have been paid by the trios to schools in all parts of Wales. A gramophone scheme ensures that a good instr. shall be placed in every elementary and secondary school in Wales. In addition to the director's lectures on melody, the schools are encouraged to obtain records selected by Council for their educational value. The dir. holds frequent conferences with teachers, directors of education, local education authorities, and inspectors of schools, for the discussion of the recognition of music as essential subject in curricula of schools. Inquiries respecting Council should be addressed: Sec., Welsh National Council of Music, Music House, Aberystwyth.—J. C. McL.

NAUJALIS, Juozas. Lithuanian compr. b. Raudondvaris, Kaunas district, 1869. In 1889, graduated at Warsaw Mus. Inst. Then orgt. at Vabalininkas, at Rietavas, and at Kaunas (Kovno). In 1894, he went to Ratisbon to the Higher Church Music School. Returned to Kaunas as cath. orgt. and lecturer at theological seminary. Formed a large choir, which sang Palestrina's and other music. From 1898, held secret practices with his Lithuanian choir (all Lithuanian gatherings being forbidden under Russian régime). Since 1919, he dir. the Kaunas Music School and now dir. of State Music School.

Mass St. Casimir, for 4-v. male choir (1895, Pustet); Mass for Virgin Mary, for 2 v. (Düsseldorf,

Schrann); Requiem Mass, for 4 v. and organ (Moniuszko Prize, Warsaw); Tres Cantus Sacri (mixed vs.); Solemn Mass (for 1 v.). His first compn. The Slav Lands have risen (1892), sung at Petrograd Theological Acad., was destroyed during a police search. From the Lithuanian press, he issued popular dainos for mixed chorus and male vs. and for solo v. and pf.; Lithuanian Church Hymn; pf. duets; organ trio; 6 vols of Maîtres contemporains de l'orgue (Warsaw, Polish coll.); etc.—H. R.

NAVARRINI, Francesco. Ital. singer; b. Cittadella (Veneto), 1858; d. Milan, 1923. One of most renowned basses of recent times. Stud. in his native city and in Milan; début at Treviso in 1880; appeared at all principal theatres of Europe and N. and S. America. His repertoire was very extensive. At La Scala in Milan he was first interpreter of Ponchielli's Marion Delorme, of Gomez's Condor, and of Verdi's Otello.—D. A.

NAYLOR, Edward Woodall. Eng. compr. and orgt. b. Scarborough, 9 Feb. 1867. Stud. with his father, who was orgt. of York Minster; organscholar, Emmanuel Coll. Cambridge, 1884–8; Mus.Doc. Cantab. 1898 (the first to take the degree under the new regulations which required residence, abolished examination and substituted orig. compn.); orgt. various London churches; returned to Cambridge where he has been orgt. and mus. lecturer Emmanuel Coll. from 1897 onwards. Has written much church music for men's voices; Hon. Fellow of the Coll. 1920; first appeared as compr. July 1892, solo-cantata Merlin and the Gleam (St. James's Hall, London). His opera The Angelus won the Ricordi Prize and was produced at Covent Garden in Jan. 1909, repeated in Feb., and was also perf. 10 times by Carl Rosa Opera Co. 1921–2.

Operas: The Angelus (Ricordi); Slaves of Liberty, comic (ms.). Pax Dei, requiem (Cambridge, 27 Feb. 1913) (Novello); Arthur the King, cantata (Harrogate, 1902; publ. Vincent); The Merry Bells of Yule (Novello, 1898); Magnificat, double choir, comp. 1903 (Curwen, 1918); 8-v. motet, Vox dicentis, comp. 1911 (Curwen, 1919); orch.: Variations on theme in B flat; Tokugawa overture in D (Tokyo, 1919); 5tet, trio, and other chamber-music (ms.). Books: Shakespeare and Music (J. M. Dent & Sons); Elizabethan Virginal Book (id.); Eng. version of Bie's History of the Piano (id.); Music and Shakespeare in Musical Antiquary; (Oxford Univ. Press, April 1910); Shakespeare Music (used by Mr. Poel in London production of Hamlet, and Ital. production of Twelfth Night in Milan; also in Weimar) (Curwen); essays on Verdi and Wagner, H. Schütz, Jac. Handl (Proceedings of Mus. Association, Novello); various arts. in Mus. Times (Bach's St. Luke Passion, April 1912; Beethoven's IX Symphony, Jan. 1912). —E.-H.

NEAL, Heinrich. Ger. compr. and teacher; b. Munich, 1870. Son of Amer. painter David Neal; pupil of Rheinberger (Munich) and Draeseke (Dresden); 1894, founder, manager and dir. of own Cons., Heidelberg. Generally publishes his own works.

Studies for teaching: 24 Studies in all Ma. and Mi. Keys as Introduction to Modern Music, op. 75; Pieces for the Young: Alpine Summer, op. 9; Children's Overture for 2 pf. op. 36; studies in expression; sonata, op. 30; In a Castle, op. 58; Consolations, op. 70; Retrospect, op. 74; Ger. Rhapsodies, pf. (several sets); songs; female and male choruses; 3 str. 4tets (E flat; A; C mi.).—A. E.

NEBUŠKA, Otakar. Czechoslovak music critic and organiser; b. Mladá Boleslav, 1875. Devoted himself first to compn. (songs, choruses publ. by Fr. A. and M. Urbánek); afterwards to

344

critical work. One of the founders of *Hudebni Revue*. Some essays were publ. in *Dalibor*. His chief efforts are given to Hudebni Matice Umělecké Besedy (see SOCIETIES) which chiefly through his guidance acquired great importance for modern Czechoslovak music.—V. ST.

NEDBAL, Karel. Czechoslovak compr. condr. *b.* Králové Dvůr, 1888. Pupil of V. Novák and J. B. Foerster; condr. of Amateurs' Symph. Orch. Prague ; then at Plzeň and Vinohrady theatres; condr. of *Vinohradský Hlahol*; since 1921, condr. and director of Opera in Olomouc.

Scenic pantomimes, *Bruncvik* (book by A. Wenig) and *The Last Laugh* (Raymann), both performed at Vinohrady Theatre, Prague. Cello sonata (Chadím); songs.—V. ST.

NEDBAL, Oskar. Czechoslovak compr. condr. *b.* Tábor, 1874. Stud. at Cons. in Prague (Bennewitz, Stecker, Dvořák); 1892, one of founders of Bohemian Quartet, in which he played vla. until 1906, and influenced their playing no little by his temperament. After moving to Vienna he cond. the new Tonkünstlerorchester very successfully until 1918. He had already cond. Philh. Concerts in Prague. Since 1918 N. has cond. occasionally in Prague (1920–21 in Suk's Philh.) and abroad. He possesses a remarkable temperament, strength, rhythm, a brilliant tone-mixture and a keen sense of gradation. In compn. N. began in an eclectic but serious manner (suite; vn. sonata; *Scherzo-Caprice* for orch.; pf. pieces), but after the success of a fine ballet, *Pohádka o Honzovi* (*The Lazy John*), Prague 1902, he sank to the operetta level, *Vinobraní* (*Vintager's Bride*), *Polská krev* (*Polish Blood*), and flimsily made ballets, *Princess Hyacinte*, *Des Teufels Grossmutter* (*The Devil's Grandmother*) (Andersen). His latest work, a comic opera *Sedlák Jakub* (*Peasant Jack*), shows a more serious tendency. Publ. Fr. A. and M. Urbánek; Simrock.—V. ST.

NEEDHAM, Alicia Adelaide. Eng. songcompr. *b.* near Dublin. Stud. R.A.M. London under Arthur O'Leary (pf.), Prout and Davenport (harmony); won song-compn. prize for 6 successive years at Irish Mus. Fest.; also £100 for best song in celebration of Coronation of King Edward VII (1902). Has publ. over 600 songs (Boosey; Chappell, etc.).—E.-H.

NEF, Albert. Condr. and compr. *b.* St. Gall, 30 Oct. 1882. Stud. at Cons. in Leipzig and Berlin, under Kretzschmar (compn.); Ph.D. 1906. Since 1907, opera-condr. at Lübeck, Neustrelitz and Rostock, where he also cond. the Singakademie; cond., since 1913, Opera at Berne.

Wrote *Das Volkstümliche Lied in der Schweiz im letzten Drittel des 18 und am Anfang des 19 Jahrhunderts*; comp. an *Academic Overture* and pf. pieces (Zurich, Hug).—F. H.

NEFF, Fritz. Ger. compr. *b.* Durlach, 20 Nov. 1873; *d.* Munich, 3 Oct. 1904. Pupil of Mottl and of Thuille; talented compr. of Munich School.

Songs; *Polish Inn* (b. and orch.); *Chorus of the Dead*, op. 5, mixed chorus with orch.; mixed choruses; *Schmied Schmerz* (op. 6); *Weihe der Nacht.*—A. E.

NEGRO SPIRITUALS. These Amer. plantation-songs are spontaneous outbursts of intense

religious fervour, which had their origin chiefly in camp-meetings and religious revivals. As the simple utterance of untutored minds, they are practically the only music in America which meets the scientific definition of Folk-Song. They must be sung reverently and impressively, for they breathe a hope and a faith in the ultimate justice and brotherhood of man. The two finest singers of Negro Spirituals are H. T. Burleigh (barit.) and Roland Hayes (t.). See arts. on them; and, for Negro music generally, see CURTIS, NATALIE; DETT, R. N.; FARWELL, ARTHUR; KREHBIEL, H. E.—H. T. B. & E.-H.

NEITZEL, Otto. Ger. compr. and author; *b.* Falkenburg, Pomerania, 6 July, 1852; *d.* Cologne, 10 March, 1920. Pupil of Kullak's Cons. and Univ., Berlin; acc. Pauline Lucca and Sarasate on concert-tour; 1878, dir. of Strasburg Mus. Soc.; 1879–81, mus. dir at Strasburg Stadttheater; also teacher at Cons.; teacher at Moscow Cons.; 1885, at Cologne Cons.; 1887, critic of *Kölnische Zeitung.*

Operas: *Angela* (Halle, 1887); *Dido* (Weimar, 1888); *The Old Man of Dessau* (Wiesbaden, 1889); *Barbarina* (Wiesbaden, 1904; Leipzig, 1913); *The Judge of Kaschau* (Darmstadt, 1916, own libretto); satirical play, *Valhalla in Distress* (Bremen, 1905); pf. concerto, op. 26; pf. pieces, op. 36. Also a wellknown *Guide to Present-day Operas* (3 vols. 1890–3, 4th ed. 1908); *Camille Saint-Saëns* (1898); *Beethoven's Symphonies explained according to their "Stimmung"* (1898); (with Ludwig Riemann) *Explanations for Hunfeld's Phonola and Dea-Künstler roll repertory* (1909); *From my Music Folio* (1913). Consult A. Dette, *Barbarina* (with biography of N.).—A. E.

NEJDANOVA, Antonina Vassilievna (*accent 2nd syll. AN*). Russ. singer; *b.* Odessa,1875. Pupil of Mazetti at Moscow Cons. Gold medallist, 1902; attached to Grand Opera House, Moscow. Sang at Grand Opera, Paris (1913), and elsewhere. In 1918, received degree of People's Artist of Russ. Republic. Repertoire of about 30 operas, Russ. and foreign.—V. B.

NEJEDLÝ, Zdeněk. Czech music critic and historian; *b.* Litomyšl, 1878. Stud. at Prague and abroad; graduated Ph.D. Prague Univ.; prof. of mus. science and æsthetics there in 1905. His intelligence in every direction, his indefatigable industry and his passionate interest in all cultural matters led him away from the purely musical sphere into that of general literature, history, and political journalism. At first he contributed to various daily and musical periodicals; since 1910 he has written for his own musical journal, the *Smetana*, which he founded. As a pupil of the æsthetician Otakar Hostinský (*q.v.*) he has introduced scientific methods into Czech musical criticism, as well as the zeal for progress, the endeavour to grasp the main essence of each problem, and a demand for a moral basis in art. The open way he goes to work, his temporary inability to distinguish the ideal intentions of work criticised from the actual artistic realisation, together with his often aggressive disposition, called forth justifiable opposition to his critical activities. As musical historian, he concentrated at first on Hussite period: *History of Pre-Hussite Vocal Music in Bohemia* (1904); *Beginnings of Hussite*

Vocal Music (1907); *History of Hussite Vocal Music during the Hussite War* (1913). The personality of Bedřich Smetana was the second subject on which his research work concentrated. He dedicated some preliminary works to this subject (*Smetana's Operas*, 1908; *Smetaniana*, I, 1922); critical editions of opera texts; and is editing a complete ed. of S.'s works, in order to write a definitive biography of this master (planned in 5 vols.; Vol. I, 1923). In addition to the books mentioned above, there are the following works (all in Czech): *Zdenko Fibich*, 1901; *Catechism of History of Czech Music*, 1903; *Catechism of Æsthetics*, 1902; *Modern Czech Opera from Smetana onwards*, 1911; *J. B. Foerster*, 1910; *Gustav Mahler*, I; *Richard Wagner*, I; *Vítězslav Novák*, 1921; *General History of Music*, I, 1921. Publ.: Hejda & Tuček; J. Otto; M. Urbánek; mus. review *Smetana* (all in Prague).—V. ST.

NĚMEČEK, Emil. Czechoslovak compr. *b.* Příbram, 1902. Pupil of Cons. in Prague; wrote some remarkably clever early compns. When twelve years, old wrote opera *Three Kisses* (Vrchlický); later on *Lucerna* (Jirásek); finally (1917–18) *The Queen's Error*, one act, perf. at National Theatre, Prague, 1922. Also sonatas for vla.; for cello; songs, choruses (ms.).—V. ST.

NERUDA, Franz Xaver. Cellist, condr. compr. teacher; *b.* Brünn, 3 Dec. 1843; *d.* Copenhagen, 20 March, 1915. A descendant of an old and well-known mus. family of Bohemia. Upon a concert-tour with his sisters (one of these being Wilma Neruda, "die Geigenfee," afterwards Lady Hallé) he came to Copenhagen, where he settled. He soon became a popular teacher and one of leading factors in mus. life of Danish capital during, and just after, the Gade period. Member of R. Chapel 1864–76. In 1868, founded the Chamber - Music Soc., which still holds its leading position. He was later one of founders of R. Chapel Soirées and founded, for his private pleasure, what later became famous as the Neruda Quartet (1st vn. Anton Svendsen), which did much to advance the cause of chamber-music in Denmark. After his sister Wilma (Lady Hallé) settled in London, he frequently visited her there and assisted in her chamber-music concerts. He was also closely allied to the mus. life of Stockholm as condr. of the leading mus. soc. there. However, he had his home in Copenhagen, and after Niels W. Gade's death he was chosen to succeed him in the leadership of the Musikforening (Music Soc.). His works, which reached op. 70, have been publ., partly by Danish firms, partly in Germany and Bohemia.

Böhmerwald, orch. suite, op. 42 (Copenhagen, Hansen); *Ballade*, vn. and orch. op. 43 (Hamburg, Rahter); *Rapsodie hongroise*, vn. op. 44 (Copenhagen, Nordisk Musikforlag); *Berceuse slave*, vn. pf. (*ib.* Hansen); cello concerto, op. 59 (Prague, Urbánek): cello and pf.: 3 *Stücke*, op. 39, and 3 *Stücke*, op. 41 (Leipzig, Kistner); Andante and Allegro de Concert (with orch.); op. 40 (Nordisk Musikforlag); *Mazurka*, op. 64 (Rahter); pf.: sonata, op. 19 (Breitkopf); Theme and variations, op. 49 (Nordisk Musikforlag); 6 *Études*, op. 53 (*id.*); Theme and variations, op. 62 (Hansen); 5 pieces, op. 65 (Urbánek); preludes and fugues, op. 78 (12 sets; Rahter); organ: Theme and variations, op. 62 (Hansen); Theme and variations, op. 72 (Rahter); Introduction, Andante and Fugue,

op. 74 (*id.*); str. 4tet, op. 35 (Hansen); *Musikal Märchen*, clar. vla. cello, op. 31 (*id.*).—A. H.

NEŠVERA, Josef. Czechoslovak compr. *b.* Praskolesy, 1842; *d.* 1914. First a teacher; then choirmaster, Olomouc Cath. (1884 till death). His style is eclectic, influenced by German Romanticism, by Smetana, and even by salon music.

Operas: *Perdita* (1897); *Lesní vzduch* (*Woodland Air*); *Radhošť* (1906); oratorio, *Job*; *De profundis* (1889, well known); series of cyclic and smaller pieces for orch.; chamber-music; pf. pieces; *Old-fashioned Songs*; *Love Songs*; 40 masses.—V. ST.

NEUHAUS. See NEWHAUS.

NEUMANN, František. Czechoslovak compr. *b.* Přerov, 1874. Stud. at Cons. in Leipzig (Jadassohn; Reinecke). For 15 years condr. of Frankfort Opera; from 1919 chief of Brno Opera, which rose quickly under his guidance, competing with Prague Opera in repertory and standard of performance. Conducts symphony concerts. His style of compn. is eclectic with Wagnerian and veristic elements.

Operas: *Námluvy* (*Wooing*) 1901, Linz; *Milkování* (*Loving*) on Schnitzler's *Liebelei* (Schott); *Equinoctium* (Berlin, Harmonie Verlag); *Beatrice Caracci* (Brno, Barvič). Cantata, *Bouře* (*The Storm*), soli, chorus, orch.—V. ST.

NEUPERT, Carl Fredrik Edmund. Norwegian pianist; *b.* Christiania, 1 April, 1842; *d.* New York, 22 June, 1888. Pupil of father, Herman Neupert, who had come from Schleswig to Norway; 1858–64, pupil of Theodor Kullak, Berlin (pf.) and of Kiel (compn.). After some concerts in Germany, the critics placed him on a level with Liszt, Rubinstein and Tausig, and his subsequent concert-tours increased his fame as a virtuoso; 1866–8 pf.-teacher at Stern's Cons. Berlin; 1868–80, at Copenhagen Cons. (establ. by Gade). In 1880, prof. at Imperial Cons. in Moscow; gave successful concerts in that city and in Petrograd, where he played, *inter alia*, Grieg's pf. concerto. After Rubinstein's death in 1881, N. gave up his post in Moscow, and returned to Norway, where he started a pf.-school; but the conditions were too restricted to enable him to make a permanent living at home. In 1882 he left Norway, gave several concerts in America (New York and Boston, 1882; in California, 1883); from 1883 prof. at newly-started Cons. in New York. As virtuoso, player of chamber-music and pf.-teacher N. enjoyed a constantly increasing reputation in the New World. N. was in his life time undoubtedly Norway's greatest pianist, a virtuoso of really international dimensions, representative of the grand style, which aimed first and foremost at clearness, strength, objectivity (as regards mus. subject-matter), and a brilliant technical equipment. As a teacher he was famed for his logically developed pf.-tuition, the "Neupert Method," which became the leading method in the North, and still forms the basis for pf.-instruction there. In a number of excellent educational works N. embodied the results of his wide experience and rare capabilities. As a compr. he also won a respected name with his pf. pieces. There is, in several of his ballades, character-pieces and studies, a touch of the romantic spirit of the

North. He frequently made use of Norwegian folk-music, but otherwise he was chiefly influenced by Schumann, Chopin and Liszt.

Norwegian Ballade, op. 58; music-picture, *Before the Battle*; 6 Improvisations on Norwegian themes; characteristic pieces; *Funeral March for Nicolas Rubinstein*; concert studies; technical studies, etc. (publ. Hansen, Copenhagen).—J. A.

NEVADA, Mignon. Soprano singer; *b.* Paris. Daughter of Emma Nevada, celebrated opera singer; *début* at Costanzi Theatre, Rome, as Rosina in *Barber of Seville*; then a whole season at San Carlos Theatre, Lisbon; Pergola Theatre, Florence; Covent Garden (autumn, 1910); Rome; Florence; Antwerp, 1912-13-14; 3 seasons under Sir Thomas Beecham's management, creating *La Jolie Fille de Perth* (Bizet); 1920, sang at Opéra-Comique, Paris.—E.-H.

NEVILLE, Charles. Eng. t. singer; *b.* Rochdale, 14 Aug. 1872. Stud. R. Manchester Coll. of Music, under John Acton, and with Ernesto Baraldi and Francis Korbay; has sung with O'Mara, Empire, J. W. Turner, Denhof, and Carl Rosa opera companies. Many song-recitals, especially Hugo Wolf's songs, which he has sung more frequently than any other Eng. singer.—E.-H.

NEVIN, Arthur Finley. Amer. compr. *b.* Edgeworth, Pa., U.S.A., 27 April, 1871. Brother of Ethelbert. Stud. from 1891-3 at New England Cons. in Boston under Bendix (pf.), Nobbs (v.), Goetschius (theory); 1893-7 in Berlin under Klindworth and Jedliczka (pf.) and Humperdinck (compn.). From 1915-20, prof. at Univ. of Kansas. Since 1920, dir. of municipal music and dramatic art in Memphis, Tenn. His Indian opera *Poia* was produced in Berlin, 23 April, 1910. A 1-act opera, *A Daughter of the Forest*, was brought out in Chicago on 5 Jan. 1918. Two orch. suites, *Lorna Doone* and *Love Dreams* (ms.); pf. trio and a str. 4tet.

Poia, 3-act opera (Fürstner, 1910); *A Daughter of the Forest*, 1-act opera (vocal score Church, 1917); *The Djinns*, cantata (Schirmer, 1913); *From Edgeworth Hills*, pf. (Church, 1903); 2 numbers from 2nd orch. suite, *Love Dreams*, transcribed for pf. (*id.* 1903); *Toccatella*, pf. (*id.* 1920). Many songs (*id.*).—O. K.

NEVIN, Ethelbert Woodbridge. Amer. compr. *b.* Edgeworth, Pa., U.S.A., 25 Nov. 1862; *d.* New Haven, Conn., 17 Feb. 1901. Stud. pf. under Von der Heide and Günther in Pittsburgh; 1877-8, pupil in singing of Boehme in Dresden. Continued stud. under Lang (pf.) and Emery (theory) in Boston. 1884-6, stud. in Berlin under v. Bülow, Klindworth and Karl Bial. After that, lived chiefly in Boston, Paris, Italy and New York, devoting himself to compn. and concert work. His compns. consist almost entirely of pf. pieces and songs, all written in the simple style that found a ready acceptance with a wide circle of admirers. His pf. piece *Narcissus* (Boston Music Co.) attained a world-wide popularity. Of his songs *The Rosary* (*id.* 1898) almost equalled *Narcissus* in popularity, and *Mighty Lak' a Rose* (John Church) also became well known. A choral work, *The Quest*, was orchestrated by Horatio Parker after N.'s death (vocal score J. Church, 1902). Also:

A Sketchbook, songs and pf. pieces, op. 2 (Boston Music Co. 1893); *Un Giorno in Venezia*, pf. op. 25 (Church, 1898); *Water Scenes*, pf. op. 13 (No. 4 is *Narcissus*) (Boston Music Co. 1891). Many vn. pieces and songs (Church; Boston Music Co; Ditson; Schirmer).—O. K.

NEWHAUS, Heinrich Gustavovitch. Russ. pianist; *b.* Elisavetgrad, 12 April (n.s.), 1890. Pupil of Godowsky in Vienna Acad. of Music (master-school) 1912-13; won the State prize; 1916-17, teacher at Tiflis (music school of Russ. Music Soc.); 1919-22, prof. at Kief Cons.; now (from 1922) prof. at Moscow Cons. A very gifted performer of Scriabin, Szymanowski, and other contemporary composers.—V. B.

NEWMAN, Ernest. Eng. writer on music; *b.* Liverpool, 30 Nov. 1868. Originally intended for Indian civil service; diverted into business at Liverpool by ill-health; 1903-5, taught music in Midland Inst. in Birmingham; 1905-6, music critic for *Manchester Guardian*; 1906-19, *Birmingham Post*; 1919-20, London *Observer*; from March 1920, *Sunday Times*, London; also weekly writer for *Glasgow Herald*, from Nov. 1923. He ed. the monthly *Piano-Player Review* from its foundation, Sept. 1912, till May 1914. N. has the largest following of all the Eng. music-critics. A deeply-read musician with a profound knowledge of orch. scores, his intense admiration of the Ger. classical and Romantic comprs. and his thorough-going study of them, makes him a severe judge of contemporary schools. His book on Hugo Wolf is one of the finest studies made of any composer; though his placing of Wolf " at the head of the song-writers of the world " (p. 153) has received little, if any endorsement.

Gluck and the Opera (Dobell, 1895); *A Study of Wagner* (Dobell, 1899); *Wagner* (" The Music of the Masters ") (Wellby, 1904); *Musical Studies* (J. Lane, 1905); *Elgar* (*id.* 1906); *Hugo Wolf* (Methuen, 1907); *Richard Strauss* (J. Lane, 1908); *Wagner as Man and Artist* (J. M. Dent & Sons, 1914); *A Musical Motley* (J. Lane, 1919); *The Piano-Player and its Music* (Grant Richards). Transls. of most of Wagner's opera-texts; of Schweitzer's *J. S. Bach*; Weingartner's *On Conducting*, etc.—E.-H.

NEWMARCH, Rosa. Eng. writer on music; *b.* Leamington Spa. Stud. painting for a time; from 1880-3, engaged in journalistic work in London; in 1897, visited Russia and came into personal contact with many of the chief Russ. comprs. (Rimsky-Korsakof, Glazunof, the critic Stassof); she has since visited Russia many times; writer of analytical notes for the Queen's Hall Promenade programmes, over a long period.

Henry J. Wood (J. Lane, 1904); *The Russian Opera* (H. Jenkins, 1914); *The Russian Arts* (*id.* 1916). Transl.: Deiter's *Johannes Brahms* (1887); Habet's *Borodin and Liszt* (Digby, Long, 1896); *Peter Ilich Tchaikovsky*, from his brother Modeste's biography (J. Lane, 1900); V. d'Indy's *César Franck* (*id.*); many arts. on Russ. music in *Dict. of Nat. Biog.* in Grove's *Dict. of Music* and in various journals.—E.-H.

NEY, Elly. Pianist; *b.* Düsseldorf, 27 Sept. 1882. Stud. at Cologne Cons. (Isidor Seiss, K. Böttcher), in Vienna (Leschetizky, Sauer); won Mendelssohn and Ibach prizes; teacher at Cologne Cons.; 1911, married Dutch violinist and condr. Willy von Hoogstraten (who was till 1919 in Crefeld; now condr. in New York).—A. E.

NICASTRO, Miguel M. Argentine violinist; *b.* Montevideo, 1888. Stud. under Massi, Scarabelli and Melani. In 1901, went to Naples to study. First violinist in several orchs. in Italy. D'Albert, at one of whose concerts he played, sent him to Berlin to perfect himself under Joachim. In 1908, N. began concert-touring in Germany and Italy. Went to Buenos Ayres in 1909, where he gave successful concerts, returning to Germany to complete his contract. Returned to S. America in 1910, settling down definitely in Buenos Ayres in 1912, to devote himself to teaching. Among his 8 famous violins are a Stradivarius and a Guarnerius del Gesù.—A. M.

NICHOLL, Horace Wadham. Eng. compr. and orgt. *b.* Tipton, near Birmingham, 17 March, 1848; *d.* New York, 10 March, 1922. Taught by his father and Samuel Prince; orgt. Dudley 1867–70; Stoke-on-Trent 1868–70; orgt. St. Pauls' Cath. Pittsburg, and later at a Presbyterian church there (1870–8); from 1878, has lived in New York; from 1883, reader for Messrs. Schirmer there; 1888–95, taught at Farmington, Conn. His organ preludes and fugues are amongst the finest written for the organ during the last hundred years. They are diatonic in the Bach style; and show a treatment of the instr. which was very advanced at the time of their composition. He was chiefly a contrapuntal compr. infusing modern harmonic feeling into the Bach style. In his choral and orch. works, he followed Liszt and Wagner.

Orch.: 2 symphonies (G mi. op. 8; C, op. 12); 2 symph. fantasias (op. 5, 7); 2 symph. poems (*Tartarus*, 11; *Hamlet*, op. 14); Suite, op. 3; pf. concerto, D mi. op. 10; *Scherzo-Fugue*, small orch. op. 15; 4 oratorios (*Abraham*; *Isaac*; *Jacob*; *The Golden Legend*); Mass in E flat; *A Cloister Scene*; sonata, cello and pf. op. 13; sonata, vn. and pf. op. 21. Organ: 12 symph. preludes and fugues (Breitkopf); 12 short preludes and fugues (Peters); sonata, A mi. op. 42); symph. poem, *Life* (*id.*); 6 short melodious pieces (*id.*); fantasia on Psalm cxxx (*id.*); *Die Pleiaden*, op. 40 (*id.*); 6 pedal studies, op. 47 (*id.*), etc.; 12 concert-preludes and fugues for organ (publ. posthumously by Schirmer, 1924); pf. pieces; songs; text-book on harmony. —E.-H.

NICHOLL, Joseph Weston. Eng. compr. and condr. *b.* Halifax, Yorks, 7 May, 1875. Stud. vn. compn. pf. organ at Berlin Cons.; then organ under Rheinberger in Munich; played R.'s concerto in F at celebration concert there in 1900; then stud. under Guilmant for a year; in 1906, condr. Yorkshire Military Band; shortly afterwards, of the Black Dyke Brass Band. In 1922, he inaugurated Halifax Competition Mus. Fest. and in 1923, Halifax Brass Band Fest.

Concert overture, organ and orch. (prize, Dover Fest. 1904); symph. poem, *Alastor*; tone-poem, *In English Seas*; *Eclogue*, orch.; 1-act music-drama, *Comala*; *Festival-Overture*, military band (Crystal Palace contest, 1913) ; tone-picture, *The Viking*, brass band (1923); choral pieces, songs, etc.—E.-H.

NICHOLLS, Agnes Harty. See Harty, Agnes.

NICHOLLS, Frederick. Eng. compr. *b.* Birmingham, 8 Jan. 1871. Stud. at Liverpool Coll. of Music; now teaches in Liverpool. His *Love-Songs of Tennyson*, op. 5 (Stainer & Bell) had a

considerable success in 1892. His pf. writing is refined.

3 orch. suites (ms.); 3 cantatas (ms.); wood-wind 5tet; 2 4tets, pf. and str. (op. 24; op. 37, *The Four Winds*); 2 trios (all ms.); over 60 songs (Cary; Curwen; Stainer & Bell); over 50 pf. pieces (Bayley & Ferguson; Curwen; Breitkopf; Larway; Wood; Weekes); *The Technique of the Pf. Pedals* (Stainer & Bell).—E.-H.

NICHOLSON, Sydney H. Eng. orgt. *b.* London, 9 Feb. 1875. Stud. at Rugby School under Dr. Basil Johnson; R.C.M. under Sir Walter Parratt and Sir Charles Stanford; Frankfort-o-M. under Ivan Knorr; orgt. and choirmaster Carlisle Cath. 1904; Manchester Cath. 1908–18; Westminster Abbey from 1918, where his mus. work is characterised by a high standard and the purest Anglican tradition, which he elects to follow.

British Songs for British Boys (Macmillan); 3 children's cantatas (Curwen); church music (Curwen; Novello; Faith Press); cantata, "1914" (Curwen); part-songs (Year Book Press); pamphlets (Church Music Soc.).—E.-H.

NICKSON, A. E. H. Australian orgt. and teacher: *b.* Melbourne. Clarke Organ Scholar, R.C.M. London, under Sir W. Parratt: orgt. St. Peter's, Melbourne, 1902: lecturer on harmony, etc. in Univ. of Melbourne. Examiner on Australian Univ. Exam. Board.—G. Y.

NICODÉ, Jean Louis. Ger. compr. *b.* Jersitz, near Posen, 12 Aug. 1853; *d.* Langebrück, 5 Oct. 1919. 1869, stud. at New Acad. of Music, with Kullak (pf.) and Würst (theory), Kiel (cpt. and free compn.) in Berlin. After several years as teacher and pianist in Berlin, and concert-tour through Galicia and Rumania with Mme. Artôt, went (1878) as pf. teacher to Dresden Cons.; 1885, took over management of Philh. Concerts; resigned same, 1888; estab. (1893) Nicodé Concerts, for which he trained Chemnitz Town Orch.; 1896, establ. the Nicodé Choir, combined it with Town Orch., thereby able to produce new and rarely heard works; 1900, retired to Langebruck, near Dresden; 1919, Member of Berlin Acad. for Art.

Symph. poems: *Mary Stuart*; *The Search for Luck*; *Gloria* (with chorus, 1904); symph. variations; 2 orch. suites (*Pictures of the South*); symphony (male chorus, solo, orch. organ), *The Sea*, op. 31, 1888; *Early Wanderings in the Mountains* (unacc. symphony for male chorus); *After Sunset* (symph. picture for male chorus unacc.); *Requiem* (from Hebbel, for male chorus unacc.); *Carnival Pictures*; sonatas for cello, op. 23 and 25; pf. sonata, op. 19; pf. studies, op. 20 and 21; songs. N.'s works are rather superficially effective. Consult Th. Schäfer's *J. L. N.* (1917).—A. E.

NICOLAU, Antonio. Span. compr. of the Catalonian group, of which he shares the leadership with his colleague Luis Millet. He is one of the 'veteran champions of mus. culture in Spain. A former dir. of Sociedad de Conciertos de Barcelona, in which capacity he gave the 1st perf. in Spain of Berlioz's *Damnation de Faust*. Teacher of Lamote de Grignon and other leading musicians of present generation. His symph. poem in 3 parts, *El Triunfo de Venus*, received its first perf. in Paris in 1882. His importance as a compr. of choral music remains unsuspected outside Spain, his best-known work in this style being *La Mort del Escolá*, a piece that ought

348

to be in the repertoire of every choral soc. throughout the world. He lives in Barcelona.

El Rapto, comic opera (Madrid, 1887); *Constanza* (Liceo, Barcelona); *La Tempestad*, dramatic scena (*ib.*), sung by Tamagno; several songs; symph. poems, *Enhora* and *Spes.*—P. G. M.

NIECKS, Frederick. Univ. prof. and author; *b.* Düsseldorf, 3 Feb. 1845; *d.* Edinburgh, 24 June, 1924. Studied violin under his father, Dr. Langhans, Grünwald, and Auer; pf. and compn. under Tausch; played in Düsseldorf orch. under Tausch (Schumann's successor); in Cologne Gürzenich orch. under Hiller; played vla. in quartet of Auer and De Swert. Career as vn. virtuoso abandoned on account of health. In 1868, made acquaintance of young A. C. Mackenzie (Sir Alexander) then visiting Düsseldorf, who suggested his going to Scotland as member of his quartet. Settled in Dumfries in 1868, removing to Edinburgh a few years later, but returning to Dumfries on medical advice; remained there teaching, writing, and travelling, until 1891 when appointed Reid Professor of Music at Edinburgh Univ. There he inst. a complete music curriculum for degrees of Mus.Bac. and Mus.Doc., personally lecturing on harmony, cpt., compn., form, history, æsthetics, instrumentation, acoustics, etc. Gave every year a series of historical concerts. Retired from chair, May 1914. Mus.Doc. Dublin *h.c.* 1898; LL.D. Edinburgh *h.c.* 1915. He contributed monthly articles to the *Monthly Musical Record* from 1876 up to 1924. Naturalised British subject, 1880.

Concise Dictionary of Musical Terms (Augener, 1884); *Frederick Chopin as a Man and Musician*, 2 vols. (Novello, 1889, 1890; Ger. ed. 1890); *Programme Music in the last 4 Centuries : A Contribution to the History of Mus. Expression* (Novello, 1907). Especially notable is his series of arts. *Supplementary and Corrective to Biography of Schumann* (*Monthly Musical Record* 1921-3).—E.-H.

NIELSEN, Carl August. Danish composer; *b.* in a village near Odense, 9 June, 1865. His father was the county fiddler, and when his young son, Carl, showed a decided taste for music he was put to play the bugle in an infantry battalion in Odense, where he made his first efforts as a composer. Amongst these was a little string quartet, which he took with him to Copenhagen, and showed to Niels W. Gade, who at once recognised his talent and arranged for him to enter the Royal Conservatoire as pupil, where he acquitted himself brilliantly, and became a violinist of Royal Chapel (1889-1905). His first ripe works date from this period. His first symphony and a string quartet at once disclosed a rising star in the Danish musical firmament. For 2 years, he was also conductor of the Opera; later, member of board of governors of Royal Conservatoire; 1915, succeeded Neruda as director of the Musikforening (Music Society).

As a composer, he stands to-day in every way among the very first Scandinavian composers of our time. He is absolutely modern, but without allying himself with any special coterie or trend. Upon a solid contrapuntal basis he builds his tonal structures that are filled with artistic spirit and an intellectual atmosphere peculiarly his own.

5 symphonies (of which No. III, *Espansiva*, and No. IV, *L'Inestinguibile*, made sensational successes); concert overture, *Helios*; choral work, *Hymnus Amoris*; 2 operas, *Saul and David* and *Mascarade* (the latter a comic opera, based upon an old Holberg text), both produced at R. Opera, Copenhagen; music to Oehlenschläger's drama *Aladdin*; vn. concerto; 4 str. 4tets; 2 vn. sonatas; many songs and ballads (Copenhagen, Hansen).—A. H.

NIELSON, Ludolf. Danish compr. *b.* Nörre Tvede, near Næstved, Zealand, 29 Jan. 1876. Pupil of R. Cons. Copenhagen. Until 1909 vice-dir. of Tivoli and Palace popular orch. concerts, where he also played the vla. Talented compr. of symph. and dramatic works.

2 symphonies; 2 suites; 3 symph. poems; concert overture; 2 str. 4tets; pf. pieces; songs; 2 operas, *Uhret* (*The Clock*) and *Isbella*; ballet, *Lakschmi*. The last two have been produced at R. Theatre, Copenhagen.—A. H.

NIEMANN, Walter. Ger. author and compr. *b.* Hamburg, 10 Oct. 1876. Son of pianist and compr. Rudolf Niemann; pupil of father and of Humperdinck, 1897; 1898, entered Univ. and Cons. Leipzig (Reinecke, Riemann); 1906-7, temporary engagement at Hamburg Cons.; 1907-17, mus. critic of Leipzig *Neueste Nachrichten*.

Music and Musicians of XIX Century (1905; *Scandinavian Music* (1906); *Short Outline of History of Pf. Music* (1907, 9th to 12th ed. 1921); *Grieg* (with Schjelderup, 1908); *Mus. Renaissance in XIX Century* (1911); *Pocket-Dictionary for Pf. Players* (1912, 4th ed. as pf. dictionary 1918); *Music of Present Day* (since Richard Wagner) (1913, 13th to 17th ed. 1921); *Jean Sibelius* (1917); *Northern Pf. Music* (1918); *Virginal Music* (1919); *Masters of the Pf.* (1919, 9th to 14th ed. 1921); *Brahms* (1st to 8th ed. 1920). Altered entirely 4th ed. of Ad. Kullak's *Æsthetic of Pf. Playing* (1905, 8th ed. 1920) and 2nd ed. of Otto Klauwell's *Forms of Instrumental Music* (1918); publ. Ph. Em. Bach's *Versuch über die wahre Art des Clavier zu spielen* (1906, 3rd ed. 1920); also ancient and modern pf. works; devoting himself now to compn.: *Crayons*, op. 5; *Dresden China*, op. 6; *Travelling Pictures*, op. 10; *Coloured Leaves*, op. 13; *Variations*, op. 20 (after Fehrs), and op. 25 (after Camoens); suites (after Hebbel, Claus Groth, Theodor Storm, Jacobsen, Hesse); *Holstein Idylls*, op. 9; *Black Forest Idylls*, op. 21; *German Country and Round Dances*, op. 26; sonatinas, op. 24; nocturnes, op. 28 and 30; *Romantic Miniatures from Jacobsen and Storm*, op. 33 and 47; *Pompeii, Romantic Miniatures in Mosaic*, op. 48; 24 preludes, op. 55; *Dresden China* (after P. Claudel, op. 63); 20 *Masks*, op. 59; melodrama, op. 27; pf. sonatas, op. 60, 75, 83, 88; pf. and vn. sonata, op. 70; *Tone-pictures*, op. 71; *Preludes, Intermezzi and Fugue*, op. 73; *The Garden of Orchids* (10 impressions), op. 76, etc.; *Rhine Serenade*, str. orch. and horns; *Anakreon*, str. orch. op. 50.—A. E.

NIETO, Ofelia. Contemporary Span. dramatic singer; *b.* Madrid. Perf. Teatro Real, Madrid; Liceo, Barcelona, La Scala, Milan; Metropolitan Opera House, New York, etc.—P. G. M.

NIETZSCHE, Friedrich. Polish philosopher; *b.* Röcken, 15 Oct. 1844; *d.* Weimar, 25 Aug. 1900. 1869-79, prof. of classical philology, Basle; then, till his mental derangement (1889), resided in Engadine or Italy. At first, most spirited adherent of Wagner. Writings: *Birth of Tragedy from the Spirit of Music*, 1872; *Richard Wagner at Bayreuth*, 1876 (*Thoughts out of Season*). Nietzsche later became an adve.sary of Wagner, showing distate for Catholic-ascetic tendency of *Parsifal* (*Der Fall Wagner*, 1888; *Nietzsche contra Wagner*, 1889), and championed Southern dances, and anti-Romantic music. Comp. songs, pf. pieces, choral works.

Consult: H. Bélart, *F. N. and R. Wagner* (1907); W. Dahms, *Manifestation of Music : an Apotheosis of F. N.* (Munich, 1922); L. Griesser, *N. and Wagner*, (1923); see particularly *Nietzsche' Letters to Peter Gast* (1908).—A. E.

NIEWIADOWSKI, Stanisław. Polish compr. music critic; *b.* Soposzryn, Galicia, 4 Nov. 1859. Stud. theory under Karol Mikuli (pupil of Chopin) at Lemberg; then in Vienna under Krenn; 1886–7, manager of Lemberg Opera; 1888–1914, teacher of theory, Lemberg Cons.; 1918–19, again manager of Lemberg Opera. Since 1919, he has remained at Warsaw as prof. of æsthetics and history of music at State Cons. Has written mus. criticism in several newspapers since 1890. Translated into Polish Hanslick's treatise *Vom Musikalisch-Schönen*. Very popular and beloved in Poland as a song-compr. His works are also publ. in foreign countries.—ZD. J.

NIGGLI, Friedrich. Pianist, compr. *b.* Aarburg (Switzerland), 15 Dec. 1875. Son of Swiss musicographer Arnold N.; stud pf. and compn. at Zurich Cons. under Rob. Freund, L. Kemptner and Fr. Hegar (1893–6), and 1 year at Odeon in Munich, under Rheinberger. Won the Mozart Scholarship in pf. competition at Frankfort, where he became pupil of Ivan Knorr and B. Scholz; in 1899 stud. under Sgambati in Rome; 1900 under Fauré in Paris; 1901 in Berlin under Urban. Since 1901, teacher at Cons. in Zurich for pf. and compn. His mus. style is founded on Swiss folk-song; he has written a great number of charming dialect-songs.

Cello sonata, op. 6; vn. sonata, op. 7; *Lasst hören aus alter Zeit* (O. v. Greyerz), Swiss folk-song play, for soli, chorus and small orch. op. 17; numerous unacc. choruses and songs (Leipzig, Hug).—F. H.

NIKISCH, Artur. Hungarian condr. *b.* Lébény Szent Miklos, 12 Oct. 1855; *d.* Leipzig, 23 Jan. 1922. Stud. Vienna Cons. In 1874, violinist, Vienna Hofkapelle; 1878, Korrepetitor, Leipzig Opera; 1879–89, 1st condr. there; 1889, Boston (Mass.) Orch.; 1893, Hofkapellmeister, Budapest Opera; 1895 (till death) condr. Gewandhaus Orch. Leipzig; also condr. Berlin Philh. Orch. One of the most brilliant condrs.; specially great in Wagner's music.—E.-H.

NIKOLAEF, Leonid Vladimirovitch (*accent the A*). Russ. compr. and pianist; *b.* Kief, 1 Aug. (o.s.), 1878. Stud. pf. under Safonof at Moscow Cons. (till 1903); lived in Moscow from 1900, taking part in the Russ. Music-lovers' Concerts, founded by the Kerzin family. In 1909, prof. at Petrograd Cons., a post he still holds, being also dean of pf. faculty there.

Orch.: *Serenade* (ms.); *Nocturne* (ms.); *The Poem* (1922, ms.); *Scherzo* (1922, ms.); cello sonata, D mi. (1922); *Tarantella*, pf. (1919). vn. sonata, op. 11; Suite, 2 pfs. 4 hands, op. 13; Variations, *id.* op. 14; songs; pf. pieces; transcriptions for pf. of Buxtehude's and Pachelbel's organ works. (Jurgenson.) —V. B.

NIN Y CASTELLANO, Joaquín. Span. pianist and publicist; *b.* Havana (Cuba), 1883. Pupil of Vidiella (Barcelona) and Moszkowski (Paris), where he also attended classes at *Schola Cantorum*, in which inst. he taught pf. in 1906, being elected afterwards hon. prof. In 1909, received a

similar distinction at the Univ. Nouvelle, Brussels. Founded a concert soc. and a mus. review at Havana in 1910. As a solo-pianist, has toured the whole of Europe. Contributor to many publications on mus. subjects. Lives in Paris.

Pour l'Art, publ. in Ger. Span. and Eng. (Reeves); *Idées et Commentaires* (Span.); set of lectures, *Las Tres Grandes Escuelas*. Has comp. pf. pieces and a 3-act mimodrama.—P. G. M.

NISSEN, Erika (*neé* Lie). Norwegian pianist; *b.* Kongsvinger, 17 Jan. 1845; *d.* Christiania, 27 Oct. 1903. Stud. pf. under sister, the noted pf.-teacher Ida Lie, and under Halfdan Kjerulf. Early in career, took part in one of Ole Bull's concerts; 1861–3, pupil of Kullak's Acad. in Berlin. Continued her studies in Paris in 1868; gave concerts in 1868–9 in London. She appeared with increasing success in Northern countries, and Germany, Holland, and Switzerland; for a short time, teacher at Cons. in Copenhagen. Subsequently she lived chiefly in Christiania as teacher. In 1889, concert with Grieg in Berlin and played his pf. concerto. In 1874, married Oscar Nissen, Christiania. The pianist Karl Nissen (*q.v.*) was her son.—J. A.

NISSEN, Karl. Norwegian pianist and condr. *b.* Christiania, 27 Feb. 1879; *d.* 14 May, 1920. Stud. pf. under mother, Erika Nissen, and Busoni (from 1898); theory under Ole Olsen and van Eycken (Berlin). Was highly-gifted pianist, in command of brilliant technique, and his mus. interpretation was stamped with taste and intelligence. From autumn of 1911 till his death, was leader of Cæcilia Soc.; from 1919 of Mercantile Choral Soc. Christiania. His most important work as condr. was with the Mus. Soc. Orch. 1913–18.—J. A.

NOBLE, Thomas Tertius. Eng. orgt. compr. *b.* Bath, England, 5 May, 1867. Stud. organ under E. Nunn in Ipswich. Orgt. of All Saints', Colchester, 1881–9, meanwhile completing his studies at R.C.M. London, under Parratt (organ) Bridge (theory) and Stanford (compn.) 1884–9. Assistant-orgt. Trinity Coll., Cambridge, 1890–2; orgt. Ely Cath. 1892–8. Went to York in 1898, founded York Symphony Orch. of which he was condr. until 1912, revived the York Fests. after a lapse of 75 years and was orgt. of York Minster from 1898–1913. In 1913 gave recitals in U.S.A. and Canada and since then orgt. of St. Thomas's, New York. Among his larger compns., some still in ms., are a suite for vn. and orch., a Communion Service for chorus, organ, horns, tps., trombones and drums (1891), music to Aristophanes' *Wasps* (1897), the *York Pageant* (1909), a comic opera *Killibegs*, perf. in York, 1911, etc.

Anthems and services (Novello; Vincent; Gray); organ pieces (Augener; Novello). Ed. (with F. H. Potter and Charles Vincent) a *Reliquary of English Song* (Schirmer, 1915).—J. M.

NOELTE, A. Albert. Ger. critic and compr. *b.* Starnberg, Bavaria, 10 March, 1885. When 16, went to America; stud. literature and music at Boston; critic on *Boston Advertiser* 2 years; 1908, returned to Munich; 1st critic of *Augsburger Abend-Zeitung*, Munich.

Songs with orch.; Prelude and fugue for str. orch.; symph. poems: *Hector's Farewell and Death*; *Lucifer*;

Rhapsody, dramatic song-scene; libretto and music of tragic operas: *Francois Villon* (Carlsruhe, 1920, Univ. Ed.); *The Duchess of Padua*.—A. E.

NOETZEL, Hermann. Ger. compr. *b.* Wiesbaden, 10 April, 1880. Pupil of Ivan Knorr, Frankfort-o-M.; then of Schröder at Sondershausen Cons.; condr. at Merseberg and Coblence short time; now devoting himself to compn. at Munich.

Symphony; orch. suite; 3 concert-overtures; pf. and orch. songs; comic opera, *Master Guido* (Carlsruhe, 1918).—A. E.

NOGUERA, Antonio. Span. compr. critic and musicologist; *b.* Mallorca (Balearic Isles). Distinguished pioneer of the religious musical reform in his country. A founder of the Capella Manacor, Mallorca, a choral inst. to encourage the exclusive use of vocal polyphony in church music. In 1887 publ. an ed. of the *Misas Corales* (choral masses) by Fray Juan Auli (*b.* Felanitx, Mallorca, 1797), preceded by a critical and biographical study. Author of *Memorias sobre los cantos, bailes y tocatas populares de la Isla de Mallorca* (1893) (an essay on folk - songs and dances of Island of Mallorca), and *Música Religiosa*, a paper read at Capella Manacor (1889).

Choral works: *La Sesta*; *Hibernenca*. Pf.: *Trois danses sur des airs de l'île de Majorque*: *Danse des Cossies, Danse de la Saint-Jean, Danse triste*. Songs, etc. (Publ.: Unión Musical Española, Madrid; Victor Berdos, Barcelona; Felipe Guasp, Palma de Mallorca.)—P. G. M.

NOLTHENIUS, Hugo. Dutch critic and compr. *b.* Amsterdam, 20 Dec. 1848. Chiefly self-taught; 1881-1915, teacher of literature at Grammar School, Utrecht; 1894-1910, mus. critic of *Utrechtsch Dagblad*; a pioneer of Wagner's music.

Many songs with pf. (Utrecht, Wagenaar; Amsterdam, Alsbach; Ghent, Willemsfonds); stage-music for Joost van den Vondel's *Lucifer* (1904) and Sophocles' *Philoctetes* (1910).—W. P.

NOORDEN, Walter van. British condr.; manager of Carl Rosa Opera Co. (1902-16); *b.* Bedford Square, London, 7 Nov. 1865; *d.* Halifax, Yorks, 14 April, 1916. Stud. at Guildhall School of Music. His best conducting was in Mozart's *Figaro* and Beethoven's *Fidelio*.—E.-H.

NOORDEWIER-REDDINGIUS, Aaltje. Dutch soprano Bach-singer; *b.* Deurne (North Brabant), 1 Sept. 1868. Famous in Bach's *St. Matthew Passion*; has sung in Holland. Berlin, Munich, Cologne, Frankfort, Leipzig, Vienna, Zurich, Basle, Paris, London, Leeds, etc. Her voice had unusual clearness and range; She has sung also the greater part of Diepenbrock's vocal works.—W. P.

NORDBERGER, Carl. Swedish violinist; *b.* Bollnäs, 22 Nov. 1885. Stud. R. Cons. Stockholm, 1903-6; Prague and Vienna under Ševčík, 1907-10; then short time under Leopold Auer. *Début* Stockholm, 1910; then concerts in Sweden, Norway, Denmark, Czecho-Slovakia and Austria; orch. leader in Hälsingborg and Malmö, 1912-14; Stockholm (Concert Soc.) 1915-16; musical critic in Stockholm many years; from 1919, manager of a concert bureau in Stockholm. Has comp. for vn. 3 Swedish dances (Copenhagen, 1913); *Alt-Wiener-Improvisation*; *Menuet*; *Airs russes*; vn. transcriptions and arrangements.—P. V.

NORDQVIST, Gustaf. Swedish compr. *b.* Stockholm, 12 Feb. 1886. Stud. R. Cons. Stockholm, 1901-10; then in Berlin, 1913. Orgt. at Adolf Fredriks Ch. Stockholm, from 1914; pf. teacher at pf. inst. of S. Carlheim-Gyllensköld from 1922. One of chief accompanists for singers.

Sonata, vn. and pf. (1916); pf. sonata; pf. suite, and other pieces; organ-pieces; hymns; choruses, etc.; about 100 songs (Abr. Lundqvist; Nord. Musikförlaget; Emil Carelius, etc.).—P. V.

NOREN, Heinrich Gottlieb. Austrian compr.; violinist; *b.* Graz, 6 Jan. 1861. Stud. vn. under Massart, Paris; Konzertmeister in Belgium, Spain, Russia and Germany; stud. compn. under Gernsheim; 1896, settled at Crefeld, founded Cons.; stud. cpt. under Klauwell, Cologne; 1902, gave up directorship of Cons.; joined Stern's Cons. as teacher. Now lives at Rottach, Tegernsee. His music is of a virtuoso. and clear-cut nature.

Orch. variations, *Kaleidoskop*, op. 30 (Dresden, 1907); symphony, *Vita*; vn. concerto, A mi. op. 38 (Dantzig Fest. 1912); cello pieces, op. 11; male choruses and songs; pf. pieces, op. 20; pieces for harmonium and vn. op. 18; pastoral sketches for harmonium, vn. and cello, op. 26; suite, E mi. vn. and pf. op. 16; pf. trio, D mi. op. 28; vn. sonata, op. 33; cello sonata; *Serenade* for orch. op. 35; *Divertimento* for 2 vns. and pf. op. 42; vn. pieces, op. 43 and 44; *Symph. Serenade*, op. 48; opera, *Beatrice's Veil*.—A. E.

NORTH AMERICAN INDIAN MUSIC. See ABRAHAM, OTTO; BAKER, THEODORE; CADMAN, C. W.; CURTIS, NATALIE; DENSMORE; FARWELL, ARTHUR; FLETCHER, ALICE C.; GILBERT, H. F. B.; HORNBOSTEL, E. M. v.; SKILTON, C. S.; WA-WAN PRESS.

NORWEGIAN FOLK-MUSIC. See ELLING, CATHERINUS; GRIEG, EDVARD; HEYERDAHL, ANDERS; LAMMERS, THORVALD; LINDEMAN, LUDVIG; SANDVIK, OLE.

NOSKOWSKI, Zygmunt. Polish composer, teacher of theory; *b.* Warsaw, 2 May, 1846; *d.* Wiesbaden, 23 July, 1909. From 1864, pupil of Stanisław Moniuszko in Warsaw. After Moniuszko's death (1872), went to Berlin to study under Kiel and soon brought out his 1st symphony there. In 1876, became condr. of choral society *Bodan* in Constance. In 1881, returned to Warsaw as dir. of Music Soc.; 1888, prof. of theory at State Cons. Since 1904, has cond. symphony concerts of Philh. and (1906) the operas. Reveals a vigorous productive talent in all branches and forms of music. His best-known orch. work is *From the Life*, which is widely played by symphony orchs. He was also a master of the polyphonic forms.

2 symphonies (the 2nd represents a programme *From Spring to Spring*, based on Polish customs); 2 concert overtures (symph. poems): *Morskie Oko* (Tatra Lake) and *The Steppe*; a Variations-Cycle, *From the Life* (on Chopin's Prelude in A ma. with a patriotic programme); 3 operas: *Livia Quintilla* (Lemberg, 1901); *The Verdict* (Warsaw, 1907); *Vengeance* (mus. comedy based on Al. Fredro's masterpiece of same name) (Warsaw, 1909); ballet, *The Fire Festival* (Warsaw, 1902). Also several vaudevilles, 4 4tets, several cantatas with orch., many pf. pieces (his numerous *Krakowiaks*—Polish dances—are well known); about 100 songs and choral compns. Also publ. in 1904 a Manual of counterpoint.—ZD. J.

NOTATIONS, Musical. Ever since Bach established the system of " equal temperament "

351

(tuning all keys alike, and dividing the octave into 12 equal parts) there have been restless attempts at a new notation which will get rid of that back-lying C-major feeling which pervades the present stave-notation. These attempts have followed one of two paths, either the improvement of the present pentagram (5-lined stave) or its complete abolition.

The most sweeping of all notational reforms is that of Angel Menchaca, an Argentine mus. theorist. In the Menchaca system the sign

represents the sound *Si*. The short and long perpendicular strokes

express high and low notes. The point . determines the length. The notation does away with the pentagram (stave), keys, ledger-lines, note-lengths, etc. The musical alphabet is:

La	Se	Si	Do	Du	Re	Ro	Mi	Fa	Fe	Sol	Nu
1	2	3	4	5	6	7	8	9	10	11	12

These signs represent the central dozen; there are 8 dozen more; 4 ascending, 4 descending:

The length of a note is represented by a point . applied thus:

For comparison, take the high B flat, in the present system:

Menchaca system:

The system is based upon the 3 fundamental units which the stave system now used lacks— the graphic unit, the unit of time-length, the unit of pitch. It is written on one line only, and dispenses with the numerous auxiliary signs, staves, octaves, ledger-lines, dots, triplets, etc. It is better adapted to the dodecuple system and harmony is simplified. The notation is alike for all instrs. The routine of the bar is suppressed and replaced by rational rules of punctuation and accentuation. It gives absolute precision to all sounds and lengths.

The Spanish compr. José María Guervós (*q.v.*) has united the bass and treble pentagrams into one stave of 10 lines which he calls the *Decagrama*. He dispenses with the G and F clefs,

replacing them by a single C clef on the 6th line of his 10-line stave.

Hermann Stephani (*q.v.*) introduced a unified notation (*Einheitspartitur*) by using the treble G clef only, with octave signs.

Walter Hampton Thelwall (*q.v.*), in his *Thelwall Notation*, uses 2 staves of 7 lines each. A great advantage of this is that the 2 staves read alike. But his invention is far more sweeping than this. It is a full acknowledgement of the dodecuple system—the complete merging of the sharp and flat into one sound to which it is desirable to give a new name. The sounds of the equal temperament series, and their mutual relations, are very simple. There are 12 notes in an octave, or, if we include, as is usual, the repetition of the 1st note at the upper end of the octave, 13 notes. It should however be remembered that this 13th note is really the 1st note of another similar octave. These notes are all of equal value and importance, and each is separated from the next by the same interval, the mean semitone, or, as Thelwall calls it, the *sem*. The sem is the unit of mus. intervals, and there are 12 sems in an octave, in much the same way that there are 12 inches in a foot. The 12 sounds may be conveniently called by the roman numbers: I, II, III, IV, V, VI, VII, VIII, IX, X, XI, XII, (I); and these numbers are adopted in the Thelwall " Note for Note " system to take the place of the alphabetical names, and signs for the sharp, flat, etc., in the old notation.

The very idea of sharps, flats, naturals, etc. has disappeared, and each note has its own name and is quite independent of its neighbours. Thelwall takes note I as equivalent to F sharp (equals G flat) in the old notation. Note VII is therefore C. The notation consists of a single stave of 7 lines and 6 spaces. The lowest line is note I, the first space, note II; the second line, note III; and so on. Note VII (C) is the middle line, and, to facilitate reading, this line is made a little thicker. This stave is repeated for every octave. When two or more octaves are used one above the other, they are written alternately with 7 full lines and 5 dotted lines, the dotted lines being drawn only where notes occur on them.

The octaves are all numbered, with arabic numbers, the bass octave being 4, the tenor 5, the treble 6, and so on, and these numbers can be used, not only to number the staves, but also to indicate, when desirable, individual notes. Thus, the lowest note on the piano keyboard is IV^2, middle C is VIII^5; the highest note on a seven-octave piano is IV^0.

The inventor appears to hedge a little, when he assumes that in music the diatonic major scale of C is the starting-point of all things, and, in order to indicate this scale in the notation, determines to adopt two new note-heads, namely an open quaver and crotchet head and a closed minim and semibreve head, and to use the open crotchet and minim heads where white notes occur and the closed or black notes where black notes on the keyboard occur; but it is only fair to say that he does this, without sacrificing the principle of equal temperament.

The illustration below shows a passage from Chopin's prelude in C sharp mi. op. 45 in the old notation, and in the Thelwall system.

From Prelude Op. 45—in the Old Notation.

The same—in the New Notation.

In the Thelwall notation the lowest and highest full lines of the stave are always note I (F sharp = G flat). The thick middle line is always note VII (C), whether the line is continuous or dotted. The open notes are white notes on keyboard, the black notes are black notes on keyboard.

The system involves the rewriting of the theory of harmony in accordance with the principle of equal temperament. Harmony thus become correspondingly simplified.

Others have dealt with the actual signs for the sharp and flat. H. Orsmond Anderton in his *Simplified Notation* uses the following:

instead of

The Belgian compr. Jean Hautstont (*q.v.*) bases his *Notation Autonome* (1921) on classification of sounds according to number of their vibrations and the physiological development of the ear. The Russ. compr. Nicolas Obukhof (*q.v.*)

invented a notation in 1915 which also democratises the notes of keyboard. He likewise abolishes the sharps and flats, christening the black notes by syllables taken from the same hymn of Guido d'Arezzo which was used for baptising our scale: *Do, Lo* (C sharp), *Re, Te* (D sharp), *Mi, Fa, Ra* (F sharp), *Sol, Tu* (G sharp), *La, Bi* (A sharp), *Si*. This led him to the reform of notation. In his system, the sharps are represented by the sign × (either in the oval, as in 2nd stave, or alone, as in top stave). Flats are unnecessary.

For an art. on Obukhof, see *Revue Musicale*, Paris, Nov. 1921.

A similar notation was discussed in the chapter on Dodecuple Scale in Eaglefield-Hull's *Modern Harmony* (London, 1913, Augener). The plan suggested there, does away much more effectively with the back-lying C-major feeling, which still pervades Obukhof's system.

With the advent of tertia-tones, a new notation, or some addition to the older one, is necessary. John H. Foulds, who has used thirds of a tone in several of his works, writes thus, in his orch. *Music-Pictures* (group 3) op. 33, produced in London, 1913. (See music ex. on next page. Foulds used tertia-tones again in parts of his *Requiem*, op. 60, 1923.)

Alois Hába in his str. 4tet in the quarter-tone system, op. 7, uses the sign > before a note to be raised a quarter-tone, and the sign < before a note to be lowered a quarter-tone. Hába demonstrated at Prague on 3 June, 1924, with a quarter-tone piano and quarter-tone wind-instruments.

The right way of reform undoubtedly lies in the direction of a completely new notation, but the great obstacle in the way is the cost of reprinting all the best of the existing music in the new notation, when the most advantageous has been found.—E.-H.

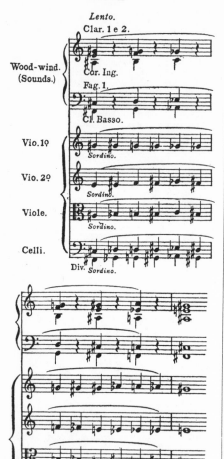

Eng.	Ital.	Fr.	Ger.
D flat	Re bemolle	Ré bémol	Des
E	Mi	Mi	E
E sharp	Mi diesis	Mi dièse	Eis
E flat	Mi bemolle	Mi bémol	Es
F	Fa	Fa	F
F sharp	Fa diesis	Fa dièse	Fis
F flat	Fa bemolle	Fa bémol	Fes
G	Sol	Sol	G
G sharp	Sol diesis	Sol dièse	Gis
G flat	Sol bemolle	Sol bémol	Ges
A	La	La	A
A sharp	La diesis	La dièse	Ais
A flat	La bemolle	La bémol	As
B	Si	Si	H
B sharp	Si diesis	Si dièse	His
B flat	Si bemolle	Si bémol	B

NOTTEBOHM, Martin Gustav. Ger. musicologist; *b.* Lüdenscheid, Westphalia, 12 Nov. 1817; *d.* Graz, 29 Oct. 1882. 1838-9 stud. under L. Berger and Dehn in Berlin; 1840, in Leipzig, stud. under Mendelssohn and Schumann; 1845, in Vienna, cpt. with S. Sechter, then private music-master, Vienna. Nottebohm was closely associated with Brahms, and specially noted as Beethoven researcher. First discovered the importance of Beethoven's sketch-books.

Beethoven's Sketch-book (1865); *Thematic Catalogue of Beethoven's Printed Works* (1864, 2nd ed. 1868, reprint with Nottebohm's biography by E. Kastner, Leipzig, 1913); *Beethoveniana* (1872); 2nd vol. 1887, publ. by Mandyczewzki; *Beethoven's Studies* (1 vol. Beethoven's lessons with Haydn, Albrechtsberger, Salieri, from original mss. 1873); *Thematic Catalogue of Franz Schubert's Printed Compositions* (1874); *Mozartiana* (1880); *A Sketch-book of Beethoven from* 1803 (1880). Comp.: pf. 4tet; several trios and pf. pieces—17 works in all.—A. E.

NOUGUÈS, Jean. Fr. compr. *b.* Bordeaux, 1876. Seeks only to write " successful " operas, thanks to commonplace formulas and a " verist" conception of musical æsthetics. His most popular opera is *Quo Vadis* (1909). He now writes music for cinematograph films, and seems thus to have found the mode of expression best suited to his temperament.

Yanna (Bourdeaux, 1897); *Le Roy du Papagey* (1901); *Thamyris* (Bordeaux, 1904); *La Mort de Tintagiles* (Paris, 1905); *Chiquito* (1909); *Quo Vadis* (Nice and Paris, 1909; Berlin, 1912); *L'Auberge Rouge* (Nice, 1910); *La Vendetta* (Marseilles, 1911); *L'Aigle* (Rouen, 1912); *L'Éclaircie* (Paris, 1914); ballet, *La Danseuse de Pompéi* (Paris, 1912); *Narkiss* (Deauville and London, 1913).—A. C.

NOVÁK, Vítĕzslav. Czechoslovak composer; *b.* Kamenice, near Lípou (Bohemia), 1870. He studied at the Conservatoire in Prague (under Knittl, Stecker and chiefly Antonín Dvořák), attending at the same time the Prague University. Until 1909 he was a private teacher of composition; afterwards lectured at Conservatoire in Prague. He refused position of professor at the Conservatoire in Vienna; in 1919 appointed professor of composition at Master-School of Prague Conservatoire, where he was rector 1919-22. He lives in Prague.

His first compositions, influenced by Liszt, Brahms and Dvořák, show Novák's chief qualities: energy, passion, love for nature-motives, an inclination to psychological sub-

NOTÉ, Jean. Belgian operatic singer; *b.* Tournai, 6 May, 1859; *d.* Brussels, 1 April, 1922. At first a railway clerk; stud. at Cons. at Ghent; prize in 1887. *Début* at Lille; sang in Antwerp, Lyons and Marseilles; entered Paris Opéra in 1893, where he stayed until his death. He possessed the *Légion d'Honneur* for preventing a railway catastrophe, and also 4 medals for saving life.—M. B.

NOTE-NAMES IN VARIOUS LANGUAGES.

Eng.	Ital.	Fr.	Ger.
C	Do	Ut	C
C sharp	Do diesis	Ut dièse	Cis
C flat	Do bemolle	Ut bémol	Ces
D	Re	Ré	D
D sharp	Re diesis	Ré dièse	Dis

jectivism. He is sound in formal construction, without falling into traditional formulas. His second stage is marked by a deep study of the Slovakian folk-music. He does not use the actual folk-tunes, though his music is full of Slovakian spirit. Characteristics : periodicity of 5 bars, church modes, striking melodic curves, harmonic relations and accented syncopations. The inner contents show quick changes from nostalgic sadness to wild joy. Novák here pictures Slovak people and nature as he sees them, or else depicts his own psychical conflicts. In his third and greatest period he stands no longer under folklore influence. His style is refined and more complicated, especially in the harmony, without breaking the line of the tradition. The form is now always dictated by the inner contents and is carefully built up. His subjectivism at times reaches real loftiness; at others the effect is achieved through tone-painting and naturalism. Not till 1914 did he start to produce dramatic works. In addition he has lately written occasional pieces in patriotic vein, and piano-music in easy style for children.

Orch.: *Slovakian Suite*, op. 32; symph. poems: *Tatra*, op. 26 (Queen's Hall, London, 1920); *O věčné touze* (*Eternal Longing*), op. 33; *Toman a lesní panna* (*Toman and the Wood-Fairy*), op. 40; *Godiva*, op. 41 (Queen's Hall, London, 1920); *Serenade*, op. 36. Chorus and orch.: 4 ballads, op. 19 and 23; *The Storm*, op. 42; *Svatební košile* (*The Wedding Shirt*), op. 48. Operas: *Zvíkovský rarášek* (*The Castle-Rogue*), op. 49; *Karlštejn*, op. 50; *Lucerna*, op. 56. 2 pf. trios, op. 1 and 27; pf. 5tet, op. 12; 2 str. 4tets, op. 22 and 35; pf. cycles: *Vzpomínky* (*Recollection*), op. 6; *Můj máj* (*My May*), op. 20; *Sonata eroica*, op. 24; *Winter-night Songs*, op. 30; *Pan*, op. 42; sonatinas, op. 54; song-cycles on words from Moravian national poetry, op. 16, 17, 21; *Melancholy*, op. 25; 2 ballads, op. 28; *Údolí nového království* (*The Valley of a New Kingdom*), op. 31; *Melancholické písně o lásce* (*Melancholy Songs of Love*), op. 39; *Notturnos*, op. 39; *Erotikon*, op. 45; *Jaro* (*Spring*), op. 51. Publ.: Simrock, Berlin; Univ. Ed. Vienna; M. Urbánek, Prague; Breitkopf, Leipzig; Hudební Matice, Prague. Consult Zd. Nejedlý, *Vít. N.* (Prague, 1921).—V. ST.

NOVELLO & CO. Ltd. Publishers, founded in 1811 by Vincent Novello (*b.* 240 Oxford Street, London, 6 Sept. 1781). His son, Joseph Alfred (*b.* 12 Aug. 1810), carried on business until 1861, when he took into partnership Henry Littleton (*b.* 1823) who had been in his employ since boyhood, and had for some years prior to 1861 been practically sole director. Henry Littleton purchased the business in 1866, and in 1867 acquired copyrights of Ewer & Co. Henry Littleton died in 1888, leaving two sons as successors—Alfred (*d.* 1914), and Augustus, the present chairman. Alfred Novello discovered that music could be published cheaply and at a profit; Henry Littleton, with great energy and enterprise, developed the idea in regard to church, choral, and school music; and to these two men is due very largely the steady growth of mus. activity in this country during past 50 years. In 1837 the piano-vocal score of *Messiah* cost a guinea; in 1887 it could be bought for a shilling! The firm has played its part, too, in the renascence of British compn.; many pages in its catalogue are devoted to important works by Parry, Stanford, Mackenzie, Sullivan, Cowen, Elgar, Walford Davies, Edward German, Benjamin Dale,

Gustav Holst, etc. They have done much, too, in the re-issue of neglected native work; 23 splendid volumes have been publ. for the Purcell Soc.—fine examples of their work as engravers and publishers.—H. G.

NOVOTNÝ, Jaroslav. Czechoslovak compr. *b.* Jičín, 1886; killed in 1918 in the Ural in a fight with Bolshevists. Stud. compn. under Vítězslav Novák, besides studies at Univ. He was a music-teacher and chorus-leader of several singing-clubs in Prague. The war forced him to become first an Austrian officer; then he was captured by Russians and entered the Czechoslovak legions in Russia. The fragility, graceful freshness, and abundance of musical ideas which characterise his first compns. gave way afterwards to his bold attempt at new expressive methods. He arrived at polytonality and atonality, but still preserved melodious fluency and strictness of form. He died just at the moment when his spontaneity of sentiment showed itself in full strength (in the choruses written in Russia).

Song-cycles: *The Eternal Wedding*; *The Ballads of the Soul* (Hudební Matice); *Children's Songs* (ms.). A str. 4tet; pf. sonata; choruses will be publ. in Hudební Matice.—V. ST.

NOVOTNÝ, Václav Juda. Czechoslovak writer on music; *b.* Vesec, 1849; *d.* Prague, 1922. Stud. at Univ. and Organ School, Prague; ed. of mus. review *Dalibor* (1873–80); later, critic of many papers. After opening National Theatre, transl. over 100 libretti. Collected national songs (Bechyňské; Libické; Řečické).—V. ST.

NOWOWIEJSKI, Feliks. Polish compr. condr. orgt. *b.* 7 Feb. 1877. Pupil of Bussler and Bellermann in Berlin, and of Haberl and Haller in Ratisbon. Gained several prizes at international competitions. Stayed in Berlin from 1900 to 1909. In 1909, dir. of Cracow Music Soc. Left that position in 1914 to return to Berlin. Since 1920, prof. of church-music and organ at Posen State Conservatoire.

2 oratorios: *The Discovery of the Holy Cross* (1906) and *Quo Vadis* (1907), after Sienkiewicz's celebrated novel. Opera, *The Compass*; symph. poem, *The Funeral of a Hero*; symphonies, A ma. and A. mi. (the latter on a devotional basis). Several songs, choral works and organ pieces.—ZD. J.

NUNN, Edward Cuthbert. Eng. compr. *b.* Bristol, 23 Nov. 1868; *d.* London 26 Nov. 1914. Stud. R.A.M. London under Sir George Macfarren, Tobias Matthay and H. R. Rose; *début* as compr. in July 1889 with orch. *Romance* at Old St. James's Hall, Piccadilly; cond. Leytonstone Orch. Soc. and Ilford Operatic Soc. N. was a composer of great merit.

Orch.: symphony in D (1 movement only); *Fête-Champêtre*, *suite de ballet*; 3 little pieces (*Marche*; *Berceuse*; *Valse*); *Petite Suite* (Withers). Fairy opera, *Kamar-al-Zaman* (Reid Bros.); children's operas: *The Fairy-Slipper* (Novello); *The Shepherdess and the Sweep* (Ambrose Abbott); mus. fairy-tale, *The Garden of Paradise*; 1-act mythological opera, *Sappho*; operatic burlesque, *William Tell*; fairy-opera, *The Wooden Bowl* (Curwen); church-cantata, *Everyman* (Ambrose Abbott); a devotion, *Via Dolorosa* (Novello); *Psalm C*; vn. pieces (Abbot, Withers); pf. pieces (Ascherberg; Lengnick; Reid; Hopwood & Crew; Stainer & Bell); church music; songs.—E.-H.

NYIREGYHÁZI, Erwin. Hungarian pianist; *b.* Budapest, 19 Jan. 1903. Lives in U.S.A.—B. B.

O

OBERHOFFER, Emil. Amer. condr. *b.* near Munich, 10 Aug. 1867. Stud. pf. and compn. under Cyril Kistler; later pf. under Philipp in Paris. Went to America and after short period in New York to St. Paul, Minnesota, as condr. of Apollo Club in 1897. In 1901, condr. of Philh. Club (choral). The orch. recruited from local musicians, which played in the club concerts, he developed into an endowed orch., the Minneapolis Symphony Orch. (50 members), which gave its 1st concert 5 Nov. 1903. At present, giving over 200 concerts annually with a personnel of over 85 players, it is a factor of recognised worth in the mus. life of America. In the autumn of 1923 O. was succeeded as condr. by Henri Verbruggen.—O. K.

OBERLEITHNER, Max von. Ger.-Czechoslovak compr. *b.* Schönberg (Moravia), 11 July, 1868. Pupil of Bruckner; lives mostly in Vienna.

Erlöst (Düsseldorf, 1899); *Ghitana* (Cologne, 1901); *Abbé Mouret* (Magdeburg, 1908; Berlin, 1910); *Aphrodite* (Vienna, 1912); *La Vallière* (Brünn, 1916); *The Iron Saviour* (Vienna, 1917); *Cecilia* (Hamburg, 1919). 3 symphonies; songs.—E. S.

OBERSTADT, Carolus. Dutch pianist and compr. *b.* Tilburg (N. Brabant), 23 June, 1871. Stud. pf. under Clara Schumann, theory under Bargiel; 1894, teacher Cons., The Hague.

Numerous songs and pf. pieces; pf. concertos, cello concerto; overtures; chamber-music: pf. 5tet; str. 4tet; trio; sonatas, vn. and pf.; cello and pf.—W. P.

OBOE FAMILY of mus. instrs., one of most important in modern orch., includes 6 members: oboe, oboe d'amore, cor anglais, oboe da caccia, bass-oboe, and heckelphone. All are wood-wind and have certain points of similarity in construction and method of tone-production. A wooden tube contains a conical air-column which is set into vibration by means of a double-reed held between the lips of the player. The instrs. usually appear in the score immediately below the flutes. Two oboes and a cor anglais are usual, the other instruments being more used for special effects. Each has a compass of about 2 octaves and a fifth, with all chromatic notes. The instrs. are all fingered in the same way, and all, except the oboe, therefore, are transposing instrs. The oboe family is evolved from the family of schalmeys used in the XVII century. The distinctive developments which the modern instrs. have undergone have been directed chiefly to (i) improvement of the intonation; (ii) refinement and ease of production of tone, largely by the use of narrower reeds than formerly; (iii) provision of a key mechanism and a system of fingering adequate for the performance of the difficult passages abounding in modern orch. music.

(1) The modern *Oboe* is a conical pipe of rosewood, blackwood, or ebonite about 2 feet long, the conical bore tapering from about $\frac{3}{16}$ inch at reed-end to $1\frac{1}{4}$ inch at lower end where it terminates in a slightly flaring bell. The compass is from

with chromatic notes, though the upper G is obtained by some players. The entire range is found in modern scores. The instr. is usually provided with about 18 keys and rings, arranged on the system introduced by Barret. The tone of the modern oboe is largely the result of use of a narrow reed, as opposed to coarser, trumpet-like quality produced in the older instrs. by a wide reed. The lower notes are full, but a little hard; from low D to the C above the stave the tone is sweet, expressive, and well suited to *cantabile* passages. The upper notes are bright, but rather thin. Though best suited to melodic *legato* phrases, the oboe is capable of considerable execution, best displayed in rapid *staccato* passages. The modern compr. makes use of the instr. in both these ways, and also takes advantage of the differing tone-colour of the various parts of the compass in the production of special tonal effects. In the earlier oboes the intonation was far from true because the sound-holes were placed with reference to the convenience of the fingers rather than to their true acoustical positions. Boehm (1794–1881) revolutionised the construction of the flute by using large sound-holes put in their correct acoustical positions and by arranging a system of rings and plates by which these holes could be brought under control of fingers. Various attempts were made, notably by Brod, by Buffet, and by Lavigne, to apply Boehm's system to the oboe, but with rather unsatisfactory results. Boehm oboes lack the distinctive oboe-tone and are rarely heard nowadays, though their intonation is nearly perfect. The oboe most used now is that designed by Barret (1804–79) and originally made by the brothers Triébert. This, with certain minor alterations, is now adopted as the Paris Cons. model. Barret, an eminent Eng. player, is chiefly responsible for (i) abolition of double finger-holes; (ii) use of tone-holes of a size proportioned to that of bore and set in acoustically correct positions, holes not being so large as to destroy characteristic timbre; (iii) the provision of a plate for left-hand thumb and a system of rings for fingers, to give middle B flat and C; (iv) double-action octave-keys; (v) additional keys and alternative fingerings for trills and passages hitherto extremely difficult or impracticable.

The Barret-system oboe as made by Triébert has for years been considered standard instr. for artists. Since the death of the Triébert brothers, their high traditions have been maintained by special manufacturers, notably by MM. Lorée and Cabart, whose oboes are widely used all over the world. The oboes of Adler and Heckel in Germany, and several makers in England are also considered excellent.

(2) The *Oboe d'Amore* is pitched a minor third lower than oboe. It is fingered in the same way and its mechanism is similar, its tube somewhat longer, its reed slightly larger. The reed is attached to a short metal crook inserted in upper end of tube; lower end of tube is expanded to form a small globular bell. The tone is rather less bright than that of oboe, the globular end modifying the tone to a rich, veiled sweetness, a little tinged with melancholy, in character suited to *legato* solos. The compass is from

written notes, sounding

The instr. in its ancient form, was known in time of Bach, who writes for it freely. At the present day it is used in rendering Bach scores and also has an important part in modern masters, notably Strauss who writes for it in *Salome* and *Sinfonia Domestica*.

(3) The *Cor Anglais* has been increasingly used since the time of Wagner, and is now a regular constituent of orch. In construction it resembles the oboe d'amore, in that it has a globular bell and a short crook to which the reed is attached. It is, however, larger in size (tube about 2 feet 8 inches long exclusive of crook) and is played with a larger reed. Owing to its greater length it emits sounds a fifth below those of oboe, to which its mechanism and fingering are similar; so that it is a transposing instr., the part for it being written a fifth above the sounded notes. It is frequently played by one of the oboists, though its modern use in combination with two oboes usually demands a third player. The compass is from

written notes, sounding

though in solo-work the upper notes are seldom used owing to their thinness. The tone is rich, veiled, and mournful, of a uniform quality over

the whole compass; it is suited to the performance of slow solo passages.

(4) The *Oboe da Caccia* in its modern form is practically a cor anglais with globular end replaced by a flaring bell of the kind used on oboe. The instr. is, in effect, an oboe a fifth lower and has a similar tone-quality. Its use is not very firmly established, but the instr. is occasionally used in the perf. of early scores in which the name of the instr., but little indication of its exact nature, appears. There is evidence to show that the old oboe da caccia was really a tenor bassoon, the cor anglais being the true tenor oboe. This latter instr. is supposed to derive its name from the corruption of the Fr. *cor anglé*, referring to the bent form of some of the earlier instruments.

(5) The *Bass-Oboe* and *Heckelphone* are both of relatively rare occurrence, even in modern scores. Both stand an octave below the oboe and have corresponding relative compass. In construction they resemble a large cor anglais with suitable modifications of the mechanism to bring the tone-holes under control of the fingers. The original bass or baritone oboe was made by Triébert, though Lorée has also manufactured the instr. Strauss, requiring a true bass for the oboe, became sensible of the imperfections of the bass-oboe. At his suggestion Heckel constructed the heckelphone in which, by careful attention to boring, accurate placing of holes with suitable mechanism, he produced a tone of good quality, louder and richer than that of the bass-oboe. Other modern comprs. have written for the heckelphone but, as yet, it is rarely heard. Heckel has also made a piccolo-heckelphone standing a fourth above the oboe. This instrument is intended for use in some of Wagner's works, and also to replace the modern trumpet in the more accurate tonal rendering of some of Bach's high trumpet parts.—J. M'D.

O'BRIEN, Charles H. F. Scottish compr. *b.* Edinburgh, 6 Sept. 1882. Pupil of late Hamish MacCunn. Is now singing-master and lecturer in mus. appreciation to R. High School, Edinburgh; examiner in theory and sight-singing to Edinburgh R. Choral Union. He early acquired in compn. a decidedly Scottish idiom, flavoured strongly with classicism; he is entirely unsympathetic to the recent new trends of mus. compn. There are few Scottish comprs. whose work is so distinctive. His recent symphony in F mi. op. 23 should mark an epoch in Scottish music.

Concert overtures, *To Spring* and *Ellangowan* (both perf. Bournemouth); *The Minstrel's Curse* (Edinburgh Amateur Orch. Soc.); pf. sonata, in E mi. op. 14; *Arabesque* (both Ricordi, London).—W. S.

OBUKHOF, Nicolas (*accent 2nd syll.*). Russ. compr. and theorist; *b.* Moscow in 1892. Stud. compn. at Petrograd Cons. under Tchérepnin and Steinberg; and (after 1919) orch. under Maurice Ravel in Paris. Has publ. (Rouart & Lerolle) settings of texts by Balmont, which are parts of a vast oratorio, *The Book of Life*, which reveal the essentially religious trend of his mind. He is, to a degree, influenced by Scriabin. His music proceeds by harmonic complexes founded upon the 12 notes of the tempered scale. In the third of his publ. fragments he gives up using sharps and flats and ascribes new names to the 5 notes to which the black keys of the keyboard correspond, in order to emphasise the final character of equal temperament. He avoids duplication of notes, and in the vocal parts he frequently resorts to *glissandi* which come into strong contrast with the strictly tempered character of the instr. parts. See art. NOTATIONS.—B. DE S.

"O CANADA" (National song). First appeared in Quebec, about 40 years ago, as a Fr.-Canadian folk-song in honour of St. John the Baptist. Composed by Calixa Lavallée, a well-known Fr.-Canadian pianist and composer of that period. Lavallée only agreed to compose the music on condition that his music should appear first and the text be adapted to it later. Original poem (in French) by the late Judge Routhier, a well-known writer and jurist. The air was in use for many years throughout the Dominion by regimental bands, as one of five official tunes authorised by the Government, and frequently played at important military and civil functions. An arrangement by the writer (for 8-v. chorus and orch.), first produced a few years ago by the Mendelssohn Choir with Pittsburg Orch. in Massey Hall, Toronto, created a profound impression. Unhappily, the allusion, in the translation, to the Holy Cross, gave rise to considerable discussion and strong sectarian feeling, with the result that over 100 " arrangements" of the text were made, in the attempt to avoid this pitfall. At the present time the song (in so far as the English-speaking section of the country is concerned) bids fair to become a national confusion, instead of a " chant national."—P. B. R.

OCHS, Siegfried. Ger. choral condr. *b.* Frankfort-o-M., 19 April, 1858. Stud. chemistry at Polytechnic, Darmstadt, and Univ. Heidelberg; then music at R. High School, Berlin (Schulze, Rudorff, Kiel, Urban). O. was founder and condr. of Philh. Choral Soc., Berlin, which he brought to quite extraordinary prominence, but had to dissolve in summer 1920 owing to unfavourable conditions; now conducting the choral class of the Berlin High School. He did much to introduce British music (Stanford especially) in Berlin.
Comic opera, *In the Name of the Law* (Hamburg, 1888); songs; duets, etc. Consult his autobiography *Geschehenes, gesehenes* (*Things acted and seen*), Berlin 1922.—A. E.

OCÓN Y RIVAS, Eduardo. Span. compr. *b.* Malaga, 12 Jan. 1834; *d.* Feb. 1901. Stud. organ under Benoit at Cons. in Paris. Founder and dir. of the Málaga Cons. Distinguished himself as an educationist, folk-lorist and compr. of many religious works, besides some secular compns. (publ. by Zozaya, Madrid), which attained popularity in Spain and abroad. His *Bolero de Concierto*, originally written for pf., was transcribed for orch. His coll. of *Cantos Españoles* (publ. Breitkopf, Leipzig), is a valuable contri-

bution to the history of the folk-lore of Spain. —P. G. M.

ODDONE SULLI-RAO, Elisabetta. Italian composer; *b.* Milan, 13 Aug. 1878. Pupil of R. Cons. in Milan. Has written 2 str. 4tets, operas. Her chief merit lies in her activity as a collector and propagandist of Ital. folk-songs. She publ. a *Canzoniere popolare italiano*, in which she brought together the beautiful melodies found and collected by her in the various regions of Italy. She herself has given perfs. of these songs, and has toured through the Ital. cities with great success. She has also devoted herself to music for children: her collection of *Canzoncine per bimbi* has been publ. by Ricordi; and *Cantilene popolari dei bimbi d' Italia* by Arti Grafiche, Bergamo. She has publ. an excellent monograph on her master *Gaetano Coronaro* (Rome, 1921, Ausonia).—D. A.

OETTINGEN, Arthur Joachim von. Physicist and musical theorist; *b.* Dorpat, 28 March, 1836; *d.* Leipzig, 6 Sept. 1920. First stud. astronomy, then physics at Dorpat Univ. 1853-9; continued physical, physiological and mathematical studies in Paris and Berlin, 1859-62; became honorary lecturer in physics at Dorpat Univ.; 1865, prof.; 1894, retired, owing to Dorpat Univ. becoming Russian; resided at Leipzig, where he became prof. Founder of so-called "dual system of harmony" and defender of "natural temperament."
Harmony System in dual development (1866; 1913, 2nd ed. entitled *Dual System of Harmony*, Leipzig, Siegel); *Principles of the Science of Music* (Leipzig, 1916, Teubner).—A. E.

OHE, aus der, Adele. Ger. pianist and compr. *b.* Hanover, 11 Dec. 1864. 1872, pupil of Franz Kullak at New Acad. of Music, Berlin; then Theodor Kullak; 1876-86, pupil of Liszt, Weimar. Undertook extensive concert-tours in America, in 1892 over all Europe.
Suites and pf. pieces; sonata, pf. and vn.; songs. —A. E.

OHLSSON, J. Richard. Swedish violinist and compr. *b.* Stockholm, 9 March, 1874. Stud. vn. at R. Cons. Stockholm, and (1896) vn. and compn. at R.A.M. London; member R.A.M. Stockholm, 1915.
Élégie and *Valse Carnaval*, vn. and orch. (1897; perf. 1922); str. 4tet, No. I, E mi. (1898); No. II in D (1899); No. II in A flat (1914); concert piece, vn. and orch. (1918); pieces for vn. and orch.—P. V.

OIREACHTAS, The (Irish Festival). Held annually and devoted to competitions in various subjects. The fest. was started in 1896 by Gaelic League, to demonstrate the Irish Revival. In the mus. part, prizes are given for solo and choral singing, only Irish words being allowed. Prizes are also offered for vn. harp and pipes. It was a good means of bringing the folk-singers from distant parts, and it is a pity that in later years this element has diminished.—W. S.

OLDROYD, George. Eng. orgt. and compr. *b.* Healey, near Batley, Yorks, 1 Dec. 1886. Stud. as articled pupil of Dr. Eaglefield-Hull; vn. under Johan Rasch and Frank Arnold; 1915, orgt. St. George's Eng. Ch., Paris; 1919, St.

Alban's, Holborn; 1921, St. Michael's, Croydon; prof. of organ and harmony, Trinity Coll. of Music. Mus.Doc. London, 1917.

Organ pieces (Augener); songs (Elkin); church music (Faith Press); singing-class music (E. Arnold). —E.-H.

O'LEARY, Arthur. Born Tralee, Co. Kerry, 15 March, 1834. Entered Cons. at Leipzig, 1847 (stud. under Moscheles); came under influence of Robert and Clara Schumann. In 1852, stud. under Sterndale Bennett at R.A.M. London; prof. there 1856–1903; ed. Sterndale Bennett's pf. works and masses by Hummel and Schubert. —W. St.

OLENIN, Alexander Alexeievitch (*accent 2nd syll.*). Russ. compr. *b.* 1865; brother of well-known Mussorgsky-singer Olenina d'Alheim. Comp. opera, *Kudejar* (perf. Moscow); many songs and pf. pieces on Russ. folk-tunes.—v. B.

OLIVIERI SANGIACOMO-RESPIGHI, Elsa. Ital. compr. *b.* Rome, 24 March, 1894. Pupil of R. Liceo Mus. di Santa Cecilia, where she stud. pf. under Sgambati, harmony and cpt. under Remigio Renzi, and compn. under Ottorino Respighi, whom she afterwards married. She has publ., through Ricordi, numerous songs and other compositions.—D. A.

d'OLLONE, Max. Fr. compr. *b.* Besançon, 13 June, 1875. Pupil at Paris Cons. under Lavignac, Lenepveu and chiefly Massenet, in whose memory he has written some articles. *Prix de Rome* in 1897. Now dir. of Amer. Cons. in Fontainebleau.

Trio, pf. vn. cello (1921); *Frédégonde* (cantata); *Jeanne d'Arc à Domrémy* (*scène lyrique*); *Saint François d'Assises* (oratorio); *Les Amants de Rimini* (*drame lyrique*); *Le Retour* (opera; Angers, 1913; Paris, 1919); *Les Uns et les Autres* (1-act, after Verlaine, 1923); *Bacchus et Silène* (pantomime, 1901). —A. C.

OLMEDA DE SAN JOSÉ, Father Federico. Span. musicologist, orgt. and compr. *b.* Burgo de Osma, 1865; d. Madrid, 11 Feb. 1909. Orgt. at Tudela Cath. (1887); Burgos Cath. (1888); and from 1903 to end of life choirmaster at Convent of Descalzas Reales, Madrid. Ed. of review *La Voz de la Música* (Madrid). Started his career as choirboy; stud. first under Don Damián Sanz and later on under Don León Lobera, who instructed him in harmony, cpt. and vn. vla. cello and d.b. Among contemporary Span. theorists he ranks next in importance to Pedrell for his research work on the art of polyphony from its early stages and his conclusions as to its relation to modern music and the origin of dissonance. This he traces (in the implied form of the chord of 7th) over 400 years before Monteverdi in the Codex attributed to Calixtus II (XII century), which is preserved at Santiago de Galicia and which nobody had thoroughly analysed before Olmeda (see BAR-BIERI). He anticipated many of the ideas embodied in the *Motu Proprio* of Pius X (1903), the interpretation of which was for him a favourite study. He possessed a valuable library on music and liturgy, acquired at his death by the bookseller Karl Hiersemann of Leipzig. His compns. numbering 350, include:

4 symphonies; symph. poem, *Paraíso Perdido* (*Paradise Lost*); *Oda*, for str. orch.; *Salve Regina*, v. and orch.; str. 4tet in E flat (1891); pf.: 32 *Rimas*, inspired by the poetical work of Becquer with same title (1890–1); sonatas; *Misa de Gloria*; *Nocturno*. (Publ. Daniel Pérez Cecilia, Burgos.)—P. G. M.

OLSEN, Ole. Norwegian compr. condr. *b.* Hammerfest, 4 July, 1850. Stud. music in Trondhjem, 1865–7; 1868, assistant-orgt. in that city. Stud. at Cons. in Leipzig, 1870–4, where he completed his nationally-tinged symphony in G. Under the influence of Wagner's music, he applied himself to production of music-dramas; during the following decades wrote numerous operas. Was condr. of Mus. Soc. in Christiania, 1878–81; choral instructor; music-instructor at Military School, 1887–1903; inspector of music to army, 1899–1919. He has given many concerts abroad; has conducted his own compns. in Stockholm, Copenhagen, Berlin, Hamburg, Leipzig, Cologne, Vienna. A very versatile compr., his symph. poems, operas and pf. pieces often bear a strongly national stamp, being in that respect influenced by Grieg and Svendsen; his amiable personality gives his works a charming touch of humour and feeling. Their tunefulness is ingratiating and taking. Warmly-coloured instrumentation and felicity of form characterise most of his orchestral works.

Operas: *Lajla* (perf. National Theatre, 1908); *Stig Hvide*; *Klippeöerne* (*The Rock-girt Isles*); *Stallo* (all to own words); music to Nordahl Rolfsen's fairy-comedy *Svein Uræd* (perf. many times in the 'nineties); music to Weilen's drama *Erik XIV*; symphony in G; symph. poem, *Aasgaardsreien*; *Alfedans* (*Fairy Dance*); oratorio, *Nidaros*; cantatas; male-voice choruses; pf. pieces; songs; adaptations of folk-melodies, etc.—J. A.

OLSSON, Otto Emanuel. Swedish orgt. compr. *b.* Stockholm, 19 Dec. 1879. Stud. R. Cons. Stockholm, 1894–1901; compn. under Josef Dente; orgt. Gustavus Vasa Ch. from 1908; teacher (harmony) R. Cons. 1908; prof.-in-ordinary, 1919; member of R. Committee for new hymn-book for the Swedish Church, 1916; well known as an organ recitalist; member R.A.M. Stockholm, 1915. As a compr. O. has a very fine polyphonic style.

Pf.: '*Fire klaverstykker* (Copenhagen, Nord. Forlag); *Vid juletid* (*At Christmas*), 5 pieces (Elkan & Schildknecht); 6 *Aquarelles* (*id.*); *Ur Skizzboken* (*Sketchbook*), 8 pieces (Th. Dahlström); 7 *Elegiska danser* (*id.*). Organ: *Meditation* (Elkan & Schildknecht); '*Adagio* (*id.*); 5 pedal-studies (Hofmeister); 5 canons (Junne); Fantasia and fugue (own ed.); 7 *Miniatures* (W. Hansen); Prelude and fugue, C sharp mi. (*id.*); Prelude and fugue, F sharp mi. (*id.*); chorale preludes (Dahlström); Gregorian melodies (Abr. Hirsch); 10 variations on Dorian plainsong; *Ave Maris Stella*, and other organ pieces (London, Augener); *Te Deum*, chorus, str. harp and organ (Musik. Konstföreningen); 6 Latin hymns *a cappella* (*id.*); 6 *a cappella* choruses; mixed choruses with organ; 3 cantatas; str. 4tet II in G (*id.*); songs for v. vn. and organ; songs with pf.; about 20 male choruses; Suite for harmonium (Dahlström).—P. V.

O'MARA, Joseph. Irish t. singer; *b.* Limerick, 16 July, 1866. In 1889, went to Milan to study singing under Moretti. In 1891, opera *début* in London; 1892, sang at the Popular Concerts; 1894, sang in Eng. and Ital. at Drury Lane and Covent Garden. On production of Stanford's *Shamus O'Brien* in 1896, made great impression in Mike's part; joined Moody-Manners Opera Co. and sang in London and provinces; successful in such widely different parts as Rodolphe (*La Bohème*) and Tannhäuser; founded an opera company which, has, for some years, toured the provinces with success.—W. ST.

OMNITONALITY. See art. on HARMONY.

ONDŘIČEK, František. Czech violinist; *b.* Prague, 1859; *d.* Milan (when on a concert tour), 1922. Stud. at Cons. Prague and Paris (Massart). Concert tours took him all over Europe and America and made him celebrated. He has a passionate and expressive temperament, and intense rhythmic feeling. Till 1918 his permanent home was Vienna, where he cond. his own music school, and (from 1908) acted as leader of his Quartet. From 1919 prof. of vn. classes at Cons. of Prague.

Publ. (with Dr. S. Mittelmann) *New Methods in Advanced Technique of Vn. Playing* (2 vol. 1908). Comp. str. 4tet; Czech Rhapsody; many vn. arrangements.—V. ST.

ONEGIN-HOFFMANN, Sigrid. Contr. singer; *b.* Stockholm, about 1885, of Ger. parents; pupil of Eugen Robert Weiss and di Raniero, Milan; 1912, concert-singer; married same year Eugen B. Onegin (compr. 1883–1919); engaged for Stuttgart and Munich Opera Houses; since 1922, concert-touring in U.S.A.—A. E.

O'NEILL, Julia A. Eng. pianist and teacher; *b.* London. Prof. of pf. Borough Polytechnic.

Guide to Theory of Music (Novello); *Exercises for Weaker Fingers* (*id.*); *Melodious Technique* (2 books) Novello; *Picturesque Technique* (Stainer & Bell, 1923). —E.-H.

O'NEILL, Norman. Eng. compr. and condr. *b.* Kensington, 14 March, 1875. Stud. under Dr. Arthur Somervell in London and Ivan Knorr at Frankfort. He has acted as mus. dir. of several London theatres (notably The Haymarket Th.) and excels as a writer of incidental music. Amongst his best music for plays are his *Blue Bird* music (1909), and his *Mary Rose* music (April 1920).

Orch.: 3 overtures (*In Autumn*, op. 8; *Hamlet*, op. 11; *In Springtime*, op. 21); Miniature Suite, op. 13; *Miniatures*, op. 25; Variations, op. 29; *Scotch Rhapsody*, op. 30; *Hornpipe*; *Overture Humoresque*; scena for barit. and orch. *La Belle Dame sans merci.* Incidental music: *A Lonely Queen*, op. 22; *A Tragedy of Truth*, op. 23; *The Last Heir*, op. 28; *King Le r*, op. 34; *Hamlet* (1905); *The Blue Bird*, op. 37 (Elkin); *The Gods of the Mountain*, op. 41; *Freedom* (New York, 1918); *Mary Rose* (1920, Schott); *Macbeth* (Nov. 1920); *Julius Cæsar* (1920); *The Snow Queen* (Kingsway, 1921); *The Merchant of Venice* (New York, 1922; H. Gray & Co.); *Stigmata* (1922); *Success* (Haymarket, June 1923); *Prisoner of Zenda* (*id.* Aug. 1923; Cramer); *Before Dawn*, a Swinburne ballet, chorus and orch.; trio in 1 movement, vn. cello, pf. op. 26 (Schott); variations for 2 pfs. (Schott); pf. pieces (Schott; Elkin; Forsyth; Anglo-Fr. Co.); songs (Keith, Prowse; Cramer; H. Gray; Forsyth; Ricordi; Weekes; Novello; Boosey); ed. *Golden Treasury of Song* (Boosey); *Song Garden for Children* (E. Arnold).—E.-H.

OPERA in Belgium, England, Germany, Hungary, etc. See under headings of various countries—BELGIAN OPERA, ENGLISH, etc.

OPÉRA-COMIQUE, THÉÂTRE DE L', Paris. The beginnings of the Opéra-Comique in Paris were very modest. The comedians of the Théâtre de la Foire, wishing to profit by the fashion for music and being hindered, by Lully's privilege, from performing entirely musical pieces, inter-

spersed their farces with couplets on well-known airs or songs specially composed. This was the origin of the type of opera composed by Philidor, Monsigny, Duny, Grétry, Boieldieu, Auber—the type which produced Bizet's *Carmen*.

The present building was constructed by Bernier in 1898 on the site of the Salle Favart burnt down in 1887. Repertory *opéras-comiques* are occasionally given there, but mostly lyric dramas such as *Louise*, *Pelléas*, *Werther*, etc. are presented. The Opéra-Comique now gives with great taste the same repertoire as the Grand Opéra, and is content to avoid the more elaborate vocal works which its stage renders impossible. It receives a subsidy from the State. The managers (1924) are Albert Carré and the brothers Isola.—H. P.

OPERA HOUSES. *ARGENTINA.*—**Buenos Ayres:** (i) *Opera.* (ii) *Teatro Colón.* (iii) *Teatro Politeama.*

AUSTRIA.—**Vienna:** (i) *State Grand Opera House* (see special art. under V). (ii) *Volksoper*, condrs. Felix Weingartner and Franz Schalk. Weingartner resigned in 1924, and was succeeded by Fritz Stiedry. (iii) *Konzerthaus*, dir. Dr. Botstiber.

BELGIUM.—**Brussels:** *Theatre de la Monnaie* (see special art. under B). **Antwerp:** *Lyrisch Vlaamsch Tooneel.* Cultivates especially Flemish comprs. (Blockx, Du Bois, P. Gilson, etc.); also Wagner, Smetana, etc.

CZECHO-SLOVAKIA.—**Prague:** The Bohemian nation built the *National Theatre* without help from Austrian state. It was burnt down in 1881, rebuilt by collected funds, and re-opened in 1883. Both drama and opera are cultivated. Dir.-condrs. 1883–1900, Adolf Čech, Moritz Auger, Adolf Vyskočil. 1900–20, Karel Kavořovic (*q.v.*) and now O. Ostrčil (*q.v.*). The Kavořovic period was most flourishing. It included model-perfs. of Smetana and Dvořák, Wagner, Strauss and many new Fr. and Russ. works. Since 1920, it comprises 2 buildings, the new large theatre, no longer suited to modern opera, and the former *Ständetheater* (built 1789) now of insufficient capacity. The present condrs. include F. Picka, R. Zamrzla, V. Brzobohotý, V. Maixner and J. Winkler. **Brno (Brünn):** *Moravian Opera House*, condr. Fr. Neumann (*q.v.*).

DENMARK.—**Copenhagen:** *Royal Opera.*

ENGLAND.—**London:** (i) *Royal Covent Garden Opera House* (orig. R. Italian Opera) See special art. The British National Opera Co. now gives a summer season and a winter one. The lessees are the Grand Opera Syndicate. (ii) Operas are very occasionally given at His Majesty's Theatre, the Shaftesbury, the Aldwych, etc. (iii) Boughton's *The Immortal Hour* has recently had a very long run at the Regent. (iv) Operas are given 3 times a week from Sept. to May at the "Old Vic."

FINLAND. — **Helsingfors:** *Opera House.* Condr. up to 1922, O. Merikanto; then T. Hannikainen. (See FINNISH OPERA.)

FRANCE.—**Paris:** (i) *Théâtre National de l'Opéra* (*q.v.*). (ii) *Opéra-Comique* (*q.v.*) Operas are also given at Marseilles, Lyons, Nancy, Lille, Nice, Monte Carlo, Cannes, etc.

GERMANY.—The German opera - houses have no " seasons " (except Bayreuth), but are permanent companies with fixed staff, changing slowly and continually replenished. **Berlin:** (i) *Staatsoper*, condrs. Schillings, Kleiber. (ii) *Deutsches Opernhaus*; the last dir. Georg Hartmann was succeeded in 1923 by Leo Blech, who is now both gen. and artistic dir. (iii) *Grosse Volksoper*, dir. Otto Klemperer. **Darmstadt:** *Landestheater*, dir. Michael Balling. **Dresden:** *Sächsisches Staatstheater* (Saxon State Theatre), dir. Fritz Busch. **Frankfort-o-M.:** *Stadttheater*, dir. Ernst Lert. **Hamburg:** (i) *Stadttheater*, dir. Siegfried Jelenko. (ii)*Volksoper*, dir. Carl Richter. **Hanover:** *Opernhaus*, dir. R. Levy. **Carlsruhe:** *Badisches Landestheater* (Baden National Theatre), dir. Fritz Cortolezis. **Cologne:** *Vereinigte Stadttheater*, dir. Eugen Szenkar. **Leipzig:** *Städtische Theater*, dir. O. Lohse. **Mannheim:** *Nationaltheater*, condr. Richard Lert. **Munich :** Operas are given in Nationaltheater, in Residenztheater (especially Mozart), and in Prinzregententheater (generally only in summer). Opera-dir. Hans Knappertsbusch. **Stuttgart:** *Württemburgisches Landestheater*, dir. C. Leonardt. **Weimar:** *Deutsches Nationaltheater*, cond. vacant. **Wiesbaden:** *Staatstheater*, condr. F. Mannstädt.

HOLLAND.—**The Hague:** *National Opera House*, founded 1916 by G. H. Koopman (dir. 1916–19); dir. W. van Korlaar, jun. 1919–22; from 1922, Jan Heythekker. 1st condr. Albert van Raalte, 1916–22. Classical operas, Wagner, d'Albert, Wolf-Ferrari, etc.

HUNGARY.—**Budapest:** *Royal Opera House.* Opened. 1881. Before that time, operas were given two or three times weekly in National Theatre (opened 1837). In this opera-house all the most important Hungarian operas and stage mus. works had their first perf., among them Erkel's operas and the stage-music of Mihalovich, Hubay, Dohnányi, Bartók, etc. Gustav Mahler was dir. 1888–91; Arthur Nikisch 1893–5. Well-known condrs. included Stephan Kerner (*q.v.*) (since 1896), and the Italian, Egisto Tango (1913–19). Among the singers have been Takács Mihály (barit.); Béla Környei (t.); Ludwig Rózsa (b.) (*qq.v.*). Best-known of present day: Ferenc Székelyhidy (t.), Erzsi Sándor (coloratura-s.), Olga Haselbeck (m.-sopr.), Rózsi Marschalkó (m.-sopr.) (*qq.v.*).

ITALY.—**Rome:** (i) *Teatro Costanzi* (see special art.). (ii) *Teatro Adriano*; very vast; recently built; privately owned; spring and autumn seasons. **Milan:** (i) *Scala* (*Teatro alla*), dir. Arturo Toscanini (see special art.). (ii) *Teatro Dal Verme*, named after the family who recently built it, and own it. **Venice:** (i) *Fenice* (*Teatro la*), well-known house, built 1792; dir. Mario Terni. (ii) *Teatro Malibran*, dir. G. Zuccani. **Turin:** *Teatro Regio*, a leading opera-house; built 1738. Entrusted by municipality to private enterprises. Seasons Carnival and Lent. *Manon Lescaut* (1 Feb. 1893) and *La Bohème* (1 Feb. 1896) were first produced

there. **Bologna:** *Teatro Comunale*, a renowned theatre, opened 1763; autumn and winter seasons. **Naples:** *Teatro San Carlo*; one of largest; built 1737; rebuilt several times; property of city, who entrust it to private enterprise. Intended for great stage spectacles. **Genoa:** *Teatro Carlo Felice.* One of best-known in Italy; built 1826; Carnival and Lent seasons.

LITHUANIA.—See LITHUANIAN MUSIC.

NORWAY.—**Christiania** has possessed a permanent opera house only during the 3 years from 1916 to 1921. The theatre was named *Opéra Comique*, and was started by a syndicate headed by Benno Singer, with Alexander Varnay as artistic leader. As Norway possesses a superfluity of brilliant vocalists, a number of the leading works, both classical and modern, were able to receive an excellent performance in this theatre, the more so because several of the most famous European artists gave "guest" performances there. The opera house ceased to exist in 1921. The various dramatic stages in Christiania, National Theatre, Central Theatre, Christiania Theatre, etc., have occasionally produced operas in addition to dramatic pieces. On initiative of the journal *Dagbladet* a fund of about 1 million kroner has been collected for establishing in the future a permanent Norwegian opera-house. In the dramatic theatres in Bergen, Stavanger and Trondhjem, operas and operettas are occasionally performed.

POLAND.—**Warsaw:** State Opera House, chief condr. Emil Młynarski. Opera is also perf. at Lwów (Lemberg), Cracow and Posen.

PORTUGAL.—**Lisbon:** (i) *San Carlos Theatre.* (ii) *Trinidade Theatre.* (iii) *Colyseu.*

RUMANIA.—**Bucharest:** *State Opera House*; dir. Georges Georgescu; 1st condr. J. N. Otescu. (See RUMANIAN OPERA.)

RUSSIA.—**Petrograd:** *State Opera House* (formerly *Imperial Opera House*). **Moscow:** *Grand Opera House*, condr. N. S. Golovanof.

SERBIA.—**Belgrade:** *National Theatre* (*New Opera House*).

SPAIN.—**Madrid:** *Teatro Real* (*Royal Opera-House*). **Barcelona:** *Liceo* (Opera House).

SWEDEN.—**Stockholm:** *Royal Opera.*

U.S.A.—**New York:** (i) *Metropolitan Opera House.* Dir. (from 1908) Giulio Gatti-Casazza. (ii) *Century Opera House* (from 1913–15). **Boston:** *Opera House*, built 1909. **Chicago:** *Opera House*, managed by an association formed in 1911.—E. H.

OPIEŃSKI, Henryk. Polish compr. violinist, condr. writer; *b.* Cracow, 13 Jan. 1870. Became an engineer in 1892. Soon left that career and began in 1894 to study music under Żeleński in Cracow; then under Stojowski and Paderewski in Paris; under Urban in Berlin, and under V. d'Indy in Paris. Was a violinist of Colonne Orch. in Paris; then in Warsaw Philh.; 1904–6, stud. musicology under Riemann in Leipzig. Ph.D. 1914. In 1911, founded in Warsaw a scientific musical review, *Kwartalnik Muzyczny*, which appeared for 2 years. During the war, O. founded in Switzerland a Madrigal Soc. to perform ancient vocal music. Since 1919, dir. of the State Conservatoire at Posen.

Symph. poems: *Lilla Weneda*, 1908 (on the tragedy of Stowacki); *Sigismund Augustus and Barbara* (received a prize, Warsaw, 1912); songs; vn. pieces. Historical works: *La Musique Polonaise, Essai historique sur le développement de l'art musical en Pologne* (Paris, 1918, Georges Crès); an art. on Polish music in the Ital. review *L'Eroica* (special number, *Polonia*, 1916); and his doctor's thesis on the ancient lutenist Valentin Greff-Bacfart.—Zp. J.

OPPEL, Reinhard. Ger. compr. *b.* Grünberg (Upper Hessia), 13 Nov. 1878. Pupil of Hoch's Cons. Frankfort-o-M.; 1903-9, orgt. at Bonn; 1911, graduated at Munich with *Study on Jacob Meiland*; 1911, teacher of compn. at Cons. Kiel.

Female and male choruses; church music; sonata and suite for vn.; pf. pieces, op. 21, 26, 27, 28; songs. In ms.: *Serenade* (flute, ob. clar. horn and bsn.), F ma. op. 30; str. trio; two 2 str. 4tets; pf. and vn. sonata; pf. sonata, A mi.; organ works. Since 1922 Oppel Soc. has been engaged in popularising his music.—A. E.

ORCHARD, W. Arundel. British compr. *b.* London; now living in Sydney, N.S.W. Dir. New South Wales State Cons. from 1923.

Music-drama, 3 acts, *Dorian Gray* (from Oscar Wilde), ms.; dramatic poem, *Ullen the Bowman*, chorus and orch. (Laudy & Co. London); *The Silent Land*, male chorus and orch.; orch. music; str. 5tet, C mi.; str. 4tet, F mi.; part-songs (Laudy; Paling & Co. Sydney).—E.-H.

ORCHESTRAL COLOUR AND VALUES. Orchestral colour, which is vital to orchestral music, is difficult to treat in a short article, not only because it is at once an intricate and a very large subject but also because it has an indefiniteness. The parallelism with painting implied by its name is incomplete. The painter's primary material consists of three colours, red, blue and yellow. When he mixes them a thousand varieties of hue result, but, for all their variety, they result definitely and in obedience to fixed rules. The maker of orchestral music may be said to work with four primaries, the strings and harp, the wood-wind instruments, the brass and the percussion instruments, these last including bells. But when he blends his primaries his results are not definite. The spacing of a chord, its doubling and its distribution among the classes of instruments can be so endlessly modified that to reach a fixed result regularly is hopeless. It is well known that some of our most experienced writers for the modern orchestra cannot hear what they write with the mind's ear. Hence the so frequent remark, "I had no idea it would sound so well."

It is impossible to make fixed rules for the blending of orchestral colour. We may, for instance, feel that strings and brass never blend, or, more forcibly, that the pianoforte and the organ do not blend with the other instruments of an orchestra. The persistently individual tone of the piano is indeed partly responsible for the continued success of the pianoforte concerto with the concert-going public. But all these and similar generalisations may at any point break down; not one of them can be erected into a rule. Skilful composers have, for instance, used organ tones, in particular the pedal tones of the organ, to the great colour-advantage of the orchestra. All combinations are part of the

individual emotion and expression of the composer and belong thereto. In every period, from Monteverdi to Stravinsky, each composer has impressed his own idiom upon the orchestra he has employed. We hear much of the greyness of Brahms's orchestration, the vermilion quality of Berlioz's dazzling brilliancy, the ethereal blue of Debussy's gossamer spinning. As we study each of these composers we find that his colour, even his lack of colour, is proper to his special language. Every note a great composer sets down is essential: its heaviness, its lightness, its very emptiness is moulded to his thought. Yet it is impossible fully to analyse his individual use of orchestral combinations, so infinitely various are they in their degrees of light and shade and in their registers of tone-quality.

It has been suggested that orchestral colour covers a multitudinous poverty of thematic and musical ideas. This is sometimes all too true, yet it cannot be admitted that all compositions for the orchestra should stand or fall by the so-called black-and-white test. The orchestral works of the older masters do indeed sound well on the pianoforte, which is a colourless instrument, because their significance is mainly a matter of form and design. It is these which are essential to them and not the orchestral colour of their simple and straightforward harmonies, and therefore their essential qualities can be rendered on the piano. This holds in spite of that rightness of colour, timbre and atmosphere which sounds in orchestral productions of the works of great classical masters, masterly adapters of the orchestras at their disposal to the idiom of their ideas.

But it cannot be fairly disputed that some of the most beautiful modern orchestral compositions convey nothing, or worse than nothing, when they are arranged as four-handed pieces for the pianoforte. The fact is that the colour, obtained from the orchestra but not from the piano, can entirely change harmonic ideas. Thus on the modern orchestra the most violent harmonic clashes, the juxtaposition of several keys at once, can give perfect æsthetic pleasure. Therefore the black-and-white test is discredited. As well judge a modern painting by a pencil sketch of it! How poor and trivial, even ugly, might the drawing be of a painting that was luminous, scintillating, ethereal by the wonder of its colour! Its whole emotional, and therefore artistic, effect may have depended upon colour. Modern orchestral composition, like modern painting, does not have form and design for its only essential elements, but is, on the contrary, mainly a matter of colour.

While, then, orchestral colour must never cover up poverty of ideas and invention, to neglect it is to incur a real and grave loss. Composers must abandon the old view that if the harmonic structure of their works be sound and the musical ideas interesting, it is impossible to have colourless orchestration. On the contrary, the subject of colour deserves special study. If one looks over modern scores, the lamentable lack of variety of colour obtained by composers without the colour-sense, even from the strings, is repeatedly apparent, and the improvement that a real orchestral colourist could bring to many of these works would surprise their authors.

The conclusion is, then, that while orchestral colouring follows rules which cannot be exactly laid down, it is a part of his work which no composer can in conscience disregard. Those of our younger composers who have no intuitive gift for orchestral tone-colour and values would be wise to hear an orchestra every day, and also to learn two or three orchestral instruments, if possible one in each of the three main groups of strings, wood-wind and brass; they should at least be able to play them in a student's orchestra. Only by thus living in a sea of orchestral sound can a musician feel and learn the varied harmonic, rhythmic and thematic sonorities. Too many of our composers still do not think their symphonic creations upon the orchestra; instead they orchestrate their musical ideas. We want orchestral thoughts, not pianistic thoughts transcribed for orchestral instruments. We want also fewer solos for wind instruments accompanied by the strings. The wood-wind has been called the flower-garden of the orchestra and the clarinet the queen thereof, but in certain works, even by composers of the last twenty years, nothing palls so much as the long-winded, barren and monotonous clarinet solos. So far, no composer has shown an intuitive grasp and a knowledge of the individual technique of every instrument of the orchestra in so masterly a way as Hector Berlioz, who died over a half century ago.

In default of fixed rules for orchestral colouring some general, guiding statements may be made.

In future instrumentation, importance will probably be given to bringing out the essential note or notes of various chordal effects. This has been neglected in many works of the great masters. Far too little attention has been paid to the balance between the vertical and the horizontal musical line.

The possibilities of doubling the three primary constituents of the orchestra—the strings, wood-wind and brass—have been far too much disregarded. In all " doubling-up " of so-called themes, the highest registers will always tell to the hearers, whereas doubling in the unison, even upon two different instruments, tends to merge the tone but gives warmer colour. It is a pity to find quite a number of modern composers employing the celesta and the pianoforte in ignorance of the fact that the tones of these instruments are very easily covered. Like harps, they only tell when they are lightly surrounded by orchestral tone.

Insufficient advantage has been taken of the possibilities of showing up a particular line of thought, or a passage, or a harmonic combination, by nuances which are often contradictory; for instance, by several *fortes* against a background of *mezzo-pianos*, and vice versa. We know the Wagnerian *hervortretend* and Debussy's *dehors*, but there are composers who expect too much of conductors in this direction and who waste the time given to the preparation of new works because they will not mark their scores with judgment. Orchestral intensity is often far too conventionally marked.

Too much stress cannot be laid on the fact that chordal spacing greatly helps variety of colour. High registers always tend to give a brilliant, luminous effect; low registers, one which is heavier and gloomier.

It is also important to remember that the string colour palls least of all, and the colour of the percussion instruments very quickly. A well-known arrangement of *God Save the King* is a devilish example of what not to do. The *grosse caisse* and cymbals are struck on every note of the melody, instead of once only, at the place which every conductor should know is their one right place, namely, the summit of the melody.

We pass to the fascinating subject of possible future developments. New technique for the orchestra offers a far wider field than the new technique for keyed instruments which attracts so much interest. It must not for a moment be imagined that Wagner and Berlioz exhausted orchestral effects and colours. The contrary is proved by Strauss and Elgar, and by Ravel, Malipiero, Stravinsky and other moderns. Ravel in his *Rapsodie espagnole*, and his later *La Valse*, uses with a masterly brush, a colour scheme which is really distinctive and subtle. In May 1924 this master's orchestral version of Mussorgsky's *Pictures from an Exhibition* was first produced in Paris. The dreamy languor and sunlit sleepiness which Debussy put into his short but immortal masterpiece, *L'Après-midi d'un Faune*, gives a quite wonderful example of truthful orchestral colouring. Yet, even by Debussy the suave, velvety, dreamy and languorous colours obtainable, for instance, from the flutes and the clarinets, have not yet been fully discovered, any more than have the dramatic, harsh, metallic and sinister hues of the orchestra by any composer. Another modern master of orchestral colour is Delius, whose *Sea-Drift*, a work for soli, chorus and orchestra, is unique in the colour of its various musical combinations which truly reflect the elusiveness of Walt Whitman's poem. But the outstanding example of what the colourist can do is given by Richard Strauss in *Don Quixote*. He obtains humorous and bizarre effects, essential to his characterisation, by using the colour of the various instruments, particularly the middle sonorities and the lower brass. Richard Strauss richly clothes his musical thought with the enormous number of combinations of timbres and the wealth of glowing colour obtainable from the modern orchestra. No composer has drawn more colour than he from each individual instrument. We need only instance the viola-solo phrases in which Sancho Panza begs for more money, or the three notes on the piccolo when he scratches his head. It is by the shape of his themes and his use of colour that Strauss reaches the grotesque. He gives an orchestral picture which may be called Goyesque. His orchestral voices seem to take on tangible form.

There is no doubt that Stravinsky, in his three important ballets, discovers many new streaks of orchestral colour. He paints from a luminous, flaring pallet, like nothing anyone else has used, but one on which the colours are vivid rather than strident and are exceptionally few, so that an elastic flexibility is maintained. His *L'Oiseau de Feu* will always remain a masterpiece of modern orchestration.

An interesting new colour effect has lately been obtained by introducing into the orchestra the human voice without words, as in Scriabin's *Prometheus*, Ravel's ballet *Daphnis et Chloé*, Delius's *Song of the High Hills* and the single vocal line in Casella's *Couvent sur l'eau*. Apart from the use of this and other new instruments, there is no doubt that orchestral values are changing. Our wood-wind players have refined their tone-quality to such an extent, and the tone of the strings has been so much enlarged, that it has become difficult to make wood-wind solos tell. In England and France the oboes and bassoons, with their beautiful scales of even quality, have almost lost their " bite." The wood-wind colour of the orchestra does not "get through," as it once did. Hence, when we go to Germany, the first thing which strikes us is the " bite " of the oboes and bassoons, even while we dislike their " throaty " quality.

The composer of the future must not only use the orchestra in its present state of development but must expect that it will be further changed; for there is much room for improvement. The most perfectly disposed concert orchestra still has some very nasty holes in it. There is no strong tenor voice in the strings; the brass-bass needs reinforcement, the quality of the bass tuba is clumsy and hooty and does not blend with the trombone timbre. It is to be hoped that someone will shortly invent a bright, clear-toned brass-bass instrument of good intonation which will carry down the bass-trombone scale chromatically, and which will blend perfectly with the trombone quality in chordal work. There is at present a great difficulty in carrying one streak or seam of colour up and down a long range.

The younger composers should go on experimenting with orchestral colour. Thinking always orchestrally, they should try to put new life into the old, and create life in the new instruments and combinations of the modern orchestra.

In spite of all that is written about orchestral effects and colours we are still only on the fringe of possibilities. The modern harmonic experiments may evolve an entirely new and yet natural system. The endeavour should be to fill up orchestral gaps and to carry oneness of tone-quality through a larger range of pitches, rather than to work with massed orchestras which thicken while they strengthen the tone

and which tend to produce heaviness and muddiness. A certain tendency towards too much economy of orchestral material, no doubt encouraged by the wish to keep the pecuniary costs of orchestras down, should however be resisted. It is true that nothing is more educative than to draw the last breath of life out of the so-called chamber orchestra, but for further progress courage and adventure are necessary. It is well that composers should throw away the old fossilised palette, and such experiments as the recent employment of an entire band of flutes are to be welcomed. It is, moreover, a mistake to think that a very large orchestra is necessarily a noisy instrument on which to play or to which to listen. Its degree of noisiness depends not on the number of its players but on the size and acoustics of the hall in which it performs and the capacity of its conductor. Two cornets can be brassier and more blatant than the full complement of Wagnerian brass as used in *The Ring*.

We look for the composer who will possess an orchestral colour-vision wider than any known to us hitherto, as well as a musical idiom worthy of his instrument and his material. The rules of academic harmony are so out of date that they have come to seem childish, and the modern orchestra will so develop that, as advantage is taken of rhythmic possibilities, the composer will be able completely to change the organism of music. British composers have in the past entirely lacked the orchestral colour-sense, but there is no reason why some of the younger of the living men should not come to equal Ravel or Roussel. They are working in a colour-medium which deserves none of the old condemnatory epithets—monotonous, too massive, too thick and muddy. Of the progress of the orchestra it is difficult to prophesy definitely. But it may become so mighty and so varied as to inspire golden colour-visions. Since more than half a century ago, at the end of his *Grand Traité de l'instrumentation et d'orchestration*, Berlioz amused himself by imagining an ideal orchestra of 467 performers, we have indeed travelled a long way. The ideal festival orchestra of the present day should indeed inspire music which would be a wonder of colour. It would, we suggest, include the following players:

    30 1st Violins
    30 2nd Violins
    20 Violas
    20 Violoncellos
    16 Double-Basses
     2 Piccolos
     3 Flutes
     1 Alto Flute (Bass Flute)
     3 Oboes
     2 Oboes d'Amore
     2 Cors Anglais
     1 Heckelphone (Baritone Oboe)
     2 Small Clarinets
     3 Ordinary Clarinets
     2 Alto Clarinets (Bassett-Horns)
     1 Bass Clarinet
     1 Pedal-Clarinet
     3 Bassoons
     2 Double Bassoons and perhaps 4 Saxophones
            (S.A.T.B.)
     8 Horns
     4 Wagner Tubas
     4 Trumpets
     1 Bass Trumpet

1 Alto Trumpet
1 Alto Trombone
3 Tenor Trombones
1 Bass Trombone
1 Contra-Bass Trombone
1 Euphonium
1 Bass Tuba in F
1 BB flat Military Brass-Bass
3 Side-Drums
1 Tenor Drum
1 Bass Drum
1 Tambourine
1 Triangle
1 pair of large Cymbals
1 very large Gong
6 Kettle-Drums
An Octave of Tubular Bells
An Octave of Mushroom Bells
A Military Glockenspiel
A Celesta
A Xylophone
6 Harps
Organ

H. J. W.

ORCHESTRAL MUSIC in Austria, Britain, Germany, etc. See under headings of the various countries—AUSTRIAN ORCH. MUSIC, BRITISH, etc.

ORCHESTRAS. *AUSTRIA.* — **Vienna:** (i) *Phil. Concerts* (see special art. under V). (ii) *Orchesterverein Haydn;* condr. Camillo Horn. (iii) *Orchesterverein of Ges. der Musikfreunde.* (iv) *Konzertverein Orch.;* condr. Ferd. Löwe, to end of 1924 season.

BELGIUM.—**Brussels:** (i) *Concerts du Conservatoire;* condr. Léon du Bois (4 concerts a year). (ii) *Concerts populaires ;* dir. Henry Le Bœuf;* condr. M. Rühlmann. A grand concert every month during winter; others with smaller orch. and partly devoted to older music. (iii) *Houdred Orch.* **Antwerp:** Two symphony orchs., one cond. by Alpaerts de Vocht, the other by Mortelmans. See also art. BELGIUM, ORCH. CONCERTS IN.

CANADA.—**Toronto:** *New Symphony Orch.* condr. L. von Kunits. **Ottawa:** *Symphony Orch.* condr. F. D. Heins.

CZECHO-SLOVAKIA.—**Prague:** *Czechische Filharmonie,* founded 1901. Original condrs. L. V. Čelanský, K. Moor, Fr. Spilka, Oskar Nedbal (*qq.v.*); 1904-18, Vilém Zemánek; then Čelanský again, for short time; now (from 1919) Václav Talich (*q.v.*).

DENMARK. — **Copenhagen:** (i) *Musikforening* (Mus. Soc.), (see HAMMERICH, ANGUL; HORNEMANN, C. F. E.; and MALLING, OTTO). (ii) *Dansk Koncertforening* (see HELSTED, G. G.). (iii) *Tivoli Concerts.* (iv) *Folkekoncerterne* (Popular Concerts).

ENGLAND.—**London:** (i) *Royal Philharmonic Society,* founded 1813; 8 to 12 orch. concerts annually (see special art.). (ii) *Queen's Hall Orch.* founded 1895 (see special art.); condr. Sir Henry Wood. (iii) *London Symphony Orch.* founded in 1904, on co-operative principles. Famous visiting condrs. (iv) *R. Albert Hall Orch.* (v) *Goossens' Orch.* **Manchester:** *Hallé Orch.* founded 1857-8; present condr. Harty (see special art.). **Liverpool:** *Philharmonic Soc.* founded 1840; 8 to 10 concerts a year, under visiting condrs. Chorus-master, Dr. A. W. Pollitt. **Bournemouth:** *Municipal Orch.* condr. Sir Dan Godfrey (see art. on SIR DAN GODFREY).

FINLAND. — **Helsingfors:** (i) *Municipal Orch.;* condr. R. Kajanus; 2nd condr. L. Madetoja. (ii) *Konsertföreningen* (Concert Assoc.) condr. G. Schnéevoigt (*q.v.*).

FRANCE.—**Paris:** (i) *Société des Concerts du Conservatoire,* founded 1792; condr, from 1909, André Messager (see SOCIETIES). (ii) *Colonne Orch.,* founded 1873 by E. Colonne; condr. from 1910, Gabriel Pierné (see special art.). (iii) *Lamoureux Orch.,* founded 1881 by C. Lamoureux; condr. from 1923, Paul Paray (see special art.). (iv) *Pasdeloup Orch.,* founded 1861; re-establ. 1920 under Rhené-Baton (see special art.). (v) *Concerts Touche* (small orch.), There are also the orchs. of the *Soc. Haydn-Mozart-Beethoven,* founded 1895; *Soc. Bach,* 1906; *Concerts spirituels de la Sorbonne,* 1900; *Concerts populaires de l'orch.* 1905; *Concerts de la Schola,* 1903; *Concerts Sechiari,* 1906; *Concerts Hasselmans,* 1908; *Concerts Chaigneau,* 1911; *Concerts Monteux,* 1914; *Concerts Rouge* (see special art.); *Concerts Golschmann,* 1919 (see GOLSCHMANN). The Russ. condr. Kussevitzky gives series of orch. concerts at Opera House with his own orch. **Bordeaux:** *Soc. Ste.-Cécile,* founded 1843. **Rennes:** *Soc. des Concerts,* founded 1874. There are also *Concerts populaires* at Angers; Lille, 1876; Nancy, 1885; Havre, 1891; Marseilles, 1887; Toulouse, 1902; Lyons, 1904; Nantes, 1904; Dijon, 1920, etc.

GERMANY. — **Leipzig:** *Gewandhaus Orch.* condr. Wilhelm Furtwängler. **Berlin:** (i) *Orch. der Staatsoper;* condrs. Fritz Stiedry, Carl Ehrenberg, Otto Urack. (ii) *Philh. Orch.* condr. Hagel. (iii) *Blüthner Orch.* condr. Camillo Hildebrand. **Dresden:** (i) *Orch. der Staatsoper;* condrs. Fritz Busch and Kutzschbach. (ii) *Philh. Orch.* condr. Edwin Lindner. **Munich:** (i) *Orch. des Nationaltheaters;* condrs. Hans Knappertsbusch, R. Heger, H. Rohn. (ii) *Konzertverein Orch.* condrs. Hausegger and Grosz. **Stuttgart:** *Orch. des Württemburg Landestheaters;* condr. Leonhardt. **Carlsruhe:** *Orch. des Badischen Landestheaters;* condr. Fritz Cortolezis. **Sondershausen:** *Loh Orch.* condr. Corbach. **Breslau:** *Orch. des Stadttheaters;* condr. Pruwer. **Weimar:** *Orch. des Deutschen Nationaltheaters* (condr. vacant). **Cologne:** *Orch. des Stadttheaters* and *Gürzenich Orch.* condr. Abendroth.

There are also permanent orchs. in Mannheim, Darmstadt, Frankfort, Hanover, Cassel, Schwerin, Wiesbaden, Hamburg, Bremen, Lübeck, Mayence, Elberfeld, Essen, Magdeburg, Aix-la-Chapelle, Crefeld, Dortmund, Duisburg, Bochum, Düsseldorf, Chemnitz, Nuremberg.

HOLLAND. — **Amsterdam:** *Concertgebouw Orch.* founded 1883; condr. 1888-95, Willem Kes; from 1895, Willem Mengelberg. The leading orchestra (100 players) of Holland.

Gives between Oct. and May 2 symph. concerts weekly at Amsterdam (Thursday and Sunday), besides 5 popular concerts in the season, and, between May and July, 10 popular concerts. In winter season also concerts at The Hague (15); Rotterdam (13); Utrecht (4); Haarlem, Arnhem, Nijmegen and Leyden. R. Strauss, Mahler, Debussy, Ravel, Casella, etc., have cond. it in their own works. Since 1920 it is cond. from Jan. to March by Dr. Karl Muck; while Mengelberg is cond. the New York Philh. The 2nd condr. is Cornelis Dopper. This orch. played in Bergen, Norway, 1898; London, R. Strauss Fest. 1903;

Brussels, Antwerp, Paris, Frankfort, Hamburg, Berlin. The soc. *Het Concertgebouw* has also given (from 1920) chamber-music perfs., and (1922) united with the *Wagnervereeniging* in opera-performances. **The Hague:** *Residentie Orkest*; 80 members; condr. Peter van Anrooy. **Utrecht:** *Stedelijk Orkest*; 65 members; condr. Evert Cornelis. **Arnhem:** *Stedelijk Orkest*; 50 members; condr. M. Spanjaard. **Groningen:** *Orkestvereeniging*; 50 members; condr. Kor Kuiler.

HUNGARY.—**Budapest:** *Philharmonic Soc.* founded 1853 by Franz Erkel (*q.v.*); after him, came his son Alexander Erkel as leader and dir.; later Stephan Kerner. Since 1917 under Ernst von Dohnányi's dir. it arranges annually at least 10 orch. concerts in Budapest.

ITALY.—**Rome:** (i) *Augusteo Orch.*; various condrs. See special art. (ii) *Unione Nazionale Concerti* gives a large number of concerts each season. **Milan:** *Società dei Concerti Sinfonici*, founded 1912; cond. mostly by Toscanini. **Palermo:** *Associazione Palermitana Concerti Sinfonici*, founded 1922.

NORWAY.—**Christiania.** The *Orch. Soc.* (*Musikföreningen*) was founded by Grieg in 1871; it dissolved in 1919. Svendsen, Selmer, Holter, and lastly Karl Nissen, were its condrs. The *Nat. Theatre's Orch.* also dissolved in 1919. Both were succeeded by the *Philh. Soc.* endowed by the shipowner A. F. Klaveness; it also receives a municipal grant. Gives about 20 concerts a month. Permanent condrs. Georg Schnéevoigt, J. Halvorsen, I. Neumark, J. Eibenschütz. **Bergen.** The mus. soc. *Harmonien* (founded 1755) secured Grieg for condr. in 1880. Since then, it has been cond. by I. Holter, P. Winge, Washington-Magnus, J. Halvorsen, and now H. Heide. Supported by municipal grant in addition to F. Sundt's endowment and Grieg Fund support. 42 players, 8 concerts a year.

POLAND. — **Warsaw:** *Philharmonic Orch.* 100 members; gives usually 4 concerts weekly in Warsaw, in hall holding 2000 people. Dir. Roman Chojnacki; condr. Jósef Oziminski.

SCOTLAND.—*Scottish Orch.* founded 1887; 4 to 8 concerts a week during the season. Various condrs. (See special art.).

SOUTH AFRICA.—**Cape Town:** *Municipal Orch.* founded 1912; 45 players; subsidy of £8000 annually from municipality; condr. Leslie H. Heward. **Durban:** *Municipal Orch.* founded 1921; condr. Lyell-Taylor.

SPAIN.—**Madrid:** (i) *Orquesta Filarmonica*, founded 1914; condr. Bartolomé Pérez Casas (*q.v.*). (ii) *Orquesta Sinfonica*; condr. E. F. Arbós (*q.v.*). (iii) *Orquestra Pau Casals*, founded in 1919 by its condr. the famous cellist Pablo Casals. **Barcelona:** *Orquesta Sinfonica de Barcelona*, founded 1910 by Mestre Lamote de Grignon, its condr. The number of concerts given up to 1923 exceed 200; at every concert there must be at least one work by an Iberian compr. By this means, and through provincial tours, this Catalonian inst. is one of the most important elements of mus. culture in Spain. **Saragossa:** *Filarmonica*.

SWEDEN. — **Stockholm:** *Konsertföreningen*, founded 1902 (Tor Aulin). Newly organised 1914; condr. from 1922 Georg Schnéevoigt. **Gothenburg:** *G.'s Orkesterförening*, founded 1905; present condr. Ture Rangström. **Gäfle.** With State-subsidy from 1912; condr. Ruben Liljefors. **Norrköping.** With State-subsidy from 1913; condr. Ivar Hellman. **Falun.** Condr. Joel Olsson. **Helsingborg:** *Nordvestra Skånes Orkesterförening.* With State-subsidy from 1912; condr. Olaf Lidner. **Boras.** Condrs. V. E. Lundqvist and Knut Håkansson. And at **Malmö** and other towns.

SWITZERLAND.—**Zurich:** *Tonhalle-Gesellschaft*, founded 1868, with Dr. Fr. Hegar as condr. of the orch. Reconstituted 1895 (inauguration of new concert hall). Hegar remained condr. till 1906. Dr. Volkmar Andreae succeeded him. Gives 12 symphony concerts, a number of popular ones and 8 chamber-music recitals every winter. Consists of 70 members; 48 of them (engaged for the whole year with title to pension) are bound to play also in the theatre (opera and operetta) and in the summer concerts (cond. by Carl Wenz). The quartet of the soc. consists of W. de Boer, H. Schroer, P. Essek, Fr. Reitz. **Basle:** *Allgemeine Musikgesellschaft*, founded in 1876. First condr. of orch. Dr. Alfred Volkland; from 1902 Dr. Hermann Suter. Gives 11 symphony concerts, a number of popular ones and chamber-music recitals. Consists of 68 members. The str. quartet of the orch. consists of Fritz Hizt, Ernst Krüger, F. Kuchler, W. Treichler. **Geneva:** (i) *Orchestre de la Suisse Romande*, founded 1918; condr. E. Ansermet; 72 members. Gives 12 symphony concerts at Geneva, 8 at Lausanne and Neuchâtel, and numerous popular concerts. (ii) *Société de Musique Symphonique*; condr. A. Paychère.

U.S.A.—The cultivation of symph. music in U.S.A. has received a decided impetus within the last few decades. Many new orchs. have been establ. in large cities. Of these many have succumbed after a few years' struggle. Others have survived. In spite of the increased numbers of concert-goers, and of a real desire on the part of the mus. public to hear good orch. music, the supply of orch. concerts in some cities (notably New York) has exceeded the demand. Few, if any, existing organisations are wholly self-supporting. The newer organisations owe their continued existence to the guarantee either of a consortium of financial backers, or the munificence of a single individual who offers to make up the annual deficit or provides an endowment outright. The oldest, the New York Philh., was aided by a bequest in 1912 of $1,000,000 from Joseph Pullitzer; while the New York Symphony Soc. has received an annual donation from Mr. H. H. Flagler who has also provided an adequate endowment for the future. The Boston Symphony Orch. was for many years the only orch. in America wholly independent of the box-office. Its members were not required to add to their income by outside work. Financial security was guaranteed by the founder, Henry Lee Higginson. In 1918 Higginson relinquished the actual control of the orch. to a board of directors. Since his death in 1919, the orch. has had to rely partly on a guarantee fund raised by its directors. The Minneapolis, Philadelphia and Detroit orchestras have also made active campaigns for guarantee or endowment funds. It should be noted that almost all of these orchestras extend their activity beyond their home cities, giving concerts in larger and smaller cities in their vicinity, and sometimes making tours to more distant points. In May and June, 1920, the New York Symphony Orch. made a European tour, playing in France, Italy, Belgium, Holland and England. The more important symphony orchs. active since 1900 are:

New York: *Philh. Soc. of New York,* founded in 1842. Its recent condrs. have been Theodore Thomas (1877–91), Anton Seidl (1891–8), Emil Paur (1898–1902), a series of guest-condrs. (1902–4), Safonof (1905–9), Mahler (1909–11), Josef Stransky (1911–1923), Willem von Hoogstraten (from 1923). Consult H. E. Krehbiel, *The Philh. Soc. of New York* (Novello, 1892) and J. G. Huneker, *The Philh. Soc. of New York, and its 75th Anniversary* (The Soc. 1917). *New York Symphony Orch.,* active under this name since 1878, although its founder Dr. Leopold Damrosch had begun his regular work with this orch. with two series of subscription concerts in 1877. On death of founder in 1885, his son, Walter Damrosch, succeeded him and has conducted ever since. *National Symphony Orch.* gave its first concerts under the name of New Symphony Orch. 11 April, 1919, with Edgar Varese as condr. In the autumn of 1919 the new name was adopted and Artur Bodanzky became condr. In Jan. 1912, Mengelberg came as guest-condr. After the season of 1920–21 the orch. was merged with the New York Philh. *Russ. Symphony Orch.* began its activity in 1903. It was founded for the special cultivation of Russ. music, and introduced many works of Russ. comprs. in America. It gave the 1st complete perf. of Scriabin's *Prometheus* with colour-keyboard on March 20, 1915, and played Stravinsky's symphony in E flat for 1st time in America in 1916. In 1919 it ceased its regular concert activity in New York. Modest Altschuler cond. from beginning. Boston: *Boston Symphony Orch.* founded in 1881 by Henry Lee Higginson. First condr. was George Henschel, followed by Wilhelm Gericke (1884–9), Arthur Nikisch (1889–93), Emil Paur (1893–8), Wilhelm Gericke (1898–1906), Carl Muck (1906–8), Max Fiedler (1908–12), Carl Muck (1912–18), Henri Rabaud (1918–19), Pierre Monteux (from 1919). Chicago: *Theodore Thomas Orch.* organised by Theodore Thomas in 1891. On the death of Thomas in 1905, he was succeeded by Frederick A. Stock, who has cond. ever since except during a short interregnum in 1918–19, when the assistant-condr. Eric Delamater directed. *American Symphony Orch.* founded in 1915 by its condr. Glenn Dillard Gunn, for the express purpose of cultivating orch. music by Amer. comprs. Cincinnati: *Cincinnati Symphony Orch.* founded in 1895. After a short series of concerts conducted by F. Van der Stucken, Anton Seidl and Henry Schradieck, Van der Stucken was the sole condr. until 1907. After a 2 years' pause, Leopold Stokowski was condr. from 1909–12. He was followed by Ernst Kunmaid (1913–17), Eugène Ysaye (1918–22) and Fritz Reiner (from 1922). Cleveland: *Cleveland Symphony Orch.* organised in 1918; condr. Nikolai Sokolof (from 1918). Detroit: *Detroit Symphony Orch.* founded 1914; condrs. Weston Gales (1914–18), Ossip Gabrilowitsch (from 1918). Hartford: *Hartford Philh. Orch.* founded 1900; condrs. Richmond P. Paine (1900–2), John S. Camp (1902–11), Robert H. Prutting (1911–21), Henry Schmitt (from 1921). Los Angeles: *Los Angeles Symphony Orch.* founded 1897; condrs. Harvey Hamilton (1897–1913), Adolf Tandler (1913–20). Disbanded 1920. The *Philh. Orch.* founded 1919 by W. F. Clark; condr., Walter H. Rothwell (1919). Minneapolis: *Minneapolis Symphony Orch.* organised 1903 by Emil Oberhoffer (*q.v.*) who cond. until 1923, when he was succeeded by Henri Verbruggen. New Haven: *New Haven Symphony Orch.* grew out of student-orch. organised by Horatio Parker at Yale Univ., and began giving regular public concerts in 1896. Parker cond. until 1919; succeeded by

David Stanley Smith. Philadelphia: *Philadelphia Orch.* organised in 1900; condrs. Fritz Scheel (1900–7), Karl Pohlig (1907–12), Leopold Stokowski (from 1912). Pittsburgh: *Pittsburgh Symphony Orch.* organised 1896; condrs. Frederic Archer (1896–8), Victor Herbert (1898–1904), Emil Paur (1904–10). Disbanded in 1910. San Francisco: *San Francisco Symphony Orch.* organised 1909; condrs. Henry K. Hadley (1909–15), Alfred Hertz (from 1915). St. Louis: *St. Louis Symphony Orch.* founded 1907; condrs. Max Zach (1907–21), Rudolf Ganz (from 1921).—E.-H.

ORDENSTEIN, Heinrich. Ger. pianist and teacher; *b.* Worms, 7 Jan. 1856; *d.* Carlsruhe, 22 March, 1921. 1871–5, pupil of Leipzig Cons. (Wenzel, Coccius, Reinecke, Jadassohn, Richter, Paul); after concert-tour with Mme. Peschka-Leutner and Leopold Grützmacher, stud. at Paris; 1879–81, music-master at Countess Rehbinder's School, Carlsruhe; 1881–2, teacher at Kullak's Acad. Berlin; 1884, establ. Grand-Ducal Cons. Carlsruhe, which he dir. till his death.
Guide to Pf. Literature (Leipzig, 1912); *History of Music at Carlsruhe* (1916).—A. E.

OREFICE, Giacomo. Ital. compr. and critic; *b.* Vicenza, 27 Aug. 1865; *d.* Milan, 22 Dec. 1922. Gained diploma in 1885 at Liceo Mus. at Bologna where he was a pupil of Luigi Mancinelli and Alessandro Busi. In 1909, prof. of compn. at Cons. of Milan, which position he occupied until his death. From 1920, mus. critic of *Il Secolo.* As a compr. one must mention his operas: *Mariska* (Turin, 1889); *Consuelo,* (Bologna, 1895); *Il Gladiatore* (publ. by Tedeschi, Milan; perf. Madrid, 1898); *Chopin* (a discussed work, interwoven with melodies of Chopin; produced at Teatro Lirico, Milan, 1901); *Cecilia* (Vicenza, 1902); *Mosè* (Genoa, 1905); *Pane altrui* (Venice, 1907); *Radda* (Milan, 1913). Nearly all these are publ. by Sonzogno, Milan. O. has also left much symph. and chamber music: symphonies, sonatas, orch. pieces, pf. music, songs, etc. He was a very cultured musician (had gained his degree in jurisprudence), and did excellent work as a teacher, propagandist, lecturer, and writer. He helped materially to elevate Ital. mus. culture. To him we are indebted for an ed. of Monteverdi's *Orfeo,* and the revival of other old Ital. music. As a writer, we mention his monograph on *Luigi Mancinelli* (Rome, 1921, Ausonia), and various important arts. in the *Rivista Musicale Italiana.*—D. A.

OREL, Dobroslav. Czechoslovak writer on music; *b.* Ronov, 1870. Ph.D.; music-teacher at a Prague school which has a fine children's choir; prof. of mus. science at Bratislava (Pressburg) Univ.; writer on Czech Middle Ages and church music.—V. St.

ORNSTEIN, Leo. Amer. pianist, compr. *b.* Krementchug, Russia, 11 Dec. 1895. Stud. at Petrograd Cons. Went to New York 1906; stud. pf. under Mrs. Thomas Tapper at Inst. of Mus. Art. *Début* as pianist in New York at New Amsterdam Theatre, 5 March, 1911. Gave recitals in Christiania, Paris and London. Attracted much attention with a series of recitals of modern and futurist pf.-music in London in 1914 and in New York, 1915. Toured U.S.A. from 1915 to 1917.

A pianist of quite unusual ability, O. has also composed much music, chiefly for pf. Among his unpubl. works are a pf. concerto, op. 44; a symph. poem, *The Fog*, op. 47; an orch. suite, *The Life of Man*. A futurist pf. piece often played by the compr. in his pf. recitals is a *Danse Sauvage* (*Wild Man's Dance*). His op. numbers rise to over 80. He has allied himself with the ultra-modernists, rivalling Schönberg and Stravinsky in the boldness of his tonal conceptions, and in the heaping up of dissonances, as well as in his repudiation of all canons of form. His later pieces, however, are more simple.

Vn. sonata, op. 31 (C. Fischer, 1915); *Three Russian Impressions*, vn. and pf. op. 37 (Ditson, 1916); cello sonata, op. 52 (C. Fischer, 1918); *7 Moments Musicals*, pf. op. 8 (Norsk Musikforlag, 1913); *6 Lyric Fancies*, pf. op. 10 (A. P. Schmidt, 1911); *2 pf. pieces*, op. 13: No. 1, *Impression de la Tamise*; No. 2, *Danse Sauvage* (*Wild Man's Dance*) (London, Schott, 1920, 1915); *6 Water Colours*, pf. op. 80 (C. Fischer, 1921); other pf. pieces: op. 4 (Ditson, 1912); op. 5, and without opus numbers (New York, Breitkopf, 1918); op. 7 (C. Fischer, 1915); op. 41 (C. Fischer, 1918); op. 11, 16, 20 (London, Schott, 1915, 1914); songs (C. Fischer, 1915). Consult F. H. Martens, *Leo Ornstein : the Man—his Ideas—his Works* (New York, Breitkopf, 1918), and C. L. Buchanan in *The Musical Quarterly*, April 1918.—O. K.

ORREGO, M. A. Chilean compr. Has utilised the forms of the national *tonados* and *zamacueca*, a species of Cordillerean *fandango*, in his music.—F. H. M.

ORSI, Romeo. Ital. clarinettist; *b.* Como, 18 Oct. 1843; *d.* Milan, 11 June, 1918. For many years, from 1873, prof. at Milan Cons. where he had been a pupil. He enjoyed great celebrity as concert-player, both in Italy and abroad. One of founders, and for 11 years vice-president, of Società Orchestrale della Scala. He founded in Milan a large mus. instr. factory, to which he gave his name. He invented and constructed new types of instrs., such as a bass clarinet in A, a bass flute, and various characteristic percussion instrs. of which modern composers have taken advantage. He publ. instructive methods and several pieces for his own instrument.—D. A.

OSELIO, Gina. Norwegian m.-sopr. singer; *b.* Christiania, 19 Nov. 1858. Stud. under Mrs. Stenhammer and Fritz Arlberg in Stockholm; under Mme. Marchesi in Paris. *Début* 1879 at R. Opera House, Stockholm, as Leonora in *La Favorita*; sang in 1882 at Padua, as Azucena in *Il Trovatore*, in a manner which made her famous in Italy. Appeared in Florence, Palermo, Rome, Venice. Concerts in Paris, 1882 and 1897; appeared 1885 and 1887, in R. Opera House in Budapest. Has since sung in large number of European theatres, at Her Majesty's Theatre in London, at the opera houses in Berlin, Leipzig, Milan, Copenhagen, Stockholm and Petrograd. Besides above rôles, she has sung Marguerite in *Faust*, in *Mefistofele* (Boito), Carmen in Bizet's opera, Elizabeth in *Tannhäuser*, Desdemona in *Otello*, Brünnhilde in *Valkyrie*, etc. Gave concerts in the Nobles' Hall in Moscow and in other cities. In Christiania, she appeared in 1891 and following years as Marguerite, Carmen,

Azucena and other rôles, and was received with enormous enthusiasm. Married in 1893 Björn Björnson, a son of the famous poet, and dir. of National Theatre in Christiania. King Oscar II conferred on her the distinction *Litteris et Artibus*, and she also holds one or two foreign orders. Since the dissolution of her marriage in 1908, she has withdrawn herself more and more from public life, and now lives in Paris. She is the most eminent vocalist Norway has hitherto possessed. At its best her voice was of unique power, brilliance and beauty, while her technique and vocalisation, as well as her histrionic abilities, were exceptionally fine. Amongst Northern vocalists she is surpassed only by the "Swedish nightingales," Jenny Lind and Christina Nilsson.—R. M.

OSTRČIL, Otakar. Czech compr. condr. *b.* Smíchov, 1879. Stud. compn. under Zdenko Fibich, 1895–1900; attended Univ. of Prague at same time; prof. at Commercial Acad. Prague, 1901; condr. (1909) of amateur orch. *Orchestrální Sdružení* (till 1922); 1914, opera dir. Vinohrady Theatre, Prague, and when this closed in 1919, dramaturg at National Theatre, Prague; on the death of Karel Kovařovic (1920) became, and is still, opera dir. Condr. Smetana Festival, Prague 1924. In his earlier works he seems to have sought his whole inspiration in Fibich. Later on the progressive modernising of the expression rendered his individuality more independent. Since his opera *Poupě*, this development has been completed. Under Mahler's influence his polyphony especially became more complicated, and this, in conjunction with the independent melodic writing for all voices and their atonality, has resulted in great harmonic intrepidity. We find in his works more of manly energy than of delicate expression of feeling. There is something objectivising about his instr. music—his feelings are sternly held in check. Among younger Czech writers he belongs to those in whom the intellectual elements play the largest part.

2 orch. suites (op. 2, 14); tone-poem, *Fairy-Tale*; 2 melodramas (op. 6, 8); ballad, *Osifelo dítě*, v. and orch. (all publ. by M. Urbánek); str. 4tet; symphony; symphonietta; *Impromptu*, orch. Operas: *Vlasta's Death*; *Kunala's Eyes*; *Poupě* (*The Bud*); *Legend of Erin* (publ. Foersterova Společnost). Choral works: *Czech Christmas Legend*; *Legend of St. Zita*; *The Stranger Guest*; 3 songs (all publ. by Hudební Matice). Consult O. Payer, *O. O.* (1912).—V. St.

ÖSTVIG, Karl Aagard. Norwegian dramatic t. singer; *b.* Christiania, 17 May, 1889. Matriculated 1908; attended Military School; stud. singing under W. Kloed; afterwards trained for 4 years in Cologne under Steinbach and Walter. *Début* 1914 at Opera House in Stuttgart, where he afterwards took an engagement for 5 years. Was offered in 1919 an engagement on generous terms at the State Opera House in Vienna, and is still working there. In Norway O. made his *début* in 1915 as concert-singer; appeared at National Theatre as Don José in *Carmen*; subsequently one or two rôles at short-lived Opéra-Comique. Every summer he visits his native land and gives concerts. Chief rôles: Lohengrin,

Parsifal and other Wagnerian heroes, Don José, Manrico, Pinkerton, etc.—R. M.

O'SULLIVAN, Denis. Barit. singer; *b.* San Francisco, 1868; *d.* 1908. Stud. singing under Vannuccini (Florence) and Santley (London) In 1895, 1st appearance, in London concerts. In opera, made his *début* in Dublin, with Carl Rosa Opera Co. As an operatic singer, was successful in Wagnerian parts as well as in Ital. opera. The success of Stanford's *Shamus O'Brien* was in great measure due to his fine singing and acting of the hero's part. He was an excellent musician, a subtle interpreter and a fine actor, and has been called " Erin's best-beloved singer." His fortune was involved in the San Francisco earthquake of 1906, and he started off on an Amer. tour, but died suddenly. In England and Ireland he was best appreciated in his vocal recitals.—W. St.

OTAÑO, P. Nemesio. Span. compr. orgt. and scholar; *b.* Azcoitia (Guipuzcoa) in 1880. Member of Jesuit Order. Pupil in compn. of Vicente Arregui. Founder of the *Schola Cantorum* of Comillas, the publ. house *Orfeo* and the review *Música Sacro-Hispana.* Publ. the *Antología de Organistas Españoles,* a remarkable coll. of both early and modern Span. organ music. He is one of leading Span. folk-lorists; and a recognised authority on the old and modern religious music of Spain.

Pf.: *Las Cavaducas*; *Remembranzas*. Chorus: *Basa Chorichu*; *La Montaña*; *Canción Montañesa*; *Negra Sombra*; *Canción del Carretero*. Songs for v. and pf. A folk-lore essay *El Canto Popular Montañés*. (Unión Musical Española.) *Orfeo* Edition, Madrid; Lazcano & Mared, Bilbao.)—P. G. M.

OTESCU, J. Norma. Rumanian compr. and condr. *b.* Bucharest in 1888. Pupil at Cons. there (under Kiriak and Castaldi), then Paris Cons. (Widor), and *Schola Cantorum* (under d'Indy). Dir. of Bucharest Cons. since 1918. A founder of the Lyric Soc. of Opera, and its president until 1922. When this soc. became a State inst., he was appointed 1st condr. of the Rumanian Opera (*q.v.*). Took Enescu Composition Prize in 1912.

All his compns. remain in ms. There are several symph. poems, three of which (*Le Temple de Gnide,* 1907; *Narcisse,* 1909; *Din bătrani*) are founded on popular Rumanian themes. Also Poem for vn. and orch. *Les Enchantements d'Armide*; music for a scene of *L'Ilderim* (by Queen Marie of Rumania); a ballet, *Ileana Cosinzeana*; many songs.—C. Br.

OTHEGRAVEN, August von. Ger. compr. *b.* Cologne, 2 June, 1864. Pupil of Cologne Cons.; scholar at Mozart Inst.; 1889, teacher of pf., choral and opera ensemble, Cologne Cons.

Fairy-play, *The Sleeping Princess* (Cologne, 1907); operettas: *Poldi's Wedding* (Cologne, 1912); *My Goddess,* op. 21 (barit., chorus, orch.); *Life of Mary* (Cologne, 1919); many songs; choral works.—A. E.

OUDRID Y SEGURA, Cristóbal. Span. compr. *b.* Badajoz, 7 Feb. 1829. Contemporary and follower of Gaztambide. Wrote many stage-works. His *El Molinero de Subiza* is one of most representative works of last period of Span. mus. decadence.—P. G. M.

OZIMIŃSKI, Józef. Polish violinist, orch. condr. *b.* Warsaw, 1877. Pupil of Stiller and Barcewicz (vn.) and Noskowski (theory) at Warsaw Cons. From 1901, 1st violinist of Warsaw Philh., of which he became conductor in 1910.—Zd. J.

P

PABLO, Vicente. Uruguay pianist; *b.* Montevideo, 1880. Stud. in Cons. La Lira, Montevideo, completing his training in Europe under Busoni and Vianna da Motta. Returning to Montevideo, he founded Cons. Uruguay (with Avelino Beños, cellist, and Edouard Fabini, violinist). This Cons. was immediately successful and to-day has 14 branches throughout Uruguay. Under initiative of P. and his associates, the Soc. of Chamber-Music was founded, a notable factor in mus. culture of the country; first concert 1910; since then over 120 perfs. (1 given at Wagnerian Association of Buenos Ayres).—A. M.

PACHECO, José Fernández. Span. compr. *b.* Madrid, 1874. Ex-assistant-condr. Teatro Real, Madrid; music-master, San Antonio de los Alemanes Ch.; chief reader for Unión Musical Española. He excels in Span. music of a light character, having to his credit some of the best and most mus. productions in that particular style. Has also written *zarzuelas* and some church music. (Unión Musical Española, Madrid; Enoch, London, etc.).—P. G. M.

PACHMANN, Vladimir de. Russ. pianist; *b.* Odessa, 27 July, 1848. First stud. under his father (prof. of Roman law at Vienna Univ. amateur violinist and author of a manual on harmony); then pf. and theory under Dachs and Bruckner at Vienna Cons. *Début,* Odessa 1869; toured Russia that year; then withdrew himself for 8 years' further study, appearing at Leipzig and Berlin, withdrawing himself again for yet another 2 years. Then appeared in Vienna, Paris and London (1882) and in U.S.A. 1892. Has toured continuously since then. Order of Danebrog from King of Denmark, 1885; R. Philh. Soc. Medal, London, 1916. Married Eng. pianist, Maggie Oakey, 1884, since divorced. His fame is due chiefly to his playing of Chopin's music, which is transfigured under his fingers by his exceptional temperament and unbridled individuality. His mastery of nuance in soft playing is unrivalled.—E.-H.

PACHULSKI, Henryk. Polish compr. pf.-teacher; *b.* Lazy, 4 Oct. 1859. Stud. pf. under Strobl and theory under Moniuszko and Żeleński at Warsaw Cons.; afterwards under Nicolas Rubinstein and Pabst in Moscow. In 1886, prof. of pf. Moscow Cons. until 1917. Has publ. many pf. works, sonatas, variations, fantasias, orch. compns. and pieces for cello and pf.—Zp. J.

PADEREWSKI, Ignacy Józef. Polish pianist and composer; eminent statesman; *b.* Kuryłówka (Podolien), 6 Nov. 1860. In 1872, pupil of Janota, Strobl and Żeleński at Warsaw Conservatoire. In 1879, became teacher of piano there. In 1881, studied under Kiel and Urban in Berlin; in 1884, went to Leschetizky in Vienna. Paderewski's renown began with his first Vienna concert in 1887. Since 1893 he has been the best-known and most highly remunerated pianist in the world. In 1910, he raised in Cracow a great monument in remembrance of the Polish victory over the Prussians in 1410. From the beginning of the war, he gave up playing at concerts and devoted himself to philanthropy and politics. He worked hard to turn public opinion and the attention of the governments of the Allied and Associated Powers to the necessity of restoring Poland. In 1919, he became President of the Polish Republic and sat at the Peace Conference at Versailles. In 1922–3, appeared again as pianist in America, Paris and London.

Opera, *Manru* (libretto by Alfred Nossig, founded on Kraszewski's romance *The Hut behind the Village*), 1901; symphony in A mi. *Poland,* with patriotic, symbolic programme, op. 20; *Polish Fantasia,* pf. and orch.: op. 19; pf. concerto, A mi. op. 17; sonata, vn. and pf. op. 13; pf. sonata, E mi. op. 21; Variations in E mi. (with a splendid final fugue), op. 23; Variations in A mi. op. 14. Many short pf. pieces and about 30 songs.—Zp. J.

PAGOLA GOYA, Beltrán. Span. compr. *b.* San Sebastian (Guipuzcoa), 28 Feb. 1878. Lecturer on modern Fr. music; adherent of folklore school. Lives at San Sebastian, where he is a prof. at the Acad. Municipal.

Sinfonía Vasca, orch.; sonata, pf. and cello; pf. sonata on Basque popular airs; *Erexia, elegia-zorzico,* left-hand study for pf.; pf. suite, *Humoradas Vascas.* —P. G. M.

PAHISA, Jaime. Contemporary Span. compr. of the Catalonian group. He represents a modern tendency based on polyphony, opposed to the Neo-Russ. school. Some of his symph. works have been perf. in Germany as well as Spain. Lives and works in Barcelona, his native town.

Orch.: *De las profundidades a las alturas; El Combate; En las Costas Mediterráneas; Estudio sinfónico;* Overture on a popular theme. V. and orch.: *Balada.* Str. orch.: *Andante.* Lyric dramas: *La Morisma; Gala Plácidia; La Prisión de Lérida; Cañigó.* Pf.: *Seis pequeñas fugas a dos voces; Preludio y grandes fugas a dos voces; Seis pequeñas fugas a tres voces; Piezas líricas.* V. and pf.: *Tres Balades.* (Unión Musical Española.)—P. G. M.

PALADILHE, Émile. Fr. compr. *b.* Montpellier, 3 June, 1844. A child-prodigy; entered Paris Cons. at 9. *Prix de Rome,* 1860 (with cantata *Ivan IV*). Member of Committee of Studies of Cons.; has a seat in the Institut. His music sometimes recalls Meyerbeer.

Symphony; 2 masses. For stage: *Le Passant* (1-act, 1872), from which is taken the *Sérénade* (well-known under title *Mandolinata*); *L'Amour africain* (1875); *Suzanne* (1878); *Patrie* (1886).—A. C.

PALLEMAERTS, Edmundo. Argentine pianist, compr. *b.* Malines, 1867. Stud. at R. Cons. Brussels, under Kufferath and De Greef. Went to Buenos Ayres in 1889, and in 1894 founded the Argentino Cons. of Music, which he directs.

Symphony in D; suite, *Fantasia Argentina;* cantata, *Bognoguat* (given at Brussels); many songs, pf. and str. pieces.—A. M.

PALMER, Sir Samuel Ernest, Bart. Eng. music patron; *b*. 28 March, 1858. Educated Malvern Coll. and in Germany; founder of the R.C.M. Patron's Fund; donor of two scholarships to the Musicians' Company at the Guildhall School of Music, besides many other gifts towards the encouragement of British comprs. and executants. Member of Council of R.C.M. and of R. Choral Soc. Committee of Management. Was presented with Honorary Freedom of Worshipful Company of Musicians, in recognition of his services to music.—E.-H.

PALMGREN, Maikki. See JÄRNEFELT-PALM-GREN.

PALMGREN, Selim. Finnish compr. pianist; *b*. Pori (Björneborg), 16 Feb. 1878. Stud. at Helsingfors Music Inst. 1895–9; later in Germany (Ansorge, Berger, Busoni) and Italy. Gave concerts in Finland and abroad. 1909–12, condr. in Turku. Now (1923) teacher of compn. at Eastman Cons., Rochester, New York. His compns. are noteworthy for their flowing melody and harmonic invention, as well as for their effective colouring. His themes are often taken from folk-music. The impressionistic pf. pieces and the fine male choruses are the outstanding features of his productivity.

Opera, *Daniel Hjort* (after J. J. Wecksell's drama); 2 pf. concertos, *The River* and *Metamorphoses*; numerous pf. pieces (Suite, op. 3; *Fantasia*, op. 6; 2 sonatas; 24 preludes; *Finnish Lyric*; *Spring*, etc.); orch. suites: *The Seasons* (*From Finland*); *Pastorale*; stage music to Larin Kyösti's fairy-play *Tuhkimo* (*Cinderella*); male choruses with orch.; numerous songs; choral works.—T. H.

PALUMBO, Costantino. Ital. pianist; *b*. Torre Annunziata (Naples), 30 Nov. 1843. Stud. at Naples Cons., taking pf. under Lanza and compn. under Mercadante. Gained much success as pianist in Italy, France and England. In 1873, appointed prof. of pf. at Cons. of Naples, and he has brought out some excellent pupils. Author of several operas, amongst which we mention *Pierluigi Farnese*, (book by Boito), a symphony, a str. 4tet, a concerto, various orch. pieces and much elegant pf. music.—D. A.

PANDER, Oskar von. Ger. condr. and compr. *b*. Agershof, Livonia, 31 March, 1883. Stud. economy and philosophy; 1908–11, theory of music at Munich (Rudolf Louis); 1911–1912, compn. under Gernsheim at Acad. for Art, Berlin; 1912–13, Korrepetitor at Ger. Opera House, Charlottenburg; 1913–14, condr. at Mayence Stadttheater; 1915, Lübeck; 1915–16, 1st condr. at Kiel; 1916–19 at Halle-o-S.; 1919–22 at Darmstadt; since 1921, condr. of Rühl Choral Soc. Frankfort-o-M.; since 1920 of Choral Union and Concert Soc. Offenbach.

Ballad, C mi. for pf. (Breitkopf); orch. arr. of Mussorgsky's *Songs and Dances of Death*. Of numerous unpubl. compns., the songs and pf. trio in A ma. have been most performed.—A. E.

PANIZZA, Ettore. Condr. *b*. (of Ital. parents) at Buenos Ayres, 12 Aug. 1875. Stud. at Milan Cons., compn. under Saladino and Ferroni, and pf. under Frugatta. He began his career as orch. condr. at the Costanzi in Rome, passing on to other leading Ital. theatres, and to La Scala, Milan. Also went to Spain, Paris and London for important seasons. Is a very capable concert condr. He has written 3 operas: *Medio evo latino* (Genoa, 1900) publ. by Ricordi; *Aurora* (Buenos Ayres, 1908); *Bisanzio* (not yet perf.); also some symph. and chamber music. We also are indebted to him for a new ed. of Berlioz's *Treatise of Orchestration*, with an appendix (Ricordi).—D. A.

PANZNER, Karl. Ger.-Czechoslovak condr. R. prof. *b*. Teplitz-Schönau, 2 March, 1866. Stud. in Dresden; condr. at Sondershausen, Elberfeld, Bremen, Leipzig, Berlin, Hamburg, Düsseldorf, at which last-named place he followed Buths and cond. the Mus. Fest. of the Ger. Soc. of Music (Allg. Deutscher Musikverein) in 1922.—E. S.

PAOLANTONIO, Francisco. Argentine compr. and condr. *b*. Buenos Ayres, 1885. Stud. at Rome and Naples. Orch. condr. at theatres in Italy. Now at La Scala, Milan. Is a sympathetic and imaginative compr. Symph. Prelude in D; many songs and pf. pieces.—A. M.

PAPIER-PAUMGARTNER, Rosa. Austrian opera singer and teacher; *b*. Baden, near Vienna, 18 Sept. 1858. The best singer at the Vienna Opera, which she left in 1891, when appointed prof. at Cons. To her, Mahler owed his call to Vienna (*cf*. his letter to P., in coll. publ. by Tal, Vienna). Married Hans Paumgartner, pianist and critic, in 1881. Her son, Bernhard Paumgartner, Mus.D., is dir. of the Mozarteum at Salzburg and comp. the opera *Das heisse Eisen* (*The Hot Iron*), perf. 1922.—P. ST.

PAPINI, Guido. Violinist; *b*. Camagiore, near Florence, 1 Aug. 1847. Pupil of Giorgetti; *début* under his direction at Florence, 1860; then leader of a chamber-music soc.; 1874, appeared in London at Mus. Union, the Crystal Palace, the Old and New Philh. etc. In 1876, played at Pasdeloup Concerts and at the Bordeaux Philh. In 1893, chief vn. prof. at R. Irish Acad. of Music, Dublin. With Esposito, he did much for chamber-music in Dublin, especially at the classical recitals of the R. Dublin Soc. His influence as teacher at the Acad. was very great in bringing forward new talent. In 1896 he resigned his post owing to ill-health, and returned to London, devoting most of his time to compn. His works include an excellent Violin School, transcriptions and smaller pieces for vn. and cello, distinguished by facile flow of melody.—W. ST.

PÂQUE, Marie Joseph Léon Désiré. Belgian compr. *b*. Liège, 21 May, 1867. Stud. Liège Cons., where he became assistant-prof. Then went abroad; taught pf., organ and compn. at Sofia, Athens, Lisbon, and later gave concerts and lectures in Switzerland, Italy, France and Germany. Settled in Paris, 1914, to compose. P. is a "musician who thinks." He is the exponent of "rational music," based on the principle of "constant joining on," a form of development in opposition to thematic unity, display of themes followed by development in sections. His music, which is very independent in character, tends towards an almost atonal polyphony in which the parts each follow their own path freely. The mus. theories which govern the compn. of his works do not however detract from their spontaneous charm. Few of his works are published:

2 symphonies; 2 overtures; pf. 5tet and 4tet; sonatas, vla. and pf. (op. 27), vn. and pf. (op. 32), pf. (op. 68, 69, 70); organ concerto; *Requiem* (op. 41); *Vaïma*, lyrical drama, etc.—C. V. B.

PARAY, Paul. Fr. compr. and condr. *b.* Tréport, 24 May, 1886. Stud. at Cons. Paris; *Prix de Rome*, 1911; since the death of Chevillard (1923) 1st condr. of Concerts Lamoureux.

Sonata for pf. and vn.; str. 4tet; symph. poems, *La Mort d'Adonis* and *Artémis troublée* (1922).—A. C.

PARELLI, Attilio. Ital. compr. and condr. *b.* Monteleone d'Orvieto (Perugia), 31 May, 1874. Gained diploma in 1899 at R. Liceo Mus. di Santa Cecilia, Rome (school of De Sanctis), and devoted himself at once to orch. conducting, giving excellent proofs of his capacity in principal Ital. cities and in Paris. He then went to America, where he was a colleague of Campanini, at Manhattan Opera House; then at Chicago, Philadelphia, and principal cities of United States with the Chicago Grand Opera Company. He also cond. successful symphony concerts. As a compr. he gained great success with his 1-act opera *I dispettosi amanti*, first perf. Philadelphia, 1912, then played at many other theatres (Covent Garden, London, 10 March, 1924) (publ. by Schirmer, New York). He has also comp. the operas *Hermes* (Genoa, 1906); *Fanfulla* (Trieste, 1921), and several orch. works.—D. A.

PARENT, Armand. Violinist; *b.* Liège, 5 Feb. 1863. Naturalised Fr. First prize, Liège Cons. Solo vn. Bilse Orch. after Thomson and Ysaye. Particularly well known in France as founder of str. quartet that bears his name. He has done much for popularisation of modern music. Gave 1st perf. of 2nd quartet and pf. and vn. sonata of Vincent d'Indy (dedicated to Parent), pf. quartet of Chausson, Magnard's trio, trios of Albert Roussel (dedicated to him) and Lekeu, and many works of Vreuls, Turina, Guy Ropartz, and Le Flem. For years, one of the very few to play the works of d'Indy, Chausson, Magnard, Ravel and Brahms. A compr. of great merit, he has written a str. 4tet; a pf. and vn. sonata; pf. compns.; songs. As a master, he gives in his *Schola Cantorum* class-instruction which combines happily classic formula with an appreciation of modern music.—M. P.

PARETTO, Graciela. Contemporary leading operatic s. singer; *b.* Barcelona, Spain. Excels in coloratura style. Perf. at Metropolitan Opera House, New York; Teatro Real, Madrid; Liceo, Barcelona; San Carlo, Naples, and all principal opera houses. First appeared in London in *La Traviata*, Covent Garden, 1919.—P. G. M.

PARIBENI, Giulio Cesare. Ital. compr. and writer; *b.* Rome, 27 May, 1881. Took degree

in arts at R. Univ. of Rome; diploma in compn. at R. Liceo Mus. di Santa Cecilia. Began career as condr.; then (1911–15) undertook the artistic dir. of the firm of Sonzogno in Milan. Since 1914, teacher of harmony and cpt. at R. Cons. in Milan. Compr. of several symph. works, also sacred and chamber-music (some publ. by Sonzogno). Amongst his books are a *Storia e teoria della antica musica greca*, (Milan, 1912, Sonzogno), and an interesting monograph on *Muzio Clementi* (Milan, 1922, Il Primato).—D. A.

PARIGI, Luigi. Ital. writer on music; *b.* Settimello (Florence), 14 July, 1883. Founded in Florence the review *La Critica Musicale*. Author of Index to first 20 years of *Rivista Musicale Italiana* (*Ital. Mus. Review*) (see PERIODICALS); of a vol. on *Il momento italiano* (Florence, 1921, Vallecchi), and numerous arts. in newspapers and reviews.—D. A.

PARIS, NATIONAL OPERA HOUSE. See THÉÂTRE NATIONAL.

PARKER, Denne. Scottish contr. singer; *b.* Edinburgh, 22 June, 1889. Stud. at R.A.M. London, and later under Sir George Henschel. Sang at Gloucester Mus. Fest. 1922; Birmingham Univ. Song-Recitals, 1922; Edinburgh Reid Orch. Concerts, 1921–3; toured America and Canada, 1923; has lectured and given frequent recitals for the Franco-Scottish Soc., the Edinburgh Bach Soc., the British Ital. League, etc.; and adjudicated at Londonderry Feis, Dublin Feis, Plymouth, Buxton, Mansfield, Cleethorpes, and other Eng. festivals.—G. B.

PARKER, George. Eng. barit. singer; *b.* Leeds, 24 Nov. 1882. Choirboy in Leeds Parish Ch.; then trained as mining engineer and held positions as colliery manager, singing during this time as an amateur; appointed to choir at Eton Coll. (6 months); then Manchester Cath. choir (1 year); Westminster Abbey as lay-vicar; later a Gentleman of His Majesty's Chapels Royal (resigned 1920); appeared at London Coliseum and in provincial music-halls as leading singer in Elgar's *Fringes of the Fleet*, the compr. conducting; created and played part of Desert Lover in Oscar Asche's *Chu Chin Chow* at His Majesty's; appeared at Hereford Fest. and leading concerts, 1921; Gloucester Fest. 1922; sang opera with Carl Rosa Co., H. B. Phillips Co. and with National Opera Co. (Amfortas and Kurwenal). A singer of great intelligence with a very even voice of good tone.—E.-H.

PARKER, Henry Taylor. Amer. journalist; *b.* Boston, 29 April, 1867. Stud. at Harvard 1886–9. From 1892–1904, correspondent and critic of various New York and Boston newspapers. Since 1905, music critic of *Boston Transcript*. Author of *Eighth Notes*, essays on music (Dodd, Mead, 1922).—J. M.

PARKER, Horatio William. Amer. compr. *b.* Auburndale, near Boston, Mass., U.S.A., 15 Sept. 1863; *d.* Cedarhurst, N.Y., 18 Dec. 1919. Son of an architect; first mus. education from his mother. Then stud. theory under Stephen Emery and G. W. Chadwick in Boston. For a time was orgt. in Dedham, Mass.; 1881–4, stud. in Munich under Rheinberger; 1885–7, orgt. and music-master at Cath. School of St. Paul's in Garden City, Long Island, New York. After a short period as orgt. of St. Andrew's in New York, was orgt. of Holy Trinity Ch. in the same city (1888–93), teaching at the same time at National Cons.; 1893–1901, orgt. of Trinity Ch. Boston. 1894, prof. of music at Yale Univ., New Haven, Conn. Under his guidance the music department of this univ. developed into one of the best in U.S.A. From the beginning, Parker laid great stress on the cultivation of symph. music among the students. He conducted regular concerts of the student orch. himself. It grew into the New Haven Symphony Orch. which, in 1917, was organised as a permanent concert organisation, giving regular concerts. In 1919, surrendered the bâton to his assistant and former pupil, David Stanley Smith, who also succeeded his master as head of music department of Univ. when Parker died in 1919.

Parker was an industrious compr. His op. 1, *The Shepherd Boy*, chorus for male vs., was written in the 'eighties. His last published work, " A.D. 1919," op. 84, for mixed vs. and orch., was written for Yale Univ. centennial celebration. He has comp. little orch. music (op. 12, 13, 46, 56; none publ.), some chamber-music; also pf. and organ pieces and songs; but his best work was done in music for the church and in choral compns. in the larger forms. In these he rose to a height not hitherto reached by any Amer. compr. His cantata, *The Dream King and his Love*, op. 31, won prize of the New York National Cons. 1893. An *a cappella* motet, *Adstant Angelorum Chori*, op. 45, won prize of Mus. Art Soc., New York, 1898. His *Morning and Evening Services in E*, op. 19, have been frequently sung in England as well as America. But his greatest work, on which his international reputation rests, is his *Hora Novissima*, op. 30, for soli, chorus and orch., first perf. by Church Choral Soc. of New York in 1893 and sung at the Three Choirs Fest. at Worcester, England, in 1899, and in 1900 at Chester, the first Amer. work of this calibre ever performed in England.

P.'s style is characterised by a serious and well-balanced loftiness, and a skill in handling vocal masses in contrapuntal design, which lends unusual depth and dignity to his larger choral works. At times he evinces an almost ascetic self-restraint, which explains why the two operas comp. in his later years, although a considerable advance over his earlier works in dramatic structure and appeal, have not held the stage, in spite of their intrinsic mus. excellence. *Mona*, op. 71, won the $10,000 prize offered by the Metropolitan Opera of New York for an Amer. opera. It was first perf. 14 March, 1912, at Metropolitan Opera House. *Fairyland*, op. 77, won an equally large prize of the National Federation of Women's Clubs. It was brought out at Los Angeles, Cal., July 1, 1915. P. was member of National Inst. of Arts and Letters. Received

degrees of A.M. *h.c.* from Yale, 1894, and Mus.D. *h.c.* from Cambridge, England, 1902.

King Trojan, soli, chorus, orch. (Schmidt, 1886); op. 30, *Hora Novissima*, soli, chorus, orch. (Novello, 1893); op. 31, *The Dream King and his Love*, t. solo, chorus and orch. (Schirmer, 1893); op. 40, *Cahal Mór of the Wine-red Hand*, rhapsody for barit. and orch. (Gray, 1910); op. 43, *The Legend of St. Christopher*, oratorio (Novello, 1898); op. 45, *Adstant Angelorum Chori (a cappella)* (Schirmer, 1899); op. 50, *A Wanderer's Psalm* for soli, chorus and orch. (Novello, 1900) (written for Hereford Fest. 1900); op. 64, *King Gorm the Grim*, ballad for chorus and orch. (Schirmer, 1908); op. 79, *Morven and the Grail*, oratorio (Boston Music Co. 1915); op. 82, *The Dream of Mary*, a morality (Gray, 1918); op. 55, concerto, organ and orch. (Novello, 1903); op. 65, sonata in E flat, organ (Schirmer, 1908); op. 35, Suite, pf. vn. and cello (*id.* 1904). Operas, *Mona* and *Fairyland* (*id.*, 1911, 1915); numerous songs (A. P. Schmidt; Schirmer; John Church Co.).—O. K.

PARODI, Lorenzo. Ital. critic and compr. *b.* Genoa, 10 Aug. 1856. Stud. first in his native city; then in Paris under Guiraud and Massenet. Settled in Genoa, where he teaches history and æsthetics of music at Civico Istituto di Musica, and directs a private mus. acad. Has comp. operas, concert and sacred music. Amongst his books is *Musicologia, tecnica e psicologia dell' arte dei suoni*, (Genoa, 1909, Libreria Moderna).—D. A.

PARRATT, Sir Walter. English orgt. *b.* Huddersfield, 10 Feb. 1841; *d.* Windsor, 27 March 1924. Educated at Huddersfield College School; organist and choirmaster successively of Armitage Bridge Church, of Great Witley, Wigan Parish Ch., Magdalen Coll. Oxford, St. George's Chapel Royal, Windsor; Prof. of Music at Oxford Univ. 1908–18; Honorary Fellow of Magdalen Coll. Oxford; Dean of Faculty of Music, London Univ. (1916–20); Master of the King's Music; prof. at R.C.M. London. Knighted in 1892; M.V.O. 1901; C.V.O. 1917; K.C.V.O. 1921. A musician of the soundly classical, inflexible type, with a widely cultivated mind, a phenomenal musical memory and great skill in organ-playing. With his natural rise to positions of great influence in church music, he was able to do (and did) more than any other musician in raising the standard of organ-playing and the status of the organist in the period from 1860–1910. He only wrote a few short occasional pieces.—H. P. A.

PARRY, Sir Charles Hubert Hastings, Bart. English composer and author; *b.* Bournemouth, 27 Feb. 1848; *d.* Rustington, 7 Oct. 1918. He spent his early life in surroundings which rarely produced a great musician, but he showed very early in life strong musical predilections. He inherited the artistic temperament from his father, Gambier Parry, whose decorative work on the nave ceilings of Ely and Gloucester cathedrals is well known.

At 8 he started on his career as a composer, with chants and hymn-tunes. When at a private school at Twyford near Winchester, he got to know Samuel Sebastian Wesley, the organist of the cathedral, and often sat with him in the organ loft. The influence of Wesley was an abiding one. Parry went to Eton in 1861, where he was regarded as a real musical prodigy. Whilst there, he was the musical leader of the school and the chief supporter of the Eton College Musical Society. A few of his compositions were published whilst he was at school, and his Service in D soon after. He took his Mus.Bac. degree at Oxford, whilst still at Eton. When he went to Exeter College, Oxford, he at once took a leading part in the college life, especially in music and games, excelling in swimming, skating, cricket and football. He was one of a set of very ardent musical enthusiasts, including Harford Lloyd, who were responsible for the founding of the Oxford University Musical Club. He had some composition lessons while he was at Oxford from G. A. Macfarren, and spent one long vacation in Stuttgart, studying there under the English composer Henry Hugo Pierson.

When he left Oxford he wanted to devote himself entirely to music; but his father opposed the wish and he entered Lloyd's in 1871, and worked there for about 3 years. About the age of 26, however, he was able to devote himself altogether to music and studied with tremendous enthusiasm under Edward G. Dannreuther, at whose concerts at 12 Orme Square most of his compositions of that period were first performed.

The first work which brought Parry into prominence was the cantata *Prometheus Unbound*, produced at Gloucester in 1880, and from that date to the end of his life, he composed a vast amount of choral music, 12 volumes of songs, a quantity of chamber-music, 5 symphonies and other orchestral works, 2 delightful string suites (the *Lady Radnor* Suite and the *English* Suite), a large number of organ works, some pf. pieces and the music to 5 Greek plays. In 1883 Parry was appointed professor of composition and lecturer in musical history at the Royal College of Music, London, then just opened. In the same year he was made Choragus of the University of Oxford, and in 1898 he succeeded Sir John Stainer as Professor of Music there. In 1894 he followed Sir George Grove as Director of the Royal College of Music. He was created a Knight in 1898 and a Baronet in 1903. He was given the honorary degree of Mus.Doc. by Cambridge in 1883, Oxford in 1884, and Dublin in 1891. His funeral at St. Paul's Cathedral, where he was buried, was attended by a huge congregation which contained many notabilities from every walk of life.

His setting of Shirley's poem, *The glories of our blood and state* (1883), was his first mature work. Four years later he produced *Blest pair of Sirens*, in which we have Parry at his best, from every point of view—in his selection of words, in his faithfulness of accentuation in setting them to music as great, producing a work in which words and music go hand in hand. The high-water-mark of Parry's use of great choral masses with the finest effect is found in *De Profundis* (*Out of the deep have I called unto Thee*). The oratorio *Job* shows Parry in a new light, for it has a dramatic significance and a range of emotion greater than any other of his works. Altogether he wrote 24 choral works on a large scale, the last one, *An Ode*

on the *Nativity* (Hereford, 1912), containing some of his most beautiful writing.

At the other end of the scale, Parry's incidental music to the Greek comedies of Aristophanes is without a rival in its own kind. Parry was a master of musical fun, and the "musical larks" are as laughter-begetting as the comedies themselves.

In the last years of his life he wrote a set of motets called *The Songs of Farewell* for unaccompanied choirs of from 4 to 8 parts. In these, especially in *There is an old belief*, we hear Parry at his greatest. Lastly, in the song called *Jerusalem* to Blake's words "And did those feet," Parry has written a new National Anthem, which has already taken deep root in Britain.

In addition to all this, he found time to write some of the best books about music which we possess, for he had above all others the mind which saw things in their true relation. It was through this and because he realised in music as in life there must be organic unity, that he was able to write such books as *The Art of Music*, his volume on the XVII century in the *Oxford History of Music*, his volume on *Style in Musical Art*, and his book on Bach. His *College Addresses*, published under the editorship of H. C. Colles, reveal the secret of his power with young people and his views on life in general. His favourite word was *Initiative*. His teaching and influence, throbbing with infectious energy, was almost miraculous. He carried the stimulus of sunshine wherever he went.

Works, with publishers and date of 1st perf.:
(Published by Novello unless otherwise stated. There are no opus numbers except in a few early instances.)
1858–65, anthems, part-songs, fugues, songs, chiefly written while studying under Sir George Elvey at Eton. 1865, anthems: *Blessed is he*; *Prevent us, O Lord* (Eton Coll. Mus. Soc. 9 Dec.). 1866, cantata, *O Lord, Thou hast cast us out* (Eton Coll. Mus. Soc. 8 Dec.) (Lamborn Cock); song, *Why does azure deck the sky?* (Eton Coll. Mus. Soc. 22 March) (Lamborn Cock). 5-pt. madrigal, *Fair Daffodils* (Royal Glee and Madrigal Union, Windsor, 12 Feb.) (Lamborn Cock). 1867, songs: *Autumn* (Lamborn Cock), *Angel hosts, sweet love, befriend thee* (Lamborn Cock); *Allegretto scherzando*, orch. (ms.); 1st str. 4tet G mi. (ms.). 1868, *Te Deum* and *Benedictus* from Service in D; *Sonnets and Songs without words*. 1st set, pf. (Lamborn Cock); *Intermezzo religioso*, orch. (Gloucester Fest.) (ms.); 2nd str. 4tet, C mi. (ms.). 1869, remainder of Service in D; songs, *Three Odes of Anacreon* (Augener, 1880). 1870, song, *The river of Life* (Lamborn Cock). 1872, 7 *Charakterbilder*, pf. (Augener). 1873, 15 variations on an air by Bach (4 Carlton Gardens, 1 April)(ms.); overture, *Vivien*, orch. (ms.); 3 songs: *The Poet's Song, More fond than cushat dove*, Music (Lamborn Cock). 1874, song, *Twilight* (Lamborn Cock); song, *A Christmas Carol*; *A Garland of old-fashioned Songs* (Lamborn Cock; later, Boosey). 1875, *Sonnets and Songs without words*, 2nd set, pf. (Lamborn Cock); 3 trios for female voices: *Hymn to Night, Hymn to Diana, Take O take those lips away* (Lamborn Cock). 1877, *Grosses Duo* in E mi. 2 pfs. (12 Orme Square, 11 April, 1873) (Breitkopf); nonet in B flat for wind instrs. (ms.); sonata in F, pf. (Lamborn Cock); *Sonnets and Songs without words*, 3rd set, pf. (Lamborn Cock). 1878, pf. trio, E mi. (12 O. Sq. 30 Jan.) (Breitkopf, 1879); sonata in A, pf. (Stanley Lucas; later, Augener); *Fantasie Sonata*, B mi. in one movt., vn. and pf. (12 O. Sq. 30 Jan. 1879) (ms.). 1879, overture, *Guillem de Cabestanh*, orch. (Crystal Palace, 15 March) (ms.); pf. 4tet in A flat (4 Carlton Gardens, 1 April). 1880, 3rd str. 4tet in G (12 O. Sq. 26 Feb.) (ms.); concerto, pf. and orch. (Crystal Palace, 3 April) (ms.); Scenes from *Prometheus Unbound*, s.a.t.b. soli, chorus and

orch. (Gloucester Fest.); sonata in A, cello and pf. (12 O. Sq. 12 Feb.). 1881, Evening Service in D. (M.S.) 1882, 1st symphony in G (Birmingham Fest.) (ms.). 1883, music to *The Birds* (Cambridge Amateur Dramatic Club, Nov.) (Stanley Lucas; later, Univ. Press, Cambridge); 2nd symphony, in F (Cambridge Univ. Mus. Soc. 11 June); ode, *The glories of our blood and state*, chorus and orch. (Gloucester Fest.). 1884, str. 5tet in E flat (12 O. Sq. 18 March); pf. trio in B mi. (12 O. Sq. 25 Nov.). 1885, Theme and 19 variations, pf. (12 O. Sq. 10 Feb.) (Stanley Lucas); English Lyrics, 1st set (Stanley Lucas; later, Novello). 1886, *Suite Moderne*, orch. (Gloucester Fest.) (ms.); Partita for vn. and pf. (12 O. Sq. 2 Dec.) (Czerny; later, Chanot); English Lyrics, 2nd set (Stanley Lucas; later, Novello). 1887, Characteristic Popular Tunes of the British Isles, pf. 2 books (Stanley Lucas; later, Augener); Four Sonnets of Shakespeare (Eng. and Ger. words) (Stanley Lucas); opera, *Guinevere* (ms.); ode, *Blest pair of sirens*, 8-pt. chorus and orch. (Bach Choir, 17 May). 1888, oratorio, *Judith*, s. a. t. b. soli, chorus and orch. (Birmingham Fest.). 1889, sonata in D, vn. and pf. (12 O. Sq. 14 Feb.) (ms.); 3rd symphony, in C (Philh. Soc. June); 4th symphony, in E mi. (Richter Concert, St. James's Hall, 1 July); *Ode on St. Cecilia's Day*, s. and barit. soli, chorus and orch. (Leeds Fest.). 1890, pf. trio in G (12 O. Sq. 13 Feb.) (ms.); *L'Allegro ed il Pensieroso*, s. and b. soli, chorus and orch. (Norwich Fest.). 1891, ode, *Eton*, chorus and orch. (Eton Celebration, 28 June); Psalm cxxx, *De Profundis*, s. solo, 12 pt. chorus and orch. (Hereford Fest.); song, *The Maid of Elsinore* (Leadenhall Press). 1892, music to *The Frogs* (O.U.D.S. Oxford, 24 Feb.); *Choric song from The Lotos-eaters*, s. solo, chorus and orch. (Cambridge, June); oratorio, *Job*, s. t. barit. and b. soli, chorus and orch. (Gloucester Fest.). 1893, incidental music to *Hypatia* (Haymarket Theatre, Jan.) (ms.); overture, *To an unwritten Tragedy*, orch. (Worcester Fest.); song, *Rock-a-bye*. 1894, Lady Radnor's Suite, str. orch. (Lady R.'s orchestra, 29 June); anthem, chorus and orch. *Hear my words ye people* (Fest. Salisbury Diocesan Choral Association, 10 May); oratorio, *King Saul*, s. a. t. barit. and b. soli, chorus and orch. (Birmingham Fest.); 1895, English Lyrics, 3rd set; *Invocation to Music*, s. t. and b. soli, chorus and orch. (Leeds Fest.); song, *Land to the leeward, Ho !*; 12 short pieces, vn. and pf. (3 books). 1896, Romance in F, vn. and pf. (R. Maver, Glasgow). 1897, English Lyrics, 4th set; Elegy for Brahms (R.C.M. 8 Nov. 1918) (ms.); 6 Lyrics from an Elizabethan Song-Book (part-songs); 6 Modern Lyrics (part-songs); *Symphonic Variations*, orch. (Phil. Soc. 3 June); *Magnificat*, s. solo, chorus and orch. (Hereford Fest.). 1898, 8 4-part songs (Windsor, 10 Dec.); *A Song of Darkness and Light*, s. solo, chorus and orch. (Gloucester Fest.). 1899, song, barit. and orch. *The North Wind* (New Brighton, 9 July) (ms.); incidental music to *A Repentance* (St. James's Theatre, Feb.) (ms.). 1900, 5-part song, *Who can dwell with greatness ?* (Windsor, 29 May); *Te Deum* in F (Latin words), s. and b. soli, chorus and orch. (Hereford Fest.); scena, b. solo and orch., *The Soldier's Tent* (Birmingham Fest.); music to *Agamemnon* (Cambridge A.D.C.); song, *Von edler Art* (Magpie Madrigal Concert, 30 May) (Boosey). 1901, *Ode to Music*, s. t. and b. soli, chorus and orch. (R.C.M. opening of Concert Hall, 13 June). 1902, English Lyrics, 5th and 6th sets. 1903, *War and Peace*, s. a. t. b. soli, chorus and orch. (R. Choral Soc., Albert Hall, 30 April); anthem, *I was glad*, and processional music (Coronation Service, Westminster Abbey, 9 Aug.); motet, *Voces Clamantium*, s. and b. soli, chorus and orch. (Hereford Fest.). 1904, sinfonia sacra, *The Love that casteth out fear*, a. and b. soli, chorus and orch. (Gloucester Fest.); song, *Newfoundland* (written for Sir Cavendish Boyle); 8-part song, *In Praise of Song* (B. B. and O. Mus. Fest. Oxford); 1905, music to *The Clouds* (O.U.D.S. Oxford, March) (Breitkopf); song, *Fear no more the heat of the sun* (Ditson Co. U.S.A.); *The Pied Piper of Hamelin*, t. and b. soli, chorus and orch. (Norwich Fest.). 1906, sinfonia sacra, *The Soul's Ransom*, s. and b. soli, chorus and orch. (Hereford Fest.). 1907, symphonic poem, *The Vision of Life*, s. and b. soli, chorus and orch. (Cardiff Fest.); Suites in D and in F, vn. and pf.; English Lyrics, 7th and 8th sets; barit. song, *The Laird o' Cockpen* (30 Nov. 1906). 1908, motet, *Beyond these voices there is peace*, s. and b. soli, chorus and orch. (Worcester Fest.); *Eton Memorial Ode*, chorus and orch. (Eton, 18 Nov.); song, *The best school of all* (Clifton Coll. 21 Dec.) (Year Book Press, 1916), 1909, 6 4-part songs; English Lyrics, 9th set;

4 unison songs (Y.B.P.); 1910, 7 part - songs for male-v. chorus. 1911, *Te Deum in D* (Coronation, Westminster Abbey); 3 school songs (Y.B.P.). 1912, *An ode on the Nativity*, s. solo, chorus and orch. (Hereford Fest.); *Soliloquy from Browning's Saul*, b. voice and organ (Browning Centenary, Westminster Abbey, 7 May) (ms.); incidental music to *Proserpine*, s. solo, female-v. chorus and orch. (Keats-Shelley Fest., St. James's Theatre) (ms.); *Symphonic Fantasia* "1912," orch. (Philh. Soc. 5 Dec.) (Goodwin & Tabb); 7 Chorale Preludes for organ, 1st set. 1913, Psalm xlvi, *God is our hope*, bass solo, double choir and orch. (Fest. of Sons of Clergy, St. Paul's Cath.); Fantasia and fugue in G, for organ; 3 unison songs (Y.B.P.); Elegy in A flat, org. (Wilton, 7 April); *Te Deum in F* (Eng. words) (Gloucester Fest.). 1914, music to *The Acharnians* (O.U.D.S. Oxford) (Breitkopf); 2 school songs (Y.B.P.); symphonic poem in 2 linked movts. *Via Mortis, Via Vitæ*, orch. (Brighton Fest. 12 Nov.) (ms.); *Shulbrede Tunes* (Augener). 1915, 3 *Chorale Fantasias*, organ; 5-pt. madrigal, *La belle dame sans merci* (Bristol, Jan.) (ms.); song, *A Hymn for Aviators* (Albert Hall, 13 May) (Boosey); carol, *When Christ was born* (R. Choral Soc. Albert Hall, Dec.); *West Downs School Song*. 1916, naval ode, *The chivalry of the sea*, 5-part chorus and orch. (Bach Choir, Albert Hall, 12 Dec.); 7 Chorale Preludes for organ, 2nd set; 4 motets from Songs of Farewell (Bach Choir, R.C.M. 22 May) (Y.B.P.); 3 songs from *Kookoorookoo Book* (Y.B.P.); choral song, *Jerusalem* (" Fight for Right " Meeting, Queen's Hall, 28 March) (Curwen). 1917, 7-pt. motet, from Songs of Farewell, *At the round earth's imagined corners* (Bach Choir, R.C.M. 22 May) (Y.B.P.); 2 carols, *Welcome Yule* and *I sing the birth* (Albert Hall, Dec.). 1918, 8-pt. motet from Songs of Farewell, *Lord, let me know mine end* (New Coll. Oxford, 17 June) (Y.B.P.); English Lyrics, 10th set (Bechstein Hall, 16 Nov.); suite, *Hands across the Centuries*, pf. (Augener); 3 school songs (Ed. Arnold). 1919, choral song, *England* (Oxford, July) (Y.B.P.). 1920, English Lyrics, 11th and 12th sets. 1921, *The Wanderer* (toccata and fugue in G ma. and E mi. for org.); An English Suite, str. orch. (Bach Choir " Parry Concert," R.C.M., 10 May).

Also a large number of compositions in ms.: songs, part-songs, short pieces for pf., org., vn., etc.—to which no dates can be assigned; and numerous hymn-tunes, many of which are published in *Hymns A. and M.*, *The Westminster Abbey Hymn Book*, *Methodist Hymn Book*, etc.

Books: *Studies of Great Composers* (1886, Kegan Paul); *The Art of Music* (1893, *ibid.*); enlarged ed. as *The Evolution of the Art of Music* (1896); *The XVII Century* (Vol. III of the *Oxford History of Music*, Oxford Univ. Press, 1902); *Summary of Musical History* (Novello's Primers); *Johann Sebastian Bach* (1909, G. P. Putnam); *Style in Musical Art* (1911, Macmillan); *College Addresses* (1921, Macmillan, edited H. C. Colles); *Instinct and Character* (typed copies, only); and a large number of lectures, articles, poems, pamphlets, etc., published and in ms.

A biography by C. L. Graves is in preparation.—H. P. A. & E. R. D.

PARSONS, Albert Ross. Amer. pianist, teacher; b. Sandusky, Ohio, U.S.A., 16 Sept. 1847. The doyen of Amer. pf.-teachers. After some years as church orgt. in his youth, stud. under Ritter in New York, 1863; from 1867-9 in Leipzig under Moscheles, Reinecke, Paul, Papperitz and Richter; 1870-2, in Berlin under Tausig, Kullak and Weitzman. Since 1872, teaching in New York and orgt. at several New York churches (Holy Trinity, Fifth Avenue Presbyterian); 1893, President of Amer. Coll. of Musicians. From 1885, for many years, head of pf.-department of Metropolitan Coll. of Music (later the Amer. Inst. of Applied Music). One of the early apostles of Wagner in America.

Pf. pieces, studies, songs (Schirmer, Silver); *The Virtuoso's Handling of the Pianoforte* (New York, Schroeder, 1917). Wrote: *Parsifal, or Finding Christ through Music* (Putnam, 1890); *The Science of Piano Practice* (Schirmer, 1886); transl. of Wagner's *Beethoven* (Boston, Lee & Sheppard, 1872; 3rd ed. Schirmer, 1883).—O. K.

PÁRTOS, Stephan. Hungarian violinist; b.

Budapest, 1 March, 1903; *d.* in Holland, 1919. Pupil of Hubay.—B. B.

PÂRVESCU, Pompiliu. See RUMANIAN FOLK-MUSIC.

PASDELOUP CONCERTS, Paris. Founded 1861 by the orch. condr. of this name (*b.* 1819, *d.* 1887); had an enormous vogue up to 1873, when the Concerts Colonne competed with them. Pasdeloup introduced Berlioz, Gounod, Saint-Saëns, Massenet, Bizet, Lalo, Brahms, Glinka, Tchaikovsky, and especially Wagner, to the Paris public. The concerts were re-established in 1920 at the Cirque d'Hiver under dir. of Rhené-Baton. In 1921 they were installed at the Opéra and in 1922 at Théâtre des Champs-Élysées, with André Caplet as 2nd condr. (for a short time), and in 1924 at the Trocadéro.—A. C.

PASINI, Laura. Ital. soprano singer; *b.* Gallarate (Milan), 28 Jan. 1894. After having completed her pf. studies at Cons. in Milan, under Appiani, and having given successful concerts as a pianist, she devoted herself to study of singing at R. Liceo Mus. di Santa Cecilia in Rome, under Di Pietro, gaining her diploma in 1921. She immediately establ. herself as a concert singer with first-class qualities; in 1922, made her *début* at the Costanzi in *Falstaff*, scoring a great success, thus beginning a very successful operatic career.—D. A.

PASODOBLES. See JUARRANZ LÓPEZ.

PASTOR, Father J. B. Span. musician. Choirmaster at Valencia Cath. from 1912.—P. G. M.

PATERSON, Robert Edward Sterling. Scottish cellist, music-seller, publisher; *b.* Edinburgh, 1872. Stud. music and painting in Berlin, where he attended the Art School; stud. cello at same time under Robert Hausmann. Then went to Paris, cello under Loeb, painting at Life School there. The death of his brother brought him back to his father's business. He is J.P. for City of Edinburgh; member of several mus. clubs there and in Glasgow.—W. S.

PATERSON, Robert Roy. Scottish compr. ♭. Edinburgh, 16 July, 1830; *d.* there, Dec. 1903. Stud. music in Leipzig under Moscheles, Mendelssohn and Richter; also pf.-making with Broadwood and with Collard, London. Second son of John Walker P. and grandson of Robert P. who founded famous firm of Paterson Sons & Co., Edinburgh and Glasgow. He had a genius for organising. Founded the Paterson Orch. Concerts given by the Scottish Orch. (then under August Manns). Has publ. some of finest colls. of Scottish songs ever compiled. Comp. many songs and pf. pieces under pen-names of " Alfred Stella," and " Pierre Pierrot."—W. S.

PATTERSON, Annie. Writer on music; *b.* Lurgan, Co. Armagh. Of Fr. Huguenot descent; received her mus. education at R. Irish Acad. of Music; Mus.Doc. Trinity Coll. Dublin; examiner in music at R. Univ. of Ireland 1892–5; re-elected in 1900; examiner in music to Irish Intermediate Board of Education, 1900–1; orgt. in some Dublin churches between 1887 and 1897, later at St. Anne's

Ch., Shandon, Cork. The idea of a national music fest. for Ireland owes its origin to her, and, under her influence, the first Feis Ceoil was held in Dublin, 1897. All her life she has striven to further the cause of Irish folk-music.

The Story of Oratorio; *Schumann* (Master Musician Series; Dent); *Chats with Music - Lovers*; *Great Minds in Music*; *How to Listen to an Orchestra*; *Beautiful Song and the Singer*; *The Music of Ireland*. *6 Original Gaelic Songs*. Ivernia series of Irish mus. arrangements.—W. ST.

PATTI, Adelina (Baroness Rolf Cederström). Operatic soprano singer; *b.* of Ital. parents, in Madrid, 19 Feb. 1843; *d.* Craig-y-Nos Castle, S. Wales, 27 Sept. 1919. Sang for first time in public (1850) at age of 7; withdrawn from public at age of 12 for 3 years; at 15½ reappeared (rôle of Lucia, 24 Nov. 1859 New York), achieving a tremendous success, singing rôles in Bellini and Donizetti for 18 months. In spring of 1861, engaged by Frederick Gye, R. Ital. Opera House, London, where she appeared as Amina in *Sonnambula*, 14 May, 1861; she repeated this part 8 times that season and appeared also as Lucia, Violetta, Zerlina, Marta, and Rosina. Italian *début* at Turin in 1876. Created rôle of Dinorah in Vienna and London; sang at Covent Garden for over 20 years; her earnings between 1861 and 1889 averaged £35,000 a year; in 1888, visited Argentina; 1889, London (for Sir Augustus Harris); sang also at many concerts and festivals. Retired from stage in 1906, but continued to sing occasionally at charity concerts, her last appearance being at Albert Hall, London, in 1911.—E.-H.

PAUER, Max. Ger. pianist; *b.* London, 31 Oct. 1866. Son and pupil of pianist Ernst Pauer; stud. theory with Vincenz Lachner, Carlsruhe, 1881–5; after 1st concert-tours, settled in London; 1887, went to Cologne Cons. as teacher; soon became celebrated as pianist of noble execution and brilliant technique; 1897, Stuttgart Cons. (teacher of advanced school); 1908, succeeded De Lange as dir. of Inst.; decorated with a title of High Order of Merit.

Pf. pieces; new ed. of Lebert and Stark's *Pf. Tutor* (1904).—A. E.

PAULUS, Olaf. Norwegian compr. orgt. *b.* Christiania in 1859; *d.* Stavanger, 29 June, 1912. Pupil of Christian Cappelen (organ) and Johan Svendsen (compn.); afterwards stud. several years at Cons. in Leipzig. From 1889, orgt. at Cath. Ch., Stavanger. For many years leader of Stavanger Mus. Soc.; was of great service for development of music in that city. As compr. P. won great esteem in his native land, through his numerous works for male chorus, of which may be mentioned *Vestanveir* and *Finshaugen*, portrayals in music of the West of Norway, instinct with Norwegian mus. feeling. In 1902 P. visited America, where he cond. concerts in Minneapolis and St. Paul.

Cantatas; compns. for male chorus; songs; pf. pieces; preludes for organ. Publ. in 1888 (collab. with Cappelen) *De tusind hjems sange* (*Songs for " The Thousand Homes "*).—J. A.

PAVLOF, Eugene Pavlovitch (*accent 1st syll.*). Russ. compr. *b.* Moscow, 8 Feb. 1894.

Son of well-known actor; pupil of Ilinsky, Sokolovsky, and Javorsky (theory). Finished course at State School of Moscow Theatre as ballet-dancer. As compr. is a follower of Scriabin, showing both talent and power. His first compositions were written in 1912.

Symph. *étude, The Sea*, op. 4; pf. preludes, op. 1, 3; 1st pf. sonata (*Heroic*), op. 5; 2nd pf. sonata, op. 8. —V. B.

PAYNE, Arthur W. Eng. violinist and condr. *b.* London 1863. Stud. R.A.M. under Weist Hill and H. C. Banister; condr. Stock Exchange Orch. Soc. 11 years; led L.S.O. for 8 years and R. Choral Soc. orch. from 1898; leader Queen's Hall Orch. for 7 years and, for some time, of London Symphony Orch. on its foundation; condr. Llandudno Pavilion Orch. (from 1900). —E.-H.

PEACAN DEL SAR, Rafael. Argentine compr. *b.* Buenos Ayres, 1884. Stud. there under Sorreus Boqui; 1910, art dir. of Centenary Exhibition; later, organised fine symphony concerts in Politeama Theatre in 1914.

8 symph. pieces; Mass; oratorio, *La Conversión de Longino*; Japanese opera, *Crisantheme*; many pf. pieces; songs.—A. M.

PEARCE, Charles William. Eng. orgt. and compr. *b.* Salisbury, 5 Dec. 1856. Stud. there under C. J. Read and T. E. Aylward; organ under W. S. Hoyte and Dr. E. J. Hopkins in London; Mus.Doc. Cantab. 1884; M.A. Dunelm. *h.c.* 1921; has had over 43 years' connection with R.C.O. and with Trinity Coll. of Music, where he has been dir. of studies from 1916. Was one of the editors (with E. J. Hopkins and C. Vincent) of *The Organist and Choirmaster.* His best qualities have been most evident on the academic side of music.

Voice-training Studies and Exercises (with late E. Behnke) (Chappell); *Voice Training Primer* (with Mrs. Behnke) (*id.*); textbooks of musical knowledge (Hammond); *The Art of the Piano Teacher* (W. Rogers); *Students' Counterpoint*; *Composers' Counterpoint* (*id.*); *Modern Academic Counterpoint* (*id.*). *The Priest's Part in Anglican Liturgy* (Faith Press). Numerous organ pieces, pf. pieces, songs, pieces for vn. and pf., vn. and organ (Rogers, Weekes, Elkin, J. Williams, Bosworth, Ashdown, Jameson, Augener, Banks, Hammond); church services, anthems, part-songs, school-songs; *Organ Acc. to Plainsong* (with George Oldroyd) (Curwen); 80 hymn-tunes in various colls.; numerous lectures, papers, arts. and reviews. —E.-H.

PECSKAI, Louis. Hungarian violinist; *b.* Fiume. Stud. R. School of Music, Budapest; *début* 1886 at Fiume; has played with leading European orchs. and has toured widely. Lives in London. Has given many concerts with the London Trio (see GOODWIN, AMINA, and WHITE-HOUSE, W. E.).—E.-H.

PEDRELL, Carlos. Compr. *b.* in Uruguay, 1878. Stud. at Barcelona and Paris. Returned to Buenos Ayres as inspector of music to Board of Education, and was entrusted with the work of verifying and establishing the true mus. form of the Argentine National Anthem, which had been subject to many unwarranted modifications. Has comp. several orch. pieces and a very large number of songs with Fr. words. His style admits of simple melody.—A. M.

PEDRELL, Felipe. Spanish composer and musicologist; *b.* Tortosa, 1841; *d.* there, 1922. Began as choir-boy at Cath. of native town; learnt elementary harmony with Antonio Nin y Serra, and subsequently acquired his vast knowledge of music and other subjects by himself. In 1873, light-opera condr. at Circo Barcelonés; taught history of music and æsthetics at Real Cons. Madrid; lecturer at Escuela de Estudios Superiores, Ateneo, Madrid; Fellow of Real Acad. de Bellas Artes, a distinction unjustly withdrawn from him in 1904 on his leaving the capital owing to bad health. Founder of the Capilla Isidoriana, the periodicals *Salterio Sacro-Hispano, Notas Musicales y Literarias* (1881), *La Música Religiosa en España* (1896) and *Ilustración Musical Hispano-Americana.* Contributed important series of arts. to *Sammelb. der I.M.G.* etc. The publication in 1894 of his 3-act opera *Los Pireneos* (finished 1892) and a Fr. transl. of his pamphlet *Por nuestra música* (on creation of a national school of mus. art) gave prominence to his name in the rest of Europe, before he obtained recognition from his countrymen. The advent of a Spanish reformer provided ample scope for the pens of such authorities as Albert Soubies, de Casembroot, R. Berger, César Cui, Arthur Hervey, C. Kobs, Van der Straeten, Tebaldini, Amintore Galli, Camille Bellaigue, Mascagni and Moszkowski, who, in the *Berliner Tageblatt*, hailed Pedrell as the Spanish Wagner. This outburst of enthusiasm abroad resounded in Spain; two bands, partisans and opponents, were soon formed, giving vent to the most exaggerated views about the master. This diversity of opinion was ¦limited to professional circles, for Pedrell, who suffered all his life the disdain of the official world, always remained an obscure figure for the public in general. According to some, the musical progress in Spain during the last 40 years, is all due to Pedrell; others hold that he was nothing but a plagiarist of Wagner's writings who failed as a practical musician. Even if *Por nuestra música* were but an adaptation of Wagner's *Opera and Drama* (as often suggested), Pedrell, in doing so, rendered a great service to Spain. *Por nuestra música* was a call to the genius of the race.

Forced by unfortunate circumstances to work under great pressure, Pedrell, too prolific with his pen, was not always a model of style, originality or accuracy; but five of his works, *Antología de organistas clásicos españoles, Teatro lírico español anterior al siglo XIX, Cancionero popular español, Hispaniæ Scholæ Musica Sacra* and *Tomæ Ludovici Victoria Opera Omnia*, constitute a monumental achievement. Their transcendental value, in a universal sense, places him not only as the first and foremost figure in the mus. renaissance of Spain, but as one of the leaders of æsthetic progress in the history of the world.

His music in the pf. editions (the form in which it is mostly available) does not afford a chance for fair judgment. Sporadic and mostly fragmentary perfs. of opera *Los Pireneos* and less important works, give the impression that its merit lies mainly in the intention of the compr. Demanding a certain knowledge of mus. history for its full comprehension, his work lacks in some measure those qualities necessary to maintain an uninterrupted current of sympathy between creator and public. For all practical purposes, Pedrell remains unknown as a compr. The unpubl. opera *La Celestina* is described by his pupil, Rafael Mitjana, as a revelation destined to astonish the world. It is the sequel to *Los Pirineos* and the second part of a trilogy (the third part, *Raimundo Lulio*, is also unpubl.) evolved from the motto of the Provençal troubadours, the upholders of the *gaya ciencia* or *gayo saber*: *Patria—Amor—Fides*. The book is an adaptation by compr. from the *Tragicomedia de Calixto y Melibea*, in 21 acts, by Fernando de Rojas (1497).

Many claim the privilege of being Pedrell's pupils; yet most of them (Albeniz included) were or are but disciples who felt the spell of his inspiring influence. Manuel de Falla is to be counted among those who studied systematically under his direction. He asserts that he owes to Pedrell all he knows. There is not a trace of Pedrell's style in de Falla's works; nevertheless the *formación espiritual* of de Falla gives ample evidence of his close association with Pedrell, who directed all his efforts to realising the fundamental principle in music of that mastermind of the XVII century—the Jesuit Antonio Eximeno: *Sobre la base del canto nacional debía construir cada pueblo su sistema* ("On the basis of its native song, every country should build its own system of musical art").

The regenerating influence of Pedrell is an undeniable fact. Spain had become the most servile slave to the Ital. school of the day. The glorious Spanish traditions were forgotten; the Ger. classics and Romantics were unknown. The disastrous effects that the theories of the pedant Pietro Cerone, and his proselyte, the blind organist of Saragossa, Fray Pablo de Nasarre (1683–1724) had in the country; the favouritism enjoyed by the singer Farinelli in the Court of Fernando VI; the long stay in Spain of Mercadante; the advent of an Ital. queen, the fourth wife of Fernando VII, to the throne; these are some of the causes which had prepared and consolidated the Ital. invasion. Pedrell, the direct successor of Bartolomé Ramos de Pareja (1500), the Benedictine Benito Jerónimo Feijóo (1600), and Fathers Antonio Eximeno and Rodríguez de Hita (1700), was the guiding light in that moment of mus. obscurantism. He investigated the past and the present, gave life to a national ideal and spread in his country the knowledge of mus. science. He has been called the Spanish Wagner, a title that hardly befits him; for Wagner was above all a compr. and secondly a theorist. Pedrell was the reverse. The inadequacy of the comparison serves only to enhance the distinct personality of the Catalonian master.

Operas: *El Último Abencerraje* (perf. Liceo, Barcelona, 1874); *Quasimodo* (Liceo, Barcelona, 1875); *Cleopatra* (awarded prize, Frankfort, 1878); *Los Pirineos* (poem by Victor Balaguer; perf. [the complete work] Liceo, Barcelona, 1902; Teatro Colón, Buenos Ayres, 1910; [prologue only] Liceo Benedetto Marcello, Venice, 1897; The Hague [Bevordering der Toonkunst] 1907; Paris, Schola Cantorum; Montpellier and Toulouse [Félibres fests.] under Charles Bordes; Pablo Casals, Conciertos Sinfónicos, Barcelona); *La Celestina*; *El Conde Arnau*; *Visión de Rauda* (*Raimundo Lulio*). Light operas (early works): *Eda, Little Carmen*; *Mara*; *Los Secuestradores*. Lyric poems and cantatas: *Mazeppa*; *Il Tasso a Ferrara*, (Madrid, 1881); *La Cançó Llatina*; *In captivitatem comploratio*; *Glosa* (sinfonía jubilar).

Religious music: *Misa de Gloria*, 3 vs. solo, chorus, orch. and organ; *Te Deum*, 4 vs. orch. organ and harps; *Requiem*, 4 vs. unacc.

Orch.: *Festa*; *Lo cant de les montanyes*; *El Rey Lear* (incidental music); *Excelsior*; *I Trionfi*. Symph. poems: *Marcha de la Coronación a Mistral* (1st perf. Madrid 1881); *Matinada*; *Otger* (marcha fúnebre). Pf.: *Escenas de niños*, 4 hands. Songs: *Orientales*; *Consolations*; *Canciones Arabescas*. A str. 4tet.

Literature: *Cartas a un amigo sobre la música de Wagner*; *Por nuestra música*; *Teatro lírico español anterior al siglo XIX*, 5 vols.; *Folk-lore musical castellano del siglo XVI*: *Cancionero popular español*, 4 vols.; unfinished: *Los músicos españoles antiguos y modernos en sus libros*, unfinished; *Diccionario histórico y biográfico de músicos y escritores de música españoles*; *Tomás Luis de Victoria*; *Thomæ Ludovici Victoria, Abulensis, Opera Omnia*; *Hispaniæ Scholæ Musica Sacra* (4 vols. on Morales, Guerrero, Victoria, Cabezón, Ginez Pérez and Diego Ortiz); *P. Antonio Eximeno* (Glosario); *Emporio científico e histórico de organografía musical antigua española*; *La Festa d'Elche*; *Indigenismo musical español del teatro del siglo XVII*; *Antología de organistas clásicos españoles*; *Lírica nacionalizada*, studies on musical folk-lore; *Catalech de la Biblioteca Musical de la Diputación de Barcelona*; *Músicos contemporáneos y de otros tiempos*; *Orientaciones*; *Musiquerías*; *Quincenas musicales* (publ. in *La Vanguardia*, Barcelona); *Musichs vells de la terra* (contributions to *Revista Catalana*); *Jornadas de Arte*, 3 vols.; *Gramática musical*; *Prácticas preparatorias de instrumentación*; *Educación musical* (transl. of Lavignac's work); *Tratado de Armonía* (transl. of Richter's work); *Diccionario técnico de la música*. Publ.: Juan Bautista Pujol, Barcelona; Breitkopf, Leipzig; Ollendorf, Paris; Ildefonso Alier, Madrid; Unión Musical Española, Madrid; Eduardo Castells, Valls, Cataluña; Canuto Berea y Cia., La Coruña. Consult art. on him by Edgar Istel, in *Mus. Quarterly*, New York, April, 1924.—P. G. M.

PEDROLLO, Arrigo. Ital. compr. *b.* Montebello Vicentino, 5 Dec. 1878. Stud. at Milan Cons. under Mapelli and Coronaro; gained diploma in 1900. He devoted himself at first to orch. conducting. Compr. of several operas, perf. with success: *Terra promessa* (Cremona, 1908); *Juana* (Vicenza, 1914); *La Veglia* (Milan, 1920); *L'Uomo che ride* (Rome, 1920); also a ballet *Giuditta*; some symph. and chamber-music. Sonzogno, Milan, publ. the operas. —D. A.

PEDROTTI, Carlo. Ital. compr. and condr. *b.* Verona, 12 Nov. 1817; *d.* by his own hand, 16 Oct. 1892. This conspicuous figure—musician, teacher, compr. and condr.—took an important part in the Ital. mus. revival which occurred during 2nd half of XIX century. After having been dir. of the Ital. Opera of Amsterdam, he went in 1869 to Regio Theatre, Turin, where he was also dir. of the Mus. Acad. He left an indelible impression as founder and 1st dir. of the Popular Concerts, which marked beginning of movement in Italy, between 1850 and 1900, in favour of symph. and concert music. P. gave up these posts in order to assume dir. of the Liceo Mus. at Pesaro. Amongst his many stage works, the best-known is *Tutti in Maschera* (first perf. Verona, 1869).—D. A.

PEEL, Gerald Graham. Eng. compr. *b.* near Manchester, 9 Aug. 1877. Educated at Harrow and Univ. Coll. Oxford; stud. under Dr. Ernest Walker; has written a large number of very successful songs (*In Summertime on Bredon; Almond, Wild Almond*), and song-cycles, *The Country Lover, The Shropshire Lad,* etc.—E.-H.

PEMBAUR, Joseph. Ger. pianist; *b.* Innsbruck, 20 April, 1875. Pupil of his father, Joseph Pembaur sen.; 1893–6, of Munich R. School for Music (Rheinberger, Thuille); 1897–1900, teacher of pf. R. School of Music, Munich; 1901–2, stud. at Leipzig Cons. (Reisenauer); afterwards teacher there; since 1921, master at Acad. of Music, Munich.
The Poetry of Pf.-Playing (1910, 1912); *L. van Beethoven's Sonatas, op. 31 ii. and op. 57* (1915). Comp. songs (Tischer & Jagenberg).—A. E.

PEMBAUR, Karl. Ger. condr. and compr. *b.* Innsbruck, 24 Aug. 1876. Son and pupil of Joseph Pembaur sen.; and at Munich R. School of Music (Rheinberger, Werner, Lang); 1901, went to Dresden as Court-orgt. and solo-repetitor, at Court Theatre; since 1903, also condr. of Choral Union; 1909, title of R. mus. dir.; 1913, 2nd condr. of Court Orch.; 1910–13, cond. Robert Schumann Acad. of Singing.
Mass, G ma. op. 10 (mixed chorus, str. orch. and organ); mass, F mi.; *Serenade,* op. 11, for male chorus and orch.; humorous male choruses, op. 15 and 16; suite, *Bergbilder,* pf. and wind instrs.; songs, op. 25 and 26; mus. comedy, *Be Careful,* op. 17. —A. E.

PEÑA Y GOÑI, Antonio. Spanish critic; *b.* San Sebastian, 2 Nov. 1846; *d.* end of xix century. Author of a large number of writings on topical mus. subjects. His most important work is *La Ópera Española y la Música Dramática en el siglo XIX* (*The Span. Opera and Dramatic Music in XIX Century*), publ. in 1885, containing historical and biographical information on comprs. and on development of Span. opera, meaning by this term the lyric stage-works called *zarzuelas.*—P. G. M.

PENILLION SINGING, also called CANU GYDA'S TANNAU, *i.e.* "singing with the [harp] strings." A peculiar mode of singing, for several centuries widely practised in North Wales, but, until its revival within recent years, hardly known in South Wales. While the harpist played a Welsh melody, the singer sang his verses, not in the notes of the air, but in a simple counterpoint to it. It was not permissible to start with the tune, but the verse had to be so fitted as to finish exactly with its last note, or, in the case of a long tune, with the close of its first section. As stanzas of very different metres, varying in number and length of lines, were sung to the same tune, the place of commencing, and rhythm of vocal part, had to vary; and as the verse, once commenced, had to run on without pause or slur, it required an extensive and accurate knowledge of the Welsh tunes and metres to secure compliance with the rules. The ability to "set" the stanzas was technically called *gosod;* and was regarded as the most important requirement for successful penillion-singing. Furthermore, a good singer

was able to vary the voice part in different verses, and to sing three-time against two-time; or three-four against six-eight time.

The repertoire of harp-tunes was a very extensive one. Leathart (1825) gives a very incomplete list of 67. As the choice of a melody did not lie with the singer but with the harpist or, in competitions, with the judges, the singer had of necessity to be familiar with all the tunes. The verses, when not extemporised, had to be sung from memory. Whether in the convivial winter evening gatherings (*Noson Lawen*), so frequent in the farmhouses, or in the competitions, the singers sang in rotation, and whoever made a mistake, or failed to follow with a *penill,* had to drop out. The result was that people's memories were well stocked with Welsh poetry. In 1789 we read of a competition which lasted all night; and in 1790 a blacksmith at St. Asaph won after a contest of 13 hours!

It is probable that this custom originated in the practice of the official bards of the Middle Ages of chanting their compositions to the accompaniment of a harp. Even to this day much of the poetry sung belongs to the elaborate *Kynghanedd* metres. (For Eng. transl. of such verse, see *Welsh Folk-Song Journal,* Vol. II, Nos. 2, 3.) In addition, there were the traditional *penillion,* comprising hundreds of short disconnected verses, or groups of verses, brimful of homely philosophy and of wit, almost like extended proverbs; all couched in direct and appealing phrases, their lines easy and natural and often full of euphony.

During the xviii century and first half of xix this mode of singing was exceedingly popular. Leathart in 1825 advertises eight houses in London where weekly *penillion*-singing gatherings were held, besides two societies meeting once a month for the same purpose. During last 20 years there has been a renewal of interest in this singing and it has been introduced into many secondary and elementary schools. Though artistically it does not seem capable of a much higher development, it possesses distinct advantages as an instr. of culture. The simplicity of its vocal passages allows of an effective declamation of the words; the minds of the singers are benefited by the poetry treasured in their memories; at the same time the harp supplies a charming mus. undercurrent to the whole. In ordinary song there is always the temptation to show off the voice and to neglect the words. Here, on the contrary, the danger is to disregard good mus. vocalisation, and to rest satisfied with mechanical accuracy in the *gosod* of the verses. —J. Ll. W.

PENNICUICK, Ramsay. Australian compr. and teacher; *b.* Goulburn, N.S.W., 1892. Now prof. State Cons. Sydney, N.S.W. Has comp. songs to poems of Yeats, Symons, Masefield, etc.—E.-H.

PENTAFONIA. New tonal effect, conceived and fixed by Domenico Alaleona (*q.v.*) in his arts. on modern harmony (*Rivista Musicale Italiana,* 1911). It is based on division of octave into 5 equal parts. He was incited to seek out this scale from the necessity, in his compns., for a tonality which should represent something still more transcendental (as compared with the normal diatonic system) than those of " neuter tonality," the sounds of which coincide with those of tempered scale, and can therefore be related to diatonic scales. Alaleona has introduced a melody in the " pentaphonic" scale in his opera *Mirra*, to express a state of complete prostration of spirit. See score of opera and (in order to observe the notation adopted) the score of the intermezzo (Ricordi). This scale must not be confused with the pentatonic, which is represented by the black notes of the piano-keyboard. Consult also *The Pentaphonic Mode*, by Eaglefield-Hull, in *Monthly Musical Record*, Sept. 1922.—E.-H.

PENTLAND, Robert W. Scottish pianist; *b.* Shawlands, Glasgow, 5 June, 1865. Entirely self-taught in music. Church-orgt. at 14; and since in three of principal city churches in Edinburgh. As an accompanist he has seldom been excelled. Associated in that capacity for 26 years with late John Kirkhope's famous Edinburgh Choir. Commenced business as music-seller in 1881 with James Graham. Started a business of his own in 1893, now one of most extensive in Scotland. Has publ. coll. of Scottish songs (notably 10 books of folk-songs, ed. by Charles Macpherson).—W. S.

PEPPERCORN, Gertrude. Eng. pianist; *b.* West Horsley, Surrey. Stud. under Tobias Matthay at R.A.M.; *début* at age of 18 with great success; toured frequently in Great Britain, Holland, Germany and America.—E.-H.

PÉREZ CASAS, Bartolomé. Span. condr. and compr. *b.* Lorca (Murcia). 1897–1911, mus. dir. of Banda del Real Cuerpo de Alabarderos (see ALABARDEROS). Prof. of harmony at R. Cons. de Música, Madrid. Condr. at Kursaal, San Sebastian, and of Orquesta Filarmónica, Madrid. Since foundation of latter (1914) he has cond. over 400 concerts in Spain, besides tours in Portugal and his collab. with the Russ. Ballet in Madrid. With the exception of *Antar*, excerpts from *Scheherazade* and some minor pieces, he is responsible for the introduction of Russ. music in Spain (including Scriabin's *Divine Poem* and Glazunof's symphonies). He has also given the 1st perf. in Madrid of:

Iberia, La Mer, Danses, Le Martyre de Saint Sébastien (Debussy); *La Valse* (Ravel); *In the South* (Elgar); *A London Symphony* (R. Vaughan Williams); and amongst others, the following works by Span. comprs.: *Salamanca*, Tomás Bretón; *Sierra de Gredos*, Laviña; *Elegía*, E. Serrano; *Goyescas* (*Intermezzo*), Granados; *Una Aventura de Don Quijote*, Guridi; *Fantasía Gitana*, A. Bretón; *Boceto Andaluz*, P. G. Morales; *Suite*, J. Gómez; *Amor Dormido*, Isasi; *Impresión Sinfónica*, María Rodrigo; *Escenas Populares*, R. Villar; *Danzas Fantásticas*, Turina; *Una Kassida*, C. del Campo.

He is considered the leading condr. in Spain, in which capacity he can claim to have rendered the greatest service in his country to the national school and the cause of modern music in general. As a compr. he is more conscientious than prolific, being specially known for his orch. *Suite Mur-*

ciana, a work revealing a mastery in mus. construction and orch. technique high above the standard of the country at the time it was written, though the author had never been abroad. It still stands by itself for its scholastic character. Awarded a prize in a competition by the R. Acad. de Bellas Artes, it has been perf. in Paris, Rome, Petrograd and Moscow. He has also written a pf. 4tet, songs, and a *Poem* for military band.—P. G. M.

PERFORMING RIGHT SOCIETIES. See, under SOCIETIES, ENGLAND (xvi), FRANCE (xix), GERMANY (ix); also CHAPÍ.

PERICON. See SOUTH AMER. DANCES.

PÉRIER, Jean. Fr. t. singer; *b.* Paris, 2 Feb. 1869, of a Belgian family of musicians. At first employed in a bank, but, attracted by theatre, presented himself at Cons. and was accepted as pupil; carried off two 1st prizes for singing, and for *opéra-comique*. *Début* in *Magic Flute*, Opéra-Comique; he left in 1895 to play at Folies-Dramatiques; then at Bouffes-Parisiennes. After 5 years, returned to Opéra-Comique and sang with triumphant success in *La Basoche* and *La Fille de Tabarin*. From that time he has been classed as a singer of exceptional ability and a comedian of great distinction. Among his most characteristic creations are: *Pelléas et Mélisande, La Reine Fiamette, Miarka, Madama Butterfly, Fortunio, L'Heure Espagnole, Marouf, La Rôtisserie de la Reine Pédauque*. In each he astonishes by his resource and his power of transformation. He has several times left the Opéra-Comique to play comedies as an actor, with very great success. The principal merit of the creator of *Pelléas* is to have been not only an incomparable actor, but to have adapted to disputable vocal abilities a unique method of singing. Having entered the Cons. as b. and left it as t., he was able to grapple with the most varied rôles without troubling about the compass. It is the mus. characterisation which he gives to the most insignificant phrases which permits him to signalise in an unforgettable way the characters which he creates.—M. B.

PERINELLO, Carlo. Ital. compr. *b.* Trieste, 13 Feb. 1877. Stud. first in his native city; then in Leipzig under Jadassohn. 1904–14, taught compn. at Cons. in Trieste; then went to Milan Cons. Has publ. a str. 5tet in B mi. (Schmidl, Trieste), a 4tet in C ma. (same publ.) and songs and pf. pieces.—D. A.

PERIODICALS, Musical. *AUSTRIA.* — (i) *Der Merker*, Vienna, half-monthly mus. and theatrical review, founded 1909 by R. Specht and R. Batka, later ed. by L. Karpath, lastly from 1918 by Jul. Bittner and D. J. Bach. (ii) *Musikblätter des Anbruch*, half-monthly review for modern music, founded 1918 by Otto Schneider, publ. by Univ. Ed. Vienna. From 1922 ed. by Paul Stefan (with Paul A. Pisk). Cultivates international relationships between young contemporary comprs. Devotes special numbers to the Salzburg International Fests. (iii) *Musica*

Divina (Univ. Ed. Vienna), Austrian journal for church music, founded 1913. Ed. by Franz Moirdl. Publ. monthly until 1922.

BELGIUM.—Le Guide Musical, founded 1854 (Schott Frères, Brussels). Ceased publication during the 1914–18 war.

CZECHO-SLOVAKIA (Prague).—The oldest, *Dalibor*, has lost much of its importance lately. There are also publ.: *Smetana* (Hub. Doležil); *Listy Hudebni Matice* (Boleslav Vomáčka); *Hudebni Výchova*; *Věstník Pěvecký*, etc. Among those which have ceased publication the most important was the monthly *Hudebni Revue* (1908–20; K. Strecker and K. Hofmeister). The new monthly *Der Auftakt* (Prague), ed. by Dr. Erich Steinhard, gives much attention to contemporary music.

ENGLAND (London).—(i) *Musical Times*, monthly, founded 1844, ed. and publ. by Novello. Since then, ed. by Henry C. Lunn, 1863; W. A. Barrett, 1887; E. F. Jacques, 1891; F. G. Edwards, 1897; Dr. W. G. McNaught, Jan. 1910; Harvey Grace from 1918. (ii) *Musical Standard*, founded 1862, first appeared fortnightly; now weekly (publ. by W. Reeves). Its editors have included T. L. Southgate, Wallace J. Crowdy, Broadhouse, Dr. Turpin, E. A. Baughan. (iii) *Monthly Musical Record*, founded by George Augener, Jan. 1871. Editors: Ebenezer Prout, 1871; Charles Ainslie Barry, 1875; John South Shedlock, 1879; Eaglefield-Hull, 1913 till present time. (iv) *Musical Opinion and Music Trades Review*, monthly, founded 1877; now ed. by A. W. Fitzsimmons. (v) *Musical News*, at first a monthly; soon became weekly; founded by Dr. E. H. Turpin and T. L. Southgate in 1891. Acquired by Curwen & Sons in 1920, absorbing the monthly *Musical Herald* (founded as *Tonic Sol-fa Reporter* 1851, changing its name to *M.H.* 1899); ed. for a year (1921) by Edwin Evans; from then until 1924 by Kenneth Curwen; then by Sir R. R. Terry. (vi) *Music Teacher* (at first *Music Student*, founded 1906, ed. by Percy A. Scholes), ed. by W. R. Anderson, and publ. by Evans Bros. (vii) *Organist and Choirmaster*, founded 1894, ed. by Dr. E. J. Hopkins, C. W. Pearce and Charles Vincent; became (viii) *The Sackbut* in 1920, ed. by Philip Heseltine until 1921, when it was acquired by Curwen & Sons and ed. by Ursula Greville. (ix) *The Chesterian*, founded Nov. 1915, ed. by G. Jean-Aubry, appears 8 times a year, publ. by Chester & Co. (x) *British Music Bulletin*, monthly, founded and ed. by Dr. Eaglefield-Hull in 1919; 1922, ed. by Dr. C. E. Wheeler; 1923, became *Music Bulletin*, ed. by Violet Balkwill; from 1924 by A. R. Reade. (xi) *National Union of Organists' Associations Quarterly Record*, founded 1916, ed. by John Brook. (xii) *Music and Letters*, a quarterly review, comparing very favourably with the *Mus. Quarterly* (New York) and *La Revue Musicale* (Paris). Founded Jan. 1920, ed. by A. H. Fox-Strangways. (xiii) *The Organ*, quarterly review, first publ. 1921 (office of *Mus. Opinion*). (xiv) *The Performing Right Gazette*, quarterly,

founded 1922, ed. by James M. Glover. (xv) *Fanfare*, ed. by Leigh Henry, a monthly devoting itself entirely to ultra-modern music, only ran for 6 numbers (Goodwin & Tabb). (xvi) *The Gramophone*, founded 1923, ed. by Compton Mackenzie.

FINLAND.—(i) *Säveleitä*, founded (1887) and edited by P. J. Hannikainen. (ii) *Suomen Musiikkilehti*, edited by L. Ikonen.

FRANCE.—(i) *La Revue Musicale*, Paris, one of leading mus. reviews of the world. Has revived the title used by Fétis in 1826 for his journal. Founded 1918; appears 11 times a year. Dir. by Henry Prunières. (ii) *Courrier Musical*, Paris, largest Fr. fortnightly. (iii) *La Semaine Musicale*, Paris, a small weekly brochure. (iv) *Le Guide du Concert*, Paris, founded 1914.

GERMANY.—(i) *Neue Zeitschrift für Musik*, Leipzig, founded 1834 by Robert Schumann; 1844–68, ed. by Franz Brendel, then (till 1892) by publisher of the journal of the Allgemeiner deutscher Musikverein; 1903–6, ed. by Arn. Schering and W. Niemann; 1906, combined with the *Musikalische Wochenblatt*; from Jan. 1910, appeared under old title; 1911–19, ed. by Fr. Brandes; 1919–20, by Max Unger; 1920, appeared under title *Zeitschrift für Musik* (publ. by Steingräber), first edited by Wolfgang Lenk; 1921, by Alfred Heusz. (ii) *Signale für die Musikalische Welt*, founded 1843 by Bartholf Senff in Leipzig; from 1908, publ. by Simrock, Berlin; from 1920, ed. by Max Chop. (iii) *Musikalische Wochenblatt*, founded 1870 by O. Paul, but after a few numbers ed. by E. W. Fritzsch in Leipzig; 1902–6, ed. by K. Kikpe; from 1907 by L. Frankenstein. (iv) *Allgemeine Deutsche Musikzeitung*, founded 1874 by Fr. Luckhardt in Cassel; 1878–80, ed. by W. Tappert; from 1883, ed. by P. Schwers as *Allgemeine Musikzeitung*. (v) *Blätter für Haus und Kirchenmusik* (Beyer & Sons, Langensalza), founded 1897, monthly, ed. by E. Rabich; discontinued since 1914. (vi) *Die Musik*, Berlin, 1901–15, a very modern fortnightly paper with portraits and mus. illustrations; ed. by Bernhard Schuster; 1922, re-appeared as monthly paper, much enlarged (Deutsche Verlags-Anstalt). (vii) *Die Musikwelt*, Hamburg, 1920; ed. by H. Chevalleh. (viii) *Rheinische Musik und Theaterzeitung*, Cologne, ed. R. Wolff from 1900; 1908–11, W. Thomas-San Galli; then G. Tischer. (ix) *Neue Musikzeitung*, Cologne, J. Tonger, 1880–6; ed. by Reiser; since then publ. by Grüninger in Stuttgart, ed. by A. Swoboda and E. Raschdorff; from 1915, Osw. Kühn; 1917–21, W. Nagel; then Dr. H. Holle. (x) *Melos* (Berlin, Neuendorff & Moll), ed. from Feb. 1920 by Hermann Scherchen, since 1921 by Fritz Windisch. (xi) *Feuer*, 1918, ed. by Guido Bagier. (xii) *Deutsche Musikerzeitung*, founded 1870, ed. by H. Mendel till 1876; then by W. Lackowitz; 1897–1905 by P. Ertel; since then by H. Schaub. (xiii) *Zeitschrift* (monthly) and *Sammelbände* (quarterly) *der I.M.G.*, from 1899 to Oct. 1914 (Leipzig, Breitkopf & Härtel); ed. by O. Fleischer and Joh. Wolf; the *Zeitschrift* from

1904, ed. by Alfr. Heusz; the *Sammelbände*
from 1904, ed. by Max Seiffert; given up in
1914. Its German successor (xiv) *Zeitschrift für
Musikwissenschaft* (from Oct. 1918), ed. by
Alfred Einstein; and (xv) *Archiv für Musik-
wissenschaft* (from Oct. 1918), ed. by Max
Seiffert, J. Wolf and M. Schneider. (xvi) The
Jahrbuch der Musikbibliothek Peters, from 1895–
1900, ed. by Emil Vogel; since then by Rud.
Schwarz.

HOLLAND.—Caecilia en het Muziekcollege,
Rotterdam; *Caecilia* founded 1844 by Dr. J. C
Kist, and *Het Muziekcollege* 1913 by Émil Wege-
lin; amalgamated Nov. 1917. Ed. committee:
W. Andriessen, P. van Anrooy, S. Dresden, J.
van Gilse, W. Landré, P. A. van Westrheene.
Monthly in the summer season, fortnightly
Oct.–May; no concert notices, but gives popular
scientific arts. and propagates Dutch-Flemish
musical union.

ITALY.—(i) Rivista Musicale Italiana, the
most authoritative review in Italy; founded in
Turin in 1898 by Giuseppe Bocca, the publisher,
who edits it. An index of the 1st 20 years, compiled by L. Parigi, has been publ. (ii) *Musica*,
publ. in Rome, founded 1907. (iii) *Il Pianoforte*,
monthly, founded 1920; publ. by Fabbrica
Italiana di Pianoforti (F.I.P.) of Turin. (iv)
La Cultura Musicale, founded 1922, ed. by
Francesco Vatielli, Bologna. (v) *L'Arte Pianistica*, Naples; ed. by Alessandro Longo (*q.v.*). (vi)
Musica d' Oggi, publ. by Ricordi, Milan. (vii)
Santa Cecilia, for sacred music, founded 1899,
publ. by Soc. Tipografica Editrice Nazionale,
Turin. (viii) *La Critica Musicale*, Florence, ed.
by Luigi Parigi. (ix) *La Prora*, Rome, founded
1924, ed. by Alfredo Casella; organ of the
Corporazione delle Nuove Musiche. (x) *Rivista
Nazionale di Musica*, founded (1920) and dir.
by Vito Raeli.

JAPAN.—Ongakukai (Musical Japan), Tokio,
founded 1902; in 1923 ed. by Y. Yamamoto.
(Partly in English, partly in Japanese.)

RUSSIA.—A number of journals, such as
Russky Muzykalny Viestnik (1880–2) and
Muzykalny Mir (1882–3) have appeared in
Russia only to vanish after a short span of existence, and a list of them would be practically
useless. The earliest to appear were the *Sankt-
Petersburgsky Muzykalnye Magazin* (1795–6) and
the Moscow *Muzykalny Jurnal* (1810). For the
investigator's practical purposes, the following
list will prove sufficient: (i) *Muzykalny Sviet*,
Petrograd (1847–78). (ii) *Muzykalny Listok, ib.*
(1872–7). (iii) *Muzykalnoe Obozrenie, ib.* (1885–9)
(iv) *Bayan, ib.* (1888–1900). (v) *Russkaya
Muzykalnaya Gazeta, ib.* (1894–1917), publ. and
ed. by N. Findeisen. Appeared as a monthly
until 1899 and thenceforth as a weekly. Is in all
respects extremely useful. (vi) *Muzyka*, Moscow
(1910–17), ed. by V. Derjanovsky. A small
weekly, giving a good deal of information on
contemporary Russ. musicians. (vii) *Muzykalny
Sovremennik*, Petrograd (1915–17). A high-class
monthly, publ. by Andrei Rimsky-Korsakof and
replete with useful materials.

SCOTLAND.—Scottish Musical Magazine,
monthly, founded Sept. 1919; publ. by Paterson
Sons, Edinburgh; ed. by William Saunders.

SPAIN.—(i) Harmonia, mus. review (Madrid).
See SAN MIGUEL. (ii) *Revista Música Sacro-
Hispana*, Madrid. [3] See OTAÑO.

U.S.A.—The rapid growth and the broad extension of mus. culture, or at any rate of mus.
interest, in the U.S.A. within the last few decades can be very well traced in the number and
the variety of mus. journals and periodicals
which have grown to maturity or come into being
during this period. Hardly a single special field
of mus. activity has been left without its official
organ or its journalistic medium.

(i) At the head of the list of serious and dignified
publications stands the *Musical Quarterly*, founded
Jan. 1915, under the editorship of Oscar G. Sonneck,
and publ. by G. Schirmer in New York. (ii) The
Chicago monthly journal *Music*, ed. by W. S. B.
Mathews, which ran through 22 vols (1891–1902), was
the nearest approach to the standard and quality of
Musical Quarterly before this time. (iii) *Church Music
Review*, begun in 1901, broadened its field and
changed its name to *The New Music Review* in 1904.
It is official organ of Amer. Guild of Orgts. Although
not a mus. journal in ordinary sense of word, the
Proceedings of Music Teachers' National Association
cannot be overlooked here. The Association has held
annual meetings since 1876 with but few omissions.
Since 1906, the *Proceedings* have been publ. under
title of *Studies in Musical Education, History and
Æsthetics*, ed. by Waldo Selden Pratt until 1915,
Charles N. Boyd 1916, Karl W. Gehrkens since 1917.
(iv) Dissemination of mus. news and information in
most energetic Amer. fashion, with portraits of comprs.
and performers, is accomplished by *Musical Courier*
(weekly, New York; founded 1880), and (v) *Musical
America* (weekly, founded 1904). (vi) The Middle
Western field has its special organ in *Musical Leader*
(monthly, Chicago; founded 1895). (vii) *Pacific
Coast Musician* (monthly, Los Angeles; founded
1912). (viii) *Musical Monitor*, monthly, Chicago
(beginning 1911 as *Musical World* and changing
its name in 1913), was until 1922 official organ of
National Federation of Mus. Clubs; publ. since 1917
in New York. With less space devoted to music
and concert news, and having therein contain instructive
arts. and essays of a more popular nature than those
of *Musical Quarterly* or *New Music Review*: (ix) The
Musician, monthly, founded by Hatch Music Co.
Boston, 1896; publ. by Oliver Ditson 1904–18, and
by Thomas Tapper (until 1907) and W. J. Baltzell
(until 1918); now publ. and ed. by Paul Kempf, New
York. (x) *The Étude*, monthly, publ. by Theodore
Presser, started in Lynchburg, Va. 1883; since 1884
in Philadelphia; present ed. J. F. Cooke. (xi)
Musical Observer, monthly, publ. since 1907 by Carl
Fischer, New York, ed. by Gustave Saenger. (xii)
Musical Digest, weekly, New York, founded 1921,
ed. by Pierre V. Key. Among the periodicals which
cover a special field: (xiii) *The Diapason*, monthly,
Chicago, founded 1910 by S. E. Gruenstein, is official
organ of National Association of Orgts. and of the
Organ Builders' Association of America. Gruenstein
still its ed. and publ. (xiv) *The American Organist*,
New York, founded 1918 by T. Scott Buhrmann on
behalf of Amer. Guild of Orgts., became independent
shortly after its foundation. (xv) Flute-players had
a periodical in *The Flutist*, monthly, begun in 1920 by
Emil Medicus in Asheville, N.C., and (xvi) harpists
are represented by the *Eolian Review*, ed. by Carlos
Salzedo, 3 times a year (first number Dec. 1921).
(xvii) The largest association of organised musicians,
the American Federation of Musicians, has for its
official journal the monthly *International Musician*,
publ. Newark, N.J., by W. J. Kerngood. The music
trades are represented by 3 weeklies, (xviii) *Presto*,
Chicago, founded 1884, (xix) *Music Trade Review*,
New York, founded 1879, and (xx) *The Music Trades*,
New York, founded 1890.

WALES.—Y Cerrdor Newydd, monthly, ed.
by W. S. Gwynn Williams.

PERKINS, Charles William. Eng. orgt. *b.*
Birmingham, 4 Oct. 1855. Stud. under Andrew

Deakin and Dr. Swinnerton Heap; various church appointments; orgt. Town Hall, Birmingham, 1887–1923; recitals all over Great Britain; orgt. Blenheim Palace (for the Duke of Marlborough) from 1894. An outstanding recital-player.—E.-H.

PEROSI, Lorenzo. Ital. priest and compr. b. Tortona, 20 Dec. 1872. One of most genial and fertile contemporary Ital. composers; has risen to high fame, particularly with his oratorios. Stud. first under his father, and very early gave proofs of great mus. aptitude and facility. Stud. for time at Milan Cons. and at Ratisbon (Regensburg) school, conducted by Haberl. Returning to Italy, P. was nominated choirmaster of Duomo at Imola, whence he passed on to Basilica of San Marco, Venice. In 1898, was appointed by Pope Leo XIII mus. dir. of Sistine Chapel. He retired from musical activies in 1915, on account of his health. In 1923 he again began conducting concerts, in which some of his new works were performed: *Psalms of David* (written in memory of his mother).

Oratorios: *La Passione di Gesù Cristo, secondo San Marco* (1897); *La Trasfigurazione di N. S. Gesù Cristo* (March, 1898); *La risurrezione di Lazzaro* (June, 1898); *La risurrezione di Cristo* (November, 1898); *Il Natale del Redentore (Birth of the Redeemer)* (1899); *L'Entrata di Cristo in Gerusalemme* (1900); *La strage degli innocenti (The Massacre of the Innocents)* (1900).
Also: *Mosè*, symphonic-vocal poem (1901); *Il Giudizio universale*, poem (1904); *Transitus animœ* (1907); *O padre nostro* (from *Divina Commedia*) (1907); *Stabat Mater* (1904); *Dies ista* (1904); *Tema can variazioni e Scherzo*, for orch. (1902); *In patris memoriam* (1910).
Further, has written much sacred music, including 20 masses; 8 orch. suites, called by names of principal Ital. cities. Various other works are still unpubl. The majority of P.'s compns. have been publ. by Ricordi; some by Capra, Turin; Bertarelli, Milan; Schwann, Düsseldorf; and Novello, London.
Consult: Romain Rolland, *Don L. P.*, in *Musiciens d'aujourd'hui* (Paris, 1908, Hachette); Agostino Cameroni, *L. P. e i suoi primi quattro oratorii* (Bergamo, 1899, Bolis); besides many arts. in reviews, including one by Adelmo Damerini in *Il Pianoforte* (Turin, April 1923).—D. A.

PERRIN, Henry Crane. Eng. orgt. compr. b. Wallingborough, in 1865. Mus.Doc. Dublin; stud. in England and on Continent. His first appointment was orgt. and choirmaster of St. Columba's Coll. Dublin. 1888–92, St. John's Ch. Lowestoft; then St. Michael's, Coventry, until 1898, when he was elected orgt. and master of choristers at Canterbury Cath. He remained there for 10 years, exercising also a valuable influence as chairman and chief organiser of Kent Competitive Mus. Fests. In 1908 he accepted position of prof. and dir. of music at McGill Univ. Montreal; in 1920 the Governors of Univ. constituted a Faculty of Music with Dr. Perrin as Dean of the Faculty. A number of his songs are publ. by Breitkopf; Stainer & Bell, etc; 2 cantatas (Breitkopf); church music (Vincent; John Church).—L. S.

PERSFELT, Bror. Swedish cellist; b. Stockholm, 27 May, 1881. Stud. R. Cons. Stockholm, 1894–99; then at Frankfort-o-M. under Hugo Becker and Bernh. Cossmann; on staff of Music Inst. at Helsingfors, 1904–9 as cello teacher;

also leading cellist of Symphony Orch. there; 2 years in Berlin as concert-player. During 1922–3 season, solo-cellist member of R. Chapel (Opera Orch.), Stockholm.
Passacaglia, vn. and cello; Introduction and fugue, cello alone; 8 concert-*études*; cello tutor.—P. V.

PERTILE, Aureliano. Ital. t. singer; b. Montagnana, Padua, 3 Nov. 1885. He has sung at principal European and Amer. theatres. In recent years, he has establ. a reputation for himself in Italy at La Scala, Milan. He is one of the most esteemed Ital. t. singers living. —D. A.

PERUTZ, Robert. Polish violinist; b. Lemberg, 1886. Pupil of Wolfsthal, Marteau and Flesch. In 1910, went to Valparaiso in Chile, where he became prof. at Cons.; returned to Europe in 1914; spent the war-years in giving concerts in Russia; in 1920 went to N. America and is living in Cleveland as prof. at the Cons. and travelling as a brilliant violinist.—Zd. J.

PESTALOZZI, Heinrich. Swiss singer, compr. b. Wädenswil, 27 Aug. 1878. Stud. compn. under R. Kahn and E. Behm and singing under Kammersänger A. Heinemann in Berlin, where he taught singing for 10 years. Since 1918, has taught singing at Cons. in Zurich. Has written over 100 songs which have become very popular in Switzerland, being extremely melodious and well written; also publ. an important essay, *Individuelle Stimmbildung*.
Songs for children (Berlin, O. Wernthal; Zurich, Orell Füssli); songs (Zurich, Hüni); 18 unacc. choruses (Zurich, Hug); vn. sonata, op. 38 (Hug); *Requiem*, soli, chorus, organ, orch.; symph. poem *Das Lied von der Sehnsucht*; chamber-music; pf. pieces.—F. H.

PETERS, Guido. Austrian pianist and compr. b. Graz, 29 Nov. 1866. Stud. Vienna Cons.; 1901-3 in Munich; from 1905 in Vienna.
3 symphonies (I, *Ländliche* in E; II, E mi; II, F sharp mi.); 2 str. 4tets (C mi.; A); 8tet (*Notturno*) in D; cello sonata, F mi.; songs.—A. E.

PETERS, Rudolf. Ger. compr. b. Gelsenkirchen, 21 Feb. 1902. Son and pupil of city mus. dir. H. Peters; then of Hugo Grüters in Bonn; since 1920 of Pauer and Haas, Stuttgart; precocious and talented composer.
Sonata for vn. and pf. C ma. op. 1; 5 fantasias for pf. op. 2; sonata for cello, C mi. op. 3; characteristic pieces for pf. op. 4; *Stimmungsbilder*, pf. op. 6; pf. fantasia, C sharp mi. op. 7; str. 4tet, A mi. op. 8.—A. E.

PETERSEN, Wilhelm. Ger. compr. b. Athens, 15 March, 1880. Stud. at Acad. of Music, Munich (Mottl and Klose); privately under Rud. Louis. 1913–14, for a short time at Stadttheater, Lubeck, but now devotes himself to compn. in Munich and Darmstadt.
Variations for pf. op. 1; pf. sonatas, op. 3 and 5; sonata, vn. and pf. op. 11; 4tet, G ma. op. 7; songs, op. 9; *Hymn*, s. and orch. op. 10; Variations, str. orch. op. 12; symph. fantasy, op. 2; *Eine Trauermusik*, op. 4; 2 symphonies, op. 6 and 8.—A. E.

PETERSON-BERGER, O. Wilhelm. Swedish compr. b. Ullånger, 27 Feb. 1867. Stud. at R. Cons. Stockholm, 1886–9; then in Dresden under E. Kretschmar and H. Scholtz; teacher at Ulmeå, 1890–2; and at Dresden, School of Music, 1892–4; returned to Stockholm, 1895; music critic on *Dagens Nyheter*, 1896–1908, and

from 1910; 1908-10, 1st *régisseur* of R. Opera, Stockholm; member R.A.M. Stockholm, 1921.
Operas (all 1st perf. Stockholm): *Sveagaldrar* (1897); *Lyckan* (1903); *Ran* (1903); *Arnljot* (1910); *Domedagsprofeterna* (1919). Orch.: *Carnival in Stockholm* (1902); Symphony No. I, *Baneret* (*The Banner*) (1904); No. II, *Sunnanfärd* (1913); No. III, *Same Åtnam*; suite, *Italiana* (1922). 2 sonatas, vn. and pf.: No. I, C mi. (1887); No. II, G (1910); Suite, vn. and pf. op. 15 (1896); cantatas, soli, chorus, orch., for Jubilees in Umeå and Luleå (1921). Songs to words by Swedish poets (*Swedish Lyrics*) and by Nietzsche; ballad, *Flor and Blancheflor*; pf. pieces, *Frösöblomster* (Abr. Lundqvist); male-v. part-songs. Also a book on music culture in Sweden (1911) and translated into Swedish some works by Wagner (1913) and Nietzsche (1902).—P. V.

PETRAUSKAS, Miskas. Lithuanian compr. Stud. at Petrograd Cons. Won fame in America, where he establ. a Lithuanian Music School and pub!. his own compns. His printed compns. are more numerous than those of any other Lithuanian compr., but unfortunately they are not widely diffused in his native country, being almost unknown except for the operettas *Birute*, *Consilium Facultatis*, and *The Lithuanian Millionaire*. To him Lithuanian-Americans owe their choirs, choir-leaders, and song-amateurs.—H. R.

PETRŽELKA, Vilém. Czechoslovak compr. *b.* Králové Pole (Moravia), 1889. Stud. compn. under L. Janáček and V. Novák; theatre-condr. (Pardubice, Bohemia); later at Brno (Brünn) as teacher; since 1919 prof. of compn. at Cons. in Brno.
2 str. 4tets; cycle of male choruses, *Zivot* (*Life*); songs: *Zivly* (*The Elements*), and *Samoty duše* (*Loneliness of Soul*); for pf.: *Písně poezie a prozy* (*Songs in Poetry and Prose*); for vn. and pf. *Z intimních chvil* (*In Intimate Hours*); mixed choir and orch. *Modlitba k slunci* (*Prayer to the Sun*); arr. of national songs (Hudební Matice, Prague).—V. ST.

PETSCHNIKOF, Alexander. Russian violin-virtuoso; *b.* Jeletz (Orel Govt.), 8 Feb. 1873. Stud. at Moscow Cons. (Hrimaly); lived in Berlin; made R. prof. 1910; teacher at R. Acad. Munich, 1913 till 1921. Gave many concerts with his wife, Mme. Lili (violinist), now divorced.—A. E.

PFEIFFER, Theodor. Ger. pianist; *b.* Heidelberg, 20 Oct. 1853. Stud. philology, then became music-seller, Stuttgart, and pupil of Seidel, Stuttgart Cons.; 1884-6, summer-pupil of Bülow at Raff Cons. Frankfort-o-M.; 1889, music-master at Baden-Baden; 1899, also teacher at Mannheim Cons.; 1905, professor.
Virtuoso Studies and *Elementary Studies to Bülow's Editions* (Berlin, Luckhardt); *Studies from Hans Bülow* (1894, 6th ed. 1909; supplement by Vianna da Motta, 1895). Comp. well-known pf. solos; *Dryaden-spiel*; *Martellato Étude*; German Mass; choruses, etc.—A. E.

PFITZNER, Hans. Composer; *b.* Moscow, 5 May, 1869. Son of German parents; pupil of father (music director and violinist at Stadttheater, Frankfort-on-Main) and of Hoch's Conservatoire there (Kwast, Knorr); 1892-3, teacher at Conservatoire, Coblenz; 1893, gave concert (own compositions) in Berlin; 1894-5, honorary conductor at Mayence Stadttheater; 1896, salaried second conductor; 1897, teacher of composition and conducting at Stern's Conservatoire, Berlin; 1903, also conductor of Theater des Westens; 1907, conducted Munich

Subscription Concerts with Kaim Orchestra till dissolution; 1908, succeeded Fr. Stockhausen as city music director, director of Conservatoire and opera manager. Pfitzner recognised that his real value lay in opera production (six books on "production" partly published by E. Mehler). Withdrew from management of Strasburg Opera, 1916; 1919-20, conducted concerts of Munich Concert Society; taught advanced classes at Berlin High School; 1913, Royal professor; Strasburg Univ. bestowed on him Ph.D.; March 1919, member of Berlin Academy for Art; 1920, Bavarian general music director. Pfitzner resides at Schöndorf on the Ammersee. He is to be accepted as one of the last disciples of that Romanticism which has its roots in Schumann's music, and in all Wagner's works, especially the earlier; in that which finds its intellectual expression in Schopenhauer and its poetical expression in Eichendorff. Pfitzner is a musician in whose ecstatic and meditative composition that spiritual tendency still lingers on.
Stage works: *Der arme Heinrich*, mus. drama in 2 (3) acts, words from legend of Middle Ages by J. Grün (Brockhaus); *The Rose in the Garden of Love*, romantic opera in 2 acts, with prelude and epilogue, words by J. Grün (Brockhaus); *Palestrina*, mus. legend, own libretto (Fürstner); *The Christmas Fairy*, op. 20, play-opera rev. with free, sometimes literal, use of text of Ilse v. Stach's *Christmas Fairy-Tale* (Fürstner).
Stage music: Music to Ibsen's *Festival at Solhaug* (Brockhaus); music to H. v. Kleist's *Käthchen of Heilbronn*, op. 17 (Ries & Erler).
For orch.: *Scherzo* (Brockhaus); pf. concerto, E flat ma. op. 31 (Fürstner); vn. concerto (1923); songs with orch. *Master Oluf*, op. 12; ballads from Herder for barit. (Bote & Bock); *The Goblins*, op. 14, b. and orch. (Brockhaus); 2 *German Songs*, op. 25: (1) *The Trumpeter*, (2) *Lamentation* (Brockhaus); *The Flower's Revenge*, female chorus, contr. solo and orch. (Ries & Erler).
Chamber-music: Sonata for cello and pf., F sharp mi. op. 1 (Breitkopf); pf. vn. and cello sonata, F ma. op. 8 (Simrock); str. 4tet, D ma. op. 13 (Brockhaus); pf. 5tet, C ma. op. 23 (Peters); pf. and vn. sonata, E mi. op. 27 (Peters).
Songs with pf.: op. 2 (Brockhaus); op. 3 (Firnberg); op. 4 (Firnberg); op. 5 (Fürstner); op. 6 (Fürstner); op. 7 (Ries & Erler); op. 9 (Brockhaus); op. 11 (Brockhaus); op. 15 (Brockhaus); op. 19 (Brockhaus); *To the Moon*, op. 18 (Brockhaus); op. 21 (Kahnt); op. 22, 24, 26 (Brockhaus), 29, 30, 32 (Fürstner).
Other works: *Columbus* (Schiller), 8-v. chorus unacc. op. 16 (Ries & Erler); *Roundelay to New Year's Festival*, 1901, b., mixed or male chorus and pf. (Brockhaus); *Song of the Bards* from Hermann's *Battle* by Kleist; *Faithlessness and Consolation*, Ger. national song (Brockhaus); 8 female choruses by Robert Schumann with instr. acc., 1 vol. (Univ. Ed.); *Undine* (E. T. A. Hoffmann), pf. score arr. from full score (Peters); *The Knight-Templar and the Jewess*, (H. Marschner), newly rev. and publ. in full and short score (Brockhaus); *Erl King*; *Odin's Ocean Ride*; ballads by Carl Löwe, arr. for full orch. Brockhaus).
Literary works: *On Musical Drama* (1915); collection of essays containing *Stage Tradition*, I, II, III; *E. T. A. Hoffmann's Undine*; *First Principles in Opera*, I, II, III; *Weber's Freischütz*; *Parsifal Material and its Formation*; *Futurist Dangers*, a reply to Busoni's *Æsthetics*; *Die neue Aesthetik der musikalischen Impotenz* (1919).
Consult: R. Louis, *H. Pf.* (1909); A. Seidl, *H. Pf.* (1921); C. Wandreg, *H. Pf.* (1922); Erwin Kroll, *H. Pf.* (1924); R. Felber, *Mus. Quarterly*, Jan. 1924.—A. E.

PFOHL, Ferdinand. Ger.-Czechoslovak author, compr. *b.* Elbogen, 12 Oct. 1863. Stud. law at Prague; 1885, at Leipzig, philosophy and music (Oskar Paul); 1892, joined editorial staff *Ham-*

burger Nachrichten; 1908, co-dir. of Vogt Cons.
(prof. of theory, æsthetics, technique, style);
1913, R. prof.; 1923, Dr. *h.c.*

Höllenbreughel as Tutor; *Bayreuth Fanfarons*; *The Nibelungen in Bayreuth* (1896); *Modern Opera* (1894); *A. Nikisch* (1900 and 1922); *Through Africa* (1891); *Travels West to East* (1902); *Richard Wagner, his Life and Work* (Berlin, 1911); *Karl Grammann, an Artist's Life* (Berlin, 1910). Songs: *Moon-Rondeau*, op. 4; *Siren Songs*, op. 9; *Tower Ballads*, op. 14; symph. poems: *Pierrot lunaire*; *The Sunken Bell*; *Frau Holle*; ballet-scene, op. 13; choral work, *Twardowsky*, op. 10 (male chorus, s. orch.); symph. fantasy (5 movements), *The Sea*; pf. pieces: *Strandbilder*; *Elegiac Suite.—A. E.*

PHILIP, Achille. Fr. orgt. and compr. *b.*
Arles, 12 Oct. 1878. Pupil of Alex. Guilmant,
Lenepveu and d'Indy; 1st prize for cpt. and
fugue, 1904; now orgt. at St.-Jacques du
Haut-Pas (Paris) and prof. at *Schola Cantorum*.

Symph. poems for orch.: *Au pays basque* (1909); *Les Djinns* (1913); *Dans un parc enchanté* (1917); *5 Études lyriques* (v. and orch. 1919); *Fantaisie orchestrale* (1919); *Nymphes et Naïades* (1920); *Messe solennelle*; *Poème des Saisons*; *L'Or du Menhir* (lyric drama, 2 acts). Also sonata, pf. and vn.; pf. pieces; 30 songs; Psalm; motets; madrigals.—A. C.

PHILIPP, Franz. Ger. compr. *b.* Freiburg-i-
Breisgau, 24 Aug. 1890. Stud. music (organ
under Adolf Hamm, Basle), literature and philosophy at Freiburg Univ. From 1914, devoted
himself to compn. Teacher of organ, theory and
mus. history and condr. of male choral soc.
Concordia at Freiburg.

Publ.: *War-Songs*, op. 5; songs, op. 7: pf. ballad, op. 6; *Germany's Hour*, chorus and orch. (Berlin, 1916). In ms.: *Mass for Peace*; symph. prelude, en-tr'actes and incidental music to Hermann Burte's *Samson*; pf. 4tet, C mi. op. 12.—A. E.

PHILIPP, Isidore. Fr. pf.-teacher and compr.
b. 2 Sept. 1863. Pupil of Georges Mathias
(Paris Cons.), of Stephen Heller, Théodore Ritter,
and Saint-Saëns. Founded (with Rémy, Berthelier and Loeb) a Soc. of Chamber-Music, which
amalgamated with the Soc. of Wind Instrumentalists, on the death of Taffanel. Philipp
has been prof. at Paris Cons. since 1903. His
educational work is considerable:

Exercices journaliers (preface by Saint-Saëns); *Exercices et Études*; *Exercices de Tenues* (4 vols.); *Études techniques* (2 vols.); *Anthologie des traits de Chopin*; *Problèmes techniques et leur solution*; 300 studies for teaching (under titles *Nouveau Gradus* and *Anthologie*). Has comp. some original suites: *Pastels, Figurines, Valses, Caprices, Fantasmagories, Féerie.—A. C.*

PHILIPPI, Maria Cäcilia. Swiss contr. singer;
b. Basle, 26 July, 1875. Stud. singing under
Stockhausen at Frankfort and Mme. Viardot-
Garcia in Paris; one of the eminent singers of
our day, possessing a strong aud admirably
trained voice, and fine musicianship. Known also
as founder of a special Bach style, all her own.
She appeared at Prom. Concerts, Queen's Hall,
London, 19 Oct. 1904.

Consult: Steinitzer, *Berühmte Gesangsmeister* (Stuttgart); articles in *Jahrbuch der Schweiz* (1921) and in *Goldene Buch der Musik* (Berlin, Spemann). —F. H.

PHILLIPS, Montague Fawcett. Eng. compr.
b. London, 13 Nov. 1885. Stud. at R.A.M. under
Frederick Corder. He is best known by his
compns. on the lighter side of music. Married
Clara Butterworth, singer and actress.

The Rebel Maid, romantic light opera in 3 acts (Chappell) Empire Theatre, London, 12 March, 1921;

symphony in C mi.; 2 overtures (*Heroic*; *Boadicea*); *Symph. Scherzo*, orch.; *Dance Suite* (Chappell); *Irish Idyll* (*id.*); pf. concertos: No. 1, F sharp mi.; No. 2, E ma.; *Phantasy* for vn. and orch. (Schott); *The Death of Admiral Blake* (Newbolt), barit. solo, chorus and orch. (Chappell); *The Song of Rosamund*, scena for s. and orch. (*id.*); Prelude and fugue in G mi. for organ (Stainer & Bell); str. 4tet, D ma.; pf. pieces (Augener); song - cycles and separate songs (Chappell).—E.-H.

PIAGGIO, Celestino. Argentine pianist, compr.
b. Concordia, in 1886. Stud. at Buenos Ayres
Cons., going to Paris in 1908 to complete
training at the *Schola Cantorum*. Has already
publ. many pf. pieces and 3 songs. Is considered to be opening a new road in Argentine
art.—A. M.

PIANOFORTE MUSIC FROM 1880. The technique of piano-playing has developed so fast and
thoroughly during the last few decades that it
seems almost impossible for any one person to
discover all the causes of development. From
1850 until 1890, certainly, the music written for
the piano was mainly Chopinesque. This is only
natural, seeing the tremendous new ground
Chopin had opened, and the immense difference
he had insisted upon in the treatment of the
piano. Until his advent, it had been used mainly
as a percussive instrument, and most of the music
written for it either demanded harsh noises from
it, or else should have been written for another
instr. or collection of instrs. He was the first
compr. to think of the beauty that it contained,
and the most emphatic in desiring it to express
the poetical side of music, so it was obvious that
until another genius was born he would have
hundreds of imitators. Claude Debussy was this
genius, and to him entirely is due the tremendous
change in the outlook of the pianist and compr.
in the way of technique. In 1890 Debussy published the *Suite Bergamasque*, a collection of 4
pieces, which, though not very startling to our
trained eyes nowadays, must have created some
stir then. The third one, *Clair de Lune*, shows us
the beginning of the use of piano-colour, which
Debussy developed so much in his later work.
In 1903 appeared another set of pieces, *Estampes*.
These are a distinct advance on all his previous
pieces. *Pagodes*, the first of the three, though
perhaps puzzling to the listener, will always be
interesting to the pianist because of the subtle
use of both pedals, particularly with the sus-
taining pedal in the long holdings of arpeggio-
seventh passages, almost producing the effect
of overtones. This becomes a feature in Debussy's pianism, and has certainly demanded
greater elasticity and freedom of arm-movement,
and prevented us from always thinking that a
note must be " struck." It is not quantity of
sound any longer; it is quality. All this is so
conclusively proved by the non-success of old-
time favourite pianists who have come back
after some years of absence and played in the
old way. The old days of percussive playing are
over. Anyone with either finger, wrist or arm-
power can produce a big tone when necessary,
but he has so many tones to think of in the interpretation of modern music, and sees so many

new channels of intimate expression in the older masters, that he cannot bring himself to concentrate on just ,strengthening the various muscles so as to strike the note with a bigger blow. After all, the modern piano is capable of producing nearly every possible colour in musical expression, and the fully equipped modern pianist has to see that he has command of this tone-colour, before he can hope to win fame. This is mainly due to Debussy, and not to the excellence of the present-day piano, which, after all, we have to thank Liszt for, and is very little better now than forty years ago. In this same set are two more remarkable pieces: *La Soirée dans Grenade*, a most attractive piece of colour-writing suggesting the glamour of a warm Mediterranean evening; and *Jardins sous la pluie*, where we find the pedal just as necessary, but used in exactly the opposite way to the previous two compositions. Here it is the percussive pedal, sharpening the short, incisive tone which is so vitally necessary to the interpretation, and enhancing the rhythmic accent. The next year we had *L'Isle joyeuse*, that wonderful example of music so befitting its title. It is a new technique that is being employed here, and yet it is mainly built on the five-finger exercise! *Reflets dans l'eau* is a superb example of Debussy's art in demanding the last atom of tone-colour. *Hommage à Rameau* is a big building-up of overtones (another favourite device of his) and *Mouvement*, with its suggestion of thousands of wheels revolving at break-neck speed, is clearly a proof of the tremendous rapidity of finger-movement which is so compulsory in the make-up of contemporary pianism. The 2 books of Preludes, 24 in all, continue this enormous development. In *La Cathédrale engloutie*, the pedal is such an important factor in the rendering that, without a special study of it, the effect is void. Here is another big stride. One has to live practically on the pedal, and on both of them. To pedal harmonically or melodically is of little use. It is used in every imaginable way. You have to pick out the important notes in chords or passages which have to stand out, although the dampers are up, and many notes are sounding. You have to hold on to notes or chords through, sometimes, great numbers of different harmonies, yet never allow them to be blurred. So the pedal has come into its own kingdom—it is as important as the fingers themselves. Maurice Ravel in his *Jeux d'eaux* (publ. in 1915) has assumed quite an individuality of his own. Here is the movement of water most ideally depicted. It has to be so clear, yet so smooth. If one played it with the same technical equipment as employed in a composition of as late a period even as Liszt, the result would be laughable. Yet it is for the selfsame instrument! It is the absence of the percussive touch, the smoothness of arm - movement, and the thorough understanding of all that the pedal is capable of, that marks the difference between old and new technique. *Ondine*, by the same compr., is another example

of this great improvement. His *Le Gibet* could never have been dreamt of by Beethoven, great genius though he was. A most remarkable piece is Déodat de Séverac's *Baigneuses au soleil*. In many respects this is one of the finest pianistic pieces ever written. It is scintillating, buoyant, full of fresh air and vitality. One can imagine the exhilaration of the surf-bather! Did you ever think of these effects in any pre-Debussy composition? It would have been impossible. The great pianists in the past could never have produced the tone-colour necessary for this type of music. During the same period, about 1906, Isaac Albeniz, a Spaniard, who lived most of his life in England, suddenly dropped the yoke of being a salon-music composer, and published 4 books, each containing 3 pieces, which he called *Iberia*. Like all modern Spanish music, they are entirely built up on the dance-rhythms of his country; but they are a very important addition to the literature of modern music. They are unaffected by any idioms of the Fr. school, yet are harmonically very modern. As legitimate pianism they are not the equal of the French works referred to above. They require greater power, are more emotional, and, not being so subtle, are more direct in their appeal. Their notation is very difficult, and one sadly misses, in their complexity. the pruning-knife of the Frenchmen. The *Goyescas* of Granados are particularly pianistic, for their compr. was an excellent player, but they say nothing new. Turina has written some excellent pieces also, but the one we expect most from in this school is Manuel de Falla, still in the prime of life. His set of *Pièces Espagnoles* (1906) established him as a man with fresh ideas, one who had the gift of expressing himself on the piano. This is an important point. There have been many fine works composed for the piano, which would have sounded equally well on another instrument, or even orchestrated. There are a great number of pieces which look wonderful on paper, but fail miserably in performance. Unless the sound of the piano can be heard in the composition, the literature of piano music can do very well without it. The Russian school is chiefly represented by Scriabin. He undoubtedly was too slavish a disciple of Chopin in his earlier works. Delightful as these are, they do not figure very much in this remarkable change in technical outlook. He was a revolutionary in all things. His ideas were big, but the piano could not stand up to what he asked of it, and his sense of pianism gradually declined. His later works cannot be labelled as true piano-music. Therefore, he need not be included in our list of comprs. responsible for the change in pf. technique. Rachmaninof's goodly number of pieces are extremely effective, but they are cast in the old mould, and offer no new ideas. Metner has been spoken of as the Russian Brahms—a safe assertion. The enormous sense of detail of the Russian is too apparent in all his work, and though it is all excellent piano-writing, it can all be played in the old, straightforward manner, and does not need the application of any new technique in performance. Prokofief and several others whom one encounters have as yet shown us nothing original in what we are seeking. In fact, since Balakiref, there have been no pioneers in Russian music. The modern Italian composers as yet are too keen imitators of the ultra-modern Frenchmen to count, though undoubtedly an Ital. school is in the making. Germany has given us nothing since Brahms—and we are beyond that period. It is curious that this nation appears so far behind all the other European countries in modern piano - music. Béla Bartók seems to be the only other representative outside France and England who is striking a new sound. Hungarian by birth, he is intensely national in his work. One is inclined to think that here is the weakness, because original music and thought cannot emanate from folk-song and folk-dance. To realise his self-expression he uses the cimbalom as the background of his writings, and naturally the piano is only thought of as an instrument to be hit. Scale-passages do not exist in any form whatsoever, whether diatonic or chromatic—all his effects are written in some form of chord. Very rarely is a passage of single notes seen, and this hardly seems fair on an instrument whose best sound is a rippling one. There is at first a suggestion of originality in his work, but when you pause to think of its foundation, you are immediately convinced that it is just a higher development of another instrument, not a new technique for the piano. The only school left for discussion is the English, which during the last 20 years has made a great bid for supremacy. Of the piano composers Cyril Scott has by far the greatest knack and facility for piano-writing, but his mould is usually so small that it is difficult to place him in any exalted position as a maker of modern technique. His earlier pieces gave promise of rare possibilities, but the French idiom had apparently too much attraction for him—and his ideas were never large enough to carry a really broad phrasing. The next in importance is John Ireland, who has much less facility but much more to say. His drawback pianistically is that he is too thick in expressing himself. Fewer notes and less harsh chords would have suited his instrument better—and perhaps a freer use of fast-moving passages, the importance of which Debussy so deftly proved, would have lighted up the whole scheme of piano-colour, and made them more grateful both to listen to and to play. However, we must include Ireland in the list of composers who count in our scheme of technical development, and as he is still in the prime of life, doubtless he will become a still greater figure. Eugène Goossens, a young man of very great gifts, has certainly the facility of piano technique at his finger-tips, and in every other department of music—but one imagines him as enjoying himself in seeing how much the modern pianist can actually do in the mere playing of notes, rather than aiming at a technical development of the instru-

ment. Our literature suffered a great loss by the death, at such an early age, of William Baines. Unmistakably he had a very great talent for piano writing. There was the influence of Chopin and Scriabin in his work, but he was only a boy when he died. He certainly showed great promise. In conclusion, modern piano technique has reached its very high standard mostly through Debussy and his contemporary compatriots. He proved that the piano can be an instrument of beauty, and he changed the methods of playing that instrument, by discarding nearly altogether the use of percussive action, and by compelling the player to think of the pedals as a component part of the piano, not just as an adjunct. Whether further development is possible on his lines, or whether a new idea of technique will have to be evolved by another original genius, time alone will prove—probably the latter, for Debussy's style was too intimate to bear imitation.

Chief books on pf.-playing since 1860: In Eng.: William Mason, *Touch and Technic*; Townsend, *Balance of Arm in Piano Technique*; T. Matthay, *The Act of Touch in all its Diversity*; C. A. Ehrenfechter, *Technical Study (Deppe Method)*; George Woodhouse, *Creative Technique*; Jacob Eisenberg, *Weight and Relaxation*; Mark Hambourg, *How to Become a Pianist*; Josef Hofmann, *Piano Playing*. In Ger.: Adolf Kullak, *Ästhetik des Klavierspiels*; Clark-Steiniger, *Die Lehre des einheitlichen Kunstmittels beim Klavierspiel*; Tony Bandmann, *Die Gewichtstechnik*; Steinhausen, *Die Physiologischen Fehler der Klaviertechnik*; Breithaupt, *Die natürliche Klaviertechnik*; M. Brée, *Die Grundlage der Methode Leschetizky*. In Fr.: Marie Jaell, *Le Mecanisme du toucher*; A. Tasset, *La Main et l'Âme au piano*; A. Marmontel, *Conseils sur l'enseignement technique et l'esthétique du piano.*—W. M.

PIATTI, Alfredo. Italian cellist; b. Bergamo, 8 Jan. 1822; d. 18 July, 1901. Pupil of Merighi at Milan Cons. Was soloist of great renown; visited all principal European cities, winning great successes everywhere. Passed greater part of his life in London, where he was a leading figure of the mus. life of the time. His influence in England may well be compared with that of Joachim. His genius influenced all living cellists of his time—Hausmann, Becker, Whitehouse, Ludwig, etc. He played for many years at Monday and Saturday Popular Concerts, St. James's Hall. Publ. interesting transcriptions of ancient music for cello.—D. A.

PIAZZINI, Edmundo. Argentine pianist; b. Missaglia, Milan, in 1857. Stud. under Angeleri at R. Cons. of Milan. In 1876, gave concerts in Milan; went to Buenos Ayres in 1878 and founded Quartet Soc. Remained on concert-platform there until 1887. In 1904, founded Cons. Thibaud-Piazzini (in collab. with Alfonso Thibaud). Has comp. several pf. pieces, an album of songs, and a Piano Method.—A. M.

PICCOLI (Teatro dei). See PODRECCA, VITTORIO; also CARABELLA, EZIO; LIUZZI, FERDINANDO; LUALDI, ADRIANO; MASSARANI, RENZO; RESPIGHI, OTTORINO.

PICCOLO-HECKELPHONE. See art. on OBOE FAMILY.

PICK-MANGIAGALLI, Riccardo. Ital. compr. b. Strakonitz (Bohemia), 10 July, 1882. Was a pupil of the Milan Cons. (pf. under Appiani; compn. under Ferroni), and took his diploma in 1903. He gained fame as a pianist and a compr. His ballets and music-dramas, *Il salice d'oro* (Scala, Milan, 1913), *Il carillon magico* (Scala, Milan, 1918), *Sumitra* (1917), have met with great success. Has also set to music the 3-act lyric comedy in Venetian dialect, *Basi e bote*, of Arrigo Boito, but it has not yet been perf. Has comp. much orch. and pf. music, publ. (as also his stage works) almost entirely by Ricordi, Milan. We mention the *Notturno e Rondo fantastico*, and the poem *Sortilegi* for pf. and orch. A str. 4tet in G mi. is publ. by Univ. Ed. Vienna.

Consult a sketch of P. M. by G. M. Gatti (in review *La Critica Musicale*, Florence, Nos. 10 and 11) and *Mus. Times* (London), May 1921.—D. A.

PICKA, František. Czechoslovak compr. *b.* Lochovice, 1873; *d.* Prague, 1918. Stud. in Prague, Organ School and Cons. He was choirmaster in Prague; from 1900 to his death condr. at National Theatre, Prague; he was also a writer. Comp. songs and church music (publ. Leuckart, Leipzig; Böhm, Augsburg; Fr. A. Urbánek, Prague).—V. ST.

PIDOLL, Carl von. Ger. compr. and condr. *b.* Luxemburg, 14 Oct. 1888. Son of painter Carl v. Pidoll; stud. music under Ed. Monod and Paul Juon, Berlin; 1907, stud. under Friedrich Klose, Felix Mottl, August Schmidt-Lindner at Munich; 1919, short time condr. of Augsburg Oratorio Society.

Str. 5tet; pf. concerto; vn. sonata; str. 4tet; symphony.—A. E.

PIEDRA, Antonio. Span. violinist; *b.* Jaén, 1890. Stud. in Madrid under Hierro, and at R.C.M. London under Arbós. Has appeared with Orquesta Sinfónica, Madrid, as leader and soloist; also in tours with the choir of the Sistine Chapel.—P. G. M.

PIERNÉ, Henri Constant Gabriel. Fr. compr. and condr. *b.* Metz, 16 Aug. 1863. Entered Paris Cons. at the early age of 8, and stud. pf. under Marmontel, organ under César Franck, and compn. under Massenet. He obtained the *Prix de Rome* in 1882, simultaneously with 1st prize for organ-playing, having previously obtained 1st prize for pf. playing (1879). In 1890 he succeeded César Franck at the organ of Ste.-Clotilde. In 1903 he was appointed assistant-condr. of the Concerts Colonne, and at Colonne's death (1910) he took sole charge of this association. His publ. works are numerous and comprise practically all orders of music. Ease and efficiency, purity and grace, characterise his writing. It is perhaps in his oratorios *La Croisade des Enfants*, *Les Enfants à Bethléem*, *Saint François d'Assises* and *Les Cathédrales*, that his poetic imagination reaches its loftiest levels, and his music assumes its most telling and original aspects.

La Coupe enchantée (1-act *opéra-comique*; new form, 1905, Astruc); *Vendée* (3-act opera, Lyons, 1897, Leduc); *La Croisade des Enfants*, mus. legend (Heugel, 1902); *Les Enfants à Bethléem*, mystery (Heugel, 1907); *On ne badine pas avec l'amour* (*opéra-comique*, Paris, 1910, Heugel); stage music for *La Princesse Lointaine*, *La Samaritaine*, *Fran-*

cesca de Rimini, *Hamlet*. Ballets: *Bouton d'Or*; *Le Docteur Blanc*; *Cydalise et le Chèvre-pied* (1923). Pf. works; organ pieces; chamber-music; songs. (Paris: Leduc; Choudens; Heugel, etc.).—M. D. C.

PIERNÉ, Paul. Fr. compr. *b.* Metz (Moselle), 30 June, 1874. Cousin of the orch. condr. Gabriel. Pupil at Paris Cons.; *Prix de l'Institut* (*Fondation Finette*) for general work in 1906.

2 symphonies; symph. poems: *Daphné*; *Andante symphonique* (1911); *De l'ombre à la lumière* (1912); *Heures héroïques* (1920). Also a str. 4tet; sonata, cello and pf.; Mass for vs. and 2 organs; *Le Diable galant* (1-act opera, 1913); *Émilie* (4-act opera); *Le Figurinaï* (ballet, 3 acts). Numerous songs and pieces for different instruments.—A. C.

PIETRI, Giuseppe. Ital. compr. *b.* Sant'Ilario (Island of Elba), 6 May, 1886. Stud. in Milan at R. Cons. under Galli and Coronaro. Principally known for his successful operettas: *Addio giovinezza* (Leghorn, 1915); *La Modella* (Rome, 1917); *Lucciola* (Leghorn, 1918); *Acqua cheta* (Rome, 1920).—D. A.

PIJPER, Willem. Dutch compr. and pianist; *b.* Zeist (Utrecht), 8 Sept. 1894. Stud. theory (Joh. Wagenaar) and pf. (Mme. van Lunteren) at Utrecht, 1911–16; mus. critic *Utrechtsch Dagblad*, 1918–23; condr. Utrecht Sextet (wind instrs.), 1922; 1918–21, teacher (harmony) at Amsterdam Music School. One of the most progressive composers of the young Dutch school.

1st symphony (*Pan*), 1917, perf. 1918, Amsterdam Concertgebouw Orch. under Mengelberg; Rhapsody, pf. and orch. (1915), perf. Utrecht under Hutschenruyter, 1916; *Divertimento*, pf. and str., 1st perf. Utrecht, 1917; songs with orch. (*Fêtes galantes* [Verlaine], 1916; *Romance sans paroles* [Verlaine], 1918), perf. Amsterdam, Concertgebouw, 1917–18–19; numerous songs with pf. (Fr. and Dutch popular songs publ. by De Haan, Utrecht); 1st vn. sonata and cello sonata (1919) (London, Chester), perf. London, Salzburg (1922); 7tet for wind instrs., d.b. and pf. (1920), perf. Amsterdam and Utrecht, 1921; *Madrigal* (ancient Dutch words) for 8 vs. (1920); 1st str. 4tet (1914); 2nd str. 4tet (1920), perf. Haarlem, 1922; 1st trio (1913); 2nd trio (1921); stage-music (melodrama) for Sophocles' *Antigone* (v. and small orch.), 1920–2; 2nd symphony (1921, Italy; perf. 1922, Amsterdam); 2nd sonata, vn. and pf. (1922); 6tet for wind instrs. and pf.; 3rd str. 4tet (1923).

Mr. Pijper is responsible for all the Dutch arts. in this Dictionary.—E.-H.

PILLOIS, Jacques. Fr. compr. *b.* in 1877. Pupil of Vierne and Widor; *lauréat* of Soc. of Composers (1907) and of Institut (1917). His writing is classic but supple in form and designedly rustic in character. He is fairly successful in the *pastiche*. Has written many vocal works and some *Bucoliques* for pf. and flute.—A. C.

PINCHERLE, Marc. French musicologist; *b.* Paris in 1891. Disciple of Lionel de la Laurencie; has specialised in the history of instrs. and principally of the vn. Publ. in 1912 a remarkable analysis of the technique of the vn. among the foremost Fr. sonatists, and in 1922 *Les Violonistes Compositeurs et Virtuoses*. Writer of the articles on Fr. violinists and cellists in this Dictionary. —A. C.

PINELLI, Ettore. Ital. violinist and condr. *b.* Rome, 17 Oct. 1843; *d.* there, 17 Sept. 1915. Was one of most esteemed Ital. musicians, for his propaganda work in spreading concert and chamber music in Rome and Italy, and in mus. education of Ital. public. To this end, he successfully devoted his long and strenuous activities as violinist, condr. and teacher. Was a pupil of Ramacciotti in Rome, and of Joachim in Hanover. In 1866 he founded in Rome the Society for Chamber-Music. In 1869, with Sgambati, he organised a school of vn. and pf. at R. Accademia di Santa Cecilia, which school constituted the beginning of present R. Liceo Mus. di Santa Cecilia. In 1867 he founded the Società Orchestrale Romana, which he cond. for many years, giving large number of concerts in Rome and elsewhere, making known the masterpieces of classical symph. art, which, until then, had been almost unknown to the public in Italy.—D. A.

PINELLI, Oreste. Ital. pianist; *b.* Rome, 1844; *d.* there, 17 March, 1924. For many years pf. prof. at R. Liceo Mus. di Santa Cecilia, Rome. Trained some excellent pupils.—D. A.

PIRRO, André. French musicologist; *b.* 12 Feb. 1869, St.-Dizier (Haute-Marne) where his father was orgt. Having stud. law and letters, he made mus. studies at Paris Cons. under Widor. Began the series of his remarkable works on J. S. Bach by writing *L'Orgue de J. S. Bach* (1894), with preface by Ch. M. Widor, crowned by the Institut (Paris, 1895, Fischbacher; Eng. transl. 1902). Member of directing committee of *Schola Cantorum* (inaugurated 15 Oct. 1896); taught history of music and the organ there, being second to Guilmant. For the latter's *Archives of the Organ* he undertook biographies of Fr. orgts. of XVI to XVIII centuries (Titelouze, A. Raison, Du Mage, etc.) Lectured at École des Hautes Études Sociales since 1904, and contributed to mus. periodicals. His second work on Bach was his Doctorate thesis *L'Esthétique de J. S. Bach* (1907), a leading work, followed by a complementary thesis, *Descartes et la Musique* (Paris, 1907, Fischbacher). The same year appeared a volume on *J. S. Bach* (Paris, Alcan); then on *Schütz* (1913, Alcan). Finally came a very important work on *Dietrich Buxtehude* (Fischbacher, 1913), the first attempted on this musician. The historic and artistic value of his works, and the spirit animating them, reveal him as one of the most striking personalities amongst musicologists. He is prof. of mus. history at the Faculty of Letters of the Univ. of Paris (following Romain Rolland). Thanks to his efforts, a special course of musicology for students was opened in 1920.—M. L. P.

PISK, Paul Amadeus. Austrian compr. musicologist ; *b.* Vienna, 16 May, 1893. Pupil of Schreker and Schönberg ; Ph.D. (musicology) of Vienna Univ.; condr. at some smaller Ger. theatres; then ed. of the *Anbruch* (together with Paul Stefan); music-critic of the *Arbeiterzeitung* (Vienna), working zealously for the people's mus. education. A compr. of great talents, of radical tendencies. His works are distinguished by clear form, impressive melody, and a very elaborate technique. As critic, he has an esteemed position.

Pf. pieces, op. 3 (Univ. Ed.); 3 books of songs to words by Stefan George (*id.*); vn. sonata (perf.

Düsseldorf Music Fest. 1922); songs with str. 4tet (perf. Salzburg Fest. 1922); *Orchesterlieder,* op. 4 (perf. Vienna); orch. suite, op. 10; *Kleine Suite,* op. 11.—P. ST.

PISKÁČEK, Adolf. Czechoslovak compr. *b.* Prague, 1873, where he died in 1919. Attended Cons.; critic and writer; condr. of *Hlahol,* Prague (1903–11).

Symph. poem *Svanda dadák*; oratorio *St. Adalbert*; operas: *Divá Bára* (*Wild Bara*); *Ughlu*; *Král a sedlák* (*King and Peasant*). Str. 4tet.—V. ST.

PITCH, Musical. The relative height or depth of a sound. Standard Pitch is the exact vibration number for a given note. The note A is taken for orchestras; the note C for piano-tuning. The presumptive pitch of the Middle Ages (Guido of Arezzo) was between C=480 and C=532. The classical pitch from Purcell to Beethoven, and partly to Spohr, Mendelssohn and Rossini, was somewhere between C=498 and C=515. The French Normal Diapason is A=435, C=522, at the usual temperature of 59 degrees Fahrenheit. Their standard fork was intended to be A=435 but as a matter of fact it is a little sharper, 435·4. This is the pitch adopted now by the leading orchestras in England, Europe and America. The highest pitch ever known was that in New York in 1881 (C=548). At the present time in Britain the military bands all play up to the absurdly high pitch of Kneller Hall Army Regulations, C=538. The Philosophical pitch, for working out abstruse problems, is C=512. The ordinary steel tuning-fork varies very slightly with changes of temperature up to the 90 degrees Fahrenheit possible in certain countries. M. Guillaume, the director of the Bureau Internationale des Poids et Mésures, states that a special alloy of nickel and steel would be quite free from temperature variation over a range of more than 300 degrees Fahrenheit.—E.-H.

PITCH, UNIVERSAL. As great inconvenience was still being felt all over Great Britain in 1920, when the British Music Soc. was holding its annual conference, a whole day was given up to the discussion of this subject (24 May). A unanimous resolution was passed that the Queen's Hall Orch. pitch—A = 435·4 at 59 degrees Fahr. —should be the one for universal adoption. This accords with the prevailing orch. pitch on the Continent. The chairman, Col. J. G. Somerville, C.M.G., C.B.E., Commandant of Kneller Hall (the training school for all the British army bands), pledged himself to do everything possible to bring the army bands, the chief offenders, down from their high pitch to the desirable one.—E.-H.

PITT, Percy. Eng. compr. and opera condr. *b.* London, 4 Jan. 1870. Stud. in Paris and at Leipzig and Munich under Carl Reinecke, S. Jadassohn, and Rheinberger; returned to England in 1893; chorus-master for the Mottl concerts, 1895; orgt. Queen's Hall orch. concerts, 1896; *maestro-al-piano,* R. Opera, Covent Garden, 1902; later mus. adviser to the Syndicate; 1906, assist.-condr. summer and autumn seasons there; followed Messager in 1907 as mus. dir. Covent Garden Grand Opera Syndicate;

condr. Beecham Opera Co. (1915–18); then artistic dir. British National Opera Co. 1920–4; chief mus. director to British Broadcasting Co. 1922; also mus. dir. Covent Garden Syndicate again in 1924. His compns., whilst not revealing any marked individuality, are pleasant and refined, and romantically coloured in harmony.

Symphony, G mi. (Birmingham Fest. 1906); symph. prelude, *Le Sang des Crépuscules* (1900); Ballad, vn. and orch. (1900); orch. suite (1895); *Fêtes galantes* (after Verlaine), orch. (1896); *Cinderella* (1899); *Dance Rhythms* (1901); clar. concerto (1897); Coronation March, orch.; *Serenade*, small orch.; symph. poem, *Anactoria*, vla. and orch.; *English Rhapsody* (on folk-songs), orch.; *Oriental Rhapsody*, orch., all produced at Queen's Hall under Sir Henry Wood; *Sakura*, ballet-pantomime; *Hohenlinden*, male chorus and orch. (1899); 5 poems, barit. v. and orch. (1902); others for m.-sopr. v. and orch. (1904); incidental music to Stephen Phillips's *Paolo and Francesca* (1902); to Alfred Austin's *Flodden Field* and to *King Richard II*; 5tet; trio; pf. pieces (Augener); songs (Novello, Boosey, etc.). —E.-H.

PIZZETTI, Ildebrando. Italian composer; *b.* Parma, 20 Sept. 1880. Was a pupil of Giovanni Tebaldini at Royal Conservatoire of his native city. In 1908 he was appointed teacher of composition there. From there he went to the Istituto Musicale of Florence, as teacher of harmony and counterpoint. In 1918, he became director of that Institute, which post he still occupies. He is one of the most remarkable and illustrious contemporary Italian composers.

His production as a composer is individual, of noble quality, and of high value. His activity is not limited to composition, but extends to teaching, lecturing and writing. In addition to various articles (in *Rivista Musicale Italiana* and elsewhere) he has written the books: *La musica dei greci* (Rome, Musica ed.); *Musicisti contemporanei* (Milan, 1914, Treves); *La musica italiana* (Florence, 1921, Vallecchi). He has given lectures on *Il dramma musicale dell' avvenire*, and *La musica nella vita italiana contemporanea*.

In 1914, together with Giannotto Bastianelli, he founded in Florence the periodical *Dissonanza*, intended for the publication of modern Italian compositions. He was co-director of the *Raccolta nazionale delle musiche italiane* (published in Milan by Istituto Editoriale Italiano), of which collection he undertook several sections. In 1910 he was music critic of newspaper *Il Secolo*, Milan; for some years he has been critic of newspaper *La Nazione*, Florence. In 1924 he was appointed dir. of Milan Cons.

Operas: *Fedra*, on tragedy by d'Annunzio (Scala, Milan, 1915; Sonzogno); *Debora e Jaéle* (Scala, Milan, 1922; Ricordi).

Symph. concert work: *Ouverture per una farsa tragica* (Milan, 1918).

Stage music: 3 *Intermezzi* for *Edipo Re* of Sophocles (Milan, 1901); music for *La Nave* of d'Annunzio; music for *La Pisanella* of d'Annunzio (1913), from which P. has also taken a suite; *Danze antiche*, orchestrated for perf. of *Aminta* of Tasso at Fiesole (1914); *Sinfonia del fuoco*, for film of *Cabiria* by d'Annunzio (1915); music for *Abraam ed Isaac* of Feo Belcari (Florence, 1917).

Chamber-music: str. 4tet, (Bologna, Pizzi); sonata for vn. and pf. (London, Chester); sonata for cello and pf. (Ricordi); many songs, amongst which we mention *I Pastori*, *La madre al figlio lontano*, *Due canti popolari greci* (Florence, Forlivesi), *Tre Sonetti di Petrarca* (Ricordi); pf. pieces. Choral music:

Tre canzoni; *Funeral Mass*, perf. at Pantheon, Rome, 1923, in memory of King Humbert I.

Consult: Renato Fondi, *I. P. e il dramma musicale italiano* (Rome, 1919); G. M. Gatti, in *Musicisti contemporanei d' Italia e fuori* (Bologna, 1920, Pizzi). The Turin review *Il Pianoforte* entirely devoted one number (15 Aug. 1921) to Pizzetti.—D. A.

PLANAL HARMONY. See art on HARMONY.

PLANCHET, D. C. Fr. compr. *b.* 25 Dec. 1857. Stud. at École Niedermeyer; is choirmaster at Sainte-Trinité, Paris; *lauréat* of the Institut; has comp. symph. poems; oratorio, *Les Mystères douloureux*; numerous motets; 2 lyrical dramas in 3 acts (*Le Grand Ferré* and *Ildis*).—F. R.

PLANQUETTE, Robert. Fr. operetta compr. *b.* Paris, 21 July, 1840; *d.* there, 28 Jan. 1903. Has written about 20 operettas, from 1873 onwards. Before that, he had written romances. In 1877, *Les Cloches de Corneville* obtained an unprecedented success. The work has already had more than 2000 perfs. in Paris alone. The next best-known are *Rip* (1882) and *Surcouf* (1887). His orchestration is always very finished. His style is allied to that of Audran. Also:

Le Serment de Mme. Grégoire (1873); *Paille d'Avoine* (1875); *Le Chevalier Gaston* (1879); *The Old Guard* (London, 1887); *Panurge* (1895); *Le Paradis de Mahomet* (posthumous, 1906).—A. C.

PLANTÉ, Francis. Fr. pianist; *b.* Orthy, in 1839. At 4, he showed an astonishing gift for music and began to study with a lady pupil of Liszt. He soon made amazing progress. At 7 he played for the first time in public; entered the Cons. in 1849; left it the following year with 1st prize for piano. He was then 11 years old. He is said to have astounded his hearers by the ease with which he read at sight the most complicated orch. scores. Eventually he gave numerous concerts in France and abroad, everywhere arousing enthusiasm by his technique, his delicacy and his interpretation. He was one of the first who dared to play Schumann in France; eventually he included in his programmes diverse composers, even moderns, like Debussy, without ever forgetting his two favourite masters, Chopin and Liszt. After having for many years ceased to play in public, he returned, for purely patriotic purposes, during the war to give recitals, which proved that he had lost nothing of his great powers.—D. L.

PLATEN, Horst. Ger. compr. and condr. *b.* Magdeburg, 14 April, 1884. Stud. music in Brussels; 1903–8, pupil of Paul Gilson (theory and compn.) and César Thomson (vn.); condr. at Magdeburg Stadttheater and Grand Opera House, Cincinnati; now lives at Hamburg.

Stage works: *Holy Morning* (Schwerin, 1918); music to Strindberg's *Folkungersage* (Hamburg, 1915); *Dance of Death* (Hamburg, 1916); Bossdorf's *De Fährkrog* (Hamburg, 1916); fairy play, *Young Dietrich's Royal Journey* (1917); mus. comedy, *On Wings of Song* (Hamburg, National Opera, 1922); comic opera, *Love-Chains*; dance-legend, *Enchanted Rose*; opera, *The Lighthouse* (1922). For orch.: Prelude to lyric drama *Flemish Rhapsody*; symph. poem for orch. and organ, *Pelleas and Melisande*; sonata, C sharp mi.; *Andante and Scherzo* for vn. and pf.; pf. pieces; songs, etc.—A. E.

PODRECCA, Guido. Ital. music critic; *b.* Vimercate (Milan), 5 Dec. 1865; *d.* Auburn (New York), April 1923. For 15 years, critic of newspaper *Avanti*; then joined paper *Il Popolo d'Italia*. Has given many propagandist lectures in Italy and America. Founded in Milan the mus. and art review *Il Primato*, with its own publishing house. The latter has publ. important works of mus. history and literature.—D. A.

PODRECCA, Vittorio. Ital. music critic; *b.* Cividale del Friuli, 26 April, 1883. Brother of Guido. He also is a devoted patron of mus. art. Was secretary to R. Liceo Mus. di Santa Cecilia in Rome. Founded and directs the Teatro dei Piccoli (Marionette Players) with which he has effected some most successful mus. perfs., reviving old operas, and having new works comp. specially for this marionette-theatre. The Teatro dei Piccoli gave their first London season at the New Scala Theatre in April, May, June, 1923, giving Respighi's *Sleeping Beauty*, Rossini's *La Gazza Ladra* (*The Magpie*), Cui's *Puss in Boots*, amongst many other pieces.—D. A.

POGGI, Alberto Santiago. Argentine violinist, compr. *b.* Buenos Ayres in 1881. Stud. under Galvani and Troiani. In 1904, organised a series of sacred concerts. Now devotes himself to teaching and compn. Chief works: Gavotte and Minuet for orch., *Berceuse* and some *Serenatas* for vn., many sacred pieces for pf. and numerous songs. His works are very popular on concert-platform in Argentina. His repertoire of Argentine national music has often been played in Europe.—A. M.

POHLIG, Carl. Ger. condr. *b.* Teplitz, 10 Feb. 1864. Pupil of Liszt at Budapest and Rome; condr. at Graz, Hamburg, London (Covent Garden), Coburg, Stuttgart (1900–7); 1907, condr. of Philadelphia Symphony Orch.; 1913, condr. of Hamburg Stadttheater; 1914, Courtcondr. at Brunswick.
Songs and choral songs; orch. works (symph. poem, *Per aspera ad astra*).—A. E.

POIRÉE, Élie. Fr. musicologist; *b.* Villeneuve Saint-Georges, 9 Oct. 1850. Custodian of the Ste.-Geneviève Library, Paris.
L'Évolution de la Musique (1884); *Essais de technique et d'esthétique musicales* (2 vols. 1898–9); *Chopin* (1907); *Richard Wagner. L'Homme : le Poète : le Musicien* (1922).—A. C.

POISOT, Charles. Fr. musicologist; *b.* Dijon, in 1822; *d.* there in 1904. Pupil of Thalberg; founder of Dijon Cons. Has publ. an estimable *Essai sur les musiciens bourguignons*; a *Histoire de la Musique en France* 1860; a *Traité d'harmonie*; a *Traité de contrepoint*. Has comp. masses and cantatas (*Jeanne d'Arc*).—A. C.

POL DAX. See POUGIN.

POLACCO, Giorgio. Ital. condr. *b.* Venice, 12 April, 1875. Began his career in Brazil; then went to Argentina, Mexico and Havana. Cond. with great success at Metropolitan in New York, Covent Garden, London; La Monnaie, Brussels, and principal Ital. theatres. Now in U.S.A. —D. A.

POLDINI, Eduard. Composer; *b.* Budapest, 13 June, 1869. Stud. R. Hungarian Cons. and later under Mandyczewski in Vienna, and with others in France and Germany. His operettas and ballets have met with success; and he is

still more characteristic in his fascinating pf. pieces (Ricordi; Augener; Lengnick, etc.). His *Swineherd and the Princess* was produced at Covent Garden, London. He lives in Switzerland.—E.-H.

POLIŃSKI, Alexander. Polish critic and music historian; *b.* Włostow, 4 June, 1845; *d.* 1915. Published many arts. on ancient Polish music in periodical *Echo Muzyczne* (Warsaw) and other reviews. His most important work is *Dzieje muzyki polskiej w zarysie* (*A Sketch of the History of Polish Music*), Lemberg, 1907. In 1904, a treatise on the oldest Polish churchsong *Boga Rodzica*, and in 1914 2 short studies on Chopin and Moniuszko. 1881–99, music critic of the *Kuryer Poranny*; thence till his death, of the *Kuryer Warszawski* (Warsaw). Contributor to the *Polish Grand Illustrated Encyclopœdia*. Since 1905, prof. of mus. history, Warsaw Cons. By his research work, P. contributed very much to the knowledge of ancient mus. monuments in Poland.—ZD. J.

POLI-RANDACCIO, Ernestina. Ital. s. singer; *b.* Ferrara. Stud. at Liceo Rossini, Pesaro. Her fame began in 1908, when Mascagni asked her to sing in his opera *Amica*. She then appeared at principal theatres in Italy and other countries, distinguishing herself as an interpreter of dramatic operas, such as *Aida*, *Gioconda*, and *Fanciulla del West*. She was first to interpret Mascagni's *La Parisina* at La Scala, Milan. —D. A.

POLISH OPERA. Although the beginning of Polish opera dates from 1635, we must consider the pieces of Mathias Kamieński of 1778 and later (*Misery made Happy* and others) as the first national works of this kind. The principal compr. of light dramatic operas and operettas for national theatre in Warsaw for first 15 years of the XIX century was Joseph Elsner (1769–1854). His successor for about 30 years was Karol Kurpiński (1785–1857), condr. of the Warsaw Opera, whose mus. style (in over 20 operas and vaudevilles) was an imitation of Rossini. Two of Kurpiński's most appreciated works (*Queen Hedwiga*, 1814, and *The Castle of Czorsztyn*, opera *buffa*, 1819) were still perf. at end of XIX and in XX century at Lemberg and Warsaw. After this preparatory epoch followed a period of evolution, thanks to the rich dramatic productiveness of Stanislaus Moniuszko (1819–1872). In his chief works, as *Halka* (1849–59), *The Countess* (1860), *Verbum nobile* (1861) and *The Terrible Court* (1865), Poland possesses his chief national operas. The extraordinary richness of his melodic invention, the national character and mus. feeling of his works, have kept them popular in Poland till the present day. None of Moniuszko's contemporary opera comprs. in Poland (as F. T. Dobrzynski, 1807–67) could be compared to him.

After Moniuszko the chief opera comprs. in Poland were: Władysław Żeleński (1837–1921), who wrote 4 romantic works: *Konrad Wallenrod* (1883); *Goplana* (1890); *Janek* (1900); *Stara*

Baśn (*The Old Tale*) (1907); and Sigismund Noskowski (1846–1909), whose 3 later works were important: *Livia Quintilla* (1900); *The Verdict* (1907); and *Vengeance* (1909). Besides these, Louis Grossmann and Adam Münchheimer belong to this period. In the last 20 years the opera productiveness in Poland has increased greatly. After I. Paderewski's only opera *Manru* (1901), 2 valuable works by Roman Statkowski, *Marya* and *Philœnis*, were perf. in 1905 and 1906. Then appeared the operas of Dłuski, Melcer, Sołtys and Gużewski. The strongest dramatic compr. of the younger generation, Ludomir Różycki, began compn. for the stage in 1909 with opera *Boleslas the Bold*, followed in 1911 by *Medusa*, in 1917 by *Eros and Psyche*, and in 1923 by *Casanova*. Being of an eclectic spirit, his works approximate somewhat to the mus. drama of Wagner and also to style of Debussy and R. Strauss. A. Wieniawski's opera *Megaë* (1913), F. Szopski's *Lilies* (1917), Joteyko's *The Player* (1919), B. Wallek-Walewski's *Fortune* (1919) and especially the first opera of the most progressive Polish compr. of to-day, Karol Szymanowski, *Hagith* (1922, written in 1912) are an expression of different currents in modern Polish dramatic music of to-day which does not restrict itself to national themes, but endeavours to place itself in line with the mus. productiveness of other Western peoples.—ZD. J.

POLÍVKA, Vladimír. Czechoslovak compr. *b.* Prague, 1896. Pupil of Vítězslav Novák at Cons. in Prague. He is known as a pianist.

2 sonatas, vn. and pf.; symph. poem, *Spring*; the *Little Symphony* (ms.).—V. ST.

POLLAIN, Fernand. Fr. cellist; *b.* Rheims, 7 Oct. 1879. Began studies at Nancy Cons.; finished them in Paris, where he obtained a 1st prize in 1896 (same year as Thibaut, and Alfred Cortot). Almost from beginning of career, was partner with Pugno and Ysaye, and soloist in all chief Fr. orchs. Very popular in America, where, after the war (in which he was seriously wounded) he made two tours, one with Mary Garden; other with Eugène Ysaye. Gave 1st perf. of many works (several dedicated to him): *Cinquième Poème* of Ysaye ; 2nd sonata of Guy Ropartz. Has also ed. large number of old works, including a charming concerto of Boccherini. Although an extremely brilliant soloist, is at same time most scrupulous in his interpretations; a worthy partner of Ysaye, Thibaut and Cortot in chamber-music. Since 1919 he has been playing a Strad. of 1701, which formerly belonged to Servais (1807-66).—M. P.

POLLITT, Arthur Wormald. Eng. orgt. and lecturer; *b.* Crompton, near Manchester, 27 Nov. 1878. Stud. R. Manchester Coll. of Music; sub-orgt. Manchester Cath. (under Dr. Kendrick Pyne); Liverpool Church and School for the Blind, 1900–17; chorus-master, Liverpool Philh. Soc. 1918; lecturer in music, Univ. of Liverpool, 1919.

Organ: Sonata in C mi. (Schott); many other organ pieces and arrs. (Schott; Augener; Stainer & Bell; Rogers; Novello; Elkin); part-songs (Stainer & Bell); *Exercises in Transposition* (Augener). Books:

The Necessity of Music in a School Curriculum (New Temple Press); *The Self-reliant Musician* (Sherratt & Hughes, Manchester); *The Enjoyment of Music* (Methuen).—E.-H.

" POLLY." A sequel to *The Beggar's Opera*. Owing to great success of latter work, Gay considered he was justified in taking Polly Peachum as heroine of a new piece. While in rehearsal, in 1729, he was informed by the Duke of Grafton (then Lord Chamberlain) that pieces in rehearsal must be submitted to him. This was done with the result that *Polly* was prohibited from being performed. No reason was assigned, but it is assumed that Gay's political enemies were at the back of this prohibition. The Duchess of Queensberry took the matter in hand and Gay, by her influence, sold the book of the play with higher profit to himself than if the piece had been performed. It was first acted in June 1777, and remained unacted after this until its recent revival on 30 Dec. 1922 (Kingsway Theatre, London). The original plot laid the scene in the West Indies, to which place Polly goes to seek her husband Macheath, who in *The Beggar's Opera* escaped hanging. He has been transported to the West Indies, but having escaped from the master to whom he has been sold, has become the leader of a band of pirates, having disguised himself as a negro and changed his name to Morano. The other characters from *The Beggar's Opera* are Jenny Diver and Mrs. Trapes. In the course of the play Polly dresses herself in male costume. The airs are of the same character as those in *The Beggar's Opera*, and number 71. In the 1922-3 revival they were reduced to about 50 and the play was largely reconstructed. It was produced by Nigel Playfair and the music arr. and composed by Frederic Austin.—F. K.

POLO, Enrico. Ital. violinist; *b.* at Parma, 1868. Stud. at Cons. in Parma; then at Hochschule, Berlin, under Joachim. Was first a teacher at Liceo Mus. at Turin; then in 1903 at Cons. of Milan. In that city he founded the quartet which bears his name, and which gained a high reputation during its tours through Ital. cities. P. has also given very successful concerts as a soloist in Germany, Spain and Switzerland. Publ. an excellent ed. of old Ital. vn. works and 4tets by Boccherini, Tartini, Viotti (Ricordi); also some original compns. and estimable teaching works.—D. A.

POLSTERER, Rudolf. Compr. *b.* Tattendorf (Lower Austria), 3 June, 1879. Stud. engineering; then cpt. under Joseph Schöpfleuthner, who interested him in organ-playing; till 1914, pupil of Otto Müller, Vienna, especially for strict vocal style. Now devoting full time to composition.

Publ. by Brockhaus, Leipzig: Prelude for organ; pf. 4tet; 12 symph. songs (*Michelangelo*); 7 songs *Of Eternal Life*; 6 songs to Virgin Mary; *Three Chinese Songs*; *Three Rückert Songs*; 3 duets; trio for vn. horn and pf.; 6tet (ob. 2 vns. vla. cello, pf.). In ms.: 2 masses (one vocal; one instr.); 8 motets for mixed chorus; songs; 6tet (fl. clar. 2 horns, bsn. and pf.).—A. E.

POLYPHONY. See COUNTERPOINT.

POLYTONALITY. Several voices, parts, or streams of harmony moving simultaneously in different keys. The term is somewhat loosely used. Polytonic procedure, according to Villermin in his *Traité d'Harmonie Ultramoderne* (1911) consists of melodic or polyphonic procedure, derived from a composite chord. The usual meaning is the effect produced by the use of 2 or more keys (tonalities, scales) being used at one and the same time. See art. on HARMONY. Consult art. on *La Musique Polytonale* in *La Revue Musicale*, Oct. 1921; also Chap. XI in Eaglefield - Hull's *Modern Harmony* (Augener, 1913).—E.-H.

POPOF, Serge Sergevitch (*accent 2nd syll.*). Russ. writer on music; *b.* Moscow, 2 Dec. 1887. Son of a merchant; pupil of Zolotaref and Gretchaninof. Chief curator of Russ. State Music Publ. Dept. The ablest connoisseur of Russ. mus. archives, mus. literature, and ms. music.—V. B.

POPPER, David. Cellist and compr. *b.* Prague, 18 June, 1876; *d.* Baden (Austria), 1913. Stud. at Prague Cons. Travelled throughout Europe as cello virtuoso, 1868–73. Solo cellist, Court Opera, Vienna. From 1886 till death, prof. of cello, R. High School for Music, Budapest, and became Hungarian citizen. Establ. with Jenö Hubay (*q.v.*) the Hubay-Popper Str. Quartet. Wrote numerous virtuoso pieces for cello. Best-known: *Gavotte*; *Spinning Song*; *Elf Dance*.—B.B.

PORTA, José. Span. vn. virtuoso; *b.* Huesca, 1890. Pupil of César Thomson. Prof. of vn. at Lausanne Cons. Tours in Switzerland, Germany, Spain, etc.—P. G. M.

PORTUGUESE OPERA SINCE 1880. The following works by Portuguese comprs. of grand opera have been given at the Theatre San Carlos since 1880: Guimarães's *Beatrice* (1882); Machado's *Laureana* (1884, 1885); V. do Arneiro's *La Derelitta* (1885); Machado's *I Doria* (1887); Keil's *Don Branca* (1888, 1889); Freitas Gazul's *Fra Luigi di Sousa* (1891); Keil's *Irène* (1896); Machada's *Maria Vetter* (1898); Keil's *Serrana* (1899, 1900, at Colyseu in 1901); Oscar da Silva's *Don Mecia* (Colyseu, 1901); Keil's *Serrano* (Oporto, 1902); Machado's *Venus* (Th. D. Amelia, 1905); Arroyo's *Amor de perdicão* (1907, 1908); Machado's *La Borghesina* (1909); his *O Espadachim do Outeiro* (Th. Trindade, 1910). —E.-H.

POTHIER, (Dom) Joseph. See SOLESMES.

POTTGIESSER, Karl. Ger. compr. *b.* Dortmund, 8 Aug. 1861. Stud. for bar; then for music under Hugo Riemann (Hamburg 1887–1890). Since 1890 at Munich, devoting himself to composition.

For orch.: Symph. poem, *Brand* (from Ibsen); symph. prologue to Hebbel's *Gyges and his Ring*; orch. variations on *O sanctissima* and Weber's *Nursery Song*; chamber-music; opera, *Heimkehr* (Cologne, 1903); fest. play, *Siegfried of Xanten and Kriemhild* (1892); *Chapter XIII of First Epistle of St. Paul to Corinthians*, for barit., mixed chorus with organ and orch.; oratorio, *God is Love*; mus. comedy, *Aldergrever's Heirs*; male chorus, *Drinking Song* (Uhland) with orch.; songs (Hebbel series); choral songs, etc.—A. E.

POUEIGH, Jean. Fr. compr. *b.* Toulouse, 24 Feb. 1876. Pupil of Toulouse Cons.; then

of Paris Cons. under Caussade and Lenepveu. His music is based on the folk-lore of his native country. He is critic of *L'Ère Nouvelle*. His habitual harshness in criticism has involved him in numerous lawsuits.

Lyric drama, *Le Meneur de Louves*; ballet, *Frivolant*; orch. suite, *Fünn*; several colls. of Languedoc folk-songs. Author of *Musiciens français d'aujourd'hui* (2nd ed. 1921, *Mercure de France*) under pen-name of Octave Séré (*q.v.*).—A. C.

POUGIN, Arthur (pseudonym "Pol Dax"). Fr. writer on music; *b.* Châteauroux (Indre), 6 Aug. 1834; *d.* Paris, 8 Aug. 1921. Pupil of Paris Cons.; devoted himself early to mus. history and criticism; ed.-in-chief of the *Ménestrel* from 1885. During his long life, publ. considerable number of studies, articles, pamphlets and works of all sorts. Among those written from 1890 onwards, are:

Méhul, sa vie, son génie, son caractère (1889–93); *L'Opéra-comique pendant la Révolution* (1891); *Essai historique sur la Musique en Russie* (1897–1904); *J. J. Rousseau, musicien* (1901); *Hérold* (1908, Paris, Laurens); *M. T. Malibran* (1912); *Giuseppina Grassini* (Paris, 1920, Fischbacher).—M. L. P.

POUISHNOF, Lef. Russ. pianist, compr. *b.* 11 Oct. 1891. Stud. at Petrograd Cons., finishing in 1910 with 1st class diploma and Gold Medal, Rubinstein Prize (concert grand piano) and £120 for a voyage to Europe. His teachers were Mme. Essipof (pf.); Rimsky-Korsakof, Liadof and Glazunof (compn.); Tchérepnin (conducting). His first appearance in London took place 2 Feb. 1921 at Wigmore Hall. Numerous orch. appearances: London Symphony Orch., Queen's Hall Orch., Albert Hall Orch., Hallé Orch., Scottish Orch., etc. Many compns. for orch. v. and pf. (ms.); 5 pf. pieces (Enoch, 1922–3–4).—E.-H.

POULENC, Francis. French composer; *b.* Paris, in 1899. He appears to be one of the most gifted composers of the new generation. His bent is fantastic; he does not seek sentimental expression, but delights in the picturesque. According to the wish of his friend, the poet Cocteau, he has tried to express the gaiety and the melancholy of public festivals. His compositions for a small orchestra of wind instruments are very singular in that they give the impression of vulgarity, without ever descending to it. There is much charm and freshness of inspiration in his *Rapsodie nègre*, his *Bestiaire* (voice and pf. London, Chester), and the humorous pieces composed for the *Mariés de la Tour Eiffel*. His piano compositions owe much to Ravel and to Erik Satie, but present also sonorous effects which are charming and very individual: *Mouvements perpétuels* (Chester), *Promenades*. He is justly reproached with his rather clumsy processes of construction and his continual repetitions; but these are defects of youth, and we must wait some time before passing judgment. His ballet *Les Biches* was prod. June 1924. He was one of the French group formerly known as "The Six."—H. P.

POULET, Gaston. Fr. violinist; *b.* Paris, 7 April, 1892; 1st prize under Lefort, at Cons. in 1910; then stud. under Maurice Hayot. Started as soloist very young at Colonne, Lamoureux and Pasdeloup Concerts. The Poulet Quartet (Poulet, Giraud, Le Guillard, L. Ruyssen) is one of the best-known. Pierné, V. d'Indy, Florent Schmitt, entrusted it with first perf. of important works. P. faithfully interprets works of all periods and schools, but excels in rendering the Romantics, particularly Schumann.—M. P.

POWELL, John. Amer. pianist, compr. *b.* Richmond, Va., U.S.A., 6 Sept. 1882. B.A. Univ. of Virginia, 1901. Stud. pf. under his sister and F. C. Hahr in Richmond; 1902–7, stud. under Leschetizky; 1904–7 compn. under Navrátil in Vienna. *Début* with Tonkünstler Orch. Vienna, Nov. 1907. Played in Berlin 1908; Paris and London, 1909. Toured Great Britain and Continent; 1st appearance (after his return to America) at Richmond (Va.) Fest. May 1912. A str. 4tet, op. 19, was played by Ševčík Quartet, London, 1910. In 1912 the compr. played his *Sonate Psychologique*, op. 15, and Moiseiwitsch played his *Sonata Teutonica* for pf. op. 24, in London. In 1912 Zimbalist played his vn. concerto in E ma. op. 23, in New York and London. In 1919, Zimbalist and the compr. first perf. his vn. sonata. His *Rapsodie Nègre*, pf. and orch., was first perf. by Russ. Symphony Orch., 23 March, 1918 (compr. at piano). An overture, *In Old Virginia*, was brought out in 1921. In style and technique his works are highly modern; in many he makes effective use of negro themes.

Rapsodie Nègre, for orch. and pf. (Schirmer, 1921); *Sonate Virginianesque*, vn. and pf. op. 7, 1st perf. Vienna, 1908 (Schirmer, 1919); *At the Fair: Sketches of American Fun*, pf.(Schott, 1912); *Suite Sudiste*, pf. op. 16 (Mathot, 1910); *Sonate Noble*, pf. op. 21 (Schirmer, 1921); songs, op. 8 and 15 (Schirmer). —O. K.

POWELL, Lloyd. Pianist of Welsh extraction; *b.* Ironbridge, Salop, 22 Aug. 1888. Stud. R.C.M.; awarded grant from Patron's Fund for study abroad; went to Berlin; later to Basle (under Busoni). In 1920, played Delius's pf. concerto at Welsh fest. with L.S.O. In 1921, gave concert of British music in Paris (with Gladys Moger); and later in the year, introduced John Ireland's pf. sonata in Melbourne, Australia; concerts in Java and Ceylon; 1919, pf. prof. R.C.M. London.—E.-H.

POWELL, Maud (Mrs. H. Godfrey Turner). Amer. violinist; *b.* Peru, Ill. U.S.A., 22 Aug. 1868; *d.* Uniontown, Pa., 8 Jan. 1920. Stud. vn. under William Lewis in Chicago, Schradieck in Leipzig, Dancla in Paris and Joachim in Berlin. First played in London, 1883. In 1885 appeared with Philh. Orch. Berlin, and same year with Philh. New York. After many Amer. tours she visited Germany and Austria again in 1892 with New York-Arion Soc. (male chorus); 1894, organised the Maud Powell Str. Quartet, which gave concerts until disbanded in 1898. Between 1899 and 1905 toured British Isles, and Continent repeatedly. In 1905 visited South Africa with concert company of her own. Death overtook her unexpectedly on one of her tours.

One of the most notable, world-famed virtuosi that America has produced, she procured a first hearing for several Amer. comprs. (H. H.

Huss, H. R. Shelley), and was the first to play in America the concertos of Arensky, Bruch (D mi.), Dvořák, Saint-Saëns (No. 2), Rimsky-Korsakof (*Fantaisie*), Sibelius and Coleridge-Taylor. A number of her excellent transcriptions were publ. by Breitkopf, Schirmer, Ditson, Carl Fischer and Schuberth.—O. K.

PRATELLA, Francesco Balilla. Ital. compr. *b.* Lugo (Romagna), 1 Feb. 1880. Stud. first under Ricci-Signorini, then at Liceo, Pesaro, under Mascagni and Cicognani. In Sonzogno 1903 Competition his opera *Lilia* was mentioned, and then successfully perf. at theatre in his native city. In 1909 he won the Baruzzi Competition in Bologna with opera, *La Sina d'Vargöun* (*Rosellina dei Vergoni*), which is full of the atmosphere of his native Romagna. This opera was then successfully perf. in Bologna at Comunale Theatre. P. directs the Istituto Musicale in his native city. A third opera, *L'Aviatore Dro*, was perf. at the Teatro Comunale, Lugo, in 1920. He is also the author of orch., vocal and instr. works (chamber-music) publ. by Fantuzzi; Bongiovanni; and Pizzi of Bologna.

P. has been the representative of the "futurist" movement in music in Italy, and has comp. and perf. futurist music and publ. manifestos. This does not prevent him from still being attached to the Ital. tradition and to the musicality of his native Romagna. Amongst his literary publications and eds. of old music, we mention:

Musica italiana : per la cultura della sensibilità musicale italiana (Bologna, 1915, Bongiovanni); *Evoluzione della musica* ; 2 small vols. : *Breviari intellettuali* (Milan, 1918–19, Istituto Ed. Italiano); *Il terzo libro delle laudi spirituali* (reprint of music of XVI century), 1916, Bongiovanni; *Oratorii di Giacomo Carissimi* (*Giona, Il giudizio di Salomone, Jefte*), in the *Raccolta Nazionale delle Musiche italiane* (Milan, 1919, Istituto Ed. Italiano); *Saggio di gridi, canzoni, cori e danze del popolo italiano* (1919, Bongiovanni).

Consult: Alceo Toni, *La Sina d'Vargöun of F. B. P.* (*Rivista Musicale Italiana*, 1910); G. M. Gatti, in *Musicisti moderni d' Italia e fuori* (Bologna, 1920, Pizzi); Giannotto Bastianelli, *Musicisti d'oggi e di ieri* (in chapters on *La musica futurista*).—D. A.

PRATT, Waldo Seldon. Amer. author, hymnologist; *b.* Philadelphia, U.S.A., 10 Nov. 1857. A.B. Williams Coll. 1878. Stud. classical philology, archæology and æsthetics at Johns Hopkins Univ. Baltimore (1878–80). A.M. Williams Coll. 1881. Assistant-dir. of Metropolitan Museum of Art, New York (1880–2). In 1882, member of faculty of Hartford Theological Seminary; since 1889, prof. of music and hymnology; 1882–91, conducted various mus. societies in Hartford. 1895–1905, lectured on music at Smith Coll., Northampton, Mass.; 1905–20 at Inst. of Mus. Art, New York. 1906–15, ed. *Proceedings of the Music Teachers' National Association*; 1906–8, President of this Association; 1912–6, President of Amer. Section of International Mus. Soc. With C. N. Boyd, publ. a valuable Amer. Supplement to Grove's *Dictionary of Music* (Macmillan, 1920), the first attempt to produce a specifically Amer. work of this kind and scope, on a sound historical basis. Received Mus.D. *h.c.* from Syracuse Univ. 1898.

Musical Ministries of the Church (Revell, 1901; enlarged ed. Schirmer, 1915); *The Church Music*

Problem (Century Co. 1887); *History of Music* (Schirmer, 1907); *The Music of the Pilgrims* (Ditson, 1921); ed. of *St. Nicholas Songs* (Century Co. 1885); mus. ed. for *Century Dictionary* (1892).—O. K.

PRILL, Emil. Ger. flautist; *b.* Stettin, 10 May, 1867. Pupil of father, Gantenberg, and Joachim Andersen: undertook concert-tour with brothers, before he finished studying at R. High School, Berlin, 1881–3; 1888, teacher at Charkof Music School; then 1st flautist, Hamburg (Laube Orch. and Philh.); 1892, 1st flautist at Berlin R. Opera; 1903, teacher R. High School for Music; 1908, R. virtuoso; 1912, professor.
Transcriptions; studies for fl.-players, op. 12; orch. studies and instructors for fl. (old system and Boehm system); *Guide to Flute Literature.*—A. E.

PRILL, Karl. Ger. violinist; *b.* Berlin, 22 Oct. 1864. Stud. under father (mus. dir.), Helmich, Wirth, and Joachim (at R. High School); solo violinist in Brenner, afterwards in Laub Orch.; 1883–5, Konzertmeister Bilse's Orch.; 1885, Konzertmeister and condr. Magdeburg; 1891, Konzertmeister Leipzig Gewandhaus Orch.; 1897, Konzertmeister Vienna R. Opera and Philh.; vn. prof. at Imperial Acad.; founder of str. quartet.—A. E.

PRILL, Paul. Ger. condr. *b.* Berlin, 1 Oct. 1860. Pupil of father, of W. Handwerg (pf.), Sturm (theory), Manecke (cello); 1879, of R. High School and Academical Meisterschule (Bargiel), Berlin; toured with brothers as cellist; 1882–5, solo cellist in Bilse's Orch.; condr. at Wallner and Belle-Alliance Theatre, Berlin; 1886–9, opera condr. Rotterdam; 1889–92, Hamburg; 1892–1901, Nuremberg; 1901–6, R. condr. Schwerin; cond. Schwerin Mus. Fest. 1903; 1906–8, Mozart Orch. Berlin; 1908–15, condr. of Concert Soc. Orch. Munich (formerly Kaim Orch.); then official condr. Cottbus; since 1922, lives at Munich.—A. E.

PRIMITIVISTA. See MOMPOU, F.

PRINGSHEIM, Heinz. German compr. and author; *b.* Munich, 7 April, 1882. Son of Alfred P. (mathematician and zealous champion of Wagner); first archæologist (Ph.D.); 1900, musician, pupil of Louis (theory), Schmidt-Lindner (pf.); Korrepetitor at Munich and Dresden R. operas; operatic condr.; now critic (on *Allgemeine Musik-Zeitung*) in Berlin.
In ms.: vn. sonata; str. 4tet; songs; *Psalm III*, barit. solo and orch.; *Rondeau*, small orch.; *Seven Dances of Life* (dance-play by Mary Wigmann, Frankfort-o-M. 1921).—A. E.

PRINGSHEIM, Klaus. Ger. dramatist; compr. *b.* Munich, 24 July, 1883. Brother of Heinz P.; pupil of Thuille and Stavenhagen, Munich, and Gustav Mahler, Vienna; 1906, repetitor Vienna R. Opera; 1907, operatic condr. Grand Theatre, Geneva; 1909, Ger. National Theatre, Prague; 1911, operatic stage-manager and dramatist there; 1914, same position Stadttheater, Breslau; 1915, Stadttheater, Bremen; 1918, engaged by Max Reinhardt as mus. condr. of Grosses Schauspielhaus, Berlin. P. is a successful concert-conductor.
Dramatic music for Reinhardt stage; opera, *Lojko Sobar*; songs with pf. and orch.; *Venice*, vs. and orch.; author of many periodical articles; *Modern Wagner Problems* (Regensburg, Bosse). Lectured at Univ. on musical social questions.—A. E.

PRIX DE ROME. A scholarship awarded every year to the pupil of the Paris Cons. whose cantata, prescribed by a jury, has been judged the most satisfactory. It permits the winner to spend 3 years at Rome, at the Villa Médicis. The system is deprecated by some who consider that it confines young talent to an academical training, without which they might have been more interesting. As will be seen by the table below, since 1880, many really good Fr. musicians have not had the *Prix.*
1880, Lucien Hillemacher; 1882, Marty; 1883, Paul Vidal; 1884, Debussy; 1885, Xavier Leroux; 1886, Savard; 1887, G. Charpentier; 1888, Erlanger; 1890, Gaston Carraud; 1891, Silver; 1893, A. Bloch; 1894, Rabaud; 1895, Letorey; 1896, Mouquet; 1897, Max d'Ollone; 1899, Levadé; 1900, Florent Schmitt; 1901, André Caplet; 1902, A. Kunc; 1903, Laparra; 1904, Pech; 1905, Gallois; 1906, L. Dumas; 1907, Le Boucher; 1908, A. Gailhard; 1909, Mazellier; 1910, Gallon; 1911, Paul Paray; 1913, Lili Boulanger and Claude Delvincourt; 1914, Marcel Dupré; 1919, Marc Delmas and Jacques Ibert; 1920, Marguerite Canal; 1921, Jacques de la Presle; 1922, J. Ibert; 1923, Jeanne Leleu. The *Prix* was not awarded in 1881, 1889, 1892, 1898, 1912, nor during the war.—A. C.

PRIX MUSICAUX (Musical Awards in France). Besides the *Prix de Rome* (*q.v.*) there exist in France numerous prizes for the encouragement of music. These prizes are of two sorts; one for comprs., other for writers on music. Amongst the former the most sought after are: *Prix de la Ville de Paris*, awarded since 1877 for an unpubl. opera, or a symph. poem with choruses. This prize has been gained by Théodore Dubois, Vincent d'Indy, Albert Doyen, Jean Cras, and others. *Prix Verley*, awarded since 1920, for an orch. work of modern tendency and for a song with orch. acc. It was gained by Arthur Honegger for his *Pastoral d' Eté* in 1921. *Prix Blumenthal*, since 1920, a purse of 12,000 francs; one of the winners was Georges Migot. *Prix Cressent*, for a dramatic work; *Prix Monbinne*, for a comic opera; *Prix Chartier*, for a chamber-music work; *Prix Lepaulle*, also for a chamber-music work; *Prix Halphen*, for the whole of a compr.'s works. Different prizes founded by musicians: *Prix Rossini*, *Prix Ambroise Thomas*, *Prix Lili Boulanger*, for encouraging young musicians. Among the prizes awarded for works of criticism and mus. history, the most important are the *Prix Bordin*, *Kastner-Boursault*, *Charles Blanc* and *J. J Weiss.*—A. C.

PROCHÁZKA, Ladislav. Real name of Lad. Prokop (*q.v.*).

PROCHÁZKA, Rudolf von, Baron. German-Czechoslovak author, compr. *b.* Prague, 23 Feb. 1864. Lawyer; pupil of Fibich and Grünberger; ministerial councillor at Prague; national reporter on music; president of Ger. State Examination Commission; was prominently active at foundation of Ger. Acad. of Music and Descriptive Art.
The Music Schools of Bohemia (1890); *Robert Franz* (1884); *Mozart in Prague* (in 3 parts, 1914); *Arpeggios* (1897); *Johann Strauss* (1900); *New Arrangement of Kothe's History of Music* (1909); *Five Centuries* (Catalogue of Exhibition of Music, 1911); *The Romantic Music of Prague* (1914); also a book on *Don Giovanni*. Comp.: opera, *Das Glück* (*Prosperity*), Vienna, 1898; mystery, *Christus*; symph.

395

songs; *Haffner Variations*, orch. (on theme of Mozart); *In Memoriam* str. 4tet; choruses; songs; pf. pieces. Consult K. Hunnius's *R. von P.* (1903).—E. S.

PROD'HOMME, Jacques Gabriel. Fr. musicologist; *b.* Paris, 28 Nov. 1871. Music critic for several newspapers. Has contributed since 1895 to a large number of reviews and periodicals, *Lauréat* of Fr. Acad. and of Acad. of Fine Arts (1907–1917), foreign member of R. Acad. of Archæology of Antwerp (1919). He has contributed to the Berlioz literature: *Le Cycle Berlioz* (*Damnation de Faust*, 1896; *L'Enfance du Christ*, 1898); *H. Berlioz, sa vie et ses œuvres* (1904; 2nd ed. 1913; Paris, Delagrave). Has also written: *Les Symphonies de Beethoven* (1920, Delagrave) and a remarkable book on *La Jeunesse de Beethoven* (1920, Payot). We owe to him the Fr. transl. of prose-works of Wagner, 13 vols. 1907–1923 (in collab. with Dr. Holl, Fr. Caillé and van Vassenhoven); a work on *Gounod* (with A. Dandelot), (Paris, Delagrave); *Écrits de Musiciens* (from xv to xviii centuries) (1912); a transl. of the *Magic Flute*, etc.—M. L. P.

PROGRAMME MUSIC. A term applied to music which is descriptive of something outside the music itself, and therefore requires a synopsis or programme in words to explain its significance. Composers have from the earliest times attempted musical descriptions of actions and events, as well as the reproduction in music of sounds of nature. Notable examples of old programme-music are Jannequin's madrigals (battles and birds' cries), the battle and weather pieces of Elizabethan virginalists, Kuhnau's *Biblical Sonatas* for the harpsichord, Dittersdorf's symphonies on the *Metamorphoses* of Ovid, Beethoven's *Battle of Vittoria* and Kotzwara's *Battle of Prague*. A different type of programme music begins with the symphonies of Berlioz and the symphonic poems of Liszt, in which emotional and psychological description is more important than representation of physical action. Liszt's system was continued by Richard Strauss in his symphonic poems. It should be pointed out that the symphonic poems of Strauss, as well as a great deal of earlier programme-music, can be analysed on purely formal lines. Many composers as a matter of fact, are inconsistent in their utterances, on the one hand professing that their music is to be listened to as music alone, and on the other issuing, or allowing others to issue for them, explanations of their music which are purely literary and descriptive. Modern composers, after passing through a phase of so-called "Impressionism" (Debussy, etc.), have rebelled violently against the sentimentalism of the older psychological programme-music, and have turned more to the reproduction and artistic treatment of purely natural physical sounds; this is naturally connected with the modern desire to avoid the emotional and associational element in music and to concentrate more upon the direct physical impression produced by musical sounds (Stravinsky, etc.).—E. J. D.

PROHASKA, Carl. Austrian compr. pianist; *b.* Mödling, near Vienna, 25 April, 1869. Stud. pf. under Eugen d'Albert, compn. under Mandyczewski and Herzogenburg; 1894–5, prof. at

Strasburg Cons.; 1901–5, condr. Philh. Orch. at Warsaw; since 1908, pf. prof. Vienna Acad.; publ. chamber-music, songs, works for male, female and mixed chorus. His cantata *Frühlingsfeier* gained Jubilee prize of Soc. of Friends of Music, Vienna.—H. B.

PROKOFIEF, Serge Sergevitch (*accent 2nd syll.*). Russ. compr. *b.* Solnzevo, in the Ekaterinoslaf government, 11/23 April, 1891. Received his education at Petrograd Cons. where his teachers were Liadof, Wihtol, and Rimsky-Korsakof (theory and compn.), Mme. Essipof (pf.). In 1910 he won the Rubinstein Prize with his 1st pf. concerto, op. 10. Left Russia in 1918; was for some years in Japan; then spent about 3 years in U.S.A.; now lives at Ettal, near Oberammergau, Bavaria.

The chief feature of his music, especially up to his op. 20 or so, is that it asserts a firm will: no passion, but a uniform terseness, continuous and almost mechanical. No shadows, no vagueness, but definite lines, sharp contours, clearly defined planes. The rhythms are always well-marked. P. invents no new rhythmic formulæ, but proceeds by constant repetition of a figure. The themes are usually short, but pregnant and plastic. The harmonies are crude and at times brutal (*e.g.* in *Sarcasmes*, his most daring work); he uses polytonality systematically. His form is clear and logical. In many respects, his mus. temperament comes near to that of the classics —especially of Scarlatti. Of late his style has become more mellow, his melodies are more abundant and broader. His *Visions Fugitives* and *Granny's Tales* reveal him in the light of a tender dreamy lyricist. He is gradually reverting to a more diatonic conception of music. He is an excellent pianist whose playing is somewhat dry, but clear, brilliant, and alive.

Operas: *Madalena* (unperf.); *The Gambler* (after Dostoievsky's novel); *The Loves of the Three Oranges* (after Carlo Gozzi) (Chicago, 1921); ballet, *Chout* (Paris, 1921); *Sinfonietta*; *Scythian Suite*; 2 tone-poems, (one of which, *They are Seven*, is choral); 3 pf. concertos (all perf. at Q. H. London, with composer at piano, the 3rd on 24 April, 1922); vn. concerto; 4 pf. sonatas; various instr. pieces, and songs.—B. DE S.

PROKOP, Ladislav (real name Lad. Procházka). Czechoslovak compr. *b.* Litomyšl, 1872. Pupil of Vít. Novák; lives in Prague practising as a physician.

3 symph. poems on Svatopluk Čech's cycle *Ve stinu lipy* (*In the Limetree's Shadow*); pf. 5tet; str. 4tet; opera, *Sen lesa* (*The Dream of the Wood*), Prague, 1907; *Otázka* (*The Question*) Prague, 1910; overture, *Osud* (*Fate*); cantata, *Staroměstský Rynk*.—V. ST.

PROLONGEMENT. See MUSTEL.

PROTHEROE, Daniel. Welsh compr. condr. and teacher; *b.* Ystradgynlais, S. Wales. Stud. under Dr. Joseph Parry. Adjudicator in principal Amer. comp. fests. and National Eisteddfodau in Wales. Mus.Doc. (New York). His compns. include many cantatas, orch. tone-poems, male-voice choruses of a high order and volumes of art-songs. He is well known in America as an experienced lecturer. Resides in Chicago. U.S.A. —D. V. T.

PROUT, Ebenezer. Distinguished English theorist and writer; *b.* Oundle, 1 March, 1835;

d. London 5 Dec. 1909. Stud. pf. under Charles Salaman; but otherwise was self-taught. Graduated at London Univ., being intended for scholastic profession; but inspired by his love for music, he followed it as a profession. In 1861, became orgt. of Union Chapel, Islington, London, where he remained until 1873. In 1862, Soc. of British Musicians awarded him 1st prize for a str. 4tet, and in 1865 for a pf. 4tet. 1871–4, ed. of *Monthly Mus. Record*; music critic of *Academy* (1874–9) and *Athenæum* (1879–89). In 1879, prof. of harmony and compn. at R.A.M. London, and in 1884 at Guildhall School of Music. His compns. were never popular on account of their stilted style and lack of melodic invention, though the str. 4tet in B flat, op. 15, has some effective writing. Far more famous were his theoretical works, which have been transl. into many languages. His *Harmony, its Theory and Practice* reached 20 eds. by 1903. In 1894 he was appointed prof. of music in the Univ. of Dublin and received an honorary Mus.Doc. in 1895. During his tenure of the professorship down to his death he not only devoted himself to his music students but gave very interesting public lectures, especially the course on the Bach cantatas illustrated by the energetic professor with the co-operation of singers trained by him. He devoted much time to editing the classics, providing additional accs. for the Handel oratorios. In 1902 he introduced to the R. Soc. of Musicians a new full score and a vocal one of *Messiah*.

2 symphonies; cantatas; organ concerto; chamber-music; church music; sonata, pf. and clar.; organ arrangements.

Educational works: *Harmony* (1889; rev. ed. 1901); *Counterpoint* (1890); *Double Counterpoint and Canon* (1891); *Fugue* (1891); *Fugal Analysis* (1892); *Form* (1893); *Applied Forms* (1895); *The Orchestra*, Vol. I (1898); Vol. II (1899). They have been transl. into many languages.—W. S.

PROUT, Louis B. Eng. writer on mus. theory; *b.* Hackney, London, 14 Sept. 1864. Son of Ebenezer P. under whose guidance he stud. at R.A.M.; prof. of Guildhall School of Music. His chief work is *Harmonic Analysis* (Augener).

Psalm XCIII, chorus and orch.; songs, etc.; *Analysis of Bach's 48 Fugues* (Weekes); *Time, Rhythm and Expression (id.)*.—E.-H.

PRÜFER, Arthur. Ger. musicologist; *b.* Leipzig, 7 July, 1860. Pupil of Friedrich Stade; stud. for Bar at Jena, Leipzig, Heidelberg, Berlin; 1886, took Dr.'s degree; then turned to music; 1887–8, at Leipzig Cons. and Univ. (Paul and Kretzschmar); 1888–9, Berlin (Spitta and Bargiel); 1890, Ph.D.; 1895, settled as Univ. teacher in science of music at Leipzig.

Publ. *J. H. Schein's Complete Works* (6 vols., Breitkopf). Wrote: *Johann Hermann Schein and Secular German Song of XVII Century* (1908); *Richard Wagner in Bayreuth* (publ. 1910); *Introduction to Richard Wagner's Opera " Die Feen."*—A. E.

PRÜMERS, Adolf. Ger. choral condr. *b.* Burgsteinfurt, Westphalia, 1 Sept. 1877. Stud. music at Weimar, Cologne, Berlin (Müller-Hartung, Kleffel, Heinrich Urban); 1903–10, opera-condr. at Basle, Metz, Bad Kreutznach and other places; 1911, condr. of male choral

soc. *Harmonia;* condr. of East Prussian Provincial Singers' League, Tilsit. Well known as compr. of male choruses. Wrote *Biography of Friedrich Silcher* (1910).—A. E.

PRUNIÈRES, Henry. Fr. musicologist; *b.* Paris, 24 May, 1886. Pupil of Roman Rolland; quickly obtained his degrees, ending in a doctorate 1913, his thesis being *L'Opéra italien en France avant Lully.* He upholds the theory, too long neglected, that erudition is worth very little unless it is put to the service of general ideas and views—in short, unless it is combined with a sense of history and philosophy. It is for this last quality, no less than for the abundance of unpubl. documents they contain, that his works are remarkable. They deal mainly with the xvii and xviii centuries. In 1910 he publ. the first critical study on *Lully* (Laurens); he succeeded in reconstructing the life of the great musician by the use of documents for the most part unpubl. With the intention of developing this subject further, he publ. two works on the origins of Fr. opera: *L'Opéra italien en France avant Lully* (Paris, 1913, Champion), and *Le Ballet de cour en France avant Benserade et Lully* (Paris, 1914, Laurens). He publ. a popular book on *Monteverdi* (Alcan, 1923), and in 1924 a more detailed work on the same subject (J. M. Dent & Sons). Has also publ. a critical ed. (with preface and notes) of *Vie de Rossini* by Stendhal (Coll. Champion). In 1914 he was secretary to Congress of *S.I.M.* in Paris. He took an active part in organisation of International Congress in History of Art, at the Sorbonne in 1921. In 1920, founded the *Revue Musicale* (see Periodicals), which he made one of the keenest and richest in musical documents of the world's musical periodicals.

P. is as well-informed on modern music as on classical, and by his articles has very largely contributed to the fame of young foreign musicians in France—G. Francesco Malipiero, Béla Bartók and Szymanowski. He founded at the Théâtre du Vieux Colombier in Paris, the *Revue Musicale* Concerts (1921), and was one of the founders of Fr. section of *S.I.M.C.,* 1923. His solid erudition, breadth of view and extraordinary energy assure him a prominent place among Fr. musicologists of this generation. Dr. Prunières is the Chairman of the Committee for the French articles in this Dictionary.

La Musique de Chambre et de l'Écurie sous le règne de François Ier (*Année Musicale*, 1911, Alcan); *Jean de Cambefort, surintendant de la Musique de la Chambre du Roy* (*Année Musicale*, 1912, Alcan); *Notes sur les origines de l'ouverture française* (*Sammelbände der I.M.G.* 12th year, No. 4); *Lecerf de la Viéville et le classicisme musical* (*S.I.M.* 1908); *Les Véridiques Aventures de D'Assoucy* (*Revue de Paris,* Dec. 1921); *La Fontaine et Lully* (*Revue Musicale,* Dec. 1921); *Le Chorégraphe Salvatore Vigano* (*Revue Musicale,* Dec. 1921); *Paolo Lorenzani à la Cour de France* (*Revue Musicale,* Aug. 1922), and a great number of arts. on the early years of Lully which are summarised in *L'Opéra italien en France.*—A. C.

PRÜWER, Julius. Austrian condr. *b.* Vienna, 20 Feb. 1874. Pupil of Arthur Friedheim and Moritz Rosenthal (pf.), of Robert Fuchs, Franz Krenn and Joh. Brahms (theory), of Richter (conducting) whom he followed to Bayreuth; condr. at Bielitz; 1894, operatic condr. at Cologne; 1896, Stadttheater, Breslau; 1923, Weimar.—A. E.

PUBLISHERS. *ARGENTINA.*—(i) The most important firm is Breyer Brothers; founded in 1882. (ii) Albert S. Poggi does some publishing; founded 1860.

AUSTRIA.—(i) Universal Edition (*q.v.*). (ii) Artaria, Ital. mus. publ. and art-dealers; settled in Vienna about 1750; publ. works of Beethoven and Schubert. (iii) Wiener Philharmonischer Verlag. (iv) E. P. Tal & Co., founded 1919; publ. literary works on music, especially contemporary composers. (v) Doblinger, Vienna.

BELGIUM.—Schott Frères, Brussels, founded orig. at Antwerp early in XIX century, later removed to Brussels. Now owned and dir. by Otto Junne. Publ. the journal *Le Guide Musical* from its foundation in 1854 to its extinction during the war.

CZECHO-SLOVAKIA.—(i) Hudební Matice (see SOCIETIES). (ii) Fr. A. Urbánek, founded 1872; his ed. includes 5000 nos. Most of Smetana's works and all Fibich's (Prague, Národní třída 1369). (iii) Mojmír Urbánek, *b.* 1873; separated from his father's business (see ii) and establ. his own which is now the largest and most important in Czecho-Slovakia. Publ. works of Novák, Foerster, Suk, etc.; owns Mozarteum concert-hall (seating 400). Address, Prague, Jungmannova 34. (iv) Em. Starý (Prague). (v) E. Wetzler (*ib.*). (vi) J. Hoffmanns (*ib.*). (vii) Fr. Chadím (*ib.*). (viii) Bravič & Novotný (Brno), (ix) O. Pozdírek (Brno).

DENMARK.—(i) Wilhelm Hansen, Danish publ. firm. Copenhagen. Founded 1857 by Jens Wilhelm H. (1821–1904); later on, through consolidation with other firms became the greatest in Scandinavia. In 1904 it was continued by his two sons, Jonas Wilhelm (*d.* 1919) and Alfred Wilhelm (*d.* 1923). The two sons of the latter, Asger and Svend Wilhelm, are the present dirs. There is a branch house in Leipzig. (ii) Nordisk Musikforlag, Copenhagen.

ENGLAND.—LONDON: (i) Abbott, Ambrose, & Co. 31 Newgate Street, E.C.; (ii) Anglo-French Music Co. 31 York Place, Baker Street, W.; (iii) Ascherberg, Hopwood & Crew, 16 Mortimer Street, Regent Street, W.; (iv) Ashdown, Edwin (*q.v.*), 19 Hanover Square, W.; (v) Augener (*q.v.*), 18 Great Marlborough Street, W.; (vi) Banks & Sons, London and York. (vii) Bayley & Ferguson, 2 Great Marlborough Street, W.; (viii) Beal, Stuttard & Co. Oxford Circus Ave., 231 Oxford Street, W.; (ix) Boosey & Co. (*q.v.*), 295 Regent Street, W.; (x) Bosworth & Co. (*q.v.*), 8 Heddon Street, Regent Street, W., (xi) Burns & Oates, 28 Orchard Street, W.; (xii) Cary & Co. 13–15 Mortimer Street, W.; (xiii) Chappell & Co. (*q.v.*), 50 New Bond Street, W.; (xiv) Chester, J & W. (*q.v.*), 11 Great Marlborough Street, W.; (xv) Clowes, Wm., & Sons (church-music), 31 Haymarket, S.W. 1; (xvi) Cramer, J. B., & Co. 139 New Bond Street, W.; (xvii) Curwen, J., & Sons (*q.v.*), 24 Berners Street, W.; (xviii) Duff,

Stewart & Co. 3 Little Marlborough Street, W.; (xix) Elkin & Co. (*q.v.*), 8 & 10 Beak Street, Regent Street, W.; (xx) Enoch & Sons, 58 Great Marlborough Street, W. 1; (xxi) Escott & Co. 64 Newman Street, W.; (xxii) Faith Press (church-music), 22 Buckingham Street, W.C.; (xxiii) Forsyth Bros. (*q.v.*), 36 Great Titchfield Street, Oxford Street, W.; (xxiv) Frederick Harris Co. 40 Berners Street, W. 1; (xxv) Goodwin, F. & B. (modern contemporary music), 34 Percy Street, W.; amalgamated with Curwen & Sons, Jan. 1924; (xxvi) Hammond & Co. (educational music), 6 Kingly Street, Regent Street, W.; (xxvii) Hawkes & Son (orch. & military band music), Denman Street, Piccadilly, W.; (xxviii) Hutchings & Romer, 28 Castle Street East, Oxford Street, W.; (xxix) John Church Co. 45 Wigmore Street, W.; (xxx) Larway, J. H. (*q.v.*), 14 Wells Street, Oxford Street; (xxxi) Laudy & Co. 8 Newman Street, W.; (xxxii) Lengnick & Co. (educational music), 14 Berners Street, W.; (xxxiii) Metzler & Co. 42 Great Marlborough Street, W.; (xxxiv) Moutrie, Collard, 52 Southampton Row, Russell Square, W.C.; (xxxv) Murdoch & Co. (*q.v.*), 23 Princes St. Oxford Circus, W. 1; (xxxvi) Novello & Co (*q.v.*), 160 Wardour Street, W.; (xxxvii) Paxton, W., & Co. 95 New Oxford Street, W.C.; (xxxviii) Reeves, W. (mostly books; publ. of weekly *Mus. Standard*), 83 Charing Cross Road, W.C.; (xxxix) Reid Bros. 26 Castle Street, Oxford Circus, W.; (xl) Reynolds & Co. 62a Berners Street, W.; (xli) Ricordi & Co. 265 Regent Street, W.; (xlii) Rogers, Winthrop (*q.v.*), 18 Berners Street, W. 1; (xliii) Rudall, Carte & Co. (military band music, and *Mus. Directory*), 23 Berners Street, W.; (xliv) Schott & Co. 63 Conduit Street, W.; (xlv) Stainer & Bell (also publ. for the Carnegie Music Trust), 58 Berners Street, W.; (xlvi) Swan & Co. 288 Regent Street, W.; (xlvii) Weekes & Co. (*q.v.*), 14 Hanover Street, Regent Street, W.; (xlviii) Williams, Joseph (*q.v.*), 32 Portland Street, W.

FRANCE.—PARIS: (i) P. de Choudens, 30 boul. des Capucines; (ii) Costallat et Cie. 60 r. de la Chaussée-d'Antin; (iii) Ch. Delagrave, 15 r. Soufflot; (iv) E. Demets, 2 r. de Louvois; (v) Durand et Cie. 4 place de la Madeleine; (vi) Édition Mutuelle (*q.v.*), 269 r. St. Jacques; (vii) Enoch et Cie. 27 boul. des Italiens; (viii) Max Eschig, 13 r. Lafitte; (ix) Fœtisch Frères, 28 r. de Bondy; (x) Fromont, 44 r. du Colisée; (xi) H. Gaillard, 18 r. Saint-Sulpice; (xii) L. Grus et Cie. 65*bis* r. de Miromesnil; (xiii) J. Hamelle, 22 boul. Malesherbes; (xiv) Hayet, 11*bis* boul. Haussmann; (xv) H. Heugel et Cie. 2*bis* r. Vivienne; (xvi) E. Leduc, P. Bertrand et Cie. 3 r. de Grammont; (xvii) Lemoine fils, 17 r. Pigalle; (xviii) A. Z. Mathot, 11 r. Bergère; (xix) G. Ricordi et Cie. 18 r. de la Pépinière; (xx) Rouart, Lerolle et Cie. 29 r. d'Astorg; (xxi) M. Senart et Cie. 20 r. du Dragon; (xxii) A. de Smit, 187 faub. Poissonnière.

GERMANY.—(i) Bote & Bock, Berlin, founded 1838; from 1847–96, publ. journal *Neue Berliner Musikzeitung*; one of first firms to introduce cheap editions of classics. (ii) Breitkopf & Härtel, Leipzig, founded 1719, still the most important publishers in Germany. (iii) Drei Masken Verlag, Munich, founded 1910, music dept. soon settled in Berlin. The Munich dept. publ. works on science and literature of music. (iv) Ernst Eulenburg, founded 1874. (v) Robert Forberg, Leipzig, founded 1862. (vi) Adolph Fürstner, Berlin, founded 1868; publ. many operas of Richard Strauss, and Pfitzner's *Palestrina* and *Von Deutscher Seele*. (vii) Heinrichshofer Musikverlag, Berlin, founded 1806; specialises on educational music and books. (viii) Hesse Verlag, founded Leipzig, 1880, now in Berlin. Specialises on Riemann's small handbooks and Ernst Kurth's books. (ix) Friedrich Hofmeister, Leipzig, founded 1807. Its monthly journal, started 1830, *Musikalisch-literarisches Monatsbericht*, is still well-known. (x) Leuckart Verlag, founded in Breslau, 1782; removed to Leipzig 1870; present owner is Martin Sander. Publ. Rheinberger, R. Strauss, Reger, Bossi, Bantock, Delius, Klose, Huber, etc. (xi) Litolff & Co. establ. by pianist H. C. Litolff, managed by his stepson Henry L. who entered the firm 1853 and establ. in 1864 the famous Litolff Edition of classics. (xii) C. F. Peters, Leipzig. The world-famous Peters Edition was started in 1867, by Dr. Abraham (then dir.). In 1893 they opened a free public music library in Leipzig. (xiii) Rahter Verlag, Hamburg, establ. by Daniel Rath (1828–91), former chief of Petrograd house of A. Bueltner; acquired works of Tchaikovsky, Arensky, Borodin, Strauss, Busoni, etc. (xiv) Kahnt Verlag, founded by Christian Friedrich K. (1823–97). Many important works by Liszt; large catalogue of books on music. (xv) Kistner Verlag, Leipzig, founded 1831. (xvi) B. Schott's Söhne, Mayence, founded 1773; orig. publ. of Wagner's *Ring*, *Parsifal*; now represent the modern German school well. (xvii) Schuberth Verlag, Leipzig, founded in Hamburg, 1826. There is still a branch there, and also in New York. (xviii) Siegel Verlag, Leipzig, establ. by C. F. W. Siegel, 1846; music and books on music. (xix) Simrock Verlag, Berlin, establ. 1790. Publ. Beethoven's op. 17, 31, 81*b*, 102, 107; chief publ. of Brahms and Dvořák. (xx) Carl Simon, Berlin. (xxi) Tischer & Jagenberg, Cologne (see TISCHER, GERHARD).

HOLLAND.—(i) Alsbach, Amsterdam. (ii) Nieuwe Muziekhandel, Amsterdam. (iii) Noske, The Hague.

HUNGARY.—(i) Rözsavölgyi & Co. Budapest (Szervita-tér, 5). Establ. 1850. Important older publications: Liszt's *Two Legendes* for pf.; Goldmark's *Sakuntala* overture and pf. pieces; Volkmann's *Visegrád*, 2 pf. trios, and pf. pieces. Since 1906 the firm has publ. many works younger Hungarian comprs. (ii) Charles Rozsnyai, Budapest (Muzeum-Körut 15). Establ. 1889. Since 1905, almost all the more important classical pf. and vn. works have been issued by this firm in a critical Hungarian edition. Publ. of works of Hungarian comprs. (Bartók, etc.).

(iii) Bárd & Sons, Budapest (Kossuth utca. 4). Establ. 1893. Among their publications are Mihalovich's opera *Eliana*; chamber-music by Leo Weiner, etc.

IRISH FREE STATE.—C. & E. Publ. Co. Dublin, founded by · Sir Stanley Cochrane and Michele Esposito.

ITALY.—(i) G. Ricordi & Co. Milan. The greatest music-publ. house in Italy; founded 1808 (see special art.) (ii) Eduardo Sonzogno, Milan, founded 1874 (see special art.). (iii) Ausonia Publ. Co. Rome; issue monographs on music. (iv) Carisch (formerly Carisch & Jänichen), Milan. (v) Pizzi, recently establ. firm, specially devoted to contemporary Ital. music. (vi) Bongiovanni, Bologna. (vii) Marcello Capra, Turin; specially church and organ music. Has publ. journal for sacred music *Santa Cecilia*, from 1889 onwards. (See art. SOCIETÀ TIPOGRAFICA, S.T.E.N.). (viii) Giuseppe Bocca, founded 1894; first in Italy to direct attention to books about music. Bocca himself (*b.* Turin, 1867) transl. Wolzogen's Wagner books and Kufferath's work on *Tristan*. (ix) Izzo, Naples. (x) Curci Fratelli, Naples. (xi) Forlivesi, Florence. (xii) Zanibon, Padua.

NORWAY.—Norsk Musikforlag, Christiania.

RUSSIA.—(i) M. P. Belaief, Moscow. (ii) Jurgenson, Moscow. (iii) Bessel & Co. Moscow. (iv) Russian Music Publ. Co. Moscow. (v) Gutheil & Co. All these have disappeared from Russia; but have centres in London, Paris, and Berlin. (vi) Russian State Music Publishing Dept. founded under the Soviet government. Publ. the works of contemporary Russ. comprs. The dir. is Paul A. Lamm (*q.v.*); the chief librarian is Serge S. Popof (*q.v.*) and the secretary V. Belaief (*q.v.*).

SCOTLAND.—(i) Paterson & Sons, Edinburgh and Glasgow. (ii) J. Pentland, Edinburgh. Both publish, amongst other music, collections of Scottish folk-songs.

SPAIN.—(i) Unión Musical Española (late Dotesio), leading Span. publishers. Head office in Madrid. (ii) Ildefonso Alier, Madrid. Publishes the reviews *Arte Musical* and *Biblioteca Sacro-Musical*. (iii) A. Matamala, Madrid. (iv) Faustino Fuentes, Madrid. (v) J. B. Pujol & Co. Barcelona.

SWEDEN.—(i) Abr. Lundqvist. (ii) Elkan & Schildknecht (now taken over by Emil Carelius). (iii) Abr. Hirsch. (iv) Julius Wibergh. (v) Carl Gehrman. (vi) M. Th. Dahlström. (vii) Carl Johnn. (viii) Musikaliska Konstföreningen. (ix) Nordiska Musikförlaget, affiliated with Nordisk Musikforlag, Wilhelm Hansen, Copenhagen.

SWITZERLAND.—(i) Fœtisch, Lausanne. (ii) Hüni, Zurich. (iii) Hug (Swiss National Ed.), Zurich (and Leipzig). (iv) Henn, Geneva. (v) Rötschy, Geneva. (vi) Chouet & Gaden, Geneva. (vii) Pohl, Basle. (viii) Verlag des Bern. Organistenverbands, Berne.

U.S.A.—(i) G. Schirmer Inc. (*q.v.*), New York. (ii) J. Fischer & Brother, New York. (iii) H. W. Gray Co. New York (*q.v.*). (iv) Carl Fischer, New

399

York. (v) Composers' Music Corporation, for works by young modernists. (vi) Boston Music Co. Boston. (vii) Oliver Ditson Co. (*q.v.*), Boston. (viii) Theo Presser Co. Philadelphia. (ix) Clayton F. Summy Co. Chicago. (x) John Church Co. Cincinnati. (xi) Wa-Wan Press, Newton Centre, Mass. (see FARWELL, ARTHUR).

PUCCINI, Giacomo. Ital. opera composer; *b.* Lucca, 23 Dec. 1858. His operas are amongst those which are most performed in theatres throughout the world. He was born from a family of musicians, and was started on his musical career by his father, Michele. He completed his studies in harmony and cpt. in his native city under the esteemed master, Angeloni. After a few first attempts at compn., he was enabled (through the generosity of Queen Margherita) to go to Milan, where he completed his studies with Bazzini and Ponchielli. A *Capriccio sinfonico*, written as a final test, revealed his extraordinary qualities. The work was publ. by the Casa Lucca, in an adaptation for two pfs. The first opera written by Puccini was *Le Villi* (libretto by Ferdinando Fontana) which was perf. with much success at Teatro Dal Verme, Milan, in May 1884. It was followed by *Edgar* (Scala, Milan, 1889). But the fullest success came to him through *Manon Lescaut* (Regio Theatre, Turin, 1893) and especially through *La Bohème* (same theatre, 1896) From that time onwards, P.'s fame continued steadily to consolidate itself, and every new opera has been regarded as an event. At present, he is working on an opera, *Turandot*, the subject taken from the fable of Carlo Gozzi. P. generally lives in retirement in his villa, Torre del Lago, near Lucca, or in Viareggio. He takes part in the most important Ital. mus. meetings, including the permanent commission of Ministry of Education.

Tosca (Costanzi, Rome, 1904); *Madama Butterfly*, a Japanese tragedy, which met with a hostile reception at La Scala in Feb. 1904, had afterwards (in a new ed. in 3 acts) a lasting success at Brescia, in May of same year; *La Fanciulla del West* (*The Girl of the Golden West*) (Metropolitan, New York, 1910); *La Rondine* (Monte Carlo, 1917); *Il Tabarro*, *Suor Angelica* and *Gianni Schicchi*, a triptych of 1-act operas, of contrasted subjects, tragic, mystic, and comic (Metropolitan, New York, 14 Dec. 1918; then at Costanzi, Rome, 11 Jan. 1919; Covent Garden, London, 1920). Apart from the theatre, he has written very little. We mention two Minuets for strings, and the *Inno a Roma* (1919), written for the pupils of the Roman schools, and first perf. at the Stadio in Rome.

His works have all been publ. by Ricordi, Milan (except *La Rondine* and the *Inno a Roma*, which are publ. by Sonzogno).

Consult: Fausto Torrefranca, *P. e l'opera internazionale* (Turin, 1913, Bocca); Giacomo Setaccioli, *Il contenuto musicale del Gianni Schicchi* (Rome, 1920, De Sanctis); Wakeling Dry, *G. P.* (London, John Lane); and numerous studies and articles in papers and reviews.—D. A.

PUCHAT, Max. Ger. compr. *b.* Breslau, 8 Jan. 1859; killed accidentally at Karwendel, Bavaria, 12 Aug. 1919. Pupil of Friedrich Kiel, Berlin; 1885, of Liszt; Mendelssohn Prize, 1884; 1886, town mus. dir. Hamm; 1896, condr. of oratorio soc. Paderborn; 1903, cond. Ger. Mus. Soc. Milwaukee; 1905, returned to Europe; 1906, dir. of Vienna Acad. of Singing; 1910, dir. Cons. Breslau.

Songs; overture; *Fuga Solemnis* for orch.: symph. poems: *Euphorion* (1888); *Life and Ideals*; *Tragedy of an Artist* (1894) (5 movements); chamber-music.—A. E.

PUDDICOMBE, Henry. Canadian pianist; *b.* London, Ontario, in 1871. Trained in Leipzig, under Krause (pf.) and Quasdorf (harmony). After 5 years there, returned to Canada and (1897) started teaching in Ottawa. In 1903 founded Canadian Cons. of Music, Ottawa, of which he is Principal. Under his *régime* the Cons. has achieved recognition as one of principal mus. colleges of Ontario (see ACADEMIES).—L. S.

PUJMAN, Ferdinand. Czech mus. critic, opera régisseur; *b.* Viškov, 1889. Became an engineer; as theatre régisseur in Prague and Brno, he displayed his modern views on the relations of music to gesture; prof. at Cons. for the same subject.

Liszt's Views; *Smetana's Breviary*; *Remarks on the Dramaturgy of Smetana's Operas*; *Osudnice lásky* (all in Czech).—V. ST.

PUJOL, Emilio. Contemporary Span. guitarist; pupil of Francisco Tárrega. Concert-tours in U.S.A., Spain, S. America, etc.—P. G. M.

PUJOL, Francesch. Contemporary Span. compr. and musicologist of the Catalonian group. Pupil of Luis Millet. He advocates nationalism in music. Lives in Barcelona. One of his best-known works is *Festa* for orch. (Unión Musical Española).—P. G. M.

PULVER, Jeffrey. Eng. violinist and writer; *b.* London, 22 June, 1884. Stud. under Ševčik (Prague), Heermann (Frankfort), Marteau (Geneva), and Moser (Berlin). Gave vn. recitals at Steinway Hall, Broadwood's, etc., besides lecturing at various places. At present chiefly engaged in research work in old Eng. music in which he has specialised. Also plays viole d'amour and XVII century tenor viol (6 str.); is an authority on obsolete instruments.

A Dictionary of Old English Music and Musical Instruments (Kegan Paul, 1923); *A Dictionary of Musical Terms* (Cassell, 1913); papers read before Mus. Assoc. and printed in the *Proceedings*: *The Ancient Dance Forms* (1st paper, 1912); *The Ancient Dance Forms* (2nd paper, 1914); *The Intermezzi of the Opera* (1917); *The Viols in England* (1920); *The Music of Ancient Egypt* (1921); arts. (biographical, bibliographical, historical, technical) in *Mus. Times*, *Mus. Opinion*, *Monthly Mus. Record*, *Mus. News*, *Sackbut*, *Strad*, *Schoolmaster*, *Mus. Quarterly*, etc. —E.-H.

QUARTER-TONES. See BAGLIONI, SILVESTRO; FOULDS, J. H.; HÁBA, ALOIS; STEIN, R. H.

QUARTETS, STRING. See CHAMBER-MUSIC PLAYERS.

QUARTETTINO. A quartet retaining many features of the classical quartet, but having the movements much more concise, often " telescoped," so to speak, as regards their form and construction. See arts. WEIDIG, WHITHORNE, etc.—E.-H.

QUEEN'S HALL ORCHESTRA. Founded and managed by Robert Newman in 1895, when first season of Queen's Hall Promenade Concerts took place. Frederic Cowen conducted the Queen's Hall Choral Soc. in 1893 at the opening of the Hall, and was followed by Randegger. Henry J. Wood was then orgt. The first condr. of the Queen's Hall Orch. was Randegger, before Wood became permanent condr. and gave unity, solidarity and character to the whole scheme. There were 49 Promenade concerts in the first season and the week was mapped out as follows: Monday, Wagner; Tuesday, Sullivan; Wednesday, "Classical"; Thursday, Schubert; Friday, "Classical"; Saturday, "Popular." From Aug. to Oct. 1896 there were 62 concerts; 1897, 43; 1898, 42; 1901-2, 106 each year. The first policy was to set apart one night a week for novelties. The Promenade Concerts had the result of forming and training a first-class orch. and creating a large Eng. public for the best orch. music. The public thronged so thickly that the term " promenade" was a delusion. In Jan. 1897, Robert Newman commenced a short series of Symphony Concerts with the orch. increased to 103, under Wood. Newman engaged the Lamoureux Orch. from Paris for a week at Queen's Hall from 13 April, 1896, again from 16 Nov. 1896, and, for the 3rd time within 12 months, from 22 March, 1897; Lamoureux cond. the Queen's Hall Orch. for the whole season (3 Nov. 1897 to 21 May, 1898), and greatly improved the standard of " bowing" in the strings. In May 1897, Robert Newman promoted the first London Festival with the Lamoureux Orch. in addition to his own. The 2 orchs. were heard alternately, dir. by their respective condrs. finishing with a concert of the 2 combined bands. At this concert, Lamoureux introduced the plan of seating the 2nd violins on his left, next to the firsts. Before the return of the Fr. orch. in 1900, Lamoureux died, and his son-in-law Chevillard took his place at the Queen's Hall second London Festival when the bands played frequently together under Wood and Chevillard alternately.

In 1901 season, the condrs. included Colonne, Ysaye, Saint-Saëns, Weingartner and Wood,

the Eng. condr. easily holding his own. In 1902 the condrs. were Weingartner, Ysaye, Saint-Saëns, Nikisch and Wood. The sensation made by Nikisch's interpretation of Tchaikovsky's 5th symphony was enormous. Henry J. Wood introduced 5 tone-poems of Strauss during the Promenade season 1902-3. At the 5th London Fest. (1911), Henry J. Wood was the principal condr. Elgar's Gerontius was given, and the 1st perf. of his 2nd symphony was played under his bâton (24 May, 1911). Besides the Promenades and the Symphony concerts, the Sunday afternoon and evening concerts were also undertaken by this orch. The evening concerts were oratorios, and have been discontinued. The Sunday concerts were orig. run by Robert Newman alone; from 11 Dec. 1898 they were under the Sunday Concert Society.

Sir Edward Speyer was chairman of the Queen's Hall Orch. from 1902 till 1915, when both hall and orch. were taken over by Messrs. Chappell & Co. The prestige of the orch. at present is greater than ever.—E.-H.

QUEF, Charles. Fr. orgt. b. Lille, 1873. Lauréat of Guilmant class at Paris Cons. 1898; succeeded his master as orgt. at La Trinité, Paris, in 1901.

Sonata, pf. and vn.; trio; Fantaisie, pf. and orch.; Funeral Prelude, organ and orch.; numerous pieces for the organ (Durand; Augener; J. Williams). —F. R.

QUILTER, Roger. Eng. compr. b. Brighton, 1 Nov. 1877. Educated at Eton; afterwards stud. at Frankfort-o-M. under Ivan Knorr. His Shakespearean and other song-settings have a great vogue. His song-cycle To Julia was first sung by Gervase Elwes in 1905; his 7 Elizabethan Lyrics by Elwes in 1908. He wrote music for the fairy-play Where the Rainbow ends (Savoy, 21 Dec. 1911); also for As You Like It (1922).

Orch.: Serenade, op. 9 (ms.); 3 English Dances, small orch. op. 11 (Boosey); Children's Overture, orch. op. 17 (Rogers); fairy-play suite, Where the Rainbow ends (Elkin); suite from As You Like It (Boosey); song-cycles and songs (Boosey; Forsyth; Chappell; Rogers; Elkin); pf. pieces (Rogers; Elkin); pieces, vn. and pf. (Rogers; Boosey); part-songs (Forsyth; Boosey); 5 old Eng. songs (arr.), 1921 (Rogers). —E.-H.

QUINET, Fernand. Compr. b. Charleroi, 29 Jan. 1898. Stud. at Brussels Cons., holder of prize for cello, 1911 and 1914. Stud. compn. under Biarent at Charleroi, and Léon Du Bois at Brussels Cons. Prix de Rome, 1921. For a time, one of Pro Arte Str. Quartet (Onnou, Halleux, Prévost, Quinet).

Le Conte d'Été, incidental music; La Guerre (cantata, gained Prix de Rome); 4tets; Suite for 3 clars.; songs.—E. C.

QUIROGA, Manuel. Span. violinist; b. Pontevedra in 1890. Stud. at R. Cons. de Música,

Madrid, and at Cons., Paris, winning the highest prizes. Recognised in England, France, America and Spain, as one of the contemporary *virtuosi*. First appearance in London, 1920.—P. G. M.

QUITTARD, Henri. Fr. musicologist; *b.* Clermont-Ferrand (Puy de Dôme) 13 May, 1864; *d.* Paris, 21 July, 1919. One of the historians whose names stand on the highest level of Fr. musicology. A *licencié-ès-lettres* at 24, he came to Paris, where he stud. under César Franck, on advice of Emmanuel Chabrier. He soon devoted himself to the history of music. Mus. critic for *Le Matin* and then for *Le Figaro* (from 1909). From 1 Jan. 1912, keeper of archives at Opéra. His first works appeared about 1898. While he was more especially interested in Fr. musicians of xvi and xvii centuries, he investigated whole domains of Fr. music since xiii century. He was also (with Michel Brenet) one of first to point out the merits of the Fr. lutenists. Lecturer at the Écoles des Hautes Études Soc. An indefatigable worker, he has unfortunately left only a few publ. works:

Un Musicien en France au XVIIe siècle, Henri du Mont (Paris, 1906, Mercure de France); *G. Bouzignac, Mélanges divers réunis au jour*; *H. du Mont, Mélanges divers remis au jour* (Paris, Schola); *Le Trésor d'Orphée, par Antoine Francique* (transcription for lute, Paris, *S.I.M.*), etc. From 1898 until his death, supplied many valuable arts. to reviews: *La Revue Internationale de Musique, La Tribune de St.-Gervais, La Revue Musicale*, the colls. of International Soc. of Music, review *S.I.M.* (*cf.* Bulletin of Fr. Soc. of Musicology, 1919, No. 5, *H. Q.*, by L. de la Laurencie). His remarkable collection, which he himself built up by copying and transcribing entire works like the *Hortus Musarum*, the pieces of J. Gallot, the airs of Lambert, Mauduit, Guédron, etc., is at present in Library of Cons. of Paris. He left (in preparation) a very important work on *Guillaume de Machaut*, of which he has given fragments to the Bulletin of Fr. Soc. of Musicology (1918), and an ed. of the *Pièces de Louis Couperin pour le clavecin.*—M. L. P.

R

RAABE, Peter. Ger. condr. *b.* Frankfort-on-Oder, 27 Nov. 1872. Nephew of actress Hedwig Niemann-Raabe; pupil of R. High School, Berlin (Bargiel); 1894–9, opera condr. at Königsberg, Zwickau, Elberfeld; 1899, 1st condr. of Dutch Opera, Amsterdam; 1903, in Munich cond. Kaim Orch.; 1906, in Mannheim as head of newly establ. Kaim Orch.; 1909, 1st R. condr. Weimar; 1910, custodian of Liszt Museum; chairman of revision-committee for a complete ed. of Liszt's works; publ. of Liszt's songs; 1920, condr. of town orch. Aix-la-Chapelle; title of Gen. Mus. Dir.; cond. in England, Belgium, Holland; 1916, graduated (Ph.D.) at Jena (dissertation, *Origin of Liszt's Orchestral Compositions*), Comp. songs and pf. pieces.—A. E.

RAALTE, Albert van. Dutch opera condr. *b.* Amsterdam, 21 May, 1890. Stud. at Amsterdam Music School and Cologne Cons.; Was vla.-player in Gürzenich Orch.; stud. under Steinbach, Eldering, von Baussnern and, at Leipzig, under Arthur Nikisch and Max Reger. Started condr.'s career 1911 (Brussels, Théâtre de la Monnaie); 1912, became 2nd condr. Leipzig; 1916, returned to Holland, 1st condr. National Dutch Opera 1916–22.—W. P.

RABAUD, Henri. Fr. compr. *b.* Paris, 10 Oct. 1873. Son of a cellist. Pupil of Massenet. *Prix de Rome*, 1895. His music, which does not disdain eloquence, is very adroitly composed and always "in the movement." Although dir. of Paris Cons. (since 1919), he associates himself with modern tendencies of Fr. music. His opéra comique *Marouf* (1911) was played with great success in all countries.

Symph. poems: *La Procession nocturne* (1899); *Divertissement sur des airs russes*; *Églogue*; oratorio, *Job* (1900); operas: *La Fille de Roland* (1904); *Marouf* (1911). Consult André Cœuroy, *La Musique française moderne* (1922, Delagrave).—A. C.

RABICH, Ernst. Ger. choral condr. publ. and compr. *b.* Herda, Valley of Werra, 5 May, 1856. Pupil of Thureau, Milde, Sophie Breymann; music-master at training college; R. orgt. and condr. at Gotha; 1889, Ducal music dir. and R. cantor.

Choral work, *Martinswand* (soli, chorus, orch.); *Spring Celebrations* (contr. chorus, orch.); *Das hohe Lied der Arbeit* (male chorus, orch.); *Columbus* (barit. male chorus, orch.); *Dornröschen* (s. chorus, orch.); publ. motet coll. *Psaltery and Harps* (5 books); the male-chorus coll. *Thuringian Choral Union*; 1897-1915, *Journal for Home and Church Music* (Langensalza, Beyer & Sons).—A. E.

RACHLEW, Anders. Norwegian pianist and compr. *b.* Drammen, 26 Aug. 1882. His mus. training was completed in Germany (Xaver Scharwenka, Carreño and others). As pianist, numerous concerts in Norway and Denmark; lives in Copenhagen, where he enjoys esteem as an excellent pf.-teacher. His compns. have attracted attention by their sound construction, and his lyric works possess much feeling and delicacy. He has comp. a vn. sonata (op. 1), songs (op. 2 and 3), as well as pf. pieces.—J. A.

RACHMANINOF, Serge Vassilievitch (*accent 2nd syll.*). Russ. compr. and pianist; *b.* Onega, 19 March/1 April, 1873. Stud. pf. first at Petrograd Cons., and later under Zvieref and Siloti, at Moscow, where his compn. teachers were S. Tanéief and Arensky. In 1892 he won the gold medal at the Cons. for composition. Has toured Europe and America. His 3 pf. concertos in F sharp mi., D mi. and C mi. are welcome additions to the repertory of concert pianists, being grateful to the soloist, and very effectively scored for orch. His style is essentially melodious, and he makes frequent use of the national idioms in his music. His music, classical in spirit and in technique, reveals a clearly defined and attractive personality. As a song-writer, R. is in the front rank of Russ. comprs. and his songs cover a wide and varied range of expression. The *Harvest of Sorrow* is frequently heard at Eng. concerts and fests. His first symphony, op. 13, was heard first in England under Nikisch at R. Philh. Soc. London, 19 May, 1909; his second symphony (E mi. op. 27) was perf. at 1910 Leeds Fest. under the composer.

His works comprise opera *Aleko* (Moscow, 1892); *The Miser Knight* (Moscow, about 1900); *Francesca da Rimini* (1906); *Bells* (chorus and orch.), perf. Birmingham Fest. Choral Soc. 1921 and Liverpool Philh. Soc. 1922, both under Sir Henry Wood; *The Rock*, orch. fantasia, op. 7; *Gipsy Capriccio*, op. 12, orch.; 2 symphonies; 2 pf. concertos; *Caprice Bohémienne* for orch.; 2 suites for pf. op. 5 and 17; 6 pieces for 4 hands, op. 11; 5 pieces for 2 hands, op. 3 (including C sharp mi. prelude); 7 pieces, op. 10; 6 *Moments Musicaux*, op. 16; Variations on theme of Chopin's Prelude in C mi. op. 22; *Elegiac Trio* (in memory of Tchaikovsky), pf. vn. and cello, op. 9 (1893); sonata, cello and pf. op. 19; 2 pieces for vn. and pf. op. 6; 2 pieces, cello and pf. op. 2; 6 choruses for female vs., op. 15; cantata, *Spring*, for chorus, solo and orch. op. 20; *Fate*, chorus (to Beethoven's Fifth Symphony), op. 17; 2 pf. sonatas; many songs. Consult J. Lipaief, *S. W. R.* (1913, Russ.).—G. B.

RADFORD, Robert. Eng. bass singer; *b.* Nottingham, 13 May, 1874. Stud. R.A.M. under Frederic King, Alberto Randegger, Battison Haynes; *début* 1899 (Norwich Mus. Fest.); since then, all the leading Eng. fests., and bass rôles in Ger., Ital., Fr. and Eng. opera at Covent Garden and elsewhere. Principal b. soloist at all the Handel Fests., Crystal Palace, since 1906. A founder and a dir. of the British National Opera Co. 1921. Has made notable successes in widely diversified rôles—Boris, Ivan the Terrible, Mephistopheles, Sarastro, Osmin, The Father (*Louise*), and the Wagnerian bass parts. In oratorio his voice is best suited to the bass parts in *The Creation* and the Handel oratorios.—E.-H.

RADICIOTTI, Giuseppe. Ital. music critic and historian; *b.* Jesi, 25 Jan. 1858. Teacher of history at the R. Liceo-ginnasio at Tivoli; devoted himself very ardently to researches in mus. history. Some important works are:
Vita di G. B. Pergolesi (Rome, 1910, Musica ed.); *Teatro, musica e musicisti in Sinigaglia* (Milan, 1893, Ricordi); *Contributo alla storia del teatro e della musica in Urbino* (Pesaro, 1899, Tipografia Nobili); *Teatro, musica e musicisti in Recanati* (1904, Tipografia Simboli); *L'Arte musicale in Tivoli nei secoli XVI, XVII e XVIII* (Tivoli, 1907); *I musicisti marchigiani dal secolo XVI al XIX* (Rome, 1909, Loescher); sketch of *Rossini* (Genoa, 1914, Formiggini).—D. A.

RADNAI, Miklós. Hungarian compr. *b.* Budapest, 1892. Stud. at R. High School for Music, Budapest; teacher of theory there since 1919.—B. B.

RADÓ, Aladár. Hungarian compr. *b.* Budapest, 26 Dec. 1882; fell in action, 1914.—B. B.

RADOUX, Charles Jean Édouard Firmin Paul. Belgian compr. *b.* Liège, 30 July, 1877. Stud. at Liège Cons. under his father Théodore Radoux. In 1907, 1st *Grand Prix de Rome* for cantata *Geneviève de Brabant.* Assistant-prof. Liège Cons. 1905; prof. since 1911. A serious musician, sacrificing no ideals to suit banal, popular taste.
Orch.: Symphony, C mi.; *La Glèbe Heureuse* (symph. triptych) etc. V. and orch.: *Les Aventures d'un Papillon et d'une Bête à Bon Dieu; Te Deum; Cantata in honour of Grétry; Adieux, absence, retour,* etc. For solo instr. and orch.: *Fantaisie* (vn.); *Variations* (pf.); *Scènes grecques* and *Choral varié* (cello); *Dans les Fagnes* (vn.), etc. Opera: *Oudelette* (4 acts, Monnaie Theatre, 1912) (Brussels, Schott); *Le Poème de Roseclaire* (1 act); *Le Sanglier des Ardennes* (incidental music). Many songs, pf. pieces, etc.—C. V. B.

RADOUX, Jean Théodore. Belgian compr. *b.* Liège, 9 Nov. 1835; *d.* there, 20 March, 1911. Pupil of Daussoigne-Méhul, Liège; of Halévy, Paris. In 1859, won the *Grand Prix de Rome* for a cantata, *Le Juif Errant.* In 1872, succeeded Étienne Soubre as principal of Liège Cons. (where he taught bsn. from 1855 onwards) until his death.
Also possessed fine literary talent, which enabled him to write an excellent monograph on *Henri Vieuxtemps* (Liège, 1891, Bénard). A posthumous perf. of his *Godefroid de Bouillon,* 1920, at Brussels Cons. showed that time had detracted nothing from value of this symph. poem, written according to traditions of Liszt and Saint-Saëns.
Operas: *Le Béarnais* (1868); *La Coupe Enchantée* (1871); *André Doria* (unfinished); *Oaïn,* lyric poem (publ. Brussels, Schott); *Patria* (*id.*); *Godefroid de Bouillon,* symph. poem; *Te Deum* (Brussels, 1904, Schott). Also choral works, songs.—C. V. B.

RAELI, Vito. Ital. pianist and critic; *b.* Tricase, 8 July, 1880. After completing pf. and compn. studies, devoted himself specially to historical research, criticism and propaganda. Since 1920 has dir. the *Rivista Nazionale di Musica,* founded by him.
Collezioni e archivi romani di stampe e manoscritti musicali (Tricase, 1919, Tipografia Raeli); *La collezione Corsini di antichi codici musicali* (*Rivista Musicale Italiana,* 1918–19). Also publ. the results of his researches in the archives of the Basilica Liberiana in Rome (Rome, 1920, Tipografia Artigianelli).—D. A.

RAGAS. See LITHUANIAN MUSIC.

RAITIO, Väinö. Finnish compr. *b.* Sortavala, 15 April, 1891. Stud. at Helsingfors Music Inst., in Moscow (1916–17), and in Germany. Particularly in his later broadly-conceived orch. works R., with a huge orch. apparatus, has developed in the direction of modern Expressionism.
Symphony; tone-poems for orch.—among them *Nocturne, Fantasia estatica, Antigone* (after Sophocles' tragedy; in 3 parts), *Moonshine in Jupiter; Poem,* cello and orch. op. 7; pf. concerto; pf. 5tet; str. 4tet; vn. sonata, op. 2.—T. H.

RALF, Oscar G. Swedish operatic t. singer; *b.* Malmö, 3 Oct. 1881. Stud. under John Forsell, G. Bratt, and Ger. and Ital. masters. Began in operetta, 1905; engaged at R. Opera, Stockholm from 1915, where he has successfully perf. many important rôles, specially those of Wagner: Lohengrin, Tannhäuser, Erik (*Dutchman*), Siegmund, Siegfried, Tristan; also Otello, Canio, Florestan, Samson, etc. He has transl. about 50 operas, operettas and plays into Swedish.—P. V.

RANALOW, Frederick Baring. Irish barit. singer; *b.* Kingstown, Ireland, 7 Nov. 1873. Stud. R.A.M. under Randegger; has appeared regularly at important concerts and in opera. Created part of Macheath in record run of *Beggar's Opera* (*q.v.*).—E.-H.

RANDEGGER, Alberto. Ital. singing teacher; *b.* Trieste, 13 Apr. 1832; *d.* London, 18 Dec. 1911. Cond. opera at Fiume, Venice, etc., 1852–4; came to London about 1854; prof. of singing, R.A.M. 1868; later R.C.M. also; condr. Carl Rosa Co. 1879–85; Norwich Fest. 1881–1905; grand opera, Drury Lane and Covent Garden; Queen's Hall Choral Soc. 1895–7.
Comp. over 600 works, now forgotten. His *Primer on Singing* (Novello) is still well-known. Consult *Mus. Times,* Oct. 1899.—E.-H.

RANDEGGER, Alberto Iginio. Ital. compr. *b.* Trieste, 3 Aug. 1880; *d.* Milan, 7 Oct. 1918. Nephew of condr. of that name. Began as violinist, under his uncle. Then condr. for Kubelík. Comp. operettas: *Il ragno azzurro* (Milan, 1916); *Sua Eccellenza Belzebù* (Rome, 1919); *Il frutto proibito* (Turin, 1919). Publ. by Ricordi.—D. A.

RANDOLPH, Harold. Amer. pianist, teacher; *b.* Richmond, Va., U.S.A., 31 Oct. 1861. Stud. pf. under Nanette Falk-Auerbach and C. Faelten; compn. under Asger Hamerik at Peabody Cons. Baltimore, Md., where he made his *début* as pianist in 1885. Orgt. of Roman Catholic Cath. Baltimore, 1885–90; of Emmanuel Episcopal Ch. Baltimore, 1890–1906. Since 1898, dir. of Peabody Cons., succeeding Hamerik.—J. M

RÄNGMAN-BJÖRLIN, Elli. Finnish pianist; *b.* Ylistaro, 21 April, 1882. Stud. at Helsingfors Music Inst. (1898–1900), at Leipzig Cons. (1900–3) and Vienna (1905). She has appeared in Finland and abroad with much success; recently again in Berlin. For a time, teacher of pf. at Helsingfors Music Inst.; 1909, married the lawyer Ilmari Björlin; now living in Helsingfors.—T. H.

RANGSTRÖM, Ture. Swedish compr. condr. *b.* Stockholm, 30 Nov. 1884. Stud. singing under Julius Hey (Berlin, Munich) 1905–7; musical critic for Stockholm journals, 1907–14 and

1920-1. 1st condr. of Orch. Soc. Gothenburg, from 1922. As compr. was mostly self-taught; is also author of poems to many of his songs, and of the text to cantata for 150-years' Jubilee of R.A.M. Stockholm (1921; music by Wilh. Stenhammar). Member R.A.M. Stockholm, 1919.

Operas: *Kronbruden* (*The Crown-Bride*, drama by Strindberg), 1915; perf. Stuttgart, 1919; Stockholm, 1922-3; *Middelalderlig* (*Medeltida* [*Middle Ages*], drama by Holger Drachmann), 1918; perf. Stockholm, 1921. Symphonies: No. I, *August Strindberg: In Memoriam* (Stockholm, 1915, Abr. Hirsch); No. II, *Mitt land* (*My Country*), 1919 (Copenhagen, Hansen). Symph. poems: *Dithyramb* (1909); *Ett Midsommarstycke* (*A Midsummer Piece*), 1910; *En höstsång* (*An Autumn Song*), 1911; *Havet sjunger* (*The sea sings*), 1913; orch. suites: *Intermezzo drammatico* (1916-18); *Divertimento elegiaco*, str. orch. (1920); *Melodier* (*Melodies*), 1919; *Scenbilder* (*Country Pictures*), 1920; *Ballade*, pf. and orch. (1909); *Ein Nachtstück*, str. 4tet (1909); 2 suites, pf. and vn.; pf. pieces. More than 100 songs (Hansen; Nord. Musikförlaget; Lundqvist). Songs with orch.: 2 *Ballades*; *The Dutchman* (Aug. Strindberg); *Notturno* (Rangström); *King Eric's Songs* (G. Fröding), part-songs, etc.—P. V.

RANZATO, Virgilio. Italian violinist and compr. *b.* Venice, 7 May, 1883. Stud. at Cons. Milan, vn. under Rampazzini, compn. under Ferroni. Several compns. were perf. successfully at concerts of Milan Cons. As violinist, has given good concerts in Italy and abroad, and was 1st violinist in important orchs. Together with Berti (cello) and Moroni (pianist), he founded the Trio Italiano. Has written various operettas: *Velivolo* (Turin, 1911); *La leggenda delle arancie* (Milan, 1916); *Quel che manca a Sua Altezza* (Rome, 1919).—D. A.

RAPPOLDI, Adrian. Ger. violinist; *b.* Berlin, 13 Sept. 1876. Son of Eduard and Laura R. Pupil of his father, Joachim and Wilhelmj; Konzertmeister of Bilse Orch. Berlin; later at Teplitz, Chemnitz, Helsingfors; now vn.-teacher at Dresden Cons.; since 1917, member of Board of Directors.—A. E.

RAPPOLDI, Eduard. Austrian violinist; *b.* Vienna, 21 Feb. 1831; *d.* Dresden, 16 May, 1903. Stud. under L. Jansa and J. Böhm (vn.), S. Sechter (theory) at Vienna Cons.; 1854-61, violinist in Vienna R. Opera orch.; 1861-6, Konzertmeister Rotterdam; 1866-70, operatic condr. Lübeck, Stettin, Prague; 1871-7, teacher at R. High School for Music, Berlin; member of Joachim Quartet; chief Konzertmeister, Dresden (till 1898); prof. of vn. at Conservatoire.

Orch. and chamber-music; songs (Simrock).—A.E.

RAPPOLDI, Laura (*née* Kahrer). Austrian pianist; *b.* Mistelbach (Lower Austria), 14 Jan. 1853. Pupil of Dachs, Dessoff (Vienna Cons.), and of Liszt, Henselt, Bülow; 1890, teacher at Dresden Cons.; R. Saxon virtuoso; 1911, prof.—A.E.

RASCH, Hugo. Ger. author and compr. *b.* Munich, 7 May, 1873. Son of painter Heinrich R.; first stud. painting, then music. Stud. singing under Resz, Garso, Sabatini (Milan); compn. under Frank Limbert (Düsseldorf), Knetsch (Berlin). Singing-master. Since 1911, permanent critic of *Allgemeine Zeitung*, Berlin, and collaborator on several other papers.

Pf. trio; *Variations sur un thème obligé*; 10 books of songs, op. 11 and 13, to words by Wilhelm Busch).—A. E.

RASCH, Johan Christoffel. Dutch violinist; *b.* Padang, Dutch East Indies, 20 April, 1882. Stud. High School of Music, Berlin, under Wirth and Joachim; led orchs. in Germany and Holland; settled in Leeds, 1905-13, where he founded the Rasch Quartet which gave many concerts in the provinces and in Ireland. In 1914 principal prof. vn. Dortmund Cons.; then settled at The Hague. Toured widely as soloist and appeared at Richter's last concert in England (at Huddersfield).—E.-H.

RASSE, François. Belgian compr. *b.* Helchin (Tournaisis), 27 Jan. 1873. Did not begin music until 20, but made rapid progress and obtained the vn. prize at Brussels Cons. under E. Ysaye, 1896. Stud. compn. under Huberti; obtained *Prix de Rome*, 1899. Leader of orch. first at La Monnaie Theatre, Brussels, then at Toulouse. Cond. at Amsterdam and Spa. From 1910, prof. of harmony at Brussels Cons. and principal of the important School of Music at St.-Josse-den-Noode and Schaerbeek (suburbs of Brussels), from 1910. Also cond. Winter Concerts at Ghent and is leader of orch. at Ostend Kursaal. Many compns. with tendency towards Modernism in a moderate form.

Operas: *Déidamia* (Brussels, 1906); " 1914 " (Brussels, 1919); ballet, *Le Maître à Danser* (Brussels, 1909). V. and orch.: *La Légende du Chevrier*; *Le Réveil*, etc. Orch.: 3 symphonies; 3 *Poèmes*; *Poème*, pf. and orch.; several suites; an overture. Chambermusic: 2 str. 4tets; 2 trios; pf. 4tet; pf. 5tet; sonatas for vn.; for cello; for pf. Many songs.—E. C.

RATEZ, Émile. Fr. compr. *b.* Besançon, 5 Nov. 1851. Pupil of Bazin and Massenet at the Cons. Paris; since 1891, dir. of Cons., Lille. From 1893 till 1906, orch. condr. of Société des Concerts Populaires de Lille. An eminent teacher, he has published:

Traité d'Harmonie; *Traité de Contrepoint et de Fugue* (Leduc). Also chamber-music, a grand cantata *Scènes héroïques* (Leduc); 3 operas: *Lyderic* (4 acts, Lille, 1895); *Le Dragon vert* (2 acts, Lille, 1907); *Paula* (4 acts, Besançon).—F. R.

RATH, Felix vom. Ger. compr. *b.* Cologne, 17 June, 1866; *d.* Munich, 25 Aug. 1905. Trained as pianist under Max Pauer (Cologne) and Reinecke (Leipzig); studied for Bar; then pupil of Thuille; became acquainted with Max Schillings and Richard Strauss; finally settled at Munich.

Vn. sonata; pf. 4tet; pf. concerto, B flat mi.; books of songs; pf. pieces.—A. E.

RATHBONE, George. English compr. and pianist; *b.* Manchester 5 Jan. 1874. Stud. privately and at R.C.M. London. In 1911 he played Macdowell's pf. concerto for 1st time in London, at a Promenade concert under Sir Henry Wood. He was for some time orgt. at Cartmel Priory Church. His cantata *Vogelweid* was given in Chicago in 1920 by a children's choir of 1500. His part-music is of a high order.

Cantatas for children's vs. in 2 parts: *Vogelweid*; *Singing Leaves* (Novello, 1913); *Orpheus*; *The Pied Piper of Hamelin* (Novello, 1923); part-songs for 2 parts; for 4 parts (Novello); unison songs (Novello; Curwen; Evans); anthems (Novello).—E.-H.

RAUGEL, Felix. Fr. choral condr. and writer on church music; *b.* Saint-Quentin, 27 Nov. 1881. Studied at Conservatoire, Lille; later at

Paris, under Albert Roussel, Henri Libert, and Vincent d'Indy; 1908, started (with the violinist E. Borrel) *La Société G. F. Haendel*, to popularise not only the oratorios of Handel, but also instrumental and vocal works of French, Italian, English and German musicians from XVII to end of XVIII century. Choir-master at St.-Eustache Church, Paris, since 1911; in 1912, elected head of the Chorale Française. Has published works on history of organ in France: *Les Orgues de l'Abbaye de Saint-Mihiel*, 1919; *Les Organistes* (1923, Edition *Musiciens Célèbres*), and many works on the oratorios of Handel. As a conductor he excels in resuscitating the works of the past. The performances of Handel's oratorios under his bâton have been some of the best ever heard.—H. P.

RAUNAY, Jeanne. Fr. operatic singer; *b.* Paris. *Début* at Opéra, 1888. Left stage to be married in 1889, but returned when a widow in 1896. At La Monnaie, Brussels, created rôle of Guillen in *Fervaal* (d'Indy); sang in same rôle at Opéra-Comique, 1898. Gained a great reputation both on concert-platform and on stage for her noble style of expression.—M. B.

RAVANELLO, Oreste. Ital. orgt. and compr. *b.* Venice, 25 Aug. 1871. One of the most capable orgts. in Italy; played a great part in revival of art of organ-playing in that country. In 1893, orgt. at Basilica of San Marco, Venice; 1897, dir. of Cappella Antoniana at Padua, also dir. of Istituto Mus. Pollini. As compr. he has a rich and estimable production of sacred music (27 masses), organ music, pf. works and songs. Author of some esteemed teaching manuals.—D. A.

RAVASENGA, Carlo. Ital. compr. *b.* Turin, 17 Dec. 1891. In addition to an opera, *Una tragedia fiorentina* (perf. Turin, 1916), has written many meritorious pieces for voice, pf., vn. and cello (publ. by Allione, Turin).—D. A.

RAVEL, Maurice. French composer; *b.* Ciboure (Pyrénées), 7 March, 1875. Educated in Paris, where his family settled. At the Conservatoire he studied piano under De Bériot and harmony under Pessard. His individuality was apparent from the outset, particularly in the dainty *Habanera* (1895), later included in the *Rapsodie Espagnole*. In 1897, he began to work at counterpoint and composition with Gédalge and Gabriel Fauré. He owed to the former his unfailing firmness in technique, and to the latter much excellent advice. In fact he resembles G. Fauré in his ability to combine respect for classical formulæ with the most extraordinary liberty of invention in harmony and rhythm. In 1898 he produced his *Sites Auriculaires* (duet for 4 hands, 2 pianos) at the Société Nationale; in 1899 the *Ouverture de Schéhérazade* (unpublished) and a charming *Pavane pour une Infante défunte*, in which one easily discerns the double influence of Gabriel Fauré and Chabrier. About this time Ravel was very much attracted by the works of Erik Satie, and found therein many sugges-

tions and ideas. Chabrier, Fauré and Satie were the musicians who exercised a greater influence in the formation of his genius than did Debussy. In 1901, Ravel carried off the 2nd *Prix de Rome* with his cantata *Myrrha*, which he had treated in operetta style—a piece of irony which his judges failed to appreciate. In the same year he introduced a perfectly new style of pianoforte composition in the *Jeux d'Eaux*, whose capricious arabesques and dazzling scales are a joy to the ear. In 1904, a quartet in F definitely brought Ravel to public notice. It is a real masterpiece on account of its combination of classical form with purely modern harmony; its emotion is delicate, and one melodic theme arises out of another without the slightest sense of mechanical effort. In the same year Ravel gained another success with his three melodies for voice and orchestra, *Schéhérazade*, a miracle of musical impressionism. In 1905, the decision of the Institut in pronouncing Ravel ineligible for the *Prix de Rome* contest, aroused the indignation of the younger musicians and their partisans, but not that of the victim, who continued to create works of increasing value: *Sonatine* and *Les Miroirs*, 1906; *Gaspard de la Nuit*, 1908; and lastly the audacious *Valses Nobles et Sentimentales*—all notable additions to pianoforte music.

In the *Histoires Naturelles*, 1907, he introduced a new humorous style in which irony and lyrical feeling, malice and emotion, alternate and combine in the most unexpected fashion. The *Rapsodie Espagnole* revealed his gift for producing local colour; he put the entire science of orchestration at the service of an inspiration sometimes gay, sometimes home-sick. *Ma Mère l'Oye* (1908) was a collection of musical interpretations of fairy tales, written first of all as pianoforte duets, then in 1919 remodelled in ballet form for the Théâtre des Arts. Meanwhile the Opéra-Comique produced the *Heure Espagnole*. Ravel revived in this work the old *opéra-bouffe*. The recitative follows the slightest inflection of the speaking voice, whilst the orchestra emphasises in an irresistibly comic manner the meaning of the words. Although incomprehensible to the public at first, this work achieved a triumph in 1921 at the Monnaie Theatre, Brussels, and in 1922 at the Opéra in Paris.

On 8 March, 1921, the Russian Ballet of Diaghilef gave a first performance of *Daphnis et Chloé* (choreography by Fokine) a work which may be considered as Ravel's masterpiece. The vigour of its rhythm, its beautiful melodies, and the force of expression in its harmonies, overcame even the most prejudiced minds. From 1912 onwards its victory was complete, and the revival of *Daphnis* at the Opéra in 1921 was a great success. About 1912, Ravel formed a friendship with Igor Stravinsky whose works *Petrushka* and *Le Sacre du Printemps* had just staggered the musical world. He also studied with curiosity Schönberg's *Pierrot lunaire*. These works did not actually exercise any influence over him, but opened up to him new points of view. One sees the general trend of his ideas at this time in his *Trois Poèmes de Mallarmé*, for voice and small orchestra, each instrument of which (string quartet, 2 flutes, 2 clarinets and piano) is treated as a soloist. Ravel was one of the first among the younger school of musicians to sense the danger of Impressionism and those flimsy methods of construction which the genius of a Debussy alone could make stable. Ravel's admirable trio, played for the first time in 1915, marks a decided return towards more solid construction and simpler outlines. The work is absolutely classical in form, in spite of the boldness of its harmonics; but this classicism has nothing pedantic about it. It is a work vibrant with life and emotion, tenderness and intelligence.

The Great War checked the creative activities of Ravel just as he had finished his trio and the *Tombeau de Couperin* (pianoforte). The musician was determined to share the dangers and discomforts of his friends, but his frail health soon collapsed under the rigours of army discipline. After his recovery, he orchestrated the delicate harmonies of the *Tombeau de Couperin*, and in 1920 wrote *La Valse*. This work interprets, with that mixture of irony and lyrical feeling which is characteristic of the composer, the dizzy, whirling intoxication of a Viennese waltz. During the summer of 1920 Ravel wrote the first part of his sonata for violin and cello for the *Tombeau de Debussy* which the *Revue Musicale* published in the month of December. He did not finish this work until 1922—it is in reality. a whole symphonic cycle reduced to miniature proportions. In 1922 he wrote a charming work for piano, violin and orchestra, dedicated to Gabriel Fauré, for a special number of the *Revue Musicale* and at the request of M. Kussevitzky he scored the *Tableaux d'une Exposition* of Mussorgsky (first prod. 8 May, 1924, Paris).

It is difficult to speak of the evolution of his genius. What he was at twenty in the *Habanera*, he still remains — witty, subtle, restrained in his emotion, always seeking to mask his deeper feelings under an ironic smile. The genius of Ravel is like some beautiful French garden where nature has been trained to the human will, where all is well-ordered, where even the most original fancy is not allowed to run riot, where the pulsing of the sap is always under control. Ravel is a French musician *par excellence*; born of the soil that produced Couperin and Rameau, like the latter he excels in using art itself to disguise art.

He visited London in 1921 to direct an orchestral concert which included *La Valse* and *Ma Mère l'Oye*; and later on for chamber concerts of his works.

Pf.: *Menuet antique* (1895, Enoch); *Pavane pour une Infante défunte* (1899, Demets); *Jeux d'Eaux* (1901); *Miroirs* (1905); *Sonatine* (1905); *Gaspard de la Nuit* (1908); *Minuet on name of Haydn* (1909, Durand); *Valses nobles et sentimentales* (1911). Pf. 4 hands, *Ma Mère l'Oye* (*Mother Goose*, suite, 1908). Vn. and pf., *Tzigane* (1st perf. London, 27 April, 1924).

V. and pf.: *Schéhérazade* (1903); *Histoires naturelles* (1906); *Sur l'herbe* (1907); *Vocalise, en forme d'Habanera* (1907); *5 Greek Folk-songs* (1907). *3 Poèmes* (pf. str. 4tet, 2 fl. 2 clar.), 1913. Str. 4tet (1902–3); sonata, cello and vn. (1922); *Introduction and Allegro* (harp, str. fl. clar.), 1906. Orch. : *Schéhérazade* (1898); *Rapsodie espagnole* (1907); *La Valse* (1922). Ballet, *Daphnis et Chloé* (1906–11; perf. Paris, 1912). Mus. comedy, 1-act, *L'Heure espagnole* (1907; perf. Paris, 1911). Consult: *R.*, brochure by Roland-Manuel (Durand); *L'Œuvre de M. R.* (by same author, *Revue Musicale*, April 1921); André Cœuroy, *Le Musique française moderne* (Delagrave, 1922); M. D. Calvocoressi, *M R.* (*Mus. Times*, Dec. 1913); R. O. Morris, *M. R.* (*Music and Letters*, July 1921). —H. P.

RAVENNA, Pia (Hjördis Tilgmann). Finnish coloratura singer; *b.* Helsingfors, 1894. Pupil of Alma Fohström and others. Has had much success in opera and concerts both in Finland and abroad.—T. H.

RAVN, Vilhelm Carl. Danish music historian; *b.* Elsinore, 19 Sept. 1838; *d.* Copenhagen, 17 May, 1905. M.A. 1857; LL.D. 1865; vice-dir. of police in Copenhagen, 1887. Besides his legal activities he assiduously cultivated musico-historical studies, and especially deserves credit for recording unprinted sources of Danish mus. history. His treatises are unfortunately not collected, but are scattered in papers and magazines. A valuable article on *Scandinavian Music* appeared in Mendel-Reissmann's *Musik-Lexicon* supplement, 1883. A comprehensive treatise upon *Concerts and Musical Societies of the Past* (*Koncerter og musikalske Selskaber i ældre Tid*) was publ. in 1886 for the Musikforening (Music Soc.) Jubilee celebration. The *Vierteljahrsschrift des I.M.G.* (Vol. VII, pp. 550-63), printed his interesting essay on *English Instrumentalists at the Danish Court in the Time of Shakespeare*, treating amongst others of Shakespeare's friend and associate William Kemp, and of the engagement in 1586 of Kemp and his troupe of actors at Kronborg Castle, Elsinore, which engagement most probably gave Shakespeare (possibly even present) the idea of laying the scene of *Hamlet* at that place.—A. H.

RAWAY, Érasme. Belgian compr. *b.* Liège, 2 June, 1850; *d.* Brussels in 1918. Began music at age of 6; later took up philosophy at Grand Seminary at Liège. After he became an abbé, he taught music and ancient geography at Coll. of St.-Trond until 1880; then choirmaster in Liège Cath. Later, became converted to rationalist philosophy, left the Church, and from that time devoted himself entirely to mus. compn., writing slowly, but gradually maturing until he reached that perfection of form which was his aim. The great ambition of his life was to produce his lyrical drama, *Freya*, unfortunately never finished; it is only known to the public in the fragment *La Fête Romaine*, which had a great success. Raway is an independent type in music; he goes straight forward, heedless of all save his own inspiration. Nevertheless he keeps his respect for old traditions, as may be seen in his enthusiasm for Weber and Schubert. Thanks to this independence of spirit, he may be regarded as one of the founders of modern music in Belgium—his songs and his *Scènes Hindoues*

(1885) struck out quite a new path in this country.

Néon, melodrama (1877); *Scènes hindoues* for orch. (pf. duet transcription, publ. Muraille, Liège); *Les Adieux,* symph. tableau (1882); *Symphonie Libre* (1885); *Scherzo-Caprice* for orch. (pf. version, Breitkopf); *Ode Symphonique* (pf. version, Breitkopf); some beautiful songs, of rare perfection of form and depth of emotion.
Consult G. Dwelshauvers, *E. R.* (*Revue de l'Université de Bruxelles,* May–June 1905).—C. V. B.

RAWLINS, Bessie. Eng. violinist; *b.* London, 1898. Stud. there under W. Sachse; recitals London, 1919–23; toured Sweden, Denmark, Holland, Switzerland, Germany, 1923. A gifted interpreter of modern as well as classical music.—E.-H.

RÉALTOR, Olivier. See CAROL-BÉRARD.

RÉBIKOF, Vladimir Ivanovitch (*accent 1st syll.*). Russ. compr. *b.* Krasnoyarsk, Siberia, 19 May/1 June, 1866; *d.* Yalta, Crimea, Dec. 1920. Began lessons in theory at Moscow Cons. under Klenovsky; later, stud. in Berlin under Mühler; 1894–8, lived in Odessa where he founded in 1897 a branch of the Soc. of Russ. Comprs. In 1898 he moved to Kishinef in S. Russia, opening a branch of the Russ. Mus. Soc. there; then he taught in Berlin, and Vienna for a time. In 1901, he was in Moscow when his *The Storm* and *The Christmas Tree* were produced at the Aquarium Theatre, 1903. The latter work went the round of Charkof, Saratof (1905), Prague, Berlin, Brünn (1906), Kief, Kazan, Laibach (1907), Novgorod, Jaroslavl, Tiflis (1908), etc. R. has been called "the father of Russ. Modernism," but this term can only refer to his new forms and novel harmonic styles, many of them frankly experimental. Occasionally he underlines melodies in fourths, in fifths, in ninths, etc. He was the first to use the "whole-tone scale" in a thoroughgoing fashion (see his *Satans Vergnügen; Moments d'allégresse; Une Fête,* etc.). His *Melomimics* (small scenes without words, or music and miming, op. 11, 15, 17) or his songs with miming (op. 1, 16, 19, 20) and his *Dramatic Fables* (after Krilof), show an art somewhat parallel to that of the Überbrettl (*q.v.*). His early works, up to op. 10, are in the Tchaikovsky manner. He transl. into Russ. Gévaert's manual on orchestration and R. Mayrberger's *The Harmony of Wagner.*

2-act opera, *The Storm* (Odessa, 1904); *The Christmas Tree,* op. 21, fairy-play in 1 act and 4 scenes, 3 solo vs. and acting groups (Moscow, 17 Oct. 1903). Musico-psychological dramas: *The Abyss* (on Andréief's story), written in Prague, 1907; *Alpha and Omega* (2 scenes), 1911 (all publ. by Jurgenson). There is also a psychological drama, *The Woman with the Dagger,* op. 41, and an opera, *Narcissus,* op. 45. A number of sacred compns. including a Liturgy of St. John Chrysostom. A very large number of pf. pieces (all publ. by Jurgenson); 4 books of pieces, op. 2, 5, 6, 7; *Rêveries d'automne,* op. 8; *Autour du Monde,* op. 9; *Melomimics,* op. 11; Suite from ballet *Mila et Nolli,* op. 14; *Les Rêves,* 5 *melomimics,* op. 15; 3 *musico-psychologics,* op. 22, 24, 25; children's pieces, op. 37; *Petite Suite de ballet; Tabatière à musique; Tristesse,* etc.; *Fables,* v. and pf. on Krilof texts, etc.—E.-H.

REBNER, Adolf. Austrian violinist; *b.* Vienna, 21 Nov. 1876. Stud. at Vienna Cons. (Grün); finished in Paris (Marsick); 1896 at

Frankfort-o-M. as 1st. vn.-master at Hoch's Cons.; succeeded Hugo Heermann as 1st violinist in Heermann Str. Quartet; Konzertmeister at Frankfort Opera; member of Museum Quartet.—A. E.

REED, William Henry. Eng. violinist; *b.* Frome, 29 July 1876. Stud. R.A.M. under Émile Sauret, E. Prout, F. Corder and H. R. Rose; leader of London Symphony Orchestra.

Orch.: *Suite Vénétienne* (Novello); *Scenes from a Ballet* (*id.*); symph. poem, *Caliban* (*id.*); *The Lincoln Imp;* vn. concerto (Augener); suite, str. orch. (Novello); 5th str. 4tet (Augener); vn. pieces (Augener; Novello); songs, part-songs (*id.*).—E.-H.

REFICE, Licinio. Ital. compr. *b.* Patrica (Rome), 12 Feb. 1885. Priest; dir. of Cappella Musicale of the Basilica Liberiana in Rome. Stud. at the R. Liceo Mus.di Santa Cecilia under Falchi; diploma in 1910. Since then has been teacher in the Pontificia Scuola Superiore di Musica Sacra. Comp. church music, and oratorios: *Maria Maddalena* (Augusteo, Rome, 1917); *Il martirio di Sant' Agnese* (Augusteo, Rome, 1919). For the Dante Centenary in 1921, he wrote mus. poem, *Dantis poetæ transitus,* perf. at Ravenna and then in Rome.—D. A.

REGER, Max. German composer; *b.* Brand (Bavaria) 19 March, 1873; *d.* Leipzig, 11 May, 1916. Son of schoolmaster, who was transferred to Weiden, 1874; first musical training from father and the Weiden organist, Adalbert Lindner, who taught him extensively from Riemann's instruction - books and editions; studied under Riemann five years at Sondershausen (1890) and at Wiesbaden (1891–5); acted till 1896 as teacher at Wiesbaden Conservatoire; then served his military year. After recovering from severe illness, he removed in 1898 to his native home; 1901 to Munich; married Elsa von Bagenski; became teacher of counterpoint (1905–6) at Royal Academy; 1907 called to Leipzig as University Music-Director and teacher of composition at Conservatoire; 1908, Royal Professor (of Saxony) and Ph.D. *h.c.* of Jena and Heidelberg Universities; Berlin University gave him title of M.D. *h.c.;* 1908, withdrew from University; 1911, Royal conductor and Hofrat (councillor); 1913, general music-director at Meiningen; at same time continued teaching at Leipzig Conservatoire; 1914, gave up Meiningen engagement and went to Jena. Characteristic of Reger's composition is firstly the exuberant richness of harmony, which stamped him as a "miniaturist" even in those compositions which demanded a huge apparatus and which necessarily resulted in a style of rhythmic atrophy, yet, with all his boldness in harmony and modulation, Reger never abandoned the ground of logic and tonality, although he expanded to an extraordinary degree all possible effects, the archaic as well as the modern. His second characteristic is his increased polyphony; his simplest ideas are polyphonically conceived. He has kept to the system of sonata-form; only it is filled with melodious "prosa"—that is to say, it renounces the uniform rhythmical development of a movement. He is happiest where a certain form forces him in a definite direction and to a natural climax (variation, fugue, choral pieces—forms he liked best to use). Particularly noticeable are his wealth of inventive power and his eminently polyphonic nature. Always remaining the "absolute" musician, he advanced from an initial dependence on Brahms, from leanings towards the archaic, to the individual freedom of works such as the C major violin sonata, D minor quartet, *Hiller Variations*, op. 100; he reached in his last compositions, after a brief inclination to Impressionism (*Eichendorff Suite*), a form of clearness and simplicity. (See arts. on GERMAN ORCH. MUSIC and GERMAN SONG).

Reger visited England in May 1909, giving 2 concerts at Bechstein Hall, London.

Op. 1, vn. and pf. sonata, D mi. (Schott); op. 2, trio, B mi. pf. vn. vla. (*id.*); op. 3, sonata, F mi. cello and pf. (*id.*); op. 4, 6 songs (*id.*); op. 5, sonata, F mi. cello and pf. (*id.*); op. 6, mixed choruses with pf. acc. (*id.*); op. 7, 3 organ pieces (*id.*); op. 8, songs (*id.*); op. 9, 12 waltz-caprices (*id.*); op. 10, 10 German dances, 4 hands (*id.*); op. 11, 7 pf. waltzes (*id.*), op. 12, 5 songs (*id.*); op. 13, *Loose Leaves*, pf. (*id.*); op. 14, 5 duets, s. and contr. (Augener); op. 15, 10 songs for m.-sopr. (Schott); op. 16, suite, E mi. organ (*id.*); op. 17, *From Youth*, pf. (*id.*); op. 18, Improvisations, pf. (*id.*); op. 19, 2 sacred songs with organ (Univ. Ed.); op. 20, 5 *Humoresques*, pf. (*id.*); op. 21, *Ode to Song*, male chorus with orch. (*id.*); op. 21 (*sic!*) pf. quartet, C mi. (published 1923); op. 22, 6 waltzes, pf. duet (*id.*); op. 23, 4 songs, v. and pf. (*id.*); op. 24, 6 pf. pieces (Forberg); op. 25, *Aquarelles*, pf. (Schott); op. 26, 7 *Fantasy-Pieces*, pf. (Forberg); op. 27, Fantasia on *A Stronghold Sure*, organ (*id.*); op. 28, cello and pf. sonata, G mi. (Univ. Ed.); op. 29, short pieces, pf. organ and v. (Beyer); op. 30, Fantasia on *Be joyful, O my Soul*, organ (Univ. Ed.); op. 31, 6 poems, v. and pf. (*id.*); op. 32, 7 characteristic pieces, pf. (*id.*); op. 33, 1st organ sonata, F sharp mi. (*id.*); op. 34, 5 picturesque pieces, pf. duets (*id.*); op. 35, 6 songs (*id.*); op. 36, *Coloured Leaves*, pf. (*id.*); op. 37, 5 songs (*id.*); op. 38, 7 male choruses unacc. (*id.*); op. 39, 3 6-v. choruses (*id.*); op. 40, 2 fantasias on chorals, organ (*id.*); op. 41, 3rd vn. and pf. sonata, A ma. (*id.*); op. 42, 4 sonatas, solo vn. (*id.*); op. 43, 8 songs (*id.*); op. 44, 10 short pf. pieces (*id.*); op. 45, 6 *Intermezzi*, pf. (*id.*); op. 46, Fantasia and fugue on B. A. C. H., organ (*id.*); op. 47, 6 trios, organ (*id.*); op. 48, 7 songs (*id.*); op. 49, 2 sonatas, clar. and pf. (*id.*); op. 50, 2 *Romances*, G and C, vn. and small orch. (*id.*); op. 51, 12 songs (*id.*); op. 52, 3 choral fantasies, organ (*id.*); op. 53, 7 *Silhouettes*, pf. (*id.*); op. 54, str. 4tets, G mi. A ma. (*id.*); op. 55, 15 songs (*id.*); op. 56, 5 easy preludes and fugues, organ (*id.*); op. 57, Symph. Fantasy and fugue, organ (*id.*); op. 58, 6 *Burlesques*, pf. duet (Simrock); op. 59, 12 pieces, organ (Peters); op. 60, 2nd organ sonata, D mi. (*id.*); op. 61, easy choral pieces for divine service (Siegel); op. 62, 16 songs (Univ. Ed.); op. 63, 12 pieces, organ (*id.*); op. 64, 5tet, C mi. pf. and str. (Peters); op. 65, 12 pieces, organ (*id.*); op. 66, 12 songs, mezzo v. (Bote & Bock); op. 67, 52 preludes, organ (*id.*); op. 68, 6 songs, mezzo v. (*id.*); op. 69, 10 pieces, organ (*id.*); op. 70, 17 songs for high v. (*id.*); op. 71, *Song of the Glorified*, 5-v. chorus and orch. (Siegel); op. 72, vn. and pf. sonata, C ma. (Bote & Bock); op. 73, Variations and fugue on original theme, organ (*id.*); op. 74, str. 4tet, D mi. (*id.*); op. 75, 18 songs (*id.*); op. 76, simple melodies, v. with pf., 6 books (*id.*); op. 77a, *Serenade*, fl. vn. and vla. (*id.*); op. 77b, str. trio (*id.*); op. 78, sonata, F ma., cello and pf. (*id.*); op. 79a, pf. pieces, 5 books (Beyer); op. 79b, organ compns., 2 books (*id.*); op. 79c, pieces for v. and pf., 2 books (*id.*); op. 79d, pieces for vn. and pf., 2 books (*id.*); op. 79e, cello and pf. pieces, 2 books (*id.*); op. 79f, 14 choral arrs., mixed chorus (*id.*); op. 79g, 3 choral arrs. for 3-v. female chorus (*id.*); op. 80, 12 organ pieces (Peters); op. 81, Variations and fugue on a theme of Bach, pf. (Bote & Bock); op. 82, *From my Diary*, pf. (*id.*); op. 83, 10 male choruses (*id.*); op. 84, vn. and pf. sonata, F sharp

mi. (*id.*); op. 85, 4 preludes and fugues, organ (Peters); op. 86, Variations and fugue on Beethoven theme, 2 pfs. (Bote & Bock); op. 87, 2 pieces, vn. and pf. (Forberg); op. 88, 4 songs (Simrock); op. 89, 2 sonatinas, pf. (Bote & Bock); op. 90, *Symphonietta*, orch. (*id.*); op. 91, 7 sonatas, vn. solo (*id.*); op. 92, suite, organ (Forberg); op. 93, vn. and pf. suite in old style (*id.*); op. 94, 6 pf. pieces (Peters); op. 95, *Serenade* in G, orch. (Bote & Bock); op. 96, Introduction, passacaglia and fugue, 2 pfs. (*id.*); op. 97, 4 songs (*id.*); op. 98, 5 songs (Simrock); op. 99, 6 preludes and fugues, pf. (Bote & Bock); op. 100, Variations and fugue on a merry theme of Hiller's, orch. (*id.*); op. 101, vn. concerto (Peters); op. 102, trio, vn. cello and pf. (Bote & Bock); op. 103a, 6 pieces, vn. and pf. (*id.*); op. 103b, 2 sonatinas, vn. and pf. (*id.*); op. 104, 6 songs, mezzo v. (Forberg); op. 105, 2 sacred songs, mezzo v. (Leuckart); op. 106, *Psalm C*, chorus and orch. (Peters); op. 107, sonata, B flat, clar. and pf. (Bote & Bock); op. 108, *Symph. Prologue*, orch. (Peters); op. 109, str. 4tet, E flat (Bote & Bock); op. 110, 2 sacred songs with organ (Leuckart); op. 111a, 3 duets, s. and contr. with pf. (Bote & Bock); op. 111b, 4-v. female choruses (*id.*); op. 111c, 3-v. female choruses (*id.*); op. 112, *The Nuns*, mixed chorus and orch. (*id.*); op. 113, pf. 4tet, D mi. (*id.*); op. 114, pf. concerto, F mi. (*id.*); op. 115, *Episodes*, pf. (*id.*); op. 116, cello and pf. sonata, A mi. (Peters); op. 117, preludes and fugues, vn. alone (Bote & Bock); op. 118, str. 6tet, F ma. (*id.*); op. 119, *The Consecration of the Night*, contr. male chorus, orch. (*id.*); op. 120, *Comedy Overture*, orch. (*id.*); op. 121, str. 4tet, F sharp mi. (Peters); op. 122, vn. and pf. sonata, E mi. (Bote & Bock); op. 123, concerto in olden style, orch. (*id.*); op. 124, *To Hope*, contr. solo and orch. (Peters); op. 125, *Romantic Suite*, orch. (Bote & Bock); op. 126, *Roman Triumphal Chant*, male chorus and orch. (*id.*); op. 127, Introduction, passacaglia and fugue, organ (*id.*); op. 128, 4 mus. poems, orch. (after A. Böcklin (*id.*); op. 129, 9 pieces, organ (*id.*); op. 130, *Ballet-Suite*, orch. (Peters); op. 131a, preludes and fugues, vn. alone (Simrock); op. 131b, 3 duos, canons and fugues in old style, 2 vns. (*id.*); op. 131c, 3 suites, cello alone (*id.*); op. 131d, 3 suites, vla. alone (*id.*); op. 132, Variations and fugue on Mozart theme, orch. (*id.*); op. 133, pf. 4tet, A mi. (*id.*); op. 134, Variations and fugue on theme of G. Th. Telemann, pf. (*id.*); op. 135a, 30 short choral preludes, organ (*id.*); op. 135b, Fantasy and fugue, D mi., organ (*id.*); op. 136, *Hymn of Love*, barit. and orch. (*id.*); op. 137, 12 sacred songs, v. and pf. (Peters); op. 138, 8 sacred songs, mixed chorus (Simrock); op. 139, vn. and pf. sonata, C mi. (*id.*); op. 140, *Patriotic Overture* (to the German army), orch. (*id.*); op. 141a, *Serenade*, G ma. str. trio (Peters); op. 141b, str. trio, D mi. (*id.*); op. 142, 5 new nursery rhymes for high v. (*id.*); op. 143, *Dreams by Fireside*, 12 short pf. pieces (Simrock); op. 144, 2 songs, mixed chorus and orch. (*id.*); op. 145, 7 pieces, organ (No. 7, Reger's last compn.) (Oppenheimer); op. 146, 5tet, A ma. for clar. and str. (Simrock); op. 147, *Andante and Rondo Capriccioso*, vn. and orch. (unfinished) (Peters). Consult Adalbert Lindner, *M. R.* (Stuttgart, 1922, Engelhorn); M. Hehemann, *M. R.* (Munich, 2 editions 1917, Piper); K. Hasse, *M. R.* (Leipzig, 1921, Siegel); G. Bagier, *R.* (Stuttgart, 1923, Deutsche Verlags-Anstalt).—A. E.

RÉGISSEUR (Fr.). The producer of an opera. The same title is used in Germany. In Ital. *direttore di scena*, or *sovrintendente dello spettacolo*.—E.-H.

REHBERG, Walter. Ger. compr. *b.* Geneva, 14 May, 1900. Son of Willy R.; pupil of father at Hoch's Cons., Frankfort-o-M., and at High School for Music, Mannheim; later of Eugen d'Albert. Comp. pf. sonatas; vn. sonata; pf. pieces.—A. E.

REHBERG, Willy. Swiss pianist and compr. *b.* Morges, 2 Sept. 1863. Son of excellent pianist Friedrich R.; stud. at Zurich Cons. (1879–1891) under Rob. Freund, Fr. Hegar and Gustav Weber, and at Leipzig Cons. (1881–4) under Reinecke and Jadassohn. Immediately after final examinations, engaged at Leipzig Cons.;

1890, principal prof. of Cons. at Geneva, where he also cond. Symphony Concerts; 1908, prof. at Frankfort Cons.; 1917, dir of Mannheim Cons. Since 1921, dir. and prof. of master-classes for pf. at Basle Cons. He is especially famous as a Brahms - interpreter, and is a remarkable teacher. Delivered many courses of lectures on mus. education, and on evolution of mus. style. His son Walter (*b.* 1900 at Geneva) ranks already amongst best pianists of the younger generation.
Str. 4tet; vn. sonata; numerous songs and pf. pieces (Breitkopf; Kistner; Siegel). Ed. of classical pf. works (Steingräber).—F. H.

REHFELD, Fabian. Ger. violinist; *b.* Tuchel, West Prussia, 23 Jan. 1842; *d.* Berlin, Nov. 1920. Pupil of Zimmermann and Grünwald, Berlin; 1868, Court-musician, Berlin; 1873–98, Konzertmeister; 1903, R. prof.; also vn. compr.; publ. 3 vols. of well-known collection *Sang und Klang.*—A. E.

REICHENBERGER, Hugo. German condr. *b.* Munich, 28 July, 1873. Stud. at Munich under V. Gluth, H. Schwartz, Eugenie Menter, Mayer, L. Thuille; condr. at Kissingen (1894), Breslau, Aix-la-Chapelle, Bremen, Stuttgart (1898–1903), Munich (1903–5), Frankfort, Vienna (since 1905); also much engaged as star conductor.
Pf. pieces; songs (3 *Marienlieder* with orch.); orch. works; chamber-music; pf. concerto; songs; opera, *Hexenfang (Capture of Witches).*—A. E.

REICHERT, Johannes. German compr. *b.* Dresden, 19 June, 1876. Stud. music under Draeseke, 1894–8 under Nicodé and Buchmayer; 1896–1906, condr. of orch. class of Dresden School of Music; 1902–6, repetitor at R. Theatre; since 1899, cond. People's Acad. of Singing (mixed chorus from among working class), founded by him. Since 1906, town music dir. at Teplitz-Schönau.
Orch works: *Concert Overture*, E ma. op. 5; *Serenade*, op. 25; *Merry Suite*, op. 30; vocal work, *Helge's Dream*, op. 11 (soli, mixed chorus, orch.); *Traumsernnernacht*, op. 18 (6-v. chorus and orch.); *Musical Art*, op. 20 (Rhapsody [Herder] for barit. mixed chorus, orch.); unacc. works for mixed chorus, male and female chorus; pf. pieces (sonata, A mi. op. 1).—A. E.

REICHMANN, Theodor. German baritone opera-singer; *b.* Rostock, 15 March, 1849; *d.* Marbach-on-Bodensee, 22 May, 1903. Sang at various Ger. theatres, 1882–9. In 1893 re-engaged at Vienna Court Opera. Best parts were Hans Heiling, Dutchman, Hans Sachs. The first Amfortas at Bayreuth (1882) where he sang often.—P. St.

REICHWEIN, Leopold. German condr. and compr. *b.* Breslau, 16 May, 1878. Condr. at Mannheim; 1909, R. Opera, Carlsruhe; 1913, cond. Vienna R. Opera; 1921, succeeded Schalk as concert-dir. of Soc. of Friends of Music and condr. of Choral Union (Singverein); 1924, succeeded Löwe as condr. of Konzertverein Orchestra.
Operas: *Vasantasena* (Breslau, 1903); *Lovers of Kandahar* (Breslau, 1907); operetta, *Hazard* (Vienna, 1919); music to *Faust* (Mannheim, 1909).—A. E.

REIDARSON, Per. Norwegian compr. condr. *b.* Bergen in 1879. Pupil in vn., harmony and cpt. of Sigurd Lie, Cath. Elling and A. Gédalge (Paris). First violinist in leading orchs. in Ber-

gen and Christiania. Music critic for *Tidens Tegn.* Condr. of Stavanger Theatre Orch. which on his initiative was transformed into a municipal orch. (1918). Has held scholarships from State and from Houen's Bequest. Much esteemed for his beautiful songs. As critic, R. combats with earnest conviction and incisive style the newest radical tendencies in music in favour of what he considers a sounder development, based upon melody and natural feeling.
Chorus with orch.: *Havet* (*The Sea*); *Haakon den godes dod* (*Death of Haakon the Good*); orch.: *Nordic Overture*; *Norwegian Rhapsody*; *Hymne*; song-play, *Sommereventyr* (*Summer Fairy-Tale*). All produced in Christiania.—R. M.

REIFNER, Vincenz. German-Czechoslovak compr. *b.* Theresienstadt, 25 Oct. 1878; *d.* Dresden, 3 Dec. 1922. Stud. Prague (Ph.D.) and at Kissingen under C. Kistler; was publ. of music in Dresden.
Symph. poem, *Spring*; 3 symph. poems, *From German Fairy Tales* (intended for first of a cycle *Fatherland*): *Dornröschen* (*Sleeping Beauty*); *Bremer Stadtmusikanten* (*Town Musicians of Bremen*); *Der Schreckenstein* (*The Stone of Terror*). National opera, *Maria*; choruses; songs.—E. S.

REINACH, Théodore. Fr. historian; *b.* St.-Germain-en-Laye (Seine et Oise). Barrister and later exclusively a historian; member of Institut; one of most active savants in domain of Hellenism. Important contributor to study of Greek music.
In *Revue des Études grecques* he has publ. (1892–1901) *Notes sur quatre problèmes d'Aristote* (with d'Eichthal, 1894); *La Guitare dans l'Art grec* (1896); *Deux fragments de musique grec* (1897), etc. Collab. in *Dictionnaire des Antiquités grecques* (*Lyra, Musica,* etc.), in *L'Ami des Monuments* (1894, *Note sur l'hymne à Apollon*; 1911, *Les Fouilles de Delphes*). The *Bulletin de Correspondance hellénique* (1893–4) contains the arts.: *Les Hymnes delphiques*; *La Musique des hymnes de Delphes*; *Un Nouvel Hymne delphique.* Contributor to *Revue Musicale* (1904–22); *Revue Critique*; *Revue de Paris*, etc. Has publ. *Plutarque*—" *De la Musique* " (transl. with H. Weil) (Paris, 1900, Leroux); is preparing a little book on *La Musique grecque* (Paris, 1923, Payot). Author of a lyric drama (after *Perses* of Æschylus), *Salamine* (music by M. Emmanuel), and of a comedy-ballet, *La Naissance de la Lyre* (after Sophocles), music by Albert Roussel.—M. L. P.

REINER, Fritz. Hungarian condr. *b.* Budapest, 19 Dec. 1888. Stud. at R. High School for Music, Budapest. Up to 1921, condr. at Dresden State Opera. Since 1922, Ysaye's successor in Cincinnati.—B. B.

REISENAUER, Alfred. German pianist; *b.* Königsberg, 1 Nov. 1863; *d.* Libau, 3 Oct. 1907; pupil of Louis Köhler and Liszt; 1881, appeared as pianist; then stud. for Bar at Leipzig; 1886, concert-career again; 1900–6, prof. of pf. at Leipzig Cons.
Comp. pf. pieces (*Reisebilder*); over 100 songs; Variations for orch. Consult: J. Schwerin, *Erinnerungen an A. R.* (1909); Felix Weingartner, *Lebenserinnerungen* (1923).—A. E.

REISS, Georg Michael Döderlein. Norwegian mus. researcher; *b.* Christiania, 12 Aug. 1861; *d.* there, 25 Jan. 1914. Graduated in law at Christiania Univ. in 1886; obtained his mus. education at home under Ludv. M. Lindeman and Otto Winter-Hjelm; from 1892 at High School in Berlin (organ under Rob. Radecke; compn. under R. Succo). From 1893 till death, orgt. at Petrus Ch. in Christiania. His songs, motets, church-choruses, *a cappella* pieces for male chorus and organ works show fine melodic inventiveness and solid construction.

R.'s principal significance for Norwegian music lies in field of musico-historical research. He was an exceedingly well-informed investigator, with keen critical powers; justly enjoyed a high reputation as an eminent scholar. He devoted himself to the study of Norwegian music in the the Middle Ages and made an extremely valuable contribution to older mus. history of the North, by his treatises *Musiken ved den middelalderlige Olavsdyrkelse i Norden* (*Music in Relation to the Mediæval Cult of St. Olav in the North*) (1912) and *Tvo norröne latinske kvæde med melodiar* (*Two Norse-Latin Lays with Melodies*) (1913). The first-named treatise obtained for R. the degree of doctor in 1913; he was thus the first in Norway to attain the dignity of Doctor of Mus. History. Of his other writings may be mentioned: *Riksarkivets middelalderlige musikhaandskrifter* (*Mediæval Music Manuscripts in the State Records*) (1908) and *To sekvenser for St. Olav* (*Two Sequences in Honour of St. Olav*) (1910). R. was also a musical critic (*inter alia*, in *Nordisk Musikrevy*). —J. A.

REISS, Józef Władysław. Polish mus. historian and theorist; *b.* Dębica, Galicia, 1879. 1901, teacher of the classical State School in Cracow; 1910, Ph.D. at Vienna Univ., for his thesis *Nicolas Gomolka and his Psalms of 1580*. Became in 1911, prof. at Cracow Cons.; in 1922, unsalaried lecturer on musicology at the Univ. there. He is music critic of the *Nowa Reforma* in Cracow.

The Musical Forms (Polish, Breitkopf, 1917); Beethoven (1920); manual of History of Music (1920; best and largest in Polish; 2nd ed. 1922); Harmony (1922). Has also written several very conscientious treatises on history of Polish music (publ. by Acad. of Sciences, Cracow).—ZD. J.

REISSIGER, Friedrich August. Norwegian compr. condr. *b.* Belzig, near Wittenberg, Germany, 26 July, 1809; *d.* Fredrikshald, Norway, 2 March, 1883. Began to study theology; soon went over to music. Pupil, chiefly, of Dehn, Berlin. 1840, condr. at Christiania Theatre (till 1850). Lived afterwards in Fredrikshald as orgt. Comp. overtures, cantatas, chamber-music, etc. Only his songs for 4-v. male chorus or quartets still live. Several of these belong to finest of their kind in the North and are still often heard at choral concerts in Scandinavia and Scandinavian America; notably, *Olav Trygvason*; *Havet er skjönt* (*Fair is the Sea*); *En sangers bön* (*A Singer's Prayer*); *Höstandagt* (*Autumn Devotion*); *Se hist ved Östersaltets vove* (*See yonder by the Baltic's waves*); *Höiest löfter jeg da guldpokalen* (*Highest lift I then the golden cup*).—U. M.

REITER, Josef. Austrian composer; *b.* Braunau, 19 Jan. 1862. Self-taught musician. Dir. of Mozarteum at Salzburg, 1908–11. Then lived in Vienna and Linz, composing. About 1890 he was considered as a great hope in dramatic music, but remained too conservative. Now only esteemed as choral compr. He

orchestrated numerous works by Handel for modern orchestra.

Opera, Der Bundschuh (perf. Vienna, 1892); Requiem; many male-chorus and chamber-music pieces. Consult Max Morold-Millenkovich, J. R. (Vienna, 1895, 1904).—P. P.

REITLER, Josef. Austrian musicologist; *b.* Vienna, 25 Dec. 1883. Stud. in Vienna and Berlin. From 1905–7, Paris theatrical correspondent for *Vossische Zeitung*; 1907 (with Korngold), critic on *Neue Freie Presse*; 1915, dir. of New Vienna Cons. On commission of the former Austrian Ministry of Education, he ed. the *Musikbuch aus Österreich* for a few years. Also wrote opera libretti.—P. ST.

REMMERT, Marta. Ger. pianist; *b.* Grossschwein, near Glogau, 4 Aug. 1864. Pupil of Liszt at Weimar; extensive concert-tours; 1900, establ. Franz Liszt Acad. Berlin, which she managed.—A. E.

REMY, Alfred. Amer. musicologist; *b.* Elberfeld, Germany, 16 March, 1870. A.M. Columbia Univ. 1905. Stud. pf. under Bruno Oscar Klein in New York (1890–6). 1895–7, music critic for *Vogue* and *The Looker-On*. 1896–8, lectured on history of music at New York Coll. of Music. Has also been a teacher of Greek (Seton Hall Coll., Orange, N.J., 1897–8), and of modern languages (Commercial High School, Brooklyn, 1899–1911); 1906–15, extension-lecturer at Columbia Univ. His 3rd ed. of *Baker's Biographical Dictionary of Musicians* (Schirmer, 1919) is the most comprehensive and thorough work of this kind hitherto written in English.—O. K.

RENARD, Marie (real name Pölzl). Austrian opera singer; *b.* Graz (Styria), 18 Jan. 1863. Graz Theatre; then Prague and Berlin Opera (1885–8); Vienna Court Opera (1880–1901); a great favourite with public, for her inimitable charm and beautiful voice. Her Manon, Mignon, Lotte (*Werther*) will live long in the memory. In 1901 she left stage and married Count Rudolf Kinsky.—P. ST.

RENARD, Rosita. Chilean pianist; *b.* 1898. Stud. under Krause in Germany; returning to Chile, gave a series of concerts; then made a successful tour through N. America in 1917.—A. M.

RENDANO, Alfonso. Ital. pianist and compr. *b.* Carolei (Cosenza), 5 April, 1853. Enjoyed great renown as a concert-player in Italy and abroad; at present lives in Rome, and is engaged in teaching. After studying at Naples Cons. for short time, began touring as a player whilst still very young; went to Paris, where (introduced by Thalberg, who took him under his protection), he met Rossini, who assisted him considerably. In Paris he gained great success as a concert-player, then at Baden and in London, where, in 1867, he played at a Philh. Soc. concert. He returned to London again, after having spent some years in Leipzig, where he stud. under Paul, Richter and Reinecke. Went back to Italy in 1874, and gave a triumphant series of concerts, rivalling Rubinstein, who was in Italy at that time. In 1880, went to Vienna, where he became the friend of Bülow and Liszt. For some time, teacher in Naples Cons. As compr. Rendano has written an opera, *Consuelo*, perf. first at Turin 1902, and played in various theatres in Germany; also a sonata, a concerto and pf. music; a 5tet, and several orch. pieces. We owe to him the invention of the Independent Pedal for pf., to which he gave his name (see below).—D. A.

RENDANO INDEPENDENT PEDAL. A third pedal applied to the piano; invented and made known by the Ital. pianist, Alfonso Rendano. Placed between the two ordinary pedals, it is furnished with a curved extension to the left, so that it can be manipulated by the heel of the left foot. Its use is to isolate one or more sounds from the rest of the strings. If one presses the key or keys of which one desires the isolated vibration, and then lowers the third pedal, it prevents the dampers of these keys from falling back on the strings. All the other dampers can be made to function normally, either by striking the keys or by putting down the right pedal. The name "Independent" originates from the fact that this pedal (as distinct from the well-known Steinway "Tonal" pedal) can, thanks to its particular construction, function whilst the right pedal also is in use.—D. A.

RENIÉ, Henriette. Fr. harpist and compr. *b.* Paris, 18 Sept. 1875. Undisputed head of Fr. school of harpists since death of Hasselmans. First came to public notice as infant prodigy; 1st prize at Cons. at age of 11; soon after, took prizes for harmony and compn. Soloist to all chief orchs. (Cons.; Colonne; Lamoureux; Sechiari, etc). First to emphasise harp as solo instr. with acc. (A timid attempt had been made in XVIII century, but had not been repeated by modern orchestras.) Numerous tours abroad. As compr. she prod. a concerto for harp and orch., at request of C. Chevillard in 1901. This work, based on a short rhythmic theme, rises far above usual level of harp concertos. Wrote *Elegy* and *Caprice* for harp and orch.: a trio for vn. cello and harp; sonata for cello and pf. and many characteristic pieces for harp alone. Numerous transcriptions for harp from old harpsichord pieces, eminently suited to harp. The Institut awarded her the *Prix Chartier*. Her lectures on virtuoso concert-playing, open to all professional artists, have been largely responsible for such harpists as Grandjany, Mme. Pignal-Régnier, Mlle. Le Dentu, and Bertile Robet.—M. P.

RENNER, Joseph. Ger. compr. of church music; *b.* Regensburg (Ratisbon), 17 Feb. 1868. Son of music-teacher Joseph R. (1832–95); pupil of Joseph Rheinberger; 1893, orgt. at Cath. Regensburg; 1896, also teacher of organ at School of Church Music; 1912, R. professor.

14 Requiems; 10 masses; offertories; religious songs, op. 55; motets; organ pieces: 2 sonatas, 3 suites, 12 trios, 20 easy preludes, etc.; secular songs; male choruses; serenades for pf. and vn.; mus. comedy, *Josef Haydn*, etc. Wrote *Modern Church Music and the Chorale*; *J. Rheinberger's Masses* (*Church Music Annual*).—A. E.

RENNER, Willy. Ger. pianist and compr. *b.* Oldisleben, Saxony, 28 May, 1883. Pupil Hoch's

Cons. (Ivan Knorr), Frankfort-o-M. whose training-class he has cond. since 1913, after short engagements as solo repetitor at Darmstadt R. Theatre.

Pf. music: Prelude and fugue, B flat mi.; suite, op. 36; *Bach-Prelude*, op. 6; *Impressions*, op. 7; pf. pieces, op. 2 and 3; Variations, op. 9; vn. sonata, op. 14; cello sonata, op. 12; *Scherzo*, orch. op. 14; 2 ballads, solo v. and orch. op. 13; Variations for 2 pfs. op. 14; songs and nursery rhymes.—A. E.

RENNES, Catharina van. Dutch compr. *b.* Utrecht, 2 Aug. 1858. Comp. more than 72 works, children's songs and cantatas, well known in Holland.—W. P.

RENZI, Remigio. Ital. orgt. and compr. *b.* Rome, 1 Oct. 1857. Is orgt. of Cappella Giulia in St. Peter's, Rome, going there from the Basilica Lateranense; since 1887, has been teacher of organ, harmony and cpt. at the R. Liceo Mus. di Santa Cecilia. As executant, concert-player and musician he is held in high esteem. As a compr. has written church music, sonatas, and organ music.—D. A.

RÉPÉTITEUR (Fr.). *Maestro - al - pianoforte* (Ital.). *Solorepetitor* (Ger.). The pianist who rehearses at the piano with the soloists of an opera. Often he is one of the junior condrs. The trainer and rehearser of the opera-chorus is called *Korrepetitor* in Germany.—E.-H.

RESPIGHI, Ottorino. Ital. compr. *b.* Bologna, 9 July, 1879. Is one of most remarkable of modern Ital. comprs. Completed studies at the Liceo in his native city (vn. under Federico Sarti, and compn. under Martucci). Then went to Russia, where he stud. under Rimsky-Korsakof, and in Berlin under Bruch. Since 1913 he been teacher of compn. at the R. Liceo Mus. di Santa Cecilia, Rome; and in Nov. 1923 was appointed its director. His orch. music is frequently perf. at Queen's Hall, London.

Operas: *Re Enzo* (Teatro del Corso, Bologna, 1905); *Semirâma* (Comunale Theatre, Bologna, 1910), Sonzogno, Milan; *Belfagor* (Scala, Milan, 1923). Also *Sleeping Beauty* (for Teatro dei Piccoli—see PODRECCA, VITTORIO).

Symph. music: *Aretusa*, symph. poem for s. and orch. (Bologna, 1911); *Sinfonia drammatica* (Augusteo, Rome, 1915); *Le Fontane di Roma*, symph. poem (Augusteo, Rome, 1917); *Ballata delle gnomidi*, symph. poem (Augusteo, Rome, 1920); *Antiche Arie e Danze italiane*.

Chamber-music: sonata, B mi. vn. and pf. (1919); 4tet, D ma. (1920); also many songs; *Concerto Gregoriano*, for vn. and orch. (Augusteo, Rome, 1922); Poem *Primavera*, for solo vs. chorus and orch. (Augusteo, Rome, 1923). R.'s music is publ. by Ricordi, Milan; Bongiovanni, Bologna; Univ. Ed. Vienna.—D. A.

RESTANO, Antonio. Argentine compr. *b.* Buenos Ayres in 1866. Stud. in Argentina and then at Cons. of Milan under Saladino, Dominiceti and Ponchielli. Obtained first success in Turin with opera *Un Milioncino* (3 acts), and later his *Margherita d'Orléans* (3 acts) firmly establ. his reputation. Now directs Weber Mus. Inst., Buenos Ayres, which he founded. First Argentine compr. whose operas were produced in European theatres.

Another opera, *Moroveldo*; orch. works: *Himno al Centenario*; overture in E flat; *Preludio*, *Intermezzo* and *Danza dei Paggi*.—A. M.

RESZKE (*phon.* Reshke), Edouard de. Polish b. singer; *b.* Warsaw, 23 Dec. 1855; *d.* Gureck,

Poland, 25 May, 1917. Brother of Jean de Reszke. *Début* in Warsaw; Ital. Theatre, Paris, 1876–8; London, 1884; Paris Grand Opéra, 1885–98. Up to 1906, sang in all the largest opera houses of Europe.—Zᴅ. J.

RESZKE (*phon.* Reshke), Jean de. Polish t. singer; *b.* Warsaw, 4 Jan. 1850. Began singing as barit. in 1874; then developed into a t. Has perf. since 1885 at the Paris Grand Opera, and as a guest in London, Petrograd, Warsaw, New York and elsewhere. His finest rôles were Faust and Romeo (Gounod); Tristan, Tannhäuser, Lohengrin and Siegfried (Wagner); Sigurd (Reyer); Samson (Saint-Saëns) and others. In 1905, he founded in Paris an operatic singing-school and soon became a celebrated teacher.—Zᴅ. J.

REUSS, August. Ger. compr. *b.* Liliendorf, near Znaim, 6 March, 1871. Pupil of Thuille, Munich, where he settled 1903; 1906–7, cond. theatres at Augsburg and Magdeburg; gave up career through ill-health; lived at Charlottenburg as teacher; now at Gräfelfing, near Munich. As compr. his first works are typical representatives of Munich (Thuille) School; shows in later works a more personal form of harmony and melody, and more clearness in form.

Many songs; some with orch. (*June Night*, op. 8; *Warm Spring*, op. 9; ballad, *Ratbod*, op. 15); male choruses: *Gotenzug*, op. 5; *Waldlied* (solo and orch.), op. 3; Christmas carol for mixed chorus, op. 6; duets; 2 melodramas (recitation and orch.), op. 21; symph. prologue, *The Fool and Death*, op. 10 (after H. v. Hofmannsthal); symph. poems, *Judith*, op. 20 (after Hebbel), and *Midsummer Night*, op. 19 (after W. Hertz); opera, ,*Duke Philip's Bridal-Journey* (Graz, 1909); pf. 5tet, F mi. op. 12; 2 str. 4tets, D mi. op. 25, and D ma. op. 31 (*Spring*); pf. trio, op. 30; 8tet for wind instrs., B ma. op. 37; vn. sonatas, op. 26 and 35 (*Romantic Sonata*); *Barcarolle*, cello and pf.; pf. sonata, C mi. op. 27; *Serenade*, small orch.; vn. concerto; several pf. pieces (op. 22).—A. E.

REYER, Ernest. Fr. compr. *b.* Marseilles, 1 Dec. 1823; *d.* Lavandou (Hyères), 15 Jan. 1909. His real name was Ernest Rey; but he added the ending -er to give it a German sound as he was in every way a convinced partisan of Wagner. Self-taught, but gifted with the most vivid .mus. sense. Received lessons in pf. and harmony from his aunt, Mme. Farrenc, while devoting himself to his career as official in Algiers. After the 1848 Revolution, which caused him to lose his post, he stud. music in Paris, and became the friend and declared defender of Berlioz. In 1850 his first public work, *Le Sélam* (symph. ode on text of Théophile Gautier), was played. Apart from this, wrote entirely for theatre. Had strong orchestral sense, but his harmonic writing was poor. Became critic for *Journal des Débats*, succeeding d'Ortigue, the successor of Berlioz. His critiques have been coll. under the title *Notes de Musique* (1875) and *Quarante Ans de Musique* (1910). He was librarian of the Opéra, and became member of the Institut in 1876 in place of Félicien David.

Messe pour l'Arrivée du Duc d'Aumale à Alger (1847); *Chœur des buveurs*; *Chœur des assiégés*; *Recueil de 40 chansons anciennes*; *Le Sélam* (4 parts, 1850); *Maître Wolfram*, 1-act *opéra-comique* (1854); *Sacountala*, 2-act ballet-pantomime, after Th. Gautier

(1858); *La Statue*, 3-act *opéra-comique* (1861); *Chant des paysans*, for Sardou's drama *Les Volontaires de 1854* (1861); *Érostrate*, 2-act opera (1862); *L'Hymne du Rhin*, cantata (1865); *La Madeleine de désert*, scena for b. and orch. (1874); *Sigurd*, 4-act opera (1884); *Salammbô*, 5-act opera, after Flaubert (1890); *Marche Tzigane*, orch.; 2 collections of songs.—A. C.

REYES, Juan. Chilean pianist; *b.* Santiago, 1899. Commenced playing at 4; later went to Europe, stud. under Desgranges in Paris, Gonzalez in Genoa, and Gutmann in Vienna, where he stayed till 1917, when he received the State diploma and the Austrian grand prize awarded to foreign students. After numerous concerts in Europe, returned to Chile, where he has been giving concerts with continuous success.—A. M.

RHEINBERGER, Joseph Gabriel. German compr. and teacher; *b.* Vaduz, Lichtenstein, 17 March, 1839; *d.* Munich, 25 Nov. 1901. Pupil of Ph. Schmutzer in Feldkirch; 1851–4, R. Music School; 1865–7, repetitor, Court Theatre; 1867, prof. of R. Music School; from 1877, R. Court condr. Teacher of an international reputation in counterpoint. As compr. R. is an epigone of the late-Romantic; he is at his best in the exquisite counterpoint of his organ compositions.

Orch. and chamber works: *Symphonische Tongemälde, Wallenstein*, op. 10; *Symph. Fantasia*, op. 79; overtures to *Demetrius* (op. 110) and *Taming of the Shrew* (op. 18); *Academical Festival Overture*, op. 195 (1908); pf. concerto, A flat, op. 94; 4 sonatas (among them *Symph. Sonata*, op. 47); pf. sonata for duet, op. 122; duo for 2 pfs., op. 15; Variations for str. 4tet, op. 61 and 93; str. 5tet, A mi. op. 82 (2 vns. 2 vlas. cello); pf. 5tet, C, op. 114; pf. 4tet, E flat, op. 38; nonet for fl. ob. clar. bsn. horn, vn. vla. cello and d.b. op. 139; 2 str. 4tets (C mi. op. 89; F, op. 147); 2 vn. sonatas (E flat, op. 77; E mi. op. 105); cello sonata in C, op. 92; horn sonata, op. 178.

Organ works: 20 organ sonatas: C, op. 27; A flat, op. 65; G (*Pastoral*), op. 88; A mi. op. 98; F sharp mi. op. 111; E flat, op. 119; F, op. 127; F mi. op. 132 (from which is derived the Passacaglia for orch. op. 132b); B flat mi. op. 142; B mi. op. 146; D mi. op. 148; D flat, op. 154; E flat, op. 161; C ma. op. 165; D ma. op. 168; G sharp mi. op. 175; B ma. op. 181; A mi. op. 188; G mi. op. 193; F ma. op. 196; 2 organ concertos with orch., op. 137 (F ma.) and 177 (G mi.); suite for organ, vn. and cello with orch. op. 149; pieces for organ: 12 trios, op. 49; 12 trios, op. 189; 12 *fughette*, op. 123; 12 characteristic pieces, op. 156; 12 meditations, op. 167; 6 pieces for organ and vn. (ob. cello), op. 150.

Choral works: Legend, *Christophorus* (chorus, soli, orch.), op. 120, one of his best compns.; *Montfort* (chorus, soli, orch.), op. 145; *Star of Bethlehem* (Christmas cantata, chorus, soli, orch.), op. 164; music to *Wundertätigen Magus* (*El Mágico Prodigioso*) by Calderón, op. 30; *Hymn to Art* (male chorus and orch.), op. 179; *Toggenburg*, op. 76; *Klärchen von Eberstein*, op. 97; *Valley of Espingo* (male chorus and orch.), op. 50; *Midsummer Night* (male chorus and orch.), op. 91; *Wittekind* (male chorus and orch.), op. 102; 12 masses; a grand *Requiem*, op. 60; a second unacc., op. 84; a third for chorus and organ, op. 194; 2 *Stabat Maters*; 9 Advent motets, op. 176; songs (Songs of old Italian poets, op. 129); vocal 4tets with pf.: *Water-Nymph*, 4-v. with pf. op. 21; *Lockung*, op. 25; *Love-Garden*, op. 80; *Dead Bride*, with solo and orch or pf. op. 81; 3-v. female chorus with organ, op. 96; 2-v. hymns for female chorus with organ, op. 118; male choruses; *Roaming*, op. 160; Turkish lyrical play *From the Golden Horn*, op. 182; pf. pieces, op. 13 (*Tarantella*), 14 (preludes), 19 (toccatina), etc., etc. Romantic opera, *The Seven Ravens*, op. 20 (Munich, 1896); comic opera, *The Little Daughter of the Tower*, op. 70 (Munich, 1873); mus. comedy, *Das Zauberwort*, op. 153.

Consult: R. Molitor, *J. Rh. and his Organ Compositions* (1904); Th. Kroyer, *J. Rh.* (Regensburg, 1916, Pustet).—A. E.

RHENÉ-BATON (real name René Baton). Fr. compr. condr. *b.* Courseulles-sur-Mer (Calvados), 5 Sept. 1879. Pupil at Paris Cons. for pf. Stud. compn. under André Bloch and André Gédalge. Chorus-condr. at Opéra-Comique, Paris; then condr. of Société des Concerts Populaires d'Angers; of Concerts de la Société Ste.-Cécile de Bordeaux; 2nd condr. of Lamoureux Concerts, Paris. Since 1916, condr. of orch. of l'Association des Concerts Pasdeloup.

Orch. suite, *Fresques antiques*; Prelude and fugue, orch.; several songs, pf. pieces (Durand), a lyric drama, a ballet (ms.).—M. L. P.

RICART MATAS, José. Span. cellist, *b.* 27 Oct. 1893. Stud. under his mother, Carmen Matas de Ricart, and under L. Millet, A. Nicolau and J. Soler at Barcelona. Tours Spain, France, Belgium and England. First appeared in London 1921, and now lives there.—P. G. M.

RICCI, Corrado. Ital. writer and critic; *b.* Ravenna, 18 April, 1858. A writer and critic of figurative art; in Rome was general dir. of Antiquities and Fine Arts; now dir. of the Istituto Archeologico. With mus. art he has a close interest and an ardent sympathy, and is author of many publications regarding history of Italian lyric theatre, and of several libretti for music, of which one is *Isora di Provenza* for Luigi Mancinelli. Among books on music: *I teatri di Bologna nei secoli XVII e XVIII* (Bologna, 1888, Monti ed.); *Arrigo Boito* (Milan, 1919, Treves); *Figure e figuri del mondo teatrale* (Milan, 1920, Treves). Also many arts. in newspapers and reviews.—D. A.

RICCI-SIGNORINI, Antonio. Ital. compr. *b.* Massa Lombarda, 22 Feb. 1867. Stud. at Liceo of Bologna, under Martucci and Busi. Author of some distinguished symph. works, and instr. and vocal chamber-music, publ. mostly by Ricordi, Carisch and Jänichen of Milan. His *Rapsodie italiane* for orch. are amongst his most successful works.—D. A.

RICCITELLI, Primo. Ital. compr. *b.* Bellante (Abruzzo), 10 August, 1880. Pupil of Pietro Mascagni at the Liceo di Pesaro. In 1916 his opera *Maria sul Monte* was perf. in Milan. In 1923, his *I Compagnacci*, comic opera in one act, at the Costanzi in Rome, met with great success.—D. A.

RICHARDS, Henry William. Eng. orgt. *b.* Notting Hill, London, 16 April, 1865. Prof. of organ, R.A.M.; lecturer and member of committee of management R.A.M.; Mus.Doc. Dunelm.; orgt. and choirmaster Christ Ch., Lancaster Gate, London, 1886–1921; representative for Music-Teachers Registration Council.

Organ Accompaniment of the Church Services (J. Williams); *Choir-Training* (id.); small vocal and instr. pieces; lectures (R.C.O. Calendar).—E.-H.

RICHARDSON, Alfred Madeley. Eng. orgt. compr. and writer; *b.* Southend-on-Sea, Essex, 1 June, 1868. Educated at Keble College, Oxford. Stud. music at R.C.M. under Parry, Parratt and Pauer. Mus.Doc. Oxon, 1897. Orgt. at Southwark Cath. London, 1897–1908. Founder and condr. of Worcester Orch. Soc., Southwark

Choral Soc., and others. In 1909 became orgt. at St. Paul's, Baltimore, U.S.A. Since 1912, instructor in theory at Inst. of Mus. Art, New York. His *Southwark Psalter* (Longmans, 1905) created a new epoch in Psalm chanting.

Choir Training (Vincent Music Co. 1899); *Church Music* (Longmans, 1904); *Modern Organ Accompaniment* (id. 1907); *The Choir-trainer's Art* (Schirmer, 1914); *Extempore Playing* (id. 1922). Also church music, services, anthems, part-songs.—J. M

RICHEZ, Céliny. See CHAILLEY, MARCEL.

RICHTER, Hans. Hungarian conductor; *b.* Györ (Raab) 4 April, 1843; *d.* Bayreuth, 5 Dec. 1916. Boy-chorister at Hofkapelle, Vienna; stud. at Acad. there 1860–5, and was horn-player of the Grand Opera orch. 1862–6. Then with Richard Wagner at Lucerne, copying for him the score of *Mastersingers*. Upon Wagner's recommendation, he went as chorus-dir. to Munich Opera (1868–9). In 1870 went to Brussels where he cond. the rehearsals for *Lohengrin*. 1871–5, was orch. condr. at Budapest (National Theatre). 1875–98, condr. at Hofoper, Vienna, and also of Soc. of Friends of Music and Philh. Concerts and, since 1878, of the Hofkapelle also; 1876, conducted the *Ring* at Bayreuth and frequently since then; being one of the most intimate members of the Bayreuth circle. Cond. Budapest Phil. concerts 1896–1897. Worked from 1897–1910 in England, where he had already cond., in association with Wagner himself, the Wagner Concerts in 1877. He dir. the Hallé Concerts at Manchester from 1900 to 1911, the music fests. at Birmingham (from 1885), the German Opera at Covent Garden and the Richter Concerts in London. From 1912 he lived at Bayreuth. Richter was not only a brilliant Wagner condr. His masterly manner, well founded on a deep knowledge of the score, was always bent on preserving the grand traditions from Mozart and Beethoven to the Romanticists as far as Brahms. He never was a "Wagnerian," but only a convinced adherent of Richard Wagner the man. His niche has not been filled, up to this day.—P. ST.

RICORDI, G. & CO. The greatest music-publ. house in Italy; owners of works of Rossini, Bellini, Donizetti, Verdi, Ponchielli and Puccini, that is to say, of nearly whole of Ital. operatic repertoire in vogue nowadays. Founded 1808 on a very modest basis by Giovanni Ricordi, who from being prompter at La Scala, became copyist and printer of music. The founder died in 1858, leaving his business to his son Tito. The latter died in 1888, leaving as heir his son Giulio (*d.* 1912), who was an outstanding figure not only as a publ. but also as an artist. A capable musician, he comp. some elegant music, particularly for pf., under pseudonym of Burgmein. Giulio enjoyed a bond of deep friendship with Giuseppe Verdi (as did also his father). His house became the meeting-place of all the principal Ital. musicians: Boito, Ponchielli, Catalani, Puccini, Perosi. Of younger musicians, the Casa Ricordi has publ. works by Zandonai, Montemezzi, Alfano, Alaleona, Pizzetti, Respighi,

Casella, Malipiero, and many others. The firm also publ. concert and chamber-music, vocal and instr., in addition to educational works and literature. The catalogue contains about 120,000 nos. The firm is a private company, managed by Carlo Clausetti (*q.v.*) and Renzo Valcarenghi. There are branches in Rome, Naples, Palermo, London, Paris, Leipzig, Buenos Ayres and New York.—D. A.

RIDOLFI, Vico. Ital. pianist; *b.* Ancona, 10 April, 1863; *d.* Rome, 31 March, 1920. Esteemed concert-player and teacher. Stud. at Cons. of Milan under Carlo Andreoli; went to Rome, where he enjoyed the esteem of Giovanni Sgambati, and gained high reputation as perfect executant and very fine interpreter.—D. A.

RIEMANN, Hugo. German musicologist; *b.* Grossmehlra, near Sondershausen, 18 July, 1849; *d.* Leipzig, 10 July, 1919. First stud. for bar at Berlin and Tübingen; later philosophy and history; not till after return from campaign 1870-1 did he turn to music; then stud. at Leipzig, besides law, music at Cons.; 1873, Ph.D. Göttingen. After many years as condr. and instructor at Bielefeld, 1878 became hon. lecturer for music at Leipzig Univ.; 1880, music-master at Bromberg; 1881-90, teacher at Cons. Hamburg; after short time at Cons. Sondershausen, 1890-5 at Cons. Wiesbaden; 1895, returned Leipzig and resumed Univ. lectures; 1901, prof.-extraordinary; 1905, prof.-in-ordinary; 1908, dir. of newly-establ. Inst. of Mus. Science (*Collegium musicum*); 1911, prof.-in-ordinary, *h.c.*; 1914, dir. of newly-establ. State Inst. for investigation of mus. science.

Theoretical works: Dissertation *On Musical Hearing* (*Musical Logic*), 1873; *Musical Syntax* (1877); *Nature of Harmonics* (1882; Eng. by Fillmore); *Manual of Harmony* (1887, 8th ed. 1920; Fr. by Calvocoressi, 1902; Ital. by Settaccioli, 1906); *Systematic Instruction in Modulation* (1887; Russ. by I. Engel, 1896); *Catechism of Harmony* (1890); *Simplified Harmony Instruction* (1893; Eng. by H. W. Bewerunge, 1895); *Problem of Harmonic Dualism* (1905); *Elementary Harmony Tutor* (Hesse, 1906); *Elementary Music Instruction* (1882); *New School of Melody* (1883); *Instruction-book for Simple and Double Counterpoint and Imitation* (1888; Eng. by Lovewell, 1904); *Catechism of Music* (1888); *Catechism of Composition* (1889); *Catechism of Fugue* (analysis of Bach's *Wohltemperirtes Klavier* and *Art of Fugue*, 3 parts, 1890-1; Eng. by Shedlock); *Catechism of Song-composition* (1891); *Composition Instructor* (1902-3; I. Homophonic Movement, II. Polyphonic Movement, III. Orchestral Movement and Dramatic Vocal Style); *Æsthetic and Formal Analysis of Beethoven's Pf. Sonatas* (3 vols. 1915-19); *Musical Instruments* (1880; also in Eng.); *Organ* (1880; *Figured-Bass* (1889); *Musical Principles* (1889); *Formation of Orchestra* (1902; Eng. 1906); *Phrasing* (4th ed. 1920); *Elements of Mus. Æsthetics* (5th ed. 1921). Riemann's most extensive work is the *Dictionary of Music* (1st ed. 1882, 8th ed. 1914-15; since then 9th ed., ed. by Alfred Einstein; Eng. by Shedlock, 1893; also in several pirated eds. in America).

Pf. educational works: *Pf. Tutor* (1883); *Expression in Music* (1883); *Musical Dynamics and Agogy* (1884); *Practical Instructions in Phrasing* (1886); *Catechism of Pf.-Playing* (1888; also Eng., Russ. and Czech); *Technical Studies for Organ* (with K. Armbrust; *Preliminary Studies for Polyphonic Playing* (Leipzig, 1888, Steingräber); *New Pf. Tutor* (Augener); *System of Musical Rhythm and Metre* (1903); *Normal Pf. Tutor* (Hesse, 1903); eds. of classical and romantic works with phrasing.

Historical works: *Studies in the History of Notation* (1878); *Development of our Notation* (1881);

Opera-Handbook (1884-93); *Catechism of Musical History* (2 parts, 1888, 7th ed. 1920; also in Eng.); *Notation Written and Printed* (1896); *History of Music-Theory from IX to XIX Century* (1898); *Eras and Heroes of Musical History* (Stuttgart, 1900); *History of Music since Beethoven* (Stuttgart, 1901); *Handbook of Musical History* (Leipzig, Breitkopf): I. 1, Ancient (1901), II. 1, Renaissance (1300-1600) (1907), II. 2, Figured-Bass Era (1600-1700) (1911), II. 3, The Great German Masters (1913); *Small Handbook of Musical History* (Leipzig, 1908); *Byzantine Script from X to XV Century* (1909); *Folklorist Study of Tonality* (1916).

Eds. of older works: *Old Chamber-music* (4 vols., Augener); *Illustrations of Musical History*; *Round Dances of Emperor Mathias' Period* (*circa* 1618); *Rococo* (*circa* 1725); Revision of Abaco's works; *Symphonies of Bavarian Palatinate School*; *Mannheim Chamber-music of XVIII Century*; *Stage Compositions of Agostino Steffani*.

Collected works as *Preludes and Studies* (3 vols. 1895-1900); *How do we hear Music?* (1886; 2 eds. as *Catechism of Musical Æsthetics*, 1903, also in Eng.); *Catechism of Acoustics* (1891); *Elements of Musical Æsthetics* (Stuttgart, 1900); *Sketches of Musical Science* (1908); *Ideas for Study of Tone-conception* and *New Contributions for Study of Tone-conception* (*Peters' Annual*, 1914-15 and 1916).

Consult the Riemann *Festival Book* (written by Mennicke (1909). All the Eng. eds. of R.'s works are publ. by Augener.—A. E.

RIETI, Vittorio. Ital. compr. *b.* Alexandria (Egypt), of Ital. parents, 1898. Stud. pf. and compn. in Milan under Frugatta, then in Rome under Respighi; has comp. an interesting piece of chamber-music.—D. A.

RIETSCH, Heinrich. Ger.-Czechoslovak writer on music, compr. *b.* Falkenon, 22 Sept. 1860. Stud. in Vienna under Hanslick and Adler (compn. Krenn, Mandyczewski, R. Fuchs). LL.D. 1895, private teacher of music in Vienna; 1900, prof. at Ger. Univ. Prague. His æsthetico-technical treatise on music in second half of XIX century is of great value.

The Mondsee-Vienna Song-MSS. and the Monk of Salzburg (in conjunction with F. A. Mayer, 1896); *Music in Second Half of XIX Century* (1900, 1906); *German Song* (1904); *Fundamentals of Music* (1907), etc. In *D.T.Ö.* he republ.: George Muffat's *Florilegium*, I, II; J. J. Fux's *Concentus instrumentalis*; *Vienna Minnesänger Fragment* 2701. Comp.: Symph. poem, *Münchausen*; *Tauferer Serenade*, orch.; *Serenade*, orch.; opera, *Walter von der Vogelweide*; 3 str. 4tets; pf. 5tet; pf. music; choruses; songs.—E. S.

RIGA, François. Belgian compr. *b.* Liège, 21 Jan. 1831; *d.* Brussels, 18 Jan. 1892. Began as chorister at Liège; stud. Brussels Cons. under Bosselet, Fétis and Lemmens. Afterwards orch. under Hanssens. He was for some time choirmaster of Church of the Minimes, and then devoted himself to teaching and compn. His numerous male-v. choruses, cleverly written, but mediocre in style and conceived especially for effect, belong to the already extinct period of choral virtuosity. They were used widely, as were also his many religious works (Brussels, Schott). He married the pianist, Clotilde Florence (*d.* 1893).—E. C.

ŘÍHOVSKÝ, Vojtěch. Czechoslovak compr. *b.* Dub (Moravia), 1871. Pupil of Skuherský at Organ School; then orgt. at different places; 1914, orgt. in Prague; later ed. to publs. Mojmír Urbánek, Prague. His speciality is church-music, melodious and easy to perform. Also instructive works. Many masses (some of them Czechoslovakian) and harmonisations of popular songs (Mojmír Urbánek, Prague).—V. Sᴛ.

RIJNBERGEN, Hendrik. Dutch violinist; *b.* Utrecht, 3 Feb. 1886. Made his first public appearance at Utrecht, when 12 years old (with Mozart and Mendelssohn concertos). Stud. at Utrecht Music School under G. Veerman (1898–1904); Carl Flesch, Berlin; Eugène Ysaye (1905) and Marsick (Paris, 1906–8); 2nd soloist in Berlin, Blüthner Orch.; State Theatre, Basle; 1911, Frankfort, soloist at Opera House and Museum Concerts; later returned to Holland; became 1st soloist at Utrecht and Amsterdam, Concertgebouw Orch. A very fine Mozart-player; moreover a pioneer of modern music (gave with Willem Pijper, first perfs. in Holland of vn. sonatas of Debussy, Darius Milhaud [second] and Willem Pijper, Feb. 1920).—W. P.

RIMSKY-KORSAKOF, Nicolas Andreievitch. Russian composer; *b.* Tikhvin, 6/18 March, 1844; *d.* Liubensk, 8/21 June, 1908. Received his first lessons in composition from his pf. teacher, Fedor Kanille, and later came under the influence of Balakiref. He served several years in the Russian navy before devoting himself to music professionally. In 1865 appeared his first symphony (the first symphony written by a Russian), which was followed by the tone-poem *Sadka* (1867), the programme-symphony *Antar* and various works of similar order. In 1871 he was appointed professor of instrumentation at the Petrograd Conservatoire. From 1874 to 1881 he was the head of the Free School of Music, and from 1886 to 1900 conductor of the Belaief Symphony Concerts. In 1872 he wrote his first opera, *The Maid of Pskof.* Shortly afterwards, considering his technical equipment inadequate, he renounced for a time composition in order to improve his capacities and specially to practise counterpoint. His first big work after this period of study was the opera *The Night in May,* and henceforth he directed his creative activities chiefly towards the lyric stage, without however relinquishing instrumental composition until a comparatively later date.

He has often been described, quite rightly, as a magician of the orchestra; and his fame rests chiefly upon the works in which he displays in richest array the outcome of his picturesque fancy and rare sense of colour. The more earnest moods of his imagination are revealed in *Antar,* in *The Maid of Pskof,* and in certain of the songs. The operas *Sadko* and *Mlada* contain some of the finest and raciest music he has written; and *The Snow-Maiden* and *The Golden Cockerel,* the former essentially lyrical, the latter humorous, illustrate in their best aspects the lighter veins of his imagination.

His influence, direct and indirect, has been considerable. Among Russian composers of repute, the following have been his pupils: Glazunof, Liadof, Arensky, Gretchaninof, A. Tanéief, Ippolitof-Ivanof, Blumenfeld, Steinberg, Wihtol, Tchérepnin, and Stravinsky.

Operas: *The Maid of Pskof* (1872, rev. 1894, Bessel)
    The Night in May (1878, Belaief)
    The Snow Maiden (1881, Bessel)
    Mlada (1893, Belaief)
    Christmas Eve (1874, *id.*)

    Sadko (1896, *id.*)
    The Tsar's Bride (1898, *id.*)
    The Legend of the Tsar Saltan (1900, Bessel)
    Servilia (1901, *id.*)
    Kashtchei the Deathless (1901, *id.*)
    Pan the Voyerod (1902, *id.*)
    The Legend of the Invisible City of Kitej (1904, Belaief)
    The Golden Cockerel (1907, Jurgenson)
Orch.: First Symphony, E mi.
    Second Symphony, *Antar* (1874, rev. 1893, Bessel)
    Third Symphony (C mi. 1873, Belaief)
    Sinfonietta, A mi. (1880, *id.*)
    Spanish Capriccio (1887, *id.*)
    Fairy-Tale, tone-poem (1887, *id.*)
    Scheherazade, suite (1888, *id.*)
    Easter Overture (1888, *id.*)
    Sadko, tone-poem (1867, rev. 1891, Bessel)
    Pf. Concerto (1887, Belaief)

He also wrote about 100 songs, a few choral works, and a small amount of chamber-music, and pf. music. His fine coll. of folk-songs appeared in 1877. After his death appeared his *My Musical Life* (Petrograd, 1909; Eng. transl. 1924, Secker), a vol. of essays on music (*ib.* 1911), and his *Treatise of Orchestration,* completed and edited by Maximilian Steinberg (Petrograd, 1913; Eng. transl. 1922).

Consult: N. Findeisen, *R. K.* (Petrograd, 1908, in Russ.); V. Karatyghin, *R. K.* (*ib.* 1909, *id.*); I. Lapshin, *Philosophical Themes in R.-K.'s Works* (*ib.* n.d. *id.*); M. Montague-Nathan, *R.-K.* (London, 1917); N. Van Gilse van der Pals, *R.-K.* (Leipzig, 1914, in Ger.); Vastrebtsef, *R.-K.* (Petrograd, 1908, in Russian).—M. D. C.

RINGNES, Inge Rolf. Norwegian pianist; *b.* Christiania, 25 Feb. 1894. Pf. pupil of Dagmar Walle-Hansen and Arthur Schnabel. First concert in Christiania in 1917; has since given concerts annually in that city. In 1923, successful concerts in Gothenburg, Copenhagen, Berlin, Dresden and Vienna. He is a gifted pianist and has done good service by producing many modern works.—J. A.

RINKENS, Wilhelm. Ger. orgt. compr. *b.* Röhn, near Eschweiler (Rhineland), 1879. Stud. at Cologne Cons. (pf. Pauer, Neitzel; compn. F. Wüllner; organ, Francke); after several years at Cologne (orgt. and teacher) became R. cantor, orgt., teacher of college and condr. of Mus. Soc. Eisenach; 1922, dir. of Training College for Music-Teachers at Thuringian National Cons. Erfurt.

Chamber-music; songs; melodrama; pf. pieces.—A. E.

RIPOLLÉS, Father Vicente. Span. compr. *b.* Valencia, 1867, where he holds the position of choirmaster at Cath. He is noted for his polyphonic works.—P. G. M.

RIPPER, Alice. Pianist; *b.* Budapest, 23 March, 1889. Stud. at National Cons. there, under Stephan Tomka and Sophie Menter. Lives at Munich.—A. E.

RISELEY, George. Eng. orgt. and condr. *b.* Bristol, 1844. Stud. under Dr. J. Corfe at the cath. there; orgt. of the cath. 1876–99; orgt. Colston Hall from its foundation; condr. of Bristol Mus. Fests.; was for many years condr. of the old Queen's Hall Choral Soc. and dir. of music at the Alexandra Palace. Lives in Bristol.—E.-H.

RISLER, Édouard. Fr. pianist; *b.* Baden-Baden, 23 Feb. 1873, of Alsatian parents who had chosen to remain Fr. citizens; came to Paris when very young; stud. pf. at Paris Cons. under Decombes and then Louis Diémer; 1st prize for pf., 1889; after completing studies with Albert Lavignac and Théodore Dubois, spent some years in Germany, especially in circle of Cosima Wagner. He was for some time singing-teacher in Bayreuth. Then he returned to Paris, where he gave series of concerts which placed him at once in the front rank of interpreters of the great classic masters. He crowned his first series by playing in full the 32 sonatas of Beethoven. To-day he has attained a technique of wonderful power and brilliance. His interpretation, always of a magnificent restraint, makes the audience forget the pianist in the work. While very eclectic and often including modern works (Chabrier, Dukas and Ravel are favourites), he is in complete sympathy with Beethoven, whom he interprets with unequalled loftiness, power and intimate feeling.—D. L.

RITTER, Alexander. Ger. compr. *b.* Narva (Russia), 27 June, 1833; *d.* Munich, 12 April, 1896. 1841, his mother Julie Ritter, patroness of Richard Wagner (*cf.* Wagner's letters to her, publ. by Siegmund v. Hausegger, Munich, 1920) moved to Dresden, where R. became school-comrade and friend of Hans v. Bülow. R. stud. there under Franz Schubert (vn.); 1849-51, visited Leipzig Cons. (David, Richter); 1854, married actress Franziska Wagner, niece of Richard Wagner. In same year went to Weimar; Bülow, Liszt, Peter Cornelius, Bronsart and Raff as friends; became compr.; 1856, condr. of Stadttheater, Stettin; 1856-60, at Dresden; 1860-62 at Schwerin, occupied with compn.; from 1863, permanently at Würzburg; 1875, establ. music-shop; 1885, sold it, having joined Bülow's Meiningen Orch. as violinist. After Bülow's departure (1886), went to Munich. R. was one of the independent partisans of North Ger. School; his symph. poems are a further development, on individual lines, of Liszt's symph. poems. His most valuable works perhaps are his short songs, which have an individual declamatory style, and are strong and masculine in feeling.

Str. 4tet, op. 1 (written 1865); 2 operas: *The Idle Hans*, 1885, and *Whose Crown?*, 1890; symph. poems: *Seraphic Fantasy*; *Erotic Legend*; *Olaf's Wedding-Dance*; *Good Friday and Corpus-Christi*; *Sursum corda*; *Emperor Rudolf's Ride to the Grave*. Consult Siegmund v. Hausegger, *Al. R.* (Leipzig, 1907, Siegel).—A. E.

RITTER-CIAMPI, Gabrielle. Fr. operatic s. singer; *b.* Paris, 2 Nov. 1886, of Ital. father and Fr. mother, both musical. Stud. pf. and gave concerts at 16; at same time was training as singer. *Début* on operatic stage in 1917, at Trianon-Lyrique (the part in *Paul et Virginie* which her mother had created). Then sang successively in *Pré aux Clercs*; *Le Barbier de Séville*; *La Traviata*; *L'Impresario* (Mozart). At request of Paul Vidal the compr. she sang in *Nozze di Figaro* (1919) at Opéra-Comique. Then in *Così fan tutte*, *Les Contes d'Hoffmann*,

Mignon, etc. With Battistini she gave 2 perfs. in Ital. of *Rigoletto* at Opéra, where she was engaged in 1921; also sang in *Faust*, *William Tell*, *Thaïs*, etc. In 1921 she revived *L'Enlèvement au Sérail* (Mozart); in 1922 *Castor et Pollux*, *Magic Flute*. Her voice is well-balanced, of very clear timbre, and easy delivery. Her remarkable style is particularly suited to s. parts in classical opera, more especially that of Mozart.—A. R.

RIVERA Y MANEJA, Antonio. Span. condr. *b.* Barcelona, 3 May, 1873. Artistic dir. of Sociedad Wagneriana, Barcelona (1901-4). Transl. of Wagner's operas into Span. and Catalonian. Formerly assistant-condr. at Bayreuth Fests. Pupil of Felix Mottl and Hugo Riemann. Has appeared as condr. at concerts and opera, Barcelona, Bayreuth, Nuremberg, Lemberg, Rome, and Lisbon. Gave first perf. in Spain of *Boris Godunof*, *Mastersingers*, and *The Marriage of Figaro*. Condr. of Orquesta d'Estudis Sinfonics, Barcelona.—P. G. M.

ROBERT, Richard. Austrian pf. teacher, writer on music; *b.* Vienna, 25 March, 1861. Stud. at Vienna Cons.; became pf. teacher there, and critic (*Sonn- und Montags Zeitung*). In 1909 dir. of New Vienna Cons., but soon resigned. President of Tonkünstlerverein (founded by Brahms). His well-known pupils include Vera Schapira, Rudolf Serkin, Therese Slottko, Wilhelm Grosz, Hans Gál, Georg Szell (chief condr. Düsseldorf), Alfred Rosé (Korrepetitor at Vienna State Opera) and many young condrs. engaged in different Ger. towns.—P. P.

ROBERTON, Hugh S. Scottish choral condr. *b.* Glasgow. Self-taught; began as a church-choir-trainer; then condr. Toynbee House Choir, Glasgow, a small body of singers, who met weekly at Toynbee Men's Social Club. He used this as nucleus for a more ambitious choir, which ultimately became the world-famous Glasgow Orpheus. R. was one of originators and pioneers of the Competition Fest. movement in Scotland, and is a frequent adjudicator both in England and Scotland. He has arr. many songs and vocal pieces for choir, including *The Red Flag*; and has written two plays.—W. S.

ROBERTS, Caradog. Welsh compr. orgt. *b.* Rhosllanerchrugog, N. Wales, 31 Oct. 1878. Stud. under Johannes Weingärtner and others; Mus.Doc. Oxon. Ed. of *Caniedydd Cynulleidfaol Newydd*, 1921; dir. of music at Univ. Coll. of N. Wales, Bangor, 1914-20. Adjudicator at National Eisteddfodau and Eng. fests.; holds a leading position in Wales as an orgt. and condr. In his literary contributions on music, is a strong advocate of establishing a Welsh school of music. His compns. include anthems; songs, etc. —D. V. T.

ROBERTSON, Alec. Eng. lecturer in music; *b.* Portsmouth, 3 June, 1892. Stud. R.A.M. London under Stewart Macpherson, Dr. H. W. Richards and Frederick Moore (1911-14); 1919, lecturer in mus. appreciation, London County

Council Evening Institutes; 1920, lecturer Education Dept. Gramophone Co.—E.-H.

ROBINSON, Edith. Eng. violinist; *b.* Manchester, 29 Oct. 1867. Stud in Manchester under Luigi Risegari, at Leipzig Cons. under Adolph Brodsky, and at Liège under César Thomson. For several seasons in Leipzig took vn. part in a series of trio-concerts with Julius Klengel and Fritz von Bose; appeared as soloist in many towns in Germany; has for many years given regular quartet concerts in Manchester. Hers is the only ladies' quartet which has played the whole of the Beethoven quartets as a series. She is prof. of vn. and 4tet-playing at R. Manchester Coll. of Music.—E.-H.

ROBINSON, Joseph. Irish condr. *b.* 20 Aug. 1815; *d.* 23 Aug. 1898. Chorister of St. Patrick's Cath.; played in Dublin Philh. Soc. In 1834 the Antient Concert Soc. was founded by him; he acted as its condr. until 1863. One of the last works of Mendelssohn, the instrumentation of *Hear my Prayer*, was written for R. to produce at the Antient Concert Soc. In 1837, Dublin Univ. Choral Soc. elected him condr. and many new works were given in Dublin for first time under him. In 1852, cond. at opening of Cork Exhibition. With his wife (Fanny Arthur) he was instrumental in reorganising the R. Irish Açad. of Music in 1856. During his 20 years' teaching there, his influence was incalculable. He wrote many songs and concert pieces and arr. Irish melodies.—W. ST.

ROBINSON, Rina. Eng. contr. singer and teacher of singing; *b.* London, 4 Aug. 1872. Stud. Metropolitan School of Music; Trinity Coll. of Music; Guildhall School of Music, and privately with Sir Charles Santley and Albert Visetti; prof. of singing at Huddersfield Coll. of Music; founder and mus. dir. of Shrewsbury Amateur Operatic Soc.; well known as an oratorio singer. Now lives at Shrewsbury.—E.-H.

ROBITSCHEK, Robert. Ger.-Czechoslovak musician; *b.* Prague, 13 Dec. 1874. Pupil of Dvořák; condr. at National Theatre, Prague; of Tonkünstler Orch. Berlin; since 1914, dir. of Klindworth-Scharwenka Cons. Berlin (at first jointly with H. and Ph. Scharwenka).

Opera, *Ahasver* (*Ahasuerus*); overture to Grillparzer's *Esther*; cello *Rhapsody* (with orch.); symph. variations; chamber-music; songs.—E. S.

ROBSON, Robert Walker. Eng. orgt. and teacher; *b.* Alnwick, 2 May, 1878. Stud. under Dr. W. Rea, Newcastle, and at R.C.M. London; orgt. Crouch Hill, N.

Cantata, *Christus Triumphator*; church music and songs (Novello); part-songs, pf. pieces (Novello; J. Williams); educational works (Weekes).—E.-H.

RODE, Halfdan. Norwegian barit. singer; *b.* Porsgrund, 20 June, 1871. Trained under W. Kloed, Christiania, afterwards in Berlin, Milan and London (partly with support of State scholarship). *Début* on concert-stage 1894; as opera-singer 1900. Chief rôles at National Theatre, Christiania: Don Juan; Toreador (*Carmen*); the Consul (*Butterfly*); Lothario (*Mignon*); Mephistopheles (*Faust*). Has toured at home and abroad during past 20 years, sometimes with

the various male choirs in Christiania — The Students' Choral Union, The Mercantile Choral Soc., The Artisans' Choral Soc., etc.—R. M.

RODRIGO, María. Span. compr. *b.* Madrid, 20 March, 1868. First tuition from her father, Pantaleón R. Stud. pf. and compn. at R. Cons. Música, Madrid; and at Munich, under Anton Beer-Walbrunn. Lives in Madrid. Holds position of assistant - condr. at R. Opera House.

Opera, *Becqueriana* (book by brothers Alvarez Quintero); orch.: *Gándara*, overture; *Alma Española*; *Impresiones sinfónicas*; 2 suites, small orch.; *Caprichos de Goya*, chorus and orch.; str. 4tet; 5tet, wind instrs. and pf.—P. G. M.

RODRÍGUEZ, Ricardo. Argentine compr. *b.* Concordia, in 1877. Stud. under Melani at Buenos Ayres Cons. Then went to *Schola Cantorum*, Paris, to study under d'Indy, returning to Buenos Ayres in 1909. Has publ. an orch. overture and many pf. pieces.—A. M.

ROESCH, Friedrich. Ger. mus. organiser and compr. *b.* Memmingen, Bavaria, 12 Dec. 1862. Law student at Univ. Munich; stud. music under Andreas Wohlmuth and Rheinberger; cond. Acad. Choral Union; 1898, organised (with Richard Strauss and Hans Sommer) the Society of German Composers (profit-sharing). Part-author of idea for *Kulturabgabe* (culture-tariff); 1919, chairman of Gen. Ger. Mus. Soc.; 1913, LL.D. *h.c.* Jena University.

4-v. madrigals for male and mixed choruses; songs. Wrote *Controversial Questions on Musical Æsthetics* (1897); *Study of Alexander Ritter* (*Musikalisches Wochenblatt*, 1898).—A. E.

ROGAN, John Mackenzie. English military bandmaster and dir. of music; *b.* Isle of Wight, 1855. Bandmaster in various regiments until 1896, when he was appointed to the famous Coldstream Guards band, a post he held till his retirement in 1920. His long and brilliant mus. record is unique in the history of the British Army, and his work for military band music was of very great importance. M.V.O. 1907; C.V.O. 1920; Mus.Doc. Toronto Cons. *h.c.* 1908. See *Mus. Times*, March 1918 (p. 119).—E.-H.

ROGER-DUCASSE. Fr. compr. *b.* Bordeaux, in 1875. One of the best pupils of Gabriel Fauré; fellow-student of Florent Schmitt, Maurice Ravel, Louis Aubert, Georges Enesco, Nadia Boulanger. Stud. pf. with Bériot, harmony with Pessard, fugue with Gédalge; 1909, inspector of singing in City of Paris schools. His music is extremely sincere, and varied.

Orch.: *Suite française*; *Marche française*; *Sarabande*; *Nocturne de Printemps*; *Au jardin de Marguerite* (symph. poem); *Orphée* (mimodrama). Variations, harp; *Pastoral* (organ); str. 4tet; pf. 4tet; *Aux premières clartés de l'aube* (chorus); *Le Joli Jeu de furet* (chorus); for pf.: *Barcarolle*; 6 preludes; studies; *Arabesques*. Some songs. Consult A. Cœuroy, *La Musique française moderne* (Paris, Delagrave, 1922).—A. C.

ROGERS, Winthrop, Ltd. Publishers, London. Came into existence in 1917 when the late Winthrop L. Rogers bought the London house of G. Schirmer Inc. of New York, which in 1913 took over publ. business of Vincent Music Co. founded by Dr. Charles Vincent in 1892. The publications consist chiefly of high-class educational music and distinctive works by modern comprs.

—Frank Bridge, John Ireland, Roger Quilter, etc.—E.-H.

ROGOWSKI, Michał Ludwik. Polish compr. condr. *b.* Lublin, 3 Oct. 1881. Pupil of Statkowski, Noskowski and Młynarski at Warsaw Cons. In 1906, went to Leipzig to study conducting under Nikisch and theory under Riemann. From 1909-12 worked in Vilna and founded and cond. a symphony orch. From 1914-21, worked in France (Paris and Villefranche) where he comp. and publ. (B. Rondanez, Paris) several chamber-music works (for choice combinations, such as a fl., little bells and pf.), an opera *Tamara* (libretto by Fr. Hellens), an orch. suite *Villafranca*, several short symph. pictures for small orch. and a ballet, *The Fable*. R.'s works are modern in harmony, rhythm and colouring. In his latest compns. he utilises some ancient Oriental songs (*Phantasm*, 4 pieces for orch. and a vocal part to vowel-sounds). He now lives in Poland.—Zd. J.

ROHDE, Friedrich Wilhelm. Ger. violinist and compr. *b.* Altona, 11 Dec. 1856. Pupil of Leipzig Cons. (David, Röntgen, Schradieck, Richter, Kretzschmar); 1878-86, Chicago (Balatka Quintet), Boston (teacher at Cons.; member of Symph. Orch.); Hamburg; then Schwerin; 1914, Copenhagen. His sister Marie is a clever pianist.

Symphony, D mi. (ms.); *Serenade*, str. orch. op. 14; *Forest Calm* and *Elf Dance*, orch., op. 11; str. 4tet in G, op. 25; pf. trio, F mi. op. 21; 12 Irish National Songs, mixed chorus; 3 mixed choruses, op. 8; 2 sacred songs, op. 13; male choruses; 3 trios, female vs. and pf.; 4 canonic duets, op. 26; songs; pf. pieces (concert waltz, op. 5).—A. E.

RÖHR, Hugo. Ger. condr. and compr. *b.* Dresden, 13 Feb. 1866. Stud. at Dresden Cons. (Wüllner, Blassmann); 1887, condr. at Augsburg, Prague, Breslau; 1892, condr. of Academic Concerts, Mannheim; 1896, Court-condr. R. Opera House, Munich; 1912, condr. Teachers' Choral Union, Munich.

Songs; choral ballad; oratorio, *Ekkehard*; operas: *Our Father* (Munich, 1904; libretto by Ernst Possart); *Frauenlist* (Leipzig, 1917; libretto by Lothar).—A. E.

ROLAND-MANUEL. See MANUEL, ROLAND.

ROLLAND, Romain. Fr. musicologist and novelist; *b.* Clamency, 29 Jan. 1869. He is best known as the writer whose novel *Jean-Christophe* gained the Nobel Prize. But a great part of his time has been spent as a historian and music critic, and his activities in this direction have exercised a considerable influence on the development of musicological study in France.

An ex-pupil at École Normale Supérieure and *agrégé d'histoire*, he was passionately interested in music. During his stay at École Française de Rome, he became very enthusiastic over the scores of old Italian masters which he read in the libraries of Rome. He devoted his thesis for doctor's degree to *History of Opera in Europe before Lully and Scarlatti* (1895). This work contained the most original and provocative views on the history and evolution of opera in the XVII century. He illustrated his subject by apt comparisons with the history of art and literature and developed musical history on

the same lines as general history. This method was entirely original and startling to musicologists, who up to this time had been too rigidly confined to their own special subject. Rolland was put in charge of a course of lectures on the history of lyrical drama at the École Normale, and later at the Sorbonne. He exercised an absolute fascination over his students and over the vast audiences who literally fought to get into his lectures. He aroused curiosity afresh in the music of the past by making it live again in his lessons and writings. Unfortunately for musicology, he gave up lecturing in 1909 and devoted himself entirely to literary work.

He is not only a great historian of music— he is the pioneer who has cleared new paths for the musicologist, and also inspired others to follow him. The best among young French musicologists have been his pupils, and he has passed on to them, not only a love and respect for erudition, but also a love of music itself and a certain vivid manner of appreciating and evoking the past which is so irresistible in his *Musicians of Former Days* (Paris, 1908, Hachette; Eng. 1915, Kegan Paul), in his *Handel* (Alcan; Eng. Kegan Paul), in the *Musical Tour through Lands of the Past* (1921, Hachette; Eng. 1922, Kegan Paul). His small book *Beethoven* (1907) has had immense popularity. It is the best picture ever painted of the poignant drama of this great musician. Rolland also showed deep sympathy and keen intellect in dealing with contemporary music. His principal articles are collected in *Musicians of To-day* (Paris, 1908, Hachette; Eng. 1915, Kegan Paul). As one reads his works one cannot but regret his decision in abandoning musical history and criticism. It may even be that this section of his work will outlive the other in the memory of men.

Consult P. Seippel, *R. R., l'homme et l'œuvre* (1913); J. Bonnerot, *R. R.* (1922).—H. P.

ROMAGNOLI, Ettore. Ital. critic and historian; *b.* Rome, 11 June, 1871. Excellent Greek scholar; prof. of Greek literature at R. Univ. of Catania, then of Padua, now of Pavia; is also a very competent and devoted student of music. The merit belongs to him of having promoted perfs. in Italy of the masterpieces of ancient Greek tragedies, for which productions he himself wrote appropriate music. R. is also a capable translator and illustrator of these masterpieces of the Greek theatre. He also collab. with Luigi Illica in libretto of mus. comedy (of mythological parodistic type) *Giove a Pompei*, set to music by Giordano and Franchetti.

Important monographs: *La commedia attica* (Florence, 1912); *La lirica greca* (Florence, 1913); *Il teatro greco* (Milan, 1918, Treves); *Nel regno di Dioniso* (Bologna, 1918, Zanichelli); *Il libro della poesia greca* (Milan, 1921, Treves).—D. A.

ROMANIELLO, Louis. Argentine pianist, compr. *b.* Naples in 1860; *d.* Buenos Ayres, 1917. Stud. at Cons. there under Cesi. In 1881, successful concert-tour throughout Italy; then in principal European capitals. Was considered the equal of Cesi, and, by some critics, of Bülow. In 1896, went under contract to Buenos Ayres, where he settled to devote himself to teaching, opening a Cons. which soon became famous. The Ital. Government made him Knight of the Crown of Italy. Comp. 2 symphonies, and pieces for pf. and orch.; many pieces for pf. and also vn. pieces. His technical work, *Tecnica Pianistica* (Buenos Ayres, Breyer) is well known. He wrote many reviews.—A. M.

ROMANTIC. A term which began to be applied to music early in the 19th century. The Romantic movement in literature and the other arts, to which the initial impulse is generally held to have come from England (*Ossian*, Chatterton, Percy's *Reliques*, etc.), had its counterpart in the music of Méhul, Lesueur, Weber, Berlioz, Schumann, Chopin and Liszt. It was a revolt against the formalism of the XVIII century; in music it sought the extreme expression of emotion and the introduction of the picturesque element. Through literary influences, especially in Germany, the Romantic comprs. came to pay much attention to the supernatural, and it has been suggested that this led to modern orchestral developments, because the orchestra was required to paint the elemental forces of nature against which humanity had to struggle. The chief examples of this style are Weber, Liszt and Wagner; but it was foreshadowed in the operas of Rameau and in much of the English theatre-music of the XVII century. The XX century has brought about a violent reaction against Romanticism, which, during the XIX, was predominantly German in character, although Romanticism is eminently characteristic of the English and Celtic temperaments. Romanticism is really not confined to any one age or nation; the function of art is to strike a balance between the " romantic " and " classic " sides of every human personality—what common parlance calls " heart " and " head."—E. J. D.

RONALD, Sir Landon. Eng. condr. *b.* 7 June, 1873. Son of Henry Russell (formerly a well-known teacher of singing and compr. of songs). First appeared as solo pianist in Wormser's mus. play without words *L'Enfant Prodigue*; *maestro-al-piano* and condr. for Sir Aug. Harris at Covent Garden, 1891; cond. there, 1894; went to America with Melba, 1894; condr. Lyric Theatre, 1890; of Birmingham Promenade Concerts; Blackpool Symph. Concerts; of Albert Hall Sunday Concerts; New Symphony Orch. concerts (later called R. Albert Hall Orch.); Scottish Orch.; Albert Hall Saturday Promenade concerts (1923). Principal, Guildhall School of Music, London, from 1910. Elected a Fellow of the R.C.M. March 1924.

Orch. works (ms.); dramatic scenes, *Adonais* and *Lament of Shah Jehan* (v. and orch.); about 300 songs; pf. pieces (Enoch); incidental music to *Garden of Allah* (1921).—E.-H.

RÖNTGEN, Julius. Compr. and pianist; *b.* Leipzig, 9 May, 1855. Pupil of Louis Plaidy, Carl Reinecke and Franz Lachner. Concert-tours with singer Julius Stockhausen in Germany, Austria, Switzerland; with Johannes Messchaert in Holland, Germany, Denmark,

Norway, England, Austria; played in Vienna with Johannes Brahms; at Copenhagen and Christiania with Edvard Grieg; 1878, went to Amsterdam, pf. teacher Music School; dir. of concerts *Felix Meritis*, 1888–98; 1913, dir. of Cons. Amsterdam (succeeding Daniel de Lange).

Symphonies; 2 operas, *Agnete* (1914) and *The Laughing Cavalier* (1920); chamber-music; songs; old Dutch folk-music, etc. (mostly Breitkopf, Leipzig; Simrock; Augener, London; Noske, The Hague; Alsbach, Amsterdam).—W. P.

ROOTHAM, Cyril Bradley. Eng. condr. compr. and orgt. *b.* Bristol, 5 Oct. 1875. Son of D.W.R. (see below). Stud. St. John's Coll. Cambridge, and R.C.M. London, 1901; St. Asaph Cath. 1901; St. John's Coll. Camb. from 1901; Mus. Doc. Cantab. 1910 Cond *Magic Flute* (Camb. Theatre) 1911; condr. Camb. Univ. Mus. Soc. 1912; univ. lecturer, 1913; Fellowship, 1914.

Opera, *The Two Sisters*, founded on folk-ballad, *The Twa Sisters o' Binnorie* (Goodwin & Tabb). Orch.: rhapsody, *Pan*; *Procession in Scarlet* (Chancellor's music); Miniature Suite in G ma. pf. and str. 5tet (Goodwin & Tabb); Suite (Passacaglia, Saraband, Jig), fl. and pf. (Chester); str. 4tet in C (Murdoch); *Andromeda*, soli, chorus and orch. (Novello); *In Highland and Meadow*, 3 songs for chorus and orch. (Stainer & Bell); *Coronach*, barit. solo, male chorus (t.b.) and orch. (*id.*); *For the Fallen* (Laurence Binyon), chorus and orch. (Novello); *Brown Earth*, chorus, semi-chorus and orch. (a Carnegie award; Stainer & Bell); *Helen of Kirkconnell*, t. v. and orch. (Stainer & Bell); 4 dramatic songs, high v. and orch. (Novello); *A Vignette*, v. pf. str. 4tet (*id.*); song from 15th Idyll of Theocritus (in Greek), high v. harp and str. 4tet; numerous songs with pf. acc.; vn. and pf. pieces (Chester; Schott; Bosworth); organ pieces (Stainer & Bell); part-songs (Weekes; Novello; Curwen; Stainer & Bell); educational work, *Voice-training for Choirs and Schools* (Cambridge Univ. Press).—E.-H.

ROOTHAM, Daniel W. Eng. barit. singer and condr. *b.* Cambridge, 1837; *d.* April 1922. Lay-clerk (bass) Bristol Cath. 1852; orgt. St. Peter's, Clifton, 1866. Played an important part in the mus. development of Bristol. Condr. of Bristol Madrigal Soc. from 1865 till 1915; of Bristol Fest. Choir, 1878–96. Clara Butt began as a singer in his choir.—E.-H.

ROPARTZ, Guy. Fr. compr. *b.* Guingamp (Côtes-du-Nord), 15 June, 1864. Pupil of César Franck and Massenet; dir. of Nancy Cons. since 1894; called to Strasburg in 1919 to directorship of Cons. and Concerts, where he entirely re-organised the teaching, according to Fr. methods. Very cultured, has publ. some vols. of poems and a comedy. His music is allied to the popular songs of Brittany as well as to religious inspiration.

Orch. works: *Les Landes* (1888); *Dimanche breton* (1894); 4 symphonies (1895, 1900, 1906, 1910); *Psalm CXXXVI* (1897); Fantasia in D (1897); *La Cloche des Morts* (1902); *A Marie endormie* (1912); *La Chasse du Prince Arthur* (1912); *Soir sur les chaumes* (1913); *Divertissement* (1915). Stage-works: *Pêcheur d'Islande* (1891); *Le Miracle de Saint-Nicolas* (1905); *Le Pays* (1910). Chamber-music: 2 str. 4tets; 2 sonatas, pf. and cello; 2 sonatas, vn. and pf.; trio, vn. pf. and cello. Pf. pieces: *Ouverture*; *Variations et Finale*; 3 *Nocturnes*; *Dans l'ombre de la Montagne*; *Scherzo*; *Musiques au jardin*; *Croquis d'été*. Many organ pieces, songs and religious pieces. Consult André Cœuroy, *La Musique française moderne* (Delagrave, 1922).—A. C.

RORICH, Karl. Ger. compr. and teacher; *b.* Nuremberg, 27 Feb. 1869. Stud. at Würzburg R. Music School; 1892, teacher Grand-Ducal

Music School, Weimar; 1897, mus. dir.; 1911, member of mus. expert committee; 1904–9, cond. Philh.; 1913, dir. of Municipal Music School, Nuremberg.

Symphony, D mi.; *Introduction and Allegro* for str. orch.; *Academical Festival March*; *Hymnus solemnis*; *Fairy Overture*; *Carnival Overture*; overtures for Grillparzer's *Weh dem der lügt*; suites: *Waldleben*; *Weihnachtsbilder*; fairy-play, *Ilsa*; *Chamber Songs* for contr. with str. 4tet; 5tet for wind instrs. E mi.; str. 4tet, B mi.; str. 6tet; suite for 2 fls.; chorus; Mass, 3-v.; pf. pieces; songs; 5tet for wind instrs. and harp, op. 58; *Material for Theory Lessons* (1908).—A. E.

ROSA, Alba. Argentine violinist; *b.* Milan in 1889. Stud. at R. Cons. of Milan under Rampazzini, having to interrupt her training when 12 years old to go to Uruguay with her family. There she attracted the attention of César Thomson, on his concert-tour through S. America, and on his advice was sent to R. Cons. of Brussels. After 2 years there under Thomson, she undertook a concert-tour through France, Spain, Portugal, and Italy, being everywhere enthusiastically received. In 1907 she came to Argentina, where she gave a series of successful concerts. In 1908 she again made a tour through Europe, finally returning to settle in Buenos Ayres in 1911. Prof. of vn. at Buenos Ayres Cons. In 1924, toured in U.S.A.—A. M.

ROSATI, Enrico. Ital. teacher of singing; *b.* Rome, 9 June, 1874. Stud. compn. under Cesare De Sanctis in Rome, at R. Liceo Mus. di Santa Cecilia; devoted himself particularly to teaching of singing at Liceo at Pesaro, in Milan, and at R. Liceo Mus. di Santa Cecilia, Rome, where he has trained some excellent pupils, amongst whom were Beniamino Gigli and Benvenuto Franci. Now teaching in New York.—D. A.

ROSATI, Tito. Ital. cellist; *b.* Sant' Elpidio a Mare, in 1883. Stud. under Cremonini (cello), Pietro Mascagni (compn.) at Liceo at Pesaro. First cellist in orch. of the Augusteo since the foundation of the concerts there. After having belonged to various groups for chamber-music, at present takes part in the quartet formed at the R. Liceo Mus. di Santa Cecilia. Also much esteemed soloist, playing at the Augusteo and elsewhere.—D. A.

ROSENBERG, Hilding C. Swedish compr. *b.* Bosjökloster, 21 June, 1892. Stud. pf. under Rich. Andersson and compn. at R. Cons. Stockholm and in Dresden (pf. under Buchmayer and conducting under K. Striegler). As compr. is a modern Expressionist. Lives in Stockholm.

Symphony (1917; perf. Gothenburg, 1921); 3 Phantasy-pieces (1918; *ib.* 1919); pf. concerto (1919); Variations and Passacaglia, orch. (1922); sonata, vn. alone (1922); trio, fl. vn. and vla. (1921); str. 4tet (1920); songs; pf. pieces.—P. V.

ROSENBLOOM, Sydney. British compr. and pianist, *b.* Edinburgh, 25 June, 1889. Came to London in 1897; stud. under Charles F. Reddie, 1901; entered Blackheath Cons. with scholarship in 1902, gaining Erard Gold Medal whilst there; entered R.A.M. 1904 with Erard Centenary Scholarship, and while there, studying under Charles F. Reddie (pf.) and Frederic Corder (compn.), gained Annual awards, Heathcote

Long Prize, R.A.M. Club Prize, Macfarren Gold Medal, and Sterndale Bennett Scholarship (compn. and pf.); sub-prof. there 1907–10. First works publ. by Chappell in 1910, and first recital given the same year at Æolian Hall. First appearance as soloist, Chappell Ballad Concerts 1911, and Promenade Concerts at Queen's Hall 1913; has played at Manchester and Liverpool (with Dr. Brodsky), Birmingham, and with orch. at Bournemouth, Eastbourne, Buxton, Harrogate, etc. Prof. Blackheath Cons. 1911–16. Military service, France and Belgium, 1916–19. First concert of own compns. May 1919, Wigmore Hall (assisted by Moiseiwitsch, Daisy Kennedy, and Herbert Heyner); went to South Africa in 1920; appointed prof. Harrison Cons. of Music, Johannesburg, March 1921; 1922–4, 3rd complete tour of the Union.

Suite for 2 vns. and str. orch. op. 18 (1st perf. 21 Nov. 1922, Johannesburg Town Hall, by Durban Orch. under Lyell-Taylor); Variations and fugue for 2 pfs. op. 16 (Augener); vn. and pf. pieces (Chappell; Augener; Bosworth); pf. pieces (Augener; Ricordi; Rogers; Bosworth; Chappell); songs (W. Rogers). —E.H.

ROSENFELD, Leopold. Danish compr. *b.* Copenhagen, 21 July, 1850; *d.* there, 19 July, 1909. A talented and prolific song-compr., and a popular singing-teacher in Copenhagen. His 30-odd light. groups of songs are instinct with feeling, character and culture. They are closely allied to the Ger. Romantic school. In larger forms there are: *Henrik og Else* (*Henry and Elsie*), soli, chorus, orch. (text by Danish poet Christian Winther). He publ. a treatise *Om Textsang* (*Text-Singing*), 1887; ed. the *Uge-skrift for Teater og Musik* (*Theatrical and Musical Weekly*), 1881; was a prominent mus. critic on Copenhagen Press. Founded Dansk Koncert-forening, Copenhagen, a mus. association devoted exclusively to performing older and newer works of Danish composers.—A. H.

ROSENSTOCK, Józef. Polish pianist, compr. *b.* Cracow, 1895. Pupil of Lalewicz (pf.) and Jachimecki (theory), then of Schreker in Vienna at State Acad. of Music. Numerous concerts as pianist and condr. 1917–20. Became prof. of pf. and theory at Akademische Hochschule für Musik in Charlottenburg (Berlin) in 1920. Condr. at Stuttgart Opera, 1921.

Fugue for 2 pfs.; Variations on Chopin's Prelude in C mi.; sonata in D mi. for pf.; concerto, pf. and orch.; *Lustige Ouvertüre* (played 1922 in Berlin); several songs.—ZD. J.

ROSENTHAL, Maurycy (Moritz). Polish pianist; *b.* Lemberg (Galicia), 18 Dec. 1862. Pupil of Karol Mikuli in Lemberg, Joseffy in Vienna, Liszt in Weimar (1877). His playing always evokes the highest admiration on account of his incomparable technique and deep expression. One of the greatest potentates of the keyboard. Lives in Vienna.—ZD. J.

ROSING, Vladimir. Russ. t. singer; *b.* Petrograd, 23 Jan. (n.s.) 1890. Stud. under Marie Rosing, Sir George Power, Jean de Reszke, Kartgeva and Sbriglia; stud. for the Bar; married (1909) Marie Falle in London; 1912, leading t. Art-Opera, Petrograd, *début* (Lensky in *Onegin*) Dec. 1912; 1st appearance in London,

May 1913, in Albert Hall; 1913–14, Russia and Switzerland; Imperial Opera, Vienna, June 1914; settled in England in 1915, and gave an opera-season in London Opera House; created, in London, Herman in Tchaikovsky's *Queen of Spades*; in 1916 commenced his series of famous song-recitals in London, and repeated them yearly till 1921; toured Great Britain, March 1921; gave his 100th London recital, at Albert Hall; 1st Paris recital, 2 May, 1921; autumn, 1921, England, Belgium, Paris; 15 Nov. 1921, 1st recital in Madrid; 1922, Amer. tour; 1923, head of opera school at Eastman School of Music, Rochester, U.S.A. R. exercises the same magnetic force on his audiences as Nikisch did on his orch. players. He is at his very best in character songs. He was the first to reveal the full beauty, power and wide range of the Russ. art-songs, and one of the first to reveal the art of programme-making *per se.*—E.-H.

ROSLAVETS, Nicolai Andréivitch (*accent 1st syll.*). Russ. compr. *b.* Surai (govt. of Chernigof), 24 Dec. 1880/5 Jan. 1881. Son of a Russ. peasant; pupil of Hjimaly (vn.), Ilinsky and Vassilenko (theory) at Moscow Cons., finishing with a silver medal for his dramatic cantata *Heaven and Earth* (after Byron). One of representatives of the "extreme left" group of Russian composers.

Symphony (1922); symph. poems: *The Man and the Sea* (1921) after Baudelaire; *On the Earth's Death* (Paul Lafargue); 5tet for harp, ob. 2 vlas. cello; 5 str. 4tets; 2 pf. trios; 5 vn. sonatas; 2 cello sonatas (1921; 1922); 2 pf. sonatas; many songs. Some of them are publ. by compr. himself.—V. B.

ROSS, Hugh Cuthbert Melville. Eng. condr. orgt. *b.* Langport, Somerset, 21 Aug. 1898. Educated at Clifton Coll.; R.C.M., and New Coll. Oxon.; President of Oxford Univ. Mus. Club. 1921. Went to Canada in 1921 as condr. of Winnipeg Male Choir and orgt. Holy Trinity Church. As choral condr. he has achieved remarkable success. In 1922, founded the Winnipeg Philh. (mixed chorus) which eminent English musicians have acclaimed as among the finest of its kind. The choir has toured in Eastern Canada and U.S.A. See art. *A Trip to the Canadian Festivals*, by H. Plunket Greene in *Music and Letters*, Oct. 1923.—L. S.

ROSSOMANDI, Florestano. Ital. pianist and compr. *b.* Bovino (Foggia), 22 Aug. 1867. Since 1889, prof. of pf. at the R. Cons. di San Pietro a Maiella, Naples; has brought out some brilliant pupils. Was pupil of same Cons. for pf. (Cesi school), compn. (Serrao school). Condr. also, at important concerts in Naples. He founded, and dir. for nearly 20 years, the Associazione Scuola Rossomandi, instituted to train young people for public perf. Compr. of much pf. music (Naples, Izzo).—D. A.

ROTERS, Ernst. Ger. compr. *b.* Oldenburg, 6 July, 1892. Pupil of Georg Schumann (compn.), Meyer-Mahr (pf.); 1914–15, cond. training and seminary classes of West Prussian Cons. Dantzig. Condr. Hamburg Chamber-Plays (*Kammerspiele*).

3 *Capricci* for pf. op. 1; 6 songs, op. 2; symph.

suite, pf. and orch. op. 3; 6 variations and fugue on Breton theme for pf. op. 4 (Berlin, Simrock); *Nachtstück*, str. 4tet, op. 5 (Simrock); *Symph. Dance-Rhapsody* for full orch. op. 6; *Rhapsody*, vn. cello and pf. op. 7 (Simrock); Prelude and fugue, str. orch. op. 8; chamber-symphony, small orch. op 9; 4 songs, v. and pf. op. 10; *Legende*, full orch. op. 11; choral variations and fugue, op. 12 (Zierfuss, Nuremberg); music to *Der glückselige Meergarten* (*The Happy Sea-garden*) (R. Walter); music to *Ein Sommernachtstraum*, op. 14; 3 songs, op. 15; 5 songs, op. 16; pf. suite, op. 17; *An Oratorio* (from Bible); symphony, soli, chorus, orch. op. 18.—A. E.

ROTH, Bertrand. Ger. pianist; *b.* Degersheim (St. Gallen), 12 Feb. 1855. 1875–7, stud. at Leipzig Cons. (pf. Wenzel, Jadassohn, Reinecke); student of philosophy; 1877–80, pupil of Liszt; 1880–4, pf. teacher Hoch's Cons. Frankfort-o-M.; 1882, establ. there (with Schwarz and Fleisch) the Raff Cons.; 1884, teacher at Dresden Cons. Among pupils are Percy Sherwood, Emil Kronke, Karl Pratzsch, Joh. Thamm. Comp. pf. pieces (op. 20, Variations on own theme); songs (op. 16–19).—A. E.

ROTH, Herman. Ger. musicologist and publ. *b.* Hornberg, Baden, 15 Feb. 1882. Stud. philology and philosophy; 1902–3, pupil of Wolfrum, Heidelberg; 1905, pupil of Riemann, Leipzig; 1907–10, concert critic, Leipzig; 1910–1921, Munich; 1921, teacher at Carlsruhe, at Baden Conservatoire.

Publ. (with pf. extracts) Bach's Works (*Magnificat*, 10 cantatas, 25 songs from Schemelli's *Book of Songs*, Hymns from *Small Hymn-book* of Anna Magdalena Bach; *Choralgesängen* and *Capriccios*); 30 songs (Ger. arias) of Handel (Munich, 1920); 30 sacred songs of Ph. Em. Bach. Wrote *Heinrich Kaspar Schmid* (Munich, 1921).—A. E.

ROTHSTEIN, James. Ger. compr. *b.* Königsberg, Prussia, 23 Nov. 1871. Stud. under Leimer and K. Berneker; 1893, under Bargiel and Bruch at Academical Meisterschule, Berlin.

Choral works (*The Grave in Busento*, with orch.); chamber-music; songs: about 200 hymns, pieces for pf. and cello; double vn. and cello concerto; lyric-parody opera, *Ariadne auf Naxos* (1903); 1-act mus. comedy; *Jasmine*, 3-act light national opera, *Die Zarenbraut* (*Czar's Bride*).—A. E.

ROTTENBERG, Ludwig. Condr. and compr. *b.* Czernowitz (Bukowina), 11 Oct. 1864. Pupil of Hrimaly; of Robert Fuchs, Mandyczewski, Vienna; concert-acc. of G. Walter, H. Spies and A. Barbi; 1888, condr. of Orch. Union of Soc. of Friends of Music, Vienna; 1891–22, 1st condr. of Stadttheater, Brünn (Brno); engaged for Opera House, Frankfort-o-M.; paid special attention to modern style (notably Schreker).

Publ. a coll. of 30 songs (1914); opera, *Die Geschwister* (*Brother and Sister*), after Goethe (Frankfort-o-M. 1916); pf. and vn. sonata, 1919.—A. E.

ROUARD, Édouard. Fr. operatic barit. *b.* Nice, 22 Nov. 1876. Stud. at Marseilles under Boudouresque (b. of Opéra, Paris). *Début* at Opéra, Nice, 1900. Appeared at Opera Houses, Lyons (1903), Liège (1904–5), Geneva (1906–7), and returned to Nice (1910–11). For 3 years at La Monnaie, Brussels, where he sang in *Parsifal*, and *Les Joyaux de la Madone* (Wolf-Ferrari). Returned to France at outbreak of war and was mobilised until 1919. In 1920, *début* at Opéra, Paris in *La Légende de St. Christophe*; sang in *La Mégère apprivoisée*, 1921; *Antar*, *Hérodiade*, 1922; *La Fille de Roland*, 1922. Possesses a beautiful voice of clear timbre and good range, capable of *nuances* and skilfully used.—A. R.

ROUSSEAU, Samuel. Fr. compr. *b.* Neuvemaison, 11 June, 1853; *d.* Paris, 1 Oct. 1904. Pupil at Cons. of César Franck; *Prix de Rome,* 1878; precentor at Ste.-Clotilde; gained *Prix de la Ville de Paris* for opera *Merowig* (1891). His style recalls at the same time Gounod and Lalo, with more elegance and correctness than depth. A prolific compr. Has been music critic of *L'Éclair.*

Pf. pieces; chamber-music; songs; *Messe de Pâques; Messe de Noël; Requiem;* a *Libera;* motets; pieces for organ; for harmonium; operas: *La Cloche du Rhin* (1898); *Milia* (1904); *Leone* (1910).—A. C.

ROUSSEL, Albert. French composer; *b.* Tourcoing, 1869. Began to devote himself to music at 25. Was formerly a naval officer, and came to recognise his true vocation during lengthy cruises under Eastern skies. From them he brought back, like Baudelaire, a passion for the sea and sunlit lands, which pervades all his music. He learnt composition and harmony under Eugène Gigout, and followed the courses of V. d'Indy at the *Schola Cantorum.* His individuality is extraordinarily marked; he can scarcely be placed in any school. He is as original as Paul Dukas; yet contradictory influences (Debussy and d'Indy) helped to form him. There is a tendency to overlaud the sensuous charm and refined elegance of his ballet, *Le Festin de l'Araignée (Feast of the Spider)* (1912), and the charming *Rustiques* and *Jardin Mouillé.* The real Roussel is not to be found in these, or at least only one aspect of his genius, and that not the most important. Neither does he reveal himself in the violin sonata in D minor (1903; dedicated to d'Indy), showing signs of scholastic restrictions usually foreign to him; but he springs into full being in the marvellous *Divertissement* (piano and wind-instruments, 1906), which by the hardness of its harmony already foreshadows Stravinsky's *Sacre du Printemps;* especially does he reveal himself in the *Évocations* (chorus and orchestra, 1919), in the prelude *Pour une Fête de Printemps* (1921), and in the symphony in G minor, 1922.

Roussel is a poet. He seizes the multiple and mysterious echoes which nature evokes in the human soul and clothes them in the magic of music. His *Poème de la Forêt* is redolent with the scent of trees; his *Évocations* are a mirage in which one espies cities of the Far East, crimsoning beneath a sky of gold. His temperament is sincere, virile, sometimes harsh, but never ascetic; on the contrary, it is distinctly sensuous. But it is a straightforward sensuousness that is robust and healthy. He loves beauty of line, harmony of rhythm, life and teeming nature, and the fauns whose woodland gambols he was so apt in portraying. His whole work is impregnated with pantheism. Unlike Ravel, Roussel does not consider music as an end in itself. He looks upon it merely as a means of expression; but he has within him some secret force, some passionate

ardour, which sometimes bursts violently forth. The symphony in G minor is a vast symphonic fresco whose final scene gives one the impression of a mob in full rebellion; the music is of such power and audacity that it disconcerted many of the composer's friends, but finally won their applause as a true masterpiece. The Paris Opéra, in May, 1923, performed his *Padmavati,* an opera-ballet on an Indian subject (poem by Louis Laloy). It was finished five years before, and contains passages of arresting grandeur.

Roussel has always employed a contrapuntal technique of very original style; for some years he has worked unrestricted by any scruple for tonal construction. This evolution took place unconsciously, and Roussel appears in some respects to be intuitive, like Berlioz and Debussy, creating novelties by seeking a sincere expression, without the slightest premeditated effort to create novelties. His works are published by Durand.

Consult Roland-Manuel, *A. R.* (*Revue Musicale,* Nov. 1922); André Cœuroy (*q.v.*)—H. P.

ROWLEY, Alec. Eng. compr. and orgt. *b.* Shepherd's Bush, London, 13 March, 1892. Stud. at R.A.M. under F. Corder, Dr. H. W. Richards, Herbert Lake. His compns. are of a romantic order, and he has written much for children.

Pf. music (W. Rogers; Swan; Ashdown; J. Williams); organ (Ashdown, Paxton, Novello); vn. (Ashdown); cantatas, vocal works (Novello; Arnold; Rogers).—E.-H.

ROYAL ACADEMY OF MUSIC, London. Founded 12 July, 1822, by Lord Burghersh (afterwards Earl of Westmorland) and a party of aristocratic amateurs of music. An imposing array of directors and patrons was drawn up, with the king at their head. Premises were taken at 4 Tenterden St., Hanover Square, and work commenced, on a very modest scale, in March 1823. Dr. W. Crotch was nominated " Principal Professor," but had little share, if any, in the direction of the school. Artistic results were quickly obtained, but pecuniary support was not forthcoming from the outside for upwards of 40 years, in spite of a Royal Charter, conferred in 1830. Dr. Crotch was succeeded in 1832 by Cipriani Potter, who held office till death of the earl in 1859. In 1853 the boarding and internal residence of students was discontinued; in 1865 a Government grant of £500 per annum was obtained, and after some time made permanent. Charles Lucas succeeded Potter as Principal and was followed, in 1866, by William Sterndale Bennett. In 1868, on withdrawal of the grant, endeavours were made to wind up the School; but this was found to be a practical impossibility. Under the management of the professors the crisis was surmounted and the fortunes of the Acad. gradually improved. Bennett died in 1875, and was succeeded by G.A. Macfarren. In 1876, it was found necessary to enlarge and re-model the premises, a proper concert-room being added. The studentship was then 300 and the numbers steadily increased, being about 500 from 1896 till end of lease in 1911. In 1888 Alexander C. Mackenzie became

Principal. By this time the Acad. comprised 6 houses more or less adjacent and was wholly unsuited to the needs of a modern school. A site in the Marylebone Road was secured and the present handsome building erected, with every regard to requirements. After the necessary set-back of the war, the studentship sprang to 730, this being the limit of its accommodation. The Acad. possesses now an elaborate system of examinations, as well as a scheme of systematic training for would-be teachers of any mus. subject. Upwards of 70 scholarships and exhibitions are in operation and 65 special prizes for students. All branches of music, as well as elocution, drama and kindred arts are taught in this inst., which in 1922 celebrated the centenary of its foundation with great pomp. Sir Alexander Mackenzie retired from the directorship in 1924 and was succeeded by John McEwen.—F. C.

ROYAL COLLEGE OF MUSIC. Had its beginning in the National Training School for Music, founded in 1873, on a site near the Albert Hall, South Kensington (now occupied by the Royal College of Organists). Opened at Easter 1876. First Principal, Sir Arthur Sullivan. 82 free 5-year scholarships of £40 a year each, obtained by competitive examination. In 1882, this institution was taken over by the Royal College of Music, and formally opened by the Prince of Wales, 7 May, 1883. Principals: Sir George Grove from 1882; Sir Hubert Parry from 1894; Sir Hugh Allen from 1918. Its first professors were Parry, Parratt, Stanford, Pauer, Franklin-Taylor, Arabella Goddard, Jenny Lind(-Goldschmidt). In 1924 the staff numbered 36 teachers of singing, 18 pf., 4 organ, 6 vn., 1 cello, 6 compn., 12 harmony, classes in conducting, choir-training, dictation, opera and musical appreciation. A Patron's Fund (£27,000) was instituted by Sir Ernest Palmer in 1903, for the encouragement of composition by the younger British composers. Rehearsals and performances of their works are held in connection with this fund, and are open to the public. The College bestows Associateship (A.R.C.M.) by examination (open to students and non-students), and gives Fellowship h.c. In 1889 it joined the R.A.M. in forming the Associated Board, which examines locally all over the British Empire.—E.-H.

ROYAL COLLEGE OF ORGANISTS. The representative institution of the organist's profession; consists of Fellows, Associates and members, all of whom are either actively engaged in, or interested in the work of the orgt. The chief work has been the holding of examinations by means of which orgts. may qualify for diplomas of Associateship and Fellowship. The first step towards the formation of the Coll. was taken by R. D. Limpus, orgt. of St. Michael's Ch. Cornhill, in 1863, but the definite founding of it dates from 12 March, 1864. Limpus was elected the first hon. sec.; on his death in 1875 he was succeeded by Edmund Hart Turpin, who held office until 1907. During Dr. Turpin's secretary-

ship the Coll. made great strides. The most eminent orgts. have been and are members of the council and also of the examining boards. For many years the high value of the diplomas has been recognised all over the English-speaking world. A Royal Charter was granted in 1893. The Coll. was formerly situated in Hart Street, Bloomsbury, but in 1904 the Commissioners of the 1851 Exhibition granted the use of the fine building which it now occupies at Kensington Gore. On the death of Dr. Turpin, Dr. J. F. Sawyer became the hon. sec., but he only lived to hold the office for a few months when he was succeeded by Dr. H. A. Harding, the present hon. secretary.—F. G. S.

ROYAL DUBLIN SOCIETY. Since 1886 this society's recitals have been the most consistent effort made to educate the Dublin public in serious music. In 1866 when the art school, which the Soc. had maintained for over 130 years, had been transferred to the Government, the council decided that their energies should be directed towards encouraging serious music. Weekly recitals of the best chamber-music were held, in order that music might be systematically brought before the public as effectively as painting and sculpture in the galleries. The co-operation of the Instrumental Music Club of Dublin was obtained. In the early years the recitals were entrusted to the same musicians engaged for a whole season. It was thus possible for the public to hear the same trio or quartet perform a complete set of chamber-music works. Another feature was the practice of giving gratuitously to the audience programmes annotated by musicians such as Sir Robert Stewart or Dr. Prout. This custom has disappeared. In 1900 the Soc. began to engage more famous trios and quartets from England and the Continent as well as the best local talent, in the Soc.'s theatre (built 1896) which has conditions well-nigh ideal for ensemble music. The hall has an organ constructed by Messrs. Henry Willis.—W. St.

ROYAL OPERA HOUSE, Covent Garden, London. The modern musical history of Covent Garden Theatre, if it be extended backwards for a period of 40 years, takes us to the time when Mr. Ernest Gye was in control for a brief space. Albani and Patti were the bright particular stars, the former still in her zenith, the latter already on the wane. It has been called, by a well-known writer, the period of the decline and fall of Italian opera in London. For another year or two things were just kept going by the joint efforts of Mapleson and Signor Lago. The latter impresario gave distinction to a brief season in 1887 by producing Glinka's *La Vie pour le Czar*. In 1888, however, a new and glorious era began, with the management of Augustus Harris, and the powerful influence of many distinguished persons in Society, headed by the Prince and Princess of Wales (afterwards King Edward and Queen Alexandra). A remarkable company of star artists, new to London, was engaged, notably the Polish tenor Jean de Reszke and Melba. In 1889

Gounod's *Romeo and Juliet* was produced in French with a superb cast. In July *The Mastersingers* was performed by a company of many mixed nationalities, in Italian! In 1890 most of the great nights were reserved for opera performed in French, even *Favorita*, and the Ravogli sisters made their *début* in *Orfeo*. In 1891, during a season of 16 weeks, 20 different operas were heard, and £80,000 taken in receipts. 1892 saw the great Bayreuth artists, Alvary and Rosa Sucher, as Siegfried and Brünnhilde. In 1893, Mascagni and Leoncavallo were first given a hearing, and we are cheered to find the name of a British composer, Sir Charles Stanford, attached to the production of an opera, *The Veiled Prophet*, though even that was produced in Italian. In 1894, several new productions were heard, by Bruneau, Massenet, Cowen, Puccini and the veteran Verdi whose amazingly fine opera, *Falstaff*, showed no weakening of his genius. In 1896 the theatre suffered a heavy loss by the sudden death of Harris, who had worn his life to a thread in its service. The following year the lease was granted to the Royal Opera Syndicate, who were content to follow a safe policy of presenting familiar works by artists of high repute, year by year. 1900–1 saw a greatly needed reconstruction of the stage and yet another season of well-tried productions. In 1902, it may be noted, Mary Garden made a highly successful *début* as Manon, and among English composers, Herbert Bunning's *Princess Osra* and Ethel Smyth's *Der Wald* were heard. During these seasons, 1903 and onwards, the genius of Hans Richter dominated the great performances of the *Ring* at Covent Garden. In 1904 Ternina and Destinn were prominent and Saint-Saëns visited the theatre to witness his new opera *Hélène*. 1905 is memorable as the year which first witnessed the never-to-be-forgotten Pinkerton of Caruso. In 1906 Tchaikovsky's *Eugene Onegin* was sung in Italian and Gluck's *Armide* was added to the repertoire. The 1907 autumn season introduced Tetrazzini to London as Lucia di Lammermoor, but nothing else noteworthy occurred until 1909 when *Samson and Delilah*, *Pelléas et Mélisande* and *Louise* were first produced. 1910 saw Richter absent from the opera and the first advent of Thomas Beecham with an ambitious programme of novelties including the much-discussed *Salome* of Strauss. 1911 saw the Russian Ballet engaged in addition to the opera company, and a first presentation in England of *The Girl of the Golden West* and Massenet's *Thaïs*. 1912 lacked any special interest, but 1913 brought Nikisch to conduct German opera, and the return of Caruso after 6 years' absence. During the war years, Covent Garden Theatre was destitute of opera, and was utilised by the Government as a furniture store. In March 1919, it was released from war service and the B.N.O.C. became responsible for the performances there. In 1924, the R. Opera Synd. resumed its international policy.—H. S. W.

ROYER, Étienne. Fr. compr. *b.* Paris, 1880. Pupil of *Schola Cantorum*; is (with André

George) music critic of the Catholic review *Les Lettres*. His compns., confined almost entirely to chamber-music, are of lofty inspiration. In his poems for str. 4tet on the *Seasons* (*Pour le temps de la Maison*; *Pour les Fêtes de Mai*) he uses Fr. folk-song motives.—A. C.

ROZKOŠNÝ, Josef Richard. Czechoslovak compr. *b.* Prague, 1833; *d.* 1913. Stud. music privately; lived in Prague as bank clerk. His music is eclectic, first a copy of the Romanticists, later of Smetana, and then even of the Verists; not deep, but cleverly constructed and theatrical. Operas: *Svatojánské proudy* (1871); *Popelka* (*Cinderella*), 1885; *Stoja* (1894); *Satanella* (1898); *Černé jezero* (*The Black Sea*), 1906; brilliant pf. pieces; songs.—V. ST.

RÓZSA, Ludwig. Hungarian operatic singer (b.); *b.* 1877; *d.* Detroit, Jan. 1923. Member of R. Hungarian Opera House until 1920.—B. B.

RÓŻYCKI, Ludomir (*phon.* Roojytski). Polish composer; *b.* Warsaw, 1884. Studied first with his father, Alexander Różycki. In 1903, finished at Warsaw Conservatoire with gold medal, as pupil of Noskowski; 1904–8, studied under Humperdinck in Berlin; 1908–12, was professor at Lemberg Conservatoire. Then lived in Berlin till 1919. Since 1920, has remained in Warsaw. Różycki's appearance as composer (in 1904) together with Szymanowski, Szeluta and Fitelberg began the period of the new school known as Young Musical Poland. In his first works his vigorous talent was revealed, especially in the field of symphonic music and opera. His power is particularly shown in his characteristic themes and great variety of instrumental colour. Operas: *Boleslas the Bold* (libretto by Al. Bandrowski; Lemberg, 1909); *Medusa* (libretto by C. Jellenta, on a tale from life of Leonardo da Vinci); *Eros and Psyche* (libretto after drama of George Zulawski); *Casanova* (libretto by Krzeminski). Symph. poems: *Stanczyk*; *Anhelli* (1908, after Stowacki); *Boleslas the Bold* (1909); *Pan Twardowski*; *Mona Lisa*; *Warszawianka*; *King Cophetua*. Pf. concerto, op. 43; pf. 5tet, op. 35. Numerous pf. pieces; chamber works; about 40 songs. R. is now working on his 5th opera, *Beatrix Cenci* (libretto founded on the tragedies by Shelley and Stowacki).—ZD. J.

RUBENS, Paul A. Eng. operetta compr. and librettist; *b.* 1876; *d.* Falmouth, Feb. 1917. Trained for law; contributed songs to *Floradora* (Lyric, 1899); comp. parts of *Great Cæsar* (1900), of *A Country Girl* (1903); sole compr. of *Lady Madcap* (1904); *Miss Hook of Holland* (1907); *My Mimosa Maid* (1908); *The Balkan Princess* (1910); *The Sunshine Girl* (1912), etc.—E.-H.

RUBINSTEIN, Arthur. Polish pianist; *b.* Łódź, 1886. When a child, was pupil of R. M. Breithaupt in Berlin; then was self-taught to a large extent. One of the most celebrated pianists of our time. Has made extensive tours in Europe and America. Is particularly fine in contemporary music.—ZD. J.

RUBINSTEIN, Erna. Hungarian violinist; *b.* Nagyszeben, Hungary (now annexed by Rumania), 2 March, 1903. Stud. under Hubay at R. High School for Music, Budapest.—B. B.

RUBIO, Agustín. Span. cellist; *b.* in Murcia, 17 Feb. 1856. Stud. at Real Cons. de Música,

Madrid, under Castellanos and Miresky; later, at Hoch's Cons. Berlin, under Haussmann, chamber-music under Joachim. With Tragó and Arbós he toured Spain, the Balearic Islands and Portugal in a series of chamber-music concerts, at which works of Schumann, Schubert and other classics were first perf. in the country. Similar tours with Albeniz; also in Germany with Vianna da Motta. In 1895, first appeared in London, touring England and Ireland several times. Was supported in his youth by King Alfonso XII at recommendation of Joachim and Sarasate. Holds several Span. and Portuguese decorations. Lives in London.

Concerto in D mi.; pieces for 2 cellos, etc. (Simrock, Ries, Berlin; Giraud, Paris; Stanley Lucas, London). —P. G. M.

RÜCKAUF, Anton. Pianist and compr. *b.* Prague, 13 March, 1855; *d.* Schloss Alt-Erlaa, 19 Sept. 1903. Pupil of Proksch, and Prague Organ School; teacher at Proksch's Inst.; State Scholarship for further studies at Vienna, Nottebohm and Navrátil (cpt.) Friend of lyric-singer Gustav Walter, who influenced his song-writing.

Songs, op. 1, 2, 3, 6 (ballads), 9, 12 (5 love-songs of Walter von der Vogelweide), 14, 15, 16, 17 (Gipsy songs) 18; duets, op. 11; choral songs with pf. op. 8 (Russ. folk-poetry); vn. sonata, op. 7; pf. 5tet, F ma. op. 13; pf. pieces, op. 10 and op. 4 (preludes and dance-tunes, pf. duet); opera, *Die Rosenthalerin* (Dresden, 1897).—A. E.

RÜDINGER, Gottfried. Ger. compr. *b.* Lindau (Bavaria), 23 Aug. 1886. Pupil of Music School, Lindau; stud. philosophy and theology at Lyceum, Eichstätt, and Munich Univ.; 1907, turned to music; till July 1909, stud. under Max Reger (compn.), Leipzig Cons.; since 1916, at Berg-on-Laim, near Munich, as condr. Palestrina Soc. (*a cappella*).

Fairy Hours, 8 pf. pieces, op. 1; 3 poems from Martin Greif, 4-v. mixed chorus, op. 2; *Aus der Dachstube*, pieces for 2 vns. op. 3; 6 epigrams of Angelus Silesius, v. and pf. op. 5; 5 epigrams, 4-v. female chorus, op. 6; *Heimliche Idyllen*, pf. and vn. op. 7; 6 short pieces, pf. and cello, op. 8; *Romantic Serenade*, str. orch. op. 9 (Essen, 1914); 7 easy pieces, pf. duet, op. 10; symphony, cello and orch. op. 11; pf. sonatas, op. 12 and 28; *Martial Tunes*, op. 13; *Heldentotenlieder* (*Heroic Death-Songs*, low v. op. 16; *Spätblatt* (song-cycle), op. 30; *Truderinger Kirchweih*, pf. op. 39; *Haidl-Bubaidl* (nursery folk-song for children's chorus); 11 national songs, 2-v. children's chorus; *Puck*, for pf. op. 38, ms.: *Kriegslieder* (war-songs), 4-v. female chorus, op. 15 ; vn. concerto; Mass, s. contr. barit. and organ, op. 32. (Publ. Tischer & Jagenberg.)—A. E.

RUDNICKI, Marjan T. Polish condr. compr. *b.* Cracow, 1888. 1916, condr. of the Operetta Theatre in Cracow; 1919, passed to Warsaw State Opera. Has written many delightful songs, choral works, pf. pieces, and several orch. suites for film-dramas and theatrical pieces, such as *Antony and Cleopatra*, *The Return of Ulysses* and *Caligula* (Karol Rostworowski).—Zd. J.

RUDORFF, Ernst. Ger. compr. *b.* Berlin, 18 Jan. 1840; *d.* there, 31 Dec. 1916. 1852–7, pupil of Bargiel (pf.), then Leipzig Cons. (Moscheles, Plaidy, Rietz), then Moritz Hauptmann (compn.) and Karl Reinecke (pf.); 1865, teacher Cologne Cons.; 1869–1910, dir. of pf. at R. High School, Berlin; 1880, successor to Max Bruch as condr. Stern's Choral Union (till 1890).

Orch works: 3 symphonies (op. 31, B flat ma.; op. 40, G mi.; op. 50, B mi.); 3 overtures (to Tieck's *Märchen vom blonden Ekbert*, op. 8, to *Otto der Schütz*, op. 12, and *Romantic Overture*, op. 45); *Ballad*, op. 15; 2 serenades (op. 20, A ma., and op. 21, G ma.); Variations; choral works with orch.: *Hymn to the Stars*; *Autumn Song*, op. 43 (6-v. chorus); choral songs; pf. pieces (Variations, op. 55, duets, op. 54); songs, etc. Publ. *Letters of C. M. v. Weber to Heinrich Lichtenstein* (1900); rev. Mozart concertos and sonatas; interested in Brahms-Chopin ed.; 1866, ed. Weber's *Euryanthe* for full score. W. Altmann ed. (1907) Rudorff's *Exchange of Letters with Brahms*. His exchange of letters with Joachim publ. in 3 vols., *Letters from and to Joseph Joachim* (1912).—A. E.

RUE, A. Span. musician of the Catalonian group. Active in restoring Gregorian chant in Spain. Author of *Cooperació a la Editió Vaticana dels Llibres de Cant Liturgich* (a study of Vatican ed. of liturgical song), 1904–5 (publ. in the *Revista Catalana*).—P. G. M.

RÜFER, Philippe Bartholomé. Ger. pianist and compr. *b.* Liège, 7 June, 1844; *d.* Berlin, 5 Sept. 1919. Son of Philipp R. (orgt. *b.* Rumpenheim, Hessen, 3 May, 1810; *d.* Liège, 30 Jan. 1891); stud. at Liège Cons.; 1867, chief condr. at Essen; 1871, in Berlin; 1871–2, pf. teacher at Stern's Cons.; later at Kullak's Cons. (till 1875); from Oct. 1881, teacher of pf. and score-reading Stern's Cons. Member of senate of Berlin R. Academy.

Symphony (F ma. op. 23); 3 overtures; orch. *Scherzo*, G mi. op. 28; str. 4tets (op. 20 and 31, E flat); vn. sonata, op. 1; trio; 2 suites for pf. and cello (op. 8, 13); organ sonata (op. 16); songs; pf. pieces, etc. Operas: *Merlin* (Berlin, 1887); *Ingo* (Berlin, 1896).—A. E.

RUFFO, Titta. See TITTA.

RUHLMANN, Frans. Belgian conductor; *b.* Brussels, 11 Jan. 1868. Stud. at Brussels Cons. where he worked at ob. under Plétinckx and Guidé, and harmony under Dupont. For 7 years member of orch. of Théâtre de la Monnaie, Brussels, as oboe. *Début* as condr. in Rouen; then Liège, Antwerp, Brussels (La Monnaie), and Antwerp again. 1905–14, cond. at Opéra-Comique, Paris; 1914–20, at Opéra; 1920–1, at La Monnaie, Brussels; from 1922 at Opéra-Comique, Paris. Since 1920 Ruhlmann has also been the greatly appreciated condr. of the Popular Concerts in Brussels.—E. C.

RUMANIAN FOLK-MUSIC. A scientific collection of this material has been confined almost entirely to those Rumanian provinces which formerly belonged to Hungary, *i.e.* Transylvania and neighbouring parts. From 1909 to 1917 the folk-music of these regions has been assiduously collected, whereas the former kingdom of Rumania is all but *terra incognita* in this respect. The collection of Béla Bartók (*q.v.*) contains about 3500 phonographed melodies which have been put into mus. notation. Some of these records are in the possession of the Ethnographical Department of the National Museum, Budapest; others are in private hands. Out of the collected material the following have been published: Bartók, *Chansons populaires roumaines du département Bihar (Hongrie)* (publ. by Academia Română, Bucharest, 1913; contains 371 melodies); *Die Volkmusik der Rumänen von Maramures*, (*Archiv für vergleichende Musik-*

wissenschaft, Vol. IV, Munich, 1923, Drei Masken Verlag; contains about 450 melodies). Material collected in Rumania proper is contained in a book *Hora din Cartal* by Pompiliu Pârvescu (publ. by Academia Română, Bucharest, 1908), which includes 63 dance-melodies.

Rumanian folk-music, especially the vocal melodies, has almost invariably a very ancient character. Apparently, with the exception of Maramureş and neighbouring districts, none of these regions has produced any new melodies for centuries past. The vocal melodies fall into several groups, quite different in character, according to the occasion on which they are sung. The most important are: (*a*) so-called *colind* (Christmas songs); and (*b*) those not sung on special occasions and called *doina* (in many places called *hora*). The first are in strict time and rhythm, and the verses are of 3 or 4 lines, mostly of equal metre. The lines are preponderantly of 8 syllables, sometimes of 6. The scales vary considerably.

The second, or *doina*, melodies fall into 2 subdivisions: (1) those from the district of Maramureş, and (2) those from the other districts of Transylvania. The latter group is the more characteristic for Rumanian territory. Special features of the latter groups include: a *parlando-rubato* style of performance; a verse-form of 3 8-syllable lines; scales in which the 3rd from the final note varies between major and minor,

the long final note of the melody being

the long final note of the second line of the melody generally being

In many districts (*Banat*) the melodies, which are of similar construction, are of 4 lines.

The third important group (*c*) comprises dance-tunes, which are almost exclusively played by instrs. (vn., bagpipes, shepherd's fl., etc.; according to the different districts). For the most part they have no text and therefore cannot be sung. This group is less intact than the two preceeding, and presents types of varied character, which betray a good deal of foreign and modern influence; for instance, in the southern provinces Jugo-Slav influence is predominant.—B. B.

RUMANIAN OPERA. The first operatic performances in Rumania were given by a foreign troupe at Bucharest in 1847; but it was only from 1870 that operas have been given there, season by season, the year 1895 and the period 1910–14 excepted. The companies were generally Ital., rarely Fr. or Ger. They included such stars as Patti, Tetrazzini, Battistini, Tita Ruffo, and the condrs. Mascagni and Leoncavallo. For its part, however, Rumania gave to foreign stages more than one famous singer: Euphrosine Popescovlasta (who created at Milan Meyerbeer's *L'Étoile du Nord*), the tenor Gabrielescu, Hélène Teodorini, Nuovika, Darclée.

Four attempts were made to found a national opera. The honour of the first three efforts belongs to the compr. Stefănescu and the teacher Wachmann (1886, 1893, 1896). The last attempt was made by a committee of students in 1913. State support not being forthcoming, they closed down finally after a maximum of 18 performances for the season.

Finally in 1919 the compr. Nonna Otescu, the condr. Massini and several singers (Mme. Drăgulinescu-Stinghe (s.), Folescu (b.), Vră-biescu (t.), Atanasiu (barit.), Istratty (b.), founded the Lyric Soc. of the Opera, whose activity, patronised by Queen Marie and helped by the State, has been uninterrupted till the present time (1923). Now the State has entire charge of the Soc. and appoints the chief officers. Scarlat Cocorascu was the first gen. dir.; then (1920) G. Georgescu. Otescu, Alfred Alessandrescu and Tango were the first condrs. Apart from Massini, who has resigned, the artistic personnel still remains as at the foundation.—C. N. B.

RUMFORD, R. Kennerley. Eng. barit. singer; *b.* London, 2 Sept. 1870. Stud. in Paris under Sbriglia and Bouhy; later under Henschel, Blume, Lierhammer and Jean de Rezske. Has toured all over the world. Married Clara Butt, the famous contr. song-singer, 1900.—E.-H.

RUMMEL, Walter Morse. Pianist and compr. *b.* Berlin (of British father), 19 July, 1887. On death of his father, he went to America with his mother; but returned to Berlin in 1904 to study compn. under Hugo Kaun and pf. under Godowsky (till 1909). First appeared in 1913 in Paris where he became a close friend of Debussy. Since 1913 he has played in Germany, Holland, Belgium and in London. His readings are distinguished by subtle intuition and a strong creative power. He is also a charming compr. with a delicate, restrained expression.

Poem, vn. and orch.; str. 4tet; *From the Depths*, sonata, vn. and pf.; pf. pieces; about 40 Eng. songs (mostly Augener); has arr. some old Fr. songs of XII and XVIII centuries and transcribed for pf. several Bach pieces.—E.-H.

RUNG, Frederik. Danish compr. and condr. *b.* Copenhagen, 14 June, 1854; *d.* there, 22 Jan. 1914. Son of Henrik Rung (*d.* 1871), also an excellent compr. and founder of Cœciliaforening (Cecilia Soc.) Copenhagen. Frederik's natural talent was thus nurtured under his father's instruction. Later he was a pupil of Niels W. Gade and Hartmann at R. Cons. Already as a youth he began to assist at R. Opera, Copenhagen, where he was regularly engaged later as répétiteur, and from 1884 as 2nd condr. On death of Johan Svendsen he became chief condr., and also (on death of his father) condr. of Cœciliaforening, which produces music from XVI–XIX centuries. Under his dir. the Madrigal Choir (the pick of the Cœciliaforening Choir) gained international fame through its concerts in Paris, Berlin, Leipzig, Hamburg, Stockholm, Gothenburg.

Operas: *Det hemmelige Selskab* (*The Secret Society*), 1888; *Den trekantede Hat* (*The Cocked Hat*), 1894; ballets: *Aditi*; *En Karnevalspög i Venedig* (*A Carnival Jest in Venice*); symphony, D mi. op. 28; Suite for str. and tpt.; nonet for wood-wind; 2 str. 4tets; pf. 5tet on a Danish folk-song; vn. sonata; cantata for Handel Memorial Celebration; pf. pieces; songs (Hansen; Nordisk Musikforlag).—A. H.

RUNNQVIST, Axel C. E. Swedish violinist; *b.* Stockholm, 30 Oct. 1880. Stud. at R. Cons. Stockholm, 1893–8; then under H. Marteau at Cons. of Geneva. Taught there, 1902–4; from 1904, concert-player and teacher in Stockholm, especially in chamber-music (trio-ensemble with Märtha Ohlson [pf.] and Carl Lindhe [cello]); 1911, vn. teacher at Andersson's pf. school. From 1915, prof. of vla. at R. Cons. Stockholm. —P. V.

RUSS CERRI, Giannina. Ital. s. singer; *b.* Lodi (Milan), 1878. Dramatic s. of great renown, known at all the principal theatres of Europe and America. Stud. at R. Cons. of Milan; *début* in 1903, rapidly making her name. Her repertoire is very extensive and varied, and extends from *Norma* and *La Gioconda* to *Rigoletto* and *Le Nozze di Figaro*.—D. A.

RUSSIAN BALLET Seasons in London. See BEECHAM, SIR THOMAS; DIAGHILEF, SERGE.

RUSSIAN FOLK-MUSIC. See BALAKIREF, M.A.; BORODIN, A.P.; CUI, C.A.; KUBA, LUDVÍK; LIAPUNOF, SERGE; LISSENKO, NICOLAS; MUSSORGSKY, M.P.; RIMSKY-KORSAKOF; SCHINDLER, KURT; STRAVINSKY, IGOR.

RUST, Wilhelm. Ger. orgt., teacher and ed. *b.* Dessau, 15 Aug. 1822; *d.* Leipzig, 2 May, 1892. Pupil of his uncle Wilhelm Karl Rust; 1843–6, pupil of Fr. Schneider. Private teacher at house of Hungarian magnate; Hungarian revolt, 1848, caused his return to Dessau; 1849, music-teacher in Berlin; member of Berlin Acad. of Singing; 1850, member of Leipzig Bach Soc.; 1861, orgt. St. Luke's Ch.; 1862, condr. of Berlin Bach Soc.; 1864, R. chief-condr.; 1868, Ph.D. *h.c.*, Marburg; 1870, teacher of theory at Stern's Cons.; 1878, orgt. of St. Thomas' Ch. Leipzig and teacher at Cons.; 1880, Cantor at St. Thomas's School. Has done great service by his publication of J. S. Bach's Works (Bach Soc.), for ten years. Composed sacred choral pieces.—A. E.

RÜTHSTRÖM, Bror Olaf Julius. Swedish violinist; *b.* Sundsvall, 30 Dec. 1877. Stud. under Johan Lindberg at R. Cons. Stockholm, 1894–9; under Willy Burmester, 1900; and (1901–3) at High School for Music, Berlin, as pupil of J. Joachim. Introduced Max Reger's sonatas for vn. alone, op. 42, at his concerts in Germany, Denmark, Norway, Finland and in Sweden (1905–6). Also introduced Swedish works (vn. concerto by Kurt Atterberg) in Berlin, 1917; from 1912, vn. prof. at R. Cons., Stockholm. Condr. (leader) of a well-known str. quartet in Stockholm. Member R.A.M. Stockholm, 1912.

Passagespelets mekanik (*Mechanics of Passage-playing*) (publ. Emil Carelius, 1914); *Strakföringens konst* (*Art of Bowing*) (*id.* 1921).—P. V.

RUTZ, Ottmar. Ger. musicologist; *b.* Fürth, 15 July, 1881. Lawyer; carried out ideas which his father (singer and singing-master, Josef Rutz), first put into practice at Munich and utilised in his teaching profession, viz. the different positions of trunk-muscles in singing, according to typical character of the song.

New Discoveries of Human Voice (Munich, 1911); *Music, Words and Body as Expression of Feeling* (Leipzig, 1911, Breitkopf); *Types of Voice-training, and New Art of Expression for Stage and Concert Platforms* (with his mother Clara Rutz, 1920); *Types of Humanity and Art* (1921).—A. E.

RUYNEMAN, Daniel. Dutch compr. and pianist; *b.* Amsterdam, 8 Aug. 1886. Originally intended for marine service, and went to India; Began his mus. career when 18; principally self-taught; but stud. for short time at Cons. of Amsterdam. His development was influenced by Javanese music and the young Fr. school. In 1918 he took part in founding the Soc. of Modern Dutch Composers—Vereeniging tot Bevordering der Moderne Scheppende Toonkunst (now defunct). R. lives in Groningen.

Hieroglyphs, 3 fls. harp, cup-bells, celesta, pf. 2 mandolines, 2 guitars (London, Chester); symphony for small orch., fl. ob. clar. bsn. saxophone, horn, electrophone, cup-bells, harp, v. 2 mandolines, 2 guitars (in preparation); *L'Appel* (*Le Chant des voyelles*) 8-v. (Chester); sonatina, pf. (*id.*); *Lamentation du Mamelouk*, vn. and pf. (*id.*); *L'Absolu*, for contr. (*id.*); *Tagore Songs*, Dutch words (G. Alsbach); *Chinese Songs*, Dutch words (*id.*). Consult: *Le Monde Nouveau* (Paris, Bérard); Arthur Petronio, *D. R. et son œuvre* (Liège, Créer); *An Introduction to Modern Music* (in Dutch; Amsterdam, Constant van Wessem); *The Musical Journey* (in Dutch; *id.*); *The Chesterian* (London); *Il Pianoforte* (Turin); *Schweizer Musikpädagogische Blätter*.—W. P.

RYBNER, Peter Martin Cornelius. Compr. *b.* Copenhagen, 26 Oct. 1855. Stud. at R. Cons. in Copenhagen under Gade, Hartmann and E. Neupert, winning 1st prize in pf., vn. and compn.; at 18 went to Leipzig, pupil of Reinecke and Ferdinand David. After tours in Europe, settled at Baden-Baden as Court pianist. Subsequently dir. of Cons. at Carlsruhe and assistant to Felix Mottl, whom he succeeded as condr. of Philh. Choral Soc., a position he held for 8 years; 1904, went to America as successor of Edward Mac-Dowell at Columbia Univ. N.Y., resigning (1919) to devote himself to teaching and compn. Has also appeared in America as condr. and concert-pianist (with Boston Symphony Orch. 24 March, 1905). His larger compns. include a fairy ballet in 3 acts, *Prinz Ador* (Carlsruhe, 8 March, 1903), a vn. concerto, G mi. (played by Florian Zajič under compr.'s direction in Berlin, 1903). His daughter, Dagmar de Corval Rybner (*b.* 1890), has comp. and publ. songs (Ditson; Schirmer).

Symph. poem, Friede, Kampf und Sieg (Oertel, 1889); pf. trio, op. 9 (Kahnt); *Fest-Ouverture*, op. 27 (Oertel, 1899); Festival Cantata, op. 32 (Novello); songs and pf. pieces (Schott; Hansen; Kahnt).—J.M.

RYCHNOWSKI, Ernst. German-Czechoslovak writer; *b.* Janowitz, 25 June, 1879. LL.D. 1903, Prague, where he stud. music under Rietsch; 1905, under Tappert in Berlin. Was mus. critic in Prague.

Descriptive Catalogue of Donebauer Collection of Musical and Theatrical Autographs (1900); *Catalogue of Exhibition of Music at Prague* (1906, W. Batka); *The Petschau School of Music* (1902); *Ludwig Spohr* and *Friedrich Rochlitz* (1904); *Joh. Friedrich Kittl* (1904–5); *Leo Blech* (1905); *Joseph Haydn* (1909); *R. Schumann* (1910); *Franz Liszt* (1911); *Smetana* (1924); new ed. of F. Niemetschek's *Biography of Mozart* (1905).—E. S.

RYELANDT, Joseph. Belgian composer; *b.* Bruges, 7 April, 1870. First stud. at Univ. (philosophy); later devoted himself entirely to music, which he stud. under Tinel. Did not study at Cons., nor enter for *Prix de Rome.* He is a compr. of worth, particularly in oratorio. His style is similar to that of Tinel, only more modern.

Opera, *Sainte Cécile* (Antwerp, 1907). Oratorios: *La Parabole des Vierges; Purgatorium; De Komst des Heeren* (*The Coming of the Lord*) (London, Novello); *Maria; Agnus Dei; Christus Rex.* Cantatas: *Le Bon Pasteur: L'Idylle mystique.* Orch.: 4 symphonies; *Gethsemane,* symph. poem; overtures: *Patrie; Jeanne d'Arc.* Church music: Mass, *Ave Maria, Audi Filia* (4-v.); *Les Béatitudes* (3-v. and organ). Chamber-music: 8 pf. sonatas; 5 for vn. and pf.; 4 respectively for vla., clar., horn, ob.—with pf.; 2 sonatas and a nocturne, cello, pf.; 1 5tet and 2 trios, str. and pf.; 4 str. 4tets. Many songs.—E. C.

RYTEL, Piotr. Polish compr., music critic; *b.* Wilna, 1884. Stud. at Warsaw Cons. under Noskowski (theory) and Michałowski (pf.). Appointed prof. at Warsaw State Cons. in 1911. Since 1920, has written music critiques in the *Gazeta Warszawska.* R. occupies an important position among Polish composers.

Opera, *Ijola* (on Żuławski's drama); symphony, A mi.; symph. poems: *Grazyna* (1908, after Mickiewicz); *The Corsair* (1910, after Byron); *Dante's Dream; The Sacred Grove; Legend of St. George* (on traditional life of England's patron saint).—ZD. J.

S

SAAR, Louis Victor. Compr. *b.* Rotterdam, 10 Dec. 1868. Son of a musician who cond. opera at Covent Garden, London, and at Metropolitan, New York. After graduating from Strasburg Gymnasium in 1884, and hearing lectures on literature and history at Univ. of Strasburg, continued study of music at Munich Acad. under Rheinberger, Abell and Bussmeyer from 1886-9. In Vienna he came into contact with Brahms. In 1890-1, stud. in Berlin, winning Mendelssohn Prize in 1891. In 1892, won Tonkünstler Prize in Vienna. In 1894, engaged in New York as coach at Metropolitan Opera House. Music critic of the *Staatszeitung* and of *New York Review*; 1906-17, head of theory department and dir. of chorus at Cincinnati Coll. of Music. Since 1917, head of theory department at Chicago Mus. Coll. His compns. exceed 100. His *Ganymede* for contr. and orch. was brought out by the New York Philh. Soc. 26 Jan. 1900. His *Rococo Suite*, orig. comp. for pf. 4 hands (1898), was arr. for small orch. and played by Barrère Ensemble. Re-orchestrated for large orch. in 1915, it was first perf. by Cincinnati Symphony Soc. 19 March, 1916.

Rococo Suite for small orch. op. 27 (Schirmer, 1899); *Wechselgesang* for 6 vs. with orch. op. 41 (Rieter-Biedermann); 4tet for pf. and str. op. 39 (Siegel, 1904); vn. sonata, op. 44 (Siegel, 1904); male choruses (by above publ. and by Hug; Leuckart; Rohlfing); pf. pieces (Schmidt; Leuckart; Schirmer; Ditson; C. Fischer); songs (Breitkopf; Ries & Erler; Rieter-Biedermann; Simrock).—O. K.

SABANÉIEF, Leonid Leonidovitch (*accent the É*). Russ. compr. and writer on music; *b.* Moscow, 1871. Pupil of S. I. Tanéief at Moscow Cons. (1899); finished a mathematical course at Moscow Univ. 1908, and received degree, Master of Maths. Writer for many Moscow papers and periodicals. Author of a fine book on *Scriabin* (2nd ed. 1922), a short Debussy and a Ravel biography. After Scriabin's death, S. revised (with Rosenof and Goldenweiser) the unpubl. works of Scriabin (still in ms.). Member of Russ. Acad. of Art-Sciences and State Inst. of Mus. Science. As a compr. is much influenced by music of Scriabin, whose follower he is.

Pf. trio; pf. sonata; vn. sonata; pf. pieces, songs, etc.—V. B.

SACHS, Curt. Ger. music research scholar; *b.* Berlin, 29 June, 1881. Stud. pf. and compn. under L. Schrattenholz, clar. under Rausch; under Fleischer (at Univ.), history of music; 1904, graduated Ph.D. at Berlin; spent several years as art historian; then devoted himself to science of music and stud. again under H. Kretzschmar and J. Wolf, prof. at Berlin Univ.

Musical History of Berlin up to 1800 (Berlin, 1908); *Music and Opera at Electoral Court of Brandenburg* (Berlin, 1910); *Modern Scientific Dictionary of Musical Instruments* (1920); *Musical Instruments of India and the East; Introduction to Science of Instruments* (Berlin, 1915); *Musical Instruments of Ancient Egypt* (Royal Museum Hand-book). Songs (Ries & Erler).—A. E.

SACHS, Leo. Fr. compr. *b.* Alsace, 1868. Vice-President of Société Musicale Indépendante (with Ravel and Florent Schmitt). His work is very varied, and recalls Schumann.

Symph. poems: *Lamento; Retour des Cloches; Sur l'eau;* 5tet; 3 str. 4tets; trio; 3 sonatas, pf. and vn.; cello sonata; 24 preludes for pf.; v. and orch.: *Les Trois Sorcières; Invocation au Soleil; Silence;* duos: *Le Jour et la Nuit; L'Amant et la Mort;* some vocal 4tets.—A. C.

SADERO, Geni. Soprano singer; *b.* Trieste, 12 May, 1890. Has devoted herself passionately and successfully, both as a collector and executant, to the propaganda of Ital. folk-songs. Completed in Italy and abroad numerous successful artistic tours. Publ., through the Istituto Editoriale of Milan, an Album of 25 Ital. regional songs, coll. and harmonised by herself.—D. A.

SAERCHINGER, César. Amer. writer; editor; *b.* Aix-la-Chapelle, 23 Oct. 1884. Stud. under Benjamin Lambord, New York; but largely self-taught. Ed. (with Daniel Gregory Mason) *The Art of Music* (New York, 1915-18; 12 vols. and 2 vols. music examples). Author of *The Opera* in above series. Ed. *The International Who's Who in Music* (New York, 1918). Founded Modern Music Soc. of New York, 1913. Associate-ed. of *The International* magazine, 1913-15; of *Current Opinion* (N.Y.), 1915-19. Special correspondent *New York Evening Post* since 1919; European ed. *Musical Courier* (N.Y.) since 1919.—E.-H.

SÆVERUD, Harald. Norwegian compr. *b.* Bergen, 17 April, 1897. Stud. compn. under Borghild Holmsen in Bergen and at High School in Berlin. *Début* 1920 in Christiania with a symph. poem for full orch. Its successful production in Berlin and Gothenburg has drawn attention to his exceptionally promising talent. —R. M.

SAINT-FOIX, Marie Olivier Georges du Parc Poullain de. Fr. musicologist; *b.* Paris, 1874. Stud. music at *Schola Cantorum.* Collab. with T. de Wyzewa in an important book: *W. A. Mozart: sa vie musicale et son œuvre, de l'enfance à la pleine maturité* (2 vols. Paris, 1912, Perrin). This book, to which he devoted 15 years' work, and which takes reader up to M.'s 21st year (1777) is foremost among all works on Mozart. Additions are still being made to it. Among important studies on XVIII century (publ. in reviews) are: *Contribution à l'histoire de la symphonie française vers* 1750 (joint-author with L. de la Laurencie) (*Année Musicale,* 1911, Paris, Alcan); *La chronologie de l'œuvre instrumental de J. B. Sammartini* (*I.M.G.,* 1914); *Muzio Clementi; Un quatuor d'Airs Dialogués de Mozart; Mozart, Disciple de Bach et Haendel* (*Bulletin de la Société française de Musicologie,* 1918, 1920, 1921, Paris, Alcan; Fischbacher);

Mozart et le jeune Beethoven (1919); *Les Débuts de Gluck à Milan*. In 1922, he started in *Revue Musicale* a series of articles on foremost Parisian pianists (beginning with Jean Schobert), very important to history of pre-Mozart period. —M. L. P.

SAINT-SAËNS, Charles Camille. French composer; *b.* Paris, 9 Oct. 1835; *d.* Algiers, 16 Dec. 1922. Studied at Paris Conservatoire under Stamitz (pianoforte), Maleden (theory), Benoist (organ), Halévy and Reber (composition), and private pupil of Gounod; tried twice for *Prix de Rome* without success; 1885, organist of St.-Merry; 1858–77, organist at the Madeleine; from that time, pianist, organist, touring condr.; composed his first symphony at 16; two operas (*La Princesse jaune*, 1872, and *Le Timbre d'argent*, 1877) were unsuccessful before he produced *Samson et Dalila* (Weimar, 1877).

In spite of the fact that his death is of recent date, he is too intimately bound to the past for any place to be given, in this Dictionary, to his long and active life, and to his enormous work. We limit ourselves to a few remarks on his rôle in musical history, as far as it may be judged thus near to his death. The sources that produced his style are complex. From his earliest youth he was an insatiable reader; he had heard everything and knew exactly how to draw inspiration from a Berlioz or from a Liszt. He came under all the influences that acted so potently on the men of his generation, and yet was able to retain his own personality. His style, precise, nervous and clear-cut, is absolutely characteristic and also essentially French; it recalls that of the XVIII century French writers, particularly of Voltaire—nothing is superfluous, everything has its place. Order and clarity are supreme. Yet this composer, although a classic by temperament and choice, is no pedant; he is often cold and empty of sentiment, but he is never heavy or pretentious. In this respect he differs completely from Brahms, with whom he is often compared.

When still young he had an extraordinary gift of fresh spontaneity, as is seen in his trio in F (op. 18). As he advanced in age his style gained in purity but lost in feeling—his last compositions are of a most chilling correctness. Moreover Saint-Saëns was always inclined to write with excessive facility; the flowing ease of his pen obliterated all other considerations. For this reason, out of his enormous work there survive to-day only a few gems of the first water—his symphonic poems, the 3rd symphony with organ and *Samson et Dalila*.

For the greater part of his life Saint-Saëns showed a most subtle and intelligent appreciation of the compositions of others, never hesitating to throw down the gauntlet in defence of Liszt, Berlioz and Wagner. But towards the end of his life he allowed himself to be dominated by his patriotic sentiments. Debussy fought against the influence of Wagner because he considered it detrimental to French art, but Saint-Saëns attacked him merely because he was a German. The violent polemics which he directed against Wagner did him much more harm in the eyes of the general public than did the bitterness with which he attacked all young artists suspected of modern tendencies in music. These foibles, excusable even on account of his age, must not be allowed to blind one to the fact that here was a great man who in his youth possessed a lucid and enthusiastic intelligence, a musician who, like his master Liszt, was always ready to sacrifice himself for fellow-musicians whom he admired.

When Impressionism first made its appearance, Saint-Saëns had already written his masterpieces. As a musician he had always put reason before sentiment—it is natural, then, that he should stand aloof from this new form of art which gave the senses a primary place. The new school never felt his influence, or rather the few who did, like Henri Rabaud, were fundamentally classic, and were content to make a few minor concessions to the fashion of the day. It is possible, however, to discern the slender thread that binds Saint-Saëns, through the intervening link of his disciple Gabriel Fauré, to such an innovator in music as Maurice Ravel—both have the same faith in art for art's sake, both have a love of constructions that are delicate yet virile, while nothing can be more profound that the gulf between these two men in temperament and emotion.

To those young musicians who escaped the influence of the Impressionists, Saint-Saëns and César Franck appear as models worthy of imitation; some who are fearful even of the sentimental effusions of the Walloon musician look to Saint-Saëns alone for the secrets of faultless construction. But the influence of Saint-Saëns on the present generation is confined to these minor details of construction, whereas César Franck arouses it to mystic enthusiasm and Debussy's art has invisible threads that bind it enthralled to some enchanted island from which there is no escape.

Saint-Saëns admirably represents one of the many aspects of the French temperament—that in which the mind and intelligence supplant sentiment and even sometimes feeling, as in the case of a Voltaire or Rameau. On the other hand we have the sensuous, sensitive art of a Debussy, akin to that of La Fontaine, Racine, Claude Lorrain and Lully.

Operas: *La Princesse jaune* (1872); *Le Timbre d'Argent* (1877); *Samson et Dalila* (Weimar, 1877); *Étienne Marcel* (Lyons, 1879); *Henry VIII* (1883); *Proserpine* (1887); *Ascanio* (*Benvenuto Cellini*, 1890); *Phryné* (1893); *Déjanire*; *Les Barbares* (1901); *Hélène* (1-act lyric poem; Monte Carlo, 1904); music to many plays. Orch. tone-poems: *Le Rouet d'Omphale* (1871), op. 37; *La Jeunesse d'Hercule*, op. 50 (1877); *Danse macabre*, op. 40. Symphonies: E flat, op. 2; A mi. op. 55; C mi. op. 78 (1886); F mi. (1856); D (1859). *Suite Algérienne*, op. 49; *Jota Aragonese*, op. 64; *Coronation March, Edward VII of England*; 5 pf. concertos: op. 17, D (1858); 22, G mi.; 29, E flat; 44, C mi.; 109, F; 3 vn. concertos; 2 cello concertos; chamber works; pf.

pieces; songs; choruses; church music; oratorios: *De Noël*, op. 12; *Le Déluge*, op. 45; *Psalm CL.* Many books and articles: *Materialism and Music* (1882); *Notes on Theatre Decoration with the Ancient Romans* (1886); *Harmony and Melody* (1885; 1902; 1905); *Portraits and Souvenirs* (1900). Consult: O. Neitzel, *S.-S.* (1899); E. Baumann, *S.-S.* (Paris, 1905); L. A. Lassus, *S.-S.* (1914); J. Bonnerot, *S.-S.* (1914); O. Séré, *Musiciens français d'aujourd'hui* (1911); A. Hervey, *S.-S.* (John Lane, 1921); A. Cœuroy, *S.-S.* (*Larousse mensuel*, June 1923); G. Servières, *S.-S.* (1923).—H. P.

SALAGHI, Salvatore Emanuele. Ital. physiologist; *b.* Forli, 1850. Prof. of physical therapy at Univ. of Bologna; also devoted himself to mus. studies; publ. important arts. on mus. physiology:
Per la fisiologia musicale dell' organo uditivo (*Concerning the Musical Physiology of the Auditory Organs*) (Bologna, 1917, Gamberini & Parmeggiani); *Una fonte ignorata di temi melodici* (*An Ignored Source of Melodic Themes*) (Bologna, 1918, Pizzi); *Problemi di acustica fisiologica risoluti musicalmente* (*Problems of Physiological Acoustics solved musically*) (Bologna, 1921, Cappelli).—D. A.

SALAZAR, Adolfo. Span. critic and compr.; one of founders of Sociedad Nacional de Música (see SOCIETIES); contributor on mus. and literary subjects to Span., Fr. and Eng. reviews; mus. critic of leading Span. newspaper *El Sol.* Has translated into Span. Eaglefield-Hull's *Modern Harmony.* Through his writings and activity he has contributed very prominently to the advancement in Spain of all modern tendencies in art. Lives in Madrid.
Trois Préludes pour le piano; *Trois Chansons de Paul Verlaine* (Chester, London).—P. G. M.

SALSBURY, Janet Mary. Eng. orgt. compr. *b.* Pershore, Worcs., 13 May, 1881. Prof. of music and hon. orgt. at Ladies' Coll. Cheltenham; prof. of music (by correspondence) and examiner (theoretical) Trinity Coll. of Music, London; Mus.Doc. Dunelm. 1910.
A Ballad of Evesham for chorus (Weekes); Christmas Carols (Stainer & Bell); song-cycle, *From Shakespeare's Garden* (J. Williams); *Analysis of Mozart's Pf. Sonatas* (Weekes); *Staff-Sight-Singing Tests*, Books I & II (J. Williams).—E.-H.

SALZBURG FESTIVAL (*Salzburger Festspiele*). The summer mus. fests. at Salzburg (Tyrol) originated in perf. of Mozart's operas there under Richter and Mahler, and in foundation of the Mozarteum edifice with its rich collection of Mozart books and music. But plan of regular annual fests. was started by F. Gehmacher of Salzburg and H. Damisch of Vienna, who founded (1917) the *Salzburger Festspielhaus Gemeinde*, intending to build a stage in Salzburg. Strauss, Max Reinhardt, Schalk, Hugo von Hofmannsthal and Alfred Roller were elected on committee. The peasants of this district have a long tradition of mystery-plays; so in Aug. 1920, the fest. opened with Hofmannsthal's *Jedermann* (*Everyman*) played in open air, before the cathedral. In following winter, the peasants perf. this play in several places; it was repeated at 1921 fest. by Reinhardt. In 1922, the fest. broadened out. Chief perf. was Hofmannsthal's *Salzburger Grosses Welttheater* (given in old Kollegium Church by Reinhardt) and Mozart operas by members of Vienna Opera, under Strauss, Schalk and Alwin. In combination with the 1922 fest. the first meetings of the Inter-

national Chamber-Music Concerts took place (founded by H. Damisch, Rudolf Réti, Paul Stefan, E. Wellesz). In 1923, the latter movement developed into the International Soc. for Contemporary Music (*q.v.*).—EG. W.

SALZEDO, Carlos. Amer. harpist; *b.* Arcachon, France, 6 April, 1885. Stud. pf. at Bordeaux Cons. 1892–4; then at Paris Cons. Began study of harp under Alphonse Hasselmans, continuing pf. under Charles de Bériot and obtaining 1st prize for both in 1901. Toured France, Spain, Portugal and Switzerland as pianist and harpist. 1909–13, harpist at Metropolitan Opera House, New York. Extended tours in U.S.A. President of National Association of Harpists, Jan. 1920. Since Oct. 1920, ed. of *Eolian Review.* Has developed technical resources of harp according to modernist tendencies and comp. many works for one or more harps, including a symph. poem, *Enchanted Isles*, perf. by Chicago Symphony Orch. 24 Nov. 1919.
For harp: Variations on an old-style theme (Leduc, 1913); *Ballade* (*id.* 1913); *5 Poetical Studies* (Schirmer, 1921); pieces for cello and pf. (Costallat, 1908, 1918); 4 choruses in old sonata-form for 3 male vs. (Gray, 1918). Wrote *Modern Study of the Harp* (Schirmer, 1921).—J. M.

SAMAZEUILH, Gustave. Fr. compr. *b.* Bordeaux, 2 June, 1877. Pupil of Chausson and d'Indy; has been member of Société Nationale; music critic of *La Republique Française.* Writes with elegance and facility for orch. and chamber-music:
Symph. poem, *Nuit*; *Le Sommeil de Canope*; *Poème*, vn. and orch.; pf. suite *La Mer*; organ Variations on theme of Bach; *La Barque*, v. and orch. str. 4tet; songs.—A. C.

SAMMARCO, Mario. Ital. barit. *b.* Palermo, 13 Dec. 1873. *Début* at Palermo in *Faust.* In 1894 at La Scala, Milan; since then known to the principal audiences in Europe and America. At La Scala, created part of Gerard in *Andrea Chénier* (Giordano).—D. A.

SAMMONS, Albert Edward. Eng. violinist; *b.* London, 23 Feb. 1886. Commenced study under his father, an amateur musician; received about a dozen lessons from F. Weist Hill and John Saunders; otherwise self-taught. After 7 years of theatre, hotel-orchestras and private bands, he became leader of Beecham's Orch.; also of R. Philh. Soc. Orch. London, and of London Str. Quartet (the latter he abandoned, after 9 years' ensemble, on account of military duties 1916–18); led Russ. Ballet orch. in Berlin; then Dieppe Symphony Orch. (1913), after which he left orch. playing to devote himself to work as soloist. He made a very great reputation for concerto-playing, especially Elgar's. He is the finest solo-player amongst contemporary Eng violinists.
Virtuosic Studies (2 books); *The Secret of Fine Technique*; *Phantasy*, str. 4tet; many vn. solos (all publ. by Hawkes & Sons, London).—E.-H.

SAMPER, Baltasar. Span. pianist; native of Catalonia; pupil of Granados. His recitals in Barcelona included the 1st public perf. in Spain of Cyril Scott's pf. music.—P. G. M.

SAMPSON, George. British compr. and author. Now cath. orgt. Brisbane, Australia. Condr. of

Sampson Orch. Representative of Univ. of Queensland on Australian Univ. Exam. Board.
Berceuse, str. and organ (Schott, London); church-music (Chester, London)—a communion-service and an evening service are on the repertory at St. Paul's Cath. London; *Romance*, vn. and pf. (Chester); text-books: *The Pianoforte* (Chester); *Rhythm* (*id.*); *Elements of Music* (*id.*); *Queensland Manual of Music for Teachers* (Novello).—E.-H.

SAMUEL, Adolphe Abraham. Belgian compr. *b.* Liège, 11 July, 1824; *d.* Ghent, 14 Sept. 1898. Stud. Liège, then Brussels. 1st *Prix de Rome*, 1845, for cantata *Vendetta*. After his stay in Rome, returned to Brussels in 1848 and besides composing became music critic. As such he went to hear concerts in London, where he met Berlioz. Harmony teacher at Brussels Cons. 1860. In 1865, founded Popular Concerts of Classical Music, which still play important part in educating popular taste in music in Belgium. Dir. of R. Cons. at Ghent, 1871. Member of R. Acad. of Belgium; dir. class of Fine Arts in 1893. S. is a musician of high culture and tendencies which were revolutionary in his time. Berlioz, Liszt and Wagner strongly influenced him without overshadowing his own characteristics.
Several operas (only one perf. Brussels, 1849: *Madeleine*, op. 11 [*opéra-comique*]). Of the 7 symphonies, last two have definite programme, *i.e.* 6th, op. 44, in 4 parts (*Genesis, Eden, Cain, Lux Luceat*), publ. Junne, Leipzig; and 7th, *Christus*, op. 48. Cantatas; choral works; songs, etc. Theoretical works include *Course of Practical Harmony*, very popular. Consult brochure on A. S. by Ad. Mathieu (Brussels, 1922, Hayez).—C. V. B.

SAMUEL, Harold. Eng. pianist; *b.* London, 23 May, 1879. Stud. R.C.M. under Dannreuther and Stanford; *début*, St. James's Hall, 1894; prof. of pf. R.C.M. Specialises on Bach's music.—E.-H.

SAMUEL, Léopold. Belgian composer; *b.* Brussels, 5 May, 1883. Stud. at Brussels Cons.; pupil of Edgar Tinel. *Prix de Rome*, 1911. In 1920 appointed Inspector of Mus. Education in middle and high schools of Belgium.
Ilka, lyric drama; *Tycho Brahé*, cantata (*Prix de Rome*); *Fleurs d'après-midi*, songs with orch. acc.; symph. poem for orch.; str. 5tet; trio.—E. C.

SAMUEL-HOLEMAN, Eugène. Belgian compr. *b.* Schaerbeck, near Brussels, 3 Nov. 1863. Son of Adolphe Samuel; stud. philosophy and literature at Ghent; but soon followed music entirely; in 1894, pianist Concerts Lamoureux, Paris; 1895, municipal-condr. at Grasse; 1897, choral condr. at Monte Carlo Theatre. As a compr. he is an isolated figure, whose art is marked with great independence. His researches into technical expression have often the character of veritable anticipations. His *La Jeune Fille à la Fenêtre* (Breitkopf), written in Belgium in 1904, but not perf. till 1914 (Théâtre des Arts, Paris), is unusually daring and in certain respects quite remarkable.
Un Vendredi-Saint en Zélande, 3-act opera; *Te Deum*; *A la tombe anonyme*, etc.—C. V. B.

SANCHEZ-DEYA, Domingo. Argentine violinist, compr. *b.* Barcelona in 1852. Trained at Cons. there. Appeared as prodigy. Taught at Cons. for 18 years. Went to Buenos Ayres in 1909; founded an Acad. of Music there, which he now

directs. Many songs, pf. and orch. pieces, mostly of a light type. His Waltz for full orch., *Lettres à Émilie*, had a wide vogue.—S. G. S.

SANDBERG, Oscar T. Swedish choral condr. compr. *b.* Kristianstad, 1 Dec. 1870. Stud. R. Cons. Stockholm, 1893-9; choirmaster at Oscar Ch. from 1903; condr. of several male-v. choral societies. Founded (with colleague Patrik Vretblad, orgt. of Oscar Ch.) the "Motet Evenings," 1909. 1906-10, music critic of *Aftonbladet*. Has comp. church music in modern style (choruses, cantatas); ed. *Musica sacra*, anthems for mixed vs. (1915). Member R.A.M. Stockholm, 1921. His wife Hilma (*née* Munthe) stud. vn. under Lindberg and Lady Hallé; member of Konsertföreningen Orchestra.—P. V.

SANDBERGER, Adolf. Ger. writer on music; *b.* Würzburg, 19 Dec. 1864. 1881-7, stud. compn. at R. School of Music, Würzburg, and Munich; 1883-7, science of music, Univs. of Munich and of Berlin (Ph. Spitta); 1889, curator of mus. department of R. Court and State Library, Munich; 1894, hon. lecturer in science of music, Munich Univ.; 1900, prof.-extraordinary; 1909, prof.-in-ordinary. Directed the publication of *Monuments of Bavarian Music* (*Denkmäler der Tonkunst in Bayern*).
Songs; pf. pieces; mixed choruses, op. 3; male choruses, op. 19; trio sonata, op. 4; pf. trio, op. 20; vn. sonata, op. 10; 2 str. 4tets, D mi. op. 9 and E mi. op. 15; symph. prologue, *Riccio*, op. 16; symph. poem, *Viola*, op. 17 (suggested by *Twelfth Night*); *Königsmarsch*, op. 21; opera, *Ludwig der Springer*, op. 12 (own text; Coburg, 1895).
Publ.: *Life and Works of Poet-Musician Peter Cornelius* (1887); *Contributions to History of Bavarian Court Orch. under Orlando di Lasso* (3 vols., 1894-5, Vol. 2 unpubl.); *Selected Essays on History of Music*, 2 vols. (Munich, 1921 and 1924). Complete eds. of works of Orlando di Lasso (Breitkopf).—A. E.

SANDERS, Herbert. Brit. orgt. condr. compr. writer on music; *b.* Wolverhampton, England, 1878. Mus.Doc. McGill Univ.; orgt. Dominion Methodist Ch. Ottawa; condr. Ottawa Oratorio Soc. Is well known as compr. of anthems, songs and organ pieces (W. H. Gray; Ditson; Boston Music Co.) and on two occasions was awarded the Clemson Gold Medal for compns. by the Amer. Guild of Orgts. Is associate-ed. of the new Canadian Methodist Hymnal. Lives in Ottawa.—L. S.

SÁNDOR, Erzsi (Bosnyák). Hungarian coloratura s. singer; *b.* Kolozsvár (now annexed by Rumania), 28 Aug. 1883. Member of R. Hungarian Opera House since 1906.—B. B.

SANDVIK, Ingeborg. Norwegian singer; *b.* Hamar, 4 Dec. 1886. Pupil of Gina Hille, Emilie Kaula (Munich) and Grace Morris (London and Berlin). First independent concert in Christiania, 1913; frequent concerts in Christiania and elsewhere in Norway. She has won great recognition by her poetic and delicate rendering, especially in Norwegian lyric music (Kjerulf, Nordraak, Grieg, Sinding). Lives in Christiania. —J. A.

SANDVIK, Ole Mörk. Norwegian music-historian; *b.* Hedemarken, 9 May, 1875. Graduated in theology in 1902; afterwards master in higher schools. Took in 1922 Ph.D. with treatise,

Norwegian Folk-Music, especially Eastland Music.
In this work he upholds new views with respect
to Norwegian folk-music. Other publications:
Norwegian Church-Music and its Sources (1918)
Folk-Music in Gudbranddalen (1919). He has
supplied contributions to *Norway's Musical
History* (1921), of which he was chief ed. together
with Gerhard Schjelderup. Dr. Sandvik is the
author of the article on GRIEG in this Dictionary.
—R. M.

SANDVIK, P. Norwegian orgt. and inspector
of schools; *b.* Söndmör in 1847. From 1869,
resident at Hamar, where he founded the Hamar
Choral Soc. His efforts for promotion of school-
singing in Norway have been of fundamental
importance.—R. M.

SANJUÁN NORTES, Pedro. Span. compr. *b.*
San Sebastian (Guipuzcoa), 15 Nov. 1886.
Started career as violinist; belonged to the
Orquesta Sinfónica, Madrid, from his 20th to
28th year, when he won a position of regimental
bandmaster. Stud. under Bartolomé Pérez Casas
and Joaquín Turina, under whose influence he
became a decided follower of modern tendencies.
He writes mainly for orchestra. In Feb. 1924,
he was appointed condr. of the Orquesta
Sinfónica, Havana, Cuba.

El Dragón de Fuego, overture, inspired by Jacinto
Benavente's dramatic work of same title; *Afrodita*,
symph. poem based on Pierre Louys' novel (1st perf.
1908, Orquesta Filarmónica, Madrid); *Poema pastoral*,
words by Juan Ramón Jiménez; *Suleika*, based on
a tale from the *Thousand and One Nights*; *Cam-
pesina*, rondo, 1st perf. Feb. 1920, Orquesta Filarmónica, Madrid; *Paisajes y lugares*, 3 poems for
pf.; *Aires del Campo*, v. and pf. (Antonio Matamala,
Madrid; Schott.)—P. G. M.

SANKEY, Ira David. Amer. evangelist-singer
and composer of hymns; *b.* Edinburgh, Pa.,
U.S.A., 28 Aug. 1840; *d.* Brooklyn, N.Y., 13 Aug.
1908. Began career as choir-singer and leader in
Methodist Ch., Newcastle, Pa. 1871, resigned
position as collector of internal revenue and
joined Dwight L. Moody as an evangelistic singer.
Toured extensively in U.S.A., Canada and Great
Britain (1st visit to England 1873). With Philip
P. Bliss, James McGranahan and others, developed a particular type of Amer. hymnody, known
as " gospel hymns."

Sankey's Story of the Gospel Hymns (Philadelphia,
1906, Sunday School Times Co.); *My Life and the
Story of the Gospel Hymns* (Philadelphia, 1907, P. W.
Ziegler); *Sacred Songs and Solos* (1873, Biglow &
Main; London, 1875, Morgan & Scott); *Hallowed
Hymns* (1908, Biglow & Main); many contributions
to *Gospel Hymns*, 6 vols. (1875–91, Biglow & Main;
many later eds.). Consult J. H. Hall, *Biography of
Gospel Song and Hymn Writers*, pp. 197–201; and
his autobiography.—J. M.

SAN MARTINO DI VALPERGA, Enrico
(Count). Born Turin, 11 March, 1863. Since
1905 has been President of the R. Accademia
di Santa Cecilia in Rome, of which he became
a member in 1891. Is passionately devoted
to music, which he studied from boyhood in
Turin (pf. under Rossaro, cello under Forneris,
harmony under Bellardi). In 1888, went to
Rome, where he was President of Accademia
Filarmonica and of Circolo dei Musicisti. During
his presidency, the R. Accademia di Santa
Cecilia has achieved great development, and

to his initiative is due the institution of orch.
concerts, first in the Sala Accademica, later at
Teatro Argentina, and finally at the Augusteo
(1908). In 1911, appointed Senator. Amongst
his most interesting publications on music are:
*Saggio sopra alcune cause della decadenza della
musica italiana alla fine del secolo XIX* (Tipografia
della Pace, Rome, 1898); *La evoluzione della musica
nel secolo XIX* (Tipografia della Pace, Rome, 1900);
Sulle belle arti (Tipografia del Senato, 1914); *Note e
ricordi del Presidente* (in publ. *Venti Anni di Concerti*,
of R. Accad. di Santa Cecilia) (Rome, 1915).—D. A.

SAN MIGUEL, Mariano. Span. clarinettist
and compr. *b.* Oñate (Guipuzcoa). Clar. soloist
of Banda del Real Cuerpo de Alabarderos (see
ALABARDEROS). Former soloist, Soc. de Conciertos, Orquesta Sinfónica, Madrid. Member of
R. Chapel Orch. Founder of Soc. de Instr. de
Viento (Wind Instr. Chamber-Music Soc.), 1910.
Recognised as one of the contemporary clar. virtuosi. Author of over 200 popular works for
military band. Founder of the mus. review
Harmonía, Madrid.—P. G. M.

SAN SEBASTIÁN, Father José Antonio de.
Span. compr. *b.* San Sebastian (Guipuzcoa),
from which town he takes his name, following the
custom of the Capuchin order to which he belongs. Stud. compn. under Granados and at
Schola Cantorum, his best-known work being
Trois Préludes Basques (Unión Musical Española).—P. G. M.

SANTA CECILIA (Regia Accademia di), Rome.
The most important mus. inst. in Italy. Founded
1584 by Pope Gregory XIII, under title of *Vir-
tuosa Compagnia dei musici di Roma*; later,
assumed name of *Congregazione di Santa Cecilia
fra i musici di Roma*; only recently that of
Academy. In 1870 it obtained title of *Royal*
and lost the religious character it had formerly
preserved. One of its original features was that
of " mutual help " amongst the members; recently it has developed its artistic activity and
is now the chief Ital. mus. centre, taking the
initiative in mus. culture and conferring degrees.
To it belongs the merit of having founded
(1876) the Liceo Musicale di Santa Cecilia (see
ACADEMIES) which, after having been for several
years dependent on it, has now become an
independent State institution. It has also
promoted in Rome the symphony concerts,
which took place at first in the beautiful academic
hall, and subsequently at the Augusteo (*q.v.*).
For the older history of the Acad., see a pamphlet
—very rare—of the Abbot Tosti. Its more
recent events are illustrated in the vol. *Twenty
Years of Concerts* and the *Annuari* of the Acad.
itself (Via Vittoria 6).—D. A.

SANTLEY, Charles. English opera, oratorio
and concert singer; *b.* Liverpool, 28 Feb. 1834;
d. 22 Sept. 1922. Son of William Santley,
orgt. and oboe-player. Educated at Liverpool
Inst. As boy, sang alto in church choirs and
played vn. in orchs. His voice having broken,
he joined choir of Liverpool Philh. Soc.
as 2nd t. on his 15th birthday, taking part
in the opening concerts of the Philh. Hall,
when he heard Viardot, Lablache and others,

After working as an accountant for a time, his voice having settled down into a fine barit., he went to Milan in 1855, and placed himself under Gaetano Nava, who eventually left him his library. In Jan. 1857, operatic *début* in *Traviata* at Pavia. On his return to England in Nov. 1857, he sang Adam in *The Creation*, under John Hullah, at St. Martin's Hall, London. He pursued his studies under Manuel Garcia, and proceeded to engage in the longest, most distinguished and most versatile vocal career which history records. Most notable appearances:

Feb. 1858, 1st appearance in title-part of *Elijah* in London at Exeter Hall. (He remained identified with the part of Elijah for upwards of 50 years.) At this period he was singing with Sims Reeves, Clara Novello, Mario and Grisi. Sept. 1859, in Pyne and Harrison Eng. Opera Co. at Covent Garden. 1861, 1st appearance at Birmingham Festival. 1862, 1st appearance at Handel Fest. at Crystal Palace; also created part of Danny Man in *Lily of Killarney*; had such great success in *Il Trovatore* that he was then engaged by Mapleson for Her Majesty's Theatre, singing in Eng. opera at Covent Garden and Ital. at Her Majesty's. 1863, 1st appearance at Worcester and Norwich Fests.; had great success as Valentine, in 1st production in England of Gounod's *Faust*. 1864, Gounod wrote *Even Bravest Heart* for the Eng. perf. especially for S. In the cast with S. were Lemmens - Sherrington, Lucia, Marchesi and Sims Reeves; at the Ital. Opera, the cast included Tietjens, Trebelli, Giuglini, Gassier and S. Winter of 1864–5, at Liceo in Barcelona, playing Rigoletto for 1st time. Dec. 1865–March 1866, at La Scala in Milan. Sang *Don Giovanni* in Manchester, 1st time in 1865. Later on, appeared as Caspar in *Der Freischütz*, in London. In 1869, sang in Ambroise Thomas' *Hamlet* (with Christine Nilsson as Ophelia); in *Gazza Ladra*, at Covent Garden with Adelina Patti. 1870, he sang Vanderdecken in *Flying Dutchman* (with Irma di Murska); then appeared in *Zampa, Fra Diavolo* and *Czar und Zimmerman* (in Eng. at Gaiety). 1871, successful tour in America; autumn 1872, toured Eng. provinces for 3 months; then dropped into concert and oratorio routine, singing in ballad concerts under Boosey. His last regular appearance in opera was in 1876 in Carl Rosa Co. (*Flying Dutchman*). He made tours in Australia, New Zealand, Africa and Canada. During his career he was offered engagements at Paris, Vienna, Naples and Petrograd, which he was unable to accept owing to pre-engagements. He sang at Monday Popular Concerts, appearing with the Joachim Quartet and Mme. Schumann. In 1907, S. celebrated his jubilee, by concert at Albert Hall; same year, received knighthood. Took his farewell at Covent Garden in 1911; at matinée given for his benefit, appearing as Tom Tug in *The Waterman* (Dibdin's ballad-opera) in which he had first sung more than half a century before. In Feb. 1915, at request of the Lady Mayoress, S. sang at Mansion House concert for Belgian refugees. On that occasion, he sang with perfect intonation and an astonishing amount of his old quality of voice and vigour of style.

His voice was of singularly bright, carrying quality, with a noble silvery resonance. His compass was from the low E flat to the high G (barit.), and every note was of fine scientific quality; there was perfect evenness throughout the whole compass. A marvellous command of vocal technique, grand elocution, remarkable gift of observation, exhaustive understanding and appreciation of men and things, with a striking power of presentation, gave him a range of style, which enabled him to hold the foremost place in every branch of singing both in opera-house and on concert-platform. He sang in four languages equally well; was moreover a master of Scots and Irish enunciation in national and humorous songs.

Santley publ. 2 vols. of autobiography: *Student and Singer, Reminiscences of My Life*, and a book on *The Art of Singing*. As a man, he was simple in his tastes, very downright, and along with a certain native dignity, had a humorous and very human outlook on life. Pope Leo XIII created him a Knight-Commander of Order of St. Gregory in 1887. He had joined the Church of Rome in 1880.—J. M. L.

SANTLEY, Edith. Daughter of Sir Charles Santley; had a successful career as a s. concert-singer, before her marriage in 1884 with the Hon. R. H. Lyttelton.—J. M. L.

SANTOLIQUIDO, Francesco. Ital. compr. *b.* San Giorgio a Cremano, Naples, 6 Aug. 1883. He studied in Rome at R. Liceo di Santa Cecilia, under Falchi. He now lives in Tunis for the greater part of each year.

Operas: *La Favola di Helga* (Teatro Dal Verme, Milan, 1910; Ricordi); *Ferhuda* (Tunis, 1919); *L'Ignota* (unpubl.); *La bajadera dalla maschera gialla* (Rome, 1923). Orch. works: *La morte di Tintagiles; Paesaggi; Il profumo delle oasi sahariane; Acquarelle*; songs; pf. pieces (Ricordi, Milan; Forlivesi, Florence; Durazzano, Tunis). Writings about music: *Il dopo Wagner : Debussy e Strauss* (Rome, 1909, Modes ed.).—D. A.

SAPELLNIKOF, Vassily. Russ. pianist; *b.* Odessa, 21 Oct. 1872. First stud. music under his parents, and appeared in public as a violinist at age of 7; stud. vn. and pf. till he met Rubinstein, who persuaded him to devote himself to the pf.; then stud. for 5 years at Petrograd Cons., next appearing at Hamburg under conductorship of Tchaikovsky, and scored an immediate success. Engagements in the principal countries in Europe. In London he introduced the Tchaikovsky concerto, under the compr. himself (R. Philh. Soc.); has played for this Soc. 15 times; was chief prof. at Moscow Cons., for 2 years, but resigned this post to pursue concert work. In 1916, returned to Odessa on family matters and was caught later by the revolution, and detained in the country until he managed to escape in summer of 1922. He has comp. a number of pf. works, the most popular being 2 gavottes and a valse.—E.-H.

SARADIEF, Constantine Solomonovitch (*accent 2nd syll.*). Russ. condr. and violinist; *b.* Derbent (Darguestan district, Caucasus), 26 Sept. 1877. Son of a physician; pupil of Hrimaly (vn.) and S. I. Tanéief (theory) at Moscow Cons. (1889–98); then of Nikisch (Leipzig, 1905–6) and Ševčík (Prague, 1900–2, 1904). Vn. teacher at Synodal Music School, Moscow, 1898–1907; chairman of Moscow Soc. of Orch. Players (1908–11); chief condr. of Moscow City Symph. Concerts in the Sokolniky, 1908, 1910, 1911; chief condr. People's Opera, Moscow, 1911, 1912. One of organisers and chief condr. of Moscow Free Theatre (1913–14). Now dir. of State Inst. of Theatre Art in Moscow (formerly Musicodramatic School of Philh.); and prof. at Moscow Cons. At his City Symph. Concerts he gave many 1st perfs. of works by Russ. and foreign comprs. (Stravinsky, Miaskovsky, Prokofief, Ravel, Debussy, Fl. Schmitt, Cyril Scott, Loeffler).—V. B.

SĀRANGI. See INDIAN MUS. INSTRUMENTS.

SARASATE Y NAVASCUÉS, Pablo de. Span. violinist; *b.* Pamplona (Navarra), 10 March, 1844; *d.* at Villa Navarra, Biarritz, 20 Sept. 1908. Buried at his native town. Honours: Grand Crosses of Isabel la Católica and Alfonso XII, Carlos III, Christo de Portugal, Albrecht of Saxony, Leopold of Belgium, the Prussian Crown, Red Eagle of Prussia, the Crown of Italy, Wendische Krone of Schwerin, Zäringen-Löwe of Baden, White Falcon of Weimar, Danebrog of Denmark, Frederick of Würtemburg, Benemerentia of Rumania, Commander of the Crown of Rumania, and of Isabel la Católica, and Medals of Merit of Mecklenburg-Schwerin, Art and Science of Russia and Dessau, Officer of Légion d'Honneur; Hon. Member of Royal Philharmonic Soc. London.

Made his first appearance on concert platform in Coruña at age of 8. His father, Don Miguel de Sarasate, a military band-master, gave him first instruction on the violin. The Countess of Espoz y Mina helped him to go to Madrid in 1854, where he took lessons under Manuel Rodríguez, leader of Teatro de la Zarzuela. In 1856, played before the Span. Royal Family and gave his first concert at the R. Opera House. In same year, he left for Paris accompanied by his mother, who died on the way, at Bayonne. The Span. Consul and banker, Don Ignacio García Echevarría, a native of Pamplona, adopted the stranded boy of 12, and took him to Paris, leaving him under the direction of Alard for his studies and the personal care of M. and Mme. de Lasabathié, who looked after his general education and regarded him as their own child. Besides Señor García's protection, Sarasate had grants from the Countess of Espoz y Mina, the Diputación de Navarra and Queen Isabel II, amounting in all to about £150 a year.

But a few months elapsed before he appeared with his master Alard at a concert at Bayonne and created a sensation. By that time he had played to Rossini, who wrote of him as "a giant in talent whose modesty doubles his charm." In 1857 he obtained 1st prize for vn. at Paris Cons. and in 1858, 1st prize for harmony. His remark in a letter to his father in 1857: "Harmony will be very easy for me; I have it all in my head already," recalls his deficiency in that branch of music, so much in evidence in his compns. In 1861 he went to Spain, receiving from the Royal Family the Cross of Carlos III. In that year he made his first appearance in England (Crystal Palace), a country he visited annually almost to the end of his life. In 1867 he toured with Adelina Patti in Brazil, Chile, Argentina and Peru. It was not until 1876 that he appeared in Germany. In 1889 he returned for second and last time to U.S.A. and S. America. His public career constitutes a record of 32 years of triumphant tours, during which he received every conceivable honour and amassed a large fortune, in spite of his charitable and hospitable disposition. He possessed 2 famous Stradivarius violins: one dated 1724, known as the "Boissier de Genève," for which he paid 5000 francs

in 1866; the other dated 1713, called, on account of its brand-new red colour, "le rouge," acquired in 1888 for 20,000 francs. These he bequeathed in his will: the "Boissier" (the only one he played in public) to the Paris Cons., and the "red" to Real Cons. de Música, Madrid.

The violin in his hands was not an instrument of masculine or feminine character to give expression to human pathos, but a wand to conjure up ravishing fantasies of sound. As revealed in his music he had not the diabolical daring of Paganini, nor the temperamental exuberance of the Belgian school. He was not a violinist, musician and artist like Kreisler, nor violinist and musician like Joachim. He was purely a fiddler, but one with an unprecedented personality. He excelled in Schubert, Mendelssohn, Raff, Saint-Saëns and Lalo, besides his own music. Bach's unaccompanied sonatas only appeared in his programmes in the last years of his life, with no particular advantage to established traditions. As a tribute to the memory of the great virtuoso, Sarasate's compns. should be passed uncriticised. Nevertheless, the vn. part of his numerous works can always be stud. with benefit, being the only traces left to posterity from which to draw an idea of the æolian and fluid quality of his playing.

Vn. and pf. (or orch.): *Le Sommeil*; *Moscowienne*; *La forza del destino*; *Homenage a Rossini*; *Serenata andaluza*; *Les Adieux*; *Dame blanche*; *Rêverie*; *Fantasia sobre el Fausto*; *Romeo y Julieta*; *Freischütz*; *Caprice sur Mireille*; *Confidences*; *Aires Españoles*; *Souvenirs de Domont*; *Mosaïque de Zampa*; *Mignon-Gavota*; *Prière et Berceuse*; *Vito y Habanera*; *Jota Aragonesa*; *Zigeunerweisen*; *El canto del ruiseñor*; etc. (Publ.: Choudens, Durand, Paris; Zimmermann, Leipzig; Simrock, Senff, Berlin.)—P. G. M.

SARI, Ada (Szajerówna, Jadwiga). Polish coloratura soprano singer; *b.* Stary Sącz, Galicia, in 1888. Celebrated in rôles of Rosina, Gilda, Lakmé, Violetta, Queen of the Night, etc., in Italy, Spain, France, England, Poland and America.—ZD. J.

SARLY, Henry. Belgian compr. *b.* Tirlemont, 28 Dec. 1884. Stud. music under his father, who dir. a school of music at Tirlemont. Later under Léon Du Bois at École de Musique, Louvain. Then at Brussels Cons.: organ under Mailly; harmony under Huberti and Paul Gilson; cpt. under Tinel; compn. under Léon Du Bois. Obtained I*ère mention* in *Prix de Rome* competition, 1907. Now in charge of a harmony class at Brussels Cons. and (from 1921) inspector of mus. education to middle and high schools of Belgium. S. is one of most gifted of Belgium's young composers. His art has a solid technical basis; is more modern than classical in tendency.

Vn. and pf. sonata; 5tet, str. and pf.; about 40 songs (Schott; Chester); *Poème*, pf. vn. and cello (Chester); *Le Cœur d'Hjalmar*, v. and orch.; *Scènes brabançonnes*, orch. suite, etc.—C. V. B.

SARNECKA, Jadwiga. Polish pianist, compr. *b.* Sławuta, Wolhynia, 1878; *d.* Cracow, 1913. Stud. under Szopski in Cracow, Melcer and Leschetizky in Vienna. In several songs to her own words and in many pf. pieces she tried to express the suffering and sorrow which filled her life.—ZD. J.

SASNAUSKAS, Česlovas. Lithuanian compr. *b.* at Kapčiamiestis, in Seinai district. Stud. under his father, who was an orgt., and his uncle, Rizauskis, a well known orgt. of Naumiestis. He then graduated (1889) in organ class of Prof. Kaluzinski at Warsaw; and in that year was appointed orgt. at Vilkaviškis; later at Dvinsk; then at Petrograd (1891) in which city he had already passed through the singing section of Cons. in 1898. Subsequently he stud. harmony and fugue under J. Drozdov. For the investigation of mus. sources, he stud. palæography and semeiography at the Archæological Inst. of which he was made an active member in 1904. In 1905 he was sent by Archbishop Count Sembek to study Gregorian chant and worked at Benedictine monasteries of Prague, Würtemberg, Rome, and in Switzerland. From 1892 till his death, S. was connected with chief Catholic ch. in Petrograd, St. Catherine, Nevsky Prospect, at first as assistant orgt., and as chief orgt. from 1896. First in Petrograd to organise a Lithuanian choir; first in Russia to introduce a model Benedictine choral service. His secular compns. drawn from Lithuanian motifs, laid the foundations of Lithuanian national music.

Cantata, *Broliai* (*Brethren*), solo, chorus and orch.; 12 *Lithuanian Dainos*; church choral works; *Requiem* (Petrograd); organ fugues, etc. (Ratisbon, Gauss-Copperath; Leipzig, Otto Junne; Paris, Senart).—H. R.

SATIE, Eric (Erik) Leslie. Fr. compr. (mother English); *b.* Honfleur, 17 May, 1866. One of the most original characters in modern music. After studying for some years at the Paris Conservatoire, where he made the acquaintance of Paul Dukas, Satie, in his passion for Gregorian music, sought original effects from the use of ancient forms, and ventured to risk harmonic combinations and sequences which the boldest of his contemporaries, even a Chabrier or a Lalo, would not have dared to write. *Les Sarabandes* (1887), *Les Gymnopédies, Les Gnossiennes* (1889), introduce the harmonic style which definitely took its legitimate rank in music in the masterpieces of Debussy.

Debussy made the acquaintance of Satie about 1890 in a Montmartre cabaret where the latter was pianist. At a time when Debussy was still wavering, Satie saw clearly that Wagnerianism was dead, and that the rhetoric of the *leit-motiv* must be abandoned. In the incidental music to the *Fils des Étoiles*, he endeavoured to create a sonorous atmosphere and background. His ideas, much more than his music, seem to have helped Debussy to find himself.

Satie has remained poor and obscure all his life. Ravel, who came very much under his influence during his youth, did his utmost to secure just recognition for him, but the public refused to take him seriously. One must admit that Satie, with his whimsical humour, seemed to make mock of the public with his absurd titles, which often disguised pianoforte pieces of rare charm and originality; *e.g. Pièces froides* (*Cold Pieces*), *Morceaux en forme de poires* (*Pear-shaped Pieces*), *Préludes flasques* (*Limp Preludes* —to a dog*) (Rouart, Lerolle), etc.

Satie, who to a certain extent had foretold the coming of musical Impressionism, realised in 1913 that music was to follow an evolution similar to that of painting, and that subtleties of notation and fugitive nuances were to give way to strong outlines and poise. He himself composed an original work in this style, *Socrate* (La Sirène, 1918) consisting of fragments of Platonic dialogue in music. It is the chief work of his late period. The melody which consists of a very simple theme, rises clear above an accompaniment which is obstinately repeated. The total impression is strangely archaic. In spite of some pages of great beauty, his work has never been appreciated at its true worth, because the public insists on seeing Satie merely as a humorist. He has been adopted as a " totem " by the younger French musicians, but only Poulenc and Auric have really shown signs of his influence. In *Parade* and various orchestral works, Satie tries, as they do, to draw his inspiration from jazz and *café-chantant* music; but his last compositions in this style are very mediocre.

Consult: A. Cœuroy, *La Musique française moderne* (Paris, 1922); J. Cocteau, *Le Coq et l'Arlequin* (Eng. transl. London, Egoist Press).—H. P.

SAUER, Emil. Ger. pianist; *b.* Hamburg, 8 Oct. 1862. Pupil of Nicolas Rubinstein, Moscow Cons. (1879–81); stud. under Liszt, 1884–5; concert work since 1882; 1901–7, and from 1915, dir. of Advanced Pf. School at Vienna Cons.; 1917, ennobled; 1918, Kgl. Hofrat. An elegant player, somewhat feminine in style.

2 pf. concertos (E mi., C mi.); 2 pf. sonatas (D ma., F ma.); 24 concert-studies (1900); ed. pf. educational works of Pischna, Plaidy, Kullak, Loeschhorn, Scarlatti and Brahms (Peters). Wrote *Meine Welt* (1901). —A. E.

SAUL, Felix. Choral condr. *b.* Preussisch Stargard (Germany), 22 Dec. 1883. Stud. at seminary of Münster; choirmaster at synagogue at Düsseldorf, 1904; at synagogue in Stockholm, 1909. Naturalised Swede, 1919. Professor of theory (Riemann's method) in music schools of Richard Andersson and Karl Wohlfart. Founded Stockholm Madrigal Soc. 1917. Music critic on *Dagens Nyheter* and continental journals (*Signale; Allgemeine Musikzeitung*).—P. V.

SAUNDERS, William. Scottish writer on music; *b.* Kirkcaldy, Fifeshire, 22 May, 1877. Educated at Edinburgh Univ.; specialised in history and principles of criticism, whilst taking full course in arts and law. Took many prizes (Gray Essay; *prox. accessit* Lord Rector's Prize). Ed. U. of E. students' magazine, *The Gambolier*, which he owned for 5 years. Stud. fl., vn., pf., singing and mus. history. Came intimately under influence of Prof. Niecks and later of Prof. Tovey. In 1918, founded *The Scottish Musical Magazine*, which he edits and for which he has written many articles. He is a good linguist, and his chief mus. interests lie in the study of opera and folk-songs of all nations. He is a regular contributor to Eng. mus. journals, and the writer of many of the Scottish articles in this Dictionary.—E.-H.

SAURET, Émile. French violinist; *b.* Dunle-Roi, 22 May, 1852. Pupil of Charles de Bériot; brilliant career as soloist abroad. Toured in England, U.S.A. and Germany; his home is in Geneva. As soloist, is remarkable for the elegance of his technique. Is also a compr. and has publ. many vn. arrangements. Has had many pupils in Berlin, London and Chicago. The essence of his teaching is contained in an excellent Violin Manual.—M. P.

SAUVREZIS, Alice. Fr. compr. *b.* Nantes. Pupil of César Franck; then of P. Vidal. President of *Société artistique et littéraire de l'Ouest.* Without closely uniting itself to folklore, her music yet seeks a Celtic character.
Sonata, pf. and vn.; sonata for 2 pfs.; 50 songs; 2 symph.poems; lyric legend, *Francen-ar-Mor.*—A.C.

SAVASTA, Antonio. Ital. compr. *b.* Catania, 22 Aug. 1874. Prof. of compn. at R. Cons. di San Pietro a Maiella, Naples, where he was a pupil. An esteemed compr. of several operas, and symph. and chamber-music.—D. A.

SCALA (Teatro alla), Milan. This magnificent Milanese theatre, built to the design of the architect Piermarini di Foligno, was inaugurated 3 Aug. 1778. Without recording the important events in virtue of which its name has acquired historic importance, we will dwell merely on the outstanding facts of the last 40 years. One of the largest and most beautiful theatres in Italy, it is used exclusively for operas and symphony concerts. Since 1870, the theatre, which formerly belonged to the State, has been property of municipality of Milan, which has ceded it now to one, now to another private management, sometimes with considerable endowments. Discussions about these endowments never ceased until, after a period of enforced closing, it was re-opened in recent years, securing a new lease of life under the management of an autonomous body. Amongst important first performances at La Scala during last 40 years, are Verdi's *Otello,* 5 Feb. 1887, and *Falstaff,* 9 Feb. 1893; Catalani's *Dejanire* (1885), *Edmea* (1886), *La Wally* (1893); Puccini's *Le Villi* (1884), *Edgar* (1889), *Butterfly* (1904); Mascagni's *Ratcliff* (1895), *Silvano* (1895), *Le Maschere* (1901, and simultaneously at other theatres), *Parisina* (1913); Boïto's *Nerone* (1924); also many 1st perfs. in Italy of the more important works produced in other countries. Present artistic dir. is Arturo Toscanini. Other condrs., V. Gui and A. Lucon.
For history of La Scala, consult the valuable work of Pompeo Cambiasi, completed and brought up to date by the fine book of Carlo Vanbianchi and Guido Marangoni (publ. by Istituto Italiano di Arti Grafiche, Bergamo).—D. A.

SCALERO, Rosario. Ital. violinist, compr. *b.* Moncalieri, 24 Dec. 1870. Stud. at Liceo Musicale, Turin, then at Genoa under Camillo Sivori, and in Germany under Wilhelmj. After a series of concerts in principal European cities, settled in Rome, where in 1913 he founded the Società del Quartetto. 1919, went to New York, joining staff of Mannes Cons. Pieces for vn., pf., orch., songs (Breitkopf; Simrock).—D. A.

SCALESE, Lorenzo. Dir. of Beethoven Cons. Buenos Ayres; *b.* Serrastretta, Calabria, in 1867. Went to Argentina as a boy. Is now a well-known pf. teacher. Publ. a suite and symphony for orch. many songs and pieces for vn. and pf.—S. G. S.

SCANDINAVIAN (Northern) MUSICAL FESTIVALS. Organised in Copenhagen, 1919, and in Helsingfors, 1921, the performers being drawn from Finland, Sweden, Norway and Denmark. —E.-H.

SCHACHTEBECK, Heinrich. Ger. violinist; *b.* Diemarden, near Göttingen, 6 Aug. 1887. Stud. in Göttingen Town Orch.; 1905, pupil at Leipzig Cons. (Arno Hilf), then Walter Hausmann; 1908, member of Gewandhaus Orch.; 1909, Konzertmeister, Stadttheater Orch.; 1911-1914, soloist in Philh. (Winderstein) Orch.; 1915, founded str. quartet with Albert Patzak, A. Witter, Alfred Patzak.—A. E.

SCHADEWITZ, Carl. Ger. compr. *b.* St. Ingbert, 23 Jan. 1887. Pupil at Würzburg Cons. where he is now engaged as condr., choirmaster and teacher of piano.
Songs: *Liedsinfonie,* s. barit. vn. fl. and pf.; a second one, s. fl. horn, vla. and pf.; vn. and pf. sonata, op. 4; cello sonata, op. 9; pf. 4tet, A mi. op. 16; 3 suites, op. 10, 14 and 18; *Symph. Poem,* op. 15, orch.; Prelude and fugue, str. orch. op. 3; stage fairy-play, *Midsummer Night,* op. 8; stage music to Calderón's *Zenobia,* op. 15; opera, *Laurenca.* —A. E.

SCHÄFER, Dirk. Dutch pianist and compr. *b.* Rotterdam, 25 Nov. 1873. Stud. 1887-90 at Rotterdam Cons.; 1890-94 Cologne; 1894, Mendelssohn Prize, Berlin; 1894-1904, settled at The Hague, giving many concerts in Holland and Belgium; 1904, produced his pf. 5tet at Frankfort Fest.; 1910, his vn. sonata (with Carl Flesch) and cello sonata (with Gérard Hekking) in Berlin; 1913, began series of 11 historical concerts, playing most important works of whole piano literature—(from Byrd and John Bull to Ravel and Schönberg); 1921, played in Vienna, Berlin, London and Paris. Since 1904 has lived in Amsterdam.
2 *Lieder,* mixed vs. and orch. op. 1 (Leipzig, Leuckart); 8 *Études,* pf. op. 3 (Breitkopf); sonatas for vn. and pf.: No. I, op. 4 (The Hague, 1901, Noske); No. II, op. 6 (Breitkopf); Nos. III and IV in op. 11 (1904 and 1909; Noske); 5tet for pf. and vn. op. 5; *Javanese Rhapsody* for orch. op. 7 (Breitkopf); *Pastoral Suite* for orch. op. 8 (Noske); sonata, cello and pf. op. 13 (1909); str. 4tet, op. 14. For pf.: *Sonate inaugurale,* op. 9; 3 pieces, op. 10; 6 pieces, op. 72; 8 pieces, op. 15 (Noske); Waltz (Copenhagen, Hansen); Barcarolle; Prelude and fugue (Leuckart); 4 little pieces (Strasburg, Süddeutsche Musikverlag); *Variations* on a sequence (Leipzig, Kahnt); *Scherzo, Impromptu* and *Valse di bravura* (Noske). Consult: *Revue Musicale* (July 1921); *Arts Gazette* (March 1922); *Chesterian;* Niemann's *Klavierbuch* (enlarged ed.).—W. P.

SCHALIT, Heinrich. Austrian pianist, compr. *b.* Vienna, 2 Jan. 1886. Pupil of Josef Labor and Robert Fuchs at Vienna Cons.; now private teacher in Munich.
Lyrical pf. pieces; songs; chamber-music (pf. 5tet, 4tet, vn. sonata); *Konzertstück,* pf. and orch. —A. E.

SCHALK, Franz. Austrian condr., dir. of Vienna Opera House; *b.* Vienna, 27 May, 1863. Stud. vn. under Hellmesberger, compn.

under Bruckner. Together with his brother Josef, he conducted a zealous propaganda for Anton Bruckner and also for Hugo Wolf. 1888, condr. at Reichenberg (Bohemia); 1889-95 at Graz (where in 1894 dir. 1st perf. of Bruckner's 5th symphony). Then Prague till 1898. In spring of 1898, guest-condr. Covent Garden Opera, London; 1898-9, condr. Metropolitan Opera House, New York (succeeding Anton Seidl.) There he first cond. the *Ring des Nibelungen* (without cuts). In 1899 (in place of Josef Sucher) he was with Muck and R. Strauss as condr. of the Comic-Opera House in Berlin. In 1900, called by Mahler to Vienna Opera, where he has been dir. (with R. Strauss) since Oct. 1918. Director of Gesellschaftskonzerte, 1904-21. In 1911 he cond. the winter season at Covent Garden, London, in place of Hans Richter, with Hallé concerts at Manchester, etc. Cond. in Vienna the 1st perf. of *Tiefland*; *Rosenkavalier*; *Die Gezeichneten*; *Palestrina*; *Ariadne*; *Salome*; *Schatzgräber*. In 1919, 1st perf. of *Frau ohne Schatten*. His indefatigable work at the Vienna Opera House has recalled the days of its greatest glory.—P. St.

SCHARRER, Irene. British pianist; *b.* London. Trained at R.A.M. under Tobias Matthay (as an Associate Board scholar at age of 12); gained Potter and Erard scholarships; 1st recital Bechstein Hall at age of 16; since then, she has toured Great Britain and played with all the leading British orchs., as well as with Nikisch and with the Berlin Philh. Orch. Her style has all the beauty and finish of the Matthay school. —E.-H.

SCHARWENKA, Ludwig Philipp. Ger. compr. *b.* Samter (Posen), 16 Feb. 1847; *d.* Bad Nauheim, 16 July, 1917. 1865, pupil of Kullak's New Acad. of Music, Berlin (Würst and H. Dorn); 1870, teacher of theory at Kullak's Acad.; 1881, teacher of compn. at brother's Cons.; then dir. with Hugo Goldschmidt; Member of Berlin Acad. of Art; finally senator.

Choral work, *Harvest Celebration*, soli and orch.; *Sakuntala*, dramatic legend arr. for stage; *Arcadian Suite* for orch.; symphony, D mi.; *Sinfonia Brevis*, E flat; symph. poem, *Spring Waves*; *Dramatic Fantasy*, B flat mi.; tone-poem, *Dreams and Reality*; *Orch. Serenade*, E flat; *Festival Overture*; vn. concerto; 2 pf. trios (C sharp, op. 100; G ma. op. 112); 2 str. 4tets (D mi. op. 117; D ma. op. 122); pf. 5tet, B mi. op. 118; trio, pf. vn. and vla. op. 121; duet, vn. and vla. with pf. op. 105; 2 vn. sonatas; pf. and vla. sonata; male and female choruses; songs; short pieces for orch.; pf. and vn. duets.—A. E.

SCHARWENKA, Xaver. Pianist and compr. *b.* Samter (Posen), 6 Jan. 1850. Brother of Philipp Sch., pupil of Kullak's Acad. (Th. Kullak and R. Würst); 1868, teacher at Kullak's Acad.; 1869, début as pianist at Acad. of Singing; 1874, gave up teaching; concert-player in almost every European country; 1881, opened own Cons., Berlin; 1891, invited to New York as dir. of Cons. (named after him) there; 1893, Berlin Scharwenka Cons. united to Klindworth Cons.; 1898, returned from New York, and took over the directorship again; 1914 (with W. Petzet), opened School of Music with

pf. teachers' seminary attached; Member-in-ordinary of R. Acad. of Art; 1911, senator.

4 pf. concertos (B flat mi. op. 32; C mi. op. 56; C sharp mi. op. 80; F mi. op. 82 [1908]); 2 pf. trios (F sharp mi. op. 1; A mi. op. 42); pf. 4tet, F ma. op. 37; vn. sonata, D mi. op. 2; cello sonata, G mi. op. 46; 2 pf. sonatas (C sharp mi. op. 6; E flat ma. op. 36); 2 ballads for pf., op. 85; Variations, pf. op. 83; symphony, C mi. op. 60; short pf. pieces (*Polish Dances*, op. 3, 9, 29, 34, 58; *Polish Rhapsody*, op. 76; *Polonaises*, op. 7, 16); songs (op. 88); Studies for pf. (op. 77, 78); opera, *Mataswintha* (Berlin, 1894). Publ. *System of Pf.-playing* (1908). Consult his autobiography *Klänge aus meinem Leben*, 1922.—A. E.

SCHATTMANN, Alfred. Compr. *b.* Rytwiany, Radom govt., 11 June, 1876. Son of Ger. parents; stud. law; after 2 years' commercial activity turned to music; pupil of Julius Schaeffer, Breslau. Compr. and mus. author in Berlin, also 1st mus. critic of *Die Zeit* there.

Songs; pf. pieces; opera, *Frithjof*; mus. play, *Die Freier (The Suitor)* (Stuttgart, 1914); comic opera, *Des Teufels Pergament (Devil's Parchment)* (Weimar, 1913); burlesque opera, *Die Geister von Kranichenstein*; tragic opera, *Die Hochzeit des Mönchs (Monk's Wedding)*.—A. E.

SCHEIDEMANTEL, Karl. Ger. stage and concert-singer (barit.); *b.* Weimar, 21 Jan. 1859; *d.* there, 26 June, 1923. Attended Weimar Training College for Teachers (private pupil of Bodo Borchers); 1878-86, at Weimar Court Theatre; 1881-3, stud. under J. Stockhausen; 1886, sang at Bayreuth; 1886-1911, Dresden Court Opera House; then teacher at Grand-Ducal Music School, Weimar; 1920-2, dir. of State Opera House (Landesoper), Dresden.

Stimmbildung (Voice Production) (1907; 7th ed. 1920); *Training of Singing* (1913; Eng. by Carlyle, 2nd ed. 1913); words to E. Lindner's *Eldena* and Pittrich's *Pechvogel und Lachtaube*; 1914, won prize of Ger. Stage Soc. for transl. of *Don Juan*. Publ. a vol. of songs, *Master Melodies* (1914, 6 parts). Consult P. Trede, *K. Sch.* (1911).—A. E.

SCHEINPFLUG, Paul. Ger. compr. *b.* Loschwitz, near Dresden, 10 Sept. 1875. 1890-4 stud. at Dresden Cons. (Draeseke, Braunroth, Rappoldi); 1897-8, private tutor in South Russia; 1898, Konzertmeister of Philh., Bremen; condr. of Choral Union of Teachers' Choral Soc., and of St. Michael's Ch. choir; 1909, went to Königsberg as condr. of Mus. Soc.; 1910, condr. of Acad. of Music; 1914, condr. of Blüthner Orch. Berlin; 1920, town mus. dir. Duisburg; 1921, gen. mus. dir. there.

Pf. 4tet, E ma. op. 4; *Worpswede* (v. vn. horn and pf.), op. 5; *Spring* for orch. op. 8; *Comedy Overture*, op. 15: vn. sonata, F ma. op. 13; str. 4tet, C mi. op. 16; songs; 2 male choruses with vn. solo, op. 10; *Die Ulme von Hirsau (The Elm of Hirsau)*, for double male chorus, op. 12; *Christmas Carol of Angels* (female chorus and organ); light opera, *Das Hofkonzert (The Court Concert)* (Berlin, 1922).—A. E.

SCHELLING, Ernest Henry. Amer. pianist, compr. *b.* Belvedere, N.J., 26 July, 1876. First instruction from his father. Appeared as infant prodigy at 4½ years at Acad. of Music, Philadelphia, 1880. At 6, taken to Europe and taught by Mathias and Moszkowski at Paris Cons.; afterwards by Pruckner, Huber (Basle, 1890), Barth, J. Pfitzner, Leschetizky. In his youth played in London, Paris, Germany, Switzerland, Sweden, Denmark. From 1898-1902, completed his studies under Paderewski at Morges, Switzerland. Since 1903, toured extensively in Europe, including Spain and Russia; since 1905 in America.

As compr. S. has produced a number of larger works. Best-known is op. 7, *Suite fantastique*, pf. and orch. (1st perf. Amsterdam, 1907). Still in ms. are a suite for orch., a vn. concerto (played by Kreisler with Boston Symphony Orch. 17 Oct. 1916, in Providence, R.I.), *Impressions of an Artist's Life*, variations, pf. and orch. (perf. by Boston Symphony Orch. 31 Dec. 1916), a vn. sonata, and *The Victory Ball*, symph. poem, perf. by Philadelphia Orch., 23 Feb. 1923.

Légende Symphonique, orch. (Schirmer, 1907), perf. in Warsaw, 1903; *Suite fantastique*, pf. and orch. op. 7 (Rahter, 1908); *Thème et variations* and other pf. pieces; songs (Schirmer).—J. M.

SCHENKER, Heinrich. Austrian writer on music; *b.* Wisniowszyk, Poland, 19 June, 1868. Pupil of Anton Bruckner at Vienna Cons. Toured as accompanist to Messchaert. Then critic, voluminous writer on music.

Many pf. pieces, songs. Books (Univ. Ed.): *New Musical Theories and Phantasies*, Vol. I, Harmony (1906), II, Counterpoint (1910), III, Counterpoint, continuation (1921); *Analysis of Beethoven Pf. Sonatas* (text and new ed. of music), 1914–22: *Concerning Beethoven's 9th Symphony*; *Ornamentation*. Also publ. new ed. of pf. concerto of Ph. E. Bach; cantatas of J. S. Bach; Bach's Chromatic Fantasia; arrangements of Handel's concertos for piano, etc. —P. P.

SCHERCHEN, Hermann. Ger. condr. and compr. *b.* Berlin, 21 June, 1891. Self-taught musician; 1907–10, vla. player Blüthner and Philh. Orch. Berlin; 1911–12, concert tour with Max Schönberg; 1914, condr. of Symph. Orch. Riga. On return from Russian imprisonment (1918), founded and cond. New Mus. Soc. Berlin; 1920–1, publ. fortnightly paper for ultra-modern music called *Melos*; became lecturer for modern music at State High School for Music; 1921, condr. of newly-estabd. Grotrian-Steinweg Orch. in Leipzig; 1922, condr. of Frankfort Museum Concerts. Is one of most energetic pioneers of the new mus. styles.

Songs (op. 2, Heine songs; Berlin, Jatho Verlag); *Le Tsigane dans la lune* (contr. and vn., Jatho); pf. sonata, op. 5 (Jatho); str. 4tet, E ma. (Steingräber); pf. trio, A mi.—A. E.

SCHERING, Arnold. Ger. musicologist; *b.* Breslau, 2 April, 1877. Stud. at Berlin and Leipzig Univ. (vn. under Joachim and compn. under Succo); 1902, graduated Leipzig as Ph.D.; 1907, Univ. teacher at Leipzig in history and æsthetics of music; 1915, made prof.-extraordinary; 1920, prof.-in-ordinary (succeeded Abert) at Univ. Halle-o-S. Since 1904 has publ. *Bach Annual* of New Bach Soc.

History of Instrumental Concerto (1905); *History of Oratorio* (1911); *Musical Training and the Education of a Musical Ear* (1911, 3rd ed. 1919); *Outline of German Musical History* (1917); *Public Musical Training Method in Germany up to establishment of Leipzig Cons.* (1918); *Dutch Organ Mass in Josquin's time* (1912); *Study of Musical History in the Early Renaissance* (1914); revised A. von Dommer's *Handbook of Musical History* (1914); Hasse's oratorio, *Conversion of St. Augustine* (*D.d.T.* XX); *Instrumental Concertos of German Masters* (1700–60) (*D.d.T.* XXIX, LIX); *Church Cantatas of pre-Bach Masters at Leipzig* (*D.d.T.* LVIII, LIX); *Old Chamber-Music*; *Old Masters of Vn.-playing*; Quantz's *Flute Instructor* (1907); 1908, Schering discovered at Upsala, Heinrich Schütz's *Christmas Oratorio*, long given up as lost (1909, printed as supplement to Spitta Complete Ed.). S. comp. music to Goethe's *Faust*; sonata for solo vn.; 2 dramatic plays: *The Cantor of St. Thomas* (*Bach Annual*, 1916) and *The Young Handel* (1918).—A. E.

CHIAVAZZI, Pietro. Italian t. singer; *b.* Cagliari in 1878. Stud. at Liceo at Pesaro, where Mascagni took a deep interest in him, and successfully launched him in perf. of his (Mascagni's) most popular operas. Was first interpreter of *L'Amica*; also of t. part in *La Conchita* (Zandonai). His repertoire is very extensive, ranging from dramatic (*Gioconda*, *Pagliacci*, *Cavalleria*) to lyric (*Rigoletto*, *Bohème*, *Sonnambula*).—D. A.

SCHIEDERMAIR, Ludwig. Ger. musicologist; *b.* Regensburg, 7 Dec. 1876. Stud. at Munich, history, Germanic philology under Sandberger, science of music; 1901, Ph.D.; 1899 and 1903, passed exams. in philological history; stud. theory of music under Riemann and Kretzschmar at Leipzig and Berlin; after a long sojourn in Italy, became (1906) hon. lecturer for theory of music at Marburg Univ.; 1912, went to Bonn Univ.; 1920, professor.

Contributions to History of Opera at the turn of XVIII and XIX Century (Simon Mayr) (Vol. I, 1906; Vol. II, 1910); *Bayreuth Festival Plays* (1908); *Introduction to Study of Musical History in the Age of Absolutism* (1918); *Mozart* (Munich, 1922) *Mozart's Letters to his Family* (5 vols., Munich, 1914, George Müller).—A. E.

SCHILLINGS, Max von. Ger. compr. *b.* Duren (Rhineland), 19 April, 1868. Pupil of K. J. Brambach and O. von Königslöw (Bonn); stud. 3 years at Munich; settled there; 1903, R. prof.; 1892, acted as dir. of rehearsals for Bayreuth perf.; 1908, mus. assistant to the Intendant of Stuttgart Court Theatre; condr. of Court Orch. and Opera; then gen. mus. dir. 1911–18; Ph.D. *h.c.* Univs. of Tübingen and Heidelberg; 1912, King of Würtemberg knighted him; 1919, dir. of Prussian State Opera, Berlin. As compr. he is a tasteful follower of the modern German direction. His opera *Mona Lisa* was perf. at the Metropolitan, New York, 1924.

Op. 1, *Abenddämmerung* (*Twilight*) (Bote & Bock); op. 16, str. 4tet, E mi. (Simrock); op. 2, 4 songs (Bote & Bock); op. 3, *Ingwelde*, 3-act opera, 1895 (Leipzig, Schuberth); op. 4, 3 songs (Fürstner); op. 5, Improvisation, pf. and vn. (Fürstner); op. 6, *Ocean Greeting* and *Sea Morning*, 2 symph. fantasies, orch. (Fürstner); op 7, 4 songs (Schuberth); op. 8, *Dialogue*, small orch., vn. and cello solos (Ries & Erler); op. 9, *Kassandra*, and *Das Eleusische Fest* (Bote & Bock); op. 10, *Der Pfeifertag* (*Piper's Day*), 3-act comic opera (Bote & Bock); op. 11, symph. prologue to Sophocles' *King Œdipus*, orch. (id.); op. 12, music to Æschylus' *Orestes* (Felix Bloch); op. 13, 5 songs (Bote & Bock); op. 14, 3 songs of Anacreon (id.); op. 14b, *Letzte Bitte* (*Last Request*); op. 14c, *Intermezzo* (Munich, Bauer); op. 15, *Das Hexenlied* (Forberg); op. 16, *Ernielieder* (Bote & Bock); op. 17, 4 songs (id.); op. 18, 3 simple melodies for vn. and pf. (id.); op. 19, 4 songs (Forberg); op. 20, *Moloch*, mus. tragedy (Bote & Bock); op. 21, *Dem Verklärten* (*To the Transfigured*), hymn-rhapsody (Schiller), mixed chorus, barit. and orch. (Forberg); *Autumn Scene* (Hebbel), for v. and pf. (Kahnt); op. 22, *Glockenlieder* (*Bell Songs*) (Forberg); *Einem Heimgegangenen* (*To a Departed One*) (*in mem.* Ludwig Thuille) (C. A. Challier); op. 23, *Der Hufschmied* (*The Farrier*) (Forberg); op. 24, music to Goethe's *Faust*, I. (ms.); op. 25, vn. concerto (Simrock); op. 26, *Hochzeitslied* (*Wedding Song*), chorus, soli, orch. (Simrock); op. 27, Festival March, military band (Simrock); *Wedding Tunes*, waltz for pf. (Drei Masken Verlag); op. 28, *Young Olaf* (Wildenbruch; orch. or pf.) (Forberg); op. 29, 2 male choruses unacc. (Forberg); op. 31, *Mona Lisa*, 2-act opera (Dowsky; Univ. Ed.); op. 32, 5tet for 2 vns. 2 vlas. cello (id.); op. 33, *The Pearl* (Goethe), s. t. orch. (Jatho Verlag); op. 34, singing dialogues from

Goethe's *Westöstliche Divan* (*id.*); op. 35, *Am Abend*, pf. and vn. (Forberg); about 40 songs with pf.; produced condensed ed. of Berlioz' *Trojans* in Stuttgart; set to music the dialogues in Mozart's *Il Seraglio* (Simrock).
Consult August Richard's *Max Sch.* (Munich, 1922).—A. E.

SCHINDLER, Kurt. Amer. compr. and choral condr. *b.* Berlin, 17 Feb. 1882. Stud. pf. under Ansorge, compn. under Bussler, Gernsheim, Thuille and L. C. Wolf, and philosophy and history of art and music at Univs. of Berlin and Munich. 1902–4, condr. of Court theatres at Stuttgart and Würzburg and assistant-condr. to R. Strauss in Berlin. Went to America as assistant-condr. at Metropolitan Opera, New York, 1905–8. In 1908 founded the MacDowell Club Chorus (known since 1910 as the *Schola Cantorum*) of which he is still condr., producing many new and unfamiliar works. S. has done much mus. editorial work, specialising in Russ. and Span. vocal music. Ed. of many valuable colls. of Russ. songs and Russ. folk-songs (Schirmer; Ditson), also Finnish folk-songs (Gray).—J. M.

SCHIPA, Tito. Ital. t. singer; *b.* Lecce, 2 Jan. 1889. One of best living Ital. lyric tenors. *Début* 1911 at Vercelli; slowly gained front rank, singing at leading theatres of Italy, Europe and America.—D. A.

SCHIRMER, Friedrich. German condr. and compr. *b.* Bonn, 27 Oct. 1881. Stud. at Cologne and Leipzig Cons.; pupil of Humperdinck, R. Acad. of Art, Berlin; Meyerbeer Prize, 1912; orch. condr. of *Miracle* (Vollmöller-Humperdinck) with Max Reinhardt's company in London, Paris, Vienna, Prague, etc. Condr. and chamber-musician (cello), Königsberg.
Orch. suite; overture, *On the Rhine*; symphony, B flat mi.; *Elegy and Hymn*, mixed chorus, t. and orch.; symph. poems, *Festival of the Dead* and *Werther*; *A German Hymn*, male chorus and orch.; *Festkantate* (male chorus and orch.); 6tet for wind instruments.—A. E.

SCHIRMER, G., Inc. American music publishing firm, founded by Gustav Schirmer (*b.* Königsee, Saxony, 19 Sept. 1829; *d.* Eisenach, 6 Aug. 1893) who came to New York in 1837. In 1861 with B. Beer he took over business of Kerksieg & Breusing under name of Beer & Schirmer. From 1866 Schirmer was sole proprietor. After his death in 1893, the firm was incorporated by heirs and managed by the two sons, Rudolph E. (*b.* New York, 22 July, 1859; *d.* Santa Barbara, Cal., 20 Aug. 1919) and Gustave (*b.* 18 Feb. 1864; *d.* 15 July, 1907). In 1885 the Boston Music Co. was formed as branch of the New York firm. In 1894 began the publ. of an inexpensive but excellently ed. and printed series of classical comprs. and studies, *Library of Musical Classics.* Another series, *The Golden Treasury*, was begun in 1905. Since 1915 (under the editorship of O. G. Sonneck) this firm has publ. America's best mus. periodical, *The Musical Quarterly.*—O. K.

SCHJELDERUP, Dagny. Norwegian lyricdramatic s. singer; *b.* Christiania. Appeared in 1919 at R. Opera House, Stockholm. In 1921, soloist with Philh. Orchs. in Berlin and Warsaw. Gave concerts (chiefly with Norwegian songs)

in Copenhagen, Helsingfors, Vienna, Paris (1920). —R. M.

SCHJELDERUP, Gerhard Rosenkrone. Norwegian compr. *b.* Kristiansand, 17 Nov. 1859. Stud. philology. Went to Paris Cons. where Massenet was one of his teachers. *Début* as cellist; gave concerts in Norway together with his gifted sisters. Wrote some choral works, one of which, *Höifjeldsliv* (*Mountain Life*), has been perf. several times in Christiania and Dresden. Heard some Wagner perfs. in Carlsruhe under Mottl and wakened to his call as a compr. of music-drama. S. has written half a score of operas and stands as the most eminent musicdramatist Norway has produced. Owing to the unsettled mus. conditions, only 3 of his musicdramas have been perf. in his native land: the delicate and deeply felt 1-act opera *Vaarnat* (*Spring Night*), the boldly-conceived piece *Bruderovet* (*The Abduction of the Bride*), from Norwegian peasant life, and the Christmas drama *En Hellig Aften* (*The Holy Eve*). In Dresden, Prague, Munich and Dessau, most of his works have been perf. with great success. He writes his own words. S. receives a compr.-pension from the Norwegian State.
Also symph. poem *Brand* (from Ibsen's drama); ballads for chorus and orch.; and a number of songs. —R. M.

SCHJELDERUP, Mon (Marie Gustava). Norwegian compr. *b.* 16 June, 1870. Stud. pf. under Agathe Backer-Gröndahl, theory under Raif Succo and Bargiel (Berlin) and Massenet (Paris). First concert in Christiania, 1894.
Prelude to Ibsen's play *Vildanden* (*The Wild Duck*) (Christiania Theatre, 1891); vn. sonata (concert of her own compns. in Salle Érard, Paris, 1895). Many songs; 4-v. male choruses.—U. M.

SCHJELDERUP-PETZOLD, Hanka. Norwegian pianist; also trained as singer; *b.* at Christiansand, 1865. Pupil of Massenet and Liszt. Has given numerous concerts in Europe, America and East Asia. At present, resident in Tokio, where she is leader of the largest music school in Japan and, as such, is a Japanese official.—U. M.

SCHLOEZER, Boris de. Russ. critic and writer on music; *b.* Vitebsk in 1884. Received his education (classics and philosophy) at Paris and Brussels; stud. music at Brussels Cons. Contributor to the *Apollon* and *Muzykalny Sovremmenik* (Petrograd) and to various Russ. dailies. Settled in Paris, 1920; assistant-ed. of, and contributor to, *Revue Musicale.* Author of a critical study (in Russ.) of Scriabin's works (Berlin, 1922, Grassi, 2 vols.). Contributor of various articles on Russ. comprs. in this Dictionary.—E.-H.

SCHLUMA, Alfredo. Argentine compr. *b.* Buenos Ayres in 1885. Stud. under Romanelo. A very fertile compr. and busy concert organiser. Comp. 3 operas (*Biancofiore*, 1913; *Amy Robsart*, 1918; *La Sirocchia*, 1920); 5 symph. poems; many chamber-music pieces.—A. M.

SCHMALSTICH, Clemens. Pianist, teacher and compr. *b.* Posen, 8 Oct. 1880. Stud. philosophy Bonn, music Berlin R. High School (pf. Rudorff, compn. Humperdinck); 1906–9, condr. New Playhouse (Neue Schauspielhaus), Berlin; R. Opera House, Berlin. Comp. pf. music of a bright, taking order (*Suite de Carneval*, op. 27; *Liebeswalzer*, pf. duet; etc.).—A. E.

SCHMEDES, Erik. Danish t. opera-singer; *b.* Copenhagen, 27 Aug. 1866. Went abroad when quite young, first studying as pianist; then under Rothmühl (Berlin) and Resz (Vienna) as barit. and sang at Wiesbaden (1891), Nuremburg (1894), Hamburg operas; then stud. under Issert, Dresden, as t. and sang in 1899 at Bayreuth, as Siegfried and Parsifal. Now one of leading singers of Vienna Opera.—A. H.

SCHMID, Heinrich Kaspar. Ger. compr. *b.* Landau-on-Isar, 11 Sept. 1874. 1884–9, choir-boy at Regensburg (Ratisbon) Cath.; 1899–1903, Munich Acad. (Thuille, Kellermann, Becht, Bussmeyer); 1903, teacher at Cons., Athens (Odeon); 1905, returned to Munich, after a concert-tour (pianist) through Austria, Scandinavia, Russia; teacher at Munich Acad.; 1919, prof.; 1921, dir. of Carlsruhe Cons.

Many songs and song-cycles; 2 books, children's songs; *Turkish Song-book*, op. 19 (Tischer & Jagenberg); *Liederspiel for Lute* (Dehmel and Rückert), op. 31; 5 pieces for wind-instrs. op. 34 (Schott); male choruses, op. 23; children's choruses, op. 21; pf. pieces: op. 2, 3, 5 (Variations on a theme of Thuille), 16 (*Forest Fantasy*); Variations for 2 pfs. on Liszt theme, op. 30 (Schott); Waltzes for 2 and 4 hands, op. 36 (*id.*); Capriccio (*The Dancer*), op. 39 (*id.*); str. 4tet, G ma. op. 26 (*id.*); vn. sonata, A mi. op. 27 (*id.*); 5tet, wind instrs. op. 28 (*id.*); pf. trio, D mi. op. 38 (*id.*); 3 songs, organ acc., op. 29 (*id.*). Consult Herman Roth, *H. K. Sch.* (Munich, 1921, Drei Masken Verlag).—A. E.

SCHMID-LINDNER, August. Ger. pianist; *b.* Augsburg, 15 July, 1870. 1886–90, stud. at Munich Acad. of Music (Bussmeyer, Rheinberger); Berlin Mendelssohn scholarship (1889); also pupil of Sophie Menter; 1893, teacher at Acad.; 1903, prof.; pianist and chamber-musician, Munich; one of first champions of Reger's art, as also of contemporary pf. music. Ed. Bach's pf. clavier music (first with Reger, then alone) and of Liszt's works (Schott).—A. E.

SCHMIDT, Franz. Austrian compr. *b.* Bratislava (Pressburg), 22 Dec. 1874. Stud. cello under Ferdinand Hellmesberger, cellist in orch. of Vienna Court Opera. 1907, prof. cello, Vienna Cons.; 1910, prof. of pf. there. His works are few but remarkable. 1st symphony, in E, gained the prize of Soc. of Friends of Music (1900). The 2nd, in E flat, was publ. 1913. One opera, *Notre-Dame*, made a big success at Vienna Opera, 1914. The second, *Fredegundis*, perf. Berlin (1923), Vienna (1924), was a failure. —H. B.

SCHMIDT, Leopold. Ger. writer on music; *b.* Berlin, 2 Aug. 1860. Stud. music at R. High School for music; 1887, condr. Heidelberg; 1888–9, Berlin (Friedrich Wilhelm City Theatre); 1891, at Zurich (Stadttheater); 1895–7, at Halle-o-S.; 1895, Ph.D. at Rostock; from 1897, mus. critic of Berlin *Tageblatt*; 1900–15, prof. of mus. history Stern's Cons.; 1912, also at Klindworth-Scharwenka Conservatoire.

History of the Fairy-Opera (1895); *Meyerbeer* (1898);

Haydn (1898, 3rd ed. 1914); *Mozart* (1909, 2nd ed. 1920); *History of Music of XIX Century* (1901); *Masters of Musical Art and Science of XIX Century* (biographical sketches, 1903, 3rd ed. 1921); coll. of criticisms, Vol. I, *Musical Life of Present Day* (1908); Vol. II, *Experiences and Reflections* (1913; Vol. III, 1922).—A. E.

SCHMITT, Florent. Fr. compr. *b.* Blamont, 28 Sept. 1870. Began his mus. education at Nancy and continued it (from 1889) at Paris Cons. where his teachers were Dubois and Lavignac (harmony), Massenet and Fauré (compn.). He won the *Prix de Rome* in 1900, and in 1922 was appointed dir. of Lyons Cons. Between these two dates the only important facts are the performance and publication of his works. These are many, and so varied in character, that at first sight his individuality, although striking and distinctive, may seem difficult to define. He has been more directly influenced by Ger. Romanticism than any other Fr. compr. of his generation. He owes much to the Russians (especially Balakiref and the early Glazunof) and to Chabrier. Fullness and energy are the chief characteristics of his music.

These qualities are apparent in works such as his *Psalm XLVI* (1904, Mathot), the tone-poem, *The Haunted Palace* (1904, Durand), the pf. 5tet, (1908, Mathot) and *La Tragédie de Salomé* (1911, Durand); the incidental music for *Antony and Cleopatra* (1919, Durand). With the *Musiques de plein air* for orch. (1900–8, Mathot), the *Musiques intimes* for pf. (1st set 1897, Heugel; 2nd set 1903, Mathot) and the *Nuits romaines* for pf. (1901, Hamelle) he is nearer the Impressionistic Fr. tendencies of the period to which these works belong. He has also written a vn. sonata, songs, part-songs, a *Chant de Guerre*, an orch. suite *Mirages* (1924), and pf. pieces.

Consult bibliography in Séré (*q.v.*), and further: A. Cœuroy, *La Musique française moderne* (Paris, 1922); M. D. Calvocoressi (*New Music Review*, 1911); P. O. Ferroud (*Revue Musicale*, April 1924).—M. D. C.

SCHMITZ, Eugen. Ger. writer on music; *b.* Neuburg, on the Danube, 12 July, 1882. Stud. music at Munich (Beer-Walbrunn) and at Univ. (Sandberger and Kroyer); 1905, graduated; resided some time Leipzig; then at Munich (Starnberg) as mus. reporter of *Münchner Allgemeine Zeitung*; 1908, of *Münchner Zeitung*, and ed. of *Neue Musikalische Rundschau*; 1909, hon. lecturer at Munich Univ.; 1914, dir. of the Mozarteum, Salzburg, which position he soon resigned; 1915, went to Dresden as critic and mus. ed, of *Dresdener Nachrichten*; 1916, Univ. teacher of mus. science at Dresden Technical High School; 1918, professor.

Publ. *Selected Works of Johann Staden* as Vols. VII i and VIII i of *D.T.B.*; new ed. of *Naumann's Musical History*, 1908 and 1918; new ed. of Marx's *Instruction for playing Beethoven's Pf. Compositions* (1912); biography of *Hugo Wolf* (1906, Reclam); *Richard Strauss as Mus. Dramatist* (1907); *Max Reger's Symphonietta* (1905); *Karl von Kaskel* (1907, Kahnt); *Puccini's* "*Bohème*" (1908); *Richard Wagner* (1909 and 1918); *Theory of Harmony Instruction* (1911); *History of Secular Solo-Cantata* (1914); *Palestrina* (1914); *Manual of Music Æsthetics* (1915); *Madonna Ideal in Art* (1919); *The Pf. and Pf.-playing* (1919).—A. E.

SCHNABEL, Alexander Maria. Ger. compr. *b.* Riga, 17 Dec. 1890. 1907–12, pupil of Payr at

Vienna; also of Ohnesorg; member of board of directors of German - Baltic Music Teachers' Society. Lives at Riga.

Pf. sonatas, C, op. 1; E flat mi. op. 8; pf. and cello sonata, C sharp mi. op. 4; vn. and pf. sonata, G, op. 5; pf. trio, C mi. op. 10; *Gorm Grimme* (melo-drama), op. 11; songs. In ms.: 3 pf. sonatas, op. 19; pf. suite, *Pan*, op. 14; str. 4tet, D, op. 12; pf. 5tet, op. 18; chamber-symphony, 12 solo instrs. op. 16; Symph. Round Dance, full orch. op. 15; *Babylonian Tragedy*, full orch. op. 20; songs, op. 13 and 17. (Publ. Raabe & Plothow, Berlin.)—A. E.

SCHNABEL, Arthur. German-Czechoslovak pianist and compr. *b.* Lipnik, 17 April, 1882. Pupil of Hans Schmitt (pf.); 1888–97, at Vienna under Leschetizky; devoted himself to virtuoso-career with great success (especially as a Brahms-player); 1919, prof.; married Therese (*née* Behr), highly esteemed contr. concert-singer. Ed. (with Carl Flesch) Mozart's Vn. Sonatas (Peters). As a composer he belongs to the Expressionist school.

Str. 4tet; *Dance Suite*, pf.; sonata for vn. alone. —E. S.

SCHNÉEVOIGT, Georg. Finnish cellist, orch. condr. *b.* Viipuri (Viborg), 8 Nov. 1872. Stud. at Orch. School, Helsingfors, and abroad (Son-dershausen, Leipzig, Brussels, Dresden, Vienna). 8 years solo cellist in Philh. Orch. Helsingfors; gave concerts in Finland and abroad. Later took up conducting. Condr. in Riga (1901–9 and 1912–13) where he founded the Riga Symphony Orch.; 1904–8, condr. of Kaim Orch. Munich. In 1912 he founded in Helsingfors a new symphony orch., which amalgamated with Philh. Orch. in 1914 and was taken over by the municipality (see KAJANUS). 1914–16, condr. of the new Municipal Orch.; since 1914, also condr. of the Concert Association (Konsertföreningen) in Stockholm and later in Christiania and Scheven-ingen. S. has acquired a reputation as a condr. of great technical ability and ardent temperament; has appeared with much success in many European music centres, Berlin, London, Rome, Holland, Belgium, Switzerland.—T. H.

SCHNÉEVOIGT, Sigrid (*neé* Sundgren). Finnish pianist; *b.* 1878. Stud. at Helsingfors Music Inst. 1886–94, and for 3 years with Busoni in Berlin. Has given successful concerts—in part together with her husband, the orch. condr. Georg Schnéevoigt in Finland, Sweden, Den-mark, Germany, Russia, and Italy. Since 1910, teacher of pf. at Helsingfors Music Inst.—T. H.

SCHNEIDER, Max. Ger. writer on music; *b.* Eisleben, 20 July, 1875. 1895, stud. at Leipzig Univ. (Paul, Riemann, Kretzschmar); compn. under Jadassohn; 1897–1901, operatic condr. at Stadttheater, Halle, and at Theater des Westens, Berlin; 1904, librarian of Music-history College, Berlin Univ.; 1907–14, assistant to Kopfermann, music department R. Library; 1909, teacher at Acad. Inst. for Church Music; 1913, prof.; 1915, prof.-extraordinary at Univ. and teacher R. Inst. for Church Music, Breslau; 1920, prof.-in-ordinary.

Register of Literature on J. S. Bach (*Bach Annual*, 1905); *Catalogue of Printed Works of Joh. Seb. Bach* (*Bach Annual*, 1906); *Thematic Register of Musical Works of Bach Family* (Part I, *Bach Annual*, 1907); *The Concerto known as* "*Organ Concerto in D mi.* of

W. Fr. Bach" (*Bach Annual*, 1911); *New Edi-tion of Mattheson's "Ehrenpforte"* (Breitkopf); *Diego Ortiz' Tratado de glosas sobre clausulas* with transl.; (with H. Springer and W. Wolffheim) *Miscellanea Musicæ Bio-bibliographica* (since 1912); 1918, publ. *The Beginnings of Basso Continuo* (Figured-Bass) *and its Figuring* (Breitkopf); in *D.d.T.* XXVIII, Tele-mann's *Judgment Day* and *Ino*; XXXVII and XXXVIII, Keiser's *Crösus* and *L'Inganno fedele*. —A. E.

SCHNEIDER-TRNAVSKÝ, Mikuláš. Slovak compr. *b.* Trnava, 1881. Stud. at Cons. Prague. Music Inspector, Trnava. The most modern of the comprs. of liberated Slovakia. Publ. coll. of Slovak folk-songs (Prague, 1908, Fr. Chadím).

Collections of songs: *Slzy a úsměvy*; *Zo srdca*; choral works; vn. sonata; pf. 5tet; symph. piece, *Podtatranská Idylla*.—V. ST.

SCHNELLAR, Johann. Austrian timpanist of Vienna Philh. Orch. Constructed kettle-drums with a hole in the middle of the skin, by which equality of sound, wherever the stick touches the skin, is obtained. Famous teacher of timpani-playing.—EG. W.

SCHNERICH, Alfred. Austrian musicologist; *b.* Tarvis, 22 Oct. 1859. Ph.D. Vienna Univ. 1888. Since 1889, engaged at Library there, his speciality being the church music of the last 2 centuries.

Der Messentypus von Haydn bis Schubert (1892); *Die Frage der Reform der Katholischen Kirchenmusik* (1902); *Messe und Requiem seit Haydn und Mozart* (1909); *Unsere Kirchenmusik* (1911); *Wiens Kirchen und Kapellen* (1920); *Josef Haydn* (1922). A notable essay of his, *Das Kirchenmusikwesen in Wien*, appeared in *Die Musik* (1915). Made a facsimile ed. of Mozart's *Requiem*.—P. ST.

SCHNITZLER, Louis. The best-known Dutch accompanist; *b.* Rotterdam, 28 Nov. 1869. Stud. under Gernsheim, Rotterdam. Has also composed some songs.—W. P.

SCHOECK, Othmar. Swiss compr. *b.* Brun-nen, 1 Sept. 1886. Stud. pf. and compn. at Zurich Cons. (1905–7) under F. Niggli and Robert Freund, and one year in Leipzig under Max Reger. Lives in Zurich, where he cond. the Männerchor Aussersihl (1909–15) and the Lehrer-gesangverein (1911–17). Condr. of Symphony Concerts in St. Gall since 1917. Comp. many songs, most of them superior in melody and imaginative beauty to anything that had been written before in Switzerland; he is often called the "Swiss Schubert." His compns. show a cer-tain relationship to Schubert in their richness and melodic charm; and they also recall Mozart in their perfect structure and Hugo Wolf in expression and excellent diction. He is, above all else, a singer, and in the direction of song he rises to his best. In many of his passages there is an ecstasy that soars until lost, as it were, in the empyrean of transcendental melody. S. is the most outstanding figure amongst the younger Swiss composers.

Serenade, small orch. op. 1; vn. concerto, op. 21; *Der Postillon* (Lenau), male chorus and orch. op. 18; *Dithyrambe* (Goethe), mixed chorus and orch. op. 22; *Wegelied* (Keller), male chorus and orch. op. 24; *Trommelschläge* (*Drum-Taps*) (Whitman), mixed chorus and orch. op. 26 (Breitkopf). Operas: *Erwin und Elmire* (Goethe), singspiel, op. 25 (Breitkopf); *Don Ranudo* (Armin Rüger), comic opera, op. 27 (Breitkopf); *Das Wandbild* (Busoni), pantomime, op. 28 (Breitkopf); *Venus* (Rüger) op. 32; vn. sonata, op. 16; str. 4tet in D, op. 23; over 100

songs, op. 2 to 17 (Hug), op. 19 to 34 (Breitkopf). The majority of his,works are publ. by Hug, Leipzig. Consult: Dr. H. Corrodi in periodicals *Der Kunstwart* (Munich, July 1922), *Die Schweiz* (Zurich, June 1919), *Neue Musikzeitung* (Stuttgart, 18 July, 1918), and an article in *Sunday Times* (London, 21 May, 1922), on his opera *Venus*, perf. at International Fest. in Zurich.—F. H.

SCHOLA CANTORUM, Paris. Founded in 1896 by Vincent d'Indy, Charles Bordes and Guilmant; really an enlargement of Association des Chanteurs de Saint-Gervais (see CHORAL SOCIETIES). It gives a complete mus. education and constitutes a small Cons. which perpetuates the teaching of César Franck. This teaching has a moral and even religious character. It is generally reproached with dogmatism and artistic *intransigeance*. The personal ascendancy exercised by Vincent d'Indy over the pupils is enormous. Instruction in plain-chant holds a considerable place in the curriculum; in the same way, the study of the classics follows the pedagogic system of textual explanation.—A. C.

SCHOLES, Percy Alfred. Eng. journalist and author; *b.* Leeds, 24 July, 1877. Formerly music critic *Evening Standard*; now of *The Observer*, London (from March 1920); founder and ed. of *The Music Student* (now ed. by W. R. Anderson as *The Music Teacher*); founder and former ed. of *Music and Youth*; musical critic to British Broadcasting Company (from June 1923).

Everyman and his Music (Kegan Paul, 1917): *An Introduction to British Music* (Cecil Palmer, 1918); *The Listener's Guide to Music* (H. Milford, 1919); *The Book of the Great Musicians* (*id.* 1922); *The Beginner's Guide to Harmony* (*id.*); *Musical Appreciation, Why and How?* (*id.*); *Listener's History of Music*, Vol. I (*id.* 1923); *First Book of the Gramophone Record* (*id.* 1923); *Crotchets* (J. Lane, 1924). —E.-H.

SCHOLTZ, Hermann. Ger. pianist and compr. *b.* Breslau, 9 June, 1845; *d.* Dresden, 13 July, 1918. Pupil of Brosig; stud. Leipzig, 1865 (Plaidy, Karl Riedel and Schulz-Beuthen); 1867, on Liszt's advice stud. at Munich R. School of Music (Bülow and Rheinberger); teacher there 6 years; 1880, title of R. Saxonian chamber-virtuoso; 1910, R. professor.

Pf. concerto, E mi.; trio, F mi. op. 51; sonata, op. 44; 5 books of variations; pf. pieces, op. 60; *Ländler*, op. 64; *Balladen*, op. 66 and 78; Passacaglia, op. 74; Scherzo, op. 79; Variations on own theme, 2 pfs. op. 77; many lyrical pieces. He rev. Chopin ed. for Peters; ed. of Heller's Studies, op. 47, 46, 45; and Brahms's pf. concerto, op. 15 (London, Augener).—A. E.

SCHOLZ, Bernhard E. German compr. *b.* Mayence, 30 March, 1835; *d.* Munich, 26 Dec. 1916. Stud. under Ernst Pauer (pf.); 1855, S. W. Dehn (theory); 1856, teacher of theory at R. School of Music, Munich; 1859–65, Court-condr. at Hanover; 1871, at Breslau as condr. of Orch. Soc. Concerts; 1883, dir. Hoch's Cons. Frankfort-o-M.; 1884, also condr. of Rühl's Choral Soc.; 1908, retired and lived at Florence; 1914, at Munich. Ph.D. Breslau *h.c.* and prof.

Instruction in Counterpoint and Imitation (1897); *Whither are we drifting?* (1904); *Musical and Personal* (1899); *Memories of Past Melodies* (1911). Songs (op. 11, 22); pf. sonatinas, op. 41; chamber-music: str. 4tets, G ma. op. 46 and A mi. op. 48; 5tet, op. 47; pf. concerto, B ma. op. 57; symphony, B flat ma. op. 60; *Malinconia*, orch.; *Das Siegesfest Victory Festival* (soli, chorus and orch.); *Song of*

the Bell (*id.*); *Sylvesterglocken* (*New Year's Eve Bells*) (*id.*); 2 overtures (Goethe's *Iphigenia*), op. 15; *Im Freien* (*In the Open Air*), op. 21; *Requiem*; operas: *Carlo Rosa* (Munich, 1858); *Zietensche Husaren* (Breslau, 1869); *Morgiane* (Munich, 1870); *Golo* (Genoveva, Nuremberg, 1875); *Trumpeter of Säckingen* (Wiesbaden, 1877); *Die vornehmen Wirte* (*Fashionable Hosts*) (Leipzig, 1863); *Ingo* (Frankfort-o-M. 1898); *Anno 1757* (Berlin, 1903); *Mirandolina* (Darmstadt, 1907).—A. E.

SCHÖNBERG, Arnold. Austrian composer and theorist; *b.* Vienna, 13 Sept. 1874. Began when quite young to compose chamber-music; at early age studied violin and cello; self-taught in musical theory, only having a few months' tuition from Zemlinsky, through whom he came into contact with musicians. In 1893 made a piano arrangement of Zemlinsky's opera *Sarema*. At that period he wrote a quartet in D minor, which was performed with some alterations in the following season (1898–9) by the Fitzner Quartet. This work is lost. In 1898 he wrote many songs (of which two are published as op. 1). Others, written 1898–1900 (now op. 2 and 3), were first performed by Gärtner in Vienna, in Dec. 1900. In the summer of 1899 he composed the string sextet *Verklärte Nacht*, op. 4, in the manner of a symphonic poem. In March 1900, he began the *Gurrelieder*, a ballad-cycle for 5 soli, 3 male choruses with 4 voices, mixed chorus for 8 voices and full orchestra. The work consists of 3 parts. Composition in 1900–1 was interrupted by the necessity of scoring operettas; though the instrumentation of the 1st, 2nd and beginning of the 3rd part was finished. In 1901 he married Mathilde Zemlinsky, sister of Alexander Zemlinsky, and removed to Berlin, as conductor at the Überbrettl, a literary variety theatre. He again scored operettas for many now famous operetta-composers. In 1902–3, composed a symphonic poem, *Pelléas and Mélisande*. He returned to Vienna- in 1903 and began his career as a teacher of theory. His name was now known to a select circle of young musicians; and he formed a close friendship with Rosé and Gustav Mahler. The end of the Wagnerian line and the beginning of Schönberg's second period show a return to a new classical style, seen in the six songs with orchestra, op. 8 (1904). The summers of 1904–5 were occupied with the string quartet in D minor, op. 7, at Gmunden. During the winter 1904–5 the first performance of *Pelléas and Mélisande* was given by the Society of Creative Musicians in Vienna with Schönberg as conductor. In 1905, eight songs, op. 6; 1906–7, two ballads, op. 12; 1906, *Kammersinfonie* (*q.v.*), op. 9, and part of a second one (unfinished); 1907, 2nd string quartet, op. 10 (with voice) (1st performance Dec. 1908, Rosé Quartet, Vienna). This work marks the end of the second period.

The transition from the classical to the new period is seen in some of the Stefan George *Lieder*, op. 15. The years 1907–10 were astonishingly productive, not only in music, but for Schönberg, inspired by the new movement in painting (notably the Exhibition of the *Kunstschau* in Vienna, with works of Klimt and Kokoschka), began to paint himself. A collection of Portraits and Visions dating from this period was exhibited in Vienna in 1901. The new musical style is fully expressed in the three piano pieces, op. 11 (composed early in 1909), in the five orchestral pieces, op. 16, the monodrama *Erwartung*, op. 17, a modern form of solo-cantata for the stage (with a single acting part; adapted from a book by Mary Pappenheim). Immediately after this work Schönberg began another dramatic work, for which he wrote his own book, *Die glückliche Hand*, op. 18, finished in 1913. In 1910–11 he wrote his famous manual *Harmonielehre* and finished scoring the *Gurre-lieder*. In the autumn of 1911 he again removed to Berlin, lectured on composition and began the *Pierrot lunaire*, op. 21—a cycle of 21 tiny poems recited to music. This work, (performed by Albertine Zehme in Berlin, autumn 1912) made his name famous. It is a chamber-work for recitation, with piano, flute, clarinet, violin, cello. During the 1912–13 season he undertook a tour with *Pierrot lunaire* party, and conducted his own works in Amsterdam, Petrograd and Prague. The first Vienna performance of the *Gurrelieder* was due to Franz Schreker, then condr. of the Philharmonic Choir. In 1913–14 he composed the four songs with orchestra, op. 22. In Feb. 1914 he conducted his five orchestral pieces, op. 16, in London (first performance in London, Sept. 3, 1912, under Sir Henry Wood; 1922, under Goossens). In 1915–17 he began a grand oratorio, *Jakobsleiter* (*Jacob's Ladder*). In 1918, he founded the Society for Private Musical Performances (known as Schönberg Verein) in Vienna. In 1920–21 he lectured on composition in Amsterdam. He then returned to Mödling, near Vienna, began to teach again, to write a work on musical composition (not yet finished) and resumed teaching and composition. In 1922 he issued a new and revised edition of his *Manual of Harmony*. In 1923 he comp. a cycle of pf. pieces, a 5tet and a 7tet for various instrs. These works seem to be the beginning of a new period of his evolution.

Works (publ. by Univ. Ed. Vienna, unless otherwise marked):

Op. 1. 2 songs, barit. (*Thanks, Parting*)
    2. 4 songs (*Expectation, Give me, Exaltation, Forest Sun*)
    3. 6 songs (*From the Youth's Magic Horn, The Excited Ones, Warning, Wedding-song, A Skilled Heart, Freihold*)
    4. Str. 6tet, *Verklärte Nacht*
    5. *Pelléas and Mélisande*, symph. poem for orch.
    6. 8 songs
    7. Str. 4tet in D mi.
    8. 6 songs with orch.
    9. Chamber-symphony, E flat
    10. Str. 4tet in F sharp mi. (with v.)
    11. 3 pf. pieces
    12. 2 ballads (*Jane Grey, Deathbound Squad*)
    13. *Friede auf Erden* (Tischer & Jagenberg)
    14. 2 songs (*I may not, In Winter Days*)
    15. 15 songs from Stefan George
    16. 5 orch. pieces (Peters)
    17. *Erwartung* (monodrama)
    18. *The Lucky Hand* (drama with music)
    19. 6 little pf. pieces
    20. *Herzgewächse* (s., celesta, organ, harp)
    21. *Pierrot lunaire* (London perf. 20 Nov. 1923)
    22. *Gurrelieder*
    23. 7tet (various instruments)
    24. Pf. suite

Consult: *A. Sch.* (by 11 pupils and friends) (Munich, 1912, Piper & Co.); E. Wellesz, *A. Sch.* Vienna, 1921, Tal); E. Wellesz, *A. Sch.* (J. M. Dent & Sons, London, 1924); art. by Cecil Gray, in *Music and Letters*, Jan. 1922.—EG. W.

SCHOOLS OF MUSIC. See ACADEMIES.

SCHRAMMEL, Johann. Austrian compr. *b.* Vienna, 22 May, 1850; *d.* there, 17 June, 1897. The last *Old Viennese* musician, of a long line of musicians. Stud. at Cons., and founded in 1877 the famous Quartet D'Schrammeln with his brother Josef, the clarinettist Danzer and the guitarist Strohmayer. Later on, the accordion, a typical street-player's instr., replaced the clar. By his songs (over 150), acc. by 2 vns., guitar and accordion, he became so famous that to-day nearly all the comprs. of popular Viennese comprs., especially operetta-comprs. are arr. for this combination which is called *Schrammel quartet.*—EG. W.

SCHREIBER, Adolf. German-Czechoslovak compr. *b.* Prague, 1883; *d.* by his own hand, 1 Sept. 1920, in Berlin. Stud. at Prague Cons. (under Dvořák); condr. in many Austrian and German cities; teacher at Mary Hahn's New Opera School, Berlin; and for one season, Korrepetitor at Ger. Opera House in Charlottenburg. Over 200 songs; a chorus with orch. (*Lenore*); a song-cycle, *Marienleben*, for v. clar. and vla.; a song-cycle to words by Christian Morgenstern; sonata for vn. and clar.; pf. pieces; stage music to 2 dramas of Max Brod. Consult Max Brod, *A. S. : Ein Musiker-schicksal* (*A Musician's Fate*) (1921).—E. S.

SCHREKER, Franz. Composer; *b.* Monaco, Riviera, 23 March, 1878. Pupil of Robert Fuchs, Vienna; founder (1911) and conductor of Philharmonic Choral Society, and since 1911 teacher of composition at Royal and Imperial Academy, Vienna; 1920, director of Academical High School of Music, Berlin. The material of the *dramatist* Schreker is either half cinema style, and half E. T. A. Hoffmann's style, or pseudo-Renaissance art-drama (*Der ferne Klang*; *Die Gezeichneten*), or mystic, symbolic fairy-tale (*Spielwerk*; *Die Schatzgräber*). Common to all these works is the purely erotic movement of all the motives and figures, which even has its roots in sexual psychology and pathology; common is the less well-chosen, but sure theatrical effect. The *musician* Schreker proceeds by contrasts, by fascination of tone, without scorning the working-out of motives or a style of romantically coloured sensuous melody. Schreker is very influential as a master and a model.

All works, not otherwise marked, publ. in Univ. Ed., Vienna. Op. 1 missing; op. 2, *Two Songs*, v. and pf.; op. 3, *5 Poems*, v. and pf. (Robitschek); op. 4, *Five Songs*, v. and pf. (Robitschek); op. 5, *Two Songs on the Death of a Child*; op. 6, *Psalm CXVI*, 3-v. female chorus (Robitschek); *Orchesterstück*, str. orch. and harp (lost; perf. London, 1896); *Andante for Orch.* (unpubl., perf. at Cons. 1900); *Ave Maria*, v. and organ (*Der Merker*, I, 2); *Eight Songs*, v. and pf.; op. 8, *Intermezzo*, str. orch. (Bosworth); op. 10, *Flammen* (*Flames*), 1-act opera (printed privately); op. 11, *Swan Song*, mixed chorus and orch.; op. 12, *Ekke-hard*, symph. overture, orch.; *Romantic Suite*, orch.; *Fantastic Overture*, orch.; *Der Geburtstag der Infantin*, music to dance-pantomime (after O. Wilde) rev. 1923; *The Wind*, dance-allegory, orch.; *Dance Suite*, full orch. (ms.); *Der ferne Klang* (*Far-off Tone*), opera, Frankfort-o-M. 1912; *Five Songs*, v. and pf.; *Ent-führung* (*Elopement*), for v. and pf. (*Der Merker*,

III, 4); *Das Spielwerk und die Prinzessin* (*The Musical Box and the Princess*), opera, Vienna, 1913 (rev. 1915 to 1-act setting, *Das Spielwerk*, Munich, 1920); *The Red Death* (E. A. Poe); *Die Gezeichneten* (*The Branded*), opera, Frankfort-o-M, 1918; *Die tönenden Sphären* (*The Sounding Spheres*), opera-poem, 1915 (ms.); Chamber-Symphony for 23 solo instrs.; *Der Schatzgräber* (*The Treasure-Seeker*), opera, Frankfort-o-M. 1920; *Memnon*, operatic poem; *Irrelohe* (*Fitful Flames*), opera-poem, Cologne,1924. Has publ. 2 books of his *Poems for Music* (1920, Univ. Ed.). Consult: Paul Bekker, *F. Schr.: Study in Criticism of Modern Opera* (1919); R. St. Hoffmann, *F. Schr.* (Vienna, 1921, Tal & Co.); Jul. Kapp, *F. Schr.* (Munich, 1921, Drei Masken Verlag).—A. E.

SCHREYER, Johannes. Ger. ed. and teacher; *b.* Possendorf, near Dresden, 20 June, 1856. Stud. at Leipzig Cons. and R. Acad. of Art, Berlin (compn.); 1881, music-master at Dresden.
Ed. selection of Bach's organ works with phrase-marks; theoretical work, *From Bach to Wagner: Contributions to Psychology of Musical Hearing* (1903, rev. as *Instruction in Harmony*, 1905; 4th ed. 1911); *Contributions to Bach Criticism* (1911-12, 2 vols.).—A. E.

SCHRÖDER, Edmund. Ger. compr. *b.* Berlin, 1882. Pupil of Ph. Scharwenka; then of R. High School (H. v. Eyken); finally of Reger and Storck.
Over 100 songs; 3 pf. trios; suite, cello and pf.; 7 duets, vn. and pf. 3 pieces, bsn. and pf.—A. E.

SCHROEDER, Alwin. Ger. cellist; *b.* Neu-haldensleben, 15 June, 1855. Brother of Karl, pianist, pupil of father and of brother, Hermann; later of J. B. André at Ballenstedt; also violinist (pupil of de Ahna at Berlin R. High School); stud. theory under W. Tappert; taught himself the cello; 1875, 1st cellist in Liebig's Concert Orch.; 1880, Leipzig Gewandhaus Orch. (successor to his brother Karl); cello-teacher at Cons.; cellist in Petri's Str. Quartet; 1886, cellist in Kneisel Quartet, Boston, U.S.A.; 1907, succeeded Hugo Becker at Frankfort; 1908, acc. Felix Berber to Geneva; returned to Boston same year as cellist in Hess Quartet.—A. E.

SCHROEDER, Karl. Ger. cellist and condr. *b.* Quedlinburg, 18 Dec. 1848. Pupil of Drechsler at Dessau ; 1862, member of Court Orch. Sondershausen ; 1871, formed touring str. quartet with three brothers, Hermann (1st vn.), Franz (2nd vn.), and Alwin (vla.); 1872, condr. Kroll's Theatre; 1873, 1st cellist of Court Theatre, Brunswick; 1874, solo-cellist, Gewandhaus; teacher at Cons. Leipzig; 1881, Court-condr. Sondershausen ; establ. Cons. there; sold same, 1866; condr. Ger. Opera at Rotterdam one season; chief condr. Berlin Court Opera House; 1888, succeeded Sucher at Hamburg; 1890, returned to Sondershausen as Court-condr. and dir. of Cons.; 1907, retired; 1908, Frankenhausen; Dresden; since 1911 at Berlin, as teacher at Stern's Conservatoire.
For cello: concertos, op. 32, D mi. and op. 36, A mi.; *Capriccios*, op. 26; studies, op. 48; cello tutor, op. 34 (4 parts); 2 str. 4tets, op. 88 and 89; str. trio; songs; pf. pieces; operas: *Aspasia* (1892, rev. as *Die Palikarin*, Posen, 1905); *Der Asket* (*The Ascetic*) (Leipzig, 1893). Elementary books: *Time-keeping and Conducting*; *Cello - playing*; *Violin - playing* (Berlin, Max Hesse).—A. E.

SCHUBERT, Kurt. Pianist and compr. *b.* Berlin, 1891. Pf. pupil of father and of Xaver Scharwenka; 1918, teacher of pf. training class at Klindworth-Scharwenka Cons.; 1921,

teacher at State Acad. Inst. for Church Music; 1921, also vice-chairman of Berlin Tonkünstlerverein; 1922, made prof. Wrote a 5tet in 1 movement for pf. and strings.—A. E.

SCHUCH, Ernst von. Austrian condr. *b.* Graz (Steiermark), 23 Nov. 1847; *d.* Dresden, 10 May, 1914. First stud. law at Graz; finally turned to music; trained by E. Stoltz and (for short time) by O. Dessoff; 1867, chief condr. at Lobe's Theatre, Breslau; later at Würzburg, Graz and at Basle (1871); 1872 (after conducting Pollini's Ital. Opera), engaged as chief condr. at Dresden Court Opera House; 1873, R. condr. with Rietz; 1878, R. prof.; 1882 (after Rietz's death) 1st condr. Dresden Opera (for a short time); 1889, gen. mus. dir.; 1899, privy-councillor; 1875, married operatic singer, Klementine Proska (real name, Procházka), Vienna. Their daughter, Lisel, was engaged at Dresden Court Opera House as coloratura singer, 1914. Schuch was an especially sensitive condr. of Ital. opera; he cond. 1st perfs. of most of R. Strauss's operas. Consult P. Sakolowsky, *E. Schuch* (1901).—A. E.

SCHULHOFF, Erwin. Pianist and compr. *b.* Prague, 8 June, 1894. Stud. pf. under Jindřich Kaàn de Albést; 1902-4, attended Prague Cons.; 1904-8, pupil of Willy Thern, Vienna; 1908-10, of Leipzig Cons. (Teichmüller, Krehl, Reger); 1910-14, of Cologne Cons. (Uzielli, Friedberg, Steinbach, Bölsche); 1913, gained Mendelssohn Prize for pf.; 1918, same prize for compn. at Berlin High School. An excellent pianist, making propaganda for the most modern music of all countries. In his compns. he aims at natural Expressionism and the grotesque. His style is between Schönberg's and Stravinsky's.
Pf. pieces (Jatho, Berlin): preludes; fugues; inventions: variations; 2 pf. sonatas; *Six Ironies*, pf. duet; suites, vn. and pf.; sonata, vn. and pf.; sonata, cello and pf.; str. 4tet; *Divertimento*, str. 4tet; 3 pieces for double-bsn. alone; pf. concerto; 32 variations on original 8-bar theme (orch.); *Serenade* (orch.); *Lustige Ouvertüre*, orch.; *Landschaften* symphony; *Menschheit* (*Humanity*) symphony, contr. and orch.; suite in modern style for chamber-orch.; *5 Expressions* for voice and pf.; songs.—E. S.

SCHULTHESS, Walter. Swiss composer; *b.* Zurich, 24 July, 1894. Stud. compn. under Volkmar Andreae, pf. under P. Moeckel at Zurich; at Munich Cons. (1915), pupil of Courvoisier and Schmid-Lindner; 1916, in Berlin, under Ansorge. Lives at Zurich. His music shows the influence of Max Reger, and reveals great originality and strong invention.
Vn. sonata; str. 4tet; str. trio; concertino, vn. and orch. (all by Schott); pf. pieces; songs (Zurich, Hug).—F. H.

SCHULTS, Ulfert. Dutch pianist and compr. *b.* Amsterdam, 19 Nov. 1871. Dir. of Music School, Amsterdam; mus. critic of *Het Nieuws van den Dag*, 1911-22.
Pf. pieces: *Aquarellen*; *Andante and Scherzo*; *Valse*; *Papillons*; *Scherzo*; *Tambourin*; 20 smaller pieces; *Valses*, op. 13 (Amsterdam, Alsbach); Theme and variations for 2 pfs. op. 10 (Leipzig, Rieter-Biederman); many songs.—W. P.

SCHULZ, Heinrich (Schulz-Beuthen). Compr. *b.* Beuthen (Upper Silesia), 19 June, 1838; *d.* Dresden, 12 March, 1915. 1862-5, attended

Leipzig Cons.; private lessons from Karl Riedel; 1866, went to Zurich. Illness prevented him for considerable time from composing; 1881, settled at Dresden; 1893-5 at Vienna; since at Dresden again; 1911, R. prof. Compns. mostly in ms.; 8 symphonies; symph. poems; choral works; chamber-music; operas.—A. E.

SCHUMANN, Elisabeth. Austrian opera singer; b. Merseburg (Thuringia). Since 1919 at Vienna Opera (formerly at Hamburg). Her fine, easily produced s. voice is specially suited to Mozart (best parts, Susanna and Zerlina; but in other parts also she has proved an excellent soubrette and coloratura singer. Many tours (last with R. Strauss in America, 1921). Fine singer of Strauss's songs. Married the condr. Karl Alwin.—P. St.

SCHUMANN, Georg Alfred. Ger. compr. and condr. b. Königstein, Saxony, 25 Oct. 1866. Pupil of C. A. Fischer, B. Rollfuss and Fr. Baumfelder at Dresden; 1882-8, of Leipzig Cons.; 1890-6, condr. Dantzig Choral Union; 1896-9, condr. of Philh. Orch. Bremen; 1900, R. prof.; succeeded Blumner as condr. Berlin Acad. of Singing; 1913, chairman of advanced school of compn. (successor to Bruch); 1916, Ph.D. Berlin Univ. h.c.

Choral works with orch.: *Amor and Psyche*, op. 3; *Song of Praise and Thanksgiving*; *Ruth* (1908); *Death Lament* from *The Bride of Messina*, op. 33; *Longing*, op. 40; *Das Thränenkrüglein* (*The Lachrymatory*), op. 57 (soli, chorus, pf. harp, harmonium); burlesque scena, t. and contr. soli and orch. *David and Absalom*; *Serenade* (Uhland), op. 70; Prize Symphony, B mi.; 2nd symphony, F mi. op. 42; overtures: *Spring of Love* (*Liebesfrühling*); *For a Drama*, op. 45; *Joys of Life* (*Lebensfreude*), op. 54; *Serenade*, op. 32; Symph. Variations on *Wer nur den lieben Gott läszt walten*, op. 24 (organ and orch.); orch. suite, *At Carnival Time*, op. 32; orch. variations and double fugue on a merry theme, op. 30; orch. variations and fugue on a Bach theme, op. 59; Variations and fugue on a Beethoven theme, 2 pfs.; organ Passacaglia on B.A.C.H., op. 39; pf. 5tets, op. 18, E mi. and op. 49, F. ma.; pf. 4tet, F mi. op. 29; trios, F ma. op. 25 and F ma. op. 62; 2 vn. sonatas, op. 12; 55; cello sonata, op. 19; pf. pieces; songs.—A. E.

SCHUMANN, Maria. Violinist; b. Philadelphia. Began studies at G.S.M. London, continued under Brodsky and Joachim in Germany, later in Brussels and Budapest. Concert tours in U.S.A. Prof. of vn. Buenos Ayres Cons. 1893-1902. Returned to concert platform, touring in Mexico and Chile; 1909, prof. of vn. Thibaud-Piazzini Cons. Buenos Ayres.—S. G. S.

SCHUMANN-HEINK, Ernestine (*née* Rossler). Amer. contr. singer; b. Lieben, near Prague, 15 July, 1861. Received her education at Ursuline Convent, Prague, and in 1874 her training in singing from Marietta von Leclair at Graz, where she made her 1st public appearance 2 years later in contr. solo in Ninth Symphony. Immediately engaged for the Dresden Hofoper; *début* as Azucena, 13 Oct. 1878, meanwhile continuing her vocal studies under Krebs and Wüllner. Went to Berlin in 1882; appeared next year at Hamburg Stadttheater, and thereafter sang in concert, oratorio and at fests. in principal Ger. cities. Made English *début* as Erda at Covent Garden, 8 June, 1892; sang at Bayreuth, 1896;

at the Royal Opera, Berlin, 1898. Came to America, and appeared for 1st time in Chicago, 7 Nov. 1898, as Ortrud; in New York at Metropolitan Opera, in same rôle, 9 Jan. 1899. 1903-4, and again in 1904-5, undertook wide tours of U.S.A. in comic opera, *Love's Lottery*, specially written for her by Julian Edwards. In 1909 she created the part of Klytemnestra in Strauss's *Elektra*. Since then, occasional appearances in opera. Begins (1923-4) her 47th concert season. She was at her best in the great Wagnerian contralto parts, Brangäne, Erda, Waltraute, Ortrud, etc.

Married (1) Ernest Heink, (2) the actor, Paul Schumann, (3) the Chicago lawyer, William Rapp, jun. Became an Amer. citizen in 1908.—J. M.

SCHÜNEMANN, Georg. Ger. writer on music; b. Berlin, 13 March, 1884. Stud. at Stern's Cons. under Löwengard, Klatte (compn.), Schönberger (pf.), Pfitzner (cond.), Emil Prill (fl.); stud. science of music at Univ.; 1907, Ph.D.; from that time teacher and writer; 1920, deputy-dir. High School of Music, Berlin; at same time (1920) lecturer at Univ. Berlin; 1923, prof. extraordinary.

Mozart as Eight-year-old Composer (1908, Sketch-book of 1764); *History of Conducting* (1913, Breitkopf); *Berlin Soc. of Musicians* (*Tonkünstlerverein*), 1919. Publ. in *D.d.T.* (Vol. LVI) 2 oratorios of J. Chr. Fr. Bach, of whom he had written a comprehensive biography in the *Bach Annual*, 1914. As mus. authority of Phonographical Commission he made a large coll. of songs, other than European, from prisoners in the Ger. war camps. One result of this study is *Kasatatarische Lieder* (*A.f.M.* I); he graduated at Berlin Univ. with a second work on this subject, *The Songs of German Colonials in Russia* (publ. as Vol. III of *Sammelbände für vergleichende Musik-Wissenschaft*, Munich, 1922.—A. E.

SCHURÉ, Édouard. Fr. poet, philosopher and dramatic critic; b. Strasburg, 1841. Pursued in his native town classical and law studies, which he completed in Germany. There he became familiar with the popular Ger. songs, the subject of his first book: *Histoire du Lied ou la Chanson Populaire en Allemagne* (1868, Paris, Perrin; Ger. ed. 1870). Admirer and commentator of Richard Wagner, with whom he was closely connected from 1865, he was able to resist that master's supremacy and preserve his independence.

Le Drame musical. Richard Wagner (1875; 5th ed. 1902; Paris, Perrin); *Histoire du Drame musical* (1876); *Souvenirs sur Richard Wagner, la première de Tristan et Iseult* (1900, Perrin); *Tannhäuser, lettre à M. de Wolzogen sur l'execution du drame à Bayreuth en 1891* (Paris, 1892, Fischbacher), etc.—M. L. P.

SCHURICHT, Karl. Ger. condr. b. Dantzig, 3 July, 1880. Stud. at Berlin R. High School for Music (R. Rudorff, E. Humperdinck); voluntary condr. at Mayence; gained at Berlin compn. scholarships of Franz v. Mendelssohn and Paul Kuczynski Foundations. Choral and orchestral condr.; theatre condr. at Zwickau, Dortmund, Kreuznach, Goslar; succeeded Siegfried Ochs as condr. of Rühl Choral Union, Frankfort-o-M.; 1912, also chief town-condr. and condr. of Symph. Concerts, Wiesbaden. Comp. pf. sonata, op. 1; preludes, op. 4; *Herbststücke*, orchestra.—A. E.

SCHUSTER, Bernhard. Ger. compr. and ed. *b.* Berlin, 26 March, 1870. Pupil of Ludwig Gentz (pf. and vn.), Stolzenberg and Bussler (theory). Many years operatic condr. at Magdeburg and Berlin.

Songs; 3-act romantic opera, *Der Jungbrunnen* (Leipzig and Basle, 1920). In ms.: songs; str. 4tet; suite, small orch.; symphony; 2 choral works with orch. and organ; 3-act comic opera, *Der Dieb des Glücks* (*Thief of Happiness*) perf. Wiesbaden 1923; 1901, ed. *Die Musik* (Berlin, Deutsche Verlags-Anstalt); discontinued 1915; revived 1922.—A. E.

SCHWARTZ, Alexander. Compr. *b.* Petrograd, 7 July, 1874. Stud. law at Petrograd; 1899, pupil of Leipzig Cons.; 1902, went to Berlin to hear lectures on mus. science; dir. of rehearsals at R. Opera House for one year; devoted himself to composition.

Songs: op. 6 (Nietzsche); 10 (Arno Holz); 11 (Richard Dehmel); 12 (Gustav Falke); 13 (Carmen Sylva); duets, op. 15; Christmas carol for 2 children's vs. and pf.; trio; *Picture-Book without Pictures* (Andersen), recitation and pf.—A. E.

SCHWARTZ, Heinrich. Ger. pianist; *b.* Dietenhofen (Ansbach), 30 Oct. 1861. Stud. music in Munich (Rheinberger and K. Bärmann); 1885, teacher of pf. at Munich Acad.; 1891, prof.; 1900, Bavarian Court-pianist. Wrote *Aus meinen Klavierunterrichte* (*From my Pf. Teaching*) (1917; 2nd ed. 1920).—A. E.

SCHWARTZ, Rudolf. Ger. writer on music; *b.* Berlin, 20 Jan. 1859. Stud. philosophy in Berlin; 1882-7, science of music under Spitta; 1887, condr. of students' glee-club, Greifswald; 1897, went to Leipzig; 1901, succeeded Emil Vogel as librarian of Peters' Music Library and ed. of their annual periodicals; 1907, professor.

Works of Philipp Dulichius (1st pt. as Vol. XXXI, 2nd pt. as Vol. XLI of *D.d.T.*); and, as Vol. IV ii of *D.T.B.*, publ. compns. of H. L. Hasler (*Canzonet von 1590, Neue teytsche Gesang von 1596*); wrote *Die Tonkunst im XIX Jahrhundert* (1900).—A. E.

SCHWEITZER, Albert. Orgt. writer on music, theologian, medical missionary; *b.* Kayserberg, Alsace, 14 Jan. 1875. Stud. organ under Widor in Paris. Wrote *J. S. Bach, le Musicien-Poète,* 1905; enlarged ed. in Ger. 1908; Eng. transl. by Ernest Newman, 1911 (Breitkopf). The work is based on the pictorial realism of Bach's music. Ed. (with Widor) Bach's complete organ works for Schirmer (6 vols. only publ.). Orgt. Paris Bach Society till 1913, when he went to Equatorial Africa to establish his medical mission. After 4½ years returned to Europe to raise funds by his Bach organ recitals, and went back to Africa in 1924.—E.-H.

SCHWERS, Paul. Ger. ed. *b.* Spandau, 22 Feb. 1874. Pupil of R. High School, Berlin, and advanced pupil in compn. of Martin Blumner and Ludwig Bussler; 1895, orgt. and choirmaster, Berlin; 1898-1905, mus. reporter of newspaper *Germania*; 1907, ed. *Allgemeine Musikzeitung*; comp. masses; religious and secular choruses; chamber-music; about 25 books of songs and ballads.—A. E.

SCHWICKERATH, Eberhard. Ger. condr. *b.* Solingen, 4 June, 1856. Stud. law at Bonn and Leipzig; 1876-9, barrister at Cologne; music pupil of Seiss and G. Jensen; abandoned law; finished mus. studies at Vienna under A. Door

and A. Bruckner; returned to Cologne; 1882-7, cond. a large unacc. choral soc., also small soc. for sacred music; teacher at Cons.; 1887, chief town-condr. at Aix-la-Chapelle for 25 years. Cond. several Lower Rhine mus. fests.; successful condr. of unacc. choruses, establ. such a choral soc. at Aix-la-Chapelle; 1912, dir. of Munich R. Acad. of Art; condr. of choral class; cond. (till 1923) Concert Soc. for Choral Singing.—A. E.

SCHYTTE, Anna. Danish pianist; *b.* Copenhagen, 20 Nov. 1881; daughter of Ludvig Schytte; pupil of J. Röntgen and Reisenauer.—A. H.

SCHYTTE, Frida. Danish violinist; *b.* Copenhagen, 31 March, 1871. Pupil of F. Stockmarr and V. Tofte, Copenhagen, and Massart and Berthelier, Paris. *Début* 1889 in Copenhagen. Concert tours included Stockholm, Paris, Berlin, Dresden, Munich, Vienna, Budapest, London, Edinburgh, Glasgow, Petrograd, where (under professional name of Frida Scotta) she won high rank as a gifted artist. Her last appearance was in Copenhagen in 1897, in which year she married Fr. Aug. Kaulbach, the noted Ger. painter of Munich, and retired from concert platform.—A. H.

SCHYTTE, Henrik Vissing. Danish cellist, music critic; *b.* Aarhus, Jutland, 4 May, 1827; *d.* Copenhagen, 22 Feb. 1903; brother of Ludvig Schytte; 1884-93, ed. *Musikbladet*; critic on *Dagens Nyheder, Dagbladet, Berlingske Tidende.*—A. H.

SCHYTTE, Ludvig. Danish compr. *b.* Aarhus, 28 April, 1848; *d.* Berlin, 10 Nov. 1909. Followed pharmacy for a time until music finally gained the ascendancy. Pupil of Edmund Neupert in Copenhagen. His unusual pianistic talent was supplemented by one equally great for compn., and he rapidly developed both under Liszt in Weimar and later in Berlin. His real *début* took place at Carlsruhe Mus. Fest. 1885, when his pf. concerto was perf. with Arthur Friedheim as soloist. After this he settled in Vienna, as a teacher at both Horák's and Urban's Cons., composing a great deal. The latter years of his life (from 1907) he spent in Berlin, teaching at Stern's Cons. It was especially as pf. compr. that he won renown. His compns., great and small, bear witness to a fluency of mus. ideas, a sure intuition of sonorities, and an intimate knowledge and appreciation of his instrument.

Pf. concerto, op. 28, perf. Queen's Hall, London, 21 Jan. 1902; pf. sonata, op. 23; *Pantomimes,* op. 30; *Suite facile* for pf. trio, op. 132; *Pièces lyriques,* op. 15; *Promenades musicales,* op. 26; 3 *Études de Concert,* op. 48; Piano School; Pedal Studies, op. 104; pf. technical studies; scale studies; *Études* (all Nordisk Musikforlag, Copenhagen); *Children's Symphony,* op. 31 (Berlin, Simrock); *Hero,* dramatic scena for v. (Copenhagen, Hansen).—A. H.

SCONTRINO, Antonio. Italian composer; *b.* Trapani, 17 May, 1850; *d.* Florence, 7 Jan. 1922. Began as d.b.-player; devoted himself to compn. at Palermo under Platania; then in Munich; 1891, prof. of compn. at Cons. of

Palermo; then at Istituto Musicale of Florence,
until his death.

Operas: *Matelda* (Milan, 1879); *Il progettista*
(Rome, 1882); *Sortilegio* (Turin, 1882); *Gringoire*
(Milan, 1890); *Cortigiana* (Milan, 1896). Orch.:
Intermezzos for *Francesca da Rimini* (d'Annunzio);
a symphony; much vocal and instr. chamber-
music.—D. A.

SCOTT, Charles Kennedy. Eng. choral condr.
b. Romsey, 16 Nov. 1876. Stud. Brussels Cons.
(vn. under Cornélis, organ under Alphonse
Mailly, compn. under F. Kufferath and, later,
Tinel); 1st prize for organ-playing 1897; settled
in London 1898. Founded Oriana Madrigal Soc.
in 1904; Philh. Choir in 1919; Euterpe Str.
Players in 1922. Has played an important part
in choral music in London, cultivating both
old and new music, especially of Eng. schools.

Songs (Breitkopf); eds. of old carols and XVI
century vocal music; (Chester); manual of Madrigal-
Singing (Breitkopf).—E.-H.

SCOTT, Cyril Meir. Eng. compr. and poet; *b.*
Oxton, Cheshire, 27 Sept. 1879. Stud. at Hoch's
Cons. Frankfort-o-M., compn. under Ivan Knorr,
pf. under Lazarro Uzielli; at age of 20, S. went
back to Liverpool, playing and teaching for
some years. His *Heroic Suite* was played both
there and at Manchester under Richter; his
Pelléas and Mélisande shortly afterwards at
Frankfort; Kreisler played vn. in the pf. 4tet
at a Broadwood concert in St. James's Hall.
His early pf. pieces were first publ. by Boosey,
and then Forsyth; but he soon found his most
enterprising publ. in Mr. W. A. Elkin, for whom
he has written regularly ever since. Sir Henry
Wood perf. his 2nd symphony in A mi. op. 22
at the Promenades, London, 25 Aug. 1903; his
Rhapsody No. I, op. 32, 10 Sept. 1904; his
overture *Princess Maleine*, 22 Aug. 1907; his
2 Poems for orch. 26 Aug. 1913; *Britain's War
March*, 23 Oct. 1914. His 2nd symphony later
on became *Three Symph. Dances*, one of which
was perf. at a Balfour Gardiner concert in the
Queen's Hall. His 2 Passacaglias on Irish
themes were given by Beecham at a R. Philh.
concert, London. His vn. sonata was played by
Rosé in Vienna, when his *Overture* was also given
under Schreker. S. is best known in England for
his songs and pf. pieces; but abroad he is known
for his orch. and chamber-music, which represent
him more fully; and his position in music must
be decided by his larger and more serious works,
as yet too little heard. Whereas many comprs.
are mainly influenced by music itself, S. has
found his moulding forces outside music. His
friendships with the Fr. poet, Bonnier, at Liverpool, with the Ger. mystic poet, Stefan George,
and with the painter-designer, Melchior Lechter,
all had an important bearing on his music.
So, too, did his close reading of science, philosophy and especially occultism and Eastern
mysticism. Under this latter influence, he began
to rid himself of " key-tonality," time-signatures,
bar-lines, etc. He was not only a pioneer in England in this technical way; but stood in the van
of tendencies which have since then become
firmly established. Much of his music has a
strangely exotic charm; he has a horror of the

obvious in melody, harmony and even in orchestration. Occasionally, this becomes a pose; but
more than any other British compr. in the late
'nineties and first decades of the XX century, S.
stood almost alone in pf. music and songs for
what was then vaguely termed " modernism."
He has a very original way of treating the pf.;
and has contributed largely to the pianist's
repertory. His skill in pictorial writing (*Jungle
Book*; *Rainbow-Trout*, etc.) is very considerable;
and he is always sure of his expression, even in
such hazardous impressionistic pieces as *Poems*,
Vistas, etc.; some things (the pf. 5tet, the str.
4tet, etc.) have a strong masculine grip, and a
vigour not unlike that of Strauss or Reger;
albeit he always retains a distinct personality.

Opera, *The Alchemist* (Schott); ballet, *The Incom-
petent Apothecary*, ms.; *Nativity Hymn*, soli, chorus,
orch. (Stainer & Bell); *Aubade*, orch. (Schott); 2
Passacaglias on Irish themes, orch. (*id.*); pf. concerto (*id.*); 5tet, pf. and str. (1911–12); trio, vn.
cello, pf. (*id.*); vn. sonata (*id.*); str. 4tet (Elkin);
Idyllic Phantasy, m.-sopr. v. ob. and cello (*id.*); pf.
sonata (*id.*); *The Ecstatic Shepherd*, fl. alone (Schott);
Scotch Pastoral, fl. and pf. (Hansen, Stockholm);
Pierrot amoureux, cello and pf. (Schott); for pf.:
2nd Suite (Schott); Ballad; *Handelian Rhapsody*;
Prélude solennelle (Elkin); *Egypt*; *Poems*; *Jungle
Book Impressions* (Schott); 2 songs without words;
2 4tets for male vs. *The Emir's Serenade* and *The
Ratcatcher* (Boosey); British folk-songs rearranged;
numerous pf. pieces and many songs (Elkin; Schott).
Book, *My Years of Indiscretion* (1924).—E.-H.

SCOTTISH FOLK-MUSIC. See BURNETT,
ROBERT; PENTLAND, R. W.; also art. FOLK-
SONG SOCIETIES.

SCOTTISH ORCHESTRA. During the season
1887–8, the well-known music-selling firm of
Messrs Paterson & Son, Edinburgh, inaugurated
a series of orch. concerts to be run in conjunction with the Glasgow Choral Union under
August Manns. Four concerts were given during
that season, and six during each of the three
immediately succeeding seasons. The orch.
at this time was, however, of a very fluid character, and in order to place it upon a more permanent basis, the Scottish Orch. Co. was formed
in Glasgow with a capital of about £30,000. The
chief personality associated with this was James
A. Allan, the Glasgow shipowner. From that
time till the middle of the late war, the orch.
prospered exceedingly, but then the body
suffered eclipse owing to the large number of its
members which was taken for active service. It
has since been resuscitated, but since 1919, its
troubles have not so far been overcome, and a
process of reorganisation is now (1923) in progress. Its permanent condrs. have been August
Manns (1887–93), George Henschel (1893–5),
Willem Kes (1895–8), Max Bruch (1898–1900),
Frederick Cowen (1900–10), E. Młynarski (1910–
1916), Landon Ronald (1919–23), and Julius
Harrison (1920–23), after which, the plan of
varying the condrs. was adopted.—W. S.

SCOZZI, Riccardo. Ital. oboist; *b.* Venice,
27 July, 1878. Teacher at R. Liceo Mus. di
Santa Cecilia; 1st oboist in Augusteo Orch.
An artist of exceptional merit, both as regards
softness and beauty of sound and perfect
musicianship; author of several compns. and
studies for own instr. (Milan, Fantuzzi).—D. A.

SCRIABIN, Alexander Nicolaevitch (*accent the A*). Russian composer; *b.* Moscow, 1871; *d.* 1/14 April, 1915. Evinced his inclination towards music at an early age, and entered the Moscow Conservatoire, where he studied composition and piano under S. Tanéief, Arensky, and Safonof. He afterwards toured Europe, giving pianoforte recitals devoted solely to his own works. In 1898, he was appointed professor of piano at Moscow. Resigning the post in 1904, he went to live abroad and devoted himself solely to composition, returning to Moscow in 1910.

His work is unified. One idea inspires it and gives it being. The whole of his activities, from his first symphony in E op. 26 (1900–1) onwards, constitutes a series of attempts to achieve the embodiment of that idea. The unique work towards which he strives, and of which his symphonies and sonatas are but sketches or fragments, he used to call "The Mystery." It was to be a liturgy constituting a synthesis of all arts and in which the whole of humanity and nature would take part. In his mind, art was but a means of achieving a higher form of life—a purely romantic conception. The vast metaphysical and religious system created by him is analogous to Indian mysticism. It is symbolised in *L'Acte Préalable*, a cantata which was to serve as an introduction to the Mystery, but of which we possess the text only (*Propylées*, Moscow, 1920) and a few musical fragments.

His evolution followed a regular course. He was influenced by Wagner, Liszt, and Chopin, but from these joint influences derived from the very outset an idiom typically his own and of powerful originality. Glinka and the "Five" did not influence him in the least, and folk-music plays no part in his style. But the spirit of his music, European, mystical, impassioned, joyous, ecstatically lyrical, and enthusiastic, is altogether Russian. Its form is altogether classical.

His output can be divided into three groups. The first will include the opp. 1 to 25, comprising among other things the pf. sonatas, op. 6, 19, and 23, the first two symphonies (E and C, op. 26 and 29), the *Études*, op. 8; the Preludes, op. 11, 15, 17, in which the keen ardour, the wistful reverie, and graceful, aerial sensuousness which characterise his later works are already asserted. The second group comprises the fourth pf. sonata (F sharp, op. 30), the *Poème Satanique* for pf. op. 34; the eight *Études*, op. 42; the fifth sonata, op. 53, countless Miniatures, Preludes, and Poems (written from 1903 to 1909); the third symphony (in C); *Le Divin Poème*, op. 43, and *Le Poème de l'Extase*, op. 54. It is an altogether new world that Scriabin reveals us here. For him Art has become a feast, a transfiguration. Here all is pure ecstatic joy, light playing and dancing. Nothing is stable or solid; all runs, leaps and flies. The orchestral style, which in the earlier works showed many affinities with Wagner's, becomes very individual in *Le Divin Poème* and reaches its full individuality in *Le*

Poème de l'Extase, although its derivation from *Tristan* remains obvious.

Prometheus, the Poem of the Fire, op. 60, for orchestra, piano, organ, chorus and colour-keyboard; five piano sonatas, op. 62, 64, 66, 68 and 70; the *Poème Nocturne* for piano, op. 61; two dances (*Guirlandes* and *Flammes Sombres*), op. 73; *Vers la Flamme*, op. 72; *Trois Études* (in fifths, in sevenths and in ninths respectively), op. 65, and numerous miniatures for piano, constitute the output of the third period. All these works are founded on a new harmonic basis, a chord of seven sounds (" synthetic chord "), generally distributed in fourths: C, F sharp, B flat, E, A, D, G. This chord, a " thirteenth " with minor seventh and augmented ninth, reflects in its structure the series of the upper partials 8, 9, 10, 11, 12, 13, 14; so that Scriabin appears to open the way to ultra-chromaticism. But at this point, art acquires for him a mystical religious significance: it is a means of occult action, and the artist is an Orpheus who deeply modifies the nature of beings and of things.

In *Prometheus* he has attempted to achieve the synthetic art he was dreaming of. And simultaneously with his sonorous visions, he attempted to incarnate his luminous visions by means of a colour-keyboard, in accordance with a system of correspondences which he had established between colours and sounds. But the results of attempts made with this contrivance in Russia and in America proved disappointing.

Scriabin's art has exercised in Russia a profound influence, which made itself felt from 1915 onwards upon all the younger composers. It extended to arts other than the musical.

Prometheus was first given in Moscow, 2 March, 1911, under Kussevitzky. The first London perf. took place at Queen's Hall under Sir Henry Wood, who gave it twice at one concert (1 Feb. 1913). It was repeated there the following year (14 March) with the compr. at the piano.

Consult the monographs by Sabanéief (Moscow), Karatyguin (Petrograd) Gunst (Moscow), B. de Schloezer (Berlin), and the special number of the *Muzykalny Sovremmenik* (Petrograd, 1915,[?] Nos. 4, 5); A. Eaglefield-Hull, *A Russian Tone-Poet* (London, Kegan Paul; 1st ed. 1916; 3rd ed. 1922), gives full analyses of all works.—B. DE S.

SCRIPTURE, Edward Wheeler. Amer. phonetician, investigator of the voice; *b.* Mason, N.H., U.S.A. 21 May, 1864. Ph.D. (Leipzig); M.D. (Munich); formerly prof. of experimental psychology at Yale Univ. U.S.A. In the Yale Laboratory he devised an apparatus for tracing off the curves from gramophone discs (the only one ever made) with an enlargement of 500. The tracing of Caruso's *Madre infelice*, etc., shows quite unexpected peculiarities in the mechanism of his voice which gave it its special character; these were quite unknown to Caruso himself. S. has devised apparatus for registering speech and song so that the details can be studied under the microscope; has invented the *strobilion*, an instr. that shows to the eye just the pitch of the tone being sung and even the minutest variation in pitch; has also developed the *laryngostroboscope*, an instr. by which a single vibration of the vocal cords can be seen and followed by the eye. In addition to his post at King's Coll. Univ. of London, he has lately been called to Univ. of Vienna as prof. of experimental phonetics.

Elements of Experimental Phonetics (Yale Univ. Press); *Stuttering, Lisping and the Voices of the Deaf* (Macmillan Co.); *The Study of English Speech by New Methods of Phonetic Investigation* (Oxford Univ. Press); *Shakespeare's Versification in the Light of Experimental Phonetics*; *The Curves of Caruso* (1924), etc.—E.-H.

SEGOVIA, Andrés.   Span. guitar - player; *b.* Jaén in 1894.   His art represents a link between the Romantic school of xix century (Carnicer, Arcas, Tárrega) and the modern style. Tours in France, Spain, Germany and America. —P. G. M.

SEIDL, Anton. Hungarian condr. *b.* Budapest, 7 May, 1850; *d.* New York, 28 March, 1898. 1870-2, pupil at Leipzig Cons.; then assistant to Richard Wagner, Bayreuth; 1875, through Wagner's recommendation, engaged by Angelo Neumann as condr. at Leipzig; acc. Neumann to Bremen; 1885, accepted appointment at the head of Ger. Opera, New York, and soon made orch. which he cond. popular; 1886, at Bayreuth Fest.; 1897, cond. London Wagner operas (Grau's season).

Consult H. C. Krehbiel, *A. S.* (1898); also *A. S.: a Memorial by his Friends* (1899, a magnificent work, in English).—A. E.

SEIDL, Arthur.   Ger. author; *b.* Munich, 8 June, 1863.   Stud. philosophy and history of literature at Munich, Tübingen, Berlin and Leipzig: practical music and mus. science under O. Paul, Fritz Stade, Ferdinand Langer, Ph. Spitta and H. Bellermann; 1887, doctor's degree with *On the Sublime in Music, prolegomena* to mus. æsthetics (2nd ed. 1907; critic at Dresden and Hamburg; 1898-9, at Weimar (Nietzsche Archives, engaged in publ. of Nietzsche's works [Vols. I–VIII] and letters [Vol. I with Peter Gast]); later at Munich (as feuilleton-writer and edit. of periodical *Die Gesellschaft*); 1903-19, mus. manager at Dessau Court Theatre. Since 1904, teacher at Leipzig Cons.; lecturer in mus. history, literature and æsthetics. Since 1919, conducts private courses in mus. science, Dessau.

History of Ideas of the Sublime since Kant (1889); *Has Richard Wagner left a School ?* (1892); *Richard Strauss, character-study* (1895 with W. Klatte); *Modern Spirit in German Musical Art* (1900, new ed. 1913); *What is Modern ?* (1900); *Wagneriana* (3 vols. 1901-2), *Modern Conductors* (1902); *Art and Culture* (1902); *Festival Writings for Jubilee of General German Musical Society* (1911); *The Hellerau School Festivals and Training Institute of Jaques-Dalcroze* (1912); *Straussiana* (1913); *Ascania* (10 years at Anhalt) (1913); *R. Wagner's "Parsifal"* (1914); *New Wagneriana* (3 vols. 1914); *Hans Pfitzner* (1921).—A. E.

SEIFFERT, Max.   Ger. writer on music; *b.* Beeskow-on-Spree, 9 Feb. 1868. 1886, stud. in Berlin classical philology, science of music (Spitta); 1891, doctor's degree, Berlin, with *J. P. Sweelinck and his Direct German Scholars*; 1907, R. prof.; 1914, member of Acad. of Berlin.

Wrote *History of Pf. Music* (1899); arr. complete ed. of Sweelinck's works (12 vols.); ed. in the *D.d.T.* S. Scheidt's *Tabulatura nova*; Selected Works of Franz Tunder; J. G. Walther's organ works; organ works of M. Weckmann and Chr. Bernhard; works of Zachow; sacred music of Joh. Philipp Krieger; Joh. and W. H. Pachelbel's pf. works; works of Leopold Mozart (1909); collected pf. and organ works of Johann Krieger, Murschhauser and I. Ph. Krieger; Anthony van Noort's *Tabulature Book* and C. Boskoop's *Psalms of David*; eds. of Bach and Handel. 1904-14, ed. vols. of *I.M.G.* and, since 1918, of *A.f.M.* Publ. bibliographical catalogue in the prefaces to the works of Joh. Philipp and Joh. Krieger (1916 and 1919).—A. E.

SEITZ, Ernest. Canadian pianist; *b.* Hamilton, Ontario, 29 Feb. 1892. Stud. pf. under A. S. Vogt at Toronto Cons. and later for 4 years under Josef Lhévinne, Berlin. On returning to America, stud. under Ernest Hutcheson, New York. In 1916, joined staff of Toronto Cons. as teacher and examiner. As concert-pianist he is becoming well known in U.S.A. and Canada. In 1922, accompanied Mendelssohn Choir as soloist during their American tour.—L. S.

SEKLES, Bernhard. Ger. compr. *b.* Frankfort-o-M., 20 June, 1872. Stud. at Hoch's Cons. (Uzielli, Knorr, Scholz), 1893-4, theatre condr. at Heidelberg; 1894-5 at Mayence; 1896, teacher of theory at Hoch's Cons.; 1923, director.

Serenade for 11 solo instrs. op. 14; symph. poem, *From the Gardens of Semiramis*; Passacaglia and fugue for full orch. and organ (1919); *Short Suite* for orch., op. 21; *Temperaments* for orch., op. 25; Phantastic Miniatures for small orch.; 15 little chamber-pieces, fl. clar. vla. cello and percussion instr.; Passacaglia and fugue for str. 4tet, op. 23; sonata in D, cello and pf.; dance-play, *Der Zwerg und die Infantin* (Frankfort-o-M. 1913); opera, *Scaharazade* (Mannheim, 1917); burlesque dream-play, *Die Hochzeit des Faun (The Faun's Wedding)* (Wiesbaden, 1921); pf. pieces, op. 4, 5, 10; songs (s. op. 2, 3, 8, 15; t. op. 13; barit. op. 1, 7, 11); female choruses, op. 6; male choruses, op. 12 (s. solo). Wrote *Musical Dictation*. —A. E.

SELIN, Yrjö. Finnish cellist; *b.* Vaasa, 1897. Pupil of O. Fohström in Helsingfors, and Hekking and Casals in Paris. Has appeared with success in Finland and Norway. Since 1922, member of the A. Arvesen Quartet, Christiania, Norway.—T. H.

SELMER, Johan Peter. Norwegian compr. *b.* Christiania, 20 Jan. 1844; *d.* Venice, 22 July, 1910. First stud. law; but in order to overcome a chest affection he went for a long sea-voyage. The many and varied impressions he received, during his two years' wanderings, awakened his slumbering artistic temperament and he devoted himself to music. Went to Paris in 1869 and stud. there under C. Alexis Chauvet and Ambroise Thomas. As early as 1870 he made his *début* with his op. 1, *Chanson de Fortunio* (t. and orch.). He remained in Paris during the siege, joined the revolutionaries (the Commune) and even became one of their orch. condrs. His experiences in this stirring time left deep traces on his susceptible mind. The first musical fruit of this experience was the impressive orch. work *Scène funèbre* (op. 4). In 1871-3 he stud. in Leipzig under Friedrich Richter, Jadassohn and Oscar Paul. Here he wrote music to parts of Victor Hugo's *Les Orientales (The Turks' March on Athens*, orch. male chorus and solo, op. 7; *La Captive*, contr. solo with orch. op. 6, etc.). A half-year's stay in Italy for reasons of health gave him a wealth of new impressions. In 1878 his orch. work *Nordic Festal Pageant* was perf. with great success in Leipzig, Berlin and (cond. by himself) at Mus. Fest. at Erfurt. In spring of 1879 he gave a concert of his own compns. in Christiania, and Parliament granted him a composer's pension, as in the case of Grieg and Svendsen. In 1883 he wrote a magnificent cantata, *Greeting to Nidaros* (op. 23), for choral fest. in Trondhjem. From 1883 to 1886 he was leader of Mus. Soc. in Christiania. Subsequently he resided mostly abroad, but constantly visited his native land and gave many concerts there. At first Nordic Mus. Fest. in Copenhagen in 1888 he cond. his op. 5, the short but forceful *Nordens Aand* (*Spirit of the North*), male chorus and orch. At his last concert in his native country (Christiania, 1898) he produced his finest orch. work, *Prometheus* (op. 50). Altogether he has written about 60 works for orch.; orch. with chorus and solo; songs with orch. or pf.; male choruses; mixed and 3-part female choruses; duets, etc. S. holds an exceptional position amongst Northern comprs. of the last century. He is Norway's Berlioz, the pioneer in the field of programme-music. In the 'seventies and 'eighties he suffered on account of the "radicalism" of his peculiarly bluff, often bizarre harmonisation. His style is strongly individual; he paints with a broad and powerful brush and does not shrink from the fantastic or even the grotesque (see orch. work *Carnival in Flanders*). In his best moments he is absolutely sublime; for example, in *Prometheus,* when depicting the flight of Mercury and the eagle through space. His talent was so adaptive that he could, with equal felicity of characterisation, write "Norwegian"—in the famous song *Tollekniven* (*The Sheath-Knife*); "Finnish"—in the orch. work *Finnish Festal Notes;* "Nordic"—in *The Spirit of the North;* "Spanish"—in *La Captive;* and "Turkish"—in *The Turks' March on Athens.* In his songs he strictly follows the principle that the music shall illustrate the words; but in this respect he cannot be acquitted of considerable exaggeration. Of his 4-v. male choruses, *Norway, Norway* (words by Björnstjerne Björnson) has attained exceptional popularity; and *Ulabrand* is a monumental work amongst Norwegian male-chorus music. Most of his larger works are publ. by C. Warmuth, Christiania, Wilhelm Hansen, Copenhagen, or C. F. W. Siegel, Leipzig. His choruses have been publ. by himself.—U. M.

SELVA, Blanche. French pianist; *b.* Brive, 29 Jan. 1884. Attended Paris Cons. between age of 9 and 11; entered *Schola Cantorum* as pupil of V. d'Indy. Began her career as pianist at 13. At 20, perf. all Bach's works in 17 concerts. She has, since 1902, placed her remarkable talent at the service of all the modern Fr. works, of which she has played a large number, principally at Société Nationale (Paris) and at *Libre Esthétique de Bruxelles.* Has taught the pf. at *Schola Cantorum* for many years; now prof. at Cons. Strasburg, and Prague. Has written some works relating to pf. teaching and mus. inter-

pretation, *e.g.*: *La Sonate* (Paris, 1913, Rouart); *Quelques Mots sur la Sonate* (Paris, Mellotée); *L'Enseignement musical de la technique du Piano* (2 vols., Rouart); Preparatory Book to same (Rouart, 1922).—M. L. P.

SELZ, Gaston. Fr. compr. *b.* Boulogne-sur-Seine, 1873. Pupil of Paris Cons. Charged with organisation of the singing competitions in schools of Department of Seine, 1921. Operettas: *La Nuit de Mai; Amour marié; Joie d'Italie* (*poème-dansé*); songs.—A. C.

SEM, Arne van Erpekum. Norwegian teacher of singing and musical critic; *b.* Christiania, 1 May, 1873. Stud. theology, but soon devoted himself to music. Owing to an injury to his hand, gave up intention of being pianist and became singer (t.). Trained in Paris and Vienna. Engaged at Stadttheater in Bremen; afterwards at Opera House, Stuttgart. Appeared also in other Ger. theatres. Concerts in many great cities of Europe. Since 1914, resident in Christiania. Mus. critic on *Tidens Tegn* (since 1918). Leader of Opéra-Comique opera school, 1918–19. For Bach Fest. in Christiania, 1921, he wrote some very full annotations.—U. M.

SEMBRICH, Marcelina. See KOCHANSKA-SEMBRICH.

SENGER, Hugo von. Condr. and compr. *b.* Munich, 13 Sept. 1835; *d.* Geneva, 18 Jan. 1892. After having studied philosophy at Munich, devoted himself entirely to music; orch. leader at St. Gall; then condr. of opera at Zurich; prof. at Cons. and condr. of Symphony Concerts and the Société de Chant Sacré (mixed choir) at Geneva, remaining there till 1891. An eminent teacher and an excellent condr. His compns., recalling Schubert, attain great depth of expression.

2 festspiele, *Fête des Vignerons* and *Fête de la Jeunesse;* cantata, *Général Dufour; Marche funèbre;* Prelude; *Airs de ballet,* orch.; unacc. choruses; songs (publ. by Fœtisch, Lausanne; Rötschy, Geneva).—F. H.

SENILOF, Vladimir Alexeievitch (*accent 2nd syll.*). Russ. compr. *b.* 27 June/9 July, 1875; *d.* Petrograd, 1920. Stud. mus. theory under Hugo Riemann at Leipzig (1899–1901) and compn. at Petrograd Cons. under Rimsky-Korsakof, Liadof, and Glazunof. At the beginning of his career, he was strongly under Ger. influences; but has since succeeded in disengaging his individuality. This is shown clearly enough by some of his publ. works (Jurgenson), such as the settings for v. and pf. (or orch.) of poems by Sologub, Remizof, Balmont, etc.; his *Poem* for cello and pf.; his Variations upon a song of the Flagellants for pf. (Jurgenson). His chief works, such as the tone-poems (*The Wild Geese; Pan; The Scythians*), are unpubl. and not available for study at the present time. The last-named is described as particularly interesting.—M. D. C.

SENIOR, Wilfred Edward. Scottish pianist; *b.* Tillicoultry, 20 Aug. 1880. Stud. pf., vn., conducting at Dresden Cons. 1894–1900; also singing under Lamperti, privately; gained con-

cert-pianist diploma; also diploma as condr.;
appointed Korrepetitor at Dresden R. Opera
House, 1902. Settled in Glasgow, 1904, as teacher
of pf. and singing. Condr. of Glasgow Choral
Union. His arrs. of old Scottish songs are publ.
by James Kerr, Glasgow.—J. P. D.

SERAFIN, Tullio. Ital. condr. *b.* Rottanova
di Cavarzere (Venice), 8 Dec. 1878. One of best
and most brilliant of living Ital. condrs. Stud.
vn. and compn. at R. Cons. Milan. At first, vn.
and vla.-player in orch. at La Scala. Condr.
there (deputy to Toscanini); rose to front rank
as condr., both in theatre and on concert-
platform. Many important seasons at Regio
Theatre, Turin; La Scala, Milan (for 4 years);
at Paris Opéra; Covent Garden, London;
Colón, Buenos Ayres, etc.—D. A.

SERATO, Arrigo. Ital. violinist; *b.* Bologna,
7 Feb. 1877. Son of distinguished cellist, Francesco (prof. at Mus. Acad. Bologna); pupil
of Federico Sarti at same Acad. Whilst very
young began concert-tours, gaining fame as
one of most brilliant Ital. concert-players;
toured triumphantly through Europe and
America. In Germany, took part in Joachim
Quartet, and enjoyed the friendship of that renowned master; taught for several years in
Berlin; 1914, prof. at R. Liceo Mus. di Santa
Cecilia, Rome. In 1921 took up again career
of concert-player very successfully.—D. A.

SERATO, Francesco. Ital. cellist; *b.* Castel-
franco Veneto, 17 Sept. 1843; *d.* Bologna, 24
Dec. 1919. From 1871 until his death, was
most esteemed prof. of cello at Mus. Acad. at
Bologna; many of most illustrious of living Ital.
cellists have been his pupils. First cellist in
orch. of La Scala, Milan, and Teatro Comunale,
Bologna. As concert artist, gained enthusiastic
success. Took part in famous Trio Bolognese
(with Sarti and Tofano); was one of founders
of Società del Quartetto of Bologna; with
Giuseppe Martucci, was one of inspirers of the
Quartetto Bolognese (Serato, Sarti, Consolini
and Massarenti), which gained a European
reputation.—D. A.

SÉRÉ, Octave. Fr. writer on music. Pseudonym under which Jean Poueigh (*q.v.*) wrote the
book *Musiciens français d'aujourdhui* (Paris,
1911, *Mercure de France*) which so far as it
goes, is invaluable for the biographical data,
excerpts of criticisms by various authors, and
bibliography which it contains.—M. D. C.

SERIEYX, Auguste. Fr. compr. and musicologist; *b.* Amiens, 14 June, 1865. Pupil of
Barthe (harmony) and Gédalge (cpt.); then of
V. d'Indy. He counts among the first members
of the *Schola Cantorum.* Collab. with d'Indy in
the *Cours de Composition* (Durand, Vol. I, 1900;
Vol. II, 1909), and wrote the *Trois États de la
Tonalité;* a study on *Vincent d'Indy,* etc. Has
cond. compn. class at the *Schola.* His pieces
include a vn. sonata; pieces for pf.; for organ; for
v. and orch. notably *La Voie lactée* (1911).—A. C.

SEROEN, Berthe. Belgian singer; *b.* Mechlin,
27 Nov. 1882. Stud. pf. in Brussels under

Gevaerts, singing under Dina Beumer and
Seguin; *début* at Mechlin, 1900; 1907, soloist
of Flemish Opera, Antwerp, and Théâtre de la
Monnaie, Brussels; 1914, went to Holland and
gave with Evert Cornelis concerts of modern Fr.
music. She introduced in Holland the songs of
Debussy, Ravel, Roussel, Castelnuovo-Tedesco,
Pizzetti, Mussorgsky, Stravinsky (*Pribaoutki*),
Gilson, Jongen, Mortelmans, Diepenbrock, Zag-
wijn, Matthijs Vermeulen, Alex. Voormolen,
Willem Pijper, Brucken-Fock, etc.—W. P.

SERRANO, José. Span. compr. *b.* Sueca
(Valencia), 14 Oct. 1873. Writes for the stage,
in a light vein, being one of the most successful
and popular comprs. of mus. comedies (*zarzuelas*),
in spite of unevenness of style and idiom, which
are either typically Span. or strikingly Ital., as
plainly manifest in his best-known work *La
Canción del Olvido.* Lives in Madrid.

La Mazorca Roja; Alma de Dios; El Motete; La
Mala Sombra; El Amigo Melquiades; La Reina
Mora; La Canción del Olvido (publ. Antonio Mata-
mala; Unión Musical Española, Madrid).—P. G. M.

SERRANO Y RUIZ, Emilio. Span. compr.
and pianist; *b.* Vittoria (Alava), 15 March, 1850.
Stud. at R. Cons. de Música, Madrid, where he
has taught at different times theory, pf., and
compn. (1870–1920). Counts among his pupils
the modern Span. comprs. Julio Gómez, María
Rodrigo, Ricardo Villa and Conrado del Campo.
Music-master to H.R.H. the Infanta Doña Isabel.
Member of R. Acad. de San Fernando. Founder
of Círculo de Bellas Artes symph. concerts. Dir.
of R. Opera House, Madrid, 1895–8.

Operas: Mitridates, Ital. text (R. Opera House,
Madrid, 1882); Giovanna la Pazza (R. Opera House,
Madrid, 1870); Irene de Otranto, book by José
Echegaray (R. Opera House, Madrid, 1871); Gon-
zalo de Córdova, book by compr. (R. Opera House,
Madrid, 1888); La Maja de Rumbo (Teatro Colón,
Buenos Ayres, 1910). Other works: pf. concerto;
str. 4tet; La Primera Salida de Don Quijote, symph.
poem; Elegía; Canciones del Hogar, v. and orch.
(Luca, Milan, later Ricordi; Unión Musical Española;
Faustino Fuentes, Madrid.)—P. G. M.

SERRAO, Paolo. Ital. compr. *b.* Filadelfia
(Catanzaro), 1830; *d.* Naples, 17 March, 1907.
Was for many years prof. of compn. at Naples
Cons.; from his school came many excellent
pupils: Martucci, Giordano, Mugnone, Cilea,
Vessella. His opera *Pergolesi* was successful. He
also wrote some good concert and sacred
music.—D. A.

SERVAIS, Franz Mathieu. Belgian compr. *b.*
Petrograd in 1846; *d.* Asnières, near Paris,
13 Jan. 1901. Eldest son of François Servais,
the great cellist. Pupil of Ferdinand Kufferath.
Obtained *Prix de Rome,* 1873, for cantata *Le
Tasse.* Travelled in Italy, and Germany; lived
for some time at Weimar as intimate friend of
Liszt, who gave him much encouragement.
S. was determined to create a big lyrical work;
chose a poem of Leconte de Lisle, *L'Apollonide.*
The libretto had to be altered many times, and
he revised his score more than 25 times. His
extremely artistic and dreamy character, melancholy and rather lacking in firmness, coupled
with consistent ill-luck, seemed to doom all
his enterprises to failure. *L'Apollonide* was
produced at Carlsruhe (in Ger.) in 1899

under the title *Ion*; its success was only moderate. S. founded a Concert Soc. (Winter Concerts) in Brussels in 1887, producing most interesting but unsuccessful programmes. Also temporarily engaged at La Monnaie as condr. for Wagnerian works (1889–91). Cond. *Flying Dutchman*, and 1st perf. of *Siegfried* in Fr. (1891). Consult *Au Souvenir de Fr. S.* (Nicholte, 1907).—E. C.

SERVAIS, Joseph. Belgian cellist; *b.* Hal (Brabant), 23 Nov. 1850; *d.* there, 29 April, 1885. Son of cellist Adrien François Servais (1807–66); his father's pupil at Brussels Cons. Acc. his father to Russia 1866; numerous tours in different European countries; was attached for some time to the choir of Duke of Saxe-Weimar (1869–70); appointed cello prof. at Brussels Cons. 1872. A virtuoso of very high standing, universally acclaimed by European Press.—C. V. B.

SERVIÈRES, Georges. Fr. musicologist; *b.* Fréjus, 13 Oct. 1858. Has written:
Richard Wagner jugé en France (1887); *Le Tannhäuser à l'Opéra en* 1861 (1895); *La Musique française moderne* (1887); *Weber* (1906); *Chabrier* (1911); *Épisodes d'histoire musicale* (1914); *Saint-Saëns* (1923), etc.—A. C.

SETACCIOLI, Giacomo. Ital. compr. *b.* Corneto Tarquinia, 8 Dec. 1868. Teacher of harmony and cpt. and, from 1922, of compn. at R. Liceo Mus. di Santa Cecilia, Rome. There completed studies in compn. under Cesare De Sanctis; flute under Franceschini. Many years 1st flautist in orch. of Costanzi and Augusteo.
Compr. of several operatic works; symphony (perf. at Augusteo); symph. poems; 4tet (Florence, Salonoff); Requiem Mass, perf. at Pantheon in memory of King Humbert; many vocal and instr. chamber-works. Has written: *Claudio Debussy*: *È un innovatore?* (*Claude Debussy*: *Is he an Innovator?*) (Rome, 1910, Musica); numerous critical articles and didactic treatises.—D. A.

ŠEVČÍK, Otakar. Czech vn. teacher; *b.* Horaž-dovice, 22 March, 1852. Pupil of Bennewitz; 1870–3, Konzertmeister of Mozarteum, Salzburg; later in Vienna; 1874–92 in Russia, finally as prof. at Cons. Kief.; 1892, called to Prague Cons., where he had control of vn. department till 1901; in 1909, Vienna Cons.; 1919, again at Prague Cons. After Kubelík's and Kocián's successes, his pupils gathered in large numbers, forming a veritable colony at S.'s residence, Písek. His method is based on the semitone system, the fingers remaining at equal distances on all the strings during the technical studies. This leads to absolute safety, precision and remarkable fluency. Other famous pupils are Štěpán Suchý, Marie Hall, Mary Dickenson, Reznikov.
School of Vn. Technique (1st ed. 1880, 4 vols.); *School of Bowing* (1893; contains 4,000 different bowings); *Elements of Vn. Playing* (1900); *Prep. School of Vn. Technique* (1896). (Eng. publ. Bosworth; Chappell.)—V. ST.

SÉVERAC, Joseph Marie Déodat de. Fr. compr. *b.* St.-Félix de Caraman, 20 July, 1873; *d.* Céret (East Pyrenees), 27 March, 1921. Stud. music firstly at Toulouse Cons., and in 1896, came to Paris, where he entered the *Schola Cantorum*, studying cpt. under Magnard and

compn. under d'Indy. His principal works (publ. Rouart) are: *Le Chant de la Terre* (1903), *En Languedoc* (1905), *Baigneuses au soleil* (1908) and *Cerdana* (1910) for pf.; the lyric stage-piece *Le Cœur du Moulin* (Paris, 1909), *Héliogabale* (Béziers, 1910) and *Les Antibel*; songs, and a few books of collected folk-songs. A number of other works remain unpubl. It is perhaps in his pf. music that he has given the best of himself. His musical imagination, although somewhat limited in scope, is of a rare quality, and he derived particularly felicitous inspirations from the rural scenes which he often elected to translate into music.
Consult bibliography in Séré (*q.v.*) and further: articles by Eugène Rouart (*Revue Mus.*, Oct. 1921) Leigh Henry (*Mus. Times*, July 1919); W. W. Roberts (*Music and Letters*, April 1922); obituary notices in Fr. mus. periodicals (April 1921) and A. Cœuroy (*Larousse mensuel*, Nov. 1923).—M. D. C.

SGAMBATI, Giovanni. Italian pianist and composer; *b.* Rome, 28 May, 1841; *d.* there, 14 Dec. 1914. One of outstanding figures in Italian musical life of his time. Having completed studies under Barberi, Natalucci and Aldega, immediately gained fame in Rome by his qualities as a pianist to such an extent as to attract the attention of Franz Liszt, who took Sgambati under his protection. Through Liszt, S. came to know Wagner also, and became acquainted with the publisher Schott, who subsequently publ. nearly all his compositions. His career as a pianist was a very glorious one. In Rome and throughout Italy, he was a worthy propagandist of classical works, both as soloist, and by taking part in such combinations as the famous Quintetto di Corte (Sgambati, Monachesi, Masi [whom De Sanctis afterwards succeeded], Jacobacci and Ferdinando Forino). During his tours in Italy, France, England, Germany and Russia, he gained triumphant successes. In Rome, he was one of the founders of the Liceo Musicale di Santa Cecilia (see ACADEMIES), in which, from its foundation until his death, he was prof. of pf., training a large number of excellent and devoted pupils. During the last period of his life, Sgambati hardly ever left Rome, where he devoted himself almost exclusively to teaching. His production as a composer is striking and of the highest value. He stands in the very front rank of modern Ital. comprs. of chamber and symph. music, of which he was one of the leading promoters in the XIX century.
2 symphonies (D ma.; E flat, unpubl.); 2 5tets; 4tet; *Requiem*, barit. solo, chorus, orch. (1906, in commemoration of King Victor Emmanuel II); many pf. pieces (nocturnes, studies, lyric pieces); songs. Consult a study by Alberto De Angelis, in *Rivista Musicale Italiana* (1912).—D. A.

SHAPOSHNIKOF, Adrian Gregorievitch (*accent 1st syll.*). Russ. compr. *b.* Petrograd, 10 June (n.s.), 1888. Pupil of N. Sokolof and Glazunof, Petrograd Cons. (1913).
Opera, *King's Feast*; ballets, *The Poisoned Garden* (book by Sologub); symph. poem, *Charuzsa* (*Marsh-Nymphs*); pf. sonatina; songs (publ. Jurgenson; Russ. State Music Publ. Dept.; operas ms.).—V. B.

SHARP, Cecil James. Eng. collector and arranger of Eng. folk-songs and dances, lecturer;

b. Denmark Hill, London, 22 Nov. 1859; *d.* London, 22 June, 1924. Mainly self-taught. Mus.M. Cantab. *h.c.* 1923. He did very valuable work in collecting, publishing, and lecturing on Eng. folk-music. The revival of interest in folk-songs and dances is due chiefly to his work. He also collected in Appalachia.

A Book of British Song (John Murray); *English Folk Song : Some Conclusions* (Simpkin & Co.); *Folk Songs from Somerset* (with Rev. Charles Marson) Series 1–5 (Schott); *English Folk-Carols* (Novello); *English Folk-Chanteys* (Schott); *English Folk Songs for Schools* (with Rev. Sabine Baring-Gould) (Curwen); *Children's Singing Games* (with Alice B. Gomme) (Novello); *Folk Songs for use in Schools,* Sets I–X (*id.*); *Folk Songs from the Southern Appalachians* (with Dame Campbell) (Putnam's Sons); *Folk Songs collected in the Appalachian Mountains,* Series 1 and 2 (Novello); *Nursery Songs from the Appalachian Mountains,* illustrated by E. Mackinnon (*id.*); songs, dances and incidental music to *A Midsummer Night's Dream* (*id.*); 4 folk-airs, vn. and pf. (*id.*); *The Country Dance Book* (with George Butterworth and Maud Karpeles), Parts 1–6 (*id.*); *Country Dance Tunes,* Sets I–XI (*id.*); *The Morris Book* (with Herbert MacIlwaine and George Butterworth), Parts 1–5 (*id.*); *Morris Dance Tunes,* Sets I–X (*id.*); *The Sword Dances of Northern England,* Parts 1–3 (*id.*); *Sword-Dance Songs and Tunes,* Sets I–III (*id.*); *Folk Songs of England,* selected ed., 2 vols. (*id.*), etc., etc.—E.-H.

SHARPE, Cedric. Eng. cellist; *b.* London, 13 April, 1891. Son of Herbert S. (*q.v.*). Stud. first under Tennyson Werge, from age of 7; later at R.C.M. under W. H. Squire; gained scholarship there, 1907; left in 1912. Has a fine tone and good style; does valuable work as chamber-music player, especially in the Philh. Str. Quartet.—E.-H.

SHARPE, Ethel (Mrs. Hobday). Irish pianist; *b.* Dublin, 28 Nov. 1872. Pupil of R. Irish Acad. of Music; subsequently went to R.C.M. London, under Franklin Taylor; 1st recital in Prince's Hall, Nov. 1891. Received silver medal of Musicians' Company. In 1894, gave a recital at Vienna. Reappeared in London, 1895. Wife of Alfred Hobday (*q.v.*). She has given many interesting chamber-music recitals.—W. St.

SHARPE, Herbert Francis. Eng. pianist and compr. *b.* Halifax, 1 March, 1861. Gained a pf. scholarship at National Training School (now R.C.M.), South Kensington, in 1876; succeeded Eugen d'Albert as Queen's scholar there; stud. under Sir Arthur Sullivan, Ebenezer Prout, J. F. Barnett and Sir F. Bridge. Appointed prof. at R.C.M. in 1884.

3-act light opera, ms.; *Concert Overture* (ms.); Variations for 2 pfs. (Cary); pf. pieces (*Eng. Fantasias*; *Undine*; 2 preludes, etc.) (Cary; Ashdown; Beale; Ricordi); pf. duets (3 symph. pieces [Leonard]; 5 character-pieces [Cary]); *Idyll,* fl. and pf. (Cary); *Suite,* fl. and pf. (Rudall, Carte); numerous songs and part-songs (Augener; Bayley & Fergusson).—E.-H.

SHATTUCK, Arthur. Amer. pianist; *b.* Neenah, Wis., U.S.A., 19 April, 1881. Pupil of Leschetizky in Vienna for 7 years. In 1901, soloist with Philh. Orch. Copenhagen. Lived in Paris until 1911. Toured Europe, and (1911–12) America. 1912–15, again in Europe. Has appeared with many large orchs. in Europe and America. Since 1916, playing in U.S.A.—O. K.

SHAW, Geoffrey Turton. H.M. Inspector of Music; Eng. compr. and singer; brother of Martin Shaw; *b.* Clapham, 14 Nov. 1879.

Educated at St. Paul's Choir Cath. School (Sir George Martin); Derby School (J. R. Sterndale-Bennett and S. Neville Cox); Caius Coll. Cambridge (organ scholar); Univ. Stewart of Rannoch scholar; stud. at Cambridge under Dr. Charles Wood and Sir Charles Stanford. Has worked hard to help the revival of Eng. music and in the reform of church music, and to provide music for ordinary people.

3 *Hymns to Pan,* chorus and orch. (Novello); *Shakespeare Choruses* with orch. (J. Williams); part-songs and church music, school songs (E. Arnold; Boosey; Curwen; Evans; Novello; Year-Book Press); pf. music (Winthrop Rogers; J. Williams); vn. music (Ashdown); numerous hymn-tunes.—E.-H.

SHAW, George Bernard. Author, playwright, and formerly mus. critic; *b.* Dublin, 26 July, 1856. Wrote weekly arts. in *The Star,* signed *Corno di Bassetto,* from 1888 to 1890. Wrote the musical *feuilleton* in *The World* from 1890 to 1894. Also wrote *The Perfect Wagnerite* (1898; 4th ed. 1922). Since 1898, he has written a few occasional arts. on music (notably for the *British Music Bulletin,* June 1919, and *Music and Letters* on Elgar, Jan. 1920); but he retired from regular practice as a critic in 1898, in which year his book *The Perfect Wagnerite* appeared. He played a prominent part in the formation of the British Music Soc. (*q.v.*), frequently appearing as speaker and lecturer at its public meetings and conferences. —E.-H.

SHAW, Martin. Eng. compr. *b.* London, 9 March 1876. Brother of Geoffrey Shaw. Stud. at R.C.M. London under Sir Charles Stanford. Has worked hard to establish a stronger Eng. national feeling in music. Has done much to cultivate community singing; to free Eng. church music from a load of sentimentality. He has written many fine church hymn-tunes and school songs. Comp. the simple direct little operas *Brer Rabbit* and *Fools and Fairies* for the League of Arts, who perf. them in Hyde Park. His music has a bold, tuneful and manly ring.

Ballad-opera, *Mr. Pepys*; light opera, *Brer Rabbit* (J. Williams); mus. plays: *The Soul of the World* (vocal score, J. Williams); *The Pedlar* (Evans); *Fools and Fairies* (*id.*); *The Cockyolly Bird* (overture publ. Goodwin); *The Vikings*; *The Dreamer*; incidental music to *The Lord of Death* (L. N. Parker; Plymouth, 1923); *Fantasia,* pf. and orch.; *Suite,* A mi. for str. 4tet (Cramer); pf. trio; pf. album, *Brer Rabbit* (Williams); 6 *Songs of War* (Rogers); *Sing Song* (Curwen); *Kipling Songs* (Curwen); many other songs (Boosey; Curwen; Cramer; Chappell; Enoch); *Pastorals,* etc., 2-part songs (Curwen); part-songs (Novello; J. Williams; Curwen; Arnold); unison songs (Evans; Curwen; Arnold); *Tallis Funeral March,* arr. organ (Curwen); British Marches, arr. (Evans); 100 *Songs of Britain* (Boosey); *Song-time* (Curwen); Eng. *Carol Book* (Mowbray); 28 selected Songs of Britain, arr. (Boosey, 1922); *League of Nations Song-book* (Stainer & Bell); *Motherland Song-book,* Vol. II (with G. Shaw) (*id.*). Book, *The Principles of English Church Music Composition* (*Mus. Opinion* Office, 1921).—E.-H.

SHEDLOCK, John South. Eng. mus. critic and writer; *b.* Reading, 29 Sept. 1843; *d.* London, 9 Jan. 1919. Educ. partly in France, and then in London; B.A. London Univ.; stud. pf. in Paris under Ernst Lübeck, compn. under Édouard Lalo; began as a pianist and teacher in London; produced a 4tet for str. and pf. in

1886; 1879, mus. critic for the *Academy*; in 1901 for the *Athenæum*; editor *Monthly Musical Record*, 1902–12, continuing to contribute valuable articles to it until Jan. 1918.

Transl. of *Beethoven's Letters*, from Kalischer's collection (2 vols. J. M. Dent, 1909); *The Pianoforte Sonata* (Methuen, 1895); *Beethoven* (Bell, 1903); *Beethoven's Pianoforte Sonatas and Various Readings* (Augener, 1918); transl. of *Riemann's Dictionary*, with additions (Augener, 1892); arts. on Beethoven and Bach in *M.M.R.* and *Mus. Times.*—E.-H.

SHELDON, A. J. Brit. musical critic; *b.* Liverpool, 20 Aug. 1874. Educated at Glasgow; mus. amateur for 20 years; occasional critical work, 1912–13. Musical critic *Manchester Courier*, 1913–16. Regular contributor to *Mus. Opinion* from 1915. Musical critic *Birmingham Daily Post* from 1919; writer of analytical notes, City of Birmingham Orch. programmes.—E.-H.

SHELLEY, Harry Rowe. Amer. orgt. compr. *b.* New Haven, Conn., 2 June, 1858. Stud. music under Gustav J. Stoeckel at Yale Coll. and in New York under Dudley Buck and Max Vogrich. In youth, orgt. of Centre Ch. New Haven; then of Plymouth Ch. Brooklyn, N.Y. In 1887 visited Europe, stud. under Dvořák; returning to America same year, became orgt. of Church of the Pilgrims, Brooklyn, N.Y. Since 1899, orgt. of Fifth Avenue Baptist Ch. New York. His larger works have been an opera *Leila* (ms.), a vn. concerto (perf. 1891), 2 symphonies (the first, E flat, perf. New York, 1897), symph. poem, *The Crusaders*; an overture, *Francesca da Rimini*. Member of National Inst. of Arts and Letters.

Romeo and Juliet, lyric drama (Schuberth); cantatas: *The Inheritance Divine* (Schirmer, 1895); *Death and Life* (id. 1898); *Vexilla Regis* (Novello, 1893); *Psalm XCI* (Schirmer, 1921). Many pf. pieces, songs, choruses (sacred and secular) (Curwen; Schirmer).—J. M.

SHENSHIN, Alexander Alexeievitch (*accent 2nd syll.*). Russ. compr. *b.* 19 Nov. 1890. Pupil of Kruglikof, Gretchaninof, Glière and Javorsky (1907–15); 1922, prof. at Moscow State Cons.; 1920, member of Russ. Acad. of Art-Sciences; from 1920, compr. Moscow Theatre for Children.

The Poem, orch. op. 5 (ms.); pf. 5tet, D mi. (ms.); many fine songs, op. 1, 2, 4, 6, 7, 8, 9 (Jurgenson; Russ. State Music Publ. Dept.); pf. pieces; music for children's plays.—V. B.

SHERA, F. H. Eng. compr. *b.* 1882. Dir. of music, The College, Malvern; M.A. and Mus.M. Cantab.

Miniature symphony; 2 orch. pieces; pf. 5tet; songs (ms.); book, *Musical Groundwork*, a short course of aural training (Milford, 1923).—E.-H.

SHINN, Frederick George. Eng. orgt. and educationist; *b.* London, 23 Dec. 1867. Stud. at R.C.M. under Sir. Hubert Parry, Sir Walter Parratt and Sir F. Bridge; orgt. St. Bartholomew's Ch. Sydenham, since 1893. Prof. at R.A.M. and R. Normal Coll. for the Blind. Has done much fine work in advancing the cause of mus. appreciation, by means of aural training of students and sight-reading.

Mus. Memory and its Cultivation (Vincent; now Augener, 1898); *Elementary Ear-training*, Part I, Melodic; Part II, Harmonic (formerly publ. by Vincent; now Augener); *Method of teaching Harmony based on Ear-training*, Part I, Diatonic; Part II, Chromatic (Augener).—E.-H.

SHISHOF, Ivan Petrovitch (*accent 2nd syll.*). Russ. compr. *b.* Novocherkask (district of Don Cossacks), 26 Sept./8 Oct. 1888. Pupil of Kastalsky and A. Koreschenko, at music school of Moscow Philh. Soc. (finished courses in 1916).

Symphony, orch. (1923); overture, orch. (1915); songs, some with text, some wordless (Russ. State Music Publ. Dept.).—V. B.

SHORE, Samuel Royle. Eng. orgt. compr. lecturer; *b.* Edgbaston, Birmingham, 12 April, 1856. Solicitor by prof.; stud. music under Alfred R. Gaul; self-taught in compn. Held various posts as orgt.; appointed (by Bishop Gore) instructor in plain-chant for Diocese of Birmingham, 1911–13; lecturer in ecclesiastical music, Birmingham Cath. 1912–13; to Southwark Diocese Plain-song Association from 1915. Between 1906 and 1913 (in conjunction with late Edwin Stephenson, then orgt. Birmingham Cath.) publ. and perf. a series of Palestrina, Tudor and Jacobean classics. Has lectured widely on plain-chant, making a large use of modern notation and popular manuals. Has written many church services in a new form which contrasts congregational singing with that of the skilled choir.

Missa Sanctorum Meritis, op. 9, in 4- and 5-part modern vocal polyphony (Eng. Novello); *Missa Stabat Mater* (id.); *Requiem* (id.); Motet, 8 vs. Phrygian mode (Priestley, Birmingham); Madrigal, 6 vs. Hypo-æolian mode (Novello); *Te Deum* for 2 choirs (one in unison leading the congregation), Novello. Ed. *The Cathedral Series* of xvi and xvii century comprs., Mundy, Causton, Tallis, Ward, Gibbons, Anerio; *The Sarum Litany* (plain-chant and faux-bourdon), etc.; The *Diocesan Music Series*, handy manuals of church services in modern notation for the people (Novello).—E.-H.

SIAMESE MUSIC. See GRASSI, E. C.

SIBELIUS, Jean. Finnish compr. *b.* Tavastehus, 8 Dec. 1865. He soon abandoned legal studies for music; stud. under Wegelius at Helsingfors Music Institute, and later in Berlin (under Becker) and Vienna (under Fuchs and Goldmark). A life State grant from 1897 enabled him to devote himself to composition. Consequently his production is very considerable. His strong individuality made itself felt from the beginning, sometimes weird and wild, sometimes of a mysterious, penetrating sweetness, often majestic, bold, and infinitely sad. His compositions are messages from "the land of a thousand lakes and islets" with their manifold and changing tones of colour. They have, like their country, their force in beauty of shading.

To penetrate a composer's message fully we must know the atmosphere he breathes, the racial and social influences which have moulded him. In the case of Sibelius the deep melancholy of nature in Finland, and the impression of the Russian iron grip, have produced a genius, strong, original and full-blooded. He has contributed to almost every branch of music except opera; but his most important compositions are in the form of tone-poem, symphony, and song. The six symphonies represent the true character of his development. The tone-poems are full of the folk-song spirit, though not one draws on actual folk-tunes. One of his latest pieces, *The Oceanides* (written for an orchestra of 120) is a very personal work. It is a magnificent piece of colouring—the sea in various moods. It awakens, stirring under the dawn-wind's cold caressing; echoes to unseen voices proclaiming the breaking of light on the deep; Oceanus stretches his night-benumbed limbs, tingling with full remembrance of their potency, and rises to a grand tidal climax.

Sibelius ranks among the foremost living composers of to-day. He has been wholly unaffected by the work of his predecessors and contemporaries. He is concerned, first and last, in giving his own message to the world in a form that appears austere and forbidding on a first acquaintance, but which holds the attention throughout. His method of thematic development is peculiarly original. As a general rule, his symphonic movements are built up from fragmentary germs, or groups of notes, which grow and expand until the climax is reached with the complete presentation of the theme in its full splendour. He draws his inspiration direct from nature, and, though essentially a composer of absolute music, he has not neglected to make use of the opportunities afforded him by various episodes in the *Kalevala* and other legendary myths of Finland. A new orch. work, *Fantasia Symphonica*, was produced at Stockholm, March 1924.

6 symphonies: No. I, in E mi. (1899); II, D ma. (1902); III, C ma. (1907); IV, A mi. (prod. Birmingham Fest. 1912); V, E flat ma. (prod. Helsingfors on compr.'s birthday (1915); VI (1923) Symph. poems: *En Saga*, op. 9; *Spring Song*, op. 16; *The Swan of Tuonela*, and *Lemminkäinen (Homeward Bound)* from Lemminkäinen Suite, op. 22; *Finlandia*, op. 26; *Pohjola's Daughter*, op. 49; *The Night-Ride and Sunrise* op. 54; *The Bard*, op. 54; and *Oceanides*, op. 72; *Karelia Overture*, op. 10; *Karelia Suite*, op. 11; *Rakastava (The Lover)*: Suite for str. orch.; *Scènes historiques*, op. 25 and 66, both suites; *Lemminkäinen II* (suite from stage-music to Adolf Paul's drama); *Valse triste* (from stage-music to Arvid Järnefelt's *Kuolema*); stage-music to Maeterlinck's *Pelléas et Mélisande*, *Belsazar* (Procopé) and *Svanehvit* (Strindberg); also smaller orch. compns.: *The Dryads*; *Dance Intermezzo*; *Pan and Echo*; *Canzonetta*; and *In Memoriam*. Vn. concerto, op. 47; 2 sonatas, vn. and orch. op. 69; *Devotion and Cantique*, cello and orch.; *Kullervo* symphony (on episode from *Kalevala*), orch. and final chorus (1892); *Snöfrid*, chorus and orch.; *Origin of Fire (Ukko the Fire-maker)*, for dedication of Finnish National Theatre, 1902 (barit. male chorus and orch.); *The Ferry-man's Brides* (ballad by Oksanen), v. and orch.; *The Captured Queen*, choir and orch.; *Jordens sang*; *Maan virsi (Hymn to Earth)*; *Oma maa (Native Land)*, chorus and orch. Str. 4tet, *Voces intimæ*, op. 56; pf. sonatas and sonatinas; songs (*Tryst*; *Black Roses*; *Jubal*; *Spring is flying*; *Little Lassie*; *But my Bird is long in homing*; *Evening*; *Astray*; *First Kiss*; etc., etc.); choruses; also the fine *Athenian Hymn* for boy's v. and orch. (See also articles on FINNISH MUSIC).—M.-L.

SIEBEN, Wilhelm. Ger. condr. *b.* Landau, Palatinate, 29 April, 1881. In 1898, entered Munich Univ. as law-student; turned to music; pupil of Rheinberger and Thuille (theory), later of Ševčík (Prague) and Fel. Berber (vn.); 1905, vn. teacher at Munich Acad. of Music (1916, prof.); leader of a str. quartet; especially cultivated contemporary chamber-music; 1918, succeeded Brode as condr. of Symphony Concerts and of Singakademie at Königsberg; 1920, chief condr. at Dortmund.—A. E.

SIEGEL, Rudolf. Ger. compr. and condr. *b.*

Berlin, 12 April, 1878. Turned to music after law studies (LL.D.). Pupil of Thiel, Humperdinck, Berlin; L. Thuille, Munich; 1910–11, cond. Concert Soc. for choral singing, Munich; 1st perf. of Pfitzner's *Poor Heinrich (Arme Heinrich)* at Prince Regent Theatre, Munich; 1914–1917, dir. of Mus. Acad. Königsberg; 1918–19, opera stage-manager at Mannheim; 1919, chief town-condr. and condr. of Concert Soc.; 1922, gen. mus. dir. at Crefeld.

Heroische Tondichtung for orch. (Mus. Fest. Essen, 1906); opera, *Herr Dandolo* (Essen, 1914); *Apostatenmarsch* (G. Keller, male chorus and orch.); 12 Ger. national songs for pf. (3 hands); *Der Einsiedler* (Eichendorff), barit. and orch.—A. E.

SIEMS, Margarete. Ger. s. singer; *b.* Breslau, 30 Dec. 1881. Pupil of Mme. A. Orgeni (Dresden); 1902, member of Ger. Theatre, Prague; 1908–20, coloratura-s., Dresden Court Opera House; 1920, teacher at Stern's Cons. Berlin. —A. E.

SIEWERS, V. W. H. H. Norwegian jurist and music critic; *b.* in 1855. Degree in law, 1879. Since 1889, judge in Christiania Town Court. Besides publishing a juridical work in several vols., S. has done great service for Norwegian mus. history by his contributions to various dictionaries and periodicals, and especially by many years' activity as mus. critic to *Morgenbladet* in Christiania.—R. M.

SIGTENHORST MEYER, B. van den. Dutch compr. and pianist; *b.* Amsterdam, 17 June, 1888. Stud. at Amsterdam Cons. under De Pauw, pf., Dan. de Lange and B. Zweers, theory.

2 str. 4tets: No. I, 1919, perf. 10 April, Paris (Amsterdam, Alsbach); No. II, 1921, perf. 1922, The Hague); oratorio, *De verzoeking van Boeddha (Temptation of Buddha)*, 1918, perf. The Hague, Oct. 1921 (Alsbach); *Stabat Mater*, unacc. choir (1918), perf. The Hague (same year) by the Madrigaalvereeniging (Alsbach); *De bron van Badrah*, 1-act opera (1917), perf. The Hague; many songs (Dutch words of P. C. Hooft, Rient van Santen, Noto Soeroto); pf. works (Alsbach).—W. P.

SIGWART, Botho (Count of Eulenburg). Ger. compr. *b.* Berlin, 10 Jan. 1884; fell in action (Galicia), 2 June, 1915. Son of Count Philipp of Eulenburg; 1909, married concert-singer Helene Staegemann. Lived at Dresden.

Melodrama, *Hector's Burial*, op. 15; *Ode to Sappho*, op. 18; str. 4tet, B mi. op. 13; vn. sonata, op. 6; pf. sonatas op. 14 and 19; sonata for vla. d'amore and pf. op. 16; symphony, organ and orch. C mi. op. 12; songs; opera, *Songs of Euripides* (Stuttgart, 1915).—A. E.

SIKLÓS, Albert. Hungarian compr. *b.* Budapest, 26 June, 1878; prof. of compn. at Budapest High School for Music.—B. B.

SILK, Dorothy. Eng. s. singer; *b.* Moseley, Birmingham. Stud. singing under Mme. Minadieu there; then in Vienna for 2 years under Ress. Has a particularly clear and sweet voice of pure s. quality and good range; specialises in Bach's music and famous old comprs.; is at her best as a chamber-music singer; is well known both in London and the provinces.—E.-H.

SILVA, Giulio. Ital. teacher of singing; *b.* Parma, 22 Dec. 1875. Whilst studying medicine (later abandoned) took a course in compn. at R. Liceo Mus. di Santa Cecilia (De Sanctis school); first devoted himself successfully to conducting; 1913, won by competition post of singing - teacher at R. Cons. at Parma; from there to Liceo di Santa Cecilia, Rome (succeeding Antonio Cotogni). 1920, went to New York as teacher of singing in Mannes Cons. Wrote book, *Il Canto* (Turin, Bocca), and many arts. for *Rivista Musicale Italiana* and other periodicals.—D. A.

SILVA, Oscar da. Portuguese pianist and teacher; *b.* Lisbon, 1872. Stud. there under Timotheo da Silveira and others; later at Leipzig under Reinecke and Clara Schumann. Toured widely as pianist. Now lives at Lisbon. One of the best of Portuguese comprs. See art. PORTUGUESE OPERA.

Opera *Don Mecia* (produced Colyseu dos Recreios, 1901); numerous pf. pieces (*Bilder*; *Rapsodie portugaise*; *Mazurkas*; *Dolorosas*, etc.); *Mélodie* and a Suite, vn. and pf.; many songs.—E.-H.

SILVER, Charles. Fr. compr. *b.* Paris, 16 Feb. 1868. Pupil of Massenet at Cons.; *Prix de Rome* 1891, with cantata *L'Interdit*; prof. at Paris Cons. Writes almost entirely for theatre, following a rather conventional æsthetic formula; but what he writes is carefully finished.

La Belle au bois dormant (1902); *Le Clos* (1906); *Myriane* (1913); *La Mégère apprivoisée* (1922); *Neigilde* (ballet, 1913); *Tobie* (oratorio, 1902); and some orch. pieces.—A. C.

S.I.M. See SOCIETIES.

ŠIMKUS, Stasys. Lithuanian compr. *b.* Motiskiai, Seredžius district, 23 Jan. 1887. Stud. under J. Naujalis at Kaunas. At 13, played organ at Ciebeškis, Kidokelaukys, and Skirsnemune. In 1905 entered Vilna Music School; in autumn of same year, joined Warsaw Mus. Inst., graduating in 1908, in organ section. He then entered Petrograd Cons. where he finished his course in 1914. At outbreak of war, he was sent to America to collect donations for Lithuanian war-sufferers. He stayed there 5 years. In 1917, he began to publ. there his journal *Muzika* (in Lithuanian). Returned home in 1920. When the war with Poles arose, he entered army as a volunteer and organised concerts at the front. At Lithuanian Scientific Association at Vilna, 1000 folk-songs, coll. by him, await publication.

2 music-dramas: *Čigonai* (*The Gypsies*), *Išeivis* (*The Emigrant*); pf. sonata; trio (pf. vn. cello); str. 4tet hundreds of songs, duets, 4tets, choruses. Best-known choruses are *Kur bakuže samanota* (*Where the moss-grown hut*); *Plaukia sau laivelis* (*The Gliding Boat*); *Vakarine daina* (*Evening Song*).—H. R.

SIMON, James. Ger. author, compr. pianist; *b.* Berlin, 29 Sept. 1880. Pupil of Conrad Ansorge (pf.) and of Max Bruch (compn.) at R. High School of Music and advanced class at Acad.; 1904, Ph.D. Munich; 1907, teacher at Klindworth-Scharwenka Cons. Berlin. Wrote *Faust in Music* (1906, in R. Strauss's coll. *Musik*).

Many songs; pf. concerto, F ma. (ms.); Goethe's *Urworte* (soli, chorus, orch. and organ); symphony, B flat ma.; *Rhapsody and Rustic Suite* in 5 movements (orch.); trio, A ma.; str. 4tet in E; pf. and vn. sonata, E mi. op. 20; 6-v. motet, *Die Tod ist gross* (*Great is Death*) (Rilke), with organ.—A. E.

SIMONETTI, Achille. Violinist, composer; *b.* Turin, 1857. Stud. first under Francesco Bianchi; then in Milan Cons. 1872, under Giuseppe Gamba, a pupil of Polledro. The strongest in-

fluence which formed his playing style came from Camillo Sivori, under whom he stud. at Genoa. S. assimilated many qualities of this great pupil of Paganini—brilliant left-hand agility, facility for double-stops and a clear, unaffected *cantabile*. In 1880, toured through France and played in Pasdeloup Concerts; 1881, entered Paris Cons. where he stud. vn. under Charles Dancla and compn. under Massenet; 1883, went to Nice, where he establ. a quartet with D'Ambrosio; 1887, went to London where he speedily became a favourite. His first visit to Ireland was with Bottesini, the famous d.b. player. He formed the well-known London Trio with Amina Goodwin and W. E. Whitehouse and toured abroad with them. After many years' touring in Europe, became vn. prof. at R. Irish Acad. of Music in 1912. With Esposito (pf.) and Clyde Twelvetrees (cello), gave many trio-recitals and led the Dublin Orch. Soc. concerts; 1919, resigned his professorship and went to France. Has comp. some works distinguished by melodic charm and thought.

2 str. 4tets; 2 sonatas, vn. and pf.; vn. pieces (*Madrigal*; *Spinning-Wheel*; *Le Nocturne japonais*, etc.).—W. ST.

SIMPLIFIED SCORE (*Vereinfachte Partitur*). Arnold Schönberg publ. his 4 songs with orch. op. 22 in a simplified score for the use of condrs. It is easier to study and conduct from this score. The full score only serves the purpose of copy for the copyist of the parts. The beginnings and ends of the leading parts are marked ⌐ and ¬; principal parts with the sign H⁻ (*Hauptstimme*); subordinate parts N⁻ (*Nebenstimmen*).—EG. W.

ŠÍN, Otakar. Czech compr. *b.* Fryšava (Moravia), 1881. Stud. at Cons. Prague; since 1920 prof. and since 1922 administrative dir. of Cons. His compns. show serious endeavour and modern harmonic colour.

Symph. poem, *Tilottama*; *King Menkera*; str. 4tet; 2 books pf. pieces (Fr. Chadím; Hudební Matice, Prague).—V. ST.

SINCLAIR, George Robertson. Eng. organist, master of the choristers and succentor at Hereford Cath.; condr. of the Three Choirs Fests. at Hereford; *b.* Croydon, 28 Oct. 1863; *d.* suddenly at Birmingham, shortly after conducting a rehearsal of Verdi's *Requiem*, 7 Feb. 1917. At age of 8, entered the R. Irish Acad. of Music, where he stud. under Sir Robert Stewart. At 10, choral scholar, St. Michael's Coll. Tenbury; was the favourite pupil of its founder, the Rev. Sir Frederick Gore Ouseley. In 1879, went to Gloucester as assistant to Dr. C. Harford Lloyd, orgt. of the cath. At 17, orgt. of Truro Cath. In 1889, succeeded Dr. Langdon Colborne as orgt. of Hereford Cath. where he soon brought the music up to a high standard. Through his efforts the magnificent organ was rebuilt by Willis. The success of the Three Choirs Fests., 8 of which he conducted, is largely due to him. In 1889 the degree of Mus.Doc. *h.c.* was conferred on him by the Archbishop of Canterbury. After his death a memorial fund was raised for the benefit of old Hereford choristers wishing to take up music as a profession.—P. C. H.

SINDING, Christian. Norwegian composer; *b.* Kongsberg, 11 Jan. 1856. Studied violin under Gustav Böhn, Christiania; afterwards began to study the piano, but soon realised that the career of a virtuoso did not suit him. In theory, he was a pupil of Ludv. M. Lindeman; studied at Conservatoire in Leipzig, 1874–7 (teachers: Reinecke, Jadassohn, Schradieck and Kretzschmar). Returned to Norway, 1877; went again to Leipzig in 1879. Up to that time he had composed a piano sonata (F minor), a string quartet and a violin sonata (the last was played at a *soirée* at the Conservatoire). His studies at the Conservatoire did not seem to bring him an entirely satisfactory result. Therefore, when in 1880–2 he visited Dresden, Munich and Berlin (with a scholarship from the State) he pursued his musical studies on his own account. From this time on, his compositions display that freedom in form and expression which he had striven after, but not found at the Conservatoire in Leipzig. In 1882–4 Sinding was engaged upon the work with which he first made a name, the piano quintet in E minor (op. 5). After having been played, for first time in Christiania, in 1885 by Erika Nissen and Böhn's Quartet, it was performed in 1888 in Leipzig by the Brodsky Quartet with Busoni. It provoked a bitter discussion in the German Press, some critics being exasperated at the daring " parallel fifths " in the last movement, while his defenders maintained that the work was the expression of a self-reliant individuality. On the next performance of the quintet (1889) the feeling was entirely in Sinding's favour, and the work was soon being performed in all lands. This quintet inaugurated a new period, not only in Sinding's life, but also for Norwegian music. It was a fruit of the Neo-Romantic tendency, and with its combination of national tone and colouring with Wagnerian rhythm and structure, it contains elements which are afterwards frequently met with in Sinding's works. It gave the signal-note for Norwegian musical progress in those years.

After this first success the composer created a number of works, which belong to his best and most characteristic productions: the piano concerto in D major, dedicated to Erika Nissen (perf. first time Christiania Musical Society, 1890) and the 1st symphony (D minor, op. 21; performed in Christiania same year; afterwards revised and produced at symphony concert in Berlin, 1892, under Weingartner). These two works confirmed his reputation both at home and abroad, and after the publishing firm of Peters in Leipzig had in 1892 taken over publication of his works he soon won great renown. In his later production, lyric compositions take up a large space (over 200 songs, choral works, cantatas, etc.), but he has also produced many works for orchestra and for piano. Sinding's music has, like Grieg's, won its way to all parts of the world. It has little or nothing in common with the bright, ingratiating tone of Grieg's works; yet Sinding's broad, epic style, with its

optimistic and cosmopolitan tendency, has won friends in the widest circles. During a great part of his life, he lived in Berlin; has often conducted his own works both at home and abroad; was elected an honorary member of the Akademie der Künste in Berlin. Of late years he has been living in Christiania, except during 1921–2, when he was professor of composition at the Eastman Conservatoire of Music in Rochester, U.S.A.

As a composer Sinding is independent of any school. His style has often a Scandinavian strain, without its being always possible to characterise it as specifically Norwegian; but its sharp-cut rhythms, bold harmonies and vigorous tendency are characteristic of his Norwegian temperament. He finds himself more at home in the broader forms of composition than did his compatriot, Grieg. Sinding's muse is more epic than dramatic. He favours an heroic *al fresco* style which is manly and passionate in its form of expression. Side by side with the typical Sinding characteristics (restless modulation, violent harmonic movements, rhythmic monotony) we see the influence of Wagner, especially as regards melody and harmonisation. His lyrical compositions are often more Norwegian in their tone than his symphonic works; they supplement Grieg's works by their great contrast.

Opera, *Det Hellige Bjerg* (*The Holy Mount*) (Dessau, 1914); symphonies: No. I, D mi.; No. II, D ma. (1st perf. Berlin, 1907); No. III, F ma. (1st perf. Leipzig, 1921, under Arthur Nikisch); symph. poem, *Rondo infinito*; *Épisodes chevaleresques* for orch.; pf. concerto, D flat, op. 35 (publ. Hansen, Copenhagen); 2 vn. concertos (A, op. 45; D, op. 60); *Legende*, vn. and orch.; 2 romances, vn.; 2 pf. trios; 3 vn. sonatas; pf. 4tet; 5tet; str. 4tet; 3 suites, vn. and pf.; *Serenade*, 2 vns. and pf.; pf. pieces; songs; cantatas; choral work (*To Molde*), etc. A number of his pf. pieces and songs are pub. by the Norsk Musik-forlag and Wilh. Hansen, Copenhagen; but most by Peters in Leipzig.—J. A.

SINIGAGLIA, Leone. Ital. compr. *b.* Turin, 14 Aug. 1868. Stud. at Turin under Giovanni Bolzoni; then Vienna under Mandyczewski. In Vienna, became acquainted with Goldmark and Dvořák, who had some influence on his artistic tendencies. Widely known and appreciated for his orch. works, inspired by songs and dances of his native Piedmont. His *Danze piemontesi*, orch. op. 31; *Rapsodia piemontese*, vn. and orch. op. 26; *Piemonte*, suite for orch.; *Vecchie canzoni popolari del Piemonte* (*Old Folk-Songs of Piedmont*), v. and pf., have been perf. in principal European concert-halls; also overture, *Le baruffe chiozzotte*, op. 32. In addition to above, much other instr. and vocal chamber-music (leading Ital. and Ger. publishers).—D. A.

SITT, Hans. Hungarian compr. *b.* Prague, 21 Sept. 1850; *d.* Leipzig, 10 March, 1922. Son of vn.-maker Anton Sitt; stud. at Prague Cons. (Bennewitz, Mildner, Kittl and Krejčí); 1867, Konzertmeister, Breslau; 1870–3, theatre condr. Breslau and Prague; 1873–80, town condr. Chemnitz; cond. Baron P. v. Dervies' private orch., Nice; inaugurated popular concerts Crystal Palace, Leipzig; 1883, teacher R. Cons. Leipzig (retired 1921); member of

Brodsky Quartet (vla.); 1885–1903, condr. Bach Society.

Songs (op. 18, 36); pf. pieces; 3 vn. concertos (op. 11, D mi.; op. 21, A mi.; op. 111, D mi.); Concertino, op. 28, A mi.; Polonaise, op. 29, A ma.; Romance, op. 52 (vn. and orch.); *Notturno (id.)*; 2 cello concertos (op. 34, A mi.; op. 38, D mi.); vla. concerto, op. 68, A mi.; *Konzertstücke* for vla. op. 46, G mi.; vn. duets, op. 117 and 118; pf. pieces, op. 10; orch. works (overture to Leschivo's *Don Juan of Austria, Festival March*, op. 54, E flat ma.); *Festival Hymn*, op. 55 (male chorus and orch.; *Hohenzollern und Oranien* (barit. male chorus and orch.); male choruses (op. 60, 85, 86).—A. E.

SITTARD, Alfred. Ger. organ-virtuoso and condr. *b.* Stuttgart, 4 Nov. 1878. Pupil of father (mus. writer Josef Sittard), of Karl Armbrust and W. Köhler; 1896–7, orgt. of St. Petri Ch. Hamburg; 1897–1901, pupil at Cologne Cons. (Wüllner, Franke, Seiss); hon. condr. Hamburg Opera House; Mendelssohn Prize, 1902; 1903, orgt. of Kreuzkirche, Dresden; 1912, orgt. of St. Michael's Ch. Hamburg; establ. a large church choir; 1920, condr. of Hamburg Teachers' Singing Union.

Choral studies for organ; *Psalm I* for 8-v. chorus unacc.; religious and secular unacc. choral works. —A. E.

SIX (Groupe des Six). By this name is denoted the friendly group formed in 1918 by Darius Milhaud, Arthur Honegger, Francis Poulenc, Germaine Tailleffère, Georges Auric and Louis Durey. It is a popular error to attribute to "the Six" a common ideal and common tastes. These artists follow very different paths, and have nothing in common but their friendly feeling. Poulenc and Auric have a conception of music as far removed as possible from that of Honegger or of Milhaud. In practice the constitution of this group made possible the organisation of concerts in France and abroad which rapidly made known the works of these young musicians, works of very unequal value. —H. P.

SJÖBERG, Svante Leonard. Swedish compr. orgt. *b.* Karlskrona, 28 Aug. 1873. Stud. under Joseph Dente (compr.) at R. Cons. Stockholm, 1893–7; then under Max Bruch and Rob. Hausmann in Berlin, 1900–2. From 1902, condr. of Music Soc. and Orch. Soc. at Karlskrona. Orgt. from 1902 at chief church there.

Sonata, vn. and pf. op. 2 (1898; Musikaliska Konstföreningen); concert overtures, op. 3 (1899), *Gustaf Wasa*, op. 5 (1901; 1904, Breitkopf); cantatas; songs.—P. V.

SJÖGREN, J. G. Emil. Swedish compr. orgt. *b.* Stockholm, 16 June, 1853; *d.* there, 1 March, 1918. Stud. R. Cons. Stockholm, and then (1879–80) in Berlin (compn. under Fr. Kiel; organ under Haupt). Orgt. at Fr. Reformed Ch. Stockholm, 1880–4; from 1891 at Johannes Ch.; 1886, also teacher at Richard Andersson's pf. school. As compr., was a genial follower of the Romantic school. His songs belong to the best (in this style) of the period 1880–1900. His vn. sonatas and pf. pieces are much admired.

Songs with orch. op. 18, 25; nearly 100 songs with pf.; many pf. pieces (op. 10, *Eroticon*; 14, *Novellettes*; 35, 1st sonata; 44, 2nd sonata); 5 sonatas for vn. and pf.; also 2 *Fantasiestücke*, op. 27; *Poème*, op. 40; *Morceau de concert*, op. 45; sonata, cello and pf.; organ pieces, op. 4 and 49; cantatas; trios; duets; male-v. choruses.—P. V.

SKILTON, Charles Sanford. Amer. compr. *b.* Northampton, Mass., U.S.A., 16 Aug. 1868. A.B. Yale Univ. 1889. From 1891–3, stud. in Berlin under Bargiel and Boise (compn.) and Heintz (organ). From 1893–6, instructor in music in Salem (N.C.) Acad. 1897–8, stud. under Shelley and Dudley Buck in New York. 1898 to 1903, taught pf. and theory at State Normal School, Trenton, N.J. Since 1903, prof. of organ, theory and history of music at Univ. of Kansas. 1903–15, also Dean of the School of Fine Arts of this Univ.

As early as 1889 his incidental music to Sophocles' *Electra* was perf. at Smith College, Northampton, Mass. In 1897 a vn. sonata won a prize of Music Teachers' National Assoc. A number of orch. works are still unpubl. (overture, *Mount Oread*; symph. poem, *A Carolina Legend*; a suite, *East and West*). Lately he has devoted much attention to compn. based on Indian music. *Two Indian Dances* were played in str. 4tet form by Zoellner Quartet, 1915–6. In orch. form they have been given repeatedly in America and by Queen's Hall Orch. in London.

Suite Primeval on tribal Indian melodies (1921), of which Nos. 1 and 2 are orch. arr. of *Two Indian Dances* for str. 4tet (1917); *The Witch's Daughter*, cantata for soli, chorus and orch. (1918); 3 *Indian Sketches*, pf. (1919) (all publ. by C. Fischer, New York).—O. K.

SKUDUTIS. See LITHUANIAN MUSIC.

SKUHERSKÝ, František. Czechoslovak theorist, compr. *b.* Opočno, 1830; *d.* Budějovice, 1902. Stud. in Prague; 1854–65, dir. of Mus. Soc. in Innsbruck (Tyrol), then dir. of Organ School, Prague. From 1879 lecturer at Univ. Prague. His *Theory of Musical Composition* (1881), *Musical Forms* (1879) and *Theory of Harmony* (1885) are, for their time, quite revolutionary and advanced. His principles of harmony lead directly to atonality. He helped the reform of church music. Publ. an Organ School.

Operas: *Vladimír* (1863); *Lora* (1868); *Rector and General* (1873); symph. poem, *May*; pf. trio, etc. —V. ST.

SLAVONIC FOLK-MUSIC. See KUBA, LUDVÍK.

SLEZAK, Leo. Austrian opera singer; *b.* Schönberg, Moravia, 8 Aug. 1875. Pupil of Adolf Robinson at Brünn; appeared there (1896) as Lohengrin; brilliant stage-career in Olmütz, Breslau and Berlin; then Vienna Court Opera, since 1901. Tours all over Europe and America. Heroic t. with bright voice and fine stage appearance. Especially good singer of Wagner (all parts, Tristan and Parsifal excepted), of Verdi's *Otello*, etc. His autobiography *Meine sämtlichen Werke* is one of the most amusing books written by a musician (Berlin, 1921). Consult biography by Klinenberger (1910).—P. ST.

SLIWIŃSKI, Józef. Polish pianist; *b.* Warsaw, 15 Dec. 1865. Stud. under Leschetizky in Vienna and Anton Rubinstein in Petrograd. For many years, pf. prof. at Riga Cons. Has lived in Warsaw since 1918. His poetic playing is especially suited to the execution of Chopin, Schumann and Liszt.—ZD. J.

SLOVAK FOLK-MUSIC. The Slovaks, numbering about 2 millions, are a Slav people closely related to the Czechs. They live in the eastern half of Czecho-Slovakia, which formerly represented North Hungary. The extant Slovak folklore material, which consists almost entirely of vocal melody, has appeared in the following important publications: *Slovenské Spevy*, 3 vols. (publ. in Turčiansky-Svätý-Martin, Slovakia, 1880, 1890, 1899), contains nearly 1,800 melodies; Bartók's Slovakian Folk-Tunes (Slovak soc. *Matica* in Turčiansky-Svätý-Martin; to appear 1924–5). This later coll. contains about 2,500 melodies (many recorded by phonograph) and also a Preface and notes, in Slovak, French, English, German.

The Slovak melodies fall into three groups:

(*a*) Apparently the oldest melodies, with two sub-divisions: (i) so-called *valašské* (shepherd) melodies; (ii) Cradle, Harvest, Mowing, Wedding and St. John's Eve songs. The first have an improvised character and are in no particular form. They generally consist of melodies which consist of 4, 5 or 6 6-syllable lines in *rubato-parlando* rhythm and in the Mixolydian mode, with the compass of at least an octave. The latter consist of 4 6-syllable lines, with *rubato-parlando* rhythm; the compass does not exceed a fifth, very often even a fourth or third. The mode or scale varies. Often the augmented 4th follows the major 3rd. Group *a* forms by far the most original and oldest portion of Slovak folk-music.

(*b*) Melodies of unequal metre and form. They show extraordinary variety in both form and scale; specially characteristic of Slovak folk-music is the use of the Lydian mode. The rhythm is nearly always *tempo giusto*, 2–4, and the notes are nearly always crotchets and quavers; frequent rhythmic forms are:

♪ ♩   ♪ or ♫ ♩

The phrases often group themselves into three. This group contains fewer ancient melodies. It has many common types and melodies similar to the Moravian and even the Czech folk-songs. It stands also in close relation to group *c* of the Hungarian folk-songs (*q.v.*).

(*c*) Modern melodies. They betray the strong influence of Hungarian new folk-melody. The influence is shown either in a faithful assimilation of modern Hungarian melodies, or in the formation of new tunes which have been merely influenced, generally in the rhythm, by Hungarian prototypes.—B. B.

SMAREGLIA, Antonio. Italian composer; *b.* Pola, 5 May, 1854. Esteemed opera compr. Stud. at Milan Cons. under Franco Faccio, who was much attached to him. After writing some concert-music, he devoted himself to opera: *Preziosa*, Milan, 1879; *Bianca di Cervia*, Milan, 1882; *Re Nala*, Milan, 1883 (all publ. Casa Lucca); *Il Vassallo di Szigeth*, Weimar, 1889 (Vienna, Weinberger); *Cornelio Schutt*, Prague, 1893 (Hofbauer); *Nozze istriane*, Prague, 1895 (same publ.); *La Falena*, Venice, 1895 (Vienna, Herberle); *Oceana*, Scala, Milan, 1902 (Herzmensky); *Abisso*, Scala, Milan, 1914 (Heberle).

S. united in his technique the characteristics of Ital. with Ger. (Wagnerian) influences. About 1900, as result of an illness, he completely lost his sight. In 1921, head of school of cpt. and compn. at Tartini Cons. at Trieste.

Consult Adriano Lualdi, *Il musicista cieco: A. Sm.* (in review *Emporium*, Bergamo, Oct. 1919).—D. A.

SMETANA, Bedřich (*accent 1st syll.*). Czechoslovak composer, founder of modern Czechoslovak music; *b.* Litomyšl, 2 April, 1824; *d.* Prague, 12 May, 1884. Son of a brewer. Whilst attending grammar-schools in several provincial towns, especially in Plzeň (Pilsen), he became more and more fond of music and from 1843 devoted himself entirely to it. Studied piano and theory at Jos. Proksch's Music School in Prague, becoming an excellent pianist, giving many concerts at home and making several tours abroad. In 1848, founded a private music-school of his own in Prague, directing it until 1856; then went to Gothenburg (Sweden) as conductor of its Philharmonic Society. After five years abroad he settled definitely in Prague. In this period he proclaims himself a follower of Liszt, and certainly he is so in his first three symphonic poems and the piano study *Na břehu mořském* (*At the Sea-Coast*), but even then his personality is strongly penetrated by the national element, although the idea of Bohemian art had not then awaked with him to its full grandeur. (See piano polkas, which are idealised Czech national dances, and the orchestral *Valdštýnův tábor—Wallenstein's Camp*.) His full aim only came to him after his return to Prague, where he found a lively national cultural and political movement. In 1860 Smetana became chairman of Umělecké Beseda, trainer of the choir *Hlahol*; music-critic to daily paper *Národní Listy*; proprietor of a music-school; conductor of National Theatre (1866–74). But he chiefly concentrated on composition, and from that time followed the way which made him the greatest national Bohemian composer. Then the first five operas were composed, his *Prodaná nevěstá* (*The Bartered Bride*) immediately becoming the most popular work of Czechoslovak music. It is a village idyll, merry, simple and national without using or imitating the folksongs. In *Dalibor* and *Libuše* another trait appears—a sense of bigness, and a heroism full of ardour and love. *Libuše* was dedicated to the great national festivals. In *Dvě vdovy* (*Two Widows*) he is full of cheerfulness and fun in an aristocratic *milieu*. In 1874 he became deaf and had to give up all musical work, removing from Prague to Jabkenice, a little village in the valley of the Labe (Elbe). But his creative power did not lessen either in volume or value. In the two new comic operas *Hubička* (*The Kiss*) and *Tajemství* (*The Secret*) the humour is founded on a greater artistic maturity, which, together with their varied dramatic expression, puts them on an even higher plane than *The Bartered Bride*.

In symphonic music Smetana created his standard work *Má Vlast* (*My Country*), a cycle of six symphonic poems, celebrating Czech nature and history, giving an insight into the soul of the nation, being chiefly a manifestation of faith in a better future. Thus this work has always been understood and esteemed by the nation. An intimate confession is his string quartet *Z mého života* (*From my Life*). For the piano he wrote six *Rêves*, ten *Czech Dances*, which are really miniature symphonic poems in dance rhythm. His last opera, *Čertova stěna* (*The Devil's Rock*), suffers from the weakness of its libretto. The works of 1882 to 1884 showed traces of the mental disease which set a sad end to his life in 1884.

Though he was a partisan of Wagner's views, only *Libuše* was consequently composed upon Wagnerian lines. In comic opera he comes nearer to Mozart's dramatic type. His significance for Czechoslovakian music is epoch-making. He was the first musician to elevate native art, after its national reawakening, by his genius and the expanding of his thought to the European level. His music is national not by the use of folk-songs but by its intuitive penetration into the national soul, reaching from rustic merriment and idyll up to the monumental tragedy of myth and history. The portrayal of his race through a series of tone-pictures and moods is not his aim, but merely a way to the great conception of his thought. The Czechs see in his art the symbolised national idea cherished alike in periods of national oppression and in the later time of freedom. A Smetana Fest. was held in Prague, May 1924.

Operas: *Branibori v Čechách* (*The Brandenburgians in Bohemia*; first perf. 1866); *Prodaná nevěsta* (*Bartered Bride*; 1866); *Dalibor* (1868); *Libuše* (1881; Smetana waited for the opening of National Theatre); *Dvě vdovy* (*Two Widows*; 1874); *Hubička* (*The Kiss*; 1876); *Tajemství* (*The Secret*; 1878); *Čertova stěna* (*The Devil's Rock*; 1882). Symph. poems: *Richard III*; *Valdštýnův tábor* (*Wallenstein's Camp*; 1858); *Haakon Jarl* (1861); the cycle *My Country* (in six parts: *Vyšehrad, Vltava* [1874], *Šárka, In Bohemian Meadows and Forests* [1875], *Tábor, Blaník,* [1878-7]). Trio (1855); two str. 4tets (1876-83); two duos for vn. and pf. *Z domoviny* (*At Home*, 1880); polkas for pf. (from 1855, 1861, 1877); *Rêves* (1874-5); Bohemian dances (1879); 8 vols. of posthumous pieces; chorus and orch., *Česká píseň* (*Bohemian Song*; 1868); male chorus, *Rolnická* (*The Peasant's Song*; 1868); *Píseň na moři* (*A Song of the Sea*; 1877).

Consult: Ger.: Bronislaw Wellek, *Friedrich Smetana* (Prague, 1895); Ernst Rychnovsky, *Smetana* (Deutsche Verlags-Anstalt, 1924); Fr.: William Ritter, *Smetana* (Paris, 1907); Czech: Hostinský, *B. S.* (1901); F. V. Krejčí (1900); K. Hoffmeister (Prague, 1915; Library *Zlatoroh*); Zd. Nejedlý, *Smetaniana* (1922), a preparation to a great biography.

(Publ.: Hudební Matice Umělecké Besedy; Fr. A. Urbánek, Prague; Univ. Ed. Vienna).—V. St.

SMITH, David Stanley. Amer. compr. *b.* Toledo, Ohio, U.S.A., 6 July, 1877. Stud. compn. under Horatio Parker at Yale Univ. Graduated A.B. in 1900, at which time his *Commencement Ode* for barit., male chorus and orch. was perf. From 1901-3, stud. in Europe, under Thuille in Munich, d'Indy in Paris. Returning to Yale to receive degree of Mus. Bac. in 1903, was appointed instructor in theory in music department; 1909, assistant-prof.; 1916, prof. In 1919, relieved Parker as condr. of New Haven Symph. Orch.; after Parker's death made Dean of School of Music, 1920. Has composed many orch. and chamber-music works of recognised worth, fre-

quently perf. and favourably received, but few publ. His op. 11, *Ouverture Joyeuse*, was first perf. by New Haven Orch. 1904. His 1st str. 4tet, F mi. op. 19, was played by Kneisel Quartet, Chicago (1912) and elsewhere. *The Fallen Star*, for chorus and orch. op. 26, won Paderewski Prize 1909. His 1st symphony, A mi. op. 28, was brought out by Chicago Symphony Orch. 13 Dec. 1912. In same month New Haven Orch. first played his overture *Prince Hal*. A 2nd str. 4tet, in A, op. 37, was played by Kneisel Quartet, 1915. A 2nd symphony, D ma. op. 42, was first perf. at Norfolk (Conn.) Fest. 3 June, 1918. A 3rd str. 4tet, C ma. op. 46, was produced at Berkshire Chamber-Music Fest., Pittsfield, Mass., Sept. 1921. *A Poem of Youth*, op. 47, was first perf. by Boston Symphony Orch., 11 Nov. 1921. Also:

Overture, *Prince Hal*, op. 31 (Schirmer, 1915); *Rhapsody of St. Bernard*, chorus and orch. op. 3 (1st perf. Chicago North Shore Fest. 1918) (Schirmer, 1918); 3rd 4tet in C, op. 46 (Soc. for Publ. of Amer. Music; Schirmer, 1922); *Fête Galante*, orch. with fl. obbligato, op. 48; *Symphony in Miniature*, for solo-orch. op. 49; anthems, part-songs (Novello; Schirmer; Ditson).—O. K.

SMITH, Leo. Brit. cellist; writer on music; *b.* Birmingham, 26 Nov. 1881; stud. there under A. J. Priestley, and later at R. Manchester Coll. of Music and at Owen's Coll., under Carl Fuchs (cello), Adolph Brodsky (ensemble) and Henry Hiles (harmony). After taking degree of Mus. Bac. at Manchester Univ. became a member of Hallé Orch. 1905-9, member of Covent Garden Orch. In 1909, came to Toronto, and, in 1911, joined staff of Toronto Cons. of Music as prof. of cello and harmony, becoming lecturer in mus. history. A member of Toronto Str. Quartet and also for some time of Canadian Acad. Quartet. Contributing editor of *Toronto Cons. Quarterly Review* since its inception in 1918. His compns. include numerous songs, part-songs and cello pieces (Schirmer); is author of text-book on Musical Rudiments (Boston Music Co.). In 1922-3 compiled the Canadian articles for this Dictionary.—A. S. V.

SMULDERS, Carl. Belgian pianist and compr. *b.* Maestricht, 8 May, 1863. Naturalised in Belgium. Entered Liège Cons. as early as 1873; stud. pf., organ, compn. Teacher of harmony there, 1887. Once entered, in 1889, the Rome competition, and obtained 2nd prize. As virtuoso, occupied himself especially in making known the Hans keyboard (see HANS). Engaged also in mus. criticism and literature (3 novels in *Belgique artistique et littéraire*.)

Cantata, *Androméde* (for *Prix de Rome*); symph. poems: *Adieu, Absence et Retour*; *Chant d'amour*; *Aurore, Jour, Crépuscule*; *Ballade*, orch.; *Rosh-Hashana* (his most frequently perf. work) and *Yom-Kippur*, 2 pieces, cello and orch.; pf. concerto, A mi.; *Cantilena*, vn. and orch.; *Solemn March*, orch.; male choruses unacc.: *La Mer*; *La Route*; *Pater Noster*; vn. and pf. sonata; songs; pf. pieces.—E. C.

SMYTH, Dame Ethel. Compr. *b.* London, 23 April, 1858. Stud. Leipzig Cons., later under Heinrich von Herzogenberg. Her first perf. works were chamber-music at the Abonnement concerts, Leipzig, 1884; her orch. works, *Serenade* in D and overture

Antony and Cleopatra, at G. Henschel's Symphony concerts and at the Crystal Palace. Her first opera, *Fantasio*, was produced at Weimar in 1898 and later at Carlsruhe under Mottl. *Der Wald* was produced at Dresden in 1901 and Berlin in 1902. The opera *Strandrecht* was produced at Leipzig and Prague 1906, Vienna 1908, as *The Wreckers* (under Beecham) in 1909 and 1910. Her 2-act opera *The Boatswain's Mate* was produced at the Shaftesbury Theatre, London on 28 Jan. 1916, conducting it herself.

She was a militant suffragist, and comp. amongst other suffrage music *The March of the Women*, the battle-song of the W.S.P.U. Received Mus.Doc. Dunelm. 1910. In 1921 she re-orchestrated *The Boatswain's Mate* for small orch. Her 1-act opera *Fête Galante—a Dance-Dream* (Vienna, Univ. Ed.) was produced at the Repertory Theatre, Birmingham, on 4 June, 1923, and a week later by the British National Opera Co. at Covent Garden.

Her mus. personality is dual; there are scores of austere works which follow Brahms so closely (the str. 4tets and 5tets, the polyphonic overture to Act II of *The Boatswain's Mate*, for instance) that only here and there, if at all, does her own personality come through. The 4 de Régnier songs (Novello) appear to stand by themselves between the two styles. On the other hand we have the vigorous writing of *The Wreckers* (especially in the closing scene), *The Boatswain's Mate*, and such things as the dashing *Hey Nonny No*, that show the same abundant virility, combined with warm geniality, that we find in her spirited memoirs, *Impressions that Remained* (Longmans, 1919) and *Streaks of Life* (*id.* 1921). Historically, as a compr. she is important. She suffered much neglect by reason of the many political drawbacks of the period in which her main work was done.

Operas: *Fantasio* (1898); *Der Wald* (1901, Breit-kopf); *The Wreckers* (1906, *id.*); *The Boatswain's Mate* (W. W. Jacobs; London, 1918). Orch.: *Sere-nade* in 4 movements (London, 1890); overture, *Antony and Cleopatra* (*id.*); *March of the Women*. Chorus and orch.: Mass in D (London, 1893); next perf. at Birmingham under Adrian Boult, Feb. 1924); *Hey Nonny No* (Breitkopf); chamber-music (Univ. Ed.); songs (Breitkopf; Novello); pf. sonatas; sonata, vn. and pf. (1887), etc.
Consult art. *E. S.* by Rutland Boughton in *Music Bulletin*, Feb. 1923; by R. Capell on the operas, *Monthly Mus. Record*, July, 1923.—E.-H.

SOBINOF, Leonid Vitalievitch (*accent 1st syll.*). Russ. t. singer; *b.* Jaroslavl, 26 May (o.s.), 1872. Finished law course at Moscow Univ. 1894; stud. singing under Dodonof and Mme. Santa-gano-Gortschakova at music school of Moscow Philh. Soc. (1892–7); from then till now, singer at Moscow Opera House. Celebrated his 25th anniversary as artist in 1922. Has degree of People's Artist of Republic. Is best in lyric parts.—V. B.

SOBOLEWSKI, Cyrus Marjan. Polish compr. *b.* Cracow, 1884. Pupil of Żeleński. Is LL.D.
4tet for str.; 5tet with fl.; sonata for cello and pf.; sonata for vla. etc.; songs; symph. poem (pro-duced at Katowice, Polish Silesia, 1923). Publ. also a good manual of orchestration (Polish, 1923).—ZD. J.

SOBRINO, Carlos. Span. pianist; *b.* Ponte-vedra, 25 Feb. 1861. In his youth, combined study of architecture and music; finally devoted himself to pf. on which he had always shown, since a child, exceptional ability. Received his first music-lessons from his sister and a local teacher, at age of 8. When 11, he appeared at a concert in co-operation with Isaac Albeniz, at that time also a child. After some time at R. Cons. de Música, Madrid, he went abroad and became a friend and pupil of Anton Rubinstein. Has toured throughout world as concert-player, alone and in association with Ysaye (America) and Sarasate (England, France, Germany, Austria and Poland) with whom he appeared on his last European tours. Lives and works in London, his residence since the outbreak (1898) of the war between Spain and America, where he had been successfully establ. as teacher and soloist. Prof. of pf. at Guildhall School of Music, London, since 1905. Married in 1889 the well-known Wagnerian singer Luisa Sobrino, *née* Schmitz (Düsseldorf).—P. G. M.

SOCIETÀ POLIFONICA ROMANA. Choral group organised and directed in Rome by Raf-faele Casimiri (*q.v.*). It is composed of male voices, and choir-boys for s. and contr. parts. There are nearly 60 singers, belonging mostly to Cath. choirs and those of principal Roman churches. The Soc. has devoted itself to revival of masterpieces of sacred polyphonic vocal music of XVI century. It has given very successful concerts, not only in Rome and other Ital. cities, but also in the various countries of Europe and North America.—D. A.

SOCIETÀ TIPOGRAFICA EDITRICE NAZIO-NALE (S.T.E.N.). Italian publishing house, established in Turin. It has an important section devoted to music, of which the director is Marcello Capra (*q.v.*). Publishes sacred music and educational works.—D. A.

SOCIÉTÉ MODERNE D'INSTRUMENTS A VENT, Paris. Founded 1895 by Georges Barrère, flautist at the Cons. The Soc. then included Louis Aubert (pf.) Foucault (ob.), Vionne (clar.), Bultian (bsn.), Servat (horn). In 1901, there was a strengthening of ensemble by second parts for wind instrs. After Barrère went to America (1905), conductorship was entrusted to Louis Fleury (*q.v.*). Subsided by State, and having opened wide its doors to young comprs., it was able to place on its programmes over 120 works, of which it gave 1st perf. It has toured in France, and abroad. Present members: Louis Fleury, Bauduin (fls.); Gaudard, Lamorlette (obs.); Cahuzac, Delacroix (clars.); Entraigue, Levasseur (horns); Hermans, Dhérin (bsns.); Garès (pf.). —M. L. P.

SOCIETIES, CONCERT INSTITUTIONS, etc.
ARGENTINA. — *Wagnerian Association of Buenos Ayres*, founded 1913; 2000 members; general mus. culture; 4 concerts a month; presi-dent, Carlos López Buchardo.
AUSTRIA.—(i) *Gesellschaft der Musikfreunde*, founded 1812. (See special art.). (ii) *Wiener*

Tonkünstlerverein, founded by Johannes Brahms; regular concerts of modern works; now dir. by R. Robert and Julius Bittner. (iii) *Akademischer Verband für Literatur und Musik;* students' association at Vienna Univ.; did good work, especially 1911–14 by first perfs. of modern music (Schönberg, Webern, Berg, etc.). It took up the work of the Vienna *Ansorge-Verein,* which also cultivated Schönberg, Zemlinsky and Max Reger. Both are now dissolved. (iv) *Verein für Musikalische Privat-Aufführungen* (often called Schönberg-Verein after its founder [1918]). Contemporary music is rehearsed several times. In 1922, Erwin Stein dir. it on to broader lines. (v) *Schola austriaca,* founded 1913 at Klosterneuburg monastery, near Vienna; for specialists in church-music, on lines on Pontifical *Motu Proprio* of 22 Nov. 1903. It publ. periodical *Musica Divina* and the *Masterworks of Sacred Music in Austria* (Univ. Ed.).

CZECHO-SLOVAKIA. — (i) *Hudebni Matice Umělecké Besedy* (the Mus. Section of the Art Soc.), founded in Prague in 1908 to assist the publ. of Czechoslovak comprs. Publ. all Dvořák; operas of Smetana, Kovařovic, etc. (ii) *Hudebni Klub* (recitals). (iii) *Klub der czechischen Komponisten.* (iv) *Ochranné.*

DENMARK.—(i) *Chamber-Music Soc.* Copenhagen. See NERUDA, FRANZ XAVER. (ii) *Dansk Komponistsamfund (Danish Composers' Club).* See HELSTED and TOFFT.

ENGLAND.—(i) *Philharmonic Soc.* (London) (see ORCH.). (ii) *Royal Choral Soc.* (see CHORAL). (iii) *Incorporated Soc. of Musicians,* founded 1882 (at first, in Manchester) to protect professional interests, (chiefly teachers at present). (iv) *Soc. of British Composers,* founded in June 1905 by a small group of comprs. of the younger generation. Publ. new compositions in their own Avison Edition. Disbanded in 1913. (v) *British Music Soc.* founded by Dr. Eaglefield Hull 1918, for furtherance of music in Britain. (See special art.). (vi) *Music Publishers' Association.* (vii) *Music-Teachers' Association,* founded 1908. (viii) *Musical Association,* founded 1874 for lectures on musical science and art. Publ. its proceedings annually (Novello). (ix) *The Musicians' Company,* an old guild instituted by Edward IV in 9th year of his reign. (x) *The Musicians' Union* (including the *National Orch. Union* and *Amalgamated Musicians' Union)* for protecting interests of orch. players. (xi) *Tonic Solfa Association,* founded 1853. (xii) *Union of Graduates in Music,* for protection of Univ. graduates. (xiii) *Royal Soc. of Musicians,* a benevolent league founded 1738. (xiv) *Organists' Benevolent League,* founded by Sir Frederick Bridge in 1910. (xv) *Soc. of Women Musicians,* founded 1911 to encourage serious mus. compn. amongst women, and to co-operate in matters of women's mus. interests. First president, Liza Lehmann; second, Cécile Chaminade. (xvi) *Performing Right Soc. Ltd.* An association of authors, composers, publishers and other owners of musical, literary or dramatic copyrights, establ. to protect and enforce their rights, to restrain unauthorised use of their works

and to collect fees for their performance in public in Great Britain and throughout the British Empire.

FINLAND.—(i) *Finnish Music Soc. (Suomen musiikkilieteellinen seura — Musikvetenskapliga sällskapet i Finnland),* founded 1916 in Helsingfors, in place of former section of *Internationale Musikgesellschaft* (meetings, lectures, addresses and performances of ancient music). President and founder, Dr. Ilmari Krohn. (ii) *Finnish Musicians' Union (Finnisches Musikerverband—Suomen Muusikeriliitte — Finnlands Musikerförbund),* founded in Helsingfors, 1917. Local branches were founded in 1923 in Turku (Åbo), Tampere (Tammerfors) and Viipuri (Viborg). The society joined the Northern Musicians' Union in 1920, which now embraces the Musicians' Unions of Denmark, Sweden, Norway and Finland. President, Lepo Laurila. (iii) *Finnish Musicians' Association (Suomen Säveltaiteilijain Liitte—Tonkonstnärsbundet i Finnland—Finnisches Tonkünstlerverein),* organised in Helsingfors in 1917, for stimulating mus. life in Finland; it includes almost all the creative and executive musicians. President, Prof. R. Kajanus.

FRANCE.—(i) *Société Nationale de Musique,* founded in Paris, 25 Feb. 1871, by Romain Bassine (1830–99), singing prof. at Cons., and Saint-Saëns (1835-1921). Performs works of living Fr. comprs. This soc. is the laboratory where generations of Fr. musicians were fashioned. First concert, 25 Nov. 1871; first work, trio of César Franck. Since then, 9 or 10 concerts annually for 50 years. (See *Société Mus. Indépendante.*) (ii) *Société Musicale Indépendante (S.M.I.),* Paris. Founded 1910 by a committee, G. Fauré (president), Ravel, Caplet, Schmitt, Roger-Ducasse and others. Same aims as *S.N. de M.* which it judged too conservative. Gives monthly concerts from Dec. to May, devoted to *first performances* of contemporary works, not exclusively of Fr. comprs. (iii) *Société des Concerts du Conservatoire.* Sprang from same organisation as the Cons. (*q.v.*). Has existed from 1792. Produced Beethoven's works in 1810; given a definite constitution in 1828. Conservative in its choice of works. Condrs.: Habeneck, 1820; Girard, 1849; Tilmant, 1860; Haine, 1864; Deldevez, 1872; Garain, 1885; Taffanel, 1892; Marty, 1903; Messager from 1909. (iv) *Société Philharmonique de Paris,* founded 1902; dir. from 1905 by E. Rey. 12 chamber-music concerts a year. (v) *La Trompette.* A soc. founded in 1865 by Émile Lemoine; for perfect interpretation of original works before a select audience. Saint-Saëns wrote his septuor with tpts. for it. (vi) *Société Moderne d'Instruments à Vent,* Paris, founded 1895 by the flautist Georges Barrère. (See art. on this soc. under S.) (vii) *Cercle Musical Universitaire.* Univ. of Paris, club for students interested in music; founded 1919. (viii) *L'Œuvre Inédite.* Concerts of unpubl. chamber-music; founded in Paris, 1920, by the *Office Musical Français* (G. Bender and J. Baudry). It aims also at assisting publication. (ix) *Société des Instruments Anciens,* founded 1900 by Henri Casadesus, for the perf.

of ancient music: viols, lutes, clavecin, etc. (x) *La Chorale Française*, Paris, founded by the singer Charlotte Danner in 1921, for encouragement of choral singing, ancient and modern. Present condr. Félix Raugel. (xi) *Société J. S. Bach*, founded in Paris 1904 by G. Bret (*q.v.*). Regular choral and instr. perfs. of Bach's works (Paderewski, Cortot, Selva, Landowska and others). Suspended 1914. (xii) *Société Haendel*, founded 1909 by E. Borrel and F. Raugel; ceased in 1914; a choral and orch. soc. giving 4 concerts a year of Handel's works. (xiii) *Manécanterie des Petits Chanteurs à la Croix de Bois*, founded at Paris in 1907; school of liturgical chant and centre of Christian education; dir. l'Abbé Rebufat. (xiv) *La Cantoria*. Similar to above. Cond. by choirmaster of Ste.-Clotilde. Gives concerts and takes part in fests. (xv) *Chanteurs de Saint-Gervais* (*Association des*), formed in Paris, 1892, by Charles Bordes for perf. choral masterpieces from xv century to our own day. In developing, it brought the *Schola Cantorum* into being. (See ACADEMIES.) (xvi) *Chorale des Franciscains*. A soc. founded in 1906 by Canon Clément Besse at Saint-Germain-en-Laye, near Paris, for the improvement of Gregorian Chant, according to the principles laid down by Georges Houdard. The orgt. is Albert Alain. This and the *Maîtrise* of Canon Moissenet at Dijon are the two finest groups of Gregorian singers in France. (xvii) *Fêtes du Peuple*. Association founded in Paris, 1918, by Albert Doyen. Aims at establishing a closer contact between the people and the arts. Gives regular concerts. (xviii) *Société Française de Musicologie*, founded Paris, 1904, by Lionel Dauriac (*q.v.*). Publ. periodical *Bulletin de la S.F. de M.*; since 1922, *Revue de Musicologie* (Fischbacher). The soc. brings together musicologists, publishers, and enlightened amateurs. (xix) *Union Syndicale des Compositeurs de Musique*, formed in Paris, 1920, for defending the interests of Fr. comprs. President, Vincent d'Indy; secretary, Carol Bérard. (For Concerts Colonne, etc., see articles.)

GERMANY.—(i) *Allgemeiner deutscher Musikverein*, founded 1859 by F. Brenzel, L. Köhler and others under patronage of Liszt, for annual mus. fests. for producing new works, at different places every year (*Tonkünstlerversammlungen*). It has championed Wagner, Liszt, R. Strauss, M. Schillings, Mahler, 1st perf. of operas and orch. works. From 1880, Baden-Baden; 1881 Magdeburg; 1882 Zurich; 1883 Leipzig; 1884 Weimar; 1885 Karlsruhe; 1886 Sondershausen; 1887 Cologne; 1888 Dessau; 1889 Wiesbaden; 1890 Eisenach; 1891 Berlin; none in 1892; 1893 Munich; 1894 Weimar; 1895 Brunswick; 1896 Leipzig; 1897 Mannheim; 1898 Mayence; 1899 Dortmund; 1900 Bremen; 1901 Heidelberg; 1902 Crefeld; 1903 Basle; 1904 Frankfort-o-M.; 1905 Graz; 1906 Essen; 1907 Dresden; 1908 Munich; 1909 Stuttgart; 1910 Zurich; 1911 Heidelberg; 1912 Dantzig; 1913 Jena; 1914 Essen; 1919 Berlin; 1920 Weimar; 1921 Nuremberg; 1922 Düsseldorf; 1923 Cassel. Journal of Soc. is *Neue Zeitschrift für Musik*. Present dir. F.

Rösch. (ii) *Allgemeiner deutscher Musikerverband*, founded 1872 by H. Thadewaldt (dir. now by G. Fauth, P. Blanschewiski, A. Prietzel and O. Mai) to protect the interests of professional musicians. Journal of soc. is *Deutsche Musiker-Zeitung*. (iii) *Deutsche Sängerbund*, founded 1862. Its journal is *Deutsche Sängerbund-Zeitung*. (iv) *Genossenschaft deutscher Bühnenangehörigen*, founded 1871. (v) *Cäcilienverein für alle Länder deutscher Zunge*, founded 1867 by Franz X. Witt. Its journal is *Cäcilienvereinsorgan*. (vi) *Allgemeiner Richard-Wagner Verein*, founded 1883 from the *Bayreuther Patronatsverein*. (vii) *Gewandhauskonzerte*, a Leipzig concert inst. founded 1781, in the Leipzig Cloth-Hall, by Burgomaster K. W. Müller. New Gew. building opened 11 Dec. 1884. Condrs.: J. A. Hiller (1781), Schicht, Schulz, Pohlenz, Mendelssohn, F. Hiller, Gade, Rietz, Reinecke, Nikisch; and from 1922, Furtwängler. Consult A. Dörffel's *Festschrift* (1881); E. Kneschke's *Die 150 jährige Geschichte der Leipziger Gewandhauskonzerte 1743–1893* (1893). (viii) *Deutsche Musik-Gesellschaft* (Ger. Mus. Soc.), founded 20 Jan. 1918 in Berlin by Dr. Hermann Kretzschmar, as a partial substitute for the *International Soc. of Music* (dispersed at its German centre in 1914). It has a monthly journal publ. by Breitkopf and ed. by Dr. Alfred Einstein from Oct. 1918. (ix) *Genossenschaft deutscher Tonsetzer*, founded by Richard Strauss, Max Schillings, Fr. Rösch and Hans Sommer, for securing the performing rights of the music of its members.

HOLLAND.— (i) *Maatschappij tot bevordering der Toonkunst* (generally called the *Toonkunst*), founded by A. C. G. Vermeulen, 1829. (See special art. TOONKUNST.) (ii) *Wagner-vereeniging*, founded by Henri Viotta in 1883. From then till 1920 perf. Wagner, Berlioz, Liszt, Strauss, Humperdinck, etc. In 1922, amalgamated with *Concertgebouw* (see ORCHESTRAS, HOLLAND).

IRELAND. — (i) *Royal Dublin Society*, founded 1886. (See special art.). (ii) *Dublin Orch. Soc.* founded 1898 by M. Esposito to form a permanent orch. in Dublin. Started with a fund of £2500 and gave regular concerts up to 1914, when it disbanded.

ITALY.—(i) *Santa Cecilia* (*Regia Accademia di*), Rome. The most important mus. soc. in Italy. (See special art.). (ii) *Filarmonica* (*Reale Accademia*), Rome. Important mus. acad., founded 1821. Had a glorious past during the struggles for Ital. independence, and was once dissolved for political reasons. In recent years it has again flourished, giving annually interesting series of concerts in its own hall, named after Giovanni Sgambati. (iii) *Amici della Musica*. A soc. in Rome for giving concerts and promoting music. It possesses its own str. quartet: Sandri, Zerti, Raffaelli, Albini. (iv) *Unione Nazionale Concerti*. A body constituted in Rome by Regia Accademia di Santa Cecilia (*q.v.*) in 1922, for confederating all the concert-insts. of Italy, and co-ordinating their activity. During its first year of life, it organised some important concert tours. (v) *Gruppo Universitario Musicale* (*G.U.M.*). An inst. which sprang up in 1909 in Rome, and then spread through all the Ital. Univs. for promoting cult of music amongst the students, and organising concerts. The headquarters are in Rome. Domenico Alaleona (artistic adviser), Dr. Gino Rosi (sec.). There are branches in Milan, Turin, Genoa, Florence, Naples, Bologna and Padua. (vi) *Società del Quartetto* (Milan), founded 1864 by Count Lurani, for concerts of chamber-music. It is still very flourishing, over 1000 members. (vii) *Casa di Riposo per Musicisti*, Home of Rest for Musicians in Milan (Piazzale Buonarroti), founded by bequest of Giuseppe Verdi, and maintained exclusively by funds which he appointed for that purpose, and of which he speaks a great deal in his will. Verdi is buried next to his wife in this " Casa di Riposo." (viii) *Associazione Italiana degli Amici della Musica* (Milan), founded 1902 by Orefice (*q.v.*). It promotes performance and publication. (ix) *Società del Quartetto di Bologna*, founded in 1877 by the Marchese Camillo Pizzardi. At first a private soc. for chamber-music; in 1879 it became a public one. Artistic directors in the past have been Luigi Mancinelli, Giuseppe Martucci, Marco Enrico Bossi; now dir. by a committee. (x) *Risveglio Musicale* (Bologna); for promoting musical art, and organising concerts. (xi) *Società dei Concerti* (Turin), founded 1896, taking up traditions of the noteworthy *Società torinese per i Concerti popolari*. Its promoters were Giuseppe Martucci and Arturo Toscanini, who cond. the first 4 concerts. The Soc. possesses a rich library of symph. music. (xii) *Società degli Amici della Musica* (Turin), founded 1913 by Ferraria, who directs it. Shows great concert activity. (xiii) *Società pro Cultura Femminile, Sezione Musicale Autonoma* (Turin), founded 1918 by Dr. Lisetta Motta Ciaccio; numerous concerts, especially chamber-music. 1100 members. (xiv) *Società Corale Stefano Tempia-Palestrina* (Turin), founded 1923 by fusion of two choral societies, *Stefano Tempia* and *Palestrina*. The dir. is the Rev. Giuseppe Ippolito Rostagno. About 150 performers (men and women). (xv) *Società Bufaletti per Concerti di Musica da Camera* (Turin), founded by the musician whose name it bears (see BUFALETTI). (xvi) *Società Filarmonica Fiorentina*, founded in Florence, 1830. (xvii) *Società di Concerti " Amici della Musica "* (Naples), founded 1915 by Oreste De Rubertis; at present dir. by Florestano Rossomandi. Chamber and orch. music, divided into annual series. (xviii) *Società del Quartetto* (Naples), founded 1915 by Alessandro Longo. Gives concerts of chamber-music and soloists. (xix) *Associazione Alessandro Scarlatti* (Naples), founded 1919 by Signorine Maria De Sanna and Emilia Gubitosi, for the revival and spreading of old mus. masterpieces, and the presentation of the work of younger Ital. school. Concerts, mostly choral, and lectures and competitions. Present dir. Franco Michele Napolitano.

NORWAY—(i) *Norwegian Musicians' Assoc.* founded 1912. Present chairman, Alf. Hurum. (ii) *Norwegian Composers' Union*, founded 1916.

Present chairman, Eyvind Alnæs. (iii) *Norwegian Music Teachers' Assoc.* See M. MOESTUE. (iv) *Christiania Organists' Assoc.* See J. W. HUUS-HANSEN.

POLAND.—(i) *Soc. of Young Polish Composers.* See FITELBERG. (ii) *Syndicate of Musicians and Music Teachers*, Cracow. There are Musical Societies at Warsaw and Lwów (Lemberg).

SPAIN.—(i) *Academia de Bellas Artes de San Fernando (Real)*, founded by Philip V (1701–46), though its scheme dated from Philip IV (1621–65). Originally included all fine arts except music, a new section for this not being sanctioned until 1873. Formerly it consisted of 12 academicians elected by the Government (now elected by the Academicians themselves). (ii) *Sociedad Nacional de Música*, founded in Madrid, 1915 (disbanded about 1922), in place of the *Sociedad Wagneriana*, to foster the national revival and modern musical art in general. (iii) *Sociedad de Compositores*, etc. See CHAPÍ.

SWEDEN. — *Soc. of Swedish Composers*, founded 1918. See BERG, NATANAEL.

SWITZERLAND.—(i) *Swiss Music Soc.* (ii) *Association of Swiss Musicians.* See COMBE.

U.S.A.—(i) *Music Teachers' National Association*, founded 1876 at Delaware, by Theodore Poesser. (ii) *National Federation of Music Clubs.* President, Mrs. John F. Lyons. (iii) *Beethoven Association*, New York. See BAUER, HAROLD. (iv) *Amer. Guild of Orgts.* founded 1896. (v) *New York Chamber-Music Soc.* (vi) *Manuscript Soc.*; gives concerts of new works. (vii) *Composers' Music Corporation* (Boston Music Co. New York). (viii) *The Musical Alliance of America*, founded 1917 by John C. Freund of New York, for the recognition of music in national, civic and domestic life. (ix) *Amer. Federation of Musicians.* (x) *National Association of Organists.*

[See also CHORAL SOCIETIES.]—E. H.

SOHLBERG, Thorleif. Norwegian operatic singer (t.-barit.); *b.* Christiania, 11 July, 1878. Trained in Christiania and Stockholm. Attached to National Theatre, Christiania, since 1906. Best rôles: Goro Makodo (*Butterfly*); Amonasro (*Aïda*); Sebastiano (*Tiefland*); Figaro (*Barber of Seville*). Has sung at many concerts in Norway Sweden and Denmark.—U. M.

SOHY, Ch. (Mme. Marcel Labey). Fr. compr. *b.* Paris, 1887. Stud. harmony under Georges Marty; cpt. and compn. under V. d'Indy; organ under Guilmant. The Société Nationale has already produced 3 of her works—a pf. sonata (1910), *Poème*, solo, chorus and orch. (1912), *Thémé Varié*, pf. and vn. (1922). She has also publ. songs and pf. compns. (Senart; Rouart, Lerolle) and still has in ms. a symphony in C sharp (1916); *Astrid*, a 3-act lyrical drama on Scandinavian legend of Selma Lagerlöf, etc. —M. L. P.

SOKOLOF, Nicolas Alexandrovitch (*accent 3rd syll.*). Russ. compr. *b.* Petrograd, 14/26 March, 1859; *d.* there, 1922. Stud. at Petrograd Cons. under Rimsky-Korsakof and Johansen.

In 1896, was appointed teacher of theory. His works (Belaief) comprise 3 str. 4tets; ballet, *The Wild Swans*; incidental music to *The Winter's Tale*; songs.—M. D. C.

SOLESMES. Benedictine abbey in Le Mans diocese (France), founded 1010; restored by Dom Guéranger in 1837; famous for its school of Gregorian chant. As a result of restoration of Roman liturgy in France by Dom Guéranger, and under influence of the abbot, several monks dedicated themselves to restoration of the Gregorian chant, then in full decline. Dom Joseph Pothier (*b.* 7 Dec. 1835; *d.* Jan. 1924) publ. in 1880 *Les Mélodies grégoriennes*, and, in 1883, the *Liber Gradualis.* Later on he was appointed President of Pontifical Commission establ. by Pius X, for the official Vatican ed. of the chantbooks. Soon after this, one of Dom Pothier's pupils, Dom André Mocquereau, improved the work of his teacher. He founded in 1890, and supervises since that time, the *Paléographie Musicale*, for publ. of the most important mss. of Gregorian chant, and for providing archæological musicians, palæographers and liturgists with invaluable documents and authentic works. All lovers of Gregorian chant may now follow for themselves the processes used for reading neums, melodically and rhythmically. Dom Mocquereau has discovered the ancient and authentic interpretation of the Gregorian melodies; and he is now able to affirm that, in the Middle Ages, all peoples were singing in the same way in the whole Occidental Church: *Una fides unus cantus.* And he is able, with some special signs, to give the most important rules of interpretation in what is called *The Rhythmic Editions by the Benedictines of Solesmes* (publ. Desclée, Tournai, Belgium). He has expounded his principles in several vols. of the *Paléographie Musicale* (Books VII, X, XI), and also in his other work *Le Nombre Musical grégorien.* Dom Mocquereau must be regarded as the real founder of the Solesmes School, which is not *a* school, but *the* school of Gregorian Chant. At Solesmes Abbey, the monks' choir, trained by him, sings according to his principles the art-treasure which is Gregorian chant, the sung prayer of the Roman Church. The school was moved to Quarr Abbey, Isle of Wight, for some years, after the passing of the Fr. associations law.

Consult: *La Paléographie Musicale*, ed. by the Solesmes Benedictines (Desclée); Dom Mocquereau, *Le Nombre Musical grégorien (id.)*; Dom A. Gatard, *La Musique grégorienne* (Paris, 1913, Laurens); N. Rousseau, *L'Ecole grégorienne de Solesmes 1833–1910* (Desclée); C. Bellaigue, *A l'abbaye de Solesmes* (*Revue des Deux Mondes*, 15 Nov. 1898); *Revue grégorienne*, ed. under the supervision of the Solesmes Benedictines (Desclée).—J. B.

SOLOMON. Eng. pianist; *b.* 1903 in East-End of London. *Début* 30 June, 1911, as boy of 8, playing Tchaikovsky's concerto, etc., with Q.H. Orch. under Müller-Reuter; stud. under Mathilde Verne. Has toured widely and appeared with the chief orchestras.—E.-H.

SOLOMON, John. Famous Eng. trumpet; *b.* London, 2 Aug. 1856. Prof. R.A.M. London. Principal tpt. Leeds, Birmingham, Sheffield, Bristol, Three Choirs, Fests. etc. Late principal

tpt. of R. Philh. Soc., R. Choral Soc.; Fellow R.A.M. A founder and dir. of London Symphony Orch. S. has a brilliant record as a player.—E.-H.

SOLOMON, Mirrie. Australian pianist and teacher; *b.* Sydney, 1893. Stud. under Bennicke Hart; is now prof. at State Cons. of Music, Sydney.

Suite (5 impressions of *The Little Dream*, Galsworthy), orch.; *Rhapsody*, pf. and orch.; 4tet in D, pf. vn. vla. cello; trio in B mi. pf. vn. cello; *Improvisation*, vn. and pf.; many pf. pieces (Nicholson & Co., Sydney); many songs (*id.*).—E.-H.

SOŁTYS, Adam. Polish writer, compr. condr. *b.* Lemberg, 4 July, 1890. Stud. theory under his father, then under Kahn, K. L. Wolf and G. Schumann in Berlin. Ph.D. Berlin (1921), as a pupil in musicology of Kretzschmar, Stumpf and J. Wolf. His thesis for Doctorate, *Georg Oesterreich und seine Werke*, was publ. in *A.f.M.*, 1922. Prof. of theory and history of music at Lemberg Cons.; condr. of symphony concerts.

2 symphonies (D ma. and D mi.); 2 overtures; pf. sonata; vn. sonata; many songs and pf. pieces in modern style.—ZD. J.

SOŁTYS, Mieczysław. Polish compr. condr. theorist; *b.* Lemberg, 1863. Graduated Lemberg Univ. (philology); stud. theory and pf. under Mikuli there. Then under Krenn in Vienna and Saint-Saëns and Gigout in Paris. Since 1899, dir. of Lemberg Cons. Prof. of theory and condr. of symphony concerts of Musical Society.

Oratorios: *The Vows of John Casimir* (words by Duchińska); *The Queen Poland* (text by Lucyan Rydel); both perf. many times in Lemberg, Warsaw and Berlin. Operas: *Republika Babińska*; *Opowiesc Ukraińska* (on Malczewski's *Marya*); *Panie Kochanku*; *Jezioro Dusza*; *L'Inferno*. 2 symphonies; numerous pf., organ and choral works.—ZD. J.

SOMERVELL, Arthur. Eng. compr. *b.* Windermere, 5 June, 1863. Educated at Uppingham and King's Coll. Cambridge; stud. compn. under Sir Charles Stanford; and at High School for Music, Berlin (1883–5); R.C.M. London, 1885–7 (under Sir H. Parry); prof. R.C.M. 1894; cond. his own works at Leeds and Birmingham fests. (1895–1897); appointed inspector of music to Board of Education and Scottish Educational Dept. 1901; Mus.Doc. Cantab.; cond. his *Intimations on Immortality*, Leeds Fest. 1907; became Principal Inspector of Music for Board of Education 1920. S. is one of the most successful of Eng. song-writers. His best song-cycles are *James Lee's Wife* (1906) and *Maud* (1898), and his most widely popular song is *The Shepherd's Cradle Song.*

Operettas: *The Enchanted Palace*; *Princess Zara*; *King Thrushbeard*; *Knave of Hearts* (Novello); *Golden Straw* (Curwen); *Thomas the Rhymer*; *Thalassa Symphony*, orch. (Boosey); *Helen of Kirkconnel*, orch. (Novello); *In Arcady*, suite for small orch. (Donajowski); Mass; *Power of Sound*; *The Charge of the Light Brigade*; *Elegy*, chorus and orch. (Novello); *Song of Praise*, chorus and orch. (Metzler); *To the Vanguard*; *Passion of Christ*, chorus and orch. (Boosey); Mass in D mi. (Ricordi); *Concertstück*, vn. and orch. produced Aix-la-Chapelle, 1913 (Augener); symph. variations, *Normandy*, 1911, pf. and orch. (Augener); *Highland Concerto*, pf. and orch. (1920, ms.); 5tet, clar. and str. (ms.); suites, studies, pieces, vn. and pf. (Augener; Weekes; Williams; Ashdown); Variations, 2 pfs. (Augener); pieces, pf. (Augener; Williams; Leonard; Lucas; Hatzfeld; Ashdown; Boosey; Bosworth; Weekes). Song-cycles: *Maud*; *Shropshire Lad*; *James Lee's Wife*; *Love in Springtime* (Boosey); *Windflowers*, cycle for vocal 4tet, or female vs. (*id.*): part-songs (Boosey; Ashdown; Novello); songs (Boosey; Moore; Lucas; Leonard; Dunn; Gill; Ascherberg; Ashdown; Enoch; Forsyth); *Rhythmic Gradus* for pf. (Bosworth); exercises in sight-reading, etc. (Curwen); *Sight-reading*, 6 vols. (Swan); sight-reading exercises (Augener); charts of the rules of Harmony and Counterpoint (Clarendon Press).—E.-H.

SOMERVILLE, John Arthur Coghill. Commandant, R. Military School of Music; *b.* Drishane, Skibbereen, Co. Cork, 26 March, 1872. Stud. singing under Francis Harford and then J. Campbell McInnes; appointed Commandant at Kneller Hall, R.M. School of Music, 31 Jan. 1920, where he did much to raise the standard of military band-music, to induce comprs. to take the military band seriously, to establ. concerted vocal music amongst all ranks in the army, and to bring about co-operation between musicians in civil life and in the army. A massed band perf. of works expressly comp. for military band in Albert Hall in 1922 (under auspices of British Music Soc.) made a deep impression on the leading composers present.—E.-H.

SÖMME, Johanne Margrethe. Norwegian pianist; *b.* Stavanger; niece of famous Norwegian writer Alexander Kielland. Pupil of Dohnányi in Berlin. Made her *début*, 1912, in Christiania. Since 1921, living in New York, as teacher and soloist.—R. M.

SOMMER, Hans (real name Hans Friedrich August Zincke.) Ger. compr. *b.* Brunswick, 20 July, 1837 ; *d.* there, 28 April, 1922. Stud. mathematics; 1858, Ph.D. Göttingen; 1859–84, teacher at Technical High School, Brunswick; establ. there Soc. for concert-music; 1885, in Berlin; 1888, in Weimar, 1898, returned to Brunswick.

About 200 songs, among them the series: *Pied Piper of Hamelin*, *The Wild Hunter*, *Hunold Singuf*, *Sappho's Songs*, *Tannhäuser*, *Last Bloom*, *Eliland*, *Werner's Songs of Italy*; operas: *Night Watchman* (Brunswick, 1865); *Loreley* (1891); *St. Foix* (1-act, Munich, 1894); *Rübezahl und der Sackpfeifer von Neisse* (Brunswick, 1904); *Der Meermann* (1-act, Weimar, 1896); *Riquet mit dem Schopf* (Brunswick, 1907); *Der Waldschratt* (*id.* 1912); *Münchhausen*; *Augustin*; *Castle of Hearts*; *Festival Tunes*; symph. work for orch.; male chorus, op. 37, 43; *13 Soldier Songs* with orch. Establ. (with Richard Strauss, M. Schillings and Fr. Rösch) the Soc. of Ger. Comprs. (Genossenschaft deutscher Tonsetzer) for securing performing rights.—A. E.

SOMMERFELDT, Waldemar. Norwegian compr. *b.* 5 June, 1885; *d.* in 1919. Stud. pf. under Agathe Backer-Gröndahl, theory under Gerhard Schjelderup in Dresden. His very talented lyrically-conceived works include a pf. concerto and an orch. piece (both produced with great success in Christiania) and a couple of vols. of pf. pieces.—R. M.

SONG in England, Finland, France, Germany, etc. See under headings of various countries—ENGLISH SONG, FINNISH SONG, etc.

SONGS OF THE HEBRIDES. Hebridean music is racially traditional, but only a section of it, say perhaps the labour lilts, can be truly termed folk-music. Music was pursued seriously for centuries by the Gaels of the Hebrides. Not committed to notation (at a time when notation itself was in the making), it was passed on orally.

But the professional musician of the Isles having disappeared generations ago with the passing of the Clan régime, the survivals of that melodic art have been preserved by the folk. So strong a love of their own music do they evince that every scrap of the ancient melody is cherished by them.

The scales or modes, on which the airs were constructed, are of that quasi-universal order that obtained before the harmonic music of the last 300 years narrowed down the scale-choice to major and minor. But, as modern music has opened wide its gates to a richer field of tonality, Hebridean music is once more coming into its own. In using the many modes of pre-XVI century days, however, the music of the Gael had its own peculiar way. And just as Celtic line and colour art used Oriental spirals, vines and interlaced work, in its own unmistakable fashion, so Hebridean music deals with these many tonalities after its own fashion, stressing its own favourite intervals and peculiar cadences. So peculiar to itself, indeed, are its own ways of stepping about among the notes, that even the most experienced singers are apt in reading out and studying the airs to sing the wrong intervals, taking for granted, say a 5th, where Hebridean music insists on its favourite 6th; and substituting a half-tone passing-note or leading-note where Hebridean music demands a leading whole-tone.

Thus Hebridean music may be said not only to add a number of fine airs to the world's melodic heritage but to bring also an individually strong, fresh contribution to the common stock of melodic formulæ. This it seems to have inherited from different races—Iberian, Celtic, Scandinavian—and one has there the rare opportunity of studying ancient melody in the living specimen, groping one's way back through long ages to possible Oriental sources.—M. K.-F.

SONNECK, Oscar George Theodore. Amer. musicologist, librarian, music publ. *b.* Jersey City, N.J., U.S.A., 6 Oct. 1873. Educated at Gymnasium, Frankfort-o-M. (1883–93). Stud. at Heidelberg Univ. 1893; Munich Univ. 1893-7, under Sandberger (mus. history), Stumpf, Riehl, Lipps (philosophy), M. E. Sachs (compn.); 1898, stud. at Cons. Sondershausen; then at Frankfort under Kwast (pf.) and Knorr (orch.). After a visit to Italy (1899), returned to America and devoted himself to thorough and painstaking research on early mus. history of United States, on which subject he has become the foremost authority in that country. 1902, called to organise a Music Division at Library of Congress in Washington, D.C. By his energetic and far-sighted methods of acquisition and organisation and with liberal support of the Library administration, S. has made this one of the most important colls. of its kind in the world. At the Library, compiled and ed. a series of catalogues, bibliographies, some of which, like the magnificent 1674-page catalogue of opera-libretti, are monuments of scientific research and extremely valuable source-books of historical information. In 1917, re-

signed from Library of Congress to become the head of the publ. department of house of Schirmer in New York. Since 1921, Vice-President of this corporation.
The results of his researches in early Amer. music history, laid down in the 4 vols. named below, cast an entirely new light on this hitherto uncultivated field. His numerous contributions to mus. and musicological journals have been publ. in book form. Besides these he has publ. two early booklets of verse in Ger. (*Seufzer*, 1895, and *Eine Todtenmesse*, 1898). Since 1915, ed. of *Musical Quarterly*. In 1911 was official representative of United States Government at mus. congresses held in Rome and in London.

Bibliography of Early American Secular Music (privately printed, 1905); *Francis Hopkinson and James Lyon* (privately printed, 1905); *Early Concert Life in America* (Breitkopf, 1907); *Early Opera in America* (Schirmer, 1915); *Suum Cuique* (essays) (Schirmer, 1916); *Miscellaneous Studies in the History of Music* (Macmillan, 1921); and following Library of Congress publications: *Classification of Music and Literature of Music* (1904; rev. ed. 1917); *Report on* " *The Star-spangled Banner*," " *Hail Columbia*," " *America*," " *Yankee Doodle*" (1909); " *The Starspangled Banner*" (rev. and enlarged from *Report*) (1914). *Dramatic Music in the Library of Congress*: *Catalogue of Full Scores* (1908); *Catalogue of Orchestral Music* (1912); *Catalogue of First Editions of Edward MacDowell* (1917); *Catalogue of Opera Librettos printed before 1800*, 2 vols. (1914); (with W. R. Whittlesey) *Catalogue of First Editions of Stephen C. Foster* (1915). Has comp. pieces for pf. and vn. op. 8; songs, op. 9, and pf. pieces, op. 11 (Frankfort, Firnberg, 1899–1900); also songs, op. 16 (Schirmer, 1917); op. 17, 18 (Univ. Ed. 1922); others (C. Fischer, 1922).—O. K.

SONS, Maurice. Violinist; *b.* Amsterdam, 13 Sept. 1857. First appeared as soloist at orch. concert at age of 11; stud. later at Brussels under Wieniawski; afterwards sent by late King of Holland, for further study, to Dresden. After a few years in Switzerland, came to England as leader of orch. season in Scotland under August Manns. Later, leader of Scottish Orch. under its first condr. Sir George Henschel; 1903, prof. at R.C.M.; soon after, leader of Queen's Hall Orch. under Sir Henry Wood. Has frequently appeared as soloist in concertos of Mozart, Beethoven, Brahms, Dvořák, Bruch, Vieuxtemps, Mendelssohn.—E.-H.

SONZOGNO, Edoardo. Music publisher; *b.* Milan, 21 April, 1836; *d.* there 15 March, 1920. Founder and dir. of celebrated music-publ. firm. The " Casa editrice Sonzogno," restricted to literary productions, already existed in Milan. Edoardo added in 1874 a music section, which rapidly developed to great importance. The importation into Italy of large part of modern Fr. repertoire (Bizet, Thomas, Saint-Saëns, Massenet, etc., is due to him; at same time, he was one of leaders and patrons of so-called " giovane scuola " (young school) of Ital. operatic comprs., which flourished towards end of XIX century. Mascagni owed his recognition to S. through the famous " Concorso " (competition) for Ital. operas, instituted by S. in 1883, and repeated several years. In second competition, 1890, Mascagni was winner with *Cavalleria Rusticana*. Mascagni remained faithful to his publ. for all his works except *Iris*, which belongs to

Ricordi. S. directed his energies to propaganda, and was an impresario in various Ital. cities, at Paris, Vienna and elsewhere; in Milan in 1894, he dir. La Scala; then, having restored the old Canobbiana theatre, he inaugurated it as the " Teatro lirico internazionale," making it the centre of a fruitful activity. At present the firm is a limited company.—D. A.

SOOMER, Walter. Ger. b. singer; *b.* Liegnitz, 12 March, 1878. Stud. philosophy, Breslau and Berlin; then singing under Hermann Stoeckert, Josef Wolf and Mme. Anna Uhlig. Engaged 1902–3, Colmar; 1903–6, Halle-o-S.; 1906, Leipzig and Bayreuth (Kurwenal, Donner, Wotan, Wanderer, Sachs); 1909–11, 4 to 6 months' yearly absence in America (Metropolitan Opera House, New York); 1911, Dresden Court Opera House. Now at Leipzig again.—A. E.

SORABJI, Kaikhosru. Compr. *b.* in Essex, 14 Aug. 1895. Father Parsi, mother Spanish. Has lived in London all his life. Practically self-taught as regards music. Began composing in 1915, but has discarded all works prior to 1918. Since that date he has written 3 pf. sonatas, 2 concertos for pf. and orch., a symphony for chorus, pf. and orch., a 5tet for pf. and str. and some songs and shorter pf. pieces, all of which are, or will shortly be, available in print. He played his 1st pf. sonata at a " Sackbut" concert in London, Nov. 1920, and gave a recital in Vienna, Jan. 1922, the programme comprising his 1st and 2nd pf. sonatas. He also acc. Mme. Marthe Martine in a group of his songs at a concert of the Société Musicale Indépendant in Paris, June 1921. Otherwise no public perfs. of his work have yet been given, though Cortot has expressed a desire to take up one of the concertos, and the 1st pf. sonata aroused the interest of Busoni who wrote of the compr. as " *un talent naissant d'une espèce encore nouvelle qui donne à penser et à espérer.*" S.'s work is not for the amateur. The technical difficulties of his extremely individual style of pf. writing are insurmountable by any but first-rate pianists. His compns. are of great length and complexity, and when an orch. is employed it is usually of Gargantuan proportions. It is of interest to note that they are written straight down in fair copy—in the case of the orch. works, in full score. No sketches are made, nor is even the figuration of the piano music determined at the keyboard. One is reminded of Blake's methods in composing the *Prophetic Books*; but these, we are told, were dictated by angels. If we are to say the same of S.'s music we must use the word in its literal sense of " messenger " without its usual connotation of celestial origin and moral intent.

Symphony, pf. orch. chorus and organ (ms.); Prelude, interlude and fugue, pf. (ms.); 3rd pf. sonata (ms.); 1st and 2nd pf. sonatas (London & Continental Co.); 3 *pastiches* (on Chopin Valse; on Habanera in *Carmen*; on Hindoo Song in *Sadko*) (*id.*); *Fantaisie Espagnole*, pf. (*id.*); pf. concerto (*id.*); 5tet, pf. and str. (*id.*); songs to poems of Baudelaire and Verlaine.—P. H.

SÖRBY, O. J. Norwegian jurist and music-publ. *b.* Christiania in 1867. Degree in law in 1890; 1903-9, manager of Carl Warmuth's music-publishing establishment in Christiania. Since 1909, manager of the Norwegian Music Publishing Co. in same city. Concert-critic for different newspapers in Christiania. Has written a number of minor compns. and transl. several opera-texts into Norwegian.—R. M.

SORO-BARRIGA, Enrique. Chilean compr. *b.* Concepción, 1884. Began study at Santiago; then Verdi Cons. Milan. Before returning to Chile in 1905, gave concerts in Italy, France and Switzerland. Has cond. his own works in N. and S. America. Has comp. a large number of pieces for pf.; for pf. and vn.; several suites and symph. works for orch. His best-known work is the *Gran Concierto en Re Mayor* (pf. concerto in D).—A. M.

SOUBIES, Albert. Fr. musicologist; *b.* Paris, 10 May, 1846; *d.* 1918. Pupil of Guilmant at Cons. Devoted himself to rapid, and somewhat shallow description of music in different countries. His books abound in information, but do not offer a single general idea.
German Music (1896); histories of music in Russia (1897); Hungary, Bohemia, Portugal (1898); Switzerland (1899); Spain (1900); Belgium, Holland, Denmark, Sweden (1901); Norway (1903); British Isles (1904-16). With Ch. Malherbe, has publ. (since 1902) *L'Almanach des Spectacles.* Also *Histoire de l'Opéra-Comique* (with Malherbe); *Documents inédits sur le Faust de Gounod* (with de Curzon); *Massenet, historien*; *Histoire du Théatre-Lyrique.*—A. C.

SOULACROIX, Gabriel Valentin. Fr. operatic barit. *b.* Fumel (Lot et Garonne), 1855; *d.* Paris, 1906. Stud. at Cons. at Toulouse, then in Paris; two 2nd prizes, 1878; sang for 15 years at Opéra-Comique, where he created some important rôles, *e.g.* Villon in *La Basoche* (André Messager), and Falstaff in Verdi's opera. Was a singer of very sound style; also a good actor. —M. B.

SOULAGE, Marcelle. Compr. *b.* Lima (Peru), 12 Dec. 1894, of Fr. parents. Stud. at Paris Cons. where she obtained various prizes.
Suite in C mi. vn. vla. and pf. (*Prix Lepaulle*, 1918); sonata, pf. and cello (*Prix des Amis de la Musique*, 1920); sonata, pf. and vn.; sonata, vla. and pf.; Variations, pf.; pieces for harp; *Le Repos en Egypte* (female chorus); sonata, pf. and fl.; str. 4tet; songs.—A. C.

ŠOUREK, Otakar. Czechoslovak mus. writer; *b.* Prague, 1883. Contributor to many reviews, especially *Hudební Revue* (1908-1919); critic to newspapers *Samostatnost, Lidové Noviny, Venkov* (from 1919). His chief interest is centred in the work of Dvořák; published many analytical studies on Dvořák's orch. (Hudební Matice); *The Works of Dvořák,* a chronological, thematic and systematic register (Simrock); especially *Life and Work of Antonín Dvořák* (2 vols. publ. Hudební Matice; 3rd vol. not yet publ.).—V. ST.

SOUSA, John Philip. Amer. band-master; *b.* Washington, D.C., U.S.A., 6 Nov. 1854. Of Span.-Ger. parentage; 1864-7, stud. vn. under John Esputa; harmony under George Benkert. At 16 became condr. of orch. in variety-theatre; for few years led varied existence with itinerant

theatrical companies, composing incidental music, publishing arr. of light operas and producing an unsuccessful comic opera *The Smugglers* (1879), followed by a second, *Katherine,* never produced. 1880, condr. of U.S. Marine Band, a position held, with growing fame, for 12 years. He organised his subsequently famous Sousa's Band (1st concert, Plainfield, N.J., 26 Sept. 1892). With this band S. achieved great success, touring extensively and playing at principal exhibitions at home and abroad since 1893; 1910-11, undertook a tour of world. Honoured with Victorian Order by Edward VII; and commissioned lieut., senior grade, of U.S. Naval Reserve Force in 1917. His larger works for orch. are still in ms. Of his dozen comic operas 3 attained popularity: *El Capitan* (1896), *The Charlatan* (1897) (both also produced successfully in London, the 2nd as *The Mystical Miss,* 1898); *The Bride Elect* (1898). His marches, numbering nearly 100, display his talent at his best, most popular being *The Washington Post* (Coleman, 1889).—J. M.

SOUTH AFRICA, MUSIC IN. The development of music in S. Africa has always been conditioned by two important factors, the sparseness of the population (to-day there are only one and a half million white people scattered over a continent the size of Europe) and the great distance, 5000 miles, that separates it from Europe. This means that at first all mus. effort was concentrated in Cape Town, which till the discovery of gold on the Witwatersrand and the subsequent extraordinary growth of Johannesburg, was the only city large enough to support any sustained musical effort. Till 12 years ago, therefore, the music of the country was in a decidedly backward state, though excellent pioneer work was being done by men like Dr. Barrow Dowling of Cape Town, Percy Ould in Grahamstown and others in Durban, Johannesburg and Port Elizabeth, with amateur orchs. and choral societies.

The first attempt to achieve more than this was the foundation in 1909 of S. African Coll. of Music (see ACADEMIES) in Cape Town, and its recognition by Government at the end of 1911. Up to this time all tuition in music had been confined to private teaching, and to the necessarily limited, but excellent work, done at insts. like Cons. at Stellenbosch (dir. by Janasch and Hans Endler), or the music departments of larger schools like the Diocesan Coll. at Grahamstown under Percy Ould, and afterwards under Charles Wilby. Mention should be made of the excellent work being done by Miss Maud Harrison at her large Cons. at Johannesburg. Touch with the outside mus. world was kept very loosely by the very occasional visits of first-class musicians from Europe. In 1912 the Quinlan Opera Co. visited S. Africa, and made such an impression that the Cape Town municipality resolved to have its own orch. and in Feb. 1914 a professional orch. of at first 30 performers called the Cape Town Municipal Orch. (see ORCHESTRAS) was formed with Theo Wendt as its condr. Durban followed suit with the formation of an orch. in 1921 with Lyell-

Taylor as its condr. The people of S. Africa, with those of Eng. and those of Dutch extraction, are undoubtedly passionately attached to music. This is testified by enthusiasm aroused by annual tours of Cape Town Orch. in small country towns as well as by large audiences (700 to 1000) who attend weekly symphony concerts in Cape Town; while the 600-odd students on roll of S. African Coll. of Music (at least 200 going through a prof. course), are drawn not only from Cape Town, but from all over the country. Great attention to music is also given in the large secondary schools in every town, while the Univ. of Cape Town founded a chair of music in 1918, and the Univ. of Johannesburg in 1921.—W. H. B.

SOUTH AMERICAN DANCES. (i) *Zamba*, or *Zamacueca*. This dance originated in Chile among the country people. Now quite a popular ball-room dance in northern Argentine provinces. It is danced by a single couple who, handkerchief in hand, face one another, making a series of slow graceful steps and waving their handkerchiefs in time to the music. (ii) *Malambo*. A national dance of the Argentine *gauchos*, that has now practically disappeared. Of quick rhythmic movements, accompanied by guitar. The dancers, who were men, also sang. (iii) *Pericon*. This has always been the chief national country-dance of Argentina. It is danced by four couples, facing one another, standing in formation of cross. It consists of various movements, the last being the grand chain as danced in the Lancers. Invariably accompanied by guitar; dancers sing different verses for each movement. (iv) *Gato*. Argentine dance that has disappeared with the *gauchos*. It was a quick and lively measure, danced by one couple only; consisted of a series of different step-dances. (v) *Habanera*. A slow graceful dance, somewhat voluptuous, which has come to Argentina from Havana. (vi) *Tango*. This original Argentine dance is now well known throughout Europe. It is a degenerate form of the Habanera. The rhythm is elegant and attractive, although not free from vulgarity. The number of Tango pieces is extremely large. (vii) *Milonga*. A dance accompanied by song, popular among lower classes; danced to guitar and accordion.—A. M.

SOWERBY, Leo. Amer. compr. *b.* Grand Rapids, Mich., U.S.A., 1 May, 1895. Went to Chicago at 14; stud. at Amer. Cons. under Lampert and Grainger (pf.), and Anderson (theory). 1918–19, bandmaster in U.S. army; then teacher of theory, Amer. Cons. Chicago. In Nov. 1921, went to Rome as holder of first fellowship in music of Amer. Acad. in Rome (an Amer. *Prix de Rome*). His vn. concerto was perf. by Gunn's Amer. Symphony Orch., Chicago, 18 Nov. 1913. On 18 Jan. 1917, gave concert of own works, including an overture, *Comes Autumn Time* (often played by Amer. orchs.; orig. an organ piece); tone-poem, *The Sorrows of Mydath* (after Masefield); *The Irish Washerwoman*, concerto for cello; *Three Somerset Tunes*, orch.; and pf.-concerto with a part for a s. v. (revised 1919 and

voice-part left out). A str. 4tet, played by Berkshire Quartet, March 1918; 5tet for wood-wind instrs. perf. by New York Chamber Music Soc. 13 Jan. 1920. Pf.-soloist at Norfolk (Conn.) Music Fest. (1917), and with Chicago Symphony Orch. 5 March, 1920.

S. is one of most promising of younger generation of Amer. comprs. He has followed modern tendencies, though not to the latest extremes. He himself " claims affinity with the Franckd'Indy school."

Overture, *Comes Autumn Time* (Boston Music Co. 1918); *Serenade*, str. 4tet (Soc. for Publ. of Amer. Music; Schirmer, 1921); Suito, vn. and pf. (Boston Music Co. 1918).—O. K.

SPAIN, MODERN ART-SONG IN. See MORALES ; FALLA ; TURINA ; VIVES ; GRANADOS CAMPINA ; ALBENIZ ; BAUTISTA ; GUERVÓS, JOSÉ MARÍA ; MONTES ; FONT Y DE ANTA, JOSÉ. Most of the art-songs of Spain remain unpublished up to the present time.—P. G. M.

SPALDING, Albert. Amer. violinist; *b.* Chicago, Ill., 15 Aug. 1888. Stud. vn. at 7 under Chiti in Florence and Juan Buitrago in New York; then 2 years in Paris under Lefort. *Début* as professional player at Théâtre Nouveau, Paris, 6 June, 1905. Thereafter concertised in Europe, including Russia and Egypt, and U.S.A. (Amer. *début*, New York, 8 Nov. 1908, with New York Symphony). Among his unpubl. works for vn. are a concerto in F mi., a *Concerto quasi Fantasia*, a sonata with pf. acc., a str. 4tet (1922).

Suite for vn. and pf. (C. Fischer, 1916); *Etchings*, theme and variations, op. 5 (Comprs. Music Corp.), and other pieces (Hansen; Schirmer; C. Fischer; Comprs. Music Corp.).—J. M.

SPALDING, Walter Raymond. Amer. orgt. and educator; *b.* Northampton, Mass., U.S.A., 25 May, 1865. 1892, went to Europe; for 3 years stud. under Guilmant and Widor in Paris and Rheinberger and Thuille in Munich. 1895, instructor of music at Harvard Univ., Cambridge, Mass., and Radcliff Coll. (for women) at same time; assistant-prof. Harvard, 1903; succeeding Paine as head of music department in 1906; associate-prof. 1912; prof. 1921.

Tonal Counterpoint (A. P. Schmidt, 1904); (with Arthur Foote) *Modern Harmony in its Theory and Practice* (*id.* 1905); *Music, an Art and a Language* (*id.* 1920).—J. M.

SPANISH CHAMBER-MUSIC. See MONASTERIO; ARBÓS ; RUBIO ; CHAPÍ ; TRAGÓ ; CAMPO Y ZABALETA, CONRADO DEL; TURINA ; GUERVÓS, JOSÉ ; CASALS, PABLO ; FRANCÉS ; also CHAMBER-MUSIC PLAYERS.

SPANISH FOLK-MUSIC. See ALIO, FRANCISCO; BARBIERI, FRANCISCO; CALLEJA, G. R.; INZENGA, J.; MANRIQUE DE LARA; MONTES, JUAN DE; NOGUERA, ANTONIO; OCÓN Y RIVAS, E.; OTAÑO, P. N.; PEDRELL, FELIPE; TORNER, E. M.

SPANISH OPERA. See ZARZUELA ; PEDRELL ; BRETÓN, TOMÁS ; GURIDI ; USANDIZAGA ; also, CAMPO Y ZABALETA, CONRADO DEL; ALBENIZ ; GRANADOS CAMPINA ; FALLA ; MANÉN ; ARREGUI ; MORERA ; MANRIQUE DE LARA ; TURINA ; BARRIOS ; CHAPÍ.

SPANISH ORCHESTRAL MUSIC FROM 1880. See MONASTERIO ; BARBIERI ; ARBÓS ; PÉREZ

CASAS; CASALS, PABLO; LAMOTE DE GRIG-
NON; NICOLAU; LASSALLE; RIVERA Y MANEJA;
CAMPO Y ZABALETA, CONRADO DEL; ESPLÁ;
FALLA; MANÉN; PAHISA; MORERA; GURIDI;
ISASI; ARREGUI; TURINA; BACARISSE;
BAUTISTA; MARIANI GONZÁLEZ; FONT Y DE
ANTA, MANUEL; LAVIÑA; SANJUÁN NORTES;
MORENO TORROBA; MANRIQUE DE LARA;
ZAMACOIS; RODRIGO; BRETÓN, ABELARDO;
CASSADÓ, JOAQUÍN; MARRACO; MILLET;
TELLERÍA Y ARRIZABALAGA.

SPANUTH, August. Ger. author and ed. *b.*
Brinkum (Hanover), 15 March, 1857; *d.* Berlin,
9 Jan. 1920. Stud. at Hoch's Cons. Frankfort-o-M. (Heymann, Raff); then Coblence and
Bremen; 1886, to America as concert-pianist;
temporary teacher at Chicago Cons.; 1903-6,
mus. reporter; 1906, returned to Berlin;
teacher at Stern's Cons.; since 1907, wrote and
edited the *Signale* (Simrock).
    Ed.: *Preparatory Pf. Exercises; Pf. Technique;*
Liszt's pf. compns. (3 vols. by Ditson). Transl. into
Ger. Caruso's *How to sing* (1914); and wrote (with
Xaver Scharwenka) *Method of Pf.-playing* (1907).
—A. E.

SPEAIGHT, Joseph. Eng. compr. and pianist;
b. London, 24 Oct. 1868. Stud. at Guildhall
School of Music, compn. under R. Orlando Morgan, pf. under Ernst Pauer; prof. at G.S.M.
1894; at Trinity Coll. of Music, 1919. He made
a striking success in chamber-works with his
Shakespeare Fairy Characters for str. 4tet
(Hawkes).
    Pf. works; cello pieces; vn. pieces; songs (Win-
throp Rogers; Stainer & Bell; Ascherberg; Anglo-
Fr. Co.): part-songs (Curwen).—E.-H.

SPECHT, Richard. Austrian musicologist; *b.*
Vienna, 7 Dec. 1870. First stud. architecture,
but, having become acquainted with Brahms,
Goldmark, Brüll and their circle, was encouraged
by them to take up mus. and theatrical criticism
on the Vienna daily papers *Die Zeit* and *Extra-
blatt,* and the review *Die Musik.* He also founded
and ed. the *Merker* (1909). His criticisms show
a kindly disposition towards the new generation and their aims. Book on Gustav Mahler is
well known (smaller book 1906, larger monograph 1913, 16th ed. 1922). Also wrote:
    Kritisches Skizzenbuch (1900); *Johann Strauss*
(1909); *Das Wiener Operntheater: Erinnerung aus
fünfzig Jahren* (1919); *Richard Strauss und sein
Werk* (detailed analysis, 5 vols. 1921); *Julius Bittner*
(1921); *Furtwängler* (in coll. *Die Wiedergabe,* 1922);
E. N. von Reznicek (1923); *Arthur Schnitzler* (1922);
ed. of Hebbel's works (Cotta); new transl. of libretto
of Verdi's *Trovatore* (Univ. Ed. 1921); analytical
comments on Mahler's Symphonies (*id.*); introduction to Strauss's *Die Frau ohne Schatten* (1919).
S. is also the originator of a new Opera-text Library
(Univ. Ed.).—P. ST.

SPEER, William Henry. Eng. orgt. and compr.
b. London, 9 Nov. 1863. Stud. harmony under
William Haynes of Priory Church, Malvern; his
oratorio *Jonah,* comp. at age of 16, was given
in Malvern in 1880; played Prout's organ concerto in E mi. twice at Shire Hall, Gloucester, in
1880; next 3 years, pupil of Dr. Harford Lloyd;
later of Sir Walter Parratt, E. Pauer and Sir
C. V. Stanford at R.C.M.; graduated Trinity
Coll. Cambridge; Mus.Doc. 1906; cond. choral
societies, St. Albans, N.W. London, Bexhill.

His str. 4tet in B flat was perf. at British Chamber Music Concerts, St. Martin's Hall, 1894. His
cantata *Lay of St. Cuthbert* was perf. at Queen's
Hall, London, by the Edward Mason Choir, 1912.
His *Jackdaw of Rheims* has been repeatedly perf.;
his symphony in E flat over a dozen times; his
latest work is *Impressions* (given Hastings,
Bournemouth, Guildford, etc. 1922).
    The Jackdaw of Rheims, chorus and small orch.
(Novello); *The Lay of St. Cuthbert,* chorus and orch.
(*id.*); *In the Garden,* soli, female chorus and orch.
(Cary); *Festival Overture,* orch. (Novello); *Nocturne*
for str. (Stainer & Bell); str. 4tet, B flat (Simrock);
sonata, pf. and vn. in D (Breitkopf); 6 *Miniatures,*
pf. and vn. (Stainer & Bell); pf. sonata in D (Breitkopf); *The Children's Hour,* 9 easy pf. pieces (Augener); other pf. pieces; organ sonata, F mi. (Augener);
14 songs (various publ.).—E.-H.

SPENA, Lorenzo. Argentine compr. *b.* Naples
in 1874. Went to Buenos Ayres, 1901; opened
Cons. Clementi, 1907. Many chamber-music and
symph. works. Pf. and vn.-pf. works, publ. by
Breyer.—S. G. S.

SPENDIAROF, Alexander (*accent on the A*).
Russ. compr. *b.* Kakhof, 1871. Pupil of Rimsky-
Korsakof, and one of the followers of New Russ.
school, in whose works the Oriental character,
made familiar by many Russ. works of the XIX
century, plays the chief part. He now lives in
the Crimea and is working on an opera *Almast.*
    Concert overture, op. 4; *Crimean Sketches,* op. 9
(2 series); tone-picture, *The Three Palm-Trees;* many
songs (Belaief).—V. B.

SPICKER, Max. Ger. condr. and teacher;
b. Königsberg, 16 Aug. 1858; *d.* New York,
Oct. 15, 1912. Pupil of Louis Köhler and of
Leipzig Cons. (Wenzel, Richter); theatre condr.
at Heidelberg, Ghent, etc.; 1882-8, cond.
Beethoven Male Choir, New York; till 1895
dir. of Brooklyn Cons.; then teacher of theory
National Cons. New York. Comp. many pf.
pieces and songs; ed. educational pf. works.
—A. E.

SPIELGELD (Ger.). (Ital. *Paga.*) Singers'
salaries at Ger. opera-houses are usually divided
into so much a month down and so much a performance, the number of performances a month
being stipulated. They are paid for a certain
number whether they sing or not, and any performances over or above this number are paid
for in addition. This extra payment is the
Spielgeld. Three days' absence from the cast
through illness, even though one may be sche-
duled to sing only once during those days, is
counted as one Spielgeld.—E.-H.

SPIERING, Theodore. Amer. violinist, condr.
teacher; *b.* St. Louis, 5 Sept. 1871. Pupil of
father, Ernst Spiering; 1886-8 of Schradieck,
Cincinnati; till 1892, Berlin, R. High School
(Joachim); also private pupil of G. Vierling;
1892-6, member of Thomas's Orch. Chicago;
1893, organised str. quartet which for 12 years
toured U.S.A. and Canada, introducing works by
Fr. comprs.; 1898-9, teacher at Chicago Cons.;
1899-1902, managed own Vn. School; till
1905, co-dir. of Chicago Mus. Coll.; also orch.
and operatic condr.; 1905, Berlin, teacher
at Stern's Cons.; 1909, America, leader of
New York Philh. Soc. (under Mahler); 1912-

1914, condr. and artistic adviser of the *Neue Freie Volksbühne*, Berlin; 1914–16, prof. at the New York Coll. of Music and condr. of the Woman's Orchestral Club of Brooklyn.

Songs; vn. studies, op. 4; 5 impressions for pf. op. 5.—A. E.

SPILKA, František. Czechoslovak compr. condr. *b.* Štěkěn, 1877. Stud. at Prague Cons.; then choirmaster and (for short time) condr. of Czech Philh. Till 1922 teacher of choral song and theory at Prague Cons., being (from 1918) also its administrative manager. In this function he took a leading part in its reorganisation. In 1908 he founded (on the model of Moravian Teachers' Choir) Singers' Society of Prague Teachers, and brought them up to the same level. In France and England they were as successful as the older Moravian Club.

Songs; choruses; pf. sonata (Fr. A. Urbánek); opera, *Selská práva* (*The Peasants' Rights*).—V. ST.

SPINDLER, Fritz. Ger. pianist and compr. *b.* Wurzbach, near Lobenstein, 24 Nov. 1817; *d.* Lössnitz, near Dresden, 26 Dec. 1905. Pupil of Fr. Schneider (Dessau); settled at Dresden, 1841, as teacher. Comp. over 300 works, mostly brilliant salon-pieces for pf.; 2 symphonies, pf. concerto, sonatinas for teaching, str. 4tet op. 62, C mi., pf. 4tet, trios, etc.—A. E.

SPITTA, Friedrich. Ger. writer on music; *b.* Wittingen (Hanover), 10 Jan. 1852. Brother of Philipp Spitta; 1887, prof.-in-ordinary of theology at Strasburg; 1919, at Göttingen; 1896, publ. (with J. Smend) *Monatsschrift für Gottesdienst und kirchliche Kunst* (monthly magazine for church music), containing many of his studies; interested in Evangelical liturgy of Heinrich Schütz and H. v. Herzogenberg. President of Evangelical Church Singers' Soc., Alsace-Lorraine, since 1898.—A. E.

SPITTA, J. August Philipp. Ger. writer on music; *b.* Wechold, near Hoya, Hanover, 27 Dec. 1841; *d.* Berlin, 13 April, 1894. Stud. philology at Göttingen; teacher at Ritter School and Cath. School, Reval (1864–6); at Grammar School, Sondershausen (till 1874); at Nicolai Grammar School, Leipzig; 1875, called to Berlin as prof. of mus. history and permanent secretary of R. Acad. of Art; teacher at R. High School of Music; administrative dir. of same; 1891, member of Governing Board.

Biography of J. S. Bach (1873–80, 2 vols., Breit-kopf); ed. *Organ Works of Dietrich Buxtehude* (1875–1876, 2 vols.); *Complete Ed. of Works of Heinrich Schütz* (16 vols.); *Musical Works of Frederick the Great* (1889); *Zur Musik* (16 essays, 1892); *Essays on Musical History* (1894). Edited with Chrysander and Guido Adler, 1885–94, *Quarterly Journal for Musical Science* (*Vierteljahrsschrift für Musik-Wissenschaft*). Spitta's exchange of letters with Brahms was publ. by the Ger. Brahms Soc. (Vol. 15). Spitta and Chrysander are the Old Masters of Ger. musico-historical research.—A. E.

SPRINGER, Hermann. Ger. writer on music; *b.* Döbeln (Saxony), 9 May, 1872. Stud. Romance philology and mus. history in Leipzig, Berlin and Paris; 1894, took doctor's degree; 1899 in Prussian Library, now head librarian in Prussian State Library; 1914, R. prof.; 1895, also mus. reporter *Deutsche Allgemeine Zeitung*; member of board of Association of Ger. Critics

(Verband deutscher Musikkritiker). He paid special attention to history of music-typography and to Ital. mus. literature.

Canzonette da Battello (with Edwin Buhle; Leipzig, C. F. W. Siegel). 1912, with Max Schneider and Werner Wolffheim, *Miscellanea musicæ bio-bibliographica*.—A. E.

SPRINGER, Max. Compr. critic; *b.* Schwendi, Würtemberg, 19 Dec. 1877. Stud. under Schach-leitner (abbot of Benedictine monastery of Emaus, near Prague), Dvořák, Klička and Fibich. Orgt. at Emaus, excellent organ-player (extemporiser). His manual *Kunst der Orgelbegleitung* (in Eng., New York) treats of the Gregorian chant and its acc. Also *Der Liturgische Choral in Hochamt und Vesper, Choralsolfeggien, Orgelschule*. Since 1910, prof. of sacred music, Vienna State Acad. (Klosterneuburg, near Vienna) for organ and composition.

Sacred music: *Missa resurrexi*, op. 27, and *Missa puer natus est*, op. 30, both in a new style, influenced by the rhythmic recitation of Gregorian chant and modern harmony; other masses; 2 Psalms; *Abend auf Golgatha*; *Auferstehung*; stage-music for Calderón's *Weltfrauen*; *Graduale Parvum* (a rhythmic organ arr. for practical use); songs; chamber-music; 2 symphonies.—P. ST.

SPURLING, Clement Michael. Eng. dir. of music, Oundle School, Northants; *b.* London, 28 Sept. 1870. Stud. Guildhall School of Music under J. F. Barnett; R.C.M. under Stanford, Bridge, Cliffe, Gladstone, Higgs. He has raised the music of Oundle School to a unique state, one which enables the whole school to perform Handel's *Messiah*, Bach's B mi. Mass, etc.

Stately Dance, small orch. (Ashdown); easy educational pf. pieces (Augener; Novello; Arnold); songs; carols (Boosey; Novello).—E.-H.

SQUIRE, William Barclay. Eng. mus. research scholar; *b.* 1855. Librarian R.C.M. London. Educated in Germany and at Pembroke Coll. Cambridge; in charge of Printed Music, Brit. Museum, 1885–1920; mus. critic, *Saturday Review*, 1888–94; *Westminster Gazette*, 1893; *Globe*, 1894–1901. Writer of many historical arts. in Grove's *Dictionary of Music*, *Dictionary of Nat. Biogr.*, *Encyc. Brit.*, etc. Became sec. of the Purcell Soc. in 1888 (till 1923) and his untiring labour has done much for the revival of interest in Purcell in recent years. His generous help in all matters of mus. research has earned him the gratitude of scholars throughout the world.

Catalogue of Printed Music in R.C.M. 1909; of Old Printed Music in Brit. Museum, 2 vols. 1912; ed. Palestrina's *Stabat Mater*; Purcell's harpsichord music, 4 vols, 1918; Byrd's Masses; Fitzwilliam Virginal Book (with J. A. Fuller-Maitland) 1894–9 (Breitkopf); R. Jones's *Muses' Garden for Delights*; *Ausgewählte Madrigali* (30 nos.), etc.—E. J. D.

SRB, Josef (pseudonym, Debrnov). Czech writer on music, *b.* Prague, 1836; *d.* there, 1904. Devoted himself to organisation of mus. life in Prague. Maintained a constant intercourse with Smetana, whose diary he partly publ. in 1902. Chief works (all in Czech):

Short History of the Prague Conservatorium (1877); *Instrumentation* (1883); *History of Music in Bohemia and Moravia*, (1891).—V. ST.

STAATSTHEATER. A theatre or opera in Germany subsidised by the State. Not to be confused with Stadttheater, one subsidised by the municipality.—E.-H.

STABILE, Mariano. Ital. barit. *b.* Palermo, 12 May, 1888. Has attained position of one of principal Ital. lyric artists; made an unusual success in *Falstaff* at La Scala, Milan. Created there the chief character in Respighi's opera *Belfagor.*—D. A.

STADTTHEATER. A city or town theatre or opera in Germany subsidised by the municipality. Not to be confused with Staatstheater, one subsidised by the State.—E.-H.

STAEGEMANN, Max. Ger. barit. singer; *b.* Freienwalde-on-Oder, May 10, 1843; *d.* Leipzig, 29 Jan, 1905. Stud. at Cons. Dresden; 1862, Bremen as actor; 1863, Hanover, barit.; 1876, dir. Königsberg Stadttheater; 1879, went to Berlin as concert-singer and singing-master; 1882, dir. Leipzig Stadttheater. Married violinist Hildegard Kirchner (*d.* 16 June, 1913). His son, Waldemar, originally member of R. Playhouse, Berlin, became (1913) member (barit.) of Dresden Court Opera House. His daughter, Helene, is concert-singer (s.). She married the compr. Botho Sigwart (Count of Eulenburg).—A. E.

STAGIONE. A yearly visit or a season, especially of an operatic company; as opposed to a permanent company.—E.-H.

STAGNO BELLINCIONI, Bianca. Ital. .s. singer; *b.* Budapest, 23 Jan. 1888. Daughter of two famous artists, Gemma Bellincioni and Roberto Stagno (one of most famous Ital. tenors at end of xix century), she inherited from her mother, under whom she stud., her high qualities as artist and interpreter. *Début* in Florence at the Pergola; has appeared at leading theatres in Italy and in Europe. Amongst her chief parts we mention those of *Conchita* (Zandonai) and of *Pélleas et Mélisande* (Debussy).—D. A.

STANCHINSKY, Alexei Vladimirovitch (*accent 2nd syll.*). Russ. compr. *b.* 1888; *d.* 25 Sept./ 6 Oct. 1914. Pupil of Jilaief and S. I. Tanéief. A very highly gifted musician who died before his talent was fully revealed. He left a pf. sonata, and several pf. pieces. Only op. 1 (*Sketches*) for pf. is publ. (Jurgenson, Moscow).—V. B.

STANFORD, Sir Charles Villiers. Irish composer; *b.* Dublin, 30 Sept. 1852; *d.* London, 29 March, 1924. The son of John Stanford (an amateur singer, devoted to the Law as profession but to music as recreation), he heard and assimilated good music from his earliest days, and became a pupil of Arthur O'Leary and Sir Robert Stewart. At 10 years he had heard one of his youthful efforts at composition played in the Theatre Royal, and his later career showed many more pronounced points of contact with the Theatre. One can think of his life up to now as having roughly three phases, dominated by three spheres of activity: Dublin (1852–70), Cambridge (1870–92) and London (1892 onwards). To musicians, his earliest significance must date from his entry into Cambridge as an undergraduate. He went there, ordinarily, in search of a classical education, and he took honours in his stride (1874) while at

Trinity. But Cambridge meant more than this. It offered him—and his extraordinary abilities made it possible for him to accept—rare opportunities for distinctive musical work, When Dr. J. L. Hopkins resigned the Trinity organistship, Stanford succeeded him (1873); and it was in Cambridge that his influence was first felt along one of the main lines of his activities— that of conducting — through his leadership of Cambridge Univ. Mus. Soc. (1874). Against the dull-coloured background of British music in those days, Stanford's work as composer and conductor was already providing one of the very few high-lights. Thoroughly alive, he left nothing as he found it. Neglected works were revived (Astorga's *Stabat Mater* for instance, in 1878); he looked abroad for important works, sometimes for one not well-enough known here (Schumann's *Faust*, Part III), sometimes for one quite new (Brahms's *Alto Rhapsody*); he gave the second English performance of Brahms's *Requiem*. In line with another " live " young British composer—Hubert Parry—he scorned the reactionary critics with a prompt second performance of *Prometheus Unbound* (1881). He was sanely modernist. From his early teachers in Dublin he learned to respect the traditional best; out of his own progressive spirit he looked for the newest; by his travels on the Continent in search of further education (he was with Reinecke in Leipzig, and Kiel in Berlin, at intervals during 1874–6) he acquired a cosmopolitan outlook. At a time when " English music is no music " was on almost every foreign lip, his first opera, *The Veiled Prophet of Khorassan*, was produced at Hanover (1881); when the Macfarrens and Davisons and Joseph Bennetts in this country still were ridiculing the messages from Bayreuth, he was openly espousing the cause of Wagner and showing instructed enthusiasm for his operas. As a young man he produced a new work (*Festival Overture*) for Gloucester in 1877, and another (*Serenade* in G) for Birmingham, in 1882, and by these and other early choral and orchestral works won a publicity which has grown ever since.

From Cambridge his influence was felt increasingly, and in more directions than one. His conducting meant practical leadership there, and this sphere of his activity became widened by his appointment as conductor of the Bach Choir (1885), of the R.C.M. Orchestra (1887), and later (1901) of the Leeds Festival. His work as a teacher, beginning in Cambridge and leading to the Professorship of Music in the University (1887) spread enormously through his being given charge over composition at the R.C.M. (1887), where there came to study with him a great many of the most promising scholars in Britain. It is as difficult to over-emphasise the responsibility of the post which he filled at the Royal College as it is to stress too much the importance of his influence over the work of his pupils. No other creative musician in the history of British music can point to anything like as significant a record of composer-pupils as his. His other (and chief) activity, as composer, can be only referred to here in the briefest way. From his earliest Cambridge days his output was remarkable. The early festival compositions mentioned above were the first of a long line of works richly varied and interesting. An unusually complete technique enabled Sir Charles Stanford to handle surely very diverse forms of composition. His operas number seven, of which *The Travelling Companion* (1917) still awaits performance in its own country. In allied works for the theatre must be noticed incidental music for Tennyson's *Queen Mary* and *Becket*, and for Greek plays at Cambridge. In purely orchestral music there are seven symphonies, with the *Irish* for the most characteristic; the four *Irish Rhapsodies*, and many other large-scale works. Among concertos, that for the clarinet (ms.) is an epitome of felicitous writing for that instrument. The chamber-music is of relative importance with the rest of his output, though less fully known.

More than any of his other works, those which are mainly choral must have contributed to making their composer's fame so wide. They have been in (roughly) two classes: those actually concerned with or closely allied to the church services, or for the great festivals; and those others which are secular. In each class there are conspicuous examples. His early B flat Service brought a new outlook to the choristers' world. The *Stabat Mater* (Leeds Fest. 1907) is on the high plane of religious musical expression. The *Songs of the Sea* and *Songs of the Fleet* are everywhere popular; and the short cantatas *Phaudrig Crohoore* and the early *Revenge* are remarkable examples of works that make strong appeal to diverse tastes, and do it with the utmost economy of means. In one other important sphere also—that of song—he made himself one of the outstanding figures in British music; and the very significant revival of interest in native folk-music in recent years found in him a powerful champion.

Sir Charles Stanford held the honorary degree of Doctor of Music in the Universities of Oxford and Cambridge, and received the honour of knighthood in 1901.

Operas: *The Veiled Prophet of Khorassan*; *Savonarola*; *The Canterbury Pilgrims*; *Shamus O'Brien*; *Much Ado About Nothing*; *The Critic* (all Boosey); *The Travelling Companion* (Carnegie award; Stainer & Bell); incidental music to *Queen Mary* (Augener); to *The Eumenides* and *Œdipus Rex* (Stainer & Bell). Choral works: *Psalm XLVI*; *The Revenge*; *Carmen Sœculare*; *The Voyage of Maeldune*; *Eden* (oratorio); *The Battle of the Baltic*; *Mass in G*; *East to West* (all Novello); *Cavalier Songs*; *Elegiac Ode*; *Three Holy Children*; *The Bard*; *Phaudrig Crohoore*; *Requiem*; *Last Post*; *The Lord of Might*; *Songs of the Sea*; *Stabat Mater*; *Wellington*; *Welcome Song*; *Ode to Discord*; *Magnificat*; *Mass*; *Via Victrix* (all Boosey); *Ave atque Vale*; *Songs of the Fleet*; *Fairy Day*; *Thanksgiving Te Deum*; *Merlin and the Gleam* (all Stainer & Bell); *The Resurrection* (Chappell); *Psalm CL* (Forsyth). 4 publ. symphonies: *Irish* (Novello); No. IV (*id.*); *L'Allegro ed il Pensieroso* (Carnegie award; Stainer & Bell); No. VII (*id.*). *Irish Rhapsody*, No. I, orch. (*id.*); IV, vn. and orch. (Boosey); *Serenade*, orch. (*id.*); 4 Irish dances, orch. (Stainer & Bell); concerto, vn. and orch. (Breitkopf); Suite, vn. and orch. (Novello); con-

certo, pf. and orch. (Stainer & Bell); 10 dances, pf. and orch. (Boosey); Variations on an Eng. theme, pf. and orch. (*id.*). Chamber-music: 1st and 5th str. 5tets (Stainer & Bell); 1st and 2nd str. 4tets (Eulenburg); 3rd str. 4tet (Augener); pf. 5tet (Novello); pf. 4tet (Bote & Bock); 3 pf. trios (Novello; Bosworth; Augener); sonata, vn. and pf. (Ries); *Irish Fantasies*, vn. and pf. (Boosey); pieces, vn. and pf. (*id.*); easy pieces, vn. and pf. (Williams); 2 sonatas, cello and pf. (Bote & Bock; Simrock); *Intermezzi*, clar. and pf. (Novello); sonata, clar. (or vla.) and pf. (Stainer & Bell). Pf. pieces (Chappell; Boosey; Stainer & Bell; Williams; Augener; Willcocks); 6 Regimental Marches (Novello); March, military band or organ (Stainer & Bell); organ sonatas (Stainer & Bell; Augener); organ pieces (Stainer & Bell; Schirmer); 4 organ *intermezzi* (Novello); 3 preludes and fugues, organ (*id.*); *Six Eng. Songs*, 2 sets; *50 Songs of Old Ireland*; Moore's *Irish Melodies*; *Songs of Erin*, and others (all Boosey); *Cushendall*; *Four Songs*, 2 sets; *Biblical Songs*; *Leinster Songs*, etc. (all Stainer & Bell); *Songs of Heine* (Augener); *Songs of Bridges* (*id.*); songs from *The Spanish Gypsy* (Novello); *30 Irish Songs and Ballads* (Novello); many other songs; unison and part-songs (Year-Book Press); part-songs (Novello; Boosey; Stainer & Bell); Unison Church Service in D (Oxford Univ. Press). In ms.: opera; incidental music to *Becket*; *Attila the Hun*; *Drake*; 2 masses; symphonies; overtures; rhapsodies; orch. marches; concertos for clar. and orch., pf. and orch., vn. and orch.; 2 str. 5tets; *Serenade*, str. and wind; pf. 4tet; sonatas, vn. and pf.; pf. pieces. Books: *Studies and Memories* (1908); *Musical Composition* (1911); *Pages from an Unwritten Diary* (1914); *Interludes* (1922).—H. H.

STANGENBERG, Harry. Swedish opera-producer; *b.* Stockholm, 27 April, 1893. Stud. under Reinhardt, Berlin, 1914–15; and at Court Opera in Munich, 1915–16. 1st *régisseur*, R. Opera, Stockholm. Married Göta Ljungberg (*q.v.*), 1922. Produced:

In Berne: *Tales from Hoffmann*, *Tristan and Isolde*, *Tannhäuser*, *Valkyrie*, *Don Juan*, *Otello*, *Rigoletto*, *Bohème*; in Frankfort-o-M.: *Merry Wives of Windsor*, *Frauenlist*, *Venezia*, *Barber of Seville*, *Traviata*; in Riga: *Magic Flute*, *Figaro's Wedding*, *Carmen*, etc.; in Stockholm: *Härvard Harpolekare*, *Iphigenia in Tauris*, *Rosenkavalier*, *Die toten Augen*, *Manteln*, *Angelica*, *Gianni Schicchi* (Puccini), *Medeltida* (Rangström), *Alvorna* (N. Berg), *Kronbruden* (Rangström), *Figaro's Wedding*.

STANKEVIČIUS. See LITHUANIAN MUSIC.

STANLEY, Albert Augustus. Amer. educator; *b.* Manville, R.I., U.S.A., 25 May, 1851. Stud. (1871–5) Leipzig Cons. (Richter, Wenzel, Paul, Papperitz). Orgt. of Grace Ch., Providence, R.I., 1876–88. Prof. of music, Univ. of Michigan, since 1888; dir. of Univ. of Michigan School of Music since 1903. Cond. Ann Arbor May Fests. since 1893. Retired from all these positions, 1921. Symph. and choral works; symphony; *The Awakening of the Soul* (1896); symph. poem, *Attis* (1898); perf. in Ann Arbor and elsewhere. M.A. *h.c.* of Univ. of Michigan, 1889; Mus.D. *h.c.* of Northwestern Univ., 1916. Author of *Greek Themes in Modern Musical Settings* (*Univ. of Michigan Humanistic Studies*, Vols. XV, XVII, 1920).—O. K.

STARCZEWSKI, Feliks. Polish compr. and mus. writer; *b.* Warsaw, 27 May, 1868. Stud. in Warsaw, Berlin and Paris. Since 1894, teacher, organiser and writer in Warsaw. Now prof. of pf. at Warsaw State Conservatoire.

2 pf. sonatas; Variations, pf.; vn. sonata; music to vaudevilles and national dances; many songs. Has written a treatise on *Polish Dances* (Sammelb. d. I.M.G. 1901), and, in Warsaw reviews, *The Schola Cantorum and Vincent d'Indy* (1905) and *Jan Karlowicz*.—ZD. J.

STARMER, William Wooding. Eng. orgt., expert on bells, lecturer; *b.* Wellingborough, 4 Nov. 1866. Stud. at R.A.M. London; lecturer on Campanology, Birmingham Univ. 1924; has publ. church and organ music and part-songs. Lectures: *Bells and Bell Tones; Carillons and Bell Music ; Choruses and Chime Tunes* (Eng.); *Chimes* (continental); *Clock Jacks of England* (all publ. in Proceedings of Mus. Association). Has contributed arts. on BELLS, etc., to this Dictionary.—E.-H.

STATKOWSKI, Roman. Polish compr. *b.* Szczypiorno, 24 Dec. 1859. Pupil of Żeleński in Warsaw, and of Solovief in Petrograd. Since 1906, prof. of mus. history and instrumentation at Warsaw Cons. and also its vice-dir. His works are distinguished by exceeding purity of style.

Operas: *Philœnis* (libretto by H. Erler; 1st prize, International Opera Competition, London, 1903); *Marya* (on Malczewski's romantic poem; 1st prize, Warsaw, 1905); 3 str. 4tets; several orch. compns.; 11 pf. pieces and 5 for vn.—ZD. J.

STAVENHAGEN, Bernhard. Ger. pianist; *b.* Greiz (Reuss), 25 Nov. 1862; *d.* Geneva, 26 Dec. 1914. Pupil of Kiel, Rudorff and Liszt; 1880, Mendelssohn Prize; 1885, in Berlin; then Weimar (pupil of Liszt); 1890, Grand-Ducal Court-pianist; 1885, Court-condr.; 1898, Court-condr. Munich; 1901, dir. of Acad. of Mus. Art; 1904, resigned; 1907, condr. of Subscription Concerts at Geneva. Comp. 2 pf. concertos (No. 1, op. 4, in B mi.; and No. 2 in A, 1912); pf. pieces. Many pf. recital tours.—A. E.

STCHERBACHEF, Vladimir Vladimirovitch (*accent 3rd syll.*). Russ. compr. *b.* 24 Jan. (n.s.), 1889. Pupil of M. Steinberg at Petrograd Cons. of Music.

2 symphonies; 2 pf. sonatas; nonet for str. 4tet, harp, pf. solo v. solo dance and Light; some pf. pieces and songs. Some of his pieces are publ. (Russ. State Music Publ. Dept.).—V. B.

STECKER, Karel. Czechoslovak compr. writer; *b.* Kosmonos, 22 Jan. 1861; *d.* Prague, 15 Oct. 1918. From 1885 prof. at Organ School; from 1889 prof. of history of music, compn. and organ at Cons. Prague, where most of Czechoslovak comprs. were both his and Dvořák's pupils. Wrote *Musical Forms* (1905); *General History of Music* (2 vols. 1892–1903); *Thematic Improvisation* (all in Czech). 1908–18, ed. *Hudebni Revue.* From 1888, mus. lecturer at Univ. There are some songs by him—*Květy lásky (Flowers of Love); Písně milostné (Love Songs)* — but his church works are more significant : *Missa solemnis;* 16 motets for the chief festivals, etc. (Fr. A. Urbánek.)—V. ST.

STEFAN, Paul. Austrian writer on music; *b.* Brünn, 25 Nov. 1879. Since 1898 has lived in Vienna. Writer on music, with great zeal for the propaganda of modern music. Co-founder of Verein für Kunst und Kultur. President of Akademische Verband für Literatur und Musik. Organised at Vienna the first concerts at which Reger, Mahler, Zemlinsky, Schönberg have been played. Now chief ed. of *Musikblätter des Anbruch* (see PERIODICALS). Of Stefan's works dealing with music, the most famous are the essays

and books on Mahler, whose importance he was one of the first to assert. *G. Mahlers Erbe* (polemic against Weingartner, 1908); *Dedications to Mahler's 50th Birthday* (1910); biography of *Mahler* (1st ed. 1910; 7th ed. 1920; Eng. trans. 1913); study on *Oskar Fried* (1911); *History of the Vienna Opera* (1922). Very interesting is his chronicle *Das Grab in Wien* (1913) dealing with the period 1903–11 and its artistic events. St. is an excellent writer, who always fights for new talent with great vivacity and energy. He has written many of the Austrian articles in this Dictionary.—EG. W.

STEFĂNESCU, G. See RUMANIAN OPERA.

STEGGALL, Reginald. Eng. compr. and orgt. *b.* London, 17 April, 1867. Stud. R.A.M. (compn. under Sir G. A. Macfarren and E. Prout; pf. under H. R. Eyers and O. Beringer; organ under his father, Dr. Charles Steggall); Balfe R.A.M. Scholar for compn. 1887; organ prof. R.A.M. 1895 up to the present; succeeded his father as orgt. Lincoln's Inn Chapel, London, in 1905; has produced many choral works there (Parry, Elgar, Brahms, Schumann [*Requiem*], Holst). Hon. Fellow, R.C.O. 1920. As a compr. his works between 1899 and 1907 show the influence of Wagner; but since then, that influence can hardly be traced. His 1st Suite and the contr. *scena Alcestis* were produced at Crystal Palace under Manns; *Elaine* at Queen's Hall at Granville Bantock's concert, Dec. 1896 (since then, frequently in Germany and elsewhere); *Concertstück*, orch. and organ, at Leipzig and at Paris (1911). Of the later works, the best are the Variations for orch. (1908; Bournemouth) and *Phantasy-Overture* (1914; *ib.*). The 5tet for wood-wind and horn has not yet been performed.

Concertstück, organ and orch. (Breitkopf); *Elaine*, scena for contr. and orch. or pf. (*id.*); *Magnificat and Nunc Dimittis*, solo, chorus, orch. and organ (Novello); 3 pieces, pf. (Rogers); 5 pieces, pf. (Stainer & Bell); Suite, organ (Schott); 4 Shakespeare songs; *Lullaby* (Novello). In ms.: Dramatic Prelude; Variations, orch.; 2 suites; symphony; overture; symph. poem, orch.; *Agnus Dei*, s. pf. vn. harp; scena, contr. and orch.; *Festival Te Deum*, vs. and orch.; wind 5tet; str. 4tet; pf. trio (produced by London Trio in 1920).—E.-H.

STEIN, Erwin. Austrian condr. theorist; *b.* Vienna, 7 Nov. 1885. Pupil of Arnold Schönberg in 1905; then condr. at various Ger. theatres. Lives now in Vienna; first coach of Verein für musikalische Privataufführungen (Soc. for Private Mus. Perfs.). Condr. of Schönberg's *Pierrot lunaire* (alternately with Sch. himself). Publ. an Introduction (*Leitfaden*) to Schönberg's *Harmony* (for teaching use) (1923, Univ. Ed.). Also arts. on Schönberg for the *Merker* (Vienna), on Alban Berg and Webern in *Chesterian* (London, 1922).—P. ST.

STEIN, Fritz. Ger. condr. and writer on music; *b.* Gerlachsheim, Baden, 17 Dec. 1879. Stud. theology and science of music; 1902, music exclusively; assistant to Philipp Wolfrum, Heidelberg; then stud. at Leipzig Cons. and privately under Straube; 1906, successor to Ernst Naumann as dir of mus. Jena Univ.; 1910, doctor's degree at Heidelberg; 1913, prof.; 1914, succeeded Max Reger as Court-condr. at Meiningen, till dissolution of orch.; 1918, orgt. of St. Nicolai Ch. Kiel; prof.-extraordinary of mus. science at Univ. Condr. orch. concerts of Soc. of Friends of Music and Oratorio Soc. there. Discovered the orch. parts of a symphony which he attributed to the young Beethoven and publ. as *Jena Symphony*, for which consult Stein's explanation in *I.M.G.*, Vol. XIII : *An Unknown Youthful Symphony of Beethoven*. Publ. *History of Music in Heidelberg*, 1912; new ed. (1921) as *History of Musical Life at Heidelberg up to end of XVIII Century.*—A. E.

STEIN, Richard H. Ger. author and compr. *b.* Halle-o-S., 28 Feb. 1882. Stud. law in Berlin; then music at R. High School; graduated at Erlangen, 1911, with *Psychological Foundations of Ethics*; wrote pamphlet *La Musica Moderna* (Barcelona, 1918, Ger.-Span.); monograph on Grieg (1921, Deutsche Verlags-Anstalt); one on Tchaikovsky in preparation. Composed numerous pf. pieces and songs; endeavoured to introduce quarter-tone intervals in music; wrote on this subject in mus. journals; publ. compns. on this system (op. 26, 2 pieces for cello and pf.); has had a quarter-tone clar. and a small quarter-tone pf. constructed for his experiments.—A. E.

STEINBACH, Emil. Ger. condr. *b.* Lengenrieden (Baden), 14 Nov. 1849; *d.* Mayence, 6 Dec. 1919. 1867-9, pupil of Leipzig Cons.; 1869-71, of Hermann Levi, Carlsruhe; 1871-4, 2nd condr. Mannheim, temporary 1st condr. Hamburg; till 1877, Court-condr. at Darmstadt; town condr. at Mayence; 1899, condr. of Stadttheater; 1893 at Covent Garden, London; 1910, retired from conducting. Comp. chamber-music, orch. works (several symph. poems and overtures) and songs.—A. E.

STEINBACH, Fritz. Ger. condr. *b.* Grünsfeld (Baden), 17 June, 1855; *d.* Munich, 13 Aug. 1916. Brother of Emil St.; pupil of brother and of Leipzig Cons. (1873), of Lachner, Carlsruhe, and of Nottebohm, Vienna; gained Mozart scholarship; 1880-6, second condr. Mayence; 1886, Court-condr. Meiningen; 1902, succeeded Wüllner at Cologne as town-condr. and dir. of Cons. As condr. of Meiningen Court Orch., Steinbach undertook numerous concert-tours; was a celebrated Brahms condr.; 1914, resigned Cologne position and went to Munich. Comp. 7tet (op. 7), cello sonata, songs, etc.—A. E.

STEINBERG, Maximilian Osseievitch. Russ. compr. *b.* 7 July (n.s.), 1883. Pupil of Rimsky-Korsakof at Petrograd Cons. (1908); now prof. there (from 1908). His early works show the influence of Glazunof, even more strongly than that of Rimsky-Korsakof, and a great technical ability combined with a not unoriginal but essentially classical temperament.

Op. 2, Variations, orch. (1906); op. 3, 1st symphony, D, (1906); op. 4, *Russalka (Water-Nymph)*, cantata, solo, female chorus, orch. (poem by Lermontof); op. 5, str, 4tet, A; op. 8, 2nd symphony, B flat mi. (1910); op. 9, *Dramatic Fantasy*, orch. (1911); op. 10, ballet, *Metamorphoses* (after Ovid), perf. by Diaghilef troupe, Paris, London; oratorio, *Heaven and Earth*, on themes written for it by Rimsky-Korsakof, text by Bielsky after Byron (1916), ms.;

songs, etc. (Belaief; Jurgenson). Has completed Rimsky-Korsakof's *Handbook of Orchestration* and seen it through the press (Eng. transl. by Agate; London, 1922, Russ. Music Co.).—M. D. C.

STEINHARD, Erich. German-Czechoslovak compr. *b.* Prague, 26 May, 1886. Stud. music under dir. of Cons. (Knittl) and Vítězslav Novák in Prague; science of music under Rietsch (Prague), Kretschmar, Friedlaender, Wolf (Berlin); 1911, Ph.D. (for treatise on *Organum*); resides in Prague. 1911, Univ. librarian; 1918, member of Ger. State Commission for music examinations; 1920, prof. of history of music and æsthetics at Ger. Acad. of Music and Descriptive Art; 1921, chief ed. of *Auftakt* (a mus. journal for the Czechoslovak republic, dedicated in the first place to modern music). Dr. Steinhard is responsible, with Dr. Václav Štěpán, for the Czechoslovak articles in this Dictionary.

The Early History of Part-Singing (Archives of Science of Music, 1921); Report of First Congress of Æsthetics and Gen. Science of Art (Archives of Psychology, 1914); Andreas Hammerschmidt (Prague, 1914); Studies of Modern Music : Schönberg, Keussler, Finke, Zemlinsky ; Expressionism (Neue Musikzeitung, 1912, 1916, 1917, 1922); Auftakt (1921, 1922); Mus. Almanac of Czechoslovak Republic, 1922; Die Musik (1922), etc.—V. ST.

STENHAMMAR, K. Wilhelm E. Swedish compr. pianist, condr. *b.* Stockholm, 7 Feb. 1871. Stud. under Richard Andersson (pf.), Emil Sjögren, Dente, Hallén and at R. Cons. Stockholm; was orgt. at Fr. Reformed Ch. in Stockholm, 1890-2; then stud. pf. under Barth (Berlin, 1892-3). *Début* with his first pf. concerto in Stockholm, 1893; then distinguished himself as solo-pianist and chamber-music player. Member of Tor Aulin Str. Quartet. As compr. appeared (1892) with cantata *Prinsessan och svennen (Princess and Page)*; 1897-1900, condr. of Philh. Soc. Stockholm; 1900-1, of R. Theatre (Opera); 1904-6, of New Philh. Soc.; stud. in Italy, 1906-7; from 1907, 1st. condr. of Gothenburg Orch. Soc. Member R.A.M. Stockholm, 1900. Ph.D. *h.c.* Gothenburg, 1916. His 2nd pf. concerto was perf. at Queen's Hall, London, under Sir Henry Wood in 1924.

Operas: *Tirfing* (Stockholm, 1898); *Gildet på Solhaug* (Stuttgart, 1899; Stockholm, 1902). Symphonies: No. I in F (1903), No. II, G mi. (1915); overture, *Excelsior* (1897); pf. concertos: No. I, B mi. (1894); No. II, D mi. (1909); cantatas and songs with orch.: *Prinsessan och svennen* (1892); *Flor and Blancheflor* (1895); *Snöfrid* (1896); cantata for Stockholm Exhibition, 1897; *Ett folk* (including popular song *Sverige*), 1905; *Ithaka* (1905); *Midvinter* (1909); vn. sonata (1901); 5 str. 4tets; pf. sonata; pf. pieces; songs.—P. V.

ŠTĚPÁN, Václav. Czechoslovak compr. pianist; *b.* Pečky, 1889. Stud. Univ. Prague; Ph.D ; also privately, pf. with J. Čermak, compn. with Vít. Novák. Further studies in Berlin and Paris; 1919-22, prof. of æsthetics, Cons. Prague; writer of essays and criticism in *Hudebni Revue*; *Naše Doba*; *Revue Musicale*, etc. As a pianist, has given first performances of many Czech compns. Has played in Germany, Austria, England, and chiefly in France. Author of *The Musical Symbolism in Programme Music* (1914). Dr. Štěpán is responsible, with Dr. Steinhard, for the Czechoslovak articles in this Dictionary.

Pf. 5tet, *Prvni jara (First Springs)*; pf. trio; pf.

fantasy, *Teskliné sny* (*Glowing Dreams*); str. 6tet;
Pohoda života (*Harmony of Life*), pf. and cello; 5 vols.
free arrs. of national songs (publ. Rouart, Lerolle,
Paris; Univ. Ed. Vienna; Hudební Matice, Prague).
—E. S.

STEPHAN, Rudi. Ger. compr. *b.* Worms,
29 July, 1887; killed in action, 29 Sept. 1915.
Pupil of Karl Kiebitz; later of Bernard Sekles
(at Frankfort-o-M.) and Heinrich Schwartz
and Rudolf Louis (at Munich), in which city
he settled. Stephan was a forerunner of German
"Expressionism" in music.
 Music for 7 str. instrs. (pf. harp, 5 strs.), Dantzig
Music Fest. 1912; *Music for Orch.* (Jena Music Fest.
1913); *Liebeszauber* (*Love-Magic*), barit. and orch.
(words by Hebbel); *Music for Vn. and Orch.*; pf.
pieces; opera, *Die ersten Menschen* (*The First
Beings*), after O. Borngräber's erotic mystery (perf.
Frankfort-o-M. 1920). Publ. Schott. Consult Karl
Holl, *R. St.* in monthly journal *Feuer*, Vol. I, Nos.
9-12 (1920); also publ. separately (1921).—A. E.

STEPHANI, Hermann. Ger. writer on music,
compr. *b.* Grimma, Saxony, 23 June, 1877.
Stud. jurisprudence; turned to music, private
pupil of Ad. Hempel, Munich; then of Leipzig Cons. (Jadassohn, Reinecke, Homeyer,
Reckendorff); took Ph.D. Munich, 1902 (dissertation, *The Sublime, particularly in Music,
and the Problem of Form in the musically Beautiful and Sublime*, new ed. 1907). In 1903, establ.
Oratorio Soc. at Sonderburg; condr. of Teachers'
Singing and Orch. Soc., Flensburg, 1905; orgt.
of St. Andrew's Ch.; condr. of Town Choral
Union and Bach Soc. Eisleben, 1906; 1913-14,
condr. of Philh. Choral Soc. Leipzig; 1921,
mus. condr. of Marburg Univ. Publ. compns.,
choruses, songs, etc.; since 1905 he has been
endeavouring to limit mus. notation to the
treble G clef as the only clef, by using octave-
signs; as example of which he publ. the Overture to Schumann's *Manfred*, in *Einheitspartitur* (unit-score) (*q.v.*), 1905,—A. E.

STEPHEN, David. Scottish compr. and
teacher; *b.* Dundee. The most representative
Scottish musician of first decades of xx century.
His work has been accomplished entirely in his
own country and his creative spirit is really
Scottish. He began as assistant-teacher of music
in Dundee schools; held various posts as orgt.;
cond. Arbroath and Dundee Choral Unions;
gave many organ recitals. When in 1905 the
Carnegie Trust of Scotland instituted their Music
School in Dunfermline, S. was appointed its dir.
and still holds the post. He is a prolific compr.:
Mass; cantatas; chamber-music; part-songs,
etc.—W. S.

STERNBERG, Constantine Ivanovitch von.
Amer. compr. pianist; *b.* Petrograd, 9 July,
1852. Stud. 1865-7 Leipzig Cons. under
Moscheles, Reinecke, Brendel, Richter. 1867,
condr. Brühl Theatre, assistant chorus-master,
Stadttheater, Leipzig; subsequently condr. in
Ger. opera houses; 1872-4, resumed studies as
a pupil of Kullak and Dorn in Berlin and, for a
short time, of Liszt. 1875, Court-pianist and
dir. of music-school at Mecklenburg-Schwerin;
1877, dir. of Coll. of Music, Atlanta, Ga., U.S.A.;
1885, toured Germany, Russia, Asia Minor,
Central Asia and U.S.A. In 1890, establ. own
Cons. in Philadelphia.

Trios, pf. and str.: No. I, op. 69 (Junne, 1895):
No. II, op. 79 (Leuckart, 1898); No. III, op. 104 (*id.*
1912); *Aus Italien*, op. 105 (*id.* 1912). Pf. pieces
(Dieckmann; Hainauer; Rohlfing; Schuberth:
Simon; Ditson; Pond; Schirmer). Author of
Ethics and Esthetics of Piano-Playing (Schirmer,
1917); *Tempo Rubato, and Other Essays* (*id.* 1920);
ed. *Modern Russian Piano Music*, 2 vols. (Ditson,
1915).—J. M.

STEWART, Humphrey John. Amer. compr.
b. London, 22 May, 1856. Received his mus.
instruction there. Orgt. in San Francisco from
1886 to 1901; later at Trinity Ch. Boston; St.
Dominic's, San Francisco; 1915-6, official orgt.
Panama-California Exposition, San Diego, Cal.,
where under favourable climatic conditions the
experiment was made of giving open-air organ
recitals. Appointed permanently to this position in 1917 and has since given a long series of
recitals with an unusually large repertoire. Has
written romantic opera *Bluff King Hal* (J.
Fischer), 2 comic operas (produced San Francisco), *His Majesty* (1890) and *The Conspirators*
(1900). For Bohemian Club of San Francisco,
wrote music for open-air perf. in famous Red-
wood Groves: *Montezuma* (1903), *The Crema-
tion of Care* (1906) and *Gold* (1916).—O. K.

STEWART, Robert Prescot. Irish compr.
condr. *b.* Dublin, 16 Dec. 1825; *d.* there, 24
March, 1894. Son of librarian to King's Inns,
Dublin. Appointed orgt. (1844) of Christ Church
Cath. and Trinity Coll., Dublin; 1846, condr.
of Trinity Coll. Choral Soc. Vicar-choral at St.
Patrick's Cath. in 1852; in 1861, prof. of music,
Trinity Coll.; also prof. of theory at R. Irish Acad.
of Music; his boundless energy and enthusiasm
did much to raise mus. standard there. For the
Cork 1852 Exhibition he wrote a special ode; at
1870 Birmingham Fest. his *Ode on Shakespeare*
was given. In 1876, ed. *Irish Church Hymnal*.
Few musicians of xix century in Ireland were of
such commanding personality. In Trinity Coll.
it was his influence that raised the value of
the mus. degrees, and imposed a literary test.
Knighted in 1872; Mus.Doc. 1851.
 Consult biography by O. J. Vignoles (1898) and
J. C. Culwick's *Works of R. P. S.* (Dublin, 1902).
—W. ST.

STNIBER, Paul. Ger.-Czechoslovak compr.
b. Nepomuk, 1887. Stud. in Leipzig, and worked
in Germany as condr. at several theatres; now
condr. of Ger. Choral Soc. in Prague.
 Str. 4tet, A ma.; vn. and pf. sonata, F ma.; songs
with orchestra.—E. S.

STOCK, Frederick August. Amer. condr.
compr. *b.* Jülich, Germany, 11 Nov. 1872. Son
of a bandmaster from whom he received his
early training; 1886-90, attended Cologne Cons.;
vn. under Japha, and compn. under H. Zoellner,
Humperdinck, F. Wüllner; 1891-5, member of
municipal orch. Cologne; 1896, went to America
as 1st vla. in Thomas Orch., Chicago; 1901-5
was Thomas' assistant. When Thomas died in
1905, S. was chosen as successor. His methods
of systematic training and conscientious drill
have maintained the orch. (now known as
Chicago Symphony Orch.) on the high plane of
excellence to which Thomas raised it. S. has
comp. works for orch. (2 symphonies; varia-

tions; symph. poem, *Life*; 3 overtures); a vn. concerto; chamber-music for str. (4tet, 5tet, 6tet); songs, vn. and piano pieces. His 1st symphony (written 1906–8) was 1st perf. by Chicago Orch. 31 Dec. 1909. On 3 June, 1915, at Litchfield County Choral Union Fest. in Norfolk, Conn., Zimbalist played S.'s vn. concerto written for this festival. His work, *Psalmodic Rhapsody*, for solo, chorus and orch., was perf. at North Shore Music Fest., Evanston., Ill., 1921. 1915, Mus.D. *h.c.* from North Western Univ.; 1918, member of National Inst. of Arts and Letters.

Str. 4tet, op. 6 (Rahter, 1910); symph. variations, orch. and organ, op. 7 (*id.* 1910); symphony, op. 18 (Breitkopf, 1912).—O. K.

STOCKHAUSEN, Franz. Ger. choral condr. *b.* Gebweiler, 30 Jan. 1839. Brother of Julius Stockhausen; pupil of Alkan, Paris; 1860–2, of Leipzig Cons. (Moscheles, Richter, Hauptmann); 1863–6, chief condr. at Thann, Alsace; 1866–8 at Hamburg (with brother); 1868, condr. of Société de Chant Sacré and of Strasburg Cath.; 1871, dir. Strasburg Cons. and Town Concerts; 1879, gave up direction of Church Choral Soc.; 1892, R. prof.; 1907, retired from public life.—A. E.

STOCKHAUSEN, Julius. Singer and teacher of singing; *b.* Paris, 22 July, 1826; *d.* Frankfort-o-M., 22 Sept. 1906. Son of harp virtuoso Franz St.; pupil of Paris Cons. and of Manuel Garcia, London; 1862–7, cond. Philh. Concerts and Singakademie, Hamburg; 1869–70, Kammersänger, Stuttgart; 1874, dir. Stern Choral Union, Berlin; 1878–9, singing-master at Hoch's Cons. Frankfort-o-M.; then dir. of own school of singing there. Publ. *Method of teaching Singing* (2 vols. 1886–7; Eng. Novello). St. was one of the first interpreters of Brahms' songs.—A. E.

STOCKMAN, David G. Swedish t. operatic singer; *b.* Gothenburg, 30 Nov. 1879. Stud. under H. Hoffmann in Breslau; *début* R. Opera, Stockholm (1906–7), as Wilhelm Meister (*Mignon*) Lionel (*Marthe*) and Fernando (*La Favorita*); then engaged regularly. S. has a very clear, high lyric t. voice, much intelligence and a large repertoire: Romeo, Faust, Raoul, Lohengrin, Walther, Tristan, Parsifal, Tamino, Fra Diavolo, Alfredo (*La Traviata*). He created in Stockholm the parts of Marouf, André Chénier, Herman (*Pique-Dame*) and Gennaro (*Jewels of the Madonna*).—P. V.

STOCKMARR, Johanne. Pianist to Danish Court; *b.* Copenhagen, 21 April, 1869. Comes of well-known Danish mus. family; pupil of Edvard Helsted and R. Cons. of Music, Copenhagen. Later stud. under Fissot (Paris), and Fr. Neruda (Copenhagen). *Début* 1889, at chamber-music concert given by R. Danish Chapel, Copenhagen; at once secured a position amongst the foremost pianists by her great technical ability and beauty and purity of style. Has played often in England (with Lady Hallé, London, 1900; also the Monday Popular Concerts, London). Subsequently numerous concerts in London as

recitalist and as soloist under Edvard Grieg, Henry J. Wood and Hans Richter in London, Manchester and the provinces. She has been decorated with the Danish *Ingenio et Arti*, the Mecklenburg Gold Medal of Merit, etc.—A. H.

STOESSEL, Albert Frederic. Amer. violinist, condr. *b.* St. Louis, Mo., U.S.A., 11 Oct. 1894. Stud. vn. under Willy Hess and Emanuel Wirth at Hochschule, Berlin. Afterwards member of Willy Hess Str. Quartet. First appeared in America, 19 Nov. 1915, with St. Louis Symphony Orch. During European war was teacher of conducting at Amer. Expeditionary Force Bandmasters' and Musicians' School, Chaumont, France. Since 1921, condr. of Oratorio Soc. New York. Head of mus. dept. New York Univ. in 1923. *Officier de l'Académie.*

Sonata in G, vn. and pf. (Boston Music Co. 1921); *Hispania*, suite for pf. (C. Fischer, 1922); pieces for vn. (C. Fischer; Boston Music Co.). Unpubl.: str. 4tet, D ma. (perf. Berlin, 18 May, 1914); str. 5tet, C mi. (perf. Boston Music Co.). Author of *The Technic of the Bâton* (C. Fischer, 1920).—J. M.

STÖHR, Richard. Austrian compr. *b.* Vienna, 11 June, 1874. Graduated Doctor of Medicine in 1898. Then followed a mus. career. Stud. under Robert Fuchs. Assistant-teacher (1901), prof. (1904) at Cons. (now Acad. of Music) for harmony and compn. Many pf. works; chamber-music, songs; symph. choruses; fairy-operas and instruction-books. Belongs to the old classical school.—H. B.

STOJOWSKY, Sigismund Denis Antoine. Polish pianist; *b.* Strzelce, 14 May, 1870. Stud. pf. under Żeleński in Cracow. 1887–9 at Paris Cons. under Diémer (pf.) and Dubois and Delibes (compn.). Later a pupil of Paderewski; 1891, gave concert of own compns. with Colonne Orch. in Paris, producing pf. concerto in F sharp mi. and Ballade for orch. Thereafter lived chiefly in Paris; recitals in France, Belgium, England and Poland; 1905, went to New York where, until 1911, was head of pf. department of Inst. of Mus. Art; 1911–17, taught at Von Ende School. 1913, an extended tour in Europe, performing his own works (playing his 2nd pf. concerto under Nikisch in London).

Suite in E flat, orch. op. 9 (Stanley Lucas, 1893); symphony in D mi. op. 21 (Peters, 1901); 1st pf. concerto, F sharp, op. 3 (S. Lucas, 1893); *Rapsodie Symphonique*, pf. and orch. op. 23 (Peters, 1907); Prologue, Scherzo and Variations, pf. and orch. op. 32 (2nd pf. concerto) (Heugel, 1914); vn. concerto in G, op. 22 (Schmidt, 1908); Variations and fugue, str. 4tet, op. 6 (Lucas, 1891); vn. sonata in G, op. 13 (*id.* 1894); 2nd vn. sonata in E, op. 37 (Heugel, 1912); cello sonata, op. 18 (Schott, 1898); *Le Printemps* (after Horace), chorus and orch. op. 7 (full score, Lucas, 1895; vocal score [Eng.], Novello, 1905); *Prayer for Poland*, chorus and orch. op. 40 (Schirmer, 1916); *Euphonies*, 6 songs, op. 33 (*id.* 1921). Many pf. pieces (Heugel; Peters; Lucas; Schmidt).—O. K.

STOKOWSKI, Leopold Anton Stanisław. Condr. *b.* London, 18 April, 1882, of Polish parentage. Stud. vn., pf. and organ in England, France and Germany. From 1905–8, orgt. St. Bartholomew's, New York. Condr. of Cincinnati (O.) Orch. 1909-12. Since 1912, condr. of Philadelphia Orch., introducing many new works: Mahler's 8th symphony and *Das Lied von der Erde*, Rabaud's 2nd symphony, Schönberg's

Kammersinfonie and *Fünf Orchesterstücke*, etc. His own *Dithyrambe*, for fl. cello, harp, was played in Philadelphia, 15 Nov. 1917. Married pianist Olga Samarof in 1911. Mus.Bac. Oxon.; Mus. Doc. *h.c.* Univ. of Pennsylvania 1917; F.R.C.M. *h.c.* 1924.—J. M.

STORCHIO, Rosina. Ital. s. singer; *b.* Mantua, 19 May, 1876. One of most esteemed living Ital. lyric sopranos. Pupil of Cons. of Milan. *Début* in Milan at the Dal Verme Theatre in *Carmen*. Has sung at the principal theatres in Italy and America (for 10 seasons at La Scala). Repertoire is very extensive, ranging from *Sonnambula* to *La Traviata*, *Mignon* and *Don Giovanni*.—D. A.

STORM, Katinka. Norwegian operatic and concert-singer (m.-sopr.); *b.* Nes, Upper Romerike, 18 Nov. 1887. Pupil of W. Kloed and Ellen Gulbranson, Christiania. Stud. in winter 1913–14 under C. Kittel, Bayreuth; afterwards under Wilhelm Herold, Copenhagen. *Début* on stage at Bayreuth Fest., summer of 1914 (Ortlinde in *Valkyrie*); first concert, autumn of 1914 in Christiania. Has sung several Wagnerian parts at Stuttgart Opera House, *Carmen* in National Theatre, Christiania; was engaged at Opéra-Comique in that city, 1918–20. Best rôles: Recha (*The Jewess*), Venus (*Tannhäuser*), and *Fidelio*. Married in 1920 Arthur Squire Foxall. Lives at Hartlepool, England.—U. M.

STORM, Nanne. Norwegian pianist; *b.* Horten, 31 Aug. 1873. Pupil of Copenhagen Cons.; of Agathe Backer-Gröndahl, Christiania; of Busoni, Berlin; of Delaborde, Paris. *Début-concert* in Christiania, 1900. Concerts in Norwegian cities, in Paris, London, Copenhagen and Stockholm. A zealous worker for improvement of position of Norwegian music-teachers.—U. M.

STORTI, Riccardo. Ital. compr. *b.* Warsaw (Poland), 26 Jan. 1873. Pupil of Milan Cons.; teacher of compn. in Rome at Istituto Nazionale di Musica. Compr. of operas, *Venezia* (Palermo, 1907); *Sobeys*; and *Leonardo* (not yet perf.); much symph. and chamber-music.—D. A.

STRACCIARI, Riccardo. Italian baritone; *b.* Bologna in 1875. One of best-known living Ital. baritones. Stud. at Liceo at Bologna. Has sung at all principal theatres of the world, and has a very extensive repertoire. Created the barit. part in *Il Segreto di Susanna* (Wolf-Ferrari).—D. A.

STRADAL, August. Ger.-Czechoslovak pianist and compr. *b.* Teplitz, 1860. Pupil of Bruckner and Liszt; teacher; resides at Schönlinde (North Bohemia).

Pf. arr. of Liszt's orch. works, and clavier music of Bach, Handel, Buxtehude, Frescobaldi, etc. Songs; pf. pieces. Biography of Liszt (in preparation).—E. S.

STRAESSER, Ewald. Ger. compr. *b.* Burscheid, 27 June, 1867. Pupil of Wüllner, Cologne Cons.; teacher of cpt. at Inst.; 1918, R. prof.; 1921, teacher at Cologne Univ.; 1921, teacher of compn. at Stuttgart Acad. As compr. he belongs to the Brahms school.

Str. 4tets (op. 12 [I, II], 15, 42); pf. 5tet, F sharp mi. op. 18; clar. 5tet, G ma. op. 34; symph. fantasy

(1892); vn. concerto, D ma. op. 36; symphonies (G ma. op. 22; D mi. op. 27; A ma.; G ma. op. 46); orch. suite, *Spring*, op. 28; pf. suite, D ma. op. 23; · *Rhapsody*, op. 21; pf. and vn. sonata, op. 32; pf. trio, D ma.; works for pf. and for str. instrs.; female choruses op. 24; songs op 13*b*, 20, etc.—A. E.

STRANGWAYS.—See FOX-STRANGWAYS.

STRANSKY, Josef. Condr. *b.* Humpoléč, Bohemia, 9 Sept. 1872. Stud. medicine at Univs. of Prague, Vienna and Leipzig. Pursued music contemporaneously under Fibich and Dvořák in Prague, Jadassohn in Leipzig, Fuchs and Bruckner in Vienna. Qualified in medicine, 1896; but thereafter devoted himself wholly to music; 1898, condr. in Angelo Neumann's Ger. opera in Prague; 1900, went to Stadttheater, Hamburg; 1909, cond. concerts of Blüthner Orch. in Berlin; 1910–11, of Verein der Musikfreunde, Dresden. 1911, called to succeed Mahler as condr. of New York Philh. Soc. Resigned 1923 and became condr. of State Symphony Orch. in New York.

2 *Symph. Songs* for medium voice and full orch. (Simrock, 1913); songs (Simrock, 1896; Harmonieverlag, 1908).—O. K.

STRAUBE, Karl. Ger. orgt. and condr. *b.* Berlin, 6 Jan. 1873. Pupil of Heinrich Reimann (organ), Ph. Rüfer and Albert Becker; 1894, appeared as organ-virtuoso; 1897, orgt. at St. Willibrord's Cath. Wesel; 1902, orgt. St. Thomas' Ch. Leipzig; 1903, dir. of Bach Soc. Leipzig; 1904, cond. 2nd Ger. Bach Fest.; 1908, Leipzig Bach Fest. as well as later Bach Fests. (1911, 1914, 1920); 1907, organ-teacher at Cons.; 1908, R. Saxonian prof.; 1918, Precentor of St. Thomas' School; 1919, brought about union of Gewandhaus Choir and Bach Soc. One of first to produce Max Reger's organ works.

Publ. (all by Peters): New ed. of Liszt's organ works (arr. by Straube); *Old Organ Masters* (1904); 45 *Choral Preludes of the Old Masters* (1907); Bach's *Magnificat* (1909); Handel's *Dettingen Te Deum* (1913); new ed. of Bach's organ works (only partly publ.). Consult G. Robert-Tornow, *Max Reger and K. Str.* (1907).—A. E.

STRAUS, Oscar. Austrian compr. *b.* Vienna, 6 April, 1870. Pupil of Grädener (Vienna) and Max Bruch (Berlin); condr. of many provincial theatres from 1895 to 1900. Chief condr. and compr. at the cabaret *Überbrettl* (*q.v.*), founded by E v. Wolzogen, whose members included the famous poets, Frank Wedekind and O. J. Bierbaum. For their stage-pieces, St. wrote many musical numbers. Formerly a serious compr. (orch. works) he turned to light compn., and is now one of the most widely known operetta-composers. His style is different from that of Lehár and Fall. He began with satirical stories in the Offenbach manner, where he makes fun of the classical music-tragedies; then he wrote some Viennese waltz operettas; now he makes much use of the modern dances (shimmy, fox-trot). His work is pleasing and artistic.

Serious works: Overture to Grillparzer's *Der Traum ein Leben* (orch.); *Serenade* (str. orch.); vn. sonata, op. 33 (A mi.). Comic operas: *Der Schwarze Mann* (*The Black Man*), 1903; *Die galante Markgräfin* (1919). Serious opera, *Colombine*, perf. Berlin, 1904. Operettas (publ. Doblinger, Vienna): *Die lustigen Nibelungen*, parody (Berlin, 1905); *Hugdietrichs Brautfahrt* (Vienna, 1906); *Ein Walzertraum* (*A Waltz Dream*), his best work (1907); *Der tapfere Soldat* (Vienna, 1908); *Rund um die Liebe* (1914).

Modern: *Liebeszauber* (Berlin, 1916); *Der letzte Waltzer* (Vienna, 1920; as *The Last Waltz*, London, 1922–3); *Nixchen* (Berlin, 1921), and many others. Ballet, *Die Prinzessin von Tragant* (1912).—P. P.

STRAUSS, Edmund von. Ger.-Czechoslovak musician; *b.* Olmütz, 1869. Musician in orch. of Royal Opera, Berlin.—E. S.

STRAUSS, Eduard. Austrian composer; *b.* Vienna, 15 March 1835; *d.* there 28 Dec. 1916. Son of Johann Strauss, sen. Stud. under Sechter (theory) and Parish-Alvars (harp). Began as condr. 1859 at a triple ball, where 3 bands played, each conducted by a Strauss. Until 1870 cond. the orch. together with his brother Josef, after whose death he carried on alone; but dissolved the famous *Strauss-Kapelle* in 1901, and in 1906 burned the valuable orch. material, containing the special arrs. of the Strauss family written for their own band—an immeasurable loss to the historian of dance-music in xix century Vienna. Eduard was the least talented of the family, and with him the tradition ended.—EG. W.

STRAUSS, Johann, jun. Austrian compr. *b.* Vienna, 25 Oct. 1825; *d.* Vienna, 3 June, 1899. Son of Johann Strauss, sen., who created (with Josef Lanner) modern Viennese dance-music. Johann Strauss, jun., with his brothers Josef and Eduard, continued this tradition and made the Viennese waltz world-famous. On his father's death (1849) he took charge of his orch. and visited Berlin, London, Paris, America, conducting his own works. Stimulated by Offenbach, he comp. an operetta in 1871 (*Indigo*; 1st perf. 10 Feb. 1871, Vienna, Theater an der Wien; new libretto, 1901, under the name *Thousand and One Nights*). It failed on account of its poor book. *Fledermaus* (1874; revised as *La Tsigane*, Paris, 1877) succeeded. 1876, went to America. Perf. *Donauwellen Valse* in Boston with chorus of 20,000 singers. Next great operetta success, *Der Zigeunerbaron* (1885; libretto by Schnitzer). In 1892, *Ritter Pasman*, an opera which failed on account of its book. *Fürstin Ninetta* (1893), *Jabuka* (1894), *Waldmeister* (1895) *Die Göttin der Vernunft* (1897) had little success, though the dances from them became popular.

479 waltzes, polkas and quadrilles. Op. 1 was *Sinngedichte Valse* (1844); the most famous are: *Windsor-Klänge*, op. 104 (dedicated to Queen Victoria, 1851); *An der schönen blauen Donau* (Blue Danube), op. 314 (1867); *Wein, Weib, und Gesang*, op. 333 (1869); *Frühlingsstimmen*, op. 410 (1881); *Klänge aus der Raimundzeit*, op. 479 (1898). Consult biographies by Eisenberg (Leipzig, 1894), Procházka (1900), E. Decsey (Stuttgart, 1922).—EG. W.

STRAUSS, Josef. Austrian compr. *b.* Vienna, 22 Aug. 1827; *d.* there, 21 July, 1870. Brother of Johann Strauss, jun. Started as an engineer, but left that calling for music. His first waltz, 1853. From 1863, cond. his brother's band during the latter's absences from Vienna. As a compr. he is not inferior to Johann, only his waltzes are more sentimental and romantic. An operetta, *Frühlingsluft*, with music arr. from his tunes, was produced in Vienna, 1905.—EG. W.

STRAUSS, Richard. German composer; *b.* Munich, 11 June, 1864. Son of Franz Strauss

(*b.* 26 Feb. 1822; *d.* 31 May, 1905), Royal Kammermusikus (horn-player) in Munich Court Orchestra. Pupil of Benno Walter (violin), Court Kapellmeister F. W. Meyer in Munich. In 1885, Hans von Bülow brought him as Court music director to Meiningen, where Alexander Ritter won him over to the ideals of the "Music of the Future." When Bülow left (end of 1885), Strauss himself took over the orchestra; but 1886, he was called to Munich as 3rd Kapellmeister (Hofmusikdirektor), going, 1889, to Weimar as Court conductor (along with Lassen). 1894, went as Court conductor to Munich, and in the same capacity to Berlin in the autumn of 1898, becoming, 1908, general music director, and, 1917–20, director of an academic advanced school of composition at the Royal High School for Music. 1919, was called to Vienna as director of the State Opera. In 1894, Strauss married the s. singer Pauline de Ahna, who created the rôle of Freihild in *Guntram*. Richard Strauss is, in a certain objective sense, the most representative composer of latter times. He is one of the most natural and fertile musicians that ever lived—an artist who discovered for music quite new artistic means, and whose far-renowned and eminent skill in instrumentation is simply the natural expression for his polymelodic, harmonic, rhythmic ventures. Above all, Strauss has raised the art of thematic development to the very highest virtuosity, without ever in principle forsaking the basis of tonality, or rational principles generally. Strauss's limitations lie in the sphere of the psychological. He is in the finest and highest sense of the word a composer depending on externals. His development passed from a classical beginning (Mendelssohn, Brahms) to a neo-Wagnerian style (*Guntram*), while in his programme-music he raised the Berlioz-Liszt to still further heights. In opera Strauss proceeds from the orchestral opera (*Feuersnot*, *Salome*, *Elektra*) *via* musical comedy to his fairy-opera, *The Woman without a Shadow*. His best works are those in which intellect and wit, rather than pure sentiment, are pre-eminent, as in the symphonic poem *Till Eulenspiegel*, sparkling with wit; and in the field of opera, the fine, artistic musical parody *Ariadne in Naxos*.

(Univ. Ed. unless otherwise indicated.) Fest. March, E flat ma. op. 1; str. 4tet, A flat ma. op. 2; D mi. symphony (ms.); 5 pf. pieces, op. 3; pf. sonata, op. 5 (B ml.); *Stimmungsbilder* for pf. op. 9; fugue, A mi. for pf. (without op.); *Burlesque*, D mi. for pf. and orch. (without op. 1886): cello sonata, F ma. op. 8; horn concerto, op. 11; *Wanderers Sturmlied*, op. 14 (for 6-v. mixed chorus with orch.); *Taillefer*, soli, chorus and orch. (1903); pf. 4tet, op. 13; overture, C mi. op. 4, orch.

Symph. poems: *Don Juan*, op. 20 (1889); *Death and Transfiguration*, op. 23 (1890); *Macbeth*, op. 24 (1891); *Till Eulenspiegel*, op. 28 (1895); *Thus spake Zarathustra*, op. 30 (1896); *Don Quixote*, op. 35 1898); *Ein Heldenleben*, op. 40 (1899; 1st perf. in England, Queen's Hall Symph. Concert, 6 Dec. 1902, under compr.); symphony, F mi. op. 12; programme-symphony in 4 movements, *Aus Italien*, op. 16; *Sinfonia Domestica*, F ma. op. 53 (1904); and *Alpine Symphony*, op. 64 (1915; 1st perf. in England, 1923).

Operas: *Guntram*, op. 25 (Weimar, 1894); *Feuersnot*, op. 50 (Dresden, 1901); *Salome*, op. 54 (1-act, Dresden, 1909; text by Oscar Wilde); *Elektra*, op. 58

(Dresden, 1909; text after Sophocles by Hugo von Hofmannsthal, who thenceforward collaborated with Strauss as librettist); *The Rosenkavalier*, op. 59 (Dresden, 1911); *Ariadne in Naxos* (Interlude to Molière's *Bourgeois Gentilhomme*), op. 60 (Stuttgart, 1912; re-arr. 1917, Dresden); *Joseph Legend*, op. 63 (pantomime, Paris, 1914; 1st Ger. perf. Berlin, 1921); *The Woman without a Shadow*, op. 65 (Vienna, 1919); comic play-opera, *Intermezzo* (text by Strauss); ballet-pantom. *Schlagobers* (*Whipped Cream*; Vienna, 1924). 2 songs for 16-part mixed chorus unacc. (op. 34); 2 military marches, op. 57 (Peters); *Festival Prelude* for orch. op. 61; *German Motets*, op. 62; songs, op. 10, 15, 17, 19, 21, 26, 27, 32, 36, 37, 67, 68, 69, 71, *Der Krämerspiegel* (1921 publ.). Str. also ed. Gluck's *Iphigenia in Tauris*, and co-ed. with H. Rüdel 2 vols. of his father's posthumous works (Studies for horn, Leipzig, Eulenburg). A complete catalogue of the works of Str. has been publ. by R. Specht (1911), the author of the most comprehensive appreciation of Str.—*R. Str. and his Work* (2 vols., Vienna, 1920, E. P. Tal). Consult: A. Seidl and W. Klatte, *R. Str.* (1896); G. Brecher, *R. Str.* (1900); E. Urban, *Str. contra Wagner* (1902); Max Steinitzer, *R. Str.* (4 eds. 1911), and *R. Str. and his Time* (Leipzig, 1914); O. Bie, *Modern Music and R. Str.* (1906 and 1916); Eugen Schmitz, *R. Str. as Music-Dramatist* (1907); H. W. von Waltershausen, *R. Str.* (Munich, 1921); E. Newman, *R. Str.* (London, 1908), and his *Musical Studies* (London, J. Lane).—A. E.

STRAVINSKY, Igor Fedorovitch (*accent 2nd syll.*). Russian composer; *b.* Oranienbaum, 5/17 June, 1882. Son of a bass singer in the Imperial Opera, Petrograd. Studied composition as a private pupil of Rimsky-Korsakof. His first work, a symphony (1906), was followed by a *Fantastic Scherzo*, the tone-picture *Fireworks*, and a *Dirge in Memory of Rimsky-Korsakof*, all three for orchestra (1908). In 1910 his first ballet, *The Fire-Bird*, was successfully produced at Paris by Diaghilef's Russian company; *Petrushka* (1912), the opera *The Nightingale* (1912), and *The Rite of Spring* (1913) followed, the last-named giving rise, by its extraordinary novelty, to enthusiastic praises and vehement protests. (In 1915–16 he visited America.) Similar has been the fate of all Stravinsky's later works, among which should be named, especially, *Renard* (1915), *L'Histoire du Soldat* (1917) the *Symphonies d'Instruments à Vent à la mémoire de Claude Debussy* (1920), *Mavra* (1921) and *Noces* (1923). It is difficult to describe here Stravinsky's evolution, and to give even the substance of the debate which is still raging around his works from *The Rite of Spring* onwards. In the early music, in *The Fire-Bird*, in *Petrushka*, his fundamental originality rests content with means of expression in which there is nothing which can be described as incompatible with the traditions of Russian music as exemplified in the works of Rimsky-Korsakof, Borodin, and Mussorgsky; therefore, nothing which calls for particular argument. Even in *The Rite of Spring*, despite certain peculiarities of structure, of idiom, and of colour, there is nothing to render a revision of the current standards—or more simply, customs—imperative (*e.g.* compare this work with the *finale* of Borodin's second symphony). But it is precisely for a revision of this kind that the enthusiastic partisans of his later manner call, explaining, for instance, that " unity between metres which have no common measure resides in a certain rhythmical unit which remains understood," or that when his music is no longer tonal, nor modal, " different harmonies

occurring simultaneously are made clear by an element of contact which is endowed with all the virtues of a tonic, fulfilling the function of a pole from which the harmonies radiate " (E. Ansermet in *Revue Musicale*, July 1921). Problems of this or similar order arise from the study of other contemporary composers such as Schönberg, Bartók, etc. There is no doubt that Stravinsky has undergone Schönberg's influence, but only in a very general manner. His recent innovations are described by certain writers as extremely pregnant; by others (*e.g.* Ernest Newman, *Musical Times*, Nov. 1920, and in various other articles) as transparent and devoid of further significance.

Besides the aforementioned works, Stravinsky has written:

Pulcinella (ballet with v.-part); symphony, E flat (1906, ms.); pieces for str. 4tet (1915); *Concertino* for str. 4tet (1920); *Astral Cantata* (1911); *The Shepherdess*, suite, pf. and v.; 3 Japanese songs for v. piccolo, fl. clar. str. pf.; *Rag-Time* for 11 instrs.; *Les Noces villageoises*, *divertimento* for soli, chorus, orch.; a 1-act comic opera *Mavra* (on a novel of Pushkin); 8tet for wind instrs. (Paris, Oct. 1923); pf. concerto (Paris, May 1924), etc.—M. D. C.

STREICHER, Theodor. Austrian compr. *b.* Vienna, 7 June, 1874, of an old family of musicians. An ancestor of his helped Schiller to fly from the Karlsschule after having written his play *Die Räuber*, and afterwards founded a pf. factory at Vienna. He stud. acting at first; then singing; did not begin his theoretical education till 1896, at Dresden, and afterwards at Vienna. In the beginning of a new mus. era in Vienna (about 1900) he attracted attention by his songs and choruses, which have a personal character and show a rich but uncultivated talent. They lack technique. All publ. by Breitkopf.—Eg. W.

STRIEGLER, Kurt. Ger. compr. *b.* Dresden, 7 Jan. 1886. The son of a Court musician of Dresden Opera; at 8, choir-boy at Catholic Court Church Inst.; then stud. at Dresden Cons. (under Draeseke, Urbach, Kutzschbach); orch. condr. and teacher of conducting at High School; succeeded Draeseke as dir. of theatrical dept. and master of compn. classes. Began career as condr. under Schuch; 1912, condr. of Dresden Opera; for 5 years also condr. of Dresden People's Singakademie.

Symphonies: A mi. op. 12; B mi. op. 16; C sharp mi. op. 44; chamber-symphony, op. 14; vn. concerto, op. 15; *Rondo capriccio*, vn. and orch. op. 40; *Symph. Prelude*, full orch. op. 30; *Scherzo* for 6 solo tpi. with orch. op. 34; symphony, G mi. organ, op 31; pf. and vn. sonata, E mi. op. 5; Theme and variations, A mi. for pf. and vn. op. 13; pf. 5tet, op. 28; str. 4tet, op. 38; sonata, pf. and fl. op. 47; many songs and ballads; choral works; pf. pieces; fairy-tales *Snow-white*, *Mother Goose*, op. 20; music to Hebbel's *Herod and Mariamne*; operas: *The Cantor of St. Thomas*; *Hand and Heart* (after Anzengruber).—A. E.

STRIFFLING, Louis. Fr. musicologist; *b.* Dijon, 1886; *d.* 1915. Promised to become one of best historians of music in young Fr. school. *Quelques musiciens français* : *Rameau, Berlioz, Franck* (1910); *Esquisse d'une histoire du goût musical en France au dix-huitième siècle* (1912); *Musique et musiciens de France* (posthumous, 1921).—A. C.

STRING QUARTET (Players). See CHAMBER-MUSIC PLAYERS.

STROBILION. See SCRIPTURE, EDWARD W.

STRUVE, Carl. Norwegian t. singer; *b.* Fredrikshald, 12 April, 1887. Pupil of Wilhelm Kloed, Christiania. *Début* in that city in 1908. Scholarships from State and from Henrichsen's Bequest. Stud. in 1911 under F. H. von Dülong in Berlin; in 1914 under von Zur Mühlen in London; afterwards under N. Bratt in Stockholm. For several years attached to National Theatre in Christiania as one of its leading vocalists. Principal rôles: Faust; Don José (*Carmen*); Wilhelm Meister (*Mignon*), and the leading parts in *Rigoletto, Tosca, Madame Butterfly, Lakmé*, etc. Has appeared with success in R. Opera House in Stockholm, as well as in Bergen, Stavanger and Trondhjem. His voice is a lyric t. of considerable power and brilliancy.—R. M.

STRÜVER, Paul. Ger. compr. *b.* Hamburg, 12 Feb. 1896. Pupil of R. High School (under Juon), and Univ. of Berlin; 1915-17, military service; later, pupil of W. Courvoisier for compn. and Hugo Röhr for conducting, in Munich.

Songs; pf. sonata (1919); str. 4tet, E flat, op. 25 (Weimar Mus. Fest. 1920); 1-act opera, *Diana's Wedding* (text by O. Spengler).—A. E.

STUART, Elsa Marianne. Swedish musicologist; *b.* Stockholm, 26 April, 1889. B.A. 1909; stud. history of arts at Stockholm Coll.; history of music at R. Cons.; pf. under Lundberg and K. Strömberg. Musical critic on *Dagligt Allehanda*, etc. Publ. in Swedish, monographs on J. S. Bach (1922) and K. Atterberg (1924).—P. V.

STUMPF, Carl. Ger. music-investigator and psychologist; *b.* Wiesentheid in Unterfranken, 21 April, 1848. Stud. at Würzburg and Göttingen; 1870, private tutor of philosophy; prof. at Würzburg, 1873; at Prague 1879; at Halleo-S. 1884; at Munich 1889; in Berlin from 1893 till present day.

Psychology of Sound (2 vols. 1883, 1896); *The Pseudo-Aristotelian Problems* (1897); *History of the Idea of Consonance in Antiquity* (1897); contributions to *Acoustics and Science of Music*, 1898, *et seq.* (Vol. VI, *Consonance and Concordance*; VIII, *New Researches in Acoustics*); *The Beginnings of Music* (Leipzig, 1911). Shorter studies include those in collab. with E. M. v. Hornbostel (*Extracts for Comparative Science of Music* (Munich, Drei Masken Verlag, 1921).—A. E.

STYHR, Magnhild. Norwegian pianist; *b.* Kristiansand. Made her *début* at Christiania, 1915. Has since given numerous concerts throughout country. Is specially interested in modern French music.—R. M.

SUCHER, Joseph. Condr. *b.* Döbör, Hungary, 23 Nov. 1843; *d.* Berlin, 4 April, 1908. Originally stud. law (Vienna), but changed to music; Korrepetitor of Court Opera, Vienna and dir. of Acad. Choral Soc.; later condr. of Comic Opera; 1876, went to Leipzig Stadttheater as condr.; married Rosa Hasselbeck (really Haslbeck; *b.* Velburg in Oberpfalz, 23 Feb. 1849), and was engaged with her for Hamburg in 1878. In 1888, engaged as chief. condr. Berlin, and Frau Sucher as *prima-donna*; retired in 1899. Both were excellent interpreters of Wagner. Frau Sucher wrote her reminiscences in 1914. Since 1909 she had taught singing in Vienna.—A. E.

SUCHÝ, Štěpán. Czech violinist; *b.* Arad, 1872; *d.* Prague, 1920. Took private lessons and was member of several orchs. (including one at Kimberley in 1892). In 1893 joined Prague Cons. under Prof. Ševčík, being the best teacher of all his pupils. Prof. there in 1897 until his death. From 1899 for several years a member of Czech Trio.—V. ST.

SUDA, Stanislav. Czech compr. *b.* Plzeňec, 30 April, 1865. Trained for music at Blind Institute, Prague; is music-teacher at Plzeň.

Operas: *U Božích muk* (1897); *Lešetinský kovář* (*The Smith of Lešetín*) (1903, Fr. A. Urbánek); *Bar Kochba* (1905), perf. at Plzen and Prague.—V. ST.

SUGGIA, Guilhermina. Cellist. Of Portuguese and Ital. descent; *b* Oporto, 27 June, 1888. First lessons from age of 5 to 15, from father, Augusto S. In 1904 stud. Leipzig under Klengel (by the patronage of Queen Amélie). *Début* at 17 at Leipzig Gewandhaus concerts (under Nikisch). Then played in every European country in various kinds of mus. activity. In 1900 (at age of 12) was leading cellist of Oporto Orch. and in local str. 4tet. In 1906, married Pablo Casals (from whom she received some lessons) and gave up concert-playing for 7 years. Resumed her prof. career in 1912 and toured widely. The perfection of her playing of works of the old masters has never been equalled. She possesses two magnificent cellos, one by Montagnana, the other by Stradivarius. A remarkable portrait of her was painted by Augustus John in 1923. In May of the same year, the Govt. of Portugal conferred the highest order of Santiago da Espada on her. Resides in London.—E.-H.

SUK, Josef. Czechoslovak composer; *b.* Křečovice, 4 Jan. 1874. Studied violin and composition at Prague Conservatoire under Bennewitz, Stecker, Dvořák. One of founders of Bohemian Quartet (2nd vn.), remaining with it until now; since 1922 professor at Master-School for Composition at Prague Conservatoire. In his early works his expression is based on Dvořák, though there is a greater gentleness, a softer sentiment and richer rhythm. He has a great fund of melody, a sense for beauty of sonority and an uncommon technical maturity. His own joys and troubles are reflected oftener and more clearly than in most authors; the chief trend of his work is a kind of poetical autobiography. His love for Dvořák's daughter, his marriage and early artistic success, imparted for a long time a happy, cheerful, loving, mischievous tone to Suk's music. From the death of his wife, and then of his father-in-law, the world of Suk's creation became quite changed. Deeper thoughts and a higher spontaneity set in. The majesty and dread of death and elegiac meditations then inspired his music. Gradually there is a slow recovery, again new susceptibilities arise; Nature consoles; his love of mankind deepens, and all this is comprised in his last works. In this period Suk's melody is free from periodicity and symmetry of bars. The rhythm is enriched by a free elaboration of each voice, partly by the diverse functioning of polyrhythm. The harmony escapes all tonality, develops itself very quickly, the polyphony of several different harmonic progressions affording further enrichment. The instrumentation is finely cut in chamber-music manner; the form, though free from all set scheme, is monumental and logical.

First period: *Serenade*, str. op. 6; pf. 5tet, op. 8; str. 4tet, op. 11; music to scenic fairy-tales *Raduz and Mahulena*, op. 13; *Under the Apple-tree*, op. 20; symphony, op. 14 ; *Fantasy*, vn. and orch. op. 24 (given Q. H. London); *Fantastic Scherzo*, op. 25, and symph. poem *Praga*, orch. op. 26 ; 6 pf. cycles, 3 choral cycles. Second period: for orch: *Asrael*, op. 27 ; *Pohádka léta* (*A Summer Tale*), op. 29 ; *Zráni* (*The Ripening*), op. 35. Pf.: *O matince* (*My Mother*), op. 28; *Životem a snem* (*Through Life and Dream*), op. 30; *Ukolébavky* (*Lullabies*), op. 33; *Meditation*, str. 4tet; 2nd str. 4tet, op. 31.—V. ST.

SULLIVAN, Arthur Seymour. Eng. compr. *b.* London, 13 May, 1842; *d* there, 22 Nov. 1900. Buried in St. Paul's Cath. Chorister, Chapel Royal, under Helmore in 1854. Publ. a song as early as 1855. Was the first Mendelssohn scholar elected, 1856. Stud. at R.A.M. under Bennett and Goss from 1857, and Leipzig Cons. under Moscheles, Hauptmann, Richter, Plaidy 1858–61. Amongst his fellow-students were J. F. Barnett, Franklin Taylor, Carl Rosa, Dannreuther and Grieg. The production of *Kenilworth* at Birmingham Fest. 1864, in spite of its poor libretto, was received very enthusiastically, the interpolated scene from *The Merchant of Venice*, " How Sweet the Moonlight," taking a firm place in the repertoire of all glee-societies. The overture to *Lalla Rookh* was perf. in Leipzig in 1860; that to *The Tempest* at Crystal Palace in 1862. He cond. many series of concerts, the London Philh. 1885–7; Leeds Fest. from 1880. Was principal of the National Training School for Music (1876–1881) which afterwards became the R.C.M. London. Received Mus.Doc. *h.c.* from Cambridge (1876) and from Oxford (1879); Chevalier of the Legion of Honour, 1878; knighted by Queen Victoria in 1883.

The genius of Arthur Sullivan was unique. It may well be questioned if attributes of such rare quality and a versatility so extraordinary will ever again be found in combination. Especially remarkable was the eternal spring of melody of which he was the creator. It was as unfailing as the fine sense of humour—often subtle but always sure—which distinguished so much of his lighter work. Oratorio, opera, church music, orchestral and dramatic music, ballads—all came fluently from his pen—all were marked by clarity of expression. In everything he wrote he betrayed no foreign influence; he was essentially a British composer with an individuality that was unmistakable. Many musicians hold that his finest music is contained in the big and serious choral works; others take the view that it is to be found in his purely orchestral works and dramatic music. That he was a master in both branches of the art is an acknowledged fact, and he is respected accordingly. Probably, however, it was those sparkling, refined, irresistible and entirely inspired melodies from his comic operas that

established him firmly in public esteem and endeared him to the great majority of music lovers. Here was art quite as sincere as in the more severe works; for there is all the difference between light *good* music and light *bad* music! His melodies were beloved by the people, and he created for them an almost bewildering number. They accepted him as their leader, and he never betrayed the trust; on the contrary, he consistently raised their appreciation for pure, artistic and refreshing melody. Moreover, it was melody so deftly woven and wedded to such delightful harmony that public appreciation remains to-day more real than ever. As in our own country, so it is throughout most of the civilised world.

How is this enduring popularity to be accounted for? It is by the fact that Sullivan possessed so complete and unassailable an equipment. An inspired melodist, a master of harmony, counterpoint, orchestration and choral writing in every form — aided by a resolute application of his genius, Sullivan accomplished where lesser men merely attempted. Another gift was his almost uncanny sense of rhythm: it enabled him, when he willed, to turn into a swinging melody a lyric, the novel or complex rhythm of which would have driven many another composer to despair. This unquestionably is one of the secrets connected with the living success of the great Gilbert and Sullivan series.

Sullivan has left an imperishable memory for all that is healthy, masterly and inspired in the art of music.

Dramatic works: *Cox and Box*; *The Contrabandista*; *Thespis*; *Trial by Jury*; *The Zoo*; *The Sorcerer*; *H.M.S. Pinafore*; *The Pirates of Penzance*; *Patience*; *Iolanthe*; *Princess Ida*; *The Mikado*; *Ruddigore*; *The Yeomen of the Guard*; *The Gondoliers*; *Ivanhoe* (grand opera); *Haddon Hall*; *Utopia*; *The Chieftain* (revision of *The Contrabandista*); *The Grand Duke*; *The Beauty-Stone*; ballets: *L'Ile enchantée*; *Victoria*; incidental music to *The Tempest*, *The Merchant of Venice*, *Merry Wives of Windsor*, *Henry VIII*, *Macbeth* and *King Arthur*. Oratorios and cantatas: *Kenilworth*; *The Prodigal Son*; *On Shore and Sea*; *The Light of the World*; *The Martyr of Antioch*; *The Golden Legend*; a *Festival Te Deum*; ode, *I wish to tune my quiv'ring Lyre*, barit. solo with orch. For orch.: Symphony in E; overtures: *In Memoriam*; *Marmion*; *Di Ballo*; *The Sapphire Necklace*; cello concerto. Also a *Te Deum*, *Jubilate and Kyrie in D*; anthems and hymn-tunes; pf. pieces; songs.—E. G.

SUÑOL, Father Gregorio María. Contemporary Span. musician; *b.* in Catalonia. One of leaders of movement for restoration of Gregorian chant in Spain. Author of a *Méthode Complète de Chant Grégorien*; *Analecta Montserratensia* (1917), a transcription of the XIV century codex called *Llibre Vermell*.—P. G. M.

SUOMEN LAULU (Finland's Song). An important Finnish choral soc. founded in 1900 by H. Klemetti (*q.v.*).—T. H.

SUPER-HARMONICS. Those overtones of a note which are furthest out of tune with the tempered system of tuning. They start with number 11 of the harmonic series of overtones. See arts. on HARMONY and HARMONICS.—E.·H.

SUPPÉ, Franz von. Austrian compr. *b.* Spalato (Illyria), 18 April, 1819; *d.* Vienna 21 May, 1895. Stud. at Vienna Cons. (Sechter, Seyfried).

Condr. Theater in der Josefstadt; then Theater an der Wien and Carl-Theater. Wrote about 200 short operettas (1-act) and overtures to comedies, perf. in the theatre. Also a symph. Mass, *Requiem* and well-known overture to *Dichter und Bauer* (*Poet and Peasant*). At the Carl-Theater he had great success with his 3-act operettas. He transmitted the Offenbach style to the Viennese, and his gay and merry tunes and rhythmic marches caught the ear of the man in the street. All the later operettas show his influence. He has a monument in Vienna and a fine street is named after him.

1-act operettas: *"Paragraph 3"* (1858); *Zehn Mädchen und kein Mann* (*Ten Girls and no Man*) (1862); *Flotte Bursche* (*Merry Boys*) (1863); *Pique Dame* (1864); *Die schöne Galathée* (*Charming Galatea*) (1865); and 175 more. 3-act operettas: *Boccaccio* (with local colour of his Italian native country) (1879); *Donna Juanita* (Spanish burlesque music) (1880); *Die Jagd nach dem Glück* (1888); and 28 others. Consult O. Keller, *Fr. v. S.* (Vienna, 1905).—P. P.

SURETTE, Thomas Whitney. Amer. lecturer; *b.* Concord, Mass., U.S.A., 7 Sept. 1862. A.B., Harvard, 1891. Stud. under Arthur Foote (pf.), and J. K. Paine (theory). Held several church organ posts, 1883-96; thereafter devoted himself to lecturing on music. Dir. of music at Bryn Mawr Coll. 1921. A 2-act operetta, *Priscilla* (Schirmer), often perf. A romantic opera, *Cascabel*, 1st perf. Pittsburgh, 1899. *The Eve of Saint Agnes*, dramatic ballad, soli, chorus, orch., produced 1899 (Novello).

Course of Study on the Development of Symphonic Music (Nat. Fed. of Mus. Clubs, 1915); *Music and Life* (Houghton Mifflin, 1917); (with D. G. Mason) *The Appreciation of Music* (Gray, 1907).—O. K.

SURZYŃSKI, Józef (*phon.* Soojynski). Polish music-historian, ed. and compr. of church music; *b.* Srem, 15 March, 1851; *d.* at Koscian as parish priest and prelate in 1918. In 1879, became Catholic priest and Doctor of Theology in Rome; then stud. church music in Ratisbon. In 1881, condr. of church music in Posen Cath. In 1884, ed. of the review *Muzyka Koscielna* (*Church Music*), in which he publ. an immense number of arts. and compns. In 1885, began to publ. *Monumenta musices sacræ in Polonia*, containing most valuable works of Polish comprs. of XVI and XVII centuries. Publ. in 1891 an important book on *Polish Songs of the Catholic Church*. Also publ. *Magister Choralis*; *Directorium Chori*; *Cantionale Ecclesiasticum ad Normam*; *Ritualis Sacramentorum Petricoviensis* (1897). His compns. are among the best modern Polish church music.—ZD. J.

SURZYŃSKI, Mieczysław. Polish organ compr. and theorist; *b.* Sroda, 1886. Since 1904, prof. of organ, Warsaw Cons. Much appreciated as organ virtuoso; 1909, orgt. of Warsaw Cath. Has publ. compositions for organ.—ZD. J.

SUTER, Hermann. Swiss condr. compr. *b.* Kaiserstuhl, 28 April, 1870. Stud. organ, pf. and compn. at Stuttgart and Leipzig; 1894, orgt. and condr. at Zurich; since 1902, condr. of Symphony Concerts, the Liedertafel (male choir) and the Gesangverein (mixed choir) at Basle. Dir. of Cons. at Basle, 1918-21. Without doubt

the most eminent Swiss condr. His oratorio performances have justly become famous; he is a real pioneer of modern music. Strauss and Reger have dedicated to him several of their best works. In 1912, the Univ. of Basle honoured him with the Doctorate *h.c.* His compns., showing relationship to Brahms, are admirably written as regards construction and depth of invention. His most attractive and charming unacc. choruses figure in repertoire of every male choir of Switzerland and Germany.

2 str. 4tets (2nd publ. in Swiss National Ed); str. 6tet; *Swiss Symphony* (S.N.E.); *Legende*, orch.; *Walpurgisnacht*, chorus and orch. Numerous songs and unacc. choruses. Mostly publ. by Hug, Leipzig.—F. H.

SVENDSEN, Anton Plum. Danish violinist; *b.* Copenhagen, 23 June, 1846. Pupil of Fritz Schram and Valdemar Tofte (Copenhagen), Lauterbach and Joachim (Berlin), and Massart (Paris). 1868, member of R. Chapel, Copenhagen; from 1895-1910 its leader; 1st vn. in Neruda Quartet; 1904, prof. at R. Cons.; dir. 1915; chairman of Chamber-Music Association; vice-chairman of Musikforening (Music Soc.). Has appeared in Sweden and Russia (Petrograd). His excellent technique and fine feeling for style has given him a leading rôle in Copenhagen musical life.—A. H.

SVENDSEN, Johan Severin. Norwegian composer and conductor; *b.* Christiania, 30 Sept. 1840; *d.* Copenhagen, 15 June, 1911. Received his first musical instruction from his father, the violinist and military musician Gudbrand Svendsen. From 1855, earned his own living as military musician and orchestral player (flute, clarinet and violin); made concert-tours as violinist in Sweden and North Germany, 1861-2. In 1863-7, pupil of Conservatoire in Leipzig (Hauptmann, David, Reinecke and Richter), where he composed his string quartet in A minor, the octet, the D major symphony and the quintet, all of which attracted general attention. In 1867 he gave a concert of his own compositions in Christiania; then went abroad again; in 1868, violinist at Odéon Theatre, Paris; continued work as composer. Conducted in 1870-1 his D minor symphony at Gewandhaus, Leipzig, and won a brilliant success; 1871, conductor of Euterpe Concerts, Leipzig; made in 1872 Wagner's acquaintance at Bayreuth, where he composed his fanciful music-picture *Carneval de Paris*; 1872, returned to Norway. In 1872-7 and 1880-3 he and Grieg alternately conducted the Musical Society's concerts; in this period he displayed a rich productivity; 1877-80, conducted his new works in Leipzig, London and Paris; gave in 1882 two concerts in Copenhagen. These aroused so much attention that in summer of 1883 he was appointed conductor of orchestra at Royal Theatre, Copenhagen. He settled permanently in that city, where he was until 1908 conductor of the Court Orchestra and of Philharmonic Concerts.

Svendsen is not only the greatest conductor Norway has produced, but, next to Grieg and Sinding, the most eminent Norwegian composer.

His productions embrace all fields except opera, and they have already become quite classic, his art (in spite of the national elements and the personal characteristics it contains) having received the impression of the form and style of his time. The school in which Svendsen was trained, set its stamp upon his musical form, which does not, like Grieg's, represent any awakening of the new Norwegian tone-feeling based upon the lyrical note of the folk-music. The national element in Svendsen finds stronger expression in his rhythm and harmony than in his melody. Svendsen cultivated pre-eminently the larger forms (symphony and chamber-music) and is inclined to let the lyrical give place to the epic style, chiselling out clear and pure-lined themes in a classically simple form. His luxuriant melody suits his breezy joy of life, charming naturalness and sound realism; he never transgresses the established rules of traditional form, finding a harmonious balance between content and form. His orchestral treatment is masterly and especially charming in its sonorous clang. He often emphasises the cosmopolitan spirit; then there may frequently be traced the influence of Mendelssohn, Wagner and Schumann, and, in his symphonic poems *Zorahayda* and *Romeo and Juliet*, of Berlioz and New-German tendencies.

Symphonies: No. 1 in D, op. 4; No. 2 in B, op. 15; orch. legend, *Zorahayda*, op. 11; orch. fantasy, *Romeo and Juliet*, op. 18; *Carneval de Paris*, op. 9; *Norwegian Artists' Carnival*; Festal Polonaise, op. 12; symph. introduction to *Sigurd Slembe*; vn. concerto, op. 6; cello concerto, op. 7; Romance, vn. and orch. op. 26; 2 str. 4tets (A mi. op. 1; op. 20); 8tet, op. 3; 5tet, op. 5; male chorus, op. 2; 2 vols. of songs, op. 23, 24; 4 *Norwegian Rhapsodies*, orch. op. 17, 19, 21, 22; adaptations of folk-songs for str. orch. Consult: A. Grönvold, *Norwegian Musicians*; O. M. Sandvik and Gerh. Schjelderup, *Norway's Musical History*, Vol. II, pp. 107–20; *Svensk Musiktidning (Swedish Musical Journal)*, 1883, 1902 and 1911; *Tidningen för Musik (Journal of Music)*, 1910. Letters from Sv. were publ. by G. Hauch in *Tilskueren (The Spectator)* in 1913.—J. A.

SVERÉNUS, Olav. Norwegian t.-barit. singer; *b.* Christiania, 6 April, 1883. Pupil of Jens Berntsen, Christiania; of Armin, Berlin; of Clutsam, London; and of Moritz's Opera School, Berlin. *Début* as concert-singer, Berlin, 1913; appeared in Dresden Opera House, 1914. Concerts in own country, in Copenhagen, Stockholm, Gothenburg and Paris. Lives in Christiania.—U. M.

SWAAP, Sam. Dutch violinist; *b.* Amsterdam, 15 Oct. 1888. Stud. under Hofmeester and Carl Flesch at Amsterdam Cons.; 1908–12, violinist Concertgebouw Orch.; 1913–17, soloist and 2nd condr. Symph. Orch. Åbo (Finland); 1917, soloist Residentie Orch., The Hague. 1st violinist of The Hague Str. Quartet.—W. P.

SWAN & CO. Music-publ. firm, founded in London in 1849; present managing-dir. W. Bowker Andrews. Publ. of the *Magnus Pf. Albums* (100 vols.), Swan Ed. of art-songs, and other works chiefly by British comprs.—G. B.

SWIERZYŃSKI, Michał. Polish compr. *b.* Cracow, 25 Oct. 1868. Pupil of Żeleński. Since 1916, teacher of theory in Cracow Cons. Numerous short light pieces for pf.; about 200

songs; also small operas and easy symphonies for students. His melodious operettas had success in Cracow, Warsaw and Lemberg.—ZD. J.

SWINSTEAD, Felix Gerald. Eng. pianist and compr. *b.* London, 25 June, 1880. Stud. at R.A.M. London under Matthay and F. Corder. Successful compr. of pf. music, especially easy teaching-pieces and studies.

Easy (Anglo-Fr. Co. London; Ashdown; Augener; Ricordi; Murdoch); mod. difficult: 6 studies after Scarlatti, etc. (Augener; J. Williams; Anglo-Fr. Co.); difficult: *Polonaise*, op. 46; *Concert-Study*, op. 21 (J. Williams); *Fantasie*, B flat mi.; Variations on theme by Concone (Anglo-Fr. Co.).—E.-H.

SYCHRA, Josef Cyril. Czechoslovak compr. *b.* Ústí, near Orlicí, 1859. From 1889 choirmaster in Ml. Boleslav.

Church compns.: 30 masses; oratorios: *Messias*; *Golgotha*.—V. ST.

SZABADOS, Béla. Hungarian compr. *b.* Budapest, 3 June, 1867. Prof. at R. High School for Music, Budapest.—B. B.

SZÁNTÓ, Theodor. Hungarian pianist and compr. *b.* Vienna, 3 June, 1877. Entered Vienna Cons. as pupil of Dachs (pf.), and Fuchs (compn.); 1893–7, stud. at R. High School for Music, Budapest, under K. Chován (pf.) and Koessler (compn.). 1898–1901, had finishing lessons with Busoni in Berlin. 1901–4, gave concerts, mostly in Germany; settled (1905) in Paris, where he soon won recognition. At Liszt Fest., 1911, was pianist with Colonne and Cons. Orch. in Paris. Delius' pf. concerto (dedicated to him) was played by him in England, Germany and Hungary. 1914–21, lived in Switzerland; since 1921 in Budapest.

Orch.: Symphony, *Land and Sea*, in 2 movements (with mixed chorus), 1908–9 (ms.); *Symph. Rhapsody* in 4 movements (with male chorus), 1916–17 (ms.). Pf. and orch.: *Carmen Paraphrase*, 1905 (ms.). Vn. and pf.: *Magyarország*, concert sonata, 1905–6 (Berlin, Harmonie Verlag). Cello and pf.: Suite (also with harp, small orch. and organ), 1910 (Paris, Hamelle); *Poème religieux*, 1910 (*id.*). Pf.: 2 *Lamentations*, 1903 (Leipzig, Kahnt); *Ballade*, 1903 (*id.*); *Dramatic Elegy*, 1904 (*id.*); *Berceuse of Death*, 1910 (Paris, Demets); Choral Phantasy and Finale, 1910 (ms.); *Contrastes*, 4 pieces, 1911 (Paris, Durand); 17 Variations and Finale on a Hungarian folk-song, 1915 (Vienna, Univ. Ed.); *Essays in Japanese Harmonies*, 1918–19 (London, Elkin). Organ: *Cantus choralis*, 1912 (Paris, Hamelle). Transcriptions of works of Bach: Prelude and fugue, G mi. 1902 (Leipzig, Kahnt); Fantasia and fugue, G mi. 1904 (*id.*); 4 choral preludes, 1905 (*id.*); Prelude and fugue, A mi. 1911 (Vienna, Univ. Ed.); Prelude, fugue with andante, 1906 (Berlin, Harmonie); Prelude and fugue, C mi. 1912 (Demets, Paris); Passacaglia in C mi. 1922 (ms.); of works of Stravinsky: *Chinese March*, 1915; *Petrouchka Suite*, 1922 (Russischer Musikverlag).—Z. K.

SZÉKELYHIDY, Franz. Hungarian t. singer; *b.* Tövis, Hungary (now annexed by Rumania), 4 April, 1885. Member of R. Hungarian Opera House since July 1909.—B. B.

SZELUTA, Apolinary. Polish compr. *b.* in 1884. Pupil of Noskowski at Warsaw Cons. Began to publ. his compns. in 1905, together with Szymanowski and Różycki, and showed considerable promise as a compr. He then passed more than 10 years in the depths of Russia (Ufa). In his works publ. there, he has not attained the high level of his first compns.

He now lives in Warsaw and has some new works, including an opera, in preparation.

Variations in E, op. 2; pf. sonata in A, op. 3; cello sonata in F, op. 4; many fugues; several songs. —ZD. J.

SZENDY, Árpád. Hungarian pianist and compr. *b.* Szarvas, 1863; *d.* Budapest, 10 Sept. 1922. Stud. under Liszt in Budapest. From 1890, teacher of pf. at R. High School for Music, Budapest.—B. B.

SZIGETI, Josef. Hungarian violinist; *b.* Budapest, 2 Sept. 1892. Pupil of Hubay; *début* in Berlin, Dresden and London (1905–6). Toured and lived in England, 1906–1913. Hamilton Harty dedicated his D mi. concerto to him; S. did a great deal toward popularising Busoni's vn. concerto and other modern works. Is constantly touring in Europe. Since 1917, prof. of master-classes at Geneva Conservatoire.—F. H.

SZIRMAI, Albert. Hungarian operetta compr. *b.* Budapest, 2 July, 1880.—B. B.

SZOPSKI, Felicjan. Polish compr. *b.* Krzeszowice, Galicia, 5 June, 1865. Pupil of Żeleński (1885–92); then of Urban in Berlin. From 1894 to 1908, teacher of pf. and harmony in Cracow Cons. and music critic of the *Czas*. Since 1908, has lived in Warsaw. Teacher of theory at Music School of Mus. Soc. Critic for various newspapers. Since 1918, has been mus. adviser at Ministry of Public Instruction. His chief work is opera *Lilies* (after ballad by Mickiewicz), written 1900–12, in which he follows Wagner's methods. It was produced in Warsaw in 1916.

Several pf. pieces; melodious songs; coll. of transcriptions of Polish popular songs, all in easy and simple style. In the latest works (songs, orch. compns. etc.) his style is quite modern.—ZD. J.

SZULC, Bronisław (*phon.* Shults). Polish condr. compr. *b.* Warsaw, 24 Dec. 1881. Pupil of Noskowski at Warsaw Cons.; then stud. in Berlin. 1899–1908, 1st trumpeter at Warsaw Opera; 1909–11, stud. under Riemann (theory) and Nikisch (conducting). Since 1911, has cond. symphony concerts in Warsaw and Lódź, and in England (Liverpool Philh. Soc.). Much esteemed as condr. Has written 2 symph. poems and several pieces for vn. and cello.—ZD. J.

SZYMANOWSKA-BARTOSZEWICZ, Stanisława. Polish soprano operatic and song-singer; sister of the compr. Szymanowski; *b.* in Ukraine, 1887. Stud. under Kozłowska in Lemberg. Since 1907, singing in Polish operas, also in Italy, Vienna, Berlin, Prague and Paris. Is a gifted interpreter of modern vocal music, especially of the songs of her brother; also very brilliant as Violetta, Gilda, Lakmé. Lives in Warsaw.—ZD. J.

SZYMANOWSKI, Karol. The most eminent Polish composer of the present time; *b.* Tymoszówka, Ukraine, 1882. He began to write his first piano pieces and songs in 1901 (op. 1, *Nine Preludes*, and op. 2, *Four Songs*), before he commenced his studies under Noskowski in Warsaw (1903). These preludes announced the most beautiful inventive power in the field of instrumental music shown by any Polish composer since Chopin. Besides several songs and the piano *Études*, op. 4, Szymanowski's succeeding works up to op. 9 were mostly scholastic elaborations, but none the less interesting and valuable (Variations for piano, op. 3; piano sonata, op. 8; violin sonata, op. 9). Quite personal and valuable from every point of view were his Variations for piano, op. 10 in A minor (after a popular Polish melody of the Tatra mountains) and his songs, op. 13. In 1907 he wrote in Berlin his 12 songs, op. 17, which were at that date the proof of an exceedingly bold evolution of his musical tongue. From them it was seen that the conventional limits would not suffice for his aims. Similar signs were found in his orchestral composition with an obbligato vocal part to Wyspianski's words, *Penthesilea*, written in 1909. The most perfect works of his early period are the second symphony in B major, op. 18, and the piano sonata, op. 21, in A major. Both these compositions have the same form: first, a sonata form; then a theme and variations; at the end a great fugue (in the symphony, with five subjects). Also a *Romance* for violin in D major, op. 23. *The Songs of Many Colours*, op. 22, and six songs to words by the Persian poet, Hafiz, make a splendid end to the first period.

A transitional work is the opera *Hagith* to a libretto by Felix Dörmann. It was written in 1912, and performed in Warsaw in 1922 and 1923 in Dortmund. In style it is an evolution of Richard Strauss's *Salome* and *Elektra*; but Szymanowski's personality shines forth in the most beautiful parts of the work. In all these works the talent of Szymanowski is recognised not only in the beauty and depth of his lyrical themes, but also by the incomparable mastery of his polyphonic and instrumental technique.

In his latest works (written since 1914) Szymanowski shows a new aspect; the harmony is quite atonal and its character is descriptive. He stands to-day in the first rank of the pioneers of musical progress, where he holds a place of his own. His chief compositions of this period are: Third symphony, with chorus and tenor solo, op. 27; violin concerto, op. 35; *Demeter*, for alto solo, female chorus and orchestra, op. 38; *Agave*, cantata for soprano solo, chorus and orchestra, op. 41; *Myths* (*The Fountains of Arethusa*; *Narcissus*; *Pan and the Dryads*), for violin and piano, op. 30; *Masques*, for piano, op. 34; third piano sonata, op. 36; *The Songs of the Mad Muezzin*, op. 42; songs to Rabindranath Tagore's words, op. 41, etc.

An article on Szymanowski by Jachimecki appeared in the *Musical Quarterly*, New York, Jan. 1922; and one by Alex. Tansman in the *Revue Musicale*, Paris, May 1922.—ZD. J.

TAFALL, Santiago. Span. orgt. and compr.; member of the Church; *b.* Santiago de Compostela (1858); orgt. at Cath. of his native town, and in 1895 choir-master. Lives at Santiago, where in 1899 he was raised to the dignity of Canon. He is one of the pioneers of the religious music *risorgimento* initiated by Villalba, Otaño, Monasterio, Pedrell, etc. His works are unpublished, as is generally the case with religious music in Spain.—P. G. M.

TAFFANEL, Paul. Fr. flautist and condr. *b.* Bordeaux, 16 Sept. 1844; *d.* Paris, 22 Nov. 1908. Flautist without an equal; pupil in class of Dorus at Paris Cons.; 1st prize, 1865; stud. harmony with Reber; played in Opéra orch. from 1861. Solo flautist there 1864–90, as well as Société des Concerts (from 1867). Renounced career of virtuoso for that of condr., and dir. (in accordance with tradition) the two orchs. of Opéra and Cons. from 1890. Founded Soc. of Chamber-music for Wind Instrs. (1879); prof. at Cons. (1893) where his class became a nursery from which issued a generation of excellent French flautists: Gaubert, Fleury, Blancard, and others.—M. L. P.

TAGLIACOZZO, Riccardo. Italian violinist; *b.* Naples, 28 Dec. 1878. Stud. at Naples Cons. under Angelo Ferni; teacher of vn. at Istituto Musicale, Florence; author of several compns. and revisions of vn. works.—D. A.

TAILLEFÈRE, Germaine. French compr. *b.* Pau St.-Maur, near Paris, 19 April, 1892. A brilliant student of harmony and counterpoint at the Paris Conservatoire. Her *Pastorale, Les Jeux de plein air* (Chester, London); her quartet (Durand), her *Ballade* for piano and orchestra (Chester, 1923), her ballet *Le Marchand d'Oiseaux* (*Ballets suédois*, Paris, 1923) and especially her sonata for violin and piano (Durand) (played 1922 by Thibaut and Cortot at *Revue Musicale* concerts), give proof of an exquisite feminine sensibility and rare good taste. Although she belongs to the "Group of Six" (*q.v.*), she has no revolutionary tendency; but follows the tradition of Gabriel Fauré, Debussy and Ravel, and can write harmonies full of savour, without outraging the ears.—H. P.

TAKÁCS, Mihály. Hungarian barit. singer; *b.* Nagybánya, Hungary (now annexed by Rumania), 1861; *d.* Keszthely, Hungary, Aug. 1913. Stud. at R. High School for Music, Budapest. Since 1884, member of R. Hungarian Opera House. In response to Cosima Wagner's invitation, appeared in 1894 and succeeding years at Bayreuth festivals.—B. B.

TALAT-KELPŠA, Juozas. Lithuanian compr. condr. *b.* Kalnukai, 20 Dec. 1888. Educated

at Ylakiai, where his father payed the organ alternately with him. Stud. under Rudolf Limon (a Czech, who dir. the Tyzenhausus School at Rokiškis); later at Treskin Music School in Vilna, where he played at St. Michael's Ch. When the Vilna *Kankles* Association staged Fromas' *Egle*, *žalčiu karaliene* (*Egle, Queen of the Vipers*), T.-K., then only 17, wrote the music for it. Father Tumas immediately gave him a 2-year scholarship and sent him to Petrograd Cons. where he matriculated in the compn. section in 1916. Whilst still at the Cons. he brought out his song *Ne margi sakaleliai* (*The Falcons*) in 3 languages. During the war, he issued a coll. *Lakštute* (*The Nightingale*) on folk-tunes adapted for schools; also a coll. of soldiers' songs, *Kariagos Aidai*. In 1919, he entered the Berlin Acad., where he comp. his Variations on the *daina Oi*, *griežle* (*O Corncrake*) and an orch. suite. In 1920, dir. of Naujalis Music School (now Music School of Lithuanian Art Producers), where he worked hard for the staging of the first Lithuanian opera. He now conducts at the Opera. In 1921, the Švyturys Publ. Co. brought out several of his choruses (*Song of Regret*; *Asperges*, etc.). (See also LITHUANIAN MUSIC.)—H. R.

TALEN, Björn. Norwegian lyric and dramatic t. singer; *b.* Christiania, 8 Sept. 1890. Matriculated 1908. 1st-lieut. 1913. Stud. singing in Milan and Naples; also in London and Copenhagen. *Début* in autumn 1914 at concert in Christiania; in opera as Radamès (*Aida*) at National Theatre. Has since appeared in leading theatres in Stockholm, Milan, Madrid. Engaged in 1921 as 1st t. at the State Opera House, Berlin. Chief rôles: Tannhäuser; Faust; Cavaradossi (*Tosca*); Pinkerton (*Butterfly*); Canio (*Pagliacci*); Alfred (*Traviata*); the Duke (*Rigoletto*), etc.—R. M.

TALICH, Václav. Czechoslovak condr. *b.* Kroměříž (Moravia), 1883. Stud. vn. at Cons. Prague; Leipzig (Reger, Nikisch); Milan. Violinist at Philh. Orch. Berlin; Konzertmeister in Odessá; prof. in Tiflis (Russia), where he began to conduct; for some time choirmaster and condr. in Prague; 1908–12, cond. at theatres in Lublanjá (Laibach, Jugoslavia); 1912–15 in Plzeň (Bohemia). 1918, chief condr. of Czech Philh. Orch. Prague, with which he made a tour in Italy (1921), Vienna, London, Liverpool, etc. T. is one of best Czech condrs. Under his guidance the Czech Philh. became a first-rate orchestra.—V. ST.

TAMBURA. See INDIAN MUS. INSTRUMENTS.

TANÉIEF, Alexander Sergeievitch (*accent the É*). Russ. compr. *b.* Petrograd, 5/17 Jan. 1850. Stud. music at Dresden under Reichel; at a later date received advice from Balakiref; in 1886 became a pupil of Rimsky-Korsakof.

3 symphonies; 2 suites for orch.; 1-act opera, *Cupid's Pranks*; 3 str. 4tets; songs; choruses; various instr. pieces.—M. D. C.

TANÉIEF, Serge Ivanovitch (*accent the É*). Russ. compr. *b.* 13/25 Nov. 1856; *d.* Moscow, 5/18 June, 1915. Stud. at the Moscow Cons., where his teachers were Hubert and Tchaikovsky. Later he became prof. and ultimately dir. of this inst. His works comprise a good deal of chamber-music, songs, 3 symphonies, the music to trilogy *Orestes* (after Æschylus), and a remarkable treatise on *Counterpoint*. He was one of the greatest of theorists and teachers. The list of his pupils comprises the names of Scriabin, Rachmaninof, and many other Russ. comprs. —V. B.

TANGO. See SOUTH AMER. DANCES.

TANSMAN, Alexander. Polish compr. *b.* Lódź, 1900. Has publ. pf. pieces and orch. compns. in a bold modern style. Contributes to *Revue Musicale*. Lives in Paris.—ZD. J.

TAPPERT, Wilhelm. Ger. musicologist; *b.* Upper Thomaswaldau, near Bunzlau, 19 Feb. 1830; *d.* Berlin, 27 Oct. 1907. First a schoolmaster; turned to music in 1856; stud. at Kullak's School of Music (theory); 1858, went to Glogau as teacher and critic. From 1866, teacher and mus. writer in Berlin; ed. the *Allgemeine deutsche Musikzeitung* (1870–80).

Music and Musical Education (1866); *Musical Studies* (1868); *The Law against Consecutive Fifths* (1869); *R. Wagner* (1883); *Wagner-Lexicon: Dictionary of the Impolite* . . . (1887, 2nd ed. 1903); *Wandering Melodies* (1890); *54 Erl-king Compositions* (1898, 2nd ed. 1906); *Song and Sound of Olden Times* (100 lute pieces, 1906); *Catalogue of Special Exhibition: Development of Music Script from A.D. 800. to Present Time* (1898).—A. E.

TARNAY, Alajos. Hungarian compr. *b.* Jászberény, 22 Oct. 1870. Prof. R. High School for Music, Budapest. Has written many songs.—B. B.

TAROGATÓ. See HUNGARIAN MUS. INSTRS.

TÁRREGA, Francisco. Span. guitarist and compr. *b.* Villarreal (Castellón), 29 Nov. 1852; *d.* 1909. Head figure of the modern school of guitar-playing; continued classical tradition of XVIII century players, Costa, Ferrer and the old masters Aguado, Sors (1778), etc. Author of many compns. and adaptations of classical works for guitar. Prof. of guitar at R. Cons. de Música, Madrid, and at Barcelona.—P. G. M.

TARTAGLIA, Lydia. Ital. pianist; *b.* Rome, 20 Oct. 1898. Capable concert-artist; pupil of R. Liceo Mus. di Santa Cecilia, Rome, under Sgambati and Casella. Has given good concerts in Rome at Augusteo, in various Ital. cities, and in Germany and London.—D. A.

TATE, Henry. Australian compr. *b.* Prahran, Australia, 1873. Stud. under G. W. L. Marshall-Hall at Melbourne. Contributor to Australian journals, *The Argus, The Herald, Australian Mus. News, Theatre Magazine, New Outlook*, etc., on the subject of a distinctive Australian music, on which he publ. a pamphlet in 1917 entitled *Australian Musical Resources*.

The Dreams of Diaz, Australian myth-operetta; *Dawn*, orch. rhapsody, symbolising discovery of Australia; *Bush Miniatures*, 11 light orch. pieces; *Inspiration*, romantic ballet, orch. and dancers; str. 4tet in D mi.; sonata, vn. and pf. (developed from a call of the Australian thrush); *Tragic Study*, and *The Australian* (cycle of 16 pieces) for pf.; several Australian songs.—G. Y.

TAUBMANN, Otto. Ger. compr. *b.* Hamburg, 8 March, 1859. At first commercial training, then scholar at Dresden School of Music (Wüllner, Rischbieter, Nicodé, Blassmann); theatre-condr.; 1886–9, dir. of Wiesbaden School of Music, after which he went to Berlin; 1891–2, theatre-condr. Petrograd; 1895, dir. of Cäcilien-verein in Ludwigshafen; 1920, compn. teacher at Berlin High School of Music; R. prof. 1910.

Psalm XIII (solo, choir, orch.); *German Mass* (solo, choir, orch. and organ, 1898); *Tauwetter* (male chorus and orch.); 2 poems for 6-v. chorus; *Sängerweihe* (Songs of Inspiration) (choral drama, Elberfeld 1904); cantata, *War and Peace*; symphony, A mi.; opera, *Porzia* (1916, Frankfort-o-M.).—A. E.

TAWSE, William. Scottish t. singer; *b.* Aberdeen, 29 March, 1889. Stud. under late Alfred C. Young, later under Frederick King, London. Gold medal in open competition for all vs. at 1st Edinburgh Mus. Fest. Has sung with conspicuous success in Edinburgh Opera Co.'s *Trovatore, Cavalleria Rusticana, Pagliacci*; *Daughter of the Regiment*; *Ernani*. Widely popular in oratorios and songs.—W. S.

TAYLOR, COLERIDGE-. See COLERIDGE-TAYLOR.

TAYLOR, Colin. Eng. compr. pianist; *b.* Oxford, 21 Feb, 1881. Stud. R.C.M. London, 1900–4. Assistant music master, Eton College, 1904–14; war service 1914–19; joined staff of South African Coll. of Music, Cape Town, 1920. Publ. compns. are chiefly songs, pf. music and part-songs.—E.-H.

TAYLOR, Joseph Deems. Amer. compr. *b.* New York, 22 Dec. 1885. B.A. New York Univ. 1906. Stud. harmony under Oscar Coon, New York, 1908–9 and 1913; 1917–19, associate-ed. of *Collier's Weekly*. Since 1921, mus. critic of *New York World*. His op. 2, a symph. poem, *The Siren Song*, won prize of National Federation of Mus. Clubs, 1912. This, as well as op. 12, *Through the Looking Glass*, suite for str., wind and pf. (1918), is still unpubl. *The Chambered Nautilus*, cantata with orch. (Ditson, 1914), 1st perf. by *Schola Cantorum* in New York 1915. Cantata, *The Highwayman*, (Ditson) was produced at Peterboro (N.H.) Fest. 1914. Many excellent transl. of Russ., Fr., Ger., and Ital. songs.—O. K.

TCHAIKOVSKY, Peter (*accent syll. OV*). Russian composer; *b.* Kamsko Votinsk, 25 April/7 May, 1840; *d.* Petrograd, 25 Oct./7 Nov. 1893. Began to study theory in 1859, and in 1862 entered the newly-founded Conservatoire of Petrograd, where he studied counterpoint and form under Zaremba and orchestration under Anton Rubinstein. In 1866 he was appointed professor of theory at the Moscow Conservatoire, where he received much aid and encouragement from Nicholas Rubinstein. He also came into contact with Balakiref, and for a time underwent his influence. It is at Moscow that he composed his first opera, *The Voyevod* (the score of which he afterwards suppressed), and his first symphony, which bore the title *Winter Dreams*. In 1877 his health failed him, and a few months later he resigned his professional post. He found himself able, owing to the readiness of the publisher Jurgenson to publish all his works, and to the generosity of his admirer Nadejda von Meck, who made him an allowance, to devote himself entirely to composition. From that time on, he spent his life partly in Russia, and partly abroad, and became famous as a conductor as well as a composer. He died of cholera at Petrograd, a few days after conducting the first performance of his *Pathetic* Symphony.

As a composer Tchaikovsky has enjoyed, from the very outset of his career, far greater success at home and abroad than any other Russian. Even nowadays, many writers, and by far the greater part of the musical public of most countries, agree in considering him as one of Russia's greatest composers. A balance has not yet been struck between his many admirers and the few who determinedly go to the other extreme, objecting to what they describe as his facile emotionalism, lack of self-criticism, and looseness of style. Midway, however, stand writers such as César Cui, who in his book *La Musique en Russie* (Paris, 1880) considers that "Tchaikovsky excels in the domain of chamber-music and symphony, but fails in that of opera and the lyric drama."

10 operas, of which the best-known are *Evghen Onieghin* (*Eugene Onegin*), *The Queen of Spades* and *The Oprichnik* (*The Body-Guard*); ballets: *The Nutcracker*; *The Swan's Lake*; 6 symphonies; programme-symphony, *Manfred*; tone-poems: *Francesca da Rimini*; *The Tempest*; *Hamlet*; *Romeo and Juliet*; overture, "1812"; 3 pf. concertos; 3 str. 4tets; trio; 6tet; songs; pf. pieces; a small quantity of church music. Consult: M. Tchaikovsky, *Life and Letters of P. Tch.* (Moscow, 1900); Eng. transl. by R. Newmarch, London, 1906); R. Newmarch, *Tch.* (London, 1900); E. Markham Lee, *Tch.* (*ib.* 1905), and all standard books on Russ. music.—M. D. C.

TCHÉREPNIN, Alexander Nicholaievitch (*accent 3rd syll.*). Son of Nicolas (*q.v.*). Russ. compr. pianist; *b.* Petrograd, 1899. Stud. compn. under his father, Liadof, Sokolof; pf. under Mme. Essipof. In 1921, settled in Paris, continuing his stud. under Gédalge (compn.) Philippe (pf.). An orch. overture was perf. in London by Goossens. There is also a pf. concerto; vn. and pf. sonata; several pf. pieces (*Toccata*; *Petite Suite*; *Danse et Nocturne*; *Étude de concert*; *Novellettes*; *Bagatelles*). His ballet *Ajanta* was perf. in London in 1923. His personality is not yet completely free from the influence of others, especially Prokofief. His works, fresh, spontaneous, and sure in style, contain brilliant promise.—B. DE S.

TCHÉREPNIN, Nicolas Nicolaevitch (*accent 3rd syll.*). Russ. compr. and condr. *b.* Petrograd, 2/15 May, 1873. Stud. music under Van Arck (pf.) and Rimsky-Korsakof (compn.) at Petrograd Cons. 1895–98. Whilst still at the Cons. he gave numerous concerts in the city and provinces; 1907, cond. the Cons. orch. class and was

also condr. at the Marinsky Opera. 1908, went to Paris to direct the perfs. of Rimsky-Korsakof's *Snegourotchka* (*Snow-Maiden*) at the Opéra-Comique. From 1909–14, dir. the works of the Diaghilef Russ. troupe in Paris, London, etc. 1918, left Petrograd and went to Tiflis as dir. of the Cons. there. 1921, settled in Paris.

His first works, the 1st symphony, the overture for *La Princesse lointaine* (Rostand), *Fantaisie dramatique*, and the songs to words by Tioutchef, show the influence of Rimsky-Korsakof, and even of Tchaikovsky. His own personality began to emerge in 1904 with his ballet-scores, *Le Pavillon d'Armide*, op. 29, which followed the piano concerto, op. 30, and a series of songs on words by Hafiz and others. Tch. is lyrical, but is guided by a sure taste which preserves him from the occasional banalities and sentimentality of Tchaikovsky, from whom he is distinguished by a strong decorative and pictorial feeling derived from Rimsky-Korsakof. He also came under the Fr. Impressionist influences (Debussy, Ravel), thus freeing himself from the academical formulæ. This new style is seen in the ballets *Narcisse*, *The Masque of the Red Death*; the fable of the princess *Oulyba*; the *Sinfoniette* (in memory of Rimsky-Korsakof); the symph. poem, *Le Royaume enchanté* (*The Enchanted Kingdom*); the *Contes de fée* (songs on Balmont's poems); 2 masses; *Le Poisson d'or*—6 sketches for orch. on a poem by Pushkin, etc. There are also the ballets *Dionysius* (1921), *Russian Fairy-Tale* (1923); the symph. poem *Macbeth*; dramatic fantasy *From Land to Land*, op. 17; str. 4tet in A mi. etc. His melodic writing is inspired by Russ. folk-songs, without any direct use of them. The last works, the symphony and some unpubl. songs, reveal both a national and mystical feeling at the same time.—B. DE S.

TCHERNOF, Michael (*accent 2nd syll.*). Russ. compr. *b.* 10/22 April, 1879. Pupil of Rimsky-Korsakof and Glazunof at Petrograd Cons.; now a professor at that institution.

Symphony; 2 overtures; a few other orch. works, including incidental music to plays by Raffalovich and Julavsky; operetta, *Topsy, the Black Maid*; songs; pf. pieces.—M. D. C.

TCHESNOKOF, Alexander. Russ. compr. *b.* in 1877. Stud. under Rimsky-Korsakof at Petrograd Cons.; has written a number of works in which he evinces ingenuity rather than actual originality.—M. D. C.

TEBALDINI, Giovanni. One of most cultured Ital. musicians living, and one of the most praiseworthy contributors to mus. progress in Italy; *b.* Brescia, 7 Sept. 1864. Stud. at Cons. Milan, under Ponchielli. Was obliged to abandon studies owing to journalistic controversies, and took to a wandering life; orgt. in Sicily, then travelled to the Wagnerian perfs. at Bayreuth; subsequently went to Kirchenmusikschule, Regensburg, stud. under Haberl and Haller; 1889, elected master of the *Schola Cantorum* attached to the choir of St. Mark, Venice; 1894, dir. of Cappella Antoniana, Padua; 1897, appointed by competition, dir. of R. Cons. at Parma; 1902, became choirmaster at Loreto, which position he still occupies. T. has been one of most energetic and combative promoters of reform of sacred music in Italy. Has comp. much sacred music (principal Ital. and European publ.). Praiseworthy are his revivals of old Ital. music: *Rappresentazione di Anima e di Corpo* of Emilio del Cavalieri (Turin, S.T.E.N.). Has cond. revivals of this music at important concerts in Rome (Augusteo and elsewhere).

Has written: *L'Archivio della Cappella Antoniana di Padova* (Padua, 1895); *L'Archivio musicale della Santa Casa di Loreto* (Loreto, 1920); many articles in the *Rivista Musicale Italiana* and other reviews. Also a *Metodo di studio per l'organo moderno*, in collab. with M. E. Bossi (Milan, Carisch). As a lecturer, he has helped greatly in spreading musical appreciation.—D. A.

TEDESCHI, Luigi Maurizio. Ital. harpist; *b.* Turin, 7 June, 1867. Stud. at R. Cons. Milan, where he is at present an esteemed teacher. Successfully completed many concert-tours in Italy and through Europe; author of important revisions of didactic works, compr. of an opera, *Jocelyn* (perf. with success at San Remo in 1908), and pieces for his own instrument.—D. A.

TEICHMÜLLER, Robert. Ger. pf. teacher; *b.* Brunswick, 4 May, 1863. Stud. at Leipzig Cons. (Zwintscher, Reinecke, O. Paul, Jadassohn); 1907, dir. of training-classes at Leipzig Cons.; 1908, prof. Publ. revisions of pf. works (Rubinstein). Consult A. Baresel, *R. T. as Man and Artist* (Leipzig, 1922).—A. E.

TEILMAN, Christian. Norwegian compr. orgt. *b.* Tomgaard, Smaalenene, 31 July 1845; *d.* Christiania in Dec. 1909. Pupil of Arnold, Christiania, and Berens, Stockholm. From 1870 music-teacher in Christiania; afterwards orgt. at Garrison Ch. there. An enormously productive compr. His pieces in the lighter style have become extremely popular on account of their catching melody (pf. pieces, dances, paraphrases, etc.).—J. A.

TEKERŐ. See HUNGARIAN MUS. INSTRS.

TELLERÍA Y ARRIZABALAGA, Juan. Contemporary Span. compr. *b.* Zegama (Guipuzcoa), 1895. Pupil of Conrado del Campo, Madrid. Best known for his symph. poem, in two parts, *La Dama de Aitzgorry* (1st perf. Orquesta Sinfónica, Madrid, Nov. 1917.)—P. G. M.

TELMÁNYI, Emil. Violinist; *b.* Arad, Hungary (now annexed by Rumania), 22 June, 1922. Stud. under Hubay, R. High School for Music, Budapest. Lives now at Copenhagen.—B. B.

TEMESVÁRY, János. Hungarian violinist; *b.* 12 Dec. 1891. Pupil of Hubay at R. High School for Music, Budapest. Second vn. in Hungarian Str. Quartet (Waldbauer, Kornstein, Kerpely).—B. B.

TERÁN, Tomás. Span. pianist; *b.* Valencia, 1895. Pupil of José M. Guervós. In 1909, 1st prize at R. Cons. de Música, Madrid, obtaining a great success at San Sebastian the same year, at a concert in which he played Chopin's E mi. concerto. Excels as an interpreter of Bach, the

" classics " and modern Span. comprs. Tours in Spain, Portugal, France, S. and N. America. —P. G. M.

TERRASSE, Claude. Fr. compr. *b.* La Côte St.-André, 1866; *d.* Paris, 30 June, 1923. Specialised in operetta and *opéra-bouffe*. His mus. invention, less fine than Lecocq's, had more buffoonery, and was more directly comic. If his melodic imagination had been more varied he would have been one of the most remarkable representatives of humorous music. Most of his librettos were written by de Flers and Caillavet, some, such as *La Fiancée du Scaphandrier*, by Franc-Nohain, the librettist of *L'Heure Espagnole* of Ravel. As *opéras-bouffes* of mythological times or the Middle Ages, *Les Travaux d'Hercule* (1901), *Le Sire de Vergy* (1903), *Mr. de la Palisse* (1904), *Le Mariage de Télémaque* (1910) are worthy of special mention.—A. C.

TERRY, Charles Sanford. Eng. writer on music; *b.* Newport Pagnell, Bucks, 1864. Educ. at St. Paul's Cath. choir-school, London, King's Coll. School, Lancing Coll. and Clare Coll. Cambridge. Litt.D. Cantab.; specialises in history in which he has attained great eminence; lectureships at Newcastle-on-Tyne; Cambridge; from 1903, Burnett-Fletcher prof. Univ. of Aberdeen. Inaugurated first mus. (competitive) fest. in Scotland, 1909 (in Aberdeen). Mus.Doc. Edinburgh *h.c.* 1921.

Bach Chorales, Part I, *Hymns and Hymn-Melodies of Passions and Oratorios* (Cambridge Univ. Press, 1915); Part II, *H. and H.-M. of Cantatas and Motets* (*id.* 1917); Part III, *H. and H.-M. of Organ Works* (*id.* 1921). *J. S. Bach's Original Hymn-Tunes for Congregational Use* (Oxford Univ. Press, 1922); a *Bach Hymnbook of XVI century Melodies* (Stainer & Bell, 1923). Has transl. Forkel's book on J. S. Bach into English (Constable, 1920).—E.-H.

TERRY, Sir Richard Runciman. Eng. orgt., choir-dir. and researcher; *b.* Ellington, Northumberland, 1865. Educated at Oxford and Cambridge (choral scholarship, King's Coll.); orgt. and choirmaster Elstow School (1890), St. John's Cath., Antigua, West Indies (1892), and Downside Abbey (1896); then orgt. and dir. of music, Westminster Cath. (1901–24). There he raised the choral music to a unique position. He systematically revived whole schools of forgotten church compns.—masses, services, motets, carols, etc. of the XVI century polyphonic composers, chiefly England (Byrd, Taverner, Tye, Tallis, Munday, Morley, White, Philips, Deering, Parsons, Fayrfax, Shepherd and others). This work was inaugurated two years before the issue of the famous *Motu Proprio* demanding the purification of church music. He has always encouraged modern compn. in the modal style (Howells, Oldroyd). He was, for some time, Chairman of the *Tudor Church Music* Publication under the Carnegie Trust. He has lectured widely and also examined in music at Univs. of Dublin and Birmingham. He received the Mus. Doc. *h.c.* from Durham Univ. in 1911 and was knighted in 1922. Now devotes himself to writing and research work. Editor of *Musical News*, 1924.

5 masses; a Requiem; many motets; a book on *Catholic Church Music*; *Old Rhymes with New Tunes*

(Curwen). Besides being mus. ed. of *Westminster Hymnal*, the official Catholic hymn-book for England, he has ed. a large number of editions of early Eng. church music, and a *Shanty Book* (Curwen. 1920). Consult art. in *Mus. Opinion*, Jan. 1920.—E.-H.

TERTIS, Lionel. Eng. vla.-player; *b.* West Hartlepool, 29 Dec. 1876. Brought to London when 3 years old. Started pf.-study at a very early age. Later, took up vn. as principal study at Leipzig. Continued at R.A.M. London. Str. quartet music drew his attention to vla. One of the finest vla.-players; lives in London; has inspired many comprs. York Bowen, J. B. McEwen, A. Carse, A. Bax, B. J. Dale have written concertos for him. The following works for vla. and pf. were also inspired by his fine playing:

2 sonatas (York Bowen); sonatas by E. Walker, W. H. Bell and A. Bax; a Suite and Phantasy by B. J. Dale; Fantasia by Cyril Scott; 2 pieces by Frank Bridge; 2 by Farjeon; concert piece by Bax; *Arab Love Song* by W. H. Bell. Other works: duet for vlas. (Fr. Bridge), *Romance* for vla. and organ (York Bowen), *Poem* for vla. harp and organ (York Bowen), Fantasy-4tet for 4 vlas. (York Bowen), 6tet for 6 vlas. (B. J. Dale), *Nocturne* for vla. ob. d'amore and pf. (Holbrooke).—E.-H.

TERVANI (ACHTÉ), Irma. Finnish contr. singer; *b.* Helsingfors, 4 June, 1887. Sister of Aino Achté. At first, stud. under her mother, the opera-singer, Emmy Strömer-Achté; later in Paris, 1904–6 (Duvernoy), and in Dresden, 1907. Since 1907, engaged at Dresden Court Theatre (now State Theatre). Numerous tours as operatic and concert-singer in Germany and Scandinavia. Has frequently appeared in concerts and operas in Finland. She has a magnificent voice and a highly individual style. Her most noted rôle is Carmen. Married (1916) the theatre-dir. Paul Wiecke; lives in Dresden.—T. H.

TERZIANI, Raffaele. Ital. compr. teacher; *b.* Rome, 23 April, 1860. Son of celebrated compr. and condr., Eugenio Terziani. For many years has been teacher, and is now vice-dir. of R. Liceo Mus. di Santa Cecilia, Rome, where his dir. important concerts. Comp. a *Messa da Requiem*, perf. at the Pantheon, 1896, and vocal and instrumental works.—D. A.

TETRAFONIA. New tonal effect obtained by dividing the octave into 4 perfectly equal parts, expounded by Domenico Alaleona (*q.v.*) in his *I moderni Orizzonti della Tecnica Musicale* (Turin, 1911, Bocca).—E.-H.

TETRAZZINI, Eva. Ital. s. singer; *b.* Milan, March 1862. Sister to Luisa T. (*q.v.*). Stud. in Florence; *début* there in 1882, singing Margherita in *Faust*; then principal opera houses of Europe and America. 1890, married Cleofonte Campanini and settled in New York. Her repertoire extended from *Aida* and *Norma* to *Mefistofele* and *L'Africana*.—D. A.

TETRAZZINI, Luisa. Italian operatic s. singer; *b.* Florence, 29 June, 1871. On completing studies in Florence, made *début* 1890 in *L'Africana*. In 1898, in Buenos Ayres, entered lyric and comic opera company of Raffaele Tomba; became one of its most admired members. She gained memorable successes in *Lucia*, *La Sonnambula*, *I Puritani* and others. On

returning to Italy, her successes continued, and grew still further when, in 1905, she went to North America, which became the chief field of her triumphs and monetary successes. Also appeared in London at Covent Garden. Now lives in Rome. In 1921, publ. in London a book of reminiscences entitled *My Life of Song*.—D. A.

TEYTE, Maggie. Eng. s. singer; *b.* Wolverhampton, Staffs, 17 April, 1890. Stud. under Jean de Reszke at age of 15 and made her *début* as Mélisande in Debussy's opera in May 1908, Opéra-Comique, Paris; 1st London appearance, Oct. 1909, Queen's Hall; 1910, sang in Beecham season at His Majesty's and Covent Garden (Cherubino, Marguerite, Mélisande, Antonia); 1911–13, seasons in America; 1913, Eng. tour and Riviera; Oct. 1913—March 1914, Amer. season; 1914–22, Paris, etc.; created the Princess in Holst's *Perfect Fool* (B.N.O.C. Covent Garden, May 1923).—E.-H.

THÉÂTRE NATIONAL DE L'OPÉRA (Paris Grand Opera House). The first public theatre for opera was opened in Paris, 19 March, 1671, by the poet Pierre Perrin, who was assisted by the musician Cambert. In the following year he sold the privilege he had obtained from the King, to Lully, who must be considered the true founder of French opera. The royal privilege of presenting grand opera was completely reserved for this theatre up to the second part of the xviii century. It had then to compete with the *Bouffons italiens* who were much assisted by the Queen and the *Encyclopédistes*. The privilege disappeared after the Revolution, but the Académie Nationale de Musique, being subsidised by the State, preserved its official character. It includes a free dancing school where the tradition of the classic dance is preserved. From 1874 the Académie Nationale de Musique has been housed in the sumptuous edifice built by the architect Charles Garnier. From 1914, under the manager, Jacques Rouché, who has introduced many happy innovations, it has enriched its repertoire with many important modern works.—H. P.

THEIL, Fritz. Ger. condr. and compr. *b.* Altenburg, Saxony, 6 Oct. 1886. Stud. at Leipzig Cons. (Nikisch, Sitt, Quasdorf and v. Bose); Kapellmeister of former Court Theatre, Altenburg; also of theatre, Sondershausen, and of Stadttheater, Plauen (Vogtland), Thorn and Würzburg. Recently has devoted himself exclusively to concert-work (condr., Hamburg, Hanover, Cologne, Chemnitz, Weimar, Wiesbaden, Magdeburg, etc.). Lives in Magdeburg.

Tone-poems for full orch.: *King Lear*; *Judith*; *Triumph of Life*; *Struggle of Life*; *Intermezzo* for str. orch.; vn. concerto; 2 songs for barit. and orch.: *The Fight* (text by Schiller), and *The Gravediggers* (text by Karl Mehnert).—A. E.

THELWALL, Walter Hampden. Eng. engineer; *b.* London. M.Inst.C.E.; his education and life-work as a civil engineer disposed him to study the scientific as well as the artistic branch of music. In 1893, 2 arts. written by him on the subject of "Descriptive Music" appeared in

Macmillan's Magazine. In these, certain general principles as to the province and capabilities of music were laid down, and these arts. led to a further study of Helmholtz and other acoustical authorities, and led him to the inevitable conclusion that the whole of modern music is based on the facts of Equal Temperament so strongly insisted on by Bach, facts which T. enunciated in these terms:

Let V = the vibration number of any musical note we please. Then $2V$ = the vibration number of its octave. Between these 2 notes there are 11 intermediate notes used in music, making 13 notes in all in the octave (including the 13th note, which is the octave to the 1st, and is really the 1st note of a second precisely similar octave). All these notes are of equal value and importance, and all are separated, each from each, as Euclid would have said, by a common ratio, which we may call R. The series of vibration numbers is then $V \times R^0$, $V \times R^1$, $V \times R^2$, $V \times R^3$, $V \times R^4$, $V \times R^5$, $V \times R^6$, $V \times R^7$, $V \times R^8$, $V \times R^9$, $V \times R^{10}$, $V \times R^{11}$ $V \times R^{12}$. But $V \times R^{12} = 2V$; Hence $R = \sqrt[12]{2}$. By means of this formula every succession and combination of mus. sounds can be expressed in terms of the vibration ratios of the notes. R is the ratio of the mean semitone. From this series he derived the "Note for Note" system of music, which for the first time, truly represents to the eye, and through the eye to the mind, the sounds really used in modern music. It aims at the simplification of notation and theory (see art. NOTATIONS).—E.-H.

THIBAUD, Alfonso. Argentine pianist; *b.* Paris in 1867. Appeared as prodigy; stud. Paris Cons. Toured France, England, Belgium, Holland. Joined Piazzini (*q.v.*) in founding the Cons. at Buenos Ayres, which bears their names, in 1903. Marmontel, in his *Histoire du Piano*, numbers him amongst the brilliant players of our day.—S. G. S.

THIBAUT, Jacques. Fr. violinist; *b.* Bordeaux, 27 Sept. 1880. The most representative of the Fr. school of living violinists. Stud. first under his father, then at Paris Cons., where he obtained 1st prize in 1896 after brilliant studies under Marsick. T. was discovered playing in the Café Rouge by Ed. Colonne, who engaged him for his orch. During winter of 1898, T. appeared at these concerts 54 times as solo violin. His rise to fame from this date was very rapid, and he soon devoted himself entirely to a virtuoso's career. Made numerous tours and seemed more and more attracted towards America, where he spent nearly a year. Returned to Europe and gave, at École Normale de Musique in Paris, a series of courses in advanced mus. interpretation. In technique he represents, not the almost acrobatic virtuosity of a Kubelik, to which he could easily have laid claim, but rather the wide and pure technique of the great classical school, passed down to him through Marsick and Ysaye, themselves disciples of Léonard and Vieuxtemps and thus linked up with Baillot-Rode, Viotti, Pugnani, Somis and Corelli. His tone has gained in power without losing that peculiar charm and distinction which is his characteristic. His style, formerly criticised as being slightly effeminate, has for years been a model of firmness, accuracy and eloquence. His recent rendering, with Alfred Cortot, of Germaine Taillefère's Sonata is a proof that the young Fr. school has no more able or virile an advocate.—M. P.

THIÉBAUT, Henri. Belgian compr. *b.* Brussels, 4 Feb. 1865. Stud. at Brussels Cons. vn. and compn. under Kufferath. Received the advice of Blockx. In 1893, gave harmony lectures at Cons.; 1894, founded School of Music and Declamation at Ixelles (suburb of Brussels), a first attempt in Belgium in mus. teaching accompanied by general culture. In 1899, retired from Cons. in order to devote himself entirely to his school, where he started (1899) most interesting courses of literary and mus. lectures. He also introduced into Belgium the Dalcroze system of Eurhythmics. 1907, founded an *Institut des hautes études musicales et dramatiques* at Ixelles, an annexe of the School of Music.

La Passion du Christ, sacred mus. drama; Le Juré, lyrical monodrama on words of Edm. Picard; Le Bourgeois Gentilhomme, mus. comedy on Molière's play; cantatas for solo, chorus and orch.; Fantaisie orientale, orch.; str. 4tets; pf. pieces.—É. C.

THIEL, Karl. Choral condr. *b.* Klein-Öls, Silesia, 9 July, 1862. Stud. at R. Inst. for Sacred Music, Berlin, and W. Bargiel's Acad. class; travelled in Italy with a public scholarship; received Mendelssohn Prize 1894; orgt. at Sebastian Ch. Berlin; master at R. Inst. for Sacred Music, whose *a cappella* choir he brought to a high standard; 1903, R. prof.; 1922, Ph.D. *h.c.* Breslau Univ.; successor to Kretzschmar as dir. of High School for Sacred Music.

Motets, masses (Missa choralis, Loreto Mass); Penitential Psalms (choir and orch.): cantata Maria (solo, chorus, orch.), etc.; new publ. of old unacc. music.—A. E.

THIESSEN, Karl. Ger. compr. *b.* Kiel, 5 May, 1867. Stud. at the Weimar and Würzburg Schools of Music; condr. of the Ostfriesland (Emden, Aurich) Choir; teacher and compr. in Zittau (Saxony).

Pf. solos and duets; choruses, male and female vs.; pieces for cello, and for vn.; Suite for strs., op. 9; symph. poem, King Fyalar, orch. op. 11; Romance, str. orch. and horn 4tet, op. 38; Suite in Olden Style, vn. and pf. op. 43.—A. E.

THIRION, Louis. Fr. compr. *b.* Baccarat (Meurthe et Moselle), 18 Feb. 1879. Teacher of organ and pf. at Nancy Cons. since 1898. All his work shows solid and brilliant workmanship, with a great wealth of harmony and rhythm.

Several sonatas; trio; str. 4tet; 2 symphonies (perf. at Concerts Colonne).—F. R.

THOMÁN, Stephan. Hungarian pianist; *b.* Homonna, Hungary (now annexed by Czecho-Slovakia), 4 Nov. 1862. Stud. 1881-5 under Liszt. Pf. prof. R. High School for Music, Budapest, 1881-1906. Amongst pupils were Ernst v. Dohnányi, Béla Bartók and Imre Keéri-Szántó.—B. B.

THOMAS, David Vaughan. Welsh compr. condr. and teacher; *b.* Ystalyfera, Glamorganshire, 15 March, 1873; educated Llandovery

Coll. and Exeter Coll. Oxford; M.A.; Mus.Doc. Oxon.; scholastic posts United Services Coll. Westward Ho, Devon; Monkton Combe School, Bath; Harrow School; specialist inspector in music under Central Welsh Board. His compns. have a fine individual quantity and are beautifully finished. He is a most effective lecturer on music and well known as an adjudicator and condr. Lives in Swansea. Dr. Vaughan Thomas has contributed some of the Welsh arts. for this Dictionary.

Cantatas, soli, chorus, orch.: *The Bard* (Breitkopf); *A Song for St. Cecilia's Day* (Curwen); *Llyn y Fan* (*The Van Lake*) (Novello). Settings of poems by George Meredith, solo v. and orch.: *Enter these Enchanted Woods*; *Dirge in Woods*; *Song in the Songless*; *When I would image her Features*. Settings of Welsh poems in the Cywydd metre, for solo v. harp, str.; many part-songs; anthems; songs, etc. (Swan & Co., London; Snell, Swansea.)—E.-H.

THOMPSON, Herbert. Eng. music critic; *b.* Hunslet, Leeds, 11 Aug. 1856. Educated at Wiesbaden (private school); St. John's Coll. Cambridge; M.A., LL.M.; Inner Temple, barrister-at-law (1879); critic of music and art, *Yorkshire Post* (Leeds) from 1886. More than any other writer he has consistently over a long period exercised a strong influence on the improvement of musical taste in the North of England.—E.-H.

THOMSON, César. Belgian violinist, teacher; *b.* Liège, 18 March, 1857. Stud. at Liège Cons. when 7—vn. under Léonard; finished brilliantly with Gold Medal. Solo vn. at private chapel of Baron von Dervies, then in orch. of the Bilse Philh. in Berlin. Prof. of vn. Liège Cons. 1882, and at Brussels Cons. 1897. Various tours in Europe, North and South America. In Italy he was called "Paganini redivivus." He has comp. very little; is responsible for practical eds. of great musicians of XVII and XVIII centuries, especially Ital. masters for whom he had a special affection. He upholds by active example the high traditions of greatest Belgian violinists, men like Léonard and Vieuxtemps.—C. V. B.

THRANE, Carl. Danish music historian; *b.* Fredericia, 2 Sept. 1837; *d.* Copenhagen, 19 June, 1916. Stud. law at Univ. Copenhagen; took degree in 1863; Secretary of Justice in the Supreme Court, Copenhagen, 1878. His mus. interests brought him into musico-literary field; already when young he attracted notice as critic on the fashionable Copenhagen weekly, *Illustreret Tidende* (*Illustrated News*). His first book, *Danske Komponister* (*Danish Composers*), 1875, gave vivid biographical sketches of C. E. F. Weyse, Fr. Kuhlau, J. P. E. Hartmann and Niels W. Gade. It was followed in 1885 by *Rossini og Operaen* (*Rossini and the Opera*) where the Ital. master is viewed in a new and interesting light. Also his work *Cœciliaforeningen og dens Stifter* (*Cecilia Soc. and its Founder*), 1901, deals with H. Rung and his services to music in Copenhagen in middle of XIX century. T.'s chief work is his book on history of R. Chapel of Copenhagen from 1648–1848, called *Fra Hofviolonernes Tid* (1908), where he makes an important contribution to the mus. history of Denmark during 2

centuries. *Weyses Minde* (*In Commemoration of Weyse*), 1916; treatises on *Napoleon og Musiken* (*Napoleon and Music*), 1897; *Fra Klavikordiets Tid* (*From the Time of the Clavichord*), 1898, must be mentioned. An interesting article by him (in Ger.) upon *Sarti in Copenhagen* may be found in *Sammelbände der I.M.G.* III (Leipzig, 1902).—A. H.

THREE CHOIRS FESTIVALS. A combined festival of Gloucester, Worcester and Hereford choruses, held at these 3 cathedrals in rotation. Secular concerts are given in the Shire Halls. First held 1724. The fests. were suspended in 1914 at the outbreak of war, and resumed in 1920 at Worcester. Hereford followed in 1921, Gloucester in 1922, and the rotation is now again fully established. For many years they have been cond. by the respective orgts. Dr. Herbert Brewer (Gloucester), Sir Ivor Atkins (Worcester) and (since Dr. Sinclair's death) by Dr. Percy Hull (Hereford).—E.-H.

THUE, Hildur Fjord. Norwegian operatic and concert-singer (s.); *b.* Christiania, 26 Jan. 1870. Pupil of Barbara Larssen, Christiania. *Début* as concert-singer in Christiania, 1892. Afterwards stud. in Paris under Artôt, Viardot, etc. At *Figaro* concert in 1895 she introduced Norwegian songs in Paris. Subsequently gave many concerts throughout France. Appeared in operas at Covent Garden, London. From 1907 to 1917 she lived in Shanghai, in the mus. life of which city she took a great part. Now living in Christiania.—U. M.

THUILLE, Ludwig. Ger. compr. *b.* Bozen (Tyrol), 30 Nov. 1861; *d.* Munich, 5 Feb. 1907. Pupil of his father, 1871–9 of Joseph Pembaur, Innsbruck, and of Rheinberger, Munich. Mozart Scholar, 1883, and in the same year teacher of pf. and theory at Munich School of Music, where he exerted remarkable influence on a number of young and talented students, the so-called "Munich Tonschule"; 1890, R. prof. Consult F. Munter, *A. Th.* (Munich, 1922).

6tet for pf. and wind instrs. B flat ma. op. 6; organ sonata; romantic overture for orch., *Midsummer Night's Dream*; male choruses; 5tet, E flat ma. for pf. and strs. op. 20; 2 vn. sonatas (op. 1 and op. 30); cello sonata, op. 22; organ sonata, E mi. op. 2; songs; pf. pieces; operas: *Theuerdank* (awarded a prize at Munich, 1897); *Lobetanz* (Carlsruhe, 1898); *Gugeline* (Bremen, 1901); made pf. arr. of Peter Cornelius' *Cid*. Publ. with R. Louis *Text-book on Harmony* (Stuttgart, 1907, Grüninger).—A. E.

THUREN, Hjalmar. Danish music historian; *b.* Copenhagen, 10 Sept. 1873; *d.* there 13 Jan. 1912. Took his theological degree at Copenhagen Univ.; studies of Danish mus. history and folk-lore; wrote interesting treatises upon his research work, namely:

Dans og Kvaddigtning paa Færöerne (*Dances and Poetical Lays of the Faroese*), 1901; *Folk-Song in the Faroe Islands* (with excerpt in Ger.), his principal work, 337 pages (F. F. Publ., Northern Series No. 2, Copenhagen, 1908); *The Eskimo Folk-Lore* (collab. with W. Thalbitzer), Eskimo language phonetically investigated on a journey in North Greenland 1900–1 (in Eng.; printed in *Meddelelser om Grönland*, Vol. XXXI, Copenhagen, 1904); *Vore Sanglege* (*Our Song-Games*) in *Danske Studier*, Copenhagen, 1908; *J. G. Naumann's Opera "Orfeus"* (in *Fra Arkiv og Museum*, Copenhagen, 1909).—A. H.

TIBETAN MUSIC. Is of two kinds: the folk-music and the developed music of the Lamas (priests). Both kinds are entirely founded on the pentatonic scale. See chapter XIV in Hon. C. G. Bruce's *The Assault on Mount Everest* (E. Arnold, 1923) and art. by T. H. Somervell in *Mus. Times*, London, Feb. 1923: also chapter I, sect. 4 of Jacques Bacot's *Le Tibet Révolté* (1912), pages 44–49.—E.-H.

TIERSOT, Julien. Fr. musicologist and compr. *b.* Bourg (Ain), 5 July, 1857. Pupil of Paris Cons. in 1877, under Massenet, Franck and Savard. Librarian of the Cons. 1883–1919. President of the Société Française de Musicologie (see SOCIETIES). His *Histoire de la Chanson populaire en France* (1885) took the *Prix Bordin.* It was publ. in 1889.

Rouget de Lisle (1892); *Chansons populaires* (from the Vivarais and Vercors districts), with d'Indy (1892); *Les types mélodiques dans la chanson populaire française* (1894); *Les Fêtes et les chants de la Révolution française* (1908); *Notes on Musical Ethnology* (1905); *Gluck* (1910); *Jean Jacques Rousseau* (Alcan, 1912; 1918); *History of the Marseillaise* (Delagrave, 1915); *Correspondence of Berlioz*; *Les Années romantiques*; *Le Musicien errant*; *La Musique dans la Comédie de Molière* (Paris, 1922). *Mélodies populaires des provinces de France* has extended to 8 series; also 45 *French Folk-songs* (Schirmer, New York); 60 *Folk-songs of France* (Ditson, Boston). Collab. with Saint-Saëns for *Pelletan Ed.* of Gluck's works. Compns.: *Rhapsody on Folk-tunes of La Bresse* (orch.); *Hellas* (after Shelley; chorus and orch.); symph. legend, *Sir Halewyn* (1897); orch. suite; songs, choruses, etc.—M. L. P.

TIESSEN, Heinz. Ger. compr. *b.* Königsberg, 10 April, 1887. Stud. law in Berlin and attended scientific, literary and philosophical lectures; 1906–9, pupil of Ph. Rüfer, and of W. Klatte. Now works in Berlin as critic and compr. Tiessen is a modern, full-blooded and sturdy East-Prussian composer.

2 symphonies (op. 15, C ma.; op. 17, F mi. *Death and Creation*); pf. sonata, op. 12; *Nature Trilogy*, pf. op. 18; 7tet, G ma. str. 4tet, fl. clar. and horn, op. 20; songs, op. 8 10, 22–23; *Songs of the Gallows* (*Morning Star*), op. 24; orch. piece, *Eine Ibsenfeier*, op. 7; *Rondo*, orch. op. 21; *Love Song*, orch. op. 25; *Death Dance Melody*, vn. and pf. (from music of Carl Hauptmann's *The Poor Broom-maker*); music for Immermann's *Merlin* (Berlin, 1918); 3 orch. pieces, op. 31 (from music to Shakespeare's *Hamlet*) (Berlin, 1920); guide to R. Strauss's *Legend of Joseph* (1914).—A. E.

TILINKÓ. See HUNGARIAN MUS. INSTRS.

TILMAN, Alfred. Belgian compr. *b.* Brussels, 3 Feb. 1848; *d.* Brussels, 20 Feb. 1895. Stud. at Cons. 1866–70. Was given charge by Gevaert of a course of harmony based on a new principle, but retired as his official nomination was delayed. In 1873 obtained 2nd *Prix de Rome*. Comp. many choral works, religious music, songs. His male-v. pieces enjoyed a great vogue during period of greatest choral activity in Belgium.—E. C.

TINEL, Edgar. Belgian composer; *b.* Sinay (East Flanders), 27 March, 1854; *d.* Brussels, 28 Oct. 1912. First music lessons from father, an organist in Sinay. 1863, entered Brussels Conservatoire under Fétis, Brassin, F. Kufferath, Mailly, Ad. Samuel and Gevaert. At first destined for a career as pianist, and played with success in London, 1876. Soon attracted by composition, to which he devoted himself

entirely. *Prix de Rome* in 1877, and from that moment his multiplied. 1881, director of School of Religious Music, Malines (succeeding Lemmens); 1896, succeeded F. Kufferath as professor of counterpoint at Brussels Conservatoire. Finally, in 1909, became director of the Conservatoire (succeeding Gevaert). He was a member of the Royal Academy. He was an ardent spirit, highly cultivated, with a great conscientiousness. His boyhood had been extremely hard. In his early student years in Brussels, he had lodged in a garret, subject to privations of every kind, singing in churches and teaching to provide his own wants and those of a younger brother with him. His works are distinguished by a perfect musical science, but their style is resolutely conservative and a little antiquated. In form, melody and bold development, they might be compared to the classic Romanticists. The choral writing is excellent; the orchestration somewhat massive. The influences (even reminiscences) of Mendelssohn, Schumann and Brahms appear clearly in his works. Their chief characteristics are ardour, conviction, and religious fervour, in which there is no genuine mysticism, but rather a kind of solidity which is very Flemish. On account of its character, and the excellent choruses, his *Franciscus* (*St. Francis*) may be considered the best oratorio written since Mendelssohn, thus possessing historical significance. The religious operas *Godelieve* and *Katharina* are of same character, but inspiration is not sufficiently sustained. We must also note the cantata *Kollebloemen*, a charming youthful work; *Adventlieder* (mixed chorus); the organ sonata and the *Te Deum*.

Stage works: *Godelieve* (Brussels, 1897), and *Katharina* (id. 1909). Vs. and orch.: *De Drie Ridders*, ballad, solo barit., chorus and orch.; *Kollebloemen*, lyric poem; *Franciscus* (1888); *Te Deum*; *Messe* (1898). Orch.: Overture and 2 symph. sketches for *Polyeucte*. Vs., organ: *Alleluia*, *Te Deum*, sundry motets, *Psalm CL*. Vs., pf.: *Adventlieder*. Organ sonata; pf. pieces. Wrote *Le Chant grégorien*, *théorie sommaire de son exécution* (1890). Consult E. T. by Paul Tinel (1922).—E. C.

TIRINDELLI, Pier Adolfo. Ital. violinist, compr. *b.* Conegliano, Veneto, 5 May, 1858. Stud. vn. under V. Corbellini; compn. under Boniforti at Milan Cons. 1870–6; under Grün in Vienna; and (1881–3) under Massart in Paris; 1883, toured Italy; 1884, prof. of vn. at Liceo Benedetto Marcello, Venice, and dir. in 1893. Appeared in U.S.A. as soloist with Boston Symphony Orch. 16 Dec. 1895; settled in Cincinnati as vn. teacher at Cons. 1895–1922. Two operas: *Atenaide* (Venice, 19 Nov. 1892); *Blanc et Noir*, (Cincinnati, 15 Dec. 1897). Chevalier of the Crown of Italy.

Concerto, vn. and orch. (Schmidt, 1900); pieces for vn. and pf. and songs (Ricordi; Brocco; Mariani; Schirmer).—J. M.

TISCHER, Gerhard. Ger. ed. and publ. *b.* Lübnitz, near Belzig (Brandenburg), 10 Nov. 1877. Stud. philosophy and theory in Berlin; 1903, Ph.D. (thesis, *Aristotelian Mus. Problems*); 1904, teacher of history, Handel High School, Cologne; 1906, ed. of *Rheinische Musik- und*

Theater-Zeitung, and head of publ. firm Tischer & Jagenberg, Cologne, which acquired, in 1921, the Wunderhorn Verlag (Munich) copyrights.—A. E.

TITTA, Ruffo. Ital. operatic barit. *b.* Pisa, 9 June, 1877. One of most celebrated living Ital. singers. Of humble origin; stud. in Rome at R. Liceo Mus. di Santa Cecilia, under Persichini. Then went to Milan, and, after a difficult period, made his *début* in Rome as the Herald in *Lohengrin* in 1898. His fame grew rapidly, and very soon was sought after by the most important opera houses in Europe and America. He is also a capable interpreter, and his renderings of *Amleto, Barbiere di Siviglia, Rigoletto* and other leading barit. parts are famous.—D. A.

TOCH, Ernst. Austrian accompanist (pf.); *b.* Vienna, 7 Dec. 1887. Stud. medicine and philosophy; self-taught musician; won Mozart Exhibition, 1909; Mendelssohn Exhibition, 1909; Austrian State prize for compn. four times. Until 1909, lived at Frankfort-o-M.; stud. pf. under Willy Rehberg; 1913, teacher at High School of Music, Mannheim.

12 str. 4tets; chamber-symphony; sonatas for various instrs.; symphony, *To my Fatherland* (soli, chorus, organ); pf. concerto; pf. pieces; vn. pieces; stage-piece, *The Children's New-Year Dream.*—A. E.

TOFFT, Alfred. Danish compr. *b.* Copenhagen, 2 Jan. 1865. Destined for business, but taught himself mus. compn. His pf. pieces and songs enjoy widespread popularity (Augener; Breitkopf; Wilhelm Hansen); also organ compns. and pieces for ob. and vn. His opera *Vifandaka* (an Indian subject arranged by compr.), was perf. with great success at R. Theatre, Copenhagen (publ. Wilhelm Hansen). Wrote music to Drachmann's play *Bonifacius Skœret* (*The Reef of St. Boniface*), given at Dagmar Theatre, Copenhagen; mus. critic of leading Copenhagen paper, *Berlingske Tidende*; inspector of military music in Denmark; chairman of Danish Composers' Club and of Soc. for Publ. of Danish Music.—A. H.

TOMÁŠEK, Jaroslav. Czechoslovak compr. *b.* Koryčany (Moravia), 1896. Pupil of Vít. Novák, studying mus. science at Prague Univ. A rich invention and a quite new accent of eroticism distinguished him from the first.

Chorus and orch.: *Štědrovečerní romance* (*Romance of Christmas Eve*); a str. 4tet; song-cycles: *Ženě* (*To Woman*); *Prosté srdce* (*A Simple Heart*) (Hudebni Matice, Prague).—V. ST.

TOMMASINI, Vincenzo. Italian composer; *b.* Rome, 17 Sept. 1880. Stud. in Rome, under Ettore Pinelli (vn.) and Stanislao Falchi (compn.), then in Germany under Max Bruch. One of the most notable young Ital. comprs. Comp. several operas: *Medea* (Trieste, 1906); *Uguale fortuna* (Costanzi, Rome, 1913; publ. Milan, Sonzogno); *Le donne di buon umore* (*The Good-humoured Ladies*), 1-act choreographic comedy on motifs of Domenico Scarlatti, written for Diaghilef's Russ. Ballet (London, 1919, Chester). Also various orch. works, amongst which *Chiari di luna* (Ricordi), successfully perf. at the Augusteo and elsewhere, and instr. and vocal

chamber compns. Has publ. various articles in the *Rivista Musicale Italiana.* Consult art. by G. Gatti in *Mus. Times* (London) Nov. 1921, —D. A.

TONALITÀ NEUTRE (*Neutral Tonalities*). Expression adopted by Domenico Alaleona (*q.v.*) in his arts. on modern harmony (publ. in *Rivista Musicale Italiana* in 1911) to indicate certain new tonal directions of an indefinite and suspended nature; and, in particular, certain æsthetic effects of the grouping of sounds resulting from division of octave into equal parts. (See ARTE DI STUPORE.)—E.-H.

TONER, Jean Baptiste. Scottish pianist; *b.* Glasgow, 11 June, 1891. Displayed marked gifts of improvisation at an early age; stud. in London and Germany; came under influence of Pachmann, who predicted a brilliant career. Specialises in Chopin.—J. P. D.

TONI, Alceo. Ital. compr. and writer; *b.* at Lugo (Romagna), 22 May, 1884. Pupil of Pratella (*q.v.*) at Lugo. Went to Milan, where he successfully devoted himself to composition, conducting and to mus. revivals. In 1921 cond. a series of concerts of Ital. music. at Bucharest, and also dir. other important concerts at the Augusteo, Rome. Comp. much vocal and instr. chamber - music (2 sonatas, a 4tet, a 5tet, songs, etc.), sacred music, and operas. His activity in reviving old music is important. Has held the technical direction of the *Raccolta nazionale delle musiche italiane*, publ. by Istituto ed. Milan; many sections of this collection being undertaken by him. Has also publ. other interesting eds. of old Ital. music through Ricordi (the principal concertos of Corelli), and some interesting studies in the *Rivista Musicale Italiana.* Now mus. critic of *Il Popolo d' Italia*, Milan.—D. A.

TONWORTMETHODE. See EITZ, CARL A.

TOONKUNST, Maatschappij tot bevordering der. This, the greatest Dutch mus. society, founded 1829 by A. C. G. Vermeulen, had in 1924, 37 independent local departments in 37 cities; altogether 8000 members. All departments have local choral societies (Amsterdam Toonkunstkoor of 600 voices, dir. by W. Mengelberg, is famous); some of them music-schools too (Amsterdam, dir. Ulfert Schults; Rotterdam, dir. Wouter Hutschenruyter; Utrecht, dir. Ant. Averkamp). The Amsterdam Toonkunst has since 1884 had, besides the music-school, a well-known Cons. (dir. 1884–95, Frans Coenen; 1895-1913, Daniel de Lange; from 1913 till 1924, Julius Röntgen, sen.). The company has a considerable library and examines music-students yearly (at Utrecht). United with this Soc. are the *Nederlandsche Koorvereeniging* (ed. of popular choral works), 1865, and the *Vereeiniging voor Nederlandsche Muziekgeschedenis* (ed. of ancient Dutch masterpieces of Sweelinck, Obrecht, Josquin des Près, etc.), 1868. The Soc. formerly gave frequent music-fests. (famous Rotterdam fest. 1864). Last Toonkunst fest. took place

1912, Amsterdam, cond. by Willem Mengelberg. —W. P.

TORCHI, Luigi. Ital. compr. and critic; *b.* Mondano (Bologna), 7 Nov. 1858; *d.* Bologna, 18 Sept. 1920. One of most praiseworthy musicians and writers of the last period. Stud. in his native city, and then at Naples Cons. under Serrao (compn.). Then went on some important journeys through Germany and France, for the purpose of study. 1885, was appointed teacher of history and æsthetics of music at Liceo at Pesaro; 1891, went to the Liceo at Bologna, where he was librarian and prof. of compn., which post he held until the last few years of his life. T. was the first translator and propagator in Italy of the literary works of Wagner.

L'Arte musicale in Italia, a national coll., in 7 large vols., of unpubl. and little-known Ital. mus. works from XIV to XVII century (Ricordi); *Eleganti canzoni ed arie italiane del secolo XVI (id.);   A Collection of Pieces for the Violin, composed by Italian Masters of the XVII and XVIII Centuries, harmonised and arranged with pianoforte accompaniment* (London, Boosey & Co.). His writings have mostly been publ. in the *Rivista Musicale Italiana;* some are of a historic character, and others critical, dealing with contemporary mus. productions; also a monograph on Richard Wagner (Bologna, 1890, Zanichelli). As a compr. he has left several operas and some symph. and sacred music. Consult Francesco Vatielli, *L. T.* (*Rivista Musicale Italiana,* 1920, No. IV).—D. A.

TORJUSSEN, Trygve. Norwegian compr. and music critic; *b.* Drammen, 14 Nov. 1885. Stud. pf. under Rosati in Rome; under Wiehmayer in Stuttgart; compn. at Cons. in latter city. Pf.-teacher at Cons. in Christiania. From 1913–23 music critic on *Verdens Gang.* He has won great popularity with his charming, tuneful lyrics and his pf. pieces, as well as his orch. pieces with their clever instrumentation.

Suite for orch. (1st perf. Christiania, 1920); *Norwegian Poems* for organ; vn. sonatas; pf. pieces (about 75); songs (including the charming *Silent Snow*).—J. A.

TORNER, Eduardo Martínez. Span. pianist and compr. *b.* Oviedo. Best-known for his *Cancionero musical de la lírica popular asturiana* (1919), one of the finest works on folk-lore produced in Spain. He stud. at *Schola Cantorum* under d'Indy, returning to Spain in 1914. —P. G. M.

TÖRNUDD, Axel. See FINNISH CHORAL MUSIC.

TORREFRANCA, Fausto. Ital. critic and music historian; *b.* Monteleone Calabro, 1 Feb. 1883. Graduated as an engineer in 1905; subsequently devoted himself to the history and æsthetics of music; stud. harmony and cpt. in Turin under Cesare Lena; 1915, became reader of mus. history at Rome Univ.; 1914, won by competition post of prof. of mus. history in the R. Cons., Naples; 1915, librarian there. Has been mus. critic of *L'Idea Nazionale,* Rome; is contributor to many Ital. and foreign reviews. Has publ. *La vita musicale dello spirito* (Turin, 1910, Bocca); *Giacomo Puccini e l'opera internazionale* (Turin, 1912, Bocca); also a rich series of studies in the *Rivista Musicale Italiana* and other reviews, on subjects of theory, criticism and mus. history with

special reference to Ital. music of XVIII century, showing the Ital. origin of the sonata and of the symphony; particularly noteworthy are studies on Venetian cembalo-players, Giovanni Platti and Baldassare Galuppi. His theoretical studies are concerned with mus. alliteration and development of tonality; his critical studies with various modern operas, amongst them Strauss's *Elektra, Rosenkavalier* and *Ariadne auf Naxos.*—D. A.

TORRES, Father Eduardo. Span. compr. *b.* Albaida (Valencia), 1872. In 1897, choirmaster of Tortosa Cath. Since 1910, choirmaster of Cath. of Seville; devotes much time to the study of modern Russ. music. Amongst his publ. works are to be found more than 100 pieces for organ, a mass and several choral works. (Editorial Orfeo ; Unión Musical Española, Madrid ; Senart ; Rouart, Paris).— P. G. M.

TORRINGTON, Herbert Frederic. Brit. orgt. violinist, condr. *b.* Dudley, Worcestershire, in 1837; *d.* Toronto, 20 Nov. 1917. His first appointments were at Bewdley and Kidderminster as orgt. and violinist. In 1858, went to Montreal, Canada, as orgt. of St. James's Street Methodist Ch., till 1869, when he went to Boston as teacher at New England Cons. of Music, and condr. of various societies, orgt. of King's Chapel, and violinist in Harvard Symphony Orch. In 1873 went to Toronto as orgt. of Metropolitan Ch. and condr. of Toronto Philh. Soc. In 1886 he organised the Toronto Mus. Fest., one of the landmarks in history of the mus. life of the city. The chorus consisted of 1000 and the orch. numbered 100 (Gounod's *Mors et Vita;* Handel's *Israel in Egypt,* etc.). In 1888 he organised and founded the Toronto Coll. of Music, which became affiliated with Univ. of Toronto and became known not only as a teaching coll. but also as examining body (see ACADEMIES) until its absorption by Canadian Acad. of Music. Torrington's work was of the kind known as mus. pioneering and as such it was of great importance to Canada. He received Mus.Doc. *h.c.* from Trinity (Toronto) University.—L. S.

TOSCANINI, Arturo. Ital. condr. *b.* Parma, 25 March, 1867. Stud. at the Parma Cons. where he gained his diploma in cello and compn. in 1885. After a first period of activity as a cellist, began his career as a condr. in 1886 at Rio de Janeiro, suddenly being called upon to replace another condr. in opera *Aida.* His reputation rapidly gained ground. In Turin, where he remained for several years, he dir. the 1st perf. in 1886 of Catalani's *Edmea* (of which compr. Toscanini was a fervent apostle), and founded and cond. the municipal orch. reviving again the popular concerts instituted by Pedrotti (*q.v.*). During the Exhibition of 1898, he cond. in Turin a long and memorable series of concerts. In same year, was appointed to La Scala, Milan, where he effected an artistic reform, remaining there until 1907, in which year he was nominated condr. of the Metropolitan, New York. He returned to La Scala in 1921, and is now the artistic dir. The concerts cond. by him at the Augusteo in Rome have become memorable. In 1920, toured in North America, with triumphant success. Many operatic seasons were cond. by him at principal opera houses all over the world: especially the Costanzi, Rome, in 1911, and at Busseto (Verdi's native place) in the year of the Verdi Centenary, 1913. Many new Ital. operas were presented for first time by Toscanini, amongst them *Pagliacci* and *Zazà* (Leoncavallo), *La Bohème* and *Fanciulla del West* (*The Girl of the Golden West*) (Puccini), *Germania* (Franchetti), *Gloria* (Cilea). Consult G. M. Ciampelli, *A. T.* (Milan, 1923, Modernissima ed.).—D. A.

TOSTI, Francesco Paolo. Ital. compr. *b.* Ortona a Mare (Abruzzi), 9 April, 1846; *d.* Rome, 2 Dec. 1916. Popular all over the world for his songs. Until 11 years old, he stud. in his native city; afterwards at Cons. San Pietro a Maiella, Naples. When about 30 years old, he went to London, where he gained great renown; for many years held the position of singing teacher at R.A.M. and became one of Queen Victoria's favourite comprs.; he was knighted by her in 1885. His songs to Ital., Fr. and Eng. words are counted by hundreds. His early compns. recalled the folk-songs of his native Abruzzo. Afterwards his music became richer and somewhat more elaborate.—D. A.

TOURNEMIRE, Charles. Fr. compr. and orgt. *b.* Bordeaux, 22 Jan. 1870. Pupil of César Franck, but more independent in style than his other pupils (*e.g.* P. de Bréville, Samuel Rousseau). Orgt. Ste.-Clotilde, Paris, since 1898; has given recitals in France, Berlin, Moscow, Switzerland, Brussels, Turin, Holland, etc. Gained *Prix de la Ville de Paris* for dramatic legend *Le Sang de la Sirène*. Prof. of chamber-music class, Paris Conservatoire.

Organ works: op. 2, 3, 10, 16, 19, 24 (Leduc; " Noël," Paris); notably *Triple Choral*, op. 41 (Janin). Chamber-music: pf. 4tet; pf. trio; 6tet, pf. and wind instrs.; pieces for cello, for horn, for vla., for ob., etc.; coll. of songs; 2 poems, v. and pf.; *Sagesse*, v. and pf.; *Triptyque*, op. 39; 5 symphonies.—A. C.

TOURNIER, Marcel. Fr. harpist; *b.* Paris, 5 June, 1879. Prof. of harp at Paris Cons., where he gained 1st prize for harp in 1899; *Prix de Rome* in 1909; *lauréat* of Institut. Succeeded his master Hasselmans in 1912. Is author of many pieces for harp; and also of a 2-act ballet.—F. R.

TOVEY, Donald Francis. Eng. compr. pianist, condr. *b.* Eton (Berks), 17 July, 1875. Reid Prof. of Music Edinburgh Univ. since 1914; B.A. Oxon.; M.Mus. Birmingham, *h.c.*; Mus. Doc. Oxon. by decree. Second son of the Rev. D. C. Tovey, rector of Worplestone, Surrey. Trained at home by Miss Weisse. Stud. compn. under Sir Walter Parratt, Higgs, and Sir Hubert Parry. Entered Balliol Coll. Oxford, 1894. First holder of Lewis Nettleship Memorial Scholarship in Music. From early childhood was associated with Joachim, who took a great personal interest in his mus. education. In 1900, gave chamber-

music concerts in London, Berlin and Vienna. At various later dates, gave a series of 6 historical pf. recitals of the works of Beethoven. Author of some 40 arts. on music and musicians in *Encyclopædia Britannica* (11th ed.); also of numerous essays and pamphlets on mus. analysis, issued in connection with concerts. In 1917, he founded the Reid Orch. of local orch. players and students, as a concert-giving organisation and an essential part of the course for degrees in music at Edinburgh University. In 1924, he was elected Hon. Fellow of R.C.M.

T.'s music is distinguished by high and serious aims. Though he shows marked regard for classic form and style, he is also an earnest and successful explorer of new forms, abundant evidence of which fact is to be found in his chamber-music. He is most happy in his treatment of the variation form. His pf. and str. 4tets have not yet received the attention they deserve. Personal acquaintance with the music is desirable; and actual performance leads to a deeper appreciation of the compr.'s style and method, revealing a sympathetic and highly organised imagination that disdains any sensational appeal. Those who seek for truth and beauty in musical expression will find much reward in a close study of his work.

As a pianist, T. must be placed in the front rank. His interpretations of Bach, Beethoven and Brahms are of great value, and exhibit not only remarkable powers of memory and physical endurance, but illuminate the music with a noble and lofty understanding. His technique is sure and virile, and shows a rare intelligence.

As condr. of the Reid Orch. at Edinburgh, he has obtained very gratifying results. Starting with raw, unpromising material, he has, within a few years, trained the players to a state of efficiency which enables him to produce, with highly creditable results, such works as Beethoven's Choral Symphony, and standard works of classical and modern composers.

But it is as a teacher, and an exponent of his art, that T. is perhaps regarded with the greatest esteem and affection. Tall and striking in appearance, he often seems to be treading the earth with his head in the clouds. He has a keen sense of humour, a deep reverence for the classics and a broad generous mind capable of inspiring others with enthusiasm. He is ever tolerant of adverse opinions, and sympathetic to all who are devoted sincerely to their art.

Opera: *The Bride of Dionysus* (Schott); symphony in D (ms.); pf. concerto in A (Schott); 5tet in C, pf. and str. (Schott); 4tet in E mi. pf. and str. (Schott); 3 str. 4tets; 4 pf. trios (2 with wind instrs.); sonata in G for 2 cellos; sonata in B flat, pf. and clar.; sonata in F, pf. and cello; and sonatas for solo instrs. (all Schott); songs and rounds (Augener; J. Williams).—G. B.

TOWNSEND, William. Scottish pianist; author; *b.* Edinburgh, 26 Nov. 1847. Stud. at R.A.M. London, and Cons. of Leipzig, 1865–72. Since domiciled in Edinburgh. One of most successful and progressive artists.

Books: *The Pianoforte*; *Balance of Arm in Pf. Technique*; *Piano Exercises*; *Modern Pianoforte Teaching*.—J. P. D.

TOYE, John Francis. Eng. musical critic and writer; b. Winchester, 27 Jan. 1883. Educated Winchester and Trinity Coll. Cambridge. Stud. under S. P. Waddington and Edward J. Dent; musical critic for various papers; visited, for purpose of comparative study, Germany, France, Italy, Austria and America, 1923–4.

Diana and Two Symphonies, a musical novel (Heinemann, 1913); 6 songs (Elkin, 1919); 2 songs (Curwen, 1921).—E.-H.

TRAGÓ Y ARANA, José. Span. pianist; b. Madrid, 25 Sept. 1856. At the age of 14, as a pupil at R. Cons. de Música under Eduardo Compta (one of Isaac Albeniz's teachers), obtained 1st prize for pf.-playing. Entered the Paris Cons. at 1875, obtaining also the highest distinction. In 1880, made his *début* in public at the Salle Pleyel, Paris. Indifferent to the opportunities opened to him as a virtuoso, he has devoted his life mostly to imparting his knowledge to others. His appearances in public have always constituted a mus. event in the Span. capital, where he is senior pf. teacher at R. Cons. de Música, and member of R. Acad. de Bellas Artes.—P. G. M.

TRAPP, Max. Ger. compr. b. Berlin, 1 Nov. 1887. Pupil of Paul Juon (compn.) and Ernst von Dohnányi (pf.); pf. teacher and condr. in Benda Acad. Berlin.

Str. 4tet, D mi. op. 1; pf. pieces, op. 2; pf. 4tet, op. 3; pf. 4tet, C mi. op. 4; cello sonata, op. 5; songs, op. 6; pf. 4tet, F ma. op. 7; *Sinfonia giocosa*, op. 8; pf. 4tet op. 9; *Rhapsody*, pf. op. 14; *Nocturne*, small orch. (for Shakespeare's *Timon of Athens*); music for magic-lantern play by Mörike, *The Last King of Orplid* (Königsberg, 1922).—A. E.

TREE, Charles. Eng. barit. singer and lecturer; b. Exmouth, 22 Aug. 1868. Has sung with most of the chief choral societies; has a repertoire of 80 oratorios, etc. ; also specialises on folk-songs and lectures on singing.

How to acquire Ease of Voice-production (own publ.); *Exercises in the Bel Canto* (1922).—E.-H.

TRÉGLER, Eduard, Czechoslovak organist, compr. b. Louny (Bohemia), 1868. Stud. in Prague, where 1890–8 he was choirmaster; 1898–1901, court-orgt. in Dresden; afterwards gave concerts all over Europe, often as pianist in chamber-music. Now prof. at Cons. Brno.

Church compns.; organ pieces; choruses; songs. (Fr. A. Urbánek; M. Urbánek, Prague.)—V. ST.

TREND, John Brande. Eng. writer; b. Southampton, 17 Dec. 1887. Educated at Charterhouse and Cambridge; assistant-ed. *Country Life*, 1910–12; travelled in Germany, Italy, Austria, Hungary, Scandinavia and Spain; served in army in Belgium and France, 1914–17; correspondent of *The Athenæum* in Spain, 1919.

The Mystery of Elche (*Music and Letters*, 1920, I, 2); *The Dance of the Seises* (*ib.* 1921, II, 1); *Modern Spain: Men and Music* (Constable, 1921); *Manuel de Falla* (*Music and Letters*, 1922, III, 2); *The Music of Spanish Galicia* (*ib.* 1924, V, 1) and other papers on history of Spanish music.—E.-H.

TRIFONIA. New tonal effect obtained by dividing the octave into 3 perfectly equal parts, expounded by Domenico Alaleona (*q.v.*) in his *I moderni Orizzonti della Tecnica Musicale* (Turin, 1911, Bocca).—E.-H.

TRIMITAS. See LITHUANIAN MUSIC.

TRNEČEK, Hanuš. Czechoslovak composer; b. Prague, 1858; d. there, 1914. 1882–8, in Schwerin, Germany; 1888, prof. of pf. and harp, Prague Conservatoire.

Operas: *The Violin-makers of Cremona*; *Amaranta*; *Andrea Crini*; 2 symphonies; Dance-suite; concertos for different wind-instrs.; pf. 4tet; sonata, vn. and pf.; harp compns.; many transcriptions for harp (Smetana); *Piano School* (together with Hofmeister).—V. ST.

TROIANI, Cayetano. Argentine pianist, compr. b. Castiglione Marino (Abruzzi), in 1873. Went to Buenos Ayres as a child. Stud. Naples Cons., returning to Buenos Ayres giving concerts of his own works. Prof. pf. Santa Cecilia Inst. there; then co-dir. with Hector and Hercules Galvani. Several orch. and pf. pieces—his latest, *Impressioni*, publ. by Ricordi.—S. G. S.

TROMBONE "FLUTTER" or Tongueing (Ger. *Flatterzunge*). Used for first time by A. Schönberg in his 5 *Orchestral Pieces* (1909). See full score (Peters), page 11:

Used later by R. Strauss, in opera *Die Frau ohne Schatten*.—EG. W.

TROMBONE GLISSANDO. Used for 1st time by A. Schönberg in his symph. poem *Pelléas and Mélisande* (1902), full score, p. 51:

Here the note E and its octave are fixed as basis of 6th position by the lips, and the tube is pushed through all the positions in such a way that the intervals of half- and quarter-tones can be clearly heard.—EG. W.

TROMPETTE, LA, See SOCIETIES.

TRONITZ, Jo (Phillip Jonas). Norwegian pianist; b. Christiania, 1 Aug. 1879. Stud. pf. under Christian Johnson, Erika Nissen and Martin Knutzen, Christiania, and J. Kwast, Berlin; theory under Gustav Lange and Otto Winter-Hjelm, Christiania. *Début* in Christiania in 1902; 1906–15, head-teacher of pf. at Cons. in Sherman, Texas; 1915–19, had his own pf.-school in Dallas, Texas. Numerous concerts throughout Norway; has perf. at concerts in New York, Brooklyn, Chicago, etc.—U. M.

TROTTER, Thomas Henry Yorke. Eng. teacher and writer on music; b. 6 Nov. 1854. M.A. New Coll. Oxford, 1887; Mus.Doc. 1892; stud. under Dr. F. E. Gladstone and Sir Frederick Bridge; cond. 1st perf. of Schumann's *Manfred* and Mendelssohn's *Athalie* in England; principal of Incorp. London Acad. of Music, from 1915. Has specialised on a new teaching of music, founded on ear-training and rhythmic culture.

Constructive Harmony (Bosworth) ; *Rhythmic Gradus* (*id.*); *Ear-training and Sight-reading Gradus* (*id.*); *The Making of Musicians* (H. Jenkins, 1922); *Music and Mind* (Methuen, 1924).—E.-H.

TROWELL, Arnold. Eng. cellist and compr. *b.* Wellington, New Zealand, 25 June, 1887. First stud. there under his father ; then under Hugo Becker in Frankfort-o-M. and later at Brussels Cons. where he won the prize for cello-playing. *Début* in Brussels; first appearance in London 1907, in a series of recitals; has specialised on old-time masterpieces, and has toured extensively. His cello concerto in D mi. op. 33, was first perf. at Liverpool Symph. March 1909 (London, Crystal Palace, July 1911). He plays a Domenico Montagnana cello (1720).

A large number of orch. works and cello pieces (Schott, London).—E.-H.

TRUMAN, Ernest. British orgt. and compr. *b.* Weston-super-Mare, England, 29 Dec. 1869. Now city-orgt. Town Hall, Sydney, Australia.

Magnificat (Latin words), soli, chorus, orch. (Paling & Co. Sydney); cantata-grotesque, *The Pied Piper*, soli, chorus, orch. (*id.*); *Song of Tribute*, barit. v. (*id.*); *Concert Prelude and Fugue*, organ (*id.*); much chamber and solo music, ms.—E.-H.

TRUNK, Richard. Ger. compr. *b.* Tauber-bischofsheim, Baden, 10 Feb. 1879. 1894–5, stud. at Hoch's Cons. Frankfort-o-M. (pf. and theory under Knorr); 1896–9, pupil of Rhein-berger, Kellermann, Bach, Günzburg, Buss-meyer and Erdmannsdörffer at Munich Acad. Accompanist of Eugen Gura; 1907, condr. of Munich Citizen Singers' Guild and of People's Choral Union; 1912, condr. of choral and orch. soc. *Arion*, New York; condr. of *Arion* at Newark at same time; 1914, returned to Munich; 1918, condr. Citizen Singers' Guild again.

Songs, op. 9, 16, 22, 26, 40, 41, 42 (12 songs from poems by Paul Verlaine); male choruses; mixed choruses (also with full orch.); orchestral grotesque, *Walpurgis Night*; vn. and pf. pieces; pf. 5tet; operetta, *Herzdame* (*Queen of Hearts*), (Munich, 1917); mostly publ. by Otto Halbreiter, Munich.—A. E.

TUA, Teresina. Ital. violinist; *b.* Turin, 24 May, 1867. Of humble origin; after a wandering life with her parents, who were travelling musicians, her unusual talent was so striking that she found help and protec-tion which enabled her to enter the Paris Cons. to study under Massart. The results were very brilliant; Tua became one of most admired of European violinists. After several triumphant tours through Europe, she settled in Italy in 1889, where she married the music critic, Count Franchi - Verney (1848 – 1911), not, however, giving up her career. In Berlin she had the support and praise of Joachim. Her concert activity continued, especially in Rome, where she had taken up her residence. After Franchi-Verney died, she contracted a second marriage in 1914 with Count Emilio Quadrio De Maria Ponteschielli. She also took the post of teacher at the Cons. in Milan.—D. A.

TURCZYŃSKI, Jósef. Polish pianist; *b.* Zytomierz, Wolhynia, 1884. Pupil of his father, then (1907–8) of Busoni in Vienna. *Début* in 1908. In 1911, 1st prize at pf. competition in Petrograd. Has played in all the European capitals; 1915–19, prof. at Kief Cons. Since 1920, prof. of the concert-pianists' class at Warsaw State Conservatoire.—ZD. J.

TURICCHIA, Giovanni. Ital. violinist; *b.* Alfonsine (Ravenna), 21 May, 1886. Stud. under his uncle Antonio T. (orch. leader at Monte Carlo); then at Liceo Mus. di Bologna. Concerts in Italy. 1907–11, teacher at Cons. of Malmö (Sweden); co-founder of Malmö Chamber-Music Soc.; 1911–12, orch. leader in Helsingborg; 1912, orch. leader at R. Chapel in Stockholm. Wrote *Contributo alla tecnica del violino* (ms., diploma at Copenhagen, 1909).—P. V.

TURINA, Joaquín. Spanish composer and pianist; *b.* Seville, 9 Dec. 1882. Began his studies early in life in his native town under Don Evaristo García Torres, choirmaster of Cath. (harmony and counterpoint), and Don Enrique Rodríguez (piano); also studied piano under Tragó, Madrid, and Moszkowski, Paris, where he lived 1905–14, studying composition under d'Indy at *Schola Cantorum*. His name is often associated with that of de Falla (compare the case of Albeniz and Granados), no doubt because for a number of years they were the two representatives of the young generation of Spanish musicians who became most prominent in the artistic circles of Paris. Their progress was very keenly followed by Debussy, Ravel, d'Indy, Florent Schmitt and others from whom they received great encouragement and valuable advice; also, their return to Spain in 1914, when the Spanish people became properly acquainted with the modern tendencies of their works (otherwise quite distinct from each other), was almost simultaneous. Another bond of union between these two composers is their Andalusian origin, which accounts for a certain affinity of colour, but not of construction, in their earliest works. Turina has a distinct and unmistakable personality of his own. His works vibrate with the vigorous picturesqueness of the landscape, the city and even the spirit of domestic life of Seville. He is a pianist of uncommon ability, and appears often as a soloist, being the pianist of the Quinteto de Madrid (also known as Quin-teto Turina), of which he is one of the founders. Was for a time one of the conductors of the Russian Ballet in Spain, and on special occasions has acted in the same capacity at some of the Madrid theatres and symphony concerts. Lives and teaches in Madrid. Through his unselfish and unsparing efforts to displace obsolete routine in teaching theory and composition, he is acknow-ledged, with Conrado del Campo, as a regenerating influence in Spanish musical education.

Stage works: *Margot*, lyric comedy, book by Martínez Sierra (prod. Teatro de la Zarzuela, Madrid, Oct. 1914); *Navidad*, book by Martínez Sierra (Teatro Eslava, Madrid, Dec. 1916); *La Adúltera Penitente*, Martínez Sierra's adaptation of Moreto's work (Teatro Novedades, Barcelona, June 1917); *Jardín de Oriente* (first perf. Madrid, 1923).

For orch.: *La Procesión del Rocío*, symph. picture (perf. Orquesta Sinfónica, Madrid, March 1913; 1st perf. in England under Sir Henry Wood, Queen's Hall, and Pedro G. Morales, Wigmore Hall, 1918); *Evangelio de Navidad*, symph. poem (Orquesta Sin-fónica, Madrid, April 1915); *Sinfonía Sevillana*, awarded a prize in a competition at Gran Casino, San Sebastian, Sept. 1920; *Danzas Fantásticas* (Orquesta Filarmónica, Madrid, Feb. 1920; 1st perf. in England under Sir Henry Wood, Queen's Hall, 1922).

Chamber-music: pf. 5tet (1st perf. Quatuor Parent, Salle Æolian, Paris, May 1907; 1st perf. in England, Cambridge Univ. Mus. Soc. concert of Span. music under P. G. Morales, 1919); str. 4tet (Quatuor Touche, Société National, Paris, March 1911; 1st perf. in England, London Str. Quartet) ; *Escena Andaluza*, for vla. pf. and str. 4tet (Société National Indépendant, Paris, Feb. 1912; 1st perf. in England Cambridge Univ. Mus. Soc. concert of Span. music under P. G. Morales, 1919, soloist Lionel Tertis); *Poema de una Sanluquena*, suite for vn. and pf. (1st perf. London, 24 June, 1924, Angel Grande's recital).

Vocal: *Rima de Becquer* (Æolian Hall, London, May 1911); *Poema en forma de canciones* (Teatro de la Republica, Lisbon, March 1918); *Tres Arias*. Pf. (1st perf. by compr.) : *Sevilla*, picturesque suite (Quatuor Parent Concerts, Paris, 1909); *Sonata Romántica* (Salon d'Automne, Paris, Oct. 1909); *Rincones Sevillanos* (Ateneo, Seville, Jan. 1911); *Tres Danzas Andaluzas* (Filarmónica, Malaga, Nov. 1912); *Recuerdos de mi Rincón*, tragi-comedy (Ateneo de Madrid, Jan. 1915); *Album de Viaje* (Sociedad Nacional, Madrid, May 1916); *Cuentos de España* (Sociedad Nacional Filarmónica, Malaga, Nov. 1918); *Niñerias*; *Sanlúcar de Barrameda* (Sanlúcar de Barrameda, Spain, Sept. 1922); *Mujeres Españolas* (Sociedad Nacional, Madrid, Dec. 1917, soloist Ricardo Viñés).

Books: *Enciclopedia abreviada de Música*, 2 vols.; *Colección de Artículos y Criticismos* (*Revista Musical*, Bilbao; *La Tribuna*, Madrid).

(Publ: Unión Musical Española; Biblioteca Renacimiento, Madrid; E. Demets; Rouart, Lerolle; A. Z. Mathot; Ed. Mutuelle, Paris; Schott.)—P. G. M.

TURNER, Walter James. Eng. poet and music-critic; *b.* Shanghai, China, 13 Oct. 1889. Stud. under his father W. J. T. (orgt. of St. Paul's Cath. Melbourne, Australia); and privately in Dresden, Munich and Vienna. Music critic for *The New Statesman*. His views on music appear to rule out the Romantic school which introduced literary and other external influences into the tonal art. From Bach and Mozart, he seems thus to leap to Debussy, Ravel and the moderns,

regarding the Romantic school (Beethoven, Schumann, Wagner) as a side-track from the genuine line of musical evolution.

Several books of poems; *Music and Life*, coll. of essays (Methuen, 1921); *Variations on the theme of Music* (Heinemann, 1924).—E.-H.

TUSCH (Ger.). The term is related to Tucket. A flourish for tpts. on State occasions. Weber wrote one of 4 bars for 20 tpts. The term is now used for the custom in Ger. orchs. of giving on special occasions, at rehearsals or concerts, a welcome to a condr. or compr. to whom they desire to show honour. When the enthusiasm of the audience has reached a certain pitch, the tpts. horns and trombones blow a *Tusch*.—E.-H.

TYRER, Anderson. English pianist; *b.* 17 Nov. 1893. Stud. R. Manchester Coll. of Music, winning a County Council 4 years' scholarship; served in the army 1914–18; *début* at Beecham Promenade concert in 1919 (Rachmaninof concerto No. 2); gave a series of orch. concerts in Queen's Hall, London, and played concertos by Beethoven, Rachmaninof, Grieg, Tchaikovsky, Arensky, Liszt, and Mackenzie. Has played the pf. part in Scriabin's *Prometheus* several times.—E.-H.

TYRWHITT, Gerald. See BERNERS.

TYSOE, Albert Charles. Eng. orgt. *b.* Northampton, 12 Jan. 1884. Stud. under C. J. King there; later under Dr. Cuthbert Harris and Dr. Iggulden; Mus.Doc. Dunelm. 1915. Orgt. Leeds Parish Ch. from 1920; chorus-master Leeds Mus. Fest. 1922; condr. Halifax Choral Soc. 1923.—E.-H.

U

UBEDA, José María. Span. orgt. *b*. Gandía. Orgt. at the Real Colegio Corpus Christi, Valencia. Dir. of Valencia Cons. (founded 1880). The best Span. orgt. of his time. Author of *Psalmodie organica*; *Estudios Progresivos* and other works on organ technique.—P. G. M.

ÜBERBRETTL. A series of scenic miniatures brought out in beginning of 1901 by the poet and author Ernst von Wolzogen, with object of raising artistic standard of variety and speciality theatre. Besides Wolzogen, O. J. Bierbaum and Franz Wedekind were active representatives of Überbrettl, while Oscar Straus undertook the mus. arrangements. This movement had a lasting effect on the literary cabaret in Germany.— A. E.

UDBYE, Martin Andreas. Norwegian compr. *b*. Trondhjem, 18 June, 1820; *d*. there, 10 Jan. 1889. As compr. was at first self-taught, but in the beginning of the 'fifties he went to Leipzig and stud. theory under Hauptmann, organ under C. F. Becker. On returning home, became orgt. in Trondhjem; afterwards also headmaster of an elementary school and singing-master at the Cath. School. Has written about 50 works. Of his chief work, *Fredkulla* (*The Maid of Peace*), only fragments have been perf. The overture was played at the Musical Fest. in Christiania, 1914. The work was taken up for production at Christiania Theatre and the rehearsals were in full swing, when the burning down of the theatre in 1877 put a sudden end to all opera productions.

Operetta, *Junkeren og Flubergrosen* (perf. in Christiania); 2 mus. plays; 3 str. 4tets (2 printed); cantatas; organ preludes, op. 37; works for cello and pf.; songs; chorales. Fragments of the last and most important cantata (Music Fest. Trondhjem, 1883) are still heard. A book of school-songs with 166 songs arr. for 3 vs. enjoyed in its time considerable popularity.—U. M.

UGARTE, Floro M. Argentine compr. *b*. Buenos Ayres in 1885. Stud. at Paris Cons. under F. Fourdrain. His chief work is the ballet *Sigolene* (in collab. with Fourdrain), given at Tolosa Variety Theatre. Also prod. in Argentina *Entre las Montañas*, a symph. poem, and 2 orch. suites (*Paisajes de Estio*; *Escenas infantiles*). An operetta *Saika* (Colón Theatre, July 1920) was very successful. Also many songs, and chamber-music pieces.—A. M.

UIMONEN-JÄNNES, Annikki. Finnish m.-sopr. singer; *b*. Kuopio in 1891. Stud. at Helsingfors Music Inst., and in Vienna. Opera singer in Czernowitz, 1912–13; guest-singer at opera houses of Prague, Weimar and Hamburg; 1914–17 at the Finnish Opera. Has given concerts in Finland, Stockholm, Copenhagen and Petrograd.—T. H.

ULVESTAD, Marius Moaritz. Norwegian compr. *b*. Aalesund, 11 Sept. 1890. Pupil of Cons. in Christiania. Afterwards went for study to Germany, France and Italy. Gave in 1919 in Christiania a successful concert of his own works, in which his original lyrical qualities won great appreciation. Started in 1921 in Christiania a music-acad. in which he himself teaches theory and compn. Musical critic on *Arbeiderpolitiken*, 1921; on *Morgenposten* from 1922.

Cantatas; 2 orch. suites; 52 songs and ballads; a choral work with solo and orch.; male-v. choruses; 110 songs for mixed and male chorus.—J. A.

UNEQUAL TEMPERAMENT. A method of tuning which leaves a few keys perfectly tuned (with the intervals free from "beats"); that is, in Just Intonation; but leaving the other, more remote, keys badly out of tune. This method is also called the Mean-tone System. It has now been superseded by the Equal Temperament.— E.-H.

UNGER, Hermann. Ger. compr. and author; *b*. Kamenz (Saxony), 26 Oct. 1886. Stud. Germanic and classical philology, Freiburg, Leipzig and Munich; music with Edgar Istel and Joseph Haas at Munich; 1911–13 with Max Reger at Meiningen. Music critic of *Rheinische Musik-zeitung*, Cologne.

Pf. miniatures and other works; songs; *Hymn of Life* (Verhaeren), barit. solo, chorus, orch. op. 25; orch. songs, op. 31; *Totenfeier*, unacc. chorus, op. 12; *Ancient German Songs*, mixed chorus, op. 30; for orch.: *Night*, 3 sketches, op. 8; *German Dances*, op. 16; *Pictures from the East*, op. 18; *Levantine Rondo*, op. 22; *Country Scene*, op. 24; symph. suite, *The Seasons*, op. 26; symphony, D mi. op. 27. In ms.: *Jester's Songs*, barit. (Bierbaum); pf. clar. and vla. trio; str. trio; vn. sonata; *Divertimento*, str. 4tet; Variations on original theme, 2 pfs.; *Night*, Japanese operetta, mixed chorus and full orch.; Goethe's *God and Bayadere*, recitation, chorus and full orch.; stage-music to Hofmannsthal's *The Jester and Death* and Schnabel's *Return*; songs for contr., s. and t. vs. and mixed unacc. choruses. Books: *The Musical Layman's Breviary* (1920); *The Layman's Primer of Music Theory* (1922); *Max Reger* (1921).—A. E.

UNIVERSAL EDITION, Vienna. The most important of Austrian music-publishing firms. Founded 1901 for editing classical and standard mus. compns. independent of the Ger. market. In 1904 the firm acquired Munich publ. house of J. Aibl, comprising many works of R. Strauss and Reger, as well as von Bülow's arrs. The U.E. acquired the complete works of Bruckner and Mahler; later of Schönberg, Marx, Schreker, Bittner, Zemlinsky. Also publ. works of contemporary comprs.: Wellesz, Hába, Křenek, Petyrek, Webern, Pisk; Paul Graener, Braunfels, Kaminsky; Bartók and Kodály; Delius, Ethel Smyth; Milhaud; Casella, Malipiero and Respighi; Szymanowski, etc. Also publ. new Catholic church music (Springer, Goller, Wöss) and periodical *Musica Divina*. Their *Denkmäler der Tonkunst in Österreich* (ed. by Guido Adler) numbers 56 vols. The modern mus. journal *Musikblätter des Anbruch* (ed. by Paul Stefan) is also their publication. Their stage works comprise the operas of Schreker, Bartók, Bittner, Braunfels, Delius, Rezniček, Zemlinsky, etc. The total output of the U.E. numbers over 7000 vols. Thanks to the circumspection and energy of its managing dir., Emil Hertzka, the firm plays an important rôle in the development of contemporary music.—EG. W.

UNIVERSITIES. *AUSTRALIA.*—**Adelaide:** Prof. Dr. Harold E. Davies.

ENGLAND. — **Birmingham:** The Richard Peyton Chair of Music was founded by donor in 1905, first holder being Sir Edward Elgar, who resigned in 1908. His successor was Granville Bantock, who initiated the present course for the degrees of B.Mus. and M.Mus. The course, after matriculation, includes study of all branches of theory ; and special attention to particular subjects, such as development of the art-song, folk and national music, early Greek music, the Elizabethan period, the organ works of Bach, the pf. works of Beethoven and Chopin, the orchestra, choral music, opera, etc. The first B.Mus. was admitted to degree, after a 3-year course, in July 1912. Since then, an Honours School in Music has been instituted, and music has been constituted a subsidiary subject for B.A. degree, and Honours School of Mathematics. As a new development in requirements for Honours School of B.Mus. and as alternative to compn., candidates may submit, at the third year's examination: (a) A literary thesis on one of the following subjects: (i) an important mus. work; (ii) an historical period of music; (iii) the theoretical development of music; or (b) Research work in transcription, editing, and rendering available for public use, important mss. in an Eng. or foreign library. **Cambridge:** Originally gave degrees, B.Mus. and D.Mus. (1st Bac. given in 1463, 1st Doctor 1463 or earlier). In 1893 (with 5 and 7 years' grace), residence was required, and the degree of Master of Music (M.Mus.) instituted in order to qualify mus. graduates for membership of Senate. Only one person has taken it by examination during the 30-odd years since its institution (F. H. Shera). It has been given as an hon. degree to P. P. David (Uppingham) and to Cecil J. Sharp (1923). The Mus.D's under the old Regulations since 1893 are G. J. Bennett 1893, G. F. Huntley 1894, Laurence Walker 1897, H. Walford Davies 1898, J. Eaton Faning 1900 (all these non-resident) ; and still on the old regulations, though they resided : C. Wood 1894, E. Markham Lee 1899, R. Vaughan Williams 1901. Only seven have passed under the New Regulations (1893): E. W. Naylor 1899, A. Somervell 1904, W. H. Speer and H. Blair 1906, C. B. Rootham 1910, F. W. Wadeley 1915, H. D. Statham 1923. The Univ. bestowed hon. Mus.D.'s in 1893 on Saint-Saëns, Max Bruch, Tchaikovsky and Boito; in 1894 on Grieg; 1900 on Cowen and Elgar, 1902 on

Horatio Parker, 1907 on Glazunof, 1910 on Sir Walter Parratt. There was a non-resident Prof. of Music, Sir Charles Stanford, from 1887 (succeeding Macfarren) until 1924, when he resigned. Dr. Charles Wood was appointed Professor under new conditions in June 1924. **London :** First degree in Music, 1879. Candidates required to pass Matriculation. The professorship dates from 1902. In 1924, the King Edward Prof. of Music was Sir Frederick Bridge. The examiners were Dr. C. W. Pearce and Prof. C. H. Kitson. Instruction courses are recognised at R.C.M., R.A.M., Trinity Coll. of Music, Battersea Polytechnic, Chelsea Polytechnic. T. F. Dunhill is Dean of the Faculty of Music. **Manchester:** A lectureship in harmony was founded in Owen's Coll. in 1880. The Faculty of Music was instituted in connection with federation of Univs. of Manchester, Leeds, Liverpool, in 1891, Dr. Hiles being then appointed. He was retained in this position when the Faculty was incorporated in new charter in 1903. The present holder (1924) is Dr. Brodsky, Principal of R. Manchester Coll. of Music. The present lecturer in harmony is Dr. Keighley (appointed 1920); in history of music, Dr. Wilcock; in acoustics, Prof. W. L. Bragg, M.A., F.R.S., Nobel Prizeman. Students are required to have passed matriculation or some recognised equivalent. The lectures and practical work all take place at R. Manchester Coll. of Music, and cover the usual subjects. Up to 1922 the Univ. admitted 16 Doctors and 22 Bachelors in Music. **Oxford:** Gives degrees of B.Mus. and D.Mus. First Bac. was R. Widow (1499) ; first Doctor, Robert Fairfax (1511). In 1862, Sir F. Gore Ouseley reformed the faculty and instituted formal examinations for both degrees. In 1870, candidates were required to matriculate, and in 1877 to pass Responsions or a recognised equivalent. In 1890, this was reduced to a special Prelim. Exam. for Students in Music. In 1890, Sir J. Stainer instituted various lectures in music; these were continued by Sir Hubert Parry (Prof. 1901-8), Sir Walter Parratt (1908-18) and the present Prof. Sir Hugh Allen (from 1918). **Sheffield:** There is no Chair of Music, but there is a lectureship (present holder, G. E. Linfoot). The work carried on in day and evening courses does not cover the more advanced aspects of the art, and the Univ. does not, therefore, award a degree or diploma. **Southampton:** A Chair of Music was founded in 1920. The present holder is F. J. Leake, B.Mus.

SOUTH AFRICA.—**Cape Town:** Chair of Music founded in 1918. Arts course in Music (I and II), Mus.Bac. and Mus.Doc. degrees instituted 1921. Prof.W.H.Bell. Lecturer,V. Hely-Hutchinson. (S.A. Coll. of Music incorp. 1923.) **Johannesburg:** Arts course and Mus.Bac. degree instit. 1921. Prof. Percival Kirby (formerly mus. adviser to educational department of Natal).

WALES.—The Univ. of Wales was constituted in 1894. There are now 4 constituent colleges, and music has played its part as an educational factor in each. **Aberystwyth:**

The senior coll., opened Oct. 1872; two years later Dr. Joseph Parry came over from Danville in America to Aberystwyth as Prof. of Music. This was probably the first attempt in Wales to put mus. education on a recognised basis. Dr. Parry continued for sessions 1874–8. Prof. David Jenkins succeeded him and held post till his death in 1914. Dr. D. J. de Lloyd, present lecturer in music, was his pupil, and the first mus. graduate of Univ. For a short time a str. quartet from Paris under Mme. Barbier was connected with the Coll. **Cardiff:** When the Coll. was opened in 1883, Clement Templeton M.A. was appointed lecturer in music. In session 1885–6 a mus. soc. was formed, and chamber-music concerts instituted. In 1888 Dr. Joseph Parry was appointed lecturer, and the music course extended. In 1903 Dr. David Evans succeeded Dr. Parry, and in 1908 a Chair of Music was founded and Dr. David Evans appointed Prof. As a result of report of a Royal Commission on Univ. Education in Wales, the National Council of Music was formed, and the acceptance by Sir Walford Davies in 1919 of the dual posts of Dir. of Music for Univ. and Prof. of Music at Aberystwyth Coll. marked a new era. Since advent of National Council of Music (q.v.), the aim and policy have been to concentrate not so much on granting degrees, as upon making music a vital factor in Univ. life, giving facilities to students of arts, science, law and agriculture constantly to hear, and study good music. In this policy the Council of Music include the permanent institution • of weekly college concerts throughout each session; college choral unions; college orch. unions; open lectures weekly. Special facilities are offered to students becoming teachers, to learn an instr. A feature of college mus. life at Aberystwyth has been the annual 3-days orch. fest. **Bangor:** The music has been at various times under dir. of Dr. Roland Rogers, Dr. J. Lloyd Williams, Mr. Harry Evans and Dr. Caradog Roberts. There was no music department formed until Mr. T. E. Davis was appointed, and the sessions 1921–2 gave Bangor the first experience of a fairly complete music department. **Swansea:** There is as yet no complete music department in this the youngest of the colleges, but the Dir. of Music visits the Coll. to lecture, and weekly concerts are run by Coll. Mus. Club. Degrees and diplomas in music are granted at Aberystwyth and Cardiff Colleges; residence is required for both. At Bangor, diplomas are granted but not degrees, All 3 colleges have an efficient staff to provide tuition in various branches of mus. education.

U.S.A.—The Univs. of Michigan, Wisconsin, Illinois, Kansas, and Oklahoma have been foremost in musical development. Pennsylvania, Indiana, California, and Colorado have very thoroughly organised departments for musical theory.—E.-H

URBACH, Otto. Ger. compr. *b.* Eisenach, 6 Feb. 1871. Pupil of Müller-Hartung and Stavenhagen in Weimar; Bernhard Scholz,

Knorr and Humperdinck in Frankfort; Draeseke in Dresden and Klindworth in Berlin. Liszt scholar, 1890; Mozart scholar, 1893; 1898, pf. teacher at Dresden Cons.; 1911, professor.

Comic opera, *The Miller of Sans-Souci* (Frankfort, 1896); overture, *Mountain Excursion (Bergfahrt)*; str. 4tet, *Horsila*; 7tet for wind instrs.; Suite for vn.; pf. pieces and songs.—A. E.

URBAN, Heinrich. Ger. compr.; pf. teacher; *b.* Berlin, 27 Aug. 1837; *d.* there, 24 Nov. 1901. Pupil of Hubert Ries, Laub, Hellmann; since 1881, teacher at Kullak's Acad. Among his pupils were Siegfried Ochs, Arthur Bird, Paderewski and others.

Symphony, *Spring*, A flat ma. op. 16; overtures: *Fiesko*, op. 6; *Scheherezade*, op. 14, and *To a Carnival Play*; fantasy-piece, *The Pied Piper of Hamelin*; vn. concerto; vn. pieces; songs, etc.—A. E.

URETA, Rojo Osvaldo. Chilean pianist; *b.* Quilpué, 1897. Stud. in Chile; in 1913 his 1st concert at Valparaiso obtained an immediate success.—A. M.

URIARTE, Father Eustaquio de (O.S.A.). Span. musical scholar; *b.* Durango (Vizcaya), 2 Nov. 1863; *d.* Motrico, 17 Sept. 1900. Joined Augustinian order in Colegio de Agustinos Filipinos, Valladolid, 1878. In 1888, sent to the Abbey of Silos (Burgos), then in charge of a community of Fr. Benedictines, with a view to mastering the Fr. language. There, impressed by the way in which liturgical music was sung by those monks who had learned Gregorian chant in the school of Solesmes (France), he conceived the idea of restoring the Gregorian chant to its original purity. To this end, he devoted all the efforts of his life, doing much valuable writing and congress work. Started his career as a writer in the *Revista Agustiniana*. His most important arts. were written, later on, for review *La Ciudad de Dios*, publ. by the community of the R. Monasterio de San Lorenzo, Escorial, Madrid. He made himself prominent as pioneer of his cause at the Congreso Católico Español, held in Madrid in 1888; he helped materially in the creation in Spain of the Asociación Isidoriana de la Reforma de la Música Religiosa. In 1891 appeared his most important work, the *Tratado teórico-práctico de canto gregoriano, según la verdadera tradición* (Imprenta de Don Luis Aguado, Madrid). He never saw the ambition of his life fulfilled.—P. G. M.

URIBE, Guillermo. Columbian compr. Pupil of Vincent d'Indy in Paris; dir. of National Cons. in Bogotá. Comp. songs; sonata, vn. and pf.; str. 4tet; and other pieces with a decidedly modern flavour.—F. H. M.

URLUS, Jac. Dutch t. singer; *b.* Herckenrath, Limburg, in 1867. His unusually fine voice was accidentally discovered by the opera-director De Groot. He stud. singing in Utrecht under Averkamp, Nolthenius and Cornelis van Zanten, 1888–94; engaged at Dutch Opera, 1894–1900; went to Germany in 1900 and rose suddenly to fame with Wagnerian parts; sang in *Lied von der Erde* at Mahler Festival, Amsterdam, 1920.—W. P.

URSPRUCH, Anton. Ger. compr. and pf. teacher; *b.* Frankfort-o-M. 17 Feb. 1850; *d.* there, 11 Jan. 1907. Pupil of Ignaz Lachner and M. Wallenstein; later of Liszt and Raff; sometime pf. teacher in Frankfort Acad.; then at Raff Acad. since 1887.

Pf. sonata for 4 hands; pf. concerto; Variations and fugue on a theme of Bach, for 2 pfs.; symphony, E flat ma. op. 14; pf. 4tet; trio; choral songs; 2 operas: *The Storm* (Frankfort, 1888); *The Most Impossible of All* (Carlsruhe, 1897). He wrote a work on the Gregorian Choral (1901).—A. E.

URTEÁGA, Luis. Span. orgt. and compr. of religious music; *b.* at Villafranca (Guipuzcoa), 1882. Lives at Zumaya.—P. G. M.

U.S.A. MUSICAL FESTIVALS. Although the U.S.A. can boast of no such insts. as great choral fests. of England or Lower Rhine Fests. or fests. of Allgemeiner Deutscher Musikverein in Germany, there are some sufficiently regular to establish a tradition, which have not failed to exercise a wholesome influence. Emphasis is laid on choral part, but orch. side is not neglected. The orch. is generally professional, symphony orch. of seat of fest. or of some near-by city. In many cases the regular condr. of symphony orch. directs purely instr. part of fest. Some of more important are:

(i) *Worcester Musical Festival,* annually at Worcester, Mass. No fest. in 1918, because of an influenza epidemic. First was held 1858. Condrs.: Carl Zerrahn (1866–97), George W. Chadwick (1898–1901), Wallace Goodrich (1902–7), Arthur Mees (1908–19), Nelson P. Coffin (from 1920).

(ii) *Cincinnati May Festivals,* biennial. Begun 1873 by Theodore Thomas who cond. until 1904. Followed by Frank Van der Stucken (1906–12), Ernst Kunwald (1914–16), Eugène Ysaye (1918–20). No fest. in 1922.

(iii) *Springfield Music Festival* of Hampden County Mus. Association, started 1889. George W. Chadwick cond. 1889–99. Then, after interval of a year, C. S. Cornell cond. 1901, 1902. In 1903 the Association was reorganised and with John J. Bishop as condr. has held its reunions ever since.

(iv) *Ann Arbor Festival* at Univ. of Michigan in Ann Arbor, founded 1893 and cond. by Albert A. Stanley 1893–1921. In 1922 Earl V. Moore was condr.

(v) *Norfolk Festival* of Litchfield County Choral Union at Norfolk, Conn. begun in 1899. Condrs.: R. P. Paine (1899–1915), Arthur Mees (1900–21), R. P. Paine and H. P. Schmidt (1922). There is no admission fee and the entire expenses are borne by Mr. and Mrs. Carl Streckel of Norfolk, who in 1904 erected the "Music Shed" seating over 1400. Consult J. H. Vaill, *Litchfield County Choral Union,* 2 vols. (Norfolk, 1912, privately printed).

(vi) *Bach Festivals* of Bethlehem Bach Choir, held in old Moravian town of Bethlehem, Penn.; organised in present form by J. Fred Wolle in 1900. Suspended 1905; resumed on a grander scale with the financial support of steel-magnate, Charles M. Schwab, in 1912. Wolle is still condr. Consult Raymond Walter's *The Bethlehem Bach Choir* (Boston, 1918, Houghton Mifflin).

(vii) *Chicago North Shore Festivals,* held in gymnasium of Northwestern Univ. at Evanston, Ill.; begun 1909, P. C. Lutkin, Dean of Music School of Northwestern Univ. being chief condr. from beginning.

(viii) *Peterboro Festival* of MacDowell Colony at Peterboro, N.H., dating from 1910, is gradually becoming a regular inst., although it has hitherto varied from elaborate pageants (1910 and 1919) to simple outdoor perfs. of miscellaneous programmes composed mostly by members of colony.

(ix) *Berkshire Festivals of Chamber-Music,* Pittsfield, Mass., in Berkshire Hills, are the creation of Mrs. Elizabeth Coolidge who, beginning in 1918, has annually engaged chamber-music organisations of repute, European as well as Amer., and eminent soloists, to give a series of chamber-music concerts for 3 days, before an audience of invited guests. An annual prize of $1000 has been offered for a chamber-music compn., which was won in 1918 by Tadeusz Jarecki, in 1919 by Ernst Bloch, in 1920, by Francesco Malipiero, in 1921 by Waldo Warner, and in 1922 by Leo Weiner.—O. K.

USANDIZAGA, José María. Span. compr. *b.* San Sebastian (Guipuzcoa), 31 March, 1887; *d.* Oct. 1915. Stud. pf. under Planté, and compn. under d'Indy, at *Schola Cantorum,* Paris. The long-standing and unfulfilled ambition to create and establish Basque opera, as a regional institution, had reached its climax in 1910, when Usandizaga, on his return from Paris, gave to the newly-born Basque stage his opera *Mendy-Mendiyan* (Bilbao, May 1910). The occasion proved a complete success. Yet it was not long before U. turned his attention to Madrid as a national centre in which he could work to more advantage, without necessarily deserting the Basque opera ideal. On 5 Feb. 1914, his opera *Las Golondrinas (The Swallows),* the libretto (by Martínez Sierra) founded on the story of Pierrot, with its universal appeal, was produced at Teatro Price, Madrid. The outburst of enthusiasm it raised has seldom been equalled in the history of the Span. theatre. In 24 hours the young compr. became not only a celebrity but a national hero. His province acclaimed him as the greatest hope for the definite establishment of regional opera, and the whole country, forgetting with characteristic Latin impetuosity, its old idols and more than one illustrious name, hailed him as the long expected reformer of Span. lyric art.

The analysis of the score of *Las Golondrinas* would show that its compr. was fully equipped as a modern musician and knew how certain emotional elements, found in Wagner, Franck and mostly Puccini, could be blended with national folk-lore to suit the public taste. He had the gift of melody and, above all, an inborn sense of the theatre. These talents might have led him very far, but he died at 28. His native town, San Sebastian, has erected in the Plaza de Guipúzcoa a monument to his memory. He has a well-deserved place amongst the modern Span. symphonists.

Operas: *Mendy-Mendiyan*; *Las Golondrinas*; *La Llama* (posthumous work). Orch. and chorus: *Ume Zurtza.* Orch.: *Pantomine* (from *Las Golondrinas*); *Fantasía Danza.* Str. 4tet; pf. pieces. (Unión Musical Española, Madrid.)—P. G. M.

USIGLIO, Emilio. Ital. compr. and condr. *b.* Parma, 8 Jan. 1841; *d.* Milan, 8 July, 1910. One of most esteemed condrs. of his time; besides being a well-known compr. especially of comic operas. Among these, *Le educande di Sorrento* and *Le donne curiose* were very successful, and are still in the opera repertoire. Other operas are: *La locandiera*; *L'eredità in Corsica*; *La scommessa*; *Le nozze in prigione*; *La secchia rapita.* In Parma an Usiglio Prize for a comic opera was instituted by his will, in memory of him.—D. A.

V

VACH, Ferdinand. Czechoslovak choirmaster; *b.* Jažlovice, 1860. Stud. at Organ School, Prague; then condr. at Brno theatre; from 1886 condr. of choir *Moravan* in Kroměříž, which became famous by giving Dvořák's oratorios. He also taught singing at Pedagogium, and from among his pupils formed the Moravian Teachers' Choir (*Pěvecké sdružení Moravských učitelů*) (see CHORAL SOCIETIES) in 1903, with which he has ever since been connected. Since 1905, prof. at Teachers' School in Brno; prof. at Organ School; dir. of Philh. Soc. in Brno (one year), and prof. at Cons. Brno. Has written many choruses and church compositions.—V. ST.

VALDERRAMA, Carlos. Peruvian compr. Has given concerts in U.S.A. His florid pf. elaborations of Inca and Quichua melodies in form of *Inca Rhapsodies, Cashuas, Inca Dances,* are based on his 5-tone scale.—F. H. M.

VALDÉS GOICOECHEA, Father Julio. Span. musician of the Basque nationalist group; compr. of religious music; *b.* Vittoria, 1877; *d.* 1916 at Valladolid, where he was a canon. *Requiem; Miserere; Te Deum,* etc.—P. G. M.

VALEN, Fartein Olav. Norwegian compr. *b.* Stavanger, 25 Aug. 1887. Matriculated at Christiania Univ. 1906. In 1908 began his mus. studies at Christiania Cons. under Catharinus Elling (compn.) and 1909-11 stud. at R. High School, Berlin. Received in 1913 a scholarship from Houen's Bequest. One of the most talented Norwegian representatives of the newest tendencies. His works show original harmonic feeling, polyphonic talent and mastery of form. *Legend* for pf., op. 1 (1909); sonata for pf. op. 2 (1914); sonata, vn. and pf. op. 3 (1920); *Ave Maria* (v. and orch.).—J. A.

VALLE-RIESTRA, José. Peruvian compr. *b.* Lima, 1859. Pupil of Gédalge, Paris. Uses old Inca themes in his operas (*Ollanta,* Lima, 1901; *Atahualpa*) as well as in his numerous pf. pieces.—F. H. M.

VALLOMBROSA, Amédée de. Fr. orgt. *b.* Cannes, 24 March, 1880; pupil of Ch. M. Widor, Louis Vierne and Henri Libert. In 1910, orgt. at St.-Leu, Paris. Compr. of motets and a coll. of organ pieces.—F. R.

VALLON, Paul. Singer and teacher; *b.* Southport, Lancs, 21 June, 1862. Educated at Rossall School, and Oxford Univ.; stud. singing in London, Sweden, Dresden, Milan, Florence, Brussels, and Paris. From 1915, prof. of singing at R. Manchester Coll. of Music.—E.-H.

VALVERDE, Joaquín. Spanish composer of *zarzuelas*; his name is always associated with the famous Chueca, his collaborator, the combination being known as Chueca y Valverde (see CHUECA). Died at end of XIX century.—P. G. M.

VALVERDE, Joaquín, jun. Span. compr. of *zarzuelas* and light music. Usually known as Quinito Valverde. Establ. himself in Paris where he cultivated with great success the Span. *genre.* Died at the beginning of XX century.—P. G. M.

VAN AERDE, Raymond Joseph Justin. Belgian musicologist; *b.* Malines, 6 June, 1876. Secretary, librarian and teacher of mus. history at Malines Cons. Author of works on local history which show a very scientific outlook:
Life and Works of Cyprien de Rore (Malines, 1909, Godenne); *Public Minstrels and Instrumentalists either itinerant or attached to Malines from 1311 to 1790* (Malines, 1911, Godenne); brochure, *Carillon in Belgium and particularly that of Malines* (Malines, 1910, Dierickx-Beke); *The Tuerlinckx Family, Lutemakers of Malines* (Malines, 1914, Godenne).—C. V. B.

VAN DEN BORREN, Charles Jean Eugène. Belgian musicologist; *b.* Ixelles, near Brussels, 17 Nov. 1874. Began by studying law. After obtaining his LL.D. in 1897, entered the Bar at Brussels and practised as barrister for 8 years. Then abandoned law to devote himself entirely to music and musicology. Took up music criticism and gave courses of lectures on history of music, principally at Université Nouvelle de Bruxelles (from 1919 Institut des Hautes Études de Belgique.)
Dramatic Work of César Franck (Brussels, 1907, Schott); *Les Origines de la Musique de Clavier en Angleterre* (Brussels, 1912, Groenveldt) (*The Sources of Keyboard Music in England,* London, 1913, Novello, a rev. ed., transl. by James E. Matthew); *Belgian Musicians in England at the time of the Renaissance* (Brussels, 1913, Groenveldt); *Orlande de Lassus* (Coll. *Les Maîtres de la Musique,* Paris, 1920, Alcan).
Appointed librarian to Brussels Cons. in 1920 and honorary member of Mus. Association, London, in 1921. Before 1914 he contributed to the *Guide Musical,* the *Art Moderne,* the *S.I.M.,* the *Z. der I.M.G.;* from 1918 onwards wrote for the *Revue Musicale,* the *Musical Quarterly* (New York), *Musical Times* (London), *Rivista Musicale Italiana* and the *Bulletin de l'Union Musicologique* (The Hague).

Dr. Van den Borren is responsible (with Dr. E. Closson) for the Belgian articles in this Dictionary.—E. C.

VAN DEN EEDEN, Jean. Belgian compr. *b.* Ghent, 26 Dec. 1842; *d.* Mons, in 1917. Began studies at Ghent Cons.; finished at Brussels under Fétis. 1st *Grand Prix de Rome* (1869) for cantata *Faust'laatste nacht.* Later travelled in Germany, Austria, Italy and France. In 1878 succeeded Gustave Huberti as dir. of Mons Cons., a post he occupied until his death.
Oratorios: *Jacqueline de Bavière; Brutus; Le Jugement Dernier;* symph. poem, *La Lutte au XVIe siècle;* opera, *Rhena* (Paris, 1912, Enoch), produced at La Monnaie Theatre, Brussels, 15 Feb. 1912, and enjoyed a long success owing to excellent libretto by Michel Carré and also to sane, fresh and distinguished character of music.—C. V. B.

VAN DER STRAETEN, Edmond. Belgian musical critic, musicologist; *b.* Oudenarde, 3 Dec. 1826; *d.* there, 25 Nov. 1895. Stud.

philosophy at Ghent Univ.; settled in Brussels, 1857. Wrote mus. criticism and was attached to department of National Archives. Made various tours abroad, making researches in documents relating to old Belgian musicians. His works on music and musicians, numerous and varied in character, give evidence of great correctness of detail, but are unfortunately sometimes lacking in order and method, so that they are difficult to use.

Music of the Netherlands before the XIX Century (8 vols. 1867–88, and a 9th vol, in ms. belonging to library of Brussels Cons. The 6th vol. publ. under title of *Netherland Musicians in Italy* [*Les Musiciens Néerlandais en Italie*]; vols. 7 and 8 as *Netherland Musicians in Spain*). Also wrote *Voltaire as a Musician* (1878); *Minstrels of the Netherlands* (1878); and *The Village Drama in Flanders* (1881). The library of Brussels Cons. contains a coll. of bibliographical notes by him.—C. V. B.

VAN DER STUCKEN, Frank Valentin. Amer. compr. condr. *b.* Fredericksburg, Texas, U.S.A., 15 Oct. 1858. In 1866 settled with his family in Antwerp where he ·stud. under Benoit. 1876–8, stud. in Leipzig under Reinecke, Grieg, Langer. 1881–2, condr. Stadttheater, Breslau. 1883, lived in Rudolstadt where he again came in contact with Grieg; in Nov. 1883, gave concert of own works in Weimar under Liszt's protection. 1884, returned to America, condr. of New York Arion (male chorus) until 1895. Gave orch. concerts, with special prominence to works of Amer. comprs. Also gave similar concerts in Germany, and (12 July, 1889) an Amer. programme at Paris Exposition. 1895–1901, dir. of Cincinnati Coll. of Music; 1895–7, condr. of Cincinnati Symphony Orch. 1906–12, succeeding Theodore Thomas, cond. biennial Cincinnati May Fests. Since 1908, has lived mostly in Europe (Hanover; Copenhagen). Opera, *Vlasda*, and Symph. Prologue to Heine's tragedy *William Ratcliff* (Oertel, 1899), were produced Weimar 1883. Member of National Inst. of Arts and Letters.

Orch.: Prelude Act II of *Vlasda*, op. 9 (Leuckart, 1891); *Pagina d'Amore*, op. 10 (*id.* 1891); *Festzug*, march, op. 12 (*id.* 1891); symph. fest. prologue, *Pax Triumphans*, op. 26 (Oertel, 1902) (1st perf. Brooklyn Fest. 1900); *Souvenir*, op. 39 (*id.* 1911); · 2 songs with orch. (Feuchtinger, 1912). Male choruses; songs (Kistner; Breitkopf).—O. K.

VAN DOORSLAER, Georges. Belgian musicologist; *b.* Malines, 27 Sept. 1864. Although actively pursuing his profession as doctor, he has always taken a great part in the mus. life of Malines; he ransacked its archives with indefatigable curiosity and thus discovered a quantity of seemingly unimportant facts which have contributed to the progress of mus. science. He is responsible for a series of arts. on the carillon and carillonneurs, rood-screens, choir-schools and organ-makers of Malines; also of old Malines musicians, which are of the greatest interest. The most important are: *Life and Works of Philippe de Monte* (Brussels, 1921); *René del Mel* (Antwerp, 1922).—C. V. B.

VAN DUYSE, Florimond. Belgian compr. and musicologist; *b.* Ghent, 4 Aug. 1843; *d.* there, 18 May, 1910. Son of Flemish poet, Prudens Van Duyse (*d.* 1859). Stud. law, philosophy,

literature at Univ. of Ghent, and music at Cons. (under K. Miry). Took his degree as LL.D. in 1867, practised at Bar. Clerk of Bar to Court of Appeal at Ghent, 1869–76; military auditor of Hainaut (Mons), 1879, and of East Flanders at Ghent, 1882. Elected corresponding member of Classe des Beaux Arts of R. Acad. of Belgium, 1894; acting member, 1905. His light duties as magistrate left him leisure for compn. and for musicological works which are among the most remarkable written in Belgium. In his numerous works on folk-song in the Netherlands, he is a specialist of first rank, by reason of the severity of his scientific mind and his vast general culture.

Het eenstemmig fransch en nederlandsch wereldlijk lied in de belgische gewesten, van de XIe eeuw tot heden (Ghent, 1896, Vuylsteke); *De melodie van het nederlandsche lied en hare rythmische vormen* (The Hague, 1902, Nijhoff); *Een duytsch Musyck Boeck naar de uitgave van 1572 in partituur gebracht* (Amsterdam, 1903, Müller); *Het oude nederlandsche lied* (The Hague, 1903–8, Nijhoff). This last work, of nearly 3000 pages, is a veritable encyclopædia of Netherland songs, with complete history of words and music of 714 songs.

Comp.: Various cantatas; a *Feest-Cantate* (comp. on visit of English Riflemen to Ghent in 1872); *Torquato Tasso's dood* (2nd *Prix de Rome*, 1873); 11 dramatic works, all perf. at Antwerp or Ghent; choral works; songs, in Fr. and Flemish, etc.—C. V. B.

VAN DYCK, Ernest Marie Hubert. T. singer; *b.* Antwerp, 2 April, 1861; *d.* Berlaer-lez-Lierre (Antwerp) 31 Aug. 1923. First stud. at Univs. of Louvain and Brussels; later made a name as journalist in Paris. Began as singer at Lamoureux Concerts in Paris, where he sang 1883–7. In 1887 he sang *Lohengrin* (title-rôle) in Paris in one memorable perf. Engaged same year at Bayreuth. Sang in *Parsifal* (1888–1912) and in *Lohengrin*. Later became attached to Imperial Opera House, Vienna, where he remained 11 years (chief rôles in *Werther*, *Manon*, *Paillasse*, *Evangelimann*, *La Navarraise*, etc). Since 1901, returned each spring to Paris to sing in Wagnerian opera, *Lohengrin*, *Valkyrie*, etc. Also belonged for 4 years to Metropolitan Opera, New York. 1891–1907, sang at Covent Garden, London, and was manager for a short winter season there. Also manager of Champs-Élysées Theatre, Paris. Numerous engagements in all principal European countries. Retired from opera in 1914 after singing *Parsifal* at Opéra, Paris. Then devoted himself to teaching. Recently was giving singing courses at Brussels and Antwerp Cons. The extraordinary beauty of his t. v., his power of emotional interpretation and his gifts as an actor made him one of foremost singers of his time, and his name is inseparably connected with the history of Wagnerian opera. As an author, he was responsible for a new transl. of *Lohengrin* (Choudens) and several dramas, *Matteo Falcone* (Volkstheater, Vienna) and *Carillon*, (ballet, music by Massenet, produced at Opera House, Vienna).—E. C.

VAN ELEWYCK, le Chevalier Xavier Victor. Belgian writer on music; *b.* Ixelles, near Brussels, 24 April, 1825; *d.* Louvain, 28 April, 1888. Although an amateur, he fulfilled the duties of choirmaster at St. Peter's Ch. Louvain (from 1868).

Discours sur la musique religieuse en Belgique (Louvain, 1861); *Matthias Van den Gheyn* (Paris, 1862); *De l'état actuel de la musique en Italie*, report for Belgian Govt. (Paris, 1875, Heugel). Colls. of works for organ and harpsichord, by Belgian comprs. of XVIII century: *Collection d'œuvres . . . de clavecinistes flamands* (2 vols.; Brussels, Schott); *Morceaux fugués de M. Van den Gheyn* (id.); *Recueil de productions légères pour clavecin composées par M. Van den Gheyn* (id.). The library of Brussels Cons. contains ms. coll. of works of M. Van den Gheyn, copied by Van Elewyck, of which an important part is for carillon (see CARILLON MUSIC).—C. V. B.

VAN GHELUWE, Léon. Belgian compr. *b.* Wanneghem-Lede, near Oudenarde, 15 Sept. 1835; *d.* Ghent, 20 July, 1914. Stud. at Ghent; appointed National Inspector of Schools of Music. 1870, principal of Bruges Cons. (succeeding Waelput).

Cantatas: *De Wind*; *Het Woud*; *Van Eyck-Cantate*; *Callia*; *Hulde aan Laurent*; *Venise sauvée.* Also a Treatise on Harmony (in Flemish) and a Flemish solfeggio of folk-songs.—E. C.

VAN HOUT, Léon. Belgian vla.-player; *b.* Liège, 28 Nov. 1864. Stud. Liège Cons. In 1886, Gold Medal for vla. Since 1889, solo vla. at La Monnaie Theatre, Brussels. 1888–94, one of famous Ysaye Quartet; 1893, prof. of vla. at Brussels Cons. Best vla.-player in Belgium. Has publ. some sonatas of old Ital. masters for vla. or vla. d'amour (Brussels, Oertel).—C. V. B.

VAN MALDEGHEM, Robert Julien. Belgian musicologist; *b.* Denterghem, 1810; *d.* Ixelles (Brussels), 13 Nov. 1893. Famous for his *Trésor musical*, a vast compilation of polyphonic vocal works of Belgian comprs. of Renaissance (publ. by him 1865–93). In spite of its incontestable worth, this coll. shows a complete lack of scientific method; the absence of any indication of source and the misrepresentation of some texts are so serious that it should be used with caution.—C. V. B.

VANZO, Vittorio Maria. Italian compr. *b.* Padua, 29 April, 1862. Having completed studies in compn. at the R. Cons. at Milan, gained high reputation as a condr. Settled then in Milan, and devoted himself especially to teaching of singing. Comp. songs and pf. music. (publ. Ricordi, Lucca and Fantuzzi).—D. A.

VÁRKONYI, Béla. Hungarian compr. *b.* Budapest, 5 July, 1878. Prof. at R. High School for Music, Budapest.—B. B.

VARNEY, Louis. Fr. compr. *b.* Paris, 1844; *d.* Cauterets, 19 Aug. 1908. Son and pupil of author of *Chant des Girondins*; founded his reputation, as compr. of operettas, on *Les Mousquetaires au Couvent* (1880). His style approaches the *opéra-comique* of the XVIII century. Among his operettas, the chief are:

Fanfan la Tulipe (1882); *L'Amour mouillé* (1887); *Riquet à la Houppe* (1887); *Le Papa de Francine* (1896). He produced some ballets (*La Princesse Idéa*, 1895).—A. C.

VASSEUR, Léon. Fr. compr. *b.* Bapaume, 28 May, 1844. Pupil of École Niedermeyer; has turned principally to operetta, of which most popular and best written has been *La Timbale d'argent* (1872). Then:

Le Roi d'Yvetot (1873); *La Cruche Cassée* (1878);

Le Petit Parisien (1882); *Madame Cartouche* (1887); *La Famille Vénus* (1891). Founded Théâtre Nouveau Lyrique (1879), which failed almost immediately. Has also written works for organ; for pf.; masses; offertories, etc.—A. C.

VASSILENKO, Serge Nikiforovitch (*accent 3rd syll.*). Russ. compr. *b.* Moscow, 1872. Pupil of S. I. Tanéief and Ippolitof-Ivanof, Moscow Cons. (1896–1901); at first, stud. law at Moscow Univ. (till 1896); 1903–4, condr. of Private Opera House, Moscow. For some years, organiser and condr. of Historic Concerts of Russ. Mus. Soc. Now prof. at Moscow Cons. An earnest compr., whose work reveals a strong tendency towards mysticism, and deserves to be better known than it is outside Russia.

Opera, *Tale of the Great City of Kitej*, op. 5; 1st symphony, E mi. op. 10; 2nd symphony, F ma. op. 22; *Epic Poem*, orch. op. 4; symph. poems: *Garden of Death*, op. 12; *Hyrcus Nocturnus* (*Flight of Witches*), op. 15; *Au Soleil*, op. 17 (perf. London, Sir H. Wood, 1913); vn. concerto, op. 14; str. 4tet op. 1, ms.; songs; incidental music for plays. Is now working on ballet *Noïa* (from Arapof). (Mostly publ. by Jurgenson.)—M. D. C.

VAUGHAN WILLIAMS, Ralph. English composer; *b.* Down Ampney, near Cirencester, 12 Oct. 1872. Educated at Cambridge (Trinity Coll.) where he took the degrees of Mus.Bac. in 1894, B.A. in 1895, and Mus.Doc. in 1901. He stud. music under a number of teachers of widely different schools, but those who look for any traces of their influence in his mature work will look in vain, for the only influences that have appreciably contributed to the formation of his peculiarly individual style are those of Eng. folksong and of old Eng. music from the Tudor period to that of Purcell. He joined the R.A.M.C. at the outbreak of war in 1914, and later obtained a commission in the artillery. He now holds a position as professor of composition at the R.C.M. London. Apart from his compositions, he has done very valuable work in collecting folk-songs and carols, chiefly in East Anglia and in Herefordshire, and arranging them for publication. His first big success as a compr. was achieved by his setting of Walt Whitman's *Toward the Unknown Region* (Leeds Fest. 1907). This was followed 3 years later by *A Sea Symphony*, also based on poems by Walt Whitman, which placed V.-W. definitely in the front rank of living British comprs. The *London Symphony* (for orch. alone) was produced in London in 1914 at a concert given by the late F. B. Ellis, Geoffrey Toye conducting. Like many another work of this compr., it was withdrawn for revision after the 1st perf. and reappeared in 1920 in a considerably altered form. The string quartet in G minor was comp. in 1909 and revised in 1921. The *Pastoral Symphony*, undoubtedly V.-W.'s greatest achievement up to the present time, was first perf. at a Philh. concert in London, under the direction of Adrian Boult, in 1922. The Mass, for unacc. vs., was given at Westminster Cath. by Sir Richard Terry in Holy Week 1923. In the same year it was sung in Toledo Cath., and at the Thomaskirche, Leipzig. All V.-W.'s works are characterised by strong melodic invention (often traceable to folk-song sources), and a most original fund of contrapuntal resource in which there is nothing even faintly reminiscent of scholasticism. With the purely harmonic developments of the xx century V.-W. shows but little sympathy in his work. We certainly find extremely novel combinations of sounds in some of his later compositions, but they are almost invariably conditioned by the movement of individual parts, of which the line is often seen in a higher dimensional aspect, so to speak, through the addition to each note of the two other notes necessary to complete the common chord. It is easy to realise that lines of 5–3 or 6–3 chords handled contrapuntally as though they were lines of single notes may lead logically to what seem to be most surprising harmonic combinations, though the methods by which such chords are arrived at are radically different from those of the deliberate harmonist. The influence of V.-W. is much in evidence in the work of several British comprs., notably in that of Gustav Holst.

Chorus and orch.: *Towards the Unknown Region* (Breitkopf); *Willow-wood* (*id.*); *A Sea Symphony* (Stainer & Bell); *Mystical Songs* (*id.*); Fantasia on Christmas carols (*id.*). Unacc. chorus: Mass (1920, Curwen); arrs. of folk-songs (Stainer & Bell). Orch.: *A London Symphony* (*id.*); *Pastoral Symphony* (F. & B. Goodwin); Fantasia for str. on a theme by Tallis (*id.*); music to *The Wasps* of Aristophanes, Cambridge 1909; suite, *The Wasps*. Chamber-music: Phantasy 5tet for str. (Stainer & Bell); str. 4tet. Organ: 3 preludes on Welsh hymn-tunes (Stainer & Bell). Songs: *On Wenlock Edge*, song-cycle for v. str. 4tet and pf.; 3 rondels of Chaucer for v. and str. trio (1920, Curwen); *The House of Life*, cycle of sonnets by Rossetti for v. and pf. (Boosey); *Songs of Travel* and other settings of poems by R. L. Stevenson, for v. and pf. (*id.*); numerous arrs. of folk-songs for v. and pf. (Novello). In ms.: 2 music-dramas, *Hugh the Drover* (based on Eng. folk-songs) and *The Shepherds of the Delectable Mountains*, described as " a pastoral episode—after Bunyan "; a ballet, *Old King Cole*, and a suite for military band, both based on Eng. folk-songs; 3 *Norfolk Rhapsodies* and a symph. impression *In the Fen Country*, for orch.; *The Lark Ascending*, for vn. and orch. This list does not include certain early works which have been discarded by the composer.
Consult arts. by Edwin Evans in *Modern British Composers* (Kegan Paul) originally publ. in *Mus. Times*, 1919, and by A. H. Fox-Strangways and Herbert Howells in *Music and Letters*, April 1920 and April 1922 (on the *Pastoral Symphony*).—P. H.

VAURABOURG, Andrée. French composer and pianist; *b.* Toulouse, 1894. Commenced her mus. studies at Toulouse Cons. 1st prize for pf. (1902); came to Paris where she was pupil of Raoul Pugno (1908–13); entered Cons. for compn. and gained (1919) a prize for cpt. Pupil of Nadia Boulanger, Caussade, Dallier and Widor. She belongs to the group of young modern revolutionary comprs. Her music shows a delicate sensibility and at the same time a power uncommon in a feminine temperament. As pianist, she specialises in interpretation of modern music.

For orch.: *Intérieur*; and an important *Prélude*. Little pieces for 4tet; also for pf.; sonata for pf. and vn.; songs.—A. C.

VECSEY, Ferencz. Hungarian violinist and compr. *b.* Budapest, 23 March, 1893. Stud. under Jenő Hubay at R. High School for Music, Budapest. As 10-year-old prodigy aroused the interest of Joachim. Travelled through the whole

civilised world on innumerable concert tours. Has composed many virtuoso vn. pieces.—B. B.

VEGA MANZANO, Luis. Span. compr. and condr. *b.* Madrid, 25 March, 1877. In 1905, bandmaster of Ciudad Real County Council's Band. 1907, condr. of Valencia Municipal Band, one of most important in Spain; 1911, music-dir. of Real Cuerpo de Alabarderos, the King's Private Guard (see ALABARDEROS).

Credo, 6-v, for the Capilla Isidoriana; *Rapsodias de la Mancha*, orch. (perf. Orquesta Sinfónica and Orquesta Filarmónica, Madrid); *Serenata Manchega*; many military-band transcriptions of classical and modern works.—P. G. M.

VEGGETTI, Alberto. Italian flautist; *b.* Bologna, 23 April, 1874. Teacher of fl. at R. Liceo Mus. di Santa Cecilia, Rome; first flautist in the Augusteo orch. Pupil of the Liceo at Bologna. Revised studies for his own instr., for which he has also written educational works and original compns. in addition to a historical monograph.—D. A.

VENDLER, Bohumil. Czechoslovak compr. *b.* Rokycany, 1865. Pupil of Fibich; lives in Prague. His compns. are influenced by Dvořák and national motives; chiefly successful in choruses.

Májová; *Věrná milá* (*Truthful Sweetheart*); *Koleda*; *Modlitba na Řípu* (*Prayer*); choral arr. of national songs. (Fr. A. Urbánek, Prague.)—V. ST.

VENEZIANI, Vittore. Ital. chorus-master; *b.* Ferrara, 25 May, 1878. Pupil of Liceo di Bologna; for 9 years, teacher of choral-singing at Liceo Mus. Benedetto Marcello, Venice; then at Scuola Corale Municipale, Turin; now chorus-master at La Scala, Milan. Is also a good compr., having written operas, *melologhi* (poems by Domenico Tumiati), choruses, ballads, etc. —D. A.

VENTURI, Aristide. Ital. chorus-master; *b.* Finale (Emilia). Pupil of Liceo Mus. di Bologna. In chorus training he is considered one of leading Ital. professionals. Engaged in principal opera houses; for many years at La Scala, Milan.—D. A.

VENU. See INDIAN MUSICAL INSTRUMENTS.

VERBRUGGEN, Henri. Belgian violinist and condr. *b.* Brussels, 1874. Stud. under Hubay and Ysaye at Cons. there; compn. under Gevaert. Led Scottish Orch. (under Henschel) 1893; Lamoureux Orch. Paris, 1894; mus. dir. Colwyn Bay for some time; returned to Scottish Orch. as leading vn. 1902; led Queen's Hall Prom. concerts for 4 years; taught Glasgow Athenæum; succeeded Coward as condr. Glasgow Choral Union; leader of a str. quartet in Scotland, 1914; Principal of Cons. of Music, Sydney, Australia, 1918; condr. of first Australian State Orch. there; condr. Minneapolis Symphony Orch. U.S.A. from 1923.—E.-H.

VERDI, Giuseppe. Italian opera-composer; *b.* Roncole, near Busseto, 1 Oct. 1813; *d.* Milan, 27 Jan. 1901. The greater part of Verdi's life lies outside the period of this Dictionary; but his last works, *Otello* (Milan, 5 Feb. 1887), *Falstaff* (Milan, 9 Feb. 1893) and the *Quattro Pezzi Sacri* (Paris, 7 April, 1898) are among the most important landmarks in the history of XIX century music. They have even converted those who, regarding all opera from the Wagnerian standpoint, would not deign to acknowledge the earlier Verdi. But Verdi must not be judged only by his later works; his whole development must be taken into account. In the very banality which is often betrayed in *Nabucco*, *Lombardi*, *Ernani* and others, there is at times a power containing the germ of what was to follow. Verdi the rough youth, but absolutely sincere and passionately impelled to express himself through the medium of the stage, is the necessary forerunner of Verdi the accomplished musician. The works of the middle period, *Rigoletto*, *Trovatore*, *Traviata* (1851-3) are still hampered by the inheritance of Rossini, Bellini and Donizetti. The change which came later was due largely to the influence of Arrigo Boito, whom Verdi first met in Paris in 1862. In the mind of this self-critical man, who kept sharp watch—indeed too sharp a watch—upon himself as a composer, Shakespeare and Wagner had already taken deep root. Verdi greatly admired Wagner, but found his own independent dramatic style. In *Otello*, dramatic expression reaches the highest degree of emotional truth and the orchestra acquires a fuller power of speech. *Falstaff* is the greatest of modern comic operas. The sensuousness of Italian melody is no longer dominant, but every kind of recitative is developed to the utmost. Verdi there assimilates all the technical and structural achievements of European music of the time and yet by virtue of his marvellous creative vitality, even in old age, remains absolutely individual, absolutely Italian. These latest works of Verdi have exercised a profound influence on contemporary and foreign operatic composers; indeed it is clear that *Falstaff* can still teach something to composers who have definitely abandoned the school of Wagner.

Verdi spent the last years of his life partly at his country house at St. Agata, where he devoted himself to the pursuit of agriculture, and partly at Milan. The *Casa di riposo* (Home for destitute musicians) which he founded and endowed in his will is a lasting memorial to his noble humanity.

Consult: Biographies by Gino Monaldi, Aut. Giulio Barrilli, Arthur Pougin, Camille Bellaigue, Carlo Perinello ; Arnaldo Bonaventura, Andrea D'Angeli, Bragagnola and Bettazzi, Michel Brenet, Eugenio Checchi, Oscar Chilesotti, Clément, Colombani, Filippi, Franchi-Verney, Jullien. Abramo Basevi, *Studio sulle opere di G. V.*; facsimile letters of G. V., publ. and illustrated by Gaetano Cesaro and Alessandro Luzio (preface by Michele Scherillo); Italo Pizzi, *Ricordi verdiani inediti*; Nino Perfetti, *Giuseppe Verdi a Como*; Alessandro Pascolato, *Re Lear e Ballo in Maschera*; Ildebrando Pizzetti, *Musicisti contemporani*; Gino Monaldi, *Saggio iconografia verdiana*; Domenico Alaleona, *G. V. l'artista, l'uomo, il cittadino*, and *L'evoluzione della partitura verdiana* in *Nuova Antologia*, 16th Oct. 1913. Essays by Edgar Istel and Richard Specht (in Verdi numbers of *Musik* [1913]); *Falstaff* number of *Illustrazione Italiana* (1893) ; Verdi number of *Gazette Musicale* (1901); essays in *Rivista Musicale Italiana*, in *Nuova Antologia*, and by Eduard Hanslick in *Salon*. Also Adolf Weissmann, *Verdi* (1922).—A. W. & D. A.

VEREINFACHTE PARTITUR. See SIMPLIFIED SCORE.

VERMEULEN, Matthijs. Dutch music critic and compr. *b.* Helmond, N. Brabant, 1888. Critic of *De Amsterdammer*, 1909-13; of *De Telegraaf*, 1913-20. Now lives in Paris.
3 symphonies (No. I, perf. Arnhem, 1917); cello sonata (perf. Amsterdam, 1919).—W. P.

VESELÝ, Roman. Czech pianist; *b.* Chrudim, 1879. Stud. at Organ School, Prague; at Leipzig (Jadassohn); pf. at Prague (Adolf Mikeš); for long time bank-official at Prague; since 1919 prof. at Cons. there. One of best pf. arrangers of modern Czech operas and symph. works.—V. ST.

VESSELLA, Alessandro. Italian compr. and band-master; *b.* Piedimonte d' Alife (Caserta), 31 March, 1869. An outstanding musical figure, to whom we owe the creation in Italy of a true modern art in military bands. On leaving Naples Cons., where he stud. compn. under Serrao and pf. under Palumbo, V. began his career as a compr. and pianist. In 1885 won post of condr. of Banda Municipale of Rome, with which his name has since been indissolubly linked; he carried it to such a pitch of technical development and artistic perfection as to create for it the reputation of a " model " band, one of the best in the world. With this band, he carried out in Rome a lengthy and memorable work of popular propaganda for good music, especially in the classics and in Wagner. In this task, he met many obstacles, which he successfully overcame; and he took a large part in the organisation of the Italian military bands. His band-transcriptions are models of their kind, just as the assemblage of instrs. adopted by him is also considered an ideal one.

V. is also a teacher of band-orchestration at R. Liceo Mus. di Santa Cecilia; has publ. (Ricordi) a much appreciated *Trattato di istrumentazione per banda (Treatise of Instrumentation for Bands)*.

From 1905-7 he cond. popular orch. concerts, instituted by the Commune of Rome. These concerts formed the foundation for the present magnificent institution, the Augusteo. V.'s band-transcriptions (numbering about 50) are publ. in an ed. of his own (Beethoven's symphonies and sonatas, and famous pieces of Bach, Chopin, etc.). He also composes many pieces for band, for chorus, and for orchestra.

Consult: A. De Angelis, *A. V. (Rivista Romana*, Nov. 1914); A. De Gubernatis, *Dizionario dei contemporanei*; G. Biagi, *Annuario biografico*.—D. A.

VEUVE, Adolphe. Swiss pianist; *b.* Neuchâtel in 1872. Stud. first at Hochschule in Berlin, later under Leschetizky (pf.) and K. Navrátil (compn.) in Vienna. One of best Swiss pianists; possesses an excellent technique and a fluent tone; has given many concerts, particularly in Paris, Brussels and Berlin. Pf. sonata; numerous pieces for pf. (Lausanne, Fœtisch; Leipzig, Hug); songs (Geneva, Henn).—F. H.

VIDAL, Paul. Fr. compr. *b.* Toulouse, 16 June, 1863. *Prix de Rome*, 1883; condr. at Paris Opéra; at Opéra-Comique; prof. at Paris Cons. Eclectic and flexible in spirit; particularly happy in songs (*Le Jeu du Sabot*; *La Meneuse du Jeu*); less original as a symphonist (*La Vision de Jeanne d'Arc*), and as compr. for stage:

Pierrot assassin (ballet, 1888); *La Maladetta* (ballet, on Pyrenees airs, 1893); *La Dévotion à Saint André* (mystery, 1894); *Guernica* (*opéra-comique*, 1895); *La Burgonde* (opera, 1898); *Ramsès* (opera, 1908). Also pf. and orch. acc. to old music.—A. C.

VIDALITA (sometimes called VIDALA). A slow melancholy Argentine part-song with acc. of pf. and guitar, the theme being either " absence " or "past loves." For a fine modern setting of one, for solo v. and pf., see Vicente Forte's *Vidalita* (Buenos Ayres, N. H. Pirovano, 1923).—E.-H.

VIEIRA, José Antonio. Portuguese pianist; *b.* Lisbon, 1852; *d.* there, 1894. Was pf. teacher at Cons. Lisbon from 1882.—E.-H.

VIENNA PHILHARMONIC CONCERTS. Founded 1842. Name given by Dr. August Schmidt (ed. of *Wiener Allgemeine Musikzeitung*) who announced 1st concert of opera-orch. (under cond. of Otto Nicolai, compr. of *The Merry Wives of Windsor*) as *Philharmonic Academy.* The concert took place 28 March, 1842, in Grossen Redoutensaal of Imperial Palace. One of Nicolai's first achievements was a fine, elaborate perf. of Beethoven's 9th Symphony. The concerts did not become permanent until 1860 when a subscription was opened (Carl Eckert, dir. of Imperial Opera House as condr.). Fortunately he was soon replaced by the gifted Otto Dessoff, who brought concerts to their high fame, in Kärnthnerthor-Theater. In 1870, they were removed to new building of Gesellschaft der Musikfreunde, where they are held to this day. Dessoff's successor was Hans Richter. For splendour and warmth of tone as well as for brilliancy of execution the Vienna Philh. Orch. (same as Vienna opera-orch.) has probably no rival. Complete list of condrs.: Otto Nicolai (1842–7), Georg Hellmesberger (1847–8), Wilhelm Reuling (1849), Heinrich Proch (1850), Carl Eckert (1854–7 and 1860), Otto Dessoff (1860–75), Hans Richter (1875–82, 1883–98), Wilhelm Jahn (1882–3), Gustav Mahler (1898–1901), Josef Hellmesberger (1901–3), Franz Schalk (1903, 1905–8), Ernst v. Schuch (1903), W. J. Safonof (1903), Arthur Nikisch (1903), Karl Muck (1904–6), Felix Mottl (1904–7), Richard Strauss (1906–8), and Felix Weingartner (since 1908).—H. B.

VIENNA STATE OPERA HOUSE. The new opera-house, built by Siccardsburg and Van der Null, was finished 1869. The orch. (mainly the Philh. orch.) was increased to 111, the chorus to 80. In addition to operas, they give 8 concerts a year (12.30, Sundays). A 9th one is usually given to opera pension fund (Beethoven's 9th Symphony usually included). 1870–5, Herbeck as dir. of K.K. Hofoper; 1875–80, Franz Jauner dir.; Richter cond. orch. 1880–96, Wilhelm Jahn dir.; Richter became more and more the leading force (Wagner, Gluck, Mozart) with ensemble of exquisite singers (Winkelmann, Reichmann, Materna, Scaria, Schläger, Renard, Van Dyck, Dippel). This period, dominated by

Wagner, shows a rising Fr. school (*Manon, Werther*), rise of Verdi, and some veristic Ital. operas (*Cavalleria, Pagliacci*). 1896–1907, its most glorious period; Gustav Mahler as dir. built up a real repertory, a fine ensemble, including many young artists (Anna Mildenburg, Marie Gutheil, Selma Kurz, Lucy Weidt, Edyth Walker, Erik Schmedes, Leo Slezak). As condrs. he engaged Bruno Walter, Franz Schalk. Created Wagner cycle (3 or 4 times a year), Mozart cycle, and most new operas. With Alfred Roller, created new style of scenery for Mozart's operas. The orch. rose to high a standard. 1907, followed by Weingartner, very different in temperament; much of M.'s reform destroyed; took in new works, Bittner's *Rote Gred*, Strauss's *Elektra*. 1911, Hans Gregor dir. (Debussy's *Pelléas*; R. Strauss's *Salome, Ariadne, Rosenkavalier*). The last Imperial Intendant of Hoftheater was Baron Andrian, whose chief merit was the engagement of R. Strauss after cycle of his works perf. in spring 1918. Strauss and Franz Schalk have since been the leaders of the Opera. Chief events of their régime: 50th anniversary, spring, 1919; opera fest. 1920; Strauss's *Josephs Legende* and *Frau ohne Schatten*; Pfitzner's *Palestrina*; Schreker's *Die Gezeichneten*, and *Der Schatzgraber*; Korngold's *Die Tote Stadt*; Bittner's *Kohlhaymerin*; Strauss's *Schlagobers* (1924).

Consult R. Wallaschek, *Die Theater Wiens*; R. Specht, *Das Wiener Operntheater* (1919); P. Stefan, *Die Wiener Oper* (1922).—EG. W.

VIENNESE OPERETTA. The development of this form of music comedy, since 1880, proceeds from two sources: the Parisian operetta founded by Offenbach, and the Viennese local mus. farce. This latter sprang from the old *Singspiel*, which had degenerated in a rude, farcical manner. The oldest operatic compr. of this period, Franz von Suppé (*q.v.*), did not achieve real success until he approximated his style to that of the parodic and satirical forms of the Offenbach *burlesque*. The manner of Johann Strauss with his winning tunes and rhythmic dances was thrown aside. After that, many local dances (especially the Waltz) were inserted between the action, regardless of plot. The followers of Strauss emphasised local colour and the dance element; but there are also many who continue the Offenbach manner. Since 1900, national melodies (especially Hungarian and Slavonic) have assumed prominence, and Amer. dances (Shimmy and Fox-trot) have been imported into the Viennese operettas. The latest developments proceed in two directions. The first (Lehár, Kalman, Fall, etc.), by its finer instrumentation, broader ensembles and more developed songs, attaches this *genre* to the comic and lyric operas (despite the poor sentimental manner). The second (Eysler, Granichstädten, Stolz, Benatzky) prefers short songs and dances and is really a musical drollery. The last embers of the old Viennese dancing operetta are also to be seen in Ziehrer's and Reinhardt's works.

In the first class, it was Emerich Kalman (a Hungarian who stud. at Budapest Cons. with Kessler) who inspired the new national manner. He had great success in Vienna, since 1908, with *Herbstman-over, Zigeunerprimas, Czardasfürstin, Bajadere.* The Croatian Felix Albini's *Madame Troubadour* (1909) belongs to the same order. The merry, cabaret element, with many couplets and rag-times, is represented by Ralph Benatzky (*Liebe im Schnee,* 1916; *Die tanzende Maske,* 1918; *Die Verliebten,* 1919; *Apachen,* 1920); Bruno Granichstädten (*Der Kriegsberichterstatter*) and especially Robert Stolz (*Lang ist's her; Du liebes Wien,* 1913; *Die Liebe geht um,* 1921). The local piece, *Sperrsechserl,* perf. hundreds of times, is the best example of folk-buffoonery. Viennese local colour was emphasised before Eysler and Ziehrer (*qq.v.*) by Heinrich Reinhardt, critic on *New Viennese Journal,* in his operetta, *Das süsse Mädel.* Between 1900–4, Carl Zeller (*Der Vogelhändler; Vagabund; Kellermeister*), Herrmann Dostal (*Der fliegende Rittmeister,* 1912; *Urschula* 1916) and Charles Weinberger are in this rank. Lately a new method has been invented by Heinrich Berté who arranged Schubert's airs to an operetta (woven round incidents in Schubert's life) called *Dreimäderlhaus,* 1915 (produced in London as *Lilac Time,* 1922). This was followed by C. Lafite's *Hannerl* (on Schubert's tunes), 1917; and Josef Klein's *Die Siegerin,* 1922, (on Tchaikovsky's). The Berlin operetta type of Jean Gilbert came to Vienna in 1920. (His charming *The Lady of the Rose* was produced in London in 1922.) Much of the attraction of the Viennese operettas came from the wonderful actors and singers: the original comic Alexander Girardi (*d.* 1916), Carl Blasel, Wilhelm Gottsleben. Later, Max Pallenberg, Josef König, Ernst Tautenhayn, Max Brod. Tenors: Karl Streitmann, Louis Treumann, Hubert Marischka. Soprani and soubrettes: Betty Fischer, Mizzi Günther, Mizzi Zwerenz, Rosy Werginz, Louise Kartusch.—P. P.

VIERLING, Georg. Ger. compr. *b.* Frankenthal (Palatinate), 5 Sept. 1820; *d.* Wiesbaden, 1 May, 1901. Son of orgt. Jacob V. (1796–1867); pupil of father and H. Neeb, Frankfort-o-M. (pf.); organ pupil of J. H. Chr. Rinck, Darmstadt; 1842–5, compn. pupil of A. B. Marx, Berlin; 1847, orgt. of Upper Ch. Frankfort-on-Oder; dir. of Singakademie; establ. subscription concerts; 1852–3, cond. Glee-Club, Mayence; then went to Berlin, founded Bach Soc.; cond. it for 6 years and at same time subscription concerts at Frankfort-on-Oder and concert-soc. at Potsdam; 1882, prof. and member of Berlin Acad. Later, devoted himself entirely to compn. and teaching.

Songs, duets; part-songs for female, male and mixed choruses; motets; *Psalm C,* unacc.; *Psalm CXXXVII* (t. solo, chorus and orch.); *Drinking Cantata* and *Zur Weinlese* (*Vintage*) (chorus and orch.); choral works: *Hero and Leander; The Rape of the Sabines; Alaric's Death; Constantine,* op. 64. Instr. works: Symphony, C ma. op. 33; overtures: *The Tempest* (Shakespeare); *Mary Stuart; In Spring,* op. 24; *Battle of Hermann* (Kleist); tragic overture to *Fitger's Hexe,* op. 61; Capriccio, pf. and orch.; pf. trio; 2 str. 4tets, op. 56 and 76; *Fantasiestücke,* pf. and cello; *Fantasiestücke* and a grand Fantasia, pf. and vn.; pf. solo pieces.—A. E.

VIERNE, Louis Victor Jules. Fr. orgt. and compr. *b.* Poitiers, 8 Oct. 1870. Stud. at Paris Cons. under César Franck and Widor, and has proved active both as orgt. (Notre-Dame Cath., Paris) and compr. His symphonies and other works for organ are well known, but his choral and chamber-music works have not yet attracted the attention which they deserve. His poems for v. and orch. also deserve notice. His music, earnest and substantial, lacks neither poetic feeling nor originality in conception and treatment. He played in England first in Jan. 1924.

4 symphonies, organ, op. 14, 20, 28, 32; 24 *Pièces en style libre,* organ, op. 31; *Tantum Ergo,* chorus and orch. op. 4; *Missa Solemnis,* chorus and orch. op. 16; *Praxinoë,* soli, female chorus and orch. op. 22; 3 poems, v. and orch.: *Psyché,* op. 36; *Les Djinns,* op. 37; *Éros,* op. 31; str. 4tet, op. 12; sonata, vn.

and pf. op. 23; sonata, cello and pf. op. 27; *Les Chants de la Danse,* pf.—M. D. C.

VIERNE, René (not to be confused with *Louis* Vierne). Fr. orgt. *b.* Lille, 1876; pupil of Guilmant; was orgt. at Notre - Dame - des-Champs, Paris, when war broke out in 1914; he died for his country on 29 May, 1918. Has left numerous organ pieces, which show delicacy of feeling and magnificent composition; also an excellent *Méthode d'harmonium* which has already become a classic.—F. R.

VIEUILLE, Felix. Fr. operatic *b.* singer; *b.* Saugeon (Charente-inférieure), 15 Oct. 1872. On leaving school, was engaged in chorus at Opéra-Comique, and obtained a small part in *Egmont.* Entered Cons. in 1894 under Achard and Giraudet. 1st prize, *opéra-comique,* 1897 (in *Don Juan*). Engaged at Opéra-Comique; sang in *Beaucoup de bruit pour rien* (1900), *Louise, Le Juif Polonais, Pelléas et Mélisande* (1902), *La Fille de Roland* (1904), *Le Pêcheur de St.-Jean* (1905), *Le Clos* (1906), *Chiquito* (1909), *Macbeth* (1910), *La Jota* (1911), *La Lépreuse,* and *La Danseuse de Pompei* (1912), *Bérénice, Le Pays, Le Carillonneur* (1913), *Marouf* (1914) and *Dans l'ombre de la Cathédrale* (1921). He possesses an extraordinary range and timbre, a perfect diction, and a natural gift for acting. Has been associated with productions at Opéra-Comique for last quarter of century, particularly with *Pelléas et Mélisande* in which he took the orig. part of Arkel.—A. R.

VIEUX, Maurice. Fr. vla.-player; *b.* Savy-Berlett, 14 April, 1884. 1st prize at Cons. 1902; soloist at Opéra and at Cons. Concerts. Is remarkable as a virtuoso. His tone is similar to that of Casals the cellist, and his style extremely pure. Takes great interest in history of lute; possesses some very fine violas and a viol of historic value.—M. P.

VIGLIONE BORGHESE, Domenico. Italian barit.; *b.* Mondovi (Piedmont), 3 July, 1877. Stud. at the Liceo Rossini, Pesaro. After an early adventurous period of life, his triumphal career began in 1907 at the Regio Theatre, Parma, in *Aida.* Since then, has risen to the position of one of the best Ital. baritones living, and has appeared at all principal European and Amer. opera houses.—D. A.

VILLA, Luis. Span. cellist; *b.* Madrid, 1874. Stud. at R. Cons. de Música, where he was pupil for chamber-music, with his fellow-student Pablo Casals, of Don Jesús de Monasterio. Member and founder of Soc. de Conciertos de Madrid (now Orquesta Sinfónica) and of the Cuarteto Francés and Quinteto de Madrid.—P. G. M.

VILLA, Ricardo. Span. condr. and compr. *b.* Madrid, 23 Oct. 1873. Stud. at R. Cons. de Música, Madrid. Began as violinist, but abandoned that instr. to become one of condrs. at R. Opera House, Madrid, a position he still holds, as well as condr. of Madrid Municipal Band organised by him in 1909 (see BANDA MUNICIPAL, MADRID).

Misa Solemne, 4 v. and orch.; *La Visión de Fray Martin,* symph. poem (1st perf. R. Opera House,

Madrid, condr. Campanini); *Escenas montañesas*, male chorus; *Impresiones sinfónicas*, orch.; *El Cristo de la Vega*, Span. opera (see ZARZUELA); *El Patio de Monipodio*, light opera; *El Minue Real*, light opera. All these are in ms. The following are publ.: *Cantos Regionales Asturianos*, suite for orch. (1st prize, Soc. de Conciertos, Madrid); *Raimundo Lulio*, opera in 3 acts and an epilogue (1st perf. Teatro Lírico, Madrid, cond. by compr.); *Rapsodia Asturiana*, vn. and orch. (1st perf. Pamplona, soloist Sarasate, cond. by compr.); *Fantasia Española*, pf. and orch. (1st perf. Berthe Marx Goldschmidt, Saragossa). (Faustino Fuentes; Mariano San Miguel; Unión Musical Española, Madrid; Jul. Heinz Zimmermann, Leipzig).—P. G. M.

VILLALBA MUÑOZ, Father Antonio. Span. compr. *b.* Valladolid. Comp. *Oraciones* and *El Poema de la Noche*, two lengthy works in 1 movement for pf. (26 and 44 pages respectively), very ambitious in scope (publ. E. Neumann, Lima). In them he exhibits a style of untraceable origin. Lives in Lima (Peru); belongs to Augustinian order.—P. G. M.

VILLALBA MUÑOZ, Father Luis. Span. mus. scholar, critic and compr. *b.* Valladolid in 1873. *d.* Madrid, 9 Jan. 1921. Is the best-known member of a family of musicians, being the son of Alvaro Villalba, a music-teacher, and brother of compr. of light and religious music, Marcelino Villalba, and the Fathers Alberto and Enrique Villalba, both members of the Church and comprs. Luis entered at 14 the Order of St. Augustine. Ph.D., D.Litt. at Univ. Central, Madrid. 1898–1917, choirmaster of Chapel at Real Monasterio del Escorial; prof. of history and rhetoric, Colegio de Alfonso XII, Escorial; ed. of Augustinian literary and scientific review *La Ciudad de Dios* and the *Biblioteca Sacromusical* (religious music-periodical), Madrid, and, for a time, of *Ilustración Española y Americana*. Member of *Corpus Scriptorum*, Germany. He abandoned the Augustinian order but remained always a priest, and at the time of his death was a candidate for the R. Acad. de Bellas Artes and for the chair of history and æsthetics of the R. Cons. de Madrid.

La Música de Cámara en España, set of lectures; *Últimos Músicos Españoles del siglo XIX*; *Enrique Granados*; *Cuentos de Navidad*; *Cosas de la Vida*; *La Música en Solfa*; *Historia del Rey de los Reyes*, 3 vols.; *El P. Honorato del Val*; *La Inocentada*; *José María Usandizaga*; *Felipe Pedrell*; *Historia del Piano*; *El Órgano, su invención e historia y su cultivo en España por los organistas del siglo XV y primera mitad del siglo XVI*; *La Educación Artística*; *Programa explicativo y sumario de estética general aplicada a la música*; *Programa explicativo e índice sumario de historia general de la música*; *Lo Bello*. Compns.: *Canciones españolas* (10) *de los siglos XV y XVI*, v. and pf. (Span. and Fr.); *Cantiga X de Alfonso el Sabio*, v. and organ; *Antología de organistas clásicos españoles*; *Repertorio de los organistas*, 2 vols.; *Folías*; 2 sonatas, vn. and pf.; 2 str. 4tets. (No. I in F; No. II in C). This is only a small selection from a prolific list of transcriptions of old music, masses, motets, carols, religious hymns, secular songs, entr'actes, military-band and dance music, including *pasodobles toreros*, one-steps and a fox-trot, *The Best Charming* (sic). (Ildefonso Alier; Imprenta Helenica; Viuda de Pueyo, Madrid; Enrique Villalba, Segovia).—P. G. M.

VILLAR, Rogelio. Span. compr. and critic, *b.* León, 1875. Stud. at R. Cons. de Música, where he is now a prof. of chamber-music. Mus. critic to the review *Illustración Española y Americana*; ed. of several mus. periodicals and

author of a number of books and pamphlets as well as lecturer on musical subjects.
Str. 4tets; works for orch.; pf. sonatas; vn. and pf. sonatas; songs with pf.; symph. poems; pieces, for pf., for cello, for vn., for military band. (Ildefonso Alier; Antonio Matamala; Unión Musical Española, Madrid.)—P. G. M.

VILLERMIN, Louis. Fr. compr. and theorist; *b.* Baccarat, 16 July 1877. Stud at *Schola Cantorum*, Paris; after having written some works in the classical style, he devoted himself to the research of ultra-modern harmonic coloration, and later classified the modes, neuter, unitonic and polytonic and their relationships. His compns. are very clear and neat, and the harmony is never overcharged.
Orch.: *La Coupe enchantée* (Paris, 1914); *La Danse des Sirènes* (Concerts Lamoureux, 1916); *Estampe* (Théâtre Mogador, May 1922); *Première Rhapsodie Chinoise* (Havre, June 1914); *Méditation de Watteau* (Concerts Rouge, 1918); polonaises and marches for military band; book, *Traité d'Harmonie ultramoderne* (Rouhier, Paris).—E.-H.

VĪNĀ. See INDIAN MUS. INSTRUMENTS.

VINCENT, Charles J. Eng. compr. and publ.; *b.* Houghton-le-Spring, Durham, 19 Sept. 1852. Chorister Durham Cath. 1863–8; pupil of Dr. Philip Armes 1870–3; stud. Leipzig Cons. under Reinecke, Richter and Maas, 1876–7; Mus.Doc. Oxon. 1884; orgt. Christ Ch. Hampstead, 1883–1892; joint-ed. (for 25 years), *Organist and Choirmaster*; joint-ed. new ed. *Hymnal Companion*; founder of firm Vincent Music Publ. Co. (later Schirmer & Co.; later still, Winthrop Rogers).
Overture, *The Storm*; numerous songs, part-songs, anthems, services, cantatas; organ music and pf. pieces. Author of: *Harmony : Diatonic and Chromatic* (W. Rogers); *Scoring for an Orchestra* (id.); *The Brass Band and how to write for it* (id.); *Form and Design* (id.). Ed. of: *Fifty Songs by Shakspear* (Ditson); *Reliquary of English Songs*, Series I & II (Schirmer); *Vocalisation Studies*, 4 books; *Trinity Coll. Song-books*, 6 vols. (Schirmer).—E.-H.

VINÉE, Anselme. Fr. theorist and compr. Pupil of Guiraud in Paris; compr. of:
2 orch. suites (*Paysage*; *Bretagne*); 6tet for pf. and wind; *Trio-Serenade*, pf. (or harp), fl. and c.a. (or ob.); *Lamento*, cello and orch.; vn. sonata; clar. sonata; cello sonata; sonata, vn. alone; duets for str.; Variations, pf. and tpt.; songs. Wrote *Essai d'un système général de musique* (1901); and *Principes du système musical* (Paris, 1909, Hamelle), a very valuable work.—A. C.

VIÑÉS, Ricardo. Span. pianist, *b.* Lérida, 5 Feb. 1875. Stud. under orgt. Terraza; later at the Barcelona Cons. as pupil of Pujol; obtained 1st prize for pf. at 12. In 1894 obtained a similar distinction at the Paris Cons. as pupil of Charles de Bériot, Lavignac and Benjamin Godard. His success at concerts of Société National de Musique, *Schola Cantorum*, Salon d'Automne, Société des Concerts du Cons. and at Lamoureux and Colonne Concerts, was only the beginning of his brilliant career as solo-pianist in all European countries. The prominence of his name in the history of modern music cannot be sufficiently emphasised. He was the first virtuoso who placed his art at the service of the new school of Debussy, Ravel, Séverac and others who were to be acknowledged later as the leaders of an universal mus. revolution. He was one of the first to understand, and make others understand, the new Fr. school, through his wonderful exposition of its pf. works which for a long period he monopolised. The new school of Spain and, to a great extent, that of Russia, owe him a similar debt. He lives in Paris.—P. G. M.

VIOLOTTA. A large kind of viola with strings tuned G-d-a-e

constructed by Alfred Stelzner (d. Dresden, 1906). It is used in some German opera-orchestras. (See BEHM, E.).—A. E.

VIOTTA, Henri. Dutch condr. b. Amsterdam, 16 July, 1848. Stud. under Hol, Merlen and Hiller (Cologne); stud. law at Leyden and graduated in 1877. Founded, 1883, Wagner-vereeniging (see SOCIETIES); 1903–17, condr. Symph. Orch., The Hague (Residentie Orch.).
Songs; concerto, cello and orch.; Mass. Wrote numerous studies on different comprs.; Handbook of mus. history; a Wagner biography.—W. P.

VITALE, Edoardo. Ital. condr. b. Naples, 1872. Stud. at R. Liceo Mus. di Santa Cecilia under Eugenio Terziani (compn.), and was prof. of harmony there for seven years. His growing successes as a condr. led him to abandon teaching in order to devote himself completely to a career of conducting; occupied very important positions in the leading European and Amer. opera houses (La Scala, Milan; Costanzi, Rome; San Carlo, Naples; Colón, Buenos Ayres; Municipale, Rio de Janeiro, etc.). Has successfully " godfathered " very many operas, such as La Via della Finestra (Zandonai), Mirra (Alaleona), and many other modern operas which have been produced in Italy for the first time under his direction.—D. A.

VITALI, Mario. Ital. pianist; b. Pausula (Macerata), 29 Jan. 1866. Stud. at R. Cons. Naples, under Palumbo (pf.) and D'Arienzo (compn.). Whilst still very young, was appointed pf. teacher at Liceo Rossini at Pesaro where he has remained, training some excellent pupils. With Frontali and Cremonini, he formed a trio, which has become famous. Has given numerous concerts, which have been much appreciated. Is compr. of an opera, La bella del bosco dormente (The Sleeping Beauty), mentioned in one of the Sonzogno competitions. Has also written several orch. pieces, also vocal and instr. chamber-music, in addition to some accurate revisions of pf. works.—D. A.

VITERBINI, Sergio. Ital. cellist; b. Viterbo (Rome), 30 Sept. 1890. Stud. at the R. Cons. Naples; gained diploma in 1906; then teacher, which position he still occupies. He perfected himself in Berlin under Hugo Becker. Is a concert artist who is much appreciated, and is 1st cello in the orch. of the Teatro San Carlo. Recently founded and conducts a string orchestra for the diffusion of string music.—D. A.

VITOLS, Jozefs. Latvian compr.; dir. of Cons. in Riga; b. Valmiera (Livonia, formerly a

Russ. province), 26 June, 1863. Stud. (1880–6) compn. under Johansen and Rimsky-Korsakof at Petrograd Cons. In 1886, prof. of theory there, and after death of Rimsky-Korsakof (1908) took place of latter as prof. of mus. compn. After the proclamation of independent Latvia (1918), V. was entrusted with organisation and direction of the State-supported Cons. at Riga. He excels in nearly all branches of music, except opera. His compns. are refined, exquisite works, but have little national character.
Orch.: Symphony, E mi.; Ligo, op. 4; Ouverture dramatique, op. 21; overture, Spriditis; Suite of Latvian folk-tunes, op. 29; suite, Princesse Gundega; vn. and orch.: Fantaisie, op. 42; Rhapsody, op. 39; str. 4tet; pf.: Variations, op. 6; Portraits, op. 54; sonata; variations; arrs. of folk-tunes; many preludes, miniatures, etc.; many choral songs, a cappella and with orch.; songs for v. and pf.—K. P.

VITTADINI, Franco. Ital. compr. b. Pavia, April 1884. Stud. at Milan Cons. (under Galli and Ferroni (compn.) and Andreoli (pf.). Choirmaster at Varese ; has composed various masses and other sacred music (Milan, Bertarelli; Monza, Centemeri). His reputation is due to his opera Anima allegra (Costanzi, Rome, 1921), publ. by Ricordi. Another opera, Il Mare di Tiberiade (in 4 acts, libretto by Illica), he had written earlier for Sonzogno.—D. A.

VIVES, Amadeo. Span. compr., native of Catalonia. Successor of famous compr. Tomás Bretón as prof. of compn. at R. Cons. de Música, Madrid. Has attained great reputation and popularity as writer and lecturer, as well as one of leading contemporary comprs. for Span. stage. The outstanding feature of his music is clearness of construction and melody.
Zarzuelas: La Balada de la Luz; Bohemios; La Generala; Don Lucas del Cigarral; El Duquesito; El Pretendiente; El Parque de Sevilla; Pepe Conde o el mentir de las estrellas; Lola Montes; Maruxa, lyric comedy in 2 acts (perf. R. Opera House, Madrid; Liceo, Barcelona, etc.). V. and pf.: Canciones epigramáticas, a coll. of 13 mus. settings to poems of popular character by Span. classics. (Unión Musical Española, Madrid.)—P. G. M.

VIVIER, Albert Joseph. Belgian harmonist and acoustician; b. Huy, 16 Dec. 1816; d. Brussels, 3 Jan. 1903. Stud. under Fétis at Brussels Cons. (1842). His 1-act comic opera, Padillo le Tavernier, was perf. at La Monnaie. Two other operas in ms. Later on, he inclined towards mus. theory and publ. a treatise on harmony. Then he busied himself with acoustics. The Museum of the Brussels Cons. possesses two instrs. constructed according to his directions, a sonometer with 13 strings, which he called duodédicorde (Catal. No. 2256) and a harmonium in which are united two stops tuned a fifth of a tone from each other (No. 2408).
Traité d'harmonie théorique et pratique (reprinted 5 times, 1862–90); Mémoire sur les vrais rapports des sons musicaux (1893); Transformations des instruments à cordes (1893); Éléments d'acoustique musicale (1897); Acoustique musicale (1896); Questions d'acoustique musicale (n.d.).—E. C.

VOGEL, Emil. Ger. music historian and bibliographer; b. Wriezen-on-Oder, 21 Jan. 1859; d. Nikolassee, near Berlin, 18 June, 1908. Stud. philology at Berlin and Greifswald Univ.; mus. history in Berlin (Spitta); 1883, scholarship from Prussian Government, which enabled him

to accompany (as assistant) Fr. X. Haberl on his Palestrina study-tour to Italy. After return to Germany, graduated Ph.D. at Berlin Univ. 1887.
In *Vierteljahrsschrift f. M.-W.*, 1887, monograph *Claudio Monteverdi*; 1889, *Marco da Gagliano and Musical Life at Florence from 1570 to 1600*; 1890, catalogue, *Manuscripts and Early Printed Works of Music Department of Ducal Library at Wolfenbüttel*; 1892, 2 vols. *Library of Printed Secular Vocal Music of Italy from 1500 to 1700*. 1893–1901, V. was librarian of Peters' Mus. Library, Leipzig, which he organised; also publ. the *Annual* of this library. He was hon. member of R. Acad. Florence.—A. E.

VOGL, Heinrich. Ger. t. singer; *b.* Au, suburb of Munich, 15 Jan. 1845; *d.* Munich, 21 April, 1900. Schoolmaster at Ebersberg (1862–5); 1865, member of Munich R. Opera; was especially a Wagner singer; after death of Schnorr of Carolsfeld, for long time, the only Tristan available. With own opera *The Stranger* (Munich, 1899) he had no luck. Also comp. songs and ballads. Consult H. v. der Pfordten, *H. V.* (1900).—A. E.

VOGLER, Carl. Swiss orgt. compr. *b.* Oberrohrdorf, 26 Feb. 1874. Stud. organ under F. T. Breitenbach at Lucerne; then under Fr. Hegar and L. Kemptner (compn.) at Zurich, 1893; 1895, entered R. Acad. of Music at Munich; 1897, orgt. and condr. of mixed choir (Oratorio Concerts) at Baden; since 1915, has taught theory at Zurich Cons.; co-dir. there since 1919 with Volkmar Andreae; 1908, president of the Swiss Music-Pedagogical Society.
Totenzug (Isabella Kaiser), contr., chorus and orch.; *Rübezahl* (Loewenberg), fairy-opera; *Festmarsch*, orch.; 22 preludes for organ; numerous songs and unacc. choruses (Leipzig, Hug).—F. H.

VOGRICH, Max. Ger. compr. *b.* Hermannstadt, 24 Jan. 1852; *d.* New York, 10 June, 1916. 1866–9, stud. at Leipzig Cons. (pupil of Wenzel, Reinecke, Moscheles, Hauptmann and Richter). 1870–8, toured widely as pianist; 1878 in New York; 1882–6 in Australia. 1886–1902 he resided in New York as compr., then lived in Weimar till 1908 and in London till 1914; then returned to New York.
Operas: *Wanda* (Florence, 1875); *King Arthur* (Leipzig, 1893); *The Buddha* (Weimar, 1904); music to Wildenbruch's *Song of Euripides* (Weimar, 1905). Pf. concerto, E mi.; vn. concerto, *E pur si muove* (1913); cantatas. Ed. Schumann's complete pf. works and Clementi's *Gradus ad Parnassum* (Schirmer). —A. E.

VOGT, Augustus Stephen. Canadian organist and conductor; *b.* Washington, Ontario, 14 Aug. 1861; stud. music at New England Cons. Boston, and at Leipzig Cons. After holding the position of orgt. and choirmaster at First Methodist Ch., St. Thomas, he came to Toronto to Jarvis Street Baptist Ch. In 1888, joined staff of Toronto Coll. of Music as teacher of organ and pf., but in 1892 severed his connection in order to become associated with Toronto Cons. of Music. In 1894, he founded the Mendelssohn Choir (see CHORAL SOCIETIES) and remained condr. of this until 1917. In 1906 received Mus.Doc. *h.c.* from Toronto Univ.; became Dean of the Faculty of Music there, 1919. In 1913, Principal of Toronto Cons. of Music, which position he now holds. He was the first to achieve the dis-

tinction of making Canada, musically speaking, an " exporting " country; for the visits of the Mendelssohn Choir to the U.S.A. showed for the first time in the history of Canada that a home-made product could equal or surpass that of older countries. As Principal of Cons. he has brought about a much closer union between mus. education and the Univ. His tutor, *Modern Pianoforte Technique*, is now in its 20th ed.; choral works; songs, church music.—L. S.

VOLBACH, Fritz. Ger. compr. and writer on music; *b.* Wipperführt, Rhineland, 17 Dec. 1861. Stud. at Cologne Cons.; stud. philosophy at Heidelberg and Bonn. 1886, pupil of R. Inst. for Church Music, Berlin; also pupil of Grell (compn.); 1887, teacher at Inst. for Church Music; condr. Acad. Glee-Club and Klindworth chorus; 1892, condr. of Glee-Club and Ladies' Singing Soc., Mayence; 1907, acad. mus. dir. at Tübingen; 1919, prof. at Univ. Münster, Westphalia.
Symph. poems: *Easter* (organ and orch.); *Two Royal Children*; *Old Heidelberg, thou Beautiful!*; symphony, B mi.; 5tet for wind instrs. and pf. E flat (1901); pf. 5tet, D mi. op. 36 (1912); ballads: *Vom Pagen und der Königstochter*; *Raffael*, (chorus, orch. organ); *At Siegfried's Fountain*, male chorus and orch.; *King Laurin's Rose-Garden*, barit. male chorus, orch. op. 38; *Hymn to Virgin Mary* (Dante), chorus, solo instrs. organ (1921); comic opera, *Art of Loving* (Düsseldorf, 1910), etc. Wrote *Textbooks for Accompaniment of Gregorian Chant*; *Handel* (1898); *Orchestral Instruments* (Leipzig, 1915, 2nd ed. 1921); *Development of Modern Orchestra* (Leipzig, 1910, 2nd ed. 1919); *Beethoven* (1905); *German Music in XIX Century* (Kempten, 1909). Consult G. Schwake, *Fr. V.'s Works* (1921).—A. E.

VOLLERTHUN, Georg. German compr. *b.* Fürstenau (district of Elbing), 29 Sept. 1876. Pupil of Tappert, R. Radecke, Gernsheim; 1899–1905, theatre condr. at Prague, Berlin (Theater des Westens), Barmen and Mayence. Since then (1908–10 at Paris) teacher of singing in Berlin; also musical critic.
Songs: 4 duets, op. 11; opera, *Veeda*, words by G. Kiesau (Cassel, 1916).—A. E.

VOLPE, Arnold. Amer. condr. compr. *b.* Kovno, Russia, 9 July, 1869. Stud. vn. 1884–7 in Warsaw under Isidor Lotto; Petrograd Cons. 1887–1891 under Leopold Auer; 1893–7, compn. under Nicholas Solofief. Went to America in 1898; 1904, founded Volpe Symphony Soc., New York, an expansion of his Young Men's Symphony Orch. (organised 1902). For many years regular symph. concerts, and open-air symphony concerts at City College Stadium, New York, 1918–19, etc. 1916, opened Volpe Inst. of Music, New York; 1922, called to Kansas City (Mo.) Cons. as director. Songs; vn. pieces (Schirmer; Leuckart; C. Fischer).—J. M.

VOLPILAURI, Giacomo. Ital. lyric t. singer; *b.* at Rome. Stud. at the R. Liceo Mus. di Santa Cecilia, Rome, under Antonio Cotogni. *Début* at Viterbo in *I Puritani*, and definitely establ. himself in 1920 at the Costanzi, Rome, in Massenet's *Manon*. Since then his services have been sought after by the principal European and American opera houses.—D. A.

VOMÁČKA, Boleslav. Czechoslovak compr. *b.* Mladá Boleslav, 1887. Stud. compn. at Cons. Prague, under Stecker and Novák. For several years a solicitor in Czech provinces; since 1919 Social Welfare Ministry official in Prague. Mus. critic of newspapers *Čas* and *Lidové Noviny*. His own music has energetic features, occasionally reaching a stubborn hardness. Feeling is rare but very intense when present. Humour and high spirits are his characteristics. His first works approach the second-period style of Schönberg; but afterwards he became less complicated and nearer to tradition. This development is based on his critical views, maintaining that the period of an extremely subjective music is finished and that the new expression must be universal in content.

Symph. poem, *Mládí* (*Youth*); sonata, vn. and pf.; pf. sonata; pf. cycles, *Hledání* (*The Quest*); song-cycle, " 1914 "; choruses (all Hudební Matice, Prague).—V. ST.

VON KUNITS, Luigi. Violinist, compr. writer on music, condr. *b.* Vienna, Austria, in 1870. Stud. vn. under J. M. Král and O. Ševčík; compn. under Anton Bruckner, mus. history under Edward Hanslick. Graduated at Univ. of Vienna in jurisprudence and philosophy; 1893, came to America, residing in Chicago until 1896. In 1897, leading violinist of Pittsburgh Symphony Orch.; prof. at Cons. In 1910 returned to Europe for 2 years' extensive concert tours. In 1912, came to Toronto as head of vn. dept. of Canadian Acad. of Music, which position he now holds, exercising a profound influence as player and teacher, becoming widely known through his scholarly articles in *Canadian Journal of Music*, as leader of a str. quartet, condr. of New Symph. Orch. Toronto and by his chamber-music compns. During his sojourn in Vienna he appeared in many notable chamber-music perfs. with Johannes Brahms.—L. S.

VOORMOLEN, Alex. Dutch compr. *b.* Rotterdam, 3 March, 1895. Stud. in Holland under Wagenaar, Paris under Maurice Ravel, Albert Roussel and Rhené-Baton. The Fr. Impressionists and the Symbolists have influenced his style considerably. V. lives at The Hague.

Symphonietta for orch. in 3 movements, perf. Amsterdam, under Mengelberg, 1920; *Scène et danse érotique* (ms.); melodrama, *Beatrys* (words by P. C. Boutens), v. and pf., often perf. (The Hague, 1920, Van Eck); 30 songs, Dutch and Fr. words (Paris, Rouart, Lerolle), including 2 *Moralités* (words by Ch. Perrault), v. and pf.; 3 *Poèmes* (René Chalupt); 1st pf. suite (Rouart, Lerolle); *Falbalas* (3 dance movements (*id.*); *Eléfants, étude* (*id.*); 3 *Tableaux des Pays Bas* (*id.*); 2 *Offrandes* (*id.*); *Suite de clavecin* (Amsterdam, Alsbach); *Le Souper clandestin* (Brussels, Ysaye). Chamber-music (all publ. Rouart, Lerolle): Suite, cello and pf.; sonatina, cello and piano; sonata, vn. and pf.; *Sicilienne et Rigaudon*, vn. and pf.; trio, pf. vn. cello: str. 4tet.—W. P.

VRĂBIESCU, R. See RUMANIAN OPERA.

VRETBLAD, Viktor Patrik. Swedish compr. orgt. and music critic; *b.* Svartnäs (Dalarne), 5 April, 1876. Stud. at R. Cons. Stockholm, 1895–1900 (compn. under Joseph Dente and pf. under Hilda Thegerström); and in Germany, 1901. Orgt. at Fr. Reformed Ch. of Stockholm, 1900–7; and of Oscar Ch. from 1907. Has given many organ-recitals in this church and (together with his colleague, Dr. O. Sandberg [*q.v.*], condr.) many " Motet Evenings " with national and historical programmes. Music critic for *Social-*

Demokraten. Secretary of Soc. of Swedish Comprs. from its foundation, 1918. Member R.A.M. Stockholm, 1921. Ph.D. 1922. Publ. in 1914, *Johan Helmich Roman, svenska musikens fader* (*J. H. R., the Father of Swedish Music*) and (1918) *Konsertlivet i Stockholm, 1700 - talet* (*Concert-life in S. during XVIII Century*). Contributor to music journals (*Musik*, Copenhagen; *Ménestrel*, Paris).

Pf. pieces (op. 3, 5, 8, 10, 12, 13); songs with pf. (op. 4, 6, 7, 17, 20); organ pieces (op. 11, 14, 16); *Phantasy*, cello and pf.; pieces, vn. and pf.; cantata, soli, chorus and orch. (1909) (publ. Abr. Lundqvist, Elkan & Schildknecht, M. Th. Dahlström). Publ. works by J. H. Roman (2 sonatas for vn. and pf.; Nord. Musikförlaget), Beethoven (*Adagio*, vn. and piano, not publ. before) and Berwald (symph. poem).

His wife, Karin Bodman-Vretblad (*b.* Stockholm, 29 Dec. 1883) stud. vn. at R. Cons. Stockholm (under F. Book), 1895–1901; then under L. Zetterqvist, and (1903–5) under H. Marteau at Cons. of Geneva; member of Gothenburg Orch. Soc. and (from 1914) of Stockholm Concert Soc. (Konsertföreningen).

Dr. Vretblad is responsible for the Swedish articles in this Dictionary.—E.-H.

VREULS, Victor. Belgian compr. *b.* Verviers, 4 Feb. 1876. Stud. at École de Musique, Verviers, and at Liège Cons. under Th. Radoux and Dupuis. 1896, on advice of V. d'Indy, went to Paris and finished studies under him. For several years prof. of solfeggio, harmony and vla. at *Schola Cantorum*, Paris; also cond. the Parisian soc. *La Chanterie*. Since 1906, dir. of Luxembourg Cons. He has cond. concerts in Belgium, France and Germany. As compr. belongs to Belgian group of that French school which follows César Franck.

Olivier le Simple, lyric drama (Brussels, 1921); orch.: *Werther*; *Jour de Fête*, symph. poems; *Cortège héroïque*; symphony, orch. and solo vn.; *Poème*, cello and orch.; pf. 4tet; trio; vn. and pf. sonata; *La Guirlande des dunes*, songs on poems of Verhaeren. —E. C.

VRIESLANDER, Otto. German compr. *b.* Münster, Westphalia, 18 July, 1880. Music-seller; then pupil of C. Steinhauer (1891–4), Julius Buth (1896–1900), Düsseldorf; 1901–2, pupil of Cologne Cons. (Klauwell, M. van der Sandt); 1904, in Munich; 1911–12, in Vienna, pupil of Heinrich Schenker; 1912 at Ebersberg, near Munich.

Songs: *Pierrot lunaire* (46 poems by Conrad Ferdinand Meyer, 4 vols.); 12 *Goethe Songs* (1905); 12 songs and ballads (1910–11); 22 songs from *Des Knaben Wunderhorn* (*The Boy's Magic Horn*) (1905). Essay and monograph on *Ph. Em. Bach* (Munich, 1923); ed. works of Ph. Em. Bach.—A. E.

VUIDL, Theodore. Ger.-Czechoslovak compr. author; *b.* Wysotschan, near Saaz, 28 Oct. 1876. Ph.D. Stud. under Stecken, Proksch and Rietsch in Prague, where he now lives.

Comic opera, *Rural Love-Oracle* (1-act, words by Batka); opera, *Brothers and Sisters* (from Goethe, arr. by Paul Schiller); symphony, E ma.; song-cycle with orchestra.—E. S.

VUILLEMIN, Louis. Fr. compr. *b.* Nantes, 1873. His art is based on Breton folk-lore. Is music critic of *La Lanterne*. Compr. of stage-music for *Double Voile* and *Scylla*; *Danses*, pf. 4 hands; *Soirs armoricains*.—A. C.

VUILLERMOZ, Émile. Born at Lyons in 1879. Undoubtedly one of the most remarkable of French musical critics at the present time. Studied music at Lyons, also literature and law; pf. and organ, under Daniel Fleuret. Later, at Paris Conservatoire, in the class of Gabriel Fauré, where he studied with Ravel and Florent Schmitt. Although he gave ample proof of his powers as a composer (by writing songs of a delicate charm, by harmonising old folk-songs with exquisite taste, and by producing operettas and light music of extraordinary fineness under various *noms de plume*) he abandoned composition for criticism. He was a vigorous champion of the modern school and fought for Fauré, Debussy, Ravel and Schmitt. He was one of the first in France to appreciate the works of Stravinsky, Schönberg, Bartók, Malipiero, and Szymanowski. V. wrote articles for the *Mercure Musical*; also for *Revue Musicale S.I.M.* (of which he became the chief editor in 1911); for *Comœdia* and the *Éclair*. Now writes regularly for the *Temps*, *Excelsior* and the *Revue Musicale*.

A number of his arts. have been collected in a book, *Musiques d'aujourd'hui* (Crès, 1923).—H. P.

VYCPÁLEK, Ladislav. Czechoslovak compr. b. Vršovice, 1882. Doctor of philology. Stud. compn. under Vít. Novák; secretary of Univ. Library, Prague. Is also a critic. His compns. (chiefly vocal), though small in quantity, are, by reason of their depth of thought, originality and seriousness, amongst most important by living Czechoslovak comprs. At first, he was slightly influenced by Impressionism; but soon became independent. His style is consistently polyphonic, thematic, never shrinking from any harmonic hardness resulting from the linear cpt. His moods are of a soft and discreet sensibility, inclining towards religious themes.

Cantata, soli, chorus, orch., *O posledních věcech Člověka (Of Man's Last Things)*. Song-cycles: *Světla v temnotách (Light in Darkness)*; *Tuchy a vidiny (Divination and Vision)*; *V Boží dlani (In God's Hand)*; *Moravské balady* (very free harmonisations of Moravian national songs); *Vojna (The War)*. Choruses (for male and mixed chorus): *Tuláci (Tramps)*; *Sirotek (The Orphan)*; *Boj nynější (The Struggle of the Present)*. Publ.: Hudební Matice Umělecké Besedy; Chadím (Prague).—V. ST.

W

WACHMANN. See RUMANIAN OPERA.

WACHTMEISTER, Axel Raoul (Count).
Swedish compr. *b.* in London, 2 April, 1865.
Stud. *Schola Cantorum,* Paris, in which city
he lives.

Symphony, D mi.; cantata, *Sappho* (New York);
sonata, vn. and pf. (Novello); for cello and pf. (John
Church Co.); *Fantasietta,* vn. and pf. (*id.*); *Redowa*
(cello and pf.); choruses; songs, etc.—P. V.

WADDINGTON, Sidney Peine. Eng. compr.
b. Leicester, 1869. Stud. R.C.M. London,
1883-8; also in Germany and Vienna; Mendelssohn scholar, 1890-92; prof. of harmony at
R.C.M.; completed the score of Goring Thomas's
Golden Web.

John Gilpin, cantata, orch. and chorus (Novello);
Whimland, operetta for children (*id.*); chamber-
music; pf. music, etc.—E.-H.

WAELPUT, Henri. Belgian compr. *b.* Ghent,
26 Oct. 1845; *d.* there, 8 July, 1885. When
quite a child, had the precocity to compose a
quantity of pieces, even for orch. Was entrusted
to Karel Miry, who gave him lessons in harmony. About the age of 15, he had already
written a series of pieces (especially under
pseudonym of Lubner). His parents intended
him for the Bar; he gained at Univ. diploma
in philosophy and literature. However, he had
decided to become a musician and entered the
Brussels Cons., working under Fétis and Hanssens. In 1865, his comic opera *La Ferme du
Diable* was perf. in Ghent. In 1866-7 he cond.
orch. of Flemish Theatre in Brussels and introduced some of his own works. 1867, gained
Prix de Rome. After spending a year and half
in Germany, he accepted (1869) the office of
dir. of Bruges Cons. 1870, founded in Brussels
popular classical concerts and became dir. of
orch. of theatre. Vigorously attacked for political
reasons, he gave up (1871) his various posts and
(1872-5) travelled as orch. condr. (The Hague,
Dijon, Ghent, Liège, Antwerp), without neglect-
ing mus. compn. In 1876, commissioned by city
of Ghent to compose cantata for celebration of
3rd centenary of Peace of Ghent, he produced
his best work. 1879, teacher of harmony at
School of Music, Antwerp. Was entrusted with
compn. of important works for special occasions.
His works were unanimously praised and became
known abroad. However, he did not obtain the
official recognition to which he aspired, and he
was affected to such a degree that his health
failed. From 1884-85, he again cond. the theatre-
orch. at Ghent, but this was his last engagement.
His numerous works, in spite of something
reminiscent of other comprs., show a vigorous
personality and abundant inspiration. The harmony, polyphony and orchestration are masterly.
The style is connected with Ger. Romanticism,
but is resolutely progressive. He was the only
Belgian musician of this period who ventured
into the domain of "absolute" music.

La Ferme du diable, comic opera (Ghent, 1865);
Stella, lyrical drama (Brussels, 1881); *Berken de
diamantslijper,* opera (unpubl.); cantatas: *Het Woud*
(1867); *Memling-Cantate* (1871); *De Zegen der
Wapens* (1872); *De Pacificatie van Gent* (1876);
male-v. choruses with brass band; 5 symphonies,
3 overtures; suite for orch.; str. 5tet; male-v.
choruses unacc.; many songs; also a series not
publ., but of which proof-sheets have been kept;
pf. pieces. Consult P. Bergmans, *H. W.* (1886).—E. C.

WAGENAAR, Bernard. Dutch violinist and
compr. *b.* Arnhem, 18 Aug. 1894. Stud. vn. under
Veerman (Utrecht), theory under Dr. Joh.
Wagenaar; 1920, went to New York, where he
is violinist in New York Philh. Orchestra.

Numerous songs (Amsterdam, De Nieuwe Muziekhandel); pieces for vn. and pf.; for cello and pf.;
Serenade, str. and pf. (1915), often perf.; 2 melodramas with orch., *Das tote Kind* (Hoffmann von
Fallersleben) and *De blinden* (Schürman); symph.
poem, *Niobe;* *Concertstück,* cello and orch.; trio; 4tet;
vn. sonata; cello sonata; choral works; songs with fl.,
harp and pf. (Bethge, *Chinesische flöte,* 1919).—W. P.

WAGENAAR, Johan. Dutch composer; *b.*
Utrecht, 1 Nov. 1862. Stud. under Hol (Utrecht)
and Herzogenberg (Berlin); 1888, orgt. of
Utrecht Cath.; 1904, dir. of Music School,
Utrecht; choral condr. Utrecht (1904), Arnhem
(1908), Leyden (1910); 1919, dir. of R.A.M.,
The Hague; 1916, Doctorate *h.c.* from Utrecht
University.

Frithjof's Meerfahrt, overture for orch. (1886);
De Schipbreuk (*The Shipwreck*), humorous cantata
(1899); *Romantic Intermezzo* for orch. (1894); opera,
The Doge of Venice (1901); overture, *Cyrano de Bergerac* (Rostand), publ. Leuckart, Leipzig (1905);
Saul and David, symph. poem for orch. (1906); overture, *The Taming of the Shrew* (Shakespeare), 1909;
opera, *The Cid* (1914); *The Fortune Box,* vaudeville
(1916) (pf. score J. A. H. Wagenaar, Utrecht); madrigal for 5 v. (1916); *Sinfonietta* for orch. (1917);
Avondfeest (*Evening Feast*) for orch. (1922); songs, etc.
Consult: *Eigen Haard,* 1906 (No. 30); 1912 (No.
44); 1916, (No. 17); *Elseviers Geïllustreerd Maand-
schrift,* 1913 (No. 3); *Revue Musicale,* 1921 (No. 1).
—W. P.

WAGHALTER, Ignaz. Ger. composer. 1910,
condr. at Komische Oper, Berlin; since 1912,
condr. at Ger. Opera House, Charlottenburg.

Operas: *Der Teufelsweg* (*The Devil's Road*)
(Berlin, 1912); *Mandragola* (Charlottenburg, 1914);
Jugend (*Youth*) (words from Max Halbe by R.
Weinhoeppel; Berlin, 1917); *Der späte Gast* (*The Late
Guest*) (Berlin, 1912 and 1922); *To Whom does
Helene belong?* (Berlin, 1914); *Satani* (P. Milo),
Charlottenburg, 1923. Vn. concerto, op. 15; str. 4tet,
op. 3; vn. sonata, op. 5.—A. E.

WAGNER, Erika von. Actress and singer; *b.*
Zabern (Courland), 23 March, 1890. In 1907,
Hoftheater, Meiningen; 1910, Burgtheater;
afterwards in Berlin. Since 1912 a popular
heroine at Deutsches Volkstheater, Vienna.
From 1919 she has appeared in public as a concert singer also, and sings almost exclusively
contemporary songs. Her most renowned appearance was in the recitative part of Schönberg's

Pierrot lunaire. She has made concert-tours with the *Pierrot lunaire* party (cond. by the composer) since 1921.—P. St.

WAGNER, Wilhelm Richard. German composer-poet; *b.* Leipzig, 22 May, 1813; *d.* Venice, 13 Feb. 1883. Nominally the son of the Leipzig police-actuary, Friedrich Wagner, but actually son of the Dresden Court actor Ludwig Geyer (who later became his stepfather) and of Johanna Rosine, *née* Bätz; spent his youth in Dresden, where his parents settled in 1814. After a short stay in Eisleben attended 1822 the Kreuz Schule, Dresden. During this period his first attempts at poetry were made (*Leubald*), and from 1817 onwards, he received from C. M. von Weber his first serious impressions of opera. Towards the end of 1827 the family again settled in Leipzig, where he entered the Nikolaischule. The local theatre, at which his sister Rosalie was engaged as actress, exercised a strong influence on him, and in particular the intercourse with his uncle, the noted philologist, Adolf Wagner. From the Nikolaischule he went in 1830 to the Thomasschule, and six months later to the University. Hitherto self-taught, he now received regular instruction in music from the Thomaskirche Cantor, Theodor Weinlig (1780–1842). Prior to this, he had produced an overture in B flat (unsuccessfully performed at the Gewandhaus), four piano works (sonata, B flat; polonaise, D ma.; sonata, A ma.; fantasy, F sharp mi.); concert overtures, D mi. and C ma., an overture to Raupach's *King Enzio*; seven compositions to Goethe's *Faust*; and a symphony, C ma. A journey to Vienna and Prague occasioned the sketch of an opera, *Die Hochzeit*, of which some fragments remain. In 1833, Wagner began his career as conductor, by going as chorusmaster to Würzburg Stadttheater, where his brother Albert was already engaged as singer and producer. Here he finished his first opera, *Die Feen* (taken from Gozzi's *La Donna Serpente*), a work in the style of Marschner and of Weber's *Euryanthe*, in which already the "redemption" motive had been clearly treated (first performance 29 July, 1888, Munich). Returning to Leipzig (1834) Wagner soon fell under the influence of the so-called "Young Germany" (Laube, Heine, Gutzkow); the fruit of this was the opera *Das Liebesverbot*, after Shakespeare's *Measure for Measure*, which had one performance, Magdeburg (1836), where he had been conductor since 1834. In Magdeburg Wagner made the acquaintance of his future wife, Minna Planer (*b.* 5 Sept. 1809), with whom he entered on a fateful marriage, 24 Nov. 1836, at Königsberg. During the Magdeburg period appeared a *New Year's Cantata* and an overture to Apel's drama *Columbus*. After brief activity in Königsberg (1837) and a summer visit to Dresden, during which Wagner secured divorce from his wife, he proceeded in the autumn to Riga, where he developed a serious and zealous activity as opera and concert conductor, and performed as his own compositions the overtures *Rule Britannia* and *Polonia*. The sketch of an opera-text

(later completed for Wagner's friend, J. F. Kittl, the director of the Prague Conservatoire), *Die hohe Braut*, and the writing of a second libretto, *Die glückliche Bärenfamilie*, belong to the Riga period; also the libretto and the beginning of the composition of his grand opera *Rienzi*, which Wagner had already proposed to perform in Paris. Wagner left Riga for Paris, 1839, and broke his sea-voyage for three weeks in London and several weeks in Boulogne, where he met Meyerbeer. Wagner's three years in Paris belong to the most trying and difficult of his whole life. All hopes of a performance of *Das Liebesverbot* came to nothing. In order to live he had to undertake all kinds of humble musical work; but necessity made of him a writer. He finished *Rienzi* (Nov. 1840) and began at Meudon (spring and summer 1841) the text of his first characteristic Wagner opera: *The Flying Dutchman*, wherein he inwardly finds the way back to national German art. In 1840 appeared his first mature orchestral work, *Faust Overture* (1855 slightly altered and performed). Wagner left Paris 7 April, 1842, proceeding to Dresden, where his *Rienzi* has been accepted and was performed 20 Oct. Its huge success procured Wagner the post of Court conductor, a post which he accepted 2 Feb. 1843, after his *Flying Dutchman* had its first performance on 2 Jan. As early as the summer of 1842, Wagner had sketched the *Tannhäuser Saga* for an opera libretto. Text and music of this work was completed in the spring of 1845, and the first performance was on 19 Oct. *Lohengrin* followed on *Tannhäuser*, but Wagner was not to hear it in Dresden. His activity as Hofkapellmeister was remarkable for a series of noteworthy successes, among them performances of Gluck's *Iphigenia in Aulis*, which he arranged in a form somewhat questionable for modern ideas, and Beethoven's 9th Symphony. He was also instrumental in bringing over Weber's remains from London to Dresden. Composed a biblical scene for male choir and orch. *Das Liebesmahl der Apostel* (specially for the Dresden *Liedertafel*). In spite of this successful activity, Wagner belonged to the political malcontents of the time. He longed for political revolution which at the same time promised him the fulfilment of artistic reforms. Heavily involved in the Dresden May disturbances of 1849, he was in danger of merciless punishment on the part of the victorious reactionary party. He fled first to Franz Liszt at Weimar, and later to Zurich, where he was to remain in exile for the next nine years. These Zurich years, broken only by two journeys to Paris, were devoted to theoretical self-reflection, to which we are indebted for Wagner's æsthetic formulation of a national combined art-work (*Gesamtkunstwerk*): *Art and Revolution*; *The Art-work of the Future*; *Art and Climate*; *Judaism in Music*; *Opera and Drama* (his most important work); *A Communication to my Friends*. But after this phase of theoretical activity came a new period of creative energy. Wagner produced *Siegfried's Death*, a drama already begun in 1848, which gradually developed into the tetralogy when, through the *Young Siegfried*, *Valkyrie* and *Rhinegold* he had given it the necessary dramatic and philosophical foundation. The complete poem of the *Nibelung Ring* was finished in Nov. 1852. A deep love-affair with Mathilde Wesendonk (the wife of a friend and patron) resulted in the poem and music of *Tristan and Isolde* (1857–9). This episode led to the separation from his wife Minna, who died 17 Jan. 1866. Wagner then went to Venice (1858) and later to Lucerne, from which town he made a second journey to Paris. Here the first performance of *Tannhäuser* was given (24 March, 1861) with such ill-success that Wagner was forced to look for fresh sources of assistance. Following the general amnesty, Wagner then went to Biebrich near Mayence, taking with him the *Mastersingers of Nuremburg*, on the composition of which he had been engaged in Paris (1861–2). Later, after a short stay in his native country, he proceeded to Vienna. The accumulation of pressing debts again drove him to Switzerland (Mariafeld). Then he went to Stuttgart, where he received an invitation from the young Bavarian king, Ludwig II, to proceed to Munich and there realise his artistic projects. In Munich, Wagner elaborated his plan of a Festival Theatre (Festspielhaus), which was designed by Gottfried Semper; he gathered together friends like Hans von Bülow, Peter Cornelius and others, wrote articles on reform, and pursued the composition of *Siegfried*. *Tristan* was first performed 10 June, 1865. However, already towards the end of 1865, Wagner, as the result of Bavarian intrigues, was driven out of Munich. After travelling about for a time, he took up residence in Triebschen near Lucerne, where he completed the *Mastersingers* (first performance Munich, 23 June, 1868). Here he wrote *German Art and Politics* and *Beethoven*, and became intimate with the wife of his friend, Cosima von Bülow, *née* Liszt (*b.* 25 Dec. 1835), whom he married later. To this period belong also the *Siegfried Idyll* (1870) and the *Kaisermarsch*. In 1871 Wagner definitely settled in Bayreuth, where at Whitsuntide 1872 the foundation-stone of the Festival Playhouse was laid. The *Nibelung Ring*, now completed, was first performed, 13–30 Aug. 1876. The financial loss on these first festival performances forced Wagner to renew his journeys and seek fresh means of livelihood. In the meantime his last work, *Parsifal*, was completed (13 Jan. 1882) and was first performed in the summer of 1882.

As an artist Wagner represents the culmination of German romanticism—he became the creator of romantic "combined art" (*Gesamtkunstwerk*). After his early romantic operas, *Die Feen*, *Das Liebesverbot*, and the great historical opera, *Rienzi*, he wrote *The Flying Dutchman*, *Tannhäuser* and *Lohengrin* — works in which he first gives evidence of the unity of music and drama, and in which the *opera* evolves more and more into *music-drama*.

Formal melody gradually becomes a freely-flowing *melos* over an orchestra held together by a texture of "motives." This development finds its completion in works of the post-Zurich period. The old opera divided the melodic and dramatic elements: it chose the former for the full music of arias and ensembles, and the latter for the half-music of the recitatives. In Wagner's treatment of the two elements there lie both musical expansion and dramatic movement. He brought his "spoken song" (*Sprechgesang*) into a new relation with his symphonic orchestra, which he endeavoured to elevate to a significance not merely musical, but symbolical and metaphysical as well. Hence Wagner, however great a musician, is not to be estimated only as a musician: he represents a whole spiritual, intellectual and artistic epoch. No other artist has exerted such influence on the musico-dramatic as well as on the purely musical productivity and general cultural outlook of his time. Even to-day many artistic phenomena are determined, directly or indirectly, by that influence.

Literature (in Ger.): Wagner's own works (*Schriften und Dichtungen*) in 10 vols., 1871–83; his autobiography *Mein Leben* (1911) Eng. transl. *My Life* (Constable, 1911); his Letters (to Uhlig, Fischer and Heine, 1888; to Th. Apel, 1910); the Correspondence with Liszt (1900), Mathilde Wesendonk (1904), Minna Wagner (1908), Otto Wesendonk (1898), Eliza Wille (1894), August Röckel (1894), Hans v. Bülow (1916), Julie Ritter (1920); Correspondence with his publs. (1911); family letters (1907); Bayreuth letters (1907); letters to artists (1908); to friends and contemporaries (1909), etc. See W. Altmann, *R. W.'s Letters in chronological order and classified* (1905). A complete ed. of the letters (undertaken by J. Kapp and E. Mastner) never went beyond 2 vols. Biographies: C. F. Glasenapp (6 vols., Leipzig, 1911); H. S. Chamberlain, *R. Wagner* (1894). Monographs: Guido Adler, *R. W.* (1904 and 1922); P. Moos, *W.'s Æsthetics* (*R. W. als Ästhetiker*), 1906; O. Walzel, *R. W. in his Time and After* (*R. W. in seiner Zeit und nach seiner Zeit*), 1913; Friedrich Nietzsche, *R. W. in Bayreuth* (1876); also Nietzsche's other writings on W. Bibliography: N. Oesterlein, *Catalogue of a Wagner Library*, 4 vols. 1882–95.
Literature (in Eng.): F. Hueffer, *R. W. and the Music of the Future* (London, 1874); H. E. Krehbiel, *Studies in the Wagnerian Drama* (London, 1891); F. Praeger, *W. as I knew him* (London, 1892); H. T. Finck, *W. and his Works* (2 vols. New York, 1893); Hon. Mrs. Burrell, *R. W.'s Life and Works*, 1813–34 (London, 1898); G. B. Shaw, *The Perfect Wagnerite* (London, 1898); E. Newman, *A Study of W.* (London, 1899); W. Ashton Ellis, *Life of R. W.* (London, 1902–1908); E. Newman, *Wagner* (Music of the Masters, London, 1904); G. D. Gribble, *The Master-works of R. W.* (Everett, 1913); C. A. Lidgey, *Wagner* (Dent, 1921). Transls. into Eng.: *R. W.'s Letters on Liszt's Symph. Poems* (transl. by Hueffer, London, 1881); *The Music of the Future* (transl. by E. Dannreuther, London, 1873); *R. W. on Beethoven* (id. 1880); *On Conducting* (id. 1885); H. S. Chamberlain's *R. W.* (London, 1900); *Opera and Drama* (transl. E. Evans, sen., London, 1910); *My Life* (London, 1911).
Literature (in Fr.): A. Jullien, *R. W.* (Paris, 1886); Ed. Schuré, *Le Drame musical* (5th ed. 1903); A. Ernst, *L'Œuvre de W.* (1893); A. Lavignac, *Le Voyage artistique à Bayreuth* (1897); H. Lichtenberger, *R. W. poète et penseur* (2nd ed. 1901); E. Poirée, *R. W.* (1922).—A. E.

WAGNER, Siegfried. Ger. compr. *b.* Triebschen, near Lucerne, 6 June, 1869. Son of Richard Wagner; stud. at Charlottenburg and Carlsruhe for career of architect; trained finally under Engelbert Humperdinck and J. Kniese for music; 1894, assistant-condr. Bayreuth; 1896, became associate-condr. of Bayreuth

Fests. He cultivates the folk-element, taking material for operas from Ger. myths and fairy-tales. As musician, he is an *epigone* of his father. In 1924, cond. in U.S.A.

Symph. poem, *Longing* (1895); concerto for fl. and small orch. (1913); vn. concerto (1915); male chorus with orch. and organ, *Der Fahnenschwur* (*Oath to the Colours*), 1914; operas: *Der Bärenhäuter* (*Lazy Fellow*) (Munich, 1899); *Herzog Wildfang* (*Duke Madcap*) (Munich, 1901); *Der Kobold* (*The Goblin*) (Hamburg, 1904); *Bruder Lustig* (*Brother Merry*) (1905); *Sternengebot* (*Star Offering*) (Hamburg, 1908); *Banadietrich* (Carlsruhe, 1910); *Schwarzschwanenreich* (*Kingdom of the Black Swans*) (Carlsruhe, 1918); *Sonnenflammen* (*Sun-Glow*) (Darmstadt, 1918). Ready for performance: *Der Heidenkönig* (*King of Heathens*) (1915); *Der Friedensengel* (*Angel of Peace*) (1915); *An allen ist Hütchen Schuld* (*It is all the fault of Hütchen*) (1916); *Der Schmied von Marienberg* (1920). Wrote his own libretti. Consult: Glasenapp, *Siegfried Wagner and his Art* (1911), new series, I and II, on *Kingdom of Black Swans*, and *Sun-Glow* (1914 and 1919); B. Götz, *Siegfried Wagner's Banadietrich* (1912); Paul Pretzsch, *Siegfried Wagner's Art* (1919).—A. E.

WALDBAUER, Emerich. Hungarian violinist; *b.* Budapest, 12 April, 1892. Stud. under Jenő Hubay, R. High School for Music, Budapest. Founder and leader of Hungarian Str. Quartet (Temesváry, Kornstein, Kerpely), 1909.—B. B.

WALENN, Arthur. Eng. barit. singer and teacher; *b* London. Stud. at R.A.M.; then singing under Santley and Henschel; *début* 28 Nov. 1905, Q. H.; has toured widely.—E.-H.

WALENN, Herbert. Eng. cellist; *b.* London. Stud. at R.A.M. and R.C.M. and privately under Hugo Becker in Frankfort; appeared as solo cellist in 1902, Monday Popular Concerts; for 4 years, cellist of Kruse Quartet; founder of the Walenn Quartet; prof. at R.A.M.; dir. of London Violoncello School.—E.-H.

WALES, National Council of Music for. See under N.

WALKER, Edyth. Amer. operatic s. singer; *b.* New York, 1870. Stud. there and at Dresden; *début*, R. Opera House, Vienna; then Metropolitan Opera House, New York; played Kundry and Ortrud at Bayreuth; in 1912 at Munich; the title-rôle in Strauss's *Elektra* is one of her most notable parts. She appeared again in it at Covent Garden when it was produced.—E.-H.

WALKER, Ernest. Eng. compr. and writer on music; *b.* Bombay, India, 15 July, 1870. Educated Balliol Coll. Oxford; Mus.Doc. 1898; chiefly self-taught in music; now lecturer in harmony, Univ. of Oxford, and dir. of music, Balliol Coll. His music has a singularly pure Eng. feeling, though it is mostly formed on the models of the XIX century classics. It is scholarly, sound, individual and restrained. His finely conceived and outspoken *History of Music in England* is a very valuable contribution to musical literature.

Orch.: Concert overture (ms.); *Intermezzo*, str., clars. and pf. (Rogers); *Hymn to Dionysus* (Euripides) chorus and orch. (Novello); *Ode to Nightingale* (Keats), barit. solo, chorus and orch. (*id.*); *Neptune's Empire*, chorus and orch. (ms.); *Stabat Mater*, soli, 8-v. chorus and orch. (ms.). Chamber-music (all ms.); 5tet in A, pf. and str.; 5tet in B flat mi. horn and str.; 4tet in C mi. pf. and str.; a second one in D ma.; Fantasia in D ma. str. 4tet (Fischer); trio, C mi. pf. and str.; sonata, A mi. op. 8, vn. and pf. (J. Williams); sonata in C, op. 29, vla. and pf. (Schott);

sonata in F mi. cello and pf. (ms.); Prelude and fugue for organ (Stainer & Bell); songs and part-songs (Acott; Elkin; Boosey; J. Williams; Stainer & Bell; Curwen); Variations on a Norwegian air, pf. (J. Williams). Books: *History of Music in England* (Clarendon Press), Oxford, 1907; 2nd ed. 1923); *Beethoven* (J. Lane, 1913, 2nd ed. 1920); part-author of *Recent Developments in European Thought* (Oxford Univ. Press, 1920); arts. in dictionaries, periodicals and analytical programmes.—E.-H.

WALL, Alfred Michael. Eng. violinist and compr. *b.* London, 29 Sept. 1875. Stud. at R.C.M.; member of chief London orchs.; prof. Newcastle Cons. of Music; dir. chamber-concerts in Newcastle for 12 years.

Overture, *Thanet*, orch. (Bournemouth Mus. Fest. 1922); *Bagatelles*, orch. (ms.), 1922; *Two Legends* (ms.; 1923); tone-poem, *Lucretius* (Eastbourne Fest. 1923); vn. concerto (Newcastle Philh. 1920), ms.; str. 4tet (ms.), 1922; 4tet, pf. and str. 1921 (Stainer & Bell, a Carnegie award); trio in B flat, pf. vn. cello (Goodwin); sonata in A, vn. and pf. (ms.), 1921; choruses, songs, etc.—E.-H.

WALLACE, William. Scottish compr. *b.* Greenock, 3 July, 1860. Educated at Fettes Coll. Edinburgh; exhibitioner to Edinburgh Univ. which exhibition he resigned and entered Glasgow Univ.; graduated M.D. with honours for research work in department of ophthalmology which at the time had been little explored; continued studies in ophthalmology in Glasgow, Vienna, Paris and was on staff of eye-hospitals in Glasgow and London. For private reasons, abandoned this work and entered the R.A.M. London, where he was elected successively A.R.A.M. and F.R.A.M. From the first, a writer of orch. music. His *Passing of Beatrice* (1892) was the first " symphonic poem " by a British compr. It was perf. by Manns at Crystal Palace and was followed by other orchestral works. Was occasional condr. at New Brighton during Granville Bantock's seasons, with one programme devoted to his own works. Cond. his 5th symph. poem, *Villon*, at its 1st perf. by New Symphony Orch., and later at Leeds Fest. It has been given at all the important orch. concerts in the country, at Boston and New York, and by most orchs. in U.S.A, and on the Continent. Was hon. sec. of Soc. of British Comprs. and of R. Philh. Soc. During his term of office with the latter, the Soc. obtained the Royal designation. Was active on behalf of the legal position of comprs. and was a witness before the R. Commission on Copyright. Also served on composers' sub-committee of Soc. of Authors. Has publ. works on the development of the art of music and on its psychological aspects—*The Threshold of Music* and *The Musical Faculty* (Macmillan). Transl. operas, *Muguette* (Missa); *Le Chemineau* (Leroux), *Feuersnot* (Strauss), *Faust* (Berlioz), cantatas and about 50 songs. Served in the war from August 1914, first as medical officer to British Red Cross Soc., then as lieut. R.A.M.C. 1915–16, capt. 1916–1919, entirely as specialist and inspector of ophthalmic centres, and on the War Office Board.

Orch.: Symphony No. I, *The Creation*; symph. poems: I, *The Passing of Beatrice* (Schott); II, *Anvil or Hammer* (on Goethe's *Kophthisches Lied*); III, *Sister Helen* (on Rossetti); IV, *To the New Century* (Philh. Soc.); V, *Wallace, A.D. 1305–1905*; VI, *Villon* (Schott); suite, *The Lady of the Sea* (on Ibsen); suite, *A Scots Fantasy*; suite, *Moidart*;

overture, *In Praise of Scottish Poesy*; symph. prelude to Æschylus' *Eumenides*; *The Rhapsody of Mary Magdalene*; 2 suites in olden style, small orch. (Ashdown); *O Hie Honour*, str. and organ (Schott); 4 pieces for solo v. and orch. Many songs (*The Jacobite; Creation Hymn; Villon's Prayer*); songcycle, *Freebooter Songs*; 3 songs by Blake; *Spanish Improvisations*, s.a.t.b. and pf. *The Massacre of the Macpherson*, male chorus and orch. (Publ. Cramer, Boosey, Stainer & Bell; Paterson, Bosworth, Schott, Ricordi, Enoch, Elkin, etc.)—E.-H.

WALLASCHEK, Richard. Austrian writer on music; *b.* Brünn, 16 Nov. 1860; *d.* Vienna, 14 April, 1917. Doctor of law, then of arts; 1886, private lecturer in philosophy, Freiburg Univ. (Baden). In that year he turned to the æsthetics and psychology of music. 1890–5, stud. mus. coll. at British Museum, London. Private lecturer in music, Vienna Univ. 1896; and in rhetoric, 1908; also at Cons. (æsthetics). Mus. critic on *Die Zeit*.

Æsthetik der Tonkunst (1886); *Die Bedeutung der Aphasie für die Musikvorstellung* (1893, Z. für Physiologie und Psychologie); *The Origin of Music* (London, 1891); *Natural Selection and Music* (London 1892); *Difference of Time and Rhythm in Music* (London, 1893); *How we think of Tones and Music* (London, *Contemporary Review*, 1894); *Primitive Music* (London, 1893; Ger. amplified ed. *Anfänge der Tonkunst*, 1903); *Musikalische Ergebnisse des Studiums der Ethnologie* (1895, Globus); *Anfänge unseres Musiksystems* (1897); *Urgeschichte der Saiteninstrumente* (1898); *Entstehung der Skala* (1899); *Psychologie und Pathologie der Vorstellung* (Vienna, 1905); *Geschichte der Wiener Hofoper* (1907–8).—W. F.

WALLE - HANSEN, Dagmar. Norwegian pianist; *b.* Christiania, 24 Aug. 1871. Trained under Otto Winter-Hjelm and Agathe Gröndahl, Christiania, and for 4 years under Leschetizky, Vienna. From 1893 to 1914 she was the latter's assistant; 1914, again living in Christiania. Numerous concerts in Scandinavia and Central Europe.—U. M.

WALLEK - WALEWSKI, Bolesław. Polish compr. and condr. *b.* Lemberg, 1885. Pupil of Sołtys and Niewiadowski in Lemberg, then of Żeleński in Cracow and later of Riemann in Leipzig. Has been condr. of the Univ. Students' Choir in Cracow, of the choral soc. *Echo*, and of the Opera in Cracow. For 1 year (1918) was also condr. at Warsaw Opera. Hás written and publ. many excellent choral works, several songs and 3 symph. poems. In 1919, his opera *Dola* (*Fortune*), to his own libretto, was perf. in Cracow, later in Warsaw.—ZD. J.

WALLGREN, Åke. Swedish barit. operatic singer; *b.* Resteröd (Bohuslän), 9 Nov. 1873. Stud. under Julius Günther at R. Cons. Stockholm 1896–8; *début* in Gothenburg (Tonio, *Pagliacci*) 1898; engaged R. Opera, Stockholm, from 1900, where he is one of the most important artists. His b.-barit. is of a charming quality and great volume. Repertoire: Wotan, Wanderer, Gunther, Hans Sachs, Pogner, the Landgrave (*Tannhäuser*), King (*Lohengrin*), King Mark (*Tristan*), Gurnemanz, William Tell, Saint Bris, Escamillo, Ramphis (*Aïda*), etc.—P. V.

WALLNÖFER, Adolf. Austrian singer and compr. *b.* Vienna, 26 April, 1854. Pupil of Waldmüller, Krenn and O. Dessoff, (compn.), Rokitansky (singing); b.-barit. concert singer at Vienna; 1880, became t. at Stadttheater,

Olmütz; 1882, toured with Neumann's Wagner Company; settled at Stadttheater, Bremen, under Neumann; 1885, Prague; 1895, dir. of Stettin Theatre; 1896, toured in America; Russia (1896–7), etc.; long time at Nuremberg; 1906, Vienna Volksoper; now at Munich.

Songs and ballads: *Earl Eberstein; Overseer of Tenneberg; Schön Rothtraut*; pf. pieces; choral works with orch.: *Die Grenzen der Menschheit* (*Limits of Humanity*), op. 10; *Gersprenz*, op. 25; *The Flower's Revenge*, op. 31; *Universal Divine Service*, (soli, chorus, orch., organ, female choruses, op. 106, 107); opera, *Eddystone* (Prague, 1889).—A. E.

WALTER, Bruno. Ger. condr. and operatic manager; *b.* Berlin, 15 Sept. 1876. Pupil at Stern's Cons. (Ehrlich, Bussler, Rob. Radeke); operatic condr. at Cologne, Hamburg, Breslau, Pressburg, Riga, Berlin (R. Opera House), Vienna (Court Opera, 1901–12); 1911, condr. of Singakademie, Vienna; 1913–22, gen. mus. dir. Munich; now independent cond. Cond. *Ring* and *Rosenkavalier*, Covent Garden, London, May 1924. Pupil and friend of Gustav Mahler.

2 symphonies; *Das Siegesfest* (*Victory Festival*) (chorus, soli, orch.); str. 4tet.; pf. 5tet; pf. trio; vn. sonata; songs.—A. E.

WALTERSHAUSEN, Hermann Wolfgang, Baron. Ger. compr. *b.* Göttingen, 12 Oct. 1882. Pupil of M. J. Erb, Strasburg; 1900 of Ludwig Thuille, Munich, at which town W. settled; 1917, establ. Practical Seminary for Advanced Music-students, where he gave lectures on music, æsthetics, opera, etc.; 1920, representative dir. of Munich Acad. of Mus. Art; 1923, director.

Else Klapperzehen, 2-act mus. comedy (Dresden, 1909); *Colonel Chabert*, 3-act mus. tragedy (Frankfort-o-M., 1912); *Richardis*, 3-act romantic opera (Carlsruhe, 1915); *The Rauenstein Wedding* (Carlsruhe, 1919); songs: 8 songs with orch.; 7 songs from Ricarda Huch; song-cycles (all 1913); 3 *Weltgeistliche Lieder*, op. 13 (all Drei Masken Verlag); *Sinfonia apocalyptica*, full orch. (1923). Wrote: *Style in Individual Interpretation* (up to now, 4 vols. on *Magic Flute, Siegfried Idyll, Freischütz*) (1920); Gluck's *Orpheus and Eurydice* (1922); monograph on Richard Strauss (1921).—A.E.

WALTHEW, Richard Henry. Eng. compr. *b.* Islington, London, 4 Nov. 1872. Stud. R.C.M. under Sir Hubert Parry and Sir Charles Stanford; his cantata *Pied Piper* was perf. by Highbury Philh. in 1893, and repeated at Crystal Palace and elsewhere. The Strolling Players gave his pf. concerto in 1894. He was mus. dir. of Passmore Edwards Settlement 1900–4; prof. at Queen's Coll., later condr. of Univ. of London Mus. Soc.; cond. opera class at Guildhall School of Music, 1905; in 1909, condr. South Place Orch. Finsbury. His chamber-music is amongst his best work.

Orch.: Variations in B flat; 3 *Night Scenes*; 2 entr'actes and overture to *Aladdin*; overture to *Friend Fritz* (all ms.); pf. concerto in E flat; *Caprice Impromptu*, vn. and orch. (Ascherberg); cantatas: *Ode to a Nightingale* (Boosey); *The Pied Piper* (Novello); *The Fair Maids of February* (J. Williams); *John-a-Dreams* (Boosey); operettas: *The Enchanted Island; The Gardeners* (Boosey); chamber-music: 5tet, F mi. pf. and str.; 5tet, pf. vn. vla. cello and d.b. (Stainer & Bell); 5tet, clar. and str.; 4tet, G mi. pf. and str.; str. 4tet I in E; II in B flat; III in E flat; 6 *Lyrical Pieces*, str. 4tet; trio in C mi. pf. vn. clar. (Boosey); trio in G, pf. vn. cello (*id.*); Prelude and fugue for 2 clars. and bsn.; 5 *Diversions*, str. trio; sonata in A flat, pf. and vn.; *Serenade-Sonata*, vn. and pf.; sonata, cello and pf.; several pieces, clar. and pf. (Boosey); *Idyll*, fl. and pf. (Stainer & Bell); cantatas (Novello); vocal duets

(Boosey; Stainer & Bell); songs and part-songs (Novello; Stainer & Bell; Curwen; Boosey; Chappell; Williams; Laudy); pf. pieces (Augener; Boosey; Cary; Anglo-Fr. Co.; Stainer & Bell); booklet, *The Development of Chamber-Music* (Boosey, 1909).—E.-H.

WALTON, Herbert. Eng. orgt. *b.* Thirsk, Yorkshire, 1869. Stud. at R.C.M. London, under Sir Walter Parratt, Sir Hubert Parry, and Frederick Cliffe. Until 1897, private orgt. to Earl of Aberdeen, at St. Mark's Ch. Leeds; 1897, became orgt. of Glasgow Cath. where his recitals have created a new epoch in mus. appreciation in that city. Much organ music, including *Rhapsodic Variations* (Bayley & Ferguson).—W. S.

WALTON, William Turner. Eng. compr. *b.* Oldham, Lancs, 29 March, 1902. Won a probationership at age of 10, in Christ Ch. Cath. Oxford; at 16 became an undergraduate of Christ Ch.; passed first two examinations for Mus. Bac. at ages of 16 and 17; stud. under Sir Hugh Allen and E. J. Dent; but latterly has worked almost entirely by himself. His *Façade* to a series of poems by Edith Sitwell was perf. with the poet as reciter at Æolian Hall, 12 June, 1923. His str. 4tet was given at Salzburg International Music Fest. Aug. 1923. His present style is complex and atonal and is marked in the str. 4tet by deep seriousness.

Dr. Syntax, a pedagogic overture, full orch. (1921); 4tet, pf. and str. (1918); str. 4tet, 1920–2 (Salzburg Fest. 1923; Carnegie award, 1924); *Toccata,* vn. and pf. (1921–2); *The Passionate Shepherd,* t. v. and small orch. (1920); *Façade,* recitation, fl. clar. saxophone, tpt. cello, percussion (1922–3) (all in ms.). His 2 songs *The Winds* and *Tritons* are publ. by Curwen. —E.-H.

WAMBACH, Émile. Belgian compr. *b.* Arlon, 26 Nov. 1857; *d.* Antwerp, 6 May, 1924. Stud. under his father (prof. at Antwerp, School of Music), then Brussels Cons., again at Antwerp Music School; finally stud. compn. under Gevaert and Tinel. Inspector of Music Schools for Walloon provinces, 1902. Succeeded Jan Blockx as Dir. of Antwerp Cons. 1913.

Operas, *Quinten Matsys* (Antwerp 1900), *Melusina;* poème lyrique, *Joan of Arc;* cantatas, *Rubens, Vaderland, Kindercantate;* oratorio, *Moïse sur le Nil;* légende lyrique, *Yolande;* songs; pf. pieces.—E. C.

WARLOCK, Peter. Pen-name of Philip Heseltine (*q.v.*).

WARNER, H. Waldo. Eng. vla.-player and compr. *b.* Northampton, 4 Jan. 1874. Stud. at Guildhall School of Music, London, under Alfred Gibson (vn.) and Orlando Morgan (pf.). Whilst there, he wrote an opera, *The Royal Vagrants,* which was perf. by the opera class. A pf. trio of his gained a Cobbett Prize. After a few vn. recitals, took up vla. and joined in 1907 the London Str. Quartet, with which he toured Holland, France, Spain (2), Scandinavia (3), U.S.A. and Honolulu. Another pf. trio gained the Coolidge (Pittsfield Fest.) Prize of $1000 in 1921. Now devotes all his time to the L.S.Q.

Orch. suite, 3 *Elfin Dances* (Chappell); Phantasy in F, str. 4tet (Novello); Phantasy in D, str. 4tet (Cary); str. 4tet in C mi. (Ricordi); Folk-song Phantasy, str. 4tet (*id.*); fairy-suite, *The Pixy Ring,* str. 4tet (*id.*); trio, pf., vn. and cello (Coolidge Prize) (*id.*); *Elégie* and *Scherzo,* vn. and pf. (Novello); *Lullaby, Serenade, Intermezzo,* vn. and pf. (Ashdown); numerous songs and part-songs (Ricordi; Novello; Boosey; Schmidt [U.S.A.], etc.).—E.-H.

WARWICK-EVANS, Charles. Eng. cellist; *b.* Bayswater, London, 26 April, 1885. Stud. 6 years at R.C.M.; then principal cello in Beecham Opera Co.; later, leading cello in Queen's Hall Orch. a position he resigned to devote himself to rôle of cello in London Str. Quartet.—E.-H.

WATSON MUSIC LIBRARY, Manchester. Presented to City of Manchester, Libraries Committee in 1899 by Henry Watson, Mus.D. Cantab. (1846–1911). Originally numbering 16,700, the Library now contained some 40,000 vols., 16,000 copies of sheet music, 118,000 part-songs and anthems. The literature, 5000 vols., includes almost every standard work in Eng. and many foreign. Other sections of the Library contain complete eds. of the great masters (*Denkmäler Tonkunst,* and Society publications), 2000 full scores, 1000 vols. of periodicals, 800 operas, 6500 pf. works, chamber-music, etc. In many cases duplication is resorted to. The inst. is a lending library, with reservations in the case of rare and valuable works, and has 7000 borrowers in Manchester and district. The issues increased from 59,000 in 1911 to 168,229 in 1923. Chief librarian, L. Stanley Jast; music librarian, John F. Russell.—J. F. R.

WATTS, Winter. Amer. compr. *b.* Cincinnati, Ohio, U.S.A., 14 March, 1886. Stud. painting and architecture in Cincinnati; singing in Florence, Italy. In mus. theory, pupil of Goetschius in New York. A tone-pageant for orch., *Young Blood,* won Morris Loeb Prize ($1000) 1919. Two *Etchings* for orch. were perf. at Stadium Concerts, New York, under Hadley, 9 July, 1922. Incidental music for *Alice in Wonderland,* produced at Little Theatre, New York, April 1920. Dramatic ballads and songs with orchestra.

About 50 songs (Schirmer; Ditson), best-known being a cycle, *Vignettes of Italy; Wings of Night; Like Music on the Water.*—O. K.

WEATHERILL, Nellie G. Australian compr. *b.* Geelong, Victoria, 11 May, 1878.

Numerous songs and pf. pieces (some publ. Paling & Co. Sydney); pf. teaching pieces (Allan & Co. Melbourne).—E.-H.

WEBB, Dorothea. Eng. singer; *b.* Hammersmith, 6 July, 1886. Stud. R.A.M. under Theo Lierhammer and Stewart Macpherson; prof. of singing, R.C.M. from Jan. 1921; elected Fellow of R.A.M. 1922; many song-recitals; also sings unacc. songs. A very musicianly and interesting interpreter.—E.-H.

WEBER, Carl. Pianist; *b.* in St. James's Palace, London, 10 Dec. 1860. Stud. under Leschetizky; has played and taught in London from 1884. Dir. of Hampstead Cons. from 1904; condr. of orch. there. Now a dir. of Incorp. London Acad. of Music.

Cantata, *Rival Queens* (W. Rogers); *A Practical Pf. School* (Cary); pf. pieces.—E.-H.

WEBER, Ludwig. Ger. compr. *b.* Nuremberg, 13 Oct. 1891. Principally self-taught, receiving valuable advice from Courvoisier and Abendroth; one of most talented of modern composers.

Symphony, B mi.; *Hymn to Night* (chorus with orch.); 2 str. 4tets; 5tet for wind instrs.; 12 female choruses, some unacc.; pf. and organ pieces; songs with various accs. New arr. of national songs; 1-act opera, *Midas.*—A. E.

WEBERN, Anton von. Austrian compr. *b.* Vienna, Dec. 3, 1883. Disciple of Guido Adler; took his degree as Ph.D. (musicology), Vienna Univ. at the same time as Carl Horwitz. The first disciple of Schönberg, in whose immediate neighbourhood at Mödling near Vienna he now devotes himself to compn., after having been for a few years condr. of various theatres. From the end of his apprenticeship dates his Op. 1—Passacaglia for large orch., perf. 1921 at Bochum and 1922 at Düsseldorf Fest. Peculiarity of melody and harmony, strictness of form, and profound knowledge are already characteristics of this first work. Op. 2 is a mixed unacc. chorus (*Entflieht auf leichten Kähnen*). It is followed by songs, some (op. 8 and op. 13) with orch. acc.; others, op. 14–16, for v. 2 clar. vn. and cello. Op. 16 is 5 *Geistliche Lieder* for s. fl. clar. tpt. harp and double-bass. Also 4 *Stücke* for vn. and pf. op. 7; 5 *Stücke* for cello and pf. op. 11; 2 str. 4tets, op. 5 and 9; and 5 *Stücke* for orch. op. 10. The name *Stücke für* (Pieces for . . .) is characteristic of Webern's style. His ideas are very short, sometimes a few bars only; but with all their seemingly reckless shaping of harmony and form, they give, when heard, a strong impression. He is the compr. of the *pianissimo espressivo*. His infinitely delicate instrumentation makes his music glide by, as if by magic—the very shadow of a tune. Of present-day Viennese comprs. Webern is the one endowed with the strongest and noblest gifts. Of his works op. 1–3 and 5–7 are publ. (Univ. Ed.). Consult Stein's art. in *Chesterian* No. 26; also Paul Stefan's *Neue Musik und Wien* (Tal).—P. ST.

WECKERLIN, Jean Baptiste. Fr. compr. and musicologist; *b.* Alsace, 9 Nov. 1821; *d.* Gebweiler, 10 March, 1910. At first a chemist; then pupil of Paris Cons. under Halévy; prof. of singing and librarian of Cons. in 1876; also archivist of Soc. of Music Composers.
Dramatic works: *L'Organiste dans l'embarras*, 1853; *Après Fontenoy*, 1877. Some in Alsatian dialect: *Die dreifache Hochzeit*, 1867; *D'r verhäxt Herbst*, 1868. Symph. works: *Les Poèmes de la Mer* (1860); *L'Inde*; *Symphonie de la Forêt*. Coll. of folksongs (*Échos du temps passé*, 3 vols.; *Échos d'Angleterre* (1877); *Rondes populaires*; *Les Poètes français mis en musique*; *Chansons populaires des provinces de France* (in collab. with Champfleury); *La Chanson populaire* (1886); *Musical Curiosities* (*Musiciana*, 3 vols.); *Histoire des Instruments*.—A. C.

WEEKES & CO. Ltd. Publishers, founded in London, Sept. 1869, by Amos T. Weekes who served an apprenticeship with Cramer, Beale & Wood; in 1870, joined by Frederick Watt as partner, who took over the publishing. Two sons were admitted later, Robert Weekes in 1900, Eric Watt 1905. Specialises in educational works, church-music, modern pf. music, ballads.—E.-H.

WEGELIUS, Martin. Finnish compr. teacher; *b.* 1846; *d.* 1906. As organiser of the Helsingfors Music Inst. (Conservatoire), of which until his death he was dir., W. developed an activity of the highest importance for mus. life of Finland. Stud. for many years in Vienna and Leipzig; already in the 'seventies he was well known in Helsingfors as a versatile and highly

cultured musician. The foundation of the Music Inst., which was his real life's work, took place in 1882. W. publ. many serviceable educational and historical textbooks on music. Comp. cantatas (*Runeberg Cantata*, 1878), and some highly artistic choral works and songs. Many contemporary comprs. and musicians in Finland were his pupils—among them Sibelius, Järnefelt, Melartin, Kuula and others.—T. H.

WEHRLI, Werner. Swiss compr. condr. *b.* Aarau in 1892. Stud. at Cons. of Zurich and Frankfort under C. Kemptner, Fr. Hegar and Ivan Knorr; won Mozart Prize with str. 4tet at Leipzig; cond. Cäcilienverein (Oratorio Concerts) at Aarau. One of most talented Swiss comprs. of younger generation. His works are very poetically conceived and skilfully written. *Das heisse Eisen* (H. Sachs), comic opera; *Chilbizite*, fantasy for orch.; 2 str. 4tets; trio for vn. vla. and fl.; numerous songs (Leipzig, Hug).—F. H.

WEIDIG, Adolf. Amer. compr. *b.* Hamburg, 28 Nov. 1867. Stud. at Cons. in Hamburg under Bargheer (vn.) and Riemann (theory). Won a Mozart Stipend in Frankfort, 1888, with str. 4tet. Stud. until 1891 at Munich Acad. under Abel (vn.) and Rheinberger (compn.). 1892, settled in Chicago; 1892–6, member of Chicago Orch.; 1892–1901, played 2nd vn. in Spiering Quartet. 1898, assistant-dir. of Amer. Cons. of Music, Chicago. Cond. concerts (including own works) Chicago and Minneapolis; also (1908–9) Hamburg, Berlin, Munich and Frankfort. Besides works listed below, has comp. 2 symphonies, a symph. poem *Semiramis*, a symph. suite, 3 overtures, a str. 5tet, 3 4tets.
Quartettino, suite, str. 4tet, op. 11 (Schott, 1897); *Capriccio*, orch. op. 13 (*id.* 1913); 3 *Episodes*, orch. op. 38 (*id.* 1910); concert overture, op. 65 (Summy, 1921); *Serenade*, str. 4tet, op. 16 (*id.* 1899); trio, pf. vn. vla. op. 9 (Augener, 1902; Schott, 1911); Suite, vn. and pf. op. 22 (Schott, 1902); *Italian Suite*, vn. and pf. op. 40 (Summy, 1914); *A Little Suite*, pf. op. 60 (Schirmer, 1921). *O sing unto the Lord*, motet, mixed vs. op. 120 (Summy, 1900); songs (Summy; Ditson).—O. K.

WEIGL, Bruno. Ger.-Czechoslovak compr. and author; *b.* Brünn, 16 June, 1881.
Mandragola (3-act mus. farce); compns. for organ; *Psalm CXLIV*, male chorus and organ; *Serenade* for orch.; songs for orch.; *Handbook of Cello Literature*.—E. S.

WEIGL, Karl. Austrian compr. *b.* Vienna, 6 Feb. 1881. Stud. under Zemlinsky. 1899–1902, pupil of the Cons. (Door, Fuchs). Prize and silver medal of Music Society. Mus.Doc. 1903. From 1904 to 1906, repetitor of the soloists in Opera House, assistant of Gustav Mahler, with whom he worked till M.'s death. 1910, Beethoven Prize of Music Soc. for str. 4tet (A ma.). Since 1918, teacher at New Cons.; 1922, prize of Philadelphia Mendelssohn Choir for unacc. church chorus. He prefers linear cpt. and large dimensions. Despite a certain dryness in harmonic development, he is one of best known of younger comprs. of Vienna.
Symph. phantasy; 2 symphonies (E ma. and D mi.); symph. cantata, *Weltfeier*; 2 cycles of orch. songs; 3 str. 4tets (1 with vla. d'amour), C mi., E ma. A ma.; str. 6tet (D mi.); many songs; duets; vocal 4tets; *Stelldichein* for v. and str. 6tet. Some mixed choruses and some for unacc. female vs.; pf. pieces: *Bilder und Geschichten (Pictures and Tales)* (also in an

orch. version, Vienna, 1924); *Toteninsel* (*Isle of Death*); *Nachtphantasien*; 28 Variations on an 8-bar theme.—P. P.

WEINBERGER, Jaromír. Czech composer; *b.* Prague, 1896. Pupil of Jaroslav Křička and Karel Hofmeister; since 1922, prof. of compn. at Cons. at Ithaca, U.S.A. After a promising start, devoted himself more to immediate effect than to inner musical content.

Don Quixote, orch.; *Scherzo giocoso*, orch.; pantomime, *Abduction of Eveline* (1917); pf. sonata (M. Urbánek); *Colloque sentimental*, pf. (Univ. Ed.).—V. ST.

WEINER, Leo. Hungarian compr. *b.* Budapest, 16 April, 1885. Stud. compn. under Hans Koessler at R. High School for Music, Budapest. His *Serenade* for small orch., written when 21 (publ. Bote & Bock) was awarded Budapest *Lipótvárosi Kaszinó* prize. Through this work, his name became known in Hungary and other European countries. His second string quartet (Budapest, Bárd & Sons), won the Coolidge Prize in 1922. Since 1907, teacher of harmony and compn. R. High School for Music, Budapest.

Op. 4, 1st str. 4tet (Berlin, Bote & Bock); op. 5, *Fasching*, overture for small orch. (*id.*); op. 7, Prelude, Nocturne and Scherzo for pf. (*id.*); op. 9, 1st sonata for pf. and vn. (Rózsavölgyi); op. 11, 2nd sonata for pf. and vn. (Bárd & Sons).

Consult: *Della Musica in Ungheria* (*Il Pianoforte*, July 1921); *Hungarian Music of To-day* (*Monthly Musical Record*, Feb. 1922); *The Development of Art-Music in Hungary* (*Chesterian*, Jan. 1922).—B. B.

WEINGARTEN, Paul. Austrian pianist; *b.* Brünn, 20 April, 1886. Stud. theory at Vienna Acad. under Fuchs, pf. under Sauer. Gained Nicolas Rubinstein Prize. Ph.D. Vienna Univ. (musicology). Since 1921, pf. prof. at Vienna Music Acad. Extensive concert-tours in Germany, France, Spain and Holland, performing modern pf. music, (especially Debussy, Ravel, de Falla). —P. ST.

WEINGARTNER, Felix. German condr. and compr. *b.* Zara (Dalmatia), 2 June, 1863. Brought up in Graz (compn. pupil of A. W. Remy); 1881, went to Leipzig (student of philosophy); soon devoted himself entirely to music; pupil of Cons. until 1883. Then went to Weimar under Liszt; subsequently Kapellmeister in Königsberg (1884), Dantzig (1885–7), Hamburg (1887–9), Court Kapellmeister Mannheim (1889–91); 1891, Kapellmeister R. Opera and condr. of Symphony Concerts, Berlin; resigned post at Opera, though remaining condr. of Symphony Concerts, and settled in Munich as condr. of Kaim Concerts. 1908, succeeded Mahler as condr. of Vienna Opera, resigning in March, 1911, retaining conductorship of the concerts. 1912, became 1st Kapellmeister, Stadttheater, Hamburg; resigned early in 1914 and went to Darmstadt as Court Kapellmeister (gen. mus. dir.). 1919–20, dir. of Vienna Volksoper. 1891, married Marie Juillerat; 1903, second marriage with Baroness Feodora von Dreifus; 1912, married the m.-sopr. Lucile Marcel (*d.* Vienna, 25 June, 1921); 1922, married the actress Kalisch. As compr. W. is eclectic.

Symph. poems: *King Lear*; *The Abode of the Blessed*; 4 symphonies (I, G; II, E flat; III, E; IV, F);

Serenade for str. orch.; vn. concerto, G ma. op. 52; cello concerto, A mi. op. 60; overture, *Aus ernster Zeit*, op. 56; 5tet, op. 40 (2 vns. 2 obs. cello); 4 str. 4tets; pf. 6tet, op. 20; pf. 5tet, G. ma. op. 50 (with clar. vla. pf. cello); 2 vn. sonatas; *Traumnacht* and *Sturmmythus*, 8-v. mixed chorus and orch., op. 38; songs with pf. and with orch.; song-play, t. and pf. op. 63; pf. pieces; operas: *Sakuntala* (Weimar, 1884); *Malavika* (Munich, 1886); *Genesius* (Berlin, 1892); *Orestes*, a musico-dramatic trilogy after Æschylus (I, *Agamemnon*; II, *Das Totenopfer*; III, *Die Erinnyen*, Leipzig, 1902); *Spring Fairyplay* (Weimar, 1908); *Cain and Abel* (1-act opera, Darmstadt, 1914); music to *Faust* (Weimar, 1908; new arr. Chemnitz, 1917); to Shakespeare's *Tempest* (op. 65); comic opera, *Dame Cobold* (Darmstadt, 1916, own text); *Meister Andrea*, op. 66, and *Terakoya* (*The Village School*), op. 64 (both Vienna, 1920). (Publ. mostly by Breitkopf.) 1908, he publ. a poem, *Golgatha* (drama in 2 parts). Works on music include: *The Doctrine of Renascence and the Music Drama* (1895); *On Conducting* (1895, 4th ed. 1913); *Bayreuth, 1876–96* (1896, 2nd ed. 1904); *The Symphony since Beethoven* (1897, 2nd ed. 1901); *Suggestions for Performances of Beethoven's Symphonies* (1906, Eng. 1908); a similar work for Schubert and Schumann (1918); *Musical Walpurgis-Night* (1907); *Akkorde*, collection of essays, 1912. W. ed. complete ed. of Berlioz' works; also Méhul's *Joseph* with recitatives (1909), and ed. Weber's *Oberon*. Consult: Emil Krause, *W. as Creative Artist* (1904); P. Raabe, *W. as Creative Artist* (*Musik*, Jan. 1908); J. L. Lusstig, *F. W.* (1908); Felix Günther, *F. v. W.* (1918). W. began the publ. of his recollections (*Lebenserinnerungen*) in *Neues Wiener Journal*, 1919; publ. book-form 1923.—A. E.

WEINMANN, Carl. Ger. musicologist; *b.* Vohenstrauss (Oberpfalz), 22 Dec, 1873. Stud. music at Cath. School at Regensburg (Ratisbon), where he attended High School and the School of Church Music (Haberl, Haller); choirmaster (*Magister Choralis*) at Theological College, Innsbruck. After completion of Univ. studies at Innsbruck and Berlin, ordained priest, 1899; graduated under Peter Wagner at Freiburg, Switzerland, Ph.D.; went to Collegiate Ch. Regensburg, as condr. and teacher of history of music and æsthetics at School of Church Music. 1908, dean of Cath.; 1909, dir. of the Bishop's (late Proske's) Library at Regensburg. 1910 succeeded Haberl as dir. of School of Church Music; 1918, Th.D. and professor.

Hymnarium Parisiense (dissertation, 1905); *A Small History of Church Music* (1906, 2nd ed. 1913), transl. into Ital. (1908), Eng. (Bewerunge, 1910); Polish (Chybinski, 1911), Fr. (Landormy, 1912), and Hungarian (Hackl, 1914); monographs on Leonhard, Paminger (1907), and Karl Proske (1908), all in coll. *Church Music* (Regensburg, by Pustel), ed. by W.; *Stille Nacht, Heilige Nacht* (history of hymn, on its centenary), 1918, 1920; *Council of Trent and Church Music* (Breitkopf, 1919); ed. *Year-book of Church Music*, 1908–11, when it ceased; from 1911 *Musica Sacra*; ed. new eds. (Pustet, after *Editio Vaticana*) of *Roman Gradual* (1909); *Kyrie* (1911); *Office for the Dead* (1912); *Graduale Parvum* (1913); *Roman Vespers with Psalms* (1914).—A. E.

WEIS, Karel. Czech compr. *b.* Prague, 13 Feb. 1862. Stud. at Organ School and under Zdenko Fibich. At first teacher and condr., but devoted almost exclusively to compn. since 1888. His operatic work is marked by a keen sense of dramatic situation and external effects, but his music is entirely eclectic. Since 1904 he has turned to operetta.

Symphony; vn. sonata; str. 4tet; symph. poem, *The Triumphator*; a popular scene, *Přástky*, chorus and orch.; some folk-song collections, *Blatácké*. Operas: *Viola* (rev. as *The Twins*, 1892); *The Polish Jew* (1901), which also had a great success abroad; *The Storm at the Mill* (1912). Operetta, *The Revisor* (1907). Publ.: F. A. Urbánek; Brockhaus; Simrock.—V. ST.

WEISMANN, Julius. Ger. pianist and compr. *b.* Freiburg (Breisgau), 26 Dec. 1879. Pupil of E. H. Seyffart (1888–91); 1891–2 of Rheinberger and Bussmeyer, Munich; 1893–6 of H. Dimmler, Freiburg; 1898–9 of Herzogenberg, Berlin; 1899–1902 of Thuille, Munich. Now at Freiburg as compr. He is a very sensitive, romantic miniaturist.

Symphony, B mi. (op. 19); 3 orch. fantasies, op. 57; vn. concerto, D. mi. op. 36; pf. concerto; Variations and fugue on an old *Ave Maria* for pf. and vn., op. 37; cello and pf. sonata; str. 4tet, F ma. op. 14; pf. trios, D mi. op 27 and op. 77; vn. sonatas, F ma. op. 28, and F sharp mi. op. 47; sonata for vn. alone, D mi. op. 30; Variations, ob. and pf. op. 39; songs (op. 67 with trio acc.); short choral works with orch.: *Hymn to the Moon* and *Reapers' Song,* op. 10; *A Grave,* op. 11; *Fingerhütchen* (*Little Thimble*), female chorus and orch. op. 12; sacred cantata, *Macht hoch die Tür* (*Open the Gate*), s. mixed chorus, orch. op. 34; male choruses, op. 31; female choruses, op. 65; pf. pieces, op. 17, 21 (Variations and fugue), 25 (Passacaglia), 27, 32, 35 (Dance-fantasy, also for orch.), 48; Variations for 2 pfs. A ma. op. 64.—A. E.

WEISSMANN, Adolf. Critic and musicologist; *b.* Rosenberg (Upper Silesia), 15 Aug. 1873. Ph.D.; 1914, prof.; trained in Berlin; also stud. at Breslau, Innsbruck, Florence, Berne; now residing in Berlin; music critic for *Berliner Tageblatt,* 1900; for *Roland von Berlin,* 1904–10; since then, for *Montags-Zeitung, B.Z. am Mittag* and *Vossische Zeitung.* His *Music in the World Crisis* is a fine survey of the art.

Berlin as a Musical City, 1740-1911 (1911); G. Bizet (1907, in R. Strauss's coll. Music); Chopin (Berlin, 1912, 3rd ed. 1919); The Virtuoso (1918); Die Primadonna (1919); Der Klingende Garten (Impressions on the Erotic in Music) (1920); Giacomo Puccini, (Munich, 1922, Drei Masken Verlag); Music in the World Crisis (Stuttgart, 1922; Eng. J. M. Dent & Sons, 1924); Verdi (1922, Deutsche Verlags-Anstalt).—A. E.

WELLESZ, Egon. Austrian compr. writer on music; *b.* Vienna, 21 Oct. 1885. Stud. under G. Adler at Vienna Univ. (mus. science), Arnold Schönberg (cpt.) and Bruno Walter (compn.). In 1908 received degree of Mus. Doc.; in 1913 Univ. lecturer on history of music. Has publ. many scientific works, especially on the art of the baroque and rococo style (opera of XVII and XVIII century) and the old-Byzantine church music. His chief work in this little-known sphere is *Problems of Oriental Church Music* (1922). He lectured in London in 1922 on *Modern Austrian Music.* The chief virtue of Wellesz lies in his compns. His different periods and changes of style show a clear development to a new form of expression. His first songs are in the style of Reger, Mahler and especially Pfitzner. Then his harmony grows independent (diatessaron harmonies), approaching the style of Schönberg's middle period. But Wellesz soon forsakes this path entirely. In his chamber-music he attains a new mosaic-like knitting of individual themes, joined by inner continuity. In his pf. pieces (publ. before those of Schönberg) he prefers short, pregnant rhythmic forms, often resembling dance-rhythms. His lyric works were first influenced by the style of the young Fr. comprs. (followers of Debussy); then turned to an increasing concentration and religious-cosmic expression, which deepens in the

dramatic pieces. Here is not only the tragic accent, but also ascetic renunciation of outer means, with a new classical effect. The ballets, deriving from the Russ. comprs., contain dance-forms, later also transcendental expression. The latest works show a prevailing expressionism, a turning away from Romanticism, with a baroque tendency, and a more objective approach to the subject. Dr. Wellesz is the Chairman of the Committee for the Austrian articles in this Dictionary.

Operas: Prinzessin Girnara, from Jakob Wassermann (1918–19; perf. 1921, Frankfort and Hanover); Alkestis, from Hugo v. Hoffmansthal (1922). Ballets: Diana (1914); Persian Ballet (1920); Achilles at Scyros (1921). Orch.: Girls praying to the Virgin Mary (with chorus); Early Spring, symph. overture (1912). Chamber-music: 4 str. 4tets; numerous pf. pieces (1909–17); Wie ein Bild (Like a Picture) prose words from Peter Altenberg (1906); Sacred Song (1917) for str. and pf.; Aurora, song without words for coloratura voice (1922).—P. P.

WELLS, Paul. Amer. pianist; *b.* Carthage, Mo., U.S.A., 22 July, 1888; stud. pf. at Peabody Cons. of Music, Baltimore, under Ernest Hutcheson; later in Berlin under Josef Lhévinne, appearing as soloist with Berlin Philh. Orch. From there, went to Vienna to study under Leopold Godowsky. On returning to America, toured as soloist in U.S.A. (played Liszt E flat concerto with Emil Oberhoffer at Minneapolis, and with Symphony Orch. Baltimore). In 1913, came to Toronto, joining staff of Toronto Cons. of Music. Here he has become known as an eminent teacher, besides a brilliant concert-pianist.—L. S.

WELSH SONG. See HWYL; PENILLION.

WELSMAN, Frank S. Canadian pianist and condr. *b.* Toronto, 20 Dec. 1873. Stud. pf. in native city, afterwards in Germany under Martin Krause, Gustav Schreck and Richard Hofmann. Later, again visited Europe for lessons under Arnold Mendelssohn. On return to Toronto, was associated with Toronto Coll. of Music; afterwards with Toronto Cons. of Music, and toured extensively through Canada giving recitals. 1906, condr. of Toronto Symphony Orch., an organisation which he was largely instrumental in founding. Under his dir. the orch. played a prominent part in mus. life of city, until the war curtailed and finally ended its activities. In 1918, joined staff of Canadian Acad. of Music; 1922, appointed mus. dir. of that inst., which position he now holds. The Toronto Symphony Orch., while not perhaps of the standard of the great American orchs., yet must be regarded as the first real attempt to establish a professional orch. in Canada. Over 100 concerts were given in Toronto, besides many elsewhere.—L. S.

WENDEL, Ernst. Ger. condr. *b.* Breslau, 1876. Stud. vn. in Berlin (Wirth and Joachim); theory (Succo and Bargiel); 1896, on Joachim's recommendation, joined the Thomas Orch. in Chicago; 1898 (likewise at Joachim's suggestion) went to Königsberg as condr. of concerts of Soc. of Music; 1909, succeeded Panzner as dir. of Philh. Soc. Bremen; 1922, gen. mus.

dir.; also dir. of Musikalische Gesellschaft, Berlin.

Male-v. choruses with orch.: *Das Grab im Busento*, op. 9; *Das Deutsche Lied*, op. 11.—A. E.

WENDLAND, Waldemar. Ger. compr. *b.* Liegnitz, 10 May 1873. Stud. medicine; obliged to take up bank-work. Musically, for a long time self-taught; then (on Schuch's recommendation) became a free pupil of Humperdinck; was temporary Korrepetitor and condr. at theatre. Now devotes himself entirely to compn. in Berlin.

Songs; 2 pantomimes (*The Two Pierrots*, *The Dancing Fairy*); operas: *The Tailor of Malta* (Leipzig, 1912); tragic opera, *Peter Sukoff* (Basle, 1921); *Der Narr* (*The Fool*). Married the authoress, Olga Wohlbrück.—A. E.

WENDT, Theo. Condr. *b.* 1874. Stud. Cologne and R.A.M. London; appointed condr. of Cape Town Municipal Orch. in 1914; retired in 1924. His perfs. are marked by musicianly insight and the power of getting the maximum of effect with minimum of fuss. Has a wide catholicity of taste—as excellent an interpreter of Brahms and the classics, as he is of the most modern compns. A compr. of much music of a lighter order which shows considerable charm, though his duties as a condr. have precluded compn. during the last few years.—W. H. B.

WENSE, Hans Jürgen von der. Ger. compr. *b.* Ortelsburg, E. Prussia, 10 Nov. 1894. Son of an army-officer; stud. engineering; self-taught musician; is Neo-Primitive in his art; lives in Warnemünde. Comp. 5 *Klavierstücke*; songs from the *Edda*; Span. songs; Ger. songs (Novalis).—A. E.

WENTZEL, Norbert. Australian compr. *b.* Sydney, 1891. Now teaches in Sydney.

Elegy, orch.; *Scherzo*, small orch.; *Allegro and Andante*, str. 4tet; Fugue in E flat (*id.*); *Scherzo* in F (*id.*); *Scotch Airs*, vn. cello, pf.; *Scotch Fantasia*, vn. and pf.; cantata, *The Wave* (Tiedge-Longfellow), chorus and orch.; sonata in C, vla. and pf.; many part-songs and songs.—E.-H.

WERTHEIM, Julius. Polish compr. pianist; *b.* Warsaw, 1880. Pupil of Moszkowski and Sliwiński (pf.) and of Noskowski (theory), 1901, gold medal, Warsaw Cons. For some years, was prof. of instrumentation at Warsaw Cons. Now lives independently as compr. in Berlin. He has written 4 symphonies, many works for pf. in large forms (sonatas, variations, etc.), and a great number of songs. A considerable quantity of them were publ. in 1923 by Simrock, Berlin. —Zd. J.

WESTRHEENE, P. A. van. Dutch writer on music, critic; *b.* Roosendaal (Guelderland), 2 Oct. 1862. Editor of Dutch mus. review *Caecilia en het Muziekcollege*. Stud. pf. at Arnhem (under Gerbrands and Meyroos) and at Leyden (under Enderlé) where he also stud. classical philology. Was 5 years preceptor at Tiel (Guelderland) Grammar School; 1897, mus. critic of *Nieuwe Arnhemsche Courant*; cond. several choirs at Arnhem; 1919, secretary of Klokkenspel-vereeniging (soc. for development of tower-carillon playing); 1921, member of Soc. for Netherlands Mus. History. Has written a Grieg biography; a short history of Cæcilia

Soc. of Arnhem; since 1904 condr. of Bach Soc. Arnhem.

A symphony; choral works; ed. Bach cantatas and an old Dutch opera (*De triompheerende Min*); numerous songs.—W. P.

WETTON, Henry Davan. Eng. orgt. and condr. Stud. under Sir Frederick Bridge; prof. of organ R.C.M. and Guildhall School of Music; assistant-orgt. Westminster Abbey, 1881–96; head of mus. dept. Battersea Polytechnic, 1909; orgt. and dir. of music, Foundling Hospital, from 1892. Mus.Doc. Dunelm.

Much church and organ music; sacred cantata, *The Fulfilment*, soli, chorus, orch. (Curwen, 1921); *Marche Triomphale* in E flat (3rd prize Royal Air Force march competition) (Paxton, 1923); orch. overture; Suite for str. orch. (ms.).—E.-H.

WETZ, Richard. Ger.-compr. *b.* Gleiwitz (Silesia), 26 Feb. 1875. Stud. at Cons. Leipzig; private pupil of Alfred Apel and Richard Hofmann; 1899, continued studies in Munich with Thuille. After 2 years as theatre-condr. retired to Leipzig. 1906, condr. of Soc. of Music, Singakademie, later of other societies in Erfurt; 1911–21, teacher of compn. and history of music at National Cons. of Music in Erfurt. For 2 winters guest-condr. of Mus. Soc. in Gotha. 1913, elected dir. of Riedel Soc. Leipzig; retired 1915. 1913, teacher of compn. and history of music, Weimar; 1920, prof.; 1918, dir. of Engelbrecht Madrigal Chorus.

Songs; choruses (some with orch. acc.); str. 4tet, op. 43; sonatas; 3 symphonies (C mi., A, B flat); 2 operas: *The Eternal Fire* (Düsseldorf, 1907) and *Judith* (3 acts). Wrote *Anton Bruckner, his Life and Works* (1922). Consult: E. L. Schellenberg, *R. W.*; R. Querner, *R. W. als Liederkomponist* (Leipzig, Kistner); G. Arnim, *Die Lieder von R. W.*—A. E.

WETZEL, Hermann. Condr. compr. *b.* Bedlin (Pomerania), 23 Sept. 1858. Solo clarinettist of Symphony Orch. and condr. of popular Symphony Concerts at Basle, since 1905. His works, written in the style of Johann Strauss, are full of charming melodies and rhythms and finely orchestrated.

Die Wallfahrt nach Mekka, operetta (Basle, Pohl); *Humorous Serenade* for 4 wind-instrs. (Hanover, Örtel); *Serenade*, vn. and pf. (Leipzig, Hug); numerous songs.—F. H.

WETZEL, Justus Hermann. Ger. author and compr. *b.* Kyritz (Brandenburg), 11 March, 1879. Stud. natural history, philosophy and history of the arts; graduated Ph.D. 1901; took up music exclusively; 1905–7, teacher at Riemann Cons. Stettin; removed to Potsdam; in Berlin since 1910.

Pf. and other chamber-music; about 300 songs, of which song-cycle (57 songs in 10 books) has been publ. Publ. selected songs by J. Fr. Reichardt; wrote æsthetic and critical essays; publ. *Elementary Theory of Music* (Leipzig, 1911).—A. E

WETZLER, Hermann Hans. Ger. compr. *b.* Frankfort-o-M., 8 Sept. 1870. 1885–92, pupil at Hoch's Cons. (Clara Schumann, Heermann, B. Scholz, Knorr, Humperdinck); 1892, settled in New York; 1897–1901 orgt. at Trinity Ch.; 1902, organised concerts in Carnegie Hall; 1903, started the Wetzler Symphony Concerts, which concluded with the Richard Strauss Fest. in 1904; 1905–8, condr. Stadttheater, Hamburg; 1908, dir. several concerts at Imperial Opera, Petrograd; 1908, chief condr. at Stadttheater,

Elberfeld; 1909–13 at the Stadttheater, Riga; 1913–15, Stadttheater in Halle; thence to Lübeck; since 1919, Cologne Opera House.

Songs (op. 1 ballad, *Fairy Queen*, op. 2, 3, 8); pf. pieces; concert overture; Symph. Phantasy, op. 10 (Simrock); music for Shakespeare's *As You Like It* (also as orch. suite in 5 parts); organ sonata of Bach rearranged for orchestra.—A. E.

WHITE, Felix Harold. Eng. compr. *b.* London, 27 April, 1884. At 5, started learning pf. under his mother's guidance; in all other mus. respects, is self-taught. His 1st work heard in public was an overture, *Shylock*, produced by Sir Henry Wood at Queen's Hall Promenades, 26 Sept. 1907. Is one of most characteristic of the Eng. comprs. of the ten years, 1913–23.

The Mermaid Tavern, a revel for orch. (ms. 1921); *The Deserted Village*, tone-poem, orch. (ms. 1923); 2 idylls, *Indoor, Outdoor*, small orch. (ms. 1923); *To Miranda*, serenade for str. orch. (ms. 1921); *Astarte Syriaca*, orch. tone-poem (ms.); Suite (4 movements), orch. (ms.). Chamber-music: 4 *Japanese Proverbs*, fl. ob. vn. vla. cello (ms. 1922); *Dawn*, study for 12 cellos (ms.); *Arietta*, vn. vla. cello (Curwen); *Nymph's Complaint for the Death of her Fawn*, (after Andrew Marvell), ob. (or vn.) vla. pf. (Stainer & Bell; a Carnegie award, 1922); *Sweet Thoughts in a Dream*, vn. and pf. (Curwen); sonata, vn. and pf. (ms.); 5 pieces, vn. and pf. (ms.); sonata, cello and pf. (ms.), *The Deep Dirge of the Sunset*, cello and pf. (ms.). Pf. pieces (Curwen; Novello; Stainer & Bell; Keith, Prowse; Ascherberg); 40 ms. pf. pieces; 24 part-songs (6 publ. Curwen); about 250 songs (25 with orch.; 2 with vn. alone), 50 publ. (Curwen; Murdoch; Novello; Boosey; Larway; Chappell; Ricordi; Elkin; J. Church; Boston Music Co.); 4 unacc. songs (Curwen); operetta for children, *The Cockle-Boat* (*id.*); songs for children (Curwen; J. Williams; Cramer; Stainer & Bell).—E.-H.

WHITE, Mary Louisa. Eng. compr. *b.* Sheffield, 2 Sept. 1866. Showed marked mus. talent from her earliest years; in Dec. 1885, came to London to study under John Farmer; publ. her 1st compns. in 1887 (Minuet and Scherzo in A flat); evolved the *Letterless Method* for teaching music to beginners; has given frequent concerts of her own works in London and Paris.

Fairy operettas: *Beauty and the Beast*, op. 41; *The Babes in the Wood*, op. 42; songs; pf. pieces; pf. duets; part-songs (mostly J. Williams).—E.-H.

WHITEHEAD, Percy Algernon. Eng. compr. *b.* Sevenoaks, Kent, 4 Feb. 1874. Educated at Chichester Cath. under Dr. F. J. Read and Sir Hugh Allen; at R.C.M. under Dr. Charles Wood, E Dannreuther, Sir Charles Stanford; stud. pf. under Tobias Matthay; prof. of pf. R.C.M. London; teacher, Matthay Pf. School.

Albums of pf. pieces (Forsyth; Stainer & Bell); song-albums (Cramer; Boosey); book, *The Appreciation of Music* (Sidgwick & Jackson).—E.-H.

WHITEHILL, Clarence Eugene. Amer. operatic barit. *b.* Marengo, Ia., U.S.A., 5 Nov. 1871. Stud. music under L. A. Phelps in Chicago; Giraudet and Sbriglia in Paris (1896). First appeared in opera at Théâtre de la Monnaie, Brussels, as Friar Lawrence in Gounod's *Romeo and Juliet*, Nov. 1899. Engaged at Opéra-Comique, Paris, and sang for short time in New York. Returned to Europe to study under Stockhausen. Sang at Cologne Stadttheater, 1903–8; at Metropolitan Opera, New York, 1909–11; with Chicago Opera, 1911–15; then member of Metropolitan Opera, New York. Sang at Covent Garden, 1905–9, and took Wotan in Brit. Nat. Opera Co.'s season there in 1922.

Has appeared in Wagner Festspiele, Bayreuth and Munich. Particularly successful in Wagner rôles. Sang for B.N.O.C. at Covent Garden in spring 1922.—O. K.

WHITEHOUSE, William Edward. Eng. cellist; *b.* London, 20 May, 1859. Stud. under Piatti and Pezze at R.A.M.; cellist Saturday and Monday Popular concerts; the Josef Ludwig Str. Quartet; R. Philh. Soc. concerts (series at Albert Hall cond. by Wagner); toured with Joachim; in France and Italy with the London Trio (Amina Goodwin pf.; Simonetti vn.), and in Gt. Britain with Amina Goodwin and Pecskai; prof. of cello R.C.M. London; has edit. many old Italian sonatas.—E.-H.

WHITHORNE, Emerson. Amer. compr. *b.* Cleveland, O., U.S.A., 6 Sept. 1884. Stud. pf. and harmony under Joseph Hartmann and James H. Rogers in Cleveland; Leschetizky and Fuchs in Vienna; Schnabel in Berlin, and Tchérepnin. 1906–14, teacher, compr. and writer in London. Returned to U.S.A. 1914. Since then, for a time, executive ed. of Art Publication Soc., St. Louis, Mo.; now (1923) residing in New York.

Among his larger works (unpubl.) are symph. fantasy, *In the Court of Pomegranates*, op. 26, perf. by New York Philh. 12 Jan. 1922; 2 tone-poems and 2 suites for orch.; 2 str. 4tets, *Greek Impressions*, perf. by International Composers' Guild, 19 Feb. 1922, and a *quartettino*, played by Kneisel Quartet, etc.; songs; pf. pieces (C. Fischer, Schirmer; Ricordi; Comprs. Mus. Corp.; Metzler; Elkin).—J. M.

WHITING, Arthur Battelle. Amer. pianist, compr. *b.* Cambridge, Mass., U.S.A., 20 June, 1861. Stud. at New England Cons. under Sherwood (pf.) and Chadwick and Maas (theory); 1883–5, in Munich under Rheinberger, Bussmeyer, Abel. Lived in Boston until 1895; then settled in New York. 1907, began series of annual "University Concerts" at Harvard, Yale and Princeton. Since 1911 devoted himself to old music, playing harpsichord himself, often assisted by a small select ensemble using old instruments. Concert overture, op. 3, 1st perf. Boston Symphony Orch., 6 Feb. 1886; pf. concerto, D mi. op, 6, New York, 1887 (produced by Van der Stucken). The Boston Orch. played his Suite for str. and 4 horns, op. 8, 14 March, 1891; Fantasy, pf. and orch. op. 11, by same orch. in Cambridge, 12 March, 1896. Member of National Inst. of Arts and Letters.

Fantasy, pf. and orch. op. 11 (1897); songs, *The Rubaiyat*, op. 18 (1901); *Cycle of Old Scottish Melodies*, 4 solo vs. with pf. (1917); many chamber-works; *Pianoforte Pedal Studies*, 2 vols. (1904; 1912); many pf. pieces, songs. (All publ. Schirmer).—O. K.

WHITTAKER, William Gillies. Eng. compr. and condr. *b.* Newcastle-on-Tyne, 23 July, 1876. Stud. privately; pf. under John Nicholson and Dr. W. Rea; organ, C. F. Bowes; singing, Miss K. E. Behnke, Sir Charles Santley, Frederic Austin; theory, Dr. G. F. Huntley. W. is condr. of choral and orch. classes at Armstrong Coll. Newcastle-on-Tyne; and condr. Choral Union; also of Newcastle Bach Choir, which has specialised on modern British comprs. as well as Bach's works, and gave a 3-day Bach fest. in London, 1922. Mus.Doc. Dunelm. *h.c.* 1921; ed. of *Oxford Choral Songs* (H. Milford). W.'s pf.

pieces are of an advanced harmonic order (he has specialised on contemporary Fr. music); and his orig. vocal works show the influence of what has been called " modern choralism." He is one of the most alive of choral condrs. of the present day.

Among the Northumbrian Hills, pf. 5tet (Carnegie award; Stainer & Bell); pf. pieces (Rogers); choruses from the Choephorœ of Æschylus, female chorus and orch. (Curwen); unacc. settings of North Country and other folk-songs, mixed vs. (Stainer & Bell); male vs. (Stainer & Bell; Curwen; Williams); female vs. (Curwen); mixed vs. (Bayley & Ferguson); songs, 2 vs. (Chester; Arnold); songs (Curwen; Rogers); ed. arias and duets from Bach's cantatas, female vs. (Stainer & Bell); Tune Exercises for pianists (Curwen). In ms.: Prelude to the Choephorœ of Æschylus, orch.; A Lyke Wake Dirge, chorus and orch. (Carnegie award, 1924). Book, Fugitive Notes on Church Cantatas and Motets of J. S. Bach (Oxford Univ. Press).—E.-H.

WHOLE-TONE SCALE. Sometimes called TONAL SCALE. It divides the octave into 6 whole tones. The first use of it is often wrongly ascribed to Debussy. In point of fact it is an old Chinese scale. In Europe, it was used before Debussy's time, by the fathers of the Russ. school—Glinka, Dargomisky and others. In the latter's An Eastern Song, he secures Oriental feeling in this way:

Debussy made a special use of the scale and exploited its possibilities considerably in Pelléas et Mélisande; but he did not use the scale for whole pieces as Rébikof (q.v.) did in Une Fête, Les Rêves, etc. See art. on HARMONY.—E.-H.

WIBERGH, Johan Olof. Swedish pianist; b. Stockholm, 29 Dec. 1890. Stud. R. Cons. Stockholm under Lennart Lundberg, 1906–13; then in Germany, Austria (Emil Sauer, Vienna), France and Italy. Has given concerts in Sweden, Berlin, Vienna, Prague and Dresden.—P. V.

WIDÉEN, K. Ivar N. Swedish compr. and orgt. b. near Bello, 21 March, 1871. Stud. R. Cons. Stockholm, 1889–92 (compn. under J. Dente); 1892, orgt. in Laholm, and from 1900 at Skara Cath. From 1901, condr. of Music Soc. of Skara. Member R.A.M. Stockholm, 1921; member of committee for the New Hymnal.

Songs; male choruses; anthems (54); organ preludes, etc.—P. V.

WIDOR, Charles Marie. French organist, compr. and teacher; b. Lyons, 24 Feb. 1845. Pupil of Fétis père and of Lemmens. Devoted himself early to the organ. In 1870, orgt. of St.-Sulpice, Paris; then succeeded César Franck as prof. of organ at Paris Cons. In 1896, prof. of compn. at Cons. Is permanent secretary of the Académie des Beaux-Arts.

Stage-works: La Korrigane (ballet); Nerto (opera); Maître Ambros (opéra-comique); Les Pêcheurs de Saint-Jean (1905, lyric drama); Jeanne d'Arc (scènes mimées); Conte d'Avril and Les Jacobites (stage-music). Orch.: symphonies with organ; Symphonie antique; Une Nuit de Valpurgis (symph. poem with

choruses); pf. concerto; vn. concerto. Str. 4tet; pf. trio; pieces for cello and pf.; numerous organ works (especially 7 symphonies). Publ. 1904 (new ed. 1920) La Technique de l'orchestre moderne (Eng. J. Williams). Consult E. Rupp, C. M. W. (1912). —A. C.

WIEHMAYER, Theodor. German teacher; b. Marienfeld (Westphalia), 7 Jan. 1870. 1886–9, stud. at Leipzig Cons. (Coccius, Reinecke, Jadassohn); 1890, visited Sweden and Norway as pianist; 1902–6, teacher at Leipzig Cons.; 1908, teacher at Cons. at Stuttgart; 1909, prof.

Preludes and fugues for organ; mixed choruses; works for pf. Instructive pf. works: 5 Special Studies, School of Finger-Technique, School of Scales, Universal Studies, Musical Rhythm and Metre. New ed. Czerny's Virtuoso School; Tausig's Daily Studies; New and Instructive Edition of Classical Works.—A. E.

WIENIAWSKI, Adam. Polish compr. b. Warsaw, 1876. Pupil of Noskowski in Warsaw, Bargiel in Berlin and of Fauré in Paris.

Opera, Megaë (Warsaw, 1913; Petrograd, 1916; Moscow, 1920); 2 symph. poems, Kamaralmazan (Lamoureux, 1910) and Princess Boudour; Polish Suite; 2 str. 4tets; choral works; songs and transcriptions of popular Polish melodies.—ZD. J.

WIHAN, Hanuš. Czech cellist; b. Polic, 5 June, 1855; d. Prague, 3 May 1920. Stud. at Prague Cons.; engaged in France, Italy and Germany; cellist of chamber quartet of Ludwig II in Munich; prof. Prague Cons. 1888. Out of his class was formed the Czech Str. Quartet, which he himself joined after Berger's death in 1894, and which he dir. till 1913. The strain of the journeys compelled him to leave this quartet and resume his teaching at the Cons. and at the Master-School in his latter years.—V. ST.

WIHTOL, Joseph. Latvian compr. b. Volmar, 14/26 July, 1863. Stud. under Johansen and Rimsky-Korsakof at Petrograd Cons. 1880–5; from 1886 till Russ. revolution, prof. there; now dir. of Riga Cons. From 1897, he was critic on the daily St. Petersburger Zeitung. Many of his works are founded on Latvian folk-tunes.

Symph. poem, The Feast of Liho, op. 4; Dramatic Overture, orch. op. 21; Bard of Beverin, chorus and orch. op. 28; overture to Lettish fairy-tale Spriditis, op. 37; Northern Lights, solo, chorus, orch. op. 45; music to Lettish dramatic tale The King Brusuband and the Princess Hundega, op. 46; str. 4tet, G ma. op. 27; pf. sonata, B mi. op. 1; songs; choruses; harmonisations of Lettish folk-songs, etc.—V. B.

WIKLUND, Adolf. Swedish compr. condr. pianist; b. Långserud, 5 June, 1879. Brother of Victor W. Stud. at R. Cons. Stockholm from 1876; then under Joh. Lindegren (compn.), in Paris, and in Berlin (1905–7); student-condr. in Carlsruhe, 1907; Repetitor at R. Opera in Berlin, 1908; from 1911, 2nd condr. at R. Opera, Stockholm. Member R.A.M. Stockholm, 1915. Is a fine concert pianist.

Concert piece, pf. and orch. (1903); concert overture (1904); pf. concerto No. I (1908); No. II (1917); symph. poem, Sommar (1918); symphony (1922); str. 4tet; 2 sonatas, vn. and pf.; pf. pieces (Carl Gehrman); songs (id.).—P. V.

WIKLUND, Victor. Swedish condr. and pianist; b. Ånimskog, 1 March, 1874. Brother of Adolf W. Stud. R. Cons. Stockholm, 1891–4; then pf. under Rich. Andersson; teacher at Andersson's pf. school for many years; 1904, pf. prof. at R. Cons. Member R.A.M. Stockholm, 1916. Well known as pf. accompanist;

1915, succeeded Neruda as condr. of choral soc. Musikföreningen, where he has given: Handel's *Samson*, and *Alexander's Feast*; Mozart's Mass in C mi. and *Requiem*; Bruckner's Mass; Bossi's *Paradise Lost*; César Franck's *Béatitudes*; Kiel's *Christus*; Elgar's *King Olaf*; Brahms's *Requiem*; Mendelssohn's *Elijah*; Bach's *St. Matthew Passion*; Verdi's *Requiem*; Atterberg's *Requiem*; J. H. Roman's *Psalm C.*—P. V.

WILDER, Victor. Belgian writer on music; *b.* Ghent, 21 Aug. 1835; *d.* Paris, 8 Sept. 1892. Stud. philosophy and law, Univ. of Ghent. 1860, settled in Paris as mus. critic and song-translator. One of the most active authors of revival of mus. life in France, notably in triumph of Wagnerism and advent of young Fr. school. Adapted into Fr. much foreign vocal music, and thus brought a large part of modern Ger. music within reach of Fr. public (songs of Schubert, Schumann, Brahms and Grieg); was the first translator of works of Wagner. In this kind of work, so thankless, because necessarily always imperfect, he displayed remarkable ingenuity, artistic feeling and inspiration. The qualities of his translations are elegance, prosodic accuracy, and ease in singing. In contrast to Alfred Ernst, who laid greatest stress on literal rendering of meaning and exact rhythmic conformity (resulting in strange language, difficult to sing), W. turned over the original in his own mind, expressed it in his own way and was not afraid to modify the original rhythmic values to suit the Fr. language. His transl. of the *Valkyrie* is a real model. Except for this score, his adaptations are replaced to-day, in practice, by those of Ernst. W. publ. a book on *Mozart* (Paris, 1880), and one on *Beethoven* (*ib.* 1889; Eng. transl. 1908), works in popular style.—E. C.

WILHELMI, Johan Tobias Jakob. Dutch violinist and compr. *b.* Amsterdam, 7 April, 1885. Stud. in Amsterdam and Cologne; orch. leader in Leipzig, Riga, at Concert Soc. Stockholm, and (from 1921) at R. Chapel in Stockholm. A fine chamber-music player. *Ballade*, v. and orch. (1913; perf. Stockholm, 1919); *Berceuse*, vn. and pf. (1920; Elkan & Schildknecht); vn. concerto (1921); symphony in C (1922); 2 pieces for orch. (1915); songs with pf.—P. V.

WILHELMJ, August. German violinist; *b.* Usingen, Nassau, 21 Sept. 1845; *d.* London, 22 Jan. 1908. First vn. lessons with K. Fischer in Wiesbaden; 1861-4, stud. at Leipzig Cons. under David; theory under Hauptmann, Richter, and later in Wiesbaden under Raff. Appeared at concerts at the Gewandhaus, Leipzig, 1862; when his studies were completed, he started on the wandering life of the virtuoso; went to Switzerland (1865), Holland, England (1866), France, Italy (1867), Russia (1868), back to Switzerland, France, Belgium (1869), etc. In 1872 he appeared in Berlin; 1873 in Vienna; 1878-82, travelled round the world (North and South America, Australia, Asia). At the festivals in Bayreuth, leading 1st vn.; 1871, R. prof. Lived for some time at Biebrich-on-Rhine, where founded a School for Violinists; 1886-94, lived at Blasewitz, near Dresden; from there went as vn.-teacher to Guildhall School of

Music in London. In 1903 Novello publ. the 1st part of his *Modern School for Vn.*; he was also active as an editor of vn. classics. Chief compns.: str. 4tet, op. 162; Variations on theme of Schubert for str. 4tet.—A. E.

WILKES, Josué. Argentine compr. *b.* Buenos Ayres in 1883. Stud. Buenos Ayres and Paris. Then settled in Buenos Ayres. Publ. several songs, and 2 orch. pieces: *Los Espíritus de la Selva* (suite in 3 movements) and a Fugue.—S. G. S.

WILKS, Norman. Eng. pianist; *b.* Birchington, Kent, 9 June, 1885. Stud. pf. under Michaal Hambourg and Frederic Lamond; compn. under Louis Prout and Joseph Holbrooke. A pianist of a modern order, who has given many recitals in England, Holland, Belgium and Germany. In 1913 he played in U.S.A. 5 times with Boston Symphony Orch. under Muck. W. was awarded Military Cross for valour in action.—E.-H.

WILLAN, Healey. Eng. compr. and orgt. *b.* Balham, Surrey, in 1880. Mus.Doc. *h.c.* Toronto. Entered St. Saviour's Choir School, Eastbourne, 1889; stud. organ, pf., harmony, under Dr. Sangster. First appointment, orgt. St. Saviour's Ch. St. Albans. Successive posts: Christ Ch., Wanstead; St. John Baptist, Kensington. In 1913, went to Toronto as head of the theory dept. of Toronto Cons. of Music, and orgt. and choirmaster St. Paul's Ch. In 1914, examiner and lecturer to Univ. of Toronto; 1919, mus. dir. to Hart House Players' Club for which he has comp. incidental music for plays by Euripides, Shakespeare, Ben Jonson and others. In 1920, Vice-Principal Toronto Cons., which position he now holds. His compns. already number over a hundred. Much of his choral work is in the repertoire of the Toronto Mendelssohn Choir and the Toronto Orpheus Soc. His church music is becoming well known in U.S.A. The fine *Introduction, Passacaglia and Fugue* for organ (Schirmer) deserves special mention. Cantata, *England, my England*; motets: *An Apostrophe to the Heavenly Host*; *The Dead*; sonata, vn. and pf. in E; organ pieces: Prelude and fugue, B mi.; Prelude and fugue, C mi. (Schirmer; Novello). —L. S.

WILLIAMS, Albert Edward. Brit. military bandmaster and compr. *b.* Newport, Mon. 6 March, 1864. Stud. harmony under Karl Barthmann, bandmaster (a pupil of Spohr); later under Dr. John Naylor in York and Dr. C. W. Pearce in London. Bandmaster Grenadier Guards, 1897; mus. dir. 1906 (retired Oct. 1921); Mus.Doc. Oxon. M.V.O. 1908. The most highly trained military bandmaster of his day; one of the first military bandmasters to realise the potency of the military band in exercising a good influence on Eng. public taste. Arranged the chief modern orch. works (Beethoven's symphonies, Bach's fugues, Debussy) for it. Overtures: *Heloïse and Abelard* (Boosey); *Sancho Panza* (*id.*); *Heinrich von Meissen* (*id.*); various marches (*Ich Dien*; *Parade*, etc.), patrols and songs. A lecture on Military Band Inst. (R.C.O. Calendar, 1909-10).—E.-H.

WILLIAMS, Alberto. Argentine compr. and poet; *b.* Buenos Ayres in 1862. Began studies in Argentina, completing them at Cons. of Paris, under Georges Mathias, Charles de Bériot *fils*, Guiraud, Franck, and Godard. Returned to Buenos Ayres in 1899, where he gave several pf. recitals. In 1900, gave orch. concert of his works in Berlin. Founded the Cons. of Music of Buenos Ayres, which has had a wonderful success, and now has 92 branches throughout Argentina, all under the able dir. of this master, who has introduced into his native land the school of Chopin and Franck. His compns. have been placed by good critics between Schumann's and Grieg's. He has also obtained fame as a poet.

Symph. works: 2 overtures, 3 suites; 3 symphonies; a March. Chamber-music: 3 sonatas, vn. and pf.; sonata, cello and pf.; sonata, fl. and pf.; trio, vn., cello and pf. Vocal (words by compr.): 10 choruses for 4 male vs.; 10 choruses, mixed vs.; 16 songs; 146 pf. pieces; many technical studies.—A. M.

WILLIAMS, C. F. Abdy. Eng. writer on music; *b.* Dawlish, 16 July, 1855; *d.* Milford, Lymington, 27 Feb. 1923. Educated Trinity Hall, Cambridge; stud. Leipzig Cons. while orgt. of Eng. church there; comp. music in Greek modes for Greek plays at Bradfield Coll. 1895, 1898, 1900.

Books: *Historical Account of Degrees in Music at Oxford and Cambridge* (Novello); *Life of J. S. Bach* (J. M. Dent & Sons, 1900); *Life of Handel* (id. 1900); *Story of the Organ* (Walter Scott, 1903); *Story of Notation* (id. 1903); *The Rhythm of Modern Music* (Macmillan); *The Aristoxenian Theory of Musical Rhythm* (Cambridge Univ. Press); *The Rhythm of Song* (Methuen, 1924).—E.-H.

WILLIAMS, Gerrard. Eng. compr. *b.* London, 10 Dec. 1888. Self-taught by means of singing in choral societies, playing in orchs. and chamber-music and studying printed music at home and at concerts; with exception of a few " criticisms " from Richard Walthew in 1913. Began trying to compose about 1911, and, being in architect's profession, continued music and comp. in spare time until beginning of 1920. Since then, has made compn. his profession, and has had over 70 works publ. Numerous perfs. of orch., chamber and choral music, pf. works and songs in London, provinces and abroad. First recital of own compns. (chamber and pf. music and songs) Æolian Hall, London, 27 March, 1922. His music is mostly on intimate and chamber-music lines, with complete freedom of idiom, harmony and form, though it stands well the test of sound. Rhythmic developments attract him more than melody, pure and simple. His pf. music resembles Ravel's in texture.

Opera, *Kate, the Cabin-Boy*, ballad-opera, 2 acts, based on old tunes (1923, ms.); comic operetta for children, *The Story of the Willow-Pattern Plate*, 1921 (Curwen). Orch.: 3 Miniatures (after Shelley), 1918 (Chester); *Pot-Pourri*, a cycle of fragments (orch. from pf. score) (Novello); 1st str. 4tet (1915, ms.); 2nd str. 4tet (1919, Curwen); 3 Miniatures, pf. (1918, Chester); *Pot-Pourri*, pf. (1919, Novello); 3 *Preludes*, pf.; *Side-shows*, pf. (Rogers, 1922); many songs and choral works (Curwen; Novello; Paxton; Rogers; Chappell; Stainer & Bell).—E.-H.

WILLIAMS, Joseph, Ltd. Publishers, London. Founded by Lucy Williams, in Fountain Court, of old Cheapside, in 1808. The activities of this British house were at first solely concerned with music-printing; Muzio Clementi was among the firm's early customers. Joseph W. (brother of Benjamin W. another well-known music-publ.) was succeeded by his son, Joseph Benjamin (*d.* 1923). The business is now controlled

by his two sons, Florian and Ralph. The catalogues run to over 15,000 publications—songs, choral works, part-songs, pf. music, etc. Many text-books and much educational music.—E.-H.

WILLIAMS, Vaughan. See VAUGHAN WILLIAMS.

WILLIAMSON, Arthur. Australian compr. Now lives at Adelaide.

Some pf. and organ pieces; mostly songs (some publ. Breitkopf, Leipzig).—E.-H.

WILLNER, Arthur. Ger.-Czechoslovak compr. *b.* Teplitz-Schönau, 5 March, 1881. Pupil of Rheinberger and Thuille. Deputy dir. of Stern's Cons. Berlin, and also teacher of composition.

Symph. poems: *Longing*; *Days in Munich*; symphony, F ma.; *An den Tod* (barit. solo, chorus, orch.); 6tet for wind instrs. and pf.; 3 str. 4tets; 3 sonatas, vn. and pf.; pf. concerto; 3 pf. sonatas; Variations for 2 pianos; *Day and Night* (24 fugues); 2 sonatas for 2 vns. alone; *Dances* and *New Dances*, pf.; organ voluntaries; songs.—E. S.

WILM, Nicolai von. Ger. compr. *b.* Riga, 4 March, 1834; *d.* Wiesbaden, 20 Feb. 1911. Stud. Leipzig Cons. (1851-6); 1857, 2nd condr. at Stadttheater, Riga; 1860 (on Henselt's recommendation), teacher of pf. and theory, Nicolai Inst. Petrograd; 1875, retired to Dresden; 1878, settled in Wiesbaden.

Str. 6tet, B. mi. op. 27; 2 vn. sonatas, op. 83, 92; str. 4tet, C mi. op. 4; cello sonata, op 111; 2 pf. and vn. suites, op. 88, 95; pf. pieces, 2 and 4 hands; *Characteristic Pieces*; instructive works, etc.—A. E.

WILSON, Archibald Wayet. Eng. compr. *b.* Pinchbeck, Lincs, 9 Dec. 1869. Stud. at R.C.M. London under Sir W. Parratt, Sir F. Bridge and Algernon Ashton; organ scholar, Keble Coll. Oxford, 1890-4; orgt. St. Asaph Cath. 1898-1901; Ely Cath. 1901-19; then Manchester Cath.

Before the Beginning of Years, ballad for chorus and orch. (Stainer & Bell); church music, part-songs (Novello, etc.); book, *The Chorales : their Origin and Influence* (Faith Press, 1920); *The Organs and Orgts. of Ely Cath.* (Tyndal, Ely, 1911).—E.-H.

WILSON, James Steuart. Eng. t. singer; *b.* Clifton, 22 July, 1889. Educated Winchester Coll. and King's Coll. Cambridge. Member of The English Singers (*q.v.*).—E.-H.

WILSON, Mortimer. Amer. compr. *b.* Chariton, Iowa, U.S.A., 6 Aug. 1876. Stud. in Chicago from 1894 to 1900. Instructor in theory, 1901-8, at Univ. of Nebraska. Then spent 3 years in Leipzig, studying part of time under Sitt and Reger; 1912-15, cond. orch. in Atlanta, Ga.; 1913-14, dir. of a Cons. in that city; 1915-16, prof. of mus. theory at Brenau Coll., Gainesville, Ga.; 1917-18, at the Malkin School, New York.

Bagatelles, pf. op. 12 (1920); 1st vn. sonata, op. 14 (Boston Music Co. 1915); pf. trio, op. 15 (1920); 2nd vn. sonata, op. 16 (Boston Music Co. 1916); organ sonata, op. 17 (1920); *Suite Petite*, vn. and pf. op. 57 (1919); 4 songs, op. 59 (1920). (Mostly publ. by Composers' Music Corporation, New York.) In ms.: 3 symph. works for orch.; several trios and 4tets; 4 vn. sonatas, etc. Book, *The Rhetoric of Music* (Lincoln [Nebr.], Univ. Publ. Co. 1907).—O. K.

WILSON, Philip. Eng. t. singer; *b.* Hove, Sussex, 29 Nov. 1886. Originally intended for the Church. Went to Australia, 1913. Prof. of singing at State Cons. Sydney, 1915-20. Returned to England, 1920. Gave 3 historical recitals of Eng. song at Wigmore Hall, 1921, and a recital celebrating the tercentenary of Philip Rosseter (an Elizabethan compr.) 5 May, 1923, at Steinway Hall, London. Joint-editor, with Peter

Warlock, of 150 *English Ayres* of the period 1598–1622 (publ. Enoch, Chester, Novello, Harold Reeves and Oxford Univ. Press). Has lectured on old Eng. music (with vocal illustrations) at all principal stations of British Broadcasting Co.—P. H.

WINDERSTEIN, Hans. Ger. condr. *b.* Lüneburg, 29 Oct. 1856. Stud. at Leipzig Cons. (1877–80); member of Baron v. Dervies' Orch. (under Sitt) at Nice; 1884, master at School of Music and condr. of Town Orch. Winterthur; 1887, condr. of former Lenk Orch. Nuremberg; establ. Philh. Soc. there (1890–3); 1893, cond. Kaim Orch. Munich; 1896, condr. of Winderstein Orch. and of Philh. Concerts, Leipzig; 1910, prof.; 1917, councillor; 1898–9, dir. of Leipzig Acad. of Singing.

Symph. suite (5 movements); orch. pieces; vn. solos, etc.—A. E.

WINDING, August. Danish compr. pianist; *b.* on island of Lolland, 24 March, 1835; *d.* Copenhagen, 16 June, 1899. Pupil of Carl Reinecke, Dreyschock, Anton Rée and Niels W. Gade. M.A. 1855. Real *début* took place in 1857 at a Musikforening Concert under Gade's dir. in Copenhagen; later also at Gewandhaus, Leipzig, under Reinecke as condr. As pianist, he united high technical attainments with an equally high general culture. Prof. at R. Cons. of Music, Copenhagen, and member of its board of governors. Also talented and productive compr. of Romantic school with impress of Danish character.

Vn. sonata, C mi. op. 5; *Nordisk Overture*, op. 7 (Leipzig, Cranz); pf. concerto, op. 16 (Leipzig, Fritzch); concert overture, op. 14; str. 5tet, op. 23; vn. sonata, F mi. op. 35 (Breitkopf); music to ballet *Fjeldstuen* (*Norwegian Mountain Station*) by Bournonville, R. Theatre, Copenhagen; cadenzas to Beethoven's and Mozart's pf. concertos; 26 preludes in all keys (Copenhagen, Hansen; Leipzig, Steingräber); sacred songs to words by Grundtvig and Ingemann. —A. H.

WINDISCH, Fritz. Ger. editor and compr. *b.* Niederschönhausen, 20 Dec. 1897. Pupil of Hugo Venus (vn.), Richard Francke (pf. and cpt.), Hugo Riemann and Max Friedlaender (mus. science). His compns. are characterised by pure melodic line and free harmonic partwriting. Since 1921 he has been ed. of the internationally organised periodical *Melos*, as well as artistic manager of *Melos Union* for cultivation of contemporary music (Berlin).

3 pieces for str. 4tet; songs with acc. by solo instrs.; *Klangvisionen* (*Tone-visions*) (vocal solos and duets for str. and wood-wind instrs.); *Terzette* for solo instrs. and male vs.; pf. pieces; unacc. choruses. —A. E.

WINDSPERGER, Lothar. German compr. *b.* Ampfing, Upper Bavaria, 22 Oct, 1885. Son of orgt.; trained at Munich by J. Rheinberger and Rudolf Louis; lives at Mayence.

Concert overture; symphony, A mi.; symph. fantasy (*Lumen Amoris*, No. 1) for full orch.; pf. sonata, C sharp mi.; series of 12 fantasias and fantasiettes, *Lumen Amoris*; bagatelles; Rhapsody and polonaise; sonata, A ma. for vn. alone; 2 sonatas, D mi. and D. ma. for cello alone; *Ode* for vla. and pf. pieces (sonata, D ma.); short concert suite, D mi. cello and pf.; pf. trio, B mi.; str. 4tet, G mi.; pieces for organ; vn. and organ sonata, F sharp mi.; cello and organ sonata. E ma.; songs, op. 24, 25. (Publ. Schott, Mayence.)—A. E.

WINGE, Per. Norwegian compr. and condr. *b.* Christiania, 27 Aug. 1858. Stud. pf. under Otto Winter-Hjelm and Edmund Neupert, Christiania; theory under Johan Svendsen, Christiania. Stud. in Leipzig, 1883–4; in Berlin, 1884–6. Condr. at Christiania Theatre, 1894–9; leader of Female Students' Choral Soc. from 1912; leader of the Norwegian (male) Students' Choral Soc. 1915–18. Teacher of pf. at Lindeman's Music Cons. from 1895; singing-master at Cath. School, Christiania, since 1913.

Trio, pf., vn. and cello (Christiania, 1894); music to several plays; about 60 songs; several compns. for female, male, and mixed chorus; pieces for pf.; for vn.; a well-known pf. Tutor for children. (Warmuth; Norsk Musikforlag, Christiania; Wilhelm Hansen, Copenhagen.)—U. M.

WINKELMANN, Herrmann. Austrian t. singer; *b.* Brunswick, 8 March, 1849; *d.* Vienna, 18 Jan. 1912. One of the best heroic ts. of Vienna Court Opera House. Excelled especially as a pathetic hero (Florestan, Tristan). Preserved the characteristic brightness of his voice till his last years. His admirers formed the Herrmann League which often disturbed the perfs. by tumultuous acclamations of their idol.—P. St.

WINKLER, Alexander Adolphovitch. Russ. compr. and pianist; *b.* Charkof, 19 Feb./3 March, 1865. Finished students' course at Univ. there in 1887, having completed his pf. course at the Music School in 1886 (pf. pupil of Slatin). Then stud. pf. under Leschetizky in Vienna and theory under Navrátil. From 1890–6 prof. of pf. class at Charkof Music School. From 1896 till present day, pf. prof. at Petrograd Cons. His works follow the classical tendencies.

Orch.: *In Brittany*, overture, op. 13; Variations on Russ. theme op. 16; Variations on Finnish theme, vn. and orch. op. 18; str. 5tet, op. 11; str. 4tets, op..7 in C, op. 9 in D, op. 14 in B flat; pf. 4tet, op. 8; pf. trio, op. 17; vla. sonata, op. 10; cello sonata; Variations and fugue 2 pfs. 4 hands, etc. (Belaïef).—V. B.

WINTER-HJELM, Otto. Norwegian compr. condr. orgt. *b.* Christiania, 8 Oct. 1837. Stud. music in Christiania, Leipzig and Berlin (Kullak) and wrote in latter city (1857) his 1st symphony (in B), the first Norwegian symphony (produced Christiania, 1862). Condr. of Philh. Soc. Orch. Christiania 1863–5; afterwards gave orch. concerts of his own. Establ. in 1866 (together with Grieg) the first Norwegian Acad. of Music, which, however, existed only a short time. Orgt. at Trinity Ch. in Christiania from 1874, teacher of singing at Cath. School; musical critic on *Aftenposten* from 1886 (for over 20 years). An eminent teacher of theory and piano.

As compr. he belongs to the older school and his works derive from the classic comprs., but frequently reveal a lyrical quality akin to the Romanticists and the national spirit.

Cantatas; symphonies in B ma. and B mi.; str. 4tet; male-v. choruses; pf. pieces; songs; organ pieces; pf. tutor; organ tutor; arrs. of Norwegian folk-tunes, etc. Theoretical works: *Musikalsk Realordbog* (*Technical Dictionary of Music*); *Elementær Musiklære* (*Elementary Music Theory*).—J. A.

WINTERNITZ, Arnold. Ger. compr.; condr. *b.* Linz-on-Danube, 1874. 1898–1917, operatic condr. at Linz, Graz, Vienna, Hamburg, Chicago; lately devoting himself more to compn. Married the soprano, Marthe Dorda; lives at Hamburg.

Comic opera, *Meister Grobian* (Hamburg, 1918); melodrama, *The Nightingale* (from Andersen); songs (series; nursery rhymes); melodrama, *Der Fluch der Kröte* (*The Toad's Curse*) (from Gustav Meyrink); pf. pieces; dance-play, *Galante Pantomime* (Hamburg, 1920).—A. E.

WINTZER, Richard. Ger. compr. and painter; *b.* Nauendorf, near Halle-o-S., 9 March, 1866. Stud. painting at Acad. of Art, Leipzig and Berlin; then turned to music; 1888–90, pupil of Berlin R. High School of Music.

Nursery songs, op. 15; *Heitere Kinderlieder,* op. 23; 5 serious songs, op. 14; *Storm Songs,* op. 20; 6 songs and hymns, op. 26; pf. pieces (2 short preludes and fugues, op. 22); 4 pf pieces, op. 24. Operas: *Die Willis* (1895); *Marienkind* (*Child of Mary*) (words by compr.; Halle, 1905); 3-act opera, *Salas y Gomez.*—A. E.

WIRELESS BROADCASTING OF MUSIC.— The invention of the thermionic valve made wireless telephony possible. The two-electrode valve, invented by Dr. Fleming, was followed by the three-electrode. By means of this discovery, sound-modulations can be imposed upon a " carrier " wave which conducts them through the ether to be picked up by any receiver which can reverse the process. The Marconi Co. experimented at Chelmsford early in 1920, giving demonstrations and concerts. In July 1920, the ship *Victorian,* crossing to Canada, bearing many representatives of the Empire Press Union, experimented with gramophone records; ships within 800 miles heard them.

Broadcasting music as a form of public entertainment began in Feb. 1921, when the Writtle Station held regular Tuesday evening concerts under P. P. Eckersley. In May 1922, the Marconi Co. opened the London station 2LO with the same object; but difficulties prevented the establishment of regular concerts. The British Broadcasting Co., Ltd., officially commenced operations 11 Nov. 1922, and was incorporated under the Companies Act, 15 Dec. 1922. The objects for which the Company was formed may be seen in the Memorandum and Articles of Association. The Managing Dir. of the Co. is Mr. J. C. W. Reith. There are 8 main transmitting stations of the company—London, Cardiff, Bournemouth, Birmingham, Manchester, Newcastle, Glasgow and Aberdeen. In 1924, 4 relay stations (*i.e.* those which depend to a great extent on the main stations for their programmes) were in existence; there will be 10 eventually.

The musical section of the programmes is under the control of Mr. Percy Pitt (Controller of Music) and Mr. L. Stanton Jefferies (Dir. of Music), who are responsible for all the musical activities of the Co. throughout the country. The musical directors at the various stations are: London, Mr. Dan Godfrey, jun.; Bournemouth, Mr. W. A. Featherstone; Cardiff, Mr. Warwick Braithwaite; Birmingham, Mr. Joseph Lewis; Manchester, Mr. Tom Morrison; Newcastle, Mr. William A. Crosse; while the musical section of the programmes at Glasgow and Aberdeen are controlled by Mr. Herbert A. Carruthers (station dir.) and Miss Nancy Lee respectively. Each station possesses its own permanent orchestra (15 to 24 players), augmented

when occasion demands. Local artists are incorporated in programmes at provincial stations, and well-known London concert and operatic artists, under contract with the Co., also visit these stations. A number of musical institutions, etc., were antagonistic to broadcasting on its advent; but practically all these have now realised the new invention's capability of assisting rather than harming the cause of music throughout the country. The B.N.O.C. was the first organisation to throw its lot in with Broadcasting, and on 8 Jan. 1923 the opera, *The Magic Flute,* was transmitted from Covent Garden. This, perhaps, was the first occasion in the world on which an actual performance of an opera was broadcast from the theatre. Nearly every orchestra of repute throughout the country has broadcast, including the London Symphony, R. Philharmonic, R. Albert Hall, and symphony orchestras (municipal, etc.) at Birmingham, Bournemouth, Manchester and Glasgow.

Being a public institution, the programmes of the Co. are necessarily democratic, but musical enthusiasts are specially catered for on certain regular evenings throughout the week at all stations (chamber-concerts, opera, etc.). A more detailed account of the organisation may be found in *Broadcasting from Within* by C. A. Lewis (Newnes, 1924).—L. S. J.

WITHERS, Herbert. Eng. cellist; *b.* London, 31 March, 1880. Stud. at R.A.M. under Whitehouse; then under Hugo Becker at Frankfort Cons. *Début,* May 1897, Old St. James's Hall; first to play Becker's cello concerto in England (Crystal Palace); was a member of Willy Hess Quartet; afterwards of Kruse Quartet; in 1908, toured Far East and India; solo cellist of Beecham orchestra.—E.-H.

WITKOWSKI, G. M. (real name Martin). French composer; *b.* Mostaganem in 1867. Became a composer rather late in life. First a cavalry-officer, passionately fond of music. After writing, by instinct, several compositions he felt the need of a sound technique and, for 4 years, worked under Vincent d'Indy (1894–7). Then he settled in Lyons, where he founded a choral society and the Société des Grands Concerts, which he still directs at the present time. His first important compositions were a quintet (1898), a quartet (1902, Durand), a sonata for piano and violin (1907), and two symphonies (1901, 1911). These works, solidly constructed, are rather cold and rigid in form. Since the war, he has perceptibly developed. The *Poème de la Maison* (Rouart, 1920), a kind of vast secular oratorio (solo voices, chorus and orchestra), is a powerful work, full of deep feeling. *Mon lac* (1921), for pianoforte and orchestra, likewise displays qualities of the highest order. His contrapuntal style shows great boldness and occasionally this " classicist " is linked in his works to the most modern composers. As in Vincent d'Indy, Witkowski's lyricism is purposely descriptive, and the pages where he evokes nature or death by appropriate harmonies, are not the least affecting of his scores.—H. P.

WOHLFAHRT, Frank. Ger. compr. *b.* Bremen, 15 April, 1894. Stud. at Vogt Cons. Hamburg, compn. under Max Löwen, pf. under Conrad Hanns. 1913 at Stern's Cons. Berlin; continued studies for a year under Wilhelm Klatte (compn.) and Bruno Eisner (pf.); comp. 2 pf. sonatas and a book of songs. 1916–7, arr. several composition evenings at Davos, Ragaz and Berne; 1919, stud. again under Ernst Kurth, Berne; 1920, returned to Berlin and completed str. 4tet in E ma. A second str. 4tet was perf. Donaueschingen, 1923. W. is also a lyrical and dramatic poet.—A. E.

WOHLFART, Karl. Swedish compr. and teacher; *b.* Södra Vi, 19 Nov. 1874. Stud. at R. Cons. Stockholm; then compn. under J. Lindegren, E. Ellberg and W. Stenhammar; pf. under Rich. Andersson; 1901, teacher at Andersson's pf. school; 1905–6, stud. in Berlin under Barth and Pfitzner. From 1913, dir. of his own pf. school in Stockholm.

Pf. pieces; songs; *Romance*, vn. and pf. op. 6 (publ. Abr. Lundqvist). In ms.: *Swedish Rhapsody*, orch. (1903); *Andante*, orch. (1902); concert piece, pf. and orch. (1901); overture (1904); sonata, vn. and pf. (1902); pf. sonata (1906), etc. *The Technique of the Piano* (Lundqvist).—P. V.

WOLANEK, Jan Paweł. Polish violinist; *b.* Warsaw, 1895. Pupil of his father, Rudolf (prof. of vn. Warsaw Cons.); then of Boucewicz, of Rosé in Vienna and lastly of Ševčík. He worked as vn. teacher in Cracow Cons. and Lemberg Cons. In 1920, went to N. America where, having completed his studies with Kneisel, he gives numerous concerts. Lives in New York.—ZD. J.

WOLF, Bodo. Ger. compr. *b.* Frankfort-o-M., 19 Oct. 1888. Pupil of uncle, Julius W. (pf.) and of Hugo Reichenberger (score-playing); 1907–10, stud. under Friedrich Klose and Felix Mottl, Munich; 1911, Ph.D. (thesis on *Heinrich Valentin Beck : a Forgotten Master of Music*); 1920, music dir. and teacher of compn. at Saarbrücken.

Musical Epilogue to Shakespeare's Othello, orch. op. 4; *Totenfahrt*, full orch. op. 6; overture in D, op. 12; *Serenade*, small orch. op. 20; choral-prelude, *Praise the Lord*, organ, horns, tpts. and drums, op. 18; Variations, pf. and vn., op. 25; *Pf. Sketches*, op. 11, 3 sacred female choruses, 4-v. unacc. op. 15; str. 4tet, E ma. op. 16; songs.—A. E.

WOLF, Hugo. Austrian compr.; *b.* Windischgräz, 13 March, 1860; *d.* Vienna, 22 Feb. 1903. One of the most important of all song-composers. His musical talent developed early and was cultivated in his home. He attended the Gymnasium at Graz, and in 1870 began a regular musical education. From 1871–3, was educated in the monastery of Benedictines of St. Paul. 1874–1875, studied at Marburg. In 1875–7, at Vienna Conservatoire, whence he was dismissed through a quarrel with the director, Josef Hellmesberger. Then studied music and literature by himself. His chief inspiration was the performance of *Tannhäuser* in 1875. His most important work of this period is the overture *Penthesilea* (1883). In 1884–7 he was music critic of a fashionable Vienna newspaper, the *Salonblatt*, in whose

columns he attacked Brahms. In 1887 his first songs were published. In 1887 he began his *Hymnus* (soli, chorus and orchestra). It was finished in 1889 and first performed at Mannheim in 1891. In 1888 he left the town and removed to an old village, Perchtoldsdorf, near Vienna. There he wrote his 53 Mörike songs (44 of them composed in 3 months), finished the Eichendorff cycle and began the Goethe cycle of 37 songs (written between Dec. 1888 and 12 Feb. 1889). In the autumn of 1889 he commenced the *Spanisches-Liederbuch* (44 songs composed between 28 Oct. 1889, and 27 April, 1890), and then the Gottfried Keller songs. In these years his fame began rapidly to increase, especially in Germany. In 1895 he composed in a few months a comic opera, *Der Corregidor*, libretto by Rosa Mayreder after Pedro de Alarcón's novel, *The Three-cornered Hat*. This opera had no success at the theatre, in spite of its exquisite music, partly owing to the too rich scoring, partly to the Wagnerian tastes of the public, who preferred a dramatic to a lyric style. A second opera, *Manuel Venegas* (libretto by Hoernes), which Wolf wrote in 1897, is unfinished, on account of a brain disease culminating in insanity. The peculiarity of Wolf's songs, which form the chief part of his works, consists in the independence of the piano-part, which, however, never overloads the voice. His rhythmical form is very remarkable.

Cycles of songs to poems by Mörike, Goethe, Keller, Heyse (*Spanisches-Liederbuch*, *Michelangelo*); str. 4tet, D mi. (1879–80); *Italian Serenade* for small orch. or str. 4tet (1893–94); opera, *Corregidor*. His Critical Essays were published by R. Batka and H. Werner in 1911. Consult biographies: E. Decsey, 4 vols. (1903–6); in 1 vol. (1919); Ernest Newman (London, 1907, Methuen; in Ger. by H. v. Haase, Leipzig, 1910). A series of essays on H. W. are publ. as *Gesammelte Aufsätze über H. W.* by the Hugo Wolf Soc. Vienna (1898–9). A list of his works is publ. by Paul Müller (Leipzig, 1907).—EG. W.

WOLF, Johannes. Ger. writer on music; *b.* Berlin, 17 April, 1869. 1888–92, stud. Germanic and mus. science (Spitta) in Berlin; 1889, practical music at R. High School; 1893, graduated at Leipzig; 1902, univ. lecturer in music at Berlin Univ.; 1908, prof.; 1922, made hon. prof.-in-ordinary. 1907, teacher of mus. history at R. Inst. for Church Music; 1915, librarian and dir. of Music Coll. at Prussian State Library.

New ed. of "*Musica practica*" of Bartolomeo Ramis de Pareja (*I.M.G.*, 1901); *Johann Rudolph Ahle's Selected Songs*, (*D.d.T.* V, 1901); *Heinrich Isaak's Secular Works* (*D.T.Ö.* XIV, i, and XVI, 1); *Georg Rhau, New German Sacred Songs* (1544) (*D.d.T.* XXXIV); *History of Mensural Notation from 1250 to 1460, taken from theoretical and practical sources* (3 parts, Breitkopf, 1905); *Handbook of Science of Notation* (Vol. I, Leipzig, 1913; Vol. II, 1919). 1899–1904, Wolf ed. (with Oskar Fleischer) the quarterly journal of I.M.G.; prepared a complete ed. of works of Jakob Obrecht; also coll. of Dutch songs of XVI century (Soc. for North Dutch Mus. History). 1922, *Musical Tables* for teaching science of notation (ed. for Bückeburg Insts.).—A. E.

WOLF-FERRARI, Ermanno. Italian opera compr. *b.* Venice, 12 Jan. 1876. Stud. at Munich under Rheinberger. From childhood he showed very great mus. aptitude, attracting the attention of teachers and lovers of music. In 1902 was appointed dir. of the Liceo Benedetto Mar-

WOLFF WOLSTENHOLME

cello in his native city, which post he occupied until 1912. During that period he promoted in that Liceo perf. of Ital. operas of the XVIII century, and gave especial attention to the teaching of choral singing. Has comp. various operas: *Cenerentola* (Venice, 1900); *Le donne curiose* (Munich, 1903); *I quattro rusteghi* (Munich, 1906); *Il Segreto di Susanna* (Munich, 1909); *I Gioielli della Madonna* (Berlin, 1911); *Amore medico* (Dresden, 1913). Some of these operas have had a notable success; in the comic ones he has effected a successful fusion of the Ital. XVIII century type with a modern technique. Also comp. an oratorio *La Sulamite* (Venice, 1899; publ. Milan, Fantuzzi); a Canticle on Dante's *La Vita Nuova* (Munich, 1903), and some instr. concert- and chamber-music (Rahter). Consult Luigi Torchi, *W. F.* in *Rivista Musicale Italiana*, 1903, p. 597.—D. A.

WOLFF, Johannes. Dutch violinist; *b.* The Hague, 12 May, 1863. Stud. at Dresden and Paris (with a King's scholarship); appeared at Pasdeloup concerts, Paris; toured the Continent; frequently in England; taught for some years at the Guildhall School of Music; many decorations.—E.-H.

WOLFFHEIM, Werner Joachim. Ger. music researcher; *b.* Berlin, 1 Aug, 1877. Stud. law at Munich and Berlin; also mus. science (Sandberger, Fleischer) till 1898; graduated at Leipzig LL.D.; barrister, 1899; from 1906, devoted entirely to study of mus. science; stud. 3 years in Berlin under Kretzschmar, J. Wolf and O. Fleischer; theory under Wilhelm Klatte. W. lives in Berlin and possesses a valuable musical library.
Many studies, especially on J. S. Bach's circle of friends; ed. (with H. Springer and Max Schneider) *Miscellanea Bio-bibliographica.*—A. E.

WOLFRUM, Philipp. Ger. compr. and condr. *b.* Schwarzenbach-on-Wald (Upper Franconia), 17 Dec. 1854; *d.* Samaden, 8 May, 1919. Stud. at Altdorf and Munich R. School of Music (Rheinberger, Wüllner, Bärmann); 1878–84, music-master at Bamberg Training College; subsequently Univ. mus. condr. and orgt. at Heidelberg. Cond. Bach Soc., establ. by him 1885, at same time as Acad. Choral Soc., also Baden Church Choirs Fest. and Protestant Church Choral Union; 1901, Ph.D. Leipzig Univ.; 1894, Univ. condr.; 1898, prof. of mus. science; 1907, gen. mus. dir.; 1914, Geheimer Hofrat; 1910, Heidelberg Univ. bestowed on him title of Th.D. *h.c.* W. was the champion of Liszt and Strauss; also of Max Reger as an experimenter in concert reform.
Organ works: Sonatas, B flat mi. op. 1; E ma. op. 10; F ma. op. 15; 57 organ preludes for Hymn-book of Baden; 2 books *Organ Preludes on Church Melodies*, op. 25, 27; chamber-music: cello sonata, op. 6; trio, op. 24 (with vla.); pf. 5tet, op. 21; str. 4tet, A ma. op 13; overture, *Kriegerische Marschrhythmen* (1914); choral works: *Halleluja* (Klopstock); *Weihnachtsmysterium* (Xmas Mystery) (1899, also at Hereford Fest. 1903); songs; part-songs (op. 2, mixed chorus, op. 12, male chorus, and *Protestant Church Choir*, mixed chorus); pf. pieces. Wrote *J. S. Bach* (1906, 2 parts; Part I, 2nd ed. 1910, Breitkopf; Russ. by Braudo, 1912).—A. E.

WOLFURT, Kurt von. Compr. *b.* Lettin,

Livonia, 8 Sept. 1880. Educated at Petrograd; stud. natural science (1899–1903) at Dorpat, Leipzig and Munich Univs.; from 1901, music at Leipzig Cons.; 1902–5, private pupil of Max Reger (theory) at Munich and Martin Krause (pf.). 1911–12, theatre condr. at Strasburg Stadttheater; 1912–13, cond. newly establ. opera season at Kottbus Stadttheater; 1917–18 at Stockholm; now in Berlin; since 1922, critic for *Die Zeit*.
Songs (Madrigal Verlag, Berlin); choral works: *Rhapsody from Faust* (Munich, 1909); *Hymn of Moses* (Jena, 1913); *Klagelied*, mixed chorus, orch. organ; *Hymne*, male chorus and orch.; *Orch. Adagio—Hymn to Night*; *Song of the Sea*, orch.; songs for 4 solo vs.; a comic opera.—A. E.

WOLLE, John Frederick. Amer. orgt. choral condr. *b.* Bethlehem, Pa., U.S.A., 4 April, 1863. Stud. organ in Philadelphia under Dr. David Wood, 1883–4; under Rheinberger in Munich, 1884–5. Orgt. of Moravian Church, Bethlehem, Pa. (1885), and also at the Packer Memorial Ch., Lehigh Univ. (1887); 1902, orgt. First- Presbyterian Ch., Allentown, Pa.; 1905, head of music department at Univ. of California and orgt. of First Congregational Ch., Berkeley, Cal. (1907–9). Has achieved notable successes as a choral condr.; 1882, organised Choral Union, Bethlehem, Pa., devoted exclusively to perf. of Bach (1885–92). In 1898, his Moravian Church Choir formed nucleus of now famous Bach Choir of Bethlehem, Pa., which since 1900 has given annual Bach fests. on large scale. To W. belongs credit of 1st complete perf. in America of *St. John Passion* (5 June, 1888), B mi. Mass (27 March, 1900) and other Bach works. Received Mus.Doc. from Moravian Coll. and Theological Seminary. Consult Raymond Walters, *The Bethlehem Bach Choir* (Houghton Mifflin, 1918, 2nd ed. 1922).—J. M.

WOLLGANDT, Edgar. German violinist; *b.* Wiesbaden, 18 July, 1880. Stud. at Wiesbaden Cons.; then for 3 years under H. Hermann, Frankfort-o-M.; 1900, member of R. Orch. Hanover; 1903, Konzertmeister of Leipzig Gewandhaus Orch.; leader of Gewandhaus Quartet (Wollgandt, Karl Hermann, Karl Wolschke, Julius Klengel). W. is Arthur Nikisch's son-in-law.—A. E.

WOLSTENHOLME, William. Eng. compr. and orgt. *b.* Blackburn, 24 Feb. 1865. Trained at Coll. for the Blind, Worcester, and privately; orgt. King's Weigh House Congregational Ch. London, 1902; All Saints', Norfolk Square, 1904. Has made a remarkable contribution to organ literature, his sonata in F mi. being amongst finest written for the organ. The bulk of his organ music is publ. by Lengnick.
Orch.: *Phantasy* (Lengnick); *Intermezzo* (id.); *Allegretto* (Novello); str. 4tet (Laudy); sonatas, vn. and pf. (Lengnick); Polonaise, vn. and pf. (Novello); 6 lyrical pieces, vn. and pf. (Laudy); pieces, cello or vla. and pf. (Novello); pf. pieces (Lengnick; Rogers; Bosworth); organ works (Novello; Lengnick; Rogers; Ashdown; Stainer & Bell; Bosworth); songs (Lengnick); 6 national folk-songs (Cary); part-songs: mixed vs. (Lengnick; Rogers); female vs. (Novello; Rogers). In ms.: works for orch.; for str. orch.; for vla. and orch.; for military band; pf. 5tet; wind 5tet; str. 4tet; *Intermezzo* trio, 3 cellos (1922);

535

pieces for vn. and pf.; for vn. and organ; songs. —E.-H.

WOLZOGEN, Hans Paul, Baron of W. and Neuhaus. Ger. author; *b.* Potsdam, 13 Nov. 1848. 1868–71, stud. comparative philology and mythology in Berlin; resided then at Potsdam till 1877, when Wagner attracted him to Bayreuth, where he wrote *Bayreuth Pages* (*Bayreuther Blätter*).

Nibelung Myths in Legend and Literature (1876); Thematic Guides to Music of Richard Wagner's "Nibelung Ring" (1876); Tragedy and Satiric Drama at Bayreuth (1876, 5th ed. 1881); Wagner's Siegfried (1879); Parsifal (21st ed. 1914); The Language of Wagner's Poetry (1877, 2nd ed. 1861); Richard Wagner's Tristan and Isolde (1880); What is Style? What does Wagner want? (1881); Our Times and Our Art (1881); The Religion of Compassion (1882); Wagner's Heroes explained (2nd ed. 1886); Wagneriana (1888); R. Wagner and the Animal World; also Biography (1890, 3rd ed. 1910); R. Wagner's Life (1884, original of Work and Mission of My Life [under Wagner's name], publ. in North American Review, 1879); Memoirs of R. Wagner (1883, Reclam); Idealising the Theatre (1885); Great Masters of German Music (Bach, Beethoven, Mozart, Weber) (1897); Richard Wagner's Writings on State, Art and Religion from 1864 to 1881 (1902, 3rd ed. 1914); Richard Wagner on "Flying Dutchman" (1901, 2nd ed. 1914); Wagner Breviary (1904, in R. Strauss's coll. Music); Bayreuth (ib. 1904); Musico-dramatic Parallels (1906); E. T. A. Hoffmann and Richard Wagner (1906); R. Wagner (1905, in Remer's Die Dichtung); R. Wagner, Plans for the "Mastersingers," "Tristan and Isolde" and "Parsifal" (1907); Art and Church (1913); E. T. A. Hoffmann, the German Visionary (1922 in coll. Music); stage version of Hoffmann's Undine (1922).—A. E.

WOOD, Charles. Irish compr. *b.* Armagh, 15 June, 1866. Stud. compn. there under Dr. T. O. Marks, the orgt. of Cath.; went to R.C.M. London, 1883; stud. compn. under Sir C. V. Stanford and pf. under Franklin Taylor; took Morley Prize for compn.; appointed prof. of harmony, R.C.M., in 1888; settled in Cambridge; assistant condr. of Cambridge Univ. Mus. Soc. until 1894; was elected fellow of Gonville and Caius Coll. In 1897, Univ. lecturer in harmony and cpt. Took Mus.Doc. Cantab. 1894. All his music is characterised by great originality of treatment. No compr. of modern times has been so successful in the treatment of Irish folk-tunes. His book of Irish Folk-songs is deservedly popular on account of the able arr. of the melodies. The symph. variations on *Patrick Sarsfield* (Beecham Concerts, London, 1907) show his power of creating what may be called the Irish atmosphere in music. Some of his works show the influence of the Eng. school—his setting of Swinburne's *Ode on Music* (perf. opening of new building of R.C.M. London, 1894), and his *Dirge for Two Veterans* (Leeds Fest. 1901). LL.D. *h.c.* Leeds Univ. (1904). Professor of Music, Cambridge University, 1924.

Symph. variations, Patrick Sarsfield, orch.; Ode to West Wind, t. solo, chorus, orch. (Novello); Milton's On Time; Swinburne's Ode, cantata; Dirge for Two Veterans, (Boosey); Song of the Tempest, solo, chorus, orch. (Hovingham, 1902); Ballad of Dundee (Leeds, 1904). Music to Euripides' Ion (Cambridge, 1890); to Euripides' Iphigenia in Tauris (ib. 1894); Irish Folk-songs (1897); str. 4tets; many part-songs and solo songs (Ethiopia saluting the Colours).—W. St.

WOOD, Frederic Herbert. Eng. orgt. and compr. *b.* India, 10 June, 1880. Stud. in England privately; Mus.Doc. Dunelm. 1913; orgt. and condr. Blackburn, Chatburn, and Clitheroe,

and Preston Choral Soc.; orgt. Blackpool Parish Ch. from 1918. Choral adjudicator; lecturer under Liverpool Univ. Extension Board.

Ballad of Semmerwater, female vs. (1910); Lacrimæ Musarum, double chorus and orch.; part-songs: male vs., Sacramentum Supremum (Stainer & Bell, 1920; test-piece for Leicester Mus. Fest. 1920); mixed vs., The Spirit of Spring (Novello, 1922; test-piece for Leicester Fest. 1923); 10 orch. variations on My Love's an Arbutus (ms.); vn. concerto in G (ms.), 1920; orch. suite, Simon de Montfort (ms.), 1921; organ suite, Scenes in Kent (ms.), 1923.—E.-H.

WOOD, Haydn. Eng. violinist and compr. *b.* Slaithwaite, Huddersfield. Stud. at R.C.M. for 6 years under Arbós; then under César Thomson in Brussels. Made his *début* as a child at Douglas, Isle of Man (Mendelssohn's concerto). Toured with Albani.

Orch.: Suite (R.C.M. Patron's Concert); Set of Variations; Suite de Ballet; pf. concerto; String Fantasy (Cobbett Prize; Novello); numerous successful songs and solos.—E.-H.

WOOD, Sir Henry Joseph. English orchestral and choral conductor; *b.* London, 3 March, 1869. Gave organ recitals at Fisheries, Inventions and other exhibitions. 1883–9; condr. Rousby Grand Opera Co. 1889; Marie Roze concert tour, 1890; Carl Rosa Opera Co. 1891; Crotty and Burns Opera Co. 1892; Lago's Ital. Opera season 1893 (Tchaikovsky's *Onégin, Lohengrin, Oberon*, etc.); Avenue Theatre, *The Lady Slavey*, 1894 ; Q.H. Promenade concerts from 1895; Q.H. Symphony concerts from 1897; Q.H. Choral Soc. 1897; Q.H. Sunday orch. concerts from 1897; Wagner Fest. concerts, Albert Hall, 1901; Queen's Hall Orch. Saturday Symphony concerts, Crystal Palace, 1901–2; condr. Q.H. Orch. from 1905; R. Albert Hall Sunday afternoon orch. concerts; London Philh. concerts, 1908; " Shakespeare's England " Earl's Court historical concerts, 1912; *Parsifal* pictures, London Coliseum, 1913.

Sir Henry Wood has done more for orchestral work and for spreading the taste for orchestral music in England than any other man. He raised orchestral playing to a consistently high level, unattained before. This he secured partly by means of founding a stable and permanent orchestra, by securing an adequate number of re-hearsals, and by really tuning his orchestra, for his ear is unusually true and unfailing. He established the precedent for sectional rehearsals (brass, wood, str.), insisted on unanimity of bowing and introduced the French style of double-bass bowing. In 1923 he took the orchestral class at R.A.M. and kept them for a whole term on the *Oberon* overture, interchanging every part amongst the strings and amongst the wind-players. This thoroughness is characteristic of him; at Liverpool in 1922 he postponed Bach's B mi. Mass till 1923, when it was given after about 50 rehearsals. His adoption of the low Continental pitch (A=435 at 59 degrees Fahr.) in 1895 at Queen's Hall was an immense advantage. In 1912, he introduced women into the Queen's Hall Orchestra, with excellent results.

Though naturally centred in London, he has spread his good influence personally as well as subjectively through the whole country. He founded the Nottingham City Orch. (1899); conducted the Wolverhampton Fest. Choral Soc. 1900; made provincial tours with the Queen's Hall Orch. 1904–5; conducted the Birmingham Symphony concerts, 1907; Sheffield Mus. Fests. 1902–5–8–11 (also lecturing on wood-wind and choral singing); Westmorland Mus. Fests (Kendal), 1904–6–8–10–12; Norwich Fests. 1908–11; Cardiff Orch. Concerts, 1911–12–13; Gentlemen's Concerts, Manchester, 1910–11–12; Birmingham Fest. 1912; Brand Lane Concerts, Manchester, from 1912; Birmingham Fest. Choral Soc. 1919; Sheffield Amateur Mus. Soc. 1920; Leicester Philh. Soc. 1922; Hull Philh. Soc. 1923.

Internationally his importance is equally great. His co-operation with the leading continental conductors (Lamoureux, Ysaye, Nikisch, Chevillard), especially in the London Mus. Fests. 1899, etc., has had lasting effects. In 1921 he shared with Nikisch and Pierné the conductorship of the Zurich Musical Festival.

To Wood, British people owe most of their knowledge of the symphonic works of the Russian (Tchaikovsky, Scriabin, etc.), modern German (Strauss, Schönberg, etc.) and French schools (Debussy, Ravel, etc.). No less a debt do British composers owe to him; between 1895 and 1919 over 200 British works were produced, many for the first time. In the choral way, too, he has done remarkable work, and he is responsible for the tuition of numberless singers now before the public. He was knighted in 1911. Manchester Univ. bestowed an hon. Mus.Doc. on him, 24 May, 1924, and the R.C.M. an hon. Fellowship in April of the same year.

Consult Rosa Newmarch, *H. J. W.* (J. Lane, 1904), and her *Quarter of a Century of Promenade Concerts* (Baines & Scarbrook, 1920).—E.-H.

WOODALL, Doris. Eng. operatic contr. singer. Stud. at R.A.M. London; later under Frau Alken-Minor (Court singer at Schwerin), where she made her *début* as Nancy in Flotow's *Martha*; 3 years' engagement at R. Opera in Neustrelitz; joined Carl Rosa Co. in 1905; gave her first *lieder*-recital 22 May, 1912, in Bechstein Hall, London; 19 years with Carl Rosa Co.; 1923, prof. of operatic art, Glasgow Athenæum.—E.-H.

WOODFORDE-FINDEN, Amy. Eng. song compr. *b.* Valparaiso, Chile, where her father, Arthur Ward, was consul; *d.* London, 13 March, 1919. Stud. privately under Adolph Schoesser, Winter and Amy Horrocks. Compr. of many songs (best-known, *O Flower of all the World.*) Is very successful with her atmosphere in such songs as the *Indian Love Lyrics.*—E.-H.

WOODHOUSE, Charles. Eng. violinist; *b.* London, 1879. Member of London Symphony Orch.; principal first violinist Queen's Hall Orch. from 1920; formerly of R. Opera Orch. and of Saunders Quartet; member of Grimson Quartet; then Reed Quartet; Saunders Quartet; now Charles Woodhouse Quartet.—E.-H.

WOODHOUSE, George. Eng. pianist and author; *b.* Cradley Heath, near Birmingham, 16

Dec. 1877. Stud. under Dr. Swinnerton Heap there; at Dresden Cons. under Tyson-Wolff (pf.), Draeseke (compn.); in Vienna under Leschetizky. Now teaches in London, where he has establ. a Pianoforte School.

The Artist at the Piano (W. Reeves); *Creative Technique* (Kegan Paul, 1921).—E.-H.

WOODS, Francis Cunningham. Eng. compr. and condr. *b.* London, 29 Aug. 1862. Stud. National Training School (now R.C.M.) under Sullivan, Stainer, Bridge and Cowen. Orgt. Brasenose Coll. Oxford, 1883–6; Exeter Coll. 1886–95; condr. Finsbury Choral Association, 1897–1901; music-master and orgt. Highgate School, London, from 1896.

Cantatas: *King Harold*: *A Greyport Legend*; *Old May Day*; incidental music to *The Tempest*; Suite in F, small orch.; anthems, etc. (mostly Novello).—E.-H.

WOOF, Rowsby. Eng. violinist; *b.* Ironbridge, Salop, 18 Jan. 1883. Stud. R.A.M. London; professor there, 1909.

Vn. pieces (J. Williams; Cary; Anglo-Fr. Co.); *Scherzo*, pf. (Cary); book, *Violin-Playing* (E. Arnold).—E.-H.

WOOLLETT, Henry. Fr. compr. and teacher; *b.* Le Havre, 1864. In spite of his British name, he is French. His work, abundant and facile, recommends itself by its honesty without pretentiousness, principally in his many songs. He is less happy in works of musicology, *e.g.* the too elementary *Histoire de la Musique.*—A. C.

WORMALD, Lillie. Eng. s. singer; *b.* Manchester. Stud. there under Mme. Sherrington and Mme. Fillunger; *début* at Hallé concert, Manchester; 1st appearance in London 1905; for some years, a prof. at R. Manchester Coll. of Music; sings at concerts and in opera (Susanna in *Figaro*; Woglinde in *The Ring*, etc.).—E.-H.

WORMSER, André. Fr. compr. *b.* Paris, 1 Nov. 1851. Pupil, Paris Cons. (Bazin, Marmontel); *Prix de Rome*, 1875. Mostly stage works: *Adèle de Ponthieu*, 1887; *Rivoli* (Paris, 1896); *Le Fils Perdu (The Prodigal Son)*, opera without words (Paris, 1890; London; Berlin, 1903). Concert overture; orch. pieces; pf. pieces.—A. C.

WÖSS, Josef Venantius von. Austrian theorist and compr. *b.* Cattaro (Illyria), 13 June, 1863. Stud. till 1882 at Vienna Cons. under Franz Krenn. Lived 1886–9 in Weisskirchen, Moravia, teaching music; then returned to Vienna. Now mus. ed. of Univ. Ed. publ. house, and teacher. Cond. concerts of the Hietzinger Musikverein and was teacher at the Seminar der Votivkirche. Well-known as a church-compr. and author of pf. arr. of Mahler's symphonies. Publ. a fine analysis of Mahler's *Lied von der Erde* and many theoretical works. His secular music is very conservative.

7 masses; *Requiem*; motets; 2 *Te Deums* (orch. and chorus); *Sacred Song* (1910); *Trostgesang (Song of Consolation)*, 1916; symphonies; overtures (*Sakuntala*, 1901); operas: *Lenzlüge (The Illusions of Spring)*, perf. 1905, Elberfeld; *Flaviennes Abenteuer* (perf. 1910, Breslau); chamber-music; male chorus; songs. A manual on *Modulation* (Univ. Ed. 1921).—P. P.

WOTQUENNE, Alfred. Belgian musicologist; *b.* Lobbes, Hainault, 25 Jan. 1867. Librarian of

Brussels Cons. 1894–1918. Author of remarkable works of mus. bibliography:

Catalogue of the Brussels Cons., 4 vols. and supplement (opera libretti and Italian oratorios), publ. Brussels, 1898–1902, Coosemans; *Baldassare Galuppi* (Brussels, 1902, Schepens); *Thematic Catalogue of works of C. Ph. E. Bach* (1905, Breitkopf); *Zeno, Metastasio and Goldoni*: index of vocal numbers contained in their dramatic works (1905, Breitkopf); bibliographic study on *Luigi Rossi* (Brussels, 1909, Coosemans).—C. V. B.

WOUTERS, François Adolphe. Belgian compr. *b.* Brussels, 28 May, 1849. Stud. at Brussels Cons. 1861–70; pupil of A. Dupont (pf.) and Mailly (organ). Stud. compn. under Fétis. Orgt. church of Finistère; came back to the Cons. in 1871; regular prof. 1893; retired 1920. Member of commission for publ. of old Belgian mus. works. Numerous eds. of classical works under title of *Repertoire of the Brussels Conservatoire* (Brussels, Schott; Katto, etc.). Wrote much sacred music (some under pseudonym of Don Adolfo); also choral male-v. works; sonata, vn. and pf.—E. C.

WOYRSCH, Felix. Ger. compr. *b.* Troppau, Silesia, 8 Oct. 1860. Educated at Dresden and Hamburg; in music self-taught. 1894, condr. of Altona Church choir; 1895, of Altona Acad. of Singing; 1895–1903, orgt. of Church of Peace; 1903, of St. John's Ch.; 1903, condr. of Symph. Concerts, Altona; 1901, prof.; 1917, member of Berlin Academy.

Symph. prologue to Dante's *Divina Commedia*, op. 40; 2 symphonies (C mi. op. 52 [Kahnt, Leipzig]; C ma. op. 60); 3 *Böcklin-Phantasien*, orch. op. 53; overture to *Hamlet*, op. 56; vn. concerto; str. 4tets: A mi. op. 55; C mi. op. 63; E flat ma. op. 64; pf. trio, E mi. op. 58; operas: *Curé of Meudon* (Hamburg, 1886); *Woman's Strife* (1890); *Vikings' Journey* (Nuremberg, 1896); ballads: *Edward*, barit. and orch. op. 12; *Birth of Jesus*, soli, chorus, orch. op. 18; *Passion Oratorio*, soli, orch. organ, op. 45; *When Christ was on Earth*, soli, chorus, orch., organ, op. 60; *Sapphic Ode to Aphrodite*, s., female chorus, orch.; *Dance of Death*, mystery, soli, chorus, orch. organ, op. 51; *German Militia*, soli, male chorus, orch. op. 32 ; *The Vandal's Departure*, male chorus, orch. op. 31 ; *Ode to Death*, male chorus, orch. op. 57; ballad, *Beautiful Sigrid Smiles*, op. 54; songs: op. 2; *Persian Songs*, op. 6; Spanish book of songs, op. 9; *Rat-catcher's Song*, op. 16; male choruses (*Reaper Death*, op. 4); mixed choruses (3 books, arr. of old national songs); female choruses, op. 34; 10 choral-preludes, organ, op. 59; Passacaglia on *Dies Iræ*, organ, op. 62; pf. pieces (Theme with variations; Impromptus; Improvisation, *Metamorphoses*). Publ. 3 books of *Schütz's Choral Works for Practical Use.*—A. E.

WÜLLNER, Franz. Ger. condr. and compr. *b.* Münster, Westphalia, 28 Jan. 1832; *d.* Braunfels-on-Lahn, 7 Sept. 1902. Pupil of C. Arnold, Anton Schindler and F. Fessler; 1850–1 in Berlin with Dehn, Rungenhagen and Grell. Years of travel (1852–4) were spent at Frankfort-o-M., Brussels, Cologne, Bremen, Hanover, Leipzig; 1854, settled at Munich; 1856, pf. teacher at Cons.; 1858, municipal mus. dir. at Aix-la-Chapelle; 1861, R. mus. dir.; 1864, cond. (with Rietz) 45th Lower-Rhine Fest.; 1864, condr. of Hofkapelle (church choir), Munich; 1867, condr. of choral classes of R. School of Music (wrote well-known *Choral Exercises of Munich School of Music*); 1869, succeeded H. v. Bülow as condr. of R. Opera; of Acad. Concerts, and as inspector at Cons. for practical music.

W. brought the 1st perf. of *Rhinegold* and *Valkyrie* to Munich; 1870, 1st R. condr.; 1875, prof.; Ph.D. Munich, *h.c.*; 1877, left Munich for Dresden; till 1882 was Rietz's successor as R. Court condr. and dir. at Cons.; 1884, succeeded Ferdinand Hiller as head of Cons. and of Gürzenich Concerts, Cologne.

Choral work, soli and orch, *Henry the Fowler* (1864); *Flight of St. Cecilia*, 3 soli and orch. op. 13; masses; motets; *Miserere*, double chorus, op. 26; *Psalm CXXV*, with orch., op. 40; *Stabat Mater*, double chorus, op. 45; chamber-music: vn. sonatas, D mi. op. 6, E ma. op. 10; pf. trio, D ma. op. 9; Variations, pf. and cello, op. 39; songs; choral songs; pf. pieces.—A. E.

WÜLLNER, Ludwig. Ger. barit. singer; *b.* Münster, Westphalia, 19 Aug. 1858. Son of Franz Wüllner; stud. Germanics at Munich, Berlin, Strasburg; graduated Ph.D.; 1884–7, Univ. teacher at Münster Acad.; stud. singing at Cologne Cons.; condr. of church choir; 1889, actor at Meiningen; 1895, toured as reciter; 1896, as singer; lately again reciter.—A. E.

WÜRST, Richard. Compr. *b.* Berlin, 22 Feb. 1824; *d.* Berlin, 9 Oct. 1881. Stud. with Rungenhagen at Acad., vn. with Hubert Ries, later with David, Leipzig; compn. with Mendelssohn; 1845–6 student-journeys to Leipzig, Frankfort-o-M., Brussels and Paris; then settled in Berlin; 1856, R. mus. dir.; 1874, prof.; 1877, member of Acad. of Art; for several years teacher of compn. at Kullak's Cons.; 1874–5, ed. *Neue Berliner Musikzeitung* (Bote & Bock).

7 operas (*The Scarlet Cloak*; *Vineta*; *The Star of Turan*; *An Artist's Journey*; *Faublas*; *A-ing-fo-hi*; *Officers of the Empress*); lyric cantata, *The Water-Nymph*; 3 symphonies (2nd, op. 21, prize at Cologne, 1849); overtures; orch. *Serenade*, op. 55; *Fairy Tales*, orch. op. 40; Variations, orch. op. 50; *Intermezzo*, orch. op. 53; str. 4tets op. 33, i–iii; vn. concerto; *Concert Aria*, etc.—A. E.

WYZEWA (Wyzewski), Téodor de. Writer on music; *b.* Kalusik (Russian Poland), 1862. Came to France when 7; remained there until his death at the age of 55 (8 April, 1917). His talents as a writer, together with his wide culture, a perfect knowledge of seven languages and especially his keen and curious intellect, made of him one of the most critical critics of his time. In 1885, he founded (with Édouard Dujardin) *La Revue Wagnérienne* in which life, literature and art were considered from the point of view of the Wagnerian cult. In addition to books for popularising music—particularly *Beethoven et Wagner* (Perrin, 1898), in which he draws masterly portraits of Beethoven in his decline and Schubert at his *début*—he devoted his life to the study of Mozart and his contemporaries. With G. de Saint-Foix (*q.v.*) he published a work of great importance on Mozart (2 vols. Perrin, 1912), especially, emphasising the different influences under which Mozart came in his youth. He was also the first to call attention to the high merit of Muzio Clementi, of whom he published 20 sonatas, with a critical biography (Paris, 1916, Senart). Wyzewa was a man of letters who was also a great artist, and for this reason, he acted as an inspiration to all those with whom he came in contact.—H. P.

Y

YGOUW, Opol. Pseudonym of Paul Gouvy, compr. *b.* Paris, 1891. Of advanced tendencies. Symph. poem; 2 ballets; str. 4tet; cello sonata; sonata for 2 fl.; 2 sonatas, pf. and vn.; songs.—A. C.

YON, Pietro. Ital. orgt. and compr. *b.* Settimo Vittone (Turin), 1886. Stud. at Ivrea, Milan, Turin; R. Liceo Mus. di Santa Cecilia, Rome, under Renzi (organ), Bustini and Sgambati (pf.), De Sanctis (compn.); then went to America; 1917, orgt. and choirmaster at church of San Francesco Saverio, New York. 1921, appointed hon. orgt. of the Cappella Giulia of St. Peter's, Rome. A capable and successful recitalist. Organ works; sacred music (Fischer; Schirmer; Ricordi).—D. A.

YOUNG, (Alexander Bell) Filson. Irish compr. critic and writer; *b.* Ballyeaston, Ireland, 5 June, 1876. Articled pupil of Dr. Kendrick Pyne at Manchester Cath. and at R. Manchester Coll. of Music. Wrote mus. criticism for *Manchester Guardian*, 1898–1901; and from 1909–11 in the *Saturday Review*, which he edited until 1924. One of the most delightful writers on music. 5 Meredith songs; 2 Eng. songs (Forsyth); Prelude and fugue, G flat, for organ (Breitkopf); Introduction and fugue in G mi. (*id.*); 8-v motet, *From Harmony to Harmony* (*id.*); an orch. version of Schumann's *Fugue on B.A.C.H.* No. 1, with Introduction. Books: *Mastersingers* (Grant Richards, 1901); *The Wagner Stories* (*id.* 1907); *More Mastersingers* (*id.* 1911); *Opera Stories* (*id.* 1912).—E.-H.

YOUNG, Alfred C. Scottish singer; *b.* Edinburgh, 1870; *d.* there, 21 April, 1921. One of best-known singing-teachers in Scotland for over 25 years. Stud. under Sir Charles Santley and David Frangcon-Davies. His influence as a teacher is wide and lasting in the ranks of the rising generation of Northern vocalists.—W. S.

YOUNG, Dalhousie. Eng. pianist, compr. *b.* Gurdaspur (Punjab), India, 23 Nov. 1866; *d.* Brighton, 13 June, 1921. Stud. pf. under Leschetizky. His playing was marked by a wonderful tone, delicacy of thought and subtlety of rhythm. As compr. best known by his songs (*Bredon Hill* and other songs from *A Shropshire Lad*). Much of his best work is still unpubl. Orch.: *Christmas Hymn*; Suite (both perf. Bournemouth under Dan Godfrey); gesture-plays: *Prince Pierrot*; *Pierrot on Toast* (Laurence Housman); *Robe of Feathers* (produced at Court Theatre, London, by Margaret Morris); music to *Six Fairy Plays* by Netta Syrett (perf. St. James's Theatre, London); cantata, *The Blessed Damozel*, s. and t. soli, chorus and orch. (Novello); songs; pf. pieces.—C. L.

YOUNG, Gibson. Australian organiser and writer on music; *b.* Bendigo, Australia, 1888. Stud. at Manchester, R.C.M. (vn. under Brodsky, singing under Andrews, teaching under Carroll); founded Children's Concert Soc. Manchester, 1917; Newcastle-on-Tyne C.C.S. 1918;

critical work in Melbourne, 1918–23; founded Community Singing Movement in Australia; organised Music Week Fest. in Melbourne, 1921, 1922; Children's Concert League Choral Association and Orch. League, Melbourne. Lectures and writes on music.—E.-H.

YOVANOVITCH, Milan. See BRATZA.

YSAYE, Eugène. Belgian violinist; *b.* Liège, 13 July, 1858. From age of 4, taught by his father (violinist and orch. condr.). Stud. Liège Cons. under Léonard; had advice from Vieuxtemps and Wieniawski. 4 years in Berlin, as 1st vn. in Bilse's Orch.; then virtuoso in Paris; later, for 8 years, vn. prof. Brussels Cons.; resigned in order to tour abroad. Took refuge in England during 1914–18 war; went to U.S.A. in 1916; condr. of Cincinnati Symph. Orch. 1917. Returned to Belgium, 1922, and resumed Concerts Ysaye (founded 1895, replaced by chamber-music concerts in 1924).

Inheritor of the great tradition, still thoroughly imbued with the romanticism of Vieuxtemps, he refines and idealises it more and more and realises, in his playing, the most perfect union of fullness of sound, immateriality, intensity and expressive gradation of feeling. His activity has likewise been considerable in chamber-music and orch. music with advanced tendencies. The str. quartet which he founded with Mathieu Crickboom, Léon Van Hout and Joseph Jacob, and his association with Pugno for perf. of sonatas, have played a rôle which may be styled historic. So, too, his symphony concerts in Brussels have been hospitable to all novelties and have shown a spirit truly liberal and full of vitality.

Vn. and orch.: *Poème élégiaque*; *Chant d'Hiver*; *Extase*; *Divertimento*; for cello and orch., *Méditation*; str. orch. without bass, *Exil*, etc.—C. V. B.

YSAYE, Théo. Belgian pianist, compr. *b.* Verviers, 2 March, 1865; *d.* Côte d'Azur, 24 March, 1918. Brother of Eugène. Stud. at Liège Cons.; in Berlin under Kullak; compn. in Paris (from 1885). Pf. prof. at Geneva Cons. in 1889; but soon resigned, and toured as soloist. Settled in Brussels where he helped to organise the Ysaye Concerts. His pf. concerto in E flat, op. 9, was given at Q.H. London, under Sir Henry Wood, with De Greef at the pf. 29 Sept. 1921.

His delicate and distinguished talent easily assimilated the ideals of the Fr. school, and of musical Impressionism. It is this which gives his symph. work that fine and delicate atmosphere often lacking in Belgian music.

Symphony; symph. poems: *Les Abeilles*, op. 17 (Breitkopf); *La Forêt et l'Oiseau*, op. 18 (*id.*); *Le Cygne*; 2 pf. concertos; *Fantaisie* on Walloon songs, orch.; *Requiem*; 5tet, pf. and str., etc.—C. V. B.

Z

ZADEIKAS, V. See LITHUANIAN MUSIC.

ZÁGON, Géza Vilmos. Hungarian compr. *b.* Budapest, 30 Oct. 1889. Fell in action 1918. —B. B.

ZAGWIJN, Henri. Dutch compr. *b.* Nieuwer-Amstel (N. Holland), 17 July, 1878. Chiefly self-taught; founded 1918 (with Sem Dresden) Soc. of Modern Dutch Composers (now defunct); 1916, teacher (compn.) Music School at Rotterdam, where he still lives.
Der Zauberlehrling (1908), soli, chorus, orch. and organ (Breitkopf), 1st perf. Amsterdam, 9 Jan. 1914; *Fantasie*, (1903), perf. Amsterdam, Concertgebouw Orch., 24 April, 1904; 2 overtures, *Wijdingsnacht (Invitation Night)*, 1918, and *Opstanding (Resurrection)*, 1919, perf. Amsterdam, Mengelberg (ms.); Suite for wind instrs. and pf. (1913), perf. Concertgebouw Sextet; trio for pf. vn. and cello (1915); str. 4tet (1918); *Nocturne* for wind instrs., celesta and harp (1918); pf. works: *Van de Daggetyden (The Hours of the Day)* 1915 (Amsterdam, Nieuwe Muziekhandel); 3 *Klankschetsen (Sketches in Sonority)*, 1918 (*id.*); *Suite fantasque*, 1921 (*id.*); *Sylphes (Zephyros, Typhon, Danse eurythmique)*, 1921 (*id.*); works for recitation and orch.: *Jephtha* (Joost van den Vondel), 1919; *The Ballad of Reading Gaol* (Oscar Wilde), 1920; numerous songs with pf. (Dutch, Ger. and Fr. words), (Amsterdam, Nieuwe Muz.; Rotterdam, Van Esso, 1907–22); also a brochure, *Modern Movements in Music* (Rotterdam, Tydstroom). Consult Dutch reviews *Caecilia* (15 Feb. 1914) and *De Hofstad* (5 Jan. 1918).—W. P.

ZAMACOIS, J. Contemporary Span. compr. of the modern school; author of symph. poem *Los Ojos Verdes*, which gained a prize at Gran Casino competition (San Sebastian), 1920, and was perf. by Orquesta Sinfónica, Madrid (March 1922), and Orquesta Sinfónica, Barcelona. —P. G. M.

ZAMBA or Zamacueca. See SOUTH AMER. DANCES.

ZAMRZLA, Rudolf. Czechoslovak composer; *b.* Rokycany, 1869. Pupil of Skuherský at Organ School, Prague. For a long time condr. of an orch. in Russia; from 1902 condr. National Theatre in Prague.
Wedding Night (opera), *Samson* (opera), both perf. Prague; symphony, C mi., soli, chorus, orch. and organ; symph. poem, *Bacchus.*—V. ST.

ZANDONAI, Riccardo. Italian composer; *b.* Sacco (Trentino), 28 May, 1883. Pupil of Mascagni at the Liceo at Pesaro; diploma in 1902. Is one of the most esteemed of contemporary Ital. comprs. First success with the opera, *Il grillo del focolare* (Turin, 1908); followed by *Conchita*, from the novel *La Femme et le Pantin* of Pierre Louys (Milan, 1911); *Melenis*, on a Roman subject (*Milan*, 1912); *Francesca da Rimini*, on Gabriele d'Annunzio's tragedy (Turin, 1914); *La via della finestra*, comic opera (Pesaro, 1919); *Giulietta e Romeo* (Rome, 1922). Has also written a Requiem for solo vs., perf. at the Pantheon in Rome, 1916; *Primavera in Val di Sole*, and *Patria lontana*,

suites of symph. impressions; also a ·vn. concerto, and many songs (Ricordi). Consult Alessandro Benedetti, *R. Z.*, in the review, *L'Italia che scrive*, Rome, 1919.—D. A.

ZANELLA, Amilcare. Italian composer and pianist; *b.* Monticelli d'Ongina (Piacenza), 26 Sept. 1873. Stud. at the Parma Cons.; diploma, 1891. After having conducted the band in his native city, and starting his career as a pianist and orch. condr. he went to S. America, where he remained for several years. On returning to Italy he continued his activity as a pianist, compr. and condr., organising, in the last-mentioned capacity, some important perf. and revivals, particularly of Rossini's works. His opera *Aura* was perf. with success at Pesaro in 1907. Has also written symph. music (2 symphonies, symph. poem in 4 parts entitled *Vita* and many other works); instr. chamber-music (trio, 4tet, 5tet, nonet, sonatas); songs; pf. music, etc. (Ricordi, Carisch, Schmidl and Pizzi). Since 1905, has been dir. of the Liceo Mus. Rossini at Pesaro, whither he went from the Cons. at Parma, which he had directed since 1903. He is a very well known pianist and composer.—D. A.

ZARZUELA. Name given in Spain to mus. comedies or plays in which the dialogue alternates with mus. numbers. They are classified as *Género Grande* or *Zarzuela Grande*, when in 2 or more acts; *Género Chico (Petit Genre)* when in 1 act. Founding their opinion on the existence of dialogue in the original version of certain operas by Mozart and Weber, among other classics, some consider the *Zarzuela Grande* as the real *ópera española* (Spanish opera) (see CHAPÍ). Others, showing a stricter judgment, declare it to be the type from which the national opera could be evolved. From a practical point of view, the discussion is of no consequence, since the title Opera, as it is understood nowadays, could hardly be given to any of the countless *zarzuelas* which constitute the most characteristic form of mus. expression of a period (1850–80) in which the standard of mus. technique in Spain was at its worst. The *Zarzuela Grande* is similar in scope to the Ital. operetta (*opera semi-seria*) or the Fr. *opéra-comique*, the influence of both being present in the majority of cases. The works belonging to *Género Chico* can be described as mus. "curtain raisers." This type, of genuine Span. creation, lends itself to the highest artistic treatment, but is used, with rare exceptions, as a pretext for professional degradation on the part of performers and authors, a national disgrace which the famous playwrights, the brothers Quintero, strove to minimise through the influence of their wit and

540

literary art. The origin of the *Género Chico* may be traced to the *Tonadillas*, and even the *Eglogas* and *Loas* of an older period. One-act plays to finish or begin the evening programme have been always customary in Spain. In its actual form and development, the *Género Chico* is the direct outcome of a box-office device — the institution of the *teatro por hora* (theatre by the hour) so much in vogue for the last 30 years. This system consists of making an evening programme of 4 different 1-act plays, allowing the public to book for 1, 2 or more, independent of their order in the programme, the theatre being cleared or the tickets revised after each piece. Nothing has proved so profitable to impresarios, authors and comprs., and so detrimental to the cause of art and the education of the public taste.

The use of the word *zarzuela* as title of a play with music, originated in the XVII century entertainments celebrated at the Real Palacio de la Zarzuela, near Madrid, for the amusement of Philip IV's Court, at which the *Eglogas*, *Loas*, *Tonadas*, *Bailetes* and the *Comedias Armónicas* of the period were performed. These Royal entertainments became famous and known as *Fiestas de la Zarzuela*, a contracted form of *Fiestas del Palacio de la Zarzuela*. The Palace was situated in La Zarzuela, a place near Madrid, so called from the abundance of bramble (Span. *zarza*) in its vicinity, from which the Royal Palace took its name. In 1629, Calderón de la Barca wrote *El Jardín de Falerina, Fiesta de Zarzuela*, with music by José Peyró. The Span. lyric theatre can claim an ancestry still older in the poet-musician Juan del Encina (XV century).—P. G. M.

ZBOIŃSKA-RUSZKOWSKA, Helena. Polish soprano singer; *b.* Lemberg, 1878. From 1900–3, sang at Lemberg Opera; 1904–6 at Warsaw; then Vienna, Madrid, Buenos Ayres, Palermo. In 1913, sang Aïda 12 times at La Scala, Milan, during the Verdi fests. In 1916–18 she sang at Prague (Národní Divadlo), and since 1919 she has sung at Warsaw State Opera.—Zd. J.

ZEISLER, Fanny Bloomfield. Amer. pianist; *b.* Bielitz, Austria, 16 July, 1863. Went to Chicago in early childhood, where she stud. pf. under Ziehn and Wolfsohn; 1878–83, pupil of Leschetizky in Vienna; 1883–93, many Amer. concerts, and after that, Germany (1893–5), Germany, Austria, France (1902), Germany, England, France (1912). One of the most successful Amer. pianists.—O. K.

ZEITLIN, Lef Moiseievitch. Russ. violinist; *b.* 14 March (n.s.), 1881. Pupil of L. Auer, Petrograd Cons. (1901). From then till 1910, orch. player in Colonne Orch. Paris, and member of Zeitlin Str. Quartet. In 1910, leading vn. of Zimin Opera House, Moscow; then of Kussevitsky's orch.; prof. of music school of Moscow Philh. Soc. and now of Moscow Cons. and chairman of Conductor-less Orch. Moscow, from 1922. —V. B.

ŻELEŃSKI, Władysław (*phon.* Jelenski). Polish composer; *b.* Grodkowice, Galicia, 6 July, 1837; *d.* Cracow, 23 Jan. 1921. From 1883–1921, was director of Cracow Conservatoire. In all his works Żeleński remained a follower of the classical and Romantic masters. He continued composing literally till the last day of his life. Several hours before his death he finished a vigorous march for Polish soldiers.

Operas: *Konrad Wallenrod* (after Mickiewicz); *Goplana* (1896) after Stowacki's *Balladyna*; *Janek* (libretto by Ludomir German), 1900; *Stara Baśń* (libretto after Kraszewski by Alex. Bandrowski). 2 symphonies; concerto for pf. and orch. op. 60; several orch. overtures and symph. compns.; many chamber-works (including 2 sonatas for pf. op. 5 and 20); 2 vn. sonatas, on. 30 and 67; trio, op. 20; 2 4tets (op. 28 and 42). His 80 songs are among the best Polish songs of the XIX century.—Zd. J.

ZELINKA, Jan. Czechoslovak compr. *b.* Prague, 1893.

Overture to a Renaissance comedy, orch.; pf. 4tet; 1-act opera, *Dceruška hostinského* (*The Innkeeper's Daughter*); vn. sonata; pf. cycles (*Burlescamente*; *Feuilletons*); songs; choruses.—V. St.

ZEMLINSKY, Alexander von. Austrian compr. *b.* Vienna, 4 Oct. 1872. Stud. at Vienna Cons. He is the representative compr. for that synthesis of Wagnerian and Brahmsian elements which is felt in so many of the Viennese school, even in the earlier works of Schönberg. Started as condr. at Volksoper, Vienna, where he inaugurated a brilliant epoch; 1908, at Vienna Hofoper; 1909, Mannheim; then again at Vienna Volksoper. Now chief condr. Prague Opera. 3 symphonies (3rd, *Lyric*, 1st perf. Prague 6 June 1924); a symph. poem *Die Seejungfrau*; chamber-music (his 2nd str. quartet in 1 movement shows great qualities). His first opera, *Sarema* (perf. Munich, 1897), took Luitpold Prize; the 2nd, *Es war einmal*, had great success in Vienna, 1900; *Kleider machen Leute*, 1910; *The Dwarf* (libretto after Oscar Wilde), 1921; then *The Birthday of the Infanta* (Cologne). Brother-in-law of A. Schönberg and teacher of E. W. Korngold.—Eg. W.

ZENATELLO, Giovanni. Ital. tenor, one of the most esteemed lyric and dramatic singers of the present day; *b.* Verona, 22 Feb. 1876. *Début* at the Mercadante, Naples, in *Cavalleria Rusticana*. He has sung in the principal European and Amer. opera houses. His repertoire extends from *Cavalleria Rusticana, Andrea Chénier, Carmen* to *Lucia*. Created tenor rôles in *Figlia di Jorio* (Franchetti), *Siberia* (Giordano), *Madama Butterfly* (Puccini), *Gloria* (Cilea).—D. A.

ZENGER, Max. Ger. compr. *b.* Munich, 2 Feb. 1837; *d.* 16 Nov. 1911. Self-taught musician; 1860, condr. at Regensburg (Ratisbon); 1869, condr. R. Opera House, Munich; 1872, Court mus. condr. at Carlsruhe; 1878–85, condr. of Oratorio Soc. of Singakademie; teacher at Königliche Musikschule. Wrote *History of the Munich Opera*, 1923 (Theodor Kroyer).

Oratorio *Cain* (Byron, 1867); *Festival March*, orch.; over 100 songs; part-songs; duet-sonata for pf.; 2 str. 4tets; pf. trio; sonata for horn (or cello) and pf.; *Konzertstücke*, vns. clars. cello and orch.; *Konzertstücke*, harps, vns. horns and small orch.; *Festival Overture*; *Old Greek Song-plays* (solo and chorus); operas: *The Foscari* (Munich, 1863);

Ruy Blas (Mannheim, 1868); *Wieland the Smith* (Munich, 1880); rev. Munich, 1894); *Eros and Psyche* (Munich, 1901); music to both parts of Goethe's *Faust*; ballet-music: *Venus and Adonis*; *Les Plaisirs de l'île Enchantée* (both comp. 1881, for Ludwig II); an idyll, *The Girl of the Forest*, soli, female chorus and pf. (op. 11); 2 symphonies (*Tragic*); overture, op. 42.—A. E.

ZEPLER, Bogumil. Ger. compr. *b.* Breslau, 6 May, 1858; *d.* Krummhübel, 17 Aug. 1918. First a doctor of medecine; then stud. music under Heinrich Urban in Berlin.

Comic operas: *The Marriage-Market at Hira* (Berlin, 1892); *The Count of Letorières* (Hamburg, 1899); *Monsieur Bonaparte* (Leipzig, 1911); dramatic 1-act play, *Night* (Berne, 1900); operettas: *Diogenes* (Berlin, 1902); *The Baths of Lucca* (Berlin, 1905); *The Fortress of Love* (Berlin, 1905); pantomime, *The Shoe pinches the Prince* (*Prince Blondel*, Vienna, 1905); 2 ballet-suites, orch.; songs.—A. E.

ZETTERQVIST, Lars J. Swedish violinist; *b.* Tveta (Värmland), 25 March, 1860. Stud. R. Cons. Stockholm 1875-8 (under Fr. Book) then under Léonard (Paris) and Sivori 1878–80. Attached to the R. Chapel 1882; leader there, 1886–1914, and then in Concert Soc. from 1915. Teacher at R. Cons. Stockholm from 1903, prof. 1914. Condr. of many military bands 1885–1911. Member R.A.M. Stockholm, 1892.—P. V.

ZICH, Otakar. Czech compr. *b.* Králové Městec, 1879. First grammar-school master; then Univ. teacher of æsthetics, Prague; now Univ. prof. at Brno. Much occupied with collection of national songs, their analysis and publication (*Chodské písně*). His opera *Vina* (*The Crime*), based on the realistic text of Jaroslav Hilbert, taken from modern life without any alteration, excited much attention. First perf. National Theatre, Prague, 1922. Wrote numerous criticisms and æsthetic treatises on musical appreciation (*The Apperception of Music*, in Czech).

Polka jede (*Polka Drives*); *Osudná svatba* (*The Fateful Wedding*), both chorus and orch.; songs (words by Jan Neruda) and opera *Malířský nápad* (*A Painter's Downfall*).—V. ST.

ZIEHRER, Carl Michael. Austrian compr. *b.* Vienna, 2 May, 1843; *d.* there 14 Nov. 1922. Formerly condr. of military band; then dir. of Court Ball music. Famous for his Viennese waltzes. Continued and finished the line of Vienna dance-comprs.: Strauss (father and son) and Lanner. About 1880, toured with his own orch. in Russia, England, America. Died in indigent circumstances.

Operettas: *Wiener Blut*; *Der Landstreicher* (1900); *Der Schatzmeister*; *Fesche Geister*; *Die drei Wünsche*; *Das dumme Herz* (1914); and 17 others. 600 waltzes, polkas and marches.—P. P.

ZILCHER, Hermann. Ger. compr. *b.* Frankfort-o-M., 18 Aug. 1881. Son of Paul Zilcher; pupil of father (pf.) and at Hoch's Cons. Frankfort-o-M. (Kwast, Scholz and Knorr); 1901, won Mozart Prize for compn.; went to Berlin; took concert-parties to America, Spain and Scandinavia (with Petschnikof, v. Vecsey, etc.); 1905, teacher at Hoch's Cons.; 1908, prof., first pf., then compn., at Munich Acad. of Music. 1920, Dir. of Cons. of Music, Würzburg. As compr., he takes a half Brahms and half Neo-Romantic and Impressionist direction.

Songs, chiefly in cycles: Dehmel set, s. and t. op. 25; Hölderlin set, t. and orch.; 4 War Songs,

op. 30; *Gesang zu zweien in der Nacht*, op, 31; *Serenade* and *Morning Song*, barit. and orch.; *Dance Song*, s. vn. and pf.; 15 short songs; a German Folk-Song Play, solo 4tet and pf. op. 32; *Song of Solomon*, contr. barit. str. 4tet and pf. op. 38; *Hymnus* for v. and pf. op 17; *To My German Land*, prelude, orch. and choir *ad lib.* op. 48; pf. pieces; vn. sonata, op. 16; pf. 5tet, op. 42; *Symphonietta*, op. 1; suite, orch. op. 4; 2 symphonies (A, op. 17; F mi. op. 23); concerto for 2 vns. op. 9; vn. concerto, op. 11; suite, 2 vns. and orch. op. 15; cello concerto, op. 21; *Lamentation*, vns. and orch. op. 22; pf. concerto op. 20; *Night and Morning*, 2 pfs. orch. and drums, op. 24; choral work, *Reinhart*, op. 2, and *The Love Mass* (Will Vesper), op. 27, a large choral work in 3 parts (Strasburg, 1913); a dream-play, *Fitzebutze* (Dehmel, pantomime with songs, op. 19, Mannheim, 1903); incidental music, Shakespeare's *As You Like It* and *The Winter's Tale*, op. 39; mus. comedy, *Doctor Iron-Beard*, op. 45 (Mannheim, 1922). Consult Hans Oppenheim, *H. Z.* (Munich, 1921).—A. E.

ZILCHER, Paul. Ger. compr. *b.* Frankfort-o-M., 9 July, 1855. Son of Carl Zilcher; pupil of J. Schoch and J. C. Hauff. Founder of the Parlow-Zilcher School of Pf. at Offenbach-o-M. Wrote easy pf. pieces and chamber-music for teaching.—A. E.

ŽILEVIČIUS, Juozas. Lithuanian compr. and condr. *b.* Žemaitia in 1891. Stud. under Kykuskas and Sasnauskas, at same time acting as orgt. to Prince Oginski at Plunge. In 1911, stud. under Lipowski at Warsaw Mus. Inst., and privately under Suržynski. In 1914, he removed to Petrograd and in 1915 entered the Cons. there. Attended the Archæological Inst. for 2 years. In 1918, stud. at Inst. of Art History. 1919, secretary to faculty of pedagogic theory at Vitebsk Cons. Was dir. of mus. training and choir-instructor of Vitebsk district (Vitebsk, Minsk, Mohilev, Smolensk). Returned to Lithuania in 1920 and organised the theatre, and took active part in creation of school of drama, opera and music. The abnormal strain brought on partial deafness. He transferred to Ministry of Education and abandoned compn. for teaching and writing. His chief works are a symphony, based on popular themes; an Elegy; and a set of variations on the popular song *Seriau žirgeli* (*I have fed my Steed*). *Gunde mane bernuželis* (*The Young Swain tempted me*) is an air from K. Puida's operetta *Raseiniu Magde* (*The Magdalen of Raseniai*); *Močiute širdele* (*Mother darling!*) is a trio, etc.—H. R.

ZIMBALIST, Efrem. Russ. violinist; *b.* Rostof on the Don, Russia, 9 April, 1889. Stud. first under his father, then, 1901–7, at Petrograd Cons. under Auer. *Début* in Berlin, 7 Nov. 1907, with Brahms's concerto. On 9 Dec. 1907, played in London for 1st time with Landon Ronald's London Symphony Orch.; 1st heard in America with Boston Symphony Orch., 27 Oct. 1911. Married (15 June, 1914) in London the Amer. operatic and concert-soprano, Alma Gluck, at whose recitals he has frequently acted as pf. accompanist. His mus. comedy, *Honeydew*, was 1st perf. New Haven, Conn., 30 Aug. 1920, and met with success.

Suite in the Old Form, vn. and pf. (Schott, 1911); 3 *Slavic Dances*, vn. and pf. (*id.*).—O. K.

ZIMMER, Albert Jacques. Belgian violinist; *b.* Liège, 5 Jan. 1874. Stud. at Liège Cons.;

pupil of Eugène Ysaye (1893) at Brussels Cons. Started the Zimmer Quartet in 1896, to-day one of chief str. quartets in world. It is composed of MM. Ghigo, Barsen and Gaillard, besides Zimmer. In 1905 he started J. S. Bach Soc., which gave Bach concerts in Brussels up to outbreak of war in 1914. Prof. of vn. and chamber-music at Ghent Cons. until appointed to Brussels Cons. in succession to César Thomson.—C. V. B.

ZIMMERMANN, Louis. Dutch violinist; b. Groningen, 19 July, 1873. Studied under Poortman, Hans Sitt and Eugène Ysaye; 1896–99, soloist at Darmstadt; 1899–1904, soloist Concertgebouw Orchestra, Amsterdam; on 6 Dec. 1902, visited London to play in 1st Eng. perf. of Strauss's *Ein Heldenleben*, when the compr. conducted; 1904, prof. at R.A.M. London; 1911, returned to Amsterdam; since 1911, 1st soloist Concertgebouw Orchestra.

Vn. concerto (1st perf. 1921, Amsterdam); Variations for vn. and orch.; str. 4tet; smaller pieces for vn. and pf.; songs.—W. P.

ZINCKE, Hans Friedrich August. Real name of Hans Sommer (*q.v.*).

ZITEH, Otakar. Czech compr. writer; b. Prague, 1892. Stud. at Cons. and Univ. both in Prague and Vienna (Novák, Adler, Graedener). Wrote articles and criticisms for periodicals (*Hudební Revue*; *Lidové noviny*); paid special attention to questions of dramaturgical technique in opera (*Modern Opera*, in Czech, Hudební Matice); since 1921 operatic producer at National Theatre, Brno; at same time teacher at Brno Conservatoire.

Operas: *Vznešené srdce* (*The Exalted Heart*), 1918; *Pád Petra Králence* (*Fall of Peter Kralenec*), 1921. Song collections: *Melancholická pout* (1917); *Z vojny* (*From the War*), 1918; *U nás* (*With Us*) (Hudební Matice).—V. ST.

ZLICA. Professional name of Alice Everaerts, Belgian pianist; b. Brussels, 25 July, 1876. Stud. at Brussels Cons. under Gurickx, at Leipzig under Reinecke. Author of educ. works and children's pf. pieces; also school-play, *Labyrinthe musical.*—E. C.

ZOELLNER, Heinrich. Ger. compr. b. Leipzig, 4 July, 1854. 1875–7, stud. at Leipzig Cons. (Reinecke, Jadassohn, Richter, Wenzel). 1878, mus. dir. at Dorpat Univ.; 1885, condr. of Men's Choral Soc. Cologne (touring a concert-party through Italy, 1889); also teacher at Cologne Cons.; 1890, went to New York as condr. of Ger. Singing Club there. Called back to Leipzig as mus. dir. of the Univ. 1898; teacher of compn. at Cons. there 1902; 1903, mus. ed. of *Leipziger Tageblatt*. Gained title of Prof. in 1905; 1906, cancelled his Leipzig engagements; 1907, joined Stern's Cons. Berlin. 1908, went to Antwerp to conduct the Flemish Opera there. Now lives at Freiburg (Breisgau).

Operas: *Frithjof* (1884, Antwerp, 1910); *The Merry Chinese Girls* (Cologne, 1886; also New York); *Faust* (Munich, 1887); *Matteo Falcone* (1-act opera, perf. New York, 1894); *At Sedan* (Leipzig, 1895); *The Attack* (Leipzig, 1895); *The Wooden Sword* (Cassel, 1897); *The Sunken Bell* (Berlin, 1899); *The King of the Shooters* (1903); *Gipsies* (Stuttgart, 1912); cantata, *Battle of the Huns* (Leipzig, 1880); oratorio, *Luther* (1883); *Columbus* male, chorus, mixed and orch. (Leipzig, 1886); *Hymn of Love*, mixed

chorus, soli and orch. (Cologne, 1891); *The New World* (prize compn. at Singers' Fest. at Cleveland, U.S.A., 1893); *King Sigurd's Bride Voyage* (Leipzig, 1895); *The Seafarers* (1896); *Heroes' Requiem* (1895); *Review* (1901); *Boniface* (1903); *Babylon*, op. 145 (1922), all for chorus and orch.; 4 symphonies; orch. episodes, *A Summer Trip*, op. 15; *Forest Phantasy*, orch. (New York, 1894); *Serenade*, str. orch. and fls. op. 95; 5 str. 4tets; songs; choruses for male voices.—A. E.

ZOELLNER, Richard. Compr.; b. Metz, 16 March, 1896. Son of Heinrich Zoellner; stud. music under Franz Rau, Munich, and Paul Graener. Lives at Berchtesgaden; is a talented musician of modern style.

Chamber-symphony; 2 *Musiken* for orch.; *Ode to Love*, chamber-orch.; Variations on original theme, full orch.; songs; 2 sacred pieces, for 4tet.; str. 4tet; 5tet, clar. and strings.—A. E.

ZOLOTAREF, Vassily Andreievitch (*accent 4th syll.*). Russ. compr. b. Taganrog (govt. of Don Cossacks), 23 Feb./7 March, 1873; choir-boy at Court Chapel, Petrograd, 1883–92; stud. under Balakiref; then pupil of Rimsky-Korsakof at Petrograd Cons. (1898–1900); Rubinstein Prize (1200 roubles) for cantata *Paradise and the Peri*; prof. Moscow Cons.; after the revolution settled at Krasnodar (formerly Ekaterinodar), govt. Kuban Cossacks, Caucasus.

Symphony, op. 8; overture, *The Country Feast*, op. 4; *Hebrew Rhapsody*, orch. op. 7; *Overture-fantaisie*, orch. op. 22; str. 5tet, D mi. op. 19; str. 4tet I, D, op. 5; II, A, op. 6; III, D, op. 25; IV, B. flat mi. op. 33; pf. 4tet, D, op. 13; pf. trio, E mi. op. 28; pf. sonata, G, op. 10; songs; pf. pieces, etc. (Mostly Belaief.)—V. B.

ZORKA, Joran. Serbian violinist, chamber-music player, teacher; b. Belgrade, 23 April, 1881. Stud. at Moscow Cons. under Hrimaly. Since 1920, has been dir. of State School of Music, Belgrade.—T. F. D.

ZRNO, Felix. Czechoslovak compr. b. 1890. Pupil of Vít. Novák.

Vocal compns.; male choruses: *All Souls' Day*; *Sárka*; *The Tower*; *The Eternal Song*. (E. Starý; Hudební Matice, Prague.)—V. ST.

ZSOLT, Nándor. Hungarian violinist and compr. b. Esztergom, 1887. Stud. vn. under Jenő Hubay, compn. under Hans Koessler, at R. High School for Music, Budapest. His pf. 5tet was awarded Budapest *Lipótvárosi Kaszinó* Prize. This, his pf. Toccata, his *Satyr et Dryade* and *Enchaînée* for pf. and vn. are publ. by Augener; his *Libellule* by Mathot, Paris. He was a member of the Queen's Hall Orch. London for several years. Since 1920 he has been teacher of vn. at R. High School for Music, Budapest.—B. B.

ZUCCARINI, Oscar. Ital. violinist; b. Rome, 19 Feb. 1888. Stud. with success at the R. Liceo Mus. di Santa Cecilia, under Ettore Pinelli. Is an estimable concert artist; has played as solo violinist with the orch. at Riga and Kief (cond. by Schnéevoigt), and has given successful concerts at the Augusteo. Since 1913 has occupied the position of 1st violinist in the Augusteo orch. Took part in the Trio Romano and the Quintetto Cristiani. Now 1st violinist of the new Quartetto di Roma (see CHAMBER-MUSIC PLAYERS).—D. A.

ZUELLI, Guglielmo. Ital. compr. b. Reggio Emilia, 22 Oct. 1859. After a hard time when

young, he succeeded in gaining admittance to
the Liceo Mus. at Bologna, where he stud.
compn. under Busi and Mancinelli; diploma,
1882. Whilst carrying on his profession of
teacher and orch. condr. in 1883 he won the
Sonzogno Competition with his 1-act opera *La
fata del Nord*, successfully perf. at the Manzoni
Theatre in Milan, 1884 (Ricordi). Another
opera, in 4 acts, *Il Profeta del Korasan*, won the
Baruzzi competition in Bologna. After travelling
for some years in various cities as teacher and
condr., was appointed prof. of cpt. and compn.
at Cons. at Palermo in 1892, of which he afterwards became dir. Now directs the Cons. at
Parma. Also comp. 2 symphonies, a 4tet,
and many other vocal and instr. works of
concert and chamber-music (publ. partly by
Ricordi).—D. A.

ZUMPE, Hermann. Ger. condr. *b.* Tauben-
heim (Oberlausitz, Saxony), 9 April, 1850; *d.*
Munich, 4 Sept. 1903. First a general teacher;
then stud. music with A. Tottmann; engaged by
Wagner at Bayreuth (1873–6) to assist him in
finishing off the *Nibelungen* scores. After that,
cond. at theatres at Salzburg, Würzburg, Magdeburg, Frankfort-o-M. and Hamburg, 1884–6.
Condr. at Court Theatre, Stuttgart, 1891; condr.
of Kaim Concerts, Munich, 1895; condr. at
Court Theatre, Schwerin, 1897; gen. condr.
R. Opera House, Munich, 1900.

Songs; overture to *Wallenstein's Death*; fairy-
opera, *Anahra* (Berlin, 1881); romantic comic opera,
The Bewitched Princess (ms.); operettas: *Farinelli*
(Hamburg, 1886); *Karin* (Hamburg, 1888); *Polish
Household* (Hamburg, 1889; Berlin, 1891). A 3-act
opera, *Sawitri*, was discovered among his papers
after his death, finished by Rössler and perf. at
Schwerin in 1907; a second 3-act opera, *The Spectre
of Horodin*, was perf. at Hamburg in 1910.—A. E.

ZURRÓN, Vicente. Contemporary Span.
compr. His pf. 4tet in D took the prize at first
competition of Sociedad Filarmónica, Madrid.

Zarzuelas (1-act): *Bodas Reales*; *El Cazador de
Milanos* (Sociedad de Autores Españoles, Madrid).
—P. G. M.

ZUSCHNEID, Karl. Compr. *b.* Oberglogau,
Silesia, 29 May, 1854. Pupil at Stuttgart Cons.
under Lebert, Stark, Pruckner and Faisst;
1879–89, condr. of Mus. Soc. at Göttingen;
then condr. of Mus. Soc. at Minden; 1897–
1907, cond. Soller Mus. Soc. and Men's Choral
Soc. Erfurt. In 1907, dir. of High School of
Music, Mannheim. Prof. 1914; retired in 1917.
Now residing at Bad-Homburg.

For male choruses, soli and orch.: *Hermann der
Befreier*; *A Spring Trip*; *A Singer's Prayer*; for
mixed chorus, soli and orch.: *Beneath the Stars*;
The Zollern and the Kingdom; *Germany's Awakening*;
A Christmas Anthem; unacc. male chorus: *Psalm
XXIX* (op. 40), *Festival Hymn* (op. 63); unacc.
mixed chorus, op. 23, 25 and 39 (sacred); pf. pieces;
Variations and Improvisations, str. orch.; vn.
concerto; pf. tutor; *Guide to Pf. Teaching*; about
300 part-songs (*New Song Treasures*).—A. E.

ZWEERS, Bernard. Dutch compr. *b.* Amsterdam, 18 May, 1854. Started music when very
young; 1881, stud. under Jadassohn, Leipzig;
1890 – 1922, teacher (compn.) at Amsterdam
Cons. Most of the modern Dutch comprs. have
studied under him.

3 symphonies (No. III, *Mijn Vaderland*) (publ.
Noske. The Hague); choral works; songs (publ.
Alsbach, Amsterdam); stage-music to *Gijsbrecht van
Amstel*.—W. P.

ZWEYGBERG, Lennart von. Finnish cellist;
b. Jyväskylä, 25 Dec. 1874. Stud. in Orch.
School at Helsingfors under Schnéevoigt; in
Cons. at Sondershausen under Schröder; later
under Jacob in Brussels and Hugo Becker in
Frankfort. He then joined Philh. Orch. at Helsingfors (1900–1); travelled as soloist in Finland, Russia and Germany; later became
teacher at Crefeld Cons. (1903–9) in which year
he settled as a teacher at Minusio (Ticino),
Switzerland, occasionally touring as concert-
player in England, France, Italy, Germany,
Sweden, Norway, and Finland.—T. H.